Contents

Preface to the Fifth Edition

Geographical dictionaries have a long history. A number were published in Europe in the seventeenth and eighteenth centuries: a few – mostly those with greater pretensions to providing conceptual order – were described as 'Geographical Grammars'. The majority were compendia of geographical information, or gazetteers, some of which were truly astonishing in their scope. For example, Lawrence Echard noted with some asperity in his 1691 *Compendium of Geography* that the geographer was by then more or less required to be 'an *Entomologist*, an *Astronomer*, a *Geometrician*, a *Natural Philosopher*, a *Husbandman*, an *Herbalist*, a *Mechanik*, a *Physician*, a *Merchant*, an *Architect*, a *Linguist*, a *Divine*, a *Politician*, one that understands *Laws* and *Military Affairs*, an *Herald* [and] an *Historian*.' Margarita Bowen, commenting on 1981 on what she took to be Geography's isolation from the scientific mainstream in Echard's time, suggested that 'the prospect of adding epistemology and the skills of the philosopher' to such a list might well have precipitated its Cambridge author into the River Cam!

It was in large measure the addition of those skills to the necessary accomplishments of a human geographer that prompted the first edition of *The Dictionary of Human Geography*. The original idea was John Davey's, a publisher with an extraordinarily rich and creative sense of the field, and he persuaded Ron Johnston, Derek Gregory, Peter Haggett, David Smith and David Stoddart to edit the first edition (1981). In their Preface they noted that the changes in human geography since the Second World War had generated a 'linguistic explosion' within the discipline. Part of the *Dictionary*'s purpose – then as now – was to provide students and others with a series of frameworks for situating, understanding and interrogating the modern lexicon. The implicit model was something closer to Raymond Williams' marvellous compilation of *Keywords* than to any 'Geographical Grammar'. Certainly the intention was always to provide something more than a collection of annotated reading lists. Individual entries were located within a web of cross-references to other entries, which enabled readers to follow their own paths through the *Dictionary*, sometimes to encounter unexpected parallels and convergences, sometimes to encounter creative tensions and contradictions. But the major entries were intended to be comprehensible on their own, and many of them not only provided lucid presentations of key issues but also made powerful contributions to subsequent debates.

This sense of *The Dictionary of Human Geography* as both mirror and goad, as both reflecting and provoking work in our field, has been retained in all subsequent editions. The pace of change within human geography was such that a second edition (1986) was produced only five years after the first, incorporating significant revisions and additions. For the third (1994) and fourth (2000) editions, yet more extensive revisions and additions were made. This fifth edition, fostered by our publisher Justin Vaughan, continues that restless tradition: it has been comprehensively redesigned and rewritten and is a vastly different book from the original. The first edition had over 500 entries written by eighteen contributors; this edition has more than 1000 entries written by 111 contributors. Over 300 entries appear for the first time (many of the most important are noted throughout this Preface), and virtually all the others have been fully revised and reworked. With this edition, we have thus once again been able to chart the emergence of new themes, approaches and concerns within human geography, and to anticipate new avenues of enquiry and new links with other disciplines. The architecture of the *Dictionary* has also been changed. We have retained the cross-referencing of headwords within each entry and the detailed Index, which together provide invaluable alternatives to the alphabetical ordering of the text, but references are no longer listed at the end of each entry. Instead, they now appear in a consolidated Bibliography at the end of the volume. We took this decision partly to avoid duplication and release space for new and extended entries, but also because we believe the Bibliography represents an important intellectual resource in its own right. It has over 4000 entries, including books, articles and online sources.

Our contributors operated within exacting guidelines, including limits on the length of each entry and the number of references, and they worked to a demanding schedule. The capstone entry for previous editions was 'human geography', but in this edition that central place is now

THE DICTIONARY OF
Human Geography

5th Edition

LIS - LIBRARY	
Date	Fund
17/09/15	Xg-Shr
Order No.	
2 650812	
University of Chester	

Edited by

Derek Gregory
Ron Johnston
Geraldine Pratt
Michael J. Watts
and Sarah Whatmore

WILEY-BLACKWELL

A John Wiley & Sons, Ltd., Publication

This 5th edition first published 2009
© 2009 by Blackwell Publishing Ltd except for editorial material and organization
© 2009 Derek Gregory, Ron Johnston, Geraldine Pratt, Michael J. Watts, and Sarah Whatmore
Edition history: Basil Blackwell Ltd (1e, 1981 and 2e, 1986);
Blackwell Publishers Ltd (3e, 1994 and 4e, 2000)

Blackwell Publishing was acquired by John Wiley & Sons in February 2007. Blackwell's publishing program
has been merged with Wiley's global Scientific, Technical, and Medical business to form Wiley-Blackwell.

Registered Office
John Wiley & Sons Ltd, The Atrium, Southern Gate, Chichester,
West Sussex, PO19 8SQ, United Kingdom

Editorial Offices
350 Main Street, Malden, MA 02148-5020, USA
9600 Garsington Road, Oxford, OX4 2DQ, UK
The Atrium, Southern Gate, Chichester, West Sussex, PO19 8SQ, UK

For details of our global editorial offices, for customer services, and for information about how
to apply for permission to reuse the copyright material in this book please
see our website at www.wiley.com/wiley-blackwell.

The right of Derek Gregory, Ron Johnston, Geraldine Pratt, Michael J. Watts, and Sarah
Whatmore to be identified as the author of the editorial material in this work has been
asserted in accordance with the Copyright, Designs and Patents Act 1988.

All rights reserved. No part of this publication may be reproduced, stored in a retrieval system, or
transmitted, in any form or by any means, electronic, mechanical, photocopying, recording or
otherwise, except as permitted by the UK Copyright, Designs and Patents Act 1988,
without the prior permission of the publisher.

Wiley also publishes its books in a variety of electronic formats. Some content that appears
in print may not be available in electronic books.

Designations used by companies to distinguish their products are often claimed as trademarks.
All brand names and product names used in this book are trade names, service marks, trademarks or
registered trademarks of their respective owners. The publisher is not associated with any product
or vendor mentioned in this book. This publication is designed to provide accurate and authoritative
information in regard to the subject matter covered. It is sold on the understanding that the publisher
is not engaged in rendering professional services. If professional advice or other expert assistance
is required, the services of a competent professional should be sought.

Library of Congress Cataloging-in-Publication Data

The dictionary of human geography / edited by Derek Gregory ... [et al.]. – 5th ed.
p. cm.
Includes bibliographical references and index.
ISBN 978-1-4051-3287-9 (hardcover : alk. paper) – ISBN 978-1-4051-3288-6 (pbk. : alk. paper)
1. Human geography–Dictionaries. I. Gregory, Derek, 1951–
GF4.D52 2009
304.203–dc22
2008037335

A catalogue record for this book is available from the British Library.

Set in 9/10pt Plantin by SPi Publisher Services, Pondicherry, India
Printed in Singapore by Markono Print Media Pte Ltd

7 2015

taken by a major entry on 'geography', with separate entries on 'human geography' and (for the first time) 'physical geography'. The inclusion of the latter provides a valuable perspective on the multiple ways in which human geography has become involved in interrogations of the biophysical world and – one of Williams's most complicated keywords – 'nature'. Accordingly, we have expanded our coverage of environmental geographies and of terms associated with the continued development of actor-network theory and political ecology, and for the first time we have included entries on biogeography, biophilosophy, bioprospecting, bioregionalism, biosecurity, biotechnology, climate, environmental history, environmental racism, environmental security, genetic geographies, the global commons, oceans, tropicality, urban nature, wetlands and zoos.

The first edition was planned at the height of the critique of spatial science within geography, and for that reason most of the entries were concerned with either analytical methods and formal spatial models or with alternative concepts and approaches drawn from the other social sciences. We have taken new developments in analytical methods into account in subsequent editions, and this one is no exception. We pay particular attention to the continuing stream of innovations in Geographic Information Systems and, notably, the rise of Geographic Information Science, and we have also taken notice of the considerable revival of interest in quantitative methods and modelling: hence we have included for the first time entries on agent-based modelling, Bayesian analysis, digital cartography, epidemiology, e-social science, geo-informatics and software for quantitative analysis, and we have radically revised our coverage of other analytical methods. The vital importance of qualitative methods in human geography has required renewed attention too, including for the first time entries on discourse analysis and visual methods, together with enhanced entries on deconstruction, ethnography, iconography, map reading and qualitative methods. In the previous edition we provided detailed coverage of developments in the social sciences and the humanities, and we have taken this still further in the present edition. Human geographers have continued to be assiduous in unpicking the seams between the social sciences and the humanities, and for the first time we have included entries on social theory, on the humanities, and on philosophy and literature (complementing revised entries on art, film and music), together with crucial junction-terms such as affect, assemblage, cartographic reason, contrapuntal geographies, dialectical image, emotional geography, minor theory, posthumanism, representation and trust (complementing enhanced entries on performance, performativity, non-representational theory and representation). Since the previous edition, the interest in some theoretical formations has declined, and with it the space we have accorded to them; but human geography has continued its close engagement with postcolonialism and post-structuralism, and the new edition incorporates these developments. They involve two continuing and, we think, crucial moments. The first is a keen interest in close and critical reading (surely vital for any dictionary!) and, to repeat what we affirmed in the preface to the previous edition, we are keenly aware of the slipperiness of our geographical 'keywords': of the claims they silently make, the privileges they surreptitiously install, and of the wider webs of meaning and practice within which they do their work. It still seems to us that human geographers are moving with considerable critical intelligence in a trans-disciplinary, even post-disciplinary space, and we hope that this edition continues to map and move within this intellectual topography with unprecedented precision and range. The second implication of postcolonialism and post-structuralism is a heightened sensitivity to what we might call the politics of specificity. This does not herald the return of the idiographic under another name, and it certainly does not entail any slackening of interest in theoretical work (we have in fact included an enhanced entry on theory). But it has involved a renewed interest in and commitment to that most traditional of geographical concerns, the variable character of the world in which we live. In one sense, perhaps, this makes the fifth edition more conventionally 'geographical' than its predecessors. We have included new entries on the conceptual formation of major geographical divisions and imaginaries, including the globe and continents (with separate entries on Africa, the Americas, Asia, Australasia and Europe), and on Latin America, the Middle East, the global South and the West, and on cognate fields such as area studies and International Relations. But we also asked our contributors to recognize that the world of geography is not limited to the global North. In previous editions, contributors frequently commented on the multiple ways in which modern human geography had worked to privilege and, indeed, normalize 'the modern', and together they traced a genealogy of geographical knowledge in which the world beyond Europe and North America was all too often marginalized or produced as a problematic 'pre-modern'. For this edition, we asked contributors to go beyond the critique of these assumptions and, wherever possible, to incorporate more cosmopolitan geographies (and we have included a new entry on cosmopolitanism).

And yet we must also recognize that this edition, like its predecessors, remains focused on English-language words, terms and literatures. There are cautionary observations to be made about the power-laden diffusion of English as a 'global language', and we know that there are severe limitations to working within a single-language tradition (especially in a field like human geography). The vitality of other geographical traditions should neither be overlooked nor minimized. We certainly do not believe that human geography conducted in English somehow constitutes the canonical version of the discipline, though it would be equally foolish to ignore the powers and privileges it arrogates to itself in the unequal world of the international academy. Neither should one discount the privileges that can be attached to learning other languages, nor minimize the perils of translation: linguistic competences exact their price. But to offer some (limited) protection against an unreflective ethnocentrism, we have been guided by an international Editorial Advisory Board and we have extended our coverage of issues bound up with Anglocentrism and Eurocentrism, colonialism and imperialism, Empire and Orientalism – all of these in the past and in the present – and we continue to engage directly with the politics of 'race', racism and violence. All of this makes it impossible to present *The Dictionary of Human Geography* as an Archimedean overview, a textual performance of what Donna Haraway calls 'the God-trick'. The entries are all situated knowledges, written by scholars working in Australia, Canada, Denmark, India, Ireland, Israel, New Zealand, Singapore, the United Kingdom and the United States of America. None of them is detached, and all of them are actively involved in the debates that they write about. More than this, the authors write from a diversity of subject-positions, so that this edition, like its predecessor, reveals considerable diversity and debate within the discipline. We make no secret of the differences – in position, in orientation, in politics – among our contributors. They do not speak with a single voice, and this is not a work of bland or arbitrary systematization produced by a committee. Even so, we are conscious of at least some of its partialities and limitations, and we invite our readers to consider how these other voices might be heard from other positions, other places, and to think about the voices that are – deliberately or unconsciously – silenced or marginalized.

None of these changes is a purely intellectual matter, of course, for they do not take place in a vacuum: the world has changed since the previous edition, and this is reflected in a number of entries that appear here for the first time. Some reach back to recover terms from the recent past that are active in our present – including Cold War, fascism, Holocaust and Second World – but all of them are distinguished by a sense of the historical formation of concepts and the webs of power in which they are implicated. While we do not believe that 'everything changed' after the attacks on the World Trade Center and the Pentagon on 11 September 2001, one year after our last edition, a shortlist of terms that have achieved new salience within the field indicates how far human geography has been restructured to accommodate a heightened sensitivity to political violence, including its ethical, economic and ecological dimensions. While many of these terms (like the four we have just mentioned) should have been in previous editions, for the first time we now have entries on: American Empire, asylum, bare life, the camp, ethnic cleansing, spaces of exception, genocide, *homo sacer*, human rights, intifada, just war, militarism, military geography, military occupation, resource wars, rogue states, security, terrorism, urbicide and war. Human geography has made major contributions to the critical study of economic transformation and globalization too, and our entries continue to recognize major developments in economic geography and political economy, and the lively exchanges between them that seek to explicate dramatic changes in contemporary regimes of capital accumulation and circulation. The global economic crisis broke as this edition was going to press. We had already included new entries on anti-development and anti-globalization, on the International Monetary Fund and the World Social Forum, and on narco-capitalism and petrocapitalism, which speak to some of the ramifications of the crisis, but we also believe that these events have made our expanded critiques of (in particular) capitalism, markets and neo-liberalism more relevant than ever before.

A number of other projects have appeared in the wake of previous editions of the *Dictionary*: meta-projects such as the *International Encyclopedia of Human Geography* and several other encyclopedias, an indispensable *Feminist Glossary of Human Geography*, and a series devoted to *Key Concepts* in the major subdisciplines of human geography. There is, of course, a lively debate about scale in geography, but we believe that the scale (or perhaps the extent of the conceptual network) of *The Dictionary of Human Geography* continues to be a crucial resource for anyone who wants to engage with the continued development of the field. It is not the last word – and neither pretends nor wishes to be – but rather an invitation to recover those words that came before, to reflect on their practical consequences, and to contribute to future 'geo-graphings'. This makes it all the more salutary to return to Echard's original list and realize that virtually all of the fields he identified as bearing on geography have their counterparts within the contemporary discipline. The single exception is the figure of the Herald, but if this is taken to imply not the skill of heraldry but rather a harbinger of what is to come, then human geography's interest in prediction and forecasting returns us to the footsteps of our seventeenth-century forebear. Be that as it may, none of us is prepared to forecast the scope and contents of the next edition of *The Dictionary of Human Geography*, which is why working on the project continues to be such a wonderfully creative process.

Derek Gregory
Ron Johnston
Geraldine Pratt
Michael J. Watts
Sarah Whatmore

How to Use This Dictionary

Keywords are listed alphabetically and appear on the page in **bold type**: in most cases, users of the *Dictionary* should begin their searches there. Within each entry, cross-references to other entries are shown in CAPITAL LETTERS (these include the plural and adjectival versions of many of the terms). Readers may trace other connections through the comprehensive index at the back of the book.

Suggested readings are provided at the end of each entry in abbreviated (Harvard) form; a full *Bibliography* is provided between pages 818 and 956, and readers seeking particular references or the works of particular authors should begin their searches there.

Acknowledgements

In the production of this edition, we are again indebted to a large number of people. We are particularly grateful to Justin Vaughan, our publisher at Wiley-Blackwell, for his enthusiasm, support and impeccably restrained goading, and to many others at Wiley-Blackwell (especially Liz Cremona and Tim Beuzeval) who have been involved in the management and implementation of this project. We owe a special debt to Geoffrey Palmer, our copy-editor, who performed marvels turning multiple electronic files into an accurate and coherent printed volume, and to WordCo Indexing Services, Inc., who compiled and cross-checked the Index with meticulous care.

The preparation of a large multi-authored volume such as this is dependent on the co-operation of a large number of colleagues, who accepted our invitation to contribute, our cajoling to produce the entries, our prompts over deadlines and our editorial interventions: we are immensely grateful to them for their care, tolerance and patience. It is with the greatest sadness that we record the deaths of two of them during the preparation of the *Dictionary* – Denis Cosgrove and Les Hepple – and we dedicate this edition to their memory.

The authors, editors and publishers thank the following for permission to reproduce the copyright material indicated:

Martin Cadwallader for the figure reproduced in the entry for **Alonso model** from *Analytical Urban Geography*, 1985.

Blackwell Publishing Ltd with The University of Chicago Press for the figure reproduced in the entry **capitalism** from D. Harvey, *The Limits to Capital*, 1982.

Blackwell Publishing Ltd for the figure reproduced in the entry **crisis** from D. Gregory, *Geographical Imaginations*, 1993.

Blackwell Publishing Ltd for the figure reproduced in the entry **critical theory**, based on Jürgen Habermas, *The Theory of Communicative Action*, Vol. 2, Polity Press.

University of California Press for the figure reproduced in the entry **cultural landscape** from Carol O. Sauer, *The Morphology of Landscape*, 1925. © 1925 The Regents of the University of California.

Peter Haggett for the figure reproduced in the entry for **demographic transition** from *Geography: A Modern Synthesis*, 1975.

Ohio State University Press/Macmillan Publishers Ltd for the figure reproduced in the entry **distance decay** from Peter J. Taylor, 'Distance transformation and distance decay functions', *Geographical Analysis*, Vol. 3, 3 July 1971. © Ohio State University Press.

Hodder and Stoughton Publishers Ltd for the figure reproduced in the entry **Kondratieff waves** based on Marshall, 1987, from P. Knox and J. Agnew, *Geography of the World-Economy*, 1989.

Macmillan Publishers Ltd with St. Martin's Press for the figure reproduced in the entry **Kondratieff waves** from Knox and Agnew, adapted from M. Marshall, *Long Waves of Regional Development*, 1987.

Peter Haggett for the figure reproduced in the entry for **locational analysis**, from *Locational Analysis in Human Geography*, 1977.

ACKNOWLEDGEMENTS

Cambridge University Press and The University of Chicago Press for the figure reproduced in the entry for **multiple nuclei model** from Harris and Ullman in H.M. Mayer and C.F. Kohn, eds, *Readings in Urban Geography*, 1959.

Blackwell Publishing Ltd for figures 1 and 2 reproduced in the entry **production of space** from D. Gregory, *Geographical Imaginations*, 1993.

The Estate of Conroy Maddox for the figure reproduced in the entry for **reflexivity**.

Contributors

AA   Ash Amin, Professor of Geography, University of Durham, UK

AB   Alison Blunt, Professor of Geography, Queen Mary, University of London, UK

AGH   Tony Hoare, Senior Lecturer in Geography, University of Bristol, UK

AJB   Adrian Bailey, Professor of Migration Studies, School of Geography, University of Leeds, UK

AJS   Anna Secor, Associate Professor of Geography, University of Kentucky, USA

AL   Andrew Leyshon, Professor of Economic Geography, University of Nottingham, UK

AV   Alexander Vasudevan, Lecturer in Cultural and Historical Geography, University of Nottingham, UK

BA   Ben Anderson, Lecturer in Geography, University of Durham, UK

BY   Brenda Yeoh, Professor of Geography, National University of Singapore, Singapore

CB   Clive Barnett, Reader in Human Geography, The Open University, UK

CF   Colin Flint, Professor of Geography, University of Illinois, Urbana-Champaign, USA

CK   Cindi Katz, Professor of Geography, Graduate Center, The City University of New York, USA

CP   Chris Philo, Professor of Geography, University of Glasgow, UK

CW   Charles Withers, Professor of Historical Geography, University of Edinburgh, UK

DCa   David Campbell, Professor of Cultural and Political Geography, University of Durham, UK

DCl   Dan Clayton, Lecturer in Human Geography, University of St Andrews, UK

DCo   Denis Cosgrove, *formerly* Alexander von Humboldt Professor of Geography, University of California, Los Angeles, USA

DG   Derek Gregory, Professor of Geography, University of British Columbia, Vancouver, Canada

DH   Dan Hiebert, Professor of Geography, University of British Columbia, Vancouver, Canada

DL   David Ley, Professor of Geography, University of British Columbia, Vancouver, Canada

DMat   David Matless, Professor of Cultural Geography, University of Nottingham, UK

DMar   Deborah Martin, Assistant Professor of Geography, Clark University, USA

DMS   David Smith, Emeritus Professor of Geography, Queen Mary, University of London, UK

DNL   David Livingstone, Professor of Geography and Intellectual History, Queen's University, Belfast, UK

DP   David Pinder, Reader in Geography, Queen Mary, University of London, UK

EM   Eugene McCann, Associate Professor of Geography, Simon Fraser University, Canada

EP   Eric Pawson, Professor of Geography, University of Canterbury, New Zealand

ES   Eric Sheppard, Regents Professor, University of Minnesota, USA

ESch   Erica Schoenberger, Professor of Geography, the Johns Hopkins University, USA

FD   Felix Driver, Professor of Human Geography, Royal Holloway, University of London, UK

GB   Gavin Bridge, Reader in Economic Geography, University of Manchester, UK

GHa   Gillian Hart, Professor of Geography, University of California, Berkeley, USA

GHe   George Henderson, Associate Professor of Geography, University of Minnesota, USA

GK   Gerry Kearns, Professor of Government and International Affairs, Virginia Tech, USA

GP   Geraldine Pratt, Professor of Geography, University of British Columbia, Vancouver, Canada

GR   Gillian Rose, Professor of Cultural Geography, The Open University, UK

GRe   George Revill, Senior Lecturer, Department of Geography, The Open University, UK

GV   Gill Valentine, Professor of Geography, University of Leeds, UK

GW   Graeme Wynn, Professor of Geography, University of British Columbia, Vancouver, Canada

JA   John Agnew, Professor of Geography, University of California, Los Angeles, USA

JD   Jessica Dubow, Lecturer in Geography, University of Sheffield, UK

JF   James Faulconbridge, Lecturer in Human Geography, Lancaster University, UK

JGl	Jim Glassman, Associate Professor of Geography, University of British Columbia, Vancouver, Canada	**LST**	Leigh Shaw-Taylor, Senior Research Associate in Geography and Deputy Director of the Cambridge Group for the History of Population and Social Structure, University of Cambridge, UK
JGu	Julie Guthman, Associate Professor, Community Studies, University of California, Santa Cruz, USA	**LWH**	Les Hepple, *formerly* Professor of Geography, University of Bristol, UK
JH	Jennifer Hyndman, Professor of Geography, Syracuse University, USA	**MB**	Michael Brown, Professor of Geography, University of Washington, Seattle, USA
JK	Jake Kosek, Assistant Professor, University of California, Berkeley, USA	**MC**	Mike Crang, Reader in Geography, University of Durham, UK
JL	Jo Little, Professor in Gender and Geography, University of Exeter, UK	**ME**	Matthew Edney, Director of the History of Cartography Project, University of Wisconsin, Madison, USA
JM	James McCarthy, Assistant Professor of Geography, Pennsylvania State University, USA	**MH**	Michael Heffernan, Professor of Historical Geography, University of Nottingham, UK
JPa	Joe Painter, Professor of Geography, University of Durham, UK	**MM**	Mark Monmonier, Distinguished Professor of Geography, Syracuse University, USA
JPe	Jamie Peck, Professor of Geography, University of British Columbia, Vancouver, Canada	**MS**	Matthew Sparke, Professor of Geography, University of Washington, USA
JPi	John Pickles, Earl N. Phillips Distinguished Professor of International Studies and Geography, University of North Carolina, Chapel Hill, USA	**MSG**	Meric Gertler, Dean of Arts and Sciences and Professor of Geography, University of Toronto, Canada
JPJ	John Paul Jones III, Professor of Geography, University of Arizona, USA	**MSR**	Matthew Smallman-Raynor, Professor of Analytical Geography, Nottingham University, UK
JSD	James Duncan, Reader in Cultural Geography, University of Cambridge	**MT**	Matt Turner, Professor of Geography, University of Wisconsin-Madison, USA
JSh	Jo Sharp, Senior Lecturer in Geography, University of Glasgow, UK	**MW**	Michael J. Watts, Professor of Geography, University of California, Berkeley, USA
JSt	Jon Stobart, Professor of History, Northampton University, UK	**NB**	Nick Bingham, Lecturer in Human Geography, The Open University, UK
JSu	Juanita Sundberg, Assistant Professor of Geography, University of British Columbia, Vancouver, Canada	**NC**	Nigel Clark, Senior Lecturer in Human Geography, The Open University, UK
JWi	Jane Wills, Professor of Human Geography, Queen Mary, University of London, UK	**NJ**	Nuala Johnson, Reader in Human Geography, Queen's University, Belfast, UK
JWy	John Wylie, Senior Lecturer in Human Geography, University of Exeter, UK	**NJC**	Nick Clifford, Professor of River Science, School of Geography, University of Nottingham, UK
KB	Keith Bassett, Senior Lecturer in Geography, University of Bristol, UK	**NKB**	Nick Blomley, Professor of Geography, Simon Fraser University, Canada
KJ	Kelvyn Jones, Professor of Human Quantitative Geography, University of Bristol, UK	**NS**	Nadine Schuurman, Associate Professor of Geography, Simon Fraser University, Canada
KM	Katharyne Mitchell, Professor of Geography, University of Washington, Seattle, USA	**OY**	Oren Yiftachel, Professor of Geography, Ben Gurion University of the Negev, Israel
KS	Kirsten Simonsen, Professor of Geography, Roskilde University, Denmark	**PG**	Paul Glennie, Senior Lecturer in Geography, University of Bristol, UK
KWa	Kevin Ward, Professor of Geography, University of Manchester, UK	**PH**	Phil Hubbard, Professor of Urban Social Geography, Loughborough University, UK
KWo	Keith Woodard, Lecturer in Human Geography, University of Exeter, UK	**PM**	Phil McManus, Associate Professor of Geography, School of Geosciences, University of Sydney, Australia
LB	Liz Bondi, Professor of Social Geography, University of Edinburgh, UK	**PR**	Paul Routledge, Reader in Geography, University of Glasgow, UK
LK	Lily Kong, Vice President (University and Global Relations) and Professor of Geography, National University of Singapore, Singapore	**RH**	Richard Harris, Senior Lecturer in Geography, University of Bristol, UK
LL	Loretta Lees, Professor of Human Geography, King's College, London, UK	**RJ**	Ron Johnston, Professor of Geography, University of Bristol, UK

RK   Roger Keil, Professor of Environmental Studies, York University, Canada

RL   Roger Lee, Professor of Geography, Queen Mary, University of London

RMS   Richard Smith, Professor of Historical Geography and Demography, University of Cambridge, UK

RN   Richa Nagar, Professor of Gender, Women and Sexuality Studies, Department of Geography, University of Minnesota, USA

SC   Sharad Chari, Lecturer in Human Geography, London School of Economics, UK

SCh   Sanjay Chaturvedi, Professor of Political Science and Co-ordinator of the Centre for the Study of Geopolitics, Panjab University, Chandigarh, India

SCo   Stuart Corbridge, Professor of Development Studies, London School of Economics, UK

SD   Simon Dalby, Professor of Geography, Carleton University, Canada

SE   Stuart Elden, Professor of Geography, University of Durham UK

SG   Stephen Graham, Professor of Geography, University of Durham, UK

SHa   Susan Hanson, Research Professor of Geography, Clark University, USA

SHe   Steve Herbert, Professor of Geography, University of Washington, Seattle, USA

SHi   Stephen Hinchliffe, Reader in Environmental Geography, The Open University, UK

SM   Sallie Marston, Professor of Geography, University of Arizona, USA

SP   Scott Prudham, Associate Professor of Geography, University of Toronto, Canada

SW   Sarah Whatmore, Professor of Environment and Public Policy, School of Geography and the Environment, University of Oxford, UK

TJB   Trevor Barnes, Professor of Geography, University of British Columbia, Vancouver, Canada

US   Ulf Strohmayer, Professor of Geography, National University of Ireland, Galway, Ireland

VG   Vinay Gidwani, Associate Professor of Geography, University of Minnesota, USA

WMA   Bill Adams, Moran Professor of Conservation and Development, University of Cambridge, UK

Editorial Advisory Board

Nicholas Blomley
Professor of Geography, Simon Fraser University, Canada

Sanjay Chaturvedi
Professor of Political Science and Co-ordinator of the Centre for the Study of Geopolitics, Panjab University, India

Eric Clark
Professor, Department of Social and Economic Geography, Lund University, Sweden

Felix Driver
Professor of Human Geography, Royal Holloway, University of London, UK

Katherine Gibson
Professor, Department of Human Geography, Research School of Pacific and Asian Studies, Australian National University, Canberra, Australia

Michael Heffernan
Professor of Historical geography, University of Nottingham, UK

Jennifer Hyndman
Professor of Geography, Syracuse University, USA

Kelvyn Jones
Professor of Human Quantitative Geography, University of Bristol, UK

Paul Longley
Professor of Geographic Information Science, University College London, UK

Peter Meusburger
Senior Professor, Department of Geography, University of Heidelberg, Germany

Don Mitchell
Professor of Geography, Syracuse University, USA

Anna Secor
Associate Professor of Geography, University of Kentucky, USA

Joanne Sharp
Senior Lecturer in Geography, University of Glasgow, UK

Eric Sheppard
Regents Professor, Department of Geography, University of Minnesota, USA

Kirsten Simonsen
Professor of Geography, Roskilde University, Denmark

David Slater
Loughborough University, UK

Gearoid Ó Tuathail (Gerard Toal)
Professor, School of Public and International Affairs, Virginia Tech, USA

Jane Wills
Professor of Human Geography, Queen Mary, University of London, UK

Brenda Yeoh
Professor of Geography, National University of Singapore

Oren Yiftachel
Professor of Geography, Ben-Gurion University of the Negev, Israel

Yoka Yoshida
Associate Professor of Human Geography, Nara Women's University, Japan

A

abduction A form of reasoning that takes accepted knowledge and infers the 'best available' explanations for what is observed. Whereas DEDUCTION formally infers the consequences of a cause-and-effect relationship (if *a*, then *b*), and INDUCTION infers a conclusion from a number of observations (of the same patterns, for example), abductive reasoning infers relationships from observations rather than asserting them. It thus presents a 'provisional' account for what has been observed (for why *a* is related to *b*), either inviting further empirical investigation that might sustain the 'explanation' or encouraging deductive work that might put the putative causal chain on a former footing.   RJ

abjection A psychoanalytic concept that describes a psychic process through which the pure, proper and bounded body and IDENTITY emerge by expelling what is deemed impure, horrific or disgusting. The abject refers to bodily by-products such as urine, saliva, sperm, blood, vomit, faeces, hair, nails or skin, but also to impure psychic attachments, such as same-sex desire (Butler, 1997) and to entire zones of uninhabitable social life. What and who is classified as abject is socially and culturally contingent; it is that which 'upsets or befuddles order' (Grosz, 1994, p. 192). The abject thus signals sites of potential threat to the psychic and social order. Abjection is a process that can never be completed, and this is one factor that creates the intensity of psychic investment in the process. The concept is of interest because it attests to the materiality of subjectivity (the constant interplay between the body and SUBJECTIVITY); the persistent work required to maintain the fragile boundary between inside and outside, object and subject; and the intimate ways in which cultural norms inhabit the BODY. Geographers have been drawn in particular to the role that abjection plays in group-based fears manifest, for instance, in RACISM, sexism, homophobia (see HOMOPHOBIA AND HETEROSEXISM), ableism and some forms of NATIONALISM (Young, 1990a), particularly in the maintenance of borders and purification of space, and in the production of the space of the exception (see EXCEPTION, SPACE OF). As one example, Jo Long (2006) interprets the efforts of the Israeli state to defend its borders from the 'leakage' of Palestinian checkpoint births and female 'suicide bombers' through the concept of abjection; Judith Butler (2004) conceives the US-operated Guantánamo Bay detention camp as a domain of abjected beings.   GP

Suggested reading
Sibley (1995).

aboriginality A term derived from the Latin *ab origine*, meaning the original founders, or 'from the beginning'. In the nineteenth century, 'Aborigines' denoted the existing inhabitants of what Europeans called the 'New World'. Today, the terms 'aboriginal peoples' and 'aboriginality' are in official use in Australia and in Canada, and in Canada it is also common to refer to 'First Nations'. Elsewhere, it is more usual to refer to *indigenous peoples*, and hence *indigeneity*.

According to the United Nations Working Group on Indigenous Peoples, the interpretation of such expressions should reflect the historical and current situations of these colonized peoples (see COLONIALISM), as well as their manner of self-identification and search for greater degrees of self-determination. However, as a construct of European MODERNITY, 'aboriginality' was freighted with connotations of 'savagery' and lack of CULTURE (Anderson, 2000a) (see also PRIMITIVISM), and its continued use also obscures the subjectivities of the heterogeneous groups to which it is applied. Indigenous peoples often had no single name to describe themselves before there was a colonizing Other to make this necessary. The Maori (meaning 'ordinary', or 'the people') of New Zealand did not describe themselves as such until they were aware of Pakeha ('not Maori' or Europeans). They knew and named themselves as members of kin-based groups, as is still the case. Likewise, amongst the Kwara'ae of Malaita (one of the Solomon Islands) self-definition is understood in relation to PLACE, genealogy, right of access to land and the right to speak (Gegeo, 2001).

Since the 1980s, GLOBALIZATION and the architecture of NEO-LIBERALISM have presented both problems and opportunities. Marginalization and loss of control of RESOURCES continue (Stewart-Harawira, 2005), but there is also potential for insertion into transnational informational and economic networks. This can facilitate steps towards indigenous professionalization and self-determination. Participation in activities such as TOURISM, oil extraction and cattle ranching by the Cofan and Secoya peoples of the Ecuadorian Amazon has opened spaces for questioning fixed notions of indigenous identities (as 'natural' conservationists of remote territories, for example). These are often articulated in different ways and contested within communities, particularly along generational lines (Valdivia, 2005).

Despite official recognition of indigenous peoples in national legislation and constitutional LAW, the practical implementation of policy remains a problem in many parts of the world. According to the United Nations Working Group in 2003, this applies in areas ranging from rights to land and natural resources to the alleviation of POVERTY. Institutionalized discrimination is pervasive, not least through superimposed definitions of identity (e.g. for census purposes or for state entitlements). State education systems have often been structured to facilitate integration or assimilation, denying cultural and ethnic diversity. Universities may be complicit. Research on, rather than with, indigenous people is seen as reproducing colonial relations, advancing the career of the researcher rather than indigenous interests. (cf. Smith, 1999b).   EP

Suggested reading
Smith (1999); Valdivia (2005).

abstraction Methodologically, abstraction involves the conceptual isolation of (a partial aspect of) an object. During the QUANTITATIVE REVOLUTION, abstraction was seen as the starting-point for the construction of spatial MODELS, but few methodological principles were provided (Chorley, 1964). Some critics of SPATIAL SCIENCE were drawn instead to the construction of what the sociologist Max Weber called IDEAL TYPES: 'one-sided' idealizations of the world seen from particular points of view. There was nothing especially 'scientific' about them, which is presumably why they appealed to the critics, and Weber claimed that this kind of selective structuring is something that we all do all the time. Since it is possible to construct quite different ideal types of the same phenomenon, depending on one's point of view, the critical moment comes when the ideal type is compared with 'empirical reality' – but here too few methodological principles were proposed to conduct or interpret any such comparisons.

REALISM rejected both of these approaches as arbitrary and substituted what its proponents saw as a rigorous scientific methodology. According to Sayer (1992 [1984]), abstractions should identify essential characteristics of objects and should be concerned with 'substantial' relations of connection rather than merely 'formal' relations of similarity (which Chorley (1964) had called 'analogues'; cf. METAPHOR). Realism turns on identifying those INTERNAL RELATIONS that *necessarily* enter into the constitution of specific structures. Hence Sayer distinguished a *rational abstraction* – that is, 'one that isolates a significant element of the world that has some unity and autonomous force' – from a *chaotic conception* – that is, one whose definition is more or less arbitrary. It is no less important to recognize different *levels of abstraction*, a strategy of considerable importance in theoretical formations such as HISTORICAL MATERIALISM that claim to move between the general and the (historically or geographically) specific (Cox and Mair, 1989). But these prescriptions turn out to be far from straightforward in a HUMAN GEOGRAPHY where 'context' cannot be cleanly severed from objects of analysis, and recent debates over SCALE have revealed the importance of revisiting issues of EPISTEMOLOGY and ONTOLOGY that are focal to the process of abstraction (Castree, 2005b).

Abstraction is more than a formal method: it is a profoundly human and thoroughly indispensable practice, as Weber recognized, so that what matters are the consequences of *particular* modes of abstraction. Seen thus, it spirals far beyond the spheres of SCIENCE and other forms of intellectual enquiry. Many critics have drawn attention to the role of abstraction in the heightened rationalization of everyday life under CAPITALISM – what Habermas (1987b [1981]) called 'the colonization of the LIFEWORLD' – and the attendant production of an *abstract space*, 'one-sided' and 'incomplete', that Lefebvre (1991b [1974]) identified as the dominant spatial thematic of MODERNITY (see PRODUCTION OF SPACE).   DG

Suggested reading
Castree (2005b); Sayer (1982).

accessibility The standard definition is the ease with which people can reach desired activity sites, such as those offering employment, shopping, medical care or recreation. Because many geographers and planners believe that access to essential goods and services is an important indicator of QUALITY OF LIFE, measures of access are used to compare the accessibility levels of different groups of individuals and households, or of different places or locations. Most measures of accessibility entail counting the number of opportunities or activity sites available within certain travel times or distances of a specified origin (Handy and Niemeier, 1997). A simple example is

$$A_i = \sum_j O_i d_{ij}^{-b},$$

where A_i is the accessibility of person i, O_i is the number of opportunities (say, the number of job openings of a particular type or the number of grocery stores) at distance j from person i's home, and d_{ij} is some measure of the FRICTION OF DISTANCE between i and j (this measure could be distance in kilometres, travel costs in euros or travel time in minutes). This equation could also be used to assess the relative levels of accessibility of different areas, such as census tracts; in this case, A_i is the accessibility of place i, O_j is the number of opportunities in place j, and d_{ij} is a measure of separation between places i and j.

As is evident from the measure above, accessibility is affected by land-use patterns, MOBILITY and mobility substitutes in the form of telecommunications. If many opportunities are located close to someone's home or workplace, that person can enjoy a relatively high level of accessibility with relatively little mobility, and will be more likely to gain access to opportunities via walking or biking rather than via motorized modes (Hanson and Schwab, 1987). As opportunities are located at greater distances from each other and from residential areas, greater mobility is required to attain access. As the cost of overcoming spatial separation increases, all else being equal, accessibility decreases. Electronic communications such as the telephone and the INTERNET enable access without mobility, although in most cases, such as that of purchasing a book from an online vendor, the cost of overcoming distance remains in the form of shipment costs (Scott, 2000b). These relationships among accessibility, mobility and land-use patterns are central to efforts to promote the URBAN VILLAGE as an alternative to SPRAWL.

The advent of GIS technology has enabled the development of accessibility measures that recognize that a person's access changes as that person moves about, for example, over the course of a day (Kwan, 1999). In addition, there is increasing recognition that the ability to take advantage of spatially dispersed employment opportunities, medical services and shops involves more than overcoming dis-tance. Gaining access often entails overcoming barriers constructed by language and culture (as in the ability to access medical care), by lack of education or skills (as in access to certain jobs), or by GENDER ideologies (which prohibit women from entering certain places or place additional space–time constraints on women's mobility). In short, lack of access involves more than SPATIAL MISMATCH.   SHa

Suggested reading
Kwan and Weber (2003); Kwan, Murray, O'Kelly and Tiefelsdorf (2003).

accumulation   The process by which CAPITAL is reproduced on an expanding scale through the reinvestment of surplus value. Accumulation of capital is possible within a variety of social structures, but for Marx accumulation was uniquely imperative within capitalist societies and therefore constituted a definitive condition of the capitalist mode of production (see CAPITALISM).

In capitalist contexts, accumulation involves reinvesting the surplus value from past rounds of production, reconverting it into capital. Marx discussed different forms of accumulation that applied to different historical and geographical conditions of production. In early centuries of European capitalism, a crucial dimension of the accumulation process was enclosure of common lands and conversion of communal or tied labour into 'free' wage labour, through destruction of independent control over means of production. Marx described this process of primitive (or 'primary') accumulation as a historical precondition for the development of capitalism (Marx, 1967 [1867], pp. 713–41), but it has also been seen in more recent Marxist scholarship as a continuing dimension of the overall process of accumulation that Harvey (2003b, pp. 137–82) calls *accumulation by dispossession* (cf. Amin, 1974; see also MARXIAN ECONOMICS).

Within the capitalist mode of production proper, the major form of accumulation is what Marx calls 'expanded reproduction.' To remain in business, any given capitalist must at least preserve the value of the capital originally invested, what Marx calls 'simple reproduction.' But, as individual capitalists seek to more effectively extract surplus from labour, they employ new means of production (machinery and other technologies), the value of which can only be fully realized through expanding their scale of operation. This spurs competition over markets, and competition in turn comes to act as the enforcer of expanded

3

reproduction. Any capitalist who chooses only to engage in simple reproduction would soon lose market share and go out of business. As Marx put the matter, 'Accumulate, accumulate! That is Moses and the prophets!' (Marx, 1967 [1867], p. 595).

This competition-enforced dynamic of accumulation shapes the geography of capitalist development. The search for new MARKETS drives investors to intensify production and consumption within given locations, contributing to the development of the built environment and transforming social relations in ways that facilitate expanded reproduction (Harvey, 1999 [1982]). It also drives investors to seek opportunities in new locations, thus giving rise to a geographical expansion of capitalist relations of production and consumption, albeit in a highly uneven fashion when considered at a global scale (Amin, 1974; see UNEVEN DEVELOPMENT). Both intensive and extensive capitalist accumulation are fraught processes that do not occur automatically, and are shaped by numerous social struggles (Harvey, 2003b, pp. 183–211). The reproduction of capitalist social relations may or may not occur in given contexts, and may depend upon a variety of factors, including the roles played by STATES.   JGl

Suggested reading
Amin (1974); Harvey (1999 [1982], 2003b); Marx (1967 [1867]).

acid rain The deposition of sulphuric and nitric acids on to land or water by rainwater. Acid rain is one form of acid precipitation, which also includes acid snow, acid hail, dry deposition and acid fog condensation. On a pH scale of 14, a substance with a pH value of less than 7 is considered acidic, while a pH value greater than 7 is considered alkaline. Rainwater is naturally slightly acidic, with a pH value of about 5.6. Acid rain generally has an average pH range of 3–5. Acidity is greatest near the base of clouds, and is diluted by a factor of 0.5 to 1 pH during rainfall (Pickering and Owen, 1994).

The English chemist R. A. Smith discovered a link between industrial POLLUTION and acid rain in Manchester in 1852, although it was known in the twelfth century that the burning of coal caused air pollution (Turco, 1997). Smith first used the term 'acid rain' in 1872, but his ideas have only been treated seriously since the late 1950s. The studies of Swedish soil scientist Svente Oden focused attention on this international issue. In 1972 the Swedish Government presented its case at the United Nations Conference on the Human Environment in Stockholm. The term 'acid rain' has been used extensively in recent decades.

Acid rain is caused primarily by the cumulative release of nitrogen and sulphur from the burning of fossil fuels. This includes coal for power, heating and industry, petrol in automobiles, and uncontrolled fires in coalfields and coal mines, particularly in northern China (Stracher and Taylor, 2004). While acid rain may occur through natural processes such as volcanic activity, it is the cumulative impact of human activities that has caused a marked increase in acid rain over the past century. Since about 1990 various Western countries have been generally successful in reducing their generation of acid precipitation, mostly through the closure of old factories, improved pollution control measures and the phasing out of domestic coal burning, but sulphur and nitrogen oxide emissions have increased rapidly in countries such as China (Cutter and Renwick, 2004).

Acid deposition is most severe in western Europe, the Midwest of North America, in China and in countries near its eastern borders. These areas have higher generation rates. Acid rain may cross national boundaries and fall several hundred kilometres from the source, particularly when tall smokestacks displace pollution from its source area. The areas most affected by acid rain tend to be downwind of dense concentrations of power stations, smelters and cities, are often in upland areas with high levels of precipitation, and are often forest areas dissected by rivers and lakes. Acid rain kills forests when acidic particles directly damage leaves, and/or when the soil becomes acidified and the metals bound in the soil are freed. The nutrients necessary for plant growth are then leached by the water. Acid rain lowers the pH value of lakes and other water bodies, which kills fish and other aquatic forms of life. Acid rain may also corrode buildings and other structures.   PM

action research A synthesis between study of social change and active involvement in processes of change, where critical research, reflexive activism and open-ended pedagogy are actively combined in an evolving collaborative methodology.

By its very nature, action research interrogates the conventional idea of the academic researcher as an isolated expert who is authorized to produce knowledge about the marginalized 'Other'. It seeks to eliminate the dichotomy between researcher and researched by involving research subjects as intellectual collaborators in the entire process of knowledge production: from agenda formation, analysis and decisions about forms that knowledge should take, to grappling with the intended and unintended outcomes emanating from the knowledges produced. In this sense, the relevance of research for social action is not primarily about helping the marginalized to identify their problems by fostering social awareness or militancy. Rather, relevance comes from deploying analytical mediation, theory-making and critical self-reflexivity in ways that allow people who are excluded from dominant systems of knowledge production and dissemination to participate in intellectual self-empowerment by developing critical frameworks that challenge the monopolies of the traditionally recognized experts (Sangtin Writers [and Nagar], 2006; see also PARTICIPANT OBSERVATION).

To avoid slipping into a romance of undoing the dominant norms of knowledge production, however, one must recognize that 'participation,' 'transformation,' 'knowledge' and 'EMPOWERMENT' are also COMMODITIES with exchange values in the academic (and expertise) market. Rather than assuming social transformation to be the ultimate goal for a COMMUNITY, it is necessary to examine critically what motivates and legitimizes the production of social knowledge for social change or empowerment and to ask whether participation is a means or an end. Poetivin (2002, p. 34) points out that participation as a means runs the risk of becoming a manipulative device in the hands of urban researchers and social activists who can operate communication techniques and modern information systems with a missionary zeal. As an end, however, participation can become an effective democratic process, enabling intellectual empowerment and collective social agency.

Until the 1980s, action research was regarded as a largely unproblematic community-based and practice-oriented realm that was less theoretical than other forms of research. But such neat separation between action and theory has been successfully muddied by geographers whose work blends POST-STRUCTURALISM with a commitment to praxis (see APPLIED GEOGRAPHY). Such writing struggles with dilemmas of authority, privilege, voice and REPRESENTATION in at least three ways. First, it recognizes the provisional nature of all knowledge, and the inevitably problematic nature of translation, mediation and representation. Second, it underscores the

importance of being attentive to the existence of multiple situated knowledges (frequently rooted in mutually irreconcilable epistemological positions) in any given context. Thus, negotiating discrepant audiences and making compromises to coalesce around specific issues are necessary requirements for academics who seek to engage with, and speak to, specific political struggles (Larner, 1995). Third, it suggests how specifying the limits of dominant DISCOURSES can generate dialogues across difference in ways that disrupt hegemonic modes of representation (Pratt, 2004).   RN

Suggested reading
Enslin (1994); Friere (1993); Gibson-Graham (1994).

activism The practice of political action by individuals or collectives in the form of social movements, non-government organizations and so on. Within GEOGRAPHY, this is related to discussions about the political RELEVANCE of the discipline to 'real-world concerns' and to practices of RESISTANCE. With the advent of RADICAL and MARXIST GEOGRAPHY in the 1960s came a concern to facilitate the direct involvement of geographers in the solving of social problems (e.g. Harvey, 1972). Early radical geographers called for the establishment of a people's geography, in which research was focused on politically charged questions and solutions and geographers actively involved themselves with the peoples and communities that they studied (e.g. William Bunge's 1969 'Geographical Expeditions' in Detroit). The development of FEMINIST GEOGRAPHY has emphasized politically committed research, including promoting dialogue and collaboration between activist-academics and the people they study, as well as recognizing and negotiating the differential POWER relations within the research process. Another central concern has been the question of whom research is produced 'for' and whose needs it meets (Nast, 1994a; Farrow, Moss and Shaw, 1995).

Since the 1990s, geographers have lamented anew the separation between critical sectors of the discipline and activism both inside and outside the academy (e.g. Blomley, 1994a; Castree, 1999a; Wills, 2002: see CRITICAL HUMAN GEOGRAPHY). Calls have been made for critical geographers to become politically engaged outside the academy, collaborating with social movements, community groups and protests, among others, to interpret and effect social change (Chouinard, 1994b; Kobayashi, 1994; Routledge, 1996b; Fuller, 1999). Because

5

activism is gendered, classed, racialized and infused with cultural meanings depending on the context of struggle, collaboration requires theorizing and negotiating the differences in power between collaborators and the connections that they forge. Hence several authors have proposed that the differences between academic and activist collaborators are engaged in relational and ethical ways, aware of contingency and context (Katz, 1992; Slater, 1997; Kitchin, 1999; Routledge, 2002). This also demands acknowledgement of what Laura Pulido (2003) calls the 'interior life of politics': the entanglement of the emotions, psychological development, souls, passions and minds of activist-academic collaborators.

Activism is discursively produced within a range of sites, including the media, grassroots organizations and academia, and this has frequently led to a restrictive view of activism that emphasizes dramatic, physical and 'macho' forms of action. Ian Maxey (1999) has argued for a more inclusive definition of activism, as the process of reflecting and acting upon the social world that is produced through everyday acts and thoughts in which all people engage. Through challenging oppressive power relations, activism generates a continual process of reflection, confrontation and EMPOWERMENT. Such an interpretation opens up the field of activism to everybody and serves to entangle the worlds of academia and activism (Routledge, 1996b; see also THIRD SPACE).

Recent calls for activist research have argued that academics have a social responsibility, given their training, access to information and freedom of expression, to make a difference 'on the ground' (Cumbers and Routledge, 2004; Fuller and Kitchen, 2004a), although such responsibility is not necessarily restricted to the immediate or very local (Massey, 2004). Fuller and Kitchen see the role of the academic as primarily that of an enabler or facilitator, acting in collaboration with diverse communities. Radical and critical praxis is thus committed to exposing the socio-spatial processes that (re)produce inequalities between people and places; challenging and changing those inequalities; and bridging the divide between theorization and praxis. They bemoan the fact that there is still some scholarly distance between geographers' activism and their teaching, as well as between their research and publishing activities, and that critical praxis consists of little else beyond pedagogy and academic writing. They posit that the structural constraints of the desire to maintain the power of the academy in knowledge production and the desire to shape the education system for the purposes of the neoliberal status quo work to delimit and limit the work of radical/critical geographers. Under such conditions, an activist geography entails making certain political choices or committing to certain kinds of action (Pain, 2003), where commitment is to a moral and political PHILOSOPHY of social justice, and research is directed both towards conforming to that commitment and towards helping to realize the values that lie at its root (see also ACTION RESEARCH).   PR

actor-network theory (ANT)   An analytical approach that takes the world to be composed of associations of heterogeneous elements that its task it is to trace. What became known as ANT emerged out of work being done within Science and Technology Studies (STS) during the 1980s by a group of scholars including, most notably, Bruno Latour, Michael Callon and John Law. Drawing on a diversity of conceptual influences ranging from the relational thought of philosopher of science Michel Serres and materialized POST-STRUCTURALISM of philosophers Michel Foucault and Gilles Deleuze to the practice-centred ETHNOMETHODOLOGY of sociologist Harold Garfinkel and the narrative semiotics of Algirdas Greimas, these authors together produced the basis of a thoroughly empirical philosophy (Mol, 2002) that has now established itself as a serious alternative to more established SOCIAL THEORIES.

Latour (2005) suggests that what ANT offers as a 'sociology of association' is an uncertainty as to 'what counts' in a given situation, which stands in marked contrast to the approach of traditional 'sociologies of the social', where the salient factors are more or less determined in advance. The objective of ANT is thus to give things some room to express themselves such that the investigator can 'follow the actors' (to quote an oft-quoted ANT rule of method), letting them define for themselves what is or is not important. In practice, of course, such aspirations are profoundly difficult to operationalize, meaning that ANT studies rarely start from a completely blank slate and instead tend to repeatedly draw attention to a number of features of the world that are usually downplayed or ignored in classic social science accounts. This has led Law (1994) to suggest that ANT is perhaps better thought of as a 'sensibility' than a theory *per se*, an orientation to the world that brings certain characteristics into view. Most notably, these include (1) *the constitutive role of non-humans* in the fabric of social life. Whether it is as 'quasi-objects' around which groups form, 'matters of concern' that animate sociotechnical controversies or 'immutable mobiles' through which knowledge travels in the durable guise of techniques and technologies, ANT takes things to be lively, interesting and important. This move can be seen as restoring agency to non-humans as long as it is appreciated that (2) *agency is distributed*, which is to say that it is a relational effect that is the outcome of the ASSEMBLAGE of all sorts of social and material bits and pieces. It is these actor networks that get things done, not subjects or objects in isolation. Actors are thus networks and vice versa, hence the significance of the always hyphenated 'actor-network theory'. Making and maintaining actor-networks takes work and effort that is often overlooked by social scientists. Callon (1986) terms this mundane but necessary activity the 'process of translation', within which he elaborates four distinctive movements. This concern with the work of the world also helps to explain the ongoing attraction of sociotechnical controversies to ANT practitioners as sites not only of political significance, but also where science and society can be observed in real time.

Advocates of ANT often express modesty and caution regarding how far the findings of their specific case studies might be extended. However, the approach itself offers a radical challenge to the organizing binaries of MODERNITY, including nature and culture, technology and society, non-human and human and so on. Viewed from an ANT perspective, these are, at best, the outcomes of a whole range of activities (as opposed to the appropriate starting points for action or analysis). At worst, they are political shortcuts that serve to bypass the due democratic consideration that our collective 'matter of concerns' deserve.

With its combination of a transferable toolkit of methods and far reaching conceptual implications, it is perhaps not surprising that ANT has begun to travel widely, far beyond the laboratories where it started into fields as various as art, law and economics. In geography, the particular appeal of ANT has been that it speaks to two of the discipline's most long-standing concerns. On the one hand, the approach has proved helpful to those seeking to enrich and enliven understanding of the relationships between humans and non-humans whether coded 'technological' (e.g. Bingham, 1996) or 'natural' (e.g. Whatmore,

2002a; Hinchliffe, 2007). On the other hand, ANT's tendency to at once 'localise the global' and 'redistribute the local' (Latour, 2005) has been both employed and extended by geographers seeking to understand how action at a distance is achieved in a variety of contexts (e.g. Thrift, 2005b; Murdoch, 2005).

Despite internal debates about everything from the appropriateness of the term (Latour, 2005) to whether we are now 'after ANT' (Law and Hassard, 1999), there can be little doubt that the sensibility, and probably the term, is here to stay – if still very much a work in progress. One indication of this is the fact that there now exist a number of standard criticisms of ANT. These include the charges that it ignores the structuring effects of such classic sociological categories as RACE, CLASS and GENDER and that it underplays the influence of POWER in society. Whether such dissenting voices represent valid concerns or are an indication of the challenge that ANT poses to traditional social science thinking is a matter of judgement. More significant, perhaps, for the future of ANT is that a number of its most influential figures have begun to address such criticisms in more or less direct ways, armed with a newly identified set of antecedents (including Gabriel Tarde, John Dewey and Alfred North Whitehead). Prompted in part by contemporary work around the edges of ANT, such as the cosmopolitical thinking of the Belgian philosopher of science Isabelle Stengers (2000) and the 'politics of what' promoted by Dutch philosopher Annemarie Mol, recent work in the field is concerned not only with how the world is made, unmade and remade, but also with the better and worse ways in which the social is and might be reassembled. Whether this marks the start of a 'normative turn' for ANT it is too early to tell, but will be worth following. NB

Suggested reading
Law and Hetherington (2000); Latour (2005).

adaptation Derived from Darwinian and evolutionary theory (cf. DARWINISM; LAMARCKIANISM), adaptation is an enormously influential METAPHOR for thinking about the relations between populations (human and non-human) and their environment (Sayer, 1979). It is a concept with a long and robust life in the biological and social sciences. Adaptation is rooted in the question of survival, and specifically of populations in relation to the biological environments that they inhabit (Holling, 1973). Adaptation refers to the changes in

7

gene frequencies that confer reproductive advantage to a population in specific environments, and to physiological and sociocultural changes that enhance individual fitness and well-being.

Adaptation has a currency in the social sciences through the organic analogy – the idea that social systems are forms of living systems in which processes of adaptation inhere (Slobodkin and Rappaport, 1974). In geography, CULTURAL and HUMAN ECOLOGY drew heavily on biological and adaptive thinking by seeing social development in terms of human niches, adaptive radiation and human ecological succession (see Watts, 1983b). Some of the more sophisticated work in cultural ecology (Nietschmann, 1973) drew upon the work of Rappaport (1979), Wilden (1972) and Bateson (1972), who employed systems theory (cf. SYSTEMS ANALYSIS), cybernetics and ECOSYSTEMS modelling as a way of describing the structure of adaptation in PEASANT and tribal societies. Here, adaptation refers to the 'processes by which living systems maintain homeostasis in the face of short-term environmental fluctuations and by transforming their own structures through long-term non-reversing changes in the composition and structure of their environments as well' (Rappaport, 1979, p. 145). There is a structure to adaptive processes by which individuals and populations respond, in the first instance, flexibly with limited deployments of resources and over time deeper more structural (and less reversible) adaptive responses follow. Maladaptation in this account refers to processes – pathologies – by which an orderly pattern of response is compromised or prevented. In social systems, these pathologies emerge from the complex ordering of societies. Cultural ecology and ecological anthropology focused especially on rural societies in the THIRD WORLD to demonstrate that various aspects of their cultural and religious life fulfilled adaptive functions. Adaptation has also been employed however by sociologists, geographers and ETHNOGRAPHERS in contemporary urban settings as a way of describing how individuals, households and communities respond to and cope with new experiences (MIGRATION, POVERTY, VIOLENCE) and settings (the CITY, the PRISON). In the human sciences, the term 'adaptation' has, however, always been saddled with the baggage of STRUCTURAL FUNCTIONALISM on the one hand and biological reductionism on the other (Watts, 1983b). Much of the new work on RISK and vulnerability – whether to global climate change or the resurgence of infectious diseases – often deploys the language or intellectual architecture of adaptation.   MW

aerotropolis   A term introduced by Kasarda (2000) referring to urban developments focused on major airports, which increasingly act as major economic centres and urban development, for both aeronautical- and non-aeronautical-related activities: Kasarda likens them to traditional CENTRAL BUSINESS DISTRICTS, with important retail, hotel, entertainment and conference facilities, drawing on wider clienteles than those who fly into the airport at the development's core. Increasingly, land-use planning focuses on airports as major economic development cores.   RJJ

Suggested reading
http://www.aerotropolis.com/aerotropolis.html

affect   The intensive capacities of a BODY to affect (through an affection) and be affected (as a result of modifications). The concept is used to describe unformed and unstructured intensities that, although not necessarily experienced by or possessed by a SUBJECT, correspond to the passage from one bodily state to another and are therefore analysable in terms of their effects (McCormack, 2003). In contemporary HUMAN GEOGRAPHY, there is no single or stable cultural-theoretical vocabulary to describe affect. It is possible to identify at least five attempts to engage with affects as diffuse intensities that in their ambiguity lie at the very edge of semantic availability: work animated by ideas of PERFORMANCE; the psychology of Silvan Tomkins; neo-DARWINISM; Gilles Deleuze's ethological re-workings of Baruch Spinoza; and post-Lacanian psychoanalysis (see PSYCHOANALYTIC THEORY) (Thrift, 2004a).

Within these five versions, the most in-depth has been the engagement of NON-REPRESENTATIONAL THEORY with Deleuze's creative encounter with the term *affectus* in the work of the seventeenth-century philosopher Baruch Spinoza (which had been translated as 'emotion' or 'feeling'). This begins from an analytic distinction between affect and other related modalities, including emotion and feeling (Anderson, 2006b), and is organized around two claims. First, affects can be described as *impersonal* or *pre-personal*, as they do not necessarily belong to a subject or inhabit a space between an interpretative subject and an interpreted object. Rather, affects can be understood as autonomous, in that they are composed in and circulate through materially heterogeneous ASSEMBLAGES. This retains the connotation that affects come from elsewhere to effect a subject or self. Second, affect is equivalent to intensity in that it does not function like a system of signification, but constitutes a movement of qualitative difference. The relationship between the circulation and distribution of affects and signification is not, therefore, one of conformity or correspondence, but one of *resonation* or *interference*.

Unlike other versions of what affect is and does, non-representational theory's engagement with the term is based on a distinction between affect and emotion – where emotion is understood as the socio-linguistic fixing of intensity that thereafter comes to be defined as personal (cf. EMOTIONAL GEOGRAPHY). The term 'affect' has thus been central to non-representational theory's break with signifying or structuralizing versions of CULTURE. The difficulties that affect poses for social analysis – how to describe the circulation and distribution of intensities – have been engaged through the creation of new modes of *witnessing* that learn to pay attention to the inchoate, processual, life of SPACES and PLACES (Dewsbury, 2003). Alongside this development of new methodological repertoires has been a growing recognition that understanding the circulation and distribution of affect is central to engagements with a contemporary political moment in which affect has emerged as an object of contemporary forms of BIOPOWER and BIOPOLITICS (Thrift, 2004a). In response, a range of work has begun to articulate and exemplify the goals and techniques of a spatial politics and/or ETHICS that aims to inventively respond to and intervene in the ongoing composition of spaces of affect (McCormack, 2003). BA

Suggested reading
McCormack (2003); Thrift (2004a).

Africa (idea of) Geography, as an institutionalized field of knowledge, figures centrally in both the history of informal and formal colonial rule in Africa and in the ways in which Africa came to be represented in the West – and in turn how the West has represented itself to itself – especially from the eighteenth century onwards. In his important and controversial book *Orientalism* (2003 [1978]), Edward Said reveals how ideas and knowledge, while complex and unstable, are always inseparable from systems of subjection. In his case, ORIENTALISM represents a body of European knowledge, a geography of the Orient, which not only helped construct an imperial vision of particular places and subjects but displaced other voices, and indeed had material consequences as such ideas became the basis for forms of rule. In an almost identical fashion, the history of geographical scholarship, and of academic geography, in particular in the nineteenth and early twentieth centuries, was closely tied to the European imperial mission in Africa. The Royal Geographical Society (RGS) was formed in 1830 as an outgrowth of the Africa Association, and Britain's overseas expansion in the nineteenth century (in which Africa figured prominently, especially after 1870) was by and large orchestrated through the RGS. Similarly, the Franco-Prussian War (1870–1) directly stimulated an increase in French geographical societies, which helped sustain a coherent political doctrine of colonial expansion, not least in Africa. At the Second International Congress of Geographical Sciences held in 1875, and attended by the president of the French Republic, knowledge and conquest of the Earth were seen as an obligation, and GEOGRAPHY provided the philosophical justification.

Africa was central to, and to a degree constitutive of, the troika of geography, RACE and EMPIRE. European geography helped create or, more properly, invent a sort of Africanism, and relatedly a particular set of tropical imaginaries or visions embodied in the emergent field of tropical geography (see TROPICALITY). Equally, Africa played its part in the debates within geography over ENVIRONMENTAL DETERMINISM, race and CIVILIZATION, and in what Livingstone called the moral economy of climate; Africa helped invent geography. The iconography of light and darkness portrayed the European penetration of Africa as simultaneously a process of domination, enlightenment and liberation. Geography helped make Africa 'dark' in the nineteenth and twentieth centuries, as it simultaneously assisted in the means (military cartography) by which the darkness was to be lifted by the *mission civilisatrice*. In a sense, then, the study of Africa lay at the heart of academic geography from its inception.

The idea of Africa and its genealogical provenance in the West is far too complex to be sketched here. Suffice to say that Stanley Crouch is quite right when he writes that Africa is 'one of the centerpieces of fantasy of our time' (Crouch, 1990). Africa was after all, in the words of Joseph Conrad's Marlow in *Heart of darkness* (2007 [1902]), 'like travelling back to the earliest beginnings of the world'. It is no surprise that one of the most important texts

9

on contemporary Africa – Achille Mbembe's *Postcolony* (2001) – begins with the statement that Africa stands as the 'supreme receptacle' of the West's obsession with 'absence', 'non being' – in short, 'nothingness' (p. 4). The Hegelian idea that Africa was a space without history has been elaborated so that Africa's special feature is 'nothing at all'. It is against this sort of dehistoricization that so much intellectual effort has been put – by African intellectuals in particular – to account for another idea of Africa, one that approaches what Bayart (1993) calls 'the true historicity of African societies'.

A history of geographers and geographical practice in the service of colonial rule in Africa has yet to be written, but it is quite clear that geographical ideas, most obviously land use and agrarian change, population growth and mobility, and environmental conservation, run through the period from the imperial partitioning of Africa in the 1870s to the first wave of independence in 1960. Richard Grove (1993) has traced, for example, early CONSERVATION thinking in the Cape in southern Africa to the 1811–44 period, which had produced a conservation structure of government intervention by 1888, driven by a triad of interests: scientific botany, the white settler community and government concerns for security. This tradition of land use and conservation was inherited by various colonial officials in Africa, and reappeared across much of western and southern Africa in the 1930s in a debate over population growth, deforestation and the threat of soil erosion. In colonial British West Africa, the rise of a populist sentiment in agricultural policy singing the praises of the smallholder and the African PEASANT is very much part of the historiography of cultural ecological thinking in geography as a whole (see CULTURAL ECOLOGY).

The relevance of geography's concern with land use and HUMAN ECOLOGY for colonial planning in Africa (and elsewhere) was vastly enhanced by what one might call the 'invention of DEVELOPMENT' in the late colonial period. While the word 'development' came into the English language in the eighteenth century with its root sense of unfolding, and was subsequently shaped by the Darwinian revolution a century later, development understood as a preoccupation of public and international policy to improve welfare and to produce governable subjects is of much more recent provenance. Development as a set of ideas and practices was, in short, the product of the transformation of the colonial world into the

independent developing world in the postwar period. Africa, for example, only became an object of planned development after the Depression of the 1930s. The British Colonial Development and Welfare Act (1940) and the French Investment Fund for Economic and Social Development (1946) promoted modernization in Africa through enhanced imperial investment against the backdrop of growing nationalist sentiments. After 1945, the imperial desire to address development and welfare had a strong agrarian focus, specifically productivity through mechanization, settlement schemes and various sorts of state interventions (marketing reform, co-operatives), all of which attracted a good deal of geographical attention. Growing commercialization in the peasant sector and new patterns of population mobility and demographic growth (expressed largely in a concern with the disruptive consequences of URBANIZATION and rural–urban migration) pointed to land use as a central pivot of geographical study.

Geography was a central practical field in the mapping of the continent. At the Treaty of Berlin (1895) when Africa was partitioned, the maps produced by geographers were for the most part incomplete and inadequate. But the harnessing of cartography to the colonial project was an indispensable component of colonial rule and the exercise of power. Cadastral surveys were the ground on which Native Authorities and tax collection were to be based, but fully cadastral mapping proved either too expensive or too political. New critical studies in cartography have provided important accounts of the institutionalized role of mapping in colonial (and post-colonial) rule and its use as an exercise of power (see CARTOGRAPHIC REASON; CARTOGRAPHY). The mapping of Africa is still ongoing and the delimitation of new territories (whether states, local government areas or chieftaincies) remains a complex process, wrapped up with state power and forms of representation that are not captured by the purported objective qualities of scientific map production.

Colonial rule in Africa proved to be relatively short, little more than one lifetime long, and produced neither mature capitalism nor a standard grid of imperial rule. Whether settler colonies (Kenya), peasant-based trade economies (Senegal) or mine-labour reserves (Zaire), in the 1960s virtually all the emerging independent African states shared a common imperial legacy: the single-commodity economy. African economies were one-horse towns, hitched to the world market through primary export commodities such as cotton, copper and cocoa. However distorted or neo-colonial their national economies, African hopes and expectations at independence were high – indeed, in some sense almost euphoric. The heady vision of Kwame Nkrumah – of a black Africa utilizing the central-planning experience of the Soviet Union to industrialize rapidly and overcome poverty, ignorance and disease – captured the popular imagination. Indeed, among the first generation of African leaders, irrespective of their political stripe, there was an infatuation with national plans and ambitious long-term planning. Health, education and infrastructure were heavily funded (typically aided and abetted by technical foreign assistance), and government activities were centralized and expanded to facilitate state-led MODERNIZATION. In spite of the fact that state agencies extracted surpluses from the agrarian sector – peasant production remained the bedrock of most independent states – to sustain import-substitution and INDUSTRIALIZATION (as well as a good deal of rent-seeking and corruption by elites), African economies performed quite well in the 1960s, buoyed by soaring commodity prices (especially after 1967).

Not surprisingly, much of the geographical scholarship of the 1960s was framed by some variant of modernization theory, or at the very least by the presumption that the processes of MODERNITY (commercialization, urbanization and transportation) were shaping indigenous institutions and practices. From the onset of the 1970s, the complacency and optimism of the 1960s appeared decidedly on the wane. Mounting US deficits, the devaluation of the dollar and the emergence of floating exchange rates marked the demise of the postwar Bretton Woods financial order. The restructuring of the financial system coincided with the crisis of the three F's (price increases in fuel, fertilizer and food) in 1972–3, which marked a serious deterioration in Africa's terms of trade. Ironically, the oil crisis also contained a solution. Between 1974 and 1979, the balance-of-payments problems of many African states (which faced not only a quadrupling of oil prices but a general price inflation for imported goods and a sluggish demand for primary commodities) was dealt with through expansionary adjustment: in other words, through borrowing from banks eager to recycle petrodollars or from the special facilities established by the INTERNATIONAL MONETARY FUND (IMF) and the World Bank. Expansionary adjustment, however, deepened

two already problematic tendencies in African political economies. The first was to enhance the politics of public-sector expansion, contributing to waste, inefficiency and the growing privatization of the public purse. The second was to further lubricate the political machinery, which produced uneconomic investments with cheaply borrowed funds.

The crisis of the 1970s helped to precipitate two major changes in the institutional and theoretical climate of Africanist geography. On the one hand, the spectre of FAMINE in the Sahel and the Horn drew increased foreign assistance to sub-Saharan Africa as a whole and to rural development in particular. To the extent that this support translated into research and programming activities in the donor countries, academics and consultants were drawn into development and applied work, in the USA through USAID, in the UK through the Ministry of Overseas Development, and in France through the Office de la Recherche Scientifique et Technique d'Outre-Mer (ORSTOM). In the USA in particular, USAID-funded projects permitted some campuses to expand their Africanist activities and encouraged some geographers to systematically explore a number of questions relating to drought, food security and rural resource use. On the other, the bleak prospects for Africa in the face of a world recession and deteriorating terms of trade, prospects that contributed to the call for a new international economic order in the first part of the 1970s, were not unrelated to the growing critique of market-oriented modernization theory and the early growth theorists, and to the gradual emergence, beginning in the late 1960s, of radical dependency theory, and subsequently of Marxist-inspired development theory (Watts, 1983a).

The precipitous collapse in the 1980s brought on by drought, famine, AIDS, bankruptcy, civil strife, corruption, the conflation of troubles, was matched by an equally dramatic rise of neo-liberal theory (see NEO-LIBERALISM) – what John Toye (1987) has called the counterrevolution in development theory. Championing the powers of free and competitive MARKETS – and by extension the assault on the state-led post-colonial development strategies of most African states – while popular in the halls and offices of the World Bank and various development agencies, was an object of considerable theoretical debate. Some geographical scholarship had certainly been critical of state-initiated development schemes, but the myopic prescriptions for free markets were properly criticized for their impact on the poor, for their dismissal of the institutional prerequisites for market capitalism and as a basis for sustained accumulation. At the same time, the adjustment had devastating consequences on university education in Africa, with the result that research by African geographers was seriously compromised. African scholarship generally withered to the point of collapse as faculties faced the drying up of research monies, compounded by declining real wages. Many academics were compelled to engage in second occupations. The most active African geographers were those who were based outside of the continent or who acted as consultants to international development agencies.

By the new millennium two other issues had, in a curious way, come back to haunt Africa, raising difficult and profound questions about the way Africa is, and has been, inscribed through Western discourse. One is rooted in debates that stretch back to the end of the eighteenth century and the other is relatively new. The Malthusian spectre (see MALTHUSIAN MODEL) hangs over the continent and has pride of place in the major policy documents of global development agencies. Some geographers, working largely within a Boserupian problematic (see BOSERUP THESIS), had explored the relations between demographic pressure and land use during the 1980s, but the new demographic debate is driven increasingly by the presumption of persistently high fertility rates (in some cases over 4 per cent per annum), rapid environmental degradation (the two are seen to be organically linked) and what is widely held to be the extraordinarily bleak economic future in the short term for most African economies. AIDS, conversely, is of late-twentieth-century provenance, but its history has been, from its inception, linked (often falsely) to Africa. While the statistics are contested on virtually every front, work by geographers has begun to draw out the patterns and consequences of terrifyingly high rural and urban infection rates in the east and central African arc.

Whether the human geography of Africa has approached Edward Said's goal to produce a geography of African historical experience remains an open question. What the most compelling geographies of the 1980s and 1990s accomplished, nonetheless, was the addition of complexity to our understanding of African places and spaces (Hart, 2003; Moore, 2005). Since 2000, there is no question that Africa has gained a newfound international visibility. Driven in part by the debt question and the efforts of the likes of Bono, Gordon Brown in his time at the British Exchequer, the New Economic Partnership for Africa (NEPAD), and the so-called ANTI-GLOBALIZATION movement, Africa is now the focus of substantial global concern. The conjuncture of a number of forces have brought the continent to a sort of impasse: the HIV/AIDS epidemic, the limited success of the austerity and adjustment reforms, a continuing decline in their share of world trade and foreign direct investment, the failure to meet the 2005 Millennium Goals, and the rise of massive cities (mega-cities) dominated by SLUMS. The Commission on Africa ('Blair Report') and the US Council of Foreign Relations Task Force on Africa Report – both released in 2005 – speak in quite different registers to the challenges that geographical scholarship and practice must speak to. The growing significance of Africa in US 'energy security', in which the Gulf of Guinea figures so centrally, is one area in which the long-standing interest of geographers in strategic resources will continue to develop. MW

Suggested reading
Cooper (2003); Ferguson (2006); Mamdani (1995).

ageing The process of becoming chronologically older, something affecting all lifeforms, but which in the social sciences becomes significant to the study of human populations and their internal differentiation. POPULATION GEOGRAPHY reconstructs the age profiles of populations within areas, noting the relative sizes of different age cohorts, and examining the DEMOGRAPHIC TRANSITION ensuing if fertility and mortality rates *both* decline and prompt the overall ageing of a population. This latter phenomenon is an oft-remarked feature of the more-developed world, with implications such as the increasing tax burden placed on the working age cohort, allied to increasing needs for specialist social, health and personal services for the growing elderly cohort (e.g. Andrews and Phillips, 2005).

Other researchers directly tackle the worlds and experiences of older people. While the broad field of gerontology (the study of such people) has prioritized a 'medical model', concentrating on the biological facts of 'senescence' (reduced mobility, deteriorating sight etc.), social scientists – looking to *social* gerontology – increasingly favour a 'social model', emphasizing instead society's progressive withdrawal from and even exclusion of its older members (as in the Western orthodoxy of 'retiring' people at c. 60–70 years). The social model acknowledges *ageism* as discriminatory ideas and practices directed at people solely because of their age, specifically when this is *old* age, the latter being influenced by negative portrayals involving 'impotency, ugliness, mental decline, ... uselessness, isolation, poverty and depression' (Vincent, 1999, p. 141). Countering such ageism, it is argued that many societies historically and beyond the West respond respectfully to their elders, regarding them as sources of wisdom, balanced judgement and effective political leadership. Many older people shatter the stereotypes, moreover, and are healthy, active and able to lead lives that are personally fulfilling and socially worthwhile. A tension nonetheless arises between the relative bleakness of the social model (e.g. Vincent, 1999), stressing the iniquities pressing on elder life, and a vision of the 'freedoms' now enjoyed by many older people as consumers buying into a dizzying variety of cultural practices (e.g. Gilleard and Higgs, 2000). Much depends on other dimensions of social being, such as CLASS, ETHNICITY and GENDER, which differentially impact the life experiences of different elderly population segments, and there is also an emerging distinction between the 'younger old' and the 'older old' (the latter, 85 + years, now being seen as the real 'other' emblematic of old age: Gilleard and Higgs, 2000, pp. 198–9).

These issues have all figured in geographical scholarship on ageing and elderly people. While CHILDREN have recently attracted concerted geographical research attention, parallel work on elderly people remains fragmented, lodged in different corners of SOCIAL, CULTURAL, ECONOMIC, POPULATION and MEDICAL GEOGRAPHIES and various studies of DISABILITY. Some attempts have been made to delineate an overall field of 'gerontological geography' (Golant, 1979; Warnes, 1990), and to examine the intersections of ageism, other bases of identity and the socio-spatial worlds of old age (Laws, 1993; Harper and Laws, 1995; Pain, Mowl and Talbot, 2000). More specific studies have considered: the migration patterns traced out by elderly people, notably to 'amenity destinations' in coastal areas, rural 'idylls' and even purpose-built 'retirement villages' (Rogers, 1992); the daily activity spaces of elderly people, including the possible diminishing of such spaces attendant on both increasing bodily frailty and loss of social roles (Golant, 1984); the everyday environmental experience of elderly people in residential neighbourhoods, particularly those of the city, including the meanings and memories attaching to the quite mundane, peopled, object-filled places all around them (Rowles, 1978; Golant, 1984); and the growth of 'nursing homes' of different kinds, with definite locational and internal spatial configurations, which can be critiqued as zones of exclusion, putting boundaries between dependent elderly people and the rest of the population (Rowles, 1979; Phillips, Vincent and Blacksell, 1988). CPP

Suggested reading
Andrews and Phillips (2005); Golant (1984); Harper and Laws (1995); Rowles (1978).

agent-based modelling An approach to understanding DECISION-MAKING and its consequences through SIMULATION models, which require substantial computing power. Agent-based models recognize the interconnections and spatial dependencies among people and places: a large number of agents make decisions that affect others who respond in a dynamic process, the outcomes of which can be identified and – in geographical applications – mapped (cf. GAME THEORY). The collective outcomes may be unexpected, even when the individual agents' decision-making criteria are fairly simple (cf. RATIONAL CHOICE THEORY). Complex patterns 'emerge' from the interaction of a large number of simple decisions, which is one of the hallmarks of the burgeoning science of complexity (Holland, 1995). In this sense, agent-based modelling conceives of the world as being generated from the bottom up, in contrast to an earlier generation of models in the social sciences which were aggregative, working from the top down (as in GRAVITY MODELS).

A classic agent-based model of spatial patterns and processes was developed by Schelling's (1971) work on ethnic residential SEGREGATION. His agents were households that had preferences for the type of neighbourhood in which they lived – such as for whites that 'no more than half of their immediate neighbours should be black'. Individuals were randomly distributed across a chequerboard representation of an urban environment, and those whose situation did not match their preferences sought moves to vacancies where the criteria were met. Schelling showed that the equilibrium solution would almost certainly be a greater level of segregation than expressed in the preferences – for example, although whites would be content if their neighbourhoods were 50 per cent black, most of them would live in areas where whites were in a large majority. With increases in computing power much more complex models can be run, which continue to provide the somewhat counter-intuitive result that segregation is greater than people's individual preferences suggest (Fossett, 2006).

Agent-based modelling is widely used in the social sciences – in, for example, modelling the spread of diseases (cf. EPIDEMIOLOGY), traffic-generation, LAND USE AND LAND COVER CHANGE, the DIFFUSION of ideas, MIGRATION, crowding in small spaces and inter-firm competition (see http://www.econ.iastate.edu/tesfatsi/ace.htm).   RJ

Suggested reading
Batty (2005); Testfatsion and Judd (2006).

agglomeration The association of productive activities in close proximity to one another. Agglomeration typically gives rise to EXTERNAL ECONOMIES associated with the collective use of the INFRASTRUCTURE of transportation, communication facilities and other services. Historically, there has been a tendency for economic activity to concentrate spatially, the large markets associated with metropolitan areas adding to the external cost advantages. Agglomeration also facilitates the rapid circulation of capital, commodities and labour. In some circumstances, DECENTRALIZATION may counter agglomerative tendencies; for example, if land costs and those associated with congestion in the central area are very high. (See also ECONOMIES OF SCALE; ECONOMIES OF SCOPE.)   DMS

Suggested reading
Malmberg (1996); Scott (2006).

aggregate travel model A statement, often expressed as an equation, that predicts some aspect of travel (e.g. the number of trips or travel mode) for units (e.g. individuals or households) aggregated to small areas, often called 'traffic analysis zones'. The data are collected and analysed for these zones, obscuring differences that may exist within zones and, because zones do not make travel decisions, rendering impossible investigation of decision-making processes underlying travel. For example, number of trips generated by a zone may be predicted as a function of the zone's average household income and average number of vehicles per household. Aggregate travel models have been fundamental to transportation planning since the 1950s.   SHa

Suggested reading
Hanson (1995, esp. chs 1,4,5,6).

agrarian question The forms in which capitalist relations transform the agrarian sector, and the political alliances, struggles and compromises that emerge around different trajectories of agrarian change. The founding theoretical text in studies of the agrarian question is Karl Kautsky's *The agrarian question*, first published 1899 (but not translated into English until the 1980s). Kautsky's focus on the agrarian question in western Europe rested on a striking paradox: agriculture (and the rural) came to assume a political gravity precisely at a moment when its weight in the economy was waning. Agriculture's curious political and strategic significance was framed by two key processes: the first was the growth and integration of a world market in agricultural commodities (especially STAPLES) and the international competition that was its handmaiden; and the second was the birth and extension into the countryside of various forms of parliamentary DEMOCRACY. International competition in grains was driven not only by the extension of the agricultural FRONTIER in the USA, in Argentina, in Russia and in eastern Europe (what Kautsky called the 'colonies' and the 'Oriental despotisms'), but also by improvements in long-distance shipping, by changes in taste (e.g. from rye to wheat) and by the inability of domestic grain production to keep up with demand. As a consequence of massive new supplies, grain prices (and rents and profits) fell more or less steadily from the mid-1870s to 1896 (Konig, 1994). It was precisely during the last quarter of the nineteenth century when a series of protectionist and TARIFF policies in France (1885), Germany (1879) and elsewhere were implemented to insulate the farming sector. New World grain exports were but one expression of the headlong integration of world commodity and capital markets on a scale and with an intensity then without precedent and, some would suggest, unrivalled since that period.

Kautsky then devoted much time to the Prussian Junkers and their efforts to protect their farm interests. But in reality the structure of protection only biased the composition of production in favour of grains (and rye in particular) grown on the East Elbian estates. Tariffs provided limited insulation in the protectionist countries, while the likes of England, The Netherlands and Denmark actually adopted free TRADE (Konig, 1994). Protection did not, and could not, save landlordism but was, rather, a limited buffer for a newly enfranchised PEASANT agriculture threatened by the world market. The competition from overseas produce ushered in the first wave of agricultural protectionism, and in so doing established the foundations of the European 'farm problem', whose political economic repercussions continue to resonate in the halls of the European Commission, the GATT/WTO and trade ministries around the world (Fennell, 1997).

The agrarian question was a product of a particular political economic conjuncture, but was made to speak to a number of key theoretical concerns that arose from Kautsky's careful analysis of the consequences of the European farm crisis: falling prices, rents and profits coupled with global market integration and international competition. In brief, he discovered that: (i) there was no tendency for the size distribution of farms to change over time (capitalist enterprises were not simply displacing peasant farms – indeed, German statistics showed that middle peasants were increasing their command of the cultivated area); (ii) technical efficiency is not a precondition for survivorship (but self-exploitation might be); and (iii) changes driven by competition and market integration did transform agriculture, but largely by shaping the production mix of different enterprises, and by deepening debt-burdens and patterns of out-MIGRATION rather than by radically reconfiguring the size distribution of farms. The crisis of European peasants and landlords in the late nineteenth century was 'resolved' by intensification (cattle and dairying in particular in a new ecological complex) and by the appropriation of some farming functions by capital in processing and agro-industry (see also Goodman, Sorj and Wilkinson, 1987: see also AGRO-FOODSYSTEM).

Kautsky concluded that industry was the motor of agricultural development – or, more properly, agro-industrial capital was – but that the peculiarities of agriculture, its biological character and rhythms (see Mann, 1990; Wells, 1996), coupled with the capacity for family farms to survive through self-exploitation (i.e. working longer and harder in effect to depress 'wage levels'), might hinder some tendencies; namely, the development of classical agrarian capitalism. Indeed, agro-industry – which Kautsky saw in the increasing application of science, technology, and capital to the food processing, farm input and farm finance systems – might prefer a non-capitalist farm sector. In all of these respects – whether his observations on land and part-time farming, of the folly of land redistribution, his commentary on international competition and

its consequences, or on the means by which industry does or does not take hold of land-based production – Kautsky's book was remarkably forward-looking and prescient.

Terry Byres (1996) has suggested that there are three agrarian questions. The first, posed by Engels, refers to the *politics of the agrarian transition* in which peasants constitute the dominant class: What, in other words, are the politics of the development of agrarian CAPITALISM? The second is about *production and the ways in which market competition drives the forces of production* towards increased yields (in short, surplus creation on the land). And the third speaks to ACCUMULATION *and the flows of surplus*, and specifically inter-sectoral linkages between agriculture and manufacture. The latter Byres calls 'agrarian transition', a term that embraces a number of key moments; namely, growth, TERMS OF TRADE, demand for agrarian products, proletarianization, surplus appropriation and surplus transfer. Byres is concerned to show that agriculture can contribute to industry without the first two senses of the agrarian question being, as it were, activated, and to assert the multiplicity of agrarian transitions (the diversity of ways in which agriculture contributes to capitalist INDUSTRIALIZATION with or without 'full' development of capitalism in the countryside). While Byres' approach has much to offer, it suffers from a peculiar narrowness. On the one hand, it is focused on the internal dynamics of change at the expense of what we now refer to as GLOBALIZATION. On the other, the agrarian question for Byres is something that can be 'resolved' (see also Bernstein, 1996). 'Resolved' seems to imply that once capitalism in agriculture has 'matured', or if capitalist industrialization can proceed without agrarian capitalism ('the social formation is dominated by industry and the urban bourgeoisie'), then the agrarian question is somehow dead. This seems curious on a number of counts, not the least of which is that the three senses of the agrarian question are constantly renewed by the contradictory and UNEVEN DEVELOPMENT of capitalism itself. It is for this reason that we return to Kautsky, since his analysis embraces all three dimensions of the agrarian question (something seemingly not acknowledged by Byres) and because he focused so clearly on substantive issues central to the current landscape of AGRO-FOOD SYSTEMS: globalization, vertical INTEGRATION, the importance of biology in food provisioning, the application of science, the shifts of POWER off farm, the intensification of land-based activities and the new dynamisms associated

15

with agro-processing (McMichael, 1996; Goodman and Watts, 1997). Of course, Kautsky could not have predicted the molecular revolution and its implications for the role of intellectual property rights and so on. But it is an engagement with his work that remains so central to current studies of modern agriculture.

The role of SOCIALISM also stands in some tension to the agrarian question. After 1917, Russian theoreticians of rather different stripes – for example, Chayanov and Preobrazhensky – posited a type of socialist agrarian question in which peasants were collectivized into either state farms or co-operatives (Viola, 1996), sometimes in practice through extraordinary violence and compulsion. There were very different experiences across the socialist world as regards the means by which socialist agricultural surpluses were generated and appropriated by the state (here, for example, the Soviet Union and China are quite different). In the same way, the fall of actually existing socialisms after 1989 produced a circumstance in which a new sort of agrarian question emerged as agrarian socialism was decollectivized – in the Chinese case, for example, gradually producing, after 1978, several hundred million peasants (Zweig, 1997).

Kautsky was, of course, writing towards the close of an era of protracted crisis for European agriculture, roughly a quarter of a century after the incorporation of New World agriculture frontiers into the world grain market had provoked the great agrarian depressions of the 1870s and 1880s. A century later, during a period in which farming and transportation technologies, diet and agricultural commodity markets are all in flux, the questions of competition, shifting terms of trade for agriculture and subsidies remain politically central in the debates over the European Union, GATT and the NEO-LIBERAL reforms currently sweeping through the THIRD WORLD. Like the 1870s and 1880s, the current phase of agricultural RESTRUCTURING in the periphery is also marked (sometimes exaggeratedly so) by a phase of 'democratization' (Kohli, 1994; Fox, 1995: cf. CORE–PERIPHERY model). Agrarian parallels at the 'centre' can be found in agriculture's reluctant initiation into the GATT/WTO trade liberalization agreement, albeit with a welter of safeguards and, relatedly, the dogged rearguard action being fought by western European farmers against further attempts to renegotiate the postwar agricultural settlement, which reached its protectionist apotheosis in the Common Agricultural Policy (CAP) during the 1980s. It is a picture clouded, however, by the strange bedfellows that the CAP has joined in opposition, including environmentalists, food safety activists, animal liberationists, bird watchers, rural preservationists and neo-conservative free trade marketeers – all of which is to say that if agrarian restructuring has taken on global dimensions, it is riddled with unevenness and inequalities (and here claims that the agrarian question is 'dead' appear rather curious). The rules of the game may be changing, but the WTO playing field is tilted heavily in favour of the OECD sponsors of this neo-liberal spectacle.   MW

Suggested reading
Bobrow-Strain (2007).

agribusiness A term coined by economists Davis and Goldberg (1957, p. 3) at the Harvard Business School, who defined it as

> the sum total of all operations involved in the manufacture and distribution of farm supplies; production operations on the farm; storage; processing and distribution of farm commodities and items made from them.

The term emphasizes the increasingly *systemic* character of food production, in which the activities of FARMING are integrated into a much larger industrial complex, including the manufacture and marketing of technological inputs and of processed food products, under highly concentrated forms of corporate ownership and management. Agribusiness has since become used in much looser and more ideologically loaded ways as shorthand, on the Left, for the domination of capitalist corporations in the agro-food industry and, on the Right, for the role of] in the MODERNIZATION of food production capacities and practices. In this looser sense it has become a synonym of the industrialization of the AGRO-FOOD SYSTEM.

The classic model of agribusiness centres on the *vertical* INTEGRATION of all stages in the food production process, in which the manufacture and marketing of technological farm inputs, farming and food processing are controlled by a single agro-food corporation. This model was based largely on the US experience, where corporations such as Cargill and Tenneco gained control of particular COMMODITY CHAINS through a combination of direct investment, subsidiary companies and contracting relationships. Numerous studies in the 1970s drew attention to its significance for commodities such as fresh fruit and vegetables, broiler chickens and sugar cane (e.g. Friedland et al., 1981). It should be noted that a rival term, '*la complexe agro-alimentaire*', coined contemporaneously in the French research literature, proposed a much more diffuse model of the industrial development of the agro-food complex (e.g. Allaire and Boyer, 1995).

The 'US school' of agribusiness research had considerable influence over the development of AGRICULTURAL GEOGRAPHY in the English-speaking world, particularly in the 1980s. But it has increasingly attracted criticism both because of a disenchantment with its theoretical debt to systems theory, and because vertical integration proved too empirically specific to support the larger claims of agribusiness as a general model of food production today (Whatmore, 2002b).   sw

agricultural geography In the second half of the twentieth century, agricultural geography has undergone profound changes, as has its subject. Until the 1950s, agricultural geography was a subset of ECONOMIC GEOGRAPHY, concerned with the spatial distribution of agricultural activity and focusing on variations and changes in the pattern of agricultural land use and their classification at a variety of scales (see also FARMING). As the economic significance of agriculture declined in terms of the sector's contribution to GDP and employment, particularly in advanced industrial countries, so interest in the subject diminished in the geographical research community. Thus, by the end of the 1980s, leading practitioners were advocating the end of agricultural geography and the dawn of a 'geography of food' (see also FOOD, GEOGRAPHY OF).

The importation of new theoretical concepts from POLITICAL ECONOMY and a shift in the substantive focus of study to the AGRO-FOOD SYSTEM as a whole, rather than farming as a self-contained activity, renewed the field of agricultural geography. Research agendas framed in terms of the agro-food system (see, e.g., Marsden, Munton, Whatmore and Little, 1986), set the parameters for a new phase of geographical interest; the initial momentum for the shift came from encounters with interdisciplinary networks and ideas, notably those of rural sociology, as much as with conversations with the broader geographical community.

By the early 1990s, researchers had taken the field beyond the farm gate in two direc-

tions. First, it had expanded to the wider organization of CAPITAL ACCUMULATION in the agricultural and food industries, focusing on the social, economic and technological ties between three sets of industrial activities: food raising (i.e. farming), agricultural technology products and services, and food processing and retailing. Second, it now encompassed the regulatory INFRASTRUCTURE underpinning these activities, focusing on the political and policy processes by which national and supranational STATE agencies intervene in agricultural practices and food markets.

The contemporary agro-food system is a composite of these various perspectives and concepts (see Millstone and Lang, 2003), as depicted in the accompanying figure. The figure illustrates the enlargement of the scope of agricultural geography from a focus primarily on activities taking place on the farm itself (B) to one spanning the diverse sites and activities of food production and consumption (A–D). In addition to emulating economic geography's enduring emphasis on TRANSNATIONAL CORPORATIONS, this broadening focus of agricultural geography includes particular attention to the regulatory agencies and processes that are so prominent in the organization of advanced industrial food production and consumption (see Marsden, Munton, Whatmore and Little, 2000).

Research within this political economy tradition has been driven by two contradictory impulses. On the one hand, it has sought to treat agriculture and food production as just another industrial sector, like cars or steel, thus aligning it much more closely with the broader community of INDUSTRIAL GEOGRAPHY and its concerns with GLOBALIZATION, corporate CAPITALISM and the so-called transition from FORDISM to POST-FORDISM. Indeed, many concerns associated with the AGRARIAN QUESTION, such as the uneven process of capitalist development, came to preoccupy industrial geographers in the past decade. On the other hand, researchers have sought to make sense of the distinctive features of the industrial organization of farming that persist, particularly the adaptive resilience of family and PEASANT forms of production (e.g. Whatmore, 1991; Watts, 1994a), and their intimate relationship with rural LANDSCAPES and national historiographies, which magnifies their political significance in the electoral and policy processes of developed and developing countries to this day (e.g. Moore, 2005).

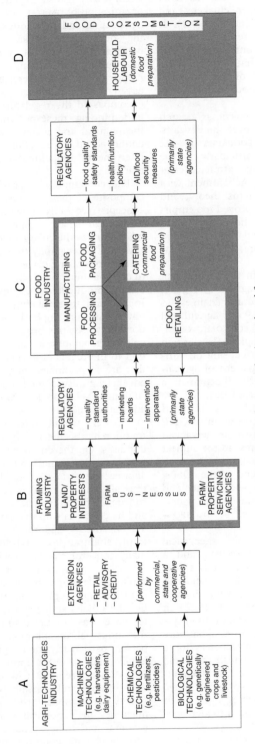

agricultural geography (reproduced from Whatmore, 2002a, p. 13)

The tensions between these two impulses have proved potentially creative, and geographers' efforts to recognize and work through them have been a major contribution to the interdisciplinary field of agro-food studies. These efforts bring quite different levels of analysis into common focus to examine the social and economic connections between, for example, global *and* local networks, corporate *and* household actors, production *and* consumption processes. The influential collection of essays *Globalising food*, edited by David Goodman and Michael Watts (1997), exemplifies these contributions. But, as this same volume indicates, the tensions between the two impulses in agricultural geography have also generated some significant analytical disagreements and silences, including a growing divergence between North American and European agro-food research in terms of theoretical influences, analytical foci and policy engagement. Crudely put, the divergences revolve around the extent to which the social, political and cultural diversity of food production and consumption processes are admitted into the compass and terms of analysis.

However, there is arguably a more widely shared sense emerging among geographers and others about the need to direct attention to (at least) three critical issues that have been eclipsed and/or marginalized by the terms of political economic analysis. First, there is the question of 'NATURE' and farming's impact on valued environments, culminating in the reorientation of agricultural subsidies (notably the European Common Agricultural Policy) towards the promotion of environmental rather than productivity outcomes (Lowe, Clark, Seymour and Ward, 1998). Second, there is the rise of CONSUMPTION as a key focus of analysis, not least in the political significance of consumer anxieties around industrial agriculture associated with a series of 'food scares' (Friedberg, 2004). Linking these two themes is a growing interest in so-called 'alternative food networks' or 'quality foods' such as fairtrade, organic and animal welfare foods. Here, attention focuses on the bodily currency of agro-food networks as they connect the health and well-being of people (both as food consumers or producers), the animals and plants that become human foodstuffs, and the ecologies that they inhabit (Stassart and Whatmore, 2003).   sw

Suggested reading
Freidberg (2004).

agricultural involution   A term coined by the anthropologist Clifford Geertz (1963) to refer to the intensification and elaboration of the agrarian labour process without substantial gains in per capita output. Based on his studies of rice paddy production in post-colonial Java and concerned with prospects for DEVELOPMENT, Geertz posited that rice production there hindered the MODERNIZATION process. Without the application of new methods, it absorbed virtually all existing labour, so that productivity merely kept up with population growth. His thesis can be contrasted with the BOSERUP THESIS (Boserup, 1965), which sees population growth as inducing technological change. (See also INTENSIVE AGRICULTURE.)   JGu

Suggested reading
Harriss (1982).

Agricultural Revolution   A collection of social, technological and productivity changes, which took place somewhere between the sixteenth and the nineteenth centuries, and which collectively revolutionized English agriculture. These changes are generally associated with the INDUSTRIAL REVOLUTION and are widely thought to have promoted INDUSTRIALIZATION, both by reducing agriculture's share of the workforce and by enabling a much larger population to be fed. The same term is also sometimes used to describe similar agricultural changes in Scotland and Wales in the eighteenth and nineteenth centuries, as well as in Continental Europe in the nineteenth century. Whilst there is general agreement amongst historians and historical geographers that an Agricultural Revolution took place in England, there is profound disagreement both as to when and where it took place, and as to what it entailed.

Writers on the Agricultural Revolution have drawn attention to one or more of three major areas of change (Overton, 1996):

(1)   A change in the social organization of agriculture, usually described as a shift from PEASANT agriculture to agrarian CAPITALISM, a process sometimes termed an 'agrarian revolution'. This process had two central features. First, there was a long-term shift away from production for use to production for sale; such commercialization clearly began in the medieval period and may have been essentially completed before 1700. Second, there was a shift away from the

dominance of small farms worked mainly by family labour to a system whereby most land was owned by large estates, let as large farms at commercial rents to capitalist tenant farmers and worked by wage labour. Both the chronology and causes of this second shift have been the subject of much debate. There is no agreement over whether the key period of change was the sixteenth, seventeenth or eighteenth century, but the primacy once accorded to ENCLOSURE is now usually displaced by causes such as population change and long-term price movements.

(2) Technical changes, particularly in the eighteenth and nineteenth centuries, have loomed large in accounts of the Agricultural Revolution. In the arable sector, the key innovation was the introduction of more complex crop rotations including clover and turnips, which provided high-quality fodder for animals, thus allowing the area of grassland to be reduced without decreasing the production of animal products. It now seems clear that these and associated changes allowed an extension of the arable area between 1750 and 1850 (Campbell and Overton, 1993; Williamson, 2002). In the pastoral sector, technical improvements were related largely to selective animal breeding aimed at increasing carcass weight, decreasing the age at maturity (slaughter) for meat animals or increasing the yields of wool or milk.

(3) Until recently, discussions of agrarian change were not informed by any direct accounts of productivity, but measurements of changes in productivity and their connection with technical change have since been placed on a more secure statistical footing (Wrigley, 1985a; Allen, 1992, 1999; Overton, 1996).

In the early twentieth century, the historiographical emphasis was on technical and social change, and the most important changes were held to have taken place in the late eighteenth and early nineteenth centuries, in parallel with what was then thought to be the key period of industrialization. Chambers and Mingay's classic (1966) account more or less repeated this framework, but its restatement coincided with a series of major revisions: Jones (1965) identified the century from 1650 to 1750 as the key period, while Kerridge (1967) argued that the Agricultural Revolution's key achievements were between 1570 and 1673. The debates have multiplied ever since.

Although recent work has generally focused on productivity, different measures of productivity have been emphasized. Wrigley (1985a) has stressed the growth of labour productivity between 1550 and 1850, and the way in which that allowed a wider restructuring of the economy through a shift in occupational structure away from agriculture towards manufacturing and services. Grain yields are known to have doubled between 1500 and 1800. Allen (1992; cf. Glennie, 1991) put the growth in wheat yields in the seventeenth century at centre stage, and in his subsequent (1999) account emphasized the growth in total food output between 1600 and 1750 and between 1800 and 1850, as well as the growth of wheat yields. Overton (1996) has emphasized three features of the century after 1750: the unprecedented increase in total food production implied by the tripling of population over any previously achieved level, a rise in overall grain yields, and the fact that these productivity changes coincided with a period of fundamental technical change. Turner, Beckett and Afton (2001) have argued that the key changes took place between 1800 and 1850, though they pay no attention to the undoubted achievements of the period before 1700.

A series of major and historically unprecedented achievements can be identified in English agriculture for every identified sub-period between 1550 and 1850, therefore, and it is probably unhelpful to isolate one particular element and identify the period of its achievement as 'the Agricultural Revolution'. Such a broad perspective sits comfortably alongside recent views of industrialization as a process that began well before 1750.   LST

Suggested reading
Allen (1992); Campbell and Overton (1991); Overton (1996); Wrigley (1988).

agro-food system According to the Organisation for Economic Co-operation and Development (OECD), 'the set of activities and relationships that interact to determine what, how much, by what methods and for whom food is produced and distributed' (Whatmore, 2002b, pp. 57–8). The most commonly acknowledged sectors/spheres that comprise the agro-food system are agrarian production itself (FARMING); agricultural science and technology products and services to farming (upstream industries); food processing, marketing, distribution and retail (downstream industries); and household food purchasing, preparation and

CONSUMPTION. In addition, those state and, increasingly, private bodies that regulate prices, TERMS OF TRADE, food quality and environmental concerns relative to food production play an integral role in shaping the agro-food system. Various analytical frameworks have been employed to specify the ways in which the multiple practices and institutions that organize the provision of food are interrelated, and even co-produced.

Among different conceptualizations of the agro-food system, one major axis of difference is whether the key organizing forces of the food system exist at horizontal SCALES or vertical FLOWS. An example of the first is the concept of *food regime*. Borrowing from REGULATION THEORY, Friedman and McMichael (1989) first employed this concept to denote the existence of national patterns of food production and trade that are periodically stabilized by distinct configurations of private, sub-national, national and supra-national regulation. An example of the latter is Fine, Heasman and Wright's (1996) 'system of provision'. In keeping with the COMMODITY CHAIN approach, they take the vertical trajectory of a given COMMODITY as the unit of analysis. In this approach, the agro-food system is best understood as a composite of all commodity systems, even though many food stuffs travel through horizontal organizations and institutions and are eaten as part of a (horizontal) diet.

A second major consideration in these differing approaches is the extent to which the natural conditions of production, the organic properties of food, and/or specific commodity characteristics are seen to shape the agro-food system. Goodman, Sorj and Wilkinson (1987) afford a good deal of explanatory power to the biological foundations of food production insofar as they posit that INDUSTRIALIZATION takes place in ways that are distinct from other key sectors (see AGRARIAN QUESTION).

A third consideration is the ontological status of the food system itself; namely, to what extent the term reifies a set of relationships that are then seen to be more determined and stable than they may be. Drawing on French convention theory, Allaire and Boyes (1995) first highlighted the importance of embedded social relations in constructing the quality of food COMMODITIES. Recently, agro-food scholars have borrowed from ACTOR-NETWORK THEORY as well, not only to recognize that food provision is more contingent, variable, fragmented and, hence, vulnerable to political change than the systemic language

implies, but also to theorize the significance of the non-human in non-binary ways. Whatmore and Thorne's (1997) discussion of alternative food networks mostly precipitated the shift from 'systems' to 'NETWORKS' as the dominant analytic in agro-food studies.   JGu

Suggested reading
Fold and Pritchard (2005); Tansey and Worsley (1995).

aid Targeted and typically conditional flows of RESOURCES aimed at alleviating specific social and economic problems and/or promoting long-term economic DEVELOPMENT. Aid may take a variety of forms, but the predominant forms, such as WORLD BANK loans and Official Development Assistance (ODA) from government agencies, are usually designed to encourage specific policy choices by recipients and are conditional upon the recipient importing specific products or services from firms connected with the donor agency.

Such forms of 'tied aid' have a long history, but have become especially important since the end of the Second World War. From that point the World Bank, which was formed along with the INTERNATIONAL MONETARY FUND (IMF) in 1945, took on a central role in providing large-scale international aid for reconstruction and long-term development (Payer, 1982; Kolko, 1988, pp. 265–77). While the World Bank was originally focused upon the reconstruction of advanced industrial economies, it came later to have as one of its main tasks the provision of aid to developing countries. Since the 1970s, World Bank loans have been offered on the condition that a number of political and economic reforms, often referred to as 'STRUCTURAL ADJUSTMENT', are implemented (Mosley, Harrigan and Toye, 1991; see also NEO-LIBERALISM). This practice has come under considerable criticism in recent years, on grounds ranging from distributional and environmental impacts to failure to involve local communities in development decisions.

Many forms of ODA have been criticized, like World Bank projects, for their effects on local livelihoods and recipient country autonomy (Gibson, Andersson, Ostrom and Shivakumar, 2005). For example, tied aid forces recipient countries to purchase goods and services from the donor country, thus subsidizing donor country exporters and forcing recipients to purchase goods.

For example, in 1990, only one of the world's 27 Development Assistance Countries (DAC),

Norway, gave more than 1 per cent of its Gross National Income (GNI) in aid (1.17 per cent), with the DAC average being 0.33 per cent of GNI. In 2003, no DAC members donated as much as 1 per cent of GNI, and the overall DAC average declined to a quarter of one per cent. For the USA, the figures were 0.21 per cent in 1990 and 0.15 per cent in 2003 (UNDP, 2005, p. 278). Other forms of emergency and short-term relief aid are provided under the auspices of a wide variety of agencies, including humanitarian and non-governmental organizations. With an endowment of nearly $40 billion in 2008, the Bill and Melinda Gates Foundation is set to become a major player among international aid agencies.   JGl

Suggested reading
Gibson, Andersson, Ostrom and Shivakumar (2005); Kolko (1988); Mosley, Harrigan and Toye (1991); Payer (1982); United Nations Development Program (UNDP) (2005).

AIDS Geographical perspectives on Acquired Immune Deficiency Syndrome, its causes and consequences, have taken three related tacks. The earliest was from the discipline's SPATIAL SCIENCE tradition (e.g. Shannon, Pyle and Bashshur, 1991). This approach treated AIDS as a newcomer in a long line of non-human infective agents (bacteria, viruses etc.), such as cholera, influenza, tuberculosis and malaria, that medical geographers could model (see MEDICAL GEOGRAPHY). Work in this tack mapped the spatial distribution, and sought to model the DIFFUSION of the disease (especially its various strains) predictively.

This approach was quickly outpaced by political and cultural geographers, who exposed the HOMOPHOBIA AND HETEROSEXISM often at work in earlier spatial science approaches, as well as reflecting a postmodern trend that challenged the primacy of science to guide geographers' approach to studying the WORLD. (For instance, this work often exposed spatial science's embarrassingly awkward encounters with culture.) Rather than reductively conceptualizing the virus as a non-human/biological entity (as spatial science had), this scholarship emphasized the virus and its syndrome as a thoroughly social, rather than biological, phenomenon. It therefore explored the multiple meanings at stake in transmission, prevention and care. It showed how various structures such as PATRIARCHY, biomedical hegemony and RACISM, in places disempower people living with HIV. It especially reframed AIDS as a POLITICAL GEOGRAPHY, raising ques-

tions of equity and SOCIAL JUSTICE in particular places. In this way, HIV-positive people were reconceptualized not as passive nodes of diffusion (with all the attendant blame), but as active agents struggling to prevent further infection, and to respond caringly and humanely to the 'glocal' dimensions (see GLOCALIZATION/ GLOCALITY) of the pandemic. In this way, geographers' complex response to AIDS was a synecdoche for the epistemological and methodological debates within/between MEDICAL GEOGRAPHY and geographies of HEALTH AND HEALTH CARE, but also the growing interest in FEMINISM and the rise of queer geography (see QUEER THEORY). It thereby accelerated and intensified links between that sub-discipline and a wide array of others. This work also broached the nature–society duality, exemplifying for some the incorporation of the BODY and disease into the exploding field of POLITICAL ECOLOGY.

Presently, work in geography continues on the SOCIAL CONSTRUCTION of the syndrome and the various social identities of SEXUALITY, RACE, CLASS and GENDER (e.g. Raimondo, 2005). In more contemporary work on HIV and AIDS, there has also been a return to a more global (or glocal) perspective (Craddock, 2000b). There has also been a much needed return to a regional focus on AIDS in AFRICA (e.g. Oppong, 1998; Kesby, 1999), but also the global South more generally, bringing the pandemic into DEVELOPMENT geography, as well as GLOBALIZATION and geographies of NEO-LIBERALISM (e.g. questions on access to expensive, life-saving drugs in the context of free trade and market hegemony; or questions of safer-sex education in the context of an ascendant social conservatism and homophobia in social and international aid policy). In this way, more recent works show a much greater appreciation of the multiplicity of social geographies of AIDS than the previous two strands of research.   MB

Suggested reading
Craddock, Oppong, Ghosh and Kalipeni (2003); Shannon, Pyle and Bashshur (1991).

algorithm A problem-solving procedure with set rules. Many algorithms can be represented as DECISION-MAKING trees and translated into computer code, allowing complex tasks to be tackled efficiently.   RJ

alienation A term derived from the Latin word *alienus*, meaning 'of or belonging to another'. Of Judeo-Christian origin, the concept became a secularized keyword in nineteenth- and twentieth-century PHILOSOPHY and SOCIAL THEORY via G.W.F. Hegel's writings, particularly his *Phenomenology of the spirit* (1808) and *Philosophy of right* (1821), and their critical adaptation by Karl Marx in his early writings (1843–5). In *Phenomenology*, Hegel contended that the object world (NATURE, RELIGION, ART etc.), which loomed independent of man's consciousness, epitomized alienation. Accordingly, absolute knowledge or freedom consisted in overcoming alienation by understanding the external world as emanation of Spirit – a facet of the human subject's *own* self-consciousness or essence. Rejecting the politically conservative implications of Hegel's philosophy, which anointed the STATE and its order of private property as the culmination of substantive freedom (i.e. as the essence and end product of man's striving for self-consciousness), Karl Marx instead proposed that capitalist production organized around state-protected private property rights and that calculative reason was *the* source of radical disharmony among individuals, who ended up estranged from their social existence; between individuals and their creative life activity or labour; and between individuals and means of production (see CAPITALISM; CLASS). The concept of alienation entered geography via the work of Bertell Ollman (1976) and his interlocutors.   VG

Suggested reading
Marx (1988 [1844]).

Alonso model   A model of the zonal structuring of land use within an urban area. Using ACCESSIBILITY (measured as transport time and cost: cf. FRICTION OF DISTANCE) as the key variable, it accounts for intra-urban variations in land values, land use and land-use intensity. Its simplest form assumes that all journeys are focused on the city centre. Land users balance transport costs to that point against those for land and property, with the highest prices being bid for the most accessible inner-city land – which only commercial and industrial enterprises can afford. The result (shown in the figure) is a DISTANCE-DECAY relationship between location-rent and distance from the centre, with residential uses (which have the lowest BID-RENT CURVES) confined to the outer zone. Alonso's now largely obsolete model of a unicentric city can be modified to accommodate a multi-centred organization of urban land use (see CENTRIFUGAL AND CENTRIPETAL FORCES; DECENTRALIZATION; EDGE CITY;

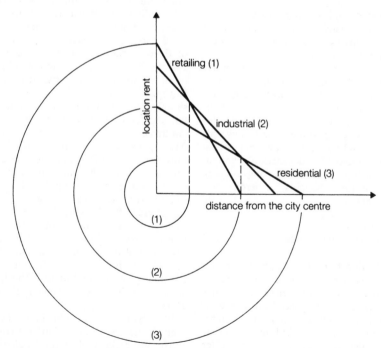

Alonso model   *Concentric intra-urban land-use zones generated by the bid-rent curves for retailing, industrial and residential land uses* (Cadwallader, 1985)

SPRAWL) and also GENTRIFICATION of inner-city, formerly non-residential areas, but is less relevant to spatial structures in which accessibility to a small number of points (usually by public transport) is a minor influence on many locational choices.   RJ

Suggested reading
Alonso (1964a); Cadwallader (1996).

alterity A philosophical term for OTHER/OTHERNESS. Rather than referring to individual differences, it more often refers to the systematic construction of classes, groups and categories. Such groups or classes are seen as 'Other' to a dominant construction of the Self (Taussig, 1993). Occupying the position of outsiders, such groups are often denied the basic RIGHTS and dignities afforded to those who are included within such cultural units as COMMUNITY, CITIZENSHIP or humanity (Isin, 2002). Alterity does not refer merely to a casting out. Instead, the logic of exclusion is such that the Other is immanent to the constitution of the dominant group.   AS

Suggested reading
Isin (2002).

alternative economies Approaches to TRADE that challenge many of the principles of CAPITALISM. As part of a broader set of critical commentaries on capitalism (see, e.g., Gibson-Graham, 1996), work on alternative economies has revealed the importance of initiatives including gift economies, charity banks and Local Exchange Trading Systems (see Leyshon, Lee and Williams, 2003). Alternative economies are often seen as a viable strategy for dealing with forms of social exclusion caused by groups being bypassed or exploited by mainstream spaces of capitalism, such as the retail banking industry (Leyshon, Burton, Knights, Alferoff and Signoretta 2004).   JF

Suggested reading
Leyshon, Lee and Williams (2003).

America(s) (idea of) The landmass in the Western Hemisphere consisting of the continents of North and South America (sometimes Central America and the Caribbean are identified as separate sub-regions). The plural form is relatively recent, providing an alternative to a singular that typically refers to either the entire landmass or the United States of America on its own. The earliest use of the name *America* for the continents of the Americas is on a globe and map created by the cartographer Martin Waldseemüller in 1507. The most popular story about the naming draws from a book that accompanied the map in which the name is derived from the Latin version of the explorer Amerigo Vespucci's name, Americus Vespucius, in its feminine form, *America*, as all of the continents were given Latin feminine names by their European namers. From this viewpoint, Vespucci (directly or indirectly) 'invented' America (O'Gorman, 1961).

Most of the inhabitants of the Americas call themselves Americans, but in the English-speaking world use of the word is often restricted to residents of the USA, a product both of the difficulty of making 'the United States' into an adjective and the political–economic weight of the USA. The majority of the population of the Americas lives in LATIN AMERICA (542 out of 851 million), named as such because the south and central regions were colonized mainly by Spain and Portugal, in distinction from North America colonized initially by the British and French. As the largest and most developed economy, the USA has long dominated economically and frequently manipulated politically the STATES and peoples in the rest of the landmass.

The discovery of America by Europeans is usually put down to Christopher Columbus in 1492, though the existence of lands to the west of Europe was mooted in medieval Europe. Effectively, however, in terms of political, economic and intellectual consequences, it is the European encounter after 1492 that is most significant, even though it was not until the late eighteenth century that the shape of the landmass as a whole was finally established. The appearance of America in the mental universe of fifteenth-century Europeans represented a crucial early moment in the creation of the sense of a geopolitical world (see GEOPOLITICS) that was increasingly to match the physical Earth. The 'discovery' was more than just the discovery of a new RACE of non-Europeans. More particularly, it was the discovery of a previously unknown landmass and with it the recognition that ancient Greek cosmology, which had divided the Earth into three parts, had been mistaken (Kupperman, 1995).

Initially, at least, as John Elliott (1972) has argued, the discovery of America encouraged European intellectuals and officials to enlarge their concept of humanity. Eventually, though, the new variety of patterns of human behaviour made for some difficulty in retaining the natural law belief in an essential and universal human nature. The increasing sense of absolute cultural difference from the natives and the impulse to exploit the new-found lands of America combined, however, to create propitious circumstances for the expansion of settlement by Europeans. To the English philosopher John Locke, writing in 1689 and providing an early example of the backward-modern conception of the stages of human social development, the Roman law known as *res nullius* applied to the 'empty lands' not put to active agricultural use by the native inhabitants and thus justified their takeover: '*America*', he wrote, 'is still a pattern of the first Ages in *Asia* and *Europe*, whilst the Inhabitants were too few for the Country, and want of People and Money gave Men no temptation to enlarge their Possessions of Land, or contest for wider extent of Grounds' (Locke, 1960 [1689], pp. 357–8; see also TERRA NULLIUS).

America was EUROPE's first 'new world'. As such, it was regarded as a *tabula rasa* for European efforts at bringing the whole world into the European world economy (Armitage, 2004). In this respect, North and South America parted company over how this was done. If from 1492 to 1776 the North was increasingly dominated by an EMPIRE in ascendancy, the British, the South was subject to two empires, those of Spain and Portugal, in long-term decay. By the late eighteenth century, local settler elites in both parts were in revolt against distant rule. As a result of their relative success, they were able by the early nineteenth century to imagine an America autonomous of Europe in which their 'political independence was accompanied by a symbolic independence in the geopolitical imagination' (Mignolo, 2000, p. 135). If on the US side this led to the Monroe Doctrine of 'America for the Americans', on the southern side it led to a developing sense of a 'Latin America' increasingly dominated by its northern neighbour, particularly as the USA emerged as a global power towards the century's end. The struggle to expropriate or qualify the labels 'America' and 'American', therefore, cannot be separated from the wider political conflict over the geopolitical consequences for the whole world of the discovery and subsequent rising significance of the 'Americas'. JA

Suggested reading
Agnew (2003); Burke (1995); Pagden (1993).

American empire As an informal form of imperial rule mediated by market mechanisms as much as by military might, American EMPIRE has traditionally proved to be an elusive object of analysis and critique (but see Williams, 1980). In the context of the Iraq war this elusiveness has declined, afflicted by the spectacle of US dominance and the protests ranged against it (*RETORT*, 2005). In the media, liberal apologists joined conservatives in promoting the Iraq adventure explicitly as a way of expanding American empire (e.g. Boot, 2003; Ignatieff, 2003), and, in the streets, amongst the millions marching against the war in 2003, many held placards that just as explicitly decried the violence and hubris of empire. However, as the playwright Harold Pinter reminded audiences when he received his Nobel Prize in 2005, the norm has more generally been silence on the topic. 'The crimes of the United States have been systematic, constant, vicious, remorseless,' he complained, 'but very few people have actually talked about them' (Pinter, 2005). One explanation for this silence is that in political DISCOURSE two kinds of 'exceptionalism' continually conspire to make talk of American empire somehow seem inappropriate. On the one hand, there is the exceptionalism of imperial denial that developed out of the anti-imperial origins of American CAPITALISM and the Jeffersonian idea of the USA as an 'empire of liberty'. Having started with the national origin stories about independence from imperial rule, this is the popular discourse that extends today to arguments that American dominance in the MIDDLE EAST is exceptional in its emphasis on freedom, free enterprise and liberal rights. On the other hand, there is the illiberal connotation that makes exceptions in the name of American 'leadership' or 'sovereignty': a discourse that argues that unique global circumstances require the USA to make exceptions and break global rules (such as the Geneva Conventions) in order to maintain global order. There is a wealth of scholarship addressing how the contradiction between these two discourses exposes the exclusions and obscured authoritarian underpinnings of liberal universalism (Cooper, 2004; Lott, 2006; Singh, 2006). By also mapping the geographies of dominance that are at once concealed and enabled by the appeals to exceptionalism, CRITICAL HUMAN GEOGRAPHY has simultaneously sought to make American empire itself less obscure (see El Fisgón, 2004).

Challenging the liberal capitalist dissembling of empire, Neil Smith has underlined how the exceptionalist RHETORICS of imperial denial have also been predicated on a form of flat-world disavowal of geography (Smith, 2003c, 2005b; see also Sparke, 2005). By promoting the US model of liberal-democratic capitalism in the terms of an 'American Century' (as Henry Luce, the publisher of *Time* magazine, did in 1941) and by recently attempting to renew and expand this world historical dominance with a 'Project for a New American Century' (as neo-conservative advocates of a PAX AMERICANA have done in the past decade), Smith argues that a focus on making global history has helped to hide the global geography of American empire. Advanced today with a-geographical appeals to GLOBALIZATION, Smith suggests that American dominance abroad is also ironically vulnerable to nationalist reaction at home (cf. Pieterse, 2004). Focusing further on the capitalist contradictions in the global system on which these vulnerabilities turn, other geographers have emphasized that American global HEGEMONY has been centrally related to the country's role as the incubator, exporter and regulator of free-market NEO-LIBERALISM on the world stage (Harvey, 2004b, 2005; Agnew, 2005a). Such work suggests that just as this hegemony was underpinned by America's centrality to twentieth-century capitalism, so too will it be undermined by the changing economic organization of the world, including the USA's increasing indebtedness in the twenty-first century.

While the political-economic geography of globalization exposes forms of American dominance that lie beneath the flat appeals of liberal exceptionalism, cultural-political geographies of American empire have in turn showed how the illiberal exceptionalism illustrated by America's contravention of laws protecting liberty has also created spaces of exception (see EXCEPTION, SPACE OF) on the ground. Derek Gregory's account of the 'colonial present' thus explores how imaginative geographies tied to ORIENTALISM have helped to legitimize the US-led re-colonization of the Middle East, turning the local inhabitants into outcasts and depriving them of human rights in the name of spreading freedom (Gregory, 2004b; see also Mitchell, 2002; Vitalis, 2002). Similarly, recent work by the American intellectual historian Amy Kaplan has provided a scrupulous legal geography of the Guantánamo military base as another space of exception that is at once inside and outside the empire of American liberty (Kaplan, 2005; see also Gregory, 2006).

Pinter the playwright argued that the double standards represented by such spaces are normally hidden backstage: 'you have to hand it to America,' he concluded. 'It has exercised a quite clinical manipulation of power worldwide while masquerading as a force for universal good. It's a brilliant, even witty, highly successful act of hypnosis.' But what comes after the wit and hypnosis when the whole world can see the torture and abuse that go on backstage? One answer is simply the end of empire, or, as the *RETORT* group put it, 'real strategic failure' (*RETORT*, 2005, p. 5). But before this happens another development, indicated by the work of Gregory, Kaplan and a host of other scholars examining American GEOPOLITICS, is an almost religious re-mapping of American grand strategy as a Manichean double vision: a world in which core capitalist countries are seen as deserving of universal RIGHTS while a supposedly dysfunctional set of exceptional spaces are seen as sites where freedom must be suspended and people dispossessed in the name of spreading freedom (see Roberts, Secor and Sparke, 2003; Sparke, 2005; Dalby, 2006; Smith, 2006b). Following this neo-liberal geopolitical script – which has a precedent in imperial British liberalism (Mehta, 1999) – American empire can continue the hypnotic 'god-trick' of universalism in the spaces of the core by masquerading as an overarching force for good.   MS

analogue   The world is too complex to represent in its entirety. Analogue MAPS or other devices produce scaled-down MODELS of the world using lines and areas to represent selected features. This is different from digital models (cf. DIGITAL CARTOGRAPHY), which can be edited and transformed using GIS and other computer programs. In analogue maps or diagrams, for instance, information is fixed. The data cannot be viewed through a different MAP PROJECTION, nor can the SCALE be changed. Analogue maps literally use analogies (lines for roads, blocks for houses, circles for towns, etc.) to represent the Earth. By contrast, digital maps display information on the screen but the properties, such as scale and projection, are not fixed and can be displayed in different formats.   NS

analytical Marxism   Scholarship using the logic and language of mathematics to interrogate Karl Marx's theory of CAPITALISM (and other MODES OF PRODUCTION) for theoretical and/or empirical analysis (see MARXISM). In the three volumes of *Capital*, Marx drew at times extensively on mathematical examples to explicate his theory of value, as well as on quantitative information about poverty and capital–labour relations in nineteenth-century Britain. Marx has been criticized by mainstream economists for mathematical incompetence, particularly for errors in his 'transformation problem', which sought somewhat unsuccessfully to show that prices of production (long-run market prices) are determined by labour values. Sraffa (1960) demonstrated, however, that neo-classical macroeconomics had the same mathematical limitations, being only logically correct if production technologies are identical in every sector of the economy. Morishima showed that Marx's theory of exploitation can be deduced mathematically from his theory of capitalism: capitalists can only make positive monetary profits if labour is exploited in labour value terms. This triggered scholarship in analytical Marxism.

In economics and sociology, analytical Marxism stressed developing deductive theories consistent with Marx's theorization of capitalism. Much of this work, pioneered by John Roemer, John Elster, George Cohen and Erik Olin Wright, is grounded in RATIONAL CHOICE THEORY – the belief that macro-features of society are the consequence of the self-interested actions of informed, rational economic actors. Taking the same starting point as NEO-CLASSICAL ECONOMICS, remarkably they show that under Marxian assumptions a very different view of capitalism emerges. Exploitation occurs, the opposed economic interests of workers and capitalists generate CLASS struggle over the economic surplus, capitalism is unstable, and individuals choose to join exploiting and exploited classes because of initial wealth and endowment differences. These scholars have rejected Marx's labour theory of value. Empirically, however, observed long-term market prices are indeed closely correlated with labour values, suggesting that such rejection is premature. These rational choice Marxists are criticized for their grounding in rational choice behaviour, and insistence on deductive reasoning, which are seen as inconsistent with Marx's dialectical logic (see DIALECTIC: see also Roemer, 1982, 1986b; Carver and Thomas, 1995).

Geographers have applied mathematical reasoning to a Marxian analysis of the capitalist SPACE-ECONOMY, without grounding this in individual rational choice. Like Harvey's dialectical analysis, Sheppard and Barnes (1990) demonstrate that the incorporation of

SPACE complicates some of Marx's theoretical propositions. Space further destabilizes the capitalist dynamics of UNEVEN DEVELOPMENT, increases the likelihood that the interests of individual capitalists are in conflict with class interests and catalyses conflict between places that can undermine class dynamics. Equilibrium analysis is thus of little value, as equilibria are most unlikely and always unstable. Unlike Harvey, it is deduced that space undermines labour value as the foundation of Marxian analysis. Empirically, Webber and Rigby (1996) show that FORDISM was not the golden age of postwar capitalism, *contra* regulation theory. Recent advances in COMPLEXITY THEORY suggest that mathematical analysis of complex systems such as capitalism approximates many aspects of dialectical reasoning, suggesting that Marx's own resort to mathematics was not in tension with his philosophical approach. ES

Suggested reading
Roemer (1986); Sheppard and Barnes (1990).

anarchism A political PHILOSOPHY that is anti-authoritarian, seeking the elimination of the STATE and its replacement by a decentralized social and political self-governing social order. Anarchist social order is not the absence of government, but a form of self-government that does not demand obedience. It is a mixture of libertarian, utopian and SOCIALIST ideas that counters POWER and hierarchy through voluntary, and usually local, decentralized COMMUNITIES. Cook (1990) identified five different forms of anarchism – individualism, collectivism, anarchist COMMUNISM, anarcho-syndicalism and pacifism. Anarcho-feminism and SITUATIONISM are also relevant varieties of anarchism that have been utilized by geographers. Geographers Peter Kropotkin and Elisée Reclus were among the early proponents of anarchist COMMUNISM. Both were active members of the academic geography community in the late 1800s and early 1900s (Kearns, 2004), though their political leanings were ignored as 'baggage' by the geography establishment, which was focused upon imperial and national projects (MacLaughlin, 1986). Kropotkin's belief that 'the duty of socially-concerned scientists lay in articulating the interests of subordinate social classes and combating poverty, underdevelopment and social justice' (quoted in MacLaughlin, 1986, p. 25) lay at the heart of the RADICAL GEOGRAPHY that emerged in the late 1970s. However, the initial identification of anarchism as a philosophical basis for radical geography was short-lived, and in the late 1970s its influence declined (Peet, 1977b; Peet and Thrift, 1989). More recently, Blunt and Wills' (2000) identification of radical geography's attention to anarchism as facilitating the 'breakthrough' to MARXISM echoes Peet's sentiments, but they also highlight Emma Goldman's contribution to anarcho-feminism and its role in stimulating FEMINIST GEOGRAPHIES.

However, there has been renewed interest in the philosophy and practice of anarchism in explaining contemporary human geography. Sibley (2001) has identified the importance of anarchist theory in promoting the challenge to binary thinking that has developed into the concept of THIRD SPACE. Bonnett's (1996) study of SITUATIONISTS (a political force that was particularly active in the 1960s, seeking a 'new human geography' by critiquing contemporary URBANISM, PLANNING and architecture) focuses upon the creation of politicized urban spaces as a way of challenging authority. Economic geographers interested in contemporary resistance to neo-liberalist GLOBALIZATION have identified the creation of autonomous geographies that are underpinned by anarchist principles. Chatterton's (2005) study of workers' co-operatives in Argentina defines three autonomous geographies: a territorial geography of networked autonomous NEIGHBOURHOODS, a material geography of mutual aid, and a SOCIAL GEOGRAPHY of daily practice and interaction. Following the tension in anarchism between individual freedom and social action, Chatterton shows how the groups try to manage their interaction with the rest of the world while simultaneously creating a network of autonomous places. Taylor (2004a) has taken a more structural approach to anarchism in identifying GLOBAL CITIES as a basis for resisting state power. Blunt and Wills' claim that anarchist ideas have 'spawned only the outlines of a tradition of geographical scholarship and there is plenty of scope for further elaboration' (2000, p. 2) is still true, but there are signs that urban, economic and political geographers find contemporary changes a catalyst for elaboration.   CF

Suggested reading
Blunt and Wills (2000); Peet (1977).

androcentricity Viewing the world from a male perspective. Some feminist theorists view mainstream scholarship or science such as geography as androcentric, in that what is presented as a gender-neutral analysis or method, in practice embodies masculine values and assumptions (e.g. Rose, 1993; see also FEMINIST GEOGRAPHIES). Eichler (1988) outlines six types of androcentricity: male frame of reference; locating men as agents and women as objects; female invisibility; maintaining male over female interests; misogyny; and defending male dominance. She also traces five manifestations of androcentricity in the research process (see MASCULINISM).   SW

Suggested reading
Eichler (1988); Rose (1993).

Anglocentrism An attitude that unreflexively assumes the superiority of KNOWLEDGE produced in Anglo-American contexts (see also ETHNOCENTRISM; EUROCENTRISM). In contemporary geography it refers to a debate – in particular, within CRITICAL HUMAN GEOGRAPHY – addressing the social and epistemological mechanisms that construct an 'international' writing space imbued with Anglo-American HEGEMONY. The debate mostly has been performed at International Conferences of Critical Geography and in commentaries and editorials in 'international' journals (e.g. Berg and Kearns, 1998; Minca, 2000; Braun, Vaiou, Yiftachel, Sakho, Chaturvedi, Timar and Minca, 2003; Geoforum, 2004).

This Anglo-American hegemony does not work as an intentional domination of debates, nor is it something to be accepted as inevitable – it is the outcome of a series of POWER-constituting practices. One of these is LANGUAGE. To an increasing extent, English has become the lingua franca of 'international' academic (and other) discourses, a practice giving precedence to some while putting 'others' in a position where they have to cope with the burden of translation and struggle to communicate thoughts and concepts in an idiom that to them is a secondary skill. This is not only about translation in a literal sense, because no language is a neutral medium; the adoption of any language has a range of cultural and conceptual consequences. The question of language therefore folds into a much broader power–knowledge system, which constitutes geographical writing spaces including Anglophone journals, books, conferences, seminars and so on. In these writing spaces, power and knowledge connect, through the media of language, institutional arrangements and social practices of inclusion/exclusion and through the political economy of international publishing, to produce a 'centre–periphery' imaginary with regard to the relationship between

Anglo-American and non-Anglo-American writers. Notwithstanding an increased sensitivity to SITUATED KNOWLEDGE in contemporary geography, these practices, connected to an implicitly supposed neutrality of concepts and categories, tend to conceal the partiality and local character of Anglo-American theoretical production and reproduce it as 'unlimited', 'universal' or at least 'transferable'. The 'master-subject' of geographical theory is constructed as Anglo-American, with more inferior subject-positions left open to writers from 'other' places. Contributions from outside the Anglophone world are at one level welcome, but the authors tend to be seen, not as theory-producing subjects, but rather as providers of 'case-studies-from-another-place'. The non-Anglo-American writer is constructed as a mediator or translator, often in a double sense; on the one hand 'translating' travelling Anglo-American theory and putting it into use in 'other' contexts, and on the other one 'translating' the unknown and exotic 'other' and making it accessible to the powerful knower in the centre.

Geographical writings based in FEMINISM and POST-COLONIALISM have in many ways identified and challenged this power–knowledge system. Even they, however, are not immune from the charges made in the debate. Like any dominant DISCOURSE, they have difficulties destabilizing their own power position. But the very existence of the debate can be seen as a promising opening; in particular, to the extent that it is based on common recognition and works against the hegemony from 'inside' and 'outside' alike.   KS

Suggested reading
Gregson, Simonsen and Vaiou (2003); Paasi (2005).

animals Once of marginal concern to geography, animals, their places, welfare, relationships and spatialities have recently become areas of debate and innovation. Attention has been buoyed by growing social concerns for animals and the, albeit problematic, growth in animal rights literature. Moreover, developments in SOCIAL THEORY that have (a) deconstructed the human, exposing the indistinct character of the divides between humans and animals (Agamben, 2002), and (b) reconstructed animals, affording them active roles in constituting their environments, bodies and relationships (see ACTOR-NETWORK THEORY, NON-REPRESENTATIONAL THEORY), have started to unsettle the human of HUMAN GEOGRAPHY.

While antecedents of this new animal geography certainly existed in CULTURAL ECOLOGY and studies of DOMESTICATION (Tuan, 1984), the most important shift in the place of animals in geography occurred in the 1990s, through a series of innovative papers that aimed to bring the animals back in (Wolch and Emel, 1995, 1998; Philo and Wilbert, 2000). This work covered a range of topics focusing on spaces of exclusion of, and human cohabitation with, animals. One difficulty in this work was to devise means of talking about animals themselves, rather than reducing non-human animals to having bit parts in human history (and thereby inadvertently reproducing the Cartesian and Kantian notions of non-human animals as automata, and as means to human ends). It is here that the work of a whole range of approaches that share something with POST-STRUCTURALISM has been most productive in affording animals their own histories and geographies. The work of anthropologists, particularly that of Tim Ingold, highlighted the similarities between human and non-human animals' dwelling practices (Ingold, 2000). DE-CONSTRUCTION of the terms 'human' and 'animal' afforded insights into the role that the singular noun 'the animal' has played in what Jacques Derrida has called the sacrificial structure of human supremacy (Derrida, 2003). Finally, work informed by understandings and tracings of the material and cultural associations of human and non-human animals has demonstrated complex histories and geographies of sharing (molecules, viruses, flesh), accommodating, adapting, hostilities and hospitalities (Haraway, 2003). The resulting HYBRID forms are multiple, leading not to some undifferentiated human/non-human amalgam, but to worlds wherein non-human and human animals differentiate themselves at the same time as they form close relationships (Whatmore, 2002a).   SJH

Suggested reading
Wolch and Emel (1998); Wolfe (2003).

Annales School An interdisciplinary school of French historians established by Lucien Febvre and Marc Bloch, co-founders in 1929 of the journal *Annales d'histoire économique et sociale* (now *Annales. Économies. Sociétés. Civilisations*). The *Annalistes*, originally based in Strasbourg (a German city from 1871 to 1918) developed an integrative, synthesizing and distinctively French style of 'total history', in opposition to German historical methods. Drawing ideas from sociology,

29

anthropology and HUMAN GEOGRAPHY, the *Annalistes* insisted that short-term political events must be understood in relation to long-term structural economic, social and environmental change. The writings of Fernand Braudel (1902–85) exemplify this approach, which continues to be significant in both French social science and in the (stylistically very different) transatlantic development of WORLD-SYSTEMS ANALYSIS.   MJH

Suggested reading
Baker (1984); Clark (1999b); Friedman (1996).

anthropogeography A school of HUMAN GEOGRAPHY closely associated with the German geographer Friedrich Ratzel (1844–1904: see Bassin, 1987b). Ratzel had trained in the natural sciences and, like many of his contemporaries, was taken by the ideas of DARWINISM (see also LAMARCK(IAN)ISM). Following an extended visit to the USA, however, it was clear that his imagination had also been captured by anthropology. On the marchlands between the natural sciences and anthropology, he now 'sought to lay out the conceptual foundations of a new discipline – human geography' (Livingstone, 1992, p. 198). Its central statement was in the two volumes of his *Anthropogeographie*, published in 1882 and 1891, the first subtitled 'Geography's application to history' and the second 'The geographical distribution of mankind'. These volumes have to be placed in the context of the contemporary debates within the German intellectual community over the place of the cultural sciences and their relation to the natural sciences (Smith, 1991). Ratzel's achievement was to put 'the human' back into GEOGRAPHY: in his view, the discipline could not be assimilated to the natural sciences but, on the contrary, had to explore the reciprocal relations between 'CULTURE' and 'NATURE'. It also had to set those relations in motion by recognizing the dynamics of spatial formations (notably DIFFUSION and MIGRATION).

Ratzel's project was thus not ENVIRONMENTAL DETERMINISM, as some commentators have suggested, but it was distinguished by the attempt to elaborate a series of nominally scientific concepts whose significance extended beyond the formalization of an academic discipline. For Ratzel, writing in the middle of what Bassin (1987c) describes as an 'imperialist frenzy', the development of a STATE could not be separated from its spatial growth. Natter (2005) is thus surely right to say that Ratzel's *Anthropogeographie* 'bleeds

into' his *Politische Geographie*, published in 1897. Indeed, Ratzel himself saw *Anthropogeographie* as only a preliminary stage in the foundation of 'the science of POLITICAL GEOGRAPHY'. In his *Politische Geographie*, Ratzel accordingly described the state as 'a living body which has extended itself over a part of the Earth and has differentiated itself from other bodies which have similarly expanded'. The object of these extensions and expansions was always 'the conquest of SPACE', and it was this that became formalized in the concept of *LEBENSRAUM* ('living space'): 'the geographical area within which living organisms develop'. Ratzel was keenly aware of the dangers of organicism, but even so insisted that: 'Just as the struggle for existence in the plant and animal world always centres about a matter of space, so the conflicts of nations are in great part only struggles for TERRITORY' (see also GEOPOLITICS).

Wanklyn (1961) treats *Lebensraum* as 'a fundamental geographical concept', and in her eyes Ratzel's writings were directed primarily towards 'thinking out the scope and content of biogeography'. This is to understand BIOGEOGRAPHY in a highly particular way, but there is a more general tradition of biogeographical reflection within human geography that suggests affinities between Ratzel's *Lebensraum*, Paul Vidal de la Blache's *genre de vie* and the concept of *rum* ('room') developed in Torsten Hägerstrand's TIME-GEOGRAPHY. If these affinities are recognized, then Dickinson's (1969) view of Ratzel's original formulation, stripped of its subsequent distortions by the Third Reich, as 'one of the most original and fruitful of all concepts in modern geography', becomes peculiarly prescient. But such a purely 'scientific' reading does scant justice to the context in which Ratzel was working and, in particular, ignores the fact that his vision of human geography not only had political implications but also rested on – and indeed was made possible by – a series of political assumptions (Bassin, 1987b). Crucially, Farinelli (2000, p. 951) insists that through Ratzel's reformulations 'the state takes possession of geography, and becomes its supreme object'.   DG

Suggested reading
Farinelli (2000); Natter (2005).

anti-development A body of work and practice that is fundamentally opposed to mainstream conceptions of DEVELOPMENT. Standard accounts of development assume that people's lives will be improved to the extent that they are linked to others by efficient systems of economic production and exchange, and by capable systems of government. Development presumes an extension of scale in social life. With this comes a surrender of POWER to experts and more abstract social forces such as the financial system or the STATE. Anti-developmentalists have opposed these notions for several reasons. As early as 1908, Mohandas Gandhi raged against the introduction of manufacturing into India in his essay *Hind Swaraj* (Gandhi, 1997 [1908]). It was dehumanizing, he said, and removed the possibility of living a virtuous life, which revolved around self-provisioning and religious contemplation in a village setting. There are echoes of this complaint in Tolstoy and Ruskin and other parts of the Western pastoral tradition.

Modern anti-developmentalism continues to draw on Gandhi, but it also draws on more contemporary critiques by Schumacher, Illich, Berry and others. For the Indian public intellectual Ashis Nandy (2003), developmentalism is a violent set of social practices that denies space to other accounts of being human. The violence that Nandy refers to is an originary violence that resides in the will to power that development must embody. By this yardstick, efforts to promote human development or SUSTAINABLE DEVELOPMENT are oxymoronic. Development is opposed to humanity and to forms of life lived in harmony with other beings, and hence the call for its negation. Other versions of anti-development strike a more populist note. Development is condemned less for its intrinsic violence – for creating what Esteva and Prakash (1998) call the 'cold calling-card mentality of the modern West' – than for its self-satisfied service on behalf of the global rich. In the words of Gustavo Esteva, 'If you live in Rio or Mexico City, you need to be very rich or very stupid not to notice that development stinks.'

Critics of anti-development believe that it is all but impossible to opt out of some version of development, and/or that some versions of development have empowered poorer people in countries as diverse as Costa Rica, Botswana and Taiwan (Kiely, 1999). Life expectancies in India and China increased by more than twenty-five years over the period from 1950 to 2000, the so-called 'Age of Development'. If there is room for criticism of 'the' development DISCOURSE, it needs to be promoted within the framework of POST-DEVELOPMENT, or as a series of alternatives to mainstream conceptions of development. SCO

Suggested reading
Nandy (2003); Power (2003).

anti-globalization A set of political positions that articulate RESISTANCE and alternatives to neo-liberal or capitalist GLOBALIZATION. A range of international initiatives have cohered since the 1970s, such as the international anti-corporate boycott of Nestlé between 1977 and 1984, the riots against INTERNATIONAL MONETARY FUND (IMF) STRUCTURAL ADJUSTMENT programmes throughout the global South during the 1980s and the formation of *Via Campesina* – an international farmers' network (Starr, 2005). A key moment was the emergence in 1994 of the *Zapatista* rebellion in Chiapas, Mexico, which has demanded indigenous rights and the democratization of Mexican civil and political society, as well as articulating both a critique of the globally dominant economic process of NEO-LIBERALISM, and a vision of an alternative politics (Routledge, 1998).

The emergence of neo-liberal globalization as the globally hegemonic economic model has prompted the upscaling of previously local struggles – between citizens and governments, international institutions and transnational corporations – to the international level, as marginalized groups and SOCIAL MOVEMENTS have begun to forge global networks of action and solidarity. 'Anti-globalization' is a misnomer, since such groups struggle for inclusive, democratic forms of globalization, using the communicative tools of the global system such as the INTERNET. What they are expressly against is the neo-liberal form of globalization. Hence a more accurate term is 'grassroots globalization' (Appadurai, 2000), although other popular names have included 'globalization-from-below' (Brecher, Costello and Smith, 2000), 'movement of movements' (Mertes, 2004) and the global justice movement (see www.globaljusticemovement.net).

By taking part in grassroots globalization NETWORKS, activists from participant movements and organizations embody their particular places of political, cultural, economic and ecological experience with common concerns, which lead to expanded spatiotemporal horizons of action (Reid and Taylor, 2000). Such coalitions of different interests are necessarily contingent and context-dependent, forms of solidarity being diverse, multiple, productive and contested (Braun and Disch,

2002; Featherstone, 2003; Mertes, 2004). They are dynamic, negotiated 'convergence spaces' of multiplicity and difference, constructed out of a complexity of interrelations and interactions across all spatial scales (Routledge, 1998).

Grassroots globalization networks have been manifested in 'global days of action', which have consisted of demonstrations and direct actions against targets that symbolize neo-liberal power, such as the G8 (e.g. protests in Genoa, Italy, in 2001 and Gleneagles, Scotland, in 2005), the WORLD TRADE ORGANIZATION (protests in Seattle, USA, in 1999, Cancun, Mexico, in 2003 and Hong Kong in 2005) and the World Bank and the IMF (e.g. protests in Prague, Czech Republic, in 2000 and Washington, USA, in 2002 and 2005). Such protests have been characterized by a convergence of interests and concerns in the particular place of protest, and solidarity protests that have occurred in cities across the globe at the same time. The symbolic force generated by protests in such places has contributed to further mobilizations and the creation of common ground amongst activists.

Another important manifestation has been the establishment in 2001 of the WORLD SOCIAL FORUM (WSFM) – an annual convergence of NGOs, trades unions, social movements and other resistance networks in Porto Alegre, Brazil (2001–3), and subsequently in Mumbai, India (2004). The WSF attempts to engender a process of dialogue and reflection, and the transnational exchange of experiences, ideas, strategies and information concerning grassroots globalization. The WSF (which attracted tens of thousands of participants in 2003) has decentralized into regional and thematic forums that are being held in various parts of the world, such as the European Social Forum in Florence, Italy (2002), the Asian Social Forum in Hyderabad, India (2003), and the Thematic Forum on Drugs, Human Rights and Democracy in Cartagena, Colombia (2003) (Sen, Anand, Escobar and Waterman, 2004).

Mary Kaldor (2003) posits that such developments represent the emergence of a 'global CIVIL SOCIETY' that includes at least six different types of political actor that are 'anti-globalization' in outlook: more traditional social movements such as trades unions; more contemporary social movements such as women's and environmental movements; NGOs such as Amnesty International; transnational civic networks such as the International Rivers Network; 'new' nationalist and fundamentalist movements such as *Al Qaeda*; and the anti-capitalist movement. Meanwhile, Amory Starr (2000) identifies at least three different strategic foci within the 'anti-globalization movement': (i) *Contestation and Reform*, which involves social movements and organizations that seek to impose regulatory limitations on corporations and or governments, or force them to self-regulate, mobilizing existing formal democratic channels of protest (e.g. Human Rights Watch and the Fair Trade network); (ii) *Globalization from Below*, whereby various social movements and organizations form global alliances around such issues as environmental degradation, the abuse of HUMAN RIGHTS and labour standards, to make corporations and governments accountable to people instead of elites (e.g. the *Zapatistas*, labour unions or the WSF); and (iii) *De-linking, Relocalization and Sovereignty*, whereby varied initiatives articulate the pleasures, productivities and rights of localities and attempt to de-link local economies from corporate-controlled national and international economies (e.g. permaculture initiatives, community currency, community credit organizations, sovereignty movements – especially those of indigenous peoples – and various religious nationalisms; see also Hines, 2000).

Despite such diversity, certain key areas of agreement have emerged, such as demands for (i) the cancellation of foreign debt in the developing world (which amounted to US $3,000 billion in 1999); (ii) the introduction of a tax on international currency transactions, and controls on capital flows; (iii) the reduction in people's working hours and an end to child labour; (iv) the defence of public services; (v) progressive taxation to finance public services and redistribute wealth and income; (vi) the international adoption of enforceable targets for greenhouse emissions and large-scale investment in renewable energy; (vii) policies that ensure land, water and food sovereignty for PEASANT and indigenous people; and (viii) the defence of civil liberties (Callinicos, 2003; Fisher and Ponniah, 2003). At the root of such demands is the perceived necessity to reclaim and protect common RESOURCES and RIGHTS seen as directly under threat of erasure or appropriation by the processes and agents of neo-liberal globalization. PR

anti-humanism A critique of HUMANISM that seeks to displace the human subject as the centre of philosophical and social enquiry. Knowledge and understanding, morality and ethics, and interpretation are all challenged by a rethinking of notions of agency, rationality and subjectivity. While 'anti-humanism' is a term that can encompass a range of different perspectives, it generally takes its philosophical basis from Friedrich Nietzsche's thinking through of the death of God. For Nietzsche, it was not enough to replace God at the centre with the human but, rather, the implications needed to be thought through more fundamentally. Martin Heidegger's 1947 'Letter on Humanism' (see Heidegger, 1991[1947]) was a major influence on a generation of French writers such as Michel Foucault (1970 [1966]) and Jacques Derrida (1982b), collectively identified under the sign of POST-STRUCTURALISM, whose reformulations proved influential in the Anglophone academy. The white, male, heterosexual adult who is generally a cipher for the 'human' of classical humanism has also been criticized from a range of perspectives. Not all of these take the strong anti-humanist perspective that denies agency and responsibility, which is often seen as politically disabling, but the challenge to the universalizing tendencies of classical humanist reasoning has been pervasive. In HUMAN GEOGRAPHY, this critique has led to a broadly understood POSTHUMANIST tradition.   SE

Suggested reading
Soper (1986).

apartheid A political and legal system of racial classification, spatial separation and discrimination against black South Africans. Associated with the white minority National Party that came to power in 1948, apartheid policies built on pre-existing forms of racial SEGREGATION and DISPOSSESSION, but took them in new directions.

Dismissing presumptions of South African exceptionalism, Mamdani (1996) maintains that apartheid was simply a variant of indirect rule through which colonial power operated in other parts of AFRICA (see COLONIALISM). While acknowledging these continuities, Alexander (2002, p. 140) insists that 'the fact of a large population of European descent [...] *does* make all the difference'. So, too, do the interconnections between institutionalized RACISM and forms of CLASS exploitation that characterized apartheid.

Apartheid officially died in 1994, when the African National Congress (ANC) received overwhelming support in South Africa's first non-racial election, which marked the transition to liberal DEMOCRACY. Yet apartheid retains a powerful afterlife in terms of persistent racial, spatial and economic inequalities in South Africa, and as emblematic of ongoing forms of racialized oppression around the world.

Gross violations of HUMAN RIGHTS committed during the apartheid era were the focus of the Truth and Reconciliation Commission (TRC), which has become a model for countries all over the world seeking to come to terms with histories of violence. Between 1996 and 1998, the TRC received 20,000 statements from victims and nearly 8,000 applications for amnesty from perpetrators. In her compelling account of the TRC, Krog (2000) illuminates its accomplishments, limitations and ambiguities, along with chilling testimonies of many who bore the brunt of state-sanctioned violence. The final report of the TRC, submitted in 2003, recommended that the government pay some US $375 million in reparations, and that businesses that had benefited from apartheid policies make reparations through a special wealth tax. President Thabo Mbeki authorized a one-time payment of R30,000 (approximately US $5,000) to each of about 22,000 people defined as victims of apartheid, but refused to impose a tax on businesses.

The debate over apartheid reparations overlaps with the ANC government's controversial embrace of a conservative package of neoliberal macro-economic policies in 1996 (Bond, 2000; see NEO-LIBERALISM). The post-apartheid era has seen the rapid emergence of an African middle class and a small but extremely wealthy corporate black elite. Yet huge numbers of black South Africans remain in impoverished conditions in poorly serviced and densely populated townships, rural reserves and slum settlements. Persistent poverty and inequality have prompted some critics to argue that there has been a shift from RACE to CLASS apartheid, while others contest this formulation. Since 2001 many oppositional movements have arisen demanding access to resources, and fierce protests have erupted in many different parts of the country. Despite these challenges, the ANC continues to exercise considerable hegemonic power – a testimony, perhaps, to the ongoing importance of NATIONALISM, grounded partly in histories and memories of the struggle against apartheid.

Global apartheid, some maintain, is a more adequate description of the current world order than apparently race-neutral terms such as GLOBALIZATION or neo-liberalism, and can also bolster efforts to transform global minority rule. Experience in post-apartheid South Africa has much to contribute to struggles aimed at deepening democracy and challenging inequality. GHa

Suggested reading
Beinart (2001); Hart (2003); Marais (2001).

applied geography This is a notion that necessarily operates at a number of different levels. On the one hand, geographical research and the production of geographical knowledge are activities that necessarily relate to the 'real world'. Geographers are attempting to understand the physical and human world, and their knowledge is produced in a DIALECTIC with the world around them. In addition, their knowledge is disseminated to others – and particularly students – in a way that is likely to shape people's beliefs and behaviour. In this regard, all knowledge is potentially applied.

On the other hand, however, there are particular strands of geographical enquiry that prioritize the production of knowledge that can be applied to solving pressing issues or concerns in society. There are strong strands of geographical research in the fields of environmental policy, DEVELOPMENT and URBAN AND REGIONAL PLANNING that have been more applied. It is also important to note that any field of HUMAN GEOGRAPHY and PHYSICAL GEOGRAPHY can potentially be applied to the development of policy. Geographers might be contracted to do research about a social concern and highlight the potential policy implications of their findings. They may also be consulted as experts in order to draw on their knowledge in the production of public policy. Yet further, geographers might highlight their own views about potential policy-making by the STATE, corporations or CIVIL SOCIETY as a result of their own research or insights. There is clearly a place for geography to be applied through policy engagements of various kinds and there have long been vocal calls to do more of this work – for the debate in the 1970s, see Coppock (1974) and, more recently, see Martin (2001b) and Ward (2005a).

It is useful to distinguish this focus on policy from a wider set of engagements and applications that we can call PUBLIC GEOGRAPHIES. Echoing recent debates in the discipline of sociology (see Burawoy, 2005), a number of geographers are beginning to rethink the way in which academics engage with, and even create, audiences through their research, teaching and in their roles and performances as intellectuals in the wider society (Murphy,

2006; Ward, 2006). In this model, the discipline itself comprises different interlocutors such as students and fellow academics with whom there is an ongoing dialogue over the production and dissemination of ideas. In addition, there are multiple publics with whom academics might engage with as part of their own work, exploring new developments, testing out ideas and putting research into action. The explosion of interest in ACTION RESEARCH and PARTICIPANT OBSERVATION methodologies that seek to empower research groups and participants is in part a reflection of this shift towards public collaborative engagement through our research (see Hale and Wills, 2005). Furthermore, the practice of research can itself constitute audiences, however fleetingly, through activities such as holding a workshop or conference to disseminate findings, publishing research material and papers on the Internet, or taking part in media coverage of events.

Geography and geographers can add significantly to understanding the contemporary human and physical world at a time when issues of geography are increasingly pressing. There is clearly a place for applying such knowledge on a whole range of fronts, from the most powerful intellectual interventions about contemporary NEO-LIBERALISM and WAR (Gregory, 2004b; *RETORT*, 2005), to ongoing engagement in the problems of civil society and the development of policy for particular 'clients'. Our notion of applied geography thus needs to be widened far beyond the traditional focus on policy, to incorporate the discipline's relevance to multiple audiences and political forces for change. JWi

Suggested reading
Murphy (2006); Ward (2005, 2006).

area studies Academic programmes that cut across disciplinary boundaries to develop a relatively comprehensive body of knowledge about given REGIONS – or areas – of the world. There is a history of such regionally based, interdisciplinary studies that pre-dates the Second World War (Said, 2003 [1978]), including within geography. Contemporary area studies, however, and the world regions that they have taken as objects of study, are largely a post-Second World War phenomenon.

At the end of the Second World War, the US government took on a leading role in funding area studies programmes within US universities in order to develop the academic expertise necessary for effective management of the national project of world leadership (Gendzier, 1985). In the COLD WAR era, some of the first areas of major concern were in EUROPE, but area studies programmes were also quickly developed for regions of ASIA (including the MIDDLE EAST) and the rest of the so-called THIRD WORLD (Cumings, 1998). Although the intention of the US government in funding such programmes clearly had to do with the need to develop knowledge useful to the maintenance of imperial power (see AMERICAN EMPIRE), the kinds of work done within area studies came to vary widely, both methodologically and politically (Wallerstein, Juma, Keller et al., 1996).

Methodologically, area studies programmes brought together scholars from a range of social sciences – including anthropology, applied economics, geography, history, political science and sociology – as well as various HUMANITIES and physical sciences disciplines. This spurred a significant amount of interdisciplinary collaboration and is credited by some scholars with having helped erode disciplinary boundaries in the post-Second World War academy (Wallerstein, Juma, Keller et al., 1996, pp. 36–48).

While many early Cold War studies were animated by a desire to serve the US government's overseas projects – even leading in some cases to considerable controversy within disciplines over the appropriate role of scholarship – many area studies programmes also came to serve as the home base for a range of critical scholarly endeavours that questioned these same US policies (Anderson, 1998, pp. 11–12). This was the case, for example, in Asian studies, where a group called the 'Concerned Asian Scholars' came together during the Vietnam War, challenging the views of Asianist scholars who supported the US war effort. Likewise, scholarship critical of US foreign policy agendas has frequently emanated from fields such as Latin American and Middle Eastern studies.   JGI

Suggested reading
Anderson (1998); Cumings (1998); Gendzier (1985); Said (2003 [1978]); Wallerstein, Juma, Keller et al. (1996).

areal differentiation The study of the spatial distribution of physical and human phenomena as they relate to one another in REGIONS or other spatial units. Also sometimes referred to as CHOROLOGY, it is, with LANDSCAPE and SPATIAL ANALYSIS approaches, often

regarded as one of the three main conceptions of HUMAN GEOGRAPHY. Of the three, it is the oldest Western tradition of geographical enquiry, tracing its beginnings to the Greeks Hecateus of Miletus and Strabo, although the term itself only dates from the 1930s. In Strabo's words, the geographer is 'the person who describes the parts of the Earth'. Description, however, has never been just taking inventory of the features of regions. The purpose was always to relate the features to one another to understand how PLACES differ from one another and how this has come about. As the theoretical justification for studying REGIONS and REGIONAL GEOGRAPHY, use of areal differentiation has waxed and waned down the years, with different proponents using distinctive concepts and language.

The 'classic' epoch of regional geography, to use Paul Claval's (1993, p. 15) turn of phrase, was reached in the late nineteenth and early twentieth centuries, when much of the theoretical debate in geography was devoted to the concept of the region. The most important modern statement of geography as areal differentiation was made in Richard Hartshorne's *The nature of geography* (1939). Though often viewed as an argument for the uniqueness of regions, the logic of the presentation suggests that recognizing regions requires investigating similarities as well as differences over space. In the 1950s and 1960s, critics of regional geography succeeded in marginalizing the focus on areal differentiation as they pushed a redefinition of the field in terms of spatial analysis. In the 1980s, however, the approach made something of a comeback. But the revival is neither directly connected to older debates such as that between Hartshorne and his critics, nor is it monolithic. Three positions can be distinguished. One involves a focus on place-making as an essential human activity. A second sees regional differences in terms of processes of UNEVEN DEVELOPMENT that are forever rearticulating the global DIVISION OF LABOUR under CAPITALISM. A third attempts reconciliation between the first two by seeing places or regions as settings for the interpellation of HUMAN AGENCY and the conditioning effects on it of social and environmental context.

Persisting dilemmas limit the possibility of unifying these positions. For one thing, the question of whether regions are 'real' or exist solely in the mind of the observer continues to wrack debate (Agnew, 1999). There are also important differences over narrative versus analytic modes of thinking and presentation, the relevance of regional divisions in an increasingly 'networked' world, and the best terminology (such as that of place versus region).   JA

Suggested reading
Entrikin and Brunn (1989); Sack (1997).

art Geography has a long-standing and multifarious relationship with art. GEOGRAPHY'S literal meaning as 'earth writing' and its concern with visual REPRESENTATION have often brought the discipline into close involvement with artistic practices, with geographical knowledge frequently being dependent upon skills of visual survey and graphic recording such as sketching, drafting and painting, especially during the period of European EXPLORATION (Cosgrove, 1999). The significance of an aesthetic sensibility continued through much CULTURAL GEOGRAPHY and RE-GIONAL GEOGRAPHY in the early twentieth century; for example, in Carl Ortwin Sauer's studies of CULTURAL LANDSCAPES and in the pictorial language with which Paul Vidal de la Blache referred to landscape description. Geographical interest in visual art has taken many forms. These include studies of representations of spaces, places and environments in a range of artistic media, especially in terms of the politics of representation, ideology, identity and the construction of IMAGINATIVE GEOGRAPHIES. Also important is geographical research on art production (e.g. the formation of local, regional and national artistic traditions; the role of arts industries in economic and urban change; the spaces of artistic creativity); on art dissemination and reception (including through artistic networks, institutions, audiences, and public engagement with and contestation of works of art); and on art practices (as embodied creative processes, as expressions and forms of geographical knowledge, as interventions in and performances of spaces and places).

Geography's reconstitution as a SPATIAL SCIENCE in the 1950s and 1960s sidelined such artistic considerations, although a concern with visualization and the aesthetics of order can be discerned in geometric spatial modelling (Gregory, 1994). HUMANISTIC GEOGRAPHY brought an interest in the expressive and emotional engagement of art with places through its emphasis on subjectivity and human experience. The emergence of a politicized cultural geography in the 1980s, influenced by MARXISM as well as social histories of art and broader currents of cultural theory, turned critical attention to the social conditions and power relations through which art is produced as part of a concern with the politics of representation. Significant studies focused on the constitution of the Western idea of landscape as a 'way of seeing', and on its role in naturalizing class and property relations, in articulating visions of national identity, and in legitimating colonial interests (e.g. Daniels, 1993; Cosgrove, 1998 [1984]). Feminist critics also emphasized the importance of gender relations and SEXUALITY in discussions of visuality and landscape (see also VISION AND VISUALITY).

Recent geographical interest in art has become more extensive and diverse. While much work remains focused on visual and ICONOGRAPHIC readings of artefacts such as paintings, drawings, MAPS, photographs, landscapes, architecture, MONUMENTS and sculptures, research has also addressed the spatialities of sound art, land art, street art, MUSIC, video, FILM, performance and dance, among other fields. Attention has turned in particular to artistic practices and to the embodied, processual and performative elements of art (see PERFORMANCE). Studies have thus drawn out the bodily practices and sensory immersion in places involved in visual art production (Crouch and Toogood, 1999), and to a lesser extent viewing and reception. They have also explored the ways in which modern and contemporary artistic practices have directly engaged with urban and rural geographies, from attempts by twentieth-century avant-gardes such as the dadaists, surrealists and SITUATIONISTS to break down divisions between art and everyday spaces, to more recent 'works' and interventions by performance artists, conceptual artists, community artists and others. The latter often take collectivist, collaborative, ethnographic or dialogical approaches, based not on the individualized production of aesthetic objects but on practices such as URBAN EXPLORATIONS, walks, participatory events, investigations of social spaces and sites, and interactions with groups and communities. They are also frequently politicized or activist, forging public arenas for political discussion and critical engagement with the processes through which spaces are produced (Deutsche, 1996b; for examples, see Cant and Morris, 2006; and the 'Cultural geographies in practice' section of the journal *Cultural Geographies*). Alongside researching such art, a number of geographers are collaborating with artists (e.g. Driver, Nash, Prendergast and Swenson, 2002). Some are further experimenting themselves with artistic and performative practices as a critical and imaginative means of addressing geographical concerns.   DP

Suggested reading
Cosgrove (1999); Deutsche (1996b).

artificial intelligence Computerized DECISION MAKING that simulates human expert decision-making. In its simplest form, artificial intelligence (AI) consists of a body of procedural rules (e.g. the linear *IF THEN ELSE* rules that are the mainstay of computer programming). Or it can describe a heuristic type of intelligence that surpasses simple procedural instructions. Artificial intelligence can relieve humans of tedious tasks such as addition of grocery prices. For such simple tasks, it often surpasses humans in speed and accuracy but can fall short when asked to codify knowledge in a holistic manner. Since the early 1990s, more sophisticated AI has sought to emulate human thinking using parallel computing (e.g. NEURAL NETS and genetic ALGORITHMS). These techniques have been more successful than traditional linear rule-based systems in classifying area types or identifying regional zones. They have also been used for MAP generalization – a task that requires processing of multiple decision-making facets including context, intention, SCALE and contiguity. In each case, neural nets and genetic algorithms teach themselves based on positive or negative reinforcement during 'training'. In the case of neural nets, a series of images corresponding to a given classification may be 'fed' into the net. Subsequent training rewards the net for choosing the right classification. At the present, AI is only able to emulate very simple human decision-making though the promise of truly intelligent computing.   NS

Suggested reading
Openshaw and Openshaw (1997); Weibel (1991).

Asia (idea of) Considered the world's largest CONTINENT but actually part of a single landmass with Europe (the conventional dividing line being the Ural and Caucasus mountains), Asia lays claims to being the 'cradle of human civilization' as it is home to important ancient CIVILIZATIONS – including those of China, India, Japan and Persia – that generated major developments in agriculture, urbanism, religion and other fields of human expression (Parker, 1994, p. 4).

Derived from Greek and first used to describe the region later known as Asia Minor, 'Asia', like other related terms such as the 'Orient' or the 'Far East', is a cartographic construct imposed from the outside rather than a pre-existing geographical reality. Depicted on EUROCENTRIC maps of the world as the 'east', European colonizers tended to frame Asia in oppositional terms to Europe: as culturally degenerate, environmentally debilitating and inherently backward, in contrast to Europe's civilizational progress and ENLIGHTENMENT (Weightman, 2006). As a conceptual category, the term 'Asia' has continued to evolve, often in response to external categorization. The term for the sub-region of South East Asia, for example, has only gained currency since the Second World War, when the region gained visibility in military and strategic terms under the South East Asia Command established in 1943, and consequently achieved legitimacy in international eyes (Savage, Kong and Yeoh, 1993). 'Asia' as a construct is also subject to internal pressures. For example, the term 'Asiatic' to refer to the inhabitants of Asia or as an adjective pertaining to Asia has now been superseded in common usage by 'Asian': the former nomenclature fell out of favour in the postwar era, as it had become laden with pejorative implications during European COLONIALISM.

Today, Asia's 3.6 billion people account for about three-fifths of the world's population. China, the most populous nation in the world, has a current population of more than 1.2 billion people, followed closely by India, with a population of slightly over a billion (United Nations, 2005). Although the world's population growth rate is now generally declining, and in Asia it is likely to fall even further below the global rate, nonetheless, the developing countries of Asia will still be major contributors to world population growth for many decades to come. More than a third of Asia's population live in urban areas, including some of the largest megacities in the world.

Considering Asia as one geographical entity, however, belies the diversity in cultures and peoples, as well as a wide range of economic, political and demographic structures. Migration, trade, war and European colonization in the past had contributed to contact, exchange and syncretism in many spheres of life within the region. Despite the new sense of Asian solidarity expressed during the Bandung Conference of 1955 to sever ties of dependency on the West, different approaches to decolonization and nationalism in the mid-twentieth century led the countries in Asia down divergent pathways (Parker, 1994, p. 10). The more recent pursuit of modernity and global futures has also been characterized by uneven and different trajectories for countries in Asia. Optimism about the region based on the runaway success of some East and South East Asian 'miracle' economies (see ASIAN MIRACLE / TIGERS) was suddenly brought up short as the region floundered in crisis in the closing years of the twentieth century (Chapman and Baker, 1992; Forbes, 2005).   BY

Suggested reading
Weightman (2006).

Asian miracle/tigers A popular description of East and South East Asian countries that had exceptionally high rates of ECONOMIC GROWTH from the 1960s until the Asian economic crisis of 1997. Some lists of the Asian miracle economies include Japan, but most early discussions focused on Hong Kong, Singapore, South Korea and Taiwan, also called the 'first tier' Asian newly industrializing countries (NICs). After the economic boom extended to Southeast Asia in the 1980s and 1990s, authors began to speak of Indonesia, Malaysia and Thailand as part of the miracle, and some discussions of China's rapid growth since the 1990s also place it on the list of tigers/miracle economies.

The World Bank's *East Asian Miracle* report (1993) put an official seal on the language of miracles, though the bank's analysis argued that the rapid growth of these economies was not in fact miraculous and could be replicated by other countries. The report was met with varied forms of criticism, however, and there have been analysts who question whether the performance of the Asian NICs is replicable or should be celebrated as uncritically as it often has been.

The *East Asian Miracle* report generally credited neo-liberal policies with responsibility for the boom, including maintenance of export-oriented trade regimes, though it acknowledged some benefits from policies of 'financial repression', such as state-imposed below-market interest rates for loans to specific exporting industries. Various institutionalist analysts criticized the bank for overlooking a range of other state policies that facilitated growth, but that do not fit the tenets of NEO-LIBERALISM (Wade, 1996).

Other analysts have criticized celebration of the Asian NICs performance, regardless of the specific role of states in their growth. Criticisms have included concerns about the political repressiveness of Asian states and environmental destruction caused by rapid growth. After the economic crisis hit many of the tigers in 1997, some analysts also began to question the economic sustainability of the Asian NIC growth model (Hart-Landsberg and Burkett, 1998). In addition, some authors have noted that the Asian miracle has much to do with the development of a networked, COLD WAR era, regional production hierarchy, led by Japan, which is both geographically and historically specific – and thus not readily replicated even if it does present a desirable model (Cumings, 1984; Bernard and Ravenhill, 1995).   JGl

Suggested reading
Bernard and Ravenhill (1995); Cumings (1984); Hart-Landsberg and Burkett (1998); Wade (1996); World Bank (1993).

assemblage The process by which a collective asian miracle/tigers entry entity (thing or meaning) is created from the connection of a range of heterogeneous components. A translation of the French word *agencement*, the solidity of the English term tends to make it sound more static, rational and calculated than the original term signifies. In fact, it is precisely the sense of an aggregate with a certain consistency being created from an active, *ad hoc* and ongoing entanglement of elements that has made the notion so attractive to authors working in a POST-STRUCTURALIST vein. The concept has been put to work notably in science and technology studies (STS) (see Law, 2004), the work of Jacques Derrida, and – most significantly – the combined writings of Gilles Deleuze and Félix Guattari (1998).   NB

assimilation A particular form of the social integration of people into a new SOCIETY, typically after they have migrated from another country (cf. MIGRATION). There are many forms of integration, which include SOCIAL EXCLUSION (denying migrants basic social rights), assimilation, *laissez-faire* approaches (leaving migrants alone to choose their own mode of social engagement with mainstream society) and PLURALISM (allowing migrants to retain their cultural traditions and live separately from mainstream society). Assimilation is a process whereby migrants give up their cultural traditions, including attire, language, cuisines and ways of thinking, and take on the cultural traditions of the society in their destination country (Gordon, 1964; Glazer and Moynihan, 1970). The classic IMMIGRATION-based countries – the USA, Canada,

Australia and New Zealand – all expected migrants to assimilate for most of their history. Recently, Canada and Australia have adopted the policy of MULTICULTURALISM as a new mode of migrant integration, which is a kind of hybrid between assimilation and pluralism (Hiebert and Ley, 2003). Several European countries also adopted multicultural policies in the latter decades of the twentieth century, notably the Netherlands, Sweden and the UK. Other European countries, such as France and Germany, have been wary of multiculturalism and continue to expect migrants to assimilate. In the aftermath of terrorist incidents and several episodes of social unrest, those European countries that adopted multiculturalism appear to be reconsidering that decision, and may be returning to assimilation as a means of integration (Vasta, 2005). These debates have been highly politically charged, and critics of the return to assimilation have argued that it reflects an Islamophobic agenda.   DH

Suggested reading
Massey and Denton (1993).

asylum Asylum has two distinct meanings in HUMAN GEOGRAPHY. One stream of work has been directed towards the (historical) geography of institutions for mental illnesss (Philo, 2004; and see MEDICAL GEOGRAPHY). Another body of work examines asylum as the displacement of REFUGEES from one state to another, in which they seek sanctuary from violence and political persecution (Hyndman, 2000). The two are very different, but both of them raise searching questions about marginalization and the production and location of 'outsiders'. JH

Austral(as)ia, idea of The term 'Australasia' is a construct of IMPERIALISM. As a means of delineating and denoting a diversity of far-flung colonial TERRITORIES, it had wide currency in the nineteenth century, both in the metropole and regionally. If it retains some utility in the former context, it is 'a repressed memory' in the latter (Denoon, 2003). This is despite continually evolving regional NETWORKS of economy, MIGRATION and, to a lesser extent, collective MEMORY.

'Austral' means 'belonging to the south', so 'Australasia' is literally to the south of, but distinct from, ASIA. The term was coined in 1756 by the Frenchman Charles de Brosses for one of his three divisions of the great southern continent. Belief in the existence of this CONTINENT – also known as *Terra Australis* – entered the European GEOGRAPHICAL IMAGIN-ATION from sources in classical CARTOGRAPHY. The search for it was one of the purposes of James Cook's voyages to the Pacific; what eventually emerged were the islands of the Pacific and continental Australia.

'Australasia' came to have flexible meaning, but usually encompassed the British colonies on the Australian mainland along with Tasmania, New Zealand, Fiji, British New Guinea (Papua), the Solomon Islands, the Cook Islands and Tonga. The construct reflected the shared interests of British colonists and capital in the region, their security dependent on the imperial navy and their political legitimacy on the imperial parliament. The continuing popularity in Australia of Blainey's book *The tyranny of distance* (1966) indicates that (western) EUROPE remains for many a cardinal cultural reference point.

But shared interests were also undercut by other, conflicting, perspectives. The eventual outcome of the 1890 Australasian Federation Conference was the federation, in 1901, of the Australian colonies alone. The term 'Australasia' became tainted, particularly in New Zealand, one of whose representatives at the 1890 meeting had underlined its concern about Australian dominance by describing his homeland as a 'rather remote part of Australasia' (in Mein Smith, 2003, p. 312). There were also anxieties, in New Zealand and the Pacific islands, that matters of 'native administration' would be silenced in an Australian-dominated Federal parliament. This reflected the particularities of relations with indigenous peoples in the different territories.

In the 1920s 'Australia Unlimited' was promoted by boosters who envisaged population capacities of 100–500 million and saw a dominant Australia as 'the future pivot of white settlement in a secure and revivified empire' (Powell, 1988, p. 131). The geographer Griffith Taylor, whose prediction of a population of only 20 million in 2000 was prescient, challenged this vision cartographically, labelling much of the Australian interior as 'uninhabited' and 'almost useless'. This echoed another colonial imaginary, that of Australia as *TERRA NULLIUS*, or no one's land, prior to European settlement. Not until the Mabo judgement of 1992 was native (or aboriginal) title recognized in Australian common LAW (Whatmore, 2002c) (cf. ABORIGINALITY). Mabo has 'unsettled' Australia, bringing to the fore contestations over national aspirations that also characterize the other countries of what was 'Australasia'. The past has also returned to haunt the present in another guise: whereas Australasia was originally used to mark a separation from Asia, in recent years regional GEOGRAPHICAL IMAGINARIES have been both dislocated and reoriented by deepening economic and cultural connections between the two.   EP

Suggested reading
Denoon (2003); Whatmore (2002c).

authenticity The genuineness, trustworthiness and accuracy of an object or an account. Human geographers have addressed the issue of authenticity in relation to a whole raft of questions from IDENTITY politics (e.g. the gendered self) to our understanding of and relationship with NATURE. In all cases there has been a shift away from an essentialist concept of the authentic (cf. ESSENTIALISM) to a more partial, constructed and situated notion of what passes as authentic (Whatmore, 2002a). Rather than presenting a foundationalist account of authenticity, human geographers are tracing how particular versions of authenticity get played out in the knowledge-making practices of specific times and places (Livingstone, 2003c).   NJ

Suggested reading
Livingstone (2003c).

azimuth The azimuth is the horizontal ('on the ground') angle between a given direction and some line of reference (a meridian). Imagine that you stand looking northwards along the Grand Meridian (zero degrees longitude) at Greenwich, England – the official starting point for each new day. A bird flies nearby and you turn your feet towards its shadow on the ground. The angle you have rotated defines the azimuth. Because that angle usually is measured with a compass, azimuth is synonymous with bearing. But be warned if travelling to the North Pole – the azimuth you should follow is not magnetic north!   RH

Suggested reading
Robinson, Morrison, Muehrcke, Guptill and Kimerling (1993).

B

back-to-the-city movement A term usually indicating repopulation of cities by former suburban residents. The perception of a back-to-the-city movement has, since the 1990s, been influenced by media reports and some research studies that indicate, advocate, and/or celebrate the return of mostly affluent CLASS fractions to some inner-city neighbourhoods (Florida, 2002). The term is, then, closely associated with discussions of GENTRIFICATION. Recent research in the USA cautions that most residential MIGRATION still involves SUBURBANIZATION or COUNTER-URBANIZATION and notes that we are far from seeing a widespread back-to-the city movement (Kasarda, Appold, Sweeney and Sieff, 1997).   EM

Suggested reading
Kasarda, Appold, Sweeney and Sieff (1997).

balkanization The fragmentation of a larger political entity into smaller, mutually hostile units. The term originates from the GEOPOLITICS of national SELF-DETERMINATION in a context of continental POWER rivalries in the Balkans at the end of the nineteenth century. The term returned to prominence with the break-up of Yugoslavia in the 1990s, and was brought to bear upon other states, especially Russia. Balkanization has been used as a METAPHOR for IMMIGRATION patterns into the USA producing a spatial and social segmentation of the population (Frey, 1996: see SEGREGATION). Such usage has been contested for its negative connotations (Ellis and Wright, 1998).   CF

bare life ('naked life') Life that is excluded from political participation, and so can be abandoned to VIOLENCE and death without recrimination or penalty. The emphasis on exclusion and abandonment is vital: 'bare life' is not a given but is socially produced. Agamben (1998) claims that classical Greek philosophy made a vital distinction between political life (*bios*) and merely existent, biological life (*zoe*): and, as he uses the term, bare life is actively poised between the two. To show how vulnerable such a position is, Agamben locates the production of bare life at the intersection of two distinctive modalities of power: SOVEREIGN POWER and BIOPOWER.

His thesis is a double critique of Michel Foucault's theses on BIOPOLITICS, DISCIPLINARY POWER and GOVERNMENTALITY.

(1) Agamben refuses Foucault's historical trajectory. Foucault (1981a[1976], p. 141) argued that a crucial junction between MODERNITY and CAPITALISM was the novel 'entry of life into history' that took place in eighteenth-century Europe, whereas Agamben insists that 'the inclusion of bare life in the political realm constitutes the original – if concealed – nucleus of sovereign power': in other words, for Agamben this is a process with a much longer history (which is why he returns to classical philosophy). What characterizes political modernity for Agamben is then the 'coincidence' of bare life with the political realm, but a coincidence that is profoundly contradictory: bare life is no longer at the margins of the political order, in fact it becomes a central object of political calculation, but it is also excluded from its deliberations (Mills, 2004, p. 46). It is by no means clear that Foucault and Agamben mean the same thing by 'life', but the bearers of Agamben's 'bare life' are political objects not political subjects: they are wilfully exposed to violence and death because they are treated as though they do not matter so that, collectively, they become so many versions of HOMO SACER.

(2) Agamben twists Foucault's spatial template. His account turns not on strategies through which the normal order contains and confines its 'outside' – the sick, the mad, the criminal, the deviant – but on strategies through which the 'outside' is *included* 'by the suspension of the juridical order's validity – by letting the juridical order withdraw from the exception and abandon it'. Agamben argues that this space of exception (see EXCEPTION, SPACE OF) is typically produced through martial LAW and a state of emergency, which then become the ground through which sovereign power constitutes and extends itself.

41

Agamben treats the CAMP as the exemplary locus of the production of bare life. He does not confine the camp to particular locations, but other writers have seen the production of bare life in the plight of refugees in Kosovo (Edkins, 2003), in the contemporary 'war on terror' in Afghanistan, Palestine and Iraq and its global war PRISON (Gregory, 2004b, 2006b), in post-colonial violence in Rwanda and Zimbabwe (Sylvester, 2006), and in post-Katrina New Orleans (Braun and McCarthy, 2005). The disposition to abandon people in this way, visible in early and late capitalism, has economic and well as political coordinates, and these imperatives have been vigorously reasserted under the sign of NEO-LIBERALISM (cf. Bauman, 2004). DG

Suggested reading
Sylvester (2006).

barrio A Spanish word meaning 'neighbourhood'. The term's various significations in the Americas are rooted in Spanish COLONIALISM. Colonial cities were laid out in a grid pattern radiating out from a central plaza, church and government buildings (Bakewell, 2004). Residence near the plaza was reserved for the city's principal *vecinos*, or citizens. Poorer residents, with varying CITIZENSHIP status, lived in *barrios* on the outskirts of the town. Thus, urban location signified social, political, economic and racial status. In LATIN AMERICA today, '*barrio*' may signify a neighbourhood or a squatter settlement (see SQUATTING); the actual cultural signification assigned to the term varies widely (Clawson, 1997, p. 319).

In the Mexican states annexed by the USA in 1848 after the Mexican–American War, the term referred to the neighbourhoods inhabited by Mexican-Americans. Raúl Homero Villa (2000, pp. 4, 7) proposes the terms *barrioization* to refer to the external legal and ideological structures that contribute to the formation of segregated *barrios* and *barriology* to describe the internal processes of PLACE-making that facilitate the creation of Mexican-American communities. For Mexican-Americans, 'barrio' is associated with both the poverty resulting from dispossession and the 'feeling of being at home' (Griswold del Castillo, 1979, p. 150). JSU

Suggested reading
Villa (2000).

base and superstructure The metaphor that Marx uses to express the idea that the economic structure of society (its 'base') conditions corresponding legal and political superstructures and forms of consciousness. As Marx succinctly puts it in the Preface to his 1859 work *A contribution to the critique of political economy*, 'The mode of production of material life conditions the social, political and intellectual life process in general' (see MARXISM; MODE OF PRODUCTION).

The relationship is more complicated than it appears. Marx and Engels subsequently denied that this formulation implied a simple economic determinism, and insisted that there were many forms of reciprocal effect between base and superstructure. This did not prevent the hardening of the distinction in the often mechanical interpretations that were systematized in textbooks by Marx's immediate followers (such as Plekhanov). The tendency amongst Marxists in the more recent past has been to downplay the METAPHOR as too crude to capture the complexity of interrelationships that Marx was trying to encapsulate (interactions between base and superstructure are more evident in some of his historical analyses, such as 'The Eighteenth Brumaire of Louis Napoleon'). It has also proved difficult to maintain a simple base/superstructure distinction when many superstructural elements – such as legal conceptions and scientific knowledges – clearly enter into the economic base.

Cohen (1978) has provided a sophisticated, modern restatement in functionalist terms that tries to clarify these issues (see FUNCTIONALISM). On his reading, the economic base comprises relations of production (but not forces of production), and the superstructure is much smaller than is often supposed, comprising only those non-economic institutions, such as legal systems and the STATE, that are functionally necessary to the reproduction of the economic base (art, for example, is thus largely excluded).

Althusser (see Althusser and Balibar, 1970) tried to resolve the problem in a different way by developing a further distinction that Marx made between 'determination' and 'domination' in his claim that politics played the *dominant* role in the ancient world and religion in the Middle Ages. Althusser interprets this to mean that the economic structure is only 'determinant in the last instance', and may not itself play the dominant role in many social formations, although it *determines* which of the other levels assumes that dominant role. For Althusser, therefore, the social system is thus a complex totality 'structured in dominance'. Following Althusser, 'anti-essentialist' Marxists such as Resnick and

Wolff (1987) and Gibson-Graham (2006b [1996]) have gone further in dissolving the very notion of the economy as a separate space with deterministic effects, replacing base and superstructure with the notion of a decentred, over-determined totality with no essential, determining structure (cf. ESSENTIALISM).

Harvey (1999 [1982]), on the other hand, continues to emphasize the classical role of the economy and the dynamics of capital ACCUMU-LATION in shaping social (and, crucially, CLASS) structures under capitalism, but avoids simple base/superstructure distinctions by conceptu-alizing economic and superstructural elements as 'moments' in the total circulation process of capital.

In summary, although the base/superstructure distinction is too crude to provide an answer, it does point towards the key question of the nature of 'the ECONOMY' in capitalist systems and its influence on, and interaction with, wider social, cultural and political structures.   KB

Bayesian analysis A type of statistical mod-elling and estimation deriving from the early ideas of the Reverend Thomas Bayes, who developed his 'doctrine of chances' in 1763 (Bayes, 1763 [1958]). The Bayesian perspec-tive differs from traditional or 'orthodox' stat-istical inference in giving explicit recognition to the role of prior ideas and probabilities and so is sometimes labelled as a 'subjective' ap-proach to probability and statistics. Much of the probability theory was developed by 1939, when Jeffreys wrote his classic text (Jeffreys, 1998 [1939]), but the implementation of Bayesian methods as a practical statistical technique is much more recent, and had to await modern computer technology and the invention of some very clever new devices.

Bayes' central idea is that prior probabilities are updated by confrontation with data to pro-vide posterior probabilities. For example, sup-pose we want to make inferences about a parameter θ (which might be a mean or a REGRESSION coefficient). Our prior probability distribution for θ is $p(\theta)$. The observed data are represented by the likelihood function $p(y|\theta)$. Using Bayes' rule on conditional prob-abilities gives us the posterior density or distri-bution $p(\theta|y)$ as follows:

$$p(\theta|y) = p(\theta)p(y|\theta)/p(y),$$

where $p(y) = \sum_{\theta} p(\theta)p(y|\theta)$, the sum over all possible values of θ, which acts as a normalizing constant. This term may be ignored in many instances (though not in MODEL comparison) to give the unnormalized posterior density:

$$p(\theta|y) \propto p(\theta)p(y|\theta).$$

This expression defines the core of Bayesian inference. Note that this method derives a posterior probability distribution for θ, whereas classical (or standard) inference uses the sample data to make inferences about the unknown, but assumed fixed, parameter value of θ. Where there are several parameters in question, such as θ_1 and θ_2, then $p(\theta|y)$ is a joint distribution, and the Bayesian statistician converts this to two marginal posterior distri-butions by integrating across the range of the other θ:

$$p(\theta_1|y) \propto \int p(\theta)p(y|\theta)d\theta_2.$$

In this framework, inferences about θ_1 are made taking account of the full distribution of θ_2, whereas classical inference is based just on the optimal point estimates and local curvature around that location.

Opinions about the potential of Bayesian methods have differed sharply. Some have seen them as a way of broadening the scope of quantitative analysis, whilst others have rejected the notion of bringing SUBJECTIVITY into statistical inference. In practice, Bayesian methods were little used except for circum-stances under which they were equivalent to classical results and so there was no computa-tional difference, only one of interpretation. More direct implementation depended on the facility to do the numerical integrations required to get the marginal distributions, and modern computing provided this. In the social sciences, the work of the Chicago econometrician Arnold Zellner was very important in this process (Zellner, 1971). Modern Bayesian analysis is usually based on 'uninformative' or 'diffuse' prior information, reflecting prior ignorance or a determination not to introduce subjective prior inform-ation into the analysis; Bayesian estimation is then used very much as a technical device to estimate posterior distributions.

Bayesian methods have taken a further leap forward in the past decade with the construc-tion of Markov Chain Monte Carlo, or 'MCMC', techniques (Gilks, Richardson and Spiegelhalter, 1996). It has been shown that complete sets of joint and marginal posterior distributions may be constructed by this SIMU-LATION method. Starting from the (diffuse) prior distributions, the conditional distributions of the θ-parameters are sampled using random SAMPLING (hence the 'Monte Carlo' part of the name) and these sampled θ values are then brought together with the data to estimate the likelihood. This information is then used to update the conditional distributions, and the process is repeated many hundreds or thousands of times, gradually building up samples representing the posterior distribution. The sampling at any stage t is based on updating from the conditionals at time $t - 1$, and hence it is a (first-order) MAR-KOV CHAIN PROCESS. This remarkable method can be developed for very complicated models with many parameters and difficult structures, and is being used in many disciplines. Models in both SPATIAL ECONOMETRICS and MULTI-LEVEL MODELLING may now be estimated by these Bayesian methods.

Bayesian methods have been applied in several areas of geographical and SPATIAL AN-ALYSIS. The specific version of 'empirical Bayes' estimation is widely used in spatial interpolation and in disease mapping and spatial EPIDEMIOLOGY. Other applications include population and economic forecasting, crime 'hotspot' modelling, and hierarchical Bayes estimation to lend insight into the problem of ECOLOGICAL INFERENCE. Brunsdon (2001) provides a case-study using MCMC in a Bayesian model predicting school performance figures for pupil-tests. In SPATIAL ECONOMETRICS, Bayesian methods, both numerical integration and MCMC, have been used to estimate models with spatial ENDOGENEITY and more complicated forms (Hepple, 1995; LeSage, 1997). The geographer Peter Congdon has written two major statistical texts on Bayesian statistical modelling (Congdon, 2001). Opinions still differ about the role of subjective prior information, but modern Bayesian methods are one of the fastest developing areas of quantitative analysis.   LWH

Suggested reading
Withers (2002).

behavioural geography A sub-discipline emphasizing the psychological underpinnings of individual spatial behaviour; in particular, the cognitive and decision-making processes that intervene between a complex environment and human action. In its earliest expression this work was more humanistic, exemplified in the historical musings of J.K. Wright in the 1940s (Keighren, 2005), and the influential essays of Lowenthal (1961) and Brookfield (1969) on ENVIRONMENTAL experience and PERCEPTION. While this tradition led into HUMANISTIC GEOGRAPHY, behavioural geography was typically more formal and analytic, drawn into the POSITIVIST paradigm of LOCATIONAL ANALY-SIS. Its characteristic question was: Given the assumption of rational behaviour, why did an actual location or pattern of spatial behaviour depart from an optimal form? (See LOCATION THEORY.) The answer was seen to be a product of DECISION-MAKING, and notably the human tendency to have only incomplete information, to make imperfect choices, and to be satisfied with sub-optimal options. Applications included Wolpert's (1964) study of Swedish farmers and Pred's (1967) analysis of industrial location. In each instance, behaviour was seen to be *satisficing* rather than optimizing as predicted, for decision-makers were not only incapable but even unwilling to compromise other values in order to maximize their utility functions. Similar work examined the journey to shop, and showed again how, both in terms of retail location and shopping behaviour, cognitive variables intervened to complicate geographically rational behaviour (see RETAILING). A particular emphasis was upon preference structures in spatial behaviour, modelling such topics as place utility and residential search. The most celebrated work was conducted by Peter Gould and his students who examined the MENTAL MAPS, or preference surfaces, within different countries held, usually by students, and which might permit the prediction of subsequent MIGRA-TION (Gould and White, 1993 [1974]).

One of the most interesting and applied aspects of behavioural geography was work examining human perception of ENVIRONMEN-TAL HAZARDS. Typically, this research addressed itself to a seemingly anachronistic location decision. Why did people or industry locate in unpredictable sites such as flood-plains or areas of earthquake or avalanche hazard? How was such irrational behaviour to be explained? The pioneering work by Robert Kates and Gilbert White on floodplain hazards inspired many subsequent studies, which included increasing methodological sophistication. For example, Saarinen's (1966) innovative study of the perception of drought hazard by farmers on the Great Plains postulated the existence of a distinctive personality disposition, which he explored using the thematic apperception test, a personality assessment measure. A range of related personality assessments, such as personal construct theory and the semantic differential, were employed, and in this work geography and psychology became close neighbours (Aitken, 1991; Kitchin, Blades and Golledge, 1997). During the 1970s, in particular, this productive interdisciplinary relationship was developed through the annual meetings of the Environmental Design Research Association and in the pages of the new journal, *Environment and Behavior* (see ENVIRONMENTAL PSYCHOLOGY).

Since that period, behavioural geography has continued to diversify, even if its position has been less elevated than in the 1960s and 1970s when many disciplinary leaders worked in this sub-discipline. More recent research has included analysis of environmental learning, spatial search, developmental issues in spatial cognition and cartography and Golledge's (1993) important work with the disabled and sight-impaired (see DISABILITY). But some of the lustre has left the field. In part, this may be related to the methodological sensibilities of post-positivist human geography. In part, it is due to the growing conviction of the inherently socialized nature of geographical knowledge, which challenges the individualism of psychological models. In part, it emanates from a suspicion of the adequacy of an EPISTEMOLOGY of observation and measurement that may leave unexamined non-observable and non-measurable contexts and ideological formations. Nonetheless, behavioural geography has a continuing legacy, comprehensively itemized and integrated in the massive compilation of Golledge and Stimson (1997).   DL

Suggested reading
Gold (1980); Golledge and Stimson (1997); Walmsley and Lewis (1993).

Berkeley School American CULTURAL GEOGRAPHY was dominated until the 1980s by Carl Sauer, his colleagues at the University of California at Berkeley and their students. While this type of cultural geography is no longer important in Berkeley, it remains a research tradition carried on by former Berkeley students and their students scattered throughout the world.

Arguably, no geographer had more influence on American geography in the twentieth century than Carl Ortwin Sauer (1889–1975). He received his PhD in 1915 from the University of Chicago, where he came under the influence of the ENVIRONMENTAL DETERMINISM

of Ellen Churchill Semple. In 1923 he moved to Berkeley, and under the influence of the anthropologists A.L. Kroeber and R.H. Lowie was exposed to a concept of CULTURE that was to replace his earlier environmentalist ideas. In 1925 Sauer wrote what is perhaps his best known essay, 'The MORPHOLOGY of LANDSCAPE', which strongly denounced environmental determinism and suggested a method by which cultural geographers should conduct their FIELDWORK (Sauer, 1963b [1925]). Shortly after arriving at Berkeley, Sauer developed what was to become a life-long interest in LATIN AMERICA, and there remains a strong connection with the REGION in the work of subsequent generations of his students. Cultural geography, for Sauer, was the study of the relationship between humans and the land (see also CULTURAL LANDSCAPE). During the latter part of his career, he pursued two broad, rather speculative historical themes. The first focused on such questions as early humans' use of fire and the seashore as a primeval habitat, while the second explored the condition of America when Europeans first encountered it.

While giving Sauer his due, it must be remembered that most of the ideas that he introduced into the field – historical reconstruction, CULTURAL HEARTH and DIFFUSION amongst them – were current at the time in German geography (see ANTHROPOGEOGRAPHY) and American cultural anthropology. His intellectual debt to Friedrich Ratzel, Otto Schluter, Eduard Hahn and A.L. Kroeber was immense. Sauer and his students placed a greater emphasis upon human relationships with the physical environment than did the anthropologists, whose interests not only included human–environment relations but whose focus was on human behaviour more generally. Wagner and Mikesell (1962) identify three principal themes that define the work of the Berkeley School. The first is the diffusion of culture traits, such as plants, ANIMALS and house types. The second is the identification and evolution of culture regions through material and non-material traits (cf. SEQUENT OCCUPANCE). The third is CULTURAL ECOLOGY, usually also studied in historical perspective. Sauer's persistent insistence on the importance of an historical perspective ensured that many American geographers referred to a distinctively hybrid cultural–historical geography.

It has been argued that the Berkeley School adopted a reified 'superorganic' conception of culture from the anthropologist A.L. Kroeber (Duncan, 1980). After the 1980s, the Berkeley School served as a counterpoint for New

Cultural Geographers of a more theoretical bent. In the past decade, however, some cultural geographers who feel that New Cultural Geography had been too discursive and human in its focus, paying insufficient attention to NATURE, have come to a new appreciation of some of the more environmentally focused contributions of the Berkeley School (Price and Lewis, 1993).   JSD

Suggested reading
Leighly (1963); Wagner and Mikesell (1962).

bid-rent curve A plot of the RENT that people are prepared to pay against distance from some point, usually the city centre. Rent bids generally decrease with increasing distance from a city or its centre where land values are highest, so a bid-rent curve slopes down in a diagram with rent on the vertical axis and distance displayed horizontally (see ALONSO MODEL; DISTANCE DECAY). The curve is sometimes shown as convex to the graph's origin, to reflect sharp decreases in rent with short distances from the city (centre), levelling off with increasing distance. Bid-rent curves are an important element in models of both urban and agricultural land use (cf. VON THÜNEN MODEL).   DMS

biodiversity A term defined in the United Nations Convention on Biological Diversity (CBD) as 'the variability among living organisms from all sources including *inter alia* terrestrial, marine and other aquatic ECOSYSTEMS and the ecological complexes of which they are part; this includes diversity within species, between species and of ecosystems' (Article 2). The stated objectives of the Convention are 'the conservation of biological diversity, the sustainable use of its components and the fair and equitable sharing of the benefits arising out of the utilization of genetic resources' (Article 1).

As Jeffries (1997) points out in his account of the rise of biodiversity as a matter of scientific and policy concern, the term was barely used in scientific or policy communities before the 1980s. He tracks its rise to the development of a scientific infrastructure associated with the new field of conservation biology, including a learned society (the Society for Conservation Biology), a scientific journal (*Conservation Biology*) and an undergraduate teaching programme (at the University of California, Berkeley), all established in 1985. This body of work focused on recording and accounting for the observed and hypothesized

decline in the variety of living organisms in any number of contexts – a decline represented as a human-driven process of extinction. Defined by its sense of urgency, biodiversity CONSERVATION readily took on the mantle of a global environmental crisis in both scientific and popular imaginations through such totemic (and telegenic) spaces as the Amazonian rainforest. The rapid uptake of this new scientific agenda in the world of international environmental policy-making, centred on the United Nations, is attributed by Takacs (1996) to the influential efforts of some of its leading scientific sponsors – whom he collectively labels the 'rainforest mafia', notably the eminent US biologist E.O. Wilson.

Efforts to reduce the rate of decline in biological diversity associated with global and local management practices fostered under the CBD, such as Biodiversity Action Plans, are bound up with the rather different agendas of those concerned with exploiting biodiversity as a new form of natural RESOURCE (Bowker, 2000; see also GENETIC GEOGRAPHIES). Among a number of problematic tensions inherent in these management regimes, two have drawn significant and persistent political fire. First, the CBD regime sets biological diversity apart from, and at odds with, human society and activity. This is contradicted by the historical record of co-evolution between humans, plants and ANIMALS, which has left its mark, through processes such as DOMESTICATION, on the genetic and phenotypic diversity of our biological heritage today. Second, the CBD regime has generated some highly contested management arrangements, such as those permitting the slaughter of animals belonging to mammal species threatened with extinction in order to generate income to invest in the protection of the remaining species population.   SW

Suggested reading
Bowker (2000); Jeffries (1997); Takacs (1996); United Nations Environment Programme (1992).

biogeography One of the oldest sub-fields of the discipline, concerned with describing and explaining the spatial patterns of the distribution of living organisms: where they are, where they are not and why. While this field of concern has now become tightly bound up with the rise of scientific and policy effort to manage species extinctions and conserve biological diversity (see BIODIVERSITY), the study of biogeography represents an important and generative common ground between human and physical geographers, both historically and today (see Spencer and Whatmore, 2001).

In the late nineteenth and early twentieth centuries, biogeography was a focus of analysis across disciplines such as GEOGRAPHY, anthropology and archaeology, both for those concerned with the development of human societies and for those concerned with the distribution and viability of ANIMAL or plant populations. Cultural geographers such as Carl Sauer, for example, framed their accounts of societal development in terms of the ecological fabric of a region or landscape in which it was situated (see BERKELEY SCHOOL). While these concerns fell from favour in CULTURAL GEOGRAPHY as divisions between natural and social science perspectives and practices became more entrenched (see ENVIRONMENTAL DETERMINISM), they have gained new impetus from the popular science writing of sociobiologists such as Jared Diamond, in his account of the connections between the social and ecological collapse in the historical demise of any number of CIVILIZATIONS (Diamond and LeCroy, 1979). As a result, for much of the late twentieth century biogeography became, in effect, a subspecialty within PHYSICAL GEOGRAPHY, as represented by the leading academic publication, the *Journal of Biogeography*. This subdiscipline has fared unevenly in the research agendas and teaching curricula of the discipline in different parts of the world.

In its twenty-first century incarnation, biogeography has regained its status as a generative common ground that takes life as its central concern, inspired by two currents (see Thrift, 2005a). The first of these is the rise of the life sciences and their potency in reworking the genetic fabric of living kinds, including humankind. The second is a renewed interest in the resources of BIOPHILOSOPHY that informs academic and popular concerns about the social and ecological implications of the biotechnologies that are proliferating at the interface between life and computer sciences (see Greenhough and Roe, 2006). Between the policy investment in biodiversity and the intellectual re-investment in the question of life, biogeography has become an important focus of transdisciplinary work between social and natural scientists.   SW

Suggested reading
Diamond (1979); Greenhough and Roe (2006); Quamen (1996); Spencer and Whatmore (2001); Thrift (2005).

biophilosophy A term associated with a long history of deliberations in Western thought from Aristotle, through natural history and evolutionary theory to post-genomic biology, on the question 'What is life?' (Margulis and Sagan, 2000). Two aspects of these deliberations are particularly influential today in academic – and, to some extent, popular – debates about the always urgent business of living. The first is the PHILOSOPHY of biology (or the philosophy of organism), in which theoretical biologists and philosophers since the nineteenth century have been concerned with elucidating the principles of organization that characterize life informed by the changing practices and paradigms of biological knowledge (see Doyle, 1997). These principles primarily concern the processes of growth, decay, reproduction, development and ADAPTATION. Here, the question 'What is life?' is frequently articulated as an EPISTEMOLOGICAL question about how and why the study of biology (living things) differs from other fields of study.

Biophilosophy, on the other hand, represents a critique of the philosophy of biology in the sense that it is more interested in posing the same question in ONTOLOGICAL terms that interrogate the precarious register of 'life' as a means of thinking past human/animal/machine categorical divisions. In this, it is less concerned with describing the universal essence of life than with tracing through its ceaseless multiplicity. Here, the focus is on the NETWORK of relations that always take the living organism outside itself and the morphogenic impulses of replication and differentiation, multiplicity and singularity through which the flux of worldly becomings takes, holds and changes shape. It is now most closely associated with a 'vitalist' current that runs through Leibniz and Spinoza, Bergson and Whitehead to Deleuze (see Ansell-Pearson, 1999), and is concerned with the life force that 'insinuates itself into the habits and repetitions of matter without becoming contained by materiality' (Bergson, 1983 [1907], p. 126). This is one of a number of important threads weaving through NON-REPRESENTATIONAL THEORY that has become so influential in GEOGRAPHY and other social sciences over the past five years or so.   SW

Suggested reading
Ansell-Pearson (1999); Bergson (1983 [1907]); Doyle (1997); Margulis and Sagan (2000); Whitehead (1929).

biopolitics, biopower Terms coined by French philosopher Michel Foucault in his writings on medicine, discipline and SEXUALITY (see Foucault, 1978 [1976], 2003 [1997], 2008 [2004]), which refer to power over life. Foucault traces the emergence of this particular practice to Europe in the seventeenth century, where instead of political rule being primarily over territories (see TERRITORY) and only secondarily over the people within them, it moved to being over individuals and the populations of which they were part, particularly in terms of their biological and physical characteristics. Power is exercised over the individual body and the collective body of the population. Instead of the SOVEREIGN POWER to *take* life, this new biopower is the power to *make*, sustain or remove life. Foucault was particularly interested in how, as political rule becomes increasingly medicalized, it is simultaneously mathematicized, with the development of measures and statistical techniques. Biopower is the tool by which the group of living beings understood as a population is measured in order to be governed, which is in turn closely connected to the political rationality of LIBERALISM (see GOVERNMENTALITY). Under the broad term of biopower, Foucault examined a range of institutional practices and knowledges, including public health, housing campaigns, mechanisms for control of disease and famine, sexual behaviour, work patterns, and the treatment and organization of social, sexual and physical abnormality. His writings on this topic are part of a wider project understanding rationalities of government and the birth of the modern SUBJECT, and are interested in how power produces and shapes individuals as subjects of knowledge.

Since his death, there have been several significant extensions of Foucault's theses. Although most of his work concentrated on EUROPE, his lectures on RACE (2003) have proved influential in thinking about colonial and post-colonial modalities of power and political violence, including WAR (see Stoler, 1995; Agamben, 1998; Mbembe, 2003). Several scholars have focused on the bio-political implications of contemporary biomedical and genomic research for the intensifying medicalization of society (see Rabinow and Rose, 2006b; Rose, 2006b: cf. MEDICAL GEOGRAPHY). As their work shows, developments in the life sciences now spiral far beyond questions of health to address species-being, and this has prompted several scholars to argue that SECURITY practices are being driven by

a 'toxic combination' of GEOPOLITICS and biopolitics (Dillon, 2007; Dillon and Lobo-Guerrero, 2008).

An important stream of work on contemporary biopolitics seeks to show how the advance of particular techniques, notably biometrics, has profound political and politico-geographical consequences. *Biometrics* – literally the measurement of life – takes unique physical or behavioural traits such as DNA, fingerprints, iris scans or gait (the manner of walking) in order to build up a profile of an individual to enhance the workings of security systems. Much work has been done to extend these insights in analyses of the 'war on terror' and its derivatives (see TERRORISM) (Amoore, 2006; Reid, 2006; Dauphinee and Masters, 2007; Gregory, 2008a).   SE

Suggested reading
Dillon and Lobo-Guerrero (2008); Esposito (2006); Gregory (2008a); Rabinow and Rose (2006b).

bioprospecting The exploration, collection and testing of biological materials in search of genetic, biochemical, morphological or physiological features that may be of value for commercial development. In certain senses it is an extension of age-old practices by which people have learned to benefit from their biophysical (and especially plant) environments. However, the 'social and spatial dynamics' (Parry, 2004) that underlie such activity have changed so dramatically in the past 30 years that bioprospecting can today be most usefully regarded as a significantly new articulation of that entanglement.

Specifically, three related but distinguishable developments have provided new opportunities for business and science to come together to detach biological materials and associated knowledges from their contexts, so as better to exploit them elsewhere. First, a series of economic developments has served to make bioprospecting profitable. With the emergence of BIODIVERSITY as an organizing trope and its framing as a valuable resource through the rhetoric of 'green developmentalism', the notion of 'selling nature to save it' has become legitimized. Second, a series of technical developments has served to make bioprospecting practical. In particular, the transformation of biology associated with the emergence of information technologies has made the manipulation of the genetic code of organisms the basis of its value. Finally, a series of developments in international PROPERTY law has served to make bioprospecting legal. In two major multilateral agreements – the 1992 Convention of Biological Diversity (CBD) and the 1994 Agreement on Trade-related Aspects of Intellectual Property Rights (TRIPS) – much of the world's biological material has been designated as ownable in various senses, and thus a legitimate object for transaction and exchange.

The situation that has emerged from these three developments is profoundly politicized (Dutfield, 2004). For advocates, bioprospecting can deliver assistance ranging from the financial to the educational to those communities in which it takes place, as well as contributing to the production of new pharmaceutical and other products. For critics, bioprospecting is biopiracy (Shiva, 1998 [1997]), in that it fails to adequately recognize or reward the traditional knowledge of the peoples who have cultivated of modified the properties that make a given organism valuable. Questions of what should be ownable (even in a temporary form) are another matter. Only by tracing the sorts of benefit-sharing agreements in a particular case is one likely to get beyond the terms of this increasingly polarized debate (Castree, 2003a). NB

bioregionalism An ecological philosophy and movement advocating the new ecological politics of place, born in San Francisco in the 1970s. Bioregions are defined by two kinds of mapping. First, the tools of climatology, geomorphology and natural history are used to map 'geographic terrains' with distinctive ecological characteristics. Second, descriptions of SENSE OF PLACE or 'terrains of consciousness' by those who live within them refine the BOUNDARIES of these bioregions. Both the approach and practice of bioregionalism have been widely criticized as analytically and politically misconceived in the context of global social and environmental problems and processes. SW

Suggested reading
List (1993); Sale (1991).

biosecurity Biosecurity is a STATE and intra-state response to the cross-boundary movements of non-human living things, particularly those organisms that are considered a threat to human, ecological and economic welfare. It has at least three elements. First, there is the attempt to manage the movements of pests and diseases (cf. DISEASE, DIFFUSION OF).

Attention is focused on nation-states and their disease statuses. These regional disease zones sometimes map on to other distinctions between North and South or Rich and Poor, mappings that are far from accidental and not without consequence (Davis, 2005). Within the state, specific sites are earmarked for biosecurity measures: these include airports, seaports and increasingly farms (Donaldson and Wood, 2004). Second, there are the attempts to reduce the effects of invasive species on so-called indigenous flora and fauna (Bright, 1999). Third, there are the attempts to reduce the risks of microbiological materials being used as weapons. All three practices link together GEOPOLITICS and BIO-GEOGRAPHY, throwing up real tensions between movement and stasis, nations and natures (Clark, 2002). SJH

biotechnology The term is perhaps most usefully defined by a phrase as simple as 'the uses of life' (to quote the title of one history of the concept: see Bud, 1993). Those searching for more technically precise versions should refer to Bains' (2003) A–Z on the subject. Although vague, this formulation has the virtue of getting across two of the more important things about biotechnology; namely, that it is both a very broad term and one that is confused and contested. Starting with the latter point, when one reviews the literature on the subject, it swiftly becomes apparent that there is nothing like an agreed definition of biotechnology. For some the notion covers everything from the ancient art of brewing through plant breeding and chemical engineering all the way to modern techniques of genetic manipulation, because all of these activities result from a coming together of human ingenuity, technical intervention and biological materials. For others, biotechnology is a frontier technology that should restrict the term to only the most recent elements of this long history; namely the proliferation of technical possibilities in the late twentieth/early twenty-first century around the convergence of an informational biology, a NEO-LIBERAL economic context and extensive legal protections on INTELLECTUAL PROPERTY. What is perhaps most significant about these competing positions is how they are mobilized during the many debates pertaining to biotechnology. One hears more of the former if the aim is reassurance and when long track records of safety are involved and more of the latter if the aim is to boost or debunk the technology by invoking its revolutionary novelty. Both accounts can be heard at the same time (as in some discussions of GM crops in the USA) when the aim is to make products appear at once 'substantially equivalent' to what has gone before *and* radically new and worthy of patents and payment. Even if one sticks with the restricted take on biotechnology, the term is used to cover a diverse range of activities. The colour-coded categorization of biotechnology in common use gives some sense of this:

(1) Red signifies biotechnology as applied to medical processes. This can include the genetic modification of bacteria and yeast in the development of drugs or the direct manipulation of a person's genome in an attempt to prevent or cure disease.

(2) Green signifies biotechnology as applied to agricultural processes. Most notably (and controversially), this includes the development of transgenic plants specifically designed (for example) to express or be resistant to a certain pesticide.

(3) White (sometimes) grey signifies biotechnology as applied to industrial processes. Examples here include growing organisms engineered to produce a useful chemical, or bacteria that help break down certain chemicals (as used to clear up oil spills).

(4) Blue, finally, signifies biotechnology as applied to aquatic, coastal or marine processes. Little used as yet but a rapidly expanding field, applications here focus on extracting useful substances from water-dwelling bacteria and other organisms.

Biotechnology in all its hues has long been identified as an area that provides both challenges and opportunities for GEOGRAPHY (Katz and Kirby, 1991). Following a series of more recent provocations (e.g. Castree, 1999c; Whatmore, 1999a; Spencer and Whatmore, 2001), a body of literature is now finally emerging within the discipline that is taking these opportunities and challenges seriously – see, for example, the articles collected in special issues edited by Bridge, Marsden and McManus (2003) and Greenhough and Roe (2006). Even more encouragingly, the best of this work is eschewing the familiar temptations of economic reductionism or technological determinism in favour of developing conceptually informed, empirically rich accounts of what happens when something new (an object or a

technique) is added to an already full world. Thus attention is paid at once to the new spaces of transformation and circulation involving biotechnology and also the questions of coexistence of existing and novel ways of life that such new spaces raise.   NB

Suggested reading
Bingham (2006); Parry (2004).

blockbusting A tactic engaged by American land speculators to buy housing units and then rent or sell them at inflated prices. In cities such as Chicago, INDUSTRIALIZATION, African-American MIGRATION to northern cities and racial SEGREGATION resulted in a growing, but spatially contained, African-American population (Philpott, 1991 [1978]). In White neighbourhoods adjacent to this African-American GHETTO, real estate agents would sell or rent a vacant unit to an African-American household, then use fear tactics about lower home values and racial change to persuade white homeowners to sell. Units would then be sold or rented to African-American households at grossly inflated prices. The result spatially expanded the GHETTO (Hirsch, 1983).   DGM

Suggested reading
Hirsch (1983).

body A rapidly growing field within GEOGRAPHY deals with social and spatial conceptions of the human body – often located in the tension between the body as a social and a biological phenomenon. This upsurge of interest in the body does not confine itself to geography, but occurs all over the social sciences and HUMANITIES. The background might be found in a mixture of circumstances. Some authors refer it to changes in the cultural landscape of late MODERNITY, involving a rise of consumer culture and self-expression. Others regard it primarily as a theoretical intervention, rectifying a former deficiency in social theory. And for still others, FEMINISM is held responsible for putting the body on the intellectual map. Initially, there is a division in the SOCIAL THEORY of the body, one that is often attributed to Maurice Merleau-Ponty and Michel Foucault, respectively. On the one side stand analyses of the body as lived, active and generative, and on the other side studies of the body as acted upon, as historically inscribed from without. Still other approaches are informed by PSYCHOANALYTIC THEORY. These different approaches are mostly translated into geography by means of feminist writings. A major source is Judith Butler's Foucauldian theory of PERFORMATIVITY, understood as 'the reiterative and citational practice by which discourse produces the effect that it names' (1993a, p. 2). For Butler, the body is socially constructed, embodying possibilities both conditioned and circumscribed by historical convention. Moi (1999), following Simone de Beauvoir, forwards a concept of the body as a 'situation' – a situation amongst many other social ones, but fundamental in the sense that it will always be a part of our lived experience and our coping with the environment. Grosz (1994) argues for a sexed corporeality in which ALTERITY is constitutive of (material, psychological and cultural) bodies and emphasizes the volatile boundaries of the bodies, permeated by bodily flows and fluids (see also ABJECTION).

Within geography, the degree to which TIME-GEOGRAPHY dealt with the body is a contested matter, but two approaches to human geography in the 1970s and 1980s did contain traces of the body. In HUMANISTIC GEOGRAPHY, lived and sentient body-subjects appeared, and in MARXIST GEOGRAPHY the body was implicitly present in notions of the material reproduction of labour power. The real upsurge of interest in the body, however, occurred in the 1990s, not surprisingly led by FEMINIST GEOGRAPHIES. This work can be summarized around three themes.

The first one is the body as *the geography closest in*. It includes the SPATIALITY of the body, drawing on PHENOMENOLOGY or on Lefebvre's theory of the PRODUCTION OF SPACE, including both the generative spatializing body and the historical confinement of the body in abstract space (Simonsen, 2005). Mostly, however, the literature has dealt with the inscription of POWER and resistance on the body, concurrently involving issues of performativity, body politics and the body as a site of struggle. Due to her processual, non-foundational approach to IDENTITY, many have incorporated Butler's notion of performativity into their work on the intersections between GENDER, SEXUALITY, SPACE and PLACE – for example, the performance of gay skinheads and lipstick lesbians in sexualized spaces (Bell, Binnie, Cream and Valentine, 1994), or gendered performances of work identities within the finance industry (McDowell and Court, 1994). The notion is, however, contested. For example, Nelson (1999) criticizes the translations of the language of performativity into geography for not being aware of

what she sees as its radical representational notion of body and SUBJECTIVITY, in this way initiating a lively discussion of the limits of performativity.

The second, related, theme is *other bodies*. Taking off from the insights of FEMINISM, POST-STRUCTURALISM and POST-COLONIALISM, it tackles the necessity of acknowledging differences and power in embodiment. The body is central in the process where dominant cultures designate certain groups (disabled, elderly, homosexual, fat, female, people of colour, people of other nations and so on: see AGEISM; DISABILITY; ETHNICITY; HOMOPHOBIA AND HETEROSEXISM; RACISM; SEXUALITY) as Other. Subordinate groups are defined by their bodies and according to norms that diminish and degrade them as ugly, loathsome, impure, deviant and so on, while privileged groups, by imprisoning the Other in her/his body, are able to take on the position as disembodied subjects. This 'scaling of bodies' has provoked analyses that on the one hand expose processes of domination and socio-spatial exclusion (Sibley, 1995) and on the other explore struggles for recognition and appropriation of space. A well-developed area within this group is QUEER THEORY, which explores negotiations and conflicts over symbolic and material spaces marked by exclusionary imperatives and politics.

Third, philosophies on the body have inspired theorists to *dismantle dualisms* that have long troubled Western thought and culture. Primarily, the mind/body dualism is addressed, subsequently leading to the ones of subject/object, CULTURE/NATURE, SEX/GENDER and ESSENTIALISM/constructionism. Feminists have shown how such dualisms have been strongly gendered, connecting the female body to nature, emotionality, non-consciousness and irrationality. Substantially, the dismantling of dualisms has worked as a means to expose the instability and fluidity of bodily-ascribed identities. Epistemologically, it has enforced the acknowledgment that not only the objects of analysis but also the geographer her-/himself are embodied. Many geographers have, at least in principle, adopted the notion of embodied or SITUATED KNOWLEDGE as a substitute for decontextualized, disembodied, 'objective' knowledge.

As pointed out by several authors (e.g. Callard, 1998), the first wave of body-literature within geography favoured particular ways of understanding the body. A wealth of studies was devoted to body-inscriptions, body regimes and discourses on bodies, while practices of material and fleshy bodies attracted less attention. This gap has, however, started to be filled: Longhurst (2001) implements Grosz's theory of the volatile materiality of the body through ideas of body boundaries, body fluids, ABJECTION and (im)pure spaces; studies on illness, impairment and DISABILITY explore 'body troubles' in everyday coping with the environment; and theories of PRACTICE and NON-REPRESENTATIONAL THEORY focus on moving bodies and the performative and material nature of embodiment. The latter also dissolves the distinction between the human and non-human, the organic and non-organic (see also CYBORG).   KS

Suggested reading
Bell and Valentine (1995); Butler and Parr (1999); Longhurst (2001); Nast and Pile (1998).

border A form of BOUNDARY associated with the rise of the modern NATION-STATE and the establishment of an inter-state GEOPOLITICAL order, founded – most famously with the foundational myths of the 1648 Treaty of Westphalia (Teschke, 2003) – on the political norms of national states claiming and using terror to control TERRITORY (as the etymology is also sometimes interpreted: see Hindess, 2006). Both on maps and on the ground, borders make spaces of national SOVEREIGNTY, and are thus key sites where the 'inside versus outside' distinctions of TERRITORIALITY and modern INTERNATIONAL RELATIONS are at once reproduced, reinforced, contested and transcended (Walker, 1993; Agnew, 2003a). Thus, as the French philosopher Etienne Balibar suggests, borders are 'overdetermined, and in that sense, sanctioned, reduplicated and relativized by other geopolitical divisions' (Balibar, 2002, p. 79). It is for this same reason that political geographers have increasingly focused on what many call 're-(b) ordering' (Newman, 2002; Kolossov, 2005; Van Houtum, 2005; Van Houtum, Kramsch and Zierhofer, 2005).

Borders appear in geopolitical discourses that at once reproduce and reinforce the nation-state. In media ranging from the legal and pedagogic to the prosaic and banal – from court-case cartography, school maps and museums, to murals, cartoons and even weather forecasts – IMAGINATIVE GEOGRAPHIES script and thereby sanction the divisions of national borders (Paasi, 2005a; Sparke, 2005; Anderson, 2006a; Painter, 2006). These cultural geographies of border construction in turn inform the actual enforcement of borders on the ground through both social practices and state practices of border control (Nevins, 2002; Coleman, 2005). Many border-buttressing social practices are xenophobic, and remain animated today in many parts of the world by provincial, racist and/or masculinist fantasies about foreign 'floods' overwhelming homeland defenses (see Theweleit, 1987; Darian-Smith, 1999; Wright, 1999b; Price, 2004). However, while such social reinforcement continues to reduplicate twentieth-century divisions produced by liberal regimes of ethno-racial and sexual GOVERNMENTALITY, contemporary state practices of border control are simultaneously being shaped by the new CLASS divisions and related but context-contingent recombination of neo-liberal governmentality with neo-liberal GOVERNANCE. It is in this way that the borders inside and around various free trade regions are being both softened and hardened simultaneously. Within the EU (Sparke, 2000a; Walters, 2002), the NAFTA region (Bhandar, 2004; Coleman, 2005; Gilbert, 2007), and diverse, smaller scale cross-border free market development zones (for which the Malaysia–Indonesia–Singapore growth triangle is the prototype; see Sparke, Sidaway, Bunnell and Grundy-Warr, 2004), governments are attempting to bifurcate border management: facilitating fast crossing for business travellers and increasing punitive policing of working class 'others' deemed dangerous to the neo-liberal free market order.

The neo-liberal class-divided relativization of borders is not happening in the same way everywhere. Within the NAFTA zone there remain all sorts of informal cross-border economies (see Staudt, 1998), and in Europe, while the old Cold War East German/West German border has turned into an Ossie/Wessie social class divide (Berdhal, 1999), the Iron Curtain border of the COLD WAR past has not been bifurcated but, rather, subsumed into an EU growth and integration zone (Scott, 2002; Smith, 2002a). And these kinds of complexities seem minor in contrast to the ways in which the new border between Israeli-occupied enclaves and Palestinian-controlled parts of the West Bank reduplicates the geopolitics of religious and ethnic divisions with a vengeance, all the while relativizing the old Green Line and hopes of a 'good border' by imposing a monumental and militarized class divide with the new concrete curtain of the colonial present (Gregory, 2004b; Newman, 2005; see also Falah and Newman, 1995).

Contextual contingencies noted, the emergence of a transnational business class with increasingly global RIGHTS to own PROPERTY, make contracts and move freely has clearly been marked at and on borders the world over. State border management is becoming increasingly transnationalized in its global co-ordination, with border-relativizing reliance being placed on individualized biometric codes rather than traditional national passports (Adey, 2004; Salter, 2007). Meanwhile, as the US continues to wage its so-called war on terror, the soft-COSMOPOLITANISM of the border-crossing kinetic elites seems set to be accompanied by the creation of a carceral cosmopolitanism for those border-crossers deemed a threat to the free world (Sparke, 2006). Within these developments we can see – to return to a term of Balibar's – the 'other scene' of borders today: a scene in which the sovereignty system supposedly established at Westphalia is superseded by a new kind of global 'terrortory', delinked from the nation-state and its geographical borders (cf. Kelly, 2005; Hindess, 2006).   MS

borderlands A key term in two contemporary literatures, the concept-METAPHOR of borderlands is employed alternatively as either a research re-focusing concept for scholars who study cross-border regional development (e.g. Pratt and Brown, 2000), or as a meaning re-making metaphor designed to disrupt normalizing notions of NATION and the NATION-STATE (e.g. Anzaldúa, 1999). Both uses of the term refer back to the geographical REGIONS surrounding international BORDERS, and both also frequently involve attempts to describe the lives and IMAGINATIVE GEOGRAPHIES of people whose daily practices, economic activities and cultural connections cross the borders that define nation-states. But whereas research on cross-border regional development tries to draw analytical comparisons between different models of borderlands GOVERNANCE, work on the multiple meanings of borderlands seeks to find antidotes to nationalist chauvinism and attendant forms of ethnic absolutism in the cross-cultural intermixing of everyday borderland life. This does not mean that the disruptive uses of the term are always focused on just cultural HYBRIDITY. There are some brilliant borderlands studies that underline how everyday economic, social and political ties across border regions are just as disruptive of normative assumptions about nation-states and related forms of gendered, racialized and/or

ethnicized identity (Staudt, 1998; Berdahl, 1999; Darian-Smith, 1999, Price, 2004). Likewise, there are also many usefully sobering studies that show how, in all too many cases, such disruptions still continue to be exploited, controlled and/or destroyed through various combinations of state- and market-mediated VIOLENCE (Wright, 1999b; Nevins, 2002; Lindquist, 2004; Coleman, 2005).

Inspired in part by the studies that highlight how POWER relations become particularly evident in borderlands, and catalysed by an emerging governmental interest in cross-border regional planning, there has been a recent explosion of articles and edited volumes on border-region development that are increasingly attuned to the ways in which such regions make manifest diverse political geographies of reterritorialization (Eskelinen, Liikanen and Oksa, 1999; Perkmann and Sum, 2002; Nicol and Townsend-Gault, 2005; van Houtum, Kramsch and Ziefhofer, 2005). While a few contributions to this literature seek to emulate a corporate TRANSNATIONAL-ISM and promote branded borderlands for capitalist development (e.g. Artibise, 2005), other works critically chart the ways in which such place promotionalism feeds into and out of the cross-border regional entrenchment of NEO-LIBERALISM (Perkmann, 2002; Nicol and Townsend-Gault, 2005; Sparke, 2005). But borderlands continue to be shaped by a multitude of other forms of reterritorialization too, and whether these take geographical shape as geopolitics (see Scott, J.W., 2002, 2005b; Brunn, Watkins, Fargo and Lepawsky, 2005; Edwards, 2005), hybrid natures (Sletto, 2002; Fall, 2005) or post-colonial sovereignties (Mbembe, 2000; Kramsch, 2002; Sidaway, 2002; Sparke, Sidaway, Bunnell and Grundy-Warr, 2004), borderlands provide usefully prismatic lenses on to the changing geography of power in the context of GLOBALIZATION. MS

Boserup thesis Classical political economists, and Malthus and Ricardo in particular, developed in the early stages of DEMOGRAPHIC TRANSITION in Europe a macroeconomic theory of the relations between population growth and agriculture. Ricardo (1817) distinguished between intensive and extensive agricultural expansion: *extensive expansion* presumed the extension of cultivation into new lands that were marginal and therefore subject to diminishing returns to labour and capital, whereas *intensive expansion* enhanced the output of existing lands through the application of better

53

weeding, fertilizer, drainage and so on, which was also subject to diminishing returns to labour and capital. Ricardo, like Malthus (1803), assumed that population growth increases would be arrested by a decline in real wages, by increases in rents and by per capita food decline.

There is a third form of intensification that rests upon the deployment of the increasing labour force to crop farmland more frequently (i.e. to increase the cropping intensity or to reduce the fallow). The *reduction of the period of fallow* (the period of non-cultivation or recovery in which the land is allowed to regenerate its fertility and soil capacities) was a major way in which European agriculture increased its output during periods of population growth, as observed at the time when Ricardo and Malthus were writing. Fallowing does not imply poorer or more distant land, but as the fallow length is reduced greater capital and labour inputs are required to prevent the gradual decline of crop yields and the loss of fodder for animals.

Esther Boserup (1965, 1981) made fallow reduction a central plank of her important work on agrarian intensification. While fallow reduction is also likely to yield diminishing returns, these are more than compensated for by the additions to total output conferred by increased cropping frequency.

In the eighth century the two-field system predominated in Western Europe, but by the twelfth and thirteenth centuries the three-field system had come to displace its two-field counterpart in high-density regions (see FIELD SYSTEM). By the eighteenth and nineteenth centuries, the fallow had begun to disappear entirely. Boserup (1965) saw this fallowing reduction as the central theme in agrarian history and the centrepiece around which the Malthusian debates over overpopulation and famine ultimately turned (cf. MALTHUSIAN MODEL). In her view, output per person–hour is highest in the long-fallow systems – for example, the shifting or swiddening systems of the humid tropical forest zone, in which diverse polycropping of plots for one or two seasons is then followed by a fallow of 15–25 years (depending on local ecological circumstances: cf. SHIFTING CULTIVATION) – and population growth is the stimulus both for reduction in fallow and the innovations associated with intensified land use.

Boserup envisaged a progressive series of fallow reductions driven by the pressure of population (and the threat of exceeding the CARRYING CAPACITY). Long-fallow systems

that are technologically simple (associated only with the digging stick and the axe) are displaced by bush fallow (6–10 year fallow) and short fallowing (2–3 year fallow) in which the plough is a prerequisite. Annual, and finally multiple, cropping appear as responses to continued population pressure. Across this progression of intensification is a reduction in output per person–hour, but a vast increase in total output. The shift to annual and multiple cropping also requires substantially new forms of skill and investment, however, which typically demand STATE-organized forms of investment and surplus mobilization. Boserup saw much of Africa and Latin America as occupying an early position in a linear model of intensification in which output could be expanded by fallow reduction. The 'Boserup thesis' refers to the relationship between population growth and agrarian intensification, measured through fallow reduction and a decreasing output per person–hour.

Implicit in the Boserup thesis, although she did not develop these implications, is the changing role of LAND TENURE, the increasing capitalization of the land and the more complex forms of state–society interaction. Indeed, Boserup's work has been taken up by a number of archaeologists and anthropologists, who have charted patterns of state formation and social development in terms of agrarian intensification.

Boserup's anti-Malthusian theory lays itself open to all manner of charges, including a non-linear form of techno-demographic determinism and a general lack of attention to the ECOLOGICAL limits of intensification (Grigg, 1980; cf. TELEOLOGY). It is not at all clear how or whether Boserup's thesis can be applied to MARKET economies. Indeed, her thesis does not seem to be much help, for example, in the English case: in its essentials, the agricultural technology of the eighteenth century (the Norfolk four-course rotation) had been available since the Middle Ages, and although the eighteenth century was a period of population growth, the previous period of sustained demographic growth from the mid-sixteenth century had witnessed no intensification as such (Overton, 1996: see AGRICULTURAL REVOLUTION). Processes of intensification are naturally on the historical record and the reduction of fallowing in the THIRD WORLD – whether driven by demographic growth or not – has been and continues to be documented (see Guyer, 1997). But intensification is a socially, culturally and politically complex process. To the extent that fallow reduction involves someone working harder and differently, the question of who works, when and for what return (a question played out in terms of age, gender and CLASS in the PEASANT household) is not posed by Boserup. Here, newer work on household dynamics has more to offer (Carney and Watts, 1990). 　　　　　MW

boundary At once a geographical *marker* and a geographical *maker* of regulative authority in social relations. As markers of authority, boundaries range considerably in SCALE, significance and social stability. From international boundaries that mark the BORDERS between NATION-STATES to the barbed-wire boundaries that mark the perimeters of export-processing zones, to the racially, religiously and/or sexually exclusive boundaries that still mark the privileged places of decision-making occupied by straight, white, Christian, men of property in America, boundaries take many different forms. But whether boundaries are the product of international conventions, economic expedience or cultural conservatism, a key point highlighted in the work of geographers is that boundaries are also geographically constitutive makers as well as markers of regulative power relations. In other words, international boundary lines actively operate to create and consolidate the global norms of nation-state TERRITORIALITY and the national identities forged under the resulting aegis of state sovereignty (Paasi, 1996). Barbed-wire fences around EXPORT-PROCESSING ZONES serve directly to carve off such spaces from wider political geographies of civil interaction, labour organization and democratic oversight, thereby depriving workers inside of numerous citizenship rights (Klein, 2002). And the invisible but often impenetrable boundaries referred to by terms such as the 'glass ceiling' also clearly help enable and enforce spaces of privileged authority (Berg, 2002).

Nevertheless, not all boundaries create their regulative effects through binary 'us–them' partitions. In many cases of state boundary drawing *inside* modern nation-states – including the boundaries drawn to delineate electoral districts, schools districts, police districts, public health districts and so on – the act of inscribing a boundary on a MAP and enforcing it with routinized bureaucratic state actions on the ground helps create the larger singular effect we call 'the state'. As Timothy Mitchell (1991) has argued, following Foucault, STATE effects can thereby be said to emerge through the everyday acts of spatial organization created by government. This is also no doubt

why the publishers of a book such as *Seeing like a state* (Scott, J.C., 1998b) saw fit to put an everyday image of a distinctly right-angled turn in a road on the cover, an apparently arbitrary turn, presumably produced by some jurisdictional boundary marked on a state map. But since a scholar such as Mitchell argues *vis-à-vis* traditional state theories (including the highly anthropomorphized and sovereigntist kind advanced by Scott), the lesson of such geographical boundary making is not that there is a king-like state whose boundary-drawing is a sign of top-down state dominance. Rather, the point is that along with all the state practices that the boundaries enable, the process of boundary drawing is itself a disciplinary dynamic that helps consolidate the authority of the state. Mitchell applies this argument most directly to theorizing the emergence of nation-state power, but it can equally be argued to apply to sub-national and transnational forms of state-making too (Sparke, 2005). Once examined in such venues as courtrooms and free trade tribunals, boundary drawing can also be seen as a highly contested mediation process through which the power relations of everyday social life, and the power relations of government themselves begin to reappear as if divided by a stark state/SOCIETY boundary. However, as work by geographers on everything from electoral GERRYMANDERING (Forest, 2005) to community policing (Herbert, 2006) shows, the concept of such a clear-cut state/society boundary is better reinterpreted as a site of fraught political–geographical struggles, struggles which in the very process of blurring the abstract state–society distinction often end up creating new jurisdictional boundary lines on the ground. 　　　　　MS

Brenner thesis A thesis proposed by historian Robert Brenner (1976) as a contribution to a running debate within primarily Marxist scholarship about the transition from FEUDALISM to CAPITALISM. Brenner emphasized the ways in which CLASS, and more specifically PROPERTY relations, served as a 'prime mover' of economic change. His basic premise is that the relationship between landlord and tenant was exploitative and depended on 'non-economic compulsion'. Thus relations of production in thirteenth- and fourteenth-century England were dominated by the institution of serfdom, which was buttressed by the manorial system and the common LAW that excluded serfs from access to royal courts (which were reserved for those who were legally free). Hence lords could act arbitrarily in their dealings with their unfree tenants. The power of this exploitative relationship provided a ready explanation for low and declining productivity within the peasant sector before the Black Death, which in this analysis has little if anything to do with a population-RESOURCE imbalance as proposed in the POSTAN THESIS. Not only was this relationship inimical to the maintenance of effective husbandry within the peasantry, but it also led to a build-up of tenants on the land, since it curtailed the MIGRATION of serfs to areas where their labour could be more effectively deployed.

The struggle between lords and PEASANTS had different outcomes in different regions, which Brenner argues accounts for macrogeographical variations in the move towards agrarian CAPITALISM in EUROPE: in England lords were the victors, since tenants never gained absolute property rights, whereas in France peasants were far more successful. Brenner contends that landlord capacity was diminished in the period of demographic depression after the Black Death, but that when population growth resumed in the sixteenth century, lords who still retained their power were able to evict peasant producers and install entrepreneurial tenants who farmed larger holdings with the increasing use of wage labourers. In this way, Brenner explains how agrarian capitalism emerged earlier in England than in the rest of Europe.

The thesis has been subject to considerable debate in history and HISTORICAL GEOGRAPHY (Aston and Philpin, 1985). Many now claim that serfdom did not operate in the manner proposed by Brenner, since custom gave unfree tenants much protection from market forces – and, indeed, benefited this group in the period of price and rent inflation in the thirteenth and early fourteenth centuries (Hatcher, 1981; Kanzaka, 2002; Campbell, 2005). Furthermore, English customary LAW may have been greatly influenced by the common law to the extent that lords were in no position to operate their courts arbitrarily to their advantage (Razi and Smith, 1996b). While Brenner purports to treat the landlord–tenant relationship as an endogenous component, he is reluctant to admit the impact of exogenous forces associated with demographic change driven by epidemiological movements that have little to do with human agency (Hatcher and Bailey, 2001). Others have argued that changes in the distribution of land and the stimulus of land markets came as much from within the tenantry as it did from landlord initiatives (Glennie, 1988; Hoyle, 1990; Smith, 1998b). Likewise, it has been claimed that middling sized owner-occupied farms were the principal source of an early modern AGRICULTURAL REVOLUTION (Allen, 1992). Even within Marxist circles, there are those who would stress the emergence of a WORLD SYSTEM in which international trade and colonial expansion served to advantage England and its near neighbour Holland, leading to the emergence of large urban centres, which in turn stimulated demand for foodstuffs and the move towards capitalist FARMING. Such arguments have loomed large in the writings of Pomeranz (2001), who also stresses the importance of access to the 'ghost acres' of the AMERICAS as fundamental to English economic success.   RMS

Suggested reading
Aston and Philpin (1985); Brenner (1976).

C

cadastral mapping A system of SURVEYING and recording the BOUNDARIES, structures and salient features of land parcels in order to confirm ownership, support the buying and selling of land, promote the assessment and taxation of landed PROPERTY, and delineate the territorial privileges of tenants and others assigned limited RIGHTS. In addition to its traditional role in the commodification of land, a modern multi-purpose cadastre provides an efficient framework for URBAN AND REGIONAL PLANNING, land-use regulation, and the management of publicly and privately owned INFRASTRUCTURE such as sewers and distribution pipelines for water and natural gas (National Research Council Panel on a Multipurpose Cadastre, 1983). Where data-sharing arrangements and a common plane-coordinate system permit, a GEOGRAPHIC INFORMATION SYSTEM can readily integrate land-record data with street-address information, terrain data, CENSUS results, and environmental and natural-HAZARDS data, including flood-zone boundaries.

Allied with notions of private property, cadastral MAPS are among the oldest cartographic forms (see CARTOGRAPHY, HISTORY OF), in use at least as early as 2300 BCE, when the Babylonians described land boundaries and structures on clay tablets (Kain and Baigent, 1992, p. 1). The Egyptians and the Greeks were less inclined to map property surveys than the Romans, who used maps to tax private holdings and differentiate them from state lands. The collapse of the Roman Empire in the fifth century AD temporarily ended property mapping in Europe, but Renaissance CAPITALISM revived the map as a management tool for private estates and precipitated the development of intricate state cadastres during the ENLIGHTENMENT. Cadastral mapping was essential to European colonization of the New World, where land grants and orderly settlement depended on map-based land registration (see COLONIALISM).

Cadastral mapping has an important role in the THIRD WORLD, where comprehensive land-record systems can promote land reform by validating traditional holdings, minimizing boundary disputes, promoting CONSERVATION of NATURAL RESOURCES, and reducing land fragmentation, which can undermine agricultural productivity. However promising, cadastral reform easily fails if poorly planned or not fully implemented (Ballantyne, Bristow et al., 2000).

In the more developed world, online cadastres have heightened the innate conflict between personal privacy and open access to public records (Monmonier, 2003). Public access to cadastral information is a fundamental right in the USA and other countries in which local officials base evaluations of taxable real property on the parcel descriptions and sale prices of nearby or similar properties. Without access, citizens cannot judge the fairness of their assessments and present an informed challenge to an inequitable evaluation. By making transaction data far more readily available, the INTERNET has undermined the expectation of privacy among buyers reluctant to disclose their purchase price. Even so, benefits clearly trump injuries insofar as ready disclosure promotes a more knowledgeable real-property market and arguably fairer tax assessments. MM

Suggested reading
Jeffres (2003); Kain and Baigent (1992).

camp 'The hidden matrix ... of the political space in which we are living' (Agamben, 1998, p. 166). Agamben's controversial thesis focuses on the juridico-political structure (or *NOMOS*) that produced the concentration camp. These camps were introduced by European colonial regimes in Cuba and South Africa at the close of the nineteenth century, but Agamben is most interested in those established by the Nazis during the Second World War. Unlike many writers, Agamben does not see these as aberrations from the project of MODERNITY – paroxysmal spaces – but, rather, as *paradigmatic* spaces. What took place in them was made possible, so Agamben claims, because the camps were materializations of the space of exception (see EXCEPTION, SPACE OF) in which the state withdrew legal protections from particular groups of people (Jews, gays and Romanies among them). By this means, millions of victims of FASCISM could be reduced to BARE LIFE (cf. Agamben, 1999). But the camp is neither peculiar to fascism

57

nor limited to an enclosed space. For Agamben, 'the camp is the space that is opened when the state of exception begins to become the rule', and he insists that 'we find ourselves virtually in the presence of a camp every time such a structure is created' (Agamben, 1988, p. 174). Seen thus, it is by no means absent from liberal-democratic societies. Hence Agamben draws formal parallels between concentration camps and the sites where states now hold illegal immigrants or REFUGEES (cf. Perera, 2002), and he claims that the juridico-political structure through which prisoners taken during the 'war on terror' are held confirms that the global generalization of the state of exception is intensifying (cf. Gregory, 2006b, 2007). 'The normative aspect of LAW can be thus be obliterated and contradicted with impunity,' he continues, through a constellation of SOVEREIGN POWER and STATE violence that 'nevertheless still claims to be applying the law.' In such a circumstance, he concludes, the camp has become 'the new biopolitical *nomos* of the planet' (see BIOPOLITICS) and 'the juridico-political system [has transformed] itself into a killing machine' (Agamben, 1988).

That Agamben's thesis is concerned with the *metaphysics* of power and the logic of juridico-political structures needs emphasis. Bernstein (2004) objects that what then becomes lost from view is the complex of institutions, practices and people through which these reductions to bare life are attempted: in the case of Auschwitz, for example, the gas chambers, the guards, the huts, the watch-towers, the railways, the police, the round-ups – in short, the whole apparatus of VIOLENCE that produced the HOLOCAUST. But this is precisely Agamben's point: 'Instead of deducing the definition of the camp from the events that took place there, we will ask: What is a camp, what is its juridico-political structure, that such events could take place there?' In his view, the urgent political task is to disclose 'the juridical procedures and deployments of power by which human beings could be so completely deprived of their RIGHTS and prerogatives that no act committed against them could appear any longer as a crime' (1998, pp. 166, 171). Even so, it is not at all clear that Agamben is much interested in the details of those other 'deployments of power' or the spaces that are produced through them, and nor does he register the ways in which RESISTANCE to the production and proliferation of camps is mobilized. DG

Suggested reading
Agamben (1998, pp. 166–76); Minca (2004).

capital In everyday parlance, capital is an asset to be mobilized by a group, individual or institution as wealth. This economic sense of capital has, according to Raymond Williams (1983 [1976], p. 51), been present in English since the seventeenth century and in a fully developed form since the eighteenth – derived from its general sense of 'head' or 'chief'. Capital in this sense might be a stock of money (invested to secure a rate of return), a pension fund or a piece of property. In the broadest sense – often deployed as such by conventional forms of economics – capital is an asset of whatever kind capable of yielding a source of income for its owner (which is typically, depending on the asset and the legal rights to it, a claim on interest, on RENT or on profits). In classical economics, capital was assumed to be one of a trio of factors of production (land and labour being the others), distinguished by the fact that it was produced (*contra* land), could not be used up in the course of production as might a RESOURCE and could be used in the production of other goods. Both Adam Smith and David Ricardo referred to a distinction between fixed and circulating forms of capital. Capital goods are already produced durable goods, available for use as a factor of production. In this classical (and indeed neo-classical) sense, capital was a stock, in contradistinction to investment over time (a flow). Implicit in all of these definitions is a twofold sense of capital being trans-historical (it applies to every society) and it posits the fact of inanimate objects (land) being generative (of income). Over the past half-century there have been many efforts to classify capital beyond its narrow economic meaning. The list is now very long (see Putnam, 2001; Bourdieu, 2002): human capital (skills, competences, education), cultural capital (the symbolic and hermeneutic CLASS powers deployed in the political and economic realm), SOCIAL CAPITAL (the social networks and social agencies deployed in economic development), political capital (political resources deployed within different domains of politics – for example, the state, the family) and finance capital (originally developed a century ago by Hilferding to address the increasing integration of industrial and banking enterprises).

The Marxist conception of capital stands in sharp contradistinction to these sorts of claims and to all conventional definitions. Capital is first a social form that pre-dates CAPITALISM but dominates in, and is generic to, capitalism as a system of generalized commodity production. Capital is not a thing, but is a 'social relation' that appears in the form of things (money, means of production). Capital does indeed entail making money or creating wealth but, as Marx (1967) pointed out, what matters are the relations by which some have money and others do not, how money is put to work, and how the PROPERTY relations that engender such a social world are reproduced. Capital, said Marx, 'is a definite social production relation belonging to a definite historical formation of society which is manifested in a thing and lends this thing a specific social character' (Marx, 1967, vol. III, p. 48). Under capitalism, capital is 'value in motion'; that is to say, it is an expansionary social value that drives, and arises from, the production process. The process – multifaceted and unstable – by which money is converted into labour, raw materials, capital goods, commodities and back into money again is what Marx called 'the general formula of capital'. Capital arises from the social labour organized for generalized COMMODITY production – that is to say, a competitive system in which commodities produce commodities. The enormous complexity of the category is bound up with the ways in which the meaning of the word 'capital' shifts and transforms itself in Marx's work, leading some to note that a word such as capital is bat-like: one can see in it both birds and mice.

Capital comes to dominate in a capitalist MODE OF PRODUCTION. Capitalist societies are marked by the fact that capital is socially owned and organized in particular ways – by a capitalist class. Contemporary forms of capitalism have, however, vastly complicated this class map, not least by the ways in which shareholder capital (pension funds, individual shareholders and government ownership of stock) has refigured the cartography of the ownership of capital. Geographers have largely focused on the ways in which capital as a social relation has spatial and ecological expressions – for example, the geography of ACCUMULATION or INDUSTRIAL DISTRICTS, and the relations between value in motion and global climate change – and on the prismatic ways in which capital attaches natural characteristics to things that are socially produced (see Harvey, 1999 [1982]; Smith, 1982; *RETORT*, 2005). MW

capitalism   As a word denoting a distinctive economic system, 'capitalism' began to appear, according to Raymond Williams (1983 [1976], p. 50) in English, French and German from the early nineteenth century (although the *Oxford English Dictionary* cites its first use by Thackeray in 1854). 'Capitalist' – as a key actor in a capitalist system – has a longer semantic history, dating back a half-century earlier, but this term too was clearly being used to describe an economic system – sketched by Adam Smith and the Scottish political economists among others – for which the word capitalism had not yet been invented. Capital and capitalist, says Williams, were technical terms in any economic system but gradually became deployed to account for a particular stage of historical development, and out of this shift in meaning crystallized the term capitalism. Marx, who did not use the term until the 1870s, was the central figure in distinguishing CAPITAL as an economic category from capitalism as a specific social form in which ownership of the means of production was centralized (through a capitalist CLASS), and that depended upon a system of wage-labour in which a class had been 'freed' from property. Capitalism in this sense, again as Williams observed, was "a product of a developing bourgeois society' (1976, p. 51). The term gained some traction in the 1880s in the German socialist movement and was then extended to non-socialist writing, though its first extensive English and French usages seem to not have been until the early twentieth century. In the wake of 1917, and most especially after the Second World War, capitalism was rarely used as a descriptor by its promoters, and was deliberately replaced by such terms as free or private enterprise and, more recently still, the MARKET or free market system (as part of the neo-liberal discourse of the 1980s and 1990s).

What, then, are the defining qualities of capitalism, understood as a distinctive MODE OF PRODUCTION? It is a historically specific form of economic and social organization and in its industrial variant can be roughly dated to mid-eighteenth century Britain, but the theorization of its conditions of possibility and its internal dynamics have necessarily been an object of intense debate. Classical POLITICAL ECONOMY – Adam Smith and David Ricardo – and its Marxian critique both accepted that capitalism was a class system, that labour and capital were central to its operations, and that capitalism as a system was expansive, dynamic and unstable. These accounts fasten upon the economy – or, more properly, the political economy – and the centrality of PROPERTY relations, the market–commodity nexus, the separation of the workers from the means of production and the centralization of capitalist control under the figure of the capitalist-entrepreneur. These claims – to the extent that they reflect some common ground – are subsequently elaborated in radically different ways. Some cling to a narrow definition of ECONOMY (theorized in different ways) as central to the intellectual enterprise; others seek to link economy, CULTURE, politics and SOCIETY into a more elaborated sense – what Max Weber called a 'cosmos' – of a capitalist system. In general, the development and institutionalization of the critical social sciences has seen a massive proliferation of opinion – and of conceptual apparatuses – for the examination of actually existing capitalist systems.

Some of this diversity of opinion can be appreciated by a consideration of a quartet of theorists. Adam Smith, like other classical political economists, was concerned with the distribution and accumulation of economic surplus and the problems of wage, price and employment determination. Writing at the birth of industrial manufacture, the key to the *Wealth of nations* (see Smith, 2003) is the concept of an autonomous self-regulating market economy described as CIVIL SOCIETY. Smith's genius was to have seen the possibility of an autonomous civil society, its capacity for self-regulation if left unhindered and its capacity for maximizing welfare independent of state action. Smith located capitalism at the intersection of the DIVISION OF LABOUR and the growth of markets. Furthermore, in this system self-interested individuals indirectly and inadvertently promoted collective interest through the functions of self-regulating markets. The growth of commerce and the growth of liberty reinforce one another under capitalism. In its neo-classical variant, labour markets are seen as no different than any commodity market and capitalist markets are assumed, if unimpeded by the state or other distortions, to function to produce a general equilibrium. Friedrich von Hayek's (1944) account of liberal capitalism took this reasoning to its limit. Capitalism was conceived of as a unity of liberty, science and the spontaneous orders that co-evolved to form modern society (the 'Great Society', as he termed it). It is a defence of the liberal (unplanned) market order from which the preconditions of civilization – competition and experimentation – had emerged. Hayek, like Weber, saw this modern world as an iron cage constituted by impersonality, a loss of community, individualism and personal responsibility. But, *contra* Weber,

these structures, properly understood, were the very expressions of liberty. From the vantage point of the 1940s this (classical) liberal project was, as Hayek saw it, under threat. Indeed, what passed for liberal capitalism was a travesty, a distorted body of ideas warped by constructivist rationalism, as opposed to what he called 'evolutionary rationalism'. Milton Friedman (2002 [1962]), in the realm of economic theory, waged this battle from the 1960s onwards.

For Max Weber, the capitalist cosmos was guided by systems of calculability and rationality – this is what gave Western capitalism its specificity – which grew in part as an unintended consequence of Protestantism (see Weber, 2001 [1904–5]). Formal rationality produced a capitalist society characterized by large-scale industrial production, centralized bureaucratic administration and the 'iron cage' of capitalism that shapes individuals' lives with 'irresistible force'. *Contra* Smith's roseate vision of capitalism – though always wary of the costs of class oppression, in his view dished out by corrupt government – Weber's vision of capitalism was ultimately bleak, always operating in the shadow of the 'totally administered society'.

Karl Polanyi was a Hungarian economic historian and socialist, who believed that the nineteenth-century liberal capitalist order had died, never to be revived (see Polanyi, 2001 [1944]). By 1940, every vestige of the international liberal order had disappeared, the product of the necessary adoption of measures designed to hold off the ravages of the self-regulating market; that is, 'market despotism'. It was the conflict between the market and the elementary requirements of an organized social life that made some form of collectivism or planning inevitable. The liberal market order was, *contra* Hayek, not 'spontaneous' but a planned development, and its demise was the product of the market order itself. A market order could just as well produce the freedom to exploit as the freedom to associate. The grave danger, in Polanyi's view, was that liberal utopianism might return in the idea of freedom as nothing more than the advocacy of free enterprise, in which planning is 'the denial of freedom', and the justice and liberty offered by regulation or control just 'a camouflage of slavery'. LIBERALISM on this account will always degenerate, ultimately compromised by an authoritarianism that will be invoked as a counterweight to the threat of mass DEMOCRACY. Modern capitalism, he said, contained the famous 'double-movement' in which markets were serially and coextensively disembedded from, and re-embedded in, social institutions and relations. In particular, the possibility of a counter-hegemony to the self-regulating market resided in the resistance to (and reaction against) the commodification of the three fictitious commodities – land, labour and money – that represented the spontaneous defence of society.

Marx's account identifies a fundamental contradiction at the heart of capitalism – a contradiction between two great classes (workers and owners of capital) that is fundamentally an exploitative relation shaped by the appropriation of surplus. Unlike FEUDALISM, in which surplus appropriation is transparent (in the forms of taxes and levies made by landowners and lords, backed by the power of the church and Crown), surplus value is obscured in the capitalist LABOUR PROCESS. Marx (1967) argues that labour is the only source of value and value is the embodiment of a quantum of socially necessary labour. It is the difference between the sale of a worker's labour power and the amount of labour necessary to reproduce it that is the source of surplus value. The means by which capital extracts this surplus value under capitalism – through the working day, labour intensification and enhancing labour productivity – coupled to the changing relations between variable and constant capital determine, in Marx's view, the extent, degree and forms of exploitation. In the first volume of *Capital*, Marx identifies the origins of surplus value in the organization of production (the social relations of production so-called). In volume II, Marx explains how exploitation affects the circulation of capital, and in volume III he traces the division of the total product of exploitation among its beneficiaries and the contradiction so created. In Marxist theory two kinds of material interests – interests securing material welfare and interests enhancing economic power – are linked through exploitation (exploiters simultaneously obtain greater economic welfare and greater economic power by retaining control over the social allocation of surplus through investments). Members of a class, in short, hold a common set of interests and therefore have common interests with respect to the process of exploitation (see also MARXISM).

In the wake of Marx's work, the central debates over capitalist exploitation have turned on (i) whether the labour theory of value is a necessary condition for any truth claim about exploitation, (ii) whether exploitation can be made congruent with the complex forms of class differentiation associated with modern industrial society, and (iii) whether there are non-Marxist accounts of exploitation. In NEO-CLASSICAL ECONOMICS, for example, exploitation under capitalism is seen as 'the failure to pay labour its marginal product' (Brewer, 1987, p. 86). Exploitation in this view is micro-level and organizational. That is to say, using micro-economic theory exploitation is a type of market failure due to the existence of monopoly or monopsony. In more developed versions of this organizational view, exploitation can be rooted in extra-market forces; for example, free-riding or asymmetric information (the so-called principal–agent problem). A more structural account of exploitation from a liberal vantage point would be the ideas of Henry George or John Maynard Keynes, for whom land owners or rentier classes (non-working owners of financial wealth) produce not exploitation in the Marxist sense, but exploitation as waste and inefficiency due to 'special interests'.

In the Marxian tradition, there has been in general an abandonment of the labour theory of value – away from the view of Elster (1986) that 'workers are exploited if they work longer hours than the number of hours employed in the goods they consume' (1986, p. 121) – towards John Roemer's notion that a group is exploited if it has "some conditionally feasible alternative under which its members would be better off" (Roemer, 1986a, p. 136). Perhaps the central figure in developing these arguments is Erik Olin Wright (1985), who sought to account for the contradictory class location of the 'middle classes' (in that they are simultaneously exploiters and exploited). Building on the work of Roemer, Wright distinguishes four types of assets, the unequal control or ownership of which constitute four distinct forms of exploitation under capitalism: labour power assets (feudal exploitation), capital assets (capitalist exploitation), organization assets (statist exploitation) and skill assets (socialist exploitation). While pure modes of production can be identified with single forms of exploitation, 'actually existing capitalism' consists of all four, opening up the possibility of the simultaneous operation of exploiter/exploitee relations (e.g. managers are capitalistically exploited but are organizational exploiters).

A long line of Marx-inspired theorizing has attempted to grasp the relations between (European or transatlantic) capitalism, EMPIRE and the non-capitalist (or developing) world. This is the heart of theories of IMPERIALISM

61

(Lenin, 1916), whether as the coercive extraction of surplus through colonial states (Fanon, 1967 [1961]), through unequal exchange (Arrighi and Pearce, 1972), or through the imperial operation of transnational banks and multilateral development institutions (the World Bank and the INTERNATIONAL MONETARY FUND). The so-called 'ANTI-GLOBALIZATION' movement (especially focusing on institutions such as the World Trade Organization) and the 'sweatshop movements' (focusing on transnational firms such as Nike) are contemporary exemplars of a politics of exploitation linking advanced capitalist state and TRANS-NATIONAL CORPORATIONS with the poverty and immiseration of the global SOUTH against a backdrop of NEO-LIBERALISM and free TRADE (Harvey, 2005; Starr, 2005).

It is axiomatic that there has been enormous controversy over the operations, the merits and the costs of the capitalist system since the nineteenth century. Much ink has also been spilled attempting to provide periodization or classifications of actually existing capitalisms and the origins of capitalism in the transformation from feudalism. The pluralization of the word capitalism – capitalisms – highlights enormous geographical, temporal, institutional and cultural diversity of what is now a global and integral form of political economy. The originary question hinges in large measure on engaging with Marx's account of PRIMITIVE ACCUMULATIONS and the British ENCLOSURES, and the extent to which the feudal system was transformed by the corrosive effects of the markets and/or urban-based merchants, by demography or by internal contradictions within the feudal system (reflections in class and other struggles between tenants, lords, the Church and merchants). The periodization of capitalism turns on similar theoretical tensions: Was 'early' capitalism characterized by expansionary trade and the dominance of merchants' capital? Was this early mercantile capitalism actually in the business of inventing new systems of capitalism production (e.g. the PLANTATION)? What was – or is – the relation between forms of unfree labour (some of which still exist, although not as organized mass slavery) and the development of industrial capitalism? To what extent were the accumulations associated with differing phases of the development of the world system – SLAVERY, informal empire, and the first age of empire – integral to the rise of industrial capitalism in Britain or elsewhere in Europe? These questions have produced a vast body of scholarship and theorizing. What can

be said, with some trepidation, is that while the trajectories of capitalism in EUROPE and elsewhere have some substantive diversity, there is some agreement that the rise of industrial manufacture in Britain in the eighteenth century, the growing concentration of capitals (and the linking of industrial and bank capital) at the end of the nineteenth century, the institutionalization of a sort of Keynesian capitalism in the wake of the First World War, and the genesis of a resurrected 'liberal capitalism' (dubbed neo-liberalism, echoing the late nineteenth century) as a force driving the post-1945 globalization of transnational capitalism are key moments – or watersheds – in the long march of modern capitalism. The national and local forms in which the great arch of capitalist development has been institutionalized – sometimes theorized as systems of regulation or social accumulation (see REGULATION THEORY), sometimes as national capitalisms, sometimes as models or cultures of capitalism – has generated a very substantial and sophisticated body of work over the past three to four decades, including an important dialogue over the differences between the first and 'late' developers (e.g. the so-called ASIAN TIGERS).

Geographers, particularly since the 1970s, have been especially concerned to address the relations between SPACE, environment and the reproduction of the capitalist system. The most elaborated account in the English language is the body of work of David Harvey (1999 [1982]) – but one might easily point to an equally expansive and synoptic account in the work of Henri Lefebvre (2003 [1970]). Harvey's work began as a critical account of the city in the advanced capitalist states, but quickly developed into a magisterial re-reading of capital in which the friction of space – and what he termed the 'spatial fix' – provided a key theoretical ground on which to understand the circuits of capital (see figure) and the built environment, the changing geography of capitalist accumulation and the environmental costs of – and, more recently, the relations between – AMERICAN EMPIRE and primitive accumulation (what he calls *accumulation by dispossession*). Other geographers have naturally contributed to the space–nature–capitalism triumvirate: Doreen Massey on spatial divisions of labour, Neil Smith on UNEVEN DEVELOPMENT, Richard Walker on regional and agrarian capitalism, Ash Amin on INDUSTRIAL DISTRICTS, Gillian Hart on trajectories of capitalism, Stuart Corbridge and Richard Peet on neo-liberalism and DEVELOPMENT, and so on.

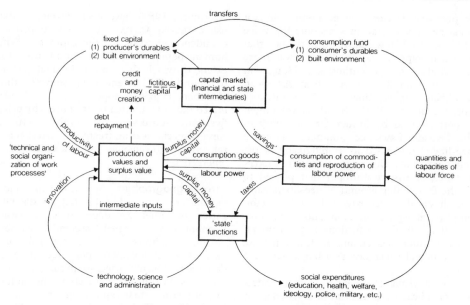

capitalism   *Circuits of capital* (Harvey, 1999 [1982])

Since the 1990s, the spectacular rise of NEO-LIBERALISM as a specific form of capitalist development and its relation to questions of empire, development and environment has drawn much critical attention. David Harvey's *A brief history of neoliberalism* (2005) attempts to map the dismantling of the social democratic world, with a special focus on the British form of national Keynesianism, inflected by the COMMAND ECONOMY of the Second World War, but whose roots lay earlier in the response of the managers of North Atlantic capitalism to the Depression, and which came in the form of welfare safety nets, income redistribution, domestic industry protection, state-financed public works and capital controls – 'embedded liberalism' of the Polanyian sort.

The rise of neo-liberal capitalism was in a sense the victory of Friedrich von Hayek's *The road to serfdom*. It was Margaret Thatcher, after all, who pronounced, at a Tory Cabinet meeting, 'This is what we believe', slamming a copy of Hayek's *The constitution of liberty* onto the table at 10 Downing Street. His critique of collectivism – that it destroys morals, personal freedom and responsibility, impedes the production of wealth, and sooner or later leads to totalitarianism – is the ur-text for market utopians. Collectivism was by definition a made rather than a grown order; that is, a 'taxis' rather than a 'cosmos'. Collectivism

was, Hayek said, constructivist rather than evolutionary, organized not spontaneous, an economy rather than a 'catallaxy', coerced and concrete rather than free and abstract.

As Antonio Gramsci might have put it, there has been a Hayekian 'passive revolution' from above, in which we have witnessed what Perry Anderson has dubbed a 'neoliberal grand slam' (2000c). The vision of the Right has no equivalent on the Left; it rules undivided across the globe and is the most successful ideology in world history.

The process by which neo-liberal capitalist hegemony was established, and its relation to forms and modes and sites of resistance, remains a story for which, even with Harvey's synoptic survey at hand, we still have no full genealogy. Neo-liberalism was a class reaction to the crisis of the 1970s (Harvey talks of a 'restoration of class power'); on that much, Milton Friedman and David Harvey are agreed. But we are still left with many paradoxes and puzzles. Why, for example, did the LSE and Chicago – once the respective centres of Fabianism and a certain version of (American) liberalism under Robert Hutchins – become the forcing houses of neo-liberalism? What were the facilitating conditions that fostered the arrival of the maverick Ronald Coase in Chicago, marking a neo-liberal turning point? How did the World Bank – a bastion of post-war development economics and, it must be said, of statism – become the voice of *laissez faire*? How can we grasp the fact that 'shock therapy' in eastern Europe was more the product of the enthusiastic Hungarian reformers than of the more reticent American neo-liberal apparatchiks? It is sometimes noted that the 1991 World Development Report (shaped by former US Secretary of the Treasury Lawrence Summers) marked a neo-liberal watershed in its refiguring of the role of the state. But it was AFRICA (not LATIN AMERICA or eastern Europe) that proved to be the first testing ground of neo-liberalism's assault on the over-extended public sector, on physical capital formation and on the proliferation of market distortions by government. There is much that remains unclear in the rise of neo-liberal hegemony as a particular force of capitalism.

As Polanyi might have anticipated, three decades of radical neo-liberalism culminated in the autumn of 2008 with a spectacular and massive implosion of the US financial sector, turning quickly into a deeper and systemic crisis of capitalism itself. The catastrophic collapse of US investment banks – which ramified globally producing *de facto* bank nationalizations in much of western Europe – was triggered by a classic housing bubble. During the 1990s, however, this bubble was, unlike the past, driven by new and dubious financial and mortgage instruments, and by the utter failure of the financial regulatory institutions (the credit rating agencies and the Securities and Exchange Commission in particular). By late 2008, in spite of a massive $700 billion bailout by the US Treasury, credit and the banking sector remained in effect frozen and the prospect of a massive global recession loomed. The great experiment in free market utopianism - the so-called 'neo-liberal grand slam' - had put Keynesianism back on the political agenda. In the US and much of Europe, a Polanyian counter-revolution - in the US there is talk of a new New Deal – is now in the offing.   MW

capture–recapture methods A SAMPLING technique that was developed in ECOLOGY to estimate population size and vital rates (including survival, movement and growth). A search is made in a defined area and identified ANIMALS are captured and marked or recorded in some way. Visits are made on subsequent occasions and the proportion of unmarked animals is recorded; this allows, given assumptions, the estimation of the total population. Model-based approaches

(Cormack, 1989) have been developed that use CATEGORICAL DATA ANALYSIS to provide confidence intervals for the estimates. With human populations, the method uses the extent to which the same individuals are to be found in different data sources; thus Hickman, Higgins, Hope et al. (2004) estimated the total number of drug users by using five data sources – community recruited survey, specialist drug treatment, arrest referral, syringe exchange, and accident and emergency   KJ

carceral geographies Spaces in which individuals are confined, subjected to SURVEILLANCE or otherwise deprived of essential freedoms can be termed 'carceral'. The most obvious examples of these are jails and PRISONS, which are STATE-sponsored spaces of detention, typically used to punish criminal offenders. Prisons are relatively young, in historical terms, first appearing in Western Europe in the eighteenth century. These spaces were designed to maximize surveillance, and to encourage self-monitoring and possible rehabilitation.

In geography, much interest in carceral institutions flows from Michel Foucault's influential study, *Discipline and punish: the birth of the prison* (1995 [1975]). There, Foucault traced the logics that underlay early prison designs, and sought to illustrate how these logics were deployed by other social institutions, such as schools and military organizations. Foucault's description of POWER as diffuse and capillary has influenced considerable work across HUMAN GEOGRAPHY, much of which demonstrates how social control is mobilized through the construction and regulation of SPACE.

Such geographies of control are widespread. From its birth in EUROPE, the use of incarceration as a punishment practice diffused widely and quickly. Indeed, in some former colonial states, prisons built decades ago by the colonial powers are still in use (Stern, 1998). Today, there is evidence that the harsh punishment practices common in the USA are diffusing through much of the rest of the world. Although prisons and their operative conditions vary across the globe, certain characteristics are common: their populations are dominated by members of lower economic classes and ostracized social groups; their environments are commonly overcrowded, dirty, disease-ridden and violent; and their everyday realities make elusive personal security, privacy and dignity.

Just as prisons restrict the mobility of individuals inside their walls, they are central to the regulation of movement of people across boundaries, particularly given concerns about security in this age of panic about TERRORISM. The most obvious example here is the USA, which operates a separate set of prisons for those accused of IMMIGRATION violations. These detention centres are run by the executive branch of the federal government, and thus lie largely outside judicial review. Detentions can be indefinite, and detainees left bereft of legal representation. Such detention centres reportedly house many suspected of plotting terrorist acts (Dow, 2004). Beyond its own territory, the USA operates CAMPS and so-called 'black sites', part of a global war prison where practices of torture and otherwise inhumane detention take place outside the constraints of international LAW (Gregory, 2007).

Incarceration thus becomes implicated in wider processes of CITIZENSHIP, MIGRATION and national SECURITY. Borders become heavily policed (Nevins, 2002) and those arrested crossing illicitly are subject to indefinite detention and possible deportation. Those who do manage to cross illegally come to inhabit 'spaces of non-existence' (Coutin, 2003), invisible to legal and other authorities, and thus deprived of the benefits of formal recognition. Full citizenship, however, hardly leaves one outside of places that are heavily monitored and tightly controlled: in a world of increasing surveillance and security consciousness, the scope of carceral geographies promises to widen.   SKH

Suggested reading
Foucault (1995 [1975]); Nevins (2002).

carrying capacity A concept developed mainly in population biology and ECOLOGY that commonly refers to the maximum number of a given species that a given environment can support indefinitely. Developed with respect to animal populations that grow quickly and then crash precipitously when they exceed their environment's carrying capacity, it has been widely but controversially applied to human-environment relations (e.g. efforts to quantify the maximum number of park visitors compatible with conservation, or the maximum human population that the Earth can support). Such applications frequently neglect more relevant questions regarding the complex social dynamics of RESOURCE use, particularly issues of distributive justice and technological change.
JM

Suggested reading
Harvey (1974a); Meadows, Meadows and Randers (1992).

Cartesianism In order to provide a firm and permanent structure for the sciences, the philosopher René Descartes (1596–1650) outlined a method of enquiry based on certain and indubitable knowledge. The kind of knowing learned from hearsay, teachers and parents was seen to be suspect, marked by the uncertainties of opinion (*doxa*). Only knowledge derived from reason and method (*episteme*) provided adequate foundations for scientific knowledge, and clear and explicit criteria for demarcating scientific from non-scientific claims (Bernstein, 1983, p. 23). For LOGICAL EMPIRICISM and LOGICAL POSITIVISM, such methods were seen to offer the possibility of developing a universal SCIENCE that would share common foundations and principles. Such Cartesian science was to be disinterested, objective, value-free, universal and abstract, and it was based on a firm belief that science represented NATURE in a direct manner, serving – as Rorty (1979) suggested – as 'the mirror of nature' (cf. MIMESIS). Bernstein (1983) referred to this history of scientific efforts to found basic statements in direct observation of an external reality as the *Cartesian Anxiety*, a term that Gregory (1994, pp. 71–3) extended to the cartographical and geographical project (see CARTOGRAPHIC REASON).

In the 1960s, the growing power and reach of universal science, hypothetico-deductive methodologies and mathematical ABSTRACTION in the natural and social sciences led to a series of disciplinary *methodenstreiten* ('struggles over method'). The 'Positivist dispute in German sociology' (see Adorno, 1976) was particularly influential in this struggle, bringing together the views of a broad group of philosophers of science, including Thomas Kuhn, Karl Popper, Imre Lakatos, Paul Feyerabend, Jürgen Habermas and Theodor Adorno, on the limits of disinterested, value-free and universalist understandings of science. In HUMAN GEOGRAPHY, a critique of Cartesianism, and the clearest reflection of this broader *methodenstreit*, was provided by Gregory (1978a), who argued against positivism and spatial analytic claims to a privileged form of knowledge production. Instead, geographical science was never disinterested or innocent, but always a social activity framed by determinate interests. Habermas (1987a [1968]) had argued that knowledge claims must be understood in terms of such interests (see also PHENOMENOLOGY),

65

and Gregory elaborated these claims for geography. In the place of a single privileged scientific method, Gregory outlined a plurality of scientific epistemologies, each one determined by the specific knowledge-constitutive interests that give rise to them (he identified three: technical, interpretative and emancipatory). Corresponding to each knowledge-constitutive interest was a particular form of science: empirical, HERMENEUTIC and critical (see CRITICAL THEORY). Since then, it has become commonplace to treat geographical enquiry, like all forms of intellectual enquiry, as an irredeemably social practice, although this has been understood in ways that often differ significantly from Habermas' original theses, and the rise of a CRITICAL HUMAN GEOGRAPHY has been accompanied by a series of searching enquiries into the effects produced through REPRESENTATION and other modes of apprehending the world (see NON-REPRESENTATIONAL THEORY). JPI

cartogram A customized MAP PROJECTION that adjusts area or distance to reveal patterns not apparent on a conventional base MAP. For area cartograms this adjustment might be specific, as when the areas of countries or provinces are made proportional to their populations (Dorling, 1993), or expedient, as when small places such as Luxembourg or Rhode Island are rendered sufficiently large so that their symbols on a CHOROPLETH map are readily visible. Similarly, distance cartograms might adjust distances to reflect TRANSPORT COST relative to a particular place (Monmonier, 1993, pp. 198–200) or rearrange transport routes to promote clarity, as on the widely imitated London Underground map.   MM

Suggested reading
Gastner and Newman (2004).

cartographic reason The belief that cartographic and geographical representations are direct representations of an external and independent world or, as the philosopher Richard Rorty (1979) put it more generally, they are the 'mirror of nature' (see also CARTESIANISM; OBJECTIVITY). In this view, the task of CARTOGRAPHY and GEOGRAPHY is to represent the external world faithfully, and the criterion for success and hence 'truth' is the degree to which this correspondence is achieved. This view of REPRESENTATION depends upon a cartographic theory of correspondence in which, to take the METAPHOR at its most literal, information about the world is accurately

transmitted (primary sense data) through a medium (the MAP) to a receiver (the map reader) (for a critical reading, see Pickles, 1992). The accuracy of the transmission of the information from the real world to the reader is a measure of the accuracy and hence effectiveness of the mapping process. This representational notion of SCIENCE presumed that the world was external and independent of the observer and that the nominally scientific observer could describe the world in ways that corresponded directly to the reality of the world. Such foundational and objectivist epistemologies have variously been referred to as observer epistemologies or, in an acknowledgement of the effects that they produce, the 'god-trick' (Haraway, 1991d) and the 'Cartesian Anxiety' (Bernstein, 1983). It was this latter term that Gregory (1994) adapted as the cartographic anxiety to characterize a particular mode of GEOGRAPHICAL IMAGINATION.

Some commentators have associated such critiques of cartographic reason with the influence of POSTMODERNISM on HUMAN GEOGRAPHY, but some of the most telling interventions have been inspired by MODERNISM and its sustained interrogation of representational practices. Thus for Olsson (2007, p. 4), the thought of such a *tabula rasa*, a pristine 'world' uncontaminated by the act of knowing, is literally unimaginable, and theories of human knowledge that presume such a beginning point or possibility are deeply flawed. Instead, for Olsson, the drawing and interpreting of a line is the cartographic act exemplified. It is always an act that creates meaning; every drawing of a line is the creation of a distinction, the delimiting of an identity, and the creation of a BOUNDARY. As Pickles (2004) shows, by inscribing lines, creating distinctions, and drawing borders, cartography and, by extension, geography, can be seen as a part of a diverse array of cultural practices and politics that are constantly producing and reproducing worlds (see also Farinelli, Olsson and Reichert, 1994). JPI

cartography (1) The design and production of MAPS by individuals or organizations; (2) the scientific study of the technology of mapmaking and the effectiveness of maps as communication devices; and (3) the scholarly examination of the societal role and impact of maps. The term's association with mapmaking reflects lexical roots in *carte* (French for map) and *graphie* (Greek for writing). Although mapmaking is an ancient art, *cartography* is a nineteenth-century word, introduced in 1839 by Portuguese scholar Manuel Francisco de Barros e Sousa, Viscount of Santarém, who used it to describe map study in the same way that *historiography* refers to the history of historical writing (Wolter, 1975). Although Santarém referred only to early maps, the word evolved to include contemporary maps and mapping as well as ancient artefacts (Harley, 1987, p. 12).

As a synonym for mapmaking, cartography is often construed to include the collection of geographical information through systematic surveys, formal or otherwise, of the physical landscape or its human occupants. In an institutional context, cartography might refer narrowly to the production of artwork for printed maps (also called 'map finishing') or more broadly to the overall mission of a commercial firm such as Rand McNally or a government agency such as the Ordnance Survey. Although individuals working as freelance mapmakers or non-faculty staff members of an academic geography department are still content to call their work cartography and themselves cartographers, the term's other institutional connotations declined markedly in the final years of the twentieth century, when new technologies (see DIGITAL CARTOGRAPHY; GEOGRAPHIC INFORMATION SYSTEMS; REMOTE SENSING) and new business models undermined the paper map's traditional role in storing and distributing geographical information, and organizations at different levels replaced 'cartography' as a descriptor with more fashionable labels based on 'geospatial' or 'geographical information'.

As a scientific endeavour focused on the increasing efficiency in mapmaking, improving the reliability of map communication, or enhancing the understanding of cognitive processes involved in decoding and using maps, cartography remains an active if somewhat retrenched sub-discipline of GEOGRAPHY. Moreover, its boundary with GEOGRAPHIC INFORMATION SCIENCE is blurred insofar as many (perhaps most) academics trained as cartographers not only understand the power and limitations of geospatial technology but know how to use GI software. Similarly, many (but probably not most) academics trained as GI scientists not only appreciate the map as an interface and display device but also recognize the inadequacy of current GI software as a design tool. Labelling became especially important in the 1990s, as older faculty retooled and academic departments converted course titles and job descriptions from cartography to GIS. *The American Cartographer* became *Cartography and Geographic Information*

Systems in 1990, only to reposition itself as *Cartography and Geographic Information Science* nine years later. Despite this blatant but apparently successful attempt to retain market share through re-branding, the journal remains committed to improving the practice and understanding of map communication, albeit with a clear emphasis on electronic and digital cartography.

Map-design research has theoretical, technical and more ostensibly scientific–empirical themes, with the latter often relying on subject-testing to improve pedagogical approaches to map reading, enhance understanding of how the human eye-brain system processes map information (MacEachren, 1995), and evaluate the effectiveness of competing solutions to design problems (Montello, 2002). In the latter three empirical realms, academic cartographers constitute a numerical and philosophical majority only in design-related cartographic research, which also includes work on dynamic and interactive maps, multi-sensory cartographic interfaces (see VISUALIZATION), and tactile maps for persons with impaired vision (Perkins, 2002). Not surprisingly, educational psychologists and cognitive psychologists dominate explorations of map-reading and cognitive mapping, respectively.

Arthur Robinson's *The look of maps* (1952) was the seminal work in empirical map-design research, a topic taken up in various guises by Robinson's graduate students and their intellectual offspring. Robinson held that effective map design required an appreciation of the design's impact on map viewers, whose ability to decode cartographic symbols was understandably impaired if they could not read labels or detect crucial differences in line thickness, greytones or colour. Aligned philosophically with the LOGICAL POSITIVISM of the QUANTITATIVE REVOLUTION, map-design researchers uncritically adopted psychophysics, a PARADIGM in experimental psychology that treats the magnitude of a response as a power function of the magnitude of the activating stimulus (Montello, 2002, pp. 288–9). A succession of empirical studies attempted to 'rescale' graduated circles, line weights and greytones to the perceptual prowess of a hypothetical average map reader, an attractive concept undermined by variations in cognitive style, training and prior knowledge as well as by the unavoidable distractions of nearby symbols in the 'map environment'. Although less ambitious studies of 'just noticeable differences' among lines, greytones and colours provided reliable guidance for mapmakers, map-design research lost momentum in the 1980s, when the shortcomings of psychophysical rescaling became apparent. Despite this disappointment, subject-testing remains a useful strategy for evaluating solutions to problems in map design, and empirical studies experienced a revival in the 1990s, when the computer proved a valuable tool for testing subjects and QUALITATIVE METHODS such as FOCUS-GROUP interviews offered further insights (Suchan and Brewer, 2000).

Computers fostered numerous technical advances as well, including automated strategies for placing labels in non-overlapping locations, generalizing linear features, classifying data for CHOROPLETH maps, interpolating ISOLINES, generating oblique views of three-dimensional SURFACES, and creating visually effective animated and interactive maps (Monmonier and McMaster, 2004). Although the computer was ostensibly an instrument of mapmaking, these techniques clearly functioned as tools for map design insofar as the map author could readily experiment with thresholds, parameters and methods of symbolization. Although the limitations of psychophysics were readily apparent in the 1980s, interactive maps that the user could query with a cursor further undermined the need to improve value estimation by rescaling map symbols.

Two other theories prominent in cartography in the 1970s were the communication model and a conceptual framework called visual variables. Derived from feedback-loop models in INFORMATION THEORY, the cartographic communication model in its simplest form treated the map as a channel connecting a map author (source) with a percipient (destination). A more elaborate version treated the map author as a filter that helped form the percipient's view of the world and added a reverse flow (FEEDBACK), which encouraged a modification of the map's design or content to promote a more accurate transmission of the map author's intended message. Particularly noteworthy was a comparatively sophisticated modification by Antonín Koláčný (1969), whose model described the cartographer's reality and the map user's reality as overlapping but not completely coincident subsets of a larger reality. Although the communication PARADIGM received considerable attention in the academic press and no doubt heightened awareness of communication among academic cartographers, the notion that all maps, or even most maps, contained a specific message was largely viewed as naïve or trivial by the 1980s, when computer-assisted cartography began to command

increased attention (Antle and Klinkenberg, 1999). By contrast, French semiologist Jacques Bertin's (1983) notion of visual variables, especially the six retinal variables (size, shape, hue, value, pattern and orientation) under the map author's control, proved more relevant to map design, and remains a significant theory in cartography.

The third definition of cartography, focused on the societal impact of maps, recognizes that the map is not only a descriptive medium and a problem-solving tool but also a TEXT, as that term is used in textual studies, cultural studies and CRITICAL THEORY, and that MAP READING is thus a situated cultural practice. Although academic cartographers had at least a vague awareness of the map's rhetorical clout, especially in GEOPOLITICS (Tyner, 1982), the 1980s witnessed a renewed interest in cartographic propaganda. Particularly influential were the writings of J.B. Harley, a map historian acutely aware of the map's role in asserting HEGEMONY and justifying exploitation and also its vulnerability to manipulation as an instrument of warfare, colonization and diplomacy. Harley's most important contribution was the notion of cartographic silences, whereby the deliberate omission of features or PLACE NAMES might advance a government's territorial claims or promote an illusion of benevolence or efficiency (Harley, 2001a). These ploys succeeded largely because the public understands the need for selective generalization – the map works as a communication device only when the mapmaker consciously avoids graphic clutter – and widely accepts the map as an ostensibly objective, factual representation of reality. And because most maps work, or appear to, the public generally accepts the map author's view of reality, however flawed or one-sided. That many maps in the media and the political arena contain discernible biases made the label 'social construction' particularly appropriate (Vujakovic, 1999; Schulten, 2005).

Harley challenged scholars to question the motives of mapmakers by 'deconstructing' contemporary as well as historic maps (cf. DECONSTRUCTION). Although the studies that followed sometimes bordered on mild paranoia in their disdain for evidence of intent or impact – Pickles' (2004, pp. 60–71) critique of exaggerated claims for the 'power of maps' includes some good examples – other scholars combined an insightful examination of the map author's mindset with a careful appraisal of the institutional context in which maps were produced. For example, Herb (1997) tied the development of strident late-1930s German propaganda maps, which probably convinced few people who were not already Nazi sympathizers, to a post-First World War collaboration between scholars and activist politicians eager for a 'Greater Germany'. Similarly, Cosgrove and della Dora (2005) offer a perceptive interpretation of the vivid pictorial Second World War maps of *Los Angeles Times* cartographer Charles Owens, a self-trained newspaper artist fascinated with aviation, cinema and photojournalism. Cloud (2002), whose work is similarly grounded in archives and interviews, studied the 'military–industrial–academic complex' during the Cold War and provides numerous insights on the intelligence community's contributions to private-sector GIS and remote sensing, including the use of classified satellite imagery to update domestic TOPOGRAPHIC MAPS and the paradox of conceptual details of top-secret research and development efforts 'hidden in plain sight' in readily available cartographic and photogrammetric journals.

Research on the societal impacts of mapping is also concerned with public access to geographical information, including the role of government and other institutions in producing and distributing maps, influencing their content, and restraining or promoting their use. In this context, the map becomes not only an artefact or tool, but also a piece of intellectual property or an opportunity for international collaboration (Rhind, 2000). Moreover, growing use of the INTERNET as a medium for delivering and integrating geographical information has not only altered the appearance and usability of maps but substantially altered relationships between public and private sectors as well as between map author and map viewer (Taylor, 2006a). The increasingly eclectic nature of maps and mapping promises to make map study a fascinating and challenging geographical endeavour, whatever one calls it.   MM

Suggested reading
Harley (2001a); MacEachren (1995); Monmonier (2004); Montello (2002); Pickles (2004); Taylor (2006).

cartography, history of The study of the processes whereby people in all cultures and in all periods have variously made and used MAPS to comprehend, organize and act in space and place, together with their motives for and effects of doing so. A primary element of HUMAN GEOGRAPHY and the HISTORY OF GEOGRAPHY, the history of CARTOGRAPHY is

also widely recognized across the HUMANITIES and social sciences as an intellectually vibrant and exemplary interdisciplinary field of study that draws on and makes significant contributions to many historical fields. Note that 'historical cartography' *per se* is the practice of representing past distributions or events in maps; as such, it constitutes a particular topic for historians of cartography (Skelton, 1972).

Librarians, professors, lawyers and lay scholars (notably collectors and their dealers) have studied maps as historical phenomena since the 1700s. Traditionally, such studies have elucidated the content of old maps in order to generate locational and morphological data for use by other historians, notably those of geography, exploration and COLONIALISM, but also historical geographers, geomorphologists, lawyers, archaeologists and students of cities and landscapes. Even so, there was little disciplinary identity for such 'map history' before the twentieth century: map historians were few in number, widely dispersed and they were constrained within national schools by differential physical and linguistic access to primary sources. The viscount de Santarém's 1839 neologism of 'cartography', to mean the study of old maps, accordingly could not take root; it was instead quickly appropriated by professional map-makers. A more coherent scholarly community coalesced around *Imago Mundi*, founded in 1935 by Leo Bagrow; this is still the leading journal in the field and has since 1967 given rise to biennial international conferences (Skelton, 1972; Harley, 1986, 1987; Edney, 2005a).

The successful promotion after 1945 of cartography as an academic subject entailed the expansion and consolidation of a previously minor, sporadic and internalist history of cartographic techniques. The new concern for such a 'history of cartography' was truly innovative in that it focused on map form rather than on map content, and on archival and contextual research rather than on cartobibliography and map analysis. It generated significant studies, for example of the histories of map printing and thematic mapping. From this perspective, academic cartography provided historians of cartography – however briefly – with both an intellectual framework (Woodward, 1974) and an institutional home (Harley and Woodward, 1989; Edney, 2005b).

Both 'map history' and the 'history of cartography' were thoroughly intertwined with the modern ideology of cartography. Indeed, that ideology has in large part depended upon cartographic history for legitimation: the historians' narratives of past cartographic progress, whether in content or in form, validate the modern convictions that maps are unproblematic replications of geographical data (see CARTOGRAPHIC REASON) and that cartography is an inherently moral practice aimed at improving the human condition. Map history has thus served as a surrogate for the triumphs of modern Western SCIENCE and CIVILIZATION generally. These EMPIRICIST and POSITIVIST ideals were further perpetuated by the historical narratives constructed in order to justify an academic status for cartography (Edney, 2005b), and they further underpin a rapidly growing popular literature that allies the powerful myth of cartographic progress to the equally powerful myth of the lone scientific genius.

Paradoxically, the 'history of *cartography*' ended up establishing the broader intellectual potential of map studies and led to the proliferation of a '*history* of cartography' that has taken map studies far beyond the confines of academic cartography and geography (Edney, 2005a,b). Several factors contributed to the shift: attention to the larger historical record revealed many more cartographic activities than were encompassed by the established canon; detailed archival studies increasingly suggested that maps must be considered as humanistic as well as technological/scientific documents; academic cartography's adherence to models of communication made some historians aware of the need to study how maps were used as well as made; and academic cartography's claims to intellectual autonomy were matched by arguments that the history of cartography should no longer be subservient to other fields (esp. Blakemore and Harley, 1980). A triumphal, empiricist history of cartographic progress was increasingly recognized as intellectually bankrupt. In 1977, Denis Wood could accordingly present a structuralist reinterpretation of the history of cartography as part of a larger critique of academic cartography (see STRUCTURALISM). For Wood, the history of cartography replicated the development of spatial cognition in the individual; he has subsequently clung to this argument, even as he has made truly significant distinctions between the necessarily social processes of 'map making' and individual processes of cognitive 'mapping' (Wood and Fels, 1992).

By the late 1970s, Brian Harley and David Woodward had set out to create a new, autonomous discipline of the history of cartography by unifying the widely dispersed literature within a multi-volume *History of cartography*. Even with only three of six volumes published to date, the series has already proven enormously influential in promoting the catholic and humanistic study of cartographic history. The extensive consideration given to non-Western and pre-modern cartographies has loosened the WEST's putative stranglehold on 'proper' cartography and has seriously undermined the conviction that maps must be geometrically consistent, measured and graphic in nature. The series has demonstrated unequivocally not only that the history of cartography is a valid field of study in its own right but also that it cannot hope to make significant contributions as long as it adheres to modern cartographic IDEOLOGY (Harley and Woodward, 1987–continues; see Woodward, Delano Smith and Yee, 2001, esp. pp. 23–9; Edney, 2005b).

Harley also set out to create a new intellectual identity for the field. His initial foray, with Michael Blakemore, drew on the art-historical principles of ICONOGRAPHY to demonstrate the manner in which maps necessarily bear cultural and social significance in addition to factual and locational data (Blakemore and Harley, 1980). Subsequently, and largely influenced by the work of philosopher–historian Michel Foucault, Harley advanced a series of essays on the inherently political nature of all maps (Harley, 2001b). Harley's essays from the 1980s were crucial in that they crystallized the intellectual concerns with modern cartographic ideology already expressed by many scholars across several disciplines, waved the flag for more critical map studies and served as prominent vehicles for human geography's adoption of approaches informed by POST-STRUCTURALISM. His essays were nonetheless incomplete. Harley succeeded brilliantly in exposing modern cartographic ideology by wrenching off its mask of OBJECTIVITY, but he was ultimately unable to theorize a new, critical PARADIGM (Edney, 2005a).

Parallel to, drawing on, and at the same time motivating Harley's theoretical exposés were studies by scholars in other fields who, unburdened with any disciplinary baggage, recognized (or simply ignored) the traditional shortcomings of map history. These scholars included sociologists and political scientists as well as historians (e.g. Winichakul, 1994; see GEO-BODY), but most were literary scholars who began to consider maps as simply one more strategy of REPRESENTATION within spatial discourses. For example, Carter (1987) exposed the 'spatial history' of the shifting configuration of Australia in texts, graphics and cartographics, and Helgerson (1992) explored the early modern construction of 'England" as a site of national desire.

Today, the history of cartography features several potentially conflicting elements. Its practitioners are distributed across several disciplines and its institutional situation suffers accordingly. But it has a strong intellectual core in the rejection of traditional map history and the concomitant recognition that maps are cultural documents: maps are not the TER-RITORY, in that they do not represent the land and its essential characteristics in an unproblematic manner, yet maps emphatically are the territory, in that they are intellectual constructions through which humans have organized, comprehended and manipulated spaces and places. Critical histories of cartography have tended to examine the functioning of maps as texts within specific spatial DISCOURSES, especially those of NATIONALISM and Western rationalism, to elucidate how cartographic expression has contributed, often crucially, to associating particular meanings and configurations of identity with certain territorial entities (especially STATE and EMPIRE) and peoples (especially NATIONS). Such studies feature a renewed emphasis on MAP READING, now with the goal of elucidating the discursive meanings that would likely have been read into maps by their readers; particular success in this respect has attended the study of map forms previously deemed marginal or ephemeral, such as maps in ART, modern road maps or maps in educational texts. These studies have approached, *inter alia*, British and modern India, early modern Europe and Japan, the modern USA and Turkey, and nineteenth-century Mexico and Thailand; classical historians currently debate the extent to which Greek and Roman conceptions of territory were cartographically constructed. Critical histories of cartography have also addressed: the instrumental deployment of maps to create and maintain states and empires, overtly underpinning the application of juridical POWER, with recent explorations of thematic cartography's contributions to modern GOV-ERNMENTALITY in Europe and North America; the articulations of spatial discourses with cartographic practices, whereby distinctive cartographic modes can be discerned; the intersections of Western and indigenous peoples, which tend to break down the neat boundaries with which 'text' and 'graphic'

have been habitually circumscribed; and the patterns of map consumption, particularly in terms of 'print culture', in order to delimit the social limits of specific discourses in which maps figured and to explore the interconnections between maps and other representational strategies (Edney, 2006). All told, critical histories of cartography have promoted cartographic studies into a significant component of research in the humanities and social sciences.

Yet there is need for caution. Modern cartographic ideologies continue to infect much supposedly critical work. Whereas the very concept of 'map' is itself culturally determined (Jacob, 2006) and the making of maps is distributed across several modes that are not necessarily connected (Edney, 1993), there remains a tendency to treat 'map' as a self-evident category that is constant across cultures and to understand 'cartography' as a singular endeavour; discourse analysis based on such misconceptions inevitably fails. Again, a reading of Harley's essays without consideration of the larger stream of post-structuralist thought has led many scholars to continue to understand map meaning as being determined solely by mapmakers working for socially privileged patrons: in this arrangement, a map's meaning is bifurcated into a culturally insensitive 'factual' layer and a 'symbolic' layer that is manipulated by the map's maker to achieve some kind of effect on its readers. Such an approach denies the agency of the map-reader and so fails to realize fully the conventions of cartographic discourses and their constructions of spatial meaning. In this respect, the transition to a coherent critical paradigm of cartographic history remains incomplete.

Furthermore, critical theory does not provide by itself a sufficient basis for the history of cartography. Rigorous analysis of a spatial discourse requires a clear grasp of the forms of maps involved in the discourse, of the social and geographical patterns of that discourse, and of the relevant political and economic contexts. That is, critical studies must be competently grounded in an empirical archive. Much scope accordingly remains for carto-bibliographies to elucidate the patterns of map availability (e.g. Krogt, 1997–), although the carto-bibliographies need to be carefully designed and implemented.

The history of cartography might thus at present be described as a three-layer intellectual palimpsest. Traditional approaches have not been completely erased: they are still quite visible, especially within popular writing, and it is hard to escape the restrictions of the progressivist canon and its underlying presumptions. Academic cartographers continue to pursue an internalist history, now reconfiguring it to account for the new directions being taken by digital technologies (Slocum, McMaster, Kessler and Howard, 2008). Intellectually, the future clearly lies with the new catholic and critical history of cartography; its challenge is to turn the older strains of cartographic historiography to its own ends, remaining empirically strong but consolidating a coherent and interdisciplinary intellectual presence.   MHE

Suggested reading
Edney (2005a); Harley (1987, 2001b); Jacob (2006). See also http://maphistory.info/

case study The case study epitomizes a PROCESS or complex set of processes in context, thereby demonstrating how theoretical tools can be applied to the social world. The idea of the case study emerged in the 1930s through attempts to make the human sciences a parallel enterprise to the biophysical sciences, specifically in trying to see instantiations of sociological theory in the manner of medical case histories. Urban sociologists, mainly from the CHICAGO SCHOOL, saw the case study as the ideal method to produce hypotheses. For instance, Whyte's *Street corner society* (1943) is a classic case study of life, gangs, work and politics in a working-class Italian neighbourhood in Boston. By the late 1960s, the sociological approach of Grounded Theory advocated building theory through case studies, as a kind of stylized empiricism.

However, sociological thought has paid much longer attention to what Max Weber called 'configurations' of seemingly objective regularities or hypothetical laws, which only become intelligible in specific, concrete situations (Weber, 1949). Considered as a Weberian configuration, the case study separates contingent from necessary causes and context from structuring process, to show how both elements come together in concrete conjunctures. The Weberian approach, it would seem, provides more durable analytical tools than some of its successors in urban sociology.

Contemporary critiques from scholars such as Dipesh Chakrabarty of the Subaltern Studies Collective question the underlying presumption to objectify lived histories in cases that conceal the translation of local into expert knowledge (see SUBALTERN STUDIES). This insight would suggest that as long as disciplinary authority is itself part of the object of analysis, case studies can remain efficacious in engaging concrete interactions between expert knowledges and forms of belonging. Such an interactive conception of the case study is particularly useful from the perspective of a HUMAN GEOGRAPHY that strives to show how broader processes work through specific constellations of social space. Through Massey's notion of an extroverted SENSE OF PLACE (Massey, 1994b), one can conceive of 'case geographies' as intersections of dynamic, mobile, constructed and contested spatial processes. Another constructive critique of case studies emerges from Mary Poovey's (1998) interrogation of the boundaries between descriptive and interpretive evidence in the making of the modern fact. Poovey's analysis contrasts the kind of evidence that makes for case studies against the seemingly non-evaluative numerical and statistical indices that surround such objects of evidence. The useful insight in thinking of particular geographical cases is to ask what work the division of NOMO-THETIC and IDIOGRAPHIC forms of knowledge accomplishes in maintaining or undermining the coherence of actual cases.   SC

caste An endogamous social hierarchy of enduring political significance, believed to have emerged some 3500 years ago around highly questionable categories of Aryans and non-Aryans in the Indian subcontinent. The former – comprising *brahman, kshatriya* and *vaishya* – emerged as dominant occupational castes of so-called *dvija* (twice-born). The *shudra* caste(s) – regarded as non-Aryan and 'mixed' – were occupationally marginalized and racialized, as was also the case later with the 'outcastes' (Dalit), whose touch was deemed polluting (Thapar, 1966). This order was challenged from the sixth century BCE, but all major religions in India came to bear the social imprint of caste. Brahman social dominance was bolstered by a British neo-Brahmanical ruling IDEOLOGY, and provoked a backlash (Bose and Jalal, 1997). Significantly, leaders such as Lohia analytically separated the high castes from women, *shudra*, Dalit, Muslim and *adivasi* ('indigenous') and underscored the political necessity of marriages between *shudra* and *dvija*, while disrupting the rift between manual and brain work, which contributed to the formation, rigidification and violence of caste.   RN

Suggested reading
Lohia (1964).

catastrophe theory A branch of 'bifurcation theory', which is itself a branch of non-linear dynamic systems theory. Bifurcation theory studies how, in certain non-linear systems, there may be paths and shifts in behaviour dependent on small changes in circumstances or the current position of the system. One type is the sudden jump or catastrophe, where a dramatic change results from a small change in the parameters. Other forms of bifurcation include 'hysteresis', where the reverse path to some point is not the same as the original path, and 'divergence', where a small change leads the system towards a very different state (but not in a 'jump').

Bifurcation and catastrophe theory were developed by the French mathematician René Thom in the early 1970s (Thom, 1975). In HUMAN GEOGRAPHY, several studies suggested that it could be used to understand settlement pattern changes, both in terms of the sudden emergence and growth of cities and the sudden collapse of layers in a central place system (for a review of these and other studies, see Wilson, 1981). The difficulty with these, and with many other suggested applications in the social sciences, is that they were speculative and one had to assume particular non-linear relationships and parameters to generate a system subject to catastrophes, and the perspective has not been as productive as many originally hoped. The most detailed and analytical developments in human geography have been those by Wilson, which add dynamics in the classic retail, GRAVITY and urban structure models and explore potential bifurcations. Like its relative CHAOS THEORY, catastrophe theory is now treated as part of the wider COMPLEXITY THEORY. LWH

Suggested reading
Wilson (1981).

categorical data analysis A family of QUANTITATIVE METHODS in which the variables are gauged at a low scale of MEASUREMENT. Such variables may be binary categories (male/female; rich/poor), ordered multiple categories (as in a Likert scale such as, unhappy, neutral, happy), unordered multiple categories (travel to work by car, foot, train, cycle), or a count (the number of crimes in an area). Such data often arise through SURVEY ANALYSIS in which answers to questions are limited to a number of categories. Until the 1970s, analysis of such

data was limited to simple description in a cross-tabulation, testing for independence of variables through such procedures as chi-square, and assessing association with a range of measures of CORRELATION such as Cramer's V and Yule's Q. More recently, a full-scale modelling approach has been developed for such data in a regression-like framework.

All REGRESSION models consist of three components: the response or outcome variable; a function of the predictor or explanatory variables; and a random term that represents the STOCHASTIC variation in the outcome variable that is not accounted for by the predictors. In a standard regression model the response is a continuous variable that is related to the predictors in a linear (straight-line) fashion (the so-called 'identity link'). With such a continuous outcome, the random term is usually assumed to follow a normal distribution and is summarized by an estimate of the unexplained variation, such as the variance. In categorical data analysis, in what are known as GENERALIZED LINEAR MODELS, the response is not continuous but discrete, the link between outcome and predictors is non-linear, and the random distribution is not normal but takes an appropriate distribution, depending on the scale of measurement of the dependent variable.

A number of key members of the family are defined by different types of measurement for the response variable. One that is binary or a proportion with a relatively small absolute denominator (e.g. the unemployment rate for small areas) requires a logit link and a binomial distribution; this is known as the logit regression model. Multiple categories are usually analysed with logit link and a multinomial distribution. Responses which are counts are usually analysed with a logarithmic link and a Poisson distribution: this is known as the POISSON REGRESSION MODEL. Such models also offer a very flexible approach to LONGITUDINAL DATA ANALYSIS, called discrete time analysis, in which the response is whether or not an event (e.g. marriage/separation/divorce) occurred in a specified time-period.

This model-based approach allows assessment of the relationship between an outcome and a predictor variable (which may be continuous or categorical), taking account of other predictor variables. It is possible to test for relationships, derive overall goodness-of-fit measures and use diagnostic tools as part of EXPLORATORY DATA ANALYSIS for assessing whether the model's assumptions have been met. There is now a wide range of SOFTWARE

FOR QUANTITATIVE ANALYSIS. This is vital, as the procedures used to calibrate models do not permit exact analytical solutions as in standard regression, but require an iterative approach, which can be computationally expensive. KJ

Suggested reading
Agresti (2002); Power and Xie (2000); Wrigley (1985b).

cellular automata Models of spatial phenomena, usually comprising a RASTER grid of cells, each of which has a value representing its present 'state' on a variable of interest. ALGORITHMS with theoretically derived rules are applied to the initial system configuration to simulate changes. Run many times (each run is termed a 'generation'), the algorithm produces an evolving pattern. A classic example is the well-known 'game of life', in which all cells are initially identified as either alive or dead (Conway, 1970); its algorithm's rules specify that, for example, if any cell has fewer than two live neighbours, it too will die.

Cellular automata have been used for several decades in HUMAN GEOGRAPHY to simulate spatial patterns and change – as in Torsten Hägerstrand's original work on the DIFFUSION of INNOVATIONS (see Morrill, 2005). Developments in computer technology, especially GEOGRAPHIC INFORMATION SYSTEMS and GEOCOMPUTATION, have enabled large-scale use of cellular automata models to simulate a wide range of environmental and other geographies (cf. AGENT-BASED MODELLING). RJ

census An enumeration, usually undertaken within the STATE APPARATUS, to provide needed data for STATE purposes. The Latin word census translates as 'tax', giving a clear indication of the purpose of such enumerations, the first of which are believed to take been taken in Egypt some 3,000 years ago. Many *ad hoc* censuses were taken before the nineteenth century – as with the 1086 *Domesday book* in England. Since then, an increasing number of countries have conducted regular (usually decennial) censuses as part of the development of statistics to inform the ever-widening range of government decision-making (Cullen, 1975). Censuses of population and housing are the most common, but separate censuses of, for example, agriculture, construction, (local) governments, manufacturing, mining and retailing have been held. A few countries – mainly in Scandinavia – have replaced censuses by continuously updated, GEOCODED population registers.

Censuses are constitutionally mandated in some countries. In the USA, for example, Section Two of the First Article states that 'Representatives and direct taxes shall be apportioned among the several states ... according to their respective numbers': the first census was to be conducted within three years of the constitution's acceptance, and 'within every subsequent term of ten years'. They have been conducted decennially since 1790, and their findings have sometimes been hotly disputed because of their implications – as with the allocation of seats to the US House of Representatives after the 2000 census (Johnston, 2002: on the history of the US Census, see Eckler, 1972).

Although the primary role of a census is to collect factual information to inform PUBLIC POLICY – both current and future (such as POPULATION PROJECTIONS) – nevertheless they cannot be considered 'neutral' tools. The data that they collect all refer to categories (occupational CLASS, ETHNICITY etc.) that are social constructions, whose nature is determined by some theory of what should be measured, and how – as with the main ethnicity categories now used in the US Census (White; Black or African-American; American Indian and Alaskan Native; Asian; Native Hawaiian and Other Pacific Islander; Hispanic or Latino Origin) which dominate discourse about RACE and ethnicity there (Robbin, 2000; Yanow, 2002). Early US censuses generated considerable conflict between northern and southern states over counting slaves: southerners wanted to count them, because they would boost their entitlements to federal revenues and representation; northerners opposed to SLAVERY were against. Eventually a compromise was reached, and slaves were counted as three-fifths only of 'all other persons' until after the Civil War. 'Indians not taxed' were excluded entirely until 1936. A similar situation obtained in Australia, whose original constitution – passed in 1900 – included 'In reckoning the numbers of the people ... aboriginal natives shall not be counted'. This remained the case until 1967, when voters overwhelmingly approved (91 per cent in favour: voting is compulsory in Australia) a referendum including the requirement that Aboriginals 'be counted in reckoning the population'.

Just as there is a politics and a sociology of official statistics, including censuses (on which see several chapters in Alonso and Starr, 1987), so there is also a politics and sociology of their use. Data can be deployed in a variety of ways to sustain particular cases, including partisan political projects – as illustrated by the use of 2001 census data in the UK to portray the country's changing ethnic geography in ways that, while not wrong, emphasize findings that sustain a particular case (Dorling, 2005; Johnston and Poulsen, 2006).

The conduct of censuses is a major administrative task involving the distribution to and collection of forms from every address in the country, followed by the collation of large volumes of data. That administration is in almost every case geographical in nature: the country is divided into small areas (variously termed 'collectors' districts', 'enumeration districts', etc.) in each of which data collection is overseen by a trained administrator (a role partly eliminated in some cases by use of postal and/or on-line QUESTIONNAIRES). Those small areas may also be deployed as reporting units, with data made available to users at very fine spatial scales. (The average collection district at the 2001 New Zealand census contained 106 persons, for example.) Elsewhere, the smallest reporting units are specially designed to provide information about NEIGHBOURHOODS in urban and separate settlements in rural areas, as with CENSUS TRACTS in the USA. For the 2001 UK census, geographers were involved in designing a three-level hierarchy of *output areas* which are relatively homogeneous on two criteria – dwelling type and tenure – as well as meeting size and shape constraints and fitting within local authority boundaries: their average populations were 297, 1,513 and 7,234 persons, respectively (Rees, Martin and Williamson, 2002).

Although an increasing number of census authorities release data at such small spatial SCALES, thereby facilitating detailed geographical analyses (cf. FACTORIAL ECOLOGY; SEGREGATION; SOCIAL AREA ANALYSIS) – some of value to policy-makers, as in the identification of areas of SOCIAL EXCLUSION within cities towards which programme money may be directed – a major purpose of a census is to provide information about and for sub-national governmental and administrative units. These then form the context of much geographical analysis although geographers have been employed to define other spatial architectures for data dissemination that are commensurate with the contemporary spatial structure of economy and society, which may not be the case with administrative areas: examples are the use of COMMUTING data to define METROPOLITAN AREAS in several countries.

Although the nature of the data collected and the spatial units for which they are released are important constraints to SPATIAL ANALYSIS, nevertheless censuses provide a wealth of information that has been deployed by geographers and others to portray many aspects of SOCIETY – not least through the production of atlases (e.g. Dorling and Thomas, 2004) notably, though not only, in POPULATION, SOCIAL and URBAN GEOGRAPHY. In addition, census authorities are increasingly providing a wider range of material: public-use micro-samples of entirely anonymized individual records are released in some countries, for example, which may be linked across censuses to facilitate LONGITUDINAL DATA ANALYSES. In some countries, too, the original manuscript census returns are made available (including on the INTERNET), perhaps 100 years after they were collected, allowing detailed analyses in HISTORICAL GEOGRAPHY not previously feasible.   RJ

Suggested reading
Alonso and Starr (1987); Eckler (1972); Openshaw (1995); Rees, Martin and Williamson (2002).

census tract   A small areal unit, containing a few thousand residents, used to collect and report CENSUS data. The first tracts were defined by the US Bureau of the Census in 1920 to approximate natural areas or NEIGHBOURHOODS, providing useful data for analysing urban social geography (cf. SOCIAL AREA ANALYSIS). Many censuses now use a similar spatial architecture – with varying terminology; some report data for areas with only a few hundred residents. Most tracts and comparable areas are designed for logistical convenience, although those for the 2001 England and Wales census were defined by geographers to produce areas with different housing characteristics (Martin, 2002).   RJ

Suggested reading
US Bureau of the Census, *Census Bureau Geography*: http://www.census.gov/geo/www/GARM/

central business district (CBD)   The nucleus of an urban area around its most accessible point, containing an internally differentiated concentration of retail and office establishments. In cities where most workers and shoppers travel by public transport, the CBD has the highest density land uses, most valuable land and is the focus for most intra-urban journeys. With greater reliance on private transport, DECENTRALIZATION and deconcentration trends are eroding the CBD's role: most are now declining both absolutely and relatively as shops and offices move to more accessible suburban locations (cf. EDGE CITY; RETAILING; SPRAWL). RJ

Suggested reading
Carter (1995); Murphy (1972).

central place theory A theoretical statement of the size and distribution of settlements within an URBAN SYSTEM in which marketing – especially RETAILING of goods and services – is the predominant urban function. The theory assumes that both customers and retailers are UTILITY-maximizers, making it a NORMATIVE statement against which actual patterns can be compared.

Of the two separate central place theories developed, Christaller's (1933) has been most influential. It was based on two concepts: *the range of a good* – the maximum distance that people will travel to buy it; and *the threshold for a good* – the minimum volume of sales necessary for a viable establishment selling that good (or a bundle of linked goods, such as groceries). In order to maximize their utilities, retailers locate establishments to be as near their customers as possible and customers visit the nearest available centre: in this way, expenditure on TRANSPORT COSTS is minimized and spending on goods and services maximized.

On a uniform plane with a uniformly distributed population, Christaller showed that application of these two concepts produced a hexagonal NETWORK of central places housing the establishments, organized in a hierarchy whose number of levels reflected the number of goods/services with similar range and threshold values (he identified seven). Each was centrally located within its HINTERLAND, with those at the hierarchy's lowest level having the smallest number of establishments and serving the smallest hinterlands, and thus most widely distributed. The ways in which smaller settlements nested within the hinterlands of larger ones depended on a further set of principles. Christaller identified three (as shown in the figure). The *marketing principle* ($k = 3$: a in the figure) minimizes the number of settlements so that each is at the meeting-point of three hexagonal hinterlands for centres at the next hierarchical level up: the number of centres in each order is 1, 2, 6, 18, 54, 162 and 486. According to the *transport principle* ($k = 4$: b in the figure) the goal is to minimize the length of roads joining adjacent places. Each settlement is located centrally on the boundary line between the hexagonal

hinterlands of two places in the next highest order hierarchy, and the number of centres is in the ratio 1, 2, 8, 32, 128, 512 and 2,048. Finally, the *administrative principle* ($k = 7$: c in the diagram) has each lower-order settlement and its hinterland nested exclusively within the hinterland of a single settlement in the next highest order, producing a much larger number of places in the ratio 1, 6, 42, 294, 2,058, 14,406 and 100,842.

Lösch's (1940) model was much less restrictive than Christaller's. Rather than bunch all functions into seven 'orders' he treated each as having a separate range, threshold and hexagonal hinterland. Where feasible, functions were clustered into settlements but all central places with certain functions in them need not – as in Christaller's scheme – also contain all of the functions with smaller ranges and thresholds. This produced a much wider range of settlements in terms of size and complexity of business profiles: whereas Christaller's theory produced a stepped hierarchical urban system, Lösch's was consistent with a more continuous distribution of urban sizes.

Central place theory was a major stimulus to work in the early years of geography's QUANTITATIVE REVOLUTION: it was described by Bunge (1968, p. 133) as 'geography's finest intellectual product'. Christaller's work, in particular, was the basis of much research into the size and spacing of settlements and into consumer behaviour (both inter- and intra-urban), and also as the basis for planning settlement patterns – not only in the anodyne cases of new settlements in the Dutch polders and the distribution of new shopping centres in cities, but also in the violent resettlement of Eastern Europe as part of the Nazi HOLOCAUST.

With greater mobility and customer choice available in many, more developed, societies, the underlying assumptions are increasingly irrelevant and the theory remains more as an exemplar of modelling during that period of geography's history than as a PARADIGM for understanding contemporary settlement patterns, although it is one of the theories 'rediscovered' in the NEW ECONOMIC GEOGRAPHY. (See also PERIODIC MARKET SYSTEMS.) RJ

Suggested reading
Beavon (1977); Berry and Parr (1988); Fujita, Krugman and Venables (1999).

centrifugal and centripetal forces Terms adapted from physics by C.C. Colby (1932) to describe two counteracting forces generating intra-urban land-use changes. Centrifugal

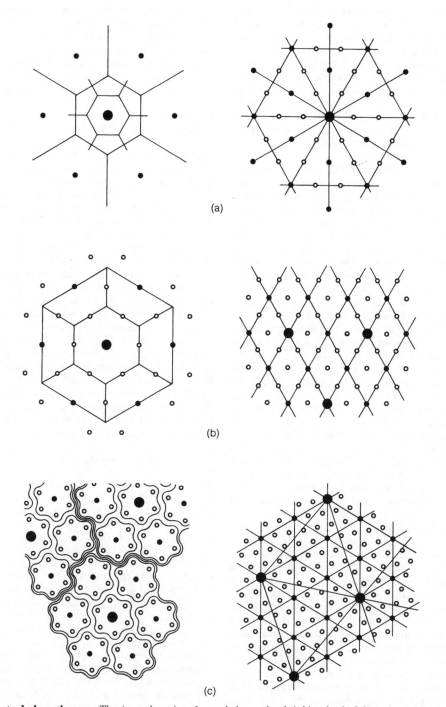

central place theory   *The size and spacing of central places, plus their hinterlands (left) and routes (right), according to three variants of Christaller's model: (a) the market principle, which minimizes the numbers of centres: (b) the transport principle, which minimizes the road length: and (c) the administrative principle, in which hinterlands are nested hierarchically*

forces push residential, business and other users away from the congested, polluted, high-density and expensive inner-city areas towards the SUBURBS and beyond (cf. decon-centration: see COUNTER-URBANIZATION; DECENTRALIZATION; SPRAWL), whereas centri-petal forces attract them towards the centre for the benefits of ACCESSIBILITY and AGGLOM-ERATION (cf. GENTRIFICATION). The balance of these two forces at any time determines the changing urban MORPHOLOGY.   RJ

chain migration A term used to describe MIGRATION that occurs in a sequence, when the movement of one person causes others to follow. It is a major component of NETWORK-based theories of migration. Chain migration typically begins at the family scale, with a single person moving to a new place in search of better opportunities. Once settled, that person facilitates the migration of other members of the nuclear or extended family (Hugo, 1994). In time, the migration network extends to friends and acquaintances as well. As this occurs, migration becomes self-perpetuating. New arrivals are assisted by those who have already learned to cope in the receiving society (Castles and Miller, 2003). This is particularly effective in the process of finding shelter and work, and newcomers generally live in close proximity, and take similar jobs to those who help them. This process leads to the develop-ment of immigrant ENCLAVES in housing and labour markets, as Banerjee (1983) has shown in the case of internal migration in India (cf. SEGREGATION and segmented LABOUR MARKET). Chain migration also fosters financial trans-fers, or remittances, between immigrants and family members who are still residents of the source country, as well as other forms of TRANS-NATIONALISM (Levitt and Glick Schiller, 2004).

From the point of view of receiving coun-tries, the chain migration process can be thought of as an 'IMMIGRATION multiplier', in the sense that each individual immigrant is likely to generate the entry of several others over time (Jasso and Rosenzweig, 1986). Once established, these networks develop routinized systems of movement that can even circum-vent STATE authority (Bocker, 1994). It is widely believed, for example, that chain migration has been an essential ingredient in the entry of the approximately 12 million undocumented immigrants residing in the USA. This insight has often been used by critics of immigration, who argue that the combination of the self-perpetuating nature of chain migration and the multiplier effect will cause a geometric increase in immigration (cf. Goering, 1989). However, it is worth remembering that social networks are just one contributing factor in migration, and that other factors, notably economic differentials between countries and various forms of VIO-LENCE, are structural causes of migration. DH

Suggested reading
Castles and Miller (2003); Hugo (1994).

chaos theory A branch of non-linear math-ematical theory dealing with dynamic systems which exhibit aperiodic behaviour that is sen-sitive to initial conditions and is unpredictable in detail. Such sensitivity to initial conditions is often referred to as the 'butterfly effect', with the illustration that the flapping of a butterfly's wings in one part of the world might, through tiny impacts on the atmosphere, have major impacts elsewhere in the world. The behaviour of systems that exhibit chaos may appear to be random, even though the system is deter-ministic in the sense that it is well defined and contains no random parameters. This tech-nical use of the word 'chaos' is at odds with everyday language, which suggests complete disorder. Chaotic systems are 'orderly' in being deterministic, and also usually have well-defined system structure and statistics. A very simple example of such a system is provided by May (1973) in his standard logis-tic model of population growth:

$$X_{t+1} = aX_t[1 - bX_t/a],$$

where next year's population X_{t+1} is depen-dent on the current population X_t and par-ameters a and b. The system exhibits very different behaviours depending on the values of a: if $1 < a < 3$, then X_t tends towards a stable equilibrium population. If $a > 4$, then there is a divergence to minus infinity (a total collapse of the system), but for values of a between 3 and 4, there are interesting dynam-ics: if $3 < a < 3.8495$, then X_t oscillates with a regular, periodic frequency, but if $3.8495 < a < 4$, then the oscillations are chaotic, with no regular frequency.

Chaos theory was a popular and much-vaunted term for a time, but, like the related mathematical systems of CATASTROPHE THEORY, it is usually now treated as part of the wider arena of COMPLEXITY THEORY, and further read-ing will be found under this term.   LWH

Chicago School The first sociology depart-ment in the USA (founded in 1892), located at the University of Chicago, where scholars including Robert Park, Louis Wirth and Ernest Burgess established an agenda, approach (HUMAN ECOLOGY) and METHODOLOGY for the study of urban areas. From the 1910s through to the 1930s, the scholars at the Chicago School set out to study the CITY as 'a product ... of human nature' (Park, 1967 [1925], p. 1). Indeed, the Chicago School sociologists saw the city as 'the natural habitat of civilized man [sic]' (Park, 1967 [1925], p. 2). Fundamental to their theories about urban life was an expectation of social organization and control. They anticipated that land use patterns in a city would reflect 'an orderly and typical grouping of its population and institutions' (Park, 1967 [1925], p. 1), and sought to study these systematically. Chicago School sociologists developed detailed descriptions of urban life based on field observations of Chicago. In doing so, they advocated that ETHNOGRAPHIC methods drawn from anthropology be applied to urban cultures (Park, 1967 [1925]). Their in-depth observations were hindered by a tendency to generalize from the single Chicago case, but their emphasis on observation remains influential in COMMUNITY research.

The Chicago sociologists drew upon Darwin's theories of order and 'cooperative competition' among species in a shared TERRITORY and applied them to humans in urban environments (Park, 1936). The concept of community articulated the biotic level of social organization, which correlated for the Chicago School scholars with RACE and ETHNICITY (Theodorson, 1961; Knox, 1994). Social communities as defined by ethnicity formed 'natural areas' that were segregated from one another (Park, 1967 [1925]). By applying biological METAPHORS to sociology, Park and his colleagues were creating a scientific justification and legitimation for the study of social phenomena (Entrikin, 1980). At the same time, however, their naturalizing of racialized social communities fostered and reinforced notions of a GHETTO that was both voluntary and temporary: 'they never saw the difference between the ethnic enclave and the black ghetto' (Philpott, 1991 [1978], p. 141). Further, Philpott argues that with the exception of the 'Black belt' African-American ghetto, the natural areas (social communities) about which the Chicago sociologists wrote were never as homogeneous as some of their writings suggested.

Well-known and influential studies of 'natural areas' that were developed by the Chicago

School faculty and their students include Zorbaugh's *The gold coast and the slum* (1929) and Frazier's 'Negro Harlem: an ecological study' (1937). Perhaps the most famous among the writings of the Chicago School, however, is that of Ernest Burgess on 'The growth of the city' (1967 [1925]). In it, he offered a descriptive MODEL of urban structure to explain land use, urban growth and NEIGHBOURHOOD change. He posited urban expansion based on differentiation of land uses and competition among those uses (a basic premise also articulated in the VON THÜNEN MODEL and also other land-use models by Hoyt (1939) and Alonso (1960), among others). His ZONAL MODEL represented the city as a series of 'concentric circles', or zones. The central zone at the core of the city was the CENTRAL BUSINESS DISTRICT (CBD), called the 'loop' in his model due to the influence of Chicago as the empirical case study. Successive zones were described as residential areas, differentiated from one another based on categories of ethnicity, social CLASS and housing type.

The process of urban expansion was explained by Burgess (1967 [1925]) in terms of the INVASION AND SUCCESSION of one zone (predominant land use) into the next outer zone adjacent to it, with physical expansion of the city the result. The MOBILITY assumed in the model to be inherent to urban expansion was seen by Burgess to be both a stimulus to urban growth and the source of instability, especially in lower-income and immigrant communities. Thus, CRIME, POVERTY, HOMELESSNESS and social and psychological instability were seen as naturally occurring phenomena in the zone of transition just outside of the expanding CBD (Burgess, 1967 [1925], p. 54).

Burgess' model, and the overall goals of the Chicago School to study urban life, community and organization, have been extremely influential in urban studies generally, including URBAN GEOGRAPHY. The inherent (and explicit) SPATIALITY of Burgess' model of urban growth is appealing to geographers. Terms such as CBD are ubiquitous in the field. Yet the assumptions underlying the model and its theory of growth, particularly the naturalization of RACE, ETHNICITY and social problems such as CRIME and HOMELESSNESS, limit its use and applicability.

The Chicago School is clearly situated in and thus limited by its time and place – because of its reliance on human ecology and Darwinian METAPHORS, and upon the city of Chicago as the main CASE STUDY. Yet Park's (1967 [1925]) original description of an agenda for research included POPULATION and DEMOGRAPHY, LAND USE, patterns of home ownership and MIGRATION, community development and character, neighbourhood history, occupational and class mobility, social unrest and social control (including POLICING and urban policies). Many of these topics remain of vital interest to urban geographers, and draw upon ideas from the Chicago School about PATTERN, PROCESS and community, although our contemporary approaches to and theories of these topics are necessarily different.   DGM

Suggested reading
Dear (2002); Entrikin (1980); Jackson and Smith (1984); Park, Burgess and McKenzie (1925).

children A burgeoning area of scholarship in HUMAN GEOGRAPHY that encompasses notions of children as active producers of SPACE, as geographical subjects and as environmental agents, at the same time as it recognizes children's limited MOBILITY, the peculiarities of their exposure to various environmental degradations and HAZARDS, and the mediated nature of their spatial engagements.

The earliest work in the field, pioneered by James Blaut and the psychologist David Stea, addressed the 'ontogeny of environmental behavior' by looking at children's geographical learning, especially their understandings of spatial relationships, mapping skills and PLACE knowledge (Blaut and Stea, 1971, p. 387). Their *Place Perception Project* (1968–71) spurred much generative work in the field, including Roger Hart's (1979) landmark study of children's place experience, Denis Wood's fascinating research on the relationship between young people's spatial behaviour and their cognitive MAPS, and research on such issues as children's differentiated access to the outdoor environment or 'home range,' their understanding of environmental processes and human–environment interactions, and their ability to negotiate aerial photographs. At about the same time as Blaut, Stea and their colleagues at Clark University were researching children's acquisition of environmental knowledge, William Bunge (see Bunge et al., 1971) was launching the Detroit Geographical Expedition, which examined the effects of noxious and deteriorated environments on children's well-being, and developed projects of environmental ACTIVISM around the uneven geographies of people's everyday lives and children's exposure to problems rooted in these geographies. These

two streams of work – not, coincidentally, by radical geographers – set the stage for much subsequent scholarship on children's geographies and the geographies of children, even as some of their key practitioners were marginalized from the field.

As geographers have continued to address the development of spatial cognition, mapping skills and environmental learning, there has been an ongoing debate about whether mapping represents a cultural universal that children share from earliest childhood, as Blaut and Stea and their colleagues have argued, or is dependent on cognitive development, as Roger Downs, Lynn Liben and their colleagues have argued. While much of this debate has concerned children's relative preparedness for acquiring spatial concepts and mapping skills (and thus was an argument about the role of geographical EDUCATION at different ages), it was animated by the principals' understandings of the nature of Piagetian developmental psychology and what Blaut considered its IDEALIST underpinnings. Both sides recognized children's embrace of geographical concepts, and advocated their being taught mapping and spatial skills in all phases of their education, agreeing that it would not only be a cornerstone of enhanced geographic literacy but contribute to cognitive development and learning in other arenas (Blaut, 1997; Liben and Downs, 1997; cf. Matthews, 1992). Despite this conclusion and the decades of scholarship that support it, there remains a surprising disconnection between the work of scholars interested in geographical or environmental EDUCATION and those who look at children's place experience and their acquisition of environmental knowledge and spatial skills.

Work on children's geographies has been developmental, ecological, milieu focused, comparative and concerned mostly with the global North. As the field evolved, its concerns expanded to include children's understanding and experience of place (Hart, 1979; Matthews, 1992; Wood and Beck, 1994), their knowledge of environmental processes and human–environment relations (Kates and Katz, 1977; Hart, 1997; Katz, 2004), the social ecologies of their environmental interactions (Ruddick, 1996; Valentine, 1997; Aitken, 2001) and studies of particular children's environments, such as playgrounds, schools, parks and NEIGHBOURHOODS (e.g. Skelton and Valentine, 1998; McKendrick, 1999). In tandem with broader disciplinary concerns, research focused on children and geography has shifted to address new arenas of experience and has recognized the socially constructed nature of childhood. Recent work has examined children and the electronic environment (Holloway and Valentine, 2000); children as environmentalists (Hart, 1997; Holloway and Valentine, 2000); aspects of place experience, such as fear, constriction and SURVEILLANCE, which have peculiar ramifications for young people (Valentine, 1997; Katz, 2005; Pain, Grundy, Gill et al., 2005); the EMOTIONAL GEOGRAPHIES of youth and childhood; IDENTITY formation and issues of DIFFERENCE; landscapes of CONSUMPTION; and questions of youth participation and RIGHTS (Hart, 1997). A growing number of geographers are attending to children's geographies in the global SOUTH and addressing the questions of DIFFERENCE that they raise (Holloway and Valentine, 2000; Katz, 2004).

In geography as in other disciplines associated with the 'new social studies of childhood,' children are recognized as SUBJECTS and social actors in their own right at the same time as they are both becoming something else and subject to structural forces beyond their control. Children and young people are seen to shape their own and others' lives, the SOCIAL FORMATIONS in which they live and the social construction of childhood itself. While children's experiences are often cast in relation to adults, geographers and others are clear that age and LIFE COURSE are not the only differences that structure young people's experiences. Geographers examine how differences of GENDER, CLASS, NATION, RACE, embodiedness and SEXUALITY separately and in conjuncture affect young people's experiences and understandings of the world (Skelton and Valentine, 1998; Holloway and Valentine, 2000). Childhood is now recognized as a SOCIAL CONSTRUCTION that varies historically and geographically, and scholars seek to understand it for itself rather than as a stage on the road to adulthood. If research only recently moved away from the latter perspective and its focus on the practices and processes of socialization, it has long been the case that scholarship on children's geographies has treated children methodologically as social actors rather than as objects of learning or vessels for knowledge. This perspective can be readily seen in the METHODOLOGIES adopted – and invented – for studying children's geographies. Beginning with the early work of Blaut and Stea and their students and colleagues, children have been asked to navigate actual and representational geographies, make MAPS, engage in landscape modelling, enact 'geodramas', take photographs and make FILMS, keep journals, write narratives, lead walks and – more recently – shape the research itself. These strategies have long complemented research methods such as SURVEYS, INTERVIEWS, PARTICIPANT OBSERVATION and the like in children's geographies.

In the past decade, children's geographies has been recognized as a vibrant sub-field of the discipline. This achievement was marked by the inauguration of an international journal, *Children's Geographies*, the online revival of the *Children's Environments Quarterly* as *CYE (Children, Youth, and Environments)*, the establishment of an IBG/RGS Working Group on the geographies of children, youth and families; the publication of a number of edited collections (e.g. Skelton and Valentine, 1998; Holloway and Valentine, 2000) and monographs (e.g. Matthews, 1992; Ruddick, 1996; Aitken, 2001; Katz, 2004); and the proliferation of specialized international workshops, conferences and special sessions at geography meetings. Perhaps the significance of this sub-field to the broader discipline, as much as its own 'coming of age', can best be seen in how a growing number of geographers have refracted issues such as GLOBALIZATION, GENTRIFICATION, MIGRATION or HOMELESSNESS, and theoretical constructs such as SCALE, SOCIAL REPRODUCTION or the PRODUCTION OF SPACE through the lens of childhood and youth (e.g. Ruddick, 1996, 2003; Katz, 2004).   CK

Suggested reading
Holloway and Valentine (2000); McKendrick (2000, 2004); Skelton and Valentine (1998).

Chinatown Chinese peoples living in cities beyond China have formed compact and comparatively exclusive settlements known as Chinatowns, in which they have resided, worked and traded (Benton and Gomez, 2003). Following the classic IDEAL-TYPE Chinatown formulated by Lawrence Crissman (1967) based on studies of Chinese societies in South East Asia and North America, scholars of the overseas Chinese such as William Skinner and Wang Gungwu have portrayed Chinatown as an extension of HOMELAND practices, where principles of social organization based on descent, locality and occupation that had ordered rural life in China were transplanted to overseas urban settings. In many countries, Chinatown demography was fuelled by an initial phase – taking place during the nineteenth and the first half of the twentieth centuries – characterized by either indentured labour systems or kinship-based CHAIN MIGRATION (predominantly of men), followed by a post-Second World War phase during which a 'bachelor society' was gradually transformed by the presence of more female migrants and family immigration (Chen, 1992; Benton and Gomez, 2003). Largely self-organizing entities, socio-political life and the provision of cradle-to-grave services in these transplanted communities were anchored, to different extents in different communities, by Chinese associations based on clan, surname, dialect or provenance. Portrayed as an immigrant neighbourhood or an ethnic ENCLAVE, Chinatown is identified as a reception area for newcomers, an agglomeration of ethnic businesses (including 'illegal' or 'immoral' practices such as drug trafficking, gambling and prostitution) serving its 'own kind', and the focal point of a well-knit COMMUNITY in a foreign land. The Chinatown depicted in this vein is essentially an outpost of a foreign country, comprising a DIASPORA of unassimilable foreigners.

Recent scholarship has challenged our understanding of Chinatown in at least three ways. First, Chinatown is not just an exported structure, but the product of host society reception, including colonial labour policies in some instances and racial discriminatory and discursive practices more generally. In colonial cities of South East Asia, Chinatown as a racial categorization and spatial container to accommodate the Chinese emerged as part of colonial urban planning, and often featured in colonial DISCOURSES as a landscape of filth, pestilence and moray decay (Yeoh and Kong, 1994). In Western contexts, by placing the idea of Chinatown at the centre of RACE-definition processes, Anderson (1987, p. 581) argues that 'Chinatown is a social construction with a cultural history and a tradition of imagery and institutional practice that has given it a cognitive and material reality in and for the West.' More than a PLACE-NAME or a social community, Chinatown is also part of the IMAGINATIVE GEOGRAPHIES underpinning white European cultural HEGEMONY (see CHINATOWN).

Second, using Chinatown as a spatial reference for an essentialized Chinese IDENTITY or 'chopsticks culture' fails to recognize differences of class, sub-ethnic affiliation and cultural history among members of Chinese communities. Social and economic mobility, generational change and the influx of later arrivals from different parts of mainland China, Hong Kong, Taiwan and other Chinese communities have transformed closed social structures and introduced diversity in terms of CLASS, occupations, educational backgrounds, political affiliations and even ethnic consciousness among those identified with Chinatown (Chen, 1992; Kwong, 2001; Christiansen, 2003).

Third, against portrayals of Chinatown as an enclave economy that defies integration into the mainstream, Zhou (1992) argues that immigrant Chinese in Chinatowns in the US context are able to draw upon social capital and networks to surmount structural barriers and facilitate socio-economic mobility. From this perspective, Chinatown as an ethnic enclave provides a mechanism for eventual immigrant incorporation into mainstream society.

Chinatown landscapes are also increasingly revitalized for the purposes of HERITAGE TOURISM or promoted as gentrified, conservation settings to enhance urban aesthetics in globalizing cities. Along with other ethnic neighbourhoods ranging from Koreatown to Little India, Chinatown as the inscription of race in place has continued to evolve in tandem not only with IMMIGRATION dynamics but with the politics of PLACE.   BY

Suggested reading
Anderson (1992); Yeoh and Kong (1994); Zhou (1992).

chorology/chorography The study of the variation in the Earth's surface from place to place (see also AREAL DIFFERENTIATION). Chorology represents the oldest tradition of Western geographical enquiry. It was first codified by Hecataeus of Miletus in the sixth century BCE and systematized by Strabo in the seventeen books of his *Geography*, probably written between AD 18 and 24. The geographer, he wrote, is 'the person who attempts to describe the parts of the earth' (in Greek, *chorographein*). The two key words were 'describe' and 'parts': in effect, Strabo was recommending what would now be called REGIONAL GEOGRAPHY as the core of geographical reflection. He was not interested in chorography for its own sake, but intended it to serve a higher purpose. The production of geographical knowledge was an indispensable complement to political and moral PHILOSOPHY, because it provided a material ground for understanding truth, nobility and virtue. For this reason, Strabo's geography was fundamentally concerned with human activities. It was also directed towards political and social ends, and paid considerable attention to the interests of the political ruler and the military commander. Although Strabo was born in Greece, he enjoyed the patronage of Augustus and did most of his work in Rome, so that his *Geography* can be read as an attempt to explain the post-Republican world (the inhabited world, or ECUMENE) to the citizens of the new Roman Empire (Dueck, 2000). Chorography was not supposed to provide a comprehensive gazeteer or regional inventory: it was partial and purposive, and Strabo focused on Rome and began with EUROPE because 'it is admirably adapted by nature for the development of excellence in men and governments' (van Paassen, 1957, pp. 1–32).

Strabo's conception of geography was challenged by Claudius Ptolemaeus (or Ptolemy) round about AD 150. In his view, the purpose of geography was to provide 'a view of the whole head' and this meant that he separated geography from chorography, which had the purpose 'of describing the parts, as if one were to draw only an ear or an eye'. As this passage implies, for Ptolemy, *graphein* did not mean describing but drawing and, specifically, mapping. Ptolemy's 'geography' was geodesy and CARTOGRAPHY, and he preferred to leave out everything that had no direct connection with that aim: 'We shall expand our "guide" for so far as this is useful for the knowledge of the location of places and their setting upon the map, but we shall leave out of consideration all the many details about the peculiarities of the peoples' (van Paassen, 1957, p. 2).

The distance between Strabo and Ptolemy could not be plainer, and it is indelibly present in the modern constitution of GEOGRAPHY too. As late as the seventeenth century, Strabo and Ptolemy continued to provide the main models for European geography. The usual distinction was between a *Special Geography*, devoted to a description of particular regions, and a *General Geography*, mathematically oriented and concerned with the globe as a whole. The premier illustration is the work of Bernhard Varenius, who published both studies in Special Geography and his famous *Geographia generalis*, in which, for the first time, geography sought to engage with the ideas of Bacon, Descartes and Galileo (Bowen, 1981).

The modern case for geography as chorology was argued most forcefully by Hartshorne (1939), and following the subsequent debate over EXCEPTIONALISM in geography – and despite the nuances and qualifications that Hartshorne had registered – chorology was often used in polemical opposition to SPATIAL SCIENCE (cf. Sack, 1974a). But the temper of the original version, with its acknowledgement of the importance of POWER and philosophical reflection (cf. Casey, 2001, p. 683), is a forceful reminder of the continuing need to attend to the politics of geographical enquiry, while Koelsch (2004) has insisted that contemporary attempts to understand the heterogeneous geography of the world still have much to learn from 'the place-based, cultural–historical model' of Strabo.   DG

Suggested reading
Koelsch (2004).

choropleth A MAP that portrays a single distribution for CENSUS TRACTS, counties or similar areal units; portrays each areal unit as homogeneous; divides the data into discrete categories; and typically describes spatial variation of intensity data with a darker-means-more sequence of greytones. Readily rendered by mapping software, choropleth maps can present misleading patterns when based on count data, highly heterogeneous areal units, inappropriate CLASS INTERVALS or illogical sequences of colours (Brewer and Pickle, 2002; Monmonier, 2005). Although most choropleth maps depict quantitative distributions such as median income or the percentage rate of population growth, qualitative choropleth maps are useful for showing distributions such as dominant religion or form of government.   MM

Suggested reading
Monmonier (1993).

chronotope Translated as 'time–space' from its origins in Greek, the term is used to designate the spatio-temporal contexts and categories embedded within a text or other cultural artefact. The term was devised by Russian literary theorist and philosopher Mikhail Bakhtin (1895–1975) in the 1920s, partly influenced by the revolutionary transformation of physics by Einstein, Planck and others, and it was subsequently imported into literary history and cultural studies. In the most general terms, the idea of a chronotope acknowledges the inseparability of TIME and SPACE while deploying their unity to materialize concrete cultural formations. It is perhaps best to think of a chronotope as a kind of matrix that allows cultural analysts to situate a work within its historico-geographical setting in order to facilitate its interpretation.

Bakhtin (1984, p. 246) offered the concrete example of the French literary *salon* as a key nineteenth-century chronotope, 'where the major spatial and temporal sequences of the novel intersect' in the works of Balzac and Stendhal. Not surprisingly, the term has been influential in theatre studies, with the stage providing an intuitive location for the observation of chronotopes in action, and theories of PERFORMANCE have developed these immanently geographical tropes still further by insisting on the contextual boundedness of human actions. In HUMAN GEOGRAPHY, Folch-Serra (1990) proposed a dialogical conception of LANDSCAPE that derived directly from Bakhtin and promised to reconstruct the power-laden interactions 'that alternately "anchor" and destabilize the "natural harmony" of a region'. This focus on the narration of landscape resurfaces in interdisciplinary studies of landscape and IDENTITY (Lehman, 1998), but the sense of diversity, dialogue and disputation that is crucial for any Bakhtinian approach is best exemplified by O'Reilly's (2007) study of the unfolding micropolitical relations between competing voices and the co-production of gendered time–spaces of participation in development projects in North India. As she shows, and as the concept of a chronotope strongly suggests, struggles over meaning are also and reciprocally struggles over the production of distinctive time–spaces. US

Suggested reading
Holloway and Kneale (1999); O'Reilly (2007).

citizenship The rights and duties relating to an individual's membership in a political COMMUNITY. In the past several centuries, the boundary of this community has been the NATION-STATE and membership has implied some degree of integration into a common national HERITAGE. In its early formulations, however, citizenship was understood as a set of RIGHTS and freedoms located primarily at the local scale. The expansion of individual freedoms (such as the right to work and *habeas corpus*) into a national institution was one of the key components of the growth of modern citizenship. It reflected a shift from local, communal relations and social rights rooted in village membership into a sense of a national community and of individual rights guaranteed by a STATE. This shift in scale from the local to the national and from communally sanctioned rights to those protected by the state is an absolutely fundamental aspect

of modern citizenship, and one that is profoundly intertwined with the growth of industrial CAPITALISM, LIBERALISM and MODERNITY in the West (Weber, 1978 [1922]; Turner, 1993; Marston and Mitchell, 2004).

As it has developed in British and North American societies, citizenship owes its modern legacy to a succession of legal and political rights and responsibilities originating in Britain mainly in the seventeenth century and continuing through to the present. According to T.H. Marshall, citizenship can be usefully periodized in terms of: (a) the eighteenth-century development of *civil* citizenship, which encompasses civil and legal rights, especially PROPERTY rights; (b) the nineteenth-century expansion of *political* citizenship, which involves the rights to vote, to associate and to participate in government; and (c) the rise of twentieth-century *social* citizenship, which involves entitlements such as provisions for health, housing and education (see Mann, 1987, p. 339; Marshall and Bottomore, 1992). Marshall envisioned a continuous positive trajectory for citizenship in terms of the ongoing inclusiveness and expansion of universal rights, as well as the evolution of those forms of state welfarism (social citizenship) that guaranteed all members the chance to access those rights and participate in the politics of the community. Although his framework remains influential, Marshall has been criticized for his lack of attention to the experiences of women (Vogel, 1994; Walby, 1994), for the linear and evolutionary qualities of his model (Giddens, 1982), and for his unquestioned liberal assumptions relating to the positive integrative capacity of citizenship itself (see LIBERALISM).

Like many mid-twentieth-century liberals, Marshall was a strong nationalist who conceptualized citizenship as corresponding with a specific state territory and as fundamentally linked with its economic development and cultural narratives. For him and many others, citizenship necessarily assumed both a sense of belonging and identity rooted in a shared national past and a commitment to the production and defence of its territorial borders. Over the past few decades, however, these types of assumptions have been overturned. As a result of the powerful new forces of GLOBALIZATION and TRANSNATIONALISM, both the national narratives of heritage and community and the state's discrete and autonomous jurisdiction over TERRITORY and population have been called into question. One of the many new kinds of tensions that have erupted in this period involves the meaning and practices of contemporary citizenship.

With the ever-increasing volume and speed of the flows characteristic of globalization, including those of trade, finance, commodities, information, ideas, culture and human beings, the ability of state actors to control and regulate BORDER-crossings and their increasingly mobile populations has greatly diminished. At the same time, most states have maintained various kinds of power through new types of geopolitical alliances, new forms of disciplining and regulation of people across borders, and the development of new transnational or supranational institutions and practices of rule. In all of these ASSEMBLAGES of power, the meaning, status and practice of citizenship has remained a crucial and much sought-after prize, and it has been at the centre of multiple hegemonic struggles worldwide over the past two decades.

The scholarship on citizenship has burgeoned over the same time period, with hundreds of titles on different forms of citizenship, such as post-national, transnational, dual and multicultural. Those with an empirical bent have tracked the transformations in citizenship LAW in different national sites over this period and/or the numbers of immigrants or denizens who have become citizens, or whose status or benefits or rights have changed. Those leaning towards POST-STRUCTURALISM have written about the cultural qualities of contemporary citizenship, emphasizing in particular its multi-layered nature and/or the ways in which belonging and IDENTITY are morphing into something quite different from earlier nation-based understandings and assumptions. Many have also remarked on the different scales of citizenship, from supra-national (e.g. the EU) to sub-national (e.g. Basque) citizenship possibilities. Soysal (1994) argues that the development of both of these forms manifests the declining importance of national citizenship and the rise of new forms of post-national membership in EUROPE.

Almost all current scholarship engages with citizenship as a constantly evolving, non-linear formation that is tied to the development of modern nation-states as well as to the evolution of contemporary economic systems. In the WEST, it is inevitably interrelated with the form and logic of capitalist development. This said, it should be noted that the ways in which citizenship takes shape at different historical periods and in different places always reflect the actions of those to whom its transformation matters. State and economic restructuring responding to civic or popular action – whether it is of resistance or accommodation – shifts the terrain of rights, responsibilities and belonging on which citizenship is based, leading inexorably to new formations through time.   KM

Suggested reading
Castles and Davidson (2000); Hall and Held (1989); Turner (1986).

city The etymological roots of the term lie in the Latin *civitas*; it is related to the Greek *polis*, the Latin *urbs*, the French *la cite, la ville*, the Italian *la città* and the German *die Stadt*. Today, a more generic usage of the term refers to an urban demographic, economic and above all political and jurisdictional unit, usually bigger than a town. In the USA, cities are considered to have self-government granted by the states. In Canada, where municipal autonomy is more restricted, cities are under the constitutional jurisdiction of provinces. In the UK, reference is to a large town that has received title from the Crown.

Cities are usually trading centres and marketplaces. Their emergence is linked to the historical separation of non-agricultural work from the land (see URBAN ORIGINS). Ancient cities in the Indus valley, in Mesopotamia, Egypt and China were based on a hydrological agricultural economy, and were the seats of religious and military POWER, and the STATE. The built environment developed around a temple or ziggurat, and was walled for defence and internal control of the population. In ancient Greece and Rome, city-states (Athens, Rome) were cores of larger empires (Mumford, 1961; Benevolo, 1980). Medieval cities in Europe are often seen as the Western archetype of urban socio-spatial organization and the core of an urban-based network of trade systems (e.g. the German *Hansa*). During that period, cities were municipal corporations of free citizens embedded in – usually feudal – larger territorial units. Cities were seats of church power and of the emerging bourgeoisie, as well as the tightly organized artisan trades. Many cities became the location of the first universities.

Today's most common image of cities is influenced by the industrial age. The INDUSTRIAL REVOLUTION led to the large-scale demographic concentration of working-class populations around manufacturing plants or industrial complexes, and housed in the typical tenement and rowhouse settlements of the nineteenth-century city. Industrial core regions such as the British Midlands or the German Ruhr area became sites of rapid URBANIZATION, creating regional agglomerations of industrial cities. In the USA, Chicago stands in as the prototypical industrial city that grew explosively around the turn of the twentieth century.

Improved transportation allowed longer commuter distances and suburbanization at the beginning of the twentieth century. The planned suburbanization and automobilization, as well as functional separation of land uses in particular, were ultimately considered a major contributor to the 'fall' of the modern city (Jacobs, 1992 [1961]; see SUBURB). The twentieth century saw metropolitanization and the rise of the MEGALOPOLIS, a supercity stretching across several urban areas. City life now encompasses most areas of society as 'urbanism as a way of life' (see URBANISM) becomes pervasive. POST-INDUSTRIAL CITIES now characterize most Western nations, as industries first moved to suburban locations and then to developing countries where – as in Korea, Brazil or China – renewed waves of urbanization and industrialization seem to repeat the history of the industrial city in Europe and North America.

In the global SOUTH, cities have often grown from colonial outposts into global trading centres (Hong Kong and Singapore). In Africa, Asia and Latin America today, cities grow dramatically, often largely on the basis of large-scale squatter settlements (see SQUATTING) and informal urbanization. Cities have recently enjoyed renewed attention as a post-Westphalian system of global GOVERNANCE has restructured the role of NATION-STATES, and as new types of GLOBAL CITIES and MEGACITIES have begun to exert territorial, economic and political POWER at a global scale.

The city has been the object of much scholarly debate in GEOGRAPHY and the social sciences. As David Harvey (1973, p. 196) has noted: 'Urbanism may be regarded as a particular form or patterning of the social process. This process unfolds in a spatially structured environment created by man [sic]. The city can therefore be regarded as a tangible, built environment – an environment which is a social product.' Urban theory of the twentieth century, strongly influenced by the work of German sociologist Max Weber (1958 [1921]) and the CHICAGO SCHOOL of sociology (Park, Burgess and McKenzie, 1925; Wirth, 1938), tended to fetishize the city spatially as something that appeared distinct from SOCIETY. Neo-Marxist and neo-Weberian critiques led to a new phase of studying the city in the 1960s and 1970s (Castells, 1972; Harvey, 1973; Smith, 1979b; Saunders, 1986; Lefebvre, 2003 [1970]), pointing to the notion that the modern city is an economic or administrative part of capitalist society and cannot be studied in separation from it. Castells influentially defined the city as the site of COLLECTIVE CONSUMPTION and a site for SOCIAL MOVEMENT mobilization (Castells, 1972, 1983). A related strand of thought redefined the city as a product of urban growth machines and governing regimes interested in the increase in property values (Logan and Molotch, 1987). Whereas in the 1970s and 1980s 'the city' often became synonymous with the site of social crisis, pathology and delinquency, the postmodern turn in geography and urban studies reinvigorated the discussion on the city in the 1990s, as Los Angeles was temporarily viewed as the new 'Chicago': a distinct and pervasive model of urbanization in a globalized capitalist system (Scott and Soja, 1996; Dear, 2002; see POSTMODERNISM). As China's cities grow in size and significance as global players, they have become the focus of increased attention at the beginning of the twenty-first century, while the sprawling megacities of the global South are considered to be on a trajectory different from the ones in the West and in the North.

Although the death of the city had been predicted as a consequence of the development of transportation and information technologies that allegedly make AGGLOMERATION less necessary and less likely, the opposite has occurred in the past decade: economic power has been re-concentrated in cities as a new wave of re-centralization of people and economic activities has led to a 'fifth migration' to urban centres (Fishman, 2005). Much of this had to do with a distinct process of 'metropolitanization', a state growth strategy that concentrates specifically on cities. As a consequence, cities have been rediscovered as the site of 'creative industries', but also as the contested space of social struggles, GENTRIFICATION and displacement.   RK

Suggested reading
Amin and Thrift (2002); Harvey (1989c); LeGales (2002); Parker (2004).

civil society Understood as a domain of associations autonomous from the STATE, this concept has been critical to the history of Western political thought. Originally posited in EUROPE in the eighteenth century to denote a realm of social mutuality, the idea of civil society increasingly came to signify aspects of social existence that occur beyond the state. In its different uptakes, the concept of civil society has been central to the development of both the liberal-parliamentary tradition and the socialist-Marxist one. Although demarcated differently by theorists of the French, German and Scottish ENLIGHTENMENTS, all attempts to articulate a notion of civil society shared the perceived tensions between the public and the private, the social and the individual, collective responsibility and self-interest, and state prerogatives and individual freedoms. But Italian Marxist Antonio Gramsci offered an alternative perspective. In his *Prison Notebooks* (1971 [1929–35]), he explored aspects of the state and civil society that liberal theory ignores – namely, the relations of power and influence between political society (what liberal theorists call 'state' or 'government') and civil society (the 'private sector' in liberal vocabulary), which mutually reinforce each other to the advantage of certain strata and groups. *Contra* LIBERALISM, Gramsci recognized civil society as the terrain of HEGEMONY rather than freedom.

The contemporary revival of the idea of civil society within academia and policy circles is a curious event. It appears to be correlated to the demise of the Soviet Union and the MARKET triumphalism that followed (see NEO-LIBERALISM). For advocates of economic GLOBALIZATION – an institutionalized project of market deregulation – the term 'civil society' functions as placeholder for an array of signifiers that are used almost interchangeably: *private sphere, free market, free society, democracy, social capital* and so on. In short, civil society denotes that desirable zone of activities and associations that is putatively free from state intervention.

Contrast this usage with that by communitarians and left liberals, who worry about the expansion of administrative and economic mechanisms into virtually all spheres of life under late CAPITALISM. For them, the concept of 'civil society' represents a fading terrain of DEMOCRACY that must be preserved and resuscitated. Thus, civil society appears in their writings as the sphere of social interaction composed of 'the intimate sphere (especially the family), the sphere of associations (especially voluntary associations), social movements, and forms of public communication' (Cohen and Arato, 1992, p. ix). It is differentiated from both a political society of 'parties, political organizations and political publics

(in particular, parliaments)' and an economic society 'composed of organizations of production and distribution, usually firms, cooperatives, partnerships, and so on' (ibid.).   VG

Suggested reading
Buttigieg (1995); Cohen and Arato (1992); Edwards (2004); Ferguson (1995 [1767]); Seligman (1992).

civilization (1) A complex sociocultural formation. (2) An evolutionary process of cultural development, most often associated with the German sociologist Norbert Elias (1897–1990), who traced a 'civilizing process' in post-medieval Europe. The two have often been connected through the distortions of a colonialist imaginary that treats the 'WEST' as coterminous with 'civilization', divides the world into superiors and SUBALTERNS (often described as 'barbarians' or 'savages'), and advances its own 'civilizing mission' to 'enlighten' or 'develop' them (cf. PRIMITIVISM). It is scarcely surprising to find that the term 'civilization' originated in Europe in the middle of the eighteenth century, when EUROPE was so busily encountering its 'OTHERS' (Mazlish, 2005). In the course of the twentieth century, anthropologists, archaeologists, ancient historians and other scholars recognized multiple civilizations, however, and increasingly treated civilizations as complex, adaptive SYSTEMS (Butzer, 1980). These more technical concepts were put to work in comparative HISTORICAL GEOGRAPHY: for example, in studies of URBAN ORIGINS it is common to distinguish the Harappan civilization in the Indus Valley or the Mayan civilization in Meso-America.

But the older colonial distortions have also resurfaced through polemical arguments about a contemporary *'clash of civilizations'*. The most detailed version of this thesis was proposed by American political scientist Samuel Huntington (1993, 1997; see also Kreutzmann, 1998). Huntington argued that questions of collective IDENTITY – 'Who are we?' and 'Who are they?' (cf. IMAGINATIVE GEOGRAPHY) – assumed a special force under the pressures of GLOBALIZATION. He saw these as intrinsically cultural questions, whose answers were almost invariably provided by RELIGION. Far from the secular world of MODERNITY carrying all before it Huntington believed that the world was witnessing a global religious revival. For this reason he used religion to identify seven or eight major civilizations and to explain the conflicts emerging on the 'fault-lines' between them. His thesis was a generalization of a polemic by British Orientalist Bernard Lewis on 'The roots of Muslim rage' and had the same destination (see ORIENTALISM). 'The overwhelming majority of fault-line conflicts,' Huntington concluded, 'have taken place along the boundary looping across Eurasia and Africa that separates Muslims from non-Muslims'. Huntington attributed this to what he called, with offensive disregard, 'the Muslim propensity toward violent conflict', and argued that since the Iranian revolution that toppled the Shah in 1979, a 'quasi-war' had been in progress between Islam and the West. Huntington's ideas gained a new lease of life following 9/11 (Salter, 2002), but they have been sharply criticized both for their conceptual crudity – in particular, Huntington's unsophisticated rendition of cultural interaction and identity formation (Said, 2000; Sen, 2006) – and for their unreflective demonization of Islam, or *Islamophobia*.   DG

Suggested reading
Kreutzmann (1998); Robertson (2006).

class In *The communist manifesto* (2002 [1848]), Karl Marx and Friedrich Engels asserted that '[t]he history of all hitherto existing society is the history of class struggles'. This declaration marks the foundations of class analysis. Although the concept of class has since come into wide usage, it remains contested. There is disagreement on how best to define it, on its general role in SOCIAL THEORY and on whether it remains relevant to the analysis of contemporary societies. For some, classes have become largely redundant in today's societies; for others, class persists as one of the fundamental forms of social inequality and POWER. Some view class as a narrow economic phenomenon, while others embrace a more elastic conception that spans cultural dimensions and economic conditions. In its most persistent popular sense, class refers to a social division or system of rank order, evident in the phrase 'upper, middle and lower classes', that is associated with position, privilege and hereditary advantage (or the lack thereof). Class is also construed as distinctive bodily practices, such as attire, carriage, speech, diet, habitation and forms of lifestyle consumption – all linked to underlying unequal structures of material resources.

Uses of the term 'class' are always evaluative, whether positive or pejorative. Hence, the upper classes are sometimes the 'aristocracy' – endowed with a natural authority and disposition to rule – or else the 'leisured class' – parasitic on society's surpluses and given to ostentatious consumption. Correspondingly, the middle classes are sometimes the 'enterprising' classes, who embody individual initiative, toil and prudence, and form the mainstay of civil society. Alternatively, they are the *bourgeoisie* – merchants, traders, entrepreneurs and professionals, committed to defending the inequalities and privileges of private property and to organizing the exploitation of the working classes. The lower classes are sometimes the 'working classes' or the 'working poor' – simple, hard-working and law-abiding people, who can claim no inherited privileges – or, alternatively, the 'lower orders' – uncivilized and unruly (and in some renderings, criminal and sexually promiscuous), who court idleness and are a drag on economic progress. The eventful 'discovery' of an UNDERCLASS by US-based conservative academics and commentators in the 1980s added a gendered and racial twist to these negative portraits. In this 'culture of poverty' discourse, which significantly influenced the 1990s policy shift in the US from welfare to workfare, the underclass came to signify a disaffected layer of work-shy, feckless, criminal, undeserving and semi-detached poor people, typically black and from disorganized households headed by single mothers, who had grown accustomed to surviving on excessively generous handouts from government-run welfare programmes.

From an academic standpoint, the analysis of class has taken two dominant forms, sorted by historical lineage. The first set of approaches, deriving from Karl Marx, pivots around the concepts of *class relations* and *class structure* (see MARXIST ECONOMICS). Other adjectival uses of the term class – class location, class conflict, class interests, class formation and class-consciousness – obtain their meanings from their link to class relations and class structure. Sociologist Erik Olin Wright contends that class relations should be viewed, *sensu stricto*, as a specific form of prevailing *social relations of production* (Wright, 2005). These, he says, designate the different kinds of rights and powers of persons in society who participate in production. When the rights and powers of people over productive RESOURCES are unequally distributed – when some people in a society have greater RIGHTS and powers with respect to certain productive resources than do others – these relations can be described as *class relations* (see CAPITALISM). It is important to note that the rights and powers in question do not pertain to the ownership or control of things in general, but specifically to resources or assets *as they are deployed in production*. The fundamental contrast in capitalist societies, for example, is between owners of means of production (machines, inputs, space etc.) and owners of labour power, where each category of owner – the capitalist and the labourer – deploys the resource that they own *in production*. That said, it is worth emphasizing that class relations as defined are elastic enough to recognize PATRIARCHY within the household and beyond and racial discrimination within society (see RACISM) as concurrent class processes. Meanwhile, work in RADICAL GEOGRAPHY has convincingly shown that exploitative class relations are fundamentally spatial and that this spatial organization is critical to understanding the nature of UNEVEN DEVELOPMENT.

The ambiguity of class location – or location within social relations of production – is forcefully illustrated by managers within corporations, who exhibit the rights and powers of both capital (they can hire and fire workers, make decisions about new technologies and changes in the labour process, etc.) *and* labour (they cannot sell a factory, they have limited discretion in the use of surplus or profit, they can be fired from their jobs if the owners are unhappy, etc.). Workers as corporate shareholders (via an employee stock ownership plan, for example) provide another vivid illustration of ambiguity, since they simultaneously occupy two class locations. Other instances that complicate the empirical exercise of class location include persons who work at two jobs, one as a worker in a firm and the other as a self-employed tradesman; professional women, who employ a full-time housemaid; or historically, working-class sepoys stationed in colonies who, by virtue of racial difference, found themselves in positions of class superiority *vis-à-vis* natives (one imagines a similar phenomenon at work in today's imperial outposts). In short, class relations, class structure and class location in societies are complex – as such, we should presuppose neither unity of purpose (class interest) nor consciousness (class agency) within a given class category (see Marx, 1963 [1852]).

The German sociologist Max Weber's analysis of class is the primary alternative to Marxist class analysis. In Weber's scheme, classes are distinguished by positions of relative advantage and disadvantage in terms of wealth and income. He writes: 'We may speak of a "class" when (1) a number of people have

in common a specific causal component of their life chances, in so far as (2) this component is represented exclusively by economic interests in the possession of goods and opportunities for income, and (3) is represented under the conditions of the commodity or labor markets' (Weber 1968 [1946], p. 181). While there are overlaps here with Marx's understanding of class, there are also clear differences. Weber, for instance, emphasizes 'personal life experiences' and 'life chances' as critical aspects of 'class situation', and takes class to be 'any group of people that is found in the same class situation' (ibid.). Thus, whereas for Marx class is an objective set of social relations, for Weber subjective elements become key. Also in contrast to the Marxist view of *class as relational*, the Weberian view emphasizes *class as market position*. Classes are hierarchical arrangements, but potentially dynamic ones because MARKET position may be changed by collective strategies in the labour market (e.g. through professional associations or trades unions). In underscoring the 'life chances' that accompany 'class situation', Weber draws attention to individuals' prospective 'personal life experiences': 'the probabilities of social and occupational mobility; of educational access and achievement; of illness and mortality' (Clarke 2005, p. 40). While classes, in Weber's view, derive unambiguously from economic interest, they are linked to political organization (party) and social position (status), both of which may be shaped by non-economic processes and may influence 'class-consciousness'. The French sociologist Pierre Bourdieu is a prominent example of a scholar who has creatively fused the Marxist and Weberian perspectives of class in his analysis of various forms of CAPITAL.   VG

Suggested reading
Bourdieu (1984); Massey (1995); Weber (1968 [1946]); Wright (2005).

class interval   A key element in the design of a quantitative MAP that partitions the range of data values into discrete categories, each assigned a unique symbol. Common on CHOROPLETH maps, class intervals are also used for maps of linear and point phenomena and embedded in maps on which ISOLINES divide the data into categories or layers. Typically, a map key links the class intervals to their respective symbols, which may vary in size, greytone value or colour. Because different class intervals can yield radically different depictions of the same data, viewers should be wary of ill-informed, careless or biased map authors (Evans, 1977; Monmonier, 2005).   MM

Suggested reading
Monmonier (1993).

classification and regionalization Procedures – most of them quantitative – for grouping individuals into categories. *Classification* involves splitting a population into mutually exclusive categories on pre-determined criteria, either deductively (using a previously determined set of classes, such as town size-groups) or inductively (finding the best set of classes, on predetermined criteria, for the data set being analysed: cf. DEDUCTION; INDUCTION). Some procedures start with the entire population and divide it; others start with individuals and group them into classes. Most proceed hierarchically, generating classes that nest within each other at various scales. The goal is to produce classes whose members are more like other members of their class than they are members of other classes: classes are internally homogeneous and externally heterogeneous. A range of classification algorithms is available in standard statistical packages.

Regionalization (cf. REGION; REGIONAL GEOGRAPHY) is a special case of classification in which the individuals classified are spatially defined units (usually areas) and the resulting classes (regions) must form contiguous spatial units. Because of this constraint, regions may not be as internally homogeneous as would be classes generated for the same set of areas but without the insistence on contiguity. These latter form regional types, areal units grouped without a contiguity constraint, so that similar areas may be spatially discontinuous (e.g. areas with Mediterranean climates).

Recent work has argued that classifications should not impose firm boundaries, and suggested instead the use of FUZZY SETS to indicate the probability that an individual belongs to any particular class. (See also DISTRICTING ALGORITHM; GEODEMOGRAPHICS; MODIFIABLE AREAL UNIT PROBLEM; REDISTRICTING.)   RJ

Suggested reading
Johnston (2005c); Heckman, King and Tracy (2005); Openshaw and Openshaw (1997).

climate Conventionally understood to comprise the meteorological elements – rainfall, wind, temperature, insolation, humidity and so on – which characterize the general atmosphere over a zone of the Earth's surface for a period of time. The Intergovernmental Panel on Climate Change (IPCC) (2003) thus identifies climate, in its *Glossary of terms*, as 'average weather' or 'more rigorously as the statistical description of the mean and variability of relevant quantities over a period of time ranging from months to thousands or millions of years'. To this, the IPCC glossary adds that the World Meteorological Organization specifies 30 years as the 'classical' temporal period for determining average conditions. The crisp clarity of this definition, however, masks the concept's contested historical lineage. During the period of the European ENLIGHTENMENT, for example, Diderot and d'Alembert's celebrated *Encyclopédie* identified as one of its definitions of climate a REGION with characteristic seasons, soils and cultural mores (Feldman, 1990). The Victorian geologist Samuel Haughton (1880, p. 74) similarly typified climate as the 'complex effect of external relations of heat and moisture upon the life of plants and ANIMALS', including the human species. Given these associations, it is not surprising that the study of climate has routinely embraced matters of social, moral and political concern.

HUMAN GEOGRAPHY′S engagements with climate have thus been manifold. Among the most conspicuous have been a noticeable inclination amongst its advocates to reduce ENVIRONMENTAL DETERMINISM to climatic determinism; the incorporation of climatic conditions into studies of the perception of ENVIRONMENTAL HAZARD and RISK; discussion about the role of human agents in inducing climate change and GLOBAL WARMING; medical geography's earlier interest in the role of climate-correlated pathologies; and imperial debates about human capacities to adapt to different climatic regimes. Each of these domains has witnessed controversy. Amongst early-twentieth-century environmental determinists, for example, climate was often called upon to justify various racial ideologies that attributed excellence to the temperate zones and explained the historical trajectory of civilization in the vocabulary of climatic circumstance (Livingstone, 1994: see also RACE). Controversy has also attended proposals over the steps that need to be taken to curb the influence that human society has had in climate change and over the degree to which the Earth's planetary atmosphere can be understood as a self-regulating system: this has immediate political implications, since individual states have been reluctant to bear the political consequences of prioritizing environmental restraint over economic growth

(Fleming, 1998). Amongst early medical geographers, debates about climate revolved around whether disease should be understood in miasmic–ecological terms or in the language of the new germ theory (Rupke, 2000: see also MEDICAL GEOGRAPHY). Debate raged too amongst colonists over whether human acclimatization was possible and, if so, under what conditions it could be effected.

Other human dimensions of climatic discourse and practice have also recently been the subject of geographical investigation. The realization that climate has often been conceived of in moral categories has established it as a significant component in a range of MORAL GEOGRAPHIES. Thus historians of SCIENCE, for example, have demonstrated how the study of meteorological conditions was rooted in a suite of discourses about the prediction of ominous social and political happenings (Jankovic, 2000). The ways in which climate was used to pathologize whole zones of the GLOBE by resorting to it as the explanation for debility as well as parasitic fecundity have also been exposed (Naraindas, 1996). At the same time, enquiries within historical geography have revealed how climate was culturally constructed to serve various, often racial, interests among philosophers, geographers, medical practitioners, travel writers and artists (Livingstone, 2002a). These pronouncements contributed directly to the production of the idea of TROPICALITY by castigating the tropical world as medically and morally degraded, and by providing a naturalistic justification for various labour practices in the colonial world and IMMIGRATION policies in the West. Read in this register, climate has persistently surfaced as a cultural category that has been deployed as a HERMENEUTIC resource to advance moral, political and social interests.

The practices of meteorological instrumentation have also raised significant geographical questions. Weather conditions are derived from a variety of instrumental devices, such as anemometers, hygroscopes, thermoscopes, barometers and pluviometers (see SCIENTIFIC INSTRUMENTATION). At centres of calculation, such as the Meteorological Office, the aggregate mensural yield of widespread meteorological networks is assembled as affiliated observation stations return standardized records to weather information centres. As Anderson (2005a, p. 290) puts it: 'Philosophically, the science of meteorology was global; in practice, global science developed in distinctively different political and geographical landscapes, and contemporaries insisted on the importance of the differences.' The inherently geographical nature of this process of knowledge production as information moves from specific sites into general circulation has been the subject of interrogation by both historians and geographers, who have examined this scientific impulse to escape the bounds of the local (Jankovic, 2000; Naylor, 2006). The significance of missionaries in the gathering of climatological data has also attracted scrutiny, as their records provide information on the weather history of locations in which they worked (Endfield and Nash, 2002). Such work has drawn attention to issues congregating around the standardization of measurement practices, the social geography of who can be trusted to deliver reliable climatic information, the regulation and management of distant observers, and the cultural politics of shifting boundary lines between amateur and professional.

Matters of climate are thus profoundly implicated in a range of discourses. The racial politics of climatic determinists, the apocalyptic tincture of certain strands of climatic prophecy, the economic geography of weather-related insurance, and the social constitution of climatological knowledge are just a few of the ways in which climate is clearly disclosed as a cultural construct.   DNL

Suggested reading
Jankovic (2000); Livingstone (2002a).

clusters A concept usually associated with the work of Michael Porter, from Harvard Business School's Institute for Strategy and Competitiveness. Porter defines clusters as '... geographic concentrations of interconnected companies, specialized suppliers, firms in related industries, and associated institutions (for example universities, standards agencies, and trade associations) in particular fields that compete but also cooperate' (Porter, 1998c, pp. 197–8). According to Porter's work, within a cluster: (1) information flows increase between related and supporting industries; (2) market awareness of firms improves thanks to the concentration in the cluster of demanding clients; (3) peer pressure/competition drives INNOVATION as rivals seek to out-compete one another; and (4) local 'factor conditions', such as the availability of skilled labour in a particular area, are exploited to make firms globally competitive. These four forces form part of Porter's 'diamond model' for successful clusters. In addition, as Porter also points out, the social foundations of a cluster are vital because success is reliant on '... social glue that binds clusters together, contributing to the value creation process. Many of the competitive advantages of clusters depend on the free flow of information, the discovery of value-adding exchanges or transactions, the willingness to align agendas and to work across organizations, the strong motivation for improvement. Relationships, networks, and a sense of common interest undergird these circumstances' (Porter, 1998c, p. 225).

The concept of the cluster mirrors in many ways ideas contained in a wider set of literatures. Dating back to Marshall's (1890) work on INDUSTRIAL DISTRICTS and, more recently, through studies of what have been called LEARNING REGIONS and innovative milieux (Asheim, 1996; Malmberg and Maskell, 2002), emphasis has been placed on the importance of geographically distinctive arrangements of firms in one industry for knowledge production and circulation. This has become especially important in light of recent debates about the KNOWLEDGE ECONOMY and the need for cities and regions to be globally competitive centres of INNOVATION. It is Porter's cluster concept that has gained most traction in policy circles, with regional authorities throughout the world employing Porter and his followers to develop a cluster strategy for their local industries. Many are, however, critical of this approach. For geographers, the main concern with the cluster concept has been its apparent geographical fuzziness and the way in which the boundaries of a cluster are never defined in existing work. In addition, the way in which iconic spaces such as Silicon Valley are used to produce 'elastic' theoretical models that can be turned into fashionable development concepts has also caused concern, particularly because of the questionable levels of success of such models (see Martin and Sunley, 2003). JRF

Suggested reading
Martin and Sunley (2003); Porter (1998b).

co-evolution In biology and ECOLOGY, co-evolution refers to the reciprocal changes that occur between populations of species as they interact. In one sense all evolution is co-evolution, as all species are considered to affect and be affected by changes to other species and their environments. In more specific terms, co-evolution is understood to apply to those interactions where there has been mutual, symbiotic or parasitic changes that have affected both parties that are temporally and spatially proximate. In HUMAN GEOGRAPHY and the social sciences, the term

has been used loosely to understand the complex relationships between, for example, technology and place (Graham, 1998), economy and environment (Costanza, 2003) and humans and companion species (Haraway, 2003). The shared aim is to avoid reductionism and determinism, and point to the relational character of change. SJH

co-fabrication An orientation towards research and intervention emphasizing the ontological and political requirement of 'working together' (Whatmore, 2003). Derived from the work of the philosopher Isabelle Stengers (1997), the implications and practices involved in co-fabrication have best been exemplified in SCIENCE and technology studies and ACTOR-NETWORK THEORY, where the production of reality is demonstrated to be something other than a zero-sum game. Rejecting discourses of either pure human invention or discovery of already existing reality, co-fabrication enacts a relational understanding of ONTOLOGY, suggesting that the more activity there is from a researcher, the more – if they are to be successful – activity there is from the researched (Latour, 1999c). This maxim applies as much to human–microbe ASSEMBLAGES in the laboratory as it does to studies of, or with, social groups. In terms of the latter, co-fabrication leads to something akin to ACTION RESEARCH, though with the added implication that all participants in the research process are treated less as informants and more as colleagues (Stengers, 1997). For social science, this requires a change of stance, away from distanced, expert critique and towards the crafting of co-operative ventures. SJH

Suggested reading
Whatmore (2003).

cohort A group of people with a common demographic vintage. Cohorts are most often defined on the basis of being born in the same year or years (i.e. *birth cohorts*, such as the US 'baby boom' born in the US between 1946 and 1964), although marriage, divorce, MIGRATION and graduation events also define groups whose life experiences and biographies can be analysed over time. Adopting a *cohort approach* has deepened understanding of very low levels of FERTILTY (Lestheage and Willems, 1999) and spatial variations in MIGRATION (Plane, 1992), and supplements *period approaches* that analyse changes occurring between two points in time. AJB

Suggested reading
Weeks (1999, Chs 5 and 8).

Cold War The period of international diplomatic, political and military rivalry between the United States of America (USA) and the Union of Soviet Socialist Republics (USSR), conventionally understood as lasting from the end of the Second World War in 1945 to the fall of the Berlin Wall in 1989. As with other periods of international transformation, the Cold War is subject to a variety of different interpretations, each highlighting different causes.

The conventional historiography of the Cold War understands the period as one of realist GEOPOLITICS, in which the balance of power and spheres of influence were historical necessities (Halle, 1991). Although allies during the defeat of Nazi Germany, the USA and the USSR approached the postwar order with different visions, the USA backing a market-oriented liberal order (see CAPITALISM; DEMOCRACY), while the USSR sought friendly regimes on its borders and the spread of COMMUNISM internationally. At the 1945 Yalta summit, President Roosevelt, General Secretary Stalin and Prime Minister Churchill outlined plans for zones of MILITARY OCCUPATION in defeated Germany, with the liberated territories to be democratic. But with Soviet forces occupying the east and the allies dominant in the west, EUROPE was divided by what Churchill called an 'Iron Curtain'. This produced two competing military alliances – the North Atlantic Treaty Organization (NATO, est. 1949) organized by the USA in the west, and the Warsaw Pact (est. 1955), dominated by the Soviets in the east, with the former seeking to contain or roll back the latter.

These 'ideological blocs' (see IDEOLOGY) became the basis for the organization of international politics for more than 40 years, with their enmity symbolized by the nuclear arms race and materialized in a number of global events, including the building of the Berlin Wall in 1961 and the Cuban Missile Crisis of 1962, amongst many others. Although many flashpoints were in Europe, the Cold War was a global geopolitical formation that produced the 'THIRD WORLD' as a non-aligned group of states that declined to side with either the 'First World' (the USA and its allies) or the 'Second World' (the USSR and its allies). Although the Cold War did not erupt into direct 'hot' WAR between the two superpowers, there were numerous proxy conflicts between their allies, largely in AFRICA and ASIA, often piggybacking on indigenous struggles, in which millions perished. The enmity between the blocs was eased by diplomacy, especially the period of 'détente' in the 1970s, and ended by the early 1990s when a variety of forces intersected to remove the Soviet hold over eastern Europe and the eventual demise of the USSR as a superpower.

Revisionist accounts of the Cold War have detailed the economic forces driving American expansionism, with the conflictual IMAGINATIVE GEOGRAPHIES of capitalism and communism having existed prior to the geopolitics of the post-Second World War era. Perspectives from CRITICAL GEOPOLITICS (e.g. Campbell, 1998; Glassman, 2005) argue that the Cold War was a discursive formation as much as a geopolitical condition. This 'architecture of enmity' (Shapiro, 1997) materialized political identities that have survived the demise of the Soviet Union and helped constitute new enemies.   DCA

Suggested reading
Gaddis (2006); Gregory (2004b).

collective consumption Basic public services such as schools, health services and utilities, usually provided by the STATE, which facilitate or enable the reproduction of labour power (Castells, 1977) (see SOCIAL REPRODUCTION). The notion of collective consumption developed within Marxist urban theory, with the spheres of production (of goods and services) and labour reproduction as defining elements (Pinch, 1989). It is an effort, therefore, to theorize social relations in capitalist SPACE; specifically, the means by which labour is reproduced 'on a daily and intergenerational basis' (Pinch, 1989, p. 47). Castells (1977) identified collective consumption as the basis for a framework for the analysis of labour reproduction in a specific sphere of social and spatial life, that of the urban (Saunders, 1986, p. 172). According to Castells' (1977) framework, since housing, recreational and health facilities, for example, are provided to people in specific locations on the basis of their collective use, investigation of collective consumption constitutes a fixed territorial setting for empirical analysis (Saunders, 1986). Thus, Castells (1977) argued that he had identified a specifically urban space with the specification of the labour reproductive and collective consumption processes. However, these processes do not occur exclusively in urban PLACES, and the challenges of reproduction and collective consumption are also evident in RURAL areas or small towns (Saunders, 1986).

Castells refined his approach to collective consumption in his influential *The city and the grassroots* (1983). In it, he argued that the increasing role of the state in collective consumption, as part of efforts to resolve the contradictions of CAPITALISM, did not solve those contradictions but, instead, led to an increasingly contentious and political consumptive sphere (Castells, 1983; Saunders, 1986). The result is collective ACTIVISM: URBAN SOCIAL MOVEMENTS organized against or as a challenge to the state over its management of and provisions for collective consumption.

Pinch (1989) argued that, with the state posited as the provider of goods and services for collective consumption, the concept is too narrow, since many collective goods can be privately provided. Indeed, with increasingly NEO-LIBERAL states, collective consumption seems an outdated concept. The problem and question of the reproduction of labour – such as how to provide for childcare or HEALTH services – however, remains salient (Pinch, 1989). Contemporary scholars concerned with these issues focus less on the state and more on its role as one element in PUBLIC-PRIVATE PARTNERSHIPS, and the responses in and effects on various communities (see COMMUNITY).   DGM

Suggested reading
Castells (1983); Herbert (2005).

collinearity A statistical problem associated with the GENERAL LINEAR MODEL, especially multiple REGRESSION analysis. If two or more of the independent variables are substantially correlated, the resulting regression coefficients will provide unreliable statements of the true relationships and be difficult to interpret. Statistical tests can identify the extent and impact of collinearity in an analysis.   RJ

colonialism An enduring relationship of domination and mode of dispossession, usually (or at least initially) between an indigenous (or enslaved) majority and a minority of interlopers (colonizers), who are convinced of their own superiority, pursue their own interests, and exercise POWER through a mixture of coercion, persuasion, conflict and collaboration (cf. Osterhammel, 1997, pp. 14–20). The term both denotes this relationship and serves as an interpretation of it – customarily one in which the experiences of colonizers and the colonized are at odds. Derived from the Latin word *'colonia'* (estate, distant settlement), and typically promulgated within the framework of an EMPIRE, 'colonialism' was first used as a term of disapprobation in eighteenth-century debates about the morality of SLAVERY, and has since been conceptualized as a distinctly Western modality of power that has been closely connected to the evolution of CAPITALISM, MODERNITY and EUROCENTRISM.

(1) *Concept and imagery.* Colonialism is commonly viewed as the chief variant and consequence of IMPERIALISM: the tangible means by which disparate parts of the world became subordinated to the drives and dictates of a separate and distant imperial centre (metropole or mother country), and struggles over territory, resources, markets and national prestige became displaced overseas (cf. WORLD-SYSTEMS theory). The term 'colonization' denotes the array of expansionist projects – EXPLORATION, WAR, geopolitical rivalry, military conquest and OCCUPATION, commerce, MIGRATION, settlement, state formation and cultural representation – from which particular colonialisms arise.

A common – and not inaccurate – image of colonialism is of a STATE-centred system of power characterized by brute exploitation, astonishing cultural arrogance and RACISM, which reached its heyday in the early twentieth century, when European colonial empires spanned the GLOBE (the British Empire covering 20 per cent of the world's land surface), and colonial rule (then justified as a 'civilizing mission') seemed secure to its protagonists, in spite of widespread anti-colonial resistance. Colonialism has also been viewed as symptomatic of an epistemological malaise at the heart of Western MODERNITY – a propensity to monopolize and dictate understanding of what counts as right, normal and true, and denigrate and quash other ways of knowing and living. Yet it is more than just a will to exercise dominant control, or a proprietary project that constructs the world as the WEST's bequest – although it is surely both of these things. Nor has it simply been a hierarchical and diffusionist process, solidified in a CORE–PERIPHERY relationship, which spawned what Frantz Fanon (1963 [1961], pp. 37–8) described as 'a world cut in two' and a colonial world 'divided into compartments' – with the colonized enjoined to emulate the West. Colonialism has also been characterized by subversion and, some argue, by inherent flux and contradiction, ambivalence and HYBRIDITY. Not feeling at home in empire was a visceral experience for the colonizer the world over.

It has become commonplace to observe that colonialism involves a mutual interdependence of forms, at root because colonial identities are constructed in relation to both a metropolitan core and indigenous/colonized lands and peoples. Identities are formed and stretched across both metropolitan/colonial and colonizer/colonized divides, creating what Edward Said (1993, pp. 3–61) – a key thinker and influence on geographers – dubs 'overlapping territories' and 'intertwined histories'. The interdisciplinary critical project of POST-COLONIALISM, which is inspired, in part, by a 'desire to speak to the Western paradigm of knowledge in the voice of otherness', has sought to show that Western/metropolitan SUBJECTIVITY has not been constituted in a self-contained box, but through this long, stretched and often violent process of colonial exchange, and tries to expose and destabilize the way in which Western and non-Western, and colonial and post-colonial, identities have been shaped by potent binaries – of 'CIVILIZATION' and 'savagery', 'modernity' and 'tradition' and so on (Goldberg and Quayson, 2002, p. xiii).

This critical reconfiguration of Western history and CULTURE is intrinsically linked to what many see as the cornerstone of colonialism's SPATIALITY: the importance of displacement for both colonizer and colonized (and for both their knowledge systems and ways of life), and the subsequent difficulty of ever going back to some pristine or authentic connection between PLACE and IDENTITY that is uncontaminated by the experience of colonization. 'Just as none of us is outside or beyond geography,' Said (1993, p. 7) writes in an influential passage, 'none of is completely free from the struggle over geography. That struggle is complex and interesting because it is not only about soldiers and cannons but also about forms, about images and imaginings'. Colonialism can be distinguished from IMPERIALISM in terms of the local intensity and materiality of this geographical struggle, centrally over home and territory. Said spurred interest in how colonialism works as a *cultural discourse* of domination animated by images, narratives and representations – and mediated by CLASS, RACE, GENDER, SEXUALITY, NATION and RELIGION – as well as a material project and feat of power. Over the past twenty years, colonialism has been studied as a 'cultural technology of rule' imperilled by various 'investigative modalities' (Cohn, 1996).

Said (1978, pp. 49–73, 327) deploys the term IMAGINATIVE GEOGRAPHY to capture the connective imperative between geography and DISCOURSE within the unequal framework of empire: the 'dramatisation' of difference between 'us' and 'them', and 'here' and 'there', with texts 'creat[ing] not only knowledge but also the very reality they appear to describe'. In famously showing how the Orient was produced, its meaning regulated and Western dominance over it shaped, by Western knowledge, institutions and scholarship (by a discourse of Orientalism), Said does not collapse the distinction between representation and reality. Rather, he underscores how ORIENTALISM and other colonial discourses exert authority by creating asymmetrical relationships between Western and 'other' knowledge systems. It is through this process of 'knowledgeable manipulation' that distorted images and stereotypes of foreign lands and peoples become taken-for-granted, traits of difference become ascribed to particular spaces, places, environments and natures, and 'other' peoples are deemed unable to represent or govern themselves. This is what Said (1978, p. 63) means when he describes 'the Orient' as 'an enclosed space' and 'a stage affixed to Europe', and David Arnold (2005, p. 225) when he describes how British observers 'affixed' India to alien European ideas of landscape and nature – as part of the Tropics (see TROPICALITY). While Said has been criticized for obscuring how non-Western peoples responded to this epistemological onslaught, he revealed how colonialism revolves around grammars of difference, othering and exclusion that are acutely spatial – that function as 'trait geographies' (Gregory, 2001b).

(2) *History and interpretation.* As much of the above implies, there is more than one MODEL of colonialism. Indeed, it is important to recognize how different meanings and models of colonialism have evolved and operate *a posteriori*. Important distinctions have been drawn between different types of colonies: exploitation colonies (e.g. British India, French Indochina; slave colonies, 'protectorates' and 'dependencies'), which were established primarily for the purpose of capitalist economic extraction, where tiny expatriate colonial elites often governed large subject populations, and ideologies of RACE and paternalism played a pivotal role in colonial rule; settler colonies (e.g. North America and AUSTRALASIA), whose political economies were premised on the availability of extensive tracts of cultivable and resource-rich land, and where indigenous peoples were systematically displaced by

colonists and native populations plummeted due to disease; and maritime enclaves (e.g. Aden, Hong Kong, Jakarta and Malacca), which served as commercial and military nodes in encompassing imperial networks. While these are ideal types – for instance, French Algeria and Spanish Peru were both extraction and settler colonies – a large literature identifies the distinct power relations pertaining to these different colonial formations. The close association of colonialism with European/white minority rule has meant that the term has been deemed inapplicable to some situations – until recently, the colonial period of US history, where colonists along the Atlantic seaboard soon outnumbered native people. And the 'salt water' association between colonialism and distant overseas possession explains why expressions such as 'internal colonialism' have been used to describe situations in which colonialist relationships exist within the borders of, or contiguous to, an imperial state or kingdom (e.g. between England and its 'Celtic fringe', especially Ireland).

The history of colonialism has also been divided into distinct periods: Spain and Portugal's initial sixteenth-century conquest of the New World; the seventeenth-century creation of an 'Atlantic world' revolving around the circulation of people and commodities, and centred on SLAVERY and the racialized PLANTATION economies of the Caribbean; the eighteenth-century extension of European (especially British and Dutch) trade and dominion in Asia; the nineteenth-century building of European land empires in Africa and Asia and the emergence of the USA as a significant empire-builder; the maturation of colonial export economies between 1900 and 1945; and a postwar welfare-minded colonialism that became entangled with independence struggles and DECOLONIZATION.

Since the 1980s work on colonialism – much of which is either aligned with, or sees itself as a response to, POST-COLONIALISM – stems from the recognition that the postwar break-up of Europe's colonial empires did not quickly or necessarily put once colonized regions on a par with the West – at any level. In 1965, Kwame Nkrumah coined the term NEO-COLONIALISM to describe how the West (and especially the USA) was perpetuating colonialism while upholding ideals of independence and liberty, the contradiction being as apparent in DEVELOPMENT models, which were the vehicles of a new cultural imperialism, as it was blatant in new international investment and trade relations (Young, 2001, pp. 44–56; cf. DEVELOPMENT GEOGRAPHY; THIRD WORLD; TRANSNATIONAL CORPORATION). Some remarkable theoretical treatments of colonialism from this era – for example, the work of Fanon and Aimé Césaire – alight on the enduring and nefarious psychological influence of colonial categories of thought and social pathologies on post-independence politics and NATIONALISM. And if, as this suggests, the colonial past was not over, then Derek Gregory (2004b, pp. 6, 117), adds what now seems an obvious rider: that the colonial past 'is not even past'. EMPIRE is being revived through the creation of new 'colonizing geographies' of division, partition and enmity (the war-torn MIDDLE EAST currently bearing the brunt of them) that displays many affinities with past colonial ideas and practices. The United Nations has declared the period 2001–10 the 'Second International Decade for the Eradication of Colonialism'.

Indeed, there is now arguably a greater range of opinion about colonialism than there has been for 50 years, including burly affirmations of its supposed benefits that feed on imperial nostalgia. On the other hand, there has been a radical re-reading of the West's conception of its cultural evolution, and much academic soul searching, not least within European and North American geography, which has strong ties with empire, blasting apart disciplinary allegories of OBJECTIVITY, progress and self-contained development (cf. GEOGRAPHY, HISTORY OF). Many discourses and practices that have been deemed central to geography's make-up and heritage – EXPLORATION, mapping, surveying, ENVIRONMENTAL DETERMINISM, geopolitical model-building and latterly GIS – have been pressed into (and are still designed for) imperial service.

CARTOGRAPHY has been a colonizing tool *par excellence*. Maps brought 'undiscovered' lands into spatial existence, emptying them of prior (indigenous) meanings and refilling them with Western PLACE-NAMES and borders, priming 'virgin' (putatively empty land, 'wilderness') for colonization (thus sexualizing colonial landscapes as domains of male penetration), reconfiguring alien space as absolute, quantifiable and separable (as property), drawing mapped space into the unifying framework of Western knowledge and reason, and, along with the clock and calendar, effecting a fundamental reorganization (standardization) of the relations between time and space (Edney, 1997; cf. TIME-SPACE DISTANCIATION). Little wonder, then, that concepts and METAPHORS of mapping and location have a seminal place in post-colonial theory.

(3) *Critical problematics.* While recent work on colonialism eludes simple characterization, it can usefully be located within a series of inter-related spatial poles of interpretation, which grapple with whether colonialism, *in extremis,* can and should be treated as uniform or diverse, coherent or fragmentary, centred or decentred, and whether it put in train a cultural history of affinity or difference, con-nection or separation, inclusion or exclusion. These analytics can be traced through two pairs of watchwords that infuse work in the field of colonial studies and the wider project of post-colonialism.

With regard to *diversity and specificity,* recognition of the historical–geographical di-versity of colonialism is often registered as a warning about the perils of generalizing about 'it' from particular locations (Algeria, India and the Caribbean being the crucibles of much theorizing). Colonialism is conceived as less amenable to ABSTRACTION than imperial-ism, as more localized and differentiated than models suggest, and in need of more compara-tive research. This critical impulse to extend what Fanon (1963 [1961], p. 239) called 'the will to particularity' – to expose the duplicity of Western universals and absolutes – has been manifested in calls to bring metropole and colony into 'a unitary analytical field' (Cooper and Stoler, 1997a, p. 1), to conceptu-alize colonialism as a 'forged concept' involving both similitude and difference (Lloyd, 1999, p. 7), and to re-examine those processes (both violent and intimate) that colonizers and the colonized shared, as well as those that set them apart.

A range of recent scholarship on struggles over 'who was inside and who was outside the nation or colony, who were subjects and who were citizens', demonstrates the importance of escaping older scholarly containers and 'map-ping … difference across nation and empire' (Hall, 2002a, p. 20; Lambert and Lester, 2006). Starting from an analytical standpoint of liminality (how colonialism operates in terms of what it excludes and places outside its domain of comprehension and action), and from the premise that significant gaps existed between metropolitan/imperial prescriptions of power and the daily realities and pressures of colonial rule, a feminist-inspired literature examines how colonialism involves incessant struggles over the making and protection of cultural boundaries and frontiers – struggles that are gendered, sexualized and racialized, and that work to demarcate the foreign from the domestic, the civilized from the wild or savage and home from away (Stoler, 2002; Blunt, 2005).

Emphasis is now routinely placed on the SPATIALITY of such struggles and dynamics, and geographers have been particularly con-cerned with how colonialism operates through: (i) particular sites and contact zones, such as ships, forts, plantations, trade posts, ports and cities, native reserves, mission stations, museums and exhibitions; (ii) the networks and institutions – such as the London-based Royal Geographical Society and Seville-based Council of the Indies – that coordinated the flows of people, goods, orders and information connecting this array of places and spaces; and (iii) the inscription devices and systems of REPRESENTATION – forms of recording, writing, and calculating distance and measuring differ-ence, such as maps, journals, ledgers, paintings and despatches; practices of exploration, observation, FIELDWORK, CLASSIFICATION and synthesis; and discourses justifying colonialism – that both shaped and were shaped by such sites, domains and networks (Driver, 2001a; cf. CENTRE OF CALCULATION; CLIMATE; TROPICAL-ITY). This body of work emphasizes that Europeans' ability to know, physically reach and govern distant and far-flung lands was something made, practiced and performed (and thus amenable to criticism and re-inven-tion) rather than given (and was not some innate and distinguishing European quality and mark of its superiority).

However, such site-specific and de-centred readings can arguably lose sight of colonial-ism's trans-historical traits and general effects – such as (for some) its propensity to racialize difference the world over, and (for others) the way in which the STATE is deemed to be the bearer of the most rational and civilized practices of rule – and thus undermine an anti-colonial politics that is responsive to the commonalities of experience among the col-onized. Anti-essentialist and non-teleological approaches to colonial history that refuse to generalize and conceptualize colonialism *in extremis,* or as a totality, can trivialize its impact, and can serve divisive ethnic and nationalist agendas in the post-colonial world that 'repeat … colonialism's own strategy … to regionalize, split up, divide and rule' (Young, 2001, p. 18). Conceptual and ethical tensions also arise when critical affiliation with the colonized (and other so-called 'injured identities') is derived from a critical stance that

97

underscores colonialism's inherently fragmentary character, and sees both colonialism's civilizing mission and 'THIRD WORLD' NATIONALISMS and revolutionary movements as doomed to failure and self-interest. One the other hand, geographers operating at the former margins of empire complain about the metro-centric focus of both older imperial histories, and newer critical accounts of the colonizing impact that metropolitan-based initiatives (such as cartography and travel) had on outlying regions. Viewing the colonized world from the (former) imperial centre – which is where a good deal of critical work on geography and empire emanates from – can blunt understanding of the specific and changing composition of colonial power in particular localities (Harris, 2004).

With regard to *discursivity and dislocation*, geographers have considered how a wide range of spatial practices and representations of space work as colonizing discourses – as textual and visual 'scriptings' and 'spaces of constructed visibility' that have shaped what Europeans understood to be 'out there' and framed how interaction was to proceed and be recorded (Duncan and Gregory, 1999). In prosecuting such ideas – TRAVEL WRITING being a prime focus – geographers have been critical of the reduction of colonialism to issues of DISCOURSE and representation, and a concomitant erasure of historical–geographical specificity, which has characterized much (especially literary) work in this area, and have coined expressions such as 'spaces of knowledge' and 'geographies of truth and trust' to underscore the materiality of discourse and the situated and embodied nature of colonial knowledge and power (Gregory, 2001b). Nevertheless, much of this literature has been preoccupied with the agency and texts of European/Western/colonizing projects and actors, and either overlooks native agency or subordinates indigenous knowledge to the gaze of the Western/metropolitan/post-colonial critic by representing it as the background noise against which the colonizing West stakes its claims to truth and power. While the difficulties involved in bringing native agendas and 'other' voices back into the colonial spotlight should not be underestimated, work that aims – laudably – to expose and question previously undisclosed connections between discourse and domination runs the risk of reinforcing the ideas, images and categories (of, for example, exoticism, primitivism and race) that it sets out to challenge. It does so, in part, Nicholas Thomas (1993) has pointed out, by obfuscating how colonial encounters operate as two-way and intersubjective (albeit still unequal) processes rather than as a one-way projection of desire and fear, or as a unitary imposition of power (see also TRANSCULTURATION).

All of this helps to dispel the illusion of a seamless or ineluctable process of Western expansion, and makes the current promulgation of a 'post-colonial geography' that seeks to assess what about geography (as a discipline, discourse and practice of power) might need decolonizing more than a belated or ironic gesture, as some have suggested.   DCl

Suggested reading
Blunt and McEwan (2002); Cooper (2005); Gregory (2004); Said (1993, 2003 [1978]).

command economy An economy in which the means of production are owned and controlled by the STATE and in which central planning prevails. The term is used to distinguish economies, such as those in Eastern Europe until the early 1990s, from either CAPITALISM or a mixed economy. The dismantling of command economies in Eastern Europe reflected an inability to produce goods in the quantities that people had come to expect, as a result of difficulties of coordination and the lack of efficiency incentives. However, the economies that replaced them have their own imperfections, including large-scale criminalization, reflecting the difficulty of creating market-regulated economies in former socialist states (cf. SOCIALISM).   DMS

commercial geography A forerunner of ECONOMIC GEOGRAPHY concerned with describing, tabulating and cartographically representing the geographical facts of commerce for practical, business ends. Coined by the philosopher Immanuel Kant (1724–1804) in the late eighteenth century as one of his six divisions of GEOGRAPHY, commercial geography was systematically taken up by German geographers from the middle of the nineteenth century. In Britain, the Scottish geographer George Chisholm (1850–1930) provided the first English-language version of the project in his 1889 tome, *A handbook of commercial geography*, and identified three sections: how commodities are produced, what commodities are produced and where commodities are produced. Chisholm provided no indication of the complexity of the concept of COMMODITY, however, and seven years before his book was published the German geographer Götz had already recognised a new sub-discipline, economic geography, that was to be a SCIENCE rather than an encyclopaedia of facts for improving the bottom line (Sapper, 1931, p. 627).   TJB

commodity With its price tag, said the great German critic Walter Benjamin, the commodity enters the MARKET. The *Oxford English Dictionary* defines a commodity as something *useful* that can be turned to *commercial advantage* (significantly, its Middle English origins invoke profit, property and income); it is an article of TRADE or commerce, a thing that is expedient or convenient. A commodity, in other words, is self-evident, ubiquitous and everyday; it is something that we take for granted. Marx (1967 [1867]) said that commodities were trivial things but also bewildering, 'full of metaphysical subtleties and theological capers'.

Commodities are everywhere, and in part define who and what we are. It is as if our entire cosmos, the way we experience and understand our realities and lived existence in the world, is mediated through the base realities of sale and purchase. Virtually *everything* in modern society *is* a commodity: books, babies (is not adoption now a form of negotiated purchase?), debt, sperm, ideas (intellectual property), pollution, a visit to a national park and human organs are all commodities. Even things that do not exist as such appear as commodities. For example, I can buy a 'future' on a basket of major European currencies, which reflects the average price (the exchange rate) of those national monies at some distant point in time. Other commodities do not exist in another sense; they are illegal or 'black' (heroin, stolen organs). Others are fictional (e.g. money scams and fraud). Visible or invisible, legal or illegal, real or fictive, commodities saturate our universe.

Commodity-producing societies – in which the dominating principle is commodities producing commodities – are a quite recent invention, and many parts of the world, while they may produce for the market, are not commodity societies. Socialist societies (and perhaps parts of China and Cuba today) stood in a quite different relationship to the commodity than so-called advanced capitalist states (cf. SOCIALISM). Low-income countries, or the THIRD WORLD so-called, are 'less developed' precisely because they are not mature commodity-producing economies (their markets are undeveloped or incomplete, as economists might put it) – they are not fully *commoditized*.

So the full commodity form as a way of organizing social life has little historical depth: it appeared in the West within the past 200 years. And over large parts of the Earth's surface the process of *commodification* – of ever greater realms of social and economic life being mediated through the market as a commodity – is far from complete. Perhaps there are parts of our existence, even in the heart of MODERNITY, that never will take a commodity form.

A peculiarity of a commodity economy is that some items are traded as commodities but are not intentionally produced as commodities. Cars and shoes are produced to be sold on the market. But labour – or, more properly, labour power – is also sold and yet it (which is to say me as a person) was not conceived with the intention of being sold. This curious aspect of labour as a commodity under capitalism is as much the case for land or Nature. These sorts of curiosities are what Karl Polanyi, in his book *The great transformation* (2001 [1944]), called *'fictitious commodities'*. Polanyi was of the opinion that market societies that do not regulate the processes by which these fictitious commodities become commodities will assuredly tear themselves apart. The unregulated, free-market, commodity society would eat into the very fabric that sustains it by destroying NATURE and by tearing asunder the most basic social relationships (see CAPITALISM).

The commodity raises the tricky matter of price, which after all is the *meaning* of the commodity in the capitalist marketplace: how it is fixed, and what stems from this price fixing. For example, the running shoes that a poor inner-city kid in the USA yearns for are Air Nike, which cost slightly more than the Ethiopian GNP per capita and perhaps more than his mother's weekly income. Or consider the fact that a great work of art, Van Gogh's *Wheat field*, is purchased for the astonishing sum of $57 million as an investment. The problem of the determination of prices and their relations to *value* lay at the heart of nineteenth-century classical POLITICAL ECONOMY, but it is an enormously complex problem that really has not gone away or in any sense been solved. The 'metaphysical subtleties' that Karl Marx refers to are very much about the misunderstandings that arise from the way we think about prices, and what we might call the sociology or social life of commodities. But if there is more to commodities than their physical properties and their prices, which are derived from costs of production or supply and demand curves, then there is a suggestion that commodities are not what they seem. Commodities have strange, perhaps 'metaphysical', effects. For example, the fact that a beautiful Caravaggio painting is a commodity – and correlatively, that it is private property and only within the means of the extravagantly rich – fundamentally shapes my experience of the work, and of my ability to enjoy its magnificent beauty in some unalloyed way. Its commodity status has tainted and coloured my appreciation of it.

A commodity, then, appears to be a trivial thing but it is in fact bewildering, even theological. The commodity, said Walter Benjamin, has a phantom-like objectivity, and it leads its own life after it leaves the hands of its maker. What on earth might this mean?

One way to think about the commodity is derived from Karl Marx, who begins his massive treatise on capitalism (Volume 1 of *Capital*) with a seemingly bizarre and arcane examination of the commodity, with what he calls the 'minutiae' of bourgeois society. The commodity, he says, is the 'economic cell form' of capitalism. It is as if he is saying that in the same way that the DNA sequence holds the secret to life, so the commodity is the economic DNA, and hence the secret of modern capitalism. For Marx, the commodity is the general form of the product – what he calls the generally necessary form of the product and the general elementary form of wealth – *only* in capitalism. A society in which the commodity is the general form of wealth – the cell form – is characterized by what Postone (1993, p. 148) calls 'a unique form of social interdependence': people do not consume what they produce and produce and exchange commodities to acquire other commodities.

But the commodity itself is a queer thing, because while it has physical qualities and uses, and is the product of physical processes that are perceptible to the senses, its *social* qualities – what Marx calls the social or value form – are obscured and hidden. 'Use value' is self-evident (this is a chair that I can use as a seat and that has many fine attributes for the comfort of my ageing body) but value form – the social construction of the commodity – is not. Indeed, this value relation – the ways in which commodities are constituted, now and in the past, by social relations between people – is not perceptible to the senses. Sometimes, says Marx, the social properties that things acquire under particular circumstances are seen as inherent in their natural forms (i.e. in the obvious physical properties of the commodity). The commodity is not what it appears. There is,

then, a hidden life to commodities and understanding something of this secret life might reveal profound insights into the entire edifice – the society, the culture, the political economy – of commodity-producing systems. It is possible to construct a diagrammatic 'biography' of the broiler from production to consumption, which depicts many of the actors involved in the commodity's complex movements and valuations. This is a *commodity circuit* or a COMMODITY CHAIN (in French, it is referred to as a *filière*). Commodity circuits can depict different types of commodity chains and contrasting commodity dynamics.

Marx invoked *commodity fetishism* to describe the ways in which commodities have a phantom objectivity. The social character of their making is presented in a 'perverted' form. By this, he meant a number of complex things: first, that the social character of a commodity is somehow seen as a natural attribute intrinsic to the thing itself; second, that the commodities appear as an independent and uncontrolled reality, apart from the producers who fashioned them; and, third, in confusing relations between people and between things, events and processes are represented as timeless or without history, they are naturalized. Another way to think about this is that commodity production – the unfathomable swirl of commodity life – produces particular forms of alienation and reification. In his book *Society of the spectacle* (1977), Guy Debord argues that in a world of total commodification, life presents itself an as immense accumulation of SPECTACLES. The spectacle, says Debord, is when the commodity has reached the total occupation of social life and appears as a set of relations mediated by images. The great world exhibitions and arcades of the nineteenth century were forerunners of the spectacle, celebrating the world as a commodity. But in the contemporary epoch, in which the representation of the commodity is so inextricably wrapped up with the thing itself, the commodity form appears as spectacle, or as a spectacular event, whether four men trying to play chicken or a chef playing football with a frozen broiler. Whatever else it may be, the terrifying events of 11 September 2001 and the collapse of the twin towers of the World Trade Center represented an enormous spectacle in the Debordian sense; and a spectacle for which there could be no spectacular response of equal measure. Necessarily, this spectacle of spectacles was a product of commodification and necessarily it has become a commodity itself. Within weeks of the attacks,

Ground Zero in New York City had become a small marketplace for 9/11 T-shirts and other mementos, just as shirts bearing the image of Osama Bin Laden and the falling towers were selling like hot cakes in Bangkok, Jakarta and the West Bank as icons of anti-imperialism.

We began with the commodity as a trivial thing and have ended with a world of commodities that 'actually conceals, instead of disclosing, the social character of private labour, and the social relations between the individual producers' (Marx, 1976 [1867], pp. 75–6). But this hidden history of the commodity allows us to expose something unimaginably vast; namely, the dynamics and history of capitalism itself. The commodity as its 'cellular form' is surely one of the keys to unlocking the secrets of what Max Weber (2001 [1904–5]) called the 'capitalist cosmos'.   MW

Suggested reading
Taussig (1978).

commodity chain/*filière* A collection of interrelated economic activities and industries that produce a particular kind of product or service. While COMMODITY chains connote 'vertical' coordination among firms, from design to assembly to final distribution, the term seems to have first been used by Hopkins and Wallerstein in 1977 in a programmatic call to de-centre the NATION-STATE in international political economy. Coming from the perspective of world systems theory (see CORE–PERIPHERY MODEL), they argued for attention to be paid to 'the widespread commodification of processes' by 'tak[ing] an ultimate consumable item and trac[ing] it back to the set of inputs that culminated in this item – the prior transformations, the raw materials, the transportation mechanisms, the labor input into each of the material processes, the food inputs into the labor' (p. 128). The alternative – and more common – usage of this concept seems to have independent origins in French industrial economics. Montfort and Dutailly (1983) used the term *filière* to refer to a set of firms linked vertically in the creation of a single product. The organizational structure of an economy is then best understood and described as a collection of constituent *filières*, or commodity chains. This approach has been used in ECONOMIC GEOGRAPHY to discuss technological and economic interdependencies between spatially proximate buyers and suppliers, as well as firms linked horizontally in relations of co-operation. The approach also appears to have

independent origins in agro-food studies (see AGRO-FOOD SYSTEM), representing a rare case in which AGRICULTURAL GEOGRAPHY led the way in economic geography. Friedland, Barton and Thomas (1981) first use of the term 'commodity systems analysis' to focus on the mutual interaction of agricultural production practices, grower organization, labour, science and extension, and marketing and distribution systems, which was quickly followed by the actor-oriented variant associated with Wageningen University to emphasize how the specificity of farm labour processes can give rise to different styles of FARMING (van der Ploeg, 1985).

For some scholars, the utility of commodity chains is largely descriptive, a lens through which to examine industrial organization and/ or economic geography. For instance, the global commodity chain approach, most associated with Gary Gereffi and his colleagues, focuses on the transnational reach of inter-firm networks of manufacturers, suppliers and subcontractors to each other, and to markets. In respect to the strong coordination role that apparel design firms started to play in the 1980s, they also suggested an epochal shift from producer-driven to buyer-driven chains. Recently, they have posited the existence of regulation- or consumer-driven commodity chains, in light of the increased salience of ethical products and the increasing power of private systems of regulation to construct and ensure quality in certain spheres of commodity production (see Gereffi, Humphrey and Sturgeon, 2005).

One variation on this approach is value chain analysis, which draws attention to how surplus distribution along a given chain is a function of rent-generating barriers to entry, which are in turn a function of chain governance (Kaplinsky, 2004). Kaplinsky and others have argued that that national DEVELOPMENT prospects can be improved by industrial 'upgrading' to higher value-added processes.

For another set of scholars, the commodity chain approach is a tool of radical scholarship, in that it has the potential to make the workings of CAPITALISM more transparent, particularly because GLOBALIZATION seems to make most commodities inscrutable as to how they are made and distributed (Hartwick, 1998). Other geographers, notably Leslie and Reimer (1999), are critical of the notion that commodities can be 'unveiled'. Leslie and Reimer have also remarked that commodity chains privilege FLOWS relative to SCALE.   JGu

Suggested reading
Gereffi and Korzeniewicz (1994); Hughes and Reimer (2004).

common pool resources RESOURCES, usually natural, from which it is difficult to exclude users, and whose use reduces resource availability for others (Ostrom, Dietz, Dolsak, Stern, Stonich and Weber, 1999). *Contra* the TRAGEDY OF THE COMMONS thesis and its calls for privatization or centralized state control, common pool resources have often been governed sustainably by COMMON PROPERTY REGIMES, whose rules are structured around the resource's size, mobility, renewability and other characteristics. Common pool resources thus differ from true open access resources. It is unclear, though, whether and how these lessons can be 'scaled up' to address contemporary problems at larger scales, with more users and greater rates of change.   JM

Suggested reading
Dietz, Ostrom and Stern (2003); Ostrom, Dietz, Dolsak, Stern, Stonich and Weber (2002).

common property regimes Forms of ownership and access whereby all or parts of a local environment are owned and managed by a COMMUNITY. This differs from private ownership, state ownership and open access regimes, where nobody owns the environment.

Common PROPERTY regimes have existed for thousands of years. They have become more popular as indigenous practices are recognized and validated, and the limitations of state ownership, top-down management and private property become increasingly apparent. Common property regimes may be particularly suited to 'RESOURCES' where it is possible to restrict access, but private ownership, while possible, is a very costly way to manage the resource.   PM

communication(s) The geography of communication treats the sending, receiving and exchange of information and messages face-to-face or via other means (letters, media, telephone, Internet). Because communication is essential to social relations, it is central to many of the processes of interest to human geographers, such as the construction of DIFFERENCE, the definition of COMMUNITY, the causes and consequences of SEGREGATION and the conduct of SOCIAL MOVEMENTS. At issue is who has access to what information, and how SPACE, PLACE and NETWORKS shape this access.

Despite the power of information technology to enable communication at a distance (see TIME–SPACE COMPRESSION; TIME–SPACE CONVERGENCE; TIME–SPACE DISTANCIATION), face-to-face communication is still prized in many theories in HUMAN GEOGRAPHY. In ECONOMIC GEOGRAPHY, for instance, the spatial AGGLOMERATION of certain types of industry (such as software development, the film industry or watchmaking) in INDUSTRIAL DISTRICTS is seen as a prime facilitator of INNOVATION: the key motivation for such agglomerations is believed to be the ease of face-to-face communication, which many see as necessary to the development of TRUST in social interactions (Murphy, 2006). In URBAN GEOGRAPHY, the desire for relatively easy face-to-face communication is seen as the main rationale for the clustering (see CLUSTERS) of PRODUCER SERVICES in dense urban areas. Information exchanged face-to-face in SOCIAL NETWORKS is also important to the functioning of labour and housing MARKETS, because large numbers of people learn about and evaluate employment and housing options via such channels. Because the nature of the information exchanged, including its locational dimensions, depends in part on the characteristics of the people in a social network, the social IDENTITY of network constituents is important. In sum, the process of face-to-face communication plays an important role in concentrating certain types of human activity in certain places and in certain groups of people.

Because telecommunications permit communicating over great distances, questions arise as to the power of such technologies to support the dispersal of human activity. Will information technologies such as the INTERNET and video conferencing undermine the *raison d'être* for urban agglomerations and industrial districts (i.e. the need for face-to-face contact)? In addressing this question, geographers have examined the extent to which communication via technology is a *substitute* for face-to-face interaction (in which case one might expect greater dispersal of human activity), a *stimulus* to face-to-face interaction (in which case one would expect information technologies to lead to a greater demand for face-to-face contact and therefore increased agglomeration effects) or a *complement* to personal contact (in which case one might expect information technologies to have little impact on the concentration or dispersal of human activity) (Janelle, 2004).   SHa

Suggested reading
Wheeler, Aoyama and Warf (2000).

communism A tradition of thought based on the principle of the communal ownership of PROPERTY (primitive communism) and common ownership of the means of production (full communism). Although traceable back to ancient Greece, in its modern form it is most widely associated with the writings of Karl Marx, especially *The communist manifesto* (Marx and Engels, 2002 [1848]). Writing at the height of the INDUSTRIAL REVOLUTION, Marx observed the increasing exploitation of newly urbanized wage labourers (the proletariat), and the widening gulf between the rich and the poor. He argued that the socio-economic system known as CAPITALISM was responsible for the exploitation and ALIENATION of these labourers, and that only by transcending it through revolutionary struggle could society advance to a better system, that of communism. In communism, all private property is abolished, there are no discernible classes and the people are self-governing. In pure communism the STATE is unnecessary, but according to Marx and most of his followers, communism will be preceded by a transitional stage called SOCIALISM, in which the state plays a major role.

Although pure communism has never been implemented, Marxist theories were central in galvanizing workers' movements in Europe in the late nineteenth century, and socialist governments became important players on the world stage following the Russian Revolution of 1917. After the Second World War, many more communist parties came to power and established regimes in Eastern Europe under the aegis of the Communist Party of the Soviet Union. The victory of Mao Zedong and the establishment of the People's Republic of China in 1949 was another major turning point in the growth and spread of communist ideology. Other countries in Asia and Africa, including Vietnam, North Korea, Laos, Mozambique and Angola, adopted some form of communist principles of government over the following years.

With the expansion of new forms of NEO-LIBERAL governance and the introduction of *glasnost* (openness) by the Soviet leader Mikhail Gorbachev in the 1980s, communist ideology began to wane. Over the past decade numerous geographers have explored the social and spatial repercussions of the transition to a post-communist world, especially in the former satellite countries of the USSR (see especially Pickles and Smith, 1998; Rainnie, Smith and Swain, 2002: see POST-SOCIALISM). Others have interrogated the implications of communism's disintegration

for theory and intellectual movements (see Burawoy, 2000). In both cases, the break-up of state planned and regulated societies has had enormous ripple effects, with ongoing ramifications in the context of increasing American dominance on the global stage. KM

Suggested reading
Marx and Engels (1972 [1845]).

communitarianism Both a political and an intellectual programme, communitarianism affirms the values and procedures of COMMUNITY, and rejects the political and analytical premises of individualism, while worrying at the effects of INDUSTRIALIZATION and URBANIZATION on community life (Smith, D.M.J 1999a). Under the direction of writers such as Amitai Etzioni (1994), as well as critics of LIBERALISM, such as Michael Sandel, communitarianism has enjoyed a resurgence in the past decade. However, one can find precedent in the work of those such as Emile Durkheim, who also traced the disorganizing effects of MODERNITY. Contemporary communitarians argue for a new moral and social order based on shared values that bridge tradition, such as moral ties of family, with modern norms of tolerance and inclusion. NKB

community A group of people who share common CULTURE, VALUES and/or interests, based on social IDENTITY and/or TERRITORY, and who have some means of recognizing, and (inter)acting upon, these commonalities. The definition is contentious, however, and Joseph (2002) has suggested that community is less about social identity and more related to practices of production and consumption under CAPITALISM. Community is frequently used to connote a SCALE at which people can easily interact and recognize one another, although as Anderson (1991a [1983]) argued in relation to NATIONS, community can be 'imagined' and actualized through MEDIA and culture rather than interpersonal interaction.

The CHICAGO SCHOOL of sociologists saw community as the basis for social organization, and their usage fostered a connotation with NEIGHBOURHOOD. The use and propagation of community as related to URBANISM by the Chicago School drew upon, but also reinterpreted, notions of community from German sociologists such as Ferdinand Tönnies (1855–1936). Tönnies envisioned community (*Gemeinschaft*) as one's family and intimate life, while SOCIETY (*Gesellschaft*) was an 'imaginary and mechanical structure' (Tönnies, 1955 [1887], p. 37). For Tönnies and the Chicago School, urban neighbourhoods could provide the kind of mutual support required for a community such as that found in a 'rural village' (Tönnies, 1955 [1887], p. 49; Park, 1967 [1925]). Nonetheless, in Tönnies' formulation, community was being replaced by society through URBANIZATION and INDUSTRIALIZATION. Although Tönnies acknowledged a possibility of community in urban neighbourhoods, his formulation situated community primarily in pre-industrial rural settings. Equating community with the intimacies of village life, however, fails to acknowledge the political and economic inequalities inherent to such a setting – Joseph (2002, pp. 4–5) cites Williams (1973) on this point.

Tönnies' (2001 [1887]) conceptualization of community as a traditional 'rural' phenomenon sets it in opposition to or pre-dating industrial capitalism (Bender, 1978; Joseph, 2002). This conceptualization fosters and supports claims such as that of communitarians – exemplified by Etzioni (1993) and Bellah, Madsen, Sullivan, Swidler and Tipton (1985). These scholars see community as missing from, or left behind by, MODERNITY. They seek a return to mutual support and responsibility, which, they argue, form the basis of community and social values (Bellah, Madsen, Sullivan, Swidler and Tipton, 1985). Such notions of community have been important to the GOVERNANCE strategies of the neoliberal STATE (Herbert, 2005: see also NEOLIBERALISM). These strategies – such as welfare reform and community POLICING – transfer to individuals or groups of citizens' activities and roles that were formerly assumed by the STATE. But Herbert (2005) argued that many communities – often conflated with neighbourhood from Chicago School formulations in these state devolutions – are unable and unwilling to assume these tasks, thus fostering a disconnect between ideals of community and actual experiences of them in neoliberalism.

The failure of community to act in lieu of the state highlights its status under capitalism. Seeking to challenge the notion of community as antecedent of and potentially in opposition to the individualization of capitalism, Joseph (2002) argued that capitalism actually produces community. In her view, community is not merely or primarily a set of shared social identities, although it is often depicted as such in identity politics (for an example, see Young, 1990a). Instead, community is performed (see PERFORMATIVITY) and practiced through relations and practices of production and CONSUMPTION: 'Marx articulates the necessary role that historically particular and differentiated social formations play as the bearers of capital, as the medium within which capital circulates …' (Joseph, 2002, p. 13). Community is a way that people articulate use values within the circulation of production and consumption, thereby supplementing and particularizing the abstractness of CAPITAL. Joseph's (2002) formulation of community as operating in and through capitalism forces reconceptualization of it as a positive reaction or antidote to capitalism. It may support or disrupt capital, but neither outcome is evident a priori (Joseph, 2002). Instead, scholars need to attend to the particularities of community; how it is produced and performed discursively and in practices, and to what end.   DGM

Suggested reading
Herbert (2005); Joseph (2002); Williams (1973); Young (1990a).

commuting The daily journey to work, implying a repetitive daily trip from a fixed home location to a fixed work location. The term dates to the mid-nineteenth century, when wealthy businessmen began travelling from their suburban dwellings to their urban worksites via railroad: the 'commutation' of their daily tickets to lower-priced monthly fares led to the term 'commuter' (Muller, 2004). The peaking of journeys to and from work during the morning and evening rush hours and associated road congestion have been a prime focus of transportation planning since the 1950s. *Telecommuting* involves using information technology to work while the worker is not physically in the workplace.   SHa

compact city A policy goal associated with advocates of SUSTAINABILITY in Western-world URBAN PLANNING. Proponents seek to mitigate automobile-related energy use, urban air pollution, and SPRAWL-related farmland and habitat loss by promoting the re-use of urban brownfield sites, high-density and mixed-use development, and public transit. The compact city ideal permeates discussions of urban SPRAWL, smart growth, QUALITY OF LIFE and questions of urban housing availability and affordability. A range of opinions exist on the veracity, feasibility and acceptability of the compact city as a model for achieving urban sustainability, from outright advocacy, to considered evaluation (Breheny, 1995), to strong scepticism (Neuman, 2005).   EM

Suggested reading
Breheny (1997).

comparative advantage The principle whereby individuals (or territories) produce those goods or services for which they have the greatest cost or efficiency advantage over others, or for which they have the least disadvantage. The outcome tends to be specialization across places. A gifted individual or RESOURCE-rich region may be able to produce everything more efficiently than others that are less well endowed, but as long as some comparative advantage exists, specialization may benefit all. An example is that of the best lawyer in town who is also the best typist: it pays the lawyer to concentrate on the lucrative practice of the law and hire a typist (who has a comparative advantage in typing relative to knowledge of the law). One region may be able to produce two goods more efficiently than another region, but it pays to concentrate on the good for which there is greatest comparative advantage and buy the other from the second region.

The notion of comparative advantage is important in understanding regional specialization, whereby all REGIONS gain from the interchange of products even if they could satisfy their own needs (cf. COMPLEMENTARITY). A condition for realizing the benefits of comparative advantage is free TRADE. At the international scale, MARKET imperfections such as TARIFF barriers can impede specialization based on comparative advantage, protecting domestic production of goods that could not withstand open competition. The objective may be to ensure more 'balanced' economic development and to avoid problems associated with narrow product specialization.   DMS

competitive advantage The relative ability of firms in the same MARKET to win above-average profit levels, through either cost or product differentiation advantages. These may result from either a superior RESOURCE base (e.g. better facilities, superior quality of workforce), greater capability to utilize its available resources (capability advantages) and/or a better-quality product. That competitive advantage may be only transient; it is sustainable if it cannot be challenged by other firms.

Competitive advantage is also used to account for the emerging DIVISION OF LABOUR, rather than the theory of COMPARATIVE ADVANTAGE. Places may compete for employment – as, for example, in many service industries, including leisure and tourism – on the basis that what they have to offer is superior to that available in other places, so that spatial differentiation results from competitive success rather than differential resource availability or efficiency.   RJ

Suggested reading
Ancien (2005); Porter (1998).

complementarity The existence of complementarity between two REGIONS implies that one produces (or has the potential to produce) goods or services for which the other suffers from a deficit (or potential deficit). Ullman (1956) used the term to describe one of the bases of SPATIAL INTERACTION, arguing that complementarity may arise either from AREAL DIFFERENTIATION (in resource endowment, or in social, economic and cultural conditions) or as a result of ECONOMIES OF SCALE (cf. COMPARATIVE ADVANTAGE).   RJ

complexity theory A term for the study of 'complex systems' that is used in both mathematical systems modelling and in qualitative and discursive work. Complex systems are non-linear, interdependent and strongly coupled systems with FEEDBACK loops, and may exhibit scale-effects, together with sensitivity to initial conditions and path-dependence. The original use of the term is for the mathematical properties and analysis of such non-linear interdependent systems, and embraces both CHAOS THEORY and CATASTROPHE THEORY as sub-branches. Many studies identify three divisions of mathematical complexity theory: algorithmic or computational complexity; deterministic complexity; and 'aggregate complexity'.

Algorithmic complexity deals with the relative computational difficulty of computable functions. This may appear the least relevant division for HUMAN GEOGRAPHY, but is important in understanding the difficulties of solving large-scale spatial OPTIMIZATION problems and other aspects of GEOGRAPHIC INFORMATION SYSTEMS and SPATIAL ANALYSIS. *Deterministic complexity* examines the properties of non-linear systems and subsumes both chaos theory and catastrophe theory as particular subsets. The third division of *aggregate complexity* considers systems of linked components or subsystems and examines the ways in which order and structure may emerge at higher levels

105

from the interactions. A classic example is the highly organized termite hill that emerges out of the interaction of countless highly specialized individual termite activities. Such properties of 'self-organization' and 'emergence' are central to aggregate complexity.

Several different attempts have been made to develop and apply the mathematical theory to urban and regional systems, such as Allen (1997) and Portugali (2000). One difficulty is defining the objects within the system and its boundaries. Reviews of these issues and their relevance for human geography may be found in Manson (2001) and O'Sullivan (2004). Wilson (2000) takes a pragmatic approach, using complexity theory as a framework within which to link various urban sub-models, arguing that such linkage is vital to understand urban structure; however, this cannot be done in analytical terms, but only through computer simulation and sensitivity analysis.

Complexity theory has also been adopted by cultural geographers (see CULTURAL GEOGRAPHY) as an analogical and metaphorical tool: as the 'CULTURAL TURN' emphasized the importance of DIFFERENCE, contingency and context, so the various concepts, MODELS and terms within mathematical complexity theory provided useful language and METAPHORS with which to examine space and society. Within human geography, this use of complexity theory outnumbers the mathematical applications. A well-developed example is provided by Urry's study of 'global complexity' (Urry, 2003), in which complexity is used to link together local and global, the emergence of global 'order' from regional 'disorder', the role of feedbacks and path dependence in how regions engage with global society, and the challenge for how social theory is constructed. Thrift (1999b) gives a wide-ranging survey of the take-up of the complexity metaphor in both business and the social sciences.   LWH

Suggested reading
Manson (2001); O'Sullivan (2004); Thrift (1999b).

confirmatory data analysis Quantitative statistical procedures used to evaluate HYPOTHESES, usually involving the use of SIGNIFICANCE TESTS (cf. EXPLORATORY DATA ANALYSIS).   RJJ

conflict At its most general, 'conflict' can mean anything from a personal disagreement between two people to a world war. It is now widely understood that conflict is part of the human condition, although only some of it results in overt VIOLENCE or combat. Conflict theory in sociology emphasizes struggles over RESOURCES and the formation of groups and social cleavages that may lead to organized conflict. Coercion, resistance, revolt and political violence within states, and warfare between states, are dynamic processes in which escalation, violence, conflict resolution and peace-making are all vitally important. In political science and economics, conflict is sometimes discussed in terms of GAME THEORY and strategic calculation, an approach that has not been frequently invoked by geographers.

Themes of conflict run through numerous facets of contemporary enquiry in HUMAN GEOGRAPHY, even though they are often not theorized as such. Marxist approaches emphasize the importance of structural conflict between classes and especially in cities under CAPITALISM, where the geography of CLASS struggle is literally built into the urban structure (see MARXISM). More recently, feminist analyses have investigated numerous conflicts generated by patriarchal structures and the strategies of resistance used by women (Staeheli, Kofman and Peake, 2004: see also FEMINISM; PATRIARCHY). MIGRATION brings peoples and cultures into conflict as newcomers and established populations negotiate coexistence, frequently in situations of considerable economic change and against a backdrop of class and gender struggles. Identity conflicts are part of the urban mosaic in most metropolitan centres, where diasporic populations (see DIASPORA) are now the subject of numerous geographical analyses inspired by POST-COLONIALISM (Jacobs, 1996).

Classic GEOPOLITICS focused on the geography of war and international rivalry, a topic that has undergone a revival of interest since the 1980s. Most recently, conflict is at the heart of a series of geographical analyses of matters of WAR and peace, where TERRITORY, IDENTITY, national independence, EMPIRE and violence have all come under scrutiny in the aftermath of the events of 11 September 2001 and the launch of the 'global war on terror' by the Bush administration in the USA (see TERRORISM). Here, conflict is discussed at the largest scales as matters of clashes between CIVILIZATIONS and cultures, but CRITICAL GEOPOLITICS also reveals the multiple ways in which these struggles are socially constructed and reach into the lives of ordinary people (Gregory, 2004b). These terms are heavily laden with both implicit and explicit geographical thinking, a matter that has gained considerable attention by geographers (Flint, 2005).   SD

Suggested reading
Flint (2005).

conflict commodities Across the global South, the dependence upon a strategic natural RESOURCE (OIL, diamonds, copper) has been associated with a cluster of poor human, economic and political DEVELOPMENT indices, an association that has been called the 'resource curse'. These pathologies appear especially robust in extractive economies; for example, the petro-states of the Gulf of Guinea, which are classic rentier economies marked by deplorable corruption, poor economic performance, authoritarian politics, miserable social achievement and civil CONFLICT (including civil WAR), against a backdrop of enormous oil wealth. Paul Collier and his colleagues at the World Bank (2003) developed a model of what they called the 'economics of civil war' in which resource-dependent economies (especially minerals) could be sought out and looted by rebel groups. The ease with which resources such as diamonds and oil could be extorted, stolen or tracked down by groups were driven, in their view, by greed and criminality rather than grievance. Civil conflict always surrounded resource-dependent economies in which the character of the resource – point or diffuse, proximate or remote (see Le Billon, 2005) – determined the particular forms of violent politics (*coup d'état* versus secessionist movements). Conflict commodities refer to the association between state dependence upon particular COMMODITIES and the ease with which rebels could plunder the resource in order to fund their war (organized crime in the World Bank's account) against the state. The case of '*blood diamonds*' gained international attention because of the ways in which alluvial diamonds and their trade could be easily controlled by rebel groups in the extraordinarily violent civil conflict in Sierra Leone. As a result of the pressure by activist groups such as Global Witness, the Kimberly Process Certification Scheme was set up in January 2003 as an international governmental certification system to prevent the trade in diamonds that funded or sustained civil conflict (see Global Witness, n.d.).   MW

Suggested reading
Collier, Elliott, Hegre, Hoeffler, Reynal-Querol and Sambanis (2003); Le Billon (2005). See also Global Witness, *The Kimberly process* (http://www.globalwitness.org/pages/en/the_kimberley_process.html).

conservation A term that implies the keeping or preservation of something for future use and human benefit. The word can be applied to buildings or to food, but it is mostly used to refer to the natural environment, natural RESOURCES, and particularly species and habitats. Concern for non-human NATURE has a long history; for example, in classical Mediterranean societies, and in the early European tropical colonial EMPIRE (Grove, 1995). In its modern form, conservation became established as a body of thought and social action towards the end of the nineteenth century.

Two aspects of the conservation of the environment have been important since the late nineteenth century. The first concerns the rate at which resources, particularly renewable resources (such as living species), are consumed. The second concerns the desire to ensure the survival of species and habitats. The distinction between these two is commonly exemplified by the sharp debate in the USA in the early years of the twentieth century between the utilitarian view of conservation of Theodore Roosevelt's adviser, the forester Gifford Pinchot, and the more romantic preservationist arguments of the Sierra Club and John Muir (Hays, 1959). However, these two aspects of conservation are still in tension today; for example, between those who argue that safari hunting and a legal trade in ivory are an appropriate and effective way of conserving species such as elephants in AFRICA, and those who feel that such hunting and trade can never be controlled in a way that guarantees sustainable harvests and that does not promote illegal killing.

The technical basis of ideas about conservation of renewable resources draws on a number of areas of natural science, particularly the science of fisheries management. In the late nineteenth century, fish catches began to decline systematically in Europe and the USA as fishing became industrialized with the advent of steam-driven boats and other innovations. The International Conference for the Exploration of the Sea in 1899 proposed scientific enquiries to promote rational exploitation. By the 1930s the idea of a maximum sustainable yield was established, and through the first half of the twentieth century a series of international institutions were established to try to regulate fishing, including the Overfishing Convention agreed in London in 1946, and the International Whaling Commission established in Washington in 1946. Neither these, nor their successors, achieved the sustained exploitation of any significant open-water stock of fish or marine mammals. The boom–crash cycle of sealing in the nineteenth century, and of the herring fishery in the North Sea, ocean whaling and Atlantic cod fishing in the twentieth century, provide ample evidence of both the desirability of conservation and the political and economic difficulty of making conservation strategies work (Cushing, 1988).

The language of fisheries science suggests the considerable influence of economics: stocks were renewed or depleted, and calculations included estimates of catch per unit effort. In turn, economics reflected evolving understanding of the dynamics of resources, particularly in the distinction between renewable (flow) and non-renewable (stock) resources (Ciriacy-Wantrup, 1952). Such ideas have been widely applied; for example, in soil erosion and FORESTRY. The US Dust Bowl stimulated concern about the management of soil resources in a way that could sustain production around the world; for example, in tropical Africa, where it provided the legitimization for widespread and unpopular compulsory terracing (Beinart and Coates, 1995). The concept of sustained yield forestry is long established, although its application to old-growth temperate forests (where 'tree farming' is regarded as environmentally highly destructive), and the failure to apply its principles to tropical REGIONS forests remain highly controversial.

At the end of the nineteenth century, the extinction of species such as the quagga (a barely striped plains zebra from the African Cape) and the North American passenger pigeon, and the near-extinction of others such as the American bison, became the rallying points for a species conservation movement in the USA, Europe and the colonial world (Sheail, 1976; Adams, 2004). This movement drew in particular on ZOOS (notably the New York Zoological Society, founded in 1895), and on the support of hunters turned conservationists; for example, in the Society for the Preservation of the Wild Fauna of the Empire (founded in London in 1903). It campaigned for the establishment of game reserves, nature reserves and eventually NATIONAL PARKS, and on the establishment of national legislation for protected species (e.g. designating closed hunting seasons and protected species),

and for international treaties for conservation; for example, the 1918 Anglo-American Convention for the Protection of Migratory Birds and the 1973 Convention on Trade in Endangered Species (CITES).

Wildlife conservation expanded rapidly after the Second World War, with the establishment of organizations such as the Conservation Foundation (1948) and the Nature Conservancy (1951) in the USA, and the IUCN – the World Conservation Union (1956) – and the Worldwide Fund for Nature (1961). The membership, capacity and number of conservation organizations grew with the wider ENVIRONMENTAL MOVEMENT, developing from a series of small patrician interest groups in a few industrialized countries into a global movement.

By the 1990s, the power and sophistication of conservation had grown, with the establishment of new and strongly corporate organizations, such as Conservation International (Brosius, 1999). The development of conservation biology as a science lent growing confidence to conservation planning; for example, in the definition of BIODIVERSITY 'hotspots' and protected area selection. The social impacts of conservation came under increasingly close scrutiny (Brechin, Wilhusen, Fortwangler and West, 2003; Neumann, 2004a). However, the erosion of living diversity through the operation of global CAPITALISM and patterns of CONSUMPTION continued unchecked (Jenkins, 2003). The factors that created conservation in the nineteenth century remain strong.   WMA

consumption Conventionally, the act of purchasing and using COMMODITIES, although some commentators insist that the term should also refer to their transformation, resale and exchange (Gregson and Crewe, 2003). Although ECONOMIC GEOGRAPHY has traditionally focused on spaces of PRODUCTION, there has been a significant rise of interest in consumption since the 1980s, accompanied by increased dialogue between economic and SOCIAL GEOGRAPHY. One reason for this is the putative shift to a POST-INDUSTRIAL SOCIETY, where RETAILING, LEISURE and TOURISM are widely identified as major engines of growth (in the WEST, at least). Another is the theorized importance of consumerism as a locus for IDENTITY: in the consumer society, what we buy has seemingly become more important in defining our sense of self than what we produce. Finally, the rise of interest in consumption appears to be related to important trends in GLOBALIZATION, with place-related consumer cultures (such as national cuisines or musics) having been largely replaced by a landscape of hybrid commodity flows (see FOOD, HYBRIDITY, MUSIC, TRANSCULTURATION).

Some of the features taken to be characteristic of contemporary consumption are likely facets of MODERNITY (Glennie and Thrift, 1992). Indeed, some argue that the consumer revolution actually preceded the INDUSTRIAL REVOLUTION, with innovation in production being fuelled by changes in consumer tastes and mores. Historical geographies of retailing thus reveal a remarkable series of INNOVATIONS in the design, advertising and selling of goods through the eighteenth and nineteenth centuries, with a succession of carefully orchestrated spaces – including market halls, arcades and department stores – playing a major role in imbuing products with an aura of desirability (Wrigley and Lowe, 2002). In the era of high MODERNISM, cultures of consumption were also very much associated with the attainment of security and comfort, with the idealization of the SUBURBS reflected in a plethora of products that no HOME could possibly be without. The domestication and suburbanization of consumption was mirrored in the de-centring of consumption, with retailing and leisure following the middle classes into the SUBURBS; simultaneously, however, mass transportation allowed the city centre to enhance its role as a space of consumption, with CINEMA-going, nightclubbing and eating out becoming key urban rituals, maintaining the myth that city centres provided a vibrant PUBLIC SPHERE.

The mid-twentieth century has thus often been characterized as an era of 'high mass consumption'. Nonetheless, Bauman (2001a) suggests that consumption remained subordinate to work throughout this period. As he describes, work served as the link holding together individual motivation, social integration and systemic reproduction, with consumer goods primarily regarded as *rewards* for work. Furthermore, in industrial producer societies, the STATE provided some of these rewards to workers through collective provision, so even the unemployed could participate in rituals of consumption. However, in POSTMODERN, deindustrialized societies, the state has little interest in tending to this 'reserve army of labour'. Hence, the WELFARE STATE 'safety net' has gradually eroded, with individuals forced to search for security in the *marketplace*. (see NEO-LIBERALISM. Luckily (at least for some), contemporary consumerism

implies that for every human problem there is a solution that can be purchased: even problems of over-consumption (e.g. obesity) fuel the marketing of new commodities (e.g. diet products, health club subscriptions, plastic surgery).

The second consumer revolution has thus heralded an era in which consumption, not work, is the hub around which identity revolves. Yet, as Appadurai (1996, p. 38) insists, 'consumption has now become serious work', and it is wrong to imply that consumer-led societies are any less disciplined than industrial ones. Indeed, consumerism has arguably bequeathed a new mode of social control, where the fundamental social divide is not between bourgeois and proletariat, but between the creditworthy *seduced* – those whose appetite for consumption fuels a huge leisure, recreation and service sector – and the *repressed* – those 'flawed consumers' who are unable to enjoy a life of conspicuous consumption (Clarke, 2003). While the former are drawn into purchases through a panoply of subtle (and not so subtle) marketing, it also requires SURVEILLANCE to exclude the repressed from spaces of leisured consumption. CCTV, security guards, credit-rating mechanisms and consumer profiling are all significant in this process, maintaining the order of consumer spaces designed for the affluent.

The way in which shopping malls combine such mechanisms of social control with a carefully orchestrated ambience has led many geographers to proclaim them as paradigmatic consumer settings:

> Developers have sought to dissociate malls from the act of shopping. That is, in recognition of the emptiness of the activity for which they provide the main social space, designers manufacture the illusion that *something else other than mere shopping is going on*. The product is effectively a pseudo-space that works through spatial strategies of dissemblance and duplicity. (Shields, 1989)

Given that the acquisition of COMMODITIES has become so central to developing a sense of self, exclusion from such spaces must be regarded as a significant dimension of SOCIAL EXCLUSION (Williams and Hubbard, 2001). However, accounts focusing on seductive spaces of consumption perhaps ignore the more routine spaces where the majority of consumption occurs (e.g. supermarkets, corner shops, takeaways). Likewise, the emergence of new spaces of 'second-hand' consumption (e.g. eBay) also raises important questions about the relationship between repressed and seduced.

Alongside the attention devoted to the socialities of consumption, there is significant work by geographers on the subjectivities created through acts of consumption. For instance, the centrality of consumption in constructions of the BODY is of growing interest (Valentine, 1999), as is the emotional connection forged between people and the things that they consume. Some are even beginning to explore the emotional labour required to dispose of old goods, noting they may be incorporated into our personal biographies in profound ways (Gregson and Crewe, 2003). The fact that consumer goods may have long and complex lives is also something that geographers have explored through attempts to chart global COMMODITY CHAINS and the 'traffic in things' (Jackson, 1999). Transcending simple distinctions between production and consumption, tracing webs or networks of commodity circulation not only offers an important perspective on TRANSNATIONALISM; it also draws attention to the range of technologies, spaces and bodies involved in practices of consumption.

Although consumption was once regarded as marginal to geographical enquiry, the sheer variety of recent studies suggests that it is now impossible to ignore the SPATIALITY of consumption. Indeed, perhaps the main impediment to the development of geographical theories of consumption is the current ubiquity of consumer studies. Having quickly reached a point at which a bewildering range of activities are understood to involve consumption, a key challenge facing human geographers is to decide whether consumption remains a useful concept around which to orient a vast and complex literature.   PH

Suggested reading
Clarke, Doel and Housiaux (2003); Mansvelt (2005).

contextual effect The impact of local environments on individuals' attitudes and behaviour. Much social science is based on *compositional effects*, whereby attitudes and behaviour are influenced by individuals' non-geographical position within society, such as their social CLASS: within any society, people from similar backgrounds are assumed to behave in similar ways, wherever they live. According to arguments regarding *contextual effects*, however, because attitudes and behaviour patterns are to a considerable extent learned through social interaction in PLACES (such as households and NEIGHBOURHOODS), similar people living in different sorts of places may think and act differently as a result of interactions with their neighbours. Furthermore, many patterns associated with compositional effects may themselves be the results of aggregating contextual effects. If behavioural norms are learned from local models, national patterns are simply summations of those local practices over all places: the national is an aggregation of the local.

The terminology regarding contextual effects varies across disciplines. In economics, for example, Brock and Durlauf (2000) distinguished among: *endogenous effects*, whereby one individual's behaviour is causally influenced by that of other group members (cf. ENDOGENEITY); *exogenous effects*, according to which individual behaviour varies with the observed attributes that define group membership; and *correlated effects*, on the argument that individuals in an area tend to behave in similar ways because they either have similar characteristics or face similar opportunities and constraints.

The contrast between compositional and contextual effects strongly influenced thinking within HUMAN GEOGRAPHY in the 1980s, as characterized by Thrift's (1983) seminal paper in which he deployed the STRUCTURATION approach to appreciate various forms of behaviour (such as the 'life path') as compositional orderings within contextual fields. Citing Therborn, he argues that 'being in the world' involves both *inclusive* (being a member of a meaningful world) and *positional* (having a particular place in the world as defined by characteristics such as GENDER, ETHNICITY etc.) characteristics and that the processes of becoming – learning about one's positional situations – are structured contextually in LOCALES.

Contextual effects underpinned much of the early work on DIFFUSION, notably through Torsten Hägerstrand's operationalization of social contact and influence through the concept of the MEAN INFORMATION FIELD, and their production was central to his conception of TIME-GEOGRAPHY. More recently they have been widely explored within ELECTORAL GEOGRAPHY, with studies showing that people are very likely to share political attitudes with and to vote in the same way as (the majority of) their neighbours, irrespective of their social positions (cf. NEIGHBOURHOOD EFFECT). They have also been identified in other fields, as in studies of morbidity and mortality in MEDICAL GEOGRAPHY and of school effects on student development (cf. EDUCATION). Although empirical studies have identified behaviours consistent with contextual effects, however, the PROCESSES assumed to produce them – for example, the role of social interaction in the spread of attitudes and behavioural norms – is less well understood. Indeed, in some situations it may be impossible to identify the causal impact of a local context because of an endogeneity effect whereby (some at least) individuals select their interaction contexts (as with working-class people who aspire to middle-class status and so choose to live in middle-class areas and send their children to local schools).

Jencks and Mayer (1990) suggested five mechanisms which can generate outcomes consistent with contextual effects:

(1) *epidemic effects*, whereby peer influences within an area spread to neighbours;
(2) *collective socialization*, whereby local role models are important ingredients in attitude development;
(3) *institutional models*, in which local institutions rather than people provide the influences;
(4) *competition models*, whereby neighbours compete for scarce resources; and
(5) *relative deprivation models*, which involve individuals comparing their situations relative to their neighbours' and act accordingly.

Two or more of these may be relevant in any particular situation.   RJ

Suggested reading
Agnew (1987); Johnston and Pattie (2006).

contextuality The situated character of social life, involving coexistence, connections and 'togetherness' as a series of associations and entanglements in time–space. The concept of context has deep historical roots. It is initiated in relations of language, and it has always contained some double sense of 'circumstances' and 'connections'. Like TEXT, context is a METAPHOR derived from the Latin *texere*, 'to weave', and in traditions of interpretation, context came to refer to the coherence of the text, the connections between the parts and the whole.

The term was translated into GEOGRAPHY by the Swedish geographer Torsten Hägerstrand as part of the ontological and epistemological basis of TIME-GEOGRAPHY. Hägerstrand (1974) distinguished between *compositional* approaches,

which proceed by splitting up their objects into structural categories derived via formal–logical method, and *contextual* ones, in which objects and events are treated in their immediate spatial and temporal setting and attributed a property of 'togetherness' that must not be split asunder. In time-geography, trajectories of individual entities are represented in time–space, not as movements in an empty Cartesian time–space, but as bundles of activities together constituting a web of trajectories. Hägerstrand saw the idea of such a web as a basic postulate of the contextual approach. It should ensure an understanding of TIME and SPACE as RESOURCES 'drawn upon' in the conduct of life. It does, however, remain debateable whether his reduction of human action to moving entities and his graphical illustrations still retained a sense of time and space as external frameworks.

Stripped of their connotations of 'physicalism', Hägerstrand's ideas eventually intersected with threads in modern SOCIAL THEORY and social PHILOSOPHY pursuing ontologies of PRACTICE and understandings of the 'situation' for social action. In STRUCTURATION THEORY, introduced by the British sociologist Anthony Giddens (1984), for example, contextuality does not denote boundaries of social life but, rather, features that are inherently involved in its construction. 'All social activity', it says, 'is formed in three conjoined moments of difference: temporally, structurally and spatially; the conjunction of these express the *situated* character of social practices' (Giddens, 1981, p. 30). Giddens provides a set of concepts that describe contextuality as inherently involved in the connection of social integration and system integration; of face-to-face interaction and more extensive relations of mediated interactions. One of them is the concept of LOCALE, describing 'settings' of interaction connected to different social activities. Many geographers have worked in critical dialogue with these formulations. Pred (1984), for instance, pursues a 'theory of PLACE as historically contingent process that emphasizes institutional and individual practices as well as the structural features with which those practices are interwoven'. Simonsen (1991) adds a more phenomenological aspect by emphasizing the 'situated life story' in an approach to the constitution of social life involving the interaction between different modes of temporality and SPATIALITY. In these, and other, contributions, a central point is that contexts are not passive backdrops. They are 'performative social situations, plural events which are more or less spatially extensive and more or less temporally specific', and they are 'productive time–spaces which have to be produced' (Thrift, 1996).

Another thematic corresponds to EPISTEMOLOGY. Several philosophical sources inform these discussions. Central are Martin Heidegger's PHENOMENOLOGY and Ludwig Wittgenstein's ideas of language games, somehow intertwining with Michel Foucault's ideas of historically constituted and spatially formed 'POWER–knowledge'. But also important is Karl Mannheim, a pioneer of the sociology of knowledge, who was one of the first to treat ideas as socially situated (*Situationsgebunden*). Part of these ideas, often mediated through Donna Haraway's notion of SITUATED KNOWLEDGE, has induced a new understanding of the production of geographical knowledge. Knowledge production is seen as a practical activity that literally takes place and intervenes within specific contexts. Different versions of contextual knowledge circulate, but what generally connects them is a rather modest attitude towards the powers of theory (cf. Thrift, 1996). Theories are of course vital and indispensable accounts, but at the same time they are always limited and partial: they are marked by the contexts from which they emerge and the circumstances that they are intended to meet.

Common to contextual approaches is their reference to dynamic, connected time–spaces. More recent contributions both accentuate and develop this point. Schatzski (2002), for example, in what he calls a 'site ONTOLOGY', connects to practice and human coexistence. Social sites, in this account, are contexts where 'practices and orders form an immense, shifting, and transmogrifying mesh in which they overlap, interweave, cohere, conflict, diverge, scatter and enable as well as constrain each other'. In another way, Massey (2005), without using the term, opens to a radically dynamic vision of contextuality. She discusses space in terms of interrelations, heterogeneity and process, and connects it to time through a double determination as 'discrete multiplicity' and 'dynamic simultaneity'. This allows for a conception of different time–spaces (or contexts) as relational; as ever-shifting constellations of trajectories, constructed out of their interrelations and 'throwntogetherness'. KS

Suggested reading
Massey (2005); Simonsen (1991); Thrift (1996).

contiguous zone A zone of special jurisdictional purposes contiguous to the TERRITORIAL SEA, which a coastal STATE may claim up to 24 nautical miles from the baseline for measuring the territorial sea. The coastal state may, in such a zone, exercise the control necessary to: (1) prevent infringement of its customs, fiscal, IMMIGRATION or sanitary LAWS and regulations within its territory or territorial sea; and (2) punish infringement of such laws and regulations committed within its territory and territorial sea (United Nations, 1983, Art. 33). This enables foreign nationals to exercise numerous prerogatives, including rights of navigation, overflying, fishing, conducting research and laying submarine cables. sch

Suggested reading
Valega (2001).

continental shelf The Third United Nations Conference on the Law of the Sea (UNCLOS III) defines the continental shelf as 'the natural prolongation of the land TERRITORY to the outer edge of the continental margin, or to a distance of 200 nautical miles from the baselines from which the breadth of the TERRITORIAL SEA is measured' (United Nations, 1983, Art. 76). Where the continental margin extends beyond 200 nautical miles from the baseline, the coastal STATE must establish its outer edge with the highly technical methods stipulated in Article 76 of the Convention. The coastal state exercises over the continental shelf 'sovereign rights for the purpose of exploring it and exploiting its natural RESOURCES' (United Nations, 1983, Art. 77). sch

Suggested reading
Valega (1992).

continents Usually defined as 'large, continuous, discrete masses of land', the identification of continents is both conventional and contingent, because it is closely bound up with the histories of EXPLORATION, GEOGRAPHY and GEOPOLITICS. Contemporaries divided the Graeco-Roman world into three continents – EUROPE, ASIA and 'Libya' (see AFRICA) – but as early as the fifth century BCE Herodotus was puzzled 'why three distinct women's names should be given to what is really a single landmass' (Lewis and Wigen, 1997, p. 22). In medieval Europe, cosmographers and cartographers retained this tripartite division but saw the three as parts of a single 'world island', or *Orbis Terrarum*. The European 'discovery' of the AMERICAS from the late fifteenth century followed by 'the Great Southern Continent' of AUSTRALIA in the early seventeenth century

Modern continental systems

Antarctica	Australia	South America	North America	Europe	Asia	Africa
Antarctica	Australia	South America	North America	Eurasia		Africa
Antarctica	Australia	America		Eurasia		Africa

displaced these ETHNOCENTRISMS and allowed for a heightened sense of global division and distinction.

In English, the word 'continent' was not used to denote major divisions of the GLOBE until the early seventeenth century. In the course of the eighteenth and nineteenth centuries, those differences were calcified by doctrines of ENVIRONMENTAL DETERMINISM: the continents were distinguished by the supposedly intimate, and even causal, connections between their physical and human geographies. The categories of the emergent 'continental system' were thus naturalized, 'coming to be regarded not as products of a fallible human imagination but as real entities that had been "discovered" through empirical inquiry' (Lewis and Wigen, 1977, p. 30). The arbitrary nature of the continental schema is revealed by the different systems in contemporary use (see table), but while these have little or no scientific merit they nonetheless often retain considerable popular and geopolitical significance. (See also META-GEOGRAPHY.)   DG

contrapuntal geographies   The NETWORKS through which people and events in different places around the world are connected in a complex, dynamic and uneven web that *both* maintains their specificity *and* mobilizes their interactions. Contrapuntal geographies thus reject two conventional prejudices: the uniqueness of PLACE and the universality of SPACE. Places are not closed and self-sufficient, but neither is (global) space open and increasingly self-similar.   The term derives from the work of Edward Said (1935–2003), a literary critic with a lively GEOGRAPHICAL IMAGINATION. He regarded 'contrapuntal reading' as an indispensable part of cultural critique, and particularly of the critique of COLONIALISM. Said argued that EUROPE – and the 'WEST' more generally – relied on a myth of auto-genesis (self-production) that represented MODERNITY as the unique product of the actions of Europeans, who then had both the right and the responsibility to reach out to bring to others the fruits of progress that would otherwise be beyond their grasp. He objected to this

not only for its narcissism but also for its ESSENTIALISM: in his view, all cultures are hybrids, 'contrapuntal ensembles'. This was partly a matter of material fact – networks of commodity exchange, of MIGRATION and the like – and partly a matter of cultural construction: 'No IDENTITY can ever exist by itself and without an array of opposites, negatives, oppositions' (Said, 1993, p. 58: see also IMAGINATIVE GEOGRAPHIES). It was therefore essential to bring these 'overlapping territories [and] intertwined histories' together.

Said was an accomplished musician and his root METAPHOR was a musical one: 'In the counterpoint of Western classical music, various themes play off one another, with only a provisional privilege being given to any particular one; yet in the resulting polyphony there is concert and order, an organized interplay that derives from the themes, not from a rigorous melodic or formal principle outside the work. In the same way, I believe, we can read and interpret English novels …' (Said, 1993, p. 51). There are three crucial points about such a project as it spirals beyond literary criticism:

(1) Contrapuntal geographies are rarely transparent and their disclosure requires both theoretical and analytical acuity. Another literary critic, Frederic Jameson, regarded contrapuntal reading as vital to the interpretation of the colonial world by virtue of 'the systematic occultation of colony from metropolis' but argued that GLOBALIZATION has produced an 'epistemological transparency'. This is precisely the universality rejected by Said's conception (cf. Gregory, 2004b, pp. 11–12).

(2) Contrapuntal geographies may disclose 'concert and order', but this must not be mistaken for harmony or equilibrium: their movements are orchestrated through differential relations of POWER (see also TRANSCULTURATION). Said's (1993, p. 279) own account focused on a particular modality of power, by seeing 'Western and non-Western experiences as belonging together because they are connected by imperialism'.

(3) Third, contrapuntal geographies require reading from multiple sites and points of view: not only from the point of view of the dominant DISCOURSE but also from the perspective of subaltern knowledges (cf. Featherstone, 2005a: see also SUBALTERN STUDIES).

Contrapuntal geographies have been invoked to wire the discourse of TERRORISM and SECURITY mobilized by the USA in its 'war on terror' in Afghanistan and Iraq to heightened Israeli military action in occupied Palestine (Gregory, 2004) and to campaigns by the Hindu Right against Muslims in India (Oza, 2007): like Said's original proposal, both studies revealed the reactivation of colonial tropes to characterize 'the common enemy'.

Other projects have been directed towards similar ends without invoking Said: Gilroy's (1993) 'Black Atlantic' is one, particularly prominent example of a transnational spatial formation composed through an intricate interplay of connection and DIFFERENCE. Said himself preferred demonstration to theoretical elaboration, but in HUMAN GEOGRAPHY there have been several attempts to develop a more insistently materialist theorization of these ideas. Thus Katz (2001a) substituted a cartographic metaphor – a *countertopography* – for Said's musical one:

I want to imagine a politics that maintains the distinctiveness of a place while recognizing that it is connected analytically to other places along contour lines that represent not elevation but particular relations to a process (e.g. globalizing capitalist relations of production). This offers a multifaceted way of theorizing the connectedness of vastly different places made artifactually discrete by virtue of history and geography but which also reproduce themselves differently amidst the common political-economic and socio-cultural processes they experience. This notion of TOPOGRAPHY involves a particular precision and specificity that connects distant places and in so doing enables the inference of connection in uncharted places in between ... Such connections are precise analytical relationships not homogenizations. Not all places affected by capital's global ambition are affected the same way ... The larger intent is to produce countertopographies that link different places analytically and thereby enhance struggles in the name of common interests. (Katz, 2001a, pp. 1229–30)

These geographies are in constant and often disjunctive motion, and Sheppard (2002) borrowed the concept of a *wormhole* from relativity theory to accentuate the complex TOPOLOGIES involved:

The POSITIONALITY of two places should be measured not by the physical distance separating them, but by the intensity and nature of their interconnectedness ... Like networks, wormholes leapfrog across space, creating topological connections that reduce the separation between distant places and reshape their positionality ... Wormholes are a structural effect of the long historical geography of globalization, reflective of how globalization processes reshape space/time. The existence of such wormholes may also have highly asymmetric consequences for the places that are connected ...' (Sheppard, 2002, pp. 323–4)

Whatever vocabulary is preferred, however, mapping these volatile geographies involves more than a CARTOGRAPHY of connections: the implication of differentials and differences in time–space is vital (cf. POWER-GEOMETRY). And Said's original metaphor conveys an equally crucial sense of dynamics: of movement, variation and change.   DG

conurbation A term coined by Patrick Geddes (1854–1932) to describe a built-up area created through the coalescence of two or more once-separate settlements, probably initiated through RIBBON DEVELOPMENT along the main inter-urban routes. With greater urban SPRAWL the term has largely been replaced by terms such as MEGALOPOLIS, METROPOLITAN AREA and METROPOLITAN LABOUR AREA, in which the built-up area may be discontinuous.   RJ

convergence, regional The tendency for regional incomes or levels of living within a country to become more equal over time. That this should be the case is a prediction derived from NEO-CLASSICAL ECONOMICS, which portrays labour, CAPITAL and other FACTORS OF PRODUCTION moving from one REGION to another seeking the best possible returns (in the form of wages or profits), until there is nothing to gain from further movement because returns are the same in all regions. Thus a competitive free-market economy under CAPITALISM should tend towards regional equality, subject to constraints on the spatial mobility of factors of production.

Evidence for individual nations shows that this prediction does not necessarily hold true. For example, regional incomes in the USA show steady convergence from the latter part of the nineteenth century up to the 1970s. However, individual regions had their own trajectory, reflecting their historical experience of greater or lesser movement towards the national average income, which complicates a simple picture of regular convergence. In addition, the convergence thesis depends on the geographical SCALE adopted: the trend towards reduced inequality at a broad regional scale can be contradicted more locally; for example, between CORE AND PERIPHERY and within the city. Thus in the USA convergence at a broad regional scale has been accompanied by local divergence between city and countryside and among NEIGHBOURHOODS.

Regional convergence is not confined to capitalist economies and, indeed, may be more marked under a SOCIALIST system that has the equalization of regional living standards as an explicit objective. For example, a strong convergence tendency could be observed among the republics of the former Soviet Union, although this may have been reversed during the so-called 'era of stagnation' that preceded *perestroika* and the eventual collapse of COMMUNISM.

There is evidence also of reversals of convergence in the capitalist world, including the USA, with inter-regional inequality increasing since the 1970s. In the UK, divergence can be observed among regions since the early 1980s, in GDP per capita and other measures of income. The fact that this has ocurred during an era of dedication to the free MARKET suggests limits to the extent of regional convergence towards perfect equality under capitalism, in practice if not in theory. Indeed, the earlier era of more positive regional PLANNING may have taken the country further in the direction of EQUALITY than would have been the case under less restrained market forces. This suggests that, after a certain level in the convergence process has been reached, state intervention in the form of REGIONAL POLICY is a necessary if not sufficient condition for further convergence. DMS

Suggested reading
Caselli and Coleman (2001); Martin (2001a); Sokol (2001); Williamson (1966).

co-operative An enterprise formed by an association of members with the aim of promoting their common economic interests. Historically, co-operatives have formed to enhance the selling power of independent, family-based producers; thus they have been most prevalent in the FARMING sector (Moran, Blundern and Bradley, 1996). Sellers' co-operatives share MARKET and pricing information, and may act as a single seller to secure better prices. The co-operative form has also been used to enhance purchasing power (bulk purchases) and to share the costs of food processing. In recent years, producer co-operatives have formed hand in glove with FAIR TRADE initiatives to improve the working conditions and income of peasant producers. JGU

Suggested reading
Cobia (1989).

core–periphery model A model of systematic patterns of UNEVEN DEVELOPMENT in the geography of human activity, based on uneven distribution of POWER within and between societies. Cores and peripheries can be analysed at a variety of geographic SCALES, including uneven regional development within national economies and uneven development at a global scale.

The development of cores and peripheries within national ECONOMIES was a topic of considerable concern to national development planners and urban and regional geographers in the early post-Second World War period. Particularly in developing countries, unbalanced growth between dominant, typically highly primate, urban centres and agrarian regions of the country led to a variety of exercises in promoting regional and secondary city development (see DUAL ECONOMY). However, the strength of existing economic cores and the failure of many decentralization projects has led in recent decades to less enthusiasm for state policies that attempt to overcome core–periphery structures at a national level, while uneven development is increasingly seen as central to the dynamics of CAPITALISM (Smith, 2008 [1984]).

The notion of cores and peripheries at a global scale is associated with the work of a variety of DEVELOPMENT economists, but has been an especially pronounced feature of approaches such as DEPENDENCY THEORY (Frank, 1967) and WORLD-SYSTEMS ANALYSIS (Wallerstein, 1979). Assessments of core–periphery dynamics at a global scale have typically taken national states and economies as important constituents of the global system, and have thus identified some STATES as being part of the global core and others as part of the global periphery. Core states are those with the highest value-added industrial manufacturing and service sectors, while peripheral states are more dependent on agricultural and raw materials exports – and, more recently, on lower value-added manufactured goods. WORLD-SYSTEMS theorists identify states that are semi-peripheral in that their exports comprise a mix of higher and lower value-added goods (Wallerstein, 1979, pp. 66–94).

Many core–periphery models, such as that of Andre Gunder Frank, connect core–periphery structures at a national scale with the global core–periphery structure (Frank, 1967, pp. 8220). In particular, such models have seen primate cities in developing countries as nodal points connecting national economies to the global system, and as 'suction pumps' from which surplus is siphoned out of peripheral societies and into global circuits of CAPITAL (Armstrong and McGee, 1985). Recent processes of GLOBALIZATION have called into question the degree of coherence of national political economies, making the variants of core–periphery theory that hinge on a hierarchy of states more problematic. But the models that emphasize crucial roles for cities in the developing world retain considerable relevance. JGl

Suggested reading
Armstrong and McGee (1985); Frank (1967); Smith (2008 [1984]); Wallerstein (1979).

corporatization The spread of business objectives, methods and DISCOURSES into the non-profit and STATE sectors of SOCIETY. Schools and universities, hospitals, welfare offices and so on are increasingly held to the operating standards of private enterprise, despite differing reasons for their existence, resources and relationship to SOCIETY. Talk of 'cost centres', 'customers', 'products', 'markets' and even 'profitability' (in relation, for example, to university spin-offs of private companies) grows more common. Non-business organizations should strive for efficiency and respond to changing social needs. But the meaning of efficiency and responsiveness in these organizations ought perhaps to be evaluated on different grounds than we would apply to a corporation. ESCH

Suggested reading
Steck (2003).

correlation The degree of association between two or more variables. In statistical analyses, correlation coefficients varying between $+/-1.0$ are measures of the goodness-of-fit of a relationship: a value of 1.0 indicates a perfect relationship. If values less than 1.0 are squared, they indicate the proportion of the variation in one variable that can be accounted for statistically by the other(s): a correlation of 0.8 indicates that 0.64 of the variation can be accounted for. Positive correlations indicate that as one variable increases in value, so does the other: negative correlations that as one increases in value, the other decreases. In several variants of the GENERAL LINEAR MODEL, notably REGRESSION analysis, the correlation between two variables is denoted by r and the (multiple) correlation among three or more variables by R. A correlation coefficient is merely an indicator of covariation among two or more variables and is not a measure of causality, although a high correlation may have important theoretical implications. RJ

cosmography The unified study of the Earth in relation to the heavens, cosmography arises from geocentric assumptions and a belief in homologies between the spatial order of terrestrial and celestial spheres. The spherical geometry of celestial poles, great circles, hemispheres and ecliptic can be projected on to both Earth and sky and illustrated by the armillary sphere, whose spherical lattice of the five great circles, poles, axis and colures makes it the symbol of cosmographic science (still to be found on the flag of Portugal). *Mathematical cosmography* had practical significance for oceanic navigation, and early in modern EUROPE cosmographers were often influential court appointees (Fiorani, 2005). Cosmographic order has given rise in many belief systems to ideas of divinely ordered, cosmic harmony, reproduced at varying SCALES, including the human microcosm, and to attempts to steer influences believed to flow through the cosmos, often by manipulating cosmographic diagrams and images. *Descriptive cosmography* was the classification and description of the contents of the created cosmos, assumed to have an order that reflected mathematical relations. Incorporating both the mathematics of order and description of contents, cosmography eludes easy definition and courts intellectual incoherence.

Cosmographic science peaked in early modern Europe, where cosmographies took the form of illustrated books and maps that may be regarded as precursors of the modern atlas. Cosmographies became increasingly encyclopaedic in seeking to systematize spatially and illustrate the whole of universal knowledge. The dazzling 'marvels' of the worlds newly encountered by Renaissance Europeans meant that cosmography often failed to distinguish reality from fable, and the cosmographic project's grand synthetic goals became increasingly unwieldy (Grafton, 1992; Lestringant, 1994). Cosmography's assumption of a closed universe meant that acceptance of Copernicus' world system, especially after Galileo and Newton, led to its decline as an active field of knowledge, being replaced by astronomy and geography as distinct enquiries (see also GEOGRAPHY, HISTORY OF), although mathematical cosmography remained a critical science during the eighteenth-century establishment of accurate meridians on an oblate globe and the development of geodetic survey (Edney, 1993). Non-Western and premodern cosmologies find graphic expression in diverse cosmographic maps and diagrams (see CARTOGRAPHY, HISTORY OF).   DCO

Suggested reading
Besse (2003); Cosgrove (2006a).

cosmopolitanism Across the centuries, political philosophers and social commentators have argued over the desirability and possibility of social organization and affiliation on a cosmopolitan scale. Cosmopolitans, blaming NATIONALISM for many of the ills of the world, have argued that universal attachments and RIGHTS offered at transnational SCALE are desirable for human progress and emancipation. For example, the ancient Greeks emphasized the global responsibility of the citizen, while during much of modernity the cosmopolitan ideal has been driven by Kant's desire for governments to have obligations beyond their own TERRITORIES (Delanty, 2005b). In contrast, Adam Smith stressed the role of sympathy as a bridge between individuals and among nations in a world differentiated by MARKET laws, and the French revolution sought to extend the principles of liberty, equality and fraternity as universal values, while Marx insisted on the necessity of a socialist commons under the guidance of the international workers' movement.

In recent years, the cosmopolitan ideal has evolved in new directions, to include proposals such as global government, binding international charters, corporate social responsibility, enhanced HUMAN RIGHTS, global environmental stewardship and various international commitments to poor countries, as a response to growing international inequality and planetary damage (Held and Koenig-Archibugi, 2003). Global CITIZENSHIP and political action in general has come to be placed at the heart of the cosmopolitan ideal as a necessary adjunct to the process of GLOBALIZATION in economic, social, institutional and cultural life, involving the rise of planetary organization, transnational flows and cross-national interdependencies. Global citizenship and global government are seen to be required by the rise of global society.

The critics of cosmopolitanism have long argued, however, that collective AFFECT and affiliation have always depended on strong territorial loyalty and identification, as have the processes and institutions of political expression and action, most commonly around ethno-national communities. Thus, cosmopolitan ideals have been judged to be elitist, as reflections of only the values and cultural practices of intellectuals, the itinerant upper echelons and territorially disaffected minorities, with mass or majority affiliation held to be gathered around enduring national and local communities. The critics – past and present – have also dismissed the cosmopolitan ideal as utopian, naïve or unworkable, on the grounds that it is a fictive aspiration that fails to excite affect and loyalty on the ground, that in a world ordered around local, national and regional SOVEREIGNTY its institutional proposals have little chance of uptake and survival, and that as a symbol of progress it is undermined by a human condition that is increasingly wary of universalistic or teleological aspirations (Bauman, 2003).

Undercutting these normative disputes, lies the claim that contemporary social reality is becoming thoroughly cosmopolitan, regardless of questions of consciousness. Ulrich Beck (2004), for example, stresses the need to distinguish cosmopolitanism as a credo from *cosmopolitanization* as a multidimensional process of trans-territorial transformation that demands more than national or STATE-centred response. Beck provides four examples. The first is 'risk cosmopolitanism', a fear shared by all around the world of heightened RISK – military, climatic, epidemiological, environmental, sociobiological – viewed as a global threat that requires new commonalities and interconnected action. Consequently, the second is a 'postnational politics' driven by a global sense of unlimited threats and uncertainties that are much harder to identify and calculate on the basis of traditional state measures, forcing new approaches to inter-state regulation and the rise of many non-state policy networks. The third example he gives is the globalization of inequality as a consequence of entangled national and transnational processes (from state welfare decisions to global NEO-LIBERALISM and the acts of TRANSNATIONAL CORPORATIONS and financial institutions); a phenomenon requiring transnational interventions, but all too frequently treated by national elites as a domestic issue (see also TRANSNATIONALISM). Finally, Beck refers to 'banal cosmopolitanism' based around the everyday consumption of products and images from around the world, and the increasing formation of cultural practices and affiliations through world engagement.

The sum of these few examples of a multi-dimensional process is the claim that 'the experiential space of separate national societies, each with its own uniform language, identity and politics, is becoming more and more of a myth', as what counts as national becomes 'in its essence increasingly trans-national or cosmopolitan' (Beck, 2004, p. 153). This does not in any way mean that we are all becoming cosmopolitans, but it does question how far accounts of what goes on within NATIONS can afford to ignore the world at large. These considerations have prompted some geographers to revisit the history of geography (see GEOGRAPHY, HISTORY OF), not to condemn its contributions *tout court* but to offer nuanced readings of its engagement with cosmopolitan ideals (Cosgrove, 2003; cf. Harvey 2000a), while others have sought to energize the contemporary project of a CRITICAL HUMAN GEOGRAPHY by reflecting on the implications of cosmopolitanism for ETHICS (e.g. Popke, 2007) and for political action (e.g. Gidwani, 2006). AA

cost structure The division of the total cost of production into its constituent parts, or the cost of individual inputs. For example, the cost structure of the iron and steel industry would indicate absolute (or relative) amounts of expenditure on iron ore, coking coal, limestone, labour, capital equipment and so on. The cost structure thus reveals whether a particular activity is material intensive, CAPITAL intensive, labour intensive and so on, with respect to expenditure on inputs. This information can provide an initial clue to the inputs likely to have the greatest bearing on the location of the activity in question. DMS

cost–benefit analysis An analytical procedure for the comprehensive, frequently *ex ante*, economic evaluation of major public-sector projects, embracing their full positive and negative societal consequences, sometimes over the range of project options and geographical SCALES (e.g. Turner, Adger and Doktor, 1995). As such, cost–benefit analysis (commonly 'CBA') covers a wider range of considerations than the profit-and-loss accounting of private-sector decision-making. Originally applied to public river and harbour projects in the USA, CBA's contemporary uses extend to such diverse issues as urban air quality, dam and irrigation schemes, refuse recycling, medical and veterinary procedures, transport deregulation, roadway maintenance, disposal of hazardous waste, energy generating and conservation and job creation schemes (Armstrong and Taylor, 2000; see also Mishan and Quah, 2007).

Cost–benefit analysis involves three stages. First, costs and benefits associated with public projects have to be identified, including intangible EXTERNALITIES such as noise, habitat loss, POLLUTION and raising human HEALTH and lifespans. Second, these must be quantified, including their discounting to a common base date, since the various costs and benefits can arise over very different time periods. Finally, the resulting cost–benefit ratios are incorporated into the decision-making, or project-evaluation, stage, alongside political and other judgmental inputs (Turner, 2007).

Economists differ as to the best application of these general principles in particular cases, and over the validity of the exercise as a whole. Defining all costs and benefits is one such: how to be comprehensive without double-counting. Not all variables have an obvious MARKET value, and some 'estimates' may be little more than guesses. The discount rate can also be crucial to the outcome, and endangers undervaluing the welfare of future generations. Finally, distributional issues are important – a $1 million benefit to poor residents from one freeway route should outweigh the same gain to rich citizens from an alternative.

Recent extensions of cost–benefit analysis to large-scale environmental issues, such as GLOBAL WARMING, are now at the forefront of international debate (Stern, 2007) but have proved particularly controversial. Not only are such potential environmental changes irreversible, but the cost and benefits vary internationally, raise sharp ethical valuation judgements (e.g. over LANDSCAPE, wildlife and human life) and questions of inter- and intra-generational fairness – the already poor are likely to suffer most, while the future generations who feel the sharp end of global changes may also have the technology to combat them.   AGH

Suggested reading
Elins (2000).

counterfactuals Literally contrary to the facts: determining what might have been had the facts been different. What if the Rhine River never existed? What if in Florida in November 2000, fewer chads were left hanging? And, perish the thought, what if *The dictionary of human geography* had never been written? Posed as subjunctive conditional, counterfactuals focus attention on comparing the known case, the historical geographical record, with what might have been the case in a different possible world. Discussions of counterfactuals are found in PHILOSOPHY, social psychology, political science, some branches of economics and perhaps most prominently in history (and through it, HISTORICAL GEOGRAPHY). Also termed *virtual history*, historians use counterfactuals to facilitate clearer explanation of past events. For example, to understand the rise of German Nazism, Ferguson (1998) imagines twentieth-century Europe without the First World War. On that basis, he cannot conceive of the emergence of the Third Reich, and so concludes that the First World War must be its cause. For a number of historians, however, this is not history, but a form of fiction. The economic historian M.M. Postan declared that 'the might-have-beens of history are not a profitable subject for discussion' (quoted in Gould, 1969, p. 195). With POSTMODERN and POST-STRUCTURAL scepticism about the separation of fact and fiction, this kind of objection is less convincing, and virtual histories burgeon both in academia and in literature (Ferguson, 1999).   TJB

Suggested reading
Ferguson (1999).

counter-urbanization Population deconcentration away from large urban areas and their SUBURBS, first identified in the USA in the 1970s, where many metropolitan areas were losing population through net MIGRATION to non-metropolitan areas. The growing areas were generally relatively small settlements, which were either increasingly accessible for COMMUTING or offered attractive environments for retirees and home-based workers. This changing population distribution was paralleled by employment deconcentration

to smaller towns that offered cheaper, more extensive tracts of land, more pliant (usually non-unionized) labour forces, plus pleasanter and less-congested environments and were more accessible as TRANSPORT COSTS were reduced both absolutely and relatively (cf. FOOTLOOSE INDUSTRY). Similar patterns of counter-urbanization were identified in many other countries in the late twentieth century, though there has been some 'BACK-TO-THE CITY' recently, which has made the patterns of change less clear-cut. (See also EDGE CITY; SPRAWL.)   RJ

Suggested reading
Champion (1991); Champion and Hugo (2004).

creative destruction The general notion that only through the demise of existing entities can new ones be brought into the world. While associated with thinkers such as Nietzsche and Hegel, creative destruction as a distinct phrase is best known to geographical audiences through the work of the economist Joseph Schumpeter. In his hands, it is both a description of CAPITALISM's disequilibrium dynamics and a historical argument regarding the passage to social democratic WELFARE STATES. Against the marginalist concerns of twentieth-century NEO-CLASSICAL ECONOMICS, Schumpeter (1942) took up macro-economic questions in the classical tradition (see POLITICAL ECONOMY). He argued that capitalist competition induces entrepreneurs to innovate (and to maintain a stable of scientists for the purpose), resulting in qualitative changes to production technologies that are fundamentally disruptive to the existing economic landscape. As opposed to the smooth unfolding of technological INNOVATION, the equilibrium provided by the market's 'hidden hand', and theories of disruption caused by exogenous forces (e.g. weather, war), Schumpeter saw capitalism as inherently unstable, a condition that its citizens would ultimately find intolerable. Schumpeter's ideas are often likened to those of Marx, important differences being that the latter desired capitalism's demise and located its chronic instability less in competition than in ACCUMULATION as such (CLASS-based extraction and investment of surplus value: see Storper and Walker, 1989). It is, of course, in the spirit of the latter that Harvey so often invokes 'creative destruction' in his construction of an explicitly historico-geographical materialism and his critical analyses of LANDSCAPES of capital accumulation (see, e.g., Harvey, 1989b: see also MARXIST GEOGRAPHY).   GHe

crime The geographical study of crime seeks to: explain the spatial clustering of criminal behaviour; consider how the construction and monitoring of spaces might reduce the incidence of criminality; and explain how wider social and political dynamics shape the fear of crime and societal responses to it.

Like many other social phenomena, criminal behaviour is unevenly distributed. Much work in GEOGRAPHY attempts to account for this variation, typically by elaborating the demographic characteristics and common social patterns in places where crime is concentrated. Often taking inspiration from the 'social disorganization' theory developed by CHICAGO SCHOOL sociologists, these accounts take aim at several factors arguably common to places characterized by concentrated disadvantage: the comparative lack of economic opportunity, the likelihood of high residential mobility, the high percentage of single-parent households, and the general cultural acceptance of crime (Smith, S.J., 1986a; Sampson, Raudenbush and Earl, 1997). Some geographical work focuses more on the common practices of criminal offenders, and how their time–space patterns make opportunities for crime more or less available to them (Rengert, 1997). A related, and highly popular, criminology of place concentrates on the alleged effects of so-called 'broken windows' as incubators of crime. Places where broken windows are not fixed signify a lack of informal social control that invites the criminally minded into their midst (Wilson and Kelling, 1982; for a critique, see Harcourt, 2001). In recent years, the geographical clustering of crime has been mapped by police departments using GEOGRAPHIC INFORMATION SYSTEMS (GIS) technologies: these help isolate 'hot spots' of criminality for targeted enforcement.

For some, this clustering of 'hot spots' is connected to the built environment. Various related approaches – 'situational crime prevention', 'defensible space', 'environmental criminology' – suggest that crime's geographies are significantly a consequence of whether spaces deter crime through effective defensibility and SURVEILLANCE. Places can thus be constructed to repel crime if they make entry difficult or monitoring easy. Such monitoring takes conspicuous form in the UK, and increasingly in other places, through closed-circuit television (CCTV) units that monitor much of public space (Fyfe and Bannister, 1998). These surveillance practices ostensibly reduce criminality by increasing the threat of capture.

Other work in the geography of crime focuses on how crime is commonly constructed, socially and politically. There is now, for instance, an extensive literature on the fear of crime, and its variation across social groups and across space (see Koskela and Pain, 2000). Such fear is more prevalent amongst the elderly and amongst females, especially when they are in unfamiliar public places. Fear of crime is also a political construct, used as a means to legitimate 'get tough' policies for reducing crime. These political processes are sometimes tied to the wider practices of NEO-LIBERALISM, through which welfarist approaches to social problems are delegitimized, in favour of policies that emphasize social control.   SKH

Suggested reading
Smith, S.J. (1986a).

crisis A potentially complete failure in the reproduction of systemic relations. The term appears in multiple DISCOURSES, being used to describe threatened failures in the reproduction of socio-economic structures, political institutions, representational conventions, ecological systems and more. Its connotations are largely negative: describing the failure to reproduce relations as a crisis carries some implication that continuity in those relations is desirable or necessary. Crises of social relations are often viewed as having positive aspects as well, though, inasmuch as they present windows of opportunity for progressive change.

Relevant work in HUMAN GEOGRAPHY has focused mainly on crises of capitalism. Human geographers influenced by HISTORICAL MATERIALISM have viewed CAPITALISM as a socio-economic system whose internal contradictions make it inherently unstable and prone to periodic crises that lead to the reconfiguration and greater socialization of relations of production and reproduction. Such a trajectory ultimately calls into question the reproduction of capitalism itself, making this perspective fundamentally different from more mainstream accounts of the 'business cycle'. Briefly, capitalism is prone to crisis because its endogenous dynamics frequently and characteristically produce situations in which: (i) workers, collectively, cannot afford to buy the COMMODITIES they produce (a crisis of underconsumption); (ii) more commodities are produced than can be absorbed by all available purchasing power (a crisis of overproduction); (iii) capitalists accumulate more capital than they can invest in profitable

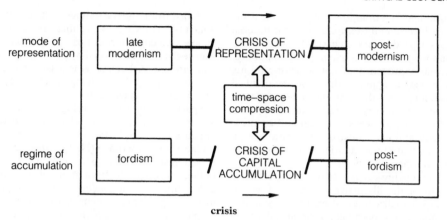

crisis

enterprises (a crisis of over-ACCUMULATION); or (iv) a large portion of the total labour force cannot be profitably employed in the production of commodities (a crisis of unemployment or underemployment). These various manifestations of crisis are closely related, with one often leading to or accompanying another.

Human geographers, most prominently David Harvey, have built upon and refined Marx's original work to develop a more coherent and geographical theory of the dynamics of capitalist crises. In work central to MARXIST GEOGRAPHY, Harvey (1999 [1982]) has proposed a threefold theory of capitalist crises. His 'first cut' explains how the crisis tendencies above are inherent to capitalism. His 'second cut' focuses on their temporal displacement via fiscal and monetary arrangements that stave off crises by laying the seeds of larger problems in the future (e.g. increased household reliance on credit cards, or ballooning national deficits). His 'third cut' explores the ways in which geography can be used to combat crisis tendencies (see also Harvey, 2001); for example, by massive investments in new locations or the opening of new MARKETS, and suggests that crises of capital accumulation are culturally mirrored in crises of REPRESENTATION that materially affect the ways in which TIME and SPACE are constructed and construed (Harvey, 1989b) (see figure: see also TIME–SPACE COMPRESSION). The STATE plays critical roles in the above processes. Collectively, these theoretical refinements help to explain how capitalism has survived and expanded despite regular crises, contrary to the predictions of classical Marxism. Similar questions have been taken up in REGULATION THEORY, which explores the role of minimally necessary fits between narrowly 'economic'

activities (*regimes of accumulation*) and broader social and political conventions and institutions (*modes of regulation*) in producing and overcoming periodic crises (Walker, 1995). Meanwhile, ecological Marxism has sought to bring NATURE into crisis theory, pointing out that severe environmental degradation and other failures of environmental regulation may both precipitate a crisis, and be important objects of political struggle during one (O'Connor, 1998).   JM

Suggested reading
Harvey (1999 [1982], 2001).

critical geopolitics The emergence of critical geopolitics within POLITICAL GEOGRAPHY situates power not in the hands of a sovereign state or individual, but in more relational ways that traverse a spectrum of scales of social life. Influenced by POST-STRUCTURALISM and responding to the realist approaches of international relations in conventional geopolitical discourse, critical geopolitics has not simply contested the claims of INTERNATIONAL RELATIONS (IR) theory and international political economy (IPE), but taken them apart by exposing the assumptions of each and challenging the taken-for-granted categories of analysis within IR in particular. Drawing inspiration from the work of Michel Foucault, Jacques Derrida and Gayatri Spivak, critical geopolitics is a less a theory of how SPACE and politics intersect than a taking apart – a deconstruction – of the normalized categories and narratives of conventional GEOPOLITICS. Such an approach challenges seemingly commonsense understandings and practices of 'peace', 'VIOLENCE' and 'WAR' within the STATE system (Dalby, 1991).

Critical geopolitics is defined by its deconstructive impulse (see DECONSTRUCTION),

121

questioning assumptions in a taken-for-granted world and examining the institutional modes of producing such a world *vis-à-vis* writing about the world, its geography and politics. Such an approach does not subscribe to any one mode of apprehending the geopolitical world; it eschews the idea that any GEOGRAPHY can be fully finalized or authoritative (Sparke, 2005). Rather, it seeks to reveal and examine the assumptions, constructions and POWER relations that are foundational to such apprehension (Shapiro, 1997).

A central project for critical geopolitics is analysis of the discursive practices by which scholars spatialize international politics: it asks why and how a particular geopolitical narrative is normalized and accepted (Ó Tuathail, 1996b) (see DISCOURSE; cf. Müller, 2008). Critical geopolitics thus seeks to politicize knowledge production through DISCOURSE ANALYSIS of dominant geopolitical practices, such as foreign policy and techniques of representing war (Shapiro, 1997; Gregory, 2004b). Within geography, '[c]ritical geopolitics is one of many cultures of resistance to Geography as imperial truth, state-capitalized knowledge, and military weapon. It is a small part of a much larger rainbow struggle to decolonize our inherited GEOGRAPHICAL IMAGINATION so that other geo-graphings and other worlds might be possible' (Ó Tuathail, 1996b, p. 256). Sparke (2005, p. xiv) adds that 'any assumption about geography either as a result of or as a basis or container for other social relations always risks fetishizing a particular spatial arrangement and ignoring ongoing processes of spatial production, negotiation, and contestation'.

Ó Tuathail's (1996b) agenda-setting call for *critical geopolitics* was a central text in the unravelling of dominant geopolitical discourse. It provided compelling critiques of geopolitics, but through its distance from alternative epistemological ways of knowing how to 'geo-graph' the world (see EPISTEMOLOGY) or from ontological commitments to it (see ONTOLOGY), critical geopolitics risked becoming disembodied critical practice and suffered from 'a dearth of commentary on the prospects for resistance' (Sparke, 2000b, p. 378; cf. Routledge, 1996a). Even as he argued against positions that are unmarked, unmediated and transcendent, then, Ó Tuathail unwittingly became part of this category. How dominant geopolitical scripts can be destabilized and recast to take account of people and places represented as the orientalized Other (see ORIENTALISM), for example, or

excluded from understandings of SECURITY and POLITICAL ECONOMY altogether, represents a major challenge for critical geopolitics. To expose the subjects effaced by realist geopolitics and international relations is a laudable goal, but how might political change be effected once power relations have been exposed?

Sparke (2005) seeks to bridge this gap in his analysis of the ways in which a Canadian organization – the National Action Committee on the Status of Women (NAC) – displaced the masculinist and state-sponsored 'big picture' politics through the formation of a *counterpublic*. Sparke's analysis of the material, political and gendered dimensions of geopolitics employs a feminist politics of location that goes beyond a purely discursive exegesis. Dalby (1994) noted the lack of attention to GENDER at the intersection of IR theory and critical geopolitics, reiterating important issues that had long been raised by feminists. He examined the ways in which geopolitical categories of security are gendered and the gender-blind analysis of much IR theory. His overview of gender and FEMINISM in IR underscored the broader absence of feminist voices in geopolitics during the 1990s, with notable exceptions (Kofman and Peake, 1990; Kofman, 1996). Since then, conversations between feminist geography and geopolitics have considerably increased, and much of the work that fills these silences is directed towards an explicitly feminist geopolitics (Staeheli, Kofman and Peake, 2004; Hyndman, 2004, 2007).

Critical geopolitics is not limited to the orthodox trinity of gender, RACE and CLASS. Sharp (2000a) took critical geopolitics in new directions in exploring the underdeveloped connections between politics, popular culture and SEXUALITY, and studies like hers have also extended the engagement of critical geopolitics with the visual rather than narrowly textual (cf. Hughes, 2007; Strüver, 2007). The agenda of critical geopolitics has been further enlarged through explorations of discourses of danger and security (Megoran, 2005), generosity and nationalist identity (Carter, 2006) and AFFECT, fear and emotion (Pain and Smith, 2008). None of these studies is limited to the analysis of discursive effects. These extensions, and others like them, have opened up the field of critical geopolitics and forged a series of connections that involve far more than political geography; critical geopolitical perspectives now reach deep into human geography at large and, as befits their interdisciplinary orientations, across a still wider interdisciplinary space. It is now difficult to imagine critical analysis of, say, AMERICAN EMPIRE, COLONIALISM, IMPERIALISM or TERRORISM that does not touch on critical geopolitics at some point. These are vital developments, at once political and intellectual, because they disclose a series of intersections between biopolitics (see BIOPOWER), geopolitics and geoeconomics that lie at the heart of the contemporary political moment and that urgently require critical analysis (cf. Sparke, 2007).   JH

critical human geography   Theoretically informed geographical scholarship, committed to Leftist politics, SOCIAL JUSTICE and liberation through scholarly enquiry. Critical geography is one variant of the rich tradition of critical enquiry in social science and the humanities that embraces Marx's call not only to interpret the world, but to change it. Fay defines contemporary critical science as the 'attempt to understand in a rationally responsible manner the oppressive features of a society such that this understanding stimulates its audience to transform their society and thereby liberate themselves' (1987, p. 4). Agger (1998) identifies several features of critical social theory, as practiced in fields such as GEOGRAPHY. These include: a rejection of positivist enquiry (see POSITIVISM); an endorsement of the possibility of progress; a model of society characterized by structural domination produced, in part, through myth and IDEOLOGY; and a rejection of revolutionary expediency with a concomitant faith in the agency of everyday change and self-transformation.

Critical human geography emerged from a long tradition of dissent. Although its predecessors include the anarchist geography of scholars such as Reclus and Kroptkin (see ANARCHISM), Anglo-American critical geography's roots are to be found in the RADICAL GEOGRAPHY that emerged in the 1970s (see Peet, 2000). A self-identified field of critical geography began to emerge in the late 1980s. Important departures included a rejection of some of the structural excesses of MARXISM (in line with a general POST-MODERN turn), and a sharpening interest in questions of CULTURE and REPRESENTATION, as opposed to the economic focus of radical geography. Radical and critical geography, while closely related, are not interchangeable. Some observers (Castree, 2000) worry at the eclipse of the former by the latter.

One important consequence of the post-modern turn has been that critical geography is remarkably varied in its commitments. For Hubbard, Kitchin, Bartley and Fuller

(2002), critical geography is diverse in its EPISTEMOLOGY, ONTOLOGY and METHODOLOGY, and lacks a 'distinctive theoretical identity' (p. 62). That said, certain common themes can be discerned (Blomley, 2006). These include:

(1) A commitment to SOCIAL THEORY and a rejection of EMPIRICISM: critical geographers draw from a number of theoretical wells, including POLITICAL ECONOMY, QUEER THEORY, POST-COLONIALISM and FEMINISM.

(2) Self-consciously oppositional enquiry: scholarship that seeks to unmask POWER, demonstrate INEQUALITY, uncover RESISTANCE and foster emancipatory politics and social change.

(3) An emphasis on REPRESENTATION as a site for domination and resistance: given a general interest in DISCOURSE and meaning, one common focus is the ways in which representations of space serve to sustain power (or conversely, can be used to challenge power).

(4) An optimistic faith in the power of critical scholarship: critical geography can both undo oppressive forms of social power, and provide transformative insights. In speaking truth to power, in other words, the scholar can undo domination, and free the oppressed: 'Dissentient thoughts and norm-challenging information can, as history shows, be as potent as armies given the right conditions', Castree and Wright (2005, p. 2) argue.

(5) A commitment to progressive praxis: critical geographers claim common-cause with movements committed to SOCIAL JUSTICE. The precise nature of the relation, and the appropriate focus for, and locus of, ACTIVISM has been much debated (Fuller and Kitchin, 2004b).

(6) SPACE as a critical tool: a particular attention to the ways in which spatial arrangements and representations can serve to produce inequality and oppression and opposition. To varying degrees, critical geographers note the ways in which space can serve as both a tool and veil of power.

Some important and unresolved questions remain. For example, relatively limited discussion has occurred over the shared commitments, if any, of critical geographers (though cf. Harvey, 2000b). What are geographers critical of? Why? And to what end? To borrow from Barnes (2002), critical geographers are better at the 'explanatory-diagnostic' than the 'anticipatory-utopian'. Critical geography, for Barnes, needs 'an imaginative capacity to reconfigure the world and our place within it' (p. 12). This should not entail enforced political conformity, of course. However, too often, the politics that informs critical geography remains implicit and inchoate. More generally, what are the assumptions implicit to critical scholarship? Agger (1998), in a supportive critique of critical social science, raises concerns that it posits a view of human capacity that is predicated on 'an inflated conception of the powers of human reason and will' (p. 9).

Another important question concerns the institutionalization of critical geography. While critical geographers like to think of themselves as rebels and outsiders (and were certainly treated as such by the disciplinary establishment fifteen years ago), critical enquiry has become pervasive in geography (Byles, 2001). Critical geography, Castree (2000, p. 958) notes 'has insinuated itself into the very heart of the discipline'. While this may reflect its analytical strengths and insights, others worry that institutionalization has entailed co-optation. Has critical enquiry lost not only its verve, but also its commitment to political change?

Such charges have come, in part, from critical geographers outside the Anglophone world. For it should be noted that critical geography is practiced (often in distinct ways) across the globe. The particular insights of, for example, Hungarian (Timar, 2003) or Japanese (Mizuoka, Mizuuchi, Hisatake, Tsutsumi and Fujita, 2005) critical geography needs to be better acknowledged (Bialasiewicz, 2003). Better linkages should also be forged with critical scholars in other disciplines.

On this point, the formation of the International Critical Geography group should be noted. This is a loose network of like-minded geographers from Europe, Asia and North America who embrace internationalism and critical enquiry (Desbiens and Smith, 1999). A series of innovative workshops and conferences have been held, beginning with a gathering in Vancouver in 1998.   NKB

Suggested reading
Blunt and Wills (2000); Castree and Gregory (2006).

critical rationalism   A PHILOSOPHY of SCIENCE developed by Karl Popper (1902–94), asserting the progressive growth in knowledge through continued rational criticism. Nothing should be sacrosanct; everything should be open to scrutiny. While Popper believed that knowledge in the traditional sense of certainty, or justified true belief, was unobtainable, sustained rational criticism would allow us to get 'nearer to the truth' (Popper, 1945, vol. 2, p. 237).

Popper ranged enormously in his philosophical interests over a long life, but two are particularly germane for critical rationalism. First, his thesis of FALSIFICATION was developed in opposition to the verifiability principle of LOGICAL POSITIVISM. Verification, Popper argued, required that the truthfulness of a scientific statement be unambiguously proven for every conceivable instance: past, present and future. This could never happen, said Popper (1959). Instead, he proposed that scientific statements are defined by their potential to be falsified. Science advances not by knowing what is true, but by knowing what is false.

Second, we have Popper's ideas about the growth of human knowledge: he claimed that scientists begin work not with bare facts (again logical positivism's contention), but with problems to be solved. The starting points are HYPOTHESES, hunches, conjectures about potential solutions and then comparisons with existing theory (Popper, 1963). Should the new conjecture remain unfalsified and possess greater 'empirical content' than the old theory, the new should replace the old. By greater empirical content Popper meant the ability of the hypothesis to account for hitherto anomalous results, solve as yet unsolvable problems or make (correct) predictions about phenomena not so far predicted. When Einstein's theory of relativity was conjectured, for example, it could not be falsified and made correct predictions that went beyond Newton's old theory. Consequently, the cosmos became Einsteinian, science progressed and human knowledge grew. Behind the latter lay the strategy of critical rationalism: *critical* in that any theory demonstrably false was eliminated; and *rational* in that the best theory, the one with the most explanatory force and predictive power, was chosen among those that remained. There was qualified progress, but progress nonetheless.

It is odd that critical rationalism, and Popper's writings more generally, were only barely taken up in GEOGRAPHY. Popper's belief in realism, rationality and progress, as well as in the importance of critique, conjecture and scepticism about ultimate truth, were made for the discipline at least in its guise as science during the QUANTITATIVE REVOLUTION. Instead, geographers clung to various forms of

POSITIVISM, the very philosophy that Popper thought he had demolished in 1935. Programmatic statements were made on the behalf of critical rationalism by some geographers including Wilson (1972), one of the key proponents of a scientific approach to geography during the 1960s, and by Bird (1975, 1989), and Chouinard, Fincher and Webber (1984) used Lakatos' critique and reformulation of Popper's proposals to outline the conduct of research programmes in a nominally scientific human geography. But critical rationalism was never realized in practice within geography. Indeed, the very idea of such a NORMATIVE philosophical scheme set out in advance to generate scientific progress became increasingly unattractive, especially in the social sciences, after Kuhn's (1970 [1962]) writings on PARADIGMS, which stressed the messiness of scientific practice and the role of ruptures and revolutions in scientific advance. Further, as human geography moved towards POSTMODERNISM and POST-STRUCTURALISM and their various commitments to anti-REALISM, RELATIVISM and incommensurability, the prospects of Popper's critical rationalism gaining hold in the discipline became ever more remote. TJB

Suggested reading
Bird (1975). See also Critical rationalism study page: http://www.geocities.com/criticalrationalist/

critical theory A primarily European tradition of social and political thought centrally concerned with critical reflection on CAPITALISM and MODERNITY. It is closely associated with the work of the so-called *Frankfurt School*, which emerged in Germany in the 1920s. The School formed amidst the defeat of left-wing parties in western Europe, the degeneration of the Russian revolution into Soviet Stalinism and the rise of FASCISM. The members of the School expanded classical MARXISM, drawing upon ideas from Freud, Weber and others outside the Marxist tradition, and in particular sought to supplement the orthodox focus on POLITICAL ECONOMY with concepts drawn from the spheres of aesthetics, culture and PHILOSOPHY. Its key members were Theodor Adorno (1903–69), Max Horkheimer (1895–1973) and Herbert Marcuse (1898–1979); another scholar associated with the School, Walter Benjamin (1892–1940), committed suicide fleeing Nazi-occupied France. By then, most members of the School had already moved to the USA, returning to Germany in the 1950s. The

key postwar representative of critical theory is Jürgen Habermas (1929–).

Horkheimer (1975) defined critical theory in contrast to traditional theory (the neutral, objective stance claimed in the natural sciences). Unlike traditional theory, critical social theory had to be reflexive and account for its own social origins and purposes. Its attitude was one of distrust towards the social rules and conventions encountered by individuals in their daily lives. The critical theorists identified new trends in capitalism with the emergence of monopolies, the closer association of STATE and capital, the growth of bureaucracy, and the rationalization of social life linked to the dominance of instrumental reason. They explored issues of IDENTITY, authoritarianism, the spread of commodity production, reification and ALIENATION. They were concerned with the way in which CULTURE had become an industry, with popular cultural forms serving to distract workers from the increasingly repetitive nature of their daily work, thus promoting a sense of fatalism and blocking the potential for resistance. Their conclusions on the ideological barriers to revolution in an increasingly one-dimensional society tended to confirm a logic of domination that led to a pessimistic political immobility that they found it difficult to break out of.

Jürgen Habermas has carried on the tradition of critical theory in the postwar period, but has also modified it in important ways. His early work presents a theory of *knowledge-constitutive interests* (technical, practical and emancipatory) that guide different types of science – empirical–analytical, hermeneutic and critical (Habermas, 1987). Here, critical theory takes on the role of a therapeutic critique, modelled on Freudian PSYCHOANALYTIC THEORY and directed towards freeing society from ideologically distorted perceptions.

Problems with this formulation led Habermas to take an important 'communicative turn' in the formulation of critical theory in the 1970s (Habermas, 1984, 1987). Social life requires co-operative, communicative interaction and Habermas undertakes the 'rational reconstruction' of the underlying system of rules that speakers must master in order to communicate. Speakers uttering a sentence necessarily (though usually implicitly) make certain validity claims (to truth, rightness, sincerity, intelligibility). A genuine rational consensus on the basis of these validity claims can emerge only under conditions of free and unconstrained debate that Habermas

125

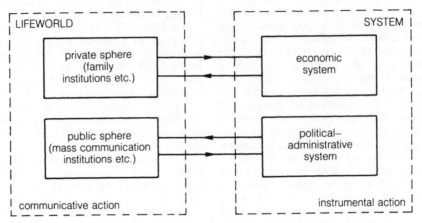

critical theory *Lifeworld and system*

summarizes as 'the ideal speech situation'. This serves as a basis for the critique of IDEOLOGY as distorted communication and false consensus. Critical theory can thus be shown to be grounded on normative standards that are not arbitrary, but that are inherent in the very structure of LANGUAGE and communication.

Habermas links these ideas to an evolutionary, developmental model of social evolution as a learning process. As societies evolve, 'SYSTEM' (which is to say those areas of social life coordinated through the steering mechanisms of money and power) becomes differentiated and uncoupled from 'LIFEWORLD' (the storehouse of background convictions and world views against which individuals come to a mutual understanding) (see figure). Capitalist MODERNIZATION can then be criticized as a process of one-sided rationalization, involving the 'colonizing' of the lifeworld through the over-extension of steering mechanisms of markets, bureaucracy and technological rationality.

Habermas sees his work as an attempt to continue the ENLIGHTENMENT tradition in the face of the irrational challenges of POSTMODERNISM (Habermas, 1990 [1985]). However, his own views have been criticized for presenting an ETHNOCENTRIC view of evolution and rationality, and many have found his foundationalist arguments for an 'inherent telos of speech' oriented towards consensus unconvincing.

Others have taken up the challenge posed in his writings in new ways. Thomas McCarthy, for example, is a leading figure in attempts to build links between Habermas' critical theory and elements of American PRAGMATISM. McCarthy's book-length exchange with David Hoy over the relative merits of a critical theory based on the work of Habermas and the genealogical approach of Foucault brings out superbly the relative strengths and weaknesses of the critical theory tradition (Hoy and McCarthy, 1994). Hoy argues that Foucault actually provides an alternative way of continuing the tradition of critical theory by developing an internal, genealogical critique that brings to light the historicity of our reason and self-understanding. In response, McCarthy continues to defend Habermas' aim of constructing a systematic theory of reason and context-transcending truth claims as a necessary basis for critique. This aim also serves to differentiate Habermas' engagement with pragmatism from the more extreme constructivist and ethnocentrist views of Richard Rorty (see Habermas' exchange with Rorty in Brandom, 2000).

Two further caveats are necessary. First, it is obviously the case that this particular tradition of critical theory does not have a monopoly on the concept of 'critical'. Habermas and Popper famously tussled over the critical claims of CRITICAL RATIONALISM, for example, while REALISM asserts its critical potential on the basis of a distinction between surface appearances and underlying, causal mechanisms in a stratified view of reality. Similarly, although the project of a CRITICAL HUMAN GEOGRAPHY has invoked critical theory in the sense discussed here (see Gregory, 1978a, 1994), it is a much more heterodox tradition. In part – and the second caveat – this is because neither Habermas nor his critics have paid much attention to the spatialities implicit in his formulations. Yet his work is, inevitably, a SITUATED KNOWLEDGE: his writings have been a response to the dilemmas of postwar Germany seeking to come to terms with the ghosts of its fascist past, and many of his arguments are centred on a particular, even privileged, view of EUROPE. More than this, however, the colonization of the lifeworld that Habermas claims to identify mirrors, in a radically different register, Lefebvre's account of the superimposition of abstract space over concrete space (Gregory, 1994: see also PRODUCTION OF SPACE), and may be glimpsed in an earlier form in the spatial impress of European colonial systems on the lifeworlds of native peoples (Harris, 1991). Of all those who have been associated with critical theory, however, it has probably been the tragic figure of Benjamin who has left the most enduring mark on HUMAN GEOGRAPHY: his experimental renderings of the city, in text and as montage, are powerful reminders that MODERNISM was a critique of modernity and not merely a celebration of it, and have inspired conceptual elaborations (e.g. Latham, 1999) and eloquent investigations (e.g. Pred, 1995).   KB

Suggested reading
Bernstein (1995b); Rush (2004).

cultural capital   A concept coined by the French sociologist Pierre Bourdieu, cultural capital is one among many forms of CAPITAL that figure prominently in his intellectual project; namely, to elaborate 'a general science of the economy of practices' that would explain the 'economic logic' behind apparently non-economic and therefore disinterested practices such as gift exchange or cultural consumption. Cultural capital is closely linked to and functions in conjunction with *economic capital* (the conventional and most crudely material form of CAPITAL that inhabits economic theory) and SOCIAL CAPITAL. The inter-convertibility of various forms of capital is a critical rather than incidental element in Bourdieu's theory of practice; but Bourdieu is careful to note that the fungibility of cultural and social capital into economic capital is conditional rather than guaranteed, and frequently partial (in short, not without risk). Two additional concepts, *symbolic capital* and *academic capital*, which have close affinities with the concept of cultural capital, also appear in Bourdieu's writings. That said, academic capital may be regarded as a subset of cultural capital and symbolic capital as a superset.

In his instructive treatise, *Distinction: a social critique of the judgment of taste* (1984), Bourdieu deploys the concept of cultural capital to great effect to show how bourgeois practices of cultural CONSUMPTION – via the arts, education, cuisine, attire and so on – consolidate an aesthetic that 'consciously and deliberately or not ... fulfill[s] a social function of legitimating social differences'. But his clearest discussion of the concept is in a short, often-overlooked essay called 'The forms of capital', where Bourdieu identifies three states in which cultural capital can exist: 'in the *embodied* state, i.e. in the form of long-lasting dispositions of mind and body; in the *objectified* state, in the form of cultural goods (pictures, books, dictionaries, instruments, machines, etc.) which are the trace or realization of theories, problematics, etc.; and in the *institutionalized* state [as educational qualifications] ...' (1985, p. 243).

Key aspects of cultural capital differentiate it from economic capital: principal among these are its necessarily embodied form, which makes it both less fungible and less easily acquired than economic capital; and the more overtly social and disguised conditions of its transmission. Economic logic dictates the efficacy of cultural capital: hence, the symbolic profits of distinction (e.g. the ability to read in a society of illiterates) that accrue from cultural capital depend on the scarcity value of that capital, which in turn depends on its distribution within society. The more ill-distributed a particular form of capital, the greater is its value. In a circular argument, Bourdieu maintains that inequalities in the distribution of capital – in short, CLASS divisions – are reproduced intergenerationally by those very forms of capital that demarcate class status in the first instance: ultimately, he writes, 'the means of appropriating the product of accumulated labor in the objectified state which is held by a given agent [i.e. various forms of capital], depends for its real efficacy on the form of distribution of the means of appropriating the accumulated and objectively available resources...' (1985, pp. 245–6).   VG

Suggested reading
Guillory (1993); Lane (2000).

cultural ecology   An important, if somewhat under-appreciated, precursor to contemporary POLITICAL ECOLOGY. Cultural ecology has been primarily concerned with the relationships among the transformation of NATURE, social

127

reproduction and cultural processes within particular social formations. Emerging from North American anthropology in the mid-twentieth century, cultural ecology has mostly concerned itself with non-industrial societies, typically pastoralists, hunter–gathers, fishing cultures and small-scale cultivators, with an emphasis on ethnographic field methods. Cultural ecology in this sense is most closely associated with the work of Julian Steward and the Chicago school, particularly after the publication of Steward's *Theory of culture change* (1955). Work done or influenced by Steward in this tradition emphasized a close relationship between symbolic culture (values, religious beliefs and traditions) on the one hand, and the material, ecological basis of a society on the other. Steward in particular developed the notion of a 'cultural core' shaped in a possibilist sense by the ways in which critical environmental RESOURCES (crops, ANIMALS, energy sources etc.) were used by a culture. It would be fair to say that Steward's primary interest was cultural formation and change, but cultural ecology more generally was at the forefront of scholarly attention to questions about the social bases of environmental change, how cultures respond or adapt to environmental change and also how cultures influence the management of critical environmental resources. Moreover, considerable theoretical and methodological diversity characterizes self-described cultural ecologists (Netting, 1986).

As the name would suggest, cultural ecology was heavily influenced by the rise of ecology. This is true not only in terms of a focus on the relationship between environmental conditions and cultural processes, but also in some of the conceptual emphasis on systems, ADAPTATION, homeostasis, resilience, stability and so on, all hallmarks of an earlier phase of ecology (see ECOLOGY). It would be unfair to attribute the kind of telos so evident in Clementsian ecology to cultural ecology. But some work in cultural ecology took on a cybernetic character, conveying a sense that all the pieces of a culture meshed into a coherent, smooth-running, well-adapted and stable machine-like whole, with CULTURE functionally linked to environmental conditions and resource availability. This is apparent, for example, in Roy Rappaport's (1968) work on wild pigs, and the spiritual beliefs and rituals surrounding these resources in New Guinea.

At the same time, strict adherence to traditional ETHNOGRAPHY in cultural ecology at times meant that particular SOCIAL FORMATIONS were conceptualized rigidly as such,

independent and isolated from the rest of the world, with little or no consideration of or facility for the ways in which these ostensibly remote cultures articulate with social processes at broader SCALES of analysis. This, in turn, meant that cultural ecology provided little capacity for understanding POWER, the appropriation of surplus and valuation in the context of a global political economy, even when important linkages along these lines were recognized by cultural ecologists themselves (Robbins, 2004). This is a theme articulated well by one of Steward's students, Eric Wolf (1982), in his argument for the relevance of POLITICAL ECONOMY, and of the need for attention to the articulation of local social formations with broader social processes.

Cultural ecology's influence goes far beyond localized studies of non-industrial societies, however. As among the first fields to reverse academic specialization, and to seriously consider environmental change within a social science framework, and with an emphasis on careful, empirical observation and analysis, cultural ecology had an important influence in translating and reinforcing ENVIRONMENTALISM in the Anglo-American academy. Cultural ecologists in numerous instances have documented the high levels of sophistication and sustainability in many 'traditional' settings, questioning the apparent 'advancement' of market-guided and/or state-managed resource appropriation (e.g. Geertz, 1963). And some cultural ecologists, before even talk of a first world political ecology, began to apply their approaches in more industrialized settings, with important results (see, e.g., Bayliss-Smith, 1982). SP

cultural economy In mainstream economics, CULTURE and ECONOMY are kept largely apart, in the belief that economic activity follows its own rules and rationality. In contrast, heterodox approaches, tapping deep into the history of classical economics, have long argued that the economy draws on cultural inputs or is culturally embedded. Thus, attention has been drawn, *inter alia*, to such phenomena as the rise of the cultural industries, the role of SPECTACLE, advertising and desire in sustaining CONSUMPTION, the lubrication of economic relationships by TRUST and reciprocity, varieties of CAPITALISM explained by differences in national institutional and business cultures, and the role of culturally inflected routines and habits in influencing economic evolution. These various approaches acknowledge the existence of a tight link between culture and economy, but still continue to treat the two domains as separate entities, arguing that logics governing the two should not be conflated (Ray and Sayer, 1997). Indeed, many writers sympathetic to these approaches insist on the continued primacy of POLITICAL ECONOMY over cultural economy.

More recently, however, a second generation of cultural economy theorization has emerged, one that sees only a singular plane holding together hybrid inputs including abstract rules, historical legacies, symbolic and discursive narratives, social and cultural habits, material arrangements, emotions and aspirations (Callon, 1999; Du Gay and Pryke, 1999; Hetherington and Law, 1999). Still struggling for an exact vocabulary and dispersed across the social sciences, this approach sees economy as a cultural act and culture as an economic act, so that meeting material needs and making a profit or earning a living can be seen as part and parcel of seeking symbolic satisfaction, pleasure and power. Accordingly, in explaining the economics of production, for example, corporate values, workplace cultures, conventions of welfare and rituals of creativity can be shown to shape competitive potential, along with various rules of technological, organizational and market ordering. Similarly, in the economics of MARKETS, rules of value based on price and other forms of rating can be shown to weave in with consumer tastes, the seductions of organized spectacle and the market power of some economic actors.

This variant of the cultural economy approach is marked by a number of conceptual orientations with long histories in classical economic thought (for a synthesis, see Amin and Thrift, 2004). One concerns the absolute centrality of passions in the economy, from the libidinal energies and spectacle of consumption and possession that drive 'fast capitalism', through to the love of objects that now so powers wants and needs. A second orientation, which can be traced back to Adam Smith's emphasis on the role of empathy in making the market economy work, highlights the pivotal significance of moral values, as manifest in the market ethic itself and in the social conventions that justify particular mores of economic behaviour (hedonism, individualism, fast food as bad/good food, trade versus aid). Third, there is new work on the economics of knowledge that recognizes the centrality of creativity based on unconscious neural mobilizations, MATERIAL CULTURES and learning-by-doing in small communities of practice. A fourth orientation is to explain generalized trust in ways that supersede the emphasis on interpersonal dynamics found in earlier variants of cultural economy. For example, Seabright (2004) has argued that the option of intimacy among strangers in the market economy, in which multitudes of economic actors who do not know each other constantly jostle, is lubricated by many cultural institutions that have evolved over time, including the facility of laughter. A fifth orientation is to explain economic POWER less as a force possessed or wielded by some actors and institutions than as a diffuse and subtle form of cultural enrolment, scripted in the standards, rules and accounting measures that daily produce disciplined subjects and regulate economic life, or through particular narratives of what counts as significant in business journals, advertising scripts and stories of corporate prowess. Finally, the cultural-economy approach, following a long lineage of projection from particular situations (e.g. Marx's projections on capitalist futures based on the British experience) explores the integrative work done by readings of the economy (e.g. Daniel Bell on the service economy or Manuel Castells on the information economy).

This new body of thought, in summary, rethinks the economy as a culturally infused entity, based on the potentialities of passion, moral sentiments, soft knowledge, instituted trust, symptoms of normality and discursive forms of power. These are considered to drive economic life at all levels and manifestations. AA

Suggested reading
Amin and Thrift (2007).

cultural geography One of the most rapidly growing and energetic sub-fields in Anglophone GEOGRAPHY over the past 20 years. Many have written of a CULTURAL TURN in geography paralleling those in other social sciences. Often the subject of controversy over its approaches, claims and methods cultural geography has seen the reinvigoration of some topics and the development of whole new topics of geographic enquiry. Indeed, it may be that we can identify a recent 'culturalization' of many branches of geography, rather than simply a field of 'cultural geography' – thus, it is not always clear if the field is defined by CULTURE as the content of study, and what its limits might be, or the approach used. There is also a long history of the study of the geography of cultures that has had an

129

often-troubled relationship with the recent surge in interest in the field. So, for the sake of clarity, we shall start with these legacies, then move to the explosion of work in the 1990s and finally point to current fragmentations in the field.

Throughout most of the twentieth century, cultural geography existed as a sub-field in different traditions of geography that addressed 'the existence of a variegated landscape of differentially adapted human groups to their immediate environment' (Archer, 1993, p. 500). To draw out three approaches to this topic:

- In North American geography, the dominant tradition was the BERKELEY SCHOOL, built around the work of Carl Ortwin Sauer (1889–1975). So powerful was this tradition that around the middle of the twentieth century cultural geography was often used to label all HUMAN GEOGRAPHY in US universities. Drawing on the work especially of emerging anthropological perspectives on MATERIAL CULTURE, from the likes of Franz Boas (1858–1942), Sauer added a geographical focus on landscape, drawn from German geography's work on LANDSCHAFT. His most famous formulation on the MORPHOLOGY of LANDSCAPE (in his essay of that name in 1925) described the CULTURAL LANDSCAPE, where culture was the agent and landscape the medium. Work in this tradition charted the origins and DIFFUSION of cultures around the globe from CULTURAL HEARTHS. In this, it tracked the movement mostly via material artefacts, taken as metonyms of cultures in which they were embedded. Some work developed a notion of cultural areas dominated by one cultural group occupying an area. The focus on culture as an agent led to accusations that it was inventing a 'superorganic' entity rather than focusing on the mixed, changeable and contested experience of people (Duncan, 1980). Despite its empirical attention to processes of DIFFUSION and change in cultures contacting different environments, it tended to a singular view of culture held by and defining a group.
- The focus on the mutual shaping of people and place was echoed in European traditions in cultural geography. The ANNALES SCHOOL that developed in France from the work of Paul Vidal de la Blache (1845–1918) is claimed by cultural, and by SOCIAL and HISTORICAL GEOGRAPHY. It paid close attention to linkage of people and place through 'GENRES DE VIE'; that is, the ways of everyday life. Exemplary works such as Le Roy Ladurie's (1966) Les Paysans de Languedoc charted the intimate connections of the rhythms of daily life and the environment over the long durée, creating a 'seamless robe' of people and place. Vidal de la Blache (1903) summarized this process as follows:

It is man who reveals a country's individuality by moulding it to his own use. He establishes a connection between unrelated features, substituting for the random effects of local circumstances a systematic cooperation of forces. Only then does a country acquire a specific character, differentiating it from others, till at length it becomes, as it were, a medal struck in the likeness of a people.

The focus was on ordinary folk and everyday cultures rather than high culture. Perhaps the greatest studies building from these traditions, that are still causing controversy, were those of Fernand Braudel (1902–85), whose magisterial works of the shared development of a Mediterranean culture (see Braudel and Reynolds, 1975 [original French 1949]) – based around olives, wine and grain, and the long-term patterns of trade – remain scholarly landmarks. These works echoed the studies of Frédéric le Play (1806–82), who developed a geographical account of France around the categories of Place–Work–Folk. His work was picked up by the British planner and biologist Patrick Geddes, and led to the foundation of the Le Play Society that sponsored a range of geographical expeditions during the mid-twentieth century. They share the vision of groups creating a cultural HOMELAND as 'an area carved out by axe and plough, which belongs to the people who have carved it out' (Olwig, 1993, p. 311).

- In British geography, a regional approach was inspired by Hettner's Länderkunde schema (see Hettner, 1907) of natural base up to social and finally cultural superstructure – starting from geology, then TOPOGRAPHY, CLIMATE, natural RESOURCES and finally leading to settlement and human culture adapted to those circumstances (Heimatkunde). A similarly CHOROLOGICAL approach in Swedish geography focused on hembydsforskning (home area studies), and drew upon ethnological studies of material culture and LANGUAGE to define cultural regions (Crang, 2000). In Britain, Geddes' influence produced a regional survey approach that emphasized a visual integration of the landscape as a method of finding unity (Matless, 1992), while the local history work on landscapes of W.G. Hoskins focused on studies that sought to capture the identity and spirit of specific regions through their landscapes.

These classic traditions focused upon the commonalities in the landscape and rural, historical or traditional forms. Criticism of this tendency mounted through the last quarter of the twentieth century. First, HUMANISTIC GEOGRAPHY challenged the lack of concern with, and scope for, individual interpretation and actions. Authors looked at the meaning of places for specific people, and the EMOTIONAL GEOGRAPHIES of cultures found in the bond with specific places and their GENIUS LOCI (e.g. Pocock, 1982). Second, RADICAL, FEMINIST and MARXIST GEOGRAPHY criticized the assumptions of organic wholeness given to cultures, and pointed to the internal divisions, contradictions and conflicts while, moreover, pointing to more contemporary and urban formations. Third, the political context and implications of European traditions has been examined. Thus the work of a German geographer such as Franz Petri, writing between the world wars, examined the spread of Germanic culture from a supposed ancestral cultural hearth around post-Roman Frankish peoples. Based upon an examination of field and PLACE NAMES, taken as indicators of Germanic culture, he could label '[t]he character of Frankish settlement in Walloon and Northern France [as] utterly Germanic' (Ditt, 2001, p. 245) – a highly charged verdict, given the territorial disputes around Germany. This highlights the problematic relationship of artefact to cultures – choosing certain things as indicators of a culture, but leaving other things as analytically insignificant, reveals political dimensions and choices in the analysis.

To these issues was added engagement with other sub-disciplines and fields outside geography, which – in the last two decades of the twentieth century – were also undergoing their own cultural turns. We might, for the sake of argument, characterize the work that followed in two strands, the first tending to respond to developments in social geography and sociology, and the second as drawing from the radical ends of the arts and humanities. Together, they have often been labelled the 'New Cultural Geography', which began as something of a rebellion to the above traditions but rapidly swept on to transform other sub-disciplines as well.

The first strand drew on work from BEHAVIOURAL GEOGRAPHY, to which it added the long tradition of ETHNOGRAPHY from the CHICAGO SCHOOL of urban sociology, and arguments over the sociology of culture emerging in the 1970s and through the 1980s. This inspired a rich vein of work on urban cultures and subcultures in modern EVERYDAY LIFE. The latter were seen as resistance or TRANSGRESSION, contesting the categories of the majority culture. Culture was no longer seen as somehow a 'natural' property of a group but, rather, the medium of power, oppression, contestation and resistance. Much of this work grew from an engagement with the Birmingham Centre for Contemporary Cultural Studies, and worked to look at the role of culture in securing and maintaining the HEGEMONY of dominant groups. It began to push at the cultural construction of social categories (such as age, RACE, CLASS, SEXUALITY or GENDER) and the ways in which these came to signify particular meanings and be connected with specific ways of life (e.g. Bell and Valentine, 1995; Kofman, 1998; Skelton and Valentine, 1998; Pred, 2000).

The second strand of work was differentiated not so much by topic as by method, drawing from the arts and HUMANITIES. Work here drew on critical studies of often high cultural artefacts such as ART and LITERATURE, but moved these techniques to include more popular cultural forms such as FILM or other MEDIA. Rather than using these cultural forms as sources of 'data' about what occurred in places, or as rich evocations of emotional resonance (which had been the tendency in HUMANISTIC GEOGRAPHY; e.g. Pocock, 1981), it unpacked the spatialities of the materials to examine what work they did in representing and shaping cultures. Thus landscape paintings were examined not just for content, but the way in which they framed the landscape – indeed, created 'landscape' as a visual category. Often using a linguistic approach, studies treated cultural artefacts as TEXTS that could be read and interpreted to uncover hidden meanings and the imprints of the POWER that shaped them and which they embodied. In this, it drew from the techniques of DECONSTRUCTION and POST-STRUCTURALISM, which focused on how texts shape meaning through processes of exclusion or repression, whereby they downplay or negate some possible interpretations while foregrounding others. The

131

recovery of these hidden meanings was thus linked to recovering the voices and views of silenced and oppressed groups, especially in studies informed by POST-COLONIALISM (Blunt and McEwan, 2002). This latter work also inspired studies of cultural definition and difference (e.g. Anderson, 2007), especially the creation of OTHERNESS. Here, the focus became how cultural artefacts were not simply indicators of cultural belonging, waiting to be analysed by academics, but were actively used to signal and create identities by ordinary people.

These two approaches often fused and cross-pollinated. For instance, work on urban ETHNICITY moved from SEGREGATION analyses, of distributions of peoples, to studies of the lived experience of those cultures, how they signified belonging and how they signified exclusion. Rather than now examining the distribution of cultures seen as discrete entities occupying more or less exclusive TERRITORIES, cultural geography engaged with the study of connections, movements and circulations of meanings in TRANSNATIONALISM and DIASPORIC cultures created in the modern global world. These often form examples of cultural HYBRIDITY and hybridization, which confound the exclusions and repressions of hegemonic cultures that sought to maintain a link of people (singular) and territory. Studies saw the multiple categories of identity connected and inflected by people's local milieu (e.g., on youth, class and race, Nayak, 2003), or looked at the fluidities and fixities of labelling and categorization in transforming urban milieux (Pred, 2000).

Beyond issues of ethnicity, cultural geography moved to explore many other aspects of IDENTITY politics (Keith and Pile 1993; Pile and Keith, 1997), such as SEXUALITY and DISABILITY, which became ever more salient in the closing years of the twentieth century. The main focus was on practices of inclusion or exclusion, belonging, resistance and identity. A major strand of work emerged around the different forms and modalities of CONSUMPTION and how this related to people's identities.

The focus on identity and the meaning of social activities was transplanted into other formerly discrete sub-disciplines. Thus it became increasingly common to see studies of rural cultural geographies, concerning issues of Otherness and identity (e.g. Cloke and Little, 1997), and urban geographies of cultures, political geographies about identity or using similar methods in deconstructing

key texts in a CRITICAL GEOPOLITICS. In ECONOMIC GEOGRAPHY there was a double focus, both on cultural forms in the CULTURAL ECONOMY (e.g. Amin and Thrift, 2003) and on 'enculturing' approaches – focusing upon processes of meaning and belonging within both firms and markets. In some cases this blurring into other fields has been controversial and has met with hostility from those who regard with suspicion the topical focus (as not being of great importance) or the methods as lacking in either rigour or the appearance of rigour sufficient to persuade policy-makers. There have thus been arguments about the cultural turn going 'too far' and undermining former assumptions and unities (Martin and Sunley, 2001). The incorporation of cultural issues has had an energizing effect on other sub-fields, but has also meant that cultural geography's own distinctiveness has become less clear. As a sub-discipline it has been relatively unconcerned, if not antipathetic, to policing the boundaries of enquiry, especially given how it has shown that definitions enact power relations and often work to exclude groups. Likewise, it has continued to draw catholically from other disciplines, blurring the edges of geography.

Within the sub-discipline, a recent series of debates have begun to challenge some of the sureties that have emerged over the past 20 years. First, while criticisms of IDEALISM have long been levelled at cultural geography, often in the name of re-prioritizing other categories of analysis in the name of HISTORICAL MATERIALISM, a new set of theorizations of MATERIALISM have emerged within the sub-field itself. These often refuse the CARTESIAN divide into SUBJECT and object, and look at thinking as a material process embedded in the world. They also attempt to provide renewed senses of AGENCY for the material world, rather than just focusing on human agency. Some work challenges the anthropocentric basis of *human* geography, and culture as a human artefact, drawing on POSTHUMANISM and driving renewed studies into ANIMAL geographies. Second, debates have contested the focus upon signification and meaning within cultural geography. Instead, recent work flags up the role of habit and routine focusing on the unconscious and preconscious shaping of identities and actions. Third, the focus on the textual mode of interpretation has been argued to privilege REPRESENTATION as a social process. Instead, NON-REPRESENTATIONAL THEORY focuses upon the PERFORMANCE and enactment of identities. This rematerialization and rethinking of cultural geography often returns to issues of dwelling and the relationship of people, but not peoples, to places drawing inspiration from post-Heideggerian and Deleuzian philosophy. It challenges a preoccupation with representational forms and meaning leading to the social construction of identities. Instead, it focuses upon the connection of material and social process in forging identities in practices and actions. These current debates promise to be as unruly as previous developments, drawing widely from outside the discipline and speaking to topics across sub-disciplines.   MC

Suggested reading
Anderson, Domosh, Pile and Thrift (2002); Atkinson, Jackson, Sibley and Washbourne (2007); Blunt, Gruffudd, May. and Ogborn (2003); Crang (1998); Mitchell (2000); Shurmer-Smith (2002).

cultural hearth   The place of origin of a cultural system. This concept was introduced into American CULTURAL GEOGRAPHY by Carl Ortwin Sauer (1952; see also 1969) and was important in the early work of the BERKELEY SCHOOL. Sauer borrowed it from late-nineteenth-century German ANTHROPOGEOGRAPHY, along with the related notions of culture area, CULTURAL LANDSCAPE and cultural diffusion. For many in the Berkeley School, the term was used primarily to refer to the originary point of agricultural systems that had subsequently diffused outwards. For others, it represented the heart of cultural regions more broadly defined (Wagner and Mikesell, 1962).   JSD

Suggested reading
Leighly (1969).

cultural landscape   Conventionally, a principal object of study in CULTURAL GEOGRAPHY. The classic definition is Carl Ortwin Sauer's (1963b [1925] – see figure):

> The cultural landscape is fashioned from a natural landscape by a cultural group. Culture is the agent, the natural area the medium, the cultural landscape is the result. Under the influence of a given culture, itself changing through time, the landscape undergoes development, passing through phases, and probably reaching ultimately the end of its cycle of development.

This definition reflects not only Sauer's personal context and scholarly concerns (see BERKELEY SCHOOL), but also theoretical issues that remain critical to discussions of cultural landscape. His description of cultural landscape as subject to evolutionary change echoes W.M. Davis' cycle of natural landscape evolution, but Sauer was explicitly concerned to counter ENVIRONMENTAL DETERMINISM and drew upon German studies of *Kulturlandschaft* that stressed the mutual shaping of people (*Volk*) and land in the creation of dwelling (*Heimat*) (Olwig, 2002). Sauer thus stressed CULTURE as a geographical agent, although the physical environment retained a central significance as the medium with and through which human cultures act (see CULTURE AREA). Hence such elements as TOPOGRAPHY, soils, watercourses, plants and ANIMALS were incorporated into studies of the cultural landscape insofar as they evoked human responses and ADAPTATIONS, or had been altered by human activity.

Today, Sauer's neat distinction between NATURE and CULTURE has been largely abandoned in favour of a 'social nature' (see also PRODUCTION OF NATURE): the *tabula rasa* of a 'natural landscape' upon which 'culture' inscribes itself ignores the constancy of environmental change, and the dialectic of 'nature' and 'culture' is historically constructed. All LANDSCAPES are at once natural and cultural (Cosgrove, 1998 [1984]). Furthermore, contemporary CULTURAL ECOLOGY has deepened our understanding of the complexities of cultural landscape change, and POST-COLONIAL-ISM has reworked perspectives on the landscape impacts of COLONIALISM (Sluyter, 2001, 2002; Mitchell, 2002e [1994]). In consequence, greater attention is now given to grids of POWER, to cultural contestation and to the active role played by the diverse 'insiders' of landscape, so that Sauer's idea of a climax cultural landscape swept away by a rejuvenated one has been replaced by notions of a more mediated, HYBRID and transcultural landscape (see also TRANSCULTURATION).

The emphasis on landscape's representational and semiotic qualities, particularly in studies informed by art history and ICONO-GRAPHY, has led to calls for renewed attention to its substantive aspects: its materialities and continued significance for LIFEWORLDS. While cultural landscape remains closely identified with the tangible, visible scene, landscapes are increasingly read by geographers as moments in a networked process of *social* relations that stretch across TIME and SPACE (see also SENSE OF PLACE). Closely connected to these developments, a nuanced use of PHENOMENOLOGY is apparent in some recent studies of landscape in which narrative

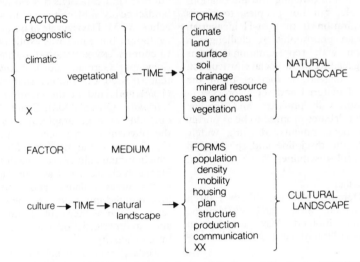

cultural landscape *Natural landscape and cultural landscape* (after Sauer, 1963 [1925])

strategies are used to explore and express the co-constitution of material and experiential space (Wylie, 2002b). Attention to myth, MEMORY and 'haunting' embodied in the material landscape is another expression of the retreat from an exclusive focus on REPRESENTATION in cultural landscape studies, but this is also another insistent restatement of the importance of historical apprehension that was the hallmark of Sauer's original prospectus: but now understood in radically different terms.   DEC

Suggested reading
Béguin (1995); Duncan, Johnson and Schein (2004).

cultural politics The processes through which 'meanings are negotiated and relations of dominance and subordination are defined and contested' (Jackson, 1989, p. 2). An insistence that the cultural *is* political, involving relations of POWER and conflicting interests between different groups, has been central to much work in cultural studies and, more recently, CULTURAL GEOGRAPHY. It depends upon a view of CULTURE as plural, as socially produced and struggled over. Attention has focused in particular on the role of SPACE and PLACE in the construction of meanings and identities as well as processes of RESISTANCE and TRANSGRESSION, in recognition that '[c]ulture wars are real wars' (Mitchell, 2000, p. 287).   DP

Suggested reading
Mitchell (2000).

cultural turn A set of intellectual developments that led to issues of CULTURE becoming central in HUMAN GEOGRAPHY since the late 1980s. The renewed interest in questions of culture is not confined to human geography, but within the discipline the cultural turn usually refers a number of related trends:

(1) the emergence of a 'new' CULTURAL GEOGRAPHY;
(2) the increasing attention to culture in sub-fields such as economic, environmental, historical and social geographies;
(3) claims that culture has become a more important factor in the world itself – for example, in economic processes or in driving political conflict.

Theoretically, the cultural turn has promoted a greater degree of pluralism in human geography, drawing on concepts from other disciplines and focusing attention on multiple dimensions of difference (including GENDER, RACE and SEXUALITY). Methodologically, the cultural turn has encouraged the use of a wider range of interpretative and QUALITATIVE METHODS. Epistemologically, the cultural turn has underwritten a commitment to investigating the contingent and constructed qualities of phenomena. It has also gone hand in hand with a 'geographical turn' across the HUMANITIES and social sciences more generally.

But the cultural turn has also been criticized for distracting geographers from undertaking research that is useful for policy-makers, and for retreating from the 'materialist' analysis of power under CAPITALISM. As these objections show, the cultural turn is embedded in wider disputes about the relevance of human geography research and teaching (Barnett, 2004a), but both these criticisms underestimate the ways in which cultural turns have been pursued far beyond the academy and in the very two spheres that the (different) critics identify. Thus CULTURAL ECONOMY has demonstrated multiple ways in which 'fast capitalism' has taken a cultural turn that involves not only the commodification of culture but also the enrolment of cultural knowledges in economic activities, and still more recently the US military has pursued a 'cultural turn' in its search for a new counter-insurgency strategy in its continued military operations in Afghanistan and Iraq (Gregory, 2008b). CB

Suggested reading
Barnett (2004c).

culture Famously described by Raymond Williams (1981) as one of the most complex words in the English language, culture is also one of the most influential, yet elusive, concepts in the HUMANITIES and social sciences. Williams' METHODOLOGY, almost philological in its attention to the historical accretion of meaning around words, is indicative of a distinctive style of conceptualization that any account of culture could do well to respect. Rather than look for a single, essential meaning behind the complexity of usages of 'culture', Williams (ibid., p. 92) held that the complexity 'is not finally in the word but in the problems which its variations of use significantly indicate'. These problems include the relationship between the general and the particular, individual and society, structure and agency, autonomy and authority. What emerges from the history of 'culture' is not a word that designates an ONTOLOGICAL entity, but a complex noun of PROCESS, whose simplest derivation is related to the idea of cultivation. In short, culture best thought of as *a process, not a thing*. Accordingly, Williams identified three broad usages of culture: (i) a general process of intellectual, spiritual development; (ii) culture as 'a way of life' characteristic of particular groups, whether nations, classes or subcultures; and (iii) works and practices of intellectual and artistic activity, such as music, opera, television and film, and literature (ibid., p. 90). This final sense is derived from the first, since these works and practices are the means of sustaining the process of development designated in (i).

In HUMAN GEOGRAPHY, the concept of culture has had a variable history. In the tradition of American cultural geography associated with Carl Ortwin Sauer, culture was rarely an object of explicit conceptual reflection. This approach concentrated upon the empirical scrutiny of MATERIAL CULTURE, understood as expressions of unified cultural systems. Such a view was criticized by Duncan (1980) for holding a 'superorganic' understanding that reified culture as an independent entity with explanatory force (see BERKELEY SCHOOL). This critique helped inaugurate the development of a so-called *new cultural geography*, and a broader CULTURAL TURN in human geography that drew on concepts of culture from a range of disciplines such as anthropology, semiotics, cultural studies, art history and literary theory. There have been two broad stages in this centring of culture as an object of conceptual debate in human geography. The first stage involved the assertion of the relevance of cultural or broadly interpretative approaches in the discipline. This stage ushered in a number of approaches that emphasized the representational dimensions of cultural processes, and which also tended to be strongly holistic, even functionalist, in their understandings of the relationships between culture and other processes. The second stage of theorizing culture in human geography has concentrated on overcoming the closures inadvertently set in place by the relative success of the first stage.

The new cultural geography that emerged in the 1980s, and the cultural turn that followed in the wake of this and debates around POSTMODERNISM, saw the concept of culture subjected to explicit conceptual reflection by geographers. In one strand of research, LANDSCAPE was re-conceptualized as a 'way of seeing', or a 'TEXT', or a 'symbolic form' or in terms of ICONOGRAPHY (see Cosgrove and Daniels, 1988). These moves were often inflected by traditions of MARXISM, but specifically by Marxist *cultural theory* that extended beyond the confines of the Marxist *political economy* that predominated in human geography (cf. CRITICAL THEORY). This relationship has become increasingly strained, however, as the difficulties of theorizing relationships of agency, determination and meaning from within the Marxist tradition have become more acutely obvious. One outcome of this reconceptualization of landscape has been an anchoring of the concept of culture around a notion of REPRESENTATION understood by analogy with seeing, imagination and vision. This visual account of landscape and culture has

135

been the occasion for sustained critical thought (Rose, 1993), but this debate about culture and visuality has done little to contest the narrowly visual construal of representation bequeathed by this strand of the new cultural geography (see also VISION AND VISUALITY).

A second strand of research, emerging from SOCIAL GEOGRAPHY, drew on concepts of culture from the new field of cultural studies. Jackson (2003 [1989]) explicitly drew on Williams' *cultural materialism* to outline a programme for a revivified cultural geography. Cultural materialism derives from Williams's argument that 'culture is ordinary', and builds on the notion that culture should be understood as a 'whole way of life'; that is, an active, lived tradition of meanings or 'structure of feeling'. Williams drew on diverse sources (e.g. conservative philosopher Edmund Burke and liberal critic F.R. Leavis), but gave them a populist twist. Cultural materialism was intended as a contribution to, but also a move beyond, Marxist understandings of the determinate relationships between ECONOMY and culture. Rather than formulating the differing degrees of relative autonomy of levels of a SOCIAL FORMATION, Williams simply collapsed the BASE/SUPERSTRUCTURE distinction of classical Marxism altogether. He did so by extending the notion of 'MATERIALISM', understood by analogy as any process of active making, to cultural life as well, arguing that culture was the practical activity of *producing* meanings. This move effectively brackets rather than resolves the key problem referred to by Marxist accounts of materialism, which is not the problem of the ontological status of culture or economy at all, but the problem of theorizing complex causal relations between different practices. Cultural materialism also informs the idea of a 'circuit of culture', which has also been influential in human geography. This model integrates different aspects of cultural processes – production and distribution, the 'text', CONSUMPTION and EVERYDAY LIFE – into a series of discrete but related 'moments' in an ongoing circulation of meaning-making (du Gay, Hall, Janes, McKay and Negus, 1997). Theoretically, the 'circuit of culture' privileges meaning as the essential quality of cultural processes. Methodologically, it provides a practical means of undertaking empirical work on specific cultural practices while remaining true to the axiom of cultural practices that need to be understood in relation to the totality of other practices of which they are a part.

These two strands of thought on culture (in terms of visual representation and in terms of meaning-making) have served as an important route towards a widespread engagement with POST-STRUCTURALISM in human geography, with its emphasis on exposing the contingency of supposedly natural forms through the deployment of interpretive methodologies. Culture has been consistently construed in representational terms by geographers (and according to an impoverished understanding of representation at that); or in terms of the intangible or ideational aspects of processes that are somehow realized or materialized in some concrete form. This first stage of theorizing culture in geography has therefore been supplanted by a second, more critical stage in which the limitations of these concepts of culture have been challenged. One feature of this second stage has been the ascendancy of an ontological register of theory, involving the abstract delimitation of the 'the cultural' from 'the economic', 'the representational' from 'materiality', or 'the human' from 'the non-human', followed by the assertion of their inevitable entanglement.

The starkest example of this ontologization of theory is Mitchell's (2000) argument that 'there is no such thing as culture'. This claim selectively invokes an ESSENTIALIST criterion of definition to assess the validity of the concept of culture, which – it is supposed – must refer to an ontologically independent thing-like entity in order to have any salience. On these grounds, Mitchell concluded that ' "culture" has no ontological basis' (ibid., 12), and that culture 'represents no identifiable process' (ibid., 74). Mitchell also argues that the concept of culture is used as an explanatory category in both cultural studies and in human geography. This claim wilfully overlooks the processual, action-oriented and practice-focused conceptualizations of culture in both fields. In place of these, Mitchell recommends an explicitly reductionist model of culture understood as merely a medium for symbolizing more fundamental economic, political and social processes. There is really just 'a very powerful *ideology* of culture' (ibid., 12), developed and deployed to control, order and define 'others' 'in the name of power and profit' (ibid., 75). Despite its ostensibly Marxist credentials, this approach to culture negates a long-tradition of Western Marxism, one in which IDEOLOGY and culture are explicitly defined against this sort of explanatory REDUCTIONISM (see also CRITICAL THEORY). The idea that culture is merely a medium through which the prevailing order of things is naturalized (i.e. a mode of *reification*) is a throwback to the nineteenth century, and does not stand up after the reorientation of questions of culture and ideology away from 'consciousness' towards 'SUBJECTIVITY' that the twentieth-century tradition of Western Marxism did much to inaugurate.

Mitchell's materialist *correction* of what he claims are politically quiescent concepts of culture is just one example of the vocabulary of 'materiality' coming to the fore in recent theorizations of culture in human geography. Calls for the 'rematerializing' of cultural geography (Jackson, 2000) now abound. This usually means looking more closely at material cultures of artefacts and objects; at issues of embodiment; and at the entanglement of 'the cultural' and 'the economic'. The ascendancy of this ontological register goes along with attempts to supersede the narrow understandings of representation, vision, meaning and textuality that geographers constructed through their initial engagements with post-structuralism. But the 'materialist' turn compounds the limitations of that construal, reinstalling dualisms between ideal and material, subject and object, and the representational and the non-representational. Calls for the rematerialization of culture, or indeed of human geography in general, give the impression that the value of a concept lies in its ability to disclose some level of ontological existence. But culture is not really an ontological category at all; it is a functional category of attribution, in the sense that to call something cultural is to ascribe a particular set of purposes and qualities to it, not to attribute a finite set of characteristics that define its essence.

The challenge to concepts of culture in human geography is not a matter of getting the correct ontology. It lies, rather, in loosening the hold exerted by *holistic* conceptions of culture that allow various sorts of exorbitant claims of political relevance to be ascribed to cultural analysis. Culture is often ascribed a *particular* sense (as one aspect of meaning of human affairs), and a very *general* and even *totalizing* (in which it is assumed that whole ways of life are unified and integrated through norms, meanings and values). The idea of 'CULTURAL POLITICS' often rests on claims that social totalities are in some way integrated, refracted or mediated through culture. There is a paradox here: holistic concepts of culture as meaning and symbolization help to acknowledge the political salience of cultural processes, but only at the cost of invoking undifferentiated concepts of POWER. By conflating politics with culture, this leads to the

failure to think about the consequences of what it might mean if politics needs to be *supplemented* (cf. DECONSTRUCTION) by cultural processes of symbolization, representation or mediation in the first place. What is left aside as a result is the question of what sorts of *powers* are intrinsic to cultural processes themselves – powers such as authority, charisma, desire, feeling or seduction.

Three overlapping trends are likely to inflect the conceptualization of culture in human geography in the near future. In each case, it is by returning to a sense of culture as practice that progress is likely to be made. First, there is interest in concepts of culture that draw on Foucault's ideas of GOVERNMENTALITY. In this approach, culture is defined as a set of aesthetic practices for cultivating the capacities for self-regulation (Bennett, 1998). This approach explicitly builds upon a genealogical analysis of the accretion of meanings of 'culture' as an independent and autonomous field. It reads this as an index of the practical deployment of culture as a medium for 'acting on the social'. This line of thought is open to an instrumentalist interpretation in which culture is understood as a medium for legitimizing or resisting the power of the STATE or CAPITAL (see INSTRUMENTALISM). But its real potential lies in disclosing some of the powers that are specific to cultural processes. One feature of the modern concept of culture that this approach focuses upon is the antithetical and self-divided structure of modern definitions of the term: not only is culture defined against SOCIETY, anarchy or NATURE; but it is also internally divided against itself, into high and low, elite and popular or mass. This 'splitting of culture' (Bennett, 1998, p. 82) is crucial to understanding the *powers of culture*: it defines a range of resources that can be deployed to transform conduct and behaviour (e.g. a canon of great works, or various repertoires of cultural judgement); and it also defines a range of domains that can be transformed through the application of these resources (e.g. 'cultures of poverty', 'institutional cultures', 'the culture of schooling'). This analysis of culture as both a medium and object of transformation owes a great deal to a tradition of anti-colonial and post-colonial cultural theory (see POST-COLONIALISM: see also Said, 1993). However, the strong Foucauldian inflection of the concept of culture implies a less holistic imagination of the relationship between culture and power than is implied by concepts such as cultural IMPERIALISM, HEGEMONY and ideology (Barnett, 2001).

A second area in which the powers of culture are foregrounded follows from and develops Stuart Hall's seminal analysis of the concept of *articulation*. Grossberg (1993, p. 4) develops an explicitly 'spatial materialism' that also builds on Deleuzian thought to argue that the concept of culture needs to be changed from that of 'the field in which power is symbolized to a set of practices which apply power'. This is related to a shift from the interpretative apprehension of meanings to a consideration of the production of relations, and recasts cultural studies as 'a theory of contexts'. There is considerable potential here for geographical research, as there is in the closely related reorientation of cultural analysis away from narrowly construed issues of meaning towards embodied practices of feeling, shame and compassion (e.g. Berlant, 2004). The third area of growing interest lies in moves to rethink culture as a field of PER-FORMANCE and action (e.g. Hastrup, 2004). Here, again, there is a move away from holistic accounts of how culture symbolizes and integrates other social relations, towards an emphasis on the specific powers of cultural practices, and suggesting new models of relations and agency in the process (Strathern, 1995).

The odyssey of the concept of culture in human geography is likely to continue awhile yet, but do not expect anyone to arrive at a singular, ontologically robust definition. Duncan and Duncan (2004a) recommend the self-consciously eclectic combination of theories of culture backed up by empirical analysis, and this seems more in the spirit of the traditions of cultural studies and anthropology from which human geographers have drawn so much inspiration. Flexibility is one of the reasons why 'culture' can serve as a useful *lingua franca* between otherwise disparate and disconnected fields. But the continuing influence of cultural analysis in the discipline depends on the acknowledgement that there is more to culture than meaning and representation; and more to culture than the reproduction of or resistance to power relations constituted by more fundamental processes. Above all, it requires a greater degree of concern with what cultural studies can teach us about how to *do* theory itself – that theory is not about arriving at essentialist criteria or the vain search for ontological clarity, but is about appreciating the *essentially contested* qualities of concepts, and analysing what is most at stake in these disagreements.   CB

Suggested reading
Frow (1997); Johnson, Chambers, Raghuram and Tincknell (2004); Mulhern (2000); Robbins (1993); Williams (1981); Yudice (2003).

culture area A geographical REGION over which homogeneity in measurable cultural traits may be identified. Contiguous zones identified within a culture area are *core*, over which the culture in question has exclusive or quasi-exclusive influence, *domain*, over which the identifying traits are dominant but not exclusive, and *realm*, over which the traits are visible but subordinate to those of other culture groups. The classic study is Meinig's (1965) identification of a Mormon culture area centred on the Great Basin of Utah. Today, the concept is little used in GEOGRAPHY, as culture is identified more closely with PROCESS, connection and NETWORK than with the areal boundedness of mappable cultural markers.   DCO

cybernetics Derived from the Greek '*kybernetes*', meaning 'steersman', it sees systems as learning and self-regulating. The term 'cybernetics' was first used by the INFORMATION THEORY pioneer Norbert Wiener in his 1948 book *Cybernetics: or control and communication in the animal and the machine*. The term has often impacted on geography through compound forms such as 'cybernetic organism', abbreviated to CYBORG, and 'cybernetic space', abbreviated to CYBERSPACE. However, two specific inflections of the term in GEOGRAPHY are worth noting in themselves.

First, the term has literal and metaphoric resonance with work that has used MODELS and algorithmic programming to simulate geographical phenomena. The weaker version of this is an EPISTEMOLOGICAL inclusion of FEEDBACK in models. ALGORITHMS as series of calculations or procedures can be sequences where each step depends upon the previous ones. Sophisticated AGENT-BASED MODELLING thus has co-dependent multiple calculations. The stronger version is an ONTOLOGICAL statement that sees the world as operating as, or analogous to, a NEURAL NETWORK. Thus the world can be seen as operating like information passing through a system. Cybernetics focuses upon the relationships of these parts to see how the whole system is controlled or governed. This has the virtue of moving away from a CARTESIAN division of thought and the world, by insisting on seeing the world as a thinking, REFLEXIVE entity. However, it also risks reducing thought to a communication system and providing a mechanistic view of the world.

Second, cybernetic space has been used in distinction to the abridged CYBERSPACE to emphasize the way in which electronic communication and information processing capacities interact with the real world (Mitra and Schwarz, 2001). Far from creating a separate virtual realm, information processing capacities are regularly embedded in everyday devices so that they are able to respond and either be programmed or learn about patterns of use – offering the prospect of a world of 'ubiquitous computing' (sometimes abbreviated to 'ubicomp'). Increasingly, life in the urbanized WEST depends on these embedded processors, which regulate temperatures, elevators, traffic and an array of taken-for-granted processes. With the variety of wireless technologies, devices can communicate with each other without the user necessarily being aware that an automated electronic conversation is occurring. They use 'soft' adaptive computational processing that creates 'a technical substrate of unconscious meaning and activity' embedded in the environment (Thrift and French, 2002, pp. 312, 322). These devices would create 'smart' environments or 'ambient intelligence' that can keep track of users and will tailor interactions to suit the users. Thus they will communicate and remember past purchases, preferences, previous visits and past actions. This, the designers believe, will be used to provide customized menus or facilities. Cybernetics points out that this builds adaptive, reflexive capacity into the very environment, rather than vesting it solely in human agents.   MC

Suggested reading
Andrejevic (2003, 2005); Cuff (2003); McCullough (2004); Thrift (2004).

cyberspace   A term that has followed a rapid arc from subcultural obscurity to media ubiquity, and is now often seen as academically misleading. It was famously coined in the novel *Neuromancer* by William Gibson, first published in 1984 (see Gibson, 1986). In his novel, he offered a futuristic vision:

> Cyberspace. A consensual hallucination experienced daily by billions of legitimate operators, in every nation, by children being taught mathematical concepts ... A graphic representation of data abstracted from banks of every computer in the human system. Unthinkable complexity. Lines of light ranged in the nonspace of the mind, clusters and constellations of data. Like city lights, receding into the distance ...

Gibson was writing (on a Remington typewriter, before the first widely available Graphical User Interfaces even appeared on desktop computers) about the emergence of a networked and immersive environment. Gibson's vision is replete with spatial METAPHORS and imaginaries for interactive fora created out of data and information. In other novels, he models online worlds on the walled city of Kowloon (*Idoru*) or a variety of urban dystopias.

The use of cyberspace in this phase was connected to dystopian cyberpunk science fiction that broke from conventions of seeing technology as promising an ever-brighter and cleaner MODERNITY (Burrows, 1997; Featherstone and Burrows, 1997; Kitchin and Kneale, 2002), to one that saw it as connected to or enabling social and personal fragmentation, woven amidst LANDSCAPES striated by effects of POWER and INNOVATION, but also decay and dispossession.

This gave impetus to seeing flows and exchanges of data and information not merely through SPACE but as creating online worlds where data were manipulated as virtual artefacts (see also VIRTUAL REALITY). The representations and MAPS of cyberspace created by programmers and writers did indeed precede the TERRITORY in Baudrillard's sense (see also SIMULACRA) – they were vital in its creation, in giving information specific forms and idioms for use. The mapping of cyberspace spawned new technologies to locate and understand data, and set up an intriguing dialogue with cartographic concepts now applied to imagined objects (see Crampton, 2003; Dodge and Kitchin, 2001a).

From this beginning, cyberspace entered wider academic and popular parlance, along with a string of other spatial metaphors for information NETWORKS. Thus the 1990s saw the rise of discourses imagining what Kitchin (1998) called the 'world in the wires' through spatial metaphors such as 'chat rooms', informational highways, 'electronic frontiers' and 'cybersalons' (see VIRTUAL GEOGRAPHIES). Indeed, new virtual worlds were designed where 'avatars' or online representations of users could interact in virtual realms (see, e.g., Anders, 1998). The possibilities for new realms of interaction attracted a great deal of attention in the mid-1990s. The possibilities of playing with IDENTITIES such as GENDER ascriptions were pursued alongside questions of the formation of online COMMUNITIES without spatial proximity in the real world. Far from the cyberpunk chaos of early accounts, many online worlds developed in the new millennia became mainstream, and quite suburban and conventional (with popular online environments such as Second Life having more than seven and half million users in 2007, and a slogan 'Your world. Your imagination' suggesting that most users had fairly conventional imaginations), while others retained a focus on gaming. Meanwhile, online sources of information have become as usual and familiar as traditional MEDIA – with online versions of conventional media and alternative media rescaling audiences, while the 'blogosphere' provides alternative fora (see, e.g., Chang, 2005). Other new media are woven into our everyday lives as part and parcel of our normal, material lives (see, e.g., Morley, 2003; Yoon, 2003):

> The 1990s were about the virtual. We were fascinated by the new virtual spaces made possible by computer technologies. Images of an escape into a virtual space that leaves physical space useless, and of cyberspace – a virtual world that exists in parallel to our world – dominated the decade. ... By the end of the decade, the daily dose of cyberspace (using the internet to make plane reservations, check email using a Hotmail account, or download MP3 files) became so much the norm that the original wonder of cyberspace – so present in the early cyberpunk fiction of the 1980s and still evident in the original manifestos of VRML evangelists of the early 1990s – was almost completely lost. The virtual became domesticated. (Manovich, 2006, p. 220)

By the millennium, even as these online worlds expanded their users, the notion of an immaterial or ethereal set of worlds as a MODEL for informational landscapes seemed to miss many dynamics. Most especially, it missed the increasing mixture of the virtual into both EVERYDAY LIFE and also everyday spaces. Far from entering a world online, the informational world began to permeate our lived environment. Increasingly, processing power was located in the environment around us, not just in discrete artefacts called computers. As mobile telephones, 'smart' devices and electronic sensors led automated responses, the separation of an online and offline world seemed anachronistic.   MC

Suggested reading
Adams (1997); Crampton (2003); Dodge and Kitchin (2001a); Kitchin (1998); Nunes (1997).

cyborg The shackling together of 'cybernetic' and 'organism' in the term 'cyborg' is designed to convey the combination of ANIMAL (usually humans) and technology. Initially drawn from science fiction, it has been taken on to critique technological futures based on a CARTESIAN division of mind and BODY. It was popularized and developed by Donna Haraway (1991a) to criticize what she called a MASCULINIST fantasy of second birthing in technological UTOPIAN writing. This technological fantasy suggested an ideal of a transcendent union of human and machine, with people uploading their consciousness into machines. The aim would be eternal life in a disembodied state in the realm of CYBERSPACE. In cyberpunk writing, this was often depicted as fusion of hardware and software escaping the limits of the 'meatware' (aka the human body).

This imaginary builds on deep-seated divides of mind and body. Cartesian PHILOSOPHY had powerfully divided thought and world (*res cogitans* and *res extensa*, respectively). This compounded medieval Christian tradition, which had developed the model of the Manichean divide of the spirit and the flesh, the former being divine and the latter earthly, sins being located with the body and virtue with the mind. Feminist critics (see FEMINISM) have long pointed out that these divisions become gendered to associate women with the body and the material, while men were associated with logic and thought. The technological fantasies of escaping the body simply restaged these debates.

The concept of the cyborg linked flesh and body to emphasize the materiality of lives and technological transformations, and to show that humans are always part of the world and entangled in technologies. The perspective links with POSTHUMANISM in challenging an autonomous and FOUNDATIONAL humanity. It implies that human intelligence and consciousness shape, but also are shaped by, technologies. While 'such FEEDBACK loops may be reaching new levels of intensity as our environments become smarter and more information rich, ... the basic dynamic is as old as humans' (Hayles, 2002, p. 303).

The term is also used to point to accelerating vectors of technological development in technoscience and BIOTECHNOLOGY that are directly fusing technical implants with animals, often to restore lost capacities. In benign ways, this is seen as augmenting the capacities of bodies. Rather than transcending the body, it is about prostheses that expand our reach or capacities. More critical accounts point out that work on 'human augmentation' has been most enthusiastically supported by the military–industrial complex, in efforts to create advanced soldiers (Gray, 1995, 2003). The figure of the cyborg is thus often used to highlight the powerful myths of technology and humanity, and the investments in them by medical and military discourse.   MC

Suggested reading
Gray (1995, 2003); Haraway (1997).

cycle of poverty The idea that POVERTY and deprivation are transmitted from one generation to the next. The work of Oscar Lewis in the 1960s (see Lewis, 1969b) presented the victims of poverty as the authors of their own misfortune. Members of poor families were said to place little value on education, hard work or sexual responsibility. The empirical evidence for this behavioural view of poverty is slight, although it feeds into talk of an UNDERCLASS. Other poverty cycle models pay more attention to NEIGHBOURHOOD EFFECTS (bad schools, lack of jobs, danger), or the determining effects of social divisions structured around CLASS, GENDER and RACE.   SCO

Suggested reading
Wilson (1990).

D

Darwinism Narrowly construed, Darwinism refers to the theory of evolution developed by Charles Darwin (1809–82) and initially published in *The origin of species* (1859). The term itself was coined by Thomas Henry Huxley in his 1860 review of *The origin* to identify the central component of the theory; namely, the mechanism of natural selection, according to which organisms born with any advantageous feature have selective advantage over rivals in the struggle for life. Yet Darwinism, more broadly understood, conveys numerous associated ideas including common organic descent, gradualism and the multiplication of species, and such additional mechanisms of evolutionary transformation as sexual selection, group selection and correlative variation (Bowler, 1989).

At the same time, Darwinism is also associated with at least two further suites of ideas – social Darwinism and neo-Darwinism. *Social Darwinism* is usually taken to refer to the application of Darwinian principles and mechanisms to human SOCIETY, and often is thought to have justified anti-interventionist, *laissez-faire* economic policies on the basis of a survival of the fittest IDEOLOGY. Trading on organic analogies, the idea is that human societies and institutions are subject to the laws of evolution by selection and struggle, and that human intrusion constitutes unwarranted interference in the processes of natural development. Such perceptions need modifying in at least two respects. First, there are good grounds for supposing that social thinking, notably in the form of Malthusian demography (see MALTHUSIAN MODEL), was integral to Darwin's theory from the beginning and it is thus not simply a case of extending its application *from* the natural *to* the social world (Young, 1969). Darwinism, in this reading, always was social (Greene, 1977). Second, revisionist social evolutionists could equally mobilize the theory, sometimes drawing on its Lamarckian counterpart, to justify interventionism and political reform (Jones, 1980). *Neo-Darwinism* (or the neo-Darwinian synthesis as it is usually known), refers to the classical theory of evolution that emerged during the 1930s when R.A. Fisher, J.B.S. Haldane and Sewall Wright – building on T.H. Morgan's earlier chromosomal

theory of inheritance – combined Darwinian natural selection with a quantitative approach to population genetics that served to show the compatibility between Mendelian genetics and Darwin's mechanism (Smocovitis, 1996). This synthesis rescued Darwinism from the attacks to which it had been subject in the decades around 1900 from figures such as William Bateson and Hugo DeVries, who had argued that evolution took place by saltation; that is, by discontinuous variation (Bowler, 1983).

Within GEOGRAPHY, Darwinian thinking in its various guises – sometimes in association with LAMARCK(IAN)ISM – has exerted considerable influence. Stoddart (1966) identified ideas of change through time, organization and ECOLOGY, selection and struggle, randomness and chance, as key Darwinian influences on geography, though some of these were already established in the tradition prior to Darwin's intervention and were, in any case, compatible with Lamarckism. Whatever the precise genealogy, evolutionary thinking in one form or another found expression in almost every sub-disciplinary specialism of geography. W.M. Davis' cycle of erosion gave an evolutionary reading of LANDSCAPE development – though hardly in any specifically Darwinian sense, given the absence of sexual reproduction and inheritance as the drivers of change, as Darwin envisaged it (see also PHYSICAL GEOGRAPHY). Frederick Clements' plant geography displayed his fascination with organic modes of thought, and the Russian geographer and ichthyologist Lev Semyonovich Berg developed a Darwinian theory of 'nomogenesis' that, by emphasizing mutations, allowed for evolutionary 'jumps' (see also BIOGEOGRAPHY). Friedrich Ratzel's ANTHROPOGEOGRAPHY disclosed an organismic conception of the STATE and translated into HUMAN GEOGRAPHY Moritz Wagner's Lamarckian-inspired MIGRATION theory. Derwent Whittlesey's scheme of SEQUENT OCCUPANCE and H.J. Fleure's geographical anthropology and anthropometric CARTOGRAPHY were also evidently imbued with evolutionary thinking. In the latter case, the interplay of racial type, evolutionary mechanisms, anthropometric localization and psycho-social factors were of central importance.

Besides these individuals, a variety of key issues within the geographical tradition drew heavily on evolutionary *motifs*. Statements of ENVIRONMENTAL DETERMINISM by figures such as Ellen Semple, Elsworth Huntington and Griffith Taylor were invariably couched in evolutionary categories, with CLIMATE, migration and natural selection routinely playing the leading roles. From a more radical perspective, Peter Kropotkin found in a modified Darwinism the grounds for championing collectivism, opposing Spencerian individualism and connecting up the philosophy of natural science with ANARCHISM. This essentially Russian reading of evolution drew inspiration from the St Petersburg naturalists, all of whom had conducted FIELDWORK in Siberia, in conditions markedly different from the tightly packed-in niches of the tropical world – in particular, from the work of Karl Kessler, who set out the law of mutual aid. The transference of ideas about COMMUNITY between sociology and ECOLOGY, couched within an evolutionary POLITICAL ECONOMY, also found expression in geography in the tradition of HUMAN ECOLOGY (Mitman, 1992). Debates about acclimatization were likewise connected up to questions about heredity and ADAPTATION (Livingstone, 1987a; Anderson, 1992). And early theoretical statements about REGIONAL GEOGRAPHY, such as those of Herbertson and Geddes, were supported by appeals to the need for elucidating evolutionary mechanisms in specific contexts (Livingstone, 1992).

Within contemporary human geography, issues raised by Darwinism continue to surface. The legitimacy of transferring biological categories to the social order, for example, continues to be the subject of debate (cf. BIO-POWER), as are matters rotating around the understanding of how NATURE and CULTURE – to employ two abstractions – are to be conceptualized. Recently too, enquiries have been undertaken into the geography *of* Darwinism, with the aim of ascertaining the ways in which evolutionary theory circulated around the world and was differently embraced, mobilized and resisted in the light of local CULTURAL POLITICS (Livingstone, 2006).   DL

Suggested reading
Bowler (1989); Livingstone (2006); Stoddart (1966).

data archive A central repository of accessible data sets. Researchers are encouraged to deposit original data sets (e.g. survey data) there to enable others to conduct SECONDARY DATA ANALYSES. Many countries now have such archives (usually sponsored by research funding agencies that encourage – in some cases require – researchers to deposit data sets to encourage social scientific advances through the re-analysis of existing data sets alongside the creation of new sources). These archives are increasingly used to store and disseminate not only original data sets collected by academic researchers but also those collected by public-sector bodies (such as CENSUSES). Although most of those archives focus on quantitative data, other types are now stored in formats that allow them to be made readily available to other researchers – as in Qualidata, part of the UK Data Archive housed at the University of Essex (see SOFTWARE FOR QUALITATIVE RESEARCH) – and archives that store maps in digital form, and the INTERNET has facilitated linking archives to enable international data-sharing. As well as storing data, most archives offer training and other forms of user support to facilitate analyses of the data sets held.   RJ

Suggested reading
See the *Guide to primary social science data and related resources available on the Internet* (http://www.chass.utoronto.ca/datalib/other/) and the *Social science data archives* (http://www2.fmg.uva.nl/sociosite/databases.html)

data mining Computer-based automated procedures for searching large and complex data sets in order to identify spatial patterns and relationships, either to confirm existing or to generate new HYPOTHESES. In SPATIAL ANALYSIS, Openshaw's GEOGRAPHICAL ANALYSIS MACHINE and GEOGRAPHICAL EXPLANATION MACHINE exemplify data mining algorithms, as do some aspects of GEODEMOGRAPHICS. Some term these practices 'data dredging', since they are based on little prior knowledge and exemplify inductive thinking (see INDUCTION) whereby explanations are sought after patterns are identified (cf. EXPLORATORY DATA ANALYSIS): however, they can also be abductive (cf. ABDUCTION; GEOCOMPUTATION). Many of the structured algorithms for data mining use ARTIFICIAL INTELLIGENCE approaches.   RJ

Suggested reading
Berry and Linoff (1997).

decentralization A process of spatial change generated by centrifugal forces (cf. CENTRIFUGAL AND CENTRIPETAL FORCES). Within urban areas (see URBANIZATION), demands for space and to avoid the congestion, POLLUTION and land costs of high-density areas stimulate decentralization into SUBURBS and beyond, whereas at larger scales the negative EXTERNALITIES of large cities encourage movement to smaller settlements (cf. COUNTER-URBANIZATION). Decentralization is facilitated by reliance on roads for the movement of goods and individuals.   RJ

decision-making The process whereby alternative courses of action are evaluated and a decision taken. The decision-making perspective attracted great interest after it was introduced to GEOGRAPHY during the 1960s as part of the behavioural movement (see BEHAVIOURAL GEOGRAPHY). It broadened traditional perspectives, making them more realistic with respect to human practice.

The crux of the decision-making perspective is the recognition that real-world location decisions are seldom if ever optimal in the sense of maximizing profits or minimizing RESOURCES used. Similarly, consumer behaviour hardly ever accords with the rational calculus of utilities assumed in conventional economic formulations. The all-knowing and perfectly able economic actor of NEO-CLASSICAL ECONOMICS bears only slight resemblance to actual human beings.

Sub-optimal location decision-making may be incorporated into conventional LOCATION THEORY by the use of *spatial margins to profitability* within which some profit is possible anywhere and the business is free to locate away from the optimal (profit-maximizing) location at some pecuniary cost. However, this tells us nothing about how actual choice of location is arrived at within the economically determined constraints.

A step further was taken by Allen Pred (1967, 1969) in his concept of the *behavioural matrix*. According to this, decision-makers have a position in a matrix with the information available on one axis and the ability to use it on the other. The more information and the greater the ability, the higher is the probability of a 'good' location within the spatial margin; that is, near the optimal location on cost/revenue grounds. Decision-makers with very limited ability and information are more likely to locate beyond the margins and fail, but a good location could still be chosen by chance.

Pred was greatly influenced by H.A. Simon's (1957) concept of SATISFICING BEHAVIOUR, as an alternative to the unrealistic optimizing capacity attributed to 'economic man' (sic). Decision-makers were viewed by Simon as considering only a limited number of alternatives, choosing one that is broadly satisfactory rather than optimal. The introduction of a more realistic perspective on location decision-making corresponded with a similar move in the study of business behaviour in general, within a broad context of industrial organization.

The decision-making perspective in LOCATIONAL ANALYSIS followed two routes: theoretical and empirical. The search for a theoretical framework for studies of location behaviour under conditions of RISK and UNCERTAINTY led geographers and regional scientists into such fields as GAME THEORY and organization theory, and more recently to use large-scale SIMULATION models, as in AGENT-BASED MODELLING (cf. ARTIFICIAL INTELLIGENCE). The light shed on actual decision-making was very limited, however.

An empirical approach promised more, in a field where the emphasis is so much on individual practice. There was a tradition of SURVEY ANALYSIS in industrial location studies well before the behavioural movements penetrated the subject. Such research often revealed the importance of 'purely personal' factors. Later empirical research preferred to take sets of firms and examine the actual process of decision-making. Some perceived problem (such as undercapacity) sets in motion a sequence of decisions beginning with whether to expand *in situ*, to set up a branch or to acquire an existing plant; the sequence continues with the process of searching for a site, the evaluation of alternatives, the final decision and the FEEDBACK of the learning experience into some subsequent decision of a similar nature. This empirical approach held out the prospect of generalizations that relate the process of location decision-making to the nature of the organization concerned (cf. SEARCH BEHAVIOUR).

After many years of behavioural studies of industrial location decision-making, the findings seemed to promise more than it was able to deliver. A critique was mounted by Doreen Massey (1979), who pointed to objections on epistemological grounds (see EPISTEMOLOGY) to the practice of adopting IDEAL TYPE constructs (whether 'economic man' or some 'satisficing man') and of making a distinction between behaviour that accords with the ideal type and that which must be attributed to other factors. Massey argued that the focus on individual decision-making distracts attention from the structural features of the ECONOMY to which firms react, and that what

144

firms actually do with respect to the setting up or closure of plants is best understood in this broader context of POLITICAL ECONOMY. There has recently been a revival of interest in aspects of location decision-making, however, including the learning process and corporate strategy with respect to RESTRUCTURING. The work of Schoenberger (1997) emphasizes recognition of the significance of cultural factors to the operation of the firm.

Other aspects of HUMAN GEOGRAPHY in which the decision-making perspective assumed importance include response to ENVIRONMENTAL HAZARDS (e.g. Kates, 1962), residential choice (e.g. Brown and Moore, 1970), shopping behaviour (e.g. Rushton, 1969: see also REVEALED PREFERENCE ANALYSIS) and the decision to migrate (e.g. Wolpert 1965). Again, NEO-CLASSICAL ECONOMICS was originally influential, the concept of *place utility* being an obvious geographical extension of the theory of consumer behaviour. While qualities of PLACE as people evaluate them do influence decisions including locational choice or movement, there are many other considerations of a fortuitous and seemingly irrational nature. Indeed, geographers can easily exaggerate the spatial element in decision-making.

Research involving QUALITATIVE METHODS has sought a more sensitive understanding of how people assign meaning to various aspects of life and how decisions follow from this. For example, the decision to seek HEALTH CARE, involving the coverage of distance, is influenced by culturally specific conceptions of the meaning of illness, personal and shared experience of being ill, assessment of the benefit likely to be derived from the doctor's advice based on past contacts, the felt need for treatment or reassurance, and so on. Such work helps to set the spatial aspects of decision-making and taking in a broader context, getting away from crude notions of human behaviour as some stimulus–response mechanism and allowing greater scope for the way meaning is interpreted and translated into action. Work in the earlier tradition is now part of the discipline's history rather than important to contemporary practice.   DMS

Suggested reading
Chapman and Walker (1991); Hayter (1997); Malmberg (1997); Smith (1981 [1971], Ch. 5); Wolpert (1964).

decolonization The process, often long, tortuous and violent, by which colonies achieve their national aspirations for political independence from the colonial metropolitan POWER (cf. NATIONALISM). Decolonization can be understood as the period of later colonialism (Chamberlain, 1985). Modern COLONIALISM covers the period from the fifteenth to the twentieth centuries, and hence decolonization is uneven in its geography and history. In the New World, which had been subjected to Spanish, French, Portuguese and Dutch colonial rule in the *First Age of Colonialism*, the first wave of decolonization occurred in the eighteenth century. In this regard, the so-called *Classical Age of Imperialism* in the last quarter of the nineteenth century was short, the first decolonizations of the second wave being achieved after the end of the Second World War. The two cycles of IMPERIALISM both concluded with a limited phase of decolonization, followed by the rapid collapse of EMPIRES and an irresistible push to political independence (Taylor, 1994b).

The first challenge to the first wave of imperialism came in 1776, as British North American colonies declared independence. While Britain maintained its Caribbean and Canadian colonies, the Napoleonic upheavals in Europe so weakened Spain and Portugal that European settlers from Mexico to Chile expelled their imperial masters. By 1825, the Spanish and Portuguese empires were dead (cf. LATIN AMERICA). In the subsequent 115 years up to the Second World War, decolonization was limited to Cuba in 1898 and two groups of British colonies: the white settler colonies (Canada, Australia, New Zealand and South Africa) granted internal autonomy and finally full sovereignty in 1931, and Egypt and Iraq after the First World War. The Second World War marked the death knell for EUROPEAN colonization: India's separation from the British, Indonesia from the Dutch, and the remaining Arab mandated territories and Indo-China from the French. The independence of Ghana in 1957 marked an avalanche of liberations in AFRICA, though the process was not complete until 1990 (Namibia). Between 1945 and 1989, over one hundred new independent STATES were created.

Decolonization is a process marked by the achievement of political independence, but the duration, depth and character of decolonization movements vary substantially. In some African colonies, colonization was barely accomplished, and resistance movements of varying degrees of organization and institutionalization attended the entire colonial project. In other cases, an organized anti-colonial and nationalist movement came late, accompanied by a rapid and hastily assembled set of political negotiations in which it is clear that the metropolitan power wished to hand over the reins of POWER with utmost expedience (Nigeria). In others, it took a WAR of liberation, a bloody armed struggle by leftist guerillas or nationalist agitators pitted against white settlers or intransigent colonial states (as in Laos, Vietnam and Zimbabwe).

One of the problems with analysing decolonization, as Fred Cooper notes (1997, p. 6), is that the story 'lends itself to be read backwards and to privilege the process of ending colonial rule over anything else that was happening in those years'. It should also be said that any account of decolonization presumes an account, or a THEORY, of colonialism itself: top-down interpretations take colonial projects at face value, whereas the nationalist account denies any reality to the goal of MODERNIZATION that the colonial STATE purported to bring. In general, decolonization is seen as either (i) *self-government as an outcome of negotiated preparation and vision from above* by a colonial STATE APPARATUS, or (ii) as a *nationalist triumph from below*, in which power is wrested (violently or otherwise) from recalcitrant colonizers. In practice, decolonization was an enormously complex process involving something of each, and shaped both by the peculiarities of colonialism itself and the particular setting in world time in which the nationalist drive began.

There are two forms of decolonization that rest on what one might call nationalist triumph. The first is built upon social mobilization in which a patchwork of anti-colonial resistances and movements (many of which are synonymous with colonial conquest itself) are sown together into a unified nationalist movement by a Western-educated elite (Malaysia, Ghana or Aden). Mobilization occurred across a wide and eclectic range of organizations – trades unions, professional groups, ethnic associations – bringing them into political parties and propelled by a leadership focused on RACISM, on liberation and the sense of national IDENTITY of the colony, given its own history and CULTURE. The second is revolutionary – Franz Fanon (1967 [1952]) is its most powerful and articulate spokesman – in which the vanguard is not Western-educated elites or indeed workers, by the PEASANTS and lumpenproletariat. It rested upon VIOLENCE and rejection of any semblance of NEO-COLONIALISM. Decolonization rejected bourgeois nationalism (of the first sort); rather, as Fanon put it, 'the last shall be first

and the first last. Decolonization is the putting into practice of this sentence' (1967, p. 30).

Both views depict nationalism as subsuming all other struggles and hence obscures and misses much history; both posit a True Cause, as Cooper (1997, p. 7) puts it, in which there is little truck with opposition. Mamdani's (1996) enormously influential book on Africa makes the important point that decolonization posed the possibility of breaking with the traditional of European colonial indirect rule (what he called 'decentralized despotism') in which African custom granted enormous powers to local systems of traditional (and therefore cultural) authority, and developing instead a sort of civic nationalism in which cultural politics did not play a key role. Most African states continued the colonial model in which African colonial subjects were granted racial equality and CITIZENSHIP rights, but in which 'indigenes' were simultaneously a sort of bonus. In the historiography of the period, the nationalist road to self-government tends to take for granted the depth and appeal of a national identity (cf. IDENTITY POLITICS). It is precisely the shallowness of these nationalisms in the post-colonial period that reveals how limited is the simple nationalist account of decolonization itself. In practice, decolonization occurred in the context of all manner of contradictions and tensions between the national question and other social questions.

There is also a narrative of decolonization that has a singular vision, but from the side of the colonial state. It was the colonial bureaucracy, long before nationalist parties arose, that shaped self-government on a calculus of interest and power derived from an older conception of colonial rule (New Zealand and Canada) as a stepping stone to Independence. In this view, Africa by 1947 had already been set on the road to decolonization – this is a classic instant of Whig history – in spite of the fact that the Colonial Offices typically saw early African leaders as schoolboys or demagogues (Cooper, 1997). Another version of the dirigiste theory is rendered through the cold calculation of money and cost. It was the decision-making rationale of accountants estimating costs and gains – and who in particular gained – against the backdrop of imperial power's economic performance after the Second World War that sealed the fate of the colonies.

In all of these accounts – for India as much as Indonesia or Iraq – colonialism is as monolithic as the explanations themselves. There is a reduction involved in seeing Indians or

Kenyans as colonial subjects or as national or proto-nationalist actors. An alternative approach pursued by the so-called Subaltern School (Guha and Spivak, 1988; see SUBALTERN STUDIES) sees colonialism as a *contra* metropolitan project, moving against trends to exercise power under universal social practices and norms. It was 'dominance without HEGEMONY'. In other words, the hegemonic project of colonialism fragmented as colonial rule attached itself to local idioms of power. From this experience characterized by hybrid forms of identity, blurred boundaries and contradictory practices, the process of decolonization must necessarily look more complex than simply self-rule managed from above by the colonial state or mobilized from below by nationalist forces (cf. HYBRIDITY). MW

deconstruction A tradition of philosophical analysis and textual criticism begun by the French philosopher Jacques Derrida (1930–2004). Derrida engages the canon of Western PHILOSOPHY from Plato through G.W.F. Hegel to Martin Heidegger, modern LITERATURE and ART, and key social and political thinkers including Karl Marx, Sigmund Freud and Ferdinand de Saussure.

The general significance of Derrida's work cannot be detached from the distinctive style of his writing: deconstruction works through the *elaboration* of particular TEXTS, rather than creating concepts or general systems. The concepts associated with deconstruction – dissemination, parasites, pharmakon, trace and others – are like found objects, terms that turn out to have ambivalent meanings in particular textual traditions. As a 'method' of analysis, or a way of reading, deconstruction exposes unacknowledged implications in existing traditions. This systematically parasitical dependence of deconstruction on other texts makes the application of any particular deconstructive motif a hazardous affair of partial validity.

Derrida's own work can be divided into an early phase of 'critical' deconstruction and a later phase of 'affirmative' deconstruction. Deconstruction first came to prominence in the 1960s and 1970s. Although Derrida is often thought of as the quintessentially 'French' theorist, deconstruction has been most influential in the English-speaking academy. In *Of grammatology* (Derrida, 1976), the basic lineaments of deconstructive 'method' are established. Derrida's notorious claim that 'there is nothing outside the text' is really an interpretative rule, according to which reading is meant to follow the immanent patterns of

texts rather than impose external criteria of interpretation (Barnett, 1999). In readings of Saussure, Claude Lévi-Strauss and Jean-Jacques Rousseau, Derrida identified a recurrent tendency to render writing as a secondary, contingent medium for the expression of pure thoughts properly expressed in direct speech. Derrida calls this privileging of expressive speech over the risks of mediated communication *logocentrism*. He claims that it embodies a deep prejudice in Western thought in favour of the ideal of a disembodied, isolated SUBJECT hooked up to the external world by the fragile and untrustworthy medium of referential LANGUAGE. In 'classical' deconstruction, this inherently normative evaluation of the relationship between speech and writing, orality and literacy, is subjected to critical analysis that leads to apparently perverse conclusions. If writing is able to act as a *supplement* to the pure form of expressive speech, then this logically implies that something essential must be absent from the pure form; it turns out that far from being a *mere supplement*, writing is a *necessary supplement* to the supposedly pure form of speech. The analysis of speech and writing in *Of grammatology* exemplifies a general theme in deconstruction, whereby what is secondary, accidental or contingent is shown to be fundamental to the working of identities, meanings and systems. The point of this demonstration is not meant to be disobliging but, rather, to encourage a reordering of the terms of normative evaluation through which concepts are developed and deployed.

Derrida calls the assumption that phenomena such as meaning or IDENTITY must have singular ESSENTIALIST forms the *metaphysics of presence*. This term indicates the relevance of deconstruction to geography's concern with SPATIALITY and temporality. Deconstruction is indebted to Heidegger's argument that Western thought has consistently privileged the present tense when trying to apprehend the nature of being, or ONTOLOGY. By affirming the irreducible role of writing in the expression of thought, Derrida is arguing that all those aspects for which writing or TEXTUALITY stands – spatial and temporal extension, and the dimension of difference that these imply – are constitutive components of apparently free-standing entities such as the unified, self-identical subject of philosophical reason. This is articulated by one of Derrida's most important neologisms, the notion of *différance* (Derrida, 1982a), which refers to the movement of spatial differentiation and temporal deferral that Derrida holds is the condition of possibility for any and all identity, punctuality or unity.

Although Derrida's work is most often thought of as a post-structuralist radicalization of structuralist accounts of signification (see POST-STRUCTURALISM), the concern with issues of presence, TIME and SPACE indicates the degree to which deconstruction engages critically with PHENOMENOLOGY as well, including the works of Edmund Husserl, Heidegger and Emmanuel Levinas. Deconstruction points up the limitations of internalist, monological accounts of the self typical of phenomenology that privilege 'experience' as the primary modality of subjectivity. Moreover, rather than thinking of deconstruction as merely concerned with the instabilities of meaning and signification, it is better to think of it as part of a broader revival of interest in RHETORIC. For example, one of Derrida's most influential contributions has been to popularize the writings of J.L. Austin on the PERFORMATIVITY of language-in-use across social sciences and HUMANITIES.

Deconstruction reached its institutional zenith in the 1980s, having become an orthodoxy in literary studies in the USA especially, although it was less well received in mainstream English-language philosophy. There is an identifiable shift in Derrida's work from the late 1980s onwards towards a more 'affirmative', although no less arcane, register of deconstruction. Less concerned with calling Western philosophy to task for its blindnesses, Derrida turned to the task of mining this same tradition for the traces of an alternative vocabulary of ethical concern and political responsibility (see also ETHICS). This shift coincided with a series of public scandals concerning Heidegger's Nazi affiliations and the anti-Semitic wartime writings of Paul de Man, Derrida's close friend and leading deconstructionist critic in the USA. In the wake of these controversies, Derrida's writing undergoes an explicit ethical and political turn, focusing on a set of topics such as the gift, animality, hospitality, ghosts, friendship and forgiveness; as well as political topics such as SOVEREIGNTY, DEMOCRACY and COSMOPOLITANISM. There has also recently been a degree of rapprochement between deconstruction and 'analytical' traditions of philosophy.

In GEOGRAPHY, deconstruction has had a variable reception-history. Derrida is rarely cited as a 'key thinker' on issues of space and PLACE, yet he is a background presence in a number of intellectual developments in the discipline in the past decade and a half.

Deconstruction first came to prominence as part of debates about POSTMODERNISM, when it was invoked as an authoritative reference point for critiques of essentialism and foundationalism in epistemology. This *epistemological* reading saw deconstruction externally applied to support arguments about the contingency of knowledge-claims and the constructedness of phenomena. This construal of deconstruction owed a great deal to Richard Rorty's PRAGMATISM. In a number of fields, such as ECONOMIC GEOGRAPHY or CRITICAL GEOPOLITICS, deconstruction is appealed to as a variant of IDEOLOGY-critique to help in debunking claims of OBJECTIVITY and naturalness (see also CARTOGRAPHY, HISTORY OF).

The predominant anti-essentialist, epistemological framing of deconstruction has been supplanted by the more sophisticated focus on ontological issues. Doel (1999) provides the most systematic engagement with the spatial and temporal metaphysics of deconstruction, laying out an alternative spatial grammar of mobility, relations and foldings. POST-COLONIALISM in geography has also been heavily inflected by deconstruction. Derrida's concern with issues of reading, interpretation and context are intimately related to a wider critique of Western HISTORICISM (Young, 1990b). And, most recently, geographers have begun to engage seriously with the ethical and political aspects of deconstruction's treatment of themes such as hospitality, responsibility, RADICAL DEMOCRACY, cosmopolitanism and sovereignty (Popke, 2003; Barnett, 2004b, 2005).

The ethical and political turn in deconstruction indicates that what is most at stake in deconstruction is neither epistemology nor ontology *per se* but, rather, a challenge to rethink the inherent normativity of theoretical reasoning. Certainly, any temptation to deploy deconstructive ideas as if they were social-theoretical concepts is best avoided, not least because Derrida's engagement with various traditions of metaphysical reflection is almost completely devoid of any mediation by sociological or historical conceptualization that any such usage would require. In short, deconstruction might be much less new, original or disruptive than is often supposed. Deconstruction is not best thought of as either postmodernist nor post-structuralist; rather, it lays is a practice of reasoning governed by the imperative of working through inherited traditions in critical, inventive and responsible ways. Deconstruction therefore continues a tradition of ENLIGHTENMENT critique, but with a distinctive flourish.   CB

148

Suggested reading
Critchley (1999); Derrida (1976, 2002); Royle (2000).

deduction A form of reasoning which – as the reverse of the sequence deployed in INDUCTION – moves from the general to the particular. It takes what is known (or assumed) as given, and deduces possible consequences from those axioms. In an empirical situation – which is the normal context for the application of deductive reasoning in HUMAN GEOGRAPHY – the deductions are normally expressed as HYPOTHESES, statements of expectations on the basis of prior knowledge. Formal procedures are then deployed to test the validity/falsifiability of those statements (cf. FALSIFICATION), most of which involve the 'scientific methods' normally associated with POSITIVISM. (See also ABDUCTION.) RJ

Suggested reading
Harvey (1969).

deep ecology A radical form of ENVIRON-MENTALISM that argues that NATURE has an inherent right to exist, that humans are part of nature and that our ecological awareness comes from experiencing ourselves within nature (Devall and Sessions, 1985). Deep ecology is both a philosophy and a practice associated with the Western ENVIRONMENTAL MOVEMENT. Although it draws on earlier ideas, the term emerged when the Danish philosopher Arne Naess (1973) distinguished between 'shallow' and 'deep' ecology. The former approach was seen as technocentric, anthropocentric and reformist. In contrast, deep ecology has emerged and developed as a PHILOSOPHY that is ecocentric; advocates dismantling the dominant socio-economic systems through which humans appropriate nature; and argues for biocentric equality, so that the desire by humans to dominate nature is eliminated in favour of humans, as one species, living in nature. Humans, like other species, must respect nature's limits and thresholds in order for all forms of life to live on a sustainable basis.

There is diversity in both the thought and practice of deep ecology. The practice includes very radical, single-issue, deep ecology organizations such as the Animal Liberation Front, which is dedicated to ANIMAL welfare, through VIOLENCE and other means if necessary, and groups such as Earth First!, which was promoted as the ACTIVIST version of deep ecology.

In addition to local site-defence groups, the philosophy has also influenced formally organized activist organizations and Green political parties in many developed countries (Luke, 2002). Within geography, while there has been more engagement with deep ecology by human geographers, Haigh (2002) advocates that deep ecology guide the teaching, research and practice of PHYSICAL GEOGRAPHY.

Deep ecology has been critiqued as romanticism, fundamentally flawed in its conception of non-human parts of nature having intrinsic value, and ANTI-HUMANIST in its approach (this was a major debate in the 1980s with social ecologists led by Murray Bookchin). Deep ecology has also been critiqued for its inability to distinguish between different parts of humanity (men and women, rich and poor, different cultural beliefs and practices) and its celebration of outdoor experiences in nature, which Luke (2002) labelled 'sportspersonism' and claimed was a potentially dangerous form of 'UTOPIAN ecologism'. The danger partly arises from the lack of a transition strategy in deep ecology, other than individual action, to move from the present situation to a future deep ecology state of 'harmony' with nature (Luke, 2002). Despite the critiques, deep ecology has been influential and cannot be ignored. It has encouraged a wider appreciation of nature and modern humanity's often destructive relations with it. PM

defensible space A concept associated with Oscar Newman (1972, 1996), who identified MODERNIST design of high-rise buildings in 'park-like' settings as a key factor increasing residents' vulnerability to CRIME. Studying crime statistics for public housing in New York City, he argued that crimes such as rape increased dramatically in anonymous interior public spaces. He argued that high-density housing can be safe if designed according to principles of defensible SPACE, which allow residents to claim TERRITORY, provide opportunities for resident self-surveillance, reduce the stigma and isolation of public housing, and connect public housing to other safe spaces by orienting buildings to public streets rather than interior pathways. These ideas were taken up and tested more rigorously in the UK by Coleman (1985), and have been extended into situational crime prevention programs such as Crime Prevention Through Environmental Design (CPTED) and Safe Cities Programs (Wekerle and Whitzman, 1995). These more recent programmes focus on public space (rather than the semi-public spaces of public housing) and address perceptions and fear of crime as well as actual crime. The Safe Cities Program in particular emphasizes a broad community-oriented approach to problem-solving. Recent efforts to control crime through SURVEILLANCE, such as security cameras, are distinct from the concept of defensible space, which emphasizes the need to create the architectural framework to enable residents to control their own environment.   GP

Suggested reading
Wekerle and Whitzman (1995).

deindustrialization A sustained decline in industrial (especially manufacturing) activity and capacity (cf. INDUSTRIALIZATION). It may involve the absolute and/or relative decline of industrial output, employment and other means of production. Such changes are quite normal in the course of economic DEVELOPMENT. However, when they are linked to the declining competitiveness of industrial production to meet extra-regional, domestic and international demand within reasonable levels of employment and a sustainable balance of payments, deindustrialization represents a process of UNDERDEVELOPMENT. The causes of deindustrialization are complex. In the contemporary global economy, they lie in a combination of local circumstances and locational adjustment to global conditions. In a CAPITALIST economy, the rate of profit and its determination must lie at the centre of any explanation of these changing spatial configurations of industrial activity. (See also RUSTBELT.)   RL

Suggested reading
Bluestone and Harrison (1982); Martin and Rowthorne (1986).

deliberative mapping The collaborative creation of MAPS by multiple authors who share a common interest or complementary expertise. Also known as 'collaborative mapping', 'participatory mapping' or 'geocollaboration', deliberative mapping is a form of distributed mapping supported by GEOGRAPHIC INFORMATION SYSTEMS and online software designed for group decision-making in map design, environmental planning, political REDISTRICTING or emergency response (MacGillavry, 2003). Collaboration can be in real time or asynchronous, over a period of days, weeks or even years (Schafer, Ganoe, Xiao, Coch and Carroll, 2005). The dialogue is both verbal and graphic, as participants at adjoining

workstations or continents apart suggest applications as well as modifications.   MM

Suggested reading
MacEachren and Brewer (2004).

democracy The term 'democracy' has a simple meaning: 'Rule by the people'. But the meaning of 'people' and 'rule' are far from straightforward. The HISTORICAL GEOGRAPHY of democracy is therefore the ongoing process of finding answers to various *practical* problems: *who* should rule, *how* rule should be organized, and over *what* scope of activities. But these practical issues are internally related to questions of *justification*, which means that democracy is a highly contested concept in both theory and practice. As a result, the empirical analysis of democratic politics cannot avoid issues of normative democratic theory.

Modern democratic theory depends on a distinctive GEOGRAPHICAL IMAGINATION. It assumes that democracy is framed by bounded TERRITORIES, involving a nested hierarchy of SCALES contained within the NATION-STATE (see also BOUNDARY). Key thinkers of this tradition have focused considerable attention on the geographical organization of democratic politics in complex, spatially extensive territories (Dahl, 1989). The limitations of this territorial framing of democracy are increasingly subjected to critical investigation in political science (Shapiro and Hacker-Cordón, 1999).

Until very recently, there has been little explicit focus in HUMAN GEOGRAPHY on the normative questions that are at the core of debates about the relationship between democracy and SPATIALITY. This is the result of POLITICAL GEOGRAPHY's avoidance of reflection on the normative basis of political issues. However, the 1990s saw a shift in various sub-disciplines towards investigating the entwinement of practical issues with normative issues central to democratic theory; for example, issues of *participation* in development geography, issues of *deliberation* in urban planning, and issues of *citizenship* in environmental studies. Aspects of democratic theory are now present across human geography (Barnett and Low, 2004).

ELECTORAL GEOGRAPHY is the sub-field in which the geographies of democracy have always been a concern. Much of this has focused on mapping distributions of votes, but recent attention has focused on developing more sophisticated, spatially sensitive explanations for voting behaviour (Agnew, 1996). The spatial organization of electoral systems effects how votes are translated into representative majorities in liberal democracies (see LIBERAL-ISM). The spatial organization of formal democracy therefore has consequences for democratic outcomes in terms of basic criteria of equality and representativeness. Research on this process has broadened out to include the geographies of campaigning, party-formation and political communication. This has also involved more explicit considerations of the normative issues at stake in the traditional issues such as GERRYMANDERING, re-districting and representation (Johnston, 1999; Hannah, 2001).

The past two decades have seen the global 'DIFFUSION of democracy', in the wake of the collapse of COMMUNISM in Eastern Europe, political transitions away from authoritarianism in LATIN AMERICA, AFRICA and ASIA, and the application of norms of 'Good Governance' in the GEOPOLITICS of Western international engagements. Geographers have investigated the degree to which the adoption of democratic forms of governance can be accounted for by specifically geographical factors (O'Loughlin, Ward, Lofdahl et al., 1998), contributing to renewed debates concerning whether democracy can only be established and sustained after various socio-economic and cultural prerequisites have been met (Przeworski, 1995). The theoretical assumptions and the practical devices through which liberal forms of electoral democracy have been circulated as the global norm have also been critically interrogated (Bell and Staeheli, 2001). Debates about *democratization* raise fundamental questions regarding the degree to which the norms of Western, liberal, representative democracy can and should be practically applied in non-Western contexts and deployed as normative benchmarks of critical analysis (see ETHNOCENTRISM; EUROCENTRISM: see also Slater, 2002). The geographical mobility of democratic practices suggests that the devices through which different imperatives of democratic rule are enacted can be combined, adapted and reordered in different geographical contexts (Saward, 2003). This points to the importance of issues of temporal sequencing and spatial organization to the successful institutionalization of the complex, competing imperatives of democratic deliberation, decision-making, accountability, participation and revision (Dryzek, 2005).

Criticisms of liberal, representative democracy that assume the nation-state as the natural container of democratic politics have encouraged geographers to pay increasing attention to various alternative models of democracy. In contrast to the focus of electoral geography on the formal democratic procedures of elections, voting and parties, geographers have turned to notions of PARTICIPATORY DEMOCRACY and RADICAL DEMOCRACY to consider the diverse practices and sites where questions of accountability, CITIZENSHIP, justice and participation are contested (Young, 2000). One feature of these explorations is a commitment to thinking of democracy as more than simply a procedure for legitimizing the decisions of centralized bureaucracies. Models of *deliberative democracy* are now in the ascendant in democratic theory, implying a much more active role for citizens in all facets of decision-making, as well as the extension of democratic norms to a far wider array of activities. These sorts of arguments are often associated with calls for the *decentralization* of DECISION-MAKING and political participation to sub-national scales of regions and cities. At the same time, there is increasing attention given to emergent forms of transnational democracy (Anderson, 2002a), focusing on the degree to which systems of globalized economic and political governance can be subordinated to democratic oversight (Held, 1996). In this work in particular, there is increasing attention given to the diverse 'agents of justice' through which democratic justice can be pursued and secured (O'Neill, 2001), moving beyond an exclusive focus on states as the privileged containers of democratic politics (cf. Low, 2003). This emphasis on the global dimensions of democratic politics has two important implications for geographical research in these areas. First, it indicates that rather than opposing representative to participatory forms of democracy, any viable form of democratic polity is likely to combine aspects of these practices in different ways. For both practical and normative reasons, representation seems an irreducible aspect of any viable, pluralistic model of democracy. Not only do representative procedures enable the TIME-SPACE DISTANCIATION of democratic politics, but they also embody important principles of DIFFERENCE and non-identity within the *demos* (Barnett, 2003, Ch. 1). Representation is also an unavoidable mechanism for the integration of so-called 'mute interests' – for example, future generations or non-human actors – which concerns with environmental futures has made a much more imperative consideration for democratic theory (Goodin, 2003). The second reason why the GLOBALIZATION of democracy is significant is that it suggests a move beyond the predominant territorial framing of the spatiality of democracy. Rather than thinking simply in terms of the need to articulate sub-national and national scales with global scales, discussions of these topics increasingly focus on the diverse spatialities of democracy, ones which articulate territorial and non-territorial practices, scalar and non-scalar conceptualizations of space (Low, 1997).   CB

Suggested reading
Barnett and Low (2004); Dunn (2005); Held (1996); Mann (2005).

demographic transition A framework that explores the historical sequence of changes in FERTILITY, MORTALITY, MIGRATION and AGE STRUCTURE. This cornerstone of research in DEM-OGRAPHY (see also HISTORICAL DEMOGRAPHY) uses widely accessible data (typically, time series records of vital rates), proposes that stages of economic development have particular demographic signatures and suggests that population policies encourage zero population growth.

Its foundational concepts drew on French and western EUROPEAN experience in the nineteenth and early twentieth centuries, and described a linked reduction in mortality rates that helped to trigger sustained declines in birth rates. According to the 'classic' transition model (see figure), (national) populations began at a high stationary phase, with both death rates and birth rates high, and overall population growth rates low. Improvements in fresh WATER supply and sanitation, public HEALTH and nutrition (characteristics of the *epidemiological transition*) begin to support a downward trend in death rates. As this occurred at the same time as birth rates remained high, population growth accelerated

during the next 'early expanding' phase. During the third 'late expanding' phase, population growth continued but annual rates of increase slowed down as the linked 'fertility transition' kicked in and birth rates fell in response to diverse factors including urbanization, decreased infant mortality, the changing roles of children and women in society, contraception, and new patterns of NUPTUALITY (Sanderson and Dubrow, 2000). Finally, populations entered a 'low stationary' phase, where both birth and death rates are low, and natural increase is again close to zero.

Considerable research has examined the degree to which, given time, all REGIONS of the world will exhibit vital signs and demographic mechanisms that 'converge' on this IDEAL TYPE (Coleman, 2002). For example, across contemporary sub-Saharan AFRICA, there is evidence to both support the DIFFUSION of the transition and question the transition's assumption of universalism (see Gould and Brown, 1996). Indeed, sensitivity to both historical and spatial variations in linked demographic transitions has led to calls for a reformulation of the classic framework. Noting very high levels of AGEING and below-replacement FERTILITY across a number of more developed nations, advocates of a new and distinctive *second demographic transition* discuss how new links between demographic drivers are being shaped by the changing relationships between parents and CHILDREN in SOCIETY, new living arrangements (including increased rates of cohabitation, mixed marriages and divorce) and sexual behaviours (including later parenting and high fertility outside marriage) (see, e.g., Ogden and Hall, 2004). In turn, the rise of IMMIGRATION

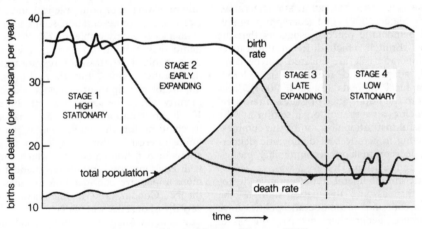

demographic transition   (Haggett, 1975)

(e.g. in response to below replacement fertility) may promote new modes of BELONGING and family strategies, and create the conditions for another distinctive transition. AJB

Suggested reading
Kirk (1996); Van de Kaa (1987).

demography The science of human populations. For much of the preceding 400 years, the field has concerned itself with the size, distribution and composition of populations, and how changes in these are connected with the three population processes of MORTALITY, FERTILITY and MIGRATION (Greenhalgh, 1996). While *formal demography* has developed mathematical and actuarial techniques to model and project changes in population (see LIFE TABLE; POPULATION PROJECTION), the interdisciplinary field of *population studies* examines demographic change within its broader societal setting and makes use of a wide range of approaches (see, e.g., HISTORICAL DEMOGRAPHY; LIFE COURSE). Despite its keen interest in population distribution, its interdisciplinary niche and its strong connections with sociology and economics, DEMOGRAPHY has had a relatively limited engagement with GEOGRAPHY. Although the development of POPULATION GEOGRAPHY between the 1960s and the 1980s and the growth of *spatial demography* drew attention to the study of mortality, fertility and particularly migration, many geographical analyses of issues including POVERTY, gender roles, social exclusion, URBANIZATION and environmental degradation underplay population factors (but for a recent exception, see Gould, 2005).

Descriptions of changes in population size and distribution make use of empirical data on deaths, births, moves and the ages at which these events occur, mostly obtained from population CENSUSES, social surveys or registers of population. Population growth within an area is most simply expressed through the balancing equation as follows:

$$P_{t2} = P_{t1} + (B_{t1-t2} - D_{t1-t2})$$
$$+ (I_{t1-t2} - E_{t1-t2}),$$

where P is the population size, B is births, D is deaths, I is in-migrants to an area, E is out-migrants from an area, $t2$ is time 2, $t1$ is time 1 in the past, and $t1 - t2$ is the time interval between time 1 and time 2. Knowledge of the ages at which vital events occur allows age-specific rates to be used to create *synthetic* or *model* populations that approximate actual AGE COMPOSITIONS of populations, and may be used to project future population scenarios (see POPULATION PROJECTION). Such *stable population theory* is at the basis of LIFE TABLES that are used to calculate LIFE EXPECTANCY by age, the number of survivors by AGE, and thus the impact of the three population processes upon the age structure, and vice versa. Armed with such data, research on changes in population growth and distribution has centred on efforts to build, critique and extend the DEMOGRAPHIC TRANSITION model; for example, through work on differentials in MORTALITY, the onset of FERTILITY decline and, more recently, its recovery (Bongaarts, 2002; Case and Paxson, 2005).

The field has long enjoyed an extremely close – some have argued, too close – relationship with social policy, whether at the international scale such as the League of Nations' commissioning of the Office of Population Research's work on transition theory in the 1940s, or in informing the US administration's laissez-faire position on family planning at the 1984 International Conference on Population and Development, or more recently in assessing the impact of immigration policy or welfare reform measures upon the life chances of low-income family members (Büche and Frick, 2005). A good deal of research effort continues to debate new dimensions of the population–RESOURCE–well-being nexus in light of the likely global DIFFUSION of low fertility and AGEING, and the short-termism of replacement migration policies (Meyerson, 2001). Connected to this, studies in family demography describe factors behind changes in the timing and nature of decisions about marriage and partnering, divorce and household dissolution, leaving and rejoining the parental home, cohabitation, and transitioning from full-time to part-time and unpaid work (Holdsworth and Elliot, 2001). The diversification and plurality of HOUSEHOLDS is a theme in work on, for example, mixed marriages, and variations in intergenerational relations and resource flows by CLASS, GENDER, RACE and ETHNICITY (Gershuny, 2000). Many analyses link family demography to well-being, with an increasing emphasis upon children (Eloundou-Enyegue, 2004). Applied research includes the development of GEOGRAPHICAL INFORMATIONAL SYSTEMS and GEODEMOGRAPHIC techniques; both are used by marketing firms to target launch new products and design sales areas, and by local authorities to deliver services more efficiently. AJB

Suggested reading
Greenhalgh (1995); Kent and Haub (2005); Lutz, Sanderson and Scherbov (2004).

density gradient The rate of falling-off in some value with distance from a central point, as with the DISTANCE-DECAY relationships showing land values and population densities declining away from a city centre (cf. ALONSO MODEL; VON THÜNEN MODEL). Such relationships are often associated with patterns of social contact, DIFFUSION and spatial spread. RJ

dependency ratio The number of persons aged 0–14 and 65 and over, divided by the number of persons aged 15–64. This *total dependency ratio* assesses the dependency or reliance of one group upon another, and is one of a suite of measures summarizing AGE COMPOSITION in a population (see also the *child dependency ratio*, or the number of persons aged 0–14 divided by the number of persons aged 15–64, and the *aged dependency ratio*, or the number of persons aged 65 and older divided by the number of persons aged 15–64). The assumptions that all persons under 15 and over 65 are (equally) dependent, and that all persons within the working ages of 15–64 are (equally) independent are problematic, and are partly based on particular ideas of work and production in CAPITALIST societies. Other measures reflect broader interest in the links between generations. For example, the caretaker ratio divides the number of females aged 50–64 by the number of persons aged 80 and older, and informs analyses of changing care relations (Teo, 1996). Overall, these measures do help expose differences in population composition that have profound social and economic implications, including the future provision of pensions and social support, patterns of economic demand and labour supply, and GENDER relations. (See also AGEING; POPULATION PYRAMID.) AJB

Suggested reading
Shryock and Siegel (1973).

dependency theory A complex body of THEORY with somewhat varied political orientations, presenting versions of CORE–PERIPHERY models that purport to explain the UNDERDEVELOPMENT of countries in the global SOUTH as a consequence of their relationships with the countries of the global NORTH. Central to these relationships have been forms of economic, political and cultural dependence on the products of the global North, including advanced manufactured goods, political models and sociocultural norms.

The earliest major variants of dependency theory developed in LATIN AMERICA and are especially associated with the Argentinean structuralist economist Raúl Prebisch, for years the head of the United Nations (UN) Economic Commission on Latin America (ECLAC) and a founder of the UN Commission on Trade and Development (UNCTAD). Prebisch presented evidence for declining long-term terms of TRADE for global South exporters of agricultural products and raw materials, resulting in their having to pay relatively more over time for manufactured imports from the global North (Kay, 1989, pp. 31–5). This line of argument, institutionally supported by ECLAC and UNCTAD, contradicted certain features of Ricardian, neo-classical trade theory that argued for the benefits to all countries of trade based on comparative advantage (see NEO-CLASSICAL ECONOMICS). Structuralists thus legitimized state policies of import-substitution industrialization (ISI) that had been attempted in Latin America since the 1930s. The goal of these ISI policies was to reduce the import of expensive manufactured goods by producing such goods domestically under high protective tariffs.

While Prebisch and other structuralists quickly recognized the limits of ISI strategies (Kay, 1989, pp. 36–41), they nonetheless came under sustained attack from economists who favoured export-oriented INDUSTRIALIZATION based on COMPARATIVE ADVANTAGE and the maintenance of minimal tariff barriers. At the same time, more politically radical versions of dependency theory came to the fore by the 1960s, including the widely read works of Andre Gunder Frank (1967). Gunder Frank, influenced in part by the Cuban revolution, argued that only a world-wide SOCIALIST revolution – not mere shifts in state trade policies – could undercut dependency in the global South and eliminate underdevelopment, which he saw as an inevitable result of CORE–PERIPHERY relationships under global CAPITALISM.

Radical dependency theories gained currency beyond Latin America in the 1970s, especially in AFRICA, but this decade also saw the formulation of less radical versions of the dependency thesis, including 'dependent development' (Evans, 1979) and WORLD-SYSTEMS ANALYSIS (Wallerstein, 1979), that more readily allowed for the possibility of some movement upwards from the global periphery. By the 1980s, however, many DEVELOPMENT theorists claimed to see considerable problems with any sort of dependency approach (Corbridge, 1986). Nonetheless, central arguments put forward by dependency theorists continue to haunt many DEVELOPMENT debates today (Gwynne, Klak and Shaw, 2003). JGl

Suggested reading
Corbridge (1986); Evans (1979); Frank (1967); Gwynne, Klak and Shaw (2003); Kay (1989); Wallerstein (1979).

desertification A term coined in 1949 to refer to an extreme form of 'savannization', the conversion of forest into savanna, involving severe soil erosion and the invasion of dryland plants. The Sahel drought and FAMINE of the early 1970s triggered concern about advance of the Sahara, and extensive scientific debate about bio-geo-physical FEEDBACK (the effect of land-use changes on atmospheric processes because of dust, surface reflectance or other factors). This environmental narrative had great power with policy-makers (Swift, 1996). Current understanding (e.g. in the UN Convention to Combat Desertification, 1994) distinguishes between long-term large-scale climatic processes that create desert conditions, and local causes of ecological degradation and poverty (Mortimore, 1998). WMA

development A central keyword of twentieth-century POLITICAL ECONOMY and social policy, which can broadly refer to processes of social change or to CLASS and STATE projects to transform national economies, particularly in formerly colonized or THIRD WORLD geographies. Cowen and Shenton (1996) provide a genealogy of these conceptions of intentional and immanent development emerging from an eighteenth-century European intellectual history concerned with secularized progress in the wake of social disorder. Such a genealogy must be pluralized and grounded in intertwined spatial, natural and cultural histories of improvement, colonization, commodification, discipline, predation, government, transformation, destruction and renovation. A category that carries such enormous and variable analytical weight is inevitably contentious, and the idea of 'development' has always been subject to critique (Cooper and Packard, 1997), long before the efficacy of the idea itself was called into question at the end of the twentieth century, whether for its allegedly inevitable EUROCENTRISM (Escobar, 1995) or for its scepticism of the invisible hand of the MARKET (Lal, 1985). One way to frame

the long history of development before the concept's use is through four key intellectual traditions: (1) political and economic liberalism and the defence of 'free markets'; (2) Marxist critique of class, class struggle and IMPERIALISM; (3) social Darwinist notions of evolution through racially hierarchized environments; and (4) anti-colonial defence of cultural difference and the possibility of national self-determination. These four currents have provided content, and contention, to what would be thought of as 'development', as well as to the technocratic and statist enterprise that came together in the wake of mid-twentieth-century DECOLONIZATION.

The narrower conception of international or intentional development came to its own after the Second World War, in an ensemble of institutions, policies, disciplinary formations and, most importantly, practices of intervention in the alleviation of POVERTY in the Third World recently decolonized nations, as they sought to steer a tenuous path through the GEOPOLITICS of the COLD WAR. Development now signified intervention by governments, rich and poor, and by an array of international institutions and organizations in CIVIL SOCIETY (Cooper and Packard, 1997). Intentional development was shaped by proximal legacies: ideas of 'late development' in Bismarck's Germany and the nascent Soviet Union, inter-war arguments for state intervention either to manage CAPITALISM, as envisioned by Keynes, or to resist the destructive aspects of commodification through some form of democratic SOCIALISM (as in Polanyi, 2001 [1944]). US political scientists were crucial to the emerging doctrine of MODERNIZATION theory as a disciplinary formation in the US academy (Gilman, 2003) tied to the conceit that the right kinds of social and economic planning would bring Third World countries in line with Western capitalist norms of social transformation. Development economics and new STATE capacities fueled the Promethean visions of Third World states, many of whom used modernization theory to navigate through the Cold War, controlling diverse and often undemocratic polities, while forging shifting economies from reliance on primary-product exports to import-substitution INDUSTRIALIZATION.

This orthodoxy of modernization, statism and developmentalism was soon called into question through oppositional forces of the 1960s and early 1970s, which sought to redefine 'development' in more radical terms. These forces were sometimes inspired by radical anti-colonial thinkers such as Fanon

(1963 [1961]), or they were spontaneous guerrilla or squatter movements critical of the failures of anti-colonial nationalists in power. Latin American structuralists and dependency theorists saw 'peripheries' revert to UNDER-DEVELOPMENT and forced stagnation through trade relations with 'metropoles' (see CORE–PERIPHERY MODEL and DEPENDENCY THEORY). Others turned to PEASANTS neglected by the systematic and global dumping of US grain surpluses. A series of 'Third Worldist' schools of development studies, along with journals such as *Monthly Review* and the *Journal of Peasant Studies*, represented this wider climate of what Emannuel Wallerstein calls the 'anti-systemic movements' of the 1960s (see Watts, 2001).

The 1970s saw the response from states and multilateral institutions to the oppositional movements of the 1960s, manifest in neopopulist discourses of incorporation and participation within the development establishment. The WORLD BANK spoke of 'basic needs'. GREEN REVOLUTION transformations reshaped agrarian geographies and associated livelihoods and expectations. Research and policy interest in the INFORMAL SECTOR intensified, while development institutions sought to integrate women in development in areas of food production and fertility. The 1970s was also a period of deepening global CRISIS and transformation in the US's hegemonic role in relation to the geopolitics of finance, currencies and energy. The OPEC oil-price hike and the subsequent flood of Eurodollars into offshore US banks led to reckless lending and borrowing by increasingly indebted Third World countries, and the Debt Crisis of the early 1980s was 'resolved' through geopolitical realignments, allowing new forms of intervention in sovereign states to ensure repayment to metropolitan banks. Development theory and practice shifted abruptly into a period of forced austerity and STRUCTURAL ADJUSTMENT, justified through a reinvention of liberal economic doctrine, in what John Toye dubbed 'the neo-liberal counterrevolution'. The onset of NEO-LIBERALISM coincided with the demise of the USSR – the massive experiment in state socialism – whose birth and death marked hopes and laments of many Leftist development thinkers and Third Worldist nationalisms, while making space to rethink anti-imperialist, democratic socialist alternatives to Cold War verities (Nove, 2005 [1983]).

By the 1990s, the focus of development had shifted to East Asia, to economies that had come through years of crisis, and to remarkable transformations in China: a kind of capitalism with Maoist characteristics, combining fast growth with piling social and environmental costs (see ASIAN MIRACLES/TIGERS). The twenty-first century has in several senses borne the continuing importance of development questions after the highpoint of neo-liberal and POST-DEVELOPMENT critiques, as well as the continued salience of its four long-term themes of LIBERALISM, MARXISM, social DARWINISM and anti-colonial radicalism. Neo-liberalisms are now seen in relation to state interventions, imperial MILITARISM and CLASS projects of regional elites as well as their adversaries. A revival of interest in Polanyi (2001 [1944]) comes at a time when the social costs of market fundamentalism are clearer, and a key task of development geography is to track its local articulations, as Hart (2001) demonstrates in South Africa. Hart's work exemplifies the importance of continuing to trace development processes in their spatial diversity, and in relation to development models abstracted from elsewhere. Taking the South African government's arguments about East Asia as exemplar, Hart argues that Chinese capitalism has relied on histories of land reform and state investment in a social wage, precisely that which has been eroded in the decade following APARTHEID. This is a powerful call to a development geography engaged with concrete policy problems and popular aspirations that is also careful about tactics.   SC

devolution The transfer of POWER or authority from one person or body to another, and specifically the transfer of governmental powers from the central or federal government to lower tiers. Devolution may involve the transfer of functions to unelected regional or local administrative bodies, but the term is more commonly used to refer to the transfer of some legislative powers to provincial elected assemblies, which are often established for the purpose.

Devolution thus involves a division of powers (administrative, judicial or legislative) between the central government and sub-national institutions. Devolution is sometimes distinguished from FEDERALISM in which the division of powers is determined by the constitution, whereas under devolution the powers are conferred by the centre, which retains the capacity to revoke them. However, the practical operations of federal and devolved systems are often similar.

The extent of devolution varies between countries, but sub-national institutions typically have responsibility for policy fields such as planning, economic DEVELOPMENT, HEALTH CARE and environmental protection, while defence and foreign affairs remain the responsibility of the central state. Devolved institutions may also have revenue-raising powers. Devolution may also be 'asymmetrical' with some territories having more autonomy and greater power than others within the same NATION-STATE.

Devolution has been an important STATE strategy for the management of territorial political and cultural differences and the political claims associated with them (Keating, 1998: cf. TERRITORY; TERRITORIALITY). It has also been an important demand of territorial (especially regionalist) political movements, whether as an end in its own right or as a step towards either independence or political separation (see REGIONALISM).

Regional devolution has been a notable feature of the political geography of the European Union since the 1970s. For example, of the six largest EU countries, different forms of regional autonomy were introduced in Spain in 1978, in France after 1982, in Italy during the 1990s and in Poland after 1999. In the UK in 1999, a devolved parliament with some tax-raising powers was established in Scotland, along with elected assemblies of more limited scope in Wales and Northern Ireland (Germany had adopted a federal constitution in 1949: see EU Committee of the Regions, 2003).   JPA

Suggested reading
Jones, Goodwin and Jones (2005); Swenden (2006).

dialectic(s)   The perpetual resolution of binary oppositions, a metaphysics most closely associated in European PHILOSOPHY and social thought with G.W.F. Hegel (1770–1813) and Karl Marx (1818–83). In HUMAN GEOGRAPHY, a simple example would be the following, essentially Hegelian reading of August Lösch's LOCATION THEORY. There:

a perfectly homogeneous landscape with identical customers, working inside the framework of perfect competition, would necessarily develop, from its inner rules of change, into a heterogeneous landscape, with both rich, active sectors and poor, depressed regions. The homogeneous regional system negates itself and generates dialectically its contradiction as regional inequalities appear. (Marchand, 1978)

This is a helpful first approximation, but the dialectic is usually deployed outside the framework of NEO-CLASSICAL ECONOMICS that contains traditional location theory. In fact, it is a characteristic of the Löschian system that once the heterogeneous landscape has emerged, it is maintained in equilibrium rather than convulsed through transformation. As such, it is really an example of a *categorical paradigm* – one in which change is simply the kaleidoscopic recombination of the same, ever-present and fixed elements – rather than a fully *dialectical paradigm*.

The most developed dialectical paradigms in human geography have been derived from Marx's HISTORICAL MATERIALISM. A formal statement of principles has been provided by Harvey (1996, pp. 48–57; cf. 1973, pp. 286–302). Its key propositions include the following:

- Dialectical thinking emphasizes PROCESSES, flows and relations.
- The formation and duration of SYSTEMS and structures is not the point of departure (these 'things' are not treated as givens) but, rather, the problem for analysis: processes, flows and relations constitute – form, shape, give rise to – systems and structures.
- The operation of these processes, flows and relations is contradictory, and it is the temporary resolution of these contradictions that feeds into the perpetual transformation of systems and structures. All systems and structures thus contain possibilities for change.
- Spaces and times (or, rather, 'space–times') are not external coordinates but are contained within – or 'implicated in' – different processes that effectively produce their own forms of space and TIME.

Particular importance is attached to the identification of contradictions. Formally, a *contradiction* is a principle that both (i) enters into the constitution of a system or structure, and also (ii) negates or opposes ('contradicts') the stability or integrity of that system or structure.

These principles seem abstract when set out in this form, but they have been used to considerable analytical effect by Harvey in his explorations of the contradictory constitution and restless transformation of CAPITALISM as a system of COMMODITY production: hence his insistence on the crucial, dialectical concept of 'creative destruction'. Harvey wires this to the dialectical PRODUCTION OF SPACE itself (see Barnes 2006a; Sheppard, 2006a). Indeed, SPACE has occupied centre-stage in many dialectical geographies, but several of these owe as much to Lefebvre's reading of Marx as they do Harvey's: hence Soja (1980, 1989) proposed a 'socio-spatial dialectic' (see also TRIALECTICS) and Shields (1999) described Lefebvre's work as a 'spatial dialectics'. Other writers, indebted in different ways to different historical materialisms, have shown how other geographical concepts may also be approached dialectically: thus Pred (1984) emphasized the dialectics of PLACE and practice; Mitchell (2002a) traced a series of ways in which LANDSCAPE may be interrogated as a dialectical formation; and Castree (2003b) examined the prospects (and problems) of treating what he called 'NATURE in the making' dialectically.

In Harvey's own writings, as elsewhere, dialectics functions as both a mode of explanation and a mode of representation (Castree, 1996). REPRESENTATION is not confined to writing, of course, and there has been considerable interest in combining the textual and the visual in the tense constellations of what Marxist cultural critic Walter Benjamin called the DIALECTICAL IMAGE. Historical materialism is rich with close readings of Marx's canon – attending not only to what he said but how he said it – and it was famously claimed that Marx's words are 'like bats: one can see in them both birds and mice'. In human geography, however, this attentiveness to the slippery subtleties of language and to the powers released by words has occasioned a series of reflections that have taken many critics a considerable distance from Harvey's own base in historical materialism. Thus Olsson (1974) argued that the categorical paradigm fails to recognize the interpenetrations of form and process, subject and object, so that its propositions reveal more about the language we are talking in, whereas 'statements in dialectics will say more about the worlds we are talking about'. Olsson's subsequent work has taken him far from Marx and into a sustained interrogation of Western philosophical thought (Olsson, 1980, 1991, 2007). To be sure, 'words' and 'worlds' are connected, as Olsson (and for that matter Harvey) constantly accentuate, and in order to explore the ways in which they are folded into one another, a number of human geographers have made two further moves. One has been to follow the linguistic turn in the humanities and social sciences, and so challenge the metaphysics of binary oppositions on which classical dialectics depends (Doel, 1992, 2006: see also DECONSTRUCTION). Another has been to take seriously Harvey's emphases on materiality, practice and transformation, but to develop these through

an avowedly NON-REPRESENTATIONAL THEORY. Here too, the accent is on practices, and on the provisional and the incomplete, but Whatmore (1999b, p. 25; see also 2002a) insists that dialectical reasoning is 'insufficiently radical' to convey the sensuous openness of 'world-making': there is thus a studied refusal to render processes through binary oppositions or to convene them within a plenary totality. But some perceptive critics have wondered whether, in practice, this agenda (its 'relational ontology') really is so different from the approach practiced by Harvey and others (Demeritt, 2005).   DG

Suggested reading
Demeritt (2005); Harvey (1996, pp. 48–57); Sheppard (2006).

dialectical image A leitmotif in the work of Walter Benjamin, the dialectical image is best described as an aesthetics of historical montage, or as a method for disrupting a linear or progressivist logic of history and historical understanding. Opposed to all forms of TELEOLOGY and totality, the dialectical image rests on a spatio-temporal paradox. On the one hand, all *images* must be torn from their immediate contexts and their chronological movement 'frozen' in order to become legible. On the other, DIALECTICS, in both the ancient sense of continuous disputation and the Marxian theoretic of contradiction, works to ensure constant mobility and mutation. So understood, the dialectical image reconfigures the relationship of the past to the present. Refusing all temporal continuity in which the present illuminates the past or the past casts its light on the present, the dialectical image constitutes the scene in which TIME and SPACE are out of joint; in which the 'then' and now', like the 'here' and 'there', combine in an explosive flash or 'constellation'. From this emerges a cognitive shock, without which rigorous conceptual thinking cannot occur. JD

Suggested reading
Benjamin (1973, 1999); Buck-Morss (1989); Dubow (2007).

diaspora A scattering of people over SPACE and transnational connections between people and places. The term was first used to describe the forced dispersal of the Jews from Palestine in the sixth century BCE, and often continues to refer to forced MIGRATION and exile. More recently, and particularly since the 1990s, diaspora studies have come to encompass wider notions of transnational migration, resettlement, connection and attachment, often closely associated with post-colonial and 'new ethnicities' research (see TRANSNATIONALISM). For Kalra, Kaur and Hutnyk (2005), there is a broad distinction between the use of diaspora as a descriptive tool and mode of categorization (including lists of various criteria that characterize diasporas) and more critical understandings of diaspora as a contested process. Whilst some accounts identify different types of diaspora, including victim, labour, trade, imperial and cultural diasporas on a global scale (Cohen, 1997), other studies theorize diaspora and its implications for understanding space, IDENTITY, CULTURE and the politics of HYBRIDITY (including Hall, 1990; Kalra, Kaur and Hutnyk, 2005). Rather than analyse diaspora solely in terms of 'RACE' and ETHNICITY, geographers and others working across the humanities and social sciences have explored the GENDER, CLASS and sexual spaces of diaspora. Geographers have also stressed the importance of studying the grounded politics of diaspora (including Mitchell, 1997b). Both the conceptual study of diaspora and the substantive study of different diasporas develop critical perspectives on GLOBALIZATION, NEO-LIBERALISM, MULTICULTURALISM and COSMOPOLITANISM.

Both ideas about diaspora and studies of particular diasporas are inherently geographical, revolving around space and PLACE, MOBILITY and locatedness, the NATION and transnationality. The diasporic lives of transnational migrants, for example, are often interpreted in terms of 'roots' and 'routes' (Clifford, 1997). Whilst 'roots' might imply an original HOMELAND from which people have scattered, and to which they might seek to return, a focus on 'routes' complicates such ideas by tracing more mobile, transcultural and deterritorialized geographies of migration and resettlement. As Paul Gilroy explains, the spatialities of diaspora represent 'a historical and experiential rift between the locations of residence and the locations of belonging' (2000b, p. 124). A wide range of research explores diasporic attachments to homelands that might be remembered, imagined, lost or are yet to be achieved, and the political, economic and cultural materialization of such attachments through political activism, the transfer of remittances and diverse cultural practices. Other research unsettles the idea that people living in diaspora are bound to a homeland or nation of origin and identification. Avtar Brah, for example, proposes the notion of 'diaspora space' to encompass the 'intersectionality of diaspora, BORDER, and dis/location as a point of confluence of economic, political, cultural and psychic processes' (1996, p. 181). As Brah explains, 'diaspora space as a conceptual category is "inhabited" not only by those who have migrated and their descendants but equally by those who are constructed and represented as indigenous. In other words, the concept of *diaspora space* (as opposed to that of diaspora) includes the entanglement of genealogies of dispersion with those of "staying put"' (p. 181). AB

Suggested reading
Brah (1996); Clifford (1997).

difference The concept of 'difference' has become an increasingly prominent concern in GEOGRAPHY over the past two decades. Geographers have looked at how socio-spatial boundaries of inclusion and exclusion are produced on the basis of categories such as RACE, CLASS, GENDER, SEXUALITY or DISABILITY. Most agree that these and other such categories are socially constructed. This is not to say that differences do not exist or are illusory but, rather, to point out that the ways in which we categorize ourselves and others are the result of social practices. Further, these socially constructed differences have very real political effects. As Audrey Kobayashi (1997, p. 3) writes, 'The concept of difference allows the social creation of categories of people subordinate to a dominant norm, and allows the continuation of cultural practices that reinscribe difference as differential values placed upon human life.'

In that difference arises from social practice, it is also spatial. David Harvey (1996) argues that SPACE and TIME work to individuate and identify people through the production of differences along multiple axes. In other words, geographically inscribed inequalities position people and groups differently in relation to political, cultural, ecological and economic RESOURCES. Spatial practices such as SEGREGATION and the POLICING of BORDERS work to enforce and consolidate difference. As David Delaney (1998) shows in his work on race, LANDSCAPE and LAW, the complex legal geographies of PROPERTY and public/private distinctions are inseparable from the relations of POWER and domination that are associated with difference. This means that some people have more access to RIGHTS in certain spaces than others.

While ideas about difference often work to delimit hierarchies and inequalities, difference is also a powerful element of IDENTITY POLITICS. Race, class, gender, sexuality and other differences can provide the basis for solidarities and RESISTANCE. Arguments that point out the constructed nature of such categories and that highlight the divisions *within* groups (such as racial differences within feminist movements, or class differences within racial politics) can seem to threaten the basis of political struggles forged around identities such as 'Black' or 'Woman'. In response, some feminists have adopted 'strategic ESSENTIALISM', choosing to emphasize the commonalities across women's experiences in order to unite women for political purposes.

Difference poses political problems for those who wish both to value diversity and to dismantle the structures of discrimination and oppression that scaffold ideas about difference. The question of how to recognize and make space for the very real effects of difference, or POSITIONALITY, and at the same time to dismantle hierarchies based on difference is of ongoing concern to political theorists and geographers. Iris Marion Young (1990a), for example, has advocated for the celebration of diversity within an overarching political unity. Such a project is not, however, without its difficulties in the context of ever shifting axes of difference and alliance.   AJS

Suggested reading
Fincher and Jacobs (1998); Women and Geography Study Group (1997).

diffusion The spread of a phenomenon (including ideas, objects and living beings) over SPACE and through TIME. There is a long tradition of diffusion studies in American CULTURAL GEOGRAPHY, most closely associated with the work of Carl Ortwin Sauer (1889–1975) and Fred B. Kniffen (1900–93). According to Sauer (1941), it was Friedrich Ratzel (1844–1904) who 'founded the study of the diffusion of cultural traits, presented in the nearly forgotten second volume of his *Anthropogeographie*' published in 1891 (see ANTHROPOGEOGRAPHY). In Sauer's view, diffusion – 'the filling of the space of the earth' – was a 'general problem of social science': 'A new crop, craft or technique is introduced to a culture area. Does it spread, or diffuse vigorously or does its acceptance meet resistance?' The specific contribution of GEOGRAPHY was to reconstruct diffusion pathways and to evaluate the influence of physical barriers (Sauer, 1952; Wagner and Mikesell, 1962). Both tasks were pursued by various members

of the BERKELEY SCHOOL, but they reappeared in a starkly different guise in the much more formal study of innovation diffusion inaugurated by Torsten Hägerstrand (1916–2004).

One of Sauer's closest associates introduced Hägerstrand's Swedish monograph to Anglo-American geography: 'No one who essays in the future to interpret the distribution of culture elements in the process of diffusion can afford to ignore Hägerstrand's methods and conclusions' (Leighly, 1954). Even so, it was some fourteen years before an English translation of Hägerstrand's *Innovation diffusion as a spatial process* appeared (Hägerstrand, 1967; see Duncan, 1974). Hägerstrand's work had two catalytic consequences: it set in motion the frozen worlds of SPATIAL SCIENCE, and it opened the door to sophisticated computer modelling of spatial processes. The theoretical structure of his original MODEL is shown in the figure. An interaction matrix provides the contours of a generalized or MEAN INFORMATION FIELD, which structures the way in which information circulates through the population in a regional system. These flows are modulated by physical barriers and individual resistances, which together check the transformation of information into INNOVATION and so shape the successive diffusion waves that break on to the final adoption surface.

Most immediate discussion focused on the operationalization of the model – on the use of SIMULATION methods, the comparison of 'observed' and 'predicted' patterns of adoption, and the detection of a localized NEIGHBOURHOOD EFFECT. Within this modelling tradition, the most important developments included the following:

- A formalization of the mathematical relationships between the structure of the mean information field and the form and velocity of diffusion waves, revealing the connections between different DISTANCE-DECAY curves and the classic neighbourhood effect (although it is scarcely surprising that a distance-bound interaction matrix should generate a contagious pattern of adoptions).

- A demonstration that the Hägerstrand model is only a special instance of the *simple epidemic model*, and the subsequent derivation of more complex EPIDEMIC models, particularly through the remarkable contributions of Cliff, Haggett, Ord and Versey (1981), whose replication of a range of 'spatial processes' (see PROCESS) confirmed:

- the recognition of *hierarchical diffusion*, typically through CENTRAL PLACE systems, and frequently operating alongside the distance-bound, *contagious diffusion* of the classical model (Hudson, 1969; Pedersen, 1970);
- the incorporation of rejection and removal processes and the modelling of competitive diffusions (Webber, 1972).

These changes entailed a move away from simulation techniques towards more analytical methods, which have been of immense importance in the increased traffic between EPIDEMIOLOGY and MEDICAL GEOGRAPHY (see DISEASE, MODELLING OF). This is now the major focus of diffusion theory in human geography, although spatial models of information circulation and innovation diffusion are important in marketing research too.

Haggett (1992) claimed to see parallels between Sauer's original prospectus and the contemporary modelling of disease, particularly his use of 'controlled speculation' and his focus on 'hearths and pathways'. Ironically, however, it was precisely these features that caused diffusion theory to fall from grace in most other areas of HUMAN GEOGRAPHY. There were several brilliant studies that wired diffusion into larger social transformations (e.g. Pred, 1973; Blaikie, 1975), but these were the exception to a cascade of studies using available data sets merely to 'fit' or 'test' diffusion models. Just ten years after the translation of Hägerstrand's *magnum opus*, Blaikie (1978) could speak of a 'crisis' in diffusion research, which he said arose from its preoccupation with spatial form and space–time sequence, while Gregory (1985) attributed the 'stasis' of diffusion theory to a pervasive unwillingness to engage with SOCIAL THEORY and social history to explore the *conditions* and the *consequences* of diffusion processes. Critics argued that the spatial circulation of information remained the strategic element in most applications of the Hägerstrand model and its derivatives, and while flows of information through different propagation structures and contact NETWORKS were exposed in more detail, the primacy accorded to the reconstruction of these spatial pathways obscured a crucial limitation of the Hägerstrand model: it operated within what Blaut (1977) called a 'granular region', 'a sort of Adam Smithian landscape, totally without macrostructure'. In particular:

(1) The Hägerstrand model begins with a pool of 'potential adopters' and does not explain the selective process through which they are constituted in the first place. This suggests the need for a model of *biased innovation*, where (for example) CLASS or GENDER circumscribes access to innovations. 'Non-diffusion' is then not a passive but an active state arising directly from the structures of a particular society (Yapa and Mayfield, 1978). Critiques of this sort required diffusion theory to be integrated with fields such as POLITICAL ECONOMY and FEMINIST GEOGRAPHY that pay attention to the social as well as the spatial.

(2) The Hägerstrand model assumes a 'uniform cognitive region' and does not explain the selective process through which information flows are interpreted. This matters because 'resistance' to innovation is not invariably a product of ignorance or insufficient information: it may signal a political struggle by people whose evaluation of the information is strikingly different to that of the 'potential adopters'. Critiques of this sort required diffusion theory to be reconnected to a more general cultural geography (Blaut, 1977).

These critiques served largely to divert attention to other projects, however, and there has been little advance in the architecture of diffusion theory in recent years. Interest in the detailed reconstruction of specific diffusion sequences as key moments in processes of economic and cultural transformation has continued in cultural–historical geography and ENVIRONMENTAL HISTORY (e.g. Jordan, 1993; Overton, 1996), and there is also a growing interest in the circulation of information, including the transmission of scientific knowledge and the formation of creative economies (Kong, Gibson, Khoo and Semple, 2006). But these enquiries rarely refer to, let alone rely on, classical diffusion theory. The tension between diffusion modelling on the one side and cultural-historical and politico-economic studies of diffusion on the other (and the versions of human geography that each represents) is exemplified by the study of AIDS. Mapping and modelling the spread of the disease has been a major focus of geographical enquiry, but this has been undertaken largely in isolation from studies of its social and cultural geography (cf. Brown, 1995). It is in the space between these two intellectual traditions that diffusion theory currently languishes, but some small steps

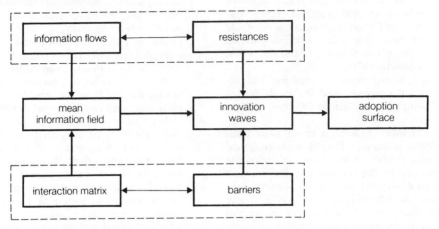

diffusion *The structure of Hägerstrand's diffusion model*

towards bridging the gap have been made in studies of disease diffusion and WAR (e.g. Smallman-Raynor and Cliff, 2004). DG

Suggested reading
Blaikie (1978); Blaut (1977); Haggett (1992).

digital cartography The use of numerical coding, electronic MEDIA and digital computers to collect, manipulate, manage and display geographical data. Coined in the 1970s, the term has largely replaced the older rubric 'computer-assisted cartography', because almost all production CARTOGRAPHY is now computer-assisted. 'Digital cartography' seems destined for obsolescence insofar as most geospatial data are now 'born digital'; that is, originally captured as numbers using a GLOBAL POSITIONING SYSTEM (GPS) receiver, aerial photogrammetry or REMOTE SENSING, rather than converted from an existing MAP image by scanning or a process of electronic tracing known as DIGITIZING. In this sense, geographical data acquired by updating, transforming or otherwise enhancing the attributes (descriptions) of cartographic objects such as street segments and land parcels are also born digital. Because hard-copy, analogue maps have become more the exception than the rule, 'digital cartography' seems likely to survive only when writers need an opposite for 'analogue cartography'. Even so, born-digital materials, especially useful because they are readily searchable and easily updated, challenge conventional practices of map preservation and copyright (Varian, 2005).

As an endeavour, digital cartography is closely related to GEOGRAPHIC INFORMATION SYSTEMS (GIS). In general, the former focuses on data acquisition, data management and the generation of reproducible images, while the latter emphasizes data retrieval and specialized analysis. These overlapping disciplines share a common interest in automated map generalization and the display of terrain data. In addition, digital cartography has a dynamic, interactive component linked to scientific VISUALIZATION and computer animation. Other shared concerns include standardized terms and definitions, flexible exchange formats, efficient methods for ensuring reliability, and the development of metadata describing a file's origin, contents and fitness for use (Nogueras-Iso, Zarazaga-Soria, Lacasta, Béjar and Muro-Medrano, 2004).

As with GIS, digital cartography recognizes two principal types of data, RASTER and VECTOR. Examples of raster data include land-cover data acquired from space with a multi-spectral scanner, digital elevation models (DEMs) consisting of surface elevations sampled for a grid with rows and columns spaced 30 m apart, and images scanned from historical TOPOGRAPHIC MAPS and nautical charts. The spatial quality of a raster data set is described by the spatial resolution of the sensor or scanner. By contrast, vector data rely on lists of point coordinates to describe the shape and position of BOUNDARY lines, streets and other linear features, as well as lists of linkages or adjacencies to specify the boundaries of polygons representing, for example, counties or CENSUS TRACTS. In addition, attribute data describe the type of feature, its name or identifying number, and specialized characteristics such as the population of a CENSUS TRACT or the width and left- and right-hand address ranges of a street segment.

Each format has particular advantages. Maps in raster format, for instance, are well suited for print-on-demand distribution as well as dissemination over the INTERNET (Evans and Vickers, 1995). By contrast, vector data are especially useful for creating map displays at different scales on diverse projections (see MAP PROJECTION). Mathematical formulae afford ready conversion between spherical and plane coordinates or from one projection to another. Indeed, tailored map projections that control distortion for a region of interest or provide insightful views, including dynamic oblique views or flyovers, are a prime asset of digital cartography.

Digital cartographic research has also produced ALGORITHMS for map generalization and map labelling, both of which support the dynamic, interactive change of scale for street maps, topographic maps and electronic atlases. Generalization is especially relevant for maps displayed at SCALES smaller than that for which the data were originally acquired (McMaster and Shea, 1992). Because map symbols are more likely to overlap as scale decreases, a generalization algorithm must first identify areas where overlap will occur and then avoid aesthetically awkward (and sometime confusing) graphic conflict by suppressing less important features or shifting them apart – one of several ethically responsible trade-offs that human mapmakers call 'cartographic license' (Li and Su, 1995). Generalization must also smooth out intricate coastlines and streams with tight meander loops, both of which can yield ambiguous and unappealing blobs at substantially reduced scales. Automated map labeling is similar to map generalization insofar as the algorithm must determine potential conflict between the allegedly ideal positions of map labels (Zoraster, 1997). If the conflict cannot be resolved by moving one or more labels to a less desirable location, the algorithm might need to leave a feature unlabeled or use a thin leader line to link a symbol with a label that cannot be adjacent. More straightforward is the attachment of text to curved features such as roads and streams.

Another common display task in digital cartography is the realistic viewing of digital elevation models. Typical strategies include low-angle oblique views, which require a geometric transformation as well as the identification and suppression of symbols where the surface is hidden from view (De Floriani and Magillo, 2003) and the addition of shadows, or hill shading, in areas not illuminated by a hypothetical light source located in the upper left or upper right (Tuhkanen, 1987). More intriguing are maps formed by draping satellite imagery, land-cover classifications or topographic symbols over obliquely viewed digital elevation models (Banerjee and Mitra, 2004).

Although digital cartography has largely displaced its non-electronic counterpart as the principal means of acquiring and storing geospatial data, paper maps thrive in diverse ways: in newspapers, magazines, atlases and geography textbooks; as mass-marketed wayfinding and recreation maps; and as customized, one-off artefacts downloaded over the Internet (Peterson, 2003) or created using commercial, off-the-shelf mapping software (Longley, Goodchild, Maguire and Rhind, 2005, pp. 157–75). Everyday experience suggests, not without irony, that the majority of paper maps nowadays are specially tailored renderings based on digital data and produced on a laser or ink-jet printer. MM

Suggested reading
DeMers (2002); Longley, Goodchild, Maguire and Rhind (2005); McMaster and Shea (1992); Peterson (2003).

digitizing The process of converting IMAGES, TEXTS, MODELS, MAPS, sounds and data into digital and computer readable forms, with an expectation of 'value added' but a risk of information loss. A paper map is easily digitized into bitmap or JPEG format using a conventional, desktop scanner. However, the user may be disappointed by the result. First, the original image will be converted into a series of discrete (RASTER) pixels. The blocky nature of these will be evident in words or labels copied from the original document; the severity will depend on the resolution of the scanner (its dpi – dots per inch). Second, loading the image into a GEOGRAPHIC INFORMATION SYSTEM will not leave it positioned correctly with other maps and data on screen. The reason is that although the digital image may show a map, no information has been encoded such that the computer can interpret it geographically. Providing a 'world file' assigns GEOCODES to the corners of the image and therefore locates it. Yet, if the user's goal is to select all schools within a certain distance of a major road, for example, then s/he will still be left wanting: the original map has been digitized 'en masse' without encoding the two specific features of schools and roads.

The general point is that digitizing may appear straightforward, but producing an outcome that is fit for purpose requires more careful thought. For example, it is easy to scan a manuscript and therefore archive it in an online depository. But unless some metadata about the document are also provided (year of publication, title, abstract etc.), then it will be hard for potential users to search the depository and extract what they are looking for. It may also be beneficial to convert the scanned image using text recognition software, permitting all documents to be searched for key words. However, this all takes time and money, as well as the development of standards and protocols to ensure consistency in how information is stored, catalogued and updated – such as those developed for the JSTOR scholarly journal archive (www.jstor.org) that allow searching of the author, title, abstract and/or full text for all or a subset of the journals archived, for all or particular dates, and for all or specific types of journal content (e.g. article, review or opinion piece) (Schonfeld, 2003).

There is also the issue of error management. Using manual digitizing tables and software to capture the geographies of schools and roads from a paper map assumes that the map is of reasonable quality, having not shrunk or stretched, and requires concentration from the person digitizing who may easily make mistakes (from a slight hand shake or from fatigue or boredom!). A lack of attention could lead to road sections that do not meet (an undershoot) or the creation of a new spur when the road is drawn past the intended intersection (an overshoot). If not detected, the errors could propagate and lead to misleading analyses of the data concerned.

Digitization is always a change to the original. Whether it matters depends on the nature of the change and how the digital version is applied. It could be argued that MP3s are inferior to vinyl records because they have a lower frequency range. But then have you ever tried to carry a thousand seven-inch singles?   RH

Suggested reading
Clarke (2003); Schonfeld (2003).

disability Conventionally understood as the state of being physically and/or mentally different from some assumed 'norm' of human corporeal and/or psychological functioning, the term applies to people with an *impairment* that supposedly limits their ability to perform activities in the manner taken as 'normal' for a human being. Disability is often framed negatively, couched as 'loss' (e.g. of a limb or vision) or 'lack' (e.g. of mobility or reasoning skills), with scant attention paid to the experiences and aspirations of the people affected.

Proponents of the *medical model* of disability stress the apparently 'damaged' BODY or mind of an individual, and invite a personal narrative of 'tragedy' followed by 'heroic' efforts at self-adjustment (Golledge, 1997). Those of the *social model* stress not the individual but, rather, a wider SOCIETY that fails to accommodate impairment, thus embracing a critical stance on the underlying *ableism* of a non-disabled society (Chouinard, 1997). The latter model, casting light on 'disabling social and *environmental* barriers' (Barnes and Mercer, 2004, p. 2; emphasis added) and advocating a critical 'politics of access', is inherently geographical in its alertness to the social and physical placing of disabled people within non-disabled settings. This model also examines both the political-economic forces impacting upon disability, as in the discriminatory dynamics of labour and housing MARKETS, and the deeper roots of oppression occasioned by the stigmatization of 'imperfect' bodies (Hahn, 1989). It has itself been criticized for remaining *too* distanced from embodied realities, and thereby neglecting subjective experience as revealed in personal stories of pain, fatigue, rejection and simply 'getting by'. Some theorists hence call for a third way, a *biosocial model*, allowing BODIES and experiences into the picture while still retaining the critical sharpness of the social model (Watson, 2004).

These debates have played out within geographical research on disability (Hall, 2000b), which has become a recognizable sub-field exemplified in review articles and edited book collections (Park, Radford and Vickers, 1998; Butler and Parr, 1999). Early work considered the wheelchair-user or visually impaired person negotiating the environmental obstacle course of streets, curbs and buildings fronted by steps (Golledge, 1993; Vujakovic and Matthews, 1994). The focus upon 'stairs' was then supplemented by a concern for 'stares' (Pain, Burke, Fuller and Gough, 2001, p. 177), so that the issue becomes not just physical accessibility but also the extent to which disabled people are marked as different, fundamentally unwanted and 'out of place' in public space (Butler and Bowlby, 1997). The broader context of 'disabling environments' here attracts critique, implicating architects, planners and building control officers (designers and 'the state') for producing spaces that effectively 'lock out' disabled people (Imrie, 1996). The longer-term historical perspective reveals how modern CAPITALISM has initiated an ongoing process of spatially marginalizing disabled people from meaningful economic roles and the normal rounds of SOCIAL REPRODUCTION (Gleeson, 1999). Other geographical enquiries now use QUALITATIVE METHODS such as in-depth interviewing to excavate the experiential dimensions of being 'out of place', detecting how the axes of disability, CLASS, ETHNICITY, GENDER and SEXUALITY meld together in (the enduring of) exclusionary spaces.

Disability geography deals with both physical and mental impairments, where the latter entail both people with mental health problems (the 'mentally ill' in a medicalized vocabulary, including the 'depressed', 'schizophrenic' etc.) and people with learning or intellectual disabilities (the 'mentally handicapped' or 'mentally retarded' of now disfavoured vocabularies). There is a vibrant tradition of mental health geography (Smith and Giggs, 1988), exploring spatial–epidemiological subjects as well as looking at both the emergence of the 'lunatic asylum' and, more recently, processes of 'deinstitutionalization', 'community care' and the sites of everyday survival today for people with mental health problems (see contributions to Philo, 2000c). Less extensive is work on geographies of intellectual disability, although historical and contemporary studies can be identified (see contributions to Metzel and Philo, 2005). There is potential for building theoretical, substantive and ethico-political bridges between the different strains of disability geography tackling physical and mental difference, and perhaps too with parts of HEALTH geography exploring the circumstances of people with long-term chronic illness (Moss and Dyck, 2002). CPP

Suggested reading
Butler and Parr (1999); Gleeson (1999); Imrie (1996); Philo (2000c).

disciplinary power A form of POWER analysed in the work of Michel Foucault (1926–84) that in his analysis follows from classical sovereignty. Foucault claims that power is dispersed throughout SOCIETY rather than coming from a centralized source, and that is therefore important to analyse it within institutional and social practices. Disciplinary power emerged in Foucault's published works with *Discipline and Punish* (1976), but was also analysed in his earlier lectures at the *Collège de France* that are now being published (see, e.g., Foucault, 2003 [1999], 2006 [2003]).

While SOVEREIGNTY may showcase its power through individual events of spectacular VIOLENCE, such as the fighting of battles or the torture of attempted regicides – like the gruesome description of the measures meted out to Damiens at the beginning of *Discipline and punish* – discipline works in an entirely other way. Power is constantly exercised, over the smallest transgression, with repetition, certainty and consistency, key elements in establishing control. Its model is the modern army, with the training of individual bodies into collective ones, a process that Foucault describes as 'dressage'. The mechanisms can be found in schools, hospitals, factories and PRISONS. The model of spatial organization in a town affected by the plague is another of Foucault's recurrent examples, which he finds taken to its ideal form in Jeremy Bentham's plan for the PANOPTICON.

A number of key themes emerge in Foucault's analyses: the control of the BODY and its ritualized training and conditioning; the continuous nature of the exercise of disciplinary power; the control and partitioning of TIME – particularly illustrated by the modern mechanized factory – and spatial organization and distribution. Spatial control works both on the level of architectural or urban planning, and on the ordering of individual bodies. Discipline is a distribution of bodies, of their actions, of their behaviour: a spatial strategy and analysis. These spatial strategies can be understood as enclosure or confinement; subdivision or partitioning of this SPACE; designation of a purpose or coding to these sites; and CLASSIFICATION or ranking of them. These spaces of power have their concomitant knowledges, which Foucault designates by the power–knowledge relation in a series of pairings: 'tactics, the spatial ordering of men; taxonomy, the disciplinary space of natural beings; the economic table, the regulated movement of wealth' (1976a [1975], pp. 148–9).

In Foucault's early work on SEXUALITY (1978 [1976], 2003 [1999]), he utilized and developed these ideas about disciplinary power, and analysed how power over life itself could be understood as BIOPOWER. In his later writings on GOVERNMENTALITY, Foucault developed an understanding of how liberal governments tried to govern as little as possible and to open up spaces for the circulation of goods, people and wealth (see LIBERALISM). Although many

165

have found Foucault's work on power generally unremittingly bleak, the critique of individual agency and the analysis of the process by which SUBJECTS are formed – a process that Foucault calls *assujettissement*, meaning both subject-formation and subjectification – have been extremely influential.   SE

Suggested reading
Crampton and Elden (2007); Driver (1992a).

discourse A specific series of representations and practices through which meanings are produced, identities constituted, social relations established, and political and ethical outcomes made more or less possible. Although different fields in the HUMANITIES and social sciences have worked with varying accounts of discourse, all grow out of the decades of debates about LANGUAGE, interpretation and understanding in the natural and social sciences (Howarth, 2000). As such, discourse is a concept that departs from the traditional PHILOSOPHY of language's relationship to the world. Instead of seeing the world as independent of ideas about it, with language transparently reflecting a pre-existing reality, theories of discourse understand reality as produced via practices of interpretation deploying different modes of representation.

Although philosophically well established, especially in POST-STRUCTURALISM, discourse remains controversial in the social sciences. Those employing the concept are often said to be claiming that 'everything is language', that 'there is no reality' and that, consequentially, a general inability to take a political position and defend an ethical stance abounds. These objections demonstrate how understandings of discourse are bedevilled by the view that interpretation involves only language, in contrast to the external, the real and the material. These dichotomies of IDEALISM/MATERIALISM and REALISM/idealism remain powerful conceptions of understanding the world. In practice, however, a concern with discourse does not involve a denial of the world's existence or the significance of materiality. This is well articulated by Laclau and Mouffe (1985, p. 108): 'the fact that every object is constituted as an object of discourse has *nothing to do* with whether there is a world external to thought, or with the realism/idealism opposition ... What is denied is not that ... objects exist externally to thought, but the rather different assertion that they could constitute themselves as objects outside of any discursive condition of emergence.' This means that

while nothing exists outside of discourse, there are important distinctions between linguistic and non-linguistic phenomena. There are also modes of REPRESENTATION that are ideational though strictly non-linguistic, such as the aesthetic and pictorial. It is just that there is no way of comprehending non-linguistic and extra-discursive phenomena except through discursive practices.

These philosophical debates are implied by different uses of discourse even when they are not overtly discussed. They lead to an appreciation of the fact that *discourses are performative*. This means that although discourses have variable meaning, force and effect, they constitute the 'objects' of which they speak and produce notions of 'the social' and 'the self' (see PERFORMATIVITY). The meanings, identities, social relations and political assemblages that are enacted in these performances combine the ideal and the material. As a consequence, appreciating that discourses are performative moves us away from a reliance on the idea of (social) *construction* towards *materialization*, whereby discourse 'stabilizes over time to produce the effect of BOUNDARY, fixity and surface' (Butler, 1993a, pp. 9, 12).

The performativity of discourse calls attention to the *discursive formations* that are produced over time by the stabilization of some interpretations at the expense of others. Discursive formations – such as NEO-LIBERAL notions of 'competitiveness' (Schoenberger, 1998), GENTRIFICATION and the racialization of Puerto Rican youth in Chicago (Wilson and Grammenos, 2005) or COLD WAR-derived GEOPOLITICAL discourses of 'danger' in Central Asia (Megoran, 2005) – are the culmination of discursive economies at work. In a discursive economy, investments have historically been made in certain interpretations; dividends can be drawn by those interests that have made the investments; representations are taxed when they confront new and ambiguous circumstances; and participation in the discursive economy is through social relations that embody an unequal distribution of power.

Within HUMAN GEOGRAPHY, the use of the concept of discourse can be characterized by a number of dimensions, though by no means would all scholars would accept every one of them:

● *Discourses are heterogeneous*: discourses are not the product of a single author or institution, and neither are they confined to literary texts, archives, scientific statements or political speeches. They come to have a dominant form over time, but they never eradicate alternatives or end resistance, and are thus constantly having to be reproduced.

- *Discourses are regulated*: discourses have coherence and systematicity, though they often contain contradictions, and are marked by their own 'regimes of truth' that police the boundaries that legislate inclusions and exclusions and establish criteria of acceptability.
- *Discourses are embedded*: discourses are not free-floating constructions produced by thought alone, but are performances that materialize social life; they are embedded in institutions, practices and subject-positions, but typically cut across and circulate through multiple institutions and subject positions.
- *Discourses are situated*: discourses, their formations and economies are the product of historical practices and geographical location. As such, they provide SITUATED KNOWLEDGES, characterized by particular constellations of power and knowledge always open to contestation and negotiation, even as they seek to obscure their historicity and specificity.

Discourses thereby shape the contours of the TAKEN-FOR-GRANTED WORLD, naturalizing and universalizing a particular subject formation and view of the world. Theories of discourse have thus greatly enlarged the interpretive horizon of human geography. Insofar as CRITICAL HUMAN GEOGRAPHY is concerned with the connections between power, knowledge and spatiality, discourse will be a vital concept.

Discourse has also altered the self-understanding of the field. It has revivified the HISTORY OF GEOGRAPHY in which 'great men' or 'paradigmatic schools' have given way to a concern with the discursive production of geographical knowledge. It has made obvious the complicity of human geography in COLONIALISM and IMPERIALISM (see POST-COLONIALISM) and the way in which traditional geographical knowledge effaced the contribution of non-Western SUBJECTS (Barnett, 1998). Theories of discourse have also played an important part in exposing the asymmetries of power that are inscribed within contemporary geographical discourses (notably ETHNOCENTRISM and PHALLOCENTRISM), elucidating the role of RHETORIC – and of poetics more generally – in legitimizing intellectual practice (Crush, 1991) and in allowing IDEOLOGY to congeal as 'unexamined discourse' (Gregory, 1978a).   DCA

Suggested reading
Foucault (1984); Howarth (2000).

discourse analysis The analysis of DISCOURSE; methodologies for studying the production and meaning of discourses. Discourse analysis involves a wide array of approaches to the construction and interpretation of meaning. These approaches understand LANGUAGE as a social practice, and are concerned with language use beyond the semantic units that are the domain of linguistics. The differences between the approaches to discourse analysis depend on the extent to which they (a) understand themselves to be a formal METHODOLOGY (hence the sometimes capitalized term 'Discourse Analysis') as opposed to a critical interpretative approach; and (b) the extent to which the formal components and properties of linguistic representations, as opposed to the social practices made possible by language, are the primary concern

The more formal, methodological approaches that comprise Discourse Analysis focus on the structure of spoken or written TEXTS, and confine their study to those texts – often in terms of content analysis – leaving questions of context and how much can be inferred from the linguistic data to others (see van Dijk, 1997). One prominent approach deals with the role that METAPHORS play in social life, and highlights the frames of reference through which problems are understood; for example, 'WAR' versus 'CRIME' in the struggle against TERRORISM, or 'choice' in the debates about public services and reproductive rights (Lakoff and Johnson, 2003 [1980]).

Critical Discourse Analysis (CDA), exemplified in the work of Fairclough (2001), extends the range of interpretive concern beyond the structures of language to the social and political context. While beginning with an analysis of language texts, CDA also includes the processes of text production, distribution and consumption in its approach. Finally, CDA is concerned with the way in which sociocultural practice is comprised of discursive events. As such, CDA argues that linguistic and social resources are controlled institutionally and access to them is unequal.

While CDA extends the concern with language to the social, it perhaps does not go as far as more interpretive and less formal approaches to discourse analysis. Allied with the conception of discourse as PERFORMATIVE, these approaches largely shun the idea of discourse analysis as a specific methodology, because they argue that all analysis

167

necessitates an encounter with the discursive given the impossibility of apprehending an extra-discursive realm beyond language and other modes of REPRESENTATION (see Howarth, Norval and Stavrakakis, 2000). Here, although few of these authors would present their thought in these terms, Roland Barthes' examination of mythologies, Jacques Derrida's notion of DECONSTRUCTION and Michel Foucault's account of GENEALOGY would all count as critical analyses of discourse, even if they could not be understood as Discourse Analysis. Nor is this broadly defined critical approach to discourse limited to questions of language or text (even if they are understood as social practices). As Rose (2007 [2001]) makes clear, discourse analysis is an important methodology for the study of visual culture (see VISUAL METHODS). DCA

Suggested reading
Fairclough (2003). See also the journal *Discourse and Society*.

disease, diffusion of An area of MEDICAL GEOGRAPHY that is concerned with mapping and modelling the spread of infectious diseases and their causative agents (e.g. viruses, bacteria and protozoa) over SPACE and through TIME. The approach is characterized by the application of QUANTITATIVE TECHNIQUES to decipher the spatial and temporal properties of EPIDEMIC waves in terms of their timing, intensity, rate and geographical corridors of spread (*descriptive models*), and to apply this understanding to the prediction of future disease distributions (*predictive models*). Particular concern with the topic stems from a need to intervene in the spread of epidemic waves (e.g. through the implementation of quarantine or vaccination) as part of public HEALTH policy

Geographical interest in the spread of infectious diseases was stimulated by a broader disciplinary concern with spatial DIFFUSION that followed from the influential studies of Torsten Hägerstrand in the 1950s (see Haggett, 2000). Within the tradition of diffusion modelling initiated by Hägerstrand, geographers have sought to identify the nature of the diffusion processes by which infectious diseases are propagated spatially, and to incorporate elements of these processes into formal mathematical MODELS of epidemic transmission. Two basic types of spatial diffusion process have received particular attention in the literature. A *contagious process* describes the wave-like spread of a disease from its point of introduction to geographically proximal

centres. Alternatively, a *hierarchical process* describes the spread of a disease through an ordered sequence of classes or places (e.g. an urban settlement hierarchy). Spatial diffusion processes of the contagious, hierarchical and related forms have been modelled for a wide variety of diseases in different historical and geographical settings; the classic studies of Pyle (1969) on cholera in the nineteenth-century USA and Cliff, Haggett, Ord and Versey (1981) on measles in twentieth-century Iceland are illustrative of the work undertaken.

Mathematical models of epidemic diffusion processes can be divided into two broad types. In *time series models* the past record of a disease in a regional system is used to model its future behaviour. In *process-based models* the person-to-person transmission of an infectious agent is simulated according to the parameters of the disease and the population at risk. Cliff, Haggett and Smallman-Raynor (1993, pp. 359–410) provide a review of the principal categories of model, along with a summary of their relative merits as tools for epidemic forecasting. The insights offered by such modelling approaches are increasingly being used in the monitoring and control of vaccine-preventable diseases, with the prospect of the construction of global early warning systems for the transmission of PANDEMIC events. MSR

Suggested reading
Cliff, Haggett, Ord and Versey (1981); Pyle (1979).

Disneyfication A process through which a PLACE becomes marketed primarily as a tourist destination, through standardized LANDSCAPE symbolization. The term derives from the Walt Disney theme parks that originated in California in 1955. Disneyland offered highly organized SPACE with themed areas, united by the central 'Main Street' (Avila, 2004). It celebrates order, cleanliness and predictability as part of the tourist-in-playground experience (Sorkin, 1992a; Avila, 2004). Sorkin (1992a, pp. 216–17) argues that Disney spaces celebrate travel and consumerism in a simulated experience and landscape that mimics reality, but is never quite real. The term 'Disneyfication' suggests a critique of this commodification of PLACE. DGM

Suggested reading
Warren (1994).

distance decay The attenuation of a pattern or process with distance from a central point.

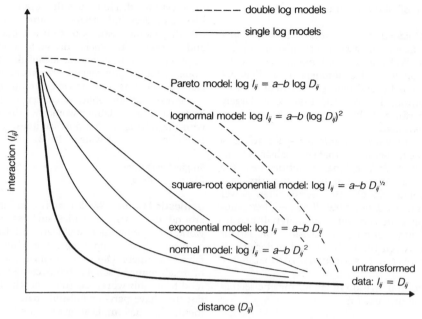

distance decay *Distance-decay curves and transformations* (Taylor, 1971)

Its importance in the evolution of spatial patterns was enshrined in Tobler's (1970) famous 'first law of geography': 'everything is related to everything else but near things are more related than distant things'. Distance-decay relationships underpin much of the work on SPATIAL STRUCTURES undertaken within SPATIAL ANALYSIS and SPATIAL SCIENCE, because the costs of SPATIAL INTERACTION are related to the distance travelled (cf. GRAVITY MODEL). Empirical studies have identified a range of distance-decay relationships in which the degree of attenuation with distance is much greater in some situations than others (see figure), in part because of the characteristics of the geometric configurations of the SPATIAL STRUCTURES within which they are set (Cliff, Martin and Ord, 1975–6).   RJ

Suggested reading
Sheppard (1984); Taylor (1971).

districting algorithm A computer procedure for defining the BOUNDARIES of electoral constituencies. Such procedures became widely used in the USA after the outlawing of MALAPPORTIONMENT in Congressional Districts and other constituencies in the 1960s: they are deployed to explore the number of ways in which constituencies can be defined which meet 'equal population' and other criteria (cf. GERRYMANDERING; REDISTRICTING).   RJ

Suggested reading
Altman, MacDonald and McDonald (2005).

division of labour The separation of tasks within the LABOUR PROCESS and their allocation to different groups of workers. Two forms are commonly identified:

(1) *Social division of labour* – the division of workers between product sectors (e.g. 'car workers' or 'textile workers').

(2) *Technical division of labour* – the division of the production process into tasks, and the specialization of workers in one or a small number of these (e.g. managers, supervisors and assembly workers).

The division of labour tends to be greater in more complex and industrialized societies and is a central component of the production systems of FORDISM. On the other hand, the putative emergence of POST-FORDISM has been associated with more flexible forms of work organization and the limited re-integration of previously separated tasks (cf. FLEXIBLE ACCUMULATION).

Other applications of the concept of the division of labour include:

(3) *Gender division of labour* – in which specific jobs are assigned to men or women: in Western societies nurses tend to be women, and coalminers men. This extends beyond paid employment, so that unwaged DOMESTIC LABOUR is largely performed by women (see GENDER; PATRIARCHY).

(4) *Cultural division of labour* – according to the theory of internal colonialism (Hechter, 1975), regional minorities bear the same relationship to the majority as a colony does to the metropolitan power under COLONIALISM. The periphery supplies the core with raw materials and labour, forming a division of labour between the minority and majority cultures (see CORE-PERIPHERY MODEL).

The cultural division of labour may be seen as a special instance of:

(5) *Ethnic division of labour* – in colonized and other ethnically divided societies, employment is frequently stratified according to ETHNICITY.

(6) *International division of labour* – characteristically, less-developed countries produce raw materials and developed countries produce manufactured goods. More recently, a NEW INTERNATIONAL DIVISION OF LABOUR has involved the development by TRANSNATIONAL CORPORATIONS of production facilities in less-developed countries. Initially, such facilities concentrated on routine and lower-skill manufacturing tasks. Subsequently, technological advances and the availability of large numbers of higher-skill (but still relatively low paid) workers in poorer countries have seen a major growth in the outsourcing of business and professional services to countries such as India.

The international division of labour is a special case of:

(7) *Spatial division of labour* – a concept developed by Massey (1984) involving the concentration of particular sectors and/or production tasks in specific geographical areas.

According to Sayer (1995), the significance of the division of labour in the organization of economic activity has been systematically underestimated. He argues that the complexities of modern industrial economies are such that they cannot feasibly be centrally planned, and nor can the social division of labour be abolished. For Sayer, this means that traditional Marxist approaches to geographical change (see MARXISM) must be rethought to recognize that the political challenges posed by the division of labour would not disappear with the transition to a post-capitalist society (see also Sayer and Walker, 1992). JPa

Suggested reading
Massey (1995a).

domestic labour Work that is done in and around the HOME: activities such as housework, food preparation, childcare and the care of disabled, sick and ageing household and family members. Domestic labour is the focus of much feminist scholarship because women tend to do this work, regardless of whether or not they have part- or full-time paid employment. This has implications for the location, type and hours of many women's paid employment, and is an important factor contributing to the persistence of women's ghettoization in 'female-dominated occupations', and the disparity between men's and women's wages (Hanson and Pratt, 1995: see FEMINISM; FEMINIST GEOGRAPHIES). Whilst many women in industrialized countries do this 'double shift' of domestic labour and paid employment, some middle-class women hire other women – typically racialized, working-class women or migrants from the global South – to do this work for them (Momsen, 1999; Pratt, 2004). GENDER oppression is thus layered on to other forms of social and GEOPOLITICAL domination. In some cases, domestic labour is then stretched over very great distances, as women caring for middle-class CHILDREN in the global NORTH strive to mother their own children still residing in the global SOUTH, through daily or weekly emails and telephone calls

Domestic labour is ambivalently valued in feminist analyses, viewed simultaneously as a burden and constraint, and as invaluable practices of care and social co-operation. Feminists have developed different strategies to remedy the unequal gender division of domestic labour. One strategy is to un-gender domestic labour, by striving towards equal contributions by men and women, as well as more collective options such as socialized childcare. A second, complementary, approach is to revalue domestic labour by demonstrating its importance to the economy. Within MARX-ISM, domestic labour is seen as necessary to the SOCIAL REPRODUCTION that supports and sustains economic production; periodically, MARXIST GEOGRAPHERS have had to be reminded of this importance (Mitchell, Marston and Katz, 2004). Other attempts to bring domestic labour within the ECONOMY – to make it more visible and highlight its value – have included 'wages for housework' campaigns, and efforts to include questions about domestic labour on QUESTIONNAIRES related to national CENSUSES. The latter allow the extent and worth of such labour to be measured and potentially figured into calculations of national economic activity, such as GROSS NATIONAL PRODUCT (Domosh and Seager, 2001, p. 45). Cameron and Gibson-Graham (2003) argue that the second set of strategies (which they characterize as 'adding on' and 'counting in') 'fall short of generating a feminist politics of transformation' (p. 151), because they seek to include domestic labour within existing ways of thinking about the economy, rather than using domestic labour as a vehicle for thinking about the economy differently. Rather than incorporating domestic labour into a broader conception of the capitalist economy, these authors urge that domestic labour be rethought within a diverse economy of MARKET/non-market, paid/unpaid, CAPITALIST/non-capitalist relations. England and Lawson (2005) caution that the category itself maintains troubling conceptual borders by reinforcing a distinction between domestic and other kinds of work.   GP

Suggested reading
Domosh and Seager (2001).

domestication The process by which plant or ANIMAL species are reshaped through the social and economic uses to which they are put by human SOCIETIES in particular cultural and historical contexts. As this implies, human societies have altered the genetic composition of plants and animals by influencing their reproduction and life histories so as to make them better fitted to human needs and designs (see Clutton-Brock, 1999). In his theory of evolution, Darwin (1998 [1868]) called this process 'artificial' (as opposed to 'natural') selection and illustrated it with the example of pigeon-fanciers (see DARWINISM). Some domesticated species and organisms can become adapted to the point of dependency on human relations – for example, garden plants and companion animals or agricultural crops and livestock – and would have difficulty surviving outside of that domesticated context.

Domestication is strongly bound up with the centrality of cultivation to Western ideas of CIVILIZATION and the advancement of human societies from the STATE OF NATURE. Here, the process of domestication is understood as consequential not only in terms of altering the physiognomy of plants and animals, but also the sociocultural practices of what is taken to define human beings (Anderson, 1997). The historical realization of these ideas in the political and legal practices of COLONIALISM finds echoes in those of the POST-COLONIAL present through the persistent imperatives of the scientific management and technological improvement in the efficiency and productivity of NATURAL RESOURCES. In an era of BIOTECHNOLOGY, this historical legacy informs new GEOPOLITICAL investments in the meaning and practice of domestication. In forums such as the Food and Agriculture Organization and the WORLD TRADE ORGANIZATION, for example, Western countries have asserted claims to INTELLECTUAL PROPERTY RIGHTS in biological resources on the basis of scientific interventions in what are presented as previously 'natural' materials (see PATENTING). By contrast, countries in the global SOUTH have sought to assert the claims of farmers and indigenous peoples to equivalent rights in recognition of their transformative ecological relations with plants and animals time-out-of-mind.   SW

Suggested reading
Harlan (1995).

domesticity Home life and home-making practices within and beyond the household and/or family. Closely tied to understandings of HOME, house and HOUSEHOLD, domesticity encompasses paid and unpaid domestic work (including cooking, cleaning and caring; see DOMESTIC LABOUR), the home life of people who live alone or with others, and a wider sense of what is familiar and homely rather than 'foreign' and unhomely. The study of domesticity dates back to attempts to formalize, rationalize and teach its principles from the mid-nineteenth century. Within GEOGRAPHY, the work of feminist geographers has been particularly influential in studying domesticity since the 1970s (see FEMINIST GEOGRAPHIES). In their analysis of SOCIAL REPRODUCTION within the domestic sphere, socialist feminists have explored the ways in which domesticity, as a site of contested and unequal gender relations, is inseparably bound up with CAPITALISM and PATRIARCHY (Gregson and Lowe, 1994). Feminist geographers have studied the GENDER, CLASS and racialized POWER relations of paid and unpaid domestic work, and the ways in which the transnational MIGRATION of domestic workers, particularly women, binds household to global economies and inequalities (including Pratt, 2004). A wide range of other geographical research has explored domestic technologies and rationalities, domestic interiors, embodied domestic practices and domestic MATERIAL CULTURES (for an overview, see Blunt and Dowling, 2006). Important themes include the ways in which domestic practices reproduce, recast and resist ideas about the home and/or family and the ways in which domesticity is closely bound up with MODERNITY, power and IDENTITY.

Geographies of domesticity also extend far beyond the household. As Amy Kaplan (2002) observes, the term 'domestic' has a double meaning, referring both to the SPACE of the NATION and to the space of the household. Both of these meanings are closely bound up with shifting ideas about the 'foreign,' and are imagined and materialized through a range of domestic politics and practices. Rather than view domesticity as confined to a PRIVATE SPHERE of influence, it is a crucial site of reproduction and resistance that is intimately bound up with the world beyond, as well as within, the household. Historical studies reveal the ways in which domesticity was explicitly and intimately tied to wider national and imperial politics through, for example, DISCOURSES and practices concerning maternity, CONSUMPTION and child-rearing (including Stoler, 2002). Other research has shown the importance of domesticity in anti-imperial nationalist politics, often focusing on the politicization of women within and beyond the home (including Legg, 2003).

Studies of domesticity in both historical and contemporary contexts usually focus on the material and symbolic importance of women. Whilst a wide range of research documents the oppression of women through domestic work and domestic VIOLENCE, other research explores domesticity as a site of potential creativity, power and resistance. Other researchers have begun to investigate the domestic lives of men and the relationships between domesticity and masculinity (see, e.g., Tosh, 1999).   AB

domination The physical or cultural assertion of POWER over an individual, social group or TERRITORY. The term refers to the practice and manifestation of power relationships, especially in terms of the construction of territory and spaces as a means of control

Domination was originally perceived in a classical GEOPOLITICAL sense of territorial control. In the late nineteenth and early twentieth centuries, geopolitical theories advocating the expansion of state BORDERS at the expense of 'inferior' cultures were the basis for the FRONTIER expansion of the USA and Russia, Germany's desire for territory in eastern Europe, and the establishment of European empires. In this period, domination was viewed as the ability of a STATE to control territory – and hence its residents – on the basis of cultural superiority. In the COLD WAR period, domination was also seen as a matter of the power of states to define and attain their own self-interests.

However, critical scholarship began to define other forms of domination. The Marxist Antonio Gramsci (1971 [1929–35]) noted that the ideas of the ruling CLASS are mainly accepted by the whole of society, producing acquiescence in national projects of capital accumulation that benefit a few (cf. HEGEMONY). Edward Said's (2003 [1978]) exposition of ORIENTALISM illustrated the cultural practices by which colonial powers created a sense of superiority over their subjects through literature and the arts. The practices of cultural domination have been addressed by geographers at a number of SCALES, from the construction of EMPIRE to the normative understanding of PLACES that exclude particular people, groups and behaviours (Cresswell, 1996).

Feminist and queer studies (see FEMINIST GEOGRAPHIES; QUEER THEORY) have emphasized the HETERONORMATIVE and PATRIARCHAL character of SPACES ranging from the HOUSEHOLD to the nation-state (Staeheli, Kofman and Peake, 2004). In addition, the racial domination of whites is gaining increasing attention (see WHITENESS). However, criticism remains that many human geography studies tend to ignore questions of RACE, GENDER and SEXUALITY (Staeheli, Kofman and Peake, 2004). Still, the emphasis placed upon cultural domination has been connected to the creation of material spaces of racial SEGREGATION in the city, hate CRIME activity in gay NEIGHBOURHOODS and patriarchal practices. In a separate vein of work, the role of the USA as hegemonic power has attracted the attention of geographers, especially its role in dominating the global political agenda and its massive military power.   CF

Suggested reading
Flint (2004); Staeheli, Kofman and Peake (2004).

domino theory A THEORY of GEOPOLITICS orig- inally proposed by the USA in the 1950s, claim- ing that if one country joined or was forced to join the Soviet Union's sphere of influence, then its neighbours would inevitably follow. The theory rested upon an analogy of toppling dominoes and was used to justify the military and political involvement of the USA in other countries, especially in South East Asia, in the 1950s and 1960s, but also in Central America in the 1990s (see also COLD WAR). O'Sullivan (1982) critiques the theory for ignoring the unique history and internal politics of different countries (the dominoes).   CF

dry farming   A set of FARMING techniques for crop cultivation without irrigation, used in areas with variable or little rainfall (Heathcote, 1983). Dry farming requires both water and soil conservation measures, such as mulching, frequent weeding and summer fallowing in alternate years. A long-established practice in the Near East, North Africa and north-west India, dry farming can only produce a narrow range of crops and low yields. These methods were instrumental in the extension of crop cultivation into the semi-arid areas of the AMERICAS and AUSTRALIA by European settlers in the nineteenth century. Dry farming is see- ing a minor resurgence among followers of sustainable agriculture.   JGu

Suggested reading
Hargreaves (1992).

dual economy   An ECONOMY made up of two supposedly distinct parts: the modern econ- omy and the pre-modern economy. The term was probably first used by Dutch economist J.H. Boeke, in his account of Indonesia as a dual society (Boeke, 1953). Boeke maintained that parts of Indonesian society had already become modern: some urban enterprises were organized according to recognizably scientific and capitalist principles, and were situated in neighbourhoods that seemed 'Western' to Boeke. Most of Indonesia, however, was 'Eastern' or pre-modern: life and work here were loosely organized and geared to the pro- duction of things for household consumption or local exchange.

Boeke's work on Indonesia was meant to contribute to PUBLIC POLICY debates. The question he raised was the classic mid-twenti- eth-century question of how to get from A to B, or from a traditional society to a modern society (see MODERNIZATION). As in many of these MODELS, cultural change was thought to

be driven by economic DEVELOPMENT. This was certainly the case in W. Arthur Lewis' (1954) account of 'economic development with unlimited supplies of labour'. Lewis argued that vast pools of unproductive rural labour could be decanted to the urban–indus- trial sector without affecting levels of FOOD production. Scarce resources could then be channelled into the 'commanding heights of the economy', much as the Indian government tried to do in its Second and Third Five Year Plan periods (1956–66). Even better, urban real wage rates would not rise in the short run. Rural–urban MIGRATION served an equili- brating function, and helped to ensure that the modern economy would slowly take the place of the pre-modern economy.

In the 1960s and 1970s, the logic of this version of the dual economy model was turned upside down. Michael Lipton (1977) famously argued that most of the POVERTY of the THIRD WORLD was in the countryside, along with most of the low-cost sources of economic advance. To neglect the rural sector in the name of an abstract model of economic modernity was inequitable and inefficient. It installed urban bias as public policy and stalled the process of human development. Other critics sympa- thized with some parts of Lipton's critique – noting also the growth of urban SLUMS and shanties – while challenging the dual economy model to which he still subscribed. Recent thinking has focused on the complicated ways in which 'rur-urban households' put together livelihood strategies across the town/country divide. Such thinking is focused on the eco- nomic costs of barriers to MOBILITY, rather than on the presumed integrity of the urban or rural sectors (Ellis and Harris, 2004). Still other critics have gone further. Radical development theorists argued that the production of pre- capitalist spaces in an economy was a legacy of COLONIALISM, rather than a state of original sin (see DEPENDENCY THEORY). In any case, the two sectors were linked to the advantage of the 'modern' sector. Finally, and perhaps most pertinently, recent work has emphasized that MODERNITY is not a singular condition. There are many forms of modernity, all of which are structured by a high degree of path depend- ence. It is a fantasy to suppose that 'Eastern' parts of a dual economy can be made 'Western' in the sense of the mid-twentieth-century USA, and a fantastical abuse of public policy to push for this.   SCO

Suggested reading
Ellis and Harris (2004); Hart (2001).

E

ecofeminism An umbrella term for a wide variety of environmental concerns and approaches that integrate diverse feminist and environmentalist perspectives. Ecofeminism is both THEORY and praxis, building on the intellectual foundations of ecological and feminist political movements where these intersect as, for example, in popular mobilizations in the name of peace and nuclear disarmament (Seagar, 1993), animal WELFARE (Gaard, 1993) or ENVIRONMENTAL JUSTICE (Shiva, 1988). There are different accounts of the origin of the term itself, but it is most frequently attributed to the 1980 work of the French author François D'Eaubonne.

The thematic connection linking diverse ecofeminist currents is the notion that women are closer to NATURE. This putative connection is woven into the mainstream intellectual, religious and social fabric of many cultures, and has been an important focus of feminist critique (see FEMINISM). For several decades, feminists sought to distance the analysis of women's position in society from any bodily or biological referent, labelling any such reference 'ESSENTIALIST' and, thereby, unspeakable (see Fuss, 1989). As a consequence, ecofeminist concerns and arguments were cold-shouldered by the feminist academy for some years when they found their most powerful expression in works of the imagination as, for example, in the science fiction writing of Ursula le Guin or Marge Piercy.

While ecofeminism's conservative tendencies to reduce the heterogeneity of women's experience to the singular figure of Woman and the mutability of nature to an unchanging primordial Nature remain, since the late 1980s ecofeminist work has found new consonance with developments in feminist philosophy and social theory (see, e.g., Plumwood, 1993). These developments centre on concerns with (i) the MATERIALISM of social life and its connectedness beyond the human (see also BIOPHILOSOPHY) and (ii) the situatedness of knowledge production associated with the rise of feminist SCIENCE STUDIES. As Donna Haraway, one of the leading proponents of this latter project, has argued, 'Ecofeminists have perhaps been the most insistent on some version of the world (nature/body) as active subjects, not as RESOURCES to be mapped or appropriated in bourgeois, MARXIST or MASCULINIST projects' (1991, p. 199).   SW

Suggested reading
Fuss (1989); Gaard (1993); Haraway (1991c); Plumwood (1993); Seagar (1993); Shiva (1988).

ecological fallacy A problem that may arise when inferring characteristics of individuals from aggregate data referring to a population of which they are part. It was first highlighted by Robinson (1950), who found CORRELATIONS of 0.773 in a REGRESSION of the percentage of African-Americans in a state's population against its percentage illiterate, but only 0.203 when using data on individuals from the same source. The fact that African-Americans were concentrated in states with high illiteracy rates did not necessarily mean that African-Americans had high illiteracy rates (hence the necessity not to confuse correlation with causality).

Alker (1969) identified six related fallacies:

- *the ecological fallacy* – assuming that relationships identified using aggregate data apply to the individuals concerned;
- *the individualistic fallacy* – assuming that the whole is no more than the sum of its parts (the inverse of the ecological fallacy);
- *the cross-level fallacy* – assuming that a relationship identified in one aggregation of a population applies to other aggregations (cf. MODIFIABLE AREAL UNIT PROBLEM);
- *the universal fallacy* – assuming that relationships identified among some individuals applies to all members of the population from which they have been selected, but not as a random SAMPLE;
- *the selective fallacy* – in which data from carefully chosen cases are used to 'prove' a general point; and
- *the cross-sectional fallacy* – assuming that what is observed at one data applies to others as well.

All are problems of ECOLOGICAL INFERENCE, as is the more recently identified *cross-time fallacy*, whereby relationships that hold at one time are fallaciously assumed to hold at others as well.   RJ

ecological imperialism In his seminal account of 'the biological expansion of

EUROPE' Crosby (1986) described ecological imperialism as the environmental destruction of large tracts of the Earth by European colonization. Crosby chose to emphasize the imperial project largely in biological terms (rather than, say, military or economic) and the 'encounters' between hitherto largely separated regions of the earth now linked together by new systems of TRADE, production and forms of cultural interchange and settlement. As he put it, 'the success of European imperialism has a biological and an ecological component' (p. 7) (see ECOLOGY). Crosby traced the European settlement in the 'Neo-Europes' (North and South AMERICA and AUSTRALASIA), a process in which their temperate agricultures thrived and local indigenous systems and ECOSYSTEMS collapsed. The introduction of Old World pathogens decimated native populations (e.g. the Spanish devastated the indigenous populations of the Canaries by introducing pneumonia and dysentery). Smallpox decimated the Americas. In addition, Crosby charts the impact the introduction and dispersion of European 'weeds' and the transformative effects of, for example, the proliferation of new domesticated animals (see DOMESTICATION).

The term has been deployed in other more critical and expansive ways. In the activist world – and the so-called 'movement of movements' (see WORLD SOCIAL FORUM) – ecological IMPERIALISM is sometimes held to be 'the imposition of a set of ecological values held by one individual or group onto another individual or group without their consent' (Okonski, 2003). In this account the causes of eco-imperialism are multilateral agreements, foreign AID and the romanticization of the poor. A different, and more theorized and rigorous, account draws from Marxian theory, in which ecological imperialism is the product of the intersection of an expansionary CAPITALISM on the one side and what Karl Marx called a 'metabolic rift' (Foster, 2000). The dispossession of PEASANTS from the land, the creation of a pool of landless labourers and the concentration of the means of production (see PRIMITIVE ACCUMULATION) historically left a deep ecological footprint. Land was reduced to a level of being 'a venal object' and this whole process operated on a global (imperial) SCALE. Marx's notion of a 'metabolic rift' was derived from his analysis of Liebig and other German chemists of the soil, and the fact that an expansionary capitalism shipped nutrients far away, to cities and the imperial centre. A body of work has attempted to draw connections between an expansionary world system,

the transition from FEUDALISM to capitalism, the differing forms of EMPIRE (and rule) and the distribution of ecological costs (Grove, 2003). Ecological imperialism in this sense is quite different from Crosby's interpretation, and turns on the recursive aspect of primitive ACCUMULATION as it takes hold of and transforms different natural systems. In the current moment, the global search for germ plasm by private pharmaceutical companies – and relatedly the commodification of plant breeding rights – would be an example of ecological imperialism in action (cf. BIOPROSPECTING). None of this is to suggest, however, that the 'older' forms of primitive accumulation – peasant dispossession and the ecological destruction that stems from it (e.g. the Three Gorges dam project in China) – are not still proceeding apace.   MW

ecological inference Drawing conclusions about individuals from data about the populations to which they belong, in the absence of any information about the individuals themselves. The data deployed almost invariably refer to population aggregates defined by territorially bounded areas, such as those used in the production of CENSUS data. In a classic case, analysts have wanted to know election turnout rates by different ethnic groups in the USA, but the only available information indicates the total turnout in each area and its population's ethnic composition. Various QUANTITATIVE METHODS have been used to estimate separate turnout rates for each group from that information, but technical problems cast doubt on their validity. Recent developments offer possible solutions in certain circumstances, with the potential of providing more reliable estimates of unknown values. (See also ECOLOGICAL FALLACY; ENTROPY-MAXIMIZING MODELS; MICROSIMULATION.)   RJ

Suggested reading
King, Rosen and Tanner (2004); Sui et al. (2000).

ecology A SCIENCE primarily concerned with the non-human world and, more specifically, with the complex relations between organisms and their environment. As such, ecology is considered something of a holistic and synthetic science, drawing on population and evolutionary biology, soil science, hydrology, earth systems, oceanography, chemistry, conservation biology and other sciences in attempting to understand how individual organisms and populations interact with other species and, more generally, how organisms are linked to their biotic and abiotic environments. Some view ecology as the science of environment, although ecology may be distinguished from environmental science in its primary emphasis on understanding living organisms, not only at the individual, population and species levels, but in terms of identifiable communities of plant and ANIMAL species in relatively proximate interactions. The term 'oecologie' is most often seen as a neologism coined by German biologist Ernst Haeckel, who first used it in 1866, in part inspired by Darwin's *Origin of Species*. But the word draws directly on an older notion of 'oeconomy', which refers to management of the 'household' in a broad sense (Worster, 1994: see ECONOMY). This links the etymology of ecology and economics in intriguing ways, but also conveys something of the broad scope of ecological enquiry, encompassing the world of living things. In this sense, the lineage of ecology is much older and more diverse, drawing on the natural history of figures such as Gilbert White (1720–93) and Linnaeus (1707–78) (Worster, 1994), and linked by some to Aristotle's writings on environmental changes in Greece. Significantly, modern ecology and GEOGRAPHY have been closely linked, not least in drawing on the early BIOGEOGRAPHY of Alexander von Humboldt. More generally, ties between ecology and geography have been forged and renewed based on shared concerns and perspectives, including the spatial organization and foundation(s) of biodiversity and how it is affected by human action, the implications of human action on the non-human world more generally, and the use of synthetic, relational and holistic reasoning to understand how ostensibly discrete entities are connected (not least in spatial terms).

Since the late nineteenth century, ecology in the Anglo-American world has been closely linked to environmental politics. During a first generation of ecology, exemplified by Stephen Forbes's (1887) singular publication 'The lake as a microcosm', ecology was animated by concern with the implications of forestry, fisheries and agriculture (Schnieder, 2000). In the post-Second World War period, this link between environmental politics and ENVIRONMENTALISM on the one hand and ecology on the other was consolidated through scientific enquiry into such matters as the ecological effects of radiation from nuclear technologies and the persistence of synthetic organic compounds in the environment (the latter is most famously associated with Rachel Carson and her signature work, *Silent spring*). Close

association between environmentalism and ecology has continued, as was clearly evident in the way ecological enquiry was used to mediate the northern spotted owl controversy of the 1990s (Prudham, 2005). Not surprisingly, the close association of ecology and environmentalism has had a major impact on intellectual and scholarly work inside and around geography, helping to inspire the emergence of a distinct interwoven field of ENVIRONMENTAL HISTORY and HISTORICAL GEOGRAPHY preoccupied with the human origins and implications of environmental change, and drawing upon such changes as the basis of critique (see, e.g., Cronon, 1991; for a discussion linking environmental history and historical geography, see Williams, M., 1994a). POLITICAL ECOLOGY, as the name would suggest, has been similarly concerned with mobilizing ecological theories and methods in exploring the local and regional origins and implications of environmental degradation (however defined) in the context of uneven POWER relations.

During the middle of the twentieth century, particularly after the work of Frederic E. Clements, ecological research and theory generally emphasized predictability, stability, homeostasis and climax communities in the development of self-contained ECOSYSTEMS whose development, when unimpeded by human action, would tend towards increasing biological diversity. Clementsian ecology in particular stressed the recovery of 'disturbed' ecosystems from less to more diverse communities, culminating in highly stable climax ecosystems characteristic of particular REGIONS (Clements, 1936). Later, this was augmented by the development of an increasingly formal, abstract and often highly mathematical SYSTEMS ecology, emphasizing the modelling of populations, energy and material flows within ecosystems, and predicated on the assumption that discrete populations of organisms compete to fill exclusive ecological niches. Stability and homeostasis remained core principles of systems ecology.

Key concepts from Clementsian as well as systems ecology informed modernist RESOURCE MANAGEMENT paradigms. This includes the Lotka–Volterra equations used to model interconnected and predictable oscillations of predator and prey species in closed systems of mutual dependence, and the characteristic logistic growth curve underpinning maximum sustained yield management prescriptions in fisheries and FORESTRY. In each case, populations are seen to converge on stable carrying capacities defined by limits on key RESOURCES (e.g. FOOD) in closed systems. These are generalizations, in some sense crude, but they generally point to an ecology dominated by generalizable ideas about discrete, ontologically real ecosystems whose behaviour is predictable, and whose tendencies are towards increasing biological diversity and stability if left undisturbed by human action.

Yet if twentieth-century environmentalism and ecology have shared an affinity, ecology's attempt to define and speak for a strictly non-human nature has raised some difficult issues that ecology has been, as yet, unable to resolve. These issues are in part invoked by the transition from Clementsian and systems ecology to the so-called 'new ecology' achieved by degree over approximately the past two decades. New ecology has numerous facets, but is generally characterized by an embrace of complexity, history and path dependence (see COMPLEXITY THEORY); an appreciation of interconnected geographical SCALES in ecological relationships; a retreat from the broad law-like generalizations of systems ecology; and, critically, an embrace of change, not constancy, as the new normal (Botkin, 1990). Ecosystems in this PARADIGM are increasingly seen as open to the point at which defining them robustly becomes increasingly problematic. Moreover, disturbances from volcanic eruptions, fires, storms, pest outbreaks and the like are seen as endemic. Empirical studies of ecological succession following disturbance – for example, in the aftermath of the Mount St Helens eruption in Washington State, USA – also demonstrate that 'recovery" does not necessarily tend towards pre-disturbance communities, nor does the strict lineage of succession posited by Clementsian ecology strictly apply (Swanson, 1987). Rather, 'recovery' depends somewhat on initial conditions, including the legacy of pre-disturbance communities.

For these and other reasons, the new ecology is typically more agnostic about what communities of organisms may be characterized as 'normal' in any given location. Many implications follow from this, including a significantly diminished capacity for ecology to provide the baseline against which environmental degradation is defined. And with this, more overtly political ecologies become necessary, based for instance, on the increase or decrease in LANDSCAPE functions of various kinds (e.g. fuelwood production, hydrological recharge). At the same time, new ecology is much less able to sharply and categorically delineate between natural dynamics and those influenced by anthropogenic processes because of the acceptance that change is just as endemic in nature as is stability (for discussion, see Demeritt, 1994a; Worster, 1994). This in turn has made ecology a much less reliable foundation for environmental policies that would strictly delineate NATURE and CULTURE; for example, conventional WILDERNESS-oriented parks and protected areas, aimed at biodiversity CONSERVATION (Zimmerer, 1994a). The new ecology has also more generally prompted considerable ONTOLOGICAL soul searching among ecologists. And yet, as ecology has struggled to come to terms with complexity, context, path dependence, scale and the basis of inter-subjective knowledge claims about the non-human world, there remain strong parallels and linkages between ecology and geography, not least in embrace of the pervasiveness of HYBRIDS that transgress formerly stable categories, be they ecosystem boundaries or nature–society dualisms (Zimmerer, 2000; Whatmore, 2002a). SP

ecometrics A term coined by Stephen Raudenbush (see Raudenbush and Sampson, 1999) to assess the nature of ecological settings, using the QUANTITATIVE METHODS of multi-level (see MULTI-LEVEL MODELLING) and spatial MODELS to exploit spatial dependence in order to improve the reliability and validity of measures of neighborhood social processes (cf. CONTEXTUAL EFFECT; NEIGHBOURHOOD EFFECT). Unlike traditional factorial ecology (see FACTOR ANALYSIS), which uses aggregate, usually census, data to characterize places, ecometrics uses data on individuals plus systematic social observation as repeated measures of PLACE characteristics. It is also concerned with how places change over time. KJ

Suggested reading
Raudenbush and Sampson (1999); Raudenbush (2003).

economic base theory A THEORY that explains urban and regional growth in terms of a division of employment into basic and non-basic sectors. The *basic sector* (B) comprises those industries that meet external or export demand, and the location and growth of this sector is viewed as a function of national and international forces. The *non-basic sector* (S) is locally oriented employment, servicing the total local population (P). The total population is a function of total employment (E) and the economic base relationships are as follows:

$$E = S + B, \quad P = \alpha E, \quad S = \beta P.$$

The coefficients α and β can be obtained by REGRESSION using observations for a SAMPLE of cities or for one city or region over time. Growth (or decline) in local population and employment is controlled by changes in the basic sector, and the impacts (MULTIPLIERS) of such changes can be calculated from the economic base equations:

$$E = (1 - \alpha\beta)^{-1}B,$$

$$P = \alpha(1 - \alpha\beta)^{-1}B,$$

$$S = \alpha\beta(1 - \alpha\beta)^{-1}B.$$

A unit increase in B generates $\alpha/(1-\alpha\beta)$ units of additional local population.

Economic base theory is very simplistic in its assumptions, but because its data demands are simple it has been widely employed in regional economic analysis. It is used, for example, in activity allocation models and Lowry models. Correct identification of the basic sector is crucial, and LOCATION QUOTIENTS are frequently used for this purpose. Either industries with high indices of specialization are defined as basic industries, or the quotient is used to define a proportion of employment in an industry as basic; so that, for example, one-third of employment in an industry with a quotient of 1.5 is designated as basic employment. A more sophisticated approach is to use INPUT–OUTPUT analysis to trace actual inter-industrial linkages, but this is very data-demanding and expensive.

The major limitations of economic base theory spring from its aggregative nature: the difficulties of sector definition; the dubious assumption that the aggregate MULTIPLIERS will remain constant; and an inability to trace the impact of particular basic sector shifts, such as a rise in OIL exports, on specific sectors of the local ECONOMY.   LWH

Suggested reading
Glickman (1997).

economic geography A sub-field of HUMAN GEOGRAPHY concerned with describing and explaining the varied PLACES and SPACES where economic activities are carried out and circulate. The discipline was institutionalized in the late nineteenth century in both Western Europe and the USA, and remains one of the core sub-fields of Anglo-American GEOGRAPHY. There have been repeated attempts to forge links with its seeming intellectual soul mate, economics, but none have held. Economic geography from the beginning was more empirically grounded, concerned with context and conceptually open-minded, and at the same time less abstract and less formally theoretical than economics. There were moments when the two became close, but mostly they held themselves apart at a distance (as they do now; cf. NEW ECONOMIC GEOGRAPHY). Further, unlike economists, economic geographers never settled on a single METHODOLOGY, set of techniques, list of venerated luminaries, disciplinary problematic or definitive definition. Change has been incessant, the field continually reinventing itself. It makes for an exciting, dynamic, open subject, one that never looks back, and a frequent conduit for new ideas into the rest of human geography, but there is a nagging sense that before old promises are realized, new ones are made. Economic geography sometimes seems like Penelope's shroud: spun during the day, and unravelled the same night.

Existing in embryonic form as COMMERCIAL GEOGRAPHY, the discipline was formally defined in Germany in 1882 by Götz. While commercial geography 'chiefly served practical ends', the purpose of economic geography was 'the scientific task of dealing with the nature of world areas in their direct influence upon the production of commodities and the movement of goods' (Götz, quoted in Sapper, 1931, p. 627). By the 1890s, economic geography courses appeared for the first time in US university calendars (Fellmann, 1986). The first Professor of Economic Geography in Britain was Lionel Lyde, appointed in 1903 at University College London. Five years later, the University of Edinburgh created a lectureship for George Chisholm, who was author of the first English-language economic geography text, *Handbook of commercial geography* (1889). Economic geography was up and running.

Chisholm's book (published in 20 editions), and J. Russell Smith's later American version, *Industrial and commercial geography* (1913), set out an initial disciplinary agenda and intellectual style that still resonates. The original colonial context of the two books no longer applies, but continuing to remain germane were their concern with empirical detail, their celebration of numbers, their predilection for geographical categorization made visible by the MAP, their tracing of relations among places through economic flows especially of the commodity, their emphasis on the geographical effects of technological change and their suspicion of theory (although presumably no contemporary economic geographer would go as far as Chisholm 'to wish ... th[e] love of pure theory to the devil'; quoted in Wise, 1975, p. 2).

Chisholm's and Smith's emphasis was on the COMMODITY, though neither appreciated the conceptual richness of the concept, with geography coming second. The American geographer R.H. Whitbeck (1915–16, p. 197) argued that it should be the other way around: 'the unit should be the country and not the commodity'. The consequence was an increasingly regional focus, at least in economic geography in the USA, where the REGION was defined as unique, and represented by using one typological scheme or another. Clarence Fielden Jones' (1935) textbook *Economic geography*, for example, used an eight-fold typology.

Hartshorne's (1939) *The nature of geography* later provided at least a splash of scholarly respectability to an IDEOGRAPHIC regionalism. But it did nothing to connect the discipline to the fundamental changes that were about to transform a number of social sciences, and even some HUMANITIES, especially in the USA, turning on the widespread use of scientific methods and PHILOSOPHY (and propelled by the Second World War and later the COLD WAR). Economic geography initially resisted that impulse, but by the mid-1950s it too joined in. The resulting QUANTITATIVE REVOLUTION profoundly altered the discipline, bringing the systematic application of scientific forms of theorizing and rigorous statistical techniques of description and analysis (Barnes, 2001).

The discipline over the period 1955–75, sometimes labelled SPATIAL SCIENCE, was defined by:

(1) Formal THEORY and MODELS, many begged, borrowed and stolen from NEOCLASSICAL ECONOMICS (RATIONAL CHOICE THEORY, general and partial equilibrium, LOCATION THEORY), and physics (SPATIAL INTERACTION THEORY and later ENTROPY-MAXIMIZING MODELS) (Pooler, 1977).

(2) QUANTITATIVE METHODS, which were initially taken off-the-peg from inferential statistics, but later designed in-house to meet the peculiar features of economic geographical data (cf. SPATIAL AUTOCORRELATION; Gould, 1969a).

(3) The use of computers, at first very crude and limited, but within a decade performing hitherto unimaginable calculations for instrumental purposes.

(4) A philosophical justification based on some form of POSITIVISM, the idea that only scientific knowledge is authentic knowledge (see SCIENCE).

(5) A focus on abstract SPATIALITIES and geometrically defined location (cf. LOCATIONAL ANALYSIS, SPACE-ECONOMY). Consequently, the ECONOMY was conceived as an independent spatial object, with its own causative powers, morphological form and internal generative processes.

Regions remained part of the economic geographical lexicon, but conceived utterly differently: as explanatory, theoretical and instrumental, a spatial unit to achieve functional objectives (cf. REGIONAL SCIENCE). The consequence was that people like Clarence Fielden Jones (and his book) were no longer recognisable as part of the discipline. They were not in the same field, not on the same planet.

This often abstract, closed and narrowly conceived discipline did not last. It was out of synch with its own disciplinary history, and increasingly out of synch with its own historical moment (see RELEVANCE). RADICAL GEOGRAPHY emerged during the 1970s, propelling economic geography in a different direction. Harvey's (1999 [1982]) classical Marxist theorizing of capitalist ACCUMULATION and CRISIS was important (see MARXISM), but even more so was Massey's (1984) work on industrial RESTRUCTURING, which was philosophically underpinned by REALISM and culminated in the LOCALITY project that dominated British economic geography during the late 1980s (Cooke, 1989) (although disavowed by both Massey and Harvey). Across the Atlantic, a group of radical economic geographers in California carried out important empirical and theoretical work – not on cases of CAPITALISM's decline (as in studies of DEINDUSTRIALIZATION in the UK), but on its successes, such as high-tech industries (Scott, 1988b; Saxenian, 1994). Merging British and American interests from the late 1980s produced discussions around the transformation of an old, disintegrating FORDISM into a new, emerging POST-FORDISM (Tickell and Peck, 1992). Heavily influenced theoretically by French REGULATION THEORY, which was more open-ended, and less abstract and deterministic than classical Marxism, the economy remained central, but it was softened by recognition of the social institutions, and even the culture, in which it was embedded.

CULTURE and 'embeddedness' became keywords of the 'CULTURAL TURN' entering economic geography from the mid-1990s (Thrift and Olds, 1996). Often drawing upon POST-STRUCTURALISM, there was an attempt to rethink both the larger nature of the discipline – its EMPIRICIST EPISTEMOLOGY, its entrenched MASCULINISM, its economistic logic (Barnes, 1996; Gibson-Graham, 2006b [1996]) – as well as particular substantive topics that could benefit from the new conceptual armature, such as labour and work (McDowell, 1997a: see LABOUR GEOGRAPHY), financial and business services (Thrift, 2005b: see MONEY AND FINANCE), CONSUMPTION and RETAILING (Miller, Jackson, Holbrook, Rowlands and Thrift, 1998) and the firm (Schoenberger, 1997). Such a turn, its proponents argued, also allowed economic geographers to denaturalize the object of investigation, the economy. Rather than treating the economy as 'out there', as a single inviolable object, it had to be conceived as a cultural product, fragile, performed and capable of realization in a variety of forms. In this conception, the line between culture and economy is not just hard to see, but is no longer there (see also CULTURAL ECONOMY).

The 'cultural turn' is far from dominant, however, and already criticisms have mounted, and new alternatives or versions of old alternatives proposed. In truth, there is still no received view, orthodoxy or standard PARADIGM within economic geography. The current discipline is like a palimpsest, with past versions of the discipline still partially visible, not completely erased and continuing to contribute to the discipline's present form. While there is no single leading approach, several areas of the discipline are marked by energetic research and debate:

(1) Discussion of methods is one (Tickell, Sheppard, Peck and Barnes, 2007). In the beginning economic geography was heavily indebted to EMPIRICISM (and still is), assiduously collecting numbers and statistics. Even during economic geography's least numerate period, regionalism, Hartshorne (1959, p. 161) could claim that 'objectivity ... can best be accomplished ... by quantitative measurements'. That was taken to an extreme during the quantitative revolution, but as that movement broke up during the 1970s it facilitated the proliferation of new QUALITATIVE METHODS and techniques, including intensive CASE-STUDY research (Sayer and Morgan, 1985), in-depth interviews, oral histories (Schoenberger, 1996), ETHNOGRAPHIES, PARTICIPANT OBSERVATION, DISCOURSE ANALYSIS (Barnes, 1996) and action research (Gibson-Graham, 2006b [1996]). It is

an approach to methods in which nothing is proscribed and everything is permitted. The upside is diversity and rapid change – most of the methodological techniques listed would have been viewed as beyond the pale, or at best, suspiciously avant-garde, even in the mid-1980s. The downside, though, is a preoccupation with the instant of disclosure rather than the slower processes of substantiation and extension (Martin and Sunley, 2001).

(2) Hand-in-hand with permissive methodology has gone permissive theory. Thrift and Olds (1996, p. 313) speak of a 'polycentric' economic geography consisting of a 'set of narrative communities' that 'celebrate a qualitative multiplicity of "economic" TIMES and SPACES'. Those communities include an older mathematical modelling tradition, sometimes refurbished for the new economic TIMES and SPACES (e.g., Webber and Rigby, 1996) (but often not); varieties of POLITICAL ECONOMY, loosely grouped around MARXISM, and frequently focused on the STATE (most recently, its role in NEO-LIBERALISM: Peck, 2008); various stripes of FEMINISM that sometimes intersect with political economy, and often turning on BODIES of both men and women (McDowell, 1997a); a range of institutional approaches linked to economic anthropology and sociology (Polyanyi's and Granovetter's works are especially important) emphasizing embeddedness, NETWORKS and social CAPITAL (Saxenian, 1994); and selective theories drawn from SCIENCE STUDIES (particularly the work of Bruno Latour and Donna Haraway), used to understand the brute materialities of economic geographical activities, from the use of machines to the lurching movement of primary resources along the COMMODITY CHAIN (Cook, 2004). The absence of a single approach is liberating (no authority to which to kow-tow), but slightly disconcerting (the discipline continually starts anew with a clean slate).

(3) Both permissive theory and methods have been used to understand an issue increasingly preoccupying economic geography from the late 1980s, GLOBALIZATION, and forming a body of research as energetic as its focus of study. Globalization was made for economic geographical study. And in the beginning it was economic geography. Although they did not use the term, Chisholm and Smith were students of globalization. That focus was lost, however, as economic geography became the study of only WESTERN industrial economies, and the rest of the world was parcelled up and given over to either REGIONAL GEOGRAPHY or DEVELOPMENT

GEOGRAPHY. Processes beginning from the 1970s, such as the emergence of a NEW INTERNATIONAL DIVISION OF LABOUR, the increasing HEGEMONY OF MULTINATIONAL CORPORATIONS, the growth of international financial capital, and new forms of COMMUNICATION and long-distance transportation, showed economic geographers that they needed to deal with whole world. Further, under globalization the old intellectual division of labour in geography was not just redundant but obstructive. Dicken's (1988) work on the geography of multinational corporations (now in its fourth edition) was one of the first to make this point. But he made another, just as important – that globalization was no seamless process, eradicating geographical difference. Globalization represented not 'the end of geography', as economists portrayed it (O'Brien, 1992b, p. 3), but another form of its continuing importance. Geographical differentiations were the very preconditions for globalization's possibility and achievement. Dicken and a former student, Yeung (2002), sharpened the point for firms, but similar conclusions were reached for the study of global commodity chains (Hughes and Reimer, 2004), international finance, world-wide mega-project property development (Olds, 2001), and the international migratory circuit of professional elites looking for elite jobs.

(4) Finally, and perhaps surprisingly, primary RESOURCES and NATURE have become the focus of an animated disciplinary discussion. For a long period the topic was a backwater, and was almost lost altogether under spatial science. The simplifying assumptions required for spatial modelling meant that the uneven and lumpy nature of resources were treated as complicating factors, the analysis of which was promised but indefinitely postponed. Harvey (1974a) made a powerful case for considering nature along with the economy, but this was not nature 'red-in-claw' but social-nature, 'the production of nature', as Smith (2008 [1984]) put it. The PRODUCTION OF NATURE did not mean creating something where before there was nothing. Nature pre-existed, but how it was exploited, used, thought about and represented once market capitalism arrived was utterly altered. The original Marxist approach emphasized the centrality of social relations in constituting the economic resource, and in doing so joined discussions with POLITICAL ECOLOGY. In a classic paper, Watts (1994b) brilliantly showed how social relations in Nigeria made the natural resource of OIL neither natural nor a resource;

instead, it created mal-development, social discord and political mayhem (see also PETROCAPITALISM). Since then, discussions of nature and resources have centred around two axes. One turns on HYBRIDITY, a notion drawn from science studies and extending what counts as social relations, and connoting the inseparability, their mixing and blending, of nature and the social – for example, Swyngedouw's (1999) work on the political economy of WATER in Spain, and Morgan, Marsden and Murdoch's (2006) on food. The other turns on the influence of discursive and regulatory regimes, particularly neo-liberalism, in defining nature and resources – for example, Bakker's (2003) work on water, and the edited collection by Heynen, McCarthy, Prudham and Robbins (2007).

Economic geography is a discipline that is intellectually open, eclectic, pluralist, possibly chaotic and anarchic, and subject to temporary whims and fancies. Inconstancy is the only constant, inconsistency the only consistency. Over the past two decades the boundaries between economic geography and other subfields have become increasingly muddied and indistinct, as the very idea of a separate discipline, and a separate empirical object of study, has been contested (as reflected in the new textbooks for the discipline; e.g., Coe, Kelly and Yeung, 2007). Almost anything can now be fodder for its enquiry. Critics from outside have complained of a hopeless 'fuzziness' and slapdash approach (Markusen, 1999), while even inside there have been grumblings of a lack of rigour, focus and policy RELEVANCE (Martin, 2001b). The unusual challenge for the discipline will be less breaking new ground, which it seems to do on a daily basis, than holding its existing ground.　　TB

Suggested reading
Amin and Thrift (2000); Barnes (2001); Coe, Kelly and Young (2007); Scott (2000a); Sheppard and Barnes (2000).

economic growth A sustained increase in the production of goods and services, usually measured at the national level as the change in the GROSS DOMESTIC PRODUCT (GDP) of a country's economy. Economic growth is, at the same time, one of the most fundamental and perplexing issues in economic theory. There are still no conclusive answers to the questions of what causes economic growth and to what extent it can be sustained, which have been hotly debated since the time of Adam Smith and Thomas Malthus. Smith believed that the ultimate engine of growth was the DIVISION OF LABOUR, the increasing elaboration of which drives productivity, which in turn determines growth (or the 'size of the market'). Larger MARKETS would sustain higher rates of growth, and therefore growth would continue indefinitely. Malthus, for his part, was much more pessimistic. He argued that the human population would expand geometrically, while the supply of land (and therefore FOOD) could only grow slowly, resulting not only in a slowing rate of growth, but in catastrophic vulnerability to POVERTY and FAMINE (see MALTHUSIAN MODEL). Karl Marx also identified limits to the long-run rate of growth, caused in his analysis by the tendency of the rate of profit to fall and rising class conflict (see MARXIAN ECONOMICS). For Marx, economic growth would also be inherently unstable, following boom and bust cycles, along with periodic (and gradually increasing) bouts of unemployment (his 'reserve army' of labour). While Marx may have over-estimated CAPITALISM's inherent tendency to system failure, his forecast of significant fluctuation in rates of growth, combined with spatially UNEVEN DEVELOPMENT, has been borne out by the historical record (see Bluestone and Harrison, 2001; Duménil and Lévy, 2004).

'Growth is the pivot on which INDUSTRIAL GEOGRAPHY turns', Storper and Walker (1989, p. 36) have argued, 'and change is the only constant in a world of persistent disequilibrium generated by the very nature of capitalist development'. There is no evidence of sustained convergence towards an equilibrium or natural rate of growth; indeed, there is a growing awareness that there are incipient, if not urgent, social and environmental *limits to growth*. But the search for the ultimate economic causes of growth continues. Often, it appears that the simple fact of growth is taken as a sign of causality. So, during the 1980s, the relatively strong performance of the German and Japanese economies prompted widespread debate around the essence of these apparently superior models of capitalism (see Albert, 1993). During the 1990s, when economic growth in both these economies faltered and American growth surged, this was held up as a validation of the brand of market-driven, technology-intensive growth found in the USA (Friedman, 2000 [1999]), the generic form of which is often described as NEO-LIBERALISM.

The late 1990s also witnessed the emergence of 'new growth theory', developed by economists Robert Lucas and Paul Romer, which posits that the ultimate causes of growth are endogenous (i.e. internal), the rate of growth being a function of the aggregate stock of CAPITAL (both human and physical), together with the degree of technological sophistication of the ECONOMY (e.g. the rate of investment in research and development). The policy implications of this MODEL, which include accelerating the long-term rate of investment in technology and skills, have been explored by Bluestone and Harrison (2001). Here, they draw unfavourable contrasts with the prevailing ideology of neo-liberal growth, which favours short-term measures of market performance and an ethos of governmental deregulation.

Evidently, the search for the ultimate causes of growth continues, and with some urgency. Since the 1970s, growth rates across many of the advanced industrial nations have declined markedly, compared to the so-called 'Golden Age' of FORDISM, while the experience of less-developed countries (with the notable exceptions of India and China) has been decidedly uneven. This has led some to conclude that the 'Golden Age' of high growth has given way to a 'Leaden Age' of generally slower, and less sustainable, economic growth. JPe

Suggested reading
Dicken (2003, see especially 'The changing global economic map', pp. 32–81); Scott and Storper (2003); Storper and Walker (1989).

economic integration A term often coupled with GLOBALIZATION, and typically associated with claims about the virtues of free trade and unregulated capital MARKETS. If one searches for 'economic integration' on the website of the INTERNATIONAL MONETARY FUND (IMF), for example, some 3,350 documents appear – the bulk of which are concerned with defining the enabling conditions for expanding TRADE and CAPITAL flows, and documenting their beneficial effects. Such claims have been subject to intense contestation, exemplified most dramatically by the protests that erupted in Seattle in November 1999 at the time of the WORLD TRADE ORGANIZATION (WTO) ministerial meeting (see ANTI-GLOBALIZATION).

Some scholars question the extent and novelty of contemporary global economic integration, thereby casting doubt on efforts to portray it as an inexorable linear process. In the mid-1990s, for example, Hirst and Thompson (1996) observed that the international economy was actually *less* open and integrated than in the early years of the twentieth century under the Gold Standard regime. They also pointed to the concentration of trade, investment and capital flows among Europe, Japan and North America. Since then, China has emerged as a major site of trade and investment flows, as well as the single largest holder of US debt.

Burgeoning US debt underscores the structural asymmetries that have propelled the liberalization of financial markets since the 1970s. A widely held view is that the collapse of the Bretton Woods system of international monetary and financial arrangements in 1971 represented a defeat for a weakened US capitalism, unleashing market forces that quickly gained ascendance over nation-state power (see MONEY AND FINANCE). New information technologies and a 'space of FLOWS' also figure prominently in this account of intensified economic integration (e.g. Castells, 1996a).

In a revisionist analysis of the shift to what he calls the Dollar–Wall Street regime, Peter Gowan maintains that the liberation of international financial markets was part of a deliberate strategy by the Nixon administration, 'based on the idea that doing so would *liberate the American state from succumbing to its economic weaknesses and would strengthen the power of the American state*' (Gowan, 1999, p. 23; italics in original). Cutting the link between the dollar and gold in 1971 meant that the USA could force revaluation on other states through its own policy for the dollar. In a second key set of moves, closely linked to the OPEC OIL-price rise, the USA insisted that petrodollars be recycled through the private banking system and devised a set of incentives for commercial banks to lend to governments in the South. These included the abolition of capital controls, scrapping the ceiling on bank loans to a single borrower and repositioning the IMF to structure bailout arrangements that shifted the risk of such loans to the populations of borrowing countries. While ensuring the banks would not lose, these arrangements have also meant that financial crises in the SOUTH provoked capital flight of private wealth-holders that ended up strengthening Wall Street (see NEO-LIBERALISM). While the banks and Wall Street benefited in the period after 1973, the continual liberalization of the financial markets came screeching to a halt in 2008 with the collapse of over-extended US investment banks and insurance houses, and the crippling of a global financial system made excessively vulnerable by a massive housing bubble driven by excessively leveraged banks deploying risky financial instruments (credit default swaps, for example) in a fiscal environment characterized by corruption, fraud and virtually non-existent regulation and oversight.

Neo-liberal forms of economic integration emerge from this analysis *not* as a set of inexorable technological and market forces increasingly divorced from state-political controls, but as integrally linked with what Harvey (2003b) calls 'the new IMPERIALISM'. Such understandings are crucial in a post-9/11 world in which economic integration and military force are becoming closely intertwined.   GHa

Suggested reading
Barnett (2004); *RETORT* (2005).

economies of scale The cost advantages gained by large-scale production, as the average cost of production falls with increasing output. Total production costs usually increase less than proportionately with output, up to a point where *diseconomies of scale* (cost disadvantages) set in.

Economies of scale generally arise from conditions internal to the operation of the plant in question. Some important internal sources of scale economies are: (a) *indivisibilities*, where plant is built to a certain capacity below which the average cost of production will be higher than at full capacity, and the plant cannot be divided up into smaller units working with the same efficiency as the larger one; (b) *specialization and division of labour* associated with expansion of scale, which can increase efficiency and hence lower costs; and (c) *overhead processes*, such as the design of a product, which must be undertaken and paid for irrespective of scale, so that the larger the output, the lower is the overhead cost per unit. Certain EXTERNAL ECONOMIES may also be associated with expansion of scale of output; for example, if the growth of an entire industry reduces costs in each individual firm.

The existence of economies of scale encourages the expansion of productive capacity up to the point at which diseconomies eventually pull the cost of the additional (marginal) unit above the price that it will fetch. In some modern industry, it may be that this point is reached only at a very high volume of output, so that average cost continues to fall with rising output well beyond the level at which diseconomies might be expected to arise. However, in other activities a trend towards more flexible and differentiated production may lead to diseconomies at relatively small scale of output. (See also ECONOMIES OF SCOPE.)   DMS

economies of scope The cost advantages that may arise when performing two or more activities together within a single firm rather than performing them separately. When economies of scope exist, firms have an incentive to internalize (i.e. perform in-house) the production of goods or services that otherwise would be acquired through transactions with external suppliers (see TRANSACTIONAL ANALYSIS). This incentive is normally expressed in terms of reductions in production costs as result of internalization (see TRANSACTION COSTS). Hence, economies of scope may arise where the goods or services in question share inputs to their production (e.g. by using excess capacity in power generation or indivisible machinery), are related to one another through INPUT–OUTPUT relations (one good being an input to the production of the other good), draw upon common technical or manual skills for their production, or can be most efficiently produced at roughly the same scale of output. This concept, when combined with the idea of ECONOMIES OF SCALE, provides an understanding of the forces that determine firm size and the nature of inter-firm relations in localized CLUSTERS of producers (Scott, 1988c). (See also PRODUCTION COMPLEX.) MSG

economy Economy is practice and object. As human practice, Aristotle defined *oikos* as operating the household (on patriarchal principles) to meet daily needs. Over time, as the meaning of economy migrated from the domestic to the public sphere within POLITICAL ECONOMY, it came to mean 'seeking a desired end with the least possible expenditure of means'. As object, it refers to the hypothesis that practices of economy, now in the public domain, can be separated from the remainder of societal endeavour: as *the* economy. Economy has become central to social DIS-COURSE as a result of this separation: human practices are thought of as reducible to means/ends rationality, and the (capitalist) economy is thought of as central to human well-being.

The GENEALOGY of this separation of economy from related societal and biophysical processes is not yet clear. The question of how to organize society on secular principles, as a substitute for (Christian) religious mores, was a preoccupation of the ENLIGHTENMENT in France and Scotland. French Physiocrats constructed the first model of an economy as a self-sustaining entity. In 1758, François Quesnay built a *tableau économique*, forerunner of Marx's theory of the circulation of capital and of post-1945 INPUT–OUTPUT MODELS, depicting the flow of net product from its presumed agricultural source, via landlords, 'unproductive' industrialists, and back to agriculture. British political economists concerned themselves with the benefits of organizing SOCIETY around economy. It was held that the STATE could not rein in human passions, implying that the key was harnessing self-interest for this purpose. Avarice became constructed as a beneficial and mild interest rather than a passion, capable of taming other passions deleterious to society. Adam Smith solved the puzzle of how self-interest could create a society beneficial to all. He reduced self-interest to economic calculation, and articulated the principle of the *invisible hand*, whereby MARKET competition would translate individual self-interested practices of economy into mutual benefit. Smith's argument was geographical: the invisible hand and free trade would benefit Britain. These justifications gradually transformed into the abstract argument that self-interested practices of economy were universal, and generally socially beneficial.

Seventeenth- and eighteenth-century political economy focused on the relationship between economic processes and the national polity. Karl Polanyi (1944) argues that the economy was *disembedded* from society during Britain's 'Great Transformation' to liberal CAPITALISM in the early nineteenth century, and increasingly, the economy was placed in a national frame. By 1841 Friedrich List, influenced by American economic policy, was proposing protectionist policies for the German national economy, facing the debilitating consequences of free trade with Britain.

After the 1890s, European and then American economists completed a marginalist, subsequently neo-classical, revolution reinforcing the principle of the invisible hand. Assuming a world of autonomous self-interested individuals of equal political power engaged in perfect competition, NEO-CLASSICAL ECONOMICS created a level playing field, on which equilibrium market prices would track the marginal utility of each COMMODITY; ensure that capitalists, landlords and workers are fairly paid (reflecting their marginal contribution to production); and maximize social utility, in a self-regulating market. It was also extended as a normative principle to broad areas of social life. RATIONAL CHOICE THEORY, the broadly influential idea that social structures and dynamics are the result of the rational economic choices of autonomous self-interested individuals, essentially grounds all social processes in practices of economy – and equates such actions with capitalist markets. This vision of a harmonious self-regulating capitalist economy, grounded in self-interested practices of economy, and governed by rules of perfect competition, came to dominate social thought.

After 1945, as the formal end of COLONIALISM created a world largely divided up into autonomous NATION-STATES, each with acknowledged SOVEREIGNTY over their economies (controlling BORDERS, managing economic activities within the border), the idea of the national economy became commonplace. Indeed, much of the statistical knowledge produced about the economic aspects of society appears in reams of national statistics, produced using universally agreed practices of measurement (such as the Gross National Product; grounded in mainstream Anglophone economic theory), and collected and published by supra-national agencies. Timothy Mitchell (2002d) dates 'the making of the economy' to this POST-COLONIAL era; this is certainly when the discourse globalized.

ECONOMIC GEOGRAPHY has at times aligned itself with such arguments – for example, during the 1960s – but even then serious reservations were expressed about the adequacy of this discourse. Earlier eras of COMMERCIAL GEOGRAPHY and REGIONAL GEOGRAPHY created an awareness of different, non-capitalist and non-individualist practices of economy in different places, that are perfectly adequate to the social and biophysical context in which they operate. For example, slash and burn and SHIFTING CULTIVATION remain highly functional for subsistence-based societies in delicate ecological environments (see SUBSISTENCE AGRICULTURE), now being destroyed by the clear-cutting of forest ecosystems to undertake cash-crop monoculture.

SPATIAL SCIENCE offered a nascent critique of capitalism's self-sufficiency and social optimality, even under the extreme assumptions presupposed by neo-classical economics. It was shown that while neo-classical theory works well on the head of a pin, it breaks down in the real world of a geographically extensive SPACE ECONOMY. Perfect competition turns into monopolistic competition, the level playing field disappears and prices no longer approximate marginal utilities.

Marxian political economy, gaining popularity in economic geography during the 1970s and 1980s, offered much deeper criticisms: that CAPITALISM entails exploitation of labour and NATURE, generates social and political conflict and UNEVEN DEVELOPMENT, and is incapable of resolving these problems

internally (see MARXISM). The space economy poses difficulties and complexities for Marxist theory too, but these only exacerbate capitalism's internal contradictions. Capitalism thus *cannot* be disembedded from its non-economic context, as it depends on state intervention, biophysical processes with their own logic, social and legal norms, and CIVIL SOCIETY for its own reproduction (see also CULTURAL ECOLOGY). POST-STRUCTURALISM has pushed economic geography away from analyses that begin with even political economic processes, towards a view in which these are co-implicated with cultural, gendered and biophysical processes, and non-capitalist economic practices.

Geographical economy is inseparable from and constituted through societal and biophysical processes, and is variegated rather than simply capitalist. There is no single economy applicable to all places, with advanced capitalism constituting a ubiquitous best practice for all, but room for geographically differentiated possibilities and imaginaries.   ES

Suggested reading
Dumont (1977); Gibson-Graham (1996); Hirschman (1977); Sheppard and Barnes (2000).

ecosystem The concept of the ecosystem was proposed by the British ecologist A.G. Tansley in 1935, to describe the interaction of living things and their non-living surroundings, with which they interact. Tansley's paper attacked the notion that the plant community was an 'organic unity', and vegetation succession a process of development to a 'climax' state (Sheail, 1987). Tansley suggested that CLIMATE, soils, plants and ANIMALS interacted together as parts of a SYSTEM, nested within a host of other physical systems (Sheail, 1995).

The ecosystem concept allowed a reductionist approach to the analysis of forests, fields, WETLANDS and other environments in terms of flows of energy and matter. It allowed metaphors from engineering, cybernetics and control theory to be applied to such environments, such as system, feedback, equilibrium, balance and control. Ecosystems are not dimensionally defined: they can be defined at any SCALE from pond, to ocean or biosphere. Classic studies, such as those of Odum on the energetics of Silver Springs in Florida (in 1956), involved small naturally bounded systems. Much of the claim of ECOLOGY as an experimental SCIENCE can be traced back to the power of the ecosystem approach.

The ecosystem, and the wider science of ecology, provided a framework for the analysis and management of human impacts on non-human NATURE. In the mid-twentieth century, ecological 'managerialism' underpinned the expansion global policy ideas about issues such as overgrazing, DESERTIFICATION, deforestation and the problem of 'fragile environments'. Ecologists sought to apply the 'lessons' of their interdisciplinary science to DEVELOPMENT; for example, in *Ecological principles for economic development* (Dasmann, Milton and Freeman, 1973). The ecosystem as a frame for understanding human impacts on the biosphere was fundamental to the ENVIRONMENTAL MOVEMENT of the 1970s and 1980s (at that time, often called the 'ecology movement') and to the expansion of CONSERVATION.

The ecosystem concept has had a significant impact on GEOGRAPHY, first in describing vegetation patterns on global (biome) or local scales, and second as a framework for analysing the interaction of SOCIETY and nature. Organism and ecosystem were discussed by David Stoddart (1967) in Chorley and Haggett's *Models in geography*, both for their utility in explaining how the world worked and also as indicators of the value of the SYSTEMS approach and GENERAL SYSTEMS THEORY as a 'unifying methodology' for geography.

Despite the explosion of interest by human geographers in all aspects of the social construction of nature, the ecosystem continues to be central to natural scientific explanations of processes and patterns in the living environment, and human interactions with them. Moreover, recent ecological work on ecosystem disturbance and resilience has maintained interest in the ecosystem as a holistic frame for understanding human impacts on non-human nature. WMA

ecumene A term used to mean 'inhabited world' or 'dwelling place'. It generally refers to the historical process and cultural forms of human settlement, and to those parts of the Earth where people have made their permanent home, and to the economic activities that support that permanent occupation and use of land. It derives from the Greek *oecumene*, which referred specifically to the civilized world as it was known to the ancient Greeks (and, later, Romans) and centred on the Mediterranean (see CIVILIZATION). In some historiographies of GEOGRAPHY, 'ecumene' is presented as the unifying concept and distinctive concern of the discipline (James, 1972; see also GEOGRAPHY, HISTORY OF). In practice, it was in most active use by cultural geographers

in the nineteenth and early twentieth centuries, along with the allied scholars in anthropology and archaeology, who were then concerned with the imperatives and distribution of human settlement (see CULTURAL GEOGRAPHY).

Ecumene was adopted as the title of a new journal launched in 1991 that sought to showcase the work of the 'new cultural geography' and the fields of study with which it was in conversation. That this journal was re-launched in 2005 under the more straightforward title *Cultural Geography* is perhaps indicative of a declining intellectual purchase and resonance of 'ecumene' at the start of the twenty-first century. SW

Suggested reading
Ecumene; James (1972).

edge city An urban form in the USA, identified by Garreau (1991) and addressed by others (e.g. Beauregard, 1995). An edge city contains the industry, commerce and residences of traditional cities, but in less compact form (see EXOPOLIS; SPRAWL). Edge cities are new (largely emerging post-1970) and contain high levels of office and retail space. They have also become generally perceived as places in themselves, or 'new downtowns', on the edge of urban areas (e.g. Tyson's Corner, Virginia). According to Garreau, these are not only 'edge cities' because of their peripheral location, but also because they are major centres of innovation. EM

Suggested reading
Garreau, 1991.

education Studies of the *geography of education* focus on spatial variations in the provision, take-up, quality of and outputs from educational resources. Many of those RESOURCES are provided in facilities at fixed locations, so the provision of, for example, play-centres for pre-school CHILDREN may involve differential ACCESSIBILITY, with implications for SOCIAL JUSTICE. The majority of facilities are PUBLIC GOODS in most countries, so their spatial allocation is a political process, as is public expenditure on education (cf. POSITIVE DISCRIMINATION).

Spatial variations in educational outputs are related not only to the quality of the facilities and institutions' learning systems, but also their social milieux. Students' aspirations and performance reflect not only their innate abilities and home situations and the quality of the school they attend, but also the characteristics of their school and NEIGHBOURHOOD peers. Strong NEIGHBOURHOOD EFFECTS operate (Wöllmann, 2001: see also CONTEXTUAL EFFECT; MULTI-LEVEL MODELLING). Their existence was the basis for challenges to the 'separate but equal' schooling systems once operated in many US states, whereby African-Americans and whites were allocated to separate schools: after the classic *Brown v Board of Education of Topeka* Supreme Court decision in 1954, many school districts were required to integrate their schools to remove the unequal treatment suffered by the former group (Johnston, 1984). A commonly deployed strategy to achieve this was 'bussing', whereby students were transported from segregated neighbourhoods to mixed schools: this was increasingly countered by whites who either sent their children to private schools or moved to suburban school districts where housing was too expensive for most African-Americans ('white flight'). Similar patterns have been observed regarding school choice in English cities (Johnston, Burgess, Wilson and Harris, 2006).

With the adoption of NEO-LIBERALISM in many countries, although education remains a public good, parental and student choice is promoted – as against the territorially structured school catchment areas that characterized earlier eras, when the composition of a school, and thus the contextual effects operating therein, reflected the neighbourhoods that it served. To facilitate this choice, information on schools – such as the performance of their students in public examinations and their truancy rates – are published, leading to the creation of school 'league tables'.

Studies of *geographical education* focus on the provision and nature of instruction in the discipline in schools and universities. Special interest groups – including GEOGRAPHICAL SOCIETIES such as the Geographical Association in the UK – lobby relevant authorities to ensure, for example, that GEOGRAPHY is in the school curriculum and that departments offer degrees in the discipline at universities, with varying success across countries. Leading GEOGRAPHICAL SOCIETIES – such as the Association of American Geographers and the Royal Geographical Society/Institute of British Geographers – include specialty groups whose purpose is to promote pedagogy, as do journals such as the *Journal of Geography in Higher Education*.

Within universities, there is a growing trend of regularly assessing their performance – notably at research (as with the UK's Research Assessment Exercise, which grades every university department every five years on average: Johnston, 1994, 2006) – and then allocating funds according to the results, which has the consequence of concentrating research in selected institutions only.   RJ

Suggested reading
Bednarz, Downs and Vender (2003); Kong (2007); Walford (2001).

egalitarianism The view that all people are of equal fundamental moral or social worth, and should be treated as such. Egalitarianism can take a number of forms related to different types of EQUALITY: equality of opportunity, equality of outcome, equality of wealth or POWER, equality of respect, equality before the LAW or equality before God. Egalitarianism implicitly informs much research on the geographies of inequality, including those associated with differences of GENDER, CLASS, ETHNICITY, SEXUALITY, age, corporeality and nationality (cf. NATIONALISM). The mitigation of SPATIAL INEQUALITY has been an important normative concern for geographical scholarship since the early 1970s (Harvey, 1973). JPa

Suggested reading
Lee and Smith (2004).

electoral geography The study of geographical aspects of the organization, conduct and results of elections. Pioneering studies were conducted early in the twentieth century, but most of the literature – produced by a small number of specialists – dates from the 1960s on.

Because voting in national and local elections is almost invariably PLACE-bound (i.e. people have to cast their vote in a specified area, usually that containing their home) and the results are published for those places, a great deal of data that can be subject to geographical (i.e. spatial) analysis is created. Merely mapping election outcomes suggests that geography is 'epiphenomenal', however: that there is nothing inherently geographical about the processes producing the outcome, which just happens to be produced and displayable in spatial form. For geographers such as Agnew (1987a) and Cox (1969), however, the DECISION-MAKING processes underpinning those mapped patterns are inherently geographical. The socialization of voters is a contextual process (cf. CONTEXTUAL EFFECT) and much of the social interaction that precedes a voting decision is locally based, in the household and NEIGHBOURHOOD – hence the considerable emphasis in electoral geography on the NEIGHBOURHOOD EFFECT. In addition, the mobilization of voters is also at least partly a spatially specific activity, with political parties focusing their electioneering on those places where they expect to get the best returns.

Much analysis in electoral geography uses ecological data – often combining electoral returns for places with census data on the characteristics of their inhabitants – and thus faces problems associated with ECOLOGICAL INFERENCE (cf. ECOLOGICAL FALLACY; MODIFIABLE AREAL UNIT PROBLEM). Geographers have also added spatial information to survey data, facilitating analyses that at least partially circumvent those problems, although in the USA studies of patterns of voting by state and Congressional District have produced substantial insights into the political economy of elections there (Archer and Taylor, 1991).

In many electoral systems – especially those based on single-member constituencies (the so-called first-past-the-post system, deployed in both the UK and the USA) – the translation of votes into seats in the relevant legislature is an inherently geographical process, with the membership of such bodies determined by who wins most votes in each of a set of territorial constituencies. Constituency-delimitation (cf. REDISTRICTING) can thus be highly politicized in some countries, with district boundaries defined to promote the interests of one party over those of another, although similar outcomes may result without any such activity when redistricting is undertaken by independent, non-partisan, bodies (Gudgin and Taylor, 1979: cf. DISTRICTING ALGORITHM; GERRYMANDERING; MALAPPORTIONMENT).

As part of their continued mobilization of support in places, parties and/or candidates may influence the allocation of PUBLIC GOODS towards favoured areas, both to reward those who have supported them at past contests and to solicit support from others there (cf. PORK BARREL). The geography of election results is thus a potential foundation for a GEOGRAPHY of political POWER. (See also DEMOCRACY.) RJ

Suggested reading
Johnston (2005a); Johnston and Pattie (2006); Johnston, Pattie, Dorling and Rossiter (2006).

emigration A particular form of MIGRATION: the term is usually reserved for migration that occurs between countries. To emigrate is to leave a place, the opposite of IMMIGRATION, to enter a new place. Emigration was defined as a basic HUMAN RIGHT in Article 12 of the 1966 UN International Covenant on Civil and Political Rights (which came into force in 1976): 'Everyone shall be free to leave any country, including his [or her] own' (United Nations, n.d.). Note that the right to emigrate is not matched by the right to immigrate, or to enter the country of one's choice. The value of this right is therefore debatable. Furthermore, countries vary widely in their observance of this right. During the COLD WAR period, STATES within the Warsaw Pact typically prohibited their citizens from leaving, especially after walls were built to separate the CAPITALIST and state SOCIALIST countries of Europe. The number of countries that currently prohibit emigration is limited, but all NATION-STATES regulate exit to a degree through the granting, or withholding, of passports (Torpey, 2000). Countries also differ in their practices of monitoring emigration: some track their citizens abroad through registration systems, and collect detailed statistics on all entries and departures, while others are only interested in citizens who are actually resident in the nation-state (see also CITIZENSHIP). DH

Suggested reading
Castles and Miller (2003).

emotional geography The study of the dynamic, recursive relation between emotions and PLACE or space. Emotional geography includes diverse ways of understanding the differential TOPOLOGIES and TOPOGRAPHIES of emotion. As a body of work it responds, on the one hand, to the claim that emotions are an intractable aspect of life and thus potentially a constitutive part of all geographies (Anderson and Smith, 2001) and, on the other, to the recognition that emotions have long been manipulated and modulated as a constitutive part of various forms of POWER (Thrift, 2004a). As such, work on emotional geographies elicits the multiple ways in which different emotions emerge from, and re-produce, specific sociospatial orders and engages with how emotions become part of the different relations that make up the lived geographies of place (Davidson, Bondi and Smith, 2005). Consequently, the term 'emotional geography' does not designate a sub-discipline limited to the study of a set of emotions (such as fear, boredom or anxiety). Rather, it is composed of ways of considering how emotions, along with linked modalities such as feeling, mood or AFFECT, are constitutive elements within the ongoing composition of SPACE–TIME, and exploring how learning to respond to and intervene in such modalities could or perhaps should disrupt HUMAN GEOGRAPHY's methodological and theoretical practices.

Attention to emotions, or at least calls to attend to emotions, have a long history in human geography, being central, for example, to the expansive version of what a human is and does that was articulated by humanistic geographies in the 1970s and, in particular, to feminist interventions in social geography (e.g., on fear, Pain, 2000). Current work on emotional geographies is animated by two intertwined sources – both of which resonate with the attention in HUMANISTIC GEOGRAPHY to the LIFEWORLD and the TAKEN-FOR-GRANTED WORLD, and perform a sensibility that attends to the ebb and flow of everyday life. First, and most prominently, there is the careful attention in FEMINIST GEOGRAPHIES to the silencing or repressing of differential, often gendered, emotional experience and the subsequent attempts to reclaim and give voice to emotional experiences. Second, attention is paid in NON-REPRESENTATIONAL THEORIES to the emergence, or individuation, of emotions from within more or less unwilled ASSEMBLAGES that gather together human and non-human BODIES in broad fields of affect. These are by no means mutually exclusive or internally coherent perspectives – indeed, what is shared between them is a commitment to the relationality of emotions and thus an assumption that emotions are not contained by, or properties of, an individual mind. Yet the resulting theoretical and methodological pluralism raises questions about how to understand the role of the SUBJECT in what an emotion is and does, as well as broader questions of how to develop conceptual vocabularies attentive to differential emotional geographies. Both questions have been responded to through the recent experimentations with techniques such as practical psychotherapies (cf. PSYCHOANALYTIC THEORY) and performative methods (see PERFORMATIVITY) that aim to witness different emotional or affectual geographies (cf. Tolia-Kelly, 2006). The importance and interest of this new body of work is reflected in the publication of a new interdisciplinary journal, *Emotion, Space and Society* (2008–). BA

Suggested reading
Anderson and Smith, (2001); Bondi (2005); Davidson, Bondi, and Smith (2005).

empire An extensive TERRITORY and polity, encompassing diverse lands and peoples, that is ruled, more or less directly and effectively, by a single person (emperor/empress), sovereign STATE or centralized elite, and without the formal consent of all its peoples (cf. Lieven, 2005). The term is also used colloquially to denote great POWER and transcendent influence (as in 'corporate empire' and 'reason's empire'), and the adjectives 'imperial' and 'colonial' are commonly used to characterize actions and processes befitting empire.

Empire has taken diverse forms and eludes a single meaning or explanation. Parallels have been drawn between the evolution of EUROPE's modern colonial empires, which reached their heyday in the early twentieth century, and since Roman times the ability to stretch power over space has figured centrally in debates about empire (see TIME-SPACE DISTANCIATION). There have been over 70 empires in history – including those created by the Romans, Incas, Habsburgs and Ottomans, and by Britain, Japan and the Soviet Union – and Niall Ferguson (2004, p. 11) typologizes them in terms in their metropolitan foundations, declared aims, economic and political systems, social character, and perceived benefits and drawbacks. Important distinctions have been drawn between ancient and modern, Western and non-Western, maritime and land, and formal and informal empires. And histories and theories of empire have long varied in accordance with: (a) the relative importance given to six sources of power (economic, military, political, geopolitical, demographic and ideological); (b) the ways and extent to which SOVEREIGNTY is seen as unified or divided, and power as centralized and totalizing or limited and localized; and (c) the impact that empire has on the IDENTITY of colonizing and colonized peoples (Pomper, 2005).

The term derives from the Latin word *imperium*, meaning 'sovereign authority', and since the nineteenth century has been closely associated with IMPERIALISM and treated as pivotal to the globally UNEVEN DEVELOPMENT of CAPITALISM. Empire has long been used as a term of abuse – as quintessentially exploitative, and the duplicitous means by which the WEST has sought to impose its values and institutions (of reason, CIVILIZATION, progress, DEMOCRACY and so forth) on others. But over time, and still today, empire has also been viewed in a more affirmative light – as tolerant of DIFFERENCE, as a civilizing and modernizing influence, and as the harbinger of global order and a higher (perpetual) peace.

In recent years there has been a major revival of interest in empire, which is tied to three sets of (interrelated) factors. First, there has been a resurgence of scholarly interest in the history and legacies of COLONIALISM – one marked by a comparative turn in the study of world history that questions both EUROCENTRIC and nation-centred histories of empire, and a heightened concern with the 'CULTURE of empire' (Hall, 2000). Second, there has been vigorous debate, particularly since 9/11, about whether the USA should be regarded as an empire – 'empire lite' and 'empire in denial' being important slogans in the debate (*Dædalus*, 2005: (see AMERICAN EMPIRE)). Third, this debate feeds into a wider discussion of whether GLOBALIZATION is better characterized as what Michael Hardt and Antonio Negri (2000, pp. xii–xiii) see as a new age of empire that 'establishes no territorial center of power and does not rely on fixed boundaries and barriers ... a decentred and deterritorializing apparatus of rule that progressively incorporates the entire global realm within its open, expanding frontiers' (cf. BIOPOLITICS).

Since the late 1980s, an increasingly diverse geographical literature has critically examined the historical links between GEOGRAPHY (as both a discipline and DISCOURSE) and empire, sensitizing geographers to the Western-imperial-white-male biases and assumptions embedded in their disciplinary fabric. Close critical attention has been paid to how 'geography's empire' (Driver, 2001a) was fashioned at the level of knowledge and REPRESENTATION – as a form of EPISTEMOLOGICAL VIOLENCE – through practices of exploration, mapping and landscape representation, and deterministic and divisive discourses on CLIMATE and RACE (Clayton, 2004; cf. GEOGRAPHY, HISTORY OF). But geographers have also taken on board a wider interdisciplinary attempt to complicate understanding of empire's rigid geography of CORE AND PERIPHERY by recovering a community of struggles over who was included and excluded in definitions of empire and NATION, how lines and boundaries of difference were drawn between citizen and subject (see CITIZENSHIP), and the specific – and CLASS-, RACE- and GENDER-inflected – imperial and colonial locations (from museums to plantations) in which such dynamics were enacted and settled (Proudfoot and Roche, 2005).

Recent geographical research bears witness to the contemporary liaison between geography and empire in two further – if contrary – ways: first, through geohazards research and an emboldened MILITARY GEOGRAPHY, which are fired by GIS technologies and government contracts, and which serve the perceived SECURITY and SURVEILLANCE needs of Western states; and, second, through geographers' oppositional engagement with America's so-called 'WAR on terror' (see TERRORISM). In two important studies of the historical and contemporary geography of American imperialism, Neil Smith (2003c) uses the political influence of Isaiah Bowman – 'Roosevelt's geographer' – to question TELEOLOGICAL accounts of the passage from empire to NATION-STATE to globality, and recover the imperial spatiality of American visions of global development; and Derek Gregory (2004b) explores the spatial strategies and tactics – 'colonising geographies' – created and deployed by the USA and its allies in the MIDDLE EAST, showing how the USA now bestrides a 'colonial present' in which it exempts itself from international LAWS, institutions and limits on behaviour, creating 'spaces of exception' (of confinement, banishment and punishment) that strip people of their dignity and most basic HUMAN RIGHTS (cf. BIOPOLITICS; EXCEPTION, SPACE OF).

Three important insights that can be gleaned from this range of recent work are that: (a) past empires were less state-centred than was previously thought, and current US imperialism is more centred on the projection of nation-state power than contemporary theorists such as Hardt and Negri have proposed; (b) it is possible to analyse empires as both unitary and fragmentary, and as potent yet vulnerable apparatuses of power; and (c) historical work on empire, and the recognition it brings of the diverse ways in which power has and can be exercised, is key to understanding the nature and limits of empire today.   DCl

Suggested reading
Howe (2002); Kirsch (2003); Lester (2006); Lieven (2005).

empiricism A PHILOSOPHY originating with the Greeks, and later formally codified by the English philosopher John Locke (1632–1704), that privileges experience of the outside world above all else as the basis of knowledge, truth and method. The contrast is with philosophies that favour intuition, or self-revelation, or rationalism; that is, philosophies underpinned by internal mental processes independent of external senses. Empiricism most overtly entered HUMAN GEOGRAPHY through the discipline's use of the standard scientific method, which was most self-conscious during the 1960s, but which existed both before and after in less explicit forms. This method is unabashedly empiricist, averring that scientific THEORIES and HYPOTHESES are verifiable only against the gold standard of empirical data; that is, data observed though the senses. Nothing else counts. During the 1960s, this version of the scientific method and its concomitant empiricist philosophy was explicitly introduced into geography as part of the QUANTITATIVE REVOLUTION (Harvey, 1969). Ironically, though, what was so novel about 'the revolution' was the introduction of rationally derived THEORY, exactly the kind of pursuit most anathema to empiricism. This eventually clarified a crucial distinction between *empiricist* enquiry, which assumes that 'the facts' (observations) somehow speak for themselves and are independent of theory, and *empirical* enquiry, a substantive study that may be (and usually is) sensitive to the interdependence of theory and observation. TB

empowerment Defined by alternative DEVELOPMENT thinkers (Friedmann, 1992) as a process by which HOUSEHOLDS and their members wield greater socio-political and psychological POWER (e.g. knowledge, skills, voice, collective action, self-confidence) to reshape the actions affecting their own lives, empowerment has come to mean different things for different players. While mainstream development agencies regard empowerment as a tool to improve efficiency, more alternative agencies claim it as a metaphor for fundamental social transformation. Still, 'empowerment as praxis' retains its localized, personal emphasis as a phenomenon that necessitates individuals and collectives to struggle towards new consciousness and actions (Parpart, 2002) (see also POST-DEVELOPMENT and ANTI-DEVELOPMENT). RN

enclave A small piece of TERRITORY that is culturally distinct and politically separate from another territory within which it is located. 'Enclave' originally referred to a territory situated within a STATE but outside its political jurisdiction, such as the Vatican City in Italy. The term is also used to denote areas in which a minority population that identifies with one state is located in the territory of a neighbouring state, such as Ngorno Kharabach, which is an enclave within Azerbaijan but has an Armenian population. The term is increasingly used to refer to a city NEIGHBOURHOOD displaying distinctive economic, social and cultural attributes from its surroundings. (See also EXCLAVE.) CF

Suggested reading
Aalto (2002); Parks (2004).

enclosure In HISTORICAL GEOGRAPHY, enclosure refers to the extinction of 'common rights' and the replacement of open or common fields, pastures and meadows with 'enclosed' fields free of such rights. Across large swathes of medieval and early modern EUROPE, much agricultural land was *common land* that was subject to various forms of use by all individuals holding 'common-rights' (De Moor, Shaw-Taylor and Ward, 2002). These included rights to graze ANIMALS on common pasture and sometimes the right to gather fuel; rights over common fields, where individual cultivators might own a large number of scattered strips of arable land that alternated seasonally between private cultivation of the strips and communal grazing by those with common rights; and rights over common woodlands. Such common rights were not available to everyone, and were regulated by institutions such as manor or village courts. Enclosure replaced common land with fully *private land* that in some regions was physically 'enclosed' by a hedge, wall or ditch – within its boundaries, the owner or tenant normally has exclusive rights to use that land.

In England, the parliamentary enclosures of the eighteenth and nineteenth centuries are the best known, but enclosure began in the Middle Ages. It become an important process during the fifteenth century and probably peaked during the seventeenth century. Elsewhere in Europe, enclosure tended to come much later, principally during the nineteenth and twentieth centuries (as in the Soviet Union), though some common land still survives. In England, much medieval enclosure may have taken place by seigniorial edict, and is often associated with the conversion of arable to pasture and the destruction of villages (there are over 3,000 deserted medieval village sites known to archaeologists), but certainly by the early seventeenth century, and probably by the early sixteenth century, tenurial security had improved to the point at which it was legally necessary to secure the written consent of all proprietors, giving even the smallest owner an effective veto. Such enclosures by agreement became increasingly difficult to secure and during the eighteenth century, particularly after 1750, enclosure by agreement generally gave way to *parliamentary enclosure*. This required an Act of Parliament that allowed the larger landowners to override the vetoes of small owners, though not to appropriate their property. By 1500, around half of England's surface area was either already enclosed or had never been common. Perhaps 20–25 per cent was enclosed during the seventeenth century and a similar amount between 1750 and 1830 (Wordie, 1983).

The importance of enclosure in England has been stressed in three major historical processes. First, enclosure reshaped the LANDSCAPE. Second, enclosure was entangled with the destruction of the English peasantry (see PEAS-ANT) and the rise of agrarian CAPITALISM, though its importance remains a matter of debate (Humphries, 1992; Neeson, 1993; Shaw-Taylor, 2001). Third, enclosure played an important role in raising agricultural product-ivity during the AGRICULTURAL REVOLUTION (Overton, 1996). By allowing farmers to spe-cialize in the most profitable crops, enclosure facilitated regional specialization and thus higher overall productivity, and enclosure was also a precondition for certain techno-logical changes in agriculture; for example, installing under-drainage or the selective breeding of animals.

While enclosure has been subject to long-standing *historical* scrutiny, more recent work has also begun to reinterpret the concept of enclosure as a means of exploring the *contem-porary* forms and processes of NEO-LIBERALISM (see *RETORT*, 2005). Human geographers have seized upon enclosure as an ongoing feature of capital ACCUMULATION. Whereas traditional historical accounts of enclosure emphasized its relationship to 'the commons', recent work has proposed a more complex spatial formation operating across a number of SCALES, sites and practices, from special economic zones to genetic modification and biometrics (see BIOPOWER). Three major axes of investigation have been identified (Vasudevan, McFarlane and Jeffrey, 2008). The first focuses on the role of enclosure as a technology of contemporary NEO-LIBERALISM. Narratives of enclosure help illuminate the reconfiguration of political SOVEREIGNTIES, modes of subjectification and neo-liberal eco-nomic norms through a variety of TERRITORIES and NETWORKS. The second explores the role of LAW as a key instrument through which both old and new forms of enclosure are legitim-ized, regulated and policed. The third addresses the significance of enclosure as a key dimension of our colonial present. While studies of COLONIALISM underline the import-ance of land tenure as a precondition for par-ticular forms of displacement, dispossession

and discipline, contemporary instances of imperial enclosure have also mutated into new forms of the ENCLAVE capitalism that has accompanied the securitization of global mineral extraction (see Ferguson, 2006). Such an expansive re-conceptualization of enclosure has highlighted not only a complex set of logics of spatial inclusion and exclusion, but increasingly urgent forms of RESISTANCE that centre on a messy and highly conflicted reclaiming of the 'commons'.   LST/AV

Suggested reading
De Moor, Shaw-Taylor and Warde (2002); Mingay (1997); Vasudevan, McFarlane and Jeffrey (2008).

endogeneity The property that a variable is determined within a MODEL or geographical system, rather than being 'exogenous' or determined outside the model and so taken as fixed. In statistical models such as REGRES-SION and the GENERALIZED LINEAR MODEL, the right-hand side or independent variables are assumed to be exogenous, but situations arise where they are in fact endogenous, creating problems for model estimation. One widely applied example is in fiscal competition and 'tax-mimicking' between neighbouring local or regional governments (such as states within the USA): a state or local government's expenditure (or tax-rate) is determined by sev-eral (exogenous) characteristics of the state but also by the expenditure (or tax-rate) behaviour of neighbouring states, so that there is spatial endogeneity; such models are an important topic in SPATIAL ECONOMETRICS. A second example is where school pupil per-formance levels are influenced by the average income levels of families within the school catchments: the family income levels are assumed to be exogenous, but affluent families may have moved to the catchments of high-performance schools, and so not be exogenous after all, the so-called 'selection problem' in estimation. There are several methods for tak-ing endogeneity into account in the estimation process, including INSTRUMENTAL VARIABLES, maximum likelihood and BAYESIAN ANALYSIS, all of which are employed in spatial economet-rics. For studies employing individual-level data (as in some pupil performance analyses), there is a technique of 'matching' the charac-teristics of individuals between areas to elim-inate endogeneity bias.   LWH

Suggested reading
Manski (1995).

energy The capacity of a physical system for doing work. All species harness energy. Human beings harness, convert, release and (re)deploy energy to do work and yield goods and services. This is the basis for the material evolution of human societies. While all life forms ultimately depend on solar energy, since the INDUSTRIAL REVOLUTION developed countries have increasingly relied on non-renewable RESOURCES for energy.

Worldwide energy consumption is increasing. This is partly due to increases in global population, high levels of energy consumption in developed countries, and rising energy use in rapidly developing economies such as China and India. Per capita energy consumption varies significantly throughout the world. It is also important to recognize patterns of economic activity; for example, energy is consumed in developing countries to make cheap products for export to wealthier countries. Despite increased efficiencies in energy consumption in most developed countries, redistribution in energy consumption has occurred. Reducing material consumption, reusing existing materials and RECYCLING may achieve reductions in energy demand. Human geographers have studied cultural and urban aspects of energy use, including transitions to more sustainable cities (Pacione, 2001a).

Reduction in the use of energy through improved design, greater insulation and changes in use patterns can lower economic costs to an organization. Businesses have worked with parts of the ENVIRONMENTAL MOVEMENT on energy efficiency since the oil crises of 1973 and 1979. These crises signalled the end of cheap, abundant OIL and highlighted the dependency of industrialized countries on the Organisation of Petroleum Exporting Countries (OPEC), and the vulnerability of economies in some developing countries (see von Weizsacker, Lovins and Lovins, 1997).

Major concerns about energy include the continued supply of oil and the cumulative impacts of fossil-fuel consumption (see GLOBAL WARMING). Predictions of 'peak oil' at the scale of individual oilfields, countries and the globe highlight the finite nature of this NATURAL RESOURCE (Deffeyes, 2001). Every year, the world consumes billions of barrels of oil more than are discovered. Estimates of known reserves in various countries are not always reliable. Therefore, regardless of the environmental impacts of oil consumption, other sources of energy are required to continue present levels of economic activity. Natural gas (the cleanest-burning fossil fuel) is gaining importance, wind power is increasing rapidly from a low base and 'hybrid' cars are gaining popularity. The nuclear industry is advocating nuclear energy as an alternative to fossil fuels to combat global warming.

The dependence on fossil fuels inhibits the transition to renewable forms of energy such as solar, wind, biomass, hydrogen fuel cells and wave power. While fossil fuels are subsidized (Riedy and Diesendorf, 2003), the cost of renewable energy forms is not reduced significantly, due to inadequate research funding and difficulties in achieving ECONOMIES OF SCALE in production processes. Total world energy demand is anticipated to grow, despite efforts at reduction through greater efficiency. SUSTAINABILITY is crucial, including the use of appropriate technologies and energy sources in developing countries, transitions to benign energy sources throughout the world and reductions in energy use in developed countries. PM

Enlightenment In traditional interpretations, *the* Enlightenment is held to be that period of intellectual enquiry, broadly synonymous with the 'long' eighteenth century in EUROPE (*c*.1680–1820), in which 'modern' ideas of rationality, public criticism and the emancipation of CIVIL SOCIETY through reasoned reform took shape. Thus considered, the Enlightenment was distinguished by challenges to established ideas of 'ancient authority' and by the rejection of Classical and Renaissance conceptions of the world and of 'traditional' scholarship. PHILOSOPHY and SCIENCE were widely believed to be the basis to universal social betterment. Secular tolerance would overcome religious intolerance. In sum, humankind would free itself from ignorance and error.

Other interpretations are current. Indeed, even during its development and certainly since, the Enlightenment has been the subject of detailed scrutiny as to what it was, why it happened and what its consequences have been. Conventional views of the Enlightenment as a largely philosophical and uniform phenomenon evident in urban Europe especially in the lives and writings of great men, have been decisively challenged (Schmidt, 1996; Kors et al., 2003). Conceptions of the Enlightenment as a 'moment' of philosophical critique for a European elite (which still endure: see Darnton, 2003) have been supplemented by views of it as a SOCIAL MOVEMENT. Ideas of *the* Enlightenment as a uniform intellectual movement with particular national expression have been challenged by work that stresses Enlightenment, even enlightenments, as a social PROCESS or processes. As study of the Enlightenment has become more diverse – embracing, for instance, medical knowledge, questions of GENDER, exoticism, RACE and SEXUALITY – so studies of the Enlightenment have diversified (Outram, 2005). Questions of GEOGRAPHY are central to these revised and revitalized conceptions of the Enlightenment (Livingstone and Withers, 1999).

In traditional interpretation, little attention was paid to the geography of the Enlightenment. Where it was, emphasis was given to its distinctive features and differences at the level of the NATION-STATE, chiefly within Europe. Attention concentrated upon the idea of the Enlightenment's originating CULTURAL HEARTH or its 'core' NATIONS – France, England, Scotland, Holland, Germany – and to a 'periphery' where the Enlightenment was evident later or in different form: in Russia, for example, or in the Scandinavian countries. Relatively limited attention was given to the Enlightenment in the AMERICAS and to its presence and making in Portugal, Spain or the Greek-speaking countries of Eastern Europe (Porter and Teich, 1981). More recent work has moved beyond these concerns and scales of analysis. Three distinct but interrelated themes may be noted.

The first is *geographical knowledge and the Enlightenment*. Geographical knowledge, gleaned through oceanic navigation, terrestrial EXPLORATION, mapping and natural history survey, was crucial in the Enlightenment to new ideas about the shape and size of the Earth, terrestrial diversity and the nature of human cultures. In this first sense, the Enlightenment depended upon new geographical knowledge about the extent of what European contemporaries understood as TERRA INCOGNITA and then called the 'fourth world', the Americas, and, crucially, about the 'fifth division' of the world, the Pacific world or, in modern terms, AUSTRALASIA. For example, one distinctively Enlightenment idea (and ideal), that of society's development through a series of stages, was profoundly shaped by the 'discovery' of new peoples on the islands of the Southern Oceans, and by the extent of human cultural difference. Contemporaries referred to these geographies of human DIFFERENCE as 'The Great Map of Mankind' and devoted considerable time to theories explaining the development of human SOCIETY in relation to factors such as CLIMATE, the role of custom and commercial capacity. In such ways, Enlightenment was closely connected with EMPIRE (see also TRAVEL WRITING).

We may secondly think in terms of *geography in the Enlightenment*. Geography as one form of modern intellectual endeavour was itself shaped by the evolving encounter with new peoples and lands during the Enlightenment. This was apparent in terms of emphases upon realism in description, systematic classification in collection and comparative method in explanation. Geography in the Enlightenment was a DISCOURSE, a set of practices by which the world was revealed and ordered, and it was a discipline and a scale of study, the whole Earth, in which formal education was possible, in schools and universities. It was also a popular subject, taught in academies and in public lectures alongside history, astronomy and mathematics, in order to educate citizens about the extent and content of the GLOBE (Mayhew, 2000). In these ways, geography in the Enlightenment was part of what thinkers then called 'The Science of Man', that concern to understand the human world through the same observational and methodological principles as the natural world (see also GEOGRAPHY, HISTORY OF).

Finally, it is now commonplace to refer to the different *geographies of the Enlightenment*. These different geographies are distinguished by attention to the intrinsic diversity of the Enlightenment, to the social processes and contradictions underlying its intellectual and practical claims and, above all, by sensitivity to the importance of geographical SCALE in locating and explaining the Enlightenment and its constituent practices. Although the Enlightenment continues to be much studied in national context, greater attention than before is now paid to its global expression and consequences, to the local institutional sites and social settings in which the Enlightenment's defining ideas were produced and debated, to the uneven transmission of those ideas across geographical SPACE and to the variant nature of their reception (Clark, Golinski and Schaffer, 1999; Livingstone and Withers, 1999; Cañizares-Esguerra, 2001).

Questions to do with the 'where' of the Enlightenment are thus as important as those of its 'what', 'why' and 'who'. Many of the architects of POSTMODERNISM have speculated on the end of what, ignoring its diversity, they have sometimes clumsily termed the 'Enlightenment Project' (Geras and Wokler, 2000). Whilst initially critical of Enlightenment writers' emphases upon rationality, reform and the power of critical argument, many such theorists would now confirm the enduring significance of the Enlightenment as a set of critical political issues and as an object of historical and geographical study. cw

Suggested reading
Clark, Golinski and Schaffer (1999); Kors et al. (2003); Livingstone and Withers (1999); Outram (2005).

enterprise zone An area in which special policies apply to encourage economic DEVELOPMENT. Enterprise zones typically offer tax concessions and reduced planning and other regulations to private companies. Critics argue that their effect is often to move existing jobs rather than to create new ones, and that they produce a concentration of POWER in the central STATE and a loss of control by the LOCAL STATE over DEVELOPMENT strategies. Enterprise zones are common in the USA and the UK, but similar arrangements are found in many countries, including export-processing zones, special economic zones (notably in China and India) and tax- and duty-free zones. JPa

Suggested reading
Ong (2000).

entrepreneurship The geography of entrepreneurship explores the relationship of entrepreneurship to SPACE and PLACE; to date, interest has focused mainly on identifying the characteristics of places that foster the formation of businesses in high-technology industries. This kind of entrepreneurship has interested ECONOMIC GEOGRAPHERS because of its presumed importance to INNOVATION and to regional economic growth and development. In his review of the literature on entrepreneurs, NETWORKS and economic DEVELOPMENT, Malecki (1997) points to the importance of regional industrial mix, skilled labour, the spatial concentration or AGGLOMERATION of similar industries, and networks that provide access to technology and capital. He concludes, however, by noting how relatively little is known about the relationship between entrepreneurship and territory. (For the entrepreneurial behaviour of places, see URBAN ENTREPRENEURIALISM.)

The culture of entrepreneurship is another place-based characteristic that affects economic development trajectories. In her comparison of the high-technology CLUSTERS of Route 128 outside Boston, Massachusetts and Silicon Valley in the San Francisco Bay Area of California, Saxenian (1994) underlines the importance of cultural difference (in patterns of networking, in degrees of hierarchy in organizations, and in the amount of formality expected in the organization of work, for example) in shaping economic outcomes (growth versus stagnation).

In view of the degree to which social structures are gendered and racialized, characteristics of the entrepreneur affect the relationship of entrepreneurship to place. Feminist geographers have pointed to the importance of the GENDER of the entrepreneur and the ways in which gender shapes the meaning of innovation (what is considered innovative in a place) as well as an entrepreneur's access to resources; female-owned businesses often contribute to the development of places differently from male-owned businesses, and women entrepreneurs have greater difficulty obtaining bank loans, although this difficulty varies significantly from place to place even within a metropolitan area (Blake and Hanson, 2005). Entrepreneurship among members of ethnic groups is facilitated by ethnic ties, some of which may stretch to other countries, which enhance access to RESOURCES (Zhou, 1998; see ETHNICITY).

Much remains unknown about the relationship of entrepreneurship to place and space. For example, how does local context relate to the formation and nurturing of firms in non-high-technology industries? How do different kinds of businesses and business owners contribute to local economic and social well-being? How does local context enable and constrain the process of business ownership for different kinds of people? sHa

Suggested reading
Blake and Hanson (2005); Malecki (1997).

entropy A measure of the amount of UNCERTAINTY in a probability distribution or a SYSTEM subject to constraints. The term originated in thermodynamics, but has been used in a wide variety of contexts, notably in INFORMATION THEORY and as the basis for ENTROPY-MAXIMIZING MODELS of SPATIAL INTERACTION.

The concepts of macrostate and microstate are central to entropy analysis. Consider the distribution of 100 people into 10 regions: individual B to region six, individual K to region four and so on. A *macrostate* is an aggregate frequency distribution of people across regions. Several different *microstates* may correspond to or give rise to the same macrostate: different individuals go to different regions, but the frequency distributions are the same. Entropy measures the relationship between a macrostate and the possible microstates that correspond to it. At one extreme, one macro-state (all 100 people in one region) has only one associated microstate, whereas the macro-state with 10 people in each region corresponds to a large number of different microstates. The number of microstates corresponding to a macrostate is denoted here by *W*, and finding the entropy measure is a combinatorial calculation, given by

$$W = N! / \prod_i n_i!,$$

the factorial of the total number of individuals *N*, divided by the product of the factorials for each n_i (the number in each region). An alternative, but equivalent, measure is that used in information theory. LWH

Suggested reading
Wilson (1970).

entropy-maximizing models Statistical MO-DELS for identifying the 'most likely' spatial allocation pattern in a system subject to constraints. The approach was introduced into geographical modelling by A.G. Wilson (1967) as the basis for a more rigorous interpretation of the GRAVITY MODEL, and has been extensively used since for SPATIAL INTERACTION modelling in urban regions and for modelling inter-regional flows of traffic and commodities. It is based on the concept of ENTROPY, a measure of the uncertainty or 'likelihood' in a probability distribution. A journey-to-work model illustrates the method. For a city divided into *k* zones, we wish to calculate the best estimate of interzonal commuting flows T_{ij}, without knowing the detailed information of each individual movement. Assume that there are *N* total commuters. Any specific trip distribution pattern T_{ij}, known as a 'macrostate' (see ENTROPY), can arise from many different sets of individual commuting movements, or 'microstates', and entropy measures the number of different microstates that can give rise to a particular macrostate. In the absence of detailed microstate data, we assume that each microstate is equally probable, and that the macrostate with the maximum entropy value is the most probable or most likely overall pattern. Additional information is also normally available, notably the number of commuters originating from each zone, the total number of jobs available in each zone, and estimates of the average or total travel expenditure for the city, *C* (usually based on survey data). The entropy-maximizing method then consists of maximizing the entropy measure subject to these constraints.

This maximization is a non-linear optimization problem, and must be solved by iterative search methods. These models not only fit empirical trip-distributions well, but also facilitate easy calculation of the effects of new housing or jobs (by altering the constraints), and so have been widely used in more general urban models. Wilson and his Leeds colleagues have extended the model in many ways, making it dynamic, linking it to industrial and urban LOCATION THE-ORY, and including several types of disaggregation (e.g. by mode of travel). LWH

Suggested reading
Gould (1972); Thomas and Huggett (1980); Wilson (1970).

environmental audit Environmental auditing originated in the 1970s as a management tool to evaluate how well a corporation was complying with the complex array of environmental legislation that was emerging as a result of the ENVIRONMENTAL MOVEMENT. It is an important part of environmental management systems (EMS).

Environmental audits are an 'official examination and verification of accounts and records to assess how close the situation comes to meeting a set requirement' (Thomas, 2005, p. 236). They are a one-off collection of data, and therefore differ from ongoing monitoring activities. Environmental audits may be internal to a corporation, produced externally, undertaken voluntarily or to fulfil legal requirements, and may check compliance with regulations or focus on a company's systems to achieve and maintain compliance (de Moor and de Beelde, 2005). Environmental audits may be undertaken for governments, aid agencies, financial institutions and community groups. Internal environmental auditing helps companies meet regulations and their own environmental goals in a cost-effective manner. Mandatory, external auditing verifies and encourages compliance with environmental regulations. Who undertakes the environmental audit and who has access to the resulting document are questions about the regulation of industry and commerce. Environmental auditing is situated within larger debates about how to achieve and maintain high environmental quality. PM

environmental determinism A type of reasoning that holds that the character and form of a SOCIETY, CULTURE or BODY can be explained by the physical conditions within which it has developed. Determinism is a form of explanation that finds no place for other factors, outside forces or random features. All creativity and productivity is assigned to first causes, in this case to environmental conditions. Social and human diversity is explainable, this doctrine would hold, solely in terms of the environments within which they develop. In this sense there is a strong assumption that NATURE and CULTURE exist as a dualism, and that cultures are shaped by Nature. While it is accepted that cultures interact with environments, and may alter them, it is nevertheless argued that the conditions for doing so are shaped by the larger environment. There are two major forms of critique of environmental determinism. The first is a form of HUMANISM, arguing that far from being reduced to their physical conditions, human beings can transcend those conditions through, variously, ingenuity, spirit, technology and social organization. However, such arguments tend to reproduce rather than overcome the Nature/Culture dualism, and can result in forms of voluntarism and IDEALISM. The second is a more MATERIALIST argument, suggesting that people and environments continuously evolve in relation to one another, and in doing so necessarily co-produce one another. In these versions, determinism is debunked not because of any transcendent human capacity, or any mysterious element, but through the sheer randomness of matters in relation.

Environmental determinism has a long and varied history, from the ancient Greeks (notably Aristotle's climatic zones), the Renaissance (notably Montesquieu's Heaven and Earth), to post-Darwinian writers (Glacken, 1967). From the late nineteenth to the mid-twentieth century, it is often argued that GEOGRAPHY was complicit, through its environmental determinism, with a north European supremacism that linked human 'achievement' and DEVELOPMENT to environmental conditions (Livingstone, 1992). Friedrich Ratzel in Germany and Ellen C. Semple in the United States perhaps best captured this geographical tradition. Yet even here, and certainly in later writings of other environmental determinists, the arguments were rarely as clear cut as might be supposed. Ó Tuathail (1992) demonstrates Halford Mackinder's partial FOUNDATIONALISM, wherein he ceded to humans the POWER to transcend formative environmental conditions. Twentieth-century schools sought to blur the lines of explanation, giving rise to such terms as POSSIBILISM and PROBABILISM. The latter terms are most often associated with the French

school of geography, most famously Paul Vidal de la Blache. Yet, rather like the BERKELEY SCHOOL and later forms of Marxist and Russian geography, the notion that nature conditioned subsequent actions remained. Despite this recurrent NATURALISM and its essentialist and FOUNDATIONAL tones, many of these works repay close scrutiny in a discipline that has been all too keen to leave non-human matters aside. The task is now to avoid any lurch to the cultural in an attempt to leave environmental determinism behind once and for all, and instead to return to the indeterminate question of how it is that human and non-human histories and geographies are intertwined. Finally, how to account for the longevity of this form of explanation is itself a complex question, one that would require attention to processes as varied as scientific authority and forms of reasoning (see SCIENCE), COLONIALISM and academic discipline building.   SJH

Suggested reading
Livingstone (1992).

environmental economics A branch of MARKET-based economics that advocates applying economic instruments to solve environmental problems. Although environmental economics can be traced to earlier work in the 1920s, it emerged at the same time as the ENVIRONMENTAL MOVEMENT in the 1960s. At that time most academic, government and corporate economists were insensitive to the environmental impacts of economic growth. Environmental economists claim that the economic system, when the wrong price signals are given, is a major cause of environmental problems. The main solution pursued by environmental economists is to send the right price signals via market mechanisms. This approach is now among the most dominant approaches to diagnosing and managing environmental problems in developed countries. It is increasingly popular given the pro-market orientation of NEO-LIBERALISM that exists globally and dominates in particular countries.

Environmental economics is closely associated with NEO-CLASSICAL ECONOMICS and RESOURCE MANAGEMENT. It expands the reach of the market to factor in what environmental economists label an 'EXTERNALITY', thereby changing the pricing signals for existing market transactions or creating new COMMODITIES and markets. WATER trading, carbon credits (see GLOBAL WARMING) and pollution credits are all examples of environmental economics applied to environmental issues. Bosetti and Pearce (2003) demonstrate the application of environmental economics to conflicts between fishing and seal CONSERVATION interests in south-west England.

Geographers have been concerned about the pricing of the environment, and particularly about how monetary values are attached to environmental 'goods' and 'services' through CONTINGENT VALUATION. Pricing approaches include willingness to pay (WTP) and willingness to accept compensation (either WTA or WAC). Clark, Burgess and Harrison (2000) highlight the weaknesses in contingent valuation, particularly a lack of understanding by many respondents of what they were valuing and how this information would be used. This is crucial because environmental economists rely on approaches that translate 'human preferences' into monetary values in order to create pricing signals and operate a market (see Thampapillai, 2002).

Environmental economics has been subject to considerable criticism. Some critics believe that pollution taxes are licences to pollute, and do not relate to the absorptive capacities of the environment or ethical questions about perpetuating POLLUTION. It is seen as reformist, or tinkering, with markets. At best, it reduces the worst excesses of market forces, but it also justifies some environmental damage and it perpetuates market expansion through the commodification process. It does not call for an economic overhaul, as in the tradition of the more radical ecological economics approach, and it does not treat the environment as having existence in its own right. However, the approach is increasingly influential, and so it cannot be ignored.   PM

environmental hazard Sometimes known as a 'natural hazard', or popularly as a 'natural disaster', this item generally refers to geophysical events such as earthquakes, tsunamis, volcanoes, bushfires, drought, flooding, lightning and high winds that can potentially cause major economic damage and physical injury or death. Such events, for example earthquakes, will have differing impacts depending on their magnitude and the character of the affected area (e.g. a heavily populated area versus a sparsely settled area). Given the long-term involvement of humans as part of NATURE, a detailed analysis of so-called 'environmental hazards' often reveals significant human input (see HAZARD). The characteristics of an environmental hazard are that it was not directly caused by humans, it directly affects humans (unlike an extreme natural event in nature that does not directly affect humans) and it is often accompanied by a violent release of energy. The United Nations declared the 1990s the 'International Decade for Natural Disaster Reduction' (Mauro, 1995). The use of the terminology 'natural' perpetuates the false perception that humans play no part in these disasters. Geographical research in the 1990s increasingly stressed 'disaster' rather than 'hazard', thereby emphasizing the social and cultural issues and humanitarian response needed when disaster occurs (White, Kates and Burton, 2001).

The distinction between environmental hazard and a human-made hazard has blurred. It can only be maintained if humans are seen as being separate from NATURE, rather than a species that has been part of nature for thousands of years. Today we experience physical events, the impacts of which are influenced by the actions of humans and other species, which in turn influence the character of future physical events.

Work in the United States on hazards and disasters emerged in the context of the nuclear threat and the COLD WAR. Geographical research found that despite heavy spending on dams, losses due to floods were increasing. This environmental hazard research was critiqued from MARXIST GEOGRAPHY. Smith and O'Keefe (1980) claimed that geographers in the tradition of POSITIVISM displayed three major ways of dealing with nature, and demonstrated this through 'natural hazards' research. The three major approaches are nature being seen as separate from human activity; where nature is seen as neutral but becomes hazardous when it intersects with human activity; or where humans are dissolved into nature. The first approach focuses attention on 'natural causes' of disasters, rather than human vulnerability. The second approach is seen as a technocratic agenda to control nature. The third approach is seen as Malthusian (see MALTHUSIAN MODEL), because it blames the victims.

Today, many geographers question a 'natural hazard' and highlight the difference between a natural event (e.g. drought, which may be partly caused by human activity) and the consequences (FAMINE). These differences are usually attributed to the structure and performance of social systems. Recent Deleuzian-inspired work by Nigel Clark (2005b) expands the notion of systems by considering the Earth as an open system when exploring conceptions of nature, RISK SOCIETY, and the construction of catastrophic events and their counterpoint, the notion of order in nature.   PM

environmental history Environmental histories reflect a basic desire to understand the relations between people and NATURE through time. Over the years, scholars have approached this broad and important topic from several disciplines. Anthropologists conducted ETHNOGRAPHIC studies of the ways in which particular peoples conceived of, utilized and interacted with the natural (and supernatural) world. Archaeologists seeking the origins of DOMESTICATION explored the earliest relations among people, plants and ANIMALS. Ecologists and other scientists sought to understand how human actions affected natural systems. Students of mythology, RELIGION, and LAW traced expressions of human attitudes towards and concern for nature in medieval and Mesopotamian times. And after generations of philosophers had pondered the ways in which individuals living in different epochs conceived of the natural world, some among them came, late in the twentieth century, to argue against the very idea that 'nature' and 'society' are separate, distinct entities. In general, however, historians and geographers have led scholarship in this area.

In a manner reflected epigrammatically in the title of Marjorie Nicolson's book, *Mountain gloom and mountain glory* (1959), historians such as Keith Thomas (1996 [1983]) and Roderick Nash (1967) traced changes in the ways that individuals and societies regarded nature or WILDERNESS through the centuries. Others, including William Cronon (1983), Timothy Silver (1990) and Richard White (1980), considered what LANDSCAPES reflected of human endeavours, or found, with Mart Stewart (1996) and Harold Innis (1927), fruitful topics for enquiry in the ways in which economic DEVELOPMENT rested, in considerable degree, upon the natural endowments (that people thought of as RESOURCES) of particular TERRITORIES. Geographers long held the study of human–environment relations to be one of the central 'traditions" of their field, and many of those with ecological and historical inclinations wrote at some length about the mutual shaping of lands and lives over time. In France, Paul Vidal de la Blache (1926), Albert Demangeon (1942) and Jean Brunhes (1952) all pursued investigations along these lines, and were among the giants of HUMAN GEOGRAPHY early in the twentieth century. In the UK, some of the leading exponents of the developing subject, including Emrys Jones (1951–2, 1956), Estyn Evans (1960) and Harold

J. Fleure (1951), were primarily interested in the relations between human societies and the natural environment (see also Langton, 1988). And in the USA, Clarence Glacken produced a classic work, *Traces on the Rhodian shore: nature and culture in Western thought from ancient times to the end of the eighteenth century* (1967), while Carl Ortwin Sauer, one of the convenors of the 1955 symposium on 'Man's Role in Changing the Face of the Earth', led the study of human-induced landscape changes (Sauer, 1963a [1925]; Thomas, 1996 [1983]; Kenzer, 1986: see BERKELEY SCHOOL).

Still, the characterization of a particular field of enquiry as 'environmental history' is relatively new. By common North American assessments, it dates back to the rise of the ENVIRONMENTAL MOVEMENT in the 1960s. There is merit in this view. As popular interest in environmental questions climbed, the spate of historical scholarship on the relations between people and nature through time – particularly in the USA – reached new heights. In addition, the parallelism between the coinage 'environmental history' and public anxieties about 'environmental issues' – which waxed and waned, but often seemed to be rooted in past practices (even if these were relatively recent) – served, brilliantly, to draw attention to the field. Quickly, the phrase 'environmental history' was adopted as a euphonious and readily understood label for a widely diverse and rapidly expanding body of work, even as it served to veil regional, national and disciplinary differences in emphases, origins and approaches to the study of human–environment relations. The field is now too large and varied to be encompassed in any single assessment, although a number of scholars have attempted to limn its developing dimensions (see, e.g., White, 1985; McNeill, 2003; Evenden and Wynn, 2009).

From the mid-1970s onwards, there were challenges to the dominant (American-centred) construction of the field. Three among these warrant brief notice. English-educated Richard Grove took issue with the common tendency, given particular substance by David Lowenthal, to identify the 'Versatile Vermonter' George Perkins Marsh as the fountainhead of the CONSERVATION movement, arguing in *Green imperialism* (1995) that awareness of human-induced environmental changes long predated Marsh's work and was sharpened by observation of the effects of colonial expansion on 'tropical island Edens' (Lowenthal, 1958, 2000; Marsh, 1965 [1864]; Grove, 1995). In 1989, the Indian scholar Ramachandra Guha offered an important 'Third world critique' of American environmentalists' fascination with wilderness

199

preservation and their embrace of DEEP ECOL-OGY. Arguing against the anthropocentric/ biocentric distinction that marked current thinking on these matters, Guha (1989) insisted that efforts to extend wilderness protection worldwide had many harmful consequences for indigenous peoples, and urged environmentalists to place 'a far greater emphasis on equity and the integration of ecological concerns with livelihood and work'. Meanwhile, anthropologists and geographers working on questions of DEVELOPMENT and UNDERDEVELOPMENT in the global SOUTH coined the term POLITICAL ECOLOGY to describe their interest in the linkages between political ECONOMY and CULTURAL ECOLOGY (broadly, the relations between human societies and their natural environments). Political ecology is a broad church that has attracted many geographers – including, for example, Karl Zimmerer (Zimmerer and Bassett, 2003), Paul Robbins (2004), Roderick Neumann (2005) and Philip Stott (Stott and Sullivan, 2000), amongst others – for whom contemporary issues were more pressing than historical enquiry, *sensu strictu*, but many reached into the past to understand current circumstances, and the *Journal of Political Ecology*, established in 1994, promised 'Case Studies in History and Society' in its subtitle.

All of this made for something of an identity crisis in environmental history. A decade after Australian historical geographer Joe Powell suggested that the field reflected its practitioners' collective will to believe in the field, American historian of SCIENCE Harriet Ritvo described it as 'an unevenly spreading blob' (Powell, 1996; Ritvo, 2005). Responding to such challenges and seeking to define their enterprise, several environmental historians found order in diversity. According to one prominent American authority, environmental history proceeds on three levels. The first documents 'the structure and distribution of natural environments of the past'. The second 'focuses on productive technology as it interacts with the environment'. The third is concerned with the 'patterns of human perception, ideology and value' and the ways in which they have worked in 'reorganizing and recreating the surface of the planet' (Worster, 1990b). Another specialist claims that environmental historians 'study how people have lived in the natural systems of the planet ... how they have perceived nature [and how] they have reshaped it to suit their own idea of good living' (Warren, 2003). A third American scholar differentiates environmental

histories by the extent of their concern with material, cultural/intellectual or political matters (McNeill, 2003). Studies of the first type focus upon 'changes in biological and physical environments, and how these changes have affected human societies'. Cultural/intellectual environmental history is concerned with 'representations and images of nature in arts and letters', and political environmental history examines 'law and state policy as it relates to the natural world'. In a rather different vein, the English geographer Ian Simmons has given shape to his own form of environmental history in a number of sweeping book-length essays (Simmons, 1993, 1997, 2001).

CHAOS THEORY and POST-STRUCTURALISM have also contributed to the (re)definition of environmental history. Thanks in part to the contributions of geographers such as David Demeritt (1994b, 1998, 2001a), Bruce Braun (2003), Noel Castree (1995) and Braun and Castree together (Braun and Castree, 1998; Castree and Braun, 2001), a field that rested, at its inception, upon a particular conception of scientific ECOLOGY (predicated on notions of stability and climax vegetation complexes), and upon a dichotomized view of nature and culture, has been forced, in recent years, to grapple with the question of '*which* nature and *which* conceptions of science should be brought in' (Asdal, 2003: but see also, and more importantly, Worster, 1990a; Cronon, 1995). At the same time, a new awareness of the relations between knowledge and POWER (and an associated concern with questions of ETHICS and SOCIAL JUSTICE) has rendered less satisfying the once-common declensionist narratives of environmental despoliation attributed to CAPITALIST greed or human hubris. All of this has greatly complicated the stories that environmental historians tell. The field *is* broad and diffuse. It is also inherently interdisciplinary, and many of its practitioners are interested in providing perspective upon and contributing understanding to contemporary debates about human use of the Earth. Thus the field forms 'a locus for exploration and intellectual adventure', offering humans a spirited, reflexive understanding of themselves and their world (Weiner, 2005).   GW

Suggested reading
Cronon (1991); Evenden and Wynn (2009); Langton (1988); McNeill (2003); Worster (1983); Wynn (2007).

Environmental Impact Assessment A process of systematically identifying and assessing anticipated environmental impacts prior to a proposed project, policy, programme or plan being implemented. The identification of significant negative impacts may prevent the proposal (which is usually a project) from going ahead. This is very unusual. More likely, it results in the modification of the original proposal, or the introduction of measures to ameliorate the anticipated negative environmental impacts. A proposal may generate positive environmental impacts, particularly if the site is already severely degraded, and these must be considered in the process.

Environmental Impact Assessment (EIA) was introduced in the USA in 1969 under the National Environmental Policy Act (NEPA). It is now a legal requirement in many countries, provinces/states and in some cities. International institutions such as the World Bank and international aid agencies also require an EIA process on particular development proposals. Initially, assessments were limited to federal departments in the USA, but EIA has expanded to include provincial/state and private development proposals, and developed from environmental protection to include SUSTAINABLE DEVELOPMENT, a concept that emerged after EIA began.

There are numerous definitions of EIA. One succinct definition is 'an assessment of the impact of a planned activity on the environment' (in Glasson, Therivel and Chadwick, 2005, p. 4). The terminology varies between countries, and often causes confusion. For example, in some places EIA is simply known as 'Impact Assessment', because it is broader than a narrow definition of the physical environment. Elsewhere it is known as Environmental Assessment (EA) because of the perceived negative connotations of 'impact'. In the USA, an EA is a preliminary study undertaken within the EIA process to identify the likelihood of significant impacts, which then require the preparation of a full EIS (Burris and Canter, 1997).

The process of EIA has become standardized and incorporated into planning and development processes in many countries. Under some legislative frameworks, the EIA document may be required to address issues such as sustainable development, biodiversity, social impacts and economic considerations. There are also legal requirements for public participation. Some jurisdictions include Social Impact Assessment (SIA) within EIA, while in other places it is a separate activity (see Glasson, Therivel and Chadwick, 2005; Thomas and Elliot, 2005).

Environmental Impact Assessment is sometimes seen as an important process that prevents the worst aspects of proposals from being implemented. It does not necessarily guarantee high-quality development. In contrast, other people perceive the process to be a way of legitimizing controversial development proposals. In their view, it does very little to maintain environmental quality. They argue that many of the key decisions have already been taken at the policy level, and that the individual character of EIA often fails to consider the cumulative impacts of each development. In some locations these concerns are partly being addressed by Strategic Environmental Assessment (SEA) at the policy and programme level (see Caratti, Dalkmann and Jiliberto, 2004) and Cumulative Impact Assessment (CIA). Glasson, Therivel and Chadwick (2005) and others advocate that an Integrated Environmental Assessment (IEA) addresses all of these considerations.　　PM

environmental justice　The right of everyone to enjoy and benefit from a safe and healthy environment, regardless of RACE, CLASS, GENDER or ETHNICITY. More specifically, environmental justice is a SOCIAL MOVEMENT that takes SOCIAL JUSTICE and environmental politics as fundamentally inseparable. The movement has many divergent roots, such as the labour struggles of Cesar Chavez and Delores Huerta, and their crusade against the use of pesticides, in the 1960s; the community-based struggles of Lois Gibbs and others that arose from the dumping of toxic chemicals in lower-middle-class neighbourhoods at Love Canal, New York, in the 1970s; and in the responses of various offshoots of the civil rights movement to placing of toxic waste dumps, most famously in Warren County, North Carolina, in the early 1980s. Others contend that the most accurate date for the founding of the North American environmental justice movement is 1492. Whenever its origins, the movement currently stresses three major tenets. First, it gives attention to unequal exposure to HAZARDS through specific policies and practices that intentionally or unintentionally discriminate against individuals, groups or communities based on race, ethnicity, class or gender (Bullard, 1994). Second, it has become more broadly attentive nationally and internationally to the ways in which these same communities are differentially denied access to and control over both RESOURCES and decision-making processes by institutions, CORPORATIONS and individuals both in the USA and abroad (Neumann, 1998). Third, it has

201

become engaged in CULTURAL POLITICS involving the very framing of the key terms of the debate (acceptable RISK, waste, race and environmental health) that conditions the political possibilities of the struggle for environmental justice (Fortun, 2001). The movement is known for its creative, engaged ACTIVISM, its deep commitment to grassroots approaches to social change and its irreverence towards bureaucracy in-action.   JK

Suggested reading
Cole and Foster (2001); Peet and Watts (2003); Pulido and Peña (1998); United Church of Christ (1987).

environmental movement A term that has been used to describe any social or political movement directed towards the preservation of natural RESOURCES, the prevention of POLLUTION or the control of land use with the goal of CONSERVATION, restoration or improvement of the material environment. Though practices of environmental protection have been conducted in many places around the world for centuries, the movement as a modern phenomenon has its sources in different currents and critiques of MODERNITY. Some of the main currents have their sources in critiques of industrial CAPITALISM's treatment of land and labour as COMMODITIES, others in transcendental, religious and aesthetic thought, still others in the practices of modern rationalist scientific knowledge, and yet others in a troubling search for nature's 'purity'. These and other tributaries have led to a deeply heterogeneous movement that has proven to be, in the best of times, a broad coalition of caring engaged critics and thoughtful visionaries of alternative futures and, in the worst, a deeply divided, exclusionary and even reactionary force for the reproduction of elitist and racist fears. Given this diverse history, it is no surprise that the movement has many current expressions, including political parties such as the Green Party, community non-profit organizations, international lending organizations, radical affinity groups, mainstream environmental organizations, legal advocacy firms, green corporations, and consumers, who operate through just as many diverse political techniques, including lobbying, scientific research, legislation, education, organizing and direct action. Regardless of its exact origins, members and strategies, the movement's most powerful contemporary expressions seem to be found in international grassroots communities and organizations that challenge the violent effects of early twenty-first-century GLOBALIZATION. JK

Suggested reading
Gelobter, Dorsey, Fields et al. (2005); Gottlieb (2001); Kosek (2003); Guha and Martinez-Alier (1998); Shellenberger and Nordhaus (2004); Shutkin (2000).

environmental perception A general term referring to the myriad ways in which actors (usually human) perceive, engage with and symbolically represent environments. ENVIRONMENT in this sense encompasses both the 'natural' and the 'built', and includes other people and ANIMALS as key elements. Equally, perception should be understood in the widest sense, referring to both the bio-psychological idiosyncrasies of individual sensing, information-processing and cognition, and the issue of collective cultural beliefs, values and aesthetic judgements concerning natural and built environments.

Although the study of environmental perception has never been a sustained core element of human geographical research, the topic has been investigated by writers from often quite different intellectual traditions. Early work on perception in GEOGRAPHY, in the 1940s and 1950s, was concerned to highlight the importance of human perceptions, attitudes and values in shaping beliefs, understandings and decisions concerning the environment. Here, an acknowledgement of the nuance and complexity of human perception (and consequent behaviour) was intended as a corrective to human geographies that either ignored the human, or sought to understand human behaviour in solely rational or objectivist terms. The notion that human geographers should delve into the realms of human perception, meaning and value was further clarified in Kevin Lynch's (1960) *The image of the city*, which sought to programmatically investigate the relationship between an urban built environment and the mental perceptions of its inhabitants. Lynch's work was seminal for BEHAVIOURAL GEOGRAPHIES through the 1970s and 1980s, especially insofar as these elaborated the notion of the MENTAL MAP (Gould and White, 1993 [1974]) as a key element of environmental perception. For the most part scientific, quantitative and empirical in approach, these behavioural geographies connect with broader, interdisciplinary enquiries regarding the role of environmental perception and 'value' *vis-à-vis* the design and planning of urban and rural landscapes.

In contrast to the instrumental and objective approach to environmental perception characteristic of much work in the planning and design fields, Yi-Fu Tuan's (1974) *Topophilia: a study of environmental perceptions, attitudes and values* articulated a humanistic (see HUMANISTIC GEOGRAPHY), interpretative and mythopoetic approach to the topic. Tuan was mostly concerned with environmental perception at the collective cultural level and, in particular, with illustrating how symbolically meaningful and keenly felt relationships with the environment resonated deeply in both Western and non-Western cultures.

The humanistic approach advocated by Tuan and others fell from favour with the advent of critical and radical approaches emphasizing the study of socio-economic structures, and the salience and viability of subjective and emotional geographies of environmental perception was at risk through much of the 1980s and 1990s. However, over the past ten years, with the emergence of new, non-representational approaches to embodiment, practice and PERFORMANCE, and with the development of vitalist geographies of nature and environment, environmental perception has re-emerged as a substantive issue (see NON-REPRESENTATIONAL THEORY). A key text here has been the anthropologist Tim Ingold's (2000) *The perception of the environment*. Ingold queries what he terms the 'building perspective' commonly adopted by academics examining questions of environmental perception and cognition, and imputed to those being studied. This perspective is, he argues, structured around the mistaken assumption of 'an imagined separation between the human perceiver and the world, such that the perceiver has to reconstruct the world, in consciousness, prior to any meaningful engagement with it' (2000, p.191). According to Ingold, both cognitivist accounts of mental mapping and the humanistic interpretations of writers such as Tuan equally fall into this EPISTEMOLOGICAL trap.

Ingold's alternative approach to environmental perception – which he terms 'the dwelling perspective' – draws heavily upon the phenomenological PHILOSOPHY of Martin Heidegger and Maurice Merleau-Ponty (see PHENOMENOLOGY). Here, environmental perception is pictured as an ongoing, reciprocal, bodily process of engagement and involvement, a process in which 'perceiver' and 'world' are enrolled, and from which they are continuously emergent. This approach to environmental perception, and to self– LANDSCAPE and CULTURE-NATURE relations more generally, has begun to exert considerable influence upon cultural geographers attending to questions of perception and embodied practice. JWY

environmental psychology An interdisciplinary and disparate field of study, enrolling researchers from psychology, GEOGRAPHY, anthropology, sociology, planning and design, environmental psychology examines perceptual, cognitive and embodied relationships between humans and the environment, both 'natural' and 'built'. Environmental psychology is most closely and commonly associated with forms of BEHAVIOURAL GEOGRAPHY, prominent in the 1970s and 1980s (though recently renascent; see Kitchin and Blades, 2001). In contrast to the cognitivist and representational approach to human–environment relations usually adopted in this area, phenomenologically inspired forms of ecological psychology (e.g. Gibson, 1979) emphasize human(and animal)–environment relations in terms of a rolling nexus of conjoined embodied action, perception and affordance. JWY

environmental racism Environmental racism includes differential exposure to harm and limiting of access to RESOURCES that are reliant on, or that reproduce forms of, racial differentiation. The term is commonly attributed to the Reverend Ben Chavis, who in 1982 was the director of the United Church of Christ's Commission for Racial Justice when toxic chemicals were sited in Warren County, Virginia, because it was predominantly poor and black. Chavis understood this action as part of a broader institutional history of RACISM in America, and coined the term *environmental racism* to call attention to the official sanctioning of the life-threatening presence of poisons and pollutants in communities of colour, including those of African-Americans, Native Americans, Asian-Americans, Chicanos/ Latinos and others (Chavis, 1991). This definition has been amended to include not just the actions of institutions, industries and governments, but also their failure to act, as in the case of the federal government's lack of response to Hurricane Katrina (Sze, 2005). In addition, the current definitions hold institutions and individuals accountable whether their acts are intentional or not (Bullard, 1994). Examples include the military–industrial complex's disproportionate exposure of Native Americans to nuclear fallout and waste dumps, creating large 'national sacrifice zones' in the Southwest (Kuletz, 2001). This, for example, may not be an intentional act, but is still widely considered an example of environmental racism because of the notions of RACE inherent in decisions that make dumping in some sites – rural reservations, poor urban areas, immigrant communities – more 'logical' than dumping in upperclass white communities. Finally, still rare but growing trends in the definitions of environmental racism are both attention to ENVIRONMENTAL JUSTICE beyond the USA and attention to the ways in which racism is culturally formed or reproduced through the efforts and exclusions of the ENVIRONMENTAL MOVEMENT itself (Gelobter et al., 2005). JK

Suggested reading
LaDuke (1999); Pulido (1996); Romm (2002).

environmental refugees A term that became used in environmental debates, starting in the 1980s, to refer to people displaced as a result of immediate environmental change, but also including those forced to move as a result of floods and the other indirect effects of global change. The category carries the rhetorical force of the word 'REFUGEE', but not the international legal status of a person forced to cross a state boundary. 'Ecological refugee' is a synonym, but has also been used in the narrower sense of people displaced by the expansion of commercial FARMING and FORESTRY operations to feed the expanding metropolitan economy of India and elsewhere. SD

Suggested reading
Gadgil and Guha (1995); Jacobsen (1988).

environmental security As the COLD WAR ended in the late 1980s, policy-makers and scholars argued that environmental change was now a major threat to international SECURITY: advocates of this 'environmental security' perspective argued that it required top priority from STATES because of the potential for serious disruptions caused by ENVIRONMENTAL REFUGEES and likely future RESOURCE WARS. Policy advocacy on these themes was part of the rationale for holding the Rio de Janeiro Earth Summit in 1992.

Sceptical scholars were unconvinced that the causal mechanisms between environmental change, disruption and conflict were proven, however frequently they were asserted as fact. Some suggested that, given the broad generality of both terms, scholarly research should be focused more narrowly on acute conflict and resources. In the 1990s, scholarly research established that there were some plausible possible links between environmental scarcities and CONFLICT, but suggested that simple causal

mechanisms were lacking (Homer-Dixon, 1999). It was also concluded that the likelihood of wars between states as a result of environmental change was small, despite numerous public pronouncements that WATER wars in particular were an imminent danger in many parts of the world. More generally, the literature on the causes of WAR also suggests that environment has rarely been a direct cause of inter-state conflict – and, indeed, might present considerable opportunities for cross-BORDER co-operation and peace-building.

Subsequent critical work has pointed out that many of the more alarmist public discussions lack necessary analyses of either the history of RESOURCE appropriations in rural areas, or of the disruptions caused by the processes of DEVELOPMENT, and fail to adequately take these important contextual factors into account (Dalby, 2002). Critics have also argued that linking military understandings of security to environmental matters is confusing, both because military solutions are not the appropriate measures to deal with environmental difficulties and because military activities are themselves especially damaging to environments.

Geographical scholarship has recently connected insecurity with HAZARD vulnerability assessments and the literature on POLITICAL ECOLOGY has engaged the discussion linking the global economy directly to social change. This shows that insecurity, environment and their interconnections are much more complex social phenomena than was initially assumed in the 1980s (Peluso and Watts, 2001). Despite these conceptual ambiguities, and the difficulties of establishing links between environmental change and conflict, the discussion of environmental security continues apace in policy and academic circles (Dodds and Pippard, 2005). SD

Suggested reading
Dalby (2002); Dodds and Pippard (2005).

environmentalism The ways in which the relationships between people and their surroundings are understood and acted upon. These have varied greatly through time and within and across cultures. One, undoubtedly Western, typology for understanding some of these shifts is provided by Glacken (1967). Three environmentalisms are developed from an exhaustive history of understandings of human–environment relations. First, there is the notion that the Earth exists by design, one fitted in particular for human purposes. Such an environmentalism is evident in

Graeco-Christian and Hebraic theologies, wherein creation for human purpose can lead to a legitimization of human domination over the non-human world. There are strong echoes of this form of environmentalism in contemporary thoughts and practices, which tend to be human centred (*anthropocentric*). The second environmentalism is underpinned by the notion that environments act as the major influence on human affairs (ENVIRONMENTAL DETERMINISM). The REDUCTIONISM and sometime racist inflections of this mode of thinking have been discredited in REGIONAL GEOGRAPHY (Livingstone, 1992), yet it is a form of environmentalism that has enjoyed a new life at a global scale and as a normative DISCOURSE. The physical RESOURCE limits of a finite planet and the capacities of global systems to adapt to human activities became major environmentalist debates and causes in the 1960s and 1980s, respectively. The third environmentalism that Glacken traces is the attempt to understand human–environment relations in more dynamic and co-evolutionary ways. It involves an understanding of the Earth and its inhabitants – including humans – as unfinished matters. Furthermore, any human change involves changes to environments and vice versa. The three environmentalisms are complex and overlap historically and culturally, but can be summarized as human mastery over nature, environmental determinism and co-evolution. In turn, these can be roughly mapped on to contemporary inflections, including (1) anthropocentrism and technocentrism, (2) ecocentrism and (3) mutualism. O'Riordan (1976) gave particular attention to the contrast between technocentrism, which posited faith in the ability of human technical ingenuity to transcend earthly limits, and ECOCENTRISM, which cautioned people to live within their environmentally determined conditions (see also DEEP ECOLOGY; POPULATION GEOGRAPHY). The utility of the distinction can instantly be recognized in debates over FOOD and ENERGY technologies (genetic modifications versus organics, renewables versus nuclear energies and so on). The third stream is perhaps where most energies have been invested in geography in recent years. This is in part a reflection of the proliferation of humans and non-humans in recent centuries, making firm human–environment distinctions more difficult. Transgenic ANIMALS, genetically modified foodstuffs, holes in stratospheric ozone layers and climate change all undermine any firm distinction between people and environment, CULTURE and NATURE, politics and science. Human–environment DIALECTICS (Harvey,

1996) and FEMINIST and POST-STRUCTURALIST informed reformulations of human–environment relations (Haraway, 1991c; Ingold, 2000) have produced a range of writing that attempts to pair together humans and environments through such varied endeavours as POLITICAL ECOLOGY (Robbins, 2004), ECOFEMINISM and cosmopolitics (Latour, 2004; Hinchliffe, Kearnes, Degen and Whatmore, 2005). There is a good deal of variety in these literatures, but to varying degrees they all move away from a firmly fixed or FOUNDATIONAL view of environment and towards accounts where the mattering of environments (which include humans), their contribution to human and non-human vulnerabilities and to life chances, become central concerns. There is recognition in all these non-foundational accounts of uneven environments, of the need for ENVIRONMENTAL JUSTICE, of shifts in local and global patterns of DEVELOPMENT and CONSUMPTION. Finally, in this gradual move towards a non-foundational environmentalism there are huge dangers and debates. The reliability of SCIENCE as an ally to environmentalism comes under scrutiny once the fixity of environments has been unsettled, and once uncertainties and indeterminacies of scientific ways of knowing become more widely understood. The ability of science to mediate nature and act as an authority on environmental concerns has become a matter for heated debate (see RISK SOCIETY). Environmentalism is therefore currently in a crucial political moment as it negotiates between the uncertainties of socio-ecological dynamics and the calculations and arguments required for a shift in the ways in which humans dwell in the world.   SJH

Suggested reading
O'Riordan (1976).

epidemic A term (derived from the Greek *epi-*, upon + *demos*, people) used in the health sciences to describe the unusually high incidence of a specified illness, health behaviour or other health-related event in a given community or region; 'unusually high' is defined relative to the usual frequency, or *expectancy*, of the health event in the population under examination (Benenson, 1995). The term is often used to describe the rapid spread of an infectious disease (e.g. 'an epidemic of measles') and may be applied to a range of geographical scales, from small and highly localized outbreaks to global PANDEMIC episodes. Epic events, such as the Black Death (AD 1346–53) or the Spanish influenza pandemic (AD 1918–19), are extreme examples from the many tens of thousands of historically recorded disease outbreaks to which the term 'epidemic' can properly be applied (Kohn, 1998).   MSR

Suggested reading
Haggett (2000).

epidemiology The branch of medical science that is concerned with the study of the causes, distribution and control of health-related events in a specified population. GEOGRAPHY and epidemiology have a long association that can be traced back to the nineteenth century and the use of disease maps to analyse the causes of EPIDEMIC events (Gould, 1985). Today, the association between geography and epidemiology finds expression in a cross-disciplinary branch of MEDICAL GEOGRAPHY known as *spatial epidemiology* (Elliott and Wartenberg, 2004). Spatial epidemiologists map, analyse and model the distribution and spread of health-related conditions and their biological, environmental, behavioural and socio-economic determinants over space and through time. (See also DISEASE, DIFFUSION OF.)   MSR

Suggested reading
Cliff and Haggett (1988).

episteme A term introduced into modern thought by the French thinker Michel Foucault (1926–84) in his book *Les mots et les choses*, translated as *The order of things* (1970 [1966]). The term is based on the Greek word for knowledge or science, and for Foucault an episteme is a system of thought that conditions the particular sciences or knowledges (*savoirs*) that emerge at a particular time. He identifies three main epistemes: the Renaissance, the classical age and the modern. It is within an episteme that we find the criteria not just of individual pieces of knowledge, but the rules that govern the production of truth and reality as such. Foucault discounts an understanding of absolute, atemporal, aspatial knowledge, and instead analyses historically specific forms of understanding that are the conditions of possibility of knowledge (see Foucault, 1972b [1969]). In this sense, he can be understood as historicizing Kant's work (see GENEALOGY). Foucault rarely used the term in his later work, but introduced the notion of a *dispositif* (1980c), which he described as 'a thoroughly heterogeneous ensemble consisting of

discourses, institutions, architectural forms, regulatory decisions, laws, administrative measures, scientific statements, philosophical, moral and philanthropic propositions'. The notion of the episteme is now seen as 'a specifically discursive *dispositif*' (cf. DISCOURSE).   SE

Suggested reading
Gutting (1989); Han (2002).

epistemology Concerned with defining knowledge and explaining how it works. While ONTOLOGY attempts to account for what is in the world, epistemology asks how it is possible to *know* the world. Although often considered in tandem, particularly in describing the constituent elements of a body of thought, ontology and epistemology more properly should be thought of as overlapping, as there may be elements of 'what is' that are not knowable, and knowledge may contain ideas that do not correspond to existing things in the world. Their conceptual complications were made most explicit during the epistemological 'turn' in the HUMANITIES and social sciences, which was inspired by the linguistic 'turn' developed under the POST-STRUCTURALISM of Michel Foucault, Jacques Derrida and Judith Butler, among others. These connected movements rejected Platonic epistemology, which took knowledge to be innate and discoverable by profound illumination, and made it the product of circulating DISCOURSES and dispersed POWER relations, which were naturalized over time through their popular uptake and transformation into common notions (see HEGEMONY). Among the political consequences of this take on knowledge was a dethroning of the notion of Truth, particularly in its *a priori*, universal articulation, as the lofty goal of all acts of knowing. With the new, rising wave of feminist, anti-racist and anti-colonialist perspectives and ACTIVISM in and beyond the academy, the classical notion that there are absolute, knowable Truths that correspond to things in the world was increasingly critiqued as an ENLIGHTENMENT invention that reflected the privileged position of white, Western masculinity, the historical subjectivity holding scientific, social and political knowledge-power (Haraway, 1988; Rose, 1993). Rooted in FEMINISM, *standpoint epistemology* recognizes the partiality of knowledge, but goes further by arguing that the 'worked-for' or 'struggled-for' knowledge generated by members of oppressed GENDERS, RACES and CLASSES is more likely to capture truths than the uncritical and comfortable epistemologies that evolve out of privileged experience (Hartsock, 1983; Harding, 2004; see also SITUATED KNOWLEDGE).

Such concerns have made for lively debate within HUMAN GEOGRAPHY, but epistemology is also implicit within much historical theorizing in the discipline. One of the most important threads throughout the long history of geography (see GEOGRAPHY, HISTORY OF) and its attendant PHILOSOPHY has been an argument over the relative merits of generality and particularity. This seemingly abstract binary relates to concrete knowledge production insofar as 'general geography' is distinct from 'specific geography' (as Bernhardus Varenius, 1622–50, termed it: see CHOROLOGY), and on that distinction rests the question of how much emphasis should be given over to the search for trans-contextual scientific LAWS. The answer hinges to some extent on whether GEOGRAPHY can claim to be a mature science, one whose knowledge is objective, explanatory, rational and orderly. In the 1950s and 1960s, adherents to SPATIAL SCIENCE and REGIONAL GEOGRAPHY fought over various aspects of these qualities (see NOMOTHETIC and IDIOGRAPHIC), but that debate was eclipsed by HUMANISTIC GEOGRAPHY's outright reversal of the polarities fastened on to the OBJECTIVITY–SUBJECTIVITY opposition. Through its attention to HERMENEUTICS, the interpretation of subjective experience and concepts such as SENSE OF PLACE, humanistic geographers reversed direction on decades of 'scientism' in geography, and paved the way for geographical critiques informed by feminism and post-structuralism.

key epistemological binaries

Objectivity	Subjectivity
Explanation	Interpretation
Order	Complexity
General	Particular
Rational	Emotional

Most recently, post-structuralist geography has seen a shift in epistemological emphases, from (1) a trenchant critique of knowledge claims that puts all matter into question through a constructivist epistemology to (2) a materialization of epistemology through an anti-essentialist assertion of ontology (cf. ESSENTIALISM):

(1) Through the exploration of foreign CONTINENTS, the naming of their spaces after Westerners and other Western spaces, and the mapping of those spaces in such a way that Western prejudices and power relations became inscribed upon their landscapes (see also ORIENTALISM), attention has long focused on the role that CARTOGRAPHY, EXPLORATION and GEOGRAPHY played in processes of Western COLONIALISM during Enlightenment and post-Enlightenment MODERNITY (Mitchell, 1988; Gregory, 1994). Pervasive within the latter, mapping practice (Pickles, 2004) came to be based on a detached or 'bird's eye' (Schein, 1993) *perspectivalism* that Dixon and Jones (1998) summarize as follows:

- *Cartesian perspectivalism*, 'which lineates the world with respect to a central point' (see also CARTESIANISM);
- *ocularcentrism*, 'which privileges vision from an elevated vantage point from which the world may be surveilled in its totality' (see also SURVEILLANCE; VISION AND VISUALITY); and
- *the epistemology of the grid*, 'a procedure for locating and segmenting social life so that it may be captured, measured, and interrogated' (see CARTOGRAPHIC REASON).

Epistemologically, this view lent itself to a conceit of REPRESENTATION and to what Mitchell (1988) and Gregory (1994) call *the world as exhibition*: the power to know and control space rests in the capacity to visualize, demarcate and survey, all parts of a grid epistemology that colonizes spaces just as it dominates mainstream geography. These epistemological inquiries led many in the 1990s to debate the relative importance of MATERIALISM and DISCOURSE in the production of social space. In many cases, post-structuralism's representational instabilities and uncertainties trumped the apparently self-evident bedrock ontologies found in materialist theories such as MARXISM.

(2) Recently, some thinkers have begun to investigate how knowledge works beyond representation. In many ways, this work harkens back to the studies of emotional and sensational connections to places highlighted under humanistic geography, though these tended to connect interiorized and subjectivized feelings to the representational idea of place. Instead, the current work draws heavily upon Gilles Deleuze's critique of representation as a hindrance to understanding the world, which, ontologically, articulates processes of 'pure difference' beyond, prior or even contrary to the orders or similitude and resemblance at work in representation.

Human geography's exemplars here are AFFECT and NON-REPRESENTATIONAL THEORY, two areas concerned with the possibilities of 'presubjective knowledge' derived from differential bodily capacities, functions and experiences that, if only fleetingly, occur beyond the knowledge-as-representational-idea framework. The challenges to this body of theory are: (1) that it must invariably bring us, as researchers, *back* to representation through the presentation of results; and (2) that it is still largely unclear what practical political value lies within the domain of the politically unrepresentable. At present, responses to these challenges are still in the early stages (Anderson, 2006b; Thrift, 2008).   KWO / JPJ

Suggested reading
Cloke and Johnston (2005); Dixon and Jones (1998); Gregory (1994); Pickles (2004); Rose (1993).

equality A political ideal promoting the equal treatment, standing or status of people in certain respects. Equality has a close, though complex, connection to justice. While equality is a central ideal within liberal democracies (see LIBERALISM), often enshrined as a formal RIGHT, its precise meaning and scope remain controversial. Different and often competing contexts for equality exist that variously answer the question: What is the relevant respect in which people are to be compared?

(1) *Administrative equality.* The requirement that existing laws (see LAW) be administered equally to everyone. This minimal view of equality concerns the application of law, not the content. As Bakan (1997, p. 46) notes, it would be met even in a system that made explicit distinctions between people, such as APARTHEID, so long as laws were equally applied to all members of an oppressed group.
(2) *Political equality.* Equality in respect to formal political rights (such as voting or running for office). This issue, of course, has proved controversial, as in the case of the struggle for the extension of the franchise to women, for example. The disenfranchisement of convicts in many US states, or the scalar politics of non-citizen voting (Varsanyi, 2005), attests to the continued relevance of this issue.
(3) *Formal equality.* The Aristotelean principle to treat like cases as like: when two persons have equal status in relation to one relevant aspect, they must be treated equally with

regard to this aspect. Thus the content of law, rather than its implementation, must not draw distinctions between people on inappropriate grounds. This, of course, begs the question: Which distinctions are legitimate? Modern liberal sensibilities forbid distinctions on the basis of GENDER, or RACE, for example. However, CHILDREN and the insane are treated differently from adults of sound mind. For a law to meet the requirements of formal equality, however, requires only that it not draw illegitimate *formal* distinctions between people: its *effects* may still be unequal between people. A law that forbids all citizens from begging in PUBLIC SPACE treats all equally: however, given that only the poor beg, its effects are invidious. Moreover, interventions that seek to redress INEQUALITY through REDISTRIBUTION (such as social welfare or progressive taxation) compromise formal equality.

(4) *Substantive or social equality.* The absence of 'major disparities in people's resources, political and social power, well-being and of exploitation and oppression' (Bakan, 1997, p. 47). Attaining social equality is fundamental to some movements for SOCIAL JUSTICE. Advocates for social equality note that people may attain formal, political and administrative equality, yet any resultant benefits are cancelled out by their manifest social inequality. In 1929, upon learning that women could, for the first time, be appointed to the Senate, the Canadian feminist Nellie McLung asked: 'Now that we are persons [in law], I wonder if we will notice any difference?' (http://www.abheritage.ca/famous5/leadership/legal_social_equality.html). In other words, political equality was of limited utility while women faced the inequalities of PATRIARCHY. Feminists have also struggled with the tension between equality and difference. For some, feminist struggle should seek to erase differences between men and women, as it is a basis for discrimination. Others argue that the differences between men and women should be acknowledged in any adjudication of rights.

As noted, the promulgation of social equality can also conflict with formal equality (as in the case of positive discrimination, for example). For some, social equality can be attained through equality of opportunity: that is, all should be allowed the same chance to compete for social goods and resources. Others insist on the need to attain equality of outcome or results. The parameters of social equality are, however, uncertain: Are people to attain equality in RESOURCES, material goods, well-being or capabilities, for example (Gosepath, 2005)?

Equality, particularly social equality, is an important though rarely articulated principle that underlies some geographical scholarship, particularly of a critical orientation (see Smith, 2000a: see also CRITICAL GEOGRAPHY).   NKB

equilibrium   A state in which the forces making for change are in balance. This concept is central to NEO-CLASSICAL ECONOMICS, where a free MARKET working perfectly is supposed to tend towards a state of equilibrium. If the forces of supply and demand for all goods and services and all FACTORS OF PRODUCTION are balanced in such a way that all supply is consumed and all demand is met, and no participant(s) in the economy can derive any further income or satisfaction from doing anything other than what is presently done, this would constitute a state of equilibrium which would be maintained until a change took place, response to which would eventually restore equilibrium.

Suppose that, in a perfectly competitive economy in equilibrium, either the extraction of coal becomes more difficult or resources are depleted, and that the coal owners put up the price of coal so as to meet the rising cost of mining. As the consumption of coal is to some extent sensitive to its price, demand for coal is reduced. The mine owners may then find that they have coal unsold and reduce its price a little to get rid of it. Eventually, the balance of forces of supply and demand will be regained by these market adjustments, at a point at which the prevailing price just clears the stocks of coal supplied. Equilibrium will have been restored. This process may, of course, involve bringing back into balance other elements of the economy disturbed by change in the coal market; for example, if there is less coal produced than before, under the new state of equilibrium this may affect employment in mining, coal delivery and so on – while if the new market price is higher, some customers may substitute other sources of fuel for coal.

In reality, an ECONOMY will be in a process of perpetual adjustment to change. Equilibrium is an ideal state that is never achieved in practice but is helpful as a concept in the understanding of a market-regulated economy (on which, see Plummer and Sheppard, 2006; Fowler, 2007). A distinction is sometimes made between *general equilibrium*, which relates to the entire economy, and *partial equilibrium*, which refers to a single market or limited set of related activities.

Spatial equilibrium refers to balance in a spatially disaggregated economy. Change in such a system can be spatially selective; the rise in the price of coal may be confined to a specific region, and restoration of equilibrium involves change and its repercussions working their way from place to place as well as from one market to another. The spatial version of neo-classical economics suggests the equalization of income as a feature of spatial equilibrium, since regional disparities in wages should encourage labour to move to regions where wages are highest and/or CAPITAL to move to regions where wages are lowest until equality is achieved and no advantage is to be obtained from further movement (see CONVERGENCE, REGIONAL). Just as imperfection in market mechanisms can frustrate the achievement of equilibrium in general so, in geographical space, obstacles to the free mobility of labour, capital and so on impede adjustment to wage and price differentials.

The concept of spatial equilibrium has been partly responsible for some misconceptions in regional development theory and planning practice. The terms 'equilibrium' and 'balance' have desirable connotations, and the idea of a self-regulating SPACE-ECONOMY tending towards equalization of incomes encourages a view that market mechanisms are capable of promoting more even development if planners somehow harness them to a public purpose. However, the tendency of market economies under CAPITALISM in reality is more one of concentration and centralization, characterized by UNEVEN DEVELOPMENT and inequality of living standards, especially in the undeveloped world.   DMS

e-social science   An approach to social science research that takes advantage of powerful NETWORKS of computers sharing resources and processing power. These are often compared to electricity grid systems: people generally do not mind where electricity is being generated; they just want to use its power. The same could be true of accessing a computational grid, be it for quantitative modelling and SIMULATION, or for more QUALITATIVE METHODS (such as running online discussion groups). Origins of grid computing include the Search for Extraterrestrial Intelligence@Home project, whereby signals from outer space are distributed to PC users to be analysed using spare resources on their machines. A similar project, supported by the BBC, was used in 2006 to model climate change. Other developments of e-social science in the UK have been stimulated by a major research initiative in e-science, with the Economic and Social Research Council establishing a National Centre for E-Social Science at the University of Manchester (http://www.ncess.ac.uk/). There are links between e-social science and GEO-COMPUTATION. Geographers are involved in this work through the development of large-scale simulation models (as in MICROSIMULATION), by 'grid-enabling' *spatial statistics* (specifically GEOGRAPHICALLY WEIGHTED REGRESSION) and the development of two- and three-dimensional virtual environments (cf. VISUALIZATION). RJ

Suggested reading
See www.ncess.ac.uk and http://www.bbc.co.uk/sn/climateexperiment/

essentialism The doctrine that holds that it is possible to distinguish between the essential and non-essential aspects of objects or phenomena. Fuss (1989, p. xi) defines it as 'a belief in the real, true essences of things, the invariable and fixed properties which define the "whatness" of a given entity'. Essentialism is usually used as a pejorative term, but it is important to distinguish at least three different senses:

(1) Epistemological essentialism is related to FOUNDATIONALISM, and proposes that the aim of investigation is to discover the true nature or essence of things, and to describe these by way of categorical definitions (see also EPISTEMOLOGY). Essentialism in this sense assumes that essences are unchanging, that objects have single essences and that it is possible to gain certain knowledge of these essences. Rorty (1979) repudiates this sense of essentialism, arguing that it depends on a correspondence theory of truth that offsets reality and representation. In contrast to a picture of objects with intrinsic qualities, he affirms an ONTOLOGY of contingent relations that go 'all the way down' (see PRAGMATISM).

(2) Philosophical critiques of essentialism have been invoked to question the validity of explanatory SOCIAL THEORIES and METHODOLOGIES (see also PHILOSOPHY). The argument here is that any claim that X is a cause of Y is equivalent to, or founded on, essentialism in sense (1)

above. However, the argument that social phenomena have relatively stable, durable features, and that these might be ascribed some degree of causal power, is not necessarily essentialist or determinist at all. Social science methodologies and explanation tend to be *fallibilistic*, rather than claiming to establish absolute truth about facts or absolute foundations to knowledge.

(3) A third sense of essentialism is derived from critiques of the idea that racial, ethnic, sexual or gender IDENTITIES are premised on unifying, shared dimensions of experience, embodiment or social position. Criticism of essentialism is here associated with the claim that identities and norms are *relational*, socially *constructed* and historically *contingent*.

Anti-essentialist perspectives often run together these three senses, claiming that various harms or risks of essentialism in sense (3) are legitimized by epistemological essentialism (1) and notions of explanatory causality (2).

In HUMAN GEOGRAPHY, essentialism became an explicit focus of debates alongside debates about POSTMODERNISM. An influential reference point was the anti-essentialist MARXISM of Resnick and Wolff (1987), according to whom any causal account of social processes is inherently suspect. They propose instead a notion of *overdetermination*, derived from Marxist philosopher Louis Althusser, which they define as the mutual constitution of each PROCESS by all others. This anti-essentialist view of causality seems to imply that in order to be able to say anything meaningful about the relationships between processes, one must be able to provide a complete account of all existing relationships relevant to the case at hand. The anti-essentialist response to this problem is to select arbitrary *entry-points*, such as CLASS or GENDER, into the totality of social processes, claiming a pragmatist justification for this theoretical strategy. What is being confused here is the reasonable claim that one might not want to presume *in advance* the existence of a necessary causal relationship with the idea that one can legitimately proffer tentative, partial, empirically grounded, and theoretically justified claims about causal relationships in the course of ongoing, fallibilistic enquiry.

If the grand philosophical claims made on behalf of anti-essentialism in GEOGRAPHY do not stand up to serious scrutiny, then anti-essentialist perspectives have nonetheless been a boon to forms of social constructionist and relational theorizing in the discipline. The strong political impulse behind anti-essentialism has factored in issues of gender, race, culture and the like alongside the predominant focus on economic processes and class (Gibson-Graham, 2006b [1996]). However, there has not been much explicit geographical conceptualization from this anti-essentialist perspective, despite the fact that Althusser's original critique of essentialism in Marxism was oriented by an innovative attempt to think through the non-coincident temporalities of different processes (Althusser and Balibar, 1970, pp. 94–118). The potential herein for theorizing spatiality in a fully conjunctural and relational fashion has, however, been pursued by Massey (2005).

Discussions of essentialism in geography have become stuck in easy juxtapositions of 'bad' essentialism and 'good' *social constructionism*. There is a tendency to conflate cultural essentialism with biological reductionism, causal explanation with epistemological foundationalism; and to affirm simplistic notions of constructed realities and contingent knowledge-claims (Sedgwick, 2003). Anti-essentialism presents a false choice between knowledge with certain guarantees and knowledge with nothing to back it up other than arbitrary persuasive force. In contrast, recent treatments of theories of practice suggest a reorientation of theoretical energy away from essentialist definitions of fundamental, ontological qualities, towards a greater appreciation of the ways in which concepts accrete overlapping degrees of *family resemblance* without ever converging around a finite number of criteria. CB

Suggested reading
Hacking (1999); Sayer (1997).

ethics That part of PHILOSOPHY concerned with the worthiness of human actions and of systems of belief regarding what people ought or ought not to do. Questions regarding our duties, obligations and responsibilities fall within the purview of ethics. While there is no universal agreement regarding which of our acts are subject to moral evaluation and argument, the actions that affect the well-being of other human beings, ourselves and/or non-human beings, within our midst or distant from us, are most pertinent. Ethics concerns not only the actions of individual people but social, economic and political structures and arrangements that also affect human and non-human beings. In this sense, ethics and SOCIAL JUSTICE are intrinsically related to each other, if they are separable at all.

The study of ethics may be descriptive or normative, or may fall into the category of meta-ethics (see Smith, D.M., 1994a). The purpose of *descriptive ethics* is to understand what people actually do, and what they actually believe, with regard to RIGHTS, wrongs, duties and so on; it is not necessarily concerned with evaluating those actions and beliefs. Within *normative ethics*, the goal is to develop arguments or justifications for acting in particular ways and not others; normative ethics wishes to settle moral dilemmas by applying some theoretical argument to a particular case; for example, whether the US war in Iraq meets the criteria for a 'JUST WAR' (cf. NORMATIVE THEORY). *Meta-ethics* has a broader provenance than either of these; it is the field that takes on questions pertaining to the ethical as such; that is, it takes up the issue of what sort of territory ethics should cover. Examples of meta-ethical questions include the following: What actions call for ethical judgement? (I should exercise more frequently, but it is probably not an ethical matter if I do not.) What entities should be given moral consideration at all? (It would not be ethical to kick a dog for the fun of it, but I need not worry about kicking a soccer ball.) Can there be any moral universals? (Some people would argue that every society gives special consideration to the needy, but what counts specifically as a need may differ from one society to another.) Can moral views be objective or only subjective? (There are some philosophers who have argued there are verifiable moral facts in more or less the same way there are objective, scientific facts.)

Moral philosophers, in asking why a particular act, decision or belief is ethical, typically distinguish between consequentialist and deontological notions of ethics (Smith, D.M., 1994a). *Consequentialism* argues that an act (or decision or belief) must be judged against its consequences. The process is one of weighing the probable effects of one course of action as opposed to others. One makes the choice on the basis of the morally best effects. A best effect, for example, might be that the greatest good is brought to the greatest number of people: UTILITARIANISM, in other words, is a consequentialist theory of ethics. *Deontological* theories of ethics evaluate actions on their own merits, independent of their consequences. They see duties and obligations as inherently good; even if a different course of action would bring pleasure to a great many people. Thus, a deontological theorist might encourage me to give preference to the care of my own sick child over the care of other CHILDREN elsewhere, even if those resources might go further in another part of the world.

Geographers' concern with ethics and VALUES is long-standing (Kropotkin, 1885; Sauer, 1956). To a degree, the fit between GEOGRAPHY and ethics is an intuitive one, without necessarily saying anything about what kind of norms have emerged or in whose favour they work. The field's attention to cultural differences between places and peoples attunes it to the fact of differing systems of values in those PLACES, but also to the prospects for COSMOPOLITANISM (see Popke, 2007). Likewise, geographers' interest in interactions and FLOWS (of people, commodities, ideas, capital) between places has made the issue of *fair* interactions and distributions a natural one to think about. The same could be said regarding the discipline's focus on NATURE–SOCIETY relationships: debates over the proper stance towards the environment, towards access to land, WATER and other natural RESOURCES, and towards the distribution of environmental RISKS and HAZARDS are central to contemporary ENVIRONMENTALISM. Also, the propensity of places, regions, states and other territorial arenas to be marked off from one another by BOUNDARIES – material, symbolic or both – has led to questions of who is included and who is excluded, and to what extent these determinations are ethically justifiable (Sibley, 1995; Creswell, 1996). Geography, as Sack (1997) has argued, would seem to be intrinsically morally significant and so one need not look far to see that geographers have thought so, for better and worse, for centuries (e.g. Livingstone, 1992).

What makes recent work in human geography significant is the willingness to tap moral and political thought more directly and extensively than in the past. This willingness is of a piece with the emergence of alternative – RADICAL, FEMINIST, QUEER and CRITICAL HUMAN – GEOGRAPHIES in the past 30 years. Two reasons for greater attention to moral and political thought may be ventured. First, the social revolutions of the post-Second World War period (e.g. movements for political independence, civil rights, gender parity, peace and security, sexual liberation) came to have an enormous impact on geography, eventually leading to disciplinary moves against a geography in service to the status quo. One could say, as Harvey (1972) did, that real-world social revolutions extended into the academy, where the struggle for disciplinary space ensued (cf. Blunt and Wills, 2000). The struggle for new disciplinary spaces within geography involved delving into literatures on politics and ethics (e.g. Harvey, 1973). Second, debates *among* these alternative geographies have been fuelled by a similar sort of exploration, as proponents of various persuasions (say MARXISM or FEMINISM) have sought to make their cases to each other, or despite each other (cf. Harvey, 1992). In any event, the past thirty years has seen something of a 'moral turn' in the geographical literature. A particularly strong indication of this turn is the publication of surveys of moral philosophy written specifically for geographical audiences (e.g. Smith, D.M., 1994a; cf. Low and Gleeson, 1998). Smith's efforts in particular may be viewed as a search for common ground in the struggle for greater EQUALITY globally and locally. Although his contributions are to all three fields of ethics (descriptive, normative and meta-ethics), the main thrust of his work is to see through the many differences in moral theory towards an argument (deontological) for 'the more equal the better' at every geographical SCALE. Another indication of the moral turn is the elaboration of moral arguments and concepts for purposes of advancing specific issues of concern to geographers. Examples include arguments for why the welfare of distant strangers should matter (Corbridge, 1993b; but cf. Barnett and Land, 2007); 'care' as a ethical–political practice, and the notion of 'responsibility' within a globalizing world (Brown, 2004; Massey 2004; Lawson, 2007; Popke, 2007); the application of theories of ethics to a wide range of geographical topics from place and self, to DEVELOPMENT practice and climate change (Whatmore, 1997; Proctor and Smith, 1999a; Smith, 2000a); and a burgeoning interest in the ethics of ACTIVISM and research practices (Lynn and Pulido, 2003).

The moral turn in geography has been strengthened by a continuing effort to reach into new literatures. The adoption of feminist ethics and geographical reworkings of the ethical positions taken by a number of poststructuralist thinkers are good examples. Although hardly new, feminist ethics shapes the uptake of ethics in geography in important ways. Standpoint EPISTEMOLOGIES, which are embraced by a number of strands of FEMINISM, emphasize the embodied and therefore partial quality of knowledge (as against disembodied universal 'truths'), including partiality of moral convictions – meaning that moral systems are always systems that come from somewhere, that somewhere often being a privileged, masculine sphere (e.g. the state, the church) (see also SITUATED KNOWLEDGE). At the same time, a feminist geographical perspective, because of its concern for social justice and the righting of wrongs, may argue explicitly in favour of partial, as opposed to impartial, decisions regarding distribution of scarce resources – thus the enormous influence in the geography of the 1990s of philosopher Iris Marion Young's work on group rights (as opposed to individual rights) (Young, 1990a).

Feminist-standpoint epistemologies share with POST-STRUCTURALISM a scepticism towards, or even wholesale rejection of, the notion of universal truths, including the idea of universally applicable moral principles (see UNIVERSALISM). For this reason, the ethical and the moral are sometimes distinguished from each other, as when Cornell (1995, p. 78) states: 'The ethical as I define it is not a system of behavioral rules, nor a system of positive standards [morality] by which to justify disapproval of others. It is, rather, an attitude towards what is other to oneself.' This shying away from the enunciation of rules and opting instead to cultivate a considered REFELEXIVITY (although the difference between the two can be overdrawn) is what has drawn some geographers towards thinkers such as Emmanuel Levinas, Jacques Derrida and Jean Luc Nancy. The aim is to develop an ethics that is responsible to the need for openness and difference, as against an ethics built upon foundational, universal certainties (see Popke, 2003; see also Gibson-Graham, 2003). Whether an ethics can properly be built upon the notion of HUMAN RIGHTS, for example, is a case in point. Extending from the philosophies of Gilles Deleuze, Giorgio Agamben, Donna Haraway, Baruch Spinoza and others, a concept of 'POSTHUMANISM' has emerged in recent years in human geography and elsewhere that challenges the boundaries and the identity of the human SUBJECT upon which the idea of human rights relies (see Braun, 2004a). The specific interest in post-structuralism as a resource for ethics and geography should not necessarily be construed as a radical break: it is, instead, a tool or tools for grappling with what it means to think and act in terms of relationality and in alliance with struggles for a better world. At the same time, it should be noted that there are streams of ethical thought relatively untapped by human geographers.

These would include ethical systems beyond the Judeo-Christian legacy (see Esteva and Prakash, 1998), as well as the thought of 'Western' thinkers, such as Friedrich Nietzsche and Alain Badiou, for whom responsibility to the 'other' is not the objective of ethics (cf. Dewsbury, 2007). GHe

Suggested reading
Badiou (2001); Smith, D.M. (1994a); Whatmore (1997).

ethnic cleansing The forced removal of an ethnic group from a particular territory or political space by deportation, forced EMIGRATION or GENOCIDE. Examples of ethnic cleansing include the HOLOCAUST (in which six million Jews and millions more Roma and other groups were killed), the German resettlement of western Poland during the Second World War and the attempts of the South African state to relocate blacks during APARTHEID. While the practice is anything but new, the term itself gained widespread use in the 1990s, when it was used to refer to Serbian attacks on Muslims in Bosnia and Albanians in Kosovo. Political geographers have shown how the idea of ethnic cleansing is an outgrowth of the ideology of NATIONALISM, which promotes a unity between the BOUNDARIES of the STATE and the IDENTITY of the population (Flint and Taylor, 2007 [1985]). Ethnic cleansing thus attempts to create a territorial order based on 'an idealized convergence of identity and space' (Dahlman and Ó Tuathail, 2005a, p. 273). Kevin Cox (2002, p. 188) writes that ethnic cleansing 'is a solution that arises in particular geographic situations', such as when a minority population is dispersed within the dominant national population of the state and so cannot easily secede from the larger political unit.

Ethnic cleansing involves not only the removal of populations, but also the destruction of PLACE and COMMUNITY through 'the erasure of "other" CULTURAL LANDSCAPES, the renaming of locales and the repopulation of the land by a new group' (Dahlman and Ó Tuathail, 2005a, p. 273). Marcus Doel and David Clarke (1998, p. 57), in their discussion of the Holocaust, show how ethnic cleansing seeks to configure 'social, physical, moral, and aesthetic *space*' through desires for 'purity'. Ethnic cleansing can thus be seen as a violent policing of the boundaries between the Self and the Other (see OTHER/OTHERNESS). In their work on Bosnia-Herzegovina, Carl Dahlman and Gearoid Ó Tuathail (2005a) show how

213

ethnic cleansing, with its emphasis on borders and separation, becomes a means to consolidate a POLITICAL GEOGRAPHY of SECURITY. They raise important questions about the legacy of ethnic cleansing, and what happens when the displaced attempt to return to the territories from which they were removed. AJS

Suggested reading
Dahlman and Ó Tuathail (2005a); Naimark (2001).

ethnic democracy An ethnically differentiated form of DEMOCRACY articulated by sociologist Sammy Smooha during the early 1990s (see ETHNICITY). 'Ethnic democracy' (ED) is characterized by the allocation of equal political and civil RIGHTS on an individual level to all citizens (see CITIZENSHIP) *and the parallel preservation of collective political rights of the dominant majority only*. Ethnic democracy underscores the structural inequality that characterizes some formally democratic but ethnically dominated nation-states (see DEMOCRACY). The ED model maintains that the allocation of equal individual rights qualifies this regime as a democracy – even in the absence of minority collective rights – and claims that this explains its relative political stability. The ED model has sparked a lively debate both theoretically and substantively in relation to Israel/Palestine (Ghanem, 1998; Shafir and Peled, 1998; Smooha, 2002). OY

ethnicity Ethnicity is one of the most difficult concepts in the social sciences to define: researchers disagree on the meaning of the term; social groups differ in their expressions of ethnicity; and some theorists challenge the credibility of the concept in the first place (see Banks, 1996). The etymology of this term dates back to ancient Greece, where the word *ethnos* was used to refer to a distinct 'people'. The word *ethnic* originally entered the English language as an adjective applied to non-Judeo-Christian peoples. The first instance of the word *ethnicity* used as a noun occurred in the early 1940s, when researchers sought to find a replacement for the word 'RACE' once it had become associated with the genocidal policies of the Nazi party (see GENOCIDE). In contemporary usage, ethnicity is seen as both a way in which individuals define their personal identity and a type of social stratification that emerges when people form groups based on their real or perceived origins. Members of *ethnic groups* believe that their specific ancestry and CULTURE mark them as different from

others. As such, ethnic group formation always entails both inclusionary and exclusionary behaviour, and ethnicity is a classic example of the distinction people make between 'us' and 'them' (cf. DIFFERENCE; OTHER/OTHERNESS; SUBJECT).

While much attention was given to theories of ethnicity and the nature of ethnic groups in the early twentieth century, especially in the USA (see CHICAGO SCHOOL), interest waned in the postwar period. The LIBERALISM that came to dominate the intellectual climate by mid-century was predicated on a belief in the autonomy of individuals. Within the discourse of liberal individualism, the notion that people modify their actions because of their ethnic loyalties is suspect, and generally considered a fading remnant of pre-modern times. The version of MARXISM that challenged liberalism in the late 1960s was equally dismissive of ethnicity, claiming that ethnic attachments were fostered by capitalists and the state in order to divide the working class (e.g. Bonacich, 1972). By the 1970s, many leading social theorists had abandoned the study of ethnicity, associating it with antiquated views of society and conservative politics. This dismissive attitude began to change in the 1980s, however, when it became clear that ethnicity was not losing its salience; on the contrary, IDENTITY POLITICS were on the rise, and ethnic NATIONALISM had become a primary force in the most violent struggles around the world, especially in the post-COLD WAR era – a turn of events unanticipated by liberal and Marxist scholars alike (Berking, 2003). The fact that over 90 per cent of the world's nation-states are poly-ethnic suggests that this type of conflict is likely to continue (see also MULTICULTURALISM).

It is worth reflecting upon this point. Historically, the idea of a NATION-STATE was founded on the principle of ethnic homogeneity in the form of a people or NATION, which held control over a bounded TERRITORY, or STATE. It is debatable whether this simple correspondence between people and territory ever existed, but it is certainly clear that contemporary nation-states are characterized by multiplicity rather than mono-ethnic singularity. This has led to much discussion of the relationship between ethnicity, the nation and NATIONALISM (e.g. Banton, 2004). As Dunn (2003b) and Amin (2004a) point out, national cultures continue to reflect outmoded assumptions of ethnic homogeneity, to the detriment of minority groups (cf. Chow, 2002). This leads to one of two prominent confusions surrounding the concept of ethnicity. *Many use the term only to refer to minority groups*, assuming that people in the majority are 'normal' while everyone else is 'ethnic'. While this usage of the term was considered acceptable in the nineteenth century, it is no longer correct. In fact, *everyone* has an ethnic background, whether or not it is acknowledged. In most situations, people can only afford to be unaware of their ethnicity when they are in a privileged position (see WHITENESS).

A second ambiguity arises *when the terms ethnicity and race are used interchangeably*, or when they are seen as variants of the same classification system. For example, it is often thought that people can be divided into three or four broad racial groups and that each has a number of ethnic subdivisions (e.g. race = Caucasian, ethnicity = Italian). However, it is exceedingly difficult – many believe impossible – to discern discrete 'races': the genetic mixing of human populations defies such a simplistic classification system (see RACE). While there are obvious phenotypical and genetic differences between people, there is only one human race, a point emphatically made by the United Nations. Throughout history, though, people have been *racialized* by others for particular reasons. Most commentators agree that RACIALIZATION is necessarily a negative process, where one group chooses to define another as morally and/or genetically inferior in order to dominate and oppress it: racialization is always an *imposed* category. Phenotypical features, such as skin colour or facial structure, are then interpreted as evidence that the two groups are indeed separate 'types' of people and are used strategically to demark the boundaries between groups (cf. APARTHEID). Once defined, such boundaries are extremely difficult to cross. Racialized minorities become ethnic groups when they achieve social solidarity on the basis of their distinct culture and background. Racialization therefore facilitates the development of ethnic consciousness, which may be harnessed by minorities in their struggle against discrimination (e.g. the Black Power movement of the 1960s in the USA or the Palestinian INTIFADA), but does not necessarily lead to ethnic group formation. While external forces are important in the generation of ethnic consciousness, the most basic difference between race and ethnicity is that ethnic affiliation arises from inside a group; ethnicity is a process of self-definition.

However, ethnicity is not uniformly important to all people: the degree of ethnic identity and attachment varies strongly between and within societies. Many of the most cohesive ethnic groups have emerged after the conquest of a TERRITORY by an external power. In these cases, ethnic attachment and nationalism are powerfully fused as people affiliate to ensure the survival of their culture, religious practices and access to employment opportunities. The goal in these struggles is usually political independence. Occasionally, tensions in poly-ethnic states become so extreme that ethnic loyalty becomes the overriding social force shaping the polity. The genocide of Jews in Nazi Germany is a repugnant example of this tendency, as are the recent attempts at 'ETHNIC CLEANSING' (the forced removal of all minorities from an area) in parts of the former Yugoslavia and elsewhere. MIGRATION is another impetus for the development of heightened ethnic consciousness. Immigrants often face hostility within the societies they enter, and form ethnic bonds and associations to increase their political credibility, economic viability and sense of social belonging. Whereas conquered groups tend to fight for independence, DIASPORIC groups fight for the right to be included in their new societies as equal participants.

Acknowledging the variability of ethnic affiliation, theorists have long debated the causes of ethnic identity and division. Two distinct views dominate the literature: ethnicity as primordial, or absolute, versus ethnicity as constructed, as the outcome of other social processes (Jenkins, 1996; Hale, 2004). Those advocating the former see ethnicity as a basic form of affiliation that naturally emerges as people are socialized into cultures with long histories; CHILDREN are born into ethnic groups and develop deep-seated attachments to them. The most extreme primordial position is taken by sociobiologists, who believe that ethnicity is a legacy of the struggle for FOOD and shelter (Van den Berghe, 1981). In this controversial perspective, ethnic solidarity is seen as an extension of the biologically driven feelings that link individuals to their nuclear family and kin. These researchers find it difficult to explain why some people place little value on their ethnic origin and culture while others choose to express their ethnicity even when it is disadvantageous to do so.

Researchers advocating constructionist views, conversely, assert that ethnic attachments arise in specific contexts, for specific reasons. Marxists, as mentioned, often minimize the importance of ethnicity by arguing that it is a displaced form of CLASS consciousness. In its crudest form, this argument implies a rigid INSTRUMENTALISM wherein the STATE, viewed as a tool of the capitalist class, enacts colonial and immigration policies designed to create differences within the working class in order to fragment its solidarity (Bonacich, 1994; cf. COLONIALISM). More sophisticated Marxist treatments of ethnicity have emerged in light of growing ethnic and nationalist movements in the late twentieth century: even these, however, tend to portray ethnicity as a regressive force deflecting people from their 'real' material interests (Williams, R.M., 1994b).

Another variant of the constructionist view emphasizes the relational causes of ethnic identification – that is, ethnic groups acquire their identity not alone, but in relation to one another. For example, early-twentieth-century immigrants from the southern Italian peninsula to North America brought the parochial loyalties of their village origins (see CHAIN MIGRATION); in their new, displaced context, however, these local affiliations were united into a broad consciousness of being 'Italian'. This emergent ethnicity was the product of a host of factors, including similar religious expressions, common languages, geopolitical events, occupational segmentation, residential SEGREGATION and the way in which these immigrants were perceived and categorized as Italians by others around them (Yancey, Ericksen and Juliani, 1976). The constructionist view is also best suited to explain the ways that identity shifts as circumstances change. For example, a person can legitimately identify her/himself as English in the UK, British in other European countries, European in Asia and 'white' in Africa. However, while constructionist theories help us understand the variability of ethnic attachments and identities, their very flexibility makes it impossible to develop a systematic account of ethnicity. In fact, the very factors that cause ethnic consciousness to emerge in some contexts impede it in others, which tends to make theorization inherently difficult and incomplete.

Over time, ethnic solidarity may be perpetuated or may dissipate. The processes governing the dynamic between cultural retention versus ASSIMILATION are exceedingly complex, but researchers generally agree that the nature of the social boundaries between ethnic groups is critical. Boundaries are maintained when individuals maximize their interactions with those within their ethnic group while minimizing their interactions with others. This occurs when separate social, political and educational institutions are established within different groups. According to Fredrik Barth (1969), boundaries created between groups can be resilient even when the cultural practices of the groups are no longer distinctive. In many cases, ethnic boundaries become entrenched in space, such as in the formation of ethnic neighbourhoods in cities.

Geographers have shown a long-standing interest in documenting the causes and consequences of urban ethnic segregation. Much of this work stems from the conceptualization of human ecology articulated by Robert Park and other members of the CHICAGO SCHOOL in the early twentieth century. During the 1960s, attention focused on plotting ethnic 'GHETTOS', devising ways to measure the degree of ethnic segregation (see INDICES OF SEGREGATION), and formulating PUBLIC POLICY to integrate ethnic and racialized groups across the city. By the end of the decade, a concern for ethnic residential patterns entered the mainstream of urban theory and increasingly sophisticated models of urban land use were devised. This type of work came under intense criticism after the 1970s. On the one hand, the relationship between the degree of social tolerance and residential patterns is not entirely clear; that is, a high level of segregation is not necessarily the result of discrimination, just as residential mixing does not necessarily indicate the absence of discrimination (see Peach, 1996b). On the other hand, studies of segregation have relied almost exclusively on census data. Ethnicity is defined in most censuses by respondents' national or 'racial' origin, and is therefore a poor indicator of ethnic affiliation (e.g. all those of Polish descent are lumped into the same category, whether or not they identify with that cultural heritage; see Petersen, 1997). Furthermore, such classification of people perpetuates the idea that there are distinct races, and the CENSUS itself may be implicated in the racialization of minorities. Given these criticisms, the number and significance of data-intensive, quantitative studies of ethnicity declined in the 1980s. However, this type of work has been revived subsequently as the number of immigrants in European and North American cities has increased and as immigration policy has become more intensely debated.

Geographers have also devoted considerable energy studying the racialization process, especially as it impinges on people's access to housing and the labour market (e.g. Anderson, 1991b; Jacobs, 1996). The regulatory practices of government are highlighted in this work because immigration, housing, employment equity and other policies directly affect the way in which individuals experience discrimination and ethnic or racial difference. While this research has led to important insights, it has tended to ignore social processes operating within groups; that is, discrimination and racialization are emphasized without a corresponding interest in the agency of individuals to create ethnic consciousness and use this to struggle against domination (Leitner, 1992 – for examples of geographical work that explores the relationship between racialization and agency, see Ley, 1995; Mitchell, 1998; Gibson, Law and McKay, 2001; Kelly, 2002; also see IDENTITY POLITICS).

Geographers and other social scientists have also begun to examine the intersections between ethnicity and other forms of personal identity and stratification, notably CLASS and GENDER (e.g. Anthias, 2001). Here, emphasis is placed in which each dimension of identity affects all others; for example, masculinity and femininity may well be defined and lived differently in different ethnic groups (cf. FEMINIST GEOGRAPHIES). This type of investigation is both conceptually difficult, since researchers must study many facets of experience and social structure simultaneously, and controversial, since it destabilizes traditional definitions of class and gender.   DH

Suggested reading
Amin (2004a); Banton (1983); Mason (1995); Pincus and Ehrlich (1994); Smaje (1997); Smith (1989); Sollors (1996).

ethnoburb A term popularized by Li (1998) to describe the residential patterns of Asian migrants to Australian, Canadian, New Zealand and US cities in recent decades. Traditional models of ethnic residential patterns (following the CHICAGO SCHOOL) link them to processes of economic, social and cultural ASSIMILATION, whereby over time ethnic groups lose their separate IDENTITY and merge into the wider population, at the same time becoming dispersed through the urban fabric away from their original concentrations in GHETTO-like areas. Contemporary MULTI-CULTURALISM policies, on the other hand, promote economic integration alongside cultural DIFFERENCE, so that ethnic group members retain their separateness.

Ethnoburbs reflect this changed situation, involving migrant groups comprising more skilled and wealthier populations than was the case in the first half of the twentieth century – alongside continued streams of low-status immigrants (such as Hispanics to the USA and Pacific Islanders to New Zealand). These new – predominantly Asian – groups tend to cluster in suburban areas, but rarely dominate the local population, although perhaps being more visible in the LANDSCAPE (because of their housing and retail businesses) than their numbers suggest. And, Li argues, such concentrations may be much more permanent elements of the residential matrix than the enclaves associated with earlier migrant streams.   RJ

Suggested reading
Li (2006).

ethnocentrism Most cultures and peoples have historically inscribed themselves at the centre of the world. 'Ethnocentrism' refers to the practice of taking one's own subject position as the central reference point in relation to which all others can be arrayed with regard to their DIFFERENCE (see also OTHERS/OTHERING). Like anthropologists and sociologists, geographers have worked to uncover and counter the ethnocentric UNIVERSALISM implicit within much geographical practice and analysis (Godlewska and Smith, 1994; Agnew, 1998) (cf. ANGLOCENTRISM; EUROCENTRISM).   AS

Suggested reading
Robinson (2003).

ethnocracy A type of regime conceptualized by geographer Oren Yiftachel during the mid-1990s, in which a dominant ethno-national group appropriates the STATE APPARATUS to expand and deepen its control over contested TERRITORY and power structures (Yiftachel and Ghanem, 2004). Ethnocracies typically represent themselves as democracies (see ETHNIC DEMOCRACY), but are characterized by high levels of unequal segregation between rival ethnic nations and by structural inequalities between ethno-classes within each NATION. Driven by a hegemonic project of ethnicization and internal colonization, ethnocracies are neither democratic nor authoritarian. They can be found in states such as Sri Lanka, Latvia, Israel and Sudan. Ethnocracies typically lack equal CITIZENSHIP, separation of religion and state, or proportional minority representation and RIGHTS, and have suffered chronic political instability (Kedar, 2003).   OY

ethnography From the Greek *ethnos* (the nation) and *graphē* (writing), ethnography is

217

most closely associated with the discipline of sociocultural anthropology, and with PARTICIPANT OBSERVATION and long-term, in-depth engagement with specific COMMUNITIES or SOCIETIES. It refers to both a set of research methods and to the written product.

Ethnography has often come under attack for its role in British colonial efforts to produce detailed knowledges about native populations in order to govern and control them. Yet the meanings, practices and uses of ethnography are multiple and contentious, and have shifted radically over time. In recent years, sociologists, historians and geographers have joined with anthropologists to focus on how ethnography can be used to forge politically enabling understandings of processes glossed by the term 'GLOBALIZATION' and to illuminate the possibilities for social change. Relational conceptions of the PRODUCTION OF SPACE and SCALE associated with Henri Lefebvre (1991b) are becoming increasingly important in efforts to construct a project of critical ethnography.

During the 1980s, ethnography came under sharp attack from within anthropology. In *Writing culture* (1986), Clifford, Marcus and others challenged presumptions of 'ethnographic authority', and propelled what has been termed the reflexive turn (see REFLEXIVITY). Instead of simply discovering or reflecting culture, they argued, ethnographers actually write or produce it. Since the 1980s there have also been a number of feminist critiques of ethnography, some of them simultaneously critical of the sort of experimental writing and textual strategies promoted by authors of the reflexive turn (e.g. Behar and Gordon, 1995). In another set of anthropological critiques, Appadurai (1988) and others condemned traditional ethnographies through which mobile anthropologists produce knowledge that incarcerates 'natives' in bounded localities, and map essentialized cultures onto bounded TERRITORIES. He insisted on ethnography that is not so resolutely localizing, while others proposed the METAPHOR of travel as a means of escape for the ethnographer from the 'incarceration of the local' and the supposed stasis of SPACE.

By the 1990s, growing numbers of anthropologists were calling for critical understandings of space, PLACE and culture that went beyond metaphors of travel, FLOWS and deterritorialization. In *Culture, power, place: explorations in critical anthropology*, Gupta and Ferguson pointed to the necessity of 'exploring the processes of *production* of DIFFERENCE

in a world of culturally, socially and economically interconnected and interdependent spaces' (1997, p. 43), and the ethnographic essays in their volume exemplify that argument. In *Ethnography through thick and thin* (1998), Marcus sought to update his earlier critique of cultural anthropology with a call for multi-sited ethnography. The bringing together of ethnography and history by the Comaroffs (1992), Cooper and Stoler (1997b) and others was also an important development in the 1990s. Relational understandings of space and place are implicit in some of this work.

From within sociology, a significant strand of scholarship that is moving towards critical understandings of SPATIALITY is the project of global ethnography spearheaded by Michael Burawoy and his students (2000). While ethnography has generally occupied a marginal position in sociology, it formed the basis of the CHICAGO SCHOOL of urban sociology that goes back to the 1920s. A partial descendant of the Chicago School, Burawoy has shifted sociological deployments of ethnography in radically new directions. In their 'Manifesto' that launched the journal *Ethnography*, Willis and Trondman (2000) echo Burawoy's emphasis on THEORY as a 'precursor, medium and outcome of ethnographic study and writing'. They propose TIME (theoretically informed methodology for ethnography) as an appropriate acronym, as well as being relevant in a non-acronym sense.

These moves to redefine ethnography are further enriched by more explicit attention to a conception of space (or space–time) and SCALE as actively produced through situated, embodied material practices and their associated DISCOURSES and POWER relations (Lefebvre, 1991b). For example, there remains a widespread tendency to conceive of 'place' as concrete, and 'space' as abstract – in other words, a notion of place as space made meaningful. A Lefebvrian understanding of the PRODUCTION OF SPACE decisively rejects this distinction. Instead, space and place are *both* conceived in terms of embodied practices and processes of production that are simultaneously material and discursive. From this perspective, place is most usefully understood as nodal points of connection in wider NETWORKS of socially produced space – what Massey (1994b) calls an extroverted sense of place. If spatiality is conceived in terms of space–time and formed through social relations and interactions at all scales, then place can be seen as neither a bounded enclosure nor the site of meaning-making, but rather as 'a subset of the interactions which constitute [social] space, a local articulation within a wider whole' (Massey, 1994b, p. 4). Places are always formed through relations with wider arenas and other places; BOUNDARIES are always socially constructed and contested; and the specificity of a place – however defined – arises from the particularity of interrelations with what lies beyond it, that come into conjuncture in specific ways.

A conception of place as nodal points of connection in socially produced space enables a non-positivist (see POSITIVISM) understanding of generality. In this conception, particularities or specificities arise through *interrelations* between objects, events, places and IDENTITIES; and it is through clarifying how these relations are produced and changed in practice that close study of a particular part can generate broader claims and understandings. Such an approach underscores the fallacies inherent in notions that concrete studies deal with what is local and particular, whereas abstract theory encompasses general (or global) processes that transcend particular places. This conflation of 'the local' with 'the concrete' and 'the global' with 'the abstract' (see LOCAL-GLOBAL RELATIONS) confuses geographical scale with processes of ABSTRACTION in thought (Sayer, 1991).

Critical conceptions of spatiality are central to relational comparison – a strategy that differs fundamentally from one that deploys IDEAL TYPES, or that posits different 'cases' as local variants of a more general phenomenon (Hart, 2006). Instead of comparing pre-existing objects, events, places or identities, the focus is on *how* they are constituted in relation to one another through power-laden practices in the multiple, interconnected arenas of everyday life. Ethnographic studies that clarify these connections and mutual processes of constitution – as well as slippages, openings and contradictions – help to generate new understandings of the possibilities for social change.   GHa

Suggested reading
Chari (2004); Katz (2004); Mitchell (2004).

ethnomethodology An approach to studying social order and practical reason that discloses how people or 'members' produce everyday situations, deploying concepts that neither ironicize nor stipulate those found *in situ*. The concern is the routine practices through which situations 'occasion' said members, and vice versa, thus catching the self-rendering and self-describing of these situations as exactly what they *are* in the immediate flow of their conduct. Attention alights on the 'how' of this conduct – just how the people involved do what they do – and on recovering both the 'skills' exhibited by members and the situated, local, changeable 'orders' whose 'rules' they knowingly follow. Ethnomethodologists resist importing theoretical constructs that derive from 'elsewhere' or are specified at a level of ABSTRACTION removed from the situation in question. They retain a sustained commitment to the empirical, but reject the taken-for-grantedness of 'social facts' typifying EMPIRICIST or POSITIVIST social science, preferring instead to ascertain how a supposed 'social fact' has come about, become recognized and then entered the situated practical knowledge of people in the grain of their everyday lives. Central here is the REFLEXIVITY of the researcher, not so much through continually interrogating their own POSITIONALITY, but through gauging the 'how' of their *own* conduct; that is, how they do what they do themselves when researching as a practical activity.

Ethnomethodology has intellectual roots in Alfred Schutz's constitutive PHENOMENOLOGY and Erving Goffman's micro-sociology of the everyday, both of which have figured in versions of HUMAN GEOGRAPHY post-1970. The key figures here, though, are: Harold Garfinkel (e.g. 1967), who declared that the researcher must *learn* from members 'what their affairs consist of as locally produced, locally occasioned, and locally ordered, locally described, locally questionable, counted, recorded, observable phenomena of order' (Garfinkel and Weider, 1992, p. 186); and Harvey Sacks (e.g. 1992), who developed *conversation analysis* (CA), taking seriously the 'analysis' that we all do while conversing as well as the timing, spacing and 'indexicality' (the significance of immediate contexts to the progress) of any conversation. There has been no concerted attempt to create an ethnomethodological geography, although ethnomethodological 'policies' have filtered into the discipline through ETHNOGRAPHY and also brushes with the likes of SYMBOLIC INTERACTIONISM, ACTOR-NETWORK THEORY (ANT) and NON-REPRESENTATIONAL THEORY (NRT).

In various studies – on mobile phone use in cars, EVERYDAY LIFE in coffee-houses, practices with pets – Laurier (1998, 2004) has worked *between* geography and ethnomethodology, highlighting how such a position differs from 'the requirements of the PERFORMANCE of "doing competent CULTURAL GEOGRAPHY"' (Laurier, 2001, p. 486). Unlike NRT's wariness of spoken communication, he follows the impetus of CA in foregrounding 'talk' as social action, within which members undertake 'representational work' as it occurs in the immediacy of the here-and-now. He recognizes the objection that ethnomethodology appears not to tackle what theorists take as larger, more enduring 'social structures', responding on the one hand (with ANT) that such structures cannot just be the fragile accomplishment of countless interlinking peoples, conducts and situations, and on the other by seeking commonalities with the 'archaeological' method pioneered by Michel Foucault when dealing with the (seemingly grander) operations of DISCOURSE and POWER (Laurier and Philo, 2004).   CP

Suggested reading
Laurier (2001, 2004).

Euclidean space The metric space defined by the geometric system devised by the Greek mathematician Euclid of Alexandria. Euclidean space (sometimes called Cartesian space: see CARTESIANISM) is the SPACE typically presumed in everyday discussion and in more formal accounts of distance, interaction or spatial distribution in HUMAN GEOGRAPHY. Euclidean space is based on five axioms:

- Any two *points* can be joined by a *straight line*.
- Any *straight-line segment* can be extended indefinitely in a straight line.
- Given any straight-line segment, a *circle* can be drawn having the segment as *radius* and one endpoint as centre.
- All *right angles* are *congruent*.
- The *parallel postulate*. If two lines intersect a third in such a way that the sum of the *inner angles* on one side is less than two right angles, then the two lines inevitably must intersect each other on that side if extended far enough.

From the 1970s, geographers explored both the power and the limits of Euclidean space for mapping the Earth (see CARTOGRAPHY), recognizing that the surface of the GLOBE is not Euclidean but a two-dimensional surface of constant positive curvature. Spatial analytical modelling often presupposes Euclidean space, although there have been some experiments with non-Euclidean spaces, such as Riemannian and Lobachevskian geometries and multi-dimensional spaces (see also SPATIAL SCIENCE).

Euclidean space has long been treated as absolute and homogeneous, properties that for Lefebvre (1991b) guarantee its social and political utility. This utility emerges first as 'NATURE's space' and later as all of social life is reduced to Euclidean space. The result is a double reduction of complex three-dimensional realities to a two-dimensional space, and to the space of two-dimensional objects that can be 'naively' mapped or represented. At this point, the spaces of lived experience are normalized and seen as reducible to abstract and transparent spaces: the god-trick has rendered the world as something to be looked at from a distance, as a world-as-picture or *world as exhibition*, where complex social and natural worlds have become intelligible to the eye, to be read and represented (Heidegger, 1962 [1927]: see also EPISTEMOLOGY; PRODUCTION OF SPACE).   JPi

Eurocentrism A world-view that places 'Europe' at the centre of human history, social analysis and political practice. These three spheres are closely connected, and revolve around the constitution of 'Europe' as subject and object of enquiry, as architect and arbiter of method, and as exemplar and engineer of progress. Thus:

(1) 'Europe' is placed at the centre of human history through the assumption that it provides the model and master-narrative of world history: that its histories (and geographies) are the norm and the rule, from which others learn or deviate.

(2) 'Europe' is placed at the centre of social analysis through the assumption that its theoretical formulations and methods of analysis provide the most powerful resources for all explanation and interpretation.

(3) 'Europe' is placed at the centre of political practice through the assumption that its cultural and political systems act as the bearers of a universal Reason that maps out the ideal course of all human history (see ENLIGHTENMENT).

EUROPE appears in scare-quotes throughout the preceding paragraph to draw attention to its cultural construction. The very idea of 'Europe' has a long and far from unitary history. Eurocentrism has a long history (or rather historical geography) too, through which it has been so closely entwined with the projects of COLONIALISM and IMPERIALISM (Blaut, 1993) that it cannot sensibly be confined to the CONTINENT of Europe. In the course of those discursive expansions, 'Europe' has turned into 'the WEST' (cf. ORIENTALISM), which has more recently been turned into the global 'NORTH' (cf. SOUTH). Each one of these transitions has been freighted with its own cultural and political baggage, but their general burden is clear. 'Eurocentrism is not merely the ETHNOCENTRISM of people located in the West', Dhareshwar (1990, p. 235) notes, but rather 'permeates the cultural apparatus in which we participate': it is a global IDEOLOGY. It follows from these characterizations that it is possible to study Europe without being Eurocentric, and that it is equally possible to study non-European societies in thoroughly Eurocentric ways.

Geography has a particular and a general interest in Eurocentrism. Historians of the modern discipline have argued that it is a constitutively 'European science' (Stoddart, 1986). Critics have objected that this erases the contributions of other geographical traditions (Arab, Chinese and Indian among them) and that GEOGRAPHY in its modern, transnational and hegemonic forms (see HEGEMONY) is more accurately described as a 'Eurocentric science' (Gregory, 1994; see also Sidaway, 1997). Work in the history of geography (see GEOGRAPHY, HISTORY OF) has drawn attention to these issues through an interrogation of geography's complicity in the adventures of colonialism and imperialism and, in particular, of the reciprocities between the intellectual formation of the discipline and the political trajectory of European expansion, exploitation and dispossession (Driver, 1992b). During the nineteenth and early twentieth centuries, the discipline invested heavily in activities that had considerable instrumental value (some historians have suggested that it was precisely these practical contributions that helped secure the formal incorporation of the modern discipline within the Western academy). Its strategic contributions included mapping and surveying other territories, compiling RESOURCE inventories, and producing IMAGINATIVE GEOGRAPHIES of other peoples and places. These investments contributed to the formation of the modern discipline as a 'white mythology' that: (a) postulated a racially unmarked subject-position as the condition of objective truth and scientific discourse; (b) effaced alternative subject-positions; and (c) appropriated other forms of knowledge – all three gestures are diagnostics of Eurocentrism (Barnett, 1998; see also WHITENESS).

In the course of the twentieth century, Eurocentrism bled into what Peet (2005) describes as the 'even more virulent geocultural form' of Americentrism. There are

crucial differences as well as affinities between the two (Slater, 2004, pp. 13–16), but both cultural formations have underwritten and been propelled by military force and capitalist GLOBALIZATION. Their conjunction was registered within the modern discipline by the designation of a singular 'Anglo-American geography' in the 1960s and 1970s, but this was a double exclusion: apart from some key contributions from German and Swedish writers, non-Anglophone European geographers were marginalized (Eurocentrism had contracted to an ANGLOCENTRISM), and classical SPATIAL SCIENCE offered a series of supposedly general MODELS that were in fact predicated on specifically European and American cases (Christaller's Germany, Burgess's Chicago) (cf. McGee, 1995). Since then, however, while the intellectual corpus of 'Anglo-American geography' has become increasingly fractured – here too there are differences as well as affinities – Slater (1992) could still argue that much of it continued to rely on a Euro-Americanism that projected its own situations as 'lineages of universalism'. Slater claimed that the dependence of an ostensibly CRITICAL HUMAN GEOGRAPHY on European and American traditions of CRITICAL THEORY, HISTORICAL MATERIALISM and POSTMODERNISM (the list could now be extended: FEMINIST GEOGRAPHY and POST-STRUCTURALISM have been exercised by the same questions) tacitly licensed assumptions of 'universal applicability' that concealed 'a particularity based to a large extent on the specific experiences of the USA and the UK'. Geographies written under the sign of POST-COLONIALISM have been directly interested in these issues – in the need to 'provincialize' the assumptions of Euro-American geography, to attend to other voices and to 'learn from other regions' – but they also often draw directly on European high theory, and Slater (2004) has demonstrated that they have much to learn from other politico-intellectual traditions too (cf. TRICONTINENTALISM).

Geography is scarcely alone in these predicaments, and in the sense of DISCOURSE rather than discipline it has a more general involvement in Eurocentrism. Gregory (1998) has drawn attention to four conceptual strategies – 'geo-graphs' – that entered directly into the formation of a colonial MODERNITY:

(1) *Absolutizing time and space:* the construction of concepts through which European metrics and meanings of history and geography were taken to be natural and inviolable, as marking the centre

around which other histories and other geographies were to be organized (cf. Young, 1990b).

(2) *Exhibiting the world:* the production of a space within which particular objects were made visible in particular ways, and by means of which particular claims to knowledge made by viewing subjects were negotiated and legitimized.

(3) *Normalizing the subject:* the production of spaces of inclusion and exclusion that treated the subject-position of the white, middle-class, heterosexual male as the norm.

(4) *Abstracting culture and nature:* the production of 'nature' as a realm separate from 'culture', in which European CULTURE had made NATURE yield its secrets and its resources, and in which temperate nature was 'normal nature' (cf. Blaut, 1999).

This argumentation-sketch is more than an exercise in historical reconstruction. 'In elucidating the conceptual orders of Eurocentrism,' Gregory argues, 'it becomes much more difficult to assume that we have left such predicaments behind, and much more likely that we will be forced to recognise that Eurocentrism and its geo-graphs continue to invest our geographies with their troubling meanings.' DG

Suggested reading
Slater (1992); Gregory (1998a).

Europe, idea of   The REGION that we now call Europe is the western part of the Eurasian landmass. Europe has no clearly defined borders, particularly in the east, but the region's history can be read as an ongoing attempt to define what it means to be European and to fix that IDENTITY on the map (Heffernan, 1998). This process has generated a series of non-European 'others', against whom Europeans have defined themselves.

The term 'Europe' is derived from *Europa*, a female character in Greek mythology. The word had no geographical meaning for the Classical civilizations centred on the MIDDLE EAST and the Mediterranean basin, and little significance in the Roman Empire. It is absent from the Bible, but was used alongside 'Christendom' in the early medieval period to describe the area where Christianity prevailed and where a literate elite shared a common Latin language. On medieval world MAPS, Europe was depicted as a small, internally undifferentiated area, vulnerable to incursion from the Islamic regions of ASIA and AFRICA,

which were Europe's first constituting 'others' (Hay, 1968; Wilson and van den Dussen, 1993).

The expansion of Europe into the AMERICAS from the late fifteenth century was both a cause and a consequence of the intellectual and technological changes associated with the European Renaissance, and provoked a major reassessment of Europe's place in a world still seen as divinely created (Wintle, 1999, 2008). The opening of the Americas also generated a new economic system based on long-distance Atlantic TRADE and a new political system based on competitive European NATION-STATES, whose interests clashed repeatedly in Europe and the Americas during the collapse in the fragile unity of the Christian church following the Reformation. As 'Christendom' disintegrated into a complex mosaic of Catholic and Protestant communities in the Old and the New Worlds, the word 'Europe' lost its religious connotation. In the wake of the Treaties of Westphalia (1648), which ended the European WARS of RELIGION, Europe was defined as the region in which a 'balance of power' might operate between rival nation-states by mutual consent (Pagden, 2002).

The geographical limits of this arrangement were famously outlined in the Duc de Sully's mid-seventeenth-century Grand Design for European unity. For Sully, the Ottoman Empire had no part in the 'concert of Europe', because international agreements ultimately rested on Christian values. Christian Russia was also excluded, because the Russian people were deemed essentially Asiatic and hence culturally inferior. Europe now had two constituting 'others', a traditional religious enemy in the Islamic south and a new cultural enemy in the Asiatic east. Sully's cultural definition of Europe highlights a fundamental irony at the heart of the European debate. At the very moment when Europe was defined politically in the most enlightened terms as an area where permanent peace might be established by international agreement, it was also defined geographically to exclude the peoples of other regions who were deemed unworthy on cultural or civilizational grounds (Heater, 1992; Wolff, 1994; Neumann, 1996: see also CIVILIZATION; NOMOS).

The legitimacy of imposing geographical limits on supposedly universal HUMAN RIGHTS was hotly debated during the eighteenth-century ENLIGHTENMENT, but the freedom educated Europeans (including those who had settled beyond Europe) claimed for themselves in their hard-won battles against the tyranny of unelected rulers in Europe was never extended to the native peoples of Asia, Africa and the Americas. The fate of these people was to be decided by the colonizing Europeans. The values of enlightened DEMO-CRACY shone brightly in eighteenth-century Europe and the newly independent European North America, partly because the rest of the world had been simultaneously darkened.

During the nineteenth century, the high point of European IMPERIALISM, the cultural criteria used to define Europe were recast yet again, this time in racial and biological terms inspired by the prevalent theories of social DARWINISM and ENVIRONMENTAL DETERMIN-ISM. The European peoples were deemed not merely to have *acquired* a superior level of civilization but, rather, to possess an *inherent* racial superiority, a consequence of their uniquely benevolent physical environment (see RACE). This both explained and justified the European domination of the world.

As the last remaining uncolonized regions of the world gradually diminished, so the tensions between different European nations increased, unleashing a more or less continuous period of intra-European warfare from 1914 to 1945. This ended with the attempt by the Nazi authorities in Germany to eradicate long-estab-lished European communities, notably the Jews, in the name of a racially 'pure' Europe. If a 'dark continent' has ever existed, it was surely Europe between 1914 and 1945 (Mazower, 1998: see also GENOCIDE; HOLOCAUST).

Europe was divided in 1945, the western and eastern parts of the region dominated by the opposing military superpowers of the USA and the Soviet Union, respectively. New meas-ures to foster economic integration developed on both sides during the COLD WAR from the 1950s to 1980s, most successfully through the European Economic Community (EEC) and its successor the European Community (EC), which eventually encompassed most of the national economies of western Europe. This generated remarkable economic success but little additional discussion about the essential meaning of Europe, mainly because the REGION previously regarded as Europe seemed permanently divided. The word 'Europe' had little currency in eastern Europe in this period and acquired only a limited economic mean-ing in western Europe (Judt, 1996, 2005).

The realignment of central and eastern Europe after the collapse of the Soviet Union and the reunification of Germany has been achieved with remarkable speed, and amid continuing economic success. The enlarged European Union (EU) now includes 27 coun-tries with a combined population approaching 500 million. Twelve countries, with a total population in excess of 300 million, share a single currency (the euro), established in 1999. These seismic developments have begun to generate new reflections on the fun-damental idea of Europe, but it remains to be seen whether an enlarged Europe will develop a distinctive identity in the twenty-first century and emerge as a political and economic coun-terbalance to the USA. Whether the new Europe needs such a 'nation-like' identity is a moot point, however, for it might more usefully be defined as a set of values and aspir-ations that consciously reject the exclusive geographies of the past (Delanty, 1995, 2005a; Amin 2004a; Levy, Pensky and Torpey, 2005; Beck and Grande, 2007; Heffernan, 2007: see also COSMOPOLITANISM).   MJH

Suggested reading
Amin (2004a); Heffernan (1998).

everyday life   A realm associated with ordin-ary, routine and repetitive aspects of social life that are pervasive and yet frequently overlooked and taken-for-granted. For many commenta-tors, the everyday is inherently ambiguous and indeterminate, something that is both every-where yet nowhere, familiar at the same time as it escapes (Blanchot, 1993 [1969]). The term 'everyday life' is often used to evoke the lived qualities of a range of activities such as cooking, eating, drinking, shopping, playing, walking, commuting, nurturing children, working for wages and so on, through which people experience and interact with the world and with others. Henri Lefebvre (1991b, p. 97) suggests that it may be defined negatively as ' "what is left over" after all distinct, superior, specialized, structured activities have been singled out by analysis'. Yet he insists that it is related to all activities as their common ground or bond, and he likens it to a 'fertile soil' that 'has a secret life and a richness of its own' (p. 87).

From the perspective of everyday life, 'geog-raphy is everywhere' (Cosgrove, 1989), its subject matter found in even the most seem-ingly ordinary streets, homes, malls, offices, factories, parks, playgrounds and the like. As a distinct formulation, 'everyday life' has been widely referenced and problematized in recent years within GEOGRAPHY and many of the social sciences and HUMANITIES, where it has been seen as offering an important perspective on social, cultural, political and economic

223

processes and practices, one whose provenance lies between STRUCTURALISM and PHENOMENOLOGY, and one that raises lived experience to the level of a critical concept (Kaplan and Ross, 1987). The subject crosses disciplinary boundaries and indeed brings them into question, as suggested by references to an emerging 'everyday life studies' (Highmore, 2002). It has also found prominence in recent arts and cultural practice. Important for understanding the spaces and places of everyday life have been theorists such as Walter Benjamin, Michel de Certeau and Lefebvre, whose belated translation into English has been a significant spur to Anglophone scholarship. But geographical interest in the subject is long-standing, and other significant approaches in recent decades are associated with HUMANISTIC GEOGRAPHY and FEMINIST GEOGRAPHY.

Recovering everyday geographical experiences against their erasure within SPATIAL SCIENCE concerned many humanistic geographers who, influenced by phenomenology and writings by Edmund Husserl and Maurice Merleau-Ponty, turned attention to the LIFEWORLD and to emotional and subjective encounters with and attachments to places, often privileging notions of HOME. In the process, they stressed the *work* involved in interpreting geographies of the everyday, including the need for self-REFLEXIVITY. But while humanistic geographers debated the necessity for philosophical rigour, with some preferring a looser constitutive phenomenology derived from Alfred Schutz to concentrate on how the lifeworlds of ordinary social groups are intersubjectively constituted in particular places, and with others distancing themselves from THEORY to embrace 'experience' as such, feminists and Marxists criticized their neglect of the POWER relations that structure everyday experiences of PLACES, including within the home, and hence their inability to advance deeper critiques of exploitation and oppression. It is with that in mind that many feminist geographers have focused on ordinary activities and repetitive social interactions, considering how they are bound into structures that discriminate against women and reinforce gender hierarchies (cf. STRUCTURATION THEORY).

According to Susan Hanson (1992), finding significance in the everyday is a core analytic tradition shared by FEMINISM and geography. She shows how this focus can undermine the common opposition between home and work, for example, by demonstrating their interconnections at the level of everyday lives and practices with important implications for understanding local LABOUR MARKETS and gender divisions of work in both. To bring daily activities into focus, many feminists have employed TIME-GEOGRAPHY, which was developed by Torsten Hägerstrand and colleagues at the University of Lund during the 1960s and 1970s, in a context in which ideas about everyday life had been central to Swedish welfare and urban planning. Plotting women's daily space–time paths enabled insights into the role of GENDER relations in the temporal and spatial structuring of social action, and hence into 'the reproduction of PATRIARCHY in the banal activities of everyday life' (Rose, 1993, p. 25). Gillian Rose nevertheless criticizes time-geography's universal depiction of space and its claim to exhaustiveness, which she depicts as MASCULINIST, along with its inability to address differential embodiment, emotion and passion. Her concerns relate to those frequently raised more generally about the appropriateness or otherwise of different ways of apprehending the everyday, the actuality of which always exceeds attempts at capture.

Feminist interest in the geographies of the everyday is also often connected with debates about SOCIAL REPRODUCTION, which for Cindi Katz (2004, p. x) is 'as much the fleshy, messy, and indeterminate stuff of everyday life as it is a set of structured practices that unfold in DIALECTICAL relation to production, with which it is mutually constitutive and in tension'. Yet she insists that social reproduction must be understood as a critical practice marked by the refusal to see the process as inevitable or natural, and by attentiveness to resilience as well as to possibilities of reworking, resistance and even revolution. In that sense, Katz likens it to Lefebvre's influential double-sided concept of everyday life, which he developed over many decades and which is central to his writings on URBANISM and the PRODUCTION OF SPACE. On the one hand, Lefebvre used the terms 'the everyday' and 'everydayness' critically as referring to the entry of daily life into MODERNITY, as he developed Marx's account of ALIENATION to address how everyday life has been colonized by the COMMODITY and the STATE through the imposition of an abstract space. But he also sought redemptive possibilities within the everyday, arguing that it harbours traces of more authentic living as well as the potential for radical change and for the production of other differential spaces. It is therefore a key terrain of struggle.

Challenges to characterizations of everyday life as self-evident, immutable and universal have also come through place-specific studies of changing everyday worlds and LANGUAGE under conditions of modernity that are attentive to multiple practices and power relations (Pred, 1990), and cross-cultural enquiries into everydayness and its conceptualization as a means of figuring cultural experiences of modernity and capitalist modernisation (Harootunian, 2000). Lefebvre's own critique needs situating within a French tradition of everyday life theorizing that developed especially during the 1960s and 1970s in the context of rapid MODERNIZATION and processes of decolonization, and that included de Certeau, Roland Barthes, Georges Perec and the SITU-ATIONISTS, as well as the surrealists before them. This tradition's influence is apparent in much current HUMAN GEOGRAPHY, where it has been taken up alongside phenomenological and feminist writings to inform studies of PRAC-TICE, PERFORMANCE and embodiment as well as narrative and rhythm in the construction of space and time (Simonsen, 2004; see also BODY). A concern with drawing out the extra-ordinary within the ordinary and what Lefebvre called 'the minor magic in everyday life' has also occupied many geographers, including those influenced by NON-REPRESENTATIONAL THEORY, who have sought new means of noticing the practical knowledge, skilled improvisation and intuition involved in 'the elusive, phantasmic, emergent and often only just there fabric of everyday life' (Thrift, 2000d, p. 407). While much work on everyday life has emphasized the resistant and subversive tactics of ordinary people, drawing especially on de Certeau (1984) in the process, some writers are seeking to re-evaluate repetition, habit, familiarity and the non-intentional aspects of the corporeal as demanding fuller attention in their own right. For others, it is the utopian impulse concerned not simply with describing everyday life but also with transforming it for the better that remains so compelling (see also UTOPIA).   DP

Suggested reading
Highmore (2002); Katz (2004); Lefebvre (2008 [1947, 1961, 1981]); Sheringham (2006).

evidence-based policy Evidence-based policy has been developed in reaction to interventions based on inertia, expediency, opinion, subjectivity and short-term political pressures. The term refers to an approach to policy development and implementation that uses rigorous techniques to develop and maintain a robust, high-quality, valid and reliable evidence base.

The approach began in HEALTH CARE (the term 'evidence-based medicine' first appeared in 1992) and has become a world-wide movement in the Cochrane Collaboration (http://www.cochrane.org/index0.htm), which aims to provide 'the reliable source of information in health care'. Particular emphasis is placed on randomized trials in which the recipient is randomized to the new intervention (cf. SAMPLING): the epidemiologist Archie Cochrane had famously argued that researchers should 'randomise until it hurts'. The approach has been extended into the social arena with the Campbell Collaboration (http://www.campbellcollaboration.org/), named after the distinguished social science methodologist Donald T. Campbell. This aims to answer the question 'What harms, what helps, based on what evidence?' and a Centre for Neighbourhood Research was created as part of the UK Network for Evidence-based Policy and Practice (http://www.evidencenetwork.org/).

The orthodox approach to evidence-based policy is based on a systematic review finding all the relevant studies including grey literature, weeding these for methodological flaws and inconsistencies, ranking the evidence so that the greatest reliance is placed on well-designed randomized trials, and then combining valid evidence quantitatively in a meta-analysis to provide the 'weight of evidence' supporting best practice. A heterodox view is provided by Ray Pawson (2006), who argues for what he terms 'realist synthesis' that stresses generative mechanisms and causal contingency, so that data analysis aims to find 'what works for whom in what circumstances' (cf. PRAGMATISM). Consequently, there is not a single 'best buy' for all situations, but a tailored, 'transferable theory' that works in these respects, for these subjects, in these kinds of contexts.   KJ

Suggested reading
Davies, Nutley and Smith (2000); Torgerson (2003).

exception, space of A topological SPACE produced when a SOVEREIGN POWER invokes the LAW in order to suspend the law. Its modern formulation is closely associated with right-wing political philosopher Carl Schmitt (1888–1985), who declared: 'Sovereign is he who decides the exception.' Italian political philosopher Giorgio Agamben radicalized Schmitt's work to argue that it is the act of deciding the exception that defines the sovereign: that this is the ground and origin of sovereign power (rather than vice versa) (Agamben, 1998). This crucial decision – in the original German sense of 'a cut in life' – is at once performative and paradoxical. It is PERFORMATIVE because it draws a boundary between politically qualified life and merely existent life wilfully exposed and abandoned to violence and death ('BARE LIFE') that has the most acutely material consequences. And it is paradoxical, and all forms of life are thereby made precarious, because the boundary is mobile and indistinct (cf. ZONE OF INDISTINCTION).

Agamben writes about both a 'state' of exception and a 'space' of exception, and his argument bears on SPATIALITY in at least three ways.

(1) Agamben uses Set Theory to argue that the exception – from the Latin *ex-capere*, which literally means that which is 'taken outside' – is a paradoxical spacing because it 'cannot be included in the whole of which it is a member and cannot be a member of the whole in which it is always already included' (1998, p. 25). This limit-figure must be captured topologically (see TOPOLOGY), he concludes, because only a twisted CARTOGRAPHY of POWER is capable of folding such propriety (the invocation of the law) into such perversity (the suspension of the law).

(2) Many analyses of the space of exception focus on enclosed sites (the Nazi concentration camp at Auschwitz, IMMIGRATION and REFUGEE detention centres, and the US war prison at Guantánamo Bay, Cuba: see, e.g., Gregory, 2006b) or territorialized configurations of power (the shattered fragments of occupied Palestine: see, e.g., Gregory, 2004b), but by their very nature, spaces of exception may be much more indeterminate than these exemplary spatial formations imply.

(3) The state of exception is typically associated with the declaration of a national emergency and the imposition of martial law by a STATE, and Agamben argues that the growth of a national security state and the intensification of its sovereign powers through the GLOBALIZATION of the 'war on terror' has turned the state of exception into a new PARADIGM of late modern government (Agamben, 2005, pp. 1–31: cf. GOVERNMENTALITY). But these *national* framings are also affected by *transnational* GEOPOLITICS and geo-economics, and by *international* law (Gregory, 2007). **DG**

Suggested reading
Gregory (2006b); Mbembe (2003); Pratt (2005).

exceptionalism The view that 'geography is quite different from all the other sciences, methodologically unique' (Schaefer, 1953, p. 231). The term was coined by Fred K. Schaefer to disparage this, the dominant conception of American GEOGRAPHY codified by Hartshorne (1939) in his enormously influential prospectus for *The nature of geography*. Instead, Schaefer argued that geography was just like every other science, sharing a methodology based on identifying and mobilizing universal laws (see LAW, SCIENTIFIC).

Hartshorne's position was based on the writings of nineteenth- and early twentieth-century German geographers. They did not merely influence Hartshorne's interpretation: they were his interpretation. The nature of geography was determined 'in light of the past'. That past, or at least the past on which Hartshorne drew, was strongly influenced by neo-KANTIANISM that separated geography and history from other sciences because they were concerned with the unique and non-repeatable. Geography and history, Hartshorne argued, were IDEO-GRAPHIC, not NOMOTHETIC. While geography was a SCIENCE, in that it provided 'organized, objective knowledge' (Hartshorne 1939, p. 130), the geographical units in which facts were organized, of which the most important were REGIONS, were unique and non-repeatable. Geography was 'the study of areal differentiation' and was 'most clearly expressed in REGIONAL GEOGRAPHY' (Hartshorne, 1939, p. 468). Methodologically, what followed – and marked geography as exceptionalist in Schaefer's sense – was an inability to deploy scientific laws, because laws were predicated on generalization and repetition of phenomena. Hartshorne (1939, p. 446) wrote, 'We arrive, therefore, at a conclusion similar to that which Kroeber has stated for history: "the uniqueness of all historical phenomena. ... No laws or near laws are discovered." The same conclusion applies to the particular combination of phenomena at a particular place.' Geographers, therefore, were not able scientifically to explain, or predict or knowingly intervene, but only describe: 'Regional geography, we conclude, is literally what its title expresses: ... [I]t is essentially a descriptive science concerned with the description and interpretation of unique cases ...' (Hartshorne, 1939, p. 449).

In contrast, Schaefer, who was an economist and statistician before and during the Second

World War, and influenced during his tenure at the University of Iowa by the LOGICAL POSITIVIST and former Vienna Circle member, Gustav Bergmann, believed in the unity of science, and a single, common scientific methodology resting on law-based explanation. In his contrary view, geography was not exceptionalist, but a chip off a uniform scientific block: to explain phenomena within or beyond geography 'means always to recognize them as instances of laws' (Schaefer, 1953, p. 227). Schaefer argued that geography should pay particular attention to morphological laws taking the form, 'If geographical pattern (morphology) A, then geographical pattern (morphology) B' (see MORPHOLOGY).

In his reply, Hartshorne (1955) pulverized Schaefer, even though Schaefer had been dead for two years. While Hartshorne (necessarily) won that battle, Schaefer won the war, as HUMAN GEOGRAPHY increasingly rejected exceptionalism, first during the formalization of SPATIAL SCIENCE during the QUANTITATIVE REVOLUTION and later through its embrace of SOCIAL THEORY. Geography was to be ordinary, not exceptional.   TB

Suggested reading
Barnes and Farish (2006).

exchange As an activity, exchange has played a more or less critical role in virtually all societies. It has allowed them to exceed the constraints of subsistence, intensify production and diversify patterns of CONSUMPTION (although by no means equitably), form social alliances and spatial networks of association, organize and reproduce social hierarchies by expanding the reservoir of material surpluses, and generate new layers of social COMMUNICATION through the symbolic dimensions of exchange. Exchange is a precursor to commerce and therefore to a MARKET economy involving transactions of goods and services between buyers and sellers (see CAPITALISM). Hence the central claim of Adam Smith's influential 1776 treatise, *The wealth of nations* – that a growing social DIVISION OF LABOUR and specialized production of goods generates economic prosperity without causing society itself to disintegrate – is premised on the possibility of ubiquitous exchange; in other words, markets. But this is hardly a given. Some things (use-values) may never enter the realm of exchange, because society considers it profane to sell them. Additionally, some exchanges may remain individualized and sporadic, and not result in a market (new INSTITUTIONAL ECONOMICS has shown, for example, how prohibitive TRANSACTIONS COSTS can hinder individualized exchange from expanding into a market). Contrarily, exchange may not occur as a COMMODITY transaction, or it may occur, as in situations of barter, as a commodity transaction not mediated by the money-form. Finally, the good or service purveyed may take the social form of a gift, with or without expectation of reciprocity. The writings of the Hungarian anthropologist Karl Polanyi (1972) are particularly illuminating in these matters.

Wherever reciprocity is assumed or implied – commercial, barter or gift – there is the further issue of value. In one sense, the issue is straightforward: it seems reasonable to assume that in a dyadic transaction where individuals A and B exchange a good or service, they do so because A has something B wants and vice versa. In short, both A and B have something that the other *values*. At least two complications arise here. First, there can be no presumption of a transaction of equivalent value without reference to a third, transcendent standard or measure – whether this takes the guise of: (a) a subjective marginal utility principle (hence A and B transact if at least one of them is better off from the transaction in terms of marginal utility and neither is worse off – the so-called Pareto principle of NEO-CLASSICAL ECONOMICS); or (b) a principle of equilibration of labour time (A and B transact goods containing equal amounts of socially necessary labour time – the historically grounded Marxist scenario of non-exploitation: see LABOUR THEORY OF VALUE; MARXIAN ECONOMICS).

This already hints at the second complication; namely, that exchange can occur despite the absence of equivalence because of the unequal circumstances of transactors. Take the case of distress sales of crop in a drought year by a cash-strapped farmer. Given the choice between not selling and starving and selling at a loss, the second option is Pareto-superior in terms of marginal utility for both the farmer who sells and the merchant who buys. But it appears to pervert any notion of equivalence. Similarly, take two other examples: the unemployed person who sells plasma to a for-profit corporation or the runaway boy who performs sexual favours in return for money. It is possible to argue in either instance (and economists do) that the transactors are better off in terms of their respective marginal utilities (in the corporation's case, its marginal utility of profit) – but only, it seems, by compromising on a notion of equivalence that enjoins some sense of symmetry. In short, the

227

mediation that is required to explain why exchange occurs yields equivocal answers: all we can categorically say is that finite availability of a thing in TIME and SPACE and actual or anticipated social use-value are general underlying conditions for exchange.

Gifts are a subset of exchange. They involve neither mediation by money nor barter. But like these more conventional forms of transactions, they supply individuals with incentives to collaborate in a pattern of exchanges that performatively reproduce society and validate the status of participants as social beings. In *The gift: the form and reason for exchange in archaic societies* (1990 [1925]), the French scholar Marcel Mauss built on the ideas of Emile Durkheim to show how gifts function as a mechanism by which individual interests combine to make a social SYSTEM – a 'gift economy' – in the absence of market exchange. Because the gift is embedded in the economic, moral, religious, political and aesthetic dimensions, Mauss termed it a 'Total social phenomenon'. Mauss' essay has been extended in generative ways by social anthropologists such as Claude Lévi-Strauss, Mary Douglas, Pierre Bourdieu and Marilyn Strathern in their efforts to identify non-market logics that cement SOCIETY. It goes without saying that the gift economy, far from being an archaic social mechanism, remains a constitutive force in contemporary market societies.   VG

Suggested reading
Appadurai (1986); Bourdieu (1990); Davis (1992); Mauss (1990 [1925]); Polanyi (1972).

exclave A small piece of a STATE that is physically separate from its main territorial body but remains within its political jurisdiction despite being surrounded by the TERRITORY of another state. Robinson (1959) identified five exclave types by degree of separation from the HOMELAND: *normal*, as per the definition above; *pene-*, territories barely connected to the main state in such a way that access must occur via another state's territory; *quasi-*, technically disconnected but connected in practical terms; *temporary*, as the result of an armistice; and *virtual*, areas treated as exclaves without meeting the strict legal definition. (See also ENCLAVE.)   CF

Suggested reading
Aalto (2002); Robinson (1959).

existentialism A PHILOSOPHY that flourished in the middle to late twentieth century as a radical defence of human freedom. It emerged partly in reaction to TELEOLOGICAL and deterministic theories of human nature that saw human beings as determined by their biology, by the environments in which they found themselves, or by their social status or economic position. It also emerged in direct response to the racialized ideologies and GEOPOLITICS of a colonial (see COLONIALISM) and COLD WAR world. Against notions of human subjects, peoples and CULTURES determined by their 'nature', constrained by their 'essence' or being the mere 'bearers' of their class functions, existentialism argued that human beings were free subjects, whose existence defined who and what they were. For Heidegger (1962 [1927]), the 'essence' of this finite SUBJECT, this 'being-in-the-world', was that it was thrown into a world not of its own making and radically oriented to this world through projects, mood, will and other dispositions. The ONTOLOGY of finitude was, for the existential subject, a life to be lived, with 'no-exit' but death and along the way a profound anxiety and, at times, dread in the face of the individual's immense responsibility for his or her own life.

Existentialism emerged in HUMAN GEOGRAPHY in the 1970s, as part of a desire to refocus geographical enquiry away from the reductive abstractions of SPATIAL ANALYSIS and structural MARXISM. It focused on the capacities of HUMAN AGENCY, and in so doing sought to be a corrective to the overly essentialist arguments of much CULTURAL and HISTORICAL GEOGRAPHY (see ESSENTIALISM), to the structural arguments of POLITICAL ECONOMY and to the abstractions of SPATIAL SCIENCE. It focused on how human beings at once live in and make the SPACES, PLACES and LANDSCAPES that they inhabit (Samuels, 1978, 1981). Far from being an abstract science of spatial relations, existential geographies were concrete descriptions of everyday LIFEWORLDS, and were engaged with the ETHICS and VALUES of what human beings understand to be the meaning of their lives and worlds (Entrikin, 1976; Tuan, 1976b; Relph, 1981, pp. 187–91).

Radical geographers have been sceptical of existentialism, tending to see it as overly focused on the subjective experiences of individuals; a kind of IDEALISM that treated lived experience (with its anxieties and feelings of loss, uncertainty or dread) as indicative of a universal condition of existence instead of a concrete situation produced by a historical and oppressive SOCIETY. In Marcuse's (1972, p. 161) view, by hypothesizing determinate historical conditions of human existence as ontological and metaphysical characteristics, existentialism became part of the IDEOLOGY it attacked: its radicalism was illusory (cf. CRITICAL THEORY). JPi

exit, voice and loyalty A theory of consumer influence on the quality of PUBLIC GOODS developed by Hirschman (1970), who argued that service quality is likely to be lower in monopoly conditions than in situations where consumers have a choice. With the latter, the following options are available to consumers who consider a service either inefficient or ineffective:

- *exit* – consumers transfer to an alternative supplier;
- *voice* – consumers complain about the service, threatening exit if they are not satisfied with the response; or
- *loyalty* – consumers remain with their current supplier, without either exercising voice or threatening exit.

The higher the (exit) costs of switching suppliers, the lower the potential impact of voice, because suppliers can assume loyalty; under monopolies, voice need have little impact on service quality. Although individual voice may be ineffective, however, collective voice through organized pressure groups may have more POWER over suppliers; such power may be unequally distributed, however, with wealthier people better able to mobilize support and sustain their cause.

Hirschman's ideas have been developed by governments in recent decades by one or more of: PRIVATIZATION policies, placing former PUBLIC SERVICES in the private sector, believing that competition will lead to improved quality; creating quasi-MARKETS within public services (among health care providers, for example), with the same general expectation; or by promoting choice, through providing information (as in school performance league tables), which consumers can use in considering exit strategies. (See also NEO-LIBERALISM; PUBLIC–PRIVATE PARTNERSHIPS; TIEBOUT MODEL.) RJ

exopolis A new city located beyond existing urban forms (see EDGE CITY). Soja (1996a) defines it as representing a new form of URBANISM. The exopolis turns 'the city inside-out and outside-in at the same time', he suggests (p. 239). In this conception, functions formerly associated with CENTRAL BUSINESS DISTRICTS and commuter SUBURBS are not merely transposed, but their character and relationships are reconfigured. 'Exopolis' and 'edge city' are terms that indicate attempts to understand cities beyond the traditional framework of the CHICAGO SCHOOL (cf. LOS ANGELES SCHOOL) and to analyse urban processes at the city-regional scale (Brenner, 2002). EM

Suggested reading
Soja (1996).

explanation A statement that identifies the essential reasons for the occurrence of a given event or phenomena. Reasons can be physical causes, mental states, contextual circumstances or even beneficial consequences. For each of these different kinds of reasons to count as an explanation, they must be linked to the event or phenomena by set of general rules (and at the extreme by universal laws). For example, to explain why my copy of the *Dictionary of human geography* just fell off the desk, I must connect that specific event to a wider set of laws governing motion and gravity. Once the reasons behind the occurrence of a phenomenon or event are determined, the world is revealed as it really is. As Pierre Duhem (1962 [1906], p. 19) put it: 'To explain is to strip the reality of the appearances covering it like a veil, in order to see the bare reality itself.'

Geographers have been trying to discern 'bare reality' ever since the nineteenth century, when the discipline was first institutionalized. ENVIRONMENTAL DETERMINISM was initially a favoured explanatory form in which variations in CLIMATE were posited as the reason for geographical variation in human behaviour, beliefs and institutions. Discussions of explanation *as an idea*, however, did not emerge until the QUANTITATIVE REVOLUTION in the 1960s. In contrast to those who insisted that GEOGRAPHY, like history, had to be conducted under the sign of EXCEPTIONALISM, the proponents of SPATIAL SCIENCE insisted that their 'new' geography was a science like any other, and thus had to meet the strictures of scientific explanation established by PHILOSOPHY. Those strictures were originally formalized by Hempel and Oppenheim in 1948, and known as the *Deductive–Nomological (D–N) model*. Scientific explanation rested on applying a deductive syllogism to a combination of general LAWS and initial empirical conditions. For example, explaining why the *Dictionary* just fell off my desk would involve linking by means of a deductive syllogism the particularities of that event to a scientific law (e.g. the law of gravity).

Within the PHILOSOPHY of SCIENCE, the D–N model provoked, and continues to provoke, significant discussion, an there have been several refinements and alternatives (Salmon, 1990). Harvey (1969) made the D–N model the gold standard for explanation in geography, but even at the time he recognized that few geographical events could be located within such a stringent framework, given the absence of geographical laws on which explanation would have to depend. By the late 1970s there was a movement away from the D–N model of explanation. Geographers were still concerned to explain events and phenomena, but they cast around for less narrowly conceived approaches, ones that recognized that the discipline centred on specific and contingent CASE STUDIES rather than a larger statistical universe of events. For many human geographers in the 1980s the philosophy of REALISM, with its conceptual vocabulary of causal powers and liabilities, and contingent and necessary relations, offered a consistent explanatory framework couched in terms of causation and contingency. While realism is still in use, there is a sense that even its definition of explanation remains too closely defined by a natural scientific sensibility. Consequently, it is inappropriate for those forms of human geography that draw upon interpretive, non-ESSENTIALIST and even NON-REPRESENTATIONAL THEORY. The task is to re-conceive explanation in a form appropriate to HUMAN GEOGRAPHY's new guise.   TB

Suggested reading
Harvey (1969).

exploration At its basic level, exploration is usually taken to refer to the growth of knowledge of the GLOBE that resulted from various voyages of discovery and scientific expeditions. But the very vocabulary of *discovery* and *exploration* is contested by revisionists, who query its appropriateness in contexts where it is more morally responsible to speak of *invasion, conquest* or *occupation*. The reason is that these labels unmask the pretended innocence and ethical neutrality that the standard scientific-sounding idioms convey (see ETHICS).

Whatever the allocation of moral accountability, there can be no doubting the significance of what Driver (2001) calls the 'cultures of exploration' on the scientific enterprise in general and the development of geography in particular (see also GEOGRAPHY, HISTORY OF). Traditional chroniclers of these exploits have tended towards a progressivist interpretation of scientific knowledge, cartographic history

and global awareness (Baker, 1931). The vast maritime expeditions of Chêng Ho from 1405 to 1433, for example, have been commended for their contributions to Chinese marine CARTOGRAPHY and descriptive geography, although, in contrast to later voyages, the purpose of the mission was neither the garnering of 'scientific' information nor commercial conquest (Chang, 1971). Similarly, the writings of Ibn Battuta during the late Middle Ages have been read as an encyclopaedic conspectus of the Islamic world (Boorstin, 1983).

It is, however, with the European voyages of Reconnaissance during the fifteenth and sixteenth centuries that putative connections between scientific 'progress' and geographical 'exploration' begin to be more closely associated (see also SCIENCE; TRAVEL-WRITING). Writers such as Hale (1967), Parry (1981) and O'Sullivan (1984) suggest that the first scientific laboratory was the world itself and that 'the voyages of discovery' were in a fundamental sense experiments to test the validity of Renaissance geographical concepts. In such scenarios, the names of Bartholomew Dias, Vasco da Gama, Christopher Columbus, Ferdinand Magellan and, perhaps most of all, 'Prince Henry the Navigator' assume heroic status.

Indeed, the reciprocal links between voyages of exploration and scientific enterprises were deep and lasting. Francis Bacon reflected in his *Novum organum* of 1620 (§ lxxxiv) that the opening up of the geographical world through such expeditions foreshadowed the expansion of the 'boundaries of the intellectual globe" beyond the confines of 'the narrow discoveries of the ancients'. Support for this interpretation has come from those attaching crucial significance to the Portuguese encouragement of navigational science and mathematical practice through the work of the Jewish map- and instrument-maker Mestre Jacome. This Jewish tradition of Mallorcan cartography, instrumentation and nautical science was perpetuated by Abraham Zacuto and Joseph Vizinho, while Francesco Faleiro, Garcia da Orta and Pedro Nuñes did much to further medicinal botany, cartography and natural history during the first half of the sixteenth century (Goodman, 1991). Such accomplishments have been canvassed to substantiate the claim that this *Jewish* style of sixteenth-century Portuguese science provided the catalyst for 'the emergence of modern science in Western Europe' (Hooykaas, 1979; Banes, 1988, p. 58).

Nevertheless, even partisan commentators concede that the scientific advances of the

'Age of Discovery' were by-products of commercial, evangelistic and colonial motives. Ostensibly more scientific were the Pacific exploits of Enlightenment figures such as Louis Antoine de Bougainville, James Cook, Joseph Banks, the Forsters, Jean François de la Pérouse and George Vancouver (Beaglehole, 1966). And yet with them too political factors loomed as large as scientific ones: pre-voyage briefings on settlement possibility, RESOURCE inventory and the staking of colonial claims all revealed the strategic significance of everything from cartographic survey to ethnographic illustration (Frost, 1988). Still, the scientific achievements were substantial – Cook, for instance, took with him astronomers, surgeons and naturalists, and successfully completed an accurate recording of the transit of Venus. Precisely the same was true of later explorations in South America and Central Africa. Alexander von Humboldt and Aimé Bonpland, for example, used their South American findings at the turn of the nineteenth century to break the bonds of the static taxonomic system of Linnaeus, and ultimately to create a distinctive mode of scientific investigation – what Cannon labelled 'Humboldtian science' – in which 'the accurate, measured study of widespread but interconnected real phenomena' was interrogated 'in order to find a definite law and a dynamic cause' (Cannon, 1978, p. 105; cf. Dettelbach, 1996). Again, Roderick Murchison, who has been dubbed England's scientist of EMPIRE, virtually orchestrated the British colonial assault on Central Africa in the Victorian period through his oversight of the Royal Geographical Society, and used a variety of explorers to test his own geological theories there (Stafford, 1989).

There is not space here to delineate in any detail the scientific contributions of a host of other exploratory ventures: the Napoleonic survey of Egypt, Baudin's deadly mission to 'New Holland', the succession of Russian voyages into the Pacific by Krusentern, Kotzebue and Lütke, the Royal Geographical Society's efforts to reduce the Australian outback to cartographic enclosure, Lewis and Clark's western territorial expedition, Darwin's *Beagle* circumnavigation, the United States Exploring Expedition under Charles Wilkes, the voyage of T.H. Huxley on *The Rattlesnake*, a variety of late Victorian ventures to West Africa, A.R. Wallace's sojourn in Borneo, the oceanographic survey of *The Challenger*, and expeditions to the poles in the early decades of the twentieth century, to name but a very few. Chief among their scientific achievements were the discovery of numerous unknown species of plants and ANIMALS, new theories of organic dispersal, novel interpretations of human cultures, the mapping of fossils and strata on a global scale, cartographic intensification and advances in astronomical observation. The power of this scientific legacy is so engrained in the discipline's collective memory that various expeditionary ventures continue to receive the sponsorship of institutions such as the Royal Geographical Society and the National Geographic Society, and to provide a language in which to speak of geographical excursions into other threatening environments, such as urban ethnic 'no-go' areas.

The acquisition of scientific knowledge by explorers was a multifaceted enterprise and raised critical epistemological questions that have persisted up to the present day (see EPISTEMOLOGY), not least in settings where expeditionary SPACE is itself experimental space (Powell, 2007). The accumulation of scientific knowledge required careful management. First, the crying need to discipline distant observers in the effort to standardize their findings found expression in works such as the Admiralty's 1832 *Hints for collecting animals and their products*, Richard Owen's *Directions for collecting and preserving animals* (1835) and later the RGS's *Hints to travellers* (1854). Works of this stripe continued a long-standing tradition that included John Woodward's *Brief instructions for making observations in all parts of the world* (1696). The production of manuals such as these was part of an exercise in what might be called the geography of TRUST; namely, how to ensure observational reliability and disciplined data-gathering (Carey, 1997, 2006). Second, the scientific knowledge gleaned from explorations involved not only the assemblage and movement of objects, both natural and cultural, around the world, but their reconceptualization and reclassification according to some prevailing norm or taste (Thomas, 1991; Dritsas, 2005; Hill, 2006a, b). Third, the transformation of local data into universal knowledge that was critical to exploration science involved metrological standardization and thus the production and calibration of precision instruments (see INSTRUMENTATION).

The significance of expeditionary exploits, however, cannot be restricted to matters of cognitive 'progress'. And merely stating that the growth of these scientific knowledges was situated within the framework of IMPERIALISM is to pay scant attention to a whole suite of issues to do with the construction of Western identity, the representations of 'exoticism', the inscription of 'otherness', the reciprocal constitution of scientific DISCOURSE and colonial praxis (see COLONIALISM) and the DECONSTRUCTION of cartographic ICONOGRAPHY.

CULTURES of exploration were thus woven with political, artistic and literary, as well as scientific, threads. It was, for example, as a consequence of the European Age of Exploration/Reconnaissance/Conquest that the idea of the 'WEST' and 'Western-ness' received its baptism. EUROPE's sense of distinctiveness from the regions that the navigators encountered was embedded in a discourse about identity that represented 'the West' and 'the Rest' in the categories of superiority–inferiority, power–impotence, enlightenment–ignorance and civilization–barbarism (Hall, 1992b). Seen in these terms, Europe's rendezvous with the New World in the fifteenth and sixteenth centuries was as much a moral event as a commercial or intellectual one, and induced a sense of 'metaphysical unease' because it confounded standard conceptions of human nature (see also Pagden, 1993).

The construction of this 'discourse of the West', of course, depended crucially on the idioms in which the new worlds were represented. The categories, vocabularies, assumptions and instruments that the explorers brought to the encounter were, understandably, thoroughly European, and so the worlds of 'the other' were interrogated, classified and assimilated according to European norms. That the language of the engagement was frequently gendered, moreover, facilitated the representation of new LANDSCAPES in the exotic categories of a potent sexual imagery intended to indicate mastery and submissiveness.

If the foundations of Western discourse were laid during the fifteenth and sixteenth centuries, they were reinforced during the following centuries when EUROCENTRIC modes of REPRESENTATION continued to constitute regional identities. One such construction was what Edward Said termed 'ORIENTALISM' – a discursive formation through which 'European culture was able to manage—and even produce—the Orient politically, sociologically, militarily, ideologically, scientifically and imaginatively' (Said, 1978, p. 3). And, indeed, the idea of the Oriental or Asiatic type certainly gripped Western imaginations. In nineteenth-century Britain, for example, what was termed 'oriental vice' in the very heart of England – 'heathenism in the inner radius' as it was

called – expressed anxieties about the moral authority of Christian England (Lindeborg, 1994).

The procedures facilitating the marginalization of the Oriental realm, and – at the same time – its critical role in European self-definition, were also perpetuated in other places and in other terms. The variety of representational devices that Cook and his coterie of naturalists and draughtsmen deployed – whether Banks' abstract taxonomics or Parkinson's evocation of anthropological variety – succeeded in encapsulating the Pacific world within the confines of European epistemologies. Moreover, their penchant for designating names – the naming of places (see PLACE NAMES), peoples and individuals – at once invented, brought into cultural circulation and domesticated the very entities that were the subjects of their enquiries (Carter, 1987). That Cook's team was engaged in what Salmond (1991, p. 15) terms 'mirror-image ETHNOGRAPHY' is beyond dispute. But just because their modes of categorization were suffused with the expectations of eighteenth-century society should not be permitted to gainsay the remarkable accuracy of their accounts of physical phenomena.

The CULTURAL POLITICS embedded in these various ventures were further reinforced by the artistic and literary crafts of Western exploration. The evocation of distant peoples and places owed much to the supposedly realist works of visual ART produced by painters such as Jean-Léon Gérôme (Nochlin, 1991). Indeed, the standard scholarly practices of science, history and comparative literature were themselves profoundly indebted to artistic representation (Smith, 1960; Stafford, 1984). In the tropical world, for example, travelling artists such as William Hodges and Johann Rugendas gave visual form to the changing discourse of TROPICALITY in which scientific observation and aesthetic preference reinforced one another (Driver and Martins, 2005). In similar vein, the use of photographic technology to 'capture' distant sites and sights, served no less to constitute than to represent imperial subjects and spaces (Ryan, 1997). At the same time, overseas escapades provided writers of fiction with resources to stimulate readers' imaginations. In some cases, this took the form of adventure stories that fostered new senses of heroic masculinity and projected European fantasies onto non-European worlds (Phillips, 1997). In others, evocations of faraway realms were shaped by UTOPIAN or dystopian literary tropes, which were deployed by writers not only to imagine foreigners but to re-imagine themselves (Fulford, Lee and Kitson, 2004).

Evocations such as these contributed massively to the generation of global IMAGINATIVE GEOGRAPHIES (Gregory, 1994). Thus the AMERICAS, in one way or another, were constructed according to European predilections (Harley, 1990; Mason, 1990; Greenblatt, 1991); later, the Pacific was re-composed as a coherent geographical entity (MacLeod and Rehbock, 1994) – as was 'darkest AFRICA' (Brantlinger, 1985) – as these toponymic labels were brought into cultural currency. The same can also be said of the tropical world – a conceptual space that came into being courtesy of the conjoined forces of geographical exploration, colonial administration and tropical medicine (Arnold, 1996b; Livingstone, 1999; Stepan, 2001). Moreover, exploration and exhibition frequently went hand in hand, as in the case of Egypt, which found its people and places enframed, ordered and exhibited to suit European curiosity (Mitchell, 1988).

Space does not permit further elucidation of such motifs in other regions. Suffice to note that in the African context, according to the Comaroffs (1991, p. 313), European colonization 'was often less a directly coercive conquest than a persuasive attempt to colonize consciousness, to remake people by redefining the taken-for-granted surfaces of their everyday worlds'. Yet here too the temptation towards 'monolithizing' the encounter must be resisted: the moral significance of African environments became a source of endless debate about the effects of a tropical CLIMATE on white constitution and the connections between black racial character, biological make-up and PHYSICAL GEOGRAPHY (Livingstone, 1991). In South America, it was Humboldt's 'interweaving of visual and emotive language' that contributed so powerfully towards what Pratt (1992) calls the 'ideological reinvention' of 'América' – a re-imagining so vivid and so vital that Humboldt's writings provided founding visions for *both* the older elites of northern Europe *and* the newer independent elites of Spanish America.

If these machinations, however tangled their genealogies, satisfied a European sense of superiority through constituting the peripheral regions of the globe in its own terms, those self-same arenas were soon to become pivotal laboratories for scrutiny into human prehistory. In this way, the threat that resided in 'alien' human natures could be rendered benign if those RACES turned out to be the persistent remnants of earlier phases in the story of human evolution. Just as earlier Scottish and French ENLIGHTENMENT thinkers, such as Smith, Ferguson and Buffon, regularly crafted their image of the bestial or noble savage into evolutionary schemes depicting a transition from barbarism to CIVILIZATION, so early-twentieth-century students of human archaeology used 'the peoples defined as living at the uttermost ends of the imperial world as examples of living prehistory' (Gamble, 1992, p. 713: see also PRIMITIVISM). Thereby their identities remained engulfed within the imperatives of Western scientific scrutiny. They also remained subordinated in the cartographic representations that invariably accompanied the exploratory process. Whether in their use as military tools, in their advocacy of colonial promotion, in their marginal decorations, in their systems of hierarchical classification or in their imposition of a regulative geometry that bore little reference to indigenous peoples, maps became the conductors of imperial power and Western ideology (see CARTOGRAPHY, HISTORY OF).

Imperial readings of exploration, however, can serve to obscure as much as they reveal when presented with monolithic tenacity. Treating ETHNICITY as simply the invention of missionary activity, colonial officialdom or early anthropology, for example, is insufficiently flexible to take the measure of exploration encounters. Such scenarios are not sufficiently subtle to discern the complex role of the missionary movement – to take one activity too easily typecast as the servant of cultural imperialism – in emerging senses of nationhood. Thus we are only beginning to appreciate how, in the African context, a missionary passion to render indigenous languages into written form (for the purpose of Bible translation) provided mother tongue cultures with a vernacular literacy that in turn cultivated nascent senses of nationhood. Through translation, written languages were created and a vocabulary for national self-consciousness fostered (see Sanneh, 1990; Hastings, 1997).

The history and geography of 'exploration', then, turns out to be far from antiquarian chronology. Rather, it focuses centrally on the IDENTITY of people, the wielding of power and the construction of knowledge; and it is precisely because these are entangled in such complex and intricate ways that their elucidation is of crucial importance to the future course of human history. DNL

233

Suggested reading
Ballantyne (2004); Burnett (2000); Driver (2001a);
Fernandez-Armesto (2006).

exploratory data analysis (EDA)   An attitude to QUANTITATIVE METHODS that encourages and licences a 'trial-and-error' approach. The term was popularized by the statistician John Tukey, who recognized two approaches to data analysis. Exploratory approaches uncover patterns and anomalies in the data – he likened this to numerical detective work whereby evidence is gathered. CONFIRMATORY DATA ANALYSIS, in contrast, equates to SIGNIFI-CANCE TESTING and probabilistic inference, as in a trial where evidence is put in a formal manner and a judicial decision made 'beyond reasonable doubt'. The exploratory approach is based on the notion that 'better a good answer to a vague question than a precise answer to the wrong one' and that 'by assuming less you learn more'. It has encouraged the use and development of smoothing proced-ures that reveal patterns in data, of diagnostic, often graphical, tools for exposing where assumptions are not met, and of procedures that are robust/resistant to anomalies (out-liers) in data. Johnston (1986a, ch. 6) argues that such data analysis should be an integral part of a non-POSITIVIST, REALIST approach to doing geography. Exploratory spatial data analysis (ESDA) extends EDA to detect spatial properties of data.   KJ

Suggested reading
Cox and Jones (1981); Haining, Wise and Ma (1998).

export processing zone (EPZ)   A geograph-ically delimited TERRITORY providing special facilities for foreign branch plants, using imported inputs to manufacture commodities for export. Plants locating within the territory are subsidized with some combination of infrastructure, tax advantages, relaxed labour regulations, and eased imports and exports. EPZs provide incentives to attract foreign investment to low-wage countries, but also high-wage countries (there are 300 in the USA). EPZs typically locate near the periph-ery of countries, reinforcing external orienta-tion. Workers are predominantly women in non-skilled jobs, often under draconian labour relations. Since the first EPZ in Ireland in 1956, there has been an explosion since the mid-1970s to over 5,000 zones, with employ-ment exceeding 40 million, in more than 100 countries.   ES

extensive research   Research strategies directed towards discovering common proper-ties and empirical regularities and making gen-eralizations about them. Sayer (1992 [1984]) argued that extensive research is typically con-ducted under the signs of EMPIRICISM or POSI-TIVISM and relies on QUANTITATIVE METHODS, including descriptive and inferential statistics and numerical analysis, and on QUESTION-NAIRES and formal INTERVIEWS. As such, it is concerned with 'representative' studies or samples and privileges a logic of replication: Can the results of the study be repeated? Sayer regarded extensive research as weaker than INTENSIVE RESEARCH, which is typically con-ducted under the sign of REALISM, because it elucidates *formal* relations of similarity or correlation rather than *causal* or *structural* relations.   DG

external economies   Closely related to the concept of EXTERNALITIES, external economies are economic benefits that derive from sources outside an organization, such as a firm. These benefits, which can include the contributions of specialist suppliers, subcontractors or skilled workers hired from the local LABOUR MARKET, accrue to individual companies even though they are generated elsewhere. In cases where they are not available, companies must bear the costs of producing them internally.

The benefits of external economies are often captured locally, declining with distance. An early formulation of this argument came in the shape of the GROWTH POLE theory developed by the French economist François Perroux in the late 1940s (see Darwent, 1969), which was influential in REGIONAL POLICY debates in the 1960s and 1970s. Growth poles were geo-graphical concentrations of economic activity, often dominated by a single industry or a closely related group of industries, in which local firms yielded the economic benefits (or positive externalities) of co-location with other firms. In this context, the growth of individual firms might stimulate business amongst sup-pliers (through so-called backward LINKAGES) and/or amongst users of outputs or services (through forward linkages). Driven by propul-sive industries, successful growth poles are characterized by mutually beneficial, cumula-tive economic growth. These arguments recall Alfred Marshall's account of 'INDUSTRIAL DIS-TRICTS' in nineteenth-century England: in Sheffield's cutlery quarter, for example, firms clustered together to capture benefits of shared access to critical factors of production such as skilled labour and technical knowledge that circulated, Marshall observed, as if 'in the air' (see Krugman, 1991).

These arguments have been vigorously rejoined in recent years in discussions of industrial CLUSTERS, AGGLOMERATION economies, and FLEXIBLE ACCUMULATION. Allen Scott (1988b), for example, has argued that the tendency towards vertical disintegration – in which firms increasingly turn to the market to supply key inputs and services, rather than organizing these internally – is a defining characteristic of the contemporary form of POST-FORDIST capitalism. As firms become increasingly reliant on external inputs, the competitive imperative of minimizing TRANSACTION COSTS induces geographical clustering, which in turn accounts for the continuing significance of localized centres of production such as Hollywood and the City of London, even in highly globalized industries such as movie production and finance. Likewise, Storper and Walker (1989) contend that the process of capitalist INDUSTRIALIZATION is increasingly driven by external ECONOMIES OF SCALE and ECONOMIES OF SCOPE which in the contemporary phase of growth accrue to entire industries rather than just individual firms. In this analysis, technological INNOVATION (such as the development of integrated circuits or the INTERNET) assumes the character of a *shared* resource, with spillover benefits for the economy as a whole. In contemporary INDUSTRIAL DISTRICTS, such as the Emilia-Romagna region of Italy, it is also argued that even rival firms reap external economies from a climate of TRUST and reciprocity, resulting in collaborative initiatives in areas such as training, design, marketing and research. These are what Michael Storper (1997b) calls 'untraded interdependencies', which are increasingly salient in the contemporary era of vertically disintegrated, flexible CAPITALISM. JPe

Suggested reading
Scott and Storper (2003).

externalities Costs or benefits borne by an individual not directly involved in the activity; or, in broader terms, the social or environmental consequences of private choices. *Positive externalities* (sometimes known as EXTERNAL ECONOMIES) represent benefits accruing to third parties; for example, those arising from a bee-keeper located next to an apple orchard, or a group of residents living near to high-quality local schools. *Negative externalities* (which are also known as external diseconomies) refer to the downstream costs of choices or activities for third parties, the classic illustration of which is POLLUTION. This is a key concept in ENVIRONMENTAL ECONOMICS, exposing some of the limits of purely MARKET-based systems of coordination, since negative externalities are costs that fall on actors other than those directly involved in the activity. A TRAGEDY OF THE COMMONS may result, in which individually motivated actors 'free-ride' on collective or shared resources, capturing individual benefits, but with a net detriment for society as a whole, as shared resources are depleted or degraded (see Hardin, 1968). Responses to these dilemmas can include governmental regulation such as 'green taxes', or market-mimicking strategies such as pollution pricing.

In ECONOMIC GEOGRAPHY, an example of negative externalities is the common problem of firms under-investing in skills training: these costly and risky investments can be evaded by individual firms if they poach skilled workers from other firms, or otherwise plunder the resources of urban LABOUR MARKETS. The aggregate outcome is an under-investment in skills across the urban labour market, as even scrupulous employers are deterred from training their own workers for fear of poaching (see Peck, 1996). Meanwhile, examples of positive externalities include those 'agglomeration economies' captured by firms locating near to suppliers and customers. Scott (1988c) reveals how many so-called 'flexible firms' are narrowly redefining the boundaries of their organizations, focusing on core competences while buying in an increasingly broad array of goods and services from other firms (e.g. contract catering, management consultancy, temporary-agency labour). In order to minimize the TRANSACTION COSTS associated with such activities, flexible firms are induced to cluster together in space, generating the dense networks of inter-firm relations that characterize 'new industrial spaces' such as Silicon Valley.

Take the example of Wal-Mart, the world's largest retailer and the USA's biggest employer (see Wrigley, 2002; Brunn, 2006). The long-running debate around the local community impacts Wal-Mart centres on externalities. Critics of the company allege that its practice of paying low wages is a form of free-riding on public welfare systems, since many of Wal-Mart's employees qualify for government programmes designed for the poor, such as food stamps, subsidized housing and publicly funded healthcare. Other negative externalities follow from Wal-Mart's ability to hold down prices (due to its market power), which often drives smaller, neighbourhood retailers out of business. On the other hand, defenders of the company counter that most of the externalities are positive ones: Wal-Mart contributes to local social welfare by generating employment (particularly by locating in low-income neighbourhoods that have been largely abandoned by large employers) and by reducing prices for customers, many of whom also tend to be poor. A major store can also generate additional sales for a range of local companies such as restaurants and gas stations, another form of positive externality.   JPe

F

factor analysis A statistical procedure for transforming a (variables by observations) data matrix into a new matrix whose variables are uncorrelated. Unlike PRINCIPAL COMPONENTS ANALYSIS, the number of variables in the new matrix is less than in the original as the unique variance associated with each original variable is excluded. The new variables – termed *factors* – are composites of the original variables: the factor *loadings* (interpreted in the same way as CORRELATION coefficients) indicate the relative strength of the relationship between the original and new variables; the factor *scores* provide a measure for each observation on the new variables (weighted according to the factor loadings). The matrices of factor loadings may be rotated in order to enhance interpretation of the new variables. Most rotations aim to maximize the relationship of the original variables to just one factor; they may be either *orthogonal* – retaining the uncorrelated nature of the factors – or *oblique* – allowing intercorrelations among factors.

Factor analysis may be used either inductively, to identify groups of interrelated variables (cf. EXPLORATORY DATA ANALYSIS), or deductively, to test HYPOTHESES about interrelationships. Factor analysis and the associated principal components analysis (the two are often treated – although wrongly – as the same procedure) have been extensively used within geography since its QUANTITATIVE REVOLUTION, in two ways: as a means of identifying socio-spatial order in large data sets (not least in the automated treatment of the raw data in REMOTE SENSING); and to produce composite variables that could be used to represent and map general concepts – such as economic DEVELOPMENT. It is still widely used in ecological studies (cf. FACTORIAL ECOLOGY). RJ

Suggested reading
Johnston (1978).

factorial ecology The application of either FACTOR ANALYSIS or PRINCIPAL COMPONENTS ANALYSIS to matrices of socio-economic and other data for areal units. Generally used inductively (cf. INDUCTION), most factorial ecologies have been applied to data for small areas within cities (cf. CENSUS TRACT), to identify patterns of residential SEGREGATION. It is a relatively sophisticated technical procedure for describing the main elements of urban socio-spatial structure (cf. SOCIAL AREA ANALYSIS). RJ

Suggested reading
Davies (1984).

factors of production The ingredients necessary to the production process; that is, those things that must be assembled at one place before production can begin. The three broad headings conventionally adopted are land, labour and CAPITAL. Sometimes the fourth factor of 'enterprise' is added, to recognize the contribution of the 'entrepreneur' or risk-taker and the legitimacy of a special return to this participant in the productive process. However, in the current complexity of economic organization, it is hard to distinguish enterprise from general management functions, so this factor is more appropriately subsumed under labour. The combination of factors of production reflects the state of technology applied in the activity in question; for example, whether it is capital-intensive or labour-intensive.

Land is necessary for any productive activity, whether it is agriculture, mining, manufacturing or services. Land may be a direct source of a raw material, as with mining, or it may be required for the cultivation of a crop or to support the physical plant of a manufacturing activity. Modern industry requires increasing quantities of land, as factory sites and for such associated uses as storage, roadways and parking.

Labour requirements vary with the nature of the activity in question. Some need numerous unskilled workers while others require more skilled operatives, technicians, office personnel and so on. The availability of particular types of labour can have an important bearing on the location of economic activity. Despite the growing capital-intensity of modern industry, cheap labour with a record of stability is still an attraction. That the value of production can ultimately be traced to the factor of labour is central to the LABOUR THEORY OF VALUE.

237

Capital includes all things deliberately created by humans for the purpose of production. This includes the physical plant, buildings and machinery (i.e. *fixed capital*: cf. SUNK COSTS) plus the *circulating capital* in the form of stocks of raw materials, components, semi-finished goods and so on. Private ownership of capital and land is the major distinguishing feature of the capitalist MODE OF PRODUCTION, which carries with it important implications for the distribution of income and wealth (see MARXIST ECONOMICS; NEO-CLASSICAL ECONOMLCS).

The conventional categories of land, labour and capital (and enterprise) can serve an ideological role in legitimizing the differential rewards of the various contributors to production under CAPITALISM. The concept of productive forces is preferred in SOCIALIST economics. In any event, for practical purposes these broad categories tend to be subdivided into the individual inputs actually required in particular productive activities.   DMS

Suggested reading
Smith (1981).

fair trade The demand that producers from poorer countries should not be denied the legitimate maximum rewards from their sales by the actions of richer countries or other powerful agents. Fair trade campaigns go back a long way and embrace several related issues. Indian nationalists complained about a system of Imperial Preferences and asked for a measure of protection to help set up infant industries in areas such as iron and steel. In the 1950s, Oxfam took a lead in promoting fair trade ideas under the slogan 'Helping by Selling'. Similar ideas were taken up in the 1960s, when many African countries demanded 'TRADE not AID'. This slogan became the motif of the first UN Conference on Trade and Development, held in Geneva in 1964. Other trade justice campaigns have complained about export dumping by richer countries. Still others worry about pressures being placed on developing countries to liberalise their own markets too quickly. Ha-Joon Chang (2002) has charged that almost all of today's advanced industrial economies benefited from protection. Now, however, they and their representatives in the INTERNATIONAL MONETARY FUND (IMF) and WORLD TRADE ORGANIZATION (WTO) want to kick away that ladder to success in the developing world (see NEO-LIBERALISM).

Campaigns to ensure more open and equitable access to richer MARKETS for developing world producers continue to be important in the fair trade pantheon. Developing countries pressed for liberalization of agricultural markets in the European Union and North America during the World Trade Organization talks held in Hong Kong in 2005 (Stiglitz and Chorlton, 2006). The fair trade issue was also pushed strongly by the Make Poverty History campaign. Sugar producers in West Africa or the Caribbean will not receive a fair return for their crop when countries in the richer world offer large subsidies to domestic producers of sugar cane or beet. More recently, fair trade campaigners have put the spotlight on trade negotiations that link small producers to some of the world's largest or most powerful companies. Take the case of coffee. How are small producers in Central America meant to strike fair deals with giant coffee purchasers when those same companies can use their immense purchasing power to strike better deals for themselves with producers in Brazil or Vietnam? The answer, in part, is for small producers to form CO-OPERATIVES. They can then work with campaigning groups to persuade Starbucks and other coffee giants of the commercial value of selling 'fair trade' brands in their outlets. At this point, fair trade campaigns rub shoulders with calls for ethical CONSUMPTION (Nicholls and Opal, 2005).

Questions of market access and fair trade also take shape within poorer countries. Many small producers in the developing world are hurt by governments that saddle them with paperwork. It has been reported that some banana growers in the Central African Republic take over 110 days to get their bananas on a ship to Europe, and need more than 35 signatures to get them on board. Each signature creates an opportunity for corruption, or rent-seeking behaviour. Trading structures remain distorted, rather than open or developmental, and primary producers continue to lose out.   SCO

Suggested reading
Stiglitz and Charlton (2006). See also www.makepovertyhistory.org

falsification The criterion proposed by the philosopher of science Karl Popper (1902–94) to demarcate science from non-science. In Popper's view, only statements capable of falsification – that is, those possessing the capability of empirical refutation – were scientific. Statements that could not be falsified – that is, those unable to be proved wrong – were non-scientific. For Popper, the division between falsifiable and non-falsifiable statements was inviolate, allowing consistent separation of SCIENCE from non-science

Popper first proposed falsification in his 1935 book *Logik der Forschung* (translated as *The logic of scientific inquiry*; Popper, 1959). It was written as a response to discussions at the Vienna Circle of LOGICAL POSITIVISM that he attended, although it was a group to which he was never admitted as a full member. Logical positivists argued for the principle of *verification*, according to which the truth of a scientific statement was given by its correspondence to real-world observations. Popper, dubbed by one member of the Vienna Circle, Otto Neurath, as 'the official opposition', claimed to the contrary that scientific statements were never verified, only falsified. Because no one is omnipotent, it is impossible to know whether in the future a scientific claim will be disproved by a disconfirming instance (and a single disconfirming instance is all that is required to refute a general claim). For example, the verified truth of pre-eighteenth-century natural scientists in EUROPE that all swans were white was invalidated when Captain Cook sailed to AUSTRALIA and found black swans. The growth of scientific knowledge, as Popper (1963) would later claim, was based not on verifying theories, but on falsifying them, and in the process developing alternatives that were less worse; that is, not yet falsified. This was one of the basal propositions of Popper's development of CRITICAL RATIONALISM.

In *The Structure of Scientific Revolutions*, Kuhn (1970 [1962]) provided the root of a trenchant critique of Popper's position. Kuhn portrayed the trajectory of science as punctuated by periods of fundamental change he called PARADIGM shifts; for example, the move from Newtonian to Einsteinian celestial mechanics. During such shifts, everything was in flux, Kuhn argued, *including criteria of falsification*. Popper had made such criteria fixed and constant and yet, as Bernstein (1983, p. 71) later put it, 'data or evidence do not come marked "falsification".' Criteria of falsification are moving elements, not existing outside of debate, and settled only after change has happened.

Falsification should have been an important criterion for geographers during the period of the QUANTITATIVE REVOLUTION, when the discipline modelled itself most explicitly on the natural sciences. But it wasn't. If anything, that disciplinary move was backed by logical positivism, the very philosophy Popper thought he had dispatched in the 1930s. Alan Wilson (1972, p. 32), one of the leaders of geography's quantitative revolution, did suggest the importance of falsification in a 1972 statement: 'The essence of the scientific method ... is an attempt to disprove theory – to marshall observations to contradict the predictions of the theory.' But it was programmatic, and never realized in Wilson's practice, or the practices of anyone else in geography. This was precisely Kuhn's point, and later developed in SCIENCE STUDIES: falsification could never be realized.   TB

Suggested reading
Popper (1963, pp. 33–9).

family reconstitution A method used in HISTORICAL DEMOGRAPHY to create measurements in the absence of data on demographic stocks and flows made available through censuses and vital registration that applies nominative linkage techniques to baptisms, marriages and burials recorded in parish registers (see Fleury and Henry, 1965). The technique can also be adapted for use with genealogies (see Henry 1956). It starts from a marriage and links baptisms and burials of children born to the couple as well as their subsequent marriages. Family reconstitution rules devised originally for use with French parish registers by Louis Henry have been adapted for use with registers elsewhere, with a view to establishing a population at risk or under observation so that age-specific MORTALITY and FERTILITY rates can be calculated. Marriage age can be derived by linking baptisms and marriage dates and information can be extracted that will enable fecundity, birth and pre-nuptial pregnancy rates to be computed (see Wrigley, 1966a). Linkage is far more successful where MIGRATION is low, and consequently cities and large towns have rarely benefited from the technique, which has been used primarily to reconstruct the population of villages and smaller market towns (see Wrigley, Davies, Oeppen and Schofield, 1997).   RMS

Suggested reading
Wrigley (1966a); Wrigley, Davies, Oeppen and Schofield (1997).

famine A relatively sudden event involving mass MORTALITIES from starvation within a short period. Famine is typically distinguished from chronic hunger, understood as endemic nutritional deprivation on a persistent basis (as opposed to seasonal hunger, for example). Definitions of famine are fraught with danger because (i) cultural, as opposed to biological, definitions of starvation vary around diverse, locally defined norms, and (ii) deaths from starvation are frequently impossible to distinguish from those from disease

Nearly all societies have periodically suffered from the consequences of famine. The earliest recorded famine, which occurred in ancient Egypt, dates to 4000 BCE; famine conditions currently threaten parts of the Horn of Africa and parts of North Korea. The dynamics and characteristics of mass starvation in modern times have similar structural properties, however; typically, such famines involve sharp price increases for STAPLE foodstuffs, decapitalization of household assets, gathering of wild foods, borrowing and begging, petty CRIME and occasionally food riots, and out-MIGRATION. According to the Hunger Program at Brown University, the trend in famine casualties has been downward since 1945, but in the late 1980s STATES with a combined population of 200 million failed to prevent famine within their national borders. Hunger, and famine in particular, is intolerable in the modern world, however, because it is unnecessary and unwarranted (Dreze and Sen, 1989).

Famine causation has often been linked to natural disasters, population growth and WAR, which produces a reduction in the food supply (Malthus, 1970 [1798]). But some major famines (e.g. Bengal in 1943) were not preceded by a significant decline in food production or absolute availability, and in some cases have been associated with food export. Recent analyses have focused on access to and control over food resources – sometimes called the *food availability decline hypothesis*. Sen (1981) argues that what we eat depends on what food we are able to acquire. Famine, therefore, is a function of the failure of socially specific entitlements through which individuals command bundles of COMMODITIES. Entitlements vary in relation to property rights, asset distribution, CLASS and GENDER. Famine is therefore a social phenomenon rooted in institutional and political economic arrangements, which determine the access to FOOD by different classes and strata (Watts, 1983a). Mass POVERTY and mass starvation are obviously linked via entitlements. Mass poverty results from long-term changes in entitlements associated with social production and distribution mechanisms; famines arise from short-term changes

in these same mechanisms. Famine and endemic deprivation correspond to two forms of public action to eradicate them: famine policy requires entitlement protection to ensure that it does not collapse among vulnerable groups (i.e. landless labourers, women). Chronic hunger demands entitlement promotion to expand the command that people have over basic necessities (Dreze and Sen, 1989). Since 1945 India has implemented a successful anti-famine policy, yet conspicuously failed to eradicate endemic deprivation. China, conversely, has overcome the structural hunger problem (even during the socialist period), but failed to prevent massive famine in the 1950s. AFRICA has witnessed a catastrophic growth in the incidence of both mass starvation and chronic hunger (de Waal, 1997).

The role of STATE policy and of humanitarian AID figures centrally in the discussions of famine and famine causation. While the public sphere is key in understanding how and why the right to food and the right not to be hungry are made effective, the recent history of famine shows clearly how the state can use famine and humanitarian aid for explicitly political purposes. The case against Stalin and the Ukrainian famine is clear in this regard, and the catastrophic Chinese famine of the late 1950s is a compelling instance of how inept state policies to achieve rapid INDUSTRIALIZATION backfired, but also how an authoritarian state ignored famine signals and colluded in the deaths of 20 million people (Becker, 1997). Sen (1981) has argued that famines rarely occur in societies in which there is freedom of the press (and in which states are therefore held to be accountable in some way). Humanitarian assistance has also been an object of critique insofar as it itself becomes politicized (and rendered as a business), and often fails to be more than a short-term palliative (rather than assisting in the rehabilitation and reconstruction of famine-devastated COMMUNITIES; de Waal, 1997). MW

Suggested reading
Davis (2001).

farming Most literally, the land-based, human-managed production of FOOD and fibre by the transformation of seed into crops and/or the raising of livestock (the latter of which is also referred to as pastoralism or ranching). Farming is of general significance for all social scientists, because it is the most routine and widespread way in which humans directly interact with NATURE, and because adequate food production and consumption has proven to be crucial for the stability of SOCIAL FORMATIONS.

Farming as a capitalist enterprise preceded England's INDUSTRIAL REVOLUTION, as tenant farmers began cultivating wool for the nascent textile industry (see AGRICULTURAL REVOLUTION). Since the Second World War, the world has seen massive transformation of farming sectors. In the industrialized counties, these transformations began with the proliferation of technologies of INTENSIVE AGRICULTURE, especially those that relied on the development of petrochemical inputs; these technologies were extended to some areas of the THIRD WORLD, with the idea that high-yielding agriculture (see GREEN REVOLUTION) and INDUSTRIALIZATION were keys to DEVELOPMENT (Goodman and Redclift, 1991). Since the 1980s, however, rural populations have substantially declined (see URBANIZATION). The 1970s was a period of farm expansion, owing to the USA selling massive amounts of grain to the Soviet Union, which caused a temporary food shortage and high prices for farmers. The collapse in prices that followed contributed to the international debt crises of the 1980s, which forced many farmers out of business who could no longer pay the farm mortgages they acquired in the previous expansion (Friedmann, 1993). Recent free TRADE agreements have allowed low-cost producers, such as the USA, to dump surplus crops in cash-poor regions and countries, undermining the livelihoods of PEASANTS and small farmers, contributing to even more displacement.

Categorizing patterns of farm land use was a staple feature of traditional AGRICULTURAL GEOGRAPHY (Tarrant, 1974). Farm size has continued to be a major analytic in empirical studies of farming, owing in part to the availability of census data, which are often reported as acres/hectares in production and/or gross sales. As the POLITICAL ECONOMY of agriculture TRADITION came to dominate agricultural geography in the 1980s, more effort was put into developing more theoretically informed typologies of farm business organization and to help explain changes in farming practice (see, e.g., Whatmore, Munton, Little and Mardsen, 1987). These efforts engaged with a long sociological tradition concerned with the CLASS location of farmers and the social organization of farming relative to STATE and CAPITAL (see Buttel and Newby, 1980). LAND TENURE, capital ownership, labour relations, family LIFE-CYCLE and RENT-seeking thus

became primary analytics, and the persistence of the family farm, defined as that where FAMILY members provide all or most of the agricultural labour regardless of the extent of its commercial orientation (cf. SUBSISTENCE AGRICULTURE) became a central theoretical question. One widely cited theorization of this UNEVEN DEVELOPMENT of capitalist agriculture was Goodman, Sorj and Wilkinson (1987). CAPITALISM has developed around farming, they argued, because with its basis in land and biology, farming itself remains risky, while the processes that serve farming are more easily commodified and sold back to the farmer (see AGRARIAN QUESTION; SUBSTITUTIONISM). Watts (1994a) drew on these arguments in his work on contract farming, noting that the degree to which buyer firms specify required processes and inputs in their contracts has made many peasants equivalent to wage labourers on their own land. Sachs (1996) added that the enduring family basis of farming in most parts of the world has in large part depended on highly gendered divisions of labour within peasant HOUSEHOLDS. In some sectors and regions, however, farming operations themselves are large-scale, capitalist enterprises (Heffernan and Constance, 1994). Highly mechanized corporate farms should be differentiated from PLANTATIONS that, while corporately owned and managed and large in scale, employ many manual labourers.

In the early 1990s, agro-food scholars began to take note of divergent trends in farming and food production. Heightened pubic concern with food safety and quality, the ecological effects of agriculture and the changing countryside (in some cases depopulation, in others urbanization) seemed to support a turn towards farming that would be more sensitive to ecological concerns and protective of rural livelihoods. In addition, growth in part-time and hobby farming, a resurgence of back to the land sensibilities among those seeking alternative lifestyles, along with a putative shift in national forms of farm regulation away from commodity supports seemed to indicate a 'post-productivist' transition in agriculture (Marsden, 1992). While the dramatic rise in organics, for example, seems to provide support for this claim, the European and US farming sectors are state-supported more than ever, albeit in different ways to different ends. Meanwhile, many Third World farming sectors are producing high-value fruits and vegetables under conditions of STRUCTURAL ADJUSTMENT.

Technology-driven INTENSIVE AGRICULTURE has hardly gone away, in spite of increased incidences of biological 'blowback' from industrial food production – such as bovine spongiform encephalopathy (BSE), or 'mad cow' disease. Driven in part by the twin revolutions in information science and BIO-TECHNOLOGY, farming itself seems to be moving in directions that belie the opening definition of this entry. Already, surplus commodities, such as corn and oil seed, which have long been a source of livestock fodder, are being deployed for industrial uses. Precision agriculture uses satellite data to determine local variation in soil conditions and plant development, and information technologies to track and fine-tune applications of farm inputs. Genetic engineering has been used to improve crop protection by, for example, engineering natural pesticides or frost protection into plants. The use of genetically engineered livestock or plants to produce medically useful crops – or 'gene pharming' – is just in the pipeline, as is the introduction of nutrients or vaccines into existing food crops. These sorts of developments are drawing geographers to new questions and theorizations, many borrowed from the toolkits of SCIENCE and technology studies.

At the same time, many of these technologies carry ecological RISKS and are also leading to unprecedented degrees of PRIVATIZATION. Therefore, they have become a major galvanizing feature of contemporary SOCIAL MOVEMENTS. Since most of these trends point to a continued decline in rural populations, the family farm seems to have achieved heightened IDEOLOGICAL status. Thus, the distinctions between peasant, family and corporate forms are not just academic, but are relevant to political practice, particularly given the re-emergence of discourses of agrarian POPULISM within both institutions of DEVELOPMENT and social-justice oriented social movements (Wolford, 2003). JGU

Suggested reading
Bell (2004); Duncan (1996); Guthman (2004).

fascism A political IDEOLOGY that formed the basis of political parties and social movements that emerged in EUROPE between the two world wars. The nationalist governments of Adolf Hitler in Germany (1933–45) and Benito Mussolini in Italy (1922–43) are the most notable examples, but fascism was a political force across Europe at the time, including Oswald Mosley's 'black shirts' in Britain,

the Iron Guard in Romania and the Croix de Feu in France (Laqueur, 1996). Despite the lack of a seminal intellectual text, the following characteristics of the ideology can be identified: extreme racist NATIONALISM; a desire for a 'pure' NATION-STATE that contains just one national group; goals of territorial expansion to include all members of a NATION within the borders of the state (cf. LEBENSRAUM); anti-COMMUNISM and other forms of working-class organization; VIOLENCE represented as necessary for the survival of the nation and as a pathway to fulfilling innate human needs; a glorification of manliness and gender roles, promoting men as defenders of the nation and women's primary role in the biological reproduction of the nation (cf. MASCULINISM); and a mass politics in which the STATE and the party fuse and mass participation in politics (based upon a cult of the leader) is encouraged. Elements of these ideologies exist in contemporary nationalist political parties across the world, as extreme nationalism is mobilized in the wake of social dynamics (such as IMMIGRATION and a decline in the power of the state) that are identified as 'threats'. Political parties in Russia and Serbia display some of these traits, as do the British National Party and some extremist right-wing movements in the USA.

The RACISM of fascist movements is often, but not necessarily, anti-Semitic. Jews are frequently targeted as enemies because, prior to the establishment of the state of Israel, they lacked connection to a particular TERRITORY. Hence, they were seen as disloyal to the nation or inimical to the idea of territorial nation-states. The foreign policy of the Nazi Party was partially informed by the ideas of GEO-POLITIK, which saw territorial expansion as a strategy related to the HOLOCAUST and the extermination of Jews (as well as gypsies, communists and homosexuals), to create a political geography of a 'pure' and 'greater' Germany (Clarke, Doel and McDonough, 1996: see also GENOCIDE).

Social scientists and historians have debated the social bases of fascism. The idea that the middle classes were the main source of support dominated until recent years, when the notion of a cross-CLASS support for the Nazis emerged. The geography of fascism shows that support is based upon different class coalitions in different localities, within the broader context of economic RESTRUCTURING and inter-state competition (Flint, 2001). Recent scholarship has argued that the support for inter-war fascism was more widespread than had been believed (Goldhagen, 1996), with 'ordinary citizens" rather than committed party members carrying out much of the killing in the Holocaust. This controversial work has contemporary implications as geographers have turned their attention to GENOCIDE, under the label of 'ETHNIC CLEANSING', in the former Yugoslavia and in Africa. CF

Suggested reading
Larsen, Hagtvet and Myklebust (1980); Laqueur (1996).

fecundity An individual's capacity to reproduce (as distinct from FERTILITY, an individual's actual reproductive performance). A physical (biological) component varies with age and SEX, with women reaching peak fecundity between menstruation and menopause, and male fecundity decreasing, but less rapidly, with old age. Infecundity increases with poor nutrition and ill health: the ongoing HIV/AIDS epidemic has reduced fertility levels in many regions both because of the premature deaths of potential parents and because fecundity is impaired (Gregson, 1994). Research also recognizes a social component when, for example, women believe they cannot give birth, and when medical practitioners expressly counsel against giving birth. AJB

Suggested reading
Weeks (1999, Ch. 5).

federalism A form of government in which POWER and functions are divided between central and regional authorities with the goal of providing autonomy to regional units (Wheare, 1963). Federal forms of government vary widely, but require a written constitution to delimit the roles of different levels of government. Federalist STATES usually experience a continual political process of defining the degree of centralization and regional autonomy. In states with geographically concentrated ethnic groups (see ETHNICITY), federalism can reinforce ethnic differences, but it also provides a political solution to ethnic competition for control of the state (Ikporukpo, 2004). CF

Suggested reading
Smith (1995).

feedback A reciprocal effect within a SYSTEM, whereby change in one variable (A) influences changes in others (B, C), which may then stimulate further change in A. *Negative feedback* generally maintains the system's EQUILIBRIUM: an increase in the number of ANIMALS in an ECOSYSTEM may stimulate growth in the number of their predators, whose actions then reduce the number of animals to the previous level. Such systems are *morphostatic*, in dynamic equilibrium; the period between any shock to the system and the return to its equilibrium state is termed its relaxation time. With *positive feedback*, an increase in A may stimulate increase in B, which in turn stimulates further growth in A, as in the MULTIPLIER processes associated with INPUT-OUTPUT MODELS. Such systems are *morphogenetic*. RJ

Suggested reading
Langton (1972).

feminism A diffuse political movement, which has varied over space and time, that aims to identify and dismantle systematic GENDER inequality, and the myriad ways in which gender differentiation, HETERONORMATIVITY, MASCULINISM, and PHALLOCENTRICISM naturalize, anchor and relay all kinds of SOCIAL EXCLUSION, and physical and symbolic violence. It struggles to improve women's lives across a range of issues: VIOLENCE against women; sexual harassment; access and equity in schools, workplaces, before the law and within political life; the division of DOMESTIC LABOUR; and reproductive rights, among others. It seeks to revolutionize thought in daily life and throughout the arts and sciences, and to undo and reconceptualize the many naturalized qualities attributed to women and men, what counts as knowledge, and the relation between knowledge and practice. Feminist struggles have been important not only for their substantive achievements and goals, but for the process through which these have been sought; Dietz argues that feminist movements in the USA are a living repository of democratic norms and practices that have 'nearly ceased to be part of the politics of the United States' (1987, p. 16). Historical accounts of Anglo-American feminism typically distinguish between first-wave (late nineteenth century to the First World War), second-wave (1960–1980s) and third-wave (1980s–) feminisms, although this periodizing risks simplification. For instance, although first-wave feminism is known for campaigns to win women's right to vote, these were part of broader concerns about women's RIGHTS to education, paid employment, sexual freedom and financial self-sufficiency (Blunt and Wills,

243

2000). Periodizing risks a second tendency: this is to code these stages within a narrative of progress or development, against which feminisms in other parts of the world can be judged as advanced or, more typically, backwards (Shih, 2002).

Modern Western feminism was constituted in relation to the abstract INDIVIDUALISM that is the basis for social and political inclusion within LIBERALISM. Women have been excluded from many of the supposedly universal norms and claims of liberalism, but have used these norms to struggle for inclusion within them. Insofar as they have shared this experience of exclusion with other social groups, this has offered grounds for alliances. Nonetheless, Western feminism has been criticized for its own exclusions, concealed by its universalizing claims about women's experience. Criticisms of feminism as white, middle-class, heterosexist and Western were prominent in the 1980s and 1990s, and have led to attempts to understand both the specificity and diversity of women's experiences. It is not simply that women's experiences differ depending on other aspects of their social locations; feminism as a political movement takes a different trajectory in different places, depending on how it articulates with other political struggles. In the Philippines, as one example, the 'second wave' of women's liberation dating from 1970 was closely articulated with the nationalist struggle against the collusion between US imperialists and landlord–comprador–bureaucrat capitalist allies within the Philippines (West, 1992). As Morris (2006) writes: ' "Politics" is irreducibly plural ... What I have in mind is not simply the diversity of [feminist] groups, movements and "positions" that can be mapped as active at any given time around the world, but rather the intrinsically dynamic, unpredictably complex and *consequential* nature of political struggle itself; in failing as well as in succeeding, political practices alter the contexts in which they occur ... [W]e have little to gain from polemically reducing our vision to one project ... We have too rich a past from which to learn, and too much to do in the future.' But this also means that the translatability across these myriad feminist struggles can no longer be taken for granted, and that Western feminists must 'stop positing themselves as objects of MIMESIS' (Shih, 2002, p. 116) and do the hard work of fully contextualizing the specificity of feminist SOCIAL MOVEMENTS in particular times and places.

Feminism has always been a spatial practice: to disrupt traditional organizations of SPACE, to forge productive dislocations and to reconfigure conventions of SCALE: 'The dichotomy between the private and the public is central to almost two centuries of feminist writing and political struggle; it is, ultimately, what the feminist movement is about' (Pateman, 1989, p. 118: see also PRIVATE AND PUBLIC SPHERES). The feminist slogan, 'the personal is the political', expresses a refusal to accept both conventional boundaries between public and private, and scalar distinctions between the BODY and spaces of politics (see FEMINIST GEOGRAPHIES).

The term 'postfeminist' emerged in the 1990s, in part to signal differences among women, the fluidity of GENDER categories and the challenges of building a social movement through the singular identification as women. But there are many options for reformulating feminism in terms other than postfeminism, for instance, as transnational, transversal, as a solidarity movement articulated through obligations of justice rooted in the interdependencies of material conditions in specific places, or as 'an empty signifier' that gathers struggles over the production of DIFFERENCE – through political struggle rather than identification (Pratt, 2004). It certainly would be a mistake to assume that feminist struggles have been won. Although women make up roughly half the labour force in many countries, the majority of women in most countries continue to work in traditionally female jobs, for significantly lower wages than men. Reproductive rights won through second-wave feminist activism are under attack in the USA, and the division of domestic labour is largely unchanged in many countries. The devolution of care under NEO-LIBERALISM has added to women's work responsibilities at home, and the increasing militarization of daily life (cf. MILITARISM) in many countries has led to re-masculization and intensified regulation of HETERONORMATIVITY.   GP

Suggested reading
Blunt and Wills (2000); Pratt (2004).

feminist geographies These geographies focus on how GENDER and geographies are mutually produced and transformed, and the ways in which gender differentiation and HETERONORMATIVITY permeate social life, and are interwoven with and naturalize other categorical distinctions. The tradition dates from the mid-1970s, drawing inspiration from women's movements of the 1960s (see FEMINISM); it is both a sub-field and a force that has reshaped the entire discipline. It now has a considerable institutional presence: the journal *Gender, Place and Culture* has been published since 1994 (a series of excellent reviews of sub-areas within feminist geography appeared throughout 2003 and 2004 to mark the journal's tenth anniversary); there are over 12 titles in the Routledge International Studies of Women and Place series; regular progress reports of feminist geography appear in *Progress in Human Geography* and *Urban Geography*; and there are a good number of textbooks targeted to varying levels of undergraduate and (post) graduate students (e.g. Domosh and Seager, 2001; Jones III, Nast and Roberts, 1997; McDowell and Sharpe, 1997; Moss, 2002; Sharpe, Browne and Thien, 2004; Pratt, 2004), along with several key reference texts, including *A companion to feminist geography* (Nelson and Seager, 2005), a *Feminist glossary of human geography* (McDowell and Sharpe, 1999) and *The atlas of women* (Seager, 2003a). Although there are distinguishable strands, some common tendencies cut across all feminist geographies:

(1) They are critical, not only of gender oppression and various manifestations of heteronormativity in SOCIETY, but of the myriad ways that these are reproduced in geographical knowledge. There is now a comprehensive critique of geographical traditions; for example, POLITICAL GEOGRAPHY (Staeheli, Kofman and Peake, 2004); HISTORICAL GEOGRAPHY (Domosh, 1991); HUMANISTIC GEOGRAPHY (Rose, 1993); geographies of MODERNITY and POSTMODERNITY (Deutsche, 1991); and more recent literatures on TRANSNATIONALISM (Mitchell, 1997c) and GLOBALIZATION (Nagar, Lawson, McDowell and Hanson, 2002). Rose (1993) extends her critique to the discipline as a whole, cataloguing its various and complementary forms of MASCULINISM. What the relationship between feminist geography and the discipline now is and should be remains a matter of debate: some note the lack of impact that more than two decades of vibrant feminist scholarship have had on the discipline, while others problematize the increased exchange of ideas between feminist and other strands of CRITICAL HUMAN GEOGRAPHY (for an excellent discussion of the potential for exchange between feminist geographers and NON-REPRESENTATIONAL THEORY, see Jacobs and Nash, 2003). Feminist geographers' relations with the discipline have been framed through notions of ambivalence and the METAPHORS of paradoxical and in-between space (Bondi, 2004).

(2) Sexism within geographical institutions (in the teaching of geography, the staffing of academic departments, and through the publication process) has been a persistent concern (Monk and Hanson, 1982; Rose, 1993; Bondi, 2004). In the past decade, this has been intertwined with critiques of persistent RACISM in the discipline.

(3) Nelson and Seager (2005, p. 6) position feminist geography as 'an innately interdisciplinary sub-field'. Within the discipline, feminist geographers practice this tendency by tracing the interconnections between all aspects of life, across the sub-disciplinary boundaries of ECONOMIC, SOCIAL, POLITICAL and CULTURAL GEOGRAPHY. This entails breaking down boundaries *within* sub-disciplines as well; for instance, by demonstrating the interdependencies between informal and formal aspects of the ECONOMY (see DOMESTIC LABOUR). In an associated way, feminist geographers disrupt conventional notions of SCALE, and move across scales to trace connections between similar processes in different places (Katz, 2001; Nagar, Lawson, McDowell and Hanson, 2002).

(4) Most feminist geographers share a commitment to situating knowledge, the view that interpretations are context-bound and partial, rather than detached and universal (see ACTION RESEARCH; PHALLOCENTRISM, POSITIONALITY; REFLEXIVITY; QUALITATIVE METHODS; SITUATED KNOWLEDGE). This has produced a large literature on feminist METHODOLOGIES, including four journal symposia – Farrow, Moss and Shaw (1995), Hodge (1995) and Nast (1994b) – and two books (Jones III, Nast and Roberts, 1997; Moss, 2002). It has also led to experimental writing, including various modes of self-REFLEXIVITY (for a critical evaluation of these experiments, see Rose, 1997b), and to efforts to disrupt the individualist author (e.g. the fused subject of Julie Graham and Kathy Gibson as J.K. Gibson-Graham, the Women in Geography Study Group writing collective, and collaborations between academics and community groups).

(5) Feminist geographers tend to emphasize the specificity of PROCESSES in particular PLACES. This has been tied to a critique of universalizing, masculinist knowledge claims, and a commitment to agency and an open, transformable future. Certainly, this has been an important strand of feminist geographers' criticism of masculinist knowledge, but it has been extended to (non-geographical) feminist THEORY as well (Katz, 2001a). Attending to the particularities of gendered processes in specific places can be an important means of moving beyond highly polarized academic debates and to engage a messier, more nuanced and ambivalent politics (Nagar, Lawson, McDowell and Hanson, 2002; Pratt, 2004).

(6) Feminist knowledge production is typically aligned with a political commitment to social transformation.

Despite these common themes, there is a great deal of variation within feminist geography. Bowlby, Lewis, McDowell and Foord (1989) sketched an influential history of feminist geographies, in which they identified two breaks, one in the late 1970s and the other towards the end of the 1980s (see figure on page 248). The first break was less decisive in the USA, where the influence of the geography of women approach has been stronger (for a more complete map of national variations in feminist geography, see Monk, 1994). There is also a danger that a model of stages will be read as a progress narrative, with later stages interpreted as more progressive than earlier ones. It should be noted, then, that traditions exist simultaneously and there is a great deal of heterogeneity (national and otherwise) within and outside these generalizations.

An important task for feminist geographers has been to make women visible, by developing a geography of women. The goal has been to achieve gender equality; the spatial vision one of integration (Bondi, 2004). Two points have been central: women's experiences often differ from those of (white) men, and the former have restricted access to a range of opportunities, from paid employment to services. This is largely an empirical tradition, loosely influenced by liberal feminism and WELFARE GEOGRAPHY. It has tended to focus on individuals, documenting how women's roles as caregivers and 'housewives', in conjunction with the existing spatial structures, housing design and policy, and patterns of ACCESSIBILITY to transport and other services such as childcare, conspire to constrain women's access to paid employment and other resources.

An early criticism of the geography of women approach was that gender inequality is typically explained in terms of the concept of gender roles, especially women's roles as housewives and mothers, in conjunction with some notion of spatial constraint. Foord and Gregson (1986) argued that the concept of gender roles narrows the focus to women (as opposed to male POWER and the relations between women and men), emerges out of a static social theory, and presents women as victims (as passive recipients of roles). Further, although the geography of women shows how spatial constraint and separation enter into the construction of women's position, it typically provides a fairly narrow reading of SPACE, conceived almost exclusively as distance, or as transparent, and (potentially) gender-free (Bondi, 2004). In early work in this tradition, insufficient consideration was given to variations in gender relations across places. There has been, however, a very useful planning component to this literature that outlines, for example, efforts to restructure the city so as to reduce gender inequalities and enhance quality of life (e.g. Wekerle and Whitzman, 1995). Both successes and frustrations in attempts to implement some of these reforms have led to critical reconsiderations of the limits of liberal feminism and towards a fuller institutional analysis, confirming Eisenstein's (1981) point that the practical and theoretical limits of LIBERALISM are frequently discovered – in practice – by liberal feminists themselves.

Socialist feminist geographers reworked Marxian categories and theory to explain the interdependence of geography, gender relations and economic DEVELOPMENT under CAPITALISM (see MARXIST GEOGRAPHY). One of the key theoretical debates within socialist feminist geography revolved around the question of how best to articulate gender and CLASS analyses. At its most abstract, the question was addressed in terms of PATRIARCHY and capitalism, and the relative autonomy of the two systems. Socialist feminist geographers first worked primarily at the urban and regional SCALES; arguably, it is a renewed version of socialist feminist that is now most insistent about the material effects of the globalizing forces of capitalism. At the urban scale, an early focus of Anglo-American feminist geographers was the social and spatial separation of suburban homes from paid employment; this was seen as crucial to the day-to-day and generational reproduction of workers and the development and continuation of 'traditional' gender relations in capitalist societies (MacKenzie and Rose, 1983). Given a feminist commitment to agency, efforts were made to read these processes in non-functionalist terms and as strategies to manage the effects of a capitalist economy (cf. FUNCTIONALISM). For example, MacKenzie and Rose argued that the isolation of women as housewives in suburban locations emerged from the combined influence of working-class household strategies, governmental policy and male power within families and trades unions. Socialist feminist geographers also have been attentive to the ways in which gender relations differ from place to place, and are sedimented within place-specific social and economic relations, in ways that not only reflect but partially determine local economic changes. This argument has been made at urban (Hanson and Pratt, 1995), regional (McDowell and Massey, 1984) and international scales (Pearson, 1986).

Beginning in the late 1980s, many feminist geographers moved away from an exclusive focus on gender and class systems, to consider more expansive geographies of DIFFERENCE (see IDENTITY; RECOGNITION). Feminist geographers were increasingly attentive to the differences in the construction of gender relations across races, ethnicities, ages, (dis) abilities, religions, sexualities and nationalities; to exploitative relations among women who are positioned in varying ways along these multiple axes of difference (see AGEISM; ETHNICITY; HOMOPHOBIA AND HETEROSEXISM; RACE; RACISM; SEXUALITY); and to the ways that gender classification orders the existence not just of men and women, but of animals, COMMODITIES, ideas and other entities. Gender is a powerful means of naturalizing difference. They began to draw on a broader range of social, and particularly cultural, theory, including PSYCHOANALYSIS, POST-COLONIALISM, POST-STRUCTURALISM and QUEER THEORY, in order to develop a fuller understanding of how gender relations and identities are shaped and assumed (see SUBJECT FORMATION). This led to fundamental rethinking of the category, GENDER, and attending to the contradictions and possibilities presented by the seeming instability of gender. With a focus on multiple identifications and PERFORMATIVITY, the emphasis shifted from material constraint and spatial entrapment to possibilities beyond fixity. This was articulated in

Rose's (1993) notion of paradoxical space: the sense that the multiplicity and contradictoriness of the ways in which we are positioned in space generates possibilities excessive to hegemonic heterosexual norms and spaces (for further thoughts about the ways in which performativity and space are intertwined, see also Gregson and Rose, 2000; Pratt, 2004). Metaphors of multiplicity, mobility and fluidity, of HYBRIDITY and paradoxical, in-between, spaces were immensely popular in the 1990s, including Gibson-Graham's (2006b [1996]) influential re-theorizing of capitalism and CLASS processes. A considerable amount of writing developed around gendered cultural REPRESENTATION, which extended the focus to imaginative and symbolic spaces (see FILM AND GEOGRAPHY; IMAGINATIVE GEOGRAPHIES; VISION AND VISUALITY). A small but growing number of studies of masculinities (Berg and Longhurst, 2003) began to deliver on the promise of a gender relational approach, by directing the focus away from women to a larger network of heteropatriarchal relations. The influence of identity politics and post-structural theories refocused attention on SEXUALITY and the scale of the BODY.

Nonetheless, new fault lines emerged among feminist geographers. Monk (1994) observed that national differences between American and British geographers diminished as both pursued these new directions, but divisions between feminist geographers located in the global NORTH and global SOUTH increased, an institutional schism that repeats geopolitical ones in troubling ways. By 2006, Ramon-Garcia, Simonsen and Vaiou declared that Anglophone hegemony within institutionalized feminist geography was not improving; on the contrary, it was getting worse. And by the mid-1990s, cautionary reactions to a focus on MOBILITY, identity and difference suggested the need to re-invigorate links with a renewed socialist feminism.

To a considerable extent this has happened, and a fourth strand of feminist geography could be called 'transversal' feminist geography. Connections are being drawn in many directions. Seager (2003b) reviews fruits of 'boundary breakdown' within feminist POLITICAL ECOLOGY and ANIMAL geography. The latter traces structures of oppression across gender, race, class and species, as well as exposing gendered assumptions that underlie human relations to non-humans and what is conceived as NATURE. The lessons from the debates about difference in the 1990s have

247

GEOGRAPHY OF WOMEN

Topical focus	*Theoretical influences*	*Geographical focus*
Description of the effects of gender inequality	Welfare geography, liberal feminism	Constraints of distance and spatial separation

SOCIALIST FEMINIST GEOGRAPHY

Topical focus	*Theoretical influences*	*Geographical focus*
Explanation of inequality, and relations between capitalism and patriarchy	Marxism, socialist feminism	Spatial separation, sedimentation of gender relations in place

FEMINIST GEOGRAPHIES OF DIFFERENCE

Topical focus	*Theoretical influences*	*Geographical focus*
The construction of gendered heter(sexed) identities; differences among women; gender and constructions of nature; heteropatriarchy and geopolitics	Cultural, post-structural, post-colonial, psychoanalytic, queer, critical race theories	Micro-geographies of the body; mobile identities; distance, separation and place; imaginative geographies; colonialisms and post-colonialisms; environment/nature

FEMINIST TRANSVERSAL GEOGRAPHIES

Topical focus	*Theoretical influences*	*Geographical focus*
Citizenship; migration; nationalism; transnationalism; ethnographies of the state; development; political ecology; geopolitics; state violence; relations between global North and global South; material objects; progressive possibilities for mapping and GIS; affect and emotions	Theories of transnationalism, globalization and transversal networks and circuitries; non-representational theory; political ecology; Agamben; political economy; theories of affect	Global networks and circuits; multi-scalar and multi-site focus on connections, relations and processes; constructions and disruptions of scale; space of exception; borders and border breakdowns; embodiment and connectivity; dispossession

feminist geographies *Interwoven strands of feminist geography*

been learnt, and a defining characteristic of feminist animal rights analyses (as compared to those of 'mainstream' animal rights advocates) is the tendency to theorize an ethics of care without erasing the differences between humans and non-humans. Feminist geographers continue to focus on the body, but are possibly more effective in theorizing the body at a multiplicity of 'scales' and institutional sites, especially in relation to the economy (Wright, 1999a) and the STATE. Feminist geographers are tending more and more to develop their analyses beyond their national boundaries, to understand the connections between processes and lives in the global North and global South (Katz, 2001a; Nagar, Lawson, McDowell and Hanson, 2002; Pratt, 2004). As part of this, feminist geographers

are re-inventing critical geopolitics to develop a politics of security that includes the civilian body and decentres a focus on state security (Hyndman, 2005). State violence; the rape and torture of men and civilian women as technologies of war; the production of 'the monster', 'the fag' and 'the terrorist' as figures of surveillance and criminalization (Puar and Rai, 2002); the re-masculinization and militarization of daily life; the impact of neo-liberal policies on the global gender division of labour – these are themes that press for attention in our contemporary world.   GP

Suggested reading
Domosh and Seager (2001); Moss (2002); Nelson and Seager (2005); Pratt (2004); Rose (1993); Sharp, Browne and Thien (2004).

fertility Reproductive performance, or the number of live births. Along with MORTALITY and MIGRATION, it is one of the three components of the balancing equation and, as such, an important influence upon the growth, composition and distribution of populations (see DEMOGRAPHY). Unlike mortality and morbidity, which have been the subject of long-standing interest in MEDICAL GEOGRAPHY and geographies of HEALTH AND HEALTH CARE, and migration, similarly investigated in POPULATION GEOGRAPHY, fertility (and FECUNDITY) continues to receive scant attention within GEOGRAPHY (Boyle, 2003), despite such trends as the emergence of negative population growth rates fuelled by low fertility, increasingly complex HOUSEHOLD forms and a growing emphasis upon social reproduction in the discipline.

Research on geographical variations in fertility makes use of two types of measures. Period measures focus on events that occur between a starting and ending date, and include the *crude birth rate* (the number of births in a year for every 1,000 persons in a population). COHORT measures focus on events that occur to a particular group of individuals, such as those born or married in the same year, and include the *total fertility rate*, which represents the number of live births that a woman currently aged 15 would expect by the time she reaches age 49 and assuming that current age-specific fertility rates remain constant. The fact that a large number of countries exhibit total fertility rates well below the replacement level of 2.1 has stimulated debate on the fertility and DEMOGRAPHIC TRANSITION in particular, and the changing role of CHILDREN and adults in society more generally (Greenhalgh, 1995; Waldorf and Franklin, 2002).

Research on the *politics of reproduction* explores DISCOURSES surrounding family planning, reproductive health and reproductive rights movements, particularly as they impacted upon policy recommendations from successive meetings of the International Conference for Population and Development, and the geographical nature of SOCIAL CONSTRUCTIONS surrounding, for example, teen pregnancy, childbirth and maternal mortality (Fernandez-Kelly, 1994; Grimes, 1999; Underhill-Sem, 2001). AB

Suggested reading
Bongaarts (2002); Boyle (2003).

feudalism A term used in the analysis of pre-capitalist societies, especially those of medieval Europe, but also Japan under the rule of warlords from the twelfth to the nineteenth centuries. Feudalism has a wide range of meanings, from a legal focus on the military obligations imposed through the concept of a *fief* (see below) to a more comprehensive, quintessentially political and economic characterization of feudalism as a specific MODE OF PRODUCTION or SOCIAL FORMATION. The increasing scope of the definition owes much to a growing interest in comparative history and, in particular, to studies of the geographically variable relationships between the decline of feudalism and the rise of agrarian CAPITALISM (Hilton, 1976; Kula, 1976; Martin, 1983; Dodgshon, 1987; Glennie, 1987). But this has also prompted a fear that, outside history and HISTORICAL GEOGRAPHY, ' "feudalism" seems to have become a general catch-all term denoting almost anything in the pre-modern period; it is as though all societal relationships, economies and politics of the medieval period can be defined simply by this legal term that describes the action of lords collecting a surplus through a sort of military protection racket' (Harvey, 2003b, p. 152). Such a prospect has been complicated by more recent analyses that claim to identify a resurgent feudalism within late MODERNITY, a sort of 'medieval modernity' predicated on a particular combination of fiefdom and freedom and the production of fractured and competing sovereignties associated with the aggressive advance of NEO-LIBERALISM in both the global NORTH (alSayyad and Roy, 2006; Zafirokski, 2007) and the SOUTH (cf. Murray, 2006).

In its classical sense, feudalism comprises two distinct social groups. The first is a group of *direct producers* (broadly PEASANTS) who maintain direct, which is to say non-market, access to the means of production (land, tools, seed-corn and livestock) even though they may not own them (especially land). This group is subject to politico-legal domination by a second group of *social superiors*, who form a status hierarchy headed by a monarch or sovereign (see SOVEREIGN POWER). The sovereign ultimately owns all the land, but land tenure is effectively decentralized through grants of land to feudal lords in return for their political and military support. In such a system, social relations of production are thus not defined primarily through MARKETS, as in capitalism, and the means by which a surplus is extracted from the direct producers is different from systems like SLAVERY.

The key social relationships in European feudalism were vassalage and serfdom. *Vassalage* was an intra-elite relationship by which a subordinate (vassal) *held* rather than owned landed property, the 'fief' (Latin *feodum, feudum*, hence feudalism) from a lord, ultimately the sovereign, in return for military service required by the sovereign. The sovereign's vassals were tenants-in-chief, who in turn 'subinfeudated' their estates to raise their own military service. Thus a hierarchy of feudal tenants came to hold estates of various sizes, composed of territorial jurisdictions called *manors*, in what Anderson (1974, pp. 148–9) described as a complex 'parcellization' of sovereignty.

Serfdom was the legal subjection of peasant tenants to lords through the latter's manorial jurisdictions, of which unfree tenants were legally held to be part. Dependent peasant tenants held land from their lord in return for varying combinations of services in kind, especially labour services on the lord's own land within the manor (the *demesne*) and money rents. The legal dependence of peasant tenants enabled feudal lords both to extract higher than market rents from their tenants and also to impose a range of other dues and exactions, including duties on death and licenses to marry, to migrate or to brew ale. Peasant tenants were fined at a manorial court if these activities were undertaken without appropriate licenses, and courts also exercised a degree of moral regulation.

The level of RENTS and dues was set more by lords' income requirements than by market forces, although lords gained from the latter as population growth made land scarce relative to labour. Seigneurial income requirements progressively increased as lords competed for political status through conspicuous CONSUMPTION. Moreover, since feudal lords could raise income from intensified surplus-extraction, they were comparatively indifferent to innovations to raise agricultural productivity. These claims have important implications for the explanatory value of the geography of manorialism (estate size and fragmentation, seigneurial character) and of the lord–tenant struggle in accounting for geographical variations in POPULATION DENSITY, agricultural systems and productivity, and standards of living (Hilton, 1973; Hallam, 1989; Campbell, 1990, 1991; Dyer, 1993). As lordly extraction intensified, and medieval European populations grew (for reasons as yet imperfectly understood), feudal society exhibited certain CRISIS tendencies, because the surplus removal process failed to generate any significant feedback into the productive capacity of agriculture through investment. A crisis of SOCIAL REPRODUCTION was inevitable since:

(1) Production for the market and the stimulus of competition only affected a very narrow sector of the economy.

(2) Agricultural and industrial production were based on the HOUSEHOLD unit, and the profits of small peasant and small artisan enterprises were taken by landowners and usurers.

(3) The social structure and the habits of the landed nobility did not permit accumulation for investment for the extension for production (Hilton, 1985).

Hilton's work remains an important demonstration that towns and TRADE were integral to feudal economies, not 'non-feudal islands in feudal seas', exogenous factors that undermined feudal social relations (cf. PIRENNE THESIS). But recent studies have paid more attention to the extent of commercialization within medieval agrarian economies and its impact on geographies of manorialism (Power and Campbell, 1992; Campbell, 1995).

While debate continues on the importance to medieval agrarian contraction of excessive surplus-extraction (see BRENNER THESIS) and ecological frailties (see POSTAN THESIS), there has been a general move towards more sophisticated theorizations that broaden analysis of feudal society beyond property relations. Greater attention has been paid to ACCUMULATION and differentiation within the class of direct producers (Poos, 1991; Razi and Smith, 1996a). Important developments in social technologies changed the geographical structuring of feudal society. Over time, status came to be increasingly embodied in PROPERTY rather than interpersonal relations. Notable geographical components stemmed from this shift, including new legal, fiscal and administrative technologies to control TIME and SPACE (Bean, 1989; Biddick, 1990; Clanchy, 1993). Finally, certain social continuities across the feudalism–capitalism transition, especially in the functioning of geo-demographic and cultural systems, have received serious attention (Poos, 1991; McIntosh, 1998).   PG/DG

Suggested reading
Brown (1974); Dodgshon (1987); Reynolds (1994).

field system The fields and other agricultural resource elements, such as wastes and commons, of a COMMUNITY or communities that may be regarded as functioning as an agrarian and social system (Gray, 1915; Dodgshon, 1980). In a more specific sense, the term can be applied to early patterns of landholding and husbandry that entwined groups of cultivators into communities of mutual or common interests through their use of landed RESOURCES. In studies of the HISTORICAL GEOGRAPHY of EUROPE, particular attention has focused on the manner in which the intermixture of land between landholders has taken the form of strips or parcels. Other themes that loom large in defining such systems are the extent to which the system possessed a communally regulated system of cropping, or the degree to which arable cultivators possessed RIGHTS in common over the cultivated area after harvest. Analysis of such systems has also been linked to the nature of LAND TENURE and the extent to which individual ownership of land prevailed. Debates surround the extent to which communal systems of tenure and their associated field systems are seen invariably to predate those based upon enclosed fields held in severalty. In considering *open field systems*, emphasis might be placed on the way in which individual's holdings or strips of land were distributed over larger fields subject to rule-based cropping practices that were generated internally by the cultivators themselves or imposed by outside agencies such as landlords, or formed a means of RISK minimization to ensure that cultivators had lands under different crops on variable soil types, or whether they were incompatible with effective and efficient agrarian management. Such systems have formed the basis of debates in POLITICAL ECONOMY about the benefits of individual over communal tenure. The debate over the ENCLOSURE of open field systems into enclosed fields and associated scattered free-standing farms managed without reference to communal rules and regulations has played a prominent place in the timing of the AGRICULTURAL REVOLUTION (Allen, 1992). Other scholars have focused on the supposed social consequences that may have flowed from enclosure and how the removal of access to communal grazing, post-harvest gleaning and the right to collect fuel and other food resources from commons turned smallholder peasants into rural proletarians (Neeson, 1993). RMS

Suggested reading
Neeson (1993).

fieldwork A means of gathering data that involves the researcher in direct engagement with the material world. Once based in the ENLIGHTENMENT assumption that 'reality' was out there available for straightforward apprehension, fieldwork is now recognized as a more complicated mode of learning that produces SITUATED KNOWLEDGE about people, PROCESSES and PLACES. While this perspective may be seen as a hindrance in POSITIVIST approaches to human geographical research that seek to neutralize the researcher and aspire to statistical generalizations, many now recognize the strength of self-REFLEXIVITY and the necessarily partial nature of the information collected. The two modes of scholarship endure in fieldwork, and the epistemological tensions between them can be daunting (e.g. Sundberg, 2003: see also EPISTEMOLOGY).

Field research has a long history in HUMAN GEOGRAPHY. Since antiquity, much of it has been associated with imperial projects, and thus involved EXPLORATION, mapping and the taxonomic categorization of RESOURCES – animal, plant, mineral and human. But fieldwork is also a means to examine the relationships between people and their environments, the material social practices of place-making, the PRODUCTIONS OF NATURE and the sedimentations of these relationships in diverse historical geographies. Fieldwork in this regard has had a more ambiguous and contested relationship with the discipline – pitting observational against theoretical knowledge and sometimes challenging received ways of knowing (cf. Driver, 2000). Its multiple strands include the 'stout boots' tradition of British geography and Sauerian CULTURAL GEOGRAPHY in the USA (Delyser and Starrs, 2001; cf. Withers and Finnegan, 2003). Evolving from a natural history tradition, wherein physical evidence was collected in and from the environment, fieldwork of this nature focuses on LANDSCAPES as evidence of differentiated, sequential and uneven human occupance; seeking relationships and patterns in their production and persistence. Many of the field methods associated with these traditions are rooted in observation. The taken-for-grantedness of seeing as well as its reliance on unmarked 'vantage points' has been subjected to a thorough critique as MASCULINIST, because its claims to OBJECTIVITY rest on unstated hierarchies, detached observers and distancing assumed adequate to reveal hidden dimensions of the scene (Barnes and Gregory, 1997b; Rose, 1997b; Sundberg, 2003). Given these concerns and other limits of traditional approaches to fieldwork, including its interested nature, unsustainable assumptions regarding the distinction between NATURE and CULTURE, and the tendency to focus on visual rather than more dynamic, relational and contested forms of evidence, many fieldwork practitioners developed a more critical stance to their work. Feminist geographers (see FEMINIST GEOGRAPHIES) were key in this intervention, examining the politics of REPRESENTATION that percolate through fieldwork, scrutinizing the uneven power relations that propel it and calling its epistemological claims into question (Rose, 1993; *Professional Geographer*, 1994; Sundberg, 2003).

Engaging in fieldwork of this kind raises the question of what constitutes the field. The field, as Felix Driver (2000, p. 267) reminds us, 'is not just "there"; it is produced and re-produced through both physical movement across a landscape and other sorts of cultural work in a variety of sites'. It is also the effect of discursive and spatial practices that mark it as a site of enquiry 'that is necessarily artificial in its separations from geographical SPACE and the flow of TIME' (Katz, 1994, p. 67). These distinctions and the sorts of knowledge derived from them are constituted through embodied practices such as travel, residence, visiting, conversation, observing, eating, smelling, listening and various (re)presentations of self. The field and the fieldworker are co-constructions, and the knowledge produced between them reflects the materiality and mutability of this relationship. Scholars have addressed the various and multiple connotations of movement among fields – the constitution of a field site, the way in which the site and the sorts of knowledge produced there are constructed in one's disciplinary field, and the uneven valences of POWER that energize and can confound the multiple translations – spatial, linguistic, and practical – of fieldwork (e.g. *Professional Geographer*, 1994; Pluciennik and Drew, 2000; Saunders, 2001). Questions of power affect such things as negotiating access, whether and how to conduct research in areas of CONFLICT and VIOLENCE, determining what kinds of knowledge can be shared and with whom, figuring out what cannot be said and making sense of the silences, and representing oneself in 'the field' and the field to one's audience.

The METHODOLOGY of fieldwork is capacious and eclectic, encompassing quantitative and qualitative strategies of data collection. While fieldwork is commonly associated with CASE STUDY methodologies and ETHNOGRAPHIC research, it also includes survey research, broad observational studies, mapping and measurement techniques. Among the research methods associated with fieldwork in human geography are all manner of field observation, including PARTICIPANT OBSERVATION, landscape assessment and site observation; oral techniques such as casual conversation, unstructured and structured interviews, FOCUS GROUP INTERVIEWS, oral histories and environmental autobiographies; survey and census techniques (see SURVEY ANALYSIS); digging through, collecting, sorting, classifying and interpreting records, whether in the ground, in place or in archives; measurement and mapping activities; and documenting what is observed and experienced in a variety of ways, including written, photographic, cartographic, aural and artistic means. Recent investigations of fieldwork have addressed issues such as the embodiment of the fieldworker (see BODY), bringing companions to the field, sexual relations in the field, and the ETHICS and implications of dishonesty and misrepresentation in fieldwork. As these concerns suggest, fieldwork produces knowledge that is avowedly situated, and its validity resides both in that recognition and in the disciplined REFLEXIVITY that enables researchers to expose their practices and question their findings. CK

Suggested reading
Geographical Review (2001); *The Professional Geographer* (1994); *Singapore Journal of Tropical Geography* (2003); Wolf (1995).

film An inherently spatial technology through which fragments of IMAGES and sounds from different times and spaces are reassembled, and then transported to audiences in many different locations. It can be studied as a mobile cultural REPRESENTATION, a public gathering (at the cinema or movie theatre), a political opportunity, a mode of GOVERNANCE and an economic activity. The boundaries of film now blur into television, video, MUSIC and amusement park culture.

Much film analysis focuses on the film itself – for example, the narrative structure, the sets, camera shots and editing – and it can be a means of studying how dominant social and geopolitical understandings and anxieties are expressed, produced, transmitted and resisted. US noir films of the 1940s and 1950s, for instance, have been interpreted as expressions of geopolitical and social anxieties: about nuclear WAR, the MIGRATION of southern African-Americans to northern cities, and relations between women and men. The geographies scripted into noir films (e.g. the dark and foreboding city) express and fuel these anxieties (Farish, 2005). Alternatively, as a mode of storytelling and site-seeing, film can be a medium for travelling across and juxtaposing different worlds, and rupturing dominant narratives about PLACE; Taylor (2000) assesses the ways in which *The Coolboroo Club*, a film made by and about Perth's Nyungah community (an aboriginal community that was banned from entering the central metropolitan area in the 1930s and 1940s), draws on aboriginal memories to supplement and disrupt HEGEMONIC white history of 'sunny' Perth. Because film is such a good vehicle to think with and about dominant and resistant social meanings, it can be an excellent pedagogical tool; the *Journal of Latin American Geography* instituted an extensive film reviews section for this purpose in 2005, and Cresswell (2000) chronicles his use of the film, *Falling Down*, to generate nuanced classroom discussion of RESISTANCE.

Film is more than another medium for storytelling, and a long tradition of cultural criticism and avant-garde films make larger claims about the capacity of film to stimulate novel sense experiences and generate critical thought. Close-up shots, cross-cutting, slow motion and flickering effects, montages of images that juxtapose the far and near, the present and the past, and spaces that are ordinarily segregated or otherwise kept apart – these are some of the cinematic techniques that can be used to dis-order and re-order space and time, and shock the senses. Walter Benjamin (1978) theorized film's potential to de-naturalize social relations and social SPACE; Deleuze (2001) wrote of the promise of 'pure optical' situations in (particularly neo-realist) film: to release the viewer from linear cause-and-effect perceptions and bring the senses into a new relation with time and thought. Both theorists draw connections between film and the CITY: the modern city in the case of the former, the rupture forced by devastated post-Second World War European cities for the latter. It is not just theorists who have appreciated the transformational potential of film; Olund (2006) argues that urban reformers in the early-twentieth-century USA embraced some similar ideas about the ways in which film works on sense perception, and recognized film as a powerful tool for governance, especially for assimilating immigrants into middle-CLASS norms of WHITENESS.

Aitken and Zonn speculated that geographers have been slow to make a serious study of film because of 'the geographer's traditional emphasis on the material conditions of social life wherein representation is subsidiary to "physical reality"' (1994, p. 5). Even so, there are rich opportunities for investigating the play between filmic representations and concrete spaces. Analysing the Nigerian film industry, Marston, Woodward and Jones (2007) argue that the distinctive aesthetic of 'Nollywood' films (long sequences with extensive and repetitive dialogue, and little or no action) emerges out of local material circumstances of small budgets, fast shooting schedules, small crews and reliance on readily available locations. At the same time, filmic representations have material consequences. The negative portrayal of the inner city in post-Second World War Hollywood film, it has been argued, created a popular disposition in the USA for massive demolition of inner-city neighbourhoods and urban RESTRUCTURING. The film *Chinatown*, a fictionalized rendition of political corruption, personal greed, capitalist development and WATER policy in Los Angeles, is now understood to be and deployed as the historical 'truth' by environmental groups who wish to stop contemporary dam proposals (both case studies are found in Sheil and Fitzmaurice, 2001). The Hollywood film *Entrapment* created an uproar in Malaysia when it was released in 1999, because images of the Petronas Towers in Kuala Lumpur were spliced with those of a distant shanty town, to suggest that the two geographies lie side by side. This was at odds with the impression that city boosters wished to project, that of Kuala Lumpur as a clean, modernizing 'world class' city. As the government's Information Minister complained, 'the whole world will come to believe that the scenery they saw in the movie … is real' (cited in Bunnell, 2004, p. 300). Alternatively, popular films can generate informal and formal TOURISM spin-offs, when appreciative fans seek out the sites used in movie scenes. In many cities, the film industry is a major economic activity, certainly in cities such as Los Angeles (Scott, 2005a), Mumbai and Hong Kong, but in many other cities as well, whether as a location or through the business of film festivals. The geographies of film production and reception have become increasingly complex: the transnational nature of many productions complicates debates about non-Hollywood 'national' cinemas (Acland, 2003); and DIASPORIC communities generate demand for films produced outside of the USA, whilst the heavy dependence of the US entertainment industry upon international markets disrupts simplistic assumptions about the one-way, global transmission of US CULTURE.

The cinema itself is a PUBLIC SPACE, which some have argued was particularly important for women and immigrants in the early-twentieth-century US city; Hansen understands it to be a site for the formation of a counter-public sphere. Much of this has changed with new technologies of home videos and DVDs, but Hansen (1995) has been loathe to understand these new technologies as simply leading to the diminishment of cinema as counter-public sphere. She speculates that contemporary film viewers, now used to having control over their viewing at home, are more active than they were in the classical Hollywood period of film spectatorship. Certainly the material conditions of viewing film are changing. In North America through the 1990s, there was a dramatic increase in the number of screens constructed and a simultaneous reduction in the number of theatres, reflecting the construction of multiplexes, facilities that with multiple screens, typically located in the SUBURBS. These multiplex amusement spaces generate a different timing and spacing of film spectatorship (Acland, 2003).

Film (and video) is not simply an object, but a tool for analysis. Pryke (2002, p. 473) calls up Lefebvre's notion of RHYTHMANALYSIS to introduce his video and audio montage of urban redevelopment of Potsdamer Platz in Berlin (http://www.open.ac.uk/socialsciences/geography/research/berlin/). Concerns with PERFORMANCE and life that exceeds DISCOURSE (see NON-REPRESENTATIONAL THEORY) have fuelled interest in using film and video as a means of representation, and electronic journals such as *ACME* now allow the blending of TEXT and video (e.g. Pratt and Kirby, 2003). Media literacy and video production training has been a useful methodological strategy in ACTION RESEARCH.   GP

Suggested reading
Aitken and Zonn (1994); Cresswell and Dixon (2002); Scott (2005); Shiel and Fitzmaurice (2001).

filtering A process whereby housing value and status declines over time while HOUSEHOLDS gain access to increasingly higher-quality dwellings. The theory emphasizes MARKET forces in, and identifies triggers for, changes in the allocation of housing (see HOUSING STUDIES; INVASION AND SUCCESSION). The literature includes numerous refinements to filtering MODELS (Galster, 1996) and also strong critiques of the normative element in filtering theory, which tends to legitimate

laissez-faire approaches to housing provision in which demand from wealthier households for new housing is expected to open up better housing for lower-income groups (Gray and Boddy, 1979).   EM

Suggested reading
Gray and Boddy (1979).

financial exclusion The process by which people of poor and moderate incomes are directly and indirectly excluded from the formal financial system and denied access to mainstream retail financial services (see also MONEY AND FINANCE). Financial exclusion plays an active part in the geographical production of POVERTY, because those who experience difficulty in gaining access to formal financial serves tend to belong to disadvantaged social groups undergoing multiple forms of social deprivation (Leyshon and Thrift, 1997).

Access to mainstream financial services within contemporary societies is important because many economic exchanges are now mediated through financial institutions through direct transfers between accounts. Without access to the financial system, individuals and HOUSEHOLDS may find it more difficult and expensive to pay bills, while the lack of access to products such as insurance denies them the opportunity to shield against risk. In this sense, having access to a full range of financial services at a competitive price may be taken to indicate 'financial citizenship'. In large parts of the developing world, the majority of the population may lack financial citizenship, whereas in industrialized countries such as the USA and the UK it is estimated that around 10 per cent of the population is financially excluded (cf. CITIZENSHIP).

The process of financial exclusion is a product of a broader bifurcation of the MARKET for retail financial services. Socio-technologies such as credit scoring systems sort 'prime' from 'sub-prime' customers on behalf of financial institutions. Prime financial markets are made up of individuals and households that possess socio-economic and geo-demographic profiles that make them targets of the marketing and financial strategies of retail financial services firms. These middle- and high-income customers are actively pursued by retail financial services firms, and may be described as the financially 'super-included', benefiting from intense competition between institutions for their business. One of the drivers of this strategy is the tendency towards the securitization of retail financial products, whereby lenders aggregate the loans made to low-risk customers and sell them to investors in international securities markets (Dymski, 2005). Sub-prime customers, meanwhile, have low to moderate incomes and/or financial assets, and are either excluded from mainstream financial marketing campaigns for new products or are denied access to services if they apply.

The geography of prime and sub-prime financial markets follows established geographies of income and wealth. Thus, for the most part, prime retail financial customers may be found in affluent urban and suburban areas, whereas sub-prime markets are concentrated in areas of low and moderate income, typically in inner-city areas (and, in the UK, at least, on public-sector housing estates). In the absence of mainstream financial services, which continue to close branches in such areas, a host of specialist sub-prime or 'fringe' retail financial institutions ply their trade. They provide similar services to the mainstream, but at a much higher cost. It is now possible to identify pronounced financial ecologies, made up of distinctive combinations of markets, customers and institutions (Leyshon, Burton, Knights, Alferoff and Signoretta, 2004). Public policies to counter the problems of financial exclusion were initiated with increased vigour in the late 1990s (Marshall, 2004), and the explosive growth of 'predatory lending' in sub-prime markets was a key factor in the global financial CRISIS that detonated in 2008. AL

fiscal crisis A fiscal crisis occurs when the revenue raised by the STATE is insufficient to cover the cost of its activities. All governments experience short-term financial problems as a result of routine fluctuations in tax revenues and public expenditure. The term 'fiscal crisis' is usually reserved for a more serious shortfall in the state's financial position arising from structural or systematic imbalances between the cost of providing public services and social security payments and the ability of the state to finance them through taxation.

According to O'Connor (1973), a tendency towards fiscal crisis is a logical outcome of the contradictory character of the state under CAPITALISM. O'Connor argues that the state has two main functions within capitalism: to promote ACCUMULATION by private CAPITAL, and to ensure the legitimacy of this process among the population. To do the former, the state needs to make investments in economic INFRASTRUCTURE (e.g. roads, energy supply networks, the central bank), systems of regulation (e.g. to ensure the orderly functioning of market exchange; cf. REGULATION THEORY) and the maintenance of a productive labour force (e.g. by providing education). To do the latter, the state seeks to promote social integration through expenditure on the WELFARE STATE and the maintenance of LAW and order.

O'Connor's analysis suggests that with the emergence of the monopoly form of capitalism in which MARKETS are dominated by a small number of large corporations, an increasing proportion of the costs of investment must be met by the state, while expenditure on social problems also grows. This requires the state to seek to raise extra revenue from taxation, which has the effect of discouraging private investment, thereby reducing the tax base and exacerbating the problem. This can result in a fiscal CRISIS as the state's revenue-raising capacity is reduced at the same time as demands for increased state expenditure grow. The state may seek to resolve the crisis by trying to reduce public expenditure as a proportion of the economy. However, this may result in a crisis of legitimation as welfare expenditure is cut. In some cases, however, powerful states (notably the USA) have been able to sustain very large budget deficits for extended periods and to stave off fiscal crises by borrowing from overseas. In 2006, approximately one-quarter of the total US public debt of $8,500 billion was held by foreign governments and international investors.

A tendency to fiscal crisis may be spatially differentiated, particularly where local governments have autonomous revenue-raising capacities. In the 1970s and 1980s, many US cities faced serious fiscal problems as manufacturing industry declined and higher-income residents moved out to the SUBURBS (see FISCAL MIGRATION). In 1975, New York City avoided bankruptcy only after the federal government intervened. Subsequently, many local governments have faced budgetary constraints as a result of restrictions imposed by the central state or because of poor credit ratings imposed by increasingly influential private rating agencies (Hackworth, 2006). JPa

Suggested reading
Jessop (2002, ch. 2); O'Connor (1973).

fiscal migration A process by which individuals, HOUSEHOLDS and firms relocate to secure fiscal benefits. The concept is derived from the TIEBOUT MODEL, which argues that land users will move to a local government administration that optimizes their tax and services preferences, trading off the costs of paying for public services through taxation against sacrifices in their ability to consume private services. The model has been used to explore the geographical consequences of distributed and competitive local government administrative structures (e.g. Davies, 1982). The process also operates at an international level, and underlies the creation of offshore financial centres, tax havens and EXPORT PROCESSING ZONES, all of which attract international capital INVESTMENT partly through fiscal incentives that include tax holidays and other inducements. AL

flâneur/flânerie The *flâneur* is associated with aimless urban wandering and observing, especially in nineteenth-century Paris, where it took its first steps. Yet the figure has also walked further afield, as it has been taken up more widely in social, cultural and urban studies as 'an emblematic representative of MODERNITY and the personification of contemporary urbanity' (Ferguson, 1994, p. 22). Despite becoming a common motif, the *flâneur* and activities of *flânerie* remain elusive and resist easy definition, although they usually involve a solitary and anonymous male, with the emphasis falling variously on strolling, idling, watching, writing, artistic creativity and detection. Many commentators suggest that it is most productively seen as a mythological figure, a strategy of REPRESENTATION, and thus a SOCIAL CONSTRUCTION within discourse more than a sociological reality.

First referenced in 1806, the *flâneur* received its most famous articulation in the writings of Charles Baudelaire, for whom it was a 'modern hero' and passionate spectator who derived poetic meaning from an immersion in the CITY, in the fleeting movement and electrical charge of its crowd. Baudelaire's account played an important role in Walter Benjamin's investigations of Paris as 'capital of the nineteenth century', and in his attempts to decipher the phantasmagorias of urban modernity. In these texts, the increasing commodification and rationalization of the city along with the decline of the arcades meant that the *flâneur* was already becoming a displaced and bygone figure. Benjamin's writings have remained a key source for subsequent interest in the *flâneur*, with some critics viewing Benjamin's own approach as being akin to *flânerie* in its mode of reading metropolitan spaces through attending to urban fragments and signs. There have also been multiple reinventions of *flânerie* in the arts, cultural practice and urban studies through recent interest in other forms of urban walking (see URBAN EXPLORATION).

Feminist critics have emphasized the exclusivity of *flânerie*, arguing that a female equivalent – the *flâneuse* – was rendered impossible by the ideologies and sexual divisions of nineteenth- and early-twentieth-century cities that constrained anonymous and unaccompanied movement by women. The practice of *flânerie* itself, so it is argued, was structured around a male gaze. However, critical elaborations have since questioned the extent of the exclusion of women from the public realm, revealing the intersections between public and private, and have also argued that the *flâneur* was a more insecure and marginal figure than is often supposed (Wilson, 1991). Writers have further traced out the possibilities for female *flânerie* through the development of department stores, through writing and literary texts and through early cinema, which enabled a mobile urban gaze from within the safety and respectability of a FILM audience.

Such studies have led to re-evaluations of the (in)visibility of the *flâneuse* (D'Souza and McDonough, 2006). Dissenting voices nevertheless remain, with Janet Wolff arguing that the problem with the *flâneur* lies less in its exclusivity than in the centrality it has been accorded in urban and cultural studies of MODERNITY, and in the consequent occlusion of female experiences. She therefore calls for the *flâneur*'s 'retirement' from centre stage and for attention to turn instead to the 'micro-practices of urban living, and the very specific ways in which women negotiate the modern city'. In the process, she claims, questions of female *flânerie* lose importance and 'women become entirely visible in their own particular practices and experiences' (Wolff, 2006, p. 28). DP

Suggested reading
D'Souza and McDonough (2006); Tester (1994).

flexible accumulation A REGIME OF ACCUMULATION emphasizing diversity and differentiation rather than the standardization associated with Fordist modes (see FORDISM) of ACCUMULATION. Flexible accumulation requires workers, machinery and manufacturing techniques that can quickly and regularly innovate and adapt to changes in consumer tastes, thus generating profit through ECONOMIES OF SCOPE rather than the ECONOMIES OF SCALE. As Harvey (1999 [1982]) points out, the (re-)emergence of flexibility as a dominant regime of accumulation in the late 1970s and 1980s was associated with instability in the economies of developed countries and competition from THIRD WORLD industrializing nations that could mass-produce standardized goods cheaply. For McDowell (1991), it was also a change in the basic societal conditions – such as the increasing disappearance of the nuclear family as the standard domestic unit and the increasing entrance of women into the labour force – that challenged the many of the ideals underlying the Fordist regime of accumulation and led to the growth in importance of flexible accumulation. However, Gertler (1988) cautions against assuming that this means that flexible accumulation replaced Fordist modes of accumulation; rather, flexible accumulation re-emerged in this period as the dominant regime in developed countries (see also Norcliffe, 1997).

For geographers, flexible accumulation is associated with what Storper (1997b) refers to as the 'resurgence of the REGION' in INDUSTRIAL GEOGRAPHY. Because of the need for continuous innovation and rapid adaptation to changes in consumer demands, trusting relationships with numerous suppliers who can provide components just in time and expertise that facilitates INNOVATION is important. At the same time, flexible accumulation requires producers to have access to a pool of skilled labour, something that can often be found in specialized regions or CLUSTERS, where complementary industries exist. Examples include Motorsport Valley in Oxfordshire, UK (Henry and Pinch, 2001), Silicon Valley in California, USA (Saxenian, 1994), and Santa Croche in Italy (specializing in leather production: see Amin, 1989). JF

Suggested reading
Cooke (1988).

flows A name for movements between relatively fixed nodes in NETWORKS, flows can be of COMMODITIES, MONEY, people, energy or even ideas. In the 1980s and 1990s, a series of developments in both theory and global relations made reference to 'flows' increasingly common in a wide range of academic fields.

In theoretical arguments, long-standing Marxist concerns with explaining economic processes in terms of the circuit of CAPITAL came to be critically supplemented with Foucauldian and other POST-STRUCTURALIST arguments about the need to understand IDENTITY and POWER in terms of the flow of power through social relations. Though it is often forgotten, the jargon of deterritorialization developed by the French–Italian philosophical duo Deleuze and Guattari (1983) was just such an EPISTEMOLOGICAL intervention: not an empirical claim about the geography of POSTMODERNITY, but a postmodern psychoanalytical argument about the need to follow diverse flows of desire and thereby critique containerized concepts of the human psyche in modern ego-psychoanalysis (cf. PSYCHOANALYTIC THEORY). More generally, the critical import of treating power in terms of micro-flows did have implications for theories of SPACE (see PRODUCTION OF SPACE). Just as MARXIST GEOGRAPHY had challenged absolutist and fixed assumptions about space in economics by exploring capital as value in motion in global and urban landscapes (Harvey, 1999 [1982]), so in turn did the ideas of Foucault help inspire new approaches to politics that challenged spatial yet geographically dead concepts of PLACES and individuals simply holding power over powerless multitudes (Sharp, Routledge, Philo and Paddison, 2000). Power had to be rethought relationally in terms of the flows of ideas and interactions that created people (in different ways in different spaces) as both agents and subjects, a notable implication being that sites of SUBJECTIVITY formation could thereby be reconceptualized as historical geographies of truth and power (e.g. Clayton, 2000). Applied to human–environment relations too and supplemented further by the work of FEMINIST scholars (Haraway, 1991) and SCIENCE STUDIES (Latour, 1988), even the most concrete and stilled natural LANDSCAPES – such as the dammed waterscapes of formerly flowing rivers – could be rethought this way as flows of knowledge, power, capital and energy coming together in HYBRID formations in different ways in different contexts (White, 1995; Swyngedouw, 1999, 2007).

In addition to these epistemological interests in the overdetermined landscapes of flow, worldwide events associated with recent rounds of capitalist GLOBALIZATION have also brought attention to the increasing flows of commodities, capital, information and people across BORDERS. For example, the growth of cross-border flows of international TRADE (especially their increasing size as a proportion of world GDP) provides a key index of increasing global economic interdependency, an index that is only eclipsed in its significance by the even more rapid acceleration of cross-border INVESTMENT flows (foreign direct investment) as a sign of the growing importance and independence of TRANSNATIONAL CORPORATIONS *vis-à-vis* NATION-STATES (Dicken, 2003). Other increasing and accelerating flows – transnational flows of information on the INTERNET, flows of news images and popular culture through cable and satellite TV, flows of migrants and TOURISTS over barriers big and small, flows of illegal drugs and weapons, for instance – all comprise complex component parts of the 'space of flows' that has been famously associated with the rise of a globalized so-called NETWORK SOCIETY (Castells, 1996b). But whereas Manuel Castells was careful to underline that 'the space of flows is not placeless' (Castells, 1996b, p. 416), other scholars have been prone to joining their empirical observations of globalized flows with extreme epistemological emphases on deterritorialization that tend to suggest an end to geography altogether. For example, in his otherwise astute arguments about the transnational networks of MODERNITY (and - especially of contemporary MIGRATION), anthropologist Arjun Appadurai (1996) ignores the ways in which global flows reterritorialize and create new landscapes in the same moment as they eclipse older ones (see Sparke, 2005). By contrast, geographer John Agnew approaches the problem with a keen sensitivity to the ways in which flows create geographical integration and differentiation at the very same time. 'The main novelty today,' he says in a comprehensive rebuttal to end-of-geography arguments, 'is the increasing role in economic prosperity and underdevelopment of fast-paced *cross-border flows* in relation to national states and to networks linking cities with one another and their hinterlands and the *increased differentiation* between localities and regions as a result of the spatial biases built into flow-networks' (Agnew, 2006, p. 128). MS

focus group A QUALITATIVE METHOD used to obtain opinions and experiences from between six and twelve people who participate in a group discussion organized around a series of topics or questions posed by the researcher/facilitator. Focus groups typically supplement other METHODOLOGIES, and can be useful at different points in the research process: to get oriented to a new research field; to generate HYPOTHESES that can then be tested more systematically; to gather qualitative data about experiences and opinions; and as a means of presenting preliminary interpretations to a community for validation. Focus groups are used instead of INTERVIEWS or QUESTIONNAIRE surveys if the researcher believes that the group conversation will spark ideas among participants so as to elicit a richer understanding of the issue at hand. They provide an opportunity to observe how ideas develop in context, in relation to other and sometimes contradictory opinions. Although the researcher carefully facilitates the event, it can be a less hierarchical, more negotiated research event. Focus groups can also provide an important opportunity for participants to exchange information and support each other.

Focus groups must be carefully managed and are not always appropriate. POWER hierarchies within the group will persist and can potentially silence non-dominant members. When this happens, less dominant individuals are effectively excluded from the research process. For this reason separate focus groups are often conducted for men and women, or are divided in terms of other social categories, such as RACE, especially if this is relevant to the topic under discussion. It should also be recognized that focus groups are public events in which individuals give public PERFORMANCES and may be reluctant to disclose private details. The focus group risks being exploitative if the artificiality of the situation and the legitimacy of the research context lulls individuals into revealing private details. This is especially problematic if the individuals in the group know each other or are likely to encounter each other after the event.

A focus group is not equivalent to interviews with between six and twelve individuals. A focus group is a singular conversational event. For this reason, at least five or six focus groups should be done in order to assess the thematic consistency across them. Similar to interviews, they are taped and transcribed. But they invite a different approach to analysis. Rather than focusing simply on the declarations of individuals, they provide an opportunity to study the generation of meaning, as opinions are debated, qualified and potentially modified. There also is a situational geography to focus groups that is under-explored. The rules of DISCOURSE, what and how one is told, vary with the context (Pratt, 2002). Geographers thus have the potential not simply to use this methodology, but to develop it in fascinating new directions. GP

Suggested reading
Conradson (2005a); Pratt (2002).

food The study of the spatial and environmental aspects of food production, distribution and consumption. Food is a recurring concern in several academic disciplines because of its centrality to human life for both physical and social sustenance. As a specific sub-field with identifiable concepts and scholars, however, agro-food studies has come into fruition only recently, a reflection of both the resurgence of POLITICAL ECONOMY, which found a new object of study in food systems, and the 'CULTURAL TURN' in social science that brought renewed interest in CONSUMPTION. While scholars of food draw from anthropology – foodways has long been a staple of that discipline – and sociology, owing especially to the sociology of agriculture tradition, GEOGRAPHY is in many respects at the cutting edge of food studies. Arguably, this is because geography is more ecumenical in its approaches, and because the spatial and environmental aspects of food are so critical to its theorizations. At the same time, there is a tendency to use food to illustrate other geographical topics, as demonstrated by the dozens of monographs published within the past 15 years that tell larger stories through particular food COMMODITIES.

Still, geographers have made considerable progress in producing and debating a set of meta-concepts relevant to the study of food *qua* food. They have contributed to different ways of theorizing the AGRO-FOOD SYSTEM, including systems of provision, COMMODITY CHAINS and food regimes. Recently, 'food NETWORKS' has become the favoured term in recognition of the fact that food distribution is more contingent than much of this earlier language implies, and that even long-distance trade depends on embedded social relations where TRUST must be secured (Arce and Marsden, 1994). Geographers have also looked at the SCALE dimensions of food provision and consumption (e.g. Bell and Valentine, 1997); and they have engaged in important debates regarding consumption, not only the politics of consumer purchasing in influencing the agro-food system (e.g. Cook and Crang, 1996), but also the bodily materiality of eating practices. In addition, geographers have played a leading role in developing some meso-level concepts, based largely on finely tuned empirical studies.

FAMINE, hunger and food insecurity persist as objects of study, especially as they pertain to UNEVEN DEVELOPMENT and GEOPOLITICS. Watts (1983) was one of the first geographers to develop the concept of social vulnerability as it relates to the uneven effects of famine. Geographers have since adopted the language of food SECURITY, which not only encapsulates a more objective and positive characterization than 'hunger', but also highlights that food insecurity is rooted in insufficient income, entitlement or endowment (Dreze and Sen, 1989). These ideas underlie powerful critiques of how US food AID and concessionary sales of surplus commodities undercut livelihoods and thereby contribute to food insecurity. The activist-developed notion of *community food security* (CFS) suggests that the local community is the scale at which adequate and nutritious food should be ensured. CFS movements have noted the existence of food deserts, which are areas of poor access to the provision of healthy affordable food, usually related to lack of large retailers.

The twin themes of anxiety and trust are also pervasive in the geography of food, especially in light of the policy turn towards standards, labels and private regulation as the major response to recent 'food scares'. While the broader goal of standardization is harmonization in the interest of trade – as exemplified in the *Codex alimentarus* – standards and auditing are increasingly employed to make commodity chains more transparent. Geographers have offered important criticisms of this new form of food regulation. Dunn (2003a), for example, has shown how attempts to impose harmony on an uneven geographical surface can have the effect of exacerbating differentiation among producers. Guthman (2004) has argued that organic food labels have perverse consequences for the intended goals of organic agriculture. Whether voluntary labels constitute a new sort of commodity fetish has been the source of a lively debate within geography.

The other major response to recent trouble in the food system is the creation of *alternative food networks* (AFNs). According to Whatmore, Stassart and Renting (2003, p. 389), 'what they share in common is their constitution as/of food markets that redistribute value through the network against the logic of bulk commodity production; that reconvene "trust" between food producers and consumers; and that articulate new forms of political association and market governance'. AFNs have become a part of SOCIAL MOVEMENT strategies, and thus have been theorized as both alternative forms of DEVELOPMENT and resistance to GLOBALIZATION. For example, FAIR TRADE initiatives, which tie wealthy consumers' moral concerns to the livelihood making of THIRD WORLD PEASANTS, are what Goodman (2004) calls developmental consumption. Some scholars have been less sanguine on these sorts of initiatives, which have considerable overlap with standard-based regulation. Mutersbaugh (2002) has noted that certification processes can create new work routines and new levels of SURVEILLANCE.

Another area that has seen a good deal of recent empirical work is in the transformation and consolidation of food processing, marketing and RETAILING sectors. Many have commented on the enhanced power of retailers in food chains at the same time that supermarkets themselves have been at forefront of ethical trading initiatives (Marsden and Wrigley, 1995). Changing patterns of food consumption associated with the fast food industry and multiple-job HOUSEHOLDS are becoming major objects of study, as well, articulating with public HEALTH concerns regarding a widely discussed crisis of obesity. This is an area that is likely to incite lively debate with geographers of the body, who are more sceptical of the discourse of obesity (Longhurst, 2005). This last research direction augments a growing literature attentive to the ways in which eating is simultaneously metabolic and ethical, such that the BODY is a site where various sorts of food anxieties are mediated (Stassart and Whatmore, 2003). Of course, virtually all of the above recent trends are interrelated and at the same time point to the extreme bifurcations within both food provision and consumption. For these reasons and many others, geography of food has become a rich area of enquiry indeed.   JGu

Suggested reading
Atkins and Bowler (2001); Freidberg (2004); Lang and Heasman (2004); Winter (2004).

footloose industry An industry that can operate successfully in a wide variety of locations because it has no strong material orientation or market orientation requirements and wide spatial margins to profitability. Transport usually involves only a very small proportion of its cost structure – as in the establishment of call centres in countries many thousands of miles from the customers served.   RJ

Fordism The term used to describe both the manufacturing techniques and societal conditions underlying the MODE OF PRODUCTION developed by Henry Ford in the USA during the early 1900s. Ford revolutionized the production of the motor car, as well as manufacturing more generally, through his system which was based around four main principles: (1) vertical integration, whereby all elements

of the manufacturing process take place at one site and assembly occurs on a moving production line; (2) scientific management and the principles of TAYLORISM that allow worker PRODUCTIVITY to be increased; (3) standardization and ECONOMIES OF SCALE with a limited number or only one product model offered; and (4) mass consumption as a REGIME OF ACCUMULATION, driven by the fact that workers are paid well and thus became consumers themselves and create a self-reproducing demand for goods.

As work framed under the REGULATION THEORY of POLITICAL ECONOMY has shown, Fordism was widely adopted by manufacturers in the post-Second World War period and was applied to industries as diverse as biscuit production and film. Because of the unprecedented period of economic growth and stability associated with Fordism up until the 1970s, the period became known as the 'Golden Age' of Fordism (Glyn, Hughes, Lipietz and Singh, 1991). However, the very principles upon which Fordism was founded were also responsible for its undoing in the 1970s. Consumers began to develop a disdain for the homogenization associated with the one size fits all approach of Fordist manufacturing. Scientific management and the deskilling of work led to worker dissatisfaction and frustration, because of the monotonous and time-pressurized production in factories. In addition, economic instability, particularly associated with the OPEC OIL CRISIS, led to a slow-down in wage increases, thus threatening the whole regime of accumulation upon which Fordism was founded. At the same time, workers began to rebel against the way management and workers were distinct and separate categories in Fordism. This created little opportunity for progression, but most significantly meant that wage negotiations between labour and management took place through collective bargaining, something accepted in times of large wage increases but rejected as wage increases declined. However, as Sayer and Walker (1992) point out, this does not mean that Fordism ended in this period and was replaced by POST-FORDISM. Rather, Fordism was challenged (but not necessarily displaced) by the (re-)emergence of different logics of production and ACCUMULATION.

For geographers, Fordism is often associated with the emergence of important industrial REGIONS such as the Black Country in the West Midlands of the UK (see Daniels, Bradshaw, Shaw and Sidaway, 2005); industries such as FILM production, in particular in

Los Angeles, that adopted Fordist principles at an early stage (see Christopherson and Storper, 1986); and also a gendered DIVISION OF LABOUR, in which the place of men was seen to be the factory and women the HOME (McDowell, 1991).   JF

Suggested reading
Murray (1989).

forecast The construction of an estimated value for an observation unit, where the observation might be for a place, region, individual or time-period. The forecast may be generated by several quantitative MODELS and methods (see PREDICTION), and the term is usually employed for estimates applying to observations outside the group used in the model's calibration: it is an 'out-of-sample' estimate, most likely for a future time-period, or, in a 'spatial forecast', for a region not included in the estimation process (see SPACE-TIME FORECASTING MODELS).   LWH

forestry Most commonly, forestry refers to the development and application of knowledge and practices aimed at managing forests for human use. The word has a scientific connotation befitting the evolution of specialized, increasingly technical and professionalized knowledge about trees and forests aimed at their intentional manipulation, and of the particular emergence of silviculture as the science of growing trees. As a SCIENCE, forestry emerged largely from German and French antecedents in the sixteenth and seventeenth centuries, from Japanese and Chinese precedents in the intentional growth and management of forests for wood, and from early-twentieth-century Scandinavian contributions, particularly in the areas of provenance, seed source and the intentional cultivation of seed stock for plantation forestry (Boyd and Prudham, 2003). This ostensibly technical field of knowledge, widely institutionalized under the auspices of forestry departments and programmes in universities and colleges, as well as in state agencies at various SCALES from local to national, and propagated via scientific journals, is part of what is conveyed by the term 'forestry'. However, several questions arise in the very invocation of this specialized term, not least: What is a forest (and is it merely a collection of trees)? Which particular human uses dominate in shaping the trajectory of forest management? These ostensibly simple questions lead to the realization that forests and forestry, whatever else

they are, comprise sites of struggle where interacting and contending processes of social and ecological reproduction are partially constituted. For instance, the management of forests emphasizing the reproduction of commercially valuable tree species, resolved primarily at the localized level of discrete stands of forests, has been the dominant practice of scientific forestry in the European tradition (epitomized by the German notion of *Normalbaum*). This approach was widely institutionalized in both EUROPE and North America between the mid-nineteenth and mid-twentieth centuries, and has increasingly been exported around the world. However, critical examination of this PARADIGM reveals that it is hardly ecologically or socially innocent, prescribing the elimination of older trees, for instance, as well as biological organisms whose existence depends on habitat compromised by conversion to plantations (e.g. the northern spotted owl in western North America), while at the same time privileging commercial timber interests over competing human values (e.g. hunting, fishing, trapping, gathering, RECREATION, agriculture etc.). All of this reinforces the need to avoid reifying apolitical renderings of forests that would naturalize them as non-human landscapes. Rather, as works such as E.P. Thompson's *Whigs and hunters* (1975) demonstrates, it was not so long ago even in English history that forests were decidedly populated and contested, not least by conflicting PROPERTY claims. Thus, as Willems-Braun (1997) more recently argued in the context of First Nation struggles in British Columbia, Canada, the apparently empty lands typical of scientific forestry representations are often sites of past and ongoing forced removals and exclusions. In short, despite its technical connotations and widespread professionalization, forestry is a complex categorical invocation of attempts to manage complex POLITICAL ECOLOGIES, where trees, humans and other organisms interact, and where human attempts at intentional management rely on constructions of what is desirable and useful that can be (and are) politicized all the way down to the level of what constitutes a tree, and what does and ought to count as forest cover (Robbins, 2001).   SP

Suggested reading
Demeritt (2001b); Scott (1998).

foundationalism The assumption that knowledge claims must be grounded in a source of certainty that cannot be called into question, and from which the truth value of other propositions can be inferred. Rationalist foundationalism identifies this ground of certainty in intellectual intuition of some sort; in other words, most of what we know we know by reasoning. Empiricist foundationalism identifies the grounds of certainty in sensory observation; in other words, most of what we know we know by experience (see EMPIRICISM). The key point about discussions of foundationalism is that they are concerned with *epistemic justification* – with establishing the grounds for justifying when a *belief* counts as *knowledge* (see EPISTEMOLOGY).

The most famous example of a foundationalist epistemology is Descartes' *cogito ergo sum* ('I think, therefore I am'), in which the act of thinking is identified as the foundational ground of certainty that can guarantee non-foundational beliefs. It is from the confidence of this 'I think' (specifically, in response to the question 'How do I know?') that the possibility of justified knowledge claims is derived. Descartes established the criterion of *certainty* as the basis for epistemic justification. This leads to a radical scepticism about external reality. All foundationalist epistemologies share a monological, internalist view of the (human) subject of knowledge, confronting the external world wracked with doubt. Criticisms of foundationalism therefore have a content, in that they are about more than simply the best way of justifying belief; they are fundamentally about disputed pictures of what it is to be human.

Rorty's (1979) repudiation of the idea that philosophy can ever possibly find the objective, transcendent grounds of certainty from which to justify belief informs a line of *anti-foundationalist* argument in HUMAN GEOGRAPHY. For him, what confers epistemic justification on beliefs is whether they work, whether they are useful or whether they are held valid by a community of practice. This implies that the philosophical study of knowledge as an abstract conceptual matter of justification should at least be augmented by looking at how knowledge claims work in practical contexts (see PHILOSOPHY; PRAGMATISM). This type of empirical programme can certainly help us to understand the conditions that determine *when* claims will be believed as knowledge; but it closes down the question of when they *ought* to be so believed.

In GEOGRAPHY, anti-foundationalist arguments are sometimes invoked to question the validity of explanatory social science, but it is far from clear that modern social science is

vulnerable to the charge of foundationalism as this term is used in philosophical debates (cf. ESSENTIALISM). Geographers have also engaged in wider debates about the political significance of anti-foundationalist perspectives. These centre on the degree to which it is possible to square the academic disruption of knowledge claims, by showing them to be contingent and contextual, with the assumed requirement for political movements to be based on secure grounds of identity and experience. Various formulations finesse this problem, such as Judith Butler's *contingent foundations* and Gayatri Spivak's *strategic essentialism*. White (2000) develops the idea of *weak ontology* to negotiate the fact that any argument requires making presuppositions and fundamental ontological commitments, arguing that it is nonetheless possible to adopt a degree of rhetorical reflexivity to show their contingency (see ONTOLOGY). But all of these formulas tend to rest on the 'the implicit assumption that one could think like a sceptic but act like a foundationalist' (Zerilli, 1998, p. 438), and therefore tend to misconstrue what is at stake in issues of foundationalism. The widespread assumption that anti-foundationalism involves a generalized affirmation of contingency betrays a scholastic perspective that is unable to grasp the conditions of its own critical doubt, and remains caught within the problematic of epistemic certainty. A less deceitful response to the problems of foundationalism might be derived from Wittgenstein's considerations of scepticism. He held that absolute doubt of the sort entertained by Descartes does not provide plausible grounds for understanding the way in which knowledge works in practice: 'the questions we raise and our doubts depend on the fact that some propositions are exempt from doubt, are as it were like hinges on which those turn' (1969, p. 341). The point here is two-fold: the world of human affairs is not only held together by relationships of knowledge, either of certainty or contingency; and the expression of doubt is always undertaken in context, in relation to a particular set of concerns, and against a background of beliefs and commitments that stand fast.   CB

Suggested reading
Appiah (2003); Taylor (1995a, ch. 1).

Fourth World The poorest and most vulnerable groups of people within the developing world (cf. THIRD WORLD; see also SOUTH). Fourth World people are sometimes defined as those in extreme income POVERTY and/or living in the so-called FAMINE belt of sub-Saharan Africa. Many suffer from HUMAN RIGHTS abuses (see the website for the non-governmental organization ATD Fourth World: http://www.atd-fourthworld.org). Other Fourth World peoples suffer from pervasive SOCIAL EXCLUSION on grounds of ETHNICITY, GENDER or RELIGION. Many Fourth World peoples reject efforts to mark them down as 'inferior'. For example, *adivasis* ('tribals') and *dalits* (the 'oppressed', or ex-untouchables) in India have proclaimed their First Nation status (see CASTE).   SCO

Suggested reading
See http://www.atd.quartmonde.org

fractal Fractals are irregular objects that cannot be defined by traditional geometry but which, in some cases (such as Koch snowflakes) have the property of self-similarity: their pattern appears the same regardless of the scale at which they are viewed.

The easiest way to explain fractals is by appeal to intuition. In CARTOGRAPHY we are used to zero-, one- and two-dimensional objects representing point, line and area features on a map. Simply by looking, it is obvious that each higher-dimensional object fills more of the space than a lesser one: a rectangular object fills more of the MAP than a line placed along one side of the rectangle or a point positioned at one of its corners. There is a connection between dimensionality and space filling.

Now think of a number line. Although we often count using whole numbers (1, 2, 3, ...), we also accept that the line is continuous and so provides us with fractions (1, 1.2, 1.31, 1.411 etc.). Can the same principle be applied to dimensions?

Various nineteenth- and twentieth-century mathematicians have shown that it can. Of particular interest to geographers is Benoît Mandelbrot's (1967) question, 'How long is the coast of Britain?' As he showed, there is no one answer: it depends on the precision of the measuring device – the calliper – used to trace around the islands (see MEASUREMENT). As the precision increases, more of the detail of the shoreline is included and the apparent length increases.

To imagine the problem another way, suppose that we could encode the coastline in perfect detail in a digital mapping package such as a GEOGRAPHIC INFORMATION SYSTEM. Each time we 'zoomed in' to a fixed location on the coast more of its detail would be revealed. This would happen every time, without limit, because fractals possess infinite detail. Of course, we cannot really encode this infinite detail and so the total measured length of the coastline becomes dependent on the SCALE of analysis – by how the coast is generalized. Knowing this, we can take the measurement at multiple scales, to plot the (natural log) of the coastline length against the (natural log) of the calliper used to measure it. The gradient of the line of best fit to these values is an estimate of the coastline's fractal dimension.

This may sound abstract, but fractals are evident in NATURE: leaves, trees, river networks and so forth. Their relevance is not just to the physical landscape. Within the social sciences, fractals can be used to model the processes of urban MORPHOLOGY (Batty and Longley, 1994). Reciprocally, the fractal dimension, as a measure of space filling, can be used to model the SPRAWL or compactness of cities. Fractals can be linked to CHAOS THEORY: the idea that physical or social systems that appear to be chaotic can actually be modelled by clearly defined 'laws' or theories (e.g. using economic theories to model urban development and growth: see Batty, 2005). Finally, fractals are used in REMOTE SENSING to compress (reduce the file size) of images.   RH

Suggested reading
Batty (2005); Mandelbrot (1967).

free port An ENCLAVE within a country – typically a seaport, though increasingly other areas – where import and export (customs) duties are either not imposed or are reduced. This enables both warehousing and manufacturing functions to be located there producing a local COMPARATIVE ADVANTAGE and generating employment and wealth, at a cost advantage over other locations (cf. EXPORT PROCESSING ZONE). Free ports (such as Copenhagen, Danzig and Hamburg) existed in Europe until the mid-twentieth century, and free port status was a foundation of the economic success of Hong Kong and Singapore. The concept has been adapted for some airports – as at Shannon in the Irish Republic – and was reworked into that of the urban ENTERPRISE ZONE by the geographer Sir Peter Hall in the late 1980s to promote redevelopment in run-down industrial areas through tax advantages. Special Economic Zones (SEZs) with very similar characteristics are now widespread in the global SOUTH: India initiated a programme in 2000 and by

2006 had 237 SEZs approved, with a further 306 applications pending (see http://sezindia. nic.in/). RJ

free trade area (FTA) A group of NATION-STATES that agrees to practice free TRADE (no tariffs or other restrictions) amongst themselves, while retaining trade barriers with non-members. Unlike a customs union, trade relations with non-members may differ for each state. Many link contiguous nations into a supranational regional bloc, but there are also non-contiguous FTAs. More than half of the some 200 FTAs began after 1990. Rules of origin, defining what counts as production within a member nation-state, determine which COMMODITIES are subject to free trade. For proponents, FTAs catalyse global free trade; opponents see such 'Preferential' Trade Areas as detrimental. The two largest are within the global NORTH, NAFTA and the EU, and enhance North–South trade barriers, but many SOUTH–South and North–South FTAs exist (the latter usually initiated from the North). ES

friction of distance The frictional or inhibiting effect of distance on the volume of interaction between places (including MIGRATION, tourist flows, the movement of goods and the spread of ideas and DISEASES: cf. DIFFUSION): empirical regularities in interaction patterns consistent with the effect are characterized by DISTANCE DECAY. The effect is generated by the combined impact of the time and cost involved in overcoming distance, which varies according to the available transport and communications INFRASTRUCTURE. The frictions of distance are reduced with technological improvements in that infrastructure – though not necessarily to the same extent everywhere (cf. TIME-SPACE COMPRESSION; TIME-SPACE CONVERGENCE; TIME-SPACE EXPANSION). RJ

Suggested reading
Taylor (1971).

friends-and-neighbours effect A form of CONTEXTUAL EFFECT identified in ELECTORAL GEOGRAPHY whereby voters favour local candidates (even if this means abandoning their traditional party preferences) because either they know the candidate personally or/and they believe that her/his election will promote local interests. The concept was developed in Key's (1949) analyses of intra-party voting in the US South and generalized by Cox (1969) and others. Candidates who are successful

through this strategy may reward their constituents by winning public expenditure for the area (cf. NEIGHBOURHOOD EFFECT; PORK BARREL). RJ

frontier A frontier marks a limit. It has been used in two main ways. In the first case, it refers to the limits of a STATE. The frontier of a state is its border with another state. In modern times, this frontier is thought of as a line, since the SOVEREIGNTY of a state is asserted as continuous up to its edges. In medieval EUROPE, however, feudal monarchs understood that their authority waned towards the periphery of their lands: these REGIONS were termed 'marches' and the marcher lords had significant autonomy (see FEUDALISM). The emergence of the modern atlas showing countries in different colours with distinct borders represents (and in part produces) a world very different from the early modern period and conformable with the presumptions of modern NATION-STATES (Black, 1997).

Modern state frontiers are often contentious too, and a whole branch of GEOGRAPHY developed on the pretension that borders could be settled scientifically (Curzon, 1888; Holdich, 1916). These scholars paid attention to the distribution of ethnic groups, and to the existence of regions that were difficult to settle or cross. An efficient border would clearly separate different sorts of people by a line that was in an isolated region, presenting a significant challenge to transgressors. In fact, these borders reflected the geopolitical interests of global superpowers (see GEOPOLITICS), and the first major international attempts at comprehensive border-setting served the colonial interests of European powers in Africa (at the Berlin Conference in 1884–5) and of the major global powers with regard to Eastern and Central Europe (at the Paris Peace Conference in 1919). The peoples of Africa and of Eastern and Central EUROPE were not consulted.

The second sense of frontier is as a line between settled and unsettled lands, cultivated and uncultivated. This is equally contentious. It almost always, in fact, separates one society from another and yet is presented as the separation of society from emptiness (cf. TERRA NULLIUS). The most famous of these frontiers is that about which Frederick Jackson Turner developed his FRONTIER THESIS. The settlement of North America by Europeans expelled native peoples from their lands. The Europeans persuaded themselves that only sedentary cultivation was true CIVILIZATION and that lands not used for that purpose were at best wasted, even empty. Viewed, rather, as an act of COLONIALISM or IMPERIALISM (Meinig, 1986), frontiers mark an important topic for comparative study.   GK

Suggested reading
Fawcett (1918); Lamar and Thompson (1981).

frontier thesis The argument developed by Frederick Jackson Turner (1861–1932) concerning 'The significance of the frontier in American history' (Turner, 1893). The US CENSUS had been mapping the limit of European settlement as a FRONTIER moving across the land from east to west (Paulin, 1932). In 1890, the Census announced that there was no longer a clear line separating the areas to the east settled at greater than two persons per square mile and those to the west that were more sparsely settled. Instead, there was now a patchwork of less densely settled areas in the west, and the idea of a continuous frontier between more and less densely settled parts was no longer valid. Turner took this to be the end of a distinct PROCESS. In 1892, speaking to historians gathered in Chicago on the occasion of the 400th anniversary of European entry to the Americas, Turner addressed the implications of the closing of the American frontier for democracy in the USA.

Turner claimed that, at the frontier, Europeans were forced to revert to more primitive forms of CIVILIZATION. In this way they broke their links with Europe and began to create a new and distinctly *American* society. At the frontier, society passed through all the stages from hunting up to the ultimate form of civilization, urban–industrial society. By passing through all these stages, Euro-Americans re-learned for themselves the need for DEMOCRACY, lessons that people in Europe took so much for granted as to have almost forgotten. Yet this learning was at the heart of the popular democracy that Turner cherished. With the closing of the frontier, a new way would have to be found to keep these lessons alive. Universities, he argued, would now have to act as the keepers of a truth that would no longer be learned naturally at the frontier.

These ideas have been much criticized, most notably by the so-called New Western Historians (Kearns, 1998). Limerick (1987) argues that Turner only credits Euro-American men with historical agency, and ignores issues of RACE, CLASS and GENDER. A historical process that consigns the native peoples of America to a shrinking margin makes it difficult for them to make claims about their right to a future in this land. Limerick also argues that rather than being legible as a process moving from east to west, European COLONIALISM in North America included significant movement of Spanish-Americans from the south, and of other Europeans who began not on the east coast, but on the west. The frontier that Turner speaks of is a farming frontier based on family farms, and yet large parts of the USA were taken from native peoples for large-scale ranching or mining without passing through the sort of family farms and villages that sustained Turner's nascent democracies. Finally, Turner actually misses many of the distinctive features about the American West, including the continuous role of the STATE in the ECONOMY. GK

Suggested reading
Cronon (1987); Turner (1893).

functionalism A term found across the social sciences and used to explain variously mental, behavioural and social phenomena by the role that they play – which is to say, their function – in maintaining the larger SYSTEM of which they are part. The larger system comes first, reaching back to determine the functional roles of its various parts in enabling its reproduction and development.

As an explanatory strategy, functionalism was first systematically stated in nineteenth-century Darwinian evolutionary biology. Physiological characteristics were explained by their functional role in enabling the systemic ends of species survival and reproduction (see DARWINISM). Not surprisingly, when the French sociologist Émile Durkheim (1858–1917) introduced the same idea into sociology in the late nineteenth century, he drew on a biological analogy and likened the division of labour in society to the functional role of organs within a body. For Durkheim, the larger ends of stability and survival determined how society's constituent parts functioned. Durkeheim's work influenced a group of British-based anthropologists – Bronislaw Malinowski (1884–1942), Alfred Radcliffe-Brown (1881–1952), Edward Evans Pritchard (1902–73) and Meyer Fortes (1906–83) – who developed STRUCTURAL FUNCTIONALISM. While on the surface the various cultures that they studied – the Trobianders, the Nuer, the Tallensi – seemed quite different, they proposed that a common functional operation underpinned all of them: the components of culture worked together to promote smooth equilibrium and effortless reproduction. Structural functionalism entered sociology through the work of American sociologist Talcott Parsons (1902–79) and was later developed as 'systems theory' by Parsons and by Niklas Luhmann (1927–99). Outside of the anthropology–sociology nexus, functionalism was also incorporated into some forms of Marxism, provoking new theorizing about the nature of functionalist explanation (Cohen, 1978; see also ANALYTICAL MARXISM), and in the philosophy of the mind, where mental states are conceived as a function of the cognitive system of which they are part.

Oddly, given the influence of Darwinism on geography and the magpie quality of geographical theorizing, functionalism was never prominent in the discipline. It weaved in and out of some early writings by European geographers, including Ratzel's ANTHROPOGEO-GRAPHY and Vidal de la Blache's vision of HUMAN GEOGRAPHY. There were hints of functionalism in Hartshorne's (1939) notion of the REGION as an 'element complex', and even stronger ones in the systems analysis introduced to the discipline in the 1970s (although it was mainly confined to environmental issues: see Bennett and Chorley, 1978). The most likely location for structural functionalism within the modern discipline was SOCIAL GEOGRAPHY, but by the time it became interested in theoretical formalization, the star of structural functionalism was fading in both anthropology and sociology. Functionalism was more significant in early RADICAL GEOGRAPHY. Thus Harvey (1999 [1982]) conceived space and place as functional elements in the reproduction of capitalism: capitalism reached back to ensure that its landscape regenerated the system. Even crises – the annihilation of space, the destruction of place – were functional. Similarly, the REGULATION SCHOOL advocated *a posteriori* functionalism in its analysis of capitalism (the success of the functional relation is known only after the fact of its success).

All this said, the functionalism found in human geography is often only implicit. Further, given the drubbing that functionalism has received over the past half-century – it is variously accused of determinism, of neglecting historical context, of denying individual agency, of imbuing collective entities with characteristics germane only to individuals and of neglecting causal mechanisms – it is unlikely ever to become explicit.   TB

Suggested reading
Giddens (1977, ch. 2).

fuzzy sets/fuzzy logic   Sets (categories, classes, types) for which the definitions of class membership are vague or 'fuzzy', and contrast with the sharp, clearly defined definitions used by standard logic and set theory. Thus 'deprived' and 'middle-class' are fuzzy categories in everyday life and usage, only converted into precise categories by government or other statistical definitions. Fuzziness describes a type of UNCERTAINTY, but it is not the usual uncertainty of probability (e.g. the percentage chance of a US citizen being in the 'deprived' category). It describes 'event ambiguity', the degree to which an event occurs, not whether it occurs. Most quantitative and statistical modelling assumes non-fuzzy sets, and only a few studies have developed fuzzy-set applications relevant to geography, notably Openshaw's work on SPATIAL INTERACTION using fuzzy distances ('short', 'average', 'long': Openshaw and Openshaw, 1997). Openshaw (1996) saw fuzzy logic as a key to make 'soft human geography' more scientific, but most would paint a much more modest picture of its potential.   LWH

Suggested reading
Openshaw and Openshaw (1997); Robinson (2003).

G

game theory A theory of interdependent DECISION-MAKING. Individuals ('players') choose their actions ('strategies') with limited or zero knowledge of those of the other players, but with knowledge of the 'payoffs' (costs and benefits) of different joint outcomes. The theory was taken up by von Neumann and Morgenstern in *Theory of games and economic behaviour* (1944) and has been extensively developed and applied in economics and other social sciences, notably political science and sociology. In GEOGRAPHY a pioneering study was that by Gould (1963), which showed how African farmers' agricultural strategies could be modelled as 'a game against nature', with the farmers gaining different benefits depending on what they produced and what weather NATURE chose to throw at them.

Game theory tries to deduce the EQUILIBRIUM strategies of players under rational decision-making. Games may be non-co-operative (where each player only considers their own benefits and costs) or allow co-operation between the players. A classic example where individual RATIONAL CHOICE leads to collective sub-optimality is the PRISONER'S DILEMMA. A geographical example of a simple competitive, two-person, zero-sum game is the model of two ice-cream sellers on a linear beach, with a uniformly distributed population of consumers. If consumers buy from the nearest seller, then the rational seller strategy is to locate back-to-back in the centre of the beach – any other location gives an advantage to the other seller (see HOTELLING MODEL). Yet, from the consumers' angle, this is sub-optimal. They would benefit more if the sellers located one-third from the two ends of the beach, so that consumers had to walk less. (Of course, this assumes that both sellers have identical prices for identical products: see HOTELLING MODEL.) Much of the later theory has concerned how non-co-operative games can lead to non-zero-sum payoffs under various assumptions, and this work (starting with John Nash's work in the early 1950s) lies behind much of the modern THEORY of economic MARKETS and bargaining.

Game theory has been applied to problems of interregional EXTERNALITIES, where actions in one region are interdependent with those in another, as in WATER RESOURCE development, POLLUTION strategies and environmental policy, and in economic policies within a federal state such as the USA or an economic union such as the European Union. It has also been extended to dynamic games, where learning takes place and sequences of choices are made and where there may be 'leaders' and 'followers' (the Stackelberg game), as in federal–local policies. However, most of these studies are by economists, and, as ECONOMIC GEOGRAPHY has increasingly lost contact with much of recent economics, few geographers have pursued these developments. LWH

Suggested reading
Gould (1963).

garden city A relatively spacious and small, self-contained planned settlement. Originally conceived by Ebenezer Howard (1850–1928), the concept was adopted by the British Garden City Movement, which he founded. It formed the basis for two settlements – Letchworth (1903) and Welwyn (1920) – in Hertfordshire: both are now much larger than Howard originally envisaged (c.32,000 people on a 6,000 acre [~2,430 ha] site). The idea of low-density, relatively small, high-quality settlements characterized by their 'greenness' was adopted in a number of countries during the twentieth century, as part of a planning ideology based on COMMUNITY (cf. NEIGHBOURHOOD UNIT): indeed, the garden city movement was the precursor in the UK of the Town and Country Planning Association, which remains a powerful pressure group. The general concept was transferred to other countries and influenced the planning of numerous new settlements – such as Canberra – and NEW TOWN movements, as in the USA. RJ

Suggested reading
Hall and Ward (1998).

gated communities While associated with the large US urban regions (Blakely and Snyder, 1997), gated communities are increasingly global in their distribution (Webster, Glasze and Frantz, 2002). They are residential ENCLAVES demarcated physically by walls, fences and secured gateways, which are often

267

patrolled by private security guards. They are also frequently governed by community associations that regulate residents' activities and design decisions. The proliferation of gated enclaves, private GOVERNANCE and SECURITY is generally understood to lead to the delegitimization of PUBLIC SERVICES and is a physical manifestation of growing resistance to 'democratization, social equalization, and [the] expansion of citizenship rights' (Caldeira, 2000, p. 4; but see Salcedo and Torres, 2004). Thus, gated communities have been the focus of research not only because of their global presence but also because of what they suggest about perceptions of security, COMMUNITY, CITIZENSHIP, PUBLIC SPACE, PROPERTY and the role of the STATE in contemporary urban societies (cf. SURVEILLANCE).   EM

Suggested reading
Caldeira (2000).

gender A categorical distinction between men and women; a technology of CLASSIFICATION that naturalizes sexual difference and is intertwined with other distinctions, such as nature/culture, and racial and national differentiation. PLACES become coded as masculine or feminine, and this can be one important means of naturalizing gender difference (Bondi and Davidson, 2003). Haraway (1991b) provides a thorough discussion of the history and meaning of the term 'gender' within feminist theory through to the mid-1980s (see FEMINISM). The term has a broadly similar history within GEOGRAPHY: there has been a move away from theories of relatively static gender roles to gender relations, and towards a fuller exploration of how diverse gender relations are constructed in all spheres of life. Emphasis has been placed on the variety of femininities and masculinities – ways of living gender, depending on context and intersections with RACE, CLASS, RELIGION, SEXUALITY, nationality and other social and geographical DIFFERENCES (Bondi and Davidson, 2005; see also FEMINIST GEOGRAPHIES).

Within Anglophone feminism, 'gender' is typically contrasted to 'SEX': the former is understood as a SOCIAL CONSTRUCTION, the latter has been defined by biology. The distinction has been part of an effort to denaturalize conventional understandings of women and femininity, to remove women from NATURE and place them within CULTURE as constructed and self-constituting social subjects (see PHALLOCENTRICISM). The treatment of gender within GEOGRAPHY is slightly unusual in this regard, as it has not been 'quarantined from the infections of biological sex' (Haraway, 1991b, p. 134) to the same extent as in other disciplines. In an effort to theorize PATRIARCHY, for instance, Foord and Gregson (1986) identified necessary relations that constitute gender relations. Following the analytical procedures of REALISM, they reasoned that two genders, male and female, are the basic characteristics of gender relations. In order to theorize the necessary relations between these basic characteristics, they ask 'Under what conditions do men and women require each other's existence?', to which they answer, for biological reproduction and the practice of heterosexuality. Foord and Gregson's analysis was quickly criticized, because it made it difficult to theorize how CAPITALISM structures gender relations (McDowell, 1986) and for its biologism, especially in terms of its portrayal of heterosexuality as biologically or psychologically fixed (Knopp and Lauria, 1987).

The latter criticism signalled important new ways of thinking about the relations between sex and gender. The feminist distinction between sex and gender may save gender from ESSENTIALIST or naturalizing versions of femininity, but it repeats the problems of the nature/culture dualism insofar as it posits gender as the (active) social that acts upon the (passive) surface of sex. It is itself thus vulnerable to the charge of MASCULINISM: "Is sex to gender as feminine to masculine [as nature to culture]?' (Butler, 1993a, p. 4). A further problem is that within the terms of the sex/gender dualism sex seems to disappear once it is gendered: gender absorbs and displaces sex (these tendencies within geography are discussed by Nast, 1998).

Drawing upon theories of DISCOURSE, DECONSTRUCTION and PSYCHOANALYSIS, Butler (1993a) tackled this problem by arguing that both sex and gender are socially constructed. Neither sex nor gender has ONTOLOGICAL status and neither can be theorized apart from regimes of (hetero)sexuality. For Butler, sex is neither extra- nor pre-discursive: the sexed BODY is brought into being through the regulatory regime of heterosexuality. Within HETERONORMATIVITY, we must be gendered and sexed as either male or female to be human: she argues that those who are not properly sexed are threatened by psychosis (unstable bodily and psychic boundaries) and ABJECTION. Gender is a truth effect of a discourse of a primary and stable identity: this identity emerges out of repetitive gender performances, which are instantiations of an ideal/

norm (see PERFORMATIVITY; SUBJECTIVITY). Butler does see opportunities to prise performances of sex and gender apart: the subversive potential of drag performances, for example, lies in the disjunction between (an assumed interiorized) sex and exteriorized gender performances, as well as the performance of the sexually disallowed or unperformable (e.g. men acting out conventions of femininity). The implications of this retheorization of gender and sex are far reaching: gender is recast as derivative of the regulatory norms of (hetero) sex and as repetitive and unstable practices enacted in different ways in different places and times. This invites close attention to the persistent deployment of regulatory regimes of heterosexuality, to the sexualities that operate at the margins of and exceed the boundaries of these norms, and to the geographies of both (see HOMOPHOBIA AND HETEROSEXISM; QUEER THEORY; SEXUALITY; Nash, 1998; Hubbard, 2000).

The material limits to social constructivism and a focus on life that exceeds DISCOURSE has drawn increasing attention. Another approach to the problem that the sex/gender dualism replays a phallocentric binary (one that complements rather than contradicts that of Butler) has been to emphasize the agency and dynamism of nature. Grosz (2005) articulates this strategy when she implores feminists to attend to 'matter' as 'that which preconditions and destabilizes gender and bodies, that which problematizes all identity' (p. 172). Echoing Butler, she understands gender to be a contained, represented, socialized, phallocentric ideal and, following Irigarary, she directs feminist enquiry away from gender to sexual difference, which she associates with an unbounding and proliferation of identifications, ontologies and ways of knowing.

Ramon-Garcia, Simonsen and Vaiou (2006) note that the debates about the sex/gender binary are specific to particular LANGUAGE communities: feminists theorizing within languages for which there is no distinction between sex and gender have developed non-essentialist arguments about gender without drawing on this dualism. Even within Anglophone feminism, there have been other approaches to theorizing the category of woman outside of the gender/sex binary. Bondi and Davidson (2003) call upon Wittgenstein's notion of 'family resemblance' to theorize the category 'woman' as a loose network of similarities rather than essential qualities, and Iris Marion Young (1997b) has theorized the gender of woman as a series brought together by context-specific material conditions rather than as a set of embodied characteristics or an identification.   GP

Suggested reading
Bondi and Davidson (2003).

gender and development   A contested landscape of theoretical and political approaches to gender, or *the woman question* in DEVELOPMENT, where Women in Development (WID), Women and Development (WAD) and Gender and Development (GAD) emerged as major discursive fields, broadly paralleling liberal, radical and Marxist/socialist feminist perspectives (Saunders, 2002). Of these, WID (whose beginnings can be traced to the works of Esther Boserup) has been instrumental in defining the hegemonic field of feminist development practices. Although it has enjoyed legitimacy and integration with major bi-/multilateral development agencies and the United Nations, WID has been critiqued within feminist and alternative development circles for its assumptions about sisterhood and its erasure of differences based on class, nationality and colonial histories and geographies.

For WAD theorists, inclusion and exclusion is related to hierarchical spatialization of the global CAPITALIST ECONOMY that shapes the differentiated spaces of core, semi-periphery and periphery; urban and rural; capitalist and subsistence sectors (see UNEVEN DEVELOPMENT). Since peripheral spaces are central to development's local, regional and global formations, the THIRD WORLD's poorest women are seen as an integral piece of exploitative capitalist development processes. For many theorists and collectives from the SOUTH, this understanding translates into a close correspondence between 'experience' and 'visions' in their theoretical centring of those poor Third World women whose bodies have become the objects of developmentalist interventions.

The GAD theorists centre on GENDER and CLASS relations rather than on women *per se*. They emphasize broader interlocking relationships between the rules, resources, practices and POWER through which social inequalities (gender, CASTE, class etc.) are constituted and played out in specific contexts (Kabeer and Subrahmanian, 1999). Like WID, GAD is also gynocentric. Unlike WID however, GAD's socialistic orientation is reflected in a belief in the STATE's redistributive and welfare role (see SOCIALISM). At the level of practice, the strategy of gender mainstreaming – particularly NGO-linked women's

EMPOWERMENT – has become increasingly identified with GAD.

Since the 1980s, writings by post-colonial and Third World feminists have sparked sustained reflection and debate on the political and intellectual representations of the Third World woman in Western feminist discursive practices, and underscored that 'woman' is not a 'real' but a political SUBJECT, shaped through DISCOURSES and institutional actors with high political stakes (see POST-STRUCTUR-ALISM; POST-COLONIALISM). For geographers, engagements with post-structuralist insights also translated into examination of how struggles over labour and resources reveal deeper contestations over gendered (and other) meanings in the ways that RIGHTS to RE-SOURCES are negotiated and redefined within the political arenas of HOUSEHOLD, workplace and state (Carney, 1996). Katz (2004, p. 227) further spatializes processes of development and resistance through the notion of TIME–SPACE EXPANSION, which allows a simultaneous theorizing of: (a) the expanded field within which gendered and generational subjects engage in material social practices of production and reproduction; (b) the growing distance of the Third World's villages from global centres, whose own interactions have been intensified through TIME–SPACE COMPRESSION; and (c) an acute awareness among people living in impoverished rural places, not only of being marooned in a reconfigured global SPACE, but also of what is to be had and the pain of absences created by this expansion of desire. (See also FEMINIST GEOGRAPHIES.)   RN

genealogy   A mode of historical enquiry that seeks to trace the emergence and descent of terms and categories, and the interrelation of power and knowledge in their deployment. The term is used in German philosopher Friedrich Nietzsche's 1882 work *On the genealogy of morality* (1994; see Ansell-Pearson, 1994), although it is in a key essay by the French thinker Michel Foucault (1977c [1963]) and his subsequent adoption of the term to describe his own work that it took on its modern importance.

Foucault is concerned with showing how taken-for-granted phenomena actually have complicated and often-forgotten histories. In works on DISCIPLINARY POWER (1976a [1975]), sexuality (1978 [1976]) and political rationalities (see GOVERNMENTALITY), Foucault sought to undermine – in the sense of excavate and challenge – standard accounts and interpretations. He suggested that genealogy did

not confuse itself with a quest for origins, but rather looked to the moment of emergence of a problematic and to trace its descent through all the circuitous paths it may have taken. Words have not remained with the same meanings, and so etymology may reveal much about a subject – an approach favoured by Nietzsche, and his fellow German philosopher Martin Heidegger – nor have established logics always been seen the same way.

Foucault claimed that his purpose in writing was not to write a history of the past, but a history of the present, in order to illuminate how we have arrived where we are, which will open up future possibilities of change and resistance. Foucault's earlier writings had been described as archaeologies, and although the two approaches are sometimes seen as opposites, it makes more sense to see them as complementary, as Foucault often intimated. In Foucault's usage, *archaeology* tended to look at the logics that conditioned the formations of knowledge in a given epoch (see EPISTEME), while *genealogy* introduced a complementary analysis of POWER, of the practices that follow from, and enable, knowledge.

Critics have charged Foucault's approach as too negative, with Nigel Thrift (2000b, p. 269) claiming that 'in Foucault country it always seems to be raining'. However, Foucault's analysis of power sought to *decentre* it from concentration in the hands of a monarch, a STATE or a dominant CLASS, and to show how power flowed throughout SOCIETY, was not simply repressive and worked in complex interrelations – what he called 'games of power'. In his terms, 'where there is power, there is the possibility of resistance', which his genealogical works sought to exploit. It was in this period that Foucault himself became much more politically active in campaigns around PRISONS, SEXUALITY and in journalism on the Iranian revolution.

Foucault refused any kind of TELEOLOGY in history, suggesting that there was no preordained logic to the course of events. Things could have been otherwise, and could be otherwise in the future. Geographers have made use of these ideas to take into account the spatial and well as temporal aspects (see, e.g., Driver, 1993; Philo, 2004), to which Foucault himself was generally attentive (see Elden, 2001). A whole range of historical analyses have been undertaken that are inspired by Foucault's genealogical work, which are informed by a political and critical sensibility, an attentiveness to small details and textual analysis, and to deployments of power and constructions of IDEN-TITY and SUBJECTIVITY.   SE

Suggested reading
Dean (1994); Elden (2001, chs. 4, 5).

general linear model (GLM) A family of statistical procedures, used in the analysis of two or more variables, based on the covariation among those variables – the degree to which the pattern for one variable across a set of observations is replicated in another. Techniques based on this model are at the core of much SPATIAL ANALYSIS, as well as in the analytical procedures of comparable disciplines (cf. SPATIAL ECONOMETRICS), and operational algorithms are available in most computer statistical software packages (cf. SOFTWARE FOR QUANTITATIVE ANALYSIS).

The core of GLM is the technique of REGRESSION, which identifies relationships among variables, one or more specified as the independents (or causes, where causality is implied in the modelling) and another as the dependent (or effect): the associated CORRELATION coefficient evaluates the regression's goodness-of-fit. Other commonly used techniques include FACTOR ANALYSIS and PRINCIPAL COMPONENTS ANALYSIS, which seek underlying common patterns in the correlations among groups of variables.

Data deployed in GLM techniques can be at any one of the four different levels of MEASUREMENT – nominal, ordinal, interval and ratio – and variables of each type can be used in techniques incorporated within GLM, each having particular technical issues that may need resolution for it to be validly deployed. (Some ratio variables have pre-defined upper and lower values – such as percentages and proportions – and have to be transformed in order to meet the GLM requirements, as in CATEGORICAL DATA ANALYSIS, LOGIT REGRESSION MODELS and POISSON REGRESSION MODELS: see also COLLINEARITY.) Spatial data raise the particular problems of SPATIAL AUTOCORRELATION.

Apart from regression using interval and/or ratio data for both the independent and dependent variables, commonly used GLM techniques include the following:

- *Analysis of variance* (ANOVA), in which the dependent variable is either interval or ratio and the independent variables are nominal or ordinal (although nominal variables can be incorporated within a regression framework using dummy variables and continuous – interval and ratio – variables can be placed in ANOVAs using covariates).

- Binomial and multinomial regression, in which the dependent variables are nominal or ordinal (in binomial regression, there are only two possible outcomes; in multinomial there are more than two) and the independents are also nominal/ordinal – although continuous variables can also be incorporated as independent variables.
- MULTI-LEVEL MODELLING, a form of regression (with either continuous or nominal/ordinal variables), in which the observations are clustered into nominal categories.
- Factor and principal components analysis.
- Discriminant analysis, in which the dependent variable is either nominal or ordinal and the independent variables are factors/components comprising groups of related continuous variables (with the groupings derived empirically rather than predetermined).

Many techniques in spatial analysis (such as GEOGRAPHICAL WEIGHTED REGRESSION: see also LOCAL STATISTICS) are based on the GLM. RJ

Suggested reading
O'Brien (1992).

general systems theory (GST) An attempted development of universal statements about the common properties of superficially different SYSTEMS, initiated by Ludwig von Bertalanffy (1901–72: see von Bertalanffy, 1968). GST was introduced to geographers during its QUANTITATIVE REVOLUTION as a framework that could unite various strands of work, and used by some to promote links between HUMAN GEOGRAPHY and PHYSICAL GEOGRAPHY (Haggett, 1965; Coffey, 1981): Chisholm (1967) dismissed it as an 'irrelevant distraction'. The search for isomorphisms across systems focused on three 'principles':

- *allometry* – the growth rate of a subsystem is proportional to that of the system as a whole;
- *hierarchical structuring* (as in CENTRAL PLACE THEORY); and
- ENTROPY.

Few substantial achievements resulted, however, apart from the early work on MACROGEOGRAPHY and more recent analysis of FRACTALS. RJ

genetic algorithm A search technique deployed in computers to identify solutions to large OPTIMIZATION and other problems.

Initially, a large number of possible solutions is identified using random generating PROCESSES, and by iterative processes built in to the search algorithm alternatives are generated and assessed according to a fitness function until a solution is found that meets predetermined criteria (cf. CELLULAR AUTOMATA; NEURAL NETWORKS). RJ

genetic geographies An umbrella term for the ways in which geographers, among others, have been developing critical analyses in novel theoretical and methodological directions to address some of the profound social challenges to ideas of bodily integrity and intervention (see BODY); social identity and kinship; and the distinctiveness of living, in contrast to other material kinds generated by the practices and technologies of the life sciences (see also HUMAN GENOME). Geographers have been slower than some (notably anthropologists) to rise to the new questions and analytical opportunities presented by the biotechnological capabilities, processes and products that rely on various forms of genetic engineering, data banking and commercialization (Haraway, 1997). As well as contributing to the analysis of the space–times of bio-informatic scientific practices themselves (see Hall, 2003), geographers have been involved in studying the POLITICAL ECONOMY of global struggles over corporate attempts to commercialize BIODIVERSITY (Hayden, 2003), the history of the genetic framing of ideas and practices of social 'improvement' (Flitner, 2003) and various interrogations of the bio-informatic management and manipulation of human genetic materials (see Greenhough and Roe, 2006). In this, genetic geographies can be thought of as a subset of the renewed interest in, and framing of, the project of BIOGEOGRAPHY that is distinguished by the ways in which it refocuses that project from the malleability of the world of NATURE 'out there' to the human being 'in here'. SW

Suggested reading
Flitner (2003); Greenhough and Roe (2006); Hall (2003); Haraway (1997).

genius loci The spirit of PLACE, or the distinctive atmosphere found in a place. In Roman mythology, each place was protected by a guardian deity (a 'genius'), embodied in the form of an ANIMAL or supernatural being. While resonances of this idea remain (e.g. in New Age notions of sites of mystical energy, such as Stonehenge), *genius loci* now primarily refers to the unique assemblage of cultural and physical characteristics that make a place distinctive, with a characteristic ambience. Loukaki (1997, p. 308) describes *genius loci* as 'a place's fingerprint'. Often found in literary depictions (the novelist Lawrence Durrell's works are perhaps the most well known, especially his *Alexandria quartet*), *genius loci* has enjoyed only sporadic use in HUMAN GEOGRAPHY, because it is such an imprecise, difficult to use and contested term. Early on, it was taken up by Herbertson (1915, p. 153), who viewed *genius loci* as the equivalent to the historian's *Zeitgeist* or 'spirit of the age' ('There is … a spirit of place, as well as of time'). During the 1970s, kindred versions of *genius loci*, although rarely the exact term itself, were championed in HUMANISTIC GEOGRAPHY under the guise of 'SENSE OF PLACE,' 'TOPOPHILA' and 'personality of place'. More recently, the term has been taken up critically by Loukaki (1997), who has been concerned with its implications for IDEOLOGY, and by Barnes (2004b), who links the term to recent work in SCIENCE STUDIES. TB

genocide The deliberate systematic mass killing and physical liquidation ('extermination') of a group of human beings who are identified by their murderers as sharing national origin, ETHNICITY, RACE, GENDER or other social distinction.

The term was proposed by the Polish jurist Raphael Lemkin in his *Axis rule in occupied Europe* (1944), from the Latin *genus* (birth, class, order, tribe) and *cida* (a person who kills). Lemkin defined genocide as 'the destruction of a nation or of an ethnic group' and, as the title of his book suggests, he was concerned with the mass murders carried out by the Third Reich in occupied Europe, and specifically with what came to be known as the HOLOCAUST (see also FASCISM). Lemkin proposed that the industrialized murders of millions of Jews, Romanies, Slavs, gays and others should be deemed CRIMES against humanity, which he suggested involved either 'barbarism' – acts directed at the physical elimination of a group – or 'vandalism' – acts directed at the destruction of the group's CULTURE. But these distinctions have turned out to be problematic: partly because the first almost always involves a series of cultural constructions that sustain a narrative of purification and contamination to animate and legitimate the atrocities, so that it is difficult to hold the two apart, and partly because 'barbarism' and 'vandalism' are themselves historically sedimented, racialized terms that are impregnated with a EUROCENTRISM that identifies EUROPE with a privileged sense of CIVILIZATION.

In fact, genocide has a troubling relationship to Europe's history and to the modern world more generally. Some commentators have seen the Holocaust as at once starkly modern and a hideous deformation of the project of MODERNITY, but others have insisted on its intimate connections with European modernity (Bauman, 2000b). Taking into account other genocidal regimes, Rummel (1994) estimated that during the twentieth century six times more people – 169 million – were killed by their own governments in what he called *democide* or 'murder by government' than were killed in war, and Levene (2000) has explored the logics of STATE and intra-state VIOLENCE in other directions to try to account for the twentieth century as 'the century of genocide'.

Although the term 'genocide' is modern, however, and a host of other '-cides' – politicide, 'terracide' or 'the erasure of space' (Tyner, 2008) and URBICIDE among them – have been proposed to identify other supposedly modern horrors, like its hideous kin ETHNIC CLEANSING, the practice of genocide has a much longer history. Many scholars have extended the term backwards in time (see, most comprehensively, Kiernan, 2007) and drawn attention to the role of genocide in the BIOPOLITICS of COLONIALISM and IMPERIALISM. Thus Wolfe (2006) describes a 'logic of elimination' that includes 'the summary liquidation of indigenous people' and the calculated destruction of their ways of life by settler colonialisms, and Davis (2001) identifies a global series of 'Late Victorian Holocausts'.

The attribution of the term, past or present, is always highly charged because it combines juridical, political and analytical inflections (see Jones, 2006, pp. 15–22). Its origins lie in international LAW: following Lemkin's campaign, the United Nations adopted the Convention on the Prevention and Punishment of the Crime of Genocide in 1948, but it was almost fifty years before prosecutions for genocide were brought before International Criminal Tribunals for the Former Yugoslavia (for crimes since 1991) and Ruanda (for crimes in 1994). The long interval can be explained partly by the protracted process of ratification, but partly by the implications of the term itself: 'It aims to sound the alarm and oblige action' (Stein, 2005, p. 190). In fact, Stein argues that the initial reluctance to designate clusters of mass killings as genocide has since yielded to the application of the term to

so-called 'new wars' (see WAR) and other contemporary conflicts 'in which large-scale cleansings, killings and brutalities occur … Whereas previously the problem was one of apparent singularity, currently it is that of near universality.' This is something of an overstatement, as the controversy over the crisis in Darfur revealed (Straus, 2005; de Waal, 2005; Totten and Markusen, 2006), but it is clear that the attempt to ring-fence the Holocaust – as both paradigmatic and singular, what Wolfe (2006, p. 402) calls 'the non-paradigmatic PARADIGM that, being the indispensable example, can never merely exemplify' – has given way to a determination to analyse the logics and practices of extermination and atrocity, and to understand how 'ordinary people' could have taken part in state and para-state programmes of mass murder. HUMAN RIGHTS organizations are vocal in their investigations (see, for example, http://www.genocidewatch.org) and there is now an international network of genocide scholars (see http://www.inogs.com). Geographical analysis has included the use of satellite photography and remote sensing techniques to identify mass graves (cf. Parks, 2001); studies of the destruction of PLACE and LANDSCAPE to eradicate any trace or even MEMORY of the targeted group's presence; and comparative studies of contemporary genocides (Wood, 2001).   DG

Suggested reading
Jones (2006); Wood (2001).

genre de vie A French expression meaning 'mode of life', used by Paul Vidal de la Blache, doyen of French REGIONAL GEOGRAPHY at the turn of the twentieth century, to describe the range of possible livelihoods developed by geographically bounded, socially distinctive, mainly rural COMMUNITIES. It was used alongside the related concepts of *milieu* (the geographical environment that provides a community with its resources) and *circulation* (the communications linking different communities) to make sense of traditional PEASANT societies that seemed destined to be replaced by modern, deracinated urban–industrial societies in both the developed and the developing worlds.   MJH

Suggested reading
Buttimer (1971); Vidal de la Blache (1911).

gentrification Middle-class settlement in renovated or redeveloped properties in older, inner-city districts formerly occupied by a

273

lower-income population. The process was first named by Ruth Glass, as she observed the arrival of the 'gentry' and the accompanying social transition of several districts in central London in the early 1960s. A decade later, broader recognition of gentrification followed in large cities such as London, San Francisco, New York, Boston, Toronto and Sydney undergoing occupational transition from an industrial to a POST-INDUSTRIAL economy. But more recently gentrification has been identified more widely, in smaller urban centres, in Southern and Eastern Europe and also in some major centres in Asia and Latin America (Atkinson and Bridge, 2005).

Explanation of gentrification has moved in several directions. One account focused upon HOUSING MARKET dynamics, in particular the POWER of CAPITAL to shape LANDSCAPE change (Smith, N., 1996b). Another emphasized the rapid growth of a 'new class' of private- and public-sector professionals and managers in post-industrial societies, who were drawn to urbane inner-city locations (Ley, 1996). Related to this occupational change was the movement of women into the new class workforce, and the growth of smaller adult-oriented-households well suited to central neighbourhoods. By the mid-1980s, the successful re-colonization in the older INNER CITY by the middle class was well established, and more recent developments have been the extension and intensification of gentrification in new forms, including loft conversions, the massive development of obsolete industrial land, frequently on waterfront sites, such as the London Docklands, and also the deepening of wealth in formerly gentrified areas, a process named 'super-gentrification' by Lees (2003) from studies in New York and London.

The sustained interest in gentrification research for more than a generation has resulted in part from its engagement with a number of important conceptual categories including CLASS, GENDER, and, most recently, RACE, patterns and styles of CONSUMPTION, housing and other service needs, social polarization and the GOVERNANCE practices of NEO-LIBERALISM in the GLOBAL CITY. In addition, it has been a forum where competing EPISTEMOLOGICAL and theoretical positions have met (Hamnett, 2003).

Gentrification has been seen ambivalently. Positive impacts include new investment in areas often requiring significant land use and service improvement, the enhancement of the urban tax base, and the creation of new (though typically low-income) service jobs in such fields as the restaurant and arts sectors, home renovation, cleaning and security. But against this has been the massive loss of affordable inner-city housing for lower-income groups, an integral element of the polarization of life-chances in the global city. Gentrification has become a conscious policy strategy in many cities seeking to reconfigure their urban economies and landscapes in the wake of massive DEINDUSTRIALIZATION. Regeneration policies, from Amsterdam to Vancouver, frequently seek a putative 'social mix' that includes middle-class housing in former working-class neighbourhoods. Not surprisingly, gentrification has frequently become a politicized and contested process of residential transformation.   DL

Suggested reading
Atkinson (2003); Atkinson and Bridge (2005).

geo-body The spatial expression of the modern NATION. It is the socially constructed 'territorial definition which creates effects – by classifying, communicating, and enforcement – on people, things, and relationships' (see TERRITORY). This definition is derived from the work of cultural historian Thongchai Winichakul, who coined the term in his study of the cultural construction of the Siamese/Thai nation, in which he argued that the nation's spatial extent is not unproblematic but, rather, is a naturalized and mythic construction, a component of the 'life of the nation' that is at once 'a source of pride, loyalty, love, passion, bias, hatred, reason, [and] unreason' (Winichakul, 1994, p. 17). It is important to distinguish between state mapping and the construction of the 'geo-body'. *State mapping*, the CARTOGRAPHY of the modern STATE, entails detailed medium- and large-scale topographical mapping which, along with thematic–statistical mapping, allows the STATE APPARATUS oversight over its territory and population (see GOVERNMENTALITY). The *cartographic imaginary* of the modern nation, by contrast, entails the deployment of simple and simplistic small-scale maps within emotional and nationally emotive discourses, especially those carried on through news media and primary school texts (cf. EMOTIONAL GEOGRAPHIES). It is this second cartographic practice that finds resonance in subsequent studies of the cartographic construction of national IDENTITY, whether post-colonial (e.g. Ramaswamy, 1999) or European (e.g. Herb, 1997). Indeed, Winichakul's work prompted Anderson (1991a [1983]) to extend his crucial conception of nations as 'imagined communities' to encompass the self-conscious formation of national identities through maps, and in particular through 'logo maps' that sketch in outline a simple and homogenous SPACE imbued with nationalistic sentiments: more generally, Helgerson (1992) convincingly argued that a modern nation requires a spatial self-conception and that such self-conceptions are constructed cartographically. From these studies, it seems appropriate to limit the use of 'geo-body' to the spatial embodiment of the nation and its self-imaginings, leaving each state to construct and define its territorial and political limits through markedly different cartographic practices, technologies and DISCOURSES.   MHE

Suggested reading
Winichakul (1994).

geocoding Geocoding is the act of converting paper MAPS into computer-readable form by scanning or DIGITIZING (Clarke, 2002, p. 313) or, alternatively, the act of assigning a location to information (Longley, Goodchild, Maguire and Rhind, 2005, p. 110). Despite revealing that there is no standardized nomenclature for GEOGRAPHIC INFORMATION SYSTEMS (GIS), these two meanings cover common ground. To convert or to encode geographical information digitally in a GIS requires that both the characteristics and the locations of the features of interest be stored in a database, usually in VECTOR or RASTER format. Recording what is found and where gives GIS its mapping and spatial analytical capabilities.   RH

Suggested reading
Longley, Goodchild, Maguire and Rhind (2005).

geocomputation The technique of geocomputation applies the processing power of computers to enable advanced geographical analysis and modelling. However, this broad definition conceals a diversity of methods and philosophies, leading Couclelis (1998, p. 18) to ask 'whether geocomputation is to be understood as a new perspective or paradigm in geography ... or as a grab-bag of useful computer-based tools'.

To some, the spirit of geocomputation is conveyed by Openshaw, Charlton, Wymer and Craft's (1987) GEOGRAPHICAL ANALYSIS MACHINE (GAM), designed to look for spatial clusters within child leukaemia data for northern England. As a method of spatial analysis and local pattern detection, it is characterized by iterative repeat testing, subdividing the study region into overlapping regions, within each of which a significance test of the rate of incidence (of leukaemia) is undertaken. Such a technique is often portrayed as inductive (cf. INDUCTION): drawing out ideas, inferences and working hypotheses from what is found in the data, and suggesting that the process of geographical knowledge construction is data-driven or 'avowedly EMPIRICIST' (Longley, Brooks, McDonnell and Macmillan, 1998). However, that portrayal is not entirely satisfactory given any *a priori* postulate or theorization that radiation causes leukaemia and therefore an expectation that a cluster of cases be found in proximity to a nuclear power station. Finding the cluster does not prove the theory, but it may add circumstantial evidence. In this manner, geocomputational practices are abductive (cf. ABDUCTION): interesting cases (or spatial 'hot spots') are used to support a plausible although not logically necessary conclusion, not a purely (inductive) empirical generalization.

Others pursue a more deductive tradition of scientific practice (cf. DEDUCTION), with the foundations of geocomputation established firmly in the analytical traditions of SPATIAL SCIENCE and geography's QUANTITATIVE REVOLUTION (see, for example, the history of geocomputation outlined at www.geocomputation.org). Here, the focus is on modelling, analysing and theorizing dynamic socio-economic or physical systems (cf. MODEL); on modelling spatial distributions, FLOWS, NETWORKS, hierarchies and DIFFUSIONS. In particular, there is an interest in methods of SIMULATION – from a HUMAN GEOGRAPHY perspective, of simulating the spatial patterning, causes and consequences of population change, urban MORPHOLOGY, economic cycles, transport congestion and so forth. These methods build on the idea of Monte Carlo simulation outlined by Haggett (1965). It means that the rules of the system (assumed from, say, economic theory) are played out in virtual spaces, where what came before affects what follows, but the geographical outcomes are not entirely fixed or predetermined. Instead, there is randomness in the system – the ability to generate particular chance events – albeit that the consequences of those events are often constrained by the context in which they are generated; for example, their locations and the 'state' of the system around them. Such methods include the use of CELLULAR AUTOMATA and AGENT-BASED MODELLING (Flake, 2001) to model complex SYSTEMS such as cities (Batty, 2005).

If this vision of geocomputation is NOMOTHETIC and law-seeking, does it then risk the

275

criticisms of POSITIVISM, which have been used as the stick to beat other areas of quantitative, computational and spatial scientific human geography? Not necessarily. For example, if we accept the proposition that VISUALIZATION of pattern suggests insight into the processes that generate that pattern (e.g. Batty and Longley, 1994), and if the researcher goes beyond what is empirically observable to ask questions and form concepts about the more fundamental structures and mechanisms for the events or phenomena under study, then the tenets of REALISM or critical realist philosophies are approached (Danermark, Ekström, Jakobsen and Karlsson, 2001).

Is, then, Couclelis (1998, p. 22) still right to say that geocomputation has 'no [single] philosophy (and proud of it!)'? Perhaps so. Perhaps, desirably so. For, as computers and computation develop and evolve, new opportunities are presented for innovative geographical problem solving, alternative expressions of geographical enquiry and fresh geographical theorization, EXPLANATION and understanding. A few years ago the character of geocomputation could be conveyed by specifying what it was not: it was *not* simply GEOGRAPHIC INFORMATION SYSTEMS but, rather, a reaction to the (then) limited geometric data manipulations and mapping capabilities offered by GIS. What was sought was the flexibility for more sophisticated and creative spatial statistical analysis, data visualization, process modelling and dynamic simulation that broke out of the GIS straightjacket. These various domains of geocomputation – SPATIAL ANALYSIS, geovisualization, geosimulation and the application of ARTIFICIAL INTELLIGENCE for geographical problem solving and knowledge discovery – still characterize geocomputation. But the 'definition' by COUNTERFACTUAL has begun to age, as INTEROPERABILITY and the ability to customise GIS have led to more sophisticated geocomputational methods to be implemented within a GIS environment (Maguire, Batty and Goodchild, 2005).

Nevertheless, new technologies could also yield a clearer identity for geocomputation. Computational 'grid' technologies – an allusion to electricity power grids – offer the opportunity for researchers to 'plug in' to high-performance computer networks under the rubric of 'e-' (electronic) social science. Martin (2005) identifies four essential research issues for E-SOCIAL SCIENCE: automated DATA MINING; visualization of spatial data uncertainty; incorporation of an explicitly spatial dimension into simulation modelling; and neighbourhood CLASSIFICATION (see GEODEMOGRAPHICS) from multi-source distributed data sets. These, he argues, could each be considered as important elements of a grid-enabled, geocomputational toolkit. It is this potential to contribute to the new E-SCIENCE research environments that may crystallize geocomputation as a distinct research field spanning GEOGRAPHY and related disciplines.   RH

Suggested reading
Ehlen, Caldwell and Harding (2002); Gahegan (1999); Macmillan (1998); Martin (2005).

geodemographics Geodemographics is 'the analysis of people by where they live' (Sleight, 2004) or, more precisely, by a data-based classification of residential location (although classifications have also been produced for workplace, financial services and CYBERSPACE). The origins of geodemographics include Charles Booth's POVERTY Maps of London (1898–9; see http://booth.lse.ac.uk) and the 1920s–1930s CHICAGO SCHOOL of urban sociology. During the twentieth century, the increasing availability of national CENSUS data and the development of computation permitted multivariate summaries of census zones to be produced, and for those areas to be grouped together on a like-with-like basis using clustering techniques (see CLASSIFICATION AND REGIONALIZATION).

Those methodological developments provided the foundation for modern geodemographics – a major industry used by corporate, governmental, non-profit and political groups to deliver key advertising and services to their audiences, customers and users (Weiss, 2000). Commercial applications emerged during the late 1970s with the launch of PRIZM, by Claritas, in the USA and ACORN, by CACI, in the UK. Today's classifications include not only census data, but also shopping, electoral, financial and other data about the 'objects' to be classified (commonly individuals, households, postcodes, Zip codes, CENSUS TRACTS or electoral wards). ACORN currently categorizes 1.9 million UK postcodes into one of five, seventeen or fifty-six types (plus some 'unclassified'), using over 125 demographic statistics and 287 lifestyle variables. PRIZM NE incorporates both HOUSEHOLD and census data to describe, for example, Beverley Hills 90210 as containing 'Blue Blood Estates', 'Bohemian Mix' and 'Money & Brains' (amongst other segments). There are geodemographic classifications of most of Western Europe, Northern America, Brazil, Peru, Australasia, South

Africa, parts of Asia and some of China, including Hong Kong.

Many geographers have been active in developing geodemographic classifications, including Super Profiles (Charlton, Openshaw and Wymer, 1985), GB Profiles and a freely downloadable classification of UK Census Output Areas (at http://neighbourhood.statistics.gov.uk). Others have been more critical. One concern is that for some applications the cluster groups are not sufficiently homogeneous for them to represent well the individuals (or households) allocated to them. Voas and Williamson (2001) suggest that apparent differences *between* geodemographic classes conceal a much greater diversity *within* the classes. A related concern is that the montage of variables forming a geodemographic classification creates something of a black box, making it hard to determine the key predictors of the geographical phenomena being analysed. Care needs to be taken when interpreting geodemographic outputs because they are usually indexed as rates in one cluster, relative to all others. To find that an event is of above average prevalence in one geodemographic group is no guarantee that it is common there: the result could apply to a small minority of the population but still a larger proportion than for other clusters.

Surrounding geodemographics are broader debates in HUMAN GEOGRAPHY, including those about REPRESENTATION, quantitative methodologies, EMPIRICISM, generalization, INDUCTION versus DEDUCTION, data- versus theory-led approaches to understanding, NEO-LIBERAL economies and the politics and commercialization of data collection, privacy and social discrimination. Critical theorists have cited geodemographics as an example of 'software sorting', suggesting that the sorts of labelling used in geodemographic systems can produce stigmatization of certain places and potentially deny them the same level of (e.g. banking or insurance) service given to other NEIGHBOURHOODS (Burrow, Ellison and Woods, 2005). However, the argument cuts two ways: geodemographics can also identify areas of social or material need, offering opportunity to better target the resources available to those places.

Geodemographic classifications can be used to interpolate market research and other survey data to standard administrative or ad hoc geographies allowing, as examples, estimation of: the levels of consumption of grocery products by supermarket catchment; demand for particular makes of car by dealership territory; or likely levels of diabetes by GP surgery catchment area. Whereas much academic debate centres on the accuracy (or otherwise) of geodemographics for predicting the behaviour of individuals, in practice many users are interested in aggregate behaviour – What, on average, is the most likely event, characteristic or behaviour at an area level, and how does this differ from other areas?

Increasingly, uses of geodemographics bring together academic, public policy and private-sector stakeholders, applying geographical thinking to tackle questions of social concern. Geodemographics has stimulated a renaissance in applied geographical research, being recently used for investigating the spatial distributions of family names, predicting spatial variation in pupils' school examination performances, examining inequalities in hospital admissions and for guiding local POLICING (all at www.spatial-literacy.org).   RH

Suggested reading
Charlton, Openshaw and Wymer (1985); Harris, Sleight and Webber (2005).

Geographic Information Science (GISc) In the simplest sense, Geographic Information Science (GISc, or GIScience) is the theory that underlies GEOGRAPHIC INFORMATION SYSTEMS (GIS). The latter are the collection of hardware, software, output devices and practices are that used to analyse and map spatial entities and their relationships. GIS software might be used to determine the BOUNDARIES that distinguish areas with different average income levels in a city or a map of optimal delivery routes for a courier company. These results are, however, not transparent; the process through which they are derived are known as *black box*. Geographic Information Science – or the theoretical basis for GIS – is concerned with how results are obtained in GIS and what questions can legitimately be asked.

GIScience explores how spatial objects become digital entities, what effect that transformation has on their digital ONTOLOGY, how different EPISTEMOLOGIES affect ontological REPRESENTATION, how to model relationships between spatial entities, and how to visualize them so that human beings can interpret the results (Raper, 1999). This pursuit draws on and extends developments in data modelling, computer science, cognition, VISUALIZATION and a myriad fields that have emerged in response to information systems.

For the first several decades of GIS use, little attention was given to the differentiation between geographical information systems and SCIENCE. By the beginning of the 1990s, however, there was a sense among academic researchers that GIS had forged new intellectual territory. The term 'GIScience' was first used in a keynote speech given by Michael Goodchild during the July, 1990 Spatial Data Handling conference in Zurich. Goodchild noted that the GIS community is driven by intellectual curiosity about the representational and analytical capacity of Geographic Information Systems. He argued that GIS researchers should focus on fundamental precepts that underlie the technology rather than the application of existing technology. Furthermore, he argued that there are unique characteristics of spatial data, and problems associated with their analysis, that differentiate GIS from other information systems. These properties include: the need to develop conceptual MODELS of SPACE; the sphericity of spatial data (based on the shape of the Earth); problems with spatial data capture; spatial data uncertainty and error propagation; as well as algorithms and spatial data display. Given the distinctiveness of geographical data analysis and a growing community of researchers dedicated to solving technical and theoretical problems associated with GIS, Goodchild argued that 'GIS as a field contain[s] a legitimate set of scientific questions'. Goodchild's keynote address was followed by a summary article in the *International Journal of GIS* (IJGIS) in 1992. This oft-cited article (Abler, 1993b; Dobson, 1993), was a beachhead for the very successful effort to change the meaning of the 'S' word in GIS (Goodchild, 1992).

The GIScience acronym subsequently garnered widespread support in most parts of the discipline. The name shift is manifest in other areas of geography. *Progress in Physical Geography* routinely presents updates on GIScience rather than GISystems (Atkinson, 1997). The flagship journal IJGIS was renamed *International Journal of Geographical Information Science* in January 1997; its editor, Peter Fisher, stressed that IJGIS had, in ten years of publication, predominantly reflected the development of theoretical bases that underpin subsequent systems: the science on which subsequent systems are based. Fisher turned to the (shorter) *Oxford English Dictionary* to support this distinction, noting that SYSTEMS are a collection of related objects or an assemblage while science is defined as knowledge obtain through investigation. He noted that the International Geographical Union (IGU) had developed a working group for Geograph-

ical Information *Science* in 1996, the implication being that there is broad institutional support for this designation (Fisher, 1997). Marc Armstrong, the former North American editor of IJGIS, recalls that identifying aspects of GIS as science was an acknowledgement that many GIS researchers were neither using nor developing 'systems', but were doing basic theoretical work that involved the 'systematization' of knowledge (Armstrong, pers. comm.). Despite a call for recognition of the scientific value of GIS, on the part of the academic community, the technology is indisputably social in its construction, especially at the software level.

Questions about the underlying assumptions written into the code that comprises GISystems are the basis of GIScience. GIScientists might legitimately question, for example, the premises of embedded algorithmic models. A hydrological model, for instance, might be outdated and fail to reflect current understanding of flow processes. Queries about the assumptions of the model creators, their efficacy in multiple environments, and whether they are designed for use with VECTOR (polygon) or RASTER (gridded) data all fall in the realm of GIScience. These types of questions strike at the efficiency and legitimacy of current Geographic Information Systems ALGORITHMS; their resolution is the basis for increase in the reliability of GIS for the average user. Such questions do not represent the entirety of GIScience, however.

Every stage of GISystems, from spatial data collection and input, to storage, analysis and, finally, output of MAPS, is based on the translation of spatial phenomena into digital terms. At each step of GIS, data are manipulated for use in a digital environment, and these, often subtle, changes have profound effects on the results of analysis. Each of these transformations involves a subtle shift in the representation of spatial entities, and accounting for these modifications and their implications is an important part of GIScience. Physical and social information about the world, once in digital form, is often manipulated and analysed *in order to* correspond to the researcher's interpretation of the world. Thus it is of fundamental importance that GIScience develop methods to monitor and account for the effects that possible transformations have on final representation. Finally, GIScience researchers are charged with developing methods of presenting analysis results such that their visual display is consistent with database results.

GIScience is concerned theoretically with every stage of digital representation. Spatial phenomena must be delineated and classified in preparation for input to data tables. CLASSIFICATION systems, however, must be compatible with data tables, and this acts as a constraint to the development of categories. Many spatial phenomena manifest multiple characteristics, but not all of them can be included in a database or the data would be infinite. The manipulation of data depends on the attributes that are recorded, or the objects that are defined. Different community boundaries, for instance, will render different results in an assessment of population health. Visualizing GIS results is likewise vulnerable to the vagaries of the digital environment, and must be consistent with human capacity for perception. At a small SCALE (larger area), for instance, only a limited number of attributes can be displayed or the map becomes overcrowded. At a larger scale (smaller area), a greater number of attributes can be accommodated. Each of these issues has a bearing on how spatial data are analysed and interpreted.

The GIScience research purview is the representation of spatial data and their relationships and these are ultimately expressed in terms of bits and bytes. Working in a digital environment is akin to speaking another language that uses fundamentally different building blocks. If we think of the English language as being composed of twenty-six letters that can be combined in various ways to form words, sentences and ideas, then GIS is based on two letters or digits – zeros and ones – that can be combined and manipulated to represent and analyse geographical phenomena and relationships. But the environment and rules associated with manipulating geographical objects are quite different from those we are accustomed to using for conventional TEXT and graphics. The digital environment is constrained by digital parameters and the extent of representation possible through combinations and permutations of bits and bytes.

GIScience is not limited, however, to PROCESS-oriented issues. It is engaged with how people represent their geographical environment, and who has the authority to represent space. Public Participation GIS (PPGIS) studies and engages with non-profit groups and non-governmental organizations that use GIS to represent themselves, and advocate for change (Elwood and Leitner, 2003). Other GIScientists address questions about FEMINISM and GIS, and whether the technology is inherently gendered (Kwan, 2002). Stacey Warren (2004) explains that PPGIS and feminism and GIS allow us to move the focus from analysis and representation in GIS to one that views the technology as a 'collaborative process that involves both people and machinery'. This emphasis on social interactions between users, affected populations, and technology is evident in the growing number of *Critical GIS* scholars who have merged emancipatory agendas and theory from HUMAN GEOGRAPHY with GIScience.

Developers and researchers postulate that GIScience transcends mere *information* systems and allows users to ask questions about spatial relations that were previously impossible to pose. Its champions argue that Geographic Information *Science* extends spatial analysis by virtue of enhanced processing power that allows data-intensive analyses to extend their geographical breadth. They claim that GIScience is a means of investigating previously obscured spatial relationships and contingencies. There is a tension between GIS scholars who view the technology as an emergent phenomenon, capable of initiating a shift in scientific methodology and other geographers who view it simply as a vehicle for concepts that emerge from GEOGRAPHY. It is, of course, both.   NS

Suggested reading
Longley, Goodchild, Maguire and Rhind (1999); Schuurman (2004).

Geographic Information Systems (GIS) In the simplest terms, GIS (or GISystems) is the mix of hardware, software and *practices* used to run SPATIAL ANALYSIS and mapping programs. GIS does not refer to a homogeneous entity, nor one machine or a single practice but to a collection of practices, software and hardware with the ability to collect, store, display, analyse and print information about the Earth's surface (or any other SCALE of geographical data). Each such system is able to capture, store, check, integrate, analyse and display spatially referenced data about aspects of the earth. GIS allows the combination of geographical data sets (or layers) and the creation of new geospatial data to which one can apply standard spatial analysis tools. Comprehensive GIS require a means of: (i) data input, from MAPS, aerial photos, satellites, surveys and other sources (cf. REMOTE SENSING); (ii) data storage, retrieval, and query; (iii) data transformation, analysis and modelling, including spatial statistics; and finally

(iv) data reporting, such as maps, reports and plans.

The GIS acronym has tended to focus on the software developed by specific corporations with less attention to the spatial data that are the basis for knowledge generation. Geographical information is information about *where* something is or *what* is at a certain location. For example, we may have data from a forest on where some of the few remaining spotted owls live – which is geographical information. What trees grow in the areas inhabited by the owls is also geographical information, because it has a spatial component. Spatial data are any data that have a location that can be GEOCODED. Increasingly, data from most domains include spatial data.

GIS are uniquely integrative. Where spatial data are available, GIS can offer a range of functionality. Whereas other technologies might be used only to analyse aerial photographs and satellite images, to create statistical models or to draft maps, these capabilities are all offered together within a comprehensive GIS. With its array of functions, GIS should be viewed as a PROCESS rather than as merely software or hardware. To see GIS as merely a software or hardware system is to miss the crucial role it can play in a comprehensive decision-making process.

GIS has different uses and meanings among a range of users. Municipalities, for instance, view GIS as the software that allows planners to identify residential, industrial and commercial zones – and store tax information. It maps the exact location and survey coordinates of each taxable property, and provides answers to queries such as: 'How many properties would be affected by the addition of an extra lane to Highway 1 between 170th and 194th Streets?' Population HEALTH researchers, on the other hand, may use GIS to define the boundaries of COMMUNITIES that enjoy varying health outcomes. In this instance, GIS is not a piece of software, but a scientific approach to the problem: 'How do we define crisp boundaries to demarcate fuzzy and changeable phenomena?' (cf. FUZZY SETS). The latter is a fundamentally philosophical issue that must be resolved through computing and its answer lies somewhere between GIS and the underlying theory of GEOGRAPHIC INFORMATION SCIENCE. These two types of users have different goals and experiences of GIS. One is interested in 'where' spatial entities are or might be, while the other is concerned with 'how' we encode spatial entities (e.g. communities, urban/rural areas, forests, roads, bridges and anything that

might appear on a map), and the repercussions of different methods of analysis on answers to geographical questions. The diversity of GIS use is rooted in its history.

The development of GIS began in the 1960s, when the technology and EPISTEMOLOGY that underlie it were first being developed. Methods of computerizing cartographic procedures were coincident with the realization that mapping could segue neatly into analysis. In 1962, Ian Harg, a landscape architect, introduced the method of 'overlay' that was later to become the defining METHODOLOGY of GIS. He was searching for the optimal route for a new highway that would be associated with suburban development. His goal was to route the highway such that its path would involve the least disruption of other 'layers' of the LANDSCAPE, including forest cover, pastoral valleys and existing semi-rural housing. He took multiple pieces of tracing paper, one representing each layer, and laid them over each other on a light table. By visually examining their intersections, he was able to 'see' the only logical route. Ironically, none of McHarg's initial analysis was done using a computer. The METAPHOR of overlay was, however, integrated into early GIS, and became the basis for a range of analytical techniques broadly known as 'spatial analysis'.

SPATIAL ANALYSIS is differentiated from 'mapping' because it generates more information or knowledge than can be gleaned from maps or data alone. It is a synergistic means of extracting information from spatial data. In the early development stages of GIS, however, few people recognized the power of analysis, and the technology was generically referred to as 'computerized cartography'. As such, GIS was unimpressive. Early computerized maps were very primitive compared to the exquisite maps produced through manual CARTOGRAPHY. This comparison led to reluctance among geographers to adopt GIS as a 'substitute' for traditional cartography.

The questionable aesthetic merit of traditional maps was, however, a detraction from the power of computerized spatial analysis. That power was first explored in universities in the late 1950s and early 1960s. Influenced by the QUANTITATIVE REVOLUTION and the development of computers, researchers began to develop tools that could be used to analyse and display spatial data – though not always in map form. One of the earliest computer cartography systems was developed in Canada, the brainchild of Roger Tomlinson and Lee Pratt. Tomlinson had been using aerial photography to map forest cover in order to recommend locations for new growth; Pratt worked for the Canadian Ministry of Agriculture, which wanted to compile land-use maps for the entire country, maps that would describe multiple characteristics including agriculture, FORESTRY, wildlife, recreation areas and census divisions. Tomlinson suggested that they pioneer a computerized system in which land-use zones were digitally encoded so that they could be overlaid with other relevant layers such as urban/rural areas, soil type and geology. This happenstance meeting led, in 1964, to the Canada Geographical Information System (CGIS). The name of the system was bestowed by a member of the Canadian Parliament.

There were parallel developments in Europe. Tom Waugh, for example, developed an early GIS system with the acronym GIMMS. It was a VECTOR-based GIS system with sophisticated analysis, and was eventually used in twenty-three countries (Rhind, 1998). GIMMS preceded ESRI (see below) in developing a commercial GIS and was relatively sophisticated for the 1970s and 1980s – including cartographic options and batch processing. In the USA, the Harvard Graphics Laboratory was a tinderbox of the GIS revolution. Research at the laboratory established an efficient method for computerized overlay using polygon (vector) boundaries. The laboratory was populated by a host of researchers who had a profound influence on the development of current GIS, including Nicholas Chrisman and Tom Poiker. A diaspora of researchers from the Harvard Laboratory in the 1970s contributed to the dissemination of GIS, especially into the private sector. Scott Morehouse, a junior member, left in 1981 to work for a company in California called Environmental Systems Research Institute (ESRI), where he re-developed the algorithm for vector overlay which became a cornerstone of the program ARC/INFO. This dispersion of ideas from the Harvard Laboratory was the beginning of one GIS identity: that linked to software packages, hardware systems and technology in general (Chrisman, 1988).

Institutional and governmental support for GIS was also a major impetus for its growth and adoption from the 1970s onward. In the UK, four multidisciplinary Regional Research Laboratories (RRLs) were designated by the Economic and Social Research Council. They were designed to facilitate primary functions of GIS, including spatial data management, software development, spatial analysis and training of GIS researchers (Masser, 1988). In the USA, the National Center for Geographic

Information Analysis was funded by the National Science Foundation (NSF). Three US universities with GIS expertise were chosen as primary research centres. Their role was to facilitate understanding and implementation of geospatial methodologies and develop university adoption of these techniques. The NCGIA also played an important role in hosting and responding to EPISTEMOLOGICAL and pragmatic critiques of the technology (Pickles, 1995b; Curry, 1998).

The development of GIS, however, is not rooted solely in computer laboratories and universities in the latter part of the twentieth century. It is also an outgrowth of attempts to automate calculation in the nineteenth century reflected in efforts, for example, to code population data for the US CENSUS in 1890 (Foresman, 1998). Pre-eminent GIS scholar Michael Goodchild makes the point that GIS was developed during a period when information was increasingly being translated into digital terms and disseminated widely (Goodchild, 1995). If geographers had not explored the possibilities of digital manipulation of spatial data, other disciplines would have initiated the process. As it is, many roots of GIS are in disciplines other than GEOGRAPHY including landscape architecture and SURVEYING. Like all technologies, GIS is an outcome of both social and technological developments.   NS

Suggested reading
DeMers (2000); Longley, Goodchild, Maguire and Rhind (1999); Schuurman (2004).

geographical analysis machine (GAM) An example of automated spatial data analysis catalysed by three factors: the growing availability of digital data with point (x,y) GEOCODING; a move from statistical techniques 'smoothing over' geographical variation to LOCAL STATISTICS revealing geographical patterns in data; and increased computational power to guide where to look. GAM passes a moving window of fixed radius (or population count) across a study REGION, repeatedly testing for unusual clusters of a particular feature. Successfully used to study the clustering of cancers, GAM and its primary architect – Stan Openshaw – inspired much of the research in GEOCOMPUTATION.   RH

Suggested reading
Openshaw (1998).

geographical explanation machine (GEM) Whilst the GEOGRAPHICAL ANALYSIS MACHINE discovers spatial patterns in geographical data sets, the geographical explanation machine tries to 'explain' them by identifying predictor variables with a spatial distribution matching the patterns found. As a tool for computer-assisted learning, GEM is pioneering. The problem, however, is that looking hard enough through sufficient data sets – as a computer can – will probably reveal an association although not necessarily one with scientific or rational meaning. Many geographers will baulk at an approach to social scientific explanation that is so avowedly EMPIRICIST and not guided by THEORY. Perhaps the 'E' in GEM could better be described as exploration.   RH

Suggested reading
Openshaw (1998).

geographical imaginary A taken-for-granted spatial ordering of the world. 'Imaginary' is a concept derived from PSYCHO-ANALYTIC THEORY, in particular the work of Jacques Lacan and Cornelius Castoriadis, and in its original versions it implied a sort of primitive or ur-geography: 'The imaginary is the subject's whole creation of a world for itself' (Castoriadis, 1997; cf. Gregory, 1997a). In human geography, a 'geographical imaginary' is typically treated as a more or less unconscious and unreflective construction, but it is rarely given any formal theoretical inflection. It usually refers to a spatial ordering that is tied either to the *collective object* of a series of IMAGINATIVE GEOGRAPHIES (e.g. 'the geographical imaginary of the Tropics': see TROPICALITY) or to their *collective subject* (e.g. 'the imperial geographical imaginary'). Watts (1999) brilliantly combines the two in an exceptionally careful reconstruction of the ways in which the Ogoni people of the Niger delta fashioned a precarious sense of collective identity tied to space, territory and land. Like Watts, most studies recognize the crucial importance of language, especially METAPHOR, and of VISUALITY in producing these orderings.

Geographical imaginaries involve bordering as well as ordering: the hierarchical division of the globe into CONTINENTS, STATES and other sub-categories (see SCALE), for example, and the oppositions between global NORTH/SOUTH, urban/rural, inside/outside and CULTURE/NATURE. These divisions also often act as tacit valorizations ('civilized'/'savage', for example, or 'wild'/'safe') that derive not only from the cognitive operations of reason but also from structures of feeling and the operation of AFFECT. As such, geographical imaginaries are more than representations or constructions of the world: they are vitally implicated in a material, sensuous process of 'worlding'. Thus, for example, Howitt (2001a, pp. 236–7) identified a geographical imaginary that was intimately involved in the European construction of a 'bounded self' and which, in the colonial past of AUSTRALIA and on into its present, worked to construct equally bounded spaces 'that provided certainty, identity and security' from which indigenous peoples were excluded. More generally, but closely connected, Massey (2004, pp. 9–10) attributed a pervasive 'Russian-doll geography of care and responsibility' to 'the persistence of a geographical imaginary which is essentially territorial and which focuses on the near rather than the far'. It follows that a vital critical task for HUMAN GEOGRAPHY is the disclosure of these taken-for-granted geographical imaginaries and an examination of their (often unacknowledged) effects.   DG

Suggested reading
Watts (1999).

geographical imagination A sensitivity towards the significance of PLACE and SPACE, LANDSCAPE and NATURE, in the constitution and conduct of life on Earth. As such, a geographical imagination is by no means the exclusive preserve of the academic discipline of GEOGRAPHY. H.C. Prince (1962) portrayed it as 'a persistent and universal instinct of [humankind]'. The geographical imagination as he saw it was a response to places and landscapes, above all to their co-mingling of 'CULTURE' and 'NATURE', that 'calls into action our powers of sympathetic insight and imaginative understanding' and whose rendering 'is a creative art' (cf. Cosgrove, 2006b). Prince's emphasis on ART and, by implication, on geography's place among the HUMANITIES, was in part a critical response to the reformulation of the discipline as a SPATIAL SCIENCE. To Prince, these formal abstractions were ingenious and inventive but, 'like abstract painting', they would always remain indirect approaches to a world to which the freshest, fullest and richest response was, in his view, literary (whereas Cosgrove, who was profoundly sympathetic to Prince's vision, made a compelling case for a visual and aesthetic sensibility – though he expressed this in luminous prose too). In Prince's view, it was vitally important to preserve 'a direct experience of landscape' through the art of geographical description (see also REPRESENTATION).

Some ten years later, David Harvey (1973) provided a discussion of the geographical imagination that also recognized the value of the aesthetic, but Harvey departed from Prince's account in two particularly significant ways: Harvey's critique of spatial science was much more open to formal theoretical vocabularies (indeed, it relied on them), and its characteristic emphasis was on place and space rather than landscape and nature (which had occupied a much more prominent position in Prince's discussion). In Harvey's eyes, therefore, the geographical imagination enables 'individual[s] to recognize the role of space and place in [their] own biographies, to relate to the spaces [they] see around [them], and to recognize how transactions between individuals and between organizations are affected by the space that separates them ..., to judge the relevance of events in other places ..., to fashion and use space creatively, and to appreciate the meaning of the spatial forms created by others'. Harvey wanted to contrast the geographical imagination with, but also to connect it to, what sociologist C. Wright Mills (1959) had called 'the sociological imagination', a capacity that 'enables us to grasp history and biography and the relations between the two in society'. Neither Harvey nor Mills confined the terms to their own disciplines; they both said they were talking about 'habits of mind' that transcended particular disciplines and spiralled far beyond the discourse of the academy. Nonetheless, much of the discussion that followed from Harvey's intervention was concerned with formal questions of theory and method.

A central preoccupation was the articulation of SOCIAL THEORY, broadly conceived, and HUMAN GEOGRAPHY. 'It has been a fundamental concern of mine for several years now,' so Harvey (1973) had written, 'to heal the breach in our thought between what appear to be two distinctive and indeed irreconcilable modes of analysis', and he presented his seminal *Social Justice and the City* as (in part) a 'quest to bridge the gap between sociological and geographical imaginations'. It was urgently necessary to humanize human geography, and ideas and concepts were drawn in from the humanities and (especially) the social sciences – in particular, from POLITICAL ECONOMY, SOCIAL THEORY and nominally 'cultural' disciplines such as anthropology and cultural studies. En route, however, it became clear that the reverse movement was equally important, sensitizing these other fields to a geographical imagination, because most of them took a

so-called 'compositional' approach that had no interest in place or space (cf. CONTEXTUALITY). This was a challenging project, and it involved not only geographers but also original, vital contributions from other disciplines. Indeed, some of the most intriguing and influential spatializations were produced by scholars outside the formal enclosures of Geography: Foucault and Deleuze in PHILOSOPHY, Giddens and Urry in sociology, and Jameson and Said in comparative literature. Some ten years after *Social justice*, Harvey (1984) calibrated the magnitude of the collaborative, interdisciplinary theoretical task like this:

> The insertion of space, place, locale and milieu into any social theory has a numbing effect upon that theory's central propositions ... Marx, Marshall, Weber and Durkheim all have this in common: they prioritize time over space and, where they treat the latter at all, tend to view it unproblematically as the site or context for historical action. Whenever social theorists of whatever stripe actively interrogate the meaning of geographical categories, they are forced either to make so many *ad hoc* adjustments to their theory that it splinters into incoherence, or else to abandon their theory in favour of some language derived from pure geometry. The insertion of spatial concepts into social theory has not yet been successfully accomplished. Yet social theory that ignores the materialities of actual geographical configurations, relations and processes lacks validity.

Subsequent commentators reported considerable progress in sensitizing social theory and social thought more generally to these concerns. There was (and remains) an immensely productive dialogue between MARXISM and human geography, especially through ECONOMIC GEOGRAPHY and HISTORICAL GEOGRAPHY (see also MARXIST GEOGRAPHY), and these conversations and their critiques spilled over into a number of other politico-intellectual traditions (Harvey, 1990; cf. Castree, 2007). The rise of POSTMODERNISM was hailed as emblematic of a distinctively geographical (or at any rate 'spatial') imagination (Soja, 1989), and the interest in POST-COLONIALISM and POST-STRUCTURALISM contributed in still more radical ways to the critique of abstract and universal models of SUBJECT, SOCIETY and SPACE. But three other dimensions of the geographical imagination have received close attention in recent years, and each of them works towards the production of 'impure' geographies that depart considerably from the closures and clinical approaches of Geography-with-a-capital-G.

In the first place, there has *been a renewed interrogation of academic versions of the geographical imagination*, and in particular of the two versions proposed by Prince and Harvey (above). Influenced by post-structuralism in different ways and to different degrees, and in particular by a focus on geography as DIS-COURSE, several critics have argued that geography is not simply framed by or reflective of changes in the 'real' world: on the contrary, its discourses are *constitutive of* that world. For Gregory (1994) and Deutsche (1995), drawing on Mitchell's (1989) account of the world-as-exhibition, human geography is construed as 'a site where images of the city and space more generally are set up as reality', as fabrications in the double sense of imaginative works and works that are made, and hence as 'the *effects rather than the ground* of disciplinary knowledge' (emphasis added). Thus the modern geographical imagination, in its usual HEGEMONIC form, not only 'stages the world-as-exhibition and at the same time is fabricated by the picture it creates'; it also characteristically disavows its dependence by adopting an objectivist EPISTEMOLOGY that separates itself from the picture as an autonomous, all-seeing 'spectatorial' subject (Deutsche, 1995). Such an epistemology is, as she remarks, a vehicle for 'the silent spatial production' of 'the self-possessed subject of geographical knowledge who, severed from its object, is positioned to perceive an external totality and so avoids the partiality of immersion in the world' (cf. SITUATED KNOWLEDGE).

Gillian Rose (1993) emphasizes that this is both an act of *mastery* – hence her critique of the MASCULINISM of geographical knowledge – but also an act that is shot through with *ambivalence*:

In geography, a controlling, objective distance is not the only relationship which positions the knower in relation to his object of study. There is rather an ambivalence, which produces the restlessness of the signifiers within the discipline's dualistic thinking. On the one hand, there is a fear of the Other, of an involvement with the Other, which does produce a distance and a desire to dominate in order to maintain that distance. This is central to social-scientific masculinism. On the other hand, there is also a desire for knowledge and intimacy, for closeness and humility in order to

learn, and this is the desire of aesthetic masculinity to invoke its other. (Rose, 1993, p. 77)

Rose's critique identifies the first position ('social-scientific masculinity') with projects such as Harvey's and the second position ('aesthetic masculinity') with projects such as Prince's.

Rose and Deutsche both urged that this recognition of the limits (rather than the presumed completeness) of geographical knowledge's involve an engagement with PSYCHOANALYTIC THEORY in order to grapple not with the conscious and creative exercise of the 'imagination' – something that concerned Prince (1962) in particular and HUMANISTIC GEOGRAPHY in general – but with the imaginary: in other words, with 'the psychic register in which the subject searches for plenitude, for a reflection of its own completeness' (cf. GEOGRAPHICAL IMAGINARY). By this means, Rose (1993, p. 85) suggests, it is possible 'to think about a different kind of geographical imagination which could enable a recognition of radical difference from itself; an imagination sensitive to difference and power which allows others rather than an other' (see also FEMINIST GEOGRAPHIES; QUEER THEORY). In the same spirit, experiments with NON-REPRESENTATIONAL THEORY may also be seen as creative attempts to apprehend the world in terms that are not limited to cognition and consciousness (see also AFFECT).

In the second place, and closely connected to these departures, there has been a *pluralization of geographical imaginations*. Many human geographers have become reluctant to speak of 'the' geographical imagination – unless they are referring to a hegemonic form of geographical enquiry, and then usually as an object of critique – and are much more interested in the possibilities and predicaments that arise from working in the spaces between different philosophical and theoretical traditions (see Gregory, 1994). Closely connected to the production of these 'impure' geographies, there has also been a considerable interest in geographical knowledges that are not confined to (indeed, have often been excluded from) the formalizations of the academy. The boundaries of geography have thus been called into question through the recovery of quite other IMAGINATIVE GEOGRAPHIES that can have extraordinary powerful effects (cf. PER-FORMATIVITY): for example, the geographical imaginations deployed to wage WAR (see MILI-TARY GEOGRAPHY), conveyed through TRAVEL

WRITING, or mobilized in popular culture and politics (e.g. Pred, 2000). Critical studies of these geographical imaginations are not being conducted in an annex to the central structures of geography. Not only are they informed by contemporary politico-intellectual preoccupations but they also contest the conventional partitions between 'high' and 'low' cultures and imaginations. The circulation of discourses in and out of academic institutions is of vital importance to the elucidation of the politics of geographical imaginations, but also to their conduct: hence the interest in PUBLIC GEOGRAPHIES that transcend a narrow, instrumental concern with policy formulation to address political issues within a wider public sphere. A number of these contributions have been informed by post-colonialism, which has inspired a belated recognition of the WHITENESS of dominant geographical imaginations and the importance of geographical imaginations outside the global NORTH (see ANGLOCENTRISM; ETHNOCENTRISM; EUROCENTRISM).

Third, there has been *a renewed engagement with 'nature'*. The impetus for this has come from outside the discipline as much as from within, through precisely the political engagements and public, 'popular' geographies identified in the last paragraph. And yet in the previous paragraphs 'NATURE' has effectively been displaced from the central position it was once accorded within most major traditions of geography and its place taken by SPACE. The price paid for the articulation of a distinctively 'human' geography in the wake of what many critics saw as a dehumanizing spatial science was 'a peculiar silence on the question of nature' (Fitzsimmons, 1989). This has changed dramatically in recent years. These newer formulations do not eschew the significance of space – on the contrary, often informed by ACTOR-NETWORK THEORY, they elaborate a TOPOLOGICAL 'spatial imagination' – but they do so in ways that produce a much more sensuous, lively geographical imagination. For they 'alert us to a world of commotion in which the sites, tracks and contours of social life are constantly in the making through networks of actants-in-relation that are at once local and global, natural and cultural, and always more than human' (Whatmore, 1999b, p. 33). Such an approach, as Whatmore notes, 'implicates geographical imaginations and practices both in the *purifying logic* which … fragments living fabrics of association and designates the proper places of "nature" and "society", and in the *promise of its refusal*' (p. 34; emphases added). To fulfil

such a promise, critical enquiry will require the production of radically 'impure', heterogeneous geographies. The philosopher A.N. Whitehead once famously remarked, 'Nature doesn't come as clean as you can think it.' And for the reasons spelled out in these paragraphs, many would agree that geographical imaginations are – at last – becoming much dirtier.

All that said, there are two further dimensions of geographical imaginations that have received rather less attention, and both return us to the concerns originally voiced by Prince and Harvey. On one side, there have been attempts to experiment with forms of geographical expression – to realize the imaginative capacities and creative potential of geography in something like the sense that Prince used the term, the sort of sensibility that invites a reaction of surprise, even wonder: 'I've never thought of the world like that before.' Most of these have been confined to linguistic play in the pages of academic journals or monographs, however, though some human geographers have been drawn to the possibilities of art installations and dramatic performances as ways to reach wider audiences in non-traditional, non-academic forms. Without this outreach, which will almost certainly also involve the imaginative use of new technologies of COMMUNICATION, the possibility of public geographies will remain just that – a possibility. On the other side, and closely connected to this concern, there have been remarkably few attempts to imagine other worlds in the sense that Harvey (2000b) gave the term: 'spaces of hope'. This too is crucial; the transformations and extensions of geographical imaginations described above, and throughout this *Dictionary*, reveal an extraordinary capacity within and beyond the discipline for critique, for the pursuit and even the privileging of what Benhabib (1986) identified as the explanatory-diagnostic. But, as she also shows, a genuinely critical enquiry must also include the anticipatory–utopian (see UTOPIA): without releasing and realizing our geographical imaginations in this vital sense, then, we will turn forever on the treadmills of somebody else's present.   DG

Suggested reading
Gregory (1994, ch. 2); Harvey (1990); Rose (1993, ch. 4).

geographical societies Voluntary organizations, some of them professional, whose goal is the promotion of GEOGRAPHY as a subject and/ or an academic discipline.

The early and middle nineteenth century saw the formation of several societies in the former category – both national (the Royal Geographical Society – RGS – and the American Geographical Society – AGS, for example) and local (e.g. the Manchester Geographical Society). Set within the context of a massive expansion of TRADE – associated with COLONIALISM, IMPERIALISM and MILITARISM (Driver, 1998) – the societies promoted EXPLORATION, by financing expeditions and the dissemination of their findings, and CARTOGRAPHY, to represent the 'new worlds' that were mapped. Some of that dissemination was focused on commercial and government users (cf. COMMERCIAL GEOGRAPHY), but the societies also popularized geography, through their lecture programmes and publications. Some continue both functions. In their popularizing role they have been joined by others, such as the National Geographic Society, whose *National Geographic Magazine* sells millions of copies each month: similar magazines are produced as commercial ventures, such as *New Zealand Geographical* and the *Geographical Magazine*, now called simply *Geographical*, which is owned by the RGS.

In the late nineteenth century, many of these societies identified the need for geography to be included in school curricula, as part of children's general education as world citizens as well as a means of promoting national identity (cf. NATIONALISM). They were more successful in some countries (notably the UK and several in continental Europe) than others (the USA, for example: Schulten, 2001). They then turned their attention to their countries' universities, seeking to have the discipline taught there in order to ensure an adequate supply of trained teachers and others knowledgeable about geography and its techniques: the RGS funded the initial appointments at Oxford and Cambridge, for example, and also provided support to fledgling departments at Aberystwyth, Edinburgh and Manchester (Johnston, 2003).

With the establishment of geography as a school and university subject, separate professions were created and societies formed to promote geographers' interests: for school teachers, for example, these included the Geographical Association in the UK and the National Council for Geographic Education in the USA. In the universities, the research culture was nurtured by professional learned societies such as the Association of American Geographers (AAG) and the Institute of British Geographers (IBG), whose main functions were to hold conferences and other meetings and to publish journals and monographs. These learned societies operated largely independently of the longer-established societies with their wider briefs, although the AGS provided much early support for the AAG: the IBG and RGS merged in 1996.

Identification of geography as an important subject in contemporary society and then the creation and continued existence of the academic discipline owes much to the pioneering and continued efforts of these societies – critical 'spaces of science' in Livingstone's (2003c) geographies of scientific knowledge (see SCIENCE). The societies are major nexuses in the social NETWORKS through which academic geographers collaborate and promote their discipline – especially at a national level – and their journals are widely considered as among the leading media for the dissemination of and debate over research findings. RJ

Suggested reading
Bell, Butlin and Heffernan (1995); Brown (1980); Capel (1981); Dunbar (2002); Martin (2005); Steel (1983).

geographically weighted regression (GWR)
Standard REGRESSION models, like most QUANTITATIVE METHODS, fit an average relationship across all measured units; that is, an overall global MODEL is fitted, thereby assuming that processes are constant over space. GWR, as proposed by Brunsdon, Fotheringham and Charlton (1996), is an EXPLORATORY DATA ANALYSIS technique that allows the relationship between an outcome and a set of predictor variables to vary locally across the map. The approach aims to find spatial non-stationarity and distinguish this from mere chance; as such it is a development of Casetti's (1972) expansion method. With its emphasis on the potential importance of local contextuality, GWR is similar in intent to MULTI-LEVEL MODELLING: indeed, GWR-like models can be regarded as a specific type of multilevel model, the multiple membership model (Lawson, Browne and Vidal Rodeiro, 2003). As always, however, there is the danger that the results reflect not genuine spatial non-stationarity but, rather, simple misspecification, as when important predictor variables have been omitted from the model, with these variables themselves varying geographically.

The GWR technique works by identifying spatial subsamples of the data and fitting local regressions. Taking each sampled areal unit across a MAP in turn, a set of nearby areas that form the 'local' surrounding region is selected, and a regression is then fitted to data in this region in such a way that that nearby areas are given greater weight in the estimation of the regression coefficients than those further from the sampled unit. This surrounding region is known as the *spatial kernel* or bandwidth; it can have a fixed spatial size across the map, but this could result in unstable estimation in some regions where there are relatively few areas on which to base the local regression, and possibly miss important small-scale patterns where a number of local areas are clustered together spatially. Consequently, an adaptive spatial kernel is often preferred, so that a minimum number of areas can be specified as forming the region and the kernel extends out until this number has been achieved. Changing the kernel changes the spatial weighting scheme, which in turn produces estimates that vary more or less rapidly over space. A number of techniques have been developed for selecting an appropriate kernel and testing for spatial stationarity (Leung, Mei and Zhang, 2000; Paez, Uchida and Miyamoto, 2002).

Once a model has been calibrated, a set of local parameter estimates for each predictor variable can be mapped to see how the relation varies spatially. Similarly, local measures of standard errors and goodness-of-fit statistics can be obtained and mapped. An increasing number of applications of GWR includes models of house price and educational attainment level variations. Software for GWR is available from the original developers at http://ncg.nuim.ie/GWR.   KJ

Suggested reading
Fotheringham, Brunsdon and Charlton (2002).

geography Literally, 'earth-writing' from the Greek *geo* (earth) and *graphia* (writing), the practice of making geographies ('geographing') involves both writing about (conveying, expressing or representing) the world and also writing (marking, shaping or transforming) the world. The two fold in and out of one another in an ongoing and constantly changing series of situated practices, and even when attempts have been made to hold 'geo-graphing' still, to confine its objects and methods to a formal discipline, it has always escaped those enclosures. In consequence, as Livingstone (1992, p. 28) insisted, 'The idea that there is some eternal metaphysical core to geography independent of circumstances will simply have to go'. While the history of geography (see GEOGRAPHY, HISTORY OF) is neither bounded by its disciplinary formation nor the North Atlantic, recent historians of geography have paid close attention to the institutionalization of geography as a university discipline in Europe and North America from the closing decades of the nineteenth century onwards. This focus on the academy overlooks two important considerations. First, 'the institutional and intellectual form of the university is itself a series of [situated] practices that have changed over time': the present sense of a 'discipline' was alien to the early modern university, but this did not prevent the provision of instruction in both descriptive and mathematical geography (Withers and Mayhew, 2002, pp. 13–15). Second, like Molière's M. Jourdain, who was astonished to learn he had been talking prose all his life without knowing anything about it, many scholars (and others) have produced what could be regarded as geographical knowledge in the course of enquiries that they construed in quite other ways. More than this, their reception within the discipline has been uneven. Some contributions have been recognized (and even appropriated) as geography, while others have been disavowed for nominally 'professional' reasons: so, for example, research in spatial statistics may be seen as central to the discipline by some geographers, while TRAVEL-WRITING may be rejected as the impressionistic work of the amateur. As these examples suggest, however, such evaluations are themselves necessarily historically contingent, and Rose (1995) has cautioned that disciplinary geography 'has so often defined itself against what it insists it is not, that writing its histories without considering what has been constructed as not-geography is to tell only half the story'.

All boundary-drawing exercises are fraught with difficulties, therefore, and intellectual landscapes are no exception: such projects are never 'only' about ideas, but also about the grids of POWER in which they are implicated. The boundary question became intrusive with the creation of modern disciplines, and the inclusion of modern geography among them. Its disciplinary formation was a response to political and economic concerns (most viscerally, the demand for a MILITARY GEOGRAPHY in the service of modern WAR and, in the UK at least, a COMMERCIAL GEOGRAPHY to underwrite international trade) and also to pedagogical ambitions (the desire to transmit particular, nationalistic geographical knowledges through school curricula: see

EDUCATION; NATIONALISM). These practical considerations were hardly unique to the nineteenth century. Geography had long articulated political and commercial interests – in the seventeenth century Varenius had emphasized the importance of Special Geography (or REGIONAL GEOGRAPHY) to both 'statecraft' and the mercantile affairs of the Dutch Republic, for example – and it was already deeply invested in what Withers (2001) calls 'visualizing the nation'. But its academic institutionalization raised questions about the distance between 'professional' and 'popular' geographies, and about the very possibility of geography as a field of scholarly *research* (rather than the compilation of others' observations) that continue to resonate today. Soul-searching (or navel-gazing) about the 'spirit and purpose' or 'nature' of geography has become markedly less common in recent years, however, as the contingency and fluidity of intellectual enquiry have been embraced. There has been much greater interest in charting future geographies, whose variety confirms the radical openness of geographical horizons: there is no single direction, still less a teleological path, to be pursued (cf. Chorley, 1973; Johnston, 1985).

It follows that no definition of geography will satisfy everyone, and nor should it. But one possible definition of the contemporary discipline is: *(The study of) the ways in which space is involved in the operation and outcome of social and biophysical processes.* When it is unpacked, this summary sentence provides six starting-points for discussion:

(1) As the opening brackets indicate, 'geography', like 'history', has a *double meaning*: it both describes knowledge about or study of something (most formally, a discipline or field of intellectual enquiry) and it constitutes a particular object of enquiry, as in 'the geography of soil erosion' or 'the geography of China' (so that 'soil erosion' and 'China' have geographies just as they have histories). In fact, the relations between geography and history have long exercised philosophers. Classical HUMANISM distinguished between CHOROLOGY and chronology, for example, or derings in space and orderings in time, while ENLIGHTENMENT aesthetics asserted that the object of the visual arts (painting or sculpture) was the imitation of elements coexisting in space and that of the discursive arts (narrative poetry) the expression of moments unfolding in time. In the course of the twentieth century, disciplinary geography was increasingly troubled by both ways of making the distinction.

First, Hartshorne's attempt to legislate *The nature of geography* (1939) had treated geography and history as non-identical twins born under the sign of EXCEPTIONALISM. They were held to be different from one another because they classified phenomena according to their coexistence either in space (geography) or in time (history), but this also made them both different from all other forms of intellectual enquiry, which classified phenomena according to their similarity to one another (see KANTIANISM). This, in its turn, was supposed to limit concept-formation in geography and history to particularity rather than generalization, to the IDIOGRAPHIC rather than the NOMOTHETIC (which was the preserve of the sciences). These distinctions proved to be constant provocations. Most geographers insisted that TIME and history could not be excluded from geographical enquiry, and Hartshorne eventually conceded the point. Indeed, studies of landscape evolution, physical and cultural, were regarded as such mainstays of geographical enquiry that Darby (1953, p. 11) could describe geomorphology and HISTORICAL GEOGRAPHY as its twin foundations: even then, 'space' was not understood as a static stage. More than this, however, particularly after the QUANTITATIVE REVOLUTION of the 1960s, the study of DIFFUSION, the development of dynamic modelling and the capacity to capture the modalities of environmental and social change required any rigorous analysis of the concrete specificities of geographical variation to be informed by the theories and methods of the mainstream sciences and social sciences: geography could not be separated from other fields by philosophical fiat.

Second, the emphasis on geographical change raised what Darby (1962) called 'the problem of geographical description': How was it possible for a field that placed such a premium on the visual to convey any sense of PLACE and LANDSCAPE by textual means? Darby's original sense of this reactivated that Enlightenment sensibility: 'We can look at a picture as a whole,' he wrote, 'and it is as a whole that it leaves an impression upon us; we can, however, read only line by line.' The question (and Darby's way of framing it) later seemed problematic to many human geographers, who enquired more closely into practices of REPRESENTATION and interpretation. They examined the visual ideologies of CARTOGRAPHY and the poetics of prose, for example, both the nominally objective prose of scientific enquiry that dominated geographical journals and more evocative modes of expressing places and landscapes. En route, geography's connections with the HUMANITIES spiralled far beyond history, to include ART history, dance, FILM studies, the literary disciplines, MUSIC and PERFORMANCE studies. These were more than exercises in critical interrogation or DECONSTRUCTION; they also involved creative experiments in writing (see, e.g., Harrison, Pile and Thrift, 2004; Pred, 2004) and collaborations with artists, curators, film-makers and performance artists.

(2)   These close encounters with the sciences, social sciences and humanities have ensured that there is no single PARADIGM or method of enquiry in geography. In order to elucidate the *multiple ways* in which space is involved in the conduct of life on Earth and in the transformation of its surface, geographers have been drawn into many different conversations: human geographers with anthropologists, art historians, economists, historians, literary scholars, psychologists, sociologists and others; physical geographers with atmospheric scientists, botanists, biologists, ecologists, geologists, soil scientists, zoologists and others. These conversations have varied through time, and the history of geography (see HISTORY OF GEOGRAPHY) is an important part of understanding how the contemporary field of geographical enquiry has come to be the way it is, marking both its ruptures from as well as its continuities with any presumptive 'geographical tradition' (Livingstone, 1992). These conversations have also varied over space, so that there is a 'geography of Geography' too. The same claims can be made about any discipline, but in geography they have been increasingly interconnected. Most recent studies of the history of geography have recognized the importance of the spaces in which geographical knowledge is produced and through which it circulates. This has involved attempts both to *contextualize* geography – to understand the development of geographical ideas in relation to the places and situations from which they have emerged and the predicaments to which they were responding – and to *de-territorialize* geography: to open the disciplinary ring-fence, to appreciate that geography is not limited to the academy and to interrogate the production of geographical knowledges at multiple sites (Harvey, 2004a).

These studies have produced a heightened sensitivity to the specificity and partiality of Euro-American and, still more particularly, Anglo-American geography. Contracting geography's long and global history, Stoddart (1985) proclaimed that modern geography was a distinctively *European science* that could be traced back to a series of decisive advances in the closing decades of the eighteenth century. It was then, so Stoddart argued, that 'truth' was made the central criterion of objective science through the systematic deployment of observation, classification and comparison, and in his view it was the extension of these methods from the study of NATURE to the study of human societies 'that made our subject possible'. But the critique of the assumptions that underwrote such a claim, sharpened by the rise of POST-COLONIALISM, prompted many commentators to re-situate that project as a profoundly Eurocentric and, more recently, Euro-American science (see EUROCENTRISM: Gregory, 1994). Geography has thus come to be seen as a SITUATED KNOWLEDGE that, of necessity, must enter into conversations with scholars and others who occupy quite different positions.

This is not only (or even primarily) a matter of interdisciplinary dialogue; it also implies inter-locational dialogue. The more restricted idea of an *Anglo-American geography* was largely a creature of the 1960s and 1970s when, at the height of the QUANTITATIVE REVOLUTION, it seemed that a unified and coherent MODEL-based geography was emerging on both sides of the Atlantic. 'THEORY', too, seemed to offer a universal language that held out the promise of a unified, even unitary discipline. The subsequent critique of SPATIAL SCIENCE opened up many other paths for geographers to explore, and in that sense promoted diversification, but in human geography in particular it also heralded divergence as it prised apart the commonalities that once held the Anglo-American corpus together (cf. Johnston and Sidaway, 2004). This coherence (or rigidity, depending on your point of view) has also been assailed by a growing concern about the grids of power and privilege that structure the international academy, and in particular the silences and limitations of a narrowly English-language geography. If, as Wittgenstein observed, 'the limits of my language mean the limits of my world', then a geography that privileges one language is not only limited: it is also dangerous (Hassink, 2007). This poses an obvious difficulty for dictionaries of geography such as this one (cf. Brunotte, Gebhardt, Meurer, Meusburger and Nipper, 2002; Levy and Lussault, 2003).

That said, Anglophone geographers have not been wholly indifferent to work in other languages. Hartshorne's (1939) enquiry into the nature of geography was an exegesis of a largely German-language tradition, and British and American historians of geography have long acknowledged the foundational role of figures such as Alexander von Humboldt (1769–1859), Karl Ritter (1779–1859), Friedrich Ratzel (1844–1904) (see ANTHROPO-GEOGRAPHY) and, in France, Paul Vidal de la Blache (1845–1918). From the closing decades of the twentieth century, however, as human geography took an ever closer interest in continental European PHILOSOPHY – Giorgio Agamben, Alain Badiou, Jacques Derrida, Michel Foucault, Martin Heidegger, Jürgen Habermas, Julia Kristeva and Henri Lefebvre have all occupied prominent positions in contemporary discussions – there was, until very recently, little or no equivalent interest in continental European geography (apart from the work of Nordic and Dutch geographers available in English). One of the ironies of Stoddart's thesis about geography as a European science has been the extraordinary indifference of much of the Euro-American discipline to the *multiple* European genealogies of geographical discourse (cf. Godlewska, 1999; Minca, 2007b: see ANGLOCENTRISM). COLONIALISM and IMPERIALISM continue to cast long shadows over the discipline too: outside DEVELOPMENT GEOGRAPHY there has been a comparable lack of interest in the work of geographers from the global SOUTH (cf. Slater, 2004).

It is true that conferences under the auspices of the International Geographical Union and major national GEOGRAPHICAL SOCIETIES (especially the Association of American Geographers and also the Royal Geographical Society/Institute of British Geographers) attract participants from all over the world, but being together is not the same as talking together. Smaller, more focused meetings have usually been more successful at encouraging dialogue, and the activities of the International Critical Human Geography Group, the Aegean Seminars and international conferences in HISTORICAL GEOGRAPHY and ECONOMIC GEOGRAPHY have all helped to dissolve these parochialisms. But it has proved remarkably difficult to facilitate a less episodic, global exchange of ideas, and concern continues to be expressed about the HEGEMONY of English-language geography in nominally 'international' meetings and journals (Garcia-Ramon, 2003; Paasi, 2005). It may be that physical geographers have been more successful in resolving these issues, and that their ideas travel through more effective and multi-directional channels. Their main journals attract contributions from authors in many countries, and the International Association of Geomorphologists has promoted a series of international and regional conferences. But this apparent success may also reflect a problematic conviction that 'science' is itself an international and 'interest-free' language (cf. Peters, 2006).

(3) To make '*space*' focal to geographical enquiry is not to marginalize PLACE, REGION or LANDSCAPE. These constructs have often been opposed in geography's theory-wars, but while they are certainly different concepts with different entailments, genealogies and implications (all of which need to be respected) they all also register modes of producing SPACE as a field of differentiation and integration. To say this is to recognize geography's dependence on a series of technical and theoretical devices. This was so even when geography was conducted under the sign of a supposedly naïve EMPIRICISM, what William Bunge and William Warntz once called 'the innocent science', because the production and certification of its knowledges involved a series of calculative and conceptual templates. Technically, the ongoing formation of geography has been intimately involved with the changing capacity to conceive of the Earth as a whole (Cosgrove, 2001) and to fix and discriminate between positions on its surface (in geodesy, navigation and the like), and thus with the development of CARTOGRAPHY and GEOGRAPHIC INFORMATION SYSTEMS (GIS) that provide compelling demonstrations of the relevance of 'location, location, location' to more than real estate sales (Pickles, 2004; Short, 2004). The history of these procedures is closely associated with that of EXPLORATION, the politico-economic adventures of CAPITALISM, the occupations and dispossessions of COLONIALISM and IMPERIALISM, modern WAR and the deep interest of the modern STATE in the calculation and imagination of TERRITORY. To list these entanglements is not to imply a simple history of complicity, but this in its turn is not a plea for exculpation of 'Geography Militant' (Driver, 2001a): it is merely to note that many of these technical devices can be (and have been) turned to critical account, as the development of critical or radical cartographies and critical GIS attests (Harvey, Kwan and Pavovska, 2005; Crampton and Krygier, 2006), and to underscore that the 'technical' is never far from the political. These means of knowing and rendering

the world have been reinforced by formal theories about location, spatialization and interdependence that have offered an increasingly sophisticated purchase on geographies of UNEVEN DEVELOPMENT and the variable intersections between capitalism, war and GLOBALIZATION (Smith, 2008 [1984]; Harvey, 2003b; Sparke, 2005). These formulations are themselves marked by their origins, and the privileges of location that they address – and incorporate (Slater, 1992) – have been underwritten by less formal but no less rhetorically powerful IMAGINATIVE GEOGRAPHIES that not only inculcate a 'sense of place' that is central to identity-formation and the conduct of EVERYDAY LIFE, but also work to normalize particular ways of knowing the world and to produce allegiances, connections and divisions within it (Gregory, 2004b: see also GEOGRAPHICAL IMAGINARIES).

By these various means, 'space' has been produced, at once materially and discursively, through a series of what are profoundly political technologies. Hence, for example, Pickles' (2004, p. 93) pithy sense of the PERFORMATIVITY of cartography: 'Mapping, even as it claims to be reproducing the world, produces it.' Attempts to understand these processes of production have involved historical accounts of the development of concepts and the systems of practice in which they have been embedded, in both physical and human geography (see, e.g., Beckinsale, Chorley and Dunn, 1964/1973/1991; Gregory, 2008). They have involved explorations of other versions of those spatializations too: experiments with different concepts of LANDSCAPE, PLACE, REGION and SPACE itself (see, e.g., Holloway, Rice and Valentine, 2003). In the same vein, there have been repeated forays into the vexed question of SCALE, which most physical geographers – in the wake of Schumm and Lichty's (1965) classic essay – seem to regard as the very skeleton of their subject (Church and Mark, 1980), while at least some human geographers see it as the disarticulation of theirs (cf. Sheppard and McMaster, 2004; Marston, Jones and Woodward, 2005). The interrogation of these concepts has been an increasingly interdisciplinary project – none of them is the peculiar possession of geography, even if geographers have done their most characteristic work with the tools they provide: 'Space is the everywhere of modern thought' (Crang and Thrift, 2000, p. 1) – and some commentators have identified a 'spatial turn' across the whole field of the humanities and the social sciences (Thrift, 2002).

(4) This turn has been sustained, in part, by a recognition that the *outcome* of processes differs from place to place. The variable character of the Earth's surface has long driven enquiries into AREAL DIFFERENTIATION in both physical and human geography, and contrary to the predictions of prophets and critics of MODERNITY, the transformations brought about by globalization have not planed away differences: instead, they have produced new distinctions and juxtapositions. Physical geography has always been acutely sensitive to macro- and meso-variations in landforms and processes, particularly those related to climate and geology. But we now have a clearer sense of the ways in which those variations have been culturally coded and constructed: W.M. Davis' once canonical (1899a) description of fluvial erosion in temperate regions as the 'normal' cycle of erosion (which would startle people living in other regions), for example, and the vast discursive apparatus of TROPICALITY that yoked land to life in low latitudes. Spurred on by the rapid rise of Earth Systems Science, we also have a much surer understanding of the global regimes and interdependencies in which environmental variations are enmeshed (Slaymaker and Spencer, 1998). In much the same way, human geography retains its interest in the particularity of PLACE, but now usually works with a 'global sense of place' (Massey, 1994a; cf. Cresswell, 2004). Similarly, REGIONS are now rarely seen as the independent building blocks of a global inventory; a revitalized REGIONAL GEOGRAPHY focuses instead on the porosity of regions and on the intersecting processes through which their configurations are produced and transformed (Amin, 2004b). Here too, geography is not alone in its interest: AREA STUDIES, INTERNATIONAL RELATIONS and international studies have declared interests in these issues too, though where these interests have been wired to the conduct of foreign policy they have typically provided a narrower, more instrumental framing of interdependence than is now usual in geography.

More fundamentally, however, the spatial turn has also been sustained through investigations of the ways in which space affects the very *operation* of processes. It is now widely recognized that processes are not indifferent to the circumstances and configurations in which they operate, and it is this 'thrown-togetherness' that has prompted a renewed interest in spatial ONTOLOGY (Massey, 2005). This was, in a way, precisely Hartshorne's point – and it is also the pivot around which so much of Torsten Hägerstrand's extraordinary experiments with TIME-GEOGRAPHY moved – but it is now being sharpened in radically different ways. It is also why geography has always placed such a premium on FIELDWORK (which was focal to Stoddart's account too). Unlike field sciences, laboratory sciences can, in some measure, control for disturbances and isolate parameters to create idealized states. In much the same way, spatial science was an attempt to prise apart different spatial structures – the hexagonal lattices of CENTRAL PLACE systems, the wave forms of DIFFUSION processes – and then search for commonalities within these spatializations (market areas and drainage basins as hexagons) or combine them in idealized MODELS (the diffusion of innovations through central place systems). These were all attempts to order what is now most often seen as a partially ordered world – to tidy it up. As the philosopher A.N. Whitehead warned, however, 'Nature doesn't come as clean as you can think it', and it is in this spirit that much of geography is increasingly exercised by the ways in which the coexistence of different spatializations perturbs, disrupts and transforms the fields through which social and biophysical processes operate. Physical geography was in the vanguard of attempts to find the terms for what B.A. Kennedy (1979) memorably described as 'a naughty world', and since then human geography has also recognized the non-linearity, contingency and complexity of life on Earth.

(5) The processes with which geography is concerned are conventionally and collectively identified as '*social*' (economic, cultural, political etc.) and '*biophysical*' (biological, chemical, geophysical etc.). These two realms have often been assigned to a separate HUMAN GEOGRAPHY and PHYSICAL GEOGRAPHY, and the relations between the two have frequently prompted concern, on occasion even antagonism. In some institutional systems the two are more or less completely separate – in the Nordic countries, for example, there are usually separate university departments of human and physical geography – while in others one more or less dominates to the virtual exclusion of the other (in India, human geography is considerably more prominent than physical geography, for example, while in the USA, until very recently, 'Geography' was overwhelmingly human geography). Although most major geographical societies publish general journals that include papers in both

physical and human geography – in the English-speaking world, these include the *Annals of the Association of American Geographers, Canadian Geographer, Geographical Journal, Geographical Research, Geographical Review, South African Geographical Journal* and the *Transactions of the Institute of British Geographers* – in recent years many of them have found it difficult to attract physical geographers to their pages. (In Sweden, the English-language *Geografiska Annaler* is published as separate series in physical and human geography.) There are some newer, general journals produced by commercial publishers too, notably *Geoforum, GeoJournal* and *Geography Compass*, and also technical journals such as *Geographical Analysis* and the *International Journal of Geographical Information Science*. Publishing in the same journals does not imply a common discursive community, of course, and neither does it necessarily produce one: the sheer volume of academic publication makes most readers ever more selective (and perhaps idiosyncratic). But in any case the numbers of general journals have been dwarfed by the explosion of specialized, sub-disciplinary journals such as *Earth Surface Processes and Landforms, The Journal of Biogeography, Physical Geography* and *Progress in Physical Geography* on one side, and *Antipode, Cultural Geographies, Economic Geography*, the *Environment and Planning* journals, *Gender, Place and Culture, Journal of Historical Geography, Political Geography, Progress in Human Geography* and *Social and Cultural Geographies* on the other. Many of these journals advertise themselves as 'interdisciplinary', but the two groups reach out in opposite directions – to the atmospheric, biological and Earth sciences, or to the humanities and social sciences – rather than to each other.

Openness to other disciplines is widely accepted as indispensable for intellectual vitality, but there has also been a persistent anxiety that arrangements and practices such as these make a mockery of claims that geography studies the relations *between* the human and physical worlds, and at the limit threaten geography's institutional survival when ecological awareness and demands for SUSTAINABLE DEVELOPMENT are being articulated by other disciplines and emerging interdisciplinary fields (cf. Turner, 2002). To be sure, human geographers have long had important things to say about NATURE – it was only on the isotropic planes of spatial science that the biophysical environment was erased – and a host of studies in CULTURAL ECOLOGY, ENVIRONMENTAL

HISTORY, HAZARDS research and POLITICAL ECOLOGY testify to the power of their contributions. Similarly, physical geographers have long been interested in the intersection of human and physical systems (cf. Bennett and Chorley, 1978). In geomorphology, many consultative, geotechnical projects – perhaps most obviously on flooding, soil erosion, slope stability and the like – reveal the continuing vitality of this stream of work, and the atmospheric sciences have placed considerable emphasis on their practical relevance. In the future, a revitalized BIOGEOGRAPHY (as a sort of 'living Earth science') may well make some of the most direct connections to human geography and, indeed, to green politics, while pressing issues of global environmental change and GLOBAL WARMING require a transdisciplinary approach that speaks across the sciences, social sciences and humanities (see also Turner, Clark, Kates, Richards and Mathews, 1990).

But to have important things to say – and vital questions to address – does not mean that human and physical geographers speak the same language, and translation has its own problems (Bracken and Oughton, 2006). Many commentators, inside and outside geography, have insisted on a fundamental distinction between the methods of the natural sciences (that probe an 'object-world') and those of the humanities and social sciences (that probe a 'subject-world'). Unlike pebbles rolling along the bed of a river or grains of sand cascading over the crest of a dune, human beings are suspended in webs of meaning: those meanings make a difference to conduct in ways that have no parallel in the domain of the natural sciences, and their elucidation requires radically different interpretative procedures. Proponents of HUMANISTIC GEOGRAPHY were among those most likely to advance these arguments in the 1970s and 1980s, but the rise of POSTMODERNISM and the correlative CULTURAL TURN across the humanities and social sciences in the 1990s – and in particular the so-called 'science wars' epitomized by the Sokal affair (in which physicist Alan Sokal successfully submitted a spoof 'cultural studies' article to the journal *Social Text*; cf. Ross, 1996) – must have convinced many physical geographers that their commitment to 'Science' put them at a considerable distance from many, if not most, human geographers.

There have been three major responses to such polarizing views. The first has been to appeal to science studies (see SCIENCE) to argue that physical geography, like 'science' more generally, is a social practice too; it has its own, highly formalized rules, but it constantly traffics in meanings and interpretations. Seen thus, physical geographers are caught in the HERMENEUTIC circle, and as invested in (serious) language games and qualitative modes of representation – and hence in textualization, RHETORIC and the like – as human geographers (Sugden, 1996; Spedding, 1997; Phillips, 1999, pp. 758–9; Harrison, 2001). These commonalities extend beyond the notebook or the printed page, however, and include, crucially, the performance of FIELDWORK (Powell, 2002). The second response has been to return to PHILOSOPHY and explore post-positivist philosophies of science that provide more nuanced explanations of both social and biophysical systems, and allow for a more sophisticated understanding of contingency than the objectivist canon. REALISM has played a pivotal role here, not least through its qualified NATURALISM, and following its early consideration by human geographers (Sayer, 1992 [1984]) it has been explored by a growing number of physical geographers (Richards, Brookes, Clifford, Harris and Lane, 1998; Raper and Livingstone, 2001). The third response, stimulated by attempts to theorize the PRODUCTION OF NATURE (Smith, 2008 [1984]), has been to call into question the very distinction between the 'social' and 'biophysical' (Braun and Castree 1998; Castree and Braun, 2001) and to recognize the vital importance of 'hybrid geographies' (Whatmore, 2002b). A host of new approaches has confounded the deceptively commonsensical partitions between 'culture' and 'nature', including ACTOR-NETWORK THEORY, AGENT-BASED MODELLING, COMPLEXITY THEORY and NON-REPRESENTATIONAL THEORY. With one or two exceptions, it seems that human geographers are more drawn to some of these possibilities and physical geographers to others, and they do not in themselves constitute a common intellectual language. But what C.P. Snow famously castigated as 'the two cultures' in the late 1950s, one literary-social and the other physical-scientific, has come to be recognized as an artifice, and there have been a number of attempts to conduct what the Royal Geographical Society/Institute of British Geographers called 'conversations across the divide' (Harrison, Massey, Richards, Magilligan, Thrift and Bender, 2004).

Not all observers of interventions like these are sanguine about the prospects for a plenary geography (cf. Johnston, 2005b; Viles, 2005), and at the end of the day it may not matter very much. Most physical and human geographers are probably too involved in their own teaching and research to bother very much about such meta-issues. If they are interested in (say) residential segregation in cities or the dynamics of gravel-bed rivers, most scholars pursue whatever avenues of enquiry seem most promising, and do not draw back at disciplinary borders or worry about disciplinary integrity. It is hard to say – or see – why they should. To be sure, some work is by its very nature hybrid – hence the rise of various 'environmental' geographies – but it is a mistake to identify institutional politics with intellectual substance. Funding for teaching and research has become a crucial issue for all disciplines, and its impact should not be minimized. Advertising the capacity of geography to bring together the sciences, social sciences and humanities may bring its institutional rewards, but the intellectual realization of an interdisciplinary project through disciplinary privilege is surely a contradiction in terms. Disciplines are contingent institutional arrangements, and while each has a canon of sorts, activated through courses and textbooks, students and professors, societies and journals, and while there have often been attempts to police the frontiers (or to extend them through disciplinary imperialism), the fact remains that intellectual work of any significance has never been confined by administrative boundaries. Most scholars travel in interdisciplinary space, and while geography may have been unusually promiscuous in its encounters, it is by no means alone: as Gregson (2005, p. 7) astutely remarks, 'ours is increasingly a post-disciplinary world in which the geographical is critical but not ours to possess'.

(6) The emphasis on *process-based explanations* is common to human geography, physical geography and many of the interchanges between them. Contemporary geographical enquiry does not stop at mapping outcomes – a sort of global gazetteer – and the FRICTION OF DISTANCE is no longer viewed as an adequate surrogate for the operation of the processes that produce those outcomes. Hence the focus on practices and structures, micro-processes and SYSTEMS. In human geography, the argument was put with characteristic force by Soja (1989, pp. 37–8), who identified a persistent disciplinary tendency to limit enquiry to the description and calibration of 'outcomes deriving from processes whose deeper theorization was left to others' in 'an infinite regres-

sion of geographies upon geographies'. His solution, like those of an increasing number of his peers, was not to import theorizations of processes from SOCIAL THEORY, but (much more radically) to 'spatialize' social theory *ab initio* and to think about the PRODUCTION OF SPACE in ways that eventually troubled the dualism (even the DIALECTIC) of spatial form and social process. Others followed other routes to different destinations, but the common result was to underline the importance of ONTOLOGY to human geography. Some physical geographers had started to focus on process-based explanations in the 1950s, under the influence of American geologist and geomorphologist Arthur N. Strahler (1918–2002) and his graduate students, and by the time human geographers were recoiling from SPATIAL FETISHISM, their physical colleagues were heavily invested in the measurement of atmospheric, biological and geomorphological processes. But here too there has been a concerted attempt to think about process in less mechanistic terms than those early projects allowed, and in consequence to recognize the practical importance of 'philosophical speculation about the fundamental "stuff" or *substance* of reality' for geomorphology and other fields of physical geography (Rhoads, 2006, p. 15; cf. Harvey, 1996).

This interest in PROCESS is, in one sense, a peculiarly modern fascination: in a world where, as Marx so famously put it, 'all that is solid melts into air', there is a particular premium on describing, monitoring and accounting for change. But there is also a vital interest in planning, predicting and implementing change. This has had two crucial impacts on the development of contemporary geography. The first is a renewed interest in political and ethical questions. Intervening in situations of politico-ecological catastrophe or war, where ENVIRONMENTAL JUSTICE, HUMAN RIGHTS and even our very survival as a species may be at stake, requires more than a detached, analytical gaze. In its classical, Greek form, geography was closely associated with political and moral philosophy, and the luminous writings of the gentle anarchist geographer Pyotr Kropotkin (1842–1921) provided a rare, modern insistence on the importance of such questions. These were revived most effectively by David Harvey in the second half of the twentieth century, whose forensic dissection of late CAPITALISM through a close reading and reformulation of Marx's writings did much to alert human geographers to the ineluctable politics of their enquiries. This raised a series of questions about EPISTEMOLOGY and the limits of geographical knowledge that required a critique not only of geography's technical and conceptual armatures – including those derived from its newfound interest in MARXISM – but of (for example) the MASCULINISM that was reproduced through its concepts and practices (Rose, 1993). The ongoing formation of a CRITICAL HUMAN GEOGRAPHY, including CRITICAL GEOPOLITICS and FEMINIST GEOGRAPHIES, reinforced and generalized these concerns (see also RADICAL GEOGRAPHY). Physical geographers were by no means indifferent to them, but they seem to have been more directly moved by the consideration of an explicitly environmental ETHICS. Indeed, moral philosophies more generally have assumed such prominence alongside philosophies of science in contemporary geographical enquiry that some observers have discerned a 'moral turn' across the discipline as a whole (Barnett and Land, 2007; cf. Smith, 2000a; Lee and Smith, 2004).

The second consequence of orienting geographical enquiry towards change and the future has been a recognition that geography's responsibilities extend beyond a critical involvement in PUBLIC POLICY – important though that is – to a considered engagement in public *debate* (Murphy, 2006). This involves a more rigorous REFLEXIVITY: not only a careful and constructive critique of theories, methods and materials, but also an examination of the *circumstances* in which geographies are being produced and circulated and of the *consequences* in which they are implicated. This process might well begin 'at home', in the classroom and the lecture theatre, but it cannot end there. The late-modern corporate university, with its audit culture, its vested interest in the commodification of knowledge, and its incorporation of many of the modalities of NEO-LIBERALISM, materially affects teaching and research. At the same time, however, precisely because geographical knowledges are produced at so many sites outside formal educational institutions, public responsibility also involves a willingness to learn from and engage with audiences far beyond the academy, many of whose lives have been ravaged by the unregulated intrusions of the supposedly 'free' market, by new rounds of ACCUMULATION by dispossession and by the forcible installation of radically new geographies (Harvey, 2003b; Lawson, 2007). To analyse and challenge these impositions requires more than 'earth-writing' in its literal sense; geographers neglect the art of writing at their

peril, but they also need to write in different ('non-academic') styles for different audiences, to explore new technologies and MEDIA, and to experiment with different modes of presentation. None of this is about experimentation for its own sake, because the new-found interest in PUBLIC GEOGRAPHIES is not only about producing counter-publics imbued with a critical GEOGRAPHICAL IMAGINATION: it is also, crucially, about learning from and engaging them in open and respectful dialogue. This matters because geography is not, as the old saw has it, 'what geographers do': it is, in an important sense, what we *all* do. Claims about 'the end of geography' have been made since at least the early twentieth century, but (then as now) they have also always been claims about the rise of new geographies and, less obviously perhaps, the grids of power that they forward (Smith, N., 2003c). 'Geo-graphing', whether 'professional' or 'popular', thus never works on a blank surface: it always involves writing over (superimposition) and writing out (erasure and exclusion: Sparke, 2005, p. xvi). Textbooks and dictionary entries are no exception.   DG

Suggested reading
Bonnet (2007); Castree, Rogers and Sherman (2005); Livingstone (1992); Thrift (2002) [and subsequent debate].

geography, history of The term 'GEOGRAPHY' defies simple definition. The standard, non-specialist dictionary characterization of it as 'The science which has for its object the description of the Earth's surface' fails to capture the complexity of geography's history: the disorderliness of the past, to put it another way, resists ESSENTIALIST specification. As an enterprise – whether scholarly or popular, whether in terms of disciplinary history, discursive engagements or practical operations – geography has meant different things at different times and places. In fact, geographical knowledge and practice been intimately intertwined with a host of enterprises: natural magic, imperial politics, celestial cartography, natural theology, conjectural prehistory, mathematical astronomy, speculative anthropology, TRAVEL-WRITING, national identity and various species of literary endeavour. It is therefore understandable that there is no unchallenged consensus on what it means to write geography's history. And although the task of reconstructing geography's history has had its critics, some of whom are suspicious of the entire enterprise (Barnett, 1995), it would not be unreasonable to suggest that some of the most significant interventions into recent debates on the relationships between knowledge, REPRESENTATION and POWER have emanated from those concerned with the ways in which geographical knowledge is constituted socially, historically and spatially.

As a professional *discipline*, geography's GENEALOGY is part and parcel of the story of the division of intellectual labour that delivered modern 'disciplines' around the end of the nineteenth century. It has been claimed that before this period, in particular during the period of the European ENLIGHTENMENT, the label 'geography', as the precursor of the modern discipline, had fairly specific connotations that distinguished it from other fields of endeavour through its focus on the determination of relative location and description of 'phenomena to be found in those locations' (Mayhew, 2001, p. 388). But it has been shown that boundaries around the subject were never quite so sharply delineated and that geography took various shapes in different texts, at different sites and in different practical pursuits (Withers, 2006). However that particular terminological debate is to be resolved, histories of geography as a DISCOURSE continue to be written without the definitional constraints that recent history and contingent institutional arrangements necessarily impose on the modern-day discipline. To be sure, the histories of geography as discourse and discipline are interrelated in intimate ways, and there is good evidence to suppose that recent practitioners of these enterprises deploy similar historiographical tactics, though there do remain differences of substance and style in the conduct of these two enterprises. The increasing acknowledgement too that geographical pursuits in the public sphere – popular geographies – are in need of further scrutiny parallels, in some respects, the surge of interest in social studies of popular science.

So far as the modern *discipline* of geography is concerned, then, those chronicling the course of historical change have conducted their investigations in a variety of ways. A range of different strategies has been pursued. First: institutional history. Those dwelling on the history of geography's institutions have concentrated on the subject's organizational expression, and accordingly have produced narratives of a range of GEOGRAPHICAL SOCIETIES, or have enquired into the evolution of geography in different national traditions. Such projects have tended to concentrate on geography's modern narrative, but even in its pre-professional guise, the subject's institutional manifestation was significant. Its presence in university curricula, for example, has been traced back to the period of the SCIENTIFIC REVOLUTION, when it was taught in conjunction with practices such as astronomy and practical mathematics (Withers and Mayhew, 2002; Livingstone 2003c). Yet there remains significant work to be done. For the English-speaking world, to take a single example, the dimensions of the Royal Geographical Society's influence on the mutual shaping of geographical knowledge and Victorian society still remain to be charted. In other national and provincial settings, similar questions are in need of resolution.

Second: biography. The life stories of a number of key professional geographers, including Halford Mackinder, Ellsworth Huntington, Mark Jefferson, William Morris Davis and Elisée Reclus, have been narrated. Some (though not all) of these accounts have been frankly disappointing in their lacklustre narrative line and an absence of historiographical sophistication, though N. Smith's (2003) more recent analysis of Isaiah Bowman displays a richness and depth to which other accounts could profitably aspire. Alongside these full-length studies, a suite of shorter biographical sketches of a wider range of figures continues in the serial *Geographers: Biobibliographical Studies*. Biographical treatments are also available of figures looming large in the history of the subject's pre-professional past, including more recently studies of Alexander von Humboldt (Rupke, 2005), George Perkins Marsh (Lowenthal, 2000) and Nathaniel Shaler (Livingstone, 1987b). New energy has also been injected into the biographical impulse by the pursuit of what might be called 'life geographies' or 'life spaces' – namely, by taking with much greater seriousness the sites and spaces through which human beings transact their lives (Daniels and Nash, 2004). Recent autobiographical experiments by geographers have also added to this perspective; these raise significant questions about the relative value of autobiography and biography, the difference between a 'life as it is lived' and 'a life as it is told', and the inescapable HERMENEUTIC complications involved in fusing present horizons with those of the past.

Third: histories of ideas. Alongside institutional history and biographical narrative, a number of works dwelling on the history of geographical ideas within academic geography have appeared. Some are specialist treatments of how modern geographical thought has engaged with wider theoretical currents (Peet, 1998); some rehearse the internal history of sub-disciplines (for HISTORICAL GEOGRAPHY, for instance, see Butlin, 1993); others have centred on school geography texts and their role in conveying imperial attitudes about RACE and GENDER (Maddrell, 1998). Cumulatively, works such as these demonstrate the diverse range of interests and styles employed to interrogate geography's academic history.

Contributions dealing with geographical *discourses* also come in a variety of guises and encompass a wide spectrum of topics. Beazley's (1897–1906) *The dawn of modern geography* emphasized the history of medieval travel and exploration; Eva Taylor's (1930) portrayal of Tudor geography centred on mathematical practice, surveying and navigation; and J.K. Wright's (1965 [1925]) account of the *Geographical lore of the time of the Crusades* rehearsed place description, cartographic ventures and cosmographical convictions in a project that self-confessedly covered 'a wider field than most definitions of geography' (p. 2). Newer ways of thinking about medieval geography have also recently surfaced, notably the researches of Lozovsky (2000), who explores medieval scholars' perceptions and representations of geographical space and its transmission. Glacken's (1967) monumental *Traces on the Rhodian shore* mapped the contact zone between NATURE and CULTURE, and openly acknowledged that he transcended the conventional limits of the modern discipline. Bowen's (1981) compendious survey of geographical thought from Bacon to Humboldt constitutes a sophisticated historical apologia for an ecological, anti-POSITIVISTIC vision of the subject. Alongside these treatments of geographical discourse is a range of related contributions dealing with allied subjects such as BIOGEOGRAPHY (Browne, 1983), meteorology (Anderson, 2005a), Earth and environmental science (Bowler, 1992; Rudwick 2005), CARTOGRAPHY (Edney, 1997; Burnett, 2000), oceanography (Rozwadowski, 2005) geomorphology (Davies, 1969; Kennedy, 2005), HUMAN ECOLOGY (Mitman, 1992) and ideas of Nature (Coates, 1998). In many cases, these undertakings have deepened connections between geographers and historians of SCIENCE, and opened up new and fertile lines of enquiry.

If these works are indicative of geography's long-standing location within the scientific tradition, there is equally abundant evidence for the subject's textual heritage that connects it with the HUMANITIES. Since the period of the scientific revolution, geography has also been concerned with matters of commerce and strategy, and also with regional descriptions (Cormack, 1997). This realization has led Mayhew (2000) to argue that early modern geography was deeply implicated in debates about political theology and cultural identity during the so-called long eighteenth century. The subject's intimate connections with historical scholarship, moral philosophy, speculative anthropology and various species of literary endeavour, alongside its association with natural philosophy, have thus been emphasized. One mark of this connection is the way in which geographical works depicted denominational spaces, the Dissolution of the Monasteries and political insurrection at the time of the English Civil War; thereby, the inescapably political character of regional description and geographical compilation is disclosed. Another indication is the extent to which writers such as Samuel Johnston and Shakespeare's commentators were concerned with matters of geographical sensibility (Roberts, 1991).

These relatively specialist studies are supplemented by a number of what Aay (1981) calls 'textbook chronicles' – synthetic treatments designed for student consumption that provide an overview of the field. It is now plain, however, that these surveys have all too frequently lapsed into apologetics for some particular viewpoint – geography as regional interrogation, the study of occupied space or some such. Moreover, their strategy was typically *presentist*, namely using history to adjudicate on present-day controversies (though the inescapability of certain dimensions of the present as indicated above need to be registered); *internalist*, in the sense that they paid scant attention to the broader social and intellectual contexts within which geographical knowledges were produced; and *cumulative*, portraying history in terms of progress towards some perceived contemporary orthodoxy. Scepticism about precisely these assumptions has fostered greater sensitivity to currents of historiographical thinking, and a range of strategies have therefore been deployed in the endeavour to deepen analyses of geography's genealogy.

Leaving aside their problematic reading of Kuhn, some have turned to his *Structure of scientific revolutions* (1970 [1962]) to characterize the history of geography as an overlapping succession of PARADIGMS enshrined in a number of key texts: Paul Vidal de la Blache's POSSIBILISM, Ellsworth Huntington's ENVIRONMENTAL DETERMINISM, Carl Ortwin Sauer's

LANDSCAPE MORPHOLOGY, Richard Hartshorne's AREAL DIFFERENTIATION and Fred K. Schaefer's EXCEPTIONALISM are typical candidates for paradigm status (see SCIENTIFIC REVOLUTION(S)). In such scenarios, however, a good deal of historical typecasting and editorial management has had to be engaged in. Others have taken more seriously the role of 'invisible colleges' and 'socio-scientific NETWORKS' (Lochhead, 1981). At the same time, perspectives from HISTORICAL MATERIALISM have been marshalled as a means of elucidating the way in which geographical knowledge and practices have been used to legitimate the social conditions that produced that knowledge in the first place (Harvey, 1984). Still others have seen in the philosophical literature on the cognitive power of METAPHOR a key to unlocking aspects of geography's history (Buttimer, 1982), through delineating the different uses of, say, mechanistic, organic, structural and textual analogies. The insights of Foucault on the intimate connections between SPACE, SURVEILLANCE, POWER and knowledge, and of Said on the Western construction of 'non-Western' realms (see ORIENTALISM) have also opened up new vistas to the history of geography by unmasking the pretended neutrality of spatial discourse in a variety of arenas both within and beyond the academy. The related need to open up conventional histories of geography to non-Western traditions is a real *desideratum*.

More recently, rapprochement with SCIENCE STUDIES has opened up new lines of enquiry in which the social constitution of knowledge and an empirical examination of actual knowledge-making practices have come to the fore. Barnes (1996, 1998), for example, has drawn on the methodology of social studies of scientific knowledge in his account of the history and conceptual structure of modern ECONOMIC GEOGRAPHY in general, and geography's QUANTITATIVE REVOLUTION in particular. Other applications of this general perspective within human geography are advertised in this *Dictionary*'s entry on SCIENCE (including SCIENCE STUDIES). Among these are the ACTOR-NETWORK THEORY of Bruno Latour, the so-called Edinburgh strong programme in the sociology of knowledge, a range of feminist epistemologies, the ethnographic methodologies of the micro-anthropology of science and various other constructivist perspectives. All of these combine to situate cognitive claims in the conditions of their making, and to render problematic distinctions between internal and external history of scientific knowledge.

Cumulatively, such calls for re-reading geography's history have contributed to a wide range of revisionist accounts of particular episodes, among which mention might be made of the links between magic, mysticism and geography at various times (Livingstone, 1988; Matless, 1991), geography's complicity in the shaping of imperial ambitions and national identity in the early modern period (Withers, 2001: see IMPERIALISM), the intimate connections between geography, EMPIRE, HEALTH and racial theory (Livingstone, 1991; Bell, 1993; Godlewska and Smith, 1994; Driver, 2001a), the relations between LANDSCAPE REPRESENTATION, artistic convention and denominational discourse (Cosgrove and Daniels, 1988; Mayhew, 1996), the circumstances surrounding debates over the boundary between geography and sociology in turn-of-the-century France (Friedman, 1996), the imperial mould in which early ENVIRONMENTALISM was cast (Grove, 1995), the relations between geography and TRAVEL-WRITING, and calls for feminist readings of the tradition (Domosh, 1991, Rose, 1995). There is a growing recognition too that the narrative of Western geography cannot be sequestered from its wider channels of intellectual exchange even in the early modern period. Patterns of TRADE and the transmission of knowledge between 'East' and 'West' played a major role in the shaping of various European geographies. As for practical engagements, Ryan's (1998) account of the connections between geography, photography and racial representation in the Victorian era, and feminist reflections on FIELDWORK have opened up these arenas to theoretically informed interrogation. Embedded within at least of some of these accounts is a conviction that 'geography' is a negotiated entity, and that a central task of its historians is to ascertain how and why certain practices and procedures come to be accounted authoritative, and hence normative, at certain moments in time and in certain spatial settings.

It is plain, then, that the 'history of geography' comprises a variety of enterprises that have been engaged in various ways. Nevertheless, a broad shift can be detected from the 'encyclopaedism' of earlier works (which operated in a cumulative-chronological fashion) towards a more recent 'genealogical' perspective (which aims to disclose the tangled connections between power and knowledge). The subversive character of the latter has been embraced with differing degrees of enthusiasm: some now insist that the idea of history as a single master narrative is a Western 'myth', while others, unenamoured of an altogether radical RELATIVISM (in which truth is taken to be relative to circumstance) or suspicious that the genealogist is implicated in an impossible self-referential dilemma (namely, that the thesis is self-refuting), suggest that there is more value in thinking of discourses as 'contested traditions' – socially embodied and temporally extended conversations that act as stabilizing constraints on the elucidation of meaning (MacIntyre, 1990). Insofar as 'encyclopaedia', 'GENEALOGY' and 'tradition' as modes of historical interrogation reflect differing attitudes towards what has come to be called the Enlightenment project, the history of geography – as a scholarly pursuit – has a significant role to play in debates within the discipline over the relations between knowledge, power, representation and SOCIAL CONSTRUCTION (Gregory, 1994).

Moreover, recent reassertions of the significance of PLACE and SPACE in historical investigations of human knowing (Shapin, 1998; Livingstone, 2003c) are bringing the issue of geography's own knowledge spaces to the fore. Thus attention is beginning to be directed towards understanding the different sites and spaces – at a range of SCALES – within which geographical knowledge is produced and circulates. Investigations of the PERFORMATIVE geographies in seventeenth-century court masques and triumphal processions (Withers, 1997), field sites and expeditionary settings as venues of geographical enquiry and evocation (Driver and Martins, 2005), museums as spaces of display (Naylor, 2002), archives and the construction of geographical knowledge (Withers, 2002), the use of personal diaries and field journals to reconstruct learning experiences (Lorimer, 2003), mission stations as imperial sites of local knowledge (Livingstone, 2005b), ships as instruments of geodetic survey (Sorrenson, 1996), and meteorological stations (Naylor, 2006) are illustrative of this spatial turn. The CITY itself – as a laboratory field-site – has also been investigated as an epistemic 'truth-spot' and thus fundamental to the credibility of certain scientific claims; this is exemplified *par excellence* in the CHICAGO SCHOOL of urban studies (Gieryn, 2006). Other venues such as CENSUS bureaus, GIS laboratories, botanical gardens, trading floors, art studios, fields of military operation (see WAR) and government departments – where geographical knowledge of various sorts is made and remade – are no less in need of interro-

gation. Interest too is developing on the ways in which geographical TEXTS have been read in particular locations, and of regional differences in what has been called reviewing cultures (Rupke, 1999). All this confirms that 'the history of geography' as an undertaking is now beginning (all too ironically) to take 'geography' much more seriously – namely, by reconceptualizing the enterprise as 'the historical geography of geographical knowledges and practices'.   DNL

Suggested reading
Glacken (1967); Johnston and Sidaway (2004); Livingstone (1992); Stoddart (1986).

geo-informatics Geo-informatics is the interface and collaboration between the Earth and the information sciences (notably computer science) to use geocoded data (see GEOCODING) to better model, visualize and understand the Earth's complexity. More specific topics of research that have been included at the annual international conference in geo-informatics have included: discovery, integration, management and VISUALIZATION of geoscience data; INTERNET-enabled GEOGRAPHIC INFORMATION SYSTEMS (GIS); location-based services, including GLOBAL POSITIONING SYSTEMS; spatial data modelling in HYPERSPACES; REMOTE SENSING; and INTEROPERABILITY.

Looking at the research themes listed above, it is evident that the interests of geo-informatics overlap with those of GEOGRAPHIC INFORMATION SCIENCE and GEOCOMPUTATION. To find common ground is not surprising: each has an interdisciplinary nature, bound by an interest in geographical datasets and the computational requirements to store, process and make sense of them. Each also brings a spatial perspective to answer the questions of social and physical science (and also the interactions between social and physical SYSTEMS). And each is a young field of research, born out of much older traditions. However, whereas the origins of GISc are in navigation, CARTOGRAPHY, DEMOGRAPHY, RESOURCE MANAGEMENT and SPATIAL ANALYSIS, and the roots of geocomputation lie in using high-performance computing for applied SPATIAL SCIENCE, the seeds of geo-informatics were germinated in the geodetic (e.g. SURVEYING) traditions of engineering, geology, oceanography and other geosciences.

These geodetic and geoscientific foundations are revealed by the keen focus of geo-informatics on geographical data – their storage, integration, analysis and visualization. Traditional surveying in the geosciences has involved a methodological and spatially ordered collection of data or samples of a phenomenon, in order to better understand that which is being investigated. The need for scientific rigour has not changed in research. What is new is the more extensive SURVEILLANCE of the Earth's social and natural systems (e.g. by REMOTE SENSING) that has developed over recent decades, and the huge amounts of data that routinely are collected by (or to enable) the functioning of societies (e.g. population data from GOVERNANCE, consumer data from commerce, organizational data from pubic service management and so forth).

Increased data sharing, new technologies and new techniques for analysis affect the theory and practice of handling geographical information (Goodchild and Longley, 2005). For example, storing extensive and multivariate datasets to model and represent complex systems (physical or social) is not best achieved by the sorts of simplifying assumptions commonly used to capture and to map socioeconomic data. A straightforward database design used in GIS takes the idea that geographical features have a fixed and unambiguous location which can be defined by their coordinate position in a planar space, the encoding of which is prioritized. Other information, such as the height of the Earth's surface at the feature's position, the height of the feature itself or the data/time at which the feature was observed are secondary information, stored as 'just another' attribute alongside other information about the feature (e.g. what the feature is called, its size etc.) (Worboys, 2005). Such an approach works well when mapping, for example, CENSUS information collected on a particular date, once every ten years, and describing geographical features that are fixed in TIME and SPACE (i.e. the CENSUS population, per CENSUS TRACT, on the date of enumeration). It is not suitable for storing or visualizing data about dynamic PROCESSES where the temporal component of the analysis is at least as important as the spatial, or for modelling or querying genuinely three-dimensional features – for example, rock or soil layers, or subterranean walkways (at subway stations) that can fold under themselves and therefore occupy multiple positions in multidimensional space (Raper, 2000).

To integrate and to extract meaningful knowledge from data collected for different reasons, at different times, at different SCALES, using different CLASSIFICATION frameworks and different ONTOLOGIES, is a task that bridges between science and computers and that provides the structure of geo-informatics research. It is not an easy task. As the geo-informatics portal at the Pan-American Center for Earth and Environmental Studies states, 'currently, the chaotic distribution of available data sets, lack of documentation about them, and lack of easy-to-use access tools and computer modeling and analysis codes are major obstacles for scientists and educators alike' (http://paces.geo.utep.edu). There, geo-informatics is described as the 'field in which geoscientists and computer scientists are working together to provide the means to address a variety of complex scientific questions using advanced information technologies and integrated analysis'.

Writing from an URBAN AND REGIONAL PLANNING perspective, Holmberg (1994) sums up the scope of geo-informatics which incorporates elements of computation, science, systems modelling and SOCIETY. To him, geo-informatics is the technological and scientific discipline guiding the design of systems for sensing, modelling, representing, visualizing, monitoring, processing and communicating geo-information. The 'big challenge' of geo-informatics, then, is to handle geographical information in geographically minded ways, to help understand geographical systems, to undertake geographical problem solving and to progress the development of the geographical sciences.   RH

Suggested reading
Kavanagh (2002); Wolf and Ghilani (2005).

geopiety A term coined by J.K. Wright (1947) to refer to a reverential attitude towards and caring for the Earth. After three decades of relative obscurity, the term was re-introduced to a new generation of geographers in the mid-1970s by Yi-Fu Tuan (1976a). It formed an important component of Tuan's notion of TOPOPHILIA, which in turn was one of the key concepts in HUMANISTIC GEOGRAPHY. The implied spiritual approach to NATURE, while rooted in nineteenth-century romanticism, continues to resonate for contemporary romantics, including the exponents of DEEP ECOLOGY.   JSD

Suggested reading
Tuan (1976a).

geopolitics A title of an academic journal, a catch-all category for international violence, an orphaned sub-field of late imperial geography resurrected in neo-imperial America and, simultaneously, the focus of diverse forms of demythologization and debunking by scholars of CRITICAL HUMAN GEOGRAPHY, this is a term that defies easy definition. As a category of news reporting, it is used in the media to describe VIOLENCE relating to the division, control and contestation of TERRITORY. The business pages of newspapers thus often feature references to 'geopolitical concerns' as a way of describing the impact of international politics and violence. After TERRORIST attacks on commuter trains in India and Israel's invasion of Lebanon in the summer of 2006, for instance, *The Financial Times* review of global markets read as follows: 'Gold also pushed higher on continued geopolitical concerns following bomb blasts in Mumbai and clashes around the Israel–Lebanon border' (Tassell, 2006, p. 26). Academically, however, geopolitics is a much more complex and contested term, with a long history of formal definition and redefinition.

The original definitions of the field go back to the 'classical geopolitics' of military-minded academics such as the British imperialist Halford Mackinder, the Nazi expansionist Karl Haushofer and the Dutch-American Cold War strategist Nicholas Spykman. For them, geopolitics was all about how international relations relate to the spatial layout of oceans, CONTINENTS, natural RESOURCES, military organization, political systems and perceived territorial threats and opportunities (for an excellent overview, see Foster, 2006). In this respect, a constant geopolitical focus has been the Eurasian continental meta-region stretching from Eastern Europe through Russia to Central Asia. This was the so-called 'Heartland' that Mackinder argued was key to global imperial power (see IMPERIALISM). It was some of this same territory that Haushofer argued the Nazis should seize as LEBENSRAUM, or living-space, for their self-described master race. After the Soviet Union established control over the region at the end of the Second World War, it was this same area that Americans such as George Kennan argued should be contained, an argument that underpinned US COLD WAR geopolitics aimed at controlling what Spykman had previously described as the 'Rimlands' around the 'Heartland' (Dalby, 1990). Isaiah Bowman, the US geographer and presidential advisor who, early on, advocated American dominance in and around the region, was once dubbed 'the American Haushofer' (Smith, N., 2003c). However, just

as American imperialists have traditionally talked about an American Century rather than a geographically defined AMERICAN EMPIRE, American advocates of geopolitical dominance have generally avoided talk of geopolitics because of its associations with European IMPERIALISM and FASCISM. This reticence amongst US strategists began to change after 11 September 2001: a shift towards unabashed imperial attitudes occurred that was also signalled by the return to influence of the old Cold War geopolitical grandee Henry Kissinger. But whether referring explicitly to geopolitics or not, geopolitical discourse has continued to develop apace since the end of the Cold War; the transition from President Reagan's anti-Soviet invocation of an 'Evil Empire' to President Bush's angst about an 'Axis of Evil' being just one of the more imaginative and egregious attempts to remap the terrain of Mackinder's Heartland as a way of simultaneously defining the American HOMELAND (Coleman, 2004).

While classical geopolitics continues to inform policy-making, critical geographers have over the past two decades developed a vibrant new field of CRITICAL GEOPOLITICS. Under this broad umbrella they have sought to examine the ways in which a broad range of IMAGINATIVE GEOGRAPHIES, such as the 'Evil Empire', actively shape world politics (see Ó Tuathail, 1996b; Ó Tuathail and Dalby, 1998; Agnew, 2003a). Critical geopolitics continues to grow more diverse by the year: ranging from examinations of geopolitical discourse in the history of popular culture (Sharp, 2000a), to studies of the ORIENTALISM that informs the geopolitics of both the colonial past and present (Gregory, 2004; Slater, 2004), to critiques of the geopolitical justification of torture (Hannah, 2006b), to reflections on the geopolitical preoccupations of revolutionary Islam (Watts, 2007). Thus while practitioners of classical geopolitics keep producing geopolitical representations that they claim are real, the core concern for the critics is precisely this objectivist claim on reality. Critical geopolitics instead demonstrates the ideological power of geopolitical representations to 'script' SPACE – to concoct, for example, a story about Iraq having weapons of mass destruction and then using that script to legitimate war. However, in debunking such geopolitical scriptings, the critical scholarship raises at least three further sorts of question about the relationships between geopolitics and the real world: the first concerns the relationship between imaginative geopolitical scripts and the far from imaginative death and destruction they inspire or help legitimate; the second relates to how such destructive consequences relate to the CREATIVE DESTRUCTION of GLOBALIZATION and NEO-LIBERALISM; and the third concerns the reciprocal influence of these economic mediations on the ongoing articulation of new neo-liberal geopolitical scripts that emphasize ECONOMIC INTEGRATION over Cold War containment.

Geographical scholarship on the 'war on terror' has connected critical geopolitical concerns about the US President Bush administration's fear-mongering with all three questions about the ties between geopolitics and real world relations. Derek Gregory (2004b) has shown how in Afghanistan and Iraq the people construed by the 'war on terror' script as the enemy have suffered lethal consequences as a result of the 'god-tricks' of long-distance geopolitical representations. He also has continued to argue in this way that the geopolitics has constructed spaces of exception (see EXCEPTION, SPACES OF) and legal vanishing points, where huge numbers of people are treated as outcasts from humanity and the tenuous protections of international LAW (Gregory, 2007). Focusing, by contrast, on the arrogance of the American exceptionalism that has helped create these spaces of exception, recent reflections on the ties between American imperialism and neo-liberalism have highlighted how the relationship is also highly contradictory. For example, geopolitical strategies about building American dominance over the MIDDLE EAST and its OIL spigots exist in uneasy tension with ongoing interests in maintaining transnational business, CLASS harmony and support for the dollar against the backcloth of rising concerns about American indebtedness to East Asian and OPEC owners of US bonds (Smith, N., 2003c; Harvey, 2004b). These economic contexts in which geopolitical scripts are developed and implemented have further been found to be changing the nature of the scripts themselves, leading to a neo-liberal geopolitics (Roberts, Secord and Sparke, 2003) which, with its distinctly economic emphases on globalization and connection over isolation and containment, has also been called 'geoeconomics' (Sparke, 2005).   MS

Geopolitik A school of POLITICAL GEOGRAPHY, and specifically GEOPOLITICS, disseminated in inter-war Germany by the geographer and military officer Karl Haushofer (1869–1946) and the journal *Zeitschrift für Geopolitik* (1922–

44). The term in fact originated with the Swedish political scientist Rudolf Kjellen, whose ideas, along with Ratzel's organic theory of the STATE, provided a spurious rationale to justify German expansionism (Parker, 1985: see also ANTHROPOGEOGRAPHY; LEBENSRAUM). Although *Geopolitik* was associated with Hitler's Nazi Party, however, there were important differences. Whereas *Geopolitik* was influenced by the significance of natural laws in its understanding of social and political life (cf. DARWINISM), National Socialism saw societies as determined by biological inheritance and was both predicated on and powered by RACISM (Bassin, 1987a: see also FASCISM). The term is often used to portray *Geopolitik* as a purely German phenomenon, but it should be noted that the British geographer Sir Halford Mackinder also made reference to organic or natural understandings of state and society.   CF

Suggested reading
Bassin, Newman, Reuber and Agnew (2004).

geostrategic realms The largest-scale division of the GLOBE in Cohen's (2003) geopolitics of the world system. Large enough to be of global significance, geostrategic realms serve the interests of the powers that dominate them. Held together by trading, cultural and military connections, they change as economic and military forces evolve. Reflecting longstanding concerns with land and sea POWER in GEOPOLITICAL thinking, three geostrategic realms have been identified: the Atlantic and Pacific trade-dependent Maritime realm; the Eurasian Continental Russian Heartland realm; and the mixed Continental Maritime East Asia realm. The intellectual or practical significance of Cohen's typology is far from straightforward, but the US military has developed its own geostrategic division of the world, the practical significance of which is only too clear (see Morrissey, 2008b). Different 'unified combatant commands' are assigned to different world regions:

US Africa Command (all of Africa except Egypt);
US Central Command (MIDDLE EAST and Central Asia);
US European Command (centred on Europe, including Russia);
US Pacific Command (including Australia, and South and South East Asia)
US Northern Command (North Africa)

US Southern Command (Central and South America and the Caribbean).   SD

gerrymandering   The deliberate drawing of electoral district boundaries to produce an electoral advantage for an interested party. The term was coined by enemies of Massachusetts Republican Governor Elbridge Gerry, who created a district in 1812 that his party would win: it was shaped like a salamander – hence the neologism and the widespread (if false) belief that gerrymandering necessarily involves odd-shaped district boundaries. Although gerrymandering has long been practiced in the USA, it has only recently – and in specific conditions – been interpreted by the courts there as a constitutional violation (cf. DISTRICTING ALGORITHM; ELECTORAL GEOGRAPHY; REDISTRICTING).   RJ

Suggested reading
Monmonier (2001).

ghetto   An extreme form of residential concentration: a cultural, religious or ethnic group is ghettoized when (a) a high proportion of the group lives in a single area, and (b) when the group accounts for most of the population in that area. Although the practice of ghettoization – forcing a group to live separately within a city – originated in the urban quarters of pre-classical cities, the first use of the term occurred in late medieval Venice, where city authorities required Jews to live on a separate island (called *gheto*), which was sealed behind walls and gates each night (Calimani, 1987). SOCIAL EXCLUSION was imposed by the dominant CULTURE and, as such, reflected and reinforced the marginalization of the Jewish minority. However, while the ghetto was overcrowded and prone to fire and disease, Jews also gained some benefit from their enforced isolation, especially the right to practice their RELIGION and legal system and, perhaps, a degree of protection from more drastic forms of persecution (Wirth, 1928).

Instances of complete ghettoization have been rare (two modern exceptions are the Warsaw Ghetto, established as a way-station to the Nazi HOLOCAUST and designated areas for Black residential settlement in South African cities during the APARTHEID regime). Early in the twentieth century, the term came to be used indiscriminately for almost any residential area identified with a particular group, even when it did not form a majority, and even when SEGREGATION was not the result of discrimination. This ambiguity was especially prevalent in the influential work of the Chicago sociologists (see CHICAGO SCHOOL), who even referred to a wealthy NEIGHBOURHOOD in the city as the 'gilded ghetto'.

Researchers began in the 1970s to call for more analytical precision. Philpott (1991 [1979]), for example, distinguished between 'SLUMS', areas of poverty where residents (frequently immigrants) leave as they acquire the means to do so, and ghettos, areas where residents are trapped in permanent poverty (also see Ward, 1989). Also, ghettos should not be confused with ethnic ENCLAVES, areas dominated by a single cultural group. Ghettos emerge when political and/or other institutions, such as the HOUSING MARKET, operate to restrict the residential choices of certain groups, channelling them to the most undesirable neighbourhoods (Thabit, 2003). They are the product of RACIALIZATION (see also ETHNICITY; RACE), where particular minority groups are judged by the majority to be genetically and socially inferior (Wacquant, 2001). There is always a degree of involuntary behaviour in the formation of ghettos, whereas ethnic enclaves arise when members of a group choose to live in close proximity (Boal, 1976; Peach, 1996ab).

The situation of African-Americans in the USA is typically seen as the defining example of contemporary ghettoization (see Darden, 1995; Wacquant, 2001). In the 1960s, some American social scientists began to assert that ghetto environments are so debilitating that a 'culture of poverty', associated with high CRIME rates, substance abuse, broken families and a reliance on social services, is transmitted from parents to children (cf. CYCLE OF POVERTY). These alarming views were instrumental in the 'war on poverty' declared by the US government, and were important ingredients in the inauguration of urban redevelopment programmes, increased social spending, educational reform, and heightened policing and surveillance of the INNER CITY (cf. URBAN RENEWAL). These initiatives were largely withdrawn in the conservative 1980s, but the argument that ghettos should be the focus of PUBLIC POLICY was revived later in the decade, as part of the UNDERCLASS debate. Again, proponents of this thesis believe that ghettos are not just places of grinding poverty, but also places where poverty is institutionalized (Wilson, 1987). Racialization and stigmatization combine to sharply circumscribe the opportunities available to residents of ghettos, so CHILDREN are locked into the same circumstances as their parents, if not worse. Similar arguments have surfaced in the UK (e.g. Rex,

303

1988; but see Peach, 1996ab, for an alternate view).

Current attempts by various authorities in Italy to create separate, gated 'camps' for Roma (Gypsy) people constitute one of the clearest examples of ghettoization today. Governments justify this policy of segregation on two grounds: that Roma people are nomadic and ill-adapted to 'regular' urban environments, and that they need to be protected from racist incidents in the wider society (there have been a number of violent attacks on housing occupied by Roma people). Inevitably, though, by separating Roma from other groups, this policy further racializes the population and severely limits their opportunities for integration (Sigona, 2005).

As in the original Venetian case, though, ghettos, once formed, may provide a context for the maintenance and development of minority cultures: ironically, these cultural forms are sometimes embraced by the dominant culture (e.g. the many types of music pioneered by African-Americans).   DH

Suggested reading
Peach (1996ab); Sigona (2005); Thabit (2003); Wacquant (2001).

GIS   See GEOGRAPHIC INFORMATION SYSTEMS.

global cities/world cities   Major nodes in the organization of the global economy: hubs of economic control, production and trade, of information circulation and cultural transmission, and of political power. They are often represented in a hierarchically ordered NETWORK formation that spans the globe (for several representations, see Taylor, 2004). Peter Hall has credited Scottish urbanist Patrick Geddes (1854–1932; see Geddes, 1915) with introducing the term – although German literary giant Johann Wolfgang Goethe employed it as far back as the early nineteenth century, in reference to Paris. In Hall's groundbreaking book *The world cities* ([1984] 1966), six urban REGIONS were analysed under this title. In this first systematic examination, Hall treats the world cities predominantly as internationally oriented national metropolitan centres of the industrial age. It was only during the 1980s that world cities began to be seen in a different light. Based on historical work from the ANNALES SCHOOL, theoretical insights derived from WORLD-SYSTEMS ANALYSIS and explorations of the NEW INTERNATIONAL DIVISION OF LABOUR (NIDL) (Fröbel, Heinrichs and Kreye, 1980), a new generation of urban theorists began to think of global cities as articulators of international and global economies. Accordingly, Michael Timberlake (1985, p. 3) explained that 'processes such as urbanization can be more fully understood by beginning to examine the many ways in which they articulate with the broader currents of the world-economy that penetrate spatial barriers, transcend limited time boundaries and influence social relations at many different levels'. Work on historical tendencies of global URBANIZATION had laid the groundwork for understanding city systems as global and subject to long-term and macro-geographical shifts in the capitalist accumulation process. Writing in this tradition, Christopher Chase-Dunn examined the relationships between the expanding boundaries of the world system and the system of cities since AD 800 (Chase-Dunn, 1985). In a related fashion, some global city researchers have pointed to the complex colonial and post-colonial histories as well as the long trajectories of world city formation. Economic specialization has long been known to be the basis of world market-oriented urbanization, which propelled financial nodes such as Amsterdam, London or New York or industrial centres such as Leiden, Manchester, and Houston into the rank of leading world cities in subsequent historical periods (Nestor and Rodriguez, 1986). Defying any tendency to see global cities as a product of recent shifts in the world economy, Janet Abu-Lughod, for example, has argued that New York City has been a global city from its very inception as Dutch, and later English colonial outpost, and certainly as an industrial and financial powerhouse of the nineteenth and twentieth centuries (Abu-Lughod, 1999). Similarly, Anthony King (1990) has presented the global city formation of London as a complex process of the city's history as a colonial centre.

Still, the case can be, and has been, made to see global cities in their current form as a product of today's period of GLOBALIZATION. Brenner and Keil have suggested that one could see the emergence of a New International Division of Labour and the crisis of Atlantic FORDISM in the 1970s and 1980s as the starting points for this round of world city formation (Brenner and Keil, 2006, pp. 8–10). At the outset of this line of reasoning was the publication of John Friedmann and Goetz Wolff's seminal article in 1982 under the title 'World City Formation: An Agenda for Research and Action'. In this influential piece, which arguably laid the foundation for an entire industry of global cities research, Friedmann and Wolff pointed to a network of global cities that spanned the globe as the skeleton of the global ECON-OMY. They suggested that '[t]he world city "approach" is, in the first instance, a methodology, a point of departure, an initial hypothesis. It is a way of asking questions and of bringing footloose facts into relation' (Friedmann and Wolff, 1982, p. 320). Observing the emerging globalized world economy with its central actors, the TRANSNATIONAL CORPORATIONS, Friedmann and Wolff put forth the hypothesis that there would be a hierarchical system of urban regions, in which this world economic system would find its most typical socio-spatial expression. They assumed that 'a small number of massive urban regions that we shall call world cities' would be at the apex of this hierarchy (Friedmann and Wolff, 1982). They present the world cities as a flexible and ever-changing group of command centres of the world economy. The extent and nature of their INTEGRATION into that economy can only be determined through empirical research in each city. The rapid changes that these urban regions are going through can specifically be studied in the areas of economic, social and physical RESTRUCTURING. Political conflict at various SCALES of the formation of the world city can be expected and is itself productive of the world city. In particular, the gulf between the globalized 'citadel' of the elite and the 'GHETTO' of the popular classes will continue to widen and create tension in the political landscape of the global city. In 1986, John Friedmann added a more precise taxonomy of global city development, as he presented seven interrelated theses that added up to the 'world city hypothesis':

(1) The form and extent of a city's integration with the world economy, and the functions assigned to the city in the new spatial DIVISION OF LABOUR, will be decisive for any structural changes occurring within it.

(2) Key cities throughout the world are used by GLOBAL capital as 'basing points' in the spatial organization and articulation of production and MARKETS.

(3) The global control functions of world cities are reflected in the structure and dynamics of their production sectors and employment.

(4) World cities are major sites for the concentration and ACCUMULATION of international capital.

(5) World cities are points of destination for large numbers of both domestic and/or international migrants (see MIGRATION).

(6) World city formation brings into focus the major contradictions of industrial CAPIT-ALISM – among them spatial and CLASS polarization.

(7) World city growth generates social costs at rates that tend to exceed the fiscal capacity of the state.

Friedmann also impacted the way in which from now on world cities would be viewed by proposing a powerful image of networked interconnectedness showing the articulation of primary and secondary world cities in the core and the semi-periphery. The tremendous impact of the 'world city hypothesis' was subject to an international conference in 1993, from which the first multidisciplinary collection of global city essays was drawn (Knox and Taylor, 1995). In a review of the empirical and theoretical work done since his methodological intervention from 1982, Friedmann detected a lively PARADIGM that had grown from the original propositions (1995).

In the meantime, Saskia Sassen had published *The global city: New York, London, Tokyo* (2001 [1991]), which made her instantly the most prominent scholar in the rapidly expanding field. In this and subsequent publications, Sassen drew attention to the global city as a production site of the kind of internationally oriented business services that pushed for dominance in the global economy. These producer services (finances, law, marketing, advertising etc.) relied on regional production complexes, which remained tangible and led to more metropolitanization and urbanization despite the increased availability of networked electronic means of COMMUNICATION, which suggested the growing independence from fixed spatial arrangements. While *The global city* focused on the cities at the top of the global hierarchy – New York, London, Tokyo – Sassen expanded her argument in a short but incisive book *Cities in a world economy* (2006 [2000]), which identified and isolated specific strategic places where the globalized economy is taking shape: EXPORT PROCESSING ZONES, offshore banking centres, high-tech districts and global cities. Sassen insists on the interdependence of these disparate spaces as much as on the regional economy being the basis of the global city. Scott (2001, p. 4) similarly suggests that global city-regions serve 'as territorial platforms for much of the POST-FORDIST economy that constitutes the dominant leading edge of contemporary capitalist DEVELOPMENT,

305

and as important staging posts for the operations of multinational corporations'. Sassen's work on the global city has also strongly emphasized the social and political aspects of global city formation as she has consistently asked 'whose city' the global city is: Will the constant pressure for commodified and gentrified (see GENTRIFICATION) elite space or new citizenship claims by the 'Othered' majorities of the immigrant labour forces of the typical city prevail (Sassen, 1996)?

Proponents of the world city thesis have often been criticized for not providing conclusive data on the existence of a distinct set of global cities. The GaWC (Globalization and World Cities) research group at Loughborough University was set up in the late 1990s to rectify this deficit and to produce systematic empirical research on global city interconnectedness. On the basis of this research, Peter Taylor has recently provided the synthetic *World city network* (2004), in which he painstakingly prepares a massive pool of quantitative data to produce the first comprehensively researched and thoroughly theorized study of the network of global cities from a large variety of methodological angles. As Taylor (2004b, p. 21) argues, 'The world city literature as a cumulative and collective enterprise begins only when the economic restructuring of the world-economy makes the idea of a mosaic of separate urban systems appear anachronistic and frankly irrelevant.'

The world city literature is not without its detractors. On the one hand, a group of seasoned urban theorists have criticized the exclusiveness of the global city hypothesis, which ostensibly seems to pay too little attention to the 'ordinary cities' (Amin and Thrift, 2002) that continue to be the majority of urban places. Michael Peter Smith (2001a) has denounced the structuralist bias of the world city debate and has instead proposed the notion of 'transnational urbanism', which explicitly includes reference to the grassroots processes that constitute the global city. Peter Marcuse and Ronald van Kempen have criticized the apodictic assumptions of global city research, which allegedly expects similarly polarizing socio-spatial effects everywhere, and have instead proposed a multidimensional and more diversified view of 'globalizing cities' of all sorts (2000, 2003). A younger group of post-structuralist geographers have meanwhile critiqued the global cities literature from the point of view of globalized CULTURE (Flusty, 2003) and agency (R.G. Smith, 2003d). Writing from a standpoint of urbanization in the global SOUTH, Jennifer Robinson (2002) has pointed out that the literature on world cities has a clear bias towards Western standards: 'The world city approach assumes that cities occupy similar placings with similar capacity to progress up or fall down the ranks.... A view of the world of cities thus emerges where millions of people and hundreds of cities are dropped off the map of much research in urban studies, to service one particular and very restricted view of significance or (ir)relevance to certain sections of the global economy' (Robinson, 2002). Despite these critiques, global city research is alive and well, and continues to produce a rich output of empirical work and theoretical insights. The breadth of the work produced under this banner has recently been published in a reader (Brenner and Keil, 2006).   RK

Suggested reading
Brenner and Keil (2006); Friedmann (2002); Sassen (1999, 2002). The GaWC (Globalization and World Cities) website (http:www.lboro.ac.uk/gawc/) presents a wide variety of bibliographies, research bulletins, project descriptions, data sets and web links related to research on global and world cities.

global commons This concept emerges from the traditional commons used by a local community (see COMMON PROPERTY REGIMES), but also includes elements of free market ENVIRONMENTALISM (Rose, 1999a). The notion of 'commons' is expanded to the global SCALE to address concerns about the environmental destruction of the oceans, atmosphere, forests, Antarctica and BIODIVERSITY caused primarily by open access beyond the jurisdiction of NATION-STATES. In essence, the concept seeks to make modern humans, like traditional villagers, responsible for the commons so that it does not deteriorate due to neglect or exploitation. The concept has been applied to the oceans to prevent overfishing, to Antarctica and to outer space, which recognize these locations as the 'common heritage of (hu)mankind (CHM)' (in Whatmore, 2002a, p. 104). Since the emergence of issues such as ozone depletion and global warming (see GLOBAL WARMING), the concept is also applicable to the atmosphere. Attempts have been made to construct the world's BIODIVERSITY, including gene pools, as global commons. This can be understood as an attempt to preserve original NATURE against the ENCLOSURES that enable PROPERTY rights to be exercised, but with genetic manipulation it raises questions about the distinctions between so-called 'gifts of nature' and social artefacts derived from nature.

The global commons idea is used to avoid the problems of open access, and to stop the PRIVATIZATION of the world's environment (Buck, 1998; Goldman, 1998). There are important questions about who 'owns' the environment, and who should 'own' the environment. For example, is the Amazon rainforest the property of indigenous communities, the state of Mato Grosso or the country of Brazil, to be logged for economic benefits if so desired? Alternatively, is the Amazon rainforest the 'green lungs' of the Earth – in other words, part of the global commons? The concept of the global commons is appealing in that it can avoid the dangers of open access and private ownership, but it also potentially represents a new form of conquest where indigenous peoples' rights to self-determination and their ability to survive are made subservient to what are seen as the environmental agendas of affluent Western countries.

The concept of a 'global commons' requires international agreements to be enacted in national legislation. Whatmore (2002a, p. 107) questions the global commons approach in relation to genetic material, and notes that legal arrangements for the proposed global commons, which unravelled, must be understood as emerging from 'amidst, rather than "outside", the spatial practices of national sovereignty and private property'. The necessity and the ability to include air, WATER and other environmental considerations within a form of property rights is contentious. Rose (1999a, p. 50) questions the necessity of a 'global commons' approach, when many of the so-called global problems 'have components that are much more localized'. She challenges Garrett Hardin's largest issue for the global commons – that is, population growth (see POPULATION GEOGRAPHY) – and suggests that it is the impacts of population growth (specific pressures on specific RESOURCES) that should be managed at a local level.   PM

Global Positioning Systems (GPS)   The most widely known Global Positioning System (GPS) consists of 24 satellites, orbiting the Earth twice daily at a height of 200 km, used to find locations and to geocode data (see GEOCODING). It was developed by the US Department of Defense and is managed by the US Air Force. A similar system, GLONASS (Global Navigation Satellite System), is operated by the Russian Federation. The European Union and Space Agency are developing Galileo, to be deployed in 2010 as a service independent of, but interoperable with (see INTEROPERABILITY), both GPS and GLONASS.

The basic idea of a space-borne positioning service is that at least four of the system's satellites will be above the local horizon at any given time or location on the Earth's surface. The GPS receiver identifies a signal from those satellites, which contains information about each satellite's orbital position and the time of the signal's transmission. From these data and by trilateration (triangulation), the coordinate location and the elevation of the receiver can be calculated. In practice, built structures and vegetation canopies may obscure the line of sight between GPS receivers and satellites, reducing the accuracy of the measured location. Three satellites need to be visible to calculate location; four if elevation is also required (Clarke, 2003; Longley, Goodchild, Maguire and Rhind, 2005).

GPS readings typically are accurate to about 5–25 m: horizontal accuracy is generally greater than vertical accuracy. A problem is the distortion of the satellite's signal as it passes through the atmosphere. The effects of this can be measured at fixed receivers where the locations given by the GPS are compared against their known positions, communicating any correction to calibrate GPS receivers nearby (a process known as differential GPS). An extension to this approach is to upload the information back to satellites for automatic correction (a Wide Area Augmentation System). However, no positioning service is absolute: it depends on the datum (model of the Earth's shape) that is used. For GPS, this is the World Geodetic System 1984 (WGS84). Further errors will arise as this is converted to a local datum or coordinate system (notably when the three-dimensional model is projected on to a two-dimensional grid).

GPS is popular for in-car 'satellite navigation' and likely to be integrated more fully with portable communication and computing technologies such as mobile telephones and PDAs (Personal Digital Assistants), further fuelling the growth of location-based services, including 'Where am I?' or 'Where's my nearest ...?' queries. GPS can enable personal navigation and discovery, and have clear social benefits (in search and rescue and emergency management, for example). However, because people might be tracked and located, so GPS (together with closed circuit television, radio-frequency ID chips, biometric ID cards and high-resolution REMOTE SENSING imagery technologies) is sometimes given as an example of geosurveillance, emotively described by Dobson and Fisher (2003) as threatening geoslavery – the erosion of privacy, permitting governments or other organizations the ability to locate where 'their' people are at any time of day and to monitor (or control) their time–space geographies (cf. SURVEILLANCE).   RH

Suggested reading
Brimicombe (2006); Monmonier (2004).

global warming   Global warming is the increase in global temperature resulting from human activities that 'enhance' (exacerbate) the so-called natural 'greenhouse effect'. The term 'climate change' (see CLIMATE) is used increasingly, because although the global impact is warming, impacts vary throughout the world. Human-induced CLIMATE change is seen by many environmentalists as the most serious environmental problem, because it exacerbates other environmental issues.

Greenhouse gases are mostly natural compounds (water vapour, carbon dioxide, methane and nitrous oxide) that allow the Earth's atmosphere to trap heat released as longwave ENERGY from the Earth's surface. This process, called the *greenhouse effect*, means that the earth is 33°C warmer than expected given its distance from the sun. At an average temperature of 15°C, the Earth supports many lifeforms.

The Intergovernmental Panel on Climate Change (IPCC) has provided scientific analyses of various greenhouse scenarios to inform the United Nations Framework Convention on Climate Change (1992) and the Climate Change Convention in Kyoto in 1997 (O'Neill, Mackellar and Lutz, 2001). The Kyoto Protocol came into effect in February 2005, after ratification by 55 countries that were responsible for 55 per cent of emissions in 1990. The largest emitter of greenhouse gases, the USA, and the largest emitter per capita, Australia, rejected ratification. Concerns about the Kyoto Protocol range from weak targets and an emphasis on creating trading systems (see ENVIRONMENTAL ECONOMICS), to its exclusion of rapidly developing economies such as China and India. There are also issues of 'baseline inflation'. The choice of 1990 as a base year meant that pollution from redundant heavy industry in the former East Germany was included in the base figure. Under the Kyoto Protocol, the Annex One (developed) countries agreed to an average reduction of 5.2 per cent of greenhouse gas emissions from a base year of 1990 by 2008–12. Australia secured an 8 per cent increase in emissions, including foregone land clearing (Hamilton, 2001).

There have been natural cooling and heating periods throughout the Earth's history, but the IPCC found that 'most of the warming observed over the past 50 years is attributable to human activities' (IPCC, 2001, p. 10). These include increased levels of carbon dioxide (coal burning, transport and clearing of forests), methane (burning natural gas, seepage from landfill sites, rice paddies and cattle) and nitrous oxide, mainly through agricultural activities (see Munasinghe and Swart, 2005). The impacts include rising sea levels and changes in the location, intensity and frequency of cyclones, droughts and floods. The changes are yet to be fully understood, because of the lag time between emission and cumulative impacts. While initial predictions of global warming have been lowered, there is uncertainty about the significance of clouds, the operations of ocean currents and the threshold levels of ecosystems. What is certain is that emissions of carbon dioxide and some other greenhouse gases are increasing, that they have a long lifetime, and that the average temperature of the Earth is about 0.7°C warmer than 100 years ago. While these processes are still occurring, lowering the initial predictions merely means that the impacts will be delayed by a few years.   PM

globalization   A big buzzword in political speech and a ubiquitous analytical category in academic debate, globalization operates today rather like MODERNIZATION did in the mid-twentieth century as the key term of a master DISCOURSE about the general state of the world. The most common political version of the discourse depicts globalization as an unstoppable process of global INTEGRATION, a supposedly inevitable process that while being driven by free market CAPITALISM also necessitates all the free market reforms of NEOLIBERALISM. Here, for example, is Thomas Friedman (1999, pp. 7–8), a columnist of the *New York Times* who has made a name for himself by interpreting practically any event anywhere in the world through this same simple discourse. Globalization, he says,

involves the inexorable integration of markets, nation-states, and technologies to a degree never witnessed before – in a way that is enabling individuals, corporations and nation-states to reach around the world farther, faster, deeper and cheaper than ever before. The driving idea behind globalization is free-market capitalism – the more you let market forces rule and the more you open your economy to free trade and competition, the more efficient and flourishing your economy will be.

There is both a historical irony and a logical paradox in this sort of argument.

The irony is that while Friedman and others hype the new-ness of globalization to promote free market capitalism, they forget that in the middle of the nineteenth century global economic integration was depicted in very similar ways as a prelude to advancing a defiantly anti-capitalist *Communist manifesto*. In their famously lyrical account of the globalizing activities of the capitalist business class (the 'bourgeoisie'), Karl Marx and Friedrich Engels argued thus that:

The need of a constantly expanding MARKET for its products chases the bourgeoisie over the entire surface of the globe It must nestle everywhere, settle everywhere, establish connections everywhere. The bourgeoisie has, through its exploitation of the world market, given a cosmopolitan character to production and consumption in every country. To the great chagrin of reactionaries, it has drawn from under the feet of industry the national ground on which it stood. All old-established national industries have been destroyed or are daily being destroyed. They are dislodged by new industries, whose introduction becomes a life and death question for all civilized nations, by industries that no longer work up indigenous raw material, but raw material drawn from the remotest zones; industries whose products are consumed, not only at home, but in every quarter of the globe. In place of the old wants, satisfied by the production of the country, we find new wants, requiring for their satisfaction the products of distant lands and climes. In place of the old local and national seclusion and self-sufficiency, we have intercourse in every direction, universal inter-dependence of nations. (Marx and Engels, 1998 [1848], p. 38)

Marx and Engels saw these interdependencies forged by capitalist globalization as leading ultimately to a global revolution by the workers of the world. By transcending local loyalties, increasing competition and intensifying exploitation, globalized capitalism would, they thought, create a globally united working class that would eventually revolt. This global revolution has still not happened, but the logical steps in the argument made by Marx and Engels were clear. By contrast, the contemporary argument that globalization is inexorable and yet necessitates reform is paradoxical. Global integration cannot be inexorable exactly if politicians and pundits have to keep promoting neo-liberal policies as the only way for it to function effectively. Nevertheless, this is precisely what they have been doing from the late 1970s onwards (see Harvey, 2005). 'There Is No Alternative' to free market policies, argued the British Prime Minister Margaret Thatcher in the 1980s, and, following her lead, TINA-touts the world over have endlessly repeated the mantra that globalization is inevitable and that it necessitates neo-liberal policy-making (e.g. Bhagwati, 2004; Wolf, 2004; Friedman, 2005). In the context of this instrumental use of globalization in creating a TAKEN-FOR-GRANTED WORLD for policy-makers, there have been four main academic responses.

The first and most sceptical scholarly approach to globalization has been to argue that it is nothing but hype. Hirst and Thompson (1996) have suggested in this way that globalization is a myth, and that the picture of integration proceeding farther, faster, deeper and cheaper than ever before is empirically unsound. Against the claim that globalization is new, they highlight how significant forms of globe-spanning economic integration existed in the first decades of the twentieth century as a result of IMPERIALISM and the other nineteenth-century economic developments noted by Marx and Engels. Against the claim that corporations have become stateless engines of border-crossing enterprise, they show how even large TRANSNATIONAL CORPORATIONS remain shaped by national supports and norms. And against the TINA-tout promotion of free market fundamentalism, they argue that policies that are not neo-liberal can still provide successful models of national development. However, in attempting to counter the hype, Hirst and Thompson miss many of the ways in which new NETWORKS have expanded and deepened global interdependency from the 1970s onwards.

Charting the development of global networks over time has in turn been the basis of the second main academic approach to globalization. Perhaps the most exhaustive examination available defines globalization thus in terms of the extension, acceleration and intensification of consequential worldwide interconnections (Held, McGrew, Goldblatt and Perraton, 1999). The four authors argue that if globalization is conceptualized as 'the widening, deepening and speeding up of global interconnectedness' (p. 14), it is also possible to pick it apart as 'a process which embodies a transformation in the spatial organization of social relations and transactions – assessed in terms of their extensity, intensity, velocity and impact – generating transcontinental or interregional flows and networks of activity, interaction and the exercise of power' (p. 16). The precision of this approach is useful insofar as it provides clear parameters for assessing just how far global integration dynamics have created globally shared forms of common fate. They themselves also provide tremendous amounts of empirical data showing the changing extensity, intensity, velocity and impact of different sorts of space-spanning networks over time. However, their approach has two limitations. First, it obscures the ways in which global interconnections can also create deeply divergent global fates, or what critics of COSMOPOLITANISM and other idealistic accounts of TRANSNATIONALISM describe as *discrepant cosmopolitanisms* (Robbins, 1998). These discrepant communities are all also underpinned by global interconnections, but in ways that create vastly varied fates ranging from the soft cosmopolitanism of wealthy migrants and transnational capitalists (Sklair, 2001; Calhoun, 2003; Mitchell, 2003), to the carceral cosmopolitanism of those imprisoned in global spaces of exception (see EXCEPTION, SPACES OF) (Gregory, 2004b; Sparke, 2006), to the critical cosmopolitanism of grassroots globalization activists and associated anti-neoliberal NGO networks (Routledge, 2003; Sparke, Brown, Corva et al., 2005). Part of the reason why Held and co-authors tend to downplay such discrepancies between global networks may in turn be traced to a second limitation with many network-centric accounts; namely, their relative inattention to the UNEVEN DEVELOPMENT of spatial organization itself. This weakness is often amplified in assessments of globalization that stress what the sociologist Anthony Giddens (1984) once called TIME–SPACE DISTANCIATION; that is, the establishment of space-spanning relations of regulation, TRUST and interaction between people at a distance. Commentators from across the political spectrum, Giddens himself amongst them, have thus unfortunately tended to describe globalization as some sort of end to

geography in which time–space distanciation has reached its final fulfilment in the creation of a smooth, borderless, post-national, supra-territorial global landscape or, what Thomas Friedman has recently described as a 'flat' world (see, e.g., Giddens, 1995; Ohmae, 1995; Appadurai, 1996; Hardt and Negri, 2000; Scholte, 2000; Friedman, 2005).

In response to all the pre-emptive epitaphs to geography, a third more geographically sensitive approach to globalization highlights how capitalism has created new forms of uneven development involving both deterritorialization and reterritorialization. David Harvey (1989b, 2006b) has argued thus that while capitalists shrink distance and create TIME–SPACE COMPRESSION because of their deterritorializing efforts to reduce the FRICTIONS OF DISTANCE, they also episodically require a reterritorializing *spatial fix* in which fixed CAPITAL investments are made and through which CRISES of over-ACCUMULATION can be temporarily resolved (see also Harvey, 1999 [1982]). This argument has also led him to interpret the recent resurgence of AMERICAN EMPIRE in terms of the tensions between place-transcending and place-remaking dynamics on a global scale (Harvey, 2004b). Drawing further attention to the changing shape of American global place-making in particular, many other academics have highlighted how flat-world visions of globalization obscure the asymmetries and attendant GEOPOLITICS of today's US-centric global order, including the exceptional privileges reserved by the USA within global GOVERNANCE institutions such as the INTERNATIONAL MONETARY FUND and the World Bank (Anderson, 2002b; Gowan, 2003; Peet, 2003; Agnew, 2004; Pieterse, 2004; Smith, 2004; Sparke, 2005). In a different way, research on the governance of international BORDERS has shown how the border-softening emphasis in flat-world business discourse also obscures diverse forms of contemporary border hardening (Nevins, 2002; Newstead, Reid and Sparke, 2003; Sparke, Sidaway, Bunnell and Grundy-Warr, 2004; Coleman, 2005; Sparke, 2006). Meanwhile, the ongoing need to track how business practices are themselves constantly reorganizing the geography of COMMODITY CHAINS has led yet other scholars to chart the unevenness of the global economic map of production, TRADE, distribution and CONSUMPTION (e.g. Dicken, 2003: see also Mittelman, 2000). And it is this uneven and constantly shifting map that has in turn inspired interest in GLOCALIZATION as way of exploring reciprocal LOCAL–GLOBAL RELATIONS that avoids end-state end-of-geography ideas about global flattening (Swyngedouw, 2004).

With a related repudiation of what she calls an 'impact model' of globalization, the geographer Gill Hart's recent work also illustrates a fourth form of academic response to globalization focused on how its HEGEMONY as a neo-liberal DISCOURSE both works and breaks down in practice (Hart, 2004). Hart argues that this hegemony serves amongst other things to make the forced PRIVATIZATION of public goods and spaces seem natural, and in response she suggests that ETHNOGRAPHIES of the ties between different places and people can help denaturalize such dispossession (Hart, 2006: see also Tsing, 2004). Such counter-hegemonic critiques of neo-liberal globalization discourse have now developed a diverse set of compliementary strategies for debunking TINA-tout inevitability ideology. Such strategies range from efforts to chart the emergence and marketing of globalization discourse as a form of 'Globaloney' or globalist common-sense (Steger, 2005; Veseth, 2005), to examinations of how it has been re-engineered and spread internationally by 'World Bank Literature' (Kumar, 2003), global business schooling (Roberts, 2004; Olds and Thrift, 2005) and business-funded think-tanks (Peck, 2001b, 2004), to studies of its uneven implementation in the actual organization of business practices themselves (Dicken, 2003; Ho, 2005), to research into its impact as a form of *geo-economics* that shapes both national and transnational statecraft (Smith, 2002; Roberts et al., 2003; Sparke and Lawson, 2003; Hay, 2004; Jones and Jones, 2004; Gilbert, 2005), to feminist investigations of the MASCULINISM of arguments about the inevitability of global capitalist penetration (Gibson-Graham, 1996; Massey, 2005). Such examinations of the performance of globalization discourse can bring it down to size and allow academics and their audiences to see it 'stutter' (Larner and Walters, 2005, p. 20), but, just as importantly, they also clear the way for investigations of the actual POWER-GEOMETRIES of globalization in the lived worlds beyond the buzzword and its flat-world imaginative geography (see also GEOGRAPHICAL IMAGINARY).   MS

Suggested reading
El Fisgón (2004).

globe A solid sphere; in GEOGRAPHY, the globe refers to the Earth itself or a physical model of it (although the Earth's actual form

as an oblate spheroid has been known since Newton theorized it in his *Principia* and French field scientists demonstrated it in 1736). The globe is a conventional symbol of geographical science, the geographer traditionally pictured measuring distances with dividers placed on a terrestrial globe. Celestial globes showing the pattern of forms in the visible heavens have long been paired with geographical globes. Recognition of the Earth's sphericity is dated to Eratosthenes (276–195 BCE), but only celestial globes survive from Antiquity, and were used in Chinese and Islamic science too. No terrestrial globes pre-date the European Renaissance, although it is a nineteenth-century myth that before Columbus the Earth was believed to be flat.

Construction of terrestrial globes is described in Ptolemy's second-century AD book: *Geography*, known in the West from the late fourteenth century. The earliest existing terrestrial globe dates from 1492, made by a Nuremburg merchant knowledgeable about Portuguese oceanic navigations. Circumnavigation of the globe in 1522 produced a scientific and diplomatic demand for model globes, although their bulkiness and the size required for detailed representation of seas and coasts severely limited their practical navigational use on board ship (Brotton, 1997). Globe sets of terrestrial, celestial and armillary spheres (see COSMOGRAPHY) were objects of beauty, status and display as much as scientific instruments (cf. SCIENTIFIC INSTRUMENTATION) in the early modern world, and the largest globes were made for monarchs such as Louis XIV of France, or as public SPECTACLES; for example; in the great ('world') exhibitions of the nineteenth and twentieth centuries. The globe remains an icon of POWER as much as an educational object today, signifying control over the space that it represents. Model globes or globe images are thus common in advertising and entertainment as an indicator of international reach and significance, and are used by airlines, communications corporations and at self-consciously international events such as exhibitions, fairs and sports spectacles (Pickles, 2004).

The discourse of GLOBALIZATION draws on the idea and image of the globe as a symbol of connectedness and unity, drawing on an association of the globe image with COSMOPOLITANISM. Since the appearance of satellite images of Earth, 'thinking globally' has become a mantra of environmentalist discourse, while the globe has become in some respects a banal object, appearing on balloons, key fobs and other playthings (Cosgrove, 2001).   DCO

Suggested reading
Cosgrove (2001); Woodward (2006).

glocalization This awkward adversary of spell-check programs globally has been used in three quite different ways in debates over GLOBALIZATION. First, it has proved useful for critics of what Gillian Hart calls the 'impact model' of global economic integration (Hart, 2003). Challenging the idea of global CAPITALISM simply entering and transforming local REGIONS, geographers such as Erik Swyngedouw have thus invoked glocalization to describe the dialectical LOCAL–GLOBAL RELATIONS through which local regions mediate and change global processes even as they are remade and rescaled themselves (Swyngedouw, 2001, 2004a, 2006). Second, social theorists who are interested in the development of contemporary cultural hybrids refer to glocalization as a way of examining syncretic mixes and other forms of so-called heterogenization that are obscured by visions of global cultural homogenization (Featherstone, 1995; see Hybridity). And third, the most banal appeals to glocalization are from business strategists who talk about the need to 'glocalize' big brands so that they can be better targeted at particular local markets (e.g. vegetarian Big Macs in India).   MS

governable space Geographical space shaped and organized in ways that make it amenable to technologies of government. The term was used by Rose (1999c) in his development and extension of Foucault's ideas about government and GOVERNMENTALITY. Rose argues that 'governing does not just act on a pre-existing thought world with its natural divisions'; rather, 'to govern is to cut experience in certain ways, to bring new facets and forces, new intensities and relations into being' (1999, p. 31). This involves 'the making up of governable spaces: populations, nations, societies, economies, classes, families, schools, factories, individuals' (1991, p. 31). Governable spaces are not, however, 'fabricated counter to experience'. On the contrary, they 'make new kinds of experience possible, produce new modes of perception, invest percepts with affects, with dangers and opportunities, with saliences and attractions' (1999, p. 32; cf. AFFECT). Rose distinguishes three dimensions to the analysis of governable SPACE (1999, pp. 34–40). These are:

(1) *Territorializing governmental thought* through, for example, the formation of national 'societies' and 'TERRITORIES'. Smaller-scale territorializations such as the CITY and the REGION can also be traced (cf. TERRITORIALITY).

(2) *Spatializing the gaze of governors* through technologies of VISION AND VISUALITY, and particularly CARTOGRAPHY and the use of CARTOGRAPHIC REASON (Pickles, 2004).

(3) *Modelling the space of government.* This typically takes two forms: isotropic models and depth MODELS. Isotropic models conceptualize space as 'the same everywhere'. This might involve the use of plans, grids and surveys to tame space and make it comprehensible to rationalities of government. Isotropic models are particularly important in the BIOPOLITICS of COLONIALISM, where they enabled the extension of Western forms of governmental rationality and judicial SOVEREIGNTY into the spaces of racialized 'Others' (Olund, 2002). The model of POLITICAL ECONOMY, on the other hand, involves a depth model with 'hidden' determinants, such as the 'law' of supply and demand, that can be distinguished from the surface appearance of things.

Space is thus made governable through the application of specific technologies and practices, including population monitoring, statistics, SURVEYING and CADASTRAL MAPPING. On the other hand, despite the prevalence of such abstract and calculative techniques, bodily VIOLENCE remains a widespread mechanism for the production of governable space, as shown by Watts' (2006) study of the Niger Delta.   JPa

Suggested reading
Olund (2002); Pickles (2004); Rose (1999); Watts (2006).

governance A term that is sometimes used loosely to mean simply government, but more precisely refers to the process of social and economic coordination, management and 'steering'. Under this umbrella definition may be found a number of sometimes contradictory usages. At its broadest, governance can mean any kind of coordination between organizations, parts of organizations, groups and individuals, ranging from hierarchical 'command and control' systems to decentralized forms of interaction (such as MARKET forms of EXCHANGE). Most commonly, however, governance refers to forms of inter-organizational coordination modelled neither on hierarchies nor on markets but on NETWORKS, especially where these are 'self-organizing'. For Jessop, governance is 'the "self-organization of inter-organizational relations" ' (1997, p. 59), while Rhodes defines it as 'self-organizing, interorganizational networks' (Rhodes, 1997, p. 53). Rhodes expands this definition as follows:

(1) Interdependence between organizations. Governance is broader than government, covering non-state actors. Changing the boundaries of the state meant the boundaries between public, private and voluntary sectors became more shifting and opaque.

(2) Continuing interactions between network members, caused by the need to exchange resources and negotiate shared purposes.

(3) Game-like interactions, rooted in trust and regulated by rules of the game negotiated and agreed by network participants.

(4) A significant degree of autonomy from the state. Networks are not accountable to the state; they are self-organizing. Although the state does not occupy a sovereign position, it can indirectly and imperfectly steer networks.

Such definitions make it possible to speak of a shift *from* government (coordination through hierarchy) *to* governance (coordination through networks). Like Rhodes, most writers on governance take the view that networks may include a wide variety of organizations and are not limited only to state institutions. Indeed, one of the central propositions of governance research is that those involved in the generation and implementation of public policy are not only the formal agencies of government, but may include private firms, NGOs, voluntary organizations, faith- and community-based groups and grassroots campaigns. In part, this merely recognizes that the coordination of complex social SYSTEMS and the steering of societal development have never been the responsibilities of the state alone. Most writers, though, go further and argue that the state has become less prominent and that non-state organizations have become relatively more important within the coordination process.

Reducing the role of the state has also been an important goal of efforts by international DEVELOPMENT organizations to promote what they term 'good governance'. The World Bank and the INTERNATIONAL MONETARY FUND in particular have often made development assistance to poorer countries conditional on programmes of public-sector reform. In this context, 'good governance' involves transparency and accountability in public administration, the efficient use of public resources, participation in DECISION-MAKING and respect for the rule of LAW. Critics (e.g. Evans, 2004) object that these reforms require governments in developing countries to adopt inappropriate Western models of public administration, to reduce public expenditure and to privatize the provision of goods and services, leading to detrimental impacts on the lives of poorer people (cf. PRIVATIZATION). In both developing and developed countries the shift from government to governance and the increased public role of non-state actors has raised concerns about the lack of democratic control over decision-making and policy implementation.

Research on the geographies of governance has focused on two main overlapping themes:

(1) *The role of networks.* Rhodes' own work on 'policy networks' has been adapted and supplemented by other approaches to examine, for example, processes of urban development (McGuirk, 2000). Research has also focused on the growing use of inter-agency partnerships as an institutionalized expression of networked governance (Geddes, 2006) and on inter-urban networks (Leitner, Pavlik and Sheppard, 2002).

(2) *The 're-scaling' of governance.* Early accounts of the shift from government to governance linked it to the 'hollowing-out' of the state, which was said to involve the loss of central state functions to both supra-national scales (e.g. the European Union) and sub-national scales (e.g. autonomous regions, local bodies). The nature of governance processes at sub-national spatial scales has been examined in detail in URBAN and REGIONAL GEOGRAPHY (Painter and Goodwin, 2000; Jones, 2001; Brenner, 2004). One strand of this work focuses explicitly on 'multi-level governance', highlighting relations between local or regional, national and supranational SCALES (e.g. Bulkeley and Betsill, 2005). JPa

Suggested reading
Brenner (2004); Jessop (2000); Painter (2000); McGuirk (2004).

governmentality A concept devised by the French thinker Michel Foucault (1926–84) to describe the practices of government of a population as they emerged in EUROPE in the modern period. Foucault used the term to describe the particular practices of the STATE under the organizational regime that he termed '*security*'. Government is thus not a property of the space, but the PERFORMANCE of its POWER in a historically and geographically specific way. Foucault's notion of DISCIPLINARY POWER required the enclosure, circumscription, partition and control of SPACE, while *security* was concerned with opening up spaces to allow circulation and passage. This requires regulation, but of a minimal kind. In Foucault's terms, discipline is isolating, working on measures of segmentation, while security seeks to incorporate and to distribute more widely (see also SECURITY). The practices particular to this model of governmental organization are what Foucault means by governmentality.

Foucault's researches on governmentality emerged in the late 1970s as part of his project of understanding the birth of the modern human SUBJECT. He was therefore interested in the way in which humans – both as individual BODIES and as the collective body of population – were governed. This government was both government of the self by the self, to which his last works on technologies of the self and ETHICS speak, and government by others. His works on governmentality itself, in lecture courses from 1978 and 1979 (Foucault, 2007 [2004], 2008 [2004]), from which the lecture 'Governmentality' (1991) is extracted, concentrate on government is as it is exercised in political SOVEREIGNTY, political rule.

Foucault traces the emergence of governmentality historically, suggesting three main sources: the Christian pastoral, diplomatic–military techniques in early modern Europe and the police. The first provides a model for codes of conduct and the concern for the population as a flock; the second looks at the techniques of external governmental relations; and the third at internal mechanisms of the policing or ordering of a society. Foucault understands the 'police' as something much more than a uniformed force for the prevention and detection of crime but, rather, as what allows the functioning of a SOCIETY or polity as a whole (cf. POLICING). In this sense it is closer to the analyses of Hegel, Adam Smith or Adam Ferguson, with a concern for things including public infrastructure such as roads and bridges, pricing mechanisms, and public health and property. In each, he is concerned with how government is interested in 'each and all' – individual bodies subject to governmental procedures, and the population measured and calculated through larger scale campaigns (Foucault, 1988). In both, the practices are tied to the development of knowledge, which in turn conditions the practices themselves.

In order to understand the transition from earlier sovereign models of political power to discipline and security or government, Foucault does not propose a linear narrative. Rather, he suggests that we understand this model as a triangle of sovereignty–discipline–government (governmental management), whose primary target is population, whose principal form of knowledge is POLITICAL ECONOMY, and whose essential mechanism or technical means of operating are apparatuses of security. Conceiving of these three 'societies' not on a linear model but, rather, as a space of political action allows us to inject historical and geographical specificity into Foucault's narrative. Different places and different times might be closer to one node or another, while recognizing that this is a generally useful and transferable model of analysis. Although Foucault's work is largely tied to France and Germany, and dependent on better known historical transitions such as that between FEUDALISM and CAPITALISM, the birth of modern PHILOSOPHY and schisms in the church, some writers have used his ideas to look at places that did not follow such chronologies.

Foucault's work on governmentality has been widely taken up across the human sciences, including HUMAN GEOGRAPHY. Key works by his colleagues in France have been collected in *The Foucault effect* (Burchell, Gordon and Miller, 1991) and collections of writings developing and augmenting his researches have continued to appear (see, e.g., Barry, Osborne and Rose, 1996; Dean, 1999; Walters and Larner, 2004). Geographers have looked at a range of spaces through a governmentality perspective, including those that exceed Foucault's largely EUROCENTRIC perspective (Braun, 2000; Hannah, 2000, Corbridge, Williams, Srivastava and Veron, 2005). These have largely been developments of the original lecture on the topic, and related writings (i.e. Foucault, 1988), so it is likely that the publication of the full lecture courses (Foucault, 2007 [2004], 2008 [2004]), with their rich analyses, will reinvigorate this sub-field (see Lemke, 2001; Elden, 2007b; Legg, 2007b).   SE

Suggested reading
Burchell, Gordon and Miller (1991); Dean (1999); Foucault (1988, 1991); Huxley (2007).

Grand Theory A term devised by American sociologist C. Wright Mills (1959) to attack what he took to be the obsessive concern of post-Second World War social science with empty conceptual elaboration ('the associating and dissociating of concepts') at high levels of ABSTRACTION. In his view, Grand Theory was more or less severed from the concrete concerns of EVERYDAY LIFE and largely indifferent to its immense variety in time and space. His main target was Talcott Parsons, another American sociologist and the architect of STRUCTURAL FUNCTIONALISM, against whom he insisted 'there is no "grand theory", no one universal scheme in terms of which we can understand the unity of social structure, no one answer to the tired old problem of social order'.

In GEOGRAPHY, the postwar development of SPATIAL SCIENCE made similar promises to Parsons', but about spatial rather than social order: indeed, Chorley and Haggett (1967) anticipated the construction of a 'general theory of locational relativity' and a unified spatial systems theory (see SYSTEM). The critiques of structural functionalism (in the social sciences) and spatial science (in geography) did not lead to the demise of Grand Theory, however, so much as its reformulation. By the 1980s, so many other candidates had emerged that Skinner (1985) could write of 'the return of Grand Theory'. These included CRITICAL THEORY, STRUCTURALISM, STRUCTURAL MARXISM and STRUCTURATION THEORY, all of which left their marks on human geography. Indeed, Barnes and Gregory (1997a, p. 64) claimed that much of the late-twentieth-century history of Anglo-American HUMAN GEOGRAPHY had involved 'the search for a single or tightly bounded set of methodological [and theoretical] principles that, once found, would provide unity and intelligibility to the disparate material studied. When located, such principles would function as a kind of philosopher's stone, transmuting the scattered base facts of the world into the pure gold of coherent explanation. No matter the kind of phenomenon investigated, it could always be slotted into a wider theoretical scheme. Nothing would be left out; everything would be explained.'

There have been two critical responses to this search, fastening on (i) its theoretical ambitions and (ii) its totalizing ambitions:

(1) There has been a continuing debate about the scope of THEORY in human geography. Few would advocate a return to the supposedly theory-less world of EMPIRICISM, but Ley (1989), in the spirit of Mills' original objections, nonetheless complained of a fixation upon theory (or rather Theory): of the privilege accorded to the 'theorization of theories', second-order abstractions 'doubly removed from the empirical world', whose proliferation threatened to produce a disturbing fragmentation of geographical enquiry. Yet in the same year Harvey and Scott (1989) were exercised by what they saw as a withdrawal from 'the theoretical imperative' and, in consequence, the dissolution of intellectual enquiry into a host of empirical particulars. The fragmentation that dismayed both these responses (in different ways) was often the product of theoretical work conducted outside the confines of (and in large measure working against) Grand Theory: see, for example, HISTORICISM, POSTMODERNISM and POST-STRUCTURALISM. Hence Dear's (1988) exuberant insistence that 'there can be no grand theory for human geography!' was coupled with an equally exuberant demand for human geography to engage with SOCIAL THEORY. His intention was to fashion a human geography that was at once theoretically engaged and sensitive to empirical particularity – to 'difference'. Similarly – but differently – Thrift (1996, p. 30; see also 2006) argued that a yet more 'modest' form of theorizing was needed to avoid a 'theory-centred' style of research 'which continually avoids the taint of particularity', though to his chagrin several critics plainly regard his own project of NON-REPRESENTATIONAL THEORY as yet another exorbitation of Theory with a capital T. Whether Thrift has successfully clipped the wings of Grand Theory remains an open question, but in any event Katz (1996) urged human geographers to find other ways of letting theory take flight. She recommended an openness to MINOR THEORY: subverting the claims to mastery registered by Grand Theory by working in the heterogeneous 'spaces-in-between' different traditions, by

activating the disjunctures and displacements between different voices and vocabularies, and so ensuring that theoretical work is 'relentlessly transformative' and elaborates 'lines of escape'.

(2) There has been a parallel debate about the capacity of any single theoretical system to account for the world (cf. ESSENTIALISM; FOUNDATIONALISM). Many, perhaps most, human geographers seem to accept: (a) that no single theoretical system can possibly ask all the interesting questions or provide all the satisfying answers; and (b) that most scholars necessarily work in the spaces between overlapping, often contending theoretical systems, which redoubles the importance of theoretical critique to clarify dissonances, reveal erasures and evaluate consequences (Gregory, 1994, pp. 100–6). But these nostrums have neither soothed geographers' anxieties nor dispelled their ambitions. Much of the controversy attached to Harvey's historico-geographical materialism, for example, centres on his attempt to develop a totalizing critique through what his critics see as the annexation, incorporation and marginalization of other politico-intellectual traditions (Castree and Gregory, 2006). And while few geographers have pursued the Ariadne's thread linking Humboldt's grand eighteenth-century vision of the Cosmos to Chorley and Haggett's twentieth-century vision of a unified field theory for Geography, there has been considerable interest in theoretical systems that trouble the divide between the human sciences and the natural sciences: for example, CHAOS THEORY and COMPLEXITY THEORY. If Manson and Sullivan (2006, p. 678) are right to describe complexity as 'the grand theory to end all grand theories', perhaps Grand Theory always rings twice. DG

Suggested reading
Curry (2006).

graph theory A branch of mathematics that studies topological phenomena that can be represented by NETWORK diagrams comprising nodes and the links between them: the classic pioneering work was that of Leonhard Euler (1707–83) on the Königsberg bridge problem (see http://www.contracosta.cc.ca.us/math/konig.htm). TOPOLOGY refers to spatial connections and relationships that are unchanged after distortion: for example, Canada has a border with the USA regardless of which datum and MAP PROJECTION system is used to map the Earth. Graph theory was first deployed by geographers in the study of a range of network types – such as river systems and road networks (Haggett and Chorley, 1969) – but is widely deployed through the social sciences to study the structure and functioning of a range of social networks and how information flows through them (a field known as sociometrics). (See also OPTIMIZATION.) RJ

Suggested reading
Biggs, Lloyd and Wilson (1986).

gravity model A mathematical and statistical MODEL used to represent many types of SPATIAL INTERACTION and flow patterns in HUMAN GEOGRAPHY and REGIONAL SCIENCE (such as MIGRATION and commodity flows), and subsequently extended for use as a planning tool. The original formulation, as devised by members of the SOCIAL PHYSICS school, was based on an analogy with Newton's equation of gravitational force:

$$G_{ij} = gM_iM_j/d_{ij}^2.$$

This can be interpreted as follows: the gravitational force (G_{ij}) between two masses (M_i and M_j) is proportional to a gravitational constant (g) and to the product of their masses (M_iM_j) and inversely proportional to the square of the distance between them (d_{ij}^2). The analogy for migration was therefore given as

$$F_{ij} = gP_iP_j/d_{ij}^2,$$

where the migrant flow (F) from i to j was modelled as being proportional to the product of their populations and inversely proportional to the distance between them. In such an application, the constant g was empirically determined from the data set by simple arithmetic methods. At a later stage the model was fitted by REGRESSION methods in logarithmic form, and both g and the exponent for distance were empirically determined by calibration. This basic form of the model is unconstrained, and empirical studies demonstrated that the model fitted much better if origin and destination constraints (e.g. the total numbers of people starting or ending in each region) were incorporated. This was most effectively developed by Alan Wilson in his ENTROPY-MAXIMIZING formulation of the model, based on an analogy with statistical physics rather than Newtonian equations, and in this form it is widely used today. It may be used for the assessment of likely policy impacts by projecting changes to origin and destination totals, introducing different travel mode and pricing, and making the model dynamic. The gravity model approach has come under heavy criticism because of its mimicking of equations and models from physics, rather than being rooted in social science, but much recent work has shown how the various assumptions of the models (such as DISTANCE DECAY) may be derived from concepts of ACCESSIBILITY, UTILITY THEORY and INTERVENING OPPORTUNITY. The physical analogy is just that, an analogy and no more.   LWH

Suggested reading
Fotheringham and O'Kelly (1989); Sen and Smith (1995); Senior (1979).

green belt   A designated area of land surrounding a built-up area, into which urban expansion is strictly limited by planning policies. Initially proposed as part of the GARDEN CITY movement, delimitation of green belts around all major urban areas was part of the innovatory procedures made mandatory under the UK's 1947 *Town and Country Planning Act*, both to contain urban SPRAWL and to protect high-quality agricultural land plus that used for recreational and other amenity purposes. The proportion of the land surface designated as green belts has been substantially increased since, despite opposition from interest groups – such as development companies that want to build there in response to growing pressure for new housing, which governments instead wish to focus on 'brownfield' (i.e. redevelopment) sites within existing urban areas. The policy's success has stimulated urban development beyond the green belts, leading to increased COMMUTING costs for many workers and casting doubt on the overall economic and environmental justification for the continued constraints (cf.   COUNTER-URBANIZATION). Comparable policies have been instituted in many other countries.   RJ

Suggested reading
Elson (1986).

Green Line   The most common use of the term denotes the Armistice line separating Israel and the Palestinian territories of the West Bank and the Gaza Strip. The term is occasionally used elsewhere, as in the *de*

facto partition lines in Beirut (Lebanon) and Nicosia (Cyprus). The Israeli line was demarcated in 1949 following the 1948–9 war between Israel and several Arab states over the 1947 UN partition plan for Mandatory Palestine. The Green Line separated Israel from Palestinian territories captured by Jordan and Egypt. In 1967, Israel conquered the West Bank and the Gaza Strip. There have been repeated attempts to 'erase' the Green Line, although it has remained to date the *de facto* border demarcating the limit of internationally recognized Israeli SOVEREIGNTY. The MILITARY OCCUPATION of the Palestinian territories continues, however, and Israel has also built a so-called 'separation barrier' or wall beyond the Green Line and extending deep into the Occupied Territories.   OY

Suggested reading
Biger (2004); Newman (1995).

Green Revolution   A term coined in the late 1960s to refer to the so-called miracle seeds – the high-yielding varieties (HYVs), and especially wheat and rice – that held out the prospect for spectacular increases in cereal production in the THIRD WORLD. Associated with 1970 Nobel Prize winner and crop geneticist Norman Borlaug, the term 'Green Revolution' continues to have wide currency 30 years after it was minted. Nonetheless, it remains somewhat controversial and indeed there is often little consensus on what the Green Revolution actually denotes. The adjective 'Green' implies, at least in our epoch, a sensitivity to SUSTAINABILITY (but ironically the ecological costs of the HYVs have been a purported major failing) and implicitly is opposed to 'Red' in a way which technical achievements – a technical fix – could banish not simply hunger but political unrest. In order to understand the origins and genesis of the 'heroic age' (Jirstrom, 1996, p. 15) of the Green Revolution between 1963 and 1970, the miracle seeds must be located on the earlier landscape of the COLD WAR, which embraces American IMPERIALISM in Vietnam, a Malthusian view of food shortages in the post-1945 period, and the recognition that the Green Revolution was wrapped up with US foreign policy and the perceived threat posed by poor peasants inclined towards SOCIALISM (cf. MALTHUSIAN MODEL).

The meaning of 'Green Revolution' remains a contested issue. The heart of the revolutionary thrust was quite simple: seeds plus nitrogen plus water would produce increased yields

317

per unit area. As a consequence, there is a narrow and broad interpretation of the technologies themselves. In the narrow sense, it consists primarily of the adoption of the new high-yielding varieties of wheat and rice and associated technologies. In the broad sense it includes not only this, but all other economic changes, as well as the social and cultural changes that either contributed to the technological and ecological changes or were derived from them (Leaf, 1984, p. 23).

The Green Revolution as a set of new production practices for the tropical or subtropical PEASANT or smallholder rested on the development of Mendellian genetics, applied plant breeding (led by the UK and the USA), fertilizer (the petrochemical industry) and the WATER development/irrigation technologies. The coordination between the biochemical, technological and social components embraced US philanthropic organizations, the US State Department and Third World governments. What began in the 1940s in Mexico under the auspices of the US government and the Rockefeller Foundation, focused on improving wheat, has grown in half a century to a massive multi-billion dollar NETWORK of international agricultural research centres (the Consultative Group of International Agricultural Research, CGIAR), administered by the World Bank and dealing with virtually all the major FOOD complexes. HYVs are now grown worldwide – for example, 100 per cent of rice in China and Korea, and 70 per cent in India and the Philippines is miracle rice – and there is no question that the ability of food output to exceed population growth in the Third World since 1950 has been a function of the PRODUCTIVITY gains of the Green Revolution (Lipton, 1989). But the Green Revolution, insofar as it is an example of applied plant breeding, has of course a long history – human history is synonymous with successive Green Revolutions, associated with the DOMESTICATION of plants, with the European AGRICULTURAL REVOLUTIONS in the eighteenth century, the Chinese improved rice varieties from AD 1000 and so on – and is a process (still ongoing) rather than an event (Rigg, 1989).

If the Green Revolution was facilitated by new practices associated with plant breeding, soil fertility science and hydrological development, the genesis was stimulated by the activities of the Rockefeller Foundation in conjunction with the Office of Special Operations of the US Government in Mexico during the Second World War (Perkins, 1997). Whatever the intentions of the early plant breeders in Mexico, the combination of Malthusians thinking about food CRISES and the Cold War atmosphere favouring national SECURITY and the threat of peasant insurgency contributed mightily to the Green Revolution project, and to its subsequent backing and support by the Ford Foundation, USAID and the major Western donors. In the first phase of the Green Revolution, rice and wheat were the primary crops and Mexico and India its crucibles. The International Rice Research Institute (IRRI) was founded near Manila in 1960 and the Center for Maize and Wheat Improvement (CIMMYT) in Mexico in 1963. Today, there are 16 international agriculture research centres, focusing on potatoes, germ plasm collection, agroforestry and tropical agriculture.

The research programme for HYVs brought together in university-type settings transnational congeries of scientists, which constituted sophisticated breeding programs. The IRRI, for example, built upon rice-breeding expertise and dwarf varieties from Taiwan and Japan to produce, through hybridization, new dwarf HYVs that were resistant to lodging, were sensitive to nitrogen fertilizers and that could be double or triple cropped through a reduction in the growing period. Its first success – IR-8 – was released in 1966 and spread rapidly through South and South East Asia. The DIFFUSION of the seeds and mechanical packages (pump sets, small tractors) involved strong STATE intervention, typically involving new subsidies, credit, extension services, irrigation development and national breeding programmes. By the mid-1980s, more than half of the total rice in the area of the Third World was planted in HYVs (Lipton, 1989).

There has been considerable disagreement over the productivity increases attributable to HYVs. In one of the best-known and earliest reviews by UNRISD/UNDP, Griffin (1974) painted a bleak picture of the effects of HYVs between 1970 and 1974, arguing that there had been no Green Revolution in rice. A subsequent assessment by Michael Lipton (1989) in the mid-1980s showed that the output increases in wheat and maize were indeed dramatic (at least 4 per cent per year) and that those in rice were slower but no less substantial overall. Lipton pointed, however, to regional dilemmas – AFRICA was neglected on balance – and to the problems of equity within countries, which reflected disparities in irrigation development and water control investment. In the first phase of the Green

Revolution, a number of important problems emerged: first, increasing pest and weed problems; second, problems of storage and processing; and, third, ecological deterioration (especially loss of germ plasm, water depletion and toxicity). All of these direct and indirect consequences initiated a still ongoing debate over the consequences of HYVs (see Shiva, 1991, 1996).

At the heart of the impact question are equity, POVERTY and SOCIAL JUSTICE. In the early years, the adoption of HYV packages (and the recognition that the packages were not SCALE neutral) prompted much speculation about new forms of social differentiation among peasantries, of CLASS conflict between adopters and non-adopters, of deteriorating labour conditions, as HYVs were labour-displacing rather than labour-saving – of the 'green revolution turning red'. As the Indian case shows, there was in fact no simple polarization of landholding, though there has been the consolidation of a CLASS of increasingly commercialized and organized rich peasants who have benefited from the Green Revolution (these are the heart of the New Farmers Movement in India, which has changed the face of local and national politics: see SOCIAL MOVEMENTS). The impact on LABOUR MARKETS (new forms of MIGRATION, changing forms of labour permanency and tenancy), on landholding (cf. LAND TENURE) and on social inequality is enormously complex, in part because of the linkages and off-farm employment (Hazell, 1987). On balance, the mechanization that has followed the HYV adoption has been labour displacing and has favoured those with concentrated capital displacement. New forms of inequality have emerged, but this is often attributed by the proponents of the HYVs to population growth and state rent-seeking rather than technology *per se*. The debate continues.

The Green Revolution has unquestionably increased food output per capita, but this has not necessarily increased food availability for the poor (Dreze and Sen, 1989), and nor has it improved the lot of the poor (Lipton, 1989). The first issue turns less on output than on availability and entitlements – in short, the social component of the Green Revolution (including land reform). The second speaks to the problems of both the uneven adoption of HYVs and the biases built into the breeding programmes themselves. The miracle seeds are often not pro-poor and do not speak to the circumstances of the land-poor and landless.

There is a debate over whether the Green Revolution has 'ended' in the sense that there are no new seed breakthroughs likely in the world STAPLE crops. The pessimists foresee a Malthusian nightmare of FAMINE and pestilence, compounded by the growth of Chinese staple food imports. Nonetheless, the Green Revolution has entered a second phase associated with the breakthroughs of molecular science and recombinant DNA. Here, the issue is increasingly the power of large transnational seed and pharmaceutical companies, who develop new crops with built-in requirements for particular inputs, and the intellectual property rights that attend to the concentration of power in AGRIBUSINESS companies (Shiva, 1996). Genetically modified HYVs (whether soy or corn) have become part of an embattled agricultural landscape in which environmental questions have been tied to corporate power and the pressures exerted through the WORLD TRADE ORGANIZATION by First World states to liberalize protected agricultural sectors in the global SOUTH. Many of the most vociferous of the ANTI-GLOBALIZATION movements have often expressed concerns over the ways in which the second phase of the Green Revolution is now refiguring the international food order, now dominated by corporate power and a new round of privatized agricultural and seed technologies (Rosset, 2006). The current debates over farmer breeding rights, genetically modified crops and INTELLECTUAL PROPERTY RIGHTS suggests that the next Green Revolution will be as fraught as the first.   MW

Suggested reading
Bayliss-Smith and Wanmali (1984); Grigg (1989).

greenhouse effect See GLOBAL WARMING

gross domestic product (GDP) A monetary estimate of the value (at current market prices) of final goods and services produced within an ECONOMY (usually national) during a given period. Capital expenditure, indirect taxes and subsidies are excluded, as is the value of intermediate products (such as raw materials) which is included in the value of final goods. GDP is often favoured over GROSS NATIONAL PRODUCT (GNP) as a measure of economic activity because it excludes net income from abroad. International comparisons of GDP, either in aggregate or per capita, are difficult because of fluctuations in currency values through floating exchange rates, and some attempt to standardize for this using purchasing power parities, derived from data on the costs of a 'standard basket' of goods and services. In addition, as a recent OECD (2006) report indicated, comparison of GDP levels internationally is difficult because: it takes no account of leisure time and the quality of the environment; it is not standardized for income inequality (an extra $1,000 per annum means much more to a poor than to a rich person); it does not factor in negative contributors to the QUALITY OF LIFE (such as POLLUTION); and it takes no account of the depreciation of capital stock. Unfortunately, though measures have been devised to capture these, they are not readily available for many countries.   RJ

gross national product (GNP)

A measure of economic activity in a given period of time, usually applied to national economies. It comprises GROSS DOMESTIC PRODUCT (GDP) plus the net return from profits, dividends and income earned abroad. GNP estimates are used to compare the volume of economic activity over time and space – either in aggregate or per capita – but to avoid complications introduced by inflation and exchange rate fluctuations they have to be converted to a common base. This involves the use of purchasing power parities (the costs of a 'standard basket' of goods and services at a given period) – as in the calculated rate of inflation within a country, which is taken into account when calculating a 'real terms' rate of GNP growth. GNP is not necessarily a valid measure of 'economic health' since harmful consequences (e.g. on the environment) are not taken into account, whereas the later costs of their amelioration are: increased expenditure on POLICING could stimulate GNP growth, for example, even if it was merely a response to an increased CRIME rate.   RJ

growth coalitions

Alliances of urban elites, with shared interests in local ECONOMIC GROWTH, partnered in pursuit of business-friendly and market-oriented forms of city GOVERNANCE and RESOURCE allocation (Logan and Molotch, 1987). Typically centring on the rentier CLASS (including developers, financiers and realtors), the business interests of whom are 'place-based', growth coalitions also comprise a range of auxiliary players such as universities, media and utility owners, representatives of business and civic organizations, cultural leaders and labour unions. What are sometimes called 'growth machines' or 'urban regimes' have assumed increased

significance in the context of the entrepreneurial turn in urban politics since the 1970s. JPe

Suggested reading
Jonas and Wilson (1999).

growth pole

A dynamic and highly integrated set of industries, often induced by the STATE, organized around a propulsive leading sector or industry. Growth poles are intended to generate rapid growth, and to disseminate this through spillover and MULTIPLIER effects in the rest of the ECONOMY. The concept was devised by French economist François Perroux (1903–87), who, in 1955, located the *pôle de croissance* in abstract economic space. It was translated into more concrete geographical terms by J.R. Boudeville (1966). On the bases of EXTERNAL ECONOMIES and economies of AGGLOMERATION – and hence of UNEVEN DEVELOPMENT – Boudeville argued that the set of industries forming the growth pole might be clustered spatially and linked to an existing urban area. He also pointed to the regionally differentiated growth that such a spatial strategy might generate. The precise meaning of the term 'growth pole' is difficult to pin down, however, because it is frequently used in a far looser fashion to denote any (planned) spatial clustering of economic activity.

The apparent simplicity of the notion, its suggestion of dynamism and its ability to connect problems of *sectoral* growth and planning with those of *intra- and inter-regional* growth and planning, led to its ready acceptance and widespread use in the 1970s and 1980s. Although some commentators have seen Perroux's ideas resurfacing in the NEW ECONOMIC GEOGRAPHY (Meardon, 2001), there were several persistent difficulties associated with growth poles in both theory and practice that led to its fall from grace. These included the following:

(1) *Technical problems*, notably: (a) the interdependent decisions to be made on the location, size and sectoral composition of a growth pole – this was not a serious problem for Perroux, who defined growth poles around a single propulsive industry, but more recent research on the related ideas of CLUSTERS and INDUSTRIAL DISTRICTS identifies NETWORKS of industries as central to urban and regional development; (b) the distinction between spontaneous and planned poles, with the latter requiring integrated social and physical

planning; (c) the nature of the intersectoral and interregional transmission of growth; (d) the relationship between the public provision of INFRASTRUCTURE and the success of the growth pole; (e) the relationship between the growth pole and existing city distributions; and (f) the need for monitoring and management to avoid dis-economies.

(2) *Political and policy horizons*: the appropriate time-span over which to judge success or failure of a growth pole – say, 15–25 years – is often too long in political terms, as elected governments prefer results of their policies to be evident over the length of the electoral cycle (which is usually less than four years).

(3) *Space–time path dependence*: the success of a growth pole depends upon the extent to which it is linked to, and energizes and dynamizes an existing SPACE-ECONOMY or economic LANDSCAPE. Without such conformities, the spillover effects are severely inhibited. Porter's (1998a, 2000) advocacy of CLUSTERS as a means of enhancing the competitive advantage of localities has prompted critics such as Martin and Sunley (2003) to object that such policy interventions are merely one effective geography of production that may lock out other possibilities. RL

Suggested reading
Buttler (1975).

growth theory In the wake of the Second World War, and after the experience of the Marshall Plan in assisting the recovery of war-torn EUROPE, several economists with direct experience in multilateral institutions and the Marshall Plan turned their attention to the question of economic DEVELOPMENT in the THIRD WORLD. Among these pioneers of development thinking were Finnish economist Ragnar Nurkse (1953), Austrian economist Paul Rodenstein-Rodan (1976), German-born and American-naturalized economist Albert Hirschmann (1958), West Indian Nobel Laureate Sir Arthur Lewis (1984), and American economic historian Walt Rostow (1960). Their ideas were far from identical, but they formed a loose school of thought – growth theorists – emphasizing a historically informed and practical approach to economic development, and stood at an angle to the neo-classical models of Solow and others. Rostow was something of an odd man out insofar as his simple stage theory of European industrial replication was both less analytical and less historically sophisticated than the others (cf. ROSTOW MODEL).

The growth theorists were framed by three historical dynamics: *the legacy of the Keynesian revolution* and the experience of international Keynesianism through the European recovery programme; the *political agenda of the USA* in the wake of 1945 and increasingly during the COLD WAR, which turned on the use of Bretton Woods institutions to foster development and fair dealing, as President Truman put it in 1949; and the *nationalist developmentalism* (cf. NATIONALISM) associated with the last wave of DECOLONIZATION, which also emerged during and after the Second World War. Growth theory in its emphasis on aggregate phenomena and on industrialization bred a predilection for authoritative intervention – in which the STATE was a necessary actor – which involved planning systems, the application of economic growth models and AID mechanisms.

All of the growth theorists shared some sort of affinity for Keynes. They emphasized aggregate economic processes such as rates of saving and rates of investment (cf. NEO-CLASSICAL ECONOMICS). Poor economic performance and lack of aggregate demand were related. They also revealed a preference for INDUSTRIALIZATION as a driving force – indeed, they were advocates of what in the 1930s had become import-substituting industrialization – and for short-term state interventions. MARKETS were means not ends, and like Alexander Gerschenkron (1968 – one of their contemporaries), they realized that late developers required a dirigiste state. However, as growth theorists they presumed that an economy would achieve its best results within a competitive market structure.

Each of the growth theorists is a major intellectual figure in the history of economics, but there were important commonalities and points of confluence (if not necessarily agreement), which animated their policy and theory during the 1950s.

There was the concept of *hidden development potential* in the less developed nations. As Gerschenkron had argued, there were 'advantages to backwardness', and in these advantages lay hidden COMPARATIVE ADVANTAGES:

- A recognition of *market failures* and the role of positive EXTERNALITIES in creating virtuous circle effects. Rodenstein-Rodan's (1976) emphasis on social overhead capital and the role of government was a case in point.

- The *differences and merits of balanced and unbalanced growth*, and how each was related to the necessity for a 'big push' to trigger economic growth. Nurkse (1953), like Rodenstein-Rodan, emphasized the need for coordinated increase in the amount of capital utilized in a wide range of industries if industrialization was to be achieved. Hirschmann (1958), while agreeing with Nurske and others, also argued that unbalanced growth could, through linkage effects, generate innovations created by market responses to shortage and surpluses.
- The potential, as Lewis (1984) indicated, for *surplus labour as a stimulant to growth* in so-called DUAL ECONOMIES.
- The *significance of saving* at particular historical moments in order to enter what Rostow (Rostow) called the 'take-off stage' of industrialization.

Growth theory, from the vantage point of the NEO-LIBERAL revolution of the 1980s, appears as an instance of Keynesian internationalism in which market failures, planning, social capital and some aspects of POLITICAL ECONOMY are put to the service of 'developing' the poorer nations of the world. All of these growth theorists identified key developmental issues – equilibrium, social overhead capital, planning – which have continued to be objects of debate, and each (perhaps with the exception of Rostow) contributed to both the building of postwar multilateral development institutions and to the idea, which in a way was crushed by the weight of the Cold War, of a sort of liberal developmental internationalism (see LIBERALISM). In the 1980s, a 'new growth theory' emerged in which endogenous growth can occur especially through human capital and new technologies (rather than being assumed, as in neo-classical approaches, by an exogenous savings rate or rate of progress of technical change).   MW

Suggested reading
Cypher and Dietz (1997); Preston (1996).

H

habitus A term coined by French anthropologist/sociologist Pierre Bourdieu to convey the routinized, yet indeterminate, nature of social practice. It mediates between objectivist accounts, such as from STRUCTURALISM, and individualistic accounts, such as from PHENOMENOLOGY. The former would see individual practice as determined by social factors, while the latter would emphasize the individual's intentions. In essence, then, it speaks to the oxymoronic nature of always improvised yet repetitively predictable practices of everyday life. Bourdieu himself defined habitus as the system of:

> durable, transposable dispositions, structured structures predisposed to function as structuring structures, that is as principles which generate and organize practices and representations that can be objectively adapted to their outcomes without presupposing a conscious aiming at ends or an express mastery of the operations necessary in order to attain them. Objectively 'regular' and 'regulated' without being in any way the product of obedience to rules, they can be collectively orchestrated without being the product of the organizing action of a conductor. (Bourdieu, 1990b, p. 53)

This definition, then, emphasizes that practices are not (generally) subject to the anarchy of individual intentions. He plays down the role of intention, rejecting conscious planning as a principle, in favour of routinization. He also stresses that there are collective patterns without implying there is a conscious plan or conformity.

Rather, there is adaptation to a constricted set of opportunities presented to each actor in a 'social field'. These have been variously interpreted, but usually represent a social domain in which there are shared rules of operation. These can be defined by institutions but can be more open, and are defined by the circulation of specific forms and practices. Bourdieu himself worked with the 'artistic field', or what he more broadly defined as the field of cultural production, the field of consumption and the 'educational field'. Clearly, a critique is that the edges of these can be vague and that applied mechanically they merely render a institutional

sociology. However, the virtue of his approach is that these fields are relatively autonomous from each other – thus advantage in one field does not automatically mean advantage in another. Most famously, he thus developed a notion of the accumulation of CULTURAL CAPITAL as separate from economic CAPITAL. The plurality of fields provides for multiple dimensions of POWER and status in society. Each field has its own tacit rules and continual adaptation produces ingrained dispositions. For example, in Bourdieu's study of amateur photography – a voluntary activity, in which few people have any training – he found people's pictures remarkably similar, so 'there are few activities which are so stereotyped and less abandoned to the anarchy of individual intentions' (Bourdieu, 1990a, p. 19). Bourdieu has been criticized for being reductive and emphasizing the structural side of practices, and his work has an unfashionable belief in the ability to objectify the conditions of the emergence of practices.

Within GEOGRAPHY, his work was first taken up as a way of mediating in debates between structuralism's focus on determinations of action and accounts focusing on HUMAN AGENCY (e.g. Thrift, 1983). Along with STRUCTURATION THEORY, it offered a middle way in debates of the 1980s. In the 1990s, his work on cultural capital was heavily invoked in studies of CONSUMPTION, connecting habitus to the lifestyles of different class fractions (e.g. Bridge, 2001). Finally, from the 1990s interest in his notion of habitus has focused around how tacit knowledge might connect with work on the BODY and routinized habit, and embodied MEMORY (e.g. Alsmark, 1996).   MC

Suggested reading
Alsmark (1996); Bourdieu (1995); Bridge (2001); Thrift (1983).

hazard An event or phenomenon that does harm to human lives. Today, most researchers view hazards as the joint product of RISK (the potentiality or probability of harmful events) and vulnerability (the degree to which risk-affected populations are likely to suffer from the event occurring) (Mitchell, 2003b, p. 17). The field of hazard research opened up in response to so-called 'natural disasters' – the suffering visited upon human populations by such extreme geophysical phenomena as floods, earthquakes and hurricanes (see also ENVIRONMENTAL HAZARD). These events remain core concerns. The prominence of physical forces as causes or triggers of human suffering points to the need for input from both the human and natural sciences, which would seem to present special opportunities for the discipline of GEOGRAPHY, with its constitutive concern with both social and physical processes. However, the various twists and turns in the development of hazard research thus far should caution against any sense that the field offers a straightforward or self-evident bridge between the study of the social and the natural, within geography or more generally. This is all the more so considering that the study of hazards increasingly concerns itself with more obviously human-induced harms, such as technological accidents, WAR, TERRORISM and social VIOLENCE.

Within HUMAN GEOGRAPHY, the crystallizing of a concern with hazards is usually traced to the mid-twentieth century work on floods in the USA by Gilbert White. In what became known as the HUMAN ECOLOGY tradition, White and his collaborators sought to provide an alternative to the ENVIRONMENTAL DETERMINISM of the late nineteenth and early twentieth centuries, by exploring the range of ways in which individuals or COMMUNITIES could construe and respond to hazards in their environment. However, later critics found the human ecology approach overly managerialist or technocratic – too concerned with adjustment or ADAPTATION of human populations to hazards, and not concerned enough with the social processes that rendered people vulnerable to hazards (Pelling, 2001; Mustafa, 2005).

The late 1970s and 1980s saw the rise of a perspective on hazards that viewed vulnerability as having at least as much to do with the conditions of everyday social life as with the specific physical events on which the human ecologists focused. This turn was signalled by the work of Amartya Sen (1981) and Kenneth Hewitt (1983), and further developed by input from the tradition of POLITICAL ECONOMY. Addressing issues at both local and global SCALES, the political–economic perspective draws attention to the ways in which socio-economic marginalization and powerlessness leaves some people living and working in conditions of vulnerability to hazard that the more privileged sectors of society are able to avoid. As Emel and Peet sum up: 'the geography of social relations thus determines the occurrence and extent of natural disasters' (1989, p. 68). Researchers and activists have also sought to reveal how dominant DISCOURSES serve to frame hazard as a physical problem amenable to technocratic or managerial solutions, rather than one that calls for changes in the social structure.

By reconstituting hazard as a facet of everyday existence rather than as the exception to normality, the political–economic perspective has helped resituate hazard research in the broader stream of critical social theory (see Blaikie, Cannon, Davis and Wisner, 1994; Emel and Peet, 1989). Its 'denaturalizing' of natural disasters has facilitated the extension of interest in hazard beyond events with a geophysical or biological trigger, to encompass technological accidents and other human-induced threats. Among other things, this paves the way for a convergence of hazard research with environmentalist discourses and theories of RISK SOCIETY. The growing integration of the study of natural disasters with the study of environmental problems manifests itself in a shared concern with SUSTAINABILITY, including the processes by which different social groups struggle for sustainable livelihoods and places of habitation (see ENVIRONMENTALISM; SOCIAL JUSTICE). Pursuing these leads, researchers of the political–economic camp tend to encourage a participatory approach to hazard mitigation, based on the recognition that successfully diminishing vulnerability and increasing resilience in the face of a volatile world requires input from the bottom up (Mustafa, 2005).

However, care must be taken so that emphasis on the SOCIAL CONSTRUCTION of hazard does not overshadow the significance of those aspects of the physical world or 'cosmos' that cannot be reduced to the measure of the human. As James Mitchell reminds us, 'natural hazards ... represent an "other" that can be modified by humans but is not ultimately reducible to a human construction in either the material sense or the mental one' (1999, p. 2). Moreover, the downplaying of the exceptionality of the hazard, whatever its trigger may be, can also detract attention from the very things that are most disturbing and provocative about those events that impact 'disastrously' on human life. As the philosopher Maurice Blanchot pointed out, the literal meaning of the term 'disaster' is the loss of one's star (1995, p. 2). The disaster causes us to lose our bearings, it disturbs and destabilizes, he argued, precisely because it exceeds our experience or comprehension of the world.

Viewed in this way, accounting for the disastrous dimensions of hazards calls for something more than simply the extension of our rational understanding of causes and consequences. It invites us to contemplate the limits of our knowledge and how we might respond intellectually, politically and ethically, to such limits. The terrorist attacks of 11 September 2001 prompted Judith Butler to reconsider the precariousness of human life, and to muse on 'the emergence and vanishing of the human at the limits of what we can know' (2004, p. 151). For her, such a disaster impels us to reassess the way we address others who have suffered, and to think deeply about the role of loss and mourning in modern life (see ETHICS). This is not to make light of the achievements of apprehending hazard as socially constructed, but it is a reminder to think also about the capacity of hazards to shape and define our human condition, and to raise questions about the limits of knowing, writing about and ordering the volatile worlds that we inhabit.   NHC

Suggested reading
Blaikie, Cannon, Davis and Wisner (1994); Emel and Peet (1989); Mustafa (2005); Pelling (2001).

health and health care 'The concept of "health" is open to differing interpretations' (Curtis, 2004, p. 2). It can mean 'the presence or absence of diagnosed diseases', but also many different dimensions potentially contributing to the corporeal, emotional and social well-being of people in their everyday lives. Gesler and Kearns (2002, pp. 30–2) discuss 'cultures of health', identifying the explanatory models deployed by different people (e.g. experts *contra* lay people) and drawing inspiration from 'ethnomedicine' as the study of how such MODELS (and their deeper cultural, religious, cosmological moorings) vary from place to place. Additionally, assumptions about health clearly vary within places according to CLASS, ETHNICITY, GENDER and other markers of social difference (Lewis, Dyck and McLafferty, 2001).

Acknowledging such variability in health beliefs suggests an approach to a GEOGRAPHY *of* health that squares with recent shifts in the sub-discipline of MEDICAL GEOGRAPHY. Indeed, some argue that medical geography should be widened to include not just health

defined through the lenses of Western bio-medicine, casting health in the negative sense of *not* being physically or mentally 'ill', but rather in the broader sense indicated above, of health as well-being. This orientation demands a holistic focus on the great variability of the human condition, commonly at the SCALE of populations within territories, but in principle also at that of individual people interacting with quite specific sites. One upshot is then the enlarging of what is meant by RISK, with geographers addressing the many risks to health that people face from infectious illnesses *but* also from the likes of ENVIRONMENTAL HAZARDS, interpersonal VIOLENCE and occupational stress, all of which constitute multiple 'spaces of risk' figuring in domains of human DECISION-MAKING from the STATE to the HOUSEHOLD (Curtis, 2004, pp. 5–9).

A link exists here to a long-standing geographical concern for human well-being, sometimes configured as QUALITY OF LIFE, in which a political commitment to uncovering spatial *in*justice is never far below the surface. This concern awakened in the 1970s with the contribution of WELFARE GEOGRAPHY, and has continued into more recent work on the socio-spatial constitution of 'health inequalities'. A key development has been Gesler's (1992) notion of 'therapeutic LANDSCAPES', highlighting how places in all of their complexity can foster people's senses of health*ful* well-being, and Curtis (2004, ch. 2) mobilizes this notion when fashioning new perspectives on the meeting-grounds of 'health *and* inequality'. Another link exists to the various currents now coalescing under the heading of EMOTIONAL GEOGRAPHIES, wherein varying human mind–body ASSEMBLAGES (see also Butler and Parr, 1999) are examined for how they are constituted, enacted, experienced, re-presented and perhaps politicized in relation to diverse SPACES, PLACES, environments and landscapes. Work in this vein asks about what might comprise places conducive to, or alternatively destructive of, 'emotional health'.

These new trajectories complicate what is meant by health *care*, since such care can no longer be envisaged solely as providing medical facilities of varying kinds (hospitals, clinics, GP surgeries or even conventional medical outreach and educational services). Geographers have long studied these medical facilities (see MEDICAL GEOGRAPHY), but they have now begun to consider less overtly medicalized versions of care (Parr, 2003) – elder, hospice and terminal care (Brown, 2003); complementary and alternative medicines

(Doel and Segrott, 2004); psychotherapy and counselling (Bondi with Fewell, 2003) – alongside diverse retreats and centres offering massage, yoga, nature therapies and many other healing techniques. Attention is prompted to the intimacy of embodied encounters performed through these sites of non-mainstream health care (Conradson, 2003b, 2005b), but another option is to regard the latter as servicing the new 'health consumer' who can pick and mix from whatever kinds of health care, medical or otherwise, are available to them locally (or perhaps further afield for the 'health tourist'). Gesler and Kearns (2002, ch. 8) discuss this issue of 'consumption, place and health', and a further direction might follow Michel Foucault's claims about 'technologies of the self' (Martin, Gutman and Hutton, 1988) – alighting on issues of personal, especially sexual, health – when considering myriad instances of people past and present working *on* their own health. The French Revolution's dream of complete 'dehospitalization' (Philo, 2000b) and everyone becoming 'their own physician' has arguably now come to pass – partly fuelled by governments cajoling populations into a 'care of the self', partly by CAPITALISM's courting of health consumers – and the emerging geographies of health care, exploding beyond the hospital gates, signal a challenging new frontier for critical research. (See also BIOPOLITICS.)   CPP

Suggested reading
Curtis (2004); Gesler (1992); Gesler and Kearns (2002).

heartland   Many core regions are referred to as heartlands. For example, the Midwest of the USA is often termed 'the Heartland', with the implication that it is not only central in a geographical sense but also foundational in a normative sense, the place where the core American values that come from the FRONTIER process are to be found (cf. HOMELAND).

The most important use of the term, however, was by British geographer Halford Mackinder (1861–1947). Mackinder argued against the late-nineteenth-century belief that sea-power was the basis for global supremacy. Mackinder (1904) suggested that the RESOURCES of a secure land-power could now be moved around more easily with the development of transcontinental railways. Further, he proposed that the largest basket of resources of what he termed the 'World Island' (EUROPE, ASIA, AFRICA) lay in Eastern Europe and western Russia. The core of this region was

inaccessible by ocean-going navies. Gunboat diplomacy was ineffective against it. Were Russia, Germany or an alliance of the two to prevail in this region, they could mobilize resources that would make them invincible rulers of the World Island and almost certainly ultimate rulers of a World EMPIRE. Thus, Mackinder's advice to the leaders drawing up a political map of Europe after the First World War was: 'Who rules East Europe commands the Heartland: Who rules the Heartland commands the World-Island: Who commands the World-Island commands the World' (1919, p. 194). From this followed two main strategic priorities: first, to separate the Soviet Union and Germany with a viable network of buffer STATES and, second, to prevent the Soviet - Union acquiring the string of warm-water ports that would enable it to extend its land-power on to the ocean-ways of the world. The first of these was close to the state-building that was attempted from the ruins of the empires of Eastern Europe after the First World War. The second of these was close to the policies of Soviet containment that animated the COLD WAR after the Second World War.

There have been many evaluations of Mackinder's ideas. A favourable review that emphasizes Mackinder's prescience is provided by Parker (1982), while more critical reviews of the central concepts of RACE, SPACE and history used in Mackinder's GEOPOLITICS are provided by Agnew (2003a) and Kearns (2006a; see also Kearns, 2009). Advocates of the heartland thesis believe that it expresses more or less timeless relations between resources, space and military strategy. Critics argue: that in modern WAR, land- and sea-power have ceased to be distinct modalities; that far from being impregnable, the heartland has actually been occupied by hostile forces more than once in recent history (by the French under Napoleon, and the Germans under Hitler); that forceful relations between states do not exhaust the forms of INTERNATIONAL RELATIONS and that ignoring peaceful co-operation and multilateral institutions in fact makes the resort to force more likely by presenting it as inevitable; and, finally, that as technology changes, new resources will be valued and the geography of the competition for resources will shift. Despite these criticisms, our present hydrocarbon economy seems destined to focus attention for some time to come on parts of Mackinder's heartland, with the Caspian Basin still vital in the RESOURCE WARS between the world's Great Powers.

It is clear, then, that Mackinder's heartland thesis has been very heavily cited and must rank as one of the most significant geographical theories of the twentieth century. It has been claimed as central by various nationalists and imperialists, from Nazi Germany to modern Russia and the United States.　　GK

Suggested readings
Kearns (1993); Mackinder (1919).

hegemony The capacity to exercise control by means other than coercive force; namely, through constructing a willing mass acquiescence towards, and participation in, social projects that are beneficial only to an elite. Hegemony is the dissemination of the values and cultural practices of the elite in such a way that they become unquestioned. Thus, in everyday life the beliefs and values of the elite are reinforced, and a hierarchical social order is reinforced by the everyday actions (see EVERYDAY LIFE) of those who benefit less, if at all, from its existence.

Contemporary usage of the term is derived from the writings of Italian Marxist Antonio Gramsci (Gramsci, 1971 [1929–35]) who, while imprisoned by the Italian FASCIST regime between 1928 and 1935, reflected upon how the majority of citizens gave support to a repressive social order. The Frankfurt School of Marxism described how the post-1945 consumer CULTURE was a form of hegemony, entrapping the working class in the pursuit of material possessions rather than social change. Cultural geographers have used these Marxist foundations to explore the role of LANDSCAPE and PLACE in perpetuating particular hegemonic ideals (Martin, 2000a: see CULTURAL GEOGRAPHY). Such works have extended the Marxists' original concentration upon CLASS relations to questions of RACE and PATRIARCHY. Particular attention has been paid to the practice of hegemony in colonial settings, especially how the LANDSCAPE was used to inculcate ideals of racial hierarchy (McKinnon, 2005).

The term 'hegemony' has been utilized in a complementary fashion in the analysis of inter-state politics in POLITICAL GEOGRAPHY, though with the same roots and general meaning. A hegemonic power is the single most powerful STATE in the inter-state system. Though originally conceived in terms of material POWER (productive capacity and military might), scholars increasingly looked to the integrative power of the hegemonic state, or its ability to set a global agenda that, on the whole, other states followed. Post-1945, the USA was identified as the contemporary hegemonic state. Its material power is complemented by its dissemination of a 'prime MODERNITY' (Taylor, 1999), or the definition of the ultimate modern way of life. Connecting back to the Frankfurt School, the US 'prime modernity' is the consumer culture epitomized in its SUBURBAN lifestyle. Hegemony is maintained by other states' desire to emulate this lifestyle and perceiving the adoption of particular economic and political practices as the means.

Hegemony, in both senses, is a PROCESS. Hence, discussion has arisen of the way hegemony is resisted. In the first meaning of the term, working-class and SUBALTERN groups have adopted cultural practices that run counter to hegemonic demands. In the second meaning, discussion of the decline of US power, the challenge of other states and TERRORIST groups, and the meaning of 'EMPIRE' question whether hegemonic rule is being replaced by more coercive practices. A counter-argument is found in the notion of 'imperial overstretch' in which hegemonic states are eventually bankrupted by their overseas commitments and lose their primacy (Kennedy, 1988).　　CF

Suggested reading
Agnew (2005a); Lears (1985).

heritage Although 'heritage' includes and derives from a highly individualized notion of personal inheritance or bequest (e.g. through family wills and legacies), HUMAN GEOGRAPHY is concerned with collective notions of heritage that link a group to a shared inheritance. In this context, heritage usually denotes two related sets of meanings. On the one hand, it refers to iconic CULTURAL LANDSCAPES or, usually and more specifically, to TOURISM sites with an historical theme that have often been protected or preserved in some way for the nation-state and become part of the 'heritage industry'; for example, a museum or an archaeological site (Urry, 2002 [1990]). On the other hand, heritage refers to a suite of shared cultural VALUES and MEMORIES inherited over time and expressed through a variety of cultural PERFORMANCES – for example, song or parade (Peckham, 2003). The basis of this group identification varies across time and space and can hinge on allegiance derived from, for instance, a communal religious tradition, a class formation, geographical propinquity, and a national or imperial IDENTITY (Moore and Whelan, 2007).

Traditionally, historians and geographers have viewed heritage sites as spaces for inscribing nationalist narratives of the past on to the popular imagination (see NATIONALISM). The historical perspectives transmitted through these sites were seen to be selective, partial and distorting. They offered a 'bogus' history that ignored or sanitized what are now taken to be the less savoury dimensions of the past. They therefore were contrasted with the work of professional historians, represented in textbooks and monographs, where 'testable truth is [the] chief hallmark [and] ... historians' credibility depends on their sources being open to scrutiny' (Lowenthal, 1997, p. 120).

This distinction between 'true history' and 'false heritage' has been challenged from a variety of directions. Samuel (1984) made an important case for treating heritage sites as important loci for retrieving the history of the marginal, the dispossessed and the subaltern. Samuel suggests that they can act as important spaces for representing those voices often omitted in textbooks. So, for instance, industrial heritage sites can represent the lives and practices of working-class people in ways that are provocative and interesting to a popular audience and not always found in textbook accounts. POST-STRUCTURALISM suggests that all historical narration is perspectival, and thus queries the distinction between REPRESENTATION and reality, between fake heritage and genuine history, while Urry (1990, p. 82) claims that POSTMODERNISM involves 'dissolving of boundaries, not only between high and low cultures, but also between different cultural forms, such as tourism, art, music, sport, shopping and architecture' (1990, p. 82) (see also CULTURE).

Recently, geographers have begun to tackle the performative elements of heritage production and CONSUMPTION (Duncan, 2003; Hoelscher, 2003: see PERFORMATIVITY). In this work, not only are the narrative structure and visual elements of a heritage attraction analysed, but also the impact of the other senses, and the emotional response of the audience and the 'actors' to the site become crucial parts of the analysis. This broadens the discussion beyond the purely visual element of heritage, to focus attention on the whole embodied experience involved in making and participating in a heritage site. While this work is still in its infancy, it is pointing to important new themes that human geographers can address in their analysis of the ever-increasing number of heritage places.   NJ

Suggested reading
Hoelscher (2003); Peckham (2003).

hermeneutics The study of interpretation and meaning. Hermeneutics derives from the Greek word meaning to announce, to clarify or to reveal. In this sense, hermeneutics has always been an integral part of the use of LANGUAGE. The first stirrings of hermeneutics as a formal discipline began with the elucidation of biblical texts: both clarifying God's word, and adjudicating among competing interpretations. By the end of the eighteenth century, with the work of F. Schleiermacher (1768–1834), hermeneutics broadened to include the interpretation of historical texts more generally. In claiming that to understand a TEXT required scrutiny of the intentions of its author, Schleiermacher's hermeneutics implicitly challenged the relevance of the emerging scientific method for the human sciences.

Wilhelm Dilthey's (1833–1911) writings both generalized hermeneutics and made its critique of natural science explicit. He argued that the *human sciences (Geisteswissenschaften)* required a special methodology, hermeneutics, in order to understand the meanings of its objects of study. Those certainly included texts, but under Dilthey's view they could include any entity in which human meaning was invested. In contrast, the *natural sciences (Naturwissenschaften)* were not concerned with human meaning, and consequently applied an abstract universal vocabulary: the laws of physics, chemical formulae and geometrical relations.

For Dilthey, meaning is recovered through practicing the *hermeneutic circle*. By tacking back and forth both between our presuppositions and the text itself, as well as between individual parts of the text and its whole, meaning and understanding are attained. This same procedure can be used to clarify meaning in the non-textual, such as works of art, the artefacts of MATERIAL CULTURE or CULTURAL LANDSCAPES. More generally, the hermeneutic method is intrinsically circular, indeterminate and perspectival. It is circular because it involves a constant movement from us, the interpreter(s), to the interpreted and back again, thereby implying that every interpretation is itself reinterpreted. It is indeterminate because that loop of interpretation has no end. And it is perspectival because interpreters are embedded in their situations, making their knowledge partial and incomplete (cf. SITUATED KNOWLEDGE). None of this means that interpretation is merely personal whim and fancy. Interpretations are always made against a set of socially agreed upon canons and texts (albeit interpreted ones) that are publicly accessible.

In the twentieth century, the German philosopher Martin Heidegger (1889–1976) took Dilthey's epistemological rendering of hermeneutics and transformed it into an ontological one, making its focus 'being' rather than 'knowledge' (cf. EPISTEMOLOGY; ONTOLOGY). The details are complex, but the gist is that problems of understanding unfold from our 'being in the world'. Just as the hermeneutic circle for Dilthey involved tacking between parts of a text and its whole, for Heidegger it involves a movement between an anticipatory pre-understanding, which comes from our 'being-ness'', and our role as knowing subjects. Hans-Georg Gadamer (1900–2002) subsequently took Heidegger's notion of pre-understanding and showed its relation to notions of prejudice, authority and tradition. Since the ENLIGHTENMENT, Gadamer argued, there has been prejudice against prejudice. For him, however, 'pre-judgement', or pre-judice, is what makes understanding possible. In particular, the prejudices of historical 'traditions' are vital; without immersion in traditions, there is no understanding. It is not that traditions are frozen and immutable: Gadamer's point is that we can never escape traditions and the historical perspective that they bring. Historical understanding proceeds by a movement from our prejudices (traditions) to the historical totality and back, making understanding 'an open and continuously renewed "fusion" of "historical horizons"' (Thompson, 1996, p. 381).

Gadamer's work, in turn, provoked two other formulations. First, the German critical theorist Jürgen Habermas (b. 1929) thought that Gadamer made humans too much the dupes of historical tradition. Consequently, he developed a CRITICAL THEORY of SOCIETY by setting hermeneutics against quasi-transcendental forms of 'communicative reason' that in conjunction produce the possibility of emancipation and liberation. Second, American philosophers Richard Rorty (1931–2007) and Richard Bernstein, writing under the sign of neo-PRAGMATISM, were sceptical of Gadamer's claim that hermeneutics was *the* method of the human sciences, but acknowledged its importance for the critique of GRAND THEORY and other forms of FOUNDATIONALISM (thus connecting hermeneutics to POSTSTRUCTURALISM). Both Rorty and Bernstein upheld the pragmatist ideal of 'conversation', which they believed was another version of the hermeneutic circle, in this case, juxtaposing new evidence and ideas with existing and possibly incommensurate ones.

Hermeneutics was introduced to HUMAN GEOGRAPHY to contest the EMPIRICISM and POSITIVISM found in SPATIAL SCIENCE. Buttimer's (1974) 'dialogical approach', which involved bringing together inside and outside views, was an important early contribution, as were Tuan's (1971) reflexive approach to TOPOPHILIA ('to know the world is to know oneself') and Harrison and Livingstone's (1980) 'presuppositional approach'. These early forays were codified under HUMANISTIC GEOGRAPHY, which made human meaning and intentionality the very core of its concern. Since then, the explicit working out of the hermeneutical approach has become less important, although there have been some exceptions, such as Barnes' (2001) invocation in his work on the CULTURAL TURN within ECONOMIC GEOGRAPHY and Livingstone's (2002c) writings on a distinctly 'tropical hermeneutics' (see TROPICALITY). In addition, hermeneutics has been implicitly present in the burgeoning discussions about ONTOLOGY, especially those drawing upon Heidegger, and which in turn have seeped into debates around SPATIALITY. More generally, the spirit of hermeneutical enquiry – that is, the recognition of the importance of interpretation, open-mindedness and a judicious, reflexive sensibility – is as great as it has ever been, and is certainly evident in CRITICAL HUMAN GEOGRAPHY, including those versions informed by POSTSTRUCTURALISM. TB

Suggested reading
Bernstein (1983).

heteronormativity A social regulatory framework that produces binary SEX division, normalizes desire between men and women, and marginalizes other SEXUALITIES as different and deviant. Much like WHITENESS, heteronormativity is naturalized so as to be invisible to the heterosexual population, but is a compulsory norm that itself produces NATURE; namely, BODIES sexed as male or female. Reversing the assumed relations between sex and GENDER, Butler (1990) has argued that heteronormativity is the foundation on which sexual difference is built. Predicated on the paternal law of kinship, heteronormativity 'requires conformity to its own notions of "nature" and gains its legitimacy through the binary and asymmetrical naturalization of bodies' (Butler, 1990, p. 106: see PERFORMATIVITY). Bodies outside this binary are unintelligible or monstrous. Berlant has argued that in the USA in the past 20 years, the political has collapsed into the intimate sphere of the heterosexual family, such that 'the family sphere [is] considered the moral, ethical, and the political horizon of national and political interest' (1997, p. 262); this has led to the intensified regulation of heteronormativity. Honig (1998) cites the role of IMMIGRATION in reinforcing heteronormativity. Geographers have drawn attention to the many ways in which SPACE is bound up with the processes through which sexual identities are constructed, naturalized and contested, and to the need to study the particularity of heterosexualities in specific contexts (Hubbard, 2000). 'Homonormativity' has been identified as a new strand of heteronormativity. It is a politics that emerged in the 1990s, associated with state-sanctioned same-sex marriages and other rights for gays and lesbians, and it has been criticized for upholding, rather than contesting, dominant heteronormative assumptions and institutions. The GLOBALIZATION of this trend has led to criticisms of Western cultural IMPERIALISM; Oswin (2007) questions the geographical assumption that lies behind this critique – that of the DIFFUSION of ideas from Western to other societies – and argues for the need to assess the specificity of homonormativity in context. GP

Suggested reading
Hubbard (2000).

heterotopia Literally 'another place' or 'place of otherness', a term introduced into the HUMANITIES and social sciences by French thinker Michel Foucault (1926–84). Foucault borrowed the term from medicine, and uses it in opposition to utopia. While UTOPIAS – idealized happy places – do not really exist, but function as fantasies or spaces of hope, heterotopias for Foucault are places that do exist. But in their existing they radically undermine or challenge existing spatial orderings, they disturb, they are PLACES of TRANSGRESSION or OTHERNESS.

Foucault initially uses the term to describe linguistic or visual challenges, such as the writings of José Luis Borges or the paintings of René Magritte (Foucault, 1970 [1966], 1983). For Foucault these examples destroy 'syntax' – not just the syntax we use to make sentences, but also the syntax that constructs relations between words and things and allows classification and order. Borges' fictional Chinese Encyclopaedia, with its outlandish categories, and Magritte's shoes with toes, paintings that are part of the landscape that they portray and mirrors that reflect what they conceal, all disrupt and upset the commonplace. In a 1967 lecture, only published in French in 1984, shortly before his death (in English, see Foucault, 1986), Foucault broadened the analysis to include places he described as 'counter-sites, kinds of effectively enacted utopias'. Although Foucault suggests that in the modern period space is characterized by the relation between sites generally, he concentrates on those sites that link with and contradict other sites. His examples include the boarding school or the honeymoon hotel, where transitions between stages of life are managed; care homes, hospitals and PRISONS, where deviation is placed; and a wealth of other examples, such as travelling fairgrounds, hammams, saunas, brothels, boats and colonies.

The term has been developed in a number of English-language writings in human geography and related fields (e.g. Marks, 1995; Soja 1996b). One of the most important and original analyses is found in the work of Hetherington (1997b), who understands heterotopias as 'spaces of an alternative ordering' that must be seen in relation to the sites they differ from. He uses this understanding, together with a number of historical readings of the Palais Royal, Masonic lodges and factories, to illustrate how MODERNITY is constituted through RESISTANCE and DIFFERENCE as much as through the process of ordering.

'Heterotopia' was also used by the French Marxist Henri Lefebvre (1901–91), but the meanings are not entirely congruent with Foucault (see, e.g., Lefebvre, 2003 [1970]). Lefebvre understood the city through the three terms of *utopia*, *isotopia* (the same place) and *heterotopia* (places that are other, other places, or places of the other). He uses these terms to understand the uniformity, difference, contradictions and dialectical relations of urban space. Indeed, Lefebvre thinks that urban space in the singular is restrictive, and needs to be understood as urban spaces, as the differentiated spaces and the spaces of difference found in the city (see also PRODUCTION OF SPACE). SE

Suggested reading
Foucault (1986); Hetherington (1997b, Ch. 3).

heuristic A problem-solving procedure, which may be a set of formal rules (such as an algorithm) but more likely a pragmatic or 'short-cut' approach, such as drawing a diagram or reducing the set of all possible solutions to those that seem most probable. Many heuristics involve 'intelligent guesswork' based on experience (as in games of chess) and can involve trial-and-error procedures, moving towards a 'better' solution (as with NEURAL NETWORKS). Heuristics are often deployed in OPTIMIZATION studies – as with the travelling-salesman problem – and in various forms of CLASSIFICATION (as in REMOTE SENSING).   RJ

Suggested reading
Gigerenzer and Todd (1999).

Hindutva This concept encapsulates the cultural justification for Hindu NATIONALISM, a 'Hinduness' allegedly shared by all Hindus. Its first full articulation as a Hindu nationalist manifesto was made by Vinayak Damodar Savarkar in his 1923 work *Hindutva/Who is a Hindu?* For Savarkar, *Hindutva* was the life of a great RACE; it signified the religious, cultural and racial ('blood') IDENTITY of Hindus. He claimed that the membership of the Hindu NATION depended upon an acceptance of India as both fatherland and holy land. The spatial strategies of *Hindutva*, aimed at rearticulating the link between the imagined community of Hindus and the sacred geography of its territorial domain (the nation-space), have had a significant impact on contemporary Indian society and politics.   SCH

Suggested reading
Sharma (2003).

hinterland The tributary (or catchment) area of a port, from which materials for export are collected and across which imports are distributed: its complementary area – the destination for the exports and source of the imports – is the *foreland*. In more general usage, hinterland is deployed to describe a settlement's catchment area (or that of an establishment within the settlement): it is the area for which the settlement acts as a trading nexus (as in the hexagonal hinterlands of CENTRAL PLACE THEORY).   RJ

historical demography The application of demographic methods (see DEMOGRAPHY) to data sets from the past that are sufficiently accurate for formal analysis. Such data sets may take the form of vital records and CENSUSES, but most frequently, and particularly if produced before the nineteenth century, would not have been created for the purposes of demographic enquiry. Parish registers, militia and tax lists, testamentary records and genealogies have been the most prominent among the great variety of documentary sources used by historical demographers (see Hollingsworth, 1969). *Demographic history* may subsume historical demography as a field of enquiry, but it is more wide-ranging in its subject matter, being just as concerned with charting the impact of demographic change on society and economy as with the measurement and explanation of demographic change (see Wrigley, 1969).

Historical demography first secured a formal status in France at the Institut National d'Études Démographique (INED), where Louis Henry had begun research after the Second World War on contemporary FERTILITY and FECUNDITY. His investigations were handicapped because those STATES that produced the most accurate demographic statistics were by then all controlling their fertility by family limitation, and so he was drawn to the historical study of European populations to unravel 'natural fertility'. Henry (1956) devised the technique of FAMILY RECONSTITUTION for exploiting genealogies of the Genevan bourgeoisie, and then developed detailed rules of family reconstitution using parish registers. The first published study concerned the Normandy parish of Crulai (Gautier and Henry, 1958), but the method was quickly adapted and modified for work on English parish registers by historical geographer and economic historian E.A. Wrigley (1966a). Wrigley (1966b) undertook a reconstitution of the East Devon parish of Colyton, where the population appeared to have been limiting its fertility in the late seventeenth century.

In the past thirty years, a large number of reconstitution studies have been completed and they have shown little, if any, evidence of parity-dependent fertility control, although the levels of fertility within marriage have varied enormously by region. For instance, marital fertility in Belgian Flanders was 40 per cent higher than that of eighteenth-century England, although the two regions were separated by only a few miles across the English Channel. Likewise, marital fertility was almost 50 per cent higher in Bavaria than in East Friesland. By measuring birth intervals and relating infant deaths to the time elapsed to new conceptions, family reconstitution has enabled historical demographers to show that breastfeeding practices varied greatly and thereby influenced the tempo of conceptions (see Wilson, 1982). Breastfeeding also correlated closely with infant mortality rates, which were also revealed by family reconstitutions to be very frequently in excess of 300 per 1,000 in non-breastfeeding areas and as modest, by pre-industrial standards, as 150 per 1,000 or lower in areas where women breast-fed well into the second year of the child's life (see Knodel, 1988). Such techniques have also made it possible to cast light on the geography of marriage and to test an important thesis about the distinctiveness of marriage patterns in north-west Europe proposed by Hajnal (1965), who argued that females married uniquely late in life and that a large proportion remained entirely out of marriage. Hajnal discovered this pattern from census data of the nineteenth century, and family reconstitutions of France and England, southern Scandinavia and much of the German-speaking areas of Western and Central Europe showed this marital geography to have been firmly embedded before 1600 and hence not derived from URBANIZATION or INDUSTRIALIZATION, and common to both Protestant and Catholic areas (Smith, 1990).

The Cambridge Group for the History of Population was the first centre of research exclusively devoted to historical demography, and it developed techniques for the study of early censuses and aggregative counts of baptisms, burials and marriages to recreate demographic processes without employing the time-consuming method of family reconstitution. One such technique – generalized inverse projection – is a technique that projects back from a census providing accurate data on age structures and so making it possible to obtain age structures, population sizes, EMIGRATION rates, and measurements of fertility and life expectancy. This technique was first applied to English data and showed that fertility changes were considerably more important in determining demographic growth rates from c.1600, and to some extent endorsed the more optimistic view of Malthus as presented in the second edition of his *Essay* (Wrigley and Schofield, 1989 [1981]; see MALTHUSIAN MODEL). As research by historical demographers accumulated, it became apparent that eighteenth- and nineteenth-century European demographic patterns, even in the area of the so-called north-west European marriage and household formation systems, varied greatly (see Wrigley, 1981). Furthermore the extension of formal historical demographic enquiry to ASIA, utilizing early listings of inhabitants and population registers, has cast doubt on the assumed uniqueness of certain features frequently supposed to be peculiar to historic EUROPE (Lee and Feng, 1999). RMS

Suggested reading
Hajnal (1965); Smith (1990); Wrigley and Schofield (1989 [1981]).

historical geography A sub-discipline of HUMAN GEOGRAPHY concerned with the geographies of the past and with the influence of the past in shaping the geographies of the present and the future. Before the twentieth century, the term 'historical geography' was used to describe at least three distinct intellectual endeavours: the recreation of the geographies described in the Bible and in 'classical' Greek and Roman narratives; the 'geography behind history' as revealed by the changing FRONTIERS and BORDERS of STATES and EMPIRES; and the history of EXPLORATION and discovery (Butlin, 1993, pp. 1–23). Fragmented and incoherent, these early writings had little impact on contemporary historical geography, whose intellectual roots can be traced to the late-nineteenth-century writings on regional landscape formation by French geographers such as Paul Vidal de la Blache (whose influence spread into Britain through the work of H.J. Fleure and A.J. Herbertson) and by the German school of ANTHROPOGEOGRAPHY led by Friedrich Ratzel (a perspective successfully promoted in the USA by Ellen Semple).

Historical research on LANDSCAPE change received a powerful stimulus after the First World War, when the reorganization of national boundaries in EUROPE and the creation of new ones in the MIDDLE EAST re-focused attention on regional landscapes as products of long-term economic, social and political evolution that could be analysed by the scientific interrogation of archaeological and historical evidence. The study of landscape change varied in different national contexts and was by no means always described by the term 'historical geography'. Continental European research on regional, especially rural, landscape change continued without embracing a new disciplinary terminology. In inter-war France, the ANNALES SCHOOL produced a body of interdisciplinary research that might reasonably be described as historical geography, but that is more usually regarded as a distinctively French style of History. Likewise, in Germany, historical research on rural settlement change was generally seen as continuing an existing tradition of research on the CULTURAL LANDSCAPE rather than blazing a new trail in historical geography.

The situation was different in the UK, where the term 'historical geography' was deployed more frequently under the charismatic influence of H.C. Darby. Darby's vision of historical geography exhibited many similarities with research carried out simultaneously on the history of the English landscape by social and economic historians W.G. Hoskins and Maurice Beresford, but it was distinguished by its emphasis on CARTOGRAPHY as a means to both interrogate and display the archive: by the use of historical sources to construct visually impressive and typically thematic MAPS. According to Darby, historical geography was a fundamentally geographical endeavour, one of the 'twin pillars' of the larger discipline, alongside geomorphology (Darby, 2002). Geomorphology and historical geography were both concerned with landscape formation and evolution, Darby argued, the former based primarily on field evidence derived directly from the natural environment and the latter on historical evidence gleaned indirectly from archival sources. Darby placed a special emphasis on the reconstruction of geographical patterns as cartographic cross-sections, exemplified by his seven-volume reconstruction of the human geography of medieval England, published with a series of collaborators and based on tabulations in the Domesday Book (Darby, 1977). He sought to link such cross-sections into larger sequences of landscape change (VERTICAL THEMES), encapsulated in his work on the changing fenland landscapes of eastern England (Darby, 1940).

Darby's version of historical geography spread to other parts of the English-speaking world, but the study of regional landscape change in the USA developed along distinctive lines under the influence of Carl Ortwin Sauer, doyen of the BERKELEY SCHOOL of CULTURAL GEOGRAPHY. Sauer wrote enthusiastically about historical geography, but his own work is more commonly described as cultural or cultural–historical geography, in accordance with his interest in anthropological and archaeological evidence, following in some part the German tradition of *Landschaft* research. In Sauer's view, this was a more appropriate model for the study of long-term landscape change in the New World, where the SCALE of analysis was necessarily larger (so he claimed) and where written evidence was non-existent before European colonization. It is important to note, however, that some of the most successful 'big-picture' accounts of US history since Columbus have been written by American historical geographers working outside the Sauerian tradition (notably Earle, 2003; Meinig, 1986–2004), and that a number of historical geographers studying the interrelations between European conquest and native peoples have excavated archaeological and palaeo-environmental records and attended to oral traditions in ways that could not have been anticipated by Sauer.

The diffusion of SPATIAL SCIENCE in the 1960s and 1970s challenged many of the assumptions and practices of traditional historical geography, particularly the source-determined, cross-sectional studies that, through their disregard of social theory and their inattention to social process, seemed to have little purchase on the analysis of subsequent geographical structures. A lively debate ensued, some of it conducted in the pages of the *Journal of Historical Geography*, which was established in 1975. Several different kinds of historical enquiry emerged within human geography as a consequence of this period of rethinking and reformulation.

The first was advocated by those historical geographers who had become critical of their field's source-bound EMPIRICISM, and who now welcomed a METHODOLOGY that allowed historical data to be incorporated into more complex models of geographical change (Baker, 2003, pp. 37–71). The result was a more quantitative historical geography that had been anticipated by Torsten Hägerstrand's early studies of DIFFUSION and of 'population archaeology' that issued in his TIME-GEOGRAPHY; both left enduring legacies (Pred, 1973; Dodgshon, 1998). Statistically minded historical geographers also became centrally involved in the field of HISTORICAL DEMOGRAPHY, particularly in Britain, where E.A. Wrigley was a dominant influence (Wrigley and Schofield, 1989 [1981]). In Wrigley's case, this involved an institutional move from geography to economic and social history, a well-trodden and often two-way career path. These interdisciplinary exchanges explain why some of the most important research on Britain's agricultural history has been published by scholars trained as historical geographers (Campbell and Bartley, 2006; Overton, 1996: see also AGRICULTURAL REVOLUTION; FIELD SYSTEMS). The significance of quantitative historical research within human geography is also attested by highly sophisticated studies of historical EPIDEMIOLOGY and disease diffusion, consistently identified by their authors as historical geography (e.g. Smallman-Raynor and Cliff, 2004). The emerging field of historical GEOGRAPHICAL INFORMATION SCIENCE confirms the continuing strength of the enumerative tendency within historical geography (Gregory and Ell, 2007).

Other historical geographers, particularly those who had familiarized themselves with previously unexplored literatures in CRITICAL

THEORY and SOCIAL THEORY, were less convinced by the claims made by spatial science. Some of the original advocates of a quantitative approach also shifted their position and ultimately rejected the philosophical assumptions derived from POSITIVISM that underwrote spatial science. From their perspective, statistical explanation lacked the capacity for ethical or political critique and failed to acknowledge HUMAN AGENCY, intentionality and emotion (Harris, 1971; Gregory, 1981). Traditional forms of historical geography could scarcely claim a better track record, of course, so the solution was not to defend existing methods but, rather, to create a critical, theoretically informed historical geography within a new, historically sensitive human geography.

For some, this demanded a more direct engagement with HISTORICAL MATERIALISM and a sustained analysis of the deeper economic, social and political forces determining geographical change, an approach that was strongly influenced by developments in social and economic history in general and the work of E.P. Thompson in particular (e.g. Gregory, 1982). The same concerns can be detected in other work on urbanization and the INDUSTRIAL REVOLUTION in Britain (Langton, 1979, 1984; Gregory, 1982; Dennis, 1984) and in more synoptic works such as Harvey's extended (1985) essay on nineteenth-century Paris (see also Harvey, 2003a). Since the mid-1980s, new historical geographies of SPACE, POWER and the social order have extended this style of historical research, inspired by other developments in social theory more critical of HISTORICAL MATERIALISM, notably STRUCTURATION THEORY, and a series of formulations that are conventionally identified as POST-STRUCTURALISM, notably the work of Michel Foucault (Driver, 1993; Ogborn, 1998; Hannah, 2000; Philo, 2004). Perhaps the most ambitious attempt to connect these diverse post-positivist thematics into an agenda for historical geography was Harris' programmatic essay on MODERNITY (Harris, 1991).

A somewhat different style of historical investigation arose from a second attack on spatial science. This sought to reconnect geography with a wider range of disciplines in the arts and HUMANITIES, based in part on HERMENEUTICS. While sympathetic to historical forms of geographical enquiry, the leading advocates of a broadly HUMANISTIC GEOGRAPHY refused to privilege the past as arena of investigation and therefore tended to define their work as (new) cultural geography allied to (comparative) literature, cultural studies and the visual arts rather than history. The CULTURAL LANDSCAPE has been the central preoccupation of this form of historical enquiry, which has generated a rich geographical literature, including several theoretically ambitious attempts to uncover the origins and development of landscape as social and political construction and as a way of envisioning and representing space, a project far removed from the way in which landscape was apprehended in traditional historical geography (Cosgrove, 1993; Cosgrove and Daniels, 1988; Duncan, 1990; Daniels, 1999). Investigations into the relationship between landscape, HERITAGE and TOURISM generate continuing interest (Graham, Ashworth and Tunbridge, 2000), as does the relationship between landscape and MEMORY (Johnson, 2003b), while research on twentieth-century debates about landscape, IDENTITY and social practice has been especially influential (Matless, 1998). There have also been important historical studies of cultures of travel and TRAVEL WRITING that pay close attention to the texts and the images that accompanied them (Schwartz and Ryan, 2003) and, moving historical geography still further from the seemingly obdurate physicality of landscapes, studies of ways in which the very technologies of writing were caught up in the transmission of power (Ogborn, 2007).

These distinct forms of historical research in geography, always closely related, have effectively merged in the past two decades (Graham and Nash, 1999; Withers and Ogborn, 2004). The single, hybrid term 'cultural–historical geography', originating in North America and in some measure a legacy of the Berkeley School, is now widely deployed to describe a different style of research in which three closely related themes have animated recent discussions. The study of IMPERIALISM and COLONIALISM has grown steadily more important. This has shifted the focus of historical research in geography away from the global NORTH, although the constellations of Euro-American EMPIRE, HEGEMONY and power continue to cast long shadows over many of these studies, in both their theoretical form and historical substance. This work has revealed how landscapes, identities and values in the core regions and in the colonized territories of AFRICA, the AMERICAS and ASIA were fashioned by a process of imperial interaction and TRANSCULTURATION involving the circulation of people and practices, objects and ideas on a global scale (Harris, 1997; Driver and Gilbert, 1999a; Clayton, 2000; Lester, 2001; Lambert,

2005; Legg, 2007b; Ogborn, 2007). These studies have involved a close and critical engagement with various forms of POST-COLONIALISM.

The colonial project was largely concerned with the acquisition and exploitation of NATURAL RESOURCES, and much of the new work on historical geographies of colonialism has focused on its environmental consequences. This is scarcely an unheralded development (Clark, 1949; Powell, 1988; Williams, 1989; Donkin, 1999), since the relationship between ENVIRONMENTAL HISTORY and historical geography has always been extremely close, particularly in the USA (Williams, 1994a). However, recent ENVIRONMENTALISM has generated a more politically charged historical geography that has explored the impact of natural resource exploitation on regional and urban development (Cronon, 1991), and which includes explicitly Marxist historical geographies on the interactions of CLASS, RACE and the physical environment in industrializing regions (Mitchell, 1996; Walker, 2001).

Western SCIENCE, including the science of geography, was directly implicated in the processes of agricultural and industrial transformation, urbanization and imperial expansion that historical geographers have increasingly investigated. This has prompted a renewed interest in the critical history of POST-ENLIGHTENMENT geographical and environmental thought (Livingstone, 1992; Grove, 1995). Inspired in part by the writings of the literary critic Edward Said, this work has emphasized the constitutive significance of geographical knowledge in the creation of national and imperial IDENTITIES (Smith and Godlewska, 1994; Bell, Butlin and Heffernan, 1995; Driver, 2001a; Withers, 2001: see also ORIENTALISM). It has also reconnected historical geography with the history of cartography (see CARTOGRAPHY, HISTORY OF), particularly through the seminal work of historical geographer J. Brian Harley (Harley, 2001b).

No single methodological or philosophical orthodoxy has prevailed since the 1970s, and historical geography has become increasingly eclectic. This demonstrates the growing influence of perspectives from allied disciplines but is also evidence of a wider 'historicization' of human geography that has partially compromised historical geography's status as a distinctive sub-discipline (Driver, 1988). This has generated some unease about sub-disciplinary identity, notably in the debate about the legitimacy of the terms 'historical geography' and 'geographical history' (Baker, 2007). But for all its thematic diversity, twenty-first-century historical geography has become increasingly focused on the (relatively) recent past, a trend partly determined by the need for reliable, spatially extensive data, but also influenced by the INSTRUMENTALIST assumption that historical research should have immediate relevance to contemporary issues (Jones, 2004b). That said, its continued vigour is demonstrated in the pages of the *Journal of Historical Geography* and in the steady stream of innovative work in historical geography that also appears in the pages of mainstream journals inside and, crucially, outside geography. MH

Suggested reading
Baker (2003); Butlin (1993); Harris (1991); Morrissey, Whelan and Yeoh (2008).

historical materialism The materialist conception of history, formulated by Karl Marx (1818–83) with Friedrich Engels (1820–95), and the 'guiding thread' of their joint work (see also MARXISM). Historical materialism is a theory of history incorporating a series of bold theses about the dynamics of historical change, most succinctly summarized in the 1859 'Preface' to 'A Contribution to the Critique of Political Economy'.

Social development is driven by progress in meeting social needs through the development of *productive forces* (means of production and labour power). In the process of production, men and women necessarily enter into certain *social relations of production*. These include both work relations (technical relations and forms of co-operation) and forms of ownership and control of the means of production, which are at the root of *class formation*. The totality of the relations of production constitutes the *economic structure* of society, "the real foundation, on which arises a legal and political *superstructure* and to which correspond definite forms of social consciousness'. The economic base and superstructure together constitute the *mode of production* of a society. (See also BASE AND SUPERSTRUCTURE.)

Each MODE OF PRODUCTION is subject to internal tensions and contradictions (see DIALECTIC). Thus, at a certain stage of their development, the material productive forces of society come into conflict with the dominant relations of production, which reflect entrenched forms of PROPERTY ownership and CLASS relations. The relations of production increasingly become fetters on the further development of the productive forces. 'Then begins an era of social revolution', transforming the economic structure, and with it the whole

335

immense superstructure, its institutions and forms of consciousness. In illustrating this theory of contradiction and change, Marx refers variously to the ancient, Asiatic, feudal and CAPITALIST modes of production.

The theory outlined in the 1859 Preface appears disarmingly simple, and has tended to be downplayed by Marxists who find it too close to a form of economic, or even technological, determinism. Nevertheless, Cohen (1978) has shown how it can be given a rigorous and sophisticated modern defence if one is prepared to accept the validity of functionalist forms of explanation (see FUNCTIONALISM). Wright, Levine and Sober (1992) have also shown how the basic argument for economic primacy can be disaggregated into at least six linked sub-theses, not all of which are asserted with equal force in Marx's many writings, and some of which are more defensible than others. It is thus possible to extract both 'strong' and 'weak' versions of historical materialism from Marx's writings, with the latter placing more emphasis on the role of class conflict in social change, the role of the superstructure in shaping and reacting back on the economic base, and the role of contingent factors in opening up different historical trajectories.

Adding a spatial dimension to historical materialism brings further complexities. Giddens, for example, attempted to purge historical materialism of any evolutionary, functionalist, or reductionist tendencies, and his STRUCTURATION THEORY incorporated spatial concepts such as 'time–space edges' and TIME–SPACE DISTANCIATION into what he described as a weaker 'anti-evolutionary, episodic model of social change' (Giddens, 1981). However, the work of geographer David Harvey represents the most sustained and systematic attempt to incorporate space into a more general 'historical–geographical materialism' (see, centrally, Harvey, 1999 [1982]; also Castree and Gregory, 2006), and his study of nineteenth-century Paris demonstrates what can be achieved if such a framework is used subtly and flexibly as a guiding thread for research (Harvey, 2003a).   KB

Suggested reading
Bassett (2005); Shaw (1978).

historicism Historicism has two meanings: (i) intellectual traditions that assume human history to have an inner logic, overall design or direction (a 'telos'); and (ii) critical traditions that insist on the importance of specific historical contexts to the interpretation of cultural texts and practices.

Historicism in the first sense invokes transhistorical forces to structure its explanations of human 'progress' (most visibly in the movement of the world-spirit, or *Geist*, in G.W.F. Hegel's philosophical history). The appeal of TELEOLOGY – of 'unfolding' models of social change – is now much diminished, and few scholars would see human history as predictable and susceptible to the formulation of universal scientific laws. When Karl Popper famously railed against the 'poverty of historicism' in this sense, he had a reading of Marxism as economic determinism in his sights, but subsequent versions of HISTORICAL MATERIALISM have offered a much more openended view of human history and the spaces for political action (Popper, 1960 [1945]).

The second sense of historicism is much more important to contemporary social enquiry. Historical context and historical specificity are articles of faith in HISTORICAL GEOGRAPHY, and while they were undermined by SPATIAL SCIENCE in the 1960s and 1970s, the emergence of a cultural–historical geography with a critical edge brought a closer, if largely tacit, engagement with a so-called '*New Historicism*' – an approach to literary and cultural studies that originated in the USA in the 1980s (Gallagher and Greenblatt, 2001). Among the sources on which it draws, three are particularly important for human geography:

(1) the THICK DESCRIPTION of anthropologist Clifford Geertz, which underwrites the importance of a close reading of minor events in such a way that they reveal the larger situations of which they are a part and to which they can be made to speak;

(2) the GENEALOGY of philosopher–historian Michel Foucault, which resists 'POWER's descriptions of itself' by looking to the margins and the peripheries of situations; and

(3) the CULTURAL MATERIALISM of cultural critic Raymond William, which emphasizes the materiality of cultural formations and their contradictory constitution.

New Historicism has influenced studies of colonial DISCOURSE in POST-COLONIALISM and has much in common with work in CULTURAL GEOGRAPHY and the 'contextual approach' to the history of geography (see GEOGRAPHY, HISTORY OF). It should be noted that when Soja (1989, 1996b) objects to 'historicism', he has in mind an over-valuation of historical explanation and a marginalization of a 'spatial imagination'; but there are many practitioners of New Historicism who have no problem in attending to both the historicity and the SPATIALITY of their objects of enquiry.   DG

Suggested reading
Hamilton (1996).

history of geography See GEOGRAPHY, HISTORY OF

holocaust   Most generally, the systematic deaths of large numbers of people, but most specifically the campaign of GENOCIDE pursued by Hitler's Third Reich during the Second World War (1939–45) and identified by its initial capital: the Holocaust. Both usages depend on political and cultural processes of distinction and exclusion (see RACISM) and a studied indifference to the suffering of those construed as radically 'Other' (see BARE LIFE). Thus Thornton (1990) and Stannard (1992) connect European COLONIALISM to the mass destruction of indigenous societies in the AMERICAS, Davis (2002) identifies a series of late-nineteenth-century famines across the global South as a 'cultural genocide' brought about by the logics of imperial power and free trade, and all historians of the Nazi genocide acknowledge its roots in a racial fantasy of 'Aryan' supremacy and a profound anti-Semitism (see also FASCISM).

The Nazis did not confine their predations to Jews. They also systematically murdered millions of non-Jewish Soviet and Polish citizens, hundreds of thousands of Roma and Sinti (Gypsies), mentally and physically disabled people, gay men, religious dissidents and political opponents, including trades unionists, communists and socialists; the first concentration CAMP that the Nazis established at Dachau in 1933 was for political prisoners. But the (capitalized) Holocaust is increasingly and usually reserved for their concerted murder of approximately 6 million European Jews who died through malnutrition, medical experimentation and slave labour in concentration camps, who were shot or gassed by mobile killing units, or who were killed in gas chambers. This particular usage is problematic, however: in its original Greek form, 'holocaust' denoted sacrifice by fire, and while these spiritual connotations may resonate with the role Christianity played in legitimizing the deaths visited on indigenous peoples by European colonialism, their inappropriateness to describe the mass murder of European Jews has prompted many scholars to prefer the Hebrew *Shoah* ('catastrophe') (though this in turn may evoke the biblical sense of retribution found in the book of Isaiah).

Whichever term is preferred, Cole and Smith (1995, p. 30) identified the Nazi Holocaust as 'the most remarkable blank-spot in geographical research'. It is strange that it should have attracted so little analytical attention, even by Israeli historical geographers, not merely because the Holocaust 'had' a geography – it was distributed over space and varied from place to place (Gilbert, 2009) – but more fundamentally because GEOGRAPHY as both discipline and knowledge was central to the project (Charlesworth, 1992):

(1)   Particular conceptions of SPACE and spacing were indispensable to the conception of the Nazi Holocaust. Clark, Doel and McDonough (1996) identify two crucial spatial templates. The first was developed through a racist version of *GEOPOLITIK* that asserted the right to an expanded *LEBENSRAUM* for the master-race, but such a project for 'mastery of concrete, de-populated, physical space' was inseparable from a second spacing, *Entfernung*: 'an effective removal of the Jews from the life-world of the German race' (Bauman, 1991, p. 120). To these three writers, Bauman's cardinal contribution was 'his recognition of the rupturing of the imaginary social space of the Reich by the diasporic space of the Jews'. The non-national space of the DIASPORA was 'a wholly Other conception of social space', they argue, a fundamental contradiction to the project of National Socialism and its territorial inscription of the 'Aryan' Same: in short, 'a void' (Clarke, Doel and McDonough, 1996, pp. 474–5; see also Doel and Clarke, 1998).

(2)   The realization of *Lebensraum* and *Entfernung* entailed at once a de-territorialization of physical space and its re-territorialization as social space. This involved the conjoint production of a series of physical and social spaces (a) from which Jews were excluded, (b) within which they were gathered and sequestered, and (c) through which they were subsequently transported to the camps. These spatial strategies – which might be thought of as 'a series of concentric circles that, like waves, incessantly wash up against a central non-place' (Agamben, 1999, pp. 51–2) – produced a

vast genocidal archipelago (figure 1, page 339) and can in some measure be mapped on to Hilberg's (2003 [1961]) four-stage model of the Holocaust: deprivation; expulsion; segregation; annihilation. Friedlander (1997, 2007) reworked these stages as follows (the examples given are illustrative, not exhaustive):

- *Persecution (1933–9)*: the rights of German Jews were increasingly restricted, and in 1935 they were stripped of their citizenship; they were also subject to physical attacks and, from March 1938, many were imprisoned in concentration camps at Dachau, Sachsenhausen and Buchenwald.
- *Terror (autumn 1939 to summer 1941)*: Polish Jews were confined to GHETTOES and subjected to extraordinary deprivation, and as the Reich expanded, the number of concentration camps multiplied and the use of forced labour intensified.
- *Mass murder (summer 1941 to summer 1942)*: from October 1941, German Jews were deported to the occupied eastern territories; 33,700 Kiev Jews were shot in the Babi Yar ravine outside the city, and around 27,000 Jews were taken from the Riga ghetto and shot.
- *Shoah (summer 1942 to spring 1945)*: in 1942, six concentration camps in occupied Poland – Auschwitz/Birkenau, Belzec, Chelmno, Majdanek, Sobibor and Treblinka – were designated as extermination camps, dedicated to the so-called 'Final Solution' of the 'Jewish Question', and gas chambers were used for mass killing: Jews throughout occupied Europe were arrested, deported to transit camps, and then sent to the extermination camps.

It is crucial to understand that these phases, and their correlative spaces, cannot be contained by a narrative of German policies and actions: as Friedlander (2007, p. xv) insists, 'at each step in occupied Europe the execution of German measures depended on the submissiveness of political authorities, the assistance of local police forces or other auxiliaries, and the passivity or support of the population and mainly of the political and spiritual elites'.

(3) The planning and execution of the Holocaust thus relied on extensive geographical knowledge. The Reich Foundation for Geographical Studies was instrumental in the ethnic profiling and mapping of occupied territories, particularly in eastern Europe, while Walter Christaller, the architect of CENTRAL PLACE THEORY, was closely involved in developing the *Generalplan Ost* for the east of Poland. This vast region was under direct SS administration and was to be a laboratory for a new territorial order (figure 2, page 340): Germans were to 'resettle' the area, Poles reduced to slave labour, and Jews deported to the ghetto in Lodz and ultimately to the death camps (Rössler, 1989, 2001).

As the previous citations indicate, in recent years several geographers have concerned themselves with philosophical and historiographical issues surrounding the Nazi Holocaust, but there have also been substantive studies of the enforced production of Jewish GHETTOES (Cole and Smith, 1995; Cole, 2000) and of the role of LANDSCAPE in the work of MEMORY and memorialization (Charlesworth, 1994, 2004). All of these enquiries raise profound questions about REPRESENTATION and the capacity of language to render the experience of such extreme trauma (Friedlander, 1992; Agamben, 1999; LaCapra, 2000; Waxman, 2006). These have engaged the attention of geographers too, but the analysis of the Holocaust is necessarily both an interdisciplinary and a comparative project, and the United States Holocaust Memorial Museum publishes a journal dedicated to these issues: *Holocaust and Genocide Studies*.

The Nazi genocide continues to cast long shadows over the present. It has prompted politico-intellectual campaigns against both those who deny it and those who exploit it: to fight 'for the integrity of the historical record', as Finkelstein (2000, p. 8) puts it. The Holocaust materially affects political debates, policies and practices in Germany, Israel and the MIDDLE EAST. And it still troubles continental European PHILOSOPHY and SOCIAL THEORY, not least in their understandings of MODERNITY and the very possibility of critical enquiry. Indeed, Agamben (1998, 1999) sees the Nazi concentration camp as paradigmatic of political modernity:

Auschwitz is precisely the place in which the state of exception coincides perfectly with the rule and the extreme situation becomes the very paradigm of daily life ... As long as the state of EXCEPTION and the normal situation

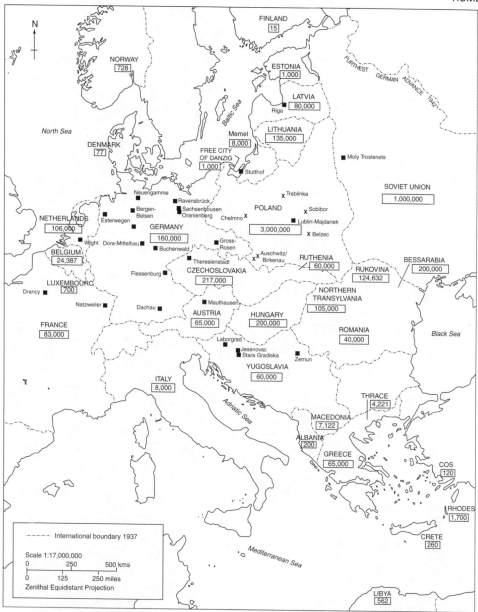

holocaust *1: The main concentration camps and estimates of the numbers murdered from each country* (from Dear, 1995)

are kept separate in space and time, as is usually the case, both remain opaque, though they secretly institute each other. But as soon as they show their complicity, as happens more and more often today, they illuminate each other ... (Agamben, 1999, pp. 49–50)

Given the spatial foundations of this state of EXCEPTION, the Nazi Holocaust should surely trouble geography too. **DG**

Suggested reading
Clare, Doel and McDonough (1996); Friedlander (2007). See also the Israeli Holocaust Museum at http://www.yadvashem.org.il and the United States Holocaust Memorial Museum at http://www.ushmm.org.

home An emotive place and spatial imaginary that encompasses lived experiences of everyday, domestic life alongside a wider

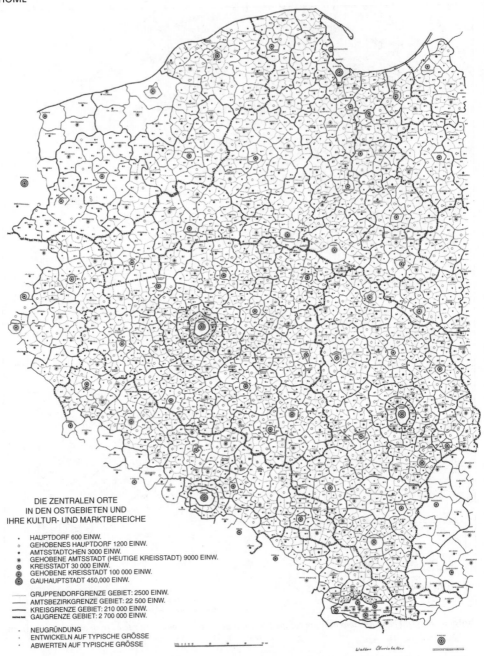

holocaust *2: Central place theory and the Generalplan Ost*

sense of being and belonging in the world. As a space of belonging and ALIENATION, intimacy and VIOLENCE, desire and fear, the home is invested with emotions, experiences, practices and relationships that lie at the heart of human life (see EMOTIONAL GEOGRAPHIES). Geographies of home span MEMORY and nostalgia for the past, EVERYDAY LIFE in the present, and future dreams and fears, and are imagined and materialized on SCALES from the domestic to the global (Blunt and Dowling, 2006). Through its internal intimacies and connections with the wider world, the home is 'perhaps the most emotive of geographical

340

concepts, inextricable from that of self, family, nation, sense of place, and sense of responsibility toward those who share one's place in the world' (Duncan and Lambert, 2004, p. 395). Although home might take the material form of a house or other shelter, it extends far beyond a material dwelling, the household and the domestic. Rather than viewing the home as a private sphere that is separate from the public world of work, CITIZENSHIP and politics, a wide range of research in historical and contemporary contexts has explored the importance of paid and unpaid work within the home, the ways in which home-making practices are tied to ideas about citizenship, and the political significance of the home and DOMESTICITY (see DOMESTIC LABOUR; PRIVATE AND PUBLIC SPHERES).

The home has long been part of a GEOGRAPHICAL IMAGINATION, as shown by early research on CULTURAL HEARTHS and the DIFFUSION of different house styles. More recently, humanistic, feminist and post-colonial geographers have been particularly influential in studying the home. *Humanistic geographers* have written eloquently about the home as a site of authentic meaning, value and experience, imbued with nostalgic memories and the love of place. In the 1970s and 1980s, humanistic geographers, in contrast to the abstractions of spatial science and inspired by the phenomenological work of Gaston Bachelard (1994 [1958]), described the home as a personal, intimate and poetical place. For Bachelard, 'a home, even though its physical properties can be described to an extent, is not a physical entity but an *orientation* to the fundamental values ... with which a home, as an intimate space in the universe, is linked to human nature' (Bunkše, 2004, pp. 101–2; original emphasis). Humanistic geographers (including Bunkše, 2004) continue to write evocative accounts of home that bind individual dwelling to the wider cosmos (see HUMANISTIC GEOGRAPHY). Other geographers have begun to study the home as a 'more-than-human' place, reflecting the entangled geographies and complex co-habitations of NATURE and CULTURE (including Kaika, 2004).

Feminist geographers have also been concerned with the relationships between the intimate relationships of home and the wider world, but in very different ways. Across a wide range of areas and contexts, feminist geographers have analysed the home as a gendered place, shaped by different and unequal relations of POWER, and as a place that might be dangerous, violent and unhappy rather than loving and secure (on home and feminist politics, see Young, 1997a). FEMINIST GEOGRAPHIES challenge the MASCULINISM that either ignores the home or overlooks the power relations that exist within it. Inspired by the work of many black feminists who have rewritten home as a site of creativity, subjectivity and resistance (including hooks, 1991), such studies also challenge a white, liberal feminism that has understood the home primarily as a site of oppression for women. For socialist feminists, the home is a site of SOCIAL REPRODUCTION – for housing, feeding and nurturing workers – and is crucial for analysing the wider interdependence of CAPITALISM and PATRIARCHY. For those geographers drawn to POST-STRUCTURALISM and POST-COLONIALISM, the home is part of a wider spatial lexicon that has become important in theorizing IDENTITY, often closely tied to ideas about the politics of location and an attempt to situate both knowledge and identity (Pratt, 1997).

Post-colonial geographers have also explored the relationships between home, NATION and EMPIRE; the material and symbolic geographies of home and homeland; and the spatialities of home, dwelling and belonging in relation to indigeneity, settlement and DIASPORA (including Blunt, 2005). A central theme within this research is the home as a site of power and RESISTANCE, as shown by studies of imperial home-making, the importance of the home in anti-imperial nationalist politics, SOCIAL JUSTICE, belonging and the politics of home for indigenous people, and the contemporary politics of homeland (in)security. Rather than viewing the home as singular and static, a wide range of research on MIGRATION and diaspora unsettles notions of fixed roots and origins (including Ahmed, Castañeda, Fortier and Sheller, 2003), revealing multiple attachments and belongings that are materially manifested in home-making practices and MATERIAL CULTURES at home (Tolia-Kelly, 2004).

Reflecting the current vibrancy of geographical interest in the home, Blunt and Dowling (2006) have developed a critical geography of home, arguing that:

- *Material and imaginative geographies of home are closely intertwined*. '[H]ome is a *relation* between material and imaginative realms and processes, whereby physical location and materiality, feelings and ideas, are bound together and influence each other ... Moreover, home is a *process* of creating and understanding forms of dwelling and belonging. Home is lived as well as imagined. What home means and how it is materially manifest are continually created and re-created through everyday home-making practices, which are themselves tied to spatial imaginaries of home' (p. 254). The materialities of home – including domestic architecture, interior design, material cultures and home-making practices – are themselves shaped by, and interpreted through, a wide range of ideas about home.

- *Home, power and identity are intimately linked.* 'Home as a place and as a spatial imaginary helps to constitute identity, whereby people's senses of themselves are related to and produced through lived and metaphorical experiences of home. These identities and homes are, in turn, produced and articulated through relations of power' (p. 256). Rather than view the home as a fixed and bounded site, grounding and containing identity, geographers have unsettled both home and identity to reflect their mutual locatedness and porosity, rootedness and mobility. The home has become an important site for studying inclusions, exclusions and inequalities in terms of GENDER, CLASS, age, SEXUALITY and 'RACE'.

- *Geographies of home are multi-scalar.* 'Home is a socially constructed SCALE that extends beyond the house and household. ... [T]he relations of domesticity, intimacy and belonging that construct home not only extend beyond, but also help to *produce* scales far beyond the household' (p. 257; also see Marston, 2004a). Ideas and lived experiences of home are located within, travel across and help to produce scales from the body to the globe, as shown by the political significance of embodied domesticity in reproducing and resisting nations and empires; the bungalow and the high-rise as transnational domestic forms; migratory transformations of home; and the employment of domestic workers in the global economy (including Pratt, 2004).

A wide range of research across the humanities and social sciences interrogates normative ideas of home as a private, bounded, autonomous, safe and comfortable place. The emotive power of home is not only evident in feelings of attachment, belonging and familiarity and their material manifestations, but also in feelings and experiences of loss, alienation and exclusion, as shown by research on domestic violence, homelessness and displacement. The term domicide, for example, has been coined by Douglas Porteous and Sandra Smith (2001) to refer to 'the deliberate destruction of home by human agency in pursuit of specified goals, which causes suffering to the victims' (p. 12). Distinguishing between its 'everyday' forms – through, for example, urban redevelopment and economic restructuring – and its 'extreme' forms – including war and the forced resettlement of indigenous people – Porteous and Smith estimate that at least 30 million people across the world are victims of domicide (cf. URBICIDE).   AB

Suggested reading
Bachelard (1994 [1958]); Blunt (2005); Bunkše (2004); Duncan and Lambert (2004); hooks (1991); Kaika (2004); Marston (2004a); Pratt (2004); Tolia-Kelly (2004); Young (1997a).

homeland An area to which a people or a political community is closely attached. 'Attachment' has a profoundly cultural and political meaning in all major uses of the term. In much of European geography, 'homeland' carries resonances of the German *Heimat*, a spiritual, even mystical and often romanticized attachment to a native land, the place to which a person is tied by blood that is also the space of the NATION. In the first half of the twentieth century, 'homeland' in this sense became infused with ideologies of racial purity and patriotism in the veneration of the Fatherland that was central to the rise of FASCISM in general and the Third Reich in particular. For others, and particularly for the peoples of the DIASPORA, 'homeland' became an object of nostalgia, desire and identification, most viscerally so for those displaced and without a home of their own: hence, for example, the project of a 'Jewish Homeland' that gained momentum after the First World War and culminated in the formation of the State of Israel in 1948. In the 1960s and 1970s, the term was cynically invoked to secure the system of APARTHEID in South Africa through the creation of 'black homelands' (Transkei was the first). These were purely instrumental attempts to confine black Africans to scattered rural areas whose delimitation bore little relation to their own cultural geographies (Butler, Rotberg and Adams, 1977).

In American CULTURAL GEOGRAPHY, 'homeland' became a term of art in the second half of the twentieth century. It too implied an historically sedimented sense of IDENTITY that derived from an intimate interaction between people and land (cf. CULTURAL LANDSCAPE), but it was invariably tied to the REGION rather than the national scale. Thus Nostrand (1992, p. 214) emphasized how inhabitants come to have 'emotional feelings of attachment, desires to possess, even compulsions to defend' their homeland. He was describing an Hispanic homeland, and cultural-historical geographers have identified other ethnically based homelands within the USA (Nostrand and Estaville, 2001). In the early twenty-first century, however, in the wake of 9/11, the USA revived the concept of homeland on a national (and nationalist) scale. The political-cultural affiliations of the term were intensified with the creation of a federal Department of Homeland Security in 2002. Its actions are directed towards BORDER SECURITY and the prevention of TERRORISM against the USA through advanced systems of SURVEILLANCE, profiling and the like, but it is also deeply invested in what Kaplan (2003) perceptively identifies as 'the cultural work of securing national borders'.   DG

Suggested reading
Kaplan (2003); Nostrand and Estaville (2001).

homelessness A complex social problem that, in the most basic terms, is defined by a lack of shelter in which to sleep and to perform basic activities such as bathing. The characteristics of homeless populations vary geographically. There are distinctions between the identities and experiences of homeless people in developed versus less developed countries, where service-dependent substance abusers sleeping rough would be an example of the former, while the latter would be exemplified by rural–urban migrants occupying squatter settlements (see SQUATTING). There are also variations in homelessness among countries, stemming from differences in national economies, welfare policies and so forth.

In developed countries, the diversity of the homeless people has increased markedly since the 1970s. For instance, middle-aged white males, who traditionally dominated homeless populations in North America, are now eclipsed numerically by ethnically diverse women, CHILDREN, and youth, including people with mental disabilities, substance abusers, victims of domestic VIOLENCE, and the elderly (Takahashi, 1996). While often regarded as largely an urban issue, homelessness among these groups is also increasing in rural areas (Cloke, Milbourne and Widdowfield, 2001). Finally, the break between being

housed and being homeless is neither sharp nor definitive. Rather, homeless people may find themselves in a cycle, moving back and forth between the streets and shelters, after a prolonged decline from cheap rental housing, through living with friends or family, to shelters and the street. This sequence also hides many homeless people, contributing to difficulties in counting the population.

The causes of homelessness are a longstanding topic of debate. Takahashi (1996) suggests that geographers largely adhere to structural explanations, which focus on interconnections between increased levels of POVERTY and decreased availability of affordable shelter (Wolch and Dear, 1993). Specifically, this perspective identifies a combination of the following factors as crucial to the rise of homelessness in developed countries: economic change, leading to the expansion of low-paid, no-benefit, insecure service-sector jobs; the decline in WELFARE STATE benefits exacerbating economic problems, coupled with other policy shifts such as the deinstitutionalization of mental health services; demographic changes, including changing family structures, the feminization of poverty, and increases in the elderly population; and the reduced availability of affordable housing, in cities experiencing upward pressures on rents as a result of a BACK-TO-THE-CITY MOVEMENT and GENTRIFICATION, in suburban and rural areas where prices are also rising, and in the wider context of declining STATE provision of social housing. The structural perspective contradicts other explanations that suggest that individual failings and vulnerabilities (e.g. drug addiction, family instability) are the primary causes of homelessness.

Solutions and responses to homelessness and their implications for social life have been another focus for geographers. The PRIVATIZATION and reorganization of PUBLIC SERVICES has had a complex impact on the geographies of homeless people's lives, as some cycle through institutional settings (DeVerteuil, 2003). Also, public stigmatization of homeless people and increasingly harsh policy responses to their presence in PUBLIC SPACES (represented by anti-panhandling ordinances and 'bum-proof' benches) have spurred ongoing investigations and interventions into questions of homeless people's RIGHTS to space (Mitchell, 2003a).   EM

Suggested reading
Mitchell (2003a); Wolch and Dear (1993).

homo sacer Literally both 'sacred man' and 'accursed man', *homo sacer* was a subject-position conferred by archaic Roman LAW on those whose lives and deaths were deemed to be of no consequence. This dismal figure has come to be of considerable significance in contemporary political PHILOSOPHY and HUMAN GEOGRAPHY. People placed in this position could not be sacrificed (because they were outside divine law – their deaths were of no value to the gods) and they could be killed with impunity (because they were outside juridical law – their lives were of no value to their contemporaries). Agamben (1998) argues that *homo sacer* emerges at the point at which SOVEREIGN POWER suspends the law, whose absence falls over a zone of abandonment. The production of this space – the space of exception (see EXCEPTION, SPACE OF) – is central to his account of modern BIOPOLITICS. Critics have dismissed Agamben's retrieval of *homo sacer* as extravagant (Fitzpatrick, 2005) and even mythical – certainly Agamben does nothing to recover the wider cultural constructions of death in early Roman society, and the ways in which (for example) figures such as the gladiator were also exposed to death – but his purpose is not primarily historical or exegetical: it is, rather, to project *homo sacer* into the present as a cipher for BARE LIFE. Agamben does so in order to claim that sovereign power has so aggressively reasserted itself that the state of exception is increasingly becoming the rule and that, in consequence, we are all potentially *homines sacri*. These arguments have been important for debates around HUMAN RIGHTS and the very definition of 'the human', where geographers have insisted on the uneven and differential distribution of vulnerability: *homo sacer* is marked by CLASS, GENDER, SEXUALITY and 'RACE' (Gregory, 2004b; Sanchez, 2004; Pratt, 2005). These analyses also reveal the importance of the BODY: *homo sacer* is thus transformed from a metaphysical sign into a corporeal materialization of political VIOLENCE. DG

Suggested reading
Fitzpatrick (2005); Pratt (2005).

homophobia and heterosexism Though interrelated, these terms refer precisely to different exercises of oppression. Homophobia refers to the fear of lesbians and gays, the existence of 'homosexuality', and sometimes other dissident or non-normative sexualities, bodily performances or political struggles. The term is used diffusely around QUEER THEORY, however, to describe sentiments ranging from the disciplining, distancing, unease, disgust or

hatred towards a queer other (who may be an embodied other or a dimension of the self: see ABJECTION; PSYCHOANALYTIC THEORY). By contrast, heterosexism (also called HETERONORMATIVITY) refers to structures or agencies in SOCIETY that privilege and normalize male–female sexual relations over same-sex (or queered) ones, as well as the gendered PERFORMANCES that accompany them (see PERFORMATIVITY). The terms may refer to structural barriers, or to HUMAN AGENCY, consciousness or subjectivity. Most if not all recent work across queer geography and SEXUALITY-and-space studies explore, document or critique the panoply of forms that either homophobia or heterosexism can take.

There are at least two ways that GEOGRAPHY is implicated in these terms. The first is that the topical interests of geographers, especially SPATIALITY and NATURE–CULTURE relations, are dimensions through which critical geographers are exposing and critiquing homophobia and heterosexism. For example, the popular spatial METAPHOR of 'the closet' to describe the concealment, denial, or erasure of gays and lesbians has been spatialized to show how homophobia and heterosexism work through spatial arrangements and practices (Brown, 2000). Scales of analyses have ranged from the BODY (how sexuality functions as a performative, and its spatial situatedness affects performance), to the global (as in questions of international TOURISM, MIGRATION and REFUGEES, and post-colonial legacies; e.g. Puar, 2002). Both place and movement can be assessed as heteronormative or homophobic.

The second way of conceiving the links between geography and homophobia involves the discipline's long and under-exposed history of internal homophobia and heterosexism, which has certainly been associated with its MASCULINISM. Yet the discipline has long been populated by lesbians, gays, bi- and omni-sexuals, even transgendered and transsexual people, some in quite prominent positions, with stellar reputations. These geographers have often experienced damaging and painful repercussions because of their sexual identities or practices (e.g. homophobia was implicated in the closure of the Harvard geography department; see also Valentine, 2000). The widest array of charges of homophobia and heterosexism have been brought by Binnie (1997), who has detected strains, not simply in conventional POSITIVIST branches of the discipline, but also in allied critical areas such as MARXIST GEOGRAPHY and FEMINIST GEOGRAPHY. MB

Suggested reading
Bell and Valentine (1995); Browne, Brown and Lim (2006).

hot money Portfolio capital INVESTMENT that is both short-term and volatile in nature (Froot, O'Connell and Seasholes, 2001). Hot money accumulates rapidly in periods of economic boom, but dissipates quickly in times of crisis, which tends to exacerbate and intensify such CRISES. Portfolio capital investment is risk averse, and is directed mainly towards property and financial COMMODITIES, for which there are well developed secondary MARKETS. These secondary markets expedite both the rapid entry and exit of money from an economy. The inflow and outflow of hot money has been associated with numerous financial crises since the beginning of the twentieth century, and recently with financial crises in South East Asia, Russia and Argentina.   AL

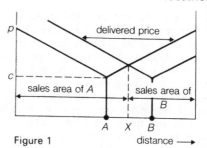

Figure 1

Suggested reading
Froot, O'Connell and Seasholes (2001); Naylor and Hudson (2004).

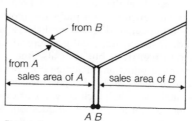

Figure 2

Hotelling model A classic model of the location strategy deployed by firms seeking to maximize their MARKET share through the size of their HINTERLANDS. The original model produced by Harold Hotelling (1895–1973: see Hotelling, 1929) identified the strategies of two firms competing in a linear market, where customers were evenly distributed, and was generalized with the example of ice-cream sellers competing on a beach (Alonso, 1964b). As formulated, the model showed that, whatever their starting locations (e.g. figure 1), the two firms would converge at the centre of the beach (figure 2), from where each would serve the half of the customers closer to them than to their competitor: those furthest from the centre would pay more for the product because of the greater TRANSPORT COSTS/time involved in making a purchase. The most efficient equilibrium distribution for two firms sharing the market equally would be that shown in figure 3, with each serving half of the beach and the total transport costs less than in figure 2. Each firm would realize, however, that if it moved closer to the centre it could capture customers from its competitor, hence the two providers congregate there.

Hotelling's model has been used to account for patterns of AGGLOMERATION under certain circumstances, and has also been applied to other competitive situations, exemplified by the large literature on the 'spatial theory of

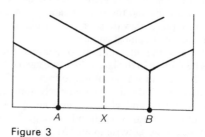

Figure 3

Hotelling model

voting' developed from Downs' (1957) classic work (cf. PUBLIC CHOICE THEORY).   RJ

household A socio-economic formation comprised of one or more individuals who share living quarters, often framed as those who 'eat from the same bowl and live under one roof'. While this notion provides some latitude against the common assumption that the household is coterminous with family, whether nuclear or extended, it lacks the spatial robustness to encompass more expansive notions, including the increasingly common formation of transnational households. Wright and Ellis (2006) frame the household 'simultaneously as a spatial SCALE and a set of practices; not situated in one place, but involving heterogeneous lives interacting with others all over town', or further afield, as recent MIGRATION research suggests.

Considering the household as a spatial SCALE can illuminate its structural relations with other scales, and bring to the fore the interconnections

345

between production and SOCIAL REPRODUC-TION at its heart. This understanding provides a corrective for the common assumption that the household is a 'natural' unit; a perspective that allows it to be disregarded in economic analyses, its substantial contributions to local and national ECONOMIES ignored or taken for granted. But without the domestic labour provided in and through the household, 'there would be no labour force and no SOCIETY' (Townsend and Momsen 1987). Not only is the household at the nexus of social reproduction, which encompasses biological reproduction – if not generational, then that associated with daily sustenance – cultural reproduction, and CONSUMPTION, but it is also the site of economic production, including both paid and unremunerated work. The balance between these activities – as much as who carries them out and for whom – is a social question. While household members manage, maintain, perpetuate, contest and sometimes change these arrangements and the social relations that hold them in place, they do so in a particular historical and geographical context.

Prior to the interventions of feminist theorists beginning in the late 1970s (see FEMINISM), the household was assumed to include affectively related individuals with largely homogenous interests, and altruistic and co-operative intentions towards each other (e.g. Folbre, 1986), but as Townsend and Momsen (1987) long ago cautioned, the household can be an 'arena of subordination'. It is a realm of differentiated and unequal social relations, structured by age, CLASS, ETHNICITY, GENDER, LIFE COURSE, nationality, RACE and SEXUALITY (e.g. Brydon and Chant, 1989). These internal divisions, which are associated with particular and shifting DIVISIONS OF LABOUR and allocations of RESOURCES, are constituted by – as they are constitutive of – broader social relations of production and reproduction. Household composition; location (whether matrilocal, patrilocal or neither); POWER dynamics, such as who heads the household and under what terms implicit or explicit; and the allocation of work and consumption practices among members are effects of this interrelationship. These differences are historically and geographically contingent. If capitalist INDUSTRIALIZATION has been associated with the separation of HOME and work, and households of individuals or nuclear families tend to predominate in the global NORTH, while extended family households are more common in the global SOUTH, it is important to remember that these differences themselves vary according to class, race,

ethnicity, sexuality and location, among other things.   CK

Suggested reading
Marston (2000); Walton-Roberts and Pratt (2005).

housing class A social group defined by its housing tenure (Rex and Moore, 1967). It suggests that tenure status shapes the material conditions of life. Rex developed a categorization of housing classes – including owners, tenants in publicly or privately owned housing, and lodgers in another household's dwelling, among others – which permitted analysis of the experiences of immigrant groups in the UK and emphasized the role of URBAN MANAGERS AND GATEKEEPERS in constraining housing market choice (see HOUSING STUDIES). Those interested in urban politics have also debated the concept, since it suggests that housing CLASS interests might be the basis for collective political action (Purcell, 2001). EM

Suggested reading
Rex and Moore (1967).

housing studies An interdisciplinary field with a wide array of research foci, dealing with aspects of housing from PROPERTY MARKET dynamics, through the provision and management of special needs accommodation, to questions of design and SUSTAINABILITY, among others. Geographical approaches to housing have frequently addressed the uneven geographies of housing production, consumption, meaning and policy. These uneven geographies reflect and produce differences in housing within cities, across countries, and between more- and less-developed countries.

One focus is the provision of housing via various mechanisms (Ball, Harloe and Martens, 1988). The production process leads to the spatial SEGREGATION of certain types of housing and therefore, certain people in specific NEIGHBOURHOODS – a process that is frequently inflected with RACISM. The nature of provision, tenure type, the cost of housing, and its quality and maintenance all vary in ways that impact its character not only as a shelter but also as a symbolic element of the LANDSCAPE (e.g. Bunnell, 2002), as an investment and as a RESOURCE that shapes residents' life chances.

For those with high incomes who can buy into neighbourhoods where the housing stock is appreciating, home ownership presents opportunities for CAPITAL gain. These opportunities are, in many countries (e.g. the USA), supported by state policies that provide subsidies and tax benefits for homeowners or that, more generally, mitigate the negative impacts of other land uses on higher-income residential neighbourhoods (cf. URBAN AND REGIONAL PLANNING; ZONING). Low-income owners, on the other hand, frequently face discrimination based on income, race and other factors (cf. REDLINING; URBAN MANAGERS AND GATEKEEPERS) and are often penalized financially as risky investments. Furthermore, they frequently face instability in their neighbourhoods as a result, for instance, of GENTRIFICATION and URBAN RENEWAL. These conditions enforce and deepen existing patterns of social polarization.

Similarly, while housing – no matter what the tenure type – is a resource that aids in access to jobs and various types of services from shops to recreational facilities, it is a socially and spatially uneven resource. For example, high-quality food at reasonable prices is often difficult to find near low-income housing, as are high-quality, safe recreational facilities for CHILDREN. These factors, among others, both reflect and reinforce inequalities relating to nutrition and health and are, in turn, directly related to housing (Smith and Mallinson, 1997).

The social, economic and geographical characteristics of housing production and CONSUMPTION are closely related to PUBLIC POLICY. In different countries and at different times, policy-makers see housing as a tool for and/or an object of policy intervention. Housing construction has been used to kick-start economies (cf. SUBURBANIZATION) and to re-shape INNER CITIES (cf. URBAN RENEWAL). It has also been central to attempts by states, charities and other organizations to improve social conditions such as health. The STATE's decreasing role in public housing provision raises new challenges in this regard, but has been paralleled by growth in alternative forms of housing tenure associated with community development (DeFilippis, 2004) and in attempts to reduce the impact of housing development on the environment.   EM

Suggested reading
Ball, Harloe and Martens (1988).

human agency The ability of people to act, usually regarded as emerging from consciously held intentions, and as resulting in observable effects in the human world. Questions about whether individuals have the freedom to act or whether their actions are constrained, or even

determined, by structural forces have been at the heart of many debates in contemporary HUMAN GEOGRAPHY.

At the turn of the twentieth century, individuals' actions were viewed by geographers as being the result of a higher logic or force, whether the imperatives of ENVIRONMENTAL DETERMINISM or the conditioning of Sauer's (1925) 'superorganic' notion of CULTURE. There were exceptions such as Vidal de la Blache's (1926) POSSIBILISM, which allowed a range of possible actions to emerge from any situation, but for most the role of the individual was secondary to process.

In the 1950s and 1960s, the introduction of SPATIAL SCIENCE allowed a DECISION-MAKING agent, but only in as far as it followed the logic of NEO-CLASSICAL ECONOMIC modelling. The adoption in geography of structural versions of MARXISM also regarded individual motivations and interpretations as necessarily secondary to the determinants of the structures of HISTORICAL MATERIALISM. HUMANISTIC GEOGRAPHY emerged in the 1970s with the stated goal of reanimating geography, to put people and their thoughts, emotions and beliefs at the heart of the discipline. It offered a challenge to structural Marxism, which humanistic geographers felt offered 'a passive model of man [sic] that is conservative and results in an obfuscation of the process by which human beings can and do change the world' (Duncan and Ley, 1982, p. 54). Focusing on issues such as dwelling, LIFEWORLD and rhythms, humanistic geographers believed that social life was constructed through human actions. For them, structure appeared due to reification, and seemed 'autonomous only because it is anonymous' (Duncan, 1980). While there were attempts by some humanistic geographers to recognise the limitations of human agency – such as Ley's (1983) focus on intersubjectivity – most tended towards epistemological IDEALISM. This led to the criticism that humanistic geography was naïve about the limitations put on individual ability to act.

STRUCTURATION THEORY and REALISM sought to explain how social structures were both outcome and medium of the agency that constitutes them. Giddens' (1984) structuration theory avoids the extremes of arguing that society is comprised of individual acts or is determined by social forces by holding these two extremes in tension with one another. It is through repetition that the acts of individual agents reproduce social structures such as institutions, moral codes, norms and conventions.

Post-structuralists (see POST-STRUCTURALISM), following Foucault (1980a [1976]), argued that the coherent, independent subjectivity required for conscious agency is an epiphenomenon of DISCOURSE: there is no prior ONTOLOGICAL self but, rather, a sense of selfhood is an effect of discourse. The 'self-contained, authentic subject conceived by humanism to be discoverable below a veneer of cultural and IDEOLOGICAL overlay is in reality a construct of that very humanist discourse' (Alcoff, 1988, p. 415). Others have critiqued the intentionality of HUMANISM and structuration theory where agency is equated with action, thus assuming intentionality and capacity to act. As a result, some have investigated PSYCHOANALYIC THEORY to expose the motivations behind actions, to reveal that SUBJECTS are not entirely self-aware and self-fashioning agents. Feminists have reacted more powerfully to POSTMODERN and post-structural pronouncements of the 'death of the subject', wondering whether this had occurred just when the male, white, subject might have had to share its status with those formerly excluded from agency (see Fox-Genovese, 1986; Mascia-Lees, Sharp and Cohen, 1989: see also GLOBAL WARMING).

The structure–agency debate continued through the discipline's CULTURAL TURN, with some fearful that the favoured discursive approach represented a new determinism that denied individual agency – see the debate between Duncan and Duncan (1996) and Mitchell (1995). For others, the privileging of discourse was an over-interpretation of agency, which regarded people as overly theoretical beings in their own decision-making. As a result, some have turned to ETHNOMETHODOLOGY and NON-REPRESENTATIONAL THEORY approaches in an attempt to record human agency without imposing the intentionality of discourse (Thrift, 1997c).

Another dimension of the debate over agency concerns the extent to which humans are the only active or creative agents. Traditional cultural geographers challenged the androcentric accounts of early agriculture by suggesting that certain plants and ANIMALS may 'elect' to live near humans rather than human subjects knowledgeably selecting species for domestication. Others have offered theoretically more sophisticated accounts of the effects of non-human actors. Haraway (1992, p. 331) suggests broadening our understanding of the place of agency, arguing that non-humans 'are not actants in the human sense, but they are part of the functional collective that makes up an actant', and has developed this in terms of the 'CYBORG' subject. Whatmore's (2002a) 'more-than-human' geography similarly highlights the agency of a variety of objects (see ACTOR-NETWORK THEORY), and has offered an image of a NETWORK of capable, but not necessarily conscious, agents.   JSh

Suggested reading
Duncan and Ley (1982); Giddens (1984); Thrift (1997c); Vidal de la Blache (1926); Whatmore (2002a).

human ecology This term is in some ways as suggestive as it is substantive, at least from the standpoint of contemporary sensibilities in the geographical tradition of studying human-environment relations. Specifically, the term carries an almost seductive appeal in promising transcendence of the pervasive NATURE-SOCIETY dualisms that are widely noted and of considerable contemporary preoccupation in explorations of the geographies of socionatures, techno-natures and the like (see, e.g., Haraway, 1997; Swyngedouw, 1999). And indeed, to the extent that the term is actually invoked by contemporary geographers, it is typically in the context of research on the human origins and implications of environmental change, and on the complex interrelations between societies and the biophysical RESOURCES and SYSTEMS on which these societies rely. For example, in their discussion of factors shaping social vulnerability to global CLIMATE change, Bohle, Downing and Watts (1994) invoke 'human ecology' to refer to highly specific relations between society and nature, but with emphasis on the ways in which '... social organizations and [social] reproduction (encompassing, for example, population growth) have direct implications for sustainability and how the environment is experienced in terms of RISK and threats ...' (p. 40). Notably, they reject the mere application of ecological concepts and methods to the study of human populations. Similarly, Bassett (1988) refers to human ecology [specifically human ecologists] in much the same way; that is, a concern with the articulations between human populations and key biophysical resources (somewhat consistent with the term 'POLITICAL ECOLOGY').

References to 'human ecology' should, however, be accompanied by knowledge of its polyvalence, not least as a product of the term's history of usage by geographers and non-geographers. This history can be traced at least to the early twentieth century, when human ecology was used to describe the object of geographical enquiry as well as in reference to the adaptation of concepts from the science of ECOLOGY for sociological analysis. Thus, in his 1922 presidential address to the Association of American Geographers, Harlan H. Barrows defined geography simply as 'the science of human ecology', a SCIENCE concerned with '... the relationships existing between natural environments and the distribution and activities of man [sic]' (Barrows, 1923, p. 3). And yet at virtually the same time, the CHICAGO SCHOOL of Sociology was placing its influential stamp on human ecology, defined by Robert E. Park (1936, p. 1) as '... an attempt to apply to the interrelations of human beings a type of analysis previously applied to the interrelations of plants and ANIMALS'. The Chicago School, of course, featured not only Park's work on the influence of racial difference in shaping the experience of newcomers and immigrants to the city of Chicago, but also Ernest Burgess and his development of a ZONAL MODEL (Park, Burgess and McKenzie, 1925).

What is perhaps critical to note here (particularly in light of the profound influence of that the Chicago School would have on the emergence of URBAN GEOGRAPHY) is that 'environment' for the likes of Park and Burgess primarily meant the built physical as well as the more general social and cultural environment of the city, including spatial configurations. This is somewhat at odds with contemporary connotations of human ecology, which tend to emphasize relations between human and non-human nature (cf. CULTURAL ECOLOGY; POLITICAL ECOLOGY). And while the Chicago School's influence on urban geography is recognized (Harvey, 1973), Park understood at the time that his version of human ecology overlapped with geography. Yet, he attempted to relegate geography to a particularistic, descriptive enterprise, leaving to sociologists the development of a more NOMOTHETIC human ecology complete with generalizations and formal theory (Entrikin, 1980).

All of this seemingly arcane intellectual history matters, because contemporary use of the term 'human ecology' can carry a fuzzy imprecision. Moreover, the term has 'baggage', associated as it is with mechanistic, POSITIVISTIC conceptions of social and cultural relationships to the environment (however conceived) based on organicist METAPHORS of social formations borrowed from ecology. These are critiques (warranted or otherwise) long directed at the Chicago School(s) (for an early example of this critique, see, e.g., Gettys, 1940). The term is still somewhat widely invoked (particularly in environmental sociology) as a synthetic, holistic approach to understanding the interrelationships of different SOCIAL FORMATIONS and their biophysical environments, including the specific and often highly complex and interactive relations governing the mobilization of key material and ENERGY resources on the one hand, and cultural (material and symbolic), institutional and technological trajectories of social development on the other. Considerable contemporary impetus is given to this line of work by attempts to understand the origins and implications of modern anthropogenic environmental problems by looking at how past societies (or non-industrial, non-Western ones) have precipitated, managed, responded to and been affected by environmental changes (Diamond, 1999; Harper, 2004). Yet fears of mechanistic, if not deterministic, renderings of the role of physical geographies in shaping social outcomes dog this line of scholarship, particularly when it comes time to formulate causal inferences and historical generalizations (Mazlish, 1999).

It also bears noting that human ecology is recognized as something of a contemporary field of holistic scholarly enquiry (complete with eponymous journal and a handful of academic departments). In this context, it is defined by Lawrence (2003, p. 31) as no less than '... the study of the dynamic interrelationships between human populations and the *physical, biotic, cultural, and social characteristics* of their environment and the biosphere' (emphasis added). All this points to the need for geographers and others to consider carefully the polyvalence of this term, and to invoke it reflexively, and with some degree of caution.   SP

human genome   The complete set of genes that make up the DNA of a human being. It is one of a number of species genomes that constitute a form of bio-information in which biological material is translated from corporeal formats, such as an organic bank, to informational formats, such as a database. Creating genomes relies on the DNA-sequencing technologies developed in the life sciences since the 1970s that make it possible to extract DNA from whole organisms and to elucidate and annotate its structure in the form of coded information. This is a laborious process, involving various methods for separating out nucleotides (the building blocks for the polymer molecules

DNA and RNA, which act as the repositories of genetic information in the cell), usually by rendering them visible as a pattern of bands in an acrylamide gel that can then be 'read' manually (with the naked eye) or scanned photographically, to translate the banding sequence into a digital code made up of four genetic digits – A, C, G, T – which can be stored in large computer databases such as the Human Genome Project Database.

The sequencing of the human genome was achieved almost simultaneously by a team at the University of Cambridge led by Peter Sanger, in competition with a team led by Craig Ventner in the USA in 2001. Not only did the methods of these two teams differ but so, crucially, did their research ethos. Whereas the Sanger team advocated that genomic databases should be a public RESOURCE, the Ventner team advocated the commercialization of such databases through the ascription of INTELLECTUAL PROPERTY RIGHTS. (See also GENETIC GEOGRAPHIES.)   SW

Suggested reading
Parry (2004); M'charek (2005).

human geography A major field of GEOGRAPHY that is centrally concerned with the ways in which PLACE, SPACE and ENVIRONMENT are both the condition and in part the consequence of human activities. The history of geography (see GEOGRAPHY, HISTORY OF) as a systematic and ordered body of knowledge was long dominated by the physical and natural sciences. This did not preclude studies focusing on the variation of human activities on the surface of the Earth (on the contrary: see AREAL DIFFERENTIATION), but the modern sense of geography as a disciplined mode of intellectual enquiry emerged through those scientific formations and their constitutive interest in 'making sense of nature' (Stoddart, 1986, p. ix). The templates of the physical and natural sciences shaped the human sciences and the social sciences as a whole, but geography's concern with the relations between peoples and their physical environments ensured that they marked human geography more than most. Those formations were not purely 'scientific': they were also philosophical, theological and irredeemably political and social. All of them were caught up in (and constituted through) relations of POWER.

A separate and distinctive human geography emerged alongside PHYSICAL GEOGRAPHY soon after the admission of geography to the mod-

ern academy towards the end of the nineteenth century, and it gained considerable momentum in the 1920s from the reaction against ENVIRONMENTAL DETERMINISM. This 'new' human geography took two main systematic forms on both sides of the Atlantic: a COMMERCIAL GEOGRAPHY that laid many of the foundations for modern ECONOMIC GEOGRAPHY (epitomized by the handbooks produced by G.G. Chisholm from 1889 through to 1928) and a POLITICAL GEOGRAPHY (dominated by F. Ratzel, H.J. Mackinder and later I. Bowman) that was primarily concerned with the STATE, TERRITORY and GEOPOLITICS. Like many other disciplines of the period, both under-laboured for CAPITALISM and EMPIRE: for the extension of European and American power abroad through NETWORKS of COMMODITY circulation and military (especially naval) might (see Smith, N., 2005a). In doing so, the two sub-disciplines also underwrote what eventually came to be recognized as CULTURAL GEOGRAPHY, which at that time was charged with inculcating a sense of national IDENTITY and NATIONALISM at home, while exhibiting the non-white world in a series of overseas tableaux.

These systematic geographies intersected in several ways, most visibly in studies of REGIONAL GEOGRAPHY, and the political, economic and cultural interests that animated them were articulated with a special force in a distinctive 'tropical geography' (cf. TROPICALITY). Regional geographies all treated the physical environment as a foundation for human activity, but none of the systematic geographies was divorced from the study of NATURE either. Much of commercial geography focused on RESOURCE inventories; securing access to those same resources was a strategic concern of political geography; and cultural geography emphasized the varying relations between peoples and environments in different parts of the world. Ratzel's ANTHROPOGEOGRAPHY had made this a touchstone of human geography, and subsequently Paul Vidal de la Blache (in France) and Carl Ortwin Sauer (in the USA) made equally cogent cases for the incorporation of the physical environment. For Vidal, this was a matter of disciplinary identity, even survival. He was no narrow disciplinarian, and geography was always closely allied to history in his vision of *la géographie humaine*. But he was taken aback by Emile Durkheim's new science of sociology, which was laying claim to much of human geography as 'social MORPHOLOGY', and Vidal insisted that this would leave society 'suspended in the air'. In his contrary view, drawing on advances in the physical sciences, it was essential to conceive of 'Nature' as providing a portfolio of opportunities within which societies and cultures made variable selections (see POSSIBILISM: Andrews, 1984). Sauer worked on the marchlands between geography and history too, and the studies produced by the first BERKELEY SCHOOL are often described as 'cultural–historical geography'. He was also keenly interested in anthropology, however, and this led him to formulate an approach in which a collective (and quasi-Durkheimian) CULTURE worked on the raw materials of the so-called 'natural landscape' to produce a climactic CULTURAL LANDSCAPE that not only evolved over time but also differed from place to place.

Human geography's interest in NATURE has continued to provide important axes of debate. The rise of SPATIAL SCIENCE after the Second World War briefly threatened to erase the physicality of human life from human geography, with many of its MODELS relying on the physical sciences for stimuli (either through physical analogies about the FRICTION OF DISTANCE or through NEO-CLASSICAL ECONOMICS, which was rooted in statistical mechanics). Many practitioners of spatial science in human geography soon returned to a consideration of environmental issues, however, through a BEHAVIOURAL GEOGRAPHY that urged the importance of ENVIRONMENTAL PERCEPTION and through a systems approach that dissected, or at any rate diagrammed, the intersections of nominally 'human' and 'physical' SYSTEMS. At that time, URBAN GEOGRAPHY was markedly less interested in these questions, and it took much longer for urban geographers to recognize that modern cities were not triumphant memorials to a human victory over 'Nature' and that the physico-ecological vertebrae of cities were crucial objects of enquiry. But it is now widely acknowledged that studies of POLLUTION, waste and WATER in cities address more than questions of public HEALTH and policy located at the crossroads of MEDICAL GEOGRAPHY and URBAN PLANNING: they also intersect with concerns about ENVIRONMENTAL JUSTICE, GOVERNMENTALITY and SOCIAL EXCLUSION that have become central to human geography more generally (see, e.g., Gandy, 2006a,c). This new agenda was advanced in part through a critique of spatial science that emphasized the material bases of CAPITALISM as a MODE OF PRODUCTION – the PRODUCTION OF SPACE was thus intimately related to the PRODUCTION OF NATURE, most

viscerally in studies of POLITICAL ECOLOGY (Watts, 1983a; Peet and Watts, 2003 [1996]; Robbins, 2004) – and in part through an engagement with other forms of SOCIAL THEORY that brought the biopolitical foundations of modern life into view (see BIOPOLITICS). The convergences between these streams of work have suggested a series of intrinsically 'hybrid geographies' (Whatmore, 2002a).

These developments reactivated and reformulated long-standing questions about the relations between human geography and PHYSICAL GEOGRAPHY, but it is only recently that the relations between the sub-disciplines of human geography have provoked equal discussion. The relative importance of the sub-disciplines has changed over time. Many of the core models of spatial science were the mainsprings for an ECONOMIC GEOGRAPHY dominated by LOCATION THEORY and driven by the search for systematic structures within a modern SPACE-ECONOMY. The subsequent critique of spatial science had many sources (Gregory, 1978a), but much of its vitality derived from a POLITICAL ECONOMY based on a close reading of Marx's analysis of CAPITALISM. This not only reshaped economic geography, where it set the space-economy in motion and allowed for more incisive analyses of (for example) the crisis-ridden dynamics of capital ACCUMULATION, spatial DIVISIONS OF LABOUR, industrial RESTRUCTURING, COMMODITY CHAINS and the circulation of CAPITAL in multiple forms. It also opened the doors to a revitalized POLITICAL GEOGRAPHY that more closely and critically engaged with the powers and practices of the STATE, and a SOCIAL GEOGRAPHY that became centrally concerned with spatial formations of CLASS and ETHNICITY. These two sub-disciplines drew on contributions to SOCIAL THEORY that spiralled far from Marx's original writings – though a diffuse Western MARXISM remained a significant source of inspiration to both of them – and these interactions issued in the rise of CRITICAL GEOPOLITICS and the emergence of vigorous FEMINIST GEOGRAPHIES that widened their horizons still further. These interdisciplinary exchanges also projected a central question for the HUMANITIES and the social sciences into the centre of human geography. Just as there were (for example) 'two anthropologies' and 'two sociologies', one emphasizing HUMAN AGENCY and the other emphasizing systems and structures, so there were two human geographies: one an avowedly HUMANISTIC GEOGRAPHY (in which IDEALISM vied with MATERIALISM) and the other much more invested in structural logics and constraints (but not reducible to a STRUCTUR-ALISM). STRUCTURATION THEORY proposed to replace this persistent dualism with a duality, but this promised to do much more than integrate 'agency' and 'structure' in explications of the conduct of social life: it also made PLACE and SPACE the pivots around which agency and structure turned. This further troubled the boundaries between contemporary and HISTORICAL GEOGRAPHY, already assailed by HISTORICAL MATERIALISM, because TIME as well as space was seen as focal to the production and reproduction of social life. In a sense, this vindicated older claims that 'all geography is historical geography' and socialized the formalism of classical DIFFUSION models, though in terms that their original protagonists would scarcely have recognized. These developments were reinforced by the 'CULTURAL TURN', which inaugurated a 'new' CULTURAL GEOGRAPHY whose development was marked by a series of theoretical 'posts' – POSTMODERNISM, POST-STRUCTURALISM and POST-COLONIALISM – though here too Marxisms in various forms continued to provide baselines for many geographers (Soja, 1989; Gregory, 1994).

This simple sequence is necessarily a caricature – human geography is not a single project and its history cannot be reduced to a linear narrative – but it does capture some of the major shifts in intellectual fashion in human geography in much of the English-speaking world since the Second World War. To describe them as fashion is not misleading; the links between CULTURAL CAPITAL, the commodification of knowledge and academic prestige ought not to be discounted. Yet they were also more than fads. While it would be misleading to plot these changes in an ascending arc of 'progress' in human geography, they have derived from intellectual debates inside and outside the discipline, and they were responses to issues of substance that required public address. This is clear from the theoretical sensibility that distinguished postwar human geography from its predecessors. Although few would welcome a return of the GRAND THEORY that preoccupied many areas of human geography as recently as the late twentieth century, *critique* as a rigorous interrogation of the ways in which concepts are freighted with relations of POWER is now firmly established as a central moment in geographical enquiry (cf. GENEALOGY). It is also clear from the success of both CRITICAL HUMAN GEOGRAPHY and RADICAL GEOGRAPHY in establishing the crucial importance of *politics* alongside the narrower and usually more instrumental focus on policy in APPLIED GEOG-

RAPHY, although Martin (2001b) complained that what he saw as 'faddishness' (in philosophy and theory) has limited the practical purchase of much of this contemporary work.

These developments have contributed to a considered blurring of the boundaries between the sub-disciplines of human geography; economic geography and political geography were brought into conversation through POLITICAL ECONOMY, for example, and both have been markedly affected by a CULTURAL TURN (see also CULTURAL ECONOMY) that requires recognition of the commodification of cultural forms and practices and their enrolment in economic and political figurations (cf. Harvey, 1989b). This 'blurring' has several sources. 'Theory' has itself become interdisciplinary, even postdisciplinary, and the same authors and texts, motifs and themes recur across the spectrum of the humanities and social sciences, while any CRITICAL THEORY worthy of the name cannot draw back when it encounters disciplinary boundaries. More than this, however, *compositional* approaches that separate 'economy', 'polity', 'society' and 'culture' – all of them at once as real and as constructed as the disciplines that have come to be identified with them: they are all fabricated rather than found objects – are confounded by geography's constitutive interest in the *contextual*: in the *coexistence* of objects, institutions and practices in time and space (cf. Hägerstrand, 1984, pp. 374–5: see also CONTEXTUALITY).

It is thus not surprising that the interactions between human geography and the other humanities and social sciences should have been a two-way street. It is perfectly true that many of the early encounters were largely derivative. Methods and theories were borrowed from other fields and put to work on the research frontier in order to stake a series of supposedly distinctive geographical claims (and, not coincidentally, to identify the adventurousness of the intellectual avant-garde). Gradually, however, a return flow was established and cross-disciplinary exchange increased:

(1) Human geographers have made substantial METHODOLOGICAL contributions. Among the most significant have been those to mathematical and statistical analysis, particularly through advances in the study of SPATIAL AUTOCORRELATION that address the problem of applying techniques associated with the GENERAL LINEAR MODEL to spatially referenced data, and the development of GEOGRAPHICAL INFORMATION SYSTEMS that have

made it possible to display and interrogate vast, spatially distributed data arrays; and to modes of visual analysis through critical readings of the spatialities of ART, CARTOGRAPHY, FILM and photography (see VISUAL METHODS). Yet these methods have been unevenly developed and deployed: QUANTITATIVE METHODS have always been most important in economic geography, where they are presently undergoing a considerable resurgence; studies in ELECTORAL GEOGRAPHY have been the principal locus of quantitative work in political geography, which has otherwise preferred qualitative methods, especially in CRITICAL GEOPOLITICS; and cultural geography has been almost entirely produced through QUALITATIVE METHODS.

(2) Human geographers have also made significant theoretical contributions. An explicit interest in theorization was a lasting achievement of spatial science: the so-called QUANTITATIVE REVOLUTION was often hailed as a local 'scientific revolution', but it was fundamentally a *theoretical* revolution, and it was the commitment to theorization that did much to constitute human geography as a research discipline (and en route to facilitate conversations with other disciplines). In the 1960s there were several calls for the development of a distinctively geographical body of THEORY: a theoretical corpus that would be the exclusive preserve of geography and thus serve to guarantee its intellectual and institutional legitimacy. At the end of that decade, Harvey concluded his prospectus for *Explanation in geography* (1969) with an injunction: 'By our theories you shall know us'. This was always an unlikely prospect at best (and a dangerous one at worst), and most human geographers – including Harvey himself (see Castree and Gregory, 2006) – became much more interested in establishing the interdisciplinary significance of place and space for social analysis. This has itself been an interdisciplinary project, not least because, as Harvey has constantly emphasized, the incorporation of such spatial concepts (the contextual) into conventional social theory (the compositional) is radically unsettling. What is sometimes called 'the spatial turn' has thus been described by more than human geographers: so much so, in fact, that accounts of LANDSCAPE, PLACE, REGION and SPACE have be-

come commonplace in many areas of the humanities and social sciences (Crang and Thrift, 2000; Hubbard, Kitchin and Valentine, 2004; Warf and Arias, 2008).

The developments summarized in the previous two paragraphs resulted in what Kwan (2004) identifies as a divide – even a 'rift' – between 'spatial–analytical geographies' invested in the development and use of quantitative techniques and geospatial technologies on one side and 'socio-cultural geographies' involved in the development and use of critical social theory and more qualitative methods on the other. Kwan insists that this is unproductive: there is no direct and immediate relation between EPISTEMOLOGY and method, she insists, so that 'the choice between critical social theory and spatial analysis is false.' She urges the development of 'hybrid geographies' that 'challenge the boundary and forge creative connections between socio-cultural and spatial–analytical geographies' (p. 758). Kwan's hybrid geographies are not (quite) Whatmore's (2002a) hybrid geographies, but they both speak of transcending the divisions between the cultural, social or 'human' sciences and the biological, physical or 'natural' sciences, and they both emphasize the role of feminist theories and FEMINIST GEOGRAPHIES in 'talking across the divide' (cf. Kwan, 2007).

In disciplinary terms, however, what matters most is the substantive work carried out under the sign of human geography. Although they are unlikely soul mates, Martin (2001b) and Harvey (2006c) have both criticized what they characterize as the deflection of human geography from rigorous, substantive inquiry through a fixation on, even an obsession with, abstract philosophical and theoretical issues. Although they were writing from opposite sides of the Atlantic, their complaints were largely addressed to a British audience and arise, in part, from recent differences in intellectual history and institutional context. It has become increasingly difficult to identify a common 'Anglo-American' human geography (cf. Johnston and Sidaway, 2004a,b), a development that has coincided with an emerging critique of Anglo-American HEGEMONY within the international discipline(s). If the coincidence seems ironic, this last critique is about more than LANGUAGE: it is about language used to privilege particular conceptual formations. And the criticisms made by Martin and Harvey also arise from opposition to equally particular philosophies and modes of theory. PHILOSOPHY was once given extraordinary legislative authority in human geography, particularly the philosophy of SCIENCE, and standard textbooks have commonly distinguished different philosophical traditions and mapped them more or less directly on to human geography (Johnston, 1986b [1983]; Cloke, Philo and Sadler, 1991; Peet, 1998) (see PHENOMENOLOGY; POSITIVISM; REALISM; STRUCTURALISM). But as human geographers were drawn away from FOUNDATIONAL philosophies like these and, coincidentally, into considerations of political and moral philosophy, so they became less impressed by exclusively scientific credentials and the power of Philosophy-with-a-capital-P to provide them (see HERMENEUTICS; PRAGMATISM; POST-STRUCTURALISM). Many of the philosophical writings that have attracted human geographers in recent years have engaged most directly with (and transformed) the core concerns of the humanities and the human sciences – see, for example, DECONSTRUCTION, DISCOURSE and PERFORMATIVITY – and in doing so they have opened up wholly new areas of geographical reflection: AFFECT, DESIRE, MEMORY and the like. This has produced a complex terrain in which different philosophical concerns have been brought into relation and juxtaposition with one another, and where philosophy has come to be treated more as a resource and less as a tribunal. Similarly, it was once possible to map human geography as a series of positions on an intellectual landscape that was, in effect, an absolute space: theoretical coordinates established the singularity of different systems of concepts. But here too there has been a sea-change, and most human geographers now accept that no one theoretical system can ask all the important questions, still less provide all the cogent answers. They thus find themselves working in (and producing) the tense space between contending and colliding systems of concepts. The result of these philosophical and theoretical innovations has been to shake the very foundations of enquiry in human geography, as they have in the other humanities and social sciences, and the oppositions that once skewered the field (such as 'agency' and 'structure', but the list is now much longer) have been called into radical question (Cloke and Johnston, 2005). A second response, then, might be that critics such as Martin and Harvey lament these tectonic shifts and yearn for solid ground (though they undoubtedly stand in different places on it).

Whatever one makes of this, however, their point remains a sharp one. It is not difficult to see why the demands of navigating this new terrain should have prompted some human geographers to become so preoccupied with philosophical and theoretical issues that these become not so much moments in as substitutes for substantive inquiry: a refuge from the capriciousness and, indeed, riskiness of the empirical. On this reading, it is symptomatic that of the 26 'key texts in human geography' identified by Hubbard, Kitchin and Valentine (2008), barely a handful focus on the results of empirical analysis. But there are many other key texts, and many writers have reactivated and reformulated sites that have long been focal to human geography – BORDERS, CITIES, industries, regions and TERRITORY, for example – and opened up new ones, such as the BODY, the HOME, the shopping mall, the PRISON and the ZOO. They have reworked traditional themes in both the past and the present, including COLONIALISM, DEVELOPMENT, IMPERIALISM, INDUSTRIALIZATION, MODERNIZATION, URBANIZATION and WAR, and explored new ones such as FILM, LAW, MONEY, MUSIC, PERFORMANCE, SEXUALITY, TERRORISM and TOURISM. And there has been a continuing stream of principled work on different places and their interconnections that collectively gives the lie to the monstrous assertion that 'the world is flat' (cf. Smith, 2005a: see GLOBALIZATION). It would take a brave or foolhardy person to issue a programmatic statement in the face of such diversity, but this has not prevented attempts to chart the future of human geography. The spirited reactions to Harvey's (1984) 'historical materialist manifesto', or Amin and Thrift's (2005a: cf. Thrift, 2002) revisionist prospectus twenty-odd years later, testify not only to the diversity of human geography, but also to a continued vitality that depends on an irreplaceable intimacy between theory and practice.   DG

Suggested reading
Cloke and Johnston (2005); Gregory (1994, chs 1 and 2); Massey, Allen and Sarre (1999).

human rights A RIGHT is an entitlement that is usually encoded in a legal context (see LAW). One can distinguish between human rights and citizenship rights. CITIZENSHIP rights are guaranteed by governments for nationals of a particular TERRITORY, whereas human rights are thought to be geographically and politically universal. Hannah Arendt (1973) warned that human rights are the least desirable rights because they imply the absence of protection by a NATION-STATE; the rights of citizens are superior to human rights because they are both applicable and enforceable. Matters are not that simple, however, because rights may be, and in fact often are, legally suspended during a 'state of emergency' (see EXCEPTION, SPACE OF).

The liberal model of rights is derived from seventeenth-century political thought that focuses on the rights accorded to individuals as well as the obligations that individuals owe society and the state (Kofman, 2003). Critics of LIBERALISM question the scale at which rights are borne – in other words, that of the individual – and highlight group or communal rights (Isin and Wood, 1999), or deconstruct political COMMUNITY as pre-given (Mouffe, 1992). Despite the limits of liberalism and rights-based political change, Blomley (1994, p. 410) argues that '[r]ights have not gone away. As such, the dismissal of rights-based struggles as incoherent or counter-progressive seems condescending.' Blomley and Pratt (2001) contend that rights are open to a variety of readings, their meaning indeterminate. Rights can be mobilized effectively at different SCALES to constructive ends.

Pratt (2004, p. 85) explores the limits and possibilities of human rights DISCOURSE, noting that any form of the universal is 'necessarily exclusionary but paradoxically holds within it the means to be challenged by those who are excluded by it'. This paradox is evident in the struggles of the Filipino caregivers who live in their employers' homes and trade their freedom and mobility for paid work. Pratt maps the ways in which rights are mobilized in different SPACES: at the scale of the BODY, between the [private] HOME and [public] Canadian SOCIETY, in the context of the Canadian state and on the GLOBAL COMMONS. Similarly, Bosco (2006, 2007) charts the ways in which human rights have been fought for by the Madres de Plaza de Mayo in Argentina through the mobilization of a series of territorially dispersed social NETWORKS.

Practically speaking, human rights have been encoded in United Nations documents and institutions, and in international law, since the Second World War. In 1948, the Universal Declaration of Human Rights was adopted, though it was not legally binding (it was a declaration, not a treaty). In 1966, two legally binding human rights instruments were created to protect civil and political rights, on the one hand, and economic, social and cultural rights on the other. These covenants depend upon the ratification of a sufficient number of STATES, which they received in 1976.

The provisions of the International Covenant on Civil and Political Rights have been privileged over those of the Covenant on Economic, Social and Cultural Rights. The first ensures respect for citizens regardless of LANGUAGE, RELIGION, SEX, political opinion and so on, as well as the right to liberty of movement and freedom. The latter includes provisions that are more applicable to developing countries than to highly industrialized ones, such as the right to FOOD, shelter, work, and basic medical and educational services. While the first covenant applies to individuals, the second refers to particular groups of people.

Tensions exist between the SOVEREIGNTY of states to govern and the human rights of their citizens. The slippage in scale between the state with its right to govern and individuals with human rights can be traced to the potentially contradictory terms enshrined in the 1945 UN Charter and the 1948 UN Declaration of Human Rights. While the 'General Assembly shall ... [assist] in the realization of human rights and fundamental freedoms for all without distinction as to race, sex, language, or religion' (Article 13 (1b)), its constituent members are states whose sovereignty and security prevail. The UN Charter has mechanisms to ensure the protection and enforcement of peace and international SECURITY, but it outlines few obligations for the protection of human rights.

Since the early 1990s, the UN Security Council has extended the meaning of what constitutes a threat to international peace and security in the Charter, and increased the conditionality of sovereignty. Developing countries have expressed concern about this interpretation as potentially interfering in internal affairs. Sovereignty is seen as a last line of defence against the will of the (largely Western) 'international community'. While the UN remains an organization comprised of member states within a framework of liberal rights and freedoms, it has challenged the abuse of sovereignty in places such as northern Iraq, Bosnia-Herzegovina, Somalia and East Timor. Sovereignty is qualified, and the abrogation of people's human rights within a given state is no longer a domestic matter, at least with a UN context.

There are many human rights instruments that have been ratified, including the Convention on the Elimination of Discrimination again Women (CEDAW) and the Convention on the Rights of the Child (CRC). The USA has signed neither of these legal instruments, illustrating that unilateralism by the world's superpower can undermine the application and monitoring of basic human rights provisions.   JH

Suggested reading
Bosco (2006); Kobayashi and Proctor (2003); Koffman (2003).

humanism A philosophical tradition that places human faculties (reason, consciousness and the like) at the centre of human action in order to account for and inform conduct. Humanism has a long history in European PHILOSOPHY, where it is usually traced back to the Renaissance, but it played a pivotal role in much later reformulations of modern HUMAN GEOGRAPHY. The architects of an explicitly HUMANISTIC GEOGRAPHY used a broadly based humanism as a crucial foundation for their critique of SPATIAL SCIENCE. To Tuan (1976b, p. 266), humanism in its various forms provided 'an expansive view of what the human person is and can do'. 'More comprehensive than science', he continued, humanism accords a central place to those uniquely human capacities that lie at the core of the humanities: consciousness, critical reflection and creativity that in turn inculcate a sense of historicity. While he did not see humanism as an alternative to 'scientific geography', Entrikin (1976, pp. 616, 632) argued that such an approach 'helps to counter the objective and abstractive tendencies of some scientific geographers' and reviewed the twin philosophies of EXISTENTIALISM and PHENOMENOLOGY to reaffirm 'the importance of the study of meaning and value in human geography'. Others insisted on the political and ethical significance of humanism. A stream of work on HUMAN AGENCY and human geography challenged the narrowly conceived and often deterministic assumptions about human action that had been incorporated into both spatial science and BEHAVIOURAL GEOGRAPHY (Ley, 1981) and reworked one of Marx's iconic statements thus: 'People make geography, but not just as they please and not under conditions of their own choosing' (Gregory, 1981). Others treated humanism as a well-spring for ethical reflection: 'The recovery of the human subject', Buttimer (1990, p. 28) concluded, allowed for what would now be called a COSMOPOLITANISM and a heightened sensitivity to what she identified as 'the "barbarism" of our times' (see also ETHICS).

Even as these claims were being registered, however, Cosgrove provided a series of compelling reconstructions of the historical trajectory of humanism that suggested a less celebratory interpretation. Focusing on the concept of LANDSCAPE, Cosgrove (1984) showed that Renaissance humanism was about certainty rather than individual subjectivity, and that it was deeply implicated not only in the geometric obsessions that the critics of spatial science sought so strenuously to repudiate, but also in a visual IDEOLOGY that underwrote a constellation of distinctively bourgeois POWER and privilege. Others took different routes to arrive at parallel conclusions. Approaches through FEMINIST GEOGRAPHY and POST-COLONIALISM revealed that the supposedly universal 'human subject' at the centre of conventional humanism was not only a SUBJECT whose class position was artfully unmarked, as Cosgrove had shown, but also a subject whose heterosexuality, masculinity and WHITENESS were concealed too. Seen thus, humanism was exposed as a normative political–ideological project. Many of these subsequent critiques were informed by POST-STRUCTURALISM, which licensed what came to be categorized as an ANTI-HUMANISM: an approach that, far from being uninterested in or dismissive of human subjects and human actions, seeks to analyse the multiple ways in which different human subjects are constituted. This project has been radicalized by a POSTHUMANISM that, critical of the *anthropocentrism* shared by humanism and anti-humanism, admits non-human actors to the production of nominally 'human' but in fact constitutively 'hybrid' geographies.

Similar critiques have been mobilized to question and contest the rise of what Douzinas (2003) calls a 'military humanism' that promotes military intervention and WAR in the name of supposedly universal HUMAN RIGHTS, or 'Humanity' more generally. These projects often promote, on their dark side, the co-production of spaces of exception (see EXCEPTION, SPACES OF), whose denizens are constructed as sub-human and hence unworthy of protection. Here, humanism functions as a sort of anthropological machine, conferring and withdrawing the status of 'human' from its objects (cf. BARE LIFE).   DG

Suggested reading
Cloke, Philo and Sadler (1991, ch. 3); Douzinas (2003).

humanistic geography An approach that seeks to put humans at the centre of GEOGRAPHY. Accounts of disciplinary history have created for humanistic geography a sense of singularity of vision that overlooks the multiple, and sometimes conflicting, approaches that humanistic geographers have adopted. They have drawn upon a wide range of humanist philosophies, which has led to a generic humanistic geography in addition to versions based around ESSENTIALISM, IDEALISM, PHENOMENOLOGY and PRAGMATISM (see also HUMANISM). Despite this, there are key similarities in terms of the reasoning behind the emergence in the 1970s of humanistic geography; it was a response to what were seen as the dehumanizing effects of both POSITIVISM and structural MARXISM, in addition to promoting a positive model of a humanistic geography. Buttimer has argued that:

> From whatever ideological stance it has emerged, the case for humanism has usually been made with the conviction that there must be more to human geography than the *danse macabre* of materialistically motivated robots which, in the opinion of many, was staged by the post-World War II 'scientific' reformation. (Buttimer, 1993, p. 47)

For many humanistic geographers, the world is primarily the sum of human experiences through their encounters with 'external reality', which cannot be accessed other than through the human mind (Cloke, Philo and Sadler, 1991). However, others were less reductionist, and recognized that the 'external' world was mediated through subjective layers of meaning in complex ways. Talking of 'body–subject' to transcend the separation of material life from thought, Seamon (1979) sought to capture the meaning of PLACE that was orchestrated through the 'pre-reflective intentionality' of 'body ballets' – the movement, often unthinking and unroutinized, of people through their environments, weaving the rich texture of place (a view echoed by recent returns to ETHNOMETHODOLOGICAL techniques and feminist theorizations of the BODY).

This is not simply an ONTOLOGICAL move in terms of focusing on individuals and their various activities, but also a philosophical one which puts human experience and understanding of the world at the centre of geography. It further insists that all human experience is articulated through geographical concepts such as SPACE, TIME and LANDSCAPE. Drawing on Husserl's PHENOMENOLOGY, Buttimer (1976) talked of the concept of the LIFEWORLD to provide a sense of this intimacy between place and people (see also Seamon, 1979). Thus, appropriate QUALITATIVE METHODS are required, as '[n]o decimal

notation of time, no geometric commandment, no camera or tape recorder could easily articulate the experience of this lifeworld' (Mels, 2004, p. 3). Phenomenological strands of humanistic geography were concerned with essences – for example, of space or experience (Tuan, 1976b) – or with the nature of existence, elucidating previously taken-for-granted ways of being in the world.

In their attempts to articulate the human experience of place and landscape, some humanistic geographers turned to the humanities, particularly ART and literature, as forms of expression that were seen to provide insights that were unavailable to the more scientific gaze of the geographer (Meinig, 1983). However, the enthusiasm of some (e.g. Pocock, 1981) for the transcendental ability of the artist or author to capture the essence of human experience has been criticized for its ignorance of the common origins of European Renaissance artistic representation with geometric knowledges of possession and control (Cosgrove, 1984), and the nature of genres in literature (Sharp, 2000b).

In addition to drawing the human as the subject of geography, humanists also turned to examine the humanity of the geographer. The emphasis on interpretation and intersubjectivity that humanistic geography propounded meant that the researcher could not be seen as 'an individual whose humanity stands outside the research process: as an individual who is nothing but a vessel for taking in information, processing it and then arriving at conclusions' (Cloke, Philo and Sadler, 1991, p. 71). Instead, the researcher had to acknowledge her or his role in the process of interpretation and the production of knowledge, and thus Buttimer (1974) stressed the importance of VALUES in geography. This necessitated the adoption of ETHNOGRAPHIC and participatory research METHODOLOGIES (e.g. Ley, 1983; Western, 1992) and experiments with writing styles to move away from sterile scientific LANGUAGE (e.g. Olsson, 1991).

Because humanistic geography emphasized experience and human SUBJECTIVITY, it tended towards idealism and voluntarism, and as a result has been criticized, particularly by MARXIST, REALIST and STRUCTURATIONIST theorists for overplaying the freedom that individuals have to act and for tending to focus on the micro-scale at the expense of important structural connections (although, in both cases, note E.P. Thompson's socialist humanism). Despite superficial similarities, the CULTURAL TURN in human geography has offered a critical challenge to humanism, and most 'new CULTURAL GEOGRAPHY' is characterized by POST-HUMANISMS of various sorts. Theorists of POST-STRUCTURALISM would further suggest that the perception of HUMAN AGENCY so promoted in humanistic geography is a product of dominant DISCOURSE. Feminist geographers have shown how these dominant discourses create an image of normal subjecthood that is white, male, bourgeois, heterosexual and able-bodied, an image that can only be maintained as coherent through the exclusion of all that is 'Other' (see FEMINIST GEOGRAPHIES). Thus, a whole range of others are denied full subjectivity and agency (Alcoff, 1988). The exposure of the fiction of coherent subjectivity has also led some to turn to PSYCHOANALYTIC THEORY to seek to understand unconscious motivations for actions, something overlooked by many humanistic geographers who regarded human agency as the result of conscious decisions (but again, there were exceptions, such as Seamon's 'body-ballets'). Recent developments of post-humanism, or what Whatmore (2004) has called 'more-than-human' geographies, have sought to populate the world with agents other than humans (see ACTOR-NETWORK THEORY).

Although these critiques have meant that the influence of humanistic geography *per se* has waned since the 1980s, many of its arguments are still key to current debates in human geography. Recent critique of the cultural turn insists that geographers' enthusiasm for discourse and REPRESENTATION have drawn them away from 'the more "thingy", bump-into-able, stubbornly there-in-the-world kinds of "matter" (the material)' (Philo, 2000a, p. 33). New cultural geographers' presentations of landscapes as already structured through discourse draw attention from the variety of corporeal practices as instances of how 'senses of landscape and self are mutually configured' (Wylie, 2005, p. 239). Wylie (2005) talks in terms of a 'post-phenomenology' in which human agency is reconnected with NETWORKS of non-human agents, through which place and experience emerge. JSH

Suggested reading
Adams, Hoelscher and Till (2001); Buttimer (1993); Cloke, Philo and Sadler (1991); Mels (2004); Seamon (1979).

humanities Emerging in EUROPE during the Renaissance from medieval scholastic study of the seven liberal arts (i.e. the *quadrivium* of arithmetic, geometry, music and astronomy, and the *trivium* of rhetoric, logic and grammar), the humanities today denotes both an approach to knowledge and a specific set of disciplines (see also HUMANISM).

As an approach to knowledge, the humanities are (still) characterized by broadly HERMENEUTIC or interpretive methods and work through cycles of criticism rather than the establishment of THEORY and scientific law (see LAW, SCIENTIFIC), although concepts, the rule of evidence and logical argument are vital to their practice. Expressions of this include privileging the monograph or essay rather than the research paper as the preferred style of scholarly communication, individual authorship, and the use of the footnote or endnote rather than the 'Harvard' referencing system, suggesting 'conversation' rather than progressive and cumulative advance of knowledge (Smith, J., 1992a). The humanities thus foreground the active role of the author in the construction of knowledge and understanding (Cosgrove and Domosh, 1993).

The humanities disciplines concern the study of distinctively human actions and works; for example history, philology (language, LITERATURE, linguistics), PHILOSOPHY, theology and studies of Antiquity. The principal goals of the humanities are both active and contemplative: they were long regarded as fundamental to the educational preparation of rulers, but their success was gauged in part by the degree of self-knowledge and self-reflection they produced in the student (Grafton and Jardine, 1986). GEOGRAPHY, sometimes characterized as the 'eye' of history, as history in turn was proclaimed 'queen' of the humanities, has a long record as a humanities discipline, initially because it based its knowledge of the world upon the authority of ancient texts and subsequently, as EXPLORATION, autopsy and EMPIRICISM displaced such authority, because it entailed the comparative study of places and peoples.

The evolution of modern geography as a university discipline has been strongly affected by both natural science and social science EPISTEMOLOGIES and methods, although HISTORICAL GEOGRAPHY's natural allegiance with history has continuously if contentiously sustained geography's connection with a key humanities discipline. The RHETORIC of 'science' within geography has long tended to subordinate a broader humanities tradition, although recent studies of SCIENCE as a social, irredeemably human practice have not only drawn in some measure from the humanities but also interrupted the authority of science understood as objectivism. The values and value of humanities scholarship have also been marginalized by geography's postwar focus on research, policy relevance and critique as opposed to pedagogy. A self-styled 'humanistic' geography in the 1970s and 1980s (Ley and Samuels, 1978) owed less to conventional humanities study than to then fashionable psychological theories and twentieth-century PHENOMENOLOGY, but it opened HUMAN GEOGRAPHY to questions of perception and interpretation that had long been associated with the humanities (see HUMANISTIC GEOGRAPHY). Probably the most productive and widely read contemporary practitioner of geography as a humanity is Yi-Fu Tuan, whose autobiography is explicit about his practice of geography as a vehicle for self-understanding through reflection on the true, the good and the beautiful in a world of PLACES and LANDSCAPES (Tuan, 1999).

Many human geographers are profoundly sceptical of the universalistic claims of 'humanity' and the humanities' focus on individual agency (both in subject matter and authorship), and indeed many contemporary scholars in the humanities have also sharply questioned such traditional orthodoxies (see POST-STRUCTURALISM). But recent critical and cultural study within human geography signals the discipline's engagement in the convergence of social sciences and humanities that has emerged with the rejection of POSITIVISM and the embrace of interpretive methods on the part of the former, and acceptance of the value of SOCIAL THEORY on the part of the latter (see also Gregory, 1994). The 'CULTURAL TURN' has thus seen human geographers working with both materials and methods conventionally associated with the humanities – for example, the interpretation of TEXTS and IMAGES – although the 'new' cultural geography represents an uneasy alliance between those pursuing a traditionally social science agenda and those who cleave to the more conventionally individualistic, reflective and pedagogical concerns of the humanities. Still, that the Association of American Geographers could convene a major interdisciplinary conference on 'Geography and the Humanities' in June 2007 says much about the salience of contemporary conversations between the two, appropriately enough, and hence about the continuing importance of the humanities in geography and geography to the humanities.   DCO

Suggested reading
Tuan (1996).

hunger The right to FOOD – and relatedly the right to not starve – represents one of the foundations of international and national human and political RIGHTS. The Universal Declaration of Human Rights (1948), the International Covenant of Economic, Social and Cultural Rights (1964) and the UN Millennium Declaration (2000) all refer to freedom from hunger as a basic and inalienable HUMAN RIGHT. The reality is, of course, very different. According to the Food and Agriculture Organization (FAO), there are 854 million people undernourished worldwide (FAO, 2006): 820 million in the developing world, 25 million in the transition (former socialist) countries and 9 million in the industrialized states. Virtually no progress has been made towards the Rome World Food Summit (1996) target of halving the number of undernourished people by 2015. There has been little change in developing-world hunger since 1990–2. It is true that the proportion of undernourished people has fallen by three percentage points, but the FAO projects that it is unlikely that the UN Millennium Goal for hunger will be met. The Near East, South ASIA and especially sub-Saharan AFRICA have seen sharp increases in the number of hungry people; currently, 33 per cent of sub-Saharan Africa is undernourished.

POVERTY and hunger are very much part of the landscape of the twenty-first century. In the period since 1980, economic growth in 15 countries has brought rapidly rising incomes to 1.5 billion people, yet one person in three still lives in poverty and basic social services are unavailable to more than 1 billion people. Nowhere is this privation more vivid and pronounced than along gender lines. Of the 1.3 billion people in poverty, 70 per cent are women. Between 1965 and 1988, the number of rural women living below the poverty line increased by 47 per cent; the corresponding figure for men was less than 30 per cent (UNDP, 1996). A key measure of poverty is the extent to which individuals are able to secure sufficient food to conduct a healthy and active life. By the conventional measure of hunger, namely the FAO's definition of household food security (HFS) ['physical and economic access to adequate food for all household members, without undue risk of losing such access' (FAO, 1996, p. 50)], millions of people are not household food secure. The FAO provides a number of measures pertaining to food, hunger and undernutrition. Currently, over 800 million consumed so little food relative to requirements that they suffered caloric undernourishment (which often leads to anthropometric deficiency and the risk of damaged human development). Malnutrition (or undernutrition) refers to physical conditions that result from the interaction of inadequate diet, poor food consumption, nutrient imbalance and illness/disease. All of these conditions – typically measured through key indicators such as infant growth, weight for height, body mass, birth weights, dietary energy supply and so on – can be the result of differing sorts of food SECURITY. Some of the rural poor may be hungry for short or long periods, but they are relatively secure that things will not deteriorate (starvation); others may have adequate nutrition or food intake but are food insecure – however, their conditions may change very rapidly and throw them into abject hunger. These differing forms of security and vulnerability are intimately wrapped up with the sorts of entitlements and protections afforded to different CLASSES, GENDERS, ages and social groups.

Currently, global food consumption provided 2720 dietary calories per person, which would have been sufficient if distributed in proportion to requirements. In global terms, then, food consumption is so unequal that caloric undernourishment is serious. It is true that the proportion of malnourished people has fallen greatly (more in the past 50 years than in the previous 3000) but hunger and undernourishment remains endemic in some regions (notably sub-Saharan Africa and South Asia). Paradoxically, there is much evidence to suggest growing hunger in some of the North Atlantic economies and within a number of post-socialist societies. According to the International Food Policy Research Institute (see Von Braun, Serova, tho Seeth and Mely 1996), agricultural production fell by 30 per cent in Russia between 1989 and 1994 and hunger was widespread during the 1990s. In California (a place where the more affluent are seemingly obsessed by eating less and losing weight), the reform of 'welfare as we know it', has produced 8.4 million who were 'food insecure' by 2000.

A conventional way to think about hunger is in terms of output or gross availability. Food security decreases accordingly as food availability declines. FAMINE, an extreme case of food insecurity, is a function of a massive collapse of food availability, a sort of Malthusian event. In contrast to the Malthusian and demographic approach, in which food insecurity arises as food output is incapable of keeping up with population growth (see MALTHUSIAN MODEL), Amartya Sen (1981) approaches hunger, and most especially how hunger and food insecurity can degenerate into famine, from a micro-economic vantage point and entitlements. Sen is able to show how gross food insecurity may occur without a decline in food availability, and how entitlements attached to individuals through a generalization of the exchange economy – through MARKETS – may shift in complex ways among differing classes, occupational groups and sections of the population.

Sen begins with the individual endowment, which is mapped into a bundle of entitlements, the latter understood as 'the set of alternative COMMODITY bundles that a person can command' (1981, p. 46) through the use of various *legal* channels of acquirement open to someone of his or her position. Such entitlement bundles confer particular capabilities that ultimately underline well-being.

Central to Sen's account of why hunger exists is the process of transforming endowments into entitlements, so-called *E-mapping*. The sorts of entitlements that Sen details are rewards to labour, production, inheritance or asset transfer, and STATE provisioning (transfers), typically through social security and food relief policies (i.e. anti-famine policies, of which the Indian Famine Codes are customarily seen as a model: Dreze and Sen, 1989). Insofar as an individual's entitlement set is the consequence of E-mapping on the endowment set, entitlements can only change through transformations in the endowment or E-mapping. Hunger and shortage occurs through a collapse or adverse change in endowment or E-mapping, or both (Sen, 1981). Entitlement, in contrast to other theories, 'draws our attention to such variables as ownership patterns, unemployment, relative prices, wage-price rations, and so on' (1993, p. 30).

Sen situates hunger, then, on a LANDSCAPE, irreducibly social, of the capabilities that individuals, and potentially classes, may mobilize. By examining mapping as an active and transformative process – how the capacity to labour, or access to land, can generate an entitlement – it dislodges a concern with output *per se* and focuses on access to and control over food. It offers a *proximate* sort of causal analysis predicated on what immediate or conjunctural forces might shift such forms of access and control, and permits a social mapping of such shifts to understand *who* dies or starves (say, artisanal craftsmen versus PEASANTS) and *why*. Entitlements – the central mechanism in his intellectual architecture – are individually assigned in virtue of a largely unexamined endowment, and are legally derived from state law (ownership, PROPERTY rights, contract). Entitlements necessitate making legitimate claims; that is to say, rights resting on the foundations of POWER (opportunity or actual command) and LAW (legitimacy and protection). A concern with entitlement failure in market circumstances leads Sen to emphasize public action through entitlement *protection* (state-funded famine protection through food for work or public food distribution) *and promotion* (a public social security net).

Sen's concern with entitlements, and relatedly the capabilities of individuals, can be extended to better grasp the conditions under which people become food secure. To begin with entitlements themselves, geographer Charles Gore has noted that 'command over food depends upon something more than legal rights' (1993, p. 433). Extended entitlements, for example, [, for example,] might include *socially determined entitlements* (a moral economy, indigenous security institutions), *non-legal entitlements* (food riots, demonstrations, theft) and *non-entitlement transfers* (charity). This highlights a rather different way of thinking about E-mapping. First, entitlements are socially constructed (not just individually conferred): they are forms of social process and a type of REPRESENTATION. Second, like all forms of representation, entitlements are complex congeries of cultural, institutional and political practice that are unstable: that is to say, they are both constituted and reproduced through CONFLICT, negotiation and struggle. Entitlements are, then, political and social achievements that are customarily fought over in the course of MODERNIZATION (in this sense, one can think about the means by which entitlements enter the political arena in the course of the differing routes to MODERNITY). And, third, social entitlements confirm Sen's unelaborated observation that the relations between people and food must be grasped as a 'NETWORK of entitlement *relations*' (1981, p. 159; emphasis added). Hunger or famine-proneness are the products of historically specific *networks of social entitlements*.

One of the great strengths of Sen's approach to food and hunger is that entitlements are part of a larger architecture of thinking about DEVELOPMENT as a state of well-being and choice or freedom. In his language, the capability of a person reflects the 'alternative combinations of functioning the person achieves and from which he or she can choose one collection' (1993, p. 3). Functionings represent parts of the state of a person, and especially those things that a person can do or be in leading a life. In seeing poverty or hunger as a failure of capabilities – rather than insufficient income, or inadequate primary goods as in the Rawlsian sense of justice – Sen shows how the freedom to lead different types of life is a reflected in the person's capabilities (see Sen, 1999).   MW

Suggested reading
Bread for the World (http://www.bread.org/learn/hunger-basics/hunger-facts-international.html) and Hunger Notes (http://www.worldhunger.org/).

hybridity A condition describing those things and processes that transgress or disconcert binary terms that draw distinctions between like and unlike categories of object – such as self/other, culture/nature, animal/machine or mind/body. Hybridity has entered popular parlance through the commercial mobilization of techno-scientific innovations (e.g. the cultivation of hybrid seeds and plants or the proliferation of hybrid vehicles), or cultural INNOVATIONS such as cyber-culture or fusion music (see CYBORG). As these examples suggest, the mixing of properties ascribed to opposing ONTOLOGICAL categories established through academic and everyday use inspires both social anxiety and excitement.

In GEOGRAPHY and the wider social sciences and HUMANITIES, hybridity has come to be used rather too loosely to mean any number of different kinds of mixing, such as the notion of 'hybrid methods' – which means little more than combining QUALITATIVE and QUANTITATIVE METHODS in the conduct of research, or what used to be called multi-method approaches. Such usages tend to treat hybridity as an intrinsically desirable quality or strategy. More theoretically or philosophically rigorous explorations of hybridity are associated primarily with two bodies of work: (i) cultural studies (see CULTURAL TURN) and IDENTITY POLITICS, particularly in the field of post-colonial studies (e.g. Bhabha, 1994; see POST-COLONIALISM) and (ii) SCIENCE and technology studies and POSTHUMANIST politics (e.g. Latour, 1993).

In the case of post-colonial studies, hybridity is associated with the interrogation of those contact spaces in which cultural differences are contingently and conflictually negotiated (see Pratt, 1992; cf. TRANSCULTURATION). In the case of science and technology studies, it is enrolled as a device to negotiate the temptations of the 'one plus one' logic or 'mixture of two pure forms' that pervade binary and DIALECTICAL modes of analysis of NATURE–CULTURE relations (see Whatmore, 2002a). The problem here, as Bruno Latour suggests, is that:

critical explanation always began from the poles and headed toward the middle, which was first the separation point and then the conjunction point for opposing resources ... In this way the middle was simultaneously maintained and abolished, recognised and denied, specified and silenced ... How? By conceiving of every hybrid as a mixture of two pure forms. (1993, pp. 77–8)

As many, particularly FEMINIST, scholars working in philosophy and science and technology studies make clear, the importance of hybridity in these terms is that it insists that questions of SOCIAL JUSTICE cannot be understood in terms of human relations or reasoning alone, and invites ETHICAL and political projects that re-frame these questions in terms of the more-than-human company of bodies, technologies and forces implicated in, and consequential for, the conduct of social life.   SW

Suggested reading
Bhabha (1994); Castree and Nash (2004); Haraway (1991); Latour (1993); Pratt (1992); Whatmore (2002a).

hyperspace Hyperspace has four or more dimensions. Geographical tradition privileges location and three (Euclidean) dimensions: (x, y, z) or (Easting, Northing and height)(see EUCLIDEAN SPACE). Yet, it is rarely just *where* something happens that is important but also *when*, giving a fourth dimension: time. Space–time is therefore a hyperspace that becomes more complex (e.g. to visualize) if variables recording *what* happened (or what is found) are treated as further dimensions of the space. The literary critic Frederic Jameson (1991, pp. 38–44) famously described multi-dimensional 'hyperspace' as the characteristic SPATIALITY of POSTMODERNITY that disrupts and exceeds conventional modes of REPRESENTATION.   RH

Suggested reading
Mlodinow (2001).

hypothesis A provisional idea requiring further assessment to test its merit. The etymological origin is from the Greek meaning 'to put under, suppose'. Within GEOGRAPHY, the formalization of hypotheses was closely associated with the QUANTITATIVE REVOLUTION, in which the 'supposed' was a scientific statement capable of empirical testing using formal statistical techniques (see also DEDUCTION).

In its early use, however, 'hypothesis' meant an imagined idea, with only a distant connection to the real. In 1616, Cardinal Bellarmine (1542–1621) warned Galileo Galilei (1564–1642) not 'to hold or defend' the idea of a heliocentric solar system, but to treat is as a 'hypothesis', not reality. And a similar sense was given to the term when Sir Isaac Newton (1643–1727) said about his theory of gravity: 'I feign no hypotheses' – that is, his work was based on observation and experiment, not speculation. By the nineteenth century, in contrast, the use of hypotheses was increasingly seen as an integral part of the very practice of SCIENCE – not at odds with it, as Newton implied. Hypotheses were where science began; with interesting but as yet unproven ideas that stemmed from scientific THEORY or MODELS. Whether hypotheses were accepted depended upon the criteria applied. Criteria have included: simplicity (the capacity to minimize new explanatory entities); scope (the power to maximize the domain of application); fruitfulness (the capability to generate future hypotheses); fit (the compatibility with other hypotheses); and, perhaps most important, empirical fidelity (the ability to match the facts).

This last criterion was taken up and formalized within the discipline of statistics from the late nineteenth century. In the late 1920s, the statisticians Jerzy Neyman (1894–1981) and Egon Pearson (1895–1980) set out what was to become the standard framework for statistical hypothesis testing that proved so influential in geography. They provided step-by-step procedures stipulating how to frame a hypothesis and how to assess its empirical merit rigorously and precisely. Formulating the *null hypothesis* was step one. Accepting the conservative supposition that it is better to assume that one is wrong rather than right, the null hypothesis stated the opposite of what one believed to be correct. The remaining steps then defined what was necessary in order either to reject or accept the hypothesis for the specified level of statistical significance.

The first widespread use of the Neyman–Pearson procedures for statistical hypothesis testing in geography occurred in the mid-1950s, at the start of the Quantitative Revolution. This transformation of the geographical agenda into SPATIAL SCIENCE was also associated with the introduction of formal theory, which generated a plethora of hypotheses to be tested. Newman (1973, p. 22) reports that in 1971, at the height of the Quantitative Revolution, 26 per cent of all papers published in the top three American geographical journals were concerned with hypothesis testing. That seems impressive, but Newman doubted whether many of the authors understood what they were doing, and whether they were doing it correctly. The point became moot, however, as human geographers increasingly abandoned formal hypothesis testing, and the very vocabulary of a hypothesis. But they have never lost sight of the importance of 'imagined ideas'.   TB

Suggested reading
Harvey (1969, 100–6).

I
---

iconography The description and interpretation of visual IMAGES in order to disclose and interpret their hermetic or symbolic meanings; a HERMENEUTIC practice, closely paralleled by semiotics in linguistic studies. Initially applied to religious icons and painted images, and theorized as a METHODOLOGY within Renaissance ART history by the cultural historian Erwin Panofsky, iconography was initially introduced into human geography by Jean Gottmann (1952) alongside 'movement' as one of two counterposing forces structuring the POLITICAL GEOGRAPHY of NATIONS: the latter acting to integrate TERRITORIES, and the former to separate them through local allegiances. While this formulation acknowledged a political efficacy on the part of cultural symbols, its impact on geographical study was limited, and only decades later was the symbolic significance of national icons such as landscapes, paintings, buildings and monuments subjected to more systematic iconographic analysis by geographers and others (Daniels, 1993; Schama, 1995).

In contemporary HUMAN GEOGRAPHY, iconography is principally used as a method of LANDSCAPE and MAP interpretation (Daniels and Cosgrove, 1988; Harley, 2001b). Landscapes, both on the ground and in their representation through various media such as maps, painting and photography, can be regarded as visible deposits of cultural meanings (see also CARTOGRAPHY, HISTORY OF; VISUAL METHODS). The iconographic method seeks to address these meanings through describing the form, composition and content of such representations, disclosing their symbolic conventions and language, and interpreting the significances and implications of their symbolism by re-immersing landscapes in their social and historical contexts. Successful iconographic interpretation requires close formal reading, broad contextual knowledge, interpretative sensitivity and persuasive writing skills: it reveals human landscapes as both shaped by and themselves active in shaping broader social and cultural processes, and thus possessed of powerful human significance. Geographical iconography today accepts that landscape meanings are unstable over time and between different groups, always negotiated and contested, and thus political in the broadest sense. Through this recognition, a connection may be made in terms of politics between current geographical uses of iconography and Gottmann's original formulation. This is exemplified by the significant body of work on landscapes, MONUMENTS, spatial images and the expression and PERFORMANCE of IDENTITY that has been produced by geographers since the early 1990s (see, e.g., Whelan, 2003). DCO

Suggested reading
Atkinson and Cosgrove (1998).

ideal type An operational construct originally proposed by the sociologist Max Weber (1864–1920) as a way of exposing the essentials of a situation to analysis for particular purposes: 'An ideal type is formed by the one-sided accentuation of one or more points of view and by the synthesis of a great many diffuse, discrete, more or less present and occasionally absent concrete individual phenomena, which are arranged according to those one-sidedly emphasized viewpoints into a unified analytical construct.' The ideal type is 'ideal' in the sense of 'idealized': it is always a partial characterization of a phenomenon that, by emphasizing particular features and ignoring others (marginalizing them, holding them constant), draws out what the analyst regards as particularly important. It is thus purposive, an ABSTRACTION, and ideal means 'pure' or 'abstract', with other elements stripped away (cf. MODEL). DG

idealism A humanist PHILOSOPHY based around the belief that the world is constructed through the human mind (see HUMANISM). Idealism's assertion that 'all reality is in some way a mental construction so that the world does not exist outside its observation and representation by the individual has long been posed against the positivistic epistemology and its emphasis on objective evidence' (Johnston, 1986, p. 55). Idealism was set in opposition to MATERIALISM, which privileged matter, rendering the import of mind or spirit secondary, dependent or invisible. In GEOGRAPHY, this is most closely associated with the work of Leonard Guelke, who drew on historian R.G. Collingwood's 'historical idealism', which insisted that 'all history is the history of human thought'. Idealism in geography regarded its aim as being one of *'rethinking the thoughts behind the actions* (the "insides" beneath the "outsides") of "human events" with tangible environmental–landscape impacts' (Cloke, Philo and Sadler, 1991, p. 70; emphasis in original). In a challenge to what he considered to be over-theorization of contemporary human geography, Guelke's idealism required a move from concern with the theories that geographers held about the world and its workings to a primary focus upon the theories used by human beings acting in the world. For Guelke, a geographer's role is to understand the theories lying behind action that essentially make up HUMAN AGENCY. As he put it, the 'intention behind an action can be regarded as the source of its power and theory in it can be considered to be the guidance system' (Guelke, 1974, p. 197).

Any insistence of the THEORY-neutrality of academic research is problematic. Moreover, Guelke's vision of geography suggests a world in which humans act 'rationally' on the basis of how they conceptualize their worlds. Thus, in many respects Guelke's idealism is an extension of BEHAVIOURAL GEOGRAPHY, rather than having a close association with the philosophically charged recovery of agency in (most) HUMANISTIC GEOGRAPHY (which focused upon notions of feeling, emotion and meaning). Guelke viewed human agency as being based upon intentional decisions, ignoring both the constraining and enabling effects of economic structures and cultural DISCOURSE. Geographies influenced by PSYCHOANALYTIC THEORY have challenged the possibility of individual agents knowing their motivations and have turned to the effects of the unconscious.

The concern of new cultural geographers with DISCOURSE and REPRESENTATION, although very different conceptually from Guelke's idealism, have nevertheless generated new debate around idealism, with both MARXIST and SOCIAL GEOGRAPHY expressing concern about the lack of attention given to issues of the material (see Mitchell, 1995; Duncan and Duncan, 1996; Philo, 2000a). Theorizations of the BODY as an inscriptive surface where the material and discursive articulate have sought to transcend the idealism–materialism debate (Nast and Pile, 1998). jsh

Suggested reading
Cloke, Philo and Sadler (1991); Guelke (1974).

identity The origins of a term that is increasingly used throughout the social sciences are somewhat obscure, but its shifts reflect changing conceptions of the human subject in the discourses of modern and late-modern thought. With its inheritance of Renaissance HUMANISM, which posited Man (sic) as the 'measure of all things', and the dramatic changes inaugurated by the Protestant Reformation, the ENLIGHTENMENT is usually identified as the context within which the identity of the modern subject definitively emerges. Based on a conception of a self-sustaining entity, possessed of the capacity of conscious reason and whose internal 'centre' was seen as essentially fixed – continuous or 'identical' with itself across time – the Enlightenment aligns identity to a decisive form of individualism. Prioritized in the seventeenth century by René Descartes ('I *think*, therefore I am'), John Locke (who equated individual identity with the 'sameness of a rational being'; see Locke, 1967 [1690]) and attenuated through the nineteenth and twentieth centuries, the individual is positioned as the author of historical development, his identity seen as the sovereign source from which all social laws and categories of knowledge are derived.

The changing formations of modern SOCIETY, and the development of sociology that sought to understand them, provided the first critique of this MODEL. Locating individual identity within group processes and submitting it to the dynamics of collective and contractual norms, sociologists such as G.H. Mead (see SYMBOLIC INTERACTIONISM) argued the ways in which identities are positioned within wider social relations and, conversely, function to sustain wider social structures. While such theories of socialization clearly break with the autonomy of the humanist self, they nonetheless continue to uphold the principle of a stable identity; the relation between the individual *and* society being an interaction between two reciprocal, but nonetheless distinct, entities.

A key revision that resolutely displaced the Cartesian and sociological subject was the reconstruction of Marxist social theory in the late 1960s. For the Marxist structuralist Louis Althusser (1970), the privileging of social formations did not just invert the relations between the individual and society, but jettisoned subjective agency from the processes of history, the concerns of ETHICS and the terms of PHILOSOPHY itself (see MARXISM; STRUCTURALISM). From this perspective, identity is not only conditional, lodged in contingency, but divested of any transcendental authority it becomes little more than the effect or 'bearer' of a social structure. 'Self-hood' thus does not derive from any faculty held in the mind, but via the mechanism of '*interpellation*'; that is, by those ideological processes that on the one hand 'speak to us' or 'hail us into place' as the social subjects of particular discourses and, on the other, produce us as subjects that can 'speak' and can be 'spoken'. To this novel understanding of identity must be added the impact of Freud on twentieth-century Western thought. Indeed, if Freud's original 'discovery' of the unconscious put paid to the humanist project of the self-knowing individual, later psychoanalytic theorists, such as Jacques Lacan, insist on identity as unresolved and irresolvable: not something that evolves organically or intentionally from inside the core of cognitive being, but via a struggle that charts the infant's difficult entry into various systems of symbolic orders, including language, culture and sexual difference. For Lacan, the agony of this 'entry' not only leaves the subject always divided in itself (the perception of wholeness being, for Lacan, as for Althusser, only an 'imaginary' or fantasized pleasure), but maintains this improper fit as an initial and continuing experience. Psychoanalytically, then, we should speak not of identity as something achieved or achievable, but of *identification* as an always imaginary search for the image of a resolved self (see PSYCHOANALYTIC THEORY).

With the de-centred SUBJECT located as the unstable core of modern and late-modern thought, identity is not only exposed as a social and psychic process, but is posed as a political problem (Pile and Thrift, 1995). With the growth of cultural studies in the 1970s, it is deployed not only a critical tool useful in the analysis of cultural forms, but as an active site of conflict and resistance within social relations fractured by divisions of GENDER, CLASS and RACE. Energized by the ferment of ideas produced by the late 1960s – the counter-culture, civil rights, feminist, anti-colonial and anti-war movements (see FEMINISM) – the 'politics of identity' emerged to mobilize new, and hitherto untheorized, individual and collective possibilities. While very different kinds of identity were examined (from working-class to sexual and gendered identities; from racial to generational identities), such analyses were determinedly committed, with a distinctively autobiographical, reflexive and strategic charge. The dialogue between identity and the 'politics of location' was to become key, especially within debates of how affective investments in the idea of a home(land) relate to the resources of history, language and culture in the production of subjective and collective allegiance. Thus various theorists (Gellner, 1983; Renan, 1990 [1882]; Balibar, 1991b; Hall, 1992a) explored the ways in which identities relate to the (relatively modern) *invention* of the NATION, which they invite us to read less as a political or territorial site than as the particular expression of cultural tradition; as an articulation of communal belonging sustained as much by myths of origin and homogeneity as it is by the supposed continuities of character, value and custom. From this perspective, national identity is decisively not a primordial gift of birth, nor even a coincidence of geographical location, but the willed incorporation into an 'imagined community' (Anderson, 1991 [1983]), a fiction continually formed and transformed by the narratives, and counter-narratives, of its telling.

By the late 1980s, this account was given fresh prominence with the explosion of post-colonial theory (see POST-COLONIALISM), which sought, amongst other things, to deconstruct the unity of the sovereign self written into European knowledge, theory and history. If at one end of the spectrum modern Western nations have produced stories of familial membership in order to negotiate internal contradictions (Matless, 1988; Cresswell, 1996) or exercise forms of territorial expansion (Daniels, 1993; Driver, 2001a), at the other end conscious assertions of identity have been mobilized as a strategy of resistance for those dispossessed by the legacy of EMPIRE (Blunt and McEwan, 2002). Yet – as in fantasies of the 'whole' self of which Lacanian psychoanalysis speaks – this often releases a regressive desire to reclaim the (lost) integrity of a 'local' or national particularity as a way of negotiating the competing pressures of existent and emergent multiplicities. In this context, identity means not only the aspiration to Selfhood, but the assumption of a fictive Otherness. Having no positive meaning, but positioned within a field of differences, identity thus entails discursive work: the binding and marking of symbolic boundaries, the defining of identity by what it produces as its negative excess or 'constitutive outside'. The crucial point, however, is not simply that identity derives its distinction from what it is not. More precariously, the 'Other' returns to breach the foreclosure that we prematurely call 'identity' (Butler, 1990).

At present, processes of MIGRATION, TRANS-NATIONALISM and DIASPORA place identity (or the project of *identification*) firmly on the theoretical agenda. In the midst of such mobilities – as much a geographical and historical reality as a theoretical benefit – new spatial metaphors of the 'out of place' and 'in-between' render identity as a performance of ambivalences, doublings and dissimulations. Various theories of the post-colonial (Said, 2003 [1978]; Spivak, 1988; Bhabha, 1990a) have all sought a more complex, non-binary mode of identity, replacing neat national and ethnic divisions with the more fluid terms of 'translation', HYBRIDITY and transgression, and using these as critical strategies for destabilizing the power, and polarities, of Western thought. As a counter-current, however, the resurgence of neo-nationalisms (Eastern Europe post 1989), the rise of religious absolutisms (from India, to the Middle East to the USA) and a renewed rhetoric of civilizational differences (the image of a 'clash of civilizations') speak directly of an anxiety at the core of our contemporary selves. Indeed, if a hardening of identities is one symptom of the contradictions of the local and the global in POSTMODERNITY, from another perspective the national frame in which people have conventionally positioned themselves has been eroded by a new social order in which the homogenizing effects of global markets has reconfigured identity as a ready-to-buy, consumer option.

All of this charges identity with questions of our present and future political and ethical practice. While recognizing its fictive nature, the disruption of conventional paradigms of social experience and analysis (the nation, ideology, gender, race, class) heralds different possibilities of identification, placing new emphasis on subjective agency in its relational negotiations and improvisations. At this point, as Stuart Hall puts it, the question is not about 'who we are' or 'where we have come from' so much as 'what we might become, how we have been represented and how that bears on how we might represent ourselves' (Hall and du Gay, 1996).   JD

Suggested reading
Duncan and Rattansi (1992).

ideology Ideology originally referred to a 'science of ideas', proposed by French rationalist philosophers at the end of the eighteenth century. It is now more widely used to refer to any system of beliefs held for more than purely epistemic reasons. Some theories of ideology are neutral when it comes to accounting for the role of ideas and beliefs in social life. Others involve normative claims about how knowledge and belief function epistemologically to reproduce power-relations. In this second set of theories, ideology is understood as a distorted, inverted, upside down or false view of reality. In this usage, ideology is therefore implicitly or explicitly counterposed to some mode of knowing that sees reality in a true and accurate way. The most influential source for this second type of understanding is Marxism.

Despite never having been clearly worked through in his own work, ideology is arguably Marx's most powerful bequest to modern social theory. In the *German ideology* of 1845, Marx and Engels argued against idealist philosophies that saw ideas as the prime movers of historical change (see IDEALISM), asserting instead that 'social being' determined people's 'consciousness'. This is a basic axiom of materialist analysis (see HISTORICAL MATERIALISM). They also argued that in class-divided societies such as those of CAPITALISM, the ruling ideas would be those of the ruling class, since they owned and controlled the means for producing and circulating the knowledge, beliefs and values through which people made sense of their own experiences. In Marx's early work, this ideological determination of people's consciousness is theorized in terms of the alienation of the working class, who come to see social relations in inverted form. The argument was subsequently later reformulated as *commodity fetishism*. In 1867, Marx argued in *Capital* that under generalized capitalist commodity production, the social dimensions of human labour and interaction take on the appearance of free-standing objects, and commodities take on apparently magical qualities independent from the labour processes that produce them. Commodity fetishism is a theory of how people come to misrecognize reality through the medium of distorted appearances. This kernel of a mature theory of ideology was further refined in 1923 by György Lukács, in *History and class consciousness*, with the concept of *reification*, whereby people appear to each other as things rather than as active agents of historical processes, which he held to be a form of *false consciousness*.

The epistemological understanding of ideology as a generalized system of misrecognition in the interests of capitalist reproduction was systematized into models of base and superstructure, in which economic processes are seen to be the prime movers shaping other aspects of social formations, such as law, religion or general modes of consciousness. The vast Marxist literature on ideology is beset by the recourse to functional explanation (see FUNCTIONALISM), drawing of loose analogies, and imputing of structural isomorphisms between economic patterns and behaviour and belief. It is not too strong to suggest that the Marxist theory of ideology is 'partly anecdotal, partly functionalist, partly conspiratorial, and partly magical' (Elster, 1982a, p. 199).

Marxist theories of ideology share two features: a formal aspect, in which ideology is understood to be a medium for the inversion or obscuring of reality; and a content, in which ideology is held to function in the interests of particular classes, by presenting their particular interests as if they were the interests of all classes. In both respects, there is a presumption that ideology is politically effective by making social relations and historical processes appear natural, inevitable, objective or a-historical. This is the strongest legacy of the Marxist heritage of theories of ideology, which lives on in a widespread assumption that the task of *critical* social science is the exposure of naturalized, de-historicized, objectified appearances as historical products and social constructs (see CRITICAL THEORY).

A recurrent theme in Western Marxism from the 1920s onwards was how to understand the means by which capitalist exploitation was legitimized through the active consent of those who were the main sources of economic value and the primary victims of injustice. The prevalence of this problem of *reproduction* helps account for the flourishing of Marxist cultural theory (Anderson, 1976). The absence of widespread political upheaval against capitalism was identified as a failure at the level of culture, attributed to the operations of ideology. In short, sophisticated theories were developed to explain capitalist reproduction on the assumption that 'people must have been got at' (Sinfield, 1994, p. 22). Some of Marxism's most important contributions emerge from this explanation of capitalist reproduction as a problem of culture and ideology. These include a shift away from focusing on false consciousness towards a consideration of the unconscious dynamics of personality formation, in the work of Herbert Marcuse for example; Theodor Adorno and Max Horkheimer's seminal account of the culture industries; Antonio Gramsci's account of cultural hegemony; and V.N. Volosinov's account of the inherently social qualities of the linguistic sign. The development of Marxist theories of ideology relied heavily on non-Marxist traditions such as psychoanalysis, Weberian sociology and semiotics. For all the sophistication of this tradition, it led to a curious 'blindspot' in Western Marxism, which came to think of cultural media such as radio, television or film primarily as ideological devices, neglecting to analyse these practices as sources for the production and distribution of surplus value (Smythe, 1978).

The nemesis of Marxist theories of ideology came in the figure of the avowedly Marxist philosopher Louis Althusser. Combining Lacanian psychoanalytic theory with Gramsci's account of hegemony, Althusser (1971) recast the concept of ideology in ways that still resonate in a range of cultural theory. He argued that ideology was not something that people could be liberated from, but was, rather, a constitutive dimension of all social formations: ideology was the mechanism through which individuals were made into subjects. The formation of subjectivity worked through the practices embodied in institutions such as churches, schools and universities. These he called Ideological State Apparatuses (ISAs). For Althusser, ideology referred to the 'representation of the imaginary relationships to their real conditions of existence'. *Imaginary* in this formulation does not mean false or unreal. It refers to the idea that this relationship is always, necessarily, mediated by way of images. In short, Althusser claimed that misrecognition was the constitutive mechanism of subjectivity in *all* societies, not just under capitalism; therefore it was not something that people could be liberated from.

Althusser's account of ISAs laid the basis for a generalized analysis of cultural practices in terms of practices of subject-formation rather than consciousness. The notion of ideological subjectification in ISAs served as a crucial way-station for the development of feminist theories of subjectivity, psychoanalytical theories of sexuality, and for the eventual supervention of 'ideology' by concepts of discourse, DISCIPLINARY POWER, GOVERNMENTALITY and other notions drawn from Michel Foucault's work (Barrett, 1991). The class content of ideology that Althusser took for granted was filled by other identities: ethnicity, gender, race and sexuality. The assertion that subjectivity was formed in ISAs was instrumental to the recognition that that struggles within civil society were a crucial dimension of counter-hegemonic political struggles (it also tended to flatter academics' sense of their own centrality to these struggles).

The traces of Althusser's account of ideology are still evident in theories of culture, discourse, governmentality and hegemony, even if the concept of ideology is rarely used in a strong analytical sense any more. There are three such traces of ideology in cultural theory, post-Marxism and post-structuralism: an emphasis on practices of subject-formation; an emphasis on the cognitive dimensions of this process, understood in terms of the naturalizing or de-historicizing of contingent relationships through the medium of representations; and an emphasis on how macro-level processes of subordination, exploitation and oppression are reproduced through this micro-level process of subject-formation. These related conceptualizations are given a geographical inflection by analysing the ways in which spatial forms (such as boundaries, scale relations or place identities) are inscribed in the representations that are supposed to function as mediums for subject-formation. The primary emphasis of post-Marxist, post-structuralist theories of discourse and hegemony remains on the ways in which people's subjectivities are *socially constructed* (see SOCIAL CONSTRUCTION). Human geographers have largely ignored the more productive turn towards analysing 'ideology' in terms of rhetoric, focusing on the relationships between active, *socially constructing* human subjects negotiating various argumentative dilemmas in everyday situations (Billig, 1996).

Marxist theories of ideology have not fared well in recent social theory. Abercrombie, Hill and Turner (1980) challenged the idea that ideology was a crucial factor in the reproduction of capitalism, calling attention to the degree to which this assumption depended on a functionalist view of society as a tightly integrated totality, whose parts contribute to the better operation of the whole. Criticisms of this sort have led to the revival of more neutral accounts of ideology. Thompson (1990) defines ideology as any system of signification that facilitates the pursuit of particular interests by a social group. Mann (1986) defines ideology as one of four sources of social power (along with economic, political and military sources), involving the mobilization of values, norms and rituals. In this sense, ideology is not false, although it does involve holding beliefs that surpass experience. These sorts of definitions see *ideology in general* as a ubiquitous feature of human affairs, while *particular ideologies* can be analysed for their practical effects and normative implications. Nevertheless, all concepts of ideology remain dogged by the problem that while it may be plausible to

assume that ideas are produced with certain intentions to influence and effect people, it is conceptually and empirically very difficult to account for just how these intended purposes actually come off successfully at all.

Theories of ideology, and their successors, are faced with two fundamental limitations. First, they emphasize the cognitive and epistemological dimensions of knowledge and belief, and assume that non-cognitive grounds for belief are at least suspect, if not false. This is an impoverished view of what it is to be a functioning human being, and it leads to a deeply problematic understanding of the politics of critique (Hanssen, 2000). Second, theories of ideology and their analogues face a persistent problem in justifying and accounting for their own epistemological claims (see EPISTEMOLOGY). The persistence of modes of 'ideological' problematization in academic analysis might even be interpreted as a symptom of scholasticism – the process by which the untheorized conditions of separation, distanciation and detachment that enable academic reflection are projected on to objects of critical analysis (Bourdieu, 2000).   CB

Suggested reading
Barrett, (1991); Billig (1996); Eagleton (1991); Thompson (1990).

idiographic Concerned with the unique and the particular (cf. NOMOTHETIC). The term originated at the end of the nineteenth century when two German philosophers, Wilhelm Windelband and Heinrich Rickert, made a famous distinction between the idiographic and the nomothetic sciences that, so they claimed, entitled history (by virtue of its central concern with the unique) to be regarded as radically different from other forms of intellectual enquiry (see KANTIANISM). Their arguments were challenged by other philosophers, but they made a forceful entry into GEOGRAPHY in the middle of the twentieth century through the Hartshorne–Schaefer debate over EXCEPTIONALISM, when traditional REGIONAL GEOGRAPHY was seen – in parallel with history – as essentially idiographic and not directed towards generalization. These claims were intensified during the QUANTITATIVE REVOLUTION, which was widely advertised as re-establishing geography within the mainstream of the sciences as a nomothetic system of knowledge 'after the lapse into ideography' (Burton, 1963). The term is rarely used today, and the idiographic/nomothetic binary has largely disappeared from most framings of geographical enquiry, but the issues it signals continue to animate geographers concerned with articulating theoretical claims with empirical particulars (see Burt, 2006). DG

image 'According to ancient etymology the word *image* should be linked to the root *imitari*' (Barthes, 1977). Thus we go to the heart of a problem first posed in Pliny's *Naturalis Historia*, later refined by Renaissance aestheticians and subsequently up-ended by modernists and postmodernists alike. Is the image (*eikon*) a particular kind of medium through which the world is most persuasively relayed to our understanding? Or is the image a graphic language that 'invisibly' encodes whole systems of value – a history, geography, a morality, an EPISTEMOLOGY? Whatever the case, to consider the image is to be aware of a trick of consciousness: an ability to see something as 'there' and as 'not there' at the same time; to appreciate that while the image might duplicate reality, it is itself not 'real'. With the status of the mimetic challenged by both the conceptualism of twentieth-century Western art and the critical charge launched by the textual or 'cultural turn' from the mid-1970s onwards, the image is now most commonly considered as a cultural encoding of a particular kind: as visual mode that involves the intervention of language and thus relies on those arbitrary, though conventionalized, signs to be accessed and read correctly. The image, in this sense, is what displays itself most and hides itself best. Accordingly, much contemporary geography (Daniels, 1993; Duncan and Duncan, 1992; Cosgrove, 1998 [1984]) has focused on the ideological force and function of the image; the ways in which by rooting itself in the apparent obviousness of the visible, the image effectively conceals the practices of its making.

But the power of the image does not consist merely in being a vehicle for interrogating what it occludes or for interpreting the relationship between expressed visual content and external or referential context. The image also interprets us. It does so in the sense that our attempts to understand the precepts and practices within we make our critical, political and epistemological choices are organized by tacit images, by a panoply of visual structures (e.g. the photographic 'freeze', cinematic mobility, digital malleability and its global relay) through which we create our orders of time, space and subjectivity (see FILM; VISION AND VISUALITY).

What emerges is a vast aggregate of things that go by the name of the image, deputized across a variety of methodologies, institutions and disciplines. Thus while some contemporary geographers have been concerned with the encoding and deciphering of pictorial or technological images (e.g. landscape painting or photography), others have examined imagery in its proper or literal sense (graphic or plastic artefacts such as MAPS, diagrams, MONUMENTS and buildings). More abstractly, geography has considered various metaphorical extensions of the concept at work within literature (the image as ornamented language in travel-writing, for example), epistemology (the image as idea in the 'eye of the mind'), physics (the image in optical theory), psychoanalysis (the image as dream, memory, fantasmata) and even, conceivably, within the possibilities of BIOTECHNOLOGY (the genetic code-as-image).

While it is impossible for so many category definitions to settle into comfortable coexistence, contemporary debates about the image share a degree of critical consensus: a rejection of truth as a matter of accurate imaging and an understanding, instead, of its cultural significance, historical circumstance and its power as epistemological constituent. All images, whether visual, graphic, textual, perceptual or psychic, are thus viewed as reflective mediations of objects, concepts and affects. Accordingly, all are disorderly and riddled with error. The misconception, then, is to think that we can know the truth about the world by knowing the right images of it. But the other misconception is to think that we can know anything about the world without images. One need not favour the postmodern conviction of reality as a depthless SIMULACRUM (Baudrillard, 1983), nor want to oppose such cynicism with a more corporeal and performative approach (see PERFORMATIVITY), to acknowledge that since the image is all we have to work with, we need to regard it not only as a site of semiotic or perceptual convention but as a starting point for a dialogue with convention that leads us to its limits. This includes investigating what might lie outside or beyond the image, as well as thinking about the relation of the image to the non-image, of vision to not-seeing, to invisibility and even to blindness. JD

Suggested reading
Crary (1990b); Melville and Readings (1995); Rose (2001).

imaginative geographies Representations of other places – of peoples and landscapes, cultures and 'natures' – that articulate the desires, fantasies and fears of their authors and the grids of power between them and their 'Others'. The concept is not confined to ostensibly fictional works. On the contrary, there is an important sense in which all geographies are imaginative: even the most formal, geometric lattices of SPATIAL SCIENCE or the most up-to-date and accurate MAPS are at once abstractions and cultural constructions, and as such open to critical readings.

The concept was originally proposed by the Palestinian/American literary critic Edward Said (1935–2003) in his influential critique of ORIENTALISM (Said, 2003 [1978]; see Gregory, 1995a). His emphasis on POWER (and in particular colonial power) was alien to the concepts of ENVIRONMENTAL PERCEPTION and MENTAL MAPS then current in BEHAVIOURAL GEOGRAPHY, and underscored the radical 'non-innocence' of REPRESENTATION. In some measure, Said's formulation anticipated ideas of SITUATED KNOWLEDGE: he was concerned to disclose the privileges that European and American authors typically claimed when representing other cultures, to chart the asymmetric grid of power within which (as he put it) 'the West' watches, 'the East' is watched, and hence to criticize the partialities of their constructions.

Said's emphasis on viewing, watching, looking, observing – on VISION AND VISUALITY – drew attention to the cultural construction of the gaze. While Said's critique of Orientalism was shot through with visual metaphors, the imaginative geographies with which he was centrally concerned were textual. Human geographers have been drawn to both the textual and the visual image, however, including art forms such as FILM and photography (Schwartz and Ryan, 2003), and they have drawn attention to viewing as an embodied, vitally sensuous practice (Martins, 2000). Unlike the other constructs of behavioural geography, therefore, none of these imaginative geographies are seen as the product of purely cognitive operations. As cultural constructs, their images are animated by fantasy, desire and the unconscious, and indeed the very idea of an 'imagination' has been extended through geographies indebted to various forms of PSYCHOANALYTIC THEORY (Pile, 1998). These images carry within them comparative valorizations – what Said called a 'poetics of space' – by means of which places are endowed with 'figurative value'. Such constructions also involve a poetics (and a politics) of NATURE, and there has been considerable interest in recovering imaginative geographies of other 'natures' as well as other cultures. At the limit, these distinguish a 'normal', temperate nature from other, intemperate natures and install their own cultural subtext about those who inhabit such 'unnatural natures' (Gregory, 1995b; Sioh, 1998; see also TROPICALITY).

Said claimed that these figurative values enter not only into the production of 'otherness' but also into the identity-formation of the viewing subject in a complex DIALECTIC. Imaginative geographies thus sustain images of 'home' as well as 'abroad', 'our space' as well as 'their space': 'Imaginative geography and history help the mind to intensify its own sense of itself by dramatizing the distance and difference between what is close to it and what is far away' (Said, 1978, p. 55). Hence Orford (2003) showed that imaginative geographies are regularly mobilized to separate the space of 'the international community' from the space of those facing security crises, so that intervention is always after the event and constructed as selflessly humanitarian; she argues that this separation is achieved through tactics of localizing and distancing ('their space') that work not only to legitimize the actions of the global North as so many virtuous efforts to find a solution, but also in many cases to obscure the active involvement of its international actors in the *generation* of the crisis. Similarly, Graham (2006) contrasts the imaginative geographies that have been used to separate HOMELAND cities from 'terror', 'target' or Arab cities during the 'war on terror', even as they are also being integrated through techno-science 'into a single, transnational battlespace'. Studies like these show why Gregory (2004b, p. 256) concludes that 'imaginative geographies are doubled spaces of articulation' whose 'inconstant topologies are mappings of connective dissonance in which connections are elaborated in some registers even as they are disavowed in others'.

'Dramatization' is not the same as 'falsification', however, and Said's discussion undercuts the distinction between 'real' and 'perceived' worlds on which behavioural geography depended. This is the most complicated and contentious part of Said's argument. There are certainly passages where he contrasted what he called 'positive geographies' with imaginative geographies produced under the sign of Orientalism. And yet, if imaginative geographies are 'fictions' in the original Latin sense of *fictio* – something made, something fabricated – this does not mean that they are necessarily without concreteness, substance and, indeed, 'reality'. On the contrary, imaginative geographies circulate in material forms (including novels, paintings, photographs and film; intelligence reports, academic geographies and popular TRAVEL WRITING; and collections and exhibitions) which become sedimented over time to form an internally structured and, crucially, self-reinforcing *archive*. This supplies a 'citationary structure' for subsequent accounts that is also in some substantial sense PERFORMATIVE: it shapes and legitimizes the attitudes and dispositions, policies and practices of its collective audience, so that in this way imaginative geographies spiral into and out of a sort of cultural paradigm of 'otherness' that has the most acutely material consequences.

Imaginative geographies thus act to both legitimize and produce 'worlds'. The circulation and sedimentation of imaginative geographies produces a sense of 'facticity' and hence of authority: the repetition of the same motifs becomes a taken-for-granted citation of Truth (Vanderbeck, 2006). In some cases, imaginative geographies work to domesticate other spaces and hence validate (for example) colonial dispossession: thus Carter's (1987) project of an avowedly *spatial history* showed how the LANDSCAPE of AUSTRALIA was brought within the horizon of European intelligibility through a series of explicitly textual and cartographic practices. In other cases imaginative geographies articulate spaces of (radical) difference, but here too, through their implication in systems of power and practice, they may be read as so many PERFORMANCES of SPACE. Thus Gregory (2004b) distinguished three strategies put to work during the 'war on terror' to bring 'the enemy' into view within three different spaces: reduced to targets in the coordinates and pixels of an abstract, geometric space; reduced to barbarians attacking the gates of CIVILIZATION from a wild, savage space; and reduced to the inhuman, lodged in a paradoxical space of exception (see EXCEPTION, SPACE OF) wherein their deaths were of no consequence (see also TERRORISM).

Strategy	Register	Space
Locating	Techno-cultural	Abstract, geometric
Inverting	Cultural–political	Wild, savage
Excepting	Politico-legal	Paradoxical, topological

Seen thus, imaginative geographies are spaces of constructed (in)visibility and it is this partiality that implicates them in the play of power.

In response, *imaginative counter-geographies* are deliberate attempts to displace, subvert and contest the imaginative geographies installed by dominant regimes of power, practice and representation. Usually produced from within the targets of representation, they seek to give voice and vision to their subjects and to undo the separations between 'our space' and 'their space': thus 'the empire writes back' and 'the subaltern speaks' to undermine the impositions of imperialism and subalternity (Slater, 1999: see SUBALTERN STUDIES). Testimonies of this sort have a long history, but today they frequently use so-called 'new media' to produce new publics: hence Gregory (2009c) explores blogs from Baghdad whose counter-geographies of everyday life contest US political and military imaginaries of Arab cities. DG

Suggested reading
Driver (2005); Gregory (1995a); Said (2003 [1978, pp. 49–73]).

immigration A form of migration that occurs when people move from one nation-state to another. Immigrants change their permanent dwelling place and are therefore distinct from *sojourners*, who relocate temporarily, usually for employment-related reasons; immigrants also move voluntarily and are therefore distinct from REFUGEES, who are forced to leave their homes because of persecution. When immigrants settle in a new country without the knowledge and approval of the government in power, they are called 'undocumented', 'illegal' or 'unauthorized' immigrants. Millions of people immigrate each year, and this form of migration is one of the most significant causes of social change in the world today (Clark, 1986; Sassen, 1996).

There have been several episodes of mass migration in history, but the decades following the Second World War have seen the largest population movements of all time. Immigration, in the sense in which the term is used today, began after the creation of nation-states and, until recently, was closely associated with colonization (cf. COLONIALISM). For example, British subjects migrated to the colonies and created *settler societies*; after colonies gained independence, this movement continued in the form of immigration. Others, at first mainly from European countries, joined them and many former colonies, such as Australia, Canada and the USA, consider themselves 'immigrant societies' in the sense that the overwhelming majority of their citizens are either immigrants themselves or the descendents of immigrants. Until recently, virtually all immigrants migrated towards what they believed to be greater economic opportunities. These historic patterns have changed in the past twenty-five years, in two key ways. First, both source and destination regions have multiplied, and immigration now is more global in scope than at any time in the past (Castles and Miller, 2003). Second, in marked contrast to past periods, a small but highly significant number of today's immigrants are wealthy. These 'designer immigrants' are especially concerned with political issues (i.e. stability) and lifestyle. They are sought by many countries for their entrepreneurial skill and capital, and have significantly changed the way in which immigrants are perceived in the places in which they settle (Skeldon, 1994; Mitchell, 2004a).

According to the influential report of the UN Global Commission on International Migration (GCIM, 2005), there are nearly 200 million people in the world who have been living, for at least one year, outside their country of birth, which translates to roughly 3 per cent of the global population. According to the GCIM (p. 2), 'The Commission concludes that the international community has failed to capitalize on the opportunities and to meet the challenges associated with international migration.' In particular, the GCIM concluded that the reception policies of destination countries do not enable immigrants to integrate efficiently.

Immigrants, wherever they settle, are usually culturally different from their receiving societies. Often, they are 'visible minorities' (i.e. of a different skin colour than the dominant population). The reception of immigrants varies widely between countries, but three types of responses are typical: isolation, ASSIMILATION and PLURALISM. Some societies believe that immigrants are necessary to fulfil certain functions – for example, when they face labour shortages – but that they should remain separate from the dominant population and, ideally, leave when no longer needed. This was the case, for example, in many Western countries in the period following the Second World War, and it is true of countries such as Japan and Singapore today (Yeoh, 2006). Countries that ascribe to this view make it difficult for immigrants to acquire full legal RIGHTS and, especially, CITIZENSHIP. Others, such as France and, to a more limited extent, the USA, expect immigrants to

conform, or assimilate, to a predefined national CULTURE. In this case, full legal rights and citizenship are often granted in stages, in step with the assimilation process. Finally, a few countries, notably Australia and Canada, have enacted legislation enshrining the concept of MULTICULTURALISM, a policy that fosters the coexistence of many forms of cultural expression. These countries typically allow immigrants to become citizens quickly and, acknowledging the complexities of IDENTITY, allow individuals to hold dual or multiple legal citizenship(s). Note, though, that the differences between these policies are easily overstated, and that countries rarely follow single immigration policies that are applied to all groups equally. Also, recall that the GCIM has concluded, generally, that reception policies are inadequate.

Traditionally, immigration has been analysed in straightforward terms as a push–pull process: people leave a country to escape problems, such as POVERTY or political CONFLICT, and are drawn to particular places that offer them a better life. In this conception, people are treated as rational individuals who are willing to cast aside their old identities and loyalties and embrace new ones if they believe it is to their advantage. Settlement is seen as a unidirectional, progressive process, where immigrants eventually become indistinguishable from the society that receives them – they become assimilated. This interpretation arose out of the research of the CHICAGO SCHOOL in the early twentieth century and continues to affect immigration research. However, recent work, drawing on different understandings of history, culture and identity, offers an alternate perspective. First, migration is seen as a collective process that occurs sequentially and in both directions. Immigrants rarely sever the links between their previous and present places and social contacts, and life in the new country is linked to life in the old (cf. CHAIN MIGRATION). As a result, immigrant culture becomes a mélange of practices, and identities are in flux rather than fixed, or in an inexorable progression from old to new. More and more, immigration studies are adopting the view of cultures as DIASPORIC – as scattered, but connected across vast distances. This realization has led to the concept of TRANSNATIONALISM, the idea that many people live in societies that stretch across – and perhaps even transcend – national boundaries (see Appadurai, 1996; Van Hear, 1998).

These new understandings of the immigration process are particularly salient given the importance of immigrants in (re)defining contemporary economic, political and cultural systems. For example, non-white people are about to become the majority of the population in the state of California, the first time in history where a white society has voluntarily become a minority in a territory under its control (Maharidge, 1996). Similar cultural transformations are occurring in large cities throughout the Western world, which are becoming more multi-ethnic and polyglot than ever before (e.g. nearly 200 languages are spoken in the area served by the municipal government of Toronto). There are few studies of the cultural dynamics of living in multi-ethnic cities (though see Jacobs, 1996; Germain, 1997), but it is clear that these new contexts raise fundamental questions about the meaning of equity, public participation, and even citizenship itself (Jacobson, 1996). DH

Suggested reading
Castles and Miller (2003); Global Commission on International Migration (GCIM) (2005); Richmond (1994); Segal (1993).

imperialism An unequal human and territorial relationship, usually in the form of an EMPIRE, based on ideas of superiority and practices of dominance, and involving the extension of authority and control of one STATE or people over another. Derived from the Latin word *imperium* ('sovereign authority'), imperialism is closely affiliated with COLONIALISM. Both are intrinsically geographical – and traumatic – processes of expropriation, in which people, wealth, resources and decision-making power are relocated from distant lands and peoples to a metropolitan centre and elite (through a mixture of exploration, conquest, trade, resource extraction, settlement, rule and representation), although the latter differs from the former in terms of the intensity and materiality of its focus on dispossession. 'Imperial' is used to denote attitudes and practices of dominance befitting an EMPIRE.

The term was originally used in the second half of the nineteenth century to describe a state-centred ethos of territorial expansion – epitomized by the imperial partition of Africa between 1885 and 1914 – that involved both aggressive national competition for prestige and a more general rationalization of imperialism as a 'civilizing mission'. This era of 'classical imperialism' drew old and new imperial powers (Britain, France, Portugal and Belgium; Germany, Italy, Japan and the USA) into an expanding and volatile capitalist world system, and two world wars that precipitated the swift disintegration of the sprawling colonial empires that had been built over the previous four centuries (Baumgart, 1982; cf. DECOLONIZATION). Geography – as both a discipline and wider discourse – forged an intimate relationship with imperialism during this period (cf. GEOGRAPHY, HISTORY OF). Projects of exploration and mapping, geopolitical models and climatic arguments for European superiority and racial difference played especially important imperial roles (Bell, Butlin and Heffernan, 1995; cf. CLIMATE; HEARTLAND).

Yet the idea and practice of imperialism has a longer history, and attempts have been made to explain it in more systematic terms. It has been traced back to Antiquity and into what David Harvey (2003b) has called 'the new imperialism' (or 'neo-imperialism') currently being expedited through American military and economic overlordship (especially in the Middle East), and justified as a 'war on terror'. The Romans left some important imperial precedents, such as the imperative to legitimize colonization by recourse to divine or secular law. However, a series of advances – initially in navigation and military technology, and then in commerce, administration and methods of knowledge production – helped European powers to create overseas empires on a SCALE never imagined or deemed feasible before; and recent work on imperialism emphasizes how the imperial prerogative of the West (and especially the USA: see AMERICAN EMPIRE) now resides in the power to circumvent international institutions and law (see, e.g., EXCEPTION, SPACE OF) and thus in some measure leave behind the moral and political legacy of Rome.

Critical approaches to imperialism emphasize its innately exploitative and dehumanizing nature (evidenced, for instance, by SLAVERY), and – at the risk of oversimplification – have come in three main forms and phases. First, and beginning with the early-twentieth-century work of J.A. Hobson, V.I. Lenin and Joseph Schumpeter, imperialism has been analysed in economic and political terms – as central to the evolution of CAPITALISM and the NATION-STATE. A large historical and geographical literature seeks to account for the specificity of imperial power, and examines how different phases of capitalist accumulation (mercantile, industrial, monopoly) have been connected to different forms of imperialism (maritime and land-based, formal and informal) and cycles of global dominance (Blaut, 1993; Taylor, 1996; Abernethy, 2000: cf. WORLD SYSTEMS THEORY). Monocausal, teleological and diffusionist explanations (including Marxist ones) of the West's rise to global dominance – encompassing 85 per cent of the Earth's surface at its 1920s peak – have been discredited in historical terms but remain culturally and politically resilient, not least in 'end of history' scenarios that see liberal capitalism as the high point and terminus of human progress (cf. NEO-LIBERALISM).

Second, since the 1980s, imperialism has been studied as a DISCOURSE – or grammar – of domination fuelled by images, narratives and representations, and shaped by categories of GENDER, SEXUALITY, RACE, nation and religion, as well as capital and CLASS. Critical energies are focused on the potency of binary and essentialist thinking – us/them and self/other stereotypes, such as the opposition between civilization and savagery – and the ways in which Western knowledge effects and secures empire and dispossession by denigrating indigenous knowledges and representing the Earth as the imperialist's rightful inheritance. Edward Said's work on ORIENTALISM, and how imperialism works as a multi-faceted 'struggle over geography', has been particularly influential in spurring interdisciplinary interest in the culturally and spatially constructed nature of Western knowledge about the 'Other' (Said, 1993, p. 7). While geographers have paid close attention to how a range of geographical ideas, practices and texts might be conceived as imperial discourses, they have warned against reducing imperialism to discourse, and insist on the need to materially ground understanding of imperialism's operations (Lester, 2000; cf. POST-COLONIALISM).

A third approach – and one currently making great headway in history and geography – is concerned with the locational basis of imperialism. It mobilizes web and network concepts to redress the residual Eurocentrism and metro-centrism (and textualism and abstraction) of much writing on imperial/colonial discourses, and guards against portraying imperialism as either rigidly hierarchical, or all seeing and knowing. Stemming from older historical debates about the ways and extent to which actions and policies emanating from the imperial core were shaped by peripheral/colonial events and pressures, this 'imperial networks' approach treats metropole and colony as mutually constitutive (rather than separate and isolated) entities, and breaks down the strict equation of imperialism with the centre/core and colonialism with the periphery/margin. This literature examines the variegated, shifting and unstable make-up of different imperial and colonial projects, and how multiple forms of affinity, difference, asymmetry and inequality became mapped across nation and empire. Imperialism can thus be seen as both unitary and highly differentiated (Lester, 2001). However, questions can be raised about how adequately this literature addresses questions of power.   DCl

Suggested reading
Lambert and Lester (2006); Said (1993); Taylor and Flint (2000); Wolfe (2004).

indigenous knowledge This term represents the understandings thought to be embedded within indigenous communities (see also ABORIGINALITY), and usually posed against universalized, Western, scientific knowledge. While indigenous knowledge was regarded as a traditionalist or backward-looking barrier to effective DEVELOPMENT in the period immediately following the 'development decade', more recently the idea of indigenous knowledge as an alternative to increasingly discredited scientific social management and developmentalism has gained significant credibility as a way out of the 'development impasse'. The valorization of indigenous knowledge represents a shift away from privileging the knowledge of 'development experts' towards the voices and experiences of the inhabitants of the global South, at whom development is usually projected, 'listening seriously to what the rural poor have to say, learning from them and respecting their realities and priorities' (Briggs, 2005, p. 100). Interest in indigenous knowledge is most often traced back to Chambers' (1983) challenge to put the last first, but there are also clear affinities with the POST-COLONIAL focus on power/knowledge. POST-DEVELOPMENT writers see indigenous alternatives as offering the only real possibilities for progressive change for the majority world. For instance, Escobar (1995, p. 98) suggests that the 'remaking of development must start by examining local constructions, to the extent that they are the life and history of the people, that is, the conditions for and of change'.

Until recently, the literature on indigenous knowledge has tended to suggest a binary between scientific and indigenous knowledge, seeing SCIENCE as a groundless set of ideas, and ignoring the HYBRID forms combining various scientific and local knowledges that emerge in the actual practice of everyday life (Agrawal, 1995). For others, the idea of indigenous knowledge as a singular concept ignores the multiplicity and POWER relations inherent in any community, and is particularly problematic in terms of GENDER relations. This has led some to talk in terms of LOCAL KNOWLEDGES (Briggs, 2005). Furthermore, a focus on knowledge can turn attention away from the material matters of development and exploitation, or the fact that while some might have knowledge, it is not always possible for them to act on it (Jewitt, 2002). Finally, some commentators have suggested caution, because the recent adoption of indigenous knowledge by development agencies such as the World Bank, while on the surface a positive move, is most often uncritical and tokenistic. In such cases, indigenous knowledge (often reduced to the singular label 'IK') is expected to be added to already existing knowledges and practices, rather than being allowed to offer a more fundamental challenge to the epistemologies of conventional development approaches (see Briggs and Sharp, 2004). JSH

Suggested reading
Agrawal (1995); Briggs (2005).

indistinction, zone of A SPACE in which nominally opposing categories not only become blurred ('indistinct') but also actively bleed into one another (cf. THIRD SPACE). This topological figure animates key claims in the political philosophy of Giorgio Agamben, which have attracted considerable attention in CULTURAL, SOCIAL and POLITICAL GEOGRAPHY. Agamben's formulation of the space of exception (see EXCEPTION, SPACE OF) identifies a space in which exclusion and inclusion, outside and inside, violence and law 'enter into a zone of irreducible indistinction' where each passes over into the other (1998, pp. 9, 32). The basis for this, he argues, is the process through which BARE LIFE is both *excluded from* and *captured within* the political order and, in its most radical form, the process through which SOVEREIGN POWER uses the law to suspend the legal (or juridical) order (1998, pp. 18–19). Agamben argues that the exception has now become generalized to the point at which it threatens to become the norm: 'The "juridically empty" space of the state of exception ... [transgresses] its spatiotemporal boundaries and now, overflowing outside them, is starting to coincide with the normal order in which everything again becomes possible' (p. 38). Whatever one makes of such a general claim, there is compelling evidence for the multiplication of particular zones of indistinction: thus, for example, Gregory (2004b, pp. 122–36) traces the ways in which the Israeli occupation of Palestine has involved the calculated proliferation of zones of indistinction, while Gandy (2006b) suggests that zones of indistinction have become characteristic of a late-modern 'anti-biotic urbanism' that is producing new modes of exclusion. DG

induction A form of reasoning that moves from the specific to the general, usually deploying information/knowledge from a small number of (possible non-representative: cf. SAMPLING) cases to develop general LAWS. Inductive reasoning is usually contrasted with deductive logics. (See also ABDUCTION; DEDUCTION.) RJ

Suggested reading
Harvey (1969).

industrial district A term developed to capture the local geography, institutional density and interlinked connectivity of productive (agro-industrial, manufacturing financial and services) activities. The common reference point is the foundational work of Alfred Marshall in his *Principles of economics* (1919), in which he referred to industrial districts as 'the concentration of specialized industries in particular localities' (see LOCALITY). In its contemporary usage, the most telling property of industrial districts turn on the dynamics of close internal (intra-district) linkages based on horizontal and vertical dis-INTEGRATION and the operations of particular customary norms and taken-for-granted rules and routines that collectively bind together firms and simultaneously provide the productive infrastructure of the district.

Marshall coined the term in an account of the Sheffield cutlery and specialized steel industry and the south-east Lancashire cotton textiles sector. He noted distinctive characteristics of the localities, what he called the 'industrial atmosphere', which collectively provided a sort of industrial hothouse with a highly competitive economic momentum. Some of the key characteristics noted by Marshall, and subsequently elaborated by others (Scott, 1988c; Amin and Thrift, 1992) included: a business structure dominated by small, locally owned firms; limited scale economies; intra-district trade among buyers and suppliers; long-term contracts and commitments between local buyers and suppliers;

a highly flexible labour market, internal to the district; a unique local cultural identity; specialized sources of finance, technical expertise and business services available within the district outside of firms; limited co-operation or linkage with firms external to the district; investment decisions made locally; labour in-migration, with lower levels of out-migration; and worker commitment to districts rather than to firms.

A contemporary example of an industrial district is 'motor sport valley' in the UK, a cluster of firms in mid-Oxfordshire in and through which has developed the world's major agglomeration of Formula 1 and Indy car engineering (see Henry and Pinch, 1997). This region is a community of knowledge sustained by and expanding through the rapid production, application and dissemination of knowledge (through observation, gossip, rumour and direct and indirect contact) among and between a network of highly secretive small and medium-size enterprises. High rates of new firm formation and knowledge transmission through a mobile workforce with a small area (a 160 km long narrow crescent, 60 km north and west of London) rests on a knowledge pool and has created a 'constant learning trajectory' (Henry and Pinch, 1997, p. 7). Integral to the district is a socially and industrially created matrix of firms.

Motor sport valley is an illustration of *new industrial spaces* (Scott, 1988), such as the Third Italy and Orange Country, California, through which the transmission of impulses around integrated and interdependent firms is both effective and flexible (hence the Marshallian argument that locality exercises a powerful influence upon productive dynamism: see Storper and Scott, 1989). In these sorts of districts, other characteristics not anticipated by Marshall are specially important, including a high incidence of exchanges of personnel between customers and suppliers; intense co-operation among competitor firms to share risk, and to stabilize market share and market instability; a collaborative system of local INNOVATION; a disproportionate share of workers engaged in design and innovation; robust trade associations providing management training, marketing, technical or financial help; and, last but not least, a strong local government role in regulating and promoting core industries. This argument is compelling in its SPATIALITY. Geography is central, in other words, to the 'untraded interdependencies' and conventions that provide the ether in which industrial districts flourish (Storper and

Salais, 1997). Amin and Thrift (1992) argue relatedly that while place constitutes social and economic practice in the City of London and Santa Croce in Tuscany, the way in which this constitution takes place is itself shaped by geographical requirements of social practice. The localization of economic geographies is not an autonomous or independent influence on productive spaces, but is also shaped by the geographical demands of increasingly global economic geographies. One of the conditions of existence of such geographies is the presence of a place or centre to act as a site of representation (a centre of authority), inter-action (a centre of sociability) and as a means of making sense of data and information (a centre of DISCOURSE). In short, industrial districts are doubly geographical: both required for and constitutive of social practice.

The industrial district is not restricted to manufacturing and financial services, but has also been productively deployed as a way of describing the GLOBALIZATION of agriculture and the changing geography associated with what has been called 'high-value agriculture'. COMMODITY CHAIN analysis has provided a powerful optic through which one can explore the emergence of key agro-industrial nodes, in which many of the properties described in the Third Italy or the Silicon Valley can be seen in the agro-export region of the Sao Francisco valley of Brazil or the wine-producing *terroires* of France (see Goodman and Watts, 1997). Here, the intersection of local specialized knowledge (often with a deep, if modernized, history), commercial and customary conventions pertaining to inter-firm interdependence (between growers, buyers, shipper and processors), and various forms of linkages to banking and the local state provide for similar forms of industrial dynamism, often draped in the cultural language of attachment to the land. The rise of the organic industry provides simply one way in which these agricultural districts are made and remade by shifts in, and as responses to, industrial agriculture (Guthman, 2004). (See also AGRICULTURAL GEOGRAPHY.)   RL/MW

industrial geography   A sub-branch of ECONOMIC GEOGRAPHY concerned with describing and explaining the spaces, PLACES and geographical circulation of industry. Interest in the discipline emerged in the early twentieth century, driven partly by theoretical arguments developed in economics. The history of industrial geography has been punctuated by moments of illuminating theory and novel methods, but the disciplinary norm tended to meticulous, empirically descriptive case studies of one firm, industry or industrial region or another. Iconic male-dominated industries such as sawmilling, iron and steel, and automobile assembly were the primary subject-matter; the field was thus marked by masculinism, reflecting the gender of the discipline's practitioners and their substantive interests (a version of 'toys for boys'), and generally uncritical methods.

In 1910, economic geographer George Chisholm drew upon the German location theorist Alfred Weber to explain 'the seats of industry'. In the late 1950s and much of the 1960s, industrial geographers rediscovered Weber and other members of the German location school (see LOCATION THEORY), and turned to NEOCLASSICAL ECONOMIC theories of RATIONAL CHOICE and maximizing behaviour (Smith, 1981a [1971]) to explain industrial location. Propelling this disciplinary intellectual move was a combination of the QUANTITATIVE REVOLUTION in human geography, which emphasized the importance of rigour and abstraction, and the influence of REGIONAL SCIENCE, which applied neoclassical theory to the SPACE-ECONOMY, including to the optimal location of industry (Isard, 1956). However, even at the time, it was unclear exactly how many industrial geographers were convinced of the need for this more formal theorization, and most of the practitioners lacked the necessary skill set to apply it. Within a decade, neoclassical formalism was criticized by: (1) a behavioural approach (following economists such as Herbert Simon), which stressed sub-optimal outcomes ('satisficing') rather than maximization (Pred, 1967, 1969: see DECISION-MAKING); and (2) an institutional approach – known initially as the 'geography of enterprise' and later 'corporate geography' – which treated the firm as a complex entity, like an organism, that evolved, adapted and struggled in a larger competitive setting, was often not rational, and whose inner workings defied formalization (McNee, 1960).

The high-water mark of the field was from the late 1970s to the end of the 1980s, when disciplinary intellectual ferment matched ferment on the ground. Not only was the intellectual environment changing, so too was the very object of investigation. It was then that seemingly entrenched Western industrial regions were beset by gales of DEINDUSTRIALIZATION, industrial restructuring and corporate hollowing-out, which both destroyed and created anew. Hitherto bread-and-butter industries of Western economies, such as iron and steel, shipbuilding and textile manufacturing, were subject to severe economic trauma as firms went bankrupt, moved offshore, or turned lean and mean. Millions of traditional manufacturing jobs were lost.

Events on the ground produced new theory and new methods in industrial geography, and even began to challenge the discipline's masculinism. Scholars began to turn to RADICAL GEOGRAPHY. In the UK, Doreen Massey's watershed book, *Spatial divisions of labour* (1984), provided original theoretical explanation and trenchant empirical analysis: in the USA, Allen Scott's (1988b) TRANSACTIONS COSTS approach to the firm was the exemplar. Both resulted in impressive empirical work: Massey's led to the British LOCALITY project (Cooke, 1989), and Scott's to case studies based in California, especially on the vibrant high-tech and FILM industries. Both bodies of work were influenced by POLITICAL ECONOMY, as well as a new methodological sensibility, CRITICAL REALISM (especially true in the UK, where critical realism became the unofficial METHODOLOGY of the discipline). Codified and circulated primarily by Andrew Sayer (1992 [1984]), critical realism suggested industrial geography proceed methodologically by 'intensive', on-the-ground, case studies of specific industries and their geographical sites.

Not everyone accepted 'critical realism', however, with critics complaining it was only another version of the old disciplinary sin of EMPIRICISM and was producing geographically parochial studies. Moreover, there was also an underlying clash between the UK version of industrial geography emphasizing capitalism's decline and fall, and the US (Californian) version highlighting capitalism's vitality. However, the UK and US versions came together in the late 1980s through REGULATION THEORY, and which set the sub-disciplinary intellectual agenda for the following decade. Developed to explain why capitalism survived in spite of Marx's best prediction of its demise, regulation theory introduced ideas of FORDIST and POST-FORDIST (see also FLEXIBLE ACCUMULATION) modes of production, and the fraught transition between them. What the distinction made clear was that while British industrial geographers had been documenting the disintegration of an older Fordist industry, US industrial geographers had been examining the formation of a brand new one, post-Fordism. They were different sides of the same Janus face of industrial capitalism (Tickell and Peck, 1992).

In unpacking the geographical character of post-Fordism during the 1990s, industrial geographers rediscovered the idea of an INDUSTRIAL DISTRICT, the propensity of firms in the same sector to cluster spatially, and to be tightly interlinked (and first recognized by the early-twentieth-century English economist Alfred Marshall). In turn, that idea was joined to 'embeddedness', a concept associated with the economic anthropologist Karl Polanyi, implying an inseparable relation between the economic and the sociocultural. It was precisely this inseparability, argued industrial geographers, that characterized and accounted for the success of post-Fordist industrial districts such as Silicon Valley, Hollywood, the Third Italy and Baden-Württemberg. They flourished because their firms were so closely embedded within the cultural institutions, relations and forms of life found in those places (Amin, 2000: see also CULTURAL ECONOMY).

An interest in GLOBALIZATION has recently defined the field, with investigations into both new geographical patterns of production and new forms of industrial organization that make them possible. Peter Dicken's *Global shift* (2007) is the exemplary text (first published in 1988, and now in its fifth edition). The reverse side of deindustrialization has been, and continues to be ever more so, rampant industrialization in the global South: certainly the post-1979 market reforms in China, but also in India, South East Asia, Central and South America and Mexico (Dicken, 2007). Industrial geography is conceptually still coming to grips with the enormous task of representing, analysing and explaining the fundamental industrial spatial transformation that is occurring. A novel conceptual vocabulary and theoretical framework is being forged, as well as new methods, which have included COMMODITY CHAIN analysis, global networks, ACTOR-NETWORK THEORY, the analytics of TRANSNATIONAL CORPORATIONS and global ETHNOGRAPHY. All have contributed, but industrial geography remains a work in progress, as is its object of enquiry.   TB

Suggested reading
Dicken (2007).

industrial organization Do a small number of large firms (*oligopoly*) or a large number of small firms dominate an industry? Why is this and what difference does it make for industrial geography, corporate behaviour, and economic and social outcomes? These are the questions of industrial organization. Oligopoly

may arise from such factors as ECONOMIES OF SCALE or collusion. The result may be spatial concentration, high profits and high wages. Competitive industries may be geographically dispersed, labour-intensive, low-margin and low-waged. Industrial organization may change due, for example, to technological shifts or the internationalization of markets. Understanding its causes and consequences illuminates the economic landscape.   ESCH

industrial revolution A transformation in the forces of production, centring on but not confined to the circuit of industrial capital (see CAPITALISM). Generally attributed to Blanqui (1837), but popularized in Britain by Arnold Toynbee, the term originally applied to a set of dramatic changes occurring in the British economy *c*.1760–1840, when the old economic order was 'suddenly broken to pieces by the mighty blows of the steam engine and the power loom' (Toynbee, 1884). Subsequent analyses identified British 'industrial revolutions' both earlier (in the sixteenth and seventeenth centuries) and later (towards the end of the nineteenth century), while the term has also been invoked to describe changes taking place across Western Europe and North America in the nineteenth century. This questions the unique nature of the classic industrial revolution, portraying it as simply another peak on the long-term waves of innovation and development (see Hudson, 1992: cf. KONDRATIEFF CYCLES). The gradualist perspective is reinforced by ideas of PROTO-INDUSTRIALIZATION and by econometric studies. The former emphasize the continuities between modern factory-based manufacturing and earlier systems of domestic production; while the latter highlight the growth of industry earlier in the eighteenth century, and question the extent and pace of structural change in the British economy before 1840. On top of these, models of dual economies – which counterpoise a small technologically dynamic sector with a much larger traditional sector – have further qualified the revolutionary nature of change.

As with other aspects of MODERNIZATION, industrialization was temporally and spatially uneven: there were periodic crises of capital accumulation and circulation, and an increasingly heterogeneous SPACE-ECONOMY. Different products and production systems were increasingly associated with particular parts of the country, creating a new REGIONAL GEOGRAPHY that was based on industrial specialization (see Langton, 1984; Langton and Morris,

1987; Hudson, 1989). There were many different routes to industrialization: in its timing, causes and manifestation, the industrial revolution varied from place to place. Much emphasis has been placed on the availability of raw materials (particularly coal) in determining both the course and geography of industrialization (Langton, 1979; Wrigley, 1988). Linked to this is the role of transport in facilitating the exploitation of mineral resources, integrating regional economies and thus promoting industrial growth. More recent analyses have highlighted the importance of a range of sociocultural factors in which economic processes were embedded (see CULTURAL TURN). These influenced access to credit and capital, determined labour mobility and discipline, and shaped attitudes to entrepreneurship (Gregory, 1990). Linked to this, neo-institutional approaches have stressed the role of networks (of people, credit, information and towns) in effectively integrating regional economies and in shaping the industrialization process (Wilson and Popp, 2003; Stobart, 2004). Ultimately, sustained development was contingent on the establishment of a critical mass of interdependent industries, services, infrastructures and communications. The varied composition of such industrial complexes and the different production systems on which they were based, led to regional variations in the experience of industrialization. Indeed, Langton (1984) argues that as regional economies became 'more specialized, more differentiated from each other and more internally unified', they found expression in coherent regional cultures. Others, though, have highlighted the varied nature of production systems, work practices, and social and cultural identities within regions: most were characterized by a symbiotic relationship between factory- and domestic or workshop-based production (Berg, 1994). Recent critiques argue that these debates are too narrow in their focus, ignoring non-industrial forms of capitalism and the wider global/imperial context of industrialization. Most influential is the 'gentlemanly capitalism' thesis which, in broadening the geographical bounds of analysis, argues that Britain's economy and overseas policy were driven not by the growth and needs of industrial capitalism, but by landed, mercantile and financial interests (Cain and Hopkins, 2001). Historical geographers have yet to engage fully in these debates, however: largely inspired by POST-COLONIALISM, work on empire has had little to say about economic processes and the global geographies of nineteenth-century British industrialization.

For individuals and communities, as well as for regions and nations, the industrial revolution had profound social and cultural repercussions (Berg and Hudson, 1992). Experiences of work were transformed as production was centralized and control was removed from the individual. Resistance to such change was occasionally dramatic, surfacing in a variety of protests across industrializing districts that often targeted new labour-saving machinery (Gregory, 1982, 1990; Hudson, 1989). More generally, the contours of the new POLITICAL ECONOMY of industrial capitalism were sharply contested as the established relationships of a so-called moral economy were replaced by those based on the market. Of particular significance was the way in which the transformation of the LABOUR PROCESS was central to the emergence of CLASS consciousness. Yet the extent to which such social identities transcended local and regional allegiances remains an area of considerable debate. Moreover, the new social relations of production were structured by GENDER as well as class. Many of the new machines were operated by women and children, creating a new sexual division of labour in which men's work was characterized as more skilled and (consequently) better paid (Hudson, 1992; Berg, 1994). Nonetheless, the earnings of all members of the household were vital in determining standards of living, conventionally seen as falling, then rising, as real incomes were first undermined, then augmented by industrialization. Living conditions and social relations were also shaped by the transformation of the urban milieu, which was both cause and consequence of industrial development (see Stobart, 2004). Towns grew both in number and size, with those in the industrializing districts experiencing the most rapid expansion. This caused a rapid deterioration in living conditions in many towns, as the construction of houses, and physical and social infrastructure, failed to keep pace with demographic growth. It also led to a restructuring of Britain's urban geography and hierarchy, and with it the geopolitical relationship between centre and periphery. London remained dominant as the focus of commercial, financial and political activity, but debates and policies were, for a brief time in the mid-nineteenth century, shaped by experiences in and the concerns of Britain's industrial towns, most notably Manchester.   JSt

Suggested reading
Berg (1994); Gregory (1990); Langton (1984).

industrialization The process whereby industrial activity comes to play a dominant role in the economy of a region or nation-state. Historically, industrialization has involved a more complex DIVISION OF LABOUR and the spread of mechanized production (*machinofacture*) in place of hand production (*manufacture*). These changes brought about a transformation in what Karl Polanyi called the form of economic integration, from the reciprocity of a moral economy to the market exchange of CAPITALISM. In certain Western societies, industrialization took place spontaneously, small-scale domestic production for local consumption being replaced by larger-scale 'factory' production aimed at more distant markets. For Adam Smith, such industrialization formed part of the 'natural progress' of economic development, founded on the production of agricultural surpluses, but ultimately leading to specialist industrial regions and to international trade. Growth was organic, and the shift to mechanized production, prompted by supply being outstripped by growing demand, was dependent upon the development of appropriate technology and the accumulation of CAPITAL for investment (Berg, 1994).

As part of modernization theory, such readings of the past were instrumental in linking industrialization with development and in its portrayal as a solution to poverty in the developing world (Power, 2003). As a result, many less-developed countries made industry central to their development strategies. This planned (rather than spontaneous or 'organic') industrialization has generally taken one of two forms: (a) import substitution, wherein governments encourage the development of indigenous manufacturing to produce consumer goods for the domestic market, or (b) export-orientated industrialization, which aims to enhance production for overseas markets. In the 1950s and 1960s, Western governments favoured import substitution as a development strategy for the THIRD WORLD. Influenced by the theories of Rostow and others (see STAGES OF GROWTH) – which accorded a pivotal role to the availability of investment capital – they provided loans to developing countries to facilitate industrial development. The problems of such strategies were thrown into stark relief by the economic crises of the 1970s. The infusion of capital, technology and business organization from outside brought with it problems of DEPENDENCY, most obviously manifest in the mounting debts of many developing countries (Schurmann, 2001). More fundamentally, Marxist scholars challenged the 'development myth' by emphasizing the inevitability of UNEVEN DEVELOPMENT under capitalism.

In recent years there has been a rearticulation of modernization theory, partly through the rhetoric of globalization, which now points to the experience of developing countries experiencing rapid industrialization. Most striking are the so-called ASIAN MIRACLE/TIGER economies of South-East Asia, where the rate of industrial growth – much of it fuelled by export-orientated industries drawing on abundant cheap labour – has far exceeded that of EUROPE during the INDUSTRIAL REVOLUTION. China has industrialized particularly rapidly and, in doing so, has highlighted many of the mounting ecological problems associated with industrial growth. In addition to those of POLLUTION of land, sea and air, is the more fundamental question of the sustainability of industrialization based on finite mineral resources (Phillips and Mighall, 2000). What the example of South-East Asia also shows is the emergence of service activities as an alternative source of employment and route to economic development (cf. SERVICES).   JST

inequality, spatial The uneven distribution across space of a particular set of attributes, over which there is a moral politics of right or wrong. So, whereas spatial *differentiation* refers to conditions over which moral questions do not arise, spatial *inequality* refers instead to those characteristics over which there is a sense that their production is the result of human agency. The uneven distribution of NATURAL RESOURCES is an example of spatial differentiation. On the other hand, variations between regions in terms of income levels or health rates would be examples of inequality. Think about the battles that have raged over the uneven distribution of access to some forms of medication, particularly between the wealthiest nations and those of the THIRD WORLD. SOCIAL MOVEMENTS of one kind or another have lobbied multinational pharmaceutical companies, in an attempt to get them to do their bit in addressing spatial inequalities in the treatment of HIV/AIDS.

WELFARE GEOGRAPHY since the 1970s has been concerned with inequality in living standards, in the broadest sense. Attention has continued to be paid to traditional concerns, such as those in differences in living standards, which remain of fundamental importance (Smith, D.M., 1994a). Additionally, however, work has focused on the spatially uneven distribution of sources of need satisfaction, reflecting a departure in welfare geography, away from narrow definitions of standards of living. While an emphasis on spatial inequalities can reveal the particular socio-economic trajectories of spatial units, it can run the risk of obscuring other factors at play. For example, we can think of inequality along the coordinates of CLASS, GENDER and RACE (Perrons, 2004). The categories cut across one another, so that we can now understand how all forms of identity and distinction – including those shaped by SPACE – in different contexts, produce situations in which individuals suffer the consequences of inequality. Moreover, the emphasis on spatial patterns risks losing sight of the structural basis of inequalities (Smith, 2008 [1984]).

While we might all think that spatial inequality is, by definition, bad, it cannot automatically be labelled as wrong. SOCIAL JUSTICE involves the conditions under which it might be possible to argue ethically and morally that spatial inequality is justified. Perhaps some groups or some spatial units are disadvantaged for the greater societal good. Given the rising inequalities, both within nations and between nations, what we can say perhaps is that the responsibility lies with those advocating inequality to justify their position in ways that do not fall back on trickle-down economics or NEO-LIBERALISM (Smith and Lee, 2004). KWA

Suggested reading
Perrons (2004); Smith and Lee (2004).

informal sector A contested term that refers to forms of employment and exchange relations that may be some combination of the following: small-scale; unregulated, poorly regulated or over-regulated (De Soto, 1989); sometimes illegal and untaxed (the black economy); precarious; family-oriented; strongly entrepreneurial; poorly remunerated; and/or based on low-level technologies. Trying to define the informal sector more precisely is unhelpful, although one can usefully consider it in relation to its assumed opposite, the formal sector.

In the context of developing countries in the 1950s, it was widely assumed that the modern sector of an economy would in time come to replace all or most of the pre-modern economy (see MODERNIZATION). It was further assumed that the formal ('Western') sector of a DUAL ECONOMY was populated by unionized, mainly male workers, who enjoyed high real wages from manufacturing and a large number of benefits, including dearness allowances and paid leave. This was the (semi-)skilled labour aristocracy that Lenin had written about. The informal sector, in contrast, described an economy made up of shoe-shiners, domestic servants and other untenured workers: women, men and children who contributed little to the economy as a whole, and who had to be encouraged into the modern (manufacturing) economy from small-scale commercial or service activities.

This teleological view of the informal sector giving way to the formal sector was sharply challenged in the 1960s and 1970s. The International Labour Organization (ILO) developed the concept of an urban informal sector in 1969, when it launched its World Employment Programme. The ILO aimed to move beyond measures of the labour force in developing countries that were restricted to the employed and the unemployed. A new generation of urban–rural MIGRATION models now appeared, which suggested that migrants to the city were faced with a choice of remaining among the urban unemployed while searching for work in the formal sector, or of accepting work and lower wages in the informal economy. Non-economists, meanwhile, led by the anthropologist Keith Hart, began to challenge the terms of the debate. Instead of emphasizing the separation of the formal and informal sectors, theorists began to focus on the ways in which 'popular entrepreneurship' (Hart, 1973) helped to reproduce capital–labour relations in the formal sector. For example, three-wheel taxi services helped to speed up circuits of exchange in city-systems not well served by freeways or mass transit systems. Micro-enterprises subcontracted intermediate goods from formal-sector firms. What marked out the informal sector was ease of access to new entrants, including migrants, both domestic and international.

Barbara Harriss-White (2003) has suggested that the hype surrounding 'hi-tech' India is blind to what she calls the India of the 88 per cent, or those men, women and children who work largely unprotected in India's agricultural, industrial and service economies. Other studies have estimated the scale of the informal sector in parts of Africa at over 50 per cent, and at over 40 per cent in Latin America and the Caribbean. The informal sector is also well entrenched in richer countries. The growth of Local Economic

Trading Systems (LETS) is evidence of this (see ALTERNATIVE ECONOMICS). So too is the growth of gardening and maid services in cities such as Miami and Los Angeles in the USA, largely staffed by labourers from Latin America. sco

Suggested reading
Roberts (1994); Tripp (1997).

information economy A term dating from the late 1960s and early 1970s, describing the growing centrality of information to the DE-VELOPMENT and RESTRUCTURING of advanced industrial economies. Pioneering work by sociologist Daniel Bell (1973) outlined the increasing significance of the distribution, production and consumption of information within what he called POST-INDUSTRIAL SOCI-ETY. Since then, human geographers – amongst many others – have made major contributions to understanding the spatial dynamics of information-intensive industries (Hepworth, 1989) and the highly uneven geographies of computer networks such as the Internet that integrate information economies (Zook, 2005: see also KNOWLEDGE ECONOMY; LEARNING REGION). sg

Suggested reading
Hepworth (1989).

information theory A mathematical approach originally developed in communication science to measure the amount of information, degree of organization or UNCERTAINTY in a SYSTEM. The measure is closely related to that for ENTROPY. The basic equation developed by Shannon (Shannon and Weaver, 1949) is as follows:

$$H = -\sum_i p_i \log (1/p_i),$$

where H is the information statistic and p_i is the probability (or proportion) of a variable in a given region. The individual p_is might be employment in different regions, the proportion of agricultural land in N counties or the probabilities of N possible outcomes in a stochastic experiment. $H = 0$ when one of the p_i is unity – all the employment is concentrated in one region – whilst H approaches a maximum (given by log N) when all the p_i are equal. H is perfectly related to log W, the entropy measure. Information theory was extensively applied to the measurement of social and economic INEQUALITY by Henri Theil

(Theil, 1967). In geography, it has been used to measure organization in settlement patterns, information in CHOROPLETH mapping techniques and in regional classification, as well as in the applications involving ENTROPY-MAXIMIZING MODELS. LWH

informational city A term coined by Manuel Castells (1989) to describe a CITY whose development is dominated by the restructuring dynamics of manufacturing and research and development (R&D) in 'hi-tech' industries (primarily information technology, defence, biotechnology and nanotechnology). Based on a detailed analysis of urban change in the USA in the late twentieth century, Castells suggested that such developments were underpinning the emergence of a global URBAN SYSTEM made up of WORLD CITIES dominated by centralized clusters of innovation in these high-technology sectors. He argued that these sectors were located in suburban complexes called *technopoles*, which tended to be associated with increasingly dualized social structures and the dismantling of welfare state systems (Castells and Hall, 1994). sg

Suggested reading
Castells (1989).

infrastructure In conventional economic theory and planning, infrastructure refers to the underlying structure of services and amenities (*social overhead capital*, or SOC) needed to facilitate *directly productive activity* (or DPA). Examples include public services, transport, telecommunications, public utilities, and social and community facilities. Infrastructure tends to be immobile, labour intensive, indivisible and open of access, and to have economy-wide effects. There is considerable argument over the extent to which infrastructural investment is a sufficient or even a necessary precondition for economic development; whether it should be provided before development in the form of excess capacity or whether scarce resources should be devoted primarily to DPA; and whether it should be publicly or privately owned. Indeed, the widespread growth of the private ownership of infrastructure and its ability to generate stable returns over long periods has led to significant financial interests in infrastructural development, not just in terms of ownership and financing, but as the basis of a range of disintermediated financial instruments.

Within MARXISM, 'infrastructure' has a more precise and theoretically charged meaning.

It refers to the forces and relations of material production that, in Marx's classic writings, provide the foundation (or 'base') for a legal, political and cultural 'superstructure' (see BASE AND SUPERSTRUCTURE). This formulation marked the site of a considerable debate within HISTORICAL MATERIALISM over the relationship between infrastructure and superstructure: some critics claimed that Marx saw this in reductive terms ('economic determinism'), while most informed scholars provided more nuanced readings of the ways in which economic practices and structures are implicated in the conduct of social and political life. RL

inheritance systems In theory, inheritance is the transmission of exclusive rights in PROPERTY at death. Such transmission is part of the wider devolution of rights between holders and heirs, and usually between generations. This process of devolution can also involve transfers between the living for education, marriage and property purchase, as well as transfer of any residual at the holder's death. In societies where production is based on the HOUSEHOLD and where property rights are vested in the domestic group, the evolution of such rights is of vital importance. In simple hoe agricultural societies, such as found over much of sub-Saharan Africa, inheritance between spouses is rare, with transfers tending to be from males to males or from females to females. In such settings, economic differentiation is limited and access to land relatively easy, with inheritance occurring within unilineal descent groups such as clans or lineage. In plough-based agrarian systems, a diverging or bisexual form of devolution is more common, and frequently involves children inheriting from both parents and parents transferring property to both daughters and sons – and not necessarily at death. One such form of *premortem* inheritance is dowry given to daughters at their marriage, which has been widespread in Eurasia. At marriage, some kind of conjugal fund is created and the property transmitted, although not in equal proportions, to the children. The different treatment of siblings depending on birth order takes the form of *primogeniture* (impartibility), *multigeniture* (partibility) or *ultimogeniture* (Borough English). Systems of impartible inheritance in which the eldest son was sole heir were common among elite groups in EUROPE, where title and position were linked to estate and income. Younger sons might seek their fortune through careers in the church or the army, to which

they had access as a result of the political power embodied in the parental estate. In European peasantries (see PEASANT), the parents might hand over the farm to a son or a daughter on the occasion of his or her marriage, reserving for themselves right to bed and board, although frequently giving rise to extended or stem family households. Such arrangements might create familial tensions, since an early transfer might weaken the authority of the elderly, and a delayed transfer might create hostility towards the elderly among the young. In CAPITALIST societies, where the majority of the population has no ownership of the means of production, inheritance is of far less significance. However, the ability to transfer privilege as well as residential property is intrinsic to family life in all economic systems. Most modern societies place a progressive tax on inherited property, which could be viewed as a means of equalizing advantage. Ways of avoiding tax on personal assets at death are found in the use of trusts, life estates and charitable giving. In the USA, where charitable gifts are tax-exempt, private foundations gain enormous benefits, and in the UK major contributions to national collections of art, buildings or land result from attempts to avoid death duties (Shoup, 1966). RMS

Suggested reading
Goody (1962, 1978); Goody, Thirsk and Thompson (1976); Shoup (1966); Smith (1984).

inner city That region of the metropolitan area consisting primarily of older residential areas in close proximity to the downtown core. By the late nineteenth century, inner-city neighbourhoods were mainly blue-collar districts, providing shelter for the families of working men employed in the wholesaling, manufacturing and transportation sectors that were located in the ring of industrial uses adjacent to port and railway terminals outside the CENTRAL BUSINESS DISTRICT. In the industrial city, then, the inner city was the home of the working poor, including immigrants, as famously described by the CHICAGO SCHOOL between 1910 and 1970 (Wirth, 1928; Suttles, 1968). In such cities, minimal land-use regulation introduced serious traffic congestion and severe air, land and water pollution, encouraging the withdrawal of the middle class to tram/streetcar and commuter suburbs. Separation bred a suspicion and even fear of the inner city by the middle class, a condition that survives in some nations to the present.

Consequently, a definition of the inner city cannot be limited to location and age of HOUS-ING alone (see HOUSING STUDIES). In the past 150 years or more, the inner city has experienced a spoiled identity. The grotesque nineteenth-century imagery of Dickensian London, Engels' poignant depictions of life in industrial Manchester, the later portrayals of Inner London by the Booths (Charles and William) and of Inner Montreal by Herbert Ames, and the photo-documentary essays of Jacob Riis in New York all consolidated a highly stigmatized image of both need and menace. In many respects, the social sciences were born into the *problem* of the inner city, with William Booth, the Pittsburgh Survey and the Chicago School all concerned with the mapping of various personal and social pathologies in inner-city districts. Not surprisingly, the influential verdict of the Chicago School was that the inner city was the natural habitat of individual and social disorganization. Such a judgement led easily to a view that demolition and rebuilding would effect social as well as urban renewal, and the nascent welfare STATE engaged in widespread clearance in older inner districts, beginning in the 1930s.

In the aftermath of DEINDUSTRIALIZATION, the inner city remains a site of social problems: Margaret Thatcher's infamous, deprecating allusion to 'those inner cities' in 1987 (Robson, 1988) revealed not only an abiding social construct but also a social reality in many declining industrial centres. Indeed, in the same year as Mrs Thatcher's declaration, William Julius Wilson (1987) published his celebrated text on concentrated and racialized urban POVERTY in American inner cities. His UNDERCLASS thesis, drawing attention both to macro-economic employment trends as well as a culture of poverty in the inner city, established an urban research agenda. In Western Europe, an explosive literature emerged in the 1990s on multidimensional SOCIAL EXCLUSION, targeted on (but not limited to) inner-city districts, some of it importing American underclass language (Mingione, 1996; Madanipour, Cars and Allen, 1998). Addressing social exclusion and deprivation in the inner city and priming urban regeneration have become significant policy directions in many European states.

However, the fusion of PLACE and identity that sees only social problems in the inner city is too rigid. For one thing, as the French 'ban-lieu' riots of 2005 revealed so clearly, deprivation and exclusion may be even sharper in suburban sites (see SUBURB). Second, the view of the inner city as a problem is an over-simplified fabrication (Ley, 2000). Just as the Chicago School displayed a patronizing sub-urban perspective on the inner city, so middle-class policy-makers and politicians through the urban renewal era and later have sustained the same stereotype. In her famous polemic against urban renewal, Jane Jacobs (1992 [1961]) contrasted the detached view of the urban bureaucrat with the view at ground level of urban residents in medium-density older neighbourhoods, extolling an insider's perspective of local vitality, diversity and self-help. Her 1961 message was prophetic and in the next decade the beginnings of GENTRIFICA-TION indicated an equally sympathetic view of the inner city by young urban professionals. In POST-INDUSTRIAL CITIES such as London, New York, Toronto or Sydney, gentrification has led to a massive middle-class make-over of many inner-city districts (Hamnett, 2003), sometimes as an objective of regeneration policies (Cameron, 2003). Frequently, gentrification has diffused outwards from the real estate anchor of existing upper middle-class districts, whose longevity over several generations also reinforces a more accurate view of inner-city diversity rather than homogeneity.   DL

Suggested reading
Ley (2000); Wilson (1987).

innovation The introduction of a new phenomenon or the phenomenon itself (which may include concepts and objects, practices and systems, variously combined in products, and processes). In HUMAN GEOGRAPHY an early stream of work focused on the origin and spread of innovations, particularly in CUL-TURAL GEOGRAPHY, and it was the study of innovations that provided the mainspring for Torsten Hägerstrand's development of the formal study of innovation DIFFUSION in SPATIAL SCIENCE (itself an example of an intellectual innovation that combined new concepts such as the MEAN INFORMATION FIELD, new objects such as the computer that enabled Hägerstrand to construct his MODEL, and new practices such as the algorithms that powered his Monte Carlo SIMULATIONS: see Hägerstrand, 1967). A more recent stream of work in ECONOMIC GEOGRAPHY has focused on the research and development processes in which commercial innovations are embedded, on spillover effects (see CLUSTERS) and on the spatial variations in productivity that may result from differential geographies of innovation (Feldmann, 2000). Taken together, these generate such complex outcomes over space that Morgan (2004) proposed a focus on *territorial innovation systems* sensitive to the multiple SCALES at which effects are registered, though most research continues to focus on the REGION (Asheim and Gertler, 2005; see also LEARNING REGIONS). DG

input–output An analytical framework developed by economist Wassily Leontieff to describe and model the inter-industry linkages within the ECONOMY, and to use this information to examine economic and policy impacts. It traces how the outputs of one sector become the inputs for others: thus the machine-tools industry uses energy, steel and other inputs, and its outputs are in turn inputs to car and aircraft industries. The model requires extensive data and estimates from surveys, and the input-output table can then be manipulated to calculate MULTIPLIERS and so model the impact of policy changes. These models were originally calculated at the national scale, but have been extended to regional and multi-regional models. LWH

Suggested reading
Miller and Blair (1985).

institutional economics Institutionalist thought has come to the fore in ECONOMIC GEOGRAPHY since the 1990s, following its revival in economic theory during the late 1980s around two very different strands. The first is *new institutional economics*, most closely associated with the work of Oliver Williamson on the theory of the firm and others such as Mancur Olson and Douglass North on the role of (public) institutions in economic regulation and evolution. In this work, the focus falls on how firms, networks and institutions arise as organizing mechanisms in the market economy, complement market transactions and generally provide stability, steer and judgment in an otherwise multi-interest and multi-directional economic space composed of competing individuals. The economy is conceptualized as a constellation of firms, markets and institutions, each working to a different logic and with specialist properties. New institutional economics does not break with mainstream economics, since it shares its core assumptions relating to individual motivation (e.g. maximization, hedonism, rational choice) and market behaviour (e.g. price as a core allocation mechanism, informational transparency).

New institutional economics has had limited impact in economic geography, having lost momentum after an initial flurry of interest sparked by extensions of Williamson's transaction cost model to explain agglomeration. For example, Scott's (1988c) work on high technology and other types of industrial agglomeration added an important spatial dimension to Williamson's model by showing how proximity in conditions of specialization and inter-firm linkage served to reduce transaction costs and transactional uncertainty. More recently, there has been a slight revival, through the work of some economic geographers engaging with the work of Paul Krugman to explain inter-regional disparities on the basis of trade differentials and national or regional institutional settings.

One reason why new institutional economics has faltered in economic geography is due to the historical dominance within the sub-discipline of heterodox economic traditions critical of the methodological individualism, rationalism, formalism and a-historicity of mainstream economics. The second strand of institutional economics – old institutionalism – fits more easily into an influential lineage that includes classical political economy accounts in the 1950s and 1960s of urban and regional growth and inequality (e.g. Nicholas Kaldor, Albert O. Hirschman and François Perroux on cumulative causation); Marxist explanations during the 1970s of uneven development and unequal exchange, based on the imperatives of capitalist accumulation and the consequences of class/gender/race exploitation and struggle; and regulation theory explanations in the 1980s of long-term economic stability, structural crisis and renewal, and capitalist variety in terms of the match or mismatch between historical regimes of accumulation and regulation.

Old institutional economics, named so in recognition of influence of US pioneers such as Thorstein Veblen, Wesley Mitchell, John Commons, Clarence Ayres, John Dewey, and later Karl Polanyi and John Galbraith, envisages the economy itself as an instituted process in all its manifestations. Thus, macroeconomic rules and institutions, markets and market practices, prices and values, production conventions and exchange norms, financial rules and economic rationalities, and corporate and regional or national standards are all conceptualized as socially instituted arrangements guiding individual action. Institutions, however defined, are not seen as a particular form of organization and distant from markets, in the way that new institutional economics does, but as the very life and substance of the economy. Institutional parameters, as Hodgson (1988) argues in his celebrated book, explain economic variety, economic impulse and organization, evolutionary change, historical specificity and rules of meaning, interpretation and action.

The term 'institution' covers a wide variety of meaning to progressively thicken the idea of the economy as an institution. Most obviously, this includes the formal institutions of economic and regulation such as firms, banks, corporate rules, business standards and government regulations that are societally specific, slow to change and significant channelling devices. It also includes informal institutions such as social conventions of power, deference, respect, trust and legitimacy, which are also highly localized, and which guide behaviour in different markets, organizations and territories. In turn, taken-for-granted economic canons such as profit maximization, market individualism, price signalling and actor rationality are read as value-laden in a dual sense: first, as embedded fictions that need to be worked at; and, second, as socially generated norms that are neither incontrovertible nor universal. Then, economic continuity and change are explained in terms of recursive routines and habits – personal, interpersonal, organizational and social – treated as the hidden hand of daily economic practice and consensus, as the social genes of economic evolution and path-dependency, and as a core determinant of learning and innovation capability. Old institutional economics, thus, rejects the premises of mainstream economics, but it also injects a considerable degree of texture, contingency and socio-institutional specificity in heterodox economic theory traditionally dominated by big-picture generalizations.

In economic geography, this variant of institutional economics has had some impact in development geography by soliciting critical work on the role of international organizations such as the World Bank or major NGOs; research on the social and institutional parameters of particular markets, such as microcredit or open-air trade; and studies of local economic potential based on an analysis of formal and informal institutions, social conventions and learning processes. The conceptual thrust, however, has come from studies of urban and regional economic dynamism and creativity in the global North. Many new concepts, such as cluster dynamics, industrial atmosphere, institutional thickness, untraded interdependencies, associational ties, industrial slack and redundancy, urban buzz and creativity, trust and reciprocity, and intelligent regionalism, have been inspired by institutional economics to account for local economic success. Researchers associated with institutionalism in this field include Annelee Saxenian, Amy Glasmeier, Michael Storper, Allen Scott, Meric Gertler, Trevor Barnes, Chris Olds, Phil Cooke, Kevin Morgan, Ron Martin, Ash Amin, Nigel Thrift, Jamie Peck, Ray Hudson, Peter Maskell, Anders Malmberg, Bjorn Asheim, Gernot Grabher, Peter Sunley and Harald Bartheld.

The work of these researchers has brought new insight into the spatial dynamics of the economy in three broad areas. The first relates to the role of spatial proximity between firms such that the full benefits of specialization, agglomeration, and trust and reciprocity can be exploited. The second relates to the different ways in which social capital developed in civic associations, institutional activism and reflexivity, and public-sector leadership can contribute to local economic vitality. The third relates to the spatial foundations of the knowledge economy and economic learning in general, where the research has highlighted the significance of localized R&D, technology transfer, learning in inter-firm networks, tacit knowledge formed in interpersonal networks of common purpose and mutual obligation. This body of work has considerably expanded understanding of how space affects the institutions of economic development and change.   AA

Suggested reading
Amin and Thrift (1994a); Hudson (2005); Martin and Sunley (2006).

institutionalism A term with many meanings in the social sciences, all intended to signal the varied ways in which institutions structure social life in time and space. It is an approach that rejects actor-centred approaches that stress individual human intention and will. It also seeks to interpret structure in terms of historically and socially embedded institutions, seen to evolve slowly, often unpredictably and sometimes inefficiently. Structures are not seen as immutable, universal, or machine-like. In POLITICAL GEOGRAPHY institutionalism has influenced the study of political institutions and their effects on ELECTORAL GEOGRAPHY, and studies of geographies of belonging, citizenship and conflict. In SOCIAL GEOGRAPHY, it has had some impact on studies of social and cultural institutions and their role in the making of space and place. But its most significant impact has undoubtedly been in economic geography, where it has forged a path between mainstream approaches and radical political economy (see INSTITUTIONAL ECONOMICS). AA

instrumental variables A statistical and econometric technique to estimate MODELS of the REGRESSION type that have problems of ENDOGENEITY. In the standard multiple regression model of the general form:

$$Y = \beta_0 + \beta_1 X_1 + \beta_2 X_2 + e,$$

where Y is the dependent variable, X_1 and X_2 are the independent variables and e is the random error term, the assumption is that the two independent variables are genuinely exogenous. Suppose, however, that X_1 is endogenous, itself determined by Y and other exogenous variables such as X_3 and X_4. An example might be if Y represents regional employment growth in 'hi-tech' services and X_1 is regional income: Y is influenced by X_1, but X_1 is itself influenced by Y, implying that X_1 is correlated with e, a violation of the assumptions of regressions.

The technique of instrumental variables works by finding a set of 'instruments', variables that are themselves exogenous and are good at predicting X_1. Such a set would include X_3, X_4 (and X_2 for the version of instrumental variables known as two-stage least-squares), other X variables and perhaps spatial or temporal lagged values of X_3 and X_4. Denoting this set of instruments as Z, one regresses X_1 against Z, obtaining the predicted or fitted estimates of X_1, denoted as $\hat{X}_1$. The estimate $\hat{X}_1$ depends only on Z, and so is uncorrelated with e, and the original regression for Y is now estimated, replacing X_1 by $\hat{X}_1$. This procedure, which thus requires two regressions, eliminates the endogeneity bias. The limitation of instrumental variables lies in the ability to find a suitable set of instruments that is both exogenous and good at predicting X_1 – weak instruments will circumvent the endogeneity but provide poor estimates of the β coefficients (for a full discussion, see Bowden and Turkington, 1990).

An interesting recent geographical example, widely publicized through *The Economist* magazine, is a study by James Feyrer and Bruce Sacerdote of the economic prosperity of 80 former-colonial islands around the globe. They argue that the current prosperity is directly related to length of colonization, but recognize that fertile and promising islands may have attracted colonists; that is, endogeneity. They then use instrumental variables with measures of wind speed and direction as instruments: before steam-ships, such variables may well have influenced the date of colonization, but are strictly exogenous. LWH

Suggested reading
Kennedy (2003). See also *The Economist*, 2 November 2006.

instrumentalism A philosophy of science concentrating on end results such that science becomes an instrument judged in terms of practical utility rather than the truth or falsity of theory. Gregory (1978a) identified instrumentalism as a feature of geography's QUANTITATIVE REVOLUTION, informed by a particular reading of POSITIVISM, the generation of models being welcomed for their potential to shape policy. Such work entailed a narrow conception of RELEVANCE, subsequently critiqued. Concerns over instrumentalism have informed debates over GEOGRAPHIC INFORMATION SYSTEMS, with calls for GIS to adopt a more critical and reflexive perspective on the conditions of its production and utilization (Pickles, 1995a). DMat

Suggested reading
Gregory (1978).

integration The creation and maintenance of intense and diverse patterns of interaction and control between formerly more or less separate social spaces. Integration involves the bringing together of different systems of meaning and action founded in different sets of social relations. It takes place in different registers – economic, political and cultural – and so is an inherently uneven process. This is compounded because integration takes place through – not merely over – TIME and SPACE: without the formation of new times and spaces, the social relations embedded in integration could not be constituted. As such, it is profoundly affected by technical change. Innovations in the movement of people and commodities, and most recently in the electronic transmission of ideas, images, information and cultural forms, have made possible new modes of interaction and new ways of being 'present' in other places (see TIME–SPACE COMPRESSION; TIME–SPACE DISTANCIATION).

Places have never been closed, cellular systems; people have always been caught up in the lives of others. But the porosity of PLACE has varied, and may be transformed forcibly (by WAR), peacefully (through agreement or negotiation), or through a mix of the two. Historically, COLONIALISM and IMPERIALISM have been powerful vehicles of integration, although the processes were highly asymmetric and shot through with differentials of POWER and profit. Today, economic integration usually depends on market mechanisms, through the circulation of capital, labour and knowledge, through the global integration of consumer practices and consumer culture, and through political interventions in international political economy (policies on trade, investment, immigration etc.), but these processes may also have violent correlates that Harvey (2003b) connects to a continuing global regime of ACCUMULATION by dispossession.

Integration does not automatically imply the erasure of difference. Economically, it may impose or allow greater degrees of specialization and promote AREAL DIFFERENTIATION (see GLOBALIZATION); politically, it may raise questions about autonomy, IDENTITY and independence within national or transnational formations; culturally, it may allow the dissemination of new hybrid cultural forms (see HYBRIDITY; TRANSCULTURATION). All three issues have surfaced in successive enlargements of the European Union and the project of a united EUROPE (see Bialasiewicz, Elden and Painter, 2005). More generally and over the longer term, Braudel (1985, p. 45) emphasizes that the integrative world economy is simply 'an order among other orders', and that the struggle between integration and differentiation/distinction has always been and remains a powerful determinant of economic, political and cultural relations.   RL

Suggested reading
Bialasiewicz, Elden and Painter (2005); Lee (1990).

Intellectual Property Rights (IPR) The collective term used to refer to the protection offered by a variety of legal instruments – most notably copyright, patents and trademarks – with respect to the use of certain intangible goods including ideas and information. Typically, the holder of such rights is entitled to a temporally or spatially limited degree of exclusivity in the use of the matter in question, an exclusivity that is designed to stimulate and reward the inventiveness involved in making it useful. Like all property rights, IPRs are very much social rights,

embodying how societies choose to recognize the claims of certain individuals and groups but not others to certain particularly significant and/or potentially limited things. As such, they have varied over time and between places on the one hand, and been the object of much debate on the other. A series of related developments over the past half-century or so has seen an intensification of the implications of these differences and contestations, bringing intellectual property rights to the very forefront of contemporary intellectual and political discussion.

First, a technologically enhanced ability on the part of scientists and others to translate, manipulate and circulate biological materials has multiplied the kinds of things which might potentially be covered by IPRs. Second, the advent of what has been called a 'KNOWLEDGE ECONOMY' has seen a scramble by relevant parties of all sorts to protect as much and as many of the intangible aspects of their products and services as possible (and thereby their profits and position). Finally, moves by global bodies ranging from the United Nations to the World Trade Organization (WTO) to harmonize and regulate how intellectual property rights are defined and practiced worldwide has publicly exposed the extent and magnitude of the issues at stake, as well as the profound disagreements that need to be overcome.

At this point, it is probably fair to say that the aspect of intellectual property rights that has most exercised geographers' interest has been the questions that they raise about the ownership of biological materials. In the 1994 Agreement on Trade-Related Aspects of Intellectual Property Rights (TRIPS) (which is administered by the WTO and is undergoing almost continuous renegotiation), provision was made for certain kinds of materials to be patentable. This reflected a trend since the 1970s of business interests (and especially the life science firms involved in producing medicines), to successfully argue that patents are essential for their ability to make a return on their investment in research and development required to discover, produce and get regulatory approval for new products. The idea that biological materials (if not animal, plants or processes themselves) should be privately owned – even in the temporary form offered by patents – has been hugely controversial. Some object that it is morally inappropriate that the legal-commercial logic of property should be extended to living things in any form. For others, what is inappropriate is the imposition of a Western model of property on to situations involving peoples who might collectively make sense of the world in very different terms. What they demonstrate is how important an understanding of the legal geographies of IPRs is likely to be for the foreseeable future (see LAW). NB

Suggested reading
Brown (2003); Coombe (1998); Dutfield (2004); Parry (2004); Whatmore (2002).

intensive agriculture Intensive agriculture is broadly characterized as repeated cultivation and/or grazing of the same area of land using supplementary energy inputs to enhance the fertility of the land: it is contrasted with *extensive agriculture*, which involves seasonal patterns of transitory land use over large areas (Simmons, 1996). As a process, intensification refers to improving the yield on land already in production, usually by efforts to speed up, enhance or reduce the risks of biological processes in agrarian production; whereas extensification refers to bringing more land into production. Boyd, Prudham and Schurman (2001) have drawn parallels between these two ideas and MARXIAN ECONOMICS concepts regarding the subsumption of labour. Food regime theorists such as Freidmann and McMichael (1989) have used regulation theory to posit a broad shift from extensive to intensive agriculture in the postwar period, although many have contested these assumptions and have noted a much more variegated landscape of extensive and intensive production.

As a historical process, intensification has been associated with the transition from feudalism to capitalism (see ENCLOSURE), and the ensuing development of markets in land, labour, credit and farm inputs. One theory of intensification is through the penetration of commodity relations into PEASANT households. What Bernstein (1995a) has called the 'simple reproduction squeeze' is when inputs and reproductive needs once produced by households need to be purchased at the same time that household members are drawn into off-farm employment, reducing the labour applied to farming and social reproduction. The prospect of declining yields and income thus forces agrarian producers to adopt more high-yielding configurations of capital, labour and technology. Blaikie's (1985) theorization as to how this squeeze can lead to soil erosion in developing countries was seminal in POLITICAL ECOLOGY. Since increased yield can be achieved with more rotations (fewer fallows),

reduced crop loss or faster-growing varieties/ animal breeds, today intensive agriculture is associated with high input use, including chemical fertilizers and pesticides, animal pharmaceuticals and growth hormones, mechanization and genetic engineering. Non-technical innovations in labour control can be considered intensification as well; for example, the use of vulnerability to ensure a timely, and compliant, labour force. Because farmers are 'price-takers', agriculture is plagued by systematic over-production, a problem that intensification only exacerbates. At the introduction of a new technology, early innovators enjoy surplus profits, based on improved productivity. As others jump in, price competition ensues, causing rates of profit to fall, until marginal returns are very low. Intensification has come to be associated with high land values, since land tends to be capitalized at the 'highest and best use' (see Guthman, 2004).

Intensive agriculture practices have become closely associated with growing public concerns about the environmental and food safety problems of industrial systems of food production. These problems range from water pollution caused by agricultural chemical runoff and the loss of biodiversity associated with monocultures, to the incubation of animal diseases such as BSE. Sometimes, the INDUSTRIALIZATION of agriculture, which can also connote corporate control, largeness or factory-like conditions, is more precisely described as intensification. JGu

Suggested reading
Kimbrell (2002).

intensive research Research strategies directed towards discovering the causal chains that connect social structures, social practices and individual agents in particular time–space contexts. Sayer (1992 [1984]) argued that intensive research is typically conducted under the sign of REALISM and relies on QUALITATIVE METHODS, including ETHNOGRAPHY. As such, it is concerned with substantial relations of connection and privileges a logic of corroboration. Sayer insisted that such studies are every bit as 'objective' as EXTENSIVE RESEARCH and, indeed, are more powerful, since their focus on causal mechanisms means that they are likely to produce 'abstract knowledge [that is] more generally applicable'. DG

internal relations Necessary relations between objects or practices that make them what they are. Formally, 'a relation AB may be defined as internal if and only if A would not be what it essentially is unless B is related to it in the way that it is' (Bhaskar, 1998 [1979]). Internal relations are of two kinds:

(1) The relation between landlord and tenant is an internal relation, for example: in this case, each presupposes the other, so that the relation is *symmetrical*.
(2) The relation between the STATE and local authority (or 'social') housing is also an internal relation: the latter presupposes the former, but the converse is not true, since it is perfectly possible to think of a state that makes no provision for social housing, so that the relation is *asymmetrical*.

These distinctions are important for the process of ABSTRACTION that is the mainspring of the philosophy of REALISM, because they guard against so-called *chaotic conceptions* that 'combine the unrelated and divide the indivisible' (Sayer, 1982).

Sets of internal relations may be termed *structures*. Thus Harvey (1973, pp. 286–314) defined a structure as 'a system of internal relations which is in the process of being structured through the operation of its own transformation rules'. In his subsequent writings, Harvey provided a more developed account of the structures of CAPITALISM as a MODE OF PRODUCTION and, in particular, of the DIALECTIC within which 'each moment is constituted as an internal relation of the others within the flow of social and material life' (Harvey, 1996, p. 81; see also Jessop, 2006). Harvey was following Marx, and his project was directed towards what he termed historico-geographical materialism (see MARXISM; MATERIALISM). In his exploration of the philosophy of internal relations, however, Olsson (1980) elected to follow a radically different direction. For Olsson, echoing Hegel in a transposed key, thought, language and action are internally related to such a degree that 'the world and our ideas are so entangled in each other that they cannot be separated'. Hence, so he claimed, 'social relations between people [are] like logical relations between propositions' and vice versa: they are all internal relations. This prompted Olsson to make a linguistic turn and embark upon a series of linguistic experiments that took him into the realms of surrealism and beyond, but always circling around the internal relations that skewer thought-and-

action through the logics of 'CARTOGRAPHIC REASON' (Olsson, 2007). DG

International Monetary Fund (IMF) One of the two international financial institutions created at the meeting of national leaders held in Bretton Woods, New Hampshire, shortly before the end of the Second World War – the other being the International Bank for Reconstruction and Development, better known as the World Bank. A third proposed Bretton Woods institution, the International Trade Organization (ITO), was stillborn because of opposition from the US Congress, and a body with the powers to be accorded the ITO did not come into existence until the founding of the World Trade Organization (WTO) in 1996.

The IMF was created with the task of promoting international TRADE through facilitating monetary co-operation, and it was allocated funds for the specific purpose of helping countries get past short-term balance-of-payments crises. This made its tasks complementary to the longer-term DEVELOPMENT funding undertaken by the World Bank. Both institutions had a somewhat Keynesian mandate. The Articles of Agreement of the IMF included among the purposes of the organization to 'facilitate the expansion and balanced growth of international trade, and to contribute thereby to the promotion and maintenance of high levels of employment and real income'. This was to be accomplished by promoting exchange rate stability among national currencies and avoiding 'competitive exchange depreciation' (Holborn, 1948, p. 172).

With the breakdown of the fixed exchange rate regime in the early 1970s, however, the IMF began to take on new and distinctly anti-Keynesian roles that mark the beginnings of NEO-LIBERALISM. The IMF is today more favourably inclined towards floating exchange rate regimes, even when this results in competitive devaluations, and its favoured policies of STRUCTURAL ADJUSTMENT have frequently sacrificed goals of high employment and wages in favour of ensuring international financial investors against the consequences of inflationary government policies such as domestic price supports (Payer, 1974; Kolko, 1988, pp. 265–9).

In its role as the dispenser of short-term funds to countries undergoing balance-of-payments crises, the IMF has increasingly demanded as its price for loans conformity by recipient governments to neo-liberal policies (see AID). This has generated criticisms from a range of popular organizations, governments and economists, making the IMF somewhat of a lightening rod for criticisms of neo-liberalism, especially in the wake of the 1997 Asian economic crisis, when many critics perceived IMF policies to have been inappropriate and to have exacerbated the crisis (see ANTI-GLOBALIZATION). In addition, because voting rights at the IMF are allocated on the basis of contributions, and because the US government is the leading contributor, the IMF has been seen by many critics as a USA-dominated institution, pushing an agenda favoured by the US Treasury Department (Stiglitz, 2002). JGl

Suggested reading
Holborn (1948); Kolko (1988); Payer (1974); Stiglitz (2002).

international relations The term has two meanings: (1) the relations between states; and (2) the study of international politics (where it is often abbreviated as IR).

(1) International relations are conventionally understood as the political issues (especially foreign, defence and security policy) that take place between states and beyond the borders of states. These 'high politics' are sometimes said to be in contrast to the 'low politics' of domestic issues. In this conception, states are understood to be bounded and sovereign, unitary and rational, and the primary actors on the international stage. World politics is thus understood as the sum of diplomatic, economic, military and political interactions between states as they prioritize their national interests and seek security by maximizing power. This view is said to be historically valid, traceable to thinkers such as Thucydides and Machiavelli, and formalized in agreements such as the 1648 Treaty of Westphalia.

This conception of world politics as international relations – which shares much with classical approaches to geopolitics – can be questioned empirically. International trade, the global circulation of capital and the movement of labour involve 'non-state' actors (e.g. corporations, markets and migrants) and traverse both 'domestic' and 'foreign' spaces, demonstrating that the varied scales of local, national and global are intertwined. Environmental issues, the transmission of disease, mobile cultural forms and fundamentalist religions are social forces that call sovereign spaces into question. They are developments that can require transnational governance that involves co-operation rather than conflict, collective interests rather than national priorities, and international organizations rather than military alliances.

(2) International Relations – especially when capitalized as IR – represents the academic study of relations between states and international politics. Although previously approached via the study of law, history and politics, as a formal discipline IR was established in the aftermath of the First World War, with positions at the University of Wales, Aberystwyth and the London School of Economics. As a predominantly Anglo-American enterprise ever since, IR has been subject to a series of paradigmatic debates that have pitched realists against idealists, scientists against historians, and globalists against statists. Only in the past 20 years or so, however, have the metatheoretical assumptions – the questions of epistemology and ontology – of all these contending positions been subject to debate. Drawing on developments in critical social theory associated with theories of discourse – which have also been behind developments in critical geopolitics – this intellectual ferment has seen questions of borders, identities and the construction of international order receive much greater attention. Approaches derived from constructivism (see SOCIAL CONSTRUCTION), FEMINISM, MARXISM, POLITICAL ECOLOGY and POST-STRUCTURALISM have taken on, but not displaced, the realist and neo-realist mainstream in the study of international politics. DCa

Suggested reading
Baylis and Smith (2004); Burchill, Devetak, Linklater, Paterson, Reus-Smit and True (2001); Dalby and Ó Tuathail (1998).

Internet A vast network of interconnected computers used to make the information, services, data and programs stored on one computer accessible to remote users, permitting them to purchase goods, download music, query databases, communicate messages and so forth.

Whilst partly developed from US defence research during the Cold War, the Internet's birth date is usually taken to be 1985, when the US National Science Foundation created NSFNet, allowing universities access to five supercomputer centres. Other networks existed at that time (e.g. the UK's Joint Academic Network and CompuServe's networking capabilities for corporate clients), but NSFNet was TCP/IP enabled: it used the protocols underpinning the Internet today, directing 'packets' of data to computers by assigning unique addresses to host networks and machines (e.g. IP address 68.142.226.55 is yahoo.com).

The Internet emerged as a public utility due to the popularity of the World Wide Web (WWW) – a series of interconnected documents (web pages). This development is credited to Tim Berners-Lee, who fused the concepts of hypertext (e.g. the ability to hyperlink pages) with the architecture of the Internet and developed the first web browser, in 1991. Amazon.com began in 1995, the same year that the Java programming language was integrated with a web browser. Google started life as a research project in 1996 – the year in which Microsoft's Internet Explorer was incorporated into Windows. *Wikipedia*, the free online encyclopaedia (and invaluable resource for this *Dictionary* entry), was launched in 2001.

Clearly, the Internet and WWW have grown rapidly in both use and scope. Whilst future trajectories and their long-term socio-economic effects are difficult to judge, recent history is suggestive. The 'dot.com bubble' may have peaked in 2000, but e-commerce (including online banking and music downloads) is still growing (e.g. downloads contributed 6 per cent of total worldwide record sales in the first half of 2005 – a 350 per cent increase in value from 2004: www.ifpi.org). If CYBER-SPACE develops as a dominant transaction space, then undoubtedly it will impact upon service- and retail-sector employment, and perhaps also on the landscapes of commerce. (Will the iconic 'high street' of shops and services be threatened by e-commerce or benefit as specialist shops are able to extend their global reach?) The Internet also contributes to alternative workspaces and practices, including home-working and 'hot-desking', and the collaboration of geographically separated persons in virtual meeting rooms and e-seminars (technologies that are being used to facilitate e-learning, taking traditionally place-bound universities into global education markets and 'knowledge economies').

It is likely that the WWW will continue to be the primary point of access to more and more information in online repositories, archives and data warehouses. Who should control or own this information? Google's Book Search facility allows the full text of books to be searched but has involved DIGITIZING the book collections of some libraries, raising copyright concerns amongst some publishers and authors. Other parties may want to restrict access to certain information for various reasons, including anti-terrorist protection or to close down undesirable websites. When Google.cn was launched in 2006, Chinese regulators required that 'sensitive information' be removed from its search results. This occasionally happens in France, Germany and the USA too (source: Google official blog).

Finally, whilst the Internet–WWW network can confidently be predicted to expand, it is unlikely to be perfectly ubiquitous. There are digital divides globally in terms of communication infrastructures, as there are nationally (e.g. broadband access is uneven across the UK, generally to the detriment of rural areas). Other geographies of cyberspace reflect on who owns the various components of the Internet–WWW (including IP addresses, content and service provision), raising social and geopolitical questions (see GEOPOLITICS). RH

Suggested reading
Dodge and Kitchin (2002); Gillies and Cailliau (2002).

interoperability The ability for something to work or interface between separate operations or systems without error or changed meaning. For example, digital downloads from online music stores to portable storage devices are facilitated by interoperability standards such as MP3 audio compression. The converse to interoperability is proprietary data formats locking the user into particular software. This was a problem with GIS, addressed by the Open Geospatial (formerly, Open GIS) Consortium leading the development of standards for geospatial and location-based services (www.opengeospatial.org) – including the Geography Markup Language (GML), a schema for the modelling, transport and storage of geographical information. RH

Suggested reading
Lake (2004).

intervening opportunities A concept developed by the American sociologist S.A. Stouffer (1940) to explain MIGRATION patterns and subsequently applied in studies of commodity flow, passenger trips, traffic movements and so on. The volume of movement between an origin and a destination is proportional to the number of opportunities at that destination, and inversely proportional to the number of opportunities between the origin and the destination. Stouffer argued that distance of itself has no effect on INTERACTION patterns and that any observed decline in the number of movements with distance (see DISTANCE DECAY) is due to the increase in the number of intervening opportunities with distance. A variant of this approach was developed in Fotheringham's (1983) 'theory of competing destinations'.   RJ

interviews and interviewing Widely used methods for learning about the experiences, attitudes and demographic characteristics of individuals, households or groups. Interviews can be structured or unstructured, and they can be administered face-to-face, over the telephone or via email. An interview using a survey QUESTIONNAIRE follows a set order of pre-established questions. Survey data underpins large scale quantitative social science, and can be effective for establishing attitudinal, demographic and socio-economic patterns across large samples representative of vast populations (see QUANTITATIVE METHODS; SAMPLING; SURVEY ANALYSIS). A CENSUS is a national survey of the entire population. Unstructured interviews are more conversational than a questionnaire, and allow interviewees to express the details and meanings of their experiences in their own terms and at their own pace. Unstructured interviews can be conducted with individuals, households or as FOCUS GROUPS, and are an appropriate QUALITATIVE METHOD for understanding complex and contradictory social processes and experiences, and when respondents need the opportunity to explain and qualify their accounts. But even the least structured ethnographic interview is very different from an ordinary conversation. It is important for an interviewer to recognize this, so as not to be caught within implicit rules of social conversation (Anderson and Jack, 1991). In contrast to ordinary conversations, the norm in ethnographic interviews is to repeat questions, ask for clarification of terms, and introduce a series of ethnographic explanations and styles of questions (Spradley, 1979: see ETHNOGRAPHY). Because they are unstructured, in-depth interviews are time-consuming (they typically last for between one and two hours), and the sample is usually much smaller (and likely less

representative of the population) than is the case for questionnaire surveys.

There has been considerable discussion of the influence of the interviewer on what is told and heard, and of the POWER dynamics between interviewers and interviewees. Although it is advisable for interviewers to dress and comport themselves so as to 'fit in', it is widely assumed to be impossible and undesirable for them to neutralize their presence. The researcher is integral to the interview process, and his or her GENDER, age, SEXUALITY, CLASS and RACE (and many other characteristics) will affect access and what they are told. In survey research, this is known as the 'interviewer effect'. There are two issues here. First, what we are told is situational, depending on the perceived social characteristics of the interviewer, the location of the interview, and many other contextual factors. Second, because most interviews are structured by 'a division of labour in which one talks and one listens', relations of oppression and domination may be unwittingly reproduced within them (Bondi, 2003, p. 70; but see England (2002) and McDowell (1998) for a different set of dynamics when interviewing elites). Both concerns have led to recommendations that interviewers reflect upon their POSITIONALITY in order to assess how they may be affecting (and affected by) the interview situation (see SITUATED KNOWLEDGE). Rose (1997b) cautions, however, that there are limits to such REFLEXIVITY, because we are not and cannot be fully conscious or transparent to ourselves; and Bondi (2003) notes that much communication within an interview is non-verbal and non-cognitive (see also NON-REPRESENTATIONAL THEORY). Power relations, and points of commonality and difference between interviewers and interviewees are also mobile and complex (McDowell, 1998; Kobayashi, 2001; Crang, 2002; England, 2002). Concerns about power relations have led to experiments training and working with community-based interviewers (Gibson-Graham, 1994; Pratt, 2004), and to calls for more activist research (Kobayashi, 2001; see also ACTIVISM, ACTION RESEARCH).

Key objectives for any unstructured interview are to create an intersubjective space in which the interviewee can express him or herself fully, and to strive to understand what is communicated as fully as possible, whilst causing no harm to the interviewee. Bondi (2003) makes a distinction between empathy and identification: the former (the recommended stance) involves the capacity to understand the interviewee's feelings

393

without becoming absorbed within and overwhelmed by them. If overwhelmed, the interviewer can move too quickly through difficult topics, or rush to comfort the interviewees without allowing them the opportunity to fully express their thoughts and feelings. Unstructured interviewing involves a process of 'learning to listen' rather than searching to confirm pre-existing ideas or theories. Anderson writes of her disappointment with the transcripts from her life history interviews with rural women, because the transcripts lacked detail and offered little insight into these women's emotional lives. Anderson closely and very usefully analyses the many moments in her interviews where she foreclosed opportunities for women to describe their lives, and thus subtlety communicated a double message: 'Tell me about your experience, but don't tell me too much' (Jack and Anderson, 1991, p. 15). She recommends that all researchers review their transcribed interviews 'to listen critically to [their] interviews, to [their] responses as well as [their] answers. We need to hear what [the interviewee] implied, suggested, and started to say but didn't. We need to interpret their pauses and, when it happens, their unwillingness or inability to respond' (Jack and Anderson, 1991, p. 17). As this quote suggests, qualitative interviews typically require textual rather than the statistical analyses typical for questionnaire surveys. The desire to extract the most meaning from transcripts has led some researchers to use transcription systems developed for conversational analysis, in which attempts are made to signal pauses and capture some of the emotional content of the interview within the transcription (England, 2002).

Domosh (2003) has criticized geographers for tending to analyse interview transcripts as if they are authentic expressions of experience. The need to examine interview data as DISCOURSE and PERFORMANCE rather than raw experience is nicely demonstrated in Visweswaran's (1994) description of her discovery that several of her interviewees had deceived her. Her analysis shows interviews to be performances in which the interviewees display limited and sometimes falsified aspects of their selves and experiences. Rather than worrying about the fact of deception, Visweswaran tries to understand why she was told particular things for specific reasons. These reasons include the fact that interviewees were unable to express some ideas or criticisms within dominant discourse. It is only

through repeated interviews, supplemented by ethnographic and archival research, that she is able to glean this. Nightingale (2003) approaches the incompleteness of in-depth interviews from another angle, stressing the advantage of mixed methods. Given the partial nature of all knowledge, she recommends that interview material be combined with other types of data, and that it be treated as no more authentic or less mediated than quantified forms of data, in the case of her research, remote sensing maps. Because survey methods are more appropriate for establishing patterns over a large population, they can be used effectively in combination with qualitative interviews.

There are many excellent methodology textbooks that introduce the basics of interviewing methodology, including Limb and Dwyer (2001) and Valentine (2005). GP

Suggested reading
Crang (2002); Limb and Dwyer (2001); Valentine (2005).

intifada A popular uprising against military occupation (see OCCUPATION, MILITARY), derived from the Arabic for a 'shaking off'. The term originated in two phases of Palestinian resistance to Israeli occupation. Israel occupied Gaza and the West Bank in 1967 and, despite United Nations Security Council resolutions and international law, encouraged its civilians to establish colonies ('settlements') there (see VERTICALITY, POLITICS OF). The First Intifada was a spontaneous uprising that began in December 1987. It involved a disengagement from systems of Israeli administration and developed into a vigorous assertion of the Palestinian right to national self-determination. After a protracted struggle, the uprising came to an end in 1993 with the signing of the Oslo accords, the promise of a phased Israeli withdrawal and the establishment of the Palestinian National Authority. The process of Israeli colonization continued unchecked, however, and in September 2000 a Second Intifada, the al-Aqsa Intifada, broke out (Carey, 2001; Gregory, 2004b). It was rooted in the failure of the 'peace process' and the accelerated dispossession of Palestinians, but it spluttered to an end during 2005. The Second Intifada was more desperate and more violent than the first: B'Tselem, the Israeli Center for Human Rights, estimates that 422 Israelis and 1,551 Palestinians were killed between 1987 and 2000, whereas 468 Israelis and 3,418 Palestinians had been killed from 2000 through to April 2006. The term 'intifada' was also invoked by some Iraqi political movements opposed to the US occupation since 2003 and by some Lebanese activists in their struggle against Syrian domination in 2005.   DG

Suggested reading
See Electronic Intifada at http://eletronicintifada. net; and the Forum on al-Aqsa Intifada, in *Arab World Geographer* (October 2001) at http://users. fmg.uva.nl/vmamadouh/awg/

invasion and succession A concept adapted from ECOLOGY by sociologists of the CHICAGO SCHOOL to describe processes of NEIGHBOUR-HOOD change within cities. Within ecology, the concept is derived from ideas regarding the 'survival of the fittest' in the competition for living space (cf. DARWINISM).

According to the Chicago School model of urban residential patterns (cf. ZONAL MODEL), the main stimulus to urban expansion is in-MIGRATION of relatively low-income groups. These are largely constrained to low-cost, high-density, relatively poor-quality housing, much of which is concentrated in the INNER CITY; in addition, many move to that area because of the presence there of family and friends who assist their initial ASSIMILATION to a new milieu (cf. CHAIN MIGRATION). The pressure that this puts on inner-city housing stock stimulates existing residents to seek housing further from the centre, initiating a ripple effect through all of the city's zones with residents on the urban edge responding by moving into new housing. Growth at the centre thus leads to expansion on the URBAN FRINGE through a process of FILTERING, whereby housing moves down the socio-economic scale as one group replaces another in a neighbourhood, whilst households move up the housing scale in terms of housing age and quality.

Given the context in which the model was developed – 1920s Chicago – many of the immigrants who initiated the invasion-and-succession sequence were members of ethnic minorities (see ETHNICITY). Their movement into areas might be challenged, causing housing stress (as densities then build up in the areas that they already occupy), until eventually pressure on an adjacent area leads to its residents yielding (cf. BLOCKBUSTING).   RJ

Suggested reading
Bulmer (1986).

investment Most commonly discussed by geographers in the context of *Foreign Direct Investment* (FDI), which Dicken defines as 'direct investment which occurs across national boundaries, that is, when a firm from one country buys a controlling investment in a firm in another country or where a firm sets up a branch or subsidiary in another country' (2003, p. 51). FDI involves either an 'organic/greenfield' strategy, in which investment is used to establish operations in an overseas country from scratch, or a 'merger' strategy, where investment is used to buy an existing operator.

When a firm or individual makes an investment, the aim is usually to reap financial benefit, either by selling the COMMODITY or RESOURCE purchased at a later date at a profit (as investment banks do through stock and commodities markets) or by extracting value-added in some other way. FDI usually follows the latter strategy, aiming to use an overseas investment to enhance long-term profitability by extracting value from presence in another country. As Dunning and Norman's (1987) 'theory of international enterprise' suggests, FDI can allow: (1) the leverage of existing assets overseas, usually resulting in increased sales and profits; and/or (2) access to new assets, again resulting in either increased sales (through innovation, for example, when the asset is skilled labour) or improved profitability (e.g. when costs are reduced because access is gained to cheap labour).

The geography of investment can be studied at two SCALES. At the macro scale it is possible to study the worldwide aggregate trends in FDI. Shatz and Venables (2000) show that: (1) the developed countries provide the dominant origin of FDI (~90 per cent), although traditional sources such as the USA and the UK are declining in their relative share because of the growing importance of Eastern European and South East Asian nations; (2) the developed nations are also the dominant receivers of FDI (~70 per cent). This does not, however, mean that developing countries are not important sources and sinks of FDI. Indeed, there are a small number of countries that are significant destinations for FDI because of the way firms seek to exploit the NEW INTERNATIONAL DIVISION OF LABOUR. Predominantly, though, FDI is used to access developed markets, in particular as a strategy to overcome trade restrictions and access consumer markets.

At the micro scale the patchiness of the geography of investment can be explored and theorized. Firms usually choose a place for investment that will bring particular market or asset benefits. For example, those seeking access to knowledge-rich workers will seek to invest in CLUSTERS, such as Silicon Valley (Saxenian, 1994), rather than rustbelt districts of a country. Those seeking access to markets will seek out AGGLOMERATIONS where demand is high, such as advertising and law producer service firms that congregate in the WORLD CITIES of London and New York (Sassen, 2006). This means, however, that those REGIONS that fail to attract investment can become backwaters of the global economy, as has been experienced to a certain extent in the North East of England since the closure of the coal mines in the 1970s and 1980s (Hudson, 2005) and the American Rust Belts, around Detroit in particular (Glasmeier, 2005).   JF

Suggested reading
Shatz and Venables (2000).

irredentism The claim by the government, or by political groups, of one country that a minority living in a neighbouring country belongs instead to it because of historical and cultural connections. Though at times the minority may live in peace within the neighbouring country, in other contexts irredentist movements may mount a campaign to 'unite' the minority, leading to BORDER disputes, active guerilla-like conflict (as in Northern Ireland), and even war. The term originated from a disputed part of Austria in 1871, which Italian nationalists called *Italia irredenta*, or unredeemed Italy. The 1990s war in the former Yugoslavia was driven by a combination of irredentist claims.   CF

Suggested reading
Ambrosio (2001).

isolines Lines on a MAP describing the intersection of a real or hypothetical SURFACE with one or more horizontal planes. On a TOPOGRAPHIC MAP, typically compiled from aerial photographs by stereocompilation (Lyon, Falkner and Bergen, 1995), each isoline, or contour, represents a constant elevation, and because the vertical interval is constant, their relative spacing is a readily visualized indicator of slope. On a statistical map, isolines may be threaded manually through a network of data points or plotted automatically by an interpolation algorithm, which provides comparative consistency and gives the map author some control over the appearance and reliability of the map (Schneider, 2001). Spot heights are occasionally added to emphasize local minima and maxima.   MM

Suggested reading
Yang and Hodler (2000).

J

just war A war whose cause and conduct can be ethically justified (see ETHICS). The desire to specify the conditions under which it is morally acceptable to resort to military VIOLENCE has a long and complicated history, in which RELIGION, GEOPOLITICS and LAW have all played central roles.

Christianity has embraced both a presumption against war and a belief that war may be justified to spread or defend the faith (the Crusades) or to combat evil. In Islam, the concept of *jihad* involves a struggle against evil, but the 'greater jihad' is a personal, spiritual struggle, while the 'lesser jihad' is reserved for armed struggles to spread or defend the faith (Devji, 2005). Much of the rhetoric surrounding the 'war on terror' (see TERRORISM) has traded on these twin versions of a supposedly 'holy war', Christian and Muslim, but within both theological traditions geopolitical and juridical issues have also loomed large.

Both theological traditions have invoked a GEOGRAPHICAL IMAGINARY in which the locations of the sacralized 'heartland' or HOMELAND and that of the enemy Other are identified. Modern geopolitics has often appropriated the language of Just War traditions too, but typically in a secularized form in order to legitimize conventional wars and, more recently, military interventions in the name of what Chomsky (1999) calls a 'new military humanism' (cf. Douzinas, 2003; see also HUMANISM). But Megoran (2008) objects that, while CRITICAL GEOPOLITICS has no hesitation in advancing all sorts of normative claims and moral judgements, it has conspicuously failed to interrogate its own ethical presuppositions in any systematic and detailed fashion. In opposing some wars and endorsing others, practitioners of critical geopolitics have implicitly adopted the categories of just war reasoning, he argues, but ironically failed to subject them to critical scrutiny. This has a number of consequences, Megoran concludes, the most important of which is a silence over the production of spaces of non-violence and 'a vision of peace and justice that explicitly eschews the resort to force' (p. 494). This is true of HUMAN GEOGRAPHY more generally, however, which has long been more invested in WAR than in peace (cf. Wisner, 1986).

Modern juridical doctrines of just war distinguish (1) law governing when a war may be fought (*jus ad bellum*) from (2) law governing how a war is to be conducted (*jus in bello*). In general, the first requires a just cause (for example, self-defence, not aggression), a declaration by a legitimate authority, a right intention (so that the motivation must be moral rather than, for example, economic: cf. RESOURCE WARS) and a reasonable prospect of success. The second requires, among other things, discrimination between military targets and civilians, the proportional use of force, and the humane treatment of prisoners of war and civilians (cf. Gregory, 2006). These two sets of requirements raise considerable philosophical and legal issues, and several commentators insist that they need to be suspended in situations of 'supreme emergency' (Walzer, 2000) (cf. EXCEPTION, SPACE OF). But they have been put under further strain by new forms of war and their geographies, including the 'war on terror', which raise complex questions about SOVEREIGN POWER and TERRITORY, and which often refuse any clear distinction between military and non-military spaces. The rhetorical power of a 'just war' depends on more than legal arguments, however: it also depends on the mobilization of IMAGINATIVE GEOGRAPHIES to legitimize the identification and characterization of the enemy – which is, of course, where theological and geopolitical claims so often make their most forceful appearance (Falah, Flint and Mamadouh, 2006). **DG**

Suggested reading
Megoran (2008).

just-in-time production A system of manufacturing in which inputs are supplied and outputs are delivered very soon after demand for a finished good has been registered. Perfected by Japanese automobile producers, and since emulated by North American and European assemblers, this set of practices has also diffused to other industrial sectors such as computer manufacturing. As one objective is to reduce the quantity of producers' capital tied up in inventories of parts and finished products, producers no longer keep large buffer stocks on hand. This has the consequent effect of forcing lower defect rates in parts supplied, and hence improves overall quality. Because suppliers are able to meet buyers' varying requirements (in both number and type) at short notice, the system allows manufacturers to respond more flexibly to changing market demands (see, more generally, FLEXIBLE ACCUMULATION and POST-FORDISM). Adoption of such practices may exert an AGGLOMERATION effect, bringing buyers and suppliers closer together to facilitate rapid delivery at short notice, but in any case transforms the dynamics of the COMMODITY CHAIN. MSG

K

Kantianism A PHILOSOPHY developed by Immanuel Kant (1724–1804) (see Kuehn, 2001). Kant's conception of the nature of GEOGRAPHY and its location within the system of knowledge as a whole provided the basis for a series of major disagreements in the twentieth-century discipline (see May, 1970). Kant considered that knowledge could be classified in two ways: either logically or physically (cf. CLASSIFICATION): 'The logical classification collects all individual items in separate classes according to similarities of morphological features; it could be called something like an "archive" and will, if pursued, lead to a "natural system"' (Büttner and Hoheisel, 1980). In a 'natural system', Kant noted, 'I place each thing in its class, even though they are to be found in different, widely separated places' (cited in Hartshorne, 1939). He assumed this to be the method of all the sciences except history and geography, which depended, in contrast, on physical classification. The physical classification collects individual items that 'belong to the same time or the same space'. In this connection, Kant asserted:

> History differs from geography only in the consideration of time and [space]. The former is a report of phenomena that follow one another (*Nacheinander*) and has reference to time. The latter is a report of phenomena beside each other (*Nebeneinander*) in space. History is a narrative, geography a description. Geography and history fill up the entire circumference of our perceptions: geography that of space, history that of time. (Kant, cited in Hartshorne, 1939)

Although Kant's views on geography were broadly similar to those of architects of the modern discipline like von Humboldt and Hettner, they appear to have had 'no direct influence' other than 'as a form of confirmation' (Hartshorne, 1958; but cf. Büttner and Hoheisel, 1980). Indeed, they were not explicitly endorsed in any programmatic statement of the scope of geography in English until Hartshorne's account of *The nature of geography* (1939), which accepted that geography's basic task was essentially Kantian:

> Geography and history are alike in that they are integrating sciences concerned with studying the world. There is, therefore, a universal and mutual relation between them, even though their bases of integration are in a sense opposite – geography in terms of earth spaces, history in terms of periods of time.

Others were more sceptical. Blaut (1961) concluded that, for Kant,

> Knowledge about the spatial location of objects is quite distinct from knowledge about their true nature and the natural laws governing them. The latter sorts of knowledge are eternal and universal, are truly scientific [whereas] spatial and temporal co-ordinates are separate and rather secondary attributes of objects, and spatial and temporal arrangement of objects is not a matter for science.

Like Schaefer (1953), therefore, Blaut saw Kant as the originator of an EXCEPTIONALISM that was inimical to the EXPLANATIONS and generalizations (rather than mere 'descriptions') required for geography to be reconstituted as a SPATIAL SCIENCE. That this was not a necessary consequence was later demonstrated by Torsten Hägerstrand, who revitalized Kant's distinction in order to demonstrate the possibility of a recognizably scientific approach to physical orderings. Although TIME-GEOGRAPHY was predicated on a rejection of divisions between 'history' and 'geography', 'time' and 'space', the contrast that Hägerstrand drew between a conventional *compositional* approach and his own *contextual* approach paralleled that between 'logical' and 'physical' classifications (see CONTEXTUALITY).

Most of the foregoing formulations depended on Kant's lectures on PHYSICAL GEOGRAPHY delivered from 1755 to 1796 and recovered from various notes, but other writers drew attention to Kant's *Critique of pure reason* (1781) and its emphasis on 'the structuring activity of the thinking subject' to develop an alternative to spatial science:

> Space is not something objective and real, nor is it a substance or an accident, or a relation, but it is *subjective* and *ideal* and

proceeds from the nature of the mind by an *unchanging law*, as a schema for co-ordinating with each other absolutely all things externally sensed. (Kant, cited in Richards, 1974; emphasis added)

This stress upon 'the epistemic structuring of the world by the human actor was the essence of the Kantian heritage', so it was claimed, and 'constitutes the common theme which has, in practice, been distilled from the variety of humanistic philosophies to which geographers of a subjectivist orientation have turned in their endeavour to transcend the dichotomy inherent in subject–object relations' (Livingstone and Harrison, 1981a: see BEHAVIOURAL GEOGRAPHY; HUMANISTIC GEOGRAPHY).

Many of these endeavours might more properly be described as neo-Kantian. *Neo-Kantianism* emerged in Germany in the closing decades of the nineteenth century. Whereas Kant had held the *a priori* to be 'externally fixed and eternally immutable' – the 'unchanging law' in Richard's quotation above – the neo-Kantians rejected the vision of a unitary scientific method that this allowed. They substituted a key distinction between:

- *the cultural and historical sciences* (the *Geisteswissenschaften*), which dealt with an intelligible world of 'non-sensuous objects of experience', which required interpretation and understanding (*verstehen*), and which were thus concerned with the IDIOGRAPHIC – this was the focus of the 'Baden School', which included Windelband and Rickert – and
- *the natural sciences* (the *Naturwissenscahften*), which dealt with the 'sensible world of science', which required explanation (*erklären*), and which were thus concerned with the NOMOTHETIC – this was the focus of the 'Marburg school', which included Cassirer.

Within HUMAN GEOGRAPHY, neo-Kantianism has been seen at work in the POSSIBILISM of the early-twentieth-century French school of geography (Berdoulay, 1976), in the programme of the CHICAGO SCHOOL of urban sociology (Park completed a doctoral dissertation under Windelband: Entrikin, 1980), and in HUMANISTIC GEOGRAPHY more generally (Jackson and Smith, 1984). In a still more fundamental sense, Entrikin (1984) proposed that Hartshorne's view of the nature of geography (above) incorporated a number of

patently neo-Kantian arguments, and that Cassirer's writings might provide a means of reinvigorating geography's various perspectives upon space (see also Entrikin, 1977).

Until recently, most geographers limited their interest in Kant to his lectures on physical geography and his first critique, largely – one suspects – because of their interest in (or objections to) the scientificity of geographies underwritten by POSITIVISM. But several writers have since reflected on Kant's second and third critiques, *Critique of practical reason* (1788) and *Critique of judgement* (1790–9). In the closing decades of the twentieth century there was a widespread (if often tacit) acceptance of an essentially Kantian distinction between three forms of knowledge or 'reason'. Following Habermas, for example, several writers associated the ENLIGHTENMENT project in particular and MODERNITY in general with the formation of three autonomous spheres (see table).

science	truth and knowledge cognitive–instrumental rationality
morality	norms and justice moral–practical rationality
art	authenticity and beauty aesthetic–expressive rationality

The task of Habermas' version of CRITICAL THEORY was, in part, to re-balance these three spheres: to guard against the inflation of 'SCIENCE' (and the detachment of its expert culture from public scrutiny) which he believed was characteristic of CAPITALISM in the early and middle twentieth century; and against the inflation of the aesthetic that he saw within late-twentieth-century POSTMODERNISM (Ingram, 1987). Certainly, Kantian aesthetics played an important part in discussions of postmodern sensibilities in human geography, and particular attention was paid to the aestheticization of politics to be found in versions of both MODERNISM and postmodernism (Harvey, 1989b).

More recently still, there been a renewed interest in Kant's view of COSMOPOLITANISM set out in 'Perpetual Peace: a philosophical sketch' (1795). To some critics, it is frankly bizarre to juxtapose Kant's essay with the ETHNOCENTRISM (at best) and at worst the 'racisms and ethnic prejudices' of his lectures on physical geography (Harvey, 2000a, p. 544). But Harvey also recognized that the 'contrast between the universality of Kant's cosmopolitanism and ETHICS and the awkward and intractable peculiarities of his geography is important' precisely because it opens a space for a crucial 'DIALECTIC between cosmopolitanism and geography' (Harvey, 2000a, pp. 535, 559). Other critics have mapped that space in radically different terms. Since the end of the COLD WAR, and even more insistently after 9/11, several hostile and usually (though by no means invariably) American commentators have described contemporary EUROPE as in thrall to Kant and his vision of 'perpetual peace', while leaving the USA the supreme task of bringing order to the Hobbesian world of 'failed states' and collapsing states, of warlords and transnational TERRORISM beyond its boundaries. That said, Elden and Bialasiewicz (2006, p. 644) argue that 'the characterisation of a "Kantian" Europe, weak, complacent, and "out of touch" with current global realities, tells us more about the United States and its imagined role than it does about Europe'.   DG

Suggested reading
Büttner and Hoheisel (1980); May (1970); Elden and Bialasiewicz (2006).

kibbutz A collective Zionist village. Over 250 rural kibbutz settlements ('kibbutzim' in the plural) have been established in Israel/Palestine since 1909. Kibbutz communities combine two ideals – SOCIALISM and Zionism. Until the 1970s, kibbutzim were considered the torch bearers of the Zionist project by embodying its main goals: colonizing, Judaizing and farming the contested frontiers, leading the Israeli army, and symbolizing the new national culture. The 'kibbutznik' became an icon of Zionist IDENTITY – the 'new Jew' – a strong, independent, settler–soldier. However, with the gradual decline of HEGEMONY held by Israel's Ashkenazi (Western) Jews and Labor Movement, the special status of the kibbutzim has eroded. Today, most kibbutzim have become urbanizing villages, and have shed many of their socialist features. OY

Suggested reading
Gavron (2000); Rosner (2000).

knowledge economy An economic regime in which knowledge-intensive manufacturing and service activities become dominant, and in which the skill and expertise of workers and the INNOVATION that this facilitates lie at the heart of the success of firms, regions and national economies. The idea of a knowledge economy derives from Drucker's (1969) account of the role of the 'knowledge worker' in manufacturing industries, and it has been developed through knowledge-based views of the firm and arguments about the centrality of knowledge to the competitiveness of national economies. The concept of a POST-INDUSTRIAL SOCIETY based on advanced, knowledge-rich services was also instrumental in attracting the attention of academics and policy-makers.

From a policy perspective, the idea of the knowledge economy has been used to foreground discussions, in the Anglo-American world in particular, about the need to invest in skills development and training for workers, and to promote the shift towards advanced knowledge-intensive industries (OECD, 2000). These debates have often been tied to discussions of national competitiveness (Dunning, 2000), which tacitly assume a spatial DIVISION OF LABOUR in which the economies of Western Europe, North America and South East Asia act as 'leaders' in the knowledge economy, whilst less developed nations will fulfil less knowledge-intensive roles, particularly in manufacturing assembly processes.

Academic debates have addressed three main issues. First, Gregersen and Johnson note that 'all economies are knowledge-based. Even so-called primitive economies depend on complicated knowledge structures' (1997, p. 481). Consequently, discussion has recognized *degrees* of knowledge-intensity. Second, the REGIONAL GEOGRAPHY of the knowledge-economy has been foregrounded in analyses of CLUSTERS, LEARNING REGIONS, INDUSTRIAL DISTRICTS and innovative milieux. But Martin and Sunley (2003) remain unconvinced that the REGION is the appropriate SCALE of analysis, while others position regions within global NETWORKS of knowledge that include both the embodied movement of personnel and the virtual circulation of knowledge through global telecommunication systems (Amin and Cohendet, 2004). Third, considerable attention has been paid to the discursive effect of the concept itself (see DISCOURSE). Thrift (1997b) posits the contemporary emergence of a 'soft CAPITALISM', whose ideologies and practices powerfully shape the ways in which policy-makers use ideas of competitiveness and innovation associated with the knowledge economy. Thus Larner (2007) shows how the New Zealand government developed policies based on the logics of the knowledge economy to harness the expertise of expatriates and emigrants in

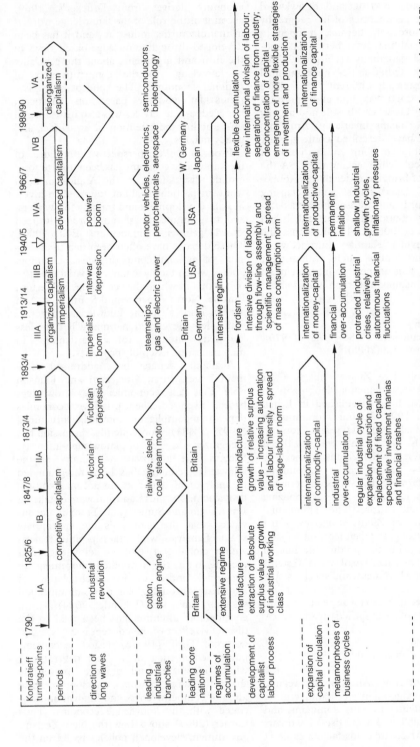

Kondratieff waves *A schematic representation of the major features associated with long-wave economic cycles* (Knox and Agnew, 1989: adapted from Marshall, 1987)

order to improve competitiveness. Peck (2005) sounds a cautionary note, however, noting that discourses surrounding the knowledge economy and a supposed 'creative CLASS' have led to the prioritization of the needs of workers with certain skill sets and the marginalization of nominally 'non-creative', 'non-innovative' workers in non-knowledge-intensive occupations (from cleaners to caterers to public transport operators), without which the knowledge economy cannot operate.   JF

Suggested reading
Dunning (2000); Gregerson and Johnson (1997).

Kondratieff waves Cycles in economic activity in the world economy, with a wavelength of 40–60 years. Shorter oscillations may be superimposed over these long waves, but Kondratieff waves imply fundamental qualitative transformations through alternating sequences of growth and stagnation rather than mere quantitative fluctuations in economic activity (see figure on page 401). Soviet economist Nikolai Kondratieff (1892–1938) claimed to have identified long waves in the 1920s, and since then there has been considerable interest in and controversy over the connections between them and the dynamics of UNEVEN DEVELOPMENT under CAPITALISM. Mandel (1980) argues that there is a systemic relationship between long waves and capitalist RESTRUCTURING, for example, while Maddison (1982) accepts the existence of major phases of capitalist growth but insists that these have been the result of 'specific disturbances of an *ad hoc* character'. Scholars who accept a systemic relationship typically fasten on technological change: technical INNOVATIONS often cluster during recessions, when they open the door to revived profits and to wider transformations in the LABOUR PROCESS, REGIMES OF ACCUMULATION and the like. On this basis, Kondratieff waves have been associated with technological revolutions (cf. INDUSTRIAL REVOLUTION) and sectoral growth – for example:

(1)   steam power and machinofacture in the textile industries;
(2)   the spread of railways and the growth of the iron and steel industries;
(3)   electricity, petroleum and the chemical and automobile industries;
(4)   electronics, synthetics and petrochemicals; and
(5)   information technology, telecommunications and biotechnology.

This is only an example; several different schemes have been proposed. Technical innovations are not only distinguished by periodicity, however, but also have distinctive geographies: spatial loci of experimentation and innovation, and networks of DIFFUSION. The complex of changes represented by these cycles and phases thus has a profound impact on and is also deeply affected by geographies of production and reproduction (see, e.g., Marshall, 1987; Hall and Preston, 1988; Dicken, 2007). Some scholars have also proposed a close association between Kondratieff waves and the global geography of WAR (see, e.g., Goldstein, 1988; Devezas, 2006).   RL

L

laboratory A laboratory is a site of experimentation. Not simply a physical space where a certain sort of scientific research takes place, the full significance of laboratories can only be appreciated if they are understood as a very particular achievement. A historically specific configuration of people, practices, machines and measurements, the laboratory is organized as an arena in which – purified of the contingencies of the field – the truth of the matter-phenomena under investigation will supposedly reveal itself. As the privileged generator of the particular form of knowledge that is the scientific fact, laboratories are thus a source of great authority and potentially power, particularly if a network allowing the extension of its results elsewhere can be built and maintained (see also SCIENCE/SCIENCE STUDIES). NB

Suggested reading
Knorr-Cetina (1999); Latour (1999b).

labour geography Straddling economic, political, social and cultural concerns, labour geography is now an established part of the geographical discipline. In its earliest manifestations, the sub-field was driven by an effort to highlight the agency of labour in making the landscape, most particularly through collective trade union organization. Rather than seeing labour as simply a factor in production, or even as an agent of a socialist dawn, labour geographers sought to document the ways in which workers' organizations developed as part of the lived experience of PLACE. As such, trade union organization is understood as being co-constituted with place. As Herod, Peck and Wills (2003, p. 176) explain in a recent overview of the field and its relationship to industrial relations:

> Axiomatic for labour geographers is the claim that spatial factors – such as the inescapably uneven geographical development of capitalist economies, the geographical scale and scope of legislation, the role of distinctive regional 'cultures' of industrial relations practices, the structure and dynamics of local labour markets, the spatial hierarchies of trade union organisation, the locally-differentiated processes of social reproduction,

gender and race relations, the shifting landscape of political activism and labour-organisational capacities – really *matter* in the practice of industrial relations and in the trajectories of workplace politics.

Hence, labour geographers argue that we cannot understand matters of work, managerial cultures, trade union organization, local politics or culture without attention to geography. Moreover, recent work in this field has highlighted the extent to which trade unionism itself has its own geography: the organizational structures and strategies deployed reflect the politics of SCALE, past and present. In responding to the challenges posed by global NEO-LIBERALISM, for example, trade unions are experimenting with new ways to find leverage and re-scale their organizations beyond the workplace to encompass COMMUNITY, regional and global dimensions (Herod, 2002; Savage and Wills, 2004; Hale and Wills, 2005).

As it has matured, labour geography has moved from its initial focus on trade union organization to speak to most of the significant debates in HUMAN GEOGRAPHY as a whole. What started as a polemical effort to put labour on the map of the discipline has become part of the mainstream. Labour geography continues to evolve, now encompassing research into matters such as LABOUR MARKETS, public policy in relation to employment and the labour market, and questions of work and IDENTITY (Castree, Coe, Ward and Samers, 2005). Contemporary research includes a focus on the dynamics of labour MIGRATION, the extent to which labour is able and willing to take its place in a multi-scalar CIVIL SOCIETY that includes the emergent global justice movement, the way in which CLASS and identity are changing, as well as questions of GLOBALIZATION and its implications for work, wealth and power relations. JWi

Suggested reading
Herod (2002); Herod, Peck and Wills (2003).

labour market The geographical arena in which labour power is bought and sold – where those looking for work (workers) and those looking for workers (employers) find each other. As such, labour markets are necessarily geographical (Martin, 2000b). These labour markets are often very local, including places such as the street corner where day labourers stand hoping for work or the town in which the local newspaper publishes adverts looking for staff. However, under conditions of neo-liberal GLOBALIZATION these transactions are being spatially stretched to incorporate MIGRANTS who might cross continents looking for work. Thus, the labour markets in some GLOBAL CITIES such as London are places where native-born Londoners are competing for jobs – at both the 'top' and 'bottom' ends of the occupational hierarchy – with workers from the rest of the world. Indeed, there is now a large literature exploring the complex labour markets of such cities and regions (May, Wills, Datta, Evans and Herbert, 2007).

Geographical understandings of the labour market were traditionally focused on mapping the geographical area from which workers travelled to work. As such, large urban connurbations often attracted workers from relatively far away, using the commuter transportation networks on which all cities depend. However, this approach to mapping the labour market tells us nothing about the POWER relations or the role of geography in the operation of labour markets. Labour power is a unique form of COMMODITY and in order to buy labour power, employers have to deal with the people who embody that power (Peck, 1996). As such, the labour market depends upon employers managing their workers through the LABOUR PROCESS in order to realize the commodity – labour power – that they buy. People come to work with their own personalities, expectations of work and political traditions, and the potential conflict between employers and workers is the root of trade union organization (see LABOUR GEOGRAPHY).

Such social relations also reflect the PLACE in which the labour market is grounded. Unequal opportunities to develop skills and different life experiences afford people varying potential to 'sell themselves' in the market for jobs; skills reflect previous opportunities for education, work and training, and the history of employment, in any location. As is well documented, workers in RUSTBELT regions that long depended on male manual work struggle to find work in the new service economy (see SERVICES). The changing nature of the economy demands new kinds of workers, with different physical and mental qualities (McDowell, 2003). There is often a spatial mismatch between the needs of employers

and the needs of those looking for work, and workers find themselves being de-skilled or having to re-train in order to secure employment. As such, the labour market has a direct relationship to and impact upon the configuration of GENDER, ETHNIC and CLASS relations in and across space. Processes of direct and indirect discrimination in labour demand further accentuate these structural divisions in labour supply. Employers view potential workers through their own characterization of the 'good worker' and employees find themselves in segregated workplaces and jobs as a result. Jobs are gendered and women are still largely concentrated in part-time, lower status and lower paid work (McDowell, 2001). Jobs are similarly racialized and socially constructed as being better suited to men and/or women from particular ethnic groups. Thus, while many minority ethnic women are nurses in the UK, they face direct and indirect discrimination in securing employment in managerial grades.

In recent years, governments have turned their attention to the labour market in order to reduce welfare receipt and 'make work pay'. In what has been called *workfare*, governments in many post-industrial economies have reduced welfare payments and/or developed active labour market strategies that demand evidence of job-search and training on the part of the unemployed. These policies have been developed without regard to the geography of labour demand or the cost of going to work. Governments have altered the supply of labour without concern for the quality of the jobs to be filled. As such, and despite national-level variations in legal minimum wages and statutory employment rights, there have been concerted efforts directed at labour market flexibility. A number of scholars have argued that these strategies are ideologically driven, seeking to create new sources of very cheap labour. As Peck puts it:

> Stripped down to its labor-regulatory essence, workfare is not about creating jobs for people that don't have them; it is about creating workers for jobs nobody wants. In a Foucauldian sense, it is seeking to make 'docile bodies' for the new economy: flexible, self-reliant and self-disciplining (2001, p. 6).

In countries such as the UK and the USA, these labour market policies are being augmented by efforts at managed MIGRATION, whereby workers are recruited to fill specific gaps in the labour market, often doing jobs that native workers are unwilling to do. This drive for labour market flexibility has fuelled the growth of the working poor in many locations, and new forms of political RESISTANCE, such as living wage campaigns, are growing as a result.   JWI

Suggested reading
McDowell (2003); Peck (1996).

labour process The means through which labour power is extracted from workers: the phrase originates in MARXISM, though it refers more broadly to the organization of work. Be they in the field, factory or filing department, when workers are employed, they enter into a labour process through which their work is organized and surplus (which is realized as CAPITAL) is extracted. As such, writers who use this phrase are often doing so with a focus on POWER relations in the workplace: they have an interest in the relationship between managerial control, technologies of work, subjectivity and workers' resistance. Research into the labour process exploded with the publication of Braverman's (1974) *Labor and monopoly capitalism*, which suggested that the de-skilling of work was the dominant tendency in the capitalist MODE OF PRODUCTION. Geographers, however, played very little part in this subsequent explosion of work on de-skilling. Instead, these ideas about the labour process have been manifest in debates about spatial DIVISIONS OF LABOUR.

In her seminal work, *Spatial divisions of labour*, Massey (1984) highlighted the ways in which the drive for profitability leads corporations to reconfigure the geography of their operations, breaking up and stretching out the labour process across space. Thus, managerial functions tend to be separated from those of manual labour and, increasingly, companies have developed complex structures of production at global dimensions. In what have been called global COMMODITY CHAINS, many of the largest TRANSNATIONAL CORPORATIONS now take advantage of a complex and fast-changing international division of labour, using subcontracted production and service delivery companies to reduce costs, minimize risk and increase flexibility (Dicken, 2003; Hale and Wills, 2005). As such, the labour process has a very clear geography, in which the map of manufacturing and, increasingly, service industries (such as call centres) is organized at a global scale. The separation of control from production raises a number of important questions about responsibility and power. Workers are generally disempowered

by this extension of corporate geography and the spatial reorganization of the labour process. As a result, trades unions are experimenting with new forms of internationalism and are attempting to forge alliances with consumers to find new sources of power (see LABOUR GEOGRAPHY).

Ultimately, geographers have sought to root understandings of the labour process in PLACE, highlighting the way in which the labour process changes social relations and political possibilities within and between different locales.   JWI

Suggested reading
Burawoy (1979).

labour theory of value A cornerstone of classical economics, prominent in the writings of Adam Smith and David Ricardo. The work of the French Physiocrats (notably François Quesnay and the elder Mirabeau) was a proximate influence on Smith's formulation of a labour theory; more distantly, the writings of the proto-liberal philosopher John Locke, especially his *Second treatise on government* (1681), were a likely influence. In his moral-political theory, Locke defended the virtues of individual labour, the sanctity of property acquired by mixing labour with objects and the natural rights of individuals – and conceived for the STATE the limited but critical role of regulating and securing private PROPERTY (see LIBERALISM).

Why have a labour theory of value at all? For one, Locke's version of the labour theory provided no indication of how to bring into equivalence different forms of private property within a generalized exchange economy. Adam Smith's version of the labour theory attempted exactly that: his purpose was to demonstrate the 'natural price ... [or] the central price, to which the prices of all COMMODITIES are continually gravitating' (1991 [1776], p. 61), or in other words, their intrinsic worth above and beyond the ephemeral fluctuations of market price. This, of course, begged the question: Which commodity served as the natural basis of all others? During the early industrial era (see INDUSTRIAL REVOLUTION), it was tempting to infer that 'labour' was the common basis of all exchanged goods. But neither Smith, nor Ricardo, who adopted his labour theory, could resolve a basic contradiction; namely, what the natural price of labour should be.

Karl Marx made the breakthrough. He drew a distinction between the 'use-value' and the 'exchange-value' of a commodity, and designated 'labour' as use-value and 'labour-power' – the actual commodity transacted between employers and employees – as 'exchange-value'. This in turn allowed him to claim, without contradiction, that in a capitalist mode of production (see CAPITALISM), 'labour-power' as a commodity had both a market price and an underlying value, which was the *socially necessary labour time necessary for its (re)production*. Capitalists purchased 'labour power' in order to consume its use-value, 'labour', which had the unique capacity to produce more value than necessary for its reproduction – in short, 'surplus-value'. Hence, in one fell stroke, Marx was able to resolve the contradiction that had plagued Smith and Ricardo, recuperate the labour theory of value, and provide a basis for capital ACCUMULATION as the accumulation of surplus-value. Notice that Marx did not seek a 'natural price' explanation; rather, he clearly inserted the adjective 'socially necessary' in order to indicate the geographical, historical and relational basis of value. Marx's labour theory of value was subsequently attacked on several fronts, most persistently around its ostensible failure to systematize the relationship between value and market price – the so-called 'transformation problem'.

Diane Elson's (1979) innovative reading of Marx's theory of value – which David Harvey endorses in *Limits to capital* (1999 [1982]) – circumvents both the critique that Marx's formulation stands – and falls – on labour being the physical substance of value as well as the transformation problem by arguing that what Marx really intended was to draw attention to *the rationalizing practices whereby labour in a capitalist mode of production is continuously enrolled in abstracted form through the wage/ money relation*. This not only involves a disciplining of labour through surveillance, monitoring, punishment and incentive contracts; but, more pointedly, these mechanisms are to be themselves viewed as symptomatic of a system of generalized commodity exchange – that is, a dominant and more-or-less competitive market system – where wealth and worth are measured in an impersonal, abstract money form. Thus, a 'value theory of labour', as Elson presents it, is a condensed expression of the imperative for capitalists to constantly cut labour costs and raise labour productivity in order to survive, and for workers to become continuously more productive at their tasks in order to not become dispensable. In Elson's words: 'My argument is that the *object* of

Marx's theory of value was labour. It is not a matter of seeking an explanation of why prices are what they are and finding that it is labour [thus, Elson sidesteps the nettlesome 'transformation problem']. But rather of seeking an understanding why labour takes the form it does, and what the political consequences are' (1979, p. 123). VG

Suggested reading
Althusser (1997 [1970]); Cohen (1978); Elson (1979); Engels (1978 [1884]); Postone (1996); Read (2003).

Lamarck(ian)ism A theory of evolutionary change originating with the French naturalist Jean Baptiste de Lamarck (1744–1829). A non-Darwinian doctrine of organic progression, early Lamarckism differed significantly from its later *Neo*-Lamarckian successor. The dynamic behind Lamarck's own scheme of evolution along separate lines of development, rather than by common descent, was the active power of nature (combining processes of environmental stimulus, the adaptive habits of organisms in adjusting to modified conditions, and the use and disuse of organs) to impel life along predetermined sequences (Burkhardt, 1977).

In the decades around 1900, when Darwinism was in eclipse as a consequence of a series of criticisms within the scientific community, the Lamarckian mechanism of the inheritance of acquired characteristics achieved considerable support as providing an alternative mechanism for evolutionary transformism (Bowler, 1983). This marginal component of Lamarck's original scheme became the central plank in Neo-Lamarckian interpretations of evolutionary change, which routinely considered that those organic modifications on which natural selection operated were environmentally induced. Particularly in the USA, but also in Britain, this alternative evolutionary theory attracted widespread support during the second half of the nineteenth century despite the absence of agreed empirical corroboration. Particularly prominent were the palaeontologists Edward Cope and Alpheus Hyatt, the geologists Joseph LeConte and Clarence King, and the Duke of Argyll and George Romanes in anthropology and psychology. In France, the *Société Zoologique d'Acclimatation* under Isidore Geoffroy St-Hilaire vigorously promulgated Lamarckism in projects on environmental adaptation that had implications for human migration and colonialism (Osborne, 1994). Most dramatic of all was the theory's official endorsement in the

Soviet Union during the 1930s, where T.D. Lysenko used Lamarckism to justify his ideas about agricultural improvement and judged that it fitted more comfortably with Marxist political ideology than did classical neo-Darwinism.

Like Darwinism, Lamarckism also had social implications. Indeed, many social evolutionists drew more inspiration from Neo-Lamarckian dogma than from standard Darwinism. For some, it provided grounds for looking to environment as the driving force behind social processes; for others, who were enthusiastic about the role it attributed to mind and will, it reserved space for psychic elements in evolution and thereby enabled them to escape the pessimism that gripped many at the beginning of the twentieth century. Either way, Lamarckism could be mobilized to justify the politics of social and political interventionism.

Given its various enthusiasms, it is not surprising that a number of geographers would find Neo-Lamarckism attractive, not least because the environment played such a key directive role in the scenario (Livingstone, 1992). In the USA during the late nineteenth and early twentieth centuries, numerous advocates of environmental determinism, such as Nathaniel Shaler, W.M. Davis, Ellen Semple, Albert Brigham and Ellsworth Huntington, displayed Lamarckian sympathies and used the theory to provide naturalistic readings of human culture. Similarly Turner's FRONTIER THESIS, which portrayed American society as recapitulating the stages of social evolution with each advance of frontier settlement, drew inspiration from Lamarckian environmentalism (Coleman, 1966). Griffith Taylor in Australia found it equally attractive, though he did not discount the significance of Mendelian genetics (Christie, 1994).

In late-Victorian Britain, similar convictions are discernible among those sympathetic to Lamarckism's emphasis on the significance of consciousness. Patrick Geddes used it to advocate various urban planning and educational reforms on the grounds that their benefits would accumulate, by social inheritance, in successive generations; Peter Kropotkin, critical of the cut-throat ethics of capitalist competitive struggle, found in Lamarckism the grounds for a more benign social order – a mix of ANARCHISM and HUMANISM – built upon mutual aid (Todes, 1989); and Andrew Herbertson and H.J. Fleure both mobilized the idea in their considerations of regional geography. Lamarckian motifs have also been discerned in Paul Vidal de la Blache's possibilism.

More generally, Neo-Lamarckism facilitated geography's transition from a natural theology framework to that of evolutionary naturalism largely due to the ease with which it could be given a teleological reading (Livingstone, 1984: see TELEOLOGY). Its impact on the evolution of geography around the time of the subject's professionalization was thus very considerable (see GEOGRAPHY, HISTORY OF). DNL

Suggested reading
Bowler (1983); Campbell and Livingstone (1983); Stocking (1962).

land tenure The practices through which land is possessed. Land tenure entails both formal PROPERTY rules and rights, sanctioned by some collective, and more symbolic and culturally coded forms of, land attachment. Land, in particular, is both an object with use value, and a symbol endowed with meaning. Scholars of land tenure tend to emphasize the latter, noting the significance of complex, ritually reproduced relations of land-holding. Land is often spoken of as an active agent, encompassing the interests of the living and the dead. Rules governing access and use rights are embedded within complex and often highly localized LIFEWORLDS (Hann, 1998). Land tenure should be distinguished from housing tenure – that is, the variegated ways in which people acquire rights in real property – hence the distinction between renters, private owners, leasehold tenants, and so on (see HOUSING CLASS).

Scholarship has tended to emphasize tenurial relations amongst peasant and hunter–gatherer communities, located in the premodern history of the West, or within the contemporary developing world. However, it should be noted that culturally laden and often collectively oriented forms of land-holding can be found within the modern West, as noted by some of the contributions in Abramson and Theodossopoulos (2000).

Land tenure, as a means through which a PLACE is known and represented, and a social order enacted and sustained, is clearly geographical. One interesting strain of scholarship concerns the ways in which LANDSCAPE – as both a material and representational resource – connects to land tenure (Olwig, 2002). Another crucial dimension concerns systematic attempts at the remaking of land tenure, of which Western colonial displacements of indigenous property (see COLONIALISM), state collectivization or individualization of landholding, the enclosure of the commons, and clashes between agrarian and hunter–gathering societies are all examples. The geographies of these often violent reworkings (Peluso and Watts, 2001), and associated forms of resistance (Peluso, 2005), have been compellingly documented.   NKB

land use and land-cover change (LULC) A component of contemporary studies of global environmental change that focuses on both land cover (i.e. the land's physical attributes, such as forest, grassland etc.) and the purpose for which those attributes are used and/or transformed by human actions. Large-scale international research programmes into land cover (making extensive use of data obtained via REMOTE SENSING) have been undertaken recently under the auspices of the International Geosphere–Biosphere Programme and related institutions. The goal is not only to establish the nature and pace of land-use cover change, at a variety of SCALES, but also to understand its causes, thereby facilitating modelling of likely future change, in the context of searches for SUSTAINABLE DEVELOPMENT (cf. SUSTAINABILITY).   RJ

Suggested reading
Gutman, Janetos, Justice et al. (2005).

landscape A cardinal term of human geography, landscape has served as central object of investigation, organizing principle and interpretive lens for several different generations of researchers. Through periods of both ascendancy and eclipse, landscape's constancy lies in its function as a locus for geographical research into culture–nature and subject–object relations.

The etymology of the English word 'landscape' is complex. Many sources (e.g. Jackson, 1984; Schama, 1995) refer to the Dutch word *landschap* as having migrated into English usage through the sixteenth and seventeenth centuries, with 'landscape' gradually coming to refer to both the visual appearance of land, most often countryside, and its pictorial depiction via perspectival techniques for representing depth and space. The association of landscape with visual art, and with rural or natural scenery, is cemented in its contemporary colloquial definition as, (a) a portion of land or scenery which the eye can view at once, and (b) a picture of it.

In partial contrast, Olwig (1996) notes that the Old Dutch *landskab* and the Germanic *landschäft* both also connote legal and administrative notions of community, region and jurisdiction: landscape as customary administrative unit. *Landschäft* was also the term adopted by American geographer Carl Ortwin Sauer (1963b [1925]) in his seminal monograph *The morphology of landscape*. This sought first to establish a definition of geography as a field science of landscape and, second, to define landscape itself in terms of interactions between human cultures and natural environments (see MORPHOLOGY). Thus landscape was conceived as a cultural entity, the distinctive product of interactions between people and topography. Sauer's argument that 'culture is the agent, the natural area is the medium, the cultural landscape the result' (1963b [1925], p. 343), oriented several decades of American cultural geography towards the historical reconstruction of cultural landscape forms through FIELDWORK and archival study.

However, Richard Hartshorne's (1939) influential *The nature of geography* notably critiqued landscape's incorporation of both objective and subjective elements (the land *and* land-as-perceived), concluding that the term could not serve as the basis of a properly scientific geography. The subsequent rise of regional and then spatial science paradigms following the Second World War thus saw something of a decline in landscape's purchase and salience as an organizing term for human geographers. In this period, most notable and innovative geographical writing on landscape appeared the journal *Landscape*, founded in 1951 by J.B. Jackson. Through his own extensive writings, Jackson defined landscape in terms of the material world of ordinary everyday or 'vernacular' life – in postwar America an often-bypassed world of garages, motels, neon-lit strips and backyards. Jackson's writing also extended the empirical emphasis of Sauerian cultural geography through attending seriously to the symbolic and iconic meanings of landscape. This vision of landscape as at once an everyday, lived-in world and a repository of symbolic value chimed with the agenda of North American humanistic geography in the 1970s, and found its clearest expression in a volume of essays on *The interpretation of ordinary landscapes* (Meinig, 1979).

A raft of innovative writing on landscape emerged in the late 1980s and early 1990s, constituting a significant element of the CULTURAL TURN in Anglo-American human geography as a whole. The work of Denis Cosgrove (1998 [1984]) and Stephen Daniels (Daniels and Cosgrove, 1988) in particular advanced an influential definition of landscape as a *way of seeing* and representing the world.

Here, landscape was largely equated with Western visual traditions of landscape painting and gardening. In drawing upon and extending the work of cultural Marxist critics such as John Berger (1972) and Raymond Williams (1973), these cultural geographies of landscape focused upon the critical interrogation of the ideological function of landscape images, arguing that landscapes worked so as to reflect and reproduce the values and norms of socio-economic elites. In pinpointing its Italian Renaissance origins, Cosgrove (1985) sought to highlight the complicity of landscape as a way of seeing with notions of objective knowledge and distanced visual authority and control. In speaking of landscape's 'duplicity', Daniels (1989) noted that the aesthetic function of artistic landscapes masked their ideological role in naturalizing socio-economic hierarchies and patterns of land ownership (see ART; ICONOGRAPHY). In defining landscape as a text to be critically read via the principles of structuralist semiotics, Duncan and Duncan (1988) argued that landscape operated as a signifying system for the production and transmission of cultural meanings.

Gillian Rose (1993) further extended and critiqued this body of work through highlighting how, for geographers and others, the landscape way of seeing was a particularly MASCULINIST gaze. Thus, in addition to systems of cultural and political power and capitalist forms of social relation, landscape visually indexed specific forms of patriarchy and disembodied, detached observation. For Rose, the academic landscape gaze involves a duality between an active masculine eye and a passive, 'naturalized' femininity. This eye, however, oscillates ambivalently between asserted rational observation and repressed visual pleasure, in the form of voyeurism and narcissism. This critique thus applied psychoanalytic principles to landscape interpretation, further aligning cultural geographies of landscape with work in visual and cultural theory (e.g. Mulvey, 1989; Nash, 1996: see VISION AND VISUALITY).

Work through the 1990s sought to inflect and extend the cultural turn focus on landscape images and texts by further apprehending landscape in terms of action, process and movement, both discursive and material. Don Mitchell's (1996, 2003) materialist analyses aim to re-invigorate Marxist understanding of landscape in terms of production as well as the cultural consumption and circulation of landscape imagery. For Mitchell, the production of actual, material landscapes such as mining towns or agricultural belts is a matter of ongoing struggle and conflict between different social and economic groups within capitalist networks of violence, inequality and profit. With a similar focus upon issues of power, but in a more discursive and interpretative vein, an influential collection edited by cultural theorist W.J.T. Mitchell (2002e [1994]) sought to define landscape as a verb, not a noun – that is, as a process, not an object or image. Here, understood in terms of culturally specific styles of moving, seeing and representing, landscape is historically identified with European imperial discourse, the visual *modus operandi* of European explorers, artists and cartographers. Extending the focus of earlier work upon landscape in national contexts, linkages between the landscape gaze, science, exploration and imperialism have been extensively discussed by cultural geographers and historians (see Pratt, 1992; Ryan, 1996; Clayton, 2000).

A further distinctive strand of current geographical writing on landscape, closely associated with the work of David Matless (1992, 1998), places emphasis upon *cultures of landscape,* most often in a British context. Drawing upon Michel Foucault's accounts of discourse, power and subjectivity, landscape practices such as walking, boating and driving are analysed here in terms of the discursive regimes (e.g. those of health and citizenship, state planning, environmental activism), through which codes of proper conduct for using, appreciating and indeed creating landscape are elaborated.

Although these various discursive, iconographic and interpretive approaches have defined cultural geographies of landscape since the 1980s, they have of late been challenged, modulated and to some degree superseded by work advocating phenomenological, corporeal and performative perspectives. The cultural anthropologist Tim Ingold (1993, 2000) in particular has argued that the definition of landscape as a way of seeing perpetuates a duality of culture and nature, and erases first-order issues of materiality, agency and embodied performance by locating landscape within a disembodied realm of cultural discourse and signification. Ingold's remedy proposes a landscape phenomenology, inspired by the writing of Martin Heidegger and Maurice Merleau-Ponty, and focusing substantively upon embodied practices of dwelling and being-in-the-world. Here, landscape is defined as a processual, material and perceptual engagement of body and world, enacted in terms of a distinctive temporality – a rich duration of inhabitation. This emphasis on bodily performance and perception is further developed in recent work on landscape from interpretive archaeology and performance studies itself (Shanks and Pearson, 2000; Tilley, 2004).

Albeit with reservations regarding both the ontological principles and topical orientations implied by terms such as 'dwelling', phenomenological and performative studies of landscape, practice and perception have emerged strongly in human geography in recent years; for example, in writing focusing on issues of inhabitation (Hinchcliffe, 2003), mobility (Cresswell, 2003), biography and memory (Lorimer, 2003) and embodied perception (Wylie, 2002a). While there has been no wholesale rejection of the critical agendas and positions associated with work on landscape as a way of seeing, Mitch Rose (2002a) has cogently identified the epistemological difficulty of, on the one hand, presenting landscapes as already ideologically structured, while, on the other, paradoxically retaining subjects with the ability to flexibly inhabit and interpret landscapes. At the same time, the development of ACTOR-NET-WORK THEORY and hybrid geographies has arguably created a lacunae within landscape studies, through providing an alternative conceptual platform from which culture–nature issues may be apprehended. Most recently, however, in an attempt to address this lacunae, the task of producing a 'post-phenomenological' account of landscape has been identified, supplementing the work of writers such as Ingold by attending to self-landscape relations via ideas of affect and narrative (Wylie, 2005) and Derridean conceptions of presence and care (Rose, 2004b).   JWY

Suggested reading
Cosgrove (1985); Rose (1993); Ingold (1993); Rose (2002); Wylie (2005).

Landschaft A German term roughly corresponding to the English 'landscape'. The scenic, pictorial and aesthetic connotations of the latter are downplayed, however, and *Landschaft* is instead more usually associated with attempts by nineteenth- and twentieth-century German scholars to fashion geography as a 'landscape science' engaged in the task of identifying and classifying distinctive natural and cultural regions. In Anglophone geography, the term *Landschaft* is closely connected with the work of Carl Ortwin Sauer and the BERKELEY SCHOOL. Sauer (1963a [1925]) in part adopted and modified the *Landschaft* approach in the development of his own morphological approach to landscape,

placing greater emphasis upon the role of human agency and culture in shaping (as well as being shaped by) landscape.   JWY

Suggested reading
Sauer (1963a [1925], ch. 16).

land-use survey The investigation and cartographic representation of land use. Large-scale surveys were launched in the UK in the 1930s by Dudley Stamp (1898–1966), based on extensive FIELDWORK and widely used as a land-use planning tool for several decades. Most surveys now deploy REMOTE SENSING and GEOGRAPHIC INFORMATION SYSTEMS for data collection, collation, display and analysis (cf. LAND USE AND LAND-COVER CHANGE).   RJ

Suggested reading
Stamp (1946).

language Study of the changing distribution and social usages of language (including dialect/idiolect) is an enduring yet varied tradition in human geography. Broadly, two main themes may be distinguished. In the first – the geography in and of language – attention focuses on studying language distributions, upon spatial and social variations in linguistic form and in the origins of and changes in place names. In the second – the language in and of geography – consideration is given to the connections between language, social power and identity and the practice of geography. Although it is not appropriate to see these two themes as mutually discrete, chronologically distinct or methodologically separate, the first is more securely rooted in certain traditions of CULTURAL GEOGRAPHY, the second more a feature of CULTURAL POLITICS and POST-COLONIALISM and contemporary interests in unequal power relations and in language as a political agency (see also DISCOURSE; QUALITATIVE METHODS; RHETORIC).

The mapping of language areas, often in association with ethnicity, has been an established feature of anthropogeographical work since the nineteenth century (see ANTHROPOGEOGRAPHY). Here, language is treated as a cultural artefact, its changing distribution a reflection of the world's shifting linguistic mosaic (and Anglicization: see Crystal, 2003), its study evident in what has been variously termed *language geography* or *language mapping*. In *linguistic geography* (sometimes termed *dialect geography*), the emphasis is upon local differentiations within speech areas, the variable distribution of given speech forms or the political authority and cultural identity rooted in certain languages (*geolinguistics*). In many such studies (but not all), the geography of language in such terms is a form of HISTORICAL GEOGRAPHY (e.g. Withers, 1984). Attempts to reverse language decline or obsolescence may involve direct language planning.

Attention to the language in and of geography is more concerned with the study of language as the medium through which inter-subjective meaning is communicated, and in the power relations intrinsic to such meaning. Thus understood, interest in the role and nature of language within geography is part of the 'linguistic turn' within twentieth-century philosophy and social theory. It is evident in work on the politics of language, in the connections between spoken and written languages and authorial power, in attempts to 'recover' or do interpretative justice to others' words and worlds in quantitative methodologies (e.g. Crang, 1992), in a recognition that the limits to our understanding of the world may indeed be the limits of our language (e.g. Farinelli, Ollson and Reichart, 1996) and, for some, in practices of resistance to an Anglo-American hegemony within geography evident in the dominance of English as the discipline's *lingua franca* (e.g. Braun, 2003; Desbiens and Ruddick, 2006: see ANGLOCENTRISM).   CWJW

Suggested reading
Crang (1992).

Latin America In conventional usage, the term refers to those countries of the American continent that share a history of Spanish, Portuguese and French colonialism. However, the term also is widely used to denote all countries south of the USA (Lewis and Wigen, 1997, p. 182). The term's ambiguity has led to academic disputes over how the category is defined and which countries properly belong within it. For instance, Quebec is not included, despite a history of French colonialism; nor are the Mexican states annexed by the USA in 1848. The problem with such debates is that they presume a natural congruence between geographical categories and an underlying social reality, which can be accurately mapped. Obscured are ontological questions concerned with how categories are constituted through intersecting DISCOURSES and interlocking POWER-GEOMETRIES.

Since its inception, the term 'Latin America' has been tangled in colonial and post-colonial contests over identity and territory (Mignolo, 2005). John Phelan (1968) attributes the term to nineteenth-century French scholars, who positioned France as the leader of a Latin 'race' engaged in a struggle for domination against Anglo-Saxon and Slavic racial blocs. According to Phelan (1968, p. 296), the term 'Latin America' was baptized in 1861 in *La revue des races Latines*, a magazine 'dedicated to the cause of Pan-Latinism'. Theories of Pan-Latinism were called upon to naturalize attempts by Napoleon III to expand imperial power in what was then commonly called *Hispanic America*.

However, the idea of pan-Latinism also circulated in Spain and Hispanic America in the mid-nineteenth century, as intellectuals from the Creole elite expressed anxiety about the imperial ambitions of Anglo-Saxon America (Ardao, 1992). Chilean scholar Miguel Rojas Mix (1986) attributes the term to Francisco Bilbao (1823–65), an exiled Chilean writer living in Paris in the mid-nineteenth century. According to Rojas Mix, Bilbao used the term in a speech in 1856. Arturo Ardao (1992) credits the Colombian writer José María Torres Caicedo (1830–89), also living in Paris, with its christening in 1856 in his poem 'The Two Americas'. In any case, both authors used the term to delineate fundamental cultural and political distinctions between a *Latin America* characterized by spirituality and a quest for independence versus a materialist, individualistic and imperialist *Anglo-Saxon America*. With the US invasion and dismemberment of Mexico in mind, Bilbao, Torres Caicedo and others echoed Simon Bolivar in calling for a union of South American nations to detain the imperialist interests of the USA.

According to the *Oxford English Dictionary*, the term 'Latin America' appears in the USA in 1890, the year of the First International Conference of American states, held in Washington, DC. A precursor to the Pan-American Union, the conference led to increased academic interest in the countries south of the Rio Grande. The first academic course on 'Spanish American History and Institutions' was offered at the University of California in 1895 (Hanke, 1964, p. 10). In 1917 the *Encyclopedia of Latin America* was published, with a foreword from the then Director General of the Pan American Union, who suggested that the spread of 'accurate information will serve Pan American solidarity and community of action and purpose' (Wilcox and Rines, 1917, p. 4). His message explicitly positions 'Latin America' as an important object of study at a time when the USA sought to bring the region in line with its policies; here, knowledge is made a key instrument of geopolitical power.

Drawing from Edward Said's understanding of ORIENTALISM, Mark T. Berger (1995) argues that ideas about Latin America in the USA are inseparable from and the effect of US imperialism in the region. Berger elaborates this argument along three lines. First, he points to the blurred boundaries between the state and Latin American studies. Not only have academics moved back and forth between academia and the various agencies of the government, but the state has also attempted to shape the kinds of research undertaken. Hence, ideas about Latin America tend to reflect and constitute state interests. For example, Santana (1996, p. 459) illustrates how US-based geographical researchers in Puerto Rico advanced a theory of 'non-viability', suggesting that the island was 'not viable as an independent state'. Such studies were used to support arguments for continued US occupation.

Second, Latin American studies scholars have used organizing concepts that facilitate reductionism and allow the region to be analysed as a coherent unit. This is especially true after the Second World War, when the US government began to promote area studies. In the newly conceived world region framework, the term 'Latin America' replaced 'South America' (Martin and Wigen, 1997, p. 162). Area studies presumed the existence of coherent, naturally bounded regions, wherein human–environment relations had produced unique cultural groups. Contemporary REGIONAL GEOGRAPHIES of Latin America continue in this tradition by seeking to delineate the core cultural traits organizing the region. Thus, Clawson's (1997, p. 7) textbook defines Latin America as a 'cultural entity' bound by 'a common Latin, or Roman, heritage'. Clawson identifies the core as that area where Latin or Hispanic culture is dominant: in fringe areas such as the US Southwest and the Caribbean, 'traditional Hispanic values are largely missing'. Such demarcations between what properly belongs inside and outside a region are deeply problematic, for they obscure differences within nations and render invisible the interconnections and interdependencies between them.

Third, Latin American studies tend to use the USA as the frame of reference or benchmark for encoding representations of, and measuring the material progress in, Latin America (Berger, 1995; Schoultz, 1998). As a result, academic knowledge tends to be underwritten by a United Statesian – Self/Latin American – Other binary, which constitutes difference and distance within a hierarchical framing. No matter the theoretical approach used in the USA, from environmental determinism in the 1930s to area studies, regional geographies and development studies from the 1940s on, Latin America is conjured to embody everything that the USA is not: handicapped by climate and geography, isolated, backward, traditional, violent, peripheral, underdeveloped and poor. Such IMAGINATIVE GEOGRAPHIES are called upon to authorize or legitimize US intervention in the region, whether to protect national interests or foster development (Santana, 1996).

When the term 'Latin America' began to have broad circulation in English and Spanish in the early decades of the twentieth century, some Spanish intellectuals decried its use. Writing in 1918, Ramón Menéndez Pidal complained that the term deprived Spain of its historical and geographical titles in the New World (Ardao, 1992, p. 17).

South of the Rio Bravo, the idea of Latin America has conjured ambivalence and passionate attachment. For Daniel Mato (1998), the continuing salience of *Latinoamericanismo* stems from its association with nationalist, anti-imperialist struggles. Thus, for example, Alonso Aguilar (1968, p. 30) contrasts the US vision of Pan-Americanism with the 'Latin-Americanism of Bolívar, San Martín, and Morelos which stood for the struggle of their people for full independence'. Appropriating such associations, ruling elites and state bureaucracies, Mato argues, repeatedly constitute and address a pan-ethnic group called *Latinoamericanos* to advance nation-building projects founded upon the myth of *mestizaje* ('racial mixing'). For instance, in *¿Existe América Latina?*, Luis Alberto Sanchez (1945, p. 239) suggests that the future of the region depends upon accepting *mestizaje* in a positive sense, as integration and creation. In Mato's view, the notion of a *mestizo* 'extended ethnic group' perpetuates the exclusion of indigenous and African-descended peoples.

The idea of Latin America has come under intense public criticism since the Columbus Quincentennial in 1992. While state officials planned elaborate celebrations – many funded by the Spanish government – indigenous and Afro-Latin American groups took to the streets throughout the region in an organized effort to posit alternative perspectives on the conquest and its aftermath. The increasing political power of such groups calls into question hegemonic views of the region's Latin heritage, which work to obscure the contributions of indigenous and African-descended peoples, as well as the many other immigrant groups involved in producing the cultural landscapes of the Americas. Since the 1990s, a number of Latin American countries have ratified new constitutions recognizing their multicultural foundations. In this context, a number of indigenous social movements have formed viable political parties.

Currently, social movements in Latin America are fostering new geographical imaginaries to contest the US-driven Free Trade Area of the Americas, which would unify all of the Americas under a single free trade agreement promising to benefit TRANS-NATIONAL CORPORATIONS. Hugo Chavez's *Bolivarian alternative for the Americas* aims to create a socially oriented trade bloc built upon effective mechanisms to eradicate the economic disparities that exist within and between countries. JSU

Suggested reading
Ardao (1980, 1992); Berger (1995); Mignolo (2005); Van Cott (2000).

law An enforceable body of rules and related norms governing social conduct. Geographers have long been interested in law, defined more or less broadly. Historically, analyses tended to divide into those, such as Ellen Semple, who sought to ground law in place, and others, like Derwent Whittlesey, who focused on what he termed the 'impress of effective central authority upon the landscape'. Whether law is explained by reference to space, or space seen as produced by law, the tendency was to impose separations on law, space and society. From the 1980s onwards, when the 'spatial turn' in social theory made such a separation untenable, such binaries came under attack. Influenced by debates within social and legal theory, critical legal geographers have developed a very different reading of law, space and their mutual relation, with scepticism towards existing legal structures and the social relations that they embody. The distinguishing feature of this perspective is its refusal to accept either law or space as pre-political or as the unproblematic outcome of external forces. Both are regarded as deeply social and political. Law is seen both as a site in which competing values, practices and meanings are fought over, and also as the means by which certain meanings and social relations become fixed and naturalized, either in oppressive or potentially empowering ways. Law is understood not only as a set of operative controls, but also as a powerful repertoire of cultural and political meanings. Similarly, space is

regarded as both socially produced and as socially constitutive, with attention being directed to the 'politics' of space. The relation between law, space and society is redefined and extended in important ways, opening up many new areas to critical geographic enquiry. This scholarship is remarkably diverse and lively, engaging with topics such as NATURE, LANDSCAPE, STATE practice, NATIONALISM and BOUNDARIES. Scholars draw from a range of theoretical sources, including QUEER THEORY, urban POLITICAL ECONOMY, ACTOR-NETWORK THEORY and cultural studies. Scholars also work across a range of SCALES, addressing not only national law (in relation to civil RIGHTS, CRIME, employment and housing, for example) but also international law (in relation to GENOCIDE, HUMAN RIGHTS, the laws of WAR and spaces of EXCEPTION). Though fluid and non-institutionalized, some foci of interest over the past decade have included the following:

(1) The analysis of the manner in which legal action and interpretation produces certain spaces. The role of the legal apparatus – especially the judiciary – is often given prominence, it being noted that court decisions have profound (and often problematic) effects within local settings in both material and discursive terms, given the manner in which legal categories and discourse can come to frame local debates (cf. Forest, 2001).

(2) The related study of the situated nature of legal interpretation, it being argued that legal practice and interpretation is often bound up in the PLACE in which it occurs (cf. Cooper, 1998; also SITUATED KNOWLEDGE).

(3) The study of the geographical claims and representations (see REPRESENTATION) contained within legal discourse: in much the same way that law relies on claims concerning history and time, so it both defines and draws upon a complex range of geographies and spatial understandings. The construction of such spaces can be seen, for example, in relation to the designation of boundaries between PRIVATE AND PUBLIC SPHERES (Pratt, 2004), struggle over the meanings of ownership and PROPERTY rights (Blomley, 2004a) or conceptions of jurisdiction (Ford, 1999).

While insightful, scholarship on law and geography requires further development. While empirical accounts abound, the theorization of the geographies of law and legal struggles is still undeveloped and somewhat ambiguous. Pressing questions include: What analytical and ethical difference does space make to the analysis of law? What sort(s) of power is law? How can space and law be brought together without succumbing to a binary logic? Are legal geographies only discursive? Finally, the 'critical' aspects of this enquiry need to be worked through more carefully. Some years ago, Vera Chouinard (1994a, p. 428) called for 'meaningful political action in and against the legal system'. While this has been embraced in some quarters (Razack, 2002; Mitchell, 2003a), the political edge to critical legal geography remains undeveloped. Whether this entails intellectual challenges to legal 'closure' or grounded and inclusionary research projects concerning law remains an important question.   NKB

Suggested reading
Blomley (1994); Blomley, Delaney and Ford (2001); Clark (1989); Holder and Harrison (2003); Sarat and Kearns (2003).

law (scientific) A statement of an invariant relationship holding between different phenomena, or between different states of the same phenomena. The best known formulation is found in orthodox philosophy of science and is represented in symbolic form as 'If A, then B'. Boyle's Law, for example, states that *if* the volume of gas at a given temperature increases, *then* pressure decreases proportionately. Similar law-like statements have been proposed for geography, of which perhaps the best known is Tobler's (1970, p. 236) *First Law of Geography*: 'Everything is related to everything else, but near things are more related than distant things.' In the orthodox rendering, scientific laws are presumed eternal, universal, absolute, true and capable of expression in formal terms. They form the basis of scientific explanation and prediction – ground zero for understanding how the universe works. Two major objections have been levelled against these conventional views. First, REALISM argues that the orthodox 'If A, then B' form of a law says nothing about causality, instead asserting only the (weak) relation of conjunctional association. A stronger statement is required assigning causation. Second, work in science studies disputes many of the characteristics attributed to scientific laws by arguing that they represent LOCAL KNOWLEDGE rather than universal knowledge, and *ex-post* rationalization rather than fundamental explanation. In this spirit, Barnes (2004a) draws on science studies to contest Tobler's First Law of Geography.   TB

Suggested reading
Barnes (2004a).

law of the sea On 10 December 1982, the third United Nations Convention on the Law of the Sea (UNCLOS III) was opened for signature in Montego Bay, Jamaica, marking the culmination of over 14 years of work. More than 150 countries participated in drafting the treaty (representing all regions of the world, legal and political systems, and degrees of socio-economic development, and including coastal, archipelagic, island and landlocked states, as well as states 'geographically disadvantageous with regard to the ocean space'; see Friedheim, 1993). The Law of the Sea entered into force on 16 November 1994. As of 16 March 2005, the number of parties to UNCLOS III, including the European Community, stood at 149 – 130 coastal and eighteen landlocked states.

The treaty aims at ensuring peace and security in the world's oceans; promoting equitable and efficient utilization of their resources; and fostering protection and CONSERVATION of the marine environment. Equally significant is its role in clarifying and balancing the rights and duties of coastal states regarding adjacent maritime areas. Several 'mini-packages' of delicately balanced compromises emerged from the lengthy negotiations. For example, the convention allows coastal states certain rights in the 'exclusive economic zone' (Articles 55–75) – up to 200 nautical miles – for the purpose of economic advantage, notably rights over fishing and exploitation of non-living resources, as well as the concomitant limited jurisdiction in order to realize those rights. At the same time, however, neighbouring landlocked and geographically disadvantaged states must be allowed access to those resources of the zones that the coastal state does not exploit.

The LOS reserves the seas and ocean for peaceful and co-operative purposes, but regional conflicts, illegal activities (piracy, maritime terrorism and drug smuggling), competitive and unsustainable exploitation of marine resources, and environmental degradation are undermining human security at an alarming pace. Despite the obvious importance of polar maritime areas, there is a lack of general international law rules or conventions dealing with polar law of the sea problems (Chaturvedi, 2000). The LOS raises difficult questions in the following areas: ice-covered waters, polar baseline, maritime zones and the deep-seabed, high-sea freedoms and navigation, and marine pollution and environmental protection.

The international community continues its efforts to strengthen the international legal framework to prevent and suppress acts of terrorism (including acts at sea), safety of navigation, maritime security and the protection of marine environment. The 1995 United Nations Fish Stocks Agreement, considered the most important multilateral legally binding instrument for the conservation and management of high-seas fisheries since the conclusion of UNCLOS III, calls upon states to establish new regional fisheries management organizations where none exist in a particular region or sub-region. Its objectives are to ensure the long-term conservation and sustainable use of straddling and highly migratory fish stocks and to protect marine biodiversity. sch

Suggested reading
Rothwell (1996).

learning regions Spatial CLUSTERS of linked industries whose continued growth is a function of permanent innovation, through inter-firm co-operation and competition. AGGLOMERATION economies were first associated with industrial districts by the economist Alfred Marshall (1890) and the role of innovation in spatially proximate linked networks of firms is usually associated with the work of Piore and Sabel (1984), who stress that the importance of both formal and informal LINKAGES within a cluster mean that the whole is more than the sum of its parts because of both the local 'industrial atmosphere' and the 'mutual knowledge and trust' resident there. Scott (2006) uses the alternative term *creative field* to describe the social relations within such a cluster, defining it as 'all those instances of human effort and organization whose *spatial and locational* attributes, at whatever scale they may occur, promote development and growth-inducing change' (p. 54). Recognition of the importance of such fields to the development of clusters such as Silicon Valley in California has stimulated many public policy initiatives aimed at creating and fostering learning regions – as with SCIENCE PARKS.   RJ

Suggested reading
Longworth (2004).

Lebensraum Literally translated as 'living space', the term was used by Friedrich Ratzel in his representation of the STATE as an organism to identify a 'geographical area within which living organisms develop' (see ANTHROPOGEOGRAPHY). The term was developed by the *Geopolitik* school and partially adopted by the Nazis to justify the extension of the borders of the German state eastwards for the benefit of Germans and at the expense of the Slavs, who were represented as inferior and 'unworthy' of the territory (Smith, W.D., 1986; Clarke, Doel and McDonough, 1996). Territorial expansion was represented as a 'natural' consequence of the survival of the fittest (cf. DARWINISM).   CF

Suggested reading
Smith, W.D. (1986b)

leisure Either freedom *from* doing some things, or freedom *to* do other things – both definitions connote an existential state that involves pleasure and enjoyment, alongside choice. In many definitions and surveys, it is construed as activities that are not biologically necessary, that are not constrained by demands of work or other social actors, but that are chosen for personal pursuits. Much analysis has looked either at the changing ways in which 'leisure' intersects with other activities or at the changing forms of leisure activities themselves.

The first approach thus looks at how leisure fits into the mix of activities that make up life. The most influential founding work in this regard is Thorsten Veblen's *Theory of the leisure class* (first published in 1899). In it, Veblen sees leisure as a positional good that shows relative status and power within a system of CONSUMPTION. For Veblen, ability to consume leisure was a signal of wealth and status. This was set within the context of long struggles in the later nineteenth and much of the twentieth century between LABOUR and CAPITAL over reductions in the working week and paid holiday time. Considerable argument has emerged over whether the deregulated economies beginning in the late twentieth century, with demands for 24/7 services, have reversed that trend (e.g. Schor, 1991) or whether people feel more stressed, and leisure is more structured, but may have increased. All these studies focus on the amount of leisure time. However, difficulties arise about definitions when one considers forms of leisure that involve 'serious leisure', such as volunteering or educational hobbies (Stebbins, 1992), or SOCIAL REPRODUCTION, such as cooking or eating, which may be for pleasure as well as necessity. These latter highlight GENDER issues in definitions, and that men in developed countries enjoy far more choice than do women with what to do with time that is free from paid work.

The second approach focuses upon the nature of leisure activities. This approach points to the significance of leisure both economically and in shaping personal identities. Classic CRITICAL THEORY argued that nothing was as abhorrent to CAPITAL as 'free time' and that leisure was its commodification into a product to be bought and sold. Originally, criticism focused on the FORDIST mass production of homogeneous leisure products. Adorno and Horkheimer, in the *Dialectic of the Enlightenment*, argued that

> amusement under late capitalism is the prolongation of work ... mechanization has such a power over man's leisure and happiness, and so profoundly determines the manufacture of amusement goods, that his experiences are inevitably after-images of the work process itself. (1979, p. 137)

Later work has argued that in a POST-FORDIST or POSTMODERN world these patterns fragment and their meaning changes. Thus many analysts point to the emergence of social groups defined not by work identities but by shared leisure activities, such as different kinds of music or skateboarding, as subcultures or neotribes (Maffesoli, 1995). Others point to the emergence of a service-led 'experience economy', where we move from selling tangible products to consuming the memory of an event or experience (Pine and Gilmore, 1998).   MC

Suggested reading
Gershuny (2000); Koshar (2002); Maffesoli (1996).

liberalism The view that individual freedom should be the basis of human life. Liberals believe that human well-being is maximized when individuals are free to pursue their own interests provided that doing so causes no harm to others. According to classical liberalism, the STATE should be as small as possible and only as strong as is necessary to maintain the conditions that will safeguard individual liberty. Liberal models of CITIZENSHIP thus emphasize the formal EQUALITY of all citizens, civil RIGHTS, the rule of law and the protection of individuals from the arbitrary exercise of state POWER. Much debate within liberalism has been concerned with how to deal with conflicts of interest between individuals. Liberal models of DEMOCRACY emphasize the expression of individual preferences through voting. In economics, liberalism favours private ownership and production

and market mechanisms of resource allocation, based on the non-coerced interactions of individual producers and consumers.

Liberalism has been highly influential. All the world's major industrialized countries are, formally at least, liberal democracies with market economies. In practice, however, their political institutions and economic systems rarely come close to liberal models, and in many places even basic civil rights are under threat in the name of the 'war on terror'. The governments of some other countries, most notably China, have explicitly eschewed liberal democracy, although market mechanisms have been widely adopted in the economic arena.

Despite its apparent global HEGEMONY, liberalism has been subject to many critiques and challenges (see, e.g., ANARCHISM; COMMUNITARIANISM; ENVIRONMENTALISM; FASCISM; FEMINISM; MARXISM; POST-COLONIALISM; - SOCIALISM). According to some contemporary defenders of liberalism, religious fundamentalism (see RELIGION) poses the principal political threat to liberalism in the early twenty-first century. For others, there are inherent limits to liberalism and it is time to chart the contours of post-liberalism (Gray, 1996) or to push the democratizing impulse in liberalism in more radical and pluralist directions (see RADICAL DEMOCRACY).

Geographers have contributed to debates about liberalism in numerous areas. Much research has focused on NEO-LIBERALISM: the widespread revival of liberal economics since the 1970s and its application to public policy by national governments and international organizations (Harvey, 2005). Work on geographies of the BODY has questioned the concept of the sovereign and autonomous individual. Geographers have also engaged extensively with debates about rights and citizenship, focusing on the differential socio-spatial distribution of rights and obligations. The fundamental liberal distinction between the PRIVATE AND PUBLIC SPHERES has been destabilized by geographical research into the fluidity and porosity of the public/private boundary. The universalizing imperatives of liberalism have been challenged by geographers charting the geopolitics of humanitarian and military intervention (Smith, 2006b). Studies of the geographies of GOVERNMENTALITY have revealed how liberal GOVERNANCE involves what Nikolas Rose (1999c) calls 'powers of freedom'. In this view, freedom is a mechanism of governance, rather than its antithesis.   JPa

Suggested reading
Gray (1995); Kelly (2005).

life expectancy The additional number of years of life that individuals who reach a certain age can anticipate. It is calculated by using current data on MORTALITY and making assumptions about future trends in growth rates within the framework of the LIFE TABLE. Life expectancy is most often reported for individuals at age zero (i.e. at birth) and shows marked variation over space and time, and by sex and ETHNICITY/RACE (Shaw, Davey and Dorling, 2005). Such variations are linked to the access that individuals and groups have to economic, social and political resources, making life expectancy a surrogate measure of SOCIAL JUSTICE within society (e.g. the *human development index* compares overall well-being between societies and is calculated using life expectancy, measures of knowledge and standard of living). AJB

Suggested reading
Weeks (1999, ch. 4).

life table An accounting framework that shows how many persons die before, and survive beyond, successive birthdays. The methodology dates to the seventeenth century and calculates, among other measures, LIFE EXPECTANCY on the basis of how many members of a hypothetical COHORT of 100,000 newly borns survive to reach each of their subsequent birthdays, assuming that the pattern of age specific death rates that prevailed at the moment of birth continues into the future. While the intermediate information on survival rates continues to be of direct interest to those calculating insurance and pension premiums, the related method of survival analysis has emerged as an important tool in longitudinal studies of migration, marriage and poverty (Plane and Rogerson, 1994). AJB

Suggested reading
Rowland (2003, ch. 8).

life course/life-cycle The notion of life course has largely replaced life-cycle in social science research, to call attention to the socially constructed nature of shifts in experience and practice associated with ageing. Research examines both the normative patterns of behaviour associated with different life stages, and the relationships among social actors at different stages, weaving together production and SOCIAL REPRODUCTION to address such issues as child and elder care, labour force participation, residential MOBILITY and MIGRATION (see McDowell, 2003;

Bailey, Blake and Cooke, 2004). While stages in the life course are associated with biological age, these associations vary across time and place, given widespread differences in life expectancy and chances depending on political economic conditions. CK

Suggested reading
Cortesi, Cristaldi and Fortuijn (2004); Katz and Monk (1993).

lifeworld Synonymous with the TAKEN-FOR-GRANTED WORLD, the everyday lifeworld of habitual actions and attitudes is the foundational setting of Schutzian PHENOMENOLOGY and the closely related SYMBOLIC INTERACTIONISM of G.H. Mead. Introduced to geographers in the HUMANISTIC GEOGRAPHY of Anne Buttimer (1976) and others, lifeworld comprised the relational and meaningful places of direct experience where intentional actions unfolded and identity was assembled. Lifeworld is socio-centric and corporeal in its range and clarity. However, it is not static but, as Buttimer stressed, dynamic, concerned with movement and rhythm that integrates parts into an experienced whole, with routines that sediment a way of life in a geographic setting (Mels, 2004). Such a fusion of intersubjective meaning and physical location is inherent to the geographies of HOME, COMMUNITY and NATION. The lifeworld is a basic building block in attempts to construct a meta-social theory by Berger and Luckmann, Giddens and others. In his influential formulation, Jürgen Habermas counters the practical intersubjective interests of the lifeworld, retrieved through HERMENEUTIC study, with the instrumentality of political and economic systems accounted for through positivist methods (see CRITICAL THEORY). DL

Suggested reading
Dyck (1995); Jackson and Smith (1984, ch. 2); Mels (2004).

limits to growth The proposition, central to much modern ENVIRONMENTALISM, that the finiteness of biophysical resources places absolute limits on demographic and economic growth. Although the idea is important in classical political economy, the phrase entered widespread modern circulation only in 1972, when it appeared as the title of a report by a group known as the Club of Rome (Meadows, Meadows, Randers and Brehens, 1972). Based on early exercises in computer modelling, the report argued that humanity was on the brink of exceeding the Earth's CARRYING CAPACITY and precipitating widespread social and ecological CRISIS. Although the report looked at resources in addition to those directly related to agricultural production, its argument was essentially a Malthusian one (see MALTHUSIAN MODEL). It was an important milestone in the development of neo-Malthusian trends in modern environmentalism, such as a concern with the 'population bomb', as well as an impetus towards calls for a 'steady-state economy' and the development of the field of ENVIRONMENTAL ECONOMICS.

Belief in absolute limits to economic growth based on material scarcity, and the politics that follow from such a position, constituted a direct challenge to the Promethean views of human activity arguably shared by neo-classical economics and classical Marxism, both of which denied the necessity of such absolute material limits to human productivity. In geography, David Harvey (1974a) and others strongly criticized resurgent neo-Malthusian models for overlooking issues of distribution, justice, scale, changes in technology and productivity, and other factors that would complicate or undermine their predictions. A significant amount of geographical work over the subsequent several decades has essentially reproduced and elaborated this debate in various arenas. Perhaps the most notable example is the rapid growth of scholarship centred on the concept of ENVIRONMENTAL SECURITY. This literature is constituted largely by debates between dominant neo-Malthusian views, which continue to articulate theories of how demographically fuelled conflicts over increasingly scarce natural resources will produce escalating violence and geopolitical instability (see RESOURCE WARS), and more critical voices, which continue to insist on attention to the social causes, contexts, and complexities of such scenarios (see Dalby, 2004).

Other work in geography, though, has revisited the question of natural limits with increasing theoretical nuance, moving beyond the simple rejection of it in much of the Marxist tradition. Theorists of natural resource industries in particular have begun to take nature's materiality seriously by attempting to understand not only the constraints, but also the affordances and surprises, that biophysical systems present to human activities in specific circumstances, developing concepts such as appropriationism, substitutionism, eco-regulation, hybridity, and the formal versus the real subsumption of nature to capital (see Boyd, Prudham and Schurman, 2001). Nat-

ural 'limits' are thus increasingly understood and investigated as differentially malleable conditions of possibility for particular forms of human activity, rather than as absolute and universal barriers. Such a perspective has proved compatible with recognition of the necessarily political and social character of any claims about natural limits, as emphasized in the literature on social constructionism.   JM

Suggested reading
Benton (1989); Boyd, Prudham and Schurman (2001).

linear programming   A type of OPTIMIZATION MODEL used to find the optimal solution to a wide variety of economic, business and geographical problems, such as the minimum total transport cost of shipping goods through a geographical network. Optimization models have an objective function (the quantity to be minimized or maximized) and a set of constraints that define the possibilities and requirements (limits on supply, demand requirements, route characteristics). In linear programming both the objective function and the constraints are linear functions and this makes solution fast and easy, even for very large problems. The TRANSPORTATION PROBLEM is a special form that has many geographical applications.   LWH

Suggested reading
Greenberg (1978); Killen (1979, 1983).

linkages   The contacts and flows of information and/or materials between two or more individuals. The term is widely used in both INDUSTRIAL GEOGRAPHY and the geography of SERVICES to indicate inter-firm interdependence and its effects on location choice (see AGGLOMERATION). A firm's linkages can be divided into: (1) *backward*, which provide goods and services for its production activities; (2) *forward*, links with customers purchasing its products; and (3) *sideways*, interactions with other firms involved in the same processes. Membership of such networks in increasingly seen as crucial to success and survival for a firm, especially a small firm. (See also INTEGRATION).   RJ

literature   Although the meanings of this term have varied widely, two have been of special interest to geographers: (a) imaginative writing, especially that deemed to be of especially high quality or status by a critical establishment; and (b) published scholarly work on a particular topic.

Literature in the sense of imaginative writing has attracted the analytical attention of cultural geographers over the past 30 years in particular. Novels, stories, poems and travel narratives have been studied for their representations of places, landscapes and nature, of regions and nations, and of geographical processes such as urbanization, migration and colonization. An interest in literature was evident in some of Alexander von Humboldt's writings, and received scattered attention at moments through the early and mid-twentieth century. Darby's essay on the regional geography of Hardy's Wessex (1948) was an early outlier, but it extracted the descriptions of LANDSCAPE from the novels and used them to reconstruct the regional geographies of Dorset in the first half of the nineteenth century: as Darby had it, placing 'the pictures that Hardy drew' in 'the sequence that stretches from John Coker's survey in the seventeenth century up to modern accounts of the land utilization of Dorset' (p. 343). Darby displayed no interest in exploring the significance of these places for the characters and events in the novels, still less in approaching these 'geographies' with the sensibility of a literary scholar (cf. Barrell, 1982). Hardy's texts were read as more or less inert sources, and Darby had no interest in (or awareness of) how, as Brosseau (1995, p. 89) later put it more generally, a novel 'has a particular way of writing its own geography.'

It was not until thirty years after Darby's essay that literature received any sustained and systematic attention in HUMAN GEOGRAPHY, as part of the growing attention to environmental perception, imagery, attitudes and values, and to consciousness as an aspect of culture. This was the product of the critique of SPATIAL SCIENCE and the flowering of a HUMANISTIC GEOGRAPHY that renewed the discipline's traditional connections with the HUMANITIES in different, more analytical, registers, and which had a particular impact on CULTURAL GEOGRAPHY (Salter and Lloyd, 1977; Pocock, 1981). These explorations intensified through the closing decades of the twentieth century and into the opening decades of the twenty-first. This was achieved, in part, through a much closer and usually theoretically informed engagement with the work of literary scholars and cultural critics – from Walter Benjamin and Mikhail Bakhtin through Edward Said and Raymond Williams to Terry Eagleton and Fredric Jameson – many of whom had an interest in SPATIALITY and the cultures of COLONIALISM, CAPITALISM and MODERNITY that was at once close to and consequential for human geography more generally. Their critical writings had a considerable impact on explorations of MODERNISM and POSTMODERNISM in the cities of the global North, of IMAGINATIVE GEOGRAPHIES produced under the signs of ORIENTALISM, TROPICALITY and similar projects, and on theorizations of POWER and CULTURE. These endeavours were reinforced through a second source of interest in literary matters: human geography's engagement with styles of contemporary PHILOSOPHY that Rorty once described as forms of cultural criticism: these included his own version of PRAGMATISM but also POST-STRUCTURALISM (the literary sensibilites of Foucault and Derrida are especially salient, though Eagleton has railed against Spivak's).

The turn to literature has raised an interesting question in a field dominated by the discourses of social science: Exactly what kind of evidence is literature? For some human geographers, it is both indicative of the capacity of human beings to make meaning and an expression of a specific meaning-filled culture (e.g. Bunkse, 2004); for others, and not mutually exclusive of other meanings, it is at once a reflection of political–economic realities and a way of thinking them through (e.g. Henderson, 1999); for others, it is part and parcel of the production of regional identity and memory (e.g. DeLyser, 2005). In human geography, the meaning of 'imaginative writing' extends to some degree to narratives of travel and exploration (see TRAVEL WRITING). While not pure figments of imagination, these writings are often structured around certain tropes and narrative conventions that give TEXTUALITY as such a constitutive role in their making: travel narratives do not simply mirror or correspond to the world (e.g. Blunt, 1994). It is probably safe to say that most contemporary geographical study of literature is not so much interested in literature *per se* than in literature as a species of REPRESENTATION, DISCOURSE and TEXT, interest in which has grown with the CULTURAL TURN in the social sciences (Barnes and Duncan, 1991). It is not entirely a one-way street, and the traffic has been marked by both interesting departures and juddering collisions: literary scholars would have no difficulty in recognizing the force and originality of Kearns' (2006b) reading of the spatial dialectics of James Joyce, for example, and the three spatial motifs he identifies (circulation, labyrinth and palimpsest) thread out on to the wider terrain of British colonialism and Irish nationalism; but most human geographers would be bemused at the traces of spatial science to be discerned in Moretti's (1998, 2005) spatialized apprehensions of the European novel and literary history.

Literature as a social and geographical phenomenon, involving the geographical spread of avowedly 'literary' forms (e.g. the novel), the emergence of publication and printing centres, literary celebrity and certain ideological effects, has been studied extensively. Few such studies have been undertaken by geographers, but the classic account of 'the coming of the book' in Europe devoted a central chapter to 'the geography of the book' (Febvre and Martin, 1984 [1958], pp. 167–215), and historians and historical geographers followed in their footsteps to study the DIFFUSION of printing, the spread of literacy, the spatial impress of censorship and other topics. These historical treatments underscore that both the forms and meanings of literature have changed dramatically. Literature's meaning as a form of imaginative writing endorsed by a critical establishment came about over time (see Williams, 1977; Eagleton, 1983). Its early meaning (into the eighteenth century) was closer to the idea of literacy; that is, it was the property or characteristic of learned, reading elites. Literature's meaning as a mark of distinction regarding what one could do (read) was then extended to what one read (books). The question of what kinds of books counted as literature then followed (Williams, 1977). There was (and there remains) no easy distinction between fiction and fact as the way to demarcate literature from other sorts of writing – witness the example of travel writing. The difference between works of, say, philosophy, history and politics as opposed to fictional writing was codified in response to industrial capitalism, which was seen as suppressing creativity. This is not to say that literature, or more specifically what cultural elites claimed counted as literature, escaped an ideological function within industrial capitalism (Eagleton, 1983). Literature as creative output was also caught up with the notion of a 'national' literature and the establishment (and struggle over) nation-state based literary canons. The formation of the literary canon carried with it a new meaning: literature exemplified for national critical establishments the best of what a nation-state could achieve and served the purposes of unifying national identity (see also NATION; NATIONALISM). (The logic of specifically regional literatures and regional literary canon formations runs in parallel. But contrast these impulses towards national and regional narratives of literary formation with the recent identification of a 'global literary space' à la world systems theory: see Casanova, 2005.)

Yet the meanings of literature have in fact remained multiple, or perhaps become multiple once again, albeit in different ways. Most of what human geographers have had to say about 'literature' has focused on the book, specifically the novel or the travel narrative, and yet many of the scholars on whose work they draw have also had important things to say about other cultural media: ART, drama, FILM, MUSIC, photography and video. Human geographers have explored these too, but they have displayed much less interest in literary dramatic works (other than their staging: see Chamberlain, 2001; Pratt and Johns, 2007) except, by analogical extension, in ideas of PERFORMANCE. This is surprising since, as the image of Shakespeare's Globe Theatre reminds us, drama has long had important things to show us about the production of human geographies (cf. Gillies, 1994).

Printed work of many kinds continues to be referred to as literature, whether this is the 'literature' produced by political campaigns, advertising literature, best-selling novels or, still, literature-capital. Within the academy, 'literature' also means the collective, published scholarly work pertaining to some field ('the geographical literature'), which typically has its own (contested) canon and its own (contentious) critical establishment. Literature as specifically scholarly work is not simply a product found on the bookshelf or downloadable as a PDF. It is a process that involves discernment, vetting, peer review, editorial negotiation and not a little politics. The scholarly literature is thus not a thing: it is a social relation out of which are wrought scholarly debate or consensus, cases for tenure (or not), new journals or lapsed subscriptions, expectations among researchers and between teachers and students, and struggles won or lost over the *lingua franca* of scholarship as such.

A much less explored resonance between geography and literature is the idea that scholarly geography *can be* literature in the creative sense of the word (cf. Bunkse, 2004), though today's human geography is no stranger to experiments with literary form, as in the work of Marcus Doel, Gunnar Olsson or Allan Pred, for example, and there are many other human geographers who write with an ear to cadence and an eye to image. But even 'geographical literature' in its radically non-experimental, more technical sense can be subject to the same disciplined processes of critical reading that literary scholars apply to poems and novels, and in as many ways. The process of theoretical critique in human geography is not only about the collision of contending concepts, therefore, but is also about its text-ures, the very languages and grammars of geographical enquiry: it can and should include the analysis of METAPHOR and RHETORIC, a disclosure of the MASCULINISM and PHALLO-CENTRISM of the formal structure of an argument or the DECONSTRUCTION of geographical texts. This ought to come as no surprise: the root meaning of 'Geo-graphy', after all, is 'Earth-writing'. GHe/DG

Suggested reading
Bunkse (2004); Thacker (2005–6).

local knowledge A term coined by the English philosopher Gilbert Ryle, and popularized by the American anthropologist Clifford Geertz (1983). Local knowledge refers to the double idea (1) that all knowledge is geographically and historically bounded, and (2) that the local conditions of its manufacture affect the nature of the knowledge produced. Note that local knowledge refers to the context in which knowledge is produced, not the geographical domain to which knowledge applies. The physicist's string theory, for example, is a piece of local knowledge even though its explanatory province is infinitely large, even beyond the known universe. To take in turn the two parts of the definition:

(1) Knowledge is historically constrained, and produced within particular material settings that include geographical site, particular kinds of human bodies, and specific types of buildings, machines and equipment. The key word is *produced*. *Producing* knowledge contrasts with the conventional view that knowledge is acquired through discovery (dis-cover, literally to uncover). In the discovery view, knowledge is assumed to be free floating and pre-existent, requiring only the right conditions to be revealed. For knowledge to be produced, however, suggests something different; that there is an active process of creative construction 'on site' according to specific local rules and conditions. An example is graduate students making vigorous use of large desk calculators in the statistics laboratory at the University of Iowa in the late 1950s, and in the process *producing* geography's QUANTITATIVE REVOLUTION (Barnes, 2004b).

(2) The material and historical setting, and associated social interests, enter into the very lineaments of knowledge. Knowledge does not come from the sky, from heavenly inspiration, but from engaging in particular kinds of social practices that are historically and geographically grounded (see SITUATED KNOWLEDGE). Knowledge is irreducibly social, never innocent, always coloured by the context of its production. This does not mean that it is singularly determined by its context. Multiple responses to any situation are possible, though their range will be constrained by the places and predicaments that have in various ways, sometimes unremarked and unconscious, both summoned and shaped them. Examples are legion: ENVIRONMENTAL DETERMINISM expressed (and helped to legitimize) the racist and imperialist impulses of late-nineteenth-century Europe; REGIONAL SCIENCE represented the INSTRUMENTAL-IST, MASCULINIST and economistic sentiments of much of mid-twentieth-century America; and POSTMODERNISM reflected a late-twentieth-century consumer capitalism constituted by flickering images and fabricated identities. In each of these cases, the knowledge that emerged is shaped by the particular, non-repeatable constellation of forces, causes and determinations found at a given time and place. One can begin to trace their effects, and they clearly travel and will be found in other times and places too, but not in the exact same combination with the same consequence. Each local context will be different, producing different knowledge. The important corollary is that universal claims to truth are unsupportable. Knowledge is always made inside the bubble of local context, with no means of moving outside for 'a god's eye view' (Haraway, 1991c, p. 193).

The issue of local knowledge has been central recently in at least two disciplines. First, in anthropology, Clifford Geertz (1988, p. 137) argues for the impossibility of 'telling it like it is', because ethnographic accounts are as much about the world of the ethnographer as the world that is represented (and transparently obvious in early ethnographies; Geertz,

1988: see also ETHNOGRAPHY). A recent complication is the effect of an increasingly fluid, mobile and hyperactive world, which seemingly undermines the idea of fixed local knowledge. The problem is that while knowledge is produced at local sites, it increasingly travels. The response has been to examine networks of knowledge, conceived as *inter-local* interactions. Local knowledge travels, but it never achieves universality.

Second, in the field of history and philosophy of science, 'telling it like it is' is also not an option, since Kuhn (1970 [1962]) devised his concept of a PARADIGM. Science is conceived as being shot full of social interests, reflecting the time and place of its manufacture: it is local knowledge. Initially the Edinburgh School, and feminists such as Haraway (1989), provided detailed, historical studies, laying bare the local social interests at play. Other work – for example, Latour and Woolgar (1979) – concentrated on specific local sites, such as the laboratory, and concomitant micro-practices of research and relations of power that produce knowledge. The point, as Rouse (1987, p. 72) writes, is that scientists 'go from one local knowledge to another rather than from universal theories to their particular instantiations'.

In spite of geography's historical concern with the local, the discipline's recent past has been dominated by a quest for universal knowledge. After the Second World War much of geography, or at any rate those areas colonized by SPATIAL SCIENCE, was bound up with the search for GRAND THEORY and its universals, predicated on ESSENTIALISM and FOUNDATIONALISM. Things have changed since the 1990s with the advent of POSTMODERNISM and POST-STRUCTURALISM. Although the term 'local knowledge' is rarely used as such, the sentiments that it expresses are now found in recent works on disciplinary history (Livingstone, 2003c: see GEOGRAPHY, HISTORY OF), around biophysical process in NATURE (Castree, 2005a) and ECONOMIC GEOGRAPHY (Gibson-Graham, 2006b [1996]). TB

Suggested reading
Rouse (1987, ch. 4).

local state The set of institutions of the STATE that have sub-national territorial remits. The local state includes elected local government as well as local agencies of public administration and public service provision and local regulatory and judicial authorities. However, it does not include all the actors involved in local GOVERNANCE, some of which are drawn from the private and voluntary sectors.

The concept of the local state came to prominence with the publication of Cockburn's *The local state: management of cities and people* (1977). Cockburn argued that the local state should be understood as an integral part of the capitalist state as a whole, and that it operates to sustain the social relations of CAPITALISM at the local level through its management of social reproduction. Rejecting this approach, Saunders (1979) proposed a 'dual state' thesis that theorized the state in terms of two distinct roles: the promotion of production (the sphere of the central state) and the maintenance of consumption (the sphere of the local state). In this view, the local state is concerned particularly with providing the means of COLLECTIVE CONSUMPTION, such as housing and local public services. These two positions were representative of a more general debate about the degree of autonomy of the local state. Is the local state merely an arm of the central state operating at the local level, or does it have at least some effective independence? All large NATION-STATES find that some system of local administration is a practical necessity to cope with the complexities of managing extensive territories. However the autonomy of local state actors varies considerably according to the legal, constitutional and fiscal framework within which local institutions operate and the extent to which they can be 'captured' by political parties or interest groups opposed to central government policies.

The concept of the local state was particularly important in geographical research during the 1980s (e.g. Clark and Dear, 1984; Duncan and Goodwin, 1988). This was in part a reflection of the conflict-ridden nature of central–local relations during the political ascendancy of the New Right. Since then, a number of factors have contributed to a decline in the use of the concept. First, the HEGEMONY of NEO-LIBERAL models of social and economic development in many countries has curtailed the scope for the local state to pursue alternative political strategies. Second, the recognition that non-state actors play important roles in shaping local areas has contributed to a shift in research focus away from theories of the state and towards theories of governance. Third, extensive research on the re-scaling of the state has drawn attention to the relational nature of SCALE, and challenged the notion that particular kinds of institutions or practices necessarily operate at particular spatial scales. Fourth, the idea that 'the' local state exists as a unified or coherent entity has been undermined by new theoretical perspectives including POST-MARXISM and various forms of POST-STRUCTURALISM.   JPa

Suggested reading
Brenner (2004); DiGaetano (2002).

local statistics A local statistic is often a numerical value describing some aspect of a locality or its population (e.g. the percentage unemployed) and offering greater detail than more aggregate regional or national statistics. The meaning is similar in SPATIAL STATISTICS, where local statistics are values obtained for geographical subsections of a larger study region, often compared to each other or to an average. Here they contrast with global methods, including REGRESSION analyses fitted for the entire region, that risk missing statistically significant and geographically localized variations in the relationships between variables. Local statistical methods include POINT PATTERN ANALYSIS, GEOGRAPHICALLY WEIGHTED REGRESSION and local indicators of spatial association (Anselin, 1995).   RH

Suggested reading
Fotheringham, Brunsdon and Charlton (2000).

locale A setting or context for social interaction, typically involving co-present actors. In STRUCTURATION THEORY (Giddens, 1979, 1984), locales provide the resources on which actors draw. Different kinds of collectivities are associated with characteristic locales (Giddens, 1981, p. 39): the locale of the school is the classroom; that of the army, the barracks; and so on. Despite his emphasis on co-presence, Giddens (1984, p. 118) also suggests that locales may range 'from a room in a house ... to the territorially demarcated areas occupied by nation states': as Thrift (1983) emphasizes, 'a locale does not have to be local'.   JPa

Suggested reading
Thrift (1983).

local–global relations A concept that seeks to capture the dialectical nature (see DIALECTICS) of the connections between global processes and local forces. The term 'local–global' resonates differently for different scholars, resulting in a number of different approaches to the intersections of local and global forces. Some scholars have pursued empirical cases in which they identify strong global forces – especially those of modernity and the market – that impact and alter local

places and customs. An example of this type of scholarship can be found in Allan Pred's (1990) work on late-nineteenth-century Stockholm, where the rapid growth of capitalist production processes greatly affected the language and symbolic codes of the city residents (see also Pred and Watts, 1992).

A second type of research investigates the ways in which local places and cultures incorporate and/or transform global processes. Particularly prevalent in the work of cultural anthropologists, this body of scholarship eschews meta-narratives of global capitalism and emphasizes instead the power of diverse local traditions in altering the meanings and workings of global processes. A good example is Watson's (1997) edited volume investigating the localization of American corporate and culinary culture (via ethnographies of McDonald's) in numerous cities of East Asia.

A third body of research attempts to combine and transcend these earlier formulations by arguing for a process of GLOCALIZATION, foregrounding the ways in which the local and the global are completely interwoven and impossible to pull apart. Economic geographers who seek to emphasize the inter-textual, multi-layered nature of SCALE have employed this concept (Swyngedouw, 1997; Brenner, 2003). It has also been used frequently by those interested in the changing nature of CITIZENSHIP and the hybrid qualities of identities formulated in conditions of transnationality (Yuval-Davis, 1999).

A number of critiques have been levelled at all three of these employments of the local–global conceit. The strongest has emerged from the feminist literature, which has interrogated the binary nature of the paired words as well as the often uncritical and ungrounded invocations of both the global and the local (see also Freeman, 2001). As Hart (2001, p. 655) notes:

In addition to active/passive and dynamic/static, these [binaries] include economics/culture, general/specific, abstract/concrete and, very importantly, dichotomous understandings of time and space, in which time is accorded active primacy while space appears as a passive container. This conflation of 'the global' with dynamic, technological-economic forces restlessly roving the globe defines its inexorable – and inexorably masculine – character. By the same token, 'the local' appears as a passive, implicitly feminine recipient of global forces whose only option is to appear as alluring as possible.

Other critiques include the observation that many of the local–global narratives that scholars employ have focused on the moment of impact between global and local processes, and as a result have underplayed the ongoing power dynamics between local–local forces (Ortner, 1995). By the same token, the actual workings and trajectories of perceived global forces such as CAPITALISM are often assumed rather than investigated empirically, leading to a blind spot with respect to global–global dynamics. This latter critique has been taken to the extent of questioning the very nature of capitalism itself (Gibson-Graham, 2006b [1996]). A final, more implicit critique has emerged with the literature on TRANSNATION-ALISM, wherein scholars have preferred to priv-ilege the ongoing movements between scales and across BORDERS rather than the perceived static conceptualization of both scales and borders that is suggested by the local–global terminology.   KM

locality   A PLACE or REGION of sub-national spatial SCALE. Locality studies were a promin-ent feature of British urban and regional re-search in the 1980s and 1990s. They developed from attempts to understand the process of socio-economic RESTRUCTURING and the role of place and spatial variation within it. Locality was a key organizing concept for three research programmes funded by the UK's Economic and Social Research Council in the 1980s: the 'Changing Urban and Regional System' initiative (CURS), the 'Social Change and Economic Life' initiative (SCELI) and the 'Economic Restructuring, Social Change and the Locality' programme. At the centre of each was a series of studies of the impact of restructuring on particular places or regions. A key concern of these 'locality studies' was to collect detailed empir-ical evidence to assist the identification of the nature, causes and consequences of spatial differentiation in processes of change (Cooke, 1989).

The research raised a series of metho-dological and theoretical issues that became bound up with wider and sometimes acrimo-nious debates. These included: the delimita-tion of localities for research; the relationship between locality studies and critical REALISM; the extent to which localities should be seen as 'pro-active' agents of their own transform-ation; the politics of the 'empirical turn'; the question of whether a concern with local dif-ference risked limiting the scope for general-ization and theoretical development (Smith,

1987); and the gendered implications (see GENDER) of most locality studies' focus on the sphere of waged labour and their limited treat-ment of cultural relations.

Since the end of the formal research pro-grammes, the concept of locality has been much less prominent in the geographical lit-erature, but two more recent developments during the 1990s may be noted. First, there has been a much stronger emphasis on rela-tional and networked concepts of locality and on the links between localities and other spatial scales. Murdoch and Marsden (1995) draw on ACTOR-NETWORK THEORY to suggest that 'localities should be seen as constituted by various networks operating a different scales' (p. 368), while Amin (2004b) has proposed a wholly non-territorial view of places as 'unbound'.

Second, many of the issues highlighted by the localities debate have been translated into new conceptual frameworks. For example, the upsurge of interest in GLOBALIZATION during the 1990s has involved a recasting of the issue of local specificity in terms of global–local relations, while the further development of CULTURAL GEOGRAPHY has seen increasingly sophisticated treatments of the relationships between politics, place and IDENTITY.   JPa

Suggested reading
Duncan (1989); *Environment and Planning A* (1991).

localization   A term often contrasted with GLOBALIZATION and meant to capture the importance of PLACE-based activities. Localization refers to the necessary embedd-edness of economic processes, which always reflect their social, political and geographical context. All activities require some degree of spatial fixity and many obtain significant advantages from being geographically local-ized. These advantages include economies of AGGLOMERATION as well as more sociocultural advantages pertaining to face-to-face contact, the formation of personal NETWORKS, and the creation of centres of innovation and know-ledge (Amin and Thrift, 1994a).   KM

Suggested reading
Amin and Thrift (1994a); Cox (1997).

location quotient   A quantitative measure used to describe the concentration of a group or an activity in a locality or region relative to that of a larger area such as the countrywide or national norm. The quotient is the ratio of the local concentration to the national figure, and location quotients have been widely used to measure regional employment specialization. For example, if locality A has 53.2 per cent of its employed population working in manufacturing and the national percentage is 28.6, then the quotient for region A is 53.2/28.6 = 1.86. A quotient greater than 1.0 indicates greater concentration in the region than the national norm, and a value less than 1.0 indicates relative absence. Location quotients provide a simple way of making ECONOMIC BASE THEORY operational. LWH

location theory A historically and intellectually varied body of THEORY and techniques concerned with the EXPLANATION and sometimes PREDICTION of the location of individual and aggregate economic activities. Until around 1980 location theory was a distinct canon, with a well-defined history, core issues and methods, and a roll-call of alumnae. No more. Location theory is less shapely, more voluminous, spilling out of its earlier constraints, but more interesting as a result.

Scott (1976a, p. 106) claims that the first location theorist was Sir James Steuart (1712–80), a Scottish political economist. Most other histories, however, start with the German location school, whose first member was Johann Heinrich von Thünen (1783–1850) (Blaug, 1979; Ponsard, 1983). A Prussian landowner, agriculturalist, political reformer and embryonic neo-classical economist (Alfred Marshall said, 'I loved von Thünen above all my masters'; quoted in Blaug, 1990, p. 23), von Thünen crafted an abstract location MODEL using a method he called '*Form der Anschaung*'. Deploying calculus and capacious observations made from his country estate, he developed a theory of concentric agricultural land use based on the variation of land RENT by location (see VON THÜNEN MODEL).

Alfred Weber (1869–1958), brother of sociologist Max, was a second member of the German school ('the true heir of von Thünen'; Blaug, 1979, p. 28). Although much of his work concerned cultural history, he also experimented with a method of establishing the most profitable location for a factory in his quest to understand the origins of AGGLOMERATION in an early twentieth-century Germany racked by a pervasive sense of crisis in its great cities. His discussion isolated the relative geographical pull of FACTORS OF PRODUCTION conceived initially on a triangular grid, and he used both a physical model (the Varignon frame) as well as complex mathematics (so complex that he needed help from Georg Pick, the mathematician who assisted Einstein in formulating relativity) to derive a solution for optimal location (minimizing costs, maximizing revenue).

August Lösch (1906–45) and Walter Christaller (1893–1969) round out the school. Christaller, who was trained as a geographer, developed CENTRAL PLACE THEORY in the 1930s both to explain the location of different kinds of services and also to undertake regional planning. Its geometries assumed a truly grotesque form when Christaller was employed by the Third Reich's Planning and Soil Office in 1940: he proposed to deploy the theory to reconfigure the geography of Poland following its depopulation by relocation, deportation and extermination (see HOLOCAUST). Lösch, an economist trained at Bonn University, independently developed his version of central place theory during the same period, but unlike Christaller couched it in mathematical terms as spatial equilibrium, with services, industry and consumers arranged within a hexagonal net of market areas. Like Christaller, there was a NORMATIVE impulse to his project, but Lösch despised Hitler (as did Alfred Weber), and died from deprivations he suffered in maintaining his values against those of the Nazis (see FASCISM).

The contributions of the German location school were rigorous, conceptually pointed and abstract. Theirs was a world apart from the a-theoretical approach that dominated ECONOMIC GEOGRAPHY until the mid-1950s, in which location was 'explained' by merely inventorying a set of *ad hoc*, unique geographical factors. Isard (1979, p. 9) recalls that economic geographers at that time had "little concern for analysis' and that they made 'no attempt' even 'to fuse ... location[al] factors into a simple cost calculus'. Isard's own REGIONAL SCIENCE movement, which for a period was symbiotically linked with economic geography, helped from the outside to push the sub-discipline into the mould of the German locational school – and which Isard (1956) was also concerned to extend. A similar move to reshape the field came from inside the discipline, with the attempt to establish human geography as SPATIAL SCIENCE during the QUANTITATIVE REVOLUTION of the late 1950s. Work at two of the earliest sites of that revolution was explicitly directed towards creating a location theory that was systematic, general and empirically exact: McCarty, Hook and Knox (1956) at Iowa drew on CORRELATION and REGRESSION techniques to explain regional industrial location, while Garrison, Berry, Marble, Nystuen and Morrill (1959), including several of his soon-to-be-famous graduate students (the "space cadets'), combined German location theory with demanding statistical analysis in their studies of highway development in Washington State.

Haggett's influential (1965) book, *Locational analysis in human geography*, summarized and solidified the new approach to location theory (see also LOCATIONAL ANALYSIS). It was to be formal, empirically rigorous, and undergirded primarily by NEO-CLASSICAL ECONOMICS (both indirectly via the German school and regional science and directly from mainstream economics). A central topic was the firm, a staple of neo-classical micro-economic analysis and underpinned by assumptions of RATIONAL CHOICE THEORY and perfect competition (many small producers, none of which control price). The theory of the firm was translated directly into spatial terms by Isard, and later in economic geography by Smith (1981a [1971]). But chinks in the armour of classic location theory were soon revealed. First, the determinacy of rational choice was shown to be unrealistic, and ideas of 'bounded rationality', or 'SATISFICING BEHAVIOUR' were preferred, producing a literature on the BEHAVIOURAL GEOGRAPHY of firm location (Pred, 1967, 1969). Second, perfect competition was demonstrably imperfect for understanding the contemporary world of TRANSNATIONAL CORPORATIONS, leading to an alternative literature on the 'geography of enterprise' (later 'corporate geography') focused on firms as institutions, decision-making hierarchies and branch plant economies (McNee, 1960; Hayter and Watts, 1983).

The disquiet only got worse. David Harvey, who earlier in his career had drawn on classical and neo-classical models of agricultural location, including von Thünen's work, and explored general models of the evolution of spatial patterns, turned to MARXISM, and particularly Marx's own writings, in the early 1970s and pursued a radically different approach. His subsequent analysis of the historical geography of CAPITALISM, brilliantly realized in *The limits to capital* (Harvey, 1999 [1982]), did not so much ignore the questions of traditional location theory as pose them in another register altogether. His emphasis was less on accounting for the locations of economic activities than in disclosing the connections between the CRISIS-ridden dynamics of capitalism and its UNEVEN DEVELOPMENT as a SPACE-ECONOMY. Doreen Massey's work around the same time was indebted to Marxism too, but it had a much more direct impact on location theory. Like Harvey, she was trained in the orthodox approach, even studying briefly with Isard. Her reformulation began in the early 1970s with a detailed internal critique of orthodoxy arguing that applying neo-classical economic theory to location generates fundamental and irreparable logical contradictions. The alternative that she constructed over the next decade or so combined the theoretical postulates of POLITICAL ECONOMY with the philosophical armature of REALISM, culminating in her watershed book, *Spatial divisions of labour* (Massey, 1984). This was crucially important because it demonstrated that location theory need be neither formal nor neo-classical, and because it considerably expanded both what could count as factors bearing on location (in her case, CLASS and GENDER, politics and culture) and what could constitute theoretical explanation (in her case, a 'geological metaphor', taking the form of *layers of investment*; Barnes, 2001). Massey's larger point was that the object of location theory – sites of economic activity – could not be separated from the wider, geographically variegated social setting of capitalism. Her argument was starkly reinforced by the setting of her own study: the massive DEINDUSTRIALIZATION of the UK during the late 1970s and early 1980s (see also DIVISION OF LABOUR; LOCALITY studies).

A similarly inspired argument emerged shortly afterwards among a group of economic geographers in California, although their context was utterly different: the study of vibrant capitalist production associated particularly with high-tech and high-end economic activities. Scott (1988b) developed what he called 'neo-Weberian' location theory drawing eclectically on the work of neo-Marxist economicst Piero Sraffa (see NEO-RICARDIAN ECONOMICS) and that of institutional economists Ronald Coase and Oliver Williamson (see INSTITUTIONAL ECONOMICS). Storper and Walker (1989) elaborated an 'inconstant geography of capitalism' roiled by technological change and social conflict. They stressed the tightly interlinked – 'NETWORK' – character of activities in which social and economic institutions cross-cut and interleaved within specific regional formations. The consequence was a rediscovery of the idea of INDUSTRIAL DISTRICTS, first recognised by Alfred Marshall at the turn of the twentieth century: dense geographical nodes of tightly knit complementary manufacturing

427

activities, sustained by strong formal and informal social connections – which Storper (1997b) labelled 'untraded interdependencies'. During the 1980s and early 1990s, 'industrial districts' seemed to be the answer to every (important) location-theoretical question. Industrial districts were variously linked to POST-FORDISM (and often presumed as its characteristic locational form); to high-tech industries and the INFORMATION ECONOMY (the stress on social connections seemed uncannily made for their study: see Saxenian, 1994); and to an emerging institutional and 'CULTURAL TURN' within economic geography itself.

But the shortcoming of the concept of industrial districts, as with Massey's geological metaphor, was its confinement to the local rather than its ability to address a SCALE increasingly on the lips of economic geographers (and everyone else's as well): the global (see GLOBALIZATION). One solution was to argue that the global was nothing more than an interlinked set of industrial districts – Scott's (1998) answer, and at one time, Amin and Thrift's (1992) too. Another was to continue with the network idea but to expand it to the whole world. Location theory's charge was to represent and explain network relations – that is, social and economic institutional linkages – wherever they were found across the globe. This approach, also called 'the relational turn', drew upon ACTOR-NETWORK THEORY and was not only concerned with social and economic relations, but with material ones too through the incorporation of COMMODITY CHAIN analysis (for examples, see Dicken, Kelly, Olds and Yeung, 2000; Dicken, 2003; Hughes and Reimer, 2004; Yeung, 2004).

Location theory, as its long history makes clear, is no autonomous creation, propelled by its own logic. The logic is only that of its human creators, reflecting their own changing circumstances: from life on an isolated farm to life in an interconnected GLOBE. The vitality of location theory is a consequence of economic geographers keeping abreast of the restless world that they inhabit.   TB

Suggested reading
Barnes (2003); Storper (1997b).

locational analysis A term best associated with Peter Haggett's (1965) seminal book, *Locational analysis in human geography*, referring to the logically and empirically rigorous investigation of the spatial arrangements of phenomena and related flow patterns. The heyday of locational analysis in GEOGRAPHY was the 1960s and early 1970s, when vigorous attempts were made to recast the discipline as SPATIAL SCIENCE, but its roots can be traced back to the first half of the nineteenth century and the formation of a German school of LOCATION THEORY. Although locational analysis is now out of fashion in contemporary geography, it has recently been reactivated in economics and advertised as a component of a NEW ECONOMIC GEOGRAPHY.

Haggett's (1965, p. 1) scrupulously ordered book was fundamentally about 'the search for order', by which he meant locational order or 'SPATIAL STRUCTURE', as it might be studied in (and as) HUMAN GEOGRAPHY. He (re)turned to the science *par excellence* of spatial order, geometry, which he described as a 'neglected tradition in geography' (p. 15). Accordingly, he organized his first five substantive chapters in geometric terms (see figure):

- movement – the interaction between points;
- networks – the lines of linkage among points;
- nodes – the convergence of links;
- hierarchies – the differential role played by different nodes;
- surfaces – the spaces among nodes.

For each of the five geometries, he deployed rigorous theory and formal numerical methods to analyse and explain associated location issues: this was locational analysis.

Haggett made it clear, though, that his approach was a continuation of the long-standing, albeit 'deviant', intellectual tradition of location theory that historically twinned geometrical reasoning with theoretical and empirical analysis. Its origins lie with the nineteenth-century Prussian landowner cum part-time geographer, Johann Heinrich von Thünen (1783–1850), who combined meticulous empiricism, theoretical innovation and a concentric geometrical sensibility to describe and explain location patterns of agricultural land use (see VON THUNEN MODEL). Later contributors to the project, and their geometries, included Alfred Weber (1869–1958) (industrial location and triangles), and August Lösch (1906–45) and Walter Christaller (1893–1969) (CENTRAL PLACE THEORY and hexagons). Walter Isard (1919–), writing in 1956, nine years before Haggett, synthesized these contributions within his own account of

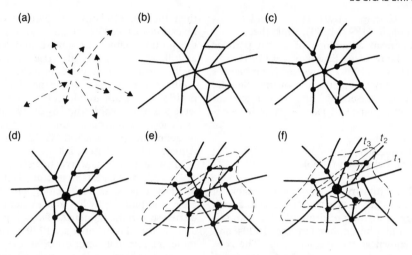

| (a) | (b) | (c) |
| (d) | (e) | (f) |

Locational analysis *Stages in the analysis of nodal regional systems: (a) interaction: (b) networks: (c) nodes: (d) hierarchies: (e) surface: (f) diffusion* (Haggett et al., 1977)

locational analysis, which he termed REGIONAL SCIENCE (although it was longer on theory and shorter on geometry than Haggett's version).

Both Haggett's and Isard's accounts of locational analysis enjoyed considerable success within human geography for a period, but their star waned from the 1970s for reasons both internal and external to the discipline (see QUANTITATIVE REVOLUTION). During the 1990s, however, the baton of locational analysis was passed to the economists in the form of a New Economic Geography (Fujita, Krugman and Venables, 1999). Unsurprisingly, it was more theoretical and mathematical, less empirical and geometrical, than in its previous version, but the basic mission was unaltered: to represent and analyse economic geographical distributions, and interactions, at all scales using exact, formal techniques and vocabularies.

The tie that binds locational analysis over its more than 150-year history is a conviction that the secrets of location are to be revealed by a ruthless pursuit of rational enquiry and methods, which takes its most perfect form in the logical structure and techniques of mathematics including geometry. The specifics of the location question vary – from point-to-point interaction to the composition of regional networks and surfaces – but the universal rationalist method is constant, thereby ensuring certainty, progress, and truth (so its protagonists claim). In contrast, Barnes (2003) argues that it is not as clear-cut: as with SCIENCE more generally, or any other form of knowledge, the historical and

geographical circumstances of the locational analysts intrude and inevitably corrupt their supposedly pure rationality (cf. LOCAL KNOWLEDGE). This does not detract from the achievements of locational analysis, but it casts them in a different light. For it requires an understanding of the peculiar historical and geographical context of their production, an emphasis ironically quite different from the one offered by locational analysts themselves.   TB

Suggested reading
Barnes (2003).

logical empiricism Sometimes used as a synonym for LOGICAL POSITIVISM, but more often used to mark the post-Second World War Anglo-American movement in PHILOSOPHY that built upon and extended it (drawing on earlier strands of POSITIVISM and EMPIRICISM). Committed to empirical verifiability and logic, the original logical positivists were sceptical of theory, because it was neither facts nor operations of logic. Such scepticism could not be sustained in the face of the massive explosion (sometimes literal) of war and postwar SCIENCE defined by theoretical construction and empirical testing. Something had to give. In this case, 'empiricism' was substituted for the troubling term 'positivism' (and the root cause of the scepticism). Those working under the banner of logical empiricism were some of the pre-war logical positivists who had immigrated to the United States and there revised their position, such as

Rudolf Carnap (1891–1970) and Hans Reichenbach (1891–1953), but there were also American adherents, of whom perhaps the best known was Ernest Nagel (1901–85). David Harvey (1969) drew heavily on Nagel's logical empiricist justification of the scientific method in presenting his own argument for the importance of EXPLANATION in geography. TB

Suggested reading
Giere and Richardson (1996).

logical positivism A particular version of the PHILOSOPHY of POSITIVISM associated with the work of a group of primarily Austrian scientists and philosophers in the 1920s and 1930s known as the *Vienna Circle*. The convenor of the discussions at the University of Vienna in 1922 was the physicist Moritz Schlick, who invited figures such as the mathematician Kurt Gödel, philosophers Rudolf Carnap and Herbert Feigl, economist Otto Neurath and physicist Phillip Frank. On the edge of the circle but not strictly members were the philosophers Karl Popper (see CRITICAL RATIONALISM), A.J. Ayer (who later popularized the movement for an English-language audience) and Ludwig Wittgenstein.

Wittgenstein was behind the defining proposal of the group, 'the verifiability principle'. It asserted that scientifically meaningful propositions are those that (1) can be verified empirically by the five senses; or (2) are true tautologically – that is, their truth arises from the very meaning of the terms in which they are expressed such as in logic or mathematics. Propositions incapable of satisfying the principle, and which included most issues that made up the history of Western philosophy until that point concerning aesthetics, morality and religion, were judged senseless if not nonsense. Carnap declared that the Circle 'reject[s] all philosophical questions, whether Metaphysics, Ethics or Epistemology'. Meaningful propositions would be found in philosophy only when it modelled itself on the natural sciences, and particularly physics.

An immediate criticism was that the verifiability principle could not itself be verified: it was neither an empirical proposition, nor a logical or mathematical tautology. The Vienna Circle's criterion of meaning was thus, disturbingly, meaningless. Additionally, Popper argued early on that even those in the Circle's Pantheon, the physicists, did not engage in empirical verification but only FALSIFICATION: that is, they sought to disprove, not prove,

their theoretical claims. As a result of these objections, as well as the physical dispersal of the group (many were Jewish and left-wing and fled Vienna with the rise of Nazism), logical positivism quickly unravelled. By the 1950s, the movement was dead. Its extreme positions were discarded, and any useful ideas were absorbed within the larger movement of analytic and empiricist philosophy that came to define the post-Second World War Anglo-American field (Reisch, 2005).

In HUMAN GEOGRAPHY, however, Guelke (1978, p. 46) suggests that 'from Hartshorne to Harvey geographical writing on methodology and philosophy has to a greater or lesser degree shown the influence of logical positivist ideas'. But Hartshorne's (1939) panegyric tome on regional description as the core of the geographical project makes no reference to logical positivism or, indeed, to a single logical positivist. It was in fact Hartshorne's methodological arch enemy, Frederick Schaefer (1953), who came under the spell of logical positivism. He was influenced at the University of Iowa in the late 1940s and early 1950s by Gustav Bergmann, one of the Vienna Circle refugees, and became the first geographer to apply formal principles of logical positivism to geography through his work on morphological LAWS that were to take the form: '*If* spatial pattern A, *then* spatial pattern B.' Watered-down versions of logical positivism were subsequently proffered by an intellectual disciple of Schaefer, William Bunge (1966), and in the form of a textbook by two former graduate students at the University of Iowa, who took the mandatory Bergmann course (Amedeo and Golledge, 1975). All three contributions were part of the QUANTITATIVE REVOLUTON, the movement towards modelling the study of geography on the natural sciences in general, and physics in particular, as part of the project of SPATIAL SCIENCE. That said, many quantitative revolutionaries were ignorant of logical positivism, and not interested anyway. Harvey's (1969) prospectus for scientific EXPLANATION in geography bears only traces of logical positivism. Its central preoccupation was the scientific method, not philosophy as such, and certainly not the philosophy of logical positivism: Harvey's understanding of the scientific method was indebted, rather, to LOGICAL EMPIRICISM. Furthermore, both Harvey and the discipline at large were subsequently to move away from this version of the scientific method, rendering discussions of the usefulness of logical positivism of only historical value. TB

Suggested reading
Guelke (1978).

log-linear modelling Procedures for analysing data at the nominal level of MEASUREMENT – that is, when the variables comprised unordered categories (such as a binary division – urban/rural – or a set of political parties – Conservative/Labour/Liberal-Democrat etc.). The goal – as in REGRESSION (hence the alternative term *logistic regression*) – is to fit an equation that estimates the values in the cells of a contingency table, where the independent variables are also measured at either the nominal (categorical) or ordinal level only; models can also be fitted if one or more of the independent variables are measured at interval or ratio level. The terms of the MODEL, presented in logarithmic form, indicate the deviations from the individual cell values of the contingency table from the grand mean for the entire sample being analysed, and can be interpreted as the odds of getting a particular outcome (e.g. the likelihood that electors in urban areas are more likely to vote for one political party than those in rural areas). (See also CATEGORICAL DATA ANALYSIS). RJ

Suggested reading
O'Brien (1992).

logit regression models These models belong to the family of techniques for CATEGORICAL DATA ANALYSIS. They are used when the response variable is either binary (e.g. a person either moved or stayed) or a proportion (the proportion who have moved). The nature of this response variable, such that it cannot exceed 0 and 1, means that the standard REGRESSION model should not be used. Instead, the logit (the logarithm of the odds of moving) is modelled and the random part of the model takes on a binomial form so that the stochastic variation (see STOCHASTIC PROCESS) around the underlying relationship is structured to be least when the values of 0 and 1 are approached. Although the modelling is undertaken on the logits, it is simple to transform these to both probabilities and odds for interpretation. The popularity of this form of the binary response model stems from the ability when the predictor is categorical of giving a relative odds interpretation, generating, for example, the relative odds of a person aged over 35 moving in comparison to someone aged under 35.

The multinomial form of the logit model is used when there are more than two possible outcomes; the conditional form is used when analysing choice alternatives and the predictor variables may include attributes of the choice alternatives (e.g. cost) as well as characteristics of the individuals making the choices (such as income); the multi-level logit (see MULTI-LEVEL MODELLING) assesses the effects of variables measured at different levels (such as individual, household and NEIGHBOURHOOD EFFECTS on an individual moving); and the nested logit model is used when there is a hierarchical structure to the outcomes (with moves broken down into short- and long-distance, for example). KJ

Suggested reading
Hensher and Greene (2004); Hosmer and Lemshow (2000).

longitudinal data analysis (LDA) A set of QUANTITATIVE METHODS that involve measures over time. In contrast to time-series analysis, in which there tends to be one entity measured a large number of times (cf. SEQUENCE ANALYSIS), LDA is usually concerned with a large number of entities (e.g. people, places or firms) measured a relatively few times. Data for such analysis come from extensive designs (see EXTENSIVE RESEARCH) such as panel or cohort studies. LDA is increasing in importance because it allows the study of development and change, including: the transition from one state to another (e.g. from single to married to separated); the time spent in a particular state (e.g. the length of unemployment); and the determinants of such duration. LDA is fundamental to adopting a life-course perspective in which people are affected by cumulative stimuli over a long period.

The value of such an approach can be seen by contrasting the data analysis of cross-sections with that of a panel. In the former, because we are measuring different people at each time point, we can only assess net or aggregate change – we can only know, for example, that the percentage of the population below the poverty line has increased from 10 to 12. But with panel data we can assess the volatility of micro-social change as individuals move in and out of poverty, thereby tackling questions about the permanent nature of an UNDERCLASS. Such questions are of particular importance in EVIDENCE-BASED POLICY when we are concerned with either affecting change or removing barriers to change. Cross-sectional analysis can also be misleading about the direction of causality, for without repeated measures over time we cannot distinguish between, say, unemployment causing

431

illness or illness causing unemployment. Measurements over time usually show strong state dependence in that individuals do not move rapidly and continually between different states, so that current behaviour is influenced by past or previous behaviour. Only LDA is capable of taking account of prior information when examining current situations. Moreover, only longitudinal data can separate age and COHORT effects – the life experiences of those aged over sixty years may be quite different between cohorts born before and after 1945. Unlike cross-sectional analysis, which analyses variation between cases, LDA also works within cases between occasions. As such, it is much better able to take account of 'unobserved heterogeneity', unexplained variation due to the omission of explanatory variables that are either un-measured or even un-measurable. LDA will improve control for such heterogeneity and help to provide a measure of the extent of its presence (Davies and Pickles, 1985).

Longitudinal data sets have a number of features that provide a challenge for analysis. Thus if the outcome has not yet occurred the sequence is censored, so that in an analysis of longevity there will be people who are still alive at the end of observation period. Standard statistical MODELS are based on the assumption of independence, but repeated measures over time are likely to be strongly autocorrelated. Missing data are also a particular problem, as the requirement of multiple follow-up often leads to attrition: this is a particularly challenging problem when the drop-out is informative, because it depends on what would have been observed if the person had not dropped out.

Technically, there are three broad sets of approaches to LDA:

- *Repeated measures analysis*, in which data on repeated occasions are seen as being nested within individuals, so that we can examine, for example, the growth of income over time and evaluate the changing gender gap; MULTI-LEVEL MODELLING is increasingly being used for such data, as it does not require the measurement of every individual on all occasions to allow between-individual, within-individual and between-occasion variation to be explicitly modelled.
- *Event history analysis* (duration analysis or hazard modelling) is concerned with the timing of transitions from one state to another, so that it is possible to test how the transition rate of moving from one state

(e.g. unemployed) to another (employed) is affected by other variables such as education level: these explanatory variables may be either time invariant (such as GENDER) and/or time varying. In such analyses, the dependent variable is the duration until event occurrence. Single non-repeatable event analysis (e.g. the transition to death) was developed first and is often called 'survival analysis', but it is now possible to analyse repeated events (e.g. multiple spells of unemployment and employment), competing risks (e.g. different reasons for leaving a job such as voluntary choosing another job, redundancy, retirement), multiple states (e.g. transitions between single, marriage and cohabitation states) and multiple processes (e.g. joint modelling of partnership and employment histories).

- SEQUENCE ANALYSIS, which works holistically to identify characteristic time-based trajectories.

These methods have been extended to model spatial choice (Wrigley, 1990), the duration of point patterns (Pellegrini and Reader, 1996) and spatial processes more generally (Waldorf, 2003). KJ

Suggested reading
Allison (1984); Blossfeld and Rohwer (2002); Dale and Davies (1994); Fitzmaurice, Laird and Ware (2004); Ruspini (2002); Singer and Willett (2003); Taris (2000); Wrigley (1986).

Los Angeles School A loose affiliation of Los Angeles-based geographers and urbanists, connected by their theorizations of the LA region and the implications of its dynamics for all cities. The School is associated with a notion of 'postmodern urbanism' and an argument that LA's complex urban form, new economic CLUSTERS and INEQUALITY signal the future of URBANISM (see POSTMODERNISM; POSTMODERNITY). Its members argue that contemporary urbanism can be understood less through the concepts of the CHICAGO SCHOOL and more through the fragmentary geography of Southern California (Dear, 2001). The School's work has been the subject of much criticism and debate continues on the efficacy of framing LA, or any single city, as an exemplar of urbanism (Dear and Dahmann, 2008; Mollenkopf, 2008; Simpson and Kelly, 2008). EM

Suggested reading
Dear (2001).

M

macrogeography The search for macro-SCALE empirical regularities in spatial distributions as a basis for generalizations about SPATIAL STRUCTURES. The approach was pioneered by a physicist, John Q. Stewart (1894–1972), and developed with William Warntz (1922–88) in a pioneering project funded by the American Geographical Society (cf. GEOGRAPHICAL SOCIETIES). Their lasting contributions to SPATIAL ANALYSIS/SPATIAL SCIENCE were (a) the concept of POPULATION POTENTIAL, a cartographic density surface that generalized point (and point-in-area) distributions and was used as a measure of ACCESSIBILITY, and (b) their research on the GRAVITY MODEL of spatial interaction and the related 'law of least effort'. (See also FRACTALS.)   RJ

Suggested reading
Warntz (1965).

malapportionment An electoral abuse in which districts are either defined or allowed to remain in use with unequal popula,tions/electorates, which thereby favours one party over another in the translation of votes into seats. The most successful malapportionment strategy for a party involves defining relatively small districts in areas where it is likely to win seats, and larger ones elsewhere, thereby enabling it to win more seats with the same total number of votes than opponents who win where seats are on average larger. Malapportionment was deemed unconstitutional by US courts in the 1960s, under the equal treatment (14th) Amendment to the Constitution, and all districts within a state must be redrawn with almost exactly the same population after each decennial census. British legislation also requires Parliamentary constituencies to be of equal size, but variations are allowed and produce malapportionment-like effects in the translation of votes into seats.   RJ

Suggested reading
Johnston, Pattie, Dorling and Rossiter (2001). See also http://www.aceproject.org/ace-en/topics/bd/bdy/bdy_us/

Malthusian model An influential and controversial MODEL of population and RESOURCES, proposed by Thomas Malthus (1766–1834). Malthus read mathematics at Cambridge and was then ordained in 1793. He published his *Essay on the principle of population* in 1798 and soon became a controversial figure. The first edition of the *Essay* was written as a counter to William Godwin's *Enquiry concerning political justice* (1793) and the radical interpretation of the science of politics and the means of social improvement associated with the French Revolution in general and the Marquis de Condorcet in particular. Malthus was far less optimistic than his antagonists, maintaining that misery and vice were the inevitable result of the fundamental law of NATURE, which was impervious to institutional and legislative change.

Malthus specified two 'postulata': that FOOD was necessary for life and that the 'passion between the sexes' could be regarded as a constant. He then gave mathematical form to his basic *Principle*: a maximum potential rate of population growth in the form of the geometric ratio (1,2,4,8,16 . . .) with an assumed arithmetic growth (1,2,3,4,5 . . .) in food supply. Malthus recognized that population growth would be curtailed either by a rise in MORTALITY associated with what he saw as 'positive checks' (WAR, DISEASE, starvation) or through a reduction in births through 'preventative checks' (adultery, birth control, abortion or infanticide), although he was inclined to regard these as all variants of 'misery and vice'. This was a deductive model, but it was given empirical substance through Malthus' interest in the population growth that had been observed in the American population, where large acreages of land were made available to settlers who had few if any subsistence constraints.

Malthus' pessimism about the prospects for England and the Old World in the first edition was tempered somewhat in the much larger and thoroughly researched second edition, published in 1803, in which he was more optimistic than other political economists such as Smith and Ricardo, and held out the possibility of a better balance between numbers and resources achieved through moral restraint, which he primarily regarded as a restraint on marriage. He was inclined to see certain

European societies as exhibiting NUPTIALITY controls, an observation that has led some to argue for a distinctive form of late and variable marriage age, particularly for women, in western EUROPE (Hajnal, 1965), and which has been used as a basis for understanding the notion of a *nuptiality valve* primarily responsible for English demographic growth rates rather than the positive check in the period between the sixteenth and early nineteenth centuries (Wrigley and Schofield, 1989 [1981]).

While the Malthusian model has been viewed as a particularly effective device through which to understand a key period in England's demographic history, it has also received much criticism. It is thought to have failed as predictor of the future, at least in its more pessimistic form, since population growth was sustained at a high rate through much of the nineteenth century, and living standards rose and fertility fell as populations resorted increasingly to marital fertility control, and at the same time infant and child mortality fell dramatically, principally as a result of eradication of infectious disease, largely through relatively low-cost public health interventions. Of course, others would argue that Malthus' arguments applied largely to an *inorganic economy* in which land was in fixed supply and the principal source of energy was the sun, and animal and human muscle power, so that when human societies began to use locked-up ENERGY in the form of coal and oil, the constraints that Malthus took as a basis for this approach were removed. A major criticism of Malthus' notion of FAMINE as a positive check brought about by OVERPOPULATION is associated with the work of Amartya Sen (1981), who has suggested that few if any FAMINES can be directly attributed to food availability declines but, rather, to institutional and MARKET failures in delivering food to those whose entitlements were not being met. Critics have also rejected Malthus' conservative acceptance of the political status quo and his objection to welfare from the collectivity in the form of poor relief, which he supposed undermined the willingness of populations to exercise moral restraint (Winch, 1998). More recently, historical demographers of ASIA in particular have taken issue with Malthus' inherent EUROCENTRISM, reflected in his portrayal of China as exemplifying a high-pressure demographic regime in which unrestricted fertility and high mortality brought about recurrent crises as populations grew to sizes far too large for their food base (Lee and Feng, 1999). Such critics emphasize the role

of breast-feeding, birth spacing and infanticide as means of constraining reproduction, notwithstanding early marriage of women, and stress the presence of effective welfare institutions, particularly controls on grain supplies and markets as insulation against harvest failure.   RMS

map A representation of all or a portion of the planet or some other vast environment: the typical map is graphic and includes discernible elements of SCALE, projection (see MAP PROJECTION) and symbolization. As this definition suggests, delineating the notion of *map* is hardly straightforward (Andrews, 1996). For one thing, not all maps are graphic, and even though the term is derived from the Latin *mappa* (the cloth-paper on which early maps were inscribed), not all graphic maps are drawn or printed on paper. Aerial photography and REMOTE SENSING gave rise to the *image map*, which has scale, projection and symbol-like tones, and readily becomes a cartographic map with the addition of line symbols or feature names. DIGITAL CARTOGRAPHY introduced the *digital map*, which can be queried and analysed by a GEOGRAPHIC INFORMATION SYSTEM (GIS) without ever creating a graphic image. Definitions that include the TERRITORY mapped are problematic insofar as telescopes and rocketry, in making possible maps of the Moon, Mars, other planets or various asteroids (not to mention representations of the solar system, galaxies and the universe), have rendered 'graphic representation of Earth' inaccurately narrow. Robinson and Petchenik (1976, p. 16), who worried that 'representation of the environment' might unduly privilege physical features, contrived the relatively neutral but rarely used 'graphic representation of the milieu'. Harley and Woodward (1987, p. xvi), in promoting the history of cartography (see CARTOGRAPHY, HISTORY OF) as a scholarly endeavour, offered the comparatively wordy definition 'graphic representations that facilitate a spatial understanding of things, concepts, conditions, processes or events in the human world', which concisely describes the focus of most contemporary scholars who claim CARTOGRAPHY as a specialization. As this last definition implies, academic cartographers study not only cartographic artefacts but also the process of mapping and its impacts.

All map IMAGES have three principal elements: scale, projection and symbolization. *Scale* is defined as the ratio of distance on the map to the corresponding distance on the ground. When recorded as a ratio or fraction, a map's scale expresses these two distances in identical units of measurement, with map distance reported first as one unit, as in 1:10,000 or 1/10,000, which means that a centimetre on the map represents 10,000 cm on the ground. (A dimensionless number, 1/10,000, also indicates that an inch on the map represents 10,000 in on the ground.) Fractional representations of scale afford a distinction between large scales such as 1/5,000 and small scales with huge denominators. Scale may be expressed verbally, as in 'one inch represents one mile', which some users might find more helpful than the equivalent ratio 1:63,360 (Goodchild and Proctor, 1997). Maps often include a graphical scale, on which a carefully measured line, perhaps subdivided with appropriately labelled ticks, portrays one or more typical distances. Unlike ratio or verbal scales, a graphical scale remains true when the map is photocopied at a larger or smaller scale.

Cartographic scale is occasionally confused with *geographical scale*, which refers to the areal extent of a physical or human process or phenomenon (see SCALE). Physical geographers study entities that range in size from the small drainage basin in which soil permeability affects stream discharge to the global stage of atmospheric circulation and climate change. Social, political and economic processes also involve a range of scales, in which a specific process or phenomenon is usually associated with a particular level in a hierarchy ranging from 'local' to 'global', perhaps with intermediate levels labelled 'provincial', 'national' and 'continental'. When a geographical phenomenon is represented graphically, cartographic scale is typically determined by the size of the page, map sheet or display screen as well as the map's *geographical scope*; that is, the area to be covered. That a map with a broad geographical scope typically has a small scale, while a map with a narrow geographical scope often has a comparatively large scale, underscores the inverse relationship between geographical scale and cartographic scale.

When a major portion of the planet is represented on a flat map, scale will vary markedly, not only from place to place but also with direction (see MAP PROJECTION). The latter distortion is particularly obvious on rectangular world maps, on which the poles are as long as the equator, while angles and small shapes are noticeably more distorted in poleward regions than at lower latitudes. A noteworthy exception is the Mercator projection, which is

conformal, meaning that scale at a point is the same in all directions, even though scale varies enormously across the map. Devised to solve a specific problem in navigation by rendering lines of constant geographical direction as straight lines, the Mercator projection famously enlarges the size of mid-latitude countries, relative to tropical nations, and because north–south scale equals east–west scale everywhere, the poles lie at infinity. While its conformality makes the Mercator projection an acceptable choice for large-scale maps with a comparatively small geographical scope, it is a poor framework for world maps that have nothing to do with navigation.

Because a map's *projection* determines the type and pattern of distortion, and thus affects the viewer's perception of size, shape, distance and direction, selecting an appropriate projection is a crucial decision for the map author (Canters, 2002). An appropriate projection is especially important for a world map, which should never include a graphical scale because extreme distortions are unavoidable. For most thematic maps, a projection that preserves relative area is desirable, although the more extreme distortions of shape found on equal-area maps of the whole world can be mollified by a compromise framework such as the Robinson projection, which attempts to balance distortions of area and angles (Ipbuker, 2004). The point or line at which a whole-world map is centred is also important, not only because distortion is usually low near the centre but also because territories thus favoured might be perceived as more important or accessible than those on the periphery. Another useful compromise is the interrupted projection, typified by Goode's homolosine equal-area projection, which partitions the world map into six lobes, for which separate, locally centred projections minimize shape distortion for continents and coastlines.

The third principal element of a map is the graphic coding of geographical features, or *symbolization*. Although labels that connote land masses, oceans and cities can expedite decoding, standardized symbols that draw on cartographic conventions, such as blue for hydrographic features and green for vegetation, are especially helpful for at-a-glance assessments of their extent. Also useful are logical linkages between a map's content and the six 'retinal variables' readily manipulated by the map author. As defined by Bertin (1983), non-verbal cartographic symbols typically vary in shape, pattern, hue, orientation, size and greytone value, each of which is especially suited for portraying a particular kind of geographical variation. For example, hue, related to wavelength of visible light and often associated with named colours such as red and green, is appropriate for representing qualitative differences among, for example, various categories of land use. Bertin's rationale was straightforward: because red, green, and yellow look different to persons with normal color vision, they are ideal for mapping differences in kind, especially for area features large enough to require discernible patches of hue. Similarly, readily recognized differences in form among point and line symbols make shape an appropriate visual variable when a map must distinguish churches from schools and footpaths from railways. By contrast, quantitative data are better represented with symbols that vary in size or greytone value; that is, relative darkness. Viewers are well served by map authors who distinguish between count or magnitude data such as total population or number of employees, and intensity data such as population density or the proportion of the labour force unemployed. With count data, for example, point symbols that vary in size support a logical larger-means-more metaphor that promotes comparisons without looking repeatedly at the map key, whereas for intensity data symbols ranging from white to black support an equally obvious darker-means-more decoding rule (Monmonier, 2005). Although symbols that vary in direction are logical for representing phenomena such as wind direction and one-way streets, pattern variation is largely limited to dashed-line symbols and area symbols, such as the arrays of dots that connote orchard land and vineyards on TOPOGRAPHIC MAPS. Dynamic cartography has produced additional visual variables, notably the duration, rate of change and order of scenes (DiBiase, MacEachren, Krygier and Reeves, 1992).

Because place and feature names use natural language to link cartographic symbols to specific locations, typography is another important part of the map's symbolic code (Wood, 2000). And because type comes in various shapes and sizes, map labels reflect conventions such as the use of italic type for hydrographic features as well as an extension of Bertin's theory of retinal variables. Although aesthetic dictates that map authors avoid using numerous typefaces to represent qualitative differences among places or features, style variations (roman/italic, all-uppercase/initial capitals, bold/plain, underlining) support the typographical coding of differences in kind, whereas type size affords a readily decoded representation of magnitude. Some reference maps use a redundant coding in which the sizes of point symbols and their labels offer a mutually reinforced treatment of population size.

Names on maps can have deep cultural–political significance, especially when conquest or revolution allows the victor to rename places and geographical features, and even install a new language or orthography (writing system). As illustrated by the renaming and re-renaming of St Petersburg in Russia, control of a country's official cartography presents an irresistible opportunity to underscore the loser's defeat by replacing its toponyms (PLACE NAMES). As pervasive symbols of domination, names on map and road signs can arouse resentment as well as inspire alternative cartographies similar to the Palestinian maps of Israel, rendered crudely in Arabic atop photographic copies of official maps (Kadmon, 2000, pp. 80–1). And because maps reveal otherwise obscure, pejorative feature names inherited from earlier, less politically sensitive times, they can trigger the belated removal of names (Monmonier, 2006). Recent disputes over cartographic labels have focused on waters separating feuding countries (e.g. Sea of Japan/East Sea, Persian Gulf/Arabian Gulf), the toponyms and orthography of indigenous peoples (e.g. in Hawaii and northern Canada) and a country's right to police the rendering of its name beyond its borders (e.g. Macedonia and Myanmar, both resisted by the USA).

Because cartographic scale is usually too small for an exact treatment of shape and other geometric relationships, maps are almost always generalized, even large-scale maps of small areas (Buttenfield and McMaster, 1991). Cartographic generalization begins with the selection of features, some of which represent the phenomenon portrayed while others provide a frame of reference linking new information to the viewer's existing understanding of the region mapped. For example, coastlines, national BOUNDARIES and highway networks are common frame-of-reference features on maps not explicitly concerned with coastal geomorphology, GEOPOLITICS or transportation. Map authors must select features carefully, because legibility often requires line and point symbols proportionately thicker than the features portrayed. For instance, a road five metres wide represented on a 1:50,000 map by a barely visible line one millimetre thick occupies a cartographic corridor corresponding to a ground swathe 50 metres across. Because the exaggeration is much greater at very small scales as well as for boundaries and contour lines, which in principle have no width, the map author must not only eliminate less significant features but also smooth out meandering streams and contorted coastlines, displace symbols that would otherwise overlap, and replace the intricate boundaries of small cities with tiny circles (Dutton, 1999). Visibility and coherence might also require, as examples, the widening of narrow entrances to important bays, the exaggeration of an important kink (jog) in a road, the amalgamation of distinct but adjoining patches for forested land, and the blurring of distinctions between diverse types of cropland. Additional accommodations are often needed to create room for important labels – although well-known abbreviations can shorten street and feature names, failure to label key features invites confusion or misinterpretation.

Generalization can be especially problematic with statistical maps, which are notorious for using aggregated counts or averages to describe trends in CENSUS data. A uniform area symbol for a large, inherently diverse NATION or county can suggest an unwarranted homogeneity as well as dilute coherent patterns obvious on maps with smaller, more reliable areal units (Crampton, 2004). Potentially troublesome are CHOROPLETH maps, readily generated with commercial, off-the-shelf mapping software that arbitrarily chops the range from lowest to highest data values into five equal intervals, which are then portrayed with a spectral sequence of hues (blue, green, yellow, orange, red) that defies the logical darker-means-more metaphor for area symbols representing intensity data (Brewer, 1997).

Maps can be categorized in numerous ways, to reflect their content (e.g., topographic map, street map), symbolization (e.g., choropleth map), intended use (e.g., CADASTRAL MAPPING, road map), publisher (e.g., government map, commercial map), format (e.g. wall map, atlas map, newspaper map) or medium (e.g. paper map, video map). Especially noteworthy are several new map forms that emerged solely or largely during the twentieth century. Image maps, rooted in the invention of the hot-air balloon and photography in the eighteenth and nineteenth centuries, became an important mapping technology with the development of fixed-wing aircraft, helicopters and artificial satellites, as well as customized cameras and electronic scanners used in remote sensing (Dahlberg, Luman and Vaupel, 1990). Also known as photomaps, image maps have become a valuable supplement to the conventional topographic 'line map', so called because features are inscribed by crisp symbols rather than inferred from tonal contrast. Although a single aerial photograph is a perspective view, with distances distorted locally by variation in elevation, photogrammetry allows the compilation of topographic maps from overlapping aerial photographs as well as the efficient generation of distortion-free, 'orthorectified' photomaps (as in Google Earth: www.earth.google.com).

Electronic technology has radically altered the appearance and usability of maps. Animated maps, first produced on film but now generated by software, treat time as a scalable entity and afford historical maps with two scales, for example, 'ten seconds represents one year' for time and 'one inch represents five miles' for distance (Harrower, 2004). Dynamic maps afford dramatic fly-by renderings of terrain or statistical surfaces, while interactive topographic maps overcome conventional treatments of scale and generalization by letting viewers zoom in or out. Interactive maps that let users retrieve additional information by clicking on or merely rolling over a symbol can remove the inherent uncertainty of categories on a choropleth map, or promote a fuller understanding of an unfamiliar country or a local hazardous waste site (see VISUALIZATION). The INTERNET not only expedites the delivery of geographic information, such as timely radar weather maps, but also affords instant access to historic maps in public archives and free, advertiser-supported route maps with supplementary verbal directions. Societal impacts are especially apparent in Web-based DELIBERATIVE MAPPING, which fosters negotiated solutions of planning or political issues by multiple authors (Wiegand, 2002), and in a 'cybercartography' that promises a wider exploitation of multi-sensor formats, an unprecedented degree of integration and customized products, and inevitable challenges for designers, politicians and scholars (Taylor, 2003). (See also MAP READING.)   MM

Suggested reading
Brewer (2005); Dorling and Fairbairn (1997); MacEachren (1995); Monmonier (1993); Peterson (2003); Southworth and Southworth (1982).

map projection A geometric transformation of the spherical world on to a flat MAP. Map

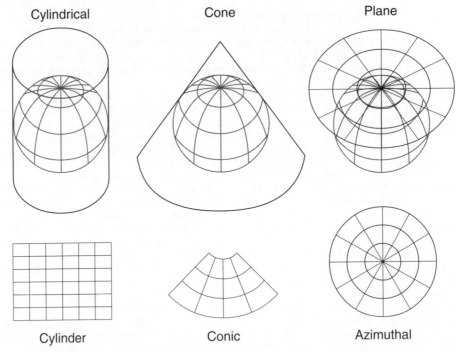

map projection *Principal developable surfaces (above) generate distinctive projection grids (below)*

projection is readily understood as a two-stage process that begins by shrinking the world to a hypothetical GLOBE, which establishes the map's stated SCALE. The second stage develops an azimuthal, a conic or a cylindrical projection by transferring meridians, parallels, coasts and boundaries on to, respectively, a plane, cone or cylinder. Each of these three developable surfaces has a distinctive grid of meridians and parallels. Sometimes a third stage readjusts locations and shapes, as when the sinusoidal projection corrects for the enlarged poleward areas on a cylindrical projection by bending meridians inward towards a central meridian.

Because of unavoidable stretching, compression or shearing, map scale generally varies from place to place across the projection as well as with direction at a point. On a cylindrical projection, for instance, scale in the north–south direction might be constant while east–west scale grows indefinitely large near the poles. In general, scale will equal the stated scale only at the point, line, or lines of contact between the globe and the developable surface. Moreover, distortion increases with distance from the tangent point or standard line, the location of which positions a zone of comparatively low distortion. Allowing the

developable surface to penetrate the globe provides a ring of low distortion on an azimuthal projection and two zones of low distortion on a conic or cylindrical projection. A map author can tailor a projection to a specific country or region by carefully selecting the developable surface and its orientation to the globe (Robinson and Snyder, 1991; Canters, 2002).

Many perspectives and orientations are possible. Although all projections distort most distances, an equidistant projection might preserve true distance from the Equator, one of the poles or some other point of interest. Similarly, an equivalent projection can preserve the true relative areas of countries and CONTINENTS, whereas a conformal projection, which preserves small shapes as well as angles around points, is especially useful on large-scale maps of small areas. Unfortunately, equidistance, equivalence and conformality are mutually exclusive.

Because the mapped area of a country or region can be seen as signifying its importance, the well-known Mercator projection, which significantly reduces the relative size of tropical nations, has been attacked as biased and EUROCENTRIC, with the most strident objections emanating from proponents of the Gall–Peters projection, an equal-area map touted as 'fair to all peoples' despite severe north–south stretching in the Tropics and comparatively reliable shapes and angles across western Europe and the northern USA (Monmonier, 2004b). Several other equal-area projections offer a more balanced pattern of shape distortion, and numerous compromise projections attempt to balance distortions of area and angles. Map authors eager to focus on people, rather than land area, can map socio-economic data on a CARTOGRAM, on which area represents population (Tobler, 1963).   MM

Suggested reading
Monmonier (2004b); Snyder (1993).

map reading The process of extracting information from a MAP, which is fundamental cartographic practice (see CARTOGRAPHY). Textbooks on the reading and use of maps and GLOBES were produced from the 1500s onwards, as a required part of a noble or genteel education. After 1650, they became a mainstay of public discourse and, after 1800, of regularized primary education in centralizing European states. Exercises in map-reading were integral to *Heimatkunde*, the initial stage of the formal curriculum in geography adopted in German primary schools after 1871 and subsequently emulated throughout western Europe and Japan. After 1900, the interpretation of larger-scale TOPOGRAPHICAL MAPS developed as a key skill for the study of landscapes within both academic geography and the military (cf. MILITARY GEOGRAPHY). Militaries have generated a variety of technical manuals, and military-orientated tasks dominated the curricula of introductory map-reading courses in many US universities after the Second World WAR. The needs of the military also drove academic research in cartography and HUMAN GEOGRAPHY into the cognitive processes of map reading to support the production of maps that could be read easily and effectively, while BEHAVIOURAL GEOGRAPHY included research into the development of map-reading skills among CHILDREN and adults (and also their production of MENTAL MAPS).

In all these circumstances, map reading has been understood as comprising four tasks, regardless of map SCALE:

(1) the identification and location of particular places;
(2) navigation, which entails route-selection, position-verification and anticipation of the future;
(3) the identification of patterns, distributions and morphologies of spatial features;
(4) the cartometric endeavours of taking measurements from maps, whether as simple as determining distances or areas or as complex as the statistical analysis of a map's geometrical accuracy (Maling, 1989).

These tasks have all been applied to old as well as modern maps (see CARTOGRAPHY, HISTORY OF). In terms of ONTOLOGY, such map-reading practices sustain the modern ideology of cartography (see also CARTOGRAPHIC REASON). Their repeated performance within authoritative STATE institutions has naturalized the expectation that maps are intended to be used *only* in such specific ways. (The automatic reaction to critical approaches to cartography is thus to appeal to the functional authority and so legitimation of the road map.)

Against this limited and only partially adequate perspective, recent critics have sought to read maps as cultural documents, to elucidate their cultural and social significance (Edwards, 2003). Two approaches are especially rewarding. Strongly influenced by art-historical studies in ICONOGRAPHY, Harley (2001b) construed maps to comprise two layers of meaning: an overt layer of factual data, directly accessed through standard map-reading techniques, and an obscured layer of cultural meaning to be elucidated through identification and consideration of a map's conventional and iconological symbolism. Wood and Fels (in Wood, 1992, pp. 95–142) advanced a more systematic analysis of maps as semiotic systems in their reading of a common road map; their essay has deservedly become the PARADIGM of critical map interpretation. Even so, their analysis of the differential and structured deployment of signs was preliminary. That is, the desideratum of a comprehensive and rigorous methodology for reading maps as cultural documents remains to be completed. (See also CULTURE.)   MHE

Suggested reading
Edwards (2003); Wood (1992, esp. pp. 95–142).

market The market is indisputably an example of what Raymond Williams (1976) called a 'keyword'. It is as a consequence rather complex, its meanings have been unstable historically, and its use and deployment always 'inextricably bound up with the problems it was being used to discuss' (p. 15). Adam Smith famously noted that there was an intrinsic human propensity to truck, barter and exchange things – in other words, to commodify the world through active participation in markets (cf. ECONOMY). Yet one of the great paradoxes of contemporary economics is that most textbooks do little to dispel the notion that markets are magical or supernatural, reflecting the extraordinary (and sometimes UTOPIAN) powers of the hidden hand. None other than Nobel Laureate Ronald Coase noted that markets had a 'shadowy role' in economic theory at least until they attracted the attention of other Nobel Laureates such as George Akerloff and Joseph Stiglitz (see McMillan, 2002).

How, then, is the term 'market' deployed? One meaning is resolutely empirical and geographical: it is a 'public place where a market is held', where the latter is 'a meeting together of people for the purpose of trade by private purchase and sale' (Online Merriam-Webster Dictionary). In this sense, of course, markets have a very deep history – commodities exchanged through some medium (money) – extending back millennia. Numismatic research suggests that while there were no formal markets as such, proto-monies facilitating exchange may date back 10,000 years; gold coins were certainly in circulation 2,500 years ago in Turkey, and the Sumerians had made use of silver bars as a money 2,000 years earlier. Markets are also in the business of commodity circulation. Markets facilitate and promote generalized COMMODITY circulation. The multiplication of markets – the purchase and sale of virtually everything – implies commodification and the expansion of the commodity frontier to every nook and cranny of the world we inhabit (Willams, 1983 [1976]). Even if some domain of our social world remains immune to the deadly conceits of the market, the extent to which the logic of the marketplace has insinuated our culture and social life is historically unprecedented: we do not as a matter of right or principle buy and sell children, and yet human organs, sperm and ova can and are part of brisk market exchanges. There can even be markets in ABSTRACTIONS and fictions – in climatic risk, in future bundles of currencies, in derivatives.

Yet this dictionary definition is superficial, because it says little of what actually constitutes – and what are the conditions of possibility of – market transactions. Most economists – influenced by TRANSACTION COST analysis, by the studies of economic norms, and by the INSTITUTIONALISM of some forms of NEO-CLASSICAL ECONOMICS (see Williamson, 1985) – identify DECISION-MAKING

autonomy and participation as key to market operations: buyers and sellers willing participate in the exchange and can veto any deal (McMillan, 2002). The purported 'freedom' of the market – buyers and sellers controlling their own resources and not acting under (extra-economic) compulsion – turns on choices and preferences subject to certain constraints (on their resources and the 'rules' of the market). Several aspects of this definition are important. First, where an authority relationship shapes the transaction, it is not a market transaction (it is another sort of transaction: administered or forced or perhaps black market). Second, for the poor the degrees of freedom, participation and choice are very constrained. Bargaining power between buyer and seller is unequal, yet economists would see the right of veto as 'a kind of freedom'. Third, while competition is not a defining feature of the market (markets might be oligopolistic), there is a presumption that adds to autonomy (by virtue of there being alternatives). As a consequence of these attributes, a market transaction is typically defined as:

> An exchange that is voluntary; each party can veto it, and (subject to the rules of the market place) each freely agrees to the terms. A market is a forum for carrying out such exchanges. (McMillan, 2002, p. 6)

Market transactions defined in this way are, of course, limited: markets are never wholly ubiquitous and there are realms in which the reach of the market is limited even in advanced capitalist states. Many of the transactions within HOUSEHOLDS, within firms and within governments are not market transactions as defined conventionally. Yet these non-market transactions take place within a universe of dominant market transactions and indeed are directly and indirectly shaped by the powerful logics of the operations of the market. It is also clear from the definition of market transaction that markets are always in a limited sense 'free'. They always have rules, more or less formal. They require patterns of TRUST and social convention. And, not least, they demand the role of government in defining PROPERTY RIGHTS, and typically providing complex bodies of LAW pertaining to contracts. All of this endorses the idea that there are many different forms of markets, that market transactions presuppose quantities and qualities of information (often unevenly unavailable – information asymmetries is the neoclassical argot), and that market transactions may be wildly different in their costs to buyer and seller alike.

When Simmel (1978) noted that EXCHANGE is one of the 'purest and most primitive of forms of human socialization', he endorsed the idea that a market is a SOCIAL CONSTRUCTION. As Stanford economist John McMillan puts it: for markets to work they must be 'well built': the field of market design, accordingly, refers to the analysis and pragmatics – the purposeful building – of institutions for transacting market exchanges. As McMillan says:

> Market design consists of the mechanisms that organize buying and selling; channels for the flow of information; state-set laws and regulations that define property rights and sustain contracting; and the markets culture, its self-regulating norms, codes and conventions governing behavior ... A workable design keeps in check transaction costs ... Transaction costs are many and varied. (2002, p. 9)

And yet even in acknowledging these properties, it is not unusual to hear the claim from economists that 'no one is in charge of the market' (McMillan, 2002, p. 7). And to this extent, as Vaclav Havel once put it, the market 'is the only natural economy'. This, of course, raises another meaning of market that is both ideological and political (see IDEOLOGY). In addition to markets and market transactions, there is the idea of 'the market', or 'the market system' or 'the free market'. It is an abstract notion – abstracted from the actual interactions and functionings of many different forms of market – but one that arises in at a particular moment – its modern founding charter is associated with Adam Smith's *The wealth of nations* – and it has a long and complex history. Smith was fully aware of the fact that markets had their limits, that government provisions and PUBLIC GOODS were indispensable to the operations of markets, and that markets left to their own devices could in fact be destructive. And yet he retained the ideological notion that markets were natural – rooted in human impulses to truck, barter an exchange. There is, of course, an alternative narrative. Even at the time of Smith's writing, his world was awash with the operations of a distinctively *moral* economy that privileged use-value above exchange-value (Thompson, 1991) and of claims for a just price. Popular reactions in defence of an arena that was seen to be beyond the market – the commons – defined much of what passed as politics (Neeson, 1993). At the very least, then, the

modern market was not so much natural as the product of struggle. And it is a struggle that is central to the operations of the market in the twenty-first century. The GLOBAL COMMONS represent a frontier of contemporary resistance to – and shaping of – the rules of the market (Saad-Filho and Johnson, 2005).

The contested nature of markets – in the details or their operations or as a utopian vision – is central to any understanding of ECONOMY, LIBERALISM and MODERNITY (Harvey, 2005). Karl Polanyi's *The great transformation* and Friedrich Hayek's *The road to serfdom* were both published in 1944. Hayek, an Austrian economist trained at the feet of Ludwig von Mises, but forever associated with a largely non-economic corpus produced at the London School of Economics and the universities of Chicago and Freiburg between 1940 and 1980, is widely recognized as one of the leading intellectual architects of the neo-liberal counter-revolution (see NEO-LIBERALISM). Margaret Thatcher pronounced that 'this is what we believe' as she slammed a copy of Hayek's *The constitution of liberty* on to the table at Number 10 Downing Street during a Tory Cabinet meeting. Hayek's critique of SOCIALISM – that it destroys morals, personal freedom and responsibility, impedes the production of wealth and sooner or later leads to totalitarianism – is the *ur* text for market utopians. Collectivism was by definition a *made* rather than a *grown* order: it was, Hayek said, constructivist rather than evolutionary, organized not spontaneous, a '*taxis*' (a made order) rather than a '*cosmos*' (a spontaneous order), an economy rather than a 'catallaxy', coerced and concrete rather than free and abstract (see Gamble, 1996, pp. 31–2). Its fatal conceit was that socialism (and social democracy for that matter) admitted the 'reckless trespass of *taxis* onto the proper ground of *cosmos*' (Anderson, 2005b, p. 16).

The other half of Hayek's project was a robust defence of Western CIVILIZATION – that is to say of liberty, SCIENCE and the spontaneous orders that co-evolved to form modern SOCIETY ('Great Society', as he termed it). It was a buttressing of the liberal (unplanned) market order from which the preconditions of civilization – competition and experimentation – had emerged. Hayek, like Weber, saw this world as an iron cage constituted by impersonality, a loss of community, individualism and personal responsibility. But unlike Weber, Hayek saw these structures, properly understood, as expressions of liberty. From the vantage point of the 1940s this (classical) liberal project was, as

Hayek saw it, under threat: what passed as liberalism was a travesty, a diluted and distorted body of ideas corrupted by constructivist rationalism (as opposed to what he called 'evolutionary rationalism'). The ground between liberalism and much of what passed as Keynesianism or social democracy was, on the Hayekian account, catastrophically slight. What was required, as he made clear at the founding of the Mont Pelerin Society in 1947, was a restoration, a purging of true liberalism (the removal of 'accretions'). There was to be no compromise with collectivism: the seized territory had to be regained. In his writing and his promotion of think-tanks such as the Institute of Economic Affairs in Britain – the brains trust for the likes of Keith Joseph and Margaret Thatcher – Hayek aggressively launched a cold war of ideas. He was part of the quartet of European theorists (Carl Schmitt, Leo Strauss and Michael Oakeshott were the others) whose ideas, while standing in a tense relationship to one another, have come to shape a large swath of the intellectual landscape of the early twenty-first century (see Anderson, 2005b). Hayek was neither a simple conservative or libertarian, nor a voice for *laissez-faire* ('false rationalism', as he saw it). He identified himself with the individualist tradition of Hume, Smith, Burke and Menger, thereby providing a bridge that linked his short-term allies (conservatives and libertarians) to classical liberals in order to make common cause against collectivism (Gamble, 1996, p. 101). To roll back the incursions of *taxis* required a redesign of the STATE. A powerful chamber was to serve as guardian of the rule of law (striking all under 45 years off the voting roll), protecting the law of liberty from the logic of popular sovereignty. As Anderson (2005a, p. 17) notes, the correct Hayekian formula was 'demarchy without democracy'.

Karl Polanyi was a Hungarian economic historian and socialist who believed that the nineteenth-century liberal order had died, never to be revived. By 1940, 'every vestige' of the international liberal order had disappeared, the product of the necessary adoption of measures designed to hold off the ravages of the self-regulating market (market despotism). It was the conflict between the market and the elementary requirements of an organized social life that made some form of collectivism or planning inevitable (Polanyi, 1944). The liberal market order was, *contra* Hayek, not 'spontaneous' but a planned development, and its demise was the product of the market order itself. A market order could just as well

produce the freedom to exploit as it could the freedom of association. The grave danger, in Polanyi's view, was that liberal utopianism might return in the idea of freedom as nothing more than the advocacy of free enterprise, the notion that planning is nothing more than 'the denial of freedom' and that the justice and liberty offered by regulation or control becomes nothing more than 'a camouflage of slavery' (1944, p. 258). Liberalism in this account will always degenerate, ultimately compromised by an authoritarianism that will be invoked as a counterweight to the threat of mass democracy. Modern CAPITALISM contained the famous 'double-movement', in which markets were serially and coextensively disembedded from, and re-embedded in, social institutions and relations – what Polanyi called the 'discovery of society'. In particular, the possibility of a counter-hegemony to the self-regulating market could be found in resistance to the commodification of the three fictitious commodities (land, labour and money): such reactions represented the spontaneous defence of society (Burawoy, 2003).

The market and anti-market mentalities of Hayek and Polanyi were both forged in the context of FASCISM, global economic depression, revolution and world WAR. To look back on the birth of *The great transformation* and *The road to serfdom* from the perch of 2008 is quite salutary: we see AMERICAN EMPIRE (military neo-liberalism), a global 'war on terror' (see TERRORISM), the dominance of unfettered global finance capital, a worldwide Muslim resurgence, a phalanx of 'failed states' (otherwise known as the failure of secular nationalist development) and a raft of so-called ANTI-GLOBALIZATION movements, and the rise of civic regulation. There has been, intellectually speaking, a consequent Polanyi boom (see Williams, 2005a) within the academy, but fewer careful readings of the Hayekian ideas that helped spawn these developments. From within the bowels of this turmoil, the Hayekian vision is triumphant – the Liberal International has come to pass. Its long march, from Mont Pelerin to the collapse of the Berlin Wall and TINA ('There Is No Alternative') took about forty years and, according to Harvey's (2005) brief history, passed through the Chicago Boys in Chile, the IMF/IBRD complex, the Reagan–Thatcher revolutions and the corporate (class) seizure of power in the 1970s against a backdrop of declining profitability and income share. Even if 'global neo-liberalism' has now assumed a neo-conservative and military cast (Saad-Filho and Johnson, 2005), nobody seems to question its HEGEMONY: as Gramsci might have put it, there has been a Hayekian 'passive revolution' from above as (Silver and Arrighi, 2003). We have witnessed what the Left's great pessimist Perry Anderson (2000c) has dubbed a 'neo-liberal grand slam', with NEO-LIBERALISM ruling undivided across the globe as the most successful ideology in world history (Anderson, 2002c). This 'fluent vision' of the Right has no equivalent on the Left: Anderson cedes that embedded liberalism (let alone something called socialism) is now as remote as 'Arian bishops', resistances are like 'chafe in the wind' and the Left can only 'shelter under the skies of infinite justice'. Of course, with the vertiginous collapse of Wall Street and a raft of financial institutions in late 2008, followed by the massive bailouts initiated by various governments in Europe and America, Anderson's grand slam now looks very different.

The very process by which neo-liberal market hegemony was established – and against which forms of RESISTANCE are to be assessed – remains a story for which at present we have no full genealogy. The cast of characters may be lined up – from the school of Austrian economics to the Reagan–Thatcher–Kohl troika – but this explains very little. Neo-liberalism can be seen as a CLASS reaction to the CRISIS of the 1970s. The global multilaterals and the Treasury–Wall Street certainly imposed brutal forms of economic discipline – STRUCTURAL ADJUSTMENT – to eradicate forever any residue of collectivism in the Third World. But beyond these general descriptions we are left with paradoxes and questions, of which I will list just a few. Why did the LSE and Chicago – the centres of Fabianism and a certain sort of American liberalism – become the forcing houses of neo-liberalism? Hayek, after all, was not associated with the Economics Department; it was the arrival of Ronald Coase at Chicago that marked a neo-liberal turning point. How did the World Bank – a bastion of postwar development economics and a certain sort of statism – become the voice of *laissez faire*? Harry Johnson (who held Chairs at the LSE and Chicago) certainly figures in the process, but how can we explain economic liberalism's capture of key sectors of the Bank (often by second-rate economists) against a backdrop of robust Keynesianism? How did the ideas of economists such as Peter Bauer and Deepak Lal gain traction? Criticism of Keynes dovetailed with the anti-statism levelled by many on the Left during the 1970s. In other words, tracing the ways in which government failures came to outweigh market failures in development thinking demands a complex picture of discursive contestations and political practices. Indeed, by the mid- to late 1970s many of neo-liberalism's intellectual architects (Milton Friedmann among them) claimed that nobody took their ideas seriously – Hayek believed that *The road to serfdom* had ruined his career and marginalized his entire project. It was the inflation of the 1970s, said Friedmann, that revealed the cracks within the Keynesian edifice. The point is that the 'neo-liberal grand slam' was preceded by decades of mediocrity, pessimism and contestation, and that the class forces around and through which embedded liberalism had been built necessarily shaped the manner and forms in which the counter-revolution could proceed (if at all). How to think about the power of *the* market now turns on how one sees this long march through institutions. The catastrophic collapse of the US investment banks and the discrediting of the various regulatory and financial rating agencies – with the prospect of a 1930s-style world depression in the offing – suggests that the neo-liberal project has come crashing to a halt. As the *New York Times* put it in early 2009, 'we are all Keynesians now'.   MW

Suggested reading
Elyachar (2005); Prasad (2006); Scabas (2007).

Markov process (or Markov chain) A type of STOCHASTIC PROCESS in which the probability of being in a particular state at time t is wholly dependent upon the state(s) at some preceding time(s). It is named after the Russian mathematician who first defined the process. The simplest form, known as a first-order Markov process, is where the dependence is entirely on just the immediately preceding state. This process can be represented by a transition probability matrix in which the rows and columns represent the different states and the cells represent the probabilities of movement between states. For example, migration movements between three regions A, B and C could be modelled as follows:

		State at time $t + 1$		
		A	B	C
State at time t	A	0.80	0.15	0.05
	B	0.08	0.90	0.02
	C	0.10	0.05	0.85

From this we may see that, between time t and time $t + 1$, 80 per cent of the population in A remain there, 15 per cent move to B and 5 per cent to C, and similarly for movements from regions B and C in rows 2 and 3. By repeated operation of the matrix, the population pattern redistributes to a stable pattern independent of the initial pattern (assuming no births, deaths or movements in or out of the total system). This Markov model has been used to study population MIGRATION, EPIDEMIC processes, the growth and movement of firms, and trends in regional economic convergence and divergence, and is a component of more sophisticated demographic modelling. LWH

Suggested readings
Collins, Drewett and Ferguson (1974); Rees and Wilson (1977).

Marxism The body of ideas and practices developed by Karl Marx (1818–83) and greatly elaborated since his death by his followers. His voluminous writings fall into several broad categories. First, there are those writings that develop a broad theory of history (HISTORICAL MATERIALISM) as a succession of MODES OF PRODUCTION, in which changes in economic and CLASS structures play a central dynamic role. Second, there are writings (such as the three volumes of *Capital*) that develop a more detailed POLITICAL ECONOMY of CAPITALISM as a mode of production, using the LABOUR THEORY OF VALUE to explore its underlying contradictions and tendencies to CRISIS. Third, there are various, more sketchy, writings on dialectical philosophy and method (see DIALECTICS). Fourth, there are a wide range of analyses of contemporary events, often designed to illustrate broader theories (such as *The eighteenth brumaire of Louis Napoleon*), polemical addresses and a mass of journalistic writings for various newpapers.

Marx did not present a single, codified version of his ideas, which in any case changed over the course of his lifetime. Some later Marxists, such as Louis Althusser (see Althusser and Balibar, 1970), have even claimed to detect a major 'epistemological break' in his work between the earlier more philosophical and 'humanist' texts, strongly influenced by Hegel, and the later, more 'scientific', analyses of political economy. Gouldner (1980) also sees a distinction between a younger and older Marx, but more in terms of a tension between a voluntaristic 'Critical Marxism' and a more deterministic 'Scientific Marxism'. Even those (the majority of commentators)

who prefer to stress the underlying continuities in his work differ in the emphases they place on different themes and texts. As a result of such multiple possible readings, Marxism has become more a family of theories with many strands than a single codified framework. This is part of its attraction and contributes to its continuing vitality.

Histories of Marxism usually identify several phases of development and divergence (McLellan, 1979). The first codified version of 'orthodox Marxism' was developed after Marx's death by Engels, Kautsky, Bernstein and Plekhanov, who published systematic expositions of historical and dialectical materialism, the nature of capitalism and the theory of revolution. Lenin subsequently adapted Plekhanov's orthodox 'stages' view of history to justify revolution in a backward capitalist state such as Russia. However, with the degeneration of the revolution and the onset of Stalinism, 'Marxism–Leninism' rapidly hardened into the official ideology of the centralized Soviet state.

The *Western Marxism* of Lukacs, Korsch, Gramsci and the Frankfurt School (Horkheimer and Adorno) was developed partly as a reaction against this dogmatism, shifting the emphasis away from political economy more towards neglected aspects of CULTURE, IDEOLOGY and ART. A return to Hegel and his influence on Marx provided an underlying philosophical thread to this work (see also CRITICAL THEORY).

The post-Second World War period has been marked by increasing internal diversity within the Marxist tradition, as Marxists have responded to, and interacted with, other developments in PHILOSOPHY and SOCIAL THEORY. Jean-Paul Sartre tried to blend a reinterpretation of Marxism with the philosophy of EXISTENTIALISM. Althusser developed a re-reading of Marxism – indebted, in part, to STRUCTURALISM – that attempted to save Marxism from what he regarded as the twin deviations of HISTORICISM and ECONOMISM. Althusserian Marxism presented a science of social systems, with a relative autonomy of levels 'structured in dominance' and an economy only 'determinant-in-the-last-instance'.

Althusser's structuralism provoked strong reactions, leading to a proliferation of new currents over recent decades. Harvey (1999 [1982]) has preferred to go back to Marx's own writings, demonstrating the continuing potential of an essentially 'orthodox' version of Marxism. The architects of ANALYTICAL MARXISM, such as Cohen, Roemer and Elster (Mayer, 1994), have sought to build micro-economic foundations for Marxism using RATIONAL CHOICE THEORY, and to displace dialectics with analytical philosophy and the labour theory of value with NEO-CLASSICAL ECONOMICS. Realist Marxists have sought to provide a stronger philosophical shell for Marxism by drawing upon recent developments in the philosophy of REALISM (Brown, Fleetwood and Roberts, 2002). Anti-essentialist Marxists have sought to expunge the last remnants of economic determinism from Althusserian Marxism (Resnick and Wolff, 1987; cf. ESSENTIALISM) and 'postmodernist Marxists' such as Laclau and Mouffe (1985) have tried to find a rapprochement with Jacques Derrida's DECONSTRUCTION (see also POSTMODERNISM; POST-STRUCTURALISM). Whether many of these lines of development are still definably 'Marxist' or whether they are 'POST-MARXIST' is an open, and perhaps irrelevant, question.

Indeed, some of the most interesting work is being generated through dialogues and critiques across boundaries, such as Deleuze and Guattari's (1984) conjunction, in *Capitalism and schizophrenia*, of Sigmund Freud, Marx and Baruch Spinoza, or *critical realist* attempts to find complementarities between Marx and Michel Foucault (Marsden, 1999) or Hardt and Negri's fusion of elements from Marx, Gilles Deleuze and Spinoza in their *Empire* (2000). There have also been vital engagements with HUMAN GEOGRAPHY. Many geographers have been influenced by the discipline's remarkably late reading of Marx: most other social sciences – notably anthropology, economics and sociology – had a much longer history of coming to terms with Marx and Marxism, but it would be a mistake to limit the influence of Marx's writings to the ongoing project of a MARXIST GEOGRAPHY, not least because so many of the other disciplines with which human geography has entered into conversation have themselves been marked by Marxism, and those traces have in turn left their own marks on geographical enquiry. There has also been a still more belated return movement, in which contemporary Marxism has started to come to terms with the core concerns of human geography. On one side, these have involved conceptual elaborations of PLACE, SPACE and NATURE that in turn require reformulations of some of Marxism's basic postulates. Harvey (1999 [1982]) in particular has sought to re-theorize Marxism as a historico-geographical materialism capable of addressing the characteristically UNEVEN DEVELOPMENT of capitalism (cf. PRODUCTION OF SPACE). On the other side, there has been

a constructive critique of the ETHNOCENTRISM of not only classical Marxism (where the formalization of an 'Asiatic' mode of production is today an embarrassment) but of the 'Westernness' of Western Marxism. This has involved an appreciation of the production of substantive geographical differences, which has been made possible by studies in REGIONAL GEOGRAPHY that have been revitalized by an engagement with a POST-COLONIALISM that has itself been inspired and provoked by Marx's legacy. As a result of these various challenges, critiques and conversations, Marxism continues to develop as a living tradition, interacting with surrounding currents in new ways, and spinning off a variety of hybrid forms.   KB

Marxist economics A heterodox field that spans the methodological gamut from structural and CLASS-centred relational and DIALECTICAL approaches to individual-centred RATIONAL CHOICE approaches. If something called 'Marxist economics' coheres, it is because of what it is not – namely, NEO-CLASSICAL ECONOMICS (however, subsets of rational choice Marxism that seek to give Marxist economics a 'micro-foundation' – these would include the projects of Adam Przeworski, Samuel Bowles, Herbert Gintis or John Roemer – veer perilously close to post-Walrasian variants of neo-classical theory). In the simplest formulation, Marxist economics, unlike its neo-classical counterpart, views individuals as *social beings*: as such, it emphasizes social structure more than individual behaviour. It draws attention to class struggle, which, it contends, is interwoven with every other aspect of society in complex and contradictory ways. The ECONOMY is understood as a terrain where class exploitation occurs and exerts its powerful influence over the rest of social life. 'Exploitation' is a key operator in most versions of Marxist economics, and refers to a 'class process in which the person who performs surplus labor is not also the person who appropriates it' (Wolff and Resnick, 1987, p. 167). Note that the description of Marxist economics so far is not confined to the analysis of CAPITALISM.

The historian Robert Brenner, for example, has offered a remarkable class-based analysis of the jagged transition from FEUDALISM to early capitalism in Western Europe and convincingly illustrated the generality of Marxist economics as a framework for understanding economic crises and growth cycles. Parting company with those rational-choice Marxists who claim that the institutional preconditions of ECONOMIC GROWTH are the outcome of (parametric or strategic) actions undertaken by sovereign economic actors (see Carver and Thomas, 1995), Brenner instead contends that it is unwarranted 'to take for granted a society of free economic actors, *rather* than one of economic actors subject to non-economic constraints' (Brenner, 1986, p. 25). Second, rationally self-interested action in such circumstances will, as a rule, exhibit the goal of maintaining existing PROPERTY relations, thereby impeding economic DEVELOPMENT; and, third, should economic development occur, it must be viewed – in light of the second premise – 'as an unintended consequence of ... conflicts between [antagonistic] classes' (ibid., p. 26).

The distinctive contribution of geographers to Marxist economics has been to show that capitalist dynamics are intrinsically GEOPOLITICAL. Thus, radical geographers such as David Harvey and Doreen Massey have demonstrated, in quite different ways, how class relations involving the extraction of surplus labour are stretched out spatially and profoundly implicated in differing patterns of UNEVEN DEVELOPMENT – whether locally, regionally or globally. Whereas studies such as those of Massey examine how PLACE-specific contingencies – including GENDER and RACE relations – mediate economic outcomes within wider SPATIAL STRUCTURES of capitalism, others such as Harvey have been more interested to elaborate how the historical and geographical dynamics of capitalism might be charted as corrective responses to recurring 'overaccumulation' crises that are generated by limits immanent to it. There is continuity here with the Marxist economics of Henryk Grossman, Ernest Mandel and James O'Connor who, in varying formulations, hitch Marx's theory of capitalist ACCUMULATION to the theory of CRISIS. (See also and MARXIST GEOGRAPHY; RADICAL GEOGRAPHY.)   VG

Suggested reading
Harvey (1985b); Massey (1995).

Marxist geography The analysis of the geographical conditions, processes and outcomes of socio-economic systems, primarily CAPITALISM, using the tools of Marxist theory. Marxist geography is significant both for its role in the evolution of the discipline and, more importantly, for its analytical claims about the world in which we live.

Marxism first became an important theoretical influence in GEOGRAPHY in the late 1960s and early 1970s. Motivated by the radical politics of that era, many younger geographers grew dissatisfied with the then-dominant vision of geography as a technocratic, POSITIVIST SPATIAL SCIENCE. They noted that: (i) a narrow focus on spatial patterns often left unexamined and unchallenged the social PROCESSES that produced the inequalities evident in those patterns; (ii) technically oriented, ostensibly neutral geographical techniques and analyses often served in practice to enable and perpetuate various relations of domination; and (iii) the 'universal laws' advanced by spatial analysts were often merely generalizations about industrialized Western societies. Marxist theory, by contrast, was DIALECTICAL, overtly political, focused on the analysis and remediation of exploitation and inequality, and internationalist. It therefore seemed to many an ideal theoretical foundation for a *critical* geography aimed at understanding and combating the production of unequal geographies. Radical geography framed in terms of Marxist theory grew quickly in the discipline: its arrival was signalled by the publication of the first issue of *Antipode* in 1969, and its theoretical architecture and points of departure from positivist spatial science were first laid out clearly in David Harvey's *Social justice and the city* in 1973.

For much of the 1970s and 1980s, Marxist approaches were the dominant ones in CRITICAL HUMAN GEOGRAPHY. Scholars working in this area developed increasingly comprehensive and detailed accounts of the geographical dynamics of capitalism, demonstrating persuasively both that Marxist theories of capitalism were incomplete without attention to spatial dynamics, and that identifiable capitalist processes and relations lay at the root of many issues of concern in contemporary human and environmental geography. Despite the fact that much of this work emerged from a critique of spatial science, some of it still bore the stamp of that theoretical tradition, inasmuch as much early Marxist geography sought to provide systematic, logical, deductive and generalizable accounts of the spatial processes and outcomes likely to result from endogenous dynamics understood as inherent to capitalism. David Harvey's *The limits to capital* (1999 [1982]) remains the single most ambitious and significant work in this vein. In this and other works, Harvey sought to build upon Marx's basic framework (see Marx, 1967 [1987]) to analyse the ways in which capitalism uses and produces space and particular geographical relationships. For instance, ongoing

UNEVEN DEVELOPMENT at multiple SCALES was interpreted as the inevitable result of the tension between the need for CAPITAL to be fixed in PLACE-bound material forms in order for production to occur on the one hand, and the imperative for it to remain liquid and mobile in the face of competition and shifting rates of profit in different places and sectors on the other. Similarly, Harvey explored how geographical relationships and strategies could be used to stave off CRISIS tendencies. Other work in this period was more historical in nature, examining the role that geographical relationships played in the origins of capitalism – whether those that concentrated large numbers of wage labourers in urban areas, thereby fostering class consciousness, or those that violently extracted and transferred labour and raw materials from colonies to industrializing core countries (e.g. Amin, 1976). Marxist geography (broadly conceived) also intersected productively with debates in THIRD WORLD Marxism in this period, leading to the development of explicitly geographical theorizations of the global capitalist economy, including WORLD SYSTEMS THEORY (Wallerstein, 1979) and DEPENDENCY THEORY (Frank, 1967), as well as critiques of the geographical imaginations underlying what often remained EUROCENTRIC conceptualizations of the global economy (Blaut, 1993). This brief review cannot do justice to the extent of Marxist geography in these decades, which also examined questions ranging from regional economic development strategies and industrial location decisions (e.g. Storper and Walker, 1989) to historical materialist interpretations of CULTURAL POLITICS (e.g. Harvey, 1989b). Marxist geographers' engagement with the discipline's NATURE–SOCIETY tradition proved highly fruitful as well: the intersection of Marxist theory, CULTURAL ECOLOGY and related work in the 1970s led directly to the burgeoning field now known as POLITICAL ECOLOGY (e.g. Watts, 1983a), while Neil Smith, focusing more on industrialized countries, made the strong claim that nature under capitalism was increasingly materially *produced* (1990). Such engagements sparked a line of work on the PRODUCTION OF NATURE that continues up to the present (e.g. Henderson, 1999), including debates about the primacy that such perspectives accord humans in general, and capitalist processes in particular, in the co-construction of nature. Much recent work in Marxist geography has focused less on structuralist MARXIST ECONOMICS, and sought instead to provide critical ETHNOGRAPHIES of capitalist societies (Postone, 1993; see, e.g.,

Chari, 2004; Wright, 2004), while at the same time re-evaluating core Marxist concepts, such as primitive accumulation, in light of contemporary geographies (e.g. Glassman, 2006).

Marxist geography itself soon became an object of critique, however, not least because of its very scope. Beginning in the early 1990s, much critical theory in geography and related fields moved strongly towards 'POST-MARXIST' theoretical frameworks that accept many basic elements of Marxist theory (e.g. the centrality of commodification and exploitation in capitalist societies) while criticizing much Marxism as fatally 'modern'; that is, as an overly ambitious and totalizing meta-theory that seeks to explain nearly all human experiences, DIFFERENCES and POWER relations via a narrow, economistic schema in which interests, conflicts, outcomes and even forms of consciousness can be deterministically read off from the position of an individual or group within relations of production (see Castree, 1999b). Whether such critiques rest upon a fair reading of all Marxist theory is debatable, but what is beyond question is that in recent years many critical geographers have found Marxism unhelpful, and sometimes even a hindrance, in attempts to analyse and combat multiple and intertwined forms of oppression. Instead, theoretical frameworks broadly characterizable as post-structuralist (see POST-STRUCTURALISM) have dominated critical geography in recent years, providing different entry points and tools with which to grapple with the problematics of GENDER, RACISM, SEXUALITY, POST-COLONIALISM and what might constitute 'Left' or radical politics in the contemporary era. Gibson-Graham (2006b [1996]), for instance, made a widely influential argument that Marxism often grants 'capitalism' far more coherence and power than it actually has, and that radical politics would be better pursued by seeking to identify and foster more modest alternatives to capitalist relations from the ground up, rather than by attempting to analyse and transform 'capitalism' as a global totality. Framings that pit these various theoretical frameworks against one another frequently rely upon quite reductive and static renderings of each; the most robust work in critical geography makes use of multiple theoretical perspectives in order to develop the fullest and most rigorous critical analyses possible. Nonetheless, Neil Smith's observation (2005a, p. 897) that Marxism, '... may be the one oppositional politics which really has not been significantly rescripted into media fodder, integrated, in greater or lesser part co-opted, but always has to be opposed', suggests at the least Marxism's enduring significance for critical geography.   JM

Suggested reading
Gibson-Graham (2006b [1996]); Harvey (1999 [1982]); Henderson (1999); Smith (1990).

masculinism The tracing of connections between cultures of masculinity, knowledge and POWER. It is located within traditions of Western scientific rationality; in particular, the dualisms between mind and BODY, and SUBJECT and object, and the presumption that scientific knowledge can and should be objective and context free. Masculinist knowledge is criticized for claiming to be exhaustive or universal, while actually ignoring women's existences or casting them within a gendered binary, framed from the perspective of men. Rose (1993) argues that GEOGRAPHY is a masculinist discipline, and that masculinism determines conventions of what is deemed worthy of geographical investigation, FIELDWORK practice, THEORY development, writing and representation, as well as everyday academic life – from conduct in seminars to job searches and promotion. She identifies two masculinities (social scientific and aesthetic) that frame this pervasive masculinism within the academic GEOGRAPHICAL IMAGINATION. (See also EPISTEMOLOGY; FEMINIST GEOGRAPHIES; PHALLOCENTRISM; POST-STRUCTURALISM.)   GP

material culture Relationships between people and things, or, more formally put, the expression and negotiation of cultural, political and economic relationships via the material world of objects. Appadurai's (1986) noted text in this area supplies a further shorthand definition: *The social life of things.* Culture has often been conceived as an immaterial and disembodied entity, composed of ideas, customs, knowledges and shared beliefs and values. One task for material culture studies – today an interdisciplinary venture, bringing together researchers from HUMAN GEOGRAPHY, archaeology, anthropology, sociology and cultural and social theory – has been to examine how cultural beliefs and values gain permanence, POWER and significance through being given material form and expression in buildings, artefacts, commodities, visual symbols, displays, rituals and so on. Beyond this, however, writers in this area have also increasingly been concerned to think through the inherent materiality of CULTURE itself. This has involved attending to the question of how cultural values are materially produced and circulated. It has further involved rethinking the categories of 'culture' and 'materiality' themselves.

The origins of material culture studies are complex. Traditionally, archaeology and anthropology have been the disciplines most clearly associated with the study of material forms of culture. Archaeology takes a realm of recovered material objects as the basis from which it seeks to reconstruct past cultures. Equally, anthropology places emphasis upon the importance of material forms and processes – objects, clothes, buildings – in the formation and communication of distinctive cultures and subcultures. However, contemporary material culture studies also draws inspiration from semiotic and interpretative analyses of the significance of particular commodity forms under CAPITALISM. In such analyses (e.g. Roland Barthes' 1957 *Mythologies*), cultural objects such as cars, wine and washing powders are understood as texts which are authored (or produced) and read (consumed) in various ways, and this is viewed as a process in which particular HEGEMONIC or IDEOLOGICAL cultural meanings are communicated and reproduced.

The study of COMMODITIES and their use and consumption has continued to be a mainstay of material culture studies (e.g. Miller, 1997), and this has further been one of the most important ways in which human geographers have contributed to and interacted with this field (e.g. Jackson, 1999). Over the past ten years, studies of the materiality of cultures and commodities have indeed flourished in human geography. In part, this has been framed in terms of an agenda seeking to 're-materialize' human geographies (Jackson, 2000), in the wake of a CULTURAL TURN which, it is argued, placed undue emphasis upon the determining role *vis-à-vis* cultural practice of IMAGINATIVE GEOGRAPHIES of TEXTS and IMAGES. This renewed geographical EMPIRICISM takes shape through studies 'following' material objects within circuits of CAPITAL and COMMODITY CHAINS (e.g. Cook, 2004), and through studies focused upon the physical materialities of particular spaces and practices. At the same time, work drawing inspiration from ACTOR-NETWORK THEORY and new vitalisms has aimed to overcome a traditional duality in which matter is viewed as dead and inanimate, and can only be given meaning and form via the conduits of human thought and DISCOURSE. Writing in this area (e.g. Anderson and Tolia-Kelly, 2004) has been explicitly concerned to rethink the EPISTEMOLOGICAL status of material objects, and has sought to develop languages and methods through which the agency and, it is argued, inherent 'liveliness' of the material world might be addressed. JWY

materialism The history of materialism as a keyword in Western PHILOSOPHY can be traced back to the Early Atomists in Greek thought, particularly Democritus, and thereon in the writings of Epicurus and Lucretius. Materialism has multiple strands, more-or-less mechanistic and more-or-less sensationalist. What each shares is the metaphysical claim that the nature, constitution and structure of reality are physical. Materialism is typically contrasted to various forms of *spiritualism* or otherworldly existence (such as belief in God or supernatural beings), or to IDEALISM – that is to say, a metaphysics that privileges mental entities – in other words, minds and their states – over physical entities. Of course, dualist metaphysics that admit as 'real' both physical and mental entities are also possible.

The Italian philologist Sebastiano Timpanaro provides one of the most forthright definitions of materialism on record. In his monograph *On materialism*, he writes:

> By materialism we understand above all acknowledgement of the priority of nature over 'mind', or if you like, of the physical level over the biological level, and of the biological level over the socio-economic and cultural level; both in the sense of chronological priority … and in the sense of the conditioning which nature still exercises on man and will continue to exercise for the foreseeable future. Cognitively, therefore, the materialist maintains that experience cannot be reduced either to a production of reality by a subject … or to a reciprocal implication of subject and object. (1976, p. 34)

Few would disagree that the physical world precedes life and consciousness, and that other life forms precede the human. But to contend that NATURE is a self-evident or even autonomous domain that unilaterally conditions 'man' is problematic. As Raymond Williams (2005b [1980]) notes, Timpanaro's separation of nature and human wilfully ignores the fact that the materials that comprise nature are extrinsic *and* intrinsic to human beings. Additionally, a diverse literature on the PRODUCTION OF NATURE within fields such as agrarian studies, MARXIST GEOGRAPHY, and science and technology studies (see SCIENCE/SCIENCE STUDIES) – armed with a retinue of concepts such as 'social

nature', 'CYBORG', 'techno-natures' and 'posthumanism' (See POSTHUMANISM) – demolishes the notion of an independent nature.

What, then, binds materialism in its various forms – historical, DIALECTICAL, linguistic, cultural and POSTMODERN? First, there is a rejection of spiritualism and idealism (indeed, radical materialists would contend that the dichotomy between idealism and materialism is itself an artefact of idealism); second, there is an emphasis on the social effects of an object- or material-world that is at least partly autonomous of humans; and, third, there is a commitment to forms of EXPLANATION that are attentive to the specific properties of materials as they influence – in often unpredictable ways – various sorts of interactions between human and non-human bodies. A specifically Marxist materialism might additionally assert that materialism is ultimately about how a MODE OF PRODUCTION constitutes matter (nature, human BODIES, language) through social labour – which then carries the implication that any being is a historical and *political* fabrication. VG

Suggested reading
Althusser (1977 [1965]); Smith (1984); Williams (2005b [1980]).

mean information field (m.i.f.) The representation of a DISTANCE-DECAY relationship by a rectangular spatial grid, used in Torsten Hägerstrand's (1916–2004) classic studies of MIGRATION and DIFFUSION (see Hägerstrand, 1967). The m.i.f. was used in SIMULATION models, in which the central square in a 5×5 grid represented a migrant's origin, and the probabilities in the other 24 squares indicated the likelihood of them being the destination: the probabilities were either obtained from empirical analyses of migration patterns or pre-defined arbitrarily. Running the MODEL many times generated an average pattern of the likely population distribution following a period of migration or the spread of an INNOVATION – such as a new practice or a disease. (See also AGENT-BASED MODELLING.) RJ

measurement A classification of data types, the characteristics of which are important in determining what quantitative analytical procedures can be deployed. Four levels are generally recognized:

• *nominal* – each individual is allocated to one selected from an exclusive list of categories;

- *ordinal* – each individual is allocated to one selected from an exclusive list of rank-ordered categories;
- *interval* – in which individuals are assessed on a continuous quantitative scale; and
- *ratio* – in which the values on a quantitative scale can be relatively evaluated.

Thus, for example, 10 million people live in either Birmingham (UK) or London – which is a nominal allocation; London is bigger than Birmingham, which is ordinal; London has 9 million residents and Birmingham 1 million, which is interval; and London is nine times larger than Birmingham, which is ratio. Data from all forms of measurement can be analysed quantitatively, but different procedures are applied to different measurement types (cf. CATEGORICAL DATA ANALYSIS; GENERAL LINEAR MODEL; REGRESSION). RJ

media Cultural technologies for the communication and circulation of ideas, information, and meaning. These are usually taken to include various mass communication media such as books, newspapers, radio, television, film and now various forms of 'new media'.

In the past two decades, research on media-related topics has flourished in HUMAN GEOGRAPHY, without adding up to a theoretically or methodologically coherent agenda for media research. In CULTURAL GEOGRAPHY, media texts are often taken as a resource for analysing various forms of REPRESENTATION (of LANDSCAPES, PLACES, IDENTITIES, CITIES etc.). In ECONOMIC GEOGRAPHY, there is also a burgeoning literature on media production, distribution and consumption, given a further boost by the growth of digital media economies and culture industries. Nevertheless, the inherent SPATIALITY of media processes has attracted surprisingly little attention from geographers. Early work by Pred (1973) reconstructed the geographies of pre-telegraphic information circulation through newspapers in the USA in suggestive ways, but his main focus was on using these DIFFUSION processes to recover the emerging system of interdependencies between cities, rather than providing a close reading of the media reports themselves. More recent work in human geography has focused on the forms of social interaction that different media help to constitute (Adams, 1998). But in the main it is scholars working outside GEOGRAPHY who have provided most insight into the spatialities of media and communications. Thompson (1995) provides the clearest articulation of

the study of media with the central concerns of SOCIAL THEORY, and in the process develops an analysis of the spatial and temporal constitution of social relations and institutions. He argues that different media and communications practices *uncouple time and space*, enabling the transmission of symbolic forms over time and space without physical transportation of objects; and they thereby enable new forms of *simultaneous co-presence* between spatially and temporally distanciated subjects and contexts (see also TIME–SPACE DISTANCIATION). This type of analysis implies thinking of 'media' as a *process of mediation* operating 'wherever human beings congregate both in real and in virtual space, where they communicate, where they seek to persuade, inform, entertain, educate, where they seek in a multitude of ways, and with varying degrees of success, to connect one to the other' (Silverstone, 1999, p. 4).

As in other disciplines, media research in geography is prone to overestimate the causal POWER of media practices, and to make functionalist assumptions about the degree to which SOCIAL FORMATIONS are held together by the mass-mediated circulation of values over integrated political, economic and cultural territories (see FUNCTIONALISM). There is a tendency to assume that SUBJECTIVITY is media-dependent, and to presume that either the content of media texts or the patterns of ownership and control of media production and distribution are highly determinate in shaping patterns of belief, knowledge and practice. Media research in geography could benefit from taking seriously Garnham's (2000, p. 5) claim that 'the central question underlying all debates about media and how we study them concerns the way in which and the extent to which humans learn and thus how through time identities are formed and actions motivated'. Combining Garnham's question of *whether* and *how* people learn through their engagements with media practices with Silverstone's idea of media as *processes of mediation* points towards a more coherent agenda for media research: one that investigates how the spatio-temporal organization of media practices helps to distribute different possibilities of agency and communicative competency (Couldry, 2006) (a project that also bears directly on recent discussions of PUBLIC GEOGRAPHIES, since a crucial question concerns precisely how publics are *produced*). CB

Suggested reading
Barnett (2003); Couldry and McCarthy (2004).

medical geography A concern for 'medical geography' has been around for centuries, since Hippocrates, the Ancient Greek scholar associated with the origins of modern medicine, stated the importance of 'airs, waters, places' as an influence on human health, achievements and history. Such an environmental perspective has prevailed in many situations over the centuries, supplemented on occasion by a spatial perspective, and nowhere more obviously than in the celebrated case of Dr John Snow in mid-nineteenth-century London. Snow ascertained from empirical observations on the spatial distribution of cholera outbreaks something about the causal factors, contaminated water from a particular pump, within the transmission of this malaise. It is easy to detect the deep historical roots of medical geography, then, as a particular way of connecting many dimensions of human ill-health to a variety of environmental preconditions through the analysis of spatial patterns (revealing something about causes or vectors of transmission).

In more recent times, formalized in the First Report of the Commission on Medical Geography to the IGU (May, 1952), a sub-discipline of medical geography has arisen within academic GEOGRAPHY and on the fringes of medical and related sciences. Prompted by contributions by the likes of May (1958) and Stamp (1964), the sub-discipline flourished, becoming the basis for research groups organized nationally (e.g. the AAG Medical Geography Speciality Group; the CAG Health and Health Care Study Group; the RGS–IBG Geography of Health Research Group) and with an international profile through the IGU Commission on Health and the Environment, International Medical Geography Symposia held since the 1980s, its own specialist journal *Health and Place* (founded 1995) and enduring prominence in the leading interdisciplinary journal *Social Science and Medicine*. Periodic worries have plagued the identity of the sub-discipline, however, with some objecting about *too* close a link with the concepts and practices of Western biomedicine, thus failing to take seriously alternative and ethno medicines rooted in quite other personnel, practices and places (Gesler and Kearns, 2002). Some (esp. Kearns, 1993; cf. Mayer and Meade, 1994) have speculated about the need for a broader characterization of the field as *health geography* or even 'post-medical geography', where health is defined as more than just the medically ascribed *absence* of *ill* health and health care as more than conventionally designated 'medical' interventions

(Gesler and Kearns, 2002, p. 9; Parr, 2002: see HEALTH AND HEALTH CARE). The conceptual borrowings and methodological practices of the sub-discipline have also varied through time, with an EMPIRICIST and POSITIVIST stream deploying quantitative, modelling and GIS techniques being gradually supplemented – and on occasion challenged – by a diversity of approaches derived from Marxian POLITICAL ECONOMY, HUMANISM, POST-STRUCTURALISM, FEMINISM and QUEER THEORY (Litva and Eyles, 1995; Philo, 1996; Milligan, 2001, Ch. 9; Parr, 2002).

It is often suggested that medical geography splits into the 'twin streams' of 'geographical EPIDEMIOLOGY' and 'health systems planning' (Mayer, 1982), or 'geography of disease/ill-health' and 'geography of health care' (Litva and Eyles, 1995); although Gesler and Kearns (2002, p. 8) respond that these streams 'have increasingly merged and … become more like a braided river'. One broad trajectory – connecting with POPULATION GEOGRAPHY's interest in MORTALITY and morbidity – has studied geographical variations in ill-health at a range of SCALES from the global to the local, examining many different manifestations of ill-health for evidence of clear patterns in maps of prevalence and impact. Initially the interest here was disease, with the earliest studies concentrating on the obvious ecologies of diseases such as malaria in tropical settings (Pelzer, 1957, pp. 335–43: with links back to the colonial origins of geography), but with subsequent studies soon considering all parts of the globe (Howe, 1977). The 'natural' environment, in all of its climatic, topographic, fluvial, pedological and vegetative complexity, was inspected for its correlations with different diseases – chiefly those known to be infectious (tuberculosis, smallpox, influenza, HIV–AIDS), but also those with less certain aetiologies (the cancers, heart conditions, bone and nervous disorders) – creating an approach to medical geography readily positioned within the orbit of tracing human–environment relations (May, 1958; Learmouth, 1988; Meade and Erickson, 2000; Curtis, 2004, Ch. 6). An offshoot here shifted to a more narrowly conceived spatial epidemiology, building from basic mapwork to more advanced spatial-statistical techniques modelling the time-space DIFFUSION of contagious illnesses (specifically influenza and HIV–AIDS) from person to person, place to place and through settlement hierarchies (Gould, 1993; Cliff, Haggett and Smallman-Raynor, 2004: for a rather different/critical take, see Brown, 1995 – and DISEASE, DIFFUSION OF). Human movements obviously shape such diffusion patterns, and some time ago Maegraith (1969) mused on what 'jet age medical geography', speeded up by the pace of worldwide travel and MIGRATION, might eventually look like.

This first stream of medical geography has been complicated by a concern with facets of ill-health for which the METAPHOR of disease is arguably less relevant, things such as malnutrition, obesity and stress, and extending to the vexed domain of 'mental illness' (as in Giggs, 1973, recognized as a classic of medical geography: see DISABILITY). Aspects of the social environment have also begun to feature, calling attention to phenomena such as employment, income, housing quality, lifestyle issues and related factors that predispose the ill-health of (certain) peoples in (certain) places, and demanding that medical geography foster dialogues with the likes of SOCIAL GEOGRAPHY, URBAN GEOGRAPHY and other sub-disciplinary geographies (a decisive point made by Hunter, 1974; also Mayer and Meade, 1994). Additionally, as Dorn and Laws (1994, p. 107) underline, it becomes important to register the human BODY as more than just 'a host to some lesion or pathology waiting to be "discovered" by the medical practitioner', and thus to recognize the variability of the human body, complete with differing material circumstances and cultural ascriptions bound up with its particular place in socio-spatial hierarchies of DIFFERENCE (Dear, Wilton, Gaber and Takahashi, 1997). Variable configurations of the body, marked by CLASS, ETHNICITY, GENDER, AGEING, SEXUALITY, being a traveller or a refugee and so on (as discussed by Curtis, 2004, chs 3 and 4; see also Gesler and Kearns, 2002, Ch. 6), explain the greater or lesser likelihood of (certain) population cohorts in (certain) places 'getting sick', being interpreted as 'sick' and in need of assistance or avoidance, or as themselves being the possible sources of 'sickness' in others (as happened with the Chinese in nineteenth-century San Francisco: Craddock, 2000a). The emerging picture hence becomes less the hypothesized causal relations between easy-to-define environments, stable resident populations and their ill-health indicators, maybe cross-cut by the migrations of people bearing diseases, and more a mosaic of 'health inequalities' traced out across diverse, multiple and fluid bodies and places, wherein ecological influences enter into entangled admixtures alongside ones more obviously social, cultural, economic and political in origin (Curtis, 2004: echoing

Eyles and Wood, 1983; Jones and Moon, 1987; Gesler and Kearns, 2002). Further challenges are posed by Smith and Easterlow (2005) when critiquing the 'strange geographies' of health inequalities research that emphasize how places determine (variable resilience to) death and disease, but *neglect* how such placed ill-health is itself bound into a more systematic operation of 'health discrimination' – notably within labour and housing markets – fundamental to 'the structuring of society and space' (a thoroughly compositional matter, not a mere contextual effect).

The second stream of medical geography, concerned with health care as linked into health systems and planning, appeared in the 1960s when researchers began to study the spatial distributions of medical facilities. Questions were asked about spatial regularities in the locating of both hospitals of various kinds (Mayhew, 1986) and surgeries run by GPs, dentists and other primary service-providers (Curtis, 2004, 133–43), as linked to the accessibility and utilization of such facilities (Joseph and Phillips, 1984), and spatial mismatches were identified between provision and demand as a potential input to the more efficient spatial planning (location-allocation modelling) of healthcare systems (Clark, 1984). More recently, it has been argued that the basic geometries of health care cannot be explained solely by the principles advanced in SPATIAL SCIENCE but, rather, by recognizing the competing pressures on health managers in choosing where to locate facilities which arise from a wider socio-economic landscape that is itself unevenly constituted at a range of spatial scales (Mohan, 2002). Beyond such decisions, moreover, researchers have explored the political economy of health care, whether delivered by the WELFARE STATE (a public sector supposedly guaranteeing equality of access to all), an emerging SHADOW STATE (comprising voluntary-sector involvement) or an increasingly NEO-LIBERAL STATE in which *all* actors are compelled to pursue private-sector principles, entering or creating MARKETS (internal or otherwise) to ensure competition and efficiency gains, and aiming at deregulation (even as legal–administrative demands are continually reinserted). More baldly, 'there has been explicit recognition by health geographers of the underlying social forces that create inequalities, often expressed in terms of the impact of the capitalist economic system on health care provision' (Gesler and Kearns, 2002, p. 51; see also Jones and Moon, 1987). Part of this story has also been the growing commodification of health care, turning it into something that 'customers' elect to 'consume', quite likely using their (or others') capital in the process, not a bundle of resources available to them as matter of right. The 'selling' of medical facilities, loosely equivalent to the marketing of places discussed by urban geographers, has become a sub-theme in the ongoing research of Kearns and co-workers (Kearns and Barnett, 1999; Curtis, 2004, pp. 125–33).

On a different but related tack, researchers have explored more cultural aspects of health care (Gesler, 1991; Kearns and Gesler, 1998; Gesler and Kearns, 2002), prompting enquiries into various cultural influences – the 'thought-worlds' of given societies, as well as everything from buried IDEOLOGIES through to the discursive scripting of health policies – that play out in the geographies of health care. Attention is paid to how agendas of POWER, control, medical authority and fiscal efficacy translate into the form, content and spaces of medical facilities, helping to explain location patterns (within overall systems), environmental associations (of particular facilities) and even architectures, decorations and layouts (of, say, hospital wards). At the latter, distinctly human scale, focus alights on the embodied relations between the 'medics' and the 'medicalized', and on how such relations are shaped by and performed across an array of in- and out-patient spaces of treatment, illuminating how both the power of the former is extended and the possible agency (maybe RESISTANCE) of the latter is expressed. This also means taking seriously the grounded experiences of the people involved, establishing how they perceive, feel about and understand what is occurring within spaces of health care, and recognizing the tensions that can fragment professional and lay judgements about what makes the best kind of 'place' for the delivery of the health care required (Milligan, 2001). Tellingly, this research strand begins to press at the limits of what is conventionally meant by 'health care', and has started to consider more ambiguous landscapes of health care – what Gesler (1992) has termed 'therapeutic landscapes' – wherein all manner of phenomena (mountains and springs, streets and malls) can be significant in how they promote or undermine senses of health*ful* well-being for those who access them. A further elaboration is work on health practices that possess an awkward relationship to Western biomedicine – that is, complementary and alternative medicines, as well as the diverse forms of psychotherapy and counselling – which then suggests a still more inclusive interest in 'geographies of care' (Conradson, 2003a) wherein the overtly *medical* element is largely left behind (and a large step is taken towards that post-medical geography speculated about by Kearns, 1993). CPP

Suggested reading
Curtis (2004); Gesler and Kearns (2002); Kearns (1993); Meade and Erickson (2000); Parr (2002).

megacities Very large, high-density urban centres, usually defined as those with populations exceeding 5 million. The International Geographical Union MegaCity Task Force (http://www.megacities.nl/) identified only four such centres in the 1950s, but 28 in 1985 and 39 in 2000: it estimates that there will be 60 by 2015. Most of these are in the 'developing world' (especially East and South Asia and LATIN AMERICA), are growing extremely rapidly, and face major problems of INFRASTRUCTURE provision and social inequalities. RJ

Suggested reading
Hall and Pain (2006).

megalopolis A Greek word (combining those for 'great' and 'city') coined by Patrick Geddes and adopted by Jean Gottmann (1915–94: see Gottmann, 1964) to describe the discontinuous urban complex of the USA's northeastern seaboard. It was also used some decades before by Lewis Mumford (1895–1988): to him, megalopolis was the end-state in the process of URBANIZATION, in which giant, fragmented cities become dysfunctional, whereas Gottmann deployed it as a descriptive label for extensive urban SPRAWL. RJ

Suggested reading
Baigent (2004).

memory An inherently geographical activity: PLACES store and evoke personal and collective memories, memories emerge as bodily experiences of being in and moving through SPACE, and memories shape IMAGINATIVE GEOGRAPHIES and material geographies of HOME, NEIGHBOURHOOD, CITY, NATION and EMPIRE. HUMAN GEOGRAPHY includes an important body of work on the role of the built landscape – museums, monuments, artefacts, heritage sites – in creating a sense of a common identity through memory, on how collective memories are made material in the landscape, and the practices of memory-making through performances and rituals of remembrance. There is also a substantial literature on HERITAGE entrepreneurship as a marketable good (see also POSTMODERNISM).

Maurice Halbwachs' book *On collective memory* (1992 [1941]) was an important early text theorizing memory as simultaneously social and spatial (as opposed to highly individualized and purely psychological) (Hebbert, 2005). Activities enhancing remembrance of a *collective past*, including commemorative rituals, story-telling, place naming and the accumulation and display of relics, trigger a *social memory* that solidifies a common shared identity. Halbwachs emphasized the importance of anchoring these memories in spatial imagery and physical artefacts, arguing that social memory endures best when there is a 'double focus – a physical object, a material reality such as a statue ... and also a symbol, or something of spiritual significance, something shared by the group that adheres to and is superimposed upon this physical reality' (1992 [1941], p. 204).

This focus on the social constitution and context of memory informed French historian Pierre Nora's (1997) influential project, which traced the development of French national IDENTITY through the analysis of a variety of '*lieux de mémoires*', or sites of memory (see also NATIONALISM). Nora (1989, p. 9) argued that with the demise of PEASANT societies, 'true memory', available 'in gestures and habits, in skills passed down by unspoken traditions, in the body's inherent self-knowledge, in unstudied reflexes and ingrained memories', has been replaced by 'modern memory' that is self-conscious, historical and archival. In modern society, we 'must deliberately create archives, maintain anniversaries, organize celebrations because such activities no longer naturally occur' (1989, p. 12). In short, the primordial memory of peasant societies embedded in *milieux de mémoires* (environments of memory) has been substituted by much more self-consciously created *lieux de mémoires*. The production of these *lieux*, or sites, has been a result of the transformations wrought by MODERNITY, including GLOBALIZATION, the rise of mass MEDIA and the institutionalization of a professional discipline of history. While Nora's distinction between true and modern memory may be overwrought, in the 1980s his work spawned widespread interest in memory and place throughout the HUMANITIES and social sciences, and it continues to provide

the impetus for a vast array of studies of different types of memory spaces (Legg, 2005).

The dominance of the NATION-STATE in framing memory has been the focus of much research on MONUMENTS and memorials. Because memory is always shadowed by forgetting, is vulnerable to manipulation and has a capacity to facilitate (or coerce) social cohesion, what is remembered and forgotten in national memory both reflects POWER relations and is of political consequence. Elite and dominant memory is typically mobilized by the powerful in the cultivation of a national imaginary, through monuments, memorials, public ritual, architectural and urban design, and through the erasure of previous PLACE NAMES or settlements of the dispossessed. However, human geographers have regularly noted the contested nature of meaning surrounding even official symbolic sites, and the production and consumption of such sites often involve CONFLICT (Till, 2001, 2005; Foote, 2003). They are neither uniformly designed nor read (and SPACE is significant in the construction of that meaning; Johnson, 2005). Nor do elites inevitably have a hold on LANDSCAPE production. Burk (forthcoming) describes the creation by grassroots groups in Vancouver of monuments to memorialize VIOLENCE against women. Recognizing the 'power of place' to repair cultural amnesia and nurture a more inclusive public memory, Hayden (1997) details a series of commemorative projects that concretize long histories of settlement of African American, Latina and Asian American families in downtown Los Angeles. Alderman (2003, p. 171) has examined how African Americans struggled to control and determine the scale of streets in which Martin Luther King Jr. would be remembered and thus the SCALE at which his memory would find public expression. He notes that the scale of memory was 'open to redefinition not only by opponents to his political/social philosophy but also people who unquestionably embraced and benefited from this philosophy'.

Memory cannot be dictated, and popular memory can be an important vehicle through which dominant, official renditions of the past and present are resisted by mobilizing groups to create subaltern and counter-memories, and alternative futures (Legg, 2005). Shared memories of loss and longing for land may form the basis for collective claims to rights or reparation: Kosek (2004) argues that shared memories of dispossession from land by Mexicans living in northern New Mexico are what make the Hispanic community in this region of the USA cohere as a social and political force. The same could be argued for Palestinians or, in Canada, First Nations groups. In diasporic and post-colonial contexts – in which memory is threatened by both nostalgia and coerced assimilation – 'cultural memory offers promise of epistemological grounding', though not necessarily within a singular national IDENTITY (Sugg, 2003, p. 469: see also DIASPORA; POST-COLONIALISM; TRANSNATIONALISM). *Counter-memories* may be assembled and transmitted through oral tradition, but also in less bureaucratized time-places: the BODY, domestic spaces (Blunt, 2003), neighbourhoods or 'temporal re-territorializations' of formal spaces (such as carnivals, festivals or rallies; Legg, 2005).

The memory projects of marginalized groups may bear the traces of trauma, such that the possibilities of memory are altered. With traumatic recall, events remain in the vivid present, resisting integration through narrativization. Though the STATE often incorporates violent or tragic events into a linear narrative of national redemption and overcoming, what Edkins (2003) calls 'trauma time' works differently, and its repetitive disruptive quality can reveal the violent foundations of SOVEREIGN POWER. Trauma thus has a relation not just to TIME but also SPACE and GEOGRAPHY; for instance, to narrations and experiences of nation and persistent claims to HOMELAND. Sugg (2003) draws on Hirsch's concept of post-memory to understand the 'suspended migration' of second-generation Cuban Americans: CHILDREN of exiled parents may inherit the collective cultural trauma of their parents and remember their parents' stories of exile as their own within a dynamic of longing and return. Alternatively, memorializing trauma in the landscape may constitute a witnessing public, setting in motion an emerging narrative (and a potential release from traumatic recall; Burk, forthcoming).

The recent tendency has been to expand the scope of memory studies by considering the role of PERFORMANCE and bodily and non-bodily practices in the making of memorial landscapes (Hoelscher, 2003), by examining the wider production of social memory beyond demarcated sites of monuments and memorials, and by considering the landscape implications of the memories of ANIMALS or other than human beings (Lorimer, 2006). NJ/GP

Suggested reading
Johnson (2003b, 2005); Legg (2007a); Till (2003).

mental maps/cognitive maps Perhaps the best-known research outcome from BEHAVIOURAL GEOGRAPHY was the retrieval of the imagined or mental maps widespread in the popular knowledge of places, mental constructs that were seen as intervening between geographical settings and human action. An early study was the simple sketch mapping of urban areas from memory supervised by Kevin Lynch in the pursuit of good urban design, which permitted an *image of the city* to be constructed, revealing districts of knowledge and ignorance, and the role of such remembered features as nodes, edges and landmarks in establishing urban legibility. Behavioural geographers, including Roger Downs and David Stea (1973), in contrast referred to *cognitive maps*, which they associated with the spatial tasks of orientation and way-finding. More formal and widely replicated were the experiments with paper and pencil tests conducted by Peter Gould and his students (Gould and White, 1993 [1974]), which were intended not so much to identify PLACE knowledge and place ignorance but, rather, to establish a surface of place preferences. From surveys in several countries, mental maps were constructed that revealed both a national preference surface and also a local surface of desirability for a home area. Subsequent work sought to establish the developmental growth of MAPS among CHILDREN of increasing age, and examined linkages between geographical preference surfaces and future residential choice and MIGRATION propensities (Gould and White, 1993 [1974]).

Mental maps were part of a broader movement in ENVIRONMENTAL PERCEPTION, which in turn has elided into an interest in the REPRESENTATION and SOCIAL CONSTRUCTION of places in a variety of disciplines using less POSITIVIST methods and emphasizing social rather than psychological factors. Nonetheless, the older analytical methods continue to generate interesting results (Kitchin, 1994), even if with interdisciplinary dissemination the links with the original work are truncated or forgotten. So a current study of the role of the MEDIA in shaping the spatial surface of fear in Los Angeles (Matei and Ball-Rokeach, 2005), contains the key words mental maps, GIS and spatial effects, but omits any reference to Gould's work, including his celebrated feature in *Time* magazine that included a map of the perceived fear of urban areas. DL

Suggested reading
Gould and White (1993).

455

metageography 'The set of spatial structures through which people order their knowledge of the world: the often unconscious frameworks that organize studies of history, sociology, anthropology, economics, political science, or even natural history' (Lewis and Wigen, 1997, p. ix). The prefix 'meta-' implies an ABSTRACTION, a concept that in some sense goes beyond the term to which it implies, so by extension a metageography is a conceptual grid that structures how geographies are ordered. These grids are cultural constructions, and the emphasis Lewis and Wigen place on the fact that they are used more or less automatically and unconsciously, without critical reflection, connects the concept to that of a GEOGRAHICAL IMAGINARY. 'Meta-' can also imply an umbrella concept, and Lewis and Wigen focus their attention on the global SCALE and the conventional division of the world into CONTINENTS. But the division of the GLOBE into a mosaic of STATES is no less commonplace and taken-for-granted, against which Beaverstock, Smith and Taylor (2000) have proposed 'a new metageography': a global NETWORK of flows between cities.   DG

metaphor For Aristotle, a metaphor 'consists in giving the thing a name that belongs to something else'. Such practice is rampant in HUMAN GEOGRAPHY, as in other disciplines: cities are plant biomes (CHICAGO SCHOOL), CULTURAL LANDSCAPES are texts, economic LOCALITIES are geological strata 'layers of investment' and non-renewable RESOURCES take on a LIFE-CYCLE.

While pervasive, some writers have criticized metaphors for being ornamental and obfuscatory. Plato said that they make 'trifle points seem important, and important points trifles', while Thomas Hobbes believed that they 'deceive others', and in geography, Harvey (1967, p. 551) argued that they 'hinder objective judgment'. In each of these cases, metaphor was attacked because it resulted in ambiguity: it is 'a sort of extra happy trick with words', as I.A. Richards (1936, p. 90) put it. More generally, such misgivings result from a particular view of LANGUAGE held by such critics: that language should be transparent, limpid and utterly dependable, all of which are undermined by metaphor.

Over the twentieth century there was an increasing recognition that language takes on none of those characteristics (see, in particular, DECONSTRUCTION) and, concomitantly, that metaphors are an indispensable part of both writing and theorizing. Metaphorical use comes in two shapes and sizes (Barnes and Curry, 1992).

Small metaphors that pepper individual writing and research are part of the very infrastructure of language construction, an 'omnipresent principle' (Richards, 1936, p. 92). Mobilizing them requires skill and sensitivity, forming an important component of RHETORIC, the attempt to persuade others of the force of one's argument by using tropes such as metaphor (Lakoff and Johnson, 2003 [1980]). *Large metaphors*, in contrast, structure entire research PARADIGMS. Some, such as 'organism' or 'mechanism', are so deeply ingrained that they become 'root metaphors' (Pepper, 1942), whereas others are only temporary, mobilized for a particular use and then discarded. However long their durability, all large metaphors operate through a process of 'metaphorical re-description' (Hesse, 1980); that is, transferring meanings and associations of one system in order to re-describe the explanandum (the part of the explanation that does the explaining) of another system. An example is Isaac Newton's metaphorical re-description of sound in terms of waves. Metaphorical re-description is ubiquitous, as well as 'potentially revolutionary' (Arib and Hesse, 1986). When Adam Smith coined the metaphor of the 'invisible hand' to describe the efficacy of the MARKET, or when Marx said 'workers have nothing to lose but their chains', or when Bunge (1966, p. 27) asked, 'Why cannot ... concepts dealing with exotic and dioric streams be applied to highways?' revolutions, albeit of different kinds, were set in motion.

There has been sporadic interest in metaphor in GEOGRAPHY since the 1960s, when the proponents of SPATIAL SCIENCE first discussed the linkages between MODELS and metaphors (Haggett and Chorley, 1967). Later, those who advocated a HUMANISTIC GEOGRAPHY, such as Tuan (1978) and Livingstone and Harrison (1981b), were drawn to metaphors because of resonances with human creativity and meaning, twin planks of the larger project (see also HUMANITIES). Most recently, critical attention has come from geographers interested in EPISTEMOLOGY. Large metaphors sometimes carry unexamined intellectual freight, resulting in unintentional and sometimes contradictory meanings. They need to be unpacked, inspected critically for their coherence, consistency and compatibility. Doing so also means scrutinizing their historical and material origins. Metaphors require 'worlding' (Smith and Katz, 1993).   TB

Suggested reading
Lakoff and Johnson (1980); Smith and Katz (1993).

methodological individualism The view that social events must be explained by reducing them to individual actions, where, in turn, those actions are explained by reference to the intentions of individual actors. For the methodological individualist, all macro-scale social entities are ultimately decomposable to the acts and underlying intentions of individuals. SOCIETY, therefore, is a chimera, something that appears real, but which is not. As a perspective, methodological individualism is usefully contrasted with, on the one hand, approaches that accentuate the importance and reality of trans-individual social structures (as found, for example, in structural Marxism, a form of MARXISM that trades on STRUCTURALISM) and, on the other hand, approaches that deny the autonomy of individual human subjects altogether (as found, for example, within POST-STRUCTURALISM).

The term 'methodological individualism' was first systematically deployed by the German sociologist Max Weber, in his book *Economy and Society* (1968 [1922]). He was keen to argue that social collectivities such as firms or governments 'must be treated as solely the resultants ... of the particular acts of individual persons, since these alone can be treated as agents in a course of subjectively understandable action' (Weber, 1968 [1922], p. 13). Weber's point was not to privilege individuals over social institutions, but to stress that understanding social phenomena should rest methodologically on action-based theory; that is, theory providing motivations for agents to act (in Weber's theory, this turned on the methodological protocols of *Verstehen* ('understanding') and IDEAL TYPES).

In subsequent versions this point was lost, however, and methodological individualism was used to privilege the individual primarily for the purpose of disparaging especially Marx's theory of HISTORICAL MATERIALISM, which rested precisely on collective social entities. This impulse is found in Friedrich von Hayek's and Karl Popper's writings of the 1940s and 1950s, and then again in Jon Elster's (1982b) work on ANALYTICAL MARXISM in the 1980s and 1990s. While there are differences among these three writers, they also have commonalities. First, Hayek and Elster, and perhaps Popper too through his model of psychological REDUCTIONISM, adhered to a RATIONAL CHOICE model of the individual derived from NEO-CLASSICAL ECONOMICS: rationality was posited as the only action-based motivation for agents. Second, all three accepted that *rational individuals* represented

'rock-bottom explanations' of social phenomena (Watkins, 1957, p. 105).

Both the specific rational choice model and the more general notion of an individualist 'rock-bottom' explanation have been criticized: the underlying intentions of an act are not always known, and so it may be impossible to provide individual action-based accounts; non-individual based forms of EXPLANATION – for example, aggregate-statistical – can in some cases provide better explanations than ones resting on individual motivations; individuals in interaction with one another produce emergent effects irreducible to individual acts; and individuals are the consequence, not the cause, of social structures and institutions ('methodological holism').

Because of the association with the rationality postulate, in HUMAN GEOGRAPHY methodological individualism was found most readily in ECONOMIC GEOGRAPHY, since it was most influenced by NEOCLASSICAL ECONOMICS, and it also reappears in REGIONAL SCIENCE and the NEW ECONOMIC GEOGRAPHY. But the CULTURAL TURN and the turn to INSTITUTIONAL ECONOMICS have resulted in the strong assertion of the importance of social phenomena on their own terms, and hence a falling away of methodological individualism from the one sub-discipline where it had gained a foothold (Lee and Wills, 1997). TB

Suggested reading
Heath (2005).

methodology The principles and assumptions underlying the choice of techniques for constructing and analysing data. Methodology should not be confused with 'methods': it is the conceptual rationale for which methods are used, and how. Methodology brings together and links the underlying philosophical and conceptual bases of a study with appropriate techniques. Good methodologies thus align the ONTOLOGY of a study, how it conceives of the world, with its EPISTEMOLOGY, how it claims to know things about the world. This is more than, though it includes, competently using one or more research 'techniques'. This *Dictionary*, for instance, lists at least 11 groups of techniques and many more analytical and representational procedures for the data thus created. Methodology is a meta-level issue about fitting techniques to research questions, rather than simply learning a method.

A weak formulation of methodology as recounting how research was done was inspired by the SCIENCES and is often a hall-mark of social *science* perspectives. This recounting of procedures offers a methodo-logical transparency that is the hallmark of scientific studies in that it allows readers the chance to 'disprove' a study's conclusions. Even beyond formally scientific studies, trans-parency is often still advocated as a way of ensuring rigour and validity across a variety of approaches. Baxter and Eyles (1997) sug-gest adapting ideas from Lincoln and Guba so that for all methods, including QUALITATIVE METHODS, the following have to be shown:

- credibility of the account (i.e. authenti-cated representation of what actually occurred);
- transferability of the material (i.e. making what occurred intelligible to the audience);
- dependability of the interpretation (i.e. that it is not illogical, or how partisan it is); and
- confirmability of the study (i.e. the ability to audit the process that made it through personal reflection, audit processes or opportunities for informants to reply).

The emphasis here is on the clear statement of procedures undertaken, the techniques and steps of analysis as a means to enable the rea-der to examine the process leading to the results and conclusions. Traditions of transpa-rency are variable across even sub-disciplinary fields where, for instance, in a comparison of the *Journal of International Business Studies* and *Economic Geography*, around 80 per cent of articles in the former had formal sections on methodology and the collection of data, while in the latter only 30 per cent or less had such sections (Poon, 2007). A degree of transparency might also be intended to enable a REFLEXIVE account that positions the research process, and allows the reader to see the contingent and situated production of knowledge. This may in fact be aimed at undercutting notions of authoritative social science by demonstrating fallibility and the limits to knowledge, and may be inspired by approaches to research ETHICS that fore-ground the contributions of research partici-pants. Thus FEMINIST methodology stretches from design to dissemination of research, but must also consider the 'relationships among people involved in the research pro-cess, the actual conduct of the research, and process through which the research comes to be undertaken and completed' (Moss, 2002, p. 12).

A stronger definition of methodology points out the different ways in which these criteria of reliability reflect theoretical approaches. For example, SAMPLING within EXTENSIVE RESEARCH would have to meet criteria of representativeness to support statistical ana-lysis of the data, while within QUALITATIVE METHODS it might aim to capture a particular group's perspective, where its validity depends on the quality of material derived from their POSITIONALITY. In this case, methodology is about joining the stages in the research from underlying PHILOSOPHY to research questions to techniques generating data to forms of an-alysis and presentation of the results.

A methodology thus involves considering how the specific techniques can be assembled and used to generate the sort of data that will enable an answer to the questions posed through a specific conceptual framework. There have been extensive arguments about whether specific conceptual frameworks dem-and specific methodological linkages and pre-clude some methods. For instance, FEMINIST GEOGRAPHY had a long debate over whether it required feminist methods, that sought to empower, give voice to women and treat them as 'subjects' who made knowledge, or whether it could use the QUANTITATIVE METHODS that feminist theorists had often critiqued for treating people as objects of knowledge and using a detached MASCULINISM in its logics. This debate has seen special issues of journals, such as the *Professional Geographer* in 1995, assessing whether a feminist method-ology can include various techniques such as GIS.

If methodology is about assessing how to create material that will answer the conceptual questions in a study, the answer may well be to use multiple methods. Thus some parts or issues might be addressed via one method while others could be addressed by another. This is often called triangulation, named metaphorically after the SURVEYING practice of taking bearings from different landmarks. Here, methodology is about combining methods to help validate each others' findings and, optimistically, integrating different forms of data in the analysis (Knigge and Cope, 2006). On the other hand, it might be argued that the different techniques, with different ONTOLOGIES, construct radically different ver-sions of the world that cannot be brought into the same EPISTEMOLOGICAL approach. How can, say, a SOCIAL CONSTRUCTIVIST account be allied to modes of statistical inference that rely on REALISM or assumptions of OBJECTIVITY? In such a case, a methodology might be about holding tensions that show these gaps and differences to offer a 'transgressive validity' that problematizes or crystallizes the issues of reliability and truthfulness between methods, rather than integrating them or using one to corroborate the other (Guba and Lincoln, 2005). An exemplary account in GEOGRAPHY is Nightingale (2003) on forest cover in Nepal, illustrating the partiality of and contradictions between both villagers' oral histories and aerial photography.

Methodology is thus about organizing research practices in relation to concepts. There is no singular way of doing this; nor is methodology simply the application of methods. It involves thinking through the connections relating concepts, topics, information-gathering and REPRESENTATION, which will inevitably vary from project to project.   MC

Suggested reading
Hoggart, Lees and Davies (2002); Limb and Dwyer (2001); Pryke, Rose and Whatmore (2003); Sharp (2005).

metropolitan area A general term for large urban settlements. Metropolitan districts were first defined by the US Bureau of the CENSUS in 1910, by grouping together large central cities (i.e. administrative districts) with their contiguous SUBURBS into a single built-up area to be used for reporting data. Over time, with continued URBANIZATION and urban SPRAWL, definitions changed and there is now a hierarchy of areas:

- *Metropolitan Statistical Areas (MSAs)* – groups of counties (or similar administrative units) with total populations exceeding 100,000, comprising a central city (with 50,000 + residents) and surrounding suburbs;
- *Consolidated Metropolitan Statistical Areas (CMSAs)* – larger units with populations exceeding 1,000,000; and
- *Primary Metropolitan Statistical Areas (PMSAs)* – separate components within CMSAs: the Detroit/Ann Arbor CMSA comprises the separate Detroit and Ann Arbor PMSAs, and the New York/New Jersey/Long Island CMSA contains ten separate PMSAs.

Analysts have also defined Metropolitan Labor Areas, which extend beyond the built-up areas to incorporate places from which at least 5 per cent of the workforce COMMUTES to a metropolitan area.

Similar schemes (with terminological variations) have been defined by the census authorities to represent and report data for the urbanized areas in a large number of other countries.   RJ

Suggested reading
See   http://www.census.gov/population/www/ estimates/metrodef.html.

micropolis A term introduced by Thomas (1989) and adopted by the US Bureau of the CENSUS in 2003, referring to urban agglomerations with total populations between 10,000 and 49,999. Each micropolis comprises a number of separate but socially and economically integrated settlements (as measured by COMMUTING patterns), one of which (the 'core centre') has a population of at least 10,000; for example, the separate settlements of Lebanon (CT), Hanover and Enfield (NH) and Norwich and Hartford (VT) in the Upper Connecticut Valley comprise a micropolis based on Hartford. Using 2001 census data, 578 separate micropoli were identified, containing about 10 per cent of the total US population. (See also METROPOLITAN AREA.)   RJ

Suggested reading
Heubusch (1997).

microsimulation Microsimulation operates at the 'micro' (not aggregate) SCALE, where the 'units' include the individual, HOUSEHOLD, firm or vehicles (International Microsimulation Association, www.microsimulation.org). These units and their socio-economic trajectories are modelled by assigning them data attributes that are altered over (simulated) time by a set of rules governing the system in which they exist. Changes may be deterministic (they *must* happen, given certain characteristics) or stochastic (see STOCHASTIC PROCESS: there is a probability that they *might* happen). In this way the impacts of, for example, government policies and economic DECISION-MAKING can be modelled. There are links between microsimulation and GEOCOMPUTATION, especially CELLULAR AUTOMATA and AGENT-BASED MODELLING.   RH

Suggested reading
Ballas, Rossiter, Thomas, Clarke and Dorling (2005).

Middle East, idea of The term has its origins in European and eventually American

DISCOURSES of diplomacy, GEOPOLITICS and SECURITY, and in a more diffuse cultural register as IMAGINATIVE GEOGRAPHIES of a largely Arab 'Orient'. The two cross-cut in complex ways, but they have their origins in Napoleon's military occupation of Egypt in 1798 (see OCCUPATION, MILITARY), in some measure part of a plan to cut Britain's lines of communication with India, and the bloody campaigns that he fought through the Levant. In invading Egypt, Cole (2007, p. 247) argues, 'Bonaparte was inventing what we now call "the modern Middle East"', and 'the similarities of the Corsican general's rhetoric and tactics to those of later North Atlantic incursions into the region tell us about the persistent pathologies of ENLIGHTENMENT republics'. Said (2003 [1978]) locates the formation of a distinctly modern ORIENTALISM in the textual and visual appropriations of Egypt made for a European audience by the scientists, scholars and artists who accompanied the French troops.

French politicians and diplomats had described the Ottoman Empire as *la Proche-Orient* ('the Near East') from the end of the eighteenth century, and for most of the nineteenth century the 'Eastern Question' that concerned high politics in EUROPE was invariably an Ottoman one. But in the course of the nineteenth century civil servants in Britain's India Office started to describe what was then Persia and its surrounding regions as 'the Middle East', and it was the geo-strategic relation to Britain's Empire in India that gave the term its eventual currency. In 1902 an American naval officer, Alfred Thayer Mahan (1840–1914), in what proved to be an extraordinarily influential essay on 'The Persian Gulf and International Relations' (Mahan, 1902), argued that Britain's control over its approaches to India via Suez and the Gulf (which is how he loosely defined 'the Middle East') was threatened by Russian advances in Central Asia and by the proposed construction of a rail link between Berlin and Baghdad; not surprisingly, he championed the importance of sea power, and recommended that the Middle East would 'some day need its Malta as well as its Gibraltar'. The term was popularized by Valentine Chirol, who published a major series of articles in the *Times*, followed by a book under the title *The Middle Eastern question, or some political problems of Indian defence* (1903). The 'Middle East' was envisioned as a security belt running from Persia through Mesopotamia and Afghanistan to Kashmir, Nepal and Tibet: as Scheffler (2003, p. 265) notes, an abstract space whose common denominator was a

strategic location across the northern and western approaches to India.

The region was redefined after the First World War, the collapse of the Ottoman Empire and the attempt by the Great Powers to divide most of the spoils between them, but it retained its strategic inflection and gained new geo-economic significance as the importance of OIL came to be recognized (at first, as the basis for naval supremacy). The European powers drew new lines on the MAP to create new STATES. In 1921, Churchill created a Middle East Department in the Colonial Office, whose area of responsibility was Iraq, Palestine, Transjordan and Aden; and during the Second World War Britain established a Middle East Command, whose area of responsibility spiralled out from Iran, Iraq, Palestine, Syria, Transjordan and the Arabian Peninsula to include Greece and Malta in the Mediterranean and Egypt, the Sudan and swathes of East Africa. After the war, the REGION was plunged back into conflict by the PARTITION of Palestine, the foundation of the state of Israel in 1948 and the dispossession of hundreds of thousands of Palestinians. By then, Britain's star was fading – a fact dramatically confirmed by the Suez Crisis of 1956 – and growing American geopolitical and geo-economic interest in the region, partly in response to the expanding Soviet sphere of influence during the COLD WAR, was signalled by the US State Department's focus on a Middle East that it now delimited as Egypt, Syria, Israel, Lebanon, Jordan, Iraq, Saudi Arabia, Kuwait, Bahrain and Qatar. This new regionalization was underwritten by financial support for AREA STUDIES and Centers for Middle Eastern Studies at major American universities.

Europe and America continued to be exercised by the region throughout the second half of the twentieth century and on into the twenty-first, and its geopolitical construction as what Sidaway (1998) called an 'arc of crisis' spanned successive WARS between Arab states and Israel, the Israeli occupation of Gaza and the West Bank after 1967, the unresolved Palestinian question and the INTIFADA, chronic crises and civil wars in Lebanon, the Iraq–Iran War (1980–8), the Iraqi invasion of Kuwait and the first Gulf War (1990–1). A key US response to these crises was the formation of a unified combatant command in 1983, US Central Command (CENTCOM), to cover 'the "central" area of the globe between the European and Pacific Commands' and which (in significant part) retraced the outlines of the former British Middle East Command.

Its importance was further increased by the terrorist attacks on the United States on 11 September 2001 and the US-led invasions of Afghanistan in 2001 and Iraq in 2003 (see TERRORISM).

CENTCOM articulates a highly particular imaginative geography of the region (Morrissey, 2009), but the invasions of Afghanistan and Iraq were underwritten by, and also extended, a series of cultural formations that could be traced back through the long history of British and American interventions in the region to a deep-seated Orientalism (Gregory, 2004b). In doing so, they confirmed that the 'Middle East' is a profoundly ethnocentric construction, as Bernard Lewis (1999) once had it, 'meaningless, colorless, shapeless, and for most of the world inaccurate'. This reached its nadir in portrayals such as this, from Fareed Zakaria, writing in *Newsweek* soon after 9/11: 'This is the land of suicide bombers, flag-burners and fiery mullahs.' In one astonishing sentence, the various, vibrant cultures of the region were fixed and frozen into one diabolical landscape (Gregory, 2004b, p. 60). And yet this (in)sensibility captured the accumulated RHETORICAL effect of constructions of the Middle East with dismal fidelity. For the 'Middle East' as a concept has been constructed, both geopolitically and discursively, largely from the 'outside': and yet its problems and predicaments are almost always assigned solely to those on the 'inside'. As Mamdani (2002) put it, within the optic of a Euro-American ETHNOCENTRISM, the world is divided into two, 'so that one part makes culture and the other is a prisoner of culture'. DG

Suggested reading
Khalidi (1998); Lockman (2004); Scheffler (2003).

migrancy The state or condition of being a migrant; 'migrancy' generally emphasizes the cultural, social and political constructions and experiences of migrant groups and displaced people (cf. MIGRATION). Historically, the slow and discontinuous process of sedentarizing populations and fixing political BORDERS and BOUNDARIES was often accompanied by a suspicion of those who remained constantly on the move. Thus, for example, the figure of the merchant forever travelling to fairs and distant MARKETS occupied an ambiguous position within the territorializations of FEUDALISM in much of medieval EUROPE, even though such movements provided essential functions for trans-regional economies. MOBILITY was often a privilege, to be sure, and it was threaded in to wider circuits of POWER and authority, so that it was (and remains) those who were HOMELESS and forced to move (through disease or POVERTY, for example) who attracted the most suspicion and even hostility. Some social groups regarded migrancy as a cultural formation constitutive of their very IDENTITY: 'travelling peoples' such as the Roma ('Gypsies'), the tramping artisans of nineteenth-century Britain (Southall, 1991) or the hobos of late nineteenth- and early twentieth-century America (DePastino, 2003).

Even though GLOBALIZATION and MODERNITY are predicated on movement and depend on migration, these capacities are still subject to social discrimination. Under neo-liberal globalization, the world may be 'flat' for business travel and international TOURISM, but those who travel under other, no less legitimate, signs are subject to policing, restriction and even detention: the Roma continue to encounter SOCIAL EXCLUSION (Sibley, 1998; Bancroft, 2005) and groups such as ASYLUM-seekers and REFUGEES, and guest-workers in EUROPE, the Gulf, Asia and Canada, find their living conditions and civil RIGHTS circumscribed by their very migrancy. The suspicion of migrancy is shared by colonial and postcolonial STATES alike, whose governments often view migrant populations as threats to their ordering design and apparatus of control. Pastoralists and shifting cultivators were (and continue to be) seen by states as lesser producers whose activities thwart efficiency, erode environments, and undercut the positive EXTERNALITIES that putatively attach to private PROPERTY and sedentary agriculture (see PASTORALISM). Lurking in these assessments is a sense that migrancy equates to vagabond conduct, an equation that is frequently sharpened through RACIALIZATION: thus the Bedouin in Israel have been constructed by the Israeli government as inimical to the PROPERTY and political regimes of the SETTLER STATE and, through their supposedly aberrant SPATIALITY, left literally 'out of place' and 'suspended in space' (Shamir, 1996; Mair, 2008).

In counterpoint to these bleak assessments, however, and the unilinear TELEOLOGY of a singular Western modernity that sustains some of them, Gidwani and Sivaramakrishnan (2003) have emphasized that the SUBJECT-positions produced through migrancy cannot be axiomatically reduce to passivity or victimhood and that, in particular circumstances, these mobilities – often marginalized in conventional accounts – may be vehicles for cultural and political assertion. To recover the complex contours of MIGRANCY and the web of DIASPORIC populations thus requires both critical analyses of the institutions that frame and facilitate, entrap and exclude migrants, but also careful and intrinsically spatialized ETHNOGRAPHIES of the migrant condition.

DG/VG

Suggested reading
Gidwani and Sivaramakrishnan (2003); Mills (1999).

migration The residential relocation of an individual, family or group from one place to another (see also MIGRANCY). It is distinct from TOURISM or other short-term visits that do not involve a change in residence. Geographers have been particularly interested in migration, since it is so clearly related to both the development of PLACES and the relationships between them (Skeldon, 1997; Black, 1998). According to the most recent figures, there are nearly 200 million migrants in the world, defined as people who are living outside their country of birth (Global Commission on International Migration, 2005). Traditionally, migration is classified according to four broad criteria: intra-national versus international; temporary versus permanent; forced versus voluntary; and legal versus illegal (Bailey, 2001; Castles and Miller, 2003). Within GEOGRAPHY and other social science disciplines, scholars tend to specialize according to these distinctions. For example, the field of intra-national migration (also known as MOBILITY) is generally distinct from that of international migration. Similarly, largely separate groups of researchers study forced migration, or the movement of REFUGEES and ASYLUM seekers, versus those who study migration arising from economic motivations. If nothing else, these categories reveal that migration is a complex phenomenon that can be generated by a number of processes. Just as there are many causes of migration, there are also many consequences. Recently, critical geographers and other progressive scholars have called these sharp distinctions into question, noting that most migrants take a variety of factors into account when making their decision to move (Bailey, 2001). While it may seem an obvious point, this is a crucial issue, since all of the systems that seek to regulate migration are based on the assumption that the causes of each individual movement are identifiable and discrete.

Ernest George Ravenstein is acknowledged as the first person to theorize migration and he introduced a number of 'laws' – in the 1880s – that he believed captured the most important processes involved (Grigg, 1977). For example, he stated that: the tendency for migration varies inversely with the distance between source and destination (i.e. there are far more short-distance moves than long-distance ones); the majority of migrants move in order to improve their economic circumstances; therefore migration is mainly directed to places of concentrated economic opportunity, particularly cities; migration accelerates when movement becomes easier (e.g. once TRANSPORTATION infrastructure is in place); women tend to move shorter distances than men; and migration in one direction eventually generates its opposite – movement in the opposite direction. These early generalizations are still seen as relevant and form the basis of the most prominent model of migration. The GRAVITY MODEL uses a simple mathematical equation to predict the amount of migration between any two places, which is projected as the product of the population size of the two places divided by the distance, squared, between them. More elaborate versions of the gravity model take more factors into consideration and are correspondingly more mathematically complex.

Migration theories today are dominated by three strands of thought. The first is a legacy of the Ravenstein approach, but informed by more recent economic theories. It posits that individuals migrate when it is in their economic interest, and will go to the place that maximizes their life-long earning potential. Meanwhile, governments create migration policies to attract the talents that they lack (cf. PUBLIC POLICY). The world is therefore seen as a kind of 'migration MARKET', much like the labour market, with rational actors and predictable outcomes (Borjas, 1989). Individuals with high levels of human capital (education and work experience) go to places that provide the highest wages for that group. Meanwhile, less-skilled individuals gravitate to countries with the least polarized wage rates and the most generous welfare policies. These types of migration are labelled, respectively, 'positive' versus 'negative selection'. There is also an emerging *new* economic theory of migration that considers families the basic unit of decision-making rather than individuals. According to this theory, families seek to enhance their survival through minimizing risk (as opposed to atomized individuals seeking to maximize their earnings), and therefore attempt to place individual family members in several countries at the same time, providing multiple possibilities should life become difficult in any particular place (Massey, Arango, Hugo, Kouaouci, Pellegrino and Taylor, 1993). Economic theories of migration, old and new, are often used to generate predictions of the SCALE and direction of migration. For this reason, they are considered to be highly relevant by governments that are interested in regulating migration. Critics charge that these models make invalid assumptions (e.g. that individuals are fully informed about opportunity structures in other countries), and produce highly simplified results.

The second major strand of migration theory is based in the logic of WORLD SYSTEMS THEORY. According to this view, migration is generated by the expansion of the CAPITALIST system throughout the world, which destabilizes traditional ways of life – both economically and environmentally – in an ever-expanding periphery (Black, 1998). People move because their livelihoods are compromised, especially when they also become captivated by the lure of high wages and consumer capitalism in affluent countries. However, affluent countries create barriers to migration in an effort to preserve their privilege. They therefore allow the selective admission of highly skilled individuals (such as trained medical professionals or high tech engineers) and relatively small numbers of individuals who are deemed to be unskilled, who are expected to accept jobs that are shunned by domestic citizens (Castles and Miller, 2003). Typically, members of the first group are granted permanent residence, while those belonging to the latter are expected to return home when their labour is no longer required (e.g. the guestworker programs in Europe from the 1950s to the 1970s). In this sense, migration is a key ingredient in the development of dual, or segmented, LABOUR MARKETS, with migrants, who are typically racialized cultural minorities, employed in '3D' jobs (dirty, dangerous and difficult) and members of mainstream society in better-remunerated jobs that are protected by professional associations or unions. Migration regulations are therefore implicated in a continuing process of DEVELOPMENT versus UNDERDEVELOPMENT, both across societies and within them (Massey, Arango, Hugo, Kouaouci, Pellegrino and Taylor, 1993).

The third major body of theory emphasizes social aspects and is especially concerned with the relationship between SOCIAL NETWORKS and migration. Individuals make migration decisions in the context of imperfect information that is shared across social networks, which often include people who have migrated (Tilly, 1990b; Weiner, 1995). Migrants tend to follow those who have gone before them, in a process that is called CHAIN MIGRATION. This is a rational process, since new migrants benefit from the experiences of their predecessors. Newcomers are also assisted when they arrive in the destination country. As this process gains momentum, immigrant communities emerge and gradually build in-group sociocultural institutions. Frequently, these communities are geographically concentrated and may be seen by mainstream society as GHETTOS, places that are both isolated from mainstream society and also disadvantaged – though there are important exceptions to this tendency (cf. UNDERCLASS). The network approach to migration has led to three particularly powerful insights. First, chain migration leads to a process of cumulative causation; that is, each move helps build pathways that facilitate additional migration. Migration begets migration (Massey, Arango, Hugo, Kouaouci, Pellegrino and Taylor, 1993). Gradually, people in the source society become convinced that migration is 'normal' and even expected as a rite of passage. Second, social networks become stretched between source and destination societies, with people who are closely connected on both sides. Echoing the point first made by Ravenstein, people begin to move back and forth across these networks in a process of circular migration. FREQUENTLY, these moves are linked to significant LIFE-CYCLE turning points, such as entering tertiary education, looking for work, raising a family and retirement. Moreover, information flows quickly across these stretched social networks, as people communicate on a regular basis and economic links also intensify. People in these TRANSNATIONAL networks develop new, combinatorial identities that include elements of both source and destination societies, and are conscious of political and social developments in both societies (Vertovec, 1993; Levitt and Glick Schiller, 2004). Geographers have contributed significantly to understanding these forms of transnational behaviour and identity. Finally, scholars who study migration networks highlight the significant differences between men and women in all aspects of migration, including: the reasons for migration; migration pathways; and the consequences of migration for the individuals involved (Pessar, 1999; Silvey, 2006; Yeoh, 2006).

463

All of these theories are much better equipped to understand voluntary migration, where people make choices about when to leave and where to go. Actually, the bulk of international migration is forced: people are compelled to leave their residence due to CON-FLICT, persecution, environmental degradation, natural disasters or development projects (Black, 1998; Hyndman, 2000). Certain types of forced migration are monitored and, to a degree, regulated by international agencies, particularly the United Nations High Commissioner for Refugees (UNHCR) and the International Organization for Migration. These organizations assist migrants by helping build and service refugee camps, facilitating repatriation when circumstances in conflict zones improve, and arranging resettlement in other countries in cases when conflict or persecution persists. In 2006, the UNHCR estimated that there were approximately 20 million 'persons of concern', or refugees, worldwide. The UNHCR and other agencies attempt to ensure that the principles of the 1951 UN Convention Relating to the Status of Refugees, and the 1967 UN Protocol Relating to the Status of Refugees are upheld. Note that other types of migration are mainly regulated by NATION-STATES rather than international agencies. That is, nation-states generally have the right to decide who can enter their BORDERS and on what terms (Castles and Miller, 2003). However, signatory states to the aforementioned UN Convention and Protocol are obligated to provide asylum to refugees.

Since the 1980s, researchers have sought to understand the ETHICAL issues involved in migration. This sub-field tends to concentrate on three major issues. First, is migration a HUMAN RIGHT? That is, should individuals have the right to live where they choose (based on an individual rights perspective; Carens, 1987), or should states have the right to control their membership by selective admission policies (based on a collective rights perspective; Weiner, 1996)? Second, who should realize the rewards of migration and, conversely, pay the costs associated with it: the migrant, the destination society, or the source society (Castles and Miller, 2003)? Generally speaking, governments of countries that receive migrants create admission policies that are intended to secure the benefits of migration for their societies, and pay little attention to migrants and virtually none to source countries. For example, affluent countries frequently encourage highly trained medical personnel to immigrate without consideration for the difficulties involved for the migrants (in re-establishing their credentials) or for the consequences for source countries (which are losing scarce individuals who have typically been trained in public education systems). Third, what should be expected of migrants once they join a new society? Should they be required to ASSIMILATE or be encouraged to retain their cultural traditions? Each of these questions has generated vigorous debate in the scholarly and policy-oriented literatures. DH

Suggested reading
Black (1998); Castles and Miller (2003); Massey, Arango, Hugo, Kouaouci, Pellegrino and Taylor (1993); Weiner (1996).

militarism The extension of military influence into civilian political, social and cultural spheres. This is achieved through both the direct extension of the immediate influence of state militaries and the indirect influence of military agendas on political institutions, social norms and cultural values (see Woodward, 2005). In his farewell address to the nation in 1961, US President Dwight D. Eisenhower warned against the 'acquisition of unwarranted influence' by what he called 'the military–industrial complex': since then, the connections between militaries, defence industries and the global arms trade have become ever more intimate, but over the same period the multiple extensions of militarism have prompted many analysts to identify an even more extensive military–industrial–media–entertainment complex (MIME). Geographically, militarism is manifest in military control of PLACE, SPACE and LANDSCAPE; military influence over civilian law enforcement and legal geographies, and the militarization of SECURITY; military research within universities and research and development organizations (for militarism in GEOGRAPHY, see Barnes and Farish, 2006; Barnes, 2008b); and military themes in popular GEOPOLITICS, linked to the dissemination of distinctive IMAGINATIVE GEOGRAPHIES through films, novels, video games, web sites, and television drama and news (see, e.g., Power, 2007; Stahl, 2006, and Stahl's documentary film on the militarization of American popular culture, 'Militainment Inc.': description and trailer at http://www.freewebs.com/apocalicious/militainmentinc.htm). In these various ways, militarism serves as an IDEOLOGY that makes particular claims on notions of CITIZENSHIP (Stahl, 2006; Cowen and Gilbert, 2008) and, not least through its appeals to particular notions of MASCULINISM, also legitimizes and even glorifies the pursuit of WAR. (See also MILITARY GEOGRAPHY.)   DG/SG

Suggested reading
Barnes and Farish (2006); Stahl (2006); Woodward (2004).

military geography The study of geographies of military activities and operations. Facilitating the military activities and operations of nation-states was central to the emergence of modern GEOGRAPHY as a formal academic discipline. The enlistment of geography in the service of EMPIRE has become a commonplace of the history of geography (see GEOGRAPHY, HISTORY OF), and the foundation of the Royal Geographical Society in Britain in 1830, for example, was closely associated with the desire to formalize geographical knowledge to be put to work in the extension and management of the British Empire through EXPLORATION and survey, often closely connected with military personnel and military objectives, and through the conduct of military campaigns (Woodward, 2005). Some historians point to the Franco-Prussian War of 1870–1 as a major spur to the institutionalization of the discipline in EUROPE: the unexpected victory of the Prussian army was attributed, in part, to its superior training in geography. Across the Atlantic, a subdiscipline identified as military geography could trace its origins to the establishment of schools of geography at military establishments such as the US Military Academy at West Point in the early nineteenth century. These versions of military geography were not only INSTRUMENTAL (as one would expect) but also largely descriptive, and they emphasized the use of geographical knowledge, particularly location – via CARTOGRAPHY and MAP READING – and physical terrain to facilitate military operations. Perhaps the closest connections between in-service military geography and the academic discipline came during the Second World War, when many professional geographers collaborated in the production of detailed REGIONAL GEOGRAPHIES, for use in identifying targets and conducting offensive campaigns (Clout and Gosme, 2003; Barnes and Farish, 2006). Geographical knowledge remained crucial to the subsequent conduct of the COLD WAR, and its 'hot' campaigns in Indochina and elsewhere. Much of the traditional function of regional intelligence in the USA was contracted to programmes in AREA STUDIES rather than

geography, while the armed forces and intelligence agencies (on both sides) placed a premium on SURVEILLANCE from air- and space-platforms, and new technologies of REMOTE SENSING, satellite photography and the like.

The repeated emphasis on regional knowledges and regional intelligence, even in more sophisticated, space-sensing technical forms, may seem to reduce military geography to what Woodward (2005) calls a 'largely a-theoretical, descriptive regional geography', divorced from intellectual developments in the academic discipline at large. There are elements of truth in this, but two caveats are crucial. First, the technical elaborations of regional intelligence could be conceptual ones too; Barnes and Farish (2006) identify a series of vital connections between these seemingly commonplace activities and the conceptual ferment of SPATIAL SCIENCE and the QUANTITATIVE REVOLUTION, and it is surely no accident that the Office of Naval Research in the USA took such a close (and often financial) interest in what might otherwise seem remarkably abstract spatial modelling and geographical research. Second, advanced militaries (and the paramilitaries that they now often find themselves fighting) have recognized the need to think of what the US Army now calls 'battlespace' as more than physical terrain. Wars have always depended on the VISUALIZATION of space, but 'battlespace' not only has a much more complex geometry than conventional battle fields or theatres of war – it is no longer possible to make clear, linear separations between fronts (even during the First World War the front line decomposed into a bewildering maze of trenches and dugouts; contemporary conflicts transpose these geometries to the large scale) – but it is also increasingly understood as a human geography. The Pentagon has become increasingly preoccupied with urban warfare, which has required the construction of new, militarized models of CITIES and URBANIZATION, particularly in the global SOUTH, a development that Graham (2009c; see also 2004a) calls 'a new military urbanism', while the experience of military occupation (see OCCUPATION, MILITARY) and the revival of counterinsurgency in the wake of the American-led invasions of Afghanistan and Iraq has prompted the US military to undertake a CULTURAL TURN of its own in order to map 'the human terrain' in ways that resonate, however awkwardly and imperfectly, with contemporary developments across the social sciences (Gregory, 2008b, 2009c).

465

All of these issues can be studied critically, as most of the references above testify. But while Palka and Galgano (2000) suggest that writings such as these have cast 'a persistent shadow on military geography as an academic discipline', critical interventions in military geography, seeking to enlarge its compass beyond military circles, have only become a significant strand of work in HUMAN GEOGRAPHY in recent years: and over that same period many advanced militaries, particularly in Europe and North America, have redoubled and rethought their interventions in the production and appropriation of geographical knowledge. Significantly, these have involved far more than the direct application of geographical methodologies and knowledges to 'kinetic' (offensive) and now 'non-kinetic' operations: they have also involved a deepening engagement with the IDEOLOGY of MILITARISM.   DG/SG

Suggested reading
Flint (2005); Woodward (2004).

mimesis Described in ancient aesthetics as the 'imitation of nature', mimesis is generally concerned with how REPRESENTATION in ART is related to truth, or how effectively a copy may mirror or make present an original scene or perception. Can the image reproduce an actual object *as it is*? Or does it merely reproduce the appearance of the object as it looks, as *semblance*? The question, famously allegorized in Pliny's tale of a contest staged between two fifth-century painters, features centrally in Plato's analysis of VISION and EPISTEMOLOGY. Plato's answer is that representation is not only antipathetic to reality, but that the degree to which it aspires to lifelikeness is the degree to which it is adulterated, or distorted. While this remarkably 'modern' position prefigures present-day debates – from Marxian critiques of COMMODITY fetishism to the unmasking, within POST-STRUCTURALISM, of 'given meaning' – the mimetic tradition has been notably resilient. From the Italian humanists onwards (see HUMANISM), it has been thought of as the desire to bring nature towards its specular perfection. As an aesthetic formulation, mimesis also has applications within political PHILOSOPHY, especially within ENLIGHTENMENT struggles between custom and reason. Thus for Edmund Burke, as for David Hume, the perpetual forging of resemblances forms the condition for all human sociality: 'It is by imitation, far more than precept, that we learn everything ... It is one of the strongest links of society;

it is a species of mutual compliance' (Burke, 1906).

If mimesis in aesthetic theory refers us to the consensual and reproductive in social terms, it is no surprise that the concept has been variously modified and attacked in contemporary cultural and critical theory. Thus Adorno (1977), Lacoue-Labarthe (1989) and Derrida (1981) not only variously demonstrate how mimetic imitation subtends all of our institutions as well as our concepts of history and LANGUAGE. They also argue the ways in which a critique of mimesis requires us to rethink the relation between NATURE and technology, and to re-conceive the mediations between lived experience and aesthetic expression. From a different perspective, Homi Bhabha's (1984) deconstructive appropriation of the mimetic principle has become a critical concept in postcolonial analysis, in which the colonized SUBJECT's mimicry of colonial knowledge systems serves to estrange the basis of an authoritative discourse and so registers as a form of counterdomination (see POST-COLONIALISM).   JD

minor theory A way of thinking that takes off from and builds upon Deleuze and Guattari's (1986) notion of minor literature. It offers a means of working with material that self-consciously refuses 'mastery' in practices and claims, striving instead for a self-REFLEXIVE scholarship that subverts 'major' THEORY from within. Minor theory is a different way of 'doing theory;' a way of reading, writing, and talking that is insistently material – embodied, sensual, positioned – and refuses to ignore the different political–economic and social conditions in which knowledge is produced and shared. It recalls Adrienne Rich's (1976) anguished call to 'think through the BODY' in the hopes of making a materialist knowledge streaked with the peculiar temporality and SPATIALITY of EVERYDAY LIFE (Katz, 1996). This SITUATED KNOWLEDGE is interstitial with and inseparable from 'major' productions of knowledge, and uses displacement to expose and chafe their limits so that they crack. In these cracks new knowledge and practice can emerge, but the process itself is transformative. In dynamic relation major theory, minor theory, and the relations that hold them in tension are reworked.

Deleuze and Guattari (1986) focus on the writings of Franz Kafka, a Czech Jew living in Prague, who wrote in German. They argue that Kafka was doubly displaced in this 'major language', which was neither his mother tongue nor the language of his community, but that he pushed this displacement to its limits to create what they call 'lines of escape'. Minor LITERATURE is about the conscious use of displacement to call into question and change dominant modes of writing and using language. By extension, minor theory is intent on making alternative SUBJECTIVITIES, SPATIAL- ITIES and temporalities. It seeks to rework major theory from within, destabilizing received modes of knowing and the power/ knowledge that produces and frames their objects. What is constituted as major or minor is historically and geographically specific. Deleuze and Guattari make clear that the major and minor are not different languages but, rather, different ways of working with the same language. This work – or play – can enliven and renovate language (and theory) so that it is made to express something new because the limits of its traditional forms are breached.

The idea of 'becoming' is crucial to Deleuze and Guattari's notion of the minor. 'Becom- ing' suggests change and mutability, but also movement that ruptures, decomposes and recomposes. 'Becoming' invokes temporality, but its space is one of betweenness. Both work against the sort of dualism that would pit major against minor, or vice versa, but if the notion of becoming is to produce a critical politics, it must be understood as positioned somewhere (Braidotti, 1994; Katz, 1996). As a mode of thinking relationally, minor theory offers a means to reframe and move through theoretical impasses between, say, MARXISM and FEMINISM or local and global (cf. Massey, Allen and Sarre, 1999; Anderson 2000b). It can be a powerful strategy for recognizing and re-imagining DIFFERENCE; of thinking RACE through CLASS through GENDER, for instance, and through the iterative displacements such work calls forth, creating new spaces of and for political practice and engagement.   CK

Suggested reading
Anderson (2000b); Massey, Allen and Sarre (1999).

mobility There are two main uses of the term in HUMAN GEOGRAPHY: (1) the movement of people, ideas or goods across TERRITORY (phys- ical mobility); and (2) change in social status (social mobility). Reflecting current interest, the journal *Mobilities* was instituted in 2006.

Human mobility occurs over varying tem- poral and spatial SCALES, with MIGRATION re- ferring to mobility that involves a change in residential location, whether within a city or across continents and daily mobility, including

COMMUTING, referring to movements that do not entail a change of residence. Involving any one of a variety of means (e.g. feet, automo- bile, train, bicycle, airplane, wheelchair), mo- bility incurs costs in both time and money. As the costs of mobility have fallen (for example, the cost of sending a letter; the cost of travel between London and Mumbai), the separation between places has shrunk, a process known as TIME–SPACE CONVERGENCE, which has contrib- uted greatly to GLOBALIZATION. In addition to incurring costs, mobility – the ability to move between and among places, whether on a daily basis or over the LIFE COURSE – also confers benefits; indeed, humans could not exist with- out some form of mobility, and at every geo- graphical scale we have been consuming ever more of it. Because mobility is important for ACCESSIBILITY, it is often considered an import- ant component of independence and quality of life (Hanson and Pratt, 1995), such that popu- lations who lack the temporal or financial re- sources required for mobility (e.g. the elderly, CHILDREN or working parents with young chil- dren) become the focus of concern and mobil- ity-enhancing programmes.

With the advent of telecommunications, physical mobility is no longer required for SPATIAL INTERACTION, and geographers have devoted considerable attention to understand- ing the complex relationship between physical mobility and virtual mobility (e.g. shopping for books on the INTERNET after browsing in a local bookstore). Whereas physical mobility does not require NETWORKS (one need not cross a meadow on a path), it is certainly enhanced by them, as movement is easier on a network than off of one. Virtual mobility does rely on network structures. For both physical and virtual mobility, networks are crucially important in channelling and shap- ing mobility patterns.

Social mobility, which refers to upward or downward changes in the socio-economic sta- tus of individuals or HOUSEHOLDS, has drawn considerable attention in URBAN and SOCIAL GEOGRAPHY. Of particular interest has been the relationship between social mobility and spatial mobility; in theories associated with the CHICAGO SCHOOL of urban sociology: for example, the upward social mobility that accompanied the assimilation of immigrants into American society took place via residential movement ever outwards from the urban core. Like other forms of mobility, social mobility also involves networks; the size, social compos- ition and spatial location of a person's network of social contacts can affect the probability of upward or downward mobility (Granovetter, 1982; Hanson and Pratt, 1991).   SHa

Suggested reading
Cresswell (2006).

mode of production Karl Marx refined 'mode of production' to explain determinate ways of harnessing social labour to the transformation of NATURE. Nonetheless, Marx and Engels use the concept variously: sometimes as a unity in tension between 'forces of production' (technology, materials, human–environment relations) that fetter the transformation of 'relations of production' (PROPERTY, work, LAW, CLASS); while elsewhere, well-known passages from the *Communist manifesto* lend weight to an epochal, teleological interpretation of successive modes, including primitive communism, SLAVERY, FEUDALISM, CAPITALISM, SOCIALISM and, finally, COMMUNISM. Marx's *Capital* systematically explores the dynamics of one mode of production, through COMMODITIES produced by 'free labor': dually freed from the means of production of necessities for survival, and free to sell all they have left, their capacity to labour, without obligations from workplace or employer. On this exploitation, *Capital* constructs ramifying, spiralling, anarchic forces of INNOVATION, class struggle, CRISIS, resolution and destruction – dynamics long debated as periodic or catastrophic (see DIALECTIC). Twentieth-century orthodox Marxists carried the burden that precise determination of the mode had vital political effects.

This orthodoxy was called into question, at least 'West' of the Iron Curtain, through the revisionist MARXISMS of the 1970s. The revival of 'modes of production' in the plural spoke to new exigencies: British Marxists broke with Stalinism and evolutionism, as social history reopened histories of transition to capitalism; scholars of DECOLONIZATION and DEVELOPMENT in AFRICA, LATIN AMERICA and ASIA questioned the politics and POLITICAL ECONOMY of peasantries (see PEASANT) in relation to capitalism and IMPERIALISM; and Marxist feminists questioned agrarian HOUSEHOLDS' internal and external relations to MARKETS (see AGRARIAN QUESTION). A translation of Marx's (1857) 'Introduction' to his *Grundrisse* exemplified a hinge between his early and late thought, calling into question an economistic, mature Marx. Passages from Marx's corpus were re-read with an eye to 'subsumption' and persisting relations *between* modes of production. In debate with radical DEPENDENCY and WORLD-SYSTEMS theorists, French structuralists (see STRUCTURALISM) – in particular, the philosophers Louis Althusser and Etienne Balibar, economic anthropologists Claude Meillassoux and Maurice Godelier, and sociologist Nicos Poulantzas – conceived of internally systematic modes 'structured in dominance'. Debates in *Economy and Society*, collected in Wolpe (1980) – including Wolpe's own classic article on South Africa – questioned the historical and political articulation between the reproduction of capitalism and that of subordinate, pre-capitalist modes within the social formation.

Eric Wolf's (1982) critique of Marxist structuralism appealed instead to consciousness and historical diversity, to show how 'people without a history' organized capitalist, tributary and kin-ordered modes of production in relation to a diffusing global capitalism. Talal Asad (1987) questions Wolf's recourse to 'permanent criteria' in distinguishing modes rather than explaining complex histories of articulation to the unequally global history of capitalism. Instead, 'articulation' would have to contend with traditions, constructions, aspirations and conditions through which people could or could not participate in 'making history'. Central to work in this vein since has been Stuart Hall's (1980) reworking of 'articulation' as both 'joining up' and 'giving expression to': a Gramscian analytic that he uses to explain state-sanctioned RACISM as one form of cultural, material and political articulation of multiple modes.   SC

model An idealized and structured representation of (part of) the world (cf. ABSTRACTION; IDEAL TYPE). Model-building has a long history in many sciences, but its formal and conscious incorporation into GEOGRAPHY is usually attributed to attempts to establish geography as a SPATIAL SCIENCE in the 1960s and 1970s. Scientificity was central to the benchmark collection of essays edited by R.J. Chorley and P. Haggett as *Models in geography* (1967). They treated models as 'selective approximations which, by the elimination of incidental detail [or 'noise'] allow some fundamental, relevant or interesting aspects of the real world to appear in some generalized form'. The accent on generalization was vital to their project, and this was achieved through visual–geometric representations of SPATIAL STRUCTURES and through mathematical–statistical generation of spatial patterns. The twentieth anniversary of the original *Models* was marked by an international conference attended by both revisionists who sought to rethink and revitalize the project and dissidents who were sceptical of its ability to address what they regarded as more important questions. On one side, Harvey claimed that 'those who have stuck with modelling since those heady days have largely been able to do so by restricting the nature of the questions they ask'. To Cosgrove, modelling was the quintessential expression of high MODERNISM, and the privilege it accorded to abstraction, functionality, generalization and simplicity was altogether incapable of responding to the challenge of DIFFERENCE in a late modern, even POSTMODERN, world. On the other side were a large number of unrepentant spatial scientists who had no time for such concerns, and who reaffirmed their faith in the central, INSTRUMENTAL importance of formal modelling. The publication of these exchanges two years later, as *Remodelling geography* (Macmillan, 1989) coincided with a radically different collection edited by R. Peet and N. Thrift entitled *New models in geography* (1989). Their subtitle indicated a tectonic shift in the foundations of model-building: 'the political-economy perspective' signalled a range of different approaches that had a common grounding in various forms of POLITICAL ECONOMY, CRITICAL SOCIAL THEORY and HISTORICAL MATERIALISM. Partly as a consequence, the original claim for analytical model-building as the central object of geographical enquiry was displaced and efforts were directed towards methods as means rather than ends in themselves.

Since then, however, the prospectus advanced by Haggett and Chorley has been renewed in two ways. First, model-building had been advanced as (at least in part) a solution to an exploding data matrix: the architects of the model-based PARADIGM insisted that geographers had no choice but to move beyond the accumulation of 'facts' that had reduced their field to an endlessly enlarging global gazetteer, with no clear logic of selection or organization. Since then, however, the development of electronic modes of data storage and retrieval, analysis and display – most visibly through GEOGRAPHIC INFORMATION SYSTEMS – has provided much more sophisticated algorithms for data management. Second, model-building was originally advertised as a necessary moment in the 'puzzle-solving' activity required for the inauguration of a new, properly scientific, paradigm for geographical enquiry: 'That there is more order in the world than appears at first sight,' Haggett and Chorley reminded their readers, 'is not discovered till the order is looked for.' Since then, many human geographers have been drawn to

forms of cultural and social theory that insist on the radical non-innocence of just 'looking', and NON-REPRESENTATIONAL THEORY, POST-STRUCTURALISM and SCIENCE STUDIES (among others) have directed attention towards the ways in which ideas and images enter directly into the very constitution – the 'ordering' – of the world.   DG

modernism Strategies of REPRESENTATION closely identified with late-nineteenth- and twentieth-century movements in the arts that challenged the conventions of romanticism and REALISM. There are many modernisms, but Lunn (1985) identified four common preoccupations:

(1) *Aesthetic self-consciousness*. 'Modern artists, writers and composers often draw attention to the media or materials with which they are working' and in doing so emphasize that their work is a fabrication in the literal sense of 'something made'; they thus seek to escape from the idea of art as a direct reflection of the world (cf. MIMESIS).

(2) *Simultaneity and juxtaposition*. Modernism often disrupts, weakens or dissolves temporal structure in favour of simultaneity: different perspectives are often juxtaposed within the same frame or narrative.

(3) *Paradox, ambiguity and uncertainty*. Modernism often explores 'the paradoxical many-sidedness of the world': instead of an omniscient narrator, for example, modernist writers may use multiple points of view.

(4) *The demise of the centred subject*. Modernism often exposes and disrupts the fiction of the sovereign individual or the 'integrated subject'.

Modernism did not emerge in a vacuum: it was a critical response to a series of crises within capitalist MODERNITY. Its coordinates included: the explosive growth of modern cities and the radical transformation of their built forms, economies and cultures; the restructuring of European CAPITALISM, especially through the Agricultural Depression at the end of the nineteenth century and the intensified technical changes brought about by a new round of INDUSTRIALIZATION; the aggressive advance of European COLONIALISM and IMPERIALISM; and the turbulence of the First World War and the Russian Revolution. This mapping has three implications of direct relevance to HUMAN GEOGRAPHY:

(1) These episodes involved significant changes in conceptions of TIME and SPACE in the WEST (Kern, 1983) which also had dramatic repercussions far beyond the shores of EUROPE and North America. Huyssen (2007) insists that modernism 'cut across' imperial and post-imperial cultures – it included Baudelaire's Paris and Joyce's Dublin, but also Borges' Buenos Aires and Kahlo's Mexico City – so that 'metropolitan culture was translated, appropriated and creatively mimicked in colonized and post-colonial countries in ASIA, AFRICA and LATIN AMERICA'.

(2) The ways in which these changes were registered in the arts, literature and elsewhere were profoundly gendered and sexualized. 'The territory of modernism,' Pollock (1988, p. 54) argues, 'so often is a way of dealing with masculine SEXUALITY and its sign, the bodies of women'. Representations of modern spaces were made to revolve around masculine subject-positions – like the mobile figure of the FLÂNEUR – and to privilege encounters 'between men who have the freedom to take their pleasures in many urban spaces and women from a class subject to them who have to work in those spaces often selling their bodies to clients or to artists'. Indeed, Lefebvre's account of the PRODUCTION OF SPACE, which was partly inspired by his encounters with surrealism and the Situationists, repeatedly draws attention to the significance of modernism for the triumph of a 'visual-phallic-geometric space'.

(3) Modernism was connected not only to experimentation in the arts, but also to new styles of philosophical reflection and to the formation of the social sciences (including CRITICAL THEORY and Western MARXISM, Lunn's primary concern). But most of these intellectual projects retained the social markings, marginalizations and exclusions written into metropolitan modernism.

Lunn's characterizations work best when applied to modern ART and LITERATURE and probably have less purchase on modern architecture, which has its own chronologies (Frampton, 1992). These architectural motifs assumed a wider significance in the 1950s and 1960s, when a *high modernism* emerged as a dominant cultural thematic, distinguished by what Bürger (1992) described as a 'pathos of purity'. 'In the same way as architecture divested itself of ornamental elements,' he argued, so 'painting freed itself from the primacy of the representational, and the nouveau roman liberated itself from the categories of traditional fiction (plot and character).' In much the same way, too, SPATIAL SCIENCE divested human geography of an interest in the particularities of AREAL DIFFERENTIATION, which became so much 'surface noise', in order to reveal the purity of geometric form and SPATIAL STRUCTURE (often, like architecture, cast in terms of FUNCTIONALISM). It would not be difficult to present other high modernist movements in social thought in much the same way, notably STRUCTURALISM.

From such a perspective, POSTMODERNISM becomes a critique of high modernism rather than of modernism *tout court*. It contains important echoes of the early-twentieth-century avant-garde, and a number of writers have urged the reclamation of that earlier modernism as an indispensable moment in the formulation of critical social theory. In fact, Berman (1983) suggests that it had its roots even earlier, in the nineteenth-century writings of Baudelaire and Marx, both of whom (in different ways) sought to come to terms with a world in which 'all that is solid melts into air'. Those human geographers most invested in these reclamation projects have paid close attention to the historical–geographical coordinates of modernism (above). Thus Harvey (1989b) sought to expose some of the connections between the cultural formations of modernism, the experience of TIME-SPACE COMPRESSION and the changing political economy of capitalism, which in turn provoked a critique of the ways in which his own representations erased the characteristic gendering and sexualization of their maps of modernity (Deutsche, 1996c). There have also been specific studies: Harvey's (2003a) excavation of modernism and its material foundations in nineteenth-century Paris, and Pinder's (2005c) exploration of forms of utopian modernism in the twentieth century (see SITUATIONISM).

But the most deliberately modernist contributions to contemporary human geography are to be found in the work of Gunnar Olsson and Allan Pred. Pred's experimental studies of European modernities (1995) and his extraordinary re-creation of a 'heart of darkness' at the very centre of 'Swedish modern' (2004) were freely informed by the example of Walter Benjamin; they beautifully exemplify all four of Lunn's diagnostics (above) and the radical, critical impulse of early modernism that

Berman so admires. In a transposed key, Olsson's (2007) critique of CARTOGRAPHIC REASON recalls those earlier modernisms too, and stages crucial encounters with the art of Duchamp, Malevich and Rothko; but its careful minimalism also reinscribes the pathos of high modernism in a newly critical register. Taken together, these thought-works show that modernism still has much to contribute to the jaded critical cultures of human geography (and much more besides). DG

Suggested reading
Brooker and Thacker (2005); Harvey (1989a, chs. 2, 16).

modernity A notoriously ambivalent and highly contested concept, the notion of 'modernity' has nonetheless acquired wide currency within HUMAN GEOGRAPHY, not the least prompted by the proliferation of ideas drawn from POSTMODERNISM in the 1980s and 1990s. Broadly speaking, the term has been used to designate a number of discrete, yet inter-related, phenomena that, in most cases until recently, place EUROPE at the centre of the world stage (see EUROCENTRISM):

(1) First and foremost, modernity is used as a means to periodize European (and, by implication, 'world') history by designating a distinct epoch. The boundaries surrounding this 'modern' epoch are unclear, starting as early as the dawn of the Italian Renaissance (fourteenth century), through the invention of the printing press (fifteenth century) to the INDUSTRIAL REVOLUTION (eighteenth and nineteenth centuries). As Bauman (1993, p. 3) put it: ' "How old is modernity?" is a contentious question ... There is no agreement on dating. There is no consensus on what is to be dated.' Common to all epochal definitions, however, is the idea of a break with the past: with established modes of REPRESENTATION, for example, with economic practices and regimes, with technologies, or with cultural and social relations.

(2) Modernity is also used to designate a particular mental attitude that seeks rationally to understand the world we live in by finding order within and achieving domination over NATURE (cf. Withers, 1996). Here, 'modernity' becomes synonymous with the notion of progress and gradually affects most areas of life, from the medicalization of bodies and environ-

ments to the rationalization of urban life through the discourse of PLANNING (see also BIOPOWER). SCIENCE and the pursuit of knowledge in the wake of the European ENLIGHTENMENT was central to this evidence-based spirit of modernity, which finds its perfect geographical expression in the notion of Cartesian, isotropic SPACE. Aspirationally, it is perhaps best captured by Kant's famous 1784 maxim, *sapere aude*, or 'dare to know'.

(3) A third dimension employs 'modernity' to designate a thoroughly secular project of liberation and emancipation that arguably culminated in the related American and French Revolutions of the late eighteenth century, and which led to the emancipation of slaves and the establishment of HUMAN RIGHTS across a range of differences. This 'political' modernity heralds a set of historical tasks that seeks the implementation of novel forms of political representation, of legal and social rights of individuals, and of justice in a host of different contexts (cf. Schama, 1989; Howell, 1993; Delaney, 2001: see also LIBERALISM).

(4) A final sense in which the concept of 'modernity' is used specifies a particular process of global incorporation that leads directly from the Age of Exploration to the European COLONIALISMS of the nineteenth and twentieth centuries. In this context, 1492 marks the dawn of a new era: the beginning of GLOBALIZATION within and through a set of clearly structured, if historically developing, CORE–PERIPHERY relationships (Taylor, 1999) and motivated, perhaps, by what Max Weber famously described as a 'protestant work ethic'. The most basic element to this notion of modernity is the NATION-STATE and its territorially expanding capacity to organize and make social processes anonymous (see also Harris, 1991).

Thus, it would seem best initially to conceptualise 'modernity' as a broad semantic field marked by tensions, contradictions and possible DIALECTICAL energies, rather than streamlining them into an organic totality. The concept is thus implicitly linked to other concepts such as CAPITALISM, 'nation-state,' MOBILITY, literacy, DEMOCRACY and URBANIZATION, to name but the most prominent. Any one of these, individually or in combination, are customarily invoked when attempting to define 'modernity,' so much so that often the

471

link is established by rendering modernity as an implicit adjectival, and thus clarifying, part of any of the nouns just listed. In other words, while 'ways of thinking', 'economic practices' or 'modes of transportation' become paradigmatically different by being prefaced and hence associated with 'modern', 'democracy' and other key concepts appear semantically to embody 'the modern' as such. Furthermore, throughout its history (however conceptualized), 'modernity' has been contested (e.g. the Counter-Reformation in the seventeenth century, the Romantic Movement in the late eighteenth century, the back-to-nature movements of the late nineteenth century, the student and worker uprisings associated with May 1968, or the current religious revival, especially in the USA).

What perhaps unites most definitions of 'modernity' is an emphasis on the notion of the 'new'. Modernity is synonymous with change and thus becomes a declared enemy of traditions. This is the root of many subsequent binary distinctions that characterize modernity: the 'new' is explicitly set apart from the 'old' – and it is the distance between the two that acquires explanatory power. The importance of this threshold is encapsulated in the different figures employed to characterize modernity: Georg Simmel's 'stranger', Max Weber's 'adventurer', or the '*FLÂNEUR*' and the 'gambler' invoked by Walter Benjamin all emphasize a border, be it between inside and outside, old and new, presence and absence or PRIVATE AND PUBLIC (Shields, 1992; Strohmayer, 1997). It is in the nature of such borderlines to invoke an 'uncanny' sense of existence where the 'new' constantly has the power to threaten or disrupt, as exemplified in Fritz Lang's 1931 film *M*.

The notion of the 'new' (and the close, intertwined relationship between modernity, and filmic and urban space: see FILM) also points us towards another geographical context surrounding modernity: its thoroughly urban, or better yet metropolitan character (Ogborn, 1998; Frisby, 2001; Pile, 2005). It is in urban settings that the 'new' materializes an exuberant side of modernity, where the 'new' is not synonymous with order but paradoxically becomes associated with a set of practices subverting traditions (Berman 1983). The undermining of sexual mores, diversification of CONSUMPTION practices, the rise in artistic freedoms and forms of expression culminating in the notion of an avant-garde, the growth in new and decidedly urbane forms of 'destructive' capital assembled in the hands of the bourgeoisie so effectively analysed by Marx, or simply the development of different lifestyles all encompass 'experiences of modernity' (Frisby, 2001, p. 2; see also Glennie and Thrift, 1992) that are not so easily, if at all, attained in non-urban spaces. Small wonder, then, that it takes another quintessentially modern and urban figure, the detective (as exemplified by virtually any film noir), to reorder a world threatening to become unreadable. The urban has become synonymous with the 'modern' in another sense as well: novelty principally also attaches to architecture, where 'order' translates into a functional approach to questions of housing and urban design (Dennis, 1994; Heynen, 1999). L.H. Sullivan's phrase that 'form (ever) follows function' (1896) and A. Loos' insistence that 'ornament is crime' (1908) together capture the architects' aspirations materialised in modern buildings. Rather crucial for any understanding of modernity is the tension emerging at the heart of this and related 'ordering' impulses: the tension between any order given or imparted upon architecture or urban design and the restless, destructive tendencies embodied by the ever-changing nature of 'the new' (Donald, 1999: see MODERNISM). As postmodernists would later lament (and remaining within Loos' dictum), 'order' thus becomes its own ornament.

A solution to this impasse is offered by a further element common to many definitions of modernity: the projection of 'progress' on to constantly developing technologies. Effectively reconciling the notion of 'the new' with the desire (or necessity) to impart order, the very idea of 'progress' imparts a sense of direction to 'modernity' and thus renders it potentially legible. Trusted or not, technological developments ranging from seafaring innovations, the invention of paper moneys, the steam engine, entertainment technologies such as panoramas or the cinema to the INTERNET of our present age all impacted upon everyday life in a way that has lent credence to the idea of an ephemeral and constantly changing; that is, a modern world that is defined by its technologically progressing nature (Asendorf, 1993). As this listing implies, these technologies have threaded different places into new conjunctions, and the intensification of multiple processes of TIME–SPACE COMPRESSION under contemporary modes of GLOBALIZATION has reworked both senses of PLACE and structures of SPACE (Entrikin, 1991; Hetherington, 1997b; Oakes, 1997).

Modernity does not, of course, merely denote a set of particular constellations characteristic of the material world. In addition to such historically contingent interpretations of modernity (or interpretations of the world through the lenses crafted by 'modernity'), a number of critiques of modernity have been formulated within PHILOSOPHY and the social sciences, themselves a direct product of modernizing tendencies within society at large. Perhaps chief amongst these is the recognition that the quest for order inherent in many modern tendencies embodies an element of systemic control that has been used historically to suppress progressive movements. Examples include the rationalization of urban space in Haussmann's Paris, seen by contemporaries as the very 'capital of modernity' (Harvey, 2003b), the BIOPOLITICS and the central function of MARKETS under NEO-LIBERALISM. Returning to the four main definitions of modernity presented above, we may thus infer a formative tension, not to say contradiction, between modernity as scientific progress and modernity as an emancipatory project. Even so, to state matters in this way may well imply an all too overt reliance on modern ways of seeing. As Bruno Latour has insisted, most attempts to infuse a clear sense of 'order' have always been implicated in non-ordered, HYBRID and networked social practices (cf. Swyngedouw, 1999).

Another critique that has gained wide currency in the geographical literature is that modernity is inherently REDUCTIONIST in its insistence on the primacy of the 'eye' over other sensual modes of connecting to the world (see also VISION and VISUALITY). Chiefly building on the work of Walter Benjamin and the writings of Guy Debord and the SITU-ATIONISTS, this strand of critique centres on the importance of optical METAPHORS and instruments in modern environments (Crary, 1990a). From René Descartes' early-seventeenth-century insistence on the importance of evidential modes of reasoning to telescopes, microscopes and cameras, through the optically structured spaces of modernity such as the arcades, boulevards and parks (Ogborn, 1998; Strohmayer, 2006), to 'ocular' writing in general with its focus on LANDSCAPES and the mappable nature of events (Guarrasi, 2001; Dubbini, 2002: see also CARTOGRAPHIC REASON), modernity is characterized as a mode of engaging with the world that favours visual relations over and against other modes of connecting with and being in the world. As before, this critique has a double edge: it attaches to a 'modern' world that has become increasingly reliant on visual modes of communication, while also being critical of modes of understanding the modern world that in turn rely on visual technologies, rhetoric and categories. The ensuing dual practice of deploying the visual both as a structuring principle informing modern spaces and as a mode of understanding such spaces has perhaps best been characterized in the notion of the SPECTACLE, as critically developed by Debord (1994). Central to this critique is the reliance common among critical social scientist and geographers alike on that which arguably requires critique itself: visual modes of existence. We 'shed light', we 'illuminate', we 'enlighten' – all the while the world we live in has become saturated with visual forms of commerce, information and entertainment. In other words: the critique of modernity all too often relies on modern modes of communication and exchange, rendering it vulnerable to the charge of being but another mode of consumption and distraction. Theodor Adorno and Max Horkheimer's earlier disenchantment with an Enlightenment, and their claims that modernity had surrendered its better impulses to an 'entertainment industry' are akin to this critique.

In all of this it is important to remember that such dis-enchantment, especially in the context of the twentieth century, was often brought about by real and often life-threatening CRISIS experiences. Nazism in particular and its thoroughly rational implementation of the HOLOCAUST, but also the Stalinist experiments, Hiroshima and the constant development of UNDERDEVELOPMENT structurally endemic to modern capitalism have all contributed (see also WAR). So too have those politico-legal responses to modern crises that have worked to produce an 'outside' to the modern, a heterogeneous and dispersed space of EXCEPTION where particular groups of people are expelled from the privileges and protections of the modern even as they are made subject to its disciplines and punishments (Minca, 2007a).

For some commentators, this disenchantment inspired the development of the concept of 'POSTMODERNITY'. Others have seen fit to speak of a *second modernity* (e.g. Beck, 1992) or of *hypermodernity* (e.g. Pred and Watts, 1992). More interesting still, given the complexities surrounding the term and its thoroughly EUROCENTRIC origins, are recent developments that attempt to broaden the linguistic field surrounding 'modernity' (Gilroy, 1993; Appadurai, 1996; Gaonkar, 2001; Venn and Featherstone, 2006: see also Martins and Abreu, 1996;

Power and Sidaway, 2005; Walton-Roberts and Pratt, 2005). The resulting post-colonial notion of 'modernity' aims to reconcile the often devastating impact that modernity has on non-Western cultures and societies with the progressive, emancipatory impulse also associated with modernity (see POST-COLONIALISM). Acknowledging that modernity has impacted unevenly across space, the focus of these often surprisingly modern investigations is chiefly on the concrete negotiations that contextualize adoptive or rejective practices locally in a global setting. Gilroy's (1993) studies of the complex formation of a 'Black Atlantic' exemplify this strand of scholarship. The main innovation of such work resides in its willingness to break with a notion of linearity that has characterized notions of modernity from Descartes to Hegel (see Duncan, 2002). At the same time, and in close analogy to other attempts to broaden analytical concepts, any gains achieved need to be measured against losses in clarity, argumentative bite and explanatory power: 'broadening' often also entails elements of diluting argumentative claims. In the case of 'modernity', with (as we have seen) its already wide semantic field, the abandonment of linearity carries the risk of no longer being able critically to differentiate if, or to what extent, societies (or elements thereof) can meaningfully be compared through the use of the conceptual apparatus developed in conjuncture with the term 'modernity'. In the absence of such comparative yardsticks, how can scholars translate findings from one geographical locale to another?

In fact, 'translation' may well be an apt term to use within modern DISCOURSES. Translations have always posed quite fundamental problems in that acts of translation tend to reduce a semantic multitude to more circumspect and singular set of equivalences. Attributing modernity to this process at least has the practical virtue of ensuring compatibility at a relatively accessible point in an argument. Traditional notions of modernity would, for instance, have firmly placed practices associated with or emanating from 'witchcraft' as being either pre-modern or outside the realm of the modern by presupposing incompatibility between the two terms. The very thought of 'alternative modernities' (Gaonkar, 2001) undermines this robust principle. By ensuring that translation between different practices can always involve or lead to a broadening of categories or non-linear historical trajectories, the notion of 'the modern' risks the loss of normative aspects associated with modernity

as an emancipatory and, in the words of Jürgen Habermas, an 'unfinished' project (see CRITICAL THEORY).

Arguably, many debates currently taking place in the first decade of the new millennium labour with precisely this point: the possibility of the universality of modern dreams, aspirations and normatively inspired practices. Can we think of 'modernity' in the absence of pre-formulated yardsticks, or clearly associated practices? Whether we invoke the notion of a 'clash of cultures', a re-investigation of notions of 'tolerance' or insist on established, modern norms (especially in the legal context) in the face of challenges, we are talking about modernity and its survival into an increasingly less certain future. Modernity may yet prove its most enduring qualities by remembering its own inherent insistence on the importance of the 'new'. In geographical terms, this 'new' translates into an insistence on the importance not of preserving a status quo but of constant experimentation and improvement (Toulmin, 1990). In other words, it involves a resolve to preserve and produce alternative spaces of modernity, rather than spaces of alternative modernities.   US

Suggested reading
Berman (1983); Gaonkar (2001); Minca (2007a); Venn and Featherstone (2006).

modernization Often conflated with DEVELOPMENT in general and Westernization in particular, modernization describes processes unleashed by the transformation of traditional societies into capitalist ones or by their incorporation through adaptation into an increasingly globally operating form of CAPITALISM. If the former process is traditionally held to characterize the transformative processes attaching to Western societies in the context of the nineteenth century, it is the latter, non-indigenous form of modernization that has come to dominate the world since the end of the Second World War. As such, notions of modernization partake in discourses of the evolutionary transformation of societies and are often deeply implicated in notions of progress, growth, liberalization and the DIFFUSION of particular values. Up until fairly recently, such processes of modernization were thought to entail a clearly legible and often TELEOLOGICAL register of changes in the economic, cultural, social and political sphere of societies undergoing transformation. Not so any more. Initially criticized for being too narrowly focused on economic forms of modernization and for disregarding the many different direct and indirect costs linked with modernization processes, attention has also moved to forms of contestation and RESISTANCE that accompany and often undermine modernization processes (Scott, 1985; Nabudere, 1997).

More recently still, the term has been recast as *reflexive modernization* in the work of Ulrich Beck and others (cf. REFLEXIVITY). Rather than following a preset and, indeed, general path (see MODERNITY), modernization is now thought to entail the ability constantly to adapt and thus to create a 'second modernity'. Where older modernization discourses argued with reference to timeless and abstract principles, a newer and reflexive practice seeks constantly to review its goals and practices in dialogue with incoming information. Key in this attempt is the geographical term 'BOUNDARY', which is seen less as a fixed entity than a conscious practice (Shields, 2006): just as boundaries emerge from processes of negotiation and remain open to future negotiations, reflexive modernization both relies on the boundedness of its practices while acknowledging their potential for change. Structurally similar to recent attempts to broaden the notion of 'modernity' by incorporating non-Western practices, reflexive modernization thus constitutes a discursive process, rather than marking the outcome of discursive practices, as older notions of modernization had attempted to do (see DISCOURSE). It is hence no surprise to see the term 'reflexive modernization' often being conflated with the notions of 'third way' or 'third (or 'new') modernity'. Likewise, the realization that modernity may well have become a problem in its own right shares the key assumption of a required dialogical openness with reflexive notions of modernization. Principally, such problematization takes place through the recognition that unintended consequences within industrial societies, which proliferate as RISKS beyond the accepted certainties, are created within modernity. In this form, 'reflexive modernization' has been heralded by many as an agency-orientated alternative to POSTMODERN discourses and attitudes (Beck, Bonss and Lau, 2003) and is related to STRUCTURATION THEORY (Beck, Giddens and Lash, 1994). **US**

Suggested reading
Alexander (1996); Beck (1997); Galloway (2005); Gleeson (2000); Nabudere (1997); Shields (2006).

modifiable areal unit problem (maup) A particular form of ECOLOGICAL FALLACY

associated with the analysis of spatial data sets, in particular those in which data on individual observation units (such as households) are aggregated into areal units (such as CENSUS TRACTS and counties) for analysis.

Robinson (1950) provided the classic exposé of the maup for social scientists (see also Gehlke and Biehl, 1934), in which he showed that a high correlation between two variables (the percentage of the population who were African-American and the percentage who were illiterate) at the state SCALE within the USA was not replicated at the individual level; in other words, whereas the aggregate data analysis showed that states with more African-Americans also had more illiterates, leading to the ecological inference that African-Americans were more likely than non-African-Americans to be illiterate, this strong claim could not be substantiated by analyses of individual level data. (The CORRELATION coefficient for the state-level analysis was 0.946, but for the individual level it was much smaller, at 0.203.)

The maup was introduced to the geographical literature by Openshaw (1977; see also Openshaw and Taylor, 1979), whose empirical studies corroborated and extended Robinson's. With one data set, for example, they showed that different aggregations (or regionalizations, since most geographical examples involve aggregations into territorial blocks) could generate correlation coefficients covering almost the entire potential range from -1.0 to $+1.0$ (in one example, the range found was -0.73 to $+0.98$), although most distributions were leptokurtic, with the majority of observed coefficients close to the median value. They showed that the problem is made up of two components. With the *scale effect*, there is a tendency for larger correlations to be associated with larger (and thus almost invariably a smaller number of) spatial units. The *aggregation effect* refers to the large number of different ways in which individual units can be combined into a set of areal units – usually with constraints such as size and contiguity (Openshaw, 1982).

The maup is important in many areas of SPATIAL SCIENCE using QUANTITATIVE METHODS, because it indicates the need for caution in inferring a relationship between two variables based on a single aggregation at a particular scale: a result identified from one such analysis may not be replicated exactly in another. Openshaw and Taylor (1981) identified three possible responses to the maup:

- it is an *insoluble problem*, and so can only be ignored;

- it is a *problem that can be assumed away*, with the results obtained from the particular available data set being accepted as 'the real ones'; or
- it is a *very powerful analytical device* for exploring various aspects of geography and spatial variations, since alternative regionalizations can be produced – this allows the creation of both frequency distributions with which one regionalization can be compared and, in some cases, optimal regionalizations for particular purposes (see CLASSIFICATION AND REGIONALIZATION).

Although the existence of the maup is widely recognized as posing a problem for much SPATIAL ANALYSIS, in very many cases researchers have had to adopt either the first or the second of these positions because they are constrained by available data sources (especially those provided by CENSUSES). Attempts have been made to develop methodologies that can take the maup into account and produce unbiased ecological estimates (as in the work of Holt, Steel, Tranmer and Wrigley, 1996, and King's, 1997, classic volume on solving the ECOLOGICAL INFERENCE problem; see also a recent overview in Swift, Liu and Uber, 2008), but few analysts have adopted the third of Openshaw and Taylor's suggested responses, preferring to accept the outcome of one aggregation as providing a reliable estimate of the 'real' relationship.

The maup is not only an issue in spatial analysis: it is also relevant to a range of practical issues – notably REDISTRICTING. Many electoral systems use territorially defined constituencies, which comprise aggregations of smaller territorial units; UK Parliamentary constituencies, for example, are aggregations of contiguous local government electoral wards with a size constraint. Johnston and Rossiter (1982; see also Cirincione, Darling and O'Rourke, 2000) have shown that there is a large number of possible solutions to the constituency-building problem in every area, which can produce different election results, so that the selection of a particular aggregation can not only lead to a particular outcome in one constituency (hence the widespread practice of GERRYMANDERING in some countries), but can also contribute to considerable bias in election results, whereby not only is the percentage of seats won by a party disproportionate to its share of the votes cast, but other parties with the same share of the votes might win very different shares of the seats

(Johnston, Pattie, Dorling and Rossiter, 2001: see ELECTORAL GEOGRAPHY).   RJ

Suggested reading
Openshaw (1982).

money and finance HUMAN GEOGRAPHY was late in recognizing the geographical significance of money and finance, with few attempts to write geographies of money and finance much before the 1980s (for exceptions, see Conzen, 1975, 1977). However, since then a new sub-field of geographical research has emerged (Corbridge, Thrift and Martin, 1994; Leyshon and Thrift, 1997; Martin, 1999; Clark, 2005a). As this work has evolved, it has followed a similar trajectory to the wider discipline, with earlier work being influenced by more abstract economic and SOCIAL THEORY, while more recent work has tended towards substantive, cultural accounts of the geographical consequences of money and finance.

The first systematic engagement with the geography of money and finance emerged from MARXIST analyses of the broader dynamics of CAPITALISM, best exemplified by the work of David Harvey (1989b, 1999 [1982]). Marx drew attention to the role that money and finance played in the financial system within capitalism, which revolves around money and the social POWER that its possession delivers in a MARKET economy. Drawing on this insight, Harvey developed the concept of TIME-SPACE COMPRESSION, which provided a propulsive element to earlier theories of a shrinking world, such as TIME-SPACE CONVERGENCE and TIME-SPACE DISTANCIATION. The social power of money increases the pace of life over TIME as part of a generalized process to reduce the turnover time of capital, and the faster realization of profits and incomes. This encourages the introduction of new space-shrinking technologies, bringing in their wake the progressive dislocation of economic and political systems. Money has become ever more mobile and fungible, and is now the most heavily traded COMMODITY in the global ECONOMY. The sheer weight of money in circulation within and between financial markets has made governments more sensitive to their operation, and economic development has been destabilized by a series of serious financial CRISES in various parts of the world, including LATIN AMERICA and Sub-Saharan AFRICA in the 1980s (Corbridge, 1993a), and South East Asia and Latin America (again) in the 1990s (Beaverstock and Doel, 2001;

Webber, 2001; Rock, 2002). These crises have often been caused by the movement of HOT MONEY, which moves in but, significantly, also out of economies at short notice in search of investment opportunities. Growing attention is being paid to such investors, such as hedge funds and pension funds, which control large volumes of CAPITAL in circulation within the global economy. For example, Clark (1999a) has argued that the current era is characterized by 'pension fund capitalism'. The rise of these institutions has coincided with the retreat of the STATE, particularly within Anglo-American economies. As voters have demonstrated their unwillingness to pay the taxes that would fund social welfare programmes and public INFRASTRUCTURE development, so large institutional investors have moved in to fill the gap, footing the bill, but for private gain. This has implications not only for what kind of infrastructure is built, but also for how it is run. Similar arguments about the growing power and influence of the financial system have been made in a body of work that emerged in the early twenty-first century, which has a focus on the process of *financialization*, which has focused on the ways in which money and finance has been colonizing economic life, both in the boardroom (Froud, Sukhdev, Leaver and Williams, 2006) and in the HOUSEHOLD (Langley, 2004, 2006).

A second area of research has focused on the regional effects of money and finance, mainly through the impacts of the reorganization of the financial services industry. Since the 1970s, and working in parallel to, and combination with, the process of financialization, there has been a process of neo-liberalization that has brought about a wave of financial re-regulation to economies in North America, Europe and South East Asia (Moran, 1991, 2003; Dymski, 1999). These developments have brought about an increase in retail financial services employment, and economic geographers have documented and explained these uneven geographies of growth (Leyshon, Thrift and Toomey, 1989; Richardson, Belt and Marshall, 2000) (see NEO-LIBERALISM).

A third area of work has focused on the urban dynamics of money. One strand of research has sought to explain the persistence of financial centres in an era of time–space compression. Geographers have sought to explain why financial centres such as the City of London and New York continue to control the majority of the world's financial activity (Thrift, 1994a; Agnes, 2000; Clark and Wojcik, 2001). The answer is to be found in the ways financial centres facilitate close interpersonal contact through episodes of co-presence. This facilitates the rapid generation, capture interpretation and representation of business information (Boden and Molotch, 1995; Boden, 2000). The financial centre may therefore be seen as a collective way of coping with the vast amount of monetary information that circulates within the global economy. It is a centre of financial expertise founded in a complex DIVISION OF LABOUR embodied in the skills of the workforce, technology, and textual material (Thrift, 1994a), and which collectively generates and disseminates financial information as well as interpretations and narratives about what this information actually means. This is the reason why it is unlikely that financial centres 'will simply melt away into a generalised "space of FLOWS" ... leaving money obligations to speed their way along the cables and through the aether [sic], to and from many different terminals located in places' across the global economy (Thrift, 1994a, p. 327). A second strand of research focuses on the urban dynamics of money upon spaces of FINANCIAL EXCLUSION, the process by which people of poor and moderate incomes are directly and indirectly excluded from the formal financial system and denied access to mainstream retail financial services (Leyshon, Burton, Knights, Alferoff and Signoretta 2004a; Dymski, 2005).

A fourth area of research has focused on geographies of money as they are played out through institutions and individual actors. A particular focus of this work has been on the BODIES that perform tasks in the service of the financial system. This work has focused in the main on the changing 'GENDER cultures' of financial institutions (Jones, 1998), such as the transformation of cultures of paternalistic masculinity within British retail banking (Halford and Savage, 1995), and analyses of LABOUR MARKET segregation within the City of London, and the ways in which highly paid jobs in corporate finance and trading are implicitly and explicitly coded as masculine.

A fifth and final area of research has been that which has focused on local currency systems, such as Local Exchange and Trading Systems (Lee, 1996; Lee, Leyshon, Aldridge, Tooke, Williams and Thrift, 2004). This work, influenced by debates on diverse or ALTERNATIVE ECONOMIES, has sought to explore the moral geographies of money and exchange, and the possibilities of local communities of creating their own systems of exchange based more on the pursuit of social and welfare gains, rather than narrow financial advantage (Williams, 1996; Williams, Aldridge, Lee, Leyshon, Thrift and Tooke, 2001; Maurer, 2003). AL

monuments Built icons of identity usually in the form of public statues or symbolic buildings that are designed and executed to evoke a sense of national and regional IDENTITY, and to induce in the collective imagination remembrance of specific events or people. Although the study of monuments has increased in HUMAN GEOGRAPHY over the past 20 years, a result of a heightened interest in the symbolic, ritualistic and performative dimensions of identity formation, historians were the first to explore the relationships between public monuments and NATIONALISM. Mosse's (1975) study of the role of the public statue in the development of German nationalism is still an exemplary analysis, while Schorske's (1979) discussion of the redevelopment of Vienna's *Ringstrasse* in the nineteenth century provides a brilliant interpretation of the role of Austria's rising middle class in impressing their political vision on the architecture of the city.

There are several reasons for studying the links between monuments and political–cultural identities. First, the erection of public monuments in PUBLIC SPACE has proliferated since the nineteenth century, and this expansion of public statuary corresponds with the heyday of nation-building projects. Second, unlike other arts such as painting or LITERATURE, monument-making is usually a collective process 'more democratic than painting because it is simpler and more solemn, more appropriate to the public square, to huge dimensions, and to emblematic figures that are both a product of, and stimulus to the imagination' (Agulhon, 1981, p. 4). Third, the rituals surrounding the unveiling of monuments and the dynamics of their reception and consumption help us to identify their role in the public consciousness. Icons in bronze or stone are made meaningful by the ways in which they visually and verbally invoke particular versions of identity. Finally, the SPATIALITY of public statuary is important in the constitution of meaning and it is here that geography has a particular contribution to make (see also MEMORY).

A seminal geographical study of a monument is Harvey's (1979) analysis of the *Basilica de Sacré Coeur* in Paris and its role in the development of class politics in the capital. Subsequent studies have pursued several different themes. Studies of the role of WAR

monuments in articulating national and sectional commemoration range from extensive surveys of memorials to the two world wars (Heffernan, 1995; Johnson, 2003b) to in-depth studies of individual statues (Till, 1999). These analyses pay close attention to the iconographic debates surrounding the use of particular motifs (see ICONOGRAPHY) and to the conflicts over identity engendered by them. The spatiality of commemorative sites has been another focus: Leib's (2002) analysis of the Arthur Ashe statue in Richmond, Virginia, for example, highlights the role of PLACE and RACE in the public discussion of the location of the monument, while Benton-Short (2006) recovers the politics of location that animated recent discussions of monuments and memorials on the Mall in Washington, DC. All of these studies focus on the visual and verbal languages surrounding public monuments, but more recently human geographers have started to address the PERFORMATIVE dimension by examining the textual and non-textual, bodily and non-bodily practices involved in the making of public icons (e.g. Howe, 2008). NJ

Suggested reading
Leib (2002); Till (1999).

moral geographies The study of the interrelationship of moral and geographical arguments. Work has considered the way in which assumptions about the relationship between people and their environments may reflect and produce moral judgements, and how the conduct of particular groups or individuals in particular spaces may be judged appropriate or inappropriate. D.M. Smith (1998a) sees moral geographies as one of six research areas linking geography and moral PHILOSOPHY, alongside the historical geography of moralities, inclusion and exclusion in bounded spaces, the moral significance of distance and proximity, questions of SOCIAL JUSTICE and environmental ETHICS. Smith extends his discussion in *Moral geographies* (2000a), a wide-ranging treatment of geography, morality, ethics and justice (see also MORAL LANDSCAPES).

The term 'moral geographies' achieved prominen within HUMAN GEOGRAPHY through Driver's study of allied 'ENVIRONMENTALISM' and 'moralism' in nineteenth-century social scientific urban studies: ' "Moral science" was ... a science of conduct and its relationship to environment, both moral and physical' (Driver, 1988, p. 279). Driver argues that such moral geographies 'permitted the birth of social science in England' (p. 276), the implication being that subsequent academic geographies may also have drawn on moralistic assumptions concerning ENVIRONMENT and SOCIETY. Jackson's account of the work of the early-twentieth-century CHICAGO SCHOOL of urban sociologists conversely shows how the identification of forms of moral order underlying 'apparent social disorganization' (1984, p. 178) may allow a critique of conventional moralistic assumptions concerning life in the modern CITY. Matless (1994) develops the theme of moral geographies of conduct by considering how the geography of a particular REGION, the Norfolk Broads in eastern England, can be understood in terms of competing formulations of appropriate behaviour in the landscape. Moral geographies are here constituted through assumptions concerning CLASS and LANDSCAPE. Such work echoes studies of SOCIAL EXCLUSION and TRANSGRESSION in highlighting the basis on which people may be labelled as in or out of PLACE FEEDBACK.

Some moral geographical work has sought a prescriptive role. Sack (1997) argues for the inherently geographical nature of moral actions in order to develop a framework through which we might improve ourselves as moral geographical subjects: 'Thinking geographically heightens our moral concerns; it makes clear that moral goals must be set and justified by us in places and as inhabitants of a world' (p. 24). Sack recognizes the complex variations of morality between different times and places, but the aim, in common with the tenor of much HUMANISTIC GEOGRAPHY, is to seek a normative framework for being human; for being, in Sack's terms, a 'geographical self'. For other work noted above, however, the term 'moral geographies' is not prescriptive, its use being informed by a philosophical and political assumption that senses of moral order are produced through environmental and spatial practices that are always bound up with relations of POWER. Here, the connection of the moral and the spatial in moral geographies is bound up with a suspicion regarding any claim to be able to define morality, and with a sceptical attitude to the social power of the moral.   DMat

Suggested reading
Driver (1988); Smith, D.M. (2000a).

moral landscapes The association of particular LANDSCAPES with schemes of moral value (see also MORAL GEOGRAPHIES). Tuan

(1989) reviews the wide-ranging historical and geographical association of particular moral values with the landscapes of city, country and garden. A moral–spatial DIALECTIC may also be identified whereby moral landscapes both reflect and reproduce senses of moral order. Work has focused on such processes in the geography of institutions, in the use of architecture and landscape design to promote particular moral principles, and in the production of consciously 'alternative' social spaces.

The institution as moral landscape is considered in Ploszajska's (1994) work on the Victorian reformatory school as an 'environment of moral reform'. Such moral landscapes are one element of a geographical interest in relations of SPACE and POWER, whereby spatial organization is shown to be not only reflective of but central to the workings of power. Daniels' (1982) study of the 'morality of landscape' in the work of Georgian landscape gardener Humphry Repton shows how aesthetic values of landscape design were at the same time moral values concerning social harmony, plebeian deference and aristocratic responsibility. The theme of moral landscapes thereby connects to aesthetic, social, political and economic issues: indeed, all of those categories are shown to be mutually constitutive. Pinder's (2005c) study of utopian URBANISM in the twentieth century similarly draws out the strong senses of moral order informing the modernist urban schemes of architects and planners such as Le Corbusier (see UTOPIA).

Studies of moral landscapes may also address the ways in which moral value is located in particular environments. Matless (1997) considers how moral debates over conduct in open-air landscape shaped cultures of landscape, LEISURE and the BODY in twentieth-century England, and served to reproduce versions of English national IDENTITY. Associations of morality and NATURE, whereby moral order may be equated with a sense of natural order, may also serve to enable particular groups or individuals to claim a moral landscape close to nature. Locating the moral in the natural is a common trope of certain forms of ENVIRONMENTALISM, which cultivate an ecological morality or environmental ethic around an assumed moral community of the human and nonhuman. Such work differs from much of the work discussed above in operating with a strongly normative sense of morality (see also MORAL GEOGRAPHIES). A normative use of the term moral landscape is also found in Ley's (1993) work on co-operative housing in Canada, presented as embodying moral principles of COMMUNITY and individuality through an oppositional POSTMODERN architectural style. Other forms of 'oppositional' moral landscape might be traced in studies of the geographies of TRANSGRESSION, where landscapes labelled by others as immoral are upheld as pointers towards the production of alternative SOCIAL SPACE.   DMat

Suggested reading
Matless (1997); Tuan (1989).

morphogenesis (The study of) change in form over time. The term derives from developmental biology, and is sometimes used as a synonym for *positive FEEDBACK* in systems analysis (see also COMPLEXITY THEORY). Its most developed use in HUMAN GEOGRAPHY to date has been in studies of LANDSCAPE change in HISTORICAL GEOGRAPHY. (See also MORPHOLOGY.)   DG

morphology Form *or* the study of form. Morphology became a contested term in the struggle between the HUMAN GEOGRAPHY of Paul Vidal de la Blache and the emerging sociology of Émile Durkheim at the turn of the twentieth century. Durkheim argued that the systematicity of the social – and thus what made its scientific study possible – was the result of its morphology, by which he meant the spatial forms through which individuals were held together as a social structure. For this reason, any account of the constitution of social life would have to include many of the propositions of human geography, which Durkheim regarded as one of the 'fragmentary sciences' that had to be drawn out of their isolation to contribute to the plenary social science of sociology (Andrews, 1993). This sense of social morphology can be traced through twentieth-century sociology in the writings of Maurice Halbwachs, Georg Simmel and others, but Vidal complained that Durkheim's view ignored the physical–ecological dimension and left society suspended in the air.

It was exactly this conjunction between 'the social' and 'the natural' that prompted Carl Sauer to insist that the morphology of LANDSCAPE was the central object of geographical enquiry. For Sauer (1963b [1925]), GEOGRAPHY was 'a science that finds its entire field in the landscape on the basis of the significant reality of chorological relation'. Sauer's conception did not neglect spatial arrangements, in his terms 'the connections of phenomena' (as these differed from place to place: see

CHOROLOGY), but his emphasis on morphology derived from J.W. Goethe's eighteenth-century interest in 'the science of forms' and registered two other claims of equal importance:

- 'NATURE' and 'CULTURE' had to be seen as interdependent in the co-production of landscapes; and
- the same basic forms recurred across the whole field of transformations.

The first of these was focal to Sauer's sense of HISTORICAL GEOGRAPHY, so that his enquiry was not confined to the morphology of landscape but was directed towards its MORPHOGENESIS; that is, the development of its forms over time. It was in this sense that Sauer described 'all geography [a]s physical geography': in its focus on physical form, on the material inscriptions of CULTURE on the surface of the Earth. This intersected with his second claim, because he insisted that 'a definition of landscape as singular, unorganized or unrelated has no scientific value' and he was concerned to develop a conception of landscape as 'a generalization derived from the observation of individual scenes'. Much later, others developed this in directions that Sauer refused to take. In particular, some early work in SPATIAL SCIENCE involved a search for geometrical and mathematical regularities in the evolution of spatial patterns of settlement (see Harvey, 1967). This too can be seen as a revivification of the science of morphology, but it usually acknowledged a debt neither to Goethe nor Sauer but to D'Arcy Thompson's *On growth and form* (1992 [1917]) and his pioneering search for 'essential similarities' between 'animate and inanimate things'.

The interest in MORPHOGENESIS has continued in both European and American geography. There has been a long-standing interest in the historical evolution of rural landscapes (e.g. Helmfrid, 1961) and urban landscapes (e.g. Conzen, 1960: see Whitehand, 2001). Much of the early work was qualitative and descriptive, but in recent years, and in conjunction with parallel studies in archaeology, there have been considerable advances in the quantitative measurement of landscape forms (*metrological analysis*), including the integration of space syntax with GIS (Bin Jiang and Claramunt, 2002; Lilley, Lloyd, Trick and Graham, 2005). *Urban morphogenesis* remains a vital area of geographical enquiry (Vance, 1990). The International Seminar on Urban Form (http://odur.let.rug.nl/ekoster/isuf2/index.html) was established in

1996 and publishes a journal devoted to *Urban Morphology*. There has been a particular interest in the POLITICAL ECONOMY of urban morphogenesis (Whitehand, 1987), and more recently in the cultural and symbolic dimensions of urban morphology (Lilley, 2004a,b). DG

Suggested reading
Lilley (2004a); Whitehand (2001).

mortality The incidence of death, or rate of dying, in a population. Along with FERTILITY, this controls natural increase which, together with MIGRATION, completes the balancing equation that is used in DEMOGRAPHY to assess population growth, decline and AGE COMPOSITION. Exploring national and regional variations in crude death rates, infant mortality rates, infanticide and LIFE EXPECTANCY has increased understandings of epidemiological transitions (Omran, 1983), UNEVEN DEVELOPMENT and gender discrimination (Rafiq, 1991) (see HEALTH GEOGRAPHY; MEDICAL GEOGRAPHY). AJB

Suggested reading
Weeks (1999, ch. 4).

multiculturalism An IDEOLOGY and STATE policy that seeks to establish a model of GOVERNANCE to permit the coexistence of culturally diverse populations. Its distinctive feature is a respect for cultural DIFFERENCE and, in contrast to ASSIMILATION, support for the maintenance of old-world cultures. While not new, cultural diversity assumes its accentuated current profile from the large movements of documented and undocumented workers from the global South to the depleted LABOUR MARKETS of the global North (see MIGRATION; NORTH-SOUTH).

Multiculturalism is not an inevitable policy response to cultural diversity; in western EUROPE, while the UK invoked some commitment to multiculturalism, France's republican model rejected reference to pre-existing immigrant cultures in favour of assimilation to a putatively egalitarian national citizen, while the German tradition of *ius sanguinis*, or ethnic exclusivity (see ETHNICITY), envisaged temporary guest-workers rather than permanent immigrants. The UK, the Netherlands and the Scandinavian states would most readily have described themselves as multicultural nations, though there has been some back-pedalling of late. More complete multicultural commitment occurs in Australia and especially Canada, the only country with a Multiculturalism Act and which includes multicultural RIGHTS within its constitution.

In an important respect, all states are multicultural inasmuch as they include culturally distinct minorities. But the existence of *demographic multiculturalism* is no basis for assuming that institutional and legal recognition of diversity will occur. A necessary development is, at minimum, a tolerance of ethnic difference, and more positively a respect and welcoming of cultural diversity that may lead to HERITAGE *multiculturalism*, where the state celebrates diversity with grants to permit the expression and survival of folk cultures, including literature, dance and religion. In the USA, the principal manifestation of multiculturalism has been the often controversial use of Spanish as a heritage LANGUAGE of instruction in schools in some districts with concentrations of Latino immigrants. But heritage multiculturalism offers no protection of CITIZENSHIP rights, and a more mature development is a *rights-based multiculturalism* that offers legal protection against group-based discrimination, where minorities can claim rights in such fields as anti-RACISM, social service delivery, employment equity, POLICING and IMMIGRATION policy.

Despite its liberal objectives, multiculturalism has attracted considerable criticism. The political right fears the escalation of an IDENTITY politics that fragments the national project (Huntington, 2004: see also NATION-STATE; NATIONALISM). The political left, in contrast, challenges the existence of a veil of cultural equality that conceals structures of economic inequality, and suspects that multiculturalism has been co-opted as a vehicle to promote neo-liberal trade and investment (Mitchell, 2004b; see NEO-LIBERALISM). To this, Ghassan Hage (1998) has charged that multiculturalism in Australia has become a tool of an older white elite to divide new immigrants, thereby maintaining traditional political privileges. But following September 2001 and subsequent TERRORIST attacks in Europe and Asia, such intellectual challenges have been superseded by a populist and media barrage that has falsely blamed multiculturalism for nurturing hostile criminal and terrorist cells within the matrix of tolerated cultural difference. In the present decade, multiculturalism is a policy forced on the defensive (Joppke, 2004). DL

Suggested readings
Mitchell (2004b); Parekh (2000).

multidimensional scaling (MDS) Methods for simplifying matrices of distances between a set of points, while as far as possible retaining their relative ordering (i.e. of the distances between the observations). Developed by psychologists for identifying similarities among individuals on a wide range of attitudes (the distances measure how much each pair differ on a set of attitudinal scales), MDS locates the individuals in a smaller number of dimensions than the original scales, so reducing a multidimensional situation to more comprehensible proportions (cf. FACTOR ANALYSIS). MDS has been adapted for simplifying MAPS on the basis of, for example, the time taken to travel between two points rather than the distance between them.   RJ

Suggested reading
Gatrell (1983).

multilateralism Foreign policy actions involving agreements, treaties and co-operative actions between more than two STATES. In contrast to actions by single states (*unilateralism*) or between two states (*bilateralism*), multilateralism involves international treaties between many parties or regional agreements between groups of neighbouring states. Multilateralism is often a strategy advocated by medium-sized states hoping to shape international agreements in their favour in the face of the greater POWER of large states. The term is sometimes used derisively by power brokers in the great powers, and as a term of virtue and aspiration by those anxious to limit the capabilities of great powers to act unilaterally.

But in fact superpowers and great powers frequently use multilateral institutions; indeed, the USA used its power after the Second World War to establish many multilateral institutions, especially through the Bretton Woods financial arrangements and alliances such as the North Atlantic Treaty Organization (NATO), which in turn were useful in the pursuit of its hegemonic international goals (Latham, 1997). Multilateralism is often directly linked to such institutions. Ruggie (1993, p. 14) suggests that the term 'multilateral' is best understood as 'an adjective that modifies the noun "institution." What distinguishes the multilateral form from others is that it coordinates behavior among three or more states on the basis of generalized principles of conduct.' This suggests that multilateralism is frequently also about building norms or rules that guide state conduct.

Currently, the most high profile multilateral institutions are the United Nations (UN) and the WORLD TRADE ORGANIZATION (WTO), which deals with most international TRADE in the global economy. Given that these organizations provide legitimacy for states, and act to censure and sanction those that violate the multilateral codes of conduct, great powers frequently use these institutions to justify their actions. The USA's use of the UN in 1990 and 1991 to justify military intervention in Iraq during the first Gulf War, and the invocation of the alliance commitments under NATO in the aftermath of the TERRORIST attacks on 11 September 2001, illustrate that multilateralism has many uses even for superpowers.

Multilateralism in European history is usually traced to the 'Concert of EUROPE' arrangements set up after Napoleon's final defeat in 1815. Designed to produce the peaceful resolution of conflicts, the Concert facilitated diplomatic agreements and, despite notable lapses such as the Franco-Prussian war of 1870–1, managed to maintain relatively peaceful relations between the European powers for a century. This system was shattered by the First World War in 1914 and replaced by the League of Nations, which in turn was replaced in 1945 after the Second World War by the UN in a further attempt to establish a multilateral institution to prevent WAR between states. The UN now includes all the states in the system as members. Among the multilateral norms that the UN system has established as ground rules for international conduct three are of particular importance: territorial integrity (see TERRITORY); non-intervention; and sovereign equality among states (see SOVEREIGNTY). In combination, these have produced a territorial order of formally sovereign states in the aftermath of the DECOLONIZATION of the European empires. This multilateral norm has also effectively fixed the BOUNDARIES of states, creating a (relative) territorial permanence to the world political map (Zacher, 2001).

Ironically, however, just as state BORDERS are becoming increasingly fixed, and thus a major source of international CONFLICTS is being removed, many major problems are spilling over those borders and require concerted international co-operation. In recent decades, multilateral action by international social movements and campaigns on HUMAN RIGHTS, GLOBAL WARMING and a host of other predicaments confronting what is sometimes described as global CIVIL SOCIETY have injected new norms into the international system and thereby added a further dimension to multilateralism (see also COSMOPOLITANISM). Arguments about humanitarian intervention in the face of state failure and environmental disasters have suggested a more activist stance for international institutions in the face of human suffering, and in the process challenged the UN norm of non-intervention. Advocates insist that all states have a responsibility to protect their citizens and that, in extreme cases when they obviously fail to do so, intervention from abroad is justified (International Commission on Intervention and State Sovereignty, 2001): a claim that is controversial precisely because it overrides the territorial integrity principle of the UN.

Simultaneously, in the aftermath of 11 September 2001, the Bush administration in the USA frequently preferred to act alone in a unilateral manner, and refused multilateral co-operation on such matters as the International Criminal Court and the Kyoto Protocol on climate change. This stance makes multilateral action more difficult on many issues, and yet, given the increasing number of international agreements on numerous matters, multilateralism as a foreign policy approach has now become a widely accepted and routine diplomatic practice. But in the process territorial sovereignty has become a more fluid principle in INTERNATIONAL RELATIONS (Agnew, 2005b). SD

Suggested reading
Ruggie (1993).

multi-level models QUANTITATIVE METHODS that can analyse research problems with a complex data structure. In a hierarchical structure, the lower-level unit is nested in one and only one unit – for example, people in neighbourhoods in a two-level structure, and people in neighbourhoods in REGIONS in a three-level structure. Other examples are repeated measures of individuals as in a panel study (cf. LONGITUDINAL DATA ANALYSIS) and a multivariate design when there is more than one response variable, so that it is possible to model several aspects of individual behaviour simultaneously. There are two types of non-hierarchical structure. In a cross-classified design, lower units may nest within more than one set of higher-level units, so that pupil performance may be affected by individual, school and neighbourhood characteristics (cf. NEIGHBOURHOOD EFFECT). Both schools and neighbourhoods are higher-level units, but

they are not nested within each other. The remaining type is a multiple membership model in which lower-level units are affected by more than one higher-level unit, so that people's voting behaviour may be affected by the different HOUSEHOLDS and neighbourhoods they have been members of, with a weight proportional to the relative time spent in each. It is possible to combine these structures in a rich fashion, so that spatial MODELS (e.g. GEOGRAPHICALLY WEIGHTED REGRESSION) can have a hierarchical structure in which individuals are affected by the area they live in, and a multiple membership relation by which they are affected by spillover effects from nearby neighbourhoods (see ECOMETRICS).

Such models can handle continuous and CATEGORICAL DATA responses and variables and, indeed, interactions between predictor variables at each level of the structure (cf. MEASUREMENT). In terms of specification, in addition to the usual REGRESSION coefficients that estimate the mean (or fixed) relationship across all structures, there is considerable development of the random stochastic part of the model (see STOCHASTIC PROCESS) so that it is possible to separate between-individual from between-neighbourhood variation and, indeed, to allow a variable to have a differential effect on the outcome in different neighbourhoods. Because of this specification, these are also known as random coefficient or mixed models (fixed and random).

Multi-level models are increasingly being used in social science research, as they have a number of advantages. Technically, they can model complex data dependencies, including spatial and temporal CORRELATION, and thereby give correct standard errors for the fixed estimates; this is particularly important for variables measured at the higher level. They also allow explicit modelling of heteroscedasticity at any level of the model. Substantively, by modelling simultaneously at the micro- and macro-levels, they overcome the atomistic fallacy of modelling individuals and ignoring context, as well as the ECOLOGICAL FALLACY, of not modelling at the individual level. Most importantly, they can incorporate an element of context so that there does not have to be a single relationship fitted for all times and places, so that the class effects on individual voting can be allowed to vary from place to place (Jones, Johnston and Pattie, 1992). KJ

Suggested reading
Jones (1991); Jones and Duncan (1998).

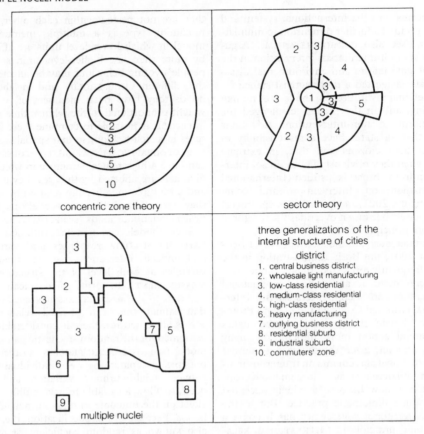

multiple nuclei model *Generalization of the internal structure of cities. The concentric-zone theory is a generalization for all cities. The arrangement of the sectors in the sector theory varies from city to city. The diagram for multiple nuclei represents one possible pattern among innumerable variations* (Harris and Ullman, 1959)

multiple nuclei model A model of intra-urban land-use patterns developed by Chauncy Harris (1914–2003) and Edward Ullman (1912–76: see Harris and Ullman, 1945) that combines and extends the features of the earlier ZONAL MODELS and SECTORAL MODELS of the CHICAGO SCHOOL. Rather than being based on a mono-nuclear city, this model has land-use patterns organized around several nodes (see figure), on the argument that different uses cluster together (in some cases to share specialized facilities) and wish to avoid other uses, thereby creating a number of nuclei around which the city is organized.   RJ

Suggested reading
Harris (1997).

multipliers A measure of the total economic impact of an investment decision, policy change or external 'shock'. This includes not just the initial, immediate impact, but also the indirect or 'knock-on' consequences. Thus a new manufacturing plant creates initial employment; this creates a demand for services in the locality, so triggering other new jobs. The manufacturing expansion also generates demand for additional inputs of energy and steel, so having ripple effects on supplying sectors. Such multiplier effects can be traced using INPUT-OUTPUT models. There is also a need to track the geography of these multiplier effects, to see what 'leaks' from the local economy into other regions, and estimating spatial multipliers undertaken in SPATIAL ECONOMETRICS.   LWH

Suggested reading
Anselin (2003); Smith (1981).

music Although GEOGRAPHY has often been dominated by visual means of REPRESENTATION, the study of music, and indeed sound more generally, has a long if discontinuous history within the discipline. The earliest work is probably that by the Finnish geographer J.G. Granö, whose studies of sonic LANDSCAPES in Finland date back to 1929 (see Granö, 1997 [1929]). However, evidence of a concerted interest in either music or sound does not exist until the early 1970s. Studies influenced by the BERKELEY SCHOOL of CULTURAL GEOGRAPHY examined musical performances, music association memberships, musical listening and musicians' birthplaces alongside a variety of other cultural artefacts. The purpose was to identify cultural hearths and trace DIFFUSIONS across space and through hierarchies, mapping out culture areas, REGIONS and LANDSCAPES. This traditional approach to the geography of music is exemplified in Carney (2003). Early studies focused substantially on rural folk cultures and regional styles in the USA. More recently, the focus has switched to consider how popular musical genres such as those based in Nashville, Seattle or Liverpool evolve within a given PLACE (Carney, 2003, pp. 1–2).

Geographical studies of music have proliferated since the mid-1990s. Developing themes and methods from the CULTURAL TURN, studies have examined issues concerned with SENSE OF PLACE, belonging, GENDER, style and IDENTITY, the politics of landscape representation, and national and transnational identities (Leyshon, Matless and Revill, 1998; Brunn and Waterman, 2006). One theoretical starting point was the concept of 'soundscapes' adopted by S.J. Smith (1994b) to bring out the inherently spatial aspects of auditory environments. However, many of these studies drew substantially from theoretical developments in related disciplines. From *sociology*, for instance, these include the functioning of institutions and organizations in the production and consumption of music and the role of sound in the fabric of EVERYDAY LIFE; from *cultural studies/anthropology*, the place of music in politics of cultural HYBRIDITY, SUBALTERN groups and alternate lifestyles; and from *critical musicology*, the social production of musical experience and critiques of conventional conceptions of popular and elite, worthy and worthless musics. The rise to prominence of CULTURE industries as a vehicle for economic regeneration has provided further impetus, resulting in studies centred on the merits of cultural policy, cultural quarters, cultural TOURISM, creative capital and festivals, as well as local and regional place marketing. The context of new digital and networked communications media has produced studies grounded in NEW ECONOMIC GEOGRAPHY primarily concerned with media synergies and with global, regional and local networks of production and marketing (Connell and Gibson, 2002).

Recent work often critiques the new cultural geography's apparent preoccupation with TEXT and REPRESENTATION. Although music can be considered a material artwork like painting or LITERATURE, the ephemeral qualities of sound make music a distinctively PERFORMATIVE cultural medium. As geographers have engaged with ART forms beyond their conventional concern for the visual, so the performative aspects of music and dance have become an increasing focus of study. Investigations of AFFECT and EMOTIONAL GEOGRAPHY have resulted in studies centred on listening practices, performing and making music, rhythm, embodiment and the dancing BODY. Much of this work explores both the subjective experience of music and its physical presence as it is embodied in objects such as instruments, recordings and sheet music; their associated organizations and infrastructures, venues, recording companies and radio stations; and the practices of performing and listening. Concerns for the co-construction of NATURE and the materiality of cultural life now produce studies that explore the multi-sensory richness of environmental experience whilst remaining sensitive to both the PHENOMENOLOGY and CULTURAL POLITICS of sound (Anderson, Morton and Revill, 2005). Such studies connect ENVIRONMENTAL HISTORY and ECOLOGY with a critical interrogation of regional and local cultures, in ways that acknowledge the pioneering work of Grano's early sonic geographies.   GRe

Suggested reading
Anderson, Morton and Revill (2005); Connell and Gibson (2002).

N

narco-capitalism It is almost impossible to assess the gross value of the global illegal drug trade – a worldwide black market in the production, processing, distribution and retailing of illegal psychoactive substances. According to the United Nations World Drug Report in 2006, the retail value of illegal drugs (including drugs seized) was $322 billion. Other sources estimate the total figure to be well in excess of $400 billion. The trans-border TRADE typically links – consistent with a much longer history of the drugging of the First World by the Third – impoverished producer states (Afghanistan, Colombia) with transatlantic economy consumers. The consumption of illegal drugs is, however, a global phenomenon (200 million people between 15 and 64 years have consumed some type of illegal drug in the past 12 months, according to the UN Drug Report in 2006). Illicit drugs are as central to the SLUM world of Rio and Jakarta as they are in the white-collar Wall Street and American GHETTOS. The massive scale of the drug business and the direct (and complex) actors in the cocaine or heroin global COMMODITY CHAIN – the PEASANT producers, the local processors, the middlemen, the wholesalers, the mules, the drug cartels, corrupt military and state security apparatuses and so on – can only be grasped as a particular sort of MARKET – albeit exceptionally violent, well-policed, often quite competitive, and of course illegal. Narco-capitalism refers to the structure and organization of the production, distribution and sale of illegal drugs, understood as a system for the production of profit; that is to say, a global system of ACCUMULATION not unlike other drugs (sugar, coffee).

It is commonplace to assume that the key illegal drugs – especially in trans-BORDER activity – are cocaine, heroin and cannabis, but narco-capitalism also includes the illegal sale of legal drugs (tobacco, for example, is often smuggled across borders, taking advantage of differential tax and tariff systems, while some prescription drugs may be available through illegal networks, thereby eliminating the need to manufacture and process the drugs). Some forms of narco-capitalism – the industrial manufacture of LSD or methadone – may be largely national or local in organization. The proliferation of small-scale marijuana production systems under hydroponic conditions may lend itself in particular to local urban markets in the same way that some centres of cannabis production (northern California; Vancouver, BC) may supply regional rather than international demand. Narco-capitalism for hard drugs such as cocaine, ecstasy, meth and heroin has a number of structural features that are especially important in understanding the dynamics of the industry. First, a number of key cartels – Cali and Medellin in Colombia, Juarez and Sonora in Mexico and Puerto Rico – are often linked through a syndicate-like organizational structure (e.g. the Mexican cartels typically traffic drugs provided by the larger Colombian cartels). Second, the cartels cannot operate without the complicity and active co-operation of corrupt governments and militaries that facilitate the transit operations by 'mules' (carriers).

To the extent that cocaine is representative of narco-capitalism in general (80 per cent of all cocaine is consumed in the USA), there have been no large US cartels discovered, and much of the drug profit is not returned to LATIN AMERICA but stays in the USA, where it is laundered for other business operations. A number of corrupt and often military THIRD WORLD states have become key actors in the global narco-capitalism system (e.g. Nigeria and Panama). What are called 'failed' or 'rogue' STATES are often the pillars for the world drug business. As a particular form of CAPITALISM, the narco-economy has two organizational forms: the spoke-and-hub model, in which a combination of violence and relations of trust draw together a central cartel and dispersed gangs and mafia-like organizations; and a vertically integrated 'corporate' form of narco-capitalism, in which the cartel controls and orchestrates the entire commodity chain through a system of force and consent, for which the Mafia may be an organizational model (and to which the drug business is in any case organically linked).   MW

Suggested reading
Clawsonn (2006); Mares (2005).

nation A product of NATIONALISM, the nation is nevertheless treated by nationalists as the naturalized geo-historical foundation for national COMMUNITY. Such FOUNDATIONAL thinking often uses GEOGRAPHY, and in particular IMAGINATIVE GEOGRAPHIES of PLACE and LANDSCAPE, to create and consolidate conceptions of primordial nationhood. Sometimes such imaginative geographies of the nation space can also be violently exclusionary, based on RACIST, ETHNICIST and/or MASCULINIST phobias about keeping the nation pure by hardening BORDERS (Gilroy, 1987; Theweleit, 1987; Parker, Russo, Sommer and Yaeger, 1992; Radcliffe, 1998; Gallaher, 2003; Flint and Fallah, 2004; Mayer, 2004). At other times, formal spatial depictions of the nation operate more subtly to encode and normalize the political geography of the NATION-STATE as it relates to international and subnational governmental practices (Schulten, 2001; Anderson, 2006a; Flint and Taylor, 2007 [1985]). And in yet other anti-colonial cases of nations without STATES, or with states that have been repeatedly undermined by COLONIALISM and neo-colonialism, imaginative geographies of the nation serve to keep alive hopes of a future national state free from occupation and external control (Gregory, 1994; Guibernau, 1999). In all these cases, innumerable geographical representations from official MAPS to LANDSCAPE depictions to monumental architecture can be drawn upon to affirm and/or question notions of national IDENTITY.

In theoretical work that is less attuned to geography, the division of the world map into a series of parcels defined by a standardized nation form tends to be ascribed to more generalized social dynamics. Conservative theorists have tended to fall back on essentializing ideas about ethno-linguistic HOMELANDS (e.g. Huntington, 2004; see also Kedourie, 1960). By contrast, LIBERAL theorists have tended to explain the abstract nation form in terms of either the global march of MODERNITY (Gellner, 1983) or the formation of the modern nation-state as a monopolist of administrative information and, in Weberian terms, the so-called legitimate use of VIOLENCE (Giddens, 1985). Subsequently, post-colonial reflections on global struggles against illegitimate imperial violence have displaced the EUROCENTRISM of the liberal accounts, all the while arguing – as in one famous case – that the assumption of a coherent nation form in the former colonies remains a 'derivative discourse' shaped as much by the performance of European nationalist norms as by the cultural complexities of the colonies themselves (Chatterjee, 1986; see also Amin, 1987).

Chatterjee advances his arguments by noting the HYBRIDITY of the historical record, but by focusing on the past, his derivative discourse thesis fails to explain how the nation form may be challenged and hybridized by extra-national FLOWS in present and future historical moments. By contrast, MARXIST accounts, with their attention to the changing SCALE of CAPITALISM's organization (e.g. Harvey, 1999 [1984]), and Foucauldian accounts, with their interest in the epistemic enframing of the nation as a container for 'the ECONOMY' amidst twentieth-century FORDISM (e.g. Mitchell, 1998), seem better placed to theorize the historical contingency of the nation form alongside its discursive PERFORMANCE. This does not mean explaining the nation in economic terms alone. As Marxist philosopher Etienne Balibar emphasizes: 'It is quite impossible to 'deduce' the nation form from capitalist relations of production' (1991, p. 89). But it does mean coming to terms with the overdetermination of the nation as part of modern twentieth-century nation-states that were once territorialized but which now seem increasingly re-territorialized amidst the political geographical tensions of global capitalism (Sparke, 2005). To ignore such changes and to continue to examine global politics with a methodological nationalism that treats the nation as a universal norm is to fall into what Agnew calls the 'territorial trap' (Agnew, 2003a) – a trap that exists in the first place because of ignorance of the geographical processes and representations through which nations are constructed.   MS

national parks The first national park was created at Yellowstone in Wyoming, USA, in 1872, although the Yosemite Valley in California (made a national park in 1890), had been a state park since 1864, and the idea of a national park was first expressed in the USA by George Catlin in 1832. The first US national parks were proposed as a way to protect the sublime and monumental LANDSCAPES of the American West, and as a reaction to the threat of the closing 'FRONTIER' and the pioneering spirit as a formative element in the American character (Nash, 1982 [1967]).

The US model of national parks was built on a conception of NATURE as WILDERNESS, pristine, separate and separable from human-transformed lands (Cronon, 1995). Yet in national parks, wilderness was created by the deliberate actions of the STATE, often involving military action: the US Army managed Yellowstone until 1918. The presence of indigenous people in these areas was systematically ignored. The same process of physical clearance and conceptual deletion of previous human presence accompanied the extension of the Yellowstone model outside the USA. It was soon copied in the British Dominions (Canada 1887, Australia 1891 and New Zealand 1894) and in colonial possessions in AFRICA (the Belgian Congo in 1925, South Africa in 1926). Following the Second World War, the model was adopted in East Africa, ASIA and eventually globally as the international CONSERVATION movement grew (Adams, 2004). The International Union for the Conservation of Nature and Natural Resources (IUCN) established a Provisional Committee on National Parks in 1958, now the World Commission on Protected Areas (www.iucn.org/themes/wcpa). The United Nations adopted a 'World List of National Parks and Equivalent Reserves' in 1962, and IUCN defined a series of protected area categories, of which US-style National Parks are widely regarded as the most important (www.unep-wcmc.org/protected_areas/categories/). The global protected area network expanded rapidly. By 2005, there were over 100,000 protected areas covering over 2 million square kilometres, more than 12 per cent of the Earth's land surface.

National parks created internationally on the Yellowstone model are imagined as places free from human settlement. Their creation has therefore often caused displacement of indigenous or other peoples, either through restrictions on access to land and RESOURCES (including cultural sites) or direct forced resettlement. Globally, there has been a persistent failure to recognize historic human occupation of and RIGHTS to land placed within national parks, or to recognize the extent of human modification of 'wilderness' (Neumann, 2004b). Partly because of opposition to such imposed parks, there has been significant emphasis in international conservation policy on 'community-based conservation' and 'park outreach projects' that seek to create local political and economic support for parks (Hulme and Murphree, 2001). There are also alternatives to the exclusive national park model; for example, British National Parks and French Parcs Régionaux, which are essentially planning designations to preserve the quality of privately owned land.WMA

nationalism A name for the modern social and political formations that draw together feelings of belonging, solidarity and

identification between national citizens and the TERRITORY imagined as their collective national homeland. The existence and coherence of a particular NATION is in this sense best understood as an ongoing product and not the primordial precursor of nationalism. But while nationalism can therefore be said to make nations, they are neither illusions nor invented like works of fiction. Although Benedict Anderson's phrase 'imagined communities' has sometimes been misinterpreted as suggesting such an inventive account, in fact, his emphasis on the politically and socially constructive work of nationalism in producing nations is the heart of his much-reprinted book (2006). Nations are imagined, he argues, because nationalism mobilizes a strong but abstract sense of COMMUNITY between distant strangers in a way that consolidates their identification with both a common historical inheritance and a shared national space. This is also why nationalism is more social than the personal passions of patriotism and less legal than the regulative norms of CITIZENSHIP, even though – as feminist and queer geographers in particular have underlined – it is clearly interwoven with each (see Bell and Binnie, 2000; Marston, 1990: see also FEMINIST GEOGRAPHIES).

In the most recent edition of his book, Anderson reviews its many translations and globe-trotting travels, further documenting how nationalism clearly fosters distinct national cultures of reading, writing, teaching and communication. He underlines too that one of his initial intentions in the book (and one that he thinks accounts for much of its global popularity) is that it shifted the geographical focus of the study of nationalism away from EUROPE (and the EUROCENTRISM that traditional Marxist accounts shared with traditional liberal accounts) and towards various post-colonial nationalisms of the global SOUTH, including not least of all what he calls the 'creole nationalisms' of the Americas (a formulation that itself also usefully undermines exceptionalist American arguments about US republicanism as the uniquely pioneering prototype of post-colonial nationalism). In making this case, however, Anderson does not directly address the many ways in which his arguments have both resonated with and been advanced by various versions of post-colonial theory (see POST-COLONIALISM). His own attention to the role of MAPS and other geographical depictions in imagining the communities of nationalism clearly resonates, for example, with Edward Said's theoretical concerns with the IMAGINATIVE GEOGRAPHIES of ORIENTALISM; one connection being the ways in which the cultures of IMPERIALISM worked CONTRAPUNTALLY to construct the modernity of Euro-American nationalism by constantly contrasting the supposedly pre-modern human geographies of their colonies with the ordered and enframed LANDSCAPES of metropolitan museums, exhibitions and textbook cartographies (Said, 1993, 2003 [1978]; cf. Mitchell, 1988; Gregory, 1994). Other post-colonial studies of nationalism have advanced these ideas by problematizing the diverse geographical arguments and assumptions that continue to create hierarchies of national belonging, national achievement and national blame in the course of imagining community. Whether it is concerned with the fate of women on the margins of the post-colonial nation (Spivak, 1992), or interest in the necessarily extra-territorial affiliations of anti-racist and anti-colonial activists (Gilroy, 1993; Singh, 2004), or reflection on the historical tragedies that have led to geographies of blame for the so-called failure of post-colonial nationalism in countries such as Haiti (Scott, 2004; see also Farmer, 1992), scholarship addressing the imagined communities of nationalism has increasingly also complicated pre-emptive EPISTEMOLOGICAL assumptions that limit national history to national geography. At the same time, work on the ways in which national geography is taught and learned in nationalist teachings themselves has also increasingly sought to unpack how the PERFORMANCE of nationalism can both close down and open up opportunities for imagining territory anew (compare Bhabha, 1994 with Brückner, 1999; Schulten, 2001; Sparke, 2005). All these post-colonial questions indicate how nationalism can be implicated in racialized imaginings of SPACE and PLACE in both dominative and resistant ways, an ambivalence that has historically been one of the reasons why defining nationalism has been so vexing for critical theorists. As Etienne Balibar puts it, with both a question and an answer of his own:

Why does it prove to be so difficult to define nationalism? First, because the concept never functions alone, but is always part of a chain in which it is both a central and weak link. This chain is constantly being enriched... with new intermediate or extreme terms: civic spirit, patriotism, populism, ethnicism, ETHNOCENTRISM, xenophobia, chauvinism, imperialism, jingoism... (1991, p. 46)

MS

nation-state The combination of national GOVERNANCE and national GOVERNMENTALITY that emerged as the norm of European state-making in the eighteenth and nineteenth centuries, and that spread across the world in the twentieth century as a basis for post-colonial state-making in the former colonies of the global SOUTH. In all these contexts, the hyphen in nation-state has traditionally symbolized the articulation of NATIONALISM with the development of the modern STATE, its sovereignty over TERRITORY, and its capacity to police and administer the spaces contained by national BORDERS (Giddens, 1985; Sparke, 2005). None of these articulations have ever been comprehensive and complete, and while most nation-states presume to govern all inhabitants as if they were a single NATION, in practice they often also dominate and marginalize populations who speak minority languages, identify with minority ethnic communities and/or who live in BORDERLANDS (Flint and Taylor, 2007 [1985]). Thus while the hyphen in nation-state is considered a conventional and quite unremarkable linguistic convention, it points to social and political practices that often put an oppressive line through the possibility of statehood for 'sub-national' nations.

The volatile and often violent two-way geographical dynamic between state-making and nationhood only really became stabilized in the mid-twentieth century, at the same time as it was extended through anti-imperial independence movements across much of the world (Blaut, 1987). At this point, Fordist REGIMES OF ACCUMULATION in core countries of the world economy tended to systematize 'official nationalism' as a basis for managing CLASS divisions through redistributive taxation, state education and welfare administration (see FORDISM). And in the global SOUTH, nationalism meanwhile served to rally popular support for new post-colonial DEVELOPMENT initiatives based on IMPORT SUBSTITUTION – albeit ironically also sometimes being twisted into neo-imperial projects of quelling the RESISTANCE of unofficial nationalism (Trouillot, 1990). But even at this high point of the nation-state as a container of politics, the hyphenated hybrid was wracked by the geopolitical tensions of the COLD WAR and global UNEVEN DEVELOPMENT (Taylor, 1994a). Even the institutions of INTERNATIONAL RELATIONS where nation-states were supposedly represented in their full normative and sovereign roles simultaneously revealed their precariousness: the United Nations was famously described in 1977, for example, as 'little more than the meeting place for representatives of disunited states' (Seton-Watson, 1977). It is scarcely surprising, therefore, that today, while we have by no means arrived at the end of the nation-state, as business-class globalists advertise (e.g. Ohmae, 1995), we are seeing nation and state being pulled apart in the context of recent rounds of GLOBALIZATION.

Macro forms of state-making are increasingly becoming transnational in their scale of organization in concert with the entrenchment of NEO-LIBERALISM as the dominant free-market model of governance (Peet, 2003; Harvey, 2005). Meanwhile, micro models of neo-liberal GOVERNMENTALITY that promote entrepreneurial forms of SUBJECTIVITY and benchmarking approaches to place-making come together in context-contingent ways with global market forces to create new ASSEMBLAGES of IDENTITY, affiliation and CITIZENSHIP that are no longer so clearly bound-up in the nation-state (Mitchell, 2004a; Ong and Collier, 2005). If the nation-state is not dead, it is clear that it is being remade in different ways in different places by both roll-out and roll-back forms of neo-liberalism; it is becoming redefined as the managed mediator of neo-liberal HEGEMONY (Peck and Tickell, 2002): on the one hand, a relentless enforcer of free trade rules and neo-liberal GOVERNANCE in arenas ranging from land management to regional development to workfare to the warfare of the coalition of the billing; and, on the other hand, a bulwark of the status quo and an excuse for business as usual when non-neo-liberal visions of development, debt relief, women's RIGHTS and environmental protection are proposed at transnational and subnational SCALES (Public Citizen, 2007). Meanwhile, social relations and identifications are themselves also becoming remade and re-territorialized by the globalizing forces. The accelerated FLOWS of tourists, migrants, money, information, movies, sports and news programmes are challenging the old print MEDIA of national consciousness, and turning the hyphen in nation-state into more of an index of disjuncture (Appadurai, 1996). All these changes have not (notwithstanding Hardt and Negri, 2000) led to the complete eclipse of the nation-state by a new global empire, but they have led to the withering of the national state as an institutional enabler of national DEMOCRACY, and they have therefore made the search for new transnational convergence spaces for of democracy all the more urgent (Routledge, 2003: see also TRANS-NATIONALISM).   MS

natural resources Conventionally, this term refers to biophysical materials that satisfy human wants and provide direct inputs to human well-being. The term may, however, be defined more broadly to include any component of the non-human world that performs a socially valuable function. Natural resources are the product of geological, hydrological and biological processes: the adjective 'natural' denotes this location *anterior* to human labour. It is for this reason that classical POLITICAL ECONOMY described as 'gifts of NATURE' the raw materials and productive energies of the non-human world.

A distinctive vocabulary is available for differentiating the qualities and properties of a vast range of natural resources. A primary distinction is between exhaustible (stock) and renewable (flow) resources, based on the potential of different biophysical materials to regenerate (see figure). For stock resources, a secondary distinction is between materials that are consumed by use and cannot be recovered (such as fuels) and those that may be recycled (most applications of metals). Flow resources may be subdivided according to whether use of the resource subtracts from the amount and/or quality of the resource base: for so-called ambient resources, use of the resource degrades neither the amount nor quality (e.g. solar radiation, wind, waves). For other flow resources, there is a threshold beyond which further consumption exceeds the capacity of the resource to regenerate: these 'critical zone' resources can be 'mined' to depletion/extinction (e.g. ground water, fish, game species). Basic distinctions such as these have underpinned the development of different MODELS for managing renewable and non-renewable resources (see RESOURCE MANAGEMENT). Recent developments in the biological sciences and the so-called 'new ECOLOGY', however, have thrown into question many of the assumptions that underlie these models, and have drawn attention to the non-linear behaviour of many ecological SYSTEMS and their capacity for 'surprise' (Botkin, 1990). At the same time, ENVIRONMENTAL ECONOMICS has re-framed many of the questions surrounding natural resources in terms of the management of 'ecological capital,' a new vocabulary that facilitates the commensurability of the non-human world.

From both an historical and a philosophical perspective, 'natural resources' are a significant misnomer. First, the practices of EXPLORATION, SURVEYING, MEASUREMENT and experimentation by which natural resources come to be known

STOCK			FLOW	
Consumed by use	Theoretically recoverable	Recyclable	Critical zone	Non-critical zone
Oil	All elemental minerals	Metallic minerals	Fish	Solar energy
Gas			Forests	Tides
Coal			Animals	Wind
			Soil	Waves
			Water in aquifers	Water
				Air

Flow resources used to extinction

Critical zone resources become stock once regenerative capacity is exceeded

natural resources *exhaustible (stock) and renewable (flow) resources (from Rees, 1991)*

('discovered') highlight their deeply social origins. Second, resources are a dynamic category: different parts of the non-human world slip into (uranium, coltan) and out of (alum, flint, osiers, guano) this category across time and place (see RESOURCES). The remarkable history of natural gas, for example, demonstrates how a single substance may be considered as variously hazardous waste, 'neutral stuff' or a valuable natural resource, depending on knowledge, price, social norms and expectations (regarding POLLUTION), and the availability of alternatives. GEOGRAPHY continues to make contributions to the practical art and science of managing natural resources, but there is also a robust tradition of critical enquiry that acknowledges how 'natural resources are not naturally resources' (Hudson, 2001).   GB

Suggested reading
Bakker and Bridge (2006); Rees (1991).

naturalism Apart from the denial of the existence of God or the rejection of the Cartesian dualism of mind and body, the term 'naturalism' is nowadays commonly used to mark one's acceptance of a scientific philosophy (see PHILOSOPHY; SCIENCE). An overwhelming majority of Anglo-American philosophers claim to subscribe to some form of naturalism. From the vantage point of contemporary philosophy, naturalism is the twofold view that: (1) everything is composed of natural entities – those studied in science – whose properties determine the properties of things, including persons and abstract

mathematical objects; and (2) that science consists essentially in the registration of (or refutation of claims about) empirical invariances between discrete events, states of affairs and the like. This view, which can be aptly termed 'scientific naturalism', argues the strong claim that natural science provides *a* true or essential picture of NATURE. More contentious versions of scientific naturalism or scientism assert that it is the *only* true picture. Thus, in the words of Wilfred Sellars, 'science is the measure of all things, of what is that it is, of what is not that it is not' (1963, p. 173). Scientific naturalism contends that the great successes of the modern natural sciences in predicting, controlling and explaining natural phenomena – mathematical physics and Darwin's theory of evolution are exemplars – imply that the natural sciences' conception of nature is very likely to be true and, moreover, that this is our only bona fide or unproblematic conception of nature.

Importantly, scientific naturalism rejects any goal of First Philosophy – which claims, as in Cartesian or Kantian thought, to provide the epistemological and metaphysical foundations for the natural sciences. Instead, scientific naturalism takes the resolutely Humean stance that the human is simply a part of nature, not set over against it. This in turn denies the possibility of a First Philosophy prior to the natural sciences, such that philosophy can no longer claim to be the master discipline that sits in judgment over the claims of natural sciences or supplies the foundations for their operation. Instead, philosophy is

491

rendered continuous with science: it *is* science in its general and abstract reaches. A further implication for the social sciences is an essential unity of method with the natural sciences and, in some formulations, an actual identity of subject matter as well.

The philosopher Roy Bhaskar, whose work has been influential for several radical geographers, counterposes 'critical naturalism' to scientific naturalism and its thesis of continuity between the social and natural sciences. He instead asserts that 'ONTOLOGICAL, EPISTEMOLOGICAL and *relational* considerations all place limits on the possibility of naturalism (or rather, qualify the form it must take); and that these considerations all carry methodological import' (1998 [1979], p. 3; author's italics). Thus, Bhaskar denies that natural and social objects are alike in their make-up; rejects *empirical realism* (Humean epistemology) in favour of *transcendental* or *critical realism* as the protocol of knowledge more appropriate to the human sciences; and offers Marx's analysis in *Capital* as paradigmatic of a substantive use of this transcendental procedure (see REALISM).

Baruch Spinoza's naturalism is worth a mention, given his current resurgence within HUMAN GEOGRAPHY and allied fields. While the renewal proximately derives from studies on Spinoza by scholars such as Gilles Deleuze, Antonio Negri, Genevieve Lloyd and Louis Althusser, their wide uptake by human geographers suggests a desire for an ETHICS and politics of interaction rooted in an immanentist ontology – that is to say, an affirmative ontology of connections between human and non-human entities that (a) denies any prior separation of NATURE and SOCIETY, (b) rejects any form of transcendence (God or otherwise) as source of an authorizing design or *telos* for society, and (c) maintains that combinations of bodies are all there *is*, and our ethical–political task is to dare to strive for sameness in ways unknown.   VG

Suggested reading
Bhaskar (1998); De Caro and Macarthur (2004); Lloyd and Gatens (1999); Negri (2000).

nature A term with three main meanings:

- the essence or defining property of something;
- a material realm untouched by human activity; and
- the entire living world, of which the human species is a part.

These meanings often overlap and are sometimes contradictory. They are used in, and reproduced through, everyday speech as well as artistic and scientific DISCOURSES. This multivalency led the cultural critic Raymond Williams to observe that 'nature is perhaps the most complex word in the [English] language' (1983 [1976], p. 221) and that a history of its changing use would amount to a history of a large part of human thought (ibid., p. 225). Something of these complexities and histories can be glimpsed by juxtaposing two Anglo-Western attitudes to nature that are 300 years apart. The leading British political commentator John Locke, writing in the late seventeenth century, as the European settlement of North America got under way, made the following observation:

> In the first ages of the world men were more in danger to be lost, by wandering from their company, in the then vast wilderness of the earth, than to be straitened for want of room to plant in. And the same measure may be allowed still without prejudice to anybody, as full as the world seems. (Locke, 1988 [1690], p. 294)

Writing in the late twentieth century, as CLIMATE change entered global public consciousness, the North American environmental observer Bill McKibben articulates a very different vision:

> An idea, a relationship, can go extinct just like an animal or a plant. The idea in this case is 'nature', the separate and wild province, the world apart from man. [...] By changing the weather, we make every spot on earth man-made and artificial. We have deprived nature of its independence and that is fatal to its meaning. (McKibben, 1990, pp. 48 and 58)

As both of these accounts suggest, there is a powerful GEOGRAPHICAL IMAGINARY associated with the idea of nature, particularly with the second of the three meanings identified above. This geographical imaginary translates the categorical opposition between things attributable to nature and those attributable to human society into a spatial purification, in which nature is understood as a pristine WILDERNESS – a space–time outside or before the presence (or taint) of human settlement or activity (Cronon, 1995). It is an imaginary with very real consequences as it is taken up and reproduced through scientific, political and legal practices (Delaney, 2003).

Alongside SPACE and PLACE, the question of nature is one of the most central and enduring of geographical concerns (Fitzsimmons, 1989). As every undergraduate knows, geography stakes its disciplinary identity on being uniquely concerned with the interface between natural environments and human cultures. Nowhere is this better epitomized than in the work of Carl Ortwin Sauer in the 1920s and the legacy of the BERKELEY SCHOOL, with its emphasis on CULTURAL LANDSCAPE in which 'culture is the agent [and] the natural area the medium' (Sauer, 1963b [1925], p. 343). However, even here, it is evident that this definitive geographical concern has tended to be cast in terms that engage the world as if it were already divided up into things belonging either to nature or to CULTURE, a division entrenched in the very fabric of the discipline and reinforced by the sometimes faltering conversation between human and physical geographers (see GEOGRAPHY; PHYSICAL GEOGRAPHY).

In consequence, as human geographers set about trafficking between nature and culture, a fundamental asymmetry in the treatment of things assigned to these categories has been smuggled in to the enterprise. Geographies, like histories, become stories of exclusively human achievement played out over, and through, a seemingly indifferent medium of matter and objects made up of everything else. Such stories percolate through diverse currents in HUMAN GEOGRAPHY. These include MARXIST accounts which advance the apparently contradictory idea of the 'PRODUCTION OF NATURE', arguing that more and more of the things we are accustomed to think of as natural – from RESOURCES to LANDSCAPES – have increasingly become refashioned as the products of human labour (e.g. Mitchell, 1996; Gandy, 2002). Such accounts identify this intensifying social capacity to produce nature as *second nature*, a distinct phase in the historical development of nature–culture relations that supersedes its original or 'God-given' state – *first nature* (Smith, 1990). Equally, they include cultural accounts that explore POSTMODERN theories to understand better the ways in which our ways of seeing nature are always mediated and shaped by representational practices and devices – from cartographic surveys to wildlife film-making (e. g. Wilson, 1992). These accounts emphasize the politics of REPRESENTATION, recognizing that representational processes are instrumental in constituting our sense of what the natural world is like, rather than merely a mirror image of a fixed external reality. In consequence, such

accounts suggest, multiple and often incompatible representations of the same natural phenomena or event can and do coexist (e.g. Cosgrove and Daniels, 1988).

Whether their emphasis has been on nature's material transformation or on its changing meaning, these are geographies whose only subject or active inhabitants are people, while everything else is consigned to nature and becomes putty in our hands. In this, human geography's long march from ENVIRONMENTAL DETERMINISM to SOCIAL CONSTRUCTIONISM seems to have brought us to the same place as that identified by the environmentalist Bill McKibben as the 'end of nature' (see Castree, 2005a). This *humanist* stance is premised on two working assumptions (see HUMANISM). The first is that the collective 'us' of human society is somehow always already removed from the rest of the world, for only by placing it *a priori* at a distance can human society be (re)connected to everything else on such asymmetrical terms as those between producer and product, or viewer and view (Ingold, 2000). The second is that in different ways the generative energies of the Earth itself, in rivers, soils, weather and oceans and the living plants and creatures assigned to 'nature', are effectively evacuated from the terms of these analyses (Haraway, 1991c). Such assumptions do not square with the anguish and infrastructure of existential concern that characterize the twenty-first century. In unimaginable and unforeseen ways, the forcefulness of all manner of things has come to make itself felt in our social lives and political agendas. From climate change to mad cow disease, there is a growing sense that our worldly interactions with, and indifference to, more-than-human forces and entities are returning to haunt us. Since the last edition of this *Dictionary* was published (2000), a major thrust of work in human, particularly cultural, geography has been to challenge these premises and rethink the 'human', and the status of the 'non-human', in the fabric of human geography (Whatmore, 2002b).

Much of this work has drawn inspiration from POST-STRUCTURALIST philosophies relatively new to geography, through intermediaries such as science and technology studies (STS) (see Hinchliffe, 2007). The argument advanced here is that what we are experiencing is less a 'crisis of nature' and more a 'crisis of OBJECTIVITY', in which the things ascribed to nature are refusing to stay passively in their boxes and are assuming their irrepressible part in the possibilities and achievements of social agency that had been falsely ascribed exclusively to humans (Latour, 2004, p. 21). Taking up this argument, human geographers have been exploring the intricate and dynamic ways in which people, technologies, organisms and geophysical processes are woven together in the making and remaking of spaces, places and landscapes. Three of the most important currents in recent work in this vein have been those addressing post-colonial, animal and bodily reframings of what matters, what must be taken into account, in the making of human geographies.

The first current is concerned with showing that the idea of nature as a pristine space outside society is an historical fallacy. This idea is so pervasive today that it is difficult for many of us to recognize it as a particular and contestable way of seeing the world. A specific concern has been to expose the ways in which the presence of native peoples was actively erased from the landscapes that came to be seen as wilderness in colonial European eyes (see COLONIALISM), and that are now revered by many environmentalists as remnants of 'pristine' nature (e.g. Braun, 2002). The second current extends this historical repudiation of the separation of human society and the natural world by paying close attention to the mixed-up mobile lives of people, plants and animals in everyday life time out of mind. Here, ANIMALS have become a vehicle for opening up the ways in which non-human creatures have long been caught up in all manner of social networks, from farming to wildlife, in ways that disconcert our assumptions about their, and our, 'natural' place in the world. The third, and perhaps most provocative, current of work in this vein explores the bodily as an important site for geographical research in which the human, quite as much as the non-human, is molten in the heat of technological achievements that recombine the qualities associated with these categories in new forms ranging from transgenic organisms to bionic enhancements (e.g. Thrift, 2005a: see also BODY; CYBORG).   SW

neighbourhood An urban area dominated by residential uses. While no fixed SCALE can be assigned, neighbourhoods have traditionally been understood to be relatively small or walkable, although they may vary considerably in terms of population (Martin, 2003). Neighbourhood has long been conflated with the notion of COMMUNITY as described in the work of the CHICAGO SCHOOL sociologists. Neighbourhood is the more explicitly *territorial*

concept of the two. Efforts at defining and using the term 'neighbourhood' fall roughly into four areas: typologies (identifying primary neighbourhood characteristics); neighbourhood change; neighbourhood effects; and as a territory for political action (Martin, 2003).

Typologies of neighbourhoods draw upon and also echo the conflation with community in the Chicago School approach. These combine physical and social features of TERRITORIES within cities in order to classify each area as some type (Hunter, 1979). The features included in such typologies include RACE and ETHNICITY, RELIGION, family status, and CLASS of the area population, housing tenure, age and other INFRASTRUCTURE characteristics. Neighbourhood types can then be correlated with *neighbourhood change* over time, drawing upon the notion of MOBILITY associated with the Chicago School and from INVASION AND SUCCESSION.

Neighbourhood change focuses on both population and INFRASTRUCTURE. Population may change by one or more measures (such as dominant ethnicity or household structure) due to residential mobility (where people move to a different area within a CITY or a different location entirely). A neighbourhood's physical INFRASTRUCTURE changes due to decline (due to age or active disinvestment) or renewed investment (as with URBAN RENEWAL or GENTRIFICATION).

'NEIGHBOURHOOD EFFECTS' approaches investigate neighbourhoods as loci of social norms that shape individual attitudes, experiences and health (Hunter, 1979; Ellaway, Macintyre and Kearns, 2001). This literature seeks to link individual outcomes with local social and physical conditions. For example, Ellaway, Macintyre and Kearns (2001) found that individuals perceive their HEALTH differently depending upon physical conditions of the neighbourhood. However, Mandanipour, Cars and Allen (2000) argued that structural exclusions of the poor (e.g. uneven access to RESOURCES, due to SEGREGATION) are more powerful forces in an individual's life chances than local cultural factors.

An approach that highlights the contingency of any definition of neighbourhood upon local context and/or scholarly purpose is that of conceptualizing *neighbourhood as a territory for political action* (Martin, 2003). In this conceptualization, neighbourhoods are constituted by practice: daily life and particular social and political claims, which are dynamic over time and space. The particular meaning of neighbourhood – as a social community or historical district, for example – will be articulated and deployed according to the people involved and issues at stake. As the other three approaches suggest, 'neighbourhood' is a term that is highly dependent upon the particular location in which it is embedded, the local political and social CULTURE, and the perspective of the individual experiencing or observing the neighbourhood.   DGM

Suggested reading
Mitchell (1993); *Urban Studies* (2001).

neighbourhood effect A type of CONTEXTUAL EFFECT whereby the characteristics of people's local social milieux influence the ways in which they think and act. Neighbours present individuals with MODELS of attitudes and practices that may either: (a) conform to their own, and so reinforce their self-IDENTITY and behaviour; or (b) contradict them and suggest alternatives that they may adopt, especially if there is considerable pressure to do so.

The search for neighbourhood effects has been especially characteristic of ELECTORAL GEOGRAPHY, with a number of studies showing greater spatial polarization of, for example, support for a political party in an area than suggested by its residents' characteristics. Most of those studies use aggregate data, however, and may involve an ECOLOGICAL FALLACY. Relatively little is known about the processes that generate the observed patterns, although the importance of interpersonal influence is often assumed, generating what is known as 'conversion through conversation'. Similar effects are postulated in the spread of other attitudes and behaviour patterns, in EDUCATION, for example.   RJ

Suggested reading
Johnston and Pattie (2006).

neighbourhood unit A relatively self-contained urban residential area. Most units are in planned residential developments, either suburban districts or NEW TOWNS and similar settlements.

The concept of a NEIGHBOURHOOD unit was first deployed in Chicago in 1916 and formalized by Clarence Perry (1872–1944) in 1929. It suggested the importance of SCALE in planning residential areas: each neighbourhood unit should be of sufficient size that it was relatively self-contained for certain functions – primary schools and daily shopping, for example – and should develop as an integrated COMMUNITY. British GARDEN CITIES were

planned with neighbourhood units of about 5,000 persons: all unit facilities were within walking distance and motorized transport largely excluded.

Although the general concept continues to underpin some URBAN PLANNING, the assumption that people wish to constrain parts of their daily/weekly lives to such relatively small bounded TERRITORIES has generated criticism, while greater reliance on personal transport has broken down the utility of such a cellular division of urban space.   RJ

Suggested reading
Hall (2002).

neo-classical economics A school of economics defined by the study of rational economic choice and the price-based optimal allocation of RESOURCES, using a body of analytically rigorous and mathematically sophisticated theory and techniques. It is *the* school of economics, at least in Anglo-America, ubiquitous, hegemonic and mainstream. The economist Roy Weintraub says, 'we are all neoclassicists now'.

Robbins (1932, p. 16) provided the iconic methodological definition of neo-classicism: 'a science which studies human behaviour as a relationship between ends and scarce means which have alternative uses'. The origins of neo-classicism are earlier, however, with the writings of a troika of late-nineteenth-century European economists: the Englishman William Stanley Jevons (1835–82), the Austrian Carl Menger (1840–1921) and the Frenchman Léon Walras (1834–1910). Alfred Marshall (1842–1924), the first economist at Cambridge, codified, systematized and elaborated their works (including inventing supply and demand diagrams: see figure) in his enormously influential textbook *Principles of economics* (published in eight editions between 1890 and 1920). After the Second World War, the centre of neo-classical economics crossed the Atlantic to the USA, taking its now familiar abstract, mathematical form. A key influence was MIT's Paul Samuelson (1915–), the second winner of the Nobel Prize in economics (1970), and author of the canonical text of formal neo-classical theory, *Foundations of economic analysis* (1947).

Neo-classical economics is neither monolithic nor static, but there are a number of core concerns that continually surface:

(1) The focus on RATIONAL ECONOMIC CHOICE, the belief that individuals have

both the mental agility and access to information to obtain the most for the least, and applying both to consumers who maximize utility, and producers who maximize profits.

(2) A concern with determining conditions for equilibrium. Rational responses by producers and consumers to MARKET signals produce equilibrium such that there is no incentive for any individual to change their decision: market equilibrium is the solution to the problem of individual maximization.

(3) An emphasis on defining competitive market efficiency such that there is an optimal allocation of resources among competing uses. If not, there is competitive market failure, requiring correction.

(4) An assertion of the methodological sovereignty of independent, rational individuals, and who form the back-stop of neo-classical explanation. Everything – institutions, firms, social classes – is reducible to the law of individual rational choice (METHODOLOGICAL INDIVIDUALISM).

Criticisms of neo-classical economics are endless. They include objections that neo-classicism is nothing but an IDEOLOGY, a sop for market CAPITALISM; that the rational choice assumption is empirically false, logically inconsistent and morally suspect; that equilibrium, with its assumption that time has stopped, holds at best in Heaven and never on Earth; that SOCIETY is always more than the sum of its rational agents (there *is* such a thing as society); and that the use of mathematics is primarily for internal sociological purposes and not for meeting scholarly ends (even Samuelson said that his intensive knowledge of mathematics made him feel like an Olympic-trained athlete with no race to run).

Neo-classical economics entered economic geography as part of the QUANTITATIVE REVOLUTION from the late 1950s, and also at the same time through an allied movement, REGIONAL SCIENCE (King, 1979). The central intellectual problem was to introduce SPACE to a theoretical system that had never systematically included it. While economic geographers and regional scientists made attempts to do so via LOCATION THEORY, there always remained fundamental problems in couching neo-classical competitive equilibrium models within an economy distributed over space (see SPACE-ECONOMY), because the spatial constitution of an economy inherently confers monopolistic advantage. Consequently, the core

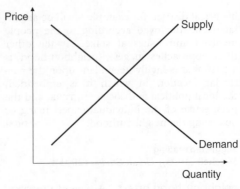

neo-classical economics *Supply and demand*

neo-classical postulate of competitive market efficiency is violated (see (3) above). This is yet another example of what Harvey (1985b, p. 142) identifies as the 'numbing effect' of space on the 'central propositions of *any* social theory'. In any case, economic geographers were never as mathematically astute as neo-classical economists, nor did most of them share their penchant for ABSTRACTION and rigour. Consequently, the importation of neo-classical theory was frequently half-hearted, incomplete and prone to mistakes. From the late 1990s, there was a second-wave attempt to link economic geography to neo-classicism through the NEW ECONOMIC GEOGRAPHY, but this has been even more unsuccessful as measured by the degree of disciplinary acceptance than in the first go-around.   TB

Suggested reading
Robinson (1962).

neo-geography A term – coined by a non-geographer – referring to the bespoke creation of MAPS using the INTERNET, involving the shared use of mapping resources (such as Google Maps and GEOGRAPHICAL INFORMATION SYSTEMS) to which information is added. Those bespoke maps can incorporate a range of other materials to illustrate the characteristics of individual places – such as photographs. It is seen as part of a movement that is de-professionalizing CARTOGRAPHY and making map construction feasible for a wide range of users. Such construction can involve the input of data from devices such as GLOBAL POSITIONING SYSTEMS – allowing, for example, the real-time mapping of journeys and tracking of movements.   RJ

Suggested reading
Turner (2006). See also http://platial.com/splash and http://neogeography.net/

neo-liberalism A doctrine, loosely conceived, that argues for the desirability of a society organized around self-regulating markets, and free, to the extent possible, from social and political intervention (Cypher and Dietz, 1997, pp. 222–32). The term came into prominence in the 1980s, especially in LATIN AMERICA, where it referred to agendas imposed by leaders such as Chilean dictator Augusto Pinochet – who, with backing from US-trained economists, opened the economy to foreign investors while pushing economic deregulation and privatization of state enterprises – and to the forms of restructuring promoted under Margaret Thatcher in the UK and Ronald Reagan in the USA (Harvey, 2005, pp. 7–9). The US government, along with the INTERNATIONAL MONETARY FUND (IMF), the World Bank and the WORLD TRADE ORGANIZATION (WTO), has aggressively promoted the policies associated with neo-liberalism; and with the collapse of socialist and communist projects since the 1980s, US leaders asserted broad agreement over neo-liberalism under the heading of 'the Washington Consensus'. Notwithstanding this geographical locus, neo-liberal policies have gained adherents around the world (Toye, 1987).

Neo-liberalism can be analysed in various ways, including as a set of theoretical propositions, as a variety of actual practices and as a manifestation of specific social interests. As a set of theoretical propositions, neo-liberalism is to its advocates an update of basic ideas about economic and social life that the classical liberal theorists of the eighteenth and nineteenth centuries put forward (see LIBERALISM). Neo-liberals cite favourably Adam Smith's contentions about the capacity of MARKETS to regulate themselves and to produce greater social prosperity than mercantilism (Smith, 1976 [1776]), as well as David Ricardo's arguments for the greater aggregate prosperity that TRADE specialization can produce, based upon COMPARATIVE ADVANTAGE and minimal tariff barriers (Ricardo, 1992). Theorists such as Friederich von Hayek and Milton Friedman (Friedman, 2002 [1962]; Hayek, 1981) reworked these ideas and used them to argue against a range of Keynesian economic policies – especially social welfare and counter-cyclical government spending policies – that had become prominent in Western countries since the Great Depression of the 1930s. Their arguments, however, did not gain substantial support in governing circles until the 1970s, when some of them came to be advertised as part of the theoretical basis

for the policies of the New Right (Harvey, 2005, pp. 19–31).

As policy, many neo-liberal practices differ from the theories (Peck and Tickell, 2002; Harvey, 2005, pp. 70–81). While neo-liberals have argued the virtues of minimalist or 'night-watchman' STATES, the states that have most aggressively promoted neo-liberalism have often been far from non-interventionist. Pinochet's military dictatorship provided a model that was to be replicated in many other developing countries undergoing IMF-mandated STRUCTURAL ADJUSTMENT policies, imposing specific forms of economic liberalization through a strong state that engaged in political repression. Similarly, neo-liberal reforms in China have been accomplished under a one-party state that exercises strict control over various aspects of social and economic life. Moreover, actual neo-liberal economic measures have typically been selective and uneven.

Contradictions between theoretical propositions and actual practice lead some commentators to argue that neo-liberalism is best seen not as a fully coherent doctrine, consistently applied, but as a reflection of the CLASS interests of particular capitalists and their allies (Duménil and Lévy, 2004; Harvey, 2005). In this view, the global economic downturn in the 1960s and 1970s led the most internationally mobile groups of investors – especially those involved in international finance – to begin attacking state policies that were seen as hindering CAPITAL mobility and reducing profit rates. Through both reinvesting capital abroad and advertising the allegedly undesirable effects of regulations on capital mobility, these investors attempted to restore profitability by driving down wages and production costs in core areas of the global economy, selectively making use of lower wages, production costs and emerging markets in countries of the global SOUTH.

These efforts to restore profitability through neo-liberal GLOBALIZATION have been partially successful, but they have also generated various forms of backlash. First, the attacks on state programmes that enhance social welfare have generated responses from popular forces that see neo-liberalism as antithetical to improved life chances for the least privileged members of society (Harvey, 2003b, pp. 137–82; Harvey, 2005, pp. 198–206). Second, neo-liberalism has come under increasing attack from within the ranks of the elite after Washington Consensus policies were seen to have been inappropriately applied during the Asian economic crisis of 1997–8

(Stiglitz, 2002, pp. 89–132). Third, the rise of neo-conservatives to power in Washington since 2000 has generated new contradictions, since many supporters of neo-conservatism claim in principle to favour free trade while openly calling for high TARIFF barriers and other forms of protection for national industries threatened by foreign competition (Harvey, 2005, pp. 81–6).

The purported hegemony of US-led global neo-liberalism – the neo-liberal grand slam as one commentator put it – came crashing to a halt in late 2008 with the failure of a number of major US investment banks, the bankruptcy of a number of insurance houses, the discrediting of the credit rating agencies and the Security and Exchange Commission (purportedly organizations designed to regulate financial institutions) and a $700 billion bailout by the outgoing Bush administration. While triggered by a US housing bubble and a crisis in the mortgage industry, the crisis quickly became global in scope. It remains unclear whether massive infusions from central banks will unfreeze the credit sector, and most commentators expect the world economy to enter into a deep recession comparable perhaps to that of the 1930s. The high tide of neo-liberalism has passed, and many of the G8 countries now openly talk of the need for Keynesianism and more government regulation.   JGl

Suggested reading
Cypher and Dietz (1997); Duménil and Lévy (2004); Friedman (2002 [1962]); Harvey (2003b, 2005); Hayek (1981); Peck and Tickell (2002); Ricardo (1992); Smith (1976 [1776]); Stiglitz (2002); Toye (1987).

neo-Ricardian economics A modern school of economics that draws upon and reworks the ideas of the English classical economist David Ricardo (1772–1823). The founding text is a slim monograph by an Italian economist at Cambridge University, Piero Sraffa (1898–1983), *The production of commodities by means of commodities* (1960). Sraffa's model of the economy consists of two components:

(1) Production is conceived as circular and interdependent where the output in one production period is used as an input for the next production period.
(2) When outputs exceed inputs, a "surplus" exists that forms the basis of the social conditions of income distribution.

Sraffa subtitled his book *Prelude to a critique of economic theory*. Although he did not engage in the critique himself, his model has provided the basis for subsequent criticisms of both NEO-CLASSICAL ECONOMICS and MARXIST ECONOMICS. These were first taken up in the 'capital controversy', where the neo-classical theory of profit (profit is the marginal product of capital) was shown to be logically untenable, and later in the 'value controversy', where the Marxist LABOUR THEORY OF VALUE was shown to be redundant in calculating prices. A number of economic geographers have elaborated Sraffa's work since Scott's (1976b) pioneering paper linking Süraffa's model of production with VON THÜNEN's theory of agricultural RENT. But the formal, minimalist style of Neo-Ricardianism is out of synch with the more expansive, empirically grounded, and less formal ECONOMIC GEOGRAPHY of today, and connections have been few, and even more rarely taken further.   TB

Suggested reading
Sheppard and Barnes (1990).

network society A term coined by Manuel Castells (1996b, 1997, 1998) in an influential trilogy of books to describe globalizing societies dominated by accelerated economic, cultural and social FLOWS, mediated predominantly by information technologies (see also GLOBALIZATION). The trilogy explored the growth of networked enterprises, global processes of SOCIAL EXCLUSION and the changing nature of TIME and SPACE, IDENTITY and STATE formation. Its key argument was that NETWORK societies are dominated by a separation of the *space of flows* – the globalized and accelerated domains that are orchestrated through new information and communications technologies – from *the space of places* – geographically confined sources of individual and collective identity.   SG

Suggested reading
Castells (1996b).

network(s) A particular kind of spatial arrangement that consists of a collection of linked elements which typically exhibit a de-centred and non-hierarchical form. With the word ever more ubiquitous in popular, business and academic usage, it is increasingly important to recognize that the proliferation of the basic topological METAPHOR of the network can conceal a range of very different analytical commitments, both explicit and implicit. At least the following approaches may be usefully distinguished, each with their different main constituents/actors, types of relation foregrounded and methods of analysis:

(1) Infrastructural technically based networks, such as electrical, road, rail, sewerage and telecommunications systems, can be described according to their density, connectedness and orientation (Haggett, 1969: see INFRASTRUCTURE).

(2) SOCIAL NETWORKS, such as kinship, friendship and communities, have historically been analysed both quantitatively by social network analysis and more qualitatively using tools derived from social anthropology (Strathern, 1996).

(3) Network-based models of organization have tended to merge the distinctive features of the previous two approaches, as the nature of collectives from the informal and local to formal and global are increasingly seen as exhibiting this kind of form (Castells, 1996b; Barry, 2001).

(4) Finally, actor-networks (Latour, 1993) are the distributed forms of agency that emerge from articulation of humans and non-humans as seen by practitioners of the conceptual approach that originated in science and technology studies (STS) and is known as ACTOR-NETWORK THEORY.   NB

neural networks Methods of finding solutions to a range of technical problems using computer ALGORITHMS based on models of the human brain. The networks are 'trained' to find solutions to new problems by being given exemplars on which to base their decisions, such as which category to assign an individual observation to when the category boundaries are fuzzy (cf. FUZZY SETS). The approach is particularly valuable in various forms of pattern recognition and classification and is widely used in REMOTE SENSING studies for classifying segments of the Earth's surface according to their LAND COVER (Foody, 1996). The spectral signatures of different land-cover types vary, and many small areas for which data are obtained contain a mixture of types. The goal is to allocate each observation unit (PIXEL) to a relatively homogeneous category. 'Training' sites are defined, using synthetic pixels with homogeneous land cover, and the neural network algorithm, through an iterative procedure, allocates all of the observed pixels to the type it most closely resembles. It is then possible to estimate the proportion of the land surface under different types of cover.

A similar approach has been suggested for CLASSIFICATION of socio-economic data. Very few small areas – such as CENSUS TRACTS – are homogeneous in their population characteristics so clear boundaries between types of area cannot be defined *a priori* on other than pragmatic grounds (e.g. use of quartiles); they are the same as pixels with mixed land uses. Using neural network approaches, IDEAL TYPES are defined (with different levels of homogeneity and mixtures, for example) and the individual tracts are allocated to those they most resemble (Mitchell, Martin and Foody, 1998).   RJ

Suggested reading
Openshaw and Openshaw (1997).

New Economic Geography An approach associated primarily with a group of American neo-classical economists (see NEO-CLASSICAL ECONOMICS) who from the early 1990s sought to apply theoretical rigour, analytical methods and econometric (statistical) techniques to a SPACE-ECONOMY. Such interest was surprising, given economists' historical attachment to an a-spatial ECONOMY, to 'a wonderland of no dimensions' (Isard, 1956, p. 25). For Paul Krugman (1995a, p. 33), however, the economist most central to the movement, the New Economic Geography was 'a vision on the road to Damascus': 'I suddenly realised that I had spent my whole professional life... thinking and writing about economic geography, without being aware of it' (Krugman, 1991, p. 1).

Krugman's epiphany was that the analytical framework he previously deployed to understand international TRADE was perfect for comprehending economic geography: 'Economic geography, like... trade theory, is largely about increasing returns and multiple equilibria. The technical tricks needed to make models tractable are often the same' (Krugman, 1995b, p. 41). That term 'MODEL' is critical. While conventional economic geography was 'a field full of empirical insights, good stories and obvious practical importance', it was 'neglected' – that is, neglected by economists – 'because nobody had seen a good way to formalize it' (Krugman, 1995b, p. 41). Krugman's project was to take works of economic geographers and to make them (as he saw it) intellectually viable by expressing them in the formal vocabulary of economic models. As he writes, 'we will integrate spatial issues into economics through clever models ... that make sense of the insights of the geographers in a way that meets the formal

499

standards of the economists' (Krugman, 1995b, p. 88). In his manifesto, Krugman (2000, p. 51) identifies 'a slogan' for his project: 'Dixit–Stiglitz, icebergs, evolution, and the computer.' Dixit–Stiglitz is the 'clever model'; icebergs refers to the 'technical trick' for introducing TRANSPORT COSTS (and hence geography), evolution points to the dynamic character of the models (as opposed to the static kind characterizing traditional LOCATION THEORY), and the computer simulates solutions for multiple equilibria (Krugman says that his laptop 'lets me produce a paper – equations, simulations and all – in a hotel room over a weekend...' (Krugman, 1995a, p. 37).

There was a precedent for the New Economic Geography in REGIONAL SCIENCE, which was established in the 1950s to apply rigour, scientific analysis and statistical methods to a space economy. Unsurprisingly, given the attempt to occupy the same terrain, the two movements have an uncomfortable relation. Krugman implies that regional scientists have yet to find 'clever models', while regional scientists dismiss Krugman's work by claiming that 'it's obvious, it's wrong, and anyway [it was] said years ago' (Isserman, 1996). The relationship between the New Economic Geography and ECONOMIC GEOGRAPHY as practised in HUMAN GEOGRAPHY is also uneasy. There was an initial flush of interest represented by the publication of a joint reader, *The Oxford handbook of economic geography* (Clark, Gertler and Feldman, 2000), and a new journal, the *Journal of Economic Geography*, which started publishing in January 2005. Both organs promoted cross-disciplinary exchange. At least as measured by citation impact scores, the new journal attracted large numbers of readers from both economic geography and economics. But being between the same covers does not prove intercourse, and Martin's (1999b, p. 70) verdict on the New Economic Geography, that it produces a 'dull sense of *déjà vu*', is still likely to be shared by many economic geographers. The more than 100-year history of economic geography is littered with failed attempts to engage economists. This is turning out to be another one.   TB

Suggested reading
Martin (1999b).

New International Division of Labour (NIDL) A recasting of the international DIVISION OF LABOUR associated with the internationalization of capital and the growth of

newly industrializing countries and regions. In one sense, the term is unhelpful, for the UNEVEN DEVELOPMENT of CAPITALISM ensures that the global division of labour is constantly changing. As Marx and Engels (2002 [1848]) put it in *The communist manifesto*, 'All that is solid melts into air.' In another sense, however, the phrase has some merit. Particularly in the heyday of the Bretton Woods system (1944–73), neither CAPITAL nor labour moved extensively across the global stage. National economies were placed squarely at the heart of an international trading system. This was partly in response to a reading of the Depression years and the Second World War. The Bretton Woods system was meant to protect national space economies in the 'First World' against undue economic and political turbulence (Corbridge, 1994). When the Bretton Woods system came undone, it gave way to high unemployment and inflation. According to Fröbel, Heinrichs and Kreye (1980), many capitalist firms in the West now had to face the consequences of the postwar corporatist settlement – a settlement that had increased returns to labour, including labour employed by the STATE, relative to those returned to capital. Firms could evaporate, innovate or emigrate. With the emigration of capital, they reasoned, came a change in the international division of labour that was distinctive – new – when viewed against the period from 1950 to 1975.

There is no doubt that the rise of newly industrialized countries such as Taiwan and South Korea came as a shock in the 1970s (see ASIAN MIRACLES/TIGERS). Some versions of DEPENDENCY THEORY maintained that the DEVELOPMENT of the core depended upon the continued non-industrialization of the periphery. Gunder Frank argued that Taiwan and South Korea were exceptions to a rule that still held. They had simply been allowed to develop by the USA for geopolitical reasons. Less blinkered theories accepted that GEOPOLITICS was part of the story, but they also noted the way in which the state in both countries had achieved a degree of relative autonomy from domestic proprietary classes. They had used this power to effect land reforms and proactive industrial policies. In the case of South Korea, industrial policy was fastened mainly around large-scale domestic capitals, including leading banks and *chaebol* such as Samsung. In Taiwan, industrial development was sponsored by networks of small-scale firms (Kohli, 2004). What NIDL theorists have added to this mix – and their work has been continued by GLOBALIZATION theorists – is close attention to the ways in which these new industrial spaces (including high-tech spaces in Indian cities such as Bangalore and Hyderabad) are linked to international capital and consumer MARKETS by firms such as IBM, Hewlett-Packard and Sony. NIDL theorists largely discounted the domestic bases of industrial success in the Asian Tiger economies and important policy differences between them. They were ahead of the game, however, in recognizing some of the global shifts set in motion by the restructuring of capitalism as it moved into an era of NEO-LIBERALISM and deepening TIME-SPACE COMPRESSION.   SCO

Suggested reading
Dicken (2003); Schatz and Venables (2000).

new town A planned town in an area that previously lacked a substantial urban settlement. Although such planned settlements can be found throughout history, the term was first widely used after passage of the British *New Towns Act 1946*. The New Town movement there, based on the earlier GARDEN CITY movement and the concept of NEIGHBOURHOOD UNITS, stimulated the creation of a number of new settlements, most of them outside London, designed to limit urban SPRAWL and protect agricultural land (see GREEN BELT), to decentralize population and economic activity and to contribute to rehousing policies necessitated by both SLUM clearance in INNER CITIES and the destruction of much housing during the Second World War. The first of those towns was Stevenage, with ten being created between 1946 and 1950. Eventually, 28 were designated and built, including major cities such as Milton Keynes, which incorporated several small existing towns.

The model set in the UK has been widely adopted over the past 60 years, and there are New Towns in a large number of countries. Although the utopian ideals of many of the movement's originators have not been met – notably with regard to the creation of relatively self-contained COMMUNITIES – most new towns represent relatively high standards of housing and urban design.   RJ

Suggested reading
Hardy (1991); Osborn (1977); Stein (1966).

NGO The acronym for Non-Governmental Organizations – not-for-profit voluntary associations that seek to act for the public good. The term covers a variety of bodies from international agencies with large professional staffs to small groups of unpaid volunteers. Their functions are diverse and include campaigning, humanitarian relief, development work, social welfare, cultural activities and CONSERVATION. Many provide services and programmes on behalf of governments and intergovernmental organizations and some have become highly dependent on government financial support. According to some accounts they operate in the space between the STATE and the private sector and are sometimes misleadingly regarded as synonymous with CIVIL SOCIETY.   JPa

Suggested reading
Townsend, Porter and Mawdsley (2004).

NIMBY The acronym for 'Not-In-My-Back-Yard', an attitude adopted by individuals resisting the siting of a source of perceived negative EXTERNALITIES (such as shelters for the homeless (see HOMELESSNESS) and those recently released from PRISON) close to their homes, and campaigning for it to be located elsewhere (cf. ZONE OF DEPENDENCE).   RJ

nodal region A REGION whose defining characteristic is the links between its component parts and one or more focal points. Nodal (or functional) regions are usually defined using flow data, as in the definition of HINTERLANDS: they form the core of Haggett's (1965) LOCATIONAL ANALYSIS schema.   RJ

nomadism A livelihood – including hunter-gathering, PASTORALISM, begging and commerce – that involves the intra-annual movements of families (or other social production units), necessitating the displacement of their dwelling(s). During the nineteenth and early twentieth centuries, the term was used more indiscriminately to refer to any livelihood associated with intra-annual human MOBILITY. Nomadism has historically elicited both fascination and revulsion (negative connotations of the terms shiftless, rootless, vagabond, vagrant, itinerant etc.) within Western CULTURE and SCIENCE (see also MIGRANCY). Cultural evolutionists have seen it as a primitive cultural trait, while environmental determinists and cultural ecologists have portrayed it as a feature inhibiting the development of complex, hierarchical political systems (see CULTURAL ECOLOGY; ENVIRONMENTAL DETERMINISM). Reflecting this history, nomadism incorrectly conjures up ESSENTIALIST notions of wandering and livelihood

501

stasis. However, studies of nomadic societies find that their mobility is neither socially nor ecologically aimless, but rather shaped by the physical availability of RESOURCES and by the SOCIAL NETWORKS required for security and maintaining access to these resources. Moreover, the degree of mobility (rate and distance of displacements) varies significantly among nomadic households, reflecting the different opportunities and constraints that they face.   MT

Suggested reading
Khazanov (1994).

nomadology Although they do not provide an explicit definition of the term, Gilles Deleuze and Félix Guattari (1987) present the discipline of nomadology as the opposite of history, which they associate with a sedentary, STATE-centric point of view. For Deleuze and Guattari, the point of nomadology is not a historical study of nomadic peoples but, rather, a study of different spatial practices. Unlike the state, the nomadic (or rhizomatic, see RHIZOME) 'war machine' is understood to occupy space without ordering, counting or surveying it. Nomadology is thus the study of what these philosophers call 'smooth space', a space of creativity, emergent properties and intensive becomings.   AJS

Suggested reading
Cresswell (1997); Deleuze and Guattari (1987).

nomos The matrix of laws, norms and conventions that orders conduct within a SOCIETY. The *nomos* is: (a) socially constructed, and so varies over space and time; and (b) generally accepted, and so serves as a template for political–moral ordering. The term emerged with the rise of democracy in fifth-century Athens, where the political structure of the classical city-state implied that the *nomos* is also (c) spatially articulated (in the sense of a distribution or assignment of powers). The term entered GEOPOLITICS through the German jurist Carl Schmitt (1888–1985), who invoked the concept to argue that in EUROPE in the sixteenth and seventeenth centuries the theological–moral model of the JUST WAR yielded to the secular–juridical model (i.e. the *nomos*) of a regulated war between sovereign STATES that claimed a monopoly of the legitimate means of VIOLENCE. Unrestrained violence was then projected 'beyond the line' into the non-European world: 'Europe sublimate[d] its animality by establishing the

AMERICAS as an extralegal zone in which bestial deeds [could] be "acted out" far away' (Rasch, 2003). Schmitt identified this zone with 'the STATE OF NATURE in which everything is possible' and with the space of exception (see EXCEPTION, SPACE OF). He argued that by the early twentieth century the line had dissolved, and the wild zones of colonial violence had appeared within the ruins of the European order (Schmitt, 2003 [1950]). Schmitt's writings have attracted renewed critical attention today, through the bearing of his *political theology* on the Bush administration's WAR on terror (see TERRORISM), and through the radicalization of his work in the political PHILOSOPHY of Giorgio Agamben (see Minca, 2006). In both cases, considerable interest has attached to Schmitt as 'above, all, a spatial thinker', where the concept of *nomos* is central (Dean, 2006, p. 7).   DG

nomothetic Concerned with the universal and the general. The term derived from the German philosopher Wilhelm Windelband who, in 1894, used it to identify one of two possible goals of concept formation:

> The theoretical interests associated with nomothetic concept formation highlight those common qualities of objects of experience that lead to the formulation of general laws of nature. The process is one of continual abstraction in which the special qualities of an object are filtered out and the object is seen as a general type that exists with certain relations to other, general types. (Entrikin, 1991)

Windelband contrasted this with IDIOGRAPHIC concept-formation, which is concerned to achieve a complete understanding of the *individual* case (see KANTIANISM; cf. IDEAL TYPE).

Windelband's views were considerably more nuanced than the caricatured oppositions between idiographic and nomothetic that were propelled into GEOGRAPHY after the middle of the twentieth century. These versions ignored Windelband's insistence that both approaches were directed towards the formation of analytical concepts. Instead, in the wake of the Hartshorne–Schaefer exchange over EXCEPTIONALISM, the proponents of SPATIAL SCIENCE ridiculed REGIONAL GEOGRAPHY in particular for its focus on the unique – its supposedly inherent inability to provide conceptual rigour or intellectual substance – and claimed that geography should focus on generalization and work towards the formulation of scientific theories and laws of spatial organization. But these caricatures have largely disappeared, not least through the critique of classical spatial science, the emergence of post-positivist geographies and the reformulation of regional geography. As Phillips (2004, p. 40) concluded, 'the debates over idiographic/regional interpretive geography versus nomothetic/quantitative/scientific geography have come and (mostly) gone; contemporary critiques emphasizing CONTEXTUALITY and contingency are with us now'.　　DG

non-place A term coined by French anthropologist Marc Augé to describe certain qualities of airports, highways, theme parks, motels, department stores and shopping centres, tourist sites and so on. These sites have in common gatherings of individuals and groups of people who temporarily come together at the same site, but who have no particular bond to each other. Rather than a social bond determining the nature of these collective gatherings, it is typically signs and texts that guide people's movements within these spaces or that direct them to other spaces. In that latter capacity, the non-place is a conduit, a potential that structures the gaze to some other site. Some interpreters take non-place to be a negation of PLACE (cf. PLACELESSNESS) but in Augé's terms 'place' works dialectically with 'non-place': 'the first is never completely erased, the second never totally completed; they are like palimpsests on which the scrambled game of identity and relations is ceaselessly rewritten' (Augé, 1995, pp. 78–9). But for some critics, Augé has not been clear about the DIALECTICS of place and non-place, and one gets the impression that a timeless passenger/commuter subject is the sole inhabitant of the non-place. Against this view is one that recognizes that those who, for example, work in these spaces have a much richer and more complicated relation to them and to one another, so that it becomes necessary to think of multiple 'placings' (of diverse people, plans, histories, blueprints) as the substantive content of 'non-places' (Merriman, 2004).　　GHe

non-representational theory A style of engagement with the world that aims to attend to and intervene in the taking-place of practices. Non-representational theory – a term first coined in HUMAN GEOGRAPHY by Thrift (1996) – emerged from a caution and a concern about the overvaluation of the 'representational-referential' dimensions of life following the discipline's CULTURAL TURN. It responds to two questions:

(1)　How to disclose and attend to life as a differential, expressive process of becoming, where much happens before and after conscious reflexive thought?
(2)　How to foster types of description or presentation that attempt to co-produce new events by engaging with and intervening in the practices that compose life?

Non-representational theory is not a new PARADIGM that would eliminate or supersede others, nor does it offer a set of rules and conventions that could form one of a number of holistic conceptions of the world; rather, it names a differentiated set of ways of learning to address these two questions. Non-representational theory is consequently composed of a multiplicity of perspectives and takes its inspiration from a range of sources, including Heideggerian theories of practice, post-PHENOMENOLOGY, various micro-sociologies, ACTOR-NETWORK THEORY, Deleuze and Guattari's heterodox version of POST-STRUCTURALISM and corporeal feminism (see figure). The plural – 'non-representational theories' – perhaps conveys a better sense of the complicated genealogy of these theories and the constantly shifting, contestable foundations of non-representational theory in human geography [compare Thrift (2008) with Thrift (1996)].

Whilst non-representational theory is, irredeemably plural, it is held together by two broad starting points – one an imperative, the other a promise – and both of which have been subject to criticisms.

First, non-representational theory affirms an *imperative* to expand the foci of ('new') CULTURAL GEOGRAPHY beyond either a focus on a sphere of REPRESENTATION or a human SUBJECT who relates to the world by representing aspects of the world through an act of interpretation (by, for example, undertaking active 'readings' of dominant or residual meanings). Each mirrors the other in that they both assume that the primary relation between an (individual or collective) subject and the world is at the level of signification. In contrast, non-representational theories are theories of *practice* in that their focus is on what humans and/or non-humans *do*, and how the reproduction and revision of practices underpin the genesis and maintenance of interpretation and thus meaning. Whilst this move resonates with the attention to practical logics of the BODY in some HUMANISTIC GEOGRAPHIES

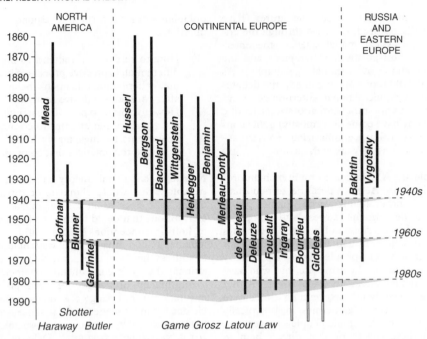

non-representational theory   *The life-time-lines of non-representational theory* (from Thrift, 1999)

and borrows from various forms of micro-sociology, a critical difference is that practices tend to be conceptualized as processually emergent compositions of human and non-human materialities (Whatmore, 2002a). From within this context, practices are understood as always embodied and composed of a set of modalities – including AFFECT and emotion (see EMOTIONAL GEOGRAPHY) – that do not have to cross over a threshold of signification to achieve political effects (see Harrison, 2000). One forceful response to this has been to claim that non-representational theory cleaves the non-representational from the representational and installs a dualism between the two by attending to the former and ignoring the varied effects of the latter. But Dewsbury, Harrison, Rose and Wylie (2002) take care to stress that non-representational theories are not anti-representation (cf. Jones, 2008) but, rather, conceptualize representations as 'presentations'. That is, representations are not understood as masks or veils that express some *a priori* system of transcendent categorizations, but are instead encountered as constitutive elements within practices (although this has raised questions about how to develop conceptual vocabularies for describing the a-signifying effects of different forms of 'presentations' that do not repro-

duce a naive psychologism or a cause/effect model). Non-representational theory, then, enacts a break with the version of CULTURE as structuralizing/signifying that defined the 'new' cultural geography. Such a move is seen as a necessary response to a contemporary political moment in which various non-representational modalities – including affect – are caught up in the emergence of new forms of SOVEREIGN POWER and BIOPOWER (Thrift, 2008; but see Barnett, 2008).

Second, non-representational theory expresses the *promise* of encountering a now expanded social as a practical achievement – an *ordering* rather than an order – emergent from multiple spatially and temporally distanciated relations. The result has been an attention to how more or less durable, differentially extensive, orderings are composed from relations between human and non-human actors – or perhaps more properly *actants* (see ACTOR-NETWORK THEORY). SOCIETY then becomes a set of partially connected NETWORKS or ASSEMBLAGES in which embodied, expressive practices act as the ongoing basis for coherence and change (Rose, 2002b). Recent work has moved to address early criticisms that such a focus on the non-representational reproduces or even celebrates a figure of the undifferentiated human (Nash, 2000) by exploring how social differences such as RACE or SEXUALITY are enacted through and disrupted by the workings of a range of non-representational modalities (e.g. Lim, 2007). However, heavily influenced by Deleuze and Guattari (McCormack, 2005) and work on PERFORMATIVITY (Dewsbury, 2000), the prefix 'non-' in 'non-representational theory' names an attunement to moments of indeterminacy and undecidability, in which new events emerge to exceed and potentially disrupt given orderings (although see Anderson (2004) and Harrison (2007a) on boredom and suffering for criticisms internal to non-representational theory around how an attention to newness can downplay relations which are, respectively, suspended and broken).

To work through the imperative and promise of non-representational theories, there has been a nascent experimentation with research methods, as well as diagrammatic and narrative forms of presentation, that take as their task to learn to witness the ongoing taking-place of life as a composite of embodied practices. THEORY is called here to act as a 'modest supplement' to life that would enable new forms of description – a move that has occasionally sat uncomfortably with the intense theoretical experimentation that has also been a mark of non-representational theory. Substantive work has begun, however, to draw this set of theories into often disruptive encounters with a range of sub-disciplines – see, for example, Wylie (2005) on LANDSCAPE or Horton and Kraftl (2006) on CHILDREN's geographies. Taking the two commonalities together, non-representational theory can be understood as a style of engagement with the world that, encountering a range of non-representational theories that exceed human geography, begins from the non-representational dimensions of practice and PERFORMANCE.   BA

Suggested reading
Dewsbury, Harrison, Rose and Wylie (2002); Lorimer (2005); Thrift (2008); Whatmore (2002a).

normative theory A theory or theoretical claim that is prescriptive, saying what ought to be. The theory of NEO-CLASSICAL ECONOMICS says that MARKETS should be competitive; the theory of MARXISM says that expropriators should be expropriated. Whenever the word 'should' appears, a normative theoretical claim is lodged. The contrast is *positive theory*, which is a claim about what is. Competitive

markets exist in China. Donald Trump is an expropriator. Positive claims (such as these) might be wrong but, if so, they can be scientifically falsified by facts. Normative theory is never falsifiable, and for that reason often engenders sharp disagreement.

The use of the distinction is most associated with economics. The early Cambridge economist John Neville Keynes (1852–1949) in his *The scope and method of political economy* (1930 [1891], pp. 34–5) distinguished between positive economics, which is 'a body of systematized knowledge concerning what is', and normative economics, 'relating to criteria of what ought to be and concerned therefore with the ideal as distinguished from the actual'. Keynes made the distinction so that economists could be scrupulously clear about their role and status: when speaking of what *is* (positive economics), they were scientists, and when speaking of what *ought to be* (normative economics), they were policy advisors. The two should never be confused.

In HUMAN GEOGRAPHY the distinction between the positive and the normative was found most often in ECONOMIC GEOGRAPHY – not surprisingly, given its origins – and connected with the period of the QUANTITATIVE REVOLUTION, when economic geographers most demanded criteria delineating scientific work (positive theory). Ironically, however, much of the LOCATION THEORY seized upon and elaborated during that period was normative rather than positive, and so did not constitute science in Keynes' terms. Location theory was underpinned by a set of 'ideal' assumptions such as an isotropic plain, transportation costs proportional to distance, equal population density and perfect rationality. August Lösch, one of the principal architects of location theory, was perfectly clear about its normative character: 'the real duty of the economist is not to explain our sorry reality, but to improve it. The question of the best location is far more dignified than determination of the actual one' (Lösch, 1954, p. 4[1940]). But this motivation was rarely registered by economic geographers at the time.

In any case, the discussion became moot as the very distinction between positive and normative theory began to unravel from the early 1970s. Olsson (1980), a former acolyte of positive theory, argued that a mainstay of economic geography's scientific approach, the family of SPATIAL INTERACTION models, was irredeemably compromised by value judgements – 'is' disguised as 'ought'. Similarly,

Harvey (1973, 1974a) found hidden normative claims lurking in every corner of positive theory: in economic theories of the city, in theories of population and resources, in quantitative techniques. All THEORY is normative theory. Our VALUES go all the way down, and we can no more escape them than avoid the smell of the air we breathe (see also ETHICS). TB

Suggested reading
Olsson (1978).

North–South The phrase gained in popularity in the 1970s as a way to describe richer, industrial countries on the one hand (the North) and poorer, mainly non-industrial countries on the other (the SOUTH). The phrase had the advantage of moving beyond the First, Second and Third Worlds. Although the South clearly referred to mainly ex-colonial or developing countries in LATIN AMERICA, AFRICA and ASIA, it seemed a more neutral term than the THIRD WORLD. It also spoke to the fact that Southern countries were reorganizing themselves politically in the 1970s. In the 1950s, the Third World referred to a group of non-aligned countries determined to forge a new way in the global political economy. In the 1960s, the meaning of the Third World was changed to define a group of countries that were marked by what was then called UNDERDEVELOPMENT. The idea that these countries might have significant GEOPOLITICAL or geo-economic POWER was not taken seriously. This changed, however, when the Organization of Petroleum Exporting Countries (OPEC) drove up OIL prices fourfold in 1973–4. The success of this action encouraged a broader group of developing countries, the Group of 77 – formed in 1964 at the first UN Conference on TRADE and DEVELOPMENT – to press for a New International Economic Order. It was partly through the Group of 77's demands for fairer and more stable trading arrangements, more AID, special financial facilities and greater voting rights in the UN that a notion of the South was born.

In the 1980s, the Americans and other Northern powers roundly defeated their demands for a New International Economic Order. However, a group of well-meaning social democrats in the North did speak back to the South's demands through the first and second reports of the Brandt Commission: *North–South* (1980) and *Common crisis* (1983). Although Brandt Commissioners tried to direct attention to the widening (and in their view dangerous) gaps between Northern and Southern countries, not much happened. Indeed, it can plausibly be argued that the end of the COLD WAR weakened Southern countries, particularly in sub-Saharan Africa (Dodds, 1999; Fawcett and Sayigh, 2005). These countries were no longer important to either the USA or the former Soviet Union. The irony, then, or the tragedy, is this: in the 1970s, a map of the world that sought to depict the global North was clumsy in the extreme. It stretched to include mainly temperate regions both sides of the Equator, pulling together North America with Australia and New Zealand. Most of the world's land mass, in any case, is north of the Equator. The South mainly occupied a more discrete space in the sub-tropical and tropical worlds. By the end of the century the conceptual integrity of the North seemed to make more sense, bolstered in part by GLOBALIZATION. The South, for its part, has found it increasingly difficult to advance a coherent political position. The Group of 77 now has 133 members, but is largely impotent in the face of the North's veto on key economic and political changes. SCO

Suggested reading
Dodds (1999); Payne (2005).

nuptuality The extent of marriage (or marriage rate) within a population. As research in DEMOGRAPHY associated being married with elevated fertility, delaying the age of marriage is argued to reduce fertility, such as occurred in some European countries in the early expanding phase of the DEMOGRAPHIC TRANSITION. However, sensitivity to the growing diversity of partnering and parenting arrangements in contemporary society complicate this thesis, and have contributed to considerable interest in family and HOUSEHOLD organization (e.g. Duncan and Smith, 2002; Wright, Houston, Ellis, Holloway and Hudson, 2003). AJB

Suggested reading
Bongaarts (1982).

O

objectivity The term 'objectivity' has at least three distinct meanings in GEOGRAPHY. The first is a relatively common everyday one, where objectivity is associated with impartiality or disinterestedness. Here, one or another approach is said not to have a particular axe to grind, or any pre-set principles or ideological positions to defend. This common-sense understanding of objectivity has a parallel in some of the HUMANITIES and professions, where objectivity derives from professionals following well-established codes to guide the careful marshalling of evidence, cross-checking of sources and accurate and unbiased presentation of information. Objectivity, in this sense, is thought to derive from careful gathering of information, mastery of the evidence and 'balance' in presenting an argument.

In a more profound sense, objectivity as an element of scientific method refers to claims about the characteristics of an object that are said to exist independent of our perception of it. In this view, objectivity presupposes some form of unmediated or direct observation – what Haraway (1985) called the 'god-trick' – and became the basis for the claims by objectivist SCIENCE that it was merely mirroring nature in a form that was unmediated and 'value-free' (see CARTESIANISM).

Since the 1970s, many human geographers have reacted against the objectivist conception of objectivity. Drawing from HERMENEUTICS, they acknowledged pre-judgements ('prejudices') as indispensable to a developing, dialogical process of understanding. Drawing on FEMINISM and MARXISM, they argued that all claims to objectivity are ideological, denying their histories, commitments and embeddedness in particular social institutions (see IDEOLOGY). As Habermas (1987a [1968]) proposed, knowledge and human interests are always necessarily connected. Critical human geography insisted on the need for an ideology critique to unmask the actors, interests and consequences of such claims to objectivity (Gregory, 1978a). A transcendental or universal 'god's eye' view of objectivity was displaced as critical human geographers turned to analyses of the role of social interests, HUMAN AGENCY and institutions in shaping existing and possible worlds (Harvey, 1974b). Thus,

a third meaning of objectivity sees knowledge (including scientific knowledge) as always historically and socially constructed out of specific projects in particular times and places: knowledge is always produced by someone; knowledge and human interests are always inextricably linked; and the production of knowledge is a social practice like any other with its own commitments, forms of embeddedness and geographies (see SITUATED KNOWLEDGE). The turn to critical human geographies of this kind marked a rejection of grand narratives, and initiated a period of rich methodological experimentation and the writing of more fallible and open geographies (Natter, Schatzki and Jones, 1996, p. 1).   JPi

Occidentalism The systematic construction of 'the WEST' ('the Occident') as a bounded and unified entity. Occidentalism is often treated as the inverse of ORIENTALISM: just as Western cultures systematically construct(ed) stereotypes of 'the Orient', so non-Western cultures produce(d) their own stereotypes of 'the Occident' (Carrier, 1995). Hence Occidentalism has been described as an *inversion* of the Western imaginary, 'the world turned upside down', or as a *counter-discourse* to Orientalism (Xiao-me Chen, 1995). Bonnett (2005) has provided one of the most sophisticated and sensitive readings of Occidentalism in these terms. Writing against those who regard the idea of ASIA as yet another exterior, European construction, he reads two authors, one Japanese and the other Indian, to show how they used their independent constructions of the WEST to explore non-Western forms of MODERNITY.

In contrast to all these versions, however, Edward Said, one of the main architects of the critique of Orientalism as a system of power-knowledge, insisted that 'no one is likely to imagine a field symmetrical to [Orientalism] called Occidentalism' because the IMAGINATIVE GEOGRAPHIES produced by non-Western cultures were not bound into a system of power-knowledge comparable to the tensile strength and span of modern COLONIALISM and IMPERIALISM (Said, 1978, p. 50). For Said, the distinctive quality of Orientalism was its structural involvement in globalizing projects of domination and dispossession. For this reason, Coronil (1996) prefers to treat Occidentalism as the condition of possibility of Orientalism itself: 'the conceptions of the West' that underwrite – that make possible – its own representations of non-western cultures. This tactic reminds us that Orientalism not only constructs 'the Orient' but also simultaneously constructs and privileges the West-as-Subject (see EUROCENTRISM).

Occidentalism in a more populist sense gained new impetus in the aftermath of the TERRORIST attacks on New York City and Washington on 11 September 2001. A common response was to ask 'Why do they hate us?' and to look for answers among 'them' rather than 'us' and, in particular, 'their' supposed hostility to the political and cultural formations of a universal MODERNITY. So, for example, Buruma and Margalit (2004) provided a thumbnail sketch of Occidentalism as 'the West in the eyes of its enemies' and sought to locate 'today's suicide bombers and holy warriors' within a larger history of 'hatred' and 'loathing' of the West and all works. Theirs was a remarkably shallow reading, which revealed more about the authors than their object of enquiry, and in this sense was another mapping of the Occidentalism that Coronil had so presciently in mind.   DG

Suggested reading
Bonnett (2005); Coronil (1966).

occupation, military The assumption of effective control through military action by a SOVEREIGN POWER over a TERRITORY to which it has no legal title. Military occupation is thus distinct from *military rule*, though both may rely on the suspension of the pre-existing rule of LAW, the imposition of martial law (cf. EXCEPTION, SPACE OF) and the violent domination of the civilian population (see, e.g., Hudson-Rodd and Hunt, 2005). Occupations have taken place throughout human history, most obviously in the expansion of EMPIRES through conquest and annexation, and these often involved transfers of population: slaves to Rome, Roman settlers to the colonies. But since the Second World War modern occupations have been governed by international LAW that both proscribes the acquisition of territory by force (so that occupations are supposed to be temporary affairs) and specifically forbids population transfers. The same body of law requires the occupying power to restore and maintain public order, to respect private PROPERTY, and to safeguard the

HEALTH and welfare of the occupied population. In practice, however, as Benvenisti's (2004) review of twentieth-century occupations reveals, these obligations have been more honoured in the breach: most either denied their status as Occupying Powers (even though international law makes it clear that occupation is a matter of fact, not intention or proclamation) or assumed wide discretionary powers.

Military occupations raise at least three sets of crucial geographical questions:

- *Strategy.* What are the objectives of military occupation? Some are the result of military success in WAR: they may be directed towards permanent annexation and the creation of tributary states for geopolitical and geo-economic reasons (e.g. the Nazi occupation of continental Europe between 1939 and 1945, or the Soviet occupation of much of Central and Eastern Europe between 1945 and 1989); or they may be temporary (but nonetheless protracted) affairs directed towards the replacement of one political system by another (e.g. the US occupation of Japan, 1945–52: see also GEOPOLITICS). Many contemporary occupations are the result of international interventions to end regional or civil war ('peace-keeping'; e.g. the NATO occupations of Kosovo and Bosnia from 1995 to the present), though some have entailed the use of military VIOLENCE on a scale that recalls Tacitus' description of the Roman occupation of Britain: 'They create a devastation and call it peace.' Still others are attempts to create buffer zones to guarantee SECURITY (e.g. the Israeli occupation of southern Lebanon, 1982–2000: and see Schofield, 1993). But many occupations have a mix of motives – occupation is rarely a coherent or transparent project – and while modern occupations often cloak themselves in the rhetoric of 'liberation', they often have long-term, transformative ends in view (Bhuta, 2005) and the presence of foreign troops often meets fierce RESISTANCE from the occupied population.
- *Logistics.* What POWER-GEOMETRIES are necessary to maintain control over an occupied population (e.g. Weizman, 2004)? Military occupations depend on the spatial circulation of information (intelligence about the occupied population and its activities, military orders and public announcements), on supply NETWORKS to provide essential resources for occupiers

and occupied, and on the capacity to mobilize troops to enforce public order. In most cases, CITIES function as the pivots for all three, but during the US occupation of Afghanistan, for example, it was (and remains) far from clear how far the authority of the USA and its proxies extended into the countryside. The crucial importance of cities also makes them centres of rebellion and resistance to military occupation (Gregory, 2007).

- *Contact zones.* Many of the relations imposed by occupying armies are intrinsically violent – including sexual violence, arrest and imprisonment, forced labour and even GENOCIDE – but the occupied also view interactions across the contact zone in complex ways: Why are some construed as collaboration, others as doing business to survive and yet others as resistance? During the US occupation of Iraq from 2003 onwards, resistance increased to the point at which it became increasingly difficult to distinguish occupation from the continuation of war (Gregory, 2004b).

It is not necessary to maintain a massive and permanent military presence to continue an occupation: Israel's continued control over Gaza and the West Bank rests on its capacity to mobilize military force at will ('incursions') and on the continuing development of colonies ('settlements') as the eyes of what Segal and Weizman (2003) call 'a civilian occupation'. DG

Suggested reading
Benvenisti (2004); Weizman (2004).

oceans Even though the decline of sea travel and diminishing dependence on self-supplied FOOD sources has removed the maritime world from the realm of landlubbers' everyday experience, the sea remains a crucial domain for the essential wherewithal that sustains humanity. Three perspectives have dominated most studies of human–marine interactions: the ocean as a RESOURCE provider, the ocean as transport surface, and the ocean as a surface for moving troops and projecting military power. Embedded in each of these analytical perspectives is a certain conception of ocean-SPACE and ocean GOVERNANCE.

The value of the oceans to mankind has political, social, economic, ecological and cultural dimensions. Marine industries include fisheries, mining, non-conventional ENERGY industries, fresh WATER production, coastal services, environmental services, TRADE, TOURISM,

sub-marine telecommunications and fibre-optic cable, safety and salvage, naval defence and ocean-related education, training and research. The economic importance of the oceans is immense. According to the Independent World Commission on the Oceans, 'one recent study suggests that the sum total of marine industries for which data are available, amounts to approximately US$ 1 trillion out of a total global GDP of US$ 23 trillion' (IWCO, 1998, p. 102).

Ecological services provided by various marine and coastal ECOSYSTEMS of the Earth include the regulation of gaseous exchange with the atmosphere (e.g. the balance between carbon dioxide and oxygen, maintenance of ozone for ultraviolet radiation protection), climate regulation, disturbance regulation (e.g. storm protection, flood control), water supply, cycling of nutrients, waste treatment, food production and raw materials supply. The value of these too is immense.

Climate change is also projected to have effects such as global sea-level rise and intensifying GLOBAL WARMING. According to a recent Arctic Climate Impact Assessment report (ACIA, 2004), the Arctic CLIMATE is warming rapidly, at almost twice the rate as the rest of the world in the past two decades. At least half the summer sea ice in the Arctic is projected to melt by the end of this century, along with a significant portion of the Greenland Ice Sheet. Climatic variations will have a large impact on marine environments and marine-related activities, including rising sea levels, changes in ocean salinity (which could strongly affect regional climate), the decline or extinction of marine species due to habitat loss, expanding marine shipping and the enhancement of some major Arctic fisheries together with the decline of others.

On 26 December 2004, the Indian Ocean tsunami devastated coastal communities. In its reports on the environmental impact of the Tsunami in Sri Lanka and Maldives, the United Nations Environmental Programme (UNEP, 2006) has noted that coastal areas where coral reefs, mangrove forests and natural vegetation had been removed suffered the greatest damage. Fishing communities were the worst hit. The challenges include not only the restoration of the livelihood of fishermen and raising the income of coastal communities above pre-tsunami levels, but also capacity building to improve skills of boat builders, enforcement of standards to reduce potential risks to fishermen, and the revival of the tsunami-hit aquaculture industry. SCH

Suggested reading
ACIA (2004); IWCO (1998); Steinberg (2001); UNEP (2006).

oil Petroleum, it is sometimes said, is the economic bedrock of our hydrocarbon civilization. The fuel of MODERNITY, oil is an archetypal global COMMODITY, the repository of unimaginable wealth ('black gold') and part of the largest business on Earth (see CAPITALISM). More than anything else, petroleum is a sort of lie: it reveals the profound mystification, the paradoxes and that contradictoriness that surround NATURAL RESOURCES in our modern world (Coronil, 1997).

If oil is a natural resource – arguably the most global, the most strategic and among the most valuable – what exactly is natural about it? It is a flammable liquid that occurs as a product of geophysical and biological processes of great historical depth. A by-product of pre-human geological history, oil is deposited in subterranean formations and consists principally of a mixture of hydrocarbons with traces of nitrogenous and sulphurous compounds. In practice, of course, the composition of what passes as petroleum varies quite considerably, as one might anticipate in view of the heterogeneous circumstances associated with its 600 million year history of sedimentation and organic decomposition. Oil's natural properties, one might say, are unstable and variegated (see NATURE).

Petroleum is customarily extracted through drilled wells, pumped along pipelines and refined into different 'fractions' or components. The science and practice by which oil is explored, located, pumped and fractionated has, in the past 150 years, deepened and proliferated to the point at which it is now part of a massive engineering and technical INFRASTRUCTURE. The oil industry is now dominated by the 'majors', a cluster of transnational and highly diversified energy companies (see TRANSNATIONAL CORPORATIONS). It is sometimes said that oil drilling was invented by E.L. Drake, when he sunk his now infamous 69 foot well in Pennsylvania in 1859. But several hundred years before the birth of Christ, the Chinese were sinking 3500 ft wells to exploit petroleum for a multiplicity of purposes. Surface oil deposits had been used as asphalt and as a sealant by Sumerians 3,000 years before the Chinese. In other words, oil's natural resource use spans a vast swathe of human history.

Currently, oil and related gas exploitation covers two-thirds of global ENERGY needs: according to the International Energy Agency,

by 2030 the figure will have fallen only marginally. Industrialized countries of the OECD account for almost two thirds of world oil demand. Global demand for oil is about 80 million barrels per day (compared to 47 million in 1970). The USA consumes by far and away the largest quantities of petroleum (roughly 25 per cent) and is extremely dependent on oil imports (largely from the MIDDLE EAST, Canada and Mexico, and increasingly AFRICA). The geology of oil and gas has a distinctive geography: two thirds of known oil reserves reside in the Middle East (which is overwhelmingly Muslim, a fact that has assumed particular significance in the context of 9/11 and the US occupation of Iraq). Saudi Arabia, Iraq and Kuwait alone account for almost 500 billion barrels of reserves. Over three-quarters of all known reserves of petroleum are found in eight oil-exporting countries. The centrality of the USA in the global oil acquisition strategy – a fact sealed by the special relationship between the USA and Saudi Arabia, made in 1945 – has meant that the GEOPOLITICS of oil have been a central plank in US foreign policy over the past 80 years. The US addiction to cheap oil – which is to say to the automobile – turned, in the postwar period, on IMPERIALIST relations with three key suppliers: Saudi Arabia, Venezuela and Iran. By 2001, this policy had proven to be a catastrophic failure – even if the US consumer had benefited from oil prices at the gas station that bore no relation to actual costs of production (which necessarily would have to include the massive expenditures on the military and the costs of global climate change and other 'EXTERNALITIES').

The structure of the oil industry is characterized by a recent (post-1970) reorganization (Yeoman, 2004). The global oil and gas industry is dominated by five transnational oil companies (ExxonMobil, Chevron, Shell, BP and TotalElfFina) with combined revenues over $1 trillion, and a number of massive national oil companies (owned by oil-producing states). The assertive petro-NATIONALISM of the 1970s saw national oil companies account for an increasingly large proportion of oil reserves, while transnational companies increasingly moved downstream to control refining and petrochemical sectors. Many of the world's most important oil producers are petro-STATES, marked by an extreme dependence (measured as a proportion of exports or GDP) derived from oil and gas. Rentier economies of this sort are plagued by what has been called the 'resource curse' (Auty, 2001):

massive corruption, CONFLICT, poor social achievement, authoritarian politics and low economic growth (see Karl, 1999: see also RENT). Oil states, transnational companies, national oil companies, international financial institutions and various sorts of military and security forces combine to produce an 'oil complex' (Watts, 2005), which operates as a powerful system for dispossession and PRIMITIVE ACCUMULATION. Industrialized oil importers have been only too happy to build warm and friendly relations with corrupt petro-states, turning a blind eye to HUMAN RIGHTS violations and failed DEVELOPMENT, provided that the oil continues to flow.

Petroleum is the quintessential modern natural resource. It is present in and produced by nature, and a material source of wealth that occurs in a natural state. But this is a contradictory and non-sensible claim on its face. Oil is natural insofar as it resides in its Jurassic bedrock. But it is not immediately accessible or useful: it presupposes human knowledge and practice (drilling, exploring, refining). Oil's wealth is not conferred solely by natural process, but rests upon an appraisal – a state of knowledge and practice – that is social, technological and historical. Petroleum is profoundly *of* nature – it is typically subterranean and has peculiar biophysical properties. And yet its naturalism is expressed and understood in quite determinate ways: how differently would the first-century BCE Chinese bureaucrat and the twentieth-century hard-rock geologist have described petroleum's natural properties! Petroleum's 'resourcefulness' is not natural at all. Its expressive form as wealth – the defining property of a resource – presupposes acts of transformation, distribution and use which, incidentally, were very different for sixteenth-century North American Indians than for a twenty-first-century Louisiana petrochemical industry. Petroleum as a natural resource rests, then, on particular meanings of natural (e.g. theories of biophysics), and particular renderings of resource (e.g. theories of wealth predicated on scarcity and natural limits).

But there is another realm in which natural resources must operate; namely, the social imaginary – in other words, how oil is rooted in the imagination of people living in the specific historical and social circumstances of its use and deployment (see GEOGRAPHICAL IMAGINARIES). Oil as a natural resource carries it own mythos, also shaped by PLACE and time. From the vantage point of the oil-importing North Atlantic economies, oil stands in a specific relationship to the mosque and the Arab world. For oil-producing states, petroleum provides the idiom for nation-building and the financial wherewithal for modern development (think, for example, of the petrolic-ambition of a great modernizer such as Shah Palavi in Iran). Oil is inextricably bound up with unimaginable personal POWER (Rockefeller, Nobel, Rothschild, the Sultan of Brunei), untrammelled corporate hegemony ('the Seven Sisters') and a history of spectacular imperial VIOLENCE and WAR. Did not the long and dark tentacles of oil appear in the catastrophic demise of the twin Trade Towers in New York? Was not Osama bin Laden a product of oil as much as of Wahabbi Islam? Was not the Ayatollah Khomeini's revolution in 1979 fuelled by oil-inspired resentments and grievances? Need one mention Enron? Oil and Islam, war and violence, corruption and power, wealth and SPECTACLE, scarcity and CRISIS are, in our times, seemingly all of a piece.

In contemporary America or Europe, oil is a particular type of commodity used, exchanged and fetishized in quite precise ways. It is a bundle of natural (biophysical), productive, cultural and economic relations. It is altogether appropriate to recall that petroleum is popularly referred to as 'black gold'. But, after all, gold isn't black. And neither are many forms of oil. They are colourless.   MW

Suggested reading
Clarke (2007); Juhasz (2008); Klare (2008).

ontology The study and description of 'being', or that which can be said to exist in the world (cf. EPISTEMOLOGY). Although ontology has many definitions and approaches in PHILOSOPHY and in GEOGRAPHY, it tends to be formulated by considering interactions between the world as-it-is and ideas or conceptions about the world. Western thought has been greatly influenced by the classical, formal ontology of essences, exemplified by Plato's Ideals (where objects in the world are imperfect copies of ideal forms) and Aristotle's categories (where all such forms emerge inductively out of the stuff of the world). Concern with ontology in the natural sciences and the human sciences typically focuses less on the *general* conditions of existence than on the objects, relations and concepts serving as the foci of their *specific* disciplines. In this vein, the main ontological hobbyhorses in HUMAN GEOGRAPHY have included the character of the relations between SOCIETY and NATURE, and concepts of PLACE and SPACE.

Ontological repositionings within human geography over recent decades have largely been a response to the scientific ontology of high MODERNISM, the belief that the world is transparently knowable to the knowledgeable observer. This approach, best exemplified by SPATIAL SCIENCE, is articulated through the philosophy of POSITIVISM and its derivatives: given enough information about objects and events in the world, it is possible to derive a series of scientific LAWS that account for or explain them. Such positions are predicated on the ontological assumption that the universe is a closed system whose movements are determined by a finite (albeit complex) set of causal forces and, further, that the objects making up the world are discrete, stable and categorizable (Dixon and Jones, 1998). This reading also holds that both the general laws pertaining to causal forces and the essences or forms that demarcate discrete objects are themselves real and objective parts of the world 'out there', awaiting discovery.

BEHAVIOURAL GEOGRAPHY and HUMANISTIC GEOGRAPHY, though sometimes falling back into versions of positivism, provided a critical response to these objectivist claims by gradually incorporating insights from non-positivist philosophies including PHENOMENOLOGY, and by paying particular attention to the importance of variations in perspective produced through the experience, perception and LIFEWORLD of the individual. Here, ontology is a matter of 'being-in-the-world', wherein the world reveals itself through the phenomena of experience. As such, the OBJECTIVITY of positivism is replaced by an experiential subjectivism. This difference has often framed the distinction between SPACE and PLACE (Entrikin, 1991).

The hints of perspectivalism within humanistic geography in particular found fuller fruition within FEMINIST GEOGRAPHIES, which critiqued spatial science for masking a masculinist EPISTEMOLOGY under the name of ontology (see MASCULINISM). While rarely making explicit ontological statements, the partial and situated standpoints of feminist theory (cf. SITUATED KNOWLEDGE) were not inconsistent with a Leibnitzian ontology of proliferated, situated DIFFERENCE. Perhaps most importantly, this resulted in the ontological notion of *relational space* (Massey, 2005), a conceptualization of co-productive SPATIALITY emerging with the mobile and mutable interactions between space and the human SUBJECT. Such entanglements point to DIALECTICS (Harvey, 1996), an ontology of INTERNAL RELATIONS rather than external relations. In contrast to positivism, therefore, dialectical thought refuses discrete objects and events as things 'in themselves', and with this denies the separation of phenomena from experience, theory and politics. An ally in this mode of thought is the philosophy of critical REALISM, an ontology of levels aimed at understanding the causal powers of necessary and contingent social relations (Sayer, 2000).

With the advance of POST-STRUCTURALISM in human geography, ontology and its cousin metaphysics were increasingly critiqued as a series of *epistemological* constructs mired in cultural, political and, most importantly, linguistic and discursive imaginaries. Thus, the ontological distinctions formed in key geographical binaries such as nature–culture, order–chaos, time–space and individual-society could, under this epistemological critique, be called out as false dichotomies that reflect more the Western bias of either/or-ness than any serious reflection on the social construction of such categories. While the post-structuralists never denied that there was a real 'out there' in the world, they denied that it was possible to know it through some form of direct, pure experience (Deutsche, 1991). By this point, ontology itself became a target: the 'real' world, it was argued, was shut out from the observer by virtue of the very knowledges that constitute the 'observer' as such, as well as by the culturally inflected modes of REPRESENTATION at hand to describe it. In a similar vein, human geographers influenced by post-structuralist renderings of PSYCHOANALYTIC THEORY, particularly those arising out of the work of Lacan and Žižek, drew from suggestions that immersion in language and symbols makes access to the 'Real' impossible.

Despite the aversion to ontology during the epistemological turn of the 1990s, however, interest in the topic has re-emerged in human geography in large measure through the growing popularity of the works of Gilles Deleuze. Drawing largely upon Baruch Spinoza, Deleuze (1994) creates a 'flat' ontology of 'pure difference' by theorizing becoming, multiplicity and differentiation as ontologically antecedent to the traditional foundations of being, categoricality and sameness, thereby rejecting long-held conceptual centrepieces. Here, being, models, structures and categories are not the stuff of ontology proper, but are rather the results of the way that thought deals with difference and continuous differentiation (i.e. by producing orders of similitude). Deleuzean ontology is not a search for transcendental objects, structures and forms making up the world, but an immanent material self-organization that allows for the possibility of new types of things to come into the world. This work has been highly influential for recent theoretical experimentations in human geography, providing perhaps the fundamental ontological support for NON-REPRESENTATIONAL THEORY (Deleuze himself had been treating the non-representational ontologically since the 1960s) and for elaborations of ACTOR-NETWORK THEORY (for re-theorizations of human–nature relationships). KWO/JPJ

Suggested reading
Cloke and Johnston (2005); Dixon and Jones (1998); Massey (2005); Sayer (2000); Tuan (2001).

opportunity costs An important concept in NEO-CLASSICAL ECONOMICS, with the costs of an action expressed as opportunities foregone – usually in monetary terms. If rural land is set aside as a nature reserve, there will be costs to both the landowner and society in terms of the net value of the agricultural products not produced: similarly, a commuter may see the cost of travel time as earnings foregone. The concept can therefore be used in explaining the allocation of productive resources between competing activities, especially where they are in short supply. It plays an important role in theories of RENT, COMPARATIVE ADVANTAGE and LINEAR PROGRAMMING. RJ

optimization models Mathematical models that are used to search for the optimal solution to a problem. These MODELS have a quantity to be either maximised or minimized, known as the 'objective function', such as the minimization of total transport costs or the maximization of a firm's profits, together with a set of constraints that limit the range of possible solutions, such as limits on supply and demand, or the capacity of transport routes. LINEAR PROGRAMMING is the most widely used form of optimization, but the models may take a great variety of mathematical forms and many spatial applications (such as optimal location decisions) involve non-linear forms. LWH

Suggested reading
Killen (1983).

Orientalism The term 'Orientalism' has three main meanings. The first two involve (i) the scholarly study of the Orient, and (ii) a more general (and especially aesthetic or cultural) interest in the Orient. But neither of them pays much attention to the possibility that the object of their interest – 'the Orient' – is itself a predominantly European and American construction produced within a specific grid of POWER and knowledge (cf. OCCIDENTALISM). This is the focus of the third definition proposed by the Palestinian/American literary critic Edward Said (1935–2003): Orientalism as (iii) both a DISCOURSE and a 'corporate institution' for the production and domination of 'the Orient' (Said, 1978, p. 3). It is this definition that has attracted most attention in HUMAN GEOGRAPHY, but it is important to notice Said's double emphasis on production *and* domination: representations of 'the Orient' often have the most acutely practical, material consequences (cf. PERFORMATIVITY).

Said acknowledged that Orientalism in this third sense has a long and tangled history, but he focused on the specifically *modern* apparatus of power-knowledge that emerged towards the end of the eighteenth century. His proxy for this was the Napoleonic occupation of Egypt (1798–1801) and, in particular, the *Description de l'Égypte* produced by the scholars who accompanied the expeditionary army. Said's emphasis on the *materiality* of power-knowledge is also significant. While he was keenly interested in the production of IMAGINATIVE GEOGRAPHIES of 'the Orient', Said insisted that Orientalism was not 'an airy European fantasy about the Orient, but created a body of theory *and practice* in which, for many generations, there has been considerable *material* investment' (1978, p. 6; emphases added). What gave Orientalism its peculiar power was that it was produced from the outside and marginalized or silenced the voices of those who were its collective subjects: 'What gave the Oriental's world its intelligibility and identity was not the result of his own efforts but rather the whole complex series of knowledgeable manipulations by which the Orient was identified by the West' (p. 40). It was this, above all else, that implicated Orientalism in the operations of colonizing POWER, because it made 'the Orient' appear as 'an essentialized realm originally outside and untouched by the West, lacking the meaning and order that only colonialism can bring' (Mitchell, 1992, p. 313). For Said, then, Orientalism operated both in advance and in conjunction with COLONIALISM, underwriting colonial power through two crucial operations:

- First, 'the Orient' was constructed as an exotic and bizarre space, and at the limit a pathological and even a monstrous space: 'a living tableau of queerness' (Said, 1978, p. 103).
- Second, 'the Orient' was constructed as a space that had to be domesticated, disciplined and normalized through a forceful projection of the order it was presumed to lack: 'framed by the classroom, the criminal court, the prison, the illustrated manual' (Said, 1978, p. 41).

It is not difficult to hear the echoes of Michel Foucault's archaeologies and GENEALOGIES in these arguments, though Said was perplexed (and vexed) by the French philosopher's metropolitan obsession and his disinterest in the operations of colonial power (Gregory, 1995b).

Said's critique of Orientalism was closely connected to his political commitment to the Palestinian cause, and his work has met with vigorous criticism from Right and Left. Theoretically, critics have been exercised by the complicity of Said's HUMANISM with the very tradition that he criticizes (Sardar, 1999, p. 73); by his conjunction of humanism with Foucault's ANTI-HUMANISM (Clifford, 1988); by his complicated relationship with HISTORICAL MATERIALISM (Ahmad, 1992); and by his seeming inability to break out from the binary oppositions of Orientalism itself (Young, 1990b). Substantively, others have criticized Said's readings and substituted more affirmative interpretations of some contributions to the Orientalist canon (Livingstone, 2004; Irwin, 2006).

Much of this discussion comprises variations on the theme of ESSENTIALISM. Said is charged with reducing the complexity of European and American engagements with other cultures to a single, totalizing essence that projects its will to power upon them. Other scholars, including Said himself, have sought to meet this objection by developing a more nuanced analysis of Orientalism. Their key propositions include the following:

(1) *Orientalism is not a synonym for colonial discourse.* There are overlaps with other colonial discourses, but different imaginative geographies were fashioned for different places and periods: see PRIMITIVISM and TROPICALITY. Indeed, Said (1993) subsequently extended his enquiries to the wider relations between CULTURE and IMPERIALISM in the nineteenth and early twentieth centuries.

(2) *Orientalism is not cut from a single cloth: there are different Orientalisms and different 'Orients'.* The substantive focus of Said's original enquiry was not 'the Orient' at large but the MIDDLE EAST in general and Egypt and Palestine in particular. It is important to recognize other versions of Orientalism developed in relation to (for example) India, China and Japan.

(3) *There are significant differences between the collective authors of Orientalism.* Said focused on British and French Orientalisms because they had such a close connection with colonialism, but other scholars have drawn careful distinctions between (for example) American, British, French and German Orientalisms.

(4) *Orientalism is not a simple projection of the will to power.* Power, including the power of REPRESENTATION, did not lie entirely with the outsider and the colonizer, and a more nuanced view of the contact zone is required that can recognize TRANSCULTURATION and the achievements of anti-colonial struggles. Said accepted this criticism, but Sardar (1999, pp. 74–5) noted that his commitment to a secular humanism allowed little space for Islam as a counter-discourse.

(5) *Orientalism is a gendered and sexualized discourse.* Said was more interested in Orientalism's feminizing metaphors ('the Orient as woman'), but feminist scholars have examined how GENDER and SEXUALITY entered into the experiences and practices of travellers, artists and writers operating under its sign (Melman, 1992; Yegenoglu, 1998).

(6) *Orientalism produced other 'natures' as well as other 'cultures'.* Like Oriental CULTURE, Oriental NATURE was often constructed as an 'unnatural nature', capricious and extreme, to be domesticated, disciplined and normalized through Euro-American cartographic, scientific and engineering projects (Gregory, 2001b).

(7) *Orientalism is not confined to texts.* Said's field was comparative literature, so it is scarcely surprising that he focused on the written traces of high culture, but other scholars have focused on other modes of REPRESENTATION (including art and photography) and its involvement in mundane practices such as travel and TOURISM (Gregory, 1999).

Most of these critical elaborations have been historical, but the spectre of Orientalism still haunts the present. Its imaginative geographies have been activated in two new rounds of demonization of the 'Oriental Other'. First, a *techno-Orientalism* has been directed against the economic rise of Japan and, more recently, China, which have both been represented as threats to the global economic power of EUROPE and the USA (Morley and Robbins, 1992). Second, a *neo-Orientalism* has been mobilized in the 'WAR on terror' against political actors, groups and organizations in the Middle East, and against Arab and Muslim communities in Europe, North America and Australia (Tuastad, 2003; Gregory, 2004b: cf. TERRORISM). These new activations have an insistently practical dimension too, which is by no means confined to grand strategies and political or military campaigns. Haldrup, Koefoed and Simonsen (2006) identified the rise of a *practical Orientalism* grounded in the corporeal encounters and routines of EVERYDAY LIFE, in which Orientalist versions of the friend/enemy distinction are reproduced through the countless 'small acts' and stories that make up the intimacies of everyday life. Seen thus, the critique of Orientalism is far more than a theoretical or textual affair: it is also a profoundly political and practical project.   DG

Suggested reading
Haldrup, Koefoed and Simonsen (2006); Said (2003 [1978]); Sardar (1999).

Other/Otherness The Other is that which is excluded from the Self and through this exclusion comes to constitute the boundaries of the Self. In *Phenomenology of spirit* (1807), G.W.F. Hegel introduced the master/slave DIALECTIC, which founded an idea of the 'Other' that has since been absorbed from continental PHILOSOPHY into the social sciences and GEOGRAPHY. Simone de Beauvoir built upon the Hegelian master/slave dialectic, in which a hierarchical dualism defines a superior position in relation to an inferior one, to show how woman has been constituted as the Other to man. As long as women remain locked in this relationship, de Beauvoir argued, they cannot become subjects in their own right (see SUBJECTIVITY). For both Hegel and de Beauvoir, true freedom requires a struggle in which the Other comes to risk her life. The MASCULINISM of the Self/Other binary has been taken up in FEMINIST GEOGRAPHIES to show how some kinds of geographical knowledge have been privileged over others.

The idea that the Self is defined in relation to Others is also a key component of PSYCHOANALYTIC THEORY. According to Jacques Lacan (2002), the 'mirror stage' of infancy occurs when the child first realizes that what he had until then experienced as fragmented is in fact his 'self'. Following this recognition comes a desire to delimit these boundaries and thereby to maintain the Self through the exclusion of the Other. Drawing upon the work of Sigmund Freud, the relationship between one's self and the objects of the world has come to be referred to as 'object relations theory'. Geographers have drawn upon these ideas to show how the Self is a cultural production that relies on socio-spatial practices of inclusion and exclusion.

The Self/Other duality has come to inform POST-COLONIALISM, FEMINISM and their intersection. In his critique of ORIENTALISM, Edward Said (2003 [1978]) showed how European and American representations of 'the Orient' have worked to constitute the self-identity of the WEST as superior to the East. Bringing Said's critique together with feminist theory, others have shown how the interlocking hierarchies of RACE, CLASS and GENDER have been constitutive of both imperial relations and domestic social structures. In other words, hierarchical dualities of Self and Other (West and East, man and woman, human and less-than-human) have been shown to be the building blocks of Western MODERNITY. '[I]t is only insofar as "Woman/Women" and "the East" are defined as *Others*, or as peripheral, that (Western) Man/Humanism can represent him/itself as the center. It is not the center that determines the periphery, but the periphery that, in its boundedness, determines the center' (Mohanty, 1991, pp. 73–4).

Geographers have shown how the Self/Other duality has worked to produce and delimit geographical knowledge. For example, Derek Gregory (2004b) has built upon Said's work to show how everyday cultural practices work to produce spaces of 'the same' and spaces of 'the other' at the global SCALE. Gregory shows how some peoples are represented as occupying a space 'beyond the pale of the modern', and therefore to have forfeited the rights and dignity associated with Western MODERNITY and HUMANISM (p. 28).   AJS

Suggested reading
McClintock (1995); Sibley (1995).

outsourcing A mode of business organization that has become increasingly common since the 1980s, in which businesses contract with third-party subcontractors to provide product components and business services such as accounting and customer relations. Whether or not it is explicitly discussed in terms of POST-FORDISM, the recent explosion in subcontracting and business-to-business ('B2B') networking is widely associated with the pressures to abandon FORDIST models of vertical integration and develop more flexible, market-mediated business practices in the context of GLOBALIZATION. For the same reason, outsourcing is often used synonymously with 'off-shoring' in political DISCOURSE. In his 2004 campaign for the US presidency, for example, Senator John Kerry assailed outsourcing by talking about 'Benedict Arnold corporations'. The implication in this analogy with the eighteenth-century American traitor (who had planned to surrender the American fort at West Point to the British) is that outsourcing by US companies is a betrayal of American independence. But outsourcing need not necessarily involve sourcing from foreign suppliers, and in fact is often based on localized regional supply networks. Indeed, economic geographers who study these NETWORKS are interested in the ways in which they both depend upon and foster forms of spatial AGGLOMERATION, because the economic ties of outsourcing supply chains necessitate diverse social and cultural ties – 'untraded interdependencies', as one leading researcher calls them (Storper, 1997b) – in order to function effectively. That said, even some of these clustering effects have been transnational in scope; for example, between Western European clothing retailers and Eastern European suppliers (see Smith, A., 2003a). More generally, the increasing turn to sourcing from foreign companies (from Infosys in India, for example) has captured the public imagination in North America and Western Europe since the 1990s (e.g. Engardio, 2006). Consequently, for critics, outsourcing has become widely associated with the downward pressures on wages and benefits that make the corporate search for sourcing efficiency synonymous with a global race to the bottom.

Since 9/11, outsourcing has been used in arguments against 'extraordinary rendition' — the clandestine US policy of sending suspected TERRORISTS abroad to be violently interrogated by third parties in countries such as Egypt and Syria (Smith, N., 2006a). There are obvious differences between this externalization of interrogation and torture by government and the externalization of business activities by transnational corporations, but NEO-LIBERAL commonalities underlie them, including the use of private logistical services (such as rented business jets) as well as the unaccountability in the use of foreign third parties (Sparke, 2006). By decrying extraordinary rendition as the 'outsourcing of torture', critics have suggested in turn that it combines a sort of penal race to the bottom with a twenty-first century betrayal of American liberty (Mayer, 2005).   MS

overpopulation The idea that the size, density or organization of an area's population is too great to be sustained. Neo-Malthusian work argues that increased population reduces an areas' resource base until the CARRYING CAPACITY is breached (see LIMITS TO GROWTH; MALTHUSIAN MODEL). However, neo-Marxist scholars have countered that overpopulation makes a structural contribution to the continuation of certain MODES OF PRODUCTION, as an increased supply of potential workers reduces wage rates (Harvey, 1974a). The associated terms *over-urbanization* and *over-ruralization* have sparked considerable debate, with recent work on China supporting a transition from an *under-urbanized* to an over-urbanized society (Shen, 2002).   AJB

Suggested reading
Cohen (1999).

P

Pacific Rim A geographical REGION stretching across the Pacific Ocean and incorporating the westernmost cities of North America in addition to Japan, Australia, and the coastal cities and city-states of East Asia. The term became prominent in the 1980s as a result of Asia's increased economic power and the intensification of cross-Pacific TRADE and financial linkages (Appelbaum and Henderson, 1992). Academic and popular writings on the region became so saturated with hyperbole that many critics began to argue that the region was itself a literary creation – one that served the economic agendas and GEOPOLITICAL VISIONS of a pro-*laissez-faire* Euro-American audience (see, e.g., Dirlik, 1993).   KM

Suggested reading
Appelbaum and Henderson (1992); Dirlik (1993).

pandemic A term (derived from the Greek *pan-*, all + *demos*, people), used in the health sciences to describe the occurrence of a specified illness, health behaviour or other health-related event that is unusually prevalent (EPIDEMIC) over an extensive geographical area. The term is often applied to periods associated with the international spread of major human infectious DISEASES such as cholera, influenza, plague and smallpox (e.g. 'pandemic influenza'; see Patterson, 1986), with the expression 'global pandemic' reserved for periods of rapid worldwide transmission of a disease agent. Global pandemic events of the past 100 years include 'Spanish' influenza (1918–19), El Tor cholera (1961–) and the Acquired ImmunoDeficiency Syndrome (AIDS) (1981–); see Kohn (1998). (See also BIOSECURITY.)   MSR

Suggested reading
Cliff, Haggett and Smallman-Raynor (2004).

Panopticon Philosopher and jurist Jeremy Bentham's design for a building, most commonly a PRISON, in which centralized power is all-seeing – *pan-opticon* – is described in his book of that title (1791; see Bentham, 1995). Bentham's design was for a circular building, with rooms arranged around the circumference, open at both ends, of one or more storeys. The individual rooms, or cells, would thus be illuminated from behind, and visible at the front to a central tower. The occupant of the tower would thus be able to look into each and every cell from a fixed position. However, it would be possible to construct a system of blinds that prevented the occupants of the cells from seeing into the control tower, and so they would be unaware if they were being observed at that point or not, or even if there was an occupant in the tower. Not only would they therefore be subject to external power, they would turn that power on to themselves, being self-disciplining. Bentham's design was suitable for any building in which it was necessary or useful to be able to continually observe individuals who would have no contact with the other occupants, such as a school, a factory, a hospital, barracks, a poor-house or, most commonly, a prison. Bentham's design was offered to the British government as a model for the prisons being constructed as transportation to the colonies became less viable in the late eighteenth and early nineteenth centuries, but was only taken up in part in model prisons such as Pentonville and the Millbank Penitentiary. Panopticons were also built outside Britain, including in Spain, the Netherlands, the USA and Cuba.

Bentham's model assumed a wider contemporary significance as a result of Foucault's 1976a [1975] analysis of the Panopticon as an exemplar of DISCIPLINARY POWER (see Patton, 1979). Foucault saw the Panopticon as the architectural conjunction of two models of dealing with social problems, which he analysed as the problem of lepers and the problem of the plague. With leprosy, victims were excluded from SOCIETY; with the plague, they were rigidly controlled from within. While 'the leper gave rise to rituals of exclusion ... the plague gave rise to disciplinary diagrams'. In a plague town there was a strict spatial partitioning, with careful SURVEILLANCE, detailed inspection and mechanisms of ordering. These illustrate two models: a pure community as opposed to a disciplined society. Both are symbols of wider models of POWER, as is the Panopticon in Foucault's analysis. It is the architectural fusion of these models, where the organization of the plague town is brought

517

to bear on the spaces of exclusion. Foucault suggested that the society that emerged in this period can be better understood as one of generalized *panopticism*, where the ideal of surveillance and ordered behaviour is spread through cities as a whole. Foucault's analysis has not been without its critics, but his account, together with his re-edition of the French text with an introductory interview (1980d), helped to bring Bentham's work back into discussion. In HUMAN GEOGRAPHY, Foucault's arguments have influenced historico-geographical studies of poverty, welfare and workhouses (Driver, 1993) and contemporary critiques of security, surveillance and incarceration (Hannah, 1997; Dobson and Fisher, 2007).   SE

Suggested reading
Bentham (1995); Foucault (1978); Wood (2007).

paradigm An old English word meaning pattern, exemplar or model, but rescued from obscurity by the American philosopher and historian of science Thomas Kuhn (1922–96) in his short monograph *The structure of scientific revolutions* (1970 [1962]), reportedly the most cited book of the twentieth century. The precise definition of 'paradigm' is contentious, with one critic counting 21 different meanings in the first edition of Kuhn's book (although the second edition offered clarification: Masterman, 1970). Roughly, a paradigm is the constellation of values, assumptions, methods and exemplars shared by a given scientific community, making it what it is. A paradigm shapes what scientists think about something before they think it.

Kuhn's use of 'paradigm' was part of his larger project to provide an alternative to the traditional history of SCIENCE that stressed science's progressive and heroic character. For Kuhn, most science was puzzle-solving, with practitioners working within a common frame of reference, shared assumptions, techniques and standards; that is, a paradigm. Consequently, the activities of scientists were run of the mill, not heroic. Within this framework of *normal science*, however, anomalies occurred that could not be explained within the prevailing paradigm. Given enough of them, a crisis eventuated, precipitating *extraordinary research* (not mere puzzle-solving). If successful, in the sense that the new research accommodated the anomalies, revolutionary change occurred in the form of a *paradigm shift*, setting the blueprint for the next period of normal science. Paradigms, however, by their very constitution, were incommensurable.

Scientific knowledge, therefore, moved not as linear progress, but as incomparable, discontinuous transformations ('scientific revolutions').

Kuhn's work garnered an enormous amount of critical attention. There were the definitional ambiguities already mentioned. Kuhn's response was to clarify 'paradigm' by separating out the global characteristics of a scientific community, labelled the 'disciplinary matrix' (Kuhn, 1970 [1962], p. 182), from 'concrete problem solutions' (Kuhn, 1970 [1962], p. 186) such as the use of a particular book or mathematical technique, termed 'exemplars' (Kuhn, 1970 [1962], pp. 186–7). Other criticisms went to his substantive claims. Toulmin (1970) argued historically that paradigm change was not revolutionary, but occurred all the time. The rarity was normal science. For this reason, Popper (1970, p. 53) thought that 'one ought to be sorry for' Kuhn's 'normal scientist'. Likewise, Kuhn's thesis of incommensurability drew fire with its implication that science does not progress. Lakatos (1978), while accepting incommensurability between 'hard cores' of rival theories, claimed that one could still meaningfully speak of progress using empirical prediction and corroboration to construct research programmes.

These are important points, but they do not help us to understand why Kuhn's book was such a runaway success. There are many reasons, but the most important was its antirationalism, and its resonance with a similar sentiment washing over a number of HUMANITIES and social sciences from the 1960s (where the book was read much more than in science), and culminating in POSTMODERNISM and POST-STRUCTURALISM. Whether he meant to or not (and the evidence is that he did not), Kuhn represented scientific knowledge not as an unsullied, abstract form of rationality (the progressive, heroic view), but relativistically as mired in context-specific cultural beliefs and ordinary practices, in paradigms. Not that this was the interpretation of paradigm by geographers who first made use of Kuhn during their own 'scientific revolution', the self-styled QUANTITATIVE REVOLUTION that was to usher in SPATIAL SCIENCE through 'extraordinary research'. Perversely Kuhn's 'paradigm' was interpreted as a justification for that movement's rationalist scientific approach (Haggett and Chorley, 1967) and paradigms were treated as scientific models (cf. Billinge, Gregory and Martin, 1984a; Mair, 1986). Some later exponents, however, tried to recoup some of the radical anti-rationalist possibilities of Kuhn's work through interpretations of the discipline's history (Barnes, 2004b). But while Kuhn's book might have been on the *Times Literary Supplement*'s list of top 100 most influential books since the Second World War, it was never on geography's top 100 list. Even so, 'paradigm' is no longer an obscure term, and is now widely used to mean 'exemplar' or, in a much looser sense than Kuhn intended, to describe a more or less systematic way of thinking about or doing something.   TB

Suggested reading
Kuhn 1970 [1962]; Mair (1986).

Pareto optimality   A situation in which it is impossible to make some people better off without making others worse off. This criterion of 'economic efficiency' was devised by the economist and sociologist V.F.D. Pareto (1848–1923), and is an important element in NEO-CLASSICAL ECONOMICS. The Pareto criterion may be applied to efficiency of RESOURCE allocation, optimality being achieved when it is impossible to reallocate resources to produce an outcome that would increase the satisfaction of some people without reducing the satisfaction of others.

The attainment of Pareto optimality is illustrated in the figure. Resources are available to generate a certain amount of income distributed among A and B – these could be individuals, groups of people or even the inhabitants of two different territories. The line AB indicates the possible distributions of the maximum total income available, ranging from all going to A and none to B (at point A) to all going to B (at B). Point X is a position of Pareto optimality, where any redistribution in the direction of either A or B (along the line) will make the other party worse off. In fact, any starting position on the line is Pareto-optimal. It would be impossible to increase A's share from X to Z (thus leaving B in the same position) because this conflicts with the resource constraint. However, point Y inside the triangle ABO is sub-optimal by the Pareto criterion because available resources are not fully utilized and it is possible to increase A's income to X, for example, without taking anything away from B. Such a move would be a 'Pareto improvement'.

The Pareto criterion figures prominently in traditional welfare economics, where it is argued that acceptance of Pareto optimality as a rule for allocative efficiency or distributive

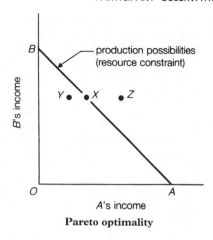

Pareto optimality

equity involves minimal ethical content. However, adoption of the Pareto criterion carries some important implications that tend to strengthen the status quo. Once society has reached the limit of production possibilities – that is, there is no more growth – then the poor cannot be made better off without conflicting with the Pareto criterion, for any such move would be at the expense of others (the rich). Thus however badly off the poor may be, they can be made better off only if more income (or whatever) is produced. In practice, the application of the Pareto criterion in a no-growth economy would prevent redistribution in the direction of the poor, no matter how unequal the existing distribution (cf. WELFARE GEOGRAPHY).   DMS

participant   observation   A research method in which the researcher aims to participate in the process under study so as to gain intimate knowledge of subjects and their habits, which insiders to a realm of practice might not otherwise reveal – or be able to reveal – in contrived situations such as interviews. Participant observation was a valued - technique for the ethnographies of the Chicago School of urban sociology, as well as for the social anthropologists Bronislaw Malinowsky and E. Evans-Pritchard, and the cultural anthropologist Margaret Mead. As Malinowsky famously put it, participant observation provides a means 'to grasp the native's point of view, his relation to life, to realize *his* vision of *his* world' (1961, p. 25), which would then have to be analysed in broader institutional terms through intellectual resources that the anthropologist considered to be 'far surpassing the natives'. This gendered and colonial defence of expertise has come under strong critique, not least within anthropology. However, attentiveness to the quality of relationships necessary to access contextual knowledge, the central concern of participant observation, remains central to a post-positivist or hermeneutic social science.

Michael Burawoy (see Burawoy, Burton, Ferguson and Fox, 1991) frames participant observation against both POSITIVISM and cultural RELATIVISM, as a method defined along two axes: a scientific or theory-data axis, which arrays objects from self-evident to subjects of theoretical scrutiny, and a hermeneutic axis, which arrays 'observer' and 'observed' across a range from estrangement to immersion. Burawoy stresses the importance of choice in locating oneself across both axes in the process of ethnographic research (see ETHNOGRAPHY). Self-consciousness about location in both these senses is crucial in analysis of what Donna Haraway (1991c) calls SITUATED KNOWLEDGES: products of perpetually tenuous relationships that cannot be resolved by claims to objectivity through familiarity or the crypto-religiosity of omniscient science.

Burawoy's analytic can be pushed farther by asking how objectification on the scientific axis presumes the translation of only some aspects of local knowledge into 'universal' science, through specifically raced and sexed practices of intimate affiliation. As Hugh Raffles (2002) eloquently argues, most local knowledge remains in the not-universal, not-scientific, ethnographic context: a realm of intimate knowledge that is embodied, spatialized, affective (see AFFECT) and relational. Raffles' challenge is to represent this broader affective geography through attention to multiple forms of participant theorization, on differentiated terms set by unequal access to broader intellectual, social and spatial resources. A key challenge of participant observation today is to find ways of representing the political economic, cultural, textual and affective resources through which knowledge is actually negotiated in context. This method can then defend the way in which specific products of participant observation become scientific evidence, not through Malinowsky's suppression of subjugated knowledges, but through norms of accountability that contend with the unequal conditions of production of scientific knowledge. Such an approach also allows for ongoing claims to responsibility and redress for human subjects and their geographies, through evidence that explicitly shows reliance on the nature of 'participation'.   sc

participatory democracy A system of government in which those being governed participate directly in decision-making and/or policy formation. It is contrasted with representative democracy, in which those being governed elect representatives to an assembly that takes decisions on behalf of the voters. Participatory democracy is usually thought to have originated in ancient Athens, where decisions were made by an assembly comprising all citizens. Although full participatory democracy is difficult to implement for large populations, popular participation in decision-making remains an aspiration for many social movements. However, COMMUNITY participation in governance has also been criticized for its association with neo-liberal policies (Herbert, 2005). (See also RADICAL DEMOCRACY.)   JPA

Suggested reading
Barber (2004).

partition In recent times, the idea of partition (connected to the interaction between competing diverse notions of statehood and nationhood) has attracted fresh attention as the inevitable, though not ideal, solution to protracted ethnic conflicts. Before the First World War, partition was a tool of the empires, dividing territories between themselves or using them to strengthen their rule. After the war, partition took place either in the devolution of authority granting independence to NATIONS or as a solution to ethnic conflicts perceived to be irreconcilable. Even then, the 'solutions' proved to be volatile and precarious since the TERRITORIES they created were not culturally homogeneous, as the partition of Palestine through the creation of the state of Israel or the successive partitions of India and Pakistan (with East Pakistan eventually becoming Bangladesh) have shown. In the 'short partitions', such as Vietnam and Germany, the nationalist journey might succeed without much difficulty, whereas in the 'long partitions', (marked by a long history of the politics of OTHERNESS and its persistence) the nation often fails the STATE. The project of harmonizing the nation with the state becomes nearly impossible.

According to a critical geopolitical perspective, 'partition' is not the end (product) of a geopolitical conflict or rivalry but, rather, a means of resolving or managing that conflict, accepted by various parties either as a matter of choice, or due to persuasion or pressure. In other words, partition is to be seen not as an inevitable consequence of actual or imagined predestined differences but, rather, as a consciously developed and deliberately deployed spatial strategy of eliminating real or imagined differences – a method preferred over other methods, including 'mutuality/consociation/power sharing'.

A comparison of partitions around the world, from British India to Yugoslavia, from Canada to Ireland, from Nigeria to Rwanda, from the Soviet Union to Palestine, appears to suggest that territory is, in fact, a crucial factor in the process of disrupting and reshaping states and loyalties. It is further revealed that the process of partition cannot be reduced to a state separation event (as in the cases of India and Pakistan, Serbia and Croatia, Ireland and Britain or potentially Canada and Quebec). This process also has to deal with additional regional sub-partitions, family divisions and religious contrasts. Partitioning British India, for instance, has generated a subsequent partition of Punjab and Bengal. Similarly, the partition of Yugoslavia has implied the sub-partition of Istria, Krajinas and Sandzak, and of Yugoslav populations and minorities.

Historically, there are very few examples of partition where violence could be avoided. Wherever and whenever partitions have been implemented, a large-scale destruction of the sociocultural landscape has invariably followed. In the vast majority of cases, violence becomes a determinant for reconfiguring political societies, where territory (or geopolitics), sources of loyalty and collective/individual psychology are forced to reshape and modify. To a certain extent, the stronger the pre-existing ties, the greater is the deployment of violence to construct new sources of identifications by redrawing maps. Among several icons of 'partitioned times' on the Indian subcontinent are millions of refugees who continue to live with bitter memories of loot, plunder, rape and murder, and in whom such memories live.   sch

Suggested reading
Pandey (2001).

pastoralism Social and economic systems of peoples who both practice and strongly identify with livestock husbandry (most commonly of camels, cattle, goats and sheep). Identities of ethnicities, castes or lineages to livestock husbandry have typically formed historically during periods of occupational specialization. Mobile forms of pastoralism require fundamentally different demands on knowledge, social connections and labour than sedentary productive pursuits. Therefore, more mobile forms of pastoralism have been most associated with the occupational specialization tied to identity formation. For this reason, common uses of the term 'pastoralism' often suggest systems of herding specialists relying on more mobile forms of animal husbandry. However, pastoralism encompasses systems of variable reliance on livestock production and on livestock mobility.

From a CULTURAL ECOLOGY perspective, pastoralism is an effective adaptation to ECOSYSTEMS that are marginal for crop agriculture due to soil, topography or climate constraints. Thus, while historically not necessarily the case, contemporary pastoralism is increasingly found largely within marginal areas, due to agricultural encroachment in productive areas. More mobile forms of pastoralism are seen as ideally suited for environments with significant spatio-temporal heterogeneity of vegetative productivity. Two axes of mobility within pastoral systems are human and livestock mobility. Nomadic pastoralism (see NOMADISM) involves the movement of pastoral families and their livestock, which does not allow the establishment of a permanent human dwelling. There are many other mobile pastoral systems, such as TRANSHUMANCE, in which the whole production unit (family, clan etc.) does not move with the animals. Studies have found that the mobility of pastoralists is highly variable (over time and between production units), making categorizations of pastoral peoples based on their mobility and that of their livestock extremely hazardous.

Despite widely held romantic visions of isolated, individualistic pastoralists relying solely on their animals to meet subsistence needs, most pastoralist societies have historically aligned themselves to broader military/political authority for security and have relied variably (depending in part on livestock ownership) on farming and/or trade to procure grain and cash. This engagement with broader political and economic systems has become more evident since the mid-twentieth century in many parts of the world. More mobile pastoral livelihoods have generally not only not had the support of NATION-STATES, but have, in certain contexts, been actively attacked and dismantled by states that see pastoral mobility as working against their DEVELOPMENT and political aims (see MIGRANCY). Resource dispossession along with the economic vulnerability of livestock producers to market and climate fluctuations has led to increased impoverishment of pastoral peoples. While many pastoralists maintain identities tied to animal husbandry,

521

their livelihoods often depend more on other economic pursuits. MT

Suggested reading
Galaty and Johnson (1990); Ingold (1980); Niamir-Fuller (1999).

patenting Patents are a category of INTELLECTUAL PROPERTY RIGHTS designed to provide inventors with legal rights for a fixed period (usually 20 years) to prevent others from using, selling or importing their innovations. An application for a patent must satisfy a national and/ or international patent office that the invention described in the application is new, useful and that its creation involved an inventive step either beyond the present state of the art or unobvious to a skilled practitioner.

Over time, more and more things (e.g. certain biological materials) have become patentable as business interests (and especially recently the life science firms involved in producing medicines) have successfully argued that patents are essential for their ability to make a return on the high R&D investment required to discover, produce and get regulatory approval for new products. Such an extension is reflected in the TRIPS (Trade-Related aspects of Intellectual Property Rights) agreement administered by the World Trade Organization (WTO) and is hugely controversial. NB

Suggested reading
Coombe (1998); Parry (2004).

patriarchy A system of social structures and practices through which men dominate, oppress and exploit women. A distinction is made between classic or paternal patriarchy, a form of household organization in which the father dominates other members of an extended kin network (including younger men) and controls the economic production of the household, and fraternal patriarchy, in which men dominate women within civil society; the latter provided a key focus for feminist theorizing and organizing during the 1960s and 1970s. By the 1980s, the utility of the concept was in doubt; critics saw it as ahistorical and insensitive to cross-cultural variation. Efforts to theorize patriarchy in relation to capitalism seemed to collapse into FUNCTIONALISM, or leave the relations between the two systems unresolved. And if patriarchy operates autonomously from capitalist relations, as posited by *dual systems theory*, did this not leave the patriarchal relations of capitalism undertheorized? In geography, efforts were made by

Foord and Gregson (1986) to resolve these dilemmas through REALISM: Walby (1989) criticized their model for neglecting paid work, the state and male violence (for other critical reactions, see GENDER and Women and Geography Study Group, 1997), and posited a dual systems theory of patriarchy at three levels of abstraction – system, structure and practice. Patriarchy, according to Walby, is composed of six structures: the patriarchal mode of production, male violence, patriarchal relations in paid work, the state, sexuality and cultural institutions. But in Acker's view (1989), the moment of theorizing patriarchy in this way had passed: the object of feminism had moved from patriarchy as a system to gender relations (and now HETERONORMATIVITY and sexual difference: see GENDER). Interest had also moved away from delineating the *cause(s)* of patriarchal relations to understanding the diversity of *effects*.

As early as 1980, Barrett suggested that patriarchy is better conceived as an adjective than as a noun. The term is still used as a noun, but typically in the plural: Grewal and Kaplan (1994, pp. 17–18) urge the need 'to address the concerns of women around the world in the historicized particularity of their relationships to multiple patriarchies as well as to international economic hegemonies', but their concern is to compare 'multiple, overlapping, and discrete oppressions' and not to construct 'a theory of hegemonic oppression under the unified sign of gender' (i.e. under the sign of patriarchy). Post-colonial theory has alerted feminists to the ways in which accusations of patriarchal relations among immigrant groups or in countries in the global South can be used to discriminatory, colonial or imperialist ends. The Bush administration's justification of the US invasion of Afghanistan in 2001 – as in part a defence and liberation of Afghan women – is one example. Young (2003a) asks Western feminists to consider how they 'laid the ground work' for the success of this appeal through their own campaigns against the Taliban and the 'stance of protector' that they sometimes adopt 'in relation to … women of the world who [Western women] construct as more dependent or subordinate' (p. 3) and more oppressed by patriarchal relations. GP

Pax Americana Also known as 'Pox Americana', this synonym for AMERICAN EMPIRE makes parallels with the ancient Roman Empire to either critically unpack (e.g. Johnson, 2003a; Foster and McChesney,

2004) or uncritically expound (e.g. Steel, 1967) the argument that US global dominance makes the world safe for long-distance TRADE, communication and DEMOCRACY. Most recently, it has been put forward by the National Intelligence Council (NIC; the US government's 'strategic intelligence' planning body) as one of four extraordinary scenarios for what the world map of GEOPOLITICS will look like in the year 2020 (National Intelligence Council, 2005). 'Mapping the global future' with a keen attention to what the strategic planners view as the long term 'mega-trend' of GLOBALIZATION, the NIC envisions *Pax Americana* as a benign extension of contemporary US military dominance alongside a faltering but still extant American ability to dominate the institutions of global GOVERNANCE. The NIC contrasts this vision of 2020 with three others: *Davos World*, which is also imagined as a relatively utopian scenario, albeit with US economic authority increasingly overshadowed by rising Asian influence; *The New Caliphate*, a very different and distinctively dystopian vision of a world rendered unstable by what is depicted (using the IMAGINATIVE GEOGRAPHIES of ORIENTALISM) as tradition-bound Muslim resistance to globalization and American influence; and, finally, the unremittingly bleak dystopia of a so-called *Cycle of Fear*, in which weapons of mass destruction circulate through globalized terror networks (see TERRORISM), in turn envisioned as spurring an authoritarian governmental backlash of which – most fearfully of all for the NIC's futurists – 'globalization may be the real victim' (NIC, 2005, p. 104).

While *Pax Americana* is imagined as a fairly unexceptional continuation of the current global order (relative to the three other 2020 scenarios), it is useful to consider what the alternative scenarios tell us about what has to be repressed by the NIC to continue with its exceptionalist imagining of America as a uniquely freedom-loving and anti-imperial NATION-STATE. *Cycle of Fear*, for example, imagines authoritarianism and the future victimization of globalization, but all the while it obscures the already existing victims of the CIA's own programmes of torture in Black Sites and other spaces of exception (see EXCEPTION, SPACES OF). *The New Caliphate* likewise dissembles the huge role of the US intelligence agencies in helping to start, arm and even train many of the key leaders of the more violent and territorially ambitious jihadist movements in Central Asia and the Arabian Peninsula. And *Davos World* meanwhile betrays the still

deeper contradictions that at once underlie and undermine the exceptionalist American idea that the spread of freedom and the spread of free enterprise are one and the same thing. If the rapid development of cadre CAPITALISM in China has not made this completely clear for the NIC, then the fiasco in Iraq that has continued unabated since the publication of the 2020 report most certainly must. Here, in what was announced by many war promoters as the inaugural battle for a new and more peaceful American century, the brutality, death and destruction of a terribly unpeaceful *Pax Americana* has been writ large on the landscape.

Even if *Pax* means peace, the more important aspect of the reference to *Pax Romana* has always been to the violence of the ancient empire and the punitive approach that the Roman army took to subduing and incorporating the periphery into a unipolar world dominated by Rome. In 1963, President Kennedy acknowledged as much when he said that the world peace that the US sought was 'not a *Pax Americana* enforced on the world by American weapons of war' (quoted in Foster and McChesney, 2004). However, by the new millennium this return to the Roman model was exactly what the administration of President Bush was openly advocating as the rationale of the Iraq war. Given the hubris of some of the advocates of this neo-conservative foreign policy, it is not surprising that their identities often remain anonymous, but the following is reporter Ron Suskind's (2004) account of one Bush aide's comments:

> The aide said that guys like me were 'in what we call the reality-based community', which he defined as people who 'believe that solutions emerge from your judicious study of discernible reality'. I nodded and murmured something about enlightenment principles and empiricism. He cut me off. 'That's not the way the world really works anymore', he continued. 'We're an empire now, and when we act, we create our own reality. And while you're studying that reality – judiciously, as you will – we'll act again, creating other new realities, which you can study too, and that's how things will sort out. We're history's actors, and you, all of you, will be left to just study what we do'

This sort of attitude clearly put the US intelligence agencies in a difficult situation – in which they had to help invent realities that helped justify the policy of attacking Iraq (Rich, 2006). The subsequent turn to scenario building at the NIC seems to be of a piece with this story-telling-cum-war-mongering geopolitical inventiveness, albeit announced instead as a peace-loving geo-economic homage to globalization. Elsewhere, though, the turn away from reality in the name of *Pax Americana* has been widely criticized. With the possible exception of fans of NON-REPRESENTATIONAL THEORY, geographers have stayed put as denizens of a reality-based community that acknowledges both the limits and possibilities of SITUATED KNOWLEDGE. Thus rather than map a futuristic scenario of *Pax Americana* for 2020, leaders in the field have instead charted the violent destruction and dispossession that constitutes Pox Americana on the ground in the colonial present (Harvey, 2004b; Johnston, 2005d; Gregory and Pred, 2007; see also Retort, 2005). And rather than counterpose globalization and fear as opposites, critical geographers have also explored the globalization of fear that has followed from the unremitting American pursuit of an informal and, as such, exceptionalist empire that is founded on ideas about peace and justice for all, but which is always also foundering in human geographies – from slave plantations to export-processing zones to Guantanamo – where exceptions are made in the name of the exceptionalist vision (Miller, 2006; Mitchell and Rosati, 2006; Sparke, 2005, 2007; Wright, 1999b). A brand name for this tortured concoction of capital and coercion is only fitting: *Pax Americana*® certain restrictions may apply.   MS

peasant   A term that was in common use in the English language from the fifteenth century, referring to individuals working on the land and residing in the countryside. By the nineteenth century, 'peasant' was employed as a term of abuse (e.g. by Marx on the idiocy of rural life), and in the recent past it has been imbued with heroic and revolutionary connotations (as in Maoism, for example). In modern usage, peasants are to be found on family farms (farming households) that function as relatively corporate units of production, consumption and reproduction (Chayanov, 1966). The particular social structural forms of the domestic unit (nuclear families, multi-generational extended families, intra-household sexual DIVISIONS OF LABOUR and property systems), the social relations between households within peasant COMMUNITIES and the ecological relations of production (the peasant ecotype) are, however, extremely heterogeneous (Wolf, 1966). The terms 'peasant' and 'peasantry' have often been employed loosely to describe a broad range of

rural producers as generic types characterized by certain social, cultural or economic traits: the backward or anti-economic peasant, the rational and moral peasant, the uncaptured peasant. These and other terms such as 'traditional', 'subsistence' or 'smallholder' detract from the important analytical task of situating peasants as specific social producers in concrete, historically specific political economies with their own dynamics and laws of motion.

Peasants are distinguished by direct access to their means of production in land, by the predominant use of family labour and by a high degree of self-sufficiency (see SUBSISTENCE AGRICULTURE). Nonetheless, all peasants are by definition characterized by a partial engagement with markets (which tend to function with a high degree of imperfection) and are subordinate actors in larger political economies, in which they fulfil obligations to holders of political and economic POWER. Peasants as forms of household enterprise rooted primarily in production on the land have a distinctive LABOUR PROCESS (the unity of the domestic unit and the productive group) and a unique combination of labour and property through partial market involvement. Peasants stand between those social groups that have lost all or most of their productive assets (proletarians or semi-proletarians), on the one hand, and farming households that are fully involved in the market (so-called petty or simple commodity producers), on the other. Seen in this way, peasants have existed under a variety of economic, political and cultural circumstances (e.g. FEUDALISM, CAPITALISM and state SOCIALISM) spanning vast periods of history, and are 'part societies'. Peasant societies are often seen as transitional – they 'stand midway between the primitive tribe and industrial society' (Wolf, 1966, p. vii) – and yet are marginal or outsiders, 'subordinate to a group of controlling outsiders' (Wolf, 1966, p. 13) who appropriate surpluses in a variety of forms (RENT, interest, unequal exchange).

In many THIRD WORLD societies in which peasants continue to constitute an important and occasional dominant stratum, a central question pertains to the fate of the peasantry in relation to growing STATE and market involvement. Peasants are invariably the victims of MODERNITY (Moore, 1966). The questions of growing commercialization and mechanization of peasant production and of the growth of off-farm income (MIGRATION, craft production, local wage labour) are reflected in the long-standing concern with internal differentiation among peasantries and hence their long-term survival (hence the debates over peasant persistence, de-peasantization and captured peasants). It is probably safe to say that the period from 1950 to 1975 witnessed an epochal shift in which peasantry became for the first time a global minority.

The proliferation of peasant studies in the past 30 years has been the source of important theoretical innovations in political economy speaking to questions of commoditization, CLASS formation, resistance and rebellion (Shanin, 1988). The study of peasants was also key to the evolution of CULTURAL ECOLOGY and POLITICAL ECOLOGY insofar as peasant knowledge and practice is an indispensable starting point for the understanding of household management of resources, and hence the processes of ecological change and rehabilitation (Watts, 1983a; Blaikie and Brookfield, 1987).

In the context of the transitions to and from capitalism, the role of peasantry is central. Barrington Moore (1966) argued that the relations between landlord and peasantry are fundamental in understanding the various routes of DEMOCRACY and dictatorship in the modern world. Peasant revolutions in Mexico, Algeria and China, for example – the antithesis of the idea of apolitical or tradition-laden peasantries – have fundamentally shaped the twentieth century (Skocpol, 1980). Kautsky (1988 [1899]) referred to the AGRARIAN QUESTION in western Europe in the nineteenth century to underscore the political ramifications of the new forms of differentiation and proletarianization associated with growing commercialization, and the political and strategic questions that arose from peasant protest and struggle. One of the major features of the period since 1989 and the decollectivization of agriculture in the former socialist bloc has been the re-emergence of millions of peasant households (re-peasantization) in China, Russia and eastern Europe. The role of peasants in post-socialist transitions has been a crucial part of the political landscape in these parts of the world and they represent intriguing cases for the study of new forms of agrarian capitalist trajectories (see Verdery, 1996; Selenyi, 1998). In other parts of the world, peasant entrepreneurial and political activism has also gained momentum in India (Gidwani, 2008), Indonesia (Li, 2006) and Mexico (Bobrow-Strain, 2007).   MW

Suggested reading
Scott (1988).

performance A concept that 'is, at this moment, one of the most pervasive metaphors in the human sciences' (Thrift, 2000a, p. 225). Its popularity has been tied to: current interest in embodiment or habits of the body; noncognitive experiences and knowledges and the production of social life through everyday practices; and desires to de-naturalize social categories and processes, create new political opportunities and emphasize the creativity of social life. Although different approaches to performance share most of these objectives, they also differ significantly in conceptions of HUMAN AGENCY, SUBJECTIVITY and POWER (Gregson and Rose, 2000), and tend to direct attention to different geographies and spaces. It is common to distinguish between four approaches: a sociological dramaturgical approach, PERFORMATIVITY (often as outlined by Butler), NON-REPRESENTATIONAL THEORY and performance studies.

The sociological, dramaturgical approach is typically traced to Erving Goffman's ideas about the codes of conduct that govern behaviour, and the various strategies that we use to manage ourselves in the presence of others. Social life is conceived as staged by conscious agents who adhere to scripts. This is a geographical narrative that distinguishes front-of-the-stage from backstage, and public from private. Gregson and Rose (2000) argue that this has been the most prevalent notion of performance in geography. A number of studies look at the performances demanded in specific, usually service-sector, workplaces (e.g. McDowell and Court, 1994). Davidson (2003) develops the dramaturgical analogy to consider agoraphobia as a kind of 'stage fright' that compels those suffering from it to restrict their public performances to obviate the need to engage in 'impression management'.

Whereas the dramaturgical analogy implies a conscious agent that exists prior to performances (Gregson and Rose, 2000), PERFORMATIVITY outlines a process through which social subjects are produced through performances. These are 'command' performances, regulated by social norms, but possibilities for subversion arise from slippages between actual performances and the norms/ideals that they cite. Although Butler largely works in a temporal rather than spatial register, she points to the importance of geographical context for the meaning of any performance: 'subversiveness is the kind of effect that *resists calculation* ... the demarcation of context is ... already a prefiguring of the result' (1993b, p. 29). Gregson and Rose (2000) have extended the notion of performativity to space, arguing that 'performances do not take place in already existing locations ... specific performances bring these spaces into being' (p. 441).

Non-representational styles of thinking bring to the notion of performativity more emphasis on creativity, what is excessive to representation, cognition and discourse, everyday skills, affect and the 'binding of bodies-with-environment' (Thrift, 2004c, p. 177). With respect to the last, Thrift writes of the 'technological unconscious', a vast 'performative infrastructure' that provides the stable ground for our practices and is producing the vast standardization of space. The spatial imaginary is that of connections, intersections, movement and ASSEMBLAGES; the temporality that of becoming and the momentary event.

Non-representational styles of thought take much from performance studies, an interdisciplinary focus with closer ties to the performing arts, especially theatre and dance. It shares the emphasis on creativity and play, the intermingling of the normative and transgressive, the limits of representation, the expressive qualities of the body beyond discourse, and the full range of the senses, including the kinaesthetic (as well as attempts to develop vocabularies to document these). Performance studies places especial emphasis on liminal times and spaces that allow the temporary suspension of norms and transitory nature of an event, which can never be fully captured, preserved or repeated.

The focus on performance has opened new ways of thinking of and about research methods. The emphasis on the extra-discursive underlines the importance of witnessing in order to understand – not just how people describe their world – but how they act in their world (see ETHNOMETHODOLOGY). Witnessing this 'doing' can offer opportunities to access a range of experiences and emotions that are not easily expressed through interview talk. It also prompts a different methodological approach to talk. Instead of asking respondents to describe their world, researchers have become more interested in listening to potential respondents talk while they are in their worlds. They are interested in the talk that does things. More and more researchers are experimenting with performative writing strategies, and expanding the boundaries of what counts as valuable research data and research products, to include theatre and video productions (see QUALITATIVE METHODS). Self-conscious research performances stretch debates about POSITIONALITY and research ETHICS in new directions (Routledge, 2002).

Despite the convergences and overlap between different approaches to performance, there are significant disagreements that warrant further debate, especially about what counts as politics and effective political strategy. Thrift (2004c) directs us to the minutiae of performativity to harness 'the energy of moments' (p. 188). Houston and Pulido (2002) have criticized the individualism of much of the work within geography influenced by the concept of performance and the tendency to reduce resistance to the scale of the body. They direct us back to historical materialism and collective politics. Jacobs and Nash (2003) are also measured in their reception of non-representational theory. They argue that the emphasis on escaping categorical fixity, in an effort to accentuate processes of becoming, risks returning the unmarked (implicitly masculine) subject. They argue as well for the need to discriminate between power relations: 'In a world in which power is understood to be radically dissimulated (as much about negotiating subjectivity or negotiating household chores, or work relations, or claiming and refusing rights), the ... research imperative becomes one of being sensitive to the relations and proximities that matter, either in their determining forces or their transforming potential' (pp. 274–5). How to make these determinations offers grounds for debate. GP

Suggested reading
Butler (1990); Jacobs and Nash (2003); Phelan and Lane (1998); Thrift (2000a).

performativity One strand of the recent thinking about PERFORMANCE: it has been an important means of theorizing the workings of POWER in the production of rules and norms. The concept is rooted in the linguistic distinction between constative and performative utterances. A performative utterance (famously exemplified by the statement: 'I pronounce you ...', uttered at the marriage ceremony) is itself an act that performs the action to which it refers. The performative 'brings to centre stage ... an active, world-making use of language' (Culler, 1997, pp. 97–8).

The concept has been worked up most thoroughly by Judith Butler in relation to GENDER and norms of heterosexuality (1990, 1993a; see QUEER THEORY). She argued that gender is a performance without ontological status: 'There is no gender identity behind the expression of gender; that identity is performatively constituted by the very "expressions" that are said to be its results' (1990, p. 25).

This is a more radical position than that of conventional feminist SOCIAL CONSTRUCTION, because she argues that biological sex is also produced: there is no interiorized, biological foundation on which gender rests. In this sense, gender norms are materialized by the BODY: they literally become matter. Butler also wrestles with a more complex SUBJECTIVITY than is evident in many social constructivist accounts, because she attempts to hold PSY-CHOANALYSIS in tension with DISCOURSE ANALYSIS. She argues that identities are not simply performed on the surface of the body: what is performed always operates in relation to what cannot be performed or said (notably homosexual relations), mediated by the unconscious. In contrast to some accounts of social performances, those analysed as performative are not seen to be freely chosen; they are compelled and sanctioned by the norms of compulsory heterosexuality (HETERONORMA-TIVITY), and the subject has no choice but to exist within gender norms and conventions of nature (i.e. binary sex difference). Performances are also historically embedded; they are 'citational chains' and their effect is dependent on conventions (i.e. previous utter-ances). Norms and identities are instantiated through repetitions of an ideal (e.g. the ideal of 'woman' or 'man'). Since we never quite inhabit the ideal, there is room for disidentifi-cation and agency (see HUMAN AGENCY).

Geographers have been divided in their reactions to performativity theory. Bell, Binnie, Cream and Valentine (1994) were among the first to deploy the concept, in their case to consider the subversive potential of particular performances of SEXUALITY. Critics have been concerned that the subject of performativity is abstracted in time and place, has little agency, is conceived within a purely dis-cursive, non-material world and is one that shares characteristics with the masculinist sov-ereign subject (for a review of these criticisms, see Pratt, 2004). Others have found the con-cept fruitful to think with: some have theorized space itself as performative (Gregson and Rose, 2000); others have drawn out the spati-alities that are under-theorized in Butler's work but necessarily underpin the process described by the concept (Thrift, 2000; Pratt, 2004). In Thrift's words: 'Social prac-tices have citational force because of the spaces in which they are embedded and through which they work' (2000, p. 677). Non-representational styles of thinking, in particular, emphasize the significance of the non-discursive and the instability of the citational process, envisioning social life 'as pro-cessually enactive, as styles and modes of per-formative moving and relating rather than as sets of codified rules' (McCormack, 2003, p. 489; original emphasis). The concept has been put to work to theorize more than gender and sexuality. Gregory (2005), for instance, brings the concept to his analysis of SOVEREIGN POWER; Thrift (2000) outlines a new 'ecology' of capitalist business practices that produce 'fast' managers with aptitudes for constant innovation and permanent high performance (see also CULTURAL ECONOMY). GP

periodic market systems The regular pro-vision of retail and other service functions at fixed points on predetermined days in the week. All of the functions may be available on certain days only: in others – as with 'market days' in British towns – additional functions to those available every day are provided on set days each week. There are analogies in their distribution with CENTRAL PLACE THEORY, as in a classic series of papers by Skinner (1964–5) on Chinese market systems. In situations with relatively low ranges and high thresholds, traders moving around markets on set days overcome problems of insufficient demand to justify permanent provision. Empirical anal-yses have identified a considerable range of ways in which such systems operate, however, often reflecting local cultural norms. RJ

Suggested reading
Bromley (1980).

petro-capitalism It has been said that mod-ern life is a form of 'hydrocarbon civilization' (Yergin, 1991). Energy, said one critic, is 'the precursor of economies' (Shelley, 2005, p. 1). OIL and gas account for over two-thirds of the world's energy supply and are indispensable to modern forms of mobility and power supply. Since the early part of the twentieth century, petroleum and industrial capitalism (and indeed industrial socialism) has been predi-cated on the availability of cheap petroleum. Petro-capitalism refers to two distinct but related ideas. The first is that petroleum is the fuel of modern industrial capitalism. In the context of contemporary debates over global climate change (see GLOBAL WARMING), addiction to (or dependency on) oil as a geo-politically risky strategy for oil-importing states and the continuing debate over whether global peak oil output has been reached, there may be the beginning of a turn to other sources of energy (biofuels, nuclear and solar).

527

But in the short and medium term, petroleum (and gas) will continue to drive the global capitalist economy. The second meaning is that oil-producing states that depend heavily on oil revenues (as a proportion of exports or as a proportion of GDP) – what are called 'oil-dependent economies' in some circles (Le Billon, 2005) – are specific sorts of capitalist economy insofar as they are not simply reliant upon oil as a source of energy but are forms of rentier economy in which oil rents (royalties, taxes, sales) are the driving the entire political economy. Petro-capitalism is a particular type of extractive economy in which oil revenues, typically under state control, undergird an ambitious programme of state-led development and modernization (an exemplary case would be the Shah's Iran in the 1970s). Nigeria, Saudi Arabia, Equatorial Guinea and Azerbaijan would be other cases of petro-capitalism – though, it needs to be said, they are customarily quite undisciplined and corrupt forms of capitalism that 'under perform' in relation to comparable non-oil states. Petro-capitalism in this second sense is associated with the 'resource curse' (Ross, 2001) (see also CONFLICT COMMODITIES). MW

Suggested reading
Kaldor and Karl (2007); Shaxon (2006); Watts (2004).

phallocentrism Placing man at the centre; a masculine way of representing and approaching the world that some theorists root in male genitalia and a masculine libidinal economy; conceiving knowledge as neutral and universal, whilst refusing alternative knowledges; knowledge that represent the interests and perspectives of men. It is intertwined with *logocentrism,* the fixing of meaning in hierarchized binary oppositions (hence the term *phallogocentrism*). Phallocentrism acknowledges women, but locates their identities only in relation to men, contained within a series of binarized concepts and terms: 'It is because sexual difference hides itself in other concepts and terms, other oppositional forms – in the distinctions between form and matter, between space and time, between mind and body, self and other, nature and culture, and so on, that it remains the latent condition of all knowledges and all social practices' (Grosz, 2005, p. 177). Critiques of phallocentrism have led French feminists such as Hélène Cixous and Luce Irigarary, and male philosophers such as Jacques Lacan and Jacques Derrida, to explore feminine (i.e. more open

and multiple) ways of writing and reading, of defining and investigating problems, including a diversity of intellectual standards for knowledge production, and diverse ways of conceiving the relations between theory and practice. Jardine (1985) terms such explorations *gynesis*. She regards the works of the male philosophers in particular with some suspicion, framing them as instances of male paranoia: such men began to desire to be woman as a way to avoid becoming the object of female desire.

Phallocentrism is an important concept within geography. Jardine (1985) attributes the critiques of phallocentrism (e.g. a disbelief in origins, master narratives, humanism and progress) that developed throughout the twentieth century to the end of European IMPERIALISM, as well as to the growing influence of FEMINISM. Critiques of phallocentrism have been important to the process of rethinking the concept of nature, because they are tied to attempts to displace 'man' from the controlling centre and to refigure nature in active, less exploitative, terms. To the extent that humanism and phallocentrism are intertwined, the critiques of that latter extend to HUMANISTIC GEOGRAPHY. Framed through the analogous concept of MASCULINISM, Rose (1993) claims that phallocentrism pervades geographical knowledge. (See also GENDER; HOMOPHOBIA AND HETEROSEXISM; SEXUALITY.) GP

Suggested reading
Grosz (2005).

phenomenology While the term 'phenomenology' was used in PHILOSOPHY by J.H. Lambert (1728–77), Immanuel Kant (1724–1804) and Ernst Mach (1838–1916), and is a vital part of G.W.F. Hegel's *Phenomenology of spirit* (1807), in the twentieth century phenomenology began with Edmund Husserl (1859–1938) and the elaborations of his work by Martin Heidegger, Roman Ingarden, Maurice Merleau-Ponty, Jean-Paul Sartre, Max Scheler, Alfred Schütz, Jacques Derrida, Emmanuel Levinas, Alain Badiou and Giorgio Agamben, among others (see Kockelmans, 1967, pp. 24–5). For Husserl, the definition of phenomenology was straightforward: it was himself and Martin Heidegger (1889–1976).

Phenomenology entered HUMAN GEOGRAPHY in the early 1970s as a reaction to and critique of the reductive and objectivist approaches of SPATIAL SCIENCE, and of the structuralism and functionalism of some versions of MARXISM then also entering the field. HUMANISTIC GEOGRAPHY in particular turned to phenomenology to redress abstract notions of people and places. This 'geographical phenomenology' focused variously on everyday practices, HUMAN AGENCY, movement, place, and social and environmental ethics (Relph, 1970; Tuan, 1971; Buttimer, 1976; Entrikin, 1976). Phenomenology was seen as a philosophical and methodological approach that was attuned to human subjectivity, and its proponents read in its claim for a return to 'the things themselves' – an argument at once opposed to scientific abstraction and in favour of a more direct social geography of everyday lives and lifeworlds (Casey, 1993).

In a major critical intervention, Pickles (1985) forcefully questioned these subjectivist readings of phenomenology. Pickles argued that 'geographical phenomenology' had overlooked Husserl's and Heidegger's critique of both objectivism *and subjectivism* in science as remaining in what Husserl called 'the natural attitude'. The real crisis of the European sciences was not that they treated the everyday world in overly abstract ways, but that they failed to recognize that their claims to OBJECTIVITY in the natural attitude had always to be clarified and situated in terms of their constitutive regional ontologies (see ONTOLOGY). Werlen (1993 [1988]) subsequently elaborated such a regional ontology of everyday life and social action through a close, creative reading of the constitutive phenomenology of Alfred Schütz (1899–1959).

Seen thus, phenomenology is not an *alternative* to the abstractive tendencies of science but a necessary *correlate* to it, seeking as it does to ground the relationship between scientific and the pre-scientific, the theoretical and the everyday, in a carefully prepared and reflective ontological analysis. Phenomenology 'does not subscribe to a "standpoint" or represent any special "direction"; for phenomenology is nothing of either sort, nor can it become so as long as it understands itself. The expression "phenomenology" signifies primarily a *methodological conception*. The expression does not characterize the what of the objects of philosophical research as a subject matter, but rather the *how* of that research. The more genuinely a methodological concept is worked out and the more comprehensively it determines the principles on which a science is to be conducted, all the more primordially is it rooted in the way we come to terms with the things themselves, and the farther is it

removed from what we call "technical devices" though there are many such devices even in the theoretical disciplines (Heidegger, 1927, p. 27: see METHODOLOGY).

It was precisely the fact that the sciences had forgotten their own histories of concepts and approaches (cf. GENEALOGY) that led to the need for phenomenology to clarify the regional ontologies of the sciences, knowledge production and the lifeworld. In Pickles' view, phenomenology is concerned not first and foremost with individualized, subjective geographies, but with the ways in which phenomena are constituted as intentional objects through complex historical and social processes of distanciation, thematization, abstraction and formalization (and sometimes mathematization) that constitute meaning-making in its many forms. Phenomenologists are, therefore, always interested in the constitution of the specific objects, with their relational nature as objects of consciousness, intention or meaning, and with the lifeworld context that always escapes all thematization but is the precondition for any such thematization. The task of phenomenology in this sense is not to assert the priority of the everyday world over the world of science, or of place over abstract spaces, but to understand through ontological investigation how each is constituted in various historical projects of abstraction and thematization (see also Gregory, 1978b).

By the 1990s and 2000s, new directions in geographical thought led to even more expanded readings of phenomenology in post-positivist geography. Phenomenology was renewed by a growing interest in POSTMODERNISM and POST-STRUCTURALISM, particularly in ways in which anti-essentialist writings questioned what Jacques Derrida called phenomenology's residual onto-theology: its specific commitments to particular interpretations of foundationalism, rationalism, and subject. More recently, growing interest amongst human geographers in the writings of Giorgio Agamben, Michel de Certeau, Jacques Derrida, Michel Foucault, Jean-Luc Nancy, Gayatri Spivak and others has led to an appreciation of the ways in which these thinkers have adapted phenomenological thought to new ends, and the advance of NON-REPRESENTATIONAL THEORY in human geography has also been achieved in part through a reading of various forms of (post-) phenomenology. JPi

Suggested reading
Pickles (1985).

philosophy The relationship between philosophy and GEOGRAPHY has been a long and interesting one. To provide examples from a broadly Western tradition: Strabo argued for a close and necessary relationship between moral philosophy and geographical knowledge; Sir Isaac Newton published his own editions of Varenius' *Geographia generalis* in 1672 and 1681; Immanuel Kant lectured on PHYSICAL GEOGRAPHY throughout his teaching career (1755–96); and in a 1976 interview Michel Foucault declared that geography 'must necessarily lie at the heart of my concerns'. Each of these authors had a different view of philosophy, of course, but also of geography and geographical knowledge. For Strabo, CHOROGRAPHY was to provide empirical particulars for reflection on truth, nobility and virtue (and also to underwrite Roman imperialism); Newton was interested in a mixed mathematical–spatial conception of geography; Kant's lectures were descriptive, comprising a series of observations about oceans, landforms and the weather, an outline of the plant, animal and mineral 'kingdoms', and a survey of the 'four parts of the world' (ASIA, AFRICA, EUROPE and AMERICA); and Foucault's remark arose from his forensic enquiries into the relationships between power, knowledge and space.

Historians of geography had been keenly aware of this historical itinerary – at least as far as Kant – and major studies in the history of geography (see GEOGRAPHY, HISTORY OF) paid close attention to philosophical reflections on the tangled relationships between 'culture' and NATURE, notably Glacken's landmark (1967) survey. But modern geography was slow to treat philosophy as a guide to contemporary enquiries, and interest in it was, at first, largely informal. Hartshorne's (1939) exegesis of *The nature of geography* repeatedly turned to Kant to underwrite a view of concept-formation in geography as IDIOGRAPHIC, concerned with the unique and the particular, but this was not the product of any rigorous engagement with Kant's lectures on physical geography or their place within his work as a whole, still less with KANTIANISM writ large. Even the repudiation of Hartshorne's views in the 1960s was less informed by philosophy than it was driven by the desire to reconstruct geography as a SPATIAL SCIENCE: its foundations in the philosophy of science (and in particular POSITIVISM) were not codified until Harvey's *Explanation in geography* (1969).

In contrast, the critique of spatial science and the formation of a series of successor projects undoubtedly depended on – and in several cases were directed by – explorations of different, avowedly post-positivist philosophies. Many of these approaches sought, like positivism or LOGICAL POSITIVISM, to identify a sort of central generating mechanism (see ESSENTIALISM) and to ground their knowledge claims in a bedrock of certainty (see FOUNDATIONALISM). Thus the first explorations of post-positivist philosophies in human geography typically found their anchors in the human subject, language or the mind (Gale and Olsson, 1979: see also HUMANISTIC GEOGRAPHY; PHENOMENOLOGY; STRUCTURALISM). But these are deep waters, and at the time many geographers navigated them by treating philosophy as a ready-made 'machine for explanation' through which geographical cases were to be fed (Barnes, 2008a); there was little sense of a *conversation* between philosophy and geography. Johnston's (1983) mapping of 'philosophy' on to the terrain of 'human geography' was typical in the privilege it accorded to philosophy, and it proved to be a template for other general surveys. Even Sayer's (1984) influential work, one of the most philosophically astute investigations of the period, limited PLACE and SPACE to context and circumstance; the architectonics of explanation were derived directly from the principles of critical REALISM. Pickles' (1985) careful reading of phenomenology (principally Edmund Husserl and Martin Heidegger) was almost alone in its recognition of SPATIALITY as a crucial concern of both philosophy and human geography. Olsson's (1980, 1991, 2007) imperturbable odyssey through philosophy (and beyond) not only had much to say to human geographers but also focused directly on some of the root-concepts in the field, especially since its reworking through spatial science: but it was conducted in such an exquisitely abstract register that many readers were probably lost en route. Part way through Olsson's quest, the rise of POSTMODERNISM in human geography (and across the spectrum of the humanities and social sciences) did much to distract attention from the sort of MODERNISM that informed projects like Olsson's. Postmodernism, in concert (and often in tension) with the other 'posts', POST-COLONIALISM and POST-STRUCTURALISM, brought new writers to the attention of human geography at large. Jacques Derrida and Michel Foucault were perhaps the most prominent, later followed by Giorgio Agamben, Judith Butler, Gilles Deleuze and others. But whether any of these figures could properly be limited to the field of 'philosophy' is an open question, and none of them would be comfortable with the legislative function that the other humanities and social sciences so often accorded to philosophy.

In fact, appeals to philosophy as judge and arbiter were subjected to two main criticisms. The first accepted the importance of philosophical reflection, but warned against its ideological deployment:

> At its best, the 'philosophy of geography' is that system of general ideas concerned with the direction and content of geographical work which practitioners elaborate during praxis ... At its worst, the 'philosophy of geography' is where those who have read philosophy in general and disciples of 'more advanced ideas in other disciplines' exercise ideological power over those who remain with practical concerns. (Peet, 1998, pp. 8–9)

Closely connected to this complaint is Marx's injunction, repeatedly invoked by those committed to CRITICAL HUMAN GEOGRAPHY and RADICAL GEOGRAPHY: 'Philosophers have only interpreted the world, in various ways; the point, however, is to change it.' That said, the development of various forms of MARXIST GEOGRAPHY was accompanied by an increasingly rigorous reading of philosophy: Louis Althusser's 'symptomatic' reading of Marx's texts had a limited audience in human geography, but Harvey's reworking of classical Marxism and Smith's (1984) dissection of the ligatures between CAPITALISM and UNEVEN DEVELOPMENT prompted a close engagement with a series of materialist philosophies to clarify not only questions of method but also questions of substance – see, for example, DIALECTICS, PROCESS and PRODUCTION OF SPACE – and even a 'symptomatic' reading of Harvey himself (Castree, 2006a; Castree and Gregory, 2006b; Harvey, 1996).

The second objection was, in some ways, even more radical. American philosopher Richard Rorty called for the wholesale demolition of 'Philosophy-with-a-capital-P' and its replacement by a post-philosophical culture. He was suspicious of those who thought philosophy could provide a single, canonical language into which all questions could be translated and through whose terms all disputes could be resolved. Rorty's PRAGMATISM acknowledged the creative capacities of DISCOURSE, and treated post-philosophical culture as a sort of 'cultural criticism' that claimed 'no extra-historical, Archimedean point' from which to offer its readings (cf. SITUATED KNOWLEDGE: see Barnes, 2008a). Rorty's prospectus did not provide a detailed model for post-foundational geographies, and nor was it intended to, but the discipline's more recent reactivation of philosophical reflection can be read as inviting a more open and dialogical relationship between philosophy and geography. There is clearly a considerable distance between the essays on philosophy *in* geography collected from geographers by Gale and Olsson (1979) and the essays from both fields published in *Philosophy and Geography* (2001–4).

Still more significantly, however, and closely paralleling Rorty's concerns, the renewed interest in philosophy extends far beyond philosophies of science to address political and moral philosophies. Indeed, a crucial focus of enquiry has been the entanglement of political and moral philosophies *with* the conduct of science: hence human geographers have effectively reactivated some of Glacken's (1976) most vital concerns through debates about the contemporary constitution of 'Nature' and life itself in ways that, at the limit, invite a re-mapping of the horizons of the social and the biological (Thrift, 2008: see also BARE LIFE; BIOPOLITICS; NON-REPRESENTATIONAL THEORY). Less epically, there have been investigations of COSMOPOLITANISM and ETHICS, dwelling and PLACE, involving critical reworkings of Heidegger, Derrida and Emmanuel Levinas (e.g. Barnett, 2005; Harrison, 2007b); investigations of EXCEPTION, law and violence, involving critical reworkings of Agamben and Foucault (e.g. Gregory, 2006; Minca, 2007a); and investigations of subjectivities and spatialities, involving critical re-readings of Butler and Foucault (Pratt, 2004). This list is indicative, not exhaustive, but it points to some of the ways in which philosophy is increasingly being treated as resource rather than writ, used to inform rather than police geographical enquiry. This does not dispense with the need for close, careful and contextual reading, and collections such as Crampton and Elden's (2007) multi-faceted readings of Foucault and geography show that the freedom to experiment with philosophical texts is not a license to ransack them.   DG

physical geography The characterization and explanation of geological, hydrological, biological and atmospheric phenomena and their interactions at, or near the Earth's surface. This is often, but not exclusively, in relation to human occupation and activity.

Physical geography is something of an intellectual chimera, whose role, relations and definition have changed as the nature and focus of the geographical enterprise itself have shifted. Throughout its modern history, physical geography has been implicated in most of the central debates within geography but, arguably, prospered from none. From formal beginnings in the early Victorian age through to the period between the two world wars, a credible case can be made that physical geography was geography. Physical geographers were part of the disciplinary elite, and geographical education and research necessarily began with the physical foundations of the Earth environment, as deployed in and across natural (geographical) regions. Somewhere in the inter-war period, all this changed. Geography was recast as a subject with an essential duality of character. For the greater part of the twentieth century, debates concerning either the curse or the virtue of this duality underscored geographical reflection, while in terms of geographical endeavour, it was physical geography that repeatedly lost its place as trend-setter in the changing geographical tradition. By the later twentieth century, geography had become an amorphous and disconnected enterprise, whose concerns were less with disciplinary identity, and more with following humanistic approaches. In what became a postmodern and post-paradigmatic world, multiple and contested viewpoints were new virtues, but intellectual largesse was not bestowed on physical geography, which was represented as the manifestation of an unyieldingly, restrictive and unwelcome positivism. In the new millennium, physical geography may, however, be on the verge of renaissance. Having fought something of a quiet rearguard action within the discipline, it may yet be revived from without: first, as a new class of environmental issues demand a new kind of scientific approach; and, second, as Earth systems science – physical geography by another name and from other places – moves in to meet this need.

Earlier nineteenth-century works provided apparently firm foundations for the contemporary discipline. For example:

Physical geography is a description of the earth, the sea, and the air, with their inhabitants animal and vegetable, of the distribution of these organized beings, and the causes of their distribution. (Somerville, 1849, p. 1)

Physical geography was thus a broad, inclusive body of knowledge, embracing the work of the great natural scholars such as Alexander von Humbolt and Charles Darwin, and claiming an intellectual heritage as Immanuel Kant's 'propaedentic of natural knowledge' (Huxley, 1877). Its project was that of geography as a whole. Its scope and its holism, however, became problems as early modern science sought sophistication and institutional organization (see Livingstone, 1992), and as more and more about a wide class of natural phenomena became both known and knowable (Dickinson and Howarth, 1933). Physical geography provided an elegant underpinning of classificatory schemes:

Few sciences offer better opportunities than physical geography for studying large units and grouping their various phenomena. (Emerson, 1909, p. vii)

Its virtues were repeatedly extolled in general education, and in support of emergent environmentalism (Marsh, 1965 [1864]). It was less secure, however, as a coherent intellectual enterprise, particularly as *EXPLANATION* of phenomena became the goals of science. Arnold Guyot, drawing a distinction between anatomy (description) and physiology (explanation) demanded that:

Physical geography ... ought to be, not only the description of our earth, but the physical science of the globe, or the science of the ... present life *of the globe in reference to their connection and their mutual dependence.* (Guyot, 1850, p. 3)

Here, then, were the seeds of a basic dilemma *within* physical geography, which provided the backdrop for the later schism within geography as a whole. Physical geography, in search of both scientific prowess and academic distinction, had somehow either to narrow its focus (and risk trespass on established fields – particularly geology), or make ambitious claim to unoccupied territory (which, as the century progressed, could draw on post-Darwinian biology). Its response, in the shorter term, was physiography – another pervasive term with tortuous associations – and in the longer term, a dalliance with environmental determinism and its nemesis, human ecology.

In some incarnations, physiography was physical geography in all its aspects:

Physiography is a description of the substance, form, arrangement and changes of all the real things of Nature in their relation to each other, giving prominence to comprehensive principles rather than isolated facts. (Mill, 1913, p. 3)

and having:

... a unique value in mental training, being at once an introduction to all the sciences and summing up of their results ... (Mill, 1913, p. 14)

In others, physiography was a more limited and scientifically precise component of physical geography, which had been:

... too often degraded into a sort of scientific curiosity shop, in which there is a vast collection of isolated facts ... without the slightest attempt ... to show how interdependent they are ... (Skertchly, 1878, p. 2)

Interdependence of natural kinds was a common theme in these early writings (see also Thornton, 1901) and recourse to the fundamental physical concepts of matter, work and energy (which seemed more at home under the label of physiography) was the common means by which this was treated. Indeed, the approach bore a striking resemblance to later attempts to rejuvenate physical geography through the applications of systems theory (see below).

Thomas Henry Huxley's volume of 1877 was different. Huxley had '... borrowed the title ... which had ... been long applied ... to a department of mineralogy ...'. Significantly, Huxley's purpose was to:

... draw a clear line of demarcation, both as to the matter and method, between it [physiography] and what is commonly understood by 'Physical Geography.' (Huxley, 1877, p. vi)

The grounds for this demarcation lay in the belief that physical geography had become too thoroughgoing a physical science! Huxley's project, of course, was the extension of general elementary education, and the comments reflect his disappointment that the unique educational value of physical geography had been lost in more specialist study. Despite Huxley's ambition to give a sense of place and purpose, where knowledge was grounded in the local and observational, his physiography was far from regional geography. Its content reflected such practicalities as how to find the North Pole or read a *Times* weather chart, alongside (by then) standard chapters on ice, sea, earthquakes and the sun. Notwithstanding Stoddart's (1986) attempt

to place it more centrally within geography, it probably held back, rather than promoted, the subject – albeit ahead of its time in educational terms and somewhat misunderstood. Certainly, more contemporary observers were able to label physiography as the elementary component of physical geography, and one more influenced (and limited) by concerns of relevance to human activity (Salisbury, 1907).

Later use of physiography confined it to the description of landscape, and placed it firmly within the geological tradition (Tarr, 1920). Indeed, according to Lobeck, physiography.

... should not be called physical geography, ... because the idea of the relation of life to physical environment is not within the scope of physiography. (Lobeck, 1939, p. 3)

Physiography was thus identified with geomorphology, and *both* terms became increasingly synonymous with physical geography. Davis (1899b) attempted to distinguish physiography from physical geography based upon a test of the presence or absence of 'causes and consequences' (p. iv) between environment and organic life. Physical geography made these connections; in their absence was pure landform study, or physiography as now cast. Davis rarely applied this prescription to his own work, and largely under his influence, physical geography become closely associated with regional landform description and evolution. In suggesting the test as a kind of prescription for study, he had, however, helped raise the spectre of environmental determinism, and to some, had thereby eased the passage of other areas of physical geography into a long, but ultimately blind, alley (Leighly, 1955).

Thus, while physiography allowed, as it were, greater room for manoeuvre in the jostling arena of nascent disciplines, it did nothing to clarify or confirm physical geography (or geography itself) as a coherent whole. On the one hand, physiography was a polyglot physical geography, whose project remained more ambitious than its achievements warranted. On the other, it was a specialism, related to geography around its circumference, along with the other applied sciences (Fenneman, 1919: see figure 1). So many circumferential fields of enquiry begged the question of what was at the centre. It was into this that physical geography was placed in uneasy alliance with the varying forms of regional enquiry.

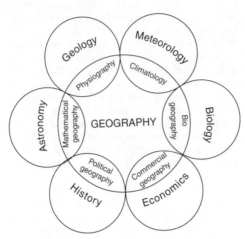

physical geography *1: The circumference of geography: '... each one of the specialized phases [spheres] of geography belongs equally to some other science ... In a loose way, the central part ... may represent regional geography'* (Fenneman, 1919, fig. 1, p. 4)

For the first half of the twentieth century, physical geography informed regional geographic enquiry. At its most obvious, physical geography provided a natural definition of regions where economic and social activity appeared adjusted to, or bounded by, the natural environment. Away from the obvious physio-climatic regions, where physical geography was merely a convenient backdrop, the degree and manner in which physical geography truly engaged the human landscape was a vexing issue. Failure to answer this satisfactorily legitimized a fundamental dualism of geography, which was never successfully reconciled. Environmental determinism ran its course rather quickly, and human ecology (Barrows, 1923) became not merely its successor, but one of the defining and prescriptive terms for geography itself (Turner, 2002). While the concern was still to find something new and unique to define the subject, there was a critical twist for physical geography, insofar as:

> I believe that the age-old subject of geography, though it has lost many specialities, still seeks to cover too much ground, and that it would benefit by frankly relinquishing physiography, climatology, plant ecology, and animal ecology. (Barrows, 1923, p. 13)

In this way, geography was not only reorientated but, with it, physical geography was

cancelled from the geographical project (for an accessible treatment of these issues, see Unwin, 1992). Physical geography was increasingly identified as a particular form of geographical activity (most frequently manifest as applied geography) rather than as a coherent intellectual field, and at best, referred to obliquely when considering the role of human–environment relations within geography as a whole.

Not all were happy with a separation of human and physical geography, of course, and displeasure or unease came from many quarters. Hartshorne (1939), for example, was at pains to draw attention to the effective elimination of physical geography, and thereby to the restriction of geography. This was not advocacy of physical geography for its own sake, but an appeal to the heritage of Humbolt and others, which held that nature was essentially unitary. Geography's mission was to disclose areal association, and *systematic study* took precedence over any particular *subject matter*. Dualism had arisen because of philosophical abstraction and a concern to study categories of phenomena in isolation (Hartshorne, 1959). Much the same sentiments were expressed by physical geographers such as Miller or Wooldridge, who maintained a belief in the foundational role of physical geography for regional study, even where connections were subtle or unclear:

> ... to hurry on content with a few shallow remarks based on perfunctory observation of the physical elements of the environment may result in overlooking or falsifying the natural intimacy of relation that nearly always exists between the physical and the cultural landscape. (Miller, 1953, p. 196)

Such convictions, although deeply situated, were rarely compellingly demonstrated, and the prevailing view of geography was one of numerous separate branches, united only in the far distant past (figure 2). Moreover, the very appeals to unity based upon identification or prescription of some essential property of geographical analysis may have contributed to the overshadowing of physical geography, both within geography and in relation to the other environmental sciences (Leighly, 1955). Leighly argued, very simply, that geographical study of *any* Earth surface phenomenon could be justified not for its own sake (as often misrepresented) but *because* its existence *in* place gave it legitimacy as the subject of geographical enquiry. By contrast, a physical geography that required a more complex geographical

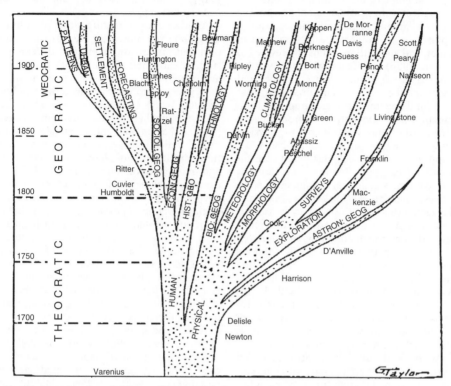

physical geography   *2: The ramifications of modern geography since 1700* (Taylor, 1953, fig. 1, p. 4)

justification for its material and methods hampered progress in achieving *scientific engagement* with the environment. This kind of physical geography (founded *either* in the disclosure of spatial associations or in the examination of human–environment relations – the contested identities of the subject: Turner, 2002) demanded a vocabulary and style of enquiry adapted to the scale and scope of landscape and regional study, which set it far apart from the other sciences, and which, throughout the latter half of the twentieth century, did not seem relevant to their increasingly reductionist methodologies.

As regionalism itself receded from the geographical stage, the role and relations of physical geography were once more examined. By this time, climatology, geomorphology and ecology were all well advanced separately, and without areal relations as a touchstone, there were uncomfortable parallels with the identity crisis of earlier generations:

It is clear that physical geography, however much it overlaps with the earth sciences, must be distinguished from disciplines which study terrestrial phenomena for their own sake, irrespective of their relevance to the spatial characterisation of man's occupancy and exploitation ... (Chorley, 1971, p. 95)

For Chorley, there were several ways forward for physical geography to avoid increasing divergence within geography and to ensure 'relevance' to science and society beyond: common application of techniques and methods (model-building and increasingly, GIS); study of resources and development; and (general) systems theory (GST), in large part adapted from Ludwig von Bertalanffy (a biologist). Of these, only the last topic was new, and for Chorley, it was only this that provided a truly integrating concept and a widely transferable approach:

... systems can be visualised as three-dimensional structures in which the very complicated flows and relationships forming the socio-economic spatial decision-making systems interpenetrate the physical process-response systems ... (ibid., p. 22)

Chorley attempted, for a modern generation, to reconnect (physical) geography with the integrative strands of natural science, and to recapture for the subject the high ground of ambition and application (brilliantly revived in Stoddart, 1986). GST was the best way to date of *representing* those elusive linkages and connections (i.e. patterns and processes) that were fundamental to geography from Victorian times. The systems approach transferred readily, and enduringly, to physical geography (see Chorley and Kennedy, 1971), but appeared overly mechanistic and control-orientated (see, e.g., Bennett and Chorley, 1978), with the ascendancy of humanistic perspectives. There quickly followed a time when, as Haggett (1990, p. 152) put it, consensus around a common nature of areal differentiation and common methodology evaporated as *human* geography was 'Cut-off from its older geographical roots ...' and drifted towards the social sciences.

Aside from the overt concerns with disciplinary definitions and coherence, the mid-to-late twentieth century was not devoid of important substantive scholarly, as well as practical achievements by physical geographers. With hindsight, these also provided important points of attachment with contemporary scientific and environmental agendas. Barry and Chorley (1968), for example, helped to keep alive synoptic climatology as a foundational strand of physical geographical study, and their book was followed by more technically and scientifically challenging texts such as Oke's on boundary layer climates (1978), and Henderson-Sellers' and McGuffie's (1989) early contribution to climatic modelling. All of these are now considered 'classics' and have run into multiple editions. With respect to climatic history, substantiating the character and scale of natural environmental change was arguably one of physical geography's greatest achievements in this period. Contributions by physical geographers remain fundamental to the sub-discipline of Quaternary studies (see Goudie, 1977, and its numerous editions for review). The traditional emphasis on human–environmental interaction was also not forgotten, with physical geographers and physical geography very well represented in the landmark text, *Man's role in changing the face of the Earth* (Thomas, 1956), and in its successors such as Manners and Mikeswell (1974) and Goudie (1981). (This latter volume offers a very accessible synthesis of the diverse geographical and non-geographical literature in its several newer editions.)

Another strong manifestation of physical geography in the later twentieth century occurred in environment and development studies, with the fusion of political–economic analysis and scientific–technical environmental expertise into what is now termed political ecology. Works by Blaikie (1985) and Blaikie and Brookfield (1987) are paradigmatic exemplars, and again offer enhanced valence with a much wider (geographical) literature and through the study of globalization, economics and uneven development. In the USA, for example, Butzer (2002) places concern for environment and development at the heart of a reinvigoration of physical geography that has been able to shape and enact globally significant agendas outside, as well as within academic circles. A good example of this is the CONSERVATION and ENVIRONMENTAL MOVEMENT, where physical geographers have been central in charting its origins and changing characteristics, and in defining and popularizing new directions – see, for example, the very different perspectives offered by Grove (1995), Pepper (1996) and Adams (2004).

Returning to a disciplinary theme, by the 1990s, geography inhabited a post-paradigmatic world (Abler, Marcus and Olson, 1992) and there seemed renewed possibilities to revisit older themes and once more to look for disciplinary coherence, if not unity. Indeed, physical geography was itself punctuated by a series of debates examining post-positivist EPISTEMOLOGIES (notably REALISM) and hence ONTOLOGICAL depth (Rhoads and Thorne, 1996). Both it and human geography might thus visit intellectual territory, if not with common purpose, then jointly armed with methodological and philosophical sophistication. There are, too, signs of more awareness of the role of physical geography and physical geographers in defining and progressing the discipline as a whole (Matthews and Herbert, 2004).

Outside the discipline, there are strong imperatives for the repositioning of academic approaches favourable to, if not reliant upon, physical geography. Systems approaches are being revisited across many disciplines, with a deeper theoretical perspective and the enhanced vocabulary of 'complexity studies' (see COMPLEXITY THEORY). Environmental debate increasingly identifies an essential linkage between science, ethics and sustainability, which necessitates both mechanistic and humanistic modes of analysis (Nordgren,

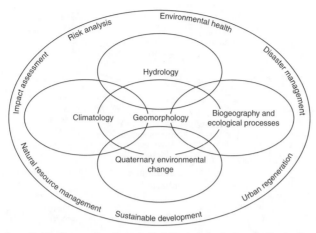

physical geography   3: *The five overlapping sub-disciplines of physical geography in the context of multidisciplinary and problem-orientated themes* (Gregory, 2005c, fig. 2, p. 83)

1997). Academic subjects are reordering, with inter- and trans-disciplinarity not merely becoming fashionable but seen as prerequisites to tackle more complex environmental and societal issues (see especially the concept and consequences of hybridity – Whatmore, 2002a). In this climate, it would seem obvious that:

> ... widening the existing divide would be a tragic mistake that would weaken the discipline at a time when ... society needs a synthetic, coherent view of how humanity uses and abuses the physical environment ... (Abler, Marcus and Olson, 1992, p. 397)

Gregory (2005c), in perhaps the most comprehensive evaluation of the recent scope and history of physical geography, provides a welter of optimistic scenarios for its engagement to this task (see figure 3).

The recent identification of sustainability science (Kates, Clark, Corell et al., 2001) is a clear example of physical geography being used to identify and coordinate trans-discplinary agendas that respond to large-scale, complex and hybrid environment–society–development issues. The growing ability of GIS to move from the realms of a research technology to practical application, particularly when used in tandem with a vastly increased information flow from a variety of remote platforms spanning observations of the human and biophysical world, would also seem to make the case for the renewed prospering of physical geography a compelling one. Nonetheless, there are warning signals,

for while Gregory reiterates one of those critical attributes defining physical geography, whose purpose:

> ... is to understand how the Earth's physical environment is the basis for and is affected by human activity. (Gregory, 2005, p. xxvii)

It is this emphasis that over a long period, has so divided and, paradoxically, often downgraded the subject outside particular 'applied' studies. Expectations are raised, to be disappointed in the follow-through. Crucially, the new millennium is a time when physical geography conducted on the margins of, or away from, the geographical arena is very strong. A new scientific network devoted to Earth systems science has developed, which claims the same human–environment agenda, and that may be better placed to take advantage of wider intellectual and analytical advances, and to fulfil societal needs (Pitman, 2005). The natural claims of physical geography to privilege as an environmental discipline thus need to show an added value that transcends that derived from the collected expertise of others. It is, for example, quite possible to view physical (and environmental) geography) as smaller components in a very broad, holistic science–environment framework that claims much of the same intellectual heritage and rationale as geography itself (see figure 4).

Once more, then, the hunt is on for a distinctive way forward, and for a more robust means of integrating physical geography into geography and science as a whole.   NJC

537

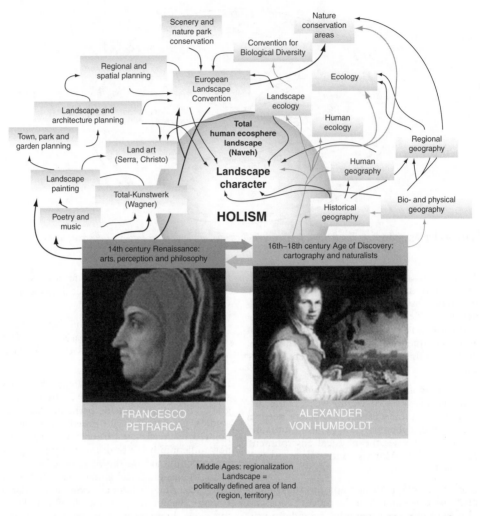

physical geography *4: The relations between landscape, conservation, geography and landscape ecology* (Wascher, 2005)

Suggested reading
Chorley (1971); Fenneman (1919); Gregory (2005), which includes a reprint of Chorley (1971); Pitman (2005); Rhoads and Thorne (1996); Turner (2002) and subsequent discussions.

Pirenne thesis A MODEL of the relations between international TRADE and URBANIZATION in post-Roman and medieval EUROPE, proposed by the Belgian historian Henri Pirenne (1862–1935) (Pirenne, 1925, 2001 [1937]). The fall of the Roman Empire in AD 476 produced a politico-military crisis, but

Pirenne argued that the major *economic* shock to the urban system came much later, from the Islamic conquest of the eastern Mediterranean and North Africa, Sicily and southern Spain (*al-Andalus*) in the eighth century. Long-distance Mediterranean trade was cut 'with the elemental force of a cosmic cataclysm', and the urban foundations of Europe crumbled as it was 'forced to live by its own resources'. Europe fractured into a series of cellular, insular regions. It was not until the tenth and eleventh centuries, so Pirenne claimed, after the Christian *Reconquista* in Spain and the military campaigns of the Crusades, that commercial recovery revived the fortunes of cities: 'Just as the trade of the west disappeared with the shutting off of its foreign markets, just so it was renewed when these markets were re-opened.' Merchants led the urban revival, spearheaded by cities in the south (especially Venice) and on the North Atlantic coast (Bruges), where they settled in grey zones close to but outside former, pre-urban fortified enclaves: the *faubourg* or *portus*.

Later work has used archaeological, numismatic and textual sources to show that the Mediterranean remained a practicable trade route throughout this period, however, though activity was concentrated in the more secure central zones, and that trade was also vigorous along the Atlantic and Baltic coasts. Still more arrestingly, McCormick (2001) argued that communications between the Frankish empire and the eastern Mediterranean surged in the final decades of the eight and ninth centuries, so that Islam did not so much 'apply the *coup de grâce* to a moribund late Roman system' as offer 'the wealth and markets which would fire the first rise of Europe' and its commercial economy (see also Hodges and Whitehouse, 1981). It is now also clear that towns 'of unambiguously commercial character' grew in north-west Europe from the seventh and multiplied in the eight and ninth centuries, with important implications for both geographies of local and long-distance trade and the role of merchants in shaping urban MORPHOLOGY (see Verhulst, 1999). DG

Suggested reading
Hodges and Whitehouse (1983); Verhulst (1989).

pixel The term 'pixel' is a corrupted abbreviation of picture element – the individual elements arranged in columns and rows to form a rectangular, composite image. For example, a 1980s VGA (Video Graphics Array) monitor had a maximum resolution of 640×480 pixels (with 16 colours), whereas a modern Super VGA monitor can have $1,024 \times 768$ pixels (and 16,777,216 colours!). Raising the number of pixels per fixed area increases the resolution of an image, but also the amount of information to be processed and stored. Consequently, RASTER images are often compressed, as are digital photographs (as JPEGs) and DVD frames (using MPEG2). RH

place In a generic sense, a place is a geographical locale of any size or configuration, comparable to equally generic meanings of AREA, REGION or LOCATION. In HUMAN GEOGRAPHY and the HUMANITIES more generally, however, place is often attributed with greater significance (cf. LANDSCAPE). It is sometimes defined as a human-wrought transformation of a part of the Earth's surface or of pre-existing, undifferentiated SPACE. It is usually distinguished by the cultural or subjective meanings through which it is constructed and differentiated, and is understood by most human geographers to be in an incessant state of 'becoming' (Pred, 1984). Place is a central concept in human geography in general and in CULTURAL GEOGRAPHY in particular, but there has also been renewed interest in the concept in ECONOMIC GEOGRAPHY, where it stands for the necessity of economic processes to be grounded in specific locales and for those locales to be proactive competitors within the global ECONOMY (Massey, 1984; Harvey, 1989b). For many geographers, place and the differences between places are the very stuff of GEOGRAPHY, the raw materials that give the discipline its warrant (cf. AREAL DIFFERENTIATION). But the potential interchangeability of place with other concepts is a sticking point. Place, region, area and so on all *can* denote a unit of space that has discrete boundaries, shared internal characteristics, and that changes over time and interacts with other similar units. What then makes place a distinctive concept? There are three arenas of discussion of special interest:

(1) *The idea that place, to be a place, necessarily has meaning.* Although there are glimmers of this idea throughout the HISTORY OF GEOGRAPHY, it grew in popularity in the modern discipline with the rise of HUMANISTIC GEOGRAPHY. Tuan (1977), Relph (1976) and a host of others approached place as a subjectively sensed and experienced phenomenon. Often taking their inspiration from PHENOMENOLOGY, humanistic geographers regarded place as not only the phenomenological ground for geography but also an irreducible component of human experience, without which human experience itself could not be constituted and interpreted. Such experiences included perceptions of place, senses of place and human dwelling in and memories of place (see ENVIRONMENTAL PERCEPTION; MEMORY). These were understood to be formative of the unique experiences of individuals, while also

being specific to different cultures. Places themselves were understood as unique, meaningful material constructions that reflected and articulated cultural perceptions and habits. With the rise of FEMINIST GEOGRAPHIES and a 'new' cultural geography in the 1980s, place was understood less through the notion of a self-adequate, intentional human SUBJECT and more through the lens of POWER-laden social relations through which human subjects were at once constituted and de-centred. That is, subjects were not understood as authors of their own intentions and meanings, but as bearers of social IDENTITIES that they did not themselves create. Place meanings came to be seen as specific to particular racial and gender-, sexual- and class-based identities (e.g. Keith and Pile, 1993; McDowell, 1997b). (This was part and parcel of the changing meanings of CULTURE in geography.) At the same time, meaning itself was cast in a new light, being viewed as much less self-evident than before. Particular attention was given to how places are represented in different cultural forms (e.g. ART, FILM, LITERATURE, MAPS), which themselves were given over to specific social uses within power-laden fields of activity (e.g. Duncan and Ley, 1993). But meaning was understood to be controlled neither by its producers nor by its consumers. Meaning had no ultimate locus: it was understood to be contestable and alterable at each point of dissemination. Another important stream of place as meaning-filled sees place as a concept that helps mark the distinction between social order/disorder, the proper/improper and so on. Place in this regard is inextricable from imposed/internalized social and cultural rules that dictate what belongs where. It denotes the (alterable) state of belonging versus exclusion, as suggested by the expression that something or someone is 'in place' or 'out of place' (Creswell, 2004) (see also HETEROTOPIA).

(2) *Place as becoming locale.* Temporal change as a constituent feature of place has long been accepted, particularly in cultural-historical geographies. It is an unexceptional (yet at times politically charged) statement that places do not remain the same. Instead, place is continually emergent. This has meant various things. It has meant that place involves a transformation of some kind; for example, the transformation of a non-human element (the physical environment) by human beings into a HYBRID of culture and nature (see CULTURAL LANDSCAPE). A different kind of transformation often spoken of is the transformation from space to place. The introduction of the notion of the PRODUCTION OF SPACE has made the space and place opposition difficult to sustain, however, as it seems to render place largely as a particular moment within produced space. More recently, the emergence of place has been understood as wrought through a process of immanence. In this sense, place is not derived from something else (as place from space); it is, rather, an always-already ongoing ASSEMBLAGE of geographically associated, ONTOLOGICALLY co-constitutive elements and relationships. (Space, one might say, is fully saturated with place.) This idea of place builds upon STRUCTURATION THEORY (e.g. Pred, 1984) and, later, on NONREPRESENTATIONAL THEORY and on the monistic thought of Gilles Deleuze and other theorists of immanence (Hetherington, 1997a; Thrift, 1999a).

(3) *The de-centred, global sense of place.* Recently, geographers and others have taken up the question of whether GLOBALIZATION has eliminated place as a social-spatial reality (in much the same way that globalization is claimed to have brought about the 'death of distance' and, still more apocalyptically, 'the end of geography'), and whether places are degenerating into 'NON-PLACES' under the signs of late MODERNITY (see also PLACELESSNESS). There seems to be broad agreement that place does still matter, and that it would be wrong to see place and globalization as negating one another. For example, places/locales continue as salient features of a globalizing economy that is still marked by the production of differences through a constitutive process of UNEVEN DEVELOPMENT. Also interesting is the way in which some geographers, notably Massey (1991), have promulgated an idea of place that takes the notion of global interconnection as a *precondition* for place or sense of place. For Massey, place is not constituted by what is internal to it, but by its distinct lines of

connection to other parts of the world. One place is different from another on the basis of its relations to the outside. This effectively renders the distinction between 'inside' and 'outside' moot. Massey's 'global sense of place' has the added virtue of a politics that looks towards the outside rather than towards a defensive localism on the basis of embattled, threatened traditions. Her sense of place nonetheless leaves open the question of whether to construe places as centres of some kind, even if only as meeting places of lines of global connectivity. Hetherington (1997), drawing upon ACTOR-NETWORK THEORY, advocates somewhat differently for place as an 'ordering process' of diffuse but connected *placings*, through which a NETWORK of potentially far flung sites are enrolled into relationship with each other. (See also CONTRAPUNTAL GEOGRAPHIES.)   GHe

Suggested reading
Cresswell (2004); Hetherington (1997a).

place-names Attaching a name to a PLACE is a way of differentiating one place from another, but place-names are more than markers in a system of differences: they are also ways of staking some sort of claim (often of rule, domination or possession) and, as such, are frequently sites of contestation. The two spatial registers, linguistic and social, are intimately connected (cf. Pred, 1990).

In HISTORICAL GEOGRAPHY, especially in EUROPE, the study of place-names or *toponyms* is a philological discipline based principally on written evidence revealing early spellings of names. Such studies have often been used to make inferences about settlement history and LANDSCAPE evolution, and have also attracted considerable controversy. Thus for Britain it was once claimed that pagan names and settlements with the element *-ingas* (e.g. Hastings) denoted the very earliest Anglo-Saxon settlement, while *-ingaham* (e.g. Birmingham) represented the next stage of settlement, and the numerous instances of *x's tun* names (e.g. Edgbaston: Ecgbald's *tun*) marked a later establishment (Gelling, 1997). Adherents to these views also believed in the so-called 'clean sweep' theory, which asserts that the Anglo-Saxons were the originators of English landscapes, since a wholesale disappearance of Celtic place-names in the eastern counties denoted a land area devoid of settlers and

settlements (cf. SETTLEMENT CONTINUITY). Almost all of these claims have been rejected in the past 40 years. The main objection is that *-ingas* and *-ingaham* place-names coincide with early Anglo Saxon archaeological remains about as little as possible, given that both occur in substantial numbers in south and east England (Dodgson, 1966). Furthermore, there are great difficulties consistently distinguishing *ham* meaning 'village' from *hamm* meaning 'land in a river bend', probably dry ground in a marsh, which opens up the possibility of mistaking topographical and habitative meanings (Dodgson, 1973). However, it is recognized that if there is one nominative form more frequently associated with the early Anglo-Saxon settlers than any other it is the topographical name. It is now supposed that *-tun* is associated with manorialization, when society was organized in a more sophisticated manner with the establishment of the powerful institutions of kingship. A stronger continuity of Celtic populations is suggested by work charting the incidence of the word *walh*, which is supposed to establish the presence of substantial Welsh-speaking populations (Cameron, 1980). Studies of Scandinavian names have, however, produced greater consensus and led to some successful integrations of philological, archaeological and landscape history. These studies consistently suggest that the Danish-named villages were located in the least desirable locations from an ecological and agricultural perspective, and imply that the victorious Danes were a militarily smaller group than once claimed and did not take over or absorb pre-existing English settlements (Fellows-Jensen, 1975).

The modern world has by no means been insensitive to the histories carried in solution in place-names. Beyond Europe, and sometimes within, COLONIALISM and IMPERIALISM exercised the power to impose new names on the landscape: naming a place coincided with the taking of place. Although the practice continues – as in Israel's colonization and settlement of Gaza and the West Bank under its military occupation (see OCCUPATION, MILITARY: Cohen and Kliot, 1992) – subject populations do not passively adopt the new nomenclatures. Indeed, the POST-COLONIAL period has usually been marked by the recovery or invention of place-names that register a pre-colonial history and an indigenous culture (Herman, 1999; Nash, 1999). Thus, for example, Salisbury, the capital of the British colony of Rhodesia, was named after a British Prime Minister, but in 1981 it became Harare, the capital of the newly independent state of Zimbabwe. Many states have attempted to fix place-names through the institution of national committees, such as the South African Geographical Names Council or the United States Board on Geographic Names (a federal institution supported by a network of committees in individual states). MODERNITY is as much an economic as it is a political project, and it is scarcely surprising that place-names have come to function not only as markers of national or cultural IDENTITY, but also as sites of commodification. A place-name, through its association with a particular regional expertise, may thus become a bearer of value for a COMMODITY (cf. INTELLECTUAL PROPERTY RIGHTS). For this reason, the European Union has attempted to regulate the attribution of regional place-names to FOOD (e.g. Roquefort cheese) and wine (e.g. Beaujolais) through a LAW on 'protected geographical indications': despite bilateral agreements, however, it has proved difficult to enforce these restrictions and protections outside the EU. In this sphere, as in so many others, place-names continue to mark sites of struggle in the present as they did in the past.   DG/RMS

Suggested reading
Gelling (1997); Nash (1999); Pred (1990, pp. 92–142).

placelessness If by one definition PLACE represents a 'fusion' of human and natural worlds that become 'significant centers of our immediate experiences' and make it possible to live authentic, original and meaning-filled lives, then placelessness represents its antithesis (Relph, 1976, p. 141). It 'describes both an environment without significant places and the underlying attitude which does not acknowledge significance of places' (Relph, 1976, p. 143). Relph devised the concept as an object of critique in a treatise that became a key text in HUMANISTIC GEOGRAPHY, particularly in those versions that were inspired by PHENOMENOLOGY. Placelessness is said to result from the tyranny of 'technique', efficiency, interchangeability and replicability, in the design and construction of the human LANDSCAPE. It is evident everywhere from suburban houses and shopping centres to tourist attractions, restaurant chains and airports. In this sense, placelessness is a distinctly modern phenomenon that is all of a piece with the rise of mass culture, mass communication, multinational corporations and overweening central governments (see also ALIENATION; MODERNITY; POSTMODERNITY).

The concept of placelessness is not without controversy. The kinds of 'places' it names (suburbs, shopping strips, tourist sites and so on) have been viewed more tolerantly, even affectionately, by students of popular and vernacular CULTURE, especially in the USA, as evinced by the writings of J.B. Jackson and his students (e.g. Jackson, 1970; Wilson and Groth, 2003). They claim an important distinction between the crass imposition of bureaucratic planning, on the one hand, and culturally original solutions to the spatial problems of everyday life, on the other. Moreover, they see in these inventive responses (not all of them 'good', but none so destructive as to undo place *as such*) a great deal of popular meaning and symbolism. More recently, geographers who study the CONSUMPTION of mass goods, including clothing, food and shelter, have argued that production does not determine consumption: thus places produced with one set of uses in mind can be claimed and hence consumed by people for quite other, often resistant, purposes (e.g. Gregson and Crewe, 2003). Placelessness has also been argued to be a necessary and important resource for the exercise of marginalized and oppressed sexual IDENTITIES, a realm of relative freedom, liberation and anonymity versus the constraints imposed by otherwise ordered places (see Knopp, 2004) (cf. HETEROTOPIA).   GHe

plantation The meaning of the term 'plantation' has changed over time. Originally a plot of ground with trees, it came to mean a group of settlers or their political units during British overseas expansion (e.g. the Ulster Plantation; see COLONIALISM). Later, 'plantation' came to mean a large farm or landed estate, especially one associated with tropical or subtropical production of 'classical' plantation crops such as sugar, coffee, tobacco, tea, cocoa, bananas, spices, cotton, sisal, rubber and palm oil (Thompson, 1975b: see FARMING). Most plantations combined an agricultural with an industrial process but technologies, labour processes, property rights and INFRASTRUCTURE have varied enormously across space and time, making a generic definition of plantation impossible (see AGRIBUSINESS). Plantations have witnessed historical transformations in labour relations between slave, feudal, migratory, indentured and free wage labour, and many plantations in LATIN AMERICA operated on a mixture of these labour forms (see LABOUR PROCESS; SLAVERY).

All definitions of plantation tend to differentiate it from other agricultural forms of production by size, authority structure, crop or labour force characteristics (low skills, work gangs, various forms of servility). The theory of plantations has had a long lineage that can be traced back to David Ricardo and John Stuart Mill in the nineteenth century through to H.J. Nieboer and Edgar Thompson in the twentieth. An important distinction has been made between old- and new-style plantations, in which the former (e.g. the *hacienda* in Central America) were essentially pre-capitalist, with surpluses directed at conspicuous consumption, while the latter were capitalist enterprises driven by the rigours of capitalist ACCUMULATION (see CAPITALISM; FEUDALISM; MARKET).

Recent work has seen plantations as 'totalizing institutions' whose historical connections with RACISM and SLAVERY have fundamentally shaped entire social and political structures (as in the Caribbean and the US South), but have also acted as powerful agents of UNDERDEVELOPMENT (Tomich, 2004; Edelson, 2006; Pons, 2007). Plantations and plantation economies and societies cannot be understood in the terms of the narrow logic of production of the enterprise alone, however. The enormously diverse forms and circumstances in which the plantation has persisted and transformed itself must be rooted in the historical forms and rhythms of capitalist accumulation under specific land, labour and capital markets.   MW

pluralism A term with more than a single distinct meaning in HUMAN GEOGRAPHY and the social sciences:

(1) In SOCIAL and CULTURAL GEOGRAPHY, anthropology and cultural studies, the term is invoked to describe a condition of societal diversity, usually (though not necessarily) along ethnic lines. In such uses, cultural pluralism can become synonymous with MULTICULTURALISM, and features prominently in discussions of the management of diversity – for example, the achievement of social cohesion in the states of the new EUROPE (Amin, 2004a). Such pluralism is usually regarded as malleable, and subject over time to the conforming forces of ASSIMILATION.

(2) More specifically, plural societies are the outcome of European COLONIALISM in the tropics, where, according to the writings of J.S. Furnivall (1948), a distinct society emerged of indigenous and marginalized labourers, Asian merchants and European elites, and where POWER was commonly held in inverse proportion to group size. Furnivall's initial work in South-East Asia was extended to the Caribbean islands by M.G. Smith, and influenced a number of studies by social geographers (Clarke, Ley and Peach, 1984). The sense of these studies is that stratification is more rigid, sustaining intergenerational divisions well into the POST-COLONIAL period.

(3) In political decision-making, 'pluralism' refers to a thesis associated with Robert Dahl concerning the mobility of power in modern DEMOCRACIES among defined interest groups. CONFLICTS are temporary rather than structural and may be addressed pragmatically, with elections forming the final court of arbitration. This optimistic thesis of self-governing checks and balances in the political arena has received sharp criticism, and has been superseded in the urban context in which it was first formulated by studies of growth coalitions (Jonas and Wilson, 1999) that revive the earlier elite theory that Dahl set out to undercut.   DL

point pattern analysis Point pattern analysis involves looking for geographical patterns in data sets that have point (*x*, *y*) GEOCODING given National Grid References, for example, of where a geographical phenomenon exists or takes place. A pattern is said to occur if the locations of the geographical feature or event are non-randomly distributed across a study REGION, meaning that they are either clustered into particular places or evenly spaced across the same.

A simple way to find patterns in point data is to plot their locations on a MAP. Reference is often made to the physician and epidemiologist John Snow, whose map of the distribution of deaths from the 1848 cholera epidemic in London provides an appealing allegory about how processes (the transmission of disease) create geographical patterns (a concentration of deaths around a water pump in Broad Street, Soho) which, when revealed (by mapping), suggest new information about how those patterns were caused (the discovery that cholera is a water-borne disease: see MEDICAL GEOGRAPHY). Whilst this popular telling is part fable – the map was not actually present in Snow's original work – the element of myth says something useful about the nature of point pattern analysis, offering an important caveat to the otherwise undoubted value of maps in supporting geographical enquiry and knowledge discovery. Shaw, Dorling and Shaw (2002) demonstrate that had Snow extended his map to include all of London, then a greater concentration of deaths would have been found south of the Thames (Soho is north of the river). Snow's map is a RHETORICAL device – centred on a particular pump in London to illustrate his pre-existing finding that cholera is harboured by polluted water. The general problem is that maps can be created for very deliberate purposes and the eye can find (or be led to find) apparent patterns that are not necessarily validated by the data.

Point patterns are therefore verified analytically against the usual statistical benchmark by asking 'Could we expect this by chance?' QUADRAT ANALYSIS overlays a RASTER grid on the study region to compare the incidence rate in each cell against the average for all. Other methods of cluster detection include calculating the distance from events to either their nearest neighbour (the earliest form of pattern analysis within quantitative geography, linked to testing hypotheses derived from CENTRAL PLACE THEORY) or to other events in the study region, and also the GEOGRAPHICAL ANALYSIS MACHINE. Assessing the significance of the patterns can use probability theory or, in an era of GEOCOMPUTATION, use random redistributions of the data to simulate the effects of geography (controlling for the fact that it is hardly surprising to find more of an event in a particular part of a study region if more people live there).

As well as in EPIDEMIOLOGY, point pattern analyses are used in environmental and CRIME mapping (Chainey and Ratcliffe, 2005), supported by a range of software that include GEOGRAPHIC INFORMATION SYSTEMS, GeoDa (Anselin, Syabri and Kho, 2006) and CrimeStat (Levine, 2006). As examples of LOCAL STATISTICS, the geographical principles of these analyses can be extended to use predictor variables to help explain what is found (see, e.g., GEOGRAPHICALLY WEIGHTED REGRESSION and the GEOGRAPHICAL EXPLANATIONS MACHINE). RH

Suggested reading
O'Sullivan and Unwin (2002); Wong and Lee (2005).

Poisson regression models These models belong to the family of techniques for CATEGORICAL DATA ANALYSIS. They are used when the response variable in a REGRESSION-like format is a count (e.g. the number of crimes in an area) and the researcher wants to relate this to other area characteristics. The nature of this response variable, which cannot be negative, means that the standard regression model should not be used. Instead, the natural log of the count is modelled and its random part takes on a Poisson distribution so that the stochastic variation (see STOCHASTIC PROCESS) around the underlying relationship has a variance constrained to be equal to the mean. The Poisson distribution is also used in LOG-LINEAR MODELLING for the analysis of multiway cross-tabulations. If the distribution of the count (having taken account of the predictor variables) has marked positive skew so that the variance of the residuals exceeds the mean, an overdispersed Poisson or Negative Binomial model is needed. An example of such a model is when hospital length of stay is the response; while the typical stay is a few days, some individuals may experience a stay of several months. The MULTI-LEVEL Poisson MODEL can accommodate spatial random effects.

An important use of Poisson regression is as part of a model-based approach to DISEASE mapping, as the Standardized Mortality Ratio is the ratio of observed count to an expected count. In the model, the log of the observed count is regressed on the log of the expected count and other predictor variables, with the coefficient associated with the expected count being treated as an offset, constrained to 1. Another important area of application is the calibration of SPATIAL INTERACTION models in which the response is the log of the number of FLOWS between areas. Guy (1987) shows how the Poisson model can be used to estimate quite complex models, including attraction and destination constraints. KJ

Suggested reading
Griffith (2006); Griffith and Haining (2006).

policing At the most general level, policing refers to practices aimed at the regulation and control of a society and its members, especially with respect to matters of HEALTH, order, LAW and safety. More specifically, policing refers to the actions of those agents of the government equipped with coercive POWER to enforce law and maintain order. Amongst the key expectations of police officers is that they will work to reduce the incidence and severity of CRIME through SURVEILLANCE and arrest. Policing is thus the first stage in a criminal process that can lead to conviction and punishment.

Most research on policing in geography focuses on the legal, bureaucratic and cultural

structures that shape the geographical imaginations (see also GEOGRAPHICAL IMAGINATION)
and tactics of police officers. This work is
largely ETHNOGRAPHIC, and emphasizes the
geographical routines through which the
police engage their work (Fyfe, 1992) and
their interest in securing territorial control
(Herbert, 1997; see TERRITORY). This research
shows that the nature of such territorial
actions by officers is strongly conditioned by
their prior definition of the spaces in which
they are operating. For instance, police construct 'no-go areas' (Keith, 1993) or 'anti-
police areas' (Herbert, 1997), places where
histories of CONFLICT with minorities cause
officers to engage in either avoidance or
heavy-handed tactics.

In recent years, police agencies have
embraced geographical techniques to isolate
and target specific locations of ongoing criminal activity, so-called 'hot spots'. Through reliance on GEOGRAPHIC INFORMATION SYSTEMS,
police departments seek to determine where
crime is perpetuated and to mobilize intensive
enforcement to reduce it. Evidence suggests
that these tactics can be successful in reducing
crime at particular places. However, such operations are expensive to conduct, and may serve
merely to displace crime to other LOCALES.

Other research on policing seeks to situate it
within broader POWER structures of the STATE
and state–SOCIETY relations. Notable here is
work on COMMUNITY policing, a contemporary
reform movement meant to increase co-
operation between officers and citizens.
Observations of community policing in action
demonstrates how officers retain authority in
defining problems and constructing solutions
(Saunders, 1999; Herbert, 2006). Research
also focuses on the blurring of the lines
between military and police in the growth of
the 'SECURITY forces'.

Analyses of policing outside the specific
context of uniformed agents of coercive state
power largely occur in the context of discussions of GOVERNMENTALITY. This refers to the
processes through which individuals and
groups are encouraged to assume responsibility for their own welfare and control. Such
'self-help' actions as creating defensible
spaces, forming neighbourhood watch groups,
and employing private security represent
instances where policing is presumed to
extend beyond the sole province of the state.
This devolution of police authority is often
criticized for exacerbating CLASS-based differences; wealthier individuals and communities
can more easily protect themselves and their

property, and thereby preserve their social
standing.   SKH

Suggested reading
Fyfe (1992); Herbert (1997).

political ecology An approach to, but far
from a coherent THEORY of, the complex metabolism between NATURE and SOCIETY (see Blaikie,
1985; Blaikie and Brookfield, 1987). The
expression itself emerged in the 1970s in a variety of intellectual contexts – employed by the
journalist Alex Cockburn, the anthropologist
Eric Wolf and the environmental scientist
Graheme Beakhurst – as a somewhat inchoate
covering term for the panoply of ways in which
environmental concerns were politicized in the
wake of the environmentalist wave that broke in
the late 1960s and early 1970s (see ENVIRON-
MENTAL MOVEMENT). In its academic, and specifically geographical, usage, political ecology
has a longer and more complex provenance –
which both hearkens back to HUMAN and CUL-
TURAL ECOLOGY, and to an earlier history of relations between Anthropology and GEOGRAPHY in
the 1940s and 1950s, and incorporates a more
recent synthetic and analytical deployment in
the early 1980s associated with the work of
Piers Blaikie (1985), Michael Watts (1983a,
1986), and Suzanna Hecht (1985). In the
1990s the core empirical concerns of political
ecology – largely rural, agrarian and THIRD
WORLD – were properly expanded, and the theoretical horizons have deepened the original
concerns with the dynamics of RESOURCE
MANAGEMENT (see Peluso, 1992; Zimmerer,
1997; Neumann, 1999). Political ecology has
also splintered into a more complex field of
political ecologies, which embraces ENVIRON-
MENTAL HISTORY (Grove, 1995), SCIENCE
STUDIES (Demeritt, 1998), ACTOR-NETWORK THE-
ORY (Braun and Castree, 1998), GENDER theory
(Agrawal, 1998: cf. FEMINIST GEOGRAPHIES; GEN-
DER; GENDER AND DEVELOPMENT), DISCOURSE
ANALYSIS (Escobar, 1995) and a reinvigorated
MARXISM (O'Connor, 1998; Leff, 1995; cf.
MARXIST GEOGRAPHY).

Two geographical monographs – *The political economy of soil erosion* (1985) by Piers
Blaikie and *Land degradation and society*
(1987), edited by Harold Brookfield and
Piers Blaikie – provided the intellectual and
theoretical foundation stones for the formalization of political ecology as such. What
Blaikie achieved in *The political economy of soil
erosion* was to systematize the growing confluence between three theoretical approaches:
cultural ecology (Nietschmann, 1973) in

545

geography, rooted in ECOSYSTEMS approaches to human behaviour; ecological anthropology, grounded in cybernetics and the adaptive qualities of living systems (see Rappaport, 1968); and the high tide of Marxist-inspired POLITICAL ECONOMY, and PEASANT studies in particular, of the 1970s. A number of people contributed to this intersection of ideas – Richards' (1985) work on peasant science, Hecht's (1985) analysis of eastern Amazonia, Grossman (1984) on subsistence in Papua New Guinea, and Watts (1983) on the simple reproduction squeeze and drought in Nigeria – but Blaikie pulled a number of disparate themes and ideas together, drawing in large measure on his own South Asian experiences. In rejecting the COLONIAL model of soil erosion that framed the problem around environmental constraints, mismanagement, OVERPOPULATION and MARKET failure, Blaikie started from the resource manager, and specifically households from whom surpluses are extracted, 'who then in turn are forced to extract "surpluses" from the environment ... [leading] to degradation' (1985, p. 124). The analytical scaffolding was provided by a number of key middle-range concepts – marginalization, proletarianization and incorporation – that permitted geographers to see the failure of soil conservation schemes in CLASS or social terms; namely, the POWER of classes affected by soil erosion in relation to STATE power, the class-specific perception of soil problems and solutions, and the class basis of soil erosion as a political issue. Blaikie was able to drive home the point that POVERTY could, in a dialectical way, cause degradation – 'peasants destroy their own environment in attempts to delay their own destruction' (1985, p. 29) – and that poverty had to be understood not as a thing or a condition, but as the social relations of production, which are realms of possibility and constraint.

In this work, political ecology came to mean a combination of 'the concerns of ECOLOGY and a broadly defined political economy' (Blaikie and Brookfield, 1987, p. 17), the latter understood as a concern with effects 'on people, as well as on their productive activities, of on-going changes within society at local and global levels' (1987, p. 21). This is a broad definition – an approach rather than a theory – which was adopted by the editors in the inaugural issue of the *Journal of Political Ecology* in 1995. Political ecology has three essential foci.

The first is interactive, contradictory and DIALECTICAL: society and land-based RESOURCES are mutually causal in such a way that poverty, via poor management, can induce environmental degradation that itself deepens poverty. Less a problem of poor management, inevitable natural decay or demographic growth (see DEMOGRAPHY), land degradation is seen as *social* in origin and definition. Analytically, the centrepoint of any nature–society study must be the 'land manager', whose relationship to nature must be considered in a historical, political and economic context.

Second, political ecology argues for regional or spatial accounts of degradation that link, through 'chains of explanation', local decision-makers to spatial variations in environmental structure (stability and resilience as traits of particular ecosystems in particular). LOCALITY studies are, thus, subsumed within multi-layered analyses pitched at a variety of regional SCALES.

Third, land management is framed by 'external structures', which for Blaikie meant the role of the state and the CORE-PERIPHERY model.

If early political ecology was not exactly clear what political economy implied, beyond a sort of 1970s DEPENDENCY THEORY, it did provide a number of principles and mid-range concepts. The first is a refined concept of marginality in which its political, ecological and economic aspects may be mutually reinforcing: land degradation is both a result and a cause of social marginalization. Second, pressure of production on resources is transmitted through social relations, which impose excessive demands on the environment (i.e. surplus extraction). And third, the inadequacy of environmental data of historical depth linked to a chain of EXPLANATION analysis compels a plural approach. Rather than unicausal theories one must, in short, accept 'plural perceptions, plural definitions ... and plural rationalities' (Blaikie and Brookfield, 1987, p. 16).

Political ecology had the advantage of seeing land management and environmental degradation (or SUSTAINABILITY) in terms of how political economy shapes the ability to manage resources (through forms of access and control, of exploitation), and through the lens of cognition (one person's ACCUMULATION is another person's degradation). But in other respects political ecology was demonstrably weak: it often had an outdated notion of ECOLOGY and ecological dynamics (including an incomplete understanding of ecological agency: Zimmerer, 1994b); it was often remarkably silent on the politics of political ecology; it had a somewhat voluntarist notion of human perception; and, not least, it did not provide a theoretically derived set of concepts to explore particular environmental outcomes or transformations. These weaknesses, coupled with the almost indeterminate and open-ended nature of political ecology, not unexpectedly produced both a deepening and a proliferation of political ecologies in the 1990s (see Hecht and Cockburn, 1989; Peet and Watts, 2003 [1996]; Bryant and Bailey, 1997). A number of studies address the question of politics, focusing especially on patterns of RESISTANCE and struggles over access to and control over the environment, and how politics as policy is discursively constructed (Moore, 1996; Leach and Mearns, 1996; Pulido, 1996; Neumann, 1998; see ENVIRONMENTAL JUSTICE). Others have taken the political economy approach in somewhat differing directions: one takes the poverty–degradation connection and explores outcomes with the tools of INSTITUTIONAL ECONOMICS (Das Gupta, 1993) and entitlements, whereas another returns to Marx to derive concepts from the second contradiction of capitalism (O'Connor, 1998). Much work has addressed the original silence of political ecology on questions of GENDER (Agrawal, 1998). And still others, often drawing upon discourse theory and social studies of science, examine environmental problems and policies – often outside the THIRD WORLD – in terms of ecological MODERNIZATION, RISK and GOVERNMENTALITY (see Leach and Mearns, 1996; Braun and Castree, 1998; Keil, Bell, Penz and Fawcett, 1998; Forsyth, 2003; Li, 2007).

Political ecology has in a sense almost dissolved itself over the past two decades as scholars have sought to extend its reach. At the same time, it has met up with the proliferations of forms of environmental studies, science studies, POST-STRUCTURALISM and new SOCIAL MOVEMENTS. Some of the most interesting work now speaks to the political ecology of CITIES (see URBAN NATURE), COMMODITIES and of forms of green rule and subject formation (Agrawal, 2005; Heynen, Kaika and Swyngedouw, 2006; Swyngedouw, 2004b) and violence (Peluso and Watts, 2001). Much of this work continues to struggle with the dialectical relations between nature and society that the early political ecology identified (see Harvey, 1996), however, and which continues to provide the central conundrum for what is now a hugely expanded and polyglot landscape of political ecology.   MW

Suggested reading
Adam (1998); Demeritt (1998); Faber (1998); Fairchild and Leach (1998); Forsyth (2003); Guha and Martinez-Alier (1997); Hajer (1995); Kuletz (1998); Moore (1996).

political economy The study of the relationship between economic and political processes. Aristotle's *Politics* distinguished between *oikos*, the operation of the HOUSEHOLD (on PATRIARCHAL principles) to meet daily needs, and the *polis*, the domain of public association and political life. In the early seventeenth century, political economy began to be used in France to discuss how economic activity might contribute to the powers of the sovereign and the prosperity of his subjects. This made economy a public rather than private activity, and located the problematic of political economy at the scale of the STATE (and implicitly as a EUROPEAN concern). *Mercantilists* explored how the sovereign/nation could prosper from running a trading surplus at the expense of other NATION-STATES. The *physiocrats*, motivated by economic crises in France, argued that the source of wealth lies in agriculture: the 'natural' fertility of the nation. Physiocrats began to argue that the sovereign should not govern the economy too much.

By the mid-nineteenth century, British political economy began to emerge, crystallized around the earlier ideas of Adam Smith (1723–90), flourishing into a school of thought of global influence throughout the nineteenth century. Experiencing Britain's shift from a society founded on landowning and rural agricultural economic activities to an urban and industrial capitalist society (see INDUSTRIAL REVOLUTION), as well as the wealth brought to Britain as a result of unequal trading networks with its colonies (see COLONIALISM) and less industrialized European neighbours, it came to be argued that national wealth was embedded in labour rather than land (a LABOUR THEORY OF VALUE), and that crucial driving forces were the DIVISION OF LABOUR, the extension of the MARKET, and free domestic and international TRADE. Smith, Thomas Malthus, David Ricardo, James and J.S. Mill conceived the relationship between economic activities and the national polity in terms that aligned political economy with Lockean LIBERALISM. Freedom was founded in men (sic) owning private PROPERTY, and political intervention into their activities was an invasion of liberty and privacy. With this geographical shift from monarchical France to democratic Britain, the political came to be equated with the national state rather than the sovereign.

By the end of the nineteenth century, political economy had split into two very different,

Marxist and liberal, schools. Refining Ricardo's labour theory of value, Marx argued that CAPITALISM exploits workers, and that the crucial relationship between political and economic processes is the way in which capitalism engenders, and is shaped by, political struggle between CLASSES (see MARXIST ECONOMICS). In his view, capitalism was an advance over previous MODES OF PRODUCTION, as it promoted the autonomous individual in the workplace and in political life, but sooner or later would founder on class conflicts that neither the market nor the state could finesse, giving way to a more collective, political economy founded on COMMUNISM or SOCIALISM.

In the 1890s, partly in response to Marx's critique of capitalism, a marginalist, subjectivist political economy emerged almost simultaneously in Britain, France, Austria, Sweden and Italy. William Stanley Jevons, Léon Walras, Carl Menger and Knut Wicksell argued that value was determined by consumers' utility, not labour value (see UTILITY THEORY). Using a pleasure/pain calculus, they argued that the marginal utility of everything – that is, the extra pleasure from obtaining an extra unit of a COMMODITY – is inversely proportional to supply. In free markets, consumers would thus pay the right amount for everything purchased: its marginal utility to them. The American John Bates Clark extended the calculus to labour and capital, concluding that labour and capital will always be paid fairly in free markets, according to their marginal productivity to society. This school of NEO-CLASSICAL ECONOMICS came to describe itself as simply 'economics', because in this view the economy, if left alone by the state, would maximize social welfare all by itself, harmoniously coordinating citizens' desires. In short, the political could be evacuated in favour of the ECONOMY, to the benefit of society.

Just as liberalism has conservative and progressive variants, so does liberal political economy. Conservative, Lockean liberalism argues that freedom is the result of maintaining a minimal 'night-watchman' state; progressive liberalism (beginning in late-nineteenth-century Britain and migrating to the USA during the twentieth century) argues that state intervention is necessary to secure the freedom and well-being of those impoverished by capitalism. The former school, now associated with the project of NEO-LIBERALISM and its architects Milton Friedman and Friedrich von Hayek, became global common sense. It still sees itself as undertaking political economy (publishing in the Chicago school's *Journal of Political Economy*), and pays close attention to political processes, but only because such processes tendentially undermine what it regards as the proper functioning of a capitalist economy. The latter school flourished in Britain and Europe during the Great Depression and until the mid-1970s, under the magisterial influence of John Maynard Keynes. As FORDISM or Keynesianism, it pursued the principle of continual state intervention to manage the contradictions of capitalism to the benefit of the nation and its least well-off citizens, and saw itself as inheriting the mantle of the 'classical' nineteenth-century political economy of Smith, Ricardo and Marx. This rapidly fell from favour in the context of the crises of postwar Fordism and the Reagan and Thatcher revolutions, although contemporary economic commentators such as Joseph Stiglitz, Jeffrey Sachs and Paul Krugman seek to keep the flame alive.

Whereas liberal political economy dominates political science and economics, at least in the global NORTH, political economy in GEOGRAPHY is usually taken to mean some variant or critical elaboration on the line of thought precipitated by Marx. During the 1970s, RADICAL GEOGRAPHY successfully displaced liberal market-oriented approaches to economic geography, associated with LOCATION THEORY and SPATIAL SCIENCE, and diversified itself. In sum: versions of MARXISM, from dialectical to analytical, articulate a political economy approach centred on class struggle. REALISM examines how the necessary economic relations and political conflicts of capitalism are complicated by differences in geographical context. REGULATION THEORY explores state-economy relations at various scales, comparing Fordist and post-Fordist regimes of ACCUMULATION across space and time. Approaches via GOVERNMENTALITY argue for more attention to everyday behaviour, the conduct of conduct, rather than the state, as shaping state-civil society relations. Approaches influenced by FEMINISM and POSTSTRUCTURALISM draw attention to GENDER and IDENTITIES other than class as emergent domains of inequality and CONFLICT under capitalism. SOCIAL MOVEMENTS approaches theorize the emergence of social contestations of capitalism (see also RESISTANCE). The CULTURAL TURN stresses the importance of discourse and representation to the dynamics and contradictions of capitalism. Diverse and community economies approaches emphasize the ongoing importance of non-capitalist economic and social relations, while approaches informed by POST-COLONIALISM pay attention to the geographically differentiated ongoing imprint of a colonial past, and question norms of progress and well-being associated with European capitalism (see also POST-DEVELOPMENT). If there is one thing shared across these different, at times hotly debated, critical approaches to economic geography, it is a resonance with Marx's political economic conception of capitalism.   ES

Suggested reading
Barnes (1996); Lee and Wills (1997); Sayer (1995); Sheppard and Barnes (2000).

political geography A subdivision of HUMAN GEOGRAPHY analysing ways in which politics and conflict create SPACES and PLACES and, in turn, are themselves partially determined by the existence and nature of geographical entities. The division of human geography into the broad spheres of economic, socio-cultural and political geography topics reflects the pre-eminence of disciplinary boundaries in academia. However, contemporary geography reflects criticism of disciplinary constraints and, in turn, political geography has become more eclectic and connected to other spheres of human geography. To understand the importance of this trend, a brief history of political geography is necessary.

At the outset of the development of modern human geography, political geography played a central role. Indeed, the term political geography was applied in a general sense to human aspects of geography and served as an adjunct of history. The establishment of geography as a university discipline created the initial subdisciplines of colonial geography, COMMERCIAL GEOGRAPHY and political geography; a reflection of the discipline's role in IMPERIALISM. The key text for the new sub-discipline was Friedrich Ratzel's (1897) *Politische geographie*, which used an organic theory of the STATE to connect cultures with environments within dynamic state BORDERS. Ratzel's influential text connected political geography to social DARWINIST ideas whereby a hierarchy of competitive cultures was defined by their differential ability to utilize the environment, with the most successful CULTURE having the right to establish a state in a particular TERRITORY. The result was the concept of *LEBENSRAUM*, or living space, which would later prescribe Germany's right to move its boundary eastwards into territory populated by Slavs.

At about the same time, Sir Halford Mackinder was both establishing political geography in universities in Great Britain and creating a political geography framework to advocate British imperialism. Also, influenced by social Darwinism and the organic theory of the state (Ó Tuathail, 1992), Mackinder is best remembered for claiming that political geography had a role in formulating grand geo-strategic plans. His 'geographical pivot of history' article (1904), later known as the HEARTLAND theory, defined a historical geography of European continental powers in perpetual conflict with maritime powers. In the context of Germany's growing challenge to Britain, Mackinder saw technological change facilitating German control of Eurasia and subsequent global dominance. His solution was a strong British Empire to counter the threat. In the USA, Isaiah Bowman promoted a political geography to serve the needs of governments defining an ever-increasing role in world politics (Smith, N., 2003c).

Mackinder and Ratzel illustrate some important features of the early political geography with contemporary implications. First, they utilized grand universal theories of dubious strength to offer academic authority to state-specific foreign policy choices. Second, they connected the establishment and vitality of political geography to national SECURITY threats and the ability to offer 'practical' advice. Third, the analysis was state-centric, identifying states as the only important actors. Fourth, the theoreticians were socially privileged, white males, but, and fifth, they still claimed to 'know' the world and classify large swathes of TERRITORY as the venues for particular behaviours or characteristics. In Haraway's (1988) phrase, they practised a 'god's eye-view'.

The relationship of political geography to foreign policy was epitomized by portrayals of General Karl Haushofer as the 'evil genius' behind Adolf Hitler's Second World War plans for world domination (Ó Tuathail, 1996b). Greatly exaggerated by American media, the end-result was a tarnished image for political geography, as it became associated with German geopolitical expansion (cf. *GEOPOLITIK*). The sub-discipline withered as a research enterprise in universities on both sides of the Atlantic, ironically at the same time that the US government was expounding geopolitical theories as it achieved the status of superpower. Political geography was pushed into the academic doldrums, although it continued to be taught in many institutions, albeit with somewhat 'dated' textbooks and approaches. Its focus became a functional view of the state that promoted national integration and the ACCUMULATION of CAPITAL. Two types of states were identified; independent SOVEREIGN states and dependent countries (colonies and other possessions) (Hartshorne, 1950). The latter were largely ignored as were the power relationships between rich and poor, or colonized and colonizing states. Without the previous environmental framework and with little political purpose, political geography lost its coherence and relevance (Claval, 1984). Instead, political geographers described political events (such as elections) or features (such as BOUNDARIES) in an attempt to oil the wheels of state integration and capital growth. Political geography remained state-centric, but inward-looking rather than geo-strategic, and normative rather than prescriptive.

Political geography, as with all academic studies, is a product of its social and intellectual contexts. Global competition between states and concepts of social Darwinism stimulated Mackinder and Ratzel, and postwar prosperity fuelled the blandness of FUNCTIONALISM. In the 1960s the global politics of the Vietnam War and internal crises manifested in RACE riots were linked to a growing intellectual engagement with the work of Karl Marx (see MARXISM). Political geography was not immune, and over time a critical political geography began to emerge. The process was a step-by-step identification of social issues and marginalized groups, adoption of new and fertile social theoretical frameworks, and the recognition of different useful methodologies.

Initially, two broad themes were explored, both relying on spatial analytical techniques: the distribution of RESOURCES and opportunities in cities (Cox, 1973), and ELECTORAL GEOGRAPHY (Taylor and Johnston, 1979). Both branches brought the belated introduction of analytical techniques to political geography. However, these were seen as inadequate in discovering the causes of social inequality. The parallel emergence of RADICAL GEOGRAPHY was seen by some as a means of identifying underlying structures that were producing social inequality and related political CONFLICTS.

The urban problems of racial strife and economic disparity and the global problems of war and gross economic inequality provoked different uses of radical literature. David Harvey's (1999 [1982]) *Limits to capital* deployed the work of Karl Marx to explain how the production of urban spaces was a necessary and contested part of CAPITALISM. On the other hand, Peter Taylor (1985) adopted the neo-Marxist WORLD-SYSTEMS THEORY of Immanuel Wallerstein to situate states within the dynamics of the capitalist world-economy. The product was a concentration on the political geography of geographical SCALE with the local/urban, nation-state and global scales being identified as interlinked.

Institutional support for political geography blossomed to match the changing intellectual climate. The journal *Political Geography Quarterly* (later *Political Geography*) was established in 1982. The first edition of Peter Taylor's (1985) textbook *Political geography: world-economy, nation-state and locality* and a host of conferences and related edited volumes (Burnett and Taylor, 1981) identified the sub-discipline as a reinvigorated component of human geography.

However, in the 1990s human geography took what has been labelled the 'CULTURAL TURN' and engaged with social theorists other than Marx (see SOCIAL THEORY). The result was a challenge to what was perceived as the existing reification of scale and the concentration upon economic structures. The politics of the production of scale was theorized with increasing sophistication, and feminist geographers and queer theorists (see FEMINIST GEOGRAPHIES; QUEER THEORY) demanded focus upon the SCALES of the BODY and the HOUSEHOLD. Political geography became increasingly eclectic as CULTURAL GEOGRAPHY emphasized the political conflicts inherent in cultural constructs and political geography included the cultural representation of politics. The boundaries of the sub-discipline became increasingly blurred (Painter, 1995).

One outcome was a renewed interest in the topic of GEOPOLITICS. Since the Second World War, political geography had defined itself as different from geopolitics. The topic of CRITICAL GEOPOLITICS (Ó Tuathail, 1996b) focused on the existing geopolitical practices of states and DECONSTRUCTED the rhetoric of politicians and 'experts' to illuminate the underlying POWER politics. Critical geopolitics also promoted a concentration on non-state actors, such as SOCIAL MOVEMENTS and indigenous groups, which also reflected calls for increased study of RACE, GENDER and SEXUALITY (Kobayashi and Peake, 2000; Staeheli, Kofman and Peake, 2004); though these topics and theoretical perspectives are not yet fully integrated into political geographical analyses.

The concentration upon the state, NATIONALISM and international politics, or formal

Politics, which had led the revival of political geography, was complemented by attention to the politics of representation and governance, or politics with a small 'p' (Flint, 2003a). The philosophies of Michel Foucault and Pierre Bourdieu, amongst others, challenged the structuralism and economism of some versions of Marxist theory, and geographers used these works to focus upon topics of GOVERNANCE (Hannah, 2000) and social constructions of space (Mohan and Mohan, 2002). Feminist scholars challenged the binary nature of existing theories and analyses (Staeheli, Kofman and Peake, 2004). In turn, the discipline saw an explosion of journals (*Space and Polity, Geopolitics, Society and Space*) as well as a surge in the publication of textbooks as political geography classes became more common in universities (Flint and Taylor, 2007 [1985]; Jones, Jones and Woods, 2004).

A coherent political geography played a key role in establishing the modern discipline of geography. However, the price of a dubious theoretical foundation was application in the name of imperialism and WAR. Contemporary political geography is eclectic and constantly engaging in self-critique challenging the prioritization of particular theories and social groups, and identifying key actors beyond the state. The result is a number of creative tensions. Within the sub-discipline, competing theoretical perspectives vie for attention. Also, as the 'war on terror' has become a dominant context (see TERRORISM), the issue of RELEVANCE has reappeared; producing a tension between social scientists critical of foreign policy, on the one hand, and administrators and politicians looking for geography to provide the tools and analysis to facilitate counter-terrorism.   CF

Suggested reading
Agnew (2002); Cox and Low (2003); Flint (1999); Painter (1995); Staeheli, Kofman and Peake (2004); Flint and Taylor (2007 [1999]).

pollution Substances released into an environment that cause harm to living organisms or built structures (e.g. roads, buildings). The substances may be human-made or natural (see ENVIRONMENTAL HAZARD; HAZARD). Harm occurs when the receiving environment cannot easily assimilate the type or quantity of substance released.

The effects of pollution range from aesthetic nuisance through to economic loss, HEALTH damage, death and long-term environmental degradation. The release of pollution may be sudden, or it may involve a slow accumulation of substances, such as the concentration of heavy metals, herbicides and pesticides in FOOD chains. The impacts of pollution may also be gradual or sudden. The impact may be short-lived or exist for a long time. It may be local, widely dispersed or far from the source of pollution (see ACID RAIN). Pollution may be described by its medium (e.g. air or water pollution), its character (e.g. noise pollution and ACID RAIN) or its source (e.g. industrial pollution).

Pollution is both physical and socially constructed (see SOCIAL CONSTRUCTION). Bickerstaff and Walker (2002) demonstrate the MORAL GEOGRAPHY of pollution, risk, responsibility and blame in an English city. Pollution may be regarded by some people as an 'accident', or understood by others as the deliberate and inevitable consequences of production processes. Sections of the ENVIRONMENTAL MOVEMENT have strongly criticized production processes that generate pollution. Increasingly, efforts are being made to 'close the circle' by using former wastes from processes as inputs into new production processes, in what is known as 'industrial ECOLOGY'. Regulations are enforced to prevent the deliberate emission of pollution that is considered unacceptable. Sometimes the pollutant must be treated to a standard before it is emitted. The setting of standards and their enforcement vary throughout the world because the receiving environments are different, and partly because of desires to maintain ECONOMIC GROWTH.

Concern about pollution rose dramatically after more than 4,000 people died in a photochemical smog in London in December 1952, and following the publication of *Silent spring* by Rachel Carson in 1962. Kates (1995) observed that the sharp decrease in pollution after the UK's Clean Air Act of 1956 was part of a longer trend to improved air quality, resulting from the displacement of coal as a source of ENERGY. Rachel Carson identified the dangers of a new pollutant, the insecticide DDT (Carson, 1962). It was the forerunner for concerns about many human-produced substances, ranging from pesticides through to nuclear industry waste. Continental- and global-scale pollutants such CFC emissions, ACID RAIN and pollutants that contribute to GLOBAL WARMING have caused most concern for governments, the environmental movement and citizens in developed countries.

Pollution is an important aspect of ENVIRONMENTAL JUSTICE in the USA (see Pastor,

Morello-Frosch and Sadd, 2005), where pollution and other differences in environmental quality are seen as discrimination, and increasingly in other countries (see Walker, Mitchell, Fairburn and Smith, 2005). In areas said to be in a state of UNDERDEVELOPMENT, it is often the local forms of pollution, such as the lack of clean drinking water, that cause the greatest immediate concern.   PM

population density The number of persons divided by the area that they occupy. Within URBAN GEOGRAPHY, neighbourhood and housing-based measures of density became part of discussions about URBANISM, which linked context to the well-being of population groups. Within DEMOGRAPHY and POPULATION GEOGRAPHY, density is mostly calculated at a national and regional SCALE, and sheds light on links between environmental conditions and population well-being (see MALTHUS MODEL; OVERPOPULATION). However, wide variations between countries in rates of URBANIZATION and the availability of cultivable land undermine the use of the simple measure in a comparative sense, and have led some to favour *physiological density*, which divides the number of persons by the area of potentially productive land (Sambrook, Pigozzi and Thomas, 1999). The availability of geo-referenced data and flexible models is supporting the further development of density-related CLASSIFICATIONS (Hugo, Champion and Lattes, 2003).   AJB

Suggested reading
Plane and Rogerson (1994, ch. 2).

population geography Scholarship on the geographical organization of, and connections between, groups. Between 1953 and the 1990s, POPULATION GEOGRAPHY defined itself as the systematic study of '(1) the simple description of the location of population numbers and characteristics ... (2) the explanation of the spatial configuration of these numbers and characteristics ... (3) the geographic analysis of population phenemona (the inter-relations among areal differences in population with those in all or certain other elements within the geographic study area)' (Zelinsky, 1966, pp. 5–6). Accordingly, the sub-discipline thought of populations as groups synonymous with political jurisdictions (e.g. urban residents, Australians), ethnic and national IDENTITIES (e.g. latino/as), phenotype (e.g. white, black), and demographic events (e.g. migrants, the elderly, families, baby boomers, REFUGEES). As links between CLASSIFICATIONS such as these

(i.e. the construction of knowledge) and the circulation of POWER became acknowledged, views on how populations were made and maintained, and for what purposes, have greatly expanded. This enlarged reading of groups also takes into account the relations and connections between groups, as with work that examines the meanings of WHITENESS in the context of blackness, or the experiences of MIGRANCY in relation to those of sedentarism. Scholarship similarly investigates more plural views of geographical organization that go beyond the one time focus upon AREAL DIFFERENTIATION in space to recover and rework ideas about PLACE and environment. For some, the widening agenda threatens the integrity of the vision for the sub-discipline first proposed by Trewartha in 1953; for others, growing plurality signals strength and the relevance of the field to other branches of GEOGRAPHY and to society more generally. The recent rebranding of the flagship journal to *Population, Space and Place* has occurred with the rise of critical accounts (see CRITICAL HUMAN GEOGRAPHY), and at a time of increasing 'post-disciplinarity' (Conway, 2004).

Contributions to population geography have long been cross-disciplinary, not least because 'geographical' EPISTEMOLOGIES (particularly those related to environment, place and space) have been variously developed as part of ENLIGHTENMENT thinking in different disciplines, including economics, sociology and demography. Classical economic thought – most notably the MALTHUSIAN MODEL – argued that population growth rates could lead to the demand for FOOD (RESOURCES) exceeding the capacity of the environment to supply necessary inputs. Neo-Malthusian work has expanded the concept of CARRYING CAPACITY to include social and cultural factors, and use has been made of large-scale SIMULATIONS and MODELS, including the LIMITS TO GROWTH model. Neo-Marxist critiques and views of a population–environment–resource–IDEOLOGY nexus have served to complicate ideas about OVERPOPULATION and drawn greater attention to political factors (see POLITICAL ECOLOGY).

While accounts concerned with environment drew attention to the links between population, scarcity and production, approaches focused upon place saw important links between population, culture and production/consumption. Reflecting the still influential ideas of the French *géographie humaine* school, Beaujeu-Garnier (1956–8) believed that by studying the 'ways of being' of populations, the field could integrate liveli-hood (or environmental and economic possi-bilities for production) with a concern for norms, values and cultural change. This inte-grative account of population and NATURE–SOCIETY links resisted the compartmentaliza-tion of population issues as separate from eco-nomic or cultural concerns, took for granted who or what constituted a population and continues to prove difficult to apply (compare Bruhnes' 1910 treatment of settlement geog-raphy with contemporary work on GLOBAL CITIES).

After the Second World War, population geography became institutionalized as a sub-discipline concerned with EMPIRICIST and POSITIVIST statements about spatial variations in the distribution, composition and growth of populations. The call to arms had been issued by Trewartha (1953), who saw a synthetic geography that existed for, and began with, people (populations) and their geographical organization. Trewartha made his case as SPATIAL SCIENCE gained prominence, ensuring that a view of space as a container through which the *order* of population phenomena could be both described and, through the development of THEORY, explained and modi-fied (see LOCATION THEORY) permeated the field. Inspired by new data and international collaborations, and drawing on the contribu-tions of DEMOGRAPHY in general, and DEMO-GRAPHIC TRANSITION and *stable population theory* more specifically, population geography contributed work on the DIFFUSION of vital transitions (notably Zelinsky's pioneering 1971 *hypothesis of the mobility* transition), spa-tial variations in the components of population change (FERTILITY, MORTALITY, MIGRATION) and composition (particularly on AGEING), and the development of more accurate and sub-national POPULATION PROJECTIONS and LIFE TABLE methods (Jones, 1981; Woods, 1982). Interest grew in the disaggregated behaviour of individuals with, for example, RATIONAL CHOICE THEORY and SOCIAL PHYSICS frameworks extended to model migration decisions at residential and regional scales (see also BEHAVIOURAL GEOGRAPHY; REGIONAL SCIENCE). The growth of studies in MEDICAL GEOGRAPHY on morbidity, mortality and geo-graphical variations in accessibility to HEALTH care combined with the relative neglect of fer-tility to leave commentators both bemoaning the migration-centred foci of much work and debating the need for continued disciplinary border-crossing to rejuvenate the field. While links with demography remain strong, the

consolidation of fields such as *spatial demog-raphy* and GEODEMOGRAPHICS (Woods, 1982; Wachter, 2005) have occurred alongside, but not to the exclusion of, alternative treatments of SPACE (White and Jackson, 1995).

The well-known critiques of Enlightenment knowledge that had taken root in HUMAN GEOGRAPHY in the 1980s impacted upon the field in at least two ways. In methodological terms, greater emphasis was placed upon QUALITATIVE METHODS and 'mixed' methods of approaching human subjects, and taking feelings, aspirations and DISCOURSES more ser-iously. LIFE COURSE frameworks extended LIFE-CYCLE explanations of, for example, HOUSE-HOLD formation, location and dissolution pat-terns to take account of interdependent spatial and temporal contexts, and better integrate accounts of structure and agency along STRUC-TURATIONIST lines (Van Wissen and Dykstra, 1999). The rapid development of MICROSIMU-LATION, AGENT-BASED MODELLING and GEO-GRAPHIC INFORMATION SCIENCE in general further exploited new data products, deepened the field's already strong engagement with PUBLIC POLICY and business planning, and fur-ther extended (some have argued, democra-tized) how population groups are defined, by whom, and for what purpose.

Indeed, the question of how knowledge about the geographical organization of popu-lation reflects and reinforces the circulation of power in society continues to shape the direc-tion of the field. In particular, a number of commentators have questioned the categories used in the study of populations and, most poignantly, the question of how populations are classified, named and legitimized as objects of study and policy. POST-STRUCTURAL views argue that populations are socially con-structed institutions that both enable and counter inequality and oppression in society. Drawing on Michel Foucault, research has examined the use of *political technology* and discourse by states to create inferior OTHERS that legitimize political projects. Examples include the deployment of RACE-based classifi-cations to underwrite ETHNIC CLEANSING and GENOCIDE, including the Nazi HOLOCAUST, and the exploitation of GENDER and SEXUALITY norms against civilians and REFUGEES in WARS. POST-COLONIAL research has investigated the link between population classifications, CEN-SUS and registry systems, and the mapping of ETHNIC populations to further COLONIAL ends, and the *neo-colonial* use of discourses of migrancy to legitimize DEVELOPMENT agen-das including STRUCTURAL ADJUSTMENT

553

programmes (Kosiński, 1984; Lawson, 2000). Drawing on FEMINIST GEOGRAPHIES and SOCIAL GEOGRAPHY, the field has re-examined the meaning of concepts of demography, including age (literatures on CHILDREN's geographies and ageing), reproduction, DISEASE, disability, death and dying (Pratt, 1999; Valentine, 2001; Kalipeni, Craddock, Oppong and Ghosh, 2004; Silvey, 2004).

The diverse readings of space, which increasingly call upon notions of environment and place, run through the field's expanding engagement with the economic, cultural and, to a lesser extent, ecological dimensions of GLOBALIZATION and NEO-LIBERALISM. Research on global cities explores patterns of skilled migration, the diversification of families and households, and variations in experiences of settlement, incorporation, ASSIMILATION and SOCIAL EXCLUSION among immigrant communities (Clark, 1998; Beaverstock, 2002; Wong, Yeoh and Graham, 2003). Balancing production-centred accounts of *family migration*, an emphasis upon gendered migration has drawn attention to factors of social reproduction and institutional context among domestic workers and persons trafficked (Boyle, Halfacree and Robinson, 1998). The growing social and spatial plurality of household living arrangements has been linked to ageing and IMMIGRATION, and has sparked new research on the demographic transition. Historically, low levels of fertility have been connected to the interplay of changes in concepts of self and a range of state policies, including housing supply and social support. Similarly, the variable ways in which states mediate TRANSNATIONAL and DIASPORIC communities, including BORDER controls, remittance management and through discourses of long-distance NATIONALISM, have witnessed a more explicitly integrative approach, combining economic, cultural and political readings (Samers, 1997; Jackson, Crang and Dwyer, 2004).

There are a number of key engagements within population geography that relate to the direction of travel and the broader influence of its scholarship. The simultaneous embrace of plurality, and the deepening methodological specialism of many approaches, ensure that time-honoured questions about intellectual coherence and vitality remain. While there is an implicit suggestion that moderation and balance (in approach, in topic and so forth) will best serve ongoing research needs and meet funding expedients, there is a tendency to define balance in terms of the long-standing demographic approach to the field. That is, migration is seen as exerting an overdue influence on research agendas, at the expense of work on fertility (and to a lesser extent mortality and composition, which are the subjects of other fields of enquiry within geography). Under post-structural and critical readings, however, this divide is artificial and problematic.

Similarly, spirited debates on methodological pluralism have supported the development of mixed methods approaches almost to the exclusion of single-method techniques, which are seen as the preserve of more specialized fields, including spatial demography. Methodological specialization has tended to exaggerate a divide between those using quantitative, qualitative and ethnographic tools at a time when many agendas require flexible and plural approaches. The growth in interest in *participatory geographies* represents another opportunity for reflection about the relationship between knowledge and power in the field.

Furthermore, it remains largely the case that analyses of RISK remain absent from debates within the field, despite increased public attention to matters of *securitization*, broadly defined (see SECURITY). Given the profound implications of well-documented ecological and cultural transitions, to name two, for the geographical organization of populations and the structure of society, work is needed to understand the roles that groups play in affecting global futures. AJB

Suggested reading
Bailey (2005); Findlay (2004); Jones (1981); Kalipeni, Craddock, Oppong and Ghosh (2004); Plane and Rogerson (1994).

population potential A measure of the nearness of a spatially distributed population to a point (developed as part of the MACROGEOGRAPHY project). The potential exerted on a point (V_i) is as follows:

$$V_i = \sum_{j=1}^{k} (P_j/d_{ij}), \quad j \neq i,$$

where P_j is the population at point j, d_{ij} is the distance between i and j and summation is over all k points (d_{ij} may be raised to some power, to reflect the FRICTION OF DISTANCE: cf. DISTANCE DECAY). The higher the potential at a point – V_i – the more accessible it is to the population concerned. Isopleth maps of population potential indicate the relative accessibility of a set of points, weighted by their populations and the distances between them (as in the GRAVITY MODEL). Population may be replaced by another variable, such as purchasing power, to give a measure of market ACCESSIBILITY for each point *i*.   RJ

Suggested reading
Stewart and Warntz (1959); Warntz (1965).

population projection A scenario about the size and composition of a population in the future (or past) that is based on a set of demographic assumptions. As 'what if' scenarios, *projections* should be distinguished from estimates (which aim to provide the most accurate picture of current populations) and *forecasts* (which aim to statistically predict the most probable scenario based on a broad range of information). The key (direct) mathematical methods for making projections include the extrapolation of demographic trends, the use of the balancing equation (see DEMOGRAPHY) and, notably, the cohort component method, which makes specific assumptions about the FERTILITY, MORTALITY and MIGRATION experiences of every five-year COHORT in a population as it ages. The increased application of population projections in business and planning has helped fuel a virtuous circle of methodological innovation, which includes developments in sub-national projections, small-area projections, multi-region models and ethnic minority projections (Wilson and Rees, 2005).   AJB

Suggested reading
Rowland (2003, ch. 12).

population pyramid A graphical depiction of the age–sex structure of a population. This provides a visual record of the current population structure and differentiates between expanding populations (pyramid shape with concave sides), stationary populations (straight-sided) and constricting populations (beehive shape with convex sides: see the US Census Bureau for contemporary pyramids that can be animated). Pyramids also provide visual clues as to prior demographic events, including the arrival/departure of sex-selective MIGRATION streams, the impact of

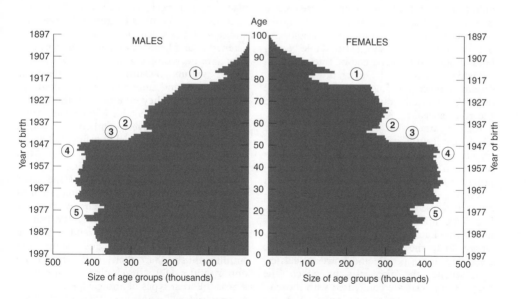

(1) Shortage in births due to the 1914–18 war ('empty classes')
(2) Passage of 'empty classes' to age of fertility
(3) Shortfall in births due to 1939–45 war
(4) Baby boom
(5) Non-replacement of generations

population pyramid *France, 1897–1997* (Lévy, 1998, p. 4)

wars upon the male population, infanticide and the movement of boom–bust cohorts (Momsen, 1991). The figure for France is typical of populations of the global North. It shows the general influence of ageing, which, because of lower male LIFE EXPECTANCY, produces a strong excess of women in the over-70 age groups. The recent decline in birth rates is also evident in the shortfall in those aged under 25 years. The demographic consequences of WAR are also apparent in the pyramid; for example, the sharp decline in births during the First World War is reflected in the shortfall in the numbers of people in their late seventies and early eighties. In countries of the global South, population pyramids are more steep-sided, reflecting higher FERTILITY (which adds more people to the base of the pyramid) and higher MORTALITY through the life course, that steadily removes them.   AJB

Suggested reading
Shryock and Siegel (1973).

populism An enormously complex term that refers to both political IDEOLOGIES and economic DEVELOPMENT strategies that are bound up with notions of the ordinary, the people, anti-industrialism and small-scale enterprise ('small is beautiful'). Populism as practice can be seen as a counter-current, a minority DISCOURSE, to the rise of industrial CAPITALISM. While certain lines of populist thinking can be traced to pre-industrial Leveller and Digger movements of seventeenth-century England, the intellectual origins are typically traced to Sismondi and the Ricardian socialists (Kitching, 1982).

Kitching notes that there are two senses in which populism is employed. One turns on its *opposition to large-scale urban manufacture* and its promotion of small-scale, moral, efficient enterprises, and the other on a particular sort of *politics in which an effort is made to manufacture a national-collective will* (see also HEGEMONY; NATIONALISM). Populist political strategies and RHETORICS reside in what Laclau (1977) calls a double articulation: first, the creation of a stable bloc consisting of the people and powerful classes; and, second, the discourses by which 'the people's' interests are configured with those of other classes (see CLASS and STATE). Populist movements can, for example, encompass farmer radicalism, agrarian SOCIALISM, populist dictatorship (Peronism), populist DEMOCRACY and URBAN SOCIAL MOVEMENTS (Canovan, 1981; see also SQUATTING). Populist, or neo-populist, development strategies can include peasant CO-OPERATIVES, the informal sector, land reform

and THIRD WORLD flexible specialization (Kitching, 1982). A powerful line of populist thinking in development geography and agrarian studies includes the work of Chayanov (see PEASANT).   MW

Suggested reading
Canovan (1981); Laclau (2006); Watts (1995).

pork barrel An American term for the unequal distribution of PUBLIC GOODS in order to promote a political party's or candidate's re-election prospects. Pork-barrelling is usually associated with legislators obtaining benefits for the spatially defined constituencies that they represent, but the term is also used more generally to refer to any apparent government favouritism of particular areas.   RJ

positionality The fact that a researcher's social, cultural and subject positions (and other psychological processes) affect: the questions they ask; how they frame them; the theories that they are drawn to; how they read – Bondi (1999) draws a distinction between intertextual and experiential reading; their relations with those they research in the FIELD or through INTERVIEWS; interpretations they place on empirical evidence; access to data, institutions and outlets for research dissemination; and the likelihood that they will be listened to and heard. Debates about positionality have been ongoing since the 1980s, especially within FEMINISM and FEMINIST GEOGRAPHIES and among those using QUALITATIVE METHODS. They emerge with the understanding that all knowledge is partial and from particular perspectives, embedded within POWER relations. In a highly influential statement, Haraway (1989) distinguished between SITUATED KNOWLEDGE and RELATIVISM, arguing that attending to positionality, as it is mediated by particular technologies for seeing (such as quantification, mapping and survey methodologies), is the route to OBJECTIVITY (rather than a sign of subjectivism), and a way of making responsible knowledge claims that simultaneously chart their limits and create opportunities for developing connections across different types of knowledges.

Approaches to positionality have changed over the years, reflecting changing theories of SUBJECTIVITY. In early discussions, positionality often took the form of self-critical introspection, through which researchers attempted to position themselves within power relations (often as middle-class, white and Western) in order to understand how this entered into their research process (see REFLEXIVITY; see also Moss, 2005). Rose (1997b) criticized these efforts to make positionality transparent. Not only is it impossible to do so, given the complexity of psychological processes, but these efforts approximate the 'god-trick' of complete vision criticized by Haraway. In a position that is now widely accepted, she argued that there is an irresolvable 'unknowability' of our own positions and those of others. From quite another direction, some have taken the position that only members of a cultural community have the right to speak for their COMMUNITY (England, 1994). This reflects concerns – especially among marginalized communities – that middle-class, often white, researchers reproduce existing patterns of domination through the research process and products. They often have access to information unavailable to marginalized groups, they treat the experiences of those they research as 'raw data' that they then interpret, they have the capacity (unavailable to marginalized groups) to present their interpretations within scholarly and sometimes policy contexts, and their research often seems to more clearly benefit them (through career advancement) than those that they study. Both the practical difficulties of IDENTITY politics and the influence of post-structural theories of the subject (see POST-STRUCTURALISM) have tended to soften this position. The understanding that subject positions are multiple and that social differences are constructed within relations of power has shifted focus away from binary thinking (i.e. the researcher is the same as or different from those studied) to understanding points of partial connection between researcher and researched, and how difference is constructed, including within the research process: '[T]he question of "Who speaks for whom?" cannot be answered upon the slippery slope of what personal attributes – what color, what GENDER, what SEXUALITY – legitimate our existence, but on the basis of our history of involvement, and on the basis of understanding how difference is constructed and used as a political tool' (Kobayashi, 1994, p. 78).

Rather than stable positionalities and relations of sameness or difference, the language has shifted to that of alliances, solidarities, collaborations, common ground and in-betweenness. Katz (1994) recommends a re-focusing of objectives, away from studying 'those poor people' to researching processes or sets of relations. Researchers can also re-deploy their privilege to access spaces of data collection and dissemination unavailable to the groups they collaborate with, support marginalized groups in their self-representation and multiply their communication resources (Butz and Besio, 2004). Rather than assuming that their research will benefit a needy group, a stance that Katz (1994) identifies as suspect because it elides the subjectivity of those researched, they can create situations in which all of the participants (academic, community partners and those researched) can appropriate the research products and use them in different ways to achieve their shared goals for social justice. Besio (Besio and Butz, 2004) cautions, however, that the capacity to position oneself in this way itself depends on positionality; in some cultural circumstances, for instance, it not a simple matter for women to enter into these kinds of research collaborations. Concerns are also raised about the hazards of over-identification with particular groups and there are good arguments for the practical and analytical benefits of scholarly distance (Brown, 1995). Finally, solidarity with ACTIVIST groups can raise ethical issues, posed most forcibly by Routledge (2002), when he performed a false identity in a duplicitous way to access information for activist allies. What are the ethical limits of this flexible positionality (see ETHICS)? This goes to the heart of what we understand as the purpose of scholarly knowledge production. GP

Suggested reading
Katz (1994); Kobayashi (1994); Rose (1997).

positive discrimination An approach that favours peoples who have traditionally suffered one or more forms of disadvantage. Positive discrimination or affirmative action programmes aim to rectify imbalances and injustices through direct intervention. In some cases, this might mean targeting policies spatially; for example, giving children from certain deprived NEIGHBOURHOODS preferential access to university places. In other cases, it might involve sector targeting; for example, in the appointment of women in senior positions in industries, in which men have traditionally dominated (Berman, 1984). The aim of both is to create a more egalitarian society, reducing if not eliminating inequalities (Leach, 1974). KWA

Suggested reading
Berman (1984).

positivism A historically variegated movement in PHILOSOPHY, affirming that only scientific knowledge is authentic knowledge, and denying validity to metaphysical (non-scientific) speculation (see also SCIENCE). The antecedents are Enlightenment thinkers such as David Hume (1711–76) and Pierre-Simon Laplace (1749–1827). But the term was first invented, and the philosophy formally codified, by the French philosopher and sociologist August Comte (1798–1851), and published in hefty instalments in his *Course in positivist philosophy* between 1830 and 1842 (six volumes). Subsequently, each future generation constructed positivism in accordance to its own ends, frequently minting a new title, perhaps the best known being LOGICAL POSITIVISM, born at discussions of the Vienna Circle during the 1920s (see also LOGICAL EMPIRICISM).

Six features characterize the different strains of positivism (Hacking, 1983):

(1) An emphasis on the importance of *observation* as the foundation for all (non-mathematical) knowledge. Scientific statements were to be grounded in immediate and accessible experience of the world, through the five senses (cf. EMPIRICISM). Such immediacy guaranteed that facts were pure, untainted by theory or value judgements; they represented the world as it really was – incorrigible and inviolate. In particular, for Comte recognition of observation as the source of knowledge was the culmination of an historical process in which the errors of previous eras, characterized by the (mistaken) dominance of first religious and later metaphysical thought, were finally overcome.

(2) A belief in either verification (using observations to prove a thesis), or its variant, FALSIFICATION (using observations to disprove a thesis). Verification or falsification is undertaken formally, using common methods and employing rigorous techniques such as statistical inference to scrupulously determine the truth or falsity of a statement.

(3) A conviction that causality seen in NATURE and SOCIETY is nothing more than the repetitive concurrence of one event followed by another. Positivism rejects the usual interpretation of cause reckoning it obscure metaphysical baggage (who has ever observed 'a cause'?). The alternative is a formulation tethered only to experience, the constant conjunction of observable events ('If event A, then event B': see LAW (SCIENTIFIC).

(4) A suspicion of theoretical entities that by definition are non-observable. Comte said that theoretical generalizations must always be regarded at best as mere HYPOTHESES, and logical positivists tried to reduce all theoretical statements to (legitimate) propositions of logic (an endeavour that ended disastrously). Even the less extreme solution of 'operationalism', that tied the meaning of a theoretical term to the empirical operations required to measure it, unravelled given the implication that each new measuring instrument defined a new theoretical term.

(5) A faith in the unity of the method allowing positivism to be as efficaciously applied to the HUMANITIES and social sciences as to the physical and life sciences. This is known as NATURALISM: one method fits all, revealing Truth wherever it is found. Comte envisioned the unity as a hierarchy in which disciplines studying more complex phenomena relied on the laws discovered in disciplines concerned with less complex phenomena (Hacking, 1983), whereas logical positivists (or at least Otto Neurath) championed the Unity of Science Movement, which cast knowledge of any discipline into the single mould of physics (the monumentally conceived *International encyclopaedia of unified science* was to show how this was to be done, but only two volumes were ever written: Reisch, 2005).

(6) The ardent denial of metaphysics (i.e. propositions bearing on the non-physical). Comte had no interest in metaphysical meaning, believing that their time literally had passed: now was the era of positivism. Logical positivists were just as extreme. A.J. Ayer (1936) titled the first chapter in his logical positivist manifesto for an English-language audience 'The elimination of metaphysics'.

Several of these six features have been found in GEOGRAPHY since its institutionalization in the nineteenth century, although sporadically, often only tacitly and never all at once. Before the Second World War, Anglo-American geography was not much of a fit. While the discipline defined itself in terms of the meticulous recording of empirical observations, often from the field, and so met positivism's first criterion, very few of the other criteria held, or at least for the reasons given by positivists.

For example, while geographers during this period were sceptical of theory, it was not because they were persuaded by philosophical arguments about the non-translation of an observation vocabulary into a theoretical one, but because theory implied a level of generalization that was deemed inappropriate to geographical subject matter (cf. EXCEPTIONALISM).

The advent of the QUANTITATIVE REVOLUTION in the late 1950s made positivism much more relevant to geography. Empirical observations continued to be central, although they were now often observations made by others and recorded in thick CENSUS volumes or on drums of magnetic tape (thereby shifting much geographical empirical enquiry from the field to the desk). Verification became a definitive pursuit undertaken using a set of ever more sophisticated formal statistical techniques (see QUANTITATIVE METHODS). Constant conjunctions were pursued, and Tobler (1970) announced the First Law of Geography: 'Everything is related to everything else, but near things are more related than distant things.' Positivism's fourth feature, suspicion towards theoretical terms, did not apply. Geography's quantitative revolutionaries were besotted by theory. In fact, the revolution had been primarily a theoretical one, especially in ECONOMIC GEOGRAPHY and URBAN GEOGRAPHY, which were transformed by importation of second-hand theory from physics, economics and sociology. The prospect of a unified method, however, was one of the quantitative revolution's strongest selling points. PHYSICAL GEOGRAPHY and HUMAN GEOGRAPHY would share a common language, and geographical science would be at one rather than a house divided. Finally, quantitative revolutionaries prosecuted less the open warfare on metaphysics that positivist philosophers urged than a continual undertone of carping about the need for greater precision, less vagueness and the importance of the exclusion of value judgements (see NORMATIVE THEORY).

All of this said, there were few explicit discussions of positivism as such until it was on the way out. Morrill (1993, p. 443), one of the pioneers of the quantitative revolution, said he 'never met a positivist'. And even Harvey's (1969) methodological compendium for scientific geography, *Explanation in geography*, barely used the word (it does not appear in the index), preferring instead 'scientific method'. The quantitative revolution was much more about getting on with the tasks of theoretical development and application, or crunching large data sets, than philosophizing about what was being done in the name of positivism. As a result, when some human geographers later vigorously attacked positivism, it did not necessarily undermine the practices of quantitative revolutionaries and spatial analysts, because the latter often neither knew nor deployed the full array of positivist tenets to begin with.

The critique of positivism was long and sustained, and in many ways still continues. Each one of the six features was criticized: (1) facts do not speak for themselves, but are always embedded in values, judgements and schemes of interpretation (see PARADIGMS); (2) truth is chimerical, and imbricated in larger social relations of POWER and knowledge (see CRITICAL THEORY; DISCOURSE); (3) constant conjunctions lead only to mindless statistical exercises, and not to explanation (see REALISM); (4) THEORY should be central to our enquiries, albeit not conceived as a mirror of the world, but as reflexive, critical, productive and provisional; (5) physical sciences offer no privileged method, but are fallible, contradictory, and limited by their historical and geographical situation (see SCIENCE); and (6) metaphysics goes all the way down, the lifeblood of our social existence and production of knowledge (see ETHICS; RELEVANCE; VALUES).

These counter-claims amount to a reassertion of the social foundations and responsibilities of intellectual enquiry, and a refusal to separate science from other discourses. Few geographers would now count themselves as positivist. Post-positivist geographies have: dimmed the enthusiasm for unbridled use of quantitative techniques; given a new slant to areas that formerly were characterized as positivist, such as economic geography and, more recently, GEOGRAPHICAL INFORMATION SYSTEMS; and opened up new fields such as FEMINISM and POST-COLONIALISM. In general, the fall of positivism in geography undermined the certainty and even optimism that the Quantitative Revolution and spatial science had promised, replacing it with what Gregory (1994) calls a 'cartographic anxiety' (see CARTOGRAPHIC REASON). Geography had grown up.   TB

Suggested reading
Gregory (1978); Kolakowski (1972).

possibilism A claim that human societies may respond in a variety of ways to the influences of the physical environment. Possibilism is primarily associated with the French School of HUMAN GEOGRAPHY that had its roots in the writings of Paul Vidal de la Blache (1845–1918), but also found favour in Britain in the early-twentieth-century work of Patrick Geddes and H.J. Fleure, and in the USA in Carl Ortin Sauer's insistence on the transformative power of human CULTURE (see also BERKELEY SCHOOL). It thus stands in contrast to ENVIRONMENTAL DETERMINISM and was classically expressed in Lucien Febvre's dictum 'There are no necessities, but everywhere possibilities; and man, as master of the possibilities, is the judge of their use' (Febvre, 1932, p. 27). Different philosophical roots of the doctrine have been identified, including neo-Kantian philosophy (see KANTIANISM: Berdoulay, 1976), probability theory associated with Poincaré (Lukermann, 1965), and Lamarckian biology (see LAMARCK(IAN)ISM: Archer, 1993). Differences between possibilism, environmental determinism and probabilism are more easily identified when taken as IDEAL TYPES rather than as operational perspectives in geographical research.   DNL

Suggested reading
Lukermann (1965).

Postan thesis A major interpretation of the dynamic of the medieval ECONOMY, proposed by historian Michael Postan (1898–1981). The thesis was first developed for England, but subsequently extended to cover much of Western EUROPE. Postan's ideas derived from classical POLITICAL ECONOMY, particularly Ricardo and Malthus, which he saw as a framework for understanding the links between population, landed RESOURCES and living standards over the long term (Postan, 1966, 1972; Hatcher and Bailey, 2001; see MALTHUSIAN MODEL). In so doing, he reacted negatively to linear interpretations of the medieval economy that were underwritten by a belief in the progressive growth of the MARKET and monetization as frameworks for understanding change. Indeed, the thesis was eventually utilized as a means of understanding both European medieval and early modern pre-industrial economies (Le Roy Ladurie, 1966; Abel, 1980).

Postan accepted classical political economic assumptions about the fixity of land supply as a factor of production, minimal technological innovation in farming and diminishing returns to increased labour inputs. As a result, he viewed population growth to be unsustainable in the long term, as it led to an oversupply of labour on the land and fragmentation of land holdings. Consequently, he argued that as a result of population growth over the thirteenth century, associated with real wage falls and shrinkage of holding sizes, an increasingly harvest-sensitive population emerged that was vulnerable to periodic crises (Postan and Titow, 1958–9). These were observable in a consistent tendency for death rates to rise with grain prices and responsible for cataclysmic phases such as the Great European FAMINE of 1315–22. Furthermore, he was inclined to see susceptibility to high death rates associated with EPIDEMIC disease such as the Black Death as a manifestation of society's vulnerability resulting from an imbalance between population and resource available per capita. Postan added other elements to this interpretation, such as a belief in the decline of soil fertility that arose as populations cropped land too frequently and nitrogen levels plummeted, driving communities to cultivate soil types that were inherently unsuitable for arable FARMING and grain production. He believed that population decline in the fourteenth century was a punishment for 'overfishing' in the previous century, and that the damage done to soil fertility was not repaired until at least the sixteenth century when population totals began again to recover.

Since Postan's death, historians and historical geographers have contested the idea that technology was unchanging and argued that the thirteenth- and early fourteenth-century economy was showing signs of developing specialization and genuine COMPARATIVE ADVANTAGES in a manner more consistent with Smithian growth theory (Britnell, 1993; Britnell and Campbell, 1995). It has also been argued, in conformity with the BOSERUP THESIS, that in densely populated areas of England grain yields were increased by an increase in labour inputs as land was cropped, weeded and fertilised more frequently (Campbell, 1983, 2000). Others have sought alternative explanations for weakness in the economy associated with seigneurial exploitation through the removal of surpluses legitimated by serfdom as a relation of production (see BRENNER THESIS). More recently, it has been claimed that the difficulties associated with harvest failure were in many instances caused by extreme natural events that would have impacted adversely on any pre-industrial economy (Bailey, 1992). It has also been argued that exogenously generated epidemic disease that brought down population levels after 1347 had little to do with the living standards of the population since rich and poor were equally susceptible (Bailey, 1996). Nonetheless, the model remains a powerful statement to which many interpreters still adhere on account of its conceptual elegance. RMS

Suggested reading
Campbell (2000); Hatcher and Bailey (2001); Postan (1972).

post-colonialism An intellectual movement originating in literary and cultural studies concerned with the diverse, uneven and contested impact of COLONIALISM on the cultures of colonizing and colonized peoples, in terms of the way in which relations, practices and representations are reproduced or transformed between past and present, as well as between the 'heart' and the 'margins' of empire and its aftermath. While the proliferation of uses and implied meanings of the term 'post-colonial' (and its conflation with other terms such as 'neo-colonial', 'ex-colonial', 'anti-colonial', 'post-independence' and 'post-imperial') has resulted in a tangled skein of intellectual threads, post-colonialism as a form of 'critical analysis of colonialism and its successor projects' takes as axiomatic the following: (1) a 'close and critical reading of colonial discourse'; (2) an understanding of 'the complicated and fractured histories through which colonialism passes from the past into the present'; (3) a mapping of 'the ways in which metropolitan and colonial societies are drawn together in webs of affinity, influence and dependence'; and (4) a sensitivity to the 'political implications' of the way history is constructed (Gregory, 2000).

Post-colonialism may refer to something tangible, with 'real political and historical referents in space and time, locating cultural as well as economic and political connections between metropole and colony' (King, 1993, p. 90). This take on post-colonialism can be distinguished in work focusing on forms of post-colonial expressions and IDENTITY such as the social, demographic, political, cultural and spatial forms, styles and identities in once-colonial societies of the periphery (Simon, 1998, p. 230). Post-colonial NATION-STATES are often 'overwhelmed with the onslaught of representational spaces' in attempts to produce the 'ideal of the post-colonial citizen' (Srivastava, 1996, p. 406). Urban forms and architecture, in particular, have been treated as 'a social and political means of representation in which a post-colonial nation forms a dialogue with its colonial past' (Kusno, 1998, p. 551). Post-colonial strivings for a new identity do not completely banish the colonial past, but involve the selective retrieval and appropriation of indigenous (see INDIGENOUS KNOWLEDGE) and colonial cultures to produce appropriate forms to represent the post-colonial present. Often 'ironic', 'contradictory' and anxious about 'inauthenticity', post-colonial identity is constituted by both a 'relatively unproblematic identification with the colonizer's culture, *and* a rejection of the colonizer's culture' (Kusno, 1998, p. 550).

Using the term 'post-colonialism' to refer to a specific period *after* colonialism is, however, problematic, as the historical reality in the second half of the twentieth century in the once-colonized world was shaped by 'a modernity that is scored by the claws of colonialism, left full of contradictions, of half-finished processes, of confusions, of HYBRIDITY, and liminalities' (Lee and Lam, 1998, p. 968). Post-colonialism must be understood in a plural sense, for there are 'quite radical differences in the "colonial" relationship between the imperial centre and the colonized in the various parts of the former empires' (Mishra and Hodge, 1991, p. 412). The term is hence less usefully tied to a specific historical moment, a political status or a concrete object. Instead, more critically, the 'post-colonial' is used to signify 'an attitude of critical engagement with colonialism's after-effects and its constructions of knowledge' (Radcliffe, 1997, p. 1331). It provides a conceptual frame that works to destabilize dominant DISCOURSES in the metropolitan West, to challenge inherent assumptions, and to critique the material and discursive legacies of colonialism (Crush, 1994; Jackson and Jacobs, 1996; Jacobs, 1996, Blunt and McEwan, 2002; McEwan, 2003). Post-colonial critique engages with 'the monumental binary constructions of East/West, traditional/ modern, natural/cultural, structural/ornamental' in order to locate 'productive tensions arising from incommensurate differences rather than deceptive reconciliations' (Nalbantoglu and Wong, 1997, p. 8).

The emancipatory radicalism and recuperative stance ascribed to the 'post-colonial' have been questioned in a number of ways. Critics argue that just as the application of the category 'pre-colonial' to societies prior to their incorporation into European political and economic systems tend to fix the 'colonial' as the main point of reference, adding the prefix 'post-' may also impose 'the continuity of foreign histories' and 'subordinate indigenous histories' (Perera, 1998, p. 6). It begs the question whether the condition of the world today has been so reconfigured as to be 'incontrovertibly *post-colonial*' (Hall, 1996, p. 256), or whether it is more likely that 'colonialism left the everyday life of many quite untouched; or that the changes it did bring often passed unrecognized as changes' (During, 1992, p. 346). Privileging 'the moment of the "post-colonial" ... [may] simply revive or re-stage exactly what the post-colonial so triumphantly declares to be "over"' (Hall, 1996b, p. 248; cf. Gregory, 2004).

Others have cautioned against the navel-gazing tendencies of certain forms of post-colonial studies – which seem reluctant to go much further beyond theorizing 'the meaning of the hyphen' (Mishra and Hodge, 1991, p. 399) – and have emphasized instead the need for post-colonial studies to engage with 'material practices, actual spaces and real politics' (Sylvester, 1999, p. 712: see also Driver, 1996; Jackson and Jacobs, 1996; Barnett, 1997, p. 137; Lester, 1998; Driver and Gilbert, 1999b). If the main limits of post-colonial theories lie in their mistaken 'attempt to transcend in RHETORIC what has not been transcended in substance' (Ryan, 1994, p. 82), then an important starting place in overcoming some of these limitations would be to dissect post-colonialism as threaded through real spaces, built forms and the material substance of everyday biospheres.

At the same time, the 'prospects of getting past the post' (Yeoh, 2001) must be tied to the larger enterprise of constructing and elaborating alternative post-colonial geographical traditions that will steer a path through what Ram (1998, p. 628) calls 'on the one hand, a sphere of the modern which is so hopelessly contaminated by its colonial origins that it seems exhausted as a source of critique and action, and on the other, a non-elite discourse which is completely unconnected with the modern and is unable to represent anything other than utter OTHERNESS'. The first steps are the most difficult, as Chatterjee (1994, p. 216) points out: "EUROPE and the AMERICAS, the only true subjects of history, have thought out on our behalf not only the script of colonial enlightenment and exploitation, but also our anti-colonial resistance and post-colonial misery.' Sidaway (2000, p. 593) also notes that 'any postcolonial geography must realize within itself its own impossibility, given that geography is inescapably marked (both philosophically and institutionally) by its location

and development as a western-colonial science'. For a post-colonial geography to aspire to significant breaks with the prescribed script, one step forward would be to view post-colonialism as a highly mobile, contestatory and still-developing arena, where opportunities for insight may be gained at multiple sites. While its redemptive features as a means of resisting colonialisms of all forms and its manipulative aspects as a vehicle for colonialism to reproduce itself cannot be totally disentangled, its critical edges may be sharpened not only to 'dismantle colonialism's signifying system', but also to articulate the silences of the native by 'liberating the suppressed in discourse', and to speak back to the centre (Alatas, 1995, p. 131: see also Rattansi, 1997; Nagar and Ali, 2003). In this vein, Robinson (2003a, citing Chakrabarty) calls for a 'provincialising' of Western scholarship, followed by a more sustained engagement with cosmopolitan practices in the production of post-colonial knowledge.   BY

Suggested reading
Blunt and McEwan (2002); Robinson (2003); Sidaway (2000).

post-development A tradition of thinking and political action that refuses to accept that DEVELOPMENT is somehow natural or innocent. Its proponents also dispute the suggestion that 'developing countries' can or should follow in the footsteps of the WEST/NORTH. Some post-developmentalists go further and argue that the DISCOURSE of development has done immense damage in the global South. Arturo Escobar (1995) has famously maintained that development produced only FAMINE, debt and increased POVERTY for the majority world. Post-1950 development had failed, he said, and other modes of being had to be discovered and worked through. In this vein, post-development refers to that set of ecological, economic and cultural experiments that will produce new and presumably better ways of being human.

Post-development thought is really a spectrum of oppositional thinking that mixes old and new insights in roughly equal measure. At one end of the spectrum is a tradition of ANTI-DEVELOPMENT thought that is frankly dismissive of development. Anti-development activists reach back to Mahatma Gandhi and Leo Tolstoy when they contend that development is violent and dehumanizing. There is more than a hint of this thinking is Escobar's book, *Encountering development*: development has failed and it must be overcome. But Escobar also draws on work produced by DEPENDENCY THEORISTS in the 1960s, including André Gunder Frank. Like many others, he maintains that the dominant MODEL of economic MODERNIZATION in the North cannot be exported to the global SOUTH. The core countries use their power to prevent balanced development. It would also be unwise, and probably impossible, for the majority world to copy the ecologically exploitative model of development pursued in the North (see also CORE-PERIPHERY MODEL).

What made Escobar's work so challenging, however, was the fact that he drew on work by Michel Foucault and the SUBALTERN STUDIES collective to think about the production of development as a form of GOVERNMENTALITY. Escobar argued that the THIRD WORLD had been invented by American AID programmes as the residual in a COLD WAR struggle between the First and Second Worlds. There is nothing natural about this SOCIAL CONSTRUCTION – nothing, save for an uncommon history of colonialism – that produced this diverse mix of countries as a singular space that henceforth would be defined by its 'mass poverty' and pathological lack of development. Escobar, in other words, argued that an IMAGINED GEOGRAPHY of UNDERDEVELOPMENT was constructed by a discourse of development that infantilized the majority world in relation to a mythical view of a perfect and benevolent West. Under the sign of development, Western experts (aid workers, technicians, military personnel) were then set free in the Third World ostensibly to secure its own dissolution. The fact that the United Nations designated the 1960s as the Development Decade speaks to the hubris that Escobar is so keen to skewer.

Escobar's work has been important in forcing a re-evaluation of the (un)productive work performed by developmentalism. By linking the study of development to GEOPOLITICS, Escobar was able to raise important questions about the meanings of COLONIALISM. Was development not simply the continuation of colonialism by another name? Did it not turn Third World men and women into a set of experimental subjects, to be dissected later in a museum or university? (See Ashis Nandy's comments on the back cover of *Encountering development*.) At the same time, there are weaknesses in Escobar's account. His suggestion that development began in 1949 ignores a history of thinking about progress and disorder (about development) that has been explored in some detail by Arndt (1981) and

Cowen and Shenton (1996). Corbridge (1998) and Kiely (1999) have further argued that Escobar's insistence on a singular discourse of development blinds him to the different governmental interventions that emerge from, for instance, the basic needs agenda, a GENDER AND DEVELOPMENT framework or NEO-LIBERALISM. At times, Escobar comes close to the anti-development position of wanting to escape from all forms of governmentality. But it is not clear how this escape will be effected; nor is it clear that Escobar has spelled out the opportunity costs of his development alternatives. In part, this is because he damns development in its entirety, failing to note that life expectancies in many parts of the world increased at a historically unprecedented rate after 1950.

If Escobar uses Foucault to moralize about developmentalism, other versions of post-development thinking are less obviously NORMATIVE. Partha Chatterjee (2004), for example, has begun to develop a POST-COLONIAL response to what he calls the 'unscrupulously charitable' gestures of neo-liberalism, and of the *new public administration* (NPA) that so often goes with it. He has repeatedly drawn attention to the different chronologies of the creation of the modern state in the West and in the countries of ASIA and AFRICA. In his view, technologies of governmentality and the creation of named populations pre-date the formation of the NATION-STATE and CIVIL SOCIETY in most of the world. NPA demands for good governance and participatory development by individuals are often wildly at odds with local realities, where people need the support of skilled brokers in political society. In an exploration of development and bureaucratization in Lesotho, James Ferguson (1990) has charged that, while individual development projects fail on a regular basis, they combine to produce an anti-politics machine that substitutes the technical jargon of development for concerted public discussion of gender relations, land rights, the nature of the STATE and so on. Ferguson's argument, in other words, is not that development has failed (*pace* Escobar). Rather, it is that a reasonably diverse range of development interventions has failed to end rural poverty in Lesotho, but has succeeded, sometimes unwittingly, in extending bureaucratic state power in the countryside.

Ferguson's work on the anti-politics machine suggests one fruitful avenue for a post-developmentalism that maintains links to radical development thinking. Similar

563

accounts of the depoliticization of development have been essayed by Peter Uvin (1998) on aid agencies in Rwanda, John Harriss (2001) on the banalities of Robert Putnam's work on SOCIAL CAPITAL theories and David Mosse (2005) on the power effects of a major UK aid project in India. It is here perhaps, and in explorations of the ways in which development thinking continues to express Western anxieties or fantasies about 'itself' (Gilman, 2003), that post-development thought has most to offer.   SCO

Suggested reading
Cooper and Packard (1998); Escobar (1995); Ferguson (1990); Watts (2003).

post-Fordism A set of production techniques that are more flexible than those associated with FORDISM and are used as part of FLEXIBLE ACCUMULATION. The techniques have three main characteristics: (1) flexibility is emphasized both in the skills of workers (who may be part-time to allow their flexible deployment as and when there is demand for a product) and in the functionality of machines that need to be reprogrammable and useable for producing a variety of different products; (2) vertical disintegration rather than vertical integration, as production relies on a close-knit NETWORK of suppliers who can quickly respond to changes in demand; and (3) an emphasis on accurate and high-quality final products because of the JUST-IN-TIME PRODUCTION and the selectivity of consumers. Post-Fordism is often said to have emerged in response to the CRISIS conditions of the 1970s, when Fordism as a MODE OF PRODUCTION and REGIME OF ACCUMULATION became unstable. However, others have pointed out that in reality many of the techniques associated with post-Fordism have existed since before the emergence of Fordism itself and were simply reinvented in the early 1980s (Gertler, 1988; Amin, 1994). Indeed, the term 'after-Fordism' was used by Peck and Tickell (1994) in recognition of the lack of a coherent set of principles underlying post-Fordism and the way in which elements of both Fordism and flexible accumulation often coexist in the production techniques and strategies of firms.

For geographers, post-Fordism is inextricably linked with the region or CLUSTER, because of the importance of AGGLOMERATION and LOCALIZATION economies for flexible production.   JF

posthumanism An intellectual and cultural style of work, evident in CRITICAL THEORY, architecture, PHILOSOPHY and the social sciences, that emphasizes the impurities involved in becoming human, oriented against a humanist tradition that has long been the dominant mode of understanding in the HUMANITIES and social sciences. Where HUMANISM supposes that humans, with their capacities for rationality, consciousness, ingenuity, soul, language and so on, stand at the centre of social action and can transcend the natural realm, posthuman work insists that all of these capacities are achieved with the help of many others (including non-humans). Two related bodies of theoretical understanding are often used to make such claims (Braun, 2004a). The first draws upon new forms of vitalism (Watson, 1998), associated with readings of Henri Bergson and Gilles Deleuze, where matters as elusive as consciousness, mind, MEMORY and other repositories often labelled quintessentially human, are taken to be nothing more and nothing less than complex movements of matter. Some of this style of working has been taken up under the label of ACTOR-NETWORK THEORY. The second intervention draws more upon DECONSTRUCTIVE traditions, and demonstrates the impossibility of a purely human subject (Badmington, 2000). In the latter the human project, or anthropological machine as Agamben (2002) has called it, can be demonstrated to be little other than an always partial differentiation of humans from non-humans, frequently taking the form of human/ANIMAL distinctions. While the prefix 'post' can sometimes be read as describing a newly emergent historical condition, wherein a once pure human is increasingly in danger of being made extinct by the growth of prosthetics, genetic technologies, new reproductive technologies and so on (Fukuyama, 2002), such HISTORICISM misses the point. The contention is that the human and humanist project has always been a fraught and heterogeneous endeavour, involving more than human beings, even if the promiscuities have achieved new forms and intensities (Hayles, 1999). The result is a challenge to re-imagine the social of social science and the human of HUMAN GEOGRAPHY. It is also a politicization of many suppressed things once left at the margins of human debate. Posthumanism, positively spun, involves 'Mixing wild imaginings with routine inventiveness, ... [heralding] a politicisation of the technologies of life in which intellectual disputes and public controversies become inextricably entangled in the event of FOOD scares, organ harvesting, genetic profiling and any number of other

BIO-POLITICAL controversies' (Whatmore, 2004, p. 1360). sjh

Suggested reading
Whatmore (2004).

post-industrial city A CITY whose economic geography has passed from a dependence on manufacturing to an emphasis on service employment (see SERVICES). Typically, its dual LABOUR MARKET is characterized by a division between well-paid private- and public-sector professional and managerial workers and lower-paid service staff. The pattern of land uses and social areas in the post-industrial city shows marked variations from the arrangement in the classic concentric-ring model of industrial cities (cf. ZONAL MODEL). The downtown skyline is now marked by new investment in office towers, public institutions, arts and sports complexes, and restaurant and LEISURE services. The brownfield sites of old industrial and transportation land uses around downtown have given way to waterfront redevelopment of condominiums and public leisure spaces, often the result of PUBLIC-PRIVATE PARTNERSHIPS. A number of INNER-CITY neighbourhoods have experienced reinvestment and GENTRIFICATION as the housing market responds to the downtown LABOUR MARKET of advanced services. New immigrants and the working poor are being displaced outwards to suburban sites, which have become the new focus of manufacturing and wholesaling, adjacent to the airport and regional highway routes. The SUBURBS are diversifying in lifestyle and social status, and with the emergence of satellite town centres (or EDGE CITIES in the largest METROPOLITAN AREAS) are assuming a more urban status themselves.

The characteristics of the post-industrial city extend beyond its population and land-use features. Canadian studies indicate that the GENDER and family traits of post-industrial cities differ from those with a manufacturing base, with smaller HOUSEHOLDS, a greater tendency for gender equality in the workplace, and lower and later marriage rates (Ley, 1996). Lifestyle LIBERALISM and higher levels of SECULARISM are among distinctive attitudinal and cultural associations.

Though typically experiencing economic and population growth, the post-industrial city faces significant challenges. Since the 1980s, NEO-LIBERAL policy has tended to trade welfare services for entrepreneurial objectives (Harvey, 1989a), accentuating social and spatial polarization (Walks, 2001). The emphasis upon QUALITY OF LIFE considerations for the middle CLASS might compromise provision of more basic services; for example, tax dollars expended on consumer attractions such as sports stadia could diminish the quality of life of more impoverished populations (Friedman, Andrew and Silk, 2004). Population growth and a large middle-class labour market are often associated with challenges to housing affordability (see HOUSING STUDIES). Under-investment in public transportation has heightened the dependence on the private car, leading to traffic congestion and severe air POLLUTION episodes. And, as the Paris *banlieu* riots of 2005 demonstrated so keenly, suburban sites may be a newly emergent zone of acute SOCIAL EXCLUSION. DL

Suggested reading
Ley (1980); Robson (1994).

post-industrial society A conceptualization of the changing conditions of ECONOMY and SOCIETY in the global NORTH, beginning approximately in the 1960s. The term was popularized by Daniel Bell's immensely influential book (1999 [1973]), and has enjoyed widespread dissemination, though not always with the specificity that Bell intended. Post-industrial society is concerned with an occupational transformation in advanced societies as, with automation and outsourcing, employment moves increasingly to a white-collar, service profile, with specialized information and information technology playing a key role in the shaping of society and economy. Beyond this, some authors see an evolutionary process, with societies passing through discrete economic and social stages from the harvesting of raw materials, to manufacturing, and finally to the provision of SERVICES aiding both consumption and production.

Through the 1970s, several variations on the theme of post-industrial society emerged. Influenced by the French student reaction against inaccessible STATE bureaucracies, Alain Touraine (1971) proposed that the holders of specialized information were becoming a privileged technocracy, extending control over growing domains of EVERYDAY LIFE. A second stream of work emphasized the holders of specialized knowledge as a new middle CLASS of professional and managerial workers, though internally fragmented by their variable access to economic and CULTURAL CAPITAL and their location in the public and private sectors (Gouldner, 1979). A third track emphasized by Manuel Castells and his followers identified

565

the role of information nodes and FLOWS in the shaping of new social configurations.

The dominant figure, however, has been Daniel Bell. Although concerned with occupational transformations to a service society, his thesis went considerably further, as he sought to trace the forward trajectory of advanced societies, using the paradigmatic case of the USA, in the three interlocking domains of social structure, politics and CULTURE. He noted a potential non-correspondence of the parts in this forward process, as, for example, a steadily more disciplined economy was tied to a steadily more antinomian culture. For Bell, a knowledge theory of value replaced a LABOUR THEORY OF VALUE, and this opened up serious disagreement with Western Marxist theorists and more doctrinaire versions in Moscow (see MARXISM). By the mid-1980s, however, leftist critics were acknowledging the accuracy of Bell's cultural and labour force projections (Wright and Martin, 1987). Nonetheless, Bell's thesis, like all SOCIAL THEORY, was a child of its time. Published as the unprecedented postwar boom was about to end, it is written from an overly optimistic and middle-class perspective, where scarcity and conflict do not deflect a track of upward social MOBILITY. But it has proven a seminal PARADIGM for subsequent research, and its basic propositions are now part of the taken-for-granted world of contemporary social science.　　DL

Suggested reading
Bell (1999 [1973]); Clement and Myles (1994).

post-Marxism Although the term 'post-Marxism' is sometimes applied to diagnose the post-Soviet era of GEOPOLITICS, this chronological usage trivializes an intellectual ferment that pre-dates the fall of the Berlin Wall by at least two decades. If calendar time is the touchstone, the year 1968 is a more precise marker of post-Marxism. Moreover, intellectual ferment neither implies a cohesive intellectual project nor necessarily an identifiable body of theory. And so it is with post-Marxism, which has instead become a convenient rubric for varying analyses of exploitation in CAPITALIST societies that depart from the rigidity and exclusivity of class-centred Marxist orthodoxy. The first explicit allegiance to a post-Marxist agenda is found in Ernesto Laclau and Chantal Mouffe's influential manifesto for RADICAL DEMOCRACY, *Hegemony and socialist strategy*, where they declare: '[I]f our intellectual project in this book is *post*-Marxist, it is also post-*Marxist*' (1985, p. 5).

In consort with other post-Marxist scholars who follow *or* precede Laclau and Mouffe, a good part of this new enterprise concerns itself with the array of DISCOURSES – that is, sign-regimes allied to institutional apparatuses – which constitute SUBJECTS and IDENTITIES in differing and differentiated ways. Indeed, if there is a common thread to 'post-Marxist' analysis, it is the insistence that there exists neither a sovereign, self-present subject who can be recognized as the centre of initiatives and the natural holder of individual rights (as in liberal political theory: see LIBERALISM); nor a collective CLASS-actor that commands ONTOLOGICAL primacy as agent of history (the proletariat in classical MARXISM). The subject is instead posited as radically incomplete or overdetermined in varying registers – psychological (Jacques Lacan, Louis Althusser), representational (Jacques Derrida, Jean-François Lyotard, Gayatri Chakravorty Spivak) or social/political (Stuart Hall, Ernesto Laclau and Chantal Mouffe, J.K. Gibson-Graham). Connected to these disavowals is a series of others – namely, rejecting a presumed primacy of the economic, CLASS, HISTORICISM, totality and a predominantly union-based labour or progressive politics.　　VG

Suggested reading
Callari and Ruccio (1996); Gibson-Graham (2006b [1996]); Laclau and Mouffe (1985); Sim (1998).

postmaterialism A generously roomy term that is suggestive rather than definitive. The prefix highlights an historical discontinuity in cultural expectations surrounding the relationship between SOCIETY and the non-human world. The term captures the elevation of aesthetic and QUALITY OF LIFE concerns over issues of production and distribution. Coined by Inglehart (1977), it describes the growth of ENVIRONMENTALISM and the decreased dominance of CLASS-based politics in the postwar era. Postmaterialism may be interpreted as an 'ECOLOGY of affluence' that is distinguishable from the 'environmentalism of the poor', whose ecological claims are rooted in the defence of livelihoods rather than quality of life (Guha and Martinez-Alier, 2000).　　GB

Suggested reading
Guha and Martinez-Alier (2000).

postmodernism An important architectural, aesthetic and intellectual movement that flourished in the latter quarter of the twentieth century. It is easily (but mistakenly) conflated with its more philosophical contemporary, POST-STRUCTURALISM, as well as with the deeper currents (economic, political, social) signalled by its epoch-defining cousin, POST-MODERNITY. And though it is sometimes indistinguishable from the intellectual trajectories of the other two 'posts', most would agree to constrain it to the cultural sphere (see CULTURE). Uncertainty exists as to whether or not postmodernism has ended, but clearly the excitement and controversy it generated has for the most part abated. While there is evidence that its roots are older, beginning in the 1960s and 1970s, many put postmodernism's apex alongside the popularization of video MEDIA and the televisualization of the Reagan presidency in the 1980s (or the politician's digital counterpart, Max Headroom).

Broadly speaking, the thematics that characterize postmodernism's artistic dimensions were said to constitute either a break from or an extension of the desire of MODERNISM to turn the everyday and the mundane into ART. Perhaps the most important result of this (dis) connection was the effort to take art out of the hands of the rich elite (historically, the main consumers of art) by collapsing the distinction between 'high' and 'low' aesthetic forms. The notorious tendency of postmodernists to blend multiple media in one work was often accomplished by combining forms that had previously been dismissed as vulgar elements of popular culture and thus marginalized in art – as in, for example, comic books, advertisements and graffiti. Modernist thematics often encouraged, if not required, reflection and contemplation about the layered meaning of a work, which was in some cases paired with the goal of faithfully recovering the artist's intentionality. In addition, many modernist works highlighted themes of ALIENATION, increased mechanization and rationalization. Postmodernism, to the contrary, often celebrated pastiche, depthlessness, multiplicity, uncertainty and fragmentation. In the hands of some postmodernists, history became less a reservoir of facts awaiting excavation than a playground of potential appropriations in which authenticity, timeless values and fealty to the truth were mocked by unceremonial gestures towards nostalgia.

Postmodern architecture concretized these concepts in the built environment. In contrast to modern architecture's allegiance to functionality and its dismissal of ornamentation (Relph, 1987), postmodern designs were playful if not exuberant, aimed at creating confusion by overlapping and juxtaposing in contiguous spaces many different aesthetic styles. As in art, postmodern architecture was to pillage rather than revere history, borrowing elements such as Greek and Roman pillars and embellishing façades with touches of Art Deco. Postmodernism's exchangeability of parts implied a relativistic approach to meaning, one that denies centres, or 'depths', of understanding (see RELATIVISM). Even the popular reflective windows of the 1980s were, according to Harvey (1989b), a flippant response to profundity, a refusal of a deeper inside that turns the gaze back upon the viewer.

That these architectural forms appeared alongside GENTRIFICATION and a raging consumerism in the 1980s and 1990s was not lost on human geographers, and for the most part their reaction was unfavourable. Harvey's (1989b) critique of the condition of postmodernity famously first situated postmodern urban forms within a set of deeper economic and political transformations (notably from FORDISM to POST-FORDISM or FLEXIBLE ACCUMULATION), and then explained what he regarded as the cultural 'response' (depthlessness, relativism, the ransacking of history etc.) as the surface-level outcome of dislodged sensibilities produced by TIME–SPACE COMPRESSION under late CAPITALISM. Among the spaces read as signs of a distinctively postmodern SPATIALITY were Baltimore's revitalized harbour (Harvey, 1989b), Los Angeles's Bonaventure Hotel (Jameson, 1984), New York's South Street Seaport (Boyer, 1992), and Los Angeles and Orange counties, in California (Soja, 1989, 1992). Whether indicted for presenting false history, structuring SPACE for maximum SURVEILLANCE, or attempting purposefully to disorient, each were tied in one way or another to the excesses of postmodernism. As Sorkin (1992b, p. 4; see also Goss, 1993) put it in describing Canada's West Edmonton Mall, 'Mirrored columns ... fragment the scene, shattering the mall into a kaleidoscope of ultimately unreadable images. Confusion proliferates at every level; past and future collapse meaninglessly into the present; barriers between real and fake, near and far, dissolve as history, NATURE, technology, are indifferently processed by the mall's fantasy machine.' Another part of the urban underbelly of postmodernism was its socio-spatial SEGREGATION, denounced by Davis (1990) as 'Fortress LA' (1992), and described by Dear and Flusty (1998) as alternating between

567

Dreamscapes of Privatopia and the Carceral City's Mean Streets. As Smith (1996b) was to make clear within the context of gentrification more generally, the new spaces of the 'revanchist' city were not simply drawn by CAPITAL, but were forged out of an unholy alliance between it and the state. Looking back on these dreary accounts of postmodern URBANISM, it is hard to remember the democratically minded intentions of one of its most influential progenitors – Robert Venturi – who reacted against the sparseness of orthodox MODERNISM by collapsing the distinction between high and low architecture in his famous book, *Learning from Las Vegas* (Venturi, Scott Brown and Izenor, 1972).

Postmodernism elicited several different responses in HUMAN GEOGRAPHY. As the foregoing suggests, many of the first responses were influenced by postmodernism in architecture and planning (rather than literature or the creative arts more generally). Some saw in postmodernism's attention to difference and specificity an opportunity to revive and refashion HUMANISTIC GEOGRAPHY as a form of irredeemably critical and affirmative LOCAL KNOWLEDGE (e.g. Ley, 1987, 1993, 2003a), while others saw an opportunity for a far more theoretically ambitious, insistently radical reconstruction of human geography writ large (Dear, 1986, 1988; Dear and Flusty, 2002). Many of these discussions were inspired in some measure by experiments in urbanism on the west coast of North America, notably Los Angeles and Vancouver, and they fostered the emergence and identification of a LOS ANGELES SCHOOL. One of its principal protagonists was Edward Soja, who straddled the

Modernism	*Postmodernism*
Compartmentalism	Holism
Individualism	Communalism
Rationalism	Spiritualism
Nationalism	Globalism
Imperatives	Tolerance

fields of GEOGRAPHY and planning. Unlike Ley and Dear, however, he had a much more positive view of HISTORICAL MATERIALISM and of the (crucial) possibility of its spatialized reconstruction through a critical engagement with postmodernism (see Soja, 1989). Against this, however, as noted above, Harvey (1989b) mobilized his own historico-geographical materialism as a vigorous critique of

postmodernism and postmodernity. These more architectonic versions of postmodernism as critical project (Soja) and critical object (Harvey) were roundly criticized by FEMINIST geographers in particular for their insensitivity to difference. These critiques were part of a growing interest in POST-COLONIALISM and post-structuralism that soon eclipsed postmodernism in human geography and beyond.

Today, the hullabaloo over postmodernism has waned, but it manages to live on in some contexts, including not only architecture but also, strangely enough, RELIGION. Part philosophical engagement inspired by post-structuralists such as Jacques Derrida (see Caputo, 1997; Caputo and Scanlon, 1999), and part a cultural wave of new Age, Eastern mysticism, this latest reconfiguration of postmodernism is paired against a disbelieving modernism, elements of which (see table) have been deployed in epic battles against religion.

How the religion–postmodernism nexus will evolve remains to be seen, but one thing is certain: whether we are in a state of MODERNITY or postmodernity, it will not take long for contemporary culture to construct nostalgia *for* postmodernism, making pastiche out of it as it did to everything else, serving up ironic quotations of the movement that gave new meaning to the term 'irony'. KWO/JPJ

Suggested reading
Dear and Flusty (1998); Harvey (1989b); Jameson (1991); Ley (2003a); Soja (1989).

postmodernity Not to be confused with the cultural and aesthetic movement POSTMODERNISM, postmodernity refers to the contemporary historical period that arguably closed the door upon MODERNITY. The advent of the historical era and its associated artistic movement occurred during roughly the same period (the mid-to-late twentieth century), but the driving forces of postmodernity operate at a longer time-scale than do those of postmodernism (particularly now that the cultural form is into its dotage). While modernity was characterized by an insistence upon the possibility and knowability of 'Truth', postmodernity replaced its FOUNDATIONAL assumptions of solvability in scientific enterprises (see SCIENCE), universality in ethical imperatives (see ETHICS) and transcendence in the essence of things (see ONTOLOGY) with uncertainty, singularity and immanence. For better or worse (and it has certainly been both), the defining elements of postmodernity arose from a series of major transformations in the social, economic and political understandings about the how the world is materialized and experienced (Jones, Natter and Schatzki, 1995).

Intellectually, postmodernity is generally considered to be a period initiated by a thorough rupture in the history of Western thought, with its confident allegiances to what Jean-François Lyotard (1984) called 'metanarratives' – grand theories of SOCIETY and human progress. These were thoroughly critiqued and often rejected by postmodernity's more philosophical wing, POST-STRUCTURALISM, which was a concurrent response to STRUCTURALISM and its endless proliferation of binarized power relations. Post-structuralism quickly extended its critical scope to the hegemonic conceptual cornerstones of Western modernity, sometimes even back to their foundational theorizations in Greek PHILOSOPHY. More broadly, postmodernity's historical break might be loosely described in terms of an avoidance of theoretical absolutism, an investment in epistemological constructivism (sometimes bastardized and mischaracterized under the slogan 'everything is relative': cf. RELATIVISM), a celebration of DIFFERENCE, a fascination with open systems and a devotion to complex relations of POWER (for a review of key thinkers, see Best and Kellner, 1991). Its rise alongside the information age inflects it away from modernity's faith in our ability to accurately and adequately represent the world, and for some, such as Jean Baudrillard (1993), postmodernity's products are not simply bad reproductions but 'simulacra', copies taken as more real than the reality that they represent (see REPRESENTATION; SIMULACRUM).

The uptake of these notions was in great part a response to the horrors that attended the rise of FASCISM and the HOLOCAUST. Often read by members of the postwar Frankfurt School (see CRITICAL THEORY) and later by post-structuralist thinkers as the logical culmination of the worst parts of modernity and as *the* political crisis to which all future ethico-political thought must respond, these events effectively signalled the end of an era. As postmodernity has progressed, its central ideas have been adopted and adapted for both progressive and quite cynical, reactionary ends.

By the late 1980s, it appeared that postmodernity and postmodernism were co-extensive, and indeed the intellectual fashions of the former fed the cultural currents of the latter. The geographer David Harvey sought to explain these connections in his 1989 book, *The condition of postmodernity* (see also Jameson, 1991;

Soja, 1989). A testament to the broader importance of both 'posts' across the intellectual and popular landscape, the book was wildly successful inside and outside HUMAN GEOGRAPHY, making Harvey one of the most well known Anglophone theorists of the twentieth century. The argument draws primarily from Harvey's reformulation of POLITICAL ECONOMY as an explicitly historico-geographical materialism, and situates both postmodernity and postmodernism within the transformations of SPACE and TIME (or, rather, time–space) brought about by the latest stage of CAPITALISM, which began to take on a new shape in the 1970s. As Harvey explained, the age of postmodernity was characterized by a series of growing CRISES in capitalism, the results of which heralded a shift from a relatively stable set of production relations, FORDISM, exemplified by the capital–state–labour contract sealed by the New Deal in the USA, to the contemporary era of POST-FORDISM. When that contract expired under the weight of international competition for low wages, Western capitalists responded with JUST-IN-TIME PRODUCTION, a credit-based economy, and the spatial fixes of capital relocation and fresh market penetration. The new economy's spatial, technological and labour processes had become, under the regime of FLEXIBLE ACCUMULATION, more nimble and quicker to change. Harvey's argument was not, however, to draw a direct line of causality from these disruptions in the economic sphere to postmodernity's seemingly similar loss of moorings in the intellectual domain. It was, rather, to couple these transformations through shifts in the 'experience of space–time'; as he put it, economic change led to TIME-SPACE COMPRESSION, which dramatically redrew our cognitive maps of the social order. Into this confusion arose postmodernity, the result of a profound disenchantment with modernity's long-held matrix of certainty and order. For its turn, postmodernism was simply a cultural blip, an ephemeral reaction in ART and architecture to the deeper anxieties brought forth by postmodernity (for an extended discussion, see Gregory, 1994, Part III, esp. pp. 406–14).

From Harvey, it follows that we should not welcome postmodernity as a new, emancipatory era that moves us beyond a confining, stodgy and conservative modernity, but see it rather as a description of forces that are deep, complex and surprising. And since 1989, arguably, things have intensified: the collapse of COMMUNISM, massive CONSUMPTION and even larger looming crises fuelled by speculation, a troubling expansion of the PRIVATIZATION of STATE functions, high levels of economic inequality alongside increased racial and ethnic tensions, and a neo-liberal excitement for free MARKETS for CAPITAL but sealed BORDERS for labour (see NEO-LIBERALISM). Meanwhile, all of these markers of instability are smoothed over with a blind, middle-class nostalgia for a media-invented image of modernity, DEMOCRACY and white HETERONORMATIVITY. Meanwhile, the exportation of cowboy capitalism to the global SOUTH serves to hide exploitative production practices and their associated environmental consequences from the eyes of Northern consumers, while simultaneously exporting jobs and hardening borders. Finally, capitalism has had its own hand in the selective deconstruction of the notion of PROPERTY, particularly in spaces in the South where indigenous rights are repeatedly trampled or simply ignored as opportunistic state leaders and corporations collude to exploit local RESOURCES in the name of the global consumer.

Within all of this we might find some optimism in the postmodern character of new SOCIAL MOVEMENTS and alternative forms of political organizing, both of which have seen radical transformation in the late twentieth century as the union-based strategies of Fordism gave way to the post-NAFTA emergence of the Zapatista rebellion in Chiapas, Mexico. To the extent that postmodernity is associated with flexibility, so too goes RESISTANCE. Characteristic of the contemporary scene are roving protests against neo-liberalism sparked by the successful disruption of the WORLD TRADE ORGANIZATION meeting in Seattle, Washington in 1999; the emergence of hundreds of globally linked collectives of indigenous peoples, operating under a common proclamation of RIGHTS while preserving the singularities of their different political projects; and the widespread attraction of youth across the world to the 'new ANARCHISM', to MINOR THEORY, to grassroots ENVIRONMENTALISM, to living beyond racial and national identifications, and to sexual freedom. These contrast markedly to mobilizations under modernity, which insisted on coherence in political IDEOLOGY and uniformity in goals for change (think global proletariat) – often topped off by rigid organizational hierarchies. In their place, and taking cues from many post-structurally inflected approaches to FEMINISM, anti-RACISM, QUEER THEORY, anti-statism and anti-capitalism, are thousands of collectives geared to produce radical change from the

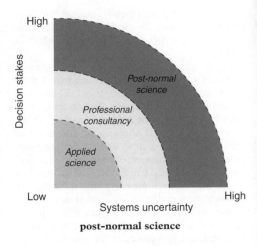

post-normal science

perspective of difference. Contemporary activists produce a continuously unfolding multiplicity of small, terminal actions that constantly work at 'expanding the floor of the cage' (in Noam Chomsky's words) within which we currently find ourselves.   KWO/JPJ

Suggested reading
Gregory (1994, pp. 406–14); Harvey (1989b); Soja (1989).

post-normal science (PNS)   Silvio Funtowicz and Jerome Ravetz (1993) contend that a new form of SCIENCE is needed when 'facts are uncertain, values in dispute, stakes high and decisions urgent'. The figure shows that where 'decision stakes' and 'systems uncertainties' are low, there is routine Kuhnian science (see PARADIGM): when both are moderate, we have consultancy, which copes with UNCERTAINTY by working within tolerances and by professional judgement. But with high stakes and high uncertainty (the 'post-normal' condition), policy has to be implemented before the evidence is certain (cf. RISK SOCIETY). This requires new ways of working based on an 'extended peer community' (all those affected by an issue who are prepared to enter into dialogue) and 'extended facts', which include anecdotal evidence, confidential information, local knowledge and ethical commitments. As such, PNS aims to provide a coherent framework for participation in DECISION-MAKING, which includes tools developed by Funtowicz and Ravetz to manage and communicate uncertainty and to allow for the qualitative assessment of quantitative information as provided by the NUSAP website (http://nusap. net/), and that goes beyond CONFIRMATORY

DATA ANALYSIS. As such, it provides an antidote to nihilistic relativism about facts, values and reality. Saloranta (2001) shows how PSN can be used in the climate change debate.　　KJ

post-socialism The various complex political and economic transformations occurring (particularly after 1989) in the former socialist states of Central and Eastern Europe and the former Soviet Union. It signals an historical break with models of social and economic development organized around a centralized bureaucratic STATE socialist project, a COMMAND ECONOMY, and the demise of the GEOPOLITICAL HEGEMONY of the Soviet Union over its satellite states. There is still debate about whether Chinese market socialism can be thought of as post-socialist with its opening of markets to foreign investment and export markets, and the expansion of private ownership in an ECONOMY still strongly controlled by the party state.

Post-socialism is also a description of a reorientation in a broader EPISTEMOLOGICAL and political structure of thought. Along with other similar 'postings' (such as POST-MODERNISM, POST-STRUCTURALISM and POST-COLONIALISM), post-socialism has signalled a conceptual break and has initiated a series of thorough-going theoretical transformations of socialist thought, as these others had with MODERNISM, STRUCTURALISM and colonial thought. With its enormous geographical scope and the depth of its impacts on regional and global economies, post-socialism has also reshaped the intellectual and institutional practices of many of the social sciences (e.g. the *perestroika* movement in political science, POST-MARXISM and rethinking MARXISM in economics, POLITICAL ECONOMY and GEOGRAPHY, and the resurgence of ANARCHIST thought and practice in SOCIAL MOVEMENTS and global justice movements).

Despite the salience of the historical changes wrought after 1989, post-socialism retains the binary nature of its origins. On the one hand, it represents one of the deepest politico-philosophical breaks of the twentieth century, the break with SOCIALISM and the return to the MARKET IDEOLOGY of Friedrich von Hayek. This break has fuelled the resurgence of NEO-LIBERALISM in former socialist states, particularly by the Bretton Woods organizations such as the IMF and World Bank. In this view, there is no alternative for reform societies but to privatize their economies, democratize their polities and liberalize their societies. De-communization must accompany structural adjustment, shock therapy and the building of open markets. On the other hand, post-socialism has also been a political–theoretical movement of socialist and social-democratic thinkers deeply concerned by the shocking deepening of social and economic inequalities produced by STRUCTURAL ADJUSTMENT and shock therapy, yet optimistic about the possibilities of what Jacques Derrida called 'DEMOCRACY-to-come' (Derrida, 1994). For such scholars, the technocratic implementation of shock therapy and the dire consequences for regional economies and livelihoods has been a cause for serious concern. From this perspective, the social and geographical contingencies of state socialism are matched by the deep complexities and contradictions of post-socialism (van Hoven, 2003). In response, geographers have explicitly challenged the dominant transition framework that examines organizational forms in Eastern Europe according to the degree to which they conform to or depart from the blueprints of already existing CAPITALISMS. In their place, they have focused on the diversity of 'actually occurring post-socialisms' (Grabher and Stark, 1997; Pickles and Smith, 1998).

With accession to the European Union, the geographies of post-socialist Central and Eastern EUROPE have become ever more focused on issues of regional and institutional INTEGRATION, the creation of common economic spaces, and issues of IMMIGRATION and LABOUR MARKET change. Here, post-socialism finally comes to mean something it probably ought to have meant much earlier; the process of regional change wrought on both sides of the Iron Curtain.　　JPi

Suggested reading
Hann (2002); Pickles (2007); Rainnie, Smith and Swain (2002); Smith (2004); Žižek (2001).

post-structuralism A post-1960s intellectual movement that countered the perceived rigidities, certainties and essentialisms thought to characterize STRUCTURALISM. Yet post-structuralism has always been indebted to its predecessor, to which it is tied in productive ways (hence 'post-' and not 'anti-' structuralism). Post-structuralism was developed first in PHILOSOPHY and later took hold in literary theory and criticism (see CULTURAL TURN). Its birth is usually marked by a 1966 conference paper by Jacques Derrida (republished in 1978; also see Derrida, 1979). Other key figures and contributions include Foucault

(1972a [1966], 1978 [1976], 1980b), Barthes (1977), Spivak (1988), Butler (1990, 1993a), Baudrillard (1993), Latour (1993), Bhabha (1994) and Badiou (2005). Often conflated with POSTMODERNITY and POSTMODERNISM, post-structuralism, while always in the mix of these theoretical and cultural currents, is more contained, analytic and philosophical. It has been, and continues to be, profoundly influential in the HUMANITIES and critical social sciences, and is noteworthy for underwriting many of contemporary HUMAN GEOGRAPHY's engagements with ACTOR-NETWORK THEORY, FEMINISM, POST-COLONIALISM, POST-DEVELOPMENT theory, POSTHUMANISM, POST-MARXISM, PSYCHOANALYTIC THEORY, QUEER THEORY and SUBALTERN STUDIES. Its influence, direct and indirect, is felt in nearly all branches of human geography, though not without critics and dissenters, especially among humanists and Marxists (cf. HUMANISM; MARXISM). Its primary effects can be felt in four theoretical shifts since the 1980s:

(1) A rethinking of the relationships between the PRODUCTION OF SPACE and its REPRESENTATION, especially through reconfigured concepts of CULTURAL LANDSCAPE and LANDSCAPE, but also in other sites of TEXT and TEXTUALITY, such as LITERATURE, FILM, the MEDIA, MUSIC and so on.
(2) New concepts of what POWER consists of, where it is 'located' and how it operates.
(3) A destabilization of FOUNDATIONALISM, leading to post-foundational accounts of IDENTITY and DIFFERENCE (including critiques of standard categories in social science, such as CLASS and DEVELOPMENT), a questioning of the binary between CULTURE and NATURE, and a suspicion towards older and less reflexive understandings of OBJECTIVITY.
(4) A somewhat more recent reversal of post-structuralists' tendency to privilege EPISTEMOLOGY over ONTOLOGY in accounts of social life.

Jacques Derrida's version of post-structuralism is fundamental to the destabilization of meaning that lies at the heart of the concept. He began with the recognition that any structure relies upon a centre, an organizing principle (e.g. God, the individual, truth, objectivity), around which the remainder of the structure is constructed. Derrida then famously unhinged the centre from its effronteries of self-actualization and independence by asserting its relational constitution with an 'other', an outside periphery that is the raw material for the centre's construction. In helping forge the identity of the centre through a process of negation (i.e. not 'other'), this 'constitutive outside' is said to leave its 'trace' within the centre, highlighting their co-dependence and providing the entry point for the post-structuralist method of DECONSTRUCTION, a form of analysis that demonstrates the reliance of the centre on its excluded other (cf. DISCOURSE ANALYSIS). Derrida's main contribution in human geography has been to help undo the security of traditional binaries, such as objectivity/subjectivity, SPACE/PLACE and nature/culture.

Foucault's brilliant contribution to post-structuralism was to trace the historical evolution – or GENEALOGY – of socially constructed categories and to ask in whose name and in what contexts certain objects became associated with certain categories. His work typically linked analyses of the interrelated production of institutions (hospitals, PRISONS: see CARCERAL GEOGRAPHIES; PANOPTICON), scientific and political discourse (see CRITICAL GEOPOLITICS) and their subjects (see DISCIPLINARY POWER). Further, it led him to envision capillaric rather than fixed sites of POWER, which operates as a difference-naming and boundary-drawing effect of DISCOURSE. Probably the most influential of the post-structuralists to date, Foucault's impact on studies of space have been plentiful: in studies of GOVERNMENTALITY (counting and placing bodies), identity (naming bodies in terms of race, deviance, health etc.) and SEXUALITY (controlling BODIES and populations: see BIO-POWER), as well as in post-structuralist studies of landscape, where discourse and space meet, and where the operation of power is concretized (see Crampton and Elden, 2007).

FEMINISM has a complicated relationship to post-structuralism. On the one hand, Butler, within the context of feminism and queer theory, described the production of the human SUBJECT as a matter of PERFORMANCE, signs acted out upon – through iteration and citation – the bodies of individuals. Like Foucault, Butler rejects any notion of an innate subject, suggesting that PERFORMATIVITY is a matter of approximating idealized imaginaries of gender, and of resisting or even satirizing such ideals. (Geographers have mostly taken up performativity by insisting on the context-specificity within which identities are formed.) On the other hand, some feminists have not welcomed the destabilization of identity that post-structuralism heralded, noting that the rise of anti-essentialist thought was curiously coincident with women's successes in demanding a voice based on SEX and GENDER (see Nicholson, 1989). In any case, a number of concepts and debates within FEMINIST GEOGRAPHIES are intimately tied to the rise of post-structuralism (see ALTERITY; BODY; DIFFERENCE; ESSENTIALISM; IDENTITY; POSITIONALITY; SUBJECTIVITY).

The above thinkers have an aversion to metaphysical or ontological speculation, and so it has been said that, in their tradition of theorizing, EPISTEMOLOGY TRUMPS ontology (Dixon and Jones, 1998). But Deleuze (1994) never refrained from attempting to develop a thoroughgoing post-structuralist philosophy that incorporated ontology. Central to this – and what makes it possible to consider Deleuze a post-structuralist – was his rejection of all conceptions of the world that relied upon transcendental or ideal objects, such as essences (see also MINOR THEORY: see Katz, 1996). Instead, he describes an immanent universe of force and AFFECT, one that organizes itself according to the matter (literally) at hand. Thus, things in the world do not correspond to a set of ideal forms, but are instead singular products of continuous material differentiation. Thought – by its very nature, but particularly so under MODERNITY – retrofits objects and relations into categories and orders of similitude, and thus keeps the thinker at a conceptual distance from the 'pure difference' expressed by the material world. As his is an approach that often has more in common with COMPLEXITY THEORY than DIALECTICS, Deleuze too has been controversial among some post-structuralists and many Marxists. Together with his colleague Félix Guattari (see Deleuze and Guattari, 1987), he developed a rich spatial vocabulary populated with concepts such as ASSEMBLAGE, NOMADOLOGY, RHIZOME, (de)territorialization, smooth and striated spaces, and the like (Bonta and Protevi, 2004; see also Doel, 1999).   KWO/JPJ

Suggested readings
Bonta and Protevi (2004); Butler (1990); Crampton and Elden (2007); Doel (1999); Foucault (1980); Harrison (2006); Murdoch (2006).

poverty A much-contested term that suggests a state of welfare/illfare in which a person cannot function in one or more respects as a capable human being. Poverty is not a term that is easily defined. In so-called 'poor' or 'developing' countries, attempts are often made to define poverty in 'absolute' or nutritional terms. The official definitions and measurements of poverty used in India highlight some of the complexities and challenges associated with this category. The Government of India tracks the number of people in the country who cannot purchase enough COMMODITIES to ensure that they get on average 2,400 calories per day in rural areas or 2,100 calories per day in urban areas. These are aggregate figures that are collected at the HOUSEHOLD level by the CENSUS authorities or by officers of the National Sample Survey. Attempts are also made to count the number of women or CHILDREN in absolute poverty, or people in female-headed households or those over 60. The Indian government maintains that the head-count ratio of people living below the poverty line has halved since 1973–4, coming down from about 55 per cent of the population to about 26 per cent of the population in 1999–2000. This still amounted to more than 260 million people. Independent scholars have challenged the India's government data and generally put the 2000 figure at 300–350 million people.

About one in five people who suffer from absolute poverty live in India, despite recent progress there. Rates of poverty are higher for females than for males. It has also been estimated (Sen, 1990) that more than 100 million women are 'missing' in South ASIA and China as a result of gendered social practices before and after birth (female abortion and infanticide, male preference in feeding and health care). Yet it is Sub-Saharan AFRICA that generally comes to mind when discussion in Northern countries turns to absolute poverty. It is here that Jeffrey Sachs, the American economist and adviser to Ban Ki-Moon at the United Nations, has demanded action to secure 'the end of poverty in our lifetime'. Sachs (2005) has called for the elimination of what he calls 'extreme poverty' by 2025. He wants the US government to impose a 5 per cent income tax surcharge on Americans earning more than $200,000 per annum. This will generate over half of the $70–80 billion per year that he reckons is necessary to kick-start economic growth in the poorest countries. The remaining funds must come from other richer countries. Such concerted spending, Sachs argues, can ensure that the first Millennium Development Goal is met – the UN-agreed target of halving between 1990 and 2015 the proportion of people whose income is less than one US dollar a day. It might also eliminate extreme poverty and HUNGER by 2025, particularly if increased AID spending is directed not only towards

ECONOMIC GROWTH, but also to better educational provision and HEALTHCARE delivery, including for HIV/AIDS patients.

Not everyone agrees with Sachs' vision of what causes absolute poverty (he directs a lot of attention to PHYSICAL GEOGRAPHY) or his suggestion that it is best addressed by massive programmes of public spending (see also DEVELOPMENT). Part of the reason for this is that Sachs is mainly concerned with calorific or income poverty. Adam Smith famously argued that a definition of poverty should include the right not to feel shame in public. In other words, he recognized that people cannot function in ways that they might want to if they are the targets of physical or verbal abuse. This tradition of thinking has been continued by John Maynard Keynes and Amartya Sen. One virtue of Sen's (2000) work is that it directs us to think about poverty in relational – and not simply absolute – terms. What matters, Sen suggests, is whether we have the capability to live our lives in ways that we consider meaningful, however differently we might define what a meaningful life is. This is partly qualified, for Sen, by the prior requirement that all human beings must have a minimal level of food intake, shelter, education and health to function as humans. One can imagine a family in Punjab, then, that is above a state-defined poverty line. Perhaps the family has benefited from rising incomes as a result of the GREEN REVOLUTION. But what if females in the family lose paid jobs to male kin, perhaps on the basis that their labour in the fields is no longer 'required'? What if this loss of earning power translates into a system of *purdah*, where women find it harder to venture into public space? For Sen, this can also be a sign of poverty, precisely because it defines a gendered system of SOCIAL EXCLUSION. The same argument can be extended to members of social groups who are not allowed to worship with others, or who cannot easily draw WATER from public wells (Erb and Harriss-White, 2002).

This way of thinking about poverty also directs attention to social norms and thus to the geographical nature of poverty. In richer countries, 'poverty' is most commonly defined as relative deprivation, and here as elsewhere it tends to be feminized (Jones and Kodras, 1990; but see also Chant, 2006). People are considered to be poor relative to some assumed bundle of goods or services, or of capabilities and functionings, that provides for at least a minimum level of access to what is considered 'normal' in a given social setting.

For example, in the USA, not having a television set might be considered an index both of social exclusion and of relative deprivation, at least where this is not an active family choice. Once the word 'normal' comes into play, however, we recognize that 'wars on poverty' are discursive constructions and not just political campaigns (Yapa, 1998: see DISCOURSE). Social scientists now pay close attention to the powers of STATE and non-state actors to define 'poverty'. They also look at the governmental effects of describing someone as poor or, as in India, as a Below Poverty Line (BPL) person or household (Corbridge, Williams, Srivastava and Véron, 2005). Work on these issues is being published alongside academic research on poverty, inequality and GLOBALIZATION in the world economy (Wade, 2004; Wolf, 2004). There is clearly room for both types of work: for studies that are sharply attentive to the cultural constructions of poverty and its effects in different locations, and for studies that carefully seek to map out what has been happening to absolute poverty in the developing world (with and without considerations of India and China, whose enormous size affects all calculations) in an age of apparently increased spatial interdependencies. SCO

Suggested readings
Gordon and Spicker (1999); Jones (2004a); Sachs (2005); World Bank (2001).

poverty gap POVERTY is conventionally measured in terms of an *Absolute Poverty Line*, expressed in monetary terms: it is the income or expenditure below which a minimum nutritionally adequate diet plus essential non-food requirements are no longer affordable (e.g. spending per capita of less than US$1.00 a day, which is the conventional measure or threshold for the Absolute Poverty Line everywhere). A poverty line distinguishes, then, the poor from the non-poor (Ravallion, 1995; UNDP, 1998). Poverty estimates are typically based on data from actual HOUSEHOLD budget or income/expenditure surveys. In this way, a proportion of a country's population or an absolute number of persons or households can be designated as living in absolute poverty: this is the *Head Count Index*. Currently, for example, it is estimated that 47 per cent of the population in Nigeria live in absolute poverty. Using this Absolute Poverty Line, it is possible to calculate what proportion of the GDP of a country would be required to lift those in absolute poverty above the poverty line (e.g. the proportion of

Nigeria's GDP that would be required to lift the 70 millions who are absolutely poor to a condition in which their basic needs were fulfilled). This is the *poverty gap*: the poorer the country and the larger the number of people in poverty, the greater is the gap (i.e. the RESOURCES that must be devoted to raise those in poverty). The poverty gap thus speaks to the scale and depth of poverty, and what it would take as a measure of national output to bring all of the population above the poverty line. The *Poverty Gap Ratio* refers to the mean distance below the $1 a day poverty line expressed as a percentage of the poverty line (currently 34 per cent for Nigeria). The *Poverty Gap Index* refers to additional money the average poor person would have to spend (in aggregate or as a proportion of total consumption) in order to reach the poverty line. The poverty gap for India is currently 4 per cent, for China 1 per cent and for eastern Europe 0.1 per cent. *The Poverty Severity Index* measures the distribution of welfare of those below the poverty line (i.e. between the poor and the ultra-poor).   MW

power A minimal definition of power would refer to the ability of one agent to affect the actions or attitudes of another. Like most concepts that are central to social science, the meanings, causes and effects of power are continually being re-assessed. One thing we know for sure is that it is trite to think of power only in negative terms. The possibility of having a conversation with someone, of running a class or seminar in which people can learn, of playing a football match, depends upon the deployment of power: of people taking turns to speak and listen, of students and teachers doing work as agreed, of players deferring to a referee. People both exercise power and are on the receiving end of power at different times every day, in all realms of life. More important than the fact that power is exercised is the way in which power is constructed and deployed. To what extent is power concentrated in certain institutions, relationships or agencies? How visible is it? What are the opportunities for power relations to be contested or rotated? Are accountability mechanisms in place, and if so how well do they work?

The idea that power is fundamentally negative continues to be a powerful one, even when it is coupled with an idea of necessary restraint. Thomas Hobbes (1968 [1651]) argued that all men (sic) acted as egoists, bent on the satisfaction of their desires through relentless power plays. Given a world of scarcity, only the sovereign could prevent these individualized acts of power from adding up to an intolerable STATE OF NATURE (cf. SOVEREIGN POWER). Contemporary work on INTERNATIONAL RELATIONS by so-called Realists presents a similar view of power, in which all states seek to maximize their self-interest and are prepared to use violence to this end. Anarchy is prevented only by the exercise of HEGEMONY by a dominant power. Some versions of MARXISM come close to this argument. Marxists argue that capitalist STATES deploy their power to guarantee the ACCUMULATION process under the rule of CAPITAL. It is not surprising, then, that many Realists and Marxists share the view that the war in Iraq was fundamentally about OIL and the protection of America's self-interest. As David Harvey puts it in *The new imperialism*, joining Marx to Mackinder, 'Whoever controls the MIDDLE EAST controls the global oil spigot and whoever controls the global oil spigot can control the global economy, at least for the near future' (2003b, p. 19).

Of course, there is more to Marxism on power than a perspective on international relations. Marxist work on power in HUMAN GEOGRAPHY first made its mark through a critique of behavioural and pluralist models of power. These models, developed by political scientists such as Robert Dahl to look at power coalitions in US cities, emphasized the overt and dispersed nature of power. Power could be observed when A made an open attempt to force B to do something that s/he would not otherwise do. If A succeeded, s/he had power in this 'issue area'. Happily, however, or so Dahl (1963) concluded, B would probably exercise power over A in another issue area. Given the nature of DEMOCRACY in the USA, power was hard to monopolize.

Radical scholars disagreed. Steven Lukes (2005) argued that this view of power was one-dimensional. The work of power was most often done in smoke-filled rooms and in the setting of agendas. Lukes referred to this as two-dimensional power, and he did not stop there. Lukes further argued, as did many Marxist geographers (see MARXIST GEOGRAPHY), that not only were agendas bent to serve certain CLASS interests (not least through the state), but also that many people at the wrong end of power were unable to see their powerlessness. In part, this is because of what Marxists call 'false consciousness'. Ordinary people cannot see their 'objective interests', because their political antennae have been deadened by years of watching sport, shopping in the mall or buying into the dream of a better life within CAPITALISM (see IDEOLOGY).

In the 1980s, cultural and political geographers began to explore some of these constructions of HEGEMONY, drawing usefully on the work of Antonio Gramsci. FEMINIST GEOGRAPHIES also explored the different ways in which relations of PATRIARCHY were embedded and understood in different parts of the world (Rose, 1993), and explored questions of RESISTANCE to power, including discussions of the weapons of the weak (Hart, 1991; see FEMINIST GEOGRAPHY). In the 1990s these explorations were significantly extended as geographers began to draw more broadly on the work of Michel Foucault, and through him the work of Edward Said and other theorists of POST-COLONIALISM or POST-STRUCTURALISM. John Allen (2003) has suggested that power can be thought of as an inscribed capacity inhering in certain agents and NETWORKS; as a RESOURCE; and as a set of strategies, DISCOURSES and technologies of government (see BIOPOWER; DISCIPLINARY POWER; GOVERNMENTALITY). This last view of power begins to hint at the richness of Foucault's legacy to the human sciences. Foucault (2001) recognized, as some of his followers have not, that power can be enabling. For the most part, however, geographers have read Foucault as a guide to the ways in which power inhabits and flows through all of the 'capillaries' of modern life. They have also taken from Foucault the notion that power is strongly territorialized. It is embedded in jurisdictions that run from the human BODY (powerfully disciplined by ideas of 'normal' SEXUALITY, for instance), through the organization of schools, hospitals, asylums (Philo, 2004) and PRISONS, and on to the construction of BOUNDARIES that express ideas of inclusion and exclusion. Power, in this view, can be challenged, critiqued and contested – this is the job of an oppositional social science – but it cannot be transcended: the line to Foucault runs through Weber and Nietzsche more strongly than it does from Marx.

The idea that power animates all spatial practices, and that power is always spatialized, is now widely understood in GEOGRAPHY. So too is the idea that power is most effective when it is least visible. CRITICAL HUMAN GEOGRAPHY seeks to denaturalize some of the most powerful discourses that are at play in the subject – ideas of DEVELOPMENT, for example, or the WEST, or WHITENESS. In so doing, it aims to reveal other ways of assembling power and knowledge. At the same time, however, as Harvey's work on the new IMPERIALISM reveals, some geographers are also concerned to keep their eyes focused on materialist conceptions of power, and the powers of CAPITAL and the STATE. When it was revealed that the Bush administration in the USA was pursuing a policy of 'extraordinary rendition' (the alleged torturing of suspected 'terrorists' in prison camps outside the USA), it became clear that work on the sovereign powers of states (Agamben, 1998: see EXCEPTION, SPACE OF) had to be linked to work on spatial strategies of demarcation, Othering and distanciation (see Gregory, 2004b, on the Israel–Palestine conflict), and to robust accounts of the deployment of US power in an age of NEOLIBERALISM (Smith, 2005a).   sco

Suggested reading
Corbridge, Williams, Srivastava and Véron (2005); Gregory (2004b); Lukes (2005); Mamdani (2004).

power-geometry The more or less systematic and usually highly uneven ways in which different individuals and groups are positioned within NETWORKS of FLOWS and interactions. These variable positions derive from the intimate connections that exist between productions of POWER and productions of SPACE: spatial modalities of power are differentially engaged such that different actors in different places have different degrees of freedom. The concept was proposed by Doreen Massey (1993) as both a critique of David Harvey's concept of TIME-SPACE COMPRESSION and an attempt to open up conventional, 'bounded' conceptions of PLACE.

Massey (1993, pp. 60–1) argued that Harvey (1989b) had emphasized CAPITALISM to such a degree that his account of time-space compression collapsed into an economism, and paid so much attention to CLASS that he failed to acknowledge the wider range of social positions that were involved, including GENDER. In short: TIME–SPACE COMPRESSION 'needs differentiating socially'. In parallel, Gregory (1994, p. 414) argued that the process also needs to be differentiated spatially: there is a complex geography to time–space compression. The concept of a power-geometry speaks to these twin concerns. It was developed independently of ACTOR-NETWORK THEORY, with which it has some affinities, but it provides a multidimensional conception of space that is intended to be unwaveringly political in its orientation.

POSITIONALITY is crucial to power-geometry (see also Sheppard, 2002). From the outset,

Massey (1993, p. 63) emphasized the politics of MOBILITY that derive directly from different positionalities within a particular power-geometry: 'We need to ask whether our relative mobility and power over mobility and communication entrenches the spatial imprisonment of other groups'. For Hyndman (1997, p. 151), this remains a promissory note, and Massey does not delve far enough into the economies of power that regulate, facilitate and disrupt transnational movement. Although her argumentation-sketches are often impressionistic and usually operate at a high level of ABSTRACTION, Massey's later writings are nonetheless directed towards the elaboration of what she calls 'a global sense of place'. For her, places are open, porous and hybrid – literally, 'meeting places' in which trajectories of all kinds (people, ideas, commodities) collide – and to represent them as containers, building blocks or objects (cf. REGIONAL GEOGRAPHY) is to foreclose the possibilities of an intrinsically spatial politics. This openness is not a peculiarity of modern GLOBALIZATION and cannot be reduced to the choreography of contemporary capitalism. Over the long term, she proposes, different places have been drawn into engagement with one another in 'a power-geometry of intersecting trajectories' (Massey, 2005, p. 64), but there is no single, plenary narrative within which these can be convened (p. 82); the outcomes of these intersections have always been open-ended (though not, of course, unconstrained) because the spatial is 'the realm of the juxtaposition of dissonant narratives', and it is out of this 'throwntogetherness' that new narratives are generated and negotiated (pp. 140–2). Seen thus, power-geometries not only shape and constrain mobility: they are themselves in constant if irregular motion, so that their analysis is necessarily both historical and geographical (cf. CONTRAPUNTAL GEOGRAPHIES). Place can then be recognized as 'woven together out of ongoing stories, as a moment within power-geometries, as a particular constellation within the wider TOPOGRAPHIES of space' (Massey, 2005, p. 131). DG

Suggested reading
Massey (1993); Sheppard (2002).

pragmatism An American tradition of PHILOSOPHY that emerged in the late nineteenth century associated with John Dewey (1859–1952), William James (1842–1910), George Herbert Mead (1863–1931) and Charles Sanders Peirce (1839–1914) (see Barnes, 2008a). The movement is best known for the idea that what counts as knowledge is determined by its usefulness. As James (1987, p. 578) wrote, 'the true is the name of whatever proves itself to be good in the way of belief'. Pragmatism is thus a philosophy of practical achievement. Ideas are labelled true when they enable humans to get things done, to cope with the world. After enjoying widespread popularity in the first half of the twentieth century, pragmatism fell out of favour after the Second World War following the ascendancy of empirical social science and analytical philosophy, a narrowly conceived, often technically abstruse form of reasoning concerned with assessing the coherence, consistency and precise meaning of an argument. The publication of Richard Rorty's *Philosophy and the mirror of nature* (1979) revived pragmatism's fortunes, however. As an ex-analytical philosopher, Rorty diagnosed with forensic precision the pathology of modern philosophy, prescribing as cure a large dose of American pragmatism. Now found in a range of HUMANITIES and social sciences, the rehabilitation of pragmatism is also a consequence of the wider interest in POST-STRUCTURALISM and POSTMODERNISM, movements with which it shares common interests.

James coined the name pragmatism in 1898 to describe the movement, but there were always strong differences among its proponents. At one point, for example, Peirce minted his own neologism, 'pragmaticism', to mark off what he was doing from his colleagues, and sufficiently 'ugly to be safe from kidnappers' (Bernstein, 1992a, p. 813). Bernstein (1992b, appendix) usefully characterizes pragmatism by five features:

(1) Anti-FOUNDATIONALISM, the belief that there are no secure anchors either in the world or in the mind that holds and guarantees the permanency of true knowledge.
(2) Fallibilism, the belief that no truth is ever final, and that knowledge should always be subject to further investigation, critical scrutiny, and questioning.
(3) Communal enquiry, the notion that scholarship takes place within a wider community involving TRUST, conversation, and shared norms and responsibilities.
(4) Radical contingency, the belief, stemming partly from Darwin's theory of evolution, that change is propelled by chance and accident, that the only certainty is uncertainty (and for this reason humans must always be ready to expect the unexpected) (cf. DARWINISM). Peirce

(1982, vol. 4, p. 544) wrote, 'Everything that can happen by chance, sometime or other will happen by chance. Chance will sometime bring about a change in every condition.'

(5) 'Radical pluralism', the belief that neither bits of the world nor of philosophy coherently fit together all of piece. Radical pluralism, as James (1977, p. 26) writes, is a 'turbid, muddled, Gothic sort of affair without a sweeping outline and little pictorial nobility'. But for James it is all we have.

The rise of analytical philosophy in America from the 1940s brought with it everything that pragmatism formerly shunned – FOUNDATION-ALISM, certainty, individual rationality, necessity and monism. Consequently, pragmatism was pushed, and sometimes shoved aside. After his death Dewey, for example, was regarded by one analytical philosopher as 'a nice old man who hadn't the vaguest conception of real philosophical rigor or the nature of a real philosophical problem' (quoted in Gouinlock, 1972, p. xi). Analytical philosophy's hold on the profession was relatively short-lived, however, and by the 1980s it was vigorously challenged by a new group of pragmatists, including Richard Rorty (1931–2007) and Richard Bernstein (b.1932).

Rorty, drawing upon the writings of Dewey and James, seeks first to dismantle from the inside out the edifice of contemporary analytical philosophy, especially the variant known as REALISM; and, second, to substitute for it, a neo-pragmatic alternative which he calls, possibly tongue-in-cheek, 'postmodernist liberal bourgeois ironism' (Rorty, 1989). Very briefly, Rorty argues that the problems of analytical philosophy stem from its appropriation of an inappropriate METAPHOR, vision or sight, or 'ocularism'. The metaphor mistakenly convinced philosophers that it was possible for the mind to mirror the world (cf. VISION AND VISUALITY). In contrast Rorty, following the pragmatists, argues for a different central metaphor, 'conversation'. Under this model there are no fixed end points, strict rules or necessary logics. This is evident by unpacking the terms of Rorty's alternative: 'POSTMODERNIST' because Rorty does not believe in the grand metanarratives of high MODERNISM that supposedly make all parts of the world commensurable; 'liberal' because for the conversation to continue there must be freedom of expression and democracy (thereby echoing Dewey's concerns); 'bourgeois' because Rorty thinks

that LIBERALISM has so far only been possible under capitalism; and 'irony' because for the conversation to continue we need to affirm certain beliefs even though there are no firm philosophical foundations for them. Rorty approvingly quotes Joseph Schumpeter (1942, p. 243), who says that one needs 'to realise the relative validity of one's convictions and yet stand for them unflinchingly'.

While sympathetic to many of Rorty's ideas, Bernstein (1992b, ch. 8) is sharply critical of his economic conservatism, and his disengagement from questions of unequal power and resources. Bernstein (1992b, p. 233), says that Rorty's version of pragmatism is 'little more than an apologia for the status quo'. In contrast, Bernstein deals with those absences by joining to pragmatism various strands of continental European philosophy, producing what he calls 'the new constellation' (Bernstein, 1992b). An important component within Bernstein's mix are writers identified with POST-STRUCTURALISM such as Foucault and Derrida, who are not economic conservatives, and who deal vitally with questions of unequal power and resources. In no small part, the renaissance of American pragmatism is a result of its resonance with the concerns of those writers.

In HUMAN GEOGRAPHY, there have been sporadic, but neither consistent nor concerted, attempts to draw upon pragmatist writers. Jackson and Smith (1984) utilize Mead's more applied prescriptions in their portrayal of SOCIAL GEOGRAPHY; Westcoat (1992) describes the relation between White's environmental outlook, and particularly Dewey's ideas; both Barnes (1996, chs. 2 and 5) and Gibson-Graham (2006b [1996]) make use of Rorty's work in countering essentialism in economic geography; and Sunley (1996) takes the ideas of another ex-analytical-philosopher-turned-pragmatist, Hilary Putnam, and puts them to work in a discussion of the relationship between the new INSTITUTIONAL ECONOMICS and ECONOMIC GEOGRAPHY. A special issue of *Geoforum* (2008) is devoted to assessing the usefulness of pragmatism for human geography and connecting it to contemporary intellectual formations: thus Allen (2008) conducts a series of radical experiments that insert pragmatism into the play of POWER, Bridge (2008) reactivates pragmatism in theorizations of PERFORMATIVITY and SPATIALITY, while Jones (2008) identifies a series of connections between pragmatism, POST-STRUCTURALISM and NON-REPRESENTATIONAL THEORY. TB

Suggested reading
Barnes (2008a); Bernstein (1992a); Menand (2001).

prediction The construction of an estimated or expected value for an observation being studied, where the observation might be for a place, region, individual or time-period. The estimate or prediction may be generated by a statistical model (e.g. REGRESSION), a mathematical model (e.g. an ENTROPY-MAXIMIZING MODEL) or a more informal SIMULATION process. The term 'predicted value' is usually employed for the 'fitted' or estimated values for observations within the data set being calibrated or modelled, and the out-of-sample extrapolation is termed the FORECAST.   LWH

pre-industrial city All cities prior to the INDUSTRIAL REVOLUTION, plus those in non-industrialized regions today. The term reflects the theory, initially advocated by Gideon Sjoberg (1960; see SJOBERG MODEL), that all pre-industrial cities, regardless of their time, place or cultural backdrop, share similar reasons for existence, social hierarchies and internal spatial structures. The term is now rarely used, as few researchers believe that the variety of urban forms created by pre-industrial and non-industrialized societies have enough in common to be considered as variations of a single category.   DH

preservation The protection, maintenance and care of relict features of the built environment, including historic buildings, archaeological sites and individual human artefacts (e.g. the Colosseum in Rome). Preservationists complement the work of conservationists, who aim to protect specific 'natural' LANDSCAPES or features of the biophysical environment (e.g. the Grand Canyon) (cf. CONSERVATION). Agencies such as the National Trust in the UK are awarded statutory powers to preserve houses and gardens of particular historical significance (see HERITAGE). This may involve the extensive restoration of buildings to bring them back to their original condition or their revival through the reproduction of past features (e.g. gardens). Human geographers have been concerned both with the practices involved in preservation projects and with the types of landscape imagery, ICONOGRAPHY and interpretation provided in preserved landscapes (e.g. Ashworth and Tunbridge, 2004). As the example of the Colosseum suggests, however, 'preservation' has a complex and often contentiously imaginative relationship with restoration (see Hopkins and Beard, 2005, chs. 1 and 6; and, more generally, Lowenthal, 1985). Relict features typically have multiple, sedimented histories inscribed in and on them: they are not the product of a single historical moment. It was for this reason that the French architect Viollet le-Duc (1814–79) argued that restoration should restore a building to an idealized state of completion, perfection 'that may never have actually existed at any given time': which is why, in turn, his 'restorations' (e.g. of the French city of Carcassonne) proved so controversial in the past and in the present.   NJ/DG

Suggested reading
Ashworth and Tunbridge (2004); Lowenthal (1985, ch. 7).

pricing policies The arrangements whereby the prices at which COMMODITIES are offered to consumers are determined. In spatial economic analysis, the important distinguishing feature of pricing policies is the extent to which price varies with distance from the origin or source of the commodity. There are two major alternative policies. The first is known as the *f.o.b. (free on board)* price system, under which there is a basic price at origin and the consumer pays the TRANSPORT COST involved in getting the commodity to the point of purchase. The second is the *c.i.f. (cost, insurance, freight)* price system, under which the producer adds insurance and shipping cost to the production cost and offers the commodity at a uniform delivered price irrespective of distance from origin. The distinction between these two policies is important, for commodities sold c.i.f. should have no bearing on locational COMPARATIVE ADVANTAGE for productive activities requiring them as inputs; similarly, distance from origin should not affect level of demand for goods offered on a c.i.f. basis (other things being equal). There is an increasing tendency for commodities to be sold at a uniform delivered price.

Various alternative pricing policies may be implemented. An f.o.b. system does not necessarily have minor incremental increases in price for small increases in distance; more often, the prevailing *freight rates* on which delivered price is based will be constant over broad zones. There may be forms of spatial price discrimination, under which customers in some areas are charged a high price (perhaps because the supplier has a local monopoly) so as to subsidize the price charged in a more competitive market elsewhere. A well-known variant is the *basing point price policy,* whereby customers are charged as if the commodity originated at a certain (base) point; this can be used to protect producers in the basing point location, for commodities actually produced elsewhere will cost more. The operation of some pricing policies may involve collusion on the part of producers to maintain an artificially high price in the industry as a whole – an increasing tendency in the advanced CAPITALIST world.   DMS

primary data analysis In contrast to SECONDARY DATA ANALYSIS, this involves data collected and analysed by the same researchers. This allows a great deal of control over what is collected and how it is collected, so that there can be high coherence between theoretical and operational concepts. Such an approach can be costly in time and resources, however, and there can be a lack of compatibility with other work in the field; use of resources such as the Question Bank (http://qb.soc.surrey.ac.uk/) and of harmonized questions in SURVEY ANALYSES can ameliorate the latter problem, while effective SAMPLING can address the former. KJ

Suggested reading
Government Statistical Service (2003).

primate city, the law of An empirical regularity identified by Mark Jefferson (1863–1949: see Jefferson, 1939). The populations of the three largest urban areas in some countries approximated the ratio sequence 100 : 30 : 20, which he attributed to the largest city's pre-eminence in economic, social and political affairs. Although the sequence is now largely ignored, the concept of primacy, implying a city's predominance within an area, is frequently deployed (cf. HEGEMONY; RANK-SIZE RULE).   RJ

Suggested reading
Vance (1970).

primitive accumulation In *Capital I*, having explained the laws of development of CAPITALISM, and the distinctive features of the capitalist MODE OF PRODUCTION, Marx turns to the process by which capitalism historically established itself (Marx, 1967 [1867]). To pose this historical question – how did CAPITALISM arise? – Marx focuses not simply upon the way in which one set of relations of production is transformed into another – the transition from FEUDALISM to capitalism – but on how one CLASS of workers, defined by their lack of property, came to confront another, capitalists, who monopolized the means of production.

The 'so-called secret', as Marx terms it, of primitive accumulation resides not in the simple expansion of the provision of the means of production in a quantitative sense but, rather, in a revolutionary reorganization of the relations of production. Primitive accumulation for Marx was, in other words, the process by which a pre-capitalist system of largely agrarian relations and small-scale property holding – a peasantry having some form of direct control over the means of production, namely land – was dispossessed. The origins of capitalism are to be found in the process by which the PEASANTS are freed – there is much irony in Marx's use of this word – to become wage labourers in agriculture (on large commercial estates) and in industry. Marx turns to the case of the ENCLOSURE movement in Britain – in effect, the violent expropriation of forms of common property – and the political and extra-economic means by which this long process of the creation and disciplining of a proletariat was achieved. Marx made it clear that this process always required the powers of the STATE and was necessarily violent – written in blood and fire, as he put it (see VIOLENCE).

In seeing the enclosure movement as paradigmatic of primitive accumulation, Marx opens up a complex debate over the transition from FEUDALISM to CAPITALISM and how other parts of EUROPE, and subsequently the colonial and post-colonial world, stood in a different relation to the 'original sin' of primitive accumulation. The debate between Dobb and Sweezy (see Hilton, 1976) turns precisely on the interpretation of other European experiences and the weight attributed to the role of EXCHANGE and MARKET transactions as the force in the disintegration of pre-capitalist relations, or whether the pre-capitalist solidity was broken by the dynamics of CLASS structure and struggle over PROPERTY (see BRENNER THESIS). These debates were, of course, central not only to the origins of capitalism in Europe but to the dynamics of capitalism at the 'periphery'; that is to say, how forms of capital took hold of agrarian societies in the context of European empire (the first age of EMPIRE) and the genesis of a mercantile world system.

The primitive accumulation question has always been central to the AGRARIAN QUESTION; that is to say, the ways in which peasant systems of production are differentiated as capital takes hold of production. Much of this work dates back to the classic studies of land, labour and markets instigated by Karl Kautsky (1988 [1899]) and Vladimir Lenin (1964) in their studies of German and Russian agriculture.

In the 1960s, the boom in peasant studies increasingly focused on the land and landed inequality question; for example, how the green revolutionary technologies were (or were not) producing an agrarian proletariat (Harriss, 1982: see GREEN REVOLUTION). Primitive accumulation has also been central to theories of IMPERIALISM, building upon Marx's observation of the ways in which COLONIALISM dispossessed Third World property holders and laid (or attempted to lay) the foundations for systematic accumulation. In so many cases, colonial capitalism proved to be dominated by merchant and other forms of capitalism, in which the speed and depth of proletarianization was often constrained (Watts, 1983a).

Against the backdrop of the counter-revolution in DEVELOPMENT theory and the rise of NEO-LIBERALISM globally in the past three decades, primitive accumulation has returned as a category of analysis. Much of this has been spurred by the new ways in which various sorts of commons – common property resources, the airwaves, human and plant genetic materials – have been subject to the violent forces of PRIVATIZATION and what Marx called 'dispossession'. Massimo De Angelis and the electronic journal *The Commoner* have been especially important in rethinking primitive accumulation in the context of GLOBALIZATION and neo-liberal hegemony (see also *RETORT*, 2005). Harvey (2005) has also returned to primitive accumulation in his account of neo-liberalism. Here he draws upon the important observation made by Arendt (1958) that primitive accumulation – the 'original sin of simple robbery' – was repeated historically as capitalism expanded into non-commodified areas, sectors, countries and frontiers. Harvey deploys this insight to show that neo-liberalism has typically operated in global terms, especially under the auspices of AMERICAN EMPIRE, as a form of dispossession – what he calls *accumulation by dispossession* – rather than intensive accumulation. The forms of dispossession are enormously varied – privatizing public housing, raiding pension funds, displacing indigenous people through dam projects, privatizing germ plasm – and throw up quite varied forms of RESISTANCE, typically articulated around the defence of the commons, which have been a fundamental force in the so-called ANTI-GLOBALIZATION movements.

In the socialist arena, a notion of primitive socialist accumulation was developed by Preobrazhensky in the 1920s, in post-revolutionary Russia (see Preobrazhensky,

1965). He emphasized that maintaining the equilibrium between the market share of industrial and agricultural output at pre-war levels meant upsetting the balance between rural effective demand and the commodity output of the town. A large increase in heavy investment was required that could not be funded internally; hence agriculture had to bear the burden. State trading monopolies would divert excess demand from the peasantry to investment from consumption. This was to be achieved by a sort of unequal exchange in which agrarian goods were underpriced and manufactures overpriced. This monopoly pricing by the state – in effect, a massive tax on peasants to kick-start heavy industry – was the socialist model of primitive (originary) accumulation. The presumption was that the terms of trade would strike the kulaks hardest. A brilliant theorist of socialist accumulation, he broke with both Trotsky and Stalin and was arrested and shot in the late 1930s.　MW

Suggested reading
De Angelis (2006).

primitivism A Euro-American DISCOURSE that represents the indigenous cultures of sub-Saharan AFRICA, South AMERICA and the Pacific islands as outside the perimeter of CIVILIZATION. It was inspired by European TRAVEL-WRITING, and in particular by the discoveries made by European explorers in the South Pacific in the closing decades of the eighteenth century. Its IMAGINATIVE GEOGRAPHIES received formal expression in post-ENLIGHTENMENT philosophy (Rousseau's 'noble savage'), in modern ART (Gauguin's Tahiti), and in early anthropology (Malinowski's *Argonauts of the Western Pacific*). In all three cases, the possessive is significant: while primitivism was often connected to a critique of MODERNITY (a 'oneness' with NATURE, for example, an intrinsic simplicity, and a celebration of the sensual and the spiritual through the fantastic), it was also closely tied to COLONIALISM. In many ways, it acted as the cultural dual to the concept of TROPICALITY, and is a powerful reminder that colonial discourse was about more than ORIENTALISM. Historically, 'primitivism has its place in the genealogy of relationships between the West and the Other: it allows one to grasp the geography by which the West has constructed itself in reference and opposition to "Elsewheres". Conversely, primitivism accounts for the geography of these "Elsewheres", in that they were transformed, and even produced by the West' (Staszak, 2004, p. 362). But primitivism continues to haunt contemporary culture (Torgovnick, 1991), and its tropes continue to be mobilized in modern TOURISM and the quest for the 'exotic'. Indeed, Li (2006) contends that it continues to be a powerful if hidden presence in critical theorizations that ostensibly seek to expose the ETHNOCENTRISM of the West. 'In order for the WEST to reflect,' he concludes, 'the savage must dance' (Li, 2006, p. 223). DG

Suggested reading
Staszak (2004).

principal components analysis (pca) A statistical procedure for transforming a data matrix so that variables in the new matrix are uncorrelated. Unlike FACTOR ANALYSIS (with which it is often confused/treated synonymously), there are as many variables (termed 'components') in the transformed as in the original matrix. Component loadings and scores are interpreted as are those derived from factor analyses, and component matrices can also be rotated. The pca procedure has been widely used in human geography: (a) to identify groups of interrelated variables inductively; (b) to simplify a data set by removing redundant information; (c) to reorganize a data set in order to eliminate COLLINEARITY; and (d) to test hypotheses. (See also FACTORIAL ECOLOGY.) RJ

Suggested reading
Johnston (1978).

prisoner's dilemma An application of GAME THEORY that illustrates the benefits of co-operative behaviour in certain situations and has been deployed to suggest a rationale for the STATE.

In the game's classic version (see Rapoport and Chammah, 1965), two men are arrested on charges of both car theft and armed robbery. The first offence can be readily proven, but the other cannot; convictions for the latter will only be obtained if one of the men confesses and implicates the other. The suspects know that if they both stay silent they will be found guilty of theft and serve a short prison sentence (one year); they also know that if both are found guilty of the armed robbery they will serve eight years. They are interrogated separately and not allowed to consult, let alone collude. Each is offered the deal that if he confesses to the robbery, resulting in the accomplice being found guilty, he will be freed and the accomplice will get ten years. The four options are set out in the following matrix:.

		Suspect B	
		Not confess	Confess
Suspect A	Not confess	1,1	10,0
	Confess	0,10	8,8

The first figure in each cell indicates Suspect A's punishment if that option is chosen by them both, and the second indicates Suspect's B punishment. Thus if neither confesses to the robbery, each serves one year in prison; if A confesses and B does not, however, then A will be freed and B will serve ten years. For each, the best option is to confess, because if either remains silent and the other confesses, he will get ten years' imprisonment. Neither dare stay silent for fear that the other will not. If the two could collude, or could guarantee that the accomplice would stay silent, then the optimal solution is for both to remain silent – a one-year sentence. But because neither can guarantee the other's choice, each selects a sub-optimal outcome and gets an eight-year sentence.

The dilemma has been used as a METAPHOR not only to illustrate that selfish behaviour may not be in an individual's best interests, but also that it is not in a person's interests to act unselfishly if everybody else takes the selfish option, particularly in issues regarding RESOURCE use and RESOURCE MANAGEMENT (cf. TRAGEDY OF THE COMMONS). In most situations involving more than a small number of actors, it is argued, unselfish behaviour can only be guaranteed if enforced by an external authority, such as the state, which exists to promote both the collective and the individual good – although there are many situations (some illustrated by more complex versions of the prisoner's dilemma game – such as the iterated prisoner's dilemma, in which the 'game' is played many times: see Axelrod, 1984) in which co-operation is sensible and can promote the collective good without state involvement. RJ

Suggested reading
Barrett (2003); Laver (1997); Poundstone (1992).

prisons Segregative institutions designed to punish, typically for criminal offences. Prisons are usually strictly regulated and tightly surveyed environments, to which offenders are confined for varying lengths of time, and sometimes for life. Often referred to as 'penitentiaries' or 'correctional institutions', prisons may also seek to reform inmates to reduce the possibility of re-offending. Although confinement is central to all prisons, incarcerative institutions vary in the types of offenders they house and the degree of security that they ensure.

The geographical literature on prisons is scant, despite the manifold geographical conditions and consequences of practices of incarceration. Imprisonment is essentially a territorialized form of punishment, a banishment from social life. In this way, it is an extreme manifestation of the territorial POWER of the STATE. Prisons can also be considered in terms of their own internal geographies, the ways in which they are constructed to maximize SURVEILLANCE and control, a process colourfully and famously outlined by Foucault (1995 [1975]). These geographies, in turn, structure a particular social order, a 'society of captives' (Sykes, 1958), who adapt to prison life and its various dangers. Prisons typically contain different levels of confinement, such that those who are viewed as especially problematic inmates can be isolated in solitary conditions. Increasingly, whole institutions – so-called 'super maximum security' (or 'supermax') prisons – are dedicated to housing those violent criminals presumed to be habitual offenders in conditions of extreme isolation (Rhodes, 2004).

More macro-oriented analyses see prisons as reflective of wider social patterns, such as economic dynamics. Since 1980, the number of people imprisoned in the USA has increased by more than 450 per cent, and Gilmore (1998, 2007) attributes this extraordinary expansion to the production of disposable or 'surplus' populations under the signs of an aggressive MILITARISM and NEO-LIBERALISM. She traces the formation of an American prison–industrial complex to state-sponsored prison construction in declining rural areas and the outsourcing and PRIVATIZATION of incarceration.

Prison populations can also be analysed in terms of their demographic characteristics. That prisons are commonly occupied by poor people of colour is suggestive of wider patterns of social differentiation and spatial exclusion: incarceration can thus be understood as yet another manifestation of racialized discrimination (see RACISM). The experience of incarceration works to increase these social divisions further still, because those convicted of crimes often face significant odds in returning to the economic mainstream. These negative consequences of incarceration can affect entire neighbourhoods where ex-convicts

cluster, and further reinforce wider social and economic divisions between different spaces within a metropolitan area (Fagan, 2004).

Prisons are also a key component of wider CARCERAL GEOGRAPHIES. These geographies promise to enlarge as concerns about TERRORISM intensify. Sites such as Guantanamo Bay are part of a carceral archipelago, a 'global war prison', used to further the 'war on terror' (Gregory, 2007). Indeed, the logic of imprisonment is arguably extended to other terrains – such as Gaza, often described as an extended 'open-air prison' – to monitor and control those deemed hostile to the particular interests of a state. SKH

Suggested reading
Gilmore (2007); Rhodes (2004).

private and public spheres Discursively constructed, contested categories that define boundaries between households, market economies, the state and political participation. The concepts are central to two distinctive, yet intertwined, discussions of: the public sphere, and ideologies and practices of separate spheres.

Jürgen Habermas' account of the bourgeois *public sphere* has been particularly influential (see CAPITALISM; CRITICAL THEORY). He argued that early capitalist societies were organized into four institutional spheres: family-consumer (private), market economy (private), the state (public) and citizen-political participation (public) – the last he identifies as the bourgeois public sphere. As both a historical phenomena and normative ideal, the bourgeois public sphere functioned as a counterweight to the state; it was where 'the public' was organized and represented, and served to mediate the relations between the STATE and SOCIETY. This liberal model of the public sphere (see LIBERALISM) was never fully achieved, he argued, but became less attainable in welfare state capitalist societies, in which the separation between the state and ECONOMY, public and private, was dissolved, and family-consumer and citizen roles were transformed. The role of citizen assumed new forms (see CITIZENSHIP): of passive recipient of publicity and social welfare client. Habermas' account is suggestive to geographers: he analyses landscape changes that concretize and reinforce both the rise and decline in active public debate (e.g. coffee houses and nineteenth-century urban culture, and the SUBURB, respectively: Habermas, 1989 [1962]). His account of the ideal of the bourgeois public sphere is nonetheless widely criticized for universalizing a model that arose within exclusionary (male, bourgeois, white) spaces in historically specific European societies (Howell, 1993; Mitchell, 2003a). Feminists have argued that GENDER exclusions are constitutive (and not simply incidental to) Habermas's idealization of the bourgeois public sphere (Fraser, 1997), and that he unwittingly reproduces a separate spheres ideology that has been the focus of so much feminist criticism and organizing (see FEMINISM; FEMINIST GEOGRAPHIES). This is an IDEOLOGY that renders domestic space as the repository of the emotions and private interest, and women 'by nature, guardians of the "household of emotions" ... a kind of sphere within [the private] sphere' (Marston, 1990, p. 456).

A notion of public sphere is nonetheless central to democratic theory and practice (see RADICAL DEMOCRACY), and there have been numerous, including important feminist, attempts to rethink it in contemporary contexts. Fraser (1997) does this by questioning four of Habermas' assumptions, including the liberal assumptions that private interests are antagonistic to the public sphere, and that one cohesive public sphere is the ideal. She argues for a theory of multiple, contending, sometimes mutually exclusive public spheres. This questioning and retheorization reflects a feminist understanding that what counts as private and public is itself the result of political struggle, and a scepticism about the ways in which concepts of 'privacy' and 'the private' often protect dominant (male) interests by de-politicizing a range of issues (such as spousal assault and child care) and legitimating the oppression of women.

Feminist retheorizing of multiple public spheres tends to emphasize the many ways in which a separate-spheres ideology continues to haunt dominant public spheres, and the persistent traffic between constructions of public and private. Fraser (1989) has described how the US state has installed a separate-spheres ideology within systems of social welfare provision, so that women are often positioned as dependents and men as deserving bearers of RIGHTS. In her analysis of a powerful coalition of women's organizations advocating the rights of women to public safety in northern Mexico, Wright (2005) notes that activists in these organizations 'face the paradox that by exercising their democratic voices through public protest, they are dismissed, by their detractors, as "unfit" citizens, based on their contamination as "public

women" ' (p. 279). And though they can challenge this 'twisted logic', 'they cannot fully escape its implications' (p. 279). Berlant argues that in the USA over the past 25 years, the public sphere has collapsed into the intimate, such that 'the family sphere [is] considered the moral, ethical, and political horizon of national and political interest' (1997, p. 262).

Geographers have sought to theorize the relations between the public sphere(s) and PUBLIC SPACE. There is a reticence simply to layer the terms on to each other, in part because much political organizing, especially for non-dominant groups, takes place in so-called private spaces, and thus there is a need to expand our thinking about the spaces of politics (or the public sphere) (Staeheli, 1996). Nevertheless, public spheres and public spaces are linked. The regulation of public space is instrumental in regulating public debate and excluding some groups from public life, and 'public spaces are decisive, for it is here that the desires and needs of individuals and groups can be seen, and therefore recognized, resisted, or ... wiped out' (Mitchell, 2003, p. 33). The distinction between spheres and spaces preserves the understanding that the concept of public sphere is in large part a democratic ideal that we strive towards, in and through the construction and use of public space. It is an ideal that can be redeployed by those who are excluded from actual political spaces – to demand inclusion within them. For this reason, some theorists have been drawn to the METAPHOR of 'empty space' to articulate the inevitably unfulfilled promise of a democratic public sphere (Pratt, 2004). GP

Suggested reading
Fraser (1997); Mitchell (2003).

private interest developments (pids) Communal housing projects in the USA (also known as *community interest developments* and *common interest communities*), in which the PROPERTY is held in common and its use governed by a homeowners' association. Those associations – many of which have considerable power over what can be done within the development – operate as 'private governments' separate from the STATE APPARATUS, although their decisions can be challenged legally. Originally associated with condominiums, the pid form of GOVERNANCE has spread to other housing types, covering more than 10 per cent of all US housing and a much higher proportion of all new housing. Most pid residents are relatively affluent, using a TERRITORIALITY strategy to distance themselves from perceived NEGATIVE EXTERNALITIES.   RJ

Suggested reading
Barton and Silverman (1994); McKenzie (1994).

privatization An increase in private ownership, control and action relative to public ownership, control and action. This may occur in three main ways. Assets and activities can be transferred from the public sector to the private sector (e.g. when a state-owned company is sold to private shareholders or the cleaning of a public building is contracted-out to a private company); private interests can increase their influence in the public sphere (e.g. when private retailers are given greater control over the uses of PUBLIC SPACE outside their shops); or private provision may grow faster than public provision (e.g. if more private than public housing is built in an area, the local housing stock becomes relatively more privatized). Privatization is often understood as one element of the rise of neo-liberal POLITICAL ECONOMY (see NEO-LIBERALISM).

Privatization has been prominent in many countries since the 1980s. Three major drivers of privatization can be identified. The rise of New Right politics during the 1980s in several Western countries (notably the USA under the Reagan administration and the UK under the government of Margaret Thatcher) was associated with economic policies that emphasized MARKET solutions and the rolling back of the STATE. This led to major sales of public assets (from utility companies to housing) and an expansion of private provision of services through contracting out and competitive tendering. A second phase of privatization was associated with the STRUCTURAL ADJUSTMENT programmes require by the INTERNATIONAL MONETARY FUND as a condition of much of its lending to low-income countries. The third driver has been the collapse of state SOCIALISM and the reintroduction of capitalist relations of production in former state socialist countries (cf. POST-SOCIALISM).

Geographers' interests in privatization focus on the unevenness of the process and its outcomes within and between countries, on the effect of privatization in generating wider processes of socio-spatial RESTRUCTURING, on its implications for understandings of state SPATIALITIES and on the privatization of space itself, through the growth of such things as semi-private shopping malls and urban GATED COMMUNITIES, and the sale of public land to private developers.

A binary view of privatization as a straight switch from public to private may be over-simplified. It risks neglecting the role of the 'third sector' of voluntary organizations, NGOS, civic associations and the social economy, which are neither wholly public nor narrowly private. In addition, marketization – the introduction of internal trading and quasi-MARKETS in the public sector, reductions in state subsidies to the private sector and the growth of user charges for public services – blurs the boundary between the public and the private, as does the widespread use of public–private partnerships in the GOVERNANCE of social and economic development.

Privatization has been an important source of capital ACCUMULATION and corporate profitability since the 1980s, but it has also been the target of major political protests. The privatization of WATER distribution in low-income countries has been of particular concern to protestors, because of the negative effect of charges on poor households' access to clean water.   JPa

Suggested reading
Han and Pannell (1999); Mansfield (2004); Painter (1991); Shiva (2002).

probabilism A thesis about the relationship between CULTURE and NATURE, which proposes that while the physical environment does not determine how human societies will react to its influence, it renders some responses more likely or probable than others. Probabilism thus aims to occupy a philosophical position somewhere between ENVIRONMENTAL DETERMINISM and POSSIBILISM. While debates over this issue were most characteristic of late-nineteenth- and early-twentieth-century GEOGRAPHY, recent reassertions about the power of the environment to channel human history in certain directions – such as those of Jared Diamond (1987) – have reopened aspects of the debate in some quarters (for a critique, see Judkins, Smith and Keys, 2008: cf. CULTURAL ECOLOGY; POLITICAL ECOLOGY). Despite its abstract clarity, in historical terms probabilism was perfectly compatible with the possibilist geographies associated with the French School of HUMAN GEOGRAPHY led by Paul Vidal de la Blache (see Lukermann, 1965).   DL

Suggested reading
Spate (1968).

probability map A probability MAP displays the estimated likelihood that a pre-defined event will occur at a specific point or defined area within a geographical space, during a particular period of time. For example, probability maps are used in meteorology to show the likelihoods of above-normal rainfall occurring around the globe (see, for example, the UK Met Office's seasonal forecasts at www.metoffice.com/research/). To interpret probability maps, it is important to know how the probabilities were calculated and interpolated across the map space, and the period for which the event is predicted (a 33 per cent chance of annual flooding being worse than a 33 per cent chance of decennial flooding). RH

process A flow of events or actions that produces, reproduces or transforms a system or structure.

It was not until the 1960s that modern geography was alerted to the complexity of the concept of a process. Blaut (1961) insisted that the standard distinction between SPATIAL STRUCTURE and temporal process derived from a KANTIANISM that had been discredited by what he called 'the relativistic revolution'. It was now clear, so he claimed, that 'nothing in the physical world is purely spatial or temporal; everything is process'. In Blaut's view, therefore, 'structures of the real world' that seemed to have a fixity and permanence were simply 'slow processes of long duration'. In principle, most formalizations of SPATIAL SCIENCE appeared to accept this claim – Golledge and Amedeo (1968) and Harvey (1969, pp. 419–32) gave 'process laws' a central place in their MODELS of EXPLANATION in geography (see POSITIVISM) – but in practice many studies simply used distance as a surrogate for process (hence 'spatial processes') and thus confirmed the geometric cast of LOCATIONAL ANALYSIS and SPATIAL ANALYSIS as these were conceived at the time (see DISTANCE DECAY).

Many of these locational–spatial models depended on *formal language systems*; that is, language systems whose elements have unassigned meanings. The *x*s and *y*s in their equations or the points and lines in their diagrams could refer to anything – they were empty of concrete content – and so analysis was governed by the relations between these abstract elements in the language system itself: by (say) the theorems of geometry, the calculus of probability theory or the mathematical theory of STOCHASTIC PROCESSES, rather than by what Olsson (1974) called 'the things we are talking *about*'. These locational–spatial

models of spatial process were reviewed in Cliff and Ord (1981).

Subsequently, however, there was a turn towards human geographies based on *ordinary language systems* whose elements have assigned meanings. This allowed more substantive conceptions of process to be utilized in human geography: cultural processes, ecological processes, economic processes, political processes, social processes and so on. Early examples included a focus on cognitive and DECISION-MAKING processes in BEHAVIOURAL GEOGRAPHY, on the dynamics of the LABOUR PROCESS and cycles of capital ACCUMULATION in ECONOMIC GEOGRAPHY, and on practices of social and symbolic interaction in CULTURAL GEOGRAPHY and SOCIAL GEOGRAPHY. This in turn, and of necessity, opened up a sustained dialogue with the other HUMANITIES and social sciences. For, as Harvey (1973) recognized, 'an understanding of space in all its complexity depends upon an appreciation of social processes [and] an understanding of the social process in all its complexity depends upon an appreciation of spatial form'. One of his most pressing concerns was thus to 'heal the breach' between the sociological and GEOGRAPHICAL IMAGINATION.

The distinction between 'formal' and 'substantive' definitions of process was cross-cut by a second distinction drawn by Hay and Johnston (1983), between 'sequences' and 'mechanisms':

(1) *Process as sequence in time and/or space.* This view of process is characteristic of the VERTICAL THEMES of traditional HISTORICAL GEOGRAPHY and of mathematical–statistical SPACE–TIME forecasting models. In both cases, the account is morphological and descriptive: compare Darby's (1951) identification of the processes that changed the English landscape ('clearing the wood', 'draining the marsh' etc.) with Bennett's simple (1979) typology of barrier, hierarchy, network and contiguity processes.

(2) *Process as mechanism.* This view of process is characteristic of both SYSTEMS analysis in geography and of geographies conducted under the sign of REALISM (which require the identification of the relations between the 'causal powers' of structures and the conditions under which they are realized). In both cases the account is interactive and explanatory: it seeks to show how – by what means, through which networks – particular outcomes materialize.

Hay and Johnston (1983) insisted that it was possible (and necessary) to reconcile these two approaches. Since their objective was also to use QUANTITATIVE METHODS to analyse spatio-temporal sequences and networks of connection and consequence, they were also seeking to employ formal language systems to substantive effect.

Through the 1980s and 1990s, most human geographers resisted such ecumenical attempts to integrate these different conceptions of process, however, and the dominant approaches focussed on describing processes through ordinary language systems and conceptualizing them as mechanisms. 'Mechanism' was soon replaced by more fluid METAPHORS, a sharper sense of agency, and a greater historical sensibility (see, e.g., STRUCTURATION THEORY). The most common focus was on POWER and *practice* and on the capacity of various forms of socio-spatial theory to elucidate their operation and outcome (see, e.g., Pred, 1984). More recently still, there has been a return to the sort of (non-Kantian) philosophical reflection recommended by Blaut forty years earlier, as a way of reworking these understandings of place, power and, crucially, practice. Much of this effort has been directed towards the elaboration of a *relational philosophy* in which 'process' takes centre stage, but in startlingly different guises. Thus Harvey (1966) turned to G.W. Leibniz (1646–1716) and A.N. Whitehead (1861–1947) to guide his theorizations of a dialectical space–time (Sheppard, 2006) and co-productions of SPACE and NATURE (Braun, 2006). Thrift (1999) and his collaborators turned to a dazzling array of European philosophers, including Ludwig Wittgenstein (1889–1951), Martin Heidegger (1889–1976), Maurice Merleau-Ponty (1908–61), and Gilles Deleuze (1925–95) and Félix Guattari (1930–92), to address similar themes, but in ways that animate an altogether different politics. Thrift's NON-REPRESENTATIONAL THEORY involves an attempt to rethink our most basic ONTOLOGY as a means of coping with an always becoming world of contingency, change and emergence (through what Thrift (2006, p. 140) calls a 'processual sensualism'); to invoke radically different conceptions of TIME as well as SPACE as a means of sensing the multiple elements that flicker into being in networks of places; and to incorporate PERFORMANCE and PERFORMATIVITY as a means of grasping the precarious, conditional and always consequential achievements of 'world-making' and 'geo-graphing' (Thrift, 1999). There are substantial disagreements between these MATERIALISMS, but they share a view of HUMAN GEOGRAPHY as incomplete project and unmastered process.   DG

Suggested reading
Pred (1984); Harvey (1996); Thrift (1999a).

producer services Services provided as inputs into the production process. This is in contrast to those SERVICES – consumer services – that are supplied to individuals or 'end' consumers, such as other firms or governments. Producer services are often characterized as intermediate inputs, before the product is completed. They include a diverse set of economic activities, such as accountancy, advertising, finance, marketing and research and development. It was in the late 1970s that geographers first became aware of the growing contribution that this type of economic activity was beginning to play towards economic growth (Dicken, 2006). Work on producer services became important in ECONOMIC GEOGRAPHY in the 1980s and early 1990s in its own right (Daniels, 1993), as well as being the basis for research into the emergence and classification of GLOBAL CITIES.

The research in the geographically UNEVEN DEVELOPMENT of producer services has revealed how and why they have important economic consequences (Bryson, Daniels and Warf, 2004). First, the supply and the demand for these services need not take place in the same place. Adverts can be produced or supplied in one place, and then e-mailed elsewhere, to the end consumer, from where there is demand. Second, and stemming from this spatial disjuncture between supply and demand, producer services are only partially dependent on the level of economic activity in their cities and regions. CLUSTERS of interconnected activity – around, for example, advertising in London (Grabher, 2001) – raise the city's profile but are not reliant on selling the product, in this case the advert, in London. Rather, the producer service is sold all over the world. The economic development to be wrung out of expanding producer services has been noted by policy-makers and politicians, and the sectors have found themselves important elements in the formation of urban and REGIONAL POLICY.   KWa

Suggested reading
Bryson, Daniels and Warf (2004); Dicken (2006).

product life cycle A concept used to connect the evolution of a product to changes in the location of its production (cf. PROFIT CYCLE). The idea is usually attributed to Vernon (1966), although its antecedents are considerably older. Vernon intended his model as an alternative to the Heckscher–Ohlin model of international TRADE, and he insisted that international INVESTMENT decisions taken by manufacturers were driven by more complex considerations than differences in factor and TRANSPORT COSTS. He proposed instead that products evolve through three distinct stages, and that manufacturers choose different locations in each of them:

(1) The *new product* tends to be unstable, since its design and production are still being modified and perfected. This usually involves considerable interaction between producers and suppliers and between producers and consumers as modifications are introduced, test-marketed and appraised. Producers thus require swift and effective access to a deep and diverse pool of suppliers and to consumers. These requirements are most likely to be met in major metropolitan industrialized economies.

(2) The *maturing product* undergoes a process of increasing standardization and, as market demand grows, the scale of production increases. Uncertainties about design and marketability diminish, so the need for flexibility is reduced. The major concern for most manufacturers becomes minimizing production costs, and they seek locations outside the most heavily industrialized economies, where labour costs are lower.

(3) The *standardized product* prompts manufacturers to turn still further afield, to less developed countries, particularly where their products are labour-intensive, have a high price elasticity of demand, and are only weakly dependent on EXTERNAL ECONOMIES for their production.

Although these ideas were directed at international trade, they enjoyed their most intensive application at the sub-national SCALE. Thompson (1968) recast Vernon's hypothesis as a 'filtering-down' theory of urban economic change. New products were supposed to originate at the top of the urban hierarchy because of the concentration of highly educated scientific and technical workers, universities and other research institutions. The earliest production of such INNOVATIONS would occur in the same REGIONS for the

reasons outlined by Vernon. With increasing standardization of the product and production process, the tie to such highly skilled labour would weaken, and cost considerations would drive manufacturers to seek out locations in intermediate urban centres where semi- and unskilled workers would be available in large numbers at lower wage rates. As products reached advanced maturity, their production would shift to the lowest tiers of the urban hierarchy or out into rural locations. Thompson's assessment of the long-term prospects for such regions was unequivocal: 'their industrial catches come to them only to die' (p. 56). When Vernon and Thompson began to work on the product life cycle concept, the long-term dominance of established industrial regions such as the Manufacturing Belt of the USA was unchallenged. For Thompson, the decline of such regions was unthinkable, because of their proven ability over the long run to continue to generate new products. The loss of manufacturing to more peripheral regions through the filter-down process was thus little cause for concern. A scant decade later, however, these assumptions were called into question by a major shift in economic activity between the regions of the USA. For Rees (1979) and Thomas (1980), the decline of the Manufacturing Belt could be explained by the accelerated rate of DECENTRALIZATION of production activities, as intensified competition from newly industrializing countries heightened the importance of cost-reduction for US-based manufacturers. And in contrast to Thompson's views, Rees and Stafford (1986) argued that previously peripheral areas such as the US Southeast could eventually achieve a critical mass once a sufficient volume of capital had been invested in production facilities in the region. At this point, they suggested, the 'incubator' functions generating new products and firms traditionally associated exclusively with the largest metropolitan regions in the Northeast and Midwest could take root in these new locations. This thesis found empirical support in studies showing that many of the largest manufacturing firms had already shifted some of their highest-order (especially research and development) functions away from their original headquarters locations to places further down the urban hierarchy (Pred, 1977: see also SUNBELT/SNOWBELT).

More recently, the product life cycle concept has been criticized for its excessive determinism and ESSENTIALISM, especially its implicit claim that all products follow a similar trajectory over time (Storper, 1985; Taylor,

1986). Critics have pointed out that even standardized and mature products can be rejuvenated through innovation in the later stages of a product's life cycle. A case in point is the automobile which, while hardly a new product, has been continuously modified and improved over time. It has also been argued that many COMMODITIES never achieve the status of cheap, standardized, mass-produced goods – especially those that, under a regime of POST-FORDISM, exhibit a high degree of variability, customization and qualitative differentiation. MSG

Suggested reading
Malecki (1991).

production complex A spatial cluster of specialized, interrelated economic activities bound together by the creation and exploitation of EXTERNAL ECONOMIES (Scott, 1988b). Such CLUSTERS offer producers the ability to establish, and easily realign, transactional LINKAGES with other local buyers and suppliers, thereby encouraging the development and maintenance of a social division of labour (see JUST-IN-TIME PRODUCTION; TRANSACTION COSTS; TRANS-ACTIONAL ANALYSIS). They also provide a local LABOUR MARKET specialized to match the needs of local producers. They are further sustained by the existence of public and quasi-public institutions developed to support specialized local economic activity and to foster non-MAR-KET forms of interaction and interdependencies between local economic actors. (See AGGLOM-ERATION; COMMODITY CHAIN/FILIÈRE; INDUS-TRIAL DISTRICT.) MSG

production of nature This rather strikingly counter-intuitive phrase comes from Neil Smith, originally in his book *Uneven development* (1984). Despite its critics, perhaps nothing attests to the power of the idea more than the fact that the phrase becomes less counter-intuitive with time.

At the simplest level, and clearly influenced by Lefebvre's understanding of the PRODUC-TION OF SPACE, Smith conveys by this phrase that NATURE is socially produced and, more specifically, that nature is increasingly an artefact of CAPITALISM in the contemporary world. At one level, this is not so counter-intuitive at all. Increasingly, at SCALES from the atmospheric to the genetic, the material natures of EVERYDAY LIFE are increasingly transformed either by intentional manipulation for the purposes of COMMODITY production (e.g. genetically modified crops), or by the myriad ecological impacts of industrial, capitalist

activities and related processes (e.g. the deposition of persistent organic pollutants in Arctic and Antarctic ecosystems). Since Smith's book, empirical processes that confirm the material production of nature to suit economic purposes have proliferated, including the onset of commercial aquaculture and the continued GLOBALIZATION of plantation FORESTRY. Moreover, empirical research has elaborated Smith's thesis, indicating that the capitalist production of nature, often in shifting and complex institutional configurations, has been ongoing for some time (Prudham, 2003). While agriculture would be the most obvious example to draw on here, under which the intentional transformation of crops and ANI-MALS is probably in excess of 10,000 years old, Smith is at pains to differentiate the capitalist production of nature from all that has come before it. This is not, as he argues, because widespread anthropogenic change is unique to capitalism (quite the opposite). Rather, it is because the particular ways that nature is transformed under capitalism are unique. This includes, for instance, the appropriation and transformation of biophysical processes as a constitutive facet of UNEVEN DEVELOPMENT under capitalism. An elaboration of this, with some qualification, can be found in Robbins and Fraser (2003), who note '... if the state can put non-commercial Scots pine woodland in the place of industrial forests, it is only, after all, because increased extraction is occurring in the Baltic states, Indonesia, and Ghana ...' (p. 113). Here, produced nature is worked through as a complex set of spatial and scalar logics that link far-flung places, not least through MARKET relations and EXCHANGE, as well as in the realm of production *per se*.

However, Smith's thesis is not only about the material transformation of nature under capitalism. Rather, he also posits that a unique feature of what might be called 'capitalist nature' is the ways in which ideas about nature are also produced in and through capitalist production, commodity circulation, and capitalist social relations and institutions. This is a complex and controversial thesis. Yet, at one level, Smith's observation is no different than those who have long recognized the rise of instrumental, utilitarian thinking alongside industrial capitalism. Smith's argument is that such an instrumentalist disposition specifically towards nature is reinforced by capitalist social relations and processes of valuation, and that these ideas become increasingly influential in the construction of meaning around nature in a capitalist society. Examples would include instrumental, utilitarian arguments for BIO-DIVERSITY conservation, which tend to both render species in terms of net present value of future benefits, while also individuating such species in relation to their ecological (and social!) context. A key facet of Smith's thesis in this respect is his anticipation of SOCIAL CONST-RUCTION debates within critical environmental geography, but his mobilization of specifically capitalist IDEOLOGIES as decisive influences on how nature comes to be known (constructed).

The production of nature thesis, despite being influential and widely cited in critical environmental geography, has arguably not been sufficiently developed or elaborated since its first publication. An exception is Castree (1995), who argues (sympathetically) that the thesis may reinforce Promethean discourses by downplaying the productive capacity of biophysical processes. Here, there is room for some sort of rapprochement with the HYBRIDITY literature (e.g. Whatmore, 2002a), which emphasizes the EPISTEMOLOGICAL and ONTO-LOGICAL co-production of nature by human and non-human alike. Another avenue not well travelled would explore the links between Smith's thesis and James O'Connor's second contradiction of capitalism (O'Connor, 1998). While O'Connor would quibble little with the notion of capitalism producing nature in this respect (it also comprises part of his theory), he places greater emphasis on this as a source of contradiction and CRISIS inherent to capital-ism because of the under-production of nature as a condition of SOCIAL REPRODUCTION.   SP

production of space A term made famous by French Marxist Henri Lefebvre (1901–91) in his 1974 book *The production of space* (trans. 1991). Lefebvre seeks to bring a Marxist analysis of production to bear on the way SPACE is created, coded and used through social, political and everyday proces-ses (cf. PRODUCTION OF NATURE). Social space is, for Lefebvre, a social product. Lefebvre came to the analysis of space through three main routes: his reworking of the PHILOSOPHY of MARXISM and in particular the notion of the DIALECTIC; work supplementing Marxist POLITICAL ECONOMY, with an experiential emphasis on EVERYDAY LIFE; and work on rural and urban sociology. Lefebvre was in his early seventies when *The production of space* was published, and had been publishing for almost 50 years: this mature work is one of the culminations of these varied interests and concerns (for overviews, see Kofman and

Lebas, 1996; Shields, 1999; Elden, 2004; Merrifield, 2006).

In the opening chapter of *The production of space*, Lefebvre suggests that we should under-stand space in three ways – as *perceived*, *con-ceived* and *lived*. The first of these, what he calls *spatial practices*, are spaces that are con-crete, material, physical. The second is what he calls *representations of space*, the space of abstract plans and mental processes. Both of these ways of thinking about space are rela-tively common within HUMAN GEOGRAPHY, but it is with the third that Lefebvre makes his key contribution. Lefebvre claims that both these spaces need to be thought together, in dialect-ical relation. But this is not a linear sense of the dialectic, in which the two terms react and form a new term that then itself comes into relation with its opposite. Rather, this is a dialectic where the third term continues to exist in relation with the other two (cf. TRIA-LECTICS). Lefebvre's third term here is what he calls *spaces of representation* – confusingly ren-dered as 'representational spaces' in the English translation – spaces that are lived, experienced and recoded through the actions of those that occupy and use them. Lefebvre therefore challenges both a crudely materialist analysis and a politically detached idealist one. For Edward Soja, whose reading of Lefebvre has been influential in Anglophone human geography, in contrast to the 'real' or 'imagined' spaces of the other two models, these are 'real-and-imagined' spaces, which he has deployed himself in readings of Los Angeles and in his construction of THIRD SPACE (Soja, 1989, 1996).

In the remainder of *The production of space*, which is a complex work that defies straight-forward summary, Lefebvre returns to this three-part model and illustrates, complicates and historicizes it. His is an analysis in the tradition of HISTORICAL MATERIALISM, and the spaces of a particular epoch are related, though not slavishly dependent on, the MODE OF PRODUCTION (see figure 1) (for a summary, see Gregory, 1994, who also emphasizes Lefebvre's suggestive reading of the changing historical modalities of the BODY, VISUALITY and space). Thus CAPITALISM produces a par-ticular political economy of space, centrally defined through the 'colonization of everyday life' through the production of abstract space (see figure 2), which Lefebvre sought to develop into a politics of space. As he declared in a 1970 essay, 'there is a politics of space because space is political'. Lefebvre was indebted to a range of thinkers who he used

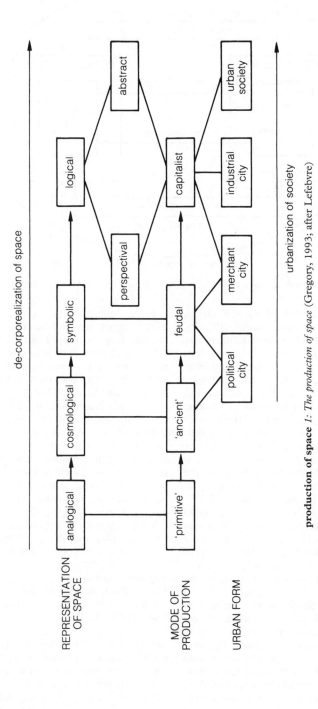

production of space 1: *The production of space* (Gregory, 1993; after Lefebvre)

591

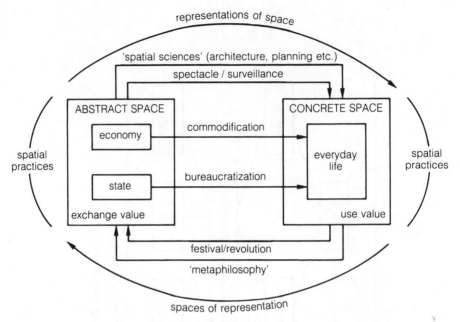

representations of space

'spatial sciences' (architecture, planning etc.)

spectacle / surveillance

ABSTRACT SPACE		CONCRETE SPACE
economy	commodification →	everyday life
state	bureaucratization →	
exchange value		use value

spatial practices

spatial practices

festival/revolution

'metaphilosophy'

spaces of representation

production of space 2: *The colonization of concrete space* (Gregory, 1993)

to supplement Marx – notably G.W.F. Hegel, Friedrich Nietzsche and, more critically, Martin Heidegger. Each of these thinkers was useful, Lefebvre contended, in adding things that Marx's analyses alone could not provide. Marx was the indispensable starting point for Lefebvre at each stage of his career, but Heidegger was particularly useful in thinking about the question of space. Heidegger's analysis of how modern thought's mathematical, geometrical sense of space is reductive and we need to recall how to dwell or live is crucial to Lefebvre's thinking through of the alienating properties of capitalist space, particularly in the city (cf. ALIENATION).

Lefebvre's work has come under sustained criticism from more orthodox Marxists, for whom his emphasis on space trembles on the edges of or, more directly, simply *is* a form of SPATIAL FETISHISM. In fact, these criticisms, and other engagements with his writings, by scholars such as Manuel Castells, David Harvey and Neil Smith, were available in English before Lefebvre's work was translated, and it was left to later commentators to explore quite other dimensions of his work. The utilization of thinkers such as Heidegger and Nietzsche brought Lefebvre into a tense proximity with the POST-STRUCTURALISM of thinkers such as Michel Foucault, but Lefebvre was strongly critical of their ANTI-HUMANISM and their use of spatial METAPHORS in the absence

of more concrete analyses (cf. Gregory, 1997b). It has largely been left to Anglophone geographers such as Soja (1989, 1996), Gregory (1994) and Dear (1997) to develop the commonalities and complementarities of their approaches (see also Gunewardena, Kipfer, Milgrom and Schmid, 2008).

Although *The production of space* remains his most influential work in human geography, Lefebvre's writings on cities (e.g. 1996), everyday life and Marxist theory are also available in English translation and provide much useful material. Lefebvre is commonly looked at as a theorist of space, yet he would have equally stressed his work on TIME and temporality (Lefebvre, 2004 [1992]: see RHYTHMANALYSIS), suggesting that space and time need to be rethought, and thought together, in any genuinely radical political action.   SE

Suggested reading
Elden (2004, ch. 5); Gregory (1994, ch. 6); Lefebvre (1991a [1974]); Merrifield (2006); Soja (1996b, ch. 1).

productivity A measure of output relative to input, usually expressed as the ratio of the returns from sales to the costs of production. The term was developed in analyses of the EFFICIENCY of manufacturing industry, where it is equivalent to the rate of surplus value or rate of exploitation in MARXIST ECONOMICS.

The higher the amount of VALUE-ADDED in the production process relative to the costs incurred (of labour, materials and fixed capital), the greater is the productivity. In primary industries, however, productivity usually implies the ratio of production per unit area of land rather than to its (imputed) cost.

With the growth of SERVICE industries in advanced CAPITALIST societies, attempts have been made to measure productivity in sectors other than manufacturing – not least in higher education! – though the concept of VALUE ADDED is not readily applied in many such situations.   RJ

profit cycle A sectoral approach to understanding changes experienced by regional economies, developed by economist Ann Markusen as an alternative to the PRODUCT LIFE CYCLE model. Instead of focusing on regularities in the changing scale of output or changes in the qualitative characteristics of a product and its production process over time, Markusen (1985) argued that the economic variable most crucial to determining industrial change is the *rate of profit*. Drawing her inspiration from both Marx and Schumpeter, she argued that change within an industry should be understood in terms of two central processes, each of which is pursued by firms to increase market power and hence profit rates: (i) INNOVATION and (ii) imperfect competition. She proposed a five-stage MODEL through which industries move:

- New industries are born and core products are being designed: a regime of *zero profits*.
- Once an innovation is commercially successful, and so long as its production is concentrated in the hands of a single (monopoly) firm, *super profits* are likely.
- As patents expire and/or imitation and innovation DIFFUSION facilitates entry by new firms, the market power once held by the monopoly firm dissipates. Profits decline to *normal profit levels* as the industry moves towards market saturation. It is only at this stage that conditions resemble perfect competition.
- If some firms increase their market shares through mergers and acquisitions, this move towards oligopoly will raise profit rates to *normal-plus* levels. But if the industry evolves along a path of predatory pricing and excessive competition, profit rates will be squeezed to *normal-minus* levels.
- Once the sector matures to obsolescence, *negative profits* will ensue.

Markusen argues that 'distinct spatial tendencies' accompany each stage of a sector's passage through the profit cycle (1985, p. 24) (see table).

Stage	Profit rate regime	Spatial tendency
1	Zero profits	Concentration
2	Super profits	Agglomeration
3	Normal profits	Dispersion
4	Normal-plus or -minus profits	Relocation
5	Negative	Abandonment

The approach is a suggestive one, but it was roundly criticized by Storper (1985) for its ESSENTIALISM. While he accepted that the MODEL was one of the most effective ways to comprehend 'multilocational, large-scale production systems and sectoral location patterns over time', he saw it as a premature formalization and argued for a much more historically informed analysis of the dynamics of geographical INDUSTRIALIZATION.   MSG

property Relationships between persons with respect to the use or benefit of valued things. Legal scholars tend to see property rights as residing in the 'jural relations' between individuals, rather than in the thing itself. If I claim a property RIGHT in a thing (such as land), what is really being asserted is that I can exclude you from access to it (Macpherson, 1978a). The LAW of property concerns itself with the legally recognized distribution of rights, benefits and responsibilities associated with the objects of property.

Variations can occur in terms of the range of objects over which property rights are recognized, the extent of rights that are recognized and the entities that can bear such rights. These can all be construed very broadly: for example, the objects of property can include not only land (LAND TENURE) and MONEY, but intangibles such as names, knowledge and shares in joint-stock companies. Despite this diversity, Western liberal societies (see LIBERALISM) tend towards a strikingly narrow view of property, summarized by Singer (2000) as the 'ownership model'. Private property, the default category here, is viewed in largely asocial terms: The owner is assumed to hold a full bundle of property rights (alienation, use, exclusion etc.), and is expected to be motivated by self-regarding behaviour. STATE intervention is presumptively suspect, and must be justified in relation to the prior and superior rights of the owner. A rich corpus of writing explores and critiques various justifications for private property (Macpherson, 1978b).

This model, it has been noted, exerts a powerful imaginative hold, shaping collective understandings of the possibilities of social life, the ETHICS of human relations and the ordering of economic life (Blomley, 2005). In response, scholars have criticized prevailing views of property: Singer (2000), for example, characterizes the ownership model as both descriptively and normatively flawed. One central argument, variously phrased, is that property is irreclaimably social and political in its constitution and effects (Alexander, 1998). Property rights, insists Underkuffler (2003), 'are not simply private interests with which the state neutrally coexists. Property rights ... are collective, enforced, even violent decisions about who shall enjoy the privileges and resources which this society allocates among its citizens' (p. 146).

Given its historical development under a liberal capitalist society (see CAPITALISM), many critics have cast property rights in a negative light, pointing to the manner in which privatized property rights instrumentally and ideologically underpin CLASS rule, PATRIARCHY and COLONIALISM. However, recent years have seen an attempt to uncover the progressive potential of property – both private and collective (Blomley, 2002).

Property is a political instrument, an element in social struggle, an object of CONSUMPTION and a site for IDENTITY formation. Given its importance, it is heartening to note some interest in GEOGRAPHY in property. Blomley has sought to uncover the ways in which conflicts over INNER-CITY GENTRIFICATION frequently invoke property claims, refracted through REPRESENTATIONS of local LANDSCAPES (Blomley, 2004b; Mitchell and Staeheli, 2005). Everyday understandings of domestic and PUBLIC SPACE are also seen to entail surprisingly complex and overlapping renderings of public and private property (Blomley, 2004a). The dynamics of COLONIALISM are also shown to entail the simultaneous reworking of space and property (Forman and Kedar, 2004). Property, of course, extends beyond claims to land: Sarah Whatmore (2002a), for example, traces the intersecting geographies of landed and INTELLECTUAL PROPERTY RIGHTS. Geographers have also expressed interest in common property: David Harvey (2003b), for example, has argued that the ENCLOSURE of the commons, rather than an episode of early capitalism, continues across the globe (see PRIMITIVE ACCUMULATION), as does political organizing in

defence of common rights (GLOBAL COMMONS; PRIMITIVE ACCUMULATION). NKB

Suggested reading
Corr (1999); Geisler and Daneker (2000); Nedelsky (1990); Rose (1994); Verdery and Humphrey (2004).

propinquity A measure of nearness or proximity, usually with reference to distance, but also to time. RJ

prostitution Broadly defined, prostitution refers to the exchange of sexual services for money or payment in kind. Though often socially marginalized, the prostitute has remained a central figure in geographical debates concerning both the gendering of SPACE and the spatial regulation of conduct. Notably, it is the place of women sex workers that has attracted most attention. While some accounts have been excessively voyeuristic and uncritical, work informed by FEMINIST theory has generated some insightful geographical commentaries on the regulation of female SEXUALITY and the role of space in the maintenance of HETERONORMATIVITY. Broadly speaking, these document the SPATIALITY of prostitution on at least three related SCALES. First, attention has been focused on the more-or-less enforced movement of women sex workers across international BOUNDARIES, a phenomena that appears to be growing as criminalized global networks extend their range and influence (Samarasinge, 2005). Reading these movements as indicative of gendered global inequalities, increasing stress is also being placed on the formation of a DIASPORIC sex workers' movement opposed to enforced prostitution (Doezema and Kempadoo, 1998: see SLAVERY). Second, on a national scale there has been a strong emphasis on the connections between prostitution LAWS and the particular concerns and anxieties projected on to the BODIES of prostitute women. This literature often has a strong historical dimension, tracking the moral and political debates encouraging the use of particular forms of SURVEILLANCE and BIOPOWER to categorize and control sex work (Howell, 2000). Finally, there is an established tradition of urban research that documents the microgeographies of sex work in RED-LIGHT DISTRICTS. One important strand of this explores the relationship between sex workers and local residents, with a particular focus on the NIMBY campaigns of displacement that are often associated with incipient GENTRIFICATION

(Hubbard, 2004). In all cases, research suggests the gendered inequalities of sexual commerce produces a series of spaces where women's sexuality can be bought and sold by men with relative impunity, albeit that these spaces may be important in the forging of new GENDER IDENTITIES and formations (Law, 1997). In this sense, the relative silence on forms of male sex work poses some interesting questions about gender inequalities within and without the discipline.   PH

Suggested reading
Hubbard (1999).

proto-industrialization   A term proposed by economic historian Franklin Mendels (1972) to denote 'the rapid growth of traditionally organised but market-oriented, principally rural industry'. Whilst the presence of such industries had long been recognized, Mendels presented proto-industrialization not merely as a description of (pre-)industrial organization, but also as an EXPLANATION of industrial change, arguing that it 'preceded and prepared for' INDUSTRIALIZATION. In emphasizing the continuities between traditional systems of domestic production and the centralized and mechanized factory system, Mendels' thesis is central to the broader reconceptualization of INDUSTRIAL REVOLUTION as an evolutionary and gradual process. Two different models have been proposed, each with its own empirical and conceptual emphasis. *Ecological models* focus on the pre-conditions for proto-industrialization, particularly the ways in which under-employed PEASANT labour was drawn into industrial production. There is little consensus on the type of agrarian economy that would favour such development, with rural industries emerging in both arable areas (with seasonal unemployment) and pastoral regions (with diurnal time-budgets). In reality, much depended upon the social and institutional environment of the area, especially land holding and the type and flexibility of labour skills. Once established, it is argued that COMPARATIVE ADVANTAGE led to a growing DIVISION OF LABOUR between specialist industrial and agricultural REGIONS. However, this not only makes unwarranted assumptions about individual and collective rationality, but also fails to acknowledge the importance of other variables, such as the presence of commercialized mercantile and urban networks (Stobart, 2004).
Economic models focus on the structural relationship between the peasant/artisan and the merchant/capitalist. The artisan HOUSEHOLD sought to balance production and consumption by adjusting the level of engagement in manufacture for the MARKET, whilst the merchant collected together the products of domestic labour and consigned them to distant markets. Although mutually dependent, the interests of these two parties were inherently contradictory. When prices fell, artisans increased production to maintain household income, thus saturating the market and worsening the recession. When prices rose, artisan households could more easily satisfy their needs and production slowed, just when merchants would seek to take advantage of increased profits. This conflict is seen as being resolved through the increasing control exercised by merchants over the production process. Initially, this involved a shift from the *Kaufsystem* of independent artisan production to the *Verlagssytem* of putting out, wherein the means of production remained in the hands of the merchant, who effectively employed dependent outworkers. This was subsequently superseded by a merchant-led centralization of production into proto-factories (Kriedte, Medick and Schlumbohm, 1981).

This version of proto-industrialization as a theory of industrial change has been challenged from three very different directions. At the level of the peasant household, de Vries (1994) has argued that consumption as well as production became ever-more market oriented, increasing household specialization and growing consumption inspiring an artisan-centred 'industrious revolution'. At a broader scale, studies of regional industrialization have emphasized that the logic of CAPITALISM was played out differently in different places: factory production was one of a range of possibilities, which included workshop-based flexible specialization as well as hybrid factory–workshop systems (Berg, 1994). More fundamentally, others have questioned whether proto-industrialization was, indeed, a necessary stage in industrial development, arguing that the switch from organic to mineral RESOURCES was the real key to industrialization.   JSt

Suggested reading
Berg, Hudson and Sonenscher (1983); Houston and Snell (1984).

psychoanalytic theory   Originating in the late nineteenth century in the work of Sigmund Freud (1986–1939), psychoanalytic theory and practice offers a distinctive way of thinking about the human mind and of responding to psychological distress. Psychoanalysis has travelled widely from its central European origins, and has evolved into a complex, multifaceted and internally fractured body of knowledge, situated at the interface between the human and natural sciences, and between clinical practice and academic theory.

Notwithstanding critiques of its EUROCENTRIC origins, psychoanalysis has been taken up in many different cultural contexts, perhaps most notably in LATIN AMERICA, but also in India, Japan and elsewhere. Its GEOGRAPHY and SPATIALITY have become topics for geographical study, albeit primarily within the Anglophone literature (Kingsbury, 2003; Cameron, 2006).

Along with the more general rise of psychological thinking, psychoanalytic ideas have had a pervasive influence on such arenas of life as child-rearing, education and popular culture. Within the academy, psychoanalytic theory has been taken up most extensively in the HUMANITIES and more sporadically in the social sciences, including HUMAN GEOGRAPHY, where a distinct sub-discipline of psychoanalytic geography has shown tentative signs of formation since around the turn of the twenty-first century.

The unconscious is perhaps the most fundamental and defining idea of psychoanalysis, albeit one that has a much longer history. For Freud, only a small proportion of the human mind is knowable through rational thought. The greater part is outside conscious awareness and full of hidden dangers. It makes its presence felt in a variety of ways, including dreams, slips of the tongue, the clinical method of 'free association' and other actions – the motivations for which are not discernible by, and are often contrary to, conscious intent. The psychoanalytic unconscious acts as the repository for experiences, thoughts and feelings that are unacceptable to, and are repressed by, the conscious mind. The unconscious therefore exemplifies a means by which rational HUMAN AGENCY is 'de-centred' in the sense of not being the driving force of human action, an idea that has been highly influential in human geography. The radical OTHERNESS, profound strangeness and disruptiveness of Freud's concept of the unconscious is emphasized by Felicity Callard (2003) in her review of geographers' engagements with psychoanalytic theory.

Freud developed his ideas over a period of nearly 50 years. Not surprisingly, there are shifts, tensions and ambiguities within his

work. Moreover, he founded an approach taken up by many others, who have variously extended, challenged, supplemented and reworked his ideas. One of the most influential lines of differentiation within the psychoanalytic tradition lies between those theorists who attach primary importance to the psychic life generated by the instinctual drives of the human organism, including especially drives towards pleasure and towards death or annihilation, and those theorists who attach primary importance to the psychic life generated by a different kind of drive or condition of existence, namely the drive to relate to others. Among the former, the French psychoanalyst Jacques Lacan (1901–81) has been especially influential, while the latter has given rise of object relations theory and other relational approaches to psychoanalysis, developed through such theorists as Melanie Klein (1882–1960) and Donald Winnicott (1896–1971).

Human geographers have engaged with different strands of psychoanalysis for a variety of purposes. One of the earliest examples in the Anglophone literature was methodological in focus and drew as much on psychoanalytic practice as theory: Jacquelin Burgess and colleagues (Burgess, Limb and Harrison, 1988) applied ideas from group analysis (a form of psychoanalysis that focuses on the relationship between individuals and their social context) to facilitate the exploration of environmental values in FOCUS GROUPS. Continuing this methodological theme, others have appealed to key ideas informing psychoanalytic practices to deepen and enrich understandings of the dynamics in play within research encounters (Bondi, 2005). Yet others have drawn on approaches derived from Carl Jung's analytic psychology to facilitate research participants to connect with unconscious childhood experience (Bingley, 2003).

Several human geographers have deployed psychoanalytic theories to develop accounts of human SUBJECTIVITY and its spatial forms. In a highly influential contribution, David Sibley (1995) examines geographies of exclusion combining Melanie Klein's object relations account of the unconscious expulsion of feared and dreaded aspects of our selves with the post-Lacanian psychoanalyst Julia Kristeva's discussion of the fascination and horror, preoccupation and repulsion, associated with that which is expelled. Using these ideas, Sibley (1995) illuminates the profound emotional power of exclusionary processes for the different groups whose members identify with each other and against others in ways that generate highly potent lines of demarcation. While Sibley's (1995) account draws primarily on object relations psychoanalysis, Robert Wilton (2003) draws on Freud's concept of castration together with Lacan's reworking to explore how the geographical exclusion of disabled people may serve to shore up illusions of 'ableism' (cf. DISABILITY). Lacanian readings of Freud are also evident in geographical accounts of topics such as RACISM (Nast, 2000) and embodied experiences of cities (Pile, 1996).

A product of nineteenth-century European culture, Freud hypothesized that the repressed unconscious contains much material of a sexual nature, which would be highly disruptive if allowed to break through into consciousness. He argued that in order to grow up in socially acceptable ways, boys and girls were called upon to repress their 'natural', sexual (or libidinal) desires. Normative heterosexual masculinity and femininity were theorized by Freud as demanding psychical achievements. Although aspects of his theories of GENDER and sexual identity have been highly controversial, his approach has also been welcomed as a resource for challenging assumptions about what is 'natural', and for elaborating a theory of subjectivity as situated in a zone of creative interplay between the 'personal' and the 'cultural'. For this reason, some feminist geographers have turned to psychoanalysis in their theorizations of the interplay between gender, SEXUALITY, subjectivity and space, and to contribute to critiques of the 'MASCULINISM' of dominant forms of knowledge (Rose, 1996; Nast, 2000: see FEMINIST GEOGRAPHIES). Against critics who consider psychoanalysis to be an intrinsically individualistic theory and practice, these applications find that it offers a powerful way of understanding how social and cultural milieux are embodied and personalized by human individuals, as well as how unconscious aspects of human life are manifest in the social world.   LB

Suggested reading
Bondi (2005); Callard (2003); Craib (1990); Sibley (2003).

psychogeography The 'study of the precise laws and specific effects of the geographic environment, consciously organized or not, on the emotions and behavior of individuals', according to Guy Debord (1981 [1955], p. 5). Psychogeography is typically traced back to this definition, and to the activities of Debord and members of the Letterist International in 1950s Paris, for whom it was a means of exploring urban spaces and EVERYDAY LIFE, and who established it as a key concern of the early SITUATIONISTS. Yet the definition's academic tone belies its politicized and playful engagement with cities, as a way of challenging dominant representations and practices, and seeking to change urban spaces and life as part of a revolutionary project. Psychogeography combined a conscious and political analysis of urban ambiences with experiments in ludic behaviour, principally through *dérives* or drifts on foot, and included the construction of 'psychogeographic maps' that challenged the values of dominant CARTOGRAPHIES.

The term was independently employed by geographers engaged in politically motivated versions of environmental psychology in the late 1960s, especially at Clark University in Massachusetts, including David Stea and Denis Wood (Wood, 1987). While influential on subsequent work in environmental psychology (see also MENTAL MAPS), that usage has been relatively sidelined in the recent resurgence of interest in psychogeography since the 1990s that has taken more inspiration from the terminology, if not always the politics, of the situationists. Much interest has been literary, involving the tracing of a longer tradition of imaginative and wayward URBAN EXPLORATION, especially in London and Paris, though writers such as William Blake, Thomas de Quincey and Charles Baudelaire, and the surrealists around André Breton (see also FLÂNEUR/FLÂNERIE). Contemporary heirs of this visionary tradition include Iain Sinclair, whose peripatetic investigations of London, especially its East End, have done much to popularize the term 'psychogeography' (Coverley, 2006).

Contemporary artists and urban explorers have also embraced the term in their engagements with emotional and psychic spaces, through urban interventions as well as new media (Pinder, 2005a). Recent years have further seen a proliferation of psychogeographical associations or organizations in Europe and North America, whose investigations of PLACES have typically been drawn by the marginal, hidden and forgotten, and whose networking has been facilitated by the INTERNET (and documented in journals such as *Transgressions*, 1995–2001). As psychogeography has moved increasingly into the mainstream, much of its early radical political edge has been lost. Yet its political ambitions as well as humour and idiosyncracies are also finding new and at times challenging modes of expression.   DP

Suggested reading
Debord (1981 [1955]).

public administration Studies of the spatial organization and management of the STATE APPARATUS (Bennett, 1990). The public administration sector comprises the different government agencies that administer, oversee and manage public programmes and that have executive, legislative or judicial authority over other institutions – such as QUANGOS – within a given spatial unit, such as a NATION-STATE or a REGION. Studies of the spatiality of public administration have explored the relationships between, on the one hand, the types of SERVICES being delivered, and, on the other, the SCALE of their delivery (Barlow, 1991).   KWa

Suggested reading
Bennett (1990).

public choice theory Using the techniques of NEO-CLASSICAL ECONOMICS, public choice theory examines issues of political decision-making and of the behaviour of government. It derives from the pioneering work of Duncan Black (1958) and James Buchanan and Gordon Tullock (1962), and was conceived to study politics on the basis of economic principles. Its original proponents argue that it should be understood as a research programme rather than as a discipline, or even a sub-discipline, of economics. It contends that elected politicians and government bureaucrats make decisions on the basis of self-interest. So, the behaviour and decisions of all individuals within the political sphere is purely instrumental. Politicians enact policies in terms of ensuring re-election, the voters remain deliberately ignorant because individually they do not understand it to be in their interest to learn more, and bureaucrats – those who put decisions into practice – do whatever is necessary to keep their jobs and get promoted. All involved strive to maximize their own welfare. At each decision, politicians, voters and bureaucrats make a RATIONAL CHOICE. Public choice theory covers a series of issues; namely, government constitutions, STATE bureaucracies and voting behaviour. While the staple diet of political scientists, these concerns, and in particular their spatial patterns and trends, have been analysed in ELECTORAL and POLITICAL GEOGRAPHY.

Within public choice theory, there are five core theoretical tensions. First, there are difficulties in aggregating individual choices and decisions to produce a collective outcome. How is it possible to produce policies on the basis of the preferences of individuals? Second, there is the range of issues that stem from the introduction of PUBLIC GOODS and market failure. There is a tendency, stemming from their monopoly POWER, for governments to extend public ownership beyond that deemed efficient by the market. Third, there is the issue of political party competition. According to public choice theory, the outcome of two vote-maximizing parties is almost identical parties. Only with three political parties vying for the votes of the electorate is policy variability introduced (cf. HOTELLING MODEL). Fourth, there is the difficulty of forming and organizing interest groups due to the free-rider problem (see GAME THEORY). Fifth, there are a number of conceptual difficulties in assuming and treating PUBLIC FINANCE as a rational exchange amongst citizens. These issues have been the subjects of much empirical and theoretical work over the past four and a half decades. As a branch of NEO-CLASSICAL ECONOMICS, public choice theory is subject to all the standard critiques of that school and, in particular, the supposition of RATIONAL CHOICE. Within GEOGRAPHY, a small number of key texts have explored the issues of public goods and market failure (Cox and Johnston, 1982) and public finance and government decentralization (Bennett, 1990).   KWa

Suggested reading
Bennett (1990); Cox and Johnston (1982).

public finance Human geographers have studied the spatial distribution of public-sector income and expenditure. In addition to producing and analysing spatial patterns, work has examined the mismatch between the geographies of public-sector revenue generation and expenditure (Bennett, 1990) – put another way (Bennett, 1980, p. ix): *who gets what, where, and at what cost?* The twin focus on spatial patterns and their consequences allows the exploration of differences between individuals and between the local governments that collect and spend the revenues (cf. COLLECTIVE CONSUMPTION). As the needs, costs and preferences for PUBLIC GOODS vary geographically, so a failure to attend to the spatial consequences of public finance matters to issues of SOCIAL JUSTICE. Once the 'who' and the 'where' are known, it is then possible to attend to the third element to the question, 'At what cost?' So, for example, how might the state-led geographical redistribution of resources alleviate SPATIAL INEQUALITY? While concern with how the STATE APPARATUS produces and can then address spatial inequality through its finance functions remains an area of interest of geographers, Bennett (1985) has argued that equity in the distribution of public goods is a UTOPIA. As such, the state should reduce its provision of public goods and services – and the role of the private and of the third sector should be increased, perhaps through PUBLIC–PRIVATE PARTNERSHIPS (Pinch, 1997). KWa

Suggested reading
Bennett (1990); Pinch (1997).

public geographies Contributions to geographical knowledge that address audiences beyond the academy and seek to intervene in public debate and PUBLIC POLICY. The formal discipline of GEOGRAPHY has a long tradition of 'applied' or 'policy relevant' work (see APPLIED GEOGRAPHY; RELEVANCE), but the recent interest in public geographies has been nurtured by a renewed interest in the NORMATIVE – in the political and ETHICAL dimensions of geographical enquiry – and by two further, more particular, considerations. First, there has been a recognition that geographical knowledge is produced at multiple sites inside and outside the academy, and the interest in 'public geographies' is thus, in part, an attempt to acknowledge the importance of those other productions and sites. This means more than an interest in 'popular geographies'. While many geographical knowledges remain undeveloped, and are often tacit and taken-for-granted, other non-academic contributions are highly developed and explicit about their intellectual and substantive basis: see, for example, the regional reports produced by the International Crisis Group, at http://www. crisisgroup.org/home/index.cfm. Second, there has been a recognition of the importance of developing and engaging audiences outside the academy, and the interest in 'public geographies' is thus also, in part, an attempt to speak in less technical vocabularies and to take advantage of non-academic publishing and the development of new media (particularly the INTERNET) to intervene in current debates in a timely and accessible fashion. These twin rationales speak to an interest in both the changing geography of the public sphere (see PRIVATE AND PUBLIC SPHERES) and the critical participation of geographical knowledges in its affairs (Gregory, 2005b), and they intersect with a renewed interest in 'public intellectuals' (Castree, 2006b; Ward, 2007). Oslender

(2007) adds a crucial rider: a focus less on public intellectuals as 'super-stars' illuminating the public sphere and more on the collaborative contributions of what he calls 'the collective intellectual' is likely to produce a genuinely public geography that is both more effective and more democratic. There have been parallel developments in other fields – public anthropology, public history and public sociology, for example – but some of the most impressive have been interdisciplinary: see, for example, the international forums on 'public issues' published by the US-based Social Science Research Council at http:// publications.ssrc.org/essays/.

Public geographies have their own geographies: Ward (2006) insists on the continuing importance of the academy as one public among many – and hence on the importance of EDUCATION and pedagogy – and it is as well to remember (as the example of the SSRC shows) that the academy and those other publics are increasingly transnational in their composition and concerns. In this sense, perhaps, public geographies can contribute to the deconstruction of the myth of the 'ivory tower' – universities are enmeshed in wider webs of political, social and economic practices –and also capitalize on the partialities of SITUATED KNOWLEDGE to articulate new collaborations, develop new conversations and forge new alliances (cf. the People's Geography Project at http://www.peoplesgeographyproject.org/). DG

Suggested reading
Oslender (2008); Ward (2007).

public goods Goods and services that are either freely available to all or provided equally to citizens of a delimited TERRITORY. Public goods are normally always provided by the STATE and fall within three main categories (Bennett, 1980, 1985). First, *pure public goods* are those that are non-excludable and non-rival in consumption. One person's consumption does not restrict another person's. These goods are freely available to all people through a state's territory. An example is national defence. However, we can also think of global public goods. The eradication of smallpox, for example, would benefit all of humanity, now and in the future. While all public goods should fall within this category, they do not. It is difficult, and sometimes impossible, to ensure the equal provision of public goods. A second type is *impure public goods*, which are provided at fixed locations or along fixed routes. A park is a public good, and so is a public transport service. However, due to DIS-TANCE DECAY, the further a person lives from these immobile public goods, the less is the usage of them, and their (potential) benefit. The CONFLICT over the production of these types of impure public goods, in the form of TURF POLITICS, is an important aspect of TER-RITORIAL JUSTICE. The third and final type are *public goods impurely distributed*, due to decisions by the STATE to vary geographical provision (Bennett, 1990). At each stage of the distribution of public goods, political DECISION-MAKING will determine how much of a good is provided, when and to whom. So, while one local government might decide not to provide one type of public good, a neighbouring authority might, producing a series of geographies of uneven provision. Moreover, there might be differences within a local or national government TERRITORY on the basis of the privileging of one geographical area's need over another (cf. PORK BARREL) (Pinch, 1997).   KWa

Suggested reading
Bennett (1990); Pinch (1997).

public policy Geographers have paid close attention to the creation, implementation, monitoring and evaluation of public policies. Work in this area has increased in recent years in capitalist countries because of: (a) the grow-ing importance of the STATE in economic and social affairs, offering enhanced opportunities for such work; (b) increased governmental recognition of environmental and spatial prob-lems awaiting resolution; (c) the desire among individual geographers to contribute to attacks on such problems; and (d) the perceived need for geographers to demonstrate the RELEVANCE of their field and so promote their discipline's claim for resources within higher education institutions in increasingly materialist situations.

Most geographical analyses have been con-cerned with evaluating policies addressed at identified 'spatial problems of environment, economy and society' (House, 1983) and with assessment of their 'geographical impact and degree of effectiveness': in the volume of essays that he edited on *United States public policy*,

> ... Critique stops short of prescription but there is some attempt to look ahead and also, in some cases, to set the problems within a theoretical, as well as an oper-ational, framework. (pp. v–vi)

He saw the benefits of such work as twofold:

> ... [T]o non-geographical academic or lay audiences ... [it reflects] a particular set of perspectives on some urgent problems which face policy-makers in our very critical times. To geographers in training, the rele-vance of applications of the discipline should be a major concern, whether to add practical purpose to their studies, or to point in the direction of possible professional car-eers outside the education field.

House identified the discipline's technocratic skills and its practitioners' ability to synthesize the many component parts of a complex prob-lem as the geographical perspectives most valuable to public policy study (see his survey of early British contributions in House, 1973); later promotions of geographers' utility have stressed their technical skills, such as those associated with GEOGRAPHIC INFORMATION SYSTEMS (see National Research Council, 1997). Others, such as C.J. Smith (1988), suggest that because many social problems are exacerbated, if not created, by environ-mental, time, place and circumstance contexts (cf. CONTEXTUAL EFFECT), then changing those contexts, through the geography of service provision and delivery, can be as influential as moves to solve the problems.

The nature of geographers' applied contri-butions has been largely pragmatic, reflecting the available opportunities and the ability of geographers to capitalise on them with their technocratic skills, hence the current promo-tion of REMOTE SENSING and GIS (Openshaw, 1989). Whereas some geographers claim that such involvement is necessary for the discip-line's survival (Berry, 1970; Abler, 1993a), others have queried this by pointing to the role of much public policy as sustaining, if not enhancing, the inequalities and exploitation that are inherent to CAPITALISM: hence Harvey's (1974b) question 'What kind of geography for what kind of public policy?' (cf. APPLIED GEOGRAPHY).   RJ

Suggested reading
Abler (1993a); Berry (1970); Harvey (1974b); House (1973, 1983); Openshaw (1989); Smith, C.J. (1988).

public–private partnership (PPPs) A collab-orative project involving the STATE APPARATUS and private companies, with the latter involved in some aspects of the provision of public services. Such partnerships have been promoted as part of the NEO-LIBERALISM agenda for two main reasons. Ideologically, private companies are presented as more efficient at managing large projects than the public sector (cf. PRIVATIZATION). Pragmatically, undertaking developments in this way can allow governments to avoid bearing the capital costs in their budgets – thereby reducing the public-sector borrowing requirement and, it is believed, interest rates and/or avoiding large increases in taxes to pay the upfront costs.

An example of such partnerships in the UK has been the Private Finance Initiative launched in the 1990s, whereby contractors undertake the capital works – building a prison, hospital, school, or road, for example – and then lease the facility to the government, which pays for the facility through its current rather than capital account. In some cases, the private contractor may either operate the new facility and pay part of the profit to the government (as with a toll road) or is given some role in its management (as with a place on a school's governing body) – this is known as the state 'contracting out' part of the provision of public services.

Examples of PPPs include New York's Central Park, which is managed for the City's Department of Parks and Recreation by the Central Park Conservancy, and an extension of California's State Route 125 south of San Diego, which was built by a private company – California Transportations Ventures Inc; the Lane Cove Tunnel under Sydney Harbour in Australia was constructed under a similar scheme, with the contractor then operating it on a 33-year lease. In the UK, the National Air Traffic Services (NATS), which control use of the country's airspace, is part-owned by the government (which has a 49 per cent stake), with most of the remainder held by a consortium of companies involved in the airline business: as with many such projects in the UK, the work of NATS is overseen by an independent regulator, which can control prices and the quality of service provision.

Whether the use of PPPs is either more efficient or more effective is open to doubt. Some claim that the overall cost of the lease-back arrangements will be greater than the initial capital costs, so that PPPs in effect involve the taxpayer creating profits for the private sector, which may be enhanced by the private companies' employment practices: in response, others argue that without such partnerships many projects would not happen, because the public sector cannot bear their cost without substantial increases in tax rates, which would deter other investment and entrepreneurship. RJ

Suggested reading
Bovaird (2004); Walzer and Jacobs (1998); Wettenhall (2003). See also http://www.hm-treasury.gov.uk/documents/public_private_partnerships/ppp_index.cfm

public services Services that are provided by (or on behalf of) the STATE according to non-MARKET criteria; that is, on the basis of the need for the services rather than the ability to pay. Although the boundaries between what counts as a 'public' or a 'private' service have historically been subject to change, together with which sector has done the providing, in general SERVICES are provided collectively because provision through the market or the third sector is believed to be either inefficient, ineffective or inequitable. Studies inside and outside of geography have tended to focus on a number of areas of public service provision and utilization, such as EDUCATION, HEALTH CARE and housing (see HOUSING STUDIES: see also Walsh, 1995). In each case a particular type of COLLECTIVE CONSUMPTION politics has been found to exist, over the provision of the public service and the conditions under which it is provided. Geographers have been particularly sensitive, not surprisingly, to the geographical aspect of provision of services, related to wider concerns over SPATIAL INEQUALITIES, TERRITORIAL JUSTICE and WELFARE GEOGRAPHY (Smith and Lee, 2004). Three arguments have been made for the need for a geographically attuned analysis of distribution of public services and the level of provision: first, that service provision varies by TERRITORY; second, that the benefits of a public service decrease the further an individual is away from its provision (cf. DISTANCE DECAY); and, third, that the location of services matters to surrounding areas and neighbourhoods, in the form of EXTERNALITIES – these are impacts that are not part of the initial DECISION-MAKING process, and can be either 'negative' or 'positive', although in many cases externalities are both, how you regard them depends on your own position.

Underpinning much geographical work on public services is an attention to the restructuring of the WELFARE STATE (Pinch, 1997). Decisions made by the STATE APPARATUS, over the provision of public services, reflect wider economic and political processes. Geographical distribution is often the outcome of a range of territorial influences. For example, politicking by local government, regional voluntary agencies, NATION-STATES and TRANSNATIONAL CORPORATIONS might produce a particular geographical configuration of public service provision. Current concern with the process of NEO-LIBERALISM, and what this process means for the qualitative restructuring of the STATE APPARATUS, lies behind recent work on public service provision and consumption (Peck, 2001). As we witness a variety of provision arrangements emerging in different countries, between governments and private-sector companies, so tensions over the defining and the use of terms such as 'equity' and 'efficiency' take on extra importance. What is meant by a 'public service'? Who has access to it and at what cost? These are questions that currently unite those working on the geographies of public services and those working on issues of state restructuring, in different regions of the world and in different areas of policy.   KWa

Suggested reading
Peck (2001a); Pinch (1997).

public space Space to which all citizens have a right of access. Public space must be juxtaposed with private space, or space over which private PROPERTY rules are in operation. Central to those rules is the right of owners to exclude others from the use and enjoyment of a space. Public space, conversely, is presumptively open to all. The archetypical public space is the plaza, street or park, the 'traditional public forum' characterized by the US Supreme Court as those places that have immemorially been used for public assembly, debate and informed dissent. An array of 'semi-public' spaces can also be identified, such as the airport or university.

To speak of public space is necessarily to speak of the public sphere, the realm of collective opinion and action that mediates between SOCIETY and STATE. Most famously, Jürgen Habermas characterized the public sphere as the site of deliberative and rational communication, within which free, rational discourse can occur between citizens (Habermas, 1989 [1962]; see also CITIZENSHIP), distanced from

the particularities of the STATE, the ECONOMY and the private domain (see PRIVATE AND PUBLIC SPHERES). While membership in the public has long been constrained by exclusions of GENDER, CLASS and RACE, it still holds normative appeal. Signalling a site of inclusion and acceptance, outsiders have long struggled for membership in the public sphere.

While the public sphere and public space are not necessarily interchangeable – publics can form in private space, as some feminist geographers (Staeheli, 1996: see also FEMINIST GEOGRAPHIES) have noted with reference to the private HOME – in general, it is in public space that the conversations and encounters of public life become physical and real. For Young (1990a, p. 240): '[p]olitics, the critical activity of raising issues and deciding how institutional and social relations should be organized, crucially depends on the existence of space and forums to which everyone has access'. These spaces serve several valuable political ends. The occupation of public space, for Mitchell (2003a), is a crucial means by which the boundaries of the public can be remade. Street protests, for example, can make visible the socially invisible. The physical designation and design of public space itself can also become avenues for the negotiation of politics (Low, 2000) and forms of public MEMORY, as well as collective forgetting (Burk, 2003). The encounters with DIFFERENCE that occur in public space can also foster the formation of an inclusionary ethos, as we learn to accommodate those people and interests beyond our own familiar contacts and ways of life.

For one constituency, however, the very diversity and unpredictability of public space undercuts the value of publicness. The rising homeless population (see HOMELESSNESS), combined with a LAW and order ethos, has prompted regulation targeted at 'disorder' in public space (such as panhandling). The exclusionary logic of such intervention has prompted some to posit the end of public space. Scholars have also traced the privatization of public space in the Western city, worrying at its effects on political activity and social life (Kohn, 2004).   NKB

Q

quadrat analysis A method of POINT PAT-
TERN ANALYSIS widely used in ECOLOGY, particularly in the analysis of plant distributions and
adopted for geographical use. A rectangular
mesh is laid across an area and the distribution
of points in each rectangle counted. That distribution can be modelled using a variety of
procedures to assess whether it: conforms to
what would occur under a random allocation
process; is significantly clustered in some
portion of the space; or is more regular than
random. CENTRAL PLACE THEORY, for example,
predicts that the distribution of settlements in a
rural area would fall into the third of those
categories, whereas theories of AGGLOMERATION
suggest that industrial plants should be significantly clustered. (cf. CATEGORICAL DATA ANALY-
SIS; POISSON REGRESSION). Quadrat analysis can
generate LOCAL STATISTICS, but artificial boundaries imposed around the study region at the
limits of each quadrat affect their utility: a more
sophisticated approach, taking a more continuous definition of space, is GEOGRAPHICALLY
WEIGHTED REGRESSION.   RJ

Suggested reading
Getis and Boots (1978); O'Sullivan and Unwin
(2002).

quadtree A procedure for compressing the
file size of geographical data sets that works by
splitting a study region into four quadrants –
as with the division of a rectangular area into
four smaller rectangles – and then recursively
splitting the quadrats until each is homogeneous on defined variables of interest that
it contains. Quadtrees are also used in GEO-
GRAPHIC INFORMATION SYSTEMS to index
phenomena within an area – such as points,
lines and areas – according to their spatial
location. The approach assumes SPATIAL AUTO-
CORRELATION in data sets and allows them –
especially those in a RASTER format – to be
efficiently sorted, explored and disseminated
(e.g. over the Internet).   RJ

Suggested reading
Wise (2002).

qualitative methods Guidelines to frame
research questions, assess what counts as
authoritative evidence and knowledge, and
collect interpretable data, and distinguished
from QUANTITATIVE METHODS. The discipline
of GEOGRAPHY has a long tradition of qualitative methods, and it has been argued that the
prioritizing of quantitative methods, associated with the QUANTITATIVE REVOLUTION of
the 1950s and 1960s, was an aberration within
the discipline's history (Winchester, 2000).
Explicit calls for qualitative methods came in
the late 1970s from HUMANISTIC GEOGRAPH-
ERS, in reaction to what was perceived as the
economic determinism, one-dimensionality
and objectification of social life within SPATIAL
SCIENCE (Ley and Samuels, 1978). There were
(at least) two methodological strands to HU-
MANISTIC GEOGRAPHY: an historical and HER-
MENEUTIC understanding of the production
and meaning of LANDSCAPE, and another
within SOCIAL GEOGRAPHY that drew upon
PHENOMENOLOGY and SYMBOLIC INTERACTION-
ISM, and sought to understand social worlds
from insiders' perspectives, often through PAR-
TICIPANT OBSERVATION or ETHNOGRAPHY
(Limb and Dwyer, 2001). Through the
1980s, FEMINIST GEOGRAPHIES took up and
expanded humanist geographers' concerns to
acknowledge and examine the VALUES, politics
and ETHICS underlying all social research, and
the need to understand and document the
plurality of coexisting and divergent social
worlds in all of their affective intensity and
complexity. Feminists have been particularly
concerned to think through implications of the
POSITIONALITY of the researcher and researched, the workings of POWER within the
research process and the responsibility of
using research to create social change. The
influence of POST-COLONIALISM and POST-
STRUCTURALISM has furthered these preoccupations. Qualitative methods are now
common and seen as appropriate in all sub-
disciplines of geography, including ECONOMIC
GEOGRAPHY, MIGRATION studies, POLITICAL
GEOGRAPHY and HEALTH GEOGRAPHY.
   By the 1990s 'a frightening array of philosophical, conceptual and theoretical terms
[were] embedded in the qualitative research
literature', and neat links between PHILOSOPHY,
theory and method were being 'unpicked'
(Smith, S.J., 2001, pp. 23–4). Nonetheless,

qualitative approaches tend to share some common understandings about ONTOLOGY and EPISTEMOLOGY: social worlds are dynamic and not fully stable or predictable; social life is produced through HUMAN (and non-human) AGENCY; there are multiple social worlds, with distinctive and sometimes competing social meanings, competencies and practices; it is important to understand social life as it is experienced; knowledge is situated and partial (see SITUATED KNOWLEDGE); theory is to be developed through empirical research rather than tested empirically; the SUBJECTIVITY of the researcher and researched is a factor in every stage of the research process; the production of knowledge is an inter-subjective, relational process between researcher and researched; and the researcher has ethical and social responsibilities to the researched (Limb and Dwyer, 2001). Smith argues that the choice of qualitative methods goes beyond these issues of ontology and epistemology, and is fundamentally a political decision: 'We choose these methods ... as a way of challenging the way the world is structured, the way that knowledges are made, from the top down ... We are ... adopting *a strategy that aims to place non-dominant, neglected knowledges at the heart of the research agenda*" (2001, p. 25; original emphasis). One part of this strategy involves making space for these other knowledges by demonstrating the constructed nature of dominant ones. Within SCIENCE STUDIES, for instance, ethnographies of the production of scientific facts trace a myriad of small translations from 'the field' to the LABORATORY (e.g. Latour, 1999a: see also FIELDWORK). Critical GIS makes explicit the genealogy and limitations of the data on which GIS maps are based. Another strand of this strategy involves subjecting dominant institutions to ethnographic study to show them to be more improvised and less powerful than supposed; Mountz's (2003) ethnography of the Canadian state is one example.

The debates about power, positionality, REFLEXIVITY and ethics are complex, and what has been called a crisis of REPRESENTATION began in the mid-1980s. Crang (2003) notes that such debates have progressed beyond the simplistic dichotomies between 'insiders' and 'outsiders' typical of earlier discussions to more nuanced considerations of 'betweenness' or working 'alongside' research participants. Concerns nonetheless linger that qualitative researchers – like all researchers – unwittingly rely upon CLASS, colonial and/or racial privilege to gain access to informants and other information, and to produce knowledge that benefits mainly themselves. For instance, Chari characterizes ethnography as 'a process of alienation, through which, for instance, ethnographers poach on working-class narratives for very different ends: like getting a job or tenure' (2003, p. 171). Such criticisms have provoked qualitative researchers to rethink their research encounters, to experiment with new ways of producing and judging knowledge and truth, and to consider a broader range of knowledges as useful and relevant. Reflecting upon their work in Pakistan, Butz and Besio (2004) consider the concept of autoethnography as one means of repositioning research subjects as active transculturally knowing subjects rather than 'native informants'. Autoethnography attends to the ways in which research subjects actively produce and represent themselves within the terms of dominant discourse, and complicates the boundary between authentic truth and manipulated (and manipulative) self-presentation or PERFORMANCE. Butz and Besio describe how they have organized their research to support their research participants' own projects of self-representation, thereby 'multiplying the communicative resources available to them' (Smith, S.J., 2001b, p. 27). Nagar has entered into another kind of collaborative research endeavour with eight development workers in Uttar Pradesh, India. Calling themselves the Sangtin Writers Collective, they have co-authored a book in which seven grassroots workers write intimately and autobiographically about their lives. This book, first published in India in Hindi in 2004, and more recently in the United States in English (2006), has created controversy in India because of its detailed critique of the politics of the non-governmental organization for which these women worked, and has become a catalyst for organizing among other grassroots workers. There are now many examples of collaborations in participatory ACTION RESEARCH (Pain, 2004), which tends to be different from, and indeed can be at odds with, the goals of APPLIED GEOGRAPHY (the latter is often more closely aligned with the priorities and perspectives of the STATE). More broadly, Smith argues that 'Qualitative research is a mode of interference. If this interference is "wrong", such approaches should be discontinued; they must be unethical. If it is "right", a lot more documentation and debate are needed on where this interference is going, whose interest it advances, what form it takes and why it is important' (2001, p. 27).

There are many different qualitative methods, and typologies for classifying them. Winchester (2000), for instance, identifies three categories of qualitative methods: oral (e.g. unstructured INTERVIEWS and INTERVIEWING, FOCUS GROUPS, and life histories), textual analysis (see TEXT and TEXTUALITY) and participant observation (or ethnography). Despite the diversity of qualitative methods used by geographers, Crang (2002, p. 650) notes a surprising tendency to favour interviews over ethnography – surprising because ethnography would seem to be more in line with field-based geographical traditions. Yet Herbert (2000) has calculated that only 3–5 per cent of journal articles draw on ethnographic research. The reasons for this are various, and include: difficulties in gaining access (McDowell, 1998); challenges of doing ethnographic fieldwork within existing institutional and funding time frames (Cook, 2001b) and disciplinary scepticism about the merits of ethnography (Herbert, 2000).

Two further methodological omissions have been noted. First, visual data tend to be under-used, relative to oral testimony or text. Crang (2003, p. 500) reasons that qualitative researchers have been influenced by critiques of vision as a medium for a detached, masculinist, objectifying gaze: 'If copresence is the privileged ground of qualitative truth claims, it is against a foil of "bad" vision' (see VISION AND VISUALITY). Especially given heightened concerns about the politics of representation, 'qualitative fieldwork almost turns away from the visual to avoid accusations of "academic tourism" and objectification' (p. 500). Rejection of the visual is, however, by no means complete, and NON-REPRESENTATIONAL THEORY and a focus on PERFORMANCE and the BODY have generated many intriguing experiments with visual data and methodologies, some of which are reviewed by Crang. In her textbook on visual methods, Rose (2007 [2001]) provides an excellent overview of a wide range of visual data; questions that can be addressed through them; and a variety of strategies for analysing them. An over-emphasis on DISCOURSE and REPRESENTATION grounds a second concern about the limitations of geographers' use of qualitative methods: this is that too little attention has been directed to how people do things, as opposed to how they see the world or what they say about it. Smith argues that this has prompted a 'second crisis of representation' that focuses on the limits of representability (Smith, S.J., 2001, p. 28), and the importance

of knowing through practice and recording fully sensual, richly emotional, momentary practices of social lives. Although qualitative methods are now widely used throughout the discipline, Thrift (2000a, p. 244) notes that even 'cultural geography still draws on a remarkably limited number of methodologies – ethnography, focus groups, and the like – which are nearly always cognitive in origin and effect'. Large claims have been made of the METHODOLOGICAL implications of non-representational theory: it is 'suggestive of nothing less than a drive towards a new methodological avant garde that will radically refigure what it is to *do* research' (Latham, 2003, p. 2000). Writing in 2005, Lorimer notes that 'the creativity [promised by non-representational theory] in research design and method still needs to be unshackled' (p. 89). Given the emphasis on knowledge through practice, there is renewed interest in symbolic interactionism, phenomenology and ETHNOMETHODOLOGY. As much as using radically different methods, it may be a matter of re-examining the potential of existing ones; for instance, to excavate everyday practices in archival evidence, or to conduct, experience and record interviews as fully embodied conversational performances in which subtle shifts in AFFECT, tone and bodily comportment are as significant as what is said. And an argument that social life exceeds discourse need not lead researchers away from discourse; as Nash (2000) has argued, even a practice such as dance – one that drew a great deal of attention in early formulations of non-representational styles of thinking – is not excessive to discourse but, rather, is a complex amalgam of discourse and embodied knowledges. Language itself has multiple relations to action: Chari (2003) draws on linguistic anthropology to consider LANGUAGE as an indexical and not just referential practice, and to consider the multiple relations between language and action.

Given an enquiring attitude about what counts as useful knowledge and recent interest in performance and the 'doing' of social life, qualitative researchers are reassessing what counts as valuable research 'products', including relatively private and fleeting ones (Thrift, 2000). For instance, whilst conducting an ethnography in a village in Pakistan, a Muslim community in which women supposedly disapproved of being photographed, Besio (Besio and Butz, 2004) was asked by some of the resident women to photograph them privately in out-of-the-way places. Besio reads these secretive photography sessions as expressions of resistance to MASCULINIST community norms. Her research thus generated a practice of RESISTANCE that could not be made public, at least at the research site. Pratt (2004, p. 193) has urged that we consider the research process itself as an important research outcome: 'We might think of it as a space ... from which to speak and perform the unspeakable ... The written traces, for example [academic] text, are but one outcome of a process that far exceeds them.' Writing and other forms of representation (such as video or photography) can be a significant part of the actual research process in qualitative research; representation is a means of doing the research, of making creative connections and developing interpretations. Different ways of understanding can be communicated through different MEDIA (Berg and Mansvelt, 2000).

Despite the widespread use of qualitative data, some scepticism remains about the credibility of qualitative data. Baxter and Eyles (1997) are concerned that qualitative geographers often have not been sufficiently transparent about their methodology. There is a danger of 'mining' qualitative interviews for enticing quotes that selectively advance the researcher's interpretation, and of presenting de-contextualized snippets of conversation. There is also a risk of stereotyping respondents by reading across interview transcripts to identify common themes rather than studying the contradictions and complexity within individual interviews. There are many different strategies for analysing qualitative data (there are 43, according to Crang, 2005). Crang (2005) distinguishes three broad approaches: developing grounded theory, analysing the formal structure of the text or transcript or image, or reading qualitative data as narrative. McDowell (1998) describes a process of repeatedly reading her transcript data, first for plot and then for representations of 'self' (also, for a strategy for analysing narrative genres, see Chari, 2003). One characteristic of the best qualitative research is the immense volume of data collected, and although there is no substitute for examining the data closely and repeatedly, a number of computer software packages are available to systematize transcript data and to assist in coding it (Peace, 2000).

Although qualitative methods have often been conceived as opposite or even opposed to quantitative methods, this is an unproductive way of conceiving the distinction. Critical REALISM was one important moment for thinking of the two approaches as compatible:

extensive methods (often quantitative) were seen to be especially useful for describing patterns, and intensive methods (typically qualitative ones) more effective for studying causal processes (cf. EXTENSIVE RESEARCH; INTENSIVE RESEARCH). More recently, the call of mixed methods has been tied to the concept of triangulation, which involves exploring processes from different angles using different methods, in order to assess the validity of each data source and method, and more fully understand the process. Nightingale (2003) links the utility of mixed methods to the concept of situated knowledge: she suggests that a mix of qualitative and quantitative methods allows the researcher to better understand the limits of knowledge acquired through any one methodological approach. Different approaches resonate with different audiences – for instance, state funding bodies and policy-makers are typically more convinced of the 'scientific merit' of quantitative techniques, which they sometimes designate as 'evidence-based' research (Mountz, Miyares, Wright and Bailey, 2003). Blending qualitative and quantitative methods may allow a researcher to reach different audiences in more authoritative ways. GP

Suggested reading
Hay (2000); Limb and Dwyer (2001).

quality of life A concept linked to that of SOCIAL WELL-BEING, which is based on the argument that the human condition should be evaluated on a wider range of indicators than just income – whether at the individual level or through national aggregates (such as GROSS NATIONAL PRODUCT and GROSS DOMESTIC PRODUCT). Work on the quality of life was introduced to geographers in the 1970s in studies of territorial social indicators (Smith, 1973; Knox, 1975), which focused on separate dimensions of collective well-being, such as income, wealth and employment, the built environment, physical and mental health, education, social disorganization, social belonging, and recreation and leisure. MAPS of these indicators, at a variety of spatial SCALES from the international to the inter-urban, provided evidence on geographical variations in well-being, with which researchers could address the question of 'who gets what, where?' (Smith, 1977).

Other concepts, such as freedom (cf. HUMAN RIGHTS) and happiness, are frequently related to measures of the quality of life that individuals and societies experience, although much work on happiness shows that – to the extent that it can be measured – it does not increase above a certain threshold income: people may be more content and live more comfortable lives with higher incomes, but they do not feel any happier (Layard, 2005).   RJ

quango   An acronym for *q*uasi-*a*utono-mous-*n*on-*g*overnmental *o*rganizations. These are established and financed by governments to perform public functions in areas of policy such as education and health care. Quango members are appointed rather than elected, and are drawn from private, public and third sectors. Since the 1970s, quangos have grown both numerically and in terms of the areas of the world in which they can be found. This growth reflects a general trend in national governments changing how they govern, involving new forms of organizations in their activities. The incorporation of these organizations into the STATE APPARATUS raises issues of accountability, DEMOCRACY and transparency in public DECISION-MAKING.   KWa

Suggested reading
Ridley and Wilson (1995).

quantitative methods   Mathematics has always been a foundation of geographical practices. For many centuries, it underpinned the development of CARTOGRAPHY, providing the techniques (notably geometrical and trigonometrical) deployed in MAP-making – in establishing exact locations (increasingly through the universally adopted graticule of latitude and longitude and the national surveying systems based on that matrix) and in portraying those locations in map form. With the latter, for example, much effort was (and still is) expended on the development of MAP PROJECTIONS with which to portray a spherical reality on to a two-dimensional surface. Increasingly, however, this work has been separated from academic geographical practices into separate disciplines (such as geodesy).

Although, as with almost all changes within a discipline, earlier exemplars can be identified, the post-1945 decades saw a major shift in geographical practices associated with a widespread adoption of quantitative methods in HUMAN and PHYSICAL GEOGRAPHY – a period widely known as the discipline's QUANTITATIVE REVOLUTION and very much linked to the adoption of an explicitly theoretical approach to the discipline's subject matter. This shift was associated with scholars located at a number of institutions, initially in the USA and then also in the UK (Johnston and Sidaway, 2004a), but the dominant core was located at the Department of Geography in the University of Washington, Seattle, in the early to mid-1950s, when a number of graduate students coalesced around two individuals – Edward Ullman and, especially, William Garrison. Their core concern was the application and development of LOCATION THEORY (especially that based in NEO-CLASSICAL ECONOMICS), with quantitative methods identified – as in other social sciences, notably economics and sociology at the time – as a means of both expressing theories in a formal language and empirically testing HYPOTHESES.

These two core activities drew on different quantitative METHODOLOGIES: the expression of THEORIES involved mathematical argumentation and representation (including MODELLING), whereas hypothesis-testing used statistical procedures, expressing the outcome of empirical research in probabilistic terms. In some cases, mathematical modelling preceded empirical work, providing the formal basis for hypothesis generation; in others, statistical analysis was either based on more informal forms of argument leading to some form of expected empirical outcome, or involved exploration of numerical data without any clear expectation as to the likely outcome (cf. EXPLORATORY DATA ANALYSIS). These two approaches (especially that involving statistical analysis) spread rapidly through the 1960s and 1970s from the core institutions in Seattle and other US centres, alongside parallel and linked developments in the UK (Barnes, 2004b, 2008b; Johnston, Fairbrother, Hoare, Hayes and Jones, 2008): according to Burton (1963), geography's 'quantitative revolution' had succeeded by the early 1960s, although circumstantial evidence suggested that it never dominated human geography (Wheeler, 2002).

Much of the mathematical modelling underpinning quantitative work in human geography has focused on either spatial patterns – such as the distribution of settlements, as in CENTRAL PLACE THEORY – or SPATIAL INTERACTION (notably various forms of MIGRATION and communication). The goal was to express the subject matter under consideration in mathematical terms. At the core of much work on spatial interaction, for example, was an analogy with Newton's famous formulation, which posited that the volume of interaction between two places was positively related to some index of the generating capacity at each place and negatively related to the distance between them (the so-called DIS-TANCE-DECAY hypothesis based on assumed FRICTIONS OF DISTANCE). This could be expressed as a simple formula (as in the well-known GRAVITY MODEL), but the formulation was later extended to present a more realistic representation through the adoption of ENTROPY-MAXIMIZING MODELS. Similar approaches presented the SPATIAL STRUCTURE being investigated as a SYSTEM, with nodes (such as TOWNS) and links (transport routes). They modelled various aspects of those systems – the optimum number and location of warehouses in a distribution network, for example, or the shortest route involving visits to three or more nodes on the network – using a variety of mathematical techniques, such as graph theory and LINEAR PROGRAMMING (cf. OPTIMIZATION MODELS). Changes of and to those structures were also analysed, notably through models of spatial DIFFUSION.

Many of these early approaches relied on a relatively simple conception of SPATIAL STRUC-TURE, in which distance was the foundational variable to which many of the key relationships were linearly related (albeit through non-linear transformations in some cases: see Cox, 1976). More sophisticated mathematical modelling procedures were later adopted, incorporating non-linear relationships between elements within the system (such as CATAS-TROPHE THEORY and CHAOS THEORY).

Most statistical analyses undertaken by human geographers are based on the GENERAL LINEAR MODEL – notably those components that identify either the relationship of one variable to another (REGRESSION, which indicates the degree of change in one variable relative to the amount of change in another) or the strength of such relationships (shown by COR-RELATION coefficients). Their introduction – as exemplified by the first textbook on using statistical methods in GEOGRAPHY (Gregory, 1962) – was initially presented by some simply as the proper way to present quantitative material and relationships (Gregory, 1971), with formal statements replacing the vagueness of ordinary language (Cole, 1969: see also PROCESS). But statistical procedures soon became the predominant means whereby analysts tested hypotheses about spatial patterns and processes, with the findings expressed as probability statements – the likelihood either that what had been observed in a sample of observations also held in the population from which that sample was drawn (cf. SAMPLING) or that the relationship identified could have occurred by chance rather than as the result of

some assumed causal sequence whereby changes in x stimulated changes in y (where, for example, x is the distance between a pair of towns and y is the number of migrants between them). Thus applications of statistical methods involved combining reasoning methods that are both DEDUCTIVE (formal hypotheses regarding the size, strength and direction of relationships among variables are stated and those expectations compared against empirical data) and INDUCTIVE (patterns are identified in data sets that suggest ordered behaviour).

By the 1960s, some geographers had become aware of potential difficulties of applying standard statistical procedures (such as those derived from the general linear model) to geographical data because of the issue of SPATIAL AUTOCORRELATION, whereby the assumed independence of observations could not be sustained. Tobler (1970), for example, had posited a 'first law of geography' that 'everything is related to everything else, but near things are more related than distant ones'. Thus the value of an observation at one place – the level of unemployment, for example – might well be related to the value at adjacent places, and incorporating all of these values into an unadjusted regression or similar model could violate its foundational assumptions and generate unreliable estimates – of, say, the relationship between unemployment levels and house values across a set of counties. Techniques for analysing spatial data that take such autocorrelation into account and provide reliable estimates were thus developed – forming the basis of an approach to spatial data analysis increasingly widely adopted across the social sciences and known as SPATIAL ECONOMETRICS. Those, and many other, approaches have been increasingly facilitated by the development and availability of GEOGRAPHICAL INFORMATION SYSTEMS.

By the 1970s, the approach to human geography widely known as SPATIAL SCIENCE or LOCATIONAL ANALYSIS was coming under increasing criticism from a number of directions. Many were associated with the assumed link between quantitative analysis and the PHILOSOPHY of POSITIVISM – the goals of spatial science, it was argued, involved a search for laws of spatial order, in terms of both patterns on the ground and the behaviour that gave rise to those patterns. Some of these criticisms emanated from adherents to a MARXIST or RAD-ICAL GEOGRAPHY, who argued that a focus on the spatial superstructure (cf. INFRASTRUC-TURE) ignored the true processes involved in the creation/re-creation of geographies of UN-EVEN DEVELOPMENT and the (CLASS-based) POWER relations that underpinned them. Other critiques emanated from what became known as HUMANISTIC GEOGRAPHY and the variety of approaches to SOCIAL and CULTURAL GEOGRAPHY that emerged in subsequent decades, which focused on spatial science's implicit characterization of decision-making as either deterministic (and thus denying the free will inherent in HUMAN AGENCY) or influenced by economic factors only, thereby ignoring the social and cultural contexts of DECISION-MAKING – not least those associated with GENDER and ETHNICITY.

To some extent, these critiques were anticipated by geographers working with quantitative methods in the spatial science genre. Many soon became aware that the complexity of contemporary SOCIETY meant that the relatively simple locational models that they were applying were insufficiently sophisticated to incorporate the wide range of contextual and other variables that can influence spatial behaviour. They therefore shifted their focus away from those models that portrayed a rigid, geometrical spatial order towards more general models of locational decision-making that emphasized context – what became known as BEHAVIOURAL GEOGRAPHY. They sought order – common patterns of decision-making – in non-deterministic situations, much as suggested in the attempt through STRUCTURATION THEORY to eliminate the binary dualism between structure and agency. Behavioural geography's core argument is not that people are irrational decision-makers but, rather, that they are boundedly (as against perfectly) rational: the boundedness reflects the limits to their information, their ability to process it and the utility functions that they apply when evaluating options. This does not mean that everybody has to be treated as both unique (having characteristics that nobody else shares in total) and singular (sharing no characteristics with others), so that no general patterns can be found and theories developed. Rushton (1969) makes this point in contrasting studies of *behaviour in space* – for example, mapping individual journey-to-work routes – with those identifying *rules of spatial behaviour*, the general patterns within all those choices that can be uncovered from the individual pieces of data using quantitative procedures, to suggest common behavioural decisions. The reasons for such commonalities can then be explored by, for example, identifying shared information underpinning such decisions, as in Peter Gould's pioneering work on MENTAL MAPS, the spatial depictions that we use when evaluating the places we want to visit, move to and so on (Gould and White, 1993 [1974]).

This general approach characterizes the contemporary use of quantitative methods in human geography. Although some have claimed that such work is now virtually absent from human geography's portfolio and prospectus, much work using quantitative methods continues to be reported in the discipline's general and specialist journals. As with its predecessors, it concentrates on aggregate patterns in space and their generating processes: the description, explanation and (in some cases) prediction of general patterns of spatial behaviour and their reflection in the landscape. (Note, however, the recent emergence of a 'NEW ECONOMIC GEOGRAPHY' within economics, and the creation of a journal – *Journal of Economic Geography* – to explore commonalities between that approach and the work of geographers who continue to undertake theoretically inspired quantitative work.)

Much contemporary work follows the behavioural geography rather than the original spatial science PARADIGM, therefore. Most of it is theory-driven, based on generalized hypotheses of how people behave, but much of the analysis involves exploring data assembled to identify patterns rather than explicit hypothesis-testing. This very largely reflects the 'immaturity' of such studies: our knowledge of how people make spatially relevant decisions and behave is limited, and so the best we can come up with at this stage is broad expectations. In ELECTORAL GEOGRAPHY, for example, there are theoretical arguments that self-interest influences how people vote, with economic concerns underpinning that self-interest. But it may be expressed in different ways: some may vote sociotropically, according to their views of the national, regional and/or local economic situation (voting for the governing party[ies] if they are optimistic about the economic situation but against if they are pessimistic); some may vote egocentrically, according to their perceived personal financial situation; and some vote altruistically, in the interests of their (geographical) neighbours even when these don't coincide with their own (Johnston and Pattie, 2006). Those theoretically based expectations generate testable hypotheses but – as with the gravity model – they cannot predict in advance the size of the relevant coefficients for each type of

609

voting, because of the many other contingent factors (some of them spatial in nature) that influence electoral behaviour.

This example illustrates the dominant focus within contemporary quantitative human geography, not – as it was 50 years ago – on the orderly arrangement of points and lines in the landscape, and of people, ideas and commodities flowing through those spatial structures (as postulated by Haggett, 1965), but rather on common patterns of behaviour in similar contexts – or common realizations of human agency within particular contextual settings. The emphasis has shifted between two of geography's fundamental concepts, from a focus on SPACE to one on PLACE. Within that changed emphasis has come the adoption of new quantitative procedures that emphasize the important role of place as context – such as GEOGRAPHICAL ANALYSIS MACHINE, GEOGRAPHICAL EXPLANATION MACHINE, LOCAL STATISTICS, GEOGRAPHICALLY WEIGHTED REGRESSION, MULTI-LEVEL MODELLING, the MODIFIABLE AREAL UNIT PROBLEM, ECOLOGICAL INFERENCE and the ECOLOGICAL FALLACY.

Contemporary use of quantitative methods in human geography entails exploring patterns and processes involving large numbers of decision-makers, seeking order in often complex situations (Haggett, 1990). Even when data are available on individual decision-makers, the goal is to distil general patterns – as in Rushton's distinction between behaviour in space and rules of spatial behaviour. Unlike other approaches to human geography, therefore, spatial science is macro/meso in SCALE, rather than micro – though it may deploy micro-scale data in its search for macro/meso-SCALE patterns. Its findings might pose questions that can only be addressed by studying individuals, but its core methodologies focus on wholes rather than parts.

This approach is the only one possible given certain subject matter. Patterns of (changing) regional development and underdevelopment, for example, can only be studied as statistical aggregates – as can many indices linked to this concept, such as inflation, unemployment rates, land values, house prices, PRODUCTIVITY and so on. Aspects of our worlds are only accessible in such formats, and are sensibly analysed quantitatively. In other cases, whereas individual-level data are available (or can be obtained through bespoke SURVEYS) – on illness, turnout at elections and so on – much can be gained from aggregating them and studying general patterns, of morbidity and mortality rates, for example. Much work in,

for example, POPULATION, MEDICAL, SOCIAL and ELECTORAL GEOGRAPHY is of this type – though such sub-disciplines are not constrained to spatial scientific approaches.

A further justification for macro-/meso-approaches lies in the probabilistic nature of much of our understanding and representation of the world. It is generally accepted that smoking causes lung cancer, for example, but not all smokers get lung cancer and not all people who get lung cancer have smoked. It is a probabilistic relationship. Part of the reason why we cannot say that smoking causes lung cancer without qualification is because other variables can either accelerate or decelerate, even block, the processes involved; part also reflects our incomplete knowledge (constrained because of the difficulties of conducting controlled experiments). Similar arguments apply to a whole range of behaviours studied by (physical and well as human) geographers: the processes involved are so complex and difficult to unravel – because we cannot conduct experiments (although a range of new techniques may be of value in such situations: Sherman, 2003; Dunning, 2008). Hence work in spatial science is almost of necessity conditional: it represents the state of our current understanding and can only be phrased in probabilistic rather than deterministic terms.

The meso-/macro-patterns in many aspects of contemporary society that are quantitatively described and analysed by social scientists are relevant to people's daily lives and experiences – the 'meaningful nature of life' explored in other geographical practices. Levels of ethnic SEGREGATION in urban neighbourhoods and schools (see URBANIZATION) provide contexts within which not only lives are (partially) lived, but also people's life chances and relationships are influenced. Geographical concentrations of POVERTY similarly structure many people's life chances, while biased election results reflect the operation of the aggregation and scale issues underpinning the modifiable areal unit problem (Johnston and Pattie, 2006).

Alongside their intrinsic interest and importance to understanding spatial patterns and behaviour, therefore, meso-/macro-scale work is relevant to PUBLIC POLICIES – either studies of their impact on geographies or analyses of geographical patterns that call for public intervention. Geographies of MORTALITY, for example, may identify areas where further investment of medical resources is warranted. Much public policy has impacts – direct and indirect – on topics of interest to human geographers and, although directed at individuals, is delivered to areas, as with the location of healthcare clinics: if the world operates through spatial aggregates, then it should be analysed accordingly (though not exclusively so).

Similarly, whatever the immense variety of human spatial behaviour, the public policy that intervenes in it in some way (and much private-sector policy too) is almost invariably phrased in aggregate terms. New highways are planned to link places where demand either currently outstrips supply or modelling suggests that it soon will. New commercial establishments are located where potential (unfulfilled) demand is deemed greatest (and usually implies some distance-decay pattern in usage, as represented by the gravity model): much APPLIED GEOGRAPHY (such as that using GEODEMOGRAPHICS and other spatial analytical procedures) is based on this aspect of Tobler's law.

Many aspects of the positivist approach have long been abandoned by almost all spatial scientists: they adopt some of its precepts – particularly that the things they study can be observed and measured; that the statements which they derive can be tested for their veracity; and that their studies can be replicated. For them, knowledge-production involves careful observation, measurement, analysis and interpretation, generating statements that identify synoptic patterns – the broad pictures that might then be decomposed to see how they are produced and what they mean for the people who live in them. They do not – as Fotheringham (2006, p. 239) puts it – ignore 'all the emotions and thought processes that are behind what is sometimes … highly idiosyncratic behaviour': they accept those as valid topics for study, calling for different approaches. For spatial scientists, a whole range of subjects can be addressed at the aggregate level using quantitative methods, from which valid generalizations can be drawn to illuminate aspects of the human condition. And these can be linked to studies using non-quantitative practices – as proponents of 'mixed-method' stress. Quantitative methods thus remain at the core of the geographical enterprise.   RJ

Selected reading
Fotheringham, Brunsdon and Charlton (2000); Haggett (1990); Wilson and Bennett (1985).

quantitative revolution The 'radical transformation of spirit and purpose' (Burton, 1963, p. 151) that Anglo-American GEOGRAPHY

experienced during the 1950s and 1960s following the widespread adoption of both inferential statistical techniques and abstract MODELS and theories. In the process, the dominance of an old IDIOGRAPHIC geography characterized by a focus on AREAL DIFFERENTIATION was displaced by a new NOMOTHETIC geography conducted as SPATIAL SCIENCE.

The quantitative revolution first emerged in the mid-1950s as a series of local affairs crystallized around one or two key individuals. In the USA, the Department of Geography at the University of Washington in Seattle was key, as was the University of Iowa in Iowa City. At Washington, it was the presence of Edward Ullman and William Garrison that was crucial, and at Iowa, Harold McCarty. In 1954 Garrison gave the first advanced course in statistics in a US Department of Geography, and the following year his Washington students, nicknamed the 'space cadets', were among the first on campus to make use of the new IBM 604 computer (also a national first). Those students subsequently proved critical in diffusing the quantitative message, which they did by quickly establishing themselves and their research agenda at several prestigious US universities during the early 1960s, including Chicago, Northwestern and Michigan. Outside the USA, Peter Haggett and Richard Chorley in the UK (affectionately described by David Harvey as the 'terrible twins' of British geography) and Torsten Hägerstrand in Sweden were central in establishing a European beachhead.

By the mid-1960s, a network was in place that connected quantitative researchers and Departments of Geography on both sides of the Atlantic. Holding it together were two new sets of geographical practices: *technique-based practices* that included computerization, and the study and application of ever more complex statistical and QUANTITATIVE METHODS; and *theory-based practices* that involved conceptualizing LOCATION and SPACE in rigorously abstract terms. Before the 1950s, human geography was resolutely a-theoretical (see also EMPIRICISM). The quantitative revolution brought a cornucopia of theoretical models typically imported from other disciplines. From physics came GRAVITY MODELS and later ENTROPY-MAXIMIZING MODELS; from economics, often by way of REGIONAL SCIENCE, came the models of a dispersed German school of LOCATION THEORY; from sociology came the urban models of the CHICAGO SCHOOL, together with urban FACTORIAL ECOLOGY and the RANK SIZE RULE; and from geometry via TRANSPORTATION studies came NETWORKS and graph theory. And from the philosophy and history of SCIENCE came a model of 'the structure of scientific revolutions' (see PARADIGM) that could be used, rhetorically at least, to legitimize the quantitative revolution as a genuinely scientific revolution. In the process the dominant stream of research in human geography moved from a field-based, craft-form of enquiry to a technical, desk-bound one, where places were analysed from afar.

Peter Gould (1978), one of the revolutionaries, labelled the era of the quantitative revolution, 'The Augean period', after the mythic Augean stables that – after thirty years of neglect – were cleaned all of a piece by Hercules. Equating quantitative revolutionaries with Hercules and an earlier non-quantitative geography with the Augean stables speaks to at least two sociological processes marking the revolution. (1) The heroic depiction points to the quantitative revolution's profound MASCULINISM (and, arguably, to its WHITENESS too). Initial proponents and expositors were all men; there were virtually no substantive studies of women; and the disembodied, totalizing knowledge produced was phallocentric (see PHALLOCENTRISM: see also SITUATED KNOWLEDGE). (2) The cleansing METAPHOR indicates how desperately keen revolutionaries were to quarantine themselves from the past. Partly this was intellectual, but, as Taylor (1976) argues, it was also for internal sociological reasons. To move ahead, to secure early promotion and status, it was necessary to do something different. For a group of very bright, young, ambitious and competitive male scholars, the quantitative revolution was the perfect vehicle.

At some point in the late 1960s, or early 1970s, the grip of the quantitative revolution on the discipline loosened. There are at least two reasons. First, a different kind of world was emerging that was more restless, and less innocent than before. Great debates were happening around issues of POVERTY, civil RIGHTS, the environment, GENDER and racial equality, and WAR, but the quantitative revolution seemed unable or unwilling to address them. The ensuing RELEVANCE debate of the early 1970s left quantifiers flat-footed. As Harvey (1973, p. 129) damningly put it, 'There is an ecological problem, an urban problem, an international trade problem, and yet we seem incapable of saying anything of depth or profundity about any of them. When we do say something, it appears trite and slightly ludicrous. In short, our paradigm is not coping well. It is ripe for overthrow.' Second, an academic generation had passed since the first quantifiers, and the time was ripe for change. A new vocabulary was forged to mark off the old from the new, in this case, one principally derived from MARXISM (Harvey, 1973). There were other, immediate contenders too, including a HUMANISTIC GEOGRAPHY that sought to develop human geography's connections with the HUMANITIES rather than the social sciences. But the important point, and why the quantitative revolution remains a watershed in geography's recent history, is that Marxism and its successor projects persisted with a theoretical vocabulary. (It is as well to remember that the humanities are every bit as 'theoretical' in their sensibility as the social sciences.) Certainly the meaning of THEORY altered, as many different avenues were explored, but the continuity of a theoretical vocabulary has proven more important in subsequently shaping the discipline than rupture. TB

Suggested reading
Barnes (2004).

queer theory A panoply of always-questioning and destabilizing theoretical and intellectual movements that centre on the significance and complexities of sexualities and genders. It emerged in the 1990s (see de Lauretis, 1991) within the humanities, but has travelled into the social sciences, and so into HUMAN GEOGRAPHY. By its very nature, the term resists being pinned down or essentialized. Above all, queer theory draws on both senses of the term 'queer'. It refers both to an array of non-normative sexualities and/or desires (lesbian/gay/bisexual/pansexual/asexual/transsexual/transgendered (see PSYCHOANALYTIC THEORY), and invokes the sense of challenging norms of sexuality by referencing the curious, odd or strange (de Lauretis, 1991; Jagose, 1996).

Two uses of the term are apparent. First, queer theory is used loosely to describe any theoretically inflected work in gay and lesbian studies. Using the term in such a way frustrates queer theorists who valorize the perspective's unabashedly and relentless push to critique. Second, and more precisely, as an instance of POST-STRUCTURALISM and POSTMODERNISM, queer theory EPISTEMOLOGICALLY challenges the ubiquity of HETERONORMATIVITY (see HOMOPHOBIA AND HETEROSEXISM). It perpetually and relentlessly destabilizes our quotidian ideas by rejecting any fixed or stable notions of SEXUALITY and GENDER, their representations or their effects (see ESSENTIALISM; FEMINIST GEOGRAPHIES; PERFORMATIVITY: see also Jagose, 1996; Sullivan, 2003).

The dilemma with any dictionary definition of this term is that it is meant to refuse fixing or defining, or delimiting a research trajectory, because such a move logically excludes facets of sexualities, or strategies to rethink them. This conundrum reflects the tendency of dominant discourses to assimilate any moves that resist or stand outside of them (see DISCOURSE). Thus there is a discernable anxiety about whether the radical potential of this term is being evacuated as its popularity grows and it is stretched to cover any work being done by or about gays and lesbians (Sothern, 2004).

Queer theory's relationship with geography has been two-directional, if rather uneven. Queer theorists demand that geographers recognize – and attend to – their own heteronormativity, but it also introduces the problematic of *homonormativity*, which is to say, the disciplining effects of privileging and imposing any sexuality or desire to the exclusion or stigmatization of others (Sothern, 2004). It has enabled geographers interested in sexuality and SPACE to maintain a focus on PLACE, yet also incorporate an appreciation and awareness of movement, MIGRATION, PLACELESSNESS and multiple SCALES (e.g. Knopp, 2004). Geographers, historians and architects have tried to point out that queer theory's roots in the humanities, often marked by a suspicion of EMPIRICISM, and penchant for discourse analysis of literary TEXTS, open it to charges of a rather unqueer GEOGRAPHICAL IMAGINATION, where the materiality of the world is sometimes lost in a sea of TEXTUALITY. While queer theorists have been willing to appreciate the significance of SPATIALITY and NATURE–SOCIETY dualities (Halberstram, 2005), they have been rather slow to acknowledge the work of geographers who themselves are informed by queer theory.   MB

Suggested reading
Jagose (1996); Sullivan (2003).

questionnaire An instrument for collecting data for SURVEY ANALYSIS. Every respondent is asked the same questions, in the same way and in the same sequence. This differs from the more open-ended, conversational format of interviews and other QUALITATIVE METHODS. Questionnaires can be used to collect information to classify respondents (e.g. gender,

income or age), to learn about their behaviour (e.g. voting practices, number of hours of television viewing per week or recycling behaviour) and to understand their attitudes. Questionnaires may be administered face-to-face, over the phone or via the INTERNET, or they can be mailed and self-administered. There are advantages and disadvantages to each mode of administering questionnaires, including cost, response rate, accuracy of responses and the level of detail that can be obtained. One mode of delivery is not superior to another: the advantages and disadvantages are weighed in relation to the research question.

Because one of the strengths of survey research is the capacity to establish patterns over large populations, questionnaires must be very carefully designed so as to be unambiguous to a large number of people. They must be unbiased and simply understood, with clear instructions of how to respond. There are standard pitfalls to avoid, such as the inclusion of double negatives and double-barrelled questions. Nevertheless, there is no avoiding the fact that questions are inevitably framed from a certain perspective and, in the case of face-to-face or telephone interviews, the presence of an interviewer will have effects that can only be understood rather than removed (see INTERVIEWS AND INTERVIEWING). A variety of types of questions can be asked, including open-ended ones. Closed-ended questions standardize responses across a given set of responses and are already structured for statistical analysis. Open-ended questions require coding before statistical analysis, but are suitable if the full range of possible responses is unknown, or the topic is a sensitive or complex one that requires some explanation or qualification. Because questionnaire design is so difficult and so important, FOCUS GROUPS can be used to understand interpretations of particular questions and questionnaires are always pre-tested.

Questionnaires are considered by some to be best suited for discovering patterns and less helpful for studying causal relationships. Marsh (1982) assesses these criticisms and provides a careful guide for questionnaire design so as to enhance the utility of questionnaires for statistical causal analysis. This involves collecting data on many different variables, beyond ones identified as independent (causal) and dependent (effect) variables, including possible confounding, antecedent and intervening variables. She also provides guidelines for asking people about their reasons for doing things. This 'reasons analysis' involves asking a series of questions that break the reasoning process down in such a way as to assist the respondent in explaining their reasons. Concerns are also expressed about the accuracy and truthfulness of survey research, and it is as well to remember that some characteristics of the survey context promote truthfulness so as to emphasize these features. These include underlining to the respondent the fact that their completion of the questionnaire is entirely voluntary, and that their responses are a valuable contribution to understanding an important research question.   GP

Suggested reading
Babbie (2001); Parfitt (2005).

R

race A historical means of social classification and differentiation that attempts to essentialize political and cultural differences by linking physical traits (i.e. skin, blood, genes) and social practices (i.e. RELIGION, VIOLENCE, passion) to innate, immutable characteristics (see ESSENTIALISM). Race as a concept presumes that characteristics (tendencies, behaviours, dispositions, interests) of an individual can be projected to understandings of essential traits of a population or that the presumed traits of a population can be discerned through the characteristics of an individual. Though these assumptions have been widely and exhaustively disproven, they still operate as 'common sense' in society with powerful and violent effects. As such, race is a SOCIAL CONSTRUCTION but RACISM is a material fact.

The contemporary meaning of 'race' has roots in older forms of hierarchy and classification, but its contemporary form as an innate physiological or genetic means of differentiating individuals and populations is largely the product of eighteenth-century social relationships associated with the European ENLIGHTENMENT and COLONIALISM (see also EUROPE). Most scholars agree that earlier forms of social differentiation and hierarchy were different from modern ideas of race. In the ancient world, for example, the Greeks distinguished between the 'civilized' and 'barbarous', the Romans between freedom and slavery, and the Christians between the savage and the saved. But in all these cases difference was not fixed: barbarians could become 'civilized' in Greek cities, Roman slaves were not determined by inherited traits, and Christians were offered the possibility of salvation through conversion.

The most powerful antecedents to the contemporary notion of race can be found in the Christian notion of the Great Chain of Being, which depicted a hierarchy in the order of things as immutably fixed by God, and the idea of succession to kingship or royalty based on a line of descent (or bloodline). These notions provided the basis for identifying populations through a fixed and defining feature such as blood. In the fifteenth century, for example, it was deemed impossible for Jews to convert to Christianity by virtue of their blood, a doctrine that helped to define the notion of a Jewish population that was supposedly distinctive and unassimilable through its shared immutable qualities. Similar appeals to a naturalized hierarchy were made in the sixteenth-century debates between Bartolomé de Las Casas and Juan Ginés de Sepúlveda, concerning the treatment of the indigenous inhabitants of the Spanish colonies in South America as either child-like human beings (who could thus be converted to Christianity) or 'savages' (whose exploitation could be justified through their lower position in the natural order of things). The Spanish Empire developed a doctrine of 'blood purity' (*limpeza de sangre*) that allowed and even required the differential treatment of those who could not be converted because of the supposed impurity of their blood, and the subsequent hierarchical classification by blood provided an influential precedent for modern formations of race (Darder and Torres, 2004).

The term 'race' came into English usage in the seventeenth century and here too it was most forcefully articulated through Anglo-American projects of colonization in the New World. In developing a concept of CIVILIZATION that was supposedly coterminous with the WEST, particularly in the eighteenth century, Europeans and Americans fabricated cultural and behavioral ('racial') traits that legitimized their own superiority and exploitative colonial practices. But these ascriptions were more than the *product* of an expansive, exploitative and European project of MODERNITY, and scholars such as Ann Stoler (1995) and Paul Gilroy (2000a) have sought to show that 'race' is *constitutive* of modernity itself.

The modern notion of 'race' thus has a complex GENEALOGY, but it has been most forcefully advanced through the claim that it is a demonstrably scientific concept. As such, 'race' is inseparable from the development of so-called 'natural history' in general and the work of the Swedish scholar Carolus Linnaeus (1707–71) in particular. Linnaeus is usually regarded as the founder of modern scientific systems of CLASSIFICATION. He divided human beings into four taxonomic sub-orders, whose distinctive traits he directly linked to skin colour. Thus the *Europeaeus* was supposedly white, gentle, sanguine, inventive and ruled by law, while *Africanus* was black, crafty, negligent and governed by caprice. In developing this taxonomy, Linneaus effectively subsumed cultural formations within the taxonomical order of NATURE. In 1745, the French naturalist Georges-Louis Leclerc Buffon (1707–88) explicitly introduced the term 'race' into natural history and, developing Linnaeus' categories, divided human beings into separate 'races'. Although Buffon acknowledged the artificiality of these divisions, they were subsequently reified by the German anthropologist and physiologist Johann Friedrich Blumenbach (1752–1840), who developed a classification of five human types based on cranial skull measurements: this system served as the 'scientific' basis for racial classification for almost 200 years – and even though it has been widely repudiated, it is still present in popular culture today.

But it was through DARWINISM and populist simplifications of Darwin's ideas of 'natural selection' and 'survival of the fittest' that the most pernicious formations of 'race' were naturalized. Most notable was Francis Galton (1822–1911), Darwin's half-cousin, who applied a version of Darwinian theories to human society and in 1883 developed the concept of *Eugenics* ('good genes') to encourage socially engineered heredity as a means of improving the human race. In the USA, the Eugenics movement found an appreciative audience in the context of increasing IMMIGRATION, POVERTY and violent labour politics, where it seemed to offer a means not only of social improvement but also of social control. The initial focus was on 'positive eugenics' through birth control, selective breeding and eventually genetic engineering to assure 'better babies'; but a 'negative eugenics' was subsequently developed, which advocated forced sterilization and segregation to preserve the purity of the white race. These concepts reached their hideous climax in Nazi Germany under the banner of 'racial hygiene', when 'Aryan' women were impregnated by SS officers, hundreds of thousands of people who were declared unfit were sterilized, and millions more 'undesirables', primarily Jews but also gypsies and homosexuals, were murdered to protect the 'purity' of the Aryan race (see HOLOCAUST). Here,

modern biological racism was taken to its 'logical' end, in which some presumed innate behavioral qualities and social status could only be addressed through the extermination of the biology of individuals who were considered the sources of the problem (Larson, 1995: cf. BIOPOLITICS).

Even after the widespread postwar repudiation of Nazi race science and Eugenics, the claim that there is an innate scientific basis to 'race', fusing physiological features to social behaviours, is still a common means of social classification, and continues to be a powerful strategy of dividing, ranking and controlling people around the world. Newer efforts from sociobiology, neo-Darwinism, evolutionary psychology, some strains of evolutionary anthropology and biology as well as some versions of genetics continue to search for a physical basis for 'racial' difference, while STATE-sponsored systems of *racial profiling* assume that such a basis has been found and can be deployed as an effective weapon against CRIME or TERRORISM.

The problem with the debates around race, as W.E.B. Du Bois pointed out over a century ago when he abandoned his efforts to show its erroneous foundation, is that the very idea of race has been so comprehensively woven into the social and psychological fabric of SOCIETY that simply revealing the fallaciousness of racial classification does little to expunge the term or diminish its extraordinary power. He wrote that 'in the fight against race prejudice, we were not facing simply the rational conscious determination of white folk to oppress us; we were facing age-long complexes sunk now largely to unconscious habit and irrational urge' (Du Bois, 1986 [1940], p. 296). This realization that constructs of 'race' are embedded within the formation of modern human SUBJECTIVITY was developed by Frantz Fanon (1925–61) who, in *Black skin, white masks* in particular, emphasized how 'race' is implicated in both how one comes to know and define a self and how that self is articulated and transformed as it acts and is acted upon in the world (Fanon, 1967 [1952]). These and other critiques prompted a shift towards an analysis of how 'race' comes into being though LAW, popular CULTURE and everyday practices of racial formation (see also POST-COLONIALISM).

The critique of race-based cultural formations has been reinforced by parallel debates within and, indeed, about the very 'nature' of SCIENCE. Most famously, Richard Lewontin and Stephen J. Gould challenged the biological and genetic basis of racial identification, arguing that there is more genetic variation within a nominally 'racial' group than between such groups. However, these and other scholars effectively placed nature outside the field of culture and politics, arguing either that 'race' was cultural and not natural or that genetic maps could not be projected on to cultural behaviours (Haraway, 1989). As such, the debate often became polarized between nature and nurture: Was race a biological category or a cultural one? Science was assumed to have the authority to speak for NATURE and, as a result, the cultural politics of the supposed 'science of race' was left largely unchallenged. More recent scholarship in science and technology studies by Donna Haraway (1989), Nancy Stepan Leyes (1990 [1986]) and Ian Hacking (1999) has help move away from the nature–culture dualism that underwrote these discussions, and has shown that nature and the voices that speak for and about race and the science of race are always already bound up in politics.

These approaches to understanding race have been echoed in contemporary black cultural studies, Chicano studies, ethnic studies and critical race theory, which have approached racial difference and affinities as constructed through social struggles, shared histories and everyday practices positioning racialized subjects and their formation within multiple relations of POWER. Rather than fixed difference, 'race' is understood as a contingent formation unevenly produced in different times and places with no invariant meaning or universal form (see, e.g., Hesse, 2000; Fregoso, 2003; Moore, Kosek and Pandian, 2003). As such, many scholars of difference have abandoned the term 'race' altogether, moving 'beyond race' to address the multiple forms and particularities of social relations, and denying any overarching integrity or coherence to race as an analytical concept while still being attentive to the ways in which racism(s) are a lived daily reality.   JK

Suggested reading
Essed and Goldberg (2002); Gilroy (2000); Miles and Brown (2003).

racial districting An aspect of REDISTRICTING within the USA intended to ensure that racial minorities – notably African-Americans and Hispanics – do not suffer from discrimination,

through such strategies as GERRYMANDERING. Under the 1965 *Voting Rights Act*, states with records of such discrimination are required to get redistricting plans pre-cleared by the Department of Justice. This usually involves ensuring that there are sufficient 'minority-majority districts' so that, for example, if 30 per cent of a state's population is African-American, then 30 per cent of its Congressional Districts should contain an African-American majority. Such schemes remain open to challenge through the courts on other grounds.   RJ

Suggested reading
Kousser (1999).

racialization A historically contingent and contested process through which racial meanings are extended in attempts to define or redefine *relationship, social practice, object, individuals* or *group*. The term has become widely used as a means of stressing that 'RACE' is a social, economic, political and psychological *process* that must be explained, rather than a biological one that is determined by inherent characteristics (Omi and Winant, 1996). Although its origins date back to the late nineteenth century, its current use can be traced to Frantz Fanon's exploration of the relational aspects of racial formation and physical and social dimensions of European domination and COLONIALISM (Fanon, 1967 [1961]). More recently, many scholars have developed reservations about the term because its overusage and vagueness has led to less rigorous attention to the specific practices and dynamics of racial formation (Goldberg, 2002).   JK

Suggested reading
Barot and Bird (2001); Essed and Goldberg (2002); Miles (1993); Murji and Solomos (2005).

racism Any act that links tendencies, affinities, behaviours or characteristics to an individual or community based on innate, indelible or physiological attributes, intended or not, is an act of racism. Racism is also the prejudice, hierarchical differentiation, discrimination and so on that results from these essentialized understandings of RACE as an innate factor that determines human traits and abilities. Racism may be manifest individually, through explicit thoughts, feelings or acts, or socially, through institutions and practices that reproduce and essentialize difference and inequities (see ESSENTIALISM; cf. APARTHEID).

Racism is now so extensively used in political discourse that it often gives the impression of being a timeless universal concept. In fact, the word did not exist in the English language until the 1930s, and only slightly before in German and French. Its rise coincides with the specific context of 1930–40s Germany. Specifically, 'racism' at the time was employed as a political critique of the German biologized understanding of race (see HOLOCAUST). Although the roots of the term have a much longer and divergent history, racism as a phenomenon was present in multiple forms before the use of the term. Among these forms were the relational differentiation of the Self and the Other in colonial practices, in which the securing of one's own positive identity was formed against the stigmatization of the inferior characteristics (often fixed through physical or biological characteristics) of an 'Other' (see COLONIALISM).

However, some critics have become wary of understanding racism as simply biological or physical, asserting that CULTURE or ETHNICITY can be reified and naturalized to the point at which they become 'functionally' equivalent to biological understandings of race (Fredrickson, 2002). The idea of cultural racism was first presented in 1952 by Frantz Fanon, who saw the emphasis on cultural differences as a modern replacement of biologically based ideas of different races (see Fanon, 1967 [1952]). Still later, Martin Barker pointed to what he called the 'new racism' that arose through the conservative political milieu in England in the late 1970s and 1980s, in which conservatives and liberals alike would criticize biological ideas of race only to naturalize ideas of community and culture (Barker, 1981). Etienne Balibar argues that this new racism in EUROPE is actually 'racism without race', in which ideas of immutable human difference are used to rigidify racial categories or assert the impossibility of coexistence (Balibar, 1991b, p. 23; see also Gilroy, 2000a). This concept of the 'new racism' was taken up by other writers, most notably a group at the Centre for Contemporary Cultural Studies in the UK, who came to understand racism, or more accurately racisms, as highly variable historical formations with shifting meanings that are temporally and spatially uneven and fiercely contested. They, and later others, emphasized the political importance of denying a universal and essentialist understanding of race or racism outside of the historically specific and intimate contexts of their formations and practices (Hall, 1980, p. 336; Gilroy, 1987, 2000: see also Goldberg, 1993; Stoler, 1995). These understandings of racisms as spatially and temporally variable, lacking any thematic unity, or that challenge intrinsic characterizations of race, have been particularly important in contemporary understandings of new forms of biological racism such as new genetic determinism as well as historical and cultural racism, such as post 9/11 racism towards Muslims, and neo-nationalist projects such as the rise of NATIONALISM in Europe.   JK

Suggested reading
Barker (1992); Fanon (1967 [1952]); Fredrickson (2002); Gilroy (2000a); Miles (1993); Miles and Brown (2003); Stoler (1997).

radical democracy A POSTMODERNIST or POST-STRUCTURALIST rethinking of modern democratic theory and practice. It takes a broad-ranging and flexible perspective on CITIZENSHIP, emphasizing capacities to 'be political' in a DEMOCRACY rather than necessarily on rights-claims or formal membership in a polity. It challenges two popular conceptualizations of the citizen. Rather than locating citizenship as one IDENTITY or PERFORMANCE alongside, but mutually exclusive to, others (such as kin, worker, consumer etc.), as is common in LIBERALISM, or heroically elevating it as the principal and optimal identity of the individual, as is common in COMMUNITARIANISM, radical democracy rethinks citizenship as a potential moment or dimension of any identity when it becomes politicized or contested (Mouffe, 1993). Radical democracy is 'radical' because it refuses closure on the questions of democracy everywhere, in all their forms. In other words, it seeks to democratize all aspects of politics, especially at sites of doxa, shared assumptions, or where things are deemed apolitical or pre-political

Radical democracy has important consequences for POLITICAL GEOGRAPHY. It has been part of a turn towards a more encompassing and theoretically informed way of understanding politics and the political. It has helped geographers broaden their focus on the STATE and sites of politics towards locations in CIVIL SOCIETY, PUBLIC SPACE and the HOME, as well as hybrid spaces such as the SHADOW STATE (Brown, 1997a). Barnett (2004b) has cautioned, however, that the spatial rhetoric in radical democratic theory desensitizes us to different temporal scales so often at work in politics. He insists that we must pay close attention to their complexity, or else UNIVERSALISM will unintentionally creep back into our thinking.

Radical democracy also has implications for SOCIAL and CULTURAL GEOGRAPHY, given its attention to multiple axes of POWER that work through multiple subject identities (see IDENTITY, SUBJECTIVITY). How identities are enabled and constrained as the subject moves through SPACE, for example, has been a point of interest for radical democratic geographers (e.g. Massey, 1995). Rejecting ESSENTIALISM, radical democracy implores a sensitivity to the openness and fluidity of the subject. It challenges the will for politics to fixate or prioritize a single identity to the exclusion or devaluation of others (e.g. where orthodox MARXISM might privilege CLASS struggle over GENDER oppression).

This has been challenged by RADICAL GEO-GRAPHY, which questions how one can have a politics without at least some ethical or political commitments that must be treated as essentialisms. A second criticism takes form around the question of the constitutive outside of the political. Simply put, even the most post-structural of scholars has questioned whether or not we can ever have a democratic politics without some form of a constitutive outside. Whenever there is a 'we' (or a 'here'), there is by definition, a 'they' (or a 'there') who are 'outside' of deliberation or perhaps even RECOGNITION. Yet logically such a border itself might be quite anti-democratic. If the promise is to always attack and render such exclusionary political geographies, the political issue at hand becomes deflected, and inevitably lost in an infinite regress of attending to exclusions. Conversely, foreclosures and boundaries around what is worthy of the appellation 'politics' or 'political' are inherently anti-democratic since they leave no space for those harmed by such foreclosures.

Addressing these paradoxes, political theorists advocate open, iterative and REFLEXIVE standpoints in order to address these tensions, but they admit these are by no means 'solutions' to the dilemma.   MB

Suggested reading
Mouffe (1993); Rasmussen and Brown (2002).

radical geography Approaches to GEOG-RAPHY committed to overturning relations of power and oppression, and to constructing more socially just, egalitarian and liberating geographies and ways of living. The term came to refer in particular to critiques of SPATIAL SCIENCE and POSITIVISM in geography during the late 1960s and early 1970s, and to attempts to chart alternatives that were socially relevant and sought fundamental change. Many geographers were radicalized by counter-culture movements and by waves of political protest at the time; in particular, struggles involving civil RIGHTS and against the Vietnam War, IMPERIALISM, POVERTY and inequality. They reacted against technocratic approaches in geography that were unable to speak to current pressing problems and that served to support the status quo, and they sought to study social issues from contrasting viewpoints, especially those based on socialist, feminist and anti-imperialist perspectives. The establishment of *Antipode: a Radical Journal of Geography* in 1969 by students and faculty at Clark University, Massachusetts, provided an important forum for Anglophone geographers, with the opening issue declaring that it was both necessary and possible to change university structures and ways of doing geography, and to revolutionize the social and physical environment

Early issues of *Antipode* were urgent, questioning, optimistic, combative in style and diverse in content. Articles addressed issues such as poverty, housing, services, planning, research methodologies, imperialism, women and war. The rediscovery of earlier radical traditions of social concern in geography – in particular, the ANARCHIST geography of Kropotkin and Reclus – inspired many. Others conducted advocacy research and experimented with taking geography into the streets, including through Bunge's 'geographical expeditions' that worked with low-income and disenfranchised communities. Organizations such as the Union of Socialist Geographers, founded in 1974, advanced a radical presence in the discipline. According to Peet, however, early radical geography was 'more relevant to social issues but still tied to a PHILOSOPHY of SCIENCE, a set of theories, and a METHODOLOGY developed *within* the existing framework of power relationships' (Peet, 1977b, p. 12). Calls for overhauling the discipline's theoretical basis to address the deep causes rather than the surface manifestations of problems led to a 'breakthrough to MARXISM' in the early to mid-1970s, as the work of Harvey and others paved the way for the analysis of CAPITALISM and CLASS struggle (Harvey, 1973, 1999 [1982]).

Marxism became central to much radical geography, which moved from an oppositional and relatively marginalized position to become a major force. Radical ideas and practices developed within FEMINIST GEOGRAPHIES, similarly committed to social change but critical of the GENDER-blindness of other radical studies, became increasingly important. Vigorous geographical debates were also stimulated by POST-COLONIALISM and concern with sexual liberation (see SEXUALITY and QUEER THEORY), as issues of CULTURAL POLITICS came to the fore, with each of these approaches being connected with political struggles inside as well as outside the academy (Blunt and Wills, 2000). In an editorial marking the twenty-fifth anniversary of *Antipode*, Walker and McDowell (1993, pp. 2–3) signalled this diversity, arguing: 'No single oppression or axis of social life can be treated as merely secondary or an afterthought of radical research or politics. While SOCIALISM and Marxism remain central to the vocabulary of the Left, we hold to no one orthodox view of radical analysis.'

Radical approaches have become increasingly accepted and influential in the discipline, yet much of the earlier optimism about the prospects for fundamental social change has receded. The idea of a 'common vision' or project in geography has also been challenged. Some have welcomed the pluralization of the Left, but others have worried about its fragmentation and depoliticization, asserting that while it is necessary to recognize the diversity of current struggles, it is also important to find points of commonality and unity between them in order to enable political change. Many now employ the term CRITICAL HUMAN GEOGRAPHY as a related and looser label for ideas and practices committed to an emancipatory politics, and considerable discussion has recently centred on the effects of institutionalization and professionalization within the academy as well as on political commitment, on ACTIVISM and on different ways of contributing to progressive social change (including through debates in *Antipode* about 'what's left?'; see also Castree, 2000). Initiatives such as the conferences of the International Critical Geography Group and the development of INTERNET forums are providing new means for developing and debating radical perspectives, and for connecting different forms of radical geography, which have their own geographies and histories. Radical perspectives in geography are further being galvanized by current political struggles against CAPITALISM, imperialism, WAR and other forms of oppression that underline the continuing need for approaches that provide '[d]issentient thoughts and norm challenging information', and that are prepared 'to bring the undiscussed into discussion; to stray beyond established perimeters of opinion; to render the familiar not only strange but, often-times, unacceptable; and to explore the depths of the meaning of "radical" itself as a conceptual rubric' (Castree and Wright, 2005, p. 2). DP

Suggested reading
Blunt and Wills (2000); Peet (1977, 2000).

rank-size rule An empirical regularity identified in the city-size distributions of some countries and regions. Generally, if the cities are ranked from 1 (the largest) to n (the smallest), then the population of any city – k – can be determined from the equation:

$$P_k = P_1/k,$$

where P_1 is the population of the largest city and P_k that of the city ranked kth. The steepness of the relationship between size and rank is incorporated by raising k to the power b; that is, k^b. No convincing explanations for the rule's existence have been developed, however, nor for variations in the parameter b between regions (e.g. why the fifth-largest city is smaller, relative to the largest, in some places than it is elsewhere). RJ

Suggested reading
Carroll (1982).

raster Raster is a GIS data structure akin to placing a regular grid over a study region and representing the geographical feature found in each grid cell numerically: for example, 1 = podsol, 2 = clay and so on. Rasters are associated with REMOTE SENSING, image processing and dynamic modelling, and are easily manipulated using map algebra (e.g. multiplying geographically corresponding cell values in two or more datasets) and neighbourhood functions (e.g. returning the sum of values in 3 × 3 cell window). Rasters are simple but often voluminous. Patterns in the data are therefore compressed using run length encoding, QUADTREES or wavelets. RH

Suggested reading
DeMers (2001).

rational choice theory A NORMATIVE THEORY of individual DECISION-MAKING, claiming that human action is motivated by getting the most for the least. On the one hand, individuals strive to achieve an unlimited set of ends where each end is associated with a different level of satisfaction or utility, but, on the other hand, they possess only a limited means to realize those ends. The role of the rationality postulate is to ensure that the best ends – that is, those yielding greatest individual satisfaction – are chosen given the constraint of limited means. Often couched in terms of the mathematics of constrained maximization, the problem of making the best choices is formally shown to reduce to a formal set of consistency requirements (Hahn and Hollis, 1979). Those requirements define rationality in the sense that if any one of them is contravened, the choice is not rational.

The historical antecedents of rational choice theory are with the British classical economists, but it is now most closely associated with their successor, NEO-CLASSICAL ECONOM-ICS, and a maverick strain of Marxism (ANA-LYTICAL MARXISM). Within economics, it is not just economic acts that are explained by rational choice. The University of Chicago, Nobel-Prize winning rational choice economist Gary Becker (1930–) uses the theory to explain all human acts from birth (the decision to have a child) to death (choosing suicide) and everything in between, including racial discrimination, committing crime, going to school, falling in love and filing for divorce (Becker, 1976). Nothing falls outside the 'lore of calculated less or more'. The rational choice assumption is deployed across the social sciences, including sociology (rational individuals choose their social CLASS), political science (scenarios of GEOPOLITICAL brinkmanship modelled via GAME THEORY) and anthropology (cultures are 'a collection of choice-making individuals'; Burling, 1962, p. 811). Within HUMAN GEOGRAPHY, rational choice theory is most frequently found in ECONOMIC GEOGRAPHY and, in particular, in the formal LOCATION THEORY associated with REGIONAL SCIENCE. Its role is to impose a determinant order on spatial arrangements, allowing the theorist to make scientific claims to precision, exact inference and predictability.

There have been many criticisms of the rationality assumption, and they frequently focus on the unrealistic characteristics attributed to the rational actor (sometimes described in the gendered language of *Homo economicus*, or 'rational economic man'): perfect knowledge; unyielding egoism; independent preferences; the ability and desire to maximize utility (minimize costs); and pursuit of a single goal (see SATISFICING BEHAVIOUR). Such criticisms are often moot, however, because the rationality postulate by its very construction is empirically untestable, a normative rather than a 'positive' theory, and therefore charges of unrealism have little purchase. More incisive are those criticisms that tackle the normative character of the postulate by arguing that it offers an unappealing vision of the world. Karl Marx (1818–83) (see Marx, 1976 [1867], ch. 6) satirizes rational choice by invoking the invidious character of 'Mr Moneybags', and the American institutional economist, Thorstein Veblen (1857–1929) (see Veblen, 1919, p. 73), makes it clear that 'economic man' is not even close to human: he is a 'homogenous globule of desire … with neither antecedent nor consequent. He is an isolated, definitive human datum, in stable equilibrium except for the buffers of the impinging forces that displace him in one direction or another' (see INSTITU-TIONAL ECONOMICS). Another line of attack is to criticize the postulate's intellectual origins and consistency. Mirowski (1989) does this by locating both the conceptual corpus of the rational actor and its associated mathematical techniques within the nineteenth-century physics of energetics. In other words, the rationality postulate was brought to social science via re-description: it is a METAPHOR. Apart from the fact that energetics itself was short-lived and quickly superseded, Mirowski argues that those economists who took up the metaphor never successfully transferred the core relations from physics to economics. The gap is of two different worlds, revealing a contradiction at the very heart of the project. TB

Suggested reading
Barnes (1996, chs 2 and 3).

realism Realism comes in many forms, and realists vary widely in what they are prepared to be realist about. At its most general, realism entails belief in an external world that exists and acts independently of our knowledge of it or beliefs about it. The weakest form of realism simply asserts this belief, but is unspecific about *what* exists. A 'common-sense realism' asserts the existence of everyday objects, such as trees, stones or chairs. All of us are probably realists at this level. In the HUMANITIES, realism identifies a broad literary movement that identified ART in general, and LITERATURE in particular, with the truthful REPRESENTATION of the world through the meticulous and dispassionate observation of contemporary life. Its central arch spanned the mid-nineteenth and early twentieth centuries – from the novels of Gustave Flaubert (who in fact rejected the label) to those of Henry James – and some writers later re-described the project as a 'naturalism'. Thus Émile Zola argued that in matters of cultural criticism and literary description 'we must imitate the naturalists'. It is this possibility of NATURALISM that has propelled realism in PHILOSOPHY, SCIENCE and the social sciences (Bhaskar, 1998 [1979])

'Scientific realism' asserts the existence of various observable and unobservable entities of which it claims to be capable of giving the best representations. Many scientific realists subscribe to an 'entity' realism, which asserts the existence of many, well-established theoretical entities (various atomic particles, for example), but not necessarily to a 'semantic' realism, or belief in the truth of any one theory about such entities that correctly represents or mirrors 'the way things really are' (Hacking, 1983). There are also profound differences amongst scientific realists on notions of truth, reference, inference and explanation (Psillos, 1999). Matters are a little simpler in the social sciences in that a particular version of realism, *critical realism*, has become dominant and the focus of most debate. This is a version particularly associated with the work of Bhaskar (1986, 1989, 1998 [1979]) and Sayer (1992 [1984], 2000).

Early formulations of critical realism typically developed its main elements by asking what reality must be like to make the existence of science and its successes possible, which leads to a critique of the impoverished assumptions underlying EMPIRICISM or positivism. Critical realists reject the possibility of basing science on a 'flat' ONTOLOGY of atomistic sense impressions. They make more complex ontological claims, distinguishing the *empirical* (events that we experience), the *actual* (events that happen whether we experience them or not) and the *real* (a deeper dimension of objects, structures and generative mechanisms that produce events).

Critical realists also reject a restricted, positivistic view of causality as the constant conjunction of observable events (a 'regularity view' of causation): 'If A, then B' (see LAW, SCIENTIFIC). Critical realists point out that the social sciences usually deal with *open systems*, rather than closed systems that can be artificially produced in a scientific laboratory. Although regularities are rare in such open systems, this does not mean that causes are not at work. Causes are thus best thought of as tendencies of objects, with distinctive powers in virtue of their essential structures, to act in certain ways. However, it is contingent whether and how those powers are activated in different combinations in different contexts to produce varying effects. Predictive success is thus difficult to achieve, but it may

be possible to identify the underlying causal mechanisms beneath the flux of surface phenomena. The distinctive mode of inference to such mechanisms is called variously ABDUCTION, retroduction or inference to the best explanation.

Powers are also often 'emergent' in the sense that the powers of objects or structures to produce effects are not reducible to those of their constituents (e.g. the powers of classes or groups may be more than the sum of the powers of their individual members). Reality is thus *stratified* in the sense that powers and mechanisms operative in one strata are not simply reducible to those of a lower strata.

Critical realists also make an important distinction between necessary and contingent properties or relations. Objects are necessarily or internally related if they are what they are by virtue of their relationships to each other (e.g. the relationship between landlords and tenants – each requires the other in order to be what it is). What we term 'structures' are made up of such networks of INTERNAL RELATIONS and define positions to be occupied by actors. However, it is often contingent who occupies these positions (landlords may be young or old, male or female etc.). ABSTRACTION is defined as the key procedure for identifying such structures by disentangling what are necessary from what are contingent relationships.

Critical realism also offers a distinctive perspective on familiar agency–structure dualisms that bedevil HUMAN GEOGRAPHY and, indeed, the humanities and social sciences more generally (see HUMAN AGENCY). Individual agency presupposes a social structure, and vice versa, but social structure and agency are ontologically distinct levels with different properties and causal powers (e.g. social structures are enabling and constraining; individuals have self-consciousness and reflexivity). Individuals may reproduce social structures through their everyday practices and understandings, but the 'critical' moment in critical realism lies in the belief that bringing underlying structures and their unconscious reproduction to the level of consciousness opens the way for emancipatory critique and social change.

Critical realism provides a philosophical framework for social science, but it does not prescribe a particular methodology. It is compatible with a range of QUALITATIVE TECHNIQUES and QUANTITATIVE TECHNIQUES that can aid the identification of causal structures, including HERMENEUTIC and interpretivist approaches.

Realism contends with various forms of anti-realism in the guise of POSTMODERNISM, PRAGMATISM and SOCIAL CONSTRUCTION. A key focus of debate concerns the meaningfulness of referring to a reality outside of the conceptual systems that we use to talk about it. From a pragmatist angle, Rorty (1979) argues that it is meaningless to talk about conceptual systems representing or 'mirroring' an extra-linguistic reality (see also REPRESENTATION). In the sociology of science, radical constructivists argue that reality is not something existing outside of scientific discourse, but is essentially a discursive construction (see SOCIAL CONSTRUCTION). Critical realists typically respond to such claims with the argument that although social reality may be highly concept-*dependent*, this does not mean that it is concept-*determined* in such an idealist way.

The division between realism and anti-realism runs through most areas of social science, including MARXISM and FEMINISM. However, the divisions should not be exaggerated. A 'realistic constructivism' would recognize both the ways in which scientific discourse is powerfully shaped by social interests and cultural values, and the constraining role of objective material realities. The relationship between DISCOURSE and reality is an interactive and reflexive one. At a more general level, Sayer (2000) has argued powerfully that critical realism occupies a 'Third Way' between the untenable extremes of empiricism on the one hand and postmodernism on the other. Certainly, critical realism was a vital intervention in the critique of SPATIAL SCIENCE and the refinement of MARXIST GEOGRAPHY in particular; it was also invoked to underwrite STRUCTURATION THEORY. There was a lively debate about 'the difference that space makes' to EXPLANATION under the sign of critical realism (Sayer, 1985). Spatial relations are clearly important in analysing the contingent circumstances, the specific combinations of conditions under which causal powers might be realized, but several geographers argued that spatial relations also enter into the very constitution of the social structures involved (see SPACE). For a time, critical realism also held out the prospect of a plenary GEOGRAPHY, drawing human geography into a conversation with PHYSICAL GEOGRAPHY through a commitment to a common and recognizably 'scientific' programme. That was never achieved: by the time most physical geographers had become interested in realism, most human geographers had started to ask critical questions about its claims and consequences (e.g. Yeung, 1997),

and many of them soon moved on to explore philosophies outside the confines of the philosophy of science, which were typically treated as resources rather than rule-books.　　KB/DG

Suggested reading
Brown, Fleetwood and Roberts (2002); Carter and New (2004); Danermark, Ekstrom, Jakobsen and Karlsson (2002); Sayer (2006).

recognition The recognition of rights and needs tied to IDENTITY became a focus of much social movement activity in the 1980s and 1990s. This is known as identity politics, and is associated with a proliferation and fragmentation of SOCIAL MOVEMENTS around identities of GENDER, RACE, DISABILITY, ETHNICITY, SEXUALITY (amongst others), taken up by some STATES as state-sponsored MULTICULTURALISM. Criticisms of politics of recognition have come from across the political spectrum. MARXISTS have expressed concern about the dissolution of the unifying CLASS struggle. Within FEMINISM, Fraser and Honneth (2003) have drawn a dichotomy between politics of recognition and redistribution, arguing that the former neglects political economic issues and geopolitical developments, as well as simplifying and reifying group identities. (But see Butler (1998) for the argument that this binary misrepresents the complexity of calls for recognition insofar as they are typically intertwined with demands for redistribution.) In a different register, feminists such as Grosz (2005) advocate a politics of imperceptibility – a politics that unleashes unexpected events and encounters without being identified with a person, group or organization. Some European intellectuals criticize the politics of identity and difference within their national context as another instance of American cultural IMPERIALISM. Mitchell (2004b) considers how this last critique converges with a growing conservative backlash against 'differentialism'.　　GP

Suggested reading
Fraser (2000).

reconstruction Meaning 'building again', reconstruction is generally used in the DEVELOPMENT community to refer to a cluster of actions to restore or re-equip economies that previously were developed or in transition to sustainable economic growth. These are distinguished from actions aimed at stimulating growth and good governance in the poorest countries, those once described as underdeveloped. This distinction goes back at least as far as the founding of the World Bank in 1944. The modern World Bank contains two institutions: the International Bank for Reconstruction and Development (IBRD) and the International Development Association (IDA). The IBRD made the first World Bank loan: $250 million to France in May 1947 for the reconstruction of its war-torn economy. The IBRD continues to be active in middle-income and transitional economies, providing loans for disaster relief purposes, in post-CONFLICT situations and to POST-SOCIALIST economies. Since 1991, The European Bank for Reconstruction and Development (EBRD) has joined the IBRD in central Europe and central Asia.

Reconstruction efforts sponsored by the IBRD and the EBRD have not been without their critics. Both institutions are committed to what they describe as democratization and MARKET-led economic growth, and the agendas of good GOVERNANCE or the new public administration feature strongly in their self-descriptions. However, good governance was not at the top of the reconstruction agenda in Russia under President Yeltsin: the shock therapy recommended by Yeltsin's advisers – including the Americans Jeffrey Sachs and David Lipton – led not only to price decontrol and currency convertibility, but also to the wholesale transfer of state assets to private monopolists. Sachs prefers to speak of 'radical reforms' rather than shock therapy (2005, p. 135) – but the shocking result of these measures (shocking, at any rate, to some mainstream economists) was a ruthless and often violent struggle for POWER, assets and TERRITORY. Far from providing an equitable restructuring of the economy of the former Soviet Union, reconstruction efforts have too often led to what David Harvey (2003b) calls 'ACCUMULATION by dispossession' (see also PRIMITIVE ACCUMULATION). Hugely widening inequalities in income levels and HEALTH-CARE provision have been just two results of reconstruction in Russia. Elsewhere, as in the Czech Republic and Poland, less dramatic reconstruction efforts have come closer to meeting the targets set by their governments and their international counterparts.   SCO

Suggested reading
Hoogvelt (2001); Ledeneva (1998).

recreation Pursuits or activities (even inactivity) undertaken voluntarily outside paid employment for the primary purpose of pleasure, enjoyment and satisfaction. Recreational activities tend to be distinguished, in academic studies, from SPORTS as not involving formal rules of competition. Such a division is also problematic, as sports may be undertaken non-competitively (e.g. one might play golf without competing), and other activities may involve more-or-less competitive elements with greater or lesser formalization (e.g. multi-player computer games contain highly formalized rules for competition, but would rarely be considered a sport). Recreational activities could be part of TOURISM, if occurring away from the place of domicile, or LEISURE, if occurring while at home, and the definitions of all the categories are very porous. A number of distinctions are often made regarding recreation's orientation and organization.

Formal and informal recreations are often differentiated. *Formal* recreation involves activities that are structured and organized by an external body in prescribed times or places. This would thus include clubs, hobby societies and other organizations. *Informal* recreation refers to self-organized activities occurring at times and/or places of the individual's own choosing. Trends to formalize more recreational activities have been linked to their commodification and the increasing sale of recreational goods – the production of which has become a major industry in the developed world. A further division often made is between passive and active recreation – playing in a band is active, while listening to one is passive. This distinction imports judgements freighted with normative values. A variety of policy initiatives around HEALTH have sought to encourage 'active' forms of recreation to increase fitness. Likewise, moral panics have often linked passive recreation to fears of youngster's becoming 'couch potatoes' or otherwise harmed by the passive enjoyment of especially digital media. The assumption of passive CONSUMPTION is contestable, since consumers may actively contribute to events and participate in numerous ways – transforming events or goods through their interpretations and reactions.

Geographies of recreation have tended to focus upon the effects on the environment and our relationship with it, and then the way in which SPACES structure the availability and nature of recreational opportunities. For instance, the development of climbing fashions both DISCOURSES and tactile or haptic ways of knowing and valuing the environment (Lorimer and Lund, 2003; Taylor, 2006b). Alternatively, looking at environmental effects (such as footpath erosion; see Liddle, 1997) or social impacts (such as contested claims and control) of recreation upon spaces might be a focus. Recreation can forge norms of appropriate conduct within spaces and lead to conflict, for instance, in parks or green spaces if different groups (in terms of age, ETHNICITY or SEXUALITY) have clashing recreational practices. A major strand of work has been disaggregating the social and physical factors affecting access to recreation in terms of income or DISABILITY or more hidden social factors. For instance, periurban woodland may be more-or-less physically accessible, but this may be compounded by fear of CRIME differentiating access by GENDER (Burgess, 1996). Work has looked to trends such as the commodification of recreation or the increasing spatial restrictions of CHILDREN's access to spaces of informal recreation in light of fears over their safety (Smith and Barker, 2001; Valentine, 2004; Department of Communities and Local Government, 2006). Recreation thus has to be seen as linked to the wider PRODUCTION OF SPACE, PRODUCTION OF NATURE and changing practices of consumption, where recent work has looked at recreational practices of dance, moving from studies of subcultures to discuss PERFORMANCE and BODY cultures, especially via NON-REPRESENTATIONAL THEORY.   MC

Suggested reading
Hall and Page (1999); Lorimer and Lund (2003); Prosser (2000); Valentine (2004).

recycling   A process that reuses the materials and energy components of an item to create another product. In most waste hierarchies, recycling sits below reducing CONSUMPTION, reusing an existing item and reprocessing, and above disposal. Although recycling uses ENERGY, it can reduce waste for disposal and the need for raw materials in production processes. Recycling was used during the two world wars, but not for environmental reasons. Although contemporary recycling may be undertaken solely for economic reasons (if recycled materials cost less than raw ones), it is usually represented as an environmental concern. Human geographers have investigated people's motivations for engaging in recycling activities (Barr, Ford and Gilg, 2003).   PM

red-light districts   While sex work has never been a solely urban phenomenon, it is in specific areas of towns and cities that it has been most visible. In most cases, these areas are particularly associated with female street PROSTITUTION, though in some instances, they are also characterized by an agglomeration of off-street work in the form of 'adult-oriented' businesses, sex clubs, theatres and peep shows. In some cities, these areas may coincide with spaces of male prostitution and gay venues, although the visibility of these in the LANDSCAPE has typically been less pronounced. The concentration of 'vice' and prostitution in specific areas has long fascinated urban geographers and sociologists, with the pioneering work of the CHICAGO SCHOOL of sociology including several detailed ETHNOGRAPHIES of the lifestyles of those occupying these areas of 'immorality' and deviance. More recent work has suggested that these areas cannot be understood merely as the outcome of supply and demand economics, but as the outcome of a complex interaction of moral codes, legal strictures and POLICING practices that encourage the containment of vice in INNER-CITY areas away from whiter, wealthier suburban populations (who, ironically, appear to be the principal clients of sex workers: Ashworth, White and Winchester, 1988; Hubbard, 1999). However, recent efforts to clean up vice areas, and the tendency for clients to contact sex workers via the INTERNET and mobile phone, means that red-light districts are becoming less numerous in Western cities (Sanchez, 2004).   PH

redistribution   A transfer of resources between groups or PLACES. Redistribution may be progressive (reducing INEQUALITY) or regressive (increasing inequality). Urban geographers emphasize the role of redistribution in the early formation of urban settlements. Harvey (1973), following the work of Karl Polanyi, argued that redistribution is one form of economic integration along with reciprocity and market exchange. Early urbanization is often assumed to have depended on the accumulation of an economic surplus, involving a shift away from reciprocity and towards redistribution (with resources being transferred from rural to urban areas).

Redistribution has been a core concern of WELFARE GEOGRAPHY with its focus on the unequal socio-spatial distribution of resources. The goal of reducing socio-SPATIAL INEQUALITY was central to the development of the WELFARE STATE which seeks to mitigate the social inequality fostered by capitalist ACCUMULATION by providing free or subsidized services such as health care and education, and cash transfers such as unemployment benefits and old-age pensions. According to Keynesian economic theory, such transfers had an economic as well as a moral rationale. It was thought that by helping to maintain the level of demand in the economy during periods of slow growth or recession, redistribution would reduce the risk of a major crisis of accumulation such as that associated with the stock market crash of 1929 (cf. FISCAL CRISIS). In practice, the extent of the redistribution provided by specific welfare states varied depending on their scope, the levels of benefits provided and the balance between universal provision and means-testing (Esping-Andersen, 1990). The rise of the New Right in the 1980s saw sustained political attacks in many high-income countries on the idea of progressive redistribution in line with the doctrines of NEO-LIBERAL economic policy. Neo-liberalism has been associated with a shift from the welfare to the workfare state, with the continuation of redistribution conditional on labour-market reform (Peck, 2001b). Work on redistribution within POLITICAL GEOGRAPHY has focused on the implications of the territorial restructuring of the STATE. For example, in devolved and federal systems, redistribution may involve 'fiscal federalism', in which the central (federal) level of the state arranges the transfer of resources between territorial units at lower levels. However, under NEO-LIBERALISM, a shift from managerial to entrepreneurial forms of urban GOVERNANCE has seen local agencies increasingly having to compete for a share of these redistributed surpluses (Harvey, 1989a). The forms of redistribution mentioned here mostly take place within the framework of the NATION-STATE, despite the fact that the greatest inequalities in income and wealth are between those living in high-income and low-income countries. In development geography, a concern with redistribution at the international scale is reflected in research on the politics of AID.   JPa

Suggested reading
Harvey (1989a); Painter (2002).

redistricting The redrawing of the boundaries of electoral districts (termed *redistribution* in the UK: see Rossiter, Johnston and Pattie, 1999). Redistricting can be manipulated to promote one party's cause over another's, as in MALAPPORTIONMENT and GERRYMANDERING. In the USA, the former was ruled unconstitutional in the 1960s, and redistricting is required after each decennial CENSUS (cf. RACIAL DISTRICTING). In most states, this is done by political parties, who deploy gerrymandering wherever possible to promote their cause. In the UK and some other countries, however, redistricting is undertaken by independent, non-partisan commissions, operating under legally defined rules.   RJ

Suggested reading
Handley (n.d.).

redlining A mortgage lenders' practice of mapping high-risk neighbourhoods by encircling them with red lines. Lenders refuse to extend loans in these 'redlined' areas because of fears of default. Redlining discriminates against ethnic minority, low-income, female-headed and 'non-traditional' households because of the NEIGHBOURHOODS in which they live. The practice has been widely prohibited but still occurs informally (e.g. estate agents/realtors 'steering' clients into select neighbourhoods). Severe consequences ensue for cities, including vacancy, dereliction and neighbourhood decline (Darden, 1980). Recent research suggests that lending discrimination is contingent on a combination of the 'RACE' of prospective borrowers and the characteristics of neighbourhoods in which they hope to buy (Holloway, 1998).   EM

Suggested reading
Darden (1980).

reductionism The methodological presumption that complex phenomena or events can be explained by their reduction to simpler, more fundamental entities. For example, rather than to talk about human behaviour it is better to talk about genes, or even more fundamentally strands of DNA molecules. Or, rather than talk about lightning, it is better to speak about an electrical discharge, or more fundamentally the flow of electrons. Reductionism as a strategy is especially common in the natural sciences that strive to decompose phenomena or events into their most basic constituents or causes. For example, under ontological reductionism, the properties of matter are reduced to sub-atomic particles, quarks and leptons. Or under methodological reductionism, the world, the universe and everything else are reduced to a single explanation, string theory.

Reductionism is also found in the social sciences, including HUMAN GEOGRAPHY. The exemplar is METHODOLOGICAL INDIVIDUALISM. In this case, the complexities of human behaviour are reduced to the single fundamental cause and typically cast as individual RATIONAL CHOICE. While it might appear that the diverse decisions involved around, say, choosing where to live, or from which retailer to buy or where to site a new factory have nothing to do with one another, in reality, say methodological individualists, they all obey the same fundamental logic of rational DECISION-MAKING. The facts and circumstances of each particular case can be eliminated because they are reducible to a more elementary set of formal axioms.

While reductionism as a methodological strategy is powerful and productive, seemingly yielding ever more secrets of nature and social life, it has been criticized on a number of grounds:

(1) The relationship among phenomena is holistic rather than reductionist. That is, the system *as a whole* determines how its parts behave. Reductionism therefore necessarily fails.
(2) Some entities, by their very nature – such as human motivations, emotions or sparks of creativity – are simply not divisible into constituent parts; there is always a 'ghost in the machine', to use Arthur Koestler's (1967) phrase. Humans cannot be reduced to Pavlovian salivating dogs or Skinnerian rats in a maze.
(3) Some phenomena or events are characterized by the property of emergence; that is, interactions of elements produce effects that cannot be predicted by examining the properties of those individual elements themselves (see also CONTEXTUAL EFFECT and COMPOSITIONAL THEORY).
(4) There is often something important in the original facts and setting that is lost when it is reduced to a different form. Translations are never perfect, and important contextual factors useful in explanation may be lost when reductionism is applied.

In human geography, reductionism was most strenuously applied during the period of the QUANTITATIVE REVOLUTION and SPATIAL SCIENCE. Then the complexities of geographical landscapes were reduced to supposedly more fundamental entities, such as the postulates of geometry or the axioms of RATIONAL CHOICE THEORY. Even after this period, reductionism remained important within the discipline. RADICAL GEOGRAPHY, for example, was often characterized by economism; that is, the reduction of spatial relationships to economic ones. Historically, however, the discipline has always emphasized the importance of context, attempting to keep geographical facts intact rather than reducing them to something else. This sensibility has taken on greater theoretical momentum in the wake of POST-STRUCTURALISM and POSTMODERNISM, movements entering geography in the 1980s and associated with an explicitly anti-reductionist agenda. Critiques of reductionism, and attempts to develop non-reductionist research strategies, are found in FEMINIST GEOGRAPHY (Pratt, 2004), CULTURAL GEOGRAPHY and ECONOMIC GEOGRAPHY (Gibson-Graham, 2006). TB

Suggested reading
Dupré (1993); Koestler and Smythies (1969).

reflexivity Reflection upon the conditions through which research is produced, disseminated and received. Emphasis on reflexivity often accompanies discussion of POSITIONALITY. Debates on reflexivity have emerged from FEMINIST research (England, 1994; Rose, 1997b), associated in particular with Donna Haraway's argument that all knowledge is SITUATED KNOWLEDGE (Haraway, 1991c), critiquing a 'god-trick' of disembodied, objective scientific neutrality. Reflexivity entails consideration of a variety of factors: personal biography, social situation, political values, situation within the academic labour structure, personal relationship to research respondents, relations of authority within the research process and so on. Reflexivity is thus a complex field, concerning EPISTEMOLOGY, politics and METHODOLOGY. Rose (1997b) critiques claims to 'transparent reflexivity', whereby an author assumes that reflexivity can produce a full understanding of researcher, researched and research context. Rose argues that such an approach risks playing a 'god-trick' of its own: 'we may be performing nothing more than a goddess-trick uncomfortably similar to the god-trick' (p. 311). For Rose, attention should instead be directed towards the uncertainties of research practice, and the emergence of DIFFERENCE through the research process, reflexivity becoming 'less a process of self-discovery than of self-construction' (p. 313). What might appear as failure from a perspective seeking transparent reflexivity becomes the spur to another mode of PERFORMATIVE reflexivity, 'webbed across gaps in understandings, saturated with power, but also paradoxically, with uncertainty' (p. 317).

In emphasizing self-conscious reflection, the term 'reflexivity' tends to downplay another meaning of the term 'reflex', namely the

Conroy Maddox, The Theorist, 1963, oil on board &
scissors, 24 × 30 in., 61 × 76 cm., Ferens Art
Gallery, Hull City Museums and Art Galleries
(Levy, 2003)

automatic or unthinking reaction to events.
Commentary on reflexivity and the situatedness of knowledge is not new, though the
vocabulary of such commentary may have
changed. In 1963 English surrealist painter
Conroy Maddox (Levy, 2003) produced
'The Theorist' (see figure), an oil painting
suggesting a particular attitude of mind, the
figure almost sculptured into the armchair, at
one remove from the external world, whose
relationship to that world is suggested by the
scissors forming the face. Maddox offers a
picture of a situated INSTRUMENTALIST, with
theory a device through which the world can
be accounted for, itemized, cut-up. Maddox's
image of the theorist personifies an outlook on
the world that has been the target of those
concerned to emphasize reflexivity, and the
situatedness of knowledge. In keeping with
surrealism's interest in the unconscious,
Maddox captures a certain image of a theoretical unconscious, whereby one whose work is
defined by THEORY risks their mind being colonized by indoor ABSTRACTION. Maddox might
have found it ironic that reflexivity can itself
on occasion be couched through abstract
theoretical language.   DMat

Suggested reading
Rose (1997).

refugees The term 'refugee' is widely used
in popular culture, legal circles and humanitarian emergencies. Broadly speaking, it means
people who have been involuntarily displaced
from their HOMES and dispossessed of their
livelihoods, normally without the protection of
their own government. The media often refer
to environmental refugees displaced from their
land by soil erosion over time, economic

refugees fleeing conditions of poverty in their
home countries, or even refugees as people
within the borders of their home country displaced by natural disasters (e.g. Hurricane
Katrina in the American South in 2005).

In international humanitarian LAW, however, the term 'refugee' is more precise. It
refers to people from one country who flee
political persecution or VIOLENCE to seek ASY-
LUM in another country. The political persecution and exodus of the Protestant
Huguenots from France during the late seventeenth century is often described as the first
modern refugee movement. Since then, refugee movements have been related to POST-
COLONIAL geographies (e.g. the PARTITION of
Pakistan from India in 1947), COLD WAR geopolitics between rival superpowers and their
allies (e.g. Cubans in the USA), geo-economic
conflict related to land and RESOURCES, and
WARS of NATIONALISM and independence.

Since the mass displacement of people in
Europe during the Second World War, the
concept of 'refugee' has taken on particular
legal meanings. The 1945 United Nations
Charter outlines a framework for the provision
of political and legal protection to refugees,
displaced persons and other vulnerable
groups. In 1951, the Convention Relating
to the Status of Refugees was drafted; it came
into effect in 1954. Along with the 1967
Protocol, these legal instruments represent
the pillars of international refugee law. The
1951 Convention definition includes anyone
who '. . . as a result of events occurring before
1 January 1951 and owing to well-founded
fear of being persecuted for reasons of RACE,
RELIGION, nationality, membership of a particular social group or political opinion, is outside the country of his [sic] nationality and is
unable or, owing to such fear, is unwilling to
avail himself of the protection of that country;
or who, not having a nationality and being
outside the country of his former habitual residence as a result of such events, is unable or,
owing to such fear, is unwilling to return to it.'

While 147 nations are party to either the
1951 Convention or its 1967 Protocol (see
below), it remains both explicitly and implicitly Eurocentric (see EUROCENTRISM). From
its conception, the Convention clearly demarcated geographical and historical limits. It
was designed to apply to refugees *in EUROPE*
displaced by events that occurred *prior to 1951*.
The Convention is characterized by its
Eurocentric focus and strategic conceptualization. The Convention definition of refugee is
spatially coded as European. Substantively, its

emphasis on persecution based on civil and political status as grounds for refugee status expresses the particular IDEOLOGICAL debates of postwar European politics, particularly the perceived threats of COMMUNISM and another HOLOCAUST. In emphasizing civil and political rights, the Convention has had the effect of minimizing the importance of other rights. The European geographical focus and emphasis on civil and political rights in the Convention have generated an exclusionary geography of asylum that is the source of contentious contemporary debate (Hyndman, 2000).

The Convention definition implicitly creates a hierarchy of RIGHTS, privileging political and civil rights of protection from *persecution* over economic, cultural and social rights and scales of violence broader than individual persecution. The definition was also an expression of Cold War geopolitics, grounded in relational identities of communist East and capitalist West. Notwithstanding the objections of several delegates from developing countries faced with responsibility for their own refugee populations, the goal of the Western states was achieved by limiting the scope of mandatory international protection under the Convention to refugees whose flight was prompted by an event within Europe before 1951. While states might opt to extend protection to refugees from other parts of the world, the definition adopted was intended to distribute the European refugee burden without any binding obligation to reciprocate by way of the establishment of rights for, or the provision of assistance to, non-European refugees.

The 1967 Protocol Relating to the Status of Refugees amended the 1951 Convention. While it rescinded the spatial and temporal restrictions of the Convention by lifting the Europe-based, pre-1951 stipulations, it merely created equal access for all member nations to a legal instrument that remained substantively Eurocentric in focus. In AFRICA, the perceived inadequacy of this pair of legal instruments resulted in the drafting of a legally binding regional policy by the Organization for African Unity (OAU). The 1969 OAU Convention Governing the Specific Aspects of Refugee Problems in Africa not only broadened but also reformulated the definition of refugee. It included the 1951 Convention definition, but added the provision that generalized violence associated with COLONIALISM and other kinds of aggression as grounds for seeking asylum.

In 1966, two legally binding HUMAN RIGHTS instruments were created to protect civil and political rights, on the one hand, and economic, social and cultural rights on the other. The International Covenant on Civil and Political Rights most closely expresses the emphasis of the Convention. It ensures respect for democratic principles and non-discrimination. The Covenant on Economic, Social and Cultural Rights includes provisions that are more applicable to developing countries than to highly industrialized ones, such as the right to FOOD, shelter, and basic medical and educational services. While the first covenant applies to individuals, the second refers to particular groups of people.

In recent years, human geographers have generated a considerable body of work on the subject of refugees, probing the GEOPOLITICS that displace them (Le Billon, 2008), the governance/governmentality of international humanitarian assistance that assists refugees and manages their mobility (Hyndman, 2000), and the politics of resettlement in a new country (Black and Koser, 1999; Dahlman and Ó Tuathail, 2005b). Those displaced by conflict and threats of persecution, but not across international BORDERS, are referred to as *internally displaced persons* (IDPs). They are conceptually and politically related to refugees, but are still technically under the legal protection of their home governments as nationals (see Brun, 2003). Geographers have been particularly active in tracing refugee participation in transnational political, economic and social circuits that traverse international borders (Al-Ali and Koser, 2002; Bailey, Wright, Mountz and Miyares, 2002; Nolin, 2006). Another emerging research focus among geographers has been the tactics of exclusion employed by states of the global NORTH [including Australia] to keep asylum seekers and other migrants at bay, away from their sovereign shores on which they could claim rights to seek asylum and other legal entitlements: references to the 'externalization of asylum' in Europe and the 'Pacific Solution' in Australia represent two cases in point (Hyndman and Mountz, 2008). Related to these tactics are geographies of containment in which displaced persons find themselves in 'protracted refugee situations' (PRS), spending years and sometimes decades in limbo, living in camps and without legal status. The United States Committee for Refugees and Immigrants (2008) calls this widespread phenomenon, which affects more than 8 million refugees, 'refugee warehousing'. (See also CAMP; EXCEPTION, SPACE OF.)   JH

629

Suggested reading
UNHCR (2006).

regime of accumulation A historically distinctive and relatively durable form of ACCUMULATION under CAPITALISM, based on complementary patterns of production and consumption, together with a supporting mode of regulation (an ensemble of organizational forms, networks, and institutions, rules, norms and patterns of conduct). Derived from French REGULATION THEORY, the concept of regimes of accumulation is most commonly associated with the analysis of FORDISM, the post-Second World War form of growth in North America and Western Europe, based on mass production/consumption and 'Keynesian-welfarist' modes of regulation (see Boyer, 1990; Jessop and Sum, 2006). Debates continue about the shape of the successor (post-1970s) regime, generically labelled POST-FORDISM.   JPe

Suggested reading
Tickell and Peck (1992).

regime theory An approach to politics that illustrates how different organizations interact in a dynamic POWER relationship under the umbrella of a larger project.

The term has become influential in urban POLITICAL ECONOMY in the emphasis upon the management of interests shared between the PRIVATE AND PUBLIC SPHERES that coalesce into the government of an urban unit (Stone, 1989). The particular nature of the regime is a function of the continually changing combination of institutions, their individually changing goals, and the manner in which they influence each other to attain self-interest within a broader project. Urban regime theory highlights the dynamic power relationships between institutions within a regime and between competing regimes. *Growth* is the usual policy common denominator that brings the regime together.

Geographers have offered constructive critiques of urban regime theory. Ward (1996) highlighted the difficulty of applying the theory in contexts other than the USA, where it was developed, and called for consideration of the mechanisms which provoke institutions to form regimes rather than concentrating on how they are maintained. Ward (1996) and Hackworth (2000) critique the localism of initial regime theory, and call for consideration of the role of the STATE APPARATUS at larger scales, such as the federal STATE (see FEDERALISM) or even the European Union (see REGIONALISM).

Urban regime theory was a response to the economism of previous state theory, but as a result lacks consideration of how regimes become agents of capital ACCUMULATION (Hackworth, 2000). Consideration of environmental policy has drawn attention to why it is easier to build regimes around particular polices and not others (Gibbs and Jonas, 2000). NEO-LIBERAL policies have placed greater emphasis upon GOVERNANCE at the urban scale. Simultaneously, supra-state institutions such as the European Union have required consideration of how regimes forge links across scales.

Regime theory also applies to co-operation between states and non-governmental institutions tackling problems beyond the purview of one state. Environmental, trade and arms-control issues are examples around which a regime of legal connections and accepted norms and behaviours are constructed. Concentration upon the idea of a GLOBAL COMMONS and COMMON POOL RESOURCES and how they should be managed in an international system of sovereign states (see SOVEREIGNTY) underlies this approach. Such a regime involves a power dynamic in which the nature of the norms and goals, and the means of maintaining them, are continually negotiated between institutions with differential power capabilities. For example, Evans (2003) illustrates how the ASEAN Regional Forum has adapted to the increase in China's economic and political capacities.   CF

Suggested reading
Lauria (1997); Rittberger and Mayer (1993).

region Most commonly used to designate: (a) an area or zone of indeterminate size on the surface of the Earth, whose diverse elements form a functional association; (b) one such region as part of a system of regions covering the GLOBE; or (c) a portion of one feature of the Earth, as in a particular CLIMATE region or economic region. The concept of the region, whichever meaning it has been given, has fallen in and out of favour, sometimes simultaneously.

The region has been subject to much examination as to its epistemological and ontological status (see EPISTEMOLOGY; ONTOLOGY). How are regions to be known and represented? Do regions exist in actuality? It is probably safe to say that most geographers who have dealt with these questions agree that regions are based on socially constructed generalizations about the world, that their delimitation and representation are artefactual but not purely fictions.

Few have disagreed, for example, that every pinpoint on the surface of the Earth is unique: the problem lies in looking past the uniqueness of mere points to say something of note about geographically bounded ASSEMBLAGES and distinctions and relations among assemblages (see also IDIOGRAPHIC). From this perspective, the artefactuality of regions is not that they are insubstantial (few geographers would claim that they are pure ABSTRACTIONS) so much as their definition demands disregarding certain details. The region in this sense is a 'way of seeing' that which exists, a device for organizing thought about the world; it is also, of course, the focus of REGIONAL GEOGRAPHY.

The above ideas have given rise to a set of specific terms used to describe regions of different kinds (see Grigg, 1965). *Formal or uniform regions* are areas defined by one or more of the features that occur within them; for example, a region of Catalan-language speakers or a mining region in some part of the world where mining dominates the economy. Formal/uniform regions are interpretive devices that some geographers have used to make sense of a fundamentally heterogeneous world. There are no purely objective measures, therefore, that dictate what proportion of Catalan speakers in an area make it a Catalan-speaking region. Nor are there universally agreed criteria about what would define a mining region – The proportion of mine workers to non-mine workers? Income generated by mining compared with non-mining income? The land area covered by mines? Criteria are set according to the purposes of designating such a mining (or Catalan-speaking) region at all. The *functional* or *nodal region* is a geographically delimited spatial system defined by the linkages binding particular phenomena in that area. Which phenomena? It depends on what kind of system we are interesting in knowing about. The paradigmatic example is the urban region, in which there is posited a spatially delimited network of transactions (e.g. trading) centring on an urban core, or central place, and spreading out into and functionally incorporating an urban periphery or hinterland. (The functional region bears a resemblance to the core and periphery of WORLD SYSTEMS THEORY, and shares some of its criticisms too.) A number of other regional terms have been experimented with, especially in the first half of the twentieth century: *single-* and *multiple-feature regions, natural regions, cultural regions, generic* and *specific regions*, and so on. The GENEALOGY of the region concept links it to related terms such as

the French *pays*. Most of these terms are not used with particular fervour any more, at least not in a disciplining defining sense, but the region nonetheless remains a core concept. Certainly, it has played a central role in suturing the different realms of HUMAN GEOGRAPHY and PHYSICAL GEOGRAPHY. And it remains a generative force in the GEOGRAPHICAL IMAGINATION (Hart, 1982; Pudup, 1988; McGee, 1991; Paasi, 2003).

The region is also an embattled concept, as Grigg (1965) pointed out several decades ago. Features that may stand in geographical relation to each other rarely spatially co-vary exactly. The grouping of different phenomena together and the drawing of boundaries around them are therefore by no means obvious. (Although BOUNDARY mapping has spawned a great deal of research, using the quantifying tools of descriptive statistics, factor analysis, and most recently GEOGRAPHIC INFORMATION SCIENCE.) There is the question too of whether the region is too static a concept, insufficiently attuned to change in the world, and whether regions have been understood too much in geographical isolation from the world. Grigg took these criticisms to mean that the region, especially its use by GEOGRAPHY, needs always to be understood as a means to an end and not an end in itself (cf. Hartshorne, 1939). The point of 'doing' the region is not ultimately to divide the world into regions and rest content. It is rather, if one wishes, to engage in classifying and modelling geographical phenomena so as to generate questions about their variability and functioning with respect to other phenomena. Indeed, for Grigg, whose essay appeared in a seminal text of the QUANTITATIVE REVOLUTION, the region *is* a MODEL.

In the 1980s and 1990s, some geographers proposed to solve the problem of the region by reframing the terms of study and ushering in a 'new regional geography' (e.g. Pudup, 1988; Thrift, 1994b; cf. Gregory, 1982). Spurred on by an interest in STRUCTURATION THEORY, SOCIAL THEORY, POLITICAL ECONOMY and LOCALITY studies, the goal was to see the region as a medium and outcome of social practices and relations of power that are operative at multiple spatial and temporal scales, among which the region might serve as a kind of fix. There was also in the new regional geography an explicit critique of an insufficiently spatialized social theory and political economy. There has been some debate as to whether the new regional geography misconstrued the concept and uses of the region during its heyday before the

Second World War, and specifically whether regional geography was an *atheoretical* geography (see Holmen, 1995). For now, debate seems to have settled down. GHe

Suggested reading
Gregory (1982); Grigg (1965); Hart (1982); Pudup (1988).

regional alliance An agreement between a group of neighbouring political units facilitating cross-BORDER co-operation. The term is particularly identified with SECURITY co-operation between STATES. NATO is the strongest such alliance, with the commitment that an attack on any one of the member states by an external aggressor is deemed as an attack against all of them. During the COLD WAR, the USA (NATO, SEATO, CENTO) and the Soviet Union (Warsaw Pact) created rival regional alliances. Since the terrorist attacks of 11 September 2001 (see TERRORISM), the USA has attempted to forge alliances with many countries, but none of the recent efforts have the intensity and breadth of the Cold War era. Post-Cold War changes and the break-up of the Soviet Union have catalysed new regional initiatives to facilitate TRADE and economic DEVELOPMENT (Pinnick, 2005) as states balance the promotion of economic interaction with cross-border security concerns, and manage security concerns no longer viewed as part of the Cold War conflict (McNulty, 1999). The increased pressure upon localities to be attractive to global INVESTMENT has also fostered local regional alliances to build transport and other forms of economic INFRASTRUCTURE that can not only enhance economic growth but also facilitate peace across international borders (Newman, 2005). The current geopolitical context shows that regional security alliances are in flux as NATO expands its border eastwards to include former Warsaw Pact members (Oas, 2005), but at the same time the European Union builds its own security apparatus that at the moment is deemed to complement NATO, but could succeed it. CF

regional cycles Fluctuations or cyclical waves in the level of a variable in a REGION. Techniques and MODELS for analysing regional cycles have been applied to both regional economic activity and to EPIDEMICS and the modelling of DISEASE. Cycles in economic activity, usually measured by industrial output or unemployment rates, can be very long-term, as with KONDRATIEFF CYCLES, or shorter-term, reflecting both seasonal variations in the demand for labour and the regional impact of national business cycles of expansion and recession. Some descriptive studies of regional cycles were undertaken in the early years of REGIONAL SCIENCE, but more recent work has focused on modelling the cycles. Economists have built regional (e.g. the State of California) and multi-regional (e.g. all the regions of France) econometric models. These relate macroeconomic variables of output, expenditure and employment at the regional level to each other, and to national economic and policy variables. Such models now exist for many countries and regions. A second approach, mainly by geographers, has studied the spatial DIFFUSION of regional cycles, tracing the timing and cyclical amplitude for different cities and regions. LWH

Suggested reading
Glickman (1997); King and Clark (1978).

regional geography The study of the variable character of places in the world, usually with an emphasis on their HUMAN GEOGRAPHY. Knowledge of world regional geography is often seen as essential to general education and a specifically 'geographical literacy', which is why it forms a mainstay of introductory survey courses in many universities. Critics frequently complain that such courses are little more than a fact-driven whirlwind tour, but regional geography has a long intellectual history and, like the larger discipline, its role, objectives and methods have changed over time. The authors of the better textbooks are very well aware of these considerations, and sensitive to the pedagogical possibilities they allow and the responsibilities they impose (e.g. Bradshaw, Dymond, White and Chacko, 2005; de Blij and Muller, 2007).

Regional geography is usually traced back to Strabo's conception of CHOROLOGY as the disciplined description of the parts of the Earth. As late as the seventeenth century, this continued to provide the model for what in early modern Europe was called *Special Geography*, founded – as Bernard Varenius (1622–50) put it – 'upon the experience and observations of those who have described the several countries'. Studies such as these may have contributed to a privileged, civic education, but they had larger purposes too. Just as Strabo's chorography informed the administration of the Roman Empire, so did Varenius recognize that Special Geography had a particular significance for both 'statecraft' and the world-empire of merchant CAPITALISM centred on the Dutch Republic and the city of Amsterdam. And both were haunted by their epistemological other: by the mathematical–locational corpus of Ptolemy's Geography and Varenius' own 'General Geography'. All three features reappear in the subsequent history of regional geography in Europe and North America: the production and circulation of regional descriptions for public audiences, the strategic application of regional intelligence, and the formalization of a spatial scientific dual to regional geography.

In the eighteenth century, a European GEOGRAPHICAL IMAGINARY treated 'EUROPE' as the master-architect of an intellectual grid, a sort of semiotic square (see table), in which 'AFRICA', 'ASIA' and 'AMERICA' were placed in distinctive and subordinate positions within a matrix of difference (Gregory, 1998b). These four cardinal orientations structured the production of regional stereotypes. These were in the main the products of European projects of EXPLORATION, whose results were circulated to a wider public through exhibitions, illustrations and published accounts of travel. In fact, TRAVEL-WRITING has been a vital source for the production of regions as bounded spaces possessing some sort of unity that makes them distinctive, 'special' or unique. Within this genre, regions are typically represented as distinctive zones set off from other regions, whose essential nature – at once a matter of 'identity' and 'authenticity' – is conveyed through both a narrativization of space (plotting the author's tracks) and an aestheticization of LANDSCAPE (producing a word-picture). Their IMAGINATIVE GEOGRAPHIES become sedimented over time, so much so that many contemporary travel writings by European and North American authors continue to sustain an elaborate textualization of regions as zones that re-inscribe eighteenth- and nineteenth-century stereotypes: 'the tropics' as a zone of excess, of primeval nature and human ABJECTION or plenitude and freedom (see TROPICALITY); 'the Orient' as a liminal zone of mystery and danger, eroticism and TRANSGRESSION (see ORIENTALISM); and 'the Arctic' as a limit-zone of solitude, silence and extremity (Lutz and Collins, 1993; Holland and Huggan, 1999). These are not (and never were) innocent representations, and similar ways of dividing up the world into regions and identifying their supposedly characteristic natures are activated within other public discourses, including the signature images associated by travel companies with places such as 'India' or 'China',

the stereotypes of 'the MIDDLE EAST' invoked by European and American media organizations, and the partitional vocabularies of 'BALKANIZATION', ENCLAVES and dominoes (see DOMINO THEORY) mobilized by contemporary GEOPOLITICS.

EUROPE	ASIA 'a space of opposition'
AMERICA 'the space of the future'	AFRICA 'a space of contradiction'

In the course of the nineteenth and early twentieth centuries, the academic discipline of GEOGRAPHY was drawn to the REGION as its central object of study. 'Object' is exactly the word: the region was seen as one of the basic 'building-blocks' of geographical enquiry. This METAPHOR clearly conveys the common sense of regionalization as both *partitional* (the world can be exhaustively divided into bounded spaces) and *aggregative* (these spaces can be fitted together to form a larger totality). This sensibility applied both to traditional regional geography and to the successor projects of SPATIAL SCIENCE. In the regional monographs written by French geographer Paul Vidal de le Blache at the turn of the nineteenth and twentieth centuries, for example, the regions (*pays*) of France owed their identity (or 'personality') to the local CULTURES that impressed themselves on the local landscapes (*differentiation*) and to their connections with other places within the system of the French NATION (*circulation*; see also AREAL DIFFERENTIATION). In the austere lexicon of LOCATIONAL ANALYSIS, regions were seen as cells within spatial grids. Thus Grigg (1965) argued that 'regionalization is similar to classification', and his account of the logic of regional taxonomy provided the basis for a series of formal region-building ALGORITHMS in which regions were treated as combinatorial, assignment or districting problems: in effect, as the product of purely technical procedures. To Haggett, Cliff and Frey (1977), therefore, the region was simply 'one of the most logical and satisfactory ways of organizing geographical information' (see also CLASSIFICATION AND REGIONALIZATION).

The regional-descriptive and the mathematical–locational impulses were both channelled into the production of regional knowledges during and after the Second World War. Indeed, one geographer claimed that 'World

War II was the best thing that happened to Geography since the birth of Strabo', because it placed renewed significance on regional geographies and regional intelligence. In the UK, a team of geographers was assembled by the Director of Naval Intelligence to produce a series of country-by-country Admiralty Handbooks, 'the largest programme of geographical writing that has ever been attempted' (Clout and Gosme, 2003). In the USA, geography's central mission within the Research and Analysis Branch of the Office of Strategic Services was to provide 'clinical' accounts of target regions, whose function was enhanced by the development of AREA STUDIES during the COLD WAR: in parallel, these regional studies were complemented by a mathematical 'Philosophy of Air Power' that was connected to the postwar development of a mathematical–statistical MACROGEOGRAPHY that heralded 'a new regional conception for geography' that was 'given purpose as part of a broader landscape of MILITARISM and WAR' (Barnes and Farish, 2006; see also Chow, 2006).

But the marriage between the regional-descriptive and the mathematical–statistical was a shotgun affair, and travel-writing and regional geography had little in common with spatial science. In the first place, they both placed a premium on FIELDWORK as the experiential ground for evocative prose, so much so that Hart (1982) hailed regional geography as 'the highest form of the geographer's art'. How many regional monographs ever reached those commanding heights remains an open question, but Lewis (1985) observed that even if few academic geographers were trained as painters or poets, there was no reason to boast about it. Spatial science found its own aesthetic in the elegance of formal analytical methods and models, and represented regions as little more than convenient ordering devices within an overwhelmingly abstract space. In the second place, travel writing and traditional regional geography sought to convey descriptions of both cultural and physical landscapes. Vidal de la Blache had assumed an intimacy between culture, landscape and region – between *paysan*, *paysage* and *pays* in rural France – that placed great demands on the sensibilities of the geographer. In contrast, spatial science was largely preoccupied with *functional regions* or regional systems in which the central organizing principle was to be found within a society largely severed from its physical landscape (see NODAL REGION). After the Second World War, for example, Dickinson (1947) proposed a focus on the city

region as 'an area of interrelated activities, kindred interests and common organizations, brought into being through the medium of the routes which bind it to urban centres', and ten years later Philbrick (1957) argued that 'the functional organization of human occupance in area' should be analysed *'independent of the natural environment'* (emphasis added) through a series of intrinsically geometric concepts: focality, localization, interconnection and discontinuity. These proposals formed a springboard for the subsequent leap towards the formal spatial analysis of regions as 'open systems' (Haggett, 1965, pp. 18–19).

Running in the depths of these different literatures and transgressing the boundaries they drew around regions was a sub-text that threatened to interrupt and prise open their compartments and closures. The journeys of explorers and traveller-writers, the capillary circulations that coursed through regions and the thematization of regions as open systems all spoke to the *porosity* of regional formations (the networks of connection between places; cf. CONTRAPUNTAL GEOGRAPHIES; POWER GEOMETRY) and to the *poetics* of regional description (the conventional, 'constructed' nature of boundary delimitation). These twin issues have since received explicit and substantial critical attention.

Even at its height, regional geography was criticized for its closures. Vidal de la Blache's celebrated *Tableau de la géographie de la France* (1903) was a portrait – some said a landscape painting – of the individual regions of pre-revolutionary France, produced through a method that critics said had little purchase on the post-revolutionary world. 'The region is an eighteenth-century concept', Kimble (1951) declared, whereas in the modern world 'it is the links in landscapes ... rather than the breaks' that matter. Similarly, Wrigley (1965) argued that the intimacy of the bonds between 'CULTURE' and 'NATURE' celebrated by regional geography was 'admirably suited to the historical geography of Europe before the INDUSTRIAL REVOLUTION', but 'with the final disappearance of the old, local, rural, largely self-sufficient way of life the centrality of regional work to geography has been permanently affected.' These twin objections were marked both by their European origins and a superficial understanding of INDUSTRIALIZATION and the dynamics of the capitalist space-economy (which produces regional differentiations rather than erasing them: see Langton, 1984; Storper and Walker, 1989). In fact, Vidal's later account of *France de l'est* (1917) was an attempt to wire the industrialization of Alsace-Lorraine to the wider geopolitical structures of France as a whole and, *en passant*, to challenge the legitimacy of its post-1871 occupation by Germany.

Recent attempts to situate regional formations and transformations as constellations or condensations within more extensive networks have been far more attentive to such concerns and in the 1980s and 1990s many of them were given a considerable fillip by WORLD-SYSTEMS THEORY and the analysis of the capitalist world-economy (see, e.g., Agnew, 1987b; Dixon, 1991; Becker and Egler, 1992). These projects were distinguished by a much greater sense of historicity – of PLACE and region as historically contingent process (Pred, 1984; Gilbert 1988) – which in turn made the 'bounded spaces' and 'building blocks' of conventional regional genres seem much less solid. To talk in this way is not merely to invoke Marx's description of capitalist MODERNITY as a world in which 'all that is solid melts into air', important though that is, because the tensions between 'fixity' and 'motion' that spasmodically interrupt and restructure regional formations are not the exclusive preserve of CAPITALISM, and are hence not contained by its history alone. Our present understanding of regions suggests that they have never been closed, cellular, bounded spaces: indeed, much of 'traditional' regional geography may turn out to have been about inventing a 'traditional' world of supposedly immobile, introspective and irredeemably localized cultures. Many anthropologists, geographers, historians and others now accept that non-capitalist worlds have also always been actively engaged in other worlds, and that they have also always been constituted through their involvement in trans-local and trans-regional networks.

In order to develop historical geographies of regional (trans)formation that are open to these possibilities, it is not enough to locate regions within progressively larger global frameworks or to identify the 'regional' as one level within an interlocking system of different SCALES. One of the persistent difficulties of such approaches is that regions become products of processes that are located 'on the outside' – in the absolute spaces of the containing frameworks and coordinate systems – so that regions become surfaces that merely register the impacts of GLOBALIZATION, of successive rounds of capital ACCUMULATION or the DIVISION OF LABOUR, or of cycles of TIME–SPACE COMPRESSION that are seen as enframing them. Against these ways of figuring the world, many scholars now argue that

such processes are also 'on the inside' – indeed, that the demarcations between 'outside' and 'inside' are deeply problematic and made more so by what Hardt and Negri (2000, pp. 194–5) call 'Empire', where 'the modern dialectic of inside and outside has been replaced by a play of degrees and intensities, of hybridities and artificiality'. Whatever one makes of this particular thesis, there is a broad consensus within human geography that regional formations are more or less impermanent condensations of institutions and objects, people and practices that are intimately involved in the operation and outcome of local, trans-local and trans-regional processes. For much the same reason, even though the 'regional' has constantly been hypostatized as the quintessential scale of geographical analysis, many writers have become much more attentive to the ways in which these scalar distinctions have been historically produced. It is through these productions, at once material and discursive, that regional structures have become sedimented in imaginative geographies, in material landscapes, and in PUBLIC POLICY.

The theorization of regional formations as partial, porous, hybrid condensations of entangled networks between human and nonhuman actants, each of different spans and with inconstant geometries, raises difficult questions of REPRESENTATION. How are these ideas and concepts to be redeemed in the fabrication of regional accounts? Part of the problem concerns the need to find ways of conveying these theoretical constructs in empirical solution: as Pudup (1988) observed, 'Anyone trying to mesh theory with empirical description [in regional geography] soon learns that movement among abstract concepts and empirical description is like performing ballet on a bed of quicksand' (see also Sayer, 1989). To some writers, the metaphor of dance subsequently seemed peculiarly appropriate: one implication of NON-REPRESENTATIONAL THEORY is that all human geographies need to become much more physically sensuous, much more expressive in their poetics. In the specific case of regional geography, there is clearly much to learn from careful, critical readings of imaginative LITERATURE, FILM and video, and from contemporary travel accounts that have tried to find the terms for the complex interpenetrations of cultures: what Iyer (1989) epigrammatically described as 'Video night in Kathmandu' (cf. TRANSCULTURATION). In doing so, authors have wrestled with some of the same demons that haunted traditional regional geography, and

635

above all with a sense of 'belatedness' – a sort of elegy for the world we have lost – that, on occasion, too readily modulates into what Rosaldo (1989) calls 'imperial nostalgia' whereby 'people mourn the passing of what they themselves have transformed'.

These issues are thus not confined to regional geography, and they admit of no easy solution. They also indicate the importance of developing an ETHICS of regional description and analysis capable of addressing both the subjects and the audiences of such accounts. The authors of regional geographies have an obligation to respond to questions of adequacy, accountability and authorization: What are their responsibilities to the people whose lives they write about? And they also have an obligation to convey places, regions and landscapes as something more than the lifeless parade of categories or the endless tabulations of statistics that loom so large in many textbooks of regional geography. There is a need to represent places and their inhabitants in ways that compel their audiences to care about them: which is why the 'openness' of regions – the sense of trans-local and trans-regional engagement and interconnection – is important not only intellectually but also politically. Whatever else regional geography is about, it surely ought to be about disclosing our involvement with the lives and needs of distant strangers. DG

Suggested reading
Barnes and Farish (2006); Paasi (2002); Thrift (1994).

regional policy Policy concerned both with the regional (normally thought of as sub-national) constitution and effectivity of ECONOMY, SOCIETY, CULTURE and polity, and with the economic, social and cultural constitution and effectivity of regions. These two aspects of policy are not binaries: they are mutually constitutive of regional policy. However, although always influentially co-present in policy initiation, design and implementation, their relative significance varies across space and time.

As objects of policy, REGIONS are subjected to attempted policy-led transformations designed to ameliorate UNEVEN DEVELOPMENT for reasons of SOCIAL JUSTICE, welfare and economic efficiency. Whilst contemporary emphases in regional policy are increasingly preoccupied with a singular concern for ECONOMIC GROWTH, these motives are not mutually exclusive. Regional policy is rarely purely redistributive. It is intended to be

transformative. Thus it may, for example, involve bringing work to (unemployed/low-productivity) workers or attempt to address the uneven distribution of cultural facilities (e.g. symphony orchestras, art galleries and theatres) or the regional availability of educational facilities (such as university disciplines, for example). Such policies are usually driven and financed from outside the region – albeit often with regional participation – by national or supra-national STATE bodies. In terms of policies attempting to address issues of welfare and social justice, what is inescapable here is fiscal redistribution and effort to direct the geographical trajectories of the circuits of value that make up economic geographies. And, in addition, national macro-economic policies are rarely region-neutral – as may be illustrated, for example, in claims for and against public expenditure in south-east England and in debates around the political and fiscal separation of the north from the south of Italy – whilst a range of policies (e.g. labour market policy, transport policy and welfare policies) have pronounced regional consequences even if articulated at the level of the nation or supra-national state.

Alternatively, regional policy may stress regional responsibilities for addressing UNEVEN DEVELOPMENT through regionally induced supply-side transformations – involving regional training, learning and innovation, for example – designed to increase regional economic efficiency, PRODUCTIVITY and dynamism. It thereby places responsibility for these transformations on local workers and firms – albeit with some support and encouragement (both positive and negative) of various kinds. Local responsibilities may also be emphasized through competitive bidding processes for major international events such as the Olympic Games, for licences to open and run casinos, or for resources to finance cultural renovation or the upgrading of institutions of higher education, or for investment in new or upgraded infrastructure – to encourage regional capacities such as public transport or cycling for a post-carbon age.

The claimed economic, political and social formative role of regions underlies their roles as subjects of policy. Economically, claims for the significance of regional context and proximity in enabling the intense development of a range of traded and untraded *interdependencies* and the emergent role of TRUST in cutting the TRANSACTION COSTS of economic activity, as well as notions of 'buzz' based around personal and face-to-face contact in enhancing the effectiveness of circuits of value and the incorporation of a wide range of local influences – including local institutions – enabling dynamic processes of learning and innovation, reveal the significance of regions in constituting productive circuits of value and hence in constituting economic geographies (cf. CLUSTER). Here, policy is based on the assumption of the critical significance of the regions in forming economic geographies and of creating the conditions of existence for the enhancement of regionally based processes of economic growth.

However, whilst such CONTEXTUAL EFFECTS are doubtless formatively important, it is easy to downplay the critical and inescapable – and hence deeply formative – material imperatives of economies and, more especially, the distinctive material objectives and dynamic geographies of CAPITALIST circuits of value in shaping regional economic geographies. Accounts of regional development focused on the geographies of global production networks held down in place by various contextual forces – including regional policy – begin to capture the essential DIALECTIC between these two sets of forces (material and contextual) that shape the economic fortune of regions.

Politically, strongly developed notions of cultural and political identity – as revealed, for example in contested relations between Macedonia and the Greek provinces of Makedonia, or in Basque and Catalonian claims for independence in Spain, and in Brittany or Corsica in France and the Chiapas in Mexico – point again to the formative significance of regions as the subjects of regional policy in wider political and cultural relations. Policy here is devoted primarily to the containment and regulation of regional aspirations. However, the geography of regional awareness, IDENTITY and imagination is itself unevenly developed.

A number of overarching issues surround the design and conduct of regional policy. First, what is the region? Territories are often contrasted to relational notions of regions. Territorial notions view regions in absolute terms – as containers – or in relative terms – as formatively interacting containers. Proponents of the latter, relational view argue that regions are porous, open and fluid. They are shaped by relations of all sorts operating in a multi-scalar universe in which SCALES themselves are socially constructed, if often powerfully defended in political terms. In this view, regions are as much a product of external relations (like flows of capital and ideas) as of

those internal relations (such as the relations between people and NATURE that were the focus of classical REGIONAL GEOGRAPHY).

In fact, however, both notions of region are mutually constitutive. Territories are themselves made up of a variety of NETWORKS, and the 'internal' characteristics of territories are simply the outcome of the historical geographies of relational links within and beyond the region. In this way, time and path dependency (but not determinancy) comes to arbitrate between TERRITORY and relationality in regional formation. At the same time, territories and regions are constructed by BOUNDARY marking (often involving powerful relations of domination and inducement) and by influential centres of calculation operating within and beyond the state (e.g. in academia) constructing statistical definitions and accounts of them. In such ways, regions may be invented in much the same way that national economies are invented through the technologies of their description and analysis.

Thus the question of who speaks for the region – who has voice in identifying the region and regional policy – becomes critically important. Given the widespread interest in the region as a long-constituted expression of distinctive and integrative social identity, it is all too easy (or convenient) in policy formulation and assessment to assume a unity of purpose and a homogeneity in regions in which diversity and contestation may be inherent. Politico-religious and class-based regional conflicts such as those in Northern Ireland during the 'troubles', or class-based conflicts of interests in regions such as the North East of England, with a long historical geography of social development based on deeply held and long-standing CLASS divisions, reveal how simplistic such assumptions may be. And, of course, speaking for the region may emanate from outside the region (e.g. from national or supra-national interests) at least as much as from within. Voice – and who has it – becomes even more significant in regions with clear aspirations to autonomy or independence.

Related to such questions around the construction of regional policy is the whole complex of issues surrounding notions of GOVERNMENTALITY and the ongoing (or not) legitimacy of the authority to govern. With the spread of DEVOLUTION around the world, the region and regional policy are deeply implicated in the emergence and negotiation of multi-level patterns of GOVERNANCE. This involves the legitimacy of different levels of government, and the distribution of resources and responsibilities between them. Such changes and the debates around them are closely related to changing notions of government – including the move from the political representation of individuals and places to the economic, social, cultural and political responsibility of individuals and places – as the distinctions between the STATE, CIVIL SOCIETY and ECONOMY are dissolved and recombined in the attempt to maintain political legitimacy in the face of such changes and the globalizing geographies (see GLOBALIZATION) that shape them. But beyond this, questions of governance open up the questions of how who gets to speak for regions and how regional policy gets to take place. Central here is the issue of expertise and the establishment of policy norms and target-setting, which enables governmental action on regions and the possibility of the emergence of creative capacity within regions. However, just as such capacities (or the lack of them) do not guarantee 'success' – whoever may define it – neither does it enhance the possibilities of more participatory forms of democracy. This is, perhaps, especially true of regions long suffering from economic decline and the withering of circuits of value. Hence the political issue of the relations and modalities of power between regional and national/supra-national governance becomes central if the question of uneven development is to be addressed head-on in policy formulation. But, of course, this does not mean that regional economic policies, for example, will be based on the pursuit of social justice rather than of economic effectivity.

Such norms and targets raise a fourth overarching issue concerning the objectives of regional policies. For example, economic policies are increasingly narrowly formatted around issues of competitiveness and PRODUCTIVITY as measured through profitability. Not only does this framing ignore a range of issues such as the work that takes place – and goes largely unmeasured – beyond the capitalist economy, as well as the diverse norms and social relations involved in materially effective circuits of value, including – but not reducible to – the social economy lying outside the mainstream, but it also tends towards reductive notions of processes such as INNOVATION defined in terms merely of contributions to profitability.

Finally, the long-standing significance of the region as a focus of distinctive identities and even loyalties – and this not least as a consequence of the crucial role of historical economic geographies in shaping a sense of belonging, albeit contested and conflicting belonging – combines in a potentially problematic fashion with the notion of the region as a formative economic, social and political entity and a constructed object of policy in which regional responsibility for development is stressed. Under these circumstances, in which the region is perceived as a REPRESENTATION of meaning and practice, blame is all too readily attached to the victim. However, this tendency may be countered from the perspective of geographical POLITICAL ECONOMY. This way of understanding is capable of recognizing not only the role of people in making their own geographies (if not necessarily under the conditions and constraints that they would choose) and the genuine material constraints on regional development (which mark the economic, political, cultural and geographical limits of regional responsibilities for the construction of geographies), but the political possibilities in the pursuit of policies capable of sustaining locally distinctive as well as materially, socially, politically and culturally effective regions. RL

Suggested reading
Amin, Massey and Thrift (2003); Coe, Hess, Yeung, Dicken and Henderson (2004); Hudson (2007); Lovering (1999); Macleod and Jones (2007); Regional Studies Association (2007); Rodriguez-Pose and Gill (2004); Scott (1998); Scott and Storper (2003).

regional science A hybrid discipline originating in the early 1950s that combined NEOCLASSICAL ECONOMICS and QUANTITATIVE METHODS to analyse spatial issues in economics, HUMAN GEOGRAPHY and planning. Regional science was the vision of a single man, the American economist Walter Isard (1919–). Isard roundly criticized the assumption of the a-spatial 'pin-head' ECONOMY found in standard economic theory, and provided an alternative version based upon LOCATION THEORY, and in 1954 he convened the first meeting of the Regional Science Association in Detroit. Partly because of Isard's indefatigable energy, and partly because of the movement's fortuitous emergence in a period of significant American regional and urban growth, regional science rapidly expanded, increasing its membership, forming new university departments, inaugurating journals such as the *Proceedings* of the Regional Science Association and then, in 1958, the

Journal of Regional Science, initiating international branches (Europe in 1961, Asia in 1963) and attracting attention from cognate disciplines. One of those was ECONOMIC GEOGRAPHY, and for a period in the 1960s – the halcyon years of the QUANTITATIVE REVOLUTION and SPATIAL SCIENCE – the agendas of the two were symbiotically linked. The 1970s began a reversal of fortunes, as former allies such as economic geography increasingly deserted regional science, its practitioners caught up in the critique of spatial science, the concomitant advance of POLITICAL ECONOMY through the sub-discipline, and the emergence of an avowedly RADICAL GEOGRAPHY. From the 1990s, competitors for the same intellectual (and artificial) turf cultivated by regional science emerged, such as the NEW ECONOMIC GEOGRAPHY, and university administrators turned sour (Isard's original Regional Science Department at the University of Pennsylvania was closed in 1994–5). Against the backdrop of two decades of intellectual and then institutional assault, regional science moved to the margins of HUMAN GEOGRAPHY and the social sciences more generally.   TB

Suggested reading
Barnes (2004c).

regionalism   A term referring to both a form of political IDENTITY and sub-national economic INTEGRATION. Attempts have been made to clarify the definition to delineate the 'old' regionalism of a political identity seeking autonomy or separation from the STATE (see SECESSION) and the 'new' regionalism of economic integration at the sub-national scale, which may include governmental administrative functions (Witt, 2005). Regionalism is seen as a theoretical and methodological vehicle to analyse new forms of GOVERNANCE within the context of neo-liberal policies (see NEO-LIBERALISM) and supra-state institutions (O'Loughlin, 1996). Further clarification is provided by Jones and MacLeod (2004), who distinguish between regional spaces and spaces of regionalism. *Regional spaces* are regional economic geographies of technological spillovers and inter-firm AGGLOMERATION that produce a regional clustering of economic assets (cf. CLUSTER). *Spaces of regionalism* are the '(re)assertion of national and regional claims to citizenship, insurgent forms of political mobilization and cultural expression and the formation of new contours of territorial government' (Jones and MacLeod, 2004, p. 435).

As governments restructure under the pressures of neo-liberalism and GLOBALIZATION, the politics of regionalism often does not distinguish between the regional economic policies and regional political identity. As Paasi (2003) has pointed out, there is an important difference between the identity of a REGION, or the classification of a space by government and other agencies, and the regional consciousness of individuals, or the degree and form of political regional attachment. Recent identification of a 'resurgence of the regions' refers to both the creation of regional economic spaces attempting to capture global investment by touting a regional COMPARATIVE ADVANTAGE as well as the political movements, such as Lega Nord in Italy, dissatisfied with membership in the existing state. Jones and MacLeod (2004) caution social scientists and policy-makers that there is no necessary relationship between regional economic spaces and regional political identity, which may cause problems for governments and the European Union promoting regional policies. Furthermore, both regional spaces and spaces of regionalism occur at various scales, and must be viewed as a political process involving conflict and negotiation rather than fixed political geographical entities. (See also REGIONALPOLICY.)   CF

Suggested reading
Allen, Massey and Cochrane (1998); Hönnighausen, Frey, Peacock and Steiner (2005).

regression   A statistical relationship between a dependent variable and one or more independent variables. The standard technique for regression analysis fits a straight-line trend through a scatter of points (as shown in the figure), with the line placed to minimize the sum of the (squared) distances between it and the individual points. In the formula for a simple regression (i.e. with one independent variable),

$$Y = a + bX \pm e,$$

Y is the dependent variable (shown on the vertical axis); X is the independent variable (shown on the horizontal axis); a is the *intercept* or *constant* term (i.e. the value of Y when X equals zero); b is the *regression coefficient* (i.e. the slope of the relationship, indicating the change in Y for each unit change in X); and e is the error term, indicating the degree of scatter of points around the line. The closer the fit of the line to all of the points, the larger the associated CORRELATION.

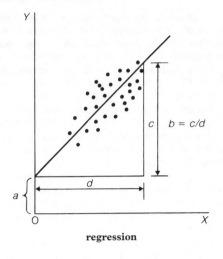

regression

Multiple regression equations have the form

$$Y = a + b_1X_1 + b_2X_2 + \ldots + b_nX_n \pm e,$$

in which each of the independent variables (X_1, X_2, ..., X_n) has an associated *partial regression coefficient* (b_1, b_2, ...) indicating the amount of change in Y for each unit change in the relevant X variable, assuming no change in any other X. (See also GENERAL LINEAR MODEL; GEOGRAPHICALLY WEIGHTED REGRESSION; LOGIT REGRESSION MODELS; MULTI-LEVEL MODELLING; POISSON REGRESSION.)   RJ

Suggested reading
O'Brien (1992).

regulation theory   A branch of contemporary political-economic theory, influenced by MARXISM, which seeks to explain the growth, crisis and transformation of CAPITALISM, with particular reference to historically, geographically and institutionally specific conditions. Regulation theorists balance a Marxian emphasis on the structures, 'laws of motion' and incipient CRISIS tendencies of capitalist economies with an appreciation of (a) the variability exhibited in forms of ECONOMIC GROWTH over time and space and (b) the complex of social and institutional forces that serve to channel and sustain particular forms of economic growth, and defer crises, over periods of decades. Here, 'regulation' does not simply denote laws and rules but, after the French *régulation*, refers to processes of social regularization.

The central concept in regulation theory is the REGIME OF ACCUMULATION, a historically distinctive and relatively durable form of growth, based on a particular nexus of production/consumption and a supporting 'mode of regulation' (an ensemble of organizational forms, networks, and institutions, rules, norms and patterns of conduct, including a distinctively capitalist STATE). Regulation theory rose to prominence in the 1980s, following the French regulationists' seminal analysis of FORDISM – the regime of mass production and mass consumption that prevailed in North America and Western Europe during the period between the mid-1940s and the mid-1970s. Fordism was accompanied by a 'Keynesian-welfarist' mode of regulation (including an interventionist NATION-STATE, a coordinated industrial relations system, a managed regime of international TRADE and finance, expansionist social welfare policies and the generalization of mass-consumption norms). Initially developed by Michel Aglietta, these arguments became well known in geography through the work of Alain Lipietz, Robert Boyer and their pre-eminent British 'translator', Bob Jessop.

Regulationist approaches became influential in GEOGRAPHY after the late 1980s, where they were invoked in debates around the decline and restructuring of Fordist manufacturing industries (paradigmatically, automobile production) and – more controversially – in the rise of putative successors to Fordism, such as flexible specialization, FLEXIBLE ACCUMULATION and POST-FORDISM (see Scott, 1988a; Tickell and Peck, 1992). For the most part, regulationists prefer to remain somewhat agnostic on the question of Fordism's successor, despite the evidence of extensive experimentation in flexible production systems and new forms of governance, since the criteria for regimes of accumulation emphasize the *medium-term* reproduction and interpenetration of these structures, most often demonstrated through historical analysis.

Subsequent regulationist-inspired work in geography has focused on emergent forms of institutional regulation and GOVERNANCE, which are evidently less centred on the national state than had been the case in the Fordist era (see MacLeod, 2001), in contrast with the rather more economistic tradition of the original French school (see Boyer and Saillard, 2002). In turn, regulationist concerns have shaped the growing body of work on NEO-LIBERALISM, raising questions about the character, origins and socio-economic implications of such MARKET-oriented modes of regulation. While strict adherence to regulationist principles has become increasingly rare in ECONOMIC GEOGRAPHY, the approach can be credited with helping to establish the widely held view that economies are socially embedded and institutionally regulated, rather than being guided by some 'hidden hand' of market forces. JPe

Suggested reading
Jessop and Sum (2006); Peck (2000).

relational database Relational databases allow tables to be joined using columns of data common to the tables in which the various data sets are stored. For example, if one table has a list of countries and population size, and a second the countries and their land areas, then relating one to another by each country's name permits calculation of population density. In GIS, the VECTOR data model is relational, storing the attributes and geography of objects in linked tables: for example, place named A [in table 1] has a boundary I [in table 2] that includes point 1 [in table 3] which has location (x, y) [in table 4]. RH

Suggested reading
Longley, Goodchild, Maguire and Rhind (2005).

relativism Understanding the production and justification of KNOWLEDGE as relative to the standards of the SOCIETY and CULTURE within which it arises. In emphasizing the social rather than individual variability of ideas and beliefs, relativism gives explanatory power to historical and geographical CONTEXTUALITY, and suggests that because knowledge is dependent upon context, truth will itself be relative. Relativism is opposed by UNIVERSALISM, which holds that true knowledge transcends context, and that reason can cut across contextual difference to judge the truth of knowledge.

HUMAN GEOGRAPHY has been concerned with both cultural and epistemological relativism. While explicit geographical arguments for relativism are rare, the term has a positive and negative presence in debate; as an approach consonant with long-standing geographical interests in cultural difference, and as an accusation levelled at those thought to be subverting the foundations of geographical enquiry. Cultural relativism is evident in anthropological enquiry concerned to understand the beliefs and practices of different societies without reducing them to some common explanatory schema. Fierce debate has proceeded over the moral and political consequences of cultural relativism. Geertz (1984)

argues for 'anti anti-relativism', criticizing the argument that challenging universal standards of cultural understanding and judgement leaves one unable to provide moral or political commentary on the world. Geertz understands the debate as an expression of anxieties, 'rather more an exchange of warnings than an analytical debate. We are being offered a choice of worries' (Geertz, 1984, p. 265). Questions of cultural relativism connect to CULTURAL GEOGRAPHY, but also to EPISTEMOLOGICAL questions concerning reason, rationalism, science and HERMENEUTICS (Hollis and Lukes, 1982; Bernstein, 1983), often raised under the heading of POSTMODERNISM. Relativism serves as a marker in the psychology of THEORY. Relativist worry is countered by the PRAGMATISM of Richard Rorty (1979), who suggests that relativism is a problem only because of the FOUNDATIONALIST vocabulary through which orthodox PHILOSOPHY condemns it. With a different vocabulary, relativism disappears as a problem. Such an argument has been regarded as political and moral evasion by those from both the political Right and Left, who present themselves as defending traditional standards and/or maintaining positions for progressive political judgement. Debates over POSTMODERNISM in geography reflect such tensions and antagonisms.

Relativism has informed debates in the HISTORY OF GEOGRAPHY, and the geographies of SCIENCE. Relativistic understandings, from PARADIGM approaches through to SCIENCE STUDIES work, have presented science as a social practice: Livingstone (1992) discusses the consequences for the status of scientific and geographical knowledge. Smith (2000a) considers the implications for the geography of ETHICS and MORAL GEOGRAPHIES, showing that relativism is a moral and philosophical impulse with its own history and geography. Whether this relativistic understanding of relativism confirms or undermines relativism is another matter. For many in human geography, the means to address or side-step such questions has been provided by arguments for SITUATED KNOWLEDGE, seen as a means to negotiate the twin perils/demons/temptations of relativism and universalism. Clear resolution of such issues is unlikely: indeed, pragmatist and/or postmodernist arguments would suggest that searching for resolution is futile, and desiring resolution misguided. DMat

Suggested reading
Geertz (1984); Smith (2000a).

relevance Concern over the relevance of GEOGRAPHY has been expressed since its foundation as a discipline; for example, in the promotion of geography as a practical science of EMPIRE. Consideration of how relevance has become a prominent word in geographical debate at specific times shows how 'relevance' can act as a marker for disciplinary disputes.

In the early 1970s, economic crisis, environmental resource debate and international conflict shaped debate on relevance, along with the sense that SPATIAL SCIENCE was becoming too abstract to gain purchase on PUBLIC POLICY issues (Johnston and Sidaway, 2004, Ch. 9). At the 1974 Institute of British Geographers conference, IBG President J.T. Coppock, building on earlier APPLIED GEOGRAPHY, outlined geography's possible relevance for governmental, planning and environmental agendas (Coppock, 1974). Among responses was David Harvey's 'What kind of geography for what kind of public policy?', questioning how definitions of relevance had been shaped by political and economic circumstances: 'The debate over relevance in geography was not really about relevance (whoever heard of irrelevant human activity?), but about whom our research was relevant to and how it was that research done in the name of SCIENCE (which was supposed to be IDEOLOGY-free) was having effects that appeared somewhat biased in favour of the status quo and in favour of the ruling CLASS of the corporate STATE' (Harvey, 1974b, p. 23). Exploring contradictions between policy demands and humanistic scholarship, Harvey sought a DIALECTICAL understanding of relevance: 'The moral obligation of the geographer, *qua* geographer, is to confront the tension between the HUMANISTIC tradition and the pervasive needs of the corporate state directly, to raise our consciousness of the contradiction and thereby learn how to exploit the contradiction within the corporate state structure itself' (p. 24).

Relevance re-emerged as a marker for debate in the late 1990s, prompted by concern over geography's CULTURAL TURN, and worries that in a period of notionally social democratic government in the UK and the USA, geography was missing a policy opportunity. A 1999 issue of the *Scottish Geographical Journal* addressed relevance in terms of recent theoretical debates (*Scottish Geographical Journal*, 1999), Michael Dear discussing POSTMODERNISM and relevance as pertinence, political commitment, and policy application, while Susan Hanson posed relevance as a feminist geographical concept, working within and across different scales (see FEMINIST GEOGRAPHIES). Martin (2001b), however, argued that particular uses of such theory were producing an increasingly irrelevant geography. With an element of envy at economists' apparent policy influence, Martin suggested that much contemporary ECONOMIC and SOCIAL GEOGRAPHY had little policy or social relevance, due in part to the cultural turn. Martin presents a particular sense of relevance, and a particular characterization, even caricature, of 'irrelevant' and theoretically indulgent cultural enquiry. The terms of debate are further explored by Staeheli and Mitchell (2005), who address 'the politics of relevance' and 'the social practices that condition relevance' (p. 357) through interviews with PUBLIC SPACE researchers and analysis of Association of American Geographers publications. The publication of Staeheli and Mitchell's article in the AAG's *Annals* underlines how relevance debates have proceeded through institutions representing the discipline.

Those wary of INSTRUMENTALISM in geography may in turn be wary of calls for relevance: pertinence may pass, commitments may wane and the relevant may become the untopical. It is important to appreciate and critique debates on relevance according to the temporality of their arguments, and to consider how geographical work not seeking immediate impact may nevertheless achieve different kinds of political and cultural influence. 　　　　　　　　　　　　　DMat

Suggested reading
Johnston and Sidaway (2004); Staeheli and Mitchell (2005).

religion Geographers approach the study of religion in a number of ways, from examining spatial patterns arising from religious influences, to the DIFFUSION of religious beliefs and organizations, the relationship between religion and population, the impact of religion on LANDSCAPE and landscape on religion, religious ecology, and the politics and poetics of religious landscapes, community and identity (Kong, 1990, 2001a).

The relationship between religion and geography may be traced to early Greek geographers, in their concern with cosmological models that reflected a world view shaped by religion (see COSMOLOGY). In the sixteenth and seventeenth centuries, the main preoccupation was 'ecclesiastical geography', the mapping of the spatial advance of Christianity in the world, propelled by the desire to disseminate the Christian faith. 'Biblical geography' also developed during this time, involving attempts to identify places in the Bible and to determine their locations. In the late seventeenth century, and particularly in the eighteenth and nineteenth centuries, nature was seen as a divinely created order for the well-being of all life. Scholars adopting the physico-theological stance ardently defended the idea that in living NATURE and on all the Earth, there existed evidence of God's wisdom. In the eighteenth and nineteenth centuries, following the lead of Montesquieu and Voltaire, the influence of the environment on religion was studied. Geographers adopted a highly deterministic approach when they sought to explain the essential nature of various religions in terms of their environments (see ENVIRONMENTAL DETERMINISM). This changed in the 1920s, when Max Weber's writings marked a turning point by inverting the earlier environmentally deterministic doctrine to focus on religion's influence on social and economic structures, and environmental and landscape change. Further, in the 1960s and 1970s, with environmental and CARRYING CAPACITY concerns, interest focused on the roots of environmental crisis, and a school of thought emerged that degradation was the result of the Christian belief that God gave humans dominion over the Earth.

Geographies of religion were sporadic for much of the twentieth century, and without major breakthroughs in perspective and approach, but especially from the 1990s onwards, the field has been reinvigorated. Kong (2001a) characterizes the emerging body of work as framed by an interest in the politics and poetics of SACRED SPACE, IDENTITY and COMMUNITY. Such research acknowledges that sacred space is contested space, just as the sacred is a contested category. Similarly, religious identity and community are subject to negotiations, embedded in relations of POWER, domination and RESISTANCE. Kong (2001a) urged geographers of religion to develop 'new' geographies of religion that emphasize different sites of religious practice beyond the 'officially sacred' (churches, temples, mosques, synagogues and the like); different sensuous sacred geographies; different religions in different historical and place-specific contexts; different geographical SCALES of analysis; different constitutions of population and their experience of and effect on religious place, identity and community; different DIALECTICS (socio-spatial, public–private, politics–poetics); and different moralities.

Since then, the terrorist attacks of 9/11 (see TERRORISM) have prompted new analytical attention to religion: most obviously to the rise of a distinctly radical or political Islam (Watts, 2007) – and here it is important to attend to the culturalist constructions of what Mamdami (2004) calls 'Good Muslim, Bad Muslim' – but also to the roles of Christianity, Hinduism and Zionism in shaping both provocations and responses to political VIOLENCE (e.g. Gregory, 2004b; Oza, 2007: see also JUST WAR). But this new interest in religion is not only political: the so-called 'moral turn' in geography, towards a renewed concern with ETHICS, has prompted Cloke (2002) and others to reflect on the place of the spiritual within HUMAN GEOGRAPHY, and Proctor (2006) and his collaborators to propose a new conversation between geographers on religion. LK

Suggested reading
Holloway and Valins (2002); Kong (2001).

remote sensing (RS) Literally, the sensing (study) of an object using instruments of observation that are remote from (not touching) the object. This includes medical scanning but, more commonly, the object is the Earth, which aerial photography and satellite-based sensors are used to observe.

The basis of RS is that different types of vegetation, landform and land cover can have distinctive spectral signatures, meaning that they emit and reflect electromagnetic radiation in different ways. The truth of this is evident by observing that features of the LANDSCAPE have different colours and temperatures. However, RS involves more of the electromagnetic spectrum than our human senses allow access to, using infrared detection, thermal scanners, radar and microwaves, for example. RS can be passive, detecting natural radiation from an object; or active, targeting energy (such as laser pulses) on to the object, from the RS device.

RS has its origins with Gaspard-Félix Tournachon, a French photographer and balloonist who took aerial photographs of Paris in 1858. It was developed during the twentieth-century world wars and the COLD WAR (a flashpoint of which was when Gary Powers' 'spy plane' was shot down over the Soviet Union, in 1960) and today is used for environmental analysis and monitoring as well as military SURVEILLANCE (see MILITARY GEOGRAPHY; WAR). In all cases, however, and despite the authority of techno-science invested in them,

RS data can be ambiguous, requiring careful interpretation.

One problem is that as RS signals pass through (for example) cloud cover and the atmosphere the signals are degraded. Second, although commercial satellites now offer very precise imagery (1–5 m resolution), if these are unavailable and if an object is smaller than the resolution offered by the sensor, then its spectral properties will be mixed with others around. Third, objects can be obscured by others above; for example, vegetation below a tree canopy.

In any case, human geographers may be less interested in land cover *per se* and more concerned with LAND USE, or the social meaning given to PLACES. A spectral signature is a co-production of NATURE and SCIENCE; the way in which places are constructed and used is infused with social praxis and signification. There is no necessary one-to-one relationship between the science and social science.

However, an interesting development within RS has been to use methods of IMAGE classification that incorporate geographical thinking. Standard methods of CLASSIFICATION generally are probability based (and Bayesian, notably the maximum likelihood approach: see BAYESIAN ANALYSIS). If it is known (from direct evidence) where various land cover types are located on some parts of the RS image, then it is possible to extrapolate and determine that the spectral signatures of other parts of the image more likely indicate one land cover type than any other. A more geographical approach is to classify PIXELS within the context of what is around them; to extract information about spatial configurations and associations that may say more about the land function than an aspatial analysis of land cover alone. Such techniques include space syntax (related to GRAPH THEORY).   RH

Suggested reading
Campbell (2002); Hillier and Hanson (1989); Lillesand, Kiefer and Chipman (2003).

rent Formally defined, rent is any payment to a FACTOR OF PRODUCTION over and above that necessary to keep it in its present use. While any factor of production can potentially accrue rent it is the analysis of only one factor – land – that dominates the discussion of rent within GEOGRAPHY. This is partly because the payment for land is pure rent (a consequence of the fact that land costs nothing to produce, and not the case for other factors), and partly because land is bound to location, thus lending itself to geographical analysis.

Rent is the price of land, and because land is differentiated by both quality and location, each land plot will have a different rent level. Two quite different approaches have been deployed to explain differential land rents. The orthodox view of NEO-CLASSICAL ECONOMICS treats land as any other COMMODITY, with rents set by forces of supply and demand. Rent is determined as in a giant auction, with rational buyers and sellers of land meeting to haggle over price. Those plots of land with characteristics most demanded given the available supply will fetch the highest rents, and in the process determine land use. In contrast, MARXIST ECONOMICS emphasizes the POWER of different social classes in determining rent levels. While land characteristics play a role in setting rent, they are always subordinate to a set of wider social relations characterizing CAPITALISM around the inequality of power and resource ownership. Without inclusion of this larger context, no analysis of rent is complete.

Both traditions have provided analyses of the role of land rent within explicitly geographical settings. The VON THÜNEN MODEL is the best known within the neo-classical tradition (Chisholm, 1979). Assuming that agricultural crops are cultivated at varying distances around a town, which is also the sole market, a competitive bidding process among farmers results in plots of land closer to the town centre receiving differentially higher rents than those farther away. In this case, the spatial pattern of land rents is explained by differential savings in TRANSPORT COSTS that allow farmers closer to the town to bid higher rents than farmers farther out. Rents are thus set by the supply and demand for plots of land differentiated by location. The von Thünen model has also been extended to explain rents within the city. William Alonso's bid-rent approach (see ALONSO MODEL) draws upon differential transportation costs of COMMUTING along incomes to explain urban land rents and residential land-use patterns.

The Marxist approach to rent is most associated with writings by David Harvey (1999 [1982]) and Neil Smith (2008 [1984]). Harvey draws directly on Marx's categories of absolute and monopoly rent to stress the role of CLASS power in determining rent levels. Landowners use their clout either to restrict INVESTMENT in the case of *absolute rent*, or to constrain the supply of land in the case of *monopoly rent*, to raise rents artificially above levels they would otherwise attain. Harvey initially applied the idea of monopoly rent to the city, but it has been Smith who has systematically worked through a Marxist analysis of urban rent. Key for him is the idea of the RENT GAP, which represents the difference between the actual rent charged for a given plot of land, and the potential rent that could be charged if that plot was developed according to its best use. For Smith, the rent gap is a result of the inherently UNEVEN DEVELOPMENT of capitalism. Only when the rent gap is significantly large will it be filled by landowners and capitalists colluding in a process of redevelopment, and producing maximum potential rents. Rent levels are not the consequence of unfettered market forces, but the deliberative power of social classes to intervene and manipulate for their utmost gain.   TJB

Suggested reading
Sheppard and Barnes (1990).

rent gap   The gap between the current RENT on a piece of land (the 'capitalized ground rent') and its potential rent under another use (the 'potential ground rent'). Developed by Smith (1979c) and emphasizing capital flows in the production of residential space, rent gap theory is a crucial element of the analysis of GENTRIFICATION. It suggests that disinvestment in inner-city NEIGHBOURHOODS reduces capitalized ground rent. When this rent is sufficiently lower than potential ground rent, opportunities for profit-making through reinvestment occur, leading to residential change. The theory has been criticized, however, for downplaying the role of individual gentrifiers' choices in shaping INNER-CITY neighbourhoods (Hamnett, 1991).   EM

Suggested reading
Clark (1995); Smith (1996).

representation   A complex concept not only because of the intricate disputes in ART and LITERATURE to which its traditional usage refers, but also because of the variety of its applications in modern and postmodern critiques of Western EPISTEMOLOGY (see MODERNISM; POSTMODERNISM). At its minimum, representation is conventionally defined as a symbol or IMAGE, or as the process of rendering something (an object, event, idea or perception) intelligible and identifiable. Bringing together the achievements of Renaissance art (the 'discovery' of perspective) and

ENLIGHTENMENT language (scientific objectivity, classificatory order), this 'NATURALIST' or 'REALIST' theory of representation is characterized by the relationship between two assumed metaphysical constants: the artist/viewer (or universal, visual experience) on the one hand, and NATURE (or the objects of external reality) on the other. From this perspective, the history of representation is the study of constant mutations reflecting the increasing sophistication of artistic execution in relation to the changing appearances of the world. However, morphology and advancing technical expertise are not by themselves history: indeed, 'history is the dimension [this understanding of representation] exactly negates' (Bryson, 1983). Recognizing this, representation is analogous to what Edmund Husserl (1859–1938) calls the 'natural attitude', a perspective whose increasingly fidelity to a reality 'out there' is as much a scientific and aesthetic practice as it is an epistemological premise. 'It is the aim of the sciences issuing from the natural attitude to attain a knowledge of the world more comprehensive, more reliable, and in every respect more perfect than that offered by the information received by experience' (Husserl, in Heath, 1972). It is Husserl's student, Martin Heidegger (1889–1976), however, who most decisively equates representation with science/knowledge and posits it as the foundation – and fateful flaw – of Western PHILOSOPHY. Manifest in what Heidegger called the modern 'age of the world picture', the representational model depends on the construal of truth as 'correspondence' or 'accordance' (Heidegger, 1962 [1927]). Representation or 'En-framing' (*Ge-stell*) thus not only assumes that the world is purely 'present-at-hand' (*vorhanden*), an object to be submitted to our pitiless and possessive gaze, but turns it into a 'standing reserve' for our technical domination and habitual instrumentalization. What such an attitude forgets, however, is that the 'world is never [that] which stands before us and can be seen' (Heidegger, 1962 [1927]). Rather, true experience for Heidegger is a matter of 'uncovering' the hidden, of revealing what might be concealed rather than accurately and anonymously representing what appears to be.

But if Heidegger's indictment of representation suggests a phenomenological critique (see PHENOMENOLOGY), other analyses insist on the historical specificity of representation and its implication in the production of knowledge. For Michel Foucault (1926–84), representation not only has a history but a precise moment of epistemic formation coincident with the onset of what he calls the Classical Age (1600–1800). Before the end of the sixteenth century, an age characterized by a theory of 'resemblances' or 'similitudes', Foucault argues, images and words were understood as decipherable hieroglyphs, as so many figural or iconic 'signatures' that bore intrinsic affinities to the things of a divinely ordained world. The result was an essential seamlessness, a 'non-distinction between what is seen and what is read ... the constitution of a single, unbroken surface in which observation and language intersect to infinity' (Foucault, 1977). For reasons that Foucault unfortunately fails to explicate, the Classical Age emerges when this unity is shattered by a growing awareness of the binary nature of representation; that is, of the discriminatory judgement of identity and difference, of the placing of things in differential relation to each other as the means to describe and systematize the manifold objects of the external world. Knowledge now begins to occupy a new space. It is the space *within* representation itself, inside the tools of its language, classificatory systems, and modes of naming and viewing. Natural history and concomitant taxonomic or tabular orderings of the world owe their triumph precisely to representation so understood. Importantly, the only thing that is not, and cannot, be included within this representational frame is the act of representation itself. Indeed, it is only in the absence of the viewing, naming and describing subject, that representation can claim its authority as infallible knowledge.

With this analysis, and Foucault's subsequent charting of the shift from a Classical to a Modern episteme, in which language becomes opaque as Man is arranged at the centre of knowledge, the stage is set for understanding representation as a discursive practice, as a kind of work (see DISCOURSE). Alternatively known as the social constructivist approach (see SOCIAL CONSTRUCTION), this perspective recognizes that while concepts and signs may have some material dimension (we do, after all, emit sounds when we speak, paint marks on a canvas, transmit electronic impulses when taking a digital photograph), the meaning of such things depends not on any pragmatic quality but on their symbolic and social function. It is for this reason that Ferdinand de Saussure (1966) preferred the word 'signify' rather than 'represent' for what words and concepts do: they do not describe a pre-existent reality, but constitute what counts and is valued *as* reality. Influenced by Saussarian linguistics and rehearsed within various registers of POST-STRUCTURALISM, the constructedness of representation is now a chief interpretive principle cutting across a wide sampling of contemporary theories, including those of human geography. Indeed, one can say that '*geo-graphy*', in its etymological connection to 'earth-writing', holds the idea of 'representation-as-text' at its practical and theoretical root (Cosgrove and Daniels, 1988; Barnes and Duncan, 1992; Duncan and Ley, 1993; Gregory, 1994).

However, acknowledging the constructed nature of representation is one thing; investigating the inherent partiality and limitations in anything constructed is another. Alongside questions of *who* and *what* it is that 'represents' (i.e. what enunciative, rhetorical or institutional position is involved in the act of representing) attention also has to be paid to the restrictions of the representational model: to not only what it excludes, but also what it inhibits in accessing the perceptual practices of our sensory and somatic lives. In recent HUMAN GEOGRAPHY, the disappearance of the textual dimension in so-called 'NON-REPRESENTATIONAL THEORY' offers one such address. Concerned to close the distance between subject and object – the very distance implied by representation as mediation, illustration or derivative sign-language – non-representational theory attends to how certain SPACES, experiences and states act directly on the BODY, addressing the manifold AFFECTS, sensations and, indeed, visibilities of the world in the subject's felt engagement with it. Here the *re* of representation, or the substitutive value that this *re* indicates, makes way for a certain intensification of presentation, for an immediacy of presence of which any secondary reproduction of the world can give no account (Dewsbury, Wylie, Harrison and Rose, 2002). JD

Suggested reading
Elkins (2002); Evans and Hall (1998); Jay (1993); Mirzoeff (1999).

resistance In HUMAN GEOGRAPHY, resistance has two distinctive meanings: political resistance, the more common usage, refers to resistance to domination or oppression; psychic resistance refers to unconscious attempts to maintain repressions of traumatic or dangerous memories (see PSYCHOANALYTIC THEORY). Pile and Keith (1997) discuss how the two concepts work in relation to each other.

Debates about political resistance crystallize key trends in CRITICAL HUMAN GEOGRAPHY. MARXIST GEOGRAPHY has a long tradition of studying collective organizing and everyday resistance to CLASS exploitation; and struggle against PATRIARCHY is well articulated in FEMINIST GEOGRAPHIES. The geographical embeddedness of political and cultural action has been explored in work on SOCIAL MOVE-MENTS, highlighting: how particularities of PLACE influence the emergence, character and strategy of movements (Routledge, 1993); what geographical dilemmas labour unions face in the age of global capital (Herod, 1998: and see LABOUR GEOGRAPHY); and the importance of social movements in shaping political and social geographies (Miller, 2000).

An interest in CULTURAL POLITICS and the persuit of the CULTURAL TURN led to two developments in the geographical study of resistance. First, the interpretative frame was enlarged to include myriad everyday symbolic and material practices, which contested not only class exploitation but also gender, racial, sexual (and other) forms of domination and oppression. James Scott's *Weapons of the weak* (1985) was a key text, in which he identified foot dragging, desertion, false compliance, pilfering, feigned ignorance, arson, sabotage and more as 'everyday resistance'. These practices required little or no coordination or planning, made use of implicit understandings and informal networks, and typically avoided any direct or symbolic confrontation with authority (1985, p. xvi). However, when almost every action is conceptualized as resistance, critical distinctions between effective and ineffective political resistance, and commitments to collective organizing and the coordination across different forms of domination, may be lost (Pile and Keith, 1997).

Second, resistant subjects were understood as authoring their political IDENTITIES in relation to multiple axes of POWER, and dominant structures, discourses and actors within society (Castells, 1997). Identity formation is thus complex in terms of both the multiplicities of identities negotiated by each individual and the HYBRIDITY of resultant resistance practices (see THIRD SPACE; Pile and Keith, 1997). Concerns with the latter have been influenced by Foucault's (1990 [1976]) version of POST-STRUCTURALISM, which views power as insinuated throughout all social activity, inherent in practically all social and political relationships. The operations of power, domination and resistance are seen as integrally rolled up

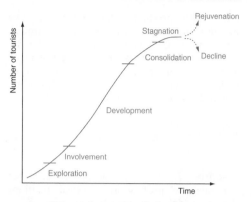

resort life-cycle model   (from Butler, 1980)

in articulations of society and SPACE, resulting in the entanglement of resisting and dominating practices; for example, through the creation of internal hierarchies, the silencing of dissent, or how various forces of HEGEMONY are internalized and reproduced within resistance practices (Sharp et al., 2000).

With the intensity of the processes of NEO-LIBERAL GLOBALIZATION, concerns over the ways in which the production of SCALE is itself an outcome of political struggle (Smith, 1993) are now turning to networked forms of politics and resistance (Grewal and Kaplan, 1994; Featherstone, 2003, 2005b; Routledge 2003; Massey, 2004). This challenges the way in which resistance has been previously theorized through bounded versions of space and PLACE, and is crucial for engaging with the dynamic transnational networks of opposition to globalization (see ANTI-GLOBALIZATION; TRANS-NATIONALISM). PR

resort life-cycle model   Originally developed by Butler (1980) (see figure), the tourist resort life-cycle MODEL depicts an almost inevitable pattern of development in five phases. First, there is a phase of *exploration* characterized by small numbers of relatively wealthy tourists 'finding' the destination. Second, local capital and populations become *involved* in developing the resort. Third, there is *development* as AGGLOMERATION effects lead to increasing returns. Thus as visitor and business numbers increase, the knowledge and skill base expands. More visitors mean more capital, which means more investment in facilities and accessibility, which makes the destination more attractive, and so on. This develops into a fourth phase of *consolidation*, where competition among increasing numbers of providers to gain large volumes of tourists

647

entails cheap products, which in turn have low margins and thus reduce further investment. The effects of expansion may also destroy the very qualities that once made the place appealing. The resort may exceed its ecological or social 'CARRYING CAPACITY', leading to a fifth phase of *stagnation*.   MC

Suggested reading
Butler (1980); Smith (1992c).

resource A deceptively peaceable term that conceals the profoundly political relations through which humans attribute value to the non-human world. 'Resource' is one of the core categories of MODERNITY: like 'NATURE' and 'CULTURE', its origins lie in the revolution of socio-natural relations associated with the emergence of CAPITALISM. The distinctions and differentiations enabled by the category of 'resources' – between productive, valued assets and unproductive 'wastes,' for example – are closely bound to notions of DEVELOPMENT and STATE formation, and play a key role in the organization of contemporary society. The 'productivist' associations that adhere to the term give it wide application beyond environmental phenomena: technology, skills and employees, for example, are frequently described as resources. These applications illustrate how the term captures a fundamentally *social* relationship: the attribution of (economic) value by a dominant group to attributes and capacities that provide functional utility for that group.

Traditionally, a 'resource' describes a product of biological, ecological or geological processes (game, soils, mineral ores, timber, water) that satisfies human wants (see NATURAL RESOURCES). The utility of these *environmental goods* and their contribution to human welfare may be experienced directly – for example, as material inputs such as FOOD and shelter that enable subsistence – or indirectly via its role in exchange. In addition to these classic productive inputs, the category of resources also includes a range of *ecosystem services*, such as carbon sequestration, flood attenuation and the maintenance of BIODIVERSITY, that are now recognized as critical to the functioning of the Earth's life-support systems (Costanza et al., 1997). Many of these provide important 'sink' functions by assimilating wastes produced during the use of environmental goods. There is also a range of non-extractive and non-utilitarian ways in which physical environments can be considered to provide 'resources': recreational amenity, aesthetic appreciation, moral worth and spiritual inspiration imply the attribution to the natural world of a complex range of value systems (see RESOURCE MANAGEMENT).

Work on resources engages with questions of value, knowledge, scarcity and SUSTAINABILITY that are at the heart of modern environmental geography. Three distinctively geographical understandings of the nature and function of resources have emerged.

(1) *Resources: neither natural nor cultural.* At the core of geographical work on resources is the recognition that resources are 'cultural appraisals' of the non-human world. This idea, which can be traced in the writings of nineteenth-century political economists such as Ricardo and Mill, is articulated most clearly by Zimmerman's (1933) aphorism that 'resources are not; they become'. In his *World resources and industries*, Zimmerman argues against the vernacular view of resources as 'material fixities of physical nature' and proposes that 'neutral stuff' acquires the status of a resource once it is recognized as having some functional value. Work by geographers has explicitly broadened the category of resources away from a restricted focus on physical stocks and flows, situating resources as an interface or boundary zone between societies and the vast range of different materials that biological, geological and atmospheric systems produce. Burton, Kates and White (1993) systematized this view of resources as an interface between human and physical systems, noting the symmetry between positive and negative social appraisals of the environment ('resources' versus 'HAZARDS'). Recent work on life sciences and BIOTECHNOLOGY questions altogether the categories 'human' and 'physical', and highlights the need for non-dualistic modes of thought within geography. To varying degrees, then, geographers have insisted that resources are hybrid forms, 'socionatures' that are neither purely natural nor purely social (Swyngedouw, 1999). By defying categorization as either nature or culture, resources highlight the insufficiency (and instability) of many of the analytical categories on

which modern GEOGRAPHY is founded (see HYBRIDITY).

(2) *Resources as relational.* Recent work by geographers starts from the premise that resources can be more productively analysed as a set of social relations between (often distant) groups rather than as discrete 'things'. This so-called 'relational approach' works against the reification of resources by turning the analytical lens back on to society: What is it about the needs and wants of a society, and the way a society is organized, that transforms a component of the non-human world into a resource in a particular time and place? (See also COMMODITY.)

At its most general, a relational approach de-naturalizes resources: it draws attention to how what counts as a resource is at least as much a matter of social, political and economic conditions as it is any intrinsic or inherent properties. More specifically, relational thinking about resources can provide a potent critique of popular assumptions that scarcity is an external physical condition setting the bounds of human possibility (Harvey, 1974a). In the face of neo-Malthusian claims about food, energy and other material shortages (see MALTHUSIAN MODEL), thinking about the social relations that define a resource highlights how access and availability are mediated by wealth and power: simply put, the rich and powerful do not starve. This insistence on the limits to resource availability being largely (although not exclusively) internal to the ECONOMY can be politically empowering, as it suggests how apparent shortages might be resolved not by increasing supply, but by changing the way in which resources are allocated within society, the uses to which they are put, and cultural expectations about the costs of use.

(3) *Resources: fighting words.* Resources have long been recognized as objects of geopolitical struggle and intrigue: control of WATER and OIL, for example, are frequently tipped to be the battlegrounds of the twenty-first century (Klare, 2002: see CONFLICT COMMODITIES; RESOURCE WARS). However, many of the most intractable contemporary political tensions surrounding resources are not struggles over a stable category, and it is the very definition of

lands *as resources* that is at stake. Thus recent work considers the cultural, economic and political processes by which parts of the non-human world are 'coaxed and coerced' from settings where they already may be valued in quite different ways (Tsing, 2004). While chimpanzees (LABORATORY experimentation), exposed uplands (wind power sites) and tropical agro-diversity (genetic diversity) are strikingly heterogeneous, what they share in common is that their status *as resources* (noted in parentheses) is achieved only in the face of opposition and resistance. The apparent objectivity and universality of the 'resource imaginary' disguises its particularity and the silencing of alternative conceptualizations of the non-human world. For example, to describe bauxite as a resource overlooks the pre-existing land uses and land ownership that must be undone to establish mines and realize the exchange value of the ore (Howitt, 2001b). It is for this reason that a number of authors refer to the 'VIOLENCE' of the resource imaginary, thereby placing resources at the centre of human geography's encounter with POSTCOLONIALISM (Braun, 1997; Peluso and Watts, 2001).   GB

Suggested reading
Bakker and Bridge (2006); Emel, Bridge and Krueger (2002); Rees (1991); Shiva (1992).

resource economics A practical art and field of study that understands NATURAL RESOURCES as a particular class of the 'scarce goods' described by NEO-CLASSICAL ECONOMICS, and that seeks to understand the opportunities and limitations of using MARKETS as the primary social mechanism for making collective decisions about their production, allocation and CONSUMPTION. Although recognizing that resource availability is finite in an absolute physical sense, a core axiom of resource economics is that any meaningful measure of a RESOURCE's availability must understand its relation to CAPITAL, labour and socio-technical knowledge – relations that can be expressed by reference to price (Barnett and Morse, 1963). A normative goal of resource economics is to improve utility maximization by attributing prices to environmental goods and services. GB

Suggested reading
Tietenberg (2005).

resource evaluation A component of the RESOURCE MANAGEMENT cycle involving physical, economic and/or cultural appraisal of NATURAL RESOURCES. Evaluation generates knowledge about a RESOURCE that is used to shape future strategies towards its use, CONSERVATION or management: it may, for example, provide a 'baseline' against which to judge the effects of human intervention; it may calculate potential commercial values of a resource for a range of possible uses; or it may be used to review the consequences and effectiveness of management strategies. Although often employed as a top-down administrative tool, participatory use of the techniques of resource evaluation can challenge 'expert' assumptions about the value, function and condition of a resource. GB

resource management The knowledges and practices associated with monitoring, evaluating, DECISION-MAKING and intervention in environments, with the objective of ensuring that these environments produce goods and services of value to SOCIETY. Resource management activities are undertaken by a wide range of actors and institutions, including private-sector organizations, national and local governments, COMMUNITY groups and HOUSEHOLDS. PEASANT studies and POLITICAL ECOLOGY highlight agriculture as the 'original' resource management activity: the farmer is a land manager who makes (highly constrained) decisions about inputs to and outputs from a plot of land.

Etymologically, 'management' conjoins two distinctive roles: the trainer or director (*managgiare*), and the careful housekeeper (*ménager*) (Williams, 1983 [1976]). Resource management is the 'applied science of possibilities' (Hays, 1959): the task of the resource manager is to ensure the orderly production of environmental goods and services over time and space. The codification of this role – and the elevation of resource management as a specialized branch of knowledge – first appeared on large European landholdings: von Thünen's work on land rent in *The isolated state* (1966 [1826]), for example, developed from a concern to determine optimal patterns of agricultural land use on his Prussian estate (see VON THÜNEN MODEL). Resource management science also developed as part of the COLONIAL project, as Europeans wrestled with unfamiliar tropical ecologies and sought ways to attain their control and maximize the yields of commercially valuable crops (Scott, 1998b). The emergence of RESOURCE management as a

distinctive social task marks a historical disjuncture: it is the point at which scarcity and abundance are recognized to be the product of social organization, and society begins the active production ('husbandry' or 'stewardship') of environmental goods and services that formerly had been taken as 'free' inputs. Recent efforts to develop planetary management regimes for global resources – BIODIVERSITY, global CLIMATE and the OCEANS – are an explicit recognition of this 'underproduction of the environment' and replicate a process that occurred earlier at the national scale for many productive resources such as timber, soils, WATER and game (e.g. the Conservation Movement of the early twentieth century in the USA).

Within GEOGRAPHY, resource management has been viewed as a promising vehicle for achieving the integration of HUMAN and PHYSICAL GEOGRAPHY (Johnston, 1983). Although geography programmes often contribute to the teaching of CONSERVATION and resource/environmental management, much recent human geography is critical of the knowledge-claims and 'utilitarian, reductionist, technocentric and market driven' practices of conventional resource management (Howitt, 2001b). Encounters between resource managers and indigenous peoples highlight the particularity and ETHNOCENTRISM of the instrumentalist 'resource imaginary', and the way in which conventional resource management works to empower those who share its EPISTEMOLOGY, while disenfranchising (and often dispossessing) those who do not. Yet there are a stunning array of other rationalities – aesthetic, spiritual, communitarian – and indigenous environmental knowledges that may provide alternative criteria and values for management. Recent work seeks to bridge the gap between expert and INDIGENOUS KNOWLEDGES via processes such as stakeholder consultation, the development of multi-actor management systems (that combine the interests of private, public and other interested parties) and community-based natural resource management. (See also NATURAL RESOURCES.) GB

Suggested reading
Bakker and Bridge (2006); Howitt (2001b).

resource wars Conflicts over the control of NATURAL RESOURCES are frequently simply called resource wars. Through much of the twentieth century, supplies of resources to feed and fuel industrial states were a matter of concern to war planners in many imperial states. During the COLD WAR, American concerns over supplies of minerals and OIL were part of its military planning. A large literature has documented the relationship between fights to control resources and GEO-POLITICS, although it has also pointed out that simple conflicts over resources are less frequently a direct cause of warfare than simplistic Malthusian assumptions of scarcity leading to conflict usually suggest (Le Billon, 2004: cf. MALTHUSIAN MODEL). The recent growth of the global economy and the ability to substitute and invent new materials in industrial processes has substantially reduced the concern with potential WARS over many resources on the large scale. However oil may yet turn out to be the 'resource war' exception that proves this rule.

Research in the 1990s gradually connected resources with contemporary VIOLENCE in many STATES in the global SOUTH. It became clear that in many places in the developing world where there were large supplies of natural resources, there was also a prevalence of violence, corruption and in some cases outright warfare (Le Billon, 2005). Research has now documented how this 'resource curse' distorts development by making the political elites who control the resource rents hugely wealthy, and in the process frequently stifles national economic innovation. It also makes clear that there are large incentives to fight to control the RENT from RESOURCE extraction, which, in the absence of a strong state and available economic alternatives, frequently fuels civil wars (Bannon and Collier, 2003).

At the largest scale, these matters are now of concern in the discussion of global oil supplies and the sometimes severely distorted political structures of oil-exporting states, in particular in the MIDDLE EAST. This now directly connects resource curse arguments with the traditional geopolitical themes of ensuring supplies for distant markets. In particular after the Iranian revolution, and during the subsequent war between Iraq and Iran in the 1980s, American military power became increasingly involved in the Gulf to control the flow of oil. This has grown dramatically as a consequence of invasion of Iraq in 2003, where the US policy in the region is now directly tied to enforcing the flow of oil, with all the potential this has for further violent conflict (Klare, 2004).   SD

Suggested reading
Klare (2004); Le Billon (2005).

restructuring Change(s) in and/or between the constituent parts of a circuit of SOCIAL REPRODUCTION, emanating from the dynamics of the circuit itself or from contradictions and crises within it.

Such changes may represent a response to changed conditions induced, for example, by TIME–SPACE COMPRESSION, technical change, or conflicts between labour and CAPITAL in the workplace, or transmitted through the competitive conditions endemic to CAPITALISM. The inherently competitive social relations of capitalism generate a permanent tendency to transformation or restructuring, but the term has come to be more widely used since the end of the long boom in the late 1960s and early 1970s (see CRISIS; MODERNITY). For some, it is a process closely associated with the transition from one KONDRATIEFF CYCLE to another or from one REGIME OF ACCUMULATION to another or with the speed of the circulation of capital and the increasing GLOBALIZATION of the world economic geography.

As such, restructuring may be thought to be synonymous with DEVELOPMENT (Streeten, 1987), or at least with certain forms of development. But it goes beyond that. Thus Laurence Harris (1988, p. 10) points out that although there is 'no easy, obvious way to distinguish structural from other changes in the abstract ... some periods seem to see greater and more significant shifts than others'. He identifies four such periods in the UK since the early nineteenth century: the 1830s and 1840s; the 1880s and 1890s; the 1930s and 1940s; and the 1970s and 1980s. But what marks these out as periods of restructuring? Apart from certain specific and system-wide components of changes (e.g. those identified by Harris, 1988, pp. 11–14), restructuring involves not just quantitative change but pronounced qualitative transformations of the ways in which CONSUMPTION, production and EXCHANGE take place and relate to each other. Furthermore, as a set of essentially qualitative changes operating on the circuit of social reproduction, restructuring necessarily involves transformations of the conditions in which such circuits create and find their conditions of existence.

At an extreme of structural change, such as occurred in the transformation of the former state socialist societies during the late 1980s (see POST-SOCIALISM), the social relations through which the dynamic, direction and mode of evaluation of social reproduction are shaped are themselves transformed and the circuit of social reproduction comes to operate on completely different principles, often associated with profound economic disruption and profound social pathologies. The parallels between *perestroika* in the former Soviet Union and capitalist restructuring are marked:

> *Perestroika* is inevitable when existing economic conditions do not respond to ... the needs of development of society and the demands of the future. Here it is necessary to change the economic system, to transform and renew it fundamentally. For this transformation restructuring is necessary not just of individual aspects and elements, but of the whole economic system. (Anganbegyan, 1988, p. 6)

This strategy for development – fatefully for Soviet SOCIALISM – presumed *uskorenie*, an acceleration of economic growth, and *glasnost*, or openness, to be achieved by the spread of DEMOCRACY and local self-management.

The more insidious, continuous and widespread social and political consequences of restructuring driven by the imposition of capitalist social relations and the norms, directions and criteria of evaluation that go with them within the THIRD WORLD are dramatically illustrated in Michael Watts' (1992) harrowing account of 'fast capitalism' and the exploitation of OIL in Nigeria.

Less dramatic but still profound changes may occur within the dynamics of particular forms of social reproduction, such as capitalism (e.g. Harris, 1988). Manuel Castells (1989, pp. 21–8) suggests that certain transformations of the capitalist MODE OF PRODUCTION on a global scale during the twentieth century are structural in form. Certainly, they serve to exemplify the point that restructuring is qualitative as well as merely quantitative. The Great Depression of the late 1920s and early 1930s and the associated disruption of the Second World War 'triggered a restructuring process that led to a new form of capitalism very different from the laissez-faire model of the pre-Depression era' (p. 21). The new model relied on restructured relations between capital and labour whereby stability in capitalist production was exchanged by the recognition of union rights, rising wages and the development of WELFARE STATES; Keynesian regulation and intervention in circuits of capital articulated primarily at the national scale; and the creation of a new set of international regulatory institutions around the INTERNATIONAL MONETARY FUND, underwritten by the POWER of the economy of the USA.

The limits of this model – manifest, for example, in rampant inflation, increases in returns to labour and FISCAL CRISES of the STATE –

were formative influences (for an attempt to assess the articulation of these formative processes, see Yergin and Stanislaw, 1998) on the creation and imposition of a restructured model of the circuit of capital involving the appropriation of an increased share of the surplus by capital based around increases in PRODUCTIVITY, changes in the LABOUR PROCESS and restructuring of LABOUR MARKETS in terms of: deregulation and reductions in the power of trades unions; a shift in the role of states from intervention to facilitation of capital ACCUMULATION; and further deregulation and opening up of local and national spaces to global competitive processes – not least through the increasing significance of globally sensitive and active spheres of reproduction (see ECONOMIC GEOGRAPHY), acting through global financial centres.

Restructuring may involve one or more of a number of transformations:

- STRUCTURAL ADJUSTMENT, which Streeten (1987, p. 1469) defines as 'adaptation to sudden or large, often unexpected changes' to an economic geography. Such changes may, however, be forced by powerful institutions such as the World Bank in, for example, making AID dependent on profound changes in macro-economic policy. Structural adjustment programmes have been designed to open up underdeveloped economies to the global economic geography in order to maximize their potential for development. In this sense, they may be viewed as a means through which the social relations of capitalism may be spread through the underdeveloped world in ways that make them secure for the future by insisting, for example on:
  - transformations in the modes of coordination and exchange within circuits of social reproduction (by, for example, opening up economies to the pressures of MARKET forces and international competition) with the objective of removing local rigidities and reducing vulnerability to shock through means such as increasing the flexibility of markets, the provision of productive INFRASTRUCTURE and the development institutions orientated to export markets;
  - switches of capital between forms of investment (direct/indirect), sphere of circulation of capital (reproduction/production/realization) and sector (e.g. DEINDUSTRIALIZATION);
  - geographical switches of capital (here/there – see NEW INTERNATIONAL DIVISION

OF LABOUR). Such changes clearly have substantial implications for the UNEVEN DEVELOPMENT of places (re/dis)incorporated from circuits of capital (see Allen and Massey, 1988; Allen, Massey, Cochrane et al., 1998).

More narrowly, the restructuring of production (e.g. Graham, Gibson, Horvath and Shakow, 1988) may have significant consequences well beyond production itself:

- changes in the process of production as a consequence of ECONOMIES OF SCALE, the concentration of centralized capital (see MARXIST ECONOMICS) or transitions from one REGIME OF ACCUMULATION to another (see REGULATION SCHOOL);
- changes in the organization of production along the production chain (see Dicken, 1998, Ch. 1);
- changes in corporate organization – such as those associated with forms of INTEGRATION within production, multidivisional organization and decentralization in the attempt to combine corporate size whilst maximizing entrepreneurial initiative within the organization;
- the development of tasking flexibility in production based, for example, upon ECONOMIES OF SCOPE or temporal flexibility based, for example, on JUST-IN-TIME forms of supply along the production chain;
- a redefinition of a firm's core activities, so redefining its sphere of activities, with profound implications for the size and status of its labour force;
- a repositioning of the firm along the production chain to deal with downstream service functions;
- a geographical reconfiguration to redefine the role and functioning of individual productive units ; and
- an organizational restructuring involving a redefinition of the firm's internal and external boundaries.

The restructuring of production in these ways has implications for, or may be undertaken through, changes in the labour process or the DIVISION OF LABOUR, but it relates to wider processes of change within which labour is necessarily caught up, and over which it has less direct influence than changes in the immediate conditions of work.

Although restructuring is a term applied mainly to economic transformation, and is frequently driven by and is obviously manifest in the activities of individual firms and capitals,

it cannot be restricted to the economic sphere. It involves, and so is predicated upon, responsiveness elsewhere in SOCIETY. Nor is restructuring reducible merely to economic dynamics. It frequently requires the support and or restructuring of the STATE or, as in the case of *perestroika* or the market-based restructuring around the discourses of monetarism in the USA ('Reaganomics') and, to a more dramatic extent, the UK ('Thatcherism') or New Zealand ('Rogernomics') cases, is driven by the transformation of regulatory practices instituted by the state and so generates a range of IDEOLOGICAL and political relationships and struggles (see, e.g., Walker, 1997). RL

Suggested reading
Allen, Massey, Cochrane et al. (1988); Castells (1989, ch. 1); Corbridge (1995, section 5); Walker (1997); Watts (1992/6).

retailing The marketing and distribution of COMMODITIES to the public. Retail geography is conventionally defined as the study of the interrelations existing between the spatial patterns of retail location and organization on the one hand, and the geography of retail consumer behaviour on the other. Retail geography is often situated at the overlap of related sub-fields, including ECONOMIC GEOGRAPHY, the geography of SERVICES and URBAN GEOGRAPHY

Work within retail geography appears to follow one of two broad trajectories. The historically dominant perspective is somewhat more applied, and neo-classical (see NEO-CLASSICAL ECONOMICS; cf. special issue of *GeoJournal*, 45 (4) (1998)). Since the late 1980s, a self-defined 'new' retail geography has emerged, in clear opposition to the former. Initially influenced by POLITICAL ECONOMY perspectives, this has subsequently become responsive to developing debates within CULTURAL GEOGRAPHY (for an overview, see Wrigley and Lowe, 2002).

Mainstream retail geography has certain general characteristics. Broadly speaking, neo-classical economic principles predominate, with considerable emphasis placed upon the structuring role of individual consumer decisions. This can be seen in the continuing influence of CENTRAL PLACE THEORY (cf. Parr, 1995), the refinement of which played an important role in the QUANTITATIVE REVOLUTION of the 1960s. With strong links to marketing (Jones and Simmons, 1993), retail geography is also applied in its emphases. Retail geography has conventionally adopted a specific spatial focus, with enquiry usually directed at the intra-urban and, occasionally, at the regional SCALE. The geographies of consumer behaviour and retail organization are also frequently theorized as some function of distance (DISTANCE DECAY), actual or perceived.

This perspective has come under challenge, as political economic and cultural perspectives have been brought to bear on retail geography. Initial insights were drawn from the allied field of INDUSTRIAL GEOGRAPHY, which saw the import of Marxist perspectives into spatial–economic analysis in the 1980s. One analysis, by Ducatel and Blomley (1990), drawing from Marxist insights into economic structure, sought to re-theorize retail CAPITAL both as a vital component of a larger capitalist system, and as characterized by its own internal logic (see MARXIST GEOGRAPHY).

Although this re-theorization has been criticized (Fine and Leopold, 1993), the call for a political economic perspective on retail capital generated a response, particularly in the UK. The 'new economic geographies of retailing', as Wrigley and Lowe (1996) styled them, paid particular attention to the phenomenon of retail restructuring. More recently, geographers have explored COMMODITY CHAINS and power relations between retailers and suppliers (Hughes, 2005).

Over the past decade or so, the 'new retail geography' has become more attentive to the cultural geographies of retailing. In line with a more generalized recognition that economic processes are culturally coded (see CULTURAL ECONOMY), retail geographers have again become interested in questions of CONSUMPTION. However, consumption is not seen simply as the unproblematic expression of consumer demands, but is understood as a critical site for the expression, reproduction and contestation of various identities (see IDENTITY). One question, in this regard, is the way in which GENDER roles are formed in retail spaces. Certain retail sites – notably the department store and the mall – have received particular attention (Blomley, 1996). However, it is interesting to see other retail spaces coming under scrutiny, including the car-boot sale (Crewe and Gregson, 1998). Excellent reviews of and commentaries on this literature are provided by Crewe (2000, 2001, 2003).   NKB

retroduction A mode of inference (particularly associated with REALISM) in which events are explained by postulating (and then identifying) the mechanisms by which they are produced. Those mechanisms realize causal powers, the potential causes of events that have to be activated (as with the striking of a match and the creation of fire): those powers may not be observable (as with gravity) and their existence has to be retroduced from appreciation of observed events.   RJ

Suggested reading
Sayer (1992 [1984]).

retrogressive approach A method of working towards an understanding of the past by an examination of the present (cf. RETROSPECTIVE APPROACH). The term achieved wide circulation through the work of Mac Bloch (see ANNALES SCHOOL), who insisted that the analysis of past landscapes required the prior analysis of the present LANDSCAPE, 'for it alone furnished those comprehensive vistas without which it was impossible to begin'. Likening history to a film, Bloch argued that 'only the last picture remains quite clear', so that 'in order to reconstruct the faded features of others' it is first necessary 'to unwind the spool in the opposite direction from that in which the pictures were taken' (see Friedman, 1996).   DG

retrospective approach A method, principally employed in HISTORICAL GEOGRAPHY, the focus of which is understanding the present, and which considers the past only insofar as it furthers an understanding of the present (cf. RETROGRESSIVE APPROACH). The retrospective approach, much advocated by Roger Dion (1949) in his study of French agrarian landscapes and similar to the historic-evolutionary approach in classical German CULTURAL GEOGRAPHY, considers that an understanding of the present LANDSCAPE poses problems of explanation that can only be solved by a retrospective search for their origins.   CW

The study of the past for the light it throws on the present (cf. RETROGRESSIVE APPROACH). The approach would make HISTORICAL GEOGRAPHY a prerequisite for contemporary analysis. Its most explicit advocate was Roger Dion (see ANNALES SCHOOL), who believed that a consideration of the present LANDSCAPE poses problems that can only be solved by a search for their origins; but the approach can evidently be extended beyond the analysis of the landscape and has much in common with 'genetic' or 'historical' EXPLANATIONS more generally.   DG

Suggested reading
Baker (1968).

revealed preference analysis Statistical methods, many based on MULTI-DIMENSIONAL SCALING, for deriving an aggregate set of decision-rules from a series of individual decisions, as in the choice of shopping centres by consumers. The individual choices are termed examples of *behaviour in space* and are particular to a given configuration (the distribution of shopping centres in one town, for example). The general rules, unconstrained by any particular arrangement, are the revealed *rules of spatial behaviour* (Rushton, 1969). Studies of other behaviours – such as voting – use similar approaches. (See also BEHAVIOURAL GEOGRAPHY.) RJJ

Suggested reading
Poole (2005).

rhetoric The term is classically defined as the art of persuasion and eloquence. The history of Western thought could be understood as a long quarrel between serious reason and rhetoric. From one perspective, ENLIGHTENMENT, rationality and SCIENCE overcome religion, superstition and magic. A counter-narrative sees in this process only the subordination of visceral, creative pluralism to soulless reason. The quarrel turns on a shared set of opposed pairs: reason versus passion, fact versus opinion, neutral versus partisan – *reason versus rhetoric*. This opposition underplays the extent to which rhetoric, as a classical discipline, was concerned with the ways in which audiences could be swayed through a combination of both reason and emotion. The epistemological significance of a consideration of rhetoric does not, therefore, lie in completely debunking the idea of truth. Rather, it requires a rethinking of the idea that the task of knowledge is for an observer to represent an independent external reality in a transparent medium: rhetoric's concern with the joint, shared aspects of gaining assent and persuading others suggests a contextual account of the justification of knowledge and belief (see also EPISTEMOLOGY).

In GEOGRAPHY, rhetoric has become a focus of attention in the wake of a more general revival of interest in this topic in PHILOSOPHY, anthropology, linguistics, literary studies and history (White, 1978; Clifford and Marcus, 1986; Nelson, Megill and McCloskey, 1987). This engagement has led to a greater degree of REFLEXIVITY towards the rhetorical strategies prevalent in the discipline, and how these inscribe particular orientations to audiences and publics. But geography's treatment of rhetoric has tended to fall into the familiar oppositional pattern noted above. The characteristic reduction of rhetoric to metaphor reinstalls the world/word binary. Interest in rhetoric has therefore been mainly restricted to debunking of the truth-claims of various research fields, as a kind of renewed IDEOLOGY-critique. On this view, the rediscovery of rhetoric helps us to see that all orthodoxies and norms are really just contingent constructs, whose reproduction is neither natural nor reasonable, but is really the effect of rhetorical strategies as part of political agendas.

There remain two areas in which a consideration of rhetoric might still have a creative impact on research agendas in HUMAN GEOGRAPHY. First, the *rhetorical-responsive* account of action, practice and subjectivity developed by Shotter (1993), and building on the tradition of Gilbert Austin, Mikhail Bakhtin, Kenneth Burke, Rom Harré, Paul Ricoeur, Lev Vygotsky, Ludwig Wittgenstein and others, retains its potential for redeeming the concept of discourse from the prevalent representational construal to which it has been subjected in geography, by returning it to a fuller sense of language-in-use and language-oriented-to-action (cf. REPRESENTATION). This in turn would have implications for methodological analysis of both archival data and talk-data generated in FOCUS GROUPS, INTERVIEWS and ethnographic situations (see ETHNOGRAPHY). Second, understanding rhetoric as the effort to move and affect audiences through various modes of appeal and persuasion points towards an alternative approach to the analysis of PUBLIC SPACE that investigates the different types of rhetorical *force* that are deployed to convene publics (Barnett, 2007). CB

Suggested reading
Fish (1995); Smith (1996).

rhizome Botanically, a rhizome is an underground system of stalks, nodes and roots through which a plant spreads horizontally and sends out new shoots. The METAPHORICAL use of the term has been associated with the philosophy of Gilles Deleuze and Félix Guattari (1987). For them, that which is rhizomatic is counterpoised to that which is arborescent, or tree-like. Unlike vertical and hierarchical arboreal structures, rhizomes are comprised of non-hierarchical NETWORKS within which there are many ways to proceed from one point to another. According to Deleuze and Guattari, such rhizomatic networks are resistant to and disruptive of ordered vertical and thus *striated* spaces, such as those of the STATE (see also POST-STRUCTURALISM). AJS

Suggested reading
Bonta and Protevi (2004); Marston, Jones and Woodward (2005).

rhythmanalysis A term coined by the French Marxist Henri Lefebvre (1901–91) to describe a mode of analysis characterized by its receptivity to temporal dimensions, particularly moments, cycles, tempo, repetition and difference (see TIME). Lefebvre (2004 [1992]) is concerned not merely with the analysis *of* rhythms – bodily, social, daily, seasonal, lunar – but also analysis *through* rhythm. In the latter case he is particularly interested in the way in which the study of rhythms can shed light on the workings of the modern CITY, EVERYDAY LIFE, the BODY and capitalist production. Lefebvre shows how SPACE and time need to be thought together rather than separately, and how a non-linear conception of time and history is a crucial balance to his famous rethinking of the PRODUCTION OF SPACE. Lefebvre's conception of rhythmanalysis may be contrasted with the more mechanical, high MODERNIST conceptualizations of Torsten Hägerstrand's TIME-GEOGRAPHY, but also can be profitably related to Ermarth's (1992) account of the crisis of representational time under POSTMODERNISM (cf. REPRESENTATION) and her own, quintessentially rhythmic sensibility that emphasizes repetition and pulse rather than linear sequence.   SE

Suggested reading
Lefebvre (2004 [1992]).

ribbon development Development strung along major roads within, on the edges of, or stretching beyond urban areas. It is generally associated with commercial establishments looking for cheap, easily accessible sites with high visibility to large volumes of passing automobile traffic. Ribbon developments are perhaps epitomized by the classic American 'highway strip', where development is often no more than one block deep on each side of the road. Celebrated by some as classic Americana, as worthwhile vernacular architecture, or as the spatial manifestation of market forces, ribbon development is increasingly criticized as an element of socially, economically and environmentally problematic urban SPRAWL.   EM

rights A right is a power or privilege to which one is justly entitled. Rights are often distinguished from duties (i.e. the behaviour expected of others, including the state) and privileges (that which can be conferred or invoked). Rights presuppose corresponding obligations upon others to do something, or to refrain from doing something. My right to freedom of speech, for example, requires the state to abstain from summarily repressing my speech. Rights are capable of several meanings, depending upon the context within which they are put to work. So, for example, moral and formal/legal rights may differ.

Within national jurisdictions (cf. HUMAN RIGHTS), formal rights can be subdivided. *Civil rights* refer to those entitlements of personal liberty given to all citizens by LAW (such as PROPERTY rights, freedom of association, religion, movement, and protection from arbitrary arrest). *Political rights* are those that bear on the establishment and operation of the state, such as the right to vote. *Social rights* entail the entitlements of citizens to social benefits, such as HEALTH or EDUCATION. The political priority accorded these different rights and their intersection is, of course, a crucial issue for any political community. Debate also turns on which entities can be legal rights-holders: Are we to include CHILDREN? ANIMALS? The insane? Ecosystems?

Rights are central to both statecraft and social life, and have become a standard feature of the constitutional apparatus of the modern STATE. Rights-claims carry special force: in ascribing rights to certain social relations, we 'shift them out of the realm of the merely desirable and into the domain of the morally essential' (Jones, 1995, p. 4). For Laclau and Mouffe (1985), a vocabulary of rights allows for the politicization of POWER relations. That which had been cast as subordination (i.e. as something that appeared natural and unchanging) can be reframed as oppression (i.e. unjust and contingent).

However, others worry at the ways in which rights can cast political SUBJECTIVITY in particular and limited ways, and reproduce contingent visions of the social and political world. For this reason, argues one strain of critical scholarship, we should be sceptical of the progressive potential of rights. Others counter by arguing that rights are 'protean and irresolute signifiers' (Brown 1997b, p. 86), whose varying and often expansionary meanings can be put to work in diverse political sites.

What, then, of the geography of rights? It is clear that SPACE shapes the ways in which rights are construed, contested and put to work (Blomley, 1994; Blomley and Pratt, 2001). Liberal rights (see LIBERALISM), most particularly, help produce, and operate within, sharply demarcated spaces. The way this 'sociopolitical map' (Walzer, 1984, p. 315) is produced may affect the ways in which subjectivity is produced, as well as shaping the political possibilities associated with rights (Marston, 2004b).

As Pratt (2004) argues, spatial REPRESENTATION can be used to close rights down as well as open them up. Representations of the spaces of the BODY, the public–private divide (see PRIVATE AND PUBLIC SPHERES) and the NATION can all serve to delimit or deny rights. And yet, Pratt argues, activists seeking to advance rights-based claims in defence of Filipino domestic workers within Canada have put other spatial representations – such as SCALE, international HUMAN RIGHTS and the 'empty space' of liberal universalism – to productive work. At an extreme, the peripheral and exclusionary locations to which marginalized groups have been assigned can also be used as a space from which to contest and challenge the ordering of rights (Chouinard, 2001; Peake and Ray, 2001).

The relation between rights and space takes on a particular dimension when it comes to PUBLIC SPACE. Public space is historically predicated on particular and related forms of territorial exclusion, with only certain subjects being deemed appropriate rights-bearers in relation, in part, to the degree to which they were imagined as fully formed citizens (see CITIZENSHIP). Yet public space, Don Mitchell (2003, p. 29) argues, is a site made through political struggle, as outsider groups, such as women, the working class and ethnic minorities, have fought their way into the public realm. Such a struggle necessarily entails rights. Again, rights can be used to deny public space to certain populations or can be used as a tool to pry public space, and thus, citizenship, open. Both rights and space, then, are said to be co-produced: social action 'always operates simultaneously to influence the production of law and the production of space' (Mitchell, 2003a).

It is because of the political valence of rights, and their spatiality, that geographers have become interested in rights in more than a descriptive sense. Lefebvre's (1996) call for a 'right to the city' has been invoked by those who seek to articulate a normative vision of space and social justice (Harvey, 2000b). However, much of this work, while interesting and even inspirational, remains under-theorized, and fails to engage the broader critical literature on rights, their politics and their geographies.   NKB

Suggested readings
Marx (1975); Purcell (2002).

risk In the first, technical, sense, risk refers to the probability of a known event (which may be a cost or a benefit) occurring. Such probabilities assume that causes and consequences can be determined, mapped and predicted. This is a highly rationalist endeavour characteristic of MODERNITY and a belief in controllability. Risk in this sense is about knowing the world, and is therefore not subject to uncertainty or indeterminacy. In order for such a probability to be calculated, the risk must be first identified (e.g. failure of an aircraft engine, the development of lung cancer, leakage of radioactive waste). The pathways to the event also need to be identified, and the likelihood of such pathways and events occurring needs to be calculated. The latter will often require some element of technical knowledge, but also an understanding of the social and institutional relations that surround a risk (e.g. the ability of a regulatory body to police possible risk pathways). In certain circumstances, probabilities can be calculated from past events (the chances of developing lung cancer from smoking can be estimated from population data). In other circumstances, where events are uncommon or where new technologies mean that there are few if any precedents, determining risk becomes more and more contentious. Not only are the occurrences or manifest dangers/benefits difficult to second-guess, but the pathways to them may be impossible to imagine prior to the event, and the institutions responsible for regulating behaviour may not be sufficiently established or experienced. Meanwhile, given the geographical, material and social complexities of everything from taking a drug to building a nuclear power station, the ability to calculate risk becomes ever more fraught with uncertainty and indeterminacy. The growing sense of the non-calculability of risks feeds in to a second, more qualitative, sense of risk. Here, risk takes on a meaning that has more akin with uncontrollability and danger. Most effectively taken up in Beck's *Risk society* (1992) and Mary Douglas' anthropology of risk and blame (Douglas, 1992), risk becomes a contestable issue in society at large. All calculations become liable to re-calculation or to rendering non-calculable. Controversies over risk become more and more common as various individuals and bodies contest each other's estimation of events and pathways, and dispute the ability of responsible or regulatory bodies to shepherd technologies, processes and markets in such a way as to minimize risk (the ongoing battles over the

657

environmental and human safety or otherwise of genetically modified foods is a case in point) (Bingham and Blackmore, 2003). The latter, institutional, element to risk debates has been taken up most effectively by those researchers who have investigated the dynamics of TRUST relationships between (expert) responsible bodies and (lay) publics (Wynne, 1992, 1996). At the same time, and partly on account of the inevitably of 'not knowing', risk enters the vernacular as something that should be encouraged, for if risks are not taken then nothing creative or new can be generated. Nevertheless, as Douglas (1992) and Lupton (1999) have argued, risk increasingly refers to the HAZARDS, dangers, threats and contingencies of actions. (See also BIOSECURITY; SECURITY.)   SJH

Suggested reading
Bingham and Blackmore (2003); Lupton (1999).

risk society An account of late modern SOCI-ETY, developed by the German sociologist Ulrich Beck in the mid-1980s (Beck, 1992), emphasizing mid- to late-twentieth-century shifts in (a) people's awareness and experience of uncertainties and dependencies, and (b) the manner in which late modern societies produce RISKS (see also MODERNITY). Beck's *Risk society* was in no way meant to suggest that life had become more dangerous; rather, it was the manner in which probabilities and uncertainties were generated and were handled that had changed. Life had become more contestable, and contested – there were more choices to be made, more matters to debate. Macnaghten and Urry (1998, p. 254) provide the following summary of these societal shifts:

(1) Public awareness of the riskiness of hitherto mundane aspects of daily life (e.g. foodstuffs, travel, work life, reproduction) had intensified.
(2) There had been a growth in the degree of uncertainty that surrounded those risks.
(3) People's sense of dependency upon the institutions and expertise responsible for managing and controlling risks had grown.
(4) At the same time, the degree of public TRUST in those institutions and in expertise to manage risks effectively had diminished.

These experiential and individualizing aspects of risk society, which have drawn on a CRITICAL THEORY tradition and which have much in common with Anthony Giddens' STRUCTURATION THEORY, have been readily taken up in sociology and geography (Beck, Giddens and Lash, 1994). However, it is the account's relevance to late modern technologies and environment that has perhaps had most geographical purchase (Beck, 1995). In the former, Beck's use of the term 'reflexive modernization' suggests a society more aware of its conditions, more able to deliberate on futures and their consequences. But this emphasis on the cognitive capabilities of human societies is undermined by another sense that Beck gives to reflexive modernization. REFLEXIVITY here refers to the 'reverberations' that actions entail (Latour, 2003). It is the realization that any action discharges a series of consequences, only some of which will be known or knowable prior to the event. Instead of more mastery through greater awareness, risk society signals a world in which 'we become conscious that consciousness does not mean full control' (Latour, 2003, p. 36). In this latter sense, Beck's use of archetypal examples of risk society technologies, including nuclear power (he was writing soon after the Chernobyl disaster of 1986) and chemical industries, emphasizes the shifts in the reach of these returns (risks involve larger swathes of SPACE and TIME; they contribute to GLOBALIZATION and affect future generations) and the entanglements that exist between what had hitherto been considered as separate spheres of SCIENCE and politics. It is here that risk society might prefigure a more progressive politics, not so much rooted in an inevitable individualization of life choices, but generating a sense of common matters of concern.   SJH

Suggested reading
Beck (1992).

rogue state A term coined in the USA in the 1990s, referring to a country that is believed to imperil world peace through its violation of international rules and norms. The US government claims to use the following objective criteria to identify a rogue state: an authoritarian regime that violates HUMAN RIGHTS; sponsorship of TERRORISM; and development of and trade in weapons of mass destruction. Critics claim that 'rogue state' is merely a rhetorical tool used to justify diplomatic and military action against a state that challenges the geopolitical goals of the USA (Hoyt, 2000), while others suggest that all three criteria rebound on the recent past and present of the USA itself.   CF

Suggested reading
Chomsky (2000); Klare (1995).

rural geography The superstructure of modern academic GEOGRAPHY was thoroughly metropolitan – London, Paris, Berlin, Chicago – but its foundations were in the countryside. Paul Vidal de la Blache developed his REGIONAL GEOGRAPHY through close (though not exclusive) attention to the peasant cultures of rural France, for example, while Carl Ortwin Sauer's vision of CULTURAL GEOGRAPHY focused on the evolution of rural and agrarian LANDSCAPES in the Americas. Even early LOCATION THEORY and SPATIAL SCIENCE looked to the countryside for their origins: VON THÜNEN's model of agricultural land use was based on records from his country estate, Christaller's CENTRAL PLACE THEORY was rooted in a stable world of southern Bavarian marketplaces rather than explosive urban–industrial growth, and Torsten Hägerstrand's DIFFUSION theory grew out of his studies of the Swedish countryside. But the distinction between CITY and countryside is a culturally constructed one (Williams, 1973), and there is an important tradition of HISTORICAL GEOGRAPHY in Europe and North America that has long been concerned with reconstructing its historical transformations (e.g. the work of the Permanent European Conference for the Study of the Rural Landscape, established in 1957: see http://www.pecsrl.org).

No less importantly, the distinction also varies over space. In Europe, and particularly in Britain, rural geography has recently been revivified as a response to a series of political and cultural concerns: the 'threat to the countryside' and to wildlife posed by URBANIZATION, the transformation of agriculture and the aggressive rise of AGRIBUSINESS (see also AGRICULTURAL GEOGRAPHY), the rise of new modes of RECREATION and the development of 'second homes' in the countryside, the changing CLASS composition of rural communities, and the ways in which all these issues are entangled in wider debates about the politics and PRODUCTION OF NATURE. These politico-intellectual responses have challenged the concept of rurality (Marsden, Murdoch, Lowe, Munton and Flynn, 1993; Cloke, 2006) and increasingly treated the rural as a series of cultural constructs rather than a set of geographically bounded spaces (Murdoch, 2003). In North America there have been comparable, historically sensitive studies of the exploitations and oppressions embedded in the production of agrarian landscapes (Mitchell, 1996) and of the IMAGINATIVE GEOGRAPHIES through which they have been domesticated, notably in LITERATURE and film (Henderson, 1999),

though probably few of those responsible would situate their work within a distinctively rural geography. Similarly, some of the most exciting work in POLITICAL ECOLOGY and environmental studies in America – Kosek's (2006) analysis of New Mexico's forests, Sayre's (2002) accounts of ranching in the Southwest, Hollander's history of the Everglades (2008) – has taken as its theatre of operations the rural broadly construed.

Still more generally, the classic AGRARIAN QUESTION has directed attention to the differentiation of rural producers, the contribution of the rural sector to capitalist accumulation, and the politics of class distinctions in the countrysides of the global SOUTH. Here, the vast literature on PEASANTS has rarely attempted to theorize rurality but has instead preferred to focus on social differentiation, the organization of work and household dynamics (Bassett, 2001; Gidwani, 2008). Analysis of the so-called urban bias (Lipton, 1977) and of rural–urban linkages has been especially fruitful in generating new questions about the formation of complex, hybrid urban–rural spaces (McGee, 1991) and about power, patronage politics and differential forms of accumulation across space (Hart, 2002; Chari, 2004). The World Bank's *World Development Report* for 2008 notes that 'three out of every four poor people in developing countries live in rural areas – 2.1 billion living on less than $2 a day, and 880 million on less than $1 a day – and most depend on agriculture for their livelihoods'. It also notes that rural POVERTY has declined over the past twenty years in East Asia and the Pacific, largely the result of improving conditions in the countryside rather than out-migration, but that the number of rural poor has continued to rise in South Asia and sub-Saharan Africa. A distinguishing characteristic of rural poverty is its disproportionate toll on women and the exposure of the rural workforce to the fragmentation of labour markets, and the impermanence and seasonality of labour contracts. Indeed, one of the central findings of the *Report* is the extent to which agricultural populations are dependent upon off-farm income, in which the structure of the rural, non-agricultural economy is crucial. The questions that dominate rural geographies in these regions include drought, FAMINE and global climate change (Watts, 1983a; see GLOBAL WARMING); the production of FOOD and access to WATER; dispossession and the politics of DEVELOPMENT; the violence of RESOURCE WARS and other forms of late-modern WAR; and the STATE regulation of MIGRANCY and MOBILITY. These issues are urgent reminders that the production and transformation of the rural is by no means confined to the global North and is everywhere enmeshed with GLOBALIZATION (cf. Woods, 2007; McCarthy, 2008). Despite the predictions of the imminent demise of the peasantry in the global South and the depopulation of the countryside in the North, the rural continues to be a site of political contestation, from debates over the agricultural policy of the European Union to the resurgence of rural protest in China.   DG/JL/MW

Suggested reading
Cloke, Marsden and Mooney (2006); Murdoch and Marsden (1994).

rural planning The attempt to organize and control the distribution of DEVELOPMENT and RESOURCES across rural areas: concerns include the management of land-use change (see LAND USE AND LAND-COVER CHANGE) in relation to the built and some aspects of the natural environment, as well as economic and social issues.

Rural planning in the developed world has two main functions: first, the strategic allocation of development through the production of frameworks and principles for resource distribution and CONSERVATION; and, second, the control of the alteration, growth and design of the built form (cf. ZONING). Tensions have frequently arisen in planning for rural areas between the many demands on rural land, particularly in the context of the changing importance of FARMING and FOOD production. In addition, pressure from COUNTER-URBANIZATION in many parts of the developed world has introduced conflicts within rural planning between the desire to conserve the natural environment and provide housing in desirable residential areas. In some rural areas, land-use designations such as NATIONAL PARKS have sought to maintain tight control on development and resource use in the most valued environments. In developing countries, emphasis is placed less on control but, rather, on the generation of economic growth in the distribution of resources and the organization of agricultural development.

The study of rural planning during the 1970s and early 1980s was largely descriptive and uncritical. From the late 1980s, however, greater attention was paid to the POWER relations within which planning operated, including the influence of social CLASS over the allocation of resources and the broader strategic direction of the planning process (Cloke and Little, 1990). Particular attention was given to the role of environmental politics in shaping planning agendas and outcomes (Williams, 2001). More recently, these discussions have been set within understandings of the shifting nature of GOVERNANCE within rural COMMUNITIES and of the relevance of new decision-making structures and responsibilities (Goodwin, 1998). Work on the emergence of new forms of rural politics has also helped to inform contemporary research on rural planning (see Woods, 2006).   JL

Suggested reading
Lapping (2006); Woods and Goodwin (2003).

rural–urban continuum A once-popular hypothesized continuous gradation of ways of life between rural areas and large cities. It assumed a polarization of attitudes and behaviours between ideal *rural* situations, on the one hand – characterized by COMMUNITIES built around kinship, attachment to place and co-operation (what Tönnies (1955) referred to as *Gemeinschaft*) – and large cities, on the other – characterized by SOCIETIES dominated by impersonal, especially market, relationships (*Gesellschaft*). Although some empirical studies found patterns consistent with the hypothesis, it was largely demolished by studies – such as Pahl's (1965) – that identified village-like communities within cities and urban traits spreading into the countryside.   RJ

rustbelt A descriptive term for the area of declining manufacturing industries in the north-east of the USA, now more widely applied to any area of industrial decline (cf. SUNBELT/SNOWBELT).   RJ

S

sacred and profane space Sacred spaces are sites imbued with a transcendent spiritual quality. They are characterized by the rituals people practice at the site, or direct towards it. Mircea Eliade, the scholar of comparative RELIGION most closely associated with the concept of sacred space, proposed that it is with sacred experience that sacred space is marked out from profane space. Whereas profane experience maintains the homogeneity of SPACE, the sacred disrupts that, creating non-homogeneous space (which is why sacred space figures so prominently in discussions of URBAN ORIGINS).

Eliade (1959, pp. 26–7) identified three ways in which sacred places are formed: when there is a hierophany (an 'act of manifestation of the sacred', such as a voice proclaiming the sacrality of a place); an unsolicited sign indicating the sacredness of a place (as when something that does not belong to this world manifests itself); or a provoked sign (e.g. using animals to help show what place or orientation to choose in setting up a village). Sacred places may also be made through the relics of holy beings.

Sacred places may occur in bio-physical or in built form. Animists, in particular, believe that some form of the divine exists in NATURE, though this is true too of some world religions. Thus, rivers, trees and mountains are religiously interpreted, and invested with symbolic meanings. For example, the bodhi tree is a sacred tree for the Buddhists, while the Ganges River is venerated by the Hindus. In built form, perhaps the most visible and obvious sacred spaces are the 'officially sacred' (Leiris, 1938) religious buildings, such as churches, temples and synagogues, though roadside shrines and home altars constitute other examples of sacred spaces too. In advanced technological societies, techno-religious spaces such as radio and television broadcasts and INTERNET-based communication also contribute to the making of sacred experiences through live telecasts of prayers and religious gatherings, for example, thus creating new conceptions of sacred space.

Chidester and Linenthal (1995, p. 6) argue that 'nothing is inherently sacred'. Sacred space is contested space. It is 'not merely discovered, or founded, or constructed; it is claimed, owned, and operated by people advancing specific interests' (ibid., p. 15), involving 'hierarchical power relations of domination and subordination, inclusion and exclusion, appropriation and dispossession' (ibid., p. 17). In these POWER relations, four kinds of politics are apparent (van der Leeuw, 1986 [1933]): a politics of position whereby every establishment of a sacred place is a conquest of space; a politics of PROPERTY whereby a sacred place is 'appropriated, possessed and, owned'; a politics of SOCIAL EXCLUSION, whereby the sanctity of sacred place is preserved by maintaining boundaries; and a politics of exile, which takes the form of a modern loss of or nostalgia for the sacred.

Sacred spaces need not always be sacred. The same space may be sacred at one time under one set of circumstances, but not sacred at other times and circumstances. For example, a house is ordinarily considered functional space, but in its design and the rituals practiced within, it may become sacralized.   LK

Suggested reading
Dunn (2005); Kong (2001a,b).

sampling Sampling involves selection from a greater whole and can be contrasted with a full enumeration or a CENSUS. However, even when a census has been undertaken, the outcomes can still be regarded as a sample of what could have occurred (another stochastic realization) – for example, on other than census day – so the concept of sampling has even wider applicability. It is an essential part of EXTENSIVE RESEARCH DESIGNS and SURVEY ANALYSIS, but is also important when qualitative data are collected and interpreted (King, Keohane and Verba, 1994). The most common reasons for sampling are the costs of measuring an entire population and the unethical intrusiveness of doing so.

Any sampling strategy is concerned with estimating an unknown parameter (such as the proportion in POVERTY, the mean income, or the total number in poverty) and its likely error, and involves trade-offs among:

- *Representation*: the ability to generalize from the sample to the (carefully defined) wider population.

661

- *Coherence*: the degree that the measured entity conforms to the theoretical construct being studied. This is particularly important in qualitative research when often necessarily small samples need to be theoretically relevant (Mitchell, 1983); consequently, for example, we need to define and sample the different mechanisms that place people in poverty (exclusion from the job market, divorce and separation, etc.) and make sure that each type is recognized and studied.
- *Bias*: the degree to which the parameter is accurately estimated, without systematic error; for example an INTERNET-based sampling strategy may seriously underestimate the extent of poverty.
- *Precision*: the degree to which the parameter is reliably measured and random, stochastic, innumerable small errors are controlled.
- *Efficiency and cost*: efficiency is the relative precision of an unbiased sample compared to others of the same size. Concern with precision can often be over-ridden by convenience, practicality and cost; moreover, it is generally much better to do a well-designed small-scale study than a botched large-scale one.

A highly convenient sample design (often used by commercial organizations) is the *quota method*, in which, for example, an interviewer approaches people on a shopping street until the desired quota of 25 each of young and old men and women is reached. This approach is simple but also open to bias, as certain types of people are not generally found in shopping streets; there can also be interviewer bias, as the interviewer may be resistant to approaching certain groups of individuals. Non-response is inevitably ignored in this approach. *Snowball sampling* is when having found a key informant (e.g. a drug user) they are asked to recommend others. While useful with hard-to-reach populations, there is again the potential for bias as isolated drug users may be missed and one circle of users may not intermix with others. A *systematic sample* is when respondents are chosen in an ordered way, such as every fourth house on a street. Such a design is highly convenient in an the field and when the total population is not known, but can produce biased results when the entity being studied has a corresponding systematic patterning, so that all even-numbered houses on one side of a street are social housing, but all odd-numbered houses are owner occupiers.

All the designs discussed so far are non-probabilistic. In *probabilistic designs* the key feature is that neither the interviewer nor the interviewed can affect the selection mechanism, which is done at random. With such samples, the likelihood of being sampled is knowable and non-zero; consequently we can use statistical theory (based on the central limit theorem) to guarantee unbiased, representative estimates and to estimate the degree of precision in those estimates. Thus we can say that the proportion in poverty is 25 per cent and that we can be 95 per cent confident, given our sample of 7,200 households, that the true underlying rate lies between 24 and 26 per cent. Non-probabilistic sampling is not necessarily biased and unrepresentative, but we lack the necessary formal framework for making any judgement.

There are three basic types of probabilistic sample:

- *Simple random sample* (SRS) requires a complete listing of the population (the sampling frame) from which a sample is chosen at random so that each and every unit has an equal chance of being selected. With such EPSEM sampling (equal probability of selection method) the standard error, which defines the precision of the sample estimate, is proportional to the square root of the absolute sample size. Consequently, the larger the sample (in absolute terms, not as a percentage of the population) the greater the precision but there are diminishing returns, as the sample size must be quadrupled to halve the standard error. This can be an expensive design as in a national survey the interviewers will be required to travel the entire country. In practice, quasi-random samples are often used; for example, the British national birth COHORTS of 1946, 1958 and 1970 were based on babies born in a particular week, while the ONS Longitudinal Study uses record linkage of individuals born on four days of a year, which equates to some 1 per cent of the national population. Indeed, providing there is no periodicity in the sampled variable, systematic sampling can be treated as quasi-random. With probabilistic sampling, an effective sample size of 10,000 respondents is needed in order to be 95 per cent confident of being ± 1 per cent of the true value, when that is 0.5. Typically, scientifically credible national opinion polls contain around 1,500 respondents. In student and other small projects, the absolute minimum is 100 and preferably 250 when subgroups (male and female; young and old) are being analysed. The aim should be a focused QUESTIONNAIRE to a lot of people, rather than a long questionnaire to few, or a recourse to SECONDARY DATA.

- *Stratified sampling* groups the population into strata so as to maximize similarity within a stratum and maximize between-strata differences. This can considerably increase the sample's efficiency if stratification is based on a variable strongly related to the estimate. If income is strongly related to region, then regions could be used for stratifying and reducing the standard error of the mean income estimate. We can also disproportionately sample from particular strata when there are important groups of the population that are numerically small and so would yield only small numbers if SRS were used within strata such as ethnic groups (see ETHNICITY) with the non-indigenous groups over-sampled to get more precise estimates. Such a strategy requires detailed knowledge of the sample frame in terms of an ethnic classification, and the analysis should be weighted to get correct estimates.

- *Multi-stage designs* involve sampling in stages. For example, a sample of constituencies may be selected at random (the so-called primary sampling units), then wards within them, then HOUSEHOLDS within wards and individuals within households. This design is often used for major scientific surveys, as it only requires a sampling frame at each stage; thus at stage one only a list of constituencies is required, while at stage two, only ward names are required for those constituencies already selected. Another advantage is the cost reduction resulting from basing a team of interviewers in the higher-level units. A variant is the *cluster design* when at some stage all the lower level units are sampled – everybody in a ward is selected, for example. A problem with these designs is that there is a tendency for people living in the same place to be somewhat similar so that the resultant sample is more alike than a random sample and standard statistical theory gives overly precise results. Clustered data lead to inefficiency and it is not unknown for an SRS a third of the size to achieve the same standard error. It is clearly vital to measure this dependency (the intra-class CORRELATION) and correct for it. The

development of MULTI-LEVEL MODELS allows this even when the sample is unbalanced with a different number of units in each higher level unit. Consequently, multistage designs are recommended for studying variation simultaneously at a number of different SCALES, with the population itself seen as having a hierarchical structure, which is itself of substantive interest (Jones, 1997). Indeed highly clustered designs are needed if survey information is to be gathered on individuals as well as their peers. With such designs, it is necessary to specify the number of units at each level; Raudenbush and Xiaofeng (2000) provide the necessary background, which is put into practice by Stoker and Bowers (2002) in their geographically sensitive designs for surveying American voting behaviour.

These three designs can be used in combination; the UK Millennium Cohort study, unlike previous birth cohorts, is spatially clustered specifically to study NEIGHBOURHOOD EFFECTS. Wards are disproportionately stratified to ensure adequate representation of all four UK countries, deprived areas and areas with high concentrations of particular ethnic groups, and then all babies aged 9 months in selected wards over a 12-month period. The resultant sample includes 19,000 infants who are being followed longitudinally.

Other probabilistic designs may be used for different circumstances; they include CAPTURE-RECAPTURE METHODS to estimate population size with mobile populations, and response-based sampling (see EXTENSIVE DESIGNS) when a numerically small but important outcome is over-sampled. In geographical studies, the standard procedures may be modified to ensure spatial coverage. Methods of random, systematic and stratified sampling of points on a MAP have been devised using coordinate systems, for example, as have methods of selecting transects (line samples) across an area (Berry and Baker, 1968). Increasingly, these designs are being used adaptively (Thompson and Seber, 2002), so that the degree of SPATIAL AUTOCORRELATION is being assessed as the survey proceeds and there is increased sampling in areas where the outcome variable is most varied and least spatially dependent.

When testing a HYPOTHESIS it is crucial to assess and control for two types of error in a probabilistic design. Type I errors, finding an effect when there really is none, are controlled by setting demanding probability levels in CONFIRMATORY DATA ANALYSIS. Type II errors – that is, having insufficient information to be able to detect a genuine effect – are managed by conducting a power analysis during the design phase. Conversely, collecting too much information is not only wasteful of resources but can be seen as an unethical intrusion. Statistical power is increased when there is little 'noise' in the system; the effect is substantial when probability levels are set leniently and when the sample size is large, and according to which statistical test is used (parametric procedures being more powerful). Consequently, researchers should choose settings/contexts that maximize the 'signal' and not as in a study of the effect of size of house on price, sample areas where all the properties are three-bedroomed ones. Power formulas and software (such as G*Power) are available but require an estimate of the size of the effect. Cohen (1988) has defined small, medium and large effects as the ratio of an effect to variation for a very large range of statistical procedures (e.g. a t-test in a multiple REGRESSION model). Thus, to be able to detect a *small* difference of 0.25 of a standard deviation between two sample means with 80 per cent power and 5 per cent significance (both these percentages being the most commonly used conventions) requires 2*253 observations in the total sample; while to be able to detect a *large* difference of 1.0 standard deviation requires only 2*17 observations. Unfortunately, academic research has paid too little attention to statistical power with, for example, Sedlmeier and Gigerenzer (1989) finding that even in a reputed journal statistical power hovered around 50 per cent. If all these studies were replicated, only half would result in an identifiable effect. The problem is actually even more widespread due to the use of non-probabilistic samples. The way forward is to use SIMULATION to judge effectiveness and efficiency, as pioneered by Snijders (1992) for snowball sampling. Indeed, simulation is a general strategy that permits great flexibility, not only allowing the assessment of power as sample size increases but also catering for missing data, non-linearity, unequal variances and other specifications of an underlying model. KJ

Suggested reading
Barnett (2002); Dixon and Leach (1977); Kish (1995); Lenth (2001); Sudman (1976). G*Power for power calculations is available from http://www.psycho.uni-duesseldorf.de/aap/projects/gpower/index.html

satisficing behaviour Behaviour that meets an actor's minimum criteria for success. The concept was developed by Herbert Simon (1916–2001: see Simon, 1956) as an alternative to the presumed OPTIMIZATION of RATIONAL CHOICE THEORY, in which actors always seek to make the best-possible choice – for example, to maximize profits. Satisficing behaviour may be appropriate either when it is impossible to calculate the maximal outcome or when actors are unprepared to make the investment necessary to identify and/or pursue that outcome (as argued by Pred, 1967, 1969). Actors will then set their own criteria that will represent a satisfactory return on their investment. (See also BEHAVIOURAL GEOGRAPHY.) RJ

Suggested reading
Gigerenzer and Selten (2001).

scale 'Scale' has no single definition, and in recent years has been the object of much theorizing (Howitt, 2003). The traditional definition in CARTOGRAPHY refers to MAP resolution. All maps represent the world by reducing the size and diversity of its component spaces for visual display, digitally or on paper. Cartographic scale expresses the mathematical relationship between the map and the Earth, usually denoted as a representative fraction. For example, the small fraction, 1:500,000, indicates that one unit of distance on the map represents 500,000 units of Earth space. Such a map would show large expanses of terrain – much more than say, the larger fraction of 1:24,000. Hence the common confusion between *large-scale* (or large-fraction) maps that show less space but typically more detail, and *small-scale* maps that show more space, but with less detail. Each type of social and environmental diversity has its own 'best resolution' in terms of cartographic REPRESENTATION; thus, the choice of cartographic scale depends on the problem at hand. To visualize US state variation in the enforcement of environmental policies, we need the familiar small-scale map of the country with state borders, while determining whether point source POLLUTION released into a river caused downstream lymphomas requires a large-scale map.

The second major definition is operational or METHODOLOGICAL. This is the scale or resolution of data collection, with the familiar cascade from micro (BODY) to macro (GLOBE). Tied to this type of scale are various analytical complexities, including the claims that: (a) social patterns and processes can be sorted according to their scale of operation and, as

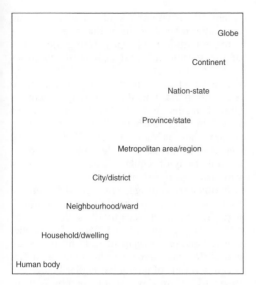

Globe

Continent

Nation-state

Province/state

Metropolitan area/region

City/district

Neighbourhood/ward

Household/dwelling

Human body

scale *A cascade of hierarchical levels*

a result, it is important to ensure an appropriate match between research questions and the scale of analysis when developing a research design (see ECOLOGICAL FALLACY); (b) some processes may operate at multiple scales at once, and as a result, attention should be paid to their operational distinctiveness at particular scales and to the mechanisms that define their modifications from one resolution to the next; and (c) any scaled process can intersect with other processes operating at any other scale, often in complex ways that attenuate, amplify or destabilize their operation. These sorts of causal complications, in which processes are conceived not only in their own terms but also in terms of their *scales of operation*, form one of the more powerful arguments for the necessity of incorporating SPACE into social science. It is also here that one finds common ground between HUMAN GEOGRAPHY and PHYSICAL GEOGRAPHY, for both deal with scalar shifts in processes. In the study of coupled social and natural SYSTEMS, the complications of (a) to (c) above may be operative.

A third aspect of scale is to recognize what has been variously called its social production or SOCIAL CONSTRUCTION (Smith, N., 1992b; Delaney and Leitner, 1997; Marston, 2000). In this view, spatial scales do not, as implied above, rest as fixed platforms for social activity and processes that connect up or down to other hierarchical levels, but are instead *outcomes* of those activities and processes, to which they in turn contribute through a

spatially uneven and temporally unfolding dynamic (Swyngedouw, 1997). This recursive relationship between social processes producing scales and scales affecting the operation of social processes is one aspect of the socio-spatial DIALECTIC: the idea that social processes and space – and hence scales – mutually intersect, constitute, and rebound upon one another in an inseparable chain of determinations (see PRODUCTION OF SPACE). Over the past two decades, this view of scale has generated some of the most productive and novel research in human geography (Cox, 1997; Herod and Wright, 2002).

Given the importance of the dialectic to HISTORICAL MATERIALISM (and the larger corpus of MARXISM) in general, and to MARXIST GEOGRAPHY in particular, it was CAPITALISM that was early on identified as the driver behind the production of scale. From the formation of working-class neighbourhoods whose residents defend 'turf' through misplaced parochialisms, to the elite spaces of cosmopolitan jet-setters who shirk their ethical responsibilities while working to expand the world economy, the inherently UNEVEN DEVELOPMENT of capitalism has been viewed as the fulcrum of the production of scale. This emphasis led Marston (2000) to critique this body of research for its privileging of production and its relative neglect of SOCIAL REPRODUCTION. There nevertheless remain several key advances in this literature, including: (a) an acknowledgement of the inherently political nature of scale production (Smith, 1996a); (b) the need to pay attention to STATE formations and various RESISTANCE movements that both deploy and construct scales (Miller, 2000; Brenner, 2004); and (c) the need to re-theorize in more complex ways the relationship between social processes and spatial outcomes as POWER comes to be understood as dispersed rather than centred. It is in part through this last point that several scale theorists over the past several years have begun to turn away from purely hierarchical – or, we might say, vertical – understandings of scale to incorporate formulations that resemble the horizontal relations of NETWORKS (Amin, 2002b; Brenner, 2004).

The latest debate revolves around the claim that scale itself, while no doubt an organizing moment in EPISTEMOLOGY, has merely a transcendent status within the domain of ONTOLOGY (Marston, Jones and Woodward, 2005). In the view of Marston and her colleagues, scale is an epistemology that, though potentially helpful in a methodological sense, is tied

665

to a global-to-local continuum that under-writes the problematic view that social processes can be detached from the grounded sites where people and objects concretely reside and social practices take place (e.g. in streets, bedrooms, boardrooms). They offer in its place a *flat ontology* that resists conceptualizing processes as operating at scales that hover above these sites (e.g. metropolitan REGIONS, NATION-STATES). This view continues to generate much debate (e.g. Leitner and Miller, 2007; Jones, Woodward and Marston, 2007). SAM/KW/JPJ

Suggested reading
Jones, Woodward and Marston (2007); Leitner and Miller (2007); Marston (2000); Marston, Jones and Woodward (2005); Sheppard and McMaster (2004).

science/science studies Science is an 'essentially contested concept' (Gallie, 1964) in the sense that it defies specification in terms of necessary and sufficient conditions. Numerous candidates have been offered by PHILOSOPHY to discriminate science from non-science – knowledge based on first-hand observation, claims and procedures warranted by predictive success, the inductive gathering of empirical data, information satisfying the principles of verification or FALSIFICATION, and so on. The efforts of Copernicus and Galileo to base knowledge on causal explanations rather than Aristotelian syllogism, Bacon's plea for inaugurating the method of INDUCTION, Newton's rejection of speculative hypotheses in favour of his own method of deduction (see HYPOTHESIS), the Logical Positivists' emphasis on the *logical* structure of theories (see LOGICAL POSITIVISM), and Lakatos' defence of what he called 'the methodology of scientific research programmes' constitute just a few of the proposals that have been made to place science on secure foundations (Oldroyd, 1986). But none of these have been adequate to catch the presumed essential features of enterprises that stretch temporally from Aristotle to Einstein, cognitively from astronomy to zoology, and spatially from medieval Arabic geodesy to Enlightenment Scottish chemistry. This recognition has led to what Larry Laudan (1988) has aptly termed 'the demise of the demarcation problem'. Uncontested mapping of the border between science and other forms of human cultural activity (see CULTURE) has simply remained elusive.

Nevertheless, the label 'science' does refer to a suite of enterprises sharing some family resemblance with the kinds of observational and experimental practices that came to characterize natural philosophy during the period of the seventeenth and eighteenth centuries (see SCIENTIFIC REVOLUTION(S)). And it was in that era that the term itself began to acquire a definition that linked it to a body of demonstrated truths and observed facts brought into coherence by their adherence to general natural laws. As Watts put it in 1725 (2, ii, §9), the word 'science' was 'usually applied to a whole body of regular or methodical observations or propositions'.

GEOGRAPHY's engagements with the scientific tradition have been multi-faceted. Terminologically, the label 'scientist' has close associations with geography via Mary Somerville, whose *Physical geography* of 1848 firmly staked geography's claims to scientific status. In fact, it was in a review of one of her earlier books that the word 'scientist' was first coined by William Whewell (that irrepressible neologist), although it did not circulate into common currency until the 1870s. Historiographically, insights from the philosophy and history of science have been used by a range of geographers to interpret the evolution of their own tradition of enquiry (see GEOGRAPHY, HISTORY OF). In particular, the perspective of Thomas Kuhn on the structure of scientific revolutions has been the subject of discussion within the discipline as to the extent to which it throws light on Geography's lineage (see also PARADIGM).

In two other substantive ways, Geography and science are tightly interwoven. First, geographical practice has routinely – though certainly not universally – adopted scientific techniques and vocabulary, and not just in PHYSICAL GEOGRAPHY with its evident roots in both field and LABORATORY science. Thus during the period of the Scientific Revolution, for example, mathematical advances were used to solve problems of MAP PROJECTION, and the subject was routinely taught in association with astronomy. In the same period, Varenius' *Geographia generalis* of 1650 advanced his own version of the mechanical philosophy to contest Aristotelianism, and William Petty began to apply the methods of the new natural philosophy to social phenomena with his development of 'political arithmetick'. Navigational expertise, requiring computational skills and knowledge of observational astronomy, was also often taught in geography courses (Livingstone, 2003b). Such projects firmly linked geography as an enterprise to practical mathematics and the scientific tradition, and this impulse has continued to animate various strands of modern geography. During the 1960s, some geographers with scientific aspirations turned to the language of logical positivism to underwrite (after the event, as a matter of fact) their project to create a SPATIAL SCIENCE grounded in natural laws of spatial relations and expressed in numerical language (see LOCATIONAL ANALYSIS; QUANTITATIVE REVOLUTION). Critics of this trajectory accused its practitioners of indifference to questions of social inequity, a lack of political engagement, and an inclination to use mathematical vernacular as a shield to deflect establishment suspicion of social science during the McCarthy era (Harvey, 1984) – though some of its advocates, such as William Bunge, mobilized spatial statistics for radical purposes.

More recently, geographers have begun to bring science within the discipline's scope both by deploying the insights and methodologies of *science studies* and by enquiring into the SPATIALITY of science as itself a cultural practice (Livingstone, 2003a). As an enterprise, science studies largely developed in the wake of Kuhn's rejection of purely logical models of scientific development and his insistence that scientific change was inherently discontinuous. By allowing a variety of social–communal factors into the understanding of the evolution of science, by emphasizing the underdetermination of THEORY by empirical data and by highlighting the role of tacit knowledge in scientific practice, Kuhn opened the door to empirical studies of scientific procedure. While he himself expressed concern about more extreme versions of RELATIVISM, his work did open the door to the social history of science. This project has taken various forms, notably the so-called Edinburgh 'strong programme' associated with writers such as Steven Shapin and David Bloor, which sought to locate the cognitive claims of science in its wider social setting; the ACTOR-NETWORK THEORY and ETHNOGRAPHIC perspectives of figures such as Bruno Latour, Michael Callon and Steve Woolgar; and the interventions via FEMINISM of figures such as Donna Haraway and Sandra Harding (Hess, 1997; Golinski, 1998). These, and numerous other strands of thought from figures such as Simon Schaffer, Michel Foucault and Joseph Rouse, have resulted in a tradition of research working with the notion of science as fundamentally *local* knowledge (see LOCAL KNOWLEDGE).

Geographers have engaged with these developments in several ways. Thus some have turned to the proposals and methods of science studies to interrogate geographical knowledge itself. Barnes' scrutiny of ECONOMIC GEOGRAPHY and the quantitative revolution (Barnes, 1996, 2004b), Demeritt's (1996) reflections on SOCIAL THEORY, science and geography, Thrift's (1996) interest in the social formations of knowledge, Whatmore's (2002a) elucidation of 'hybrid natures' and Amin and Cohendet's (2004) examination of the 'architectures of knowledge' in firms and economies are just a few investigations that are deeply informed, in one way or another, by these perspectives. At the same time, geographers have been in dialogue with practitioners of science studies in their enquiries into the part played by SPACE, PLACE and location in the production, consumption and circulation of scientific knowledge itself (Livingstone, 2003c). These latter currents in the spatiality of science stem from an interest in the role of venues such as the laboratory, the museum and the field in knowledge production; the significance of location in the reception of scientific knowledge; and the ways in which the universality of science has been accomplished through the management of various circulatory mechanisms.

Several critical statements by historians of science, such as Schaffer (2005), Ophir and Shapin (1991: see also Shapin, 1998), Kohler (2002) and Agar and Smith (1998), have firmly placed space on the science studies agenda, and this has been reinforced by the work of geographers on the geographies of scientific knowledge and on science as an inherently hermeneutic undertaking (Livingstone, 2002b: see also HERMENEUTICS). The interface that has been developing is proving to be fertile. Geographers and others have thus been variously engaged in elucidating the 'geographies of science' in a range of ways and at a range of SCALES (see also GEOGRAPHY, HISTORY OF). An indicative sampling of this work would include examinations of the geographies of ENLIGHTENMENT and scientific revolution(s); the significance of museums, lecture halls and botanical gardens in the production and display of scientific knowledge (Naylor, 2002; Johnson, 2006); the practices of making science in the field (Withers, 2004; Lorimer and Spedding, 2005: see FIELDWORK); the geography of geographical knowledge itself in the constitution of national IDENTITY (Withers, 2001); the different ways in which the glacier theory was construed in different cognitive spaces (Finnegan, 2004); the role of spatial practices in fisheries science (Evenden, 2004); the social topography of correspondence networks (Ogborn, 2002); the significance of field trials in the production of agricultural knowledge (Henke, 2000); the reciprocal connections between buildings and the building of scientific knowledge (Gieryn, 2002); and the geography of the commodification of bio-information (Parry 2004). The list could be extended *ad libitum*. Special issues of contributions by geographers to the *British Journal for the History of Science* (2005) under the guest editorship of Simon Naylor, and of *Interdisciplinary Science Reviews* (2006) on 'putting science in its place', bear witness to the interdisciplinary richness of these developments.

In the light of all this, there are good grounds for suggesting that science studies can coherently be thought of as a branch of HISTORICAL GEOGRAPHY. In keeping with this sentiment, Simon Schaffer (2005) has recently urged that it was the cartographic impulse itself that helped construct what we think of as modern science (see CARTOGRAPHIC REASON; CARTOGRAPHY). Courtesy of several 'big picture' accounts of science history (such as those of Whewell, Bernal and Needham) that sought to graphically chart scientific development, it was – as Schaffer (2005) pointedly observes – 'MAPS which invented what science was'. At a more popular level, Simon Jenkins, writing in the *Guardian* (Friday, 20 January 2006), delivers confirmatory judgment, no less provocatively quipping that 'All scientists are geographers. That is why maps are the most sacred tools of science.'   DNL

Suggested reading
Golinski (1998); Livingstone (2003c).

science park A particular form of GROWTH POLE established by property developers or, sometimes, research institutions to promote technology transfer and investment in new industries, usually in conjunction with a university and sometimes with regional and/or local government support. The goal is to capitalize on knowledge CLUSTERS in scientific and technological expertise by ensuring that INNOVATIONS are developed locally, generating jobs for the local or regional economy and contributing to the institution's costs (see also KNOWLEDGE ECONOMY).   SW

Suggested reading
Massey, Quintas and Wield (1991).

scientific instrumentation Scientific instruments are purpose-built material tools used by investigators to disclose, measure and represent aspects of the natural world. A subset of these devices devoted to SURVEYING has been used in CARTOGRAPHY, astronomy, navigation, land survey, geodesy and related geographical practices. Dating back at least to the activities of Vitruvius in the first century BCE, but particularly since the development of practical mathematics during the Renaissance, such instruments as the astrolabe, compass and theodolite were progressively refined until they were substantially replaced by the more recent use of signals from satellite systems, which deliver immediate calculations of exact locations (Bennett, 1987).

A useful distinction can be made between instrumentation *for* GEOGRAPHY and geographies *of* instrumentation. In the former case, scientific instruments have been used in the garnering of the GLOBE's geographically distributed data and, routinely, to produce MAPS. Variations in terrestrial magnetism, for example, were the subject of much concern to Edmund Halley who, it was said, set about 'the rectifying of geography', by using his own instruments to determine longitude and produce charts of magnetic variation (Fara, 2005, p. 69). Similar matters occupied the attention of Alexander von Humboldt, who travelled through South America with a remarkable range of instruments – chronometers, sextants, dipping needles, a cyanometer (for measuring the blueness of the sky), barometers, thermometers, rain gauges, aeromotors, theodolites – and used the data they delivered to construct his famous ISOLINE maps, which were designed to facilitate the interdisciplinary transfer of data (Dettelbach, 1999; Godlewska, 1999). The fundamental role of instruments in the geographical project – and its colonial preoccupations – was enshrined, during the Victorian period, in the Royal Geographical Society, which began systematic courses on surveying in 1879 (Collier and Inkpen, 2003). Of course, these practices raised a range of EPISTEMOLOGICAL problems, rotating around who could be trusted to deliver reliable information (see TRUST), how distant observers were to be regulated and what were the appropriate instruments to use in distant places. In an attempt to address such problems, the Society published its *Guide to travellers* in many successive editions, in the hope of bringing discipline and order to distant observers, and thereby to secure testimonial credibility (Driver, 2001b).

This latter concern about how to manage the harvesting of global data for geography is intimately connected with the whole subject of the geographies *of* instrumentation. The use of survey instruments and the regulation of observers in the production of geographical knowledge can be thought of as an inherently spatial strategy; it aims to conquer distance by bringing together widely distributed data and thereby integrating local knowledge into global NETWORKS. Just exactly what goes on as instrumental findings circulate from local site to global space constitutes a crucial set of questions in the geography of knowledge. During the ENLIGHTENMENT, ships' captains collected magnetic measurements and returned them to the Royal Society. In the nineteenth century, atmospheric circulation data returned from hundreds of ships to the US Navy's Depot Charts and Instruments were used by Matthew Fontaine Maury to construct his 1855 *Physical geography of the sea* (Burnett, 2005). At such key venues – centres of calculation, as Bruno Latour (1987) calls them – universality is constructed from particularity. But that conceptual circuitry is only achieved by industrious labour and careful management. The need to calibrate instruments, to normalize FIELDWORK, to discipline the senses of observers and to ensure metrological standardization are all procedures that are needed to turn instrumental readings in particular places into geographical patterns of worldwide scope (Livingstone, 2003c). And of course the standardized data, calibrated apparatus and normalized procedures that emerge from centralized nodes in the network are themselves, in turn, 'assimilated and interpreted in each local context' (Golinski, 1998, pp. 138–9). It is therefore noteworthy that historians of science have begun to speak of the 'geography of precision' (Schaffer, 2002), which identifies the inherently geographical nature of instrumental epistemology and the means by which 'universal knowledge' is made out of 'local knowledges' (see INDIGENOUS KNOWLEDGE). Further geographical scrutiny of the role of instrumental practice in the production of (geographical) knowledge is urgently needed.   DL

Suggested reading
Bourguet, Licoppe and Sibum (2002); Livingstone (2003c).

scientific revolution(s) An abrupt cognitive transformation in a tradition of scientific enquiry that radically reinterprets existing data, identifies new problems and methodologies, and establishes fertile lines of novel enquiry. By thus emphasizing discontinuities

in the history of SCIENCE, the idea of scientific revolutions runs counter to the standard *cumulative* understanding long championed by positivists and others who insisted that scientific progress comes about through the inductive accumulation of new data and the routine application of scientific method (see LOGICAL POSITIVISM; POSITIVISM). While the idea of scientific revolutions was put forward in the mid-nineteenth century by William Whewell, its most celebrated advocate was Thomas Kuhn, whose 1962 account, *The structure of scientific revolutions*, advanced a mechanism for understanding revolutionary science. To Kuhn, scientific fields embody PARADIGMS – traditions with historical exemplars that express the standard theories, concepts and practices of a particular science. At certain points in time a new paradigm arises which is incompatible, and incommensurable, with its predecessor on account of the truly radical nature of the transformation. Kuhn's model has been challenged from various quarters, and while he himself insisted that it was not applicable to the social sciences, it has nonetheless been applied in various ways to the evolution of HUMAN GEOGRAPHY and, most notably, by the architects of the QUANTITATIVE REVOLUTION that inaugurated SPATIAL SCIENCE (Mair, 1986; see also GEOGRAPHY, HISTORY OF).

But the term may also refer to a particular period in Western history, conventionally described as 'The Scientific Revolution', which has been widely regarded as of pivotal significance in the emergence of modern science. The expression was introduced in the 1930s to give unity to the period centring on the seventeenth and early eighteenth centuries, when figures such as Galileo, René Descartes, Johannes Kepler, Francis Bacon, Robert Boyle and Sir Isaac Newton transformed natural philosophy by their application of mathematical principles and experimental methods to understanding NATURE. Favouring mechanical explanations, such figures championed first-hand observation of nature over the scholastic authority of figures such as Aristotle. This typification of 'the scientific revolution', however, has been challenged more recently by scholars stressing continuities with medieval metaphysics, diversities of outlook exhibited by key figures in the period and the continuing influence of a variety of magical perspectives on practitioners of the new natural philosophy. This has led some historians to query whether there ever really was such a thing as 'the' scientific revolution. As Shapin (1996, p. 1) audaciously put it in

669

the introduction to his revisionist account, 'There was no such thing as the Scientific Revolution, and this is a book about it.'

Geographers and others working on this period have also come to stress the SPATIALITY of natural philosophy at the time, and the different ways in which what has come to be called The Scientific Revolution was constituted in different arenas (Livingstone and Withers, 2005). At the global scale of East and WEST, at the continental scale of European regionalism, and at the micro scale of dedicated scientific venues such as the LABORATORY and observatory, the new science was prosecuted in different ways. The influence of Chinese alchemy on medicine and the significance of Islamic geodetic methods on practical mathematics, the markedly different RHETORICAL spaces of the Italian court and the Royal Society, where scientific engagements were staged, the contrasts between knowledge-producing practices in the laboratory compared with the field, and differences across EUROPE in styles of patronage, pedagogic traditions, conduits of intellectual transmission and expressions of religious devotion all conspire to render troublesome the identification of something called 'The Scientific Revolution' as an essential singularity. Scientific revolutions have their own histories *and* their own geographies.   DNL

Suggested reading
Kuhn (1970 [1962]); Livingstone (2003c).

search behaviour The process of seeking out and evaluating alternative courses of action. In spatial DECISION-MAKING, searching – as in the selection of a new home – is often constrained by the FRICTIONS OF DISTANCE, so that actors operate within spatially-delimited search spaces containing a subset only of all the options available to them.   RJ

secession The transfer of political control of a piece of TERRITORY from one polity to a new or existing polity. Commonly, the term relates to a REGION within an existing STATE aiming either to become part of another state or to function as an independent state. The process may be peaceful or manifest itself through TERRORISM and guerilla WAR. Contemporary examples include northern Italy (Giordano, 1999) and Chechnya. Increasingly, the process has been explored at the local level as LOCAL STATE units seek to secede from the authority of metropolitan units (Purcell, 2001).   CF

Suggested reading
Macedo and Buchanan (2003).

Second World A term that emerged during the COLD WAR to describe the communist, industrial states of the Warsaw Pact (formerly the Eastern bloc) in contrast to the countries of NATO. In time it came to refer to the centrally planned economies and communist party states of Central and Eastern Europe (e.g. Poland, Czechoslovakia, Hungary, Romania and Bulgaria), the Former Soviet Union states from the Baltics to the Black Sea (e.g. Belarus, Estonia, Lithuania, Latvia, Estonia, Moldova and the Ukraine), Russia, the Caucuses and the former soviet states of Central Asia (e.g. Kazakhstan), as well as China and other Maoist and Marxist states in the THIRD WORLD. With the widespread collapse of COMMUNISM since 1989, however, the term has fallen out of favour. Former 'Second World' states are now members of the European Union, experimenting with liberal political and economic systems, or pursuing market socialism (see POST-SOCIALISM: see also Pickles and Smith, 1998; Smith, 2005).   JPi

secondary data analysis In contrast to PRIMARY DATA ANALYSIS, this involves data collected by different researchers than those undertaking the analysis. The advantages are potentially a great deal of saving of time and resources, and thereby it is possible to extend the scope of a study well beyond the means of a lone researcher or even small teams. The disadvantage is that concepts may not be operationalized in the manner that the secondary analyst would ideally like. There are a number of sources of such data, which include data collected for primary research that has been subsequently made available to other researchers (see DATA ARCHIVE). It is increasingly a requirement of grant awarding that this is done. Another source is when a large-scale data collection is undertaken on behalf of the wider social science community. Important examples of these are the Panel Study of Income Dynamics, begun in 1968, a longitudinal study of a representative sample of US individuals and the family units in which they reside, and the British Household Panel Survey began in 1991 which is part of the European Community Household Panel. Geographers have been able to link NEIGHBOURHOOD data to the individual data from the panels without compromising confidentiality (Bolster, Burgess, Johnston, Jones, Propper and Sarker, 2006). Researchers in the UK are also fortunate to have the birth COHORT studies, which follow individuals from birth; the most recent Millennium Cohort has a clustered design so that local geographies can be researched (www.cls.ioe.ac.uk/mcs/). Another source is through record linkage of administrative data; this is likely to become of increasing importance as part of EVIDENCE-BASED POLICY whereby data are collected and disseminated on small local areas; a substantial and growing example of this is the Neighbourhood Statistics website (http://neighbourhood.statistics.gov.uk/) which has, for example, linked claimant count data to local areas to provide an annually updated measure of income POVERTY. The potential for such administrative data is immense but is challenging because all sorts of bias are likely to be present. An important recent development has been the use of a model-based approach to the use of records from different sources. Thus Jackson, Best and Richardson (2008) were able to use an overall MULTI-LEVEL MODEL to combine detailed individual survey data from the Millennium Cohort Study with large-scale administrative data from the National births register, elaborating the model to handle a range of biases.

In Britain, the UK Data Archive (http://www.data-archive.ac.uk/) is the major repository of digital social science data; while in the USA, this role is filled by the Inter-University Consortium for Political and Social Research (http://www.icpsr.umich.edu/); globally such archives are organized into the International Federation of Data Organizations (http://www.ifdo.org/). All these websites have extensive search capabilities for identifying data being sought. King (1995) has gone further in his call that to ensure scientific integrity, replication data sets need to be made available that include *all* information necessary to reproduce empirical results; including software code for the particular analysis that has been undertaken. This is now being made manifest in the Virtual Data Centre (http://thedata.org/). Secondary analysis of qualitative data has been of less importance but its use is growing (Heaton, 1998).   KJ

Suggested reading
Boslaugh (2007); Heaton (2004).

section A territorial division of a country associated with an electoral cleavage created when a political party mobilizes support there based on policies with particular local relevance. The classic sectional cleavage occurred in the USA, where for most of the century following the Civil War the Democratic party mobilized majority support in the states that had wished to secede, against the Republican party, which granted equality of civil rights to African-Americans and ended SLAVERY.   RJ

Suggested reading
Archer and Taylor (1981).

sectoral model A model of residential patterns developed by Homer Hoyt (1895–1984: see Hoyt, 1939) for US cities, involving the segregation of housing of different quality and value into separate sectors radiating from the city centre along major routeways. Changes in the character of a residential area within a sector involved a FILTERING process whereby relatively affluent residents moved towards the urban fringe, thereby yielding their homes and neighbourhoods to lower-status in-migrants (cf. INVASION AND SUCCESSION). The model – developed for mortgage-lending applications – was presented as an alternative to the ZONAL MODEL and was later incorporated with it in a MULTIPLE NUCLEI MODEL (see figure for that entry).   RJ

secularism An IDEOLOGY in which RELIGION and supernatural beliefs are not central to understanding the world, both religious beliefs and religious institutions should not interfere with the public affairs of a SOCIETY, and are segregated from matters of GOVERNANCE. It is often associated with ENLIGHTENMENT in EUROPE, with its turn towards SCIENCE and rationalism and its move away from religion and superstition. Secularism as a philosophy owes its origins to George Jacob Holyoake (1860), who introduced the idea that life should be lived by reference to ethical principles, and the world understood by processes of reasoning, rather than by reference to God or gods, or other supernatural concepts. From the perspective of government and governance, secularism refers to a policy that separates religious authority from the STATE. The opposite of secularism is usually *theocracy*; that is, where religion has a major role in government.

The secularist movement is split between those who believe that secularism leads logically to anti-religious propaganda and ACTIVISM, and those who do not. Most modern 'Western' societies today are thought to be secular. Most would have near-complete freedom of religion. Religion does not officially dictate political decisions, though it may influence the actions of individual politicians (but see Butler, 2008).

The divergent values of the secular state and religious groups have been a source of significant conflict. The prohibition of headscarves in schools in France is one example. At the same time, different secular states are secular to different extents and in different ways. Thus, while the secular state in France prohibits headscarves, in Canada, the secular state protects rights to wear religious markers in public schools.

Geographers have mostly been concerned about the intersections of sacred and secular in the LANDSCAPE, or how sacred and secular ideologies impact on landscapes. Thus, in theory, a strictly secular ideology that underpins urban planning principles would not support the use of religious principles in the location of religious buildings, for example. However, in reality, different degrees of negotiations between sacred and secular ideologies prevail in most societies (Kong, 1993a,b).   LK

Suggested readings
Heelas (1998); Kong (1993a).

security Freedom from imagined or real danger in the present or future. Geographical orderings of security are constructed through DISCOURSE and PERFORMANCE, and play an important role in constituting political and social geographies at a wide variety of scales. Discourses of security are always highly politicized and often vigorously contested. They involve the mobilization of IMAGINATIVE GEOGRAPHIES that swirl around notions of collective IDENTITY to invoke political threats, political change and political violence. As Dalby (2002, pp. 163–4) has suggested:

> Security is about the future or fears about the future. It is about contemporary dangers but also thwarting potential future dangers. It is about control, certainty, and predictability in an uncertain world, and, in attempting to forestall chance and change, it is frequently a violent practice. [Security] is about maintaining certain collective identities, certain senses of who we are, of who we intend to remain, more than who we intend to become. Security provides narratives of danger as the stimulant to collective action but is much less useful in proposing desirable futures.

Geographies of INTERNATIONAL RELATIONS and the inter-state system are overwhelmingly constituted and re-made through realist discourses of national and international security. Through these, NATION-STATES have traditionally sought to reify and naturalize their existence as 'security containers' using discourses of 'national security' that depict them as singular actors with incontrovertible national characteristics, homogenous populations and natural BORDERS (Katzenstein, 1996). Such geopolitical discussions about national security tend to portray nation-states as facing existential threats from the incursions or ambitions of competing STATES and EMPIRES or – especially in the post-Cold War period – from non-state TERRORIST or insurgent groups. The Bush administration's 'global war on terror', launched after the terrorist attacks on New York and Washington on 11 September 2001, is a dramatic example (Kirsch, 2003). Research within CRITICAL GEOPOLITICS (Ó Tuathail, 1996b), critical international relations and security studies (Campbell, 1998) has shown how NATIONALISM, MILITARISM and WAR are constructed and entangled through the invocation of such threats to 'national security'. Imaginative geographies enlisted in the service of security typically represent the HOMELAND as virtuous and righteous whilst simultaneously demonizing the space of the enemy. That space is increasingly seen as transnational and multidimensional: at once a 'security region' that requires monitoring and surveillance and, in the case of the USA, a unified combatant command pre-assigned to military intervention there (cf. MIDDLE EAST; Morrissey, 2008b; 2009), and also a complex non-linear 'battlespace' (see MILITARY GEOGRAPHY).

These conventional imaginations of national and international security have been sharply criticized for the way in which they legitimize military VIOLENCE and neglect the environmental, social and biophysical underpinnings of the security of all human societies. In a post-COLD WAR world dominated by RESOURCE depletion, rapid population growth, intensifying URBANIZATION and a series of deepening environmental and ecological crises, all of them compounded by highly uneven configurations of MIGRATION, capital investment and environmental risk, Dalby (2002) has called for conventional discourses of national security to be challenged by broader notions of what he terms ENVIRONMENTAL SECURITY. Addressing the ecological foundations of political, social and economic security, he urges that critical discussions about national security 'need a more explicit engagement with the ecological conditions of contemporary urban existence' (p. 184; see also BIOSECURITY).

The United Nations Development Programme had already (1994) invoked the concept of 'human security' as a universally applicable notion that, crucially, shifts the referent of security studies from nation-states to peoples. This move focuses on the prevention and amelioration of a wide range of RISKS and HAZARDS facing people in all human societies within what Beck calls a global RISK SOCIETY (Beck, 1998; see also Theranian, 1999).

These proposals are important, but they also collide with a recent stream of work on BIOPOWER, if they are understood to imply a transition from geopolitical regimes that take TERRITORY as their object to biopolitical regimes that take POPULATION as their object. Inspired by Michel Foucault's lectures in the late 1970s (translated as Foucault, 2007 [2004]), researchers are now asking urgent questions about the biophysical and medicalized vocabularies in which security is being re-visioned, and the ways in which governmental technologies of contingency are entering into the very construction of life itself (Dillon, 2008). In one sense, these more recent interventions reactivate and radicalize a stream of work on the ways in which hazards, risks and fear intersect in the constitution of everyday life. In major metropolitan centres in the global NORTH and in the global SOUTH, the POLICE have become increasingly militarized, and so has architecture – to such a degree, indeed, that there is now a critical online 'field guide to military urbanism' (Subtopia, at http://subtopia. blogspot.com: see also Caldeira, 1999; Low, 2004). The 'securitization' of EVERYDAY LIFE has become so commonplace – so 'normal' – that one of the most popular, and certainly one of the edgiest, magazines on the role of technology in contemporary culture includes regular blogs on national security (Danger Room: http://blog. wired.com/defense) and on privacy, security, politics and crime (Threat Level: http://blog. wired.com/27bstroke6/). This brings us full circle, to a point at which strategic sites in cities are targeted by terrorist groups and these threats are used in turn to legitimate widespread efforts to securitize cities through installing checkpoints, defensive urban and landscape designs, and systems of intensified electronic surveillance (Graham, 2004a; Gray and Wyly, 2007; Katz, 2007).   SG/DG

Suggested reading
Bialasiewicz, Campbell, Elden, Graham, Jeffrey and Williams (2007); Dalby (2002). See also Subtopia, at http://subtopia.blogspot.com.

segregation The phenomenon of segregation is said to occur when two or more groups occupy different spaces within the same CITY, REGION or even STATE. The types of patterns identified as segregated go back to the beginnings of concentrated human settlement. Even ancient cities, for example, were usually divided internally into quarters associated with particular groups, and also characterized by a sharp separation between urban (inside the wall) and suburban (outside) groups. Human settlements have always been socially stratified and those designated as 'others' – whether based upon religion, culture, economic status or any other social division – have been relegated to specific, usually environmentally poor, places (see also OTHER/OTHERNESS). That is, social marginalization is almost always associated with spatial segregation.

The degree of segregation, or separation between groups, varies. A group may be more prevalent in one area than another: for example, people of a particular RELIGION may have a tendency to live near their place of worship but still live among people of other faiths, so that the degree of segregation is low. At the other end of the spectrum, groups may be pushed into separate areas and have their MOBILITY curtailed, as in the Jewish GHETTOS created by the Nazis during the HOLOCAUST or the segregated districts imposed by the APARTHEID regime in South Africa. The process is not merely historical: at the end of 2006, for example, several local authorities in Italy decided to designate separate spaces for Roma (Gypsy) people, complete with fences and gates regulating movement in and out.

These examples highlight another crucial element: segregation can arise from discriminatory forces outside a group and/or from the social organization and predilections of the group itself. The internal side of this dynamic was first theorized by the CHICAGO SCHOOL of urban sociologists, as they tried to understand the nature of immigrant settlement in early-twentieth-century cities in the USA. They believed that newcomers gravitated into ENCLAVES specific to their cultural group and that these segregated areas helped people to come to terms with their new society. Gradually, as individuals adapted to American CULTURE by learning English, upgrading their education and obtaining better jobs, they would move to multi-ethnic (non-segregated) neighbourhoods, typically in suburbs (see SUBURB/ANIZATION). Subsequent critics charged that the Chicago School

673

ignored powerful forces of RACIALIZATION involved in the creation and maintenance of enclaves generally, and that they particularly downplayed the RACISM that forced African-Americans into ghettos. A helpful intervention distinguished between SLUMS, neighbourhoods of POVERTY, and ghettos, places where racialized groups are trapped in poverty, which is transmitted intergenerationally (Philpott, 1979). Recent social geographers have been far more attentive to the 'constraint' side of segregation, perhaps to the detriment of understanding the degree of social organization within marginalized communities.

The consequences of urban ethnic segregation have been discussed at length by geographers and sociologists. In early statements by the Chicago School, enclaves were deemed beneficial as long as individuals only resided in them temporarily. Further, those who remained in enclaves were seen as insufficiently assimilated (see ASSIMILATION) and therefore at fault. Since then, assessments have been more complex, with several basic strands of thought. Some continue to see segregation as indicative of a reluctance to assimilate, and believe that enclaves and ghettos reproduce SOCIAL EXCLUSION because their inhabitants adopt a 'culture of poverty' associated with laziness, reliance on welfare, and crime (cf. Lewis, 1969a). Another, more critical, interpretation focuses on the institutional practices that perpetuate segregation and therefore the harm that it causes (Massey and Denton, 1993). From this point of view, segregated LANDSCAPES are both the result of inequality and also a mechanism for the reproduction of inequality. Other scholars have sought to reconcile the classic view of the Chicago School, that residents of segregated areas gain certain benefits, with these later critical perspectives, arguing that segregation can have both beneficial and deleterious effects (Peach, 1996; Logan, Alba and Zhang, 2002). Moreover, planned dispersion of marginalized residents of segregated neighbourhoods does not necessarily raise their level of opportunity or standard of living (Musterd, 2003).

The issue of segregation has become particularly charged in EUROPE, where prominent commentators have linked race riots in the UK and France to the effects of segregated urban environments (cf. Amin, 2003; Haddad and Balz, 2006). Those affiliated with the political right see concentrated minority/immigrant neighbourhoods as the result of a deliberate choice made by their inhabitants to embrace cultural isolation, an attempt to lead lives separate from mainstream society (for which the term 'parallel lives' is invoked: Amin, 2002a), while progressive critics believe that segregation is a response to racism and economic marginalization. Regardless, socio-spatial segregation is seen as an ingredient in social unrest.

The link between racialization and CLASS division, which is so obvious in the riots just discussed, is generally under-theorized in the literature on segregation. To a large degree, this omission reflects another legacy of the Chicago School. Over the past century, in geography at least, studies of segregation have been dominated by a concern for cultural forms of segregation rather than class. However, socio-spatial divisions based on class have been equally pervasive, and were first theorized in the mid-nineteenth century, as this famous statement by Friedrich Engels testifies:

> Every great city has one or more slums, where the working-class is crowded together.... And the finest part of the arrangement is this, that the members of [the] money aristocracy can take the shortest road through the middle of all the labouring districts to their places of business, without ever seeing that they are in the midst of the grimy misery that lurks to the right and the left. (Engels, 1987 [1845], pp. 70, 86)

Arguably, the situation is exactly the opposite in contemporary cities: poverty is exposed, but affluence is hidden behind walls in GATED COMMUNITIES, protected by private security systems and electronic surveillance (le Goix, 2005). As in the past, the privileged protect themselves, though the mechanisms of this process, and the detailed spatial patterns that are generated, vary.

Recently, scholars have explored the relationship between different forms of segregation, such as socio-economic class and ethnic origin (Clark and Blue, 2004). Research has also shown the relationship between residential segregation and the educational system (Burgess, Wilson and Lupton, 2005; Denton, 1996), and the fact that CHILDREN raised in highly segregated neighbourhoods experience lasting difficulty as students, even when they are in universities outside their home city (Massey and Fischer, 2006). DH

Suggested reading
Kaplan (2005); Massey and Denton (1993); Peach (1996c).

segregation, measurement of Social scientists have long tried to find ways of depicting and measuring the degree of SEGREGATION between groups in societies, especially cities. In early discussions of this topic, such as the classic studies by sociologists collectively known as the CHICAGO SCHOOL, segregation was portrayed in descriptive terms. Ernest Burgess (1967), for example, included maps that characterized areas of Chicago as the 'Deutschland Ghetto', 'Little Sicily' and the 'Black Belt'. But these terms were highly generalized and none of the areas identified on the maps held completely mono-ethnic populations. Over the past century, sociologists and geographers have struggled to find more accurate ways to visualize and analyse segregation.

The social geography of a specific group is usually depicted in MAPS that are either based on standard percentage figures or as LOCATION QUOTIENTS (LQs). These maps show areas where a group is concentrated, providing a visual demonstration of the degree of segregation involved. A group that is fully integrated into the population at large would be evenly distributed across the territory in question (with all LQ figures close to 1.0), while a completely segregated (ghettoized) group would be concentrated in a single area, with low LQ figures throughout the map except in the area of concentration.

While maps such as these are undoubtedly an improvement over the impressionistic generalizations made in early sociological studies, they remain ambiguous. More precise statistics designed to represent the degree of segregation of groups were first introduced in the late 1940s and two gained ascendancy after a crucial paper published in the mid-1950s (Duncan and Duncan, 1955). The *Index of Dissimilarity* is a measure of the degree of residential isolation between two groups and is calculated as:

$$ID_{xy} = \frac{1}{2} \sum_{i=1}^{k} [x_i - y_i],$$

where *ID* is the Index of Dissimilarity between groups *x* and *y*; x_i and y_i are the percentages of the two groups that reside in a particular spatial unit, such as a Census Tract, in a city (note that the difference in these percentages is taken as an absolute value and there are no negative numbers used in the calculation of the *ID*); and *k* is the number of spatial units that make up the whole. Arithmetically, the index shows the proportion of group *x* that would have to change its location in order to match the distribution of group *y*. An *ID* value of 0 means the two groups are precisely co-located across the city or region in question, while a value of 100 would mean that the two do not overlap at all. The *Index of Segregation* (*IS*) is calculated in much the same way, but between an individual group and all other groups in a society; *IS* values also range from 0 to 100.

Although the *ID* and *IS* have been the most enduring measures of segregation, they share a number of problems. First, there is no straightforward way to decide when an *ID* or *IS* value is significant. After considerable debate, researchers have developed a consensus that values under 25 indicate little or no segregation, while those over 60 are interpreted as indicating a high level of segregation. Second, both indices are SCALE-dependent: they tend to be higher when a city or region is divided into a larger number of administrative units (Johnston, Forrest and Poulson, 2001). For this reason, comparisons of index values over time or between cities are suspect, unless the scale of spatial units is constant (which is relatively rare, particularly in international comparisons; see Van Valley and Roof, 1976). Third, index values for groups with small populations tend to be higher than those for groups that are large. Finally, indices speak to the degree of isolation of a group but do not describe particular spatial patterns. For example, the *IS* for a group that is entirely located in one inner-city neighbourhood, which is the only group in that place, would be 100. But the *IS* would also be 100 for a group located in four different suburbs if it was the only group in those areas. The reasons for these segregated patterns could be entirely different (the first group could be impoverished while the latter could be affluent), but the *IS* values would be the same.

A number of efforts have been made to provide better measures of segregation. These are summarized by Massey and Denton (1986), who discuss five dimensions of segregation (and measures associated with each). In addition to *isolation or dissimilarity*, they describe: *concentration versus dispersion; centralization versus dispersion; clustering among groups* (e.g. individual European-origin groups may be isolated from one-another, but all European-origin groups could be in the same general area of a city that is distinct from the location of Asians, Hispanics etc.); and the degree of *exposure* between groups (also see Lieberson, 1981).

675

Despite the proliferation of indices, the *ID* and *IS* measures remain the most widely used, perhaps due to their ease of interpretation and mathematical simplicity. Also, these indices are adaptable to other types of study. For example, the same logic and formulae can be used to measure the degree of occupational segmentation, and in this case the *IS* would indicate the proportion of a group that would have to change occupations in order to have the same distribution in the LABOUR MARKET as the general population (e.g. Hiebert, 1999).　DH

Suggested reading
Massey and Denton (1986); Peach (1975).

self-determination The perceived right of a cultural group who identify with a particular piece of TERRITORY to control their political future. The concept falls within the broader political IDEOLOGY of NATIONALISM, but has a specific focus on the politics of overthrowing what is seen as unjust control of territory by an external power. Self-determination has been a rallying cry against IMPERIALISM and COLONIALISM, and is supported by the United Nations Charter. Indigenous groups, such as Native Americans and other 'first peoples', are contemporary advocates of self-determination politics, following the wave of DECOLONIZATION after the Second World War.　CF

Suggested reading
Macedo and Buchanan (2003).

sense of place This term is usually taken to refer to the attitudes and feelings that individuals and groups hold *vis-à-vis* the geographical areas in which they live. It further commonly suggests intimate, personal and emotional relationships between self and place. Thus, in early HUMANISTIC GEOGRAPHY, a 'sense of place' was understood largely in terms of positive affective qualities of place-attachment; that is, senses of affection, attachment and belonging and even 'love of place' (TOPOPHILIA: see Relph, 1976; Tuan, 1977). Such work belongs to a long-standing (and still influential; see Casey, 1998) PHENOMENOLOGICAL tradition in which place is presented as the meaningful, even potentially redemptive counter to abstract, rationalist and unlocalized notions of 'space'. However, the more critical approaches characteristic of SOCIAL and CULTURAL GEOGRAPHIES from the 1980s onwards have more often sought to highlight how such positive senses of place and IDENTITY may in fact often be based upon the symbolic and physical exclusion of those deemed to be 'out-of-place' (Cresswell, 1996).

Equally, much early work on senses of place (e.g. Relph, 1976) subscribed at least implicitly to a particular historical narrative in which supposedly authentic or original forms of place-based COMMUNITY or dwelling are seen as being progressively eroded by economic and cultural forces such as URBANIZATION, INDUSTRIALIZATION and GLOBALIZATION. These forces are understood as working to occlude the distinctiveness of particular places and cultures, so producing an increasingly 'placeless' world. But in explicit contrast to such accounts, Doreen Massey's (1994a) influential essay on a 'global sense of place' sought to advance a conception of PLACE as porous, outward-looking and progressive, as opposed to conservative, enclosed and unitary. The development of a progressive sense of place, for Massey, involves rejecting false nostalgia for pre-modern singular and coherent places, and embracing instead the culturally multiple, dynamic and connective aspects of place in a globalizing world.

While Massey's work has opened up new agendas for geographical research on senses of place, older usages of the term, in which senses of attachment and belonging are foregrounded as investigative objects, continue to be productively elaborated and refined, most notably in Feld and Basso's (1998) North American-based collection *Senses of place*. JWY

Suggested reading
Feld and Basso (1998); Massey (1994); Relph (1976).

sequence analysis An EXPLORATORY DATA ANALYSIS technique for analysing LONGITUDINAL DATA. Social behaviours, such as housing careers defined in terms of tenure and price (Clark, Deurloo and Dieleman, 2003), are likely to be patterned with many sequences that are only trivially different across different households. Unlike other techniques, such as event history analysis, the aim is not to work spell by spell, trying to account for the transition from one state to another. In contrast, sequence analysis works holistically (Pollock, 2007), classifying ordered sequences into a relatively few characteristic trajectories and then seeking to examine what determines membership of a particular trajectory. Trajectories can be defined in both time and space, so that this approach can be used to identify common time-geographic paths (Shoval and Isaacson, 2007).

A key part of the approach is that ordered sequences are clustered into a data-driven typology, according to some algorithm such as 'optimal matching' (Abbott and Tsay, 2000), which grew out of techniques developed during the 1980s and employed by biochemists to analyse DNA sequences. This works by measuring the dissimilarity of every pair of sequences by calculating the relative effort (the 'cost') needed to transform one sequence into another. Transformations are of three types – substitutions, insertions, deletions – and the user may attach a differential cost to each type of change so that, for example, moving from the rented sector to owner occupation may be given a higher cost than the opposite move. Dissimilarity is then defined as the minimum cost of transforming one sequence into another; the overall matrix of dissimilarities between all pairs can then be input to a cluster analysis, which groups together similar paths (cf. CLASSIFICATION AND REGIONALIZATION). The popularity of the approach can be expected to increase as more longitudinal data and general-purpose SOFTWARE FOR QUANTITATIVE ANALYSIS become available (Brzinsky-Fay and Luniak, 2006). KJ

Suggested reading
The publicly available software Transition Data Analysis has facilities to undertake sequence analysis (http://steinhaus.stat.ruhr-uni-bochum.de/tda.html).

sequent occupance 'The view of geography as a succession of stages of human occupance ... which establishes the genetics of each stage in terms of its predecessor' (Whittlesey, 1929; cf. SETTLEMENT CONTINUITY). As this suggests, Whittlesey – like other European and North American geographers in the early twentieth century – was strongly influenced by biological MODELS. He acknowledged that the analogy between 'sequent occupance in CHOROLOGY' and plant succession in botany would be 'apparent to all', but he insisted that his own conception of cultural–historical geography was more intricate. While 'human occupance of area, like other biotic phenomena, carries within itself the seeds of its own transformation,' such uninterrupted or 'normal' progressions would be 'rare, perhaps only ideal, because extraneous forces are likely to interfere with the normal course, altering either its direction, or rate, or both' and 'breaking or knotting the thread of sequent occupance'. Whittlesey's thesis directly resembles Frederick Jackson Turner's FRONTIER THESIS: both men

came from the American Midwest, and the transition from rural to urban societies was within living memory for them and their contemporaries. The idea was used more loosely by later cultural geographers to refer to little more than the claim that CULTURAL LANDSCAPES contain traces from the earlier stages of settlement (cf. Broek, 1932, which is usually regarded as the classic application). The biological METAPHOR was in decline in social science even as Whittlesey was writing, however, and in some ways the popularity of the thesis reflects the (then) isolation of HUMAN GEOGRAPHY among the social sciences in North America (Herbst, 1961). GK

Suggested reading
Whittlesey (1929).

services Services have historically been defined as 'activities which are relatively detached from material production and which as a consequence do not directly involve the processing of physical materials. The main differences between manufacturing and service products seems to be that the expertise provided by services relies much more directly on work-force skills, experience, and knowledge than on physical techniques embodied in machinery or processes' (Marshall, Wood, Daniels et al. 1988, p. 11). Geographers have produced a substantial and still growing corpus of work on services, one by-product of which has been to confirm the difficulty of working with these sorts of general statements. It is clear that there is no single geography of services, and there are diminishing conceptual returns of thinking of services in this way. Rather, there is a whole set of different geographies of services, which vary according to the characteristics of the specific industry. The most recent definitional work has used binaries – either/ors – to produce more specific definitions. So, terms such as PRODUCER SERVICES or consumer services, PUBLIC SERVICES or private services, and tradeable or non-tradeable services have been used. While these distinctions are an improvement on past generalizations, they pose their own problems. How to move beyond oppositional definitions? What is it that binds different services together or distinguishes them? For some, rather than seeing manufacturing and services as discrete, as separate entities, there is a need to conceptualize the COMMODITY CHAINS or production NETWORKS that link them (Henderson, Dicken, Hess, Coe and Yeung, 2001). If we trace these, then we generate a different set of insights into the service component in 'manufacturing' and the manufacturing component in 'services'.

The most recent work on the geographies of services has developed around four broad themes (Dicken, 2006). The first is the internationalization or GLOBALIZATION of service firms, with attention to why, how and to what effect they are becoming international in scope. In tandem with this emphasis on the dynamics of geographical expansion has come a widening in those industries in which geographers have performed empirical studies. We know now more about what is going on in more service industries. The second theme is the intra-organizational dynamics of the service industries; in particular, on the strategies of small and medium-sized firms. In some parts of the world it is these types of companies, and not the largest TRANSNATIONAL CORPORATIONS, that are behind the growth of urban and regional economies. The third theme is the emergence of the KNOWLEDGE ECONOMY: the rise of service activities as a function of the production and circulation of knowledge, and the growth of the knowledge industries – accountancies, business schools, consultancies of all types, law firms and so on – directed towards the construction of knowledge for economic gain. The fourth theme is PERFORMANCE and, specifically, the ways in which services are 'performed', reflecting the imprint of the CULTURAL TURN on ECONOMIC GEOGRAPHY (Thrift, 2005b).

These re-definitions and conceptual elaborations are vital because services have increased their absolute and relative importance in the ECONOMY (Bryson, Daniels and Warf, 2004). Service industries now contribute significantly to the economic performance of nations and cities and employ a growing number of workers. While geographers, and other social scientists, have been disputing how best to define services, others have been debating their economic importance, making political cases for and against particular forms of state intervention on the basis of projected economic impacts. This emphasis on service industries only reconfirms the importance of the work of geographers in this area of research.   KWa

Suggested reading
Bryson, Daniels and Warf (2004); Dicken (2006).

settlement continuity The continuity of sites of settlement and systems of territorial organization across periods of social transformation, particularly associated with the arrival of new peoples and POWER structures into an area (cf. SEQUENT OCCUPANCE). In HISTORICAL GEOGRAPHY, the term is most closely associated with a debate over the situation in Britain after the collapse of the Roman occupation and the establishment of the Anglo-Saxon kingdoms. At one extreme is the view that the sparse representation of British PLACE NAMES reflects an equally sparse Romano-British population that was rapidly overwhelmed by Anglo-Saxon immigrants who created their own distinctive LANDSCAPES. At the other is the view that the Anglo-Saxons were a small minority who rapidly acquired political control without diluting the ethnic IDENTITY of the British people. The latter is less well supported than the former, although evidence remains ambiguous for both sides of the debate. There are many instances of pre-English names adopted by the Anglo-Saxons and toponymic evidence suggests some kind of peaceful coexistence or cohabitation of British and Old English speakers (Cameron, 1980). The nature of the links to the Romano-British past clearly varied from REGION to region, but even in the Anglo-Saxon kingdom of Kent (a Roman name), founded by the middle of the fifth century, there is evidence of continuity in urban settlement and the estate structure in the countryside through a distinctive system of *lathes* (county subdivisions) centred on royal *vills* (townships) (Everitt, 1986). Similar systems are found over wide areas of northern England, suggesting that it was very old indeed. In much of the kingdom of Northumbria, the main units of authority extended over areas of c.100 square miles, centring on a royal *vill* to which all the inhabitants owed dues. Indeed, a system of this kind can be documented from later sources to have extended over a continuous belt from Wales across northern England into Scotland. It is possible that such forms of territorial organization reflect the impress of a Romano-British past that is also detectable in Kent (Jones, 1976). However, such views also have to confront the relative dearth of archaeological evidence for the Britons from the period after AD 400 in the southern and eastern areas of England. Nonetheless, there are few Anglian graves in the most northerly English regions, which certainly remained largely British. Furthermore, several Anglo-Saxon dynasties may have been partly British in origin (Wessex), suggesting that early Anglo-Saxon kingdoms were often older organizations that had come under invaders' control, while the great majority of the population stayed on to work the land (Campbell, 1982). RMS

Suggested reading
Campbell (1982).

settler society A euphemism for brutal processes of racialized dispossession, along with the decimation or subjugation of local populations. Occupation through conquest has typically been justified in terms of doctrines of TERRA NULLIUS (empty lands), and assertions of progress and redemption. Indeed, the society that is salient in the term 'settler society' is precisely that which excludes racialized others. While this definition obviously encompasses huge swathes of the world, the term is most often associated with British colonial settlement (see COLONIALISM).

Celebratory versions of liberal historiography have long been dominant in the production of knowledge about settler societies. Challenging this stance, one influential strand of scholarship argues that such societies are best understood in terms of their incorporation within the capitalist MODE OF PRODUCTION (see CAPITALISM). Denoon, for example, recognizes 'powerful strands of commonality' (1983, p. 122) among the societies encompassed by his study – New Zealand, Australia and South Africa, as well as Argentina and Chile, from 1890 to 1914 – based on their integration into the international MARKET and relations of dependency with imperial powers (see IMPERIALISM).

A subsequent body of critical scholarship insists on attention to articulations of GENDER, RACE, ETHNICITY and CLASS in the constitution and transformation of settler societies. Stasiulis and Yuval-Davis (1995), for example, bring together studies that incorporate feminist and post-colonial perspectives (see FEMINIST GEOGRAPHIES and POST-COLONIALISM) in order to 'unsettle settler societies'. Yet the range of 'settler societies' encompassed by the book – including the USA, Mexico, Peru, Algeria and Israel–Palestine, in addition to Australia, New Zealand, Canada, South Africa and Zimbabwe – raises the question of what is *not* (or has not been) a settler society. Indeed, the editors concede that their extremely broad conception of settler society underscores the difficulty of drawing a clear line of demarcation.

More recent work draws explicitly on critical conceptions of SPATIALITY. Where Stasiulis and Yuval-Davis seek to unsettle, Sherene Razack's (2002) edited collection aims at 'unmapping white settler society' – in this case, Canada. Focusing on the production of different racialized spaces, the volume is animated by 'the fervent belief that white settler societies can transcend their bloody beginnings and contemporary inequalities by remembering and confronting the racial hierarchies that structure our lives' (Razack, 2002, p. 5: see also WHITENESS). What is missing, however, is attention to the practices of counter-mapping through which native people in Canada have engaged in struggles for repossession.

Struggles for redress in situations of racialized dispossession are extremely widespread, and accelerating in some parts of the world, including Zimbabwe, South Africa and Aorteroa–New Zealand. They also underscore a crucial question regarding 'settler societies' – namely, whether and how the initial processes of settlement remain politically salient in the present. A key to grappling with this question is understanding historical geographies of racialized dispossession not as an event (or set of events) that can be consigned to some precapitalist or early colonial past, but as ongoing processes that remain actively constitutive of what Derek Gregory (2004b) calls the 'colonial present'. MW

Suggested reading
Moore (2005); Sparke (2005).

sex The term has been used historically to describe both sex differences – male/female – which are assumed to flow from anatomy, and a physical drive. Since the late 1970s both these meanings of sex, which characterize it as a biological given, have been problematized, and it has been re-theorized in increasingly complex ways. FEMINISM (Women and Geography Study Group, 1997) first introduced, and then troubled, the distinction between sex (biology) and GENDER (social meanings ascribed to biological differences). Foucault (1978 [1976]) identified sex and the related concept of sexuality as discursive constructions that are temporally and spatially specific. GV

sexuality In HUMAN GEOGRAPHY, there has been considerable interest in the mutual constitution of sexualities and space, so that most studies have focused on the SPATIALITY of the construction of sexual identities and the sexuality of SPACE. The earliest work on sexuality and geography focused on heterosexual prostitution. In the 1990s a significant body of research developed, initially on the geographies of lesbian and gay men, and latterly, on queer geographies (Bell and Valentine, 1995). This was facilitated by the development of POST-MODERN thought within human geography that promoted a sensitivity to DIFFERENCE. As a result of the impact of this research, the study of sexuality and geography is often assumed to be synonymous with the study of lesbians, gay men and bisexual and transgendered people, yet there is a growing interest in geographies of heterosexualities, and sexuality is also important in geographical writing using PSYCHOANALYTIC THEORY. The complex theoretical links between sexuality and GENDER, most notably in feminist theory, mean that the two are commonly discussed in tandem.

Work on geographies of sexualities has been most prolific within the sub-disciplinary areas of URBAN, SOCIAL and CULTURAL GEOGRAPHY, but it is also gradually spilling out into other parts of the discipline, including ECONOMIC GEOGRAPHY, POLITICAL GEOGRAPHY and MEDICAL GEOGRAPHY, in the form of research on the pink economy, sexual citizenship and HIV/AIDS, respectively (e.g. Bell and Binnie, 2000). The main strands of writing on sexuality and geography can be summarized as follows:

(1) *Geographies of lesbian, gay and bisexual lives.* Lesbians and gay men lead distinct lifestyles – defined to a lesser or greater extent by their sexuality and others' reactions to it – which have a variety of spatial expressions, creating distinct social and cultural LANDSCAPES in some contemporary cities. A number of studies have mapped gay commercial and resident districts. Knopp's (1992) work on GENTRIFICATION by gay men particularly contributed to analysing the role of sexuality within the spatial dynamics of CAPITALISM. Studies of lesbian space have suggested that women also create spatially concentrated COMMUNITIES but that these have a quasi-underground character, although having a high level of visibility among lesbians themselves (Podmore, 2001).

'Gay space' – including gay commercial and residential districts (such as the Castro District in San Francisco) as well as lesbian, gay, bisexual and transgender (LGBT) parades, have been identified as important sites of political claims-making (Johnston, 2001). Yet the very success of these LGBT claims has led to the incorporation of these previously mar-

ginalized groups through the imaging, branding and commodification of gay space as a cosmopolitan spectacle for a heterosexual market (Bell and Binnie, 2004).

While much of the work on geographies of lesbian and gay lives is located in the urban, there is an upsurge of interest in the structural limitations experienced by those living in rural areas, and the attempts of sexual dissidents to establish UTOPIAN rural communities.

(2) *The heterosexuality of everyday space.* Studies have highlighted the fact that everyday spaces are commonly taken for granted as heterosexual, and have explored the processes through which spaces are produced in this way; and the disciplinary practices that regulate 'public' PERFORMANCE of sexualities (e.g. Valentine, 1993).

(3) *Geographies of HIV/AIDS.* Mapping the transmission of the HIV virus has been at the heart of medical geographers' attempts to trace its origins and establish global typologies. This work has been criticized by sexual dissidents as irrelevant and politically dangerous. Brown (1995) has played a key role in refocusing geographical research on HIV/AIDS on to understanding sexual relations and issues of HEALTH AND HEALTHCARE promotion.

(4) *Queer geographies.* These represent a reaction against the early work about the geographies of lesbians and gay men, which adopted an uncritical, all-embracing conceptualization of lesbian and gay identity. Drawing heavily on SOCIAL THEORY from outside the discipline, queer geographies have attempted to scrutinize the desirability of IDENTITY politics and to challenge notions of fixed identities, in particular by employing the concept of PERFORMATIVITY. Attempts have also been made to utilize the insights of QUEER THEORY to think about the production of SPACE (Bell, Binnie, Cream and Valentine, 1994) and to explore the importance of MOBILITY in queer quests for identity (Knopp, 2004). There is now an emerging body of work addressing queer identities from a POSTCOLONIAL perspective – for example, focusing on queer DIASPORIC community formation – and in the context of GLOBALIZATION and TOURISM (e.g. Hawley, 2001; Binnie, 2004). Here, geographers

have contributed to interdisciplinary debates about the 'queer tourism' industry and the differential positionings of racial, sexual, gendered and national subjects (Puar, 2002).

(5) *Geographies of heterosexualities.* These are most evident in historical and contemporary work on PROSTITUTION that has looked at the role of moral representations, social DISCOURSES and practices in regulating sex work (Hubbard, 1999). Geographical writing based on psychoanalytic theory has drawn on accounts of psychosexual development, sexual differences and desire, while also challenging the heterosexism evident in the writing of authors such as Lacan (see HOMOPHOBIA AND HETEROSEXISM). There is growing interest in heterosexuality as an institution through which links between the BODY, the HOME and the public sphere are produced and negotiated (Little and Leyshon, 2003; Robinson, Hockey and Meah, 2004; see also HETERONORMATIVITY).

(6) *Critiques of the discipline.* Geographers working on sexuality share many of the concerns of feminist geographers about the MASCULINIST, heteronormative and disembodied heritage of the discipline, and about the operation of power within the academy. GV

Suggested reading
Bell and Valentine (1995); Binnie (2004); Brown (2000).

shadow state A para-STATE APPARATUS comprising voluntary, non-profit organizations providing a host of goods and SERVICES. Although the form of the shadow state varies over time and between countries, it is commonly regulated and subsidized by public funds, simultaneously creating the ability to provide services while controlling political ACTIVISM. Neo-liberal policies (see NEO-LIBERALISM) and decentralization of the STATE have increased the role of the shadow state in social service delivery and COMMUNITY development; provoking questions about the implication of unequal access to the shadow state for CITIZENSHIP (Lake and Newman, 2002), GOVERNANCE and SOCIAL JUSTICE (DeVerteuil, Lee, and Wolch, 2002). CF

Suggested reading
Wolch (1990).

sharecropping A form of land tenure in which the landowners' returns take the form of a share of the farmers' produce rather than a cash or farm RENT. Sharecropping is also known by the French as *métayage* (Wells, 1984). Sharecropping arrangements involve short-term contracts for the annual cycle of production of a specific crop in which crop raising is contracted out to labouring HOUSEHOLDS, individuals or work gangs, who thereby take on the large part of economic risks of production. These arrangements have been widely assumed to belong to the agricultural past and interpreted as FEUDAL or pre-capitalist in nature (e.g. Marx, 1964), but they remain significant in contemporary agriculture, even in modern agriculture in, for example, the USA. Sharecropping takes many forms in different contexts, but all tend to be associated with highly concentrated patterns of landownership and exploitive labour relations; for example, in the cotton-growing South of the USA between white landowners and black farmers (Mann, 1984b), or between landowners and Mexican migrant workers in California's strawberry industry (Wells, 1996). MW

shift-share model A technique for describing the relative importance of different components of growth/decline in a regional economy, widely used in REGIONAL SCIENCE. Growth may be due to a REGION having a high concentration of industries that are growing nationally, for example; because of locational shifts within certain industries towards that region; or because of differential regional trends within and across industries. Shift-share analysis splits a region's growth (in employment, for example), relative to the national norm, into: (a) *a proportionality shift*, that proportion of the growth (decline) associated with the concentration of relatively fast(slow)-growing industrial sectors there; and (b) *a differential shift*, that proportion reflecting local trends that deviate from the national. RJ

Suggested reading
Armstrong and Taylor (1978).

shifting cultivation Minimally, shifting cultivation is an agricultural system characterized by a rotation of fields rather than of crops, by discontinuous cropping in which periods of fallowing are typically longer than periods of cropping, and by the clearing of fields (usually called swiddens) through the use of slash-and-burn techniques. Known by a variety of terms (including field-forest rotation, slash and burn, and swiddening), shifting cultivation is widespread throughout the humid tropics, but was also practiced in temperate EUROPE until the nineteenth century (and sometimes later) (Conklin, 1962). It is estimated that there are over 250 million shifting cultivators world-wide, with 100 million in South-East Asia alone. Shifting cultivation is enormously heterogeneous and subtypes can be distinguished according to crops raised, crop associations and successions, fallow lengths, climatic and soil conditions, field technologies, soil treatment and the MOBILITY of settlement. Many distinguish between *integral* (shifting cultivation as an integral part of SUBSISTENCE) and *partial* (shifting cultivation as a technological expedient for cash cropping; see PEASANT) forms of shifting cultivation (Conklin, 1962). In all shifting cultivation systems, the burning of cleared vegetation is critical to the release of nutrients, which ensures field productivity. Shifting cultivation by definition is land-extensive, and is threatened by population growth and MIGRATION, and expanding land occupation (see CARRYING CAPACITY; INTENSIVE AGRICULTURE). Shifting cultivation is often stigmatized as primitive or unproductive, but it is typically predicated upon a sophisticated understanding of local environmental conditions – so-called INDIGENOUS KNOWLEDGE – and exhibits considerable flexibility and adaptiveness. MW

significance test A statistical procedure for identifying the probability that an observed event could have occurred by chance. Most statistics – such as a CORRELATION coefficient – have an associated SAMPLING distribution identifying all possible values of the coefficient for a given set of empirical observations. For example, three observations can be rank-ordered in six different ways, so that if one is correlating the rank-order of neighbourhood death rates with the local levels of lead pollution, there would be 36 different ways in which the two sets of three observations could be organized, each producing a different correlation coefficient. Those coefficients form a FREQUENCY DISTRIBUTION in which some values would appear quite frequently, others more rarely. If the observed coefficient's value would occur only rarely, this outcome was unlikely to occur by chance: it is then presented as a significant result, as a correlation with interpretative value.

In studies involving large numbers of observations – 80 neighbourhoods instead of three, say – the frequency distribution can be

predetermined and the observed statistic located within it. Most analysts operate the rule of thumb that if an observed outcome is likely to occur less frequently than five times in every 100 ways in which the data can be organized, that is a statistically significant result. Statistical significance should not be confused with substantive importance, however; it says nothing about the importance of findings and how they should be interpreted.

Statistical significance tests are used in two ways. In CONFIRMATORY DATA ANALYSIS, they assist HYPOTHESIS testing, indicating whether an observed outcome in a sample (see SAMPLING) is likely to characterize the population from which it was drawn. (If the 80 neighbourhoods were a sample from 240 within a city, a correlation coefficient statistically significant at the 0.05 level would indicate that the relationship between the two variables in the sampled areas would almost certainly be found if the whole population had been studied.) In EXPLORATORY DATA ANALYSIS, there is no sample involved and the test is used to indicate the likely importance of an observed relationship occurring: one that would occur three times in every ten ways in which the data are organized is probably less important than one that would occur only once in every 500 ways. RJ

Suggested reading
Blalock (1970). See also http://bowland-files.lancs.ac.uk/monkey/ihe/linguistics/corpus3/3sig.htm.

simulacrum A term originally derived from Platonic theory, but popularized by Jean Baudrillard. Literally, the simulacrum is a copy without an original. Baudrillard extended the argument about the modern dominance of IMAGES and IDEOLOGY by suggesting an historical *procession* of the simulacra. First, there was presence – people met and spoke – then technologies of writing allowed re-presentation of those who were not present. Now media allow the simulation of those who never existed. The term gained wide usage in discussions of themed environments such as Disneyland or shopping malls. 'Main street', Disneyland thus simulates a mythic idea of a small town community hub that has no counterpoint in reality (see DISNEYFICATION). MC

Suggested reading
Baudrillard (1983).

simulation A HEURISTIC device for solving otherwise intractable mathematical and statistical problems. There are two broad types of application: the creation of 'artificial worlds', and the use of simulation as part of the estimation of quantitative models. An early application of the former was Torsten Hägerstrand's work on the DIFFUSION of INNOVATION. He treated this as a spatial STO-CHASTIC PROCESS, in that while it had an underlying structure (adoption would decrease with distance as social interaction decreases) it could also turn out differently each time. Monte Carlo procedures were used to draw random numbers and innovation diffused outwards from initial adopters according to a probabilistic MEAN INFORMATION FIELD. Such simulation has grown rapidly in recent years and it is at the core of MICRO-SIMULATION METHODS and AGENT-BASED MODELLING. Such approaches have now developed to the extent of the SimBritain project, where as part of EVIDENCE-BASED POLICY the geographical impact of government policies can be evaluated (Ballas, Clarke, Dorling and Rossiter, 2007).

The second use of simulation, statistical model calibration, has also seen major recent developments, which have been considerably aided by increased computing power. One aspect of this is a computer-intensive approach to CONFIRMATORY DATA ANALYSIS and HYPOTHESIS testing, in which the observed data are re-sampled to characterize the empirical distribution of a test statistic. More importantly, a new method of estimation called MARKOV CHAIN Monte Carlo simulation has been developed that allows the estimation of very complex models, including MULTI-LEVEL MODELS. This methodology allows a building block approach to estimation, so that complex problems can be decomposed into lots of small ones. It is especially important for BAYESIAN ANALYSIS, for it allows the estimation of previously intractable joint posterior distribution (based on prior beliefs, data and assumptions) by iterative simulation from the much more straightforward marginal distributions (Davies-Withers, 2002).   KJ

Suggested reading
Gilbert and Troitzsch (2005); Gill (2002); Noreen (1989).

situated knowledge A term coined by the feminist cultural critic of science, Donna Haraway (1991, p. 188), to denote 'a doctrine of embodied objectivity that accommodates paradoxical and critical feminist science projects'. Situated knowledge replaces the traditional conception of SCIENCE as the pursuit of a disembodied, inviolable and neutral OBJECTIVITY with a formulation of objectivity that stresses corporeality, SOCIAL CONSTRUCTION and CULTURAL POLITICS.

Haraway argues that vision or sight is a guiding METAPHOR for Western scientists in carrying out their work: they see the world, they make observations and collect evidence (from the Latin verb, *videre*, to see) and they write down its truths. This conceit carries over into ordinary speech too when we say, for example, 'I see', meaning 'I understand'. The language of knowledge production is saturated with visual metaphors in both a technical-scientific and an everyday sense. But Wittgenstein reminds us that 'the limits of my language are the limits of my world', and in working within this language, in construing VISION AND VISUALITY in this way, scientists limit their worlds by writing themselves out of their own stories: failing to recognize their constitutive role in world-making, they reduce themselves to the status of 'modest witness' (Haraway, 1997, ch. 1). That presumption of modesty, Haraway argues, is a direct consequence of the starting point of visuality. It creates the illusory possibility of a disembodied science. She calls this illusion a 'god trick', the idea that it is possible to have 'vision from everywhere and nowhere' (Haraway, 1991, p. 191). Moreover, it is just such a trick that is the basis of one of science's most cherished ideas, objectivity, the belief in the possibility of a single, final, detached and unmarked ordering of the world. For Haraway (1991, p. 188), however, the 'gaze from nowhere', as she calls objectivity, is really a RHETORICAL move that hides and protects the interests of those who propose and benefit most from it, typically white Western men. 'Modesty pays off ... in the coin of epistemological and social power' (Haraway 1997, p. 23: see also EPISTEMOL-OGY). In this sense, then, being a 'modest witness' turns out not to be very modest at all. It is a strategy to promulgate a particular kind of knowledge and to guarantee its unassailable truth, which is often indelibly marked by HETERONORMATIVITY, MASCULINISM and RACISM (as her case studies from the life sciences testify).

Haraway (1997, ch. 4) labels scientific practices that masquerade under the cloak of objectivity 'fetishistic' because such knowledge is represented as a thing rather than a social process. Fetishism would not occur if it were recognized from the outset that all knowledge is embodied and partial; that is, 'situated'. And with that recognition comes the possibility of 'a usable, but not an innocent doctrine of objectivity' (Haraway, 1991c, p. 189). This form of 'usable objectivity' depends upon the two terms that underpin it:

(1) Embodiment means recognizing that knowledge is produced by specific bodies that always leave traces. Moreover, embodiment is not only human but also 'machinic'. Machines see and record the world and, like humans, they are more than passive observers; they construct it on the basis of particular ALGO-RITHMS and assumptions (cf. ACTOR-NETWORK THEORY). For example, software used in the computer programs of GEOGRAPHICAL INFORMATION SYSTEMS brings a systematic set of biases, hidden assumptions and *aporias*. Printouts and screenshots are not mirror copies of the world, 'the view from nowhere' but always the view from somewhere. Further, embodiment is collective not singular, mobile not fixed. Haraway (1991, p.195) writes: 'feminist embodiment ... is not about fixed location in a reified body ... but about nodes in fields, inflections in orientations, and responsibility for differences in material-semiotic fields of meaning'. Haraway's objectivity is constantly in motion, tugged and pulled among the various nodes of its constitutive field.

(2) Partial knowledge implies a recognition that no one, except gods and goddesses, possess full (objective) knowledge. There are only partial perspectives, a consequence of our own circumscribed subject location that makes us who we are, and what we know. Haraway (1991, p.193) writes: 'the knowing self is partial in all its guises, never finished, whole, simply there and original; it is always constructed and stitched together imperfectly.'

Embodiment and partiality are the conditions under which knowledge is acquired. Only when they are recognized as such is there hope of an attainable as opposed to a mythical objectivity. These are also the conditions of any politics. Embodied and partial knowledge necessitates that people literally reach out to one another and construct NETWORKS of affiliation: that is, they must engage in discussion, deliberation and evaluation; they thus come to recognize DIFFERENCE but also common beliefs and shared responsibilities. Through these 'shared conversations in epistemology', Haraway (1991, p. 191) argues, it is possible to forge 'solidarity in politics'. This does not mean that the end result is unanimity, or even that networks and conversations set us on a collective trajectory towards some final agreement. To the contrary, that was the assumption (and the failure) of the old type of objectivity. Rather, 'shared conversations' are open-ended, varied, sometimes inconsistent and paradoxical. But they are all we have, and the necessary condition for both political projects, such as FEMINISM, and epistemological ones, such as science. As a result, the traditional notion of objectivity must be recast, conceived as an incomplete process, not a final outcome. Objectivity then becomes the process of working out difference and commonality, of struggling epistemologically and politically to make connections, affiliations, and alliances. While situated knowledge is often contradictory, it contains the possibility of critical promise.

It is in exactly this spirit that Gregory (1994) argues that visions of modern GEOG-RAPHY as an intrinsically *European* science whose origins can be traced back to the late eighteenth century, and in particular to scientific expeditions beyond the shores of EUROPE (see EXPLORATION), mask its GENEALOGY as a distinctively *Eurocentric* science. Geographical knowledges, like any others, are always situated knowledges: their production often involves travel, like Cook's voyages into the South Pacific or the orbits of Earth-sensing satellites through space, and the products themselves enter into complex circuits of exchange, transfer and accumulation, but they are always marked by the situations in which and through which they are constituted (see also ETHNOCENTRISM; EUROCENTRISM; ORIENTALISM). Merrifield (1995) treats quite other, more recent and more radical 'expeditions' as exercises in the production of situated knowledge, while Cook (2001a, 2004) has used Haraway's proposals as a research method, a pedagogy, a form of writing and an exploration of MATERIAL CULTURE. In all these cases, however, it is important not to confuse situated knowledge with a form of IDEOLOGY-critique that subscribes to quite traditional notions of objectivity. For, as Rose (1997b) emphasizes, anyone claiming to fully situate their own knowledge is practising precisely the same kind of god trick that they criticize in others. All situated knowledge is partial, including the situated knowledge we have of ourselves and, of course, every entry in this *Dictionary* (cf. LOCAL KNOWLEDGE).   TB

Suggested reading
Haraway (1991, ch. 9).

situationists/situationism The Situationist International (SI) was a group of revolutionaries based in Western EUROPE between 1957 and 1972, committed to transforming dominant social and spatial relations. Their critiques of CAPITALIST as well as actually existing SOCIALIST STATES owed much to Marx as well as earlier avant-gardes such as Dada and surrealism. The group launched an uncompromising attack on the forces upholding what they believed were the alienating conditions of 'the society of the SPECTACLE', characterized by the increasing colonization of social life by the commodity. They sought to encourage existing revolts against hierarchical power by theoretically and practically articulating forms of revolutionary contestation. At the same time, they experimented with means of criticizing and freely constructing daily life. Geography was central to this endeavour, as they understood cities in particular as both key sites in the reproduction of social relations of domination, and potential realms of freedom and possibility. The situationist Guy Debord thus argued that the 'proletarian revolution is that *critique of human geography* whereby individuals and communities must construct places and events commensurate with the appropriation, no longer just of their labour, but of their total history' (Debord, 1994 [1967], thesis 178).

The SI remained small, with a total membership of 70, from 16 different countries. Developing their positions through a range of texts and artistic, cultural and political activities, the situationists were highly critical of the orthodox Left, and referred to undermining rather than contributing to specialist arenas of ART and academia. They therefore rejected the term 'situationism', claiming that it was a meaningless invention by opponents who were seeking to reduce their activities to a fixed dogma. The influence of the situationists has nevertheless been considerable and, after years of marginalization, has been increasingly recognized and reassessed. Interest has focused on their critique of the spectacle, and their associated critiques of urbanism and everyday life. Also influential have been practices of PSYCHOGEOGRAPHY as means of exploring and seeking ways to transform cities, and techniques of *détournement*, involving the hijacking of materials to create new meanings and effects (McDonough, 2002).

Situationist practices were utopian in their attempts to transform SPACE and SOCIETY through the 'construction of situations' and the production of a 'unitary urbanism', which found its most vivid expression in projects by the Dutch artist Constant for a nomadic and ludic New Babylon, and in their later concern with political–theoretical critique in the name of realizing what was hidden yet possible in modern life. Returning to the SI's utopianism and its critiques of URBANISM, is not only of historical interest, it has been argued, but can also serve to challenge how urban spaces are imagined and constructed, and to encourage struggles for alternatives (Pinder, 2005c; see UTOPIA). Resonances between situationist practices and contemporary political actions, especially over the production and contestation of space and in opposition to spectacular power, further demonstrate that, despite the 'strange respectability' that aspects of their project have recently accrued (Swyngedouw, 2002), they remain politically highly charged.   DP

Suggested reading
Pinder (2005c). See also Situationist International Online, at http://www.cddc.vt.edu/sionline/.

Sjoberg model A MODEL of social and spatial order of the PRE-INDUSTRIAL CITY, first expressed in Gideon Sjoberg's book of the same title (1960). Sjoberg's model arises from his desire to provide a critique of, and alternative to, the concentric ZONAL MODEL of the city offered by Ernest Burgess and, more generally, of HUMAN ECOLOGY as applied by prominent members of the CHICAGO SCHOOL. As such, Sjoberg's work was part of a larger project, initiated by Walter Firey (1947), to replace human ecology with STRUCTURAL FUNCTIONALISM as the central PARADIGM of urban sociology (p. 12). The major factors used to explain urban MORPHOLOGY in Sjoberg's model are social structure and technology.

Sjoberg begins by differentiating between non-urban, FEUDAL and industrial societies. He is concerned with the second of these: societies that utilize animate sources of energy, and are literate and urbanized, including all world CIVILIZATIONS prior to the INDUSTRIAL REVOLUTION as well as non-industrialized contemporary societies. He argues that feudal, or pre-industrial, societies everywhere, and through time, are characterized by similar technological achievements and a three-tiered CLASS structure that includes a small ruling class, a large lower class and outcast groups. The ruling class, comprised of those in religious and administrative authority, establishes a social order that reproduces its control over succeeding generations: URBANIZATION is both the outcome of social stratification and a means whereby HEGEMONY is perpetuated. The MORPHOLOGY of pre-industrial cities reflects this interdependence between social and spatial order: POWER is consolidated by the ruling class through its residential location in the city centre, the most protected and most accessible district. Here, residents forge a social solidarity based on their literacy, access to the surplus (which is stored in the central area of the city), and shared upperclass CULTURE, which includes distinctive manners and patterns of speech. Elite clustering in the city centre is reinforced by the lack of rapid transportation.

The privileged central district is surrounded by haphazardly arranged NEIGHBOURHOODS housing the lower class. Households in these areas are sorted by occupation/income (merchants near the centre, followed by minor bureaucrats, artisans and, finally, the unskilled), ethnic origin and extended family networks. Merchants are generally not accorded elite status, since power is achieved through religious and military control, while trade is viewed with suspicion. The model is less clear on the residential placement of outcast groups (typically slaves and other conquered peoples): some of these perform service roles and are intermingled with the rest of the urban population, while others live at the extreme periphery of the city – frequently beyond its walls.

In formulating this model, Sjoberg reverses the logic used by Burgess – who placed commercial activities at the centre of the city, and a succession of poor through wealthy residential districts around it. Sjoberg notes that the Burgess model is applicable only to industrial cities, where production and commerce propel economic growth and where capitalists are accorded high social standing. Further, he argues that human ecology incorrectly treats urbanization as an independent social force, when in reality urban growth should be seen as a 'dependent variable', as it depends on the distribution of social power, and on available technology. Empirical investigations of the Sjoberg model have been generally supportive, but caution that the model cannot account for the intricate details of urban development across different cultural contexts. Others have criticized the theoretical content of Sjoberg's work, especially his stress on the role of technology and his uncritical view of social power. Sjoberg's functionalist logic (which blurs distinctions between causes and consequences),

however, remains largely unnoticed and unchallenged (see FUNCTIONALISM).　　　DH

Suggested reading
Carter (1983); Langton (1975); Ley (1983); Morris (1994); Radford (1979); Wheatley (1963).

skid row Essentially a North American term, 'skid row' traditionally referred to areas characterized by concentrations of rooming houses and accommodation for single men working in the timber industry: over time, the term has become a more general shorthand for areas where HOMELESSNESS is evident. Often offering hostel or temporary accommodation, skid rows are thus notorious as spaces of rough sleeping, with temporary pavement encampments or 'cardboard cities' offering refuge for those who congregate in these areas. In the larger skid rows, intricate SOCIAL NETWORKS and relationships may develop within the COMMUNITY, as well as between the service-dependent and those service providers who seek to assist them with welfare, alcohol, drug and HEALTH issues (Rowe and Wolch, 1990). In many instances, dwellers of areas described as skid row districts have fought to contest this designation: despite this, the term persists in the North American social imagination as a pejorative description of the social margins of the city.

Studies by urban sociologists and geographers have suggested that the development of skid row areas in North American cities has, in some cases, been connected to policies of containment designed to remove street homeless populations from wealthier locales. Yet currently the number of skid row districts is declining markedly, as corporate gentrification of the central city squeezes homeless populations from sites that they have sometimes occupied for decades – see, for example, Smith (1996b) on the forcible removal of the homeless and itinerant population from Tompkins Square Park, New York. In such instances, anti-begging ordinances and zoning laws have been used to disperse visible homeless populations and 'sanitize' areas prior to GENTRIFICATION. Although the erasure of such 'landscapes of despair' should not be a cause for regret, it generates some significant questions about how welfare providers might best target resources to increasingly dispersed homeless populations (Lee and Price-Spratlen, 2004), as well as raising the spectre of the increased PRIVATIZATION of PUBLIC SPACE. As such, the disappearance of skid row areas is rarely taken as evidence of an improving urban quality of life, but is seen to be symptomatic of societies where the disadvantaged have less 'right to the city' (Mitchell, 1997a).   PH

slavery A condition of bondage and servitude in which one person owns another, forcibly exacts labour and services from them, and excludes them from CIVIL SOCIETY. Slavery has ancient roots in disparate parts of the world and has taken multiple forms. But up to the nineteenth century all EMPIRES were slave-owning societies, and slavery has been conceptualized by historians as a MODE OF PRODUCTION that both preceded and coexisted with FEUDALISM and with CAPITALISM. The close connections between slavery and COLONIALISM found their principal expression in the transatlantic slave trade, which reached its heyday during the seventeenth and eighteenth centuries, fed burgeoning European consumer markets with sugar, coffee, tobacco, rice and later cotton, and as Blackburn (1998) shows, was driven more by private capital and mercantile initiative than by STATE sponsorship. An estimated 11.8 million slaves – chiefly from West Africa – were put to work on plantations, and millions died of starvation and sickness in the perilous sea voyage to America. A considerable literature on PLANTATION life in Brazil, the Caribbean and the American South examines spatial strategies of POWER and RESISTANCE, modes of paternalism and HEGEMONY, and the role of GENDER, SEXUALITY and African CULTURE in the making of slave and Creole communities (see also TRANSCULTURATION).

The abolition of colonial – chattel – slavery stemmed from both metropolitan and colonial agitation, and cannot simply be explained in economic terms (e.g. in terms of the declining value of Caribbean sugar colonies). On the one hand, the British and French represented abolition as a distinctly Western triumph, and strong public sentiment created what David Brion Davis (cited in Lambert, 2005, p. 10) describes as 'a profound change in the basic PARADIGM of social geography – a conceptual differentiation between...a "slave world" aberration and a "free world" norm'. But the formal demise of slavery also stemmed from slave rebellions and struggles over CITIZENSHIP and HUMAN RIGHTS that articulated ideas of RACE, NATION and EMPIRE in complex ways (Dubois, 2004). Such struggles had a much greater impact on ENLIGHTENMENT thought than has hitherto been recognized, and recent historical and geographical work on the mutual constitution of white and black

IDENTITY, and the diasporic and transnational identities and communities shaped by slavery (a 'Black Atlantic' based on a shared history of commercial interaction and social degradation), demonstrates the need for more integrated and 'networked' (less rigidly hierarchical) understandings of the exactions and impositions bound up with this mode and phase of colonization and European commercial outreach.

The distinction between slavery and other forms of servitude has never been clear-cut, and in spite of the nineteenth-century abolition of colonial slavery, slavery-like practices have persisted, in systems of indentured labour, and state servitude in fascist Germany, communist China and the Soviet Union. The United Nations currently extends the definition of slavery to an array of widespread human rights abuses (forced labour, REFUGEE exploitation, PROSTITUTION, pornography, people trafficking and the use of children in armed conflict). Contemporary GLOBALIZATION, like the colonial and imperial globalizations that preceded it, depends on transnational flows of labour: for millions, however, the conditions of movement and the coercion of labour has transformed them into what Bales (2004) calls 'disposable people'. The crucial axis here is not RACIALIZATION but, rather, GENDER and age: most of them, perhaps 80 per cent, are female and around 50 per cent are CHILDREN. Many of these victims have been induced into crossing BORDERS to escape POVERTY and find employment; in order to pay their traffickers, they are required to work to pay off their 'debt' (many never do) in return for elemental food and shelter. Trafficking and slavery cannot simply be folded into one another – the two are conceptually and legally distinct (Manzo, 2005) – but it is clear that slavery may well occur in the course of trafficking, and that both involve extreme forms of exploitation, usually by criminal gangs. Contemporary slavery cannot entail legal ownership, but VIOLENCE nonetheless establishes a regime of control, coercion and dependence that amounts to effective ownership. More than 40 per cent of the victims are forced into the sex trades (cf. Samarasinghe, 2005), while another 32 per cent are domestic servants or construction workers. In June 2006 the US government estimated that 600,000–800,000 people were subjected to such labour bondage each year. The major destinations are Europe, North America and the MIDDLE EAST. Many millions more endure bonded labour as a means of paying off a debt or a loan in their own countries, especially in India, Pakistan, Bangladesh and Nepal. When these are included, the International Labour Organization estimates that the minimum total of people enduring some form of forced servitude is 12.3 million, while Bales (2004, p. 8) puts the figure at 27 million: both estimates are more than the total number caught up in the horrors of the Black Atlantic (Epstein, 2006). DCl

Suggested reading
Bales (2004); Drescher and Engerman (1998).

slum An area of substandard housing and inadequate provision of public utilities (especially WATER and sanitation), inhabited by poor people in high densities, who develop a distinctive culture as a means of both survival and self-respect. The term originated in Britain in the early decades of the nineteenth century. Labourers living in the countryside endured wretched conditions too, but the overcrowding of tenements in the central districts of industrial cities – the shock cities of the age – and of capital cities such as London was symptomatic of the slum. Life in these COMMUNITIES became a central object of social commentary and investigation, in studies such as Engels' *Condition of the English working class* (1844) and novels such as Dickens' *Hard times* (1854). Areas of poor housing for poor people had existed in many other periods and places too, from imperial Rome to Georgian Bath, but it was the connection forged between the built environment and the 'moral environment' – by the close of the century, fears over public order and public health were increasingly compounded by BIOPOLITICAL theses of 'urban degeneration' (cf. Luckin, 2006) – that was diagnostic of the politics of the slum on both sides of the Atlantic. The connection was both constructed and contested (Ward, 1976), so that slums were not only the product of intersections between housing and (often casual) LABOUR MARKETS but also of a particular IMAGINATIVE GEOGRAPHY (Stedman Jones, 1991 [1974]; Mayne, 1993). Their modern analysis has relied on recovering built forms and MATERIAL CULTURES, and analysing contemporary photographs and memoirs (Rose, 1997a; Mayne and Murray, 2001; cf. Roberts, 1990). Slums became targets for STATE intervention, including social regulation and URBAN RENEWAL in the nineteenth century – one of the objectives of the Haussmannization of Paris – and 'slum clearance' schemes in the

nineteenth and twentieth centuries (Wohl, 1977; Yelling, 1986, 2000).

The political salience of the term has been revived by critics such as Davis (2006), who points to the contemporary transposition of slums from the global NORTH to the global SOUTH. Colonial cities were often bipolar, with a *cordon sanitaire* between the European districts (the 'white city') and the poor, overcrowded 'native city', but the slum is primarily a product of CLASS zonation rather than the racial discriminations associated with the GHETTO. Class distinctions loom large in the rapidly growing cities of the South, and it is estimated that one-third of the global urban population now lives in slums, the vast majority of them in the South (Davis, 2006, p. 23). If the overcrowding, poverty, human degradation and exploitation are familiar from older descriptions – 'There is nothing in the catalogue of Victorian misery that doesn't exist somewhere in a Third World City today' (Davis, 2006, p. 186) – the immensity of scale is radically new. And unlike the nineteenth-century slums of the North, most of these new slums are on the edges of cities (not at the core) and their production is wired to transnational (not national) circuits of capital and to the political–economic projects of NEO-LIBERALISM. Finally, if slums have always been sites for the warehousing of what Marx called a 'surplus army' of labour, the new slums confront real armies who foresee *urban warfare* swirling around our 'planet of slums' (Davis, 2006, pp. 202–6). Although this dystopian vision is rhetorically powerful, however, it offers a remarkably undifferentiated view of a far more complex urban geography and it overlooks the crucial contribution of progressive URBAN SOCIAL MOVEMENTS (Angotti, 2006). Indeed, Roy's (2003) incisive exposure of the politics of POVERTY in Calcutta is explicitly staged as 'a satire on the very trope of the dying city' and, like Simone's (2004) brilliant study of four African cities, is a critique of the urban fantasies (and fears) of ABJECTION and failure projected on to cities of the global South by planners and theorists alike, and contained within the very concept of a 'slum'. (See also SQUATTING.) DG

Suggested reading
Davis (2006); Philpott (1991 [1978]); Ward (1976).

social area analysis A THEORY and related technique for characterizing urban residential NEIGHBOURHOODS, linking changes in urban social structure to economic DEVELOPMENT and associated URBANIZATION (termed a society's 'increasing scale': Shevky and Bell, 1955). Increasing scale (not to be confused with other uses of that term – see SCALE) involves three interrelated trends:

- Changes in the range and intensity of social relations produced by greater DIVISION OF LABOUR and reflected in the distribution of skills and rewards within society – this trend was termed *social rank* or *economic status*.
- Increasing differentiation of functions within society and its constituent HOUSEHOLDS generating new lifestyles and household forms – termed *urbanization* or *family status*.
- The concentration into cities of people from different cultural backgrounds – *segregation* or *ethnic status*.

The link between these three trends and residential differentiation was not clear in the original presentation. Shevky and Bell selected variables to represent the three trends (the percentage in certain occupations for economic status, for example), which were measured for the various CENSUS TRACTS in a city and used to produce standardized indices for each tract on each construct. The tracts were then classified into a typology of social areas depending on their values on the three indices. Although the technique was soon superseded by the more inductive approach of FACTORIAL ECOLOGY, and the theory was largely ignored within URBAN GEOGRAPHY, the three constructs remained central to much analysis of urban residential patterns.   RJ

Suggested reading
Johnston (1969).

social capital The idea that access to and participation in groups can benefit individuals and communities – the nub of contemporary social capital scholarship – is a well-established sociological insight dating to the nineteenth century writings of Karl Marx, Emile Durkheim and Ferdinand Tonnies, among others. The term itself was first invoked (and then only once) by the economist Glen Loury in a 1977 article in which he critiqued NEO-CLASSICAL theories of racial income inequality. Loury contended that by its commitment to methodological individualism, orthodox labour economics was incapable of factoring how social context – specifically, poorer connections of young black workers to the labour market and their lack of information about opportunities – impeded intergenerational mobility and reproduced race divisions rooted in economic inequality (Loury, 1977).

The sociologist Alejandro Portes (1998) attributes the first theoretically refined analysis of social capital to Pierre Bourdieu, who defined the concept as 'the aggregate of the actual or potential resources which are linked to possession of a durable network of more or less institutionalized relationships of mutual acquaintance or recognition' (Bourdieu, 1985, p. 248). Although Bourdieu's note, initially published in French in 1980, remained neglected within the English-speaking world, the concept of social capital proliferated, catalysed by a conjuncture of events. These included the publication of an article in the late 1980s by a leading American sociologist, James Coleman, in which he explored the connection between aspects of 'social structure' and 'human capital' formation (Coleman, 1988). Although Coleman's treatment of social capital lacked the rigour of Bourdieu's formulation, it garnered far more traction. Post-1989 MARKET triumphalism, accompanying receptivity within and outside academia (e.g. at powerful multinational institutions such as the World Bank) to non-*dirigiste* sources of economic DEVELOPMENT, and the linked emergence of a 'global CIVIL SOCIETY' discourse (which conflated ideas of free society and free market) undoubtedly contributed to the popularity of Coleman's thesis.

Since then, mainstream social science has operationalized the concept of social capital in a bewildering number of ways. The shared impulse has been to parlay CULTURE in a form sensible to economics and policy science. This importation of culture into the economic is sorely inadequate (see CULTURAL ECONOMY). Of the three broad categories of empirical approaches currently in vogue, the first evaluates how social relations might function as collateral or assurance that an economic transaction will occur in the manner anticipated – the distilled wisdom here is that social capital in the form of TRUST minimizes the risks (and, hence, costs) associated with transactions and boosts economic competitiveness. A second approach measures how social capital as density of strong and weak social ties and group membership acts as an insurance mechanism during periods of need or crisis – the contention being that social cohesion is positively correlated with the ability of individuals to shield themselves from idiosyncratic risks. A third approach conceptualizes social capital as a stock of accumulated obligations that can yield economic returns to the individual holder, either on an everyday basis or as investment in social relations with expected returns in the marketplace – hence, rendering the cultural into a form that is fungible with the economic.

While Bourdieu also emphasizes the fungibility of different forms of CAPITAL (academic, cultural, social, symbolic) and the reduction of all forms ultimately to economic capital, defined as accumulated human labour, his writing also reveals that 'social capital' – relations of *abstract* trust and reciprocity (displaying qualities of a quasi-PUBLIC GOOD) that inhere in society and facilitate economic transactions – as a social resource is: (a) a positive EXTERNALITY generated by a large number of individuals able to pursue conduct that they believe, given their semiotic universe, will earn them social distinction; (b) an unintended normative outcome that congeals through a long history of repeated interaction, rather than something that can be purposively manufactured in a relatively short time span (as some policy-oriented social theorists and their institutional backers are prone to claim); and (c) always anchored to a PLACE and a COMMUNITY, and as such, containing the potentially coercive elements of social SURVEILLANCE and pressure to conform, backed by the threats of SOCIAL EXCLUSION and excommunication (Gidwani, 2002). VG

Suggested reading
Bebbington, Guggenheim, Olson and Woolcock (2004); Portes (1998).

social construction The idea that the social context of individuals and groups constructs the reality that they know, rather than an independent material world. Knowledge is always relative to the social setting of the inquirers (cf. RELATIVISM), the outcome of an ongoing, dynamic process of fabrication (anti-REALISM). Further, social construction applies as much to forms of specialized understanding (e.g. high-energy physics) as it does to everyday, taken-for-granted knowledge.

Antecedents of social constructionism are found in Plato, but it was Karl Marx (1818–83) who established an intellectual agenda with his claim that the interests of the dominant social CLASS (the bourgeoisie) shaped individual beliefs (see IDEOLOGY). Marx (1904, preface) wrote: 'It is not the consciousness of men [sic] that determines their social being, but, on the contrary, their social being that determines their consciousness.' Antonio

Gramsci's (1891–1937) theory of HEGEMONY developed Marx's idea by arguing that even seemingly humdrum commonsense thinking was socially produced and, because they could not think otherwise, resulted in the working class consenting to their own domination. But the most direct statement of social construction was provided in 1966 by two American sociologists, Peter Berger and Thomas Luckman. This was significant in two ways. First, it provided a simple and remarkably popular sketch of what they called 'the social construction of reality' (there were more complicated versions: Luckmann was keenly interested in Alfred Schütz's constitutive PHENOMENOLOGY and the production of the LIFEWORLD). Second, it located social construction within the sociology of knowledge. 'Insofar as all human "knowledge" is developed, transmitted and maintained in social situations,' Berger and Luckmann (1966, p. 3) wrote, 'the sociology of knowledge is concerned with the analysis of the social construction of reality'.

Using the example of religion, Berger and Luckmann argued that social interaction, bolstered by associated institutions such as the church, constructs knowledge, taking on causal powers and entering everyday life routines. This insight was later applied by SCIENCE STUDIES to the physical world, nature, rocks and quarks (Pickering, 1984). On the surface, nature appears fixed and constant, to be 'out there', and not dependent upon social beliefs. But science studies contend that scientific knowledge is no different from any other kind of knowledge. Social context operates by shaping the scientific techniques, equipment and forms of reasoning used by scientists to erect particular constructions of NATURE (and linking with SITUATED KNOWLEDGE that also emphasizes the world-making constructions of scientists and their technology). That scientific knowledge is socially constructed does not make it wrong, however. What is wrong is belief in a science that escapes the influence of its social setting. Rocks and quarks do not express themselves in their own terms, but only in the terms of the scientists who speak for them, and thus the *social worlds that those scientists inhabit.*

Social construction has had a diffuse but, in some respects, a widespread influence in HUMAN GEOGRAPHY. The first engagements with Berger and Luckmann's theses remained close to their origins in sociology and were confined to their implications for SOCIAL GEOGRAPHY, particularly by those sailing under the flag of a HUMANISTIC GEOGRAPHY and interested in PHENOMENOLOGY, SYMBOLIC INTERACTIONISM and the constitution of meanings in the conduct of EVERYDAY LIFE. The influence of the sociology of scientific knowledge came to the discipline much later, by which time it was typically associated with POSTMODERNISM and POST-STRUCTURALISM. The latter in particular introduced the concepts of DISCOURSE and PERFORMATIVITY, which directed attention to the constitutive, 'world-making' effects of the nexus of power, knowledge and practice. In this spirit, human geographers have explored constructions of the ECONOMY (Barnes, 2005), GENDER (Pratt, 2004), NATURE (Castree and Braun, 2001) and SEXUALITY (Brown, 2000), to name but a few.   TB

Suggested reading
Hacking (1999).

social exclusion A situation in which certain members of a SOCIETY are separated from much that comprises the normal 'round' of living and working within that society. The concept is chiefly envisaged in social terms, identifying particular groupings that become excluded, but it is also recognized that the multiple factors involved in creating social exclusion may combine spatially to produce distinctive places of disadvantage and discrimination (Gough, Eisenschitz and McCulloch, 2005). Indeed, excluded groupings tend to be found outside those spaces comprising the loci of 'mainstream' social life (e.g. middle-class SUBURBS, up-market shopping malls, prime PUBLIC SPACE), congregating elsewhere as the residents of spaces largely hidden from the view of academics, politicians and policy-makers (e.g. working-class estates, homeless shelters, anonymous back streets).

The term 'social exclusion' has been popularized in policy-making across EUROPE, if less so North America, and has particularly featured in the social policies of recent UK governments. The definition favoured in the UK is broadly thus: 'the outcome of processes and/or factors which bar access to participation in CIVIL SOCIETY' (Eisenstadt and Witcher, 1998, p. 6). As a concept, social exclusion 'does not simply describe the static condition of "poverty" or "deprivation", but emphasises the *processes* by which aspects of social marginalisation are intensified over time' (Amin, Cameron and Hudson, 2002, p. 17), and it also embraces a diversity of economic, political, social and cultural dimensions. While some are sceptical, others see social exclusion as an advance over notions such as the 'underclass', originating in the USA, that effectively blame people for irresponsible lifestyles bringing their marginalized status upon themselves.

'[T]he debate on the causes and locations of social exclusion, as well as proposed solutions, has become cast in terms of geographically-defined communities', but there are snares in this 'new hegemony of the social as local' arising from a neglect of broader structural forces, whose malign impact on neighbourhoods is unlikely to be reversed by local initiatives alone (Amin, Cameron and Hudson, 2002, pp. 19–22). Many considerations ripe for critical analysis emerge, including the articulations of social exclusion with the 'social economy' of not-for-profit activity and also the possible deployment of SOCIAL CAPITAL, all of which can be traced across what Gough, Eisenschitz and McCulloch (2005) term 'spaces of social exclusion' inescapably skewered by the workings of both the local *and* the global. Relatedly, attention is drawn to the policies of social *inclusion*, designed to counter exclusionary tendencies, and new forms of CITIZENSHIP, marked by the privileging of 'active citizens' supposedly able to take responsibility for their own well-being, circumstances and neighbourhoods.

An academic geographical concern for socio-spatial exclusion pre-dates the current policy interest, though, and can be traced in a manner explicitly framed as such to Sibley's (1981) innovative *Outsiders in urban societies*. Through substantive studies of 'Gypsies', travellers and the North American Inuit, Sibley anticipated a new tradition of research into excluded minority groupings that has now greatly extended the compass of SOCIAL GEOGRAPHY. All manner of peoples standing outside of the mainstream, on whatever grounds, have now had their 'exclusionary geographies' mapped, interpreted and critiqued, with sensitivity shown to both structuring forces from without and felt experiences from within. It is possible to identify works in this vein tackling women, people of colour, REFUGEES, sexual 'dissidents', CHILDREN and elderly people, disabled and chronically ill people, welfare-dependent and homeless people, and many others (for accessible introductions, see Pain, Burke, Fuller and Gough, 2001; Panelli, 2004). These are people who are excluded because of *who* they are, how they look, and what they do and think, and who are therefore deemed 'out of place' (see also Cresswell, 1996) in a range of mainstream spaces that

691

they either choose to vacate (to avoid hostility) or because they are compelled to do so (by stigmatizing acts both symbolic and real). Various studies conceptualize the roots of such socio-spatial exclusion, notably Sibley's (1995) *Geographies of exclusion*, which borrows from PSYCHOANALYTIC THEORY to probe the inherent will of 'the Self' to distance itself from all that it perceives as 'Other' (as alien, impure, polluting and 'abject'). Sibley speculates that such psycho-dynamics, as inculcated in individual psyches, translate into wider socio-spatial configurations that materialize lines of exclusion between selves who reckon themselves to be essentially similar (the 'same') and those cast out as fundamentally 'Other'. CP

Suggested reading
Sibley (1981, 1995).

social formation In structural MARXISM, the specific combination of social relations obtaining within a particular society at a particular historical moment or conjuncture. The concept was derived from a reading of Marx's *Capital* undertaken in the 1960s and early 1970s by a group of French scholars associated with the Marxist philosopher Louis Althusser. Whereas the MODE OF PRODUCTION specifies structural combinations of relations and forces of production in general terms, identifying the diagnostic CLASS relationships involved in the production of surplus value – hence, for example, FEUDALISM or CAPITALISM – the concept of 'social formation' refers to concrete forms of social relations at a specific conjuncture (e.g. post-revolutionary France). It also takes account of social relations and forms that survive from previous conjunctures, as well as non-class modes of social exploitation and oppression (e.g. PATRIARCHY), and seeks to identify their modes of articulation with what is assumed to be the central grid of class relations. DG

social geography The sub-discipline that examines the social contexts, social processes and group relations that shape SPACE, PLACE, NATURE and LANDSCAPE. The generality of this definition indicates both the breadth of social geography and changing emphases through time, across various PARADIGMS and also in different national traditions. In France, for example, social geography has sometimes been regarded as having the range of HUMAN GEOGRAPHY itself, while in Germany it was often associated more narrowly with the landscape indicators school (see the continuing

series since 2003 on national social and cultural geographies in the journal *Social and Cultural Geography*). Three abiding theoretical concerns in the sub-discipline have been the relationship between spatial pattern and social process; the question of determinism and HUMAN AGENCY; and the engagement with a range of geographical SCALES.

Following the practice of human geography itself, early work in social geography was dominated by an emphasis on landscape form and spatial pattern. Innovative voices urging that intellectual labour should move beyond descriptive pattern studies to explanatory process included Wreford Watson's seminal chapter (1957), Max Sorre's (1957) productive engagement with French sociology, and Emrys Jones' impressive monograph (1960) on the development of social areas in Belfast. Ironically, the new paradigm of SPATIAL ANALYSIS in the 1960s did not significantly advance the explanatory ambitions of social geography but, rather, reinforced the emphasis on pattern by borrowing from HUMAN ECOLOGY to establish more rigorous quantitative descriptions of SEGREGATION patterns and classifications of social areas. While often sophisticated, only rarely did this work move into issues of EXPLANATION – as, for example, in Peach's (1996) important research on ETHNICITY and IMMIGRATION, as he considered economic and discriminatory explanations of segregation and, in earlier work, the restricted social interaction that was associated with maps of social segregation.

Akin to geomorphology's transition from form to process, social geography moved decisively into PROCESS studies in the 1970s with two significant developments. The first was David Harvey's (1973) paradigm-shaking discovery of Marxist theory (see MARXIST GEOGRAPHY), leading to his claim that CAPITALISM was the root cause of social–spatial distributions, and the two-CLASS system was the fundamental expression of social groups, a research programme that has helped to shape a continuing and vital critical tradition in social geography (e.g. Blunt and Wills, 2000). In contrast to such a POLITICAL ECONOMY, the second development was a HUMANISM that emphasized the experience and construction of PLACE, seeking inspiration from a range of theoretical and philosophical sources (Jackson and Smith, 1984; see HUMANISTIC GEOGRAPHY). Humanism was not incompatible with some forms of Marxism, as work in HISTORICAL GEOGRAPHY made clear, but contemporary humanistic approaches were much more attentive to issues of experience, IDENTITY and HUMAN AGENCY in place-making (Buttimer and Seamon, 1980). They also continued earlier resistance to ENVIRONMENTAL DETERMINISM, though by the 1970s the economic environment had replaced the physical environment as the privileged context of human action. By the 1990s, social constructionism (see SOCIAL CONSTRUCTION) had become a dominant position, and several important monographs used it to good effect (e.g. Anderson, 1991b), though sometimes risking a newer social determinism.

Humanistic and qualitative research were much more attuned to ETHNOGRAPHIC and micro-scale studies, and attempts were made to effect a theoretical convergence between agency and structure and the micro- and macro-scale, notably in the short-lived STRUCTURATION perspective. While that scaffolding has largely fallen away, the best work today continues to attempt to marry agency and structure, and micro- and macro-scale processes (e.g. Duncan and Duncan, 2004b; Mitchell, 2004a).

A number of authors have associated the explosive growth of social geography following the SOCIAL MOVEMENTS of the 1965–75 period with the newly awakened desire for RELEVANCE in HUMAN GEOGRAPHY. Aside from the theoretical issues noted above, what was at stake was also a liberal impulse towards social welfare and, for some, social ACTIVISM. A wide range of research topics came under scrutiny, beneath the initial rubric of geographies of social problems (Herbert and Smith, 1989). Some of these, including the geography of CRIME and POLICING (e.g. Herbert, 1997), and especially HEALTH geography (Gatrell, 2002), are becoming sub-disciplines in their own right. Other significant research topics include POVERTY and deprivation, social polarization and SOCIAL EXCLUSION, EDUCATION, HOUSING and, in the consumer age of NEO-LIBERALISM, geographies of LEISURE, TOURISM, SPORT and CONSUMPTION. In David Smith's work, a challenging progression has taken place from a consideration of welfare and SOCIAL JUSTICE to a more philosophical, but still activist, examination of MORAL GEOGRAPHIES and an ethic of care (Smith, 2000a).

The stratification of society in contemporary social geography follows topical as well as theoretical categories. Class, variously defined, remains a major line of demarcation, but it is far from alone. RACE and ETHNICITY have been a significant focus of attention, particularly with the growing cultural diversity in gateway cities in the global NORTH accompanying MIGRATION and REFUGEE streams from the global SOUTH. Geographers have completed research on such topics as SEGREGATION and INTEGRATION, immigrant reception and RACISM, TRANSNATIONALISM and MULTICULTURALISM as a governance policy (e.g. Anderson, 1991b; Peach, 1996a). FEMINIST GEOGRAPHERS have affected the field as a whole (Pratt, 2004), engaging structures of PATRIARCHY and diverse expressions of GENDER and SEXUALITY, among other topics. But class, race and gender are not the only divisions recognized in society by social geographers. The LIFE-CYCLE offers its own distinctive groupings, with studies of childhood, youth and the elderly, as well as varied family configurations (e.g. Aitken, 2001: see also AGEING; CHILDREN). Among cultural attributes, both religious status and aboriginal status are experiencing revived emphasis as sources of group formation (see ABORIGINALITY; RELIGION). DISABILITY studies have attracted a small but active scholarship on the spatial experience of differently abled groups (Park, Radford and Vickers, 1998). In short, the range of the social is substantial, and the POSTMODERN attention to multiple and decentred identities in cities of DIFFERENCE ensures continuing multiplication of the social groups of interest to social geographers (Fincher and Jacobs, 1998). Institutions, too, are social formations with particular rules, hierarchies and cultures, and the return of institutional approaches in the social sciences (see INSTITUTIONALISM) has encouraged more systematic study of the involvement of public and private corporations in shaping people and place (e.g. Herbert, 1997; Ley, 2003b), reinvigorating the managerial or gatekeeper approach to place-making of the 1970s.

Social geography experienced a second period of expansion in the 1990s, benefiting from the renewal and expansion of CULTURAL GEOGRAPHY. Indeed, the boundaries of the two sub-disciplines are blurred, and strict demarcation neither possible nor necessary. Today, social geography ranges widely – indeed, some might say, too widely. Like geomorphology, the preoccupation with process has sometimes led some distance from recognizable geographies of space, place, landscape or nature. Another trend has been the remarkable diffusion of QUALITATIVE METHODS as the primary and often exclusive METHODOLOGY of social geography. There would seem to be advantages to more methodological diversity to make use of large national surveys and databases that require modest quantitative skills, thereby offering a triangulation of methods that extends the range of research outcomes. These qualifications aside, social geography as a sub-discipline has entered the new millennium with considerable energy and momentum, if perhaps a less coherent subject matter.   DL

Suggested reading
Eyles (1986); Harvey (1973); Jackson and Smith (1984); Knox and Pinch (2000); Ley (1983).

social justice A standard used to assess the fairness of a SOCIETY. Justice is a central moral standard that requires the fair and impartial treatment of all. Social justice differs from other realms of justice, such as that relating to the application of LAW, being centrally concerned with the fairness of a social order and its attendant distributions of rewards and costs. Determining how fairness is to be assessed, and according to which principle, is an issue of fierce debate. Different criteria, including EQUALITY, entitlement, RECOGNITION or need, yield different principles of justice. While some scholars view social justice in essentially descriptive terms, the literature within fields such as GEOGRAPHY has been more NORMATIVE, with an emphasis on using some definition of social justice in the moral evaluation of prevailing social arrangements (see also ETHICS).

Social justice has long been a rallying cry for many SOCIAL MOVEMENTS. The arguments of poor COMMUNITIES of colour that they are disproportionately burdened by environmental EXTERNALITIES, the claim by unions for better compensation or the democratization of the workplace, or the organizing of anti-capitalist globalization (ANTI-GLOBALIZATION) movements are all motivated, in part, by the powerful claim that prevailing social arrangements should be fairer. The injustice of many social relationships, distributions and arrangements has long been the focus of a rich scholarly and activist tradition (ACTIVISM). Broadly, three perspectives can be identified:

(1) The most extensive body of scholarship is to be found in liberal political theory that seeks variously to determine the essential characteristics of a 'fair' society (see LIBERALISM). John Rawls' (1971) *A theory of justice*, for example, imagines an original position, prior to the creation of society. The just social order is that which those in this original position would agree to, he argues, if they did not know in advance whether they

would be rich or poor in the resultant society. From this, he derives a number of yardsticks to assess social justice, of which the most famous is his 'difference principle', which holds that inequality can only be justified if it benefits the least advantaged.

(2) Particularly influential within geography is a Marxist analysis of social justice (departing from one strain of MARXISM that sees social justice as an ideological construct). Since his seminal *Social justice and the city*, David Harvey (1973) has been concerned with the topic, abandoning a liberal characterization as 'a matter of eternal justice and morality' in favour of a view of social justice as 'contingent upon the social processes operating in society as a whole' (p. 15). He judged questions of spatial distribution not according to the prevailing standard of efficiency but, rather, according to some measure of distributive justice. Social justice was said to apply to the distributions of benefits and burdens, as well as the social and institutional arrangements arising from production and distribution (including power, decision-making). In sum, he sought 'a just distribution, justly arrived at' (p. 98). In subsequent work, Harvey (1996) has extended his scope to include questions of ENVIRONMENTAL JUSTICE. While he acknowledges the importance of social difference and POSITIONALITY, he continues to argue from POLITICAL ECONOMY.

(3) A POST-STRUCTURALIST reading of social justice supplements a Marxist emphasis upon CLASS and economic relationships with the inclusion of multiple axes of social differentiation – such as GENDER and RACE. For example, while recognizing the injustices of class exploitation, Iris Marion Young (1990a) constructs a pluralist reading of oppression that includes marginalization, VIOLENCE, powerlessness and cultural IMPERIALISM. She advocates a politics that 'instantiates social relations of difference without exclusion' (p. 227).

Social justice has been of occasional concern within geography since Harvey's original intervention. The collection edited by Merrifield and Swyngedouw (1997) for example, provides one example, as do recent arguments by Don Mitchell (2003a). Drawing, in part, from a Rawlsian analysis, David Smith has also written thoughtfully on the topic. In an important paper, Smith (2000b) constructs a geographically sensitive argument for EQUALITY as a basis for social justice, and articulates an argument for the morally significant aspects of human sameness as a way out of the relativism of DIFFERENCE. Smith also considers the injustices of an uneven geography of global resource endowment as a basis for a territorial social justice. In a more post-structuralist vein, Kobayashi and Ray (2000) argue for a pluralist notion of justice that embraces positionality. They eschew a calculus of RIGHTS, with its logic of impartiality, arguing instead for an emphasis upon RISK (cf. Peake and Ray, 2001). Noting that differently positioned people face differential exposure to injustice, they insist on the importance of geography to social justice. That said, social justice demands more careful and sustained attention by geographers. As Merrifield and Swyngedouw (1997, p. 2) note, it has all to often been relegated to the 'hinterlands of academic inquiry'. For while social justice is often invoked, or implicit in much geographic work, particularly of a critical bent (CRITICAL GEOGRAPHY), it is all too often left untheorized (although see the special issue of the journal *Critical Planning*, 14, 2007, which is dedicated to the theme of spatial justice: see http://www.spa.ucla.edu/critplan/).   NKB

Suggested reading
Holloway (1998); Peake and Ray (2001).

social movements The organized efforts of multiple individuals or organizations, acting outside of formal state or economic spheres, to pursue political goals. They are commonly organized around either particular *groups* – for example, the working class – or particular *goals* – for example, access to HEALTH CARE. Their demands may be focused on the state (e.g. new laws), on economic actors (e.g. wage demands), on society as a whole (e.g. the changing of norms relating to RACE or SEXUALITY) or on any combination of these. Social movements can radically transform society: consider FEMINISM or ENVIRONMENTALISM. Yet as loose NETWORKS of actors with many informal elements, they present methodological challenges: it is often difficult to show that *x* protest or NGO produced *y* effect; to determine whether a given actor is part of a movement; or to predict whether, when and how a movement will arise from given social conditions.

Early, major approaches to social movement theory conceived of social movements as phenomena within CIVIL SOCIETY, a sphere regarded as distinct from, but complementary to, the STATE and the MARKET, one containing the informal norms and institutions necessary to the ongoing reproduction of the ECONOMY and the state, as well as forms of social participation and difference not strictly tied to economic CLASS or legal CITIZENSHIP status (see Urry, 1981). MARXIST theories saw social movements, notably the labour movement, as direct results and expressions of political economic conflicts. Many early sociologists, following Emile Durkheim, adopted FUNCTIONALIST perspectives that interpreted social movements within organic, equilibrium-oriented conceptions of SOCIETY; social movements were spontaneous phenomena produced by the need for individuals and groups in the rapidly shifting geographies and economies of modern CAPITALIST societies to continually rebuild informal norms and institutions, create new relationships, and bring their material existences and expectations into alignment. From the 1960s on, liberal *RATIONAL CHOICE THEORIES* became dominant: Mancur Olson and others analysed social movements as collective action strategies by which rational individuals pursued their (calculable and known) self-interest. Interest consequently shifted from *why* social movements existed and what *effects* they produced, to a focus on *how* they pursued their goals. Questions regarding how movements mobilize resources and supporters, frame issues, identify and exploit political opportunities, and change over time dominated social movement theory for the subsequent few decades.

More recently, the 'new social movements' (NSMs) that have appeared and grown around the world since the 1960s have become central topics in the field. Theorists have argued that these NSMs, such as environmentalism and the peace movement, differ from 'old' social movements in critical respects. Posited differences include claims that NSMs: are more issue-specific; cut across class lines; use unconventional tactics; express not only instrumental goals, but meaning, identity and multiple SUBJECT positions; and are less likely to turn to established political parties and channels to achieve their goals. All of these claims warrant careful scrutiny. Most recently, geographers have begun to theorize how central geographic concerns such as SPACE, PLACE and SCALE matter in social movements' formation and operations (Miller, 2000; Wolford, 2004; McCarthy, 2005).   JM

Suggested reading
Della Porta and Diani (1999); Laclau (1985).

social network The people – especially kin, friends and neighbours – to whom an individual is tied socially, usually by shared interests and, in many cases, values, attitudes and aspirations. Most people are members of several such NETWORKS, which may overlap only slightly – in their HOME, family, NEIGHBOURHOOD, workplace and formal organizations, for example. Such networks may be spatially concentrated, as both cause and effect: people may chose to live close to others already in their network(s), and may develop ties with neighbours. Such networks are the main medium for interpersonal interaction, and therefore a core element of any social structure – hence concerns regarding the potential consequences of declines in their strength (cf. SOCIAL CAPITAL).

Social networks provide the matrices through which much information flows and is evaluated. As such they are central components in models of change that involve interpersonal interaction, much of which has a spatial component (cf. CONTEXTUAL EFFECT; DIFFUSION; ELECTORAL GEOGRAPHY; NEIGHBOURHOOD EFFECT). They are often modelled formally as graphs, with individuals represented as nodes linked by ties along which information flows (see GRAPH THEORY): those ties can be evaluated quantitatively according to the intensity of interaction between the two individuals. Such a representation enables analyses of, for example, the key roles of certain individuals as nodes linking otherwise separate networks and their potential to act as change agents by channelling new information into a network. Research on such flows has suggested that weak ties (Granovetter, 1973) are often more important than strong ones as change stimuli. Strong ties usually link people with much in common whereas weak ties (links to acquaintances rather than friends, for example) may connect people with less in common, and therefore bring new information and ideas to their contacts.

Within GEOGRAPHY, the importance of social networks has been recognized in the study of economic organization and change, as in the development of new high-technology industrial regions (such as Silicon Valley in California: see Malmberg, 1997; Scott, 2006), in electoral studies (Huckfeldt and Sprague, 1995), and also in work on the exercise of POWER within policy communities, where interest groups interact with politicians and public servants. (See also ACTOR-NETWORK THEORY; NETWORK SOCIETY.) RJ

Suggested reading
Scott (1999); Sorenson (2003).

social physics An approach that suggests aggregate human SPATIAL INTERACTION can be explained and predicted using theories and laws from physics. H.C. Carey (1858) first codified social physics when he proposed that use be made '... of the great law of molecular gravitation as the indispensable condition of ... man [sic]'. But it was primarily John Q. Stewart (1950), professor of astronomy and physics at Princeton University, together with geographer William Warntz (1965), who first systematically prosecuted social physics under the rubric of MACROGEOGRAPHY, a short-lived movement, but one that helped pave the way for the subsequent success of SPATIAL SCIENCE within HUMAN GEOGRAPHY. The Newtonian GRAVITY MODEL remains the best-known example, suggesting that humans interact over terrestrial space as do heavenly bodies in the celestial system. The model gives a good empirical fit, but its predictions are less satisfactory, and its causal explanation worse. The lack of explanatory purchase, as Lukermann (1958) pointed out in a early critique, is because the assumptions made in the physical models are not met in the human realm: 'the lacuna is of the order of two worlds' (Lukermann, 1958, p. 2). There is nothing wrong with analogies *per se*, but for them to succeed there must be certain core similarities between the analogy and the analogized. For many critics of social physics, the similarities between human and celestial movements were not just hard to find, they were simply not there to be found. TB

Suggested reading
Barnes (1996, chs 4 and 5).

social reproduction The term encompasses the daily and long-term reproduction of the means of production, the labour power to make them work and the social relations that hold them in place. It includes the 'fleshy, messy' and diffuse stuff of EVERYDAY LIFE, as well as a congeries of structured material social practices that unfold in dialectical relation with production. At its most rudimentary, social reproduction is contingent upon the biological reproduction of the labour force – both day to day and generationally – through the production, acquisition, distribution and/or preparation of the means of existence, including FOOD, shelter, clothing and HEALTH care (Katz, 2001b). But any labour force is historically and geographically contingent, and so the notion extends to the reproduction of a differentiated and differently skilled labour force and the broad range of cultural forms and practices that create, uphold and rationalize these differences. Thus EDUCATION, the legal system and mass media are arenas of social reproduction, helping to inculcate and naturalize what Pierre Bourdieu (1977) called the HABITUS.

Social reproduction is defined and secured through a fluid ASSEMBLAGE of sources associated with the STATE, CAPITAL, the HOUSEHOLD and CIVIL SOCIETY. The balance among these varies historically, geographically and by CLASS, and its precise determinants are often the outcome of struggles in the workplace, COMMUNITY and HOME. If a SOCIAL FORMATION is to continue, then CONSUMPTION, production, circulation and EXCHANGE – of goods, of knowledge, of values – must be ongoing. While social reproduction implies endurance, it should not be understood as stasis. Involving the lively practices of everyday life and the myriad efforts to secure these, social reproduction actively makes the conditions of ongoing production (cf. RESISTANCE). In this way, social reproduction is a critical concept: immanent in its material social practices is the possibility of rupture, renovation and transformation.

Social reproduction has political economic, cultural and environmental aspects. The first includes the reproduction of labour power, the material social practices that sustain class and other modes of difference, and the discursive and other work that makes these distinctions common sense. The cultural aspect of social reproduction includes the production and exchange of knowledge and skills, along with the spaces in which they are carried out and given meaning. This knowledge enables all forms of work, but also contributes to IDENTITY and social group formation as well. The environmental aspect of social reproduction refers to the making and maintenance of the forces and material grounds of production, including tools, machinery and factories, but also the environmental resources and POLITICAL ECOLOGIES that enable ongoing production.

Social reproduction has been associated with MARXISM, but much of the attention to it has come from FEMINISTS working in – or against – that tradition. This scholarship brings into critical tension the social relations of CLASS, GENDER and SEXUALITY, demonstrating the ways in which they build upon, strengthen or undermine one another under particular historical and geographical circumstances (e.g. Marston, 2000). Feminist geographers have also revealed the ways in which processes such as GLOBALIZATION, labour MIGRATION and economic RESTRUCTURING are reworked by incorporating social reproduction in their analyses (e.g. Kofman and Raghuram, 2006).   CK

Suggested reading
Dalla Costa and Dalla Costa (1999); Mitchell, Marston and Katz (2004).

social space With some notable exceptions, human geographers traditionally conceptualized SPACE as a blank canvas upon which human activities are played out. This led to the adoption of a EUCLIDIAN notion of space and technologically astute attempts to map the way space is territorialized via economic, political and social action. In the social sphere, this reinvention of geography as a SPATIAL SCIENCE triggered multiple attempts to utilize CENSUS data to identify where residents shared similar characteristics or lifestyles, with techniques of SOCIAL AREA ANALYSIS facilitating the identification of more-or-less homogeneous social areas. While some of this work perpetuated the ECOLOGICAL FALLACY (implying that all persons in a given area shared similar social characteristics), more individually centred methods of SOCIAL NETWORK ANALYSIS provided empirical evidence of the way in which individuals' social worlds characteristically revolved around a localized set of social spaces. Here, the TIME-GEOGRAPHY associated with Torsten Hägerstrand and the Lund School offered a different take on the SPATIALITY of social practice, giving some important clues as to how social activities are distributed across time and space. Elsewhere, HUMANISTIC GEOGRAPHY explored the emotional and even spiritual ties that bind societies to spaces, albeit often talking about the construction of PLACE rather than the making of social space (Cresswell, 2004).

Reacting against these types of analysis, the historical and geographical MATERIALISM that emerged in the 1970s ushered in a rather different interpretation of spatiality, whereby space was deemed to be inherently caught up in social relations, both socially produced and consumed. Perhaps most influentially, Henri Lefebvre (1991b) insisted that there can be no 'pre-social' or natural space, as, at the moment that it is occupied through social activity, it becomes relativized and historicized space. Inferring that every society – and every MODE OF PRODUCTION – creates its own space, Lefebvre further distinguished between the abstract spaces of capitalism, the SACRED SPACES of the religious societies that preceded it and the contradictory and differential spaces yet to come. In outlining this history of the PRODUCTION OF SPACE, Lefebvre implied that the division of the world into a mosaic of social spaces is in no sense natural, but is a process that needs to be understood critically (and *dialectically*): in his words, 'social space is a social product' (Lefebvre, 1991b, p. 32: see DIALECTIC).

The idea that space is not passive in the constitution of SOCIETY is now dominant in HUMAN GEOGRAPHY, manifest in numerous studies of the conflicts inherent in both the production and CONSUMPTION of social space. Key here is the notion that these conflicts are not necessarily between different groups, but are between different forms or conceptions of space (Shields, 1991). Adapting Lefebvre's terminology, it is suggested that spontaneous and fully lived 'spaces of representation' may often clash with official 'representations of space', with the former occasionally breaking through abstract capitalist logics to produce differential spaces. Studies of spatial PRACTICES as diverse as skateboarding, tagging, driving and free-running may thus point to the possibilities of producing new social spaces where human sociality is given full reign and where play is privileged over work (Thrift, 2003; Latham and McCormack, 2005). In this regard, the rise of NON-REPRESENTATIONAL THEORIES can be interpreted as an important part of geographers' ongoing attempts to elucidate the materialities rather than just the meanings of social space.   PH

Suggested reading
Holloway and Hubbard (2001).

social theory This term refers to a constellation of theories about what Giddens (1984) terms 'the constitution of SOCIETY', specifying the mechanisms or the forms of social power that lend society some overall shape and coherence, however precarious, within given territorial limits (extending in some theories to the whole globe). Callinicos (1999, p. 1) states:

Social theory ... has concerned itself ... with the three main dimensions of 'social power' – economic relations, which have

reached their furthest development in the market system known as capitalism; the ideologies through which forms of special power are justified and the place in the world of those subject to them defined; and the various patterns of political domination.

Social theory can be distinguished from PHILOSOPHY, which addresses EPISTEMOLOGICAL and ONTOLOGICAL issues pertaining to the nature of knowledge that we acquire, develop and relate about the world, its social contents included. In practice, however, social-theoretic and philosophical questions run closely together, and in many reviews of human-geographical theorizing the two are presented in an entangled (and perhaps on occasion confused) manner. Different social theories embrace a raft of varying assumptions, arguments and models about how ECONOMY, politics and CULTURE play out in social power, and perhaps too bringing in claims about psychology, mythology and many other domains of human being and endeavour. All manner of economic, political, cultural and other theories abound, deriving from diverse disciplinary fields, alongside theories about how these different domains interrelate, influence or even determine one another in the social. All of this complicated material comprises the 'house' of social theory that has been repeatedly visited, borrowed from, critiqued and reworked by geographers down the years.

The 'predisciplinary history' of social theory can be traced to EUROPE in the period 1750–1850 (Heilbron, 1995), anchored in how the ENLIGHTENMENT encouraged abstracted reflections upon the social character of the times, but its origins are usually identified with several major thinkers who continue to cast a long shadow over the contemporary academy. The pantheon here includes the 'big three' of Karl Marx, Emile Durkheim and Max Weber, the key figures of so-called 'classical social theory', as well as various others – Herbert Spencer, Georg Simmel, G.H. Mead, Talcott Parsons, the Frankfurt School theorists – bridging forward into 'modern social theory', and then another cast-list – Anthony Giddens, Richard Rorty, Ulrich Beck and various French intellectuals – deemed, if a touch misleadingly, exponents of 'postmodern social theory' (see POSTMODERNISM: for equivalent periodizations, see Lemert, 1993; Callinicos, 1999). The term 'social theory' was clearly in use by the early twentieth century, and it appeared in modern-sounding guise when Merton

(1957) talked about 'social theory and social structure'.

The level of engagement between geographers and social theorists has been highly uneven: Marx receiving far more explicit attention than, say, Durkheim and Weber; or the French 'postmodernists' (Baudrillard, Derrida, Lyotard, Foucault) more than, say, the Frankfurt 'modernists' (Adorno, Habermas, Horkheimer). Through Giddens (1979), a binary distinction is sometimes detected between the social theories on offer, cleaving a deterministic, STRUCTURAL–FUNCTIONALIST pole of explanation from a voluntaristic, interpretive–HERMENEUTIC pole of understanding, and this distinction has been usefully mapped into critical accounts of human geography's underlying social-theoretic allegiances (e.g. Thrift, 1983). In return, geographers have been injecting a spatial sensibility into the heart of social theory, a project that, while initially formulated within the latter by Giddens (1979, 1984), has now announced geography as a 'player' within social theory. The Gregory and Urry (1985) and Benko and Strohmayer (1997) collections indicate how far and quickly this project developed after the late 1970s: contributions from the likes of Soja (1989), Gregory (1994) and Massey (2005) have also been pivotal; and many other geographers, both well-known and less-heralded, have all worked on advancing space in social theory (see GEOGRAPHICAL IMAGINATION). The founding of the journal *Society and Space* in 1983, configured as a meeting-place between social theory, human geography and cognate 'spatial' disciplines, embodies how something new, social-theoretically driven, was to become (for many) what necessarily lies at the heart of a human geography escaping from disciplinary isolation.

Unsurprisingly, the pantheon of social theorists listed above has attracted criticism, in part from those objecting to a too-easy eliding of social theory with the ostensible goals and exclusions of Enlightenment: namely, its trumpeting of (certain visions of) progress, reason and scientific protocols, together with the predominantly bourgeois, white, male identities of the thinkers involved. Alternative, anti-Enlightenment social theorists of the period are hence erased from the history (Mestrovic, 1998), as too is the awkwardness that the original social theorists often felt themselves about both the emerging modern world and the intellectual tools available to them. More starkly, the classed, raced and gendered dimensions of social theory, embedded within a Euro-Americanism, are now highlighted (Slater, 1992). Lemert (1993, p. 10) dissects the issues here, linking with the 'culture wars' afflicting North America (and to an extent elsewhere in the WEST too):

There are those who insist that, whatever has changed, America and the world can still be unified around the original Western ideas that Arthur Schlesinger described as 'still a good answer – still the best hope' ... Schlesinger – white, male, Harvard, liberal, intellectual, historian – is the most persuasive of those in this camp. Against them are others who say, 'Enough. Whatever is useful in these ideas, they don't speak to me.' Audre Lorde – black, feminist, lesbian, poet and social theorist – put this opposing view sharply in an often-quoted line: 'The master's tools will never dismantle the master's house.' Between these two views, there is more than enough controversy to go around. In large part, the controversy is between two different types of social theorists *and* over how social theory ought to be done.

One result has been the rise of FEMINIST, anti-racist and POST-COLONIAL versions of social theory, perhaps deriving from 'other regions' (Slater, 1992), alert to the fundamental structuring of the social by the crisscrossing of unequal power relations at a range of spatial scales and in/through a variety of places. A further implication, resonating (if a shade ironically) with the 'postmodern social theorists', has been to challenge *all* versions of social theory (old and new) by suggesting that their claims are always too grand, totalizing, inflexible and insensitive to the specificities of (the 'real' histories and geographies of) EVERY-DAY LIFE (cf. GRAND THEORY). Consequently, 'social theory is often seen in contemporary intellectual debates as an outdated form of understanding,' which means that, '[t]hough ... no one has yet announced the end of social theory, someone is bound to get round to it sooner or later' (Callinicos, 1999, p. 1). In effect, such a move *has* occurred in recent geographical texts, with calls for 'minor theory' (Katz, 1996) and 'modest theory' (Thrift, 1996), thereby leaving social theory in an odd place, demonized but still indispensable, if only as the ever-present horizon of what needs to be argued against or at least around (the spirit of Pryke, Rose and Whatmore, 2003). In this fractured intellectual landscape, social theory does not disappear: it is not wholly redundant, but it does acquire a curious character as a resource to be quarried for cautious insights into this thing, SOCIETY, that is now acknowledged – much more than ever before – as a complicated, provisional, never-fully-formed, always becoming object.   CP

Suggested readings
Benko and Strohmayer (1997); Callinicos (1999); Giddens (1979); Slater (1992).

social well-being The degree to which a population's needs and wants are being met. In a well society operated on MARKET principles (see ECONOMIC INTEGRATION), people have sufficient income to meet their basic needs plus additional money to be used for discretionary spending, are treated with equal dignity (see HUMAN RIGHTS), have reasonable access to all PUBLIC SERVICES, and have their opinions heard and respected (cf. DEMOCRACY). Levels of social well-being vary across groups and places within societies. Measuring variations in those levels was part of the social indicators movement initiated in the 1960s and taken up by geographers with analyses of territorial social indicators. (See also QUALITY OF LIFE.)   RJ

Suggested reading
Smith (1979a).

socialism Modern socialisms have their origin largely in nineteenth-century European working-class struggles against the predatory, unequal and degrading consequences of industrial CAPITALISM and twentieth-century industrial and agrarian struggles against IMPERIALISM. Thus, if capitalism is a social and economic system in which 'the ownership and control of real capital are vested in a class of private "capitalists", whose economic decisions are taken in response to market influences operating freely under conditions of *laissez-faire*' (Crosland, 1970, p. 33), socialism seeks to change the ways in which capital–labour relations are organized and social surplus is distributed (see ANARCHISM; MARXISM).

Historically, the socialist allocation of social surplus has sometimes been organized through collective ownership or by the STATE (state socialism), and has required planning and control mechanisms to regulate the economy. Since the nineteenth century, some socialists have supported the complete nationalization of the means of production, others have been more interested in worker democracy and decentralized ownership (either in the form of COOPERATIVES or workers' councils), and yet others have proposed selective nationalization of commanding heights industries in the context of mixed economies.

Recent neo-conservative and neo-liberal theories and policies have greatly weakened the popular legitimacy of socialism in many parts of the global NORTH, but political movements in the global SOUTH (notably in South Africa, Venezuela and Bolivia) have renewed commitments to socialist parties and principles. In countries such as Portugal, Spain, Greece, Italy, Argentina and Mexico, socialist movements have emerged deeply suspicious of political projects that seek to seize the state and, instead, have articulated new claims for socialist autonomous political projects in which vanguardist theories of social action have been reworked and inflected with new alignments of socialist theory with anarchist and autonomous practices (what Derrida (1994) called the 'New International' and Hardt and Negri (2004) refer to as the new communism). Partly as a result of these broader movements in socialist practices and stimulated by the consequences of increasing integration into the global economy, reformed socialism has also emerged in former (POST-SOCIALIST) and current state-socialist societies throughout EUROPE and ASIA, perhaps most notably in China. In Europe, discussions of alternatives to NEO-LIBERALISM correspond with strong debates about the possibility of a social Europe, predicated on protections for social RIGHTS, social cohesion and a social market, while in China experiments with market socialism and Deng Xiao Ping's advice that 'To get rich is glorious' are rapidly transforming the conditions of social life and environment throughout the country.

The impact of socialist thought and practice among geographers has been significant, particularly in their analyses of the geographies of social movements and socialist politics. Geographers such as Peter Kropotkin, Élisée Reclus and others were closely engaged in debates about socialism and anarchism, while others – such as the English socialist J.F. ('Frank') Horrabin (1884–1962) – worked to construct a socialist geography through the Labour party, the Fabian Society and groups involved in working-class education, such as the Plebs League and the National Council of Labour Colleges (Hepple, 1999). In the post-war era, particularly with the emergence of strong civil rights, anti-colonial, anti-war and anti-nuclear movements, socialist geographies emerged in a wide range of arenas, generating strong interest in the institutional and intellectual development of socialist approaches to geography (through the Union of Socialist Geographers (started in 1974), *Antipode*, the Socialist Specialty Group in the Association of American Geographers, and the International Critical Geography Conference) (see Dear, 1975). At the centre of many of these developments in geography has been the towering figure of David Harvey. Since the 1970s, Harvey has systematically argued for the importance of the GEOGRAPH-ICAL IMAGINATION for understanding capitalism and socialist (Marxist) critique. From the 1990s, he increasingly extended these efforts beyond geography through his writing and speaking engagements with the *Socialist Register, New Left Review, Monthly Review* and the Brecht Forum, among many others (Castree, 2007). JPi

society A widely used term whose meaning remains frustratingly vague, but that describes the organization of human beings into forms that transcend the individual person, bringing them into relations with one another that possess some measure of coherence, stability and, indeed, identifiable 'reality'. The one-time UK Prime Minister Margaret Thatcher infamously declared 'there is no such thing as society', offering a populist version of a position in social science known as METHODOLOGICAL INDIVIDUALISM (Werlen, 1993 [1988], pp. 40–52) that ultimately lodges all social enquiry in the attitudes, goals, decisions and behaviours of individual human actors. Even within critical strands of SOCIAL THEORY/social science, however, the notion of society remains curiously taken-for-granted, under-theorized and even an embarrassing guest that certain perspectives within the contemporary theoretical landscape – various forms of POST-STRUCTURALISM, for instance, or ACTOR-NETWORK THEORY (ANT) and NON-REPRESENTATIONAL THEORY (NRT) – might wish had never arrived.

Many concepts of society set it apart from ECONOMY, politics and CULTURE, such that it (or something called 'the social') becomes a distinctive 'level' for analysis, apparently made of ontologically different stuff, with questions prompted about whether it exists in relations of influencing, co-influencing or being influenced by these other levels. More specifically, notions such as CIVIL SOCIETY have been developed to distinguish a sphere of human concern and activity that cannot be reduced to either the dynamics of economic production or the machinations of the STATE (Urry, 1981),

although debate then rages about whether a 'capital-logic' or 'state-centric' account of civil society is more appropriate (a question that arguably can only be answered by researching particular forms of [civil] society found in particular times and places). Alternatively, many social theories tackling what Giddens (1984) terms 'the constitution of society' discuss how dimensions of the economic, the political and the cultural all bolt together to create society, wherein society appears as the product, articulation or condensation of all of these dimensions rather than as something somehow separate (and separable) in its own right. Inevitably, though, different social theories suppose differing balances between these constitutive dimensions of society, with some leaning towards economic determinism and others towards what might be called political or cultural determinism. Other perspectives, meanwhile, query the very construct of 'society', regarding it as at best a name for a loose assemblage of objects – people, to be sure, but also diverse *non*-human actors (books, bullets, newspapers, telephones, hospitals, streets etc.) – that have to be constantly enlisted by people in practices that produce, sustain and render with some semblance of 'reality' a patterning that can be understood and re-presented (to others) as 'society'. Although proceeding with different (POST-STRUCTURALIST and practice-attuned) theoretical tools, Thrift (1996, pp. 30–5) draws out the implications of Copjec's (1994, pp. 8–9) psychoanalytically informed insistence that 'society never *stops realising itself*, that it *continues* to be formed over time', a claim rebounding in various ways on the static ONTOLOGIES and EPISTEMOLOGIES inherent to many conceptualizations of society.

Thrift (1996, p. 56), reflecting upon his early borrowings from Giddens' social ontology, still finds things here to praise but concludes that 'one cannot fill out all of a society in the way Giddens sometimes ... seems intent on doing'. This being said, through his STRUCTURATION THEORY, Giddens has arguably done more than most to dissect the different elements that many writers, geographers included, continue to take as indispensable for any account of something called 'society'. The elements here include: the *agency* of *individuals*, socialized into certain habits of thought, conduct and action, if always possessing the capacity to think and do things differently; *institutions*, entailing formal entities with written constitutions, regulations, memberships and so on (e.g. schools, firms, clubs) as well as informal but enduring entities such as family

701

and religion, reproduced every day by the repeated practices of many individuals (a notion of SOCIAL REPRODUCTION); *systems*, or regularized patterns of interaction between individuals often but not always functioning to keep institutions going (and in some vocabularies, 'institution' and 'system' become interchangeable); and *structures*, or 'deeper' structural forces underpinning systems, institutions and (the being and doing of) individuals, often understood in terms of unequal relations of power, status and influence traversing axes of social difference (notably of CLASS, ETHNICITY and GENDER, but also the likes of AGEING, SEXUALITY and DISABILITY). In such Giddensian theorizing, the focus is on how society arises – is 'instantiated' – in the coming together of agency and structure, made real by actions mediated through institutions and systems, and there is also a recognition that time–space relations are crucial to the precise manner in which this coming together occurs (Giddens, 1979, 1984; Gregory, 1981, 1994; Thrift, 1983; Werlen, 1993).

There has long been a relationship between geographical scholarship and notions of society, and one simple point is that geographers have often had a sharper sense than others of the exact worldly spaces to which different picturings of society commonly attach. On one reading, this means nothing more than recognizing that accounts of society are normally referencing particular territorial units (Pain, Burke, Fuller and Gough, 2001, p. 3): perhaps (NATION-)STATES with known BOUNDARIES (i.e. 'Bulgarian society'); perhaps commonly understood REGIONS large or small (i.e. 'Mediterranean society' or 'Appalachian society'); or perhaps still smaller, more local areas (i.e. London's 'West End society'). The implication of moving down spatial SCALES, as here, is to reveal that dangers accompany any identification of *one* society (with allegedly distinctive features) occupying or filling a large spatial extent, and that closer geographical scrutiny will always require a more nuanced portrayal of the *different* societies there present. On another reading, geographers have been prominent in acknowledging that urban and rural LOCALITIES possess different sorts of societies, with the classic distinction drawn by the German sociologist Ferdinand Tönnies between *Gemeinschaft* (close-knit society or COMMUNITY, based on repeated face-to-face contacts) and *Gesellschaft* (weakly bound society, based on impersonal, contractual relations) mapped on to, respectively, the countryside and the CITY. Such a mapping

has to be treated with caution, however, and many practitioners of URBAN and RURAL GEOGRAPHY would insist that any given urban or rural area, wherever located, is unlikely to possess just one, homogeneous, internally consistent society. Crucially, what emerges is the appreciation that society is not a singular entity, undifferentiated from one place to the next, and that scholars – not just geographers, but all informed intellectuals – should think in terms of many socie*ties* in the plural.

In works of geography, it is possible to find countless casual references to 'society'. As one instance, Kariel and Kariel (1972) define SOCIAL GEOGRAPHY as the 'study of the spatial aspects of characteristics of the population, social organisation, and elements of culture and *society*' (p. v, footnote; emphasis added), but never define nor explain what society means for the remainder of their text (which deals with the spatial patterns displayed by a range of phenomena such as food, buildings, language and religion). The lack of a definition of society is also true of more recent social geography texts (Valentine, 2001; Panelli, 2004), although the explicit concern here for social groupings, categories and relations means that the reader arguably emerges with a greater sense of what the social entails. One current text does provide a definition, however, noting how: ' "Society" denotes the ties that people have with others. ... Societies are usually perceived as having a distinct identity and a system of meanings and values which members share', (Pain, Burke, Fuller and Gough, 2001, p. 3, box 1.3). It is possible to find geographers leaning towards all of the theoretical positions laid out above and more, but many have been drawn to the loosely Giddensian formulation, complete with its alertness to time–space relations.

Finally, it is interesting to reflect upon how different geographical traditions have worked, unwittingly or more knowingly, with different conceptions of society, and in the process started to theorize in different ways the relations between society (the social) and space (the spatial). Tracing such differences across the twentieth-century history of human – or, more narrowly, social – geography is the task that Philo and Söderström (2004, esp. p. 106) set themselves, probing 'the work of geographers trying to make sense of "the social" by their own means, including their own *bricolage* of elements culled ... from a diversity of sources in social theory, other disciplines and popular discourses'. Environmental, REGIONAL, spatial, RADICAL, HUMANISTIC and 'culturally turned' GEOGRAPHIES are all examined, drawing from Anglophone and French literatures, and questions are asked about *how* and *why* particular scholars on particular occasions have chosen to talk about society or the social, and with what consequences for the varieties of human geography practised. More overtly, it is now possible to identify diverse strands within human geography over the past quarter century that have been explicit in seeking to theorize the relations *between* society and space. Following Soja's (1980) statement of the 'socio-spatial DIALECTIC', a range of contributions, at first chiefly based in a Marxian tradition, but subsequently enriched by insights from feminism, post-colonial theory, cultural theory, psychoanalysis and elsewhere, have illuminated the problematic of simultaneously articulating 'the societal construction of space' and 'the spatial construction of society' (see FEMINIST GEOGRAPHIES; MARXIST GEOGRAPHIES; POST-COLONIALISM; PSYCHOANALYTIC THEORY). In so doing, the very referents 'society' and 'space' have been subjected to intense questioning, in some literatures being deconstructed to the point at which the terms appear to be under permanent erasure; but they *will* persist, their names will be invoked, and the problematic of 'society-space' will continue as an unavoidable challenge to generations of geographical theorists to come.   CP

Suggested reading
Giddens (1984); Philo and Söderström (2004); Smith (2005c).

software for qualitative research Some QUALITATIVE RESEARCH METHODS generate large quantities of 'data' for which computer-based software has been developed. Most of the available software packages focus on the analysis of textual (including transcribed INTERVIEW) material and undertake various forms of content analysis through a variety of user-informed coding schemes. Among the early such packages, NUD*ist (Non-numerical Unstructured Data [for] index searching and theory-building) was particularly popular: it facilitates indexing and the structuring of indexes as well as rapid searches for words and phrases and producing statistical reports on, for example, word associations and allowing researchers to insert memos within the text. More recent developments building on that foundation include NViVo and XSight: all privilege certain approaches to textual analysis – focusing on associations and counting – and thereby to some extent constrain if not direct the enterprise. As with SOFTWARE FOR QUANTITATIVE RESEARCH, an increasing number of freeware packages is available for interrogating qualitative data – such as those made available through CAQDAS (Computer-Assisted Qualitative Data

Name	Available from	Comments
R	http://cran.r-project.org.	R is a general system for statistical computation and graphics: it offers facilities for data manipulation, calculation and graphical display either through built-in functions or add-on packages contributed by users – this includes *spdep*, which has facilities to create spatial weights, tests for spatial autocorrelation, and procedures for spatial regression.
GEODA	https://www.geoda.uiuc.edu/	This implements techniques for exploratory spatial data analysis: descriptive spatial data analysis, spatial autocorrelation tests, and some spatial regression functionality.
GeoBUGS	http://www.mrc-bsu.cam.ac.uk/bugs/winbugs/geobugs.shtml	This is a Bayesian based package that fits spatial models and produces a range of maps as output.
BAYESX	http://www.stat.uni-muenchen.de/~bayesx/bayesx.html	This has a number of distinctive features including handling structured and/or uncorrelated effects of spatial covariates. It allows non-parametric, smoothed relationships between the response and the predictors, and does this for continuous and discrete outcomes: it can manipulate and display geographical maps.
MLwiN	http://www.cmm.bristol.ac.uk/	A comprehensive package for the analysis and display of multi-level models, this uses likelihood and Bayesian approaches to estimation: it includes spatial models.

software for quantitative analysis

Analysis) – and centres have been established (such as Qualidata, part of the Data Archive at the University of Essex) to promote the shared use of qualitative data. RJ

Suggested reading
Crang, Hudson, Reimer and Hinchliffe (1997); Gibbs (2002); Richards (2005). For CAQDAS, see http://caqdas.soc.surrey.ac.uk/resources.htm and http://www.lboro.ac.uk/ research/mmethods/ research/software/caqdas_primer.html. For Qualidata, see http://www.esds.ac.uk/qualidata/.

software for quantitative analysis Software, a term invented by the statistician John Tukey, refers to the instructions executed by a computer, as opposed to the hardware, the physical device on which the software runs. Over the past 40 years, statistical software has revolutionized the way in which we approach data analysis, by allowing a much more computationally intensive approach. This has led to working with much larger data sets; using more realistic models (e.g. CATEGORICAL DATA ANALYSIS; GEOGRAPHICALLY WEIGHTED REGRESSION; MULTI-LEVEL MODELS); and better ways of visualizing data sets and models (see VISUALIZATION) as part of an EXPLORATORY DATA ANALYSIS approach. However, Ripley (2005) argues that 'software availability now drives what we do, probably much more than we consciously realize': if it is not readily available, we tend not to do the analyses. This has been particularly problematic in holding back development and adoption of geographical modeling and spatial analysis, because the widely used and otherwise reasonably comprehensive software, such as the Statistical Package for the Social Sciences (SPSS©), has limited capacity in this area. This is finally changing and a new generation of software (much of it 'freeware') has these capabilities, as in the table on page 703. KJ

Suggested reading
Anselin (2000).

South, the Invoked implicitly or explicitly in relation to its assumed opposite (the *North*), the idea of the *South* emerged as an alternative to the term THIRD WORLD for distinguishing former colonies and less industrialized nations from countries of the more affluent and industrialized North. *South* is preferred by those who see *Third World* as connoting third-ranked, rather than its original meaning of a non-aligned or third path, independent of the capitalist *First World* and the socialist *Second World*. However, the term 'South' is also problematic in that the countries of the South are (a) defined through their location with respect to the USA and Western Europe, and (b) concentrated in the tropics and sub-tropics of both the Northern and the Southern Hemispheres. To avoid such binaries, some scholars deploy the language of a 'One Third (1/3) World' - typically in conjunction with the notion of the 'First World/North' – and a 'Two Thirds (2/3) World' in conjunction with a 'Third World/South' to represent the relative fractions of global population based on quality of life (Mohanty, 2003).

The popularization of the terms 'South' and 'North' is sometimes attributed to the publication of two reports by the Brandt Commission: *North–South* (1980) and *The common crisis* (1983). Convened by Willy Brandt of the then West Germany to study critical issues arising from the economic and social disparities of the global community, this self-appointed commission highlighted a co-dependent relationship between the northern nations, which relied on the poor countries for their wealth, and the southern nations, which depended on the wealthier North for their development. With FOOD, agriculture, AID, ENERGY, TRADE, financial reform and global negotiations as their focus, the Brandt Reports sought to promote 'adequate solutions to the problems involved in DEVELOPMENT and in attacking absolute POVERTY', while also addressing issues concerning the environment, the arms race, population growth and the uncertain prospects of the global economy that the commission viewed as common to both North and South (Brandt Commission, 1980; Porter and Sheppard, 1998, p. 26).

However, it is in the post-Cold War era that the idea of the South became significant as a metaphor to define the global landscape of political and economic power. Throughout the 1980s, the two rival COLD WAR military and political systems shaped development possibilities in the Third World. While relations between either superpower bloc and the Third World frequently provided only limited development opportunities for recently decolonized nations and LATIN AMERICA, Third World leaders did have some choice of political economic system. This room for manoeuvre was at times exploited by Third World elites to resist capitalist or communist incursion, and to develop social democratic and WELFARE STATE systems (see CAPITALISM; COMMUNISM). The period after 1989 witnessed the demise of the SECOND WORLD, the rise of the USA as the dominant economic, ideological and military power, and the hegemony of neo-liberal economic discourse (see NEO-LIBERALISM). East–West rivalries have been replaced by NORTH-SOUTH tensions around such issues as the power and role of the WORLD TRADE ORGANIZATION, the United Nations and international finance institutions, global CIVIL SOCIETY and donor-driven NGOs, mobility of labour versus that of CAPITAL and COMMODITIES, and public health crises related to AIDS (Sheppard and Nagar, 2004).

However, Mamdani's (2004, p. 250) point that 'the Cold War was largely not fought in Europe but in what came to be called the Third World' serves as an important reminder that the East–West politics have been at all times North–South politics. Not surprisingly, then, while the post-9/11 'anti-TERRORISM' discourse is couched in terms of West versus radical Islam, the US war on terror has simultaneously metamorphosed into an offensive imperial WAR, in which southern nations are denied the right to defend their SOVEREIGNTY as well as the right to reform (Mamdani, 2004, p. 260).

Two noteworthy fissures in the concept of the South have emerged in this environment. First, with the emergence of the so-called newly industrializing countries (NICs), such as Taiwan and South Korea, and growing impoverishment, particularly in AFRICA, the countries of the South have become increasingly differentiated. Second, whereas East–West rivalries predominantly played out at the NATION-STATE scale, North–South tensions operate on multiple SCALES. As political and economic elites in most countries of the Third and erstwhile Second Worlds accepted the tenets of neo-liberalism, they repositioned themselves ideologically and materially alongside the more wealthy residents of the First World. At the same time, ongoing socio-economic polarization within the industrialized world (reinforced by post-9/11 reforms), together with the devolution of responsibilities for citizens' welfare from nation-states to regions and cities, has meant that livelihood possibilities in marginal localities within the former First World become more similar to those of the less well off in the former Second and Third Worlds than to the elites in their own countries. In addition, multilateral and supra-national agencies became increasingly influential proponents of the neo-liberal agenda of the global North, shaping development geographies within states (Sheppard and Nagar, 2004).

In concert, donor-driven NGOs have facilitated the co-optation of radical left and feminist politics, even as they have helped to popularize the concepts of empowerment and equity in limited but critical ways. Not surprisingly, then, the proliferation of UN conferences on women in the post-Cold War era has 'undermin[ed] nation-specific resistance in the name of international solidarity', while simultaneously creating '"the new subaltern" – the somewhat monolithic woman as victim who is the constituted subject of justice under (the now-unrestricted) international capitalism' (Spivak, 2000, p. 305).

Thus, the global North is constituted through the pathways of transnational capital and NETWORKS of political and economic elites spanning privileged localities across the globe (Castells, 1996a; Mohanty, 2003). By contrast, the global South, which theoretically inhabits the 'margins', is to be found everywhere. But this does not make all Souths 'equal'. Movements against neo-liberalism are reminders of the ways in which convergences and divergences on issues such as livelihood alternatives shape the agendas of actors operating in multiple Souths, whose visibility, in turn, is shaped by complex politics of socio-geographical locations (Glassman, 2002; Hardt, 2002; Sparke, Brown, Corva, Day and Faria, 2005).   RN

sovereign power A philosophical concept arguing that POWER is the control over individual life. The concept is a challenge to established ideas of SOVEREIGNTY that concentrate upon political authority over TERRITORY. Sovereign power focuses attention to the SCALE of the BODY, the authority to classify individuals in a particular way to grant them life or death. The roots of the concept lie in the work of Michel Foucault and his discussion of BIOPOWER, regularization and BIOPOLITICS. Foucault's analysis of nineteenth-century medicine and sexual behaviour described the way in which individual bodies and sexual practices were classified by STATE institutions as healthy/good and unhealthy/bad. The manner in which this was done led to the regulation of individual behaviour, or biopower, through classification and control, to the classification of groups of people (in terms of RACE, NATION, SEXUALITY, GENDER etc.), the political implication being that classification of people as, say, sexually deviant can be used in arguments limiting their political RIGHTS.

Usage of the concept 'sovereign power' has been promoted by the work of Giorgio

Agamben, who thought that the fate of the Jews in the HOLOCAUST ran counter to Foucault's theory. Instead, Agamben argued that at times individuals and groups may be classified in such a way that their life is deemed worthless rather than something to be regulated. For Agamben, the Nazis identified Jews as 'BARE LIFE' – life that warranted extermination. Agamben begins with the Romans, and their classification of *HOMO SACER* (from Roman law, an individual who may be killed but not sacrificed). *Homines sacri* may not be sacrificed as they are 'beyond the divine', and hence meaningless to the gods. They may be killed with impunity, however, because *homo sacer* is beyond juridical law, and hence has no value to the citizenry. While Foucault examined how power disciplined individuals to create a SUBJECT (a person behaving within imposed rules and norms), Agamben argued that sovereign power allows for the elimination of particular subjects. Foucault's biopolitics tries to define who can and should be included in a political community, while Agamben argues that sovereign power excludes individuals and groups not just from particular territorial political communities but from humanity itself.

Geographers have utilized the next logical step in Agamben's work, his identification of spaces of exception (see EXCEPTION, SPACE OF); the geographical construction of BORDERS outside which the rules and norms of established legal and political order do not apply. It is in these geographical zones that sovereign power allows and enacts the killing of *homo sacer* with impunity. The classification of territory in this way results, for Agamben, in a mapping of our world not into NATIONS, but into 'CAMPS'. In the context of the 'war on terror', Agamben's concept was used by geographers to explain the slaughter of fighters and civilians by the US military in Afghanistan and Iraq, the violence upon the Palestinians by Israeli forces, and the incarceration of 'terrorists' at the US Naval Station at Guantánamo Bay, Cuba, with no recourse to US or international LAW (Gregory, 2004b).   CF

Suggested reading
Edkins (2000); Gregory (2004b).

sovereignty A claim to final and ultimate authority over a political community. The Treaty of Westphalia (1648) codified modern politics as a system of STATES: states have sovereignty over the land and people in their territories. The term implies that no external

political entity has the authority to enact laws or exercise authority within a sovereign TERRITORY (Taylor, 1994c, 1995b). In reality, such a condition of sovereignty has never existed and has been particularly challenged by contemporary processes of GLOBALIZATION.

Sovereignty of states in an inter-state system is the result of two interrelated processes. First, *internal sovereignty* means that external powers are excluded from exercising authority within a state's territory, and that the state has authority over the whole of its territory. A distinction must be made between legal and effective sovereignty. A state may claim sovereignty over the whole of its territory but face strong opposition and resistance to its rule in particular regions to the extent that the STATE APPARATUS is ineffective and ignored. Second, *external sovereignty* means mutual recognition from other states in the system, ultimately requiring endorsement by, and membership of, the United Nations. For example, Israel's induction into the United Nations in 1947, despite protest from Arab countries, established the new state in the inter-state system.

The sub-discipline of POLITICAL GEOGRAPHY was initially focused upon issues of sovereignty, especially the precise location of the BORDERS that delimit states and their sovereignty, as well as the functional internal geography that facilitated the effective exercise of sovereignty. In addition, the fact that state sovereignty did not produce peace, as intended and expected, but has generated CONFLICTS has also provided topics for political geographers: inter-state conflicts, IMPERIALISM and SECESSION, for example. Furthermore, sovereignty over the sea and inner and outer space have emerged as important topics.

The most intriguing discussions of sovereignty have emerged in light of GLOBALIZATION, and the extreme argument, made by some, that we are facing the end of state sovereignty as it emerged in modern times (Ohmae, 1995). Before discussing globalization and sovereignty two points must be made. Sovereignty as per its definition has never existed; there have always been interdictions of external authority and challenges to internal sovereignty. Second, globalization is not an external force acting upon states, but a collection of economic, political, and cultural processes that are partially created and enacted by states. The undermining of state sovereignty by globalization is partly a result of the states themselves. This has led to the definition of 'quasi-states', those that have limited effective sovereignty, often an outcome of POST-COLONIAL relationships (Jackson, 1990).

The inter-state, or even trans-state, character of globalization has weakened the ability of states to manage their own economic affairs. Currency values and interest rates within particular countries are partially set by the decisions made by international markets rather than through domestic policy, for example. In other words, external influence is felt within sovereign territory. The outcome is a geography of 'graduated sovereignty', in which state sovereignty is spatially differentiated within a sovereign territory (Park, 2005). For example, special economic zones of reduced taxes and tariffs are established within countries that reduce the fiscal authority of the state in order to promote TRADE and INVESTMENT (cf. ENTERPRISE ZONE).

Although states have ceded sovereignty over economic processes, others, reacting to public pressure, have focused upon social sovereignty (Rudolph, 2005), defined as the states' ability to define and control access to a political community. Political CITIZENSHIP has been understood as a feature of territorial sovereignty; citizenship was attached to a particular territorially-defined community, and citizens gained RIGHTS and received duties from the sovereign state. However, processes of globalization have led to increased calls for non-territorial forms of citizenship, in effect granting sovereignty to institutions that transcend states (Russell, 2005).

Sovereignty is in a state of flux, as SOCIETY becomes increasingly organized around NETWORKS rather than territories (Castells, 1996b). Consideration of graduated sovereignty is coupled to overlapping forms of sovereignty, akin to pre-modern times, whereby a territory may be subject to a number of sovereign claims. Some of these claims may be stronger and more appealing than others as the ability to exercise authority may decline with distance from a political centre (Lake, 2003). Currently, we live in a hybrid political geography of varying forms of sovereignty within territorial and network spaces.   CF

Suggested reading
Holsti (2004); Sidaway (2002).

space The production of geographical knowledge has always involved claims to know 'space' in particular ways. Historically, special importance has been attached to the power to fix the locations of events, places, people and phenomena on the surface of the

Earth and to represent these on MAPS. The extension of these capacities involved a series of instrumental, mathematical and graphical advances, but these innovations were also *political technologies* that were implicated in the production of particular constellations of POWER (Pickles, 2004; Short, 2004). As such, they carried within them particular conceptions of space that were always more than purely technical constructions (see also CARTOGRAPHY, HISTORY OF). This recognition of an intricate connection between power, knowledge and geography has transformed the ways in which contemporary HUMAN GEOGRAPHY has conceptualized space. A suite of theories and concepts has been assembled to address what Allen (2003) describes as both 'spatial vocabularies of power' (which trace the mobilizations and effects of power *over* space) and 'lost geographies of power' (which show how power is produced and performed *through* space). These elaborations have significant repercussions for concepts such as PLACE, REGION and TERRITORY, but in what follows attention is directed towards the more general, plenary concepts of space within which these more particular concepts may be convened.

These are matters of considerable importance. Many writers have argued that the nineteenth century was the epoch of TIME, the twentieth century the epoch of space, and that as 'the modern' yielded to 'the postmodern' so there has been a marked 'spatial turn' across the spectrum of the HUMANITIES and social sciences that describes much more than the play of spatial METAPHORS (e.g. Smith and Katz, 1993; Soja, 1989). But others have insisted on the imminent 'end of geography', 'the irrelevance of space' and the 'death of distance' in ostensibly the same late, liquid or postmodern world (e.g. Bauman, 2000a). It is not difficult to reconcile these competing claims: everything depends on how 'space' is conceptualized (cf. MODERNITY; POSTMODERNITY).

Hartshorne's once influential enquiry into *The nature of geography* (1939) occupies a strange position within the history of the discipline. His view of geography was Kantian – Geography was concerned with the organization of phenomena in space (see AREAL DIFFERENTIATION; KANTIANISM) – and yet Hartshorne provided no systematic discussion of the concept on which his prospectus depended. Even his subsequent account of geography as one of the 'spatial sciences' (with astronomy and geophysics) failed to elucidate the conceptual basis of his claim. What

707

preoccupied Hartshorne (1958) was the recovery of a line of descent from Kant through Humboldt to Hettner, and yet the ways in which these writers *conceptualized* space was never allowed to become a problem. Hartshorne simply took it for granted that space (like time) was a universal of human existence, an external coordinate, an empty grid of mutually exclusive points, 'an unchanging box' *within which objects exist and events occur*: all of which is to say that he privileged the concept of *absolute space* (Smith, 1984, pp. 67–8).

Many of Hartshorne's postwar critics fastened on the way in which he had taken a specific concept of space and elevated it to the single, supposedly universal concept of space. Although Schaefer objected to the EXCEPTIONALISM of Hartshorne's views, he nonetheless agreed that 'spatial relations are the ones that matter in geography and no others'. The difference was that spatial relations were now to be defined *between objects and events* (not between the fixed points of an external coordinate system) and thereby made relative to the objects and events that constituted a spatial system or spatial structure. This substituted a concept of *relative space* whose elucidation required a more complex geometry, and for this reason SPATIAL ANALYSIS – the preferred research METHODOLOGY of many of Hartshorne's critics – involved a process of ABSTRACTION in which 'physical space [was] superseded by mathematical space' (Smith, 1984, pp. 68–73). This intellectual project promised to turn geography into a formal SPATIAL SCIENCE, predicated on a key claim: 'That there is more order than appears at first sight is not discovered till that order is looked for' (Haggett, 1965, p. 2). This was used to demarcate a new research frontier – a 'new geography' – whose explorer–scientists believed that there was an intrinsically and essentially *spatial order* to the world: that spatial science made it possible to disclose (to make visible) the spatiality of the natural and the social in ways that were literally overlooked by the other sciences.

Yet many human geographers became increasingly uncomfortable at what they saw as both SPATIAL FETISHISM (treating social relations as purely spatial relations) and SPATIAL SEPARATISM (divorcing human geography from the humanities and social sciences). The critique of spatial science was many-stranded, but many of the original objections revolved around Olsson's (1974) insight that the statements of spatial science revealed more about

the language that its protagonists were talking *in* than the world that they were talking *about*. The most general outcome was a movement towards a PROCESS-oriented human geography that explored the process-domains of POLITICAL ECONOMY and SOCIAL THEORY, and then traced the marks made by these processes and practices on the surface of the Earth. At the time, several influential writers insisted that concepts of space could not be adjudicated by appeals to the PHILOSOPHY of SCIENCE, but had to be articulated through the conduct of social practices: 'The question "what is space?" is therefore replaced by the question "How is it that different human practices create and make use of distinctive conceptualizations of space?"' (Harvey, 1973, p. 14). This introduced a *relational* concept in which space is 'folded into' social relations through practical activities. This allowed not only for the socialization of spatial analysis but also, crucially, for the spatialization of social analysis: like simultaneous equations, each was incomplete without the other (Gregory and Urry, 1985; Soja, 1989). The international journal *Society and Space* was founded in 1983 to foster the interdisciplinary conversations that were emerging in this new discursive arena.

Many of the first attempts to re-theorize 'society and space' were indebted to Harvey's re-readings of Marx. Harvey argued that Marx's critique of political economy implied a latent spatial structure that he never made explicit: CAPITALISM as a system of COMMODITY production also depends on the production of a SPACE-ECONOMY, and its spasmodic crises in turn require a precarious 'spatial fix' (Harvey, 1999 [1982]). Others preferred to explore the writings of later Marxist scholars, notably Henri Lefebvre and his suggestive yet enigmatic account of the PRODUCTION OF SPACE (Lefebvre, 1991b). Harvey had always acknowledged his interest in Lefebvre, and subsequently integrated his own work with some of Lefebvre's key propositions and, en route, diagrammed the implications of absolute, relative and relational spaces for a revitalized HISTORICAL MATERIALISM (Harvey, 2006a; see also Gregory, 1994, pp. 348–416).

Later contributions pursued the spatial implications of other thinkers with varying degrees of success (Crang and Thrift, 2000). Two diagnostics have repeatedly emerged. The first is an unwavering concern with ONTOLOGY: with grasping the significance of space not for the constitution and conduct of capitalism alone, but for being-in-the-world. Pickles (1985) was one of the first human geographers to provide a rigorous account of the implications of EXISTENTIALISM and PHENOMENOLOGY for understanding human SPATIALITY, and these themes have re-emerged in later thematizations of space (e.g. Strohmayer, 1998). The second is a persistent interest in concepts of space that are markedly less orderly than those of spatial science and its successor projects, sometimes through readings of outlaw Marxists such as Walter Benjamin (Latham, 1999; Dubow, 2004) and sometimes through POST-STRUCTURALISM: the most influential figures here have been Gilles Deleuze, Michel Foucault (Crampton and Elden, 2007) and Jacques Lacan.

Taken together, contemporary theorizations of space in human geography (and beyond) share the following features:

(1) *The integration of time and space.* Conventional social science privileged the first term (so that time was seen as change, movement and history) while marginalizing the second (so that space was seen as the site of stasis and stability). Human geography has abandoned the project of an autonomous science of the spatial, rejected conceptions of space as the fixed and frozen ground on which events take place or processes leave their marks, and is now exploring the mobile, processual fields of 'time–space' (May and Thrift, 2001; see TIME-GEOGRAPHY; TIME–SPACE COMPRESSION; TIME-SPACE EXPANSION).

(2) *The co-production of time and space.* Time and space are not neutral, canonical grids that exist 'on the outside', enframing and containing life on Earth, but are instead folded into the ongoing flows and forms of the world in which we find ourselves. Thus Thrift (1996; see also 2008) introduces the idea of *spatial formations* to figure a sensuous ONTOLOGY of practices and encounters between diverse, distributed bodies and things. This is a thoroughly MATERIALIST account, but it operates through an analytics of the surface rather than the 'depth models' of mainstream Marxism, and it refuses the oppositions between 'CULTURE' and 'NATURE' on which HISTORICAL MATERIALISM is predicated. Time–space emerges as a process of continual construction 'through the agency of things encountering each other in more or less organized circulations' (Thrift, 2003, p. 96). Similarly but differently, Rose (1999b) draws

on feminist theory, and particularly the work of Judith Butler, to insist that space is not a pre-existent void or 'a terrain to be spanned or constructed': it is instead 'a doing', a PERFORMANCE.

(3) *The unruliness of time–space.* Both spatial science and conventional social theory made too much of pattern and systematicity, labouring to solve what they called 'the problem of order', without recognizing the multiple ways in which life on Earth evades and exceeds those orders. The sense of partial ordering and incompletion is focal to many contemporary theorizations. To be sure, space is not infinitely plastic: 'certain forms of space tend to recur, their repetition a sign of the power that saturates the spatial' (Rose, 1999). And yet, while modalities of power often work to condense particular spatialities as 'natural' outcomes through architectures of SURVEILLANCE and regulation, Massey (2005) insists that space is not a coherent system of discriminations and interconnections, a grid of 'proper places'. She argues that space necessarily entails plurality and multiplicity. Hence spatial formations involve (and invite) 'happenstance juxtapositions' and 'accidental separations', so that time–space becomes a turbulent field of constellations and configurations: a world of structures and solidarities, disruptions and dislocations that provides for the emergence of genuine novelty. 'Emergence' is not necessarily progressive or emancipatory, of course, and the argument may also be put in reverse: contemporary spaces of exception (see EXCEPTION, SPACES OF) trade on paradoxical orderings of space whose very ambiguity is used to foreclose possibilities for political action. Either way, however, far from space being 'the dead', as one of Foucault's astringent critics once claimed, it is now theorized as being fully involved in the modulations of tension and transformation.

(4) *The porousness of time–space.* Constellations of power and knowledge are typically elaborated through a spatial system of inclusions and exclusions, most generally through the demarcation of a 'space of the Same' from which 'the Other' is supposedly excluded (cf. IMAGINATIVE GEOGRAPHIES). A common critical response to these measures is to call these b/ordering processes to account – to

denaturalize them by disclosing their constructedness – and to break open (literally to de-limit) the 'space of the Same'. This involves recognizing the presence of the Other within the space of the Same: the ways in which the geographical knowledges brought 'home' by European explorers relied on, appropriated and so smuggle in indigenous knowledges, for example, or the ways in which the racialized, gendered and 'pure' spaces of COLONIALISM were routinely disrupted and transgressed (cf. HYBRIDITY; TRANSCULTURATION).

Thinking about time–space in these ways invites critical readings of the ways in which LANDSCAPE, MAPS and other conceptual devices function as REPRESENTATIONS – as orderings – of space, redescribing their naturalization as the product of political technologies and cultural practices, and calling into question the discipline's claims to know the world by rendering it as a transparent space (cf. SITUATED KNOWLEDGE). But they also require other ways of grasping time–space, and there are signs of experiments with performing, plastic and media arts to subvert our taken-for-granted methods of representation, and to open new political spaces for observant participation in the making of human geographies.   DG

Suggested reading
Harvey (2006a); Thrift (2006).

space syntax An approach to studying the spatial structure of cities using mathematical tools to describe their complexity. For example, the street system may be analysed topologically by calculating the complexity distance for each street – that is, the minimum number of links needed (i.e. streets traversed) to reach all other streets in the city (see TOPOLOGY). The measures extend beyond three-dimensional descriptions of the elements of the built environment themselves to assessments of how they are integrated – as in the use of *isovists* to identify the area visible from any point, either at street level or, say, from a window on a building's fourth floor. (In GEOGRAPHIC INFORMATION SYSTEMS these are termed *viewsheds*.) Such representations, using MAPS and graphs as well as numerical indices, allow the city's 'navigability' to be assessed – how easy is it to move about and to get from one point to another? – with techniques that can be applied at any SCALE (how

easy is it to get around an airport terminal, for example?).

Using their syntactical representations of the urban built environment, workers at the Space Syntax Laboratory at the Bartlett School of Architecture, University College London have studied COMMUTING and other movements, linking flows to the urban structure and thereby providing means for predicting future traffic patterns and transport system demands.   RJ

Suggested reading
Hiller (1996); Hiller and Hanson (1984). See also http://www.spacesyntax.org/

space-economy The idea that economic processes extend across geographical SPACE, thereby influencing their operation and outcome. Walter Isard (1956) coined the term, using it as the basis for his new discipline of regional science. In his (much earlier) development of LOCATION THEORY, August Lösch (1954 [1940]) had already shown that economic competition in space does not have the same beneficial outcomes claimed in standard economic theory, because competition is monopolistic in spatially extensive MARKETS (see NEO-CLASSICAL ECONOMICS). Location theory and regional science developed a series of related claims showing how space makes a difference to economic theory, making the term popular in the 1950s and 1960s. Within this tradition, SPATIAL STRUCTURES, a consequence of rational economic DECISION-MAKING, drive equilibrium outcomes and social welfare implications that differ from those of mainstream, a-spatial economic theory. Since 1990, with a revival of this tradition of work in geographical economics, the term has regained its popularity (Fujita, Krugman and Venables, 1999; see also NEW ECONOMIC GEOGRAPHY).

A parallel usage can be found within geographical interventions in MARXISM and POLITICAL ECONOMY, particularly among theorists whose intellectual socialization was influenced by spatial science and location theory, and who subsequently became highly critical of these formulations. Thus Harvey (1999 [1982]) used the term to describe how the geographical organization of CAPITALISM shapes its dynamics and evolution, calling into question some core beliefs of the conventional a-spatial Marxist critique of capitalism, and Sheppard and Barnes (1990) took these arguments still further in their analysis of the capitalist space-economy. In this view, space qualitatively complicates the contradictions, CRISES and CLASS struggles that are characteristic of capitalism. The spaces and places produced through ACCUMULATION and competition dynamics become barriers for future accumulation; conflict between places can cut across and undermine class struggle; and individual agents find it all but impossible to undertake actions that are in their long-term as well as their immediate interests. Again, taking account of the spatial extension of economic processes requires adjustments to conventional, a-spatial political economy. In this case, however, in contradistinction to regional science and location theory, analysis focuses on the dynamical dialectical relation between economic processes and the SPATIALITY they shape and are in turn shaped by (see DIALECTIC), rather than on assumed spatial structures and their impact on spatial economic equilibria.

As economic geography has subsequently moved to a conception of economy that emphasizes the inseparability of the economic from other societal and biophysical processes, thereby calling into question any theory that seeks to separate or prioritize economic relative to these other processes, so once again the term 'space-economy' has fallen out of favour (see also CULTURAL TURN; INSTITUTIONAL ECONOMICS). ES

space–time forecasting models

Statistical models that attempt to FORECAST the evolution of variables over both TIME and SPACE (e.g. sets of regions). These models are usually of the general REGRESSION form and forecast the future value of a variable and an observation unit in terms of (a) lagged exogenous or explanatory variables, (b) its own past values and (c) the lagged values for neighbouring or influencing spatial observation-units, thus capturing the impacts of spatial DIFFUSION. These models have been used to forecast both economic and demographic changes, and in studies of EPIDEMICS and the modelling of DISEASE. LWH

Suggested reading
Bennett (1979).

spatial analysis

The application of QUANTITATIVE METHODS in LOCATIONAL ANALYSIS within HUMAN GEOGRAPHY and sometimes used as a synonym for that portion of the discipline that concentrates on the *geometry* of the LANDSCAPE (cf. SPATIAL SCIENCE). O'Sullivan and Unwin (2002) present spatial analysis as the study of the arrangements of points, lines, areas and surfaces on a MAP, and of their interrelationships. Analyses of those separate components have deployed procedures adapted from other sciences – nearest-neighbour analysis and QUADRAT ANALYSIS, for POINT PATTERN ANALYSIS; GRAPH THEORY for lines; and TREND SURFACE ANALYSIS for surfaces, for example. Whereas many geographers have undertaken analyses of the interrelationships using techniques from within the GENERAL LINEAR MODEL, others have argued that spatial analysis poses particular statistical problems because of the nature of spatial data (cf. SPATIAL AUTOCORRELATION), thus requiring special techniques.

The development of GEOGRAPHIC INFORMATION SYSTEMS is rapidly facilitating advances in spatial analysis and the greater power of computers, together with software developments, has significantly increased geographers' ability to work with large and complex spatial data sets (cf. GEOCOMPUTATION). RJ

Suggested reading
Bailey and Gatrell (1995); Haining (1990).

spatial autocorrelation

The presence of spatial pattern in a mapped variable due to geographical proximity. The most common form of spatial autocorrelation is where similar values for a variable (such as county income levels) tend to cluster together in adjacent observation-units or REGIONS, so that on average across the map the values for neighbours are more similar than would occur if the allocation of values to observation-units were the result of a purely random mechanism. This is positive spatial autocorrelation. Negative autocorrelation is where neighbouring regions are significantly dissimilar; more general and complicated forms of autocorrelation can also be defined. The presence of spatial autocorrelation is very widespread and indeed may be said to lie at the core of GEOGRAPHY, as expressed in Tobler's (1970) – light-hearted – First Law of Geography: 'everything is related to everything else, but near things are more related than distant things'.

However, the presence of spatial autocorrelation violates a basic assumption of independence in many standard statistical MODELS. Thus for REGRESSION, there is an assumption that the residuals are not autocorrelated. The issue of spatial autocorrelation was recognized early in the history of inferential statistics, but it was not until the work of Moran and Geary in the late 1940s and 1950s

711

that tests were devised, and it was the developments by Cliff and Ord that brought the topic to prominence. A mathematical representation of 'neighbours' was a stumbling-block to computing the tests, and Cliff and Ord reformulated Moran's test to employ a W-matrix of size $N \times N$, where N was the number of regions or observations, and a cell value w_{ij} of 1 indicated that regions i and j were neighbours, and 0 if they were not (Cliff and Ord, 1973). This idea opened up a whole field of research, and spatial autocorrelation is now a theme in many social sciences. Moreover, as Tobler's Law suggests, spatial autocorrelation should not just be seen as a problem but also as a reflection of SPATIAL INTERACTION and a central aspect of spatial modelling, and this has been the basis for the development of SPATIAL ECONOMETRICS. The Moran test is a global one, detecting whether there is autocorrelation on average across the set of regions; a more recent development has been the disaggregation of this measure into local measures, such as Anselin's LISA (Local Indicators of Spatial Association) to detect local clusters of positive and negative autocorrelation (Anselin, 1995). (See also LOCAL STATISTICS.)   LWH

Suggested reading
Odland (1988).

spatial econometrics An interdisciplinary research field being developed by economists, geographers and statisticians. The term was invented by Jean Paelinck (Paelinck and Klaassen, 1979), and the research focuses on the construction and application of statistical MODELS and tests explicitly designed for spatial (geographical) data, building on initial work on SPATIAL AUTOCORRELATION by Cliff, Ord and others.

The field of econometrics was developed throughout the twentieth century by economists to deal with the special statistical modelling issue posed by the non-experimental context of economics and the social sciences, often very different from the LABORATORY and agricultural field-trials context for which much statistical theory was developed. In particular, econometricians constructed methods to deal with time-series autocorrelation, time-lags and dynamics in economic relationships and simultaneity and FEEDBACK between different equations in macroeconomic models. However, it is only in recent decades that equivalent techniques for spatial data have been developed. Amongst many contributors,

Luc Anselin's work, and his computer package SpaceStat, have been particularly influential in developing both the methods and their application. The focus of the field has moved from testing for spatial autocorrelation towards the modelling of SPATIAL INTERACTION through spatial DIFFUSION, spatial lags or spillovers, and ENDOGENEITY is a major focus in the construction of the estimators and tests.   LWH

Suggested reading
Anselin (1988, 2002, 2003).

spatial fetishism Any approach that treats SPACE as sufficiently autonomous to social processes that 'no change in the social process or spatial relations could alter the fundamental structure of space' (Smith, 1981b, p. 112). The term was developed in the course of interactions between HUMAN GEOGRAPHY and MARXISM; by analogy with Marx's critique of COMMODITY fetishism, in which the conditions of production of a commodity are made invisible and the ECONOMY is reduced to exchanges between objects rather than seen as a series of unfolding social relations and practices, so it was argued that approaches such as SPATIAL SCIENCE conceptualized space as somehow exogenous to and separate from social processes (cf. Soja, 1980) (See also SPATIAL SEPARATISM.)   ES

spatial identity The ways in which identities are constituted, articulated and contested in relation to SPACE and PLACE. A wide range of research has explored the territorialized spatialities of identity in relation to, for example, a REGION, 'HOMELAND' or NATION. Other research traces the deterritorialized – and *re*territorialized – SPATIALITIES of identity in terms of MIGRATION, DIASPORA and BORDERLANDS. Whilst some research has viewed space merely as a container for IDENTITY, or as a stage on which identities are played out, other research – particularly since the 1990s – traces the mutual constitution of both space and identity and their multiple and contested articulations (including Keith and Pile, 1993). Rather than view spatial identities in ESSENTIALIST terms, this research – often inspired by POST-STRUCTURALISM, PSYCHO-ANALYSIS and POST-COLONIALISM – traces their politicized differentiation. Although spatial METAPHORS have been particularly important in conceptualizing identity, geographers have been concerned to ground and locate the material spatialities of identity, which are often closely bound up with ideas about SITUATED

KNOWLEDGE, the politics of location, and the spatial politics of identity (Yaeger, 1996; see also POSITIONALITY). In a wide variety of contexts, geographical analyses of spatial identity thereby explore the metaphorical and material relationships between space, identity and POWER.

Post-colonial and feminist theorists have been particularly influential in theorizing spatial identity. In his classic work, *Orientalism*, Edward Said (2003 [1978]) explored the IMAGINATIVE GEOGRAPHIES of 'self' and 'other' through the intensely politicized spaces of the 'Orient'. Other post-colonial theorists have explored the spatial identities bound up with MIGRATION, DIASPORA and the contested politics of HYBRIDITY, MULTICULTURALISM and COSMOPOLITANISM (including Hall, 1996a). In feminist theory, a frequently cited essay by Minnie Bruce Pratt (1984) traces her sense of identity through multiple spaces of home and MEMORY. Other feminist theorists have theorized the interplay of GENDER and other identities in place, over space, and in shaping the production of space and knowledge. In her analysis of 'locational FEMINISM', for example, Susan Stanford Friedman (1998) explores the critical interplay of space and identity through different discourses of positionality. As part of these discourses, 'situational approaches' not only 'assume that identity resists fixity, but they particularly stress how it shifts fluidly from setting to setting', whereby '[e]ach situation presumes a certain setting as site for the interplay of different axes of power and powerlessness' (p. 23).   AB

Suggested reading
Friedman (1998); Hall (1996); Keith and Pile (1993); Pratt (1984).

spatial interaction A term popularized by Edward Ullman (1980) to indicate the interdependence *between* geographical REGIONS, which he saw as complementary to the more traditional emphasis on relationships (people and their social context, people and environment) *within* each individual region. FLOWS of information, money, people and commodities thus lay at the heart of Ullman's vision, and he hoped it would provide a unifying frame for GEOGRAPHY. This has not happened, and few geographers now refer to Ullman's book or his specific ideas. However, much work in human geography in the past 30 years has taken up this theme and many would see 'spatial interaction' as central to geographers' concerns and contributions, without being aware of Ullman's work. This is true of both quantitative work on modelling spatial movements and spatial spillovers and qualitative work on local–global linkages and contexts.   LWH

Suggested reading
Ullman (1980).

spatial mismatch The notion that constraints on residential choice prevent members of certain groups from adequate access to employment (also referred to as the spatial mismatch hypothesis). Urban economist John Kain first used the term in the 1960s to describe the impacts of residential SEGREGATION and housing market discrimination on the employment opportunities and earnings of black residents of Chicago and Detroit (Kain, 1968). In a retrospective published after his death (Kain, 2004), Kain noted that he later extended the concept to include other negative impacts, such as those on home ownership and quality of education, and of discrimination in the housing market.

Following Kain's early lead, most research on spatial mismatch has sought to understand the extent to which the black–white disparity in earnings can be explained by blacks' inferior spatial ACCESSIBILITY to employment. As employment, and particularly manufacturing employment, increasingly SUBURBANIZED after the Second World War, access to such employment depended on a suburban residential location; but a variety of discriminatory practices in the housing market prevented blacks from moving to the SUBURBS. As a result, blacks were confined to inner-city neighbourhoods, which were increasingly bereft of manufacturing jobs.

Until recently, research on spatial mismatch concentrated on comparing the residential and employment patterns and COMMUTING times of black and white men; McLafferty and Preston (1997) and others have shown the importance of expanding such studies to other racialized groups such as Latinos/Latinas, and to women.

Evidence supporting the spatial mismatch hypothesis was one factor that led the US Department of Housing and Urban Development (HUD) to initiate an experimental programme, 'Moving to Opportunity', to help low-income people from high-poverty NEIGHBOURHOODS to move to racially integrated, low-poverty suburban locations. Subsequent studies have evaluated the extent to which such residential MOBILITY and the resulting change in neighbourhood context and accessibility do indeed lead to improved employment and educational opportunities (Clark, 2005c). One interesting and unanticipated outcome of this experiment has been that substantial numbers of households have subsequently moved back to their old neighbourhoods, places with which they are familiar and are where their families and friends remain (Clark, 2005). SHa

Suggested reading
Holzer (1991); Preston and McLafferty (1999).

spatial monopoly Monopolistic control over a MARKET by virtue of location. The usual meaning of MONOPOLY is that one firm or individual sells the entire output of some COMMODITY or SERVICE. This is normally the final outcome of a competitive process taking place under CAPITALIST market conditions, in which one supplier is able to produce and sell the commodity at a price favourable enough to consumers to force other suppliers out of business. Spatial monopoly is a special case, in which distance from competitors or ways of bounding space give a producer monopolistic control over a section of the market.

Spatial monopoly can arise when a producer is distributing a commodity from its point of origin, and also when consumers travel to the point of origin. In the first case, the operation of an f.o.b. pricing policy, whereby the cost of transportation is passed on to the consumer (see PRICING POLICIES), will increase delivered price with distance from the production point, so that consumers close to the production point can purchase the commodity relatively cheaply; that is, more cheaply than from alternative suppliers. The greater the elasticity of demand, or the sensitivity of the consumer to price, the greater the likelihood of local monopoly. The area within which monopoly control exists (assuming that consumers buy from the cheapest source) is bounded by a locus of points where delivered price from the supplier in question is equal to the price charged by a competitor. In the second case, consumers will tend to travel to the production point which is closest in time, effort or cost. In this case, too, the area of monopoly control will be bounded by a locus of points of consumer indifference as to whether to purchase from one point to another.

Spatial monopoly can also arise from collusion between otherwise competing firms, who may agree to a 'carve-up' of the market among themselves. As in other situations of spatial monopoly, this will enable suppliers to raise prices and exact above-normal profits in the area over which they exert exclusive control. Distance provides no absolute protection of a market, however, for some consumers may choose to purchase from high-cost sources or to travel to more distant outlets, out of preference, ignorance or other behavioural considerations.

There may be other strategies for protecting space over which monopoly control is exerted. These include the imposition of tariffs and restriction on the use of means of transportation: suppliers may use coercion to prevent competitors from entering a particular city to sell their goods, for example, as has happened in the former Soviet Union since the collapse of SOCIALISM.

In some instances, spatial monopoly may be a case of so-called natural monopoly, where the market in question is best served by a single firm because of the nature of the production process. Some public utilities are of this kind; for example, local water supply. Such public spatial monopoly may be turned into private monopoly by PRIVATIZATION. DMS

Suggested reading
Smith (1981).

spatial science The theoretical approach associated with the QUANTITATIVE REVOLUTION in Anglo-American GEOGRAPHY in the 1960s that privileged spatial analysis. During this period many human geographers turned from the integrated, descriptive and IDIOGRAPHIC analysis of specific places (i.e. the traditional forms of REGIONAL GEOGRAPHY) to the specialized, theoretically inflected and NOMOTHETIC analysis of SPATIAL STRUCTURES; that is, spatial science. EPISTEMOLOGICALLY, this stream of work, the so-called 'New Geography' of the 1960s, is usually associated with the PHILOSOPHIES of LOGICAL EMPIRICISM and LOGICAL POSITIVISM, the prevailing norms in the natural sciences and the emergent best practice in other social sciences after 1945. By aligning itself with 'normal science', and in another sense with 'extraordinary research' and 'scientific revolutions' (see PARADIGM), geography successfully sought to enhance its academic status (Ad Hoc Committee on Geography, 1965; see also Billinge, Gregory and Martin, 1984b). While rarely describing itself explicitly as positivist, it was presumed that reliable EXPLANATIONS could be achieved by constructing universal deductive causal explanations whose accuracy could be assessed by reference to independently gathered observations (Harvey, 1969).

In HUMAN GEOGRAPHY, this approach was used to develop theories of the location of human activities, the SPATIAL INTERACTIONS between places and the spatial DIFFUSION of phenomena from one place to another. Typically, research proceeded by constructing mathematical–statistical MODELS and then comparing them to observations using spatial analysis (spatial statistics and Monte Carlo SIMULATION). While some spatial science suffers from SPATIAL FETISHISM and SPATIAL SEPARATISM, these are by no means inherent shortcomings. Both the SOCIAL CONSTRUCTION of space and the THEORY-laden nature of observations were recognized within spatial science.

Given this history, it is ironic that the term 'spatial science' first appeared in English in Hartshorne's programmatic statement of *The nature of geography* (1939). This text was the *bête noire* of SPATIAL SCIENCE: Hartshorne discussed LOCATION THEORY *en passant* but ruled it out of geographical enquiry, and he located geography alongside what he called other 'spatial sciences', such as astronomy (cf. COSMOGRAPHY), only to insist that the intrinsic EXCEPTIONALISM of geography necessarily relocated it with the idiographic sensibilities of history rather than the theoretical and statistical modalities of the other, normal sciences. When the term 'spatial science' reappeared, it was not part of the rival prospectus of the quantitative revolutionaries at all but, rather, named their research as the object of critique: thus the second chapter of Gregory's *Ideology, science and human geography* (1978a) was entitled 'In place of spatial science'.

Since then, spatial science has become a catch-all characterization of forms of spatial analysis and theorization associated with the Quantitative Revolution and its derivatives. At its most general, it describes a divide within human geography and also between human and PHYSICAL GEOGRAPHY that separates those who see themselves as following the prescriptions of natural science from those who do not. Since the 1990s, as GIS has reinvigorated spatial analysis and as cognate social sciences such as economics, with stronger allegiances to the epistemologies of natural science, have rediscovered geography (see NEW ECONOMIC GEOGRAPHY), spatial science has gained new adherents. Yet the divide is based on the supposition that natural science entails different norms than the human sciences – a claim that has been increasingly questioned in contemporary geography, PHILOSOPHY and the

philosophy of SCIENCE AND SCIENCE STUDIES (cf. Harrison and Dunham, 1998; Massey, 1999). ES

spatial separatism Any geographical theory asserting that physical SPACE is an independent cause of human behaviour. Separatism has two meanings here: separating space from social processes, and separating HUMAN GEOGRAPHY from other social sciences. The term was coined by Sack (1973, 1974b) to criticize claims made specifically by Bunge (1966, 1973) in his prospectus for theoretical geography that geographical theories explain using geometric laws, thereby giving geography an exceptional status relative to the laws of other social sciences. Sack, like critics of SPATIAL FETISHISM, argued that space is relational – an emergent outcome of social processes – and that this made such separatism untenable. ES

Suggested reading
Sack (1974b).

spatial structure The organization of social and biophysical phenomena in space. The term was coined within SPATIAL SCIENCE to refer to the spatial coherence, geometric order or systematic spatial pattern (particularly spatial equilibria) generated by human activities. It implied an order in geometrical–mathematical–statistical domains characterized by degrees of symmetry, regularity and predictability. The term was subsequently used in a less restrictive, less formalist sense in HUMAN GEOGRAPHY and in SOCIAL THEORY to refer to the interdependence of human agency and spatial structures, whereby agency responds to but also reproduces and transforms its spatial templates (cf. Gregory and Urry, 1985). The term is now used more eclectically still, to refer to any more or less ordered spatial arrangement, ASSEMBLAGE or system: the orderings through which space is implicated in the operation and outcome of social and biophysical processes. The emphasis on 'ordering' rather than 'order' directs attention to the 'folding' of TIME and SPACE into the operation of processes in contingent, fluid and sensuous ways. This recognizes that practices and performances evade and exceed the symmetrical and/or logical orders proposed by classical social theory (hence its 'problem of order') and by neo-classical spatial science, and requires 'order' or 'structure' to be treated as a PROCESS rather than a thing. ES/DG

spatiality The mode(s) in which SPACE is implicated in the constitution and conduct of life on Earth. There are four main senses in which 'spatiality' has been used in HUMAN GEOGRAPHY and allied fields, but these increasingly interrupt and braid into one another:

(1) Drawing upon EXISTENTIALISM and PHENOMENOLOGY, and in particular the writings of European philosophers Martin Heidegger (1889–1976) and Edmund Husserl (1859–1938), Pickles (1985) proposed human spatiality as the fundamental basis on which 'geographical inquiry as a human science of the world can be explicitly founded'. Pickles' primary concern was ONTOLOGY: with understanding 'the universal structures characteristic of [human] spatiality as the precondition for any understanding of places and spaces as such.' Pickles objected to those views that regard the physical spaces of the physical sciences as 'the sole genuine space'. This sort of thinking was typical of SPATIAL SCIENCE but, in Pickles' view, was wholly inappropriate for a genuinely human geography. He urged in its place a recovery of our 'original experiences prior to their thematization by any scientific activity'; that is, a rigorous exposure of the TAKEN-FOR-GRANTED WORLD assumed but left unexplained by spatial science. One of its essential characteristics is what Pickles called 'the structural unity of the "in-order-to" '. Our most immediate experiences are not cognitive ABSTRACTIONS of separate objects, Pickles argued, but rather 'constellations of relations and meaning' that we encounter in our everyday activities – what Heidegger called 'equipment' – and which are 'ready-to-hand'. Such a perspective reveals the human significance of CONTEXTUALITY. For human spatiality is related 'to several concurrent and non-concurrent equipmental contexts' and 'cannot be understood independently of the beings that organise it.' Spatiality thus has the character of a 'situating' enterprise in which we 'make room' for and 'give space' to congeries of equipment. Put in this way, there are distant echoes of TIME-GEOGRAPHY, but Pickles is evoking an intellectual tradition antithetical to the physicalism of Torsten Hägerstrand's early writings and which fastens not on 'objective space' but on a fully human, social space (see also Schatzki, 1991).

(2) Drawing upon structural MARXISM of the 1960s and 1970s, a number of Francophone sociologists and economists suggested that concepts of spatiality be constructed to identify the connections and correspondences between social structures (MODES OF PRODUCTION) and SPATIAL STRUCTURES. French philosopher Louis Althusser (1918–90) had argued that different concepts of TIME or *temporalities* could be assigned to different levels of modes of production – 'economic time', 'political time', 'ideological time' – and that these had to be constructed out of the concepts of the different social practices within these domains. In much the same way, it was argued that different concepts of space or *spatialities* could be assigned to different levels of modes of production. Castells (1977) presented the most detailed analysis of CAPITALISM in these terms, but insisted that it made more sense to theorize temporality and spatiality together and to speak of distinctive *space–times* (see Gregory 1994, pp. 94–5).

(3) Drawing upon the broadly humanist Marxism of Henri Lefebvre (1901–91) and his account of the PRODUCTION OF SPACE, Soja (1985) used the term spatiality 'to refer specifically to socially produced space, the created forms and relations of a broadly defined human geography'. 'All space is not socially produced,' Soja continued, 'but all spatiality is'. In the course of his work as a whole, Lefebvre provided critiques of existentialism and phenomenology and of structuralism and structural Marxism, and so Soja insists that his 'materialist interpretation of spatiality' cannot be assimilated to either of the two traditions summarized above. For to speak of 'the production of space' in the spirit of Lefebvre is to accentuate spatiality as 'both the medium and the outcome' of situated HUMAN AGENCY and systems of social practices in a way that, so Soja argued, was broadly consonant with STRUCTURATION THEORY. Transcending his earlier claims for a 'socio-spatial dialectic' (Soja, 1980), Soja (1985) now concluded that 'spatiality is SOCIETY, not as its definitional or logical equivalent, but as its concretisation, its formative *constitution*.' And it is precisely this realization, so he subsequently argued, that was characteristic of POSTMODERNISM

and its reassertion of space – of spatiality – in critical social thought (Soja, 1989: see also THIRD SPACE; TRIALECTICS). Other human geographers working under the sign of a critical Marxism equally cognizant of Lefebvre have also conceptualized spatiality as socially produced space, and while they rarely endorse Soja's celebration of postmodernism they do accept that space is not a mere reflection of but is rather *constitutive of* capitalism as a dialectical totality (see, e.g., Sheppard, 2004; Harvey, 2006a). More than this, many of them now recognize that this implication of a produced space must incorporate non-human agency too: 'the manifold biophysical processes and technologies that shape the spatiality of the world' (Leitner, Sheppard and Sziarto, 2008, p. 158).

(4) Drawing upon POST-STRUCTURALISM – in particular, the work of Michel Foucault (1926–84) and of Gilles Deleuze (1925–95) and Félix Guattari (1930–92), together with the post-phenomenology of Alphonso Lingis (1933–) and others – a number of writers use spatiality to indicate the ways in which mobile constellations of power-knowledge and subject positions are constituted through the production and performance of space as an 'ordering' rather than a fixed and closed order (cf. Thrift, 2007, p. 55). Accordingly, they attempt to grasp space as an 'immanent spatiality', through which the world is registered as a 'multi-linear complex' whose contingent intersections and folds constantly open and present – which is to say *make* present – the emergence of 'the new' (Dewsbury and Thrift, 2005). These developing conceptions of spatiality, like those in the preceding paragraphs, have important implications for a GEOGRAPHICAL IMAGINATION that is also a profoundly *material* imagination (Anderson and Wylie, 2008) (see also NON-REPRESENTATIONAL THEORY).

These four traditions cannot be assimilated to any grand synthesis, but many writers share a subterranean dialogue with figures such as Marx, Heidegger and Foucault, and there is increasing traffic between their conceptions of spatiality: for example, Sheppard's (2008) exploration of DIALECTICAL totalities and ASSEMBLAGES. For all the differences between them, all four traditions reject the conventional separations between 'society' and 'space' (which can be traced to a persistent KANTIANISM) and in this sense can be read as four moments in the movement towards an exploration of what Smith (1990) called 'deep space': that is to say, 'quintessentially social space ... physical extent fused through with social intent'. DG

Suggested reading
Dewsbury and Thrift (2005); Pickles (1985); Soja (1989).

spectacle A term that often refers to a large-scale cultural event, festival or celebration, or to an urban scene or stage set presented for visual consumption. It has been prominent in analyses of the significance of IMAGE production and the management of appearance in strategies of urban development in recent decades, with attention focusing in particular on temporary cultural events such as carnivals, International Expositions and sporting events, including the Olympic Games (Gold and Gold, 2005), as well as on more permanent spaces of entertainment, 'theme park urbanism' and 'cities of spectacle'. The use of spectacular events has a long history, from the 'bread and circuses' of ancient times to efforts to promote European medieval city-states and metropolises of the nineteenth century. Yet the production of spectacles has become a common part of cultural strategies of economic development more recently, with studies exploring their implications for capital investment, cultural identity and TOURISM, and drawing out their multiple and contested readings by audiences. Many critics argue that such spectacles serve a diversionary function, masking underlying social and economic inequalities.

A key reference in critical discussions is Guy Debord's book *The society of the spectacle*, first published in 1967. This is concerned less with spectacles as cultural events than with *the* spectacle in a critique of an alienated and image-saturated world. Developing earlier Marxist critiques of COMMODITY fetishism and ALIENATION, Debord writes that the spectacle 'corresponds to the historical moment at which the commodity completes its colonization of social life' (1994 [1967], thesis 42). This new stage in the ACCUMULATION of capital and the domination of social life by the ECONOMY is not simply the result of mass media manipulation and visual technologies, he stresses, for 'the spectacle is not a collection of images; rather it is a social relationship

717

between people that is mediated by images' (thesis 29). URBANISM takes on particular importance within the spectacle as a technique for reshaping SPACE and ensuring the separation between people, although it is also a terrain within which struggles against the spectacle and for different relationships between people are forged.

As developed by Debord and the SITUATION-ISTS, the concept of the spectacle was part of a revolutionary project and was meant to be a weapon with which to harm spectacular society. This has not prevented it from being widely adopted within cultural, media and urban studies seeking to characterize a new cultural and mediatized era, and becoming 'a stock phrase in a wide range of critical and not-so-critical discourses' (Crary, 1989, p. 97). Yet emphasizing its original analytical force, the group *RETORT* (2005) insists that Debord's account speaks powerfully to a current 'new age of WAR', in which struggles over images and the capitalist STATE's concern with the rule of appearances are of vital political significance.   DP

Suggested reading
Debord (1994 [1967]).

spontaneous settlement A residential area developed outside the formal economy by its inhabitants, often after illegally occupying the land, and usually found in developing countries. Both the housing and INFRASTRUCTURE of public facilities are constructed outside the usual market and public service mechanisms. Although the term 'spontaneous' suggests no forethought or planning, many such clandestine settlements are the result of 'planned invasions' by the initial occupants, who subdivide the land on a pre-arranged cadastre and provide a basic infrastructure (cf. SQUATTING).   RJ

Suggested reading
Lloyd (1979).

sport(s) HUMAN GEOGRAPHY has paid increased attention to sports partly as a result of the increased economic and cultural importance given to issues of LEISURE and REC-REATION, but most especially because insights from cultural theory have been brought to bear on the performance of sports. Studies commonly take one of five approaches:

(1)   The plotting of the economic connections and organizations of sports. This follows the fortunes of 'mega-events'

such as the Olympics or soccer World Cup, and their linkage to patterns of urban development, or the competition over sport club franchises and stadia location.

(2)   The DIFFUSION and location of different sports across the globe. This tracks the relative popularity and adoption of different games, often as a cultural form in BERKELEY SCHOOL approaches to CUL-TURAL GEOGRAPHY.

(3)   The development and often hybridization of these sports in a colonial and post-colonial world (see COLONIALISM; HYBRID-ITY; POST-COLONIALISM). They become examples of contestation of meaning and adoption of cultural practices. Thus the imposition of cricket ovals across South Asia, its enthusiastic adoption and the transport of the game to the West Indies are used by C.L.R. James in his *Beyond a boundary* to suggest that it offers both insights into colonizing cultures and a stylization of resistance to that process. The postwar adoption of baseball in Japan also offers moments of cultural contact, understanding and transformation.

(4)   A HISTORICAL GEOGRAPHY of the emergence and role of sports in varying social milieu. The rise of organized mass spectator sports alongside INDUSTRIALIZA-TION, complementing or even replacing other modes of regulation, is important here, as is the construction of progressively more homogenized fields, arenas and venues as forms of abstract space. The rapid mediatization of team sport and the culture of viewing has been related to the society of the SPECTACLE, where a televisual temporality and dramatization is now driving sport.

(5)   The emergence on and off the pitch of techniques of the BODY that form exemplars of DISCIPLINARY POWER and the mobilization and channelling of collective AFFECT to create an EMOTIONAL GEOGRAPHY of support, loyalty, joy and suffering. The surging crowd at a game, or indeed around a large screen, enact changing PERFORMANCES of emotionality, RACE and GENDER. Alternatively, the body cultures in RECREATIONS and outdoor sports offer new ways to think about people's modes of engagement with landscape.   MC

Suggested reading
Bale (2002); Cronin and Bale (2002); James (2005); Roche (2000); Smart (2007).

sprawl Dispersed, low-density development on the edges of urban areas, characterized by fragmented and RIBBON DEVELOPMENT. It is often associated with EDGE CITIES and with bland, car-oriented and functionally segregated LANDSCAPES. While sprawl is often associated with a lack of planning, others suggest that government policies and public agencies, influencing decisions about road construction, housing financing and ZONING, for instance, have shaped the rise of sprawling cities (e.g. Wolch, Pastor and Dreier, 2004). 'Sprawl' is also a highly political word, framing debate over the loss of agricultural land and wildlife habitat, the costs of automobile use, and appropriate design and policy solutions (Duany, Plater-Zyberk and Speck, 2000). EM

Suggested reading
Wolch, Pastor and Dreier (2004).

squatting Dwelling in a home built on land that does not belong to the builder, typically without the consent of the land owner, in the absence of formal planning and regulation. In many countries in the world, a significant proportion of the population lives in squatter housing; for instance, this is the case for roughly half of the residents in Istanbul or Delhi. Squatter housing is typically built quickly to establish a *de facto* claim, and basic INFRASTRUCTURE for WATER, drainage, sanitation, electricity and roads is at first missing. Squatter settlements are often built on state-owned land, located on the periphery of an urban area (though relative centrality can change as cities grow up to and around them), or on unproductive land such as swamps, saline flats or steep hillsides. Although squatter housing exists outside private property relations, it can be commodified and traded (see COMMODITY; MARKET): over one-third of squatter housing in Turkey is rented, and in Hong Kong in the 1960s and 1970s the secondary housing market in squatter dwellings bore a striking resemblance to the parallel legal real estate market (Smart, 1986). Although most of the world's squatting occurs in the cities of the global SOUTH, there have been squatters' movements in European and North American cities, particularly in the 1970s and 1980s; at moments of housing shortage, squatters occupied vacant buildings without the consent of owners, to gain access to affordable housing and often as a critique of private property relations and urban restructuring (Pruijt, 2003: see also HOMELESSNESS; SLUM).

In the late 1960s, academics studying the global South began to reassess the earlier view that squatter settlements were a 'cancer on the carapace of the city' (quoted in Gonzalez de la Rocha, Perlman, Safa, Jelin, Roberts and Ward, 2004) or evidence of dysfunctional URBANISM. Studying settlements that had 'consolidated' over time, they stressed the existence of SOCIAL NETWORKS in squatter communities and began to conceive of them as rational and viable responses to rapid urbanism, as a solution to rather than a problem of massive rural to urban MIGRATION. This view continues to inform Hernando De Soto's (1989) influential celebration of the entrepreneurialism and capacity for self-organization within squatter settlements (now taken up by the World Bank). De Soto recommends that PROPERTY ownership be extended to squatters to facilitate their capacity to petition the STATE for more services and to use their property as collateral to obtain loans, which then can be used to improve their property or invest in small businesses.

A critical literature has arisen to argue, first, that consolidation and stabilization of squatter communities can happen in the absence of private property ownership (Varley, 2002) and, second, that there are serious limits to addressing issues of POVERTY and social marginalization through land titling and upgrades to housing and urban infrastructure (Roy, 2005). Extending private property ownership can lead to GENTRIFICATION and displacement, and the consolidation of PATRIARCHAL power relations (given that land title is typically granted to the male HOUSEHOLD head), and there is little evidence that land title opens assess to credit or alters employment conditions (Gonzalez de la Rocha, Perlman, Safa, Jelin, Roberts and Ward, 2004; Roy, 2005). Among scholars from LATIN AMERICA, there is less optimism now about the prospects for those living in squatter settlements. The STRUCTURAL ADJUSTMENT and austerity policies of the 1980s followed by the neo-liberal restructuring (see NEO-LIBERALISM) of the 1990s led to rising unemployment, declining opportunities in informal sectors, the devolution of the delivery of social goods to non-governmental organizations (see NGO), and increasing – often drug-related – VIOLENCE. Perlman notes of Rio de Janeiro, 'After many decades of co-existence, Rio's populous has again begun to fear and shun the *favelas* due to a sharp increase in violence. Although the *favelados* [residents of squatter communities] themselves are no longer considered marginal,

719

the physical territory of their communities has become tightly controlled by the drug dealers, who ... are known locally as "the marginality" or "the movement" ' (Gonzalez de la Rocha, Perlman, Safa, Jelin, Roberts and Ward, 2004, pp. 189–90). In other contexts, there is more optimism about the potential for squatter mobilization (Appadurai, 2001). GP

Suggested reading
Gonzalez de la Rocha, Perlman, Safa, Jelin, Roberts and Ward (2004); Roy (2005).

stages of growth The notion that SOCI-ETIES, polities or entire CIVILIZATIONS pass through stages or phases in their development, growth or maturation has a long intellectual lineage, and has been associated with very different forms of theorizing. Within certain forms of MARXISM, history as the succession of MODES OF PRODUCTION or the need to pass through particular stages of economic organization has a long pedigree (Cohen, 1978). From a very different vantage point, the theories of Arnold Toynbee (1889–1975) and Joseph Spengler (1912–91) also contained strong senses of historical progression through epochs or stages. Within twentieth-century sociology it was MODERNIZATION THEORY that exemplified the clearest instance of the suturing of evolution, TELEOLOGY and economic history as a predetermined progression through stages of social, economic and political transformation along a path blazed by capitalist powers in Western Europe. It was from within this body of work that the notion of MODERNIZATION as the culmination of a succession of stages out of backwardness received its fullest elaboration, and will be forever associated with the ideas of W.W. Rostow (1916–2003) and his foundational text *The stages of economic growth: a non-communist manifesto*, first published in 1960 (see Rostow, 1971). Like other modernization theorists, Rostow believed that the world was constituted by a fundamental rift between *'traditional'* societies – supposedly mired in anti- or non-MARKET mentalities, limited markets, pre-Newtonian science and a belief structure antithetical to self-sustaining growth – and *modern societies* that emerged in their modal form in seventeenth- and eighteenth-century EUROPE (see MODERNITY). Rostow drafted his book against a backdrop of McCarthyism, a deep ideological and political COLD WAR between East and WEST, and a massive effort by the USA to export development through USAID

and other foreign aid channels to an increasingly insurgent THIRD WORLD, led by a raft of African and Asian post-colonial (or about to become post-colonial) states (see DECOLONIZATION).

In Rostow's iteration – a MODEL explicitly presented, as Rostow's subtitle indicates, as an alternative to the idea of socialist modernization and the account of development set out by Marx and Engels in *The communist manifesto* (see HISTORICAL MATERIALISM) – modern history was the transformation of tradition via a five-stage programme, through which all societies were to pass. The first of the five stages - *the traditional society* - is characterized by 'primitive' technology, hierarchical social structures (the precise nature of which is not specified) and behaviour conditioned more by custom and ascription rather than by what Rostow takes to be 'rational' criteria. These characteristics combine to place a ceiling on production possibilities. Outside stimuli to change (including, for example, COLONIALISM and the expansion of CAPITALISM) are admitted in the transitional second stage – *the preconditions for take-off*. Here, a rise in the rate of productive investment, the provision of social and economic INFRASTRUCTURE, the emergence of a new, economically based elite and an effective centralized national STATE are indispensable to what is to follow. In short, the opportunities for profitable investment presented by the preconditions for take-off are unlikely to be ignored by CAPITAL and they pave the way for the third stage: *'takeoff' into sustained growth*. Rostow describes this stage as 'the great watershed in the life of modern societies'. It is a period of around 10–30 years during which growth dominates society, the economy and the political agenda (although the social relations which facilitate this dominance are not described) and INVESTMENT rises, especially in the leading sectors of manufacturing industry. Self-sustaining growth results in the fourth stage, *'drive to maturity'*, which is characterized by diversification as most sectors grow, imports fall and productive investment ranges between 10 and 20 per cent of national income. The increasing importance of consumer goods and SERVICES and the rise of the WELFARE STATE indicate that the final stage, the *'age of high mass consumption'*, has been reached (see also POST-INDUS-TRIAL SOCIETY).

In some respects, the determinism of Rostow's model was not too different from some of the worst excesses of structural Marxist POLITICAL ECONOMY. Whether it constitutes a THEORY or is little more than a taxonomy remains subject to debate, although Rostow certainly did knit together ideas that were found prominently among his contemporaries, such as Albert Hirschmann and Alexander Gerschenkron. Yet his insistence on placing growth in a wider historical and social context and on a disaggregated approach that reflects the uneven nature of DEVELOPMENT (cf. UNEVEN DEVELOPMENT) marks a substantial advance upon abstracted and formal theories of economic growth. And yet these same characteristics expose its universalist cast: the model of economic development derived from the stages is teleological, mechanical, a-historical and ethnocentric:

- It is *teleological* in the sense that the end result (stage 5) is known at the outset (stage 1) and derived from the historical geography of 'developed' societies, which then form the template for the 'under-developed', which are thereby denied an historical geography of their own.
- It is *mechanical* in that, despite the claim that the stages have an inner logic 'rooted in a dynamic theory of production', the underlying motor of change is not explained, so that as a result the stages become little more than a classificatory system based on data for fifteen countries only, plus outline data for others.
- It is *a-historical* in that notions of path-dependency are ignored, so that it can be assumed that the historical geographies of the underdeveloped countries are unaffected by that of the dependent, and so the intervention of the latter into the former is simply an irrelevance – this position is also profoundly a-geographical, as it is incapable of recognizing that geographical relationships are continuously formed and re-formed across the world.
- It is *ethnocentric* in espousing a future for the world based on American history and aspiring to American norms of high mass consumption (see ETHNOCENTRISM).

Capitalist society is, following Rostow's logic, a *necessary consequence* of development. By concealing the social production of the stages, capitalist societies may be reproduced and extended by apparently neutral policies advocating apparently universal processes of growth. History, in other words, is serial repetition (in the argot of the present: 'there is no alternative'). In the context of the 1950s and 1960s, the non-communist manifesto was nothing short of an IDEOLOGY for AMERICAN EMPIRE.

Rostow saw his academic work as part of a political mission, and under Presidents Kennedy and Johnson he held positions with authority over US policy towards the Third World (see Menzel, 2006). He was a brilliant student – a Rhodes scholar in the 1930s – and he gravitated towards imperial trade policy, serving briefly, after a period on the Office of Strategic Services during the Second World War, as a professor of American History at Oxford. He returned to the USA in 1947, served as an assistant to Gunnar Myrdal at the United Nations and at the tender age of 33 was appointed to the chair of Economic History at MIT. It was here, during the Korean War, that Rostow and a group of other cold warriors developed a strategy for the economic containment of COMMUNISM. Key to this strategy, which emerged more fully in the 1960s, was the sense that containment was to be achieved within the 'emerging nations' of the Third World, that external foreign assistance was key to shift poor nations from stages 2 to 3 (the alternative was the fostering of preconditions conducive to communism), an alliance with robustly anti-communist modernizing elites, and a strong state enhanced by a large military budget to push forward the long march through the stages to self-sustaining capitalist growth. Of course, it all went horribly wrong. The hubris of power was radically compromised in Vietnam (in which Rostow served a bleak and hawk-like function under President Johnson: Milne (2008) refers to him as 'America's Rasputin'), in the collapse of the Alliance for Progress in LATIN AMERICA and in the 'blowback' from supporting various dictators and psychopaths, from Mubutu to Marcos. While Rostow's career was blemished by Vietnam, it is perhaps true that his concern with the political preconditions for take-off – now the term of art is 'GOVERNANCE' – is more relevant than ever.   RL/MW

Suggested reading
Baran and Hobsbawm (1961); Keeble (1967).

staples theory The theory that national and regional economic and social development is based upon the export of unprocessed or semi-processed primary resources ('staples'). Although the theory has historical antecedents, and different (frequently truncated) versions of it have been presented (e.g. ECONOMIC BASE THEORY), staples theory is most closely associated with the work of the Canadian economic historian Harold A. Innis (1894–1952). In Innis' account, and the basis for the school of Canadian POLITICAL ECONOMY, staples production creates economic instability and hinterland dependency for staples-producing REGIONS. At least three causes are at work:

(1) MARKETS for staple COMMODITIES approximate more closely perfect competition than do those for manufactured goods. Staples regions are price-takers in markets where unpredictability is the norm, producing cycles of boom and bust.

(2) For a variety of reasons (technological INNOVATIONS that reduce resource inputs for production, the growth of synthetic substitutes, and low long-run income elasticities of demand), the terms of trade for primary commodities are increasingly less favourable to staples-producing areas.

(3) RESOURCE extraction or production tends to be undertaken by large, often foreign-owned, TRANSNATIONAL COROPORATIONS. Spry (1981) argues that this is a direct consequence of the large capital expenditures and production indivisibilities associated with staples. The presence of such firms in staples regions creates a number of potential problems for the region including: the appropriation of economic RENTS because of the undervaluing of resources by the LOCAL STATE in order to induce investment; the failure to process the staple prior to export (and where value-added occurs) because resource extraction is only one stage within a vertically integrated corporation that for reasons of internal control locates manufacture elsewhere; the low levels of technological innovation and development; the lack of local control; and finally, a weakened ability to control trade through explicit policy because of the high degree of intra-corporate transfers.

For Innis, there is thus a direct relationship between the type of TRADE in which a staples region engages and its level of social and economic development. This contradicts the orthodox neo-classical theory of trade (see NEO-CLASSICAL ECONOMICS), which would maintain that a staples NATION such as Canada benefits from specializing in and exchanging those commodities in which it possesses a COMPARATIVE ADVANTAGE, namely primary resources. But in drawing upon this theory, as Innis (1956 [1929], p. 3) wrote in the late 1920s, economists 'attempt to fit their analysis of new economic facts into ... the economic theory of old countries ... The handicaps of this process are obvious, and there is evidence to show that [this is] ... a new form of exploitation with dangerous consequences.'.

To circumscribe such exploitation, Innis developed his theory in such a way that it was peculiarly suited to the economic facts of staples regions. He brought together three types of concerns: geographical/ecological, institutional and technological (Barnes, 1996, ch. 8). Innis argued that when the right technology came together with the right geography and the right institutional structure, the result was ACCUMULATION of 'cyclonic' frenzy. In this way, virgin resource regions were transformed and enveloped within the produced spaces of the CAPITALIST periphery. Such intense accumulation, however, never lasts, and because of the very instabilities of staples production, sooner rather than later investment shifts to yet other staples regions, leaving in its wake abandoned resource sites and COMMUNITIES. As countries such as China and India rapidly industrialize, drawing in immense flows of staples commodities, transforming regions and creating shudders across the world's resources sites, Innis' theory has never been more relevant (Hayter, Barnes and Bradshaw, 2003).   TB

Suggested reading
Barnes (1996, ch. 8); Drache (1995).

state A centralized set of institutions facilitating coercive power and governing capabilities over a defined TERRITORY. No one definition of the state is adequate given the way that states have varied in their form and function over time and space. However, Michael Mann (1984a) has identified the definitional need to incorporate both institutional and functional concerns, or what the state looks like and what it does. His subsequent definition can be summarized as follows:

(1) a set of institutions and their related personnel;

(2) a degree of centrality, with political decisions emanating from this centre point;

(3) a defined BOUNDARY that demarcates the territorial limits of the state; and

(4) a monopoly of coercive POWER and LAW-making ability (Jones, Jones and Woods, 2004, p. 20).

These four points must be complemented by understanding that the state is defined in relation to two other spheres of modern life, the MARKET (or economic activity) and CIVIL SOCIETY. The functions of the state reflect the need to facilitate ECONOMIC GROWTH that generates the tax base to support a STATE APPARATUS (Tilly, 1990a), the provision of INFRASTRUCTURE and other goods to maintain a population that can serve as a workforce, the maintenance of internal order, and the capacity to defend the population from outside aggression (Mann, 1984a). The need and ability to carry out these functions constantly varies; hence the geographical variety of states and the elusiveness of a precise definition.

One approach has been to show how states have changed over time, which often falls into the developmentalist trap of assuming that states that came into existence as a result of twentieth-century DECOLONIZATION can and should take on the same form and function as the established European states that imposed their colonial subjugation. Alternatively, a structural approach defines a geographical variation in the form of the state, and differential ability to undertake the standard functions, as a product of the state's position within the hierarchy of the capitalist world-economy (Flint and Taylor, 2007 [1985]). States in the wealthy core of the world-economy have the ability to provide for most of their population and so to maintain their cohesion and strength. States in the impoverished periphery face internal challenges to their legitimacy. In the former, the state can maintain its authority through creating political consensus regarding its legitimacy. In the latter, coercive power and unstable internal politics are more common.

The geographical variation in the form of the state can be conceptualized as differences in the manner by which the state interacts with the market and civil society. FEMINIST GEOGRAPHERS discourage an understanding of the three spheres as separate. Instead, 'the MARKET and CIVIL SOCIETY involve actors and processes that help constitute the state; the procedures and actors of the state similarly influence the market and civil society' (Fincher, 2004, p. 50). The important conclusions are that the state is multi-faceted and contested. The state is manifest in the actions of the POLICE, in the prosaic sense of imposing guidelines and laws over the way people can act (e.g. seat-belt laws and smoking regulations: Painter, 2004), taxation and the military. The relative power and efficacy of these and other manifestations

is a product of a politics between social groups who seek to control or influence the institutions of the state for their own interests. In terms of coercive power, the control of the military and police may be contested between CLASS FRACTIONS or ethnic groups (see ETHNICITY). The size and direction of *redistributive* programmes is the product of conflicts between the owners of capital who seek to limit the state's taxation of their wealth and disadvantaged groups seeking security from the vagaries of capitalist economies. Of course, this is not a simple equation, as CAPITAL requires enough state involvement to allow for SOCIAL REPRODUCTION (via schools, hospitals and housing subsidies) as well as transport infrastructure and some regulation of economic activity. Feminist geographers highlight that such politics entwine the 'private' spaces of the household, the traditional site of unpaid women's work, with the male-dominated 'public' sphere in such a way that they cannot be considered a dualism (see PRIVATE AND PUBLIC SPHERES).

IDEOLOGY is a central component of maintaining states. The state is a normative ideological construction in both a general and particular sense. First, the belief that states are legitimate universal institutions with a 'right' to wield power over individuals is, generally, unchallenged. Second, the history of particular states is constructed to give them a 'naturalness' and historical permanency that is a political fiction (Krishna, 1994). The Marxist scholar Antonio Gramsci also points out that the politics within states results in a ruling class that is able to dominate through constructing an ideological consensus around its 'right' to rule and a perceived value for the whole population of decisions that greatly benefit a small elite, thus minimizing the need for coercive power (see HEGEMONY).

The state comprises institutions at various SCALES linking central and local government. The precise form varies across space and time, but the central government can use LOCAL STATES, with their sense of connectivity to a local population, as means to legitimate itself. On the other hand, local states may challenge the authority of the central state if it is believed that the latter fails to serve local needs (see REGIONALISM: Kirby, 1993). GLOBALIZATION and NEO-LIBERALISM have put greater responsibility on local governments to carry out state functions and generate their own revenue. New forms of local state GOVERNANCE are being identified that attempt to attract global investment by creating entrepreneurial local states in which many functions traditionally performed by the state are now the purview of private companies or non-state institutions (Ward, 2005b; see PRIVATIZATION). The result is a reduction in central state power, as states are not so much losing power as a result of globalization but redefining their form and function in a new climate of capital accumulation (Sassen, 1996). CF

Suggested reading
Brenner, Jessop, Jones and MacLeod (2003); Clark and Dear (1984); Painter (1995); Van Creveld (1999).

state apparatus The interacting suite of institutions and organizations through which STATE power is exercised. The state apparatus serves three broad functions: manufacturing social consensus; securing the conditions of production by facilitating investment and the reproduction of the labour force; and creating social integration by promoting the welfare of all social groups. The suite consists of manifold institutions and organizations including the police, the HEALTH service, education, fiscal regulation and elections. Neo-liberal policies (see NEO-LIBERALISM) have required changes in the relative power of different institutions to promote ECONOMIC GROWTH at the expense of welfare, with consequent geographies of uneven life opportunities (Peck, 1996). CF

Suggested reading
Clark and Dear (1984).

state of nature This phrase featured prominently in the writings of early liberal political philosophers, including most famously Thomas Hobbes, John Locke, Baruch (Benedictus) Spinoza and Jean-Jacques Rousseau (see LIBERALISM). All were concerned with establishing in their own fashion the moral basis of GOVERNANCE and a civil order based in part on their assumptions about what life in the state of nature was like. The phrase points to a kind of reference point or natural (universal) order from which to theorize about the social (Barry, 1999), but it also marks a boundary (imagined and real, historical and geographical) between a condition of being in or of nature to one of being outside of or apart from nature. Emergence from this state of nature, so these discourses suggest, establishes the need for a 'social contract', while the particular character of the state of nature (benign, violent etc.) also shapes the character of the required social contract. When taken less

literally as a specific time or place, the state of nature serves as a kind of imagined historical geography corresponding to an anarchic society, absent the rule of LAW and without a modern STATE (Smith, M., 2002b). However, the phrase is also quite telling. It points on the one hand to an emergent, modern (EUROPEAN) society concerned with distinguishing and elevating itself in relation to prior and/or culturally 'Othered' non-European peoples of the time (mid-seventeenth to early eighteenth centuries), with disquieting implications vis-à-vis IMPERIALISM. At the same time, the phrase points to a preoccupation with defining 'modern' society by separating people from nature, presumably (and in Locke, for instance, quite explicitly) legitimating the domination of nature. In addition to the telos of temporal progress, there are definite SPATIALITIES of movement invoked here, not least from the modern, colonizing core to the savage, premodern periphery, as well as from the country to the city (Whatmore, 2002a, esp. pp. 64–5; Anderson, 2003: see also MODERNITY; PRIMITIVISM). Contemporary attempts to rethink NATURE/CULTURE binaries may be informed by considerations of how and why this very binary was considered by early liberals to be foundational to modern societies, and how the same binary is constitutive of the emergence of a distinct body of 'social' theory (minus the [human] body, of course!). SP

Suggested reading
Locke and Peardon (1952 [1690]).

stochastic process A mathematical–statistical MODEL in which a sequence or pattern of outcomes is described and modelled in probabilistic terms (Bartlett, 1955). A stochastic process is one in which the outcomes are not simply independent or random draws, but a PROCESS through TIME or across SPACE in which the outcome at one time-period or location is in some way dependent on the outcomes at previous time-periods or, for a spatial stochastic process, in neighbouring locations. A MARKOV PROCESS is an elementary example of such a process. Stochastic process models have been used in spatial time-series analysis, in DISEASE modelling and EPIDEMIOLOGY and in SPATIAL ECONOMETRICS. LWH

Suggested reading
Bennett (1979); Hepple (1974).

structural adjustment A series of economic measures, often imposed on governments receiving loans from the INTERNATIONAL MONETARY FUND or the World Bank, designed to encourage exports and increase the resources that governments have available for dealing with short-term balance-of-payments crises. Typical structural adjustment programmes include measures such as reducing government spending, cutting or containing wages, liberalizing imports and reducing restrictions on foreign investment, devaluing the currency and privatizing state enterprises (see also NEO-LIBERALISM; PRIVATIZATION). JGl

Suggested readings
Bello (1994); Payer (1974).

structural functionalism A tradition of SOCIAL THEORY most closely associated with the American sociologist Talcott Parsons (1902–79), whose central proposition was that the structure of any social system cannot be derived 'from the actor's point of view', but must instead be explained by the ways in which the 'functional imperatives' necessary for the survival of any social system are met (Parsons, 1951: see also FUNCTIONALISM; SYSTEM). Parsons insisted that the analysis of any social system requires the conjunction of static ('structure') and dynamic ('function') components, and constantly accentuated the need to grasp the dynamics of social systems. He attributed crucial importance to the interchanges between systems and between subsystems, and in his later formulations developed a more formal CYBERNETIC model of SOCIETY that drew upon biology as much as it did classical social theory.

Parsons' influence on modern social theory was extraordinary, even though his views were subjected to a sustained and at times devastating critique. For all his interest in dynamics, it proved difficult to incorporate structural transformation into his model. For all his interest in generalization, his model of the social system seemed to be based on the USA as global exemplar. Today, Parsons' influence is perhaps greatest in Germany, where Luhmann (1981) and Habermas (1987) have made critical yet creative appropriations of some of his ideas. Parsons' shadow over HUMAN GEOGRAPHY has been much shorter. Systems analysis and systems theory in GEOGRAPHY had quite other sources, usually far removed from social theory. Even so, Parsons loomed large in Duncan's (1980) critique of the 'superorganic' in Sauer's CULTURAL GEOGRAPHY and WORLD-SYSTEMS ANALYSIS has been criticized as 'Parsonianism on a world scale' (Cooper, 1981). DG

Suggested reading
Alexander (1983); Duncan (1980).

structuralism A set of principles and procedures originally derived from linguistics and linguistic philosophy that seek to expose the enduring and underlying structures inscribed in the cultural practices of human subjects. There have been various structuralisms, all of them dominated by 'French' (or at least Francophone) theory, and particularly by Roland Barthes (1915–80) in literary theory, Claude Lévi-Strauss (1908–) in anthropology and Jean Piaget (1896–1980) in psychology. The ideas of all three were introduced into Anglophone HUMAN GEOGRAPHY in the late twentieth century: Harvey (1973) briefly toyed with Piaget en route to a more vigorously materialist analysis of the structures of the SPACE-ECONOMY of CAPITALISM; Gregory (1978a) drew upon Lévi-Strauss in his search for a mode of 'structural explanation' to displace the POSITIVISM on which SPATIAL SCIENCE relied; and Duncan and Duncan (1992) used Barthes as a way-station in their journey towards reading LANDSCAPE not as MORPHOLOGY but as TEXT.

As these descriptions suggest, human geography's engagement with structuralism was short-lived and functioned as a transition to other approaches that were explored in much more depth. In the most general terms, Peet (1998, p. 112) argues that 'the move towards structuralism, never complete in geographical thought, represented a search for greater theoretical coherence and rigor'. But it did not, in itself, provide a satisfying solution to the problems of EMPIRICISM that provoked human geographers to pursue it in the first place. They turned, instead, towards various forms of MARXISM, including a *structural Marxism* derived from the writings of Louis Althusser (1918–90) and Nicos Poulantzas (1936–79), whose analytics of power and process left its marks primarily in economic, political and urban geography; towards the philosophy of REALISM, whose modes of structural explanation were more sensitive to historical and geographical specificity than any structuralism; and towards various forms of POST-STRUCTURALISM, which promised a more incisive analysis of desire, DISCOURSE and SUBJECTIVITY. DG

Suggested reading
Peet (1998, pp. 112–46).

structuration theory A social theory developed by the British sociologist Anthony

Giddens (1938–) that seeks to elucidate the intersections between human SUBJECTS and the social structures in which they are involved. Giddens' original purpose was to solve the classical problem of social order. In his view, explanations of social life typically privileged either 'agency' (the intentions, meanings and actions of subjects) or 'structure' (the logics, limitations and systems of society). Instead, Giddens proposed to treat the production and reproduction of social life as an ongoing PROCESS of *structuration*. In this view, 'structure' is implicated in every moment of social interaction – 'structures' are not only constraints but also the very conditions of social action – and, conversely, structure is an 'absent' order of differences, 'present' only in the moments of social interaction through which it is itself reproduced or transformed (Giddens, 1979, 1981, 1984).

Three concepts were crucial to this model:

(1) *Reflexivity*: The production of social life is a skilled accomplishment on the part of knowledgeable and capable human subjects (see HUMAN AGENCY).

(2) *Recursiveness*: 'Structure' is both the medium and the outcome of the social practices that constitute social systems: rules and resources are drawn upon by actors from structures of signification, domination and legitimation, and these structures are in turn reproduced or transformed through those social practices (see figure).

(3) *Regionalization*: The continuity of social life depends on interactions with others who are either co-present in time and/or space (time–space routinization; cf. TIME-GEOGRAPHY) or who are absent in time and/or space (TIME–SPACE DISTANCIATION).

Giddens argued that these propositions make it possible to analyse the interconnection of routinized and repetitive conduct between actors with long-term, large-scale institutional development in a depth that is denied to both classical SOCIAL THEORY and HISTORICAL MATERIALISM.

Giddens fashioned structuration theory through a wide-ranging series of philosophical and theoretical critiques of other writers. Some of his critics complained that it was impossible to rework such radically different ideas into a coherent synthesis; others noted that Giddens worked at such a high level of ABSTRACTION that it was far from clear how his general ideas could be brought to bear on empirical enquiry (Gregson, 1989). Although the same agency–structure dualism bedevilled HUMAN GEOGRAPHY, most human geographers sought a more historically and geographically inflected version of structuration (Thrift, 1983; Gregson, 2005). Aware of parallel debates in social history, and usually more sympathetic to MARXISM than Giddens, they mapped the *variable* and *differential* intersections of 'agency' and 'structure' in the production and transformation of specific PLACES, REGIONS and LANDSCAPES (Gregory, 1982;

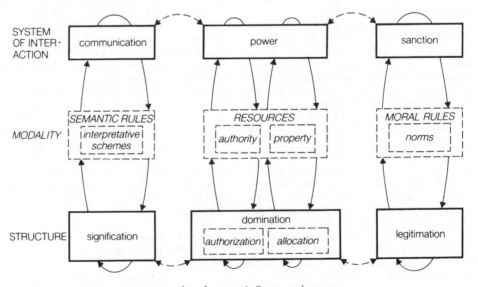

structuration theory   *1: System and structure*

Pred, 1985; Harris, 1991). For, as Hannah (2006a, p. 243) put it, 'neither term of the structure-agency duality is of much analytical use in the unmarked, abstract, universal form':

> The important thing about subjects striving to make lives and worlds is not the abstract philosophical principle according to which we are all competent actors always able to do otherwise, but the concrete, positioned and marked performances through which we (re)produce or transform specific social meanings. And the important thing about the structures that prevent differently positioned subjects from doing or being just anything we want is not their general presence and effectivity in every SOCIAL FORMATION but their specific characteristics as contested and contestable social constructions, often originating with dominant social groups.

The central term that most human geographers derived from Giddens' project was that of *practice*, at once situated and embodied, and this continues to inform much research in the field. But the concept has been extended through ideas of PERFORMANCE and the incorporation of AFFECT to such a degree that most human geographers have travelled a considerable distance from the formal corpus of structuration theory (see, for example, NON-REPRESENTATIONAL THEORY). In fact, it was always more of a 'sensitizing device' than a research programme, providing a high-level view of different positions within modern social theory – a sort of panoramic mapping – rather than a hierarchy of concepts that could inform ground-level studies. Giddens' work is now valued less for its abstract formulations than for its substantive identification of two issues that continue to haunt the world in the early twenty-first century. His early insistence on the significance of political VIOLENCE for the conduct of political and social life was remarkably prescient (Giddens, 1985: see also WAR), while discussions of GLOBALIZATION and the prospects for social democracy continue to be informed, at least in part, by his argumentation sketches of the contours of what he called 'high' MODERNITY (Giddens, 1990). DG

Suggested reading
Gregory (1994); Gregson (2005).

subaltern studies A body of historiography initiated in the late 1970s by Indian and English historians critical of 'colonialist and bourgeois-nationalist élitism' in the writing of Indian history, specifically from the Cambridge School (Guha and Spivak, 1988). Under Ranajit Guha's founding editorship, the editorial collective included Shahid Amin, David Arnold, Partha Chatterjee, David Hardiman and Gyanendra Pandey, later expanding with Gautam Bhadra, Dipesh Chakrabarty and Sumit Sarkar, all of whom had written important monographs. The first edited volume, *Subaltern studies: writings on Indian history and society*, was published in 1982. The collective drew on British social history and its renovation of Antonio Gramsci, from whom the concept 'subaltern' was adapted.

The timing of this critique of Indian NATIONALISM (particularly Marxist nationalism) – after the suppression of the Naxalbari peasant insurgency and its 'Maoist' urban allies, and after Indira Gandhi's 1975–7 dictatorial emergency – is crucial. The first volumes the collective produced explored PEASANTS' conscious agency and autonomous subaltern politics (which Cambridge historians had ignored in their emphasis on vertical 'factions' in Indian nationalism), a comment on the bankruptcy of institutionalized Indian MARXISM. From rumour and militancy under the paternalist mantle of Gandhianism to mismatches between elite and subaltern notions of political community to the disruptive effects of mill workers' religiosity on industrial discipline, the first four volumes of *Subaltern Studies* energized debate within Indian history on CLASS, subaltern/elite boundaries and popular politics (Ludden, 2002).

By the late 1980s, shifts between insiders and outsiders in the collective moved subaltern studies into a second phase of historiography, concerned less with a *sphere* of subaltern politics than with the construction of subaltern POWER/knowledge and critique of 'the ENLIGHTENMENT Project'. While one former insider, Sumit Sarkar, bemoaned 'the decline of the subaltern in *Subaltern Studies*', others saw it as serious response to outsider critiques of 'subaltern autonomy', as well as an exploration beyond Gramsci to Michel Foucault's conception of the SUBJECT of power, and to Jacques Derrida's DECONSTRUCTION (see Chaturvedi, 2000).

These intellectual shifts, combined with the edited collection by Guha and Spivak (1988), brought subaltern studies to a US – and hence global – academic audience; Edward Said's introduction to the collection ushered its arrival as the most prolific strand of postcolonial thought. Volumes to follow heightened critique from insiders and outsiders on

727

GENDER, CASTE, untouchability, charges of bias towards the Bengali intelligentsia, LAW, VIOLENCE, literary and oral traditions, DIASPORA and South India. The collective is now more intellectually eclectic than ever: it continues to be read and responded to from across the world, with a breadth of readership rare for a school of thought emerging from the SOUTH. To be sure, this is partly a consequence of the visibility of key diasporic Indian intellectuals. Subaltern studies has breathed new life into debates over colonial GOVERNMENTALITY, postcolonial nationalism, REPRESENTATION and popular histories of the present (see COLONIALISM; POST-COLONIALISM). As one instance of reception, Frederick Cooper (1994) argues against the idea of an abstract, generalized, binarist colonial rationality and for a dynamic conception of subalternity that 'put[s] the process of making history into the picture' (p. 1516). The persisting question is whether the collective remains engaged with subalterns in the noun form used by Gramsci, while also developing more sophisticated tools for engaging subaltern as an adjective, as in 'subaltern power/knowledge'. The interaction between the first two phases of the collective remains a useful and potentially radical device in understanding spatially layered politics today in the shadows of twentieth-century EMPIRES and nationalisms, and their twenty-first-century successors.   SC

subject/subjectivity   This grounds our understanding of who we are, as well as our knowledge claims. All GEOGRAPHY presumes some notion of subjectivity: even 'objective' SPATIAL SCIENCE rests on a theory of subjectivity as a foundation for 'objective' knowledge. But different theories of the subject provoke different geographical narratives (and vice versa). MARXISM assumptions about the centrality of CLASS to subjectivity have prompted studies of geographies of labour organization, as well as homeownership, residential SEGREGATION and suburbanization, many of the latter aimed at understanding the dissolution of class consciousness in Anglo-American countries in the twentieth century. HUMANISTIC GEOGRAPHY, with its emphasis on the ethical responsibility for human agency and the fullness of human experience beyond economic calculation, invites studies of the social construction of meanings in different LANDSCAPES, and the inauthenticity/authenticity of particular landscapes. Until recently, much of SOCIAL GEOGRAPHY involved locating stable, coherently formed identities (such as ETHNICITY or

RACE) in particular PLACES. This was the explicit objective of SOCIAL AREA ANALYSIS. The influences of IDENTITY politics and POSTSTRUCTURALISM from the mid-1980s led geographers to be attentive to a wider range of identifications (e.g. DISABILITY; GENDER; SEXUALITY) and problems of overgeneralization. Within FEMINIST GEOGRAPHIES, for example, there is now more sensitivity to how the experiences of different groups of women vary, within and across space. From the perspective of post-structural theories of the subject, this focus on multiplicity is not enough; identity politics (which receives credit – or takes the blame – for the proliferation of politicized identifications through the 1980s and 1990s) has been criticized for taking the fact and stability of identities for granted, and for failing to problematize the processes through which identities are created and differentiated (see RECOGNITION). The subject is even more fully de-centred in ACTOR-NETWORK THEORY, with the emphasis on the agency of non-human actants and 'a distributed and always provisional personhood' (Thrift, 2000a, p. 214). Criticizing actor-network theory for an account of subjectivity that flattens human powers of imagination and processes that are not readily reducible to an object world, Thrift (2000a) has articulated a NON-REPRESENTATIONAL style of thinking that focuses not on individual agents, but on 'a poetic of common *practices and skills*' (p. 216, original emphasis) in which 'persons become, in effect, rather ill-defined constellations rattling around in the world' (p. 220). A very different rendering of the subject through PSYCHOANALTIC THEORY has also received more attention since the mid-1990s, in what some have labelled the 'psychoanalytical turn' in geography (Philo and Parr, 2003). Callard (2003) has argued, however, that geographers have tended to assimilate psychoanalysis as yet another version of SOCIAL CONSTRUCTION to a disciplinary culture that values agency, RESISTANCE and liberatory cultural politics, and have missed what is most valuable and distinctive about psychoanalytic theory; namely, a theory of the 'intractability of the unconscious and its imperviousness to political goadings, and the anarchic and implacable movement of the drives' (p. 300).

Debates about the human subject are vast; they lie at the heart of twentieth-century Western PHILOSOPHY. They are, then, difficult to summarize (for one attempt, see Pile and Thrift, 1995). One organizational device is to distinguish between HUMANIST and

ANTI-HUMANIST conceptions of subjectivity (Soper, 1986). In geography, this distinction is often articulated through debates about agency and structure (see STRUCTURATION THEORY). Emphasizing HUMAN AGENCY, humanist versions of subject formation take identity as given in experience. 'Man' (some feminists argue that the gendering of this term is by no means incidental: see MASCULINISM; PHALLOCENTRISM) is at the centre of the world and, in order to be fully human, has the ethical responsibility to act autonomously, to claim his agency (e.g. Ley and Samuels, 1978). Anti-humanists de-centre the subject insofar as they interpret subjectivity as an outcome of subjection to societal ideologies or regulatory techniques, and question the capacity and the authority of individuals to direct their actions self-consciously and autonomously. In the most influential anti-humanist *structuralist* account of subjectivity, Althusser argued that subjectivity, especially notions of individuality and CITIZENSHIP, are ideological constructs (see IDEOLOGY; STRUCTURALISM). We are *interpellated* or 'hailed' as particular subjects through the institutions of the family, EDUCATION, RELIGION and STATE, and through our own daily practices in relation to them. Subjectivities are built up through these practices of subjection, but these are multiple and sometimes conflicting, always constituted in particular contexts. Despite the seeming role for GEOGRAPHY (as context) in Althusser's account (Probyn, 2003), in the discipline of geography his theory of the subject often has been rejected as narrowly economistic. In cultural studies, particularly FILM studies, Althusser is credited with exactly the opposite effect, for opening a realm for ideology separate from the economy. Drawing on psychoanalysis, Althusser posited a more psychologically complex subject for Marxist theory.

There is considerable variation among poststructuralist theories of subject formation, but they have two broad characteristics: they view subject formation as an effect of POWER relations; and they posit the boundaries that define identity as intertwined with processes of disidentification, such that the effect of identification is a fragile and contradictory achievement. To give a sense of the former, in Foucault's *post-structuralist* anti-humanist history of Western subjectivity, subject positions are seen to be constructed within and through DISCOURSE. He argues that, from the eighteenth century, discourses of SEXUALITY and individual RIGHTS have altered our perceptions of subjectivity and SOCIETY, and have acted as techniques of disciplinary control (see DISCIPLINARY POWER). They introduced new identities (e.g. the homosexual, the pervert, the hysterical woman), territorialized bodily pleasures as sexual, and brought the individual into new relations with the social through BIOPOWER.

The intertwined processes of identification and disidentification work differently in different theories. Psychoanalytic theories have offered rich resources for thinking about the difficulties of recognizing difference, traced from a young child's initial difficulties of registering sexual difference from a loved parent. From the perspective of POST-COLONIALISM, theorists such as Homi Bhabha have drawn on Freud's notion of the fetish (which functions as a mechanism for both recognizing and disavowing sexual difference) as a way of interpreting the ambivalences of colonial discourse and relations between colonized–colonizer. The concept of ABJECTION, which describes a process by which what is reviled in oneself is denied and relocated in another, offers another means for theorizing stigmatizing discourses of ORIENTALISM, RACISM, ableism and HOMOPHOBIA AND HETEROSEXISM. If psychoanalytic theories draw our attention to the processes whereby what is unbearable or disallowed in oneself and our loved ones is cast outside and used to stigmatize others (but imperfectly – our identity is constantly haunted and destabilized by what is disavowed or abject), DECONSTRUCTION offers a reverse perspective, of the way in which identity is always defined in relation to and inhabited by what it is not (the constitutive outside). Recognizing the exclusions that found every identity, and the necessity of keeping this process of BOUNDARY construction and the purification of space in view (Sibley, 1995), have been important ideas for recent theorizing about CITIZENSHIP and RADICAL DEMOCRACY (see PRIVATE AND PUBLIC SPHERES).

Anti-humanist accounts have been criticized for closing off the possibilities and responsibilities of agency, rights, ETHICS and politics. Four responses suggest the opposite. First, discourses are polyvalent: they structure identities without determining them. The identity of 'homosexual' can become a resource for persons thus identified when they demand rights in the name of this identity. So too, the meaning of the term 'queer' has been reworked, from a stigmatizing identity to a critique of HETERONORMATIVITY (see QUEER THEORY). Second, individuals are subject to multiple discourses and subject positions,

729

and it is at the disjuncture between various subject positions that agency can be located. Third, identities arise through repeated performates, and this opens possibilities for variation and change, ones that are closed off by positions that see identities as stable (see PERFORMANCE; PERFORMATIVITY). A fourth response is that psychoanalytic theories that explore the effects of the unconscious widen responsibilities insofar as they call into question our responsibilities for actions of which we are not conscious, such as racism and heterosexism (Culler, 1997).

A key area of contemporary theorizing explores the possibilities for new processes of subject formation whereby we come to understand ourselves and others without creating stigmatized others and hierarchies of difference (in which some groups are seen to be superior to others). The concepts of CYBORG and HYBRIDITY are two ways of disrupting ideas of pure identities and rigid boundaries. Non-representational thinking offers another model in which: 'intermediaries and mediaries multiply, so that the "human" "subject" migrates on to many more planes and is mixed with other "subjects" in increasingly polymorphous combinations' (Thrift, 2000a, p. 220; see also ASSEMBLAGE). Theorists of radical democracy, such as Mouffe, are sceptical about such possibilities and place emphasis instead on a continual questioning of the inevitable process of boundary construction that must, they argue, necessarily exclude. To evade these exclusions is impossible, but we can insist on a public sphere in which the lines that discriminate inclusion from exclusion are actively contested (for a summary of these arguments, see Pratt, 2004). Others emphasize the need to shift theorizing from 'the' subject to intersubjectivity (Rose, 1999b; Probyn, 2003). For Probyn, this draws us back to the 'hard facts', such as material inequality, that make such relations and connections difficult.

If theories of subjectivity have always informed geography, what is perhaps newer is the extent to which geography is now woven into theories of the subject. Probyn (2003) notes the interrelations between the retheorization of SPACE and subjectivity: '[t]hinking of subjectivity in terms of space of necessity reworks any conception that subjectivity is hidden away in private recesses ... Thinking about how space interacts with subjectivity entails rethinking both terms, and their relation to each other' (p. 290). Where one is located is constitutive of (and not incidental

to) perceptions of self. Thus for Foucault (1980d), the designs of European schools and homes were both reflective of and instrumental in creating the sexualized nuclear family. And one may see oneself differently in different PLACES: Blunt (1994) has argued that nineteenth-century British bourgeois women travellers were defined predominantly in terms of (a rather frail) femininity at home, but in their travels – in Africa, for example – their gendered identity receded (and their health improved), and their race and class positions came to the fore. Constructing a stable boundary for one's self is an achievement: Davidson (2001) describes the fragility of this construction for those suffering agoraphobia. The construction of coherent places and identities are intertwined social processes: Anderson (1991b) describes how the construction of CHINATOWN as a stigmatized place apart from the rest of Vancouver was instrumental in cohering a white British Columbian identity. Non-ESSENTIALIST readings of subjectivity, in which identifications are conceived as the outcome of power-laden social processes (i.e. not as natural), thus have been read back into the PRODUCTION OF SPACE. Places are conceived as open-ended sites of social contestation, and spatial politics involve attending to the moments of closure whereby the identitites of places are stabilized and particular social groups claim a natural right to that space or are entrapped within them. This can involve a dense layering of different subject positions: Anderson (1996) reworks her earlier argument about the production of Chinatown by considering how gender discourses underwrote discourses of nation and race in early-twentieth-century British Columbia.

Geographies are also at the centre of recent efforts to think about new subject formations of hybridity, multiplicity and flexible borders. Spatial metaphors of nomad, MOBILITY, travel, BORDERLAND, THIRD SPACE, NETWORKS, connectivity and viscosity, space-off and paradoxical space are some of the terms used to conceptualize these subjectivities. In some of these discussions, geography functions only as METAPHOR, but the prevalence of geographical terminology in discussions of identity also reflects processes of TRANSNATIONALISM and GLOBALIZATION, and increasingly complex geographies of subject formation, which may lead to pluri-local identifications (distributed across and located in different places) or, ironically, the intensification of localized identities (Watts, 1991).

Theories of subjectivity have led geographers to rethink EPISTEMOLOGY, METHODOLOGY, theory and representational strategy. Calls for REFLEXIVITY reflect the understanding that knowledge is a social construct contingent on social location: theories of the unconscious indicate the limits of self-reflexivity and the limits of knowledge (Rose, 1997b). Theories of mobile, fragmented identities have encouraged different mapping and writing strategies (Massey, 1997; Pred, 1997). Emphasis on AFFECT and non-cognitive aspects of experience within non-representational styles of thinking have led to many suggestions for theoretical and methodological innovation (Thrift, 2000a; see also QUALITATIVE METHODS). Her engagement with psychotherapy has led Bondi (1999) to read differently: she draws the distinction between intertextual and experiential reading practices.   GP

Suggested reading
Culler (1997); Pile and Thrift (1995); Probyn (2003).

subsidiarity The principle that authority should be exercised at the most local level consistent with effectiveness, and that higher-level institutions should have only 'subsidiary' functions. The idea originated in Catholic social teaching and became a central concept in theories of FEDERALISM. In European Union law and politics, it refers to the division of powers between the EU, member states, and regional and local authorities in a system of multi-level GOVERNANCE. Federalists argue that subsidiarity implies increased DEVOLUTION to regional bodies. In EU law, however, it mainly protects the rights of national governments *vis-à-vis* the EU's supranational institutions.   JP

Suggested reading
Jordan (2000).

subsistence agriculture A form of organizing food production such that a group (HOUSEHOLD, village, society) secures FOOD sufficient for its own reproduction over time (see SOCIAL REPRODUCTION). Subsistence production, which includes not only crop production but also hunting, fishing and PASTORALISM, is typically understood to be based on the direct exploitation of the environment, as opposed to manufacture (Neitschmann, 1973). Subsistence also suggests production for use, as opposed to for EXCHANGE, although subsistence groups might share food and other

resources for ritual, ceremonial or social reciprocity purposes. Subsistence agriculture can thereby be seen as a form of cultural ADAPTATION by which social groups adapt to and regulate ECOSYSTEMS of which they are apart (see CULTURAL ECOLOGY). In MARXIST ECONOMICS, subsistence production without market involvement of any sort is referred to as primitive economy, the earliest stage of economic development: household subsistence producers with some degree of production for sale, or who purchase some goods in markets are generally referred to as PEASANTS. Because production of surpluses and/or partial commoditization is often associated with the over-exploitation of both NATURE and direct producers (Blaikie, 1985) (see POLITICAL ECOLOGY), subsistence societies appear to be more egalitarian in their social relations, despite the fact that their organization might be highly patriarchal. Although subsistence production is rare in the modern world, it allows for the possibility of substantive group autonomy from both STATE and MARKET. For that reason, it is occasionally conjured up as a UTOPIAN ideal among communards, or invoked as something that ought to be protected in traditional societies (e.g. Norbert-Hodge, 1991).   JGu

substitutionism The products of agriculture present special obstacles and barriers for industrial production. FOOD, with its necessary links to HEALTH, well-being, sociability and CULTURE, represents impediments to the simple notion of replacement of foodstuffs by industrial products (*appropriationism*). But the growth and maturity of the food industry has witnessed a discontinuous but permanent process to achieve the industrial production of food. Goodman, Sorj and Wilkinson (1987, p. 2) refer to the rising proportion of VALUE-ADDED attributable to industrial production in the food system and the gradual replacements of agricultural by non-agricultural products (e.g. of sugar derived from sugar cane, by synthetic sugars) as the twin characteristics of what they call substitutionism. (See also AGRARIAN QUESTION; AGRO-FOOD SYSTEM.) MW

Suggested reading
Walker (2005).

suburb/anization Suburbanization is a process whereby people, housing, industry, commerce, and retailing spread out beyond traditional urban areas, forming dispersed LANDSCAPES that are still connected to CITIES

731

by COMMUTING. These are comprised of diverse suburbs with a variety of social, economic and landscape characteristics and have, as a result, been interpreted in a variety of ways. In terms of their culture and design, they have frequently been criticized for their blandness, lack of COMMUNITY and SEGREGATION. These critiques are paralleled by concerns about the environmental impact of suburban landscape forms and ways of life (see EDGE CITY; EXOPOLIS; RIBBON DEVELOPMENT; SPRAWL).

Low-density, automobile-oriented suburbs are increasingly common features of urban regions across the globe and certain elements of the suburban form, such as GATED COMMUNITIES, are springing up in numerous countries (Webster, Glaze and Frantz, 2002). The process of suburbanization is differentiated somewhat by the local or national conditions in which it operates. Lemansky (2006), for instance, describes the character of suburbanization and the creation of master-planned gated communities in post-APARTHEID South Africa and notes the complex patterns of proximity, SOCIAL EXCLUSION and connection that exist between wealthy and poor residents of suburban Cape Town. Zhou and Ma (2000), for their part, emphasize the importance of suburbanization in a number of Chinese cities. They argue that it is at a much less developed stage (with suburbs still dominated by central cities) than in the 'classic' case of the USA. They also suggest that the role of the strong Chinese STATE in shaping suburbanization has a great deal to do with the distinctiveness of this case.

Yet, the US case is worth considering as a specific and by no means easily generalizable example of the POLITICAL ECONOMY of suburbanization. The US suburbanization process accelerated in the 1920s with the explosion of automobile ownership in the 1920s. 'Automobile suburbs' such as the low-density Country Club District in Kansas City, Missouri, which included the first car-oriented shopping mall, emerged in the 1920s as private developers sought to profit from increased automobility. The Depression of the early 1930s dampened the housing market, making it an unattractive INVESTMENT for private developers. The state's subsequent intervention sought to stimulate and regulate the development industry while bolstering the ideological pre-eminence of the private PROPERTY system (Walker, 1981). By the early 1960s, half the country's urban population lived in suburbs. This trend in residential suburbanization has been paralleled by manufacturing, commerce and retail, which have all suburbanized. Contemporary authors emphasize the increasing autonomy of US suburbs from traditional central cities, and speak of a 'postsuburban' situation (cf. Zhou and Ma, 2000).

Suburbanization is, then, a process that both reflects and constitutes the political and economic geographies of contemporary cities. It is also a focus of those interested in social and cultural questions, particularly around RACE and GENDER. Ethnic suburbanization is raising important questions about the validity of arguments about the social homogeneity of suburbs and is also emphasizing the global connectedness of these places (Li, 1998). Nonetheless, suburban geographies are still marked by significant discrimination (see REDLINING; URBAN MANAGERS AND GATEKEEPERS). The shaping of gender roles and relations in and through suburban space is also a major focus of geographical enquiry. In the postwar period, suburban DOMESTICITY became a HEGEMONIC idea through which to reinforce traditional gender relations and connections between women and waged work. Analysis of contemporary relationships between gender, suburbia and work has entailed, among other things, a focus on gender differentiation in travel patterns and ACCESSIBILITY to waged work and public facilities (England, 1993).   EM

Suggested reading
Bourne (1996); Walker (1981).

sunbelt/snowbelt A popular term describing the polarization of the US SPACE-ECONOMY from the 1960s on: it contrasts areas of relative economic decline (especially in manufacturing industry) concentrated in the country's northeast (the 'snowbelt', or 'frostbelt': cf. RUST-BELT) with those, largely in the south and west, experiencing rapid economic and population growth. This change in the inter-regional DIVISION OF LABOUR reflects the COMPARATIVE ADVANTAGE and COMPETITIVE ADVANTAGES enjoyed by sunbelt states through relatively cheap and non-unionized labour, their attractive physical environments, and substantial federal government investment there – as in the aerospace and other defence industries. The term is now frequently applied in other countries: the M4 motorway corridor extending west from London through Swindon to

Bristol is sometimes referred to as the UK's sunbelt.   RJ

Suggested reading
Markusen (1987).

sunk costs Incurred costs that are invariant with output (unlike variable costs) and cannot readily be recouped. In ECONOMIC GEOGRAPHY, sunk costs include those made by a firm in a particular location which, because they cannot be recouped, act as a disincentive to either or both of RESTRUCTURING and relocation – that is, for the firm exiting either the activity or the place (cf. EXIT, VOICE AND LOYALTY). Clark and Wrigley (1995) identified three types of sunk cost: *set-up sunk costs* (initial investments in plant and machinery, for example); *accumulated sunk costs* (normal, unrecoupable, costs of doing business); and *exit sunk costs* (such as those involved not only in abandoning premises and plant, but also in making workers redundant and paying for their pensions). They identify three types of exit strategy that involve acceptance of sunk costs that might not be (fully) recovered: *strategic reallocation* – using the resources for different activities, which will incur costs (re-equipping a plant, for example, and retraining workers); *RESTRUCTURING*, which may involve either or both of plant closure and staff redundancy; and *corporate reformation*, which may involve bankruptcy or liquidation.

Clark and Wrigley (1995, p. 210) present 15 separate propositions regarding sunk costs and their importance to their 'belief that the management of sunk costs across a variety of competitive domains is a vital component in any explanation of the spatial patterns of restructuring'. The accumulation of sunk costs can reduce a firm's flexibility and thus its ability to respond to the changing pressures associated with GLOBALIZATION. Firms are rarely able to respond costlessly to those imperatives, but those that economize on their sunk costs should be better placed to respond to changing patterns and geographies of supply and demand.   RJ

Suggested reading
Baumol and Willig (1981); Clark and Wrigley (1997).

surface A surface is the exterior side of something, or the conceptual boundary from the outside to the inside of a three-dimensional object. The Earth is an irregular spheroid; its surface (of elevation) is ground or sea level. The surface is continuous but, within a study region, sampling height everywhere is impossible. Instead, the surface can be approximated by a series of discrete (x, y, z) data tuples (e.g. x and y are longitude and latitude; z is height above mean sea level), or as a mathematical model (e.g. a TREND SURFACE). The z is not limited to elevation, however: statistical surfaces are also used to visualize 'hot spots' of CRIME, DISEASE, etc., for which LOCAL STATISTICS and methods of local interpolation (such as population surface modelling: Martin, Tate and Langford, 2000) are important.   RH

Suggested reading
Burrough and McDonnell (1998).

surveillance The observation or monitoring of social behaviour by individuals and institutions. Typically, surveillance straddles or compresses the geographical distance between its subject(s) and the person(s) tasked with undertaking the monitoring (cf. TIME–SPACE COMPRESSION). Virtually all social relations involve elements of surveillance. However, initiatives involving mass or institutionalized surveillance are most often legitimized as a purported means to minimize RISK or to enforce some notion of normalization or discipline over a population or place portrayed as hazardous, deviant or pathological (see also SECURITY).

HUMAN GEOGRAPHY has shown a growing recent interest in surveillance and its imbrications with MODERNITY. A key stimulus has been the writings of French philosopher Michel Foucault, and in particular *Surveillir et punir* (1975), translated into English as *Discipline and punish* (1977a [1975]). Through an analysis of Bentham's PANOPTICON and history of French PRISONS, Foucault argued that distinctively modern societies were dominated by what he called DISCIPLINARY POWER. This operated through spatially partitioning societies into prisons, workhouses, clinics, barracks, schools and so on. At the same time, architectural techniques were applied to these institutions that allowed persistent visual inspection and control by supervisors. Foucault's crucial point was that by internalizing this possibility of scrutiny, SUBJECTS became 'normalized' by monitoring, moderating and controlling their own behaviour.

733

Since the nineteenth century, these 'fixed', architectural models of panopticism have been complemented by a widening range of surveillance machines, many of which now routinely include diffused, interconnecting, computerized devices. Human geographers and others have thus addressed the saturation of contemporary societies with sites of continuous, machinic surveillance. Early research emphasized the social implications of GEOGRAPHIC INFORMATION SYSTEMS (Pickles, 1995a) and the proliferation of Closed Circuit Television (CCTV) cameras to monitor public spaces (Koskela, 2000). The significance of these practices is not confined to the political and commercial: they also have important military applications. Late-modern WAR places a premium on persistent surveillance from aerial and space-mounted platforms, including Unmanned Aerial Vehicles (UAVs) or 'drones' that transmit real-time imagery to command and control centres and ground troops: these images can feed directly into the identification and execution of targets through what Graham (2009b) calls the 'algorithmic gaze'.

These practices have spiralled far beyond their initial spheres of application, and an important emerging strand of work in surveillance geography analyses how EVERYDAY LIFE in highly computerized societies is coming to be constituted through a burgeoning range of interlinked, digital surveillance systems. This 'calculative background', as Thrift (2004b) terms it, is increasingly automated, internationalized and organized through the active agency of computer code. This means that the geographies of life chances, MOBILITIES, access rights, BORDER crossings and service privileges are now sorted through largely invisible systems of digitized surveillance, working simultaneously across multiple geographical scales (Graham, 2005). This happens through sites as diverse as call centres, supermarket checkouts, TV viewing, digital CCTV cameras, neighbourhood GIS systems, mobile phones, webcams, web sites, computerized automobiles, and national border or airport security checkpoints. Rather than emerging as some all-seeing electronic 'Panopticon' or some dystopian 'Big Brother' drawn from Orwell's classic novel *1984*, however, these systems of surveillance remain fragmented and operate instead as multiple 'Little Brothers'. *Oligoptic* rather than panoptic, they do not monitor all spaces and behaviours at all times. Instead, their

geographies overlap, cross-cut and intersect in complex ways that are currently poorly understood.   SG

Suggested reading
Levin (2002); Lyon (2006). See also *Surveillance and Society*, an open access journal at http://www.surveillance-and-society.org.

survey analysis The various procedures involved in the collection and analysis of data from individuals, almost invariably using some sort of QUESTIONNAIRE. As such they are a type of EXTENSIVE RESEARCH design.

A survey involves several stages. The first is definition of the research problem, including the formulation of HYPOTHESES and identification of the needed information. The second includes determining the population to be studied, which includes deciding what form of SAMPLING is needed. The next stage involves deciding how the hypotheses will be tested (including the analytical techniques to be employed), and is followed by development of a questionnaire (which should include pre-test stages and pilot investigations).

After administration of the questionnaires the data are prepared for analysis: quantitative data are readily dealt with; qualitative information (such as reported occupations and responses to open-ended questions) has to be handled through the development of coding schemes, increasingly through the use of sophisticated computer software for textual analysis. To ensure statistically reliable results, it is unusual for the number of separate categorical codes (such as social class) to exceed ten, and is typically five or under. The data are then usually entered into a computer database and checked for consistency and gross errors ('cleaning' the data set) before the analyses are conducted, although increasingly the responses are entered directly to a computer by the interviewer (whether at a face-to-face interview or in an interview by telephone).

The analysis of surveys consists of four quantitative elements that need to be undertaken simultaneously:

- Evaluating the size effects between variables and by doing so taking account of other variables – what Rosenberg (1978) calls the logic of survey methodology;
- Testing as part of confirmatory data analysis whether the observed effects could have occurred by chance, or whether the lack of an effect is due to inadequate statistical power;

- Taking account quantitatively of the complex design of the survey; and
- Dealing with non-response and missing data.

To appreciate the issues concerning size of effects and the interplay between variables, consider the following 2 × 2 table in which there is a single outcome (happiness) and explanatory variable (age), each being measure on a binary scale:

		Explanatory variable		Total
		Young	Old	
Outcome	Unhappy	A	B	A + B
	Happy	C	D	C + D
Total		A + C	B + D	N

The odds ratio calculated as (A/B)/(C/D) gives the degree of association between the variables: if it is 1 there is no relationship; greater than 1 means that younger people are unhappier; less than 1 suggests that younger people are more likely to be happy. However, these results should not be taken at face value and there needs to be model elaboration (Davis, 1986) to see how the relation changes as account is taken of other variables. This can be clearly seen by examining the following set of 2 × 2 tables:

(a) Aggregated data

	Young	Old	Total
Unhappy	140	120	260
Happy	50	90	140
Total	190	210	400

(b) Relation for males

	Young	Old	Total
Unhappy	120	40	160
Happy	30	10	40
Total	150	50	200

(c) Relation for females

	Young	Old	Total
Unhappy	20	80	100
Happy	20	80	100
Total	40	160	200

In (a) there is a clear relationship in that the odds ratio of 2.1 suggest that younger people are twice as unhappy as the old. However, in (b) and (c) when the same data are disaggregated to examine the relation for men and women separately, each odds ratio is exactly

1 showing that there is no relationship between age and happiness; the apparent relationship is an artefact of the relationships between age and gender (i.e. they are confounded) and gender and happiness. The following set of 2 × 2 tables tells a different story:

(a) Aggregated data

	Young	Old	Total
Unhappy	200	200	400
Happy	200	200	400
Total	400	400	800

(b) Relation for males

	Young	Old	Total
Unhappy	170	40	210
Happy	190	80	270
Total	360	120	480

(c) Relation for females

	Young	Old	Total
Unhappy	30	160	190
Happy	10	120	130
Total	40	280	320

In (a) the aggregate relation shows no effect as there is an odds ratio of 1, but in (b) and (c) when the analysis is done separately by GENDER, the odds ratios are 1.79 for males and 2.25 for females. In this case, the effect between age and happiness has been masked by not taking account of gender. The analysis can of course be extended to more than three variables and to include continuous variables (see CATEGORICAL DATA ANALYSIS) but the underling logic of model elaboration remains the same.

Analysis also has to guard against the Type I error of finding a relation when it does not exist, and the Type II error of not finding a genuine relation (cf. SAMPLING). For the former confirmatory data analysis is used to test for the significance of a relation and to examine confidence intervals; the key here is the absolute sample size. Thus the estimated odds of 2.1 for the relation in the first aggregate analysis has 95 per cent confidence intervals that lie between 1.38 and 3.21, so there is little chance that the aggregate relation is really 1, which would indicate no effect. When no significant relationship is found this may be an outcome of too small a study. If this is the case we can perform a retrospective power analysis (Cohen, 1988) to see if the sample size was large enough to detect an effect. It would have been better, however, to do an initial power analysis before sampling.

Many surveys have a complex sampling design involving clustering, stratification and disproportionate sampling. These attributes should be taken into account during analysis so as to avoid biased estimates of standard errors and increased likelihood of Type I errors. Clustering, or multi-stage selection of sample units, typically generates dependency so that there is less information than appears. MULTI-LEVEL MODELS estimate and correct for the degree of dependency even when there are more than two sampling stages. Their results can also be substantively interesting, finding for example that members of the same HOUSE-HOLD tend to vote together (Johnston, Jones, Sarker, Burgess, Propper and Bolster, 2005). Stratification involves grouping the sampling frame into believed-to-be homogeneous groups and thereby reducing standard error. Often there is disproportionate sampling of strata so that having grouped primary sampling units into strata based on percentage ethnic minority population, ethnic areas are over-sampled. This requires at the analysis stage that the over-sampled ethnic areas are down-weighted to their correct population proportion. Sturgis (2004), using data from the 2000 UK Time Use Survey, shows how these factors should be incorporated into the estimates and illustrates the threats to inference if ignored. LONGITUDINAL DATA ANALYSIS faces its own particular analytical problems arising from the analysis of repeated measures over time.

Non-response is a growing problem with surveys. The best approach is to ensure detailed follow-up so that the issue is minimized at the design and collection phase; this is a problem where doing nothing is doing something, and where prevention is better than any cure. We can distinguish between *full, or unit, non-response* and *item non-response*, the latter being when the respondent has only answered some questions. For the former, differential *weighting* can be used to reduce bias by boosting the effective size of subgroups (such as young men) that are under-represented in the survey, but their relative size is known from other large-scale surveys or censuses. There is a danger of increasing standard errors, however, when the variance of the weights is large. Most SOFTWARE FOR QUANTITATIVE ANALYSIS automatically excludes the entire respondent when any values are missing and this is known as complete case analysis. If the data are missing completely at random (MCAR: Rubin, 1976) this will not bias the results if the observations are excluded but it will reduce the

effective sample size. If the data are missing at random (MAR) but the 'missingness' depends on recorded information, then complete case analysis can be used, but the determinants of the 'missingness' must be included in the analysis to avoid non-response bias. This suggests that at collection phase, variables that should be easier to collect are obtained alongside those that are thought to be difficult (e.g. income may be difficult so also collect information about property value). If the 'missingness' depends on unobserved predictors, even after accounting for information in the observed data, then the data are said to be not missing at random (NMAR). In this case, complete case analysis is likely to produce biased results.

There are two main approaches to 'missingness', either explicit modelling of the underlying mechanism generating the missing data or some form of imputation (or 'guessing') to replace the missing values. A number of ad hoc procedures can be used for the latter, such as carrying the last observation forward, creating an extra category for the missing observation, or replacing missing observations by the mean of the variable used. All can give unpredictable results. Consequently, the only practical, generally applicable, approach for substantial datasets is multiple imputation whereby each missing value is replaced by several (typically less than five) imputed values which come from an imputation model which also reflects sampling variability. A sensitivity analysis can then be undertaken to investigate the robustness of the estimates to differential 'missingness'.

Survey analysts are aware of criticisms that see quantitative approaches as imposing meaning on people's attitudes and behaviours. Consequently, as Marsh (1982) argued in her defence of the survey method, researchers have been highly attentive to just such issues, and developments continue to be made. One set of issues relates to whether respondents, particularly from different cultures, understand questions in different ways, or if researchers mean one thing and respondents think they mean something else. Analytical approaches to this treat survey questions as a function of the actual quantity being measured along with an element of interpersonal incomparability that is potentially different for each respondent. The new idea is to use anchoring vignettes as a common reference point (King, Murray, Salomon and Tandon, 2004; King and Wand, 2007) to measure directly and then 'subtract off' the incomparable portion. Respondents are asked for their own response to the concept being measured along with assessments, on the same scale, for each of several hypothetical benchmark situations described in the vignettes. Interpersonal incomparability is the only reason the response can differ, as the vignettes are literally the same. Statistical models have been designed to require only a small random sub-sample to correct the respondent's reply for the personal element.   KJ

Suggested reading
Groves, Fowler, Couper, Lepkowski, Singer and Tourangeau (2004); King, Honaker, Joseph and Scheve (2001); Little and Rubin (2002); Skinner, Holt and Smith (1989). Excellent practical advice on missing data can be found at http://www.lshtm.ac.uk/msu/missingdata/index. html and the Anchoring Vignettes website is at http://gking.harvard.edu/vign/.

surveying To survey is to assess or study a PLACE or population, the salient features of which might then be mapped or recorded. From a cadastral (land ownership) perspective, surveying is to apply the principles of mathematics (geometry and trigonometry) to determine points on the Earth's surface delimiting a land boundary. Alternatively, a physical scientist might apply the principles of physics, chemistry or biology to survey a site, whereas a polling company uses techniques of statistical inference to survey a population by means of a sample (see SURVEY ANALYSIS). Geographical research includes not only mathematical/scientific conceptions of surveying but also QUALITATIVE METHODS.   RH

Suggested reading
Aldridge and Levine (2001).

sustainability Sustainability, like SUSTAINABLE DEVELOPMENT, is becoming increasingly difficult to invoke with any critical weight. In fact, it would be fair to say that in critical circles, and among those interested in progressive or radical environmental politics in particular, use of the word will almost certainly elicit a cringe. This may point to an abiding cynicism, but it probably also reflects the proliferation of this term as a form of discursive gloss over disparate material and political projects, including no shortage of mobilizations in corporate 'greenwash' campaigns. Indeed, while sustainability as a buzzword does much work to enhance environmental awareness, it may just as easily be viewed as evidence of an increasingly promiscuous convergence

of capital ACCUMULATION and certain kinds of ENVIRONMENTALISM (Katz, 1998). To this may be added the concern that this word – and much more so sustainable development – has become hopelessly co-opted by an INSTRUMENTALIST and administrative connotation that takes from it any edge as a challenge to prevailing ways of thinking about and relating to one another, and to the non-human world. It is in fact difficult to argue that that any serious progress is being made in the name of this term when, by any reasonable definition and notwithstanding rosy portraits of dematerializing industrial economies, the global political economy and ecology – what Luke (2005) provocatively calls a system of 'sustainable degradation' – is characterized by more and more aggregate material and ENERGY throughput, and by greater and greater social inequality (Harper, 2004) (cf. POLITICAL ECOLOGY).

There are nevertheless good reasons to take this word and some of what it conveys seriously, and in particular to differentiate the word from the term 'sustainable development'. For one thing, sustainability is much less easily and intuitively grafted on to DEVELOPMENT orthodoxy aimed at sustaining little more than ECONOMIC GROWTH. Sustainability continues to function more as an ambiguous mantra than as a new paradigm of a POSTCOLONIAL development agenda, the latter a critique levelled at the institutionalization of sustainable development (Escobar, 1995). Instead, sustainability has been more successfully mobilized in ways that challenge conventional development paradigms – including, for example, in the notion of sustainable livelihoods – and in directing attention towards 'satisficing', or meeting basic needs (Sneddon, 2000).

Sustainability is also deployed more concretely in scientific and technical parlance. This includes efforts to develop sustainability indicators (O'Riordan, 2004) to be used as benchmarks, fixed goals by which the ABSTRACTION and obfuscation so typical of sustainability DISCOURSES might be reined in. It also includes the use of the term in policy-oriented or more applied ecological sciences (e.g. conservation biology) seeking to develop and apply notions of specifically ecological sustainability, particularly when both human and non-human systems exhibit uncertain behaviour. As thin as this literature typically is in conceptualizing human behaviour, important principles such as adaptive management and precautionary action have taken hold

(Walters and Holling, 1990: Walters, Korman, Stevens and Gold, 2000) (cf. ECOLOGY).

Attempts to define and implement principles of sustainability in planning and development policy have sometimes been pursued through the so-called 'three pillars' of sustainability, namely economic, social, and environmental or ecological. This is, for instance, a feature of local and regional planning for sustainability as pursued in the UK (Haughton and Counsell, 2004). True, the condition of sustainability in this context is still tethered (legislatively) to the maintenance of economic growth. But one advantage of at least recognizing disparate connotations of sustainability, in terms of these three pillars or otherwise, is that it leaves open the possibility that trade-offs must be made, and that not all efforts to achieve sustainability can be achieved via the win–win optimism that has been a predominant gloss on sustainable development since the Brundtland Commission, and certainly since the 1992 Rio Summit (Adams, 1995). Critical work remains to be done on the governmentalizing dimensions of particular sustainability programmes, specifically the ways in which new political subjectivities and modes of GOVERNANCE arise around the institutionalization of sustainability (see GOVERNMENTALITY). This comprises one way to bring politics into discussions and analyses concerning sustainability.

In fact, this speaks to a bigger problem of politics when it comes to sustainability and sustainable development. Seemingly endless rounds of defining the terms leads to an overriding idealism in policy and academic literatures that can actually obscure attention to changing GENEALOGIES, as predominant connotations evolve shaped in part by prevailing POWER relations. Put another way, and in the spirit of Michel Foucault, tracking the changing meaning of the term must always be situated in relation to the capacity of power to produce these changing meanings. And this is what frustrates many of a critical bent in encountering this word; it seems to preclude or leave unexamined in most iterations questions of power and politics. Revisiting the three pillars noted above, for instance, it is not clear where politics enter and how.

Thus, as opposed to more and more attempts to define the term and pin it down, it might be more useful to consider what questions it invokes. One of these, as Drummond and Marsden (1999) argue, is why sustainability literature is so much characterized by 'line drawing' exercises rather than more critical analyses of systemic tendencies for lines to be transgressed. This echoes early critics of both sustainable development and sustainability, who argued that both require direct challenges to CAPITALISM itself as an inherently unsustainable form of economic, social and political organization constituted by and productive of profound social inequalities, and predicated on the mobilization of energy and raw materials increasingly commodified for the purposes of an expanding and inherently expansionist ECONOMY (Redclift, 1987; O'Riordan, 1991; Benton, 1994).

A second question concerns the ways in which sustainability needs to be operationalized as disparate challenges in relation to the so-called environmentalism of the poor versus the environmentalism of the rich (Martinez-Alier, 2002). This would allow affluence to be challenged, while recognizing that the poverty and environmental degradation nexus requires distinct approaches (including not just policies aimed at fostering socially equitable and environmentally benign growth policies, but redistribution via genuine THIRD WORLD debt relief and reparations for COLONIAL plunders).

A third question concerns examination of real-world trade-offs and complex political ecological dynamics involved in the institutionalization of specific programmes aimed at enhancing sustainability, moving past mantras to ask the kinds of hard questions that lend themselves to social science. What, for instance, are the scaled social and environmental implications of reforestation programmes, particularly vis-à-vis reinforcing logging pressure in faraway places (Robbins and Fraser, 2003)? What happens to local level social relations, PROPERTY rights and land-use practices under the influence of international fair TRADE and organic standardization regimes (Mutersbaugh, 2004)? (See also FORESTRY.) What are the social and environmental effects – again across SCALES – introduced by regimes such as 'FOOD miles' that stigmatize distance travelled, particularly as these effects ripple through complex COMMODITY CHAINS linking First World markets and Third World agricultural systems (Friedberg, 2004)? While such critically minded, theoretically informed and empirically oriented engagements with real-world instantiations of sustainability oriented policies and programmes might seem to take some of the wind out of sustainability's sails, they also help ensure that sustainability conveys more than a lot of hot air.   SP

Suggested reading
Adams (2001); Dobson (1998); Ostrom, Burger, Field, Norgaard and Policansky (1999); Redclift (1987).

sustainable development The concept of sustainable development has become ubiquitous in global debate, but like SUSTAINABILITY, different actors use the phrase to express different visions for ECONOMY, environment and SOCIETY (Adams, 2001). The Brundtland Report of 1987 famously defined sustainable development as 'development that meets the needs of the present without compromising the ability of future generations to meet their own needs'. This cleverly captures the central paradox of the impact of ECONOMIC GROWTH on the environment, and yet the need for such growth to alleviate both present and future POVERTY (often spoken of as intra- and inter-generational equity).

Radical critiques of the unsustainable nature of DEVELOPMENT have included calls for zero economic growth and critiques of INDUSTRIAL-IZATION, consumerism and free market economics. However, mainstream thinking about sustainable development has centred on 'market environmentalism' and continued economic growth, adapted to ensure that the capacity of the planet to provide raw materials and absorb wastes is not overstretched (Low and Gleeson, 1998). This is to be achieved through the 'greening' of industry and society, 'green' consumerism and efficient production systems that minimize wastage, POLLUTION and negative social impact. Under market ENVIR-ONMENTALISM, growth and consumption are the engine that drives the creation of sustainable environments and livelihoods.

Such changes demand 'ecological MODERN-IZATION', the pursuit of rational, technical solutions to environmental problems and more efficient institutions for environmental management and control (Hajer, 1995). This involves new partnerships between STATE and private enterprise, including MARKET-based incentives, self-regulation by business, strong government and an efficient state bureaucracy. The feasibility of this approach is limited by the erosion of state power by GLOBALIZATION and free TRADE. Many developing countries in particular display significant weaknesses in governance, and powerless CIVIL SOCIETY institutions.

Mainstream thinking about sustainable development became established at the United Nations Conference on Environment and Development (UNCED, or simply the 'Rio Conference'), held at Rio de Janeiro in Brazil in June 1992 (Chatterjee and Finger, 1994). This meeting produced a vast encyclopaedia of ideas in *Agenda 21* (over 600 pages long), the Convention on Biological Diversity (http://www.biodiv.org/default.shtml) and the Framework Convention on Climate Change (http://unfccc.int/2860.php).

At Rio, sustainable development was interpreted primarily in terms of global environmental change (BIODIVERSITY depletion and CLIMATE change), reflecting the agenda of industrialized Northern countries. Complex and controversial issues of global poverty or NORTH–SOUTH inequality were discussed less effectively). However, this emphasis changed at the World Summit on Sustainable Development (WSSD), in Johannesburg, South Africa, in 2002. This followed the United Nations Millennium Summit in September 2000 and agreement on a series of Millennium Development Goals (www.developmentgoals.org/). Poverty was central to debate at Johannesburg. The Johannesburg Plan of Implementation addressed the eradication of poverty as well as issues such as unsustainable patterns of CONSUMPTION and production, the protection and management of the NATURAL RESOURCE base of economic and social development, globalization and health (www.johannesburgsummit.org/). WMA

symbolic interactionism A SOCIAL THEORY that focuses upon the SOCIAL CONSTRUCTION of the self and objects through interaction with others. Based on the theoretical formulations of the philosopher G.H. Mead (1934), its sociological implications were developed by Herbert Blumer (1969) and others. The theory posits that the self and social organization more broadly are formed by an ongoing process of the interpretation of meanings. As such, the theory is opposed to notions of structures, which are not reducible to ongoing interaction. More structurally inclined theorists have accused it of being individualistic and voluntarist. ANTI-HUMANISM in GEOGRAPHY criticizes its primary emphasis on human interaction. JSD

Suggested reading
Prus (1995).

system A set of elements organized so that each is either directly or indirectly interdependent on every other, usually in some form of network (cf. GRAPH THEORY; SOCIAL NET-WORK). Many analysts argue that systems must have a function, goal or purpose – even if this is only the maintenance of the system itself (see FUNCTIONALISM; STRUCTURAL FUNCTION-ALISM). Some have a clear, separate existence and function – as with a central heating system – but many geographical studies involve the pragmatic isolation (or ABSTRAC-TION) of linked parts from a larger whole (such as a METROPOLITAN AREA): where such abstractions are somewhat arbitrary, the system studied may yield few valuable conclusions (and be categorized as a chaotic conception).

Systems analysis involves four main decisions regarding the object of study:

- *Whether it is to be conceptualized as open or closed.* A closed system has no links to a surrounding environment – either as a source of energy (as in ECOSYSTEMS) or as a receptacle for by-products of its operation (as in POLLUTION): an open system (which is by far the commonest condition) interacts with its milieu.
- *Whether it can be divided into subsystems,* comprising separate clusters of interdependent elements weakly linked to each other.
- *Whether the links involve flows and causal relationships, or are presented as black boxes.* Systems of flows involve the movement of materials, ideas and people (as in TRADE, MIGRATION and COMMUTING); causal systems involve links that transmit clearly defined consequences (as in *A* generates *B*; e.g. assuming constant demand, an increase in the supply of a good leads to a reduction in its price): a black box incorporates links that may be causal, but for which the processes involved are not understood.
- *Whether the system involves* FEEDBACK, either positive or negative.

The concept of a system and the formal protocols of systems analysis (many of them derived from engineering) were introduced to GEOGRAPHY during its QUANTITATIVE REVOLU-TION, and were seen by some as providing both substantive and methodological links between HUMAN and PHYSICAL GEOGRAPHY (see also ECOLOGY; GENERAL SYSTEMS THEORY; HUMAN ECOLOGY; POLITICAL ECOLOGY). More generally, the concept of a system is applied descriptively in a wide range of contexts to refer to sets of interdependent phenomena, without adopting any of the more formal concepts associated with systems analysis.   RJ

Suggested reading
Bennett and Chorley (1978); Huggett (1980); Wilson (2000).

T

taken-for-granted world The realm of EVERYDAY LIFE, frequently unreflective, where convention and routine prevail, leading to the accumulation of the attitudinal norms and habitual practices that define a subculture. The taken-for-granted world was INSPIRED BY HUMANISTIC GEOGRAPHY through ETHNOGRAPHIC and other interpretative methods inspired by the philosophical traditions of German constitutive PHENOMENOLOGY and American PRAGMATISM (Ley, 1977). Also relevant is Pierre Bourdieu's concept of *HABITUS*, with its emphasis on CLASS-based subcultures with varied resources to bring to everyday social projects. The centrality of POWER in everyday life has been also been drawn out more fully by the French philosophers Michel de Certeau and Henri Lefebvre.   DL

Suggested reading
Werlen (1993, ch. 3).

tariff A tax levied by a government on the importation of a COMMODITY made abroad. Governments impose tariffs on foreign-made imports for multiple reasons, including to protect domestic producers from foreign competition, to correct a trade deficit, to give preference to imports from certain countries over others, or, contrarily, to retaliate against another country's preferential tariff regime.

Preferential tariffs designed to privilege or punish particular exporting countries date to imperial trading practices, which were often organized within networks of 'imperial preference'. But it was in the context of nineteenth-century IMPERIALISM that British industrialists began the rhetorical inflation of free trade and the political struggle to reduce tariffs (Sheppard, 2005): they wanted to sell their products to foreign and domestic markets, and also saw the advantages of tariff-free FOOD imports for feeding and maintaining a cheap workforce (Merrett, 1996). Early economists such as David Ricardo helped the industrialists make their case with academic arguments about the gains from TRADE, and until the 1930s, the cause of free trade and tariff reduction spread around the world, albeit within limits created by inter-imperial struggles (including the immense upheaval of the First World War). During the Great Depression, however, in the rush to protect their domestic capitalists from the global CRISIS of over-accumulation, governments imposed steep tariffs on foreign imports. The resultant 'tariff walls' drastically reduced world trade and created much more autarchic or self-contained national economies: this territorialization of economies set the geographical pattern for the distinctively national REGIMES OF ACCUMULATION based on FORDISM that characterized the mid-twentieth century (see Lash and Urry, 1987; Harvey, 1989b; Mitchell, 1998, 2002d).

The Fordist pattern of economic nationalization was also influenced by global politics, the rise of COMMUNISM and, most notably, the national mobilizations forced by the Second World War. However, as the war drew to a close, the cause of free trade was launched again with the American-led meetings at Bretton Woods, which led to the General Agreement on Tariffs and Trade or GATT in 1947. Some joke that GATT in fact stood for the General Agreement to Talk and Talk, because, despite unending American pressure and resulting rounds of talks, other countries were reluctant to quickly remove their tariff walls, as they faced the prospect of rebuilding their war-torn economies. The USA, by contrast, had emerged from the war with its economy unscathed and eager to expand markets for its products worldwide. American negotiators pushed for a more open global free trade system that could absorb the US trade surplus, and slowly but surely they prevailed: the crowning achievement was the establishment of the WORLD TRADE ORGANIZATION in 1994 (Peet, 2003). However, by the 1990s the US trade surplus had turned into a large and fast-growing deficit; thus, in the years since its inception the WTO has had to deal with increasing complaints by developing countries that the USA is abandoning free trade and – ironically albeit unsurprisingly – imposing tariffs on foreign products (Wallach and Woodall, 2004).   MS

Taylorism A set of workplace practices developed from the principles of 'scientific management' by the American engineer Frederick W. Taylor (1911) from his systematic time-and-motion studies of the LABOUR PROCESS in American factories. The core principle involved breaking down production activities into their simplest, standardized components and linking them in precisely coordinated, closely supervised sequences. This imposed a strictly disciplined choreography on the workplace, a sort of mechanized ballet, and workers often resisted its introduction. Taylorism was designed to enhance overall efficiency by reducing the scope of activity of individual workers and optimizing the performance of individual tasks, but the logic of distinguishing between close supervision and standardized activities also accentuated the separation of conception and execution of tasks in the workplace.

For this reason, analysts such as Braverman (1974) have associated the widespread introduction of Taylorist principles with the deskilling or degradation of work. The result is a distinctive occupational DIVISION OF LABOUR, in which unskilled workers execute simple, repetitive shop-floor fabrication functions, while skilled technical and managerial staff perform functions related to research, product design, process and quality control, coordination, finance and marketing. The economic outcomes for workers depend on the wider social and political context in which the production systems are embedded. Under the terms of classical FORDISM in the USA and western Europe, for example, the array of institutions governing collective bargaining and wage determination increased the likelihood that even unskilled workers might enjoy a decent living and enjoy tolerable working conditions. The application of Taylorist principles elsewhere, in parts of ASIA, AFRICA and LATIN AMERICA, was not normally accompanied by such institutional frameworks, however, leading to a more 'primitive Taylorization', based on the 'bloody exploitation' of labour (Peck and Tickell, 1994, pp. 286–7).

As Clark (1981) and others have observed, during the postwar period, in which Taylorist principles gained their widest acceptance, large firms organized along Taylorist lines would often segregate skilled and unskilled functions in separate plants, producing a spatial division of labour defined by the pre-existing geography of labour supply, wage rates and social relations (see also LABOUR GEOGRAPHY). Subsequent methods of work organization associated with POST-FORDISM are generally regarded as having reversed the task fragmentation and separation of conception and execution characteristic of Taylorism.

But Schoenberger (1997) and others suggest that organizational innovations such as JUST-IN-TIME PRODUCTION were developed by eliminating wasted time in production through the use of precisely the same tools of time-and-motion study pioneered by Taylor himself.   MSG

teleology   Teleological enquiry is motivated by the belief that there is an ultimate purpose or design at work within the world, and that all elements and events, whether we are conscious of it or not, are pre-configured to realize that purpose or design. The teleological end reaches back to explain everything that precedes it. The origins of teleology lie in Greek PHILOSOPHY, especially the writings of Aristotle and the concept of a final cause, which proposes that phenomena take on their peculiar properties because they enable some final end or purpose (*telos*) to be met. To use Aristotle's own example, humans do not see because of a series of prior biological processes that produce eyes; rather, eyes are produced in order to meet the purpose of seeing. The teleological end of seeing arranges biological conditions such that eyes eventuate. As Aristotle had it, 'Nature adapts the organ to the function, and not the function to the organ.'

Teleology as a form of argumentation is found in a diverse range of enquiry. It is perhaps best known within Christian theology – from St Thomas Aquinas' (1225–74) five proofs of God's existence, to recent (unsuccessful) arguments in the US court system to justify classroom teaching of 'intelligent design'. Within the HUMANITIES and social sciences, the teleological writings of the German philosopher G.W.F. Hegel (1770–1831) have been pivotal, in large part because of their influence on others, especially Karl Marx (1818–83). Hegel argued that human history was teleologically directed to the unification of spirit (*Geist*) and proceeded through a dynamic process of negation and contradiction (the DIALECTIC). At some historical juncture (which Hegel said happened to be his own time), the negations and contractions were finally comprehended by individual human minds as a unity, at which point the mandate of history was fulfilled; history's teleological purpose was reached. Marx invoked a similar teleology in his own historical scheme, also propelled also by negation and contradiction. But in Marx's view, history was moved not by contradictions of spirit becoming unified, but by a set of contradictory physical–social relationships within successive MODES OF PRODUCTION, and unification occurred not within individual minds but very much outside in the world of people's material lives and practices. Marx argued that history's teleology was marked by distinct stages of completion, with CAPITALISM, the epoch in which Marx lived, merely the penultimate one. History's ultimate purpose, the negation of all negation, would manifest in what necessarily came next, the final stage, the end of history, COMMUNISM.

Teleological arguments are criticized on many grounds, including: they are not empirically testable and are thus unfalsifiable; they reverse the temporal sequence of cause and effect (effects determine causes); causal mechanisms are either absent or not well specified; and they deny human beings free will, confining them within an iron cage of historical inevitability. Nevertheless, teleological arguments can be found in two distinct bodies of work in modern HUMAN GEOGRAPHY. The first was in studies of MODERNIZATION in the 1960s that were (mis)informed by Rostow's (1960) STAGES OF GROWTH model to depict – and predict – the inevitable spatial DIFFUSION of modernization across the landscape of a developing economy (Gould, 1969b). The second was in the early writings of some Marxist geographers who saw capitalism's CRISES as inevitable way-stations towards the end point of its final destruction and overthrow (Smith, 2008 [1984]).   TB

terms of trade   A name in economics for the ratio between a price index of a country's exports and a price index of its imports. Amongst advocates of export-led DEVELOPMENT, 'improving the terms of trade' traditionally meant increasing the ratio of profits from exports *vis-à-vis* the costs of imports. As such, it was part of the Washington consensus amongst development economists that export surpluses were better than import substitution for developing countries. But now, in the context of increasing dissensus over such axioms, a second, more literal, meaning of 'terms of trade' has come to the fore as critics of NEOLIBERALISM have sought to decode the ways in which the terminology of recent global and regional TRADE agreements obscures how they entrench neo-liberal norms of government across wide swathes of social, political and even ecological as well as economic life (Peet, Borne, Davis et al., 2003; McCarthy, 2004). Terms-of-trade legalese such as TRIPs (which in the WORLD TRADE ORGANIZATION (WTO) stands for agreements on *Trade Related Intellectual Property*) and TRIMs (*Trade Related Investment Measures*) have thereby been debunked as elements of a narrow neo-liberal, free-market fundamentalist agenda that sets constraints on democratic governance over everything from FOOD safety to DEVELOPMENT policy by giving private corporations quasi-constitutional rights to sue governments (Sparke, 2005). 'Because its terms are so broad,' argue two critics of the WTO's terms of trade, 'the WTO has managed to intervene in domestic policies all over the planet' (Wallach and Woodall, 2004, p. 2). Countering this takeover, Wallach and Woodall point out that the neo-liberal project therefore involves repeatedly expanding what were originally meant to be simple agreements on free trade into neo-liberal legal rules governing practically everything. This terms-of-trade overreach, they note, is ironically marked in the terms themselves such that 'you can identify which WTO agreements have least connection to trade by which have the "Trade Related" label slapped on them' (ibid., p. 2). It remains a credit to the critical wisdom of Marx and Engels that they foresaw precisely this terms-of-trade takeover in the *Communist manifesto*, when they described the wholesale transformation of medieval life through the free trade fetish of the capitalist business CLASS. 'The bourgeoisie,' they thereby argued, 'has drowned the most heavenly ecstasies of religious fervour, of chivalrous enthusiasm, of philistine sentimentalism, in the icy water of egotistical calculation. It has resolved personal worth into exchange value, and in place of the numberless indefeasible chartered freedoms, has set up that single, unconscionable freedom – Free Trade' (Marx and Engels, 2002 [1848]).   MS

terra nullius   A legal doctrine enshrined in eighteenth-century European LAW that legitimized the annexation of 'uninhabited lands' by settlement as an acknowledged means, alongside conquest and secession, for the proper conduct of colonization by 'civilized' nations. Such lands were not literally uninhabited; rather, the colonizers cast their existing inhabitants as too 'primitive' to merit political recognition (cf. PRIMITIVISM). *Terra nullius* was instrumental in the European dispossession of indigenous peoples in so-called settler colonies, such as Australia, which has been the subject of political COLONIALISM; struggle and legal redress ever since. (See also COLONIALISM; SETTLER SOCIETY.)   SW

Suggested reading
Simpson (1993).

743

territorial integrity A term in international LAW and, increasingly, CRITICAL GEOPOLITICS, that has two main meanings: *territorial preservation* and *territorial sovereignty*. Its meaning of territorial preservation establishes a right to the preservation of a STATE's existing BOUNDARIES, and prevents SECESSION or territorial conquest by other states. Territorial sovereignty or inviolability allows a state to exercise its power within those boundaries, without intervention or prohibition from external actors (see Akweenda, 1989). Both senses of the term are enshrined and protected by key clauses of Article 2 of the founding Charter of the United Nations.

While there is an element of necessary fiction in the idea that states are in control of, and therefore exercise SOVEREIGNTY over, their entire TERRITORY, this has provided a framework within which international law has operated. The norm of territorial preservation conditioned DECOLONIZATION in AFRICA, and helped to frame the international context of the break-up of the Soviet Union. Territorial sovereignty has been held as a guiding principle of the international system where, for actions that do not have an effect beyond its borders, a state has been held to be sovereign. This is what the European Union calls *internal competence*. Thus international law is built around three core principles: sovereign equality of all states; internal competence for domestic jurisdiction; and territorial preservation of existing boundaries. What this means is that any challenge to the 'monopoly of legitimate physical violence' that states are held to have within their territory is necessarily a challenge to territorial integrity by infringing on the spatial extent of their sovereignty.

Territorial integrity in the sense of territorial sovereignty has come under increased pressure in recent years, with humanitarian intervention or the 'responsibility to protect' civilian populations legitimating external intervention in internal jurisdiction. The doctrine of 'contingent sovereignty' promoted by the Bush administration in the 'war on terror' (Elden, 2006: see also TERRORISM; WAR) held that state sovereignty is dependent on adherence to codes of behaviour – notably not harbouring terrorists or pursuing 'weapons of mass destruction' – and violation of these norms legitimates pre-emptive action (Elden, 2005, 2007a,c). Yet at the same time territorial preservation has been held as a dominant organizing principle, with a widespread reluctance to support independence secession movements or rethink the boundaries of existing states.　　　　SE

Suggested reading
Elden (2005); Zacher (2001).

territorial justice The territorialization of the principles of SOCIAL JUSTICE. This involves examining the conditions under which wealth and SOCIAL WELL-BEING are produced, distributed and consumed (Perrons, 2004). Hence, social justice can only be giving meaning in the context of a particular set of social relations. Using territorial justice to make judgements over the justness or otherwise of societies is complicated in three ways: first, there are the difficulties posed by the ECOLOGICAL FALLACY; second, there are issues over the appropriateness of the spatial definition of the territorial units; and, third, the achievement of territorial justice has to be set against what this might mean for other forms of justice (Smith and Lee, 2004).　　　　KWa

Suggested reading
Smith and Lee (2004).

territorial sea A jurisdictional zone of the OCEAN, extending a maximum of 12 nautical miles from the baseline (United Nations, 1983, Article 3) and including air space, sea bed and subsoil. The territorial sea is the ocean zone most exposed to human pressure and RESOURCE use. The 1982 United Nations Convention on the Law of the Sea (UNCLOS) extends the SOVEREIGNTY of coastal STATES to include the territorial sea. Within the zone, other nations have few prerogatives beyond the right of 'innocent passage', which recognizes the transit right of foreign flag merchant vessels provided that it is peaceful and not prejudicial to the good order or security of the coastal state concerned.　　　　sch

Suggested reading
Valega (1992).

territoriality Either the organization and exercise of POWER, legitimate or otherwise, over blocs of SPACE or the organization of people and things into discrete areas through the use of BOUNDARIES. In studies of ANIMAL behaviour, spatial division into TERRITORIES is seen as an evolutionary principle, a way of fostering competition so that those best matched to their territory will have more surviving offspring. With human territoriality, however, spatial division is more typically thought of as a strategy used by organizations and groups to organize social, economic and political activities. From this viewpoint, space is partitioned into territorial cells or units that can be relatively autonomous (as with the division of global space into territorial NATION-STATES) or arranged hierarchically from basic units in which work, administration or SURVEILLANCE is carried out through intermediate levels at which managerial or supervisory functions are located to the top-most level, at which central control is concentrated. Alternative SPATIALITIES of political and economic organization, particularly hierarchical NETWORKS (as in the WORLD-CITY network) or reticular networks (as with the INTERNET), can challenge or supplement the use of territoriality.

Theoretically, territoriality can be judged as having a number of different origins including: (1) as a result of explicit territorial strategizing to devolve administrative functions but maintain central control (Sack, 1986); (2) as a secondary result of resolving the dilemmas facing social groups in delivering PUBLIC GOODS (as in Michael Mann's, 1984b, sociology of territory); (3) as an expedient facilitating coordination between capitalists who are otherwise in competition with one another (as in MARXIST theories of the state); (4) as the focus of one strategy among several of GOVERNMENTALITY (as in Michel Foucault's writings); and (5) as a result of defining boundaries between social groups to identify and maintain group cohesion, as in the writings of Georg Simmel (Lechner, 1991) and Fredrik Barth (1969), and in more recent sociological theories of political IDENTITY (Agnew 2003b). Whatever its origins, territoriality is put into practice in a number of different if often complementary ways: (1) by popular acceptance of *classifications* of space (e.g. 'ours' versus 'yours'); (2) through *communication* of a SENSE OF PLACE (where territorial markers and BOUNDARIES evoke meanings); and (3) by *enforcing control* over space (by SURVEILLANCE, POLICING and legitimation).

There are important cultural and historical dimensions to territoriality. Churches and polities (states, empires, federations etc.) have been the most important users of territoriality. Some churches (such as the Roman Catholic Church) and some states (such as the United States) have more complex and formally hierarchical territorialities than others. Today, TRANSNATIONAL CORPORATIONS and global businesses erect territorial hierarchies that cut across existing political ones. So, even as some users of territoriality fade away, others emerge. Though varying in precise form and complexity, therefore, territoriality seems always to be with us.   JA

Suggested reading
Amin and Thrift (1997); Brenner, Jessop, Jones and Macleod (2003).

territorialization The dynamic process whereby humans and their affairs are fixed territorially in space, by a range of actors but primarily by STATES. On the contrary, *deterritorialization* signifies a growing tendency for states, in the context of global CAPITALISM, to encounter and often encourage an uprooting of people and things with massive social, psychological, and political consequences. *Reterritorialization* is the reverse of this process.

In some usage, particularly that of Deleuze and Guattari (e.g. 1972), employment of deterritorialization seems to simply refer to the breakdown of TERRITORIALITY in thought and practice. EPISTEMOLOGICALLY juxtaposing 'State philosophy' with 'nomad thought', Deleuze and Guattari associate territorialization with the former and deterritorialization with the latter. ONTOLOGICALLY, however, there could be quite different territorial systems at play over time as, for example, with pre- and post-colonial contact between colonizers and natives leading to the breakdown of one system, followed by a period of deterritorialization before the imposition of a new territoriality. Crucial to the concept of deterritorialization with Deleuze and Guattari is the claim that 'Processes are becomings, and aren't to be judged by some final result but by the way they proceed and their power to continue, as with animal becomings, or nonsubjective individuations' (Deleuze, 1995, p. 146).

More typically, two other approaches tend to dominate contemporary usage. In the first case, TERRITORY is posed as a physical 'base' for human activities and deterritorialization is viewed as either the lessening importance of local constraints or the weakening of the impact of physical distance on EVERYDAY LIFE. The increased speed of financial and other transactions, the so-called conquest of space by time (cf. TIME-SPACE CONVERGENCE) and the advent of CYBERSPACE are frequently invoked to explain what deterritorialization is held to describe. Such ideas are part and parcel of much discussion of economic GLOBALIZATION. In the second case, territory is perceived as a spatial assemblage of POWER relations and IDENTITY strategies. From this perspective, such ideas as the 'end of territory' and the rise of network space are linked to the recent onset of a worldwide deterritorialization (e.g. Badie, 1995; Hardt and Negri, 2000: cf. NETWORK SOCIETY). Others tend to see deterritorialization in terms of the weakening of territorial identities in the face of globalization (e.g. Mitchell, 2000) or the creation of 'NON-PLACES' (Augé, 1992).

Though frequently used as a stand-alone term, deterritorialization makes most sense when used in the context of territorialization. For example, the 'disappearance' of territory at one SCALE can see its recomposition at others (Brenner, Jessop, Jones and Macleod, 2003). At the same time, deterritorialization undoubtedly has metaphorical currency (see METAPHOR) when applied, for instance, to the fading of intellectual boundaries, and some descriptive utility when used as a synonym for the instability and unravelling of territorial space. Notwithstanding the ambiguities inherent in the terms, in a world in which evidence for both territorialization (e.g. the Israel–Palestine Separation Barrier) and deterritorialization (e.g. the European Union Schengen passport zone) is not hard to come by, their usage suggests a dynamism to the forms of territories and territorialities that some writers have been all too willing to deny.   JAA

Suggested reading
Brenner, Jessop, Jones and Macleod, (2003); Doel (1996).

territory A unit of contiguous space that is used, organized and managed by a social group, individual person or institution to restrict and control access to people and places. Though sometimes the word is used as synonymous with PLACE or SPACE, territory has never been a term as primordial or as generic as they are in the canons of geographical terminology. The dominant usage has always been either political, in the sense of necessarily involving the POWER to limit access to certain places or regions, or ethological, in the sense of the dominance exercised over a space by a given species or an individual organism. Increasingly, territory is coupled with the concept of NETWORK to help understand the complex processes through which space is managed and controlled by powerful organizations. In this light, territory is only one type of SPATIALITY, or way in which space is used, rather than the one monopolizing its employment. From this perspective, TERRITORIALITY is the strategic use of territory to attain organizational goals.

Territory is particularly associated with the spatiality of the modern STATE with its claim to absolute control over a population within carefully defined external BORDERS (Buchanan and Moore, 2003, p. 6). Indeed, until Sack (1986) extended the understanding of human territoriality as a strategy available to individuals and organizations in general, usage of the term 'territory' was largely confined to the spatial organization of states. In the social sciences, such as sociology and political science, this is still mainly the case, such that the challenge posed to territory by NETWORK forms of organization (associated with GLOBALIZATION) is invariably characterized in totalistic terms as 'the end of geography'. This signifies the extent to which territory has become the dominant geographical term (and imagination) in the social sciences (Badie, 1995). It is then closely allied to state sovereignty. As SOVEREIGNTY is seen to 'erode' or 'unbundle,' so goes territory (Agnew, 1994). From this viewpoint, territory takes on an epistemological centrality (see EPISTEMOLOGY) in that it is understood as absolutely fundamental to MODERNITY. As such it can then be given an extended meaning to refer to any socially constructed geographical space, not just that resulting from statehood (Scivoletto, 1983; Bonnemaison, 1996; Storper 1997a). Especially popular with some French-language geographers, this usage often reflects the need to adopt a term to distinguish the particular and the local from the more general global or national 'space'. It then signifies the 'bottom-up' spatial context for IDENTITY and cultural difference (or place) more than the 'top-down' connection between state and territory.

The territorial state is a highly specific historical entity. It first arose in EUROPE in the sixteenth and seventeenth centuries. Since that time, political power has been seen as inherently territorial. Politics take place only within 'the institutions and the spatial envelope of the state as the exclusive governor of a definite territory. We also identify political territory with social space, perceiving countries as "state-societies"'(Hirst, 2005, p. 27). The process of state formation has always had two crucial attributes. One is *exclusivity*. All of the political entities (the Roman Catholic Church, city-states etc.) that could not achieve a reasonable semblance of sovereignty over a contiguous territory have been delegitimized as major political actors. The second is *mutual recognition*. The power of states has rested to a considerable extent on the recognition each state receives from the others by means of non-interference in so-called internal affairs (see SOVEREIGNTY). Together, these attributes have created a world in which there can be no territory without a state. In this way, territory has come to underpin both NATIONALISM and representative DEMOCRACY, both of which depend critically on restricting political membership by HOMELAND and address, respectively.

In political theory, control over a relatively modest territory has long been seen as the primary solution to the 'security dilemma': to offer protection to populations from the threats of anarchy (disorder: cf. ANARCHISM), on the one hand, and hierarchy (distant rule and subordination), on the other. The problem has been to define what is meant by 'modest' size. To Montesquieu (1949 [1748], p. 122), the ENLIGHTENMENT philosopher, different size territories inevitably have different political forms: 'It is, therefore, the natural property of small states to be governed as a republic, of middling ones to be subject to a monarch, and of large empires to be swayed by a despotic prince.' Early modern Europe offered propitious circumstances for the emergence of a fragmented political system primarily because of its topographical divisions. Montesquieu (1949 [1748], pp. 151–62) further notes, however, that popular representation allows for the territorial extension of republican government. The founders of the USA added to this by trying to balance between centralizing certain SECURITY functions, on one side, and retaining local controls over many other functions, on the other (Deudney, 2004). The recent history of the European Union can be thought of in similar terms (Milward, 2005).

Human activities in the world, however, have never conformed entirely to spaces defined by proximity as provided by territory. Indeed, and increasingly, as physical distance proves less of a barrier to movement, spatial interaction between separated nodes across networks is an important mechanism of geographical sorting and differentiation (Durand, Lévy and Retaillé, 1992). Sometimes posed today in terms of a world of FLOWS versus a world of territories, this is better thought of in terms of territories and/or networks of flows rather than one versus the other. Territories and networks exist relationally rather than mutually exclusively. If territorial regulation is all about tying flows to places, territories have never been zero-sum entities in which the sharing of power or the existence of external linkages totally undermines their capacity to regulate. If at one time territorial states did severely limit the local powers of trans-territorial agencies, that this is no longer the case does not signify that the states have lost

all of their powers: 'Territory still matters. States remain the most effective governors of populations. ... The powers to exclude, to tax, and to define political rights are those over which states acquired a monopoly in the seventeenth century. They remain the essentials of state power and explain why state sovereignty survives today and why it is indispensable to the international order' (Hirst, 2005, p. 45). JAA

Suggested reading
Agnew (2005, ch. 3); Anderson (2002); Hirst (2005); Paasi (1996).

terrorism Organized VIOLENCE that deliberately targets civilians and that is intended to sow fear among a population for political purposes. It is a deeply contested term, because many writers restrict the term to non-state actors and exclude the STATE from the (direct) use of such violence; they argue that since the state lays claim to the legitimate use of physical force, then by definition it is incapable of the deliberate targeting of a civilian population, which is an offence under international humanitarian law (see JUST WAR). It then follows that all violent challenges to the authority of the state, including armed resistance to military occupation (see OCCUPATION, MILITARY), risk being identified as terrorism. Against this, others argue more persuasively that states have often used violence to intimidate populations, either their own or those of other countries, through a systematic assault on 'enemy, 'alien', 'dissident' or 'subversive' bodies and their associated places. Indeed, the term originates in the Reign of Terror carried out by the Committee of Public Safety in 1793–4 to purge the revolutionary French republic of its 'internal enemies'. Modern state terror includes both: (i) the exemplary violence of colonial wars and counter-insurgency, Stalin's campaign of terror against dissidents in the 1930s, the German Blitz over London, the HOLOCAUST, the saturation bombing of German cities such as Hamburg and Dresden, and the nuclear bombs dropped on Nagasaki and Hiroshima during the Second World War (Hewitt, 1987: see also ETHNIC CLEANSING; GENOCIDE); and also (ii) more insidious forms of violence that work to extend the envelope of fear within their target populations through arbitrary detention, disappearance and torture (including the campaigns perpetrated by authoritarian regimes in Central and South America in the 1970s and 1980s, often with the support of the USA)

(Hewitt, 2001: see also EXCEPTION, SPACE OF). In addition, and making a distinction between its own actions and those of those states, the USA has identified selected states as 'sponsors' of international terrorism – notably Iran, Syria and North Korea.

In both cases, non-state and state, 'terrorism' functions as what Münkler (2005) calls a 'term of exclusion': its use is intended to exclude specific acts of political violence from the sphere of political legitimacy. It follows that the public attribution of the term depends on the successful mobilization of IMAGINATIVE GEOGRAPHIES that deny legitimacy (even humanity) to those who perpetrate such acts of violence (Coleman, 2004). But terrorism is itself deeply invested in public acknowledgement: it seeks to spread fear among a much wider group than those who are its immediate, physical objects of attack. It is thus a communicative strategy: 'Terrorism is a form of warfare in which combat with weapons functions as a drive wheel for the real combat with images . . . The most important feature of the recent wave of international terrorism is this combination of violence with media presentation' (Münkler, 2005, pp. 111–12; see also RETORT, 2005). Hannah (2006b, p. 627) argues that fear has become such a powerful international weapon in our late-modern world because the threat of indiscriminate, indeterminate violence at once 'acknowledges and feeds off the modern biopolitical responsibility of states' to protect the welfare of their own populations: in short, terrorism is now a biopolitial strategy (see BIOPOLITICS, BIOPOWER).

Compared to mid-twentieth-century terrorism, the terrorist organizations that Münkler, Hannah and others have in mind have been able to launch far more destructive attacks, to act across far greater distances and to make far larger political demands. The 2005 *Human security report* calculated that 'significant' international terrorist attacks increased from seventeen in 1987 to more than 170 in 2003, with a similarly clear, if uneven, upward trend in numbers killed and wounded (but see below). Terrorism continued at other SCALES too, and local and regional terrorist campaigns continued to kill and maim victims around the world: people in AFRICA, ASIA, EUROPE and South America had been living with terrorism long before 11 September 2001, and domestic terrorism in the USA also plainly pre-dates 9/11 (Nunn, 2007). But as in many other fields, the closest analytical engagement of HUMAN GEOGRAPHY with terrorism was prompted by the extraordinary reach of

al-Qaeda's attacks on the World Trade Center and the Pentagon on 9/11, and subsequent attacks by al-Qaeda and its affiliates around the world (see figure). Three geographical responses can be distinguished:

(1) A more or less 'popular' GEOGRAPHICAL IMAGINARY cast those responsible for terrorist attacks outside any space of reason, so that to try to explain their actions was to exonerate them. No cause could justify such violence: the only response to barbarians hammering at the gates of CIVILIZATION was to meet their violence with greater violence. The cry was taken up by others who dismissed any opposition to the enlarged powers of the security state as itself a form of terrorism, and who enlisted the RHETORIC of the 'war on terror' as a means of legitimizing and intensifying the apparatus of repression. At its worst, this slid into an overt RACISM that fanned the flames of hostility to Arabs and Muslims in North America and Europe. This geographical imaginary conjured up a series of 'wild spaces', 'their' spaces where deviant others supposedly scurried away in the interstices and beyond the bounds of 'our' spaces (cf. Coleman, 2004; Gregory, 2004b).

(2) An 'expert' or 'managerial' response drew on geographical technologies (that were also political technologies) to profile, predict and manage the threat of terrorism as an enduring mode of late-modern government heavily invested in logics of SECURITY. The emphasis was on geographies of RISK assessment, on geospatial data management and modelling, and on the vulnerability of biophysical and built environments to terrorist attack (Cutter, Richardson and Wilbanks, 2003; see also Sui, 2008). This geographical imaginary worked to transform 'our' spaces into 'safe spaces': the domain of HOMELAND security (cf. Kaplan, 2003).

(3) A more critical response was to map the connections between 'their' spaces and 'our' spaces, and to unsettle the partitions between them. This involved explorations of the changing political and theological ideologies of terrorist organizations, which often involved locating potential targets within distinctive geographical imaginaries (Hobbs, 2005); analyses of the relations between material conditions, recruitment zones

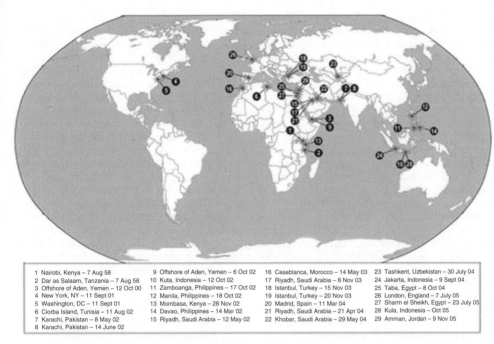

1 Nairobi, Kenya – 7 Aug 58	9 Offshore of Aden, Yemen – 6 Oct 02	16 Casablanca, Morocco – 14 May 03	23 Tashkent, Uzbekistan – 30 July 04
2 Dar as Salaam, Tanzania – 7 Aug 58	10 Kuta, Indonesia – 12 Oct 02	17 Riyadh, Saudi Arabia – 8 Nov 03	24 Jakarta, Indonesia – 9 Sept 04
3 Offshore of Aden, Yemen – 12 Oct 00	11 Zamboanga, Philippines – 17 Oct 02	18 Istanbul, Turkey – 15 Nov 03	25 Taba, Egypt – 8 Oct 04
4 New York, NY – 11 Sept 01	12 Manila, Philippines – 18 Oct 02	19 Istanbul, Turkey – 20 Nov 03	26 London, England – 7 July 05
5 Washington, DC – 11 Sept 01	13 Mombasa, Kenya – 28 Nov 02	20 Madrid, Spain – 11 Mar 04	27 Sharm el Sheikh, Egypt – 23 July 05
6 Ciorba Island, Tunisia – 11 Aug 02	14 Davao, Philippines – 14 Mar 02	21 Riyadh, Saudi Arabia – 21 Apr 04	28 Kula, Indonesia – Oct 05
7 Karachi, Pakistan – 8 May 02	15 Riyadh, Saudi Arabia – 12 May 02	22 Khobar, Saudi Arabia – 29 May 04	29 Amman, Jordan – 9 Nov 05
8 Karachi, Pakistan – 14 June 02			

terrorism *Major terrorist attacks attributed to al-Qaeda and affiliated organizations, 1998–2005* (after Hobbs and Salter, 2006)

and the locations of terrorist attacks (Enders and Sandler, 2006; Simons and Tucker, 2007; Watts, 2007); reconstructions of the fluid and fractured NETWORKS through which regional and transnational terrorist groups are organized (Ettlinger and Bosco, 2004; Hastings, 2008), including investigations of the remittance networks that have been used to scapegoat potential sources of terrorist finance (de Goede, 2003, 2007; Amoore and de Goede, 2008); and examinations of the effects of counter-terrorist strategies on the representation, built form and everyday life of CITIES (Coaffee, 2004; Graham, 2006; Gray and Wyly, 2007; Katz, 2007). These contributions are closely connected – material conditions shape but do not determine terrorist networks, for example, while transactions monitoring infiltrates multiple spheres of everyday life – and intersect with more general critiques of the 'war on terror' and its extensions (e.g. Gregory, 2004b).

The most recent *Human security brief* (2007) argues that the global incidence of terrorism has dramatically declined since 2003. Other reports and databases suggest the opposite,

but the authors of the *Brief* claim that this is in large measure a result of their inconsistent definition of 'terrorism'. While those other surveys count as victims of terrorism large numbers of civilians killed by non-state actors in Iraq's civil war, they exclude large numbers of civilians killed by non-state actors in sub-Saharan Africa's civil wars (so-called 'new WARS'). They trace this back to the US State Department, which identifies 'foreign terrorist organisations' as those that threaten the security of US citizens or the national security of the USA. This dispute focuses attention on the controversy identified in the first paragraph, and on the vexed distinctions between (for example) terrorism and insurgency. These are innately contested terms precisely because they are PERFORMATIVE: naming political violence in these and other ways has acutely real consequences for recruitment and support, legitimation and response.   DG

Suggested reading
Coleman (2004); Flint (2003b); Gregory and Pred (2007).

text The term 'text' is used in HUMAN GEOGRAPHY in both its literal sense and also in a metaphorical sense, but the boundaries between the two usages are far from clear-cut.

749

Like all academic disciplines, human geography involves the interpretation of texts, understood as a corpus of written or printed material: first-order texts such as CENSUS records, diaries and transcriptions (conventionally called 'sources' – but this is misleading, since they are complex transcriptions and codings, whose origins lie elsewhere, and they are as often as not sedimentations of multiple, sometimes contradictory layers of meanings); and second-order texts (articles, monographs, dictionaries) that offer competing interpretations of those interpretations. This may seem commonplace, but it is not: 'reading' and 'writing' are not often included in discussions of METHODOLOGY, yet they are central to the practice of geographical enquiry. They also have their own geographies, and Livingstone (2005a) has argued for an historical geography of textual circulation and interpretation. Influenced by ACTOR-NETWORK THEORY, he describes written texts as 'immutable mobiles', which means that 'knowledge does not move around the world as an immaterial entity'. Livingstone argues that the production and reception of texts are practices that *take place* in material spaces, and that geographers should attend to the geographical conditions of the engagement between texts and readers that transform interpretations and exclude as well as include audiences. In another sense, of course, this makes texts highly *mutable* mobiles: they are constantly subject to new interpretations and produce new effects (Ogborn, 2007).

These ideas have been extended still further to treat all productions of MATERIAL CULTURE as texts, including MAPS and LANDSCAPES. This work has been influenced by POST-STRUCTURALISM and sees cultural productions as unstable practices of meaning-making. Attention is focused on a multiplicity of competing meanings: hence ambiguity, volatility and a politics of interpretation. The core argument is that the principal characteristics of written discourse also describe social life: meaning in written texts is concretized through inscription, so social practices are concretized in the material landscape; as authors' intentions and the reception of texts often fail to coincide, so social practices become detached from the consciousness of agents whose collective actions constitute such practices; written texts are reinterpreted under changing circumstances just as social events are continually reinterpreted; and as the meaning of written texts is unstable and dependent on interpretations of readers, so social action and institutions are open to a multiplicity of interpretations.

Post-structuralism has had a considerable influence on the reading of maps as texts (Harley, 1989; see CARTOGRAPHY, HISTORY OF), but readings of landscape as text have a more complex genealogy (Duncan and Duncan, 1988). Although cultural geographers have long regarded landscapes as palimpsests of culture–nature interactions to be read by specialists, notably themselves, many of those who have adopted the METAPHOR of landscape as text have eschewed the role of the 'expert decoder' in favour of an ostensibly reciprocal approach to landscape interpretation that moves in a HERMENEUTIC circle. A key influence here has been the recovery of multiple layers of meaning through the THICK DESCRIPTION of American anthropologist Clifford Geertz (1926–2006) rather than their destabilization through the DECONSTRUCTION of Derrida. Geertz's hermeneutic–ETHNOGRAPHIC approach to culture as text has guided the recovery of multiple readings proffered not by experts on the history of a generic landscape type but, instead, constructed by people who inhabit a particular landscape and who mobilize different readings as part of a politics that is central to its lively production and transformation (Duncan, 1990). And yet the recovery, reproduction and transmission of those constructions and contestations for a wider public audience is hardly the work of non-experts: not only do 'first-order' and 'second-order' texts bleed into one another, but the composite textualizations provided by Geertz may be read as the articulations of 'an invisible voice of authority who declares what the you-transformed-to-a-they experience' (Crapanzo, 1986, p. 74; see also Gregory, 1994, pp. 147–8).

Many geographers have questioned the usefulness of the text metaphor altogether, arguing that it leads to an over-emphasis on communication, intentionality and the discursive rather than the material or unintended (cf. NON-REPRESENTATIONAL THEORY). Defenders of the metaphor respond by arguing that cultural productions with text-like qualities (such as landscapes) are heterogeneous, material realities that are mutually constitutive with reading practices and interact with other non-human processes. It is also argued that landscapes are normally read inattentively or subconsciously, so that the norms and values that shape the landscape become naturalized and unconsciously absorbed. There are further differences of opinion on the degree of fluidity or stability of cultural practices and productions, and on the extent to which interpretations are constrained by discourses. However, an expansive definition of text need not assume in advance of empirical investigation any particular degree of stability, instability or constraint. Fluidity versus stability is a matter of emphasis, not an either/or question.   JSD/DG

Suggested reading
Barnes and Duncan (1991); Duncan (1990); Ogborn (2007).

textuality In many versions of POST-STRUC-TURALISM, 'textuality' refers to the expansion of the term 'TEXT' to include cultural practices and material productions such as architectural forms and LANDSCAPES that may be read for meaning, connotation and contestation (cf. Barnes and Duncan, 1991; Duncan and Duncan, 1998). Such meanings are regarded as inherently unstable and incessantly recontextualized so that defined in this way textuality *is* indecidability. To investigate the textuality of the world is to investigate the PERFORMATIVITY of DISCOURSE: the ways in which meanings and objects are produced, contested, negotiated and reiterated. To view the world textually is also to see cultural productions as becoming detached from their authors and reinterpreted and recontextualized by interpreters as their relations to those productions change in often complex and unexpected ways. A textual approach thus brings into play indeterminacy, and involves both the denial of an unmediated access to the world and a critical questioning of notions of authenticity and ESSENTIALISM. It focuses attention on the relations between texts and between their multiple contexts of production, reception and reinterpretation: on the play of *intertextuality* through which texts draw on other texts which in turn draw on other texts . . .

Textuality is sometimes seen to be compromised by the danger of *textualism*. This concern has two proximate sources. First, Said's critique of ORIENTALISM has been immensely influential in HUMAN GEOGRAPHY, not least in expanding and 'worlding' texts, and asking what these cultural productions – these 'doings' – *do* in the world. Said uses the term 'textuality' in an opposite way to that described above, however, to disparage an over-emphasis on the mechanics of the text at the expense of the mechanics of the material world outside the text (cf. Smith and Katz, 1993). Second, Derrida's famous remark that 'there is nothing outside the text' has

often been used to accuse him of precisely this sort of textualism. To the contrary, however, Derrida's point was that there can be no pre-discursive, non-contextual and non-intertextual understanding of the world: context is vital to his method of reading texts (see DECONSTRUCTION). Worries about textualism are real enough, and serious questions have been raised in human geography about the limits of the text METAPHOR and the privileges that it smuggles in to critical enquiry through its focus on cognition, meaning and interpretation (see NON-REPRESENTATIONAL THEORY).   JSD

theory The term 'theory' is used in various senses in the HUMANITIES and social sciences. At its broadest, theory can be understood as any set of statements and propositions used in explanation or interpretation. From the perspective of various versions of POSITIVISM, theory is subordinated to the tribunal of empirical validation – theories generate HYPOTHESES that are tested against evidence, with the aim of generating general laws. In this tradition, the value of a theory lies in its predictive ability and explanatory power. In geography, this notion of theory was associated with the QUANTITATIVE REVOLUTION, and was distinguished by the attempt to develop uniquely *geographical theories* as the hallmark of a distinctively SPATIAL SCIENCE. The development of various post-positivist approaches has led to a shift in the meaning of theory in the discipline. These approaches all share the view that there can be no theory-neutral observation, and that the validation of any theoretical proposition is underdetermined by empirical evidence. Rather, theories are viewed as at least partly constitutive of the objects of empirical study (cf. DISCOURSE). This leads towards forms of *grounded theory*, wherein empirical observation, concrete analysis and abstraction are combined in ongoing dialogue with one another (Sayer, 1992 [1984]).

Since the 1980s, there has been a veritable explosion of theory in HUMAN GEOGRAPHY. Graff (1992, p. 53) argues that theory *breaks out* in disciplines when 'what was once silently agreed to in a community becomes disputed, forcing its members to formulate and defend assumptions that they previously did not even have to be aware of'. This idea of theory 'breaking out' is particularly pertinent to the increasing presence of cultural theory in human geography (see CULTURAL TURN). This is both a mark of heightened division within the discipline around methods and objects of research, but also of an opening out to other disciplines. The interdisciplinary or even post-disciplinary nature of the theory circulating through human geography has become incr-easingly evident in the past two decades: if in the 1980s the agenda of MARXIST-inflected human geography focused on the spatialization of SOCIAL THEORY, since the 1990s the heigh-tened GEOGRAPHICAL IMAGINATION of other dis-ciplines has generated original contributions to the theorization of traditional topics such as LANDSCAPE, PLACE, SPACE and SCALE (Gregory, 1994).

This pluralization of the sources of theory has also been associated with increasing attention to the *politics of theory*. From within geography, the growth of post-positivist ap-proaches was closely associated with Harvey's (1973) distinction between revolutionary, counter-revolutionary and status-quo theories. Geographers have also used Habermas' (1987a) analysis of the different forms of human interest sustained by distinct types of theoretical knowledge, with its explicit argu-ment that 'critical theory' best serves the causes of human emancipation (see CRITICAL THEORY). Human geographers' treatment of the relationship between theory and politics has, however, developed beyond this idea that some theories harbour inherent political virtues in themselves, towards a more REFLEX-IVE focus upon the forms of authority embed-ded in the practices of 'doing' theory. Three related issues have attracted attention:

(1) Geographers have been sensitive to the phenomenon of TRAVELLING THEORY. A great deal of theory now circulating in geography has been 'imported' from other disciplines, and this in turn allows geographers to talk across sub-disciplin-ary divisions and out to other scholars. But this raises contentions questions about expertise, competence and the ex-ternal validation of positions staked in-ternally within the discipline. Theory also has a real geography of its own. For example, most theory in the humanities and social sciences is actually produced and published in the USA, and more broadly in 'the West' (Barnett and Low, 1996). Other parts of the world are often not accorded value as sources of theoret-ical insight, being relegated to the status of sites for empirical investigation. This raises the challenge of 'learning from other regions', where this refers to the acknowledgement of versions of theoret-

ical work belonging to traditions beyond the confines of Western Europe and North America (Slater, 1992: see also ETHNOCENTRISM; EUROCENTRISM; SITU-ATED KNOWLEDGE).

(2) Building on this first issue, there is a set of concerns about the types of interper-sonal authority embedded in the preva-lent modes of theoretical commentary in human geography. Theory, and not least cultural theory, is associated with forms of mastery that construct patterns of clos-ure, emulation and influence that belie overt claims to political radicalism (cf. MAS-CULINISM). FEMINIST writers have been particularly creative in developing new *styles* of theoretical writing that challenge these prevalent forms of academic reason-ing (Katz, 1996: see also MINOR THEORY).

(3) In its self-consciously 'critical' forms in particular, theory is often understood as a tool for exposing the contingent, con-structed qualities of phenomena, as an instrument for debunking IDEOLOGIES, mythologies and misrepresentations. In turn, theory is often assumed to be an essential aspect of any practical politics of radical social transformation. This is indicative of a deeply rooted 'scholastic disposition', whereby it is assumed that the detached insights accorded to scep-tical academics provide a privileged entry-point for changing the motivations of ordinary people and the mechanics of worldly processes (Bourdieu, 2000). In response to this sort of scholastic atti-tude, Thrift (1999a, p. 304) recommends what he calls *modest theory*, understood as a 'practical means of going on rather than something concerned with enabling us to see, contemplatively, the sup-posedly true nature of what something is'. NON-REPRESENTATIONAL THEORY is meant to exemplify this notion of modest theoretical practice. However, its charac-teristic modes of presentation reiterate many of the rhetorical devices of distinc-tion and exclusion associated with con-ventional forms of GRAND THEORY.

GEOGRAPHY remains a discipline deeply sus-picious of theory, heavily invested as it is in notions such as 'the field', 'empirical work', 'politics' and 'practice'. These notions are often invoked to sustain their own forms of authority, closure and exclusion. Debates about relevance in the discipline often take the form of arguments that there is *too much* theory in geography, or too much of the *wrong sort* of theory. When faced with such arguments, it is always best to remember a simple dictum: 'Hostility to theory usually means opposition to other people's theories and an oblivion to one's own' (Eagleton 1983, p. viii). CB

Suggested reading
Bourdieu (2000, chs 1 and 2); Gallop (2002); Garber (2001); Hammersley (1995).

thick description A term coined by the philosopher Gilbert Ryle (1971) and introduced into the humanities and social sciences by the anthropologist Clifford Geertz (1973b), 'thick description' refers to rich ethnographic descriptions based on intensive investigations of informants' actions and their interpretations of their own practices placed within their cultural context. It is an intrinsically HERMENEUTIC method that recovers and represents the researcher's interpretation of informants' interpretations.

Thick description is contrasted with 'thin description' based on the tenets of behaviourism, where a detailed description of the informants' contextualized meaning systems is considered unnecessary (cf. BEHAVIOURAL GEOGRAPHY). Thick description is usually produced through grounded, long-term ethnographic research, based on (principally) QUALITATIVE METHODS applied to small-scale settings (see ETHNOGRAPHY), but it has also been used in intimate, archive-based historical research with considerable success (Darnton, 1985). Thick description is not simply about collecting details: it is about uncovering the depth of multiple, intersecting webs of meaning within which individual actors understand their own actions. Geertz conceives of individual behaviour as informed by complex, situated conceptual structures that are culturally and historically produced. As such, behavior is best interrogated contextually to reveal the systematic quality of 'cultural patternings' that are 'extra-personal institutionalized guides for behavior'. These are emphatically not 'essences' of broader cultures studied in a microcosm, the 'Jonesville is America writ small' model that Geertz dismisses as 'palpable nonsense'. An important implication of this cultural patterning is that social life has a public, TEXT-like quality to which all who share in a CULTURE interpret, negotiate and contribute. It then follows that ethnographers and other like-minded scholars must 'read over the shoulder' of those whose culture they study. Cultures as meaning systems intertextually infuse all forms of social

practice, and Geertz also saw cultural texts as literary texts to be looked at critically and not just through. Such a textual orientation (see TEXTUALITY) made him an important early figure in the cultural turn across the social sciences, and in opening up conversations between the social sciences and the HUMANITIES. Geertz's influence spread well beyond anthropology into the work of the New Historicists in literary studies and the work of the New Cultural Historians (see HISTORICISM). In CULTURAL GEOGRAPHY, his writings influenced Duncan's (2004) interpretation of the symbolic/political system of the Kandyan kingdom in Sri Lanka.

Geertz's 'cultural patterning' perspective has been critiqued in anthropology for allowing little space for the inner, private, non-cultural components of the self. Thus while Geertz was instrumental in shifting anthropology from a focus on social structure to the interpretation of meanings, his analysis remains somewhat structural. However, this is not to say his approach is at all REDUCTIONIST or determinist. He rejects tight arguments and conceptualizations 'purified of the material complexity in which they are located'. He sees structures of meaning as historically specific, fluid, fragmentary, negotiated and situational. The researcher's interpretations are interpretations of the interpretations of others and thus are always open to contestation and deeper grounding in ongoing, changing cultural meanings systems. That said, among human geographers the textual conception of culture that underpins Geertz's project has been critiqued by Gregory (1994, pp. 148–8) for its structural stasis and by Rose (2006) for its emphasis on representation, meanings and consciousness (cf. NONREPRESENTATIONAL THEORY). JSD

Suggested reading
Geertz (1973a,b); Rose (2006).

third space A space produced by processes that exceed the forms of knowledge that divide the world into binary oppositions. Bhabha (1990b) argues that third space is a consequence of HYBRIDITY, suggesting that certain forms of post-colonial knowledges challenge the division of the world into 'the WEST and the rest' by producing third spaces in which new IDENTITIES can be enacted (see POST-COLONIALISM). For Bhabha, third space is a position from which it may be possible 'to elude the politics of polarity and emerge as others of ourselves' (1994, p. 39). Some geographers have used the term to displace oppositional categories in geographical analysis, such as the opposition between academic theorizing and political activism (Routledge, 1996b; see also Pile, 1994; and see ACTIVISM). Hyndman (2003) argues that feminist GEO-POLITICS represents a third space in the context of the WAR on TERRORISM, beyond the binaries of either/or, here/there and us/them (see FEMINIST GEOGRAPHIES). Rather than promote an oppositional stance in relation to particular political principles or acts, the third space attempts to map the silences of the dominant geopolitical positions and undo these by invoking multiple SCALES of enquiry and knowledge production.

Third spaces also challenge conventional understandings of the world by reconceptualizing ways of thinking about space. For Soja (1996b), drawing on Lefebvre (1991b), the notion of third space disrupts many of the binaries through which geographers have often conceptualized space itself (see also PRODUCTION OF SPACE). The third space is simultaneously material and symbolic, and also eludes the distinction Soja detects in much Western PHILOSOPHY between dynamic TIME and static SPACE. For Soja (1996b, p. 11), third space is 'simultaneously real and imagined and more'. This 'more' is where Soja locates the critical potential of third space: it is more because it both contains binary ways of thinking about space but also exceeds them with a lived intractability to interpretative schemas that allows for potentially emancipatory practices. However, third spaces are not always emancipatory formations: Gregory (2004b) argues that detention camps such as Camp X-ray at Guantanamo Bay are extraterritorial – liminal places that are within sovereign states yet outside of those states' judicial norms.   PR

Third World   A term first used by French economist Alfred Sauvy in 1952 to locate a group of countries not formally aligned with the USA or the Soviet Union in the COLD WAR, and not always attached to CAPITALISM or SOCIALISM as defining economic models. The first Prime Minister of independent India, Jawaharlal Nehru, was a key figure in both these projects. He played a leading role in the Non-Aligned Movement, whose inaugural meetings were held at Bandung in Indonesia in 1955. He also called for a 'third way' of promoting economic DEVELOPMENT – that of planning under a system of democratic socialism – long before ideas of a Third Way were popularized by US President Bill Clinton and British Prime Minister Tony Blair.

The initial concept of a Third World as a new Third Estate has been consistently reworked since its introduction into public discourse (Mintz, 1976; Pletsch, 1981). Many of its initially positive connotations were diminished in the 1960s. They were replaced by an idea of the Third World that located a group of countries in ASIA, AFRICA and LATIN AMERICA in terms of certain presumed absences. These countries were lacking in INFRASTRUCTURE, lacking in education and healthcare systems, lacking in fiscal resources or foreign exchange, lacking in skills and so on. As such, they needed to be mended, both by their own governments and by donor agencies and military personnel from the First and Second Worlds.

This conception of the Third World has fallen from favour over the past thirty years. Peter Bauer, an economist associated with the counter-revolution in development theory and policy, argued consistently in the 1970s that the giving and receiving of foreign AID invented the Third World. Worse, in his view, it turned the Third World into a supplicant (Bauer, 1974). It deprived African and Asian countries of the motivation to pull their own peoples out of POVERTY by means of MARKET-led ECONOMIC GROWTH. In the 1990s this argument was given fresh legs by Arturo Escobar, one of the leading theorists of POST-DEVELOPMENT. Escobar (1995) argued that the Third World had been invented by American aid programmes and Cold War GEOPOLITICS. It had been infantilized and pathologized by a 'DISCOURSE of development' that 'discovered mass poverty' throughout this apparently uniform geographical and social space. Large parts of it had also been turned into battlegrounds in the struggle between the USA and the Soviet Union (literally so in various proxy WARS).

Escobar recognizes that some Third World countries have turned this form of identification to their own advantage, not least through the politics of Third Worldism. This is a common strategy of SUBALTERN social groups and it found expression in the 1970s in Southern demands for a New International Economic Order. Escobar, however, is more inclined to think outside the confines of the 'Third World/Third Worldism' categories. In his view, it is important to create new spaces for social and economic action in what he calls 'the less economically accomplished countries'. Others have suggested that the Third World should be renamed as the Two-Thirds World, and that it should not be restricted to the ex-colonial world. If poverty is a defining feature of the (Two-)Third(s) – or 'majority' - World, it is to be found in countries across the globe and not just in the global SOUTH.   SCO

Suggested reading
Gilman (2003); Power (2003).

Tiebout model An argument for dividing an area among local government units that compete for land users through the range of 'service-taxation packages' offered (see COMPETITIVE ADVANTAGE). Charles Tiebout (1924–68: see Tiebout, 1956) argued that inability to respond to the diversity of demands for PUBLIC GOODS and SERVICES (and differing willingness to pay for them) generated by a heterogeneous population makes large local governments inefficient. Fragmentation of local government within urban areas is more efficient: each unit tailors the services offered and its taxation demands to a particular population sector and people choose which they prefer (cf. FISCAL MIGRATION). The model assumes full information about the range of 'packages' on offer and no mobility constraints – which considerably limit its empirical applicability. Fragmented local government systems are frequently manipulated by the affluent and powerful to create 'tax havens' from which, however, the less well-off are excluded (cf. ZONING).   RJ

Suggested reading
See http://faculty.washington.edu/krumme/VIP/Tiebout.html and http://www.csiss.org/classics/content/43.

time The concept of time has been relegated to an implied and secondary status in discourses about the PHILOSOPHY of GEOGRAPHY ever since the path-breaking work of Immanuel Kant in the second half of the eighteenth century. Arguing that both time and SPACE are distinct and necessary *a priori* notions, rather than substances, for any understanding of human experience, Kant paved the way for the creation of separate academic disciplines addressing spatial rather than temporal questions in the nineteenth century. Advances in many of the SCIENCES during the twentieth century questioned both the validity and the wisdom of a categorical distinction between space and time, however, notably the work on 'spacetime' by Hermann Minkowski (1864-1909) and Albert Einstein (1879-1955), and on 'lived time' by Jean Piaget (1896-1980), and paved the way for more relativist and

relational accounts. Although in practice the Kantian separation between time and space advocated by Hartshorne (1939) never hindered concrete geographical research (see HISTORICAL GEOGRAPHY), a theoretical attempt to reconcile both was not launched until the 1970s and early 1980s as 'TIME-GEOGRAPHY'. Emanating chiefly from Sweden but gaining wide acceptance especially in Anglophone HUMAN GEOGRAPHY (Carlstein, Parkes and Thrift, 1978), time-geography originated in the work of Torsten Hägerstrand (1970). At its roots is the realization that the spatio-temporal choreography of individual paths through EVERYDAY LIFE is constrained in a variety of forms; their VISUALIZATION becomes a first heuristic step towards dissecting concrete POWER relations operating within society. The broad appeal of time-geography can be measured by its incorporation into the framework of STRUCTURATION THEORY (Pred, 1984).

The interrelationship between space and time can be seen in many cultural practices. It was clearly demonstrated by the establishment of Greenwich Mean Time (GMT) in 1675, which set a marker for many subsequent geographical designations and culminated in the binding arbitration of global time zones in 1884. The fact that such a system, which was both locally and globally applicable, was centrally involved in colonial conquests, the rise of CAPITALISM or in the gendering of social relations, is now well documented (Adam, 2006). Knowing where one was at any one given time was a prerequisite to ordering, hierarchically structuring and eventually commodifying daily routines, flows of goods and capital and something as mundane as travelling from A to B.

The standardization of time is connected with the rise of railroad technologies in the nineteenth century. At the beginning of that century time was still measured locally, and thus more accurately, but by the beginning of the twentieth century most NATIONS had adopted some national time or time zones (although calendars remain mired in cultural traditions to this day). Structurally akin to similar attempts to de-localize or de-nationalize spatial measurements – to wit, the standardization of the metre in 1889 – such developments ultimately paved the way for the all but universal adoption of 'clocked time', which has since held sway over modern experiences, and has perhaps most poignantly been criticized by Charlie Chaplin in his 1936 film *Modern times* (Glennie and Thrift, 2005, 2009: see also MODERNITY). However, GLOBALIZATION, and the changing geographies brought about by the spread of the Internet, have both altered the geographical experience of time and arguably led to new geographical realities. To some extent irrespective of geographical location, the experience of simultaneity may be shared by people living in most 'core' urban areas of the world – and is used by stock market traders on a 24/7 basis to further their economic gains.   US

Suggested reading
Adam (2006); May and Thrift (2001).

time-geography An approach to HUMAN GEOGRAPHY treating TIME and SPACE as RESOURCES directly involved in the constitution of social life. It was developed by the Swedish geographer Torsten Hägerstrand and his associates at the University of Lund during the 1960s and 1970s (Hägerstrand and Lenntorp, 1974). Time-geography is not supposed to be a theory, but rather an ONTOLOGICAL contribution focusing on how different phenomena are mutually modified because they coexist in time and space. As such, Hägerstrand attributed a certain NATURALISM to the approach, characterizing it as a 'topoecology' designated to grasp a society–nature–technology constellation. He acknowledged an affinity with PHENOMENOLOGY but still argued for a physical approach to the social world (Hägerstrand, 1982).

Time-geography was developed in relation to empirical work and an intensive involvement in Swedish planning. Its basic element is connections between continuous trajectories of individual entities in time–space. From these, descriptive concepts were developed, such as *paths, stations, projects, prisms, time–space bundles* and *time–space domains*. They constitute a world view on the human condition stating that everybody is subject to confinement in time–space within the limits formed by the bounded capacity of individuals to engage in more than one task at a time, by the speeds at which it is possible to move and assemble individuals, tools and materials, and by regulations of access and modes of conduct within domains of local order. Most well-known is the translation of this view into a non-linguistic notation system representing *possible* configurations in time–space (see figure). It proved a useful tool in planning and was heavily used also in early FEMINIST GEOGRAPHIES of time–space constraints in women's everyday life.

While time-geography's representational potential is widely acknowledged, its metaphysical basis has been severely criticised. Two streams

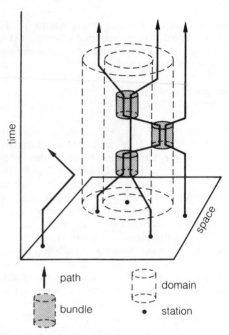

time-geography   *Hägerstrand's web model*

of criticism have prevailed. One points to a problematic relationship to SOCIAL THEORY, and especially how the naturalism or 'physicalism' of the approach leads to a defective conception of human thought-and-action and erodes the possibility of developing a social understanding of time–space (Gregory, 1985). The other line of criticism charges time-geography with MASCULINISM (Rose, 1993). It regards time-geography as a visual strategy that renders space objective and transparent (see VISION AND VISUALITY). Furthermore, the moving bodies of time-geography are seen as 'imaginary bodies'; 'universal' and deprived of social and cultural markings of 'RACE', GENDER and SEXUALITY.

Some geographers have sought to develop more socialized versions of time-geography. In the 1980s, these attempts often relied upon a convergence with STRUCTURATION THEORY. Perhaps the most prominent of these attempts came from Allan Pred (e.g. 1986), who studied agrarian and urban change in nineteenth-century Sweden as an interaction between social restructuring, everyday routines and the production of meaning. Since the 1980s interest in time-geography has been renewed on two levels. First, its descriptive capacity has been developed through GIS-based technologies and 3-D VISUALIZATIONS of human activity patterns. Second, Hägerstrand's emphasis on encountering, events

and human/non-human connectivity resonates with new ontologies with a naturalist
twist, such as ACTOR-NETWORK THEORY and
NON-REPRESENTATIONAL THEORY.   KS

Suggested reading
Dyck (1990); Hägerstrand (1985).

time–space compression An increase in the
speed of social life and a diminution in the
constraining effects of distance on human activities. Processes of this kind have a long and
varied history, but when David Harvey
(1989b) first proposed the term, his primary
purpose was to designate the product of what
Marx saw as the compulsion to 'annihilate
space by time' under CAPITALISM. Marx famously described capitalist MODERNITY as a
world in which 'all that is solid melts into
air', but Harvey showed how this extraordinary volatility – the accelerating rhythm of social change – is connected through the restless
expansion of capital ACCUMULATION to far-
reaching transformations in the structures of
an increasingly global SPACE-ECONOMY.
Harvey explained that he deliberately used
the word 'compression' because 'a strong
case can be made that the history of capitalism
has been characterized by speed-up in the
pace of life, while so overcoming barriers that
the world sometimes seems to collapse in
upon us'. These are 'processes that so revolutionize the objective qualities of space and
time that we are forced to alter, sometimes in
quite radical ways, how we represent the world
to ourselves'. Harvey thus intended the concept to have an *experiential* dimension that is
missing from related concepts such as TIME–
SPACE CONVERGENCE and TIME–SPACE DISTAN-
CIATION. He paid particular attention to the
ways in which time–space compression dis-
locates the modern *HABITUS* that gives social
life its precarious coherence: implicated in a
crisis of representation ('how we represent the
world to ourselves'), the consequences of
time–space compression are supposed to be
disturbing, even threatening; time–space compression is a 'maelstrom' and a 'tiger' that
induces 'foreboding', 'shock', a 'sense of collapse' and even 'terror' that, at the limit, translates into a 'crisis of IDENTITY' (Harvey,
1989b, 1990, 1996).

Harvey was radicalizing an argument proposed by the conservative critic Daniel Bell in
The cultural contradictions of capitalism (1978).
In Bell's view, 'physical distance' was 'compressed' by new systems of transportation and
communication at the turn of the nineteenth

and twentieth centuries, and what he called 'aesthetic distance' was in its turn compressed by a
corresponding stress on 'immediacy, impact,
sensation and simultaneity' that was characteristic of the cultural formations of MODERNISM.
Harvey took this account further by:

- wiring cultural crises of REPRESENTATION to
  basal crises of capital ACCUMULATION (see
  CRISIS); and
- reading the cultural formations of POST-
  MODERNISM as symptoms of the heightened
  intensity of a new round of time–space
  compression produced by a regime of
  FLEXIBLE ACCUMULATION at the close of
  the twentieth century (see Gregory, 1994,
  pp. 406–14).

Harvey's theses have been subjected to both
critique and development:

(1) Some FEMINIST geographers have been
    sceptical of Harvey's view of time–space
    compression as threatening, and seen his
    'cartographic anxiety' as symptomatic of a
    challenge to the confident MASCULINISM of
    mainstream theorizing (Deutsche, 1996a)
    (cf. CARTOGRAPHIC REASON). This has fed in
    to a recognition of the multiple registers
    through which time–space compression is
    socially differentiated, and Massey (1993)
    proposed a comprehensive grid of agency
    and AFFECT, position and power that she
    called the 'POWER-GEOMETRY of time–
    space compression' (cf. Bridge, 1997).
(2) These objections intersected with alter-
    native theorizations of PLACE. Some
    critics complained that the containing
    METAPHOR of time–space compression
    represented place as a bounded site
    whose 'essential identity' is hollowed
    out by the powerful forces of capitalist
    GLOBALIZATION. To Gibson-Graham
    (2006a [1996]), this scenario enacts a
    'rape- script' that 'normalizes an act of
    non-reciprocal penetration': all non-
    capitalist forms are construed as 'sites of
    potential invasion, envelopment, accumu-
    lation', victims awaiting their violation. This
    evidently militates against the very politics
    that Harvey is concerned to advance
    (but cf. Harvey, 1996, pp. 291–326).
    Others argued that the original meta-
    phor distracted attention from the pro-
    duction of more open, so-called 'global'
    conceptions of place in which the intim-
    ate and the impersonal, the virtual and
    the corporeal, the near and the far are

reassembled in new constellations. In a parallel series of essays that centred on the technical transformations in the circulation of MONEY that lie at the heart of Harvey's theses, for example, Thrift (1997a) showed that 'new forms of electronic detachment have produced new forms of social involvement': that contemporary processes of time–space compression still depend on the intimacy of interpersonal contact.

(3) These contributions emphasize that time–space compression is *spatially differentiated*. Harvey's original account of 'the shrinking world' focused on the global NORTH and was insensitive to the multiple and compound geographies of time–space compression, but since then he has provided more nuanced discussions that pay closer attention to the global SOUTH and to the politico-military carapace of contemporary *accumulation by dispossession* (Harvey, 2003b, 2005; cf. Agnew, 2001; see PRIMITIVE ACCUMULATION). Harvey continues to emphasize the POLITICAL ECONOMY of time–space compression, and while it is not necessary to accept Massey's (1993, p. 60) characterization of this as an 'economism', time–space compression does have other vital dimensions that are connected but cannot be reduced to the logics of capital. Late-modern WAR emphasizes the enhanced power of military VIOLENCE over time and space, for example, and the formation of transnational public spheres reveals the importance of global FLOWS of images and information to the formation of NETWORK SOCIETIES. All of these dimensions have their own hierarchies, margins and exclusions – hence the crucial importance of POSITIONALITY (Sheppard, 2002) – and these variable topologies imply that time–space compression operates alongside processes of TIME–SPACE EXPANSION.   DG

Suggested reading
Agnew (2001); Harvey (1989b, chs 15–17).

time–space convergence A decrease in the FRICTION OF DISTANCE between places. As this definition suggests, the concept originated within SPATIAL SCIENCE, where it was first formulated by Douglas Janelle (1968). He defined the *convergence rate* between two

locations as the average rate at which the time needed to travel between them decreases over time: the measure was supposed to be 'mathematically analogous to velocity as defined by the physicist'.

Janelle (1969) attributed time–space convergence to technical change: 'as a result of transport INNOVATION, places approach each other in time–space'. Janelle showed that time–space convergence is usually discontinuous in time – convergence curves are typically jagged, corresponding to pulses of technical innovation – and uneven over SPACE: 'Any transport improvement will tend to be of greatest advantage to the highest-ordered centre that it connects' (Janelle, 1968). Forer (1974) noted that the converse is also true – that time–space convergence is partly a function of the hierarchical structure of the settlement system – so that Janelle's model of 'spatial reorganization' entailed a double movement in which 'places define spaces' and spaces in turn progressively 'redefine' places.

Other geographers distinguished *distance-convergence* from *cost-convergence* and identified a pervasive tendency for the friction of distance to decrease under the sign of MODERNITY. Since the friction of distance is a fundamental postulate of classical CENTRAL PLACE THEORY, DIFFUSION THEORY and LOCATION THEORY – it is, after all, what makes the identification of spatial patterns possible – time–space convergence was supposed to 'scramble' and 'play havoc' with these standard geometric MODELS (Falk and Abler, 1980). Time–space convergence was thus linked to a concept of *plastic space*: 'a space defined by separation in time or cost terms, a space which the progressions and regressions of technology make one of continuous flux' (Forer, 1978).

These were simple but suggestive ideas, yet Forer (1978) suggested that most contemporary geographers had paid little attention to them because they addressed 'the larger canvas of economic history and the long-term development of society'. Ironically, however, it was precisely those links that turned out to be most important. Pred (1973) had already provided an imaginative reconstruction of the changing time-lags within the circulation of public information through major newspapers published on the eastern seaboard of the USA between 1790 and 1840. Although his studies mapped the geography of time–space convergence and its hierarchical structure, and made explicit reference to Janelle's contributions, Pred was more interested in the

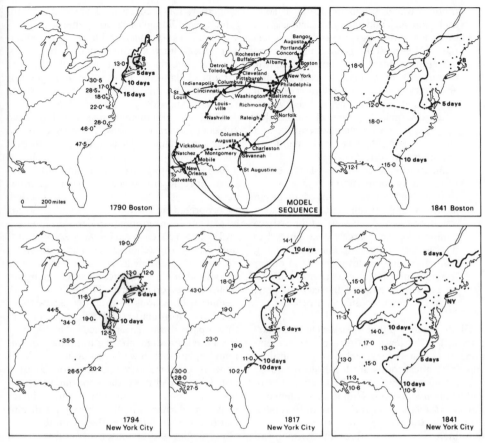

1790 Boston

MODEL SEQUENCE

1841 Boston

1794 New York City

1817 New York City

1841 New York City

time–space convergence

politico-economic and cultural implications of time–space convergence than in the geometric structures that preoccupied the original architects of the concept. For much the same reason, calibrations of time–space convergence are now more likely to be situated within the conceptual field of TIME-SPACE COMPRESSION that directly addresses such concerns.   DG

Suggested reading
Brunn and Leinbach (1991); Janelle (1969).

time–space distanciation   A term proposed by British sociologist Anthony Giddens to describe the 'stretching' of social systems across time and space. The concept played a central role in his critique of modern SOCIAL THEORY and the development of his rival STRUCTURATION THEORY. Giddens argued that conventional social theory was strongly influenced by forms of FUNCTIONALISM, which assumed that societies are coherent and bounded

SYSTEMS, and by models of social change that presumed that the basic structural dimensions of societies are internal to those systems. Time–space distanciation was intended to confound both claims: 'The nexus of relations – political, economic or military – in which a SOCIETY exists with others is usually integral to the very nature of that society' and, indeed, 'to what "societies" are conceived to be' (Giddens, 1981). Today this is a commonplace in most of HUMAN GEOGRAPHY, though it has been developed in ways that have moved far from Giddens' own formulations, but there are nonetheless affinities between time–space distanciation and concepts of TIME-SPACE COMPRESSION and TIME-SPACE CONVERGENCE. There are also two significant differences.

(1)   'Time–space distanciation' draws attention to the capacity for social life to extend over TIME as well as space in ways that are not limited to the contemplation of a

759

modern world in which 'all that is solid melts into air', and where a dizzying spiral of accelerating change sustains the 'vertigo of the modern' as a cultural dominant. For Giddens also emphasized the importance of archives, record-keeping and SURVEILLANCE to the conduct of social life, so that (in principle, at least) time–space distanciation connects more directly the roles of GOVERNMENTALITY and MEMORY in late MODERNITY than either of the other two concepts.

(2) Giddens offered an outline sketch of the historical trajectory of time–space distanciation that was also intended to be an analytical map of different types of society. In contrast, discussions of time–space compression have largely been limited to its role within contemporary CAPITALISM, while time–space convergence is a purely formal concept concerned with calibrating convergence rather than examining its constitution within different societies.

Giddens claimed that *tribal societies* are characterized by low levels of time–space distanciation – the capacity for social memory is limited and most interactions are localized – and by little substantive distinction between 'political' and 'economic' power. With the emergence of *class-divided societies* such as those of European FEUDALISM, the level of time–space distanciation increases, largely through the political powers extended to and through the STATE. The transition to the *class societies* of CAPITALISM is achieved through the greater prominence of economic power, especially through INDUSTRIALIZATION, and is marked by much higher levels of time–space distanciation. In his early texts, Giddens (1984, 1985) emphasized the mobilization of systems of writing, recording and surveillance (modalities of 'political power') and systems of monetization and commodification (modalities of 'economic power'), but in his later texts he became much more interested in the constitution of contemporary or 'high' MODERNITY. There, Giddens (1990, 1991) distinguished between:

- expert systems, which 'bracket time and space through deploying modes of technical knowledge which have validity independent of the practitioners and clients who make use of them'; and
- symbolic tokens, which are 'media of exchange which have standard value and thus are interchangeable across a plurality of contexts'.

Together, these constituted abstract systems which, so Giddens argued, penetrate all aspects of EVERYDAY LIFE and in so doing undermine local practices and LOCAL KNOWLEDGES; they dissolve the ties that once held the conditions of daily life in PLACE and recombine them across much larger expanses of SPACE (cf. GLOBALIZATION).

Giddens' argumentation-sketch has been subject to several criticisms. The most common objection is that it lacks sufficient historical and geographical specificity (cf. Harris, 1991). In treating space as a gap to be overcome, it represents space as a barrier to interaction – as a void to be transcended, incorporated and subjugated – and in doing so activates conventional conceptions of PLACE and SPACE (cf. CONTRAPUNTAL GEOGRAPHIES) and repeats the characteristic movement of Western master-narratives more generally to recover what eludes them as lacunae, margins, 'blank spaces' on the map. This intersects with sustained objections to the EUROCENTRISM of Giddens' formulations. The trajectory of time–space distanciation traces a move away from the immediate and the intimate, but this is an implausible view of non-modern societies and, as Giddens subsequently conceded, it also fails to recognize the continued importance of face-to-face interaction and intimacy in late modernity. Finally, time–space distanciation, like structuration theory more generally, privileges modalities of political and economic power and fails to explore the significance of the *cultural* formations that have been centrally involved in processes of globalization and the constitution of modernity. DG

Suggested reading
Giddens (1984, chs 4 and 5); Harris (1991).

time–space expansion A concept proposed as (1) the corollary and (2) the dual of TIME–SPACE COMPRESSION.

(1) Dodgshon (1998) proposed time–space expansion as the *corollary* of time–space compression. The modern world may be one of intensifying change and volatility, as Harvey's (1989b) original account of time–space compression suggests, but this entails more than an emphasis on the transient, the fleeting, the 'now': for the modern science that powers many of those transformations has also produced a heightened awareness of the immensity of time and of human history. For the privileged, the modern world may be

increasingly frictionless, even 'flat' as global travel and communication increases, but in consequence 'what was once thought to be an experience of the geographical world in its totality has been re-proportioned into what is simply local'. In sum, Dodgshon (1998, p. 117) insists, time–space compression means that 'culturally, we are now more aware of TIME and SPACE as dimensions that have extension'.

(2) In contrast, other writers treat time–space expansion as the *dual* of time–space compression. They recognize that POWER-GEOMETRY is highly variable, and in particular that the power to compress distance is also often the power to expand distance. The unidirectional logic of time–space compression requires distance to contract under the spasmodic compulsions of global CAPITALISM to reduce circulation time, but images of 'the shrinking world' have become so powerful and pervasive that they can obscure the ways in which, for millions of people, the imperatives of GLOBALIZATION can force their world to expand in ways that threaten to become unbearable. Katz (2001a) draws on her experience in 'Howa', a village in Sudan, to argue that:

From the vantage point of capital, the world may be shrinking but, on the marooned grounds of Howa, it appeared to be getting bigger every day. After a gruelling decade and a half of STRUCTURAL ADJUSTMENTS and political upheaval in Sudan, people in Howa survived by maintaining a semblance of the patterns and practices of production that had long sustained them . . . But this was only viable now if carried out over an extended physical arena. The terrain of social production and reproduction had expanded from perhaps five kilometres in 1980 to two hundred kilometres by 1995, the distance men routinely travelled to participate in the charcoal trade. Time–space expansion also represented a transformation of the old constellation of activities that involved men's long absences from the village. People still farmed (but also worked as agricultural laborers up to a hundred kilometres away), kept ANIMALS (by sending them out with relatives to distant pastures) and cut wood (but now in areas of the South targeted for deforestation as part of the northern government's WAR effort). (Katz, 2001, p. 1224)

For Katz, therefore, 'time–space expansion embraces, reworks and plays into the altered geographies of GLOBALIZATION'. Contemporary capitalism involves dialectical torsions of time–space compression and time–space expansion (see DIALECTIC) that produce spirals of advantage and marginalization: 'If in one way the known world expanded for people in Howa, in others their place in it receded as their village was increasingly marginalized' (p. 1225).

Time–space expansion happens not only within a relative space punctuated by the differential geographies of time–space compression, however, but also through the proliferating partitions of an intrinsically colonial MODERNITY. 'If global capitalism is aggressively *de-territorializing*, moving ever outwards in a process of ceaseless expansion and furiously tearing down barriers to capital accumulation, then colonial modernity is intrinsically *territorializing*, forever installing partitions between "us" and "them"' (Gregory, 2004a, p. 253). Those who live under military occupation (see OCCUPATION, MILITARY) know this very well, as they are caught in curfews or lockdowns and wait in line at checkpoints: TIME seems to stop, punctuated by one emergency after another, and the ordinary paths of EVERYDAY LIFE are blocked or redirected. In occupied Palestine, for example, 'as the illegal settlements are wired ever more tightly into Israel, Palestinians are made to undergo an intensified spasm of time-space expansion: families, friends and neighbours cut off from one another; farmers separated from their fields and their wells' (Gregory, 2004c, p. 604). Those who try to flee the politico-economic deformations described by Katz and the politico-military oppressions described by Gregory are peculiarly vulnerable to the despair of time–space expansion. 'The globe shrinks for those who own it,' Bhabha (1992, p. 88) remarks, but 'for the displaced or the dispossessed, the migrant or refugee, no distance is more awesome than the few feet across borders or frontiers' (cf. Hyndman, 1997: see also MIGRATION; REFUGEE). DG

topographic map A large- or intermediate-scale MAP describing the most important physical and cultural features of a PLACE or REGION. Largely a product of national or provincial governments, topographic maps support national defence, economic development, environmental science and growth management as well as providing data for compiling less detailed, smaller-scale maps. Typically compiled from aerial photography, they use contour lines (see ISOLINE) to describe the land surface and abstract symbols to represent roads, railways, political boundaries and hydrographic features such as rivers, streams and lakes (Collier, Forrest and Pearson, 2003). Toponyms (PLACE NAMES and feature names) reflect local usage as well as government efforts to standardize spelling and nomenclature (Monmonier, 2006).   MM

Suggested reading
Forrest and Kinninment (2001).

topography The detailed study and description of a PLACE as much as to the materiality of its features or landforms more generally. In recent years, topography has been mobilized as a research method, 'to carry out a detailed examination of some part of the material world, defined at any SCALE from the BODY to the GLOBE, in order to understand its salient features and their mutual and broader relationships' (Katz, 2001, p. 1228). In this sense, it has been used in CRITICAL HUMAN GEOGRAPHY to delineate the social production of localities as much as the knowledge about them, understanding both to be the contested outcomes of particular interests and actors. The intent is to discern the sedimented process of place-formation from the LOCALITY itself and in so doing, situate 'places in their broader context and in relation to other areas and geographic scales', thereby offering a means of understanding structure and PROCESS simultaneously (Katz, 2001, p. 1228). Just as TOPOGRAPHIC MAPS connect sites of equal elevation through contour lines, so too can particular relationships across localities be revealed and examined using topography. That is, the trace or effects of particular processes on various places can be demonstrated through this methodology to suggest their translocal bearing. This understanding led to the notion of 'counter-topographies', which are seen as a way to theorize the connectedness of disparate places by virtue of their relationship to a particular political–economic or social process, such as democratic inclusion, PRIVATIZATION or GENTRIFICATION. Focusing on the de-skilling of young people, for instance, Katz (2001a) produced a counter-topography linking New York City and rural Sudan. The connections drawn are analytical rather than homogenizations.

Counter-topographies are concrete ABSTRACTIONS that offer a means of recognizing the historical and geographical specificities of particular places while also enabling the inference of their connections in relation to specific material social practices. The intent in linking

different places analytically is to produce an alternative geographical and political imagination that might work translocally in the name of common interests (cf. Pratt, 2004; also CONTRAPUNTAL GEOGRAPHIES). The GEOGRAPHICAL IMAGINATION associated with topography as a method and the political possibilities of counter-topographies as concrete abstractions have been best realized by FEMINIST GEOGRAPHERS. Looking at political transformation in Mexico, Lise Nelson (2004) drew out a topographical analysis to examine the historical experiences of rural women engaging in regional and even national commerce, and the ways in which their engagements led to reconfigurations of their subjectivities along with the contours of their political practices. Her work demonstrates how 'the shifting norms and practices of GENDER and CITIZENSHIP' in a single place both propel and are propelled by changing local–global dynamics. Telling far 'more than a "local" story', the renegotiations of SUBJECTIVITY reveal as they alter the social relations of POWER and DIFFERENCE across scale (Nelson, 2004, pp. 180–2). Pratt and Yeoh (2003) use topography as a means of examining TRANSNATIONALISM with greater specificity and attentiveness to difference. Revealing the 'multistranded connections transnational subjects make' as they move across SPACE and scale, they develop the notion of 'comparative transnationalisms', and theorize their diverse but interconnected manifestations on the ground (Pratt and Yeoh, 2003, p. 164).   CK

Suggested reading
Katz (2001); Nagar and Swarr (2005).

topology A field of mathematics studying the spatial properties of an object or network that remain true when that object is stretched. These include connectivity and adjacency. Imagine stretching a rubber band between two fingers. Likening the band to a VECTOR line segment, then the start node (the one end) remains connected to the other despite the stretching. Treating the band as a polygon, the one side remains to the left of the other throughout. Topological encoding is useful in GIS for error trapping and spatial queries. NETWORKS may be represented as graphs and analysed using GRAPH THEORY.   RH

Suggested reading
Wise (2002).

topophilia A term coined by geographer Yi-Fu Tuan (1974, p. 4) to describe the 'human love of place' (see PLACE) or 'the affective bond between people and place' (cf. AFFECT). Tuan argued that this bond varies in intensity among individuals and in its cultural expression, and suggested that such attachment can be based on aesthetic appreciation, MEMORY, pride of ownership or dependence on a place for one's livelihood or security. Topophilia is not only a response *to* place, Tuan insisted, but also actively produces places for people. Its converse, *topocide*, was proposed by Porteous (1998) to describe the annihilation of those bonds and the places to which they are attached (cf. URBICIDE). Topophilia is closely associated with the HUMANISTIC GEOGRAPHY of the 1970s. JSD

tourism Tourism has been defined as 'the activities of persons traveling to and staying in places outside of their usual environment for not more than one consecutive year for leisure, business and other purposes' (UN World Tourism Organization, 1994). This relational definition positions tourism as contrasted to other travel and leisure practices. Thus travel for pleasure without staying tends to be defined as LEISURE, whilst organized activities for pleasure at home tend to be called RECREATION. Travel without return is MIGRATION, whilst temporary travel leading to residence for work over a year is to be a sojourner. The utility of this definition is enabling the counting and mapping of tourist FLOWS – arrivals, stays and departures. However, this a very limited approach to tourism. First, as a typology of travel it tidies away a wealth of practices that elide the differences of these categories. Second, there are distinctions among tourists. Third, it fails to capture the dynamic of the relationship of tourists to the people and places that they visit.

The first problem is that the practices and organization of tourism exceed its categories. It may be the largest industry on the planet, but it is a very diffuse industry. Thus tourist attractions may also serve local populations – facilities that serve tourist needs (such as restaurants or hotels) may serve local needs as well. Amidst what tourists do, there are a wealth of different interests and activities. Thus much tourist time may well be pursuing 'normal' activities (such as child care, cleaning or cooking). Equally, the edges of what is tourism are very fuzzy, so that local people might approach their local environment for pleasure like a tourist. Meanwhile, tourism has been said to develop from, and as a secular form of, pilgrimage, leaving questions over whether we

would count these spiritual practices as 'tourism' or whether we would deny any spiritual dimensions to any forms of tourism.

The second problem is that the general definition obscures differing types of tourism. One recurrent response has been to produce typologies of tourists usually defined by their motivation for travel. Popular distinctions among tourists often start by dividing them in terms of a hierarchy of serious mindedness, where the explorer charts the unknown (see EXPLORATION) and the traveller seeks to encounter difference, whilst the tourist follows the beaten track. The distinctions between these cultures of travel are social ones that are about status and cultural values.

John Urry (2002) suggests contrasting romantic and collective cultures of tourism. The latter is that which celebrates togetherness in visiting, which focuses on enjoyment and activities amongst and between visitors rather than between visitors and the environment. The former is that of the traveller, who seeks an individual encounter with the place visited – with direct contact with the locale and perhaps locals. It defines itself in opposition to the collective gaze – and in doing so sows the seeds of its own self-destruction. For once a site is found and becomes popular, is laid out in guidebooks, and develops kiosks or stalls, then it loses its appeal. The result is an expanding structure, always looking over the next hill or to the next island for the 'untouched' valley, 'pristine' beach or 'authentic' locals. This lays out tourism as what MacCannell, in his influential 1976 book *The tourist*, saw as a quest to encounter the authentically different OTHER. However, Urry's division makes clear that this is only one set of desires or motivations for tourism. He himself favours a definition that frames tourism in terms of a time and place out of the ordinary.

The notion of an 'extraordinary' time and place has been used to unpack the third issue of the dynamic of tourists and the places that they visit. Tourism as a secular kind of pilgrimage might be seen as a material semiotic process that 'sacralizes' places. In this process, various signifiers mark out sites as noteworthy to the 'tourist gaze' (Urry, 1990). These signifiers can be guidebooks, postcards, travel books, brochures, adverts and the like. These help script notions of the destination and can be seen as 'linguistic agents of touristic social control' (Dann, 1999, p. 163). Guidebooks do not just describe places, but set normative agendas of what *ought* to be seen. They emphasize, construct and delimit a geography of significant sites. Visiting these places may be part of accumulating CULTURAL CAPITAL.

The scripting may also rework the histories and geographies of places. As Jane Desmond notes, 'tourism is not just an aggregate of merely commercial activities; it is also an ideological framing of history, nature and tradition; a framing that has the power to reshape culture and nature to its own needs' (1999, p. xii). With deliberate hyperbole, the architects MVRDV speak of a Norway turned from a forest to a supervillage, the Alps becoming a park with hotel cities, France changing into a ' "Guide du Routard" landscape, in which the agricultural products became the instrument for a gastronomically oriented zone penetrated by hotels and restaurants according to special nostalgic rules' and Tuscany as an 'international villa park', where 'gigantic private gardens are maintained by the former farmers' (MVRDV, 2000, p. 57). Meanwhile, other areas become associated with 'ludic' activities – spaces where play is not only allowed but, in many cases, demanded. Tourism there forms a 'territorialized hedonism' (Löfgren, 1999, p. 269). We might think of these as liminal zones with social rituals where normal rules of conduct are suspended, in times and spaces apart from the everyday (Shields, 1991).

Critical accounts point out that touristic meanings for places can clash with or replace local ones – thus eroding an original SENSE OF PLACE and reducing it to SIMULACRUM or PLACELESSNESS. This 'erosion thesis' that sees change as diminishing original cultures and reducing global differences (Hannerz, 1996) risks presupposing a 'coercive conceptual schema' of tourism 'impacting' on local cultures seen as pitted against a global industry and cultural changes arising from tourism resulting from 'the intrusion of a superior sociocultural system in a supposedly weaker receiving milieu' (Picard, 1996, pp. 104, 110). It also echoes a tendency in academic work to denigrate tourists almost as another species – which Löfgren parodies as 'turistas vulgaris' (1999, p. 264) – who travel in 'herds', 'stampede' on to beaches, 'flock' to see places and 'swarm' around 'honey-pots'. MC

Suggested reading
Cartier and Lew (2005); Crang and Coleman (2002); Lew, Hall and Williams (2004); Löfgren (1999); Minca and Oakes (2006); Urry (2002).

town A general name for an urban place but, like both a CITY and a village, with no generally accepted criteria on which to distinguish such a settlement. Such definitional problems constrain both historical analyses (e.g. URBAN ORIGINS) and planning for urban futures. RJ

townscape The observable units of urban form that can be mapped and classified. Early work in URBAN GEOGRAPHY focused on MORPHOLOGY – the patterns of LAND USE and built form (such as street layouts and building heights), and the processes underpinning their evolution – with little reference to their visual appearance in the LANDSCAPE. A rigorous approach was developed by M.R.G. Conzen (1907–2000: see Conzen, 1969), who identified three main townscape elements: the town plan (within which the other two were largely constrained), the land-use units and the built form. His pioneer work has been developed into studies of not only the patterns of urban morphology but also of the agents who shape and re-shape it, including pioneer studies by Whitehand, Larkham and others in the University of Birmingham's Urban Morphology Research Group: the International Seminar on Urban Form launched the journal *Urban Morphology* in 1997. RJ

Suggested reading
Whitehand (1992). See also http://faculty.washington.edu/krumme/VIP/Tiebout.html

trade Under normal capitalist conditions, the transportation and exchange of COMMODITIES for money. As such, trade provides a vital link between production and consumption in capitalist COMMODITY CHAINS. It is through trade that commodities reach their markets, and it is only when commodities are sold into MARKETS that the value produced by the exploitation of workers is abstracted out and represented in the exchange values or prices generated by market trading (Harvey, 1999 [1982]). For these reasons, trade derives both its immense significance and considerable contemporary contentiousness from the ways in which it is interwoven with the wider political–economic organization of CAPITALISM.

When it occurs across national BORDERS, trade serves to create international economic ties. As a result, international trade statistics provide some of the best data available about the actual economic interdependencies underpinning GLOBALIZATION. Trade data showing global increases in international trade outstripping growth in overall global GDP provide a useful indication of the degree to which contemporary forms of capitalist development are characterized by increasingly cross-border FLOWS (Dicken, 2003). Roughly 40 per cent of international trade is actually *intra-corporate trade* – that is, border-crossing trade that nevertheless remains within the internal commodity chains of a particular TNC (Gabel and Bruner, 2003) – revealing the corporate control of these flows within the networks of global corporations (see TRANSNATIONAL CORPORATIONS (TNCS)). Meanwhile, maps of import–export data (see figure) exhibit the uneven economic integration and triadic

geographical structure of these economic FLOWS, in which over 80 per cent of trade takes place between Europe, North America and Asia. Yet while trade data can help us better map global capitalism's UNEVEN DEVELOPMENT, the contentious debates over today's TERMS OF TRADE also need to be understood in relation to the profoundly politicized DISCOURSES surrounding the asymmetries and inequities of trade-mediated interdependencies.

Many free market fundamentalists insist that trade is always good without ever pausing to consider such basic questions as: The trade of what? For whom? And under what contextual conditions? The transatlantic slave trade

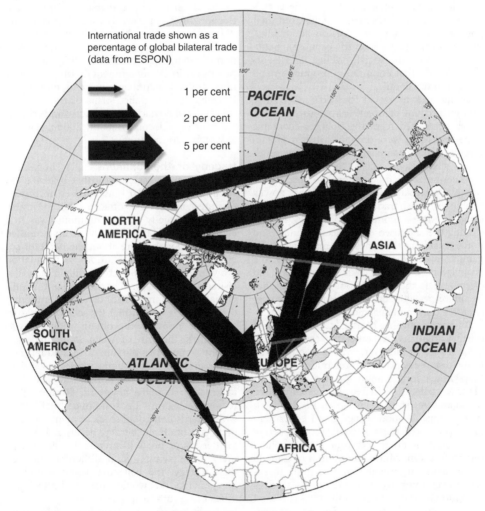

trade   *Global import and export flows*

that turned Africans into commodities, for example, can hardly be held up as an unmitigated good (see Wolf, 1982). And the recent for-profit trade in blood plasma from Haiti to the USA and Europe reveals how despite historic victories over SLAVERY, its legacies still provide a vampiric verso of economists' unending odes to free trade in the present (Farmer, 2006). But even putting such odious examples aside, studies of the political and economic geographies in which trade takes place make universal claims about the goodness of trade seem absurd (Sheppard and Barnes, 1990; Merrett, 1996; Porter and Sheppard, 1998; Gilbert, 2005). One of the major weaknesses of mainstream macroeconomics is that it continually abstracts from these geographies, mirroring but ignoring the ways in which capitalist trading relations affix prices to commodities that crystallize out their abstract value (but see Fireside and Miller, 2005). All the focus is on the economic benefits – never on the social, political and environmental ills that commodity production and trade so often entails.

Going back to David Ricardo's nineteenth-century account of COMPARATIVE ADVANTAGE – which abstracted from the political–economic imperatives that were driving British manufacturers to seek new foreign markets for their products – abstractions such as 'opportunity costs' have continually led economists to obscure the uneven international and personal POWER relations in which trade takes place. Yet notwithstanding endless economic MODELLING demonstrating the supposed efficiencies of trade, and notwithstanding the repeated emphasis on the gains from trade in economics textbooks, the geographical context of trade still matters – and often reveals the losses from trade. This has become especially clear in contemporary debates over free trade and fair trade.

When the novelist Margaret Atwood joined other Canadians in contesting the Canada–USA Free Trade Agreement, she pointed to the discursive power of free trade by underlining how it hinges on the positive association of the word 'free', 'as in free gift, free lunch, free world and free speech' (Atwood, 1993, p. 93). Against this, Atwood argued that free trade in fact represented the systematic straitjacketing of Canada's democratic autonomy and policy-setting freedom. Many other critics in Canada repeated the argument that free trade threatened everything from public health services to national development initiatives to food safety to cultural creativity. Subsequent protests from Seattle to Singapore have made similar arguments against the WORLD TRADE ORGANISATION, underlining the many areas of social, political and environmental policy-making that are straitjacketed by trade laws (Peet, 2003; Wallach and Woodall, 2004). At the heart of these criticisms is a concern with the ways in which free trade agreements create systems of rule or state effects that, while granting TNCs quasi-constitutional rights, simultaneously undermine any sort of democratic rights for the subject populations who want to question and reform the new rules (Gill, 2003; El Fisgón, 2004; Sparke, Brown, Corva et al., 2005). Based on these concerns and critiques, diverse transnational groupings from the WORLD SOCIAL FORUM to the Intercontinental Caravan are converging to deliberate and delineate diverse alternatives, including diverse forms of fair trade (Featherstone, 2003; Routledge, 2003; Sparke, Brown, Corva et al., 2005; Routledge, Nativel and Cumbers, 2006). Meanwhile, new work by feminist economic geographers points hopefully (and despite its capitalist government funding) towards non-capitalist, extra-capitalist and, most idealistically, post-capitalist forms of trade that is 'free' – from POVERTY, PATRIARCHY and corporate control (Gibson-Graham, 2006c: see also FEMINIST GEOGRAPHIES). MS

tragedy of the commons A short-hand for the popular assumption that *collective* RESOURCE MANAGEMENT – as opposed to private or state-control of RESOURCES - will inevitably fail. The 'tragedy of the commons' was first elaborated by Hardin (1968) as an extended METAPHOR for thinking about the need for social and institutional solutions to population growth. Hardin sought to highlight how decisions that are rational at the level of the individual (about family size) can yield outcomes that are far from optimal for society (what he called the 'population problem'). His aim was to 'exorcise the spirit of Adam Smith' in demography – that the pursuit of individual gain would promote the public interest – and to make the case for restrictions on 'the freedom to breed'. To make his point, Hardin asked readers to 'picture a pasture open to all' upon which herdsmen could stock as many cattle as they saw fit. Each herder, he argued, would further his or her self-interest by adding animals to the pasture, yet if all herders pursued this strategy, the collective result would be overgrazing: thus would 'freedom in the commons bring ruin to all'.

Hardin's model has travelled widely within academic and policy circles over the past four decades and is frequently invoked as a guide to renewable resource management (see Wade, 1987). Although he was not the first to draw attention to 'the dilemma of collective resources' (Gordon, 1954), Hardin 'codified into a social economic theory' the 'conventional wisdom...that private gains might hold social and ecological costs' (Robbins, 2004). Thus has the tragedy of the commons acquired the status of resource management parable, and has provided intellectual support both to calls for resource PRIVATIZATION and to demands for increased STATE control.

Since the first publication of Hardin's argument, however, a substantial body of work by both natural and social scientists has documented the remarkable diversity of contemporary PROPERTY management arrangements around the world (Berkes, 1989). This work demonstrates that successful collective management regimes cannot accurately be characterized as 'exceptions' or pre-modern relics: collective resource management regimes are widespread, are not restricted to developing countries, and can be resilient in the face of economic and environmental change. This work has shown that Hardin's error was to move too quickly from an initial observation – about the significant tensions between private and collective interests – to his conclusion that collective management must fail. In practice, 'the commons' are not the open-access, free-for-all regimes that he made them out to be; rather, what distinguishes common property from open-access regimes are the customs, rule systems and enforcement mechanisms that condition individual access to and use of the resource. Furthermore, Hardin's conclusion can only be sustained if one assumes that resource users cannot communicate with each other, share information on the condition of the resource, or coordinate their behaviour.

The past few years have seen renewed theoretical interest in the adaptive capacities, negotiated rule systems and INDIGENOUS environmental KNOWLEDGES that often characterize common property management regimes. Given the failure of many 'top-down' DEVELOPMENT and CONSERVATION initiatives, these attributes are increasingly seen as valuable components of SUSTAINABLE DEVELOPMENT and adaptive management in the face of environmental change.   GB

Suggested reading
Feeny, Berkes, McCay and Acheson (1990); Ostrom (1999).

transaction costs The costs associated with effecting an economic transaction, either through MARKET exchange between two or more legally distinct economic actors, or internally within a single organization (firm or, more generally, 'hierarchy').

Costs for *market-mediated transactions* might include:

- The cost of gathering information concerning the availability, price and quality of particular COMMODITIES (goods or SERVICES).
- The costs associated with identifying potential customers.
- The cost of determining the reliability of a supplier or the creditworthiness of a purchaser.
- The costs associated with negotiating the terms of an exchange, including price, delivery date and terms of payment (and of setting these out in the form of an agreed contract).
- The cost of completing a transaction (making or collecting payment).

Costs will also accompany *non-market transactions* within a single firm; in other words, the costs of organizing and coordinating complex, multi-step production processes in-house.

TRANSPORT COSTS associated with moving goods between transacting parties have traditionally received special attention from ECONOMIC GEOGRAPHY in general and have provided the basis for classical spatial MODELS in LOCATION THEORY but, as the following discussion shows, other forms of transaction cost have recently attracted considerable attention within INDUSTRIAL GEOGRAPHY in particular.

Williamson (1975, 1985) is generally credited with developing a comprehensive analysis of transaction costs. He sought 'to achieve a better understanding of the origins and functions of various market structures – stretching from elementary work groups to complex modern corporations' (1975, pp. 1–2). Instead of relying on technological arguments based on concepts such as indivisibilities or non-separabilities to explain why two or more functions might be performed within the same firm ('organizational hierarchy'), Williamson focused on 'transactions and the costs that attend completing transactions by one institutional mode rather than another'. He insisted that it was transactional not technological considerations that are 'typically decisive in determining which mode of organization will obtain in what circumstances and why'. Most goods require a number of semi-finished or intermediate inputs for their production. They also require a number of discrete, separate functions to be performed as part of the overall production process. Williamson argued that the extent to which all of these operations are performed within a single vertically integrated firm versus the extent to which some or all of the required inputs are produced by other firms and then acquired through a market transaction depends on which mode of organization most successfully minimizes transaction costs: 'whether a set of transactions ought to be executed across markets or within a firm depends on the relatively efficiency of each mode' (p. 8). Generally, the more difficult or expensive the task of coordination or 'governance' of the production process, Williamson proposed, the greater the likelihood that production will be vertically integrated within a single internal hierarchy.

The geographical significance of transaction costs (other than transportation costs) was first made clear by Scott (1988c), who demonstrated both theoretically and empirically that the spatial clustering of firms often serves to reduce the cost of transactions between them (see CLUSTER; INDUSTRIAL DISTRICT). Under such conditions, firms will find it cheaper and easier to acquire the requisite information concerning potential suppliers and buyers nearby. Moreover, because such firms may be managed by individuals who have come into contact with one another repeatedly over extended periods of time, they may have built up a high degree of familiarity and TRUST between them that serves to facilitate the sharing of information and the successful achievement of non-routine transactions (Harrison, 1992; Nootebloom, 2006) – what Storper (1997b) called 'untraded interdependencies'. When such circumstances prevail, Scott argued, one should expect to find a much more fully articulated social DIVISION OF LABOUR, in which individual firms specialize in the production of a relatively small number of goods and/or services and trade actively with one another. Such arrangements are likely to be specially useful in industries for which market tastes are changing rapidly, and in which PRODUCT LIFE CYCLES are short. Since input requirements for such goods will also change rapidly, spatial concentration will reduce the transaction costs associated with producers finding and assessing the performance characteristics of potential new suppliers. Similarly, when the product is complex or highly customized, it is advantageous for producers and users to interact frequently and easily. Possibilities for achieving this are enhanced when the producer and user are close to one another, thereby reducing the cost of such a complex transaction (Lundvall, 1988).

Hence, as Storper (1997, pp. 34–5) observed, this kind of analysis demonstrates 'that GEOGRAPHY figures in transaction costs in general, and hence influences the boundaries of the firm and production system'. He also concluded that 'the geography of transaction costs helps explain AGGLOMERATION and spatial divisions of labour'. However, the transaction cost approach has been criticized for its rather reductionist analysis of industrial organization – for its 'exclusive focus on the transaction rather than the relationship' (Powell, 1990, p. 323) – and for its tendency to ignore the influence of the public sector in shaping the institutions (such as markets) that mediate EXCHANGE (Harrison, 1997).   MSG

transactional analysis In ECONOMIC GEOGRAPHY, a method of determining the number of firms in an industry and the nature of exchanges between them. It is based on the proposition that 'the economic institutions of CAPITALISM have the main purpose and effect of economizing on TRANSACTION COSTS' (Williamson, 1985, p. 17). Thus it may be cheaper for a firm to produce a COMMODITY 'in-house' through an *internal transaction*, in order to exploit internal ECONOMIES OF SCOPE or to reap internal ECONOMIES OF SCALE, or it may be cheaper for a firm to acquire the same commodity through an *external transaction* (e.g. subcontracting), the cost of which may be reduced by the clustering of suppliers near to the firm (see CLUSTER). This type of analysis illuminates one of the forces said to propel the AGGLOMERATION of productive activities. Transactional analysis is also an approach used in psychology and psychotherapy; advertised as explicitly post-Freudian, transactional analysis in this second sense places its focus on interpersonal interactions (cf. PSYCHOANALYTIC THEORY). Approaches of this kind, so Bondi (1999) argued, suggest various affinities with some versions of HUMANISTIC GEOGRAPHY.   MSG/DG

transculturation The entwining and entangling of different cultural forms and practices to produce new ones (cf. HYBRIDITY). The term was originally proposed by Cuban ethnographer Fernando Ortiz (1881–1969), who contrasted transculturation to acculturation. *Acculturation* involves the adjustment of a subordinate culture to the impositions and exactions of a dominant culture, a process of learning and even 'acquiring' the idioms of the dominant culture, whereas *transculturation* involves a dialectical relation of combination and contradiction (see DIALECTIC), a process of cultural loss as well as gain, that produces new, original forms (see also CULTURE).

Ortiz developed the concept in his masterwork, *Cuban counterpoint* (1940). As the title suggests, transculturation has something in common with studies of CONTRAPUNTAL GEOGRAPHIES: it is about the interplay between different cultures situated within a global force-field. The book was a study of the colonization of his native Cuba, where Ortiz identified a series of remarkably rapid cultural readjustments forcefully made by different peoples in a stream of migrants (Spanish, African and others), 'each of them torn from [their] native moorings, faced with the problem of disadjustment and readjustment, of deculturation and acculturation – in a word, of transculturation' (1995 [1940], p. 98). This may not have been a one-sided process of adjustment and compliance, but it was none the less a violent one: 'All, those above and below, living together in the same atmosphere of terror and oppression, the oppressed in terror of punishment, the oppressor in terror of reprisals, all beside justice, beside adjustment, beside themselves. And all in the painful process of transculturation' (p. 102). The subtitle of Ortiz's text is also critical: Ortiz's analysis was a profoundly MATERIALIST one that focused on the significance of non-human actors (what ACTOR-NETWORK THEORY would call 'actants'). He described tobacco and sugar as 'the two most important figures in this history of Cuba', and showed how different groups of people exercised POWER through their alliances with them. The cultural forms and practices of colonizers and colonized were thus reworked through their material, practical involvements with these two commodities. As anthropologist Fernando Coronil puts it in his introduction to Ortiz's text, on this reading commodities are 'not merely products of human activity, but active forces which constrain and empower it' (see COMMODITY).

If Ortiz's work is not understood in relation to Cuba and LATIN AMERICA more generally, it becomes a TRAVELLING THEORY that runs the risk of losing its political force (Lund, 2001). That said, transculturation has acquired considerable significance in POST-COLONIALISM and studies of TRAVEL-WRITING, where it has allowed more subtle analyses of the considerable cultural traffic that constituted the 'contact zone' between colonizer and colonized

(Pratt, 1992). But little of this work has seized upon the materialist dimensions of Ortiz's work (cf. Coronil, 2000). DG

Suggested reading
Coronil (1995).

transfer pricing The setting of transfer prices for products (goods and SERVICES) moving between semi-autonomous divisions (cost- or profit-centres) within large organizations. The practice is most often associated with TRANSNATIONAL CORPORATIONS (TNCS), which respond to variable corporate tax regimes, to TARIFF and other barriers to TRADE, and to differential exchange rates by setting prices for internal transactions between establishments located in different national jurisdictions in ways that minimize costs or maximize gains. For example, firms may charge high prices for semi-finished products shipped for further processing to plants located in jurisdictions with high rates of tax, so that they reduce the tax take on profits generated by finishing processes.

As the GLOBALIZATION of INVESTMENT, production and trade proceeds, both the possibilities for and the extent of transfer pricing are likely to increase. Dicken (2007, p. 239) points out that 'in general, the greater the differences in levels of corporate taxes, tariffs, duties, exchange rates, the greater will be the incentive for the TNC to manipulate its transfer prices'. TNCs have a strong incentive to engage in transfer pricing and the very large, highly centralized, global TNC has the greatest potential for doing so. The problem, as Dicken recognizes, is that it is exceptionally difficult for governments (or researchers) to obtain evidence about its extent.

Transfer prices are set by and within firms and, at one level, are purely managerial, involving the monitoring and control of individual cost- and profit-centres. But at another level, the judicious use of internal transfer pricing facilitates the avoidance of tax and minimizes the cost-of-trade barriers. Firms can optimize their financial relations with the jurisdictions in which they are located and so minimize payment of TARIFFS, for example, or shift accounted profits from locations within high-tax regimes to locations with low rates of corporate taxation. TNCs can also get around difficulties associated with fluctuating exchange rates which, on the open MARKET, might tend to over- or under-pricing of products in transactions taking place between units of the same TNC located in different currency spaces. By disembedding themselves in such ways, TNCs are able to reduce their costs and increase their profitability at the expense of the jurisdictions in which they operate. RL

Suggested reading
Dicken (2007, ch. 8).

transferability One of Ullman's (1956) bases for SPATIAL INTERACTION covering both TRANSPORT COSTS, which reflect the characteristics of the transport system and the COMMODITY being moved, and commodity's ability to bear those costs. Precious metals have high transferability, for example, because they are easy to handle and transport costs are small (per unit weight) relative to their total value; plate glass has low transferability because it is difficult to handle and has relatively low value. RJ

transgression The act of crossing accepted limits, of breaking rules or exceeding BOUNDARIES. Transgression challenges but also reveals and underlines the values considered to be 'normal' and 'appropriate' in particular geographical and social settings. It works within and plays upon given spaces and conditions, rather than operating from outside them or seeking to constitute a new space or system. Through the process and the reactions to it, norms and codes about what is prohibited and considered proper are highlighted. For Bataille, whose writings have been particularly influential on understandings of the concept, the 'experience of transgression is indissociable from the consciousness of the constraint or prohibition it violates; indeed, it is precisely by and through its transgression that the force of a prohibition becomes fully realized' (see Suleiman, 1990, p. 75). Transgression and the taboo therefore coexist in a complex relationship, with the former not denying the latter but transcending and completing it (see also Foucault, 1977b [1963]; Jenks, 2003).

GEOGRAPHY is important in the constitution of limits and in demarcations of high and low, normal and deviant, clean and polluted and the like. While SPACE is used as a means of social control by the powerful, the resulting socio-spatial orderings and codings may also be potentially transgressed. Despite many celebratory accounts of transgression, Stallybrass and White (1986) insist that there is nothing inherently politically progressive – or conservative – about the process. In their investigation of the construction of European bourgeois identity that ranges across SOCIAL FORMATIONS, space and the BODY, they examine the ways in which that IDENTITY was defined through the exclusion of what it deemed 'low', and how that expelled low 'other' became a focus of desire as well as disgust. In their view, transgression is often 'a powerful ritual or symbolic practice whereby the dominant squanders its symbolic capital so as to get in touch with the fields of desire which it denied itself as the price paid for its political power' (1986, p. 210). The continual 'rediscovery' of the carnivalesque within modern CULTURE and its importance as a semiotic realm is related to its rejection in the constitution of bourgeois culture's self-identity.

Analysing transgression is therefore a significant means of understanding not only marginal acts, but also the processes by which the normal, the central and the dominant become defined. Transgression's power comes in particular from its ability to expose the constructedness of socio-spatial orderings, and hence their openness to criticism and to reconstruction. Transgression is distinct from RESISTANCE, according to Cresswell (1996), in that it does not rest on intentionality, but on its effects and on the reactions it precipitates. These cannot be defined in advance, but have to be examined in particular geographical and historical contexts. 'Transgression's efficacy lies in the power of the established boundaries and spaces that is so heretically subverts,' he states. 'It is also limited by this established geography; it is always in reaction to TOPOGRAPHIES of power' (Cresswell, 1996, p. 175). Yet, as he remarks, transgression can contain 'the seeds of new spatial orderings'. It may, through becoming part of strategic struggles, go beyond temporary tactical incursions to contribute to social and spatial transformation. DP

Suggested reading
Cresswell (1996); Stallybrass and White (1986).

transhumance Socially organized seasonal movements of livestock along altitudinal and bioclimatic gradients, usually in response to changing availability of forage or WATER. These movements differ from those associated with nomadic PASTORALISM (see NOMADISM) in that only a portion of the family (or other social unit) associated with the herd makes the journey, while the remainder of the family remains at a more permanent dwelling. The term was originally used in EUROPE (the French verb *transhumer* means to move livestock) to describe the movement of shepherds and their flocks between lowland pastures in the winter and highland pastures in the summer months, to take advantage of snow melt. Such movements are historically tied to pastoralism in mountainous areas and dryland regions with seasonal rainfall.   MT

Suggested reading
Stenning (1960).

transnational corporations (TNCs) CAPITAL moves around the globe in three forms: embodied in materials, goods and services, it enters into TRADE flows. Invested in stocks, bonds, foreign currency holdings and the like, it moves as financial capital (see FINANCE; HOT MONEY). Transnational corporations (TNCs) invest their own capital resources in other countries in order to engage in their ordinary business of extracting, producing and/or selling materials, goods and services. This is also known as *foreign direct investment* (FDI). FDI may involve the creation of an operation from the ground up – a 'greenfield investment'. More commonly, it involves buying an already existing foreign company. In either case, effective control over the offshore operation remains with the parent company, even if it does not own 100 per cent of the foreign asset. Return on INVESTMENT may be in the form of royalties, interest or profits and these may be reinvested in the offshore site, repatriated to the parent corporation or invested elsewhere altogether.

FDI grows out of the combined exigencies of international competition and the push of capital accumulation as a company amasses more capital than it can conveniently or profitably reinvest in its original market. This implies a longer term commitment of resources to a particular foreign site than either of the other forms of international capital mobility, and corporations undertake it for a number of reasons. Control over NATURAL RESOURCES is a classic motivation and the one most likely to draw a company into remote parts of the world. Tapping into low-cost and non-unionized LABOUR MARKETS is another. FDI may be a way of internalizing TRANSACTION COSTS across borders and taking advantage of ECONOMIES OF SCOPE, greater capital resources or technologies in order to gain a COMPETITIVE ADVANTAGE in foreign markets. A TNC may buy out a foreign company in order to gain access to proprietary technology or to reduce the intensity of competition in its business. Or it may be intent on gaining access to or improving its position in important foreign markets

and sees operating in the market as a better means to this end than exporting from home. This may be: because it can provide better service or respond more quickly to shifts in the market; because it will benefit politically from being perceived as a local company; because it avoids tariff barriers and TRANSPORT COSTS, or because it can keep a closer eye on the competition (Schoenberger, 1997; Dunning, 2002a; Dicken, 2003; Ietto-Gillies, 2005).

The geography of TNC investment may be counter-intuitive. Conventional economic theory supposes that capital will flow from places where it is abundant and the price correspondingly low to places where it is scarce and therefore expensive. This implies a flow from advanced industrial countries to less developed countries across the board. Other theories anticipate that capital will flow from high-cost areas to low-cost areas, again implying an outflow from advanced countries, with high labour and regulatory costs, to the Third World (see NEW INTERNATIONAL DIVISION OF LABOUR) (Dunning, 2002b; Dicken, 2003). Most non-resource FDI, however, flows among advanced industrial countries. US TNCs in manufacturing and services, for example, invest mostly in western Europe and Canada. European TNCs invest heavily elsewhere in Europe and in North America. A smaller share flows to just a handful of newly industrializing countries (NICs). Even TNCs from some NICs are investing now in North America and Europe: in 2005, a Chinese corporation, Lenovo, bought the personal computer business of IBM. Market access seems to matter more than costs. Further, since FDI is so often made via acquisition rather than as greenfield investment, it is likely to go where the largest number of potential acquisitions is located – advanced industrial countries (Schoenberger, 1997; Dicken, 2003).

Despite this skewed distribution in favour of advanced industrial countries, TNCs operating in developing regions still have a tremendous impact – in part because they may be quite large relative to the local economy. This is especially true of resource extraction operations, although even these are concentrated geographically in a relatively small number of host countries (Bridge, 2004).

Why FDI does not flow more generally across the surface of the Earth is an interesting problem. Its orientation to rich (North America and the EU) and/or fast-growing (e.g. Asia) markets is an important factor. ECONOMIES OF SCALE in many of the most important FDI industries (e.g. mining or chemicals) favour geographical concentration. Progress in automation has reduced the importance of labour costs in many sectors, making it feasible to remain in high labour cost countries. Meanwhile, poorer countries, besides having very restricted markets, also have poor physical and institutional infrastructures, which makes operations both more costly and riskier. Although usually seen to be in the vanguard of GLOBALIZATION, there are reasons to suppose that TNCs are hedging their bets. Their operations are certainly international, but they are not quite global as yet.

TNCs are the permanent object of heated political debate. Some believe that they will foster ECONOMIC GROWTH and MODERNIZATION in the developing world by importing capital, technology and managerial techniques that will then filter out into the host economy. STAGES OF GROWTH theorists see TNCs as the perfect vehicle for overcoming barriers to DEVELOPMENT and promoting REGIONAL CONVERGENCE. Others believe they are responsible for 'underdeveloping' the Third World by dominating local markets and draining capital in the form of profits from SOUTH to North – in short, that they are the modern form of IMPERIALISM and a major factor promoting DEPENDENCY and UNEVEN DEVELOPMENT. Many see them as responsible for the DEINDUSTRIALIZATION of formerly prosperous regions (Tabb, 2002; Cuyvers and DeBeule, 2005). TNCs have been charged with collaborating with oppressive governments in order to ensure access to resources and therefore being implicated in the violation of HUMAN RIGHTS and of VIOLENCE against local populations (Peluso and Watts, 2001; Frynas and Pegg, 2003). Their presence raises questions of sovereignty and the integrity of the NATION-STATE even in the most developed countries (Dicken, 2003). ESCH

Suggested reading
Dicken (2003); Harvey (1999 [1982]); Peck and Yeung (2003).

transnationalism A concept that describes a movement or set of linkages that occur *across* national BORDERS. Transnationalism is a relatively new term, and its growing popularity indicates the heightened interconnectivity of people and things that now flow across borders and BOUNDARIES in greater volume and with greater speed than ever before. While closely linked to the processes of economic GLOBALIZATION, which are often conceptualized in abstract global terms and decentred spaces, transnationalism is generally invoked to express transcendence of the specific workings of the NATION-STATE (Kearney, 1995). It is thus used most widely in the social sciences to describe phenomena in which the cultural or territorial boundaries of the NATION and/or the regulatory apparatuses of the STATE are crossed or contested in new kinds of ways.

While this notion of crossing boundaries is pertinent to many cross-border articulations, including the circulation of COMMODITIES and the flows of culture and ideas (e.g. Jackson, Crang and Dwyer, 2004), the contemporary movement of migrants is most frequently associated with the term. Unlike earlier theories of MIGRATION, which generally characterized movement across borders as either permanent rupture followed by assimilation in a new society, or as temporary sojourning followed by a return home, transnationalism describes a migration pattern of simultaneous connection to two or more nations (Basch, Glick Schiller and Blanc, 1995). In numerous case studies, migrants have been shown to construct an intricate, multi-webbed NETWORK of ongoing social relations that span their country of origin and their country (or countries) of settlement. While a pattern of transnational life has been present in past migrations to varying degrees, the new transportation, communication and computing technologies of the past few decades have greatly facilitated such arrangements in the contemporary era.

In addition to technological advances, many scholars have associated the growth of this type of migration pattern with changes in the nature of global CAPITALISM (Ong, 1999). The organization of production on a worldwide scale has affected the volume and flow of migrants across national borders, and led to a transformed culture and experience of migration and of the nation. These dynamics are implicated in the wider boundary-crossing conceptualization of transnationalism, in which the significance of national cultural narratives and the meanings and practices of state regulations are reconsidered and often reworked. One of the key signifiers of both cultural belonging and state control that is reworked under conditions of contemporary transnationality is CITIZENSHIP. The implications of transnationalism for citizenship formation are enormous, ranging from questions of state jurisdiction over borders to sociocultural considerations of IDENTITY and belonging. KM

Suggested reading
Glick Schiller and Fouron (2001); Mitchell (1997); Smith and Guarnizo (1998).

transport costs The total costs involved in moving between two places, which in the case of goods movements involves not only the *freight rate* but also the costs of documentation, packaging, insurance and inventory. Transport costs are a central element in most classical LOCATION THEORIES, being presented as a primary determinant of both agricultural land use (see VON THÜNEN MODEL) and *industrial location theories*, as well as most theories of SPATIAL INTERACTION (cf. DISTANCE DECAY): they were at the heart of arguments for geography as SPATIAL SCIENCE, or as a 'discipline in distance' (Watson, 1955: cf. LOCATIONAL ANALYSIS).   RJ

transport geography   This field of study focuses on the movement of people and goods, the transportation systems designed to facilitate such movement, and the relationship of transportation to other facets of human geography such as economic DEVELOPMENT, ENERGY, land use, SPRAWL, environmental degradation, VALUES and CULTURE. Longstanding, strong ties with the fields of civil engineering and economics have imbued transport geography with a tradition of QUANTITATIVE METHODS, particularly the use of mathematical MODELS. These ties have at once enabled transport analysts to respond to pressing planning problems and tended to limit the questions that transport geographers ask, often directing attention towards technique and away from theory (Hanson, 2000).

Studies of the movement of people and goods have sought to build predictive models of the volume of FLOWS between places; these models predict flows as a function of the *demand* for movement between nodes (usually associated with various measures of node size) and the *cost* of movement between nodes, which in turn is related to distance, the mode of travel (e.g. airplane, ship, automobile), and the ease of movement, *inter alia*. Such models of SPATIAL INTERACTION are important to a range of actors including urban transportation planners, who are responsible for providing transport facilities that will handle predicted flow volumes, and commercial airlines, which must also provide sufficient capacity to meet predicted demand. In transportation geography, the linkages among modelling, prediction and planning have been exceedingly strong.

Studies of transportation systems have focused on patterns of NETWORKS and nodes

and have often considered how these patterns affect ease of movement and therefore shape land-use and settlement patterns. In the USA, the advent of the inter-state highway system, beginning in the 1950s, led to the demise of some places by-passed by the system and to the growth of other places, whose ACCESSIBILITY was enhanced by connection to the inter-state system (Garrison, Berry, Marble, Nystuen and Morrill, 1959). More recently, the deregulation of the airlines led to the development of the hub-and-spoke system that describes the current network of air travel in the USA (O'Kelly, 1998); again, the network configuration favours certain nodes (the hubs, many of which have grown into thriving commercial centres) to the detriment of others (nodes at the extremities of the spokes, which have seen their accessibility via air decline). Transport systems studies have also examined competition between and among modes (e.g. trucking versus the railroads and waterways) and between and among routes on the same mode (e.g. among the multiple routes between Chicago and the US east coast in the early twentieth century). Of current interest is the impact of INTERNET commerce on transport: whereas such commerce might reduce the number of person–trips, it has led to an enormous increase in the demand for goods movement (Aoyama, Ratick and Schwarz, 2006).

Transport is intimately related to a host of issues that lie at the heart of HUMAN GEOGRAPHY. ENERGY consumption and environmental degradation are just two that link closely to the nature–society tradition in geography. Because transportation systems are designed to increase accessibility and accessibility is central to land-use patterns and to economic development, transport studies have much to offer the field of DEVELOPMENT. VALUES and CULTURE, which are hugely important to understandings of transport patterns and systems, have been mostly neglected by transport geographers.   SHa

Suggested reading
Black (2003); Rodigue, Comtois and Slack (2006).

transportation problem A special case of LINEAR PROGRAMMING, where the objective is to find the minimum-cost solution that transports goods from N origins to M destinations. The supplies available at each origin and the demands required at each destination define the constraints, and the transportation problem assumes that each origin is directly connected to each destination by a route with a specified unit cost. Problems with this simple SPATIAL STRUCTURE may be solved very efficiently, and the method is used in both public sector (e.g. allocating pupil to schools) and business (cheapest routing of distribution), though many recent applications use a more general network structure. LWH

Suggested reading
Hay (1977); Taaffe and Gauthier (1973).

travel writing A genre of prose about the experience of being away from home. While travel writing in EUROPE can be traced back to Homer's *Odyssey*, it has rarely been considered either serious LITERATURE or credible ETHNOGRAPHY, and was typically excluded from the conventional history of geography (see GEOGRAPHY, HISTORY OF). In the past several decades, however, the genre has been reassessed within the HUMANITIES and the social sciences, and there has been a resurgence of critical interest in travel writing. This can be traced to a number of broader changes in academic fashion. One was the rise of POSTMODERNISM, which validated the study of popular forms of CULTURE, including writing, rather than simply 'the Greats'. Within many of the social sciences, postmodernism was closely associated with a CULTURAL TURN that focused greater attention on practices of REPRESENTATION. A second, related source of interest in travel writing was the development of POST-COLONIALISM and the key role played by literary scholar Edward Said (1935–2003) in its articulation. The success of Said's (2003 [1978]) critique of ORIENTALISM created a multidisciplinary growth industry in the study of colonial representations of other places and peoples. Travel writings were seen as primary sources for the recovery of IMAGINATIVE GEOGRAPHIES. A third influence was FEMINISM, which showed that nineteenth- and early-twentieth-century travel accounts written by women were important but marginalized sites of the production of geographical knowledge (indeed, they had been marginalized by Said too) (cf. McEwan, 2000).

Within HUMAN GEOGRAPHY, interest in travel writing has had a number of different foci. Among these has been a renewed interest in records and writings produced under the signs of EXPLORATION and SCIENCE, but now read critically as TEXTS, using the resources of the literary as well as the historical disciplines to disclose the multiple ways in which the DISCOURSE of exploration and enumeration worked to produce its objects of inquiry. As the discourse of Orientalism produced 'the Orient', for example, so the discourse of TROPICALITY produced 'the Tropics' (Driver and Martins, 2005). Such studies feed into an interest in the spaces through which scientific knowledges are produced, the channels through which they circulate and the centres at which they accumulate. The same spatial thematics animate studies of travel writing outside the nominally scientific domain (Gregory, 2001a). In Europe, the distinction between 'travel' and 'TOURISM' is an historical one, freighted with assumptions about edification and independence that register a series of CLASS distinctions. But travellers and tourists throughout the nineteenth and on into the twentieth centuries had a compulsion to *write* their journeys, and the critical scrutiny of their texts has much to tell us about not only the production, and on occasion the disruption, of cultural stereotypes and processes of TRANSCULTURATION (Pratt, 1992) – few travellers arrived at their destination with their cultural baggage intact and simply unpacked it to make pre-configured sense of what they saw – but also about the formation of national IDENTITIES and the consolidation of bourgeois CULTURE (Buzard, 1993; Duncan and Gregory, 1999). Travellers did not only write diaries, journals and letters; they also sketched, painted, and took photographs, and the interrogation of this visual archive has been of considerable importance in the recovery and analysis of cultural constructions of LANDSCAPE in particular (Stafford, 1984; Osborne, 2000; Schwartz and Ryan, 2003). Travel was also historically coded through notations of GENDER and SEXUALITY, and there has been a notable interest in the ways in which travel could permit the realization of *desire* and TRANSGRESSION that was simply impossible at home (Aldrich, 1993; Boone, 1995; Gregory, 1995a).

This brief summary suggests a series of lacuna in work on travel writing that are only now starting to be addressed. First, research has been dominated by studies of European and North American travellers beyond their own shores – but what of the 'return gaze' (e.g. Burton, 1998)? Second, the texts under closest scrutiny were typically produced by those who *chose* to travel under the signs of science, culture or pleasure – but what of the experiences of those who were obliged to travel under other signs: commerce, capture or duty (e.g. Colley, 2002), or as fugitives from disaster or WAR (see REFUGEES)? Third, much of this work has fastened on historical rather than contemporary writings, a focus that forecloses questions about the complex reactivation of older, often colonial images in our own present (cf. Tavares and Brosseau, 2006) and the ways in which what Lisle (2006) calls 'the global politics of contemporary travel writing' now participates in and responds to the anxieties created by GLOBALIZATION. JSD/DG

Suggested reading
Duncan and Gregory (1989); Hume and Youngs (2002); Lisle (2006).

travelling theory Intellectual ideas that move from one location to another and, in the process, change in response to new circumstances. The original formulation was by Edward Said, who identified three critical moments:

- The first was *origination*, the circumstances within which a body of ideas emerges. Ideas are not free-floating constructions, on this reading, and their analysis requires what historians of science and of geography call a 'contextual history'. Said (1984, pp. 241–2) called for a 'critical consciousness', a 'spatial sense, a sort of measuring faculty for locating or situating theory' by understanding it 'in the place and time out of which it emerges as part of that time, working in and for it, responding to it' (cf. SITUATED KNOWLEDGE).
- The second was *institutionalization*. Said knew very well that ideas move – the circulation of ideas is an enabling condition of intellectual activity – but he was also concerned that as radical, unsettling ideas become fashionable so they are domesticated: 'Once an idea gains currency because it is clearly effective and powerful, there is every likelihood that during its peregrinations it will be reduced, codified and institutionalized' (Said, 1984, p. 239).
- The third was *revivification*. Said subsequently accepted that a theory could be reinterpreted and reinvigorated by travelling and responding to a new situation. These transgressive theorizations – his examples were Adorno and Fanon – give one a sense of 'the geographical dispersion of which the theoretical motor is capable' by pulling ideas from one region to another and realizing the productive possibility of 'actively different locales, sites, situations for theory' – a sense of active, operative, concrete differences – that allow no 'facile

universalism or over-general totalizing' (Said, 2000 [1994], p. 452).

Said's own account of ORIENTALISM has been interpreted as a classic instance of travelling theory (Brennan, 2000).

In HUMAN GEOGRAPHY travelling theory has its place in a wider landscape that includes geographies of intellectual production, dissemination and circulation, and reception. Journeying across this landscape raises important and interrelated questions about the fixation of high THEORY on fashionable thinkers; about the COMMODITY CHAINS that make up the international publishing industry; about the trafficking in metropolitan 'high theory' and the use of other regions as resource banks; about the dominance of English-language publication and the problems of translation (see ANGLOCENTRISM); and about the place of the modern corporate university and its relation to other sites at which geographical knowledge is produced (cf. PUBLIC GEOGRAPHIES).

It is not only ideas that travel, and Livingstone (2003b) sees travelling theory as part of a larger apparatus of circulation that is indispensable to the scientific enterprise: 'Ideas and instruments, texts and theories, individuals and inventions – to name but a very few – all diffuse across the surface of the earth (see SCIENCE).' Their circulation raises similar questions about the hierarchies and the NETWORKS through which they move, both inwards and outwards, and their reception and reworking also raises questions about IDEOLOGIES of respect and techniques of TRUST: 'Scientific knowledge has been expanded by circulation... [but] distance and doubt have always been close companions' (p. 178). DG

Suggested reading
Said (1984).

trend surface analysis A technique developed by Chorley and Haggett (1965) for generalizing the pattern in a set of geographical data. It usually employs a form of multiple REGRESSION in which the independent variables are the grid coordinates for the observations and the dependent variable is some item of interest measured there – such as land elevation. The aim is to identify the salient features of a complex three-dimensional SURFACE. RJ

trialectics A term proposed by the American geographer Edward Soja (1996b) as 'a mode of dialectical reasoning that is more inherently spatial than the conventionally temporally-defined dialectics of Marx or Hegel' (p. 10). In contrast to DIALECTICS, Soja identified three moments (not two), each of which is supposed to contain the others. Soja's purpose was to insist on the importance of the 'third term' in order 'to defend against any binary reductionism or totalization'. This is more than an exercise in logic, although Soja develops his argument at a high level of ABSTRACTION. He proposes two basic trialectics (see figure).

The first trialectic is primarily concerned with ONTOLOGY: Soja (1996b, pp. 71–3) describes this as the *trialectics of being*, and uses it to diagram the production of TIME, being-in-the-world and space: his argument turns on the claim that runs throughout his later writings that the 'third term', SPACE, is characteristically erased in conventional SOCIAL THEORY (cf. Soja, 1989).

The second trialectic is primarily concerned with EPISTEMOLOGY: Soja (1996b, pp. 73–82) describes this as the *trialectics of spatiality*, and uses it to diagram three approaches to SPATIALITY. These are derived from his reading of Henri Lefebvre's account of the PRODUCTION OF SPACE. Following Lefebvre, then, Soja argues that most discourses of spatiality have been confined to the realms of either:

(1) *spatial practices*, a space of OBJECTIVITY and object-ness, of 'perceived space', that Soja calls *Firstspace*; or
(2) *representations of space*, a space of signification and subject-ness, of 'conceived space', that Soja calls *Secondspace*.

Here too it is the force of the 'third term' that Soja seeks to release:

(3) *spaces of representation*, where REPRESENTATION carries both political and cultural connotations, and whose animation as 'lived space' corresponds to the subversive, radical and even revolutionary potential of what Soja identifies as *Thirdspace* (see THIRD SPACE). DG

Suggested reading
Soja (1996b, pp. 53–82); Merrifield (1996).

tricontinentalism An alternative term to POST-COLONIALISM that emphasizes the *transnational locations* and the *political implications* of critiques of COLONIALISM and IMPERIALISM. The substitution was proposed by British literary/critical theorist Robert Young, who invoked the Tricontinental Conference, the meeting of the Organization of Solidarity of the Peoples of Africa, Asia and Latin America', in Havana, Cuba in 1966 as, in effect, 'the founding moment of postcolonial theory' (Young, 2001, p. 5). Most accounts of post-colonial theory focus on three canonical figures – Edward Said, Homi Bhabha and Gayatri Chakravorty Spivak – rather than three CONTINENTS. Young acknowledges the importance of these academic writings, but the purpose of Young's redirection was twofold. First, he wanted to transcend the EUROCENTRISM of much of what passes for 'THEORY' by drawing attention to the vital importance of those 'insurgent knowledges that come from the subaltern, the dispossessed, and [which]

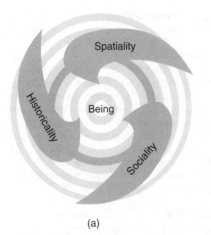

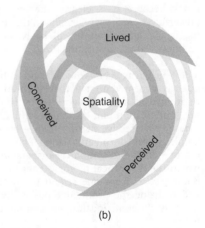

(a)   (b)

trialectics   (a) Ontology: 'trialectics of being'; (b) Epistemology: 'trialectics of spatiality'

seek to change the terms and values under which we all live': critical formulations that were rooted in the particular circumstances of exploitation and dispossession in AFRICA, ASIA and LATIN AMERICA (Young, 2003b, p. 20; cf. SUBALTERN STUDIES). Second, Young wanted to emphasize the political affinities between these knowledges and projects of popular liberation and DECOLONIZATION. In doing so, he acknowledged that Marx's writings were often a crucial inspiration, but he insisted that this was an HISTORICAL MATERIALISM that did not survive the journey from EUROPE intact: it was reworked in creative ways that were directly tied to practical, political conjunctures elsewhere in the world (see TRAVELLING THEORY).   DG

Suggested reading
Bongie (2002).

tropicality Cartographically, the Tropics are defined by the latitudinal lines of Cancer and Capricorn around the GLOBE, 23 degrees and 27 minutes north and south of the Equator, within which the sun may shine directly overhead. However, in cultural and political terms, tropicality – like ORIENTALISM – is not a fixed or a given fact of geography: it is a way of thinking in which spaces are described META-PHORICALLY, associating 'the Tropics' with a certain kind of experience, vision, LANDSCAPE or SOCIETY (Arnold, 1996a; Driver and Martins, 2005). The conceptual mapping of the 'tropical' – as defined against the 'temperate' – is one of the most enduring themes in the IMAGINATIVE GEOGRAPHIES of the globe, from classical mythology to modern LITERATURE (Cosgrove, 2001). Whether represented positively as a zone of luxuriant superabundance (as in Alexander von Humboldt's writings on tropical landscape), or negatively as a pathological space of degeneration (as in Joseph Conrad's novel, *Heart of darkness*), tropical NATURE has frequently been employed as a counterpoint to all that is modest, civilized or cultivated – or, in a word, 'normal' (cf. Gregory, 2001b). Images of tropicality have thus had a sustained impact within DISCOURSES of EXPLORATION, travel and TOURISM, and are also to be found in a wide variety of other cultural forms, from landscape painting and epic poetry to architecture and popular MUSIC. In the history of SCIENCE, they are reflected in the emergence of distinct sub-disciplinary specialisms – for example, tropical medicine, tropical climatology (see CLIMATE) or tropical geomorphology – although the

distinctiveness of the 'tropical' in these fields has always been contested. In the modern world, images of tropical difference have played a significant part in military imaginaries during WARS in ASIA and South East Asia in particular, and they continue to shape the ICONOGRAPHY of luxury tourism, global ENVIRONMENTALISM and commodity advertising more generally.

Although critical reflection on notions of tropicality is of relatively recent date (Arnold, 1996a; Driver and Yeoh, 2000), writings on the geographical characteristics of the tropical world have a long history. As the discipline of GEOGRAPHY developed in its modern form, the field of 'tropical geography' flourished for a brief period, notably in France during the mid-twentieth century, where the work of the geomorphologist Pierre Gourou (1900–99) – author of *Les pays tropicaux* (1947) – was particularly influential. Subsequent critiques of this work drew attention to its ideological blind-spots in relation to COLONIALISM and DEVELOPMENT, and its tendency to treat the impact of environment on society in a-historical terms. The history of tropical geography needs to be seen in the context of the colonial histories of the Francophone world, notably in Indochina. Recent work, however, casts new light on the ambivalent sense of tropicality within this tradition and the extent to which it supported the programmes of colonialism (Bowd and Clayton, 2005a,b). More generally, the extent to which the idea of tropicality can be understood, like Orientalism, as a form of discursive projection imposed by the West remains a matter for debate. Notions of tropicality, whether geographical, scientific or aesthetic, are not simply the product of imperial fantasy: they also contain other experiences, and other possibilities (see also Arnold, 2006).   FD

Suggested reading
Arnold (1996a); Driver and Martins (2005).

trust A quality that gives statements, individuals or organizations credibility and authority. Trust has become an important theme in areas of HUMAN GEOGRAPHY concerned to understand processes of knowledge credibility and transfer. ECONOMIC GEOGRAPHERS have addressed the ways in which economic relationships may depend upon trust between those engaged in transactions, with consequences for the value placed upon face-to-face contact, and the ways in which places may construct their economic reputation around trustworthiness. Thus Hudson's (1998) study of the offshore financial centres of Bermuda and the Cayman Islands emphasizes how the stabilization of such centres relies upon their capacity to be trusted as regulatory landscapes. Trust is here defined as 'relatively stable expectations about the actions of others, a particular level of the subjective probability with which an actor assesses whether one or more actors, with whom cooperation is envisaged, will also cooperate' (Hudson, 1998, p. 918).

Parallel concerns have shaped studies of the geographies of scientific knowledge, where the capacity for knowledge to be credible is connected to the capacity of scientists, including geographers, to be trusted. Livingstone discusses the 'techniques of trust' that developed in connection with geographical travel (2003c, pp. 147–71). Historical geographies of SCIENCE in general, and of geographical science in particular, have connected trust to issue of CLASS and GENDER, following Shapin's studies of science in seventeenth-century England (Shapin, 1994), where a particular sense of gentlemanly civility was shown to be central to the emergence of scientific CULTURE. Subsequently, Shapin (1998) directly addressed the SPATIALITY of the trust relationship in the production and validation of SCIENCE, including the finding of 'means to bring distant things near', and the ways in which 'those who have not seen these things know them by trusting those who have, or by trusting those who have trusted those who have' (Shapin, 1998, p. 8). Driver's studies of cultures of EXPLORATION and EMPIRE have shown how the trustworthiness and credibility of geographical knowledge claims concerning distant REGIONS were shaped through institutions such as the Royal Geographical Society, whether in their production of published 'Hints for Travellers', or their reception of the knowledge 'brought back' from AFRICA by figures such as Henry Morton Stanley. In the latter case, lack of trust in exploratory findings was bound up with judgements concerning the character of the explorer, with issues of 'social standing, scientific merit and moral legitimacy' becoming intertwined (Driver, 2001a, p. 129). The geographies of trust also encompass the questions of why geographers should be trusted, why the discipline should have credibility and who counts as a trustworthy geographer.   DMat

Suggested reading
Livingstone (2003c); Shapin (1994).

turf politics Political activity undertaken by residents of a NEIGHBOURHOOD to resist proposed changes that are viewed as potentially significant negative impacts upon the local COMMUNITY and also to promote changes that are perceived to carry potential positive impacts. The activity is usually locally based but is often oriented to the broader scales of local or STATE government (Ackerman, 1999). Catalysing changes usually take the form of development proposals (such as a new road), demographic change (such as the influx of a new ethnic group or social class) or investment decisions (such as continued funding for health facilities).   CF

Suggested reading
Cox and McCarthy (1982).

U

uncertainty The possibility of more than one outcome resulting from a particular course of action, the form of each possible outcome being known but the chance or probability of one particular outcome being unknown. Uncertainty differs from RISK, in that under conditions of risk it is possible to know the probability of a particular outcome. For example, in tossing a coin the probability of heads coming up is 0.5, so betting on the toss of a coin is a risk. Playing Russian roulette is a risk (also 'risky') if the pistol is known to be loaded; with a bullet in one of the six chambers, there is a one-in-six probability of death with any shot. However, if it was not known whether the gun was loaded, this would be a situation of uncertainty.

Uncertainty is part of the environment within which locational DECISION-MAKING is made. This greatly limits the practical value of theories and models that assume perfect knowledge. For example, the firm setting up a new factory or service outlet in a new territory cannot know what the reaction of competitors is likely to be. They may follow suit with new facilities of their own, they may find an alternative competitive strategy, or they may choose not to compete: there is no way of calculating the probability of each option. Residential choice is similarly made under conditions of uncertainty – for example, with respect to the stability of the neighbourhood or the sociability of the neighbours. DMS

underclass This term was introduced in the USA to refer to multiply deprived individuals who experience a form of POVERTY from which there is virtually no escape (cf. CYCLE OF POVERTY). In the USA, those classified as part of the underclass are mainly African-Americans or Latinas/os. Most lack higher education, skills that are in demand, and any apparent means of achieving upward social MOBILITY. Many are from single-parent families and are living on social assistance. There is also a geographical dimension to the underclass: it is usually identified with stigmatized NEIGHBOURHOODS that are areas of concentrated poverty and few job opportunities (Bauder, 2002). Members of the underclass experience a SPATIAL MISMATCH in that they cannot find work where they live, but also cannot afford the cost of transportation (and childcare expenses) to obtain work in more distant areas of the city (Mingione, 1996). These problems are compounded by discrimination against women and minorities in LABOUR MARKETS (see GENDER). In recent years, the term has been used to apply to extremely poor populations outside the USA, in Europe and increasingly in the developing world (see, e.g., Breman and Agarwal, 2002; Keyder, 2005; Solinger, 2006: see also DEVELOPMENT).

While liberal and radical analysts emphasize the structural causes of poverty (the nature of CAPITALISM, PATRIARCHY and RACISM – Wilson, 1987; Gans, 1995), conservative authors concentrate on the personal characteristics and lifestyles of the disadvantaged (Auletta, 1982). This latter view usually draws upon the *culture of poverty* thesis outlined by Oscar Lewis (1959) in his anthropological studies of Latin American SLUMS during the 1950s and 1960s. Lewis argued that the very poor share behavioural patterns that on the one hand allow them to cope with poverty, but on the other hand reproduce their disadvantage (e.g. a sceptical attitude towards education, that is passed on to CHILDREN). While this was unintended by Lewis, his idea of adaptation to poverty has been taken up by conservative commentators who believe that people are poor because of choices they make. This 'blame the victim' mentality permeates through much of the underclass debate, at least in the USA. Because of the frequent association of the term 'underclass' with this conservative view, many critical scholars refuse to use it.

The size of the underclass appears to be growing in North America and Europe, as governments reduce the scope and universality of social programmes, and as mental health patients are deinstitutionalized. The impact of IMMIGRATION on the underclass is also a topic of concern, and some authors believe that a new 'rainbow underclass' is forming in the USA (e.g. Portes, 2003; for an opposing view, see Waldinger and Feliciano, 2004). PUBLIC POLICY in Western countries tends to oscillate between liberal/radical and conservative views on poverty and the underclass, sometimes targeting structural problems (e.g. the 'war on poverty' of the 1970s in the USA; the creation of the Social Exclusion Unit in 1997 in the UK; see SOCIAL EXCLUSION), while at other times attempting to change the behaviour of the poor by reducing welfare payments ('welfare reform' of the 1990s in the USA) and/or providing additional funds to those who are entrepreneurially inclined (Midgley, 2001; Peck, 2001b). DH

Suggested reading
Auletta (1982); Gans (1995); Massey and Denton (1993).

underdevelopment A term used to signify a comparative absence of DEVELOPMENT, but which is now less commonly used by scholars (though it retains its popular, even populist force). It emerged as part of a postwar DISCOURSE on ECONOMIC GROWTH in the THIRD WORLD, where it functioned mainly as an adjectival noun. Underdevelopment here functioned mainly as a noun. MODERNIZATION theorists grouped together a number of countries that they described as traditional or pre-modern. These countries had not yet 'taken-off' towards an era of high mass consumption (see STAGES OF GROWTH). By the standards of the USA and other 'developed' countries, they suffered from underdevelopment (Hoselitz, 1952). Underdevelopment here defined a linked set of states that included: being mainly agricultural or rural; being religious or even fatalistic in outlook, but definitely not scientific; being poorly served by roads, railways, schools and clinics; and being beset by high rates of population growth and poor environmental conditions. The Promethean IDEOLOGY of development was meant to change all this, including in underdeveloped socialist countries. AID and planning would be the handmaidens of the transition from a state of underdevelopment to a state of development.

We now see that many of the concerns expressed by modernization theorists in the 1950s and 1960s reflected the anxieties felt by US liberals (e.g. W.W. Rostow) and conservatives (e.g. Samuel Huntington) about economic and political development in postwar America. There was particular concern about the strength of authority relations at a time of rapid social change. These concerns were allied to an extraordinary faith in the view that all countries would one day learn to be modern in the American way. Both Rostow (directly) and Huntington (indirectly) were active in promoting the USA's WAR in Vietnam in line with this secular faith. COMMUNISM was a deviant ideology that had to be defeated. PEASANTS had to be pushed (or bombed) out of the countryside, where they were coming under the influence of the Vietcong (Gilman, 2003). Significantly, however, a sparky group of Latin American scholars in the 1960s strongly challenged the idea that underdevelopment should be defined as an adjectival noun. Andre Gunder Frank (1966) famously declared that while all countries had at some stage been undeveloped, only in the 'Third World' had some countries been *made* underdeveloped. Frank, in other words, moved to redefine underdevelopment as an active verb. In his view it described not an original state of virgin forests and wilderness (see NATURE), but a grim landscape of impoverishment that had been created as part of the development of the capitalist world system. CAPITALISM, Frank suggested, created development and underdevelopment as two sides of the coin (see DEPENDENCY THEORY). Arranging countries on a straight line from underdeveloped to developed made no sense. It ignored the active creation of their very different geographies by common processes of unequal EXCHANGE and UNEVEN DEVELOPMENT. SCO

Suggested reading
Gilman (2003).

uneven development The spatially and temporally uneven processes and outcomes (socio-economic and physical) that are characteristic of, and functional to, CAPITALISM. One of the most striking features of human geographies, particularly those activities and indicators conventionally labelled as 'economic', is their unevenness at every SCALE. This is evident in the organization of the global economy (e.g. the categories of First and THIRD WORLDS, or core, peripheral and semi-peripheral countries); at regional scales within most countries (e.g. heavily industrialized or finance-centred regions versus 'laggard' or persistently poor rural areas); within metropolitan areas (e.g. 'INNER CITIES' versus SUBURBS); and within many cities at NEIGHBOURHOOD and block-by-block scales.

NEO-CLASSICAL ECONOMICS typically regards such unevenness as temporary, and assumes or predicts that capitalist DEVELOPMENT ('ECONOMIC GROWTH') will produce movement towards EQUILIBRIUM over space and time, leading to eventual CONVERGENCE (cf. modernization).

By contrast, MARXIST GEOGRAPHY views such unevenness as actually *produced* by capitalism. Neil Smith, the leading geographical theorist of uneven development, emphasizes that it is not merely a reflection of a highly heterogeneous world in which perfect uniformity is always unlikely; nor is it even solely the result of the fact that it is useful to capitalists. Rather, it is an *unavoidable consequence* of capitalism as a MODE OF PRODUCTION, '... the systematic geographical expression of the contradictions inherent in the very constitution and structure of capital' (Smith, 1990, p. xiii). If true, this would mean that that ongoing capitalist development will not eliminate unevenness; rather, it will continually recreate it. Empirically, the historical geography of capitalist MODERNITY would seem to support the latter position.

Uneven development is central to the geographies of capitalism for several reasons. Capitalist firms and states arguably *depend* upon geographical unevenness to perform functions essential to the ongoing ACCUMULATION of CAPITAL, such as displacing and ameliorating CRISIS tendencies (e.g. via the constant provision of new sites for investment) and disciplining workers or states (e.g. via threats to move jobs to lower-wage locations, or punitive disinvestment). More fundamentally, though, capitalist production *necessarily* results in uneven development, whether or not particular capitalists intend, desire or benefit from it. This is because of the unavoidable tension between the need to invest capital in the built environment in relatively fixed and enduring ways in order to engage in production, and the need for capital to remain mobile in order to circulate as value and remain available for investment in new locations and industries with higher rates of profit. As Smith puts it, 'The spatial immobilization of capital in its material form is no more or less a necessity than the perpetual circulation of capital as value. Thus it is possible to see the uneven development of capitalism as the geographical expression of the more fundamental contradiction between use value and exchange value' (1990, p. xv). The concrete implications of this rather abstract formulation are that the process of development in a particular PLACE is very likely to foster conditions that will make it a less attractive location for further investment in the not-too-distant future: wages and ground RENTS will rise, the workers concentrated there will have increased incentives and means to organize politically, and so on – all meaning that the anticipated rate of profit

on future investments there will compare unfavourably to that in less developed locations. Conversely, the consequences of underdevelopment often include conditions attractive to capital and conducive to high rates of profit: high unemployment, low wages and rents, states eager to co-operate and more. Uneven development can thus be seen as the unity of the seemingly opposed, but intimately connected, processes of DEVELOPMENT and UNDERDEVELOPMENT.

Perhaps the critical point regarding uneven development is that there is no reason to expect it to end: capital can move back and forth among places indefinitely in multiple rounds of INVESTMENT, sequentially building up, abandoning and reinvesting in the same locations. Debates over such dynamics have been central to MARXISM (see Smith, 1990): Marx himself, as well as Rosa Luxemburg and others, suggested at points that capitalist development depended on the continual incorporation of previously uncolonized areas, and that once that the global expansion of capitalism was complete, it would lead towards a homogenous LANDSCAPE of capitalist development and the preconditions for international socialism. The end of colonial expansion failed to curtail the development of capitalism, though, calling such a vision into question and leading Lenin and Trotsky to recognize and theorize the evident fact that capitalism could develop via uneven development within areas already internal to capitalism. Underdevelopment came to be understood less as a condition of neglect or exclusion from the international capitalist economy, and more as something *actively produced* though *inclusion* in that economy, often on unfavourable terms.

MARXIST GEOGRAPHY tackled the question of uneven development anew in the 1980s and 1990s, with Harvey (1999 [1982], 2001) and Smith (1990, 1996b) in particular seeking to develop a systemic theory of the geographical dynamics of capitalist development, and they and others endeavouring to delineate more precisely how uneven development works in specific types of settings. Neil Smith has introduced at least two arguments that have influenced much subsequent research in geography. The first, developed with respect to older urban areas and GENTRIFICATION, suggested that a large RENT GAP could be identified as an underlying mechanism triggering switches between periods of disinvestment and reinvestment in urban areas (Smith, 1979c, 1996a). The second was that the ongoing PRODUCTION OF NATURE under capitalism ensures that more and more of the non-human world is transformed by the dynamics of capitalist uneven development (Smith, 1990). These concepts have informed much subsequent research attempting to trace *how* capital circulates through built and natural environments, constantly recreating and undermining distinctions such as urban versus rural or suburban (e.g. Henderson, 1999; Murdoch and Lowe, 2003; Darling, 2005). Related work on INDUSTRIAL LOCATION theory has explored industrial geographies in light of theories of uneven development – theorizing, for instance, the 'windows of opportunity' for firms and sectors to dramatically change their geographies (Storper and Walker, 1989).   JM

Suggested reading
Harvey (2001); Smith (1990).

universalism   The idea that defining characteristics of phenomena, conceptual definitions or moral, aesthetic or epistemological truths hold for all times and places, transcending their immediate local circumstances (see EPISTEMOLOGY; MORAL GEOGRAPHIES). Such characteristics, definitions and truths are made on the basis of wider practices and theoretical schemes, the justification for which is given by their universal starting point. Plato first made the distinction between universals and particulars. Universals are the general referents to which words such as 'redness' or 'goodness' or 'beauty' refer, whereas particulars are their concrete instances; for example, the red serge jackets of Canadian Mounties, Mother Theresa or a Van Gogh painting. The postwar history of GEOGRAPHY can be read as the history of the invocation of different universals. So, for example, those committed to HUMAN GEOGRAPHY as SPATIAL SCIENCE appealed to the universals of QUANTITATIVE METHODS and RATIONAL CHOICE THEORY; MARXIST GEOGRAPHY looked to the universal of value as defined by the LABOUR THEORY OF VALUE; and HUMANISTIC GEOGRAPHY to a universal HUMANISM. Recent work in the HUMANITIES and social sciences, including human geography, and going under the signs of POSTMODERNISM, POST-STRUCTURALISM and POST-COLONIALISM, criticizes the use of universals, connecting their deployment to systemic POWER differentials around (for example) GENDER, CLASS and RACE. So, for example, the 'universal' SUBJECT of classical humanism turns out to have been bourgeois, male and European, but these markings were unremarked in the vocabulary of universalism to which the IDEOLOGY appealed. Universals are thus another means by which oppression and domination are realized.   TB

Suggested reading
Tsing (2004, Introduction).

urban and regional planning   The design and institution of specific policies and LAWS to guide land use in METROPOLITAN AREAS (or sub-areas), usually by or at the direction of governments. Urban and regional planning is inherently a spatial activity: the broad goal is to 'provide for a spatial structure of activities (or of land uses) which in some way is better than the pattern existing without planning' (Hall, 2002c [1975], p. 3). Planning involves predictive statistical analyses about future growth of population and economies, combined with architectural and landscape blueprints (often in the form of land-use and ZONING maps) for the physical manifestation of such growth in space. Computer technology (especially GEOGRAPHIC INFORMATION SYSTEMS) has transformed planning from blueprints for the future to a notion of 'a continuous series of controls over the development of [an] ... area' (ibid., p. 12).

UTOPIAN ideals for the physical layout and social structure of CITIES and SOCIETIES have existed for centuries (see UTOPIA), but the creation of formal planning as a profession and activity in GOVERNANCE culminated from a series of separate yet interrelated political and social concerns in the nineteenth and twentieth centuries about public health and sanitation, CRIME, POVERTY and, in the USA, immigrant ASSIMILATION (Hall, 2002b [1988]). It is rooted in the utopian ideals of MODERNISM, and a faith in the capacity for scientific and technical reason to achieve the goals of order, coherence and regulation. In the twentieth century planning was institutionalized at different SCALES of government (e.g. federal, state and municipal) to manage the growth and expansion of cities, especially in terms of land use and provision of INFRASTRUCTURE (particularly transportation and utilities). Patrick Geddes and Lewis Mumford were instrumental in reconceptualizing American and British urban or town planning into *regional* planning in the 1910s and 1920s. In the same period, ZONING was established in the USA, enabling the land-use controls that are essential to planning.

Ebenezer Howard's design for and realization of his 'GARDEN CITY' in Letchworth, England (between 1898 and 1903), was one of the first explicit attempts at urban and regional planning. One of his primary goals was to seek a balance between industry and NATURE, a goal shared with the parks movement in the USA, particularly as advocated by Calvert Vaux and Frederick Law Olmsted (Jackson, 1985; Hall, 2002a [1988]). The 'City Beautiful' movement was another response against industrialization, but one that focused primarily on physical architecture rather than land use overall (Hall, 2002a [1988]). The architect Le Corbusier's grandiose visions were influential in the creation of entirely new cities in Brasilia, Brazil and Chandigarh, India (Hall, 2002a [1988]).

With the rise of NEO-LIBERALISM, urban and regional planning is increasingly a PUBLIC-PRIVATE PARTNERSHIP, with an emphasis in some countries on self-help initiatives (Drakakis-Smith, 1997). The impact of GLOBALIZATION and competition among GLOBAL CITIES also curtail the authority of planners working at the urban and regional SCALE. The 'pillars' of modernist planning have been 'crumbling' for at least three decades for other reasons as well (Sandercock, 2003, p. 2). Jane Jacobs (1961) leveled an early and highly influential critique and alternative. More recently, Leonie Sandercock (2003) has charted 'the life and death' of modern planning, outlining alternative progressive, democratic planning practices influenced by feminist, post-colonial and postmodern theory (See FEMINISM, POSTMODERNISM, POST-COLONIALISM). DGM

Suggested reading
Hall (2002a [1988]); Jacobs (1992 [1961]); Sandercock (2003).

urban ecology Two different perspectives relating to the study of urban environments: the first, drawn from the CHICAGO SCHOOL, examines the SPATIALITY of urban land use and social groups; while the second refers to URBAN NATURE and an ECOSYSTEMS approach.

Urban ecology from the CHICAGO SCHOOL is part of the broader HUMAN ECOLOGY tradition. It treats urban land-use patterns as the result of social processes such as competition, SEGREGATION, INVASION AND SUCCESSION among social groups, resulting in a 'natural' spatial order despite constant MOBILITY and expansion of the system (Berry and Kasarda, 1977). Hawley (1950, cited in Berry and Kasarda, 1977) modified this ecological approach to emphasize interdependence among individuals and their activities, and constant ADAPTATION to the physical and social

environment (Berry and Kasarda, 1977). Scholars continue to pose research questions relating to human organization and COMMUNITY, urban form and environmental adaptation, but the urban ecology approach as derived from underneath the human ecology umbrella is not dominant. Critiques of the Chicago School's biological METAPHORS and lack of specificity in defining key terms, such as 'environment' (Berry and Kasarda, 1977, pp. 14–15), contributed to the decline, as has the rise of new approaches to concepts of NATURE and ECOLOGY itself.

The *ecosystem* perspective – often called *urban* POLITICAL ECOLOGY – is the contemporary, and dominant, approach to urban ecology (Keil, 2003). It shares with the early ecological approaches recognition of the importance of interdependence, social relations and human-environment relations (Vasishth and Sloane, 2002). But as Wolch, Pincetl and Pulido (2002) point out, the Chicago School ecologies transposed biological metaphors and ecosystem thinking on to human activity and relationships, leaving all conceptualizations of nature as separate from and outside of the urban. Contemporary urban ecology seeks to redress this omission, incorporating nature and non-human species into an approach that recognizes the interdependency and coexistence of social, political and environmental processes and events in the urban sphere. Urban political ecology examines urban and nature as interrelated, mutually constituting dynamics, rather than separate arenas (Keil, 2003). Further, urban political ecology explicitly links urban environments and problems of SUSTAINABILITY to global processes such as CAPITALISM. Urban ecology is one of a growing area of ecological scholarship, analytically linking humans and nature in LOCAL-GLOBAL RELATIONS. DGM

Suggested reading
Keil (2003); Swyngedouw and Heynen (2003).

urban entrepreneurialism A strategic and political response by urban policy-makers to the loss of income from taxes and intergovernmental fiscal transfers. It entails a shift from the management of PUBLIC SERVICES to speculative strategies intended to attract private investment and government grants through place-marketing, spectacular developments and so forth (Harvey, 1989a). Entrepreneurialism is distinguished from earlier rounds of boosterism by the local public sector's assumption of RISK associated with development through its role in PUBLIC–PRIVATE

783

PARTNERSHIPS. Jessop (1998) adds a definition of entrepreneurialism focused on INNOVATION: urban entrepreneurs devise new ways of doing urban GOVERNANCE in order to be as competitive as possible.   EM

Suggested reading
Hall and Hubbard (1998).

urban exploration Involving journeys through CITIES as a means of discovery and the construction of geographical knowledge, the term is often associated with the activities of nineteenth-century social explorers and reformers, who ventured into urban spaces in the 'heart of empire' to report on their conditions and bring them to wider public attention. As with cultures and practices of EXPLORATION more generally, such explorations have been subjected to considerable critical attention, which has focused on the colonial DISCOURSES and unequal power relations that framed them, the encounters they involved, and the ways in which their accounts were not simply neutral but had material effects – for example, scripting urban areas as 'dark', 'undiscovered' and populated by a 'race apart' (Driver, 2001a, ch. 8: cf. COLONIALISM; IMPERIALISM). The term has been appropriated for other ends, however. Among those seeking to turn around the colonialist language of exploration has been the radical geographer Bill Bunge, through his urban 'expeditions' in the late 1960s and early 1970s as part of the Society for Human Exploration. Based in Detroit and later Toronto, these aimed to be contributive rather than exploitative, democratic rather than elitist, as they worked with disenfranchised residents of INNER CITIES, planning *with* them rather than *for* them (see Merrifield, 1995; see also RADICAL GEOGRAPHY).

More recently, the term 'urban exploration' has been taken up widely by individuals and groups interested in investigating areas of cities that are 'secret', overlooked, forgotten or obscure. Such practices are also sometimes named 'infiltration' and typically focus on places off limits to the public, including abandoned buildings, ruined constructions, transit and utility tunnels, storm drains, rooftops or secure sites (Ninjalicious, 2005). Often involving photographic documentation, and imbued with a sense of play and curiosity, their profile and popularity has expanded rapidly through media attention and proliferating INTERNET sites. Modes of urban exploration have also been important in recent ARTS, cultural and writing practice through projects that seek to engage with city spaces and their potentialities beyond galleries and other formal arts institutions (Pinder, 2005b). Some of these are indebted to the earlier politicized spatial practices of the SITUATIONISTS as well as to longer visionary and literary traditions of urban wandering as they intervene in how spaces are imagined, represented and lived. (See also PSYCHOGEOGRAPHY.)   DP

Suggested reading
Driver (2001a, ch. 8); Pinder (2005b).

urban fringe Those areas around urban cores that are functionally or morphologically linked (but not necessarily contiguous) to the urban REGION and have an emerging (sub) urban settlement structure. They tend no longer to be dependent on agriculture alone and do not simply take overflow from urban industrial, transportation or commercial activities in the core. The term is a statistical category. Statistics Canada, for example, defines the urban fringe as including 'all small urban areas (with less than 10,000 population)' within census metropolitan areas that are 'not contiguous to the urban core' (http://geodepot. statcan.ca/Diss/Reference/Tutorial/UF_tut2_e. cfm).

In the 1980s and 1990s the urban fringe was the focus of much attention, as traditional urban cores lost significance to industrial and commercial competitors in SUBURBS and networked small towns close to METROPOLITAN areas. Terms such as 'EXOPOLIS' (Soja, 1992), '*Zwischenstadt*' (Sieverts, 2003) or 'EDGE CITY' (Garreau, 1991) signalled the growing significance of emerging denser nodes in the urban fringe.   RK

urban geography The geographical study of urban spaces and urban ways of being. It was the CHICAGO SCHOOL of sociology, and not geographers, who initiated the study of urban space (Fyfe and Kenny, 2005). Early urban geography was characterized by historical studies that saw physical MORPHOLOGY to be a determinant of urban development, or regional studies that looked at the different relations between towns. By way of contrast, Chicago sociologists studied HUMAN ECOLOGY, gathering data through social surveys and PARTICIPANT OBSERVATION, and producing rich urban ETHNOGRAPHIES. It was not until the mid-1950s that geographers, drawing heavily on sociology and NEO-CLASSICAL ECONOMICS, and on the LOCATIONAL THEORIES of geographers Chauncey Harris and Edward Ullman, systematized the sub-discipline of urban geography. Over the next 50 years, urban geography advanced to a central position in the discipline. By the 1960s and 1970s, urban geographers had become key players in the QUANTITATIVE REVOLUTION. Urban geographers adopted LOCATIONAL ANALYSIS, the philosophy of POSITIVISM and the methods of SPATIAL SCIENCE as the tools of their trade. The economy of cities was central to their work and a number of urban geographers sought to translate their theories into urban policy prescriptions for the revitalization of deindustrializing cities. The theoretical models associated with this SPATIAL SCIENCE, such as CENTRAL PLACE THEORY, industrial location theory, urban FACTORIAL ECOLOGY and the RANK SIZE RULE, was the backbone of a broadly (neo-)classical school of analytical urban geography. At the same time, there was other work on the city in geography that resisted the orthodoxy of spatial science. Kevin Lynch's (1960) *The image of the city*, provided a sort of BEHAVIOURAL GEOGRAPHY that looked at people's perceptions of the urban environment by analysing their MENTAL MAPS, and prefigured, in radically different form, recent work on the city as text, and the BODY and the city.

By the early 1970s, however, spatial science was being criticized for not explaining the social PROCESSES behind the spatial patterns being mapped and modelled, and two alternative theoretical frameworks emerged – one from MARXISM, espousing a radical POLITICAL ECONOMY approach, and the other from HUMANISM, drawing on the PRAGMATISM and the more interpretative methods (as opposed to the MODELS) of the Chicago School. These approaches are evident in two very different books that focused on the city – David Harvey's (1973) *Social justice and the city* and David Ley's (1974) *The black inner city as frontier outpost: images and behavior of a Philadelphia neighbourhood*. The former rejected liberal assumptions about the city and began to expose the structural logic of CAPITALISM and its role in social inequality; the latter was interested in how individuals experienced the city and the values and meanings they attached to it. Although focused on the city, these books are often seen to be studies in SOCIAL GEOGRAPHY – this mirrors the fact that studies of the urban at this time began to dominate other sub-disciplines, including also CULTURAL GEOGRAPHY, ECONOMIC GEOGRAPHY and POLITICAL GEOGRAPHY and sub-disciplinary boundaries became more blurred. Indeed, patterns of urban social and ethnic SEGREGATION were being analysed by social geographers such as Ceri Peach and Fred Boal.

From the late 1970s, global economic (and, indeed, the associated social) RESTRUCTURING significantly expanded the scope of urban geography. New research agendas emerged looking at financial capital, silicon landscapes, telecommunications networks, the new URBANISM, the new (urban) middle class and GLOBAL CITIES. Research interests moved away from the INNER CITY to the SUBURBS and EDGE CITIES and, indeed, outwards from the metropolitan to the global SCALE. Those that did choose to study the inner city looked at urban revitalization initiatives and festival marketplaces, and began to theorize processes of GENTRIFICATION. The geographical literature on gentrification that was to become so central to urban geography in the 1990s saw its genesis in the mid-1980s with the publication of Smith and William's (1986) *Gentrification of the city*. In this edited collection, theoretical debates raged between structure and HUMAN AGENCY. From this point on, urban geographers began to seek a more sophisticated conceptualization of agency in an urban geography that was dominated by political economy. In the late 1980s, Marston, Towers, Cadwallader and Kirby (1989) argued, in a chapter titled 'The urban problematic', that urban geography was suffering from a decline in its vitality due to the crippling historical legacy of outmoded approaches, but that it was beginning to move into new areas of research and expertise. In the 1980s, two distinct but overlapping developments – FEMINISM and POSTMODERNISM – began to permeate urban geography. Feminism charged urban geographers to look at the lives of women in the city and to reconsider urban theory in the light of feminist theory (McDowell, 1983), whilst postmodernism forced urban geographers to consider the privileging of one urban theory over another, the social construction of the urban, and the fact that there were differences in the city other than CLASS and RACE/ETHNICITY, such as GENDER, age, SEXUALITY and DISABILITY.

In the 1990s, the import of feminism and postmodernism forged the CULTURAL TURN in social geography and the subsequent emergence of the new CULTURAL GEOGRAPHY in the discipline as a whole. As a result of urban geography's relatively greater attachment to quantitative and applied work, the strong influence of political economy, and its long tradition of empirical and practical research, it embraced the cultural turn relatively late. This state of affairs was nowhere more apparent than in the debates over gentrification that dominated urban geography at this time. In the early to mid-1990s, debates over the causes of gentrification became stalemated between Neil Smith's political economy production explanation and David Ley's humanist CONSUMPTION – explanation – demonstrating to many geographers the necessity of challenging and (re)negotiating such metanarratives. In some respects, however, the slower import of the cultural turn into urban geography was fortuitous, as it meant that urban geography was able to avoid many of the allegedly immaterial excesses in which social and cultural geography became embroiled (Lees, 2002). Over time, interest in the IDENTITY politics of DIFFERENCE in the city grew, culminating in the notion of 'cities of difference' (Fincher and Jacobs, 1998). The hegemony of human-centred urban theories was questioned so that non-human actors, such as ANIMALS, began to be included in urban theory, leading Wolch, West and Gaines (1995) to construct a trans-species urban theory. And urban geographers began to integrate the study of LANGUAGE and CULTURE into urban geographical analysis much more fully.

In many ways symptomatic of the fact that more or less everything and everywhere had by now become urban and that urban geographers identified themselves less as urban geographers and more as feminist, postmodernist, Marxist or population geographers, in 1993 Nigel Thrift proclaimed an 'urban impasse' – the loss of the urban as both a subject and object of study. Nevertheless, refocusing on the urban as a subject and object of study, there was a proliferation of work in the 1990s on global cities and on global economic restructuring. Certain cities emerged as the command and control centres of global capitalism – cities such as New York, London and Tokyo. Sassen (1991) argued that such global cities are characterized by an hourglass socio-economic profile, with growth at the top and bottom ends and decline in the middle ranks. Hamnett (1994) refuted this claim, arguing that the outcomes of GLOBALIZATION in cities are mediated by national and city specifics. Rather than focusing on individual cities, Beaverstock, Smith and Taylor (2000) examined the NETWORKS that connect such world or global cities. Drawing on sociologist Manuel Castells' (1996b) *The rise of the network society*, they argued that global cities should be studied less as places and more as a process located in a networked space of FLOWS.

The notion of global or world cities, though, is very much from the point of view of the WEST. And urban geographers are increasingly critical of the HEGEMONY of the West in urban theory, evidence of the impact of POST-COLONIALISM on urban geography. Countering this hegemony, urban geographers are now complicating the dichotomy between the urban NORTH and SOUTH in terms of both URBANIZATIONS and URBANISM, and between First World and THIRD WORLD cities. Unlike McGee's (1971) pioneering work on Third World cities, which called for urban models to be sympathetic to the cultural and historical backgrounds of such cities, contemporary work on Third World cities argues that in an era of globalization a process of convergence has emerged such that there should now be a single urban discourse that is inclusive of all cities. Chakravorty (2000), for example, uses Calcutta to demonstrate concerns about Third World cities being viewed separately from the development of First World cities, and argues that urban development in one part of the globe cannot be understood without reference to urban development elsewhere in the world. This idea that urban processes are now converging around the globe can also be seen in the gentrification literature. For gentrification is now seen to be a process of 'new urban COLONIALISM' occurring all over the globe from Brazil to Poland to Japan. Also linked to global economic restructuring, POST-SOCIALIST cities have come under the lens of urban geographers. There has been some research on post-socialist eastern and central European cities, but more recently there has been a proliferation of research on the 'market socialism' of contemporary Chinese cities. Perhaps not surprisingly, it seems to be the economically successful cities that attract the most research. Jenny Robinson (2004) asks how it is possible to write across diverse urban contexts, which are distinctive and unique, but also interconnected and part of widely circulating practices of urbanism. She argues that suggestions that growing convergences between cities of the 'North' and the 'South' make them more comparable are a little misleading, and that the ambitions of post-colonialism suggest that simply universalizing Western accounts of cities is inappropriate. Instead, she suggests that if we are to engage in a properly comparative or transnational urbanism we need to excavate and disturb some long-standing and frequently taken-for-granted assumptions about how urban geography deals with differences among cities. She argues that two key concepts have led urban studies to this impasse – the concepts of MODERNITY and DEVELOPMENT. These have to be unpacked and urban geography allowed to learn from the diverse tactics of urban living around the world.

As urban geography entered the twenty-first century, Michael Dear (2000) proclaimed that 'the dominance of the Chicago model is being challenged by what may be an emergent "LOS ANGELES SCHOOL"'. Like the Chicago School, the LA School is not a geography school; rather, the LA School is made up of scholars largely, but not solely, based in the Graduate School of Architecture and Urban Planning at UCLA, even if many of those scholars are in fact geographers. Where Chicago was seen to be the exemplar of the old, modern, industrial city, Los Angeles is touted as the exemplar of the new, postmodern, POST-INDUSTRIAL city. With its decentred urban SPRAWL, GATED COMMUNITIES and EDGE CITIES, LA is (re)presented as the prototypical postmodern urban landscape – multinucleated, disarticulated and polarized. The city has become so unpredictable that the School represents it as a centreless urban form, a keno gameboard in place of the Chicago School's concentric rings of industry and settlement. Yet this new representation is still subject to the forces of capitalism. Dear even invents a new language for the new urban processes to be found in LA to signify the distinctiveness of postmodern urbanism – words such as 'cybergoisie' (elite executives and entrepreneurs), 'protosurps' (marginalized surplus labour), 'commudities' (commodified communities) and so on. Most geographers have been critical of claims about the PARADIGMATIC status of Los Angeles. Nijman (2000) has argued that Miami, which also experiences the same issues, but at a smaller and as a result more intense scale, is more deserving of the status of quintessential postmodern city; whilst other authors have criticized the 'thin' methodologies behind the LA School's research. In time to come, 'postmodern urbanism' may become one of the definitive statements of the LA School, 'notable more for its intellectual bravado than theoretical displacement' (Beauregard, 1999): on the other hand, all that is not solid also melts into air.

At the same time as urban geography has taken on board the interpretative turn, it has begun to move in another direction too, towards what Batty (2000) calls 'the new urban geography of the third dimension'. Here, the approach is quantitative rather than qualitative, and studies use data sets to detect fine-scale, intensive and extensive, patterns in metropolitan areas. In this work, GIS and modelling are the central techniques not textual, semiotic or DISCOURSE analysis. This reminds us that urban geography covers a large community of researchers, using different approaches to study the urban. In contrast to the LA School's representational turn, Amin and Thrift's (2002) *Cities: reimagining the urban* demonstrates a non-representational turn (see NON-REPRESENTATIONAL THEORY). Amin and Thrift argue that cities are too intricate and as such are difficult to generalize, thus voicing the limits to REPRESENTATION encountered in the HERMENEUTIC tradition. They argue that the city is a spatially open entity, cross-cut by various mobilities – people, information, commodities – and as such to properly engage with the 'multiplexity' of the city we have to recognize that cities are the 'irreducible product of mixture'. This way of looking at the city has implications for how we define urban life and for a new politics of the city.

In recent years, urban geographers have become more confident of their position again. Aitken, Mitchell and Staeheli (2002) maintain 'that [urban] geographers are [now] at the forefront not only of understanding contemporary urban space, but also of imagining and mapping its futures'. No doubt connected to this new confidence, urban geographers have begun to reflect on the postwar development of urban geography, to which the numerous special issues devoted to this in the journal *Urban Geography* over the past few years attest. Urban geographers have also begun to re-engage more clearly with questions of urban policy, and to promote an urban geography that critically evaluates urban theory and methods and has a social change and/or justice agenda. This 'new' urban geography has practical relevance and resonance, and the material engages with, and works through, substantive political engagement.   LL

Suggested reading
Allen, Massey and Pryke (1999); Bridge and Watson (2000); Fyfe and Kenny (2005); Hall (2000); Pacione (2001b, 2002).

urban managers and gatekeepers State bureaucrats (managers), such as officers in public housing and planning agencies, and private-sector professionals (gatekeepers), such as estate agents (realtors), landlords and mortgage lenders, who control access to urban resources, particularly housing (cf. HOUSING

787

CLASS; HOUSING STUDIES). Their professional norms and, in some cases, personal bias condition the access of certain social groups (often defined by RACE) to housing through DECISION-MAKING and allocation practices – withholding or providing erroneous information, differential pricing, selective advertising and REDLINING. The work of Pahl (1975) and others spurred much research, while recent work in the American context (Yinger, 1995) suggests that despite legal restrictions, non-whites continue to face discrimination in the housing market.   EM

Suggested reading
Pahl (1975).

urban nature A combination of seemingly contradictory terms: conventionally, where there is the CITY, there cannot be NATURE. In the past, urban life was decidedly built in contradistinction to rural and agricultural forms of life. Nature, like 'uncivilized' forms of life, was banned within the walls of cities. URBANIZATION, in fact, has often been understood as a process of human distancing from first nature (Lefebvre, 2003 [1970]). In cities, nature became a residual or artificial category limited to parks, ZOOS and urban – mostly ornamental – gardens. Still, twentieth-century urban theory was strongly influenced by the ways in which nature was understood by modern science. The CHICAGO SCHOOL of urban sociology organized thinking on social structures and processes around notions taken from evolutionary biology and ECOLOGY (see HUMAN ECOLOGY). These METAPHORS were so strongly criticized by human geographers and urban sociologists (Harvey, 1973; Castells, 1977; Gottdiener, 1985) that it became extraordinarily difficult to conceptualize 'urban' and 'nature' together. The impasse was broken in the 1990s, when scholars in POLITICAL ECOLOGY began to question the non-urban focus of their field and its search for 'nature' outside of cities. Some urban political ecologists began to question the non-urban focus of their field, which looked for nature outside of cities. The new field of URBAN ECOLOGY studies the specific bio-physical natures found in urban settings (Breuste, Feldman and Uhlmann, 1998). Planners and designers have taken nature into consideration when altering urban form (Hough, 2004). Urban social geographers at the same time began to take a fresh look at urban nature. Signature studies of individual cities such as Chicago (Cronon, 1991), Los Angeles (Davis, 1998) and New York City

(Gandy, 2002) placed nature in a continuum of societal relationships rather than separate from it. SOCIAL JUSTICE concerns were widened to include issues of urban ENVIRONMENTAL JUSTICE (Harvey, 1996; Bullard, 2000). By the mid-1990s, the notion of 'zöopolis' was added to acknowledge the presence of animals inside cities (Emel and Wolch, 1998; see ANIMALS). Going even further, urban geographers have now begun to speak about 'trans-human urbanism' to express the collapsing of boundaries between human and non-human nature(s) in cities (Braun, 2005). Originally used in the context of studies on urban SUSTAINABILITY (Newcombe, Kalma and Aston, 1978), the concept of 'urban metabolism' has now become central to critical explorations of urban nature (Heynen, Kaika and Swyngedouw, 2006). Urban political ecology in both the global SOUTH and the (post-)industrial NORTH has begun to acknowledge the importance of thinking urban nature as part of, rather than different from, social and cultural processes in cities.   RK

Suggested reading
Desfor and Keil (2004); Kaika (2005); Keil (2003, 2006); Swyngedouw (2004).

urban origins Most archaeologists, geographers and historians recognize five distinctive CULTURAL HEARTHS in which cities first emerged:

- Mesopotamia (modern Iraq) (3500 BCE);
- the Nile Valley (Egypt) (3000 BCE);
- the Indus Valley (modern India/Pakistan) (2300 BCE);
- the Huan He (Yellow River) Valley (China) (1500 BCE); and
- Meso-America (600 BCE).

The sites and locations differ, but so too did the process. In Mesopotamia urban trajectories were long drawn-out, for example, whereas in much of the Indus valley the transition to a distinctively 'urban phase' was much more rapid (Possehl, 1990). Gordon Childe (1946, 1950) claimed that the formation of cities was so dramatic that it constituted a veritable *urban revolution*, whereas Lewis Mumford (1963) insisted that early cities emerged through the concentration and condensation of cultural forms that pre-existed their crystallization and so preferred to speak of an *urban implosion*.

There has also been a lively debate over the importance of RELIGION: Mumford insisted that it was 'only for their gods' that people

	Physical space	Symbolic space
Religion: intervention of the gods	Sacred precinct; ziggurats; pyramids; temples	The city as sacred space ('the pivot of the four quarters')(1946, 1950)
Economy: redistribution of the surplus	Granaries, barns, cisterns; jars and vats ('a container of containers')	Writing systems (inventories then chronicles)

would have been mobilized on such a scale and for such extensive periods of time, and Paul Wheatley (1971, 1972) saw the city as not only a SACRED SPACE but also a *cosmogram*, 'the pivot of the four quarters' (see also Carl, Kemp, Laurence, Coningham, Higham and Cowgill, 2000). Others, reactivating Childe's MATERIALISM, insisted on the importance of the production and concentration of a surplus within a supra-local economy dominated by REDISTRIBUTION (Harvey, 1973). It may be, however, that the distinction between 'religion' and 'economy' owes more to our own language-systems and analytical distinctions than to the world-views of the people who made these extraordinary transitions. Focusing on the king as 'the dominant locus of spatial production in southern Mesopotamia by the Ur II period', Smith (2003b) argues that the king was *both* the guarantor of the fertility of the land, and as such responsible for constructing many of the large irrigation canals required for agricultural production on the arid plains of Sumer (see Adams, 1966), and also guarantor of the security of the city, and as such responsible for propitiating the gods through a monumental architecture of ziggurats and temples (see Gates, 2003). In short, the choice between 'gods' or 'granaries' may be a false one (see table).

Most urban geographers and historical geographers have seen the study of urban origins as little more than a platform from which to explore other, to them more pressing, issues about the nature of URBANISM (Carter, 1977). But research into the origins of URBANISM – in the canonical sites and in others – has been revitalized in recent years by new excavations, new techniques of REMOTE SENSING and reconstruction, and new ideas (in particular a move beyond the 'new archaeology' of the 1970s, which was closely modelled on SPATIAL SCIENCE, to a closer co-operation with anthropology and a correspondingly greater interest in economic, cultural and political processes). Three debates have been particularly important in opening up the trajectories through which cities first emerged in different cultures around the world:

- *'Decoupling' urbanization from agriculture.* Trading on two major excavations at Çatal Hoyuk in Anatolia by James Mellaart and Ian Hodder (see Hodder, 2006), and on a thought-experiment by Jane Jacobs (1992 [1961]) – in which Çatal Hoyuk becomes 'New Obsidian' – Edward Soja (2000b) proposed that 'Rather than an agricultural surplus being necessary for the creation of cities, it was cities that were necessary for the creation of an agricultural surplus.' It is important to recognize that the relations between subsistence, surplus and city formation were many-stranded, but the rise and fall of cities was often intimately connected to changing ecological regimes and it seems unlikely that such a global reversal can be sustained.
- *'Decoupling' urbanization from state formation.* The first cities were closely associated with the invention of writing systems, but these were usually inventories of stocks and flows of goods pivoting on the temple (rather than chronicles of kings) and so do not necessarily tie the formation of the city to the emergence of a centralized STATE (see Yoffee, 2005). In South Asia, for example, Smith (2006a, p. 109) shows that cities were tied in to larger *economic* systems and were 'long-lived regardless of the political configuration in which they were located'.
- *'Decoupling' urbanization from elites.* Cities, then as now, were more than monumental performances of power. Many scholars do still accept that the first cities 'stressed the insignificance of the ordinary person, the power and legitimacy of the ruler, and the concentration of supernatural power' (Trigger, 2003, p. 121). But Smith (2006a) insists on 'the willing presence of a population' – as Mumford (1963) had it, the first cities were 'magnets' as well as 'containers' –

789

and Smith sees these cities as 'a focal point for social, economic and ritual NETWORKS sustained and invested in by the hundreds and thousands of people who lived in them' so that the result was 'the product of negotiation, compromise and consensus among many different individuals and groups.' DG

Suggested reading
Gates (2003, pp. 29–119); Smith (2003b); Yoffee (2005).

urban renewal A term referring to a range of strategies aimed at reshaping urban LANDSCAPES and remedying social and economic problems associated with run-down INNER-CITY NEIGHBOURHOODS. These strategies, generally promoted by STATE actors and business interests, are frequently questioned and/or directly opposed by residents of central-city neighbourhoods. Nevertheless, they generally result in massive landscape change and the displacement of large numbers of existing residents. Debate around urban renewal tends to focus on the interests that drive it, the specific strategies employed to achieve it, and the impacts of renewal strategies on targeted neighbourhoods and their residents.

Urban renewal has a long history, with antecedents in the Haussmannization of Paris in the 1850s and 1860s, for instance. Yet, it generally refers to massive STATE-led building projects in the wake of the Second World War in Europe and in North America. The first phase of postwar urban renewal, in the 1950s and 1960s, was characterized by massive public works projects that razed established neighbourhoods in favour of new commercial districts, housing projects and highways in the name of MODERNIZATION (Berman, 1983). These projects were conceived and driven by powerful state bureaucracies and, in some cases, by powerful individuals such as New York's Robert Moses. Bureaucrats wielded their power not merely to address self-evident urban problems but to actually constitute specific neighbourhoods, and by extension, certain people and ways of life, as problems to be remedied. Narrow definitions of 'blight' were central to the identification of areas in need of renewal; a fact that highlights the often problematic combination of POWER, DISCOURSE and SPACE in urban renewal (Weber, 2002).

Growing criticism of these strategies – the negative impacts of which largely fell on the poor and racial minorities who were forcibly displaced – led, by the 1970s, to a wider set of renewal policies. These new approaches responded to critiques, levelled by people such as Jane Jacobs (1992 [1961]), of the high-handedness of planners and the deadened nature of the new spaces they produced.

In the next three decades, individual urban renewal projects have been marked by combinations of strategies, the relative weight of each being governed by the specific context in which each project is operationalized. Massive state-led redevelopment projects continue in some contexts while, in others, the refurbishment and preservation of older neighbourhoods, often with the involvement of neighbours in localized, participatory planning processes, has emerged as an important approach. These strategies have been accompanied by the emergence of PUBLIC-PRIVATE PARTNERSHIPS as a business-oriented, often property-led strategy, which still dominates a great deal of urban renewal and is exemplified by large-scale urban developments across Europe (Moulaert, Rodriguez and Swyngedouw, 2003).

Contemporary studies emphasize the role that the arts, TOURISM, mega-events (such as the Olympic Games) and GENTRIFICATION play in urban renewal and the uneven benefits that stem from these strategies. Others highlight alternatives to dominant public–private approaches, involving various forms of community development – from co-operative ownership models for housing to alternative methods of investing in inner-city COMMUNITIES – all of which indicate the ongoing tension and struggle that accompanies attempts to define problem areas in cities or to formulate and implement equitable solutions to those problems. EM

Suggested reading
Berman (1988); Moulaert, Rodriguez and Swyngedouw (2003).

urban social movement Collective action based on grievances that originate or are physically manifest in urban areas, such as a lack of PUBLIC SERVICES, in which the STATE is the primary target for ACTIVISM. A debate in the 1980s focused on whether there were distinctively *urban* SOCIAL MOVEMENTS, and whether these were necessarily progressive in their goals (Fincher, 1987). Castells (1983) argued that urban social movements were, more so than other social movements, oriented to grievances around COLLECTIVE CONSUMPTION, rather than around class. Yet other scholars pointed out that some urban social movements address conflicts in the sphere of production (Fincher, 1987).

A central theme of urban social movements is activism against or seeking a response from the state, which is held responsible for uneven provision of public services (Fincher, 1987). Castells (1983) identified urban social movements with very different grievances, directed at or limited by their focus on the state. Claims relating to collective consumption were exemplified by activism in France over provision of housing (Castells, 1983). Other urban social movements incorporated claims such as those around IDENTITY politics. Activists in San Francisco, for example, sought legitimation and social rights requiring state action. Castells (1983, p. 171) found these latter movements to be limited in their membership and scope, because of their adoption of social categories (identities) that defined and divided groups according to state administrative frameworks. Nonetheless, urban social movements in general could achieve some success, which may have contributed to their institutionalization, and a decline of the movements themselves (Castells, 1983; Fincher, 1987).

More recent scholarship has tended to examine social movements as a whole, with urban social movements viewed simply as territorial manifestations of broader identity, CLASS and SOCIAL JUSTICE conflicts (McAdam, Tarrow and Tilly, 2001). Activists in THIRD WORLD cities continue to seek redress for inequalities in urban service delivery, illustrating the salience of concerns oriented to collective consumption (Mitlin and Satterthwaite, 2004). Many challenges to state service provision, however, are occurring on a multi-national, multi-SCALE level, as part of broader ANTI-GLOBALIZATION efforts.   DGM

Suggested reading
Mitlin and Satterthwaite (2004); Pickvance (2003).

urban system A set of interlinked cities and towns set within a specific territory (e.g. the nation or the globe). The concept owes its origins to CENTRAL PLACE THEORY and SYSTEMS analysis approaches to economic functions, and functional DIVISIONS OF LABOUR, within national territories (Berry, 1964). While the evolution and contemporary characteristics of national urban systems remains a focus of research, a great deal of urban systems-oriented scholarship now focuses on the global scale. Contemporary GLOBAL CITIES or WORLD CITIES research seeks to understand how a NETWORK of cities, stretched unevenly across

the world, organizes the spaces of the global economy (Taylor, 2004).   EM

Suggested reading
Taylor (2003).

urban village A concept developed by Gans (1962) in his ETHNOGRAPHY of an Italian immigrant NEIGHBOURHOOD in central Boston. He identified elements of a coherent local, or 'village-like', social world – including ETHNICITY, kinship, friendship and values – that reflected and bolstered residents' identity and helped maintain it over time. Spatially, this social world is located in a clearly defined urban neighbourhood where much of the population has long-standing ties – an urban village. This argument was set against the understanding, within URBAN ECOLOGY, of URBANISM as leading to individuals' withdrawal from intimate social interactions.   EM

Suggested reading
Gans (1962).

urbanism Three common definitions for this highly contested term can be distinguished:

(1) *The typical way of life of people who live in a city or town.* In this first sense, the concept is usually traced back to Louis Wirth (1938), a CHICAGO SCHOOL sociologist who witnessed and described URBANIZATION in Chicago in the early twentieth century as a process of change to the moral order and the decline of COMMUNITY. The DIVISION OF LABOUR and sociocultural and socio-economic diversification lead to both fragmentation of individuals' lives in cities and to the normal expectation of living in the proximity of 'unknown others'. Using the criteria of size, density and heterogeneity, Wirth claimed the specificity of 'urbanism as a way of life'. Often, this quality of urbanism is confused with the notion of urbanity, which ascribes characteristics such as sophistication, refinement and courtesy to individuals or communities.

(2) *The study of life in cities and towns.* In this second sense, urbanism combines a scientific method of urban enquiry and an often linked practice of socio-spatial engineering (planning) typical of complex modern societies.

(3) *Urbanism now often refers to the way people live more generally.* Magnusson (2005) is

only one of a succession of commentators who, since Lefebvre (1970 [2003]) foresaw a modern 'urban revolution', has claimed that it is 'only recently that preponderantly modern urban societies have emerged'. The traditional split of town and countryside has been eliminated. As society becomes more urbanized, the CITY disappears as the distinct object of enquiry and practice, and urban society overall becomes the object of scientific enquiry and policy action. Critics have argued that this is both an ETHNOCENTRIC and a TELEOLOGICAL use of the term, since it equates urbanism with (and by implication normalizes) a MODEL specific to the global NORTH. Thus Robinson (2004, p. 710) insists: 'This phantasmagoria of urban experiences in the west, this western "modern," often fails to capture the inventiveness and creativity of people in poor cities, more often tied to the heroic (tragic?) resilience of urban dwellers in the face of extraordinary difficulties, rather than to the creative potential of city life.'

French philosopher Henri Lefebvre (2003 [1970]), arguably the most influential urban theorist of the past fifty years, was critical of the ideological and state-centric qualities of urbanism as a state-led project of modernization: 'Urbanism ... masks a situation. It conceals operations. It blocks a view of the horizon, a path to urban knowledge and practice. It accompanies the decline of the spontaneous city and the historical urban core. It implies the intervention of power more than that of understanding. Its only coherence, its only logic, is that of the state – the void. The state can only separate, disperse, hollow out vast voids, the squares and avenues built in its own image – an image of force and restraint' (ibid., pp. 160–1). This state-centred urbanism militates against the possibilities of the urban and against the promise of the right to the city in urban society. In Lefebvre's own notion of an urban society, which now encompasses the globe, urbanism in this sense will ultimately need to be critiqued and overcome to make way for liberated urban EVERYDAY LIFE.

If urbanism is our way of life more generally, it can also be used as a prism through which human societies and their futures can be understood. The postmodern urbanism of Los Angeles was discussed in this manner during the 1980s and 1990s (see LOS ANGELES SCHOOL). In the same sense, commentators have looked at other cities more recently as windows into a common future: 'Dubai is an extreme example of urbanism. One of the fastest growing cities in the world today, it represents the epitome of sprawling, post-industrial and car-oriented urban culture. Within it, large numbers of transient populations are constantly in flux' (Katodrytis, 2005). The term 'urbanism' has of late also been used in compound phrases to describe either real developments in the constitution of cities or normative prescriptions on how to build (better, more sustainable, more liveable) cities. Among the former is the term 'transnational urbanism', popularized by Michael Peter Smith (2001a), who believes in the establishment of cities as places through multifarious social relationships in spaces across national BORDERS (see TRANSNATIONALISM). Among the latter, the term 'urbanism' has now been resuscitated by the followers of the architectural style and practice of New Urbanism which, with its higher than usual densities and architectural features such as front porches and back alleys, is ostensibly meant to be a realistic answer to urban SPRAWL in North America. Observers have called this a 'new suburbanism', which invokes notions of density and residential community believed absent from common suburban forms of urbanism. (Lehrer and Milgrom, 1996). Similarly, Timothy Luke has appealed for 'contemporary urbanism as public ecology', which puts ecological issues into the centre of the urbanist project today (Luke, 2003). RK

urbanization   John Friedmann (2002) differentiates three meanings of urbanization. The most common use of the term is *demographic* (see DEMOGRAPHY) and it refers to 'the increasing concentration of people (relative to a base population) in urban style settlements at densities that are higher than in the areas surrounding them' (p. 3). The experience and expectation of human demographic change is ultimately the complete statistical urbanization of the world. Demographic urbanization is tied to an increase in the complexity of social life (Lefebvre, 2003 [1970]: see also URBANISM). Distinct patterns and configurations of human settlement structure growth of cities: suburbanization, exurbanization, new urbanism, metropolitanization and the emergence of city-regions. Density is not always part of urbanization, as urban regions SPRAWL across wide expanses in emerging forms of settlements as diverse as SUBURBS, excluded GATED

COMMUNITIES in natural settings and squatter settlements (see SQUATTING).

A second notion of urbanization is *economic*. Friedmann makes reference here to 'economic activities that we normally associate with cities' (2002, p. 4). While this traditionally would exclude 'rural' activities such as agriculture, FORESTRY, fishing or mining, Friedmann reminds us that many of these activities are directly related to urban forms of capitalization and organization. This observation is shared by Lefebvre, who notes: 'The *urban fabric* grows, extends its borders, corrodes the residue of agrarian life. This expression, "urban fabric," does not narrowly define the built world of cities but all manifestations of the dominance of the city over the country. In this sense, a vacation home, a highway, a supermarket in the countryside are all part of the urban fabric' (Lefebvre, 2003, pp. 3–4). Economic urbanization leads tendentially to the disappearance of 'residual' rural activities and ultimately to 'the erasure of the traditional category of rural' (Friedmann, 2002, p. 4: cf. RURAL GEOGRAPHY).

The third meaning of urbanization is *sociocultural* and 'refers to participation in urban ways of life'. This implies the embrace by populations of URBANISM as a way of life. While it is possible to identify certain developments, such as literacy, universally with sociocultural urbanization, Friedmann cautions against equating CIVILIZATION with urbanization in the tradition of the CHICAGO SCHOOL (see also Robinson, 2004). Friedmann is also quick to point out that 'sociocultural urbanization is a dimension that, like the economic, is no longer exclusively associated with the CITY as a built environment' (p. 5). While cybercafés clearly are nodes in virtual deterritorialized NETWORKS, erstwhile urban practices such as certain modes of communication are now found in the most remote parts of the world.

Friedmann employs the term 'the skein of the urban' to describe 'a new global TOPOGRAPHY of the urban, which 'steadily advances across the surface of the earth'. Its 'vertical dimensions are layered [such that] demographic, economic, and sociocultural urbanizations do not necessarily coincide in space' (2002, p. 6). The nineteenth- and twentieth-century narrative of urbanization as MODERNIZATION has been called into question since the 1980s, when GLOBAL CITY researchers detected new societal cleavages even in Western cities such as Los Angeles and New York City. Mike Davis' influential text *City of quartz* (1990) presented a dystopian view of the globalizing Pacific Rim boomtown Los Angeles. In the global SOUTH, urbanization now commonly comes with underdevelopment. The emergence of huge agglomerations – for instance, in some African contexts – has led to two counterposed narratives of urbanization: 'The first is an eschatological evocation of urban apocalypse: POVERTY, VIOLENCE, disease, political corruption, uncontrollable growth and manic religiosity ... In this nightmare vision, the city is on the brink of a cataclysm brought about by civil strife and INFRASTRUCTURAL collapse' (Gandy, 2005, p. 38). A second view is more upbeat and focuses 'on the novelties of the city's morphology ... as the precursor to a new kind of urbanism, hitherto ignored within the teleological discourses of Western modernity; one which may be perfectly adapted to the challenges of the twenty-first century' (ibid., p. 39).

Considerable controversy has now ensued as to the way in which urbanization has to be understood in a global context. Some have visualized global urbanization processes in terms of new hierarchies and networks, detected as a new class of GLOBAL CITIES or WORLD CITIES. Others have resisted this narrative as Western and potentially imperialist, and have suggested models of global urbanization less tied into notions of supremacy of certain urban centres (Marcuse and van Kempen, 2000). Differences between urbanization in the global North and the global South seem to be getting more pronounced, with rates of urbanization higher in AFRICA, ASIA and LATIN AMERICA than in EUROPE and North America. And even inside larger REGIONS and among urban areas that appear similar on the surface, differentiation occurs. Terry McGee, for example, who has identified several distinctively *Asian* features of urbanization – dominance of the population giants; immense urban increments; the prominence of megacities; and uneven globalization – has also pointed to an internal 'two-tier structure of Asian urbanization'. Using Seoul, Korea and Dhaka, Bangladesh, as examples, he presents 'two extremes' of challenges of current urbanization in Asia: one economically successful, and the other not (McGee, 2001). Similarly different models of urbanization can be identified comparing seemingly similar types of cities on different CONTINENTS in the South. Drawing on her research on African cities, Jennifer Robinson (2006) argues against 'propagating certain limited views of cities and thereby undermining the potential to creatively imagine a range of alternative urban futures' (p. 173). At the end of the twentieth century, expectations rose that cities would lose their significance in a generalized NETWORK SOCIETY of FLOWS, which would make AGGLOMERATION in PLACE an anachronism. Little evidence has been forthcoming to support such an expectation, however, even in those parts of the world where absolute urbanization rates declined (Castells, 1996b; Sassen, 2000; Storper and Manville, 2006). It is safe to say that although urbanization and the resurgence of urbanization in the West are of prime significance, the main form in which urbanization now takes place is through SQUATTING by migrant populations in the demographic hot spots of the developing world. Urbanization now leads to a 'planet of SLUMS' (Davis, 2004a). RK

Suggested reading
Amin and Thrift (2002); Brenner and Keil (2006).

urbicide Literally 'killing cities', urbicide refers to the intentional attempt to erase or destroy a CITY or cities for political purposes. The term has two main origins.

One lies in the critique of modern urban planning. Building on the work of architecture critic Ada Louise Huxtable and her 'Primer on Urbicide' (Huxtable, 1970), Berman (1996) used the term to object to modernist redevelopment strategies in American cities and their violent substitution of soulless abstraction for vibrant traditional streetscapes. Echoing Berman, Merrifield (2004) invoked the same concept in his analysis of the SITUATIONISTS' resistance to comprehensive redevelopment in Paris in the 1970s.

The term was mobilized in a second sense by Balkan scholars and architects to condemn the way in which Serbian armed forces in the WAR of the 1990s targeted the architectures and spaces of Dubrovnik, Sarajevo and other cities that were most visibly identified with a history of religious, ethnic and national pluralism and heterogeneity in what rapidly became the former Yugoslavia (Coward, 2004: see also ETHNIC CLEANSING). Since then, the analysis of urbicide through military violence has been extended both historically and geographically. Scholars have explored what W.G. Sebald called the 'natural history of destruction', the campaign of British and American strategic bombing of German cities in the Second World War, in exactly these terms (see Mendieta, 2007), for example,

while Graham (2003), Gregory (2004a), Weizman (2007) and others have analysed how Israeli armed forces have deliberately destroyed the collective INFRASTRUCTURE of Palestinian cities as part of their attacks on the Occupied Territories since 2002.

The two streams of work, the economic and the martial, forcefully collide in discussions of URBANISM in the global SOUTH, where Goonewardena and Kipfer (2006) have identified a 'post-colonial urbicide' under the sign of a new IMPERIALISM (cf. Schwartz, 2007). These later studies strongly suggest that urbicide is about more than the hollowing out of urban economies, the destruction of MEMORY or the erasure of the physical traces of past communities, important and injurious though these are. Coward (2006; see also 2007) follows Martin Heidegger to argue that 'there is more to the constitution of a *polis* than the gathering of *anthropos*': in other words, the physical fabric of the city is not incidental to, but constitutive of the possibilities of political COMMUNITY. In destroying this relational space, urbicide targets the possibility of political community and the very provocation of DIFFERENCE – of heterogeneity – that is at its core. Seen thus, urbicide is a version of political VIOLENCE that is not 'merely' corporeal and material, but also profoundly existential: 'Urbicide is a politics of exclusion aimed at establishing the fiction of a being-without-others' (p. 434) (cf. GENOCIDE). SG/DG

Suggested reading
Graham (2004); Campbell, Graham and Monk (2007).

utilitarianism A theory of ETHICS originating in nineteenth-century Britain, prescribing the greatest good for the greatest number. The good is defined by acts that promote happiness, satisfaction or pleasure of the immediate actor and those affected by the act (and making utilitarianism part of a larger philosophical approach known as *consequentialism*). Utilitarians further assume happiness is quantifiable, thereby allowing calculation over an entire population: the world is as good as it can ever be when collective pleasure is maximized. Jeremy Bentham (1748–1832) developed the theory and John Stuart Mill (1806–73) elaborated it. Both intended utilitarianism to bolster their favourite political philosophy, LIBERALISM: only when people are free to choose will the greatest good for the greatest number be achieved (Mill's 'liberty principle'). Criticisms of utilitarianism are legion and include an inability to quantify happiness (Bentham's 'felicific calculus' is chimerical), that different people's happiness is incommensurable, that the consequences of an action may take a very long time to figure (when asked in the 1980s what he thought of the French Revolution, Chou En-lai said, 'It is too early to say'), and a fixation on consequences at the expense of intentions (good utilitarian acts may be carried out for monstrous reasons). Utilitarianism only lightly brushed GEOGRAPHY. A form of utilitarianism was found in the theory of NEO-CLASSICAL ECONOMICS that was briefly taken up in ECONOMIC GEOGRAPHY.   TB

Suggested reading
Singer (1993); Sinnott-Armstrong (2006).

utility theory The basis of NEO-CLASSICAL ECONOMICS, which rests on the doctrine of consumer sovereignty and an ideological belief in both individualism and libertarianism – that individuals are the best judges of their own needs. A consumer's utility function is identified based on either assumed or revealed preferences and predicts choices, constrained within the available budget (cf. REVEALED PREFERENCE ANALYSIS). Utility theory has provided the base for much work on travel behaviour and the choice of shopping centre to patronise, referring to destination, modal split (choice of travel mode), and choice of route (cf. DISCRETE CHOICE MODEL).   RJ

Suggested reading
Golledge and Timmermans (1990).

utopia Conventionally refers to an ideal SOCIETY, STATE or commonwealth in which the problems of the present have been transcended. This is often projected as an imaginary world in another space or time, as implied by the roots of the term coined by Thomas More in his 1516 book *Utopia*, which plays upon the Greek words *eu-topos* ('good place') and *ou-topos* ('no place'). Colloquial usage tends to present utopias as impossible social and political schemes, and hence a domain of escapism, impractical dreaming or authoritarian attempts to construct perfect societies. Yet utopias take many different forms and have a variety of functions, meaning that the concept is highly contested (Levitas, 1990). Utopias find expression in fictional depictions of the good society in LITERATURE, FILM or other media; in experiments to establish ideal communities; in the desire for radical change

expressed in many political struggles as well as visions, theories, plans and performances; and, according to some commentators, in an array of everyday activities that anticipate better worlds.

Geographical concerns are central to utopia, as its etymology suggests, with many utopias being set in remote locations or based on spatial designs for cities, architecture, landscapes or environments. These utopias typically express a belief in the power of SPACE to shape human activities, whereby an ordered space becomes a means to contain social process, exclude historical change, and ensure harmony and stability (Porter and Lukermann, 1976). Such a spatial emphasis is apparent in the long association between utopia and CITIES, and in the influence of utopian thought on URBANISM (Pinder, 2005). Projecting different spaces can defamiliarize and challenge what exists, allowing imaginative exploration of alternative ways of living and being. Such utopias may function to provoke, to open senses of possibility. Their imaginative failure may also be of interest, in terms of what it reveals about current limitations and constraints. Yet attempts to realize utopias based on static spatial forms have been fraught with problems and contradictions, especially concerning their authoritarianism, required to fix geography and freeze history to create this ideal realm, and the need to reconcile this with the social processes involved in their materialization (Harvey, 2000b). The particular interests driving their visions of order have thus come under critical scrutiny (Pinder, 2005c).

Recent years have witnessed many claims about the 'end of utopia', precipitated by events such as the collapse of COMMUNISM regimes and by claims that utopian thought is necessarily authoritarian if not downright dangerous. Yet some geographers have argued for a revitalization of utopianism to counteract pronouncements that 'there is no alternative', and in the process sought to reconceptualize utopias not in terms of blueprints but in more open and process-oriented ways. For the utopian is a vital moment in CRITICAL THEORY. Benhabib (1986, p. 226) identified the task of critique as the pursuit of both the explanatory-diagnostic and the anticipatory-utopian, but for the most part even CRITICAL HUMAN GEOGRAPHY has shown more of an interest in analysis and prescription: witness the speed at which discussions of Harvey's (1973) *Social justice and the city* moved away from the first two words of the title, with their intimations of ETHICS and politics, and fastened on the last two. But Harvey (2000b, p. 196) has now returned to these themes to advocate a 'spatiotemporal' or 'DIALECTICAL utopianism' that is 'rooted in our present possibilities at the same time as it points towards different trajectories of human uneven geographical developments'. While he still insists on the need to define choices and confront issues of closure so as to define 'that port to which we might want to sail', other critics, some influenced in particular by FEMINISM and by critical debates within utopian studies, have emphasized a partial and fluid approach to utopia. This gives a central role to *desire* and to moving beyond present limits into spaces and futures that are necessarily as yet unknown. DP

Suggested reading
Harvey (2000b); Levitas (1990).

V

value-added A process that adds value (as reflected in price) to some COMMODITY. Typically, value is added when labour is applied to a material, transforming it into something more useful (cf. MARXIST ECONOMICS). Value can be added sequentially, at different stages in the production process, as material is turned into a component, which is added to others to make a finished article, which is then packaged and marketed, for example. A value-added tax usually applies a fixed percentage to the price of a good or service; this discriminates against poorer people, who pay the same tax as the rich when they purchase the same thing.   DMS

values The principles or standards informing individual or group ideas and beliefs. Geographers have considered values held by both individual geographers concerning their subject-matter, and by individuals and groups concerning SOCIETY and NATURE. The evolution of debate over values in geography reflects different associations of the term, whether social, economic, political, environmental or moral. There is, however, common rejection of the separation of fact from values; in particular, the promotion of fact as self-evident and value-free in EMPIRICISM.

Values were a central question for HUMANISTIC GEOGRAPHY in the 1970s. Anne Buttimer's *Values in geography* (1974), produced for the Association of American Geographers' Commission on College Geography, suggested that geographers consider the values motivating and informing their analyses: 'the present time is in many ways ripe for the expression of our caring presence to the world via an authentically lived profession of geography' (Buttimer, 1974, p. 15). Buttimer reflected upon her own values, informed by personal history, Christianity and EXISTENTIALISM, and their shaping of geography as 'one of the regions of my care' (Buttimer, 1974, p. 4). Discussion of values shaping earlier and current geographical thought, and their consequences for disciplinary identity and geography's engagement with the wider world, followed. Buttimer asserted PHENOMENOLOGY and existentialism as approaches placing values at the centre of human experience.

Responses from Blaut, Gibson, Hägerstrand and Tuan supplemented and critiqued Buttimer; in its presentation of debate, *Values in geography* offers a fine insight into questions then shaping human geography. In 1996, *Progress in* HUMAN GEOGRAPHY accorded it the status of a 'classic' text; Buttimer reiterated its relevance while regretting the 'extremely anthropocentric bias in the whole discussion' (Buttimer, 1996, p. 518). The human valuing of the non-human had, however, informed other humanistic geographies, as in Burgess and Gold's collection *Valued environments* (1982), which highlighted the human creation of worlds of meaning, whether around public symbols or fields of everyday care: 'the close and enriching affective bond between people and the environments they create, inhabit, manipulate, conserve, visit or, even, imagine' (ibid., pp. 4–5).

Environmental values have remained an important subject for human geography, as in recent work on ANIMALS and MORAL GEOGRAPHIES. Smith (2000a) addresses the role of intrinsic, anthropocentric and biocentric values in debates over environmental ETHICS. Harvey (1996) offers a contrasting perspective on the valuing of environment, connecting values and monetary value. Wary of conservative appeals to values as a realm of permanence and stability, Harvey seeks 'to replace the fixed idea of "values" with an understanding of "processes of valuation"' (ibid., p. 11), and pursues a DIALECTICAL understanding of values and society: 'Values inhere in socio-spatial processes, and the struggle to change the former is simultaneously a struggle to change the latter (and vice versa)' (ibid., p. 12). The process through which nature is valued – whether through supposedly inherent value, monetary value or METAPHOR – becomes a nexus for understanding and intervening in the relations of society and environment (ibid., ch. 7). Discussion of values is here, as elsewhere, shaped by the definition of the term employed, and must be understood in relation to the political and social imperatives shaping an author's work.   DMat

Suggested reading
Buttimer (1974); Harvey (1996).

797

vector data Vector is a primary data type encoding geographical phenomena in GIS (another is RASTER). It is based on recording point locations (zero dimensions) using x and y coordinates, stored within two columns of a database. By assigning each feature a unique ID, a RELATIONAL DATABASE can be used to link location to an attribute table describing what is found there. Line segments (one-dimensional) have two points: a start and end node. Polylines are connected line segments; for polygons (two-dimensional) the start and end node is the same. TOPOLOGY may also be encoded. Vector objects are discrete but sometimes represent continuous fields; for example, as contours. RH

Suggested reading
O'Sullivan and Unwin (2002).

vertical theme A method of exploring change in CULTURAL LANDSCAPES by describing the processes visibly effecting that change. Attention to 'vertical themes' is an enduring feature in HISTORICAL GEOGRAPHY, but following the template set out by H.C. Darby the traditional approach has been to identify PROCESSES in landscape terms: thus in Darby's (1951) essay on the changing English landscape, six vertical themes were identified: clearing the wood, draining the marsh, reclaiming the heath, the changing arable, laying out the landscape garden, and urban–industrial growth. It would be possible to identify quite other themes in altogether different terms – the transition from FEUDALISM to CAPITALISM, including ACCUMULATION by dispossession, for example, and civil WAR and the consolidation of the modern STATE – all of which left their marks on the landscape. But Darby was concerned to distinguish historical geography from history, and so insisted on processes that could be located directly within the LANDSCAPE. He subsequently used 'vertical themes' defined in less restrictive terms, but still expressed in cartographic-narrative form (diachronic analysis), to connect a series of cross-sections through the landscape at particular dates (synchronic analysis) in his *New historical geography of England and Wales* (1973). (See also SEQUENT OCCUPANCE.) CW/JW

Suggested reading
Darby (1951, 1962).

verticality, politics of A term devised by Israeli architect and analyst Eyal Weizman (2002) to describe the three-dimensional relations between POWER, SOVEREIGNTY and TERRITORY. Weizman's argument is both general and particular. Most generally, he argues that territory must be conceptualized not as a flat MAP in two dimensions but as a three-dimensional SPACE. Sovereignty has had a vertical dimension since at least the nineteenth century through claims over subsurface RESOURCES (Braun, 2000), and since the Convention on the Regulation of Aerial Navigation (1919) individual STATES have routinely claimed complete and exclusive sovereignty over the air space above their territory. Indeed, modern WAR has come to rely on air power to such a degree that Graham (2004b) insists that the key vector of military power is now vertical and that it is necessary to formulate a 'vertical GEOPOLITICS'.

Weizman's core argument, however, is that these general claims have assumed a particular and intense significance during the continuing Israeli occupation of Palestinian territory. He has shown how the Israeli political strategy of colonizing the West Bank has involved extraordinary three-dimensional contortions of space to separate Israeli from Palestinian areas while maintaining Israeli control over both. Weizman emphasizes the intricate partitioning of the West Bank, the grid of Israeli colonies on the hilltops, and the network of Israeli by-pass roads, tunnels and checkpoints that work to produce 'parallel geographies' of First and THIRD WORLDS, 'inhabiting two distinct planes in the startling and unexpected proximity that only the vertical dimension of the mountains can provide'. DG

Suggested reading
Campbell (2004); Weizman (2007).

violence In her essay on violence, political philosopher Hannah Arendt (1906–75) emphasizes its instrumental character. Violence appears whenever POWER is in jeopardy and 'it always stands in need of guidance and justification through the ends it pursues' (Arendt, 2004 [1969], p. 241). Hence, violence in and of itself stands emptied of strength and purpose: it is part of a larger matrix of socio-spatial power struggles (Kaur, 2005). Violence has been defined by the Norwegian peace researcher Johann Galtung (1969, 1990) as tripartite: (1) as *direct violence*, or personal injury; (2) as *structural violence*, where structures of social injustice violate or endanger the right to life of individuals or groups of people in a society; and (3) as *cultural violence*, in which any aspect of CULTURE, such as LANGUAGE,

RELIGION, IDEOLOGY, ART or cosmology, is used to legitimize direct or structural violence. In comparison to other social sciences, HUMAN GEOGRAPHY came late to theorizing violence, but Hays-Mitchell (2005) has invoked a FEMINIST analysis that draws on these diverse understandings, specifically as social, political, and economic violence.

In fact, feminist geographers have long analysed geographies of violence against women and sexual minorities, both domestic and non-domestic, as well as the built environments that engender safer spaces (Valentine, 1998; Domosh and Seager, 2001) (see FEMINIST GEOGRAPHIES). Their work has recently extended to the ways in which violence during WAR is highly gendered (Mayer, 2000; Giles and Hyndman, 2004a). In 1996, for the first time in history, the international tribunal for war crimes in Yugoslavia prosecuted rape as a weapon of war and a crime against humanity, issuing indictments for torture and enslavement. This charge moved rape from the private realm, where it was an informal aberration of war, to a public one in which can be formally prosecuted.

Modern STATES not only claim a monopoly of the legitimate means of violence; they also routinely use the threat of violence to enforce the rule of LAW. Philosopher Giorgio Agamben (1998) outlines how the state has the capacity to make and enforce laws, but also the power to suspend them in times of emergency, thereby creating spaces of exception (see EXCEPTION, SPACE OF). Anthropologist Thomas Blom Hansen (2005, p. 111) notes that within such spaces 'the law is identical with violence but it is a particular form of violence'. Hansen shows how SOVEREIGNTY is an unstable and precarious expression of power that requires constant repetition and performance, including the threat of violence, to maintain its legitimacy. It follows that political violence can assume many forms, and that TERRORISM – in the sense of mobilizing fear as a weapon to intimidate a civilian population – cannot sensibly be confined to the actions of non-state actors. The terrorist attacks on the USA on 11 September 2001 produced a stream of work exploring geographies of political violence by both state and non-state actors (Gregory and Pred, 2007), and it is also clear that violence, in the form of riots or protests, can be a response to state oppression (Kaur, 2005).

Economic violence has been a particular concern of MARXIST GEOGRAPHIES, where a primary focus of research is on modes of dispossession and exploitation. The process of capital ACCUMULATION has required repeated rounds of dispossession, in the past and in the present, and is written into the prospectus of NEO-LIBERALISM (Harvey, 2003b; Springer, 2008) (see COLONIALISM; IMPERIALISM; PRIMITIVE ACCUMULATION). Exploitation is also written in to the labour process and wreaks its own violence in multiple capitalist and non-capitalist forms and their articulations (see, e.g., SLAVERY). Violence is often inscribed in the LANDSCAPE, sometimes deliberately so to intimidate others, while Mitchell (2002b) argues that its aestheticization erases the conflict-laden work of its production and thus contributes to a generalized economy of violence. This is part of a wider process of the commodification of SPACE, and Blomley (2003) contends that physical violence is an intrinsic part of the foundation, legitimation and operation of Western PROPERTY regimes.

The real challenge is to trace the connections between these and other modes of violence: for violence cannot keep within the artificially produced and policed boundaries of the social, the political and the economic.   JH

virtual geographies   A term describing the GEOGRAPHICAL IMAGINARIES and VISUALIZATIONS made possible through the use of computer network technologies such as the INTERNET and virtual reality (VR). Propelled by the extraordinary growth and development of computerized networks such as the Internet since the mid-1990s, virtual geographies have become an increasingly important means of imagining, simulating, visualizing and representing geographical worlds. They are (re)produced through computerized and animated digital animations, GEOGRAPHIC INFORMATION SYSTEMS, immersive VR systems, video games and the three-dimensional simulation of geographical PLACES, and call forth an enormous range of virtual geographical worlds and visual metaphors as means of entertainment, projections of fantasy, and instruments for planning and controlling places in new ways.

Geographical mapping and representation of the technologies of CYBERSPACE has been an important element in the critical analysis of virtual geographies. Here, geographers have sought to explore, first, how geographical METAPHORS and representations have been widely used as means to structure and make legible the electronic services accessible over the web. Second, they have developed a range of new CARTOGRAPHIC techniques to map the complex and unequal geographies that

799

characterize the DIFFUSION and use of computer NETWORK technologies (Dodge and Kitchin, 2001b). This work has helped to undermine the widespread myths that the Internet would lead to the 'end of geography' through the sheer motive force of speed-of-light interactions (Graham, 1998; see also TIME–SPACE COMPRESSION).

The proliferation of virtual geographies raises important questions about the relationships between electronic technologies and representations and contemporary CULTURE. These questions are economic and political as much as they are cultural, and the same can be said of the ways in which virtual geographies bring processes of SIMULATION and SURVEILLANCE into very close interaction as embedded surveillance devices provide continuous data feeds to sustain virtual representations of the dynamics of geographical change. These developments have been particularly significant in late-modern WAR (Graham, 2008a,c). Consider, for example, the way in which the first 1991 Gulf War was represented through TV reportage that used digital video footage from the noses of US 'smart' bombs (Wark, 1994), or the way in which the US military has become deeply invested in computer simulations to recruit 'the digital generation' and to train troops for overseas deployment in Mission Rehearsal Exercises (Graham, 2007, 2008a,c).

Finally, this proliferation of virtual technologies blurs the boundary separating 'real' geographical worlds from electronically simulated and imagined ones. This occurs as participants and observers become less and less able to separate and distinguish between the 'real' and the 'virtual'. As truly immersive systems proliferate, and participants increasingly adopt digitally simulated avatars and 'bodies' functioning 'within' virtual geographical space, this process seems set to intensify (Hillis, 1999). Indeed, virtual geographies are already being further complicated by the transformation of computerized network devices. These are moving from being separate artefacts such as networked PCs placed within geographical spaces, with which people interact through interfaces, and are being reinvented as small and even nano-scale constructions that blend ubiquitously and invisibly into wider geographical environments. Such trends mean that new critical approaches to virtual geographies are becoming necessary, which abandon any a priori distinction of the 'real' and the 'virtual' (see REPRESENTATION).   SG

Suggested reading
Crang, Crang and May (1999); Dodge and Kitchin (2001).

virtual reality Resulting partly from an ongoing challenge to the WIMP (Windows Interface, Mouse Pointer) screen that had emerged in the late 1980s, we might see virtual reality entering GEOGRAPHY through four moments. The first moment geography encounters virtual reality is as a METAPHOR for the digital condition. Virtual reality is seen as expressing a symptomatic cultural desire to escape the messy, inevitable complications of the real world for an infantilized or perfected digital realm (Slouka, 1995). The second more technical moment is through the Virtual Reality Mark-up Language (VRML), which enabled three-dimensional browsing through screen interfaces. While it has not challenged the 'page' metaphor of the web, it has been refined into technologies to create online worlds in CYBERSPACE. Third, this has been used to produce MODELS and SIMULATIONS of geographical locations for academic, marketing and educational purposes. Fourth, it has been part of initiatives to develop immersive environments. Here, using haptic interfaces that sense user motions and head-mounted displays, a user can interact with an entirely simulated environment all around them. While the cumbersome and faintly absurd appearance of virtual reality goggles and data gloves has limited their adoption, the technology has branched into other possibilities such as 'augmented reality', which attempts to 'overlay physical objects with virtual objects in real-time and allows people to experience the virtual as if it were real' (Galloway, 2004, p. 390).   MC

virus An entity that replicates itself by infecting more complex entities and taking advantage of their reproductive systems. Biological viruses are a key agent of disease in humans and other organisms (see AIDS; EPIDEMIOLOGY; PANDEMIC). Computer viruses are self-replicating strands of code that 'infect' information systems (see INTERNET). Usually destructive, viruses can play a creative role through their capacity to initiate connections between unrelated entities. For this reason, viruses are frequently used to figure for a view of relationality – variously termed transversal, rhizomatic or hybrid (see HYBRIDITY; RHIZOME) – which is presented as an alternative to linear genealogies (Ansell Pearson, 1977; Hinchliffe, 2004).   NHC

Suggested reading
Hinchliffe (2004).

vision and visuality The distinction between vision – a biologically determined structure of seeing – and visuality – a culturally constructed way of seeing – has not been challenged in geographical work, despite sustained interest in *embodied knowledges* (see BODY; SITUATED KNOWLEDGE). Vision has been paid little attention, and questions of visuality have been most fully engaged with by cultural geographers. The starting point for much of their work is that, like any other cultural TEXT, an IMAGE draws on particular culturally constituted signs, symbols and DISCOURSES in order to make its meaning. Images are thus understood as ensembles of visual practices that structure what is visible and invisible in specific ways. Such practices are at work in both the visual content of an image – what it shows – as well as in its visual and spatial organization – how it shows what it shows, and what position it invites its audience to take in relation to it. Much attention has been paid to how images thus constitute and reconstitute social IDENTITIES and social relations by visualising SPACE, PLACE, NATURE, LANDSCAPE, the NATION, the urban and the rural in particular ways. This significant body of work has now been joined by efforts to approach images from somewhere other than entirely within the field of CULTURE.

There is now a large body of work by cultural geographers that explores the specific visualities that have contributed to a range of geographical knowledges, both popular and academic. Much attention has been paid to the emergence of the idea of 'LANDSCAPE' in the WEST during the fifteenth and sixteenth centuries, for example (Cosgrove, 1984; Olwig, 2002). This work understands landscape as a means of organizing the visual field through a specific, territorializing SPATIALITY and a single viewpoint. Such landscapes have been associated with bourgeois and masculine ways of seeing the world as PROPERTY to be owned and known (Cosgrove, 1985; Rose, 1993). The association of some landscapes with national identities has also been traced (Daniels, 1993; Matless, 1998; Olwig, 2002), and the use of certain mapping techniques and photographic practices in the creation of colonial and imperial geographical knowledges has been explored (Harley, 1989; Ryan, 1997; see also CARTOGRAPHY, HISTORY OF; COLONIALISM; MASCULINISM; POST-COLONIALISM). Indeed, Gregory (1994) has asserted the complicity of geography as an emergent academic discipline with a modern Western visuality dependent on the possibility of a 'world picture'. Images produced by newer visual media, such as FILM, GEOGRAPHIC INFORMATION SYSTEMS, and tourist and family photography have also been examined as powerful means through which more recent places and spaces are constituted (see FILM; TOURISM).

While much of this work depends on claims that particular images are given their meaning by their historically and geographically specific context, or by their embeddedness in contemporary discourses (see VISUAL METHODS), Marxist strands of work also continue. Some pursue Harvey's (1989b) claim that many visual objects reflect changes in the time–space organization of contemporary CAPITALISM, and others pursue Deutsche's (1996b) somewhat less REDUCTIONIST account of the importance of design, ART and SPECTACLE to the capital's redevelopment of cities (see GENTRIFICATION). It is, however, possible to suggest that most geographers concerned with visuality have been concerned to place specific images into their 'context', whether that context be a culture, DISCOURSE or the demands of CAPITAL. However, two other approaches to visuality are now also evident in geographical work.

First, some geographers are arguing that while certain sorts of images participate in the cultural or discursive, they can also on occasion exceed it. This claim refers to photographs quite specifically, because of the way something of what photographic technologies do is to describe the world mimetically, beyond cultural signification (see MIMESIS). Geographers such as Goin (2003) and Edensor (2005) thus insert photographs of a desert and of industrial ruins into their written text, in order to enact the intrusion of those places' non-human, non-cultural agencies into the making of geographical knowledge. Second, others are suggesting that the effects of images can only be understood as they are encountered by viewers in particular places in quite specific ways (Rose, 2004a). This argument understands images as performed in encounters with people, and is less concerned with what images mean than with what they do and what is done with them (see PERFORMATIVITY). Hence geographers and others have explored how images are put to work in different places, and the various spaces and places that such work produces (Pinney, 2003; Rose, 2004a).

These moves (back?) towards understanding images not as texts to be read but as objects to be put to use has also begun to change the way geographers discuss their own visualities. The complicity of academic geography with colonial ways of seeing has been clearly traced. But recent accounts of the messy process of FIELDWORK have emphasized the work needed to produce such authoritative ways of seeing: effort that does not always achieve its intended end (Driver, 2001b). Things in the world may remain obscure and out of focus. And even if they are visible, some theorizations of the visuality offer reminders that being visible does not always make things noticeable or knowable; both ETHNOMETHOD-OLOGY and Foucauldian work suggest that noticing what is in full-view can often be extremely difficult (Laurier and Philo, 2004). Thus, as several geographers have agreed, much about the relationship between visualities and geographical knowledges still requires attention (*Antipode*, 2003). GCR

Suggested reading
Antipode, (2003); Cosgrove (1985); Rose (2004); Ryan (1997).

visual methods The history of geographical knowledge is replete with visual IMAGES of many kinds created in order to describe particular places. Although what constituted adequate description was often debated, the recent interest in visual methods in Anglo-American geography has been prompted in part by a move away from understanding images as in some way mimetic of the world (see VISION AND VISUALITY; MIMESIS). Instead, it is argued that images are active participants in the construction of geographical knowledges; and it follows that to explore that participation requires some consideration of method.

There are a range of possible methods for interpreting visual materials (Banks, 2001; Rose, 2007 [2001]). The most common approach to understanding the production of visual geographical knowledges depends on making connections between a specific image already in circulation, and the wider context of which it is a part. Such approaches have included ICONOGRAPHY – explicating the meaning of the discrete symbolic elements of an image – and semiology – treating an image or scene as a constellation of interrelated signs. Currently, however, the most common method focuses on a range of aspects of the content of an image in order to make claims about its effect in the cultural field. This has been described as a kind of DISCOURSE analysis (Rose, 2006), and is the implicit method adopted by much of the *new* CULTURAL GEOGRAPHY.

Fewer geographers have chosen to work with images produced as part of the research process. Some, however, have used images – often photographs taken by the geographer – to supplement written argument. Here, the implication is that although photographs, like any other visual image, become meaningful in relation to the wider culture of which they are a part, they also have some ability to exceed cultural meaning. They have thus been deployed by geographers with an interest in NON-REPRESENTATIONAL THEORY or MATERIAL CULTURE to suggest the agency of the more-than-human (see, e.g., Edensor, 2005).

The second way in which geographers have created images as part of the research process is by making images that exemplify or develop their analyses. Allen and Pryke (1994), for example, created montages that brought together what they saw as the different spaces of financial corporations' headquarters that, although constitutively interrelated, were kept separate in everyday encounters. Others have systematically photographed urban environments in order to understand better the detail and texture of GENTRIFICATION.

The third way in which images may be used more centrally in geographical research has been called 'photo-elicitation' by visual sociologists. In this approach, photographs are taken by people who the geographer has been researching for some time. The photographs are then used in further INTERVIEW work, as powerful stimuli that allow the exploration of issues that might otherwise not be broached in more conventional interview situations (see, e.g., Latham, 2004). GCR

Suggested reading
Rose (2006).

visualization A means of transforming data into visual representations that, for those who work within GEOGRAPHIC INFORMATION SCIENCE, takes place at the intersection of computing graphics and mathematics. Other human geographers, particularly within CULTURAL GEOGRAPHY, locate VISION and VISUALITY within a wider techno-cultural frame, but Kwan (2002) nonetheless claims that the intersection between computing graphics and mathematics allows more intuitive analysis and can incorporate many different agendas.

Visualization in this specific sense has its roots in early three-dimensional MODELS in SCIENCE (Watson, 1969) and in the use of computer graphics to display calculation results. But there is a much longer tradition of visual display in pre-digital GEOGRAPHY, from explanatory diagrams through the elaborate visual renderings of the idealized landscapes of SPATIAL SCIENCE to the three-dimensional displays of Torsten Hägerstrand's TIME-GEOGRAPHY. That spatial-graphical tradition has been re-energized through the development of Visualization in Scientific Computing (ViSC), and now increasingly incorporates relationships between conceptual and physical entities as well as three dimensions (Turk, 1994). Visualization is now widely accepted as a means of interpreting and 'making sense' of spatial patterns as part of a revivified cartographic imagination within these avowedly scientific streams of geographical enquiry (cf. MacEachren, 1994).

GEOGRAPHIC INFORMATION SYSTEMS can be understood as an ONTOLOGY of that which can be visualized. Visualization of spatial phenomena is a delicate play between deductive and inductive techniques, a subtle shift in science that GIS promotes. Visualization provides a greater understanding, leads to effective causal variable identification and improved HYPOTHESIS formulation, and results in more reliable predictive relationships between variables (Anselin, 1988). Visualization supports a wider range of collaboration and exploration with less concern for mathematical rigour, hypotheses testing and generality (Wright, Goodchild and Proctor, 1997). Visualization is a way of making quantitative approaches less mathematical as it allows researchers to work with a large number of variables. As the number of variables increases, measures of certainty are difficult to obtain and the analysis becomes less mathematical. NS

Suggested reading
Slocum, McMaster, Kessler and Howard (2005).

von Thünen model A model for analysing agricultural location patterns, based on the pioneering work of a Prussian landowner. Johann von Thünen (1783–1850) envisaged a single MARKET for farm products and suggested that distance from that point would be a prime determinant of both what was produced where and the RENT (net profit) generated there. Based on this variable alone, the model suggested a zonal land-use model (see figure), on the assumption that farmers produced the commodity on each tract of land that would maximize their net returns. Because of variations in the costs of transporting different agricultural products, bulkier and/or more perishable items are produced closest to the market, where land rents are

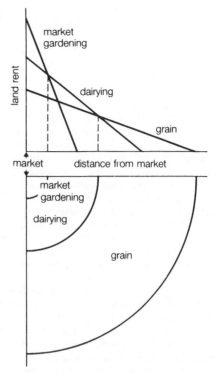

von Thünen model *Land rent variations and land-use patterns*

consequently highest, leading to a DISTANCE-DECAY gradient. This IDEAL TYPE arrangement – also suggested for urban areas (cf. ALONSO MODEL) – provides a MODEL against which reality can be compared, and can be modified to take account of variations in, for example, land PRODUCTIVITY

The von Thünen model was a central element in the promotion of HUMAN GEOGRAPHY as a SPATIAL SCIENCE, in the context of RATIONAL CHOICE THEORY and DECISION-MAKING. It was applied to land-use studies at a variety of SCALES (e.g. Blaikie, 1971; Peet, 1969; Block and DuPuis, 2001); Barnbrock (1974: see also Mäki, 2004) pointed out that many have been very partial in their use of von Thünen's ideas and fail to take account of his full project, which saw his model as an IDEAL TYPE of a spatial arrangement that would emerge under a benign form of CAPITALISM. Its means of simplifying the world in order to understand it has declined in relevance as transport costs have been reduced both relatively and absolutely, but it remains a valuable analytical framework. RJ

Suggested reading
Chisholm (1979); von Thünen (1966 [1842]).

W

war The mobilization of military or para-military VIOLENCE between political communities. Although the STATE is often defined in terms of its claim to a monopoly on the legitimate use of physical force, war is not confined to hostilities between states: *civil wars* are intra-state wars, *wars of liberation* are fought by resistance movements against (for example) COLONIALISM or military occupation (see OCCUPATION, MILITARY), and the global *'war on terror'* is waged by states against regional and international terrorist organizations. Nor is war confined to formal hostilities between the main parties ('hot wars'): the COLD WAR between the USA and the Soviet Union took many forms, including economic warfare and numerous *proxy wars*.

The history of geography (see GEOGRAPHY, HISTORY OF) has frequently intersected with the history of war: war has marked the practice of geographical enquiry and geographical knowledge has shaped the prosecution of war. Classical geography knew its strategic value – Strabo's CHOROGRAPHY was addressed to military commanders and civil administrators in the Roman Empire – while the institutionalization of geography as a university discipline owed much to the part played by MILITARY GEOGRAPHY in the unexpected victory of Prussia over France in 1870–1. Geography was instrumental in the development of a 'New Army' in Britain in the early twentieth century (Stoddart, 1992) and had a pivotal role in the formulation of modern geopolitics. Since then, geographical knowledge has been important to war in four main ways:

- *The resort to war* through the production of geo-strategic imperatives (see GEOPOLITICS).
- *The conduct of war* through the production of regional intelligence (Lacoste, 1973; Heffernan, 1996; Barnes, 2006b: see also AREA STUDIES; REGIONAL GEOGRAPHY).
- *The representation of war* through the production of IMAGINATIVE GEOGRAPHIES of 'the enemy' and the conduct of hostilities (Ó Tuathail, 1996a, 2005; Farish, 2001).
- *The memorialization of war* through the production of symbolic landscapes (Falah, 1996; Johnson, 2003b: see also MEMORY).

The importance of geography is not surprising, since war is fought over (and often about) TERRITORY, but new forms of war have introduced more complex concepts of SPACE. 'War,' Hirst (2005, p. 151) insisted, 'can never be de-spatialized.'

Yves Lacoste (1976) claimed that *La géographie, ça sert, d'abord, à faire la guerre* ('Geography's primary purpose is to make war'), and in an interview with Lacoste's journal, philosopher Michel Foucault was prompted to trace his own spatial preoccupations to a series of martial concepts (Foucault, 1976b/1980). In a course of lectures given that same year, Foucault explored the relations between SOVEREIGN POWER, DISCIPLINARY POWER and war, tracing how the post-medieval state came to assume the monopoly of legitimate violence, expelling war to its outer limits (frontiers) while 'secretly' allowing war 'to rage in all the mechanisms of power' beneath the surface of its own juridical order. Politics was thus the continuation of war by other means. Although Carl von Clausewitz (1780–1831) would eventually propose a strategic reversal in his treatise *On war* (1832) – 'War is not merely a political act but also a real political instrument, a continuation of political commerce, a carrying out of the same by other means' – Foucault saw this as a deceptive mapping of MODERNITY. Far from war being an interruption to the project of modernity, the last resort, the exception to be rationalized and regulated, war continues to saturate the social field; its strategies and modes of calculation are deployed to defend society (the imperative title of his lectures) against the dangers 'that are born in and of its own body' (Elden, 2002; Foucault, 2003: cf. GOVERN-MENTALITY). Late modern warfare is wired to POLITICAL ECONOMY – to NEO-LIBERALISM and its rounds of renewed ACCUMULATION by dispossession (Roberts, Secor and Sparke, 2003; *RETORT*, 2005: cf. RESOURCE WARS) – but on Foucault's reading it is also intimately invested in a racialized BIOPOLITICS. Both of these dimensions have been revealed with unusual clarity in the US-led 'war on terror' in the early twenty-first century (Dauphinee and Masters, 2007; Dillon and Reid, 2009: see also TERRORISM).

'New wars' (1)	'New wars' (2)
REASON – SCIENCE – LAW	UNREASON – TRADITION – CRIMINALITY
High technology: • professional, specialized armies • surveillance from air and space platforms • long-distance, precision-guided weapons	Low technology: • warlords and militias • local, ground-based knowledge • short-distance, often improvised weapons
Globalization: • the global arms trade • private (often foreign) contractors • accumulation by dispossession	Shadow globalization: • illegal and small arms trade • diasporic recruitment • traffic in conflict commodities
Strikes target combatants: • the 'erasure' of the body	Strikes target civilians: • war made flesh
The re-enchantment of war: • enforcement of international law • 'just wars' and military humanism	The dis-enchantment of war: • violation of international law • wars of economic predation

Some scholars have proposed the concept of a *mode of warfare* to characterize the 'complex of social relations through which wars are prepared, military power organized and wars fought' (Shaw, 2005, p. 42; Kaldor, 2006). Modes of warfare differ over space and time, but several writers have identified the contemporary emergence of new, global modes of warfare that are closely connected to GLOBALIZATION (cf. Bauman, 2001b) (see table).

On one side, and closely associated with the USA, is a *Revolution in Military Affairs* (RMA) and its successor projects, which promise that future wars can be fought with fewer ground troops through the intensive use of high technology by ever more professionalized and specialized armies. New systems of sensing and SURVEILLANCE from air and space platforms, advanced systems of information management ('command, control and communications' or C3), and weapons systems revolving around pilotless aircraft and robotic vehicles, precision-guided weapons and 'smart bombs', substantially rework the spatial templates of GEOPOLITICS. Crucially, the significance of physical distance is diminished though not erased: the distance over which air strikes can be launched is increased, but the global deployment of ground forces and equipment still poses logistical problems (Ek, 2000; Graham, 2008b; Singer, 2009). These developments have produced a convergence between military operations and the advanced sectors of the global economy, particularly the armaments, telecommunications and software industries, and the connections within the Military–Industrial–Media–Entertainment complex have been reinforced through the enhanced TIME–SPACE COMPRESSION made possible by NETWORK-*centric warfare*. This transforms the battle space from the conventional, linear form with its geometry of fronts and battles, advances and retreats; instead, military forces 'swarm' in complex, fluid formations through multiple theatres of war that 'will be as virtual as they will be geographic, coursing through the capillaries and conduits that comprise NETWORK SOCIETY itself' (Dillon, 2002, p. 74). The combined effect of these innovations is to institute a hypermodern form of warfare that creates what Coker (2004) calls a 're-enchantment' of war: offensive, 'surgical' strikes target combatants and supposedly minimize 'collateral damage', death virtually disappears from the battle space, and military interventions are increasingly staged as JUST WARS.

On the other side are so-called *new wars* fought by non-state and para-state actors including militias and guerrilla forces who, when they engage professional armies, resort to *asymmetric warfare*. For the most part these armed groups rely on local, ground-based knowledge and the use of cheap, light and even improvised weapons (Kaldor, 2006). Although their violence is close-range and even face-to-face, these conflicts often spill across BORDERS. Combatants take advantage of border zones, such as the tribal territories straddling the Afghanistan–Pakistan border, but their activities are also enmeshed in what Nordstrom (2004) identifies as an even wider 'shadow globalization': many of the armed groups are supported and funded (at least in part) by emigré communities; they draw their recruits from DIASPORIC populations, from REFUGEE camps and from city-dwellers who have been forcefully excluded from the global economy; and they are involved in trans-local networks that are non-state, non-formal and extra-legal, and which in many cases traffic not only in weapons but in CONFLICT COMMOD-ITIES such as drugs and diamonds. Münkler (2005, pp. 2, 36) represents these develop-ments as in some measure a throwback to the Thirty Years War (1618–48) and, in contrast to hypermodern forms of warfare, they create a rhetorical 'disenchantment' of war: they are extraordinarily savage and intensely corporeal, they deliberately target non-combatants, and they sustain an economy of lawless predation (see Gregory, 2009b).

These two modalities of war converged with extraordinary intensity in the early twenty-first century in the military operations undertaken by the USA and its allies in Afghanistan and Iraq and by Israel in southern Lebanon and occupied Palestine, where the advanced weapons systems of state militaries were met by crude missiles, improvised explosive devices, suicide bombs and guerrilla raids (Gregory, 2004b, 2006). Indeed, the two modalities have increasingly bled into each other: the US invasion of Afghanistan involved a high-tech war from the air in support of a ground war fought by US troops in close con-cert with the local militias of the Northern Alliance, for example, while the US occupation of Iraq prompted the US military to perform a 'cultural turn' that accorded local knowledge a central place within a counter-insurgency campaign that could not be waged through firepower alone (Gregory, 2008, 2009a). Critics have often claimed that American mili-tary power has been deployed in the service of a new American EMPIRE, and Münkler (2005) argues that these 'new wars' characteristically develop 'in the margins and breaches of former empires'. But the two modalities of war also increasingly converge in cities. According to Davis (2004b, p. 15), 'the poor peripheries of developing cities will be the permanent battle-fields of the twenty-first century', and urban warfare is an increasing preoccupation of mili-tary strategists (Graham, 2009a).

These two modalities of contemporary war have several mutually reinforcing effects:

- *They blur the distinctions between war and peace*: many of these conflicts are chronic with no clearly defined beginning or end, characterized by 'peace processes' rather than peace agreements.

- *They blur the distinctions between war and commerce*: the US military is not only closely connected to the global armaments industry, but it also relies on private service companies and contractors, and militia leaders and warlords often have a keen interest in the profits of war.

- *They blur the distinctions between civilian and combatant*: they make it difficult to distin-guish civilian and military spaces; conflicts increasingly spill across and in some places even constitute the spaces of EVERYDAY LIFE; and in many, perhaps most cases the majority of casualties are civilians (Giles and Hyndman, 2004b). Militias are often criti-cised for their indifference to civilian casu-alties, but Shaw (2005, pp. 71–97) insists that the RMA also involves the systematic transfer of risk to civilians whose deaths are explained away through either their own alleged complicity or accidental, 'collateral damage' (see also Gregory, 2006a).

- *They blur the distinctions between the real and the virtual*: late modern targeting and imaging systems radically transform the visual field of war, and professional armies are acutely sensitive to the effect of MEDIA images; militias are also keenly aware of the power of video coverage, and the 'war on terror' has involved the conscious deploy-ment of SPECTACLE and the mobilization of AFFECT on both sides (Ó Tuathail, 2003; *RETORT*, 2005; Gregory, 2006).

Even as the two modalities become entangled in one another, the distinctions between them have been RHETORICALLY reaffirmed to produce an imaginative geography that is also a MORAL GEOGRAPHY: thus 'our' wars are construed as humane wars because they are fought within the space of the modern – the space of Reason, Science and Law – whereas 'their' wars are inhumane because they are located outside that space. Dexter (2007, 2008) argues that this de-politicizes late-modern war – 'Western inter-vention is elevated to a position above politics' – and de-legitimizes all forms of warfare except those of the global NORTH, which then has both the obligation and the right to police the frontier between the two in the name of SECURITY.   DG

Suggested reading
Flint (2005); Gregory (2009b); Münkler (2005).

water   A prerequisite for life on Earth, water, unlike some 'natural' RESOURCES, has no sub-stitute. It is present at every SCALE, from the global atmospheric system to the individual cell, and stores, redistributes and releases about 30 per cent of the total amount of solar energy that hits the Earth (Clarke, 1993). To some extent a renewable resource, water's availability is nevertheless finite and dependent on regional variations, seasonal fluctuations and CLIMATE change, as well as being subject to sustained, and sometimes violent, local and GEOPOLITICAL disputes.

Water resources are powerfully shaped by human actions, including reduction of the Earth's storage capacity through development of the built environment (e.g. in the suburban expansion of major cities around the world); the degradation of water quality through POLLUTION (e.g. in the arsenic poisoning of groundwater wells in Bangladesh and West Bengal); and the overuse or mismanagement of water resources that makes them scarce (e.g. in the 1930s Dust Bowl in the Great Plains of the USA). Water has also attracted monumental feats of civil engineering and technological governance throughout human history, and has been frequently tied up with the constitution of NATION-STATES and national identities (see NATIONALISM). The mega-dams that became emblems of the assertion of independence of sovereign states (re)-emerging from the yoke of European IMPERIALISM in the second half of the twentieth century are one example. Another is the long history of sustained engineering that has gone, and continues to go, into stabilizing the low-lying territory of the Netherlands (Bijker, 2005).

Human geographers have made important contributions to understanding the material cultures and political economies of water use over a long period, through various theoretical perspectives. Amongst the most significant of these perspectives are ENVIRONMENTAL HISTORIES of the politics of water GOVERNANCE in situations of water scarcity and conflicting demand, such as in California (see Gottlieb and Fitzsimmons, 1991), and the constitutive role of water in the POLITICAL ECOLOGY of world cities such as New York (Gandy, 2002).   SW

welfare geography   An approach to geography where the emphasis is on SPATIAL INEQUALITY and TERRITORIAL JUSTICE. Bound up with the rise of RADICAL GEOGRAPHY in the early 1970s, welfare geography stresses the need to identify and explain the existence of CRIME, hunger, POVERTY and other forms of discrimination and disadvantage. Originally conceived by David Smith (1977), welfare geography basically sought to reveal who gets what, where and how. This early work was largely descriptive, and developed the abstract formulation used in welfare economics, grounding it empirically but maintaining the use of algebraic representations. It provided a basis for evaluation. Current welfare configurations, in terms of who gets what, where and how, could be judged against alternatives. This preoccupation with description eventually was matched, and then superseded, by work on the processes through which inequality is produced. MARXIST ECONOMICS replaced NEO-CLASSICAL ECONOMICS as the basis for explanatory analysis, which takes place at two different levels. The first involves understanding how the whole economic–political–social system functions, and teasing out generic tendencies (see MODE OF PRODUCTION). In the case of CAPITALISM, for example, this level of analysis reveals that inequality is endemic. UNEVEN DEVELOPMENT is the spatial imprint, the geographical result of the restlessness of capitalism as a system. The second level of explanation attends to the details of particular economic–social–political systems; for example, how housing policy under capitalism advantages some people in some places and disadvantages other people in other places. The analysis of the politics behind these policies has recently been reinvigorated (Staeheli and Brown, 2003), as part of renewed interest in the relationship between SOCIAL JUSTICE and the STATE. Accompanying an attention to the restructuring of the WELFARE STATE, which characterizes much of this recent work (Peck, 2001b), have been efforts to theorize a relational ETHICS of care. Drawing on FEMINIST theory, this work seeks to uncover the social relations behind constructions of care and of justice. Understanding politics as integral in the everyday doing of care, the emphasis is on the connections and relations rather than the difference between categories, such as private and public, state and MARKET (Smith and Lee, 2004).   KWA

Suggested reading
Smith and Lee (2004); Staeheli and Brown (2003).

welfare state   A social system whereby the STATE assumes primary, but not exclusive, responsibility for the welfare of its citizens – more specifically, those parts of the STATE APPARATUS involved in the direct provision or management of public services and benefits. In principle, the welfare state exists to address issues of SPATIAL INEQUALITY and TERRITORIAL JUSTICE through income and wealth redistribution policies. In areas of policy such as education, employment, health, social services and transport, the state apparatus strives to ensure the delivery of some basic levels of service. So, for example, state-funded schooling sets out to ensure that every child receives an education. Empirical studies have, however, revealed that in practice it is not easy to control who benefits. They have found that it is sometimes the case that the most affluent in society that gain from the provision of PUBLIC SERVICES.

The modern Western welfare state emerged during the 1930s and 1940s, in the context of the two world wars and significant economic and political turbulence. The precise timing differed from one country to another, as did the functions that were brought within the remit of the welfare state. Most noticeably, for example, the USA has never had a national health service, unlike most of the NATIONS of Europe. In general, welfare states were formed to address some of the fundamental social issues of the time, such as disease, inequality and POVERTY. A strong role for the state apparatus was created, in which it would it ensure a basic standard for all citizens. These decisions reflected the wider belief at the time in the ENLIGHTENMENT project, and in the enshrining of universal RIGHTS in the design and structure of the original welfare states (see also CITIZENSHIP).

However, since the 1980s the welfare state has been restructured both quantitatively and qualitatively (Pierson, 1991). Although in many countries it remains heavily involved in the lives of citizens, its size and its organization have changed considerably in recent years. Critiques from the political parties of the right have become mainstream policy in a number of countries. In a growing number of countries, we have witnessed a significant rethinking of the role assigned to the welfare state. On the one hand, some functions it previously performed have been contracted-out to private-sector providers, in the form of PRIVATIZATION, or through the formation of PUBLIC-PRIVATE PARTNERSHIPS. This growth in private-sector firms, employing their workers on private-sector terms and conditions, troubles the notion of public services (Pinch, 1997). How public is a service managed by the welfare state but delivered by the private sector, according to MARKET rules? This also challenges us to reflect carefully on where the welfare state starts and stops, where its edges are (Peck, 2001a). On the other hand, the introduction into the state apparatus of private sector-type audits, evaluations, management techniques and performance indicators has transformed its *modus operandi*. While the welfare state might continue to deliver the services, the conditions under which this is performed is as a result qualitatively different (Jessop, 2002).   KWa

Suggested reading
Jessop (2002); Pierson (1991).

West, the   The idea of the West and the concept of westernization are interwoven with a world-view that believes in the superiority of the human over the non-human, the masculine over the feminine, the adult over the child, and the modern over the traditional. Legitimized through 'anthropocentric doctrines of secular salvation, in the ideologies of progress, normality and hyper-masculinity, and in theories of cumulative growth of science and technology' (Nandy, 1997, p. 169), westernization is akin to another form of colonization – *an intimate enemy* –

> which at least six generations of the THIRD WORLD have learnt to view as a prerequisite for their liberation. This COLONIALISM colonizes minds in addition to bodies and it releases forces within the colonial societies to alter their cultural priorities once and for all. In the process, it helps generalize the concept of the modern West from a geographical and temporal entity to a psychological category. The West is now everywhere, within the West and outside; in structures and in minds. (Nandy, 1997, p. 170)

For Bhabha (1985), such omnipresence of the West (cf. EUROCENTRISM) allows opportunities for HYBRIDITY and RESISTANCE: when colonized people become 'European', the resemblance can subvert the IDENTITY of that which is being represented. The hybrid that articulates colonial and native knowledges may reverse the process of domination as repressed knowledges enter subliminally, enabling subversion, intervention and resistance (Peet and Watts, 1993).

The concept of DEVELOPMENT, with its close affinity with TELEOLOGICAL views of history, science and progress, has served as a central and dynamic theme in Western modernist discursive formations. By the end of the nineteenth century, both the colonialist as well as the radical alternative intellectual traditions became associated with 'linearity, scientism, and modernization, universalisms which carried the appeal of secular utopias constructed with rationality and enlightenment' (Peet and Watts, 1993, p. 232). With CAPITALISM, bureaucracy and SCIENCE as the holy trinity, development became MODERNITY on a planetary scale, in which the West served as the 'transcendental pivot of analytical reflection' (Slater, 1992, p. 312). Western modernity attempted to organize social life on the basis of voluntary actions of individuals whose values were supposed to be predominantly UTILITARIAN. Similarly, NATURAL RESOURCES came to mean those parts of NATURE that were required as inputs for industrial production and colonial TRADE. Technology and economics mutually reinforced the assumption that nature's limits must be broken for the creation of abundance. The concept of the NATION-STATE, moreover, displaced other surviving notions of the STATE, the latter being perceived as examples of medievalism and PRIMITIVISM (Anderson, 1991a [1983]). The process was strengthened when 'indigenous' intellectuals and activists confronting the colonial power found in the idea of the nation-state *the* clue to the West's economic success and political dominance:

> Indeed, no other idea, except probably the twin notions of modern science and development, was accepted so uncritically by the elites of old continuous civilizations like China and India. Even modern science and development became, for Third World elites the responsibility precisely of the nation-state and two new rationalizations for its predominant role. (Nandy, 1992, p. 267)

Development DISCOURSES have continued to construct the relationship between West and non-West in terms of the West being the detached centre of rationality and intelligence: the West possesses the expertise, technology and management skills that the non-West is lacking. Conversely, this lack is the chief cause of the problems of the non-West (cf. OCCIDENTALISM; ORIENTALISM). What is consistently ignored in this framework are questions of POWER and inequality, whether on the global level of international MARKETS, state subsidies and the arms trade, or the more local level of landholding, FOOD supplies and income distribution. This dominant paradigm of the West, furthermore, 'constitutes a perfectly auto-referential sphere, containing only a very limited number of elements. Need, scarcity, work, production, income, and consumption are the key concepts within an enclosed semantic field that has no need of the outside world' (Latouche, 1992, p. 254).

While the history of the 'modernizing' world is often erroneously written as one of failed imitation of the West – failures of secular DEMOCRACY, NATIONALISM, enlightened modernity or enslavement to 'tradition' – scholars working in the post-colonial paradigms have complicated such frameworks (see POSTCOLONIALISM). Conceptualizing modernity as a construct and an organizing trope, especially for the national developmentalist successors of colonial regimes, these scholars have suggested ways in which the complexities of the East–West encounters might be better apprehended through METAPHORS of translation, hybridization and dislocation, rather than more monolithic ideas of imitation, ASSIMILATION or rejection (Abu-Lughod, 1998, p. 18). Furthermore, they have complicated the very exercise of knowledge production 'in and for the West' where the very act of writing for the West about 'the other' implicates us in projects that establish Western authority and cultural difference (Abu-Lughod, 2001, p. 105).

Such intellectual projects acquire particular significance in the context of FEMINIST politics in the THIRD WORLD, which has had to negotiate a complex relationship with Marxist struggles at home, as well as with women's movements and writings in the West (Loomba, 1998, p. 253: see also MARXISM). Despite the deep scepticism to which 'feminism' and agendas associated with Western feminisms are often subjected in post-colonial contexts, women's movements have consistently challenged the assumption that women's activism in post-colonial worlds are only inspired by their Western counterparts (see FEMINIST GEOGRAPHIES). Such moves have involved rewriting indigenous histories, appropriating pre-colonial symbols and mythologies, and amplifying the voices of women themselves, each of which is ridden with its own problems and contradictions (Loomba, 1998). Grappling with 'the woman question' anywhere requires: (a) attending to the complex ways in which the West and things/concepts associated with West are embraced, repudiated and translated in contemporary politics; and (b) developing subtle ways of thinking about the CULTURAL POLITICS of past and present colonial encounter(s), and more broadly, the relationship between the constructs of East and West as they have shaped anti-colonial nationalist projects on the one hand, and the complex dynamics between processes of GLOBALIZATION and the post-colonial nation-state on the other (Abu-Lughod, 1998).   RN

Suggested reading
Mitchell (2002c); Parajuli (1991); Sachs (1992).

wetlands Covering about 6 per cent of the Earth's land area (Turner, 1991), wetlands include rivers, lakes, marshes, fens and peatlands, and intertidal and shallow-marine environments up (such as salt marshes and mangroves). Wetlands are economically important as sources of fish, crops, grazing land and other products, and provide critical ECOSYSTEM services (World Resource Institute, 2005). Key threats include dams, POLLUTION, introduced species, aquaculture, agriculture, URBANIZATION and INDUSTRIALIZATION. The 1971 Ramsar Convention promotes the CONSERVATION and 'wise use' of wetlands as a contribution to achieving SUSTAINABLE DEVELOPMENT. There are over 1500 Wetlands of International Importance, covering (129 million hectares) (http://www.ramsar.org/). WMA

whiteness A racialized IDENTITY that is bound up with POWER and privilege (see also RACE; RACIALIZATION). Although whiteness is a long-established part of a GEOGRAPHICAL IMAGINATION, it has only been subject to critical scrutiny in recent years, particularly since the 1990s. Both within and beyond geography, the power and privilege associated with whiteness has underpinned its normalization and assumed transparency, against which other racialized IDENTITIES are perceived as visible, different and/or inferior. But since the 1990s, geographers and others working across the humanities and social sciences have interrogated WHITENESS, white identities, and their normative and naturalizing power (for an influential study, see Dyer, 1997). Rather than view whiteness as a fixed and ESSENTIALIST category, geographers and others have traced more complex and differentiated racializations that are bound up with CLASS, ETHNICITY, GENDER and SEXUALITY, as shown by research on 'poor whites' in the USA and South Africa; whiteness, mixed descent and racial 'passing'; the gendered and sexualized commodification of whiteness; and the ways in which the racializations of the white working class and the Irish, for example, complicate assumptions about white privilege. Geographers have explored the power relations of whiteness and white identities in relation to racist and ANTI-RACIST politics; their spatial and temporal differentiation; and their articulation within and through both the disciplinary spaces of geography and other spaces such as the street, SUBURB, TOWN, CITY and NATION (see, e.g., Bonnett, 2000; McGuinness, 2002).

Both the normative power of whiteness and critical studies of whiteness have their own geographies. The emergence of 'White Studies' in the late 1990s brought together critical work across a wide range of disciplines, and has been largely based in the USA (including Delgado and Stefancic, 1997). Other researchers have sought to widen comparative and transnational research beyond what might be termed 'American whiteness studies' (Ware and Back, 2002, p. 14) by studying the power relations and material effects of whiteness in a wide range of different contexts. In his forceful critique of multicultural Australia, for example, Ghassan Hage (1998) analyses the ways in which 'fantasies of White supremacy' have shaped ideas about the nation. He considers ' "Whiteness" to be itself a fantasy position of cultural dominance born out of the history of European expansion' (p. 20). Alastair Bonnett (2000) analyses the 'mythologies of EUROPEAN whiteness' in relation to two, connected processes: first, 'The development of non-European (and non-racialised) white identities and their marginalisation or erasure by an increasingly hegemonic, European-identified, racialised whiteness' (p. 7); and, second, the ways in which 'the development of whiteness as a racialised, fetishised and exclusively European attribute produced a contradictory, crisis-prone, identity' (p. 8). Unlike work that not only overlooks the importance of white identities beyond the particularity of European and/or Western MODERNITY, but also fails to interrogate this particularity, Bonnett (2000) has studied whiteness and the meaning of modernity in LATIN AMERICA and Japan.

Like other research that recognizes the SOCIAL CONSTRUCTION of 'race' and ETHNICITY, the critical study of whiteness in both historical and contemporary contexts has been concerned with the risks of reifying whiteness and its normative power. As Vron Ware and Les Back explain, 'For us it is impossible to separate the act of writing about whiteness from a political project that involves not simply the fight against RACISM, but also an attack on the very notion of race and the obstinate resilience of racial identities – one of its most disastrous consequences' (2002, p. 2). AB

Suggested reading
Delgado and Stefancic (1997); Hage (1998); McGuinness (2002); Ware and Back (2002).

wilderness A condition, usually applied to a LANDSCAPE, of being wild, out of human control, uncultivated and uninhabited. Wilderness is a highly contentious term with a long history of usage. As an uninhabited land, wilderness has had both negative and positive value. Until the late eighteenth century, Euro-Americans regarded wilderness as unproductive, as wasteland, full of danger, a place to be crossed without delay. It was also land ripe for DOM-ESTICATION, for bringing into the house of human and godly order. The gendering of such landscapes (the fertile though poorly harnessed feminine wilds, set against the progressive and ordered masculine settlement) is another element to this entrenched cartography of NATURE or CULTURE. The dualism is carried forward, rather than being overturned, by more contemporary environmentalist interest in wilderness as a refuge from the ravages of modern industrial and urban SOCI-ETY. The valorization is reversed and wilderness becomes something to save. Particularly evident in the NATIONAL PARKS movement in North America, and later in AFRICA and AUSTRALASIA, conservationists have sought to protect wilderness from human incursion, producing a form of fortress CONSERVATION (Adams and Mulligan, 2003). Such enclosures are highly controversial, particularly since the advent of a series of critiques of the idea of wilderness, specifically the sense that current understandings of wilderness tend to be rooted in Western value systems and fail to adequately understand the complexities of LANDSCAPE histories and geographies. The environmental historian William Cronon produced one of the more telling critiques, arguing that current concerns over BIODI-VERSITY and endangered species continue the wilderness tradition, producing a deep fascination for remote and exotic ecosystems (the classic example being the tropical rainforest) (Cronon, 1996). As Cronon went on to suggest, protecting the forests often involved protecting them from the people who lived there (and were in fact partly responsible for the existing ecologies). The cultural myth and ECOLOGICAL IMPERIALISM of a peopleless nature resulted in forced removals akin in historical and ecological terms to the tragedy that befell the American Indians. Historical, geographical and POST-COLONIAL imaginations have started to displace wilderness, demonstrating its peculiar heritage and power as an idea, and the material consequences of emptying wild places of people. In addition, there has been work that has sought to demonstrate the material and social connections between so-called wilderness and so-called CIVILIZA-TION, particularly through figures such as wild ANIMALS which, it turns out, exist within and across a complex web of spaces, neither confined to wilderness nor ever reduced to civilizing processes (Whatmore, 2002a). The result

of this work is certainly fraught by the realization that ENVIRONMENTALISM has a good deal invested in pure categories such as wilderness. Practical manifestations such as fortress conservation are certainly not criticized across the board, even while the complexities and paradoxes of such practices are recognized (Adams and Mulligan, 2003). Meanwhile, the power of the idea is evident in its longevity and cross-cultural currency. The polarization of the civil and the wild is not confined to Western cultures. While the dynamics can be different, the place of wilderness as other to (or distance from) society often seems to be populated in different ways and at different times where it forms part of a spatial practice or rite of passage. From the recuperative desert of the Old and New Testaments, to male circumcision rituals, to contemporary safaris and gap-year treks (see also TOURISM), wilderness acts as a complex repository of values.   SJH

Suggested reading
Cronon (1996).

world city A major node in the organization of the world-economy. The term was originally coined by Geddes (1915) to denote those 'great cities in which a quite disproportionate part of the world's business is conducted'. But contemporary usages owe much more to Friedmann's much later (1986, 1996) discussions of world cities as global control centres, which gave the term both a theoretical and an analytical inflection. Those conceptual elaborations, in concert with WORLD-SYSTEMS ANALYSIS, have inspired a major programme of research into Globalization and World Cities at Loughborough University in the UK. In fact, the intimacy of the connections between 'world cities' and GLOBALIZATION have prompted many researchers to substitute the term 'GLOBAL CITY'.   RJ

Suggested reading
Taylor (2004).

World Social Forum (WSF) First convened in January 2001 in Porto Alegre, Brazil, the World Social Forum is an annual meeting held by members of the so-called anti-globalization movements – sometimes dubbed the 'movement of movements' (Mertes, 2004) – to provide a setting in which global and national campaigns can be coordinated, shared and refined. It is not an organization or a united front, but 'an open meeting place for reflective thinking, democratic debate ... by groups and movements of civil society that are opposed to neo-liberalism and to domination of the world by any capital or any form of imperialism' (see www.wsf.org). The WSF has grown substantially from its first meeting in Brazil. Subsequent meetings in 2002 and 2003 were also held in Porto Alegre, and thereafter in Mumbai (2004), Porto Alegre (2005) and Nairobi (2007). In 2006 a 'polycentric forum' was held in Bamako (Mali), Caracas (Venezuela) and Karachi (Pakistan). In 2001, 12,000 people attended the WSF; by 2007 the number had grown to 60,000 registered attendees, and 1,400 organizations representing 110 countries. The WSF has also prompted the establishment of a number of regional fora – the Asian Social Forum, the Mediterranean Social Forum, and in 2007 the first US Social Forum – though not all of them stand in a similar relation to the 'parent body'.

The genealogy of the WSF is complex. The fact that four of the WSF meetings have been held in Porto Alegre – a city with strong connections to the Brazilian Left and the Workers Party, and the home to an innovative model of local government and participatory DEMOCRACY (so-called participatory budgeting) – says much about the broad ideological thrust of the Forum. It stands ideologically against NEO-LIBERALISM and free market CAPITALISM; it is of the Left but it looks for new and different models of economic and political organization, drawing from a vast array of experiments embracing the landless workers movements, anti-dam struggles, indigenous peoples, and anti-corporate and multilateral struggles. The idea of a global convention of anti-capitalist movements was in part driven by the desire to provide a counterweight to the World Economic Forum held every year in Davos, and by the difficulty of organizing mass protest in Switzerland capable of generating sufficient media coverage to challenge the prevailing HEGEMONY of free market DISCOURSE and practice. The protests against the World Bank and INTERNATIONAL MONETARY FUND annual meetings in 1999 and thereafter – most notably in Seattle, Genoa and Washington, DC – were an important milestone in the move towards an alternative forum for civic movements opposing unfettered capitalism around the world.

It is impossible, however, to understand the WSF outside of the counter-revolution in DEVELOPMENT thinking and, relatedly, the growing dominance of neo-liberalism (free MARKETS, free TRADE, PRIVATIZATION and state cutbacks). The abandonment of Keynesian models of capitalist development – marked by the ascendancy

of Ronald Reagan, Margaret Thatcher and Helmut Kohl – and the rapid adoption of the economic ideas associated with Friedrich von Hayek and Milton Friedman and the Mont Pelerin Society, had massive and direct implications for the global SOUTH, beginning in the 1980s with the massive onslaught of STRUCTURAL ADJUSTMENT and stabilization programmes. It was out of this combination of 'economic reform' (namely, the rapid liberalization of state-led development), 'shock therapy' and in many places massive economic recession (e.g. the early 1980s and the late 1990s) that the plethora of movements, often arraigned against the privatizations of various commons (see PRIMITIVE ACCUMULATION) arose. In contradistinction to the triumphalism (and purported inevitability) of GLOBALIZATION that dominated the 1990s, the WSF stood for, in their own language, 'another world is possible' rather than 'there is no alternative'. In some circles, the WSF is held up as a shining example of what Hardt and Negri (2004) call 'the multitude'.

Inevitably, a forum embracing a massive heterogeneity of movements from around the world must confront the problem of political coherence and its strategic role. The WSF has 14 principles (laid out in Porto Alegre in 2001) as part of its Charter. These include strong statements against 'totalitarian' approaches to economy, politics and development, and a robust critique of corporate capitalist and global regulatory institutions such at the WORLD TRADE ORGANIZATION and the IBRD. But in practice the WSF has never functioned as a central or strategic decision-making body, and has often run aground on the reefs of political diversity. Popular movements often stand very differently in relationship to development than, for example, non-governmental organizations (NGOs), and there are no procedures as such for adopting consensus statements or advocacies. As it has grown in size and scope – and become something of a media event for visible anti-globalization celebrities (Tariq Ali, Vandana Shiva) – the early radicalism of the first forum has been lost and dissipated.   MW

Suggested reading
Leite (2005); Teivainen (2002). See also the official home page at http://www.forumsocialmundial.org.br

World Trade Organization (WTO) Although the idea of an international trade organization was formulated in 1944 at Bretton Woods, today's World Trade Organization was only founded in 1994 at the close of the Uruguay Round (1986–94) of the General Agreement on Tariffs and Trade (GATT) talks in Marrakesh. Its purpose is to liberalize international TRADE by enforcing free trade rules, arbitrating international trade disputes, and working to forge new global agreements on the removal of TARIFF and so-called non-tariff barriers to trade (the latter including all sorts of national rules on health and environmental protections). Unlike the International Monetary Fund (IMF) and the World Bank – which were set up at Bretton Woods to run on a 'one dollar, one vote' principle – the WTO operates on an ostensibly more inclusive model, in which the voices of individual member states are all meant to count. However, because the ground rules for inclusion are fixed as free trade rules, because the basic goal of the organization is to remove frictions on the movement of COMMODITIES, and because the organization's disputes resolution mechanism works on the assumption that it is intrinsically good to reduce both tariff and non-tariff barriers to trade, the WTO serves institutionally to expand and entrench NEO-LIBERALISM on a global scale (Peet, 2003; see also TERMS OF TRADE). Everywhere its rules apply, the WTO enables the PRIVATIZATION of formerly public goods and common property RESOURCES, whether they be medicines, government-provided HEALTH services, shared forests or clean WATER. As well as thereby facilitating ACCUMULATION by dispossession (Harvey, 2005: see PRIMITIVE ACCUMULATION), WTO rules also simultaneously undercut democratic governance insofar as they provide a powerful lever through which businesses can reduce or eliminate democratic law-making (including, for example, legislation banning carcinogenic chemicals and pesticides) by coding the resulting public interest laws as non-tariff barriers to trade (Wallach and Woodall, 2004). Another neo-liberal aspect of the WTO is that there is no possibility under its free trade rules to permit development strategies that are not neo-liberal, such as state assistance to new industries, that try to establish themselves in the face of competition from developed producers elsewhere. As a result, the WTO has been criticized for 'kicking away the ladder' (Chang, 2002) for the world's poorer countries, preventing them from following a path once taken by countries such as the USA and Japan that used industrial protectionism in their early approach to DEVELOPMENT. It has been this basic injustice, combined with the WTO's DEMOCRACY-eroding complicity in

processes of dispossession, that has led so many critics to take to the streets from Seattle in 1999 through to Hong Kong in 2006. Ironically, however, it has been yet another injustice noted by the protestors that has ultimately proved most damaging to the WTO's own attempts to expand free trade since the 'Battle in Seattle'. This injustice is the disproportionate POWER still wielded by the US government in negotiations because of the importance of the US market in global trade. The irony is that because the USA has been unwilling to fully implement free trade itself, and, most notably, because (like the EU) it has been unwilling to give up the huge subsidies given each year to domestic farmers, US officials have been moving increasingly away from the MULTILATERALISM of WTO negotiations, where they face growing demands from developing countries to eliminate such practices. As a result, American trade negotiators have preferred more recently to develop bilateral trade deals with particular countries such as Singapore, and, meanwhile, the WTO's failing attempts to expand free trade remain an important reminder that GLOBALIZATION is not so inevitable after all. MS

world-systems analysis A MATERIALIST and historical approach to the study of social change developed by Immanuel Wallerstein (1979, 1984, 1991a). The approach builds upon three research schools – DEPENDENCY THEORY, the ANNALES SCHOOL and MARXISM (see HISTORICAL MATERIALISM) – to create a unidisciplinary and holistic historical social science. The approach was integral to the reinvigoration of POLITICAL GEOGRAPHY in the 1980s and its usage in GEOGRAPHY is still largely restricted to this sub-discipline (Flint and Shelley, 1996).

World-systems analysis runs counter to mainstream social science in its definition of society. Wallerstein begins by identifying three basic MODES OF PRODUCTION, or ways of organizing production and social reproduction. The *reciprocal-lineage* mode describes a society in which production is organized around age and GENDER differences and exchanges are reciprocated within the group. The *redistributive-tributary* mode occurs in CLASS-based societies in which a large class of agricultural workers gives the surplus of their production to elites. The *capitalist mode of production* is also class based, but is defined by ceaseless capital ACCUMULATION motivated by the MARKET which sets prices through the logic of supply and demand.

Wallerstein defines society by the spatial extent of these modes of production, and not necessarily by political BORDERS. Hence, three types of society are identified: *mini-systems* are small tribal entities following the reciprocal-lineage mode; *world-empires*, such as the Roman empire or FEUDAL Europe, practice the redistributive-tributary mode; and *world-economies* are capitalist. In the broad historical purview of world systems, the contemporary capitalist world economy emerged in EUROPE in the fifteenth century and has since diffused to encompass the whole globe and eliminate all other forms of society. Thus, the modern world system is a single society, the global capitalist world-economy. Scholars have used world-systems analysis to study all types of society, but geographers have concentrated upon the modern world-system (Flint and Shelley, 1996).

The geographical expression of political borders and the spatial extent of society were matched in mini-systems and world-empires. However, in the capitalist world-economy the mode of production is defined by a global market, while the system is divided into separate STATES. It is here that Wallerstein's challenge to mainstream social science lies. He claims that social scientists equate states with society, and therefore have only a limited view of social change if they restrict analysis of cause and effect to one country. The result is the error of developmentalism (Taylor, 1989), practiced within both liberal and Marxist social science, arguing that countries move through particular stages of development; for example, individual countries were identified as 'progressing' through stages of population dynamics following the DEMOGRAPHIC TRANSITION model. Alternatively, social change occurs at the scale of the system, and changes within states occur within the broader context. Such thinking led to critique of world-systems analysis as denying the agency of states and other groups.

Geographers have attempted to address this critique through an application of geographical SCALE (Taylor, 1981). Taylor identified three key political scales; the LOCALITY, the NATION-STATE and the global. Ultimately, processes of social change can be traced to the global scale, but individual agency occurs at the local scale within the political and social limits set by states, themselves restricted by the imperatives of the global scale. Such an approach has been critiqued as structurally deterministic, but others have shown how political agency is limited within the constraints of the modern world-system (Flint, 2001).

Initially, geographers complemented their application of geographical scale with a focus upon a key feature of the modern world-system, the CORE–PERIPHERY hierarchy. The capitalist world-economy is necessarily unequal, comprised of peripheral processes (low-income and low-profit production) and core processes (high-income and high-profit). These processes cluster geographically, so that core processes may dominate (but not exclusively) in some states, and vice versa. In the UK, for example, core processes predominate, but some expression of peripheral processes is also evident in inner-city sweatshops. In addition, some states and REGIONS are identified as semi-peripheral – with a relatively even balance of core and periphery processes. Core and peripheral processes were used to map broad global geographies of equality (Flint and Shelley, 1996).

Recent analysis by political geographers has focused upon two concepts; HEGEMONY and WORLD CITIES. A hegemonic power is the one dominant state in the modern world-system. Its power rests upon economic strength, but is also expressed in the dissemination of CULTURE (Taylor, 1999). The 'war on terror' has been identified as the GEOPOLITICAL response of the USA, the current hegemonic power, in the face of violent challenge (Flint and Falah, 2004: see TERRORISM; WAR). World cities have been identified as the key nodes on a new geographical expression of power in the modern world-system, a NETWORK of economic and cultural relations that facilitates capital ACCUMULATION (Knox and Taylor, 1995). Mapping the goods and services produced within particular cities and their interconnectivity results in a hierarchy of cities, and informs geographies of SOVEREIGNTY and GLOBALIZATION.

World-systems analysis challenged liberal and Marxist approaches to social science, and has been critiqued by both – by one for being too structural and Marxist and by the other by not being these things enough! Wallerstein (1991b) has also challenged the way in which social science is organized into separate disciplines. Instead, world-systems analysis is a unidisciplinary approach, encompassing economic, political, social, and cultural processes to show how culture and politics are inseparable from economics. Although world-systems analysis was at the forefront of the revitalized political geography, it is no longer dominant, however, and instead is now one of many theories informing the sub-discipline.   CF

Suggested reading
Hall (2000c); Taylor and Flint (1999); Wallerstein (2004).

Z

zonal model A model of intra-urban spatial organization created by E.W. Burgess (1886–1966: see Burgess, 1924), a leading member of the 1920s CHICAGO SCHOOL of sociologists. To assist in understanding why certain types of social problem were concentrated in particular areas, he split an idealized city (based on Chicago) into five zones (see figure), whose dominant feature is the increase in an area's socio-economic status with distance from the CBD ('The Loop' in Chicago). Growth was propelled outwards from that point by INVASION AND SUCCESSION processes involving new immigrants to the city, who established homes in the 'zone in transition' and pressed longer-established groups to move towards the SUBURBS and beyond. Burgess' model was complemented by Hoyt's SECTORAL MODEL and combined with it to form a MULTIPLE NUCLEI MODEL in work on urban residential patterns. (cf. FACTORIAL ECOLOGY; SOCIAL AREA ANALYSIS). RJ

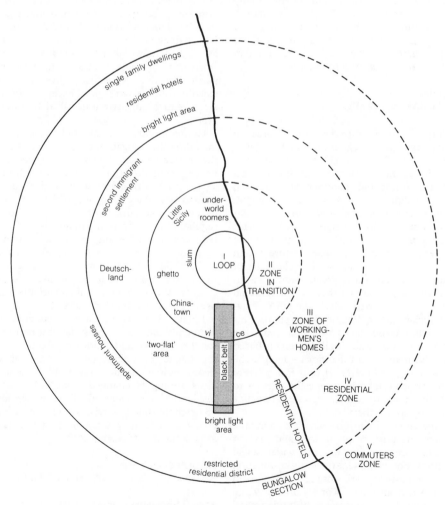

zonal model *Burgess's zonal model* (Park et al., 1925)

Suggested reading
Johnston (1971).

zone of dependence An area characterized by the spatial clustering of residential and other facilities used by those dependent on the STATE and other bodies (such as charities) for housing and other support. The importance of such facilities has been increased with the general trend involving the closure of many psychiatric and other facilities and replacing them with 'community care', with many of its facilities located in the INNER CITY, where large properties are available for conversion and there is less likelihood of resistance from established residents (cf. NIMBY). That spatial concentration encourages their users to find accommodation nearby, thereby creating an area where such dependent people, many suffering in various ways from SOCIAL EXCLUSION, dominate. As more people congregate in such zones, more facilities are placed there to serve them, and eventually a situation akin to the creation of a GHETTO emerges.   RJ

Suggested reading
Dear and Wolch (1993).

zoning A term used to describe the practice of dividing a city or region into tracts of land, or zones, for the purposes of land-use planning. Each zone is assigned a set of permitted uses (e.g. residential, commercial, industrial or some subdivision of these, such as single-family residential), often overlain by regulations on density, height and design. Regulations are codified in a comprehensive plan and, consequently, shape future urban development (Smith, 1983). The character of zoning regulations varies greatly among countries, with some framing them at the national level and others – particularly the USA – having a localized and fragmented system. This local ability to use state power to advance the general good over individual interests is based on US Supreme Court decisions – such as the famous *Village of Euclid v. Ambler Realty Co.* of 1926 – which established the right of cities to limit the uses to which private PROPERTY owners could put their land.

While zoning is, in one sense, a mundane bureaucratic practice, its history and present operation are also tied up with wider social questions. For example, ETHNIC discrimination forms the basis for early zoning regulations in North American cities. Worries among white elites about the encroachment of 'undesirable' ethnic groups such as Chinese populations led to ordinances that only permitted their businesses, such as laundries, in specific areas. Today, exclusionary zoning continues to be used, often by wealthy municipalities, to exclude low-income people. Strategies of exclusion include requirements that houses be built on large (i.e. expensive) lots and prohibitions on apartment buildings.

Proponents of contemporary zoning argue that it provides a transparent framework for DECISION-MAKING, since principles of development have been codified before decisions on particular proposals are made; that it provides predictability for landowners, investors and developers; and that it offers safeguards for residents and the environment by controlling the spread of unwanted or noxious land uses. Critics point to zoning's unequal effects and its potential for discriminatory SOCIAL EXCLUSION; criticize its restrictions on landowners; point to its tendency to produce large, environmentally damaging land-use monocultures, such as single-family suburban subdivisions; and worry about the potential for zoning decisions – particularly those regarding requests to change existing zoning or to seek an exception (a variance) – to be unfairly influenced by interest groups.

Contemporary urban policy concerns, including the mitigation of urban SPRAWL and the encouragement of compact and mixed-use developments, relate to zoning. Growth management and smart growth strategies, such as growth boundaries (beyond which, the types of permissible urban land uses are strictly regulated) are used to maintain COMPACT CITIES (Knaap and Nelson, 1992). Within cities, long-standing criticisms of single-use zoning and developers' interest in mixed use developments have led to the increased use of zoning categories that accommodate a variety of land uses in one location (Knox, 1991).

Finally, it is worth noting that zoning is frequently the object and stake of urban politics. Developers and landowners often lobby for changes in zoning to increase the value of their holdings (a tract may be more valuable if its zoning is changed from industrial to residential, for instance). Environmentalists or neighbourhood activists often oppose such changes when they seem to create negative EXTERNALITIES (McCann, 2002).   EM

Suggested reading
Knaap and Nelson (1992); Smith (1983).

zoos Enclosures where ANIMALS are held for a variety of purposes, including display, human entertainment and education, *ex situ* breeding and conservation. Initially developed from menageries of animal exotica, and designed for human consumption, zoos responded in the mid-to-late twentieth century to public anxiety, animal welfare and environmental criticisms by re-staging and re-selling animal collections as crucial to BIO-DIVERSITY CONSERVATION (Anderson, 1995). Zoos then formed NETWORKS linked by the movements of animals, reproductive tissues and records (Whatmore, 2002a). Animal lives were behaviourally enhanced, and collections shifted from the comprehensive (displaying a wide variety of specimen species) to the specialized (focused on sustainable groups of species types). Criticisms remain, especially from those who regard zoo improvements as little other than conscience and market protection devices in an increasingly competitive edu-tainment sector.   SJH

817

LIBRARY, UNIVERSITY OF CHESTER

Bibliography

Note: Square brackets refer to original publication dates. Some later editions are grouped with earlier editions for convenience.

Aalto, P. 2002: A European geopolitical subject in the making? EU, Russia and the Kaliningrad question. *Geopolitics* 7: 143–74.

Aay, H. 1981: Textbook chronicles: disciplinary history and the growth of geographic knowledge. In B.W. Blouet, ed., *The origins of academic geography in the United States.* Hamden, CT: Archon Books, 291–301.

Abbott, A. and Tsay, A. 2000: Sequence analysis and optimal matching methods in sociology: review and prospect. *Sociological Methods & Research* 29(1): 3–33.

Abel, W. 1980: *Agricultural fluctuations in Europe from the thirteenth to twentieth centuries.* London: Methuen.

Abercrombie, N., Hill, S. and Turner, B.S. 1980: *The dominant ideology thesis.* London: George Allen and Unwin.

Abernethy, D. 2000: *The dynamics of global dominance: European overseas empires, 1415–1980.* New Haven: Yale University Press.

Abler, R.F. 1993a: Desiderata for geography. In R.J. Johnston, ed., *The challenge for geography. A changing world: a changing discipline.* Oxford: Blackwell.

Abler, R.F. 1993b: Everything in its place: GPS, GIS and geography in the 1990s. *Professional Geographer* 45(2): 131–9.

Abler, R.F., Marcus, M.G. and Olson, J.M., eds, 1992: *Geography's inner worlds.* New Brunswick, NJ: Rutgers University Press.

Abrahamson, M. 2004: *Global cities.* New York and Oxford: Oxford University Press.

Abramson, A. and Theodossopoulos, D., eds, 2000: *Land, law and environment: mythical land, legal boundaries.* London: Pluto Press.

Abu-Lughod, J.L. 1989: *Before European hegemony: The world system AD 1250–1350.* New York: Oxford University Press.

Abu-Lughod, J.L. 1998: Introduction: feminist longings and postcolonial conditions. In L. Abu-Lughod, ed., *Remaking women: feminism and modernity in the Middle East.* Princeton, NJ: Princeton University Press, 3–31.

Abu-Lughod, J.L. 1999: *New York, Chicago, Los Angeles: America's global cities.* Minneapolis: University of Minnesota Press.

Abu-Lughod, J.L. 2001: Orientalism and Middle East feminist studies. *Feminist Studies* 27: 101–13.

ACIA 2004: *Impacts of a warming Arctic: Arctic climate impact assessment.* Cambridge, UK: Cambridge University Press.

Acker, J. 1989: The problem with patriarchy. *Sociology* 23: 235–40.

Ackerman, W.V. 1999: Growth control versus the growth machine in Redlands, California: conflict in urban land use. *Urban Geography* 20: 147–67.

Acland, C. 2003: *Screen traffic.* Durham, NC: Duke University Press.

Ad Hoc Committee on Geography 1965: *The science of geography.* Washington, DC: National Academy of Sciences – National Research Council.

Adam, B. 1998: *Timescapes of modernity.* London: Routledge.

Adam, B. 2006: Time. *Theory, Culture & Society* 23(2–3): 119–26.

Adams, P. 1997: Cyberspace and virtual places. *Geographical Review* 87(2): 155–71.

Adams, P. 1998: Network topologies and virtual place. *Annals of the Association of American Geographers* 88(1): 88–106.

Adams, P., Hoelscher, S. and Till, K., eds, 2001: *Textures of place: exploring humanist geographies.* Minneapolis: University of Minnesota Press.

Adams, R. McC. 1966: *Evolution of urban society: early Mesopotamia and pre-Hispanic Mexico.* London: Weidenfeld & Nicolson.

Adams, W.M. 1995: Sustainable development. In R. Johnston, P. Taylor and M. Watts, eds, *Geographies of global change: remapping the world in the late twentieth century.* Oxford: Blackwell, 354–73.

Adams, W.M. 2001: *Green development: environment and sustainability in the Third World,* 2nd edn. London: Routledge.

Adams, W.M. 2004: *Against extinction: the story of conservation.* London: Earthscan.

Adams, W.M. and Mulligan, M., eds, 2003: *Decolonizing nature: strategies for conservation in a post-colonial era.* London: Earthscan.

Adey, P. 2004: Surveillance at the airport: surveilling mobility/mobilising surveillance. *Environment and Planning A* 36: 1365–80.

Adorno, T. 1976: *The positivist dispute in German sociology.* New York: Harper & Row.

Adorno, T. 1977: *Aesthetic theory.* Minneapolis: University of Minnesota Press.

Adorno, T. and Horkheimer, M. 1979: *The dialectic of the Enlightenment*. New York: Continuum.

Agamben, G. 1998: *Homo sacer: sovereign power and bare life*, trans. D. Heller-Roazen. Stanford, CA: Stanford University Press.

Agamben, G. 1999: *Remnants of Auschwitz: the witness and the archive [Homo sacer III]*, trans. D. Heller-Roazen. New York: Zone Books.

Agamben, G. 2002: *The open: man and animal*. Stanford, CA: Stanford University Press.

Agamben, G. 2005: *State of exception*. Chicago: The University of Chicago Press.

Aganbegyan, A. 1988: *The challenge: economics of perestroika*. London: Hutchinson.

Agar, J. and Smith, C., eds, 1998: *Making space for science: territorial themes in the shaping of knowledge*. London: Macmillan.

Agger, B. 1998: *Critical social theories: an introduction*. Boulder, CO: Westview Press.

Agnes, P. 2000: The 'end of geography' in financial services? Local embeddedness and territorialization in the interest swaps industry. *Economic Geography* 76: 347–66.

Agnew, J.A. 1987a: *Place and politics: the geographical mediation of state and society*. Boston: Allen and Unwin.

Agnew, J.A. 1987b: *The United States in the world-economy: a regional geography*. Cambridge, UK: Cambridge University Press.

Agnew, J.A. 1994: The territorial trap: the geographical assumptions of international relations theory. *Review of International Political Economy* 1: 53–80.

Agnew, J.A. 1996: Mapping politics: how context counts in electoral geography. *Political Geography* 15: 129–46.

Agnew, J.A. 1998: *Geopolitics: re-visioning world politics*. London: Routledge.

Agnew, J.A. 1999: Regions on the mind does not equal regions of the mind. *Progress in Human Geography* 23: 91–6.

Agnew, J.A. 2001: The new global economy: time–space compression, geopolitics and global uneven development. *Journal of World-Systems Research* 7: 133–54.

Agnew, J.A. 2002: *Making political geography*. London: Arnold.

Agnew, J.A. 2003a: *Geopolitics*, 2nd edn. New York: Routledge.

Agnew, J.A. 2003b: Territoriality and political identity in Europe. In M. Berezin and M. Schain, eds, *Europe without borders: remapping territory, citizenship, and identity in a transnational age*. Baltimore, MD: The Johns Hopkins University Press.

Agnew, J.A. 2005a: *Hegemony: the new shape of global power*. Philadelphia: Temple University Press.

Agnew, J.A. 2005b: Sovereignty regimes: territoriality and state authority in contemporary world politics. *Annals of the Association of American Geographers* 95: 437–61.

Agnew, J.A. 2006: Globalization has a home address: the geopolitics of globalization. In D. Conway and N. Heynen, eds, *Globalization's contradictions: geographies of discipline, destruction and transformation*. New York: Routledge.

Agrawal, A. 1995: Dismantling the divide between indigenous and scientific knowledge. *Development and Change* 26: 413–39.

Agrawal, A. 2005: *Environmentality*. Raleigh, NC: Duke University Press.

Agrawal, B. 1998: The gender and environment debate. In R. Keil, D.V.J. Bell, P. Penz and L. Fawcett, eds, *Political ecology*. London: Routledge, 193–220.

Agresti, A. 2002: *Categorical data analysis*. New York: Wiley.

Aguilar, A. 1968: *Pan-Americanism from Monroe to the present: a view from the other side*, trans. A. Zatz. New York: Monthly Review Press.

Agulhon, M. 1981: *Marianne into battle: republican imagery and symbolism in France, 1789–1881*. Cambridge, UK: Cambridge University Press.

Ahmad, A. 1992: Orientalism and after: ambivalence and metropolitan location in the work of Edward Said. In his *In theory: classes, nations, literatures*. London: Verso, 159–219.

Ahmed, S., Castañeda, C., Fortier, A.-M. and Sheller, M., eds, 2003: *Uprootings/regroundings: questions of home and migration*. Oxford: Berg.

Aitken, S. 1991: Person–environment theories in contemporary perceptual and behavioural geography: 1. Personality, attitudinal and spatial choice theories. *Progress In Human Geography* 15: 179–93.

Aitken, S. 2001: *Geographies of young people: the morally contested spaces of identity*. New York: Routledge.

Aitken, S. and Zonn, L., eds, 1994: *Place, power, situation, and spectacle: a geography of film*. London: Rowman & Littlefield.

Akweenda, S. 1989: Territorial integrity: a brief analysis of a complex concept. *Revue africaine de droit international et comparé* 1: 500–6.

Al-Ali, N. and Koser, K., eds, 2002: *New approaches to migration: transnational communities and the transformation of home*. London: Routledge.

Alatas, S.F. 1995: The theme of 'relevance' in Third World human sciences. *Singapore Journal of Tropical Geography* 16(2): 123–40.

Albert, M. 1993: *Capitalism against capitalism*. London: Whurr.

Alcoff, L. 1988: Cultural feminism versus post-structuralism: the identity crisis in feminist theory. *Signs: Journal of Women in Culture and Society* 13(3): 405–36.

Alderman, D. 2003: Street names and the scaling of memory: the politics of commemorating

Martin Luther King Jr. within the African American community. *Area* 35: 163–73.

Aldrich, R. 1993: *The seduction of the Mediterranean: writing, art and homosexual fantasy.* London: Routledge.

Aldridge, A. and Levine, K. 2001: *Surveying the social world: principles and practice in survey research.* Buckingham: Open University Press.

Alexander, G. 1998: Critical land law. In S. Bright and J. Dewar, eds, *Land law: themes and perspectives.* Oxford: Oxford University Press, 52–78.

Alexander, J. 1983: *Theoretical logic in sociology.* Vol. 4: *The modern reconstruction of social thought: Talcott Parsons.* Berkeley, CA: University of California Press.

Alexander, J.C. 1996: Critical reflections on 'reflexive modernization'. *Theory, Culture & Society* 13(4): 133–9.

Alexander, N. 2002: *An ordinary country: issues in the transition from apartheid to democracy in South Africa.* Pietermaritzburg: University of Natal Press.

Alker, H.R. 1969: A typology of ecological fallacies. In M. Dogan and S. Rokkan, eds, *Quantitative ecological analysis in the social sciences.* Cambridge, MA: The MIT Press, 69–86.

Allaire, G. and Boyer, R., eds, 1995: *La grande transformation.* Paris: Institute Nationale de Recherche Agronomique (INRA).

Allen, J. 2003: *Lost geographies of power.* Oxford: Blackwell.

Allen, J. 2008: Pragmatism and power, or the power to make a difference in a radically contingent world. *Geoforum* 39: 1613–24.

Allen, J. and Massey, D. 1988: *The economy in question.* London: Sage.

Allen, J. and Pryke, M. 1994: The production of service space. *Environment and Planning D: Society and Space* 12: 453–75.

Allen, J., Massey, D. and Pryke, M., eds, 1999: *Unsettling cities.* London: Routledge.

Allen, J., Massey, D., Cochrane, A., Court, G., Henry, N., Massey, D. and Sarre, P., 1998: *Rethinking the region: spaces of neo-liberalism.* London: Routledge.

Allen, P. 1997: *Cities and regions as self-organizing systems: models of complexity.* Amsterdam: Gordon & Breach.

Allen, R.C. 1992: *Enclosure and the yeoman: the agricultural development of the South Midlands 1450–1850.* Oxford: The Clarendon Press.

Allen, R.C. 1999: Tracking the agricultural revolution in England. *Economic History Review* LII (2): 209–35.

Allison, P.D. 1984: *Event history analysis: regression for longitudinal event data,* London: Sage.

Alonso, W. 1960: A theory of the urban land market. *Papers and Proceedings of the Regional Science Association* 6: 149–57.

Alonso, W. 1964a: *Location and land use: toward a general theory of land rent.* Cambridge, MA: Harvard University Press.

Alonso, W. 1964b: Location theory. In J. Friedmann and W. Alonso, eds, *Regional development and planning: a reader.* Cambridge, MA: The MIT Press, 78–106.

Alonso, W. and Starr, P., eds, 1987: *The politics of numbers.* New York: Russell Sage Foundation.

alSayyad, N. and Roy, A. 2006: Medieval modernity: on citizenship and urbanism in a global era. *Space and Polity* 10: 1–20.

Alsmark, G. 1996: When in Sweden … immigrant encounters with Swedish culture. In J. Frykman and O. Löfgren, eds, *Force of habit: exploring everyday culture.* Lund: Lund University Press, 87–102.

Althusser, L. 1970: Ideology and ideological state apparatus. In Althusser, *Lenin and philosophy and other essays.* New York: Monthly Review Press.

Althusser, L. 1971: Ideology and ideological state apparatuses: notes towards an investigation. In *Lenin and philosophy.* London: New Left Books, 127–86.

Althusser, L. 1977 [1965]: The 'Piccolo Teatro': Bertolazzi and Brecht: notes on a materialist theatre. In *For Marx,* trans. B. Brewster. London: New Left Books, 129–51.

Althusser, L. 1997 [1970]: The merits of classical economics. In L. Althusser and E. Balibar, eds, *Reading capital.* London: Verso, 83–90.

Althusser, L. and Balibar, E. 1970: *Reading capital.* London: New Left Books, reissued Verso 1998 [originally published as *Lire le capital,* 1965].

Altman, M., MacDonald, K. and McDonald, M. 2005: From crayons to computers: the evolution of computer use in redistricting. *Social Science Computer Review* 23: 334–46.

Ambrosio, T. 2001: *Irredentism: ethnic conflict and international politics.* Westport, CT: Praeger.

Amedeo, D. and Golledge, R.G. 1975: *An introduction to scientific reasoning in geography.* New York: Wiley.

Amin, A. 1989: Flexible specialisation and small firms in Italy: myths and realities. *Antipode* 21(1): 13–34.

Amin, A. 1994: Post-Fordism: models, fantasies and phantoms of transition. In A. Amin, ed., *Post-Fordism: a reader.* Oxford: Blackwell.

Amin, A. 2000: Industrial districts. In E. Sheppard and T.J. Barnes, eds, *A companion to economic geography.* Oxford: Blackwell, 149–68.

Amin, A. 2002a: *Ethnicity and the multicultural city: living with diversity.* Report for the Department of Transport, Local Government and the Regions and the ESRC Cities Initiative.

Amin, A. 2002b: Spatialities of globalization. *Environment and Planning A* 34: 385–99.

Amin, A. 2003: Unruly strangers? The 2001 urban riots in Britain. *International Journal of Urban and Regional Research* 27: 460–4.

Amin, A. 2004a: Multiethnicity and the idea of Europe. *Theory, Culture & Society* 21(2): 1–24.

Amin, A. 2004b: Regions unbound: towards a new politics of place. *Geografiska Annaler* 86B: 33–4.

Amin, A. and Cohendet, P. 2004: *Architectures of knowledge: firms, capabilities, and communities.* Oxford: Oxford University Press.

Amin, A. and Thrift, N.J. 1992: Neo-Marshallian nodes in global networks. *International Journal of Urban and Regional Research* 16: 571–87.

Amin, A. and Thrift, N.J., eds, 1994a: *Globalisation, institutions and regional development in Europe.* Oxford University Press.

Amin, A. and Thrift, N.J. 1994b: Living in the global. In Amin and Thrift, eds, *Globalization, institutions and regional development in Europe.* Oxford: Oxford University Press, 1–22.

Amin, A. and Thrift, N.J. 1997: Globalization, socio-economics, territoriality. In R. Lee and J. Wills, eds, *Geographies of economies.* London: Arnold.

Amin, A. and Thrift, N.J. 2000: What sort of economics for what sort of economic geography? *Antipode* 32: 4–9 (plus commentaries published on the paper in *Antipode* 33(1), 2001).

Amin, A. and Thrift, N.J. 2002: *Cities: reimagining the urban.* Cambridge, UK: Polity Press.

Amin, A. and Thrift, N.J. 2004: *The Blackwell cultural economy reader.* Oxford: Blackwell.

Amin, A. and Thrift, N.J. 2005: What's left? Just the future. *Antipode* 37: 220–38.

Amin, A. and Thrift, N.J. 2007: Cultural-economy and cities. *Progress in Human Geography* 31: 143–61.

Amin, A., Cameron, A. and Hudson, R. 2002: *Placing the social economy.* London: Routledge.

Amin, A., Massey, D. and Thrift, N.J. 2003: *Decentering the nation: a radical approach to regional inequality.* London: Catalyst.

Amin, S. 1974: *Accumulation on a world scale: a critique of the theory of underdevelopment,* vols 1 and 2. New York: Monthly Review Press.

Amin, S. 1976: *Unequal development: an essay on the social formations of peripheral capitalism.* New York: Monthly Review Press.

Amin, S. 1978: *Accumulation on a world scale.* London: Harvester.

Amin, S. 1987: Democracy and national strategy in the periphery. *Third World Quarterly* 9: 1129–56.

Amoore, L. 2006: Biometric borders: governing mobilities in the war on terror. *Political Geography* 25: 336–51.

Amoore, L. and de Goede, M. 2008: Transactions after 9/11: the banal face of the pre-emptive strike. *Transactions of the Institute of British Geographers* 33: 173–85.

Ancien, D. 2005: Local and regional development policy in France: of changing conditions and forms, and enduring state centrality. *Space and Polity* 3: 217–36.

Anders, P. 1998: Envisioning cyberspace: the design of on-line communities. In J. Beckmann, ed., *The virtual dimension: architecture, representation, and crash culture.* New York: Princeton Architectural Press, 218–33.

Anderson, B. 1983: *Imagined communities: reflections on the origin and spread of nationalism.* London: Verso.

Anderson, B. 1991a [1983]: *Imagined communities,* rev. ed. London: Verso.

Anderson, B. 1998: *The spectre of comparisons: nationalism, Southeast Asia, and the world.* London: Verso.

Anderson, B. 2004: Time-stilled space-slowed: how boredom matters. *Geoforum* 35: 739–54.

Anderson, B. 2006a: *Imagined communities,* 4th edn. London: Verso.

Anderson, B. 2006b: Becoming and being hopeful: towards a theory of affect. *Environment and Planning D: Society and Space* 24(5): 733–52.

Anderson, B. and Tolia-Kelly, D. 2004: Matter(s) in social and cultural geography, *Geoforum* 35: 669–74.

Anderson, B. and Wylie, J. 2008: On geography and materiality. *Environment and Planning A*: in press.

Anderson, B., Morton, F. and Revill, G., eds, 2005: Geographies of music and sound. Special issue of *Social and Cultural Geography* 6(5).

Anderson, J., ed., 2002a: *Transnational democracy: political spaces and border crossings.* London: Routledge.

Anderson, K. 1987: The idea of Chinatown: the power of place and institutional practice in the making of a racial category. *Annals of the Association of American Geographers* 77(4): 580–98.

Anderson, K. 1991b: *Vancouver's Chinatown: racial discourse in Canada, 1875–1980.* Montreal: McGill-Queen's University Press.

Anderson, K. 1995: Culture and nature at the Adelaide Zoo: at the 'frontiers' of human geography. *Transactions of the Institute of British Geographers* 20: 275–94.

Anderson, K. 1996: Engendering race research. In N. Duncan, ed., *Bodyspace.* London: Routledge, 197–211.

Anderson, K. 1997: A walk on the wild side: a critical geography of domestication. *Progress in Human Geography* 21(4): 463–85.

Anderson, K. 2000a: 'The beast within': race, humanity and animality. *Environment and Planning D: Society and Space* 18(3): 301–20.

Anderson, K. 2000b: Thinking 'postnationally': dialogue across multicultural, indigenous, and settler spaces. *Annals of the Association of American Geographers* 90(2): 381–91.

Anderson, K. 2003: White natures: Sydney's Royal Agricultural Show in post-humanist perspective. *Transactions of the Institute of British Geographers* 28(4): 422–41.

Anderson, K. 2005a: *Predicting the weather: Victorians and the science of meteorology.* Chicago: The University of Chicago Press.

Anderson, K. 2006c: *Race and the crisis of humanism.* London: UCL Press.

Anderson, K. and Jack, D.C. 1991: Learning to listen: interview techniques and analyses. In S. Berger Gluck and D. Patai, eds, *Women's words: feminist practice of oral history.* New York: Routledge, 11–26.

Anderson, K. and Smith, S. 2001: Editorial: emotional geographies. *Transactions of the Institute of British Geographers* 26: 7–10.

Anderson, K., Domosh, M., Pile, S. and Thrift, N. 2002: *Handbook of cultural geography.* London: Sage.

Anderson, P. 1974: *Passages from antiquity to feudalism.* London: Verso.

Anderson, P. 1976: *Considerations on Western Marxism.* London: New Left Books.

Anderson, P. 2000c: Renewals. *New Left Review* 1: 5–24.

Anderson, P. 2002b: Force and consent. *New Left Review* 17: 5–30.

Anderson, P. 2002c: Internationalism: a breviary. *New Left Review* 14: 5–25.

Anderson, P. 2005b: *Spectrum.* London: Verso.

Anderson, W. 1992: Climates of opinion: acclimatization in nineteenth-century France and England. *Victorian Studies* 35: 135–57.

Andrejevic, M. 2003: Tracing space: monitored mobility in the era of mass customization. *Space and Culture* 6(2): 132–50.

Andrejevic, M. 2005: Nothing comes between me and my CPU: smart clothes and 'ubiquitous' computing. *Theory, Culture & Society* 22(3): 101–19.

Andrews, G.J. and Phillips, D.R., eds, 2005: *Ageing and place: perspectives, policy, practice.* London: Routledge.

Andrews, H. 1984: The Durkheimians and human geography. *Transactions of the Institute of British Geographers* 9: 315–36.

Andrews, H.F. 1993: Durkheim and social morphology. In S.P. Turner, ed, *Emile Durkheim: sociologist and moralist.* New York: Routledge, 112–38.

Andrews, J.H. 1996: What was a map? The lexicographers reply. *Cartographica* 33(4): 1–11.

Angotti, T. 2006: Apocalyptic anti-urbanism: Mike Davis and his planet of slums. *International Journal of Urban and Regional Research* 30: 961–7.

Anselin, L. 1988: *Spatial econometrics.* Dordrecht: Kluwer.

Anselin, L. 1995: Local indicators of spatial association – LISA. *Geographical Analysis* 27: 93–115.

Anselin, L. 1998: Exploratory spatial data analysis in a geocomputational environment. In P. Longley, S.M. Brooks, R. McDonnell and B. Macmillan, eds, *Geocomputation: a primer.* Chichester: Wiley, 77–94.

Anselin, L. 2000: Computing environments for spatial data. *Journal of Geographical Systems* 2: 201–20.

Anselin, L. 2002: Under the hood: issues in the specification and interpretation of spatial regression models. *Agricultural Economics* 27: 247–67.

Anselin, L. 2003: Spatial externalities, spatial multipliers and spatial econometrics. *International Regional Science Review* 26: 153–66.

Anselin, L., Syabri, I. and Kho, Y. 2006: GeoDa: an introduction to spatial data analysis. *Geographical Analysis* 38: 5–22.

Ansell-Pearson, K. 1994: *An introduction to Nietzsche as political thinker.* Cambridge, UK: Cambridge University Press.

Ansell-Pearson, K. 1997: *Viroid life: perspectives on Nietzsche and the transhuman condition.* London: Routledge.

Ansell-Pearson, K. 1999: *Germinal life: difference and repetition in Deleuze.* London: Routledge.

Anthias, F. 2001: The concept of 'social division' and theorising social stratification: Looking at ethnicity and class. *Sociology* 35: 835–54.

Antipode 2003: Intervention roundtable: geographical knowledge and visual practices. *Antipode* 35: 212–43.

Antle, A. and Klinkenberg, B. 1999: Shifting paradigms: from cartographic communication to scientific visualization. *Geomatica* 53: 149–55.

Anzaldúa, G. 1999: *Borderlands/la frontera.* San Francisco: Aunt Lute Books.

Aoyama, Y., Ratick, S.J. and Schwarz, G. 2006: Organizational dynamics of the U.S. logistics industry from an economic geography perspective. *Professional Geographer* 58(3): 327–40.

Appadurai, A., ed., 1986: *The social life of things: commodities in cultural perspective.* Cambridge, UK: Cambridge University Press.

Appadurai, A. 1988: Place and voice in anthropological theory. *Cultural Anthropology* 3: 16–20.

Appadurai, A. 1996: *Modernity at large: cultural dimensions of globalization.* Minneapolis: University of Minnesota Press.

Appadurai, A. 2000: Grassroots globalization and the research imagination. *Public Culture* 12(1): 1–19.

Appadurai, A. 2001: Deep democracy: urban governmentality and the horizon of politics. *Environment and Urbanization* 13: 23–43.

Appelbaum, R. and Henderson, J., eds, 1992: *States and development in the Asian Pacific rim.* London: Sage.

Appiah, K.A. 2003: *Thinking it through: an introduction to contemporary philosophy.* Oxford: Oxford University Press.

Arce, A. and Marsden, T. 1994: The social construction of international food: a new research agenda. *Economic Geography* 69(3): 293–311.

Archer, J.C. and Taylor, P.J. 1981: *Section and party: a political geography of American presidential elections from Andrew Jackson to Ronald Reagan.* Chichester: Wiley.

Archer, K. 1993: Regions as social organisms: the Lamarckian characteristics of Vidal de la Blache's regional geography. *Annals of the Association of American Geographers* 83(3): 498–514.

Ardao, A. 1980: *Génesis de la idea y el nombre de América Latina.* Caracas.

Ardao, A. 1992: *España en el origen del nombre América Latina (Spain in the origin of the name Latin America).* Montevideo: Biblioteca de Marcha.

Arendt, H. 1958: *The origins of totalitarianism.* New York: Random House.

Arendt, H. 1976: Decline of the nation-state: end of the rights of man. In Arendt, *The origins of totalitarianism.* San Diego: Harcourt, 267–302.

Arendt, H. 2004 [1969]: On violence. In N. Scheper-Hughes and P. Bourgois, eds, *Violence in war and peace: an anthology.* Oxford: Oxford University Press.

Arib, M.A. and Hesse, M.B. 1986: *The construction of reality.* Cambridge, UK: Cambridge University Press.

Armitage, D. 2004: John Locke, Carolina, and the *Two treatises of government. Political Theory* 32: 602–27.

Armstrong, H.W. and Taylor, J. 1978: *Regional economic policy and its analysis.* Deddington, Oxford: Philip Allan.

Armstrong, H.W. and Taylor, J. 2000: *Regional economics and policy,* 3rd edn. Oxford: Blackwell.

Armstrong, W. and McGee, T.G. 1985: *Theatres of accumulation: studies in Asian and Latin American urbanization.* London: Methuen.

Arndt, H. 1981: Economic development: a semantic history. *Economic Development and Cultural Change* 29: 457–66.

Arnold, D. 1996a: Inventing tropicality. In Arnold, *The problem of nature: environment, culture and European expansion.* Oxford: Blackwell.

Arnold, D. 1996b: *The problem of nature: environment, culture and European expansion.* Oxford: Blackwell.

Arnold, D. 2006: *The tropics and the travelling gaze: India, landscape and science, 1800–1856.* Seattle: University of Washington Press.

Arrighi, G. 1979: *The geometry of imperialism.* London: Verso.

Arrighi, G. 1995: *The long twentieth century,* London: Verso.

Arrighi, G. and Pearce, B. 1972: *Unequal exchange,* London: Monthly Review Press.

Artibise, A. 2005: Cascadian adventures: shared visions, strategic alliances, and ingrained barriers in a transborder region. In H. Nicol and I. Townsend-Gault, eds, *Holding the line: borders in a global world.* Vancouver: University of British Columbia Press, 238–67.

Asad, T. 1987: Are there histories of peoples without Europe? A review article. *Comparative Studies in Society and History* 29(3): 594–607.

Asdal, K. 2003: The problematic nature of nature: the post-constructivist challenge to environmental history. *History and Theory* 42 (December): 60–74.

Asendorf, C. 1993: *Batteries of life: on the history of things and their perception in modernity.* Berkeley, CA: University of California Press.

Asheim, B. 1996: Industrial districts as 'learning regions': a condition for prosperity. *European Planning Studies* 4: 379–405.

Asheim, B. and Gertler, M.S. 2005: The geography of innovation: regional innovation systems. In J. Fagerberg, D. Mowery and R. Nelson, eds, *The Oxford handbook of innovation.* Oxford: Oxford University Press, 291–317.

Ashworth, G. and Tunbridge, J. 2004: Whose tourist-historic city? Localizing the global and globalizing the local. In A.A. Lew, C.M. Hall and A.M. Williams, eds, 2004: *A companion to tourism.* Oxford: Blackwell, 210–22.

Ashworth, G.J., White, P.E. and Winchester, H.P.M. 1988: The red-light district in the West European city: a neglected aspect of the urban landscape. *Geoforum* 19: 201–12.

Aston, T.H. and Philpin, C.E., eds, 1985: *The Brenner debate: agrarian class structure and economic development in pre-industrial Europe.* Cambridge, UK: Cambridge University Press.

Atkins, P. and Bowler, I. 2001: *Food in society: economy culture geography.* London: Arnold.

Atkinson, D. and Cosgrove, D. 1998: Urban rhetoric and embodied identities: city, nation and empire at the Vittorio Emanuele II monument in Rome 1870–1945. *Annals of the Association of American Geographers* 88: 28–49.

Atkinson, D., Jackson, P., Sibley, D. and Washbourne, N., eds, 2007: *Cultural geography: a critical dictionary of key concepts.* London: I.B. Tauris.

Atkinson, P.M. 1997: Geographical information science. *Progress in Physical Geography* 21: 573–82.

Atkinson, R., ed., 2003: The gentry in the city: urban neighbourhood trajectories and gentrification. *Urban Studies* 40: 2343–584.

Atkinson, R. and Bridge, G., eds, 2005: *Gentrification in a global context.* New York: Routledge.

Atwood, M. 1993: In Nader, R. ed., *The case against 'free trade': GATT, NAFTA, and the globalization of corporate power*. San Francisco: Earth Island Press.

Augé, M. 1992: *Non-lieux*. Paris: Seuil.

Augé, M. 1995: *Non-places: introduction to an anthropology of supermodernity*. London: Verso.

Auletta, K. 1982: *The underclass*. New York: Random House.

Auty, R., ed., 2001: *Resource abundance and economic development*. Oxford: Oxford University Press.

Avila, E. 2004: *Popular culture in the age of white flight: fear and fantasy in suburban Los Angeles*. Berkeley, CA: University of California Press.

Axelrod, R. 2006: *The evolution of cooperation*, 2nd edn. New York: Perseus Books.

Ayer, A.J. 1936: *Language, truth and logic*. London: Victor Gollancz.

Babbie, E. 2001: *The practice of social research*, 9th edn. Belmont, CA: Wadsworth Thomson Learning.

Bachelard, G. 1994 [1958]: *The poetics of space*, trans. M. Jolas. Boston: Beacon Press.

Badie, B. 1995: *La fin des territoires: essai sur le désordre international et sur l'utilité sociale du respect*. Paris: Fayard.

Badiou, A. 2001: *Ethics: an essay on the understanding of evil*, trans. P. Hallward. London: Verso.

Badiou, A. 2005: *Being and event*, trans. O. Feltham. New York: Continuum.

Badmington, N., ed., 2000: *Posthumanism*. London: Palgrave Macmillan.

Baigent, E.A. 2004: Patrick Geddes, Lewis Mumford and Jean Gottmann: divisions over 'megalopolis'. *Progress in Human Geography* 28: 687–700.

Bailey, A.J. 2001: Turning transnational: notes on the theorisation of international migration. *International Journal of Population Geography* 7: 413–28.

Bailey, A.J. 2005: *Making population geography*. London: Hodder.

Bailey, A.J., Blake, M.K. and Cooke, T.J. 2004: Migration, care, and the linked lives of dual-earner households. *Environment and Planning A* 36: 1617–32.

Bailey, A.J., Wright, R., Mountz, A. and Miyares, I. 2002: Producing Salvadoran transnational geographies. *Annals of the Association of American Geographers* 92(1): 125–44.

Bailey, M. 1992: *Per impetum maris*: natural disaster and economic decline in eastern England, 1275–1350. In B.M.S. Campbell ed., *Before the Black Death: studies in the 'crisis'; of the early fourteenth century*. Manchester: Manchester University Press, 184–208.

Bailey, M. 1996: Demographic decline in late medieval England: some thoughts on recent research. *Economic History Review* 49: 1–19.

Bailey, T.C. and Gatrell, A.C. 1995: *Interactive spatial data analysis*. London: Longman.

Bains, W. 2003: *Biotechnology A–Z*. Oxford: Oxford University Press.

Bakan, J. 1997: *Just words: constitutional rights and social wrongs*. Toronto: University of Toronto Press.

Baker, A.R.H. 1968: A note on the retrogressive and retrospective approaches in historical geography. *Erdkunde* 22: 244–5.

Baker, A.R.H. 1984: Reflections on the relations of historical geography and the Annales school of history. In A.R.H. Baker and D. Gregory, eds, *Explorations in historical geography: interpretative essays*. Cambridge, UK: Cambridge University Press, 1–27.

Baker, A.R.H. 2003: *Geography and history: bridging the divide*. Cambridge, UK: Cambridge University Press.

Baker, A.R.H. 2007: Classifying geographical history, *Professional Geographer* 59: 344–56.

Baker, J.N.L. 1931: *A history of geographical discovery and exploration*. London: Harrap.

Bakewell, P. 2004: *A history of Latin America: c. 1450 to the present*. Malden, MA: Blackwell.

Bakhtin, M. 1984: *The dialogical imagination*. Austin, TX: University of Texas Press.

Bakker, K.J. 2003: *An uncooperative commodity: privatising water in England and Wales*. Oxford: Oxford University Press.

Bakker, K.J. and Bridge, G. 2006a: Material worlds? Resource geographies and the matter of nature. *Progress in Human Geography* 30(1): 5–27.

Bakker, K.J. and Bridge, G. 2006b: Resource regulation. In K. Cox, M. Low and J. Robinson, eds, *Handbook of political geography*. Newbury Park, CA: Sage.

Bale, J. 2002: *Sports geography*. London: Routledge.

Bales, K. 2004: *Disposable people: new slavery in the global economy*, rev. edn. Berkeley, CA: University of California Press.

Balibar, E. 1991a: Racism and nationalism. In E. Balibar and E. Wallerstein, *Race, nation, class: ambiguous identities*. London: Verso: 37–67.

Balibar, E. 1991b: The nation form: history and ideology. In E. Balibar and I. Wallerstein, *Race, nation, class: ambiguous identities*. London: Verso, 86–106.

Balibar, E. 2002: *Politics and the other scene*. London: Verso.

Ball, M., Harloe, M. and Martens, M. 1988: *Housing and social change in Europe and the USA*. London: Routledge.

Ballantyne, B., Bristow, M. et al. 2000: How can land tenure and cadastral reform succeed? An inter-regional comparison of rural reforms. *Canadian Journal of Development Studies* 21: 693–723.

Ballantyne, T., ed., 2004: *Science, empire and the European exploration of the Pacific*. Aldershot: Ashgate.

Ballas, D., Clarke, G., Dorling, D. and Rossiter, D. 2007: Using SimBritain to model the geographical impact of national government policies. *Geographical Analysis* 39: 44–77.

Ballas, D., Rossiter, D., Thomas, B., Clarke, G. and Dorling, D. 2005: *Geography matters: simulating the local impacts of national social policies*. York: Joseph Rowntree Foundation (or view online at www.jrf.org.uk/bookshop/).

Bancroft, A. 2005: *Roma and Gypsy travellers in Europe: modernity, race, space and exclusion*. Aldershot: Ashgate.

Banerjee, B. 1983: Social networks in the migration process: empirical evidence on chain migration in India. *Journal of Developing Areas* 17: 185–96.

Banerjee, S. and Mitra, S. 2004: Remote surface mapping using orthophotos and geologic maps draped over digital elevation models: application to the Sheep Mountain anticline, Wyoming. *American Association of Petroleum Geologists Bulletin* 88: 1227–37.

Banes, D. 1988: The Portuguese voyages of discovery and the emergence of modern science. *Journal of the Washington Academy of Sciences* 28: 47–58.

Banks, M. 1996: *Ethnicity: anthropological constructions*. London: Routledge.

Banks, M. 2001: *Visual methods in social research*. London: Sage.

Bannon, I. and Collier, P., eds, 2003: *Natural resources and violent conflict: options and actions*. Washington, DC: The World Bank.

Banton, M. 1983: *Racial and ethnic competition*. Cambridge, UK: Cambridge University Press.

Banton, M. 2004: Are ethnicity and nationality twin concepts? *Journal of Ethnic and Migration Studies* 30: 807–14.

Baran, P.A. and Hobsbawm, E.J. 1961: The stages of economic growth. *Kyklos* 14: 324–42.

Barber, B.R. 2004: *Strong democracy: participatory politics for a new age*. Berkeley and Los Angeles, CA: University of California Press.

Barker, M. 1981: *The new racism: conservatives and the ideology of the tribes*. London: Junction Books.

Barker, M. 1992: Biology and the new racism. In D.T. Goldberg, ed., *Anatomy of racism*. Minneapolis: University of Minnesota Press, 18–37.

Barlow, M. 1991: *Metropolitan government*. London: Routledge.

Barnbrock, J. 1974: Prolegomenon to a methodological debate on location theory: the case of von Thünen. *Antipode* 6: 59–66.

Barnes, C. and Mercer, G. 2004: Theorising and researching disability from a social model perspective. In C. Barnes and G. Mercer, eds, *Implementing the social model of disability: theory and research*. Leeds: Disability Press, 1–17.

Barnes, T.J. 1996: *Logics of dislocation: models, metaphors, and meanings of economic space*. New York: Guilford Press.

Barnes, T.J. 1998: A history of regression: actors, networks, machines, and numbers. *Environmental and Planning D: Society and Space* 30: 203–24.

Barnes, T.J. 2001: Retheorizing economic geography: from the quantitative revolution to the 'cultural turn'. *Annals of the Association of American Geographers* 91: 546–65.

Barnes, T.J. 2002: Critical notes on economic geography from an aging radical. Or radical notes on economic geography from a critical age. *Acme* 1: 8–14.

Barnes, T.J. 2003: The place of locational analysis: a selective and interpretive history. *Progress in Human Geography* 27: 69–95.

Barnes, T.J. 2004a: A paper related to everything, but more related to local things. *Annals of the Association of American Geographers* 94: 278–83.

Barnes, T.J. 2004b: Placing ideas: genius loci, heterotopia, and geography's quantitative revolution. *Progress in Human Geography* 29: 565–95.

Barnes, T.J. 2004c: The rise (and decline) of American regional science: lessons for the new economic geography? *Journal of Economic Geography* 4: 107–29.

Barnes, T.J. 2005: Culture: economy. In P. Cloke and R. J. Johnston, eds, *Spaces of geographical thought*. London: Sage, 61–80.

Barnes, T.J. 2006a: Between deduction and dialectics: David Harvey on knowledge. In N. Castree and D. Gregory, eds, *David Harvey: a critical reader*. Oxford: Blackwell, 26–46.

Barnes, T.J. 2006b: Geographical intelligence: American geographers and research and analysis in the Office of Strategic Services 1941–5. *Journal of Historical Geography* 32: 149–68.

Barnes, T.J. 2008a: American pragmatism: towards a geographical introduction. *Geoforum* 39(4): 1542–54.

Barnes, T.J. 2008b: Geography's underworld: the military–industrial complex, mathematical modelling and the quantitative revolution. *Geoforum* 39: 3–16.

Barnes, T.J. and Curry, M.G. 1992: Postmodernism in economic geography: metaphor and the construction of alterity. *Environment and Planning D: Society and Space* 10: 57–68.

Barnes, T.J. and Duncan, J.S., eds, 1991: *Writing worlds: discourse, text and metaphors in the representation of landscape*. London: Routledge.

Barnes, T.J. and Farish, M. 2006: Between regions: science, militarism, and American geography from world war to cold War. *Annals of the Association of American Geographers* 96: 807–26.

Barnes, T.J. and Gregory, D. 1997a: Grand Theory and geographical practice. In T. Barnes and

D. Gregory, eds, *Reading human geography: the poetics and politics of inquiry*. London: Arnold, 85–91.

Barnes, T.J. and Gregory, D. 1997b: Worlding geography: geography as situated knowledge. In T. Barnes and D. Gregory, eds, *Reading human geography: the poetics and politics of inquiry*. London: Arnold, 13–26.

Barnett, C. 1995: Awakening the dead: who needs the history of geography? *Transactions of the Institute of British Geographers*, NS 20: 417–19.

Barnett, C. 1997: 'Sing along with the common people': politics, postcolonialism and other figures. *Environment and Planning D: Society and Space* 15: 137–54.

Barnett, C. 1998: Impure and worldly geography: the Africanist discourse of the Royal Geographical Society, 1831–73. *Transactions of the Institute of British Geographers*, NS 23: 239–52.

Barnett, C. 1999: Deconstructing context: exposing Derrida. *Transactions of the Institute of British Geographers*, NS 24: 277–93.

Barnett, C. 2001: Culture, geography and the arts of government. *Environment and Planning D: Society and Space* 19: 7–24.

Barnett, C. 2003: *Culture and democracy: media, space and representation*. Edinburgh: Edinburgh University Press.

Barnett, C. 2004a: A critique of the cultural turn. In J. Duncan, N. Johnson and R. Schein, eds, *A companion to cultural geography*. Oxford: Blackwell.

Barnett, C. 2004b: Deconstructing radical democracy: articulation, representation and being-with-others. *Political Geography* 23: 503–28.

Barnett, C. 2005: Ways of relating: hospitality and the acknowledgement of otherness. *Progress in Human Geography* 29: 1–17.

Barnett, C. 2007: Convening publics: the parasitical spaces of action. In K. Cox, M. Low and J. Robinson, eds, *Handbook of political geography*. London: Sage.

Barnett, C. 2008: Political affects in public space: normative blind-spots in non-representational ontologies. *Transactions of the Institute of British Geographers* 33: 186–200.

Barnett, C. and Land, D. 2007: Geographies of generosity: beyond the moral turn. *Geoforum* 38: 1065–75.

Barnett, C. and Low, M. 1996: Speculating on theory: towards a political economy of academic publishing. *Area* 28: 13–24.

Barnett, C. and Low, M., eds, 2004: *Spaces of democracy: geographical perspectives on citizenship, participation and representation*. London: Sage.

Barnett, H. and Morse, C. 1963: *Scarcity and growth: the economics of natural resource availability*. Baltimore, MD: The Johns Hopkins University Press.

Barnett, T. 2004c: *The Pentagon's new map: war and peace in the twenty-first century*. New York: G.P. Putnam's Sons.

Barnett, V. 2002: *Sample survey: principles and methods*. London: Arnold.

Barot, R. and Bird, J. 2001: Racialization: the genealogy and critique of a concept. *Ethnic and Racial Studies* 21(4): 601–18.

Barr, S., Ford, N.J. and Gilg, A.W. 2003: Attitudes towards recycling household waste in Exeter, Devon: quantitative and qualitative approaches. *Local Environment* 8: 407–21.

Barrell, J. 1982: Geographies of Hardy's Wessex. *Journal of Historical Geography* 8: 347–61.

Barrett, M. 1980: *Women's oppression today: problems in Marxist feminist analysis*. London: Verso.

Barrett, M. 1991: *The politics of truth: from Marx to Foucault*. Cambridge, UK: Polity Press.

Barrett, S. 2003: *Environment and statecraft: the strategy of environmental treaty-making*. Oxford: Oxford University Press.

Barrows, H.H. 1923: Geography as human ecology. *Annals of the Association of American Geographers* 13(1): 1–14.

Barry, A. 2001: *Political machines*. Oxford: Blackwell.

Barry, A., Osborne, T. and Rose, N., eds, 1996: *Foucault and political reason*. London: UCL Press.

Barry, J. 1999: *Environment and social theory*. London: Routledge.

Barry, R.G. and Chorley, R.J. 1968: *Atmosphere, weather and climate*. London: Methuen (see also many later editions).

Barth, F. 1969: Introduction. In F. Barth, ed., *Ethnic groups and boundaries: the social organization of cultural difference*. Boston: Little, Brown/London: George Allen and Unwin, 9–38.

Barthes, R. 1957: *Mythologies*. London: Penguin.

Barthes, R. 1977: *Image, music, text*, trans. S. Heath. London: Fontana/New York: Hill and Wang.

Bartlett, M.S. 1955: *An introduction to stochastic processes*. Cambridge, UK: Cambridge University Press.

Barton, S.E. and Silverman, C.J. 1994: *Common interest communities: private governments and the public interest*. Berkeley, CA: University of California, Institute of Local Government Studies.

Basch, L., Glick Schiller, N. and Blanc, C. 1995: *Nations unbound: transnational projects, postcolonial predicaments and deterritorialized nation-states*. New York: Gordon & Breach.

Bassett, K. 2005: Marxian theory and the writing of urban history. *Journal of Historical Geography* 31: 568–82.

Bassett, T.J. 1988: The political ecology of peasant herder conflicts in the northern Ivory Coast. *Annals of the Association of American Geographers* 78(3): 453–72.

Bassin, M. 1987a: Race contra space: the conflict between German *Geopolitik* and National Socialism. *Political Geography Quarterly* 6: 115–34.

Bassin, M. 1987b: Friedrich Ratzel 1844–1904. In T.W. Freeman (ed), *Geographers: biobibliographical studies* 11: 123–33.

Bassin, M. 1987c: Imperialism and the nation-state in Friedrich Ratzel's political geography. *Progress in Human Geography* 11: 473–95.

Bassin, M., Newman, D., Reuber, P. and Agnew, J. 2004: Forum: Is there a politics to geopolitics? *Progress in Human Geography* 28: 619–40.

Bateson, G. 1972: *Steps to an ecology of mind.* New York: Ballantine.

Batty, M. 2000: The new urban geography of the third dimension. *Environment and Planning B: Planning and Design* 27: 483–4.

Batty, M. 2005: *Cities and complexity: understanding cities with cellular automata, agent-based models, and fractals.* Cambridge, MA: The MIT Press.

Batty, M. and Longley, P.A. 1994: *Fractal cities: a geometry of form and function.* London: Academic Press.

Bauder, H. 2002: Neighbourhood effects and cultural exclusion. *Urban Studies* 39: 85–93.

Baudrillard, J. 1983: *Simulations*, trans. P. Foss, P. Patton and P. Beitchman. New York: Semiotext(e).

Baudrillard, J. 1993: *Symbolic exchange and death*, trans. I.H. Grant. London: Sage.

Bauer, P. 1974: Foreign aid, forever? *Encounter* 42: 15–28.

Bauman, Z. 1991: *Modernity and the Holocaust.* Cambridge, UK: Polity Press.

Bauman, Z. 2000a: *Modernity and the Holocaust*, reprint with new afterword. Cambridge, UK: Polity Press.

Bauman, Z. 1993: *Modernity and ambivalence.* Cambridge, UK: Polity Press.

Bauman, Z. 2000b: *Liquid modernity.* Cambridge, UK: Polity Press.

Bauman, Z. 2001a: Consuming life. *Journal of Consumer Studies* 1: 9–29.

Bauman, Z. 2001b: Wars of the globalization era. *European Journal of Social Theory* 4: 11–28.

Bauman, Z. 2003: Utopia with no topos. *History of the Human Sciences* 16(1): 11–25.

Bauman, Z. 2004: *Wasted lives: modernity and its outcasts.* Cambridge, UK: Polity Press.

Baumgart, W. 1982: *Imperialism: The idea and reality of British and French colonial expansion, 1880–1914.* Oxford: Oxford University Press.

Baumol, W.J. and Willig, R. 1981: Fixed costs, sunk costs, entry barriers and the sustainability of monopoly. *Quarterly Journal of Economics* 95: 405–31.

Baxter, J. and Eyles, J. 1997: Evaluating qualitative research in social geography: establishing 'rigour' in interview analysis. *Transactions of the Institute of British Geographers*, NS 22: 505–25.

Bayart, J.F. 1993: *The state in Africa: the politics of the belly.* London: Methuen.

Bayes, T. 1763 [1958]: Studies in the history of probability and statistics IX. Thomas Bayes's essay towards solving a problem in the doctrine of chances. *Philosophical Transactions of the Royal Society of London* 53: 370–418.

Baylis, J. and Smith, S., eds, 2004: *The globalization of world politics*, 3rd edn. Oxford: Oxford University Press.

Bayliss-Smith, T.P. 1982: *The ecology of agricultural systems.* Cambridge, UK: Cambridge University Press.

Bayliss-Smith, T.P. and Wanmali, S., eds, 1984: *Understanding green revolutions.* Cambridge, UK: Cambridge University Press.

Beaglehole, J.C. 1966: *The exploration of the Pacific*, 3rd edn. Stanford, CA: Stanford University Press.

Bean, J. 1989: *From lord to patron: lordship in late medieval England.* Manchester: Manchester University Press.

Beaujeu-Garnier, J. 1956–8: *Géographie de la Population*, 2 vols. Paris: Presses Universitaires de France.

Beauregard, R.A. 1995: Edge cities: peripheralizing the center. *Urban Geography* 16(8): 708–21.

Beauregard, R.A. 1999: Break dancing on Santa Monica Boulevard. *Urban Geography* 20: 396–9.

Beaverstock, J.V. 2002: Transnational elites in global cities: British expatriates in Singapore's financial district. *Geoforum* 33: 525–38.

Beaverstock, J.V. and Doel, M.A. 2001: Unfolding the spatial architecture of the East Asian financial crisis: the organizational response of global investment banks. *Geoforum* 32(1): 15–32.

Beaverstock, J.V., Smith, R.G. and Taylor, P.J. 2000: World-city network: a new metageography? *Annals of the Association of American Geographers* 90: 123–34.

Beavon, K.S.O. 1977: *Central place theory: a reinterpretation.* London: Longman.

Beazley, C.R. 1897–1906: *The dawn of modern geography*, 3 vols. Oxford: The Clarendon Press.

Bebbington, T., Guggenheim, S., Olson, E. and Woolcock, M., 2004: Exploring social capital debates at the World Bank. *Journal of Development Studies* 40(5): 33–64.

Beck, U. 1992: *Risk society: towards a new modernity*, trans. M. Ritter. London: Sage.

Beck, U. 1995: *Ecological politics in the age of risk.* Cambridge, UK: Polity Press.

Beck, U. 1997: *The reinvention of politics: rethinking modernity in the global social order.* Cambridge, UK: Polity Press.

Beck, U. 1998: *World risk society.* Cambridge, UK: Polity Press.

Beck, U. 2004: Cosmopolitan realism: on the distinction between cosmopolitanism in philosophy and the social sciences. *Global Networks* 4(2): 131–56.

Beck, U. and Grande, E. 2007: *Cosmopolitan Europe*. Cambridge, UK: Polity Press.

Beck, U., Bonss, W. and Lau, C. 2003: The theory of reflexive modernization: problematic, hypotheses and research programme. *Theory, Culture & Society* 20(2): 1–33.

Beck, U., Giddens, A. and Lash, S. 1994: *Reflexive modernization*. Stanford, CA: Stanford University Press.

Becker, B.K. and Egler, C. 1992: *Brazil: a new regional power in the world-economy: a regional geography*. Cambridge, UK: Cambridge University Press.

Becker, G.S. 1976: *The economic approach to human behavior*. Chicago: The University of Chicago Press.

Becker, J. 1997: *Hungry ghosts*. London: John Murray.

Beckinsale, R., Chorley, R.J. and Dunn, A. 1964/1973/1991: *The history of the study of landforms*, 3 vols. London: Taylor & Francis.

Bednarz, S.W., Downs, R.M. and Vender, J.C. 2003: Geography education. In G.L. Gaile and C.J. Willmott, eds, 2003: *Geography in America at the dawn of the 21st century*. Oxford: Oxford University Press.

Béguin, F. 1995: *Le paysage*. Paris: Flammarion.

Behar, R. and Gordon, D.A., eds, 1995: *Women writing culture: the poetics and politics of ethnography*. Berkeley, CA: University of California Press.

Beinart, W. 2001: *Twentieth-century South Africa*. Oxford and New York: Oxford University Press.

Beinart, W. and Coates, P. 1995: *Environment and history: the taming of nature in the USA and South Africa*. London: Routledge.

Bell, D. 1973: *The coming of post-industrial society*. New York: Basic Books.

Bell, D. 1978: *The cultural consequences of capitalism*. New York: Basic Books.

Bell, D. 1999 [1973]: *The coming of post-industrial society*. New York: Basic Books.

Bell, D. and Binnie, J. 2000: *The sexual citizen: queer politics and beyond*. Cambridge, UK: Polity Press.

Bell, D. and Binnie, J. 2004: Authenticating queer space: citizenship, urbanism and governance. *Urban Studies* 41(9): 1807–20.

Bell, D. and Valentine, G., eds, 1995: *Mapping desire: geographies of sexualities*. London: Routledge.

Bell, D. and Valentine, G. 1997: *Consuming geographies: we are where we eat*. London: Routledge.

Bell, D., Binnie, J., Cream, J. and Valentine, G. 1994: All hyped up and no place to go. *Gender,* *Place and Culture: a Journal of Feminist Geography* 1: 31–48.

Bell, J.E. and Staeheli, L. 1998: Discourses of diffusion and democratization. *Political Geography* 20: 175–95.

Bell, M. 1993: 'The pestilence that walketh in darkness': imperial health, gender and images of South Africa, c.1880–1910. *Transactions of the Institute of British Geographers*, NS 18: 327–41.

Bell, M. 2004: *Farming for us all: practical agriculture and the cultivation of sustainability*. University Park, PA: Pennsylvania State University Press.

Bell, M., Butlin, R. and Heffernan, M., eds, 1995: *Geography and imperialism, 1820–1920*. Manchester: Manchester University Press.

Bellah, R., Madsen, R., Sullivan, W., Swidler, A. and Tipton, S. 1985: *Habits of the heart: individualism and commitment in American life*. Berkeley, CA: University of California Press.

Bello, W. 1994: *Dark victory: the United States, structural adjustment and global poverty*. London: Pluto Press.

Bender, T. 1978: *Community and social change in America*. Baltimore, MD: The Johns Hopkins University Press.

Benenson, A.S., ed., 1995: *Control of communicable diseases manual*, 16th edn. Washington, DC: American Public Health Association.

Benevolo, L. 1980: *The history of the city*. Cambridge, MA: The MIT Press.

Benhabib, S. 1986: *Critique, norm and utopia: a study of the foundations of critical theory*. New York: Columbia University Press.

Benjamin, W. 1973: Theses on the philosophy of history. In *Illuminations*, trans. H. Zohn. London: Collins/Fontana, 255–66.

Benjamin, W. 1978: The work of art in the age of mechanical reproduction. In *Illuminations*, trans. L. Zohn, ed. H. Arendt. New York: Schocken Books, 217–42.

Benjamin, W. 1999: *The Arcades Project*, trans. H. Leiland and K. McLaughlin. Cambridge, MA: Harvard University Press.

Benko, G. and Strohmayer, U., eds, 1997: *Space and social theory: interpreting modernity and postmodernity*. Oxford: Blackwell.

Bennett, J. 1987: *The divided circle: a history of instruments for astronomy, navigation and surveying*. Oxford: Phaidon Christie's.

Bennett, R.J. 1979: *Spatial time series: analysis – forecasting – control*. London: Pion.

Bennett, R.J. 1980: *The geography of public finance*. London: Methuen.

Bennett, R.J. 1985: *Central grants for local governments*. Cambridge, UK: Cambridge University Press.

Bennett, R.J., ed., 1990: *Decentralisation, local government and markets*. Oxford: The Clarendon Press.

Bennett, R.J. and Chorley, R.J. 1978: *Environmental systems: philosophy, analysis and control*. London: Methuen.

Bennett, T. 1998: *Culture: a reformer's science*. London. Sage.

Bentham, J. 1995: *The Panopticon writings*. London: Verso.

Benton, G. and Gomez, E.T. 2003: Essentializing Chinese identity: transnationalism and the Chinese in Europe and Southeast Asia. In B.S.A. Yeoh, M.W. Charney and C.K. Tong, eds, *Approaching transnationalism*. Dordrecht: Kluwer.

Benton, T. 1989: Marxism and natural limits: An ecological critique and reconstruction. *New Left Review* 178: 51–86.

Benton, T. 1994: Biology and social theory in the environmental debate. In M.R. Redclift and T. Benton, eds, *Social theory and the global environment*. London: Routledge: 28–50.

Benton-Short, L. 2006: Politics, public space and memorials: the brawl on the Mall. *Urban Geography* 27: 297–329.

Benvenisti, E. 2004: *The international law of occupation*. Princeton, NJ: Princeton University Press.

Berdahl, D. 1999: *Where the world ended: reunification and identity in the German borderland*. Berkeley, CA: University of California Press.

Berdoulay, V. 1976: French possibilism as a form of Neo-Kantian philosophy. *Proceedings of the Association of American Geographers* 8: 176–9.

Berg, L. 2002: Gender equity as boundary object: or the same old sex and power in geography all over again? *Canadian Geographer* 46(3): 248–56.

Berg, L. and Kearns, R. 1998: America unlimited. *Environment and Planning D: Society and Space* 16: 128–32.

Berg, L. and Longhurst, R. 2003: Placing masculinities and geography. *Gender, Place and Culture* 10: 351–60.

Berg, L. and Mansvelt, J., 2000: Writing in, speaking out: communicating qualitative research findings. In I. Hay, ed., *Qualitative research methods in human geography*. Oxford: Oxford University Press, 161–82.

Berg, M. 1994: *The age of manufactures, 1700–1820: industry, innovation and work*, 2nd edn. London: Routledge.

Berg, M. and Hudson, P. 1992: Rehabilitating the industrial revolution. *Economic History Review*, 45: 4–50.

Berg, M., Hudson, P. and Sonenscher, M., eds, 1983: *Manufacture in town and country before the factory*. Cambridge, UK: Cambridge University Press.

Berger, J. 1972: *Ways of seeing*. London: Penguin.

Berger, M.T. 1995: *Under Northern Eyes: Latin American studies and U.S. hegemony in the Americas: 1898–1990*. Bloomington: Indiana University Press.

Berger, P.L. and Luckmann, T. 1966: *The social construction of reality: a treatise in the sociology of knowledge*. New York: Doubleday.

Bergson, H. 1983 [1907]: *Creative evolution*, trans. A. Mitchell. Lanham, MD: University Press of America.

Berkes, F., ed., 1989: *Common property resources: ecology and community-based sustainable development*. London: Belhaven Press.

Berking, H. 2003: 'Ethnicity is everywhere': on globalization and the transformation of cultural identity. *Current Sociology* 51: 248–64.

Berlant, L. 1997: *The Queen of America goes to Washington City*. Durham, NC: Duke University Press.

Berlant, L., ed., 2004: *Compassion*. London: Routledge.

Berman, M. 1983: *All that is solid melts into air: the experience of modernity*. London: Verso.

Berman, M. 1984: On being a woman in American geography: a personal perspective. *Antipode* 16: 61–6.

Berman, M. 1996: Falling towers: city life after urbicide. In D. Crow, ed., *Geography and identity*. Washington, DC: Maisonneuve Press, 172–92.

Bernard, M. and Ravenhill, J. 1995: Beyond product cycles and flying geese: regionalization, hierarchy, and the industrialization of East Asia. *World Politics* 47: 171–209.

Bernstein, H. 1995a: Notes on capital and peasantry. In Harriss, J. ed., *Rural development: theories on peasant economy and agrarian change*. London: Hutchinson University Library, 160–77.

Bernstein, H. 1996: Agrarian questions then and now. *Journal of Peasant Studies* 24(1/2): 22–49.

Bernstein, J. 1995b: *Recovering ethical life: Jürgen Habermas and the future of critical theory*. London: Routledge.

Bernstein, J.M. 2004: Bare life, bearing witness: Auschwitz and the pornography of horror. *parallax* 10(1): 2–16.

Bernstein, R. 1983: *Beyond objectivism and relativism: science, hermeneutics, and praxis*. Philadelphia: University of Pennsylvania Press.

Bernstein, R.J. 1992a: The resurgence of pragmatism. *Social Research* 59: 813–40.

Bernstein, R.J. 1992b: *The new constellation: the ethical political horizons of modernity/postmodernity*. Cambridge, MA: The MIT Press.

Berry, B. and Kasarda, J. 1977: *Contemporary urban ecology*. New York: Macmillan.

Berry, B.J.L. 1964: Cities as systems within systems of cities. *Papers of the Regional Science Association* 13: 147–63.

Berry, B.J.L. 1970: The geography of the US in the year 2000. *Transactions of the Institute of British Geographers* 51: 21–53.

Berry, B.J.L. and Baker, A.M. 1968: Methods of spatial sampling. In B.J.L. Berry and D.F. Marble, eds, *Spatial analysis: a reader in statistical geography*. Englewood Cliffs, NJ: Prentice-Hall, 91–100.

Berry, B.J.L. and Parr, J.B. 1988: *Geography of retailing and market centers (second edition)*. Englewood Cliffs, NJ: Prentice-Hall.

Berry, M. and Linoff, G. 1997: *Data mining techniques for marketing, sales and customer support*. New York: Wiley.

Bertin, J. 1983: *Semiology of graphics: diagrams, networks, maps*, trans. W.J. Berg. Madison: University of Wisconsin Press.

Besio, K. and Butz, D. 2004: Autoethnography: a limited endorsement. *Professional Geographer* 56: 432–38.

Besse, J.-M. 2003: *Les grandeurs de la terre: aspects du savoir géographique à la Renaissance*. Lyon: ENS Editions.

Best, S. and Kellner, D. 1991: *Postmodern theory: critical interrogations*. New York: Guilford Press.

Bhabha, H.K. 1984: Of mimicry and man: the ambivalence of colonial discourse. *October* 28: 125–33.

Bhabha, H.K. 1985: Signs taken for wonders: question of ambivalence about authority under a tree outside Delhi. *Critical Inquiry* 12: 144–65.

Bhabha, H.K. 1990a: Interview with Homi Bhabha: the third space. In J. Rutherford, ed., *Identity: community, culture, difference*. London: Lawrence and Wishart, 207–21.

Bhabha, H.K. 1990b: The third space. In J. Rutherford, ed., *Identity*. London: Lawrence and Wishart.

Bhabha, H.K. 1992: Double visions. *Artforum* 30(5): 82–90.

Bhabha, H.K. 1994: *The location of culture*. London: Routledge.

Bhagwati, J. 2004: *In defense of globalization*. Oxford: Oxford University Press.

Bhandar, D. 2004: Renormalizing citizenship and life in Fortress North America. *Citizenship Studies* 8(3): 261–78.

Bhaskar, R. 1979: *The possibility of naturalism: a philosophical critique of the contemporary human sciences*. Brighton: Harvester / Atlantic Highlands, NJ: Humanities Press.

Bhaskar, R. 1986: *Scientific realism and human emancipation*. London: Verso.

Bhaskar, R. 1989: *Reclaiming reality: an introduction to contemporary philosophy*. London: Verso.

Bhaskar, R. 1998 [1979]: *The possibility of naturalism*, 3rd edn. London: Routledge.

Bhuta, N. 2005: The antinomies of transformative occupation. *European Journal of International Law* 16: 721–40.

Bialasiewicz, L. 2003: The many wor(l)ds of difference and dissent. *Antipode* 35: 14–23.

Bialasiewicz, L., Elden, S. and Painter, J. 2005: The constitution of EU territory *Comparative European Politics* 3: 333–63.

Bialasiewicz, L., Campbell, D., Elden, S., Graham, S., Jeffrey, A. and Williams, A. 2007: Performing security: the imaginative geographies of current US strategy. *Political Geography* 26: 405–22.

Bickerstaff, K. and Walker, G. 2002: Risk, responsibility, and blame: an analysis of vocabularies of motive in air pollution(ing) discourses. *Environment and Planning A* 34(12): 2175–92.

Biddick, K. 1990: People and things: people and power in early English development. *Comparative Studies in Society and History* 32: 3–23.

Biger, G. 2004: *Boundaries of modern Palestine*. London: Routledge.

Biggs, N., Lloyd, E. and Wilson, R. 1986: *Graph theory, 1736–1936*. Oxford: Oxford University Press.

Bijker, W. 2005: The politics of water: a Dutch thing to keep the water out or not? In B. Latour and P. Wiebe, eds, *Making things public*. Karlsruhe: ZKM/Cambridge, MA: The MIT Press, 512–29.

Billig, M. 1996: *Arguing and thinking: a rhetorical approach to social psychology*, rev. edn. Cambridge, UK: Cambridge University Press.

Billinge, M., Gregory, D. and Martin, R.L. 1984a: Reconstructions. In M. Billinge, D. Gregory and R. Martin, eds, *Recollections of a revolution: geography as spatial science*. London: Macmillan, 1–24.

Billinge, M., Gregory, D. and Martin, R., eds, 1984b: *Recollections of a revolution: geography as spatial science*. London: Macmillan.

Bin Jiang and Claramunt, C. 2002: Integration of space syntax into GIS: new perspectives on urban morphology. *Transactions in GIS* 6: 295–309.

Bingham, N. 1996: Object-ions: from technological determinism towards geographies of relations. *Environment and Planning D: Society and Space* 14(6): 635–57.

Bingham, N. 2006: Bees, butterflies, and bacteria: biotechnology and the politics of nonhuman friendship. *Environment and Planning A* 38: 483–98.

Bingham, N. and Blackmore, R. 2003: What to do? How risk and uncertainty affect environmental responses. In S. Hinchliffe, A. Blowers and J. Freeland, eds. *Understanding environmental issues*. Chichester: Wiley, 127–64.

Bingley, A. 2003: In here and out there: sensations between self and landscape. *Social and Cultural Geography* 4: 329–45.

Binnie, J. 1997: Coming out of geography: towards a queer epistemology. *Society and Space* 15: 223–37.

Binnie, J. 2004: *The globalisation of sexuality*. London: Sage.

Bird, J.H. 1975: Methodological implications for geography from the philosophy of K.R. Popper. *Scottish Geographical Magazine* 91: 153–63.

Bird, J.H. 1989: *The changing worlds of geography*. Oxford: The Clarendon Press.

Black, D. 1958: *The theory of committees and elections*. Cambridge, UK: Cambridge University Press.

Black, J. 1997: *Maps and history: constructing images of the past*. New Haven, CT: Yale University Press.

Black, R. 1998: *Refugees, environment and development*. London: Longman.

Black, R. and Koser, K., eds, 1999: *The end of the refugee cycle? Refugee repatriation and reconstruction*. New York: Berghahn Books.

Black, W. 2003: *Transportation: a geographical analysis*. New York: Guilford Press.

Blackburn, R. 1998: *The making of New World slavery: From the Baroque to the modern 1492–1800*. London: Verso.

Blaikie, P.M. 1971: Spatial organization of agriculture in some North Indian villages. *Transactions of the Institute of British Geographers* 52: 1–40; 53: 15–30.

Blaikie, P.M. 1975: *Family planning in India: a socio-geographical approach*. London: Edward Arnold/New York: Holmes and Meier.

Blaikie, P.M. 1978: The theory of the spatial diffusion of innovations: a spacious cul-de-sac. *Progress in Human Geography* 2: 268–95.

Blaikie, P.M. 1985: *The political economy of soil erosion in developing countries*. London: Longman Development Studies.

Blaikie, P.M. and Brookfield, H.C. 1987: *Land degradation and society*. London: Methuen.

Blaikie, P.M., Cannon, T., Davis, I. and Wisner, B. 1994: *At risk: natural hazards, people's vulnerability, and disasters*. London: Routledge.

Blainey, G. 1966: *The tyranny of distance. How distance shaped Australia's history*. Melbourne: Sun Books (also Sydney: Macmillan, 2001).

Blake, M. and Hanson, S. 2005: Rethinking innovation: context and gender. *Environment and Planning A* 37: 381–401.

Blakely, E.J. and Snyder, M.G. 1997: *Fortress America: gated communities in the United States*. Washington, DC: Brookings Institution Press.

Blakemore, M.J. and Harley, J.B. 1980: *Concepts in the history of cartography: a review and perspective*. Cartographica Monograph 26. *Cartographica* 17, no. 4. Toronto: University of Toronto Press.

Blalock, H.M. 1970: *Social statistics*. New York: McGraw-Hill.

Blanchot, M. 1993 [1969]: Everyday speech. In Blanchot, *The infinite conversation*, trans. S. Hanson. Minneapolis: University of Minnesota Press, 238–45.

Blanchot, M. 1995: *The writing of the disaster*. Lincoln, NE: University of Nebraska Press.

Blanqui, J.A. 1837: *Histoire de l'économie politique en Europe, depuis les anciens jusqu'à nos jours, suivie d'une bibliographie raisonnée des principaux ouvrages d'économie politique*. Paris: Guillemain.

Blaug, M. 1979: The German hegemony of location theory: a puzzle in the history of economic thought. *History of Political Economy* 11: 21–9.

Blaug, M. 1990: The economics of Johann von Thünen. In *Economic theories, true or false? Essays in the history and methodology of economics*. Aldershot: Edward Elgar, 121–43.

Blaut, J.M. 1961: Space and process. *Professional Geographer* 13: 1–7.

Blaut, J.M. 1977: Two views of diffusion. *Annals of the Association of American Geographers* 67: 343–9.

Blaut, J.M. 1987: *The national question*. London: Zed Books.

Blaut, J.M. 1993: *The colonizer's model of the world: geographical diffusionism and eurocentric history*. New York: Guilford Press.

Blaut, J.M. 1997: The mapping abilities of young children: children can. *Annals of the Association of American Geographers* 87: 152–8.

Blaut, J.M. 1999: Environmentalism and Eurocentrism. *Geographical Review* 89: 391–408.

Blaut, J.M. and Stea, D. 1971: Studies of geographic learning. *Annals of the Association of American Geographers* 61: 387–93.

Block, D. and DuPuis, E.M. 2001: Making the country work for the city: von Thünen's ideas in geography, agricultural economics and the sociology of agriculture. *American Journal of Economics and Sociology* 60: 79–98.

Blomley, N.K. 1994a: Activism and the academy. *Society and Space* 12: 383–5.

Blomley, N.K. 1994b: *Law, space and the geographies of power*. New York: Guilford Press.

Blomley, N.K. 1994c: Mobility, empowerment and the rights revolution. *Political Geography* 13(5): 407–22.

Blomley, N.K. 1996: I'd like to dress her all over: masculinity, power and retail space. In N. Wrigley and M. Lowe, eds, *Retailing, consumption and capital: towards the new retail geography*. London: Longman, 238–57.

Blomley, N.K. 2002: Mud for the land. *Public Culture* 14: 557–82.

Blomley, N.K. 2003: Law, property, and the geography of violence: the frontier, the survey and the grid. *Annals of the Association of American Geography* 93: 121–41.

Blomley, N.K. 2004a: *Unsettling the city: urban land and the politics of property*. New York: Routledge.

Blomley, N.K. 2004b: The boundaries of property: lessons from Beatrix Potter. *Canadian Geographer* 48: 91–100.

Blomley, N.K. 2005: Remember property? *Progress in Human Geography* 29: 125–7.

Blomley, N.K. 2006: Uncritical critical geography? *Progress in Human Geography* 30: 87–94.

Blomley, N.K. and Pratt, G. 2001: Canada and the political geographies of rights. *The Canadian Geographer* 45(1): 151–66.

Blomley, N.K., Delaney, D. and Ford, R.T., eds, 2001: *The legal geographies reader*. Malden, MA: Blackwell.

Blossfeld, H.-P. and Rohwer, G. 2002: *Techniques of event history modelling*. Mahwah, NJ: Lawrence Erlbaum.

Bluestone, B. and Harrison, B. 1982: *The deindustrialization of America*. New York: Basic Books.

Bluestone, B. and Harrison, B. 2001: *Growing prosperity*. Berkeley, CA: University of California Press.

Blumer, H. 1969: *Symbolic interactionism*. Englewood Cliffs, NJ: Prentice Hall.

Blunt, A. 1994: *Travel, gender and imperialism: Mary Kingsley and West Africa*. New York: Guilford Press.

Blunt, A. 2003: Collective memory and productive nostalgia: Anglo-Indian homemaking at McCluskieganj. *Environment and Planning D: Society and Space* 21(6): 717–38.

Blunt, A. 2005: *Domicile and diaspora: Anglo-Indian women and the spatial politics of home*. Oxford: Blackwell.

Blunt, A. and Dowling, R. 2006: *Home*. London: Routledge.

Blunt, A. and McEwan, C., eds, 2002: *Postcolonial geographies*. London: Continuum.

Blunt, A. and Wills, J. 2000: *Dissident geographies: an introduction to radical ideas and practices*. London: Prentice Hall.

Blunt, A., Gruffudd, P., May, J. and Ogborn, M. 2003: *Cultural geography in practice*. London: Arnold.

Boal, F.W. 1976: Ethnic residential segregation. In Herbert, D.T. and Johnston, R.J., eds, *Social areas in cities, volume 1: spatial processes and form*. Chichester: Wiley, 41–79.

Bobrow-Strain, A. 2007: *Intimate enemies*. Durham, NC: Duke University Press.

Bocker, A. 1994: Chain migration over legally closed borders: settled immigrants as bridgeheads and gatekeepers. *The Netherland Journal of Social Sciences* 30: 87–106.

Boden, D. 2000: Worlds in action: information, instantaneity and global futures trading. In B. Adam, U. Beck and J. Can Loon, eds, *The risk society and beyond: critical issues in social theory*. London: Sage, 183–97.

Boden, D. and Molotch, H. 1995: The compulsion of proximity. In R. Friedland and D. Boden, eds, *Now/here: time, space and modernity*. Berkeley, CA: University of California Press, 257–86.

Boeke, J.H. 1953: *Economics and economic policy of dual societies, as exemplified by Indonesia*. Haarlem: H.D.Tjeenk Willink and Zoon.

Bohle, H.G., Downing, T.E. and Watts, M. 1994: Climate change and social vulnerability. *Global Environmental Change* 4(1): 37–48.

Bolster, A., Burgess, S., Johnston, R., Jones, K., Propper, C. and Sarker, C. 2006: Neighbourhoods, households and income dynamics: a semi-parametric investigation of neighbourhood effects. *Journal of Economic Geography* 7: 1–38.

Bonacich, E. 1972: A theory of ethnic antagonism: the split labor market. *American Sociological Review* 37: 547–59.

Bonacich, E. 1994: Thoughts on urban unrest. In F.L. Pincus and H.J. Ehrlich, eds, *Race and ethnic conflict*. Boulder, CO: Westview Press, 404–7.

Bond, P. 2000: *Elite transition: from apartheid to neoliberalism in South Africa*. London: Pluto Press.

Bondi, L. 1999: Stages on journeys: some remarks about human geography and psychotherapeutic practice. *Professional Geographer* 51: 11–24.

Bondi, L. 2003: Empathy and identification: conceptual resources for feminist fieldwork. *ACME: an International E-Journal for Critical Geographies* 2: 64–76.

Bondi, L. 2004: 10th Anniversary Address for a feminist geography of ambivalence. *Gender, Place and Culture* 11: 3–15.

Bondi, L. 2005: Making connections and thinking through emotions: between geography and psychotherapy. *Transactions of the Institute of British Geographers* 30: 433–48.

Bondi, L. and Davidson, J. 2003: Troubling the place of gender. In K. Anderson, M. Domosh, S. Pile and N. Thrift, eds, *Handbook of cultural geography*. London: Sage, 325–43.

Bondi, L. and Davidson, J. 2005: Situating gender. In L. Nelson and J. Seager, eds, *A companion to feminist geography*. Oxford: Blackwell, 15–31.

Bondi, L. with Fewell, J. 2003: 'Unlocking the cage door': the spatiality of counselling. *Social and Cultural Geography* 4: 527–47.

Bongaarts, J. 1982: The fertility-inhibiting effects of the intermediate fertility variables. *Studies in Family Planning* 13: 179–89.

Bongaarts, J. 2002: The end of fertility transition in the developed world. *Population and Development Review* 28: 419–43.

Bongie, C. 2002: What's literature got to do with it? *Comparative Literature* 54: 256–67.

Bonnemaison, J. 1996: *Les fondements géographique d'une identité: l'arcipel du Vanuatu*. Paris: Orstom.

Bonnet, A. 2007: *What is geography?* London: Sage.

Bonnett, A. 1996: The situationist legacy. In S. Horne, ed., *What is situationism? A reader*. Edinburgh: AK Press, 192–201.

Bonnett, A. 2000: *White identities: historical and international perspectives*. London: Prentice Hall.

Bonnett, A. 2005: Occidentalism and plural modernities: or how Fukuzawa and Tagore invented the West. *Environment and Planning D: Society and Space* 23: 505–25.

Bonta, M. and Protevi, J. 2004: *Deleuze and geophilosophy: a guide and glossary*. Edinburgh: Edinburgh University Press.

Boone, J. 1995: Vacation cruises, or the homoerotics of Orientalism. *PMLA* 110: 89–107.

Boorstin, D. 1983: *The discoverers. A history of man's search to know his world and himself*. New York: Random House.

Boot, M. 2003: American imperialism? No need to run away from the label. *USA Today*, 6 May: 15A.

Borjas, G.J. 1989: Economic theory and international migration. *International Migration Review* 23: 457–85.

Bosco, F.J. 2006: The Madres de Plaza de Mayo and three decades of human rights' activism: embeddedness, emotions and social movements. *Annals of the Association of American Geographers* 96: 342–65.

Bosco, F.J. 2007: Emotions that build networks: geographies of human rights movements in Argentina and beyond. *Tijdschrift voor Economische en Sociale Geografie* 98: 545–63.

Bose, S. and Jalal, A. 1997: *Modern South Asia: history, culture, political economy*. Delhi: Oxford University Press.

Boserup, E. 1965: *The condition of agricultural growth*. London: George Allen and Unwin.

Boserup, E. 1981: *Population and technological change*. Chicago: The University of Chicago Press.

Bosetti, V. and Pearce, D. 2003: A study of environmental conflict: the economic value of grey seals in southwest England. *Biodiversity and Conservation* 12(12): 2361–92.

Boslaugh, S. 2007: *Secondary data sources for public health: a practical guide*. Cambridge: Cambridge University Press.

Botkin, D.B. 1990: *Discordant harmonies: a new ecology for the twenty-first century*. New York: Oxford University Press.

Boudeville, J.R. 1966: *Problems of regional economic planning*. Edinburgh: Edinburgh University Press.

Bourdieu, P. 1977: *Outline of a theory of practice*. Cambridge, UK: Cambridge University Press.

Bourdieu, P. 1984: *Distinction: a social critique of the judgement of taste*. Cambridge, MA: Harvard University Press.

Bourdieu, P. 1985: The forms of capital. In J. Richardson, ed., *Handbook of theory and research for the sociology of education*. New York: Greenwood Press, 241–58. [Originally published as Ökonomisches Kapital, kulturelles capital, soziales Kapital: 1983. In Kreckel, R. ed., *Soziale Ungleichheiten* (Soziale Welt, Sonderhelt 2). Goettingen: Otto Schartz and Co., 183–98.]

Bourdieu, P. 1990a: *Photography: a middlebrow art*. Cambridge, UK: Polity Press.

Bourdieu, P. 1990b: *The logic of practice*, trans. R. Nice. Cambridge, UK: Polity Press.

Bourdieu, P. 1995: *The field of cultural production*. Cambridge, UK: Polity Press.

Bourdieu, P. 2000: *Pascalian meditations*. Cambridge, UK: Polity Press.

Bourdieu, P. 2002: *Distinction*. Cambridge, MA: Harvard University Press.

Bourguet, M.-N., Licoppe, C. and Sibum, H.O., eds, 2002: *Instruments, travel and science: itineraries of precision from the seventeenth to the twentieth century*. London: Routledge.

Bourne, L. 1996: Reinventing the suburbs: old myths and new realities. *Progress in Planning* 46(3): 163–84.

Bovaird, T. 2004: Public–private partnerships: for contested concepts to prevalent practice. *International Review of Administrative Sciences* 70: 199–215.

Bowd, G. and Clayton, D. 2005a: French tropical geographies: editors' introduction. *Singapore Journal of Tropical Geography* 26: 271–88.

Bowd, G. and Clayton, D. 2005b: Tropicality, Orientalism and French colonialism in Indochina: the work of Pierre Gourou 1927–1982. *French Historical Studies* 28: 297–327.

Bowden, R.J. and Turkington, D.A. 1990: *Instrumental variables*. Cambridge, UK: Cambridge University Press.

Bowen, M. 1981: *Empiricism and geographical thought: from Francis Bacon to Alexander von Humboldt*. Cambridge, UK: Cambridge University Press.

Bowker, G. 2000: Biodiversity datadiversity. *Social Studies of Science* 30(5): 643–83.

Bowlby, S., Lewis, J., McDowell, L. and Foord, J., 1989: The geography of gender. In R. Peet and N. Thrift, eds, *New models in geography*. London: Unwin and Hyman, 157–75.

Bowler, P.J. 1983: *The eclipse of Darwinism: anti-Darwinian evolution theories in the decades around 1900*. Baltimore, MD: The Johns Hopkins University Press.

Bowler, P.J. 1989: *Evolution: the history of an idea*, rev. edn. Berkeley, CA: University of California Press.

Bowler, P.J. 1992: *The Fontana history of the environmental sciences*. London: Fontana.

Boyd, W. and Prudham, S. 2003: Manufacturing green gold: industrial tree improvement and the power of heredity in the post-war United States. In S. Schrepfer and P. Scranton, eds, *Industrializing organisms: introducing evolutionary history*. New York: Routledge, 107–42.

Boyd, W., Prudham, W.S. and Schurman, R. 2001: Industrial dynamics and the problem of nature. *Society and Natural Resources* 14(7): 555–70.

Boyer, M.C. 1992: Cities for sale: merchandising history at South Street Seaport. In M. Sorkin, ed., *Variations on a theme park: the new American city and the end of public space*. New York: Hill and Wang, 181–204.

Boyer, R. 1990: *The regulation school: a critical introduction*. New York: Columbia University Press.

Boyer, R. and Saillard, Y., eds, 2002: *Regulation theory: the state of the art*. London: Routledge.

Boyle, P. 2003: Population geography: does geography matter in fertility research? *Progress in Human Geography* 27: 615–26.

Bracken, L.J. and Oughton, E.A. 2006: 'What do you mean?' The importance of language in developing interdisciplinary research. *Transactions of the Institute of British Geographers* 31: 371–82.

Bradshaw, M., Dymond, J., White, G. and Chacko, E. 2006: *Contemporary world regional geography*. New York: McGraw-Hill.

Brah, A. 1996: *Cartographies of diaspora: contesting identities*. London: Routledge.

Braidotti, R. 1994: *Nomadic subjects*. New York: Columbia University Press.

Brandom, R., ed., 2000: *Rorty and his critics*. Oxford: Blackwell.

Brandt Commission 1980: *North–South: a programme for survival*. London: Pan Books.

Brandt Commission 1983: *Common crisis: North–South cooperation for world recovery*. London: Pan Books.

Brantlinger, P. 1985: Victorians and Africans: the genealogy of the myth of the dark continent. *Critical Inquiry* 12: 166–203.

Braudel, F. 1979–84: *Civilization and capitalism 15th–18th* century. 3 vols. Berkeley, CA: University of California Press.

Braudel, F. 1985: *Civilization and capitalism*. Vol. III: *The perspective of the world*. London: Fontana.

Braudel, F. and Reynolds, S. 1975: *The Mediterranean and the mediterranean world in the age of Philip II*. London: Fontana.

Braun, B. 1997: Buried epistemologies: the politics of nature in (post)colonial British Columbia. *Annals of the Association of American Geographers* 87(1): 3–31.

Braun, B. 2000: Producing vertical territory: geology and governmentality in late-Victorian Canada. *Ecumene* 7, 1: 7–46.

Braun, B. 2002: *The intemperate rainforest: nature, culture, and power on Canada's west coast*. Minneapolis: University of Minnesota Press.

Braun, B. 2003: Introduction: tracking the power geometries of international critical geography. *Environment and Planning D: Society and Space* 21: 131–3.

Braun, B. 2004a: Modalities of posthumanism. *Environment and Planning A* 36: 1352–5.

Braun, B. 2004b: Querying posthumanism. *Geoforum* 35: 269–73.

Braun, B. 2005: SARS and the posthuman city. Paper presented at the SARS and the Global City Workshop, York University, 29 April (www.yorku.ca/sars2003).

Braun, B. 2006: Towards a new Earth and a new humanity: nature, ontology, politics. In N. Castree and D. Gregory, eds, *David Harvey: a critical reader*. Oxford: Blackwell, 191–222.

Braun, B. and Castree, N., eds, 1998: *Remaking reality: nature at the millennium*. London: Routledge.

Braun, B. and Disch, L. 2002: Radical democracy's 'modern constitution'. *Environment and Planning D: Society and Space* 20(5): 505–11.

Braun, B. and McCarthy, J. 2005: Hurricane Katrina and abandoned being. *Environment and Planning D: Society and Space* 23: 802–9.

Braun, B., Vaiou, D., Yiftachel, O., Sakho, H., Chaturvedi, S., Timar, J. and Minca, C. 2003: Guest editorials. *Environment and Planning D: Society and Space* 21: 131–68.

Braverman, H. 1974: *Labor and monopoly capital: the degradation of work in the twentieth century*. New York: Monthly Review Press.

Brecher, J., Costello, T. and Smith, B. 2000: *Globalization from below*. Boston: South End Press.

Brechin, S.R., Wilhusen, P.R., Fortwangler, C L. and West, P.C., eds, 2003: *Contested nature: promoting international biodiversity with social justice in the twenty-first century*. New York: State University of New York Press.

Breheny, M. 1995: The compact city and transport energy-consumption. *Transactions of the Institute of British Geographers* 20(1): 81–101.

Breman, J. and Agarwal, R. 2002: Down and out: labouring under global capitalism. *Critical Asian Studies* 34: 116–28.

Brennan, T. 2000: The illusion of a future: Orientalism as traveling theory. *Critical Inquiry* 26: 558–83.

Brenner, N. 2002: Decoding the newest 'metropolitan regionalism' in the USA: a critical overview. *Cities* 19: 3–21.

Brenner, N. 2003: Glocalization as a state spatial strategy: urban entrepreneurialism and the new politics of scale. In J. Peck and H. Yeung, eds, *Remaking the global economy: economic-geographical perspectives*. London: Sage, 197–215.

Brenner, N. 2004: *New state spaces: urban governance and the rescaling of statehood*. Oxford and New York: Oxford University Press.

Brenner, N. and Keil, R. 2006: *The global cities reader*. London: Routledge.

Brenner, N., Jessop, B., Jones, M. and Macleod, G., eds, 2003: *State/space: a reader*. Oxford: Blackwell.

Brenner, R. 1976: Agrarian class structure and economic development in pre-industrial England, *Past and Present* 70: 30–75.

Brenner, R. 1986: The social basis of economic development. In J. Roemer, ed., *Analytical Marxism*. Cambridge, UK: Cambridge University Press.

Breuste, J., Feldman, H. and Uhlmann, O., eds, 1998: *Urban ecology*. Berlin: Springer-Verlag.

Brewer, C.A. 1997: Spectral schemes: controversial color use on maps. *Cartography and Geographic Information Science* 24: 203–20.

Brewer, C.A. 2005: *Designing better maps: a guide for GIS users*. Redlands, CA: ESRI Press.

Brewer, C.A. and Pickle, L.W. 2002: Evaluation of methods for classifying epidemiological data on choropleth maps in series. *Annals of the Association of American Geographers* 92: 662–81.

Brewer, J. 1987: Exploitation in the new Marxism of collective action. *Sociological Review* 35: 84–96.

Bridge, G. 1997: Mapping the terrain of time-space compression: power networks in everyday life. *Environment and Planning D: Society and Space* 15: 611–26.

Bridge, G. 2001: Bourdieu, rational action and the time–space strategy of gentrification. *Transactions of the Institute of British Geographers* 26(2): 205–16.

Bridge, G. 2004: Mapping the bonanza: geographies of mining investment in an era of neo-liberal reform. *Professional Geographer* 56(3): 406–21.

Bridge, G. 2008: City senses: on the radical possibilities of pragmatism in geography. *Geoforum* 39(4): 1570–84.

Bridge, G. and Watson, S., eds, 2000: *A companion to the city*. Oxford: Blackwell.

Bridge, G., Marsden, T.K. and McManus, P. 2003: Guest editorial: 'The next new thing?' Biotechnology and its discontents. *Geoforum* 34: 165–75.

Briggs, J. 2005: The use of indigenous knowledge in development: problems and challenges. *Progress in Development Studies* 5(2): 99–114.

Briggs, J. and Sharp, J. 2004: Indigenous knowledge and development: a postcolonial caution. *Third World Quarterly* 25(4): 661–76.

Bright, C. 1999: *Life out of bounds: bio-invasions in a borderless world*. London: Earthscan.

Brimicombe, A. 2006: *Location-based services & geo-information engineering*. Chichester: Wiley.

Britnell, R.H. 1993: *The commercialisation of English society 1000–1500*. Cambridge, UK: Cambridge University Press.

Britnell, R.H. and Campbell, B.M.S., eds, 1995: *A commercializing economy: England 1086 to c.1300*. Manchester: Manchester University Press.

Brock, W. and Durlauf, S. 2000: *Interactions-based models*. Washington, DC: National Bureau of Economic Research, Working Paper 258.

Broek, J.M. 1932: *The Santa Clara Valley, California: a study in landscape changes*. Utrecht: Oosthock.

Bromley, R.F. 1980: Trader mobility as systems of periodic daily markets. In D.T. Herbert and R.J. Johnston, eds, *Geography and the urban environment*, vol. 3. Chichester: Wiley, 133–74.

Brooker, P. and Thacker, A., eds, 2005: *Geographies of modernism: literatures, cultures, spaces*. London: Routledge.

Brookfield, H. 1969: On the environment as perceived. *Progress in Geography* 1: 51–80.

Brooks Green, D., ed., 1991: *Historical geography: a methodological portrayal*. Savage, MD: Rowman & Littlefield.

Brosius, J.P. 1999: Analyses and Interventions: anthropological engagements with environmentalism. *Current Anthropology* 40: 277–309.

Brosseau, M. 1995: The city in textual form: *Manhattan Transfer's* New York. *Ecumene* 2: 89–114.

Brotton, J. 1997: *Trading territories: mapping and the early modern world*. London: Reaktion Books.

Brown, A., Fleetwood, S. and Roberts, J., eds, 2002: *Critical realism and Marxism*. London: Routledge.

Brown, E.A.R. 1974: The tyranny of a construct: feudalism and historians of medieval Europe. *American Historical Review* 79: 1063–88.

Brown, E.H., ed., 1980: *The Royal Geographical Society – yesterday and tomorrow*. Oxford: Oxford University Press.

Brown, L.A. and Moore, E.G. 1970: The intra-urban migration process: a perspective. *Geografiska Annaler* 52B: 1–13.

Brown, M. 1995: Ironies of distance: an ongoing critique of the geographies of AIDS. *Environment and Planning D: Society and Space* 13: 159–83.

Brown, M. 1997a: *Replacing citizenship: AIDS activism and radical democracy*. New York: Guilford Press.

Brown, M. 2003: Hospice and the spatial paradoxes of terminal care. *Environment and Planning A* 35: 833–51.

Brown, M. 2004: Between neoliberalism and cultural conservatism: spatial divisions and multiplications of hospice labor in the United States. *Gender, Place, and Culture* 11: 67–82.

Brown, M.F. 2003: *Who owns native culture?* Cambridge, MA: Harvard University Press.

Brown, M.J. 2000: *Closet space: geographies of metaphor from the body to the globe*. London: Routledge.

Brown, W. 1997b: Rights and identity in late modernity: revisiting the 'Jewish Question'. In A. Sarat and T.R. Kearns, eds, *Identities*, *politics and rights*. Ann Arbor: University of Michigan Press, 85–130.

Browne, J. 1983: *The secular ark: studies in the history of biogeography*. New Haven: Yale University Press.

Browne, K., Brown, G. and Lim, J., eds, 2006: *Sexy spaces*. London: Ashgate.

Brückner, M. 1999: Lessons in geography: maps, spellers and other grammars of nationalism in the Early Republic. *American Quarterly* 51(2): 311–43.

Brun, C. 2003: *Finding a place: local integration and protracted displacement in Sri Lanka*. PhD Thesis, Department of Geography, Norwegian University of Science and Technology, Trondheim.

Brunhes, J. 1910: *La géographie humaine*. Paris: Alcan.

Brunhes, J. 1952: *Principles of human geography*. London: Harrap.

Brunn, S. 2006: *Wal-Mart world*. New York: Routledge.

Brunn, S. and Leinbach, T., eds, 1991: *Collapsing space and time: geographic aspects of communications and information*. London: HarperCollins.

Brunn, S. and Waterman, S., eds, 2006: *Geojournal* (special edition on Geography and Music) 65 (1 and 2).

Brunn, S., Watkins, J.F., Fargo, T., Lepawsky, J. and Jones, J.A. 2005: Towards a geopolitics of life and living: where boundaries still matter. In H. Nicol and I. Townsend-Gault, eds, *Holding the line: borders in a global world*. Vancouver: University of British Columbia Press, 381–99.

Brunotte, E., Gebhardt, H., Meurer, M., Meusburger, P. and Nipper, J., eds, 2002: *Lexicon der Geographie*. Heidelberg: Spektrum.

Brunsdon, C. 2001: A Bayesian approach to schools' catchment-based performance modelling. *Geographical and Environmental Modelling* 5: 9–22.

Brunsdon, C., Fotheringham, S. and Charlton, M. 1996: Geographically weighted regression – modelling spatial non-stationarity. *Geographical Analysis* 28: 281–9.

Bryant, R. and Bailey, S. 1997: *Third World political ecology*. London: Routledge.

Brydon, L. and Chant, S. 1989: *Women in the Third World: gender issues in rural and urban areas*. New Brunswick, NJ: Rutgers University Press.

Bryson, J., Daniels, P.W. and Warf, B. 2004: *Service worlds*. London: Routledge.

Bryson, N. 1983: *Vision and painting*. London: Macmillan.

Brzinsky-Fay, U.K. and Luniak, M. 2006: Sequence analysis with STATA. *Stata Journal* 6: 435–60.

Buchanan, A. and Moore, M., eds, 2003: *States, nations, and borders: the ethics of making boundaries*. Cambridge, UK: Cambridge University Press.

Buchanan, J.M. and Tullock, G. 1962: *The calculus of consent: logical foundations of constitutional democracy*. Ann Arbor: University of Michigan Press.

Büche, F. and Frick, J.R. 2005: Immigrants' economic performance across Europe – does immigration policy matter? *Population Research and Development Review* 24: 175–212.

Buck, S. 1998: *The global commons: an introduction*. Washington, DC: Island Press.

Buck-Morss, S. 1989: *The dialectics of seeing: Walter Benjamin and the Arcades Project*. Cambridge, MA: The MIT Press.

Bud, R. 1993: *The uses of life: a history of biotechnology*. Cambridge, UK: Cambridge University Press.

Bulkeley, H. and Betsill, M. 2005: Rethinking sustainable cities: multilevel governance and the 'urban' politics of climate change. *Environmental Politics* 14: 42–63.

Bullard, R. 1994: *Dumping in Dixie: race, class and environmental quality*. Boulder, CO: Westview Press.

Bullard, R. 2000: *Sprawl city: race, politics, and planning in Atlanta*. Washington, DC: Island Press.

Bulmer, M. 1986: *The Chicago School of sociology: institutionalization, diversity and the rise of sociological research*. Chicago: The University of Chicago Press.

Bunge, W. 1966: *Theoretical geography*. Department of Geography, University of Lund and Gleerup.

Bunge, W. 1968: Fred K. Schaefer and the science of geography. *Harvard Papers in Theoretical Geography, Special Papers Series A*. Cambridge, MA: Harvard University, Laboratory for Computer Graphics and Spatial Analysis.

Bunge, W. 1969: *The first years of the Detroit Geographical Expedition: a personal report*. Detroit: Society for Human Exploration.

Bunge, W. 1973: Spatial prediction. *Annals of the Association of American Geographers* 63: 566–8.

Bunge, W. et al. 1971: *Geography of the children of Detroit, field notes 1–3*. Detroit, MI: Detroit Geographical Expedition.

Bunkše, E. 2004: *Geography and the art of life*. Baltimore, MD: The Johns Hopkins University Press.

Bunnell, T. 2002: Kampung rules: landscape and the contested government of urban(e) Malayness. *Urban Studies* 39(9): 1685–701.

Bunnell, T. 2004: Re-viewing the entrapment controversy: megaprojection, (mis)representation and postcolonial performance. *GeoJournal* 59: 297–305.

Burawoy, M. 1979: *Manufacturing consent*. Chicago: The University of Chicago Press.

Burawoy, M. 2000: Marxism after communism. *Theory and Society* 29(2): 151–74.

Burawoy, M. 2003: For a sociological Marxism. *Politics and Society* 31(2): 162–83 (available at: http//sociology.berkeley.edu/faculty/ BURAWOY/).

Burawoy, M. 2005: For public sociology. *American Sociological Review* 70: 4–28.

Burawoy, M., Burton, A., Ferguson, A.A. and Fox, K.J. 1991: *Ethnography unbound: power and resistance in the modern metropolis*. Berkeley, CA: University of California Press.

Burawoy, M., Blum, J.A., George, S., Gille, Z., Gowan, T., Haney., L., Klawiter, M., Lopez, S. H., O Rian, S. and Thayer, M. 2000: *Global ethnography: forces, connections, and imaginations in a postmodern world*. Berkeley, CA: University of California Press.

Burchell, G., Gordon, C. and Miller, P., eds, 1991: *The Foucault effect: studies in governmentality*. Chicago: The University of Chicago Press.

Burchill, S., Devetak, R., Linklater, A., Paterson, M., Reus-Smit, C. and True, J. 2001: *Theories of international relations*. London: Palgrave.

Bürger, P. 1984: *Theory of the avant-garde*. Minneapolis: University of Minnesota Press.

Burgess, E.W. 1924: The growth of a city: an introduction to a research project. *Publications of the American Sociological Society* 18: 85–97.

Burgess, E.W. 1967 [1925]: The growth of the city: an introduction to a research project. In R. Park, E.W. Burgess and R. McKenzie, eds, *The city*. Chicago: The University of Chicago Press, 47–62.

Burgess, J. 1996: Focusing on fear: the use of focus groups in a project for the Community Forest Unit, Countryside Commission. *Area* 28(2): 130–5.

Burgess, J. and Gold, J., eds, 1982: *Valued environments*. London: George Allen and Unwin.

Burgess, J., Limb, M. and Harrison, C.M. 1988: Exploring environmental values through small groups. Part one: theory and practice. *Environment and Planning A* 20: 457–76.

Burgess, S., Wilson, D. and Lupton, R. 2005: Parallel lives? Ethnic segregation in schools and neighbourhoods. *Urban Studies* 42: 1027–56.

Burk, A. 2003: *A politics of visibility: public space, monuments and social memory*. PhD thesis, Simon Fraser University, Burnaby.

Burk, A. forthcoming: *Speaking for a long time: public space, monuments, and social memory*. Vancouver: University of British Columbia Press.

Burke, E. 1906: Philosophical inquiry into the origin of our ideas of the sublime and the beautiful. In *The works of Edmund Burke*, vol. 1. London: Oxford University Press.

Burke, P. 1995: America and the rewriting of world history. In K.O. Kupperman, ed., *America in European consciousness, 1493–1750*. Chapel Hill, NC: University of North Carolina Press.

Burkhardt, R.W. 1977: *The spirit of system: Lamarck and evolutionary biology*. Cambridge, MA: Harvard University Press.

Burling, R. 1962: Maximization theory and the study of economic anthropology. *American Anthropologist* 64: 802–21.

Burnett, A.D and Taylor, P.J., eds, 1981: *Political studies from spatial perspectives*. Chichester: Wiley.

Burnett, D.G. 2000: *Masters of all they surveyed: exploration, geography and a British El Dorado*. Chicago: The University of Chicago Press.

Burnett, D.G. 2005: Matthew Fontaine Maury's 'Sea of Fire': hydrography, biogeography, and providence in the Tropics. In F. Driver and L. Martins, eds, *Tropical visions in an age of empire*. Chicago: The University of Chicago Press.

Burris, R. and Canter, L. 1997: Cumulative impacts are not properly addressed in Environmental Assessments. *Environmental Impact Assessment Review* 17: 5–18.

Burrough, P.A. and McDonnell, R.A. 1998: Creating continuous surfaces from point data. In their *Principles of Geographical Information Systems*, 2nd edn. Oxford: Oxford University Press, 98–131.

Burrow, R., Ellison, N. and Woods, B. 2005: *Neighbourhoods on the net: the nature and impact of Internet-based neighbourhood information systems*. Bristol: The Policy Press (or view online at www.jrf.org.uk/bookshop/).

Burrows, R. 1997: Virtual culture, urban social polarisation and social science fiction. In B. Loader, ed., *The governance of cyberspace*. London: Routledge, 38–45.

Burt, T. 2006: General/particular. In N. Castree, A. Rogers and D. Sherman, eds, *Questioning geography: fundamental debates*. Oxford: Blackwell, 117–30.

Burton, A. 1998: *At the heart of empire: Indians and the colonial encounter in late Victorian Britain*. Berkeley, CA: University of California Press.

Burton, I. 1963: The quantitative revolution and human geography. *The Canadian Geographer* 7: 151–62.

Burton, I., Kates, R. and White, G. 1993: *The environment as hazard*, 2nd edn. New York: Guilford Press.

Buruma, I. and Margalit, A. 2004: *Occidentalism: the West in the eyes of its enemies*. New York: Penguin.

Butler, J. 1990: *Gender trouble: feminism and the subversion of identity*. New York: Routledge.

Butler, J. 1993a: *Bodies that matter: on the discursive limits of 'sex'*. New York: Routledge.

Butler, J. 1993b: Critically queer. *GLQ: a Journal of Lesbian and Gay Studies* 1: 17–32.

Butler, J. 1997: *The psychic life of power: theories of subjection*. Stanford, CA: Stanford University Press.

Butler, J. 1998: Merely cultural. *New Left Review* 227: 33–44.

Butler, J. 2004: *Precarious life: the powers of mourning and violence.* London: Verso.

Butler, J. 2008: Sexual politics, torture and secular time. *The British Journal of Sociology* 59(1): 1–23.

Butler, J., Rotberg, R. and Adams, J. 1977: *The black homelands of South Africa.* Berkeley, CA: University of California Press.

Butler, R. and Parr, H., eds, 1999: *Mind and body spaces: geographies of illness, impairment and disability.* London: Routledge.

Butler, R.E. and Bowlby, S. 1997: Bodies and spaces: an exploration of disabled people's experiences of public space. *Environment and Planning D: Society and Space* 15: 411–33.

Butler, R.W. 1980: The concept of a tourist area cycle of evolution – implications for management of resources. *Canadian Geographer – Geographe Canadien* 24(1): 5–12.

Butlin, R.A. 1993: *Historical geography: through the gates of space and time.* London: Arnold.

Butlin, R.A. 1995: *Historical geography.* New York: Wiley.

Buttel, F.H. and Newby, H., eds, 1980: *The rural sociology of the advanced societies: critical perspectives.* Montclair, NJ: Allanheld, Osmun.

Buttenfield, B.P. and McMaster, R.B., eds, 1991: *Map generalization: making rules for knowledge representation.* London: Longman.

Buttigieg, J. 1995: Gramsci on civil society. *Boundary 2* 22(3): 1–32.

Buttimer, A. 1971. *Society and milieu in the French geographic tradition.* Chicago: Rand McNally.

Buttimer, A. 1974: *Values in geography.* Washington, DC: Association of American Geographers, Commission on College Geography, resource paper 24.

Buttimer, A. 1976: Grasping the dynamism of lifeworld. *Annals of the Association of American Geographers* 66: 277–92.

Buttimer, A. 1982: Musing on Helicon: root metaphors and geography. *Geografiska Annaler* 64B: 89–96.

Buttimer, A. 1990: Geography, humanism and global concern. *Annals of the Association of American Geographers* 80: 1–33.

Buttimer, A. 1993: *Geography and the human spirit.* Baltimore, MD: The Johns Hopkins University Press.

Buttimer, A. 1996: Classics in human geography revisited: values in geography. *Progress in Human Geography* 20: 513–19.

Buttimer, A. and Seamon, D., eds, 1980: *The human experience of space and place.* London: Croom Helm.

Buttler, F.A. 1975: *Growth pole theory and economic development.* Farnborough: Saxon House/Lexington, MA: Lexington Press.

Büttner, M. and Hoheisel, K. 1980: Immanuel Kant. *Geographers: Bio-bibliographical Studies* 4: 55–67.

Butz, D. and Besio, K. 2004: The value of autoethnography for field research in transcultural settings. *Professional Geographer* 56: 350–60.

Butzer, K.W. 1980: Civilizations: organisms or systems? *American Scientist* 68: 517–23 (reprinted 1996 in J. Agnew, D. Livingstone and A. Rogers, eds, *Human geography: an essential anthology.* Cambridge UK: Blackwell, 268–81).

Butzer, K.W. 2002: The rising cost of contestation: commentary/response: Turner's 'contested identities'. *Annals of the Association of American Geographers* 92: 75–86.

Buzard, J. 1993: *The beaten track: European tourism, literature and the ways to 'culture' 1800–1918.* Oxford: The Clarendon Press.

Byles, J. 2001: Maps and chaps: the new geography reaches critical mass. *Village Voice* 1–7 August. Available at http://www.villagevoice. com/2001-07-31/art/maps-and-chaps/1

Byres, T. 1996: *Capitalism from above and below.* London: Macmillan.

Cadwallader, M. 1996: *Urban geography: an analytical approach.* Englewood Cliffs, NJ: Prentice-Hall.

Cain, P. and Hopkins, A. 2001: *British imperialism, 1688–2000,* 2nd edn. London: Longman.

Caldeira, T.P.R. 2000: *City of walls: crime, segregation, and citizenship in São Paulo.* Berkeley, CA: University of California Press.

Calhoun, C. 2003: The class consciousness of frequent travellers: towards a critique of actually existing cosmopolitanism. In D. Archibugi, ed., *Debating cosmopolitics.* New York: Verso, 86–116.

Calimani, R. 1987: *The ghetto of Venice.* New York: Evans.

Callard, F.J. 1998: The body in theory. *Environment and Planning D: Society and Space* 16: 387–400.

Callard, F.J. 2003: The taming of psychoanalysis in geography. *Social and Cultural Geography* 4: 296–312.

Callari, A. and Ruccio, D.F., eds, 1996: *Postmodern materialism and the future of Marxist theory.* Hanover, NH: Wesleyan University Press.

Callinicos, A. 1999: *Social theory: a historical introduction.* Cambridge: London.

Callinicos, A. 2003: *An anti-capitalist manifesto.* Cambridge, UK: Polity Press.

Callon, M. 1986: Some elements of a sociology of translation: domestication of the scallops and the fishermen of St Brieuc Bay. In J. Law, ed., *Power, action and belief: a new sociology of knowledge.* London: Routledge, 196–233.

Callon, M., ed., 1999: *The laws of the markets.* Oxford: Blackwell.

Cameron, J. and Gibson-Graham, J.-K. 2003: Feminising the economy: metaphors, strategies, politics. *Gender, Place and Culture* 10: 145–57.

Cameron, K. 1980: The meaning and significance of Old English *walh* in English place-names. *English Place Names Society Journal* 12: 1–53.

Cameron, L. 2006: Science, nature, and hatred: 'finding out' at the Malting House Garden School, 1924–29. *Environment and Planning D: Society and Space* 24: 851–72.

Cameron, S. 2003: Gentrification, housing redifferentiation and urban regeneration. *Urban Studies* 40: 2367–82.

Campbell, B.M.S. 1983: Agrarian progress in medieval England: some evidence from eastern Norfolk. *Economic History Review* 36: 26–46.

Campbell, B.M.S. 1990: People and land in the Middle Ages 1066–1500. In R.A. Butlin and R.A. Dodgshon, eds, *An historical geography of England and Wales*, 2nd edn. London: Academic Press, 69–122.

Campbell, B.M.S. 1991: Land, labour, livestock and productivity trends in English seignorial agriculture 1208–1450. In B.M.S. Campbell and M. Overton, eds, *Land, labour and livestock: historical studies in European agricultural productivity*. Manchester: Manchester University Press, 144–82.

Campbell, B.M.S. 1995: Progressiveness and backwardness in thirteenth and early fourteenth century English agriculture: the verdict of recent research. In J.-M. Duvosquel and E. Thoen, eds, *Peasants and townsmen in medieval Europe*. Gent: Snoeck-Ducaju and Zoon, 541–9.

Campbell, B.M.S. 2000: *English seigneurial agriculture, 1250–1450.* Cambridge, UK: Cambridge University Press.

Campbell, B.M.S. 2005: The agrarian problem in the early fourteenth century. *Past and Present* 188: 3–71.

Campbell, B.M.S. and Bartley, K. 2006: *England on the eve of the Black Death: an atlas of lay lordship, land and wealth, 1300–1349.* Manchester: Manchester University Press.

Campbell, B.M.S. and Overton, M. 1993: A new perspective on medieval and early modern agriculture: six centuries of Norfolk farming c.1250–c.1850. *Past and Present* 141: 38–105.

Campbell, D. 1998: *Writing security: United States foreign policy and the politics of identity*, rev. edn. Minneapolis: University of Minnesota Press.

Campbell, D. 2004: Construction site: architecture and politics in Israel/Palestine. *Theory and Event* 7.4, http://muse.jhu.edu/journals/theory_and_event/

Campbell, D., Graham, S. and Monk, D.B., eds., 2007: Symposium on urbicide. *Theory and Event* 10(2).

Campbell, J. 1982: The lost centuries: 400–600. In J. Campbell, ed., *The Anglo-Saxons*, London: Phaidon, 20–44.

Campbell, J.A. and Livingstone, D.N. 1983: Neo-Lamarckism and the development of geography in the United States and Great Britain. *Transactions of the Institute of British Geographers*, NS 8: 267–94.

Campbell, J.B. 2002: *Introduction to remote sensing*, 3rd edn. New York: Guilford Press.

Cañizares-Esguerra, J. 2001: *How to write the history of the new world: histories, epistemologies, and identities in the eighteenth-century Atlantic world.* Stanford, CA: Stanford University Press.

Cannon, S.F. 1978: *Science in culture: the early Victorian period.* New York: Dawson and Science History Publications.

Canovan, M. 1981: *Populism.* London: Junction Books.

Cant, S. and Morris, N., eds, 2006: Special issue: 'Geographies of art and the environment'. *Social and Cultural Geographies* 7(6): 860–993.

Canters, F. 2002: *Small-scale map projection design.* London: Taylor & Francis.

Capel, H. 1981: Institutionalisation of geography and strategies of change. In D.R. Stoddart, ed., *Geography, ideology and social concern.* Oxford: Blackwell, 37–69.

Caputo, J.D. 1997: *The prayers and tears of Jacques Derrida: religion without religion.* Indianapolis: Indiana University Press.

Caputo, J.D. and Scanlon, M. 1999: *God, the gift, and postmodernism.* Indianapolis: Indiana University Press.

Caratti, P., Dalkmann, H. and Jiliberto, R., eds, 2004: *Analysing strategic environmental assessment towards better decision-making.* Northampton, MA: Edward Elgar.

Carens, J.H. 1987: Aliens and citizens: the case for open borders. *The Review of Politics* 49: 251–73.

Carey, D. 1997: Compiling nature's history: travelers and travel narratives in the early royal society. *Annals of Science* 54: 269–92.

Carey, D. 2006: Travel, geography, and the problem of belief: Locke as a reader of travel literature. In Rudolph, J., ed., *History and nation.* Lewisburg, PA: Bucknell University Press, 97–136.

Carey, H.C. 1858: *Principles of social science.* Philadelphia: J.B. Lippincott.

Carey, R., ed., 2001: *The new intifada.* London: Verso.

Carl, P., Kemp, B., Laurence, R., Coningham, R., Higham, C. and Cowgill, G.C. 2000: Were cities built as images? *Cambridge Archaeological Journal* 10: 327–65.

Carlstein, T., Parkes, D. and Thrift, N.J. 1978: *Timing space and spacing time*, 2 vols. London: Edward Arnold.

Carney, G., ed., 2003: *The sounds of people and places: a geography of American music from country to classical and blues to bop*, 4th edn. Lanham, MD: Rowman & Littlefield.

Carney, J. 1996: Converting the wetlands, engendering the environment: the intersection of gender with agrarian change in Gambia. In R. Peet and M. Watts, eds, *Liberation ecologies: environment, development, social movements*. New York: Routledge.

Carney, J. and Watts, M. 1990: Disciplining women? *Signs* 16(4): 654–81.

Carrier, J., ed., 1995: *Occidentalism: images of the West*. Oxford: The Clarendon Press.

Carroll, G.R. 1982: National city-size distributions: what do we know after 67 years of research? *Progress in Human Geography* 16: 1–43.

Carson, R. 1962: *Silent spring*. Boston: Houghton Mifflin.

Carter, B. and New, C., eds, 2004: *Making realism work: realist social theory and empirical research*. London: Routledge.

Carter, H. 1977: Urban origins: a review. *Progress in Human Geography* 1: 12–32.

Carter, H. 1983: *An introduction to urban historical geography*. London: Edward Arnold.

Carter, H. 1995: *The study of urban geography*, 4th edn. London: Arnold.

Carter, P. 1987: *The road to Botany Bay: an essay in spatial history*. London: Faber and Faber.

Carter, S. 2006: Mobilising generosity, framing geopolitics: narrating crisis in the homeland through diasporic media. *Geoforum* 6: 1102–12.

Cartier, C. and Lew, A., eds, 2005: *Seductions of place: geographical perspectives on globalization and touristed landscapes*. London: Routledge.

Carver, T. and Thomas, P., eds, 1995: *Rational choice Marxism*. London: Macmillan/ University Park, PA: The Pennsylvania University Press.

Casanova, P. 2005: *The world republic of letters*. Cambridge, MA: Harvard University Press.

Case, A. and Paxson, C. 2005: Sex differences in morbidity and mortality. *Demography* 42: 189–215.

Caselli, F. and Coleman, W.J. 2001: The U.S. structural transformation and regional convergence: a reinterpretation. *Journal of Political Economy* 109: 584–616.

Casetti, E. 1972: Generating models by the expansion method. *Geographical Analysis* 4: 81–91.

Casey, E. 1993: *Getting back into place: toward a renewed understanding of the place-world*. Bloomington: Indiana University Press.

Casey, E. 1998: *The fate of place: a philosophical history*. Berkeley, CA: University of California Press.

Casey, E. 2001: Between geography and philosophy: what does it mean to be in the place-world? *Annals of the Association of American Geographers* 91: 683–93.

Castells, M. 1972: *La question urbaine*. Paris: François Maspero.

Castells, M. 1977: *The urban question: a Marxist approach*, trans. A. Sheridan. London: Edward Arnold/Cambridge, MA: The MIT Press.

Castells, M. 1983: *The city and the grassroots: a cross-cultural theory of urban social movements*. Berkeley, CA: University of California Press.

Castells, M. 1989: *The informational city: information technology, economic restructuring and the urban-regional process*. Oxford: Blackwell.

Castells, M. 1996a: *The information age: economy, society and culture*. Vol. 1: *The rise of the network society* (1996, 2nd edn 2000); Vol. 2: *The power of identity* (1997, 2nd edn. 2004); Vol. 3: *End of millennium* (1998; 2nd edn. 2000). Oxford: Blackwell.

Castells, M. 1996b: *The rise of the network society*. Vol. 1 of *The information age: economy, society and culture*. Oxford: Blackwell.

Castells, M. 1997: *The power of identity*. Vol. 2 of *The information age: economy, society and culture*. Oxford: Blackwell.

Castells, M. 1998: *End of millennium*. Vol. 3 of *The information age: economy, society and culture*. Oxford: Blackwell.

Castells, M. and Hall, P. 1994: *Technopoles of the world: the making of twenty-first century industrial complexes*. London: Routledge.

Castles, S. and Davidson, A. 2000: *Citizenship and migration: globalization and the politics of belonging*. London: Macmillan.

Castles, S. and Miller, M.J. 2003: *The age of migration: international population movements in the modern world*, 3rd edn. New York: Guilford Press.

Castoriadis, C. 1997: *World in fragments*. Stanford, CA: Stanford University Press.

Castree, N. 1995: The nature of produced nature: materiality and knowledge construction in Marxism. *Antipode* 27(1): 12–48.

Castree, N. 1996: Birds, mice and geography: Marxism and dialectics. *Transactions of the Institute of British Geographers* 21: 342–62.

Castree, N. 1999a: 'Out there'? 'In here'? Domesticating critical geography. *Area* 31(1): 81–6.

Castree, N. 1999b: Envisioning capitalism: geography and the renewal of Marxian political economy. *Transactions of the Institute of British Geographers* 24: 137–58.

Castree, N. 1999c: Synthesis and engagement: critical geography and the biotechnology century. *Environment and Planning A* 31: 763–6.

Castree, N. 2000: Professionalization, activism, and the university: whither 'critical geography'? *Environment and Planning A* 32(6): 955–70.

Castree, N. 2003a: Bioprospecting: from theory to practice (and back again). *Transactions of the Institute of British Geographers* 28(1): 35–55.

Castree, N. 2003b: Geographies of nature in the making. In K. Anderson, M. Domosh, S. Pile and N. Thrift, eds, *Handbook of cultural geography*. London: Sage, 168–83.

Castree, N. 2005a: *Nature*. London: Routledge.

Castree, N. 2005b: The epistemology of particulars: human geography, case studies and 'context'. *Geoforum* 36: 541–4.

Castree, N. 2006a: David Harvey's symptomatic silence. *Historical Materialism* 14: 35–57.

Castree, N. 2006b: Geography's new public intellectuals? *Antipode* 38: 396–412.

Castree, N. 2007: David Harvey: Marxism, capitalism and the geographical imagination. *New Political Economy* 12(1): 97–115.

Castree, N. and Braun, B., eds, 2001: *Social nature: theory, practice and politics*. Oxford: Blackwell.

Castree, N. and Gregory, D., eds, 2006: *David Harvey: a critical reader*. Oxford: Blackwell.

Castree, N. and Nash, C., eds, 2004: Mapping posthumanism: an exchange. *Environment and Planning A* 36: 1341–63.

Castree, N. and Wright, M.W. 2005: Home truths. *Antipode* 37(1): 1–8.

Castree, N., Rogers, A. and Sherman, D., eds, 2005: *Questioning geography: fundamental debates*. Oxford: Blackwell.

Castree, N., Coe, N., Ward, M. and Samers, M. 2004: *Spaces of work: global capitalism and geographies of labour*. London: Sage.

Chainey, S. and Ratcliffe, J. 2005: *GIS and crime mapping*. New York: Wiley.

Chakravorty, S. 2000: From colonial city to globalizing city? The far-from-complete spatial transformation of Calcutta. In P. Marcuse and R. van Kempen, eds, *Globalizing cities: a new spatial order?* Oxford: Blackwell, 56–77.

Chamberlain, M. 1985: *Decolonization*. Oxford: Blackwell.

Chamberlain, P.G. 2001: The Shakespearian globe: geometry, optics, spectacle. *Environment and Planning D: Society and Space* 19: 317–33.

Chambers, J.D. and Mingay, G.E. 1966: *The agricultural revolution 1750–1880*. London: Batsford.

Chambers, R. 1983: *Rural development: putting the last first*. London: Longman.

Champion, A.G., ed., 1991: *Counterurbanization: the changing pace and nature of population concentration*. London: Edward Arnold.

Champion, A.G. and Hugo, G.J., eds, 2004: *New forms of urbanization: beyond the urban-rural dichotomy*. Aldershot: Ashgate.

Chang, H.-J. 2002: *Kicking away the ladder: development strategies in historical perspective*. London: Anthem.

Chang, K.-S. 1971: The Ming maritime enterprise and China's knowledge of Africa prior to the age of great discoverers. *Terrae Incognitae* 3: 33–4.

Chang, W.-Y. 2005: The Internet, alternative public sphere and political dynamism: Korea's *non-gaek* (polemist) websites. *The Pacific Review* 18(3): 393–415.

Chant, S. 2006: *Gender, generation and poverty: exploring the 'feminisation of poverty' in Africa, Asia and Latin America*. Cheltenham: Edward Elgar.

Chapman, G.P. and Baker, K.M. 1992: The *changing geography of Asia*. London: Routledge.

Chapman, K. and Walker, D. 1991: *Industrial location: principles and policies*, 2nd edn. Oxford: Blackwell.

Chari, S. 2003: Marxism, sarcasm, ethnography: geographical fieldnotes from South India. *Singapore Journal of Tropical Geography* 24: 169–83.

Chari, S. 2004: *Fraternal capital: peasant-workers, self-made men, and globalization in provincial India*. Stanford, CA: Stanford University Press.

Charlesworth, A. 1992: Towards a geography of the Shoah. *Journal of Historical Geography* 18: 464–9.

Charlesworth, A. 1994: Contesting places of memory: the case of Auschwitz. *Environment and Planning D: Society and Space* 12: 579–93.

Charlesworth, A. 2004: A corner of a foreign field that is forever Spielberg's: understanding the moral landscapes of the sites of the former KL Plaszow, Kraków, Poland. *Cultural Geographies* 11: 291–312.

Charlton, M., Openshaw, S. and Wymer, C. 1985: Some new classifications of census enumeration districts in Britain: a poor man's ACORN. *Journal of Economic and Social Measurement* 13, 69–96.

Chase-Dunn, C. 1985: The system of cities, AD 800–1975. In M. Timberlake, ed., *Urbanization in the world-economy*. New York: Academic Press, 269–92.

Chase-Dunn, C. and Jorgenson, A. 2002: *Settlement systems: past and present*. Research Bulletin 73, Globalization and World Cities Study Group and Network. Available online at http://www.lboro.ac.uk/gawc/rb/rb73.html.

Chatterjee, P. 1986: *Nationalist thought and the colonial world: a derivative discourse?* London: Zed Books.

Chatterjee, P. 1994: Whose imagined community? In G. Balakhrishnan, ed., *Mapping the nation*. London: Verso, 214–25.

Chatterjee, P. 2004: *The politics of the governed*. New York: Columbia University Press.

Chatterjee, P. and Finger, M. 1994: *The Earth brokers: power, politics and world development*. London: Routledge.

Chatterton, P. 2005: Making autonomous geographies: Argentina's popular uprising and the Movimiento de Trabajadores Desocupades (Unemployed Workers Movement). *Geoforum* 36: 545–61.

Chaturvedi, S. 2000: Ocean governance and the polar regions: geopolitics, law and sustainability. In A. Chircop, E. Mann Borgese and M.L. McConnell, eds, *Ocean yearbook* 15. Chicago: The University of Chicago Press, 475–522.

Chaturvedi, V., ed., 2000: *Mapping subaltern studies and the postcolonial*. London: Verso.

Chavis, B. 1991: The historical significance and challenges of the First National People of Color Environmental Leadership Summit. In C. Lee, ed., *Proceedings of the First National People of Color Environmental Leadership Summit*. Washington, DC: United Church of Christ Commission for Racial Justice, 1992.

Chayanov, A.V. 1966: *The theory of peasant economy*, trans. R.E.F. Smith; eds D. Thorner, B. Kerblay and R.E.F. Smith. Homewood, IL: American Economic Association (first Russian edition, 1912).

Chen, H.S. 1992: *Chinatown no more: Taiwan immigrants in contemporary New York*. Ithaca, NY: Cornell University Press.

Chidester, D. and Linenthal, E.T. 1995: Introduction. In D. Chidester and E.T. Linenthal, eds, *American sacred space*. Bloomington: Indiana University Press, 1–42.

Childe, V. Gordon 1946: *What happened in history*. London: Penguin.

Childe, V. Gordon 1950: The urban revolution. *Town Planning Review* 23: 3–17.

Chisholm, G.G. 1889: *Handbook of commercial geography*. London: Longman.

Chisholm, M. 1967: General systems theory and geography. *Transactions of the Institute of British Geographers* 42: 45–52.

Chisholm, M. 1979: *Rural settlement and land use: an essay in location*, 3rd edn. London: Hutchinson.

Chomsky, N. 1999: *The new military humanism: lessons from Kosovo*. London: Pluto Press.

Chomsky, N. 2000: *Rogue states: the rule of force in world affairs*. Cambridge, MA: South End Press.

Chorley, R.J. 1964: Geography and analogue theory. *Annals of the Association of American Geographers* 54: 127–37.

Chorley, R.J. 1971: The role and relations of physical geography. *Progress in Geography* 3, 87–109.

Chorley, R.J., ed., 1973: *Directions in geography*. London: Methuen.

Chorley, R.J. and Haggett, P. 1965: Trend surface mapping in geographical research. *Transactions of the Institute of British Geographers* 37: 47–67.

Chorley, R.J. and Haggett, P., eds, 1967: *Models in geography*. London: Methuen.

Chorley, R.J. and Kennedy, B.A. 1971: *Physical geography: a systems approach*. London: Prentice Hall.

Chouinard, V. 1994a: Geography, law and legal struggles: which ways ahead? *Progress in Human Geography* 11(5): 415–40.

Chouinard, V. 1994b: Reinventing radical geography: is all that's Left Right? *Environment and Planning D: Society and Space* 12: 2–6.

Chouinard, V. 1997: Making space for disabling difference: challenging ableist geographies. *Environment and Planning D: Society and Space* 15: 379–87.

Chouinard, V. 2001: Legal peripheries: struggles over disabled Canadians' place in law, society and space. *The Canadian Geographer* 45: 187–93.

Chouinard, V., Fincher, R. and Webber, M. 1984: Empirical research in scientific human geography. *Progress in Human Geography* 8: 346–80.

Chow, R. 2002: *The protestant ethnic and the spirit of capitalism*. New York: Columbia University Press.

Chow, R. 2006: The age of the world target: atomic bombs, alterity, area studies. In *The age of the world target: self-referentiality in war, theory and comparative work*. Durham, NC: Duke University Press, 25–43.

Chrisman, N. 1988: The risks of software innovation: a case study of the Harvard Lab. *The American Cartographer* 15(3): 291–9.

Christaller, W. 1933: *Die zentralen Orte in Süddeutschland*. Jena: G. Fischer. Translated by C.W. Baskin as *Central Places in Southern Germany*. Englewood Cliffs, NJ: Prentice-Hall, 1966.

Christiansen, F. 2003: *Chinatown, Europe: an exploration of overseas Chinese identity in the 1990s*. London: Routledge Curzon.

Christie, N. 1994: Environment and race: geography's search for a Darwinian synthesis. In R. MacLeod and P.E. Rehbock, eds, *Darwin's laboratory: evolutionary theory and natural history in the Pacific*. Honolulu: University of Hawai'i Press.

Christopherson, S. and Storper, M. 1986: The city as a studio; the world as a back lot: the impact of vertical disintegration on the location of the motion picture industry. *Environment and Planning D: Society and Space* 4: 305–20.

Church, M. and Mark, D.M. 1980: On size and scale in physical geography. *Physical Geography* 4: 342–90.

Ciriacy-Wantrup, S.V. 1952: *Resource conservation, economics and policies*. Berkeley, CA: University of California Press.

Cirincione, C., Darling, T.A. and O'Rourke, T. G. 2000: Assessing South Carolina's congressional districting. *Political Geography* 19: 189–212.

Clanchy, M. 1993: *From memory to written record: England 1066–1307*. London: Edward Arnold.

Clark, A.H. 1949: *The invasion of New Zealand by people, plants and animals: the South Island*. New Brunswick, NJ: Rutgers University Press.

Clark, E. 1995: The rent gap re-examined. *Urban Studies* 32: 489–503.

Clark, G.L. 1981: The employment relation and the spatial division of labor. *Annals of the Association of American Geographers* 71: 412–24.

Clark, G.L. 1989: The geography of law. In R. Peet and N. Thrift, eds, *The new models in human geography*. London: Unwin Hyman, 310–37.

Clark, G.L. 1999a: The retreat of the state and the rise of pension fund capitalism. In R. Martin, ed., *Money and the space economy*. Chichester: Wiley, 241–60.

Clark, G.L. 2005a: Money flows like mercury: the geography of global finance. *Geografiska Annaler* 87B: 99–112.

Clark, G.L. and Dear, M.J. 1984: *State apparatus: structures and language of legitimacy*. Boston: Allen and Unwin.

Clark, G.L. and Wojcik, D. 2001: The city of London in the Asian crisis. *Journal of Economic Geography* 1: 107–30.

Clark, G.L. and Wrigley, N. 1995: Sunk costs: a framework for economic geography. *Transactions of the Institute of British Geographers*, NS 20: 204–23.

Clark, G.L. and Wrigley, N. 1997: Exit, the firm and sunk costs: reconceptualising the corporate geography of disinvestment and plant closure. *Progress in Human Geography* 21: 338–58.

Clark, G.L., Feldman, M.P. and Gertler, M.S., eds, 2000: *The Oxford handbook of economic geography*. Oxford: Oxford University Press.

Clark, J., Burgess, J. and Harrison, C. 2000: 'I struggled with this money business': respondents' perspectives on contingent valuation. *Ecological Economics* 33: 45–62.

Clark, M., ed., 1984: *Planning and analysis in health care systems*. London: Pion.

Clark, N. 2002: The demon seed: bioinvasion as the unsettling of environmental cosmopolitanism. *Theory, Culture & Society* 19: 101–25.

Clark, N. 2005b: Ex-orbitant globality. *Theory, Culture & Society* 22(5): 165–85.

Clark, S., ed., 1999b: *The Annales school*, 4 vols. London: Routledge.

Clark, W., Golinski, J. and Schaffer, S., eds, 1999: *The sciences in enlightened Europe*. Chicago: The University of Chicago Press.

Clark, W.A.V. 1986: *Human migration*. Beverly Hills: Sage.

Clark, W.A.V. 1998: *The California cauldron: immigration and the fortunes of local communities*. New York: Guilford Press.

Clark, W.A.V. 2005c: Intervening in the residential mobility process: neighborhood outcomes for low-income people. *Proceedings of the National Academy of Sciences* 102(43): 15299–300.

Clark, W.A.V. and Blue, S.A. 2004: Race, class, and segregation patterns in U.S. immigrant gateway cities. *Urban Affairs Review* 39: 667–88.

Clark, W.A.V., Deurloo, M.C. and Dieleman, F.M. 2003: Housing careers in the United States, 1968–93: modelling the sequencing of housing states. *Urban Studies* 40(1): 143–60.

Clarke, C., Ley, D. and Peach, C., eds, 1984: *Geography and ethnic pluralism*. London: George Allen & Unwin.

Clarke, D.B. 2003: *The consumer society and the postmodern city*. London: Routledge.

Clarke, D.B., Doel, M. and McDonough, F.X. 1996: Holocaust topologies: singularity, politics, space. *Political Geography* 15: 457–89.

Clarke, D.B., Doel, M.A. and Housiaux, K.M.L. 2003: *The consumption reader*. London: Routledge.

Clarke, I. 2007: *Empire of oil*. Exmouth: Profile Books.

Clarke, J. 2005: Class. In T. Bennett, L. Grossberg and Morris, M., eds, *New keywords: a revised vocabulary of culture and society*. Malden, MA: Blackwell.

Clarke, K.C. 2003: *Getting started with Geographic Information Systems*, 4th edn. Upper Saddle River, NJ: Prentice Hall.

Clarke, R. 1993: *Water: the international crisis*. Cambridge, MA: The MIT Press.

Claval, P. 1984: The coherence of political geography: perspectives on its past evolution and its future relevance. In P.J. Taylor and J.W. House, eds, *Political geography: recent advances and future directions*. London: Croom Helm, 8–24.

Claval, P. 1993: *Initiation á la géographie régionale*. Paris: Editions Nathan (English translation by Ian Thomson, published by Blackwell: Oxford, 1998).

Clawson, D. 2005: *Latin America and the Caribbean: lands and peoples*, 3rd edn. New York: McGraw Hill.

Clawson, P. 2006: *The Andean cocaine industry*. London: Palgrave.

Clayton, D. 2000: *Islands of truth: the imperial fashioning of Vancouver Island*. Vancouver: University of British Columbia Press.

Clayton, D. 2004: Imperial geographies. In J. Duncan, N. Johnson and R. Schein, eds, *A companion to cultural geography*: Oxford: Blackwell, 449–68.

Clement, W. and Myles, J. 1994: *Relations of ruling: class and gender in postindustrial societies*. Montreal: McGill-Queen's University Press.

Clements, F.E. 1936: Nature and structure of the climax. *Journal of Ecology* 24(1): 252–84.

Cliff, A.D. and Haggett, P. 1988: *Atlas of disease distributions: analytic approaches to epidemiological data*. Oxford: Blackwell.

Cliff, A.D. and Ord, J.K. 1973: *Spatial autocorrelation*. London: Pion.

Cliff, A.D. and Ord, J.K. 1981: *Spatial processes: models and applications*. London: Pion.

Cliff, A.D., Haggett, P. and Smallman-Raynor, M. 1993: *Measles: an historical geography of a major human viral disease, from global expansion to local retreat 1840–1990.* Oxford: Blackwell.

Cliff, A.D., Haggett, P. and Smallman-Raynor, M., 2004: *World atlas of epidemic diseases.* London: Arnold.

Cliff, A.D., Martin, R.L. and Ord, J.K. 1975–6: Map pattern and friction of distance parameters. *Regional Studies* 9: 285–8; 10: 341–2.

Cliff, A.D., Haggett, P., Ord, J.K. and Versey, G.R. 1981: *Spatial diffusion: an historical geography of epidemics in an island community.* Cambridge, UK: Cambridge University Press.

Clifford, J. 1988: On Orientalism. In Clifford, *The predicament of culture: twentieth-century ethnography, literature and art.* Cambridge, MA: Harvard University Press.

Clifford, J. 1997: *Routes: travel and translation in the late twentieth century.* Cambridge, MA: Harvard University Press.

Clifford, J. and Marcus, G.E., eds, 1986: *Writing culture: the poetics and politics of ethnography.* Berkeley, CA: University of California Press.

Cloke, P.J. 2002: Deliver us from evil? Prospects for living ethically and acting politically in human geography. *Progress in Human Geography* 26: 587–604.

Cloke, P.J., ed., 2003: *Country visions.* London: Pearson.

Cloke, P.J. and Johnston, R.J., eds, 2005: *Spaces of geographical thought: deconstructing human geography's binaries.* London: Sage.

Cloke, P.J. and Little, J. 1990: *The rural state?* Oxford: Oxford University Press.

Cloke, P.J. and Little, J., eds, 1997: *Contested countryside cultures: otherness, marginalisation and rurality.* London: Routledge.

Cloke, P.J., Marsden, T. and Mooney, P., eds, 2006: *Handbook of rural studies.* Sage, London.

Cloke, P.J., Milbourne, P. and Widdowfield, R. 2001: The geographies of homelessness in rural England. *Regional Studies* 35(1): 23–37.

Cloke, P.J., Philo, C. and Sadler, D. 1991: *Approaching human geography: an introduction to contemporary debates.* London: Paul Chapman.

Cloud, J. 2002: American cartographic transformations during the Cold War. *Cartography and Geographic Information Science* 29: 261–82.

Clout, H.C. and Gosme, C. 2003: The Naval Intelligence Handbooks: a monument in geographical writing. *Progress in Human Geography* 27: 153–73.

Clutton-Brock, J. 1999: *A natural history of domesticated mammals (2nd edition).* Cambridge, UK: Cambridge University Press.

Coaffee, J. 2004: Rings of steel, rings of concrete and rings of confidence: designing out terrorism in central London pre and post September 11th. *International Journal of Urban and Regional Research* 28: 201–11.

Coates, P. 1998: *Nature: Western attitudes since ancient times.* Cambridge, UK: Polity Press.

Cobia, D.W., ed., 1989: *Cooperatives in agriculture.* Englewood Cliffs, NJ: Prentice-Hall.

Cockburn, C. 1977: *The local state: management of cities and people.* London: Pluto Press.

Coe, N., Kelly, P. and Yeung, H.W.-C. 2007: *Economic geography: a contemporary introduction.* Oxford: Blackwell.

Coe, N.M., Hess, M., Yeung, H.W.-C., Dicken, P. and Henderson, J. 2004: Globalising regional development: a global production networks perspective. *Transactions of the Institute of British Geographers* 29: 468–84.

Coffey, W.J. 1981: *Geography: towards a general spatial systems approach.* London: Methuen.

Cohen, G.A. 1978: *Karl Marx's theory of history: a defence.* Oxford: The Clarendon Press/Princeton, NJ: Princeton University Press.

Cohen, J. 1988: *Statistical power analysis for the behavioural sciences.* Mahwah, NJ: Lawrence Erlbaum.

Cohen, J. 1999: *How many people can the Earth support?* New York: W.W. Norton.

Cohen, J.L. and Arato, A. 1992: *Civil society and political theory.* Cambridge, MA: The MIT Press.

Cohen, R. 1997: *Global diasporas: an introduction.* London: UCL Press.

Cohen, S. 2003: *Geopolitics of the world system.* Lanham, MD: Rowman & Littlefield.

Cohen, S. and Kliot, N. 1992: Place-names in Israel's ideological struggle over the Administered Territories. *Annals of the Association of American Geographers* 82: 653–80.

Cohn, B. 1996: *Colonialism and its forms of knowledge: the British in India.* Princeton, NJ: Princeton University Press.

Coker, C. 2004: *The future of war: the re-enchantment of war in the twenty-first century.* Oxford: Blackwell.

Colby, C.C. 1932: Centripetal and centrifugal forces in urban geography. *Annals of the Association of American Geographers* 23: 1–20.

Cole, J. 2007: *Napoleon's Egypt: invading the Middle East.* New York: Palgrave Macmillan.

Cole, J.P. 1969: Mathematics and geography. *Geography* 54: 152–63.

Cole, L.W. and Foster, S.R. 2001: *From the ground up: environmental racism and the rise of the environmental justice movement.* New York: New York University Press.

Cole, T. 2003: *Holocaust city: the making of a Jewish ghetto.* London: Routledge.

Cole, T. and Smith, G. 1995: Ghettoization and the Holocaust: Budapest 1944. *Journal of Historical Geography* 22: 300–16.

Coleman, A., with the Design Disadvantagement Team of the Land Use Research Unit King's College London 1985: *Utopia on trial: vision and reality in planned housing.* London: Shipman.

Coleman, D.A. 2002: Populations of the industrial world – a convergent demographic community? *International Journal of Population Geography* 8: 319–44.

Coleman, J. 1988: Social capital in the creation of human capital. *American Journal of Sociology* 94 (Supplement): S95–S120.

Coleman, M. 2004: The naming of 'terrorism' and evil 'outlaws': geopolitical place-making after 11 September. *Geopolitics* 8: 87–104.

Coleman, M. 2005: US statecraft and the US–Mexico border as security/economy nexus. *Political Geography* 24: 1–25.

Coleman, W. 1966: Science and symbol in the Turner frontier hypothesis. *American Historical Review* 72: 22–49.

Colley, L. 2002: *Captives: Britain, empire and the world*. London: Cape.

Collier, P. and Inkpen, R. 2003: The Royal Geographical Society and the development of surveying 1870–1914. *Journal of Historical Geography* 29: 93–108.

Collier, P., Forrest, D. and Pearson, A. 2003: The representation of topographic information on maps: the depiction of relief. *Cartographic Journal* 40: 17–26.

Collier, P., Elliott, V.L., Hegre, H., Hoeffler, A., Reynal-Querol, M. and Sambanis, N. 2003: *Breaking the conflict trap*. Washington, DC: The World Bank.

Collins, L., Drewett, R. and Ferguson, R. 1974: Markov models in geography. *The Statistician* 23: 179–210.

Comaroff, J. and Comaroff J.L., 1991: *Of revelation and revolution. Vol. 1: Christianity, colonialism, and consciousness in South Africa*. Chicago: The University of Chicago Press.

Comaroff, J. and Comaroff, J.L. 1992: *Ethnography and the historical imagination*. Boulder, CO: Westview Press.

Congdon, P. 2001: *Bayesian statistical modeling*. Chichester: Wiley.

Conklin, H. 1962: An ethnoecological approach to shifting cultivation. In P. Wagner and M. Mikesell, eds, *Readings in cultural geography*. Chicago: The University of Chicago Press, 457–64.

Connell, J. and Gibson, C. 2002: *Sound tracks: popular music, identity and place*. London: Routledge.

Conrad, J. 2007 [1902]: *The heart of darkness*. London: Penguin.

Conradson, D., ed., 2003a: Geographies of care. Special issue of *Social and Cultural Geography* 4: 451–547.

Conradson, D. 2003b: Spaces of care in the city: the place of a community drop-in centre. *Social and Cultural Geography* 4: 507–48.

Conradson, D. 2005a: Focus groups. In R. Flowerdew and D. Martin, eds, *Methods in human geography: a guide for students doing a research project*, 2nd edn. Harlow: Pearson Education, 128–43.

Conradson, D. 2005b: Freedom, space and perspective: moving encounters with other ecologies. In J. Davidson, L. Bondi and M. Smith, eds, *Emotional geographies*. Aldershot: Ashgate, 103–34.

Conway, D. 2004: On being part of population geography's future: population–environment relationships and inter-science initiatives. *Population Space and Place* 10: 295–302.

Conway, J.H. 1970: The game of life. *Scientific American* 223: 120–3.

Conzen, M.P. 1960: Alnwick, Northumberland: a study in town plan analysis. *Transactions of the Institute of British Geographers* 27.

Conzen, M.P. 1975: Capital flows and the developing urban hierarchy: state bank capital in Wisconsin, 1854–1895. *Economic Geography* 51: 321–38.

Conzen, M.P. 1977: The maturing urban system in the United States, 1840–1910. *Annals of the Association of American Geographers* 67: 88–108.

Conzen, M.R.G. 1969: *Alnwick, Northumberland: a study in townplan analysis*. London: Institute of British Geographers, Publication 27.

Cook, I. 1990: Anarchist alternatives: an introduction. In I. Cook and D. Pepper, eds, special issue: 'Anarchism and geography.' *Contemporary issues in geography and education* 3: 9–21.

Cook, I. 2001a: You want to be careful you don't end up like Ian. He's all over the place: autobiography in/of an expanded field (the director's cut). http://www.gees.bham.ac.uk/downloads/gesdraftpapers/iancook-directorscut.htm

Cook, I. 2001b: You want to be careful you don't end up like Ian. He's all over the place. In P. Moss, ed., *Placing autobiography in geography*. Syracuse, NY: Syracuse University Press, 99–120.

Cook, I. 2004: Follow the thing: papaya. *Antipode* 36: 642–64.

Cook, I. and Crang, P. 1996: The world on a plate: culinary culture, displacement and geographical knowledges. *Journal of Material Culture* 1(2): 131–54.

Cooke, P. 1988: Flexible integration, scope economies, and strategic alliances: social and spatial mediations. *Environment and Planning D: Society and Space* 6: 281–300.

Cooke, P. 1989: *Localities: the changing face of urban Britain*. London: Unwin Hyman.

Coombe, R. 1998: *The cultural life of intellectual properties*. Durham, NC: Duke University Press.

Cooper, D. 1998: *Governing out of order: space, law and the politics of belonging*. London: Rivers Oram Press.

Cooper, F. 1981: Africa and the world economy. *African Studies Review* 14: 1–86.

Cooper, F. 1994: Conflict and connection: rethinking colonial African history. *American Historical Review* 99(5): 1516–45.

Cooper, F. 1997: *Decolonization and African society*. Cambridge, UK: Cambridge University Press.

Cooper, F. 2003: *Africa since 1940*. Cambridge: Cambridge University Press.

Cooper, F. 2005: *Colonialism in question: theory, knowledge, history*. Berkeley, CA: University of California Press.

Cooper, F. and Packard, R., eds, 1997: *International development and the social sciences: essays on the history and politics of knowledge*. Berkeley, CA: University of California Press.

Cooper, F. and Stoler, A., eds, 1997a: Between metropole and colony: rethinking a research agenda. In Cooper and Stoler, eds, *Tensions of empire: colonial cultures in a bourgeois world*. Berkeley, CA: University of California Press, 1–56.

Cooper, F. and Stoler, A., eds, 1997b: *Tensions of empire: colonial cultures in a bourgeois world*. Berkeley, CA: University of California Press.

Cooper, M. 2004: Insecure times, tough decisions: the nomos of neo-liberalism, *Alternatives* 29(5): 515–34.

Copjec, J. 1994: *Read my desire: Lacan against the historicists*. Cambridge, MA: The MIT Press.

Coppock, J.T. 1974: Geography and public policy: challenges, opportunities and implications. *Transactions of the Institute of British Geographers* 63: 1–16.

Corbridge, S. 1986: *Capitalist world development: a critique of radical development geography*. London: Macmillan.

Corbridge, S. 1993a: *Debt and development*. Oxford: Blackwell.

Corbridge, S. 1993b: Marxisms, modernities, and moralities: development praxis and the claims of distant strangers. *Environment and Planning D: Society and Space* 11: 449–72.

Corbridge, S. 1994: Bretton Woods revisited: hegemony, stability and territory. *Environment and Planning A* 26(12): 1829–59.

Corbridge, S. 1995: *Development studies: a reader*. London: Arnold.

Corbridge, S. 1998: 'Beneath the pavement only soil': the poverty of post-development. *Journal of Development Studies* 34: 138–48.

Corbridge, S., Thrift, N. and Martin, R., eds, 1994: *Money, power and space*. Oxford: Blackwell.

Corbridge, S., Williams, G., Srivastava, M. and Véron, R. 2005: *Seeing the state: governance and governmentality in India*. Cambridge, UK: Cambridge University Press.

Cormack, L.B. 1997: *Charting an empire: geography at the English universities, 1580–1620*. Chicago: The University of Chicago Press.

Cormack, R.M. 1989: Log-linear models for capture–recapture. *Biometrics* 45: 395–413.

Cornell, D. 1995: What is ethical feminism? In S. Benhabib, J. Butler, D. Cornell, and N. Fraser, eds, *Feminist contentions: a philosophical exchange*. London: Routledge, 75–106.

Coronil, F. 1995: Transculturation and the politics of theory: countering the center, Cuban counterpoint. Introduction to Ortiz, F. 1995 [1940]: *Cuban counterpoint: tobacco and sugar*, trans. H. de Onís. Durham, NC: Duke University Press, ix–lv.

Coronil, F. 1996: Beyond Occidentalism: toward nonimperial geohistorical categories. *Cultural Anthropology* 11: 51–87.

Coronil, F. 1997: *The magical state*. Chicago: The University of Chicago Press.

Coronil, F. 2000: Towards a critique of globalcentrism: speculations on capitalism's nature. *Public Culture* 12(2): 351–74.

Corr, A. 1999: *No trespassing! Squatting, rent strikes and land struggles worldwide*. Cambridge: South End Press.

Cortesi, G., Cristaldi, F. and Fortuijn, J.D., eds, 2004: *Gendered cities: identities, activities, networks: a life-course approach*. Rome: Società geografica italiana.

Cosgrove, D. 1984: Prospect, perspective and the evolution of the landscape idea. *Transactions of the Institute of British Geographers*, NS 10(1): 45–62.

Cosgrove, D. 1989: Geography is everywhere: culture and symbolism in human landscapes. In D. Gregory and R. Walford, eds, *Horizons in human geography*. London: Macmillan, 118–35.

Cosgrove, D. 1993: *The Palladian landscape: geographical change and its cultural representation in sixteenth-century Italy*. Leicester: Leicester University Press.

Cosgrove, D. 1998 [1984]: *Social formation and symbolic landscape*. Madison: University of Wisconsin Press.

Cosgrove, D., ed., 1999: *Mappings*. London: Reaktion Press.

Cosgrove, D. 2001: *Apollo's eye: a cartographic genealogy of the earth in the Western imagination*. Baltimore, MD: The Johns Hopkins University Press.

Cosgrove, D. 2003: Cosmopolitanism and tolerance in early modern geography. *Annals of the Association of American Geographers* 93: 852–70.

Cosgrove, D. 2006a: Cosmographic mapping. In D. Woodward, ed., *The history of cartography*, vol. 3, *Cartography in the European Renaissance*. Chicago: The University of Chicago Press.

Cosgrove, D. 2006b: *Geographical imagination and the authority of images*. Hettner Lectures (9), Department of Geography, University of Heidelberg.

Cosgrove, D. and Daniels, S., eds, 1988: *The iconography of landscape: essays on the symbolic representation, design and use of past environments*. Cambridge, UK: Cambridge University Press.

Cosgrove, D. and Domosh, M. 1993: Author and authority: writing the new cultural geography. In J. Duncan and D. Ley, eds, *Place/culture/representation*. London: Routledge, 25–38.

Cosgrove, D.E. and della Dora, V. 2005: Mapping global war: Los Angeles, the Pacific, and Charles Owens's pictorial cartography. *Annals of the Association of American Geographers* 95: 373–90.

Costanza, R. 2003: A vision of the future of science: reintegrating the study of humans and the rest of nature. *Futures* 35: 651–71.

Costanza, R., d'Arge, R., de Groot, R., Farber, S., Grasso, M., Hannon, B., Limburg, K., Naeem, S., O'Neill, R.V., Paruelo, J., Raskin, R.G., Sutton, P. and van den Belt, M. 1997: The value of the world's ecosystem services and natural capital. *Nature* 387: 253–60.

Couclelis, H. 1998: Geocomputation in context. In P.A. Longley, S.M. Brooks, R. McDonnell and B. Macmillan, eds, *Geocomputation: a primer*. Chichester: Wiley, 17–29.

Couldry, N. 2006: *Listening beyond the echoes: media, ethics and agency in an uncertain world*. Boulder, CO: Paradigm Books.

Couldry, N. and McCarthy, A., eds, 2004: *Mediaspace: place, scale and culture in a media age*. London: Routledge.

Coutin, S. 2003: *Legalizing moves: Salvadoran immigrants' struggle for U.S. residency*. Ann Arbor, MI: University of Michigan Press.

Coverley, M. 2006: *Psychogeography*. Harpenden, Herts: Pocket Essentials.

Coward, M. 2004: Urbicide in Bosnia. In S. Graham, ed., *Cities, war and terrorism: towards an urban geopolitics*. Oxford: Blackwell, 154–71.

Coward, M. 2006: Against anthropocentrism: the destruction of the built environment as a distinct form of political violence. *Review of International Studies* 32: 419–37.

Coward, M. 2007: Urbicide revisited. *Theory and Event* 10:2.

Cowen, D. and Gilbert, E., eds, 2008: *War, citizenship, territory*. London: Routledge.

Cowen, M.P. and Shenton, R.W. 1996: *Doctrines of development*. London: Routledge.

Cox, K.R. 1969: The voting decision in spatial context. In C. Board, R. J. Chorley, P. Haggett and D. R. Stoddart, eds, *Progress in Geography, Volume 1*. London: Edward Arnold, 81–118.

Cox, K.R. 1973: *Conflict, power and politics in the city: a geographic view*. New York: McGraw-Hill.

Cox, K.R. 1976: American geography: social science emergent. *Social Science Quarterly* 57: 182–207.

Cox, K.R., ed., 1997: *Spaces of globalization: reasserting the power of the local*. New York: Guilford Press.

Cox, K.R. 2002: *Political geography: territory, state, and society*. Oxford: Blackwell.

Cox, K.R. and Johnston, R.J., eds, 1982: *Conflict, politics and the urban scene*. New York: St Martin's Press.

Cox, K.R. and Low, M. 2003: Political geography in question. *Political Geography* 22: 599–602.

Cox, K.R. and McCarthy, J.J. 1982: Neighborhood activism as a politics of turf. In K.R. Cox and R.J. Johnston, eds, *Conflict politics and the urban scene*. London: Longman, 196–219.

Cox, K.R. and Mair, A. 1989: Levels of abstraction in locality studies. *Antipode* 21: 121–32.

Cox, N.J. and Jones, K. 1981: Exploratory data analysis. In N. Wrigley and R.J. Bennett, eds, *Quantitative geography*. London: Routledge, 135–43.

Craddock, S. 2000a: *City of plagues: disease, poverty and deviance in San Francisco*. Minneapolis: University of Minnesota Press.

Craddock, S. 2000b: Disease, social identity and risk: rethinking the geography of AIDS. *Transactions of the Institute of British Geographers* 25: 153–68.

Craddock, S., Oppong, J., Ghosh, J. and Kalipeni, E., eds, 2003: *HIV and AIDS in Africa: beyond epidemiology*. Oxford: Blackwell.

Craib, I. 1990: *Psychoanalysis and social theory*. Amherst: The University of Massachusetts Press.

Crampton, J. 2003: *The political mapping of cyberspace*. Chicago: The University of Chicago Press.

Crampton, J. and Krygier, H. 2006: An introduction to critical cartography. *ACME: an International E-Journal for Critical Geographies* 4(1): 11–33.

Crampton, J.W. 2004: GIS and geographic governance: reconstructing the choropleth map. *Cartographica* 39(1): 41–54.

Crampton, J.W. and Elden, S., eds, 2007: *Space, knowledge and power: Foucault and geography*. Aldershot: Ashgate.

Crang, M. 1998: *Cultural geography*. London: Routledge.

Crang, M. 2000: Between academy and popular geographies: cartographic imaginations and the cultural landscape of Sweden. In I. Cook, D. Crouch, S. Naylor and J. Ryan, eds, *Cultural turns/geographical turns: perspectives on cultural geography*. London: Prentice Hall, 88–108.

Crang, M. 2002: Qualitative methods: the new orthodoxy? *Progress in Human Geography* 26: 647–55.

Crang, M. 2003: Qualitative methods: touchy, feely, look-see? *Progress in Human Geography* 27: 494–504.

Crang, M. 2005: Analyzing qualitative materials In R. Flowerdew and D. Martin, eds, *Methods in human geography: A guide for students doing a research project*. London: Pearson Educational, 218–32.

Crang, M. and Coleman, S., eds, 2002: *Tourism: between place and performance*. Oxford: Berghahn.

Crang, M. and Thrift, N., eds, 2000: *Thinking space*. London: Routledge.

Crang, M., Crang, P. and May, J. 1999: *Virtual geographies: bodies, space and relations*. London: Routledge.

Crang, M.A., Hudson, A.C., Reimer, S.M. and Hinchliffe, S.J. 1997: Software for qualitative research. *Environment and Planning A* 29: 771–87, 1109–24.

Crang, P. 1992: The politics of polyphony: reconfigurations in geographical authority. *Environment and Planning D: Society and Space* 10: 527–50.

Crapanzo, V. 1986: Hermes' dilemma: the masking of subversion in ethnographic description. In J. Clifford and G. Marcus, eds, *Writing culture: the poetics and politics of ethnography*. Berkeley, CA: University of California Press, 51–76.

Crary, J. 1989: Spectacle, attention, countermemory. *October* 50: 97–107.

Crary, J. 1990a: Modernity and the problem of the observer. In Crary, *Techniques of the observer*. Cambridge, MA: The MIT Press.

Crary, J. 1990b: *Suspensions of perception: attention, spectacle and modern culture*. Cambridge, MA: The MIT Press.

Cresswell, T. 1996: *In place/out of place: geography, ideology and transgression*. Minneapolis: University of Minnesota Press.

Cresswell, T. 1997: Imagining the nomad: mobility and the postmodern primitive. In G. Benko and U. Strohmayer, eds, *Space and social theory*. Oxford: Blackwell, 360–79.

Cresswell, T. 2000: Falling down: resistance as diagnostic. In J. Sharp, P. Routledge, C. Philo and R. Paddison, eds, *Entanglements of power: geographies of domination/resistance*. London: Routledge, 256–68.

Cresswell, T. 2003: Landscape and the obliteration of practice. In K. Anderson, D. Domosh, S. Pile and N. Thrift, eds, *Handbook of cultural geography*. London: Sage.

Cresswell, T. 2004: *Place: a short introduction*. Oxford: Blackwell.

Cresswell, T. 2006: *On the move: mobility in the modern Western world*. London: Routledge.

Cresswell, T. and Dixon, D., eds, 2002: *Engaging film: geographies of mobility and identity*. Lanham, MD: Rowman & Littlefield.

Crewe, L. 2000: Geographies of retailing and consumption. *Progress in Human Geography* 24(2): 275–90.

Crewe, L. 2001: The besieged body: geographies of retailing and consumption. *Progress in Human Geography* 25(4): 629–40.

Crewe, L. 2003: Geographies of retailing and consumption: markets in motion. *Progress in Human Geography* 27(3): 352–62.

Crewe, L. and Gregson, N. 1998: Tales of the unexpected: exploring car boot sales as marginal spaces of contemporary consumption. *Transactions of the Institute of British Geographers* 23: 39–53.

Crissman, L. 1967: The segmentary structure of urban Chinese communities. *Man* 2: 185–204.

Critchley, S. 1999: *The ethics of deconstruction*, 2nd edn. Edinburgh: Edinburgh University Press.

Cronin, M. and Bale, J. 2002: *Sport and postcolonialism*. Oxford: Berg.

Cronon, W. 1983: *Changes in the land*. New York: Hill and Wang.

Cronon, W. 1987: Revisiting the vanishing frontier: the legacy of Frederick Jackson Turner. *Western Historical Quarterly* 18: 157–76.

Cronon, W. 1991: *Nature's metropolis: Chicago and the great West*. New York: W.W. Norton.

Cronon, W. 1995: The trouble with wilderness: or getting back to the wrong nature. In W. Cronon, ed., *Uncommon ground: toward reinventing nature*. New York: W.W. Norton, 69–90.

Crosby, A. 1986: *Ecological imperialism: the biological expansion of Europe 900–1900*. Cambridge: Cambridge University Press.

Crosland, A. 1970: The transitions from capitalism. In R. Crossman, ed., *New Fabian essays*. London: Dent, 33–68.

Crouch, D. and Toogood, M. 1999: Everyday abstraction: geographical knowledge in the art of Peter Lanyon. *Ecumene* 6(1): 72–89.

Crouch, S. 1990: *Notes of a hanging judge*. New York: Random House.

Crush, J. 1991: The discourse of progressive human geography. *Progress in Human Geography* 15: 395–414.

Crush, J. 1994: Post-colonialism, de-colonization, and geography, In A. Godlewska and N. Smith, eds, *Geography and empire*. Oxford: Blackwell, 333–50.

Crystal, D. 2003: *English as a global language*. Cambridge, UK: Cambridge University Press.

Cuff, D. 2003: Immanent domain: pervasive computing and the public realm. *Journal of Architectural Education* 57(1): 43–9.

Cullen, M.J. 1975: *The statistical movement in early Victorian Britain: the foundations of empirical social research*. New York: Barnes and Noble.

Culler, J. 1997: *Literary theory: a very short introduction*. Oxford: Oxford University Press.

Cumbers, A. and Routledge, P. 2004: Alternative geographical imaginations: introduction. *Antipode* 36(5): 818–28.

Cumings, B. 1984: The origins and development of the Northeast Asian political economy: industrial sectors, product cycles, and political consequences. *International Organization* 38(1): 1–40.

Cumings, B. 1998: Boundary displacement: area studies and international studies during and after the Cold War. In C. Simpson, ed., *Universities and empire: money and politics in the social sciences during the Cold War.* New York: New Press.

Curry, M. 1998: *Digital places: living with geographic information technologies.* New York: Routledge.

Curry, M. 2006: Meta-theory/many theories. In N. Castree, A. Rogers and D. Sherman, eds, *Questioning geography: fundamental debates.* Oxford: Blackwell, 167–86.

Curtis, S. 2004: *Health and inequality: geographical perspectives.* London: Sage.

Curzon, G.N. 1888: The 'scientific frontier' an accomplished fact. *Nineteenth Century* 23: 901–17.

Cushing, D.H. 1988: *The provident sea.* Cambridge: Cambridge University Press.

Cutter, S. and Renwick, W. 2004: *Exploitation, conservation, preservation: a geographic perspective on natural resource use,* 4th edn. Hoboken, NJ: Wiley.

Cutter, S., Richardson, D. and Wilbanks, T., eds, 2003: *Geographical dimensions of terrorisms.* New York: Routledge.

Cuyvers, L. and De Beule, F. 2005: *Transnational corporations and economic development.* London: Palgrave Macmillan.

Cypher, J. and Dietz, J. 1997: *The process of economic development.* London: Routledge.

D'Souza, A. and McDonough, T., eds, 2006: *The invisible* flâneuse*? Gender, public space, and visual culture in nineteenth-century Paris.* Manchester: Manchester University Press.

Dædalus 2005: On imperialism. Theme Issue, no. 134.

Dahl, R. 1963: *Modern political analysis.* Englewood Cliffs, NJ: Prentice Hall.

Dahl, R. 1989: *Democracy and its critics.* New Haven: Yale University Press.

Dahlberg, R.E., Luman, D.E. and Vaupel, R.P. 1990: Development of the satellite image map genre in the United States. *International Yearbook of Cartography* 30: 165–88.

Dahlman, C. and Ó Tuathail, G. 2005a: The legacy of ethnic cleansing: the international community and the returns process in post-Dayton Bosnia-Herzegovina. *Political Geography* 24: 569–99.

Dahlman, C.T. and Ó Tuathail, G. 2005b: Broken Bosnia: the local geopolitics of

displacement and return in two Bosnian places. *Annals of the Association of American Geographers* 95(3): 644–62.

Dalby, S. 1990: *Creating the second cold war: the discourse of politics.* New York: Guilford Press.

Dalby, S. 1991: Critical geopolitics: discourse, difference, and dissent. *Environment and Planning D: Society and Space* 9: 261–83.

Dalby, S. 1994: Gender and critical geopolitics: reading security discourse in the new world order. *Environment and Planning D: Society and Space* 12: 595–612.

Dalby, S. 2002: *Environmental security.* Minneapolis: University of Minnesota Press.

Dalby, S. 2004: Exorcising Malthus' ghost: resources and security in global politics. *Geopolitics* 9(1): 242–54.

Dalby, S. 2006: Geopolitics, grand strategy and the Bush doctrine: the strategic dimensions of U.S. hegemony under George W. Bush. In C.P. David and D. Grondin, eds, *Hegemony or empire? The redefinition of American power under George W. Bush.* Aldershot: Ashgate.

Dalby, S. and Ó Tuathail, G., eds, 1998: *Rethinking geopolitics.* London: Routledge.

Dale, A. and Davies, R.B., eds, 1994: *Analyzing social and political change: a casebook of methods.* London: Sage.

Dalla Costa, M. and Dalla Costa, G.F., eds, 1999: *Women, development and labor of reproduction: struggles and movements.* Trenton, NJ: Africa World Press.

Danermark, B., Ekström, M., Jakobsen, L. and Karlsson, J.C. 2001: *Explaining society: an introduction to critical realism in the social sciences.* London: Taylor & Francis.

Danermark, B., Ekström, M., Jakobsen, L. and Karlsson, J.C. 2002: *Explaining society: critical realism in the social science.* London: Routledge.

Daniels, P., Bradshaw, M., Shaw, D. and Sidaway, J. 2005: *An introduction to human geography: issues for the 21st century,* 2nd edn. London: Pearson.

Daniels, P.W. 1993: *Service industries in the world economy.* Oxford: Blackwell.

Daniels, S. 1982: Humphry Repton and the morality of landscape. In J. Gold and J. Burgess, eds, *Valued environments.* London: George Allen and Unwin, 124–44.

Daniels, S. 1989: Marxism, culture and the duplicity of landscape. In R. Peet and N. Thrift, eds, *New models in geography,* vol. 2. London: Unwin Hyman.

Daniels, S. 1993: *Fields of vision: landscape imagery and national identity in England and the United States.* Cambridge, UK: Polity Press.

Daniels, S. 1999: *Humphry Repton: landscape gardening and the geography of Georgian England.* New Haven: Yale University Press.

Daniels, S. and Cosgrove, D. 1988: Introduction: iconography and landscape. In Cosgrove and Daniels, eds, *The iconography of landscape: essays on the representation design and use of past environments*. Cambridge, UK: Cambridge University Press, 1–10.

Daniels, S. and Nash, C. 2004: Lifepaths: geography and biography. *Journal of Historical Geography* 30: 449–58.

Dann, G. 1999: Writing out the tourist in space and time. *Annals of Tourism Research* 26(1): 159–87.

Darby, H.C. 1940: *The draining of the Fens*. Cambridge, UK: Cambridge University Press.

Darby, H.C. 1948: The regional geography of Thomas Hardy's Wessex. *Geographical Review* 38: 426–43.

Darby, H.C. 1951: The changing English landscape. *Geographical Journal* 117: 377–94.

Darby, H.C. 1953: On the relations of geography and history. *Transactions of the Institute of British Geographers* 19: 1–11.

Darby, H.C. 1962: The problem of geographical description. *Transactions of the Institute of British Geographers* 30: 1–14.

Darby, H.C., ed., 1973: *A new historical geography of England and Wales*. Cambridge, UK: Cambridge University Press.

Darby, H.C. 1977: *Domesday England*. Cambridge, UK: Cambridge University Press.

Darby, H.C. 2002: *The relations of history and geography: studies in England, France and the United States*. Exeter: Exeter University Press.

Darden, J.T. 1980: Lending practices and policies affecting the American metropolitan system. In S.D. Brunn and J.O. Wheeler, eds, *The American metropolitan system: present and future*. New York: Wiley, 93–110.

Darden, J.T. 1995: Black residential segregation since the 1948 Shelly v. Kraemer decision. *Journal of Black Studies* 25: 680–91.

Darder, A. and Torres, R.D. 2004: *After race: racism after multiculturalism*. New York: New York University Press.

Darian-Smith, E. 1999: *Bridging divides: the Channel Tunnel and English legal identity in the new Europe*. Berkeley, CA: University of California Press.

Darling, E. 2005: The city in the country: wilderness gentrification and the rent gap. *Environment and Planning A* 37: 1015–32.

Darnton, R. 1985: *The Great Cat Massacre and other episodes in French cultural history*. New York: A.A. Knopf.

Darnton, R. 2003: *George Washington's false teeth: an unconventional guide to the eighteenth century*. New York: W.W. Norton.

Darwent, D. 1969: Growth poles and growth centers in regional planning – a review. *Environment and Planning* 1: 5–32.

Darwin, C. 1998 [1868]: *The variation of animals and plants under domestication*. Baltimore, MD: The Johns Hopkins University Press.

Das Gupta, P. 1993: *An inquiry into well being and destitution*. Oxford: The Clarendon Press.

Dasmann, R.F., Milton, J.P. and Freeman, P.H. 1973: *Ecological principles for economic development*. Chichester: Wiley.

Dauphinee, E. and Masters, C., eds, 2007: *The logics of biopower and the war on terror: living, dying, surviving*. London: Palgrave.

Davidson, J. 2001: Fear and trembling in the mall: women, agoraphobia and body boundaries. In I. Dyck, N. Davis Lewis and S. McLafferty, eds, *Geographies of women's health*. London: Routledge, 213–30.

Davidson, J. 2003: 'Putting on a face': Sartre, Goffman, and agoraphobic anxiety in social space *Environment and Planning D: Society and Space* 21: 107–22.

Davidson, J. Bondi, L. and Smith, M., eds, 2005: *Emotional geographies*. Aldershot: Ashgate.

Davies, G.L. 1969: *The Earth in decay: a history of British geomorphology 1578 to 1878*. London: MacDonald.

Davies, H. 1982: Fiscal migration and the London boroughs. *Urban Studies* 19: 143–54.

Davies, H.T.O., Nutley, S.M. and Smith, P.C. 2000: *What works: evidence-based policy and practice in public services*. Bristol: Policy Press.

Davies, R.B. and Pickles, A. 1985: Longitudinal vs. cross-sectional methods for behavioural research: a first round knockout. *Environment & Planning A* 17: 1315–29.

Davies, W.K.D. 1984: *Factorial ecology*. Aldershot: Gower.

Davies-Withers, S. 2002: Quantitative methods: Bayesian inference, Bayesian thinking *Progress in Human Geography* 26: 553–66.

Davis, J. 1992: *Exchange*. Minneapolis: University of Minnesota Press.

Davis, J. and Goldberg, R. 1957: *A concept of agribusiness*. Boston: Harvard Business School.

Davis, J.A. 1986: *The logic of causal order*. Sage. QASS No. 55. New York: Sage.

Davis, M. 1990: *City of quartz: excavating the future in Los Angeles*. London: Verso.

Davis, M. 1998: *Ecology of fear: Los Angeles and the imagination of disaster*. New York: Metropolitan Books.

Davis, M. 2000: *Late Victorian holocausts: El Niño famines and the making of the Third World*. London: Verso.

Davis, M. 2004a: Planet of slums. *New Left Review* 26, March–April: 5–34.

Davis, M. 2004b: The urbanization of empire: megacities and the laws of chaos. *Social Text* 81(4): 9–15.

Davis, M. 2005: *The monster at our door: the global threat of avian flu*. New York: The New Press.

Davis, M. 2006: *Planet of slums*. London: Verso.

Davis, W.M. 1899a: The geographical cycle. *Geographical Journal* 14: 481–504.

Davis, W.M., with W.H. Snyder 1899b: *Physical geography*. Boston: Ginn.

De Angelis, M. 2006: *The beginning of history*. London: Pluto Press.

de Blij, H.J. and Muller, P. 2007: *The world today: concepts and regions in Geography*. Hoboken, NJ: Wiley.

De Caro, M. and Macarthur, D., eds, 2004: *Naturalism in question*. Cambridge, MA: Harvard University Press.

de Certeau, M. 1984 [1980]: *The practice of everyday life*, trans. S. Rendell. Berkeley, CA: University of California Press.

De Floriani, L. and Magillo, P. 2003: Algorithms for visibility computation on terrains: a survey. *Environment and Planning B: Planning and Design* 30: 709–28.

De Goede, M. 2003: *Hawala* discourses and the war on terrorist finance. *Environment and Planning D: Society and Space* 21: 513–32.

De Goede, M. 2007: Underground money. *Cultural Critique* 65: 140–63.

de las Casas, B. 1992 [1552]: *In defense of the Indians*, trans. S. Poole. DeKalb, IL: Northern Illinois Press.

de Lauretis, T. 1991: Queer theory: lesbian and gay sexualities an introduction. *Differences* 4: 1–10.

De Moor, M., Shaw-Taylor, L. and Warde, P., eds, 2002: *The management of common land in north-west Europe, c.1500–1850*. Turnhout: Brepols.

de Moor, P. and de Beelde, I. 2005: Environmental auditing and the role of the accountancy profession: a literature review. *Environmental Management* 36(2): 205–19.

De Soto, H. 1989: *The other path: the invisible revolution in the Third World*. London: I.B. Tauris/ New York: Harper & Row.

de Vries, J. 1994: The industrial revolution and the industrious revolution. *Journal of Economic History*, 54: 249–71.

de Waal, A. 1997: *Famine crimes*. London: Heinemann.

de Waal, A. 2005: Defining genocide. *Index on Censorship* 34(1): 6–13.

Dean, M. 1994: *Critical and effective histories: Foucault's methods and historical sociology*. London: Routledge.

Dean, M. 1999: *Governmentality: power and rule in modern society*. London: Sage.

Dean, M. 2006: A political mythology of world order: Carl Schmitt's *Nomos*. *Theory, Culture & Society* 23(5): 1–22.

Dear, I.C.B., ed., 1995: *The Oxford companion to World War II*. Oxford: Oxford University Press.

Dear, M.J. 1975: The nature of socialist geography. *Antipode* 7(1), February: 87.

Dear, M.J. 1986: Postmodernism and planning. *Environment and Planning D: Society and Space* 4: 367–84.

Dear, M.J. 1988: The postmodern challenge: reconstructing human geography. *Transactions of the Institute of British Geographers* 13: 262–74.

Dear, M.J. 1997: Postmodern bloodlines. In G. Benko and U. Strohmayer, eds, *Space and social theory: interpreting modernity and postmodernity*, Oxford: Blackwell, 49–71.

Dear, M.J. 2000: *The postmodern urban condition*. Blackwell: Oxford.

Dear, M.J. and Dahmann, N. 2008: Urban politics and the Los Angeles School of Urbanism. *Urban Affairs Review* 44(2): 266–79.

Dear, M.J. and Dishman, J.D., eds, 2001: *From Chicago to L.A.: making sense of urban theory*. Thousand Oaks, CA: Sage.

Dear, M.J. and Flusty, S. 1998: Postmodern urbanism. *Annals of the Association of American Geographers* 88: 50–72.

Dear, M.J. and Flusty, S., eds, 2002: *The spaces of postmodernity: readings in human geography*. Oxford: Blackwell.

Dear, M.J. and Wolch, J. 1993: *Landscapes of despair: from deinstitutionalization to homelessness*. Princeton, NJ: Princeton University Press.

Dear, M.J., Wilton, R., Gaber, S.L. and Takahashi, L. 1997: Seeing people differently: the sociospatial construction of disability. *Environment and Planning D: Society and Space* 15: 455–80.

Debord, G. 1981 [1955]: An introduction to the critique of urban geography. In K. Knabb, ed. and trans., *Situationist international anthology*. Berkeley, CA: Bureau of Public Secrets, 5–8.

Debord, G. 1994 [1967]: *The society of the spectacle*, trans. D. Nicholson-Smith. New York: Zone Books.

Deffeyes, K. 2001: *Hubbert's peak: the impending world oil shortage*. Princeton, NJ: Princeton University Press.

DeFilippis, J. 2004: *Unmaking Goliath: community control in the face of global capital*. New York: Routledge.

Delaney, D. 1998: *Race, place and the law: 1836–1948*. Austin: University of Texas Press.

Delaney, D. 2001: Running with the land: legal–historical imagination and the spaces of modernity. *Journal of Historical Geography* 27(4): 493–506.

Delaney, D. 2003: *Law and nature*. Cambridge, UK: Cambridge University Press.

Delaney, D. and Leitner, H. 1997: The political construction of scale. *Political Geography* 16: 93–7.

Delanty, G. 1995: *Inventing Europe: idea, identity, reality*. London: Macmillan.

Delanty, G. 2005a: *Rethinking Europe: social theory and the implications of Europeanization*. London: Routledge.

Delanty, G. 2005b: The idea of a cosmopolitan Europe: on the cultural significance of

Europeanization. *International Review of Sociology* 15(3): 405–21.

Deleuze, G. 1994: *Difference and repetition*, trans. P Patton. New York: Columbia University Press.

Deleuze, G. 1995: *Negotiations*. New York: Columbia University Press.

Deleuze, G. 2001 [1983]: Beyond the movement-image. In J. Orr and O. Taxidou, eds, *Post-war cinema and modernity: a film reader*. New York: New York University Press, 89–102. Original translation by H. Tomlinson and R. Galeta, from Deleuze, *Cinema 2: The time-image*. Minneapolis: University of Minnesota Press.

Deleuze, G. and Guattari, F. 1972: *L'anti-Oedipe*. Paris: Minuit.

Deleuze, G. and Guattari, F. 1983: *Anti-Oedipus: capitalism and schizophrenia*, translated from the French by R. Hurley, M. Seem and H.R. Lane; preface by M. Foucault. Minneapolis: University of Minnesota Press.

Deleuze, G. and Guattari, F. 1986: *Kafka toward a minor literature*. Minneapolis: University of Minnesota Press.

Deleuze, G. and Guattari, F. 1987: *A thousand plateaus*, trans. B. Massumi. Minneapolis: University of Minnesota Press.

Deleuze, G. and Guattari, F. 1988: *A thousand plateaus*. London: Athlone Press.

Deleuze, G. and Guattari, F. 2004: *Anti-Oedipus*. London: Continuum.

Delgado, R. and Stefancic, J., eds, 1997: *Critical white studies: looking behind the mirror*. Philadelphia: Temple University Press.

Della Porta, D. and Diani, M. 1999: *Social movements: an introduction*. London: Blackwell.

DeLyser, D. 2005: *Ramona memories: tourism and the shaping of southern California*. Minneapolis: University of Minnesota Press.

DeLyser, D. and Starrs, P.F. 2001: Doing fieldwork: editors' introduction, *Geographical Review* 91(1–2): 4–8.

Demangeon, A. 1942: *Problèmes de géographie humaine*. Paris: A. Colin.

Demeritt, D. 1994a: Ecology, objectivity and critique in writings on nature and human societies. *Journal of Historical Geography* 20(1): 22–37.

Demeritt, D. 1994b: The nature of metaphors in cultural geography and environmental history. *Progress in Human Geography* 18: 163–85.

Demeritt, D. 1996: Social theory and the reconstruction of science and geography. *Transactions of the Institute of British Geographers*, NS 21: 483–504.

Demeritt, D. 1998: Science, social constructivism and nature. In B. Braun and N. Castree, eds, *Remaking reality: nature at the millennium*. London: Routledge, 173–93.

Demeritt, D. 2001a: Being constructive about nature. In N. Castree and B. Braun, eds, 2001: *Social nature: theory, practice and politics*. Oxford: Blackwell, 22–40.

Demeritt, D. 2001b: Scientific forest conservation and the statistical picturing of nature's limits in the progressive-era United States. *Environment and Planning* 19: 431–59.

Demeritt, D. 2005: Hybrid geographies, relational ontologies and situated knowledges. *Antipode* 37: 818–23.

DeMers, M.N. 2000: *Fundamentals of Geographic Information Systems*, 2nd edn. Toronto: Wiley.

DeMers, M.N. 2001: *GIS modeling in raster*. New York: Wiley.

Dennis, R. 1984: *English industrial cities in the nineteenth century: a social geography*. Cambridge, UK: Cambridge University Press.

Dennis, R. 1994: Interpreting the apartment house: modernity and metropolitanism in Toronto, 1900–1930. *Journal of Historical Geography* 20(3): 305–22.

Denoon, D. 1983: *Settler capitalism: the dynamics of dependent development in the southern hemisphere*. Oxford: The Clarendon Press.

Denoon, D. 2003: Re-membering Australasia: a repressed memory. *Australian Historical Studies* 34(122): 290–304.

Denton, N. 1996: The persistence of segregation: links between residential segregation and school segregation. *Minnesota Law Review* 80: 795–824.

Department of Communities and Local Government 2006: *Green and public space research: mapping and priorities*. London: HMSO.

DePastino, T. 2003: *Citizen Hobo: how a century of homelessness shaped America*. Chicago: The University of Chicago Press.

Derrida, J. 1976: *Of grammatology*, trans. Gayatri Chakravorty Spivak. Baltimore, MD: The Johns Hopkins University Press.

Derrida, J. 1978: *Writing and difference*, trans. A. Bass. London: Routledge.

Derrida, J. 1979: *Limited Inc*. Evanston, IL: Northwestern University Press.

Derrida, J. 1981: The double session. In *Disseminations*. Chicago: The University of Chicago Press.

Derrida, J. 1982a: *Margins of philosophy*. Chicago: The University of Chicago Press.

Derrida, J. 1982b: The ends of man. In *Margins of philosophy*. Chicago: The University of Chicago Press, 109–36.

Derrida, J. 1994: *Specters of Marx: the state of the debt, the work of mourning, and the New International*. New York: Routledge.

Derrida, J. 2002: *Negotiations: interventions and interviews 1971–2001*. Stanford, CA: Stanford University Press.

852

Derrida, J. 2003: And say the animal responded. In C. Wolfe, ed., *Zoontologies: the question of the animal.* Minneapolis: University of Minnesota Press, 121–46.

Desbiens, C. and Ruddick, S. 2006: Speaking of geography: language, power and the spaces of Ango-Saxon 'hegemony'. *Environment and Planning D: Society and Space* 24: 1–8.

Desbiens, C. and Smith, N. 1999: The International Critical Geography Group: forbidden optimism? *Environment and Planning D: Society and Space* 18: 379–82.

Desfor, G. and Keil, R. 2004: *Nature and the city: making environmental policy in Toronto and Los Angeles.* Tucson: University of Arizona Press.

Desmond, J. 1999: *Staging tourism: bodies on display from Waikiki to Sea World.* Chicago: The University of Chicago Press.

Dettelbach, M. 1996: Humboldtian science. In N. Jardine, J.A. Secord and E.C. Spary, eds, *Cultures of natural history.* Cambridge, UK: Cambridge University Press, 287–304.

Dettelbach, M. 1999: The face of nature: precise measurement, mapping and sensibility in the work of Alexander von Humboldt. *Studies in History and Philosophy of Biological and Biomedical Sciences* 30: 473–504.

Deudney, D. 2004: Publius before Kant: federal-republican security and democratic peace. *European Journal of International Relations* 10: 315–56.

Deutsche, D. 1991: Boys town. *Environment and Planning D: Society and Space* 9: 5–30.

Deutsche, R. 1995: Surprising geography. *Annals of the Association of American Geographers* 85: 168–75.

Deutsche, R. 1996a: Boys town. In Deutsche, *Evictions: art and spatial politics.* Cambridge, MA: The MIT Press, 203–44.

Deutsche, R. 1996b: *Evictions: art and spatial politics.* Cambridge, MA: The MIT Press.

Deutsche, R. 1996c: Men in space. Reprinted in Deutsche, *Evictions: art and spatial politics.* Cambridge, MA: The MIT Press, 195–202.

Devall, B. and Sessions, G. 1985: *Deep ecology: living as if nature mattered.* Salt Lake City: Peregrine Smith.

DeVerteuil, G. 2003: Homeless mobility, institutional settings, and the new poverty management. *Environment and Planning A* 35(2): 361–79.

DeVerteuil, G., Lee, W. and Wolch, J. 2002: New spaces for the local welfare state? The case of general relief in Los Angeles county. *Social and Cultural Geography* 3: 229–46.

Devezas, T., ed., 2006: *Kondratieff waves, warfare and world security.* Amsterdam: IOS Press.

Devji, F. 2005: *Landscapes of the jihad: militancy, morality, modernity.* Ithaca, NY: Cornell University Press.

Dewsbury, J.-D. 2000: Performativity and the event: enacting a philosophy of difference. *Environment and Planning D: Society and Space* 18: 473–96.

Dewsbury, J.-D. 2003: Witnessing space: 'knowledge without contemplation'. *Environment and Planning A* 35: 1907–32.

Dewsbury, J.-D. 2007: Alain Badiou and the event of thought in thinking politics. *Transactions of the Institute of British Geographers* 32: 443–59.

Dewsbury, J.-D. and Thrift, N. 2005: 'Genesis eternal': after Paul Klee. In I. Buchanan and G. Lambert, eds, *Deleuze and space.* Edinburgh: Edinburgh University Press, 89–108.

Dewsbury, J.-D., Harrison, P., Rose, M. and Wylie, J. 2002: Enacting geographies. *Geoforum* 33: 437–40.

Dexter, H. 2007: New war, good war and the war on terror: explaining, excusing and creating Western neo-interventionism. *Development and Change* 38: 1055–71.

Dexter, H. 2008: The 'new war' on terror, cosmopolitanism and the just war revival. *Government and Opposition* 43: 55–78.

Dhareshwar, V. 1990: The predicament of theory, in M. Kreiswirth and M. Cheetham, eds, *Theory between the disciplines: authority/vision/politics.* Ann Arbor: University of Michigan Press, 231–50.

Diamond, J. 1997: *Guns, germs, and steel: the fates of human societies.* New York: W.W. Norton.

Diamond, J. and LeCroy, M. 1979: Birds of Karkar and Bagabag Islands, New Guinea. *Bulletin of American Natural History* 164: 469–531.

DiBiase, D., MacEachren, A.M., Krygier, J.B. and Reeves, C. 1992: Animation and the role of map design in scientific visualization. *Cartography and Geographic Information Systems* 19: 201–14.

Dicken, P. 2007: *Global shift: mapping the changing contours of the world economy,* 5th edn. New York: Guilford Press/London: Sage.

Dicken, P., Kelly, P.F., Olds, K. and Yeung, H.W.-C. 2000: Chains and networks, territories and scales: towards a relational framework for analysing the global economy. *Global Networks* 1: 89–112.

Dickinson, R. 1969: *The makers of modern geography.* London: Routledge and Kegan Paul/New York: Prager.

Dickinson, R.E. 1947: *City region and regionalism: a contribution to human ecology.* London: Kegan Paul, Trench Trübner.

Dickinson, R.E. and Howarth, O.J.R. 1933: *The making of geography.* Oxford: The Clarendon Press.

Dietz, M.G. 1987: Context is all: feminism and theories of citizenship. *Daedalus* 4: 1–24.

Dietz, T., Ostrom, E. and Stern, P. 2003: The struggle to govern the commons. *Science* 302: 1907–12.

DiGaetano, A. 2002: The changing nature of the local state: a comparative perspective. *Policy and Politics* 30: 61–77.

Dillon, M. 2002: Network society, network-centric warfare and the state of emergency. *Theory, Culture & Society* 19: 71–9.

Dillon, M. 2007: Governing terror: the state of emergency of biopolitical emergence. *International Political Sociology* 1: 7–28.

Dillon, M. 2008: Underwriting security. *Security Dialogue* 39: 309–32.

Dillon, M. and Lobo-Guerrero, L. 2008: Biopolitics of security in the 21st century. *Review of International Studies* 34: 265–92.

Dillon, M. and Reid, J. 2006: *The liberal way of war: the martial face of global biopolitics*. London: Taylor & Francis.

Dillon, M. and Reid, J. 2009: *The liberal way of war: killing to make life live*. London: Routledge.

Dion, R. 1949: La géographie humaine rétrospective. *Cahiers Internationaux de Sociologie* 6: 3–27.

Dirlik, A., ed., 1993: *What is in a rim? Critical perspectives on the Pacific region idea*. Boulder, CO: Westview Press.

Ditt, K. 2001: The idea of German cultural regions in the Third Reich: the work of Franz Petri. *Journal of Historical Geography* 27(2): 241–58.

Dixon, C. 1991: *South-East Asia in the world-economy: a regional geography*. Cambridge, UK: Cambridge University Press.

Dixon, C.J. and Leach, B. 1977: *Sampling methods for geographical research*. Concepts and Techniques in Modern Geography 17. Norwich: Geo Books.

Dixon, D.P. and Jones, J.P. III 1998: My dinner with Derrida, *or* spatial analysis and poststructuralism do lunch. *Environment and Planning A* 30: 247–60.

Dobson, A. 1998: *Justice and the environment: conceptions of environmental sustainability and theories of distributive justice*. New York: Oxford University Press.

Dobson, J. 1993: Automated geography. *Professional Geographer* 35: 135–43.

Dobson, J. and Fisher, P.F. 2003: GeoSlavery. *IEEE Society and Technology* 22, 47–52.

Dobson, J.E. and Fisher, P.F. 2007: The Panopticon's changing geography. *Geographical Review* 97: 307–23.

Dodds, F. and Pippard, T., eds, 2005: *Human and environmental security: an agenda for change*. London: Earthscan.

Dodds, K. 1999: Taking the Cold War to the Third World. In D. Slater and P. Taylor, eds, *The American century*. Oxford: Blackwell.

Dodge, M. and Kitchin, R. 2001a: *Atlas of cyberspace*. London: Routledge.

Dodge, M. and Kitchin, R. 2001b: *Mapping cyberspace*. London: Routledge.

Dodgshon, R.A. 1980: *The origins of British field systems: an interpretation*. London: Academic Press.

Dodgshon, R.A. 1987: *The European past: social evolution and spatial order*. London: Macmillan.

Dodgshon, R.A. 1998: *Society in time and space: a geographical perspective on change*. Cambridge, UK: Cambridge University Press.

Dodgson, J.M. 1966: The significance of the distribution of English place-names in *-ingas*, *-inga* in south-east England. *Medieval Archaeology* 10: 1–29.

Dodgson, J.M. 1973: Place-names from *ham*, distinguished from *hamm* names, in relation to the settlement of Kent, Surrey and Sussex. *Anglo-Saxon England* 11: 1–50.

Doel, M. 1992: In stalling deconstruction: striking out the postmodern. *Environment and Planning D: Society and Space* 10: 163–79.

Doel, M.A. 1999: *Poststructuralist geographies: the diabolical art of spatial science*. Edinburgh: Edinburgh University Press.

Doel, M.A. 2006: Dialectical materialism: stranger than friction. In N. Castree and D. Gregory, eds, *David Harvey: a critical reader*. Oxford: Blackwell, 55–79.

Doel, M.A. 1996: A hundred thousand lines of flight: a machinic introduction to the nomad thought and scrumpled geography of Gilles Deleuze and Félix Guattari. *Environment and Planning D: Society and Space* 14: 421–40.

Doel, M.A. and Clarke, D.B. 1998: Figuring the Holocaust: singularity and the purification of space. In G. Ó Tuathail and S. Dalby, eds, *Rethinking geopolitics*. London and New York: Routledge, 39–61.

Doel, M.A. and Segrott, J. 2004: Materialising complementary and alternative medicines: aromatherapy, chiropractic and Chinese herbal medicines in the UK. *Geoforum* 35: 727–38.

Doezema, J. and Kempadoo, K., eds, 1998: *Global sex workers: rights, resistance, and redefinition*. London: Routledge.

Domosh, M. 1991: Towards a feminist historiography of geography. *Transactions of the Institute of British Geographers*, NS 16: 95–104.

Domosh, M. 2003: Toward a more fully reciprocal feminist geography. *ACME: an International E-Journal for Critical Geographies* 2: 107–11.

Domosh, M. and Seager, J. 2001: *Putting women in place: feminist geographers make sense of the world*. New York: Guilford Press.

Donald, J. 1999: *Imagining the modern city*. London: The Athlone Press.

Donaldson, A. and Wood, D. 2004: Surveilling strange materialities: categorisation in the evolving geographies of FMD biosecurity. *Environment and Planning D: Society and Space* 22: 373–91.

Donkin, R.A. 1999: *Dragon's brain perfume: an historical geography of camphor*. Leiden: E.J. Brill.

Dorling, D. 1993: Map design for census mapping. *Cartographic Journal* 30: 167–83.

Dorling, D. 2005: Counting and measuring: happy Valentine's Day. In N. Castree, A. Rogers and D. Sherman, eds, *Questioning geography: fundamental debates*. Oxford: Blackwell, 241–57.

Dorling, D. and Fairbairn, D. 1997: *Mapping: ways of representing the world*. London: Longman.

Dorling, D. and Thomas, B. 2004: *People and places: a 2001 census atlas of the UK*. Bristol: The Policy Press.

Dorn, M. and Laws, G. 1994: Social theory, body politics and medical geography: extending Kearns's invitation. *The Professional Geographer* 46: 106–10.

Douglas, M. 1992: *Risk and blame: essays in cultural theory*. London: Routledge.

Douzinas, C. 2003: Humanity, military humanism and the new moral order. *Economy & Society* 32: 159–83.

Dow, M. 2004: *American Gulag: inside U.S. immigration prisons*. Berkeley, CA: University of California Press.

Downs, A. 1957: *An economic theory of democracy*. New York: Harper & Row.

Downs, R. and Stea, D. 1973: *Image and environment: cognitive mapping and spatial behavior*. Chicago: Aldine.

Doyle, P. and Bennett, M. 1997: Military geography: terrain evaluation and the British Western Front 1914–1. *Geographical Journal* 163: 1–24.

Doyle, R., 1997: *On beyond living: rhetorical transformation of the life sciences*. Stanford, CA: Stanford University Press.

Drache, D. 1995: Celebrating Innis: the man, the legacy, and our future. In D. Drache, ed., *Staples, markets, and cultural change: selected essays of Harold A. Innis*. Montreal and Kingston: McGill Queen's University Press, xiii–lix.

Drakakis-Smith, D. 1997: Third World cities: sustainable urban development III – basic needs and human rights. *Urban Studies* 34: 797–823.

Drescher, S. and Engerman S., eds, 1998: *A historical guide to world slavery*. Oxford: Oxford University Press.

Dreze, J. and Sen, A. 1990: *Hunger and public action*. Oxford: The Clarendon Press.

Dritsas, L. 2005: From Lake Nyassa to Philadelphia: a geography of the Zambesi expedition, 1858–64. *British Journal for the History of Science* 38: 35–52.

Driver, F. 1988: Moral geographies: social science and the urban environment in mid-nineteenth century England. *Transactions of the Institute of British Geographers* 13: 275–87.

Driver, F. 1988: The historicity of human geography. *Progress in Human Geography* 12: 397–506.

Driver, F. 1992a: Geography and power: the work of Michel Foucault. In P. Burke, ed., *Critical essays on Michel Foucault*. Aldershot: Scolar Press.

Driver, F. 1992b: Geography's empire: histories of geographical knowledge. *Environment and Planning D: Society and Space* 10: 23–40.

Driver, F. 1993: *Power and pauperism: the workhouse system 1834–1884*. Cambridge, UK: Cambridge University Press.

Driver, F. 1996: Histories of the present? The history and philosophy of geography, part III. *Progress in Human Geography* 20(1): 100–9.

Driver, F. 2000: Editorial: fieldwork in geography, *Transactions of the Institute of British Geographers* 25: 267–68.

Driver, F. 2001a: *Geography militant: cultures of exploration and empire*. Oxford: Blackwell.

Driver, F. 2001b: Hints to travellers: observation in the field. In Driver, ed., *Geography militant: cultures of exploration and empire*. Oxford: Blackwell, 49–67.

Driver, F. 2005: Imaginative geographies. In P. Cloke, P. Crang and M. Goodwin, eds, *Introducing human geographies*. London: Hodder Arnold.

Driver, F. and Gilbert, D., eds, 1999a: *Imperial cities: landscape, display and identity*. Manchester: Manchester University Press.

Driver, F. and Gilbert, D. 1999b: Imperial cities: overlapping territories, intertwined histories. In F. Driver and D. Gilbert, eds, *Imperial cities: landscape, display and identity*. Manchester: Manchester University Press, 1–17.

Driver, F. and Martins, L., eds, 2005: *Tropical visions in an age of empire*. Chicago: The University of Chicago Press.

Driver, F. and Yeoh, B., eds, 2000: Constructing the tropics. *Singapore Journal of Tropical Geography* 21: 1–98.

Driver, F., Nash, C., Prendergast, K. and Swenson, I., eds, 2002: *Landing: eight collaborative projects between artists and geographers*. Egham: Royal Holloway.

Drucker, P. 1969: *The age of discontinuity: guidelines to our changing society*. New York: Harper & Row.

Drummond, I. and Marsden, T. 1999: *The condition of sustainability*. London: Routledge.

Dryzek, J.S. 2005: Deliberative democracy in divided societies: alternatives to agonism and analgesia. *Political Theory* 33, 218–42.

Du Bois, W.E.B. 1986 [1940]: Dusk of dawn: an essay towards an autobiography of a concept. In Du Bois, *Writings*. New York: Library of America.

du Gay, P. and Pryke, M., eds, 1999: *Cultural economy: cultural analysis and commercial life.* London: Sage.

du Gay, P., Hall, S., Janes, J., McKay, H. and Negus, K., eds, 1997: *Doing cultural studies.* London: Sage.

Duany, A., Plater-Zyberk, E. and Speck, J. 2000: *Suburban nation: the rise of sprawl and the decline of the American dream.* New York: North Point Press.

Dubbini, R. 2002: *Geography of the gaze.* Chicago: The University of Chicago Press.

Dubois, L. 2004: *A colony of citizens: revolution and slave emancipation in the French Caribbean, 1787–1804.* Chapel Hill, NC: University of North Carolina Press.

Dubow, J. 2004: Outside of place and other than optical: Walter Benjamin and the geography of critical thought. *Journal of Visual Culture* 3: 259–74.

Dubow, J. 2007: Case interrupted: Sebald, Benjamin and the dialectical image. *Critical Inquiry* 33(4): 820–36.

Ducatel, K.J. and Blomley, N.K. 1990: Rethinking retail capital. *International Journal of Urban and Regional Research* 14(2): 207–27.

Dudley, O. and Duncan, B. 1955: A methodological analysis of segregation indexes. *American Sociological Review* 20: 210–17.

Dueck, D. 2000: *Strabo of Amasia: a Greek man of letters in Augustan Rome.* London: Routledge.

Duhem, P. 1962 [1906]: *The aim and structure of physical theory.* New York: Atheneum.

Duménil, G. and Lévy, D. 2004: *Capital resurgent: roots of the neoliberal revolution.* Cambridge, MA: Harvard University Press.

Dumont, L. 1977: *From Mandeville to Marx.* Chicago: The University of Chicago Press.

Dunbar, G.S., ed., 2002: *Geography: discipline, profession and subject since 1870.* Dordrecht: Kluwer.

Duncan, C. 1996: *The centrality of agriculture: between humankind and the rest of nature.* Montreal: McGill/Queen's University Press.

Duncan, J. and Rattansi, A., eds, 1992: *'Race', culture and difference.* London: Sage.

Duncan, J.S. 1980: The superorganic in American cultural geography. *Annals of the Association of American Geographers* 70: 181–98.

Duncan, J.S. 1990: *The city as text: the politics of landscape interpretation in the Kandyan kingdom.* Cambridge, UK: Cambridge University Press.

Duncan, J.S. 2002: Embodying colonialism? Domination and resistance in nineteenth-century Ceylonese coffee plantations. *Journal of Historical Geography* 28(3): 317–38.

Duncan, J.S. 2003: Representing empire at the National Maritime Museum. In R.S. Peckham, ed., *Rethinking heritage: culture and politics in Europe.* London: I.B. Tauris, 17–28.

Duncan, J.S. 2004: *The city as text: the politics of landscape interpretation in the Kandyan kingdom.* Cambridge, UK: Cambridge University Press.

Duncan, J.S. and Duncan, N.G. 1988: (Re)reading the landscape. *Environment and Planning D: Society and Space* 6: 117–26.

Duncan, J.S. and Duncan, N.G. 1992: Ideology and bliss: Roland Barthes and the secret histories of landscape. In T.J. Barnes and J.S. Duncan, eds, *Writing worlds: discourse, text and metaphor in the representation of landscape.* London: Routledge, 18–37.

Duncan, J.S. and Duncan, N.G. 1996: Reconceptualizing the idea of culture in geography: a reply to Don Mitchell. *Transactions of the Institute of British Geographers* 21(3): 576–9.

Duncan, J.S. and Duncan, N.G. 2004a: Culture unbound. *Environment and Planning A* 36: 391–403.

Duncan, J.S. and Duncan, N.G. 2004b: *Landscapes of privilege: the politics of the aesthetic in an American suburb.* New York: Routledge.

Duncan, J.S. and Gregory, D., eds, 1999: *Writes of passage: reading travel writing.* London: Routledge.

Duncan, J.S. and Lambert, D. 2004: Landscapes of home. In J.S. Duncan, N.C. Johnson and R. H. Schein, eds, *A companion to cultural geography.* Oxford: Blackwell, 382–403.

Duncan, J.S. and Ley, D. 1982: Structural Marxism and human geography. *Annals of the Association of American Geographers* 72: 30–59.

Duncan, J.S. and Ley, D., eds, 1993: *Place/culture/representation.* London: Routledge.

Duncan, J.S., Johnson, N.C. and Schein, R.H., eds, 2004: Landscapes. In J.S. Duncan, N.C. Johnson and R.H. Schein, eds, *A companion to cultural geography.* Oxford: Blackwell, 329–446.

Duncan, S. 1974: The isolation of scientific discovery: indifference and resistance to a new idea. *Science Studies* 4: 109–34.

Duncan, S. 1989: What is locality? In R. Peet and N. Thrift, eds, *New models in geography*, vol. 2. London: Unwin Hyman, 221–52.

Duncan, S. and Goodwin, M. 1988: *The local state and uneven development.* Cambridge, UK: Polity Press.

Duncan, S. and Smith, D.P. 2002: Geographies of partnering and parenting in Britain. *Transactions of the Institute of British Geographers* 27: 471–93.

Dunn, E. 2003a: Trojan pig: paradoxes of food safety regulation. *Environment and Planning A* 35(8): 1493–511.

Dunn, J. 2005a: *Setting the people free: the story of democracy.* London: Atlantic Books.

Dunn, K.M. 2003b: Using cultural geography to engage contested constructions of ethnicity and citizenship in Sydney. *Social and Cultural Geography* 4: 153–65.

Dunn, K.M. 2005b: Repetitive and troubling discourses of nationalism in the local politics of mosque development in Sydney, Australia. *Environment and Planning D: Society and Space* 23(1): 29–50.

Dunning, J. and Norman, G. 1987: Theory of multinational enterprise. *Environment and Planning A* 15: 675–92.

Dunning, J.H. 2000: *Regions, globalization and the knowledge-based economy.* Oxford: Oxford University Press.

Dunning, J.H. 2002a: *Global capitalism, FDI and competitiveness.* Cheltenham, UK: Edward Elgar.

Dunning, J.H. 2002b: *Theories and paradigms of international business activity.* Cheltenham, UK: Edward Elgar.

Dunning, T. 2008: Improving causal inference: strengths and limitations of natural experiments. *Political Research Quarterly* 61: 282–93.

Dupré, J. 1993: *The disorder of things: metaphysical foundations of the disunity of science.* Cambridge, MA: Harvard University Press.

Durand, M.-F., Lévy, J. and Retaillé, D. 1992: *Le monde: espaces et systèmes.* Paris: Presses de la Fondation Nationale des Sciences Politiques and Dalloz.

During, S. 1992: Postcolonialism and globalization. *Meanjin* 51: 339–53.

Dutfield, G. 2004: *Intellectual property, biogenetic resources and traditional knowledge.* London: Earthscan.

Dutton, G. 1999: Scale, sinuosity, and point selection in digital line generalization. *Cartography and Geographic Information Systems* 26: 33–53.

Dyck, I. 1990: Space, time and renegotiating motherhood: an exploration of domestic workplace. *Environment and Planning D: Society and Space* 8: 459–83.

Dyck, I. 1995: Hidden geographies: the changing lifeworlds of women with multiple sclerosis. *Social Science and Medicine* 40: 307–20.

Dyer, C. 1993: *Standards of living in the later middle ages: social change in England, c.1200–1520,* 2nd edn. Cambridge, UK: Cambridge University Press.

Dyer, R. 1997: *White.* London: Routledge.

Dymski, G. 2005: Financial globalization, social exclusion and financial crisis. *International Review of Applied Economics* 19(4): 439–57.

Dymski, G.A. 1999: *The bank merger wave: the economic causes and social consequences of financial consolidation.* Armonk, NY: M.E. Sharpe.

Eagleton, T. 1983: *Literary theory: an introduction.* Oxford: Blackwell/Minneapolis: University of Minnesota Press.

Eagleton, T. 1991: *Ideology: an introduction.* London: Verso.

Earle, C. 2003: *The American way: a geographical history of crisis and recovery.* Lanham, MD: Rowman & Littlefield.

Eckler, A.R. 1972: *The Bureau of the Census.* New York: Praeger.

Economist, The 2006: Winds of change. *The Economist,* 2 November.

Ecumene (journal of cultural geography) 1991–2004: London: Hodder and Stoughton.

Edelson, S.M. 2006: *Plantation enterprise in colonial South Carolina.* Cambridge, MA: Harvard University Press.

Edensor, T. 2005: *Industrial ruins: aesthetics, materiality and memory.* Oxford: Berg.

Edkins, J. 2000: Sovereign power, zones of indistinction and the camp. *Alternatives* 25: 3–25.

Edkins, J. 2003: *Trauma and the memory of politics.* Cambridge, UK: Cambridge University Press.

Edney, M.H. 1993: Cartography without 'progress': reinterpreting the nature and historical development of mapmaking. *Cartographica* 30: 54–68.

Edney, M.H. 1997: *Mapping an empire: the geographical construction of British India, 1765–1843.* Chicago: The University of Chicago Press.

Edney, M.H. 2005a: *The origins and development of J.B. Harley's cartographic theories.* Cartographica Monograph 54. *Cartographica* 40(1/2). Toronto: University of Toronto Press.

Edney, M.H. 2005b: Putting 'cartography' into the history of cartography: Arthur H. Robinson, David Woodward, and the creation of a discipline. *Cartographic Perspectives* no. 51: 14–29.

Edney, M.H. 2006: *Recent trends in the history of cartography: a bibliographical guide,* 3rd edn. *Coordinates* (journal of the Map and Geography Round Table of the American Library Association) Series B, no. 6, at http://www.sunysb.edu/libmap/coordinates/seriesb/no6/b6.pdf

Edwards, J. 2003: How to read an early modern map: between the particular and the general, the material and the abstract, words and mathematics. *Early Modern Literary Studies* (http://purl.oclc.org/emls/09–1/edwamaps.html) 9(1): 6.1–58.

Edwards, M. 2004: *Civil society.* Cambridge, UK: Polity Press.

Edwards, T. 2005: Information geopolitics: blurring the lines of sovereignty. In H. Nicol and I. Townsend-Gault, eds, *Holding the line: borders in a global world.* Vancouver: University of British Columbia Press, 26–49.

Ehlen, J., Caldwell, D.R. and Harding, S. 2002: GeoComputation: what is it? *Computers, Environment and Urban Systems* 26: 257–65.

Eichler, M. 1988: *Nonsexist research methods: a practical guide.* Winchester, MA: Unwin Hyman.

Eisenstadt, N. and Witcher, S. 1998: Social exclusion and poverty. *Outlook: The Quarterly Journal of the National Council of Voluntary Child Organisations* 1: 6–7.

Eisenstein, Z. 1981: *The radical future of liberal feminism*. New York: Longman.

Ek, R. 2000: A revolution in military geopolitics? *Political Geography* 19: 841–74.

El Fisgón, R.B.D. 2004: *How to succeed at globalization: a primer for the roadside vendor*, trans. M. Fried. New York: Metropolitan Books.

Elden, S. 2001: *Mapping the present: Heidegger, Foucault and the project of a spatial history*. London: Continuum.

Elden, S. 2002: The war of the races and the constitution of the state: Foucault's *Il faut défendre la societé. boundary 2*, 29: 125–51.

Elden, S. 2004: *Understanding Henri Lefebvre: theory and the possible*. London: Continuum.

Elden, S. 2005: Territorial integrity and the war on terror. *Environment and Planning A* 37(12): 2083–104.

Elden, S. 2006: Contingent sovereignty, territorial integrity and the sanctity of borders. *SAIS Review* 26: 11–24.

Elden, S. 2007a: Blair, neo-conservatism, and the war on territorial integrity. *International Politics* 44: 37–51.

Elden, S. 2007b: Governmentality, calculation, territory. *Environment and Planning D: Society and Space* 25: 562–80.

Elden, S. 2007c: Terror and territory. *Antipode* 39: 821–45.

Elden, S. and Bialasiewicz, L. 2006: The new geopolitics of division and the problem of a Kantian Europe. *Review of International Studies* 32: 623–44.

Eliade, M. 1959: *The sacred and the profane: the nature of religion*, trans. W.R. Trask. San Diego: Harcourt Brace Jovanovich.

Elins, P. 2000: *Economic growth and environmental sustainability: the prospects for green growth*. London: Routledge.

Elkins, J. 2002: *Visual studies: a skeptical introduction*. New York: Routledge.

Ellaway, A., Macintyre, S. and Kearns, A. 2001: Perceptions of place and health in socially contrasting neighbourhoods. *Urban Studies* 14: 2299–316.

Elliott, J.H. 1972: The discovery of America and the discovery of man. *Proceedings of the British Academy* LVIII: 101–25.

Elliott, P. and Wartenburg, D. 2004: Spatial epidemiology: current approaches and future challenges. *Environmental Health Perspectives* 112: 998–1006.

Ellis, F. and Harris, N. 2004: *New thinking about rural and urban development*. Mimeo, paper prepared for DFID, UK (see also a commentary, online at www.new-agri.co.uk/04–5/develop/dev01.html).

Ellis, M. and Wright, R. 1998: The Balkanization metaphor in the analysis of US immigration. *Annals of the Association of American Geographers* 88: 686–98.

Eloundou-Enyegue, P.M. 2004: Pregnancy-related dropouts and gender inequality in education: a life table approach and application to Cameroon. *Demography* 41: 509–29.

Elson, D. 1979: The value theory of labour. In D. Elson, ed., *Value*. London: New Left Books, 115–80.

Elson, M.J. 1986: *Green belts*. London: Heinemann.

Elster, J. 1982a: *An introduction to Karl Marx*. Cambridge, UK: Cambridge University Press.

Elster, J. 1982b: The case for methodological individualism. *Theory and Society* 11: 453–82.

Elster, J., ed., 1986: *Karl Marx: a reader*. Cambridge, UK: Cambridge University Press.

Elwood, S. and Leitner, H. 2003: GIS and spatial knowledge production for neighborhood revitalization: negotiating state priorities and neighborhood visions. *Journal of Urban Affairs* 25(2): 139–57.

Elyachar, J. 2005: *Markets of dispossession*. Durham, NC: Duke University Press.

Emel, J. and Peet, R. 1989: Resource management and natural hazards. In R. Peet and N. Thrift, eds, *New models in geography: the political-economy perspective*, vol. 1. London: Unwin Hyman, 49–76.

Emel, J. and Wolch, J., eds, 1998: *Animal geographies: place, politics and identity in the nature–culture borderlands*. London: Verso.

Emel, J., Bridge, G. and Krueger, R. 2002: The Earth as input: resources. In R.J. Johnston, P.J. Taylor and M. Watts, eds, *Geographies of global change: remapping the world*. Oxford: Blackwell, 377–90.

Emerson, F.V. 1909: *Manual of physical geography*. New York: Macmillan.

Enders, W. and Sandler, T. 2006: Distribution of transnational terrorism among countries by income class and geography after 9/11. *International Studies Quarterly* 50: 367–93.

Endfield, G.H. and Nash, D.J. 2002: Drought, desiccation and discourse: missionary correspondence and nineteenth-century climate change in central southern Africa. *The Geographical Journal* 168: 33–47.

Engardio, P. 2006: The future of outsourcing: how it's transforming whole industries and changing the way we work. *Business Week* 3969: 50–53.

Engels, F. 1978 [1884]: Preface. In K. Marx, *Capital*, vol. 2. London: Penguin, 83–102.

Engels, F. 1987 [1845]: *The condition of the working class in England*. London: Penguin.

England, K. 1993: Suburban pink collar ghettos: the spatial entrapment of women? *Annals of the Association of American Geographers* 83: 225–42.

England, K. 1994: Getting personal: reflexivity, positionality and feminist research. *Professional Geographer* 46: 80–9.

England, K. 2002: Interviewing elites: cautionary tales about researching women managers in Canada's banking industry. In P. Moss, ed., *Feminist geography in practice: research and methods*. Oxford: Blackwell, 200–13.

England, K. and Lawson, V. 2005: Feminist analyses of work: rethinking the boundaries, gendering, and spatiality of work. In L. Nelson and J. Seager, eds, *A companion to feminist geography*. Oxford: Blackwell, 77–92.

Enslin, E. 1994: Feminist practice and the limitations of ethnography. *Cultural Anthropology* 9: 537–68.

Entrikin, J.N. 1976: Contemporary humanism in geography. *Annals of the Association of American Geographers* 66(4): 615–32.

Entrikin, J.N. 1977: Geography's spatial perspective and the philosophy of Ernst Cassirer. *Canadian Geographer* 21: 209–22.

Entrikin, J.N. 1980: Robert Park's human ecology and human geography. *Annals of the Association of American Geographers* 70(1): 43–58.

Entrikin, J.N. 1981: Philosophic issues in the scientific studies of regions. In D.T. Herbert and R.J. Johnston, eds, *Geography and the urban environment: progress in research and applications*, vol. 4. Chichester: Wiley, 1–27.

Entrikin, J.N. 1991: *The betweenness of place: towards a geography of modernity*. London: Macmillan/Baltimore, MD: The Johns Hopkins University Press.

Entrikin, J.N. and Brunn, S.D., eds, 1989: *Reflections on Richard Hartshorne's* The nature of geography. Washington, DC: Association of American Geographers.

Environment and Planning A 1991: Special issue on 'New perspectives on the locality debate'. *Environment and Planning A* 23: 155–308.

Epstein, K. 2006: The new global slave trade. *Foreign Affairs* 85(6): 103–15.

Erb, S. and Harriss-White, B. 2002: *Outcast from social welfare: adult disability, incapacity and development in rural south India*. Bangalore: Books for Change.

Ermarth, E. Deeds 1992: *Sequel to history: postmodernism and the crisis of representational time*. Princeton, NJ: Princeton University Press.

Escobar, A. 1995: *Encountering development: the making and unmaking of the Third World*. Princeton, NJ: Princeton University Press.

Eskelinen, H., Liikanen, I. and Oksa, J. 1999: *Curtains of iron and gold: reconstructing borders and scales of interaction*. Aldershot: Ashgate.

Esposito, R. 2006: *Bios: biopolitics and philosophy*, trans. T. Campbell. Minneapolis: University of Minnesota Press.

Essed, P. and Goldberg, D.T. 2002: *Race critical theories: text and context*. Malden, MA: Blackwell.

Esteva, G. and Prakash, M.S. 1998: *Grassroots post-modernism: remaking the soil of cultures*. London and New York: Zed Books.

Ettlinger, N. and Bosco, F. 2004: Thinking through networks and their spatiality: a critique of the US (public) War on Terrorism and its geographic discourse. *Antipode* 36: 249–71.

Etzioni, A. 1993: *The spirit of community: rights, responsibilities, and the communitarian agenda*. New York: Crown.

Etzioni, A. 1994: *The spirit of the community*. London: Simon and Schuster.

EU Committee of the Regions 2003: *The process of decentralization in the European Union and the candidate countries*. Brussels: Committee of the Regions; www.cor.europa.eu/document/documents/decentralisationEN.pdf (updated 2005).

Evans, E.E. 1960: The peasant and the past. *Advancement of Science* 17: 293–302.

Evans, I.S. 1977: The selection of class intervals. *Transactions of the Institute of British Geographers*, NS 2: 98–124.

Evans, J. and Hall, S., eds, 1998: *Visual culture: the reader*. London: Routledge.

Evans, J.R. and Vickers, W.E. 1995: Map production using print-on-demand capabilities. *US Geological Survey Open File Report* 95–0653.

Evans, P. 1979: *Dependent development: the alliance of multinational, state, and local capital in Brazil*. Princeton, NJ: Princeton University Press.

Evans, P. 2004: Development as institutional change: the pitfalls of monocropping and potentials of deliberation. *Studies in Comparative International Development* 38: 30–53.

Evans, T. 2003: The PRC's relationship with the ASEAN Regional Forum: *Realpolitik*, regime theory or a continuation of the sinic zone of influence system? *Modern Asian Studies* 37: 737–63.

Evenden, M. 2004: Locating science, locating salmon: institutions, linkages, and spatial practices in early British Columbia fisheries science. *Environment and Planning D: Society and Space* 22, 355–72.

Evenden, M. and Wynn, G. 2009: *54:40 or fight*: writing within and across borders in North American environmental history. In S. Sorlin and P. Warde, eds, *Nature's end: history and the environment*. London: Palgrave Macmillan.

Everitt, A. 1986: *Continuity and colonization: the evolution of Kentish settlement*. Leicester: Leicester University Press.

Eyles, J. and Woods, K. 1983: *The social geography of medicine and health*. London: Croom Helm.

Eyles, J., ed., 1986: *Social geography in international perspective*. London: Croom Helm.

Faber, D., ed., 1998: *The struggle for ecological democracy*. New York: Guilford Press.

Fagan, J. 2004: Crime, law and the community: dynamics of incarceration in New York City.

In M. Tonry, ed., *The future of imprisonment.* Oxford: Oxford University Press, 27–59.

Fairchild, J. and Leach, M. 1998: *Reframing deforestation.* London: Routledge.

Fairclough, N. 2001: *Language and power,* 2nd edn. London: Longman.

Fairclough, N. 2003: *Analysing discourse: textual analysis for social research.* London: Routledge.

Falah, G. 1996: The 1948 Israeli–Palestinian War and its aftermath: the transformation and de-signification of Palestine's cultural landscape. *Annals of the Association of American Geographers* 86: 256–85.

Falah, G. and Newman, D. 1995: The spatial manifestation of threat: Israelis and Palestinians seek a 'good' border. *Political Geography* 14(8): 689–706.

Falah, G.-W., Flint, C. and Mamadouh, V. 2006: Just war and extra-territoriality: the popular geopolitics of the United States' war on Iraq as reflected in newspapers of the Arab World. *Annals of the Association of American Geographers* 96: 142–64.

Falk, T. and Abler, R. 1980: Intercommunications, distance and geographical theory. *Geografiska Annaler* 62B: 59–67.

Fall, J. 2005: *Drawing the line: nature, hybridity, and politics in transboundary spaces.* Burlington, VT: Ashgate.

Fanon, F. 1963 [1961]: *The wretched of the Earth,* trans. C. Farrington. New York: Grove Press.

Fanon, F. 1967 [1961]: *The wretched of the Earth.* London: Penguin.

Fanon, F. 1967 [1952]: *Black skin, white masks,* trans. C.L. Markmann. New York: Grove Press.

FAO 1996: *Sixth world food survey.* Rome: Food and Agriculture Organization of the United Nations.

FAO 2006: *The state of food insecurity in the world 2006.* Rome: Food and Agriculture Organization of the United Nations.

Fara, P. 2005: Mapping magnetism. In Fara, *Fatal attraction: magnetic mysteries of the Enlightenment.* Cambridge: Icon Books, ch. 4.

Farinelli, F. 2000: Friedrich Ratzel and the nature of (political) geography. *Political Geography* 19: 943–55.

Farinelli, F., Olsson, G. and Reichert, D., eds, 1996: *Limits of representation.* Munich: Accedo.

Farish, M. 2001: Modest witnesses: foreign correspondents, geopolitical vision and the First World War. *Transactions of the Institute of British Geographers* 26: 273–87.

Farish, M. 2005: Cities in shade: urban geography and the uses of noir. *Environment and Planning D: Society and Space* 23(1): 95–118.

Farmer, P. 1992: *AIDS and accusation: Haiti and the geography of blame.* Berkeley, CA: University of California Press.

Farmer, P. 2006: *The uses of Haiti.* Monroe, ME: Common Courage Press.

Farrow, H., Moss, P. and Shaw, B. 1995: Symposium on feminist participatory research. *Antipode* 27(1): 71–101.

Fawcett, C. 1918: *Frontiers: a study in political geography.* Oxford: The Clarendon Press.

Fawcett, L. and Sayigh, J., eds, 2005: *The Third World beyond the Cold War: continuity and change.* Oxford: Oxford University Press.

Fay, B. 1987: *Critical social science: liberation and its limits.* Ithaca, NY: Cornell University Press.

Featherstone, D. 2003: Spatialities of transnational resistance to globalization: the maps of grievance of the Inter-Continental Caravan. *Transactions of the Institute of British Geographers* 28(4): 404–21.

Featherstone, D. 2005a: Atlantic networks, antagonisms and the formation of subaltern political identities. *Social and Cultural Geography* 6: 387–404.

Featherstone, D. 2005b: Towards the relational construction of militant particularisms: or why the geographies of past struggles matter for resistance to neoliberal globalisation. *Antipode* 37: 250–71.

Featherstone, M. 1995: *Undoing culture: globalization, postmoderism and identity,* Thousand Oaks, CA: Sage.

Featherstone, M. and Burrows, R. 1997: *Cyberspace/cyberbodies/cyberpunk: cultures of technological embodiment.* London: Sage, 135–55.

Febvre, L. 1932: *A geographical introduction to history.* London: Kegan Paul, Trench, Trübner (originally published in 1922 as *La terre et l'évolution humaine*).

Febvre, L. and Martin, H.J. 1984 [1958]: *The coming of the book: the impact of printing, 1450–1800.* London: Verso.

Feeny, D., Berkes, F., McCay, B. and Acheson, J. 1990: The tragedy of the commons – 22 years later. *Human Ecology* 18(1): 1–19.

Feld, S. and Basso, K., eds, 1998: *Senses of place.* Washington, DC: University of Washington Press.

Feldman, T.S. 1990: Late enlightenment meteorology. In T. Frängsmyr, J.L. Heilbron and R.E. Rider, eds, *The quantifying spirit in the eighteenth century.* Berkeley, CA: University of California Press, 143–78.

Feldmann, M.P. 2000: Location and innovation: the new economic geography of innovation spillovers and agglomeration. In G.L. Clark, M.P. Feldman, M.S. Gertler and K. Williams, eds, *The Oxford handbook of economic geography.* Oxford: Oxford University Press, 373–94.

Fellmann, J.D. 1986: Myth and reality in the origin of American economic geography. *Annals of the Association of American Geographers* 76: 313–30.

Fellows-Jensen, G. 1975: The Vikings in England: a review. *Anglo-Saxon England* 4: 181–206.

Fennell, R. 1997: *The Common Agricultural Policy*. Oxford: Oxford University Press.

Fenneman, N.M. 1919: The circumference of geography. *Annals of the Association of American Geographers* 9: 3–11.

Ferguson, A. 1995 [1767]: *An essay on the history of civil society*, ed. F. Oz-Salzberger. Cambridge, UK: Cambridge University Press.

Ferguson, J. 1990: *The anti-politics machine: 'development', depoliticisation and bureaucratic power in Lesotho*. Cambridge, UK: Cambridge University Press.

Ferguson, J. 2006: *Global shadows: Africa in the neoliberal world order*. Durham, NC: Duke University Press.

Ferguson, N. 1998: *The pity of war: explaining World War I*. New York: Basic Books.

Ferguson, N., ed., 1999: *Virtual history: alternatives and counterfactuals*. London: Papermac.

Ferguson, N. 2004: *Colossus: the rise and fall of the American empire*. London: Penguin.

Ferguson, P.P. 1994: The *flâneur* on and off the streets of Paris. In K. Tester, ed., *The* flâneur. London: Routledge, 22–42.

Fernandez-Armesto, F. 2006: *Pathfinders: a global history of exploration*. New York: W.W. Norton.

Fernandez-Kelly, M.P. 1994: Towanda's triumph: social and cultural capital in the transition to adulthood in the urban ghetto. *International Journal of Urban and Regional Research* 18: 88–111.

Fincher, R. 1987: Defining and explaining urban social movements. *Urban Geography* 8: 152–60.

Fincher, R. 2004: From dualisms to multiplicities: gendered political practices. In L.A. Staeheli, E. Kofman and L.J. Peake, eds, *Mapping women, making politics*. New York: Routledge, 49–69.

Fincher, R. and Jacobs, J.M., eds, 1998: *Cities of difference*. New York: Guilford Press.

Findlay, A.M. 2004: Population geographies for the 21st century. *Scottish Geographical Journal* 119: 177–90.

Fine, B. and Leopold, E. 1993: *The world of consumption*. New York: Routledge.

Fine, B., Heasman, M. and Wright, J. 1996: *Consumption in the age of affluence: the world of food*. New York: Routledge.

Finkelstein, N. 2000: *The Holocaust industry: reflections on the exploitation of Jewish suffering*. London: Verso.

Finnegan, D. 2004: The work of ice: glacial theory and scientific culture in early Victorian Edinburgh. *British Journal for the History of Science* 37: 29–52.

Fiorani, F. 2005: *The marvel of map: art, cartography and politics in Renaissance Italy*. New Haven, CT: Yale University Press.

Fireside, D. and Miller, J. 2005: *Real world macro: a macroeconomics reader from dollars and sense*. Boston: Capital City Press.

Firey, W. 1947: *Land use in central Boston*. Cambridge, MA: Harvard University Press.

Fish, S. 1995: Rhetoric. In F. Lentricchia and T. McLaughlin, eds, *Critical terms for literary study*, 2nd edn. Chicago: The University of Chicago Press, 203–22.

Fisher, W.F. and Ponniah, T., eds, 2003: *Another world is possible*. London: Zed Books.

Fishman, R. 2005: The fifth migration. *Journal of the American Planning Association* 71(4): 357–66.

Fitzmaurice, G., Laird, N. and Ware, J. 2004: *Applied longitudinal analysis*. New York: Wiley, http://biosun1.harvard.edu/~fitzmaur/ala/

Fitzpatrick, P. 2005: Bare sovereignty: *homo sacer* and the insistence of law. In A. Norris, ed., *Politics, metaphysics and death: essays on Giorgio Agamben's* homo sacer. Durham, NC: Duke University Press, 49–73.

Fitzsimmons, M. 1989: The matter of nature. *Antipode* 21(2): 106–20.

Flake, W.G. 2001: *The computational beauty of nature: computer explorations of fractals, chaos, complex systems and adaptation*. Cambridge, MA: The MIT Press.

Fleming, J.R. 1998: *Historical perspectives on climate change*. New York: Oxford University Press.

Fleure, H.J. 1951: *A natural history of man in Britain, conceived as a study of changing relations between men and environments*. London: Collins.

Fleury, M. and Henry, L. 1965: *Nouveau manuel de dépouillement et d'exploitation de l'état civil ancien*. Paris: Institut National d'Etudes Démographiques.

Flint, C. 1999: Changing times, changing scales: world politics and political geography since 1890. In G.J. Demko and W.B. Wood, eds, *Reordering the world: geopolitical perspectives on the 21st century*, 2nd edn. Boulder, CO: Westview Press.

Flint, C. 2001: A TimeSpace for electoral geography: economic restructuring, political agency and the rise of the Nazi party. *Political Geography* 20: 301–29.

Flint, C. 2003a: Dying for a 'P'? Some questions facing contemporary political geography. *Political Geography* 22: 617–20.

Flint, C. 2003b: Terrorism and counter-terrorism: geographic research questions and agendas. *Professional Geographer* 55, 161–9.

Flint, C. 2004: *Spaces of hate: geographies of discrimination and intolerance in the U.S.A.* New York: Routledge.

Flint, C., ed., 2005: *The geography of war and peace: from death camps to diplomats*. Oxford: Oxford University Press.

Flint, C. and Falah, G.-W. 2004: How the United States justified its war on terrorism: prime morality and the construction of a 'just war'. *Third World Quarterly* 25: 1379–99.

Flint, C. and Shelley, F.M. 1996: Structure, agency and context: the contributions of geography to world-systems analysis. *Sociological Inquiry* 66: 494–508.

Flint, C. and Taylor, P. 2007 [1985]: *Political geography: world economy, nation-state and locality*, 5th edn. New York: Prentice Hall.

Flitner, M. 2003: Genetic geographies: a historical comparison of agrarian modernization and eugenic thought in Germany, the Soviet Union, and the United States. *Geoforum* 34: 175–86.

Florida, R. 2002: *The rise of the creative class: and how it's transforming work, leisure, community and everyday life*. New York: Basic Books.

Flusty, S. 2003: *De-Coca-Colonization*. New York: Routledge.

Folbre, N. 1986: Hearts and spades: paradigms of household economics. *World Development* 14(2): 245–55.

Folch-Serra, M. 1990: Place, voice, space: Mikhail Bakhtin's dialogical landscape. *Environment and Planning D: Society and Space* 8: 255–74.

Fold, N. and Pritchard, B., eds, 2005: *Cross-continental food chains*. London: Routledge.

Foody, G. 1996: Approaches for the production and evaluation of fuzzy land cover classifications from remotely-sensed data. *International Journal of Remote Sensing* 17: 1317–40.

Foord, J. and Gregson, N. 1986: Patriarchy: towards a reconceptualisation. *Antipode* 18(2): 186–211.

Foote, K. 2003: *Shadowed ground: America's landscapes of violence and tragedy*, 2nd edn. Austin: University of Texas Press.

Forbes, D.K. 2005: Asia. In *Microsoft Encarta online encyclopedia*: http://encarta.msn.com

Forbes, S.A. 1887: The lake as microcosm. *Bulletin of the Peoria Scientific Association* 1887: 77–87.

Ford, R.T. 1999: Law's territory (a history of jurisdiction). *Michigan Law Review* 97(4): 843–930.

Forer, P. 1974: Space through time. In E.L. Cripps, ed., *Space–time concepts in urban and regional models*. London: Pion, 22–45.

Forer, P. 1978: A place for plastic space? *Progress in Human Geography* 2: 230–67.

Foresman, T., ed., 1998: *The history of geographic information systems: perspectives from the pioneers*. Upper Saddle River, NJ: Prentice Hall.

Forest, B. 2001: Mapping democracy: racial identity and the quandary of political representation *Annals of the Association of American Geographers* 91(1): 143–66.

Forest, B. 2005: The changing demographic, legal and technological contexts of political representation. *Proceedings of the National Academy of Sciences* 102(43): 15331–6.

Forman, G. and Kedar, A. 2004: From Arab land to 'Israel lands': the legal dispossession of the Palestinians displaced by Israel in the wake of 1948. *Environment and Planning, A: Society and Space* 22: 809–30.

Forrest, D. and Kinninment, E. 2001: Experiments in the design of 1 : 100 000 scale topographic mapping for Great Britain. *Cartographic Journal* 38: 25–40.

Forsyth, T. 2003: *Critical political ecology: the politics of environmental science*. London: Routledge.

Fortun, K. 2001: *Advocacy after Bhopal: environmentalism, disaster, new global orders*. Chicago: The University of Chicago Press.

Fossett, M. 2006: Ethnic preferences, social distance dynamics and residential segregation: theoretical explorations using simulation analysis. *Journal of Mathematical Sociology* 20: 185–273.

Foster, J. 2000: *Marx's ecology*. New York: Monthly Review Press.

Foster, J.B. 2006: The new geopolitics of empire. *Monthly Review* 57(8): 1–18.

Foster, J.B. and McChesney, R.W. 2004: The American empire: *Pax Americana* or *Pox Americana*? *Monthly Review* 56(4): accessed at http://www.monthlyreview.org/0904jbfrwm.htm

Fotheringham, A.S. 1983: A new set of spatial interaction models: the theory of competing destinations. *Environment and Planning A*, 15: 15–36.

Fotheringham, A.S. 2006: Quantification, evidence and positivism. In S. Aitken and G. Valentine, eds, *Approaches to human geography*. London: Sage, 237–50.

Fotheringham, A.S. and O'Kelly, M.E. 1989: *Spatial interaction models: formulations and applications*. Dordrecht: Kluwer.

Fotheringham, A.S., Brunsdon, C. and Charlton, M. 2000: *Quantitative geography: perspectives on spatial data analysis*. London: Sage.

Fotheringham, A.S., Brunsdon, C. and Charlton, M.E. 2002: *Geographically weighted regression: the analysis of spatially varying relationships*. Chichester: Wiley.

Foucault, M. 1970 [1966]: *The order of things: an archaeology of the human sciences*, trans. A. Sheridan. London: Tavistock/New York: Random House.

Foucault, M. 1972a [1966]: *The order of things*. New York: Random House.

Foucault, M. 1972b [1969]: *The archaeology of knowledge*, trans. A. Sheridan. London: Tavistock/New York: Barnes & Noble.

Foucault, M. 1976a [1975]: *Discipline and punish: the birth of the prison*, trans. A. Sheridan. London: Tavistock.

Foucault, M. 1976b: Questions à Michel Foucault sur la géographie. *Hérodote* 1:

71–85. Translated as Foucault, M. 1980: Questions on geography. In *Power/knowledge*, ed. C. Gordon. Brighton: Harvester, 63–77.

Foucault, M. 1977a [1975]: *Discipline and punish*. London: Penguin (also New York: Pantheon, 1978).

Foucault, M. 1977b [1963]: Preface to transgression. In Foucault, *Language, counter-memory, practice*, ed. D. Bouchard. Ithaca, NY: Cornell University Press.

Foucault, M. 1977c [1963]: Nietzsche, genealogy, history. In Foucault, *Language, counter-memory, practice*, ed. D. Bouchard. Ithaca, NY: Cornell University Press.

Foucault, M. 1978 [1976]: *The history of sexuality*, vol. 1: *An introduction*, trans. R. Hurley. London: Penguin/New York: Random House.

Foucault, M. 1980a [1976]: *The history of sexuality*, vol. 1. New York: Vintage.

Foucault, M. 1980b: *Power/knowledge: selected interviews and other writings, 1972–1977*, ed. C. Gordon. New York: Pantheon.

Foucault, M. 1980c: The confession of the flesh. In *Power/knowledge: selected interviews and other writings, 1972–1977*, ed. C. Gordon. Brighton: Harvester Wheatsheaf.

Foucault, M. 1980d: The eye of power. In *Power/knowledge: selected interviews and other writings, 1972–1977*, ed. C. Gordon. Brighton: Harvester Wheatsheaf.

Foucault, M. 1981a [1976]: *The history of sexuality*, vol. 1. London: Penguin.

Foucault, M. 1981b [1971]: The order of discourse, trans. I. McLeod, In R. Young, ed., 1981: *Untying the text: a poststructuralist reader*. London: Routledge, 48–78.

Foucault, M. 1983: *This is not a pipe*, trans. J. Harkess. Berkeley, CA: University of California Press.

Foucault, M. 1986 [1984]: Of other spaces. *Diacritics* 16(1): 22–7. Also available in *Power*, ed. J. Faubion. *Essential works of Foucault 1954–1984*, vol. 3, series ed. P. Rabinow. New York: New Press, 2000; London: Allen Lane, 2001.

Foucault, M. 1988: Politics and reason. In *Politics, philosophy, culture: interview and other writings*, ed. L. Kritzman. New York: Routledge, 57–85.

Foucault, M. 1990 [1976]: *The history of sexuality*, vol. 1: *An introduction*, trans. R. Hurley. New York: Vintage.

Foucault, M. 1991: Governmentality. In G. Burchell, C. Gordon and P. Miller, eds, *The Foucault effect: studies in governmentality*. Chicago: The University of Chicago Press, 87–104.

Foucault, M. 1995 [1975]: *Discipline and punish*. New York: Vintage.

Foucault, M. 2001: *Power: essential works of Foucault*, vol. 3. New York: New Press.

Foucault, M. 2003 [1997]: *'Society must be defended': lectures at the Collège de France 1975–76*, trans. D. Macey. London: Allen Lane/New York: Picador.

Foucault, M. 2003 [1999]: *Abnormal: lectures at the Collège de France 1975–75*, trans. G. Burchell. London: Verso.

Foucault, M. 2006 [2003]: *Psychiatric power: lectures at the Collège de France 1973–1974*, trans. C. Burchell. London: Palgrave Macmillan.

Foucault, M. 2007 [2004]: *Security, territory, population: lectures at the Collège de France 1977–1978*, trans. G. Burchell. London: Palgrave Macmillan.

Foucault, M. 2008 [2004]: *Birth of biopolitics: lectures at the Collège de France 1978–1979*, trans. G. Burchell. London: Palgrave Macmillan.

Fowler, C.S. 2007: Taking geographical economics out of equilibrium: implications for theory and policy. *Journal of Economic Geography* 7: 265–84.

Fox, J. 1995: Government and rural development in rural Mexico. *Journal of Development Studies* 29: 610–44.

Fox-Genovese, E. 1986: The claims of a common culture: gender, race, class and the canon. *Salmagundi* 72: 119–32.

Frampton, K. 1992: *Modern architecture: a critical history*. London: Thames & Hudson.

Frank, A.G. 1966: The development of underdevelopment. *Monthly Review* (September): 27–37.

Frank, A.G. 1967: *Capitalism and underdevelopment in Latin America: historical studies of Chile and Brazil*. New York: Monthly Review Press.

Fraser, N. 1989: *Unruly practices: power, discourse and gender in contemporary social theory*. Minneapolis: University of Minnesota Press.

Fraser, N. 1997: *Justice interruptus: critical reflections on the 'postsocialist' condition*. New York: Routledge.

Fraser, N. 2000: Rethinking recognition: overcoming displacements and reification in cultural politics. *New Left Review* 3: 107–20.

Fraser, N. and Honneth, A. 2003: *Redistribution or recognition? A political–philosophical exchange*. London: Verso.

Frazier, E.F. 1937: Negro Harlem: an ecological study. *American Journal of Sociology* 43: 72–88.

Fredrickson, G.M. 2002: *Racism: a short history*. Princeton, NJ: Princeton University Press.

Freeman, C. 2001: Is local: global as feminine: masculine? Rethinking the gender of globalization. *Signs* 26(4): 1007–23.

Fregoso, R.L. 2003: *MeXicana encounters: the making of social identities on the Borderlands*. Berkeley, CA: University of California Press.

Freidberg, S. 2004: *French beans and food scares: culture and commerce in an anxious age*. Oxford: Oxford University Press.

Frey, W.H. 1996: Immigration, domestic migration, and demographic balkanization in America: new evidence for the 1990s. *Population and Development Review* 22: 741–63.

Freidberg, S. 2004: The ethical complex of corporate food power. *Environment and Planning D: Society and Space* 22: 513–31.

Friedheim, R.L. 1993: *Negotiating the new ocean regime*. Columbia, SC: University of South Carolina Press.

Friedland, W., Barton, A. and Thomas, R. 1981: *Manufacturing green gold*. Cambridge, UK: Cambridge University Press.

Friedlander, S., ed., 1992: *Probing the limits of representation: Nazism and the 'Final Solution'*. Cambridge, MA: Harvard University Press.

Friedlander, S. 1997: *Nazi Germany and the Jews*, vol. 1: *The years of persecution, 1933–1939*. New York: Harper.

Friedlander, S. 2007: *Nazi Germany and the Jews*, vol. 2: *The years of extermination, 1939–1945*. New York: Harper.

Friedman, M. 2002 [1962]: *Capitalism and freedom*, special 40th anniversary edition. Chicago: The University of Chicago Press.

Friedman, M., Andrew, D. and Silk, M. 2004: Sport and the façade of redevelopment in the postindustrial city. *Sociology of Sport Journal* 21: 119–39.

Friedman, S.S. 1998: *Mappings: feminism and the cultural geographies of encounter*. Princeton, NJ: Princeton University Press.

Friedman, S.W. 1996: *Marc Bloch, sociology and geography: encountering disciplines*. Cambridge, UK: Cambridge University Press.

Friedman, T.L. 2000 [1999]: *The lexus and the olive tree: understanding globalization*. New York: Farrar, Straus and Giroux.

Friedman, T.L. 2005: *The world is flat: a brief history of the twenty-first century*. New York: Farrar, Strauss and Giroux.

Friedmann, H. 1993: The political economy of food. *New Left Review* 197: 29–57.

Friedmann, H. and McMichael, P. 1989: Agriculture and the state system: the rise and decline of national agricultures, 1870 to the present. *Sociologia Ruralis*, 29(2): 93–117.

Friedmann, J. 1986: The world city hypothesis, *Development and Change* 17: 69–83.

Friedmann, J. 1992: *Empowerment: the politics of alternative development*. Oxford: Blackwell.

Friedmann, J. 1996: Where we stand: a decade of world-city research. In P.L. Knox and P.J. Taylor, eds, *World cities in a world-system*. Cambridge, UK: Cambridge University Press.

Friedmann, J. 2002: *The prospect of cities*. Minneapolis: University of Minnesota Press.

Friedmann, J. and Wolff, G. 1982: World city formation: an agenda for research and action. *International Journal of Urban and Regional Research* 6(3): 309–44.

Friere, P. 1993: *Pedagogy of the oppressed*. New York: Continuum.

Frisby, D. 2001: *Cityscapes of modernity*. Cambridge, UK: Polity Press.

Fröbel, F., Heinrichs, J. and Kreye, O. 1980: *The New International Division of Labor*. New York: Cambridge University Press.

Froot, K.A., O'Connell, P.G.J. and Seasholes, M.S. 2001: The portfolio flows of international investors. *Journal of Financial Economics* 59: 151–93.

Frost, A. 1988: Science for political purposes: European explorations of the Pacific Ocean, 1764–1806. In R. MacLeod and P.E. Rehbock, eds, *Nature in its greatest extent: Western science in the Pacific*. Honolulu: University of Hawaii Press, 27–44.

Froud, J., Sukhdev, J., Leaver, A. and Williams, K. 2006: *Financialization and strategy: narrative and numbers*. London: Routledge.

Frow, J. 1997: *Cultural studies and cultural value*. Oxford: Oxford University Press.

Frynas, J. and Pegg, S., eds, 2003: *Transnational corporations and human rights*. London: Palgrave Macmillan.

Fujita, M., Krugman, P.R. and Venables, A.J. 1999: *The spatial economy: cities, regions and international trade*. Cambridge, MA: The MIT Press.

Fukuyama, F. 2002: *Our posthuman future: consequences of the biotechnology revolution*. London: Profile Books.

Fulford, T., Lee, D. and Kitson, P.J. 2004: *Literature, science and exploration in the romantic era: bodies of knowledge*. Cambridge, UK: Cambridge University Press.

Fuller, D. 1999: Part of the action, or 'going native'? Learning to cope with the 'politics of integration'. *Area* 31(3): 221–8.

Fuller, D. and Kitchin, R. 2004a: Radical theory/critical praxis: academic geography beyond the academy? In Fuller and Kitchen, eds, *Critical theory/radical praxis: making a difference beyond the academy?* Vernon and Victoria, BC, Canada: Praxis (e)Press. http://www.praxis-epress.org/rtcp/contents.html

Fuller, D. and Kitchin R., eds, 2004b: *Radical theory/critical praxis: making a difference beyond the academy?* Vernon and Victoria, BC: Praxis (e)Press. http://www.praxis-epress.org/rtcp/contents.html

Funtowicz, S.O. and Ravetz, J.R. 1993: Science for the post-normal age. *Futures* 2: 735–55.

Furnivall, J.S. 1948: *Colonial policy and practice*. Cambridge, UK: Cambridge University Press.

Fuss, D. 1989: *Essentially speaking: feminism, nature and difference*. London: Routledge.

Fyfe, N.R. 1992: Space, time and policing: towards a contextual understanding of police work. *Environment and Planning D: Society and Space* 10: 469–86.

Fyfe, N.R. and Bannister, J. 1998: The 'eyes upon the street': closed circuit television surveillance and the city. In N.R. Fyfe, ed., *Images of the street: representation, experience and control in public space.* London: Routledge, 254–67.

Fyfe, N.R. and Kenny, J., eds, 2005: *The urban geography reader.* London: Routledge.

Gaard, G., ed., 1993: *Ecofeminism: women, animals, nature.* Philadelphia, PA: Temple University Press.

Gabel, M. and Bruner, H. 2003: *Global Inc.: an atlas of the multinational corporation.* New York: New Press.

Gaddis, J.L. 2006: *The Cold War.* London: Allen Lane.

Gadgil, M. and Guha, R. 1995: *Ecology and equity: the use and abuse of nature in contemporary India.* London: Routledge.

Gahegan, M. 1999: What is geocomputation? *Transactions in GIS* 3: 203–6.

Galaty, J.G. and Johnson, D.L., eds, 1990: *The world of pastoralism: herding systems in comparative perspective.* New York: Guilford Press.

Gale, S. and Olsson, G., eds, 1979: *Philosophy in geography.* Boston, MA: D. Reidel.

Gallagher, C. and Greenblatt, S. 2001: *Practicing new historicism.* Chicago: The University of Chicago Press.

Gallaher, C. 2003: *On the fault line: race, class, and the American patriot.* Lanham, MD: Rowman & Littlefield.

Gallie, W.B. 1964: Essentially contested concepts. In Gallie, *Philosophy and the historical understanding.* London: Chatto and Windus.

Gallop, J. 2002: *Anecdotal theory.* Durham, NC: Duke University Press.

Galloway, A. 2004: Intimations of everyday life: ubiquitous computing and the city. *Cultural Studies* 18(2/3): 384–408.

Galloway, J.H. 2005: The modernization of sugar production in Southeast Asia, 1880–1940. *Geographical Review* 95(1): 1–23.

Galster, G. 1996: William Grigsby and the analysis of housing sub-markets and filtering. *Urban Studies* 33(10): 1797–805.

Galtung, J. 1969: Violence, peace and peace research. *Journal of Peace Research* 6(3): 167–91.

Galtung, J. 1990: Cultural violence. *Journal of Peace Research* 27(3): 291–305.

Gamble, A. 1996: *Hayek: the iron cage of liberty.* Boulder, CO: Westview Press.

Gamble, C. 1992: Archaeology, history and the uttermost ends of the Earth – Tasmania, Tierra del Fuego and the Cape. *Antiquity* 66: 712–20.

Gandy, M. 2002: *Concrete and clay: reworking nature in New York City.* Cambridge, MA: The MIT Press.

Gandy, M. 2005: Learning from Lagos. *New Left Review* 33, May/June: 37–52.

Gandy, M. 2006a: Urban nature and the ecological imaginary. In E. Swyngedouw, N. Heynan and M. Kalka, eds, *The nature of cities: urban political ecology and the politics of urban metabolism.* London: Routledge, 63–74.

Gandy, M. 2006b: Zones of indistinction: biopolitical contestations in the urban arena. *Cultural Geographies* 13: 497–516.

Gandy, M. 2006c: Zones of indistinction: some thoughts on the bio-politics of urban space. *Cultural Geographies* 13: 1–20.

Gandhi, M.K. 1997 [1908]: *Hind Swaraj and other essays*, edited and introduced by A. Parel. Cambridge, UK: Cambridge University Press.

Gans, H.J. 1962: *The urban villagers: group and class in the life of Italian-Americans.* New York: The Free Press of Glencoe.

Gans, H.J. 1995: *The war against the poor: the 'underclass' and antipoverty policy.* New York: Basic Books.

Gaonkar, D.P., ed., 2001: *Alternative modernities.* Durham, NC: Duke University Press.

Garber, M. 2001: *Academic instincts.* Princeton, NJ: Princeton University Press.

Garcia-Ramon, M.D. 2003: Globalization and international geography: the questions of languages and scholarly traditions. *Progress in Human Geography* 27: 1–5.

Garfinkel, H. 1967: *Studies in ethnomethodology.* Englewood Cliffs, NJ: Prentice-Hall.

Garfinkel, H. and Wieder, D.L. 1992: Two incommensurable, asymmetrically alternate technologies of social analysis. In G. Watson and R.M. Seiler, eds, *Text in context: contributions to ethnomethodology.* London: Sage, 175–206.

Garnham, N. 2000: *Emancipation, the media, and modernity: arguments about the media and social theory.* Oxford: Oxford University Press.

Garreau, J. 1991: *Edge city: life on the new frontier.* New York: Doubleday.

Garrison, W.L., Berry, B.J.L., Marble, D.F., Nystuen, J. and Morrill, R.L. 1959: *Studies of highway development and geographic change.* Seattle: University of Washington Press.

Gastner, M.T. and Newman, M.E.J. 2004: Diffusion-based method for producing density-equalizing maps. *Proceedings of the National Academy of Sciences* 101: 7499–504.

Gates, C. 2003: *Ancient cities: the archaeology of urban life in the ancient Near East and Egypt, Greece and Rome.* London and New York: Routledge.

Gatrell, A.C. 2002: *Geographies of health: an introduction.* Oxford: Blackwell.

Gatrell, A.C. 1983: *Distance and space: a geographical perspective.* Oxford: The Clarendon Press.

Gautier, E. and Henry, L. 1958: *La population de Crulai, paroisse normande: etude historique.* Institut National d'Etudes Démographiques, Travaux et documents, Cahier no. 33. Paris: Presses Universitaires de France.

Gavron, D. 2000: *The kibbutz: awakening from Utopia.* Lanham, MD: Rowman & Littlefield.

Geddes, M. 2006: Partnership and the limits to local governance in England: institutionalist analysis and neoliberalism. *International Journal of Urban and Regional Research* 30: 76–97.

Geddes, P. 1915: *Cities in evolution: an introduction to the town planning movement and the study of civics.* London: Ernest Benn.

Geertz, C. 1963: *Agricultural involution: the process of ecological change in Indonesia.* Berkeley, CA: University of California Press

Geertz, C. 1973a: Deep play: notes on the Balinese cock fight. In Geertz, *The interpretation of cultures.* New York: Basic Books, 412–54.

Geertz, C. 1973b: Thick description: towards an interpretive theory of culture. In Geertz, *The interpretation of cultures.* New York: Basic Books, 3–30.

Geertz, C. 1983: *Local knowledge: further essays in interpretive anthropology.* New York: Basic Books.

Geertz, C. 1984: Anti anti-relativism. *American Anthropologist* 86: 263–78.

Geertz, C. 1988: *Works and lives: the anthropologist as author.* Stanford, CA: Stanford University Press.

Gegeo, D.W. 2001: Cultural rupture and indigeneity: the challenge of (re)visioning 'place' in the Pacific. *The Contemporary Pacific* 13(2): 491–507.

Gehlke, C.E. and Biehl, H. 1934: Certain effects of grouping upon the size of the *correlation* coefficient in census tract material. *Journal of the American Statistical Association, Supplement* 29: 169–70.

Geisler, C. and Daneker, G., eds, 2000: *Property and values: alternatives to public and private ownership.* Washington, DC: Island Press.

Gelling, M. 1997: *Signposts to the past,* 3rd edn. Chichester: Phillimore.

Gellner, E. 1983: *Nations and nationalism.* Oxford: Blackwell.

Gelobter, M., Dorsey, M., Fields, L., Goldtooth, T., Mendiratta, A., Moore, R., Morelo-Frosch, R., Shepard, P.M. and Torres, G. 2005: *The soul of environmentalism: rediscovering transformational politics in the 21st century.* Oakland, CA: Redefining Progress, http://www.soulofenvironmentalism.org/

Gendzier, I. 1985: *Managing political change: social scientists and the Third World.* Boulder, CO: Westview Press.

Geoforum 2004: Themed section: 'The spaces of critical geography', ed. L. Berg. *Geoforum* 35(5): 523–58.

Geographical Review 2001: Special issue: 'Doing fieldwork'. *Geographical Review* 91(1–2).

Geras, N. and Wokler, R., eds, 2000: *Enlightenment and modernity.* London: Macmillan.

Gereffi, G. and Korzeniewicz, M. eds, 1994: *Commodity chains and global capitalism.* London: Praeger.

Gereffi, G., Humphrey, J. and Sturgeon, T. 2005: The governance of global value chains. *Review of International Political Economy* 12(1): 78–104.

Germain, A. 1997: *Montréal: An experiment in cosmopolitanism within a dual society.* Utrecht: ERCOMER.

Gerschenkron, A. 1968: *Continuity in history.* Cambridge, MA: Harvard University Press.

Gershuny, J.I. 2000: *Changing times: work and leisure in postindustrial society.* Oxford: Oxford University Press.

Gertler, M.S. 1988: The limits to flexibility: comments on the post-Fordist vision of production and its geography. *Transactions of the Institute of British Geographers,* NS 13: 419–32.

Gesler, W.M. 1991: *The cultural geography of health care.* Pittsburgh: University of Pittsburgh Press.

Gesler, W.M. 1992: Therapeutic landscapes: medical issues in the light of the new cultural geography. *Social Science and Medicine* 34: 735–46.

Gesler, W.M. and Kearns, R.A. 2002: *Culture/place/health.* London: Routledge.

Getis, A. and Boots, B. 1978: *Models of spatial processes: an approach to the study of point, line and area patterns.* Cambridge, UK: Cambridge University Press.

Gettys, W.E. 1940: Human ecology and social theory. *Social Forces* 18(4): 469–76.

Ghanem, A., Rouhana, N.N. and Yiftachel, O. 1998: Questioning 'ethnic democracy': a response to Sammy Smooha. *Israel Studies* 3(2): 253–67.

Gibbs, D. and Jonas, A.E.G. 2000: Governance and regulation in local environmental policy: the utility of a regime approach. *Geoforum* 31: 299–313.

Gibbs, G.R. 2002: *Qualitative data analysis: explorations with NVivo.* Buckingham: Open University Press.

Gibson, C.C., Andersson, K., Ostrom, E. and Shivakumar, S. 2005: *The Samaritan's dilemma: the political economy of development aid.* Oxford: Oxford University Press.

Gibson, J.J. 1979: *The ecological approach to visual perception.* Boston: Houghton Mifflin.

Gibson, K., Law, L. and McKay, D. 2001: Beyond heroes and victims: Filipina contract migrants, economic activism and class transformations. *International Feminist Journal of Politics* 3: 365–86.

Gibson, W. 1986: *Neuromancer.* New York: Ace Books.

Gibson-Graham, J.-K. 1994: 'Stuffed if I know!': Reflections on post-modern feminist social research. *Gender, Place and Culture: A Journal of Feminist Geography* 1: 205–24.

Gibson-Graham, J.-K. 2003: An ethics of the local. *Rethinking Marxism* 15: 49–74.

Gibson-Graham, J.-K. 2006a [1996]: Querying globalization. In Gibson-Graham, *The end of capitalism (as we knew it): a feminist critique of political economy.* Oxford: Blackwell/Minneapolis: Minnesota University Press, 120–47.

Gibson-Graham, J.-K. 2006b [1996]: *The end of capitalism (as we knew it): a feminist critique of political economy.* Oxford: Blackwell/Minneapolis: Minnesota University Press.

Gibson-Graham, J.-K. 2006c: *Postcapitalist politics.* Minneapolis: University of Minnesota Press.

Giddens, A. 1977: *Studies in social and political theory.* London: Hutchinson.

Giddens, A. 1979: *Central problems in social theory: action, structure and contradiction in social analysis.* London: Macmillan.

Giddens, A. 1981: *A contemporary critique of historical materialism*, vol. 1: *Power, property and the state.* London: Macmillan.

Giddens, A. 1982: Class division, class conflict, and citizenship rights. In A. Giddens, ed., *Profiles and critiques in social theory.* London: Macmillan.

Giddens, A. 1984: *The constitution of society: outline of the theory of structuration.* Cambridge, UK: Polity Press.

Giddens, A. 1985: *A contemporary critique of historical materialism*, vol. 2: *The nation-state and violence.* Cambridge, UK: Polity Press.

Giddens, A. 1990: *The consequences of modernity.* Stanford, CA: Stanford University Press.

Giddens, A. 1991: *Modernity and self-identity.* Cambridge, UK: Polity Press.

Giddens, A. 1999: *Runaway world: how globalization is shaping our lives.* London: Profile Books.

Gidwani, V. 2002: New theory or new dogma? A tale of social capital and economic development from Gujarat, India. *Journal of Asian and African Studies* 37(2): 83–112.

Gidwani, V. 2006: Subaltern cosmopolitanism and politics. *Antipode* 38: 7–21.

Gidwani, V. 2008: *Capital interrupted.* University of Minnesota Press.

Gidwani, V. and Sivaramakrishnan, K. 2003: Circular migration and the spaces of cultural assertion. *Annals of the Association of American Geographers* 93(1): 186–213.

Giere, R.N. and Richardson, A.W., eds, 1996: *Origins of logical empiricism.* Minneapolis: University of Minnesota Press.

Gieryn, T.F. 2002: What buildings do. *Theory and Society* 31: 35–74.

Gieryn, T.F. 2006: City as truth-spot: laboratories and field-sites in urban studies. *Social Studies of Science* 36: 5–38.

Gigerenzer, G. and Selten, R., eds, 2001: *Bounded rationality: the adaptive toolbox.* Cambridge, MA: The MIT Press.

Gigerenzer, G. and Todd, P.M. 1999: *Simple heuristics that make us smart.* Oxford: Oxford University Press.

Giggs, J.A. 1973: The distribution of schizophrenics in Nottingham. *Transactions of the Institute of British Geographers* 59: 55–76.

Gilbert, A. 1988: The new regional geography in French- and English-speaking countries. *Progress in Human Geography* 12: 208–28.

Gilbert, E. 2005: The inevitability of integration? Neoliberal discourse and the proposals for a new North American economic space after September 11. *Annals of the Association of American Geographers* 95: 202–22.

Gilbert, E. 2007: Leaky borders and solid citizens: governing security, prosperity and quality of life in a North American partnership. *Antipode* 39(1): 77–98.

Gilbert, M. 2009: *The Routledge atlas of the Holocaust.* London: Routledge.

Gilbert, N. and Troitzsch, K.G. 2005: *Simulation for the social scientist.* Maidenhead: Open University Press.

Giles, W. and Hyndman, J. 2004a: Introduction: women in conflict zones. In W. Giles and J. Hyndman, eds, *Sites of violence: gender and conflict zones.* Berkeley, CA: University of California Press, 3–23.

Giles, W. and Hyndman, J., eds, 2004b: *Sites of violence: gender and conflict zones.* Berkeley, CA: California University Press.

Gilks, W.R., Richardson, S. and Spiegelhalter, D.J., eds, 1996: *Markov chain Monte Carlo in practice.* London: Chapman & Hall.

Gill, J. 2002: *Bayesian methods for the social and behavioral sciences.* Chapman & Hall.

Gill, S. 2003: *Power and resistance in the new world order.* London: Palgrave Macmillan.

Gilleard, C. and Higgs, P. 2000: *Cultures of ageing: self, citizen and the body.* London: Pearson.

Gillies, J. 1994: *Shakespeare and the geography of difference.* Cambridge, UK: Cambridge University Press.

Gillies, J. and Cailliau, R., 2002: *How the Web was born: the story of the World Wide Web.* Oxford: Oxford University Press.

Gilman, N. 2003: *Mandarins of the future: modernization theory in Cold War America.* Baltimore, MD: The Johns Hopkins University Press.

Gilmore, R. 1998: Globalisation and US prison growth: from military Keynesianism to post-Keynesian militarism. *Race & Class* 40: 171–87.

Gilmore, R. 2007: *Golden Gulag: prisons, surplus, crisis and opposition in globalizing California.* Berkeley, CA: University of California Press.

Gilroy, P. 1987: *'There ain't no black in the Union Jack': the cultural politics of race and nation.* London: Hutchinson.

Gilroy, P. 1993: *The Black Atlantic: modernity and double consciousness.* Cambridge, MA: Harvard University Press.

Gilroy, P. 2000a: *Against race: imaging political culture beyond the color line.* Cambridge, MA: Harvard University Press.

Gilroy, P. 2000b: *Between camps: nations, cultures and the allure of race.* London: Penguin.

Giordano, B. 1999: A place called Padania? The Lega Nord and the political representation of northern Italy. *European Urban and Regional Studies* 6: 215–30.

Glacken, C. 1967: *Traces on the Rhodian shore: nature and culture in Western thought from ancient times to the end of the eighteenth century.* Berkeley, CA: University of California Press.

Glasmeier, A.K. 2005: *An atlas of poverty in America: one nation, pulling apart, 1960–2003.* New York: Routledge.

Glassman, J. 2002: From Seattle (and Ubon) to Bangkok: the scales of resistance to corporate globalization. *Environment and Planning D: Society and Space* 20: 513–33.

Glassman, J. 2005: On the borders of Southeast Asia: Cold War geography and the construction of the other. *Political Geography* 24: 784–807.

Glassman, J. 2006: Primitive accumulation, accumulation by dispossession, accumulation by 'extra-economic' means. *Progress in Human Geography* 30: 608–25.

Glasson, J., Therivel, R. and Chadwick, A. 2005: *Introduction to Environmental Impact Assessment,* 3rd edn. London: Routledge.

Glazer, N. and Moynihan, D.P. 1970: *Beyond the melting pot.* Cambridge, MA: The MIT Press.

Gleeson, B. 1999: *Geographies of disability.* London: Routledge.

Gleeson, B. 2000: Reflexive modernisation: the re-enlightenment of planning? *International Planning Studies* 5(1): 117–35.

Glennie, P. 1987: The transition from feudalism to capitalism as a problem for historical geography. *Journal of Historical Geography* 13: 296–302.

Glennie, P. 1988: In search of agrarian capitalism: manorial land markets and the acquisition of land in the Lea valley, c.1450–c.1560. *Continuity and Change* 3: 11–40.

Glennie, P. 1991: Measuring crop yields in early modern England, in M. Overton and B.M.S. Campbell, eds, *Land, labour and livestock: historical studies in European agricultural productivity.* Manchester: Manchester University Press, 255–83.

Glennie, P. and Thrift, N.J. 1992: Modernity, urbanism and modern consumption *Environment and Planning D: Society and Space* 10: 423–43.

Glennie, P. and Thrift, N.J. 2005: Revolutions in the times: clocks and the temporal structure of everyday life. In D.N. Livingstone and C.W.J. Withers, eds, *Geography and revolution.* Chicago: The University of Chicago Press.

Glennie, P. and Thrift, N.J. 2009: *Shaping the day: a history of timekeeping in England and Wales 1300–1800.* Oxford: Oxford University Press.

Glick Schiller, N. and Fouron, G. 2001: *Georges woke up laughing: long-distance nationalism and the search for home.* Durham, NC: Duke University Press.

Glickman, N.J. 1997: *Econometric analysis of regional systems: explorations in model building and policy analysis.* New York: Academic Press.

Global Commission on International Migration (GCIM) 2005: *Migration in an interconnected world: New directions for action. Report of the Global Commission on International Migration.* Geneva: GCIM.

Global Witness n.d.: *The Kimberly process,* http://www.globalwitness.org/pages/en/the_kimberley_process.html

Glyn, A., Hughes, A., Lipietz, A. and Singh, A. 1991: The rise and fall of the golden age. In S. Marglin and J.B. Schor, eds, *The golden age of capitalism.* Oxford: The Clarendon Press.

Godlewska, A. 1999: From Enlightenment vision to modern science? Humboldt's visual thinking. In D.N. Livingstone and C.W.J. Withers, eds, *Geography and Enlightenment.* Chicago: The University of Chicago Press, 236–75.

Godlewska, A. 1999: *Geography unbound: French geographic science from Cassini to Humboldt.* Chicago: The University of Chicago Press.

Godlewska, A. and Smith, N., eds, 1994: *Geography and empire.* Oxford: Blackwell.

Goering, J.M., ed., 1989: The 'explosiveness' of chain migration: research and policy issues. *International Migration Review* 23: 797–888.

Goin, P. 2003: Where the pavement ends. *Geographical Review* 92: 545–54.

Golant, S.M. 1979: Rationale for geographic perspectives on aging and the aged. In Golant, ed., *Location and environment of elderly population.* Chichester: Wiley, 1–14.

Golant, S.M. 1984: *A place to grow old: the meaning of the environment in old age.* New York: Columbia University Press.

Gold, J. 1980: *An introduction to behavioural geography.* Oxford: Oxford University Press.

Gold, J.R. and Gold, M. 2005: *Cities of culture.* Aldershot: Ashgate.

Goldberg, D. and Quayson, A., eds, 2002: *Relocating postcolonialism.* Oxford: Blackwell.

Goldberg, D.T. 1993: *Racist culture: philosophy and the politics of meaning.* Oxford: Blackwell.

Goldberg, D.T. 2002: *The racial state.* Oxford: Blackwell.

Goldhagen, D.J. 1996: *Hitler's willing executioners: ordinary Germans and the Holocaust.* New York: A.A. Knopf.

Goldman, M., ed., 1998: *Privatizing nature: political struggles for the global commons.* New Brunswick, NJ: Rutgers University Press.

Goldstein, J. 1988: *Long cycles, prosperity and war in the modern age.* New Haven, CT: Yale University Press.

Golinski, J. 1998: *Making natural knowledge: constructivism and the history of science.* Cambridge, UK: Cambridge University Press.

Golledge, R.G. 1993: Geography and the disabled: a survey with special reference to vision impaired and blind populations. *Transactions of the Institute of British Geographers,* NS 18: 63–85.

Golledge, R.G. 1997: On reassembling one's life: overcoming disability in its academic environment. *Environment and Planning D: Society and Space* 15: 391–409.

Golledge, R.G. and Amedeo, D. 1968: On laws in geography. *Annals of the Association of American Geographers* 58: 760–74.

Golledge, R.G. and Stimson, R. 1997: *Spatial behavior: a geographic perspective.* New York: Guilford Press.

Golledge, R.G. and Timmermans, H. 1990: Applications of behavioural research on spatial problems I: cognition; and II: preference and choice. *Progress in Human Geography* 14: 57–100, 311–44.

Gonzalez de la Rocha, M., Perlman, J., Safa, H. Jelin, E., Roberts, B.R. and Ward, P.M. 2004: From the marginality of the 1960s to the 'new poverty' of today: a LARR research forum. *Latin American Research Review* 39: 183–203.

Goodchild, M.F. 1992: Geographical information science. *International Journal of Geographical Information Systems* 6(1): 31–45.

Goodchild, M.F. 1995: Geographic systems information and research. In J. Pickles, ed., *Ground truth.* New York: Guilford Press, 31–50.

Goodchild, M.F. and Longley, P.A. 2005: The future of GIS and spatial analysis. In P.A. Longley, M.F. Goodchild, D.J. Maguire and D.W. Rhind, eds, *Geographical Information Systems,* abridged edn. Chichester: Wiley, 235–48.

Goodchild, M.F. and Proctor, J. 1997: Scale in a digital world. *Geographical and Environmental Modelling* 1: 5–23.

Goodin, R. 2003: Representing mute interests. In Goodin, *Reflective democracy.* Oxford: Oxford University Press, 209–26.

Goodman, D. 1991: Iberian science: navigation, empire and Counter-Reformation. In D. Goodman and C.A. Russell, eds, *The rise of scientific Europe, 1500–1800.* Sevenoaks, Kent: Hodder & Stoughton, 117–44.

Goodman, D. and Redclift, M. 1991: *Refashioning nature.* London: Routledge.

Goodman, D. and Watts, M., eds, 1997: *Globalising food: agrarian questions and global restructuring.* London: Routledge.

Goodman, D., Sorj, B. and Wilkinson, J. 1987: *From farming to biotechnology.* Oxford: Blackwell.

Goodman, M. 2004: Reading fair trade: political ecological imaginary and the moral economy of fair trade foods. *Political Geography* 23(7): 891–915.

Goodwin, M. 1998: The governance of rural areas: some emerging research issues and agendas. *Journal of Rural Studies* 14: 5–12.

Goody, J. 1962: *Death, property and the ancestors.* Stanford, CA: Stanford University Press.

Goody, J. 1978: *Production and reproduction: a comparative study of the domestic domain.* Cambridge, UK: Cambridge University Press.

Goody, J., Thirsk, J. and Thompson, E.P. 1976: *Family and inheritance: rural society in Western Europe.* Cambridge, UK: Cambridge University Press.

Goonewardena, K. and Kipfer, S. 2006: Postcolonial urbicide: new imperialism, global cities and the damned of the Earth. *New Formations* 59: 23–33.

Gordon, D. and Spicker, P., eds, 1999: *The international glossary on poverty.* London: Zed Books.

Gordon, H. 1954: The economic theory of a common property resource: the fishery. *Journal of Political Economy* 62(2): 124–42.

Gordon, M. 1964: *Assimilation in American life.* New York: Oxford University Press.

Gore, C. 1993: Entitlement relations and 'unruly' social practices: a comment on the work of Amartya Sen. *Journal of Development* 29: 429–60.

Gosepath, S. 2005: Equality. In E.N. Zalta, ed., *Stanford encyclopedia of philosophy.* Stanford, CA: Stanford University Press.

Goss, J. 1993: The 'magic of the mall': an analysis of form, function, and meaning in the contemporary retail built environment. *Annals of the Association of American Geographers* 83: 18–47.

Gottdiener, M. 1985: *The social production of urban space.* Austin: The University of Texas Press.

Gottlieb, R. 2001: *Environmentalism unbound: exploring new pathways for change.* Cambridge, MA: The MIT Press.

Gottlieb, R. and Fitzsimmons, M. 1991: *Thirst for growth: water agencies as hidden government in California.* Tuscon, AZ: University of Arizona Press.

Gottmann, J. 1952: *La politique des états et leur géographie.* Paris: Armand Colin.

Gottmann, J. 1964: *Megalopolis: the urbanized northeastern seaboard of the United States.* Cambridge, MA: The MIT Press.

Goudie, A.S. 1977: *Environmental change.* Oxford: Oxford University Press (see also many later editions).

Goudie, A.S. 1981: *The human impact: man's role in environmental change.* Oxford: Blackwell (see also many later editions).

Gough, J., Eisenschitz, A. and McCulloch, A. 2005: *Spaces of social exclusion.* London: Routledge.

Gouinlock, J. 1972: *John Dewey's philosophy of value.* New York: Humanities Press.

Gould, J.D. 1969: Hypothetical history. *Economic History Review* 22: 195–207.

Gould, P. 1963: Man against his environment: a game-theoretical framework. *Annals of the Association of American Geographers* 53: 290–7.

Gould, P. 1969a: Methodological developments since the fifties. *Progress in Geography* 1: 1–49.

Gould, P. 1969b: *Spatial diffusion.* AAG Resource Paper, No. 4. Washington, DC: Association of American Geographers.

Gould, P. 1972: Pedagogic review [of Wilson, 1970]. *Annals of the Association of American Geographers* 62: 689–700.

Gould, P. 1978: The Augean period. *Annals of the Association of American Geographers* 69: 139–51.

Gould, P. 1985: Geography and medicine: an old partnership. In Gould, *The geographer at work.* London: Routledge and Kegan Paul, 225–38.

Gould, P. 1993: *The slow plague: a geography of the AIDS pandemic.* Oxford: Blackwell.

Gould, P. and White R. 1993 [1974]: *Mental maps.* London: Penguin/New York: Routledge.

Gould, W.T.S. 2005: Vulnerability and HIV/AIDS in Africa – from demography to development. *Population Space and Place* 11: 473–84.

Gould, W.T.S. and Brown, M.S. 1996: A fertility transition in sub-Saharan Africa? *International Journal of Population Geography* 2: 1–22.

Gouldner, A. 1979: *The future of intellectuals and the rise of the new class.* New York: Seabury Press.

Gouldner, A. 1980: *The two Marxisms.* London: Macmillan.

Government Statistical Service 2003: *Harmonised concepts and questions for governmental social surveys.* London: Office for National Statistics.

Gowan, P. 1999: *The global gamble: Washington's faustian bid for world dominance.* London: Verso.

Gowan, P. 2003: The American campaign for global sovereignty. In L. Panitch and C. Leys, eds, *Fighting identities: race, religion and ethno-nationalism* [Socialist Register 2003] London: Merlin Press.

Grabher, G. and Stark, D., eds, 1997: *Restructuring networks in post-socialism.* Oxford: Oxford University Press.

Graff, G. 1992: *Beyond the culture wars.* New York: W.W. Norton.

Grafton, A. and Jardine, L. 1986: *From humanism to the humanities: education and the liberal arts in fifteenth- and sixteenth-century Europe.* Cambridge, MA: Harvard University Press.

Grafton, A., with Shelford, A. and Siraisis, N. 1992: *New worlds, ancient texts: the power of tradition and the shock of discovery.* Cambridge, MA: Harvard University Press.

Graham, B. and Nash, C., eds, 1999: *Modern historical geographies.* London: Longman.

Graham, B., Ashworth, G. and Tunbridge, J. 2000: *A geography of heritage: power, culture and economy.* Oxford: Oxford University Press.

Graham, J., Gibson, K., Horvath, R. and Shakow, D. 1988: Restructuring in US manufacturing: the decline of monopoly capitalism. *Annals of the Association of American Geographers* 78: 473–90.

Graham, S. 1998: The end of geography or the explosion of place? Conceptualising space, place and information technology. *Progress in Human Geography* 22(2): 165–85.

Graham, S. 2003: Lessons in urbicide. *New Left Review* 19, January/February: 63–78.

Graham, S., ed., 2004a: *Cities, war and terrorism: towards an urban geopolitics.* Oxford: Blackwell.

Graham, S. 2004b: Vertical geopolitics: Baghdad and after. *Antipode* 36: 12–23.

Graham, S. 2005: Software-sorted geographies. *Progress in Human Geography* 29: 1–19.

Graham, S. 2006: Cities and the war on terror. *International Journal of Urban and Regional Research* 30: 255–76.

Graham, S. 2007: War and the city. *New Left Review* 44: 121–32.

Graham, S. 2008a: Imagining urban warfare: urbanization and US military technoscience. In D. Cowen and E. Gilbert, eds, *War, citizenship, territory.* London: Routledge, 33–56.

Graham, S. 2008b: Robo-war™ dreams: US military technophilia and global south urbanisation. *City* 12: 25–49.

Graham, S. 2008c: War play: practising urban annihilation. In F. von Borries, S. Walz and M. Bötther, eds, *Space time play: on the synergy between computer games, architecture and urbanism.* Basel: Birkhauser.

Graham, S. 2009a: *Cities under siege: the new military urbanism.* London: Verso.

Graham, S. 2009b: Interrupting the algorithmic gaze? Urban warfare and US military technology. In F. MacDonald, K. Dodds and R. Hughes, eds, *Observant states: geopolitics and visual culture.* London: I.B. Tauris.

Grahber, G. 2001: Ecologies of creativity: the village, the group and the heterarchic organization of the British advertising industry. *Environment and Planning A* 33: 351–74.

Gramsci, A. 1971 [1929–35]: *Selections from the prison notebooks*, ed. Q. Hoare and G.N. Smith. London: Lawrence and Wishart and New York: International.

Granö, J.G. 1997 [1929]: *Pure geography*, trans. M. Hicks. Baltimore, MD: The Johns Hopkins University Press.

Granovetter, M. 1982: The strength of weak ties: a network theory revisited. In P.V. Marsden and N. Lin, eds, *Social structure and network analysis*. Beverly Hills, CA: Sage, 105–30.

Granovetter, M.S. 1973: The strength of weak ties. *American Journal of Sociology* 78: 1360–80.

Grant, R. and Nijman, J. 2006: Globalization and the corporate geography of cities in the less-developed world. In N. Brenner and R. Keil, eds, *The global cities reader*. London: Routledge, 224–37.

Gray, C., ed., 1995: *The cyborg handbook*. London: Routledge

Gray, C. 2003: Posthuman soldiers in postmodern war. *Body & Society* 9(4): 215–26.

Gray, F. and Boddy, M. 1979: The origins and use of theory in urban geography: household mobility in filtering theory. *Geoforum* 10: 117–27.

Gray, H.L. 1915: *English field systems*. Cambridge: MA: Harvard University Press

Gray, J. 1995: *Liberalism*, 2nd edn. Buckingham: Open University Press.

Gray, J. 1996: *Post-liberalism: studies in political thought*. London: Routledge.

Gray, M. and Wyly, E. 2007: The terror city hypothesis. In D. Gregory and A. Pred, eds, *Violent geographies: fear, terror and political violence*. London: Routledge, 329–48.

Greenberg, M.R. 1978: *Applied linear programming for the socioeconomic and environmental sciences*. New York: Academic Press.

Greenblatt, S. 1991: *Marvellous possessions: the wonder of the New World*. Chicago: The University of Chicago Press.

Greene, J.C. 1977: Darwin as a social evolutionist. *Journal of the History of Biology* 10: 1–27.

Greenhalgh, S. 1995: *Anthropology and demographic inquiry*. Cambridge, UK: Cambridge University Press.

Greenhalgh, S. 1996: The social construction of population science: an intellectual, institutional, and political history of twentieth century demography. *Comparative Studies in Society and History* 38: 26–66.

Greenhough, B. and Roe, E., eds, 2006: Theme issue on 'Towards a geography of bodily technologies'. *Environment and Planning A* 38(5): 416–98.

Gregersen, B. and Johnson, B. 1997: Learning economies, innovation systems and European integration. *Regional Studies* 31(5): 479–90.

Gregory, D. 1978a: *Ideology, science and human geography*. London: Hutchinson.

Gregory, D. 1978b: The discourse of the past: phenomenology, structuralism and historical geography. *Journal of Historical Geography* 4: 161–73.

Gregory, D. 1981: Human agency and human geography. *Transactions of the Institute of British Geographers* 6: 1–18.

Gregory, D. 1982: *Regional transformation and Industrial Revolution: a geography of the Yorkshire woollen industry*. London: Macmillan and Minneapolis: University of Minnesota Press.

Gregory, D. 1985: Suspended animation: the stasis of diffusion theory. In D. Gregory and J. Urry, eds, *Social relations and spatial structures*. London: Macmillan, 293–336.

Gregory, D. 1990: 'A new and different face in many places': three geographies of industrialization. In R.A. Dodgshon and R.A. Butlin, eds, *An historical geography of England and Wales*, 2nd edn. London: Academic Press, 351–99.

Gregory, D. 1994: *Geographical imaginations*. Oxford: Blackwell.

Gregory, D. 1995a: Between the book and the lamp: imaginative geographies of Egypt, 1849–1850. *Transactions of the Institute of British Geographers* 20: 29–57.

Gregory, D. 1995b: Imaginative geographies. *Progress in Human Geography* 19: 477–85.

Gregory, D. 1997a: Lacan and geography: the *Production of space* revisited. In G. Benko and U. Strohmeyer, eds, *Space and social theory: interpreting modernity and postmodernity*. Oxford: Blackwell, 203–31.

Gregory, D. 1997b: Lefebvre, Lacan and the production of space. In G. Benko and U. Strohmayer, eds, *Space and social theory: interpreting modernity and postmodernity*. Oxford: Blackwell, 203–31.

Gregory, D. 1998a: Power, knowledge and geography. *Geographisches Zeitschrift* 86: 70–93.

Gregory, D. 1998b: Power, knowledge and geography. In Gregory, *Explorations in critical human geography*. Heidelberg: Karl-Ruprechts Universität.

Gregory, D. 1999: Scripting Egypt: Orientalism and cultures of travel. In J. Duncan and D. Gregory, eds, *Writes of passage: reading travel writing*. London and New York: Routledge, 114–50.

Gregory, D. 2000: Postcolonialism. In R.J. Johnston, D. Gregory, G. Pratt and M. Watts, eds, *The Dictionary of Human Geography*, 4th edn. Oxford: Blackwell, 612–5.

Gregory, D. 2001a: Cultures of travel and spatial formations of knowledge. *Erdkunde* 54: 297–319.

Gregory, D. 2001b: (Post)colonialism and the production of nature. In N. Castree and

B. Braun, eds, *Social nature: theory, practice and politics*. Oxford: Blackwell, 84–111.

Gregory, D. 2004a: Defiled cities. In Gregory, *The colonial present: Afghanistan, Palestine, Iraq*. Oxford: Blackwell, 107–43.

Gregory, D. 2004b: *The colonial present: Afghanistan, Palestine, Iraq*. Oxford: Blackwell.

Gregory, D. 2004c: Palestine under siege. *Antipode* 36: 601–6.

Gregory, D. 2005a: Colonial precedents and sovereign powers: a response *Progress in Human Geography* 29: 367–79.

Gregory, D. 2005b: Geographies, publics and politics. *Progress in Human Geography* 29: 182–9.

Gregory, D. 2006a: 'In another time-zone, the bombs fall unsafely': targets, civilians and late modern war. *Arab World Geographer* 9(2): 88–111.

Gregory, D. 2006b: The black flag: Guantánamo Bay and the space of exception. *Geografiska Annaler* 89B: 405–27.

Gregory, D. 2007: Vanishing points: law, violence and exception in the global war prison. In D. Gregory and A. Pred, eds, *Violent geographies: fear, terror and political violence*. New York: Routledge, 205–36.

Gregory, D. 2008a: The biopolitics of Baghdad: counterinsurgency and the counter-city. *Human Geography* 1: 6–27.

Gregory, D. 2008b: The rush to the intimate: counterinsurgency and the cultural turn in late modern war. *Radical Philosophy* 150: 8–23.

Gregory, D. 2009a: American military imaginaries and Iraqi cities: the visual economies of globalizing war. In C. Lindner, ed., *Globalization, violence and the visual culture of cities*. New York: Routledge.

Gregory, D. 2009b: War and peace. *Transactions of the Institute of British Geographers*, in press.

Gregory, D. 2009c: *War cultures*. New York: Routledge.

Gregory, D. and Pred, A., eds, 2007: *Violent geographies: fear, terror and political violence*. New York: Routledge.

Gregory, D. and Urry, J., eds, 1985: *Social relations and spatial structures*. London: Macmillan.

Gregory, I. and Ell, P. 2007: *Historical GIS: technologies, methodologies and scholarship*. Cambridge, UK: Cambridge University Press.

Gregory, K.J., ed., 2005c: *Physical geography*. London: Sage.

Gregory, S. 1962: *Statistical methods and the geographer (first edition)*. London: Longman.

Gregory, S. 1971: The quantitative approach in geography. In H.M. French and J.-B. Racine, eds, *Quantitative and qualitative geography: la nécessité d'un dialogue*. Ottawa, University of Ottawa Press, 25–33.

Gregson, N. 1989: On the (ir)relevance of structuration theory to empirical research. In D. Held and J.B. Thompson, *Social theory of the modern societies: Anthony Giddens and his critics*. Cambridge, UK: Cambridge University Press, 235–48.

Gregson, N. 2003: Discipline games, disciplinary games and the need for a post-disciplinary practice. *Geoforum* 34: 5–7.

Gregson, N. 2005: Agency: structure. In P. Cloke and R. Johnston, eds, *Spaces of geographical thought: deconstructing human geography's binaries*. London: Sage, 21–41.

Gregson, N. and Crewe, L. 2003: *Second-hand cultures*. London: Berg.

Gregson, N. and Lowe, M. 1994: *Servicing the middle classes*. London: Macmillan.

Gregson, N. and Rose, G. 2000: Taking Butler elsewhere: performativities, spatialities and subjectivities. *Environment and Planning D: Society and Space* 18: 433–52.

Gregson, N., Simonsen, K. and Vaiou, D. 2003: Writing (across) Europe: on writing spaces and writing practices. *European Urban and Regional Studies* 10: 5–22.

Gregson, S. 1994: Will HIV become a major determinant of fertility in sub-Saharan Africa? *Journal of Development Studies* 30: 650–79.

Grewal, I. and Kaplan, C., eds, 1994: *Scattered hegemonies: postmodernity and transnational feminist practices*. Minneapolis: University of Minnesota Press.

Griffin, K. 1974: *The political economy of agrarian change*. London: Macmillan.

Griffith, D.A. 2006: Beyond the bell-shaped curve: Poisson models in spatial data analysis. *Geographical Analysis* 38: iii–iv.

Griffith, D.A. and Haining, R.P. 2006: Beyond mule kicks: the Poisson distribution in geographical analysis. *Geographical Analysis* 38: 123–39.

Grigg, D. 1965: The logic of regional systems. *Annals of the Association of American Geographers* 55: 465–91.

Grigg, D. 1967: Regions, models and classes. In R. Chorley and P. Haggett, eds, *Models in geography*. London: Methuen, 461–509.

Grigg, D.B. 1977: E.G. Ravenstein and the laws of migration. *Journal of Historical Geography* 3: 41–54.

Grigg, D.B. 1980: *Population and agrarian change*. Cambridge, UK: Cambridge University Press.

Grigg, D.B. 1989: *The world food problem*. Cambridge, UK: Cambridge University Press.

Grimes, S. 1999: From population control to 'reproductive rights': ideological influences in population policy. *Third World Quarterly* 19: 373–93.

Griswold del Castillo, R. 1979: *The Los Angeles barrio, 1850–1890: a social history*. Berkeley, CA: University of California Press.

Grossberg, L. 1993: Cultural studies and/in New Worlds. *Critical Studies in Mass Communication* 10: 1–22.

Grossman, L. 1984: *Peasants, subsistence ecology and development in the highlands of Papua New Guinea*. Princeton, NJ: Princeton University Press.

Grosz, E. 1994: *Volatile bodies: toward a corporeal feminism*. Bloomington: Indiana University Press.

Grosz, E. 2005: *Time travels: feminism, nature, power*. Durham, NC: Duke University Press.

Grove, R. 1995: *Green imperialism: colonial expansion, tropical island Edens and the origins of environmentalism, 1600–1860*. Cambridge, UK: Cambridge University Press.

Grove, R. 2003: *Green imperialism*. Cambridge, UK: Cambridge University Press.

Groves, R., Fowler, F., Couper, M., Lepkowski, J., Singer, E. and Tourangeau, R. 2004: *Survey methodology*. New York: Wiley.

Guarrasi, V. 2001: Paradoxes of modern and postmodern geography: heterotopia of landscape and cartographic logic. In C. Minca, ed., *Postmodern geography: theory and praxis*. Oxford: Blackwell, 226–37.

Guba, E. and Lincoln, Y. 2005: Paradigmatic controversies, contradictions and emerging confluences. In N. Denzin and Y. Loncoln, eds, *The Sage handbook of qualitative research*, 3rd edn. London: Sage, 191–216.

Gudgin, G. and Taylor, P.J. 1979: *Seats, votes and the spatial organization of elections*. London: Pion.

Guelke, L. 1974: An idealist alternative in human geography. *Annals of the Association of American Geographers* 55: 465–91.

Guelke, L. 1978: Geography and logical positivism. In D.T. Herbert and R.J. Johnston, eds, *Geography and the urban environment*, vol. 1. Chichester: Wiley, 35–61.

Guha, R. 1989: Radical American environmentalism and wilderness preservation: a Third World critique. *Environmental Ethics* 11: 71–83.

Guha, R. and Martinez-Alier, J. 1998: *Varieties of environmentalism: essays North and South*. London: Earthscan.

Guha, R. and Martinez-Alier, J. 2000: *Varieties of environmentalism*. New Delhi: Oxford University Press.

Guha, S. and Spivak, G., eds, 1988: *Selected subaltern studies*. Oxford: Oxford University Press.

Guibernau, M. 1999: *Nations without states: political communities in a global age*. Malden, MA: Blackwell.

Guillory, J. 1993: *Cultural capital: the problem of literary canon formation*. Chicago: The University of Chicago Press.

Gunewardena, K., Kipfer, S., Milgrom, R. and Schmid, C., eds, 2008: *Space, difference, everyday life: reading Henri Lefebvre*. London: Routledge.

Gupta, A. and Ferguson, J., eds, 1997: *Culture, power, place: explorations in critical anthropology*. Durham, NC: Duke University Press.

Guthman, J. 2004: *Agrarian dreams: the paradox of organic farming in California*. Berkeley, CA: University of California Press.

Guthman, J. 2004: Back to the land: the paradox of organic food standards. *Environment and Planning A* 36: 511–28.

Gutman, G., Janetos, A.C., Justice, C.O., Moran, E.F., Mustard, J.F., Rindfuss, R.R., Skole, D., Turner II, B.L. and Cochrane, M.A., eds, 2005: *Land change science: observing, monitoring and understanding trajectories of change on the Earth's surface*. Dordrecht: Kluwer

Gutting, G. 1989: *Michel Foucault's archaeology of scientific reason*. Cambridge, UK: Cambridge University Press.

Guy, C.M. 1987: Recent advances in spatial interaction modelling: an application to the forecasting of shopping travel. *Environment and Planning A* 19: 173–86.

Guyer, J. 1997: *An African niche economy*. Edinburgh: Edinburgh University Press.

Guyot, A. 1850: *Comparative physical geography, or the Earth in relation to man*. London: Edward Gover (rev. edn, trans. C.C. Felton).

Gwynne, R.N., Klak, T. and Shaw, J.B. 2003: *Alternative capitalisms: geographies of emerging regions*. London: Arnold.

Habermas, J. 1984 [1981]: *The theory of communicative action*, vol. 1: *Reason and the rationalization of society*, trans. T. McCarthy. Boston: Beacon Press/Cambridge, UK: Polity Press.

Habermas, J. 1987a [1968]: *Knowledge and human interests*, 3rd edn. Cambridge, UK: Polity Press.

Habermas, J. 1987b [1981]: *The theory of communicative action*, vol. 2: *Lifeworld and system: a critique of functionalist reason*, trans. T. McCarthy. Cambridge, UK: Polity Press.

Habermas, J. 1989 [1962]: *The structural transformation of the public sphere: an inquiry into a category of bourgeois society*, trans. T. Burger. Cambridge, MA: The MIT Press.

Habermas, J. 1990 [1985]: *The philosophical discourse of modernity*, trans. F.G. Lawrence. Cambridge, MA: The MIT Press.

Hacking, I. 1983: *Representing and intervening: introductory topics in the philosophy of natural science*. Cambridge, UK: Cambridge University Press.

Hacking, I. 1999: *The social construction of what?* Cambridge, MA: Harvard University Press.

Hackworth, J. 2000: State devolution, urban regimes, and the production of geographic scale: the case of New Brunswick, New Jersey. *Urban Geography* 21: 450–8.

Hackworth, J. 2006: *The neoliberal city: governance, ideology and development in American urbanism*. Ithaca, NY: Cornell University Press.

Haddad, Y.Y. and Balz, M.J. 2006: The October riots in France: a failed immigration policy of the empire strikes back? *International Migration* 44: 22–34.

Hage, G. 1998: *White nation: fantasies of white supremacy in a multicultural society*. Sydney, NSW: Pluto Press (also London: Taylor and Francis, 2000).

Hägerstrand, T. 1967: *Innovation diffusion as a spatial process*, trans. A. Pred. Englewood Cliffs, NJ: Prentice-Hall.

Hägerstrand, T. 1970: What about people in regional science? *Papers of the Regional Science Association* 24: 7–21.

Hägerstrand, T. 1974: Tidsgeografisk beskrivning. Syfte och postulat. *Svensk geografisk årsbok* 50: 86–94.

Hägerstrand, T. 1982: Diorama, Path and Project. *Tijdschrift voor Economische en Sociale Geografie* 73: 323–39.

Hägerstrand, T. 1984: Presence and absence: a look at conceptual choices and bodily necessities. *Regional Studies* 8: 373–9.

Hägerstrand, T. 1985: Time-geography: focus on the corporeality of man, society and environment. In S. Aida, ed., *The science and praxis of complexity*. Tokyo: The United Nations University, 193–216.

Hägerstrand, T. and Lenntorp, B. 1974: Samhälls-organisation i tidsgeografiskt perspektiv (Social organization in a time geographical perspective). *SOU* (Swedish Government Offical Reports) 2: 221–32.

Haggett, P. 1965: *Locational analysis in human geography*. London: Edward Arnold.

Haggett, P. 1990: *The geographer's art*. Oxford: Blackwell.

Haggett, P. 1992: Sauer's 'Origins and Dispersals': its implications for the geography of disease. *Transactions of the Institute of British Geographers* 17: 387–98.

Haggett, P. 2000: *The geographical structure of epidemics*. Oxford: The Clarendon Press.

Haggett, P. and Chorley, R.J. 1967: Models, paradigms and the new geography. In Haggett and Chorley, eds, *Models in geography*. London: Methuen, 19–41.

Haggett, P. and Chorley, R.J. 1969: *Network models in geography*. London: Edward Arnold.

Haggett, P., Cliff A. and Frey, A. 1977: *Locational analysis in human geography*, 2nd edn. London: Edward Arnold.

Hahn, F. and Hollis, M., eds, 1979: Introduction. In *Philosophy and economic theory*. Oxford: Oxford University Press, 1–17.

Hahn, H. 1989: Disability and the reproduction of bodily images: the dynamics of human appearances. In J. Wolch and M. Dear, eds, *The power of geography: how territory shapes social life*. London: Unwin Hyman, 370–88.

Haigh, M. 2002: Land reclamation and deep ecology: in search of a more meaningful physical geography. *Area* 34(3): 242–52.

Haining, R., Wise, S. and Ma, J. 1998: Exploratory spatial data analysis in a Geographic Information System environment. *The Statistician* 47: 457–69.

Haining, R.P. 1990: *Spatial data analysis in the social and environmental sciences*. Cambridge, UK: Cambridge University Press.

Hajer, M.A. 1995: *The politics of environmental discourse: ecological modernization and the policy process*. Oxford: Oxford University Press.

Hajnal, J. 1965: European marriage patterns in perspective. In D.V. Glass and D.E.C. Eversley, eds, *Population in history*. London: Edward Arnold, 101–45.

Halberstram, J. 2005: *In a queer time and place*. New York: State University of New York Press.

Halbwachs, M. 1992 [1941]: *On collective memory*. Chicago: The University of Chicago Press.

Haldrup, M., Koefoed, L. and Simonsen, K. 2006: Practical Orientalism: bodies, everyday life and the construction of otherness. *Geografiska Annaler* 88B: 173–84.

Hale, A. and Wills, J., eds, 2005: *Threads of labour: garment industry supply chains from the workers' perspective*. Oxford: Blackwell.

Hale, H.E. 2004: Explaining ethnicity. *Comparative Political Studies* 37: 458–85.

Hale, J.R. 1967: A world elsewhere. In D. Hay, ed., *The age of renaissance*. London: Thames and Hudson.

Halford, S. and Savage, M. 1995: Restructuring organisations, changing people: gender and restructuring in banking and local government. *Work, Employment and Society* 9(1): 97–122.

Hall, C., ed., 2000a: *Cultures of empire: a reader*. Manchester: Manchester University Press.

Hall, C. 2002a: *Civilising subjects: metropole and colony in the English imagination, 1830–67*. Cambridge, UK: Polity Press.

Hall, C.M. and Page, S. 1999: *The geography of tourism and recreation: environment, place and space*. London: Routledge.

Hall, E. 2000b: 'Blood, brain and bone': taking the body seriously in the geographies of health and impairment. *Area* 32: 21–9.

Hall, E. 2003: Reading the maps of genes: interpreting the spatiality of genetic knowledge. *Health and Place* 9: 151–61.

Hall, P. 1984 [1966]: *The world cities*, 3rd edn. New York: McGraw-Hill.

Hall, P. 2002b [1988]: *Cities of tomorrow: an intellectual history of urban planning and design in the twentieth century*, 3rd edn. Oxford: Blackwell.

Hall, P. 2002c [1975]: *Urban and regional planning*, 4th edn. London: Routledge.

Hall, P. and Pain, K., eds, 2006: *The polycentric megalopolis: learning from mega-city regions in Europe*. London: Earthscan.

Hall, P. and Preston, P. 1988: *The carrier wave: information technology and the geography of innovation 1846–2003*. London: Unwin Hyman.

Hall, P. and Ward, C. 1998: *Sociable cities: the legacy of Ebenezer Howard*. Chichester: Wiley.

Hall, S. 1980: Race, articulation, and societies structured in dominance. In *Sociological theories: race and colonialism*. Paris: UNESCO, 305–45.

Hall, S. 1986: Gramsci's relevance for the study of race and ethnicity. *Journal of Communications Inquiry* 10(2): 5–27.

Hall, S. 1990: Cultural identity and diaspora. In J. Rutherford, ed., *Identity: community, culture and difference*. London: Lawrence and Wishart, 222–38.

Hall, S. 1992a: The question of cultural identity. In Hall, D. Held, and T. McGrew, eds, *Modernity and its futures*. Cambridge, UK: Polity Press.

Hall, S. 1992b: The West and the rest: discourse and power. In Hall and B. Gieben, eds, *Formations of modernity*. Oxford: Polity Press.

Hall, S. 1996a: Introduction: who needs identity? In Hall and P. du Gay, eds, *Questions of cultural identity*. London: Sage, 1–17.

Hall, S. 1996b: What was 'the post-colonial'? Thinking at the limit. In I. Chambers and L. Curti, eds, *The post-colonial question: common skies, divided horizons*. London: Routledge, 242–60.

Hall, S. and du Gay, P., eds, 1996: *Questions of cultural identity*. London: Sage.

Hall, S. and Held, D. 1989: Citizens and citizenship. In S. Hall and M. Jacques, eds, *New times: the changing face of politics in the 1990s*. London: Lawrence and Wishart.

Hall, T. 2000c: *Urban geography*, 2nd edn. London: Routledge.

Hall, T. and Hubbard, P., eds, 1998: *The entrepreneurial city: geographies of politics, regime, and representation*. New York: Wiley.

Hall, T.D., ed., 2000d: *A world-systems reader: new perspectives on gender, urbanism, cultures, indigenous peoples, and ecology*. Oxford: Rowman & Littlefield.

Hallam, H.E., ed., 1989: *The agrarian history of England and Wales*, vol. II: *1042–1350*. Cambridge, UK: Cambridge University Press.

Halle, L. 1991: *The Cold War as history*, revised edn. New York: Harper & Row.

Hamilton, C. 2001: *Running from the storm: the development of climate change policy in Australia*. Sydney: University of New South Wales Press.

Hamilton, P. 1996: *Historicism*. London: Routledge.

Hammersley, M. 1995: *The politics of social research*. London: Sage.

Hamnett, C. 1991: The blind men and the elephant: the explanation of gentrification. *Transactions of the Institute of British Geographers*, NS 16: 173–89.

Hamnett, C. 1994: Social polarisation in global cities: theory and evidence. *Urban Studies* 30: 401–24.

Hamnett, C. 2003: *Unequal city: London in the global arena*. London: Routledge.

Han, B. 2002: *Foucault's critical project*, trans. E. Pile. Stanford, CA: Stanford University Press.

Han, S.S. and Pannell, C.W. 1999: The geography of privatization in China, 1978–1996. *Economic Geography* 75: 272–96.

Handley, L.R., ed., n.d.: *Administration and cost of elections project*. http://www.aceproject.org/main/english/index.htm

Handy, S. and Niemeier, D.A. 1997: Measuring accessibility: an exploration of issues and alternatives. *Environment and Planning A* 29: 1175–94.

Hanke, L., ed., 1964: *Do the Americas have a common history?* New York: A.A. Knopf.

Hann, C., ed., 2002: *Postsocialism*. London: Routledge.

Hann, C.M., ed., 1998: *Property relations: renewing the anthropological tradition*. Cambridge, UK: Cambridge University Press.

Hannah, M. 1997: Imperfect panopticism: envisioning the construction of normal lives. In G. Benko and U. Strohmayer, eds, *Space and social theory: interpreting modernity and postmodernity*. Oxford: Blackwell, 344–59.

Hannah, M. 2000: *Governmentality and the mastery of territory in nineteenth-century America*. Cambridge, UK: Cambridge University Press.

Hannah, M. 2001: Sampling and the politics of representation in US Census 2000. *Environment and Planning D: Society and Space* 19: 515–34.

Hannah, M. 2006a: Politics *in suspenso*. *ACME: an International E-journal for Critical Geographies* 4: 240–8.

Hannah, M. 2006b: Torture and the ticking bomb: the War on Terrorism as a geographical imagination of power/knowledge. *Annals of the Association of American Geographers* 96(3): 622–40.

Hannerz, U. 1996: *Transnational connections: culture, people, places*. London: Routledge.

Hansen, M. 1995: Early cinema, late cinema: transformations of the public sphere. In L. Williams, ed., *Viewing positions: ways of seeing film*. New Brunswick, NJ: Rutgers University Press, 134–52.

Hansen, T.B. 2005: Sovereigns beyond the state: on legality and public authority in India. In R. Kaur, ed., *Religion, violence and political mobilisation in South Asia*. London: Sage, 109–44.

Hanson, S. 1992: Feminism and geography: worlds in collision? *Annals of the Association of American Geographers* 82(4): 569–86.

Hanson, S., ed., 1995: *The geography of urban transportation*, 2nd edn. New York: Guilford Press.

Hanson, S. 2000: Transportation: hooked on speed, eyeing sustainability. In E. Sheppard and T. Barnes, eds, *A companion to economic geography*. Oxford: Blackwell, 468–83.

Hanson, S. and Pratt, G. 1991: Job search and the occupational segregation of women. *Annals of the Association of American Geographers* 81: 229–53.

Hanson, S. and Pratt, G. 1995: *Gender, work, and space*. London: Routledge.

Hanson, S. and Schwab, M. 1987: Accessibility and intraurban travel. *Environment and Planning A* 19: 735–48.

Hanssen, B. 2000: *Critique of violence: between poststructuralism and critical theory*. London: Routledge.

Haraway, D. 1985: A manifesto for cyborgs: science, technology, and social feminism in the 1980s. *Socialist Review* 80: 65–107.

Haraway, D. 1988: Situated knowledges: the science question in feminism and the privilege of partial perspective. *Feminist Studies* 14: 575–99.

Haraway, D. 1989: *Primate visions: gender, race, and nature in the world of modern science*. New York: Routledge.

Haraway, D. 1991a: A cyborg manifesto: science, technology, and socialist-feminism in the late twentieth century. In Haraway, *Simians, cyborgs and women: the reinvention of nature*. London: Free Association Books, 149–81.

Haraway, D. 1991b: 'Gender' for a Marxist dictionary: the sexual politics of a word. In Haraway, *Simians, cyborgs, and women: the reinvention of nature*. London: Free Association Books, 127–48.

Haraway, D. 1991c: *Simians, cyborgs and women: the reinvention of nature*. London: Free Association Books.

Haraway, D. 1991d: Situated knowledges: the science question in feminism and the privilege of partial perspective. In Haraway, *Simians, cyborgs and women: the reinvention of nature*. New York: Routledge, 183–201.

Haraway, D. 1992: Promises of monsters: a regenerative politics for 'inappropriate/d others'. In L. Grossberg, C. Nelson and P. Treichler, eds, *Cultural studies*. New York: Routledge, 295–337.

Haraway, D. 1997: *Modest_Witness@Second_Millennium. FemaleMan© Meets_OncoMouse™. Feminism and Technoscience*. London: Routledge.

Haraway, D. 2003: *The companion species manifesto: dogs, people and significant otherness*. Chicago: Prickly Paradigm Press.

Harcourt, B. 2001: *The illusion of order: the false promise of broken windows policing*. Cambridge, MA: Harvard University Press.

Hardin, G. 1968: The tragedy of the commons. *Science* 162: 1243–8.

Harding, S., ed., 2004: *The feminist standpoint theory reader: intellectual and political controversies*. New York: Routledge.

Hardt, M. 2002: Porto Alegre: today's Bandung? *New Left Review* 14: 29–45.

Hardt, M. and Negri, A. 2000: *Empire*. Cambridge, MA: Harvard University Press.

Hardt, M. and Negri, A. 2004: *Multitude: war and democracy in the age of empire*. New York: Penguin and London: Hamish Hamilton.

Hardy, D. 1991: *From garden cities to new towns*. London: E.F. & N. Spon.

Hargreaves, M.M. 1992: *Dry farming in the northern Great Plains: years of readjustment 1920–1990*. Lawrence, KS: University Press of Kansas.

Harlan, J. 1995: *The living fields: our agricultural heritage*. Cambridge: Cambridge University Press.

Harley, J.B. 1986: *Imago mundi*: the first fifty years and the next ten. *Cartographica* 23(3): 1–15.

Harley, J.B. 1987: The map and the development of the history of cartography. In J.B. Harley and D. Woodward, eds, *The history of cartography*, vol. 1. Chicago: The University of Chicago, 1–42.

Harley, J.B. 1989: Deconstructing the map. *Cartographica* 26 1–20. Reprinted in T. Barnes and J. Duncan, eds, *Writing worlds: discourse, text and metaphor in the representation of landscape*. London: Routledge, 1991, 231–47.

Harley, J.B. 1990: *Maps and the Columbian encounter*. Milwaukee: The Golda Meir Library.

Harley, J.B. 2001a: Silences and secrecy: the hidden agenda of cartography in early modern Europe. In his *The new nature of maps: essays in the history of cartography*. Baltimore, MD: The Johns Hopkins University Press. 83–107.

Harley, J.B. 2001b: *The new nature of maps: essays in the history of cartography*, ed. P. Laxton. Baltimore, MD: The Johns Hopkins University Press.

Harley, J.B. and Woodward, D. 1989: Why cartography needs its history. *The American Cartographer* 16: 5–15.

Harley, J.B. and Woodward, D., 1987: Preface. In Harley and Woodward, founding eds, *The history of cartography*, vol. 1. Chicago: The University of Chicago Press, xv–xxi.

Harley, J.B. and Woodward, D., founding eds, 1987– : *The history of cartography*. Chicago: The University of Chicago Press. Vol. 1, *Cartography in prehistoric, ancient, and medieval Europe and the Mediterranean*, ed. Harley and Woodward (1987); vol. 2.1, *Cartography in the traditional Islamic and South Asian societies*, ed. Harley and Woodward (1992); vol. 2.2, *Cartography in the traditional East and Southeast Asian societies*, ed. Harley and Woodward (1994); vol. 2.3, *Cartography in the traditional African, American, Arctic, Australian, and Pacific societies*, ed. Woodward and G.M. Lewis (1998); vol. 3, *Cartography in the European Renaissance*, ed. Woodward (2007); vol. 4, *Cartography in the European Enlightenment*, eds M.H. Edney and M.S. Pedley (forthcoming); vol. 5, *Cartography in the nineteenth century* (forthcoming); vol. 6, *Cartography in the twentieth century*, ed. M. Monmonier (forthcoming).

Harootunian, H. 2000: *History's disquiet: modernity, cultural practice, and the question of everyday life*. New York: Columbia University Press.

Harper, C.L. 2004: *Environment and society: human perspectives on environmental issues*, 3rd edn. Upper Saddle River, NJ: Prentice Hall.

Harper, S. and Laws, G. 1995: Rethinking the geography of ageing. *Progress in Human Geography* 19: 199–221.

Harris, C.D. 1997: 'The nature of cities' and urban geography in the last half-century. *Urban Geography* 18: 15–35.

Harris, C.D. and Ullman, E.L. 1945: The nature of cities. *Annals of the American Academy of Political and Social Science* 242: 7–17.

Harris, L. 1988: The UK economy at the crossroads. In J. Allen and D. Massey, eds, *The economy in question*. London: Sage in association with the Open University, 7–44.

Harris, R.C. 1971: Theory and synthesis in historical geography. *Canadian Geographer* 15: 157–72.

Harris, R.C. 1991: Power, modernity and historical geography. *Annals of the Association of American Geographers* 81(4): 671–83.

Harris, R.C. 1997: *The resettlement of British Columbia: essays on colonialism and geographical change*. Vancouver: University of British Columbia Press.

Harris, R.C. 2004: How did colonialism dispossess? Comments from an edge of empire. *Annals of the Association of American Geographers* 94(1): 165–82.

Harris, R.C., Sleight, P. and Webber, R. 2005: *Geodemographics, GIS and neighbourhood targeting*. Chichester: Wiley.

Harrison, B. 1992: Industrial districts: old wine in new bottles? *Regional Studies* 26: 469–83.

Harrison, B. 1997: *Lean and mean*. New York: Guilford Press.

Harrison, P. 2000: Making sense: embodiment and the sensibilities of the everyday. *Environment and Planning D: Society and Space* 18: 497–517.

Harrison, P. 2006: Post-structuralist theories. In S. Aitken and G. Valentine, eds, *Approaches to human geography*. London: Sage, 122–35.

Harrison, P. 2007a: 'How shall I say it …?' Relating the nonrelational. *Environment & Planning A* 39: 590–608.

Harrison, P. 2007b: The space between us: opening remarks on the concept of dwelling. *Environment and Planning D: Society and Space* 25: 625–47.

Harrison, R.T. and Livingstone, D.N. 1980: Philosophy and problems in human geography: a presuppositional approach. *Area* 12: 25–31.

Harrison, S. 2001: On reductionism and emergence in geomorphology. *Transactions of the Institute of British Geographers* 26: 327–39.

Harrison, S. and Dunham, P. 1998: Decoherence, quantum theory and their implications for the philosophy of geomorphology. *Transactions of the Institute of British Geographers*, NS 23: 501–14.

Harrison, S., Pile, S. and Thrift, N., eds, 2004: *Patterned ground*. London: Reaktion Books.

Harrison, S., Massey, D., Richards, K., Magilligan, F., Thrift, N. and Bender, B. 2004: Thinking across the divide: perspectives on the conversations between physical and human geography. *Area* 36: 435–42.

Harriss, J. 1982: *Capitalism and peasant farming*. Bombay: Oxford University Press.

Harriss, J., ed., 1982: *Rural development: theories of peasant economy and agrarian change*. London: Hutchinson Library for Africa.

Harriss, J. 2001: *Depoliticising development: the World Bank and social capital*. New Delhi: Leftword.

Harriss-White, B. 2003: *India working: essays on society and economy*. Cambridge, UK: Cambridge University Press.

Harrower, M. 2004: A look at the history and future of animated maps. *Cartographica* 39(3): 33–42.

Hart, G. 1991: Engendering everyday resistance: gender, patronage and production politics in rural Malaysia. *Journal of Peasant Studies* 19: 93–121.

Hart, G. 2001: Development critiques in the 1990s: *culs de sacs* and promising paths. *Progress in Human Geography* 35(4): 649–58.

Hart, G. 2003: *Disabling globalization: places of power in post-apartheid South Africa*. Berkeley, CA: University of California Press.

Hart, G. 2006: Denaturalizing dispossession: critical ethnography in the age of resurgent imperialism. *Antipode* 38(5): 977–1004.

Hart, J.F. 1982: The highest form of the geographer's art. *Annals of the Association of American Geographers* 72: 1–29.

Hart, K. 1973: Informal income opportunities and urban employment in Ghana. In R. Jolly, E. de Kadt, H. Singer and F. Wilson, eds, *Third World employment*. London: Penguin.

Hart, R. 1997: *Children's participation: the theory and practice of involving young citizens in community development and environmental care*. London: Earthscan.

Hart, R.A. 1979: *Children's experience of place*. New York: Irvington.

Hart-Landsberg, M. and Burkett, P. 1998: Contradictions of capitalist industrialization in East Asia: A critique of 'flying geese' theories of development. *Economic Geography* 74(2): 87–110.

Hartshorne, R. 1939: *The nature of geography: a critical survey of current thought in light of the past*. Lancaster, PA: Association of American Geographers.

Hartshorne, R. 1950: The functional approach to political geography. *Annals of the Association of American Geographers* 40: 95–130.

Hartshorne, R. 1955: 'Exceptionalism in geography' re-examined. *Annals of the Association of American Geographers* 45: 205–44.

Hartshorne, R. 1958: The concept of geography as a science of space: from Kant and Humboldt to Hettner. *Annals of the Association of American Geographers* 48: 97–108.

Hartshorne, R. 1959: *Perspective on the nature of geography*. Chicago: Rand & McNally.

Hartsock, N. 1983: *Money, sex, and power: toward a feminist historical materialism*. New York: Longman.

Hartwick, E. 1998: Geographies of consumption: a commodity-chain approach. *Environment and Planning D: Society and Space* 16: 423–37.

Harvey, D. 1966: *Justice, nature and the geography of difference*. Oxford: Blackwell.

Harvey, D. 1967: Models of the evolution of spatial patterns in human geography. In R.J. Chorley and P. Haggett, eds, *Models in geography*. London: Methuen, 549–608.

Harvey, D. 1969: *Explanation in geography*. London: Edward Arnold.

Harvey, D. 1972: Revolutionary and counter-revolutionary theory in geography and the problem of ghetto formation. *Antipode* 4: 1–13.

Harvey, D. 1973: *Social justice and the city*. London: Edward Arnold.

Harvey, D. 1974a: Population, resources and the ideology of science. *Economic Geography* 50(3): 256–77.

Harvey, D. 1974b: What kind of geography for what kind of public policy? *Transactions of the Institute of British Geographers*, NS 63: 18–24.

Harvey, D. 1979: Monument and myth. *Annals of the Association of American Geographers* 69: 362–81.

Harvey, D. 1984: On the history and present condition of geography: an historical materialist manifesto. *Professional Geographer* 36: 1–11.

Harvey, D. 1985a: *Consciousness and the urban experience*. Oxford: Blackwell.

Harvey, D. 1985b: The geopolitics of capitalism. In Gregory, D. and Urry, J., eds, *Social relations and spatial structures*. London: Macmillan, 128–63.

Harvey, D. 1988: The geographical and geopolitical consequences of the transition from Fordist to flexible accumulation. In G. Sternlieb and J.W. Hughes, eds, *America's new market geography*. New Brunswick, NJ: Rutgers Center for Urban Policy Research, 101–34.

Harvey, D. 1989a: From managerialism to entrepreneurialism: the transformation of urban governance in late capitalism. *Geografiska Annaler* 71B: 3–17.

Harvey, D. 1989b: *The condition of postmodernity: an enquiry into the origins of cultural change*. Oxford: Blackwell.

Harvey, D. 1989c: *The urban experience*. Baltimore, MD: The Johns Hopkins University Press.

Harvey, D. 1990: Between space and time: reflections on the geographical imagination. *Annals of the Association of American Geographers* 80: 418–34.

Harvey, D. 1992: Postmodern morality plays. *Antipode* 24: 300–26.

Harvey, D. 1996: *Justice, nature and the geography of difference*. Oxford: Blackwell.

Harvey, D. 1999 [1982]: *Limits to capital*, 2nd edn. London: Verso.

Harvey, D. 2000a: Cosmopolitanism and the banality of geographical evils. *Public Culture* 12: 529–64.

Harvey, D. 2000b: *Spaces of hope*. Berkeley, CA: University of California Press/Edinburgh: Edinburgh University Press.

Harvey, D. 2001: The geography of capitalist accumulation. In Harvey, *Spaces of capital*. New York: Routledge, 237–66.

Harvey, D. 2003a: *Paris, capital of modernity*. London and New York: Routledge.

Harvey, D. 2003b: *The new imperialism*. Oxford: Oxford University Press.

Harvey, D. 2004a: Geographical knowledges/political powers. *Proceedings of the British Academy* 122: 87–115.

Harvey, D. 2004b: *The new imperialism*. Oxford: Oxford University Press.

Harvey, D. 2005: *A brief history of neoliberalism*. Oxford: Oxford University Press.

Harvey, D. 2006a: Space as a keyword. In N. Castree and D. Gregory, eds, *David Harvey: a critical reader*. Oxford: Blackwell, 270–93.

Harvey, D. 2006b: *Spaces of global capitalism: a theory of uneven geographical development*. New York: Verso.

Harvey, D. 2006c: The geographies of critical geography. *Transactions of the Institute of British Geographers* 31: 409–12.

Harvey, D. and Scott, A. 1989: The practice of human geography: theory and empirical specificity in the transition from Fordism to flexible accumulation. In B. Macmillan, ed., *Remodelling geography*. Oxford: Blackwell, 217–29.

Harvey, D.C. 2003: Territoriality, parochial development and the place of 'community' in later medieval Cornwall. *Journal of Historical Geography* 29: 151–65.

Harvey, D.W. 1974: Population, resources and the ideology of science. *Economic Geography* 50: 256–77.

Harvey, F., Kwan, M.-P. and Pavovska, M., eds, 2005: Theme issue: 'Critical GIS'. *Cartographica* 40(4).

Hassink, R. 2007: It's the language, stupid! On emotions, strategies and consequences related to the use of one language to describe and explain a diverse world. *Environment and Planning A* 39: 1282–7.

Hastings, A. 1997: *The construction of nationhood: ethnicity, religion and nationalism.* Cambridge, UK: Cambridge University Press.

Hastings, J.V. 2008: Geography, globalization and terrorism: the plots of *Jemaah Islamiyah. Security Studies* 17: 505–30.

Hastrup, K. 2004: *action: anthropology in the company of Shakespeare.* Copenhagen: Museum Tusculanum Press, University of Copenhagen.

Hatcher, J. 1981: English serfdom and villeinage: towards a reassessment. *Past and Present* 90: 4–39.

Hatcher, J. and Bailey, M. 2001: *Modelling the Middle Ages: the history and theory of England's economic development.* Oxford: Oxford University Press.

Haughton, G. and Counsell, D. 2004: *Regions, spatial strategies, and sustainable development.* London: Routledge.

Haughton, S. 1880: *Six lectures on physical geography.* London: Longmans, Green.

Hawley, J.C. 2001: *Postcolonial queer.* New York: State University of New York Press.

Hay, A.M. 1977: *Linear programming: elementary applications of the transportation problem.* Norwich: Geo Books CATMOG 11.

Hay, A.M. and Johnston, R.J. 1983: The study of process in human geography. *L'espace géographique* 12: 69–76.

Hay, D. 1968: *Europe: the emergence of an idea,* 2nd edn. Edinburgh: Edinburgh University Press.

Hay, I., ed., 2000: *Qualitative research methods in human geography.* Oxford/Melbourne: Oxford University Press.

Hayden, D. 1997: *The power of place: urban landscapes as public history.* Cambridge, MA: The MIT Press.

Haydon, C. 2003: *When nature goes public: the making and unmaking of bioprospecting in Mexico.* Princeton, NJ: Princeton University Press.

Hayek, F. 1944: *The road to serfdom.* Chicago: The University of Chicago Press.

Hayek, F. 1981: *The political order of a free people.* Chicago: The University of Chicago Press.

Hayles, N.K. 1999: *How we became posthuman: consequences of the biotechnology revolution.* Chicago: The University of Chicago Press.

Hayles, N.K. 2002: Flesh and metal: reconfiguring the mindbody in virtual environments. *Configurations* 10: 297–320.

Hays, S.P. 1959: *Conservation and the gospel of efficiency – the progressive conservation movement 1890–1920.* Cambridge, MA: Harvard University Press.

Hays-Mitchell, M. 2005: Women's struggles for sustainable peace in post-conflict Peru: a feminist analysis of violence and change. In L. Nelson and J. Seager, eds, *A companion to feminist geography.* Oxford: Blackwell, 590–606.

Hayter, R. 1997: *The dynamics of industrial location.* New York: Wiley.

Hayter, R. and Watts, H.D. 1983: The geography of enterprise: a reappraisal. *Progress in Human Geography* 7: 157–81.

Hayter, R., Barnes, T.J. and Bradshaw, M.J. 2003: Relocating resource peripheries to the core of economic geography's theorizing: rationale and agenda. *Area* 35: 15–23.

Hazell, P., ed., 1987: *The Green Revolution reconsidered.* Baltimore, MD: The Johns Hopkins University Press.

Heater, D. 1992: *The idea of European unity.* Leicester: Leicester University Press.

Heath, J. 2005: Methodological Individualism. In E.N. Zalta, ed., *The Stanford encyclopedia of philosophy*; available at http://plato.stanford.edu/archives/spr2005/entries/methodological-individualism/

Heath, S. 1972: *The nouveau roman.* London: Paul Elek, 13.

Heathcote, R. 1983: *The arid lands: their use and abuse.* London: Longman.

Heaton, J. 1998: Secondary analysis of qualitative data. *Social Research Update 22*; available at http://sru.soc.surrey.ac.uk/SRU22.html

Heaton, J. 2004: *Reworking qualitative data: the possibility of secondary analysis.* London: Sage.

Hebbert, M. 2005: The street as a locus of collective memory. *Environment and Planning D: Society and Space* 23: 581–96.

Hecht, S. 1985: Environment, development and politics. *World Development* 13: 663–84.

Hecht, S. and Cockburn, A. 1989: *The fate of the forest.* London: Verso.

Hechter, M. 1975: *Internal colonialism.* London: Routledge.

Heelas, P., ed., 1998: *Religion, modernity and postmodernity,* Oxford: Blackwell.

Heffernan, M. 1995: For ever England: the Western Front and the politics of remembrance in Britain. *Ecumene* 2: 293–324.

Heffernan, M. 1996: Geography, cartography and military intelligence: the Royal Geographical Society and the First World War. *Transactions of the Institute of British Geographers* 21: 504–33.

Heffernan, M. 1998: *The meaning of Europe: geography and geopolitics.* London: Arnold.

Heffernan, M. 2007: *The European geographical imagination.* Stuttgart: Franz Steiner.

Heffernan, W.D. and Constance, D.H. 1994: Transnational corporations and the globalization of the food system. In A. Bonanno, L. Busch, W. Friedland, L. Gouveia and E. Mingione, eds, *From Columbus to ConAgra.*

Kansas City: University Press of Kansas, 29–51.

Heidegger, M. 1962 [1927]: *Being and time*. New York: Harper & Row and Oxford: Blackwell.

Heidegger, M. 1991 [1947]: Letter on humanism. In D.F. Krell, ed., *Basic writings*. London: Routledge, 189–242.

Heilbron, J. 1995: *The rise of social theory*. Minneapolis: University of Minnesota Press.

Held, D. 1996: *Models of democracy*. Cambridge, UK: Polity Press.

Held, D. and Koenig-Archibugi, M., eds, 2003: *Taming globalization*. Cambridge: Polity Press.

Held, D., McGrew, A., Goldblatt, D. and Perraton, J. 1999: *Global transformations: politics, economics and culture*. Stanford, CA: Stanford University Press.

Helgerson, R. 1992: *Forms of nationhood: the Elizabethan writing of England*. Chicago: The University of Chicago Press.

Helmfrid, S. 1961: Morphogenesis of the agrarian landscape. *Geografiska Annaler* 43: 1–328.

Hempel, C.G. and Oppenheim, P. 1948: Studies in the logic of explanation. *Philosophy of Science* 15: 135–75.

Henderson, G. 1999: *California and the fictions of capital*. New York: Oxford University Press.

Henderson, J., Dicken, P., Hess, M., Coe, N. and Yeung, H.W.-C. 2001: Global production networks and the analysis of economic development. *Review of International Political Economy* 9: 436–64.

Henderson-Sellers, A. and McGuffie, K. 1987: *A climate modelling primer*. Chichester: Wiley.

Henke, C.R. 2000: Making a place for science: the field trial. *Social Studies of Science* 30: 483–511.

Henry, L. 1956: *Anciennes familles genevoises: etude démographiques XVIe–XXe siècles*. Travaux et Documents, Cahier no. 26. Paris: Institut National d'Etudes Démographiques.

Henry, L. 1956: *Anciennes familles genevoises: Etude démographiques XVIe-XXe siècles*. Institut National d'Etudes Demographiques. Travaux et documents, Cahier No. 26. Paris: Presses Universitaires de France.

Henry, N. and Pinch, S. 1997: *A regional formula for success?* Birmingham, UK: University of Birmingham.

Henry, N. and Pinch, S. 2000: Spatialising knowledge: placing the knowledge community of Motor Sport Valley. *Geoforum* 31: 191–208.

Hensher, D.A. and Greene, W.H. 2004: The mixed logit model; the state of practice. *Transportation* 30: 133–76.

Hepple, L.W. 1974: The impact of stochastic process theory upon spatial analysis in human geography. *Progress in Geography* 5: 89–142.

Hepple, L.W. 1995: Bayesian techniques in spatial and network econometrics: 2. Computational methods and algorithms. *Environment and Planning A* 27: 615–44.

Hepple, L.W. 1999: Socialist geography in England: J.F. Horrabin and a workers' economic and political geography. *Antipode* 31(1): 80–109.

Hepworth, M. 1989: *The geography of the information economy*, London: Frances Pinter.

Herb, G.H. 1997: *Under the map of Germany: nationalism and propaganda, 1918–1945*. London: Routledge.

Herbert, D. and Smith, D., eds, 1989: *Social problems and the city: new perspectives*. Oxford: Oxford University Press.

Herbert, S. 1997: *Policing space: territoriality and the Los Angeles Police Department*. Minneapolis: University of Minnesota Press.

Herbert, S. 2000: For ethnography. *Progress in Human Geography* 24: 550–68.

Herbert, S. 2005: The trapdoor of community. *Annals of the Association of American Geographers* 95: 850–65.

Herbert, S. 2006: *Citizens, cops and power: recognizing the limits of community*. Chicago: The University of Chicago Press.

Herbertson, A.J. 1915: Regional environment, heredity and consciousness. *The Geography Teacher* 8: 147–53.

Herbst, J. 1961: Social Darwinism and the history of American Geography. *Proceedings of the American Philosophical Society* 105: 538–44.

Herman, R.D.K. 1999: The Aloha State: place names and the anti-conquest of Hawai'i. *Annals of the Association of American Geographers* 89: 76–102.

Herod, A., ed., 1998: *Organizing the landscape: geographical perspectives on labor unionism*. Minneapolis: University of Minnesota Press.

Herod, A. 2002: *Labour geographies: workers and the landscapes of capitalism*. New York: Guilford Press.

Herod, A. and Wright, M., eds, 2002: *Geographies of power: placing scale*. Oxford: Blackwell.

Herod, A., Peck, J. and Wills, J. 2003: Geography and industrial relations. In P. Ackers and A. Wilkinson, eds, *Reworking industrial relations: new perspectives on employment and society*. Oxford: Oxford University Press, 176–94.

Hess, D.J. 1997: *Science studies: an advanced introduction*. New York: New York University Press.

Hesse, B., ed., 2000: *Un/settled multiculturalisms: diaspora, entanglements, transruptions*. London: Zed Books.

Hesse, M.B. 1980: *Revolutions and reconstructions in the philosophy of science*. Brighton: Harvester.

Hetherington, K. 1997a: In place of geometry: the materiality of place. In K. Hetherington and R. Munro, eds, *Ideas of difference: social spaces and the labour of division*. Oxford: Blackwell, 183–99.

Hetherington, K. 1997b: *The badlands of modernity: heterotopia and social ordering*. London: Routledge.

Hetherington, K. and Law, J., eds, 2000: After networks. Theme issue of *Environment and Planning D: Society and Space* 18(2).

Hettner, A. 1907: *Grundzüge der Länderkunde*, Band 1. Leipzig: Europa.

Heubusch, K. 1997: *The new rating guide to life in American small cities*. Amherst NY: Promoetheus Books.

Hewitt, K., ed., 1983: *Interpretations of calamity*. London: George Allen & Unwin.

Hewitt, K. 1987: The social space of terror: towards a civil interpretation of total war. *Environment and Planning D: Society and Space* 5: 445–74.

Hewitt, K. 2001: Between Pinochet and Kropotkin: state terror, human rights and the geographers. *Canadian Geographer* 45: 338–55.

Heynen, H. 1999: *Architecture and modernity: a critique*. Cambridge, MA: The MIT Press.

Heynen, N., Kaika, M. and Swyngedouw, E., eds, 2006: *In the nature of cities: urban political ecology and the politics of urban metabolism*. London: Routledge.

Heynen, N., McCarthy, J., Prudham, S. and Robbins, P., eds, 2007: *Neoliberal environments: false promises and unnatural consequences*. New York: Routledge.

Hickman, H., Higgins, V., Hope, V., Bellis, M., Tilling, K., Walker, A. and Henry, J. 2004: Injecting drug use in Brighton, Liverpool, and London: best estimates of prevalence and coverage of public health indicators. *Journal of Epidemiology and Community Health* 58: 766–71.

Hiebert, D. 1999: Local geographies of labour market segmentation: Montréal, Toronto and Vancouver, 1991. *Economic Geography* 75: 339–69.

Hiebert, D. and Ley, D. 2003: Assimilation, cultural pluralism and social exclusion among ethno-cultural groups in Vancouver. *Urban Geography* 24: 16–44.

Highmore, B. 2002: *Everyday life and cultural theory: an introduction*. London: Routledge.

Hilberg, R. 2003 [1961]: *The destruction of the European Jews*. New Haven, CT: Yale University Press.

Hill, J. 2006a: Globe-trotting medicine chests: tracing geographies of collecting and pharmaceuticals. *Social and Cultural Geography* 7: 365–84.

Hill, J. 2006b: Travelling objects: the Wellcome collection in Los Angeles, London and beyond. *Cultural Geographies* 13: 340–66.

Hiller, B. 1996: *Space is the machine: a configurational theory of architecture*. Cambridge, UK: Cambridge University Press.

Hillier, B. and Hanson, J. 1989: *The social logic of space*. Cambridge, UK: Cambridge University Press.

Hillis, K. 1999: *Digital sensations: space, identity and embodiment in virtual reality*. Minneapolis: University of Minnesota Press.

Hilton, R. 1973: *Bond men made free: medieval peasant movements and the English rising of 1381*. London: Temple Smith.

Hilton, R., ed., 1976: *The transition from feudalism to capitalism*. London: Verso.

Hilton, R., ed., 1985: *Class conflict and the crisis of feudalism: essays in medieval social history*. London: Hambledon Press.

Hinchcliffe, S. 2003: Inhabiting – landscapes and natures. In K. Anderson, M. Domosh, S. Pile and N. Thrift, eds, *Handbook of cultural geography*. London: Sage.

Hinchliffe, S. 2004: Viruses. In S. Harrison, S. Pile and N.Thrift, eds, *Patterned ground: entanglements of nature and culture*. London: Reaktion Books, 228–30.

Hinchliffe, S. 2007: *Geographies of nature: societies, environments, ecologies*. London: Sage.

Hinchliffe, S., Kearnes, M., Degen, M. and Whatmore, S. 2005: Urban wild things: a cosmopolitical experiment. *Environment and Planning D: Society and Space* 23: 643–58.

Hindess, B. 2006: Terrortory. *Alternatives* 31: 243–57.

Hines, C. 2000: *Localization: a global manifesto*. London: Earthscan.

Hirsch, A. 1983: *Making the second ghetto: race and housing in Chicago, 1940–1960*. Cambridge, UK: Cambridge University Press.

Hirschman, A.O. 1970: *Exit, voice and loyalty*. Cambridge, MA: Harvard University Press.

Hirschman, A.O. 1977: *The passions and the interest*. Princeton, NJ: Princeton University Press.

Hirschmann, A. 1958: *The strategy of economic development*. New Haven, CT: Yale University Press.

Hirst, P. 2005: *Space and power: politics, war and architecture*. Cambridge, UK: Polity Press.

Hirst, P. and Thompson, G. 1996: *Globalization in question: the international economy and possibilities of governance*. Cambridge, UK: Polity Press.

Ho, K. 2005: Situating global capitalisms: a view from Wall Street investment banks. *Cultural Anthropology* 20: 68–96.

Hobbes, T. 1968 [1651]: *Leviathan*, ed. C.B. Macpherson. London: Penguin.

Hobbs, J. 2005: The geographical dimensions of al-Qa'ida rhetoric. *Geographical Review* 25: 301–27.

Hobbs, J. and Salter, K. 2006: *Essentials of world regional geography*. Wadsworth, CA: Brooks/Cole.

Hodder, I. 2006: *The leopard's tail: revealing the mysteries of Çatalhoyük*. London: Thames and Hudson.

Hodge, D., ed., 1995. Focus: Should women count? The role of quantitative methodology in feminist geographic research. *The Professional Geographer* 47: 426–66.

Hodges, R. and Whitehouse, D. 1983: *Mohammed, Charlemagne and the origins of Europe: archaeology and the Pirenne thesis.* London: Duckworth.

Hodgson, G. 1988: *Economics and institutions.* Cambridge, UK: Polity Press.

Hoelscher, S. 2003: Making place, making race: performances of whiteness in the Jim Crow South. *Annals of the Association of American Geographers* 93: 657–86.

Hoggart, K., Lees, L. and Davies, A. 2002: *Researching human geography.* London: Arnold.

Holborn, L., ed., 1948: *War and peace aims of the United Nations: from Casablanca to Tokio Bay, January 1, 1943–September 1, 1945.* Boston: World Peace Foundation.

Holder, J. and Harrison, C., eds, 2003: *Law and geography.* Oxford: Oxford University Press.

Holdich, T.H. 1916: *Political frontiers and boundary making.* London: Macmillan.

Holdsworth, C. and Elliot, J. 2001: The timing of family formation in Britain and Spain. *Sociological Research Online* 6: U49–U72.

Holland, J.H. 1995: *Hidden order: how adaptation builds complexity.* Reading, MA: Addison-Wesley.

Holland, P. and Huggan, G. 1999: *Tourists with typewriters: critical reflections on contemporary travel writing.* Ann Arbor: University of Michigan Press.

Holling, C. 1973: Resilience and stability in ecological systems. *Annual Review of Ecology and Systematics* 4: 1–23.

Hollingsworth, T. 1969: *Historical demography.* London: Hodder and Stoughton

Hollis, M. and Lukes, S., eds, 1982: *Rationality and relativism.* Oxford: Blackwell.

Holloway, J. and Kneale, J. 1999: Bakhtin's geographies. In M. Crang and N.J. Thrift, eds, *Thinking space.* London: Routledge.

Holloway, J. and Valins, O. 2002: Placing religion and spirituality in geography. *Social and Cultural Geography* 3(1): 5–10.

Holloway, L. and Hubbard, P. 2001: *People and place: the extraordinary geographies of everyday life.* London: Longman.

Holloway, S., Rice, S. and Valentine, G., eds, 2003: *Key concepts in Geography.* London: Sage.

Holloway, S.L. 1998: Geographies of justice: preschool childcare provision and the conceptualisation of social justice. *Environment and Planning C: Government and Policy* 16(1); 85–104.

Holloway, S.L. and Valentine, G., eds, 2000: *Children's geographies: playing, living, learning.* London: Routledge.

Holloway, S.R. 1998: Exploring the neighborhood contingency of race discrimination in mortgage lending in Columbus, Ohio. *Annals of the Association of American Geographers* 88 (2): 252–76.

Holmberg, S.C. 1992: Geoinformatics for urban and regional planning. *Environment and Planning B: Planning and Design* 21: 5–19.

Holmen, H. 1995: What's new and what's regional in the 'new regional geography'? *Geografiska Annaler* 77B: 47–63.

Holsti, K.J. 2004: *Taming the sovereigns: institutional change in international politics.* Cambridge, UK: Cambridge University Press.

Holt, T., Steel, D., Tranmer, M. and Wrigley, N. 1996: Aggregation and ecological effects in geographically-based data. *Geographical Analysis* 28: 244–61.

Holyoake, G.J. 1860: *The principles of secularism.* London: IDEM.

Holzer, H.J. 1991: The spatial mismatch hypothesis: What has the evidence shown? *Urban Studies* 28(1): 105–22.

Homer-Dixon, T. 1999: *Environment, scarcity and violence.* Princeton, NJ: Princeton University Press.

Honig, B. 1998: Immigrant America? How foreignness 'solves' democracy's problems. *Social Text* 16: 1027.

Hönnighausen, L., Frey, M., Peacock, J. and Steiner, N. 2005: *Regionalism in the age of globalism,* vol. 1: *Concepts of regionalism.* Madison, WI: University of Wisconsin Press.

hooks, b. 1991: *Yearning: race, gender and cultural politics.* London: Turnaround.

Hooykaas, R. 1979: *Humanism and the voyages of discovery in 16th century Portuguese science and letters.* Amsterdam: North Holland.

Hopkins, K. and Beard, M. 2005: *The Colosseum.* London: Profile Books.

Hopkins, T. and Wallerstein, I. 1977: Patterns of development of the modern world-system. *Review* 1(2): 11–145.

Horkheimer, M. 1975: *Critical theory.* New York: Continuum.

Horton, J. and Kraftl, P. 2006: What else? Some more ways of thinking about and doing children's geographies. *Children's Geographies* 4: 69–95.

Hoselitz, B.F. 1952: *The progress of underdeveloped areas.* Chicago: The University of Chicago Press.

Hosmer, D.W. and Lemshow, S. 2000: *Applied logistic regression,* 2nd edn. New York: Wiley.

Hotelling, H. 1929: Stability in competition. *The Economic Journal* 39: 40–7.

Hough, M. 2004: *Cities and natural process,* 2nd rev. edn. London: Routledge.

House, J.W. 1973: Geographers, decision takers and policy makers. In M. Chisholm and B. Rodgers, eds, *Studies in human geography.* London: Heinemann, 272–301.

House, J.W., ed., 1983: *United States public policy: a geographical view.* Oxford: The Clarendon Press.

Houston, D. and Pulido, L. 2002: The work of performativity: staging social justice at the

University of Southern California *Environment and Planning D: Society and Space* 20: 401–24.

Houston, R. and Snell, K. 1984: Protoindustrialisation? Cottage industry, social change and industrial revolution. *Historical Journal* 27: 473–92.

Howarth, D. 2000: *Discourse*. Milton Keynes: Open University Press.

Howarth, D., Norval, A.J. and Stavrakakis, Y., eds, 2000: *Discourse theory and political analysis: identities, hegemonies and social change*. Manchester: Manchester University Press.

Howe, G.M., ed., 1977: *A world geography of human diseases*. London: Academic Press.

Howe, N. 2008: Thou shalt not misinterpret: landscape as legal performance. *Annals of the Association of American Geographers* 98: 435–60.

Howe, S. 2002: *Empire: a very short introduction*. Oxford: Oxford University Press.

Howell, P. 1993: Public space and the public sphere: political theory and the historical geography of modernity. *Environment and Planning D: Society and Space* 11(3): 303–22.

Howell, P.M.R. 2000: Prostitution and racialised sexuality: the regulation of prostitution in Britain and the British Empire before the Contagious Diseases Acts. *Environment and Planning D: Society and Space* 18: 321–39.

Howitt, R. 2001a: Frontiers, borders, edges: liminal challenges to the hegemony of exclusion. *Australian Geographical Studies* 39: 233–45.

Howitt, R. 2001b: *Rethinking resource management: justice, sustainability and indigenous peoples*. London: Routledge.

Howitt, R. 2003: Scale. In J. Agnew, K. Mitchell K, and G. Ó Tuathail, eds, *A companion to political geography*. Oxford: Blackwell, 138–57.

Hoy, D. and McCarthy, T. 1994: *Critical theory*. Oxford: Blackwell.

Hoyle, R. 1990: Tenure and the land market in early modern England. Or a late contribution to the Brenner debate. *Economic History Review* 43: 1–20.

Hoyt, H. 1939: *The structure and growth of residential neighborhoods in American cities*. Washington, DC: Federal Housing Administration.

Hoyt, P.D. 2000: The 'rogue state' image in American foreign policy. *Global Society* 14: 297–310.

Hubbard, P. 1999: *Sex and the city: geographies of prostitution in the urban West*. Aldershot: Ashgate.

Hubbard, P. 2000: Desire/disgust: mapping the moral contours of heterosexuality. *Progress in Human Geography* 24: 191–217.

Hubbard, P. 2004: Revenge and injustice in the revanchist city: uncovering masculinist agendas *Antipode* 36: 665–86.

Hubbard, P., Kitchin, R. and Valentine, G., eds, 2004: *Key thinkers on space and place*. London: Sage.

Hubbard, P., Kitchin, R. and Valentine, G., eds, 2008: *Key texts in human geography*. London: Sage.

Hubbard, P., Kitchin, R., Bartley, B. and Fuller, D. 2002: *Thinking geographically: space, theory and contemporary human geography*. London: Continuum.

Huckfeldt, R. and Sprague, J. 1995: *Citizens, politics and social communication: information and influence in an election campaign*. Cambridge, UK: Cambridge University Press.

Hudson, A. 1998: Placing trust, trusting place: on the social construction of offshore financial centres. *Political Geography* 17: 915–37.

Hudson, J.C. 1969: Diffusion in a central place system. *Geographical Analysis* 1: 45–58.

Hudson, P., ed., 1989: *Regions and industries: a perspective in the Industrial Revolution in Britain*. Cambridge, UK: Cambridge University Press.

Hudson, P. 1992: *The Industrial Revolution*. London: Edward Arnold.

Hudson, R. 2001: *Producing places*. New York: Guilford Press.

Hudson, R. 2005: *Economic geographies*. London: Sage.

Hudson, R. 2005: Rethinking change in old industrial regions: reflecting on the experiences of North East England. *Environment and Planning A* 37: 581–96.

Hudson, R. 2007: Regions and regional uneven development forever? *Regional Studies* 41(9): 1149–60.

Hudson-Rodd, N. and Hunt, M. 2005: The military occupation of Burma. *Geopolitics* 10: 500–21.

Huggett, R.J. 1980: *Systems analysis in geography*. Oxford: The Clarendon Press.

Hughes, A. 2005: Geographies of exchange and circulation I: alternative trading spaces *Progress in Human Geography* 29(4): 496–504.

Hughes, A. and Reimer, S., eds, 2004: *Geographies of commodity chains*. London: Routledge.

Hughes, R. 2007: Through the looking blast: geopolitics and visual culture. *Geography Compass* 1: 976–94.

Hugo, G. 1994: Migration and the family. *Occasional Papers Series for the International Year of the Family*, Number 12. Vienna: United Nations.

Hugo, G., Champion, T. and Lattes, A. 2003: Toward a new conceptualization of settlements for demography. *Population and Development Review* 29: 277–97.

Hulme, D. and Murphree, M., eds, 2001: *African wildlife and livelihoods: the promise and performance of community conservation*. Oxford: James Currey.

Human Security Brief 2007, available at http://www.humansecuritybrief.info

Human Security Report 2005, available at http://www.humansecurityreport.info

Hume, P. and Youngs, T., eds, 2002: *The Cambridge companion to travel writing.* Cambridge, UK: Cambridge University Press.

Humphries, J. 1990: Enclosure, common rights and women: the proletarianization of families in the late eighteenth and early nineteenth century. *Journal of Economic History* 50(1): 17–42.

Hunter, A. 1979: The urban neighborhood: its analytical and social contexts. *Urban Affairs Quarterly* 14: 267–88.

Hunter, J.M. 1974: The challenge of medical geography. In J.M. Hunter, ed., *The geography of health and disease: papers of the first Carolina Geographical Symposium.* Chapel Hill: University of North Carolina Department of Geography, Studies in Geography No. 6.

Huntington, S. 1993: The clash of civilizations? *Foreign Affairs* 72: 22–49.

Huntington, S. 1997: *The clash of civilizations and the remaking of the world order.* New York: Touchstone/Simon and Schuster.

Huntington, S.P. 2004: *Who are we? The challenges to America's national identity.* New York: Simon and Schuster.

Huxley, M. 2007: Geographies of governmentality. In J. Crampton and S. Elden, eds, *Space, knowledge and power: Foucault and geography.* London: Ashgate, 185–204.

Huxley, T.H. 1877: *Physiography: an introduction to the study of nature.* London: Macmillan.

Huxtable, A.L. 1970: *Will they ever finish Bruckner Boulevard?* Berkeley, CA: University of California Press.

Huyssen, A. 2007: Geographies of modernism in a globalizing world. *New German Critique* 34: 189–207.

Hymer, S. 1979: *The multinational corporation: a radical approach,* ed. R. Cohen. Cambridge, UK: Cambridge University Press.

Hyndman, J. 1997: Border crossings. *Antipode* 29: 149–76.

Hyndman, J. 2000: *Managing displacement: refugees and the politics of humanitarianism.* Minneapolis: University of Minnesota Press.

Hyndman, J. 2003: Beyond either/or: a feminist analysis of September 11th. *ACME: an International E-Journal for Critical Geographies* 2(1).

Hyndman, J. 2004: Mind the gap: bridging feminist and political geography through geopolitics. *Political Geography* 23: 307–22.

Hyndman, J. 2005: Feminist geopolitics and September 11. In L. Nelson and J. Seager, eds, *A companion to feminist geography.* Oxford: Blackwell, 565–77.

Hyndman, J. 2007: Feminist geopolitics revisited: body counts in Iraq. *Professional Geographer* 59: 35–46.

Hyndman, J. and Mountz, A. 2008: Another brick in the wall? Neo-refoulement and the externalization of asylum by Europe and Australia. *Government and Opposition* 43: 249–69.

Ietto-Gillies, G. 2005: *Transnational corporations and international production.* London: Edward Elgar.

Ignatieff, M. 2003: The burden? With a military of unrivalled might, the United States rules a new kind of empire. *The New York Times Magazine,* 5 January: 22–54.

Ikporukpo, C. 2004: Petroleum, fiscal federalism, and environmental justice in Nigeria. *Space and Polity* 8: 321–54.

Imrie, R. 1996: *Disability and the city: international perspectives.* London: Paul Chapman.

Inglehart, R. 1977: *The silent revolution: changing values and political styles.* Princeton, NJ: Princeton University Press.

Ingold, T. 1980: *Hunters, pastoralists, and ranchers: reindeer economies and their transformations.* Cambridge, UK: Cambridge University Press.

Ingold, T. 1993: The temporality of the landscape. *World Archaeology* 25(2): 152–71.

Ingold, T. 2000: *The perception of the environment: essays in livelihood, dwelling and skill.* London: Routledge.

Ingram, D. 1987: *Habermas and the dialectic of reason.* New Haven, CT: Yale University Press.

Innis, H. 1927: *The fur-trade of Canada.* Toronto: University of Toronto Library.

Innis, H.A. 1956 [1929]: The teaching of economic history in Canada. In M.Q. Innis, ed., *Essays in Canadian economic history.* Toronto: University of Toronto Press, 3–16.

Intergovernmental Panel on Climate Change (IPCC) 2001: *Climate change 2001.* Cambridge, UK: Cambridge University Press.

Intergovernmental Panel on Climate Change (IPCC) 2003: Glossary of terms; available at http://www.ipcc.ch/pub/gloss.htm

International Commission on Intervention and State Sovereignty 2001: *The responsibility to protect.* Ottawa: International Development Research Corporation.

Ipbuker, C. 2004: Numerical evaluation of the Robinson projection. *Cartography and Geographic Information Science* 31: 79–88.

Irwin, R. 2006: *For lust of knowing: the Orientalists and their enemies.* London: Allen Lane.

Isard, W. 1956: *Location and space economy.* Cambridge, MA: The MIT Press.

Isard, W. 1979: Notes on the origins, development, and future of regional science, *Papers and Proceedings of the Regional Science Association* 43: 9–22.

Isin, E.F. 2002: *Being political.* Minneapolis: University of Minnesota Press.

Isin, E.F. and Wood, P.K. 1999: *Citizenship and identity.* London: Sage.

Isserman, A. 1996: 'It's obvious, it's wrong, and anyway they said it years ago.' Paul Krugman on large cities. *International Regional Science Review* 19: 37–48.

IWCO 1998: *The ocean: our future.* Cambridge, UK: Cambridge University Press.

Iyer, P. 1989: *Video night in Kathmandu.* London: Abacus.

Jackson, C., Best, N. and Richardson, S. 2008: Hierarchical related regression for combining aggregate and survey data in studies of socio-economic disease risk factors. *Journal of the Royal Statistical Society, Series A* 171: 159–78.

Jackson, J.B. 1970: *Landscapes: selected writings of J.B. Jackson,* ed. E.H. Zube. Amherst: University of Massachusetts Press.

Jackson, J.B. 1984: *Discovering the vernacular landscape.* Princeton, NJ: Yale University Press.

Jackson, K. 1985: *Crabgrass frontier.* New York: Oxford University Press.

Jackson, P. 1984: Social disorganization and moral order in the city. *Transactions of the Institute of British Geographers* 9: 168–80.

Jackson, P. 1989: *Maps of meaning: an introduction to cultural geography.* London: Unwin Hyman.

Jackson, P. 1999: Commodity cultures: the traffic in things. *Transactions of the Institute of British Geographers* 24: 95–108.

Jackson, P. 2000: Rematerializing social and cultural geography, *Social & Cultural Geography* 1: 9–14.

Jackson, P., Crang, P. and Dwyer, C., eds, 2004: *Transnational spaces.* London: Routledge.

Jackson, P. and Jacobs, J.M. 1996: Editorial: post-colonialism and the politics of race, *Environment and Planning D: Society and Space* 14: 1–3.

Jackson, P. and Smith, S. 1984: *Exploring social geography.* London: George Allen and Unwin.

Jackson, R.H. 1990: *Quasi-states: sovereignty, international relations, and the Third World.* Cambridge, UK: Cambridge University Press.

Jacob, C. 2006: *The sovereign map: theoretical approaches in cartography throughout history,* trans. T. Conley; ed. E.H. Dahl. Chicago: The University of Chicago Press.

Jacobs, J. and Nash, C. 2003: Too little, too much: cultural feminist geographies. *Gender, Place and Culture* 10: 265–79.

Jacobs, J.M. 1992 [1961]: *The death and life of great American cities.* New York: Vintage Books.

Jacobs, J.M. 1996: *Edge of empire: postcolonialism and the city.* London and New York: Routledge.

Jacobsen, J.L. 1988: *Environmental refugees: a yardstick of habitability.* Washington, DC: Worldwatch Institute Worldwatch Paper no. 86.

Jacobson, D. 1996: *Rights across borders: immigration and the decline of citizenship.* Baltimore, MD: The Johns Hopkins University Press.

Jagose, A. 1996: *Queer theory: an introduction.* New York: State University of New York Press.

James, C.L.R. 2005 [1963]: *Beyond a boundary.* London: Random House/Yellow Jersey Press.

James, P. 1972: *All possible worlds: a history of geographical ideas.* Indianapolis: Bobbs-Merrill.

James, W. 1977: *A pluralistic universe.* Cambridge, MA: Harvard University Press.

James, W. 1987: *Writings, 1902–1910,* ed. B. Kuklick. New York: Library of America.

Jameson, F. 1984: Postmodernism, or the cultural logic of late capitalism. *New Left Review* 146: 53–92.

Jameson, F. 1991: *Postmodernism, or the cultural logic of late capitalism.* Durham, NC: Duke University Press.

Janelle, D. 1968: Central-place development in a time–space framework. *Professional Geographer* 20: 5–10.

Janelle, D. 1969: Spatial reorganization: a model and concept. *Annals of the Association of American Geographers* 59: 348–64.

Janelle, D. 2004: Impact of information technologies. In S. Hanson and G. Giuliano, eds, *The geography of urban transportation,* 3rd edn. New York: Guilford Press.

Janković, V. 2000: *Reading the skies: a cultural history of English weather, 1650–1820.* Manchester: Manchester University Press.

Jardine, A. 1985: *Gynesis: configurations of women and modernity.* Ithaca, NY: Cornell University Press.

Jasso, G. and Rosenzweig, M.R. 1986: Family reunification and the immigration multiplier: United States immigration law, origin country conditions and the reproduction of immigrants. *Demography* 23: 291–311.

Jay, M. 1993: *Downcast eyes: the denigration of vision in 20th century French thought.* Berkeley, CA: University of California Press.

Jefferson, M. 1939: The law of the primate city. *Geographical Review* 29: 226–32.

Jeffres, G.A. 2003: The value of cadastral surveying to efficient land administration. *Surveying and Land Information Science* 63: 253–58.

Jeffreys, H. 1998 [1939]: *Theory of probability,* 3rd edn. Oxford: Oxford University Press.

Jeffries, M. 1997: *Biodiversity and conservation.* London: Routledge.

Jencks, C. and Mayer, S. 1990: The social consequences of growing up in a poor neighborhood. In L. Lynn and M. McGeary, editors, *Inner-city poverty in the United States.* Washington, DC: National Academy Press, 111–86.

Jenkins, M. 2003: Prospects for biodiversity. *Science* 302: 1175–7.

Jenkins, R. 1996: Ethnicity etcetera: social anthropological points of view. *Ethnic and Racial Studies* 19: 807–22.

Jenks, C. 2003: *Transgression.* London: Routledge.

Jessop, B. 1997: A neo-Gramscian approach to the regulation of urban regimes: accumulation strategies, hegemonic projects, and governance. In M. Lauria, ed., *Reconstructing urban* regime theory: regulating urban politics in a global economy. Thousand Oaks, CA: Sage, 51–73.

Jessop, B. 1998: The narrative of enterprise and the enterprise of narrative: place marketing and the entrepreneurial city. In T. Hall and P. Hubbard, eds, The entrepreneurial city: geographies of politics, regime, and representation. New York: Wiley, 77–99.

Jessop, B. 2000: Governance failure. In G. Stoker, ed., The new politics of British local governance. London: Macmillan, 11–32.

Jessop, B. 2002: The future of the capitalist state. Cambridge, UK: Polity Press.

Jessop, B. 2006: Spatial fixes, temporal fixes and spatio-temporal fixes. In N. Castree and D. Gregory, eds, David Harvey: a critical reader. Oxford: Blackwell, 142–66.

Jessop, B. and Sum, N.-L. 2006: Beyond the regulation approach: putting capitalist economies in their place. Cheltenham: Edward Elgar.

Jewitt, S. 2002: Environment, knowledge and gender: local development in India's Jharkhand. Aldershot: Ashgate.

Jirstrom, M. 1996: In the wake of the Green Revolution. Lund: Lund University Press.

Johnson, C. 2003a: The sorrows of empire: militarism, secrecy and the end of the republic. New York: Henry Holt.

Johnson, N.C. 2003b: Ireland, the Great War and the geography of remembrance. Cambridge, UK: Cambridge University Press.

Johnson, N.C. 2005: Locating memory: tracing the trajectories of remembrance. Historical Geography 33: 165–79.

Johnson, N.C. 2006: Cultivating science and planting beauty: the spaces of display in Cambridge's botanical gardens. Interdisciplinary Science Reviews 31: 42–57.

Johnson, R., Chambers, D., Raghuram, P. and Tincknell, E. 2004: The practice of cultural studies. London: Sage.

Johnston, L. 2001: (Other) bodies and tourism studies. Annals of Tourism Research 28: 180–201.

Johnston, R.J. 1969: Urban residential patterns: an introductory review. London: George Bell/New York: Praeger (also London: George Bell, 1971; New York: Praeger, 1972).

Johnston, R.J. 1978: Multivariate statistical analysis in geography. London: Longman.

Johnston, R.J. 1983: Resource analysis, resource management and the integration of physical and human geography. Progress in Physical Geography 7: 127–46.

Johnston, R.J. 1984: Residential segregation, the state and constitutional conflict in American urban areas. Institute of British Geographers, Special Publication 17. London: Academic Press.

Johnston, R.J., ed., 1985: The future of geography. London: Methuen.

Johnston, R.J. 1986a: On human geography. Oxford: Blackwell.

Johnston, R.J. 1986b [1983]: Philosophy and human geography: an introduction to contemporary approaches. London: Edward Arnold.

Johnston, R.J. 1994: The 'quality industry' in British higher education and the AAG's publications. The Professional Geographer 46: 491–7.

Johnston, R.J. 1999: Geography, fairness and liberal democracy. In J. Proctor and D.M. Smith, eds, Geography and ethics. London: Routledge, 44–58.

Johnston, R.J. 2002: Census counts and apportionment: the politics of representation in the United States ... continued. Environment and Planning D: Society and Space 20: 619–28.

Johnston, R.J. 2003: The institutionalisation of geography as an academic discipline. In R.J. Johnston and M. Williams, eds, A century of British geography. Oxford: Oxford University Press for the British Academy, 45–91.

Johnston, R.J. 2005a: Anglo-American electoral geography: same roots and same goals but different means and ends? The Professional Geographer 57: 580–7.

Johnston, R.J. 2005b: Geography – coming apart at the seams? In N. Castree, A. Rogers and D. Sherman, eds, Questioning geography: fundamental debates. Oxford: Blackwell, 9–25.

Johnston, R.J. 2005c: Regionalization and classification. In K. Kempf-Leonard, J. Heckman, G. King and P. Tracy, eds, Encyclopaedia of social measurement. New York: Elsevier, 337–50.

Johnston, R.J. 2005d: Review of D. Gregory, The colonial present: Afghanistan, Palestine, Iraq. Annals of the Association of American Geographers 95(3): 719–23.

Johnston, R.J. and Pattie, C.J. 2006: Putting voters in their place: geography and elections in Great Britain. Oxford: Oxford University Press.

Johnston, R.J. and Rossiter, D.J. 1982: Constituency building, political representation and electoral bias in urban England. In D.T. Herbert and R.J. Johnston, eds, Geography and the urban environment, vol. 5. Chichester: Wiley, 113–56.

Johnston, R.J. and Sidaway, J. 2004a: Geography and geographers: Anglo-American human geography since 1945, 6th edn. London: Hodder Arnold (R.J. Johnston was sole author of the first five editions).

Johnston, R.J. and Sidaway, J. 2004b: The trans-Atlantic connection: 'Anglo-American' geography reconsidered. GeoJournal, 59: 15–22.

Johnston, R.J., Forrest, J. and Poulson, M. 2001: The geography of an EthniCity: residential segregation of birthplace and language groups in Sydney, 1996. Housing Studies 16: 569–94.

Johnston, R.J., Burgess, S., Wilson, D. and Harris, R. 2006: School and residential segregation: an analysis of variations across England's Local Education Authorities. Regional Studies 40: 973–90.

Johnston, R.J., Pattie, C.J., Dorling, D.F.L. and Rossiter, D.J. 2001: *From votes to seats: the operation of the UK electoral system since 1945*. Manchester: Manchester University Press.

Johnston, R.J., Fairbrother, M., Hoare, T., Hayes, D. and Jones, K. 2008: The Cold War and geography's quantitative revolution: some messy reflections on Barnes' geographical underworld. *Geoforum* 39: 1802–6.

Johnston, R.J., Jones, K., Sarker, R., Burgess, S., Propper, C. and Bolster, A. 2005: A missing level in the analysis of British voting behaviour: the household as context as shown by analyses of a 1992–1997 longitudinal survey. *Electoral Studies* 24: 201–25.

Jonas, A.E.G. and Wilson, D., eds, 1999: *The urban growth machine: critical perspectives two decades later*. Albany, NY: State University of New York Press.

Jones, A. 1998: (Re)producing gender cultures: theorizing gender in investment banking recruitment. *Geoforum* 29: 451–74.

Jones, A. 2006: *Genocide: a comprehensive introduction*. London: Routledge.

Jones, C.F. 1935: *Economic geography*. New York: Henry Holt.

Jones, E. 1951–2: Some aspects of the study of settlement in Britain. *Advancement of Science* 8: 59–65.

Jones, E. 1956: Cause and effect in human geography. *Annals of the Association of American Geographers* 46: 369–77.

Jones, E. 1960: *A social geography of Belfast*. London: Oxford University Press.

Jones, E.L. 1965: Agriculture and economic growth in England 1660–1750: agricultural change. *Journal of Economic History* XXV: 1–18.

Jones, G. 1980: *Social Darwinism and English thought: the interaction between biological and social theory*. London: Harvester Press/Atlantic Highlands, NJ: Humanities Press.

Jones, G.R.J. 1976: Multiple estates and early settlement. In P.H. Sawyer, ed., *Medieval settlement: continuity and change*. London: Edward Arnold, 15–40.

Jones, G.S. 2004a: *An end to poverty? A historical debate*. London: Profile.

Jones, H.R. 1981: *A population geography*. London: Harper & Row.

Jones, J.P. and Kodras, J. 1990: Restructured regions and families: the feminization of poverty in the United States. *Annals of the Association of American Geographers* 80: 163–83.

Jones, J.P. III, Nast, H. and Roberts, S. 1997: *Thresholds in feminist geography*. Lanham, MD: Rowman & Littlefield.

Jones, J.P. III, Natter, W. and Schatzki, T., eds, 1995: *Postmodern contentions: epochs, politics, space*. New York: Guilford Press.

Jones, J.P. III, Woodward, K. and Marston, S.A. 2007: Situating flatness. *Transactions of the Institute of British Geographers* 32: 264–76.

Jones, K. 1991: *Multilevel models for geographical research*. Concepts and Techniques in Modern Geography 54. Norwich: Environmental Publications.

Jones, K. 1997: Multilevel approaches to modelling contextuality: from nuisance to substance in the analysis of voting behaviour, in G.P. Westert and R.N. Verhoeff, eds, *Places and people: multilevel modelling in geographical research*. Utrecht: KNAG/Netherlands Geographical Studies.

Jones, K. and Duncan, C. 1998: Modelling context and heterogeneity: applying multilevel models, in E. Scarbrough and E. Tanenbaum, eds, *Research strategies in the social sciences*. Oxford: Oxford University Press.

Jones, K. and Moon, G. 1987: *Health, disease and society: an introduction to medical geography*. London: Routledge and Kegan Paul.

Jones, K. and Simmons, J. 1993: *Location, location, location: analyzing the retail environment*. Toronto: Methuen.

Jones, K., Johnston, R.J. and Pattie, C.J. 1992: People, places and regions: exploring the use of multi-level modelling in the analysis of electoral data. *British Journal of Political Science* 22: 343–80.

Jones, M. 2001: The rise of the regional state in economic governance: 'partnerships for prosperity' or new scales of state power? *Environment and Planning A* 33: 1185–211.

Jones, M. and MacLeod, G. 2004: Regional spaces, spaces of regionalism: territory, insurgent politics and the English question. *Transactions of the Institute of British Geographers* 29: 433–52.

Jones, M., Goodwin, M. and Jones, R., eds, 2005: Special issue on devolution. *Regional Studies* 39: 397–553.

Jones, M., Jones, R. and Woods, M. 2004: *An introduction to political geography: space, place and politics*. London: Routledge.

Jones, O. 2008: Stepping from the wreckage: geography, pragmatism and anti-representational theory. *Geoforum* 39, 1600–12.

Jones, P. 1995. *Rights*. London: Macmillan.

Jones, R. 2004b: What time human geography? *Progress in Human Geography* 28(3): 287–304.

Joppke, C. 2004: The retreat of multiculturalism in the liberal state: theory and practice. *British Journal of Sociology* 55: 237–57.

Jordan, A. 2000: The politics of multilevel environmental governance: subsidiarity and environmental policy in the European Union. *Environment and Planning A* 32: 1307–24.

Jordan, T. 1993: *North American cattle ranching frontiers: origins, diffusion and differentiation*.

Albuquerque, NM: University of New Mexico Press.

Joseph, A. and Phillips, D. 1984: *Accessibility and utilisation: geographic perspectives on health care delivery*. London: Longman.

Joseph, M. 2002: *Against the romance of community*. Minneapolis: University of Minnesota Press.

Judkins, G., Smith, M. and Keys, E. 2008: Determinism within human–environment research and the rediscovery of environmental causation. *Geographical Journal* 174: 17–29.

Judt, T. 1996: *A grand illusion: an essay on Europe*. New York: Hill and Wang.

Judt, T. 2005: *Postwar: a history of Europe since 1945*. London: Heinemann.

Juhasz, A. 2008: *The tyranny of oil*. New York: William Morrow.

Kabeer, N. and Subrahmanian, R., eds, 1999: *Institutions, relations and outcomes: a framework and case studies for gender-aware planning*. New Delhi: Kali for Women.

Kadmon, N. 2000: *Toponymy: the lore, laws and language of geographical names*. New York: Vantage Press.

Kaika, M. 2004: Interrogating the geographies of the familiar: domesticating nature and constructing the autonomy of the modern home. *International Journal of Urban and Regional Research* 28: 265–86.

Kaika, M. 2005: *City of flows: modernity, nature and the city*. London: Routledge.

Kain, J. 1968: Housing segregation, negro employment, and metropolitan decentralization. *Quarterly Journal of Economics* 82(2): 175–97.

Kain, J. 2004: A pioneer's perspective on the spatial mismatch literature. *Urban Studies*: 41(1): 7–32.

Kain, R.J.P. and Baigent, E. 1992: *The cadastral map in the service of the state: a history of property mapping*. Chicago: The University of Chicago Press.

Kaldor, M. 2003: *Global civil society*. Cambridge, UK: Polity Press.

Kaldor, M. 2006: *New and old wars: organized violence in a global era*, 2nd edn. Cambridge UK: Polity Press.

Kaldor, M. and Karl, T. 2007: *Oil wars*. London: Pluto Press.

Kalipeni, E., Craddock, S., Oppong, J.R. and Ghosh, J., eds, 2004: *HIV and AIDS in Africa: beyond epidemiology*. Malden, MA: Blackwell.

Kalra, V.S., Kaur, R. and Hutnyk, J. 2005: *Diaspora and hybridity*. London: Sage.

Kanzaka, J. 2002: Villein rents in thirteenth-century England: an analysis of the Hundred Rolls of 1279–80. *Economic History Review* 55: 593–618.

Kaplan, A. 2002: *The anarchy of empire in the making of US culture*. Cambridge, MA: Harvard University Press.

Kaplan, A. 2003: Homeland insecurities: reflections on language and space. *Radical History Review* 85: 82–93.

Kaplan, A. 2005: Where is Guantánamo? *American Quarterly* 57(3): 831–58.

Kaplan, A. and Ross, K. 1987: Introduction. *Yale French Studies*, issue on *Everyday Life* 73 (Fall): 1–4.

Kaplan, D.H. 2005: Research in ethnic segregation II: measurements, categories and meanings. *Urban Geography* 26: 737–45.

Kaplinsky, R. 2004: Spreading the gains from globalization: what can be learned from value chain analysis? *Problems of Economic Transition* 47(2): 74–115.

Kariel, H.G. and Kariel, P.E. 1972: *Explorations in social geography*. Reading, MA: Addison-Wesley.

Karl, T. 1999: *The paradox of plenty*. Berkeley, CA: University of California Press.

Kasarda, J.D. 2000: Aerotropolis: airport-driven urban development. In Urban Land Institute, *ULI on the future: cities in the 21st century*. Washington, DC: Urban Land Institute.

Kasarda, J.D., Appold, S.J., Sweeney, S.H. and Sieff, E. 1997: Central-city and suburban migration patterns: is a turnaround on the horizon? *Housing Policy Debate* 8(2): 307–58.

Kates, R. 1995: Labnotes from the Jeremiah Experiment: hope for a sustainable transition (Presidential Address). *Annals of the Association of American Geographers* 85(4): 623–40.

Kates, R.W. 1962: *Hazard and choice perception in flood plain management*. Department of Geography, Research Paper 78. Chicago: The University of Chicago.

Kates, R.W. and Katz, C. 1977: The hydrologic cycle and the wisdom of the child. *The Geographical Review* 67: 51–62.

Kates, R.W., Clark, W.C., Corell, R., Hall, J.M., Jaeger, C.C., Lowe, I., McCarthy, J.J., Shellnhuber, H.J., Bolin, B., Dickson, N.M., Faucheux, S., Gallopin, G.C., Grübler, A., Huntley, B., Jäger, J., Jodha, N.S., Kasperson, R.E., Mabogunje, A., Matson, P., Mooney, H., Moore III, B., O'Riordan, T. and Svedin, U. 2001: Sustainability science. *Science* 292: 641–2.

Katodrytis, G. 2005: Metropolitan Dubai and the rise of architectural fantasy. *Bidoun Magazine* 4, http://www.bidoun.com/4_metropolitan.ph

Katodrytis, G. and Powers, R. 1988: *Dubai: growing through architecture*. London: Thames and Hudson.

Katz, C. 1992: All the world is staged: Intellectuals and the process of ethnography. *Environment and Planning D: Society and Space* 10: 495–510.

Katz, C. 1994: Playing the field: questions of fieldwork in geography. *The Professional Geographer* 46(1): 67–72.

Katz, C. 1996: Towards minor theory. *Environment and Planning D: Society and Space* 14: 487–99.

Katz, C. 1998: Whose nature, whose culture? Private productions of space and the 'preservation' of nature. In B. Braun and N. Castree, eds, *Remaking reality: nature at the millennium.* London: Routledge, 46–63.

Katz, C. 2001a: On the grounds of globalization: a topography for feminist political engagement. *Signs: Journal of Women in Culture and Society* 26(4): 1213–34.

Katz, C. 2001b: Vagabond capitalism and the necessity of social reproduction. *Antipode* 33(4): 709–28.

Katz, C. 2004: *Growing up global: economic restructuring and children's everyday lives.* Minneapolis: University of Minnesota Press.

Katz, C. 2005: The terrors of hypervigilance: security and the compromised spaces of contemporary childhood. In J. Qvortrup, ed., *Studies in modern childhood: society, agency, culture.* London: Palgrave, 99–114.

Katz, C. 2007: Banal terrorism: spatial fetishism and everyday insecurity. In D. Gregory and A. Pred, eds, *Violent geographies: fear, terror and political violence.* London: Routledge, 349–61.

Katz, C. and Kirby, A. 1991: In the nature of things: the environment and everyday life. *Transactions of the Institute of British Geographers* 16: 259–71.

Katz, C. and Monk, J. 1993: *Full circles: geographies of women over the life course.* London: Routledge.

Katzenstein, P., ed., 1996: *The culture of national security: norms and identity in world politics.* New York: Columbia University Press.

Kaur, R. 2005: Mythology of communal violence: an introduction. In R. Kaur, ed., *Religion, violence and political mobilisation in South Asia.* London: Sage, 19–45.

Kautsky, K. 1988 [1899]: *The agrarian question,* trans. P. Burgess. 2 vols. London: Zwan.

Kavanagh, B.F. 2002: *Geomatics.* Englewood Cliffs, NJ: Prentice Hall.

Kay, C. 1989: *Latin American theories of development and underdevelopment.* London and New York: Routledge.

Kearney, M. 1995: The local and the global: the anthropology of globalization and transnationalism. *Annual Review of Anthropology* 24: 547–65.

Kearns, G. 1993: Fin-de-siècle geopolitics: Mackinder, Hobson and theories of global closure. In P. Taylor, ed., *Political geography of the twentieth century.* London: Belhaven Press, 9–30.

Kearns, G. 1998: The virtuous circle of facts and values in the New Western History. *Annals of the Association of American Geographers* 88: 377–409.

Kearns, G. 2004: The political pivot of geography. *Geographical Journal* 170: 337–46.

Kearns, G. 2006a: Naturalising empire: echoes of Mackinder for the next American century? *Geopolitics* 11: 74–98.

Kearns, G. 2006b: The spatial poetics of James Joyce. *New Formations* 57: 107–25.

Kearns, G. 2009: *Geopolitics and empire: the legacy of Halford Mackinder.* Oxford: Oxford University Press.

Kearns, R.A. 1993: Place and health: towards a reformed medical geography. *The Professional Geographer* 45: 139–47.

Kearns, R.A. and Barnett, J.R. 1999: To boldly go? Place, metaphor and marketing of Auckland's Starship hospital. *Environment and Planning D: Society and Space* 17: 201–26.

Kearns, R.A. and Gesler, W.M., eds, 1998: *Putting health into place: landscape, identity and well-being.* Syracuse: Syracuse University Press.

Keating, M. 1998: *The new regionalism in Western Europe: territorial restructuring and political change.* Cheltenham: Edward Elgar.

Kedar, S. 2003: On the legal geography of ethnocratic settler states: towards a research agenda. *Current Legal Issues* 5: 401–41.

Kedourie, E. 1960: *Nationalism.* New York: Blackwell.

Keeble, D.E. 1967: Models of economic development. In R.J. Chorley and P. Haggett, eds, *Models in geography.* London: Methuen, 248–54.

Keighren, I. 2005: Geosophy, imagination and terrae incognitae: exploring the intellectual history of John Kirtland Wright. *Journal of Historical Geography* 31: 546–62.

Keil, R. 1998: *Los Angeles: globalization, urbanization and social struggles.* Chichester: Wiley.

Keil, R. 2003: Progress report – urban political ecology. *Urban Geography* 24(8): 723–38.

Keil, R. 2005: Progress report – urban political ecology. *Urban Geography* 26(7): 640–51.

Keil, R., Bell, D.V.J., Penz, P. and Fawcett, L., eds, 1998: *Political ecology.* London: Routledge.

Keith, M. 1993: *Race, riots and policing: lore and disorder in a multi-racist society.* London: Routledge.

Keith, M. and Pile, S., eds, 1993: *Place and the politics of identity.* London: Routledge.

Kelly, M.J. 2005: Pulling at the threads of Westphalia: involuntary sovereignty waiver – revolutionary international legal theory or return to rule by the great powers? *UCLA Journal of International Law & Foreign Affairs* 10(2): 101–39.

Kelly, P. 2002: Canadian–Asian transnationalism. *The Canadian Geographer* 47: 209–18.

Kelly, P. 2005: *Liberalism.* Cambridge, UK: Polity Press.

Kennedy, B. 2005: *Inventing the Earth: ideas on landscape development since 1740.* Oxford: Blackwell.

Kennedy, B.A. 1979: A naughty world. *Transactions of the Institute of British Geographers* 4: 550–8.

Kennedy, P. 1988: *The rise and fall of the great powers*. New York: Random House.

Kennedy, P. 2003: *Guide to econometrics*, 5th rev. edn. Oxford: Blackwell.

Kent, M.M. and Haub, C. 2005: *Global demographic divide*. Washington, DC: Population Reference Bureau, December.

Kenzer, M.S. 1986: *Carl O. Sauer, a tribute*. Corvallis, OR: Oregon State University Press.

Kern, S. 1983: *The culture of time and space, 1880–1918*. Cambridge, MA: Harvard University Press.

Kerridge, E. 1967: *The agricultural revolution*. London: George Allen & Unwin.

Kesby, M. 1999: Locating and dislocating gender in rural Zimbabwe: the making of space and the texturing of bodies. *Gender, Place, and Culture* 6: 27–47.

Key, V.O. Jr 1949: *Southern politics in state and nation*. New York: A.A. Knopf.

Keyder, C. 2005: Globalization and social exclusion in Istanbul. *International Journal of Urban and Regional Research* 29: 124–34.

Keynes, J.N. 1930: *The scope and method of political economy*, 4th edn. London: Macmillan.

Khalidi, R. 1998: The 'Middle East' as a framework for analysis: re-mapping a region in the era of globalization. *Comparative Studies of South Asia, Africa and the Middle East* 18(2): 1–8.

Khazanov, A.M. 1994: *Nomads and the outside world*. Madison: University of Wisconsin Press.

Kiely, R. 1999: The last refuge of the noble savage: a critical assessment of post-development theory. *European Journal of Development Research* 11: 30–55.

Kiernan, B. 2007: *Blood and soil: a world history of genocide and extermination from Sparta to Darfur*. New Haven, CT: Yale University Press.

Killen, J.E. 1979: *Linear programming: the simplex method with geographical applications*. Norwich: Geobooks (CATMOG).

Killen, J.E. 1983: *Mathematical programming methods for geographers and planners*. London: Croom Helm.

Kimble, G.H.T. 1951: The inadequacy of the regional concept. In L.D. Stamp and S.W. Wooldridge, eds, *London essays in geography*. London: Longman.

Kimbrell, A., ed., 2002: *The fatal harvest reader: the tragedy of industrial agriculture*. Washington, DC: Island Press.

King, A. 1991: *Urbanism, colonialism and the world-economy*. New York: Routledge.

King, A.D. 1993: Identity and difference: the internationalization of capital and the globalization of culture. In Knox, P. *The restless landscape*. Englewood Cliffs, NJ: Prentice Hall, 83–110.

King, G. 1995: Replication, replication. *Political Science and Politics* 28: 443–99.

King, G. 1997: *A solution to the ecological inference problem*. Princeton, NJ: Princeton University Press.

King, G. and Wand, J. 2007: Comparing incomparable survey responses: new tools for anchoring vignettes. *Political Analysis* 15(1): 46–66.

King, G., Keohane, R.O. and Verba, S. 1994: *Designing social inquiry*. Princeton, NJ: Princeton University Press.

King, G., Rosen, O. and Tanner, M.A., eds, 2004: *Ecological inference: new methodological strategies*. Cambridge, UK: Cambridge University Press.

King, G., Honaker, J., Joseph, A. and Scheve, K. 2001: Analyzing incomplete political science data: an alternative algorithm for multiple imputation. *American Political Science Review* 95 (March): 49–69.

King, G., Murray, C.J.L., Salomon, J.A. and Tandon, A. 2004: Enhancing the validity and cross-cultural comparability of survey research. *American Political Science Review* 98(1): 191–205.

King, L.J. 1979: On neoclassicism in economic geography theory. In Hamelin, L.-E. and Beauregard, L., eds, *Retrospective 1951–76*. Montreal: Canadian Association of Geographers, 31–44.

King, L.J. and Clark, G.L. 1978: Regional unemployment patterns and spatial dimensions of macro-economic policy: the Canadian experience 1966–1975. *Regional Studies* 12: 283–96.

Kingsbury, P. 2003: Psychoanalysis, a gay spatial science? *Social and Cultural Geography* 4: 347–367.

Kirby, A. 1993: *Power/resistance: local politics and the chaotic state*. Bloomington, IN: Indiana University Press.

Kirk, D. 1996: Demographic transition theory. *Population Studies* 50: 361–87.

Kirsch, S. 2003: Empire and the Bush doctrine. *Environment and Planning D: Society and Space* 21(1): 1–6.

Kirsch, S., ed., 2003: Critical forum on *Empire*. *ACME: an International E-Journal for Critical Geographies* 2(2): 221–53.

Kish, L.T. 1995: *Survey sampling*. New York: Wiley.

Kitchin, R. 1994: Cognitive maps: what they are and why study them? *Journal of Environmental Psychology* 14: 1–19.

Kitchin, R. 1998: *Cyberspace: the world in the wires*. Chichester: Wiley.

Kitchin, R. 1999: Ethics and morals in geographical studies of disability. In J. Proctor and D. Smith, eds, *Geography and ethics: journeys through a moral terrain*. London: Routledge.

Kitchin, R. and Blades, M. 2001: *The cognition of geographic space*. London: I.B. Tauris.

Kitchin, R. and Kneale, J., eds, 2002: *Lost in space: geographies of science fiction*. London: Continuum.

Kitchin, R., Blades, M. and Golledge, R. 1997: Relations between geography and psychology. *Environment and Behavior* 29: 554–73.

Kitching, G. 1982: *Development and underdevelopment in historical perspective*. London: Methuen.

Klare, M. 1995: *Rogue states and nuclear outlaws: America's search for a new foreign policy*. New York: Hill and Wang.

Klare, M. 2002: *Resource wars: the new landscape of global conflict*. New York: Owl Books.

Klare, M. 2004: *Blood and oil: the dangers and consequences of America's growing dependence on imported petroleum*. New York: Metropolitan.

Klare, M. 2008: *Rising powers, shrinking planet*. New York: Metropolitan Books.

Klein, N. 2002: *Fences and windows: dispatches from the front lines of the globalization debate*. New York: Picador USA.

Knaap, G. and Nelson, A. 1992: *The regulated landscape: lessons in state land use planning from Oregon*. Cambridge, MA: Lincoln Institute of Land Policy.

Knigge, L. and Cope, M. 2006: Grounded visualization: integrating the analysis of qualitative and quantitative data through grounded theory and visualization. *Environment and Planning A* 38(11): 2021–37.

Knodel, J. 1988: *Demographic behaviour in the past: A study of 14 German village populations in the eighteenth and nineteenth centuries*. Cambridge, UK: Cambridge University Press.

Knopp, L. 1992: Sexuality and the spatial dynamics of capitalism. *Environment and Planning D: Society and Space* 10: 651–69.

Knopp, L. 2004: Ontologies of place, placelessness, and movement: queer quests for identity and their impacts on contemporary geographic thought. *Gender, Place, and Culture* 11: 121–34.

Knopp, L. and Lauria, M. 1987: Gender relations as a particular form of social relations. *Antipode* 19(1): 48–53.

Knorr-Cetina, K. 1999: *Epistemic cultures*. Cambridge, MA: Harvard University Press.

Knox, P.L. 1975: *Social well-being: a spatial perspective*. Oxford: The Clarendon Press.

Knox, P.L. 1991: The restless urban landscape: economic and sociocultural change and the transformation of Metropolitan, DC. *Annals of the Association of American Geographers* 81(2): 181–209.

Knox, P.L. 1994: *Urbanization: an introduction to urban geography*. Englewood Cliffs, NJ: Prentice Hall.

Knox, P.L. and Pinch, S. 2000: *Urban social geography: an introduction*. New York: Prentice Hall.

Knox, P.L. and Taylor, P.J., eds, 1995: *World cities in a world-system*. Cambridge, UK: Cambridge University Press.

Kobayashi, A. 1994: Coloring the field: gender, 'race', and the politics of fieldwork. *The Professional Geographer* 46: 73–80.

Kobayashi, A. 1997: Introduction to Part I: the paradox of difference and diversity (or, why the threshold keeps moving). In J.P. Jones III, H.J. Nast and S.M. Roberts, eds, *Thresholds in feminist geography: difference, methodology, representation*. Lanham, MD: Rowman & Littlefield, 3–10.

Kobayashi, A. 2001: Negotiating the personal and the political in critical qualitative research In M. Limb and C. Dwyer, eds, *Qualitative methodologies for geographers: issues and debates*. London: Arnold, 55–70.

Kobayashi, A. and Peake, L. 2000: Racism out of place: thoughts on whiteness and an antiracist geography in the new millennium. *Annals of the Association of American Geographers* 90: 392–403.

Kobayashi, A. and Proctor, J. 2003: Values, rights and justice. In G. Gaile and C. Willmott, eds, *Geography in America at the dawn of the 21st century*. Oxford: Oxford University Press, 721–9.

Kobayashi, A. and Ray, B. 2000: Civil risk and landscapes of marginality in Canada: a pluralist approach to social justice. *The Canadian Geographer* 44: 401–17.

Kockelmans, J., ed., 1967: *Phenomenology: the philosophy of Edmund Husserl and its interpretation*. Garden City, NY: Doubleday.

Koelsch, W. 2004: Squinting back at Strabo. *Geographical Review* 94: 502–18.

Koestler, A. 1967: *The ghost in the machine*. London: Picador.

Koestler, A. and Smythies, J.R., eds, 1969: *Beyond reductionism: the Alpbach symposium. New perspectives in the life sciences*. London: Hutchinson.

Kofman, E. 1996: Feminism, gender relations and geopolitics: problematic closures and opening strategies. In E. Kofman and G. Youngs, eds, *Globalization: theory and practice*. London: Frances Pinter, 209–24.

Kofman, E. 1998: Whose city? Gender, class and immigration in European globalizing cities. In R. Fincher and J.M. Jacobs, eds, *Cities of difference*. New York: Guilford Press, 279–300.

Kofman, E. 2003: Rights and citizenship. In J. Agnew, K. Mitchell and G. Toal, eds, *A companion to political geography*. Oxford: Blackwell, 393–407.

Kofman, E. and Lebas, E. 1996: Lost in transposition – time, space and the city. In H. Lefebvre, *Writings on cities*, trans. and ed. E. Kofman and E. Lebas. Oxford: Blackwell, 3–60.

Kofman, E. and Peake, L. 1990: Into the 1990s: a gendered agenda for political geography. *Political Geography Quarterly* 9: 313–36.

Kofman, E. and Raghuram, P. 2006: Gender and global labour migrations: incorporating skilled workers. *Antipode* 38(2): 282–303.

Kohler, R. 2002: Place and practice in field biology. *History of Science* 40: 189–210.

Kohli, A. 1994: A democracy of economic orthodoxy. *Third World Quarterly* 14: 671–89.

Kohli, A. 2004: *State-directed development: political power and industrialization*. Cambridge, UK: Cambridge University Press.

Kohn, G.C. 1998: *Encyclopaedia of plague and pestilence*. Ware, Hertfordshire: Wordsworth Reference.

Kohn, M. 2004: *Brave new neighborhoods: the privatization of public space*. New York: Routledge.

Koláčný, A. 1969: Cartographic information – a fundamental concept and term in modern cartography. *Cartographic Journal* 6: 47–9.

Kolakowski, L. 1972: *Positivist philosophy: from Hume to the Vienna Circle*. London: Penguin.

Kolko, J. 1988: *Restructuring the world economy*. New York: Pantheon.

Kolossov, V. 2005: Border studies: changing perspectives and theoretical approaches. *Geopolitics* 10: 606–32.

Kong, L. 1990: Geography and religion: trends and prospects. *Progress in Human Geography* 14(3): 355–71.

Kong, L. 1993a: Negotiating conceptions of sacred space: a case study of religious buildings in Singapore. *Transactions of the Institute of British Geographers*, NS 18(3): 342–58.

Kong, L. 1993b: Ideological hegemony and the political symbolism of religious buildings in Singapore. *Environment and Planning D: Society and Space* 11(1): 23–45.

Kong, L. 2001a: Mapping 'new' geographies of religion: politics and poetics of modernity. *Progress in Human Geography* 25(2): 211–33.

Kong, L. 2001b: Religion and technology: refiguring place, space, identity and community. *Area* 33(4): 404–13.

Kong, L., ed., 2007: The promises and prospects of geography in higher education. Special issue of *Journal of Geography in Higher Education* 31(1).

Kong, L., Gibson, C., Khoo, L.-M. and Semple, A.-M. 2006: Knowledges of the creative economy: towards a relational geography of diffusion and adaptation in Asia. *Asia Pacific Viewpoint* 47: 173–94.

Konig, H. 1994: *The failure of agricultural capitalism*. London: Routledge.

Korf, B. 2007: Antinomies of generosity: moral geographies and post-tsunami aid in Southeast Asia. *Geoforum* 38: 366–78.

Kors, A.C. et al., eds, 2003: *Encyclopedia of the Enlightenment*, 4 vols. New York: Oxford University Press.

Kosek, J. 2003: Environmental anxieties: race, nature and political ecology. In R. Peet and M. Watts, eds, *Liberation ecology*. London: Routledge.

Kosek, J. 2004: Deep roots and long shadows: the cultural politics of memory and longing in northern New Mexico. *Environment and Planning D: Society and Space* 22: 329–54.

Koshar, R. 2002: *Histories of leisure*. Oxford: Berg.

Kosiński, L. 1984: The roots of population geography. In J.I. Clarke, ed., 1984: *Geography and population: approaches and applications*. Oxford: Pergamon Press.

Koskela, H. 2000: 'The gaze without eyes': video surveillance and the changing nature of urban space. *Progress in Human Geography* 24: 243–65.

Koskela, H. and Pain, R. 2000: Revisiting fear and place: women's fear of attack and the built environment. *Geoforum* 31: 269–80.

Kousser, J.M. 1999: *Colorblind injustice: minority voting rights and the undoing of the Second Reconstruction*. Chapel Hill, NC: University of North Carolina Press.

Kramsch, O. 2002: Re-imagining the scalar topologies of cross-border governance: Euro regions in the postcolonial present. *Space and Polity* 6: 169–96.

Kreutzmann, H. 1998: From modernization theory towards the 'clash of civilizations': directions and paradigm shifts in Samuel Huntington's analysis and prognosis of global development. *GeoJournal* 46: 255–65.

Kriedte, P., Medick, H. and Schlumbohm, J. 1981: *Industrialization before industrialization: rural industry in the genesis of capitalism*. Cambridge, UK: Cambridge University Press.

Krishna, S. 1994: Cartographic anxiety: mapping the body politic in India. *Alternatives* 19: 507–21.

Krog, A. 2000: *Country of my skull: guilt, sorrow, and the limits of forgiveness in the new South Africa*. New York: Three Rivers Press.

Krogt, P. van der 1997– : *Koeman's Atlantes Neerlandici*, 2nd edn, many vols. 't Goy-Houten, The Netherlands: HES Publishers.

Kropotkin, P. 1885: What geography ought to be. *The Nineteenth Century* 18: 940–56.

Krugman, P. 1991: *Geography and trade*. Cambridge, MA: The MIT Press.

Krugman, P.R. 1995a: Incidents from my career. In A. Heertje, ed., *The makers of modern economics*, vol. II. Aldershot: Edward Elgar, 29–46.

Krugman, P.R. 1995b: *Development, geography, and economic theory*. Cambridge, MA: The MIT Press.

Krugman, P.R. 2000: Where in the world is the 'new economic geography'? In G.L. Clark, M.P. Feldman and M.S. Gertler, eds, *The*

Oxford handbook of economic geography. Oxford: Oxford University Press, 49–60.

Kuehn, M. 2001: *Kant: a biography*. Cambridge, UK: Cambridge University Press.

Kuhn, T.S. 1970 [1962]: *The structure of scientific revolutions*, 2nd edn. Chicago: The University of Chicago Press.

Kula, W. 1976: *An economic theory of the feudal system*. London: New Left Books.

Kuletz, V. 1998: *The tainted desert*. London: Routledge.

Kuletz, V. 2001: Invisible spaces, violent places. In N. Peluso and M. Watts, eds, *Violent environments*. Ithaca, NY: Cornell University Press.

Kumar, A. 2003: *World Bank literature*, Minneapolis: University of Minnesota Press.

Kupperman, K.O. 1995: Introduction: the changing definition of America. In K.O. Kupperman, ed., *America in European consciousness, 1493–1750*. Chapel Hill, NC: University of North Carolina Press.

Kusno, A. 1998: Beyond the postcolonial: architecture and political cultures in Indonesia. *Public Culture* 10: 549–75.

Kwan, M.-P. 1999: Gender, the home–work link, and space–time patterns of nonemployment activities. *Economic Geography* 75: 370–94.

Kwan, M.-P. 2002: Feminist visualization: re-envisioning GIS as a method in feminist geographic research. *Annals of the Association of American Geographers* 92(4): 645–61.

Kwan, M.-P. 2004: Beyond difference: from canonical geography to hybrid geographies. *Annals of the Association of American Geographers* 94: 756–63.

Kwan, M.-P. 2007: Affecting geospatial technologies: toward a feminist politics of emotion. *Professional Geographer* 59: 22–34.

Kwan, M.-P. and Weber, J. 2003: Individual accessibility revisited: implications for geographical analysis in the twenty-first century. *Geographical Analysis* 35: 341–53.

Kwan, M.-P., Murray, A., O'Kelly, M. and Tiefelsdorf, M. 2003: Recent advances in accessibility research: representation, methodology, and applications. *Journal of Geographical Systems* 5: 129–38.

Kwong, P. 2001: *Chinatown, N.Y.: labor and politics, 1930–1950*. New York: The New Press.

Lacan, J. 2002: *Ecrits*. New York: W.W. Norton.

LaCapra, D. 2000: Trauma, absence, loss. In LaCapra, *Writing history, writing trauma*. Baltimore, MD: The Johns Hopkins University Press, 43–85.

Laclau, E. 1977: *Politics and ideology in Marxist theory*. London: Verso.

Laclau, E. 1985: New social movements and the plurality of the social. In D. Slater, ed., *New social movements and the state in Latin America*. Amsterdam: CEDLA, 27–42.

Laclau, E. 2006: *On populist reason*: London: Verso.

Laclau, E. and Mouffe, C. 1985: *Hegemony and socialist strategy: towards a radical democratic politics*, trans. W. Moore and P. Cammack. London: Verso.

Lacoste, Y. 1973: An illustration of geographical warfare: bombing of the dikes on the Red River, North Vietnam. *Antipode* 5: 1–13.

Lacoste, Y. 1976: *La géographie, ça sert, d'abord, à faire la guerre*. Paris: Maspero; 2nd edn, La Découverte, 1988.

Lacoue-Labarthe, P. 1989: *Typography: mimesis, philosophy, politics*, ed. C. Fynsk. Stanford, CA: Stanford University Press.

LaDuke, W. 1999: *All our relations: native struggles for land and life*. Boston: South End Press.

Lakatos, I. 1978: *The methodology of scientific research programmes*. Cambridge, UK: Cambridge University Press.

Lake, D.A. 2003: The new sovereignty in international relations. *International Studies Review* 5: 303–23.

Lake, R. 2004: *Geography Mark-up Language – foundation for the Geo-Web*. New York: Wiley.

Lake, R.W. and Newman, K. 2002: Differential citizenship in the shadow state. *Geojournal* 58: 109–20.

Lakoff, G. and Johnson, M. 2003 [1980]: *Metaphors we live by*, 2nd edn. Chicago: The University of Chicago Press.

Lal, D. 1985: The misconception of 'development economics'. *Finance and Development* 22 (2): 10–13.

Lamar, H. and Thompson, L., eds, 1981: *The frontier in history: North America and South Africa compared*. New Haven, CT: Yale University Press.

Lambert, D. 2005: *White creole culture, politics and identity during the age of abolition*. Cambridge, UK: Cambridge University Press.

Lambert, D. and Lester, A., eds, 2006: *Colonial lives across the British Empire: imperial careering in the long nineteenth century*. Cambridge, UK: Cambridge University Press.

Lane, J.F. 2000: *Pierre Bourdieu: a critical introduction*. London: Pluto Press.

Lang, T. and Heasman, M. 2004: *Food wars: the global battle for mouths, minds and markets*. London: Earthscan.

Langley, P. 2004: In the eye of the 'perfect storm': the final salary pensions crisis and financialisation of Anglo-American capitalism. *New Political Economy* 9(4): 539–58.

Langley, P. 2006: Securitising suburbia: the transformation of Anglo-American mortgage finance. *Competition & Change* 10(3): 283–99.

Langton, J. 1972: Potentialities and problems of adopting a systems approach to the study of change in human geography. *Progress in Geography* 4: 125–79.

893

Langton, J. 1975: Residential patterns in pre-industrial cities. *Transactions of the Institute of British Geographers*, NS 1: 1–27.

Langton, J. 1979: *Geographical change and Industrial Revolution: coalmining in south-west Lancashire, 1590–1799*. Cambridge, UK: Cambridge University Press.

Langton, J. 1984: The Industrial Revolution and the regional geography of England. *Transactions of the Institute of British Geographers*, NS 9: 145–67.

Langton, J. 1988: The two traditions of geography: historical geography and the study of landscapes. *Geografiska Annaler* 70B: 17–25.

Langton, J. and Morris, R.J., eds, 1987: *Atlas of industrializing Britain 1780–1914*. London: Routledge.

Lapping, M. 2006: Rural policy and planning. In P. Cloke, T. Marsden and P. Mooney, eds, *Handbook of rural studies*. London: Sage, 104–22.

Laqueur, W. 1996: *Fascism: past, present, and future*. Oxford: Oxford University Press.

Larner, W. 1995: Theorising 'difference' in Aotearoa/New Zealand. *Gender, Place and Culture* 2: 177–90.

Larner, W. 2007: Expatriate experts and globalising governmentalities: the New Zealand diaspora strategy. *Transactions of the Institute of British Geographers*, NS 32(3): 331–45.

Larner, W. and Walters, W. 2005: Globalization as governmentality. *Alternatives* 29: 1–24.

Larsen, S.U., Hagtvet, B. and Myklebust, J.P., eds, 1980: *Who were the Fascists: social roots of European fascism*. Bergen: Universitetsforlaget.

Larson, E.J. 1995: *Sex, race, and science*. Baltimore, MD: The Johns Hopkins University Press.

Lash, S. and Urry, J. 1987: *The end of organized capitalism*. Madison, WI: University of Wisconsin Press.

Latham, A. 1999: The power of distraction: distraction, tactility and habit in the work of Walter Benjamin. *Environment and Planning D: Society and Space* 17: 451–73.

Latham, A. 2003: Research, performance, and doing human geography: some reflections on the diary–photograph, dairy–interview method. *Environment and Planning A* 35: 1993–2018.

Latham, A. and McCormack, D. 2004: Moving cities: rethinking the materialities of urban geographies. *Progress in Human Geography* 28 (6): 701–24.

Latham, R. 1997: *The liberal moment: modernity, security, and the making of postwar international order*. New York: Columbia University Press.

Latouche, S. 1992: Standard of living. In W. Sachs, ed., *The development dictionary: a guide to knowledge as power*. London: Zed Books, 250–63.

Latour, B. 1987: *Science in action*. Cambridge, MA: Harvard University Press.

Latour, B. 1988: *The pasteurization of France*, trans. A. Sheridan and J. Law. Cambridge, MA: Harvard University Press.

Latour, B. 1993: *We have never been modern*, trans. C. Porter. Brighton: Harvester Wheatsheaf/ Cambridge, MA: Harvard University Press.

Latour, B. 1999a: Circulating reference. In Latour, *Pandora's hope: essays on the reality of science studies*. Cambridge, MA: Harvard University Press, 24–79.

Latour, B. 1999b: Give me a laboratory and I will raise the world. In M, Biagioli, ed., *The science studies reader*. New York: Routledge, 258–75.

Latour, B. 1999c: *Pandora's hope: essays on the reality of science studies*. Cambridge, MA: Harvard University Press.

Latour, B. 2003: Is re-modernization occurring – and if so, how to prove it? A commentary on Ulrich Beck. *Theory, Culture & Society* 20: 35–48.

Latour, B. 2004: *Politics of nature: how to bring the sciences into democracy*. Cambridge, MA: Harvard University Press.

Latour, B. 2005: *Reassembling the social*. Oxford: Blackwell.

Latour, B. and Woolgar, S. 1979: *Laboratory life: the construction of scientific facts*. London: Sage.

Laudan, L. 1988: The demise of the demarcation problem. In M. Ruse, ed., *But is it science?* Buffalo, NY: Prometheus Books, 337–50.

Lauria, M., ed., 1997: *Reconstructing urban regime theory: regulating urban politics in a global economy*. Thousand Oaks, CA: Sage.

Laurier, E. 1998: Geographies of talk: 'Max left a message for you'. *Area* 31: 36–45.

Laurier, E. 2001: Why people say where they are during mobile phone calls. *Environment and Planning D: Society and Space* 19: 485–504.

Laurier, E. 2004: The spectacular showing: Houdini and the wonder of ethnomethodology. *Human Studies* 27: 377–99.

Laurier, E. and Philo, C. 2004: Ethnoarchaeology and undefined investigations. *Environment and Planning A* 36: 421–36.

Laver, M. 1997: *Private desires, political action: an invitation to the politics of rational choice*. London: Sage.

Law, J. 1994: *Organising modernity*. Oxford: Blackwell.

Law, J. 2004: *After method*. London: Routledge.

Law, J. and Hassard, J., eds, 1999: *Actor network theory and after*. Oxford: Blackwell.

Law, L. 1997: Dancing on the bar: sex, money and the uneasy politics of third space. In S. Pile and M. Keith, eds, *Geographies of resistance*. London: Routledge.

Lawrence, R.J. 2003: Human ecology and its applications. *Landscape and Urban Planning* 65: 31–40.

Laws, G. 1993: 'The land of old age': society's changing attitudes toward urban built environments for elderly people. *Annals of the Association of American Geographers* 83: 672–93.

Lawson, A.B., Browne, W.J. and Vidal Rodeiro, C.L. 2003: *Disease mapping using WinBUGS and MLwiN*. Chichester: Wiley.

Lawson, V. 2000: Arguments within geographies of movement: the theoretical potential of migrant's stories. *Progress in Human Geography* 24: 173–89.

Lawson, V. 2007: Geographies of care and responsibility. *Annals of the Association of American Geographers* 97: 1–11.

Layard, R. 2005: *Happiness: lessons from a new science*. London: Allen Lane.

Le Billon, P. 2004: The geopolitical economy of 'resource wars'. *Geopolitics* 9: 1–28.

Le Billon, P. 2005: *Fuelling war: natural resources and armed conflict*. Adelphi Paper 373. London: Routledge for the International Institute for Strategic Studies.

Le Billon, P. 2008: Diamond wars? Conflict diamonds and geographies of resource wars. *Annals of the Assocation of American Geographers* 98(2): 345–72.

le Goix, R. 2005: Gated communities: sprawl and social segregation in southern California. *Housing Studies* 20: 323–44.

Le Roy Ladurie, E. 1969 [1966]: *Les paysans de Languedoc*. Paris, Flammarion. English translation by John Day, *The peasants of Languedoc*. Urbana: University of Illinois Press, 1974.

Leach, B. 1974: Race, problems and geography. *Transactions of the Institute of British Geographers* 63: 41–7.

Leach, M. and Mearns, M., eds, 1996: *The lie of the land*. London: Heinemann.

Leaf, M. 1984: *Song of hope*. New Brunswick, NJ: Rutgers University Press.

Learmouth, A. 1988: *Disease ecology: an introduction*. Oxford: Blackwell.

Lears, T.J. 1985: The concept of cultural hegemony: problems and possibilities. *American Historical Review* 90: 567–93.

Lechner, F. 1991: Simmel on social space. *Theory, Culture & Society* 8: 195–201.

Lee, B.A. and Price-Spratlen, T. 2004: The geography of homelessness in American communities: concentration or dispersion? *City and Community* 3: 3–27.

Lee, G.B. and Lam, S.S.K. 1998: Wicked cities: cyberculture and the reimagining of identity in the 'non-Western' metropolis. *Futures* 30(10): 967–79.

Lee, J.Z. and Feng, W. 1999: *A quarter of humanity: Malthusian mythology and Chinese realities 1700–2000*. Cambridge, MA: Harvard University Press.

Lee, R. 1990: Making Europe: towards a geography of European integration. In M. Chisholm and D.M. Smith, eds, *Shared space: divided space*. London: Unwin Hyman, 235–59.

Lee, R. 1996: Moral money? LETS and the social construction of local economic geographics in southeast England. *Environment and Planning A* 28(8): 1377–94.

Lee, R. and Smith, D.M., eds, 2004: *Geographies and moralities: international perspectives on development, justice, and place*. Oxford: Blackwell.

Lee, R. and Wills, J., eds, 1997: *Geographies of economies*. London: Arnold.

Lee, R., Leyshon, A., Aldridge, T., Tooke, J., Williams, C. and Thrift, N. 2004: Making geographies and histories? Constructing local circuits of value. *Environment and Planning D: Society and Space* 22(4): 595–617.

Lees, L. 2002: Rematerializing geography: the 'new' urban geography. *Progress in Human Geography* 26: 101–12.

Lees, L. 2003: Super-gentrification: the case of Brooklyn Heights, New York City. *Urban Studies* 40: 2487–510.

Lefebvre, H. 1970: Reflections on the politics of space. *Antipode* 8(2): 30–7.

Lefebvre, H. 1991a: *Critique of everyday life*, vol. 1, trans. J. Moore. London: Verso.

Lefebvre, H. 1991b [1974]: *The production of space*, trans. D. Nicholson-Smith. Oxford: Blackwell.

Lefebvre, H. 1996: *Writings on cities*, trans. and ed. E. Kofman and E. Lebas. Oxford: Blackwell.

Lefebvre, H. 2003 [1970]: *The urban revolution*, trans. R. Bononno. Minneapolis: University of Minnesota Press.

Lefebvre, H. 2004 [1992]: *Rhythmanalysis: space, time and everyday life*, trans. S. Elden and G. Moore. London: Continuum.

Lefebvre, H. 2008 [1947, 1961, 1981]: *Critique of everyday life*, vols 1–3, trans. J. Moore and G. Elliott. London: Verso.

Leff, E. 1995: *Green production*. New York: Guilford Press.

LeGales, P. 2002: *European cities: social conflicts and governance*. Oxford: Oxford University Press.

Legg, S. 2003: Gendered politics and nationalised homes: women and the anti-colonial struggle in Delhi, 1940–1947. *Gender, Place and Culture* 10: 7–28.

Legg, S. 2005: Contesting and surviving memory: space, nation, and nostalgia and *Les Lieux de Mémoire*. *Environment and Planning D: Society and Space* 23: 481–504.

Legg, S. 2007a: Reviewing geographies of memory/forgetting. *Environment and Planning A* 39: 456–66.

Legg, S. 2007b: *Spaces of colonialism: Delhi's urban governmentalities*. Oxford: Blackwell.

Lehman, K. 1998: Geography and gender in the narrative of Argentinean national origin: the 'Pampa' as chronotope. *Revista de Estudios Hispánicos* 32(1): 3–28.

Lehrer, U. and Milgrom, R. 1996: New (sub) urbanism: countersprawl or repackaging the product. *Capitalism, Nature, Socialism* 7(2): 49–64.

Leib, J.I. 2002: Separate times, shared spaces: Arthur Ashe, Monument Avenue and the politics of Richmond, Virginia's symbolic landscape. *Cultural Geographies* 9: 286–312.

Leighly, J.B. 1954: Innovation and area. *Geographical Review* 44: 439–41.

Leighly, J.B. 1955: What has happened to physical geography? *Annals of the Association of American Geographers* 45: 309–18.

Leighly, J.B., ed., 1963: *Land and life: selections from the writings of Carl Ortwin Sauer.* Berkeley, CA: University of California Press.

Leiris, M. 1938: The sacred in everyday life. Reprinted in translation in D. Hollier, ed., 1988, *The College of Sociology 1937–39.* Minneapolis: University of Minnesota Press, 24–31.

Leite, J. 2005: *The World Social Forum.* London: Haymarket Books.

Leitner, H. 1992: Urban geography: responding to new challenges. *Progress in Human Geography* 16: 105–18.

Leitner, H. and Miller, B. 2007: Scale and the limitations of ontological debate: a commentary on Marston, Jones and Woodward. *Transactions of the Institute of British Geographers* 32: 116–25.

Leitner, H., Pavlik, C. and Sheppard, E. 2002: Networks, governance, and the politics of scale: inter-urban networks and the European Union. In A. Herod and M.W. Wright, eds, *Geographies of power: placing scale.* Oxford: Blackwell, 274–303.

Leitner, H., Sheppard, E. and Sziarto, K. 2008: The spatialities of contentious politics. *Transactions of the Institute of British Geographers* 33: 157–72.

Lemansky, C. 2006: Spaces of exclusivity or connection? Linkages between a gated community and its poorer neighbour in a Cape Town Master Plan development. *Urban Studies* 43 (2): 397–420.

Lemert, C. 1993: Social theory: its uses and pleasures. In C. Lemert, ed., *Social theory: the multicultural and classic readings.* Boulder, CO: Westview Press, 1–24.

Lemke, T. 2001: The birth of bio-politics – Michel Foucault's lecture at the Collège de France on neo-liberal governmentality. *Economy & Society* 30(2): 190–207.

Lemkin, R. 1944: *Axis rule in occupied Europe: laws of occupation, analysis of government, proposals for redress.* Washington, DC: Carnegie Endowment for International Peace, Division of International Law.

Lenin, V. 1916: *Imperialism.* Moscow: Progress Publishers.

Lenin, V. 1964: *The development of capitalism in Russia.* Moscow: Progress Publishers.

Lenth, R.V. 2001: Some practical guidelines for effective sample size determination. *The American Statistician* 55: 187–93.

LeSage, J. 1997: Bayesian estimation of spatial autoregressive models. *International Regional Science Review* 20: 113–29.

Leslie, D. and Reimer, S. 1999: Spatializing commodity chains. *Progress in Human Geography* 23(3): 401–20.

Lester, A.J. 1998: 'Otherness' and the frontiers of empire: the Eastern Cape Colony, 1806–c.1850. *Journal of Historical Geography* 24: 2–19.

Lester, A.J. 2000: Historical geographies of imperialism. In B. Graham and C. Nash, eds, *Modern historical geographies.* London: Pearson, 100–20.

Lester, A.J. 2001: *Imperial networks: creating identities in nineteenth-century South Africa and Britain.* London: Routledge.

Lester, A.J. 2006: Empire. In M. Low, K. Cox and J. Robinson, eds, *Handbook of political geography.* London: Sage.

Lesthaeghe, R. and Willems, P. 1999: Is low fertility a temporary phenomenon in the European Union? *Population and Development Review* 25: 211–28.

Lestringant, F. 1994: *Mapping the Renaissance world: the geographical imagination in the age of discovery,* trans. D. Fausett. Berkeley, CA: University of California Press.

Leung, Y., Mei, C.-L. and Zhang, W.-X. 2000: Statistical tests for spatial nonstationarity based on the geographically weighted regression model. *Environment and Planning A* 32: 9–32.

Levene, M. 2000: Why is the 20th century the century of genocide? *Journal of World History* 11: 305–36.

Levin, T., ed., 2002: *CTRL (Space): rhetorics of surveillance from Bentham to Big Brother.* Cambridge, MA: The MIT Press.

Levine, N. 2006: GeoDa: an introduction to spatial data analysis. *Geographical Analysis* 38: 41–56.

Levitas, R. 1990: *The concept of Utopia.* Hemel Hempstead, Herts: Philip Allan.

Levitt, P. and Glick Schiller, N. 2004: Conceptualizing simultaneity: a transnational social field perspective on society. *International Migration Review* 38: 1002–39.

Levy, D., Pensky, M. and Torpey, J., eds, 2005: *Old Europe, new Europe, core Europe: transatlantic relations after the Iraq War.* London: Verso.

Levy, J. and Lussault, M., eds, 2003: *Dictionnaire de la géographie et de l'espace des sociétés.* Paris: Belin.

Levy, S. 2003: *The scandalous eye: the surrealism of Conroy Maddox.* Liverpool: Liverpool University Press.

Lew, A.A., Hall, C.M. and Williams, A., eds, 2004: *A companion to tourism*. Malden, MA: Blackwell.

Lewis, A. 1984: Development economics in the 1950s. In G. Meier and D. Seers, eds, *Pioneers in development*. Oxford: Oxford University Press.

Lewis, B. 1999: *The multiple identities of the Middle East*. New York: Schocken.

Lewis, M.W. and Wigen, K.E. 1997: *The myth of continents: a critique of metageography*. Berkeley, CA: University of California Press.

Lewis, N.D., Dyck, I. and McLafferty, S., eds, 2001: *Geographies of women's health: place, diversity and difference*. London: Routledge.

Lewis, O. 1959: *Five families: Mexican case studies in the culture of poverty*. New York: Basic Books.

Lewis, O. 1969a: *On understanding poverty: perspectives from the social sciences*. New York: Basic Books.

Lewis, O. 1969b: The possessions of the poor. *Scientific American* 221: 114–24.

Lewis, P. 1985: Beyond description. *Annals of the Association of American Geographers* 75: 465–78.

Lewis, W.A. 1954: Economic development with unlimited supplies of labour. *Manchester School of Economics and Social Studies* 22: 139–91.

Ley, D. 1974: *The black inner city as frontier outpost: images and behavior of a Philadelphia neighbourhood*. Washington, DC: Association of American Geographers.

Ley, D. 1977: Social geography and the taken-for-granted world. *Transactions of the Institute of British Geographers*, NS 2: 498–512.

Ley, D. 1980: Liberal ideology and the postindustrial city. *Annals of the Association of American Geographers* 70: 238–58.

Ley, D. 1981: Behavioural geography and the philosophies of meaning. In K. Cox and R. Golledge, eds, *Behavioral problems in geography revisited*. London: Methuen, 209–30.

Ley, D. 1983: *A social geography of the city*. New York: Harper & Row.

Ley, D. 1987: Styles of the times: liberal and neoconservative landscapes in inner Vancouver, 1968–1986. *Journal of Historical Geography* 30: 14–56.

Ley, D. 1989: Fragmentation, coherence and limits to theory in human geography. In A. Kobayashi and S. Mackenzie, eds, *Remaking human geography*. London: Unwin Hyman, 227–44.

Ley, D. 1993: Co-operative housing as a moral landscape: re-examining 'the postmodern city'. In J. Duncan and D. Ley, eds, *Place/culture/representation*. London: Routledge, 128–48.

Ley, D. 1995: Between Europe and Asia: the case of the missing *sequoias*. *Ecumene* 2: 185–219.

Ley, D. 1996: *The new middle class and the remaking of the central city*. Oxford: Oxford University Press.

Ley, D. 2003a: Forgetting postmodernism? Recuperating a social history of local knowledge. *Progress in Human Geography* 27: 537–60.

Ley, D. 2003b: Seeking *homo economicus:* the Canadian state and the strange story of the Business Immigration Program. *Annals of the Association of American Geographers* 93: 426–41.

Ley, D. and Frost, H. 2006: The inner city. In T. Bunting and P. Filion, eds, *Canadian cities in transition*, 3rd edn. Toronto: Oxford University Press, 192–210.

Ley, D. and Samuels, M., eds, 1978: *Humanistic geography: prospects and problems*. London: Croom Helm/Chicago: Maaroufa Press.

Leyshon, A. and Thrift, N. 1997: *Money/space: geographies of monetary transformation*. London: Routledge.

Leyshon, A., Lee, R. and Williams, C., eds, 2003: *Alternative economic spaces*. London: Sage.

Leyshon, A., Matless, D. and Revill, G., eds, 1998: *The place of music*. London: Guilford Press/Longman.

Leyshon, A., Thrift, N. and Toomey, C. 1989: The rise of the British provincial financial center. *Progress in Planning* 31: 151–229.

Leyshon, A., Burton, D., Knights, D., Alferoff, C. and Signoretta, P. 2004: Towards an ecology of retail financial services: understanding the persistence of door-to-door credit and insurance providers. *Environment and Planning A* 36: 625–45.

Li, T. 2007: *The will to improve: governmentality, development and the practice of politics*. Durham, NC: Duke University Press.

Li, V. 2006: *The neo-primitivist turn: critical reflections on alterity, culture and modernity*. Toronto: University of Toronto Press.

Li, W. 1998: Anatomy of a new ethnic settlement: the Chinese ethnoburb in Los Angeles. *Urban Studies* 35(3): 479–501.

Li, W., ed., 2006: *From urban enclave to ethnic suburb: new Asian communities in Pacific Rim countries*. Honolulu: University of Hawai'i Press.

Li, Z. and Su, B. 1995: Algebraic models for feature displacement in the generalization of digital map data using morphological techniques. *Cartographica* 32(3): 39–56.

Liben, L.S. and Downs R.M. 1997: Can-ism and can'tianism: a straw child. *Annals of the Association of American Geographers* 87: 159–67.

Liddle, M. 1997: *Recreation ecology: the ecological impact of outdoor recreation and ecotourism*. London: Chapman & Hall.

Lieberson, S. 1981: An asymmetrical approach to segregation. In C. Peach, V. Robinson and S. Smith, eds, *Ethnic segregation in cities*. London: Croom Helm, 61–82.

897

Lieven, D. 2005: Empire, history and the contemporary global order. *Proceedings of the British Academy* 131: 127–56.

Lillesand, T.M., Kiefer, R.W. and Chipman, J.W. 2003: *Remote sensing and image interpretation*, 5th edn. Chichester: Wiley.

Lilley, K. 2004a: Cities of God? Medieval urban forms and their Christian symbolism. *Transactions of the Institute of British Geographers*, NS 29: 296–313.

Lilley, K. 2004b: Mapping cosmopolis: moral topographies of the medieval city. *Environment and Planning D: Society and Space* 22: 681–98.

Lilley, K., Lloyd, C., Trick, S. and Graham, C. 2005: Analysing and mapping medieval urban forms using GPS and GIS. *Urban Morphology* 9: 1–9.

Lim, J. 2007: Queer critique and the politics of affect. In K. Browne, G. Brown and J. Lim, eds, *Geographies of sexualities*. London: Ashgate, 53–67.

Limb, M. and Dwyer, C., eds, 2001: *Qualitative methodologies for geographers: issues and debates*. London: Arnold.

Limerick, P.N. 1987: *The legacy of conquest: the unbroken past of the American West*. New York: W.W. Norton.

Lindeborg, R.H. 1994: The 'Asiatic' and the boundaries of Victorian Englishness. *Victorian Studies* 38: 1–24.

Lindquist, J. 2004: Veils and ecstasy: negotiating shame in the Indonesian borderlands. *Ethnos* 69(4): 487–508.

Lipton, M. 1977: *Why poor people stay poor: a study of urban bias in world development*. London: Temple Smith.

Lipton, M. 1989: *New seeds and poor people*. London: Macmillan.

Lisle, D. 2006: *The global politics of contemporary travel writing*. Cambridge, UK: Cambridge University Press.

List, P. 1993: *Radical environmentalism: philosophy and tactics*. Belmont, CA: Wadsworth.

Little, J. and Leyshon, M. 2003: Embodied rural geographies: developing research agendas. *Progress in Human Geography* 27: 257–72.

Little, R.J.A. and Rubin, D.B. 2002: *Statistical analysis with missing data*. New York: Wiley.

Litva, A. and Eyles, J. 1995: Coming out: exposing social theory in medical geography. *Health and Place* 1: 5–14.

Livingstone, D.N. 1984: Natural theology and Neo-Lamarckism: the changing context of nineteenth century geography in the United States and Great Britain. *Annals of the Association of American Geographers* 74: 9–28.

Livingstone, D.N. 1987a: Human acclimatization: perspectives on a contested field of inquiry in science, medicine and geography. *History of Science* 25: 359–94.

Livingstone, D.N. 1987b: *Nathaniel Southgate Shaler and the culture of American science*. London: University of Alabama Press.

Livingstone, D.N. 1988: Science, magic and religion: a contextual reassessment of geography in the sixteenth and seventeenth centuries. *History of Science* 26: 269–94.

Livingstone, D.N. 1991: The moral discourse of climate: historical considerations on race, place and virtue. *Journal of Historical Geography* 17: 413–34.

Livingstone, D.N. 1992: *The geographical tradition: episodes in the history of a contested enterprise*. Oxford: Blackwell.

Livingstone, D.N. 1994: Climate's moral economy: science, race and place in post-Darwinian British and American geography. In N. Smith and A. Godlewska, eds, *Geography and empire*. Oxford: Blackwell, 132–54.

Livingstone, D.N. 1995: The spaces of knowledge: contributions towards a historical geography of science. *Environment and Planning D: Society and Space* 13: 5–34.

Livingstone, D.N. 1999: Tropical climate and moral hygiene: the anatomy of a Victorian debate. *British Journal for the History of Science* 32: 93–110.

Livingstone, D.N. 2002a: Race, space and moral climatology: notes toward a genealogy. *Journal of Historical Geography* 28: 159–80.

Livingstone, D.N. 2002b: *Science, space and hermeneutics*. University of Heidelberg, Hettner Lecture for 2001.

Livingstone, D.N. 2002c: Tropical hermeneutics and the climatic imagination. *Geographische Zeitschrift* 28: 65–88.

Livingstone, D.N. 2003a: British geography, 1500–1900: An imprecise review. In M. Williams and R. Johnston, eds, *A century of British geography*. London: British Academy, 11–41.

Livingstone, D.N. 2003b: Circulation: movements of science. In his *Putting science in its place: geographies of scientific knowledge*. Chicago: The University of Chicago Press, 135–78.

Livingstone, D.N. 2003c: *Putting science in its place: geographies of scientific knowledge*. Chicago: The University of Chicago Press.

Livingstone, D.N. 2004: Oriental travel, Arabian kinship and ritual sacrifice: William Robertson Smith and the fundamental institutions. *Environment and Planning D: Society and Space* 22: 639–57.

Livingstone, D.N. 2005a: Science, text and space: thoughts on the geography of reading. *Transactions of the Institute of British Geographers*, NS 30: 391–401.

Livingstone, D.N. 2005b: Scientific inquiry and the missionary enterprise. In R. Finnegan, ed., *Participating in the knowledge society: researchers beyond the university walls*. London: Palgrave, 50–64.

Livingstone, D.N. 2006: The geography of Darwinism. *Interdisciplinary Science Reviews* 31: 32–41.

Livingstone, D.N. and Harrison, R.T. 1981a: Immanuel Kant, subjectivism and human geography: a preliminary investigation. *Transactions of the Institute of British Geographers*, NS 6: 359–74.

Livingstone, D.N. and Harrison, R.T. 1981b: Meaning through metaphor: analogy as epistemology. *Annals of the Association of American Geographers* 71: 95–107.

Livingstone, D.N. and Withers, C.W.J., eds, 1999: *Geography and enlightenment*. Chicago: The University of Chicago Press.

Livingstone, D.N. and Withers, C.W.J., eds, 2005: *Geography and revolution*. Chicago: The University of Chicago Press.

Lloyd, D. 1999: *Ireland after history*. Cork: Cork University Press.

Lloyd, G. and Gatens, M. 1999: *Collective imaginings: Spinoza, past and present*. London: Routledge.

Lloyd, P. 1979: *Slums of hope?* London: Penguin.

Lobeck, A.K. 1939: *Geomorphology: an introduction to the study of landscapes*. New York: McGraw-Hill.

Lochhead, E. 1981: Scotland as the cradle of modern academic geography in Britain. *Scottish Geographical Magazine* 97: 98–109.

Locke, J. 1967 [1690]: *An essay concerning human understanding*. London: Fontana.

Locke, J. 1988 [1690]: *Two treatises on government*. Cambridge, UK: Cambridge University Press.

Locke, J. and Peardon, T.P. 1952 [1690]: *The second treatise of government*. New York: The Liberal Arts Press.

Lockman, Z. 2004: *Contending visions of the Middle East*. Cambridge, UK: Cambridge University Press.

Löfgren, O. 1999: *On holiday: a history of vacationing*. Berkeley, CA, University of California Press.

Logan, J.R. and Molotch, H. 1987: *Urban fortunes: the political economy of place*. Berkeley, CA: University of California Press.

Logan, J.R., Alba, R. and Zhang, W. 2002: Immigrant enclaves and ethnic communities in New York and Los Angeles. *American Sociological Review* 67: 299–322.

Lohia, R. 1964: *The caste system*. Hyderabad: Rammanohar Lohia Samata Vidyalaya Nyas.

Long, J. 2006: Border anxiety in Palestine–Israel. *Antipode* 38: 107–27.

Longhurst, R. 2001: *Bodies: exploring fluid boundaries*. London: Routledge.

Longhurst, R. 2005: Fat bodies: developing geographical research agendas. *Progress in Human Geography* 29(3): 247–59.

Longley, P.A., Books, S.M., McDonnell, R. and Macmillan, B., eds, 1998: *Geocomputation: a primer*. Chichester: Wiley.

Longley, P.A., Goodchild, M.F., Maguire, D.J. and Rhind, D.W., eds, 1999. *Geographic information systems: principles and techniques*, vol. 1. New York: Wiley.

Longley, P.A., Goodchild, M.F., Maguire, D.J. and Rhind, D.W. 2005: *Geographic information systems and science*, 2nd edn. Chichester: Wiley.

Longworth, N. 2004: *Learning cities, learning regions, learning communities*. London: Routledge.

Loomba, A. 1998: *Colonialism/postcolonialism*. London: Routledge.

Lorimer, H. 2003: Telling small stories: spaces of knowledge and the practice of geography. *Transactions of the Institute of British Geographers* 28: 197–217.

Lorimer, H. 2005: Cultural geography: the busyness of being 'more-than-representational'. *Progress in Human Geography* 29: 83–94.

Lorimer, H. 2006: Herding memories of humans and animals. *Environment and Planning D: Society and Space* 24(4): 497–518.

Lorimer, H. and Lund, K. 2003: Peak performance: practising walking on Scotland's mountains. In B. Szerszynski and C. Waterton, eds, *Nature performed: environment, culture and performance*. Oxford: Blackwell.

Lorimer, H. and Spedding, N. 2005: Locating field science: a geographical family expedition to Glen Roy, Scotland. *British Journal for the History of Science* 38: 13–33.

Lösch, A. 1940: *Die räumliche Ordnung der Wirtschaft*. Jena: G. Fischer. Translated by W.H. Woglom as *The economics of location*. New Haven, CT: Yale University Press, 1954.

Lösch, A. 1954 [1940]: *The economics of location*. New Haven, CT: Yale University Press.

Lott, E. 2006: *The disappearing intellectual*. New York: Basic Books.

Loukaki, A. 1997: Whose *genius loci*? Contrasting interpretations of the 'Sacred rock of the Athenian Acropolis'. *Annals of the Association of the American Geographers* 87: 306–29.

Loury, G.C. 1977: A dynamic theory of racial income differences. In P.A. Wallace and A. Lamond, eds, *Women, minorities and employment discrimination*. Lexington, MA: Lexington Books.

Lovering, J. 1999: Theory led by policy: the inadequacies of the 'new regionalism' (illustrated from the case of Wales). *International Journal of Urban and Regional Studies* 23: 379–95.

Low, M. 1997: Representation unbound. In K. Cox, ed., *Spaces of globalization*. New York: Guilford Press.

Low, M. 2003: Political geography in question. *Political Geography* 22: 625–31.

Low, N. and Gleeson, B. 1998: *Justice, society and nature: an exploration of political ecology*. London: Routledge.

Low, S. 2000: *On the plaza: the politics of public space and culture*. Austin, TX: University of Texas Press.

Low, S. 2004: *Behind the gates: life, security, and the pursuit of happiness in Fortress America*. New York: Routledge.

Lowe, L. 2001: Epistemological shifts: national ontology and the new Asian immigrant. In K. Chuh and K. Shimakawa, eds, *Orientations*. Durham, NC: Duke University Press.

Lowe, P., Clark, J., Seymour, S. and Ward, N. 1998: *Moralising the environment*. London: UCL Press.

Lowenthal, D. 1958: *George Perkins Marsh: versatile Vermonter*. New York: Columbia University Press.

Lowenthal, D. 1961: Geography, experience and imagination: toward a geographical epistemology. *Annals of the Association of American Geographers* 51: 241–60.

Lowenthal, D. 1985: *The past is a foreign country*. Cambridge, UK: Cambridge University Press.

Lowenthal, D. 1997: *The heritage crusade and the spoils of history*. London: Viking.

Lowenthal, D. 2000: *George Perkins Marsh: prophet of conservation*. Seattle: University of Washington Press.

Lozovsky, N. 2000: *The earth is our book: geographical knowledge in the Latin West ca. 400–1000*. Ann Arbor: University of Michigan Press.

Luckin, B. 2006: Revisiting the idea of urban degeneration in Britain, 1830–1900. *Urban History* 33: 234–52.

Ludden, D. 2002: *Reading subaltern studies: critical history, contested meaning, and the globalisation of South Asia*. New Delhi: Permanent Black.

Luhmann, N. 1981: *The differentiation of society*. New York: Columbia University Press.

Luke, T. 2002: Deep ecology: living as if nature mattered: Devall and Sessions on defending the Earth. *Organization and Environment* 15(2): 178–86.

Luke, T. 2003: 'Global cities' vs. 'global cities': rethinking contemporary urbanism as public ecology. *Studies in Political Economy* 70: 11–33.

Luke, T. 2005: The system of sustainable degradation. *Capitalism, Nature, Socialism* 17(1): 99–112.

Lukermann, F. 1958: Towards a more geographic economic geography. *Professional Geographer* 10: 2–10.

Lukermann, F. 1965: The 'calcul des probabilités' and the École Française de Géographie. *Canadian Geographer* 9: 128–37.

Lukes, S. 2005: *Power: a radical view*, 2nd edn. London: Palgrave Macmillan.

Lund, J. 2001: Barbarian theorizing and the limits of Latin American exceptionalism. *Cultural Critique* 47: 54–90.

Lundvall, B.A. 1988: Innovation as an interactive process: from user–producer interaction to the national system of integration. In G. Dosi, C. Freeman, R. Nelson, G. Silverberg and L. Soete, eds, *Technical change and economic theory*. London: Frances Pinter, 349–69.

Lunn, E. 1985: *Marxism and modernism*. London: Verso.

Lupton, D. 1999: *Risk*. London: Routledge.

Lutz, C. and Collins, J. 1993: *Reading* National Geographic. Chicago: The University of Chicago Press.

Lutz, W., Sanderson, W.C. and Scherbov, S., eds, 2004: *The end of world population growth in the 21st century: new challenges for human capital formation and sustainable development*. London: Earthscan.

Lynch, K. 1960: *The image of the city*. Cambridge, MA: The MIT Press.

Lynn, W.S. and Pulido, L., eds, 2003: Act of ethics: a special section on ethics and global activism. *Ethics, Place, and Environment* 6: 43–78.

Lyon, D., ed., 2006: *Theorizing surveillance: the Panopticon and beyond*. Portland OR: Willan Publishing.

Lyon, J.G., Falkner, E. and Bergen, W. 1995: Estimating cost for photogrammetric mapping and aerial photography. *Journal of Survey Engineering* 121: 63–86.

Lyotard, J.-F. 1984: *The postmodern condition: a report on knowledge*, trans. G. Bennington and B. Massumi. Minneapolis: University of Minnesota Press.

M'charek, A. 2005: *The Human Genome Diversity Project: an ethnography of scientific practice*. Cambridge, UK: Cambridge University Press.

MacCannell, D. 1976: *The tourist: a new theory of the leisure class*. London: Macmillan.

MacEachren, A.M. 1995: *How maps work: representation, visualization and design*. New York: Guilford Press.

MacEachren, A.M. and Brewer, I. 2004: Developing a conceptual framework for visually-enabled geocollaboration. *International Journal of Geographic Information Science* 18: 1–34.

Macedo, S. and Buchanan, A., eds, 2003: *Secession and self-determination*. New York: New York University Press.

MacGillavry, E. 2003: Collaborative mapping: by the people, for the people. *Society of Cartographers Bulletin* 37(2): 43–5.

MacIntyre, A. 1990: *Three rival versions of moral enquiry: encyclopaedia, genealogy, and tradition*. Notre Dame, IN: University of Notre Dame Press.

MacKenzie, S. and Rose, D. 1983: Industrial change, the domestic economy and home life. In J. Anderson, S. Duncan and R. Hudson, eds, *Redundant spaces in cities and regions*. New York: Academic Press.

Mackinder, H.J. 1904: The geographical pivot of history and discussion. *Geographical Journal* 23: 421–37, 437–44.

Mackinder, H.J. 1919: *Democratic ideals and reality: a study in the politics of reconstruction.* London: Constable.

MacLaughlin, J. 1986: State-centered social science and the anarchist critique: ideology in political geography. *Antipode* 18: 11–38.

MacLeod, G. 2001: Beyond soft institutionalism: accumulation, regulation, and their geographical fixes. *Environment and Planning A* 33: 57–89.

Macleod, G. and Jones, M. 2007: Territorial, scalar, networked, connected: in what sense a 'regional world'? *Regional Studies* 41(9): 1177–91.

MacLeod, R. and Rehbock, P.H., eds, 1994: *Darwin's laboratory: evolutionary theory and natural history in the Pacific.* Honolulu: University of Hawai'i Press.

Macmillan, B., ed., 1989: *Remodelling geography.* Oxford: Blackwell.

Macmillan, W.D. 1998: On geocomputation. *Computers, Environment and Urban Systems* 22: 1–6.

Macnaghten, P. and Urry, J. 1998: *Contested natures.* London: Sage.

Macpherson, C.B. 1978a: The meaning of property. In C.B. Macpherson, ed., *Property: mainstream and critical positions.* Toronto: University of Toronto Press, 1–14.

Macpherson, C.B., ed., 1978b: *Property: Mainstream and critical positions.* Toronto: University of Toronto Press.

Madanipour, A., Cars, G. and Allen, J., eds, 1998: *Social exclusion in European cities: processes, experiences, and responses.* London: Regional Studies Association.

Maddison, A. 1982: *Phases of capitalist development.* Oxford: Oxford University Press.

Maddrell, A.M.C. 1998: Discourses of race and gender and the comparative method in geographical school texts 1830–1918. *Environmental and Planning D: Society and Space* 16: 81–103.

Maegraith, B. 1969: Jet age medical geography. In F. Gale and G.H. Lawton, eds, *Settlement and encounter: geographical studies presented to Sir Grenfell Price.* Melbourne: Oxford University Press, 149–71.

Maffesoli, M. 1996: *The time of the tribes.* London: Sage.

Magnusson, W. 1996: *In search of political space.* Toronto: University of Toronto Press.

Magnusson, W. 2005: Urbanism, cities and local self-government, *Canadian Public Administration* 48(1): 96–124.

Maguire, D., Batty, M. and Goodchild, M., eds, 2005: *GIS, spatial analysis and modeling.* Redlands, CA: ESRI Press.

Mahan, A.T. 1902: The Persian Gulf and international relations. *National Review,* September: 27–45.

Maharidge, D. 1996: *The coming white minority: California's eruptions and America's future.* New York: Times Books.

Mair, A. 1986: Thomas Kuhn and understanding geography. *Progress in Human Geography* 10: 345–69.

Mair, A. 2008: Contemporary state discourse and historical pastoral spatiality: contradictions in the land conflict between the Israeli Bedouin and the state. *Ethnic and Racial Studies* 31: 1–21.

Mäki, U. 2004: Realism and the nature of theory: a lesson from J.J. von Thünen for economists and geographers. *Environment and Planning A* 36: 1719–30.

Malecki, E.J. 1991: *Technology and economic development: the dynamics of local, regional and national change.* London: Longman.

Malecki, E.J. 1997: Entrepreneurs, networks, and economic development: a review of recent research. In J.A. Katz and R.H. Brockhaus, eds, *Advances in entrepreneurship, firm emergence and growth,* vol. 3. Greenwich, CT: JAI Press, 57–118.

Maling, D.H. 1989: *Measurements from maps: principles and methods of cartometry.* Oxford: Pergamon Press.

Malinowsky, B. 1961: *Argonauts of the western Pacific.* New York: Dutton.

Malmberg, A. 1996: Industrial geography: agglomeration and local milieu. *Progress in Human Geography* 20: 392–403.

Malmberg, A. 1997: Industrial geography: location and learning. *Progress in Human Geography* 21: 573–82.

Malmberg, A. and Maskell, P. 2002: The elusive concept of localization economies: towards a knowledge-based theory of spatial clustering. *Environment and Planning A* 34: 429–49.

Malthus, T.R. 1970 [1798]: *An essay on the principle of population,* ed. A. Flew. London: Penguin.

Mamdani, M. 1996: *Citizen and subject: contemporary Africa and the legacy of late colonialism.* Princeton, NJ: Princeton University Press.

Mamdani, M. 2002: 'Good Muslim, bad Muslim': a political perspective on culture and terrorism. In E. Hershberg and K. Moore, eds, *Critical views of September 11: analyses from around the world.* New York: The New Press, 44–60.

Mamdani, M. 2004: *Good Muslim, bad Muslim: America, the Cold War and the roots of terror.* New York: Pantheon.

Mandanipour, A., Cars, G. and Allen, J., eds, 2000: *Social exclusion in European cities.* London: The Stationery Office and Regional Studies Association.

Mandel, E. 1980: *Long waves of capitalist development*. Cambridge, UK: Cambridge University Press.

Mandelbrot, B. 1967: How long is the coast of Britain? Statistical self-similarity and. fractional dimension, *Science* 156: 636–8.

Mann, M. 1984a: The autonomous power of the state: its origins, mechanisms, and results. *European Journal of Sociology* 25: 185–213.

Mann, M. 1986: *The sources of social power. Vol. 1: A history of power from the beginning to A.D. 1760*. Cambridge, UK: Cambridge University Press.

Mann, M. 1987: Ruling class strategies and citizenship. *Sociology* 21(3): 339–54.

Mann, M. 2005: *The dark side of democracy: explaining ethnic cleansing*. Cambridge, UK: Cambridge University Press.

Mann, S. 1984b: Sharecropping in the cotton South: a case of uneven development in agriculture. *Rural Sociology* 49: 412–29.

Mann, S. 1990: *Agrarian capitalism*. Durham, NC: University of North Carolina Press.

Manners, I.R. and Mikeswell, M.W., eds, 1974: *Perspectives on environment*. Washington, DC: Association of American Geographers.

Manovich, L. 2006: The poetics of augmented space. *Visual Communication* 5(2): 219–40.

Mansfield, B. 2004: Rules of privatization: contradictions in neoliberal regulation of North Pacific fisheries. *Annals of the Association of American Geographers* 94: 565–84.

Manski, C.F. 1995: *Identification problems in the social sciences*. Cambridge, MA: Harvard University Press.

Manson, S. and O'Sullivan, D. 2006: Complexity theory in the study of space and place. *Environment and Planning A* 38: 677–92.

Manson, S.M. 2001: Simplifying complexity: a review of complexity theory. *Geoforum* 32: 405–14.

Mansvelt, J. 2005: *Geographies of consumption*. London: Sage.

Manzo, K. 2005: Exploiting West Africa's children: trafficking, slavery and uneven development. *Area* 37: 393–401.

Marais, H. 2001: *South Africa: limits to change*. London and New York: Zed Books.

Marchand, B. 1978: A dialectic approach in geography. *Geographical Analysis* 10: 105–19.

Marcus, G. 1998: *Ethnography through thick and thin*. Princeton, NJ: Princeton University Press.

Marcuse, H. 1972: *Sartre's existentialism*, trans. J. de Bres. Studies in Critical Philosophy. London: New Left Books.

Marcuse, P. and van Kempen, R., eds, 2000: *Globalizing cities: a new spatial order?* Oxford: Blackwell.

Marcuse, P. and van Kempen, R., eds, 2003: *Of states and cities*. Oxford: Oxford University Press.

Mares, D. 2005: *Drug wars and coffeehouses*. New York: CQ Press.

Margulis, L. and Sagan, D. 2000: *What is life?* Berkeley, CA: University of California Press.

Marks, J. 1995: A new image of thought. *New Formations* 25, 66–76.

Markusen, A.R. 1985: *Profit cycles, oligopoly and regional development*. Cambridge, MA: The MIT Press.

Markusen, A.R. 1987: *Regions: the economics and politics of territory*. Totowa, NJ: Rowman & Littlefield.

Markusen, A.R. 1999: Fuzzy concepts, scanty evidence, policy distance: the case for rigor and policy relevance in critical regional studies. *Regional Studies* 33: 869–84.

Marsden, R. 1999: *The nature of capital: Marx after Foucault*. London: Routledge.

Marsden, T. 1992: Exploring a rural sociology for the fordist transition. *Sociologia Ruralis* XXXII(2/3): 209–30.

Marsden, T. and Wrigley, N. 1995: Regulation, retailing and consumption. *Environment and Planning A* 27: 1899–912.

Marsden, T., Flynn, A. and Harrison, M. 2000: *Consuming interests: the social provision of foods*. London: UCL Press.

Marsden, T., Munton, R., Whatmore, S. and Little, J. 1986: Towards a political economy of capitalist agriculture. *International Journal of Urban and Regional Research* 4: 498–521.

Marsden, T., Murdoch, J., Lowe, P., Munton, R. and Flynn, A. 1993: *Constructing the countryside*. London: UCL Press.

Marsh, C. 1982: *The survey method: the contribution of surveys to sociological explanation*. London: George Allen and Unwin.

Marsh, G.P. 1965 [1864]: *Man and nature, or, physical geography as modified by human action*. Reprint edition edited by David Lowenthal (Cambridge, MA: Belknap Press of Harvard University Press.

Marshall, A. 1890: *Principles of economics*. London: Macmillan.

Marshall, A. 1919: *Industry and trade*. London: Macmillan.

Marshall, J.N. 2004: Financial institutions in disadvantaged areas: a comparative analysis of policies encouraging financial inclusion in Britain and the United States. *Environment and Planning A* 36: 241–61.

Marshall, J.N., with Wood, P., Daniels, P.W., McKinnon, A., Bachtler, J., Damesick, P., Thrift, N., Gillespie, A., Green, A. and Leyshon, A. 1988: *Services and uneven development*. Oxford: Oxford University Press.

Marshall, M. 1987: *Long waves of regional development*. London: Macmillan.

Marshall, T.H. and Bottomore, T. 1992: *Citizenship and social class*. London: Pluto Press.

Marston, S. 1990: Who are 'the people'?: gender, citizenship, and the making of the American nation. *Environment and Planning D: Society and Space* 8: 449–58.

Marston, S. and Mitchell, K. 2004: Citizens and the state: contextualizing citizenship formation in space and time. In M. Low and C. Barnett, eds, *Spaces of democracy*. London: Sage.

Marston, S.A. 2000: The social construction of scale. *Progress in Human Geography* 24(2): 219–42.

Marston, S.A. 2004a: A long way from home: domesticating the social production of scale. In E. Sheppard and R. McMaster, eds, *Scale and geographic inquiry: nature, society and method*. Oxford: Blackwell, 170–91.

Marston, S.A. 2004b: Space, culture, state: uneven developments in political geography. *Political Geography* 23: 1–16.

Marston, S.A., Jones, J.P. III and Woodward, K. 2005: Human geography without scale. *Transactions of the Institute of British Geographers* 30: 416–32.

Marston, S.A., Woodward, K. and Jones, J.P. III 2007: Flattening ontologies of globalization: the Nollywood case. *Globalizations* 4: 1–19.

Marston, S.A., Towers, G., Cadwallader, M. and Kirby, A. 1989: The urban problematic. In G. Gaile and C. Wilmott, eds, *Geography in America*. Columbus, OH: Merrill, 651–72.

Martin, D. 2002: Output areas for 2001. In P. Rees, D. Martin and P. Williamson, eds, *The Census data system*. Chichester: Wiley, 37–46.

Martin, D. 2003: Enacting neighborhood. *Urban Geography* 24: 361–85.

Martin, D. 2005: Socioeconomic GeoComputation and e-social science. *Transactions in GIS* 9: 1–3.

Martin, D., Tate, N.J. and Langford, M. 2000: Refining population surface models: experiments with Northern Ireland census data. *Transactions in GIS* 4: 343–60.

Martin, D.G. 2000a: Constructing place: cultural hegemonies and media images of an inner-city neighborhood. *Urban Geography* 21: 380–405.

Martin, G.J. 2005: *All possible worlds: a history of geographical ideas*, 4th edn. New York: Oxford University Press.

Martin, J.E. 1983: *Feudalism to capitalism: peasant and landlord in English agrarian development*. London: Macmillan.

Martin, L.H., Gutman, F. and Hutton, P.H., eds, 1988: *Technologies of the self: a seminar with Michel Foucault*. London: Tavistock Press.

Martin, R.L. 1999a: The new economic geography of money. In R. Martin, ed., *Money and the space economy*. Chichester: Wiley, 3–27.

Martin, R.L. 1999b: The new 'geographical turn' in economics: some critical reflections. *Cambridge Journal of Economics* 23: 65–91.

Martin, R.L. 2000b: Local labour markets: their nature, performance and regulation. In G. Clark, M.P. Feldman and M.S. Gertler, eds, *The Oxford handbook of economic geography*. Oxford: Oxford University Press.

Martin, R.L. 2001a: EMU versus the regions? Regional convergence and divergence in Euroland. *Journal of Economic Geography* 1: 51–80.

Martin, R.L. 2001b: Geography and public policy: the case of the missing agenda. *Progress in Human Geography* 25: 189–209.

Martin, R.L. and Rowthorne, B., eds, 1986: *The geography of deindustrialization*. London: Macmillan.

Martin, R.L. and Sunley, P. 2001: Rethinking the 'economic' in economic geography: broadening our vision or losing our focus? *Antipode* 33(2): 148–61.

Martin, R.L. and Sunley, P. 2003: Deconstructing clusters: chaotic concept or policy panacea? *Journal of Economic Geography* 3: 5–35.

Martin, R.L. and Sunley, P. 2006: Path dependence and regional economic development. *Journal of Economic Geography*, 6: 395–437.

Martinez-Allier, J. 2002: *The environmentalism of the poor: a study of ecological conflicts and valuation*. Cheltenham: Edward Elgar.

Martins, L. 2000: A naturalist's vision of the tropics: Charles Darwin and the Brazilian landscape. *Singapore Journal of Tropical Geography* 21: 19–33.

Martins, L.L. and Abreu, M.A. 2001: Paradoxes of modernity: imperial Rio de Janeiro, 1808–1821. *Geoforum* 32(4): 533–50.

Marx, K. 1857: Introduction. In Marx, K. 1973 [1939]: *Grundrisse: foundations of the critique of political economy (rough draft)*. London: Penguin, in association with *New Left Review*.

Marx, K. 1904: *A contribution to the critique of political economy*, trans. N.I. Stone (from 2nd German edn). Chicago: C.H. Kerr.

Marx, K. 1963 [1852]: *The eighteenth brumaire of Louis Bonaparte*. New York: International.

Marx, K. 1964: *Pre-capitalist economic formations*. London: Lawrence and Wishart.

Marx, K. 1967– : *Capital*, vols I–III. London: Penguin.

Marx, K. 1967 [1867]: *Capital*, vol. 1, trans. B. Fowkes. London: Penguin.

Marx, K. 1975: On the Jewish question. In L. Colletti, ed., *Early writings*. London: Penguin.

Marx, K. 1992 [1894]: *Capital*, vol. III, trans. D. Fenbach. London: Penguin.

Marx, K. 1988 [1844]: *The economic and philosophic manuscripts of 1844 and the communist manifesto*, trans. M. Milligan. Amherst, NY: Prometheus Books.

Marx, K. and Engels, F. 1972 [1845]: *The German ideology*. New York: International.

Marx, K. and Engels, F. 2002 [1848]: *The communist manifesto*, trans. S. Moore; ed. G. Stedman Jones. London: Penguin.

Mascia-Lees, F., Sharp, P. and Cohen, C. 1989: The postmodern turn in anthropology: cautions from a feminist perspective. *Signs* 15: 7–33.

Mason, D. 1995: *Race and ethnicity in modern Britain*. New York: Oxford University Press.

Mason, P. 1990: *Deconstructing America: representations of the other*. London: Routledge.

Masser, I. 1988: The Regional Research Laboratory initiative: a progress report. *International Journal of Geographical Information Systems* 2(1): 11–22.

Massey, D. 1973: Towards a critique of industrial location theory. *Antipode* 5: 33–9.

Massey, D. 1991: A global sense of place. *Marxism Today*, June: 24–9.

Massey, D. 1993: Power-geometry and a progressive sense of place. In J. Bird, B. Curtis, T. Putnam, G. Robertson and L. Tickner, eds, *Mapping the futures: local cultures, global change*. London: Routledge, 60–70.

Massey, D. 1994a: A global sense of place. In Massey, *Space, place and gender*. Cambridge, UK and Minneapolis: Polity Press and The University of Minnesota Press, 146–56.

Massey, D. 1994b: *Space, place and gender*. Cambridge, UK and Minneapolis: Polity Press and The University of Minnesota Press.

Massey, D. 1995a [1984]: *Spatial divisions of labour: social structures and the geography of production*, 2nd edn. London: Macmillan.

Massey, D. 1995b: Thinking radical democracy spatially. *Environment and Planning D: Society and Space* 13: 283–8.

Massey, D. 1997: Spatial disruptions. In S. Golding, ed., *The eight technologies of otherness*. London: Routledge, 218–25.

Massey, D. 1999: Space–time, 'science' and the relationship between physical and human geography. *Transactions of the Institute of British Geographers*, NS 24: 261–76.

Massey, D. 2004: Geographies of responsibility. *Geografiska Annaler* 86B: 5–18.

Massey, D. 2005: *For space*. London: Sage.

Massey, D., Allen, J. and Sarre, P., eds, 1999: *Human geography today*. Cambridge, UK: Polity Press.

Massey, D., Quintas, P. and Wield, D. 1991: *High-tech fantasies: science parks in society, science and space*. London: Routledge.

Massey, D.B. 1979: A critical evaluation of industrial location theory. In F.E.I. Hamilton and G.J.R. Linge, eds, *Spatial analysis, industry and the industrial environment*, vol. I. *Industrial systems*. New York: Wiley, 57–72.

Massey, D.S. and Denton, N.A. 1986: The dimensions of residential segregation. *Social Forces* 67: 281–351.

Massey, D.S. and Denton, N.A. 1993: *American apartheid: segregation and the making of the underclass*. Cambridge, MA: Harvard University Press.

Massey, D.S. and Fischer, M.J. 2006: The effect of childhood segregation on minority academic performance at selective colleges. *Ethnic and Racial Studies* 29: 1–26.

Massey, D.S., Arango, J., Hugo, G., Kouaouci, A., Pellegrino, A. and Taylor, J.E. 1993: Theories of international migration: a review and appraisal. *Population and Development Review* 19: 431–66.

Masterman, M. 1970: The nature of a paradigm. In I. Lakatos and A. Musgrave, eds, *Criticism and the growth of knowledge*. Cambridge, UK: Cambridge University Press, 59–89.

Matei, S. and Ball-Rokeach, S. 2005: Watts, the 1965 Los Angeles riots, and the communicative construction of the fear epicenter of Los Angeles. *Communication Monographs* 72: 301–23.

Matless, D. 1991: Nature, the modern and the mystic: tales from early twentieth century geography. *Transactions of the Institute of British Geographers*, NS 16: 272–86.

Matless, D. 1992: An occasion for geography: landscape, representation and Foucault's corpus. *Environment and Planning D: Society and Space* 10(1): 41–56.

Matless, D. 1993: Regional surveys and local knowledges: the geographical imagination in Britain, 1918–39. *Transactions of the Institute of British Geographers* 17(4): 464–80.

Matless, D. 1994: Moral geography in Broadland. *Ecumene* 1: 127–55.

Matless, D. 1997: Moral geographies of English landscape. *Landscape Research* 22: 141–55.

Matless, D. 1998: *Landscape and Englishness*. London: Reaktion Books.

Mato, D. 1998: On the making of transnational identities in the age of globalization: the US Latina/o-'Latin' American case. *Cultural Studies* 12: 598–620.

Matthews, M.H. 1992: *Making sense of place: children's understanding of large-scale environments*. Hemel Hempstead: Harvester Wheatsheaf.

Matthews, J.A. and Herbert, D.T. 2004: *Unifying geography*, London: Routledge.

Maurer, B. 2003: Uncanny exchanges: the possibilities and failures of 'making change' with alternative monetary forms. *Environment and Planning D: Society and Space* 21(3): 317–40.

Mauro, A. 1995: Stop disasters: the newsletter of the UN International Decade for Natural Disaster Reduction. In T. Horlick-Jones, A. Amendola and R. Casale, eds, *Natural risk and civil protection*. London: E. & F.N. Spon, 511–15.

Mauss, M. 1990 [1925]: *The gift: the form and reason for exchange in archaic societies*, trans. W.D. Halls. New York: W.W. Norton.

Maxey, I. 1999: Beyond boundaries? Activism, academia, reflexivity and research. *Area* 31(3): 199–208.

May, J. and Thrift, N., eds, 2001: *TimeSpace: geographies of temporality*. London: Routledge.

May, J., Wills, J., Datta, K., Evans, Y. and Herbert, J. 2007: Keeping London working: global cities, the British state and London's new migrant division of labour. *Transactions of the Institute of British Geographers* 32(2): 151–67.

May, J.A. 1970: *Kant's conception of geography and its relation to recent geographical thought*. Toronto: University of Toronto, Department of Geography, Research publication 4.

May, J.M. 1952: *International Geographical Union, XVII International Congress: first report of the Commission on Medical Geography (Ecology of Health and Disease)*. Washington, DC: UNESCO.

May, J.M. 1958: *The ecology of human disease*. New York: M.D. Publications.

May, R.M. 1973: *Stability and complexity in model ecosystems*. Princeton, NJ: Princeton University Press.

Mayer, J. 2008: Outsourcing torture: the secret history of America's 'extraordinary rendition' program. In Mayer, *The dark side*, New York, Doubleday, 101–38.

Mayer, J.D. 1982: Relations between two traditions of medical geography: health systems planning and geographical epidemiology. *Progress in Human Geography* 6: 216–30.

Mayer, J.D. and Meade, M.S. 1994: A reformed medical geography reconsidered. *The Professional Geographer* 46: 103–6.

Mayer, T. 1994: *Analytical Marxism*. London: Sage.

Mayer, T., ed., 2000: *Gender ironies of nationalism: sexing the nation*. London: Routledge.

Mayer, T. 2004: Embodied nationalisms. In L. Staeheli, E. Kofman and L. Peake, eds, *Mapping women, making politics*. New York: Routledge.

Mayhew, L. 1986: *Urban hospital location*. London: George Allen & Unwin.

Mayhew, R. 1996: Landscape, religion and knowledge in eighteenth century England. *Ecumene* 3: 454–71.

Mayhew, R. 2000: *Enlightenment geography: the political languages of British geography, 1650–1850*. London: Macmillan.

Mayhew, R. 2001: The effacement of early modern geography (c.1600–1850). *Progress in Human Geography* 25: 282–401.

Mayne, A. 1993: *The imagined slum: newspaper representation in three cities 1870–1914*. Leicester: Leicester University Press.

Mayne, A. and Murray, T., eds, 2001: *The archaeology of urban landscapes: explorations in slumland*. Cambridge, UK: Cambridge University Press.

Mazlish, B. 1999: Big questions? Big history. *History and Theory* 38(2): 232–48.

Mazlish, B. 2005: *Civilization and its contents*. Stanford, CA: Stanford University Press.

Mazower, M. 1998: *Dark continent: Europe's twentieth-century*. London: Allen Lane.

Mbembe, A. 2000: At the edge of the world: boundaries, territoriality, and sovereignty in Africa. *Public Culture* 12: 259–84.

Mbembe, A. 2001: *On the Postcolony*. Berkeley, CA: University of California Press.

Mbembe, A. 2003: Necropolitics. *Public Culture* 15: 11–40.

McAdam, D., Tarrow, S. and Tilly, C. 2001: *Dynamics of contention*. Cambridge, UK: Cambridge University Press.

McCann, E.J. 2002: The cultural politics of local economic development: meaning-making, place-making, and the urban policy process. *Geoforum* 33(3): 385–98.

McCarthy, J. 2004: Privatizing conditions of production: trade agreements as neoliberal environmental governance. *Geoforum* 35: 327–41.

McCarthy, J. 2005: Scale, sovereignty, and strategy in environmental governance. *Antipode* 37(4): 731–53.

McCarty, H.H., Hook, J.C. and Knox, D.S. 1956: *The measurement of association in industrial geography*. Iowa City: Department of Geography, University of Iowa.

McClintock, A. 1995: *Imperial leather: race, gender, and sexuality in the colonial contest*. London: Routledge.

McClintock, C.C., Brannon, D. and Maynard-Moody, S. 1979: Applying the logic of sample surveys to qualitative case studies. *Administrative Science Quarterly* 24(12): 4–16.

McCormack, D. 2003: An event of geographical ethics in spaces of affect. *Transactions of the Institute of British Geographers* 4: 488–507.

McCormack, D. 2005: Diagramming practice and performance. *Environment and Planning D: Society and Space* 23: 119–47.

McCormick, M. 2001: *Origins of the European economy: communications and commerce AD 300–900*. Cambridge, UK: Cambridge University Press.

McCullough, M. 2004: *Digital ground: architecture, pervasive computing and environmental knowing*. Cambridge, MA: The MIT Press.

McDonough, T., ed., 2002: *Guy Debord and the Situationist International: texts and documents*. Cambridge, MA: The MIT Press.

McDowell, L. 1983: Towards an understanding of the gender division of urban space. *Environment and Planning D: Society and Space* 1: 15–30.

McDowell, L. 1986: Beyond patriarchy: a class-based explanation of women's subordination. *Antipode* 18(3): 311–21.

McDowell, L. 1991: Life without father and Ford: the new gender order of post-Fordism. *Transactions of the Institute of British Geographers* 16(4): 400–19.

McDowell, L. 1997a: *Capital culture: gender at work in the city.* Oxford: Blackwell.

McDowell, L., ed., 1997b: *Undoing place? A geographical reader.* London: Arnold.

McDowell, L. 1998: Elites in the City of London: some methodological considerations. *Environment and Planning A* 30: 2133–46.

McDowell, L. 2001: Father and Ford revisited: gender, class and employment change in the new millennium. *Transactions of the Institute of British Geographers* 26: 448–64.

McDowell, L. 2003: *Redundant masculinities? Employment change and white working class youth.* Oxford: Blackwell.

McDowell, L. and Court, G. 1994: Performing work: bodily representations in merchant banks. *Environment and Planning D: Society and Space* 12: 727–50.

McDowell, L. and Massey, D. 1984: A woman's place? In D. Massey and J. Allen, eds, *Geography matters.* Cambridge, UK: Cambridge University Press in Association with the Open University, 128–47.

McDowell, L. and Sharpe, J. 1997: *Space, gender, knowledge: feminist readings.* London: Arnold.

McDowell, L. and Sharpe, J., eds, 1999: *Feminist glossary of human geography.* London: Arnold.

McEwan, C. 2000: *Gender, geography and empire: Victorian women travellers in West Africa.* London: Ashgate.

McEwan, C. 2003: Material geographies and postcolonialism. *Singapore Journal of Tropical Geography* 24(3): 340–55.

McGee, T.G. 1971: *The urbanization process in the Third World: explorations in search of a theory.* London: George Bell.

McGee, T.G. 1991: The emergence of desakota regions in Asia: expanding a hypothesis. In N. Ginsburg, B. Koppel and T.G. McGee, eds, *The extended metropolis: settlement transition in Asia.* Honolulu: University of Hawaii Press.

McGee, T.G. 1995: Eurocentrism and geography: reflections on Asian urbanization, in J. Crush, ed., *Power of development.* London: Routledge, 192–207.

McGee, T.G. 2001: Urbanization takes on new dimensions in Asia's population giants. *Population Today* 29(7): 1–2.

McGuinness, M. 2002: Geographies with a difference? Citizenship and difference in postcolonial urban spaces. In A. Blunt and C. McEwan, eds, *Postcolonial geographies.* London: Continuum, 99–114.

McGuirk, P.M. 2000: Power and policy networks in urban governance: local government and property-led regeneration in Dublin. *Urban Studies* 37: 651–72.

McGuirk, P.M. 2004: State, strategy, and scale in the competitive city: a neo-Gramscian analysis of the governance of 'global Sydney'. *Environment and Planning A* 36: 1019–43.

McIntosh, M. 1998: *Controlling misbehaviour in England, 1370–1600.* Cambridge, UK: Cambridge University Press.

McKendrick, J.H. 1999: Not just a playground: rethinking children's place in the built environment. *Built Environment* 25(1): 75–8.

McKendrick, J.H. 2000: The geography of children: an annotated bibliography. *Childhood* 73(3): 359–87.

McKendrick, J.H., ed., 2004: *First steps: a primer on the geographies of children and youth.* London: Limited Life Working Party on Children, Youth and Families of the Royal Geographic Society with the Institute of British Geographers.

McKenzie, E. 1994: *Privatopia: homeowner associations and the rise of residential private government.* New Haven, CT: Yale University Press.

McKibben, W. 1990: *The end of nature.* London: Penguin.

McKinnon, K. 2005: (Im)mobilization and hegemony: 'Hill tribe' subjects and the 'Thai' state. *Social and Cultural Geography* 6: 31–46.

McLafferty, S. and Preston, V. 1997: Gender, race, and the determinants of commuting: New York in 1990. *Urban Geography* 18: 192–202.

McLellan, D. 1979: *Marxism after Marx.* London: Macmillan.

McMaster, R.B. and Shea, K.S. 1992: *Generalization in digital cartography.* Washington, DC: Association of American Geographers.

McMichael, P., ed., 1996: *Food and agrarian orders in the world economy.* New York: Praeger.

McMillan, J. 2002: *Reinventing the bazaar.* New York: W.W. Norton.

McNee, R. 1960: Towards a more humanistic geography: the geography of enterprise. *Tijdschrift voor Economische en Sociale Geografie* 51: 201–6.

McNeill, J.R. 2003: Observations on the nature and culture of environmental history. *History and Theory* 42 (December 2003): 5–43.

McNulty, M. 1999: The collapse of Zaire: implosion, revolution or external sabotage? *Journal of Modern African Studies* 37: 53–82.

Mead, G.H. 1934: *Mind, self and society.* Chicago: The University of Chicago Press.

Meade, M. and Erickson, R. 2000: *Medical geography,* 2nd edn. New York: Guilford Press.

Meadows, D.H., Meadows, D.L. and Randers, J. 1992: *Beyond the limits: global collapse or a sustainable future.* London: Earthscan.

Meadows, D.H., Meadows, D.L., Randers, J. and Brehens, W. III 1972: *The limits to growth.* London: Earth Island.

Meardon, S. 2001: Modelling agglomeration and dispersion in city and country: Gunnar Myrdal, François Perroux and the New Economic Geography. *American Journal of Economics and Sociology* 60(1): 25–57.

Megoran, N. 2005: The critical geopolitics of danger in Uzbekistan and Kyrgyztan.

Environment and Planning D: Society and Space 23: 555–80.

Megoran, N. 2008: Militarism, realism, just war or nonviolence? Critical geopolitics and the problem of normativity. *Geopolitics* 13: 473–97.

Mehta, U. 1999: *Liberalism and empire: a study in nineteenth-century political thought and practice.* Chicago: Chicago University Press.

Mein Smith, P. 2003: New Zealand Federation Commissioners in Australia: one past, two historiographies. *Australian Historical Studies* 34 (122): 305–25.

Meinig, D.W. 1965: The Mormon culture region: strategies and patterns in the American West. *Annals of the Association of American Geographers* 55: 191–220.

Meinig, D.W., ed., 1979: *The interpretation of ordinary landscapes.* Oxford: Oxford University Press.

Meinig, D.W. 1983: Geography as an art. *Transactions of the Institute of British Geographers,* NS 8(3): 314–28.

Meinig, D.W. 1986: *The shaping of America: a geographical perspective on 500 years of history,* vol. 1: *Atlantic America, 1492–1800.* New Haven, CT: Yale University Press.

Meinig, D.W. 1986–2004: *The shaping of America: a geographical perspective on 500 years of history,* 4 vols. New Haven, CT: Yale University Press.

Melman, N. 1992: *Women's Orients: English women and the Middle East 1718–1918.* Ann Arbor: University of Michigan Press.

Mels, T. 2004: Lineages of a geography of rhythms. In T. Mels, ed., *Reanimating places: a geography of rhythms.* Aldershot: Ashgate, 3–42.

Melville, S. and Readings, B., eds, 1995: *Vision & textuality.* London: Macmillan.

Menand, L. 2001: *The metaphysical club: a story of ideas in America.* New York: Farar, Straus and Giroux.

Mendels, F. 1972: Proto-industrialization: the first phase of the industrialization process. *Journal of Economic History* 32: 241–61.

Mendieta, E. 2007: The literature of urbicide: Friedrich, Nossack, Sebald and Vonnegut. *Theory and Event* 10:2.

Menzel, U. 2005: W.W. Rostow. In D. Simon, ed., *Fifty key thinkers on development.* London: Routledge.

Merrett, C. 1996: *Free trade: neither free nor about trade.* Montreal: Black Rose Books.

Merrifield, A. 1995: Situated knowledge through exploration: reflections on Bunge's 'geographical expeditions'. *Antipode* 27(1): 49–70.

Merrifield, A. 1996: The extraordinary voyages of Ed Soja: inside the trialectics of spatiality. *Annals of the Association of American Geographers* 89: 345–8.

Merrifield, A. 2004: The sentimental city: the lost urbanism of Pierre Mac Orlan and Guy

Debord. *International Journal of Urban and Regional Research* 28: 930–40.

Merrifield, A. 2006: *Henri Lefebvre: a critical introduction.* London: Routledge.

Merrifield, A. and Swyngedouw, E., eds, 1997: *The urbanization of injustice.* New York: New York University Press.

Merriman, P. 2004: Driving places: Marc Augé, non-places, and the geographies of England's M1 motorway. *Theory, Culture & Society* 21: 145–67.

Mertes, T. 2004: *A movement of movements: is another world really possible?* London: Verso.

Merton, R.K. 1957: *Social theory and social structure.* Toronto: Free Press.

Mestrovic, S. 1998: *Anthony Giddens: the last modernist.* London: Routledge.

Metzel, D. and Philo, C., eds, 2005: Theme section on 'Geographies of intellectual disability. *Health and Place* 11: 77–120.

Meyerson, F.A.B. 2001: Replacement migration: A questionable tactic for delaying the inevitable effects of fertility transition. *Population and Environment* 22: 401–9.

Midgley, J. 2001: The United States: welfare, work and development. *International Journal of Social Welfare* 10: 284–93.

Mignolo, W. 2005: *The idea of Latin America.* Malden, MA: Blackwell.

Mignolo, W.D. 2000: *Local histories/global designs: coloniality, subaltern knowledges, and border thinking.* Princeton, NJ: Princeton University Press.

Milbourne, P., ed., 1997: *Revealing rural 'others': representation, power and identity in the British countryside.* London: Frances Pinter.

Miles, R. 1993: *Racism after race relations.* London: Routledge.

Miles, R. and Brown, M. 2003: *Racism,* 2nd edn. London: Routledge.

Mill, H.R. 1913: *The realm of nature.* London: John Murray.

Miller, A. 1953: *The skin of the Earth.* London: Methuen.

Miller, B. 2006: The globalization of fear: fear as a technology of governance. In D. Conway and N. Heynen, eds, *Globalization's contradictions: geographies of discipline, destruction and transformation.* New York: Routledge, 161–95.

Miller, B.A. 2000: *Geography and social movements: comparing antinuclear activism in the Boston area.* Minneapolis: University of Minnesota Press.

Miller, D., ed., 1997: *Material cultures.* London: UCL Press.

Miller, D., Jackson, P., Holbrook, B., Rowlands, M. and Thrift, N.J. 1998: *Shopping, place and identity.* London: Routledge.

Miller, R.E. and Blair, P.D. 1985: *Input–output analysis: foundations and extensions.* Englewood Cliffs, NJ: Prentice-Hall.

Milligan, C. 2001: *Geographies of care: space, place and the voluntary sector.* Aldershot: Ashgate.

Mills, C. 2004: Agamben's Messianic politics: biopolitics, abandonment and happy life. *Contretemps* 5: 42–62.

Mills, C.W. 1959: *The sociological imagination.* Oxford: Oxford University Press.

Mills, M. 1999: *Thai women in the global labor force: consuming desires, contested selves.* New Brunswick, NJ: Rutgers University Press.

Millstone, E. and Lang, T. 2003: *The Penguin atlas of food: who eats what, where and why.* London: Penguin.

Milne, D. 2008: *America's Rasputin: Walt Rostow and the Vietnam War.* New York: Hill and Wang.

Milward, A. 2005: Review article: the European Union as a superstate. *International History Review* XXVII: 90–105.

Minca, C. 2000: Venetian geographical praxis. *Environment and Planning D: Society and Space* 18: 285–9.

Minca, C. 2004: The return of the camp. *Progress in Human Geography* 29: 405–12.

Minca, C. 2006: Giorgio Agamben and the new biopolitical *nomos. Geografiska Annaler* 89B: 387–403.

Minca, C. 2007a: Agamben's geographies of modernity. *Political Geography* 26: 78–97.

Minca, C. 2007b: Humboldt's compromise, or the forgotten geographies of landscape. *Progress in Human Geography* 31: 179–93.

Minca, C. and Oakes, T., eds, 2006: *Travels in paradox: remapping tourism.* Lanham, MD: Rowman and Littlefield.

Mingay, G.E. 1997: *Parliamentary enclosure in England: an introduction to its causes, incidence and impact 1750–1850.* New York: Longman.

Mingione, E., ed., 1996: *Urban poverty and the underclass: a reader.* Oxford: Blackwell.

Mintz, S. 1976: On the concept of a Third World. *Dialectical Anthropology* 1: 377–82.

Mirowski, P. 1989: *More heat than light. Economics as social physics: physics as nature's economics.* Cambridge, UK: Cambridge University Press.

Mirzoeff, N. 1999: *Visual culture: an introduction.* Cambridge, UK: Polity Press.

Mishan, E.J. and Quah, E. 2007: *Cost–benefit analysis,* 5th edn. London: Routledge.

Mishra, V. and Hodge, B. 1991: What is postcolonialism? *Textual Practice* 5: 399–413.

Mitchell, D. 1995: There's no such thing as culture: towards a reconceptualization of the idea of culture in geography. *Transactions of the Institute of British Geographers* 20(1): 102–16.

Mitchell, D. 1996: *The lie of the land: migrant workers and the California landscape.* Minneapolis: University of Minnesota Press.

Mitchell, D. 1997a: The annihilation of space by law: the roots and implications of anti-homeless laws in the United States. *Antipode* 29: 303–35.

Mitchell, D. 2000: *Cultural geography: a critical introduction.* Oxford: Blackwell.

Mitchell, D. 2002a: Cultural landscape: the dialectical landscape. *Progress in Human Geography* 26: 381–9.

Mitchell, D. 2002b: Dead labor and the political economy of landscape – of California living, California dying. In K. Anderson, M. Domosh, S. Pile and N. Thrift, eds, *Handbook of cultural geography.* London: Sage, 233–48.

Mitchell, D. 2003a: *The right to the city: social justice and the fight for public space.* New York: Guilford Press.

Mitchell, D. and Rosati, C. 2006: The globalization of culture: geography and the industrial production of culture. In D. Conway and N. Heynen, eds, *Globalization's contradictions: geographies of discipline, destruction and transformation.* New York: Routledge, 144–60.

Mitchell, D. and Staeheli, L. 2005: Turning social relations into space: property, law and the plaza of Santa Fe, New Mexico. *Landscape Research* 30: 361–78.

Mitchell, J.C. 1983: Case and situation analysis. *Sociological Review* 31(3): 186–211.

Mitchell, J.K., ed., 1999: *Crucibles of hazard: mega-cities and disasters in transition.* Tokyo: UN University Press.

Mitchell, J.K. 2003b: Urban vulnerability to terrorism as hazard. In S.L. Cutter, D.B. Richardson and T.J. Wilbanks, eds, *The geographical dimensions of terrorism.* New York: Routledge, 17–26.

Mitchell, K. 1993: Multiculturalism, or the united colors of capitalism? *Antipode* 25: 263–94.

Mitchell, K. 1997b: Different diasporas and the hype of hybridity. *Environment and Planning D: Society and Space* 15: 533–53.

Mitchell, K. 1997c: Transnational discourse: bringing geography back in. *Antipode* 29(2): 101–14.

Mitchell, K. 1998: Reworking democracy: contemporary immigration and community politics in Vancouver's Chinatown. *Political Geography* 17: 729–50.

Mitchell, K. 2004a: *Crossing the neo-liberal line: Pacific Rim migration and the metropolis.* Philadelphia: Temple University Press.

Mitchell, K. 2004b: Geographies of identity: multiculturalism unplugged. *Progress in Human Geography* 28: 641–51.

Mitchell, K., Marston, S.A. and Katz, C., eds, 2004: *Life's work: geographies of social reproduction.* Oxford: Blackwell.

Mitchell, R., Martin, D. and Foody, G. 1998: Estimating the social composition of enumeration districts. *Environment and Planning A* 30: 1929–41.

Mitchell, T. 1988: *Colonising Egypt.* Cambridge, UK: Cambridge University Press.

Mitchell, T. 1989: The world-as-exhibition. *Comparative Studies in Society and History* 31: 217–36.

Mitchell, T. 1991: The limits of the state: beyond statist approaches and their critics. *American Political Science Review* 85(1): 77–96.

Mitchell, T. 1992: Orientalism and the exhibitionary order. In N. Dirks, ed., *Colonialism and culture*. Ann Arbor: University of Michigan Press, 289–317.

Mitchell, T. 1998: Fixing the economy. *Cultural Studies* 12(1): 82–101.

Mitchell, T. 2002c: McJihad: Islam in the U.S. global order. *Social Text* 73: 1–18.

Mitchell, T. 2002d: *Rule of experts: Egypt, technopolitics, modernity*. Berkeley, CA: University of California Press.

Mitchell, W.J.T., ed., 2002e [1994]: *Landscape and power*, 2nd edn. Chicago: The University of Chicago Press.

Mitlin, D. and Satterthwaite, D., eds, 2004: *Empowering squatter citizens: local government, civil society and urban poverty reduction*. London: Earthscan.

Mitman, G. 1992: *The state of nature: ecology, community, and American social thought, 1900–1950*. Chicago: the University of Chicago Press.

Mitra, A. and Schwartz, R.L. 2001: From cyber space to cybernetic space: rethinking the relationship between real and virtual spaces. *Journal of Computer-Mediated Communication* 7(1), http://www3.interscience.wiley.com/journal/117979306/home

Mittelman, J. 2000: *The globalization syndrome: transformation and resistance*. Princeton, NJ: Princeton University Press.

Mizuoka, F., Mizuuchi, T., Hisatake, T., Tsutsumi, K. and Fujita, T. 2005: The critical heritage of Japanese geography: its tortured trajectory for eight decades. *Environment and Planning D: Society and Space* 23: 453–73.

Mlodinow, L. 2001: *Euclid's window: the story of geometry from parallel lines to hyperspace*. New York: The Free Press.

Mohan, G. and Mohan, J. 2002: Placing social capital. *Progress in Human Geography* 26: 191–210.

Mohan, J. 2002: *Planning, markets and hospitals*. London: Routledge.

Mohanty, C.T. 1991: Under Western eyes: feminist scholarship and colonial discourses. In C.T. Mohanty, A. Russo and L. Torres, eds, *Third World women and the politics of feminism*. Bloomington, IN: Indiana University Press, 51–80.

Mohanty, C.T. 2003: 'Under Western eyes' revisited: feminist solidarity through anti-capitalist struggles. *Signs: Journal of Women in Culture and Society* 28: 499–535.

Moi, T. 1999: *What is a woman? And other essays*. Oxford: Oxford University Press.

Mol, A. 2002: *The body multiple*. Durham, NC: Duke University Press.

Mollenkopf, J. 2008: School is out: the case of New York City. *Urban Affairs Review* 44(2): 239–65.

Momsen, J. 1999: *Women and development in the Third World*. London: Routledge.

Momsen, J., ed., 1999: *Gender, migration and domestic service*. London: Routledge.

Monk, J. 1994: Place matters: comparative international perspectives on feminist geography. *The Professional Geographer* 46: 277–88.

Monk, J. and Hanson, S. 1982: On not excluding the other half from human geography. The *Professional Geographer* 32: 11–23.

Monmonier, M. 1993: *Mapping it out: expository cartography for the humanities and social sciences*. Chicago: The University of Chicago Press.

Monmonier, M. 2001: *Bushmanders and bullwinkles: how politicians manipulate electronic maps and census data to win elections*. Chicago: The University of Chicago Press.

Monmonier, M. 2003: The Internet, cartographic surveillance, and locational privacy. In M.P. Peterson, ed., *Maps and the Internet*. Oxford: Elsevier Science, 97–113.

Monmonier, M. 2004a: *How to lie with maps*, 2nd edn. Chicago: The University of Chicago Press.

Monmonier, M. 2004b: *Rhumb lines and map wars: a social history of the Mercator projection*. Chicago: The University of Chicago Press.

Monmonier, M. 2004c: *Spying with maps: surveillance technologies and the future of privacy*. Chicago: The University of Chicago Press.

Monmonier, M. 2005: Lying with maps. *Statistical Science* 20: 215–22.

Monmonier, M. 2006: *From Squaw Tit to Whorehouse Meadow: how maps name, claim, and inflame*. Chicago: The University of Chicago Press.

Monmonier, M. and McMaster, R.B. 2004: Cartography. In G.L. Gaile and C.J. Willmott, eds, *Geography in America at the dawn of the twenty-first century*. New York: Oxford University Press, 419–41.

Montello, D.R. 2002: Cognitive map-design research in the twentieth century: theoretical and empirical approaches. *Cartography and Geographic Information Science* 29: 283–304.

Montesquieu, C.L. 1949 [1748]: The *spirit of the laws*. New York: Hafner.

Montfort, M.J. and Dutailly, J.C. 1983: *Les filières de production*. Paris: INSEE.

Moore, B. 1966: *The social origins of dictatorship and democracy*. Boston: Beacon Press.

Moore, D. 1996: Marxism, culture and political ecology. In R. Peet and M. Watts, eds, *liberation ecologies*. London: Routledge, 125–47.

Moore, D. 2005: *Suffering for territory: race, place and power in Zimbabwe*. Durham, NC: Duke University Press.

Moore, D., Kosek, J. and Pandian, A., eds, 2003: *Race, nature and the cultural politics of difference*. Durham, NC: Duke University Press.

Moore, N. and Whelan, Y., eds, 2007: *Heritage, memory and the politics of identity: new perspectives on the cultural landscape*. Aldershot: Ashgate.

Moran, M. 1991: *The financial services revolution: the USA, UK and Japan*. London: Macmillan.

Moran, M. 2003: *The British regulatory state: high modernism and hyper-innovation*. Oxford: Oxford University Press.

Moran, W., Blundern, G. and Bradley, A. 1996: Empowering family farms through cooperatives and producer marketing board. *Economic Geography* 72(2): 161–77.

Moretti, F. 1998: *Atlas of the European novel 1800–1900*. London: Verso.

Moretti, F. 2005: *Graphs, maps and trees: abstract models for a literary history*. London: Verso.

Morgan, K. 2004: The exaggerated death of geography: learning, proximity and territorial innovation systems. *Journal of Economic Geography* 4: 3–21.

Morgan, K., Marsden, T. and Murdoch, J. 2006: *Worlds of food: place, power, and provenance in the food chain*. Oxford: Oxford University Press.

Morley, D. 2003: What's home got to do with it? Contradictory dynamics in the domestication of technology and the dislocation of domesticity. *Cultural Studies* 6(4): 435–58.

Morley, D. and Robins, K. 1992: Techno-Orientalism: futures, foreigners and phobias. *New Formations* 16: 136–56.

Morrill, R. 1993: Geography, spatial analysis and social science. *Urban Geography* 14: 442–6.

Morrill, R.L. 2005: Hägerstrand and the 'quantitative revolution': a personal appreciation. *Progress in Human Geography* 29: 333–6.

Morris, A.E.J. 1994: *History of urban form: before the industrial revolutions*. New York: Wiley.

Morris, M. 2006: 'Politics' is plural. *Women's Studies Quarterly* 34(1/2): 82–6.

Morrissey, J. 2008b: The geoeconomic pivot of the global war on terror: US Central Command and the war in Iraq. In D. Ryan and P. Kiely, eds, *America and Iraq: policy-making, intervention and regional politics*. New York: Taylor and Francis, 103–22.

Morrissey, J. 2009: Bases, bodies and biopolitics: US juridical warfare in the War on Terror. In D. Grondin, ed., *War beyond the battlefield*. New York: Routledge (in press).

Morrissey, J., Strohmayer, U., Whelan, Y. and Yeoh, B. 2009: *Key concepts in historical geography*. London: Sage.

Mortimore, M. 1998: *Roots in the African Dust: sustaining the drylands*. Cambridge: Cambridge University Press.

Mosley, S., Harrigan, J. and Toye, J. 1991: *Aid and power: the World Bank and policy-based lending*. London: Routledge.

Moss, P., ed., 2002: *Feminist geography in practice: research and methods*. Oxford: Blackwell.

Moss, P. 2005: A bodily notion of research: power, difference, and specificity in feminist methodology. In L. Nelson and J. Seager, eds, *A companion to feminist geography*. Oxford: Blackwell, 41–59.

Moss, P. and Dyck, I. 2002: *Women, body, illness: space and identity in the everyday lives of women with chronic illness*. Lanham, MD: Rowan and Littlefield.

Mosse, D. 2005: *Cultivating development: an ethnography of aid policy and practice*. London: Zed Books.

Mosse, G. 1975: *The nationalisation of the masses*. New York: Howard Fertig.

Mouffe, C. 1992: Feminism, citizenship, and radical democratic politics. In J. Butler and J. Scott, eds, *Feminists theorize the political*. New York: Routledge, 369–84.

Mouffe, C. 1993: *The return of the political*. London: Verso.

Moulaert, F., Rodriguez, A. and Swyngedouw, E., eds, 2003: *The globalized city: economic restructing and social polarization in European cities*. Oxford: Oxford University Press.

Mountz, A. 2003: Human smuggling, the transnational imaginary, and everyday geographies of the nation-state. *Antipode* 35: 622–44.

Mountz, A., Miyares, A., Wright, R. and Bailey, A. 2003: Methodologically becoming: power, knowledge and team research. *Gender, Place and Culture* 10: 29–46.

Mulhern, F. 2000: *Culture/metaculture*. London: Routledge.

Müller, M. 2008: Reconsidering the concept of discourse for the field of critical geopolitics. *Political Geography* 27: 322–38.

Muller, P. 2004: Transportation and urban form: stages in the spatial evolution of the American metropolis. In S. Hanson and G. Giuliano, eds, *The geography of urban transportation*, 3rd edn. New York: Guilford Press, 59–85.

Mulvey, L. 1989: *Visual and other pleasures*. London: Macmillan.

Mumford, L. 1961: *The city in history*. New York: Harcourt, Brace.

Munasinghe, M. and Swart, R. 2005: *Primer on climate change and sustainable development: facts, policy analysis and applications*. Cambridge: Cambridge University Press.

Münkler, H. 2005: *The new wars*. Cambridge UK: Polity Press.

Murdoch, J. 2003: Co-constructing the country-side: hybrid networks and the extensive self. In P. Cloke, ed., *Country visions*. London: Pearson, 263–82.

Murdoch, J. 2006: *Post-structuralist geography: a guide to relational space*. London: Sage.

Murdoch, J. and Lowe, P. 2003: The preservationist paradox: modernism, environmentalism and the politics of spatial division. *Transactions of the Institute of British Geographers* 28: 318–32.

Murdoch, J. and Marsden T. 1995: The spatialization of politics: local and national actor-spaces in environmental conflict. *Transactions of the Institute of British Geographers* 20: 368–80.

Murji, K. and Solomos, J. 2005: *Racialization: studies in theory and practice*. Oxford: Oxford University Press.

Murphy, A.B. 2006: Enhancing geography's role in public debate. *Annals of the Association of American Geographers* 96(1): 1–13.

Murphy, J. 2006: Building trust in economic space. *Progress in Human Geography* 30(4): 427–50.

Murphy, R.E. 1972: *The central business district*. London: Longman.

Murray, R. 1989: Fordism and post-Fordism. In S. Hall and M. Jacques, eds, *New times*. London: Lawrence and Wishart.

Murray, W.E. 2006: Neo-feudalism in Latin America? Globalization, agribusiness and land re-concentration in Chile. *Journal of Peasant Studies* 33: 646–77.

Mustafa, D. 2005: The terrible geographicalness of terrorism: reflections of a hazards geographer. *Antipode* 37(1): 72–92.

Musterd, S. 2003: Segregation and integration: a contested relationship. *Journal of Ethnic and Migration Studies* 29: 623–41.

Mutersbaugh, T. 2002: The number is the beast: a political economy of organic-coffee certification and producer unionism. *Environment and Planning A* 34(7): 1165–84.

Mutersbaugh, T. 2004: Serve and certify: paradoxes of service work in organic coffee certification. *Environment and Planning D: Society and Space* 22: 533–52.

MVRDV 2000: *Costa Iberica*. Barcelona: Actar.

Nabudere, D.W. 1997: Beyond modernization and development, or why the poor reject development. *Geografiska Annaler* 79B: 203–15.

Naess, A. 1973: The shallow and the deep, long-range ecology movements: a summary. *Inquiry* 16: 95–100.

Nagar, R. and Ali, F. 2003: Collaboration across borders: moving beyond positionality. *Singapore Journal of Tropical Geography* 24(3): 356–72.

Nagar, R. and Swarr, A.L. 2005: Organizing from the margins: grappling with 'empowerment' in India and South Africa. In L.

Nelson and J. Seager, eds, *A companion to feminist geography*. Oxford: Blackwell, 291–304.

Nagar, R., Lawson, V., McDowell, L. and Hanson, S. 2002: Locating globalization: feminist (re)readings of the subjects and spaces of globalization. *Economic Geography* 78: 257–84.

Naimark, N.M. 2001: *Fires of hatred: ethnic cleansing in twentieth century Europe*. Cambridge, MA: Harvard University Press.

Nalbantoglu, G.B. and Wong C.T. 1997: Introduction. In G.B. Nalbantoglu and C.T. Wong, eds, *Postcolonial space(s)*. New York: Princeton Architectural Press, 7–12.

Nandy, A. 1992: State. In W. Sachs, ed., *The development dictionary: a guide to knowledge as power*. London: Zed Books, 264–74.

Nandy, A. 1997: Colonization of the mind. In M. Rahnema with V. Bawtree, eds, *The post-development reader*. London: Zed Books, 168–78.

Nandy, A. 2003: *The romance of the state and the fate of dissent in the tropics*. New Delhi: Oxford University Press.

Naraindas, H. 1996: Poisons, putresence and the weather: a genealogy of the advent of tropical medicine. *Contributions to Indian Sociology* 30: 1–35.

Nash, C. 1996: Reclaiming vision: looking at landscape and the body, *Gender Place and Culture* 3: 149–69.

Nash, C. 1999: Irish placenames: postcolonial locations. *Transactions of the Institute of British Geographers* 24: 457–80.

Nash, C. 2000: Performativity in practice: some recent work in cultural geography *Progress in Human Geography* 24: 653–64.

Nash, R.F. 1982 [1967]: *Wilderness and the American mind*. New Haven, CT: Yale University Press.

Nast, H. 1994a: Opening remarks on 'Women in the field'. *The Professional Geographer* 46: 54–66.

Nast, H., ed., 1994b: Women in the field: critical feminist methodologies and theoretical perspectives. *Professional Geographer* 46: 54–102.

Nast, H. 1998: Unsexy geographies. *Gender, Place and Culture* 5: 191–206.

Nast, H. 2000: Mapping the 'unconscious': racism and the Oedipal family. *Annals of the Association of American Geographers* 90: 215–55.

Nast, H.J. and Pile, S., eds, 1998: *Places through the body*. London: Routledge.

National Intelligence Council 2005: *Mapping the global future*. Washington, DC: NIC, http://www.cia.gov/nic/NIC_globaltrend2020

National Research Council Panel on a Multipurpose Cadastre 1983: *Procedures and standards for a multipurpose cadastre*. Washington, DC: National Academy Press.

Natter, W. 2005: Friedrich Ratzel's spatial turn: identities of disciplinary space and its borders between the anthropo- and political geography of Germany and the United States. In H. van Houtum, O. Kramsch and W. Zierhoger, eds, *B/ordering space*. Aldershot: Ashgate, 171–86.

Natter, W., Schatzki, T.R. and Jones, J.P., eds, 1996: *Objectivity and its other*. New York: Guilford Press.

Nayak, A. 2003: *Race, place and globalization: youth culture in a changing world*. Oxford: Berg.

Naylor, R.T. and Hudson, M. 2004: *Hot money and the politics of debt*. Montreal/Kingston: McGill-Queens University Press.

Naylor, S. 2002: The field, the museum and the lecture hall: the spaces of natural history in Victorian Cornwall. *Transactions of the Institute of British Geographers*, NS 27: 494–513.

Naylor, S. 2006: Nationalising provincial weather: meteorology in nineteenth century Cornwall. *British Journal for the History of Science* 39: 1–27.

Nedelsky, J. 1990: Law, boundaries and the bounded self. *Representations* 30: 162–89.

Neeson, J.M. 1993: *Commoners, common right, enclosure and social change in England 1700–1820*. Cambridge, UK: Cambridge University Press.

Negri, A. 2000: *The savage anomaly: the power of Spinoza's metaphysics and politics*. Minneapolis: University of Minnesota Press.

Nelson, J.S., Megill, A. and McCloskey, D.N., eds, 1987: *The rhetoric of the human sciences: language and argument in scholarship and public affairs*. Madison: University of Wisconsin Press.

Nelson, L. 1999: Bodies (and spaces) do matter: the limits of performativity. *Gender, Place and Culture* 6: 331–53.

Nelson, L. 2004: Topographies of citizenship: Purhépechan Mexican women claiming political subjectivities. *Gender, Place and Culture* 11(2): 163–87.

Nelson, L. and Seager, J., eds, 2005: *A companion to feminist geography*. Oxford: Blackwell.

Netting, R.M. 1986: *Cultural ecology*. Prospect Heights, IL: Waveland Press.

Neuman, M. 2005: The compact city fallacy. *Journal of Planning Education and Research* 25(1): 11–26.

Neumann, I. 1996: *Russia and the idea of Europe: a study in identity and international relations*. London: Routledge.

Neumann, R.P. 1998: *Imposing wilderness: struggles over livelihood and nature preservation in Africa*. Berkeley, CA: University of California.

Neumann, R.P. 2004a: Moral and discursive geographies in the war for biodiversity in Africa. *Political Geography* 23: 813–37.

Neumann, R.P. 2004b: Nature–state–territory: towards a critical theorization of conservation enclosures. In R. Peet and M. Watts, eds, *Liberation ecologies: environment, development, social movements*. London: Routledge, 195–217.

Neumann, R.P. 2005: *Making political ecology*. London: Hodder Arnold.

Nevins, J. 2002: *Operation gatekeeper: the rise of the 'illegal alien' and the making of the U.S.–Mexico boundary*. New York: Routledge.

Newcombe, K., Kalma, J. and Aston, A. 1978: The metabolism of a city: the case of Hong Kong. *Ambio* 7(1): 3–15.

Newman, D. 1995: *Boundaries in flux: the Green Line boundary between Israel and the West Bank – past, present and future*. Monograph Series, Boundary and Territory Briefings, No. 7. Durham, UK: International Boundaries Research Unit, University of Durham.

Newman, D. 2002: The lines that separate: boundaries and borders in political geography. In J. Agnew and G. Toal, eds, *A companion to political geography*. Oxford: Blackwell.

Newman, D. 2005: Conflict at the interface: the impact of boundaries and borders on contemporary ethnonational conflict. In C. Flint, ed., *The geography of war and peace*. Oxford: Oxford University Press, 321–44.

Newman, J.L. 1973: The use of the term 'hypothesis' in geography. *Annals of the Association of American Geographers* 63: 22–7.

Newman, O. 1972: *Defensible space: crime prevention through urban design*. New York: Macmillan.

Newman, O. 1996: *Creating defensible space*. Washington, DC: US Department of Housing and Urban Development, Office of Policy Development and Research.

Newstead, C., Reid, C. and Sparke, M. 2003: The cultural geography of scale. In K. Anderson, M. Domosh and N. Thrift, eds, *The handbook of cultural geography*. London: Sage, 485–97.

Niamir-Fuller, M., ed., 1999: *Managing mobility in African rangelands*. London: Intermediate Technology Publications.

Nicholls, A. and Opal, C. 2005: *Fair trade: market-driven ethical consumption*. London: Sage.

Nicholson, L.J., ed., 1989: *Feminism/postmodernism*. New York: Routledge.

Nicol, H.N. and Townsend-Gault, I., eds, 2005: *Holding the line: borders in a global world*. Vancouver: University of British Columbia Press.

Nicolson, M.H. 1959: *Mountain gloom and mountain glory: the development of the aesthetics of the infinite*. Ithaca, NY: Cornell University Press.

Nietschmann, B. 1973: *Between land and water: the subsistence ecology of the Miskito Indians, Eastern Nicaragua*. New York: Seminar Press.

912

Nietzsche, F. 1994: *On the genealogy of morality*, ed. K. Ansell-Pearson. Cambridge, UK: Cambridge University Press.

Nightingale, A. 2003: A feminist in the forest: situated knowledges and mixing methods in natural resource management. *ACME: an International E-Journal for Critical Geographies* 2(1): 77–90.

Nijman, J. 2000: The paradigmatic city. *Annals of the Association of American Geographers* 90: 135–45.

Ninjalicious [Jeff Chapman] 2005: *Access all areas: a user's guide to the art of urban exploration.* Toronto: Infilpress.

Nochlin, L. 1991: The imaginary Orient. In Nochlin, *The politics of vision: essays on nineteenth-century art and society.* London: Thames and Hudson, 33–59.

Nogueras-Iso, J., Zarazaga-Soria, F.J., Lacasta, J., Béjar, R. and Muro-Medrano, P.R. 2004: Metadata standard interoperability: application in the geographic information domain. *Computers, Environment and Urban Systems* 28: 611–34.

Nolin, C. 2006: *Transnational ruptures: gender and forced migration.* Aldershot: Ashgate.

Nootebloom, B. 2006: Innovation, learning and cluster dynamics. In B. Asheim, P. Cooke and R. Martin, eds, *Clusters and regional development: critical reflections and explorations.* London: Routledge, 137–63.

Nora, P. 1989: Between memory and history: *Les Lieux de Mémoire. Representations* 26: 7–25.

Nora, P. 1997: *Realms of memory.* New York: Columbia University Press.

Norbert-Hodge, H. 1991: *Ancient futures: learning from Ladakh.* San Francisco: Sierra Club Books.

Norcliffe, G.B. 1997: Popeism and Fordism: examining the roots of mass production. *Regional Studies* 30: 267–80.

Nordgren, A., ed., 1997: *Science, ethics and sustainability: the responsibility of science in attaining sustainable development.* Studies in Bioethics and Research Ethics 2. Uppsala: Acta Universitatis Upsaliensis.

Nordstrom, C. 2004: *Shadows of war: violence, power and international profiteering in the twenty-first century.* Berkeley, CA: University of California Press.

Noreen, E. 1989: *Computer-intensive methods for testing hypotheses.* New York: Wiley.

Nostrand, R. 1992: *The Hispano homeland.* Norman: University of Oklahoma Press.

Nostrand, R. and Estaville, L., eds, 2001: *Homelands: a geography of culture and place across America.* Baltimore, MD: The Johns Hopkins University Press.

Nove, A. 2005 [1983]: *The economics of feasible socialism revisited.* London: Taylor and Francis.

Nunes, M. 1997: What space is cyberspace? In D. Holmes, ed., *Virtual politics: identity and community in cyberspace.* London: Sage, 163–78.

Nunn, S. 2007: Incidents of terrorism in the United States, 1997–2005. *Geographical Review* 97: 89–111.

Nurkse, R. 1953: *Problems of capital formation in underdeveloped countries.* New York: Oxford University Press.

Ó Tuathail, G. 1992: Putting Mackinder in his place: material transformations and myth. *Political Geography* 11: 100–18.

Ó Tuathail, G. 1996a: An anti-geopolitical eye? Maggie O'Kane in Bosnia, 1992–94. *Gender, Place and Culture* 3: 171–85.

Ó Tuathail, G. 1996b: *Critical geopolitics: the politics of writing global space.* London: Routledge; Minneapolis: University of Minnesota Press.

Ó Tuathail, G. 2003: 'Just looking for a fight': American affect and the invasion of Iraq. *Antipode* 35: 856–70.

Ó Tuathail, G. 2005: The frustrations of geopolitics and the pleasures of war: *Behind Enemy Lines* and American geopolitical culture. *Geopolitics* 10: 356–77.

Ó Tuathail, G. and Dalby, S., eds, 1998: *Rethinking geopolitics.* New York: Routledge.

O'Brien, L. 1992a: *Introducing quantitative geography: measurement, methods and generalised linear models.* London: Routledge.

O'Brien, R. 1992b: *Global financial integration: the end of geography.* London: Frances Pinter.

O'Connor, J. 1973: *The fiscal crisis of the state.* New York: St Martin's Press.

O'Connor, J. 1998: *Natural causes: essays in ecological Marxism.* New York: Guilford Press.

O'Gorman, E. 1961: *The invention of America.* Bloomington, IN: Indiana University Press.

O'Kelly, M.E. 1998: A geographer's analysis of hub-and-spoke networks. *Journal of Transport Geography* 6(3): 171–86.

O'Loughlin, J. 1996: 'Europe of the Regions' and the federalization of Europe. *Publius* 26: 141–62.

O'Loughlin, J., Ward, M.D., Lofdahl, C.L., Cohen, J.S., Brown, D.S., Reilly, D., Gleditsch, K.S. and Shin, M. 1998: The diffusion of democracy, 1946–1994. *Annals of the Association of American Geographers* 88: 545–74.

O'Neill, B. Mackellar, F.L. and Lutz, W. 2001: *Population and climate change.* Cambridge, UK: Cambridge University Press.

O'Neill, O. 2001: Agents of justice. *Metaphilosophy* 32(1/2): 180–95.

O'Reilly, K. 2007: 'Where the knots of narrative are tied and untied': the dialogic production of gendered development spaces in

North India. *Annals of the Association of American Geographers* 97: 613–34.

O'Riordan, T. 1976: *Environmentalism*. London: Pion.

O'Riordan, T. 1991: The new environmentalism and sustainable development. *The Science of the Total Environment* 108: 5–15.

O'Riordan, T. 2004: Environmental science, sustainability and politics. *Transactions of the Institute Of British Geographers* 29(2): 234–47.

O'Sullivan, D. 1984: *The age of discovery 1400–1550*. London: Longman.

O'Sullivan, D. 2004: Complexity science and human geography. *Transactions of the Institute of British Geographers*, NS 29: 292–5.

O'Sullivan, D. and Unwin, D.J. 2002: *Geographic information analysis*. New York: Wiley.

O'Sullivan, P. 1982: Antidomino. *Political Geography Quarterly* 1: 57–64.

Oakes, T. 1997: Place and the paradox of modernity. *Annals of the Association of American Geographers* 87(3): 509–31.

Oas, I. 2005: Shifting the Iron Curtain of Kantian peace: NATO expansion and the modern Magyars. In C. Flint, ed., *The geography of war and peace*. Oxford: Oxford University Press, 395–414.

Odland, J. 1988: *Spatial autocorrelation*. Beverly Hills: Sage.

OECD 2000: *Knowledge management in the learning economy*. Paris: OECD.

OECD 2006: *Economic policy reforms: going for growth*. Paris: OECD.

Ogborn, M. 1998: *Spaces of modernity: London's geographies 1680–1780*. New York: Guilford Press.

Ogborn, M. 2002: Writing travels: power, knowledge and ritual on the English East India Company's early voyages. *Transactions of the Institute of British Geographers*, NS 27: 155–71.

Ogborn, M. 2007: *Indian ink: script and print in the making of the English East India Company*. Chicago: The University of Chicago Press.

Ogden, P.E. and Hall, R. 2004: The second demographic transition, new household forms and the urban population of France during the 1990s. *Transactions of the Institute of British Geographers* 29: 88–105.

Ohmae, K. 1995: *The end of the nation state: the rise of regional economies*. New York: The Free Press.

Oke, T.R. 1978: *Boundary layer climates*. London: Methuen.

Okonski, K. 2003: 'Ecological imperialism: a sustainable development network briefing paper', Sustainable Development Network at http://www.sdnetwork.net/main/page.php?page_id=4&p=2&publication_id=20

Oldroyd, D. 1986: *The arch of knowledge: an introduction to the history of the philosophy and methodology of science*. London: Methuen.

Olds, K. 2001: *Globalization and urban change: capital, culture, and Pacific Rim mega-projects*. Oxford: Oxford University Press.

Ollman, B. 1976: *Alienation: Marx's conception of man in capitalist society*, 2nd edn. Cambridge, UK: Cambridge University Press.

Olsson, G. 1974: The dialectics of spatial analysis. *Antipode* 6(3): 50–62.

Olsson, G. 1978: On the mythology of the negative exponential or power as a game of ontological transformation. *Geografiska Annaler* 50B: 116–23.

Olsson, G. 1980: *Birds in egg/eggs in bird*. London: Pion.

Olsson, G. 1991: *Lines of power/limits of language*. Minneapolis: University of Minnesota Press.

Olsson, G. 2007: *Abysmal: a critique of cartographic reason*. Chicago: Chicago University Press.

Olund, E. 2006: *Whitewatching: cinema, race and regulation in the progressive-era United States*. Unpublished PhD dissertation, Department of Geography, University of British Columbia.

Olund, E.N. 2002: From savage space to governable space: the extension of United States judicial sovereignty over Indian Country in the nineteenth century. *Cultural Geographies* 9: 129–57.

Olwig, K. 1993: Sexual cosmology: nation and landscape at the conceptual interstices of nature and culture; or, what does landscape really mean? In B. Bender, ed., *Landscape: politics and perspectives*. Oxford: Berg, 307–43.

Olwig, K. 1996: Recovering the substantive nature of landscape. *Annals of the Association of American Geographers* 86(4): 630–53.

Olwig, K. 2002: *Landscape, nature, and the body politic: from Britain's renaissance to America's New World*. Madison, WI: University of Wisconsin Press.

Omi, M. and Winant, H. 1996: *Racial formation in the United States*. New York: Routledge and Kegan Paul.

Omran, A. 1983: The epidemiological transition theory. *Journal of Tropical Pediatrics* 29: 305–16.

Ong, A. 1999: *Flexible citizenship: the cultural logics of transnationality*. Durham, NC: Duke University Press.

Ong, A. 2000: Graduated sovereignty in southeast Asia. *Theory, Culture & Society* 17: 55–75.

Ong, A. and Collier, S., eds, 2005: *Global assemblages: technology, politics and ethics as anthropological problems*. Oxford: Blackwell.

Openshaw, S. 1977: A geographical study of scale and aggregation effects in region-building, partitioning and spatial modelling. *Transactions of the Institute of British Geographers*, NS 2: 459–72.

Openshaw, S. 1982: *The modifiable areal unit problem*. Norwich: GeoBooks (CATMOG 38).

Openshaw, S. 1989: Computer modelling in human geography. In B. Macmillan, ed.,

Remodelling geography. Oxford: Blackwell, 273–90.

Openshaw, S. 1996: Fuzzy logic as a new scientific paradigm for doing geography. *Environment and Planning A* 28: 761–8.

Openshaw, S. 1998: Building automated geographical analysis and explanation machines. In P.A. Longley, S.M. Brooks, R. McDonnell and B. Macmillan, eds, *Geocomputation: a primer.* Chichester: Wiley, 95–115.

Openshaw, S., ed., 1995: *Census users' handbook,* Cambridge: Geoinformation International.

Openshaw, S. and Openshaw, C. 1997: *Artificial intelligence in geography.* Chichester: Wiley.

Openshaw, S. and Taylor, P.J. 1979: A million or so correlation coefficients: three *experiments* on the modifiable areal unit problem. In N. Wrigley, ed., *Statistical methods in the spatial sciences.* London: Pion, 127–44.

Openshaw, S. and Taylor, P.J. 1981: The modifiable areal unit problem. In N. Wrigley and R.J. Bennett, eds, *Quantitative geography: a British view.* London: Routledge and Kegan Paul, 60–70.

Openshaw, S., Charlton, M., Wymer, C. and Craft, A.W. 1987: A Mark I Geographical Analysis Machine for the automated analysis of point datasets. *International Journal of Geographic Information Systems* 1: 335–58.

Ophir, A. and Shapin, S., eds, 1991: The place of knowledge: the spatial setting and its relations to the production of knowledge. Special issue of *Science in Context.*

Oppong, J. 1998: A vulnerability interpretation of the geography of HIV/AIDS in Ghana, 1986–1995. *The Professional Geographer* 50: 437–48.

Orford, A. 2003: Localizing the other: the imaginative geography of humanitarian intervention. In Orford, *Reading humanitarian intervention: human rights and the use of force in international law.* Cambridge, UK: Cambridge University Press, 82–125.

Ortiz, F. 1995 [1940]: *Cuban counterpoint: tobacco and sugar,* trans. H. de Onís. Durham, NC: Duke University Press.

Ortner, S. 1995: Resistance and the problem of ethnographic refusal. *Society for the Comparative Study of Society and History* 37: 1773–93.

Osborn, F.J. 1977: *New towns: their origins, achievements and progress.* London: L. Hill.

Osborne, M.A. 1994: *Nature, the exotic, and the science of French colonialism.* Bloomington: Indiana University Press.

Osborne, P. 2000: *Traveling light: photography, travel and visual culture.* Manchester: Manchester University Press.

Oslender, U. 2007: The resurfacing of the public intellectual: towards the proliferation of public spaces of critical intervention. *ACME: an International E-journal for Critical Geographies* 6(1): 98–123.

Osterhammel, J. 1997: *Colonialism: a theoretical overview.* Princeton, NJ: Markus Wiener.

Ostrom, E., Burger, J., Field, C.B., Norgaard, R.B. and Policansky, D. 1999: Revisiting the commons: local lessons, global challenges. *Science* 284(5412): 278–82.

Ostrom, E., Dietz, T., Dolsak, N., Stern, P., Stonich, S. and Weber, E., eds, 2002: *The drama of the commons.* Washington, DC: National Academy Press.

Oswin, N. 2007: Producing homonormativity in neoliberal South Africa: recognition, redistribution and the equality project. *Signs: Journal of Women in Culture and Society* 32: 649–69.

Outram, D. 2005: *The Enlightenment,* 2nd edn. Cambridge, UK: Cambridge University Press.

Overton, M. 1996: *Agricultural revolution in England: the transformation of the agrarian economy 1500–1850.* Cambridge, UK: Cambridge University Press.

Overton, M. 1996: Re-establishing the English agricultural revolution, *Agricultural History Review* 44: 1–20.

Oza, R. 2007: Contrapuntal geographies of threat and security: the United States, India and Israel. *Environment and Planning D: Society and Space* 25: 9–32.

Oza, R. 2007: The geography of Hindu right-wing violence in India. In D. Gregory and A. Pred, eds, *Violent geographies: fear, terror and political violence.* London: Routledge, 153–73.

Paasi, A. 1996: *Territories, boundaries, and consciousness: the changing geographies of the Finnish–Russian border.* New York: Wiley.

Paasi, A. 2002: Place and region: regional worlds and words. *Progress in Human Geography* 26: 802–11.

Paasi, A. 2003: Region and place: regional identity in question. *Progress in Human Geography* 27: 475–85.

Paasi, A. 2005a: Boundaries as social practice and discourse: the Finnish–Russian border. In P. Ganster and D. Lorey, eds, *Borders and border politics in the globalizing world.* Lanham, MD: Rowman & Littlefield/SR Books, 117–36.

Paasi, A. 2005b: Globalisation, academic capitalism, and the uneven geographies of international journal publishing spaces. *Environment and Planning A* 37: 769–89.

Pacione, M. 2001a: The future of the city – cities of the future. *Geography* 86(4): 275–86.

Pacione, M. 2001b: *Urban geography: a global perspective.* London: Routledge.

Pacione, M., ed., 2002: *The city: critical concepts in the social sciences,* 5 vols. London: Routledge.

915

Paelinck, J. and Klaassen, L. 1979: *Spatial econometrics*. Farnborough: Saxon House.

Paez, A., Uchida, T. and Miyamoto, K. 2002: A general framework for estimation and inference of geographically weighted regression models: 1: location-specific kernel bandwidths and a test for locational heterogeneity; 2: spatial association and model specification tests. *Environment and Planning A* 34: 733–54, 883–904.

Pagden, A. 1993: *European encounters with the New World: from Renaissance to romanticism*. New Haven, CT: Yale University Press.

Pagden, A., ed., 2002: *The idea of Europe from antiquity to the European Union*. Cambridge, UK: Cambridge University Press.

Pahl, R.E. 1965: *Urbs in rure*. London: Weidenfeld and Nicolson.

Pahl, R.E. 1975. *Whose city? And further essays on urban society*. London: Penguin.

Pain, R. 2000: Place, social relations and the fear of crime: a review. *Progress in Human Geography* 24(3): 365–87.

Pain, R. 2003: Social geography: on action-oriented research. *Progress in Human Geography* 7(5): 649–57.

Pain, R. 2004: Social geography: participatory research. *Progress in Human Geography* 28: 652–63.

Pain, R. and Smith, S.J. 2008: *Fear: critical geopolitics and everyday life*. Aldershot: Ashgate.

Pain, R., Mowl, G. and Talbot, C. 2000: Difference and the negotiation of 'old age'. *Environment and Planning D: Society and Space* 18: 377–94.

Pain, R., Burke, M., Fuller, D. and Gough, J. 2001: *Introducing social geographies*. London: Arnold.

Pain, R., Grundy, S. and Gill, S., with Towner, E., Sparks, G. and Hughes, K. 2005: 'So long as I take my mobile': mobile phones, urban life and geographies of young people's safety. *International Journal of Urban and Regional Research* 29(4): 814–30.

Painter, J. 1991: The geography of trade union responses to local government privatization. *Transactions of the Institute of British Geographers* 16: 214–26.

Painter, J. 1995: *Politics, geography and 'political geography'*. London: Arnold.

Painter, J. 2000: State and governance. In E. Sheppard and T. Barnes, eds, *A companion to economic geography*. Oxford: Blackwell, 359–76.

Painter, J. 2004: Prosaic states. Paper presented at the Annual Conference of the Association of American Geographers. Denver, CO.

Painter, J. 2006: Prosaic geographies of stateness. *Political Geography* 25: 752–74.

Painter, J. and Goodwin, M. 2000: Local governance after Fordism: a regulationist approach. In G. Stoker, ed., *The new politics of British local governance*. London: Macmillan, 33–53.

Palka, E. and Gangano, F., eds, 2000: *The scope of military geography: across the spectrum from peace-time to war*. New York: McGraw-Hill.

Pandey, G. 2001: *Remembering Partition*. Cambridge, UK: Cambridge University Press.

Panelli, R. 2004: *Social geographies: from difference to action*. London: Sage.

Parajuli, P. 1991: Power and knowledge in development discourse. *International Social Science Journal* 127: 173–90.

Parekh, B. 2000: *Multiculturalism: cultural diversity and political theory*. London: Macmillan.

Parfitt, J. 2005: Questionnaire design and sampling. In R. Flowerdew and D. Martin, eds, *Methods in human geography: a guide for students doing a research project*, 2nd edn. London: Pearson Educational, 78–109.

Park, B.-G. 2005: Spatially selective liberalization and graduated sovereignty: politics of neo-liberalism and 'special economic zones' in South Korea. *Political Geography* 24: 850–73.

Park, D.C., Radford, J.P. and Vickers, M.H. 1998: Disability studies in geography. *Progress in Human Geography* 22: 208–22.

Park, R.E. 1936: Human ecology. *American Journal of Sociology* 42(1): 1–15.

Park, R.E. 1967 [1925]: The city: suggestions for the investigation of human behavior in the urban environment. In R. Park, E. Burgess and R. McKenzie, eds, *The city*. Chicago: The University of Chicago Press, 1–46.

Park, R.E., Burgess, E.W. and McKenzie, R.D. 1925: *The city*. Chicago: The University of Chicago Press.

Parker, A., Russo, M., Sommer, D. and Yaeger, P. 1992: *Nationalisms & sexualities*. New York: Routledge.

Parker, G. 1985: *The development of western geopolitical thought in the twentieth century*. London: Croom Helm.

Parker, S. 2004: *Urban theory and the urban experience: encountering the city*. London: Routledge.

Parker, S.P. 1994: *World geographical encyclopedia*, vol. 3: *Asia*. New York: McGraw-Hill.

Parker, W.H. 1982: *Mackinder: geography as an aid to statecraft*. Oxford: The Clarendon Press.

Parks, L. 2001: Satellite views of Srebrenica: televisuality and the politics of witnessing. *Social Identities* 7: 585–611.

Parks, V. 2004: The gendered connection between ethnic residential and labor-market segregation in Los Angeles. *Urban Geography* 25: 589–630.

Parpart, J. 2002: Lessons from the field: rethinking empowerment, gender and development from a post-(post-?)development perspective. In K. Saunders, ed., *Feminist post-development thought: rethinking modernity, post-colonialism and representation*. London: Zed Books.

Parr, H. 2002: Medical geography: diagnosing the body in medical and health geography, 1999–2000. *Progress in Human Geography* 26: 240–51.

Parr, H. 2003: Medical geography: care and caring. *Progress in Human Geography* 27: 212–21.

Parr, J.B. 1995: Alternative approaches to market area structure in the urban system. *Urban Studies* 32(8): 1317–29.

Parry, B. 2004: *Trading the genome: investigating the commodification of bio-information*. New York: Columbia University Press.

Parry, J.H. 1981: *The age of reconnaissance: discovery, exploration and settlement 1450 to 1650*. Berkeley, CA: University of California Press.

Parsons, T. 1951: *The social system*. London: Routledge and Kegan Paul.

Pastor, M. Jr, Morello-Frosch, R. and Sadd, J. 2005: The air is always cleaner on the other side: race, space and ambient air toxics exposures in California. *Journal of Urban Affairs* 27 (2): 127–48.

Pateman, C. 1989: *The disorder of women: democracy, feminism and political theory*. Stanford, CA: Stanford University Press.

Patterson, K.D. 1986: *Pandemic influenza, 1700–1900: a study in historical epidemiology*. Totowa, NJ: Rowman & Littlefield.

Patton, P. 1979: On power and prisons. In M. Morris and P. Patton, eds, *Michel Foucault: power, truth, strategy*. Sydney: Feral Publications.

Paulin, C.O. 1932: *Atlas of the historical geography of the United States*. Washington, DC: Carnegie Institution.

Pawson, R. 2006: *Evidence-based policy: a realist perspective*. London: Sage.

Payer, C. 1974: *Debt trap: the IMF and the Third World*. London: Penguin.

Payer, C. 1982: *The World Bank: a critical analysis*. New York: Monthly Review Press.

Payne, A. 2005: *The global politics of unequal development*. London: Palgrave Macmillan.

Peace, R. 2000: Computers, qualitative data and geographic research. In I. Hay, ed., *Qualitative research methods in human geography*. Oxford: Oxford University Press, 144–60.

Peach, C., ed., 1975: *Urban social segregation*. London and New York: Longman.

Peach, C. 1996a: Does Britain have ghettos? *Transactions of the British Institute of Geographers*, NS 21: 216–35.

Peach, C. 1996b: Good segregation, bad segregation. *Planning Perspectives* 11: 379–98.

Peach, C. 1996c: The meaning of segregation. *Planning Practice and Research* 11: 137–50.

Peake, L. and Ray, B. 2001: Racializing the Canadian landscape: whiteness, uneven geographies and social justice. *The Canadian Geographer* 45(1): 180–7.

Pearson, R. 1986: Latin American women and the new international division of labour: a reassessment. *Bulletin of Latin American Research* 5: 67–79.

Peck, J. 1996: *Work-place: the social regulation of labor markets*. New York: Guilford Press.

Peck, J. 2000: Doing regulation. In G.L. Clark, M.P. Feldman, and M.S. Gertler, eds, *The Oxford handbook of economic geography*. Oxford: Oxford University Press, 61–80.

Peck, J. 2001a: Neoliberalizing states: thin policies/hard outcomes. *Progress in Human Geography* 25: 445–55.

Peck, J. 2001b: *Workfare states*. New York: Guilford Press.

Peck, J. 2004: Geography and public policy: constructions of neoliberalism. *Progress in Human Geography* 28: 392–405.

Peck, J. 2005: Struggling with the creative class. *International Journal of Urban and Regional Research* 29(4): 740–70.

Peck, J. 2008: Remaking laissez-faire. *Progress in Human Geography* 32: 3–43.

Peck, J. and Tickell, A. 1994: Searching for a new institutional fix: the *after*-Fordist crisis and global–local disorder. In A. Amin, ed., *Post-Fordism: a reader*. Oxford: Blackwell, 280–315.

Peck, J. and Tickell, A. 2002: Neoliberalizing space. *Antipode* 34(3): 380–404.

Peck, J. and Yeung, H., eds, 2003: *Remaking the global economy*. London: Sage.

Peckham, R.S., ed., 2003: *Rethinking heritage: culture and politics in Europe*. London: I.B. Tauris.

Pedersen, P. 1970: Innovation diffusion within and between national urban systems. *Geographical Analysis* 2: 203–54.

Peet, J.R. 1969: The spatial expansion of commercial agriculture in the nineteenth century: a von Thünen explanation. *Economic Geography* 45: 283–301.

Peet, R., ed., 1977a: *Radical geography: alternative viewpoints on contemporary social issues*. Chicago: Maaroufa Press.

Peet, R. 1977b: The development of radical geography in the United States. In R. Peet, ed., *Radical geography: alternative viewpoints on contemporary social issues*. Chicago, Maaroufa Press, 6–30.

Peet, R. 1998: *Modern geographical thought*. Oxford: Blackwell.

Peet, R. 2000: Commentary: thirty years of radical geography. *Environment and Planning A* 32: 951–3.

Peet, R., ed., 2000: Special issue: 'Radical geography, parts 1 and 2'. *Environment and Planning A* 32(6/7): 951–1050, 1149–244.

Peet, R. 2003: *Unholy trinity: The IMF, World Bank and WTO*. London: Zed Books.

Peet, R. 2005: From Eurocentrism to Americentrism. *Antipode* 37: 936–43.

Peet, R. and Thrift, N.J., eds, 1989a: *New models in geography: the political economy perspective*, 2 vols. London: Unwin Hyman.

Peet, R. and Thrift, N.J. 1989b: Political economy and human geography. In R. Peet and N.J. Thrift, eds, *New models in geography: the political economy perspective*, vol. 1. London: Unwin Hyman, 3–29.

Peet, R. and Watts, M. 1993: Introduction: development theory and environment in an age of market triumphalism. *Economic Geography* 69: 227–53.

Peet, R. and Watts, M., eds, 2003 [1996]: *Liberation ecologies: environment, development and social movements*, 2nd edn. London: Routledge.

Peirce, C.S. 1982: *Writings of Charles S. Peirce: a chronological edition*, ed. M.H. Fisch, 6 vols. Bloomington, IN: Indiana University Press.

Pellegrini, P.A. and Reader, S. 1996: Duration modelling of spatial point patterns. *Geographical Analysis* 28(3): 219–43.

Pelling, M. 2001: Natural disasters? In N. Castree and B. Braun, eds, *Social nature: theory, practice, and politics*. Oxford: Blackwell, 170–88.

Peluso, N. 1992: *Rich forests, poor people*. Berkeley, CA: University of California Press.

Peluso, N. 2005: Seeing property in land use: local territorializations in West Kalimantan, Indonesia. *Geografisk Tidsskrift* 105: 1–15.

Peluso, N. and Watts, M., eds, 2001: *Violent environments*. Ithaca, NY: Cornell University Press.

Pelzer, K.J. 1957: Geography and the tropics. In G. Taylor, ed., *Geography in the twentieth century: a study of growth, fields, techniques, aims and trends*. London: Methuen, 311–44.

Pepper, D. 1996: *Modern environmentalism*. London: Routledge.

Pepper, S. 1942: *World hypothesis: a study in evidence*. Berkeley, CA: University of California Press.

Perera, N. 1998: *Society and space: colonialism, nationalism, and postcolonial identity in Sri Lanka*, Boulder, CO: Westview Press.

Perera, S. 2002: 'What is a camp?'; available at http://www.borderlandsejournal.adelaide.edu.au/vol1no1_2002/perera_camp.html

Perkins, C. 2002: Cartography: progress in tactile mapping. *Progress in Human Geography* 26: 521–30.

Perkins, J. 1997: *Geopolitics and the Green Revolution*. Oxford: Oxford University Press.

Perkmann, M. 2002: Euroregions: institutional entrepreneurship in the European Union. In M. Perkmann and N.L. Sum, eds, *Globalization, regionalization and cross-border regions*, London: Palgrave, 103–24.

Perkmann, M. and Sum, N.L., eds, 2002: *Globalization, regionalization and cross-border regions*. London: Palgrave.

Perrons, D. 2004: *Globalisation and social change: people and places in a divided world*. London: Routledge.

Perroux, F. 1955: Note sur la notion de pôle de croissance. *Économie Appliquée* 7: 307–20.

Pessar, P.R. 1999: Engendering migration studies: the case of new immigrants in the United States. *The American Behavioral Scientist* 42: 577–600.

Peters, M. 2006: The rise of global science and the emerging political economy of international research collaborations. *European Journal of Education* 41: 225–44.

Petersen, W. 1997: *Ethnicity counts*. New Brunswick, NJ: Transaction Books.

Peterson, M.P., ed., 2003: *Maps and the Internet*. Amsterdam: Elsevier.

Phelan, J.L. 1968: Pan-Latinism, French intervention in Mexico (1861–1867) and the genesis of the idea of Latin America. In *Conciencia y autenticidad históricas*. Mexico: UNAM, 279–98.

Phelan, P. and Lane, J., eds, 1998: *The ends of performance*. New York: New York University Press.

Philbrick, A.K. 1957: Principles of areal functional organization in regional human geography. *Economic Geography* 33: 299–336.

Phillips, D.R., Vincent, J.A. and Blacksell, S. 1988: Spatial concentration of residential homes for the elderly: planning responses and dilemmas. *Transactions of the Institute of British Geographers* 12: 73–83.

Phillips, J. 1999: Methodology, scale and the field of dreams. *Annals of the Association of American Geographers* 89: 754–60.

Phillips, J. 2004: Laws, contingencies, irreversible divergence and physical geography. *Professional Geographer* 56: 37–43.

Phillips, M. and Mighall, T. 2000: *Society and nature through exploitation*. London: Prentice Hall.

Phillips, R. 1997: *Mapping men and empire: a geography of adventure*. London: Routledge.

Philo, C. 1992: Neglected rural geographies: a review. *Journal of Rural Studies* 8: 193–207.

Philo, C. 1996: Staying in? Invited comments on 'Coming out: exposing social theory in medical geography'. *Health and Place* 2: 35–40.

Philo, C. 2000a: More words, more worlds: reflections on the 'cultural turn' and human geography. In I. Cook, D. Crouch, S. Naylor and J. Ryan, eds, *Cultural turns/geographical turns*. London: Prentice Hall, 26–53.

Philo, C. 2000b: *The birth of the clinic*: an unknown work of medical geography. *Area* 32: 11–19.

Philo, C., ed., 2000c: Theme issue on 'Post-asylum geographies'. *Health and Place* 6: 135–259.

Philo, C. 2004: *A geographical history of institutional provision for the insane from medieval times to the 1860s in England and Wales: the space reserved for insanity*. Lampeter, Wales and New York: The Edwin Mellen Press.

Philo, C. and Parr, H. 2003: Introducing psychoanalytic geographies. *Social and Cultural Geography* 4: 283–93.

918

Philo, C. and Söderström, O. 2004: Social geography: looking for society in its spaces. In G. Benko and U. Strohmayer, eds, *Human geography: a history for the 21st century*. London: Arnold, 105–38.

Philo, C. and Wilbert, C., eds, 2000: *Animal spaces, beastly places: new geographies of human–animal relations*. London: Routledge.

Philpott, T.L. 1991 [1978]: *The slum and the ghetto: immigrants, blacks and reformers in Chicago, 1880–1930*. Belmont, CA: Wadsworth.

Picard, M. 1996: *Bali: cultural tourism and touristic culture*. Singapore: Archipelago Press.

Pickering, A. 1984: *Constructing quarks: a sociological history of particle physics*. Chicago: The University of Chicago Press.

Pickering, K. and Owen, L. 1994: *An introduction to global environmental issues*. London: Routledge.

Pickles, J. 1985: *Phenomenology, science and geography: spatiality and the human sciences*. Cambridge, UK: Cambridge University Press.

Pickles, J. 1992: Texts, hermeneutics and propaganda maps. In T.J. Barnes and J.S. Duncan, eds, *Writing worlds: discourse, texts, and metaphor in the representation of landscape*. London: Routledge: 193–230.

Pickles, J., ed., 1995a: *Ground truth: the social implications of Geographic Information Systems*, New York: Guilford Press.

Pickles, J. 1995b: Representations in an electronic age: geography, GIS, and democracy. In J. Pickles, ed., *Ground truth*. New York: Guilford Press.

Pickles, J. 2004: *A history of spaces: cartographic reason, mapping, and the geo-coded world*. London: Routledge.

Pickles, J. 2007: *State and society in post-socialist economies*. London: Palgrave Macmillan.

Pickles, J. and Smith, A., eds, 1998: *Theorising transition: the political economy of post-communist transformations*. London: Routledge.

Pickvance, C. 2003: From urban social movements to urban movements: a review and introduction to a symposium on urban movements. *International Journal of Urban and Regional Research* 27: 102–9.

Pierson, C. 1991: *Beyond the welfare state? The new political economy of welfare*. Cambridge, UK: Polity Press.

Pieterse, J.N. 2004: *Globalization or empire?* New York: Routledge.

Pile, S. 1994: Masculinism, the use of dualistic epistemologies and third spaces. *Antipode* 26: 255–77.

Pile, S. 1996: *The body and the city: psychoanalysis, space and subjectivity*. London: Routledge.

Pile, S. 1998: Freud, dreams and imaginative geographies. In A. Elliott, ed, *Freud 2000*. Cambridge UK: Polity Press, 204–34.

Pile, S. 2005: *Real cities: Modernity, space, and the phantasmagorias of city life*. London: Sage.

Pile, S. and Keith, M., eds, 1997: *Geographies of resistance*. London: Routledge.

Pile, S. and Thrift, N., eds, 1995: *Mapping the subject: geographies of cultural transformation*. London: Routledge.

Pinch, S. 1989: Collective consumption. In J. Wolch and M. Dear, eds, *The power of geography: how territory shapes social life*. Boston: Unwin Hyman, 41–60.

Pinch, S. 1997: *Worlds of welfare: understanding the changing geographies of social welfare provision*. London: Routledge.

Pincus, F.L. and Ehrlich, H.J., eds, 1994: *Race and ethnic conflict*. Boulder, CO: Westview Press.

Pinder, D. 2005a: Arts of urban exploration. *Cultural Geographies* 12(4): 383–411.

Pinder, D., ed. 2005b: Theme issue: 'Arts of urban exploration'. *Cultural Geographies* 12(4): 383–526.

Pinder, D. 2005c: *Visions of the city: utopianism, power and politics in twentieth-century urbanism*. Edinburgh: Edinburgh University Press.

Pine, B.J. and Gilmore, J.H. 1998: Welcome to the experience economy. *Harvard Business Review* 76(4): 97–110.

Pinney, C., ed., 2003: *Photography's other histories*. Durham, NC: Duke University Press.

Pinnick, K. 2005: The greater Altai initiative: cross-border cooperation on Russia's southern periphery. *Regional and Federal Studies* 15: 379–99.

Pinter, H. 2005: *Art, truth and politics*. Nobel Lecture; available at http://nobelprize.org

Piore, M. and Sabel, C. 1984: *The second industrial divide: possibilities for prosperity*. New York: Basic Books.

Pirenne, H. 1925: *Medieval cities: their origins and the revival of trade*, trans. F.D. Halsey. Princeton, NJ: Princeton University Press.

Pirenne, H. 2001 [1935]: *Mohammed and Charlemagne: the birth of the Occident, the fall of Antiquity and the rise of the Germanic Middle Ages*. New York: Dover.

Pitman, A.J. 2005: On the role of geography in Earth system science. *Geoforum* 36, 137–48 (see also subsequent discussions).

Plane, D.A. 1992: Age composition change and the geographical dynamics of interregional migration in the US. *Annals of the Association of American Geographers* 74: 244–56.

Plane, D.A. and Rogerson, P.A. 1994: *The geographical analysis of population: with applications to planning and business*. New York: Wiley.

Pletsch, C. 1981: The three worlds, or the division of social scientific labor, circa 1950–1975. *Comparative Studies in Society and History* 23: 565–90.

Ploszajska, T. 1994: Moral landscapes and manipulated spaces: gender, class and space in Victorian reformatory schools. *Journal of Historical Geography* 20: 413–29.

Pluciennik, M. and Drew, Q. 2000: 'Only connect': global and local networks, contexts and fieldwork, *Ecumene* 7(1): 67–104.

Plummer, P.S. and Sheppard, E.S. 2006: Geography matters: agency, structures and dynamics at the intersection of geography and economics. *Journal of Economic Geography* 6: 619–37.

Plumwood, V. 1993: *Feminism and the mastery of nature.* London: Routledge.

Pocock, D., ed., 1981: *Humanistic geography and literature: essays on the experience of place.* London: Croom Helm.

Pocock, D. 1982: Valued landscape in memory: the view from Prebends' Bridge. *Transactions of the Institute of British Geographers,* NS 7(3): 354–64.

Podmore, J. 2001: Lesbians in the crowd: gender, sexuality and visibility along Montreal's Boul. St-Laurent. *Gender, Place and Culture: a Journal of Feminist Geography* 8: 333–55.

Poetivin, G. 2002: *The voice and the will: subaltern agency: forms and motives.* New Delhi: Manohar and Centre de Sciences Humaines.

Polanyi, K. 1972: Forms of integration and supporting structure. In H.W. Pearson, ed., *The livelihood of man: studies in social discontinuity.* New York: Academic Press.

Polanyi, K. 2001 [1944]: *The great transformation: the political and economic origins of our time.* Boston: Beacon Press.

Pollock, G. 1988: Modernity and the spaces of femininity. In Pollock, *Vision and difference: femininity, feminism and histories of art.* London: Routledge, 50–90.

Pollock, G. 2007: Holistic trajectories: a study of combined employment, housing and family careers by using multiple-sequence analysis. *Journal of the Royal Statistical Society Series A* 170(1): 167–83.

Pomeranz, K. 2001: *The great divergence: China, Europe and the making of the modern world economy.* Princeton, NJ: Princeton University Press.

Pomper, P. 2005: The history and theory of empires. *History and Theory* 44: 1–27.

Pons, F. 2007: *History of the Caribbean: plantations, trade and war in the Atlantic world.* Princeton, NJ: Markus Wiener.

Ponsard, C. 1983: *History of spatial economic theory,* trans. B.H. Stevens, M. Chevallier and J.P. Pujol. Berlin: Springer-Verlag.

Poole, K.T. 2005: *Spatial models of parliamentary voting.* Cambridge, UK: Cambridge University Press.

Pooler, J.A. 1977: The origins of the spatial tradition in geography: an interpretation. *Ontario Geography* 11: 56–83.

Poon, J.P.H. 2007: Instrumentation rigor and practice. *Environment and Planning A* 39(5): 1017–19.

Poos, L. 1991: *A rural society after the Black Death: late medieval Essex.* Cambridge, UK: Cambridge University Press.

Poovey, M. 1998: *A history of the modern fact: problems of knowledge in the sciences of wealth and society.* Chicago: The University of Chicago Press.

Popke, J. 2003: Poststructuralist ethics: subjectivity, responsibility and the space of community. *Progress in Human Geography* 27: 298–316.

Popke, J. 2007: Geography and ethics: spaces of cosmopolitan responsibility. *Progress in Human Geography* 31: 509–18.

Popper, K.R. 1959: *The logic of scientific inquiry.* New York: Basic Books.

Popper, K. 1960 [1945]: *The poverty of historicism.* London: Hutchinson / New York: Harper & Row.

Popper, K. 1970: Normal science and its dangers. In I. Lakatos and A. Musgrave, eds, *Criticism and the growth of knowledge.* Cambridge, UK: Cambridge University Press, 51–8.

Popper, K.R. 1945: *The open society and its enemies,* 2 vols. London: Routledge.

Popper, K.R. 1963: *Conjectures and refutations: the growth of scientific knowledge.* London: Routledge & Kegan Paul.

Porteous, J.D. 1988: Topicide: the annihilation of place. In J. Eyles and D.M. Smith, eds, *Qualitative methods in human geography.* Cambridge, UK: Polity Press, 75–93.

Porteous, J.D. and Smith, S. 2001: *Domicide: the global destruction of home.* Montreal: McGill-Queen's University Press.

Porter, M.E. 1998a: Clusters and the new economics of competitiveness. *Harvard Business Review,* December: 77–90.

Porter, M.E. 1998b: *Competitive advantage: creating and sustaining superior performance.* London: The Free Press.

Porter, M.E. 1998c: *On competition.* Harvard, MA: Harvard Business School Press.

Porter, M.E. 2000: Locations, clusters and company strategies. In G.L. Clark, M.P. Feldman and M.S. Gertler, eds, *The Oxford handbook of economic geography.* Oxford: Oxford University Press, ch. 13.

Porter, P. and Lukermann, F. 1976: The geography of utopia. In D. Lowenthal and M. Bowden, eds, *Geographies of the mind: essays in historical geosophy in honor of John Kirtland Wright.* New York: Oxford University Press, 197–223.

Porter, P.W. and Sheppard, E.S. 1998: *A world of difference: society, nature, development.* New York: Guilford Press.

Porter, R. and Teich, M., eds, 1981: *The Enlightenment in national context.* Cambridge, UK: Cambridge University Press.

Portes, A. 1998: Social capital: its origins and applications in modern sociology. *Annual Review of Sociology* 24: 1–24.

Portes, A. 2003: Ethnicities: children of migrants in America. *Development* 46: 42–52.

Portugali, J. 2000: *Self-organisation and the city.* Berlin: Springer-Verlag.

Possehl, G. 1990: Revolution in the urban revolution: the emergence of Indus urbanization. *Annual Review of Anthropology* 19: 261–82.

Postan, M.M. 1966: Medieval agrarian society in its prime: England. In M.M. Postan, ed., *The Cambridge economic history of Europe: the agrarian life of the middle ages.* Cambridge, UK: Cambridge University Press, 549–632.

Postan, M.M. 1972: *The medieval economy and society: an economic history of Britain 1100–1500.* London: Weidenfeld and Nicolson.

Postan, M.M. and Titow, J. 1958–9: Heriots and prices on Winchester manors. *Economic History Review* 11: 392–417.

Postone, M. 1993: *Time, labor, and social domination: a reinterpretation of Marx's critical theory.* Cambridge, UK: Cambridge University Press.

Poundstone, W. 1992: *Prisoner's dilemma.* New York: Doubleday.

Powell, J.C. 2007: 'The rigours of an Arctic experiment': the precarious authority of field practices in the Canadian High Arctic, 1958–1970. *Environment and Planning A* 39: 1794–811.

Powell, J.M. 1988: *An historical geography of modern Australia: the restive fringe.* Cambridge, UK: Cambridge University Press.

Powell, J.M. 1996: Historical geography and environmental history: an Australian interface. *Journal of Historical Geography* 22: 253–73.

Powell, R.C. 2002: The Sirens' voices? Field practices and dialogue in geography. *Area* 34: 261–72.

Powell, W.W. 1990: Neither market nor hierarchy: network forms of organization. In B. Straw and L. Cummings, eds, *Research in organizational behavior.* Greenwich, CT: JAI Press, 295–336.

Power, D.A. and Xie, Y. 2000: *Statistical methods for categorical data analysis.* San Diego: Academic Press.

Power, J.P. and Campbell, B.M.S. 1992: Cluster analysis and the classification of medieval demesne-farming systems. *Transactions of the Institute of British Geographers,* NS 17: 227–45.

Power, M. 2003: *Rethinking development geographies.* London: Routledge.

Power, M. 2007: Video wargames and post-9/11 cyber deterrence. *Security Dialogue* 38: 271–88.

Power, M. and Sidaway, J. 2005: Deconstructing twinned towers: Lisbon's Expo '98 and the occluded geographies of discovery. *Social and Cultural Geography* 6(6): 865–83.

Prasad, M. 2006: *The politics of free markets.* Chicago: The University of Chicago Press.

Pratt, G. 1992: *Imperial eyes: travel writing and transculturation.* London: Routledge.

Pratt, G. 1997: Geographic metaphors in feminist theory. In S.H. Aiken et al., eds, *Making worlds: gender, metaphor, materiality.* Tucson: University of Arizona Press, 13–30.

Pratt, G. 1999: From registered nurse to registered nanny: discursive geographies of Filipina domestic workers in Vancouver, B.C. *Economic Geography* 75: 215–36.

Pratt, G. 2002: Studying immigrants in focus groups. In P. Moss, ed., *Feminist geography in practice.* Oxford: Blackwell, 214–29.

Pratt, G. 2004: *Working feminism.* Edinburgh: Edinburgh University Press/Philadelphia, PA: Temple University Press.

Pratt, G. 2005: Abandoned women and spaces of the exception. *Antipode* 37: 1052–78.

Pratt, G. and Johnson, C. 2007: Turning theatre into law, and other spaces of politics *Cultural Geographies* 14: 92–113.

Pratt, G. and Kirby, E. 2003: Performing nursing: the B.C. Nurses' Union theatre project. *ACME: an international E-journal for critical geographies* 2: 14–32.

Pratt, G. and Yeoh, B. 2003: Transnational (counter) topographies. *Gender, Place and Culture* 10(2): 159–66.

Pratt, M. and Brown, J. 2000: *Borderlands under stress.* Boston: Kluwer Law International.

Pratt, M.B. 1984: Identity: skin, blood, heart. In E. Burkin, M.B. Pratt and B. Smith, eds, *Yours in struggle: three feminist perspectives on anti-semitism and racism.* New York: Long Haul Press, 9–64.

Pratt, M.-L. 1992: *Imperial eyes: travel writing and transculturation.* London: Routledge.

Pred, A.R. 1967: *Behavior and location: foundations for a geographic and dynamic location theory,* part 1. Lund studies in geography, series B, no. 27. Lund: C.W.K. Gleerup.

Pred, A.R. 1969: *Behavior and location: foundations for a geographic and dynamic location theory,* part 2. Lund studies in geography, series B, no. 28. Lund: C.W.K. Gleerup.

Pred, A.R. 1973: *Urban growth and the circulation of information: the United States' system of cities, 1790–1840.* Cambridge, MA: Harvard University Press.

Pred, A.R. 1977: *City-systems in advanced economies.* New York: Halstead Press.

Pred, A.R. 1984: Place as historically contingent process: structuration and the time-geography of becoming places. *Annals of the Association of American Geographers* 74(2): 279–97.

Pred, A.R. 1986: *Place, practice and structure: social and spatial transformation in southern Sweden 1750–1850.* Cambridge, UK: Polity Press.

Pred, A.R. 1990: *Lost words and lost worlds: modernity and the language of everyday life in late nineteenth-century Stockholm.* Cambridge, UK: Cambridge University Press.

Pred, A.R. 1995: *Recognizing European modernities: a montage of the present.* London: Routledge.

Pred, A.R. 1997: Re-presenting the extended present moment of danger: a meditation on hypermodernity, identity and the montage form. In G. Benko and U. Strohmayer, eds, *Social theory: interpreting modernity and postmodernity.* Oxford: Blackwell, 117–40.

Pred, A.R. 2000: *Even in Sweden: racisms, racialized spaces and the popular geographical imagination.* Berkeley, CA: University of California Press.

Pred, A.R. 2004: *The past is not dead: facts, fictions and enduring racial stereotypes.* Minneapolis: University of Minnesota Press.

Pred, A.R. and Watts, M., eds, 1992: *Reworking modernity: capitalism and symbolic discontent.* New Brunswick, NJ: Rutgers University Press.

Preobrazhensky, E. 1965: *The new economics.* London: Oxford University Press.

Preston, P. 1996: *Development theory.* Oxford: Blackwell.

Preston, V. and McLafferty, S. 1999: Spatial mismatch research in the 1990s: progress and potential. *Papers in Regional Science* 78: 387–402.

Price, M. and Lewis, M. 1993: The reinvention of cultural geography. *Annals of the Association of American Geography* 83: 1–17.

Price, P. 2004: *Dry place: landscapes of belonging and exclusion.* Minneapolis: University of Minnesota Press.

Prince, H.C. 1962: The geographical imagination. *Landscape* 11: 22–5.

Probyn, E. 2003: The spatial imperative of subjectivity. In K. Anderson, M. Domosh, S. Pile and N. Thrift, eds, *Handbook of cultural geography.* London: Sage, 290–9.

Proctor, J. 2006: Theorizing and studying religion. *Annals of the Association of American Geographers* 96: 165–8.

Proctor, J. and Smith, D.M., eds, 1999: *Geography and ethics: journeys in a moral terrain.* London: Routledge.

Professional Geographer, The 1994: Women in the field: critical feminist methodologies and theoretical perspectives (Special section), 46(1): 54–102.

Professional Geographer, The 1995: Special issue: Should Women Count?, 47(4).

Prosser, R. 2000: *Leisure, recreation and tourism.* London: Collins.

Proudfoot, L. and Roche, M., eds, 2005: *(Dis)placing empire: renegotiating British colonial geographies.* Aldershot: Ashgate.

Prudham, W.S. 2003: Taming trees: capital, science, and nature in Pacific Slope tree improvement. *Annals of the Association of American Geographers* 93(3): 636–56.

Prudham, W.S. 2005: *Knock on wood: nature as commodity in Douglas-fir country.* New York: Routledge.

Pruijt, H. 2003: Is the institutionalization of urban movements inevitable? A comparison of the opportunities of sustained squatting in New York City and Amsterdam. *International Journal of Urban and Regional Research* 27: 133–57.

Prus, R.C. 1995: *Symbolic interaction and ethnographic research: intersubjectivity and the study of human lived experience.* Albany, NY: State University of New York Press.

Pryke, M. 2002: The white noise of capitalism: audio and visual montage and sensing economic change. *Cultural Geographies* 9(4): 472–7.

Pryke, M., Rose, G. and Whatmore, S., eds, 2003: *Using social theory: thinking through research.* London: Sage.

Przeworski, A. 1995: *Sustainable democracy.* Cambridge, UK: Cambridge University Press.

Psillos, S. 1999: *Scientific realism: how science tracks truth.* London: Routledge.

Puar, J.K. 2002: Circuits of queer mobility: tourism, travel and globalization *GLQ: a Journal of Lesbian and Gay Studies* 8(1–2): 101–37.

Puar, J.K. and Rai, A. 2002: Monster, terrorist, fag: the war on terrorism and the production of docile patriots *Social Text* 72: 117–48.

Public Citizen 2007: *Global Trade Watch*; available at http://www.citizen.org/trade

Pudup, M.-B. 1988: Arguments within regional geography. *Progress in Human Geography* 12: 369–90.

Pulido, L. 1996: A critical review of the methodology of environmental racism research. *Antipode* 28(2): 142–59.

Pulido, L. 1996: *Environmentalism and economic justice.* Tucson: University of Arizona Press.

Pulido, L. 2003: The interior life of politics. *Ethics, Place and Environment* 6(1): 46–52.

Pulido, L. and Peña, D. 1998: Environmentalism and positionality: the early pesticide campaign of the United Farm Workers' Organizing Committee, 1965–1971. *Race, Gender & Class* 6(1): 33–50.

Purcell, M. 2001: Metropolitan political reorganization as a politics of urban growth: the case of San Fernando Valley secession. *Political Geography* 20: 613–33.

Purcell, M. 2001: Neighborhood activism among homeowners as a politics of space. *Professional Geographer* 53(2): 178–94.

Purcell, M. 2002: Excavating Lefebvre: the right to the city and its urban politics of the inhabitant. *GeoJournal* 58: 99–108.

Putnam, R. 2001: *Bowling alone.* New York: Simon and Schuster.

Pyle, G.F. 1969: Diffusion of cholera in the United States. *Geographical Analysis* 1: 59–75.

Pyle, G.F. 1979: Studies of disease diffusion. In Pyle, *Applied medical geography.* New York: Wiley, 123–63.

Quamen, D. 1996: *The song of the dodo: island biogeography in an age of extinctions.* London: Hutchinson.

Rabinow, P. and Rose, N. 2006: Biopower today. *Biosocieties* 1: 195–217.

Radcliffe, S.A. 1997: Different heroes: genealogies of postcolonial geographies. *Environment and Planning D: Society and Space* 29: 1331–3.

Radcliffe, S.A. 1998: Frontier and popular nationhood: geographies of identity in the 1995 Ecuador–Peru border dispute. *Political Geography* 17: 273–93.

Radford, J.P. 1979: Testing the model of the pre-industrial city. *Transactions of the Institute of British Geographers,* NS 5: 392–410.

Raffles, H. 2002: Intimate knowledge. *International Social Science Journal* 173: 325–35.

Rafiq, N. 1991: Female child mortality in Bangladesh: the discrimination against women at the root. *Oriental Geographer* 35: 21–31.

Raimondo, M. 2005: AIDS capital of the world: representing race, sex, and space in Belle Glade, Florida. *Gender, Place, and Culture* 12: 53–70.

Rainnie, A., Smith, A. and Swain, A., eds, 2002: *Work, employment and transition: restructuring livelihoods in post-communism.* London: Routledge.

Ram, K. 1998: *Na sharirram nadhi,* my body is mine: the urban women's health movement in India and its negotiation of modernity. *Women's Studies International Forum* 21: 617–31.

Ramaswamy, S. 1999: Catastrophic cartographies: mapping the lost continent of Lemuria. *Representations,* no. 67: 92–129.

Ramon-Garcia, M.D., Simonsen, K. and Vaiou, D. 2006: Does Anglophone hegemony permeate *Gender, Place and Culture? Gender, Place and Culture* 13: 1–5.

Raper, J. 1999: Spatial representation: the scientist's perspective. In P.A. Longley, M.F. Goodchild, D.J. Maguire and D.W. Rhind, eds, *Geographical Information Systems: principles, techniques, management and applications.* New York: Wiley, 71–80.

Raper, J. 2000: *Multidimensional Geographic Information Science.* London: Taylor & Francis.

Raper, J. and Livingstone, D. 2001: Let's get real: spatio-temporal identity and geographic entities. *Transactions of the Institute of British Geographers* 26: 237–42.

Rapoport, A. and Chammah, M. 1965: *Prisoner's dilemma.* Ann Arbor: University of Michigan Press.

Rappaport, R.A. 1968: *Pigs for the ancestors: ritual in the ecology of a New Guinea people.* New Haven, CT: Yale University Press.

Rappaport, R.A. 1979: *Ecology, meaning and religion.* Richmond: North Atlantic Books.

Rasch, W. 2003: Human rights as geopolitics: Carl Schmitt and the legal form of American supremacy. *Cultural Critique* 54: 120–47.

Rasmussen, C. and Brown, M. 2002: Between political theory and geography: radical democratic citizenship. In B. Turner and E. Isin, eds, *Handbook of citizenship studies.* London: Sage, 294–327.

Rattansi, A. 1997: Postcolonialism and its discontents. *Economy and Society* 26, 480–500.

Ratzel, F. 1897: *Politische Geographie.* Munich: Oldenburg.

Raudenbush, S.W. 2003: The quantitative assessment of neighborhood social environment. In I. Kawachi and L. Berkman, eds, *Neighborhoods and health.* Oxford: Oxford University Press, 112–31.

Raudenbush, S.W. and Sampson, R.J. 1999: Ecometrics: toward a science of assessing ecological settings, with application to the systematic social observations of neighborhoods. *Sociological Methodology* 29: 1–41.

Raudenbush, S.W. and Xiaofeng, L. 2000: Statistical power and optimal design for multisite randomized trials. *Psychological Methods* 5: 199–213.

Ravallion, M. 1995: *Poverty comparisons.* London: Harwood.

Rawls, J. 1971: *A theory of justice.* Cambridge, MA: Harvard University Press.

Ray, L. and Sayer, A., eds, 1997: *Culture and economy after the cultural turn.* London: Sage.

Razack, S.H., ed., 2002: *Race, space, and the law: unmapping a white settler colony.* Toronto: Between the Lines.

Razi, Z. and Smith, R.M., eds, 1996a: *Medieval society and the manorial court.* Oxford: The Clarendon Press.

Razi, Z. and Smith, R.M. 1996b: The origins of the English manorial court rolls as a written record: a puzzle. In Z. Razi and R.M. Smith, eds, *Medieval society and the manor court.* Oxford: The Clarendon Press, 36–61.

Read, J. 2003: *The micro-politics of Capital: Marx and the prehistory of the present.* Albany, NY: State University of New York Press.

Redclift, M.R. 1987: *Sustainable development: exploring the contradictions.* London: Methuen.

Rees, J. 1979: Technological change and regional shifts in American manufacturing. *Professional Geographer* 31: 45–54.

Rees, J. 1991: *Natural resources: allocation, economics and policy.* London: Routledge.

Rees, J. and Stafford, H.A. 1986: Theories of regional growth and industrial location: their relevance to understanding high technological complexes. In J. Rees, ed., *Technology, regions and policy.* Totowa, NJ: Rowman & Littlefield, 23–50.

Rees, P.H. and Wilson, A.G. 1977: *Spatial population analysis*. London: Edward Arnold.

Rees, P.H., Martin, D. and Williamson, P., eds, 2002: *The census data system*. Chichester: Wiley.

Regional Studies Association 2007: Special issue: whither regional studies? *Regional Studies* 41(9): 1143–269.

Reid, H.G. and Taylor, B. 2000: Embodying ecological citizenship: rethinking the politics of grassroots globalization in the United States. *Alternatives* 25: 439–66.

Reid, J. 2006: *The biopolitics of the war on terror: life struggles, liberal modernity and the defence of logistical societies*. Manchester: Manchester University Press.

Reisch, G.A. 2005: *How the Cold War transformed philosophy of science: to the icy slopes of logic*. Cambridge, UK: Cambridge University Press.

Relph, E. 1970: An inquiry into the relations between phenomenology and geography. *Canadian Geographer* 14: 193–201.

Relph, E. 1976: *Place and placelessness*. London: Pion.

Relph, E. 1981: *Rational landscapes and humanistic places*. London: Croom Helm.

Relph, E. 1987: *The modern urban landscape*. Baltimore, MD: The Johns Hopkins University Press.

Renan, E. 1990 [1882]: What is a nation? In H. Bhabha, ed., *Nation and narration*, trans. M. Thom. London: Routledge, 8–22.

Rengert, G. 1997: *The geography of illegal drugs*. Boulder, CO: Westview Press.

Resnick, S.A. and Wolff, R.D. 1987: *Knowledge and class: a Marxian critique of political economy*. Chicago: The University of Chicago Press.

RETORT 2005: *Afflicted powers: capital and spectacle in a new age of war*. London: Verso.

Rex, J. 1988: *The ghetto and the underclass: essays on race and social policy*. Aldershot: Avebury.

Rex, J. and Moore, R. 1967: *Race, community and conflict*. Oxford: Oxford University Press.

Reynolds, S. 1994: *Fiefs and vassals: the medieval evidence reinterpreted*. Oxford: The Clarendon Press.

Rhind, D. 1998: The incubation of GIS in Europe. In T. Foresman, ed., *The history of Geographic Information Systems: perspectives from the pioneers*. Upper Saddle River, NJ: Prentice Hall, 293–306.

Rhind, D. 2000: Current shortcomings of global mapping and the creation of a new geographical framework for the world. *Geographical Journal* 166: 295–305.

Rhoads, B.L. 2006: The dynamic basis of geomorphology re-envisioned. *Annals of the Association of American Geographers* 96: 14–30.

Rhoads, B.L. and Thorne, C.E. 1996: *The scientific nature of geomorphology*. Chichester: Wiley.

Rhodes, L. 2004: *Total confinement: madness and reason in the maximum security prison*. Berkeley, CA: University of California Press.

Rhodes, R. 1997: *Understanding governance: policy networks, governance, reflexivity and accountability*. Buckingham: Open University Press.

Ricardo, D. 1817: *The principles of political economy and taxation*. Cambridge, UK: Cambridge University Press.

Ricardo, D. 1992: *Principles of political economy and taxation*. London: Dent/New York: Dutton.

Rich, A. 1976: *Of woman born: motherhood as experience and institution*. New York: W.W. Norton.

Rich, F. 2006: *The greatest story ever told: the decline and fall of truth from 9/11 to Katrina*. New York: Penguin.

Richards, I.A. 1936: *The philosophy of rhetoric*. Oxford: Oxford University Press.

Richards, K., Brookes, S., Clifford, N., Harris, T. and Lane, S. 1998: Theory, measurement and testing in real geomorphology and physical geography. In Stoddart, D., ed., *Process and form in geomorphology*. London: Routledge, 265–92.

Richards, L. 2005: *Handling qualitative data: a practical guide*. London: Sage.

Richards, P. 1974: Kant's geography and mental maps. *Transactions of the Institute of British Geographers* 61: 1–16.

Richards, P. 1985: *Indigenous agricultural revolution*. London: Hutchinson.

Richardson, R., Belt, V. and Marshall, N. 2000: Taking calls to Newcastle: the regional implications of the growth in call centres. *Regional Studies* 34(4): 357–69.

Richmond, A.H. 1994: *Global apartheid: refugees, racism, and the new world order*. Toronto: University of Toronto Press.

Ridley, F.F. and Wilson, D. 1995: *The quango debate*. Oxford: Oxford University Press.

Riedy, C. and Diesendorf, M. 2003: Financial subsidies to the Australian fossil fuel industry. *Energy Policy* 31: 125–37.

Rigg, B. 1989: *The green revolution*. Cambridge, UK: Cambridge University Press.

Ripley, B.D. 2005: How computing has changed statistics. In A.C. Davidson, Y. Dodge and N. Wermuth, eds, *Celebrating statistics: papers in honour of Sir David Cox on his 80th birthday*. Oxford: Oxford University Press.

Rittberger, V. and Mayer, P., eds, 1993: *Regime theory and international relations*. Oxford: The Clarendon Press.

Ritvo, H. 2005: Discipline and indiscipline. *Environmental History* 10: 75–6.

Robbin, A. 2000: Classifying racial and ethnic data in the United States: the politics of negotiation and accommodation. *Journal of Government Information* 27: 129–56.

Robbins, B. 1993: *Secular vocations: intellectuals, professionalism, culture*. London: Verso.

Robbins, B. 1998: Comparative cosmopolitanisms. In P. Cheah and B. Robbins, eds,

Cosmopolitics: thinking and feeling beyond the nation. Minneapolis: University of Minnesota Press, 246–64.

Robbins, L. 1932: *Essay on the nature and significance of economic science.* London: Macmillan.

Robbins, P. 2001: Fixed categories in a portable landscape: the causes and consequences of land-cover categorization. *Environment and Planning A* 33(1): 161–79.

Robbins, P. 2004: *Political ecology: a critical introduction.* Oxford: Blackwell.

Robbins, P. and Fraser, A. 2003: A forest of contradictions: producing the landscapes of the Scottish Highlands. *Antipode* 35(1): 95–118.

Roberts, B. 1994: Informal economy and family strategies. *International Journal of Urban and Regional Research* 18: 6–23.

Roberts, J.A. 1991: *The Shakespearean wild: geography, genus and gender.* Lincoln: University of Nebraska Press.

Roberts, R. 1990: *The classic slum: Salford life in the first quarter of the century.* London: Penguin.

Roberts, S. 2004: Global strategic vision, managing the world. In B. Maurer and R.W. Perry, eds, *Globalization under construction: governmentality law and identity.* Minneapolis: University of Minnesota Press.

Roberts, S., Secor, A. and Sparke, M. 2003: Neoliberal geopolitics. *Antipode* 35(3): 886–897.

Robertson, R. 2006: Civilization. *Theory, Culture & Society* 23: 421–7.

Robinson, A.H. 1952: *The look of maps: an examination of cartographic design.* Madison, WI: University of Wisconsin Press.

Robinson, A.H. and Petchenik, B.B. 1976: *The nature of maps: essays toward understanding maps and mapping.* Chicago: The University of Chicago Press.

Robinson, A.H. and Snyder, J.P. 1991: *Matching the map projection to the need.* Bethesda, MD: American Congress on Surveying the Mapping.

Robinson, A.H., Morrison, J.L., Muehrcke, P. C., Guptill, S.C. and Kimerling, A.J. 1993: *Elements of cartography,* 6th edn. Chichester: Wiley.

Robinson, G.W.S. 1959: Exclaves. *Annals of the Association of American Geographers* 49: 283–95.

Robinson, J. 1962: *Economic philosophy: an essay on the progress of economic thought.* London: Penguin.

Robinson, J. 2003a: Postcolonialising geography: tactics and pitfalls. *Singapore Journal of Tropical Geography* 24(3): 273–89.

Robinson, J. 2004: In the tracks of comparative urbanism: difference, urban modernity and the primitive. *Urban Geography* 25(8): 709–23.

Robinson, J. 2006: *Ordinary cities: between modernity and development.* London and New York: Routledge.

Robinson, V., Hockey, J. and Meah, A. 2004: What I used to do ... on my mother's settee:

spatial and emotional aspects of heterosexuality in England. *Gender, Place and Culture: a Journal of Feminist Geography* 11: 417–35.

Robinson, V.B. 2003b: A perspective on the fundamentals of fuzzy sets and their use in geographical information systems. *Transactions in GIS* 7: 3–30.

Robinson, W.S. 1950: Ecological correlations and the behavior of individuals. *American Sociological Review* 15: 351–7.

Robson, B. 1988: *Those inner cities.* Oxford: The Clarendon Press.

Robson, B. 1994: No city, no civilization. *Transactions of the Institute of British Geographers* 19: 131–41.

Roche, M. 2000: *Mega-events and modernity: Olympics and expos in the growth of global culture.* London: Routledge.

Rock, D. 2002: Racking Argentina. *New Left Review* 2/17: 55–86.

Rodenstein-Rodan, P. 1976: The theory of the big push. In G. Meier and D. Seers, eds, *Pioneers in development.* Oxford: Oxford University Press.

Rodigue, J.-P., Comtois, C. and Slack, B. 2006: *The geography of transport systems.* New York: Routledge.

Rodriguez, N. and Feagin, J.R. 1986: Urban specialization in the world system: an investigation of historical cases. *Urban Affairs Quarterly* 22(2): 187–220.

Rodriguez-Pose, A. and Gill, N. 2004: Is there a global link between regional disparities and devolution? *Environment and Planning A* 36: 2097–117.

Roemer, J. 1982: *A general theory of exploitation and class.* Cambridge, UK: Cambridge University Press.

Roemer, J. 1986a: An historical materialist alternative to welfarism. In J. Elster and A. Hylland, eds, *Foundations of social choice theory.* Cambridge, UK: Cambridge University Press.

Roemer, J., ed., 1986b: *Analytical Marxism.* Cambridge, UK: Cambridge University Press.

Rogers, A., ed., 1992: *Elderly migration and population redistribution.* London: Belhaven Press.

Rojas Mix, M. 1986: Bilbao y el hallazgo de América latina: unión continental, socialista, y libertaria ..., *Caravelle: Cahiers du monde hispanique et luso-brésilien* 46: 35–47.

Romm, J. 2002: The coincidental order of environmental justice. In K.M. Mutz, G.C. Bryner and D.S. Kenney, eds, *Justice and natural resources.* Washington, DC: Island Press.

Rorty, R. 1979: *Philosophy and the mirror of nature.* Princeton, NJ: Princeton University Press.

Rorty, R. 1982: Pragmatism, relativism, and irrationalism. In Rorty, *The consequences of pragmatism.* Minneapolis: University of Minnesota Press, 160–75.

925

Rorty, R., 1989: *Contingency, irony, and solidarity.* Cambridge, UK: Cambridge University Press.

Rosaldo, R. 1989: *Culture and truth: the remaking of social analysis.* Boston: Beacon Press.

Rose, C. 1994: *Property and persuasion.* Boulder, CO: Westview Press.

Rose, C.M. 1999a: Expanding the choices for the global commons: comparing newfangled tradeable allowance schemes to old-fashioned common property regimes. *Duke Environmental Law and Policy Forum* 10(1): 45–72.

Rose, G. 1993: *Feminism and geography: the limits of geographical knowledge.* Cambridge, UK: Polity Press/Minneapolis: University of Minnesota.

Rose, G. 1995: Tradition and paternity: same difference? *Transactions of the Institute of British Geographers*, NS 20: 414–6.

Rose, G. 1996: As if the mirrors bled: masculine dwelling, masculine theory and feminist masquerade. In N. Duncan, ed., *BodySpace: destabilizing geographies of gender and sexuality.* London: Routledge, 56–74.

Rose, G. 1997a: Engendering the slum: photography in East London in the 1930s. *Gender, Place and Culture* 4: 277–300.

Rose, G. 1997b: Situating knowledges: positionality, reflexivities and other tactics. *Progress in Human Geography* 21(3): 305–20.

Rose, G. 1999b: Performing space in D. Massey, J. Allen, and P. Sarre, eds, *Human geography today.* Cambridge, UK: Polity Press, 247–59.

Rose, G. 2001: *Visual methodologies: an introduction to the interpretation of visual materials.* London: Sage.

Rose, G. 2004a: Family photographs and domestic spacings: a case study. *Transactions of the Institute of British Geographers* 28: 5–18.

Rose, G. 2006: *Visual methodologies,* 2nd edn. London: Sage.

Rose, M. 2002a: Landscape and labyrinths. *Geoforum* 33: 455–67.

Rose, M. 2002b: The seductions of resistance: power, politics and a performative style of systems. *Environment and Planning D: Society and Space* 20: 383–400.

Rose, M. 2004b: Re-embracing metaphysics. *Environment and Planning A* 36: 461–9.

Rose, M. 2006a: 'Gathering dreams of presence': a project for the cultural landscape. *Environment and Planning D: Society and Space* 24: 537–54.

Rose, N. 1999c: *Powers of freedom: reframing political thought.* Cambridge, UK: Cambridge University Press.

Rose, N. 2006b: *The politics of life itself: biomedicine, power and subjectivity in the twenty-first century.* Princeton, NJ: Princeton University Press.

Rosenberg, M. 1968: *The logic of survey analysis.* New York: Basic Books.

Rosner, D. 2000: *The second generation: continuity and change in the kibbutz,* vol. 2. New York: Greenwood.

Ross, A., ed., 1996: *Science wars.* Durham, NC: Duke University Press.

Ross, M. 2001: Does oil hinder democracy? *World Politics* 53: 325–61.

Ross, R. and Trachte, K. 1990: *Global capitalism: the new leviathan.* Albany, NY: State University of New York Press.

Rosset, P. 2006: *Food is different.* London: Pluto Press.

Rossiter, D.J., Johnston, R.J. and Pattie, C.J. 1999: *The Boundary Commissions: redrawing the UK's map of parliamentary constituencies.* Manchester: Manchester University Press.

Rössler, M. 1989: Applied geography and area research in Nazi society: central place theory and planning, 1933 to 1945. *Environment and Planning D: Society and Space* 17: 419–31.

Rössler, M. 2001: Geography and area planning under National Socialism. In M. Szöllösi-Janze, ed., *Science in the Third Reich.* Oxford: Berg, 59–78.

Rostow, W.W. 1960: *The stages of economic growth: a non-communist manifesto.* Cambridge, UK: Cambridge University Press.

Rostow, W.W. 1971: *The stages of economic growth: a non-communist manifesto,* 2nd edn. Cambridge, UK: Cambridge University Press.

Rothwell, D. 1996: *The polar regions and the development of international law.* Cambridge, UK: Cambridge University Press.

Rouse, J. 1987: *Knowledge and power: towards a political philosophy of science.* Ithaca, NY: Cornell University Press.

Routledge, P. 1993: *Terrains of resistance: nonviolent social movements and the contestation of place in India.* Westport CT: Praeger.

Routledge, P. 1996a: Critical geopolitics and terrains of resistance. *Political Geography* 15(6/7): 509–52.

Routledge, P. 1996b: The third space as critical engagement. *Antipode* 28(4): 399–419.

Routledge, P. 1998: Going globile: spatiality, embodiment and mediation in the Zapatista Insurgency. In S. Dalby and G. Ó Tuathail, eds, *Rethinking geopolitics.* London: Routledge.

Routledge, P. 2002: Travelling east as Walter Kurtz: identity, performance and collaboration in Goa, India. *Environment and Planning D: Society and Space* 20: 477–98.

Routledge, P. 2003: Convergence space: process geographies of grassroots globalization networks. *Transactions of the Institute of British Geographers* 28(3): 333–49.

Routledge, P., Nativel, C. and Cumbers, A. 2006: Entangled logics and grassroots imaginaries of global justice networks. *Environmental Politics* 15(5): 839–59.

Rowe, S. and Wolch, J. 1990: Social networks in time and in space: homeless women in Skid Row, Los Angeles. *Annals of the Association of American Geographers* 80: 184–204.

Rowland, D.T. 2003: *Demographic methods and concepts*. Oxford: Oxford University Press.

Rowles, G.D. 1978: *Prisoners of space? Exploring the geographical experience of older people*. Boulder, CO: Westview Press.

Rowles, G.D. 1979: The last new home: facilitating the older person's adjustment to institutional space. In S.M. Golant, ed., *Location and environment of elderly population*. London: Wiley, 81–94.

Roy, A. 2003: *City requiem, Calcutta: gender and the politics of poverty*. Minneapolis: University of Minnesota Press.

Roy, A. 2005: Urban informality: toward an epistemology of planning. *Journal of the American Planning Association* 71: 147–58.

Royle, N., ed., 2000: *Deconstructions: a user's guide*. London: Palgrave.

Rozwadowski, H.M. 2005: *Fathoming the ocean: the discovery and exploration of the deep sea*. Cambridge, MA: Harvard University Press.

Rubin, D.B. 1976: Inference and missing data. *Biometrika* 63: 581–92.

Ruddick, S.M. 1996: *Young and homeless in Hollywood: mapping social identities*. New York: Routledge.

Ruddick, S.M. 2003: The politics of aging: globalization and the restructuring of youth and childhood. *Antipode* 35(2): 334–62.

Rudolph, C. 2005: Sovereignty and territorial borders in a global age. *International Studies Review* 7: 1–20.

Rudwick, M. 2005: *Bursting the limits of time: the reconstruction of geohistory in the age of revolution*. Chicago: The University of Chicago Press.

Ruggie, J.G. 1993: *Multilateralism matters*. New York: Columbia University Press.

Rummel, R.J. 1994: *Death by government*. New Brunswick, NJ: Transaction Books.

Rupke, N. 1999: A geography of enlightenment: the critical reception of Alexander von Humboldt's Mexico work. In D.N. Livingstone and C.W.J. Withers, eds, *Geography and enlightenment*. Chicago: The University of Chicago Press, 281–94.

Rupke, N., ed., 2000: *Medical geography in historical perspective*. London: Wellcome Trust Centre for the History of Medicine.

Rupke, N. 2005: *Alexander von Humboldt: a metabiography*. Bern: Peter Lang.

Rush, F., ed., 2004: *The Cambridge companion to critical theory*. Cambridge, UK: Cambridge University Press.

Rushton, G. 1969: Analysis of spatial behavior by revealed space preference. *Annals of the Association of American Geographers* 59: 391–400.

Ruspini, E. 2002: *An introduction to longitudinal research*. London: Routledge.

Russell, J. 2005: Rethinking post-national citizenship: the relationship between state territory and international human rights law. *Space and Polity* 9: 29–39.

Ryan, J.R. 1997: *Picturing empire: photography and the visualization of the British empire*. London: Reaktion Books (also Chicago: The University of Chicago Press, 1998).

Ryan, M. 1994: *War and peace in Ireland: Britain and the IRA in the new world order*. London: Pluto Press.

Ryan, S. 1996: *The cartographic eye: how explorers saw Australia*. Cambridge, UK: Cambridge University Press.

Ryle, G. 1971: *Collected papers*, vol. 2: *Essays 1929–1968*. London: Hutchinson.

Saad-Filho, A. and Johnston, D. 2005: *Neoliberalism: a critical reader*. London: Pluto Press.

Saarinen, T. 1966: *Perception of drought hazard on the Great Plains*. University of Chicago, Department of Geography, Research paper no. 106.

Sachs, C. 1996: *Gendered fields: rural women, agriculture and environment*. Boulder, CO: Westview Press.

Sachs, J. 2005: *The end of poverty: how we can make it happen in our lifetime*. London: Penguin.

Sachs, W., ed., 1992: *The development dictionary: a guide to knowledge as power*. London: Zed Books.

Sack, R.D. 1973: The concept of physical space in geography. *Geographical Analysis* 5: 16–34.

Sack, R.D. 1974a: Chorology and spatial analysis. *Annals of the Association of American Geographers* 64: 439–52.

Sack, R.D. 1974b: The spatial separatist theme in geography. *Economic Geography* 50: 1–19.

Sack, R.D. 1986: *Human territoriality: its theory and history*. Cambridge, UK: Cambridge University Press.

Sack, R.D. 1997: *Homo geographicus: a framework for action, awareness and moral concern*. Baltimore, MD: The Johns Hopkins University Press.

Sacks, H. 1992: *Lectures on conversation*, vols 1 and 2. Oxford: Blackwell.

Said, E.W. 1984: Travelling theory. In Said, *The world, the text and the critic*. London: Faber, 226–47.

Said, E.W. 1993: *Culture and imperialism*. London: Chatto and Windus/New York: A.A. Knopf.

Said, E.W. 2000: The clash of definitions. In Said, *Reflections on exile and other essays*. Cambridge, MA: Harvard University Press, 569–90.

Said, E.W. 2000 [1994]: Travelling theory reconsidered. In his *Reflections on exile*. Cambridge, MA: Harvard University Press, 436–52.

Said, E.W. 2003 [1978]: *Orientalism*. London: Penguin.

Salcedo, R. and Torres, A. 2004: Gated communities in Santiago: wall or frontier? *International*

Journal of Urban and Regional Research 28(1): 27–44.

Sale, K. 1991: *Dwellers in the land: the bioregional vision.* Philadelphia, PA: New Society Publishers.

Salisbury, R.D. 1907: *Physiography.* London: John Murray.

Salmon, W. 1990: *Four decades of scientific explanation.* Minneapolis: University of Minnesota Press.

Salmond, A. 1991: *Two worlds: first meetings between Maori and Europeans 1642–1772.* Auckland, New Zealand: Viking.

Saloranta, T.M. 2001: Post-normal science and the global climate change issue. *Climatic Change* 50(4): 395–404.

Salter, C.L. and Lloyd, W.J. 1977: *Landscape in literature.* Washington, DC: Association of American Geographers.

Salter, M. 2002: *Barbarians and civilization in international relations.* London: Pluto Press.

Salter, M. 2007: Governmentalities of an airport: heterotopia and confession. *International Political Sociology* 1: 49–66.

Samarasinghe, V. 2005: Female labor in sex trafficking: a darker side of globalization. In L. Nelson and J. Seager, eds, *A companion to feminist geography.* Oxford: Blackwell, 166–78.

Sambrook, R.A., Pigozzi, B.W. and Thomas, R.N. 1999: Population pressure, deforestation, and land degradation: a case study from the Dominican Republic. *The Professional Geographer* 51: 25–40.

Samers, M. 1997: The production of diaspora: Algerian emigration from colonialism to neocolonialism (1840–1970). *Antipode* 29: 32–53.

Sampson, R., Raudenbush S. and Earls, F. 1997: Neighborhoods and violent crime. *Science* 277: 918–24.

Samuel, R. 1994: *Theatres of memory,* vol. 1, London: Verso.

Samuels, M.S. 1978: Existentialism and human geography. In D. Ley and M.S. Samuels, eds, *Humanistic geography: prospects and problems.* London: Croom Helm, 22–40.

Samuels, M.S. 1981: An existential geography, in M.E. Harvey and B.P. Holly, eds, *Themes in geographic thought.* London: Croom Helm, 115–32.

Samuelson, P.A. 1947: *Foundations of economic analysis.* Cambridge, MA: Harvard University Press.

Sanchez, L. 2004: The global e-rotic subject, the ban and the prostitute-free zone: sex work and the theory of differential exclusion. *Environment and Planning D: Society and Space* 22: 861–83.

Sanchez, L.A. 1945: *¿Existe América Latina?* México: Fondo de cultura económica.

Sandercock, L. 1998: *Cosmopolis.* New York: Wiley.

Sanderson, S.K. and Dubrow, J. 2000: Fertility decline in the modern world and in the original demographic transition: testing three theories with cross-national data. *Population and Environment* 21: 511–37.

Sangtin Writers Collective and Nagar, R. 2006: *Playing with fire: feminist thought and activism through seven lives in India.* New Delhi: Zubaan/Minnesota: University of Minnesota Press.

Sanneh, L. 1990: *Translating the message: the missionary impact on culture.* Maryknoll, New York: Orbis Books.

Santana, D.B. 1996: Geographers, colonialism, and development strategies: the case of Puerto Rico. *Urban Geography* 17: 456–74.

Sapper, K. 1931: Economic geography. In E.R.A. Seligman, editor-in-chief, *Encyclopaedia of the social sciences,* vol. 5. New York: Macmillan, 626–9.

Sarat, A. and Kearns, T.R., eds, 2003: *The place of law.* Ann Arbor: University of Michigan Press.

Sardar, Z. 1999: *Orientalism.* Buckingham: Open University Press.

Sassen, S. 1996: *Losing control? Sovereignty in an age of globalization.* New York: Columbia University Press.

Sassen, S. 1996: Whose city is it? *Public Culture* 8 (2): 205–23.

Sassen, S. 1999: *Globalization and its discontents.* New York: The Free Press.

Sassen, S. 2001 [1991]: *The global city: New York, London, Tokyo,* 2nd edn. Princeton, NJ: Princeton University Press.

Sassen, S. 2006 [2000]: *Cities in a world economy,* 3rd edn. London: Sage.

Sauer, C.O. 1925: The morphology of landscape. *University of California Publications in Geography* 2(2): 19–54.

Sauer, C.O. 1941: Foreword to historical geography. *Annals of the Association of American Geographers* 31: 1–24.

Sauer, C.O. 1952: *Agricultural origins and dispersals.* New York: American Geographical Society.

Sauer, C.O. 1956: The agency of man on the Earth. In W.L. Thomas, ed., *Man's role in changing the face of the Earth.* Chicago: The University of Chicago Press, 49–69.

Sauer, C.O. 1963a [1925]: *Land and life: a selection from the writings of Carl Ortwin Sauer,* ed. J.B. Leighly. Berkeley, CA: University of California Press.

Sauer, C.O. 1963b [1925]: The morphology of landscape. Reprinted in J. Leighly, ed., *Land and life: selections from the writings of Carl Ortwin Sauer.* Berkeley, CA: University of California Press, 315–50.

Sauer, C.O. 1969: *Seeds, spades, hearths and herds: the domestication of animals and foodstuffs.* Cambridge, MA: The MIT Press.

Saunders, K. 2002: Introduction: towards a deconstructive post-development criticism. In

K. Saunders, ed., *Feminist post-development thought: rethinking modernity, postcolonialism, representation*. London: Zed Books.

Saunders, P. 1979: *Urban politics: a sociological approach*. London: Hutchinson.

Saunders, P. 1986: *Social theory and the urban question*, 2nd edn. London: Hutchinson/New York: Holmes and Meier.

Saunders, R. 1999: The space community policing makes and the body that makes it. *The Professional Geographer* 51: 135–46.

Saunders, R.H. 2001: Home and away: bridging fieldwork and everyday life. *Geographical Review* 91(1–2): 88–94.

Saussure, F. de 1966: *Course in general linguistics*, edited by C. Bally and A. Sechehaye in collaboration with A. Riedlinger; translated, with an introduction and notes, by W. Baskin. New York: McGraw-Hill (an English translation of the reissued Saussure, F. de 1966: *Cours de linguistique générale*. Paris: Bibliothèque scientifique).

Savage, L. and Wills, J., eds, 2004: New geographies of trade unionism. *Geoforum* 35(1): 5–68.

Savage, V.R., Kong, L. and Yeoh, B.S.A. 1993: The human geography of Southeast Asia: an analysis of post-war developments. *Singapore Journal of Tropical Geography* 14(2): 229–51.

Saward, M. 2003: Enacting democracy. *Political Studies* 51: 161–79.

Saxenian, A. 1994: *Regional advantage: culture and competition in Silicon Valley and Route 128*. Cambridge, MA: Harvard University Press.

Sayer, A. 1979: Epistemology and conceptions of people and nature in geography. *Geoforum* 10: 19–43.

Sayer, A. 1982: Explanation in economic geography: abstraction versus generalization. *Progress in Human Geography* 6: 68–88.

Sayer, A. 1984: *Method in social science: a realist approach*. London: Hutchinson.

Sayer, A. 1989: The 'new' regional geography and problems of narrative. *Environment and Planning D: Society and Space* 7: 253–76.

Sayer, A. 1991: Behind the locality debate: deconstructing geography's dualisms. *Environment and Planning A* 23: 283–308.

Sayer, A. 1992 [1984]: *Method in social science: a realist approach*, 2nd edn. London and New York: Routledge.

Sayer, A. 1995: *Radical political economy: a critique*. Oxford: Blackwell.

Sayer, A. 1997: Essentialism, social constructionism, and beyond. *Sociological Review* 45(3): 453–87.

Sayer, A. 2000: *Realism and social science*. London: Sage.

Sayer, A. 2006: Realism as a basis for knowing the world. In S. Aitken and G. Valentine, eds, *Approaches to human geography*. London: Sage, 98–106.

Sayer, A. and Morgan, K. 1985: A modern industry in a declining region: links between method, theory and policy. In D. Massey and R. Meegan, eds, *Politics and method*. London: Methuen, ch. 6.

Sayer, A. and Walker, R. 1992: *The new social economy: reworking the division of labor*. Oxford: Blackwell.

Scabas, M. 2007: *The natural origins of economics*. Chicago: The University of Chicago Press.

Schaefer, F.K. 1953: Exceptionalism in geography: a methodological introduction. *Annals of the Association of American Geographers* 43: 226–49.

Schafer, W.A., Ganoe, C.H., Xiao, L., Coch, G. and Carroll, J.M. 2005: Designing the next generation of distributed, geocollaborative tools. *Cartography and Geographic Information Science* 32: 81–100.

Schaffer, S. 2002: Golden means: assay instruments and the geography of precision in the Guinea trade. In M.-N. Bourguet, C. Licoppe and H.O. Sibum, eds, *Instruments, travel and science: itineraries of precision from the seventeenth to the twentieth century*. London: Routledge, 20–50.

Schaffer, S. 2005: Inventing science; mapping knowledge. Paper presented at the conference on 'Big Issues in History of Science', University of Manchester, June.

Schama, S. 1989: The costs of modernity. In *Citizens*. New York: A.A. Knopf, 183–200.

Schama, S. 1995: *Landscape and memory*. London: HarperCollins/New York: A.A. Knopf.

Schatz, H. and Venables, A. 2000: The geography of international investment. In G. Clark, M. Feldman and M. Gertler, eds, *The Oxford handbook of economic geography*. Oxford: Oxford University Press.

Schatzki, T.R. 1991: Spatial ontology and explanation. *Annals of the Association of American Geographers* 81: 650–70.

Schatzki, T.R. 2002: *The site of the social: a philosophical account of the constitution of social life and change*. State College, Pennsylvania: Pennsylvania State University Press.

Scheffler, S. 2003: 'Fertile Crescent', 'Orient', 'Middle East': the changing mental maps of southwest Asia. *European Review of History* 10: 253–72.

Schein, R. 1993: Representing urban America: nineteenth century views of landscape, space, and power. *Environment and Planning D: Society and Space* 11: 7–21.

Schelling, T.C. 1971: Dynamic models of segregation. *Journal of Mathematical Sociology* 1: 143–86.

Schmidt, J.A., ed., 1996: *What is enlightenment? Eighteenth-century answers and twentieth-century questions*. Berkeley, CA: University of California Press.

Schmitt, C. 2003 [1950]: The *nomos* of the Earth in the international law of the *jus publicum Europaeum*, trans. G. Ulmen. New York: Telos.

Schneider, B. 2001: On the uncertainty of local shape of lines and surfaces. *Cartography and Geographic Information Science* 28: 237–47.

Schnieder, D.W. 2000: Local knowledge, environmental politics, and the founding of ecology in the United States: Stephen Forbes and 'The lake as microcosm' (1887). *Isis* 91(4): 681–705.

Schoenberger, E. 1997: *The cultural crisis of the firm.* Oxford: Blackwell.

Schoenberger, E. 1998: Discourse and practice in human geography. *Progress in Human Geography* 22: 1–14.

Schofield, C. 1993: Elusive security: the military and political geography of South Lebanon. *Geojournal* 31: 149–61.

Scholte, J.A. 2000: *Globalization: a critical introduction.* London: Palgrave.

Schonfeld, R.C. 2003: *JSTOR: a history.* Princeton, NJ: Princeton University Press.

Schor, J.B. 1991: *The overworked American: the unexpected decline of leisure.* New York: Basic Books.

Schorske, C.E. 1979: *Fin-de-siecle Vienna: politics and culture.* London: Weidenfeld and Nicholson.

Schoultz, L. 1998: *Beneath the United States: a history of U.S. policy toward Latin America.* Cambridge, MA: Harvard University Press.

Schulten, S. 2001: *The geographical imagination in America 1880–1950.* Chicago: The University of Chicago Press.

Schumm, S.A. and Lichty, R.W. 1965: Time, space and causality in geomorphology. *American Journal of Science* 263: 110–19.

Schumpeter, J.A. 1942: *Capitalism, socialism, and democracy.* New York: Harper & Row.

Schurmann, F.J., ed., 2001: *Globalization and development: challenges for the 21st century.* London: Sage.

Schuurman, N. 2004: *GIS: A short introduction.* Oxford: Blackwell.

Schwartz, J. and Ryan, J., eds, 2003: *Picturing place: photography and the geographic imagination.* London: I.B. Tauris.

Schwartz, M. 2007: Neo-liberalism on crack: cities under siege in Iraq. *City* 11(1): 21–69.

Scivoletto, A. 1983: *Sociologia del territorio: tra scienza e utopia.* Milan: Franco Angeli.

Scott, A.J. 1976a: Land and land rent: an interpretive review of the French literature. In C. Board, R.J. Chorley, P. Haggett and D.R. Stoddart, eds, *Progress in geography*, vol. 9. London: Edward Arnold, 101–45.

Scott, A.J. 1976b: Land use and commodity production. *Regional Science and Urban Economics* 6: 147–60.

Scott, A.J. 1988a: Flexible production systems and regional development: the rise of new industrial spaces in North America and western Europe. *International Journal of Urban and Regional Research* 12: 171–86.

Scott, A.J. 1988b: *Metropolis: from the division of labor to urban form.* Berkeley, CA: University of California Press.

Scott, A.J. 1988c: *New industrial spaces.* London: Pion.

Scott, A.J. 1998a: *Regions and the world economy: the coming shape of global production, competition, and political order.* Oxford: Oxford University Press.

Scott, A.J. 2000a: Economic geography: the great half-century. In G.L. Clark, M.P. Feldman and M.S. Gerter, eds, *The Oxford handbook of economic geography.* Oxford: Oxford University Press, 18–44.

Scott, A.J., ed., 2001: *Global city-regions.* New York: Oxford University Press.

Scott, A.J. 2005a: *On Hollywood: the place, the industry.* Princeton, NJ: Princeton University Press.

Scott, A.J. 2006: *Geography and economy.* Oxford: The Clarendon Press.

Scott, A.J. and Soja, E.W., eds, 1996: *The city: Los Angeles and urban theory at the end of the twentieth century.* Berkeley, CA: University of California Press.

Scott, A.J. and Storper, M. 2003: Regions, globalization, development. *Regional Studies* 37: 579–93.

Scott, D. 2004: *Conscripts of modernity: the tragedy of colonial enlightenment.* Durham, NC: Duke University Press.

Scott, J.C. 1985: *Weapons of the weak: everyday forms of peasant resistance.* New Haven, CT: Yale University Press.

Scott, J.C. 1998b: *Seeing like a state: how certain schemes to improve the human condition have failed.* New Haven, CT: Yale University Press.

Scott, J.P. 1999: *Social network analysis.* London: Sage.

Scott, J.W. 2002: A networked space of meaning? Spatial politics as geostrategies of European integration. *Space and Polity* 6: 147–67.

Scott, J.W. 2005b: Transnational regionalism, strategic geopolitics, and European integration: the case of the Baltic Sea region. In H. Nicol and I. Townsend-Gault, eds, *Holding the line: borders in a global world.* Vancouver: University of British Columbia Press, 90–116.

Scott, L.M. 2000b: Evaluating intra-metropolitan accessibility in the information age: operational issues, objectives, and implementation. In D.G. Janelle and D.C. Hodge, eds, *Information, place and cyberspace: issues in accessibility.* Berlin: Springer-Verlag, 22–45.

Scottish Geographical Journal 1999: Relevance in human geography. *Scottish Geographical Journal* 115(2): v–xiv, 91–165.

Seabright, P. 2004: *The company of strangers: a natural history of economic life*. Princeton, NJ: Princeton University Press.

Seagar, J. 1993: *Earth follies. Coming to feminist terms with the global environmental crisis*. London: Routledge.

Seager, J. 2003a: *The atlas of women*. London: Women's Press.

Seager, J. 2003b: Pepperoni or broccoli? On the cutting wedge of feminist environmentalism. *Gender, Place and Culture* 10: 167–74.

Seamon, D. 1979: *A geography of the life-world: movement, rest and encounter*. London: Croom Helm.

Sedgwick, E.K. 2003: *Touching feeling: affect, pedagogy, performativity*. Durham, NC: Duke University Press.

Sedlmeier, P. and Gigerenzer, G. 1989: Do studies of statistical power have an effect on the power of studies? *Psychological Bulletin* 105: 309–16.

Segal, A. 1993: *An atlas of international migration*. New Providence, NJ: Hans Zell.

Segal, R. and Weizman, E., eds, 2003: *A civilian occupation: the politics of Israeli architecture*. London: Verso.

Selenyi, I., ed., 1998: *Privatizing the land*. London: Routledge.

Seligman, A. 1992: *The idea of civil society*. New York: The Free Press.

Sellars, W. 1963: Empiricism and the philosophy of mind. In Sellars, *Science, perception and reality*. London: Routledge, 127–96.

Sen, A. 1981: *Poverty and famines: an essay on entitlement and deprivation*. Oxford: Oxford University Press.

Sen, A. 1990: More than one hundred million women are missing. *New York Review of Books* (20 December): 61–6.

Sen, A. 1993: The causation and prevention of famines: a reply. *Journal of Peasant Studies*, 21: 29–40.

Sen, A. 1999: *Development as freedom*. New York: Oxford University Press.

Sen, A. 2006: *Identity and violence: the illusion of destiny*. New York: W.W. Norton.

Sen, A. and Smith, T. 1995: *Gravity models of spatial interaction behaviour*. Berlin: Springer-Verlag.

Sen, J., Anand, A., Escobar, A. and Waterman, P., eds, 2004: *World Social Forum: challenging empires*. New Delhi: The Viveka Foundation.

Senior, M.L. 1979: From gravity modelling to entropy maximizing: a pedagogic guide. *Progress in Human Geography* 3: 179–211.

Serres, M., with Latour, B. 1995: *Conversations on science, culture, and time*. Ann Arbor, MI: University of Michigan Press.

Seton-Watson, H. 1977: *Nations and states*. London: Methuen.

Shafir, G. and Peled, Y. 1998: Citizenship and stratification in an ethnic democracy. *Ethnic and Racial Studies* 21(3): 408–27.

Shamir, R. 1996: Suspended in space: Bedouins under the law of Israel. *Law and Society Review* 30: 231–58.

Shanin, T., ed., 1988: *Peasants*. Oxford: Blackwell.

Shanks, M. and Pearson, M. 2001: *Theatre/archaeology*. London: Routledge.

Shannon, C.E. and Weaver, W. 1949: *The mathematical theory of communication*. Champaign, Il: University of Illinois Press.

Shannon, G., Pyle, G. and Bashshur, R. 1991: *The geography of AIDS: origins and course of an epidemic*. New York: Guilford Press.

Shapin, S. 1994: *A social history of truth: civility and science in seventeenth-century England*. Chicago: The University of Chicago Press.

Shapin, S. 1996: *The scientific revolution*. Chicago: The University of Chicago Press.

Shapin, S. 1998: Placing the view from nowhere: historical and sociological problems in the location of science. *Transactions of the Institute of British Geographers*, NS 23: 5–12.

Shapiro, I. and Hacker-Cordón, C., eds, 1999: *Democracy's edges*. Cambridge, UK: Cambridge University Press.

Shapiro, M. 1997: *Violent cartographies: mapping cultures of war*. Minneapolis: University of Minnesota Press.

Sharma, J. 2003: *Hindutva: exploring the idea of Hindu nationalism*. New Delhi: Penguin.

Sharp, J. 2000a: *Condensing the Cold War: Reader's Digest and American identity*. Minneapolis: University of Minnesota Press.

Sharp, J. 2000b: Towards a critical analysis of fictive geographies. *Area* 32(3): 327–34.

Sharp, J. 2005: Geography and gender: feminist methodologies in collaboration and in the field. *Progress in Human Geography* 29(3): 304–9.

Sharp, J., Browne, K. and Thien, D., eds, 2004: *Gender and geography revisited*. London: Women and Geography Study Group of the Royal Geographical Society of the Institute of British Geographers.

Sharp, J., Routledge, P., Philo, C. and Paddison, R., eds, 2000: *Entanglements of power: geographies of domination/resistance*. New York: Routledge.

Shatz, H.J. and Venables, A.J. 2000: The geography of international investment. In G.L. Clark, M.P. Feldman and M.S. Gertler, eds, *The Oxford handbook of economic geography*. Oxford: Oxford University Press, 125–45.

Shaw, M. 2005: *The new Western way of war*. Cambridge, UK: Polity Press.

Shaw, M., Davey, G.D. and Dorling, D. 2005: Health inequalities and New Labour: How the promises compare with real progress. *British Medical Journal* 330: 1016–21.

Shaw, M., Dorling, D. and Shaw, M. 2002: *Health, place and society*. London: Prentice Hall.

Shaw, W. 1978: *Marx's theory of history*. London: Hutchinson.

Shaw-Taylor, L. 2001: Labourers, cows, common rights and parliamentary enclosure: the evidence of contemporary comment c.1760–1810. *Past and Present* 171: 95–126.

Shaxon, N. 2006: *Poisoned wells*. London: Palgrave.

Sheail, J. 1976: *Nature in trust: the history of nature conservation in Great Britain*. Glasgow: Blackie.

Sheail, J. 1987: *Seventy-five years of ecology: the British Ecological Society*. Oxford: Blackwell Scientific.

Sheail, J. 1995: The ecologist and environmental history: a British perspective. *Journal of Biogeography* 22: 953–66.

Shellenberger, M. and Nordhaus, T. 2004: *The death of environmentalism: global warming politics in a post-environmental world*. Proceedings of the Environmental Grantmakers Association, October.

Shelley, T. 2005: *Oil: politics, poverty and the planet*. London: Zed Books.

Shen, J. 2002: A study of the temporary population in Chinese cities. *Habitat International* 26: 363–77.

Sheppard, E. 2002: The spaces and times of globalization: place, scale, networks and positionality. *Economic Geography* 78: 307–30.

Sheppard, E. 2004: The spatiality of *The limits to capital*. *Antipode* 36: 470–79.

Sheppard, E. 2005: Constructing free trade: from Manchester boosterism to global management. *Transactions of the Institute of British Geographers* 30: 151–72.

Sheppard, E. 2006: David Harvey and dialectical space–time. In N. Castree and D. Gregory, eds, *David Harvey: a critical reader*. Oxford: Blackwell, 121–41.

Sheppard, E. 2008: Geographical dialectics? *Environment and Planning A* 40: 2603–12.

Sheppard, E. and Barnes, T.J. 1990: *The capitalist space economy: geographical analysis after Ricardo, Marx and Sraffa*. London: Unwin Hyman.

Sheppard, E. and Barnes, T.J., eds, 2000: *A companion to economic geography*. Oxford: Blackwell.

Sheppard, E. and McMaster, R.B., eds, 2004: *Scale and geographic inquiry: nature, society and method*. Oxford: Blackwell.

Sheppard, E.S. 1984: The distance-decay gravity model debate. In G.L. Gaile and C.J. Willmott, eds, *Spatial statistics and models*. Dordrecht: D. Reidel, 367–88.

Sheppard, E.S. and Nagar, R. 2004: From east–west to north–south. *Antipode: a Radical Journal of Geography* 36: 557–63.

Sheringham, M. 2006: *Everyday life: theories and practices from surrealism to the present*. Oxford: Oxford University Press.

Sherman, L. 2003: Misleading evidence and evidence-led policy: making social science more experimental. *Annals of the American Academy of Political and Social Science* 589: 6–19.

Shevky, E. and Bell, W. 1955: *Social area analysis: theory, illustrative application and computational procedures*. Stanford CA: Stanford University Press.

Shiel, M. and Fitzmaurice, T., eds, 2001: *Cinema and the city: film and urban societies in a global context*. Oxford: Blackwell.

Shields, R. 1989: Social spatialisation and the built environment: the West Edmonton Mall. *Environment and Planning D: Society and Space* 7: 147–64.

Shields, R. 1991: *Places on the margin: alternative geographies of modernity*. London: Routledge.

Shields, R. 1992: A truant proximity: presence and absence in the spaces of modernity. *Environment and Planning D: Society and Space* 10(2): 181–98.

Shields, R. 1999: *Lefebvre, love and struggle: spatial dialectics*. London: Routledge.

Shields, R. 2006: Boundary-thinking in theories of the present: the virtuality of reflexive modernisation. *European Journal of Social Theory* 9 (2): 223–37.

Shih, S. 2002: Towards an ethics of transnational encounter, or 'when' does a 'Chinese' woman become a 'feminist'? *Differences: a Journal of Feminist Cultural Studies* 13: 90–126.

Shiva, V. 1988: *Staying alive: women, ecology and development*. London: Zed Books.

Shiva, V. 1991: *The violence of the Green Revolution*. London: Zed Books.

Shiva, V. 1992: Resources. In W. Sachs, ed., *The development dictionary: a guide to knowledge and power*. London: Zed Books.

Shiva, V. 1998 [1997]: *Biopiracy: the plunder of nature and knowledge*. Cambridge, MA: Green Books.

Shiva, V. 2002: *Water wars: pollution, profits and privatization*. London: Pluto Press.

Short, J.R. 2004: *Making space: revisioning the world 1475–1600*. Syracuse, NY: Syracuse University Press.

Shotter, J. 1993: *Conversational realities: the construction of life through language*. London: Sage.

Shoup, C. 1966: *Federal estate and gift taxes*. Washington, DC: Brookings Institution.

Shoval, N. and Isaacson, M. 2007: Sequence alignment as a method for human activity analysis in space and time. *Annals of the Association of American Geographers* 97(2): 282–97.

Shryock, H.S. and Siegel, J.S. 1973: *The methods and materials of demography*. Washington, DC: US Bureau of the Census, US Government Printing Office.

Shurmer-Smith, P., ed., 2002: *Doing cultural geography*. London: Sage.

Shutkin, W.A. 2000: *The land that could be: environmentalism and democracy in the twenty-first century*. Cambridge, MA: The MIT Press.

Sibley, B. 2001: The binary city. *Urban Studies* 38: 239–50.

Sibley, D. 1981: *Outsiders in urban societies*. Oxford: Blackwell.

Sibley, D. 1995: *Geographies of exclusion: society and difference in the West*. London: Routledge.

Sibley, D. 1998: Problematizing exclusion: reflections on space, difference and knowledge. *International Planning Studies* 3: 93–100.

Sibley, D. 2003: Geography and psychoanalysis: tensions and possibilities. *Social and Cultural Geography* 4: 391–9.

Sidaway, J.D. 1997: The (re)making of the Western 'geographical tradition': some missing links. *Area* 29: 72–80.

Sidaway, J.D. 1998: What is in a gulf? From the 'arc of crisis' to the Gulf War. In G. Ó Tuathail and S. Dalby, eds, *Rethinking geopolitics*. London: Routledge, 224–39.

Sidaway, J.D. 2000: Postcolonial geographies: an exploratory essay. *Progress in Human Geography* 24(4): 591–612.

Sidaway, J.D. 2002: *Imagined regional communities: integration and sovereignty in the global South*. London: Routledge.

Sieverts, T. 2003: *Cities without cities: an interpretation of the Zwischenstadt*. New York: Routledge.

Sigona, N. 2005: Locating 'the Gypsy problem': the Roma in Italy: stereotyping, labelling and 'nomad camps'. *Journal of Ethnic and Migration Studies* 31: 741–56.

Silver, B. and Arrighi, G.B. 2003: Polanyi's double movement: the belle époques of British and US hegemony compared. *Politics and Society* 31(2): 325–55.

Silver, T. 1990: *A new face on the countryside: indians, colonists, and slaves in South Atlantic forests, 1500–1800*. Cambridge, UK: Cambridge University Press.

Silverstone, R. 1999: *Why study the media?* London: Routledge.

Silvey, R. 2004: Power, difference, and mobility: feminist advances in migration studies. *Progress in Human Geography* 28: 490–506.

Silvey, R. 2006: Geographies of gender and migration: spatializing social difference. *International Migration Review* 40: 64–81.

Sim, S., ed., 1998: *Post-Marxism: a reader*. Edinburgh: Edinburgh University Press.

Simmel, G. 1978: *The philosophy of money*. Boston, Routledge.

Simmons, I.G. 1993: *Environmental history: a concise introduction*. Oxford: Blackwell.

Simmons, I.G. 1996: *Changing the face of the Earth*. Oxford: Blackwell.

Simmons, I.G. 1997: *Humanity and environment: a cultural ecology*. London: Longman.

Simmons, I.G. 2001: *An environmental history of Great Britain: from 10,000 years ago to the present*. Edinburgh: Edinburgh University Press.

Simon, D. 1998: Rethinking (post)modernism, postcolonialism, and posttraditionalism: South–North perspectives. *Environment and Planning D: Society and Space* 16: 219–45.

Simon, H.A. 1956: Rational choice and the structure of the environment. *Psychological Review* 63: 129–38.

Simon, H.A. 1957: *Models of man: social and rational*. New York: Wiley.

Simone, A.M. 2004: *For the city yet to come: changing African life in four cities*. Durham, NC: Duke University Press.

Simons, A. and Tucker, D. 2007: The misleading problem of failed states: a 'socio-geography' of terrorism in the post 9/11 era. *Third World Quarterly* 28: 387–401.

Simonsen, K. 1991: Towards an understanding of the contextuality of mode of life. *Environment and Planning D: Society and Space* 9: 417–32.

Simonsen, K. 2004: Spatiality, temporality and the construction of the city. In J.O. Bærenholdt and K. Simonsen, eds, *Space odysseys: spatiality and social relations in the 21st century*. Aldershot: Ashgate.

Simonsen, K. 2005: Bodies, sensations, space and time – the contribution from Henri Lefebvre. *Geografiska Annaler* 87B: 1–14.

Simpson, A. 1993: Mabo, international law, terra nullius and the stories of settlement: an unresolved jurisprudence. *Melbourne University Law Review* 19: 195–210.

Simpson, D. and Kelly, T.M. 2008: The new Chicago School of urbanism and the new Daley machine. *Urban Affairs Review* 44(2): 218–38.

Sinfield, A. 1994: *Cultural politics – queer reading*. London: Routledge.

Singer, J. 2000: *Entitlement: the paradoxes of property*. New Haven, CT: Yale University Press.

Singer, J. and Willett, J. 2003: *Applied longitudinal data analysis: modelling change and event occurrence*. Oxford: Oxford University Press.

Singer, P. 1993: *Practical ethics*, 2nd edn. Cambridge, UK: Cambridge University Press.

Singer, P. 2009: *Wired for war: the robotics revolution and conflict in the twenty-first century*. New York: Penguin.

Singh, N. 2004: *Black is a country: race and the unfinished struggle for democracy*. Cambridge, MA: Harvard University Press.

Singh, N. 2006: The afterlife of fascism. *The South Atlantic Quarterly* 105: 71–93.

Sinnott-Armstrong, W. 2006: Consequentialism. In E.N. Zalta, ed., *The Stanford encyclopedia of philosophy*; available at http://plato.stanford.edu/archives/spr2006/entries/consequentialism/

Sioh, M. 1998: Authorizing the Malaysian rainforest: configuring space, contesting claims and conquering imaginaries. *Ecumene* 5: 144–6.

Sjoberg, G. 1960: *The pre-industrial city, past and present.* New York: The Free Press (two chapters co-authored with A.F. Sjoberg).

Skeldon, R. 1994: *Reluctant exiles? Migration from Hong Kong and the new overseas Chinese.* Armonk, NY: M.E. Sharpe.

Skeldon, R. 1997: *Migration and development: a global perspective.* London: Longman.

Skelton, R.A. 1972: *Maps: a historical survey of their study and collecting,* ed. David Woodward. Chicago: The University of Chicago Press.

Skelton, T. and Valentine, G., eds, 1998: *Cool places: geographies of youth cultures.* London: Routledge.

Skertchley, S.B.J. 1878: *The physical system of the universe: an outline of physiography.* London: Daldy, Isbister and Co.

Skinner, C., Holt, D. and Smith, T. 1989: *Analysis of complex surveys.* New York: Wiley.

Skinner, Q., ed., 1985: *The return of Grand Theory in the human sciences.* Cambridge, UK: Cambridge University Press.

Sklair, L. 2001: *The transnational capitalist class.* Oxford: Blackwell.

Skocpol, T. 1980: *States and social revolution.* Cambridge, MA: Harvard University Press.

Slater, D. 1992: On the borders of social theory: learning from other regions. *Environment and Planning D: Society and Space* 10: 307–27.

Slater, D. 1997: Spatialities of power and post-modern ethics – rethinking geopolitical encounters. *Environment and Planning D: Society and Space* 15: 55–72.

Slater, D. 1999: Situating geopolitical representations: Inside/outside and the power of imperial interventions. In D. Massey, J. Allen and P. Sarre, eds, *Human geography today.* Cambridge UK: Polity Press, 62–84.

Slater, D. 2002: Other domains of democratic theory: space, power, and the politics of democratization. *Environment and Planning D: Society and Space* 20: 255–76.

Slater, D. 2004: *Geopolitics and the postcolonial: rethinking North–South relations.* Oxford: Blackwell.

Slaymaker, O. and Spencer, T. 1998: *Physical geography and global environmental change.* London: Longman.

Sleight, P. 2004: *Targeting customers: how to use geodemographic and lifestyle data in your business,* 3rd edn. Henley-upon-Thames: World Advertising Research Center.

Sletto, B. 2002: Boundary making and regional identities in a globalized environment: rebordering the Nariva Swamp, Trinidad. *Environment and Planning D: Society and Space* 20: 183–208.

Slobodkin, A. and Rappaport, R. 1974: An optimal strategy of evolution. *Quarterly Review of Biology* 49: 181–200.

Slocum, T.A., McMaster, R.B., Kessler, F.C. and Howard, H.H. 2008: *Thematic cartography and geographical visualization,* 3rd edn. Englewood Cliffs, NJ: Prentice-Hall.

Slouka, M. 1995: *War of the worlds: cyberspace and the high-tech assault on reality.* New York: Basic Books.

Sluyter, A. 2001: Colonialism and landscape in the Americas: material/conceptual transformations and continuing consequences. *Annals of the Association of American Geographers* 91: 410–29.

Sluyter, A. 2002: *Colonialism and landscape: postcolonial theory and applications.* Lanham, MD: Rowman & Littlefield.

Smaje, C. 1997: Not just a social construct: Theorising race and ethnicity. *Sociology* 31: 307–327.

Smallman-Raynor, M. and Cliff, A.D. 2004: *War epidemics: an historical geography of infectious diseases in military conflict and civil strife 1850–2000.* Cambridge, UK: Cambridge University Press.

Smart, A. 1986: Invisible real estate: investigations into the squatter property market. *International Journal of Urban and Regional Research* 10: 29–45.

Smart, B. 2007: Not playing around: global capitalism, modern sport and consumer culture. *Global Networks – a Journal of Transnational Affairs* 7(2): 113–34.

Smith, A. 1976 [1776]: *The wealth of nations.* Chicago: The University of Chicago Press.

Smith, A. 2002a: Imagining geographies of the 'new Europe': geo-economic power and the new European architecture of integration. *Political Geography* 21: 647–70.

Smith, A. 2003a: Power relations, industrial clusters, and regional transformations: pan-European integration and outward processing in the Slovak clothing industry. *Economic Geography* 79(1): 17–41.

Smith, A. 2003b: *The political landscape: constellations of authority in early complex polities.* Berkeley, CA: University of California Press.

Smith, A. 2004: Regions, spaces of economic practice and diverse economies in the 'new Europe'. *European Urban and Regional Studies* 11: 9–25.

Smith, B. 1960: *European vision and the South Pacific, 1768–1850: a study in the history of art and ideas.* Oxford: Oxford University Press.

Smith, C.J. 1988: *Public problems: the management of urban distress.* New York: Guilford Press.

Smith, C.J. and Giggs, J.A., eds, 1988: *Location and stigma: contemporary perspectives on mental health and mental health care.* London: Unwin Hyman.

Smith, D.M. 1973: *The geography of social well-being in the United States: an introduction to territorial social indicators*. New York: McGraw-Hill.

Smith, D.M. 1977: *Human geography: a welfare approach*. London: Edward Arnold.

Smith, D.M. 1979a: *Where the grass is greener: living in an unequal world*. London: Penguin.

Smith, D.M. 1981a [1971]: *Industrial location: an economic geographical analysis*, 2nd edn. New York and Chichester: Wiley.

Smith, D.M. 1994a: *Geography and social justice*. Oxford: Blackwell.

Smith, D.M. 1998a: Geography and moral philosophy. *Ethics, Place and Environment* 1: 7–34.

Smith, D.M. 1999a: Geography, community and morality. *Environment and Planning A* 31(1): 19–35.

Smith, D.M. 2000a: *Moral geographies: ethics in a world of difference*. Edinburgh: Edinburgh University Press/New York: Columbia University Press.

Smith, D.M. 2000b: Social justice revisited. *Environment and Planning A* 32: 1149–62.

Smith, D.M. and Lee, R., eds, 2004: *Geographies and moralities: international perspectives on justice, development and place*. Oxford: Blackwell.

Smith, F. and Barker, J. 2001: Commodifying the countryside: the impact of out-of-school care on rural landscapes of children's play. *Area* 33(2): 169–76.

Smith, G., ed., 1995: *Federalism: the multiethnic challenge*. London: Longman.

Smith, H.H. 1983: *The citizen's guide to zoning*. Chicago, IL: American Planning Association.

Smith, J. 1992a: The slightly different thing that is said: writing the aesthetic experience. In T.J. Barnes and J.S. Duncan, eds, *Writing worlds: discourse, text and metaphor in the representation of landscape*. London: Routledge, 73–85.

Smith, J.M. 1996a: Geographical rhetoric: modes and tropes of appeal. *Annals of the Association of American Geographers* 86(1): 1–20.

Smith, J.R. 1913: *Industrial and commercial geography*. New York: Henry Holt.

Smith, L.T. 1999b: *Decolonizing methodologies: research and indigenous peoples*. London: Zed Books.

Smith, M. 2002b: The state of nature: the political philosophy of primitivism and the culture of contamination. *Environmental Values* 11(4): 407–25.

Smith, M.L. 2006a: The archaeology of South Asian cities. *Journal of Archaeological Research* 14: 97–142.

Smith, M.P. 1979b: *The city and social theory*. New York: St Martin's Press.

Smith, M.P. 2001a: *Transnational urbanism*. Malden, MA: Blackwell.

Smith, M.P. and Feagin, J., eds, 1987: *The capitalist city*. Malden, MA: Blackwell.

Smith, M.P. and Guarnizo, L., eds, 1998: *Transnationalism from below*. New Brunswick, NJ: Transaction Books.

Smith, N. 1979c: Toward a theory of gentrification: a back to the city movement by capital not people. *Journal of the American Planning Association* 45: 538–48.

Smith, N. 1981b: Degeneracy in theory and practice. *Progress in Human Geography* 5: 111–18.

Smith, N. 1987: Dangers of the empirical turn: some comments on the CURS initiative. *Antipode* 19: 59–66.

Smith, N. 1990: *Uneven development: nature, capital and the production of space*, 2nd edn. Oxford: Blackwell.

Smith, N. 1992b: Contours of a spatialized politics: homeless vehicles and the production of geographical space. *Social Text* 33: 54–81.

Smith, N. 1993: Homeless: global: scaling places. In J. Bird, B. Curtis, T. Putnam, G. Robertson and L. Tickner, eds, *Mapping the futures: local cultures, global change*. London: Routledge, 87–119.

Smith, N. 1996b: Spaces of vulnerability: the space of flows and the politics of scale. *Critique of Anthropology* 16: 63–77.

Smith, N. 1996c: *The new urban frontier: gentrification and the revanchist city*. London: Routledge.

Smith, N. 2003c: *American empire: Roosevelt's geographer and the prelude to globalization*. Berkeley, CA: University of California Press.

Smith, N. 2005a: Neo-critical geography, or, the flat pluralist world of business class. *Antipode* 37(5): 887–99.

Smith, N. 2005b: *The endgame of globalization*. New York: Routledge.

Smith, N. 2006b: Global executioner. *The South Atlantic Quarterly* 105: 55–69.

Smith, N. 2006c: The endgame of globalization. *Political Geography* 25: 1–14.

Smith, N. 2008 [1984]: *Uneven development, nature, capital and the production of space*, 3rd edn. Athens, GA: The University of Georgia Press.

Smith, N. and Godlewska, A., eds, 1994: *Geography and empire*. Oxford: Blackwell.

Smith, N. and Katz, C. 1993: Grounding metaphor: towards a spatialized politics. In M. Keith and S. Pile, eds, *Place and the politics of culture*. London: Routledge, 67–83.

Smith, N. and O'Keefe, P. 1980: Geography, Marx and the concept of nature. *Antipode* 12 (2): 30–39.

Smith, N. and Williams, P., eds, 1986: *Gentrification of the city*. Boston: Allen & Unwin.

Smith, R.A. 1992c: Beach resort evolution – implications for planning. *Annals of Tourism Research* 19(2): 304–22.

Smith, R.G. 2003d: World city typologies. *Progress in Human Geography* 27(5): 561–82.

Smith, R.M. 1984: *Land, kinship and life-cycle.* Cambridge, UK: Cambridge University Press.

Smith, R.M. 1990: Monogamy, landed property and demographic regimes in pre-industrial Europe, in J.M. Landers and V. Reynolds, eds, *Fertility and resources.* Cambridge, UK: Cambridge University Press, 164–82.

Smith, R.M. 1998b: The English peasantry 1250–1650. In T. Scott, ed., *The peasantries of Europe from the fourteenth to the eighteenth centuries.* London: Longman, 339–71.

Smith, S.J. 1986a: *Crime, space and society.* Cambridge, UK: Cambridge University Press.

Smith, S.J. 1989: *The politics of 'race' and residence: citizenship, segregation and white supremacy in Britain.* Cambridge, UK: Polity Press.

Smith, S.J. 1994b: Soundscape. *Area* 26: 232–40.

Smith, S.J. 2001b: Doing qualitative research: from interpretation to action. In M. Limb and C. Dwyer, eds, 2001: *Qualitative methodologies for geographers: issues and debates.* London: Arnold, 23–40.

Smith, S.J. 2005c: Society-space. In P. Cloke, P. Crang and M. Goodwin, eds, *Introducing human geographies*, 2nd edn. London: Hodder Arnold, 18–35.

Smith, S.J. and Easterlow, D. 2005: The strange geography of health inequalities. *Transactions of the Institute of British Geographers* 30: 173–90.

Smith, S.J. and Mallinson, S. 1997: Housing for health in a post-welfare state. *Housing Studies* 12(2): 173–200.

Smith, W.D. 1986b: *The ideological origins of Nazi imperialism.* Oxford: Oxford University Press.

Smith, W.D. 1991: *Politics and the sciences of culture in Germany 1840–1920.* New York: Oxford University Press.

Smocovitis, V.B. 1996: *Unifying biology: the evolutionary synthesis and evolutionary biology.* Princeton, NJ: Princeton University Press.

Smooha, S. 2002: The model of ethnic democracy: Israel as a Jewish and democratic state. *Nation and Nationalism* 8(4): 475–503.

Smythe, D. 1978: Communications: blindspot of Western Marxism. *Canadian Journal of Political and Social Theory* 1(3): 1–27.

Sneddon, C.S. 2000: 'Sustainability' in ecological economics, ecology, and livelihoods: a review. *Progress in Human Geography* 24(4): 521–49.

Snijders, T.A.B. 1992: Estimation on the basis of snowball samples: how to weight. *Bulletin de Méthodologie Sociologique* 36: 59–70.

Snyder, J.P. 1993: *Flattening the Earth: two thousand years of map projections.* Chicago: The University of Chicago Press.

Soja, E.W. 1980: The socio-spatial dialectic. *Annals of the Association of American Geographers* 70: 207–25.

Soja, E.W. 1985: The spatiality of social life: towards a transformative retheorisation. In D. Gregory and J. Urry, eds, *Social relations and spatial structures.* London: Macmillan, 90–122.

Soja, E.W. 1989: *Postmodern geographies: the reassertion of space in critical social theory.* London: Verso.

Soja, E.W. 1992: Inside exopolis: scenes from Orange County. In M. Sorkin, ed., *Variations on a theme park: the new American city and the end of public space.* New York: The Noonday Press, 94–122.

Soja, E.W. 1996a: Inside exopolis: everyday life in the postmodern world. In Soja, *Thirdspace: Journeys to Los Angeles and other real-and-imagined places.* Oxford: Blackwell, 237–79.

Soja, E.W. 1996b: *Thirdspace: journeys to Los Angeles and other real-and-imagined places.* Oxford: Blackwell.

Soja, E.W. 2000a: *Postmetropolis: critical studies of cities and regions.* Oxford: Blackwell.

Soja, E.W. 2000b: Putting cities first. In Soja, *Postmetropolis: critical studies of cities and regions.* Oxford: Blackwell, 19–49.

Sokol, M. 2001: Central and eastern Europe a decade after the fall of state-socialism: regional dimensions of transition process. *Regional Studies* 35: 645–55.

Solinger, D.J. 2006: The creation of a new underclass in China and its implications. *Environment and Urbanization* 18: 177–92.

Sollors, W., ed., 1996: *Theories of ethnicity: a classical reader.* London: Macmillan.

Somerville, M. 1849: *Physical geography*, 2nd edn. London: John Murray.

Soper, K. 1986: *Humanism and anti-humanism: problems in modern European thought.* London: Hutchinson.

Sorenson, O. 2003: Social networks and industrial geography. *Journal of Evolutionary Economics* 13: 513–27.

Sorkin, M. 1992a: See you in Disneyland. In M. Sorkin, ed., *Variations on a theme park: the new American city and the end of public space.* New York: The Noonday Press, 305–32.

Sorkin, M., ed., 1992b: *Variations on a theme park: the new American city and the end of public space.* New York: The Noonday Press.

Sorre, M. 1957: *Rencontres de la géographie et de la sociologie.* Paris: Riviére.

Sorrenson, R. 1996: The ship as a scientific instrument in the eighteenth century. *Osiris*, 2nd Series, 11: 221–36.

Sothern, M. 2004: (Un)queer patriarchies, or 'what do we think when we fuck?' *Antipode* 36: 183–90.

Southall, H. 1991: The tramping artisan revisited: labour mobility and economic distress in early Victorian England. *Economic History Review* 44: 272–96.

Southworth, M. and Southworth, S. 1982: *Maps: a visual survey and design guide*. Boston: Little, Brown.

Soysal, Y. 1994: *Limits of citizenship: migrants and postnational membership in Europe*. Chicago: the University of Chicago Press.

Sparke, M. 2000a: Chunnel visions: unpacking the anticipatory geographies of an Anglo-European borderland. *Journal of Borderland Studies* 15(1): 2–34.

Sparke, M. 2000b: Graphing the geo in geo-political: *Critical Geopolitics* and the re-visioning of responsibility. *Political Geography* 19: 373–80.

Sparke, M. 2005: *In the space of theory: postfoundational geographies of the nation-state*. Minneapolis: University of Minnesota Press.

Sparke, M. 2006: A neoliberal nexus: citizenship, security and the future of the border. *Political Geography* 30(2): 151–80.

Sparke, M. 2007: Geopolitical fears, geoeconomic hopes and the responsibilities of geography. *Annals of the Association of American Geographers* 97(2): 338–49.

Sparke, M., Sidaway, J., Bunnell, T. and Grundy-Warr, C. 2004: Triangulating the borderless world: geographies of power in the Indonesia–Malaysia–Singapore growth triangle. *Transactions of the Institute of British Geographers*, NS 29: 485–98.

Sparke, M., Brown, E., Corva, D., Day, H., Faria, C., Sparks, T. and Varg, K. 2005: The World Social Forum and the lessons for economic geography. *Economic Geography* 81(4): 359–80.

Spate, O.H.K. 1968: Environmentalism. In D.L. Sills, ed., *International encyclopedia of the social sciences*, vol. 5. New York: Macmillan/The Free Press, 93–7.

Spedding, N. 1997: On growth and form in geomorphology. *Earth Surface Processes and Landforms* 22: 261–5.

Spencer, T. and Whatmore, S. 2001: Bio-geographies: putting some life back into the discipline. Editorial in *Transactions of the Institute of British Geographers* 26(2): 139–41.

Spivak, G.C. 1988: *In other worlds: essays in cultural politics*. New York: Routledge.

Spivak, G.C. 1992: Woman in difference: Mahasweta Devi's *Douloti the beautiful*. In A. Parker, M. Russo, D. Sommer, and P. Yaeger, eds, *Nationalisms and sexualities*. New York: Routledge, 96–117.

Spivak, G.C. 2000: Discussion: an afterword on the new subaltern. In P. Chatterjee and P. Jeganathan, eds, *Subaltern studies XI: community, gender, violence*. Delhi: Permanent Black, 305–34.

Spradley, J. 1979: *The ethnographic interview*. New York: Holt Reinhart and Winston.

Springer, S. 2008: The non-illusory effects of neoliberalisation: linking geographies of poverty, inequality and violence. *Geoforum*, 39: 1520–5.

Spry, I.M. 1981: Overhead costs, rigidities of productive capacity and the price system. In W.H. Melody, L. Salter and P. Heyer, eds, *Culture, communication, and dependency: the tradition of H.A. Innis*. Norwood, NJ: Ablex, 155–66.

Sraffa, P. 1960: *Production of commodities by means of commodities: a prelude to a critique of economic theory*. Cambridge, UK: Cambridge University Press.

Srivastava, S. 1996: Modernity and post-coloniality: the metropolis as metaphor. *Economic and Political Weekly*, 17 February: 403–12.

Staeheli, L.A. 1996: Publicity, privacy, and women's political action. *Environment and Planning D: Society and Space* 14: 601–19.

Staeheli, L.A. and Brown, M. 2003: Guest editorial. *Environment and Planning A* 35: 771–77.

Staeheli, L.A. and Mitchell, D. 2005: The complex politics of relevance in geography. *Annals of the Association of American Geographers* 95: 357–72.

Staeheli, L.A., Kofman, E. and Peake, L.J., eds, 2004: *Mapping women, making politics: feminist perspectives on political geography*. London: Routledge.

Stafford, B.M. 1984: *Voyage into substance: art, science, nature and the illustrated travel account 1760–1840*. Cambridge, MA: The MIT Press.

Stafford, R.A. 1989: *Scientist of empire: Sir Roderick Murchison, scientific exploration and Victorian imperialism*. Cambridge, UK: Cambridge University Press.

Stahl, R. 2006: Have you played the war on terror? *Critical Studies in Media Communication* 23(2): 112–30.

Stallybrass, P. and White, A. 1986: *The politics and poetics of transgression*. Ithaca, NY: Cornell University Press.

Stamp, L.D. 1946: *The land of Britain*. London: Longman.

Stamp, L.D. 1964: *The geography of life and death*. London: Collins.

Stannard, D. 1992: *American holocaust: Columbus and the conquest of the New World*. Oxford: Oxford University Press.

Starr, A. 2000: *Naming the enemy: anti-corporate movements against globalization*. London: Zed Books.

Starr, A. 2005: *Global revolt*. London: Zed Books.

Stasiulis, D. and Yuval-Davis, N., eds, 1995: *Unsettling settler societies: articulations of race, ethnicity, and class*. London: Sage.

Stassart, P. and Whatmore, S.J. 2003: Metabolising risk: food scares and the un/remaking of Belgian beef. *Environment and Planning A* 25: 449–62.

Staszak, J.-F. 2004: Primitivism and the other: history of art and cultural geography. *GeoJournal* 60: 353–64.

Staudt, K. 1998: *Free trade? Informal economies at the U.S.–Mexico border.* Philadelphia, PA: Temple University Press.

Stebbins, R. 1992: *Amateurs, professionals, and serious leisure.* Montreal: McGill-Queen's University Press.

Steck, H. 2003: Corporatization of the university: seeking conceptual clarity. *Annals of the American Academy of Political and Social Science* 585 (January): 66–83.

Stedman Jones, G. 1991 [1974]: *Outcast London: a study in the relationship between classes in Victorian society.* London: Penguin.

Steel, R. 1967: *Pax Americana.* New York: Viking Press.

Steel, R.W. 1983: *The Institute of British Geographers: the first fifty years.* London: Institute of British Geographers.

Stein, C. 1966: *Towards new towns for America.* Cambridge, MA: The MIT Press.

Stein, S. 2005: Conceptions and terms: templates for the analysis of holocausts and genocides. *Journal of Genocide Research* 7: 171–203.

Steinberg, P.E. 2001: *The social construction of the ocean.* Cambridge, UK: Cambridge University Press.

Stengers, I. 1997: *Power and invention: situating science.* Minneapolis: University of Minnesota Press.

Stengers, I. 2000: *The invention of modern science.* Minneapolis: University of Minnesota Press.

Stenning, D.J. 1960: Transhumance, migratory drift, migration: patterns of pastoral Fulani nomadism. In S. Ottenburg and P. Ottenburg, eds, *Cultures and societies of Africa.* New York: Random House, 139–59.

Stepan, N.L. 1990 [1986]: Race and gender: the role of analogy in science. In D.T. Goldberg, ed., *Anatomy of racism.* Minneapolis: University of Minnesota Press (originally published in *Isis* 77 (1986): 261–77).

Stepan, N.L. 2001: *Picturing tropical nature.* London: Reaktion Books.

Stern, N. 2007: *The economics of climate change: the Stern review.* Cambridge, UK: Cambridge University Press.

Stern, V. 1998: *A sin against the future: imprisonment in the world.* Boston: Northeastern University Press.

Steward, J. 1955: *Theory of culture change: the methodology of multilinear evolution.* Urbana-Champagne: University of Illinois Press.

Stewart, J.Q. 1950: The development of social physics. *American Journal of Physics* 18: 239–53.

Stewart, J.Q. and Warntz, W. 1959: The physics of population distributions. *Journal of Regional Science* 1: 99–123.

Stewart, M. 1996: *'What nature suffers to groe': life, labor, and landscape on the Georgia coast, 1680–1920.* Athens, GA: University of Georgia Press.

Stewart-Harawira, M. 2005: *The new imperial order: indigenous responses to globalization.* London: Zed Books.

Stiglitz, J. 2002: *Globalization and its discontents.* New York: W.W. Norton.

Stiglitz, J. and Charlton, A. 2006: *Fair trade for all: how trade can promote development.* Oxford: Oxford University Press.

Stobart, J. 2004: *The first industrial region: northwest England 1700–1760.* Manchester: Manchester University Press.

Stocking, G.W. Jr 1962: Lamarckianism in American social science: 1890–1915. *Journal of the History of Ideas* 23: 239–56.

Stoddart, D.R. 1966: Darwin's impact on geography. *Annals of the Association of American Geographers* 56: 683–98.

Stoddart, D.R. 1967: Organism and ecosystem as geographical models. In R.J. Chorley and P. Haggett, eds, *Models in geography.* London: Methuen, 511–48.

Stoddart, D.R. 1985: *On geography and its history.* Oxford: Blackwell.

Stoddart, D.R. 1992: Geography and war: The 'New Geography' and the 'New Army' in England, 1899–1914. *Political Geography* 11: 87–99.

Stoker, L. and Bowers, J. 2002: Designing multilevel studies: sampling voters and electoral contexts. *Electoral Studies* 21(3): 235–67.

Stoler, A.L. 1995: *Race and the education of desire: Foucault's* History of sexuality *and the colonial order of things.* Durham, NC: Duke University Press.

Stoler, A.L. 1997: Racial histories and their regimes of truth. *Political Power and Social Theory* 11: 183–206.

Stoler, A.L. 2002: *Carnal knowledge and imperial power: race and the intimate in colonial rule.* Berkeley, CA: University of California Press.

Stone, C.N. 1989: *Regime politics: governing Atlanta, 1946–1988.* Lawrence, KS: University of Kansas Press.

Storper, M. 1985: Oligopoly and the product cycle: essentialism in economic geography. *Economic Geography* 61: 260–82.

Storper, M. 1997a: Regional economies as relational assets. In R. Lee and J. Wills, eds, *Geographies of economies.* London: Arnold.

Storper, M. 1997b: *The regional world: territorial development in a global economy.* New York: Guilford Press.

Storper, M. and Manville, M. 2006: Behaviour, preferences and cities: urban theory and urban resurgence. *Urban Studies* 43: 1247–74.

Storper, M. and Salais, M. 1997: *Worlds of production.* Cambridge, MA: Harvard University Press.

Storper, M. and Scott, A. 1989: The geographical foundation and social regulation of flexible production spaces. In J. Wolch and M. Dear, eds, *The power of geography*. Winchester, MA: Unwin Hyman.

Storper, M. and Walker, R. 1989: *The capitalist imperative: territory, technology, and industrial growth*. Oxford: Blackwell.

Stott, P. and Sullivan, S., eds, 2000: *Political ecology: science, myth and power*. London: Arnold.

Stouffer, S.A. 1940: Intervening opportunities: a theory relating mobility to distance. *American Sociological Review* 5: 845–67.

Stracher, G. and Taylor, T. 2004: Coal fires burning out of control around the world: thermodynamic recipe for environmental disaster. *International Journal of Coal Geology* 59: 7–17.

Strathern, M. 1995: The nice thing about culture is that everyone has it. In M. Strathern, ed., *Shifting contexts: transformations in anthropological knowledge*. London: Routledge.

Strathern, M. 1996: Cutting the network. *Journal of the Royal Anthropological Institute* 2: 517–35.

Straus, S. 2005: Darfur and the genocide debate. *Foreign Affairs* 84: 123–33.

Streeten, P. 1987: Structural adjustment: a survey of the issues and options. *World Development* 15: 1469–82.

Strohmayer, U. 1997: Technology, modernity, and the restructuring of the present in historical geographies. *Geographiska Annaler* 79B(3): 155–70.

Strohmayer, U. 1998: The event of space: geographic allusions in the phenomenological tradition. *Environment and Planning D: Society and Space* 16: 105–21.

Strohmayer, U. 2006: Engineering vision: the Pont-Neuf in Paris and modernity. In A. Cowan and J. Steward, eds, *The city and the senses: urban culture since 1500*. Aldershot: Ashgate, 75–92.

Strüver, A. 2007: The production of geopolitical and gendered images through global aid organisations. *Geopolitics* 12: 680–703.

Sturgis, P. 2004: Analysing complex survey data: clustering, stratification and weights. *Social Research Update*, Issue 43, http://epubs.surrey.ac.uk/publsoc2/2

Suchan, T.A. and Brewer, C.A. 2000: Qualitative methods for research on mapmaking and map use. *Professional Geographer* 52: 145–54.

Sudman, S. 1976: *Applied sampling*. New York: Academic Press.

Sugden, D. 1996: The East Antarctic ice-sheet: unstable ice or unstable ideas? *Transactions of the Institute of British Geographers* 21: 443–54.

Sugg, K. 2003: Migratory sexualities, diasporic histories, and memory in queer Cuban–American cultural production. *Environment and Planning D: Society and Space* 21(4): 461–77.

Sui, D., ed., 2008: *Geospatial technologies and homeland security*. Geojournal Library. Berlin: Springer-Verlag.

Sui, D., Fotheringham, A.S., Anselin, A., O'Loughlin, J. and King, G. 2000: Book Review Forum. *Annals of the Association of American Geographers* 90: 579–606.

Suleiman, S. 1990: *Subversive intent: gender, politics, and the avant-garde*. Cambridge, MA: Harvard University Press.

Sullivan, N. 2003: *A critical introduction to queer theory*. Albany, NY: State University of New York Press.

Sundberg, J. 2003: Masculinist epistemologies and the politics of fieldwork in Latin Americanist geography. *Professional Geographer* 55(2): 180–90.

Sunley, P. 1996: Context in economic geography: the relevance of pragmatism. *Progress in Human Geography* 20: 338–55.

Suskind, R. 2004: Without a doubt. *The New York Times Magazine*, 17 October: 44–77.

Suttles, G. 1968: *The social order of the slum: ethnicity and territory in the inner city*. Chicago: The University of Chicago Press.

Swanson, F.J. 1987: Ecological effects of the eruption of Mount St. Helens: an overview. In D.E. Bilderback, ed., *Mount St. Helens 1980: botanical consequences of the explosive eruptions*. Berkeley, CA: University of California Press, 1–3.

Swenden, W. 2006: *Federalism and regionalism in Western Europe*. London: Palgrave.

Swift, A., Liu, L. and Uber, J. 2008: Reducing MAUP bias of correlation statistics between water quality and GI illness. *Computers, Environment and Urban Systems* 32: 134–48.

Swift, J. 1996: Desertification narratives; winners and losers. In M. Leach and R. Mearns, eds, *The lie of the land: challenging received wisdom on the African environment*. Oxford: James Currey, 73–90.

Swyngedouw, E. 1997: Neither global nor local: 'glocalization' and the politics of scale. In K. Cox, ed, *Spaces of globalization: reasserting the power of the local*. New York: Guilford Press, 137–66.

Swyngedouw, E. 1999: Modernity and hybridity: nature, *regeneracionismo*, and the production of the Spanish waterscape, 1890–1930. *Annals of the Association of American Geographers* 89(3): 443–65.

Swyngedouw, E. 2001: Neither global nor local: 'glocalization' and the politics of scale. In B. Jessop, ed., *Regulation theory and the crisis of capitalism*. Cheltenham: Edward Elgar, 196–225.

Swyngedouw, E. 2002: The strange respectability of the situationist city in the society of the spectacle. *International Journal of Urban and Regional Research* 26(1): 153–65.

Swyngedouw, E. 2004a: Globalisation or 'glocalisation'? Networks, territories and re-scaling.

Cambridge Review of International Affairs 17(1): 25–48.

Swyngedouw, E. 2004b: *Social power and the urbanization of water: flows of power*. Oxford: Oxford University Press.

Swyngedouw, E. 2006: *Glocalizations*. Philadelphia, PA: Temple University Press.

Swyngedouw, E. 2007: Technonatural revolutions: the scalar politics of Franco's hydro-social dream for Spain, 1939–1975. *Transactions of the Institute of British Geographers* 32(1): 9–28.

Swyngedouw, E. and Heynen, N. 2003: Urban political ecology, justice, and the politics of scale. *Antipode* 35: 898–918.

Sykes, G. 1958: *The society of captives*. New York: Rinehart.

Sylvester, C. 1999: Development studies and postcolonial studies: disparate tales of the 'Third World'. *Third World Quarterly* 20: 703–21.

Sylvester, C. 2006: Bare life as a development/postcolonial problematic. *Geographical Journal* 172: 66–77.

Sze, J. 2005: Toxic soup redux: why environmental racism and environmental justice matter after Katrina. In *Understanding Katrina: perspectives from the social sciences*. SSRC Forum: http://understandingkatrina.ssrc.org/

Taaffe, E.J. and Gauthier, H.L. 1973: *Geography of transportation*. Englewood Cliffs, NJ: Prentice-Hall.

Tabb, W. 2002: *Unequal partners: a primer on globalization*. New York: The Free Press.

Takacs, D. 1996: *The idea of biodiversity: philosophies of paradise*. Baltimore, MD: The Johns Hopkins University Press.

Takahashi, L.M. 1996: A decade of understanding homelessness in the USA: from characterization to representation. *Progress in Human Geography* 20(3): 291–310.

Tansey, G. and Worsley, T. 1995: *The food system: a guide*. London: Earthscan.

Taris, T. 2000: *Longitudinal data analysis*. London: Sage.

Tarr, R.S. 1920: *College physiography*. New York: Macmillan.

Tarrant, J. 1974: *Agricultural geography*. Newton Abbot: David and Charles.

Tassell, T. 2006: Global overview. *Financial Times*, 13 July: 26.

Taussig, M. 1978: *The Devil and commodity fetishism in South America*. Chapel Hill, NC: University of North Carolina Press.

Taussig, M. 1993: *Mimesis and alterity*. London: Routledge.

Tavares, D. and Brosseau, M. 2006: The representation of Mongolia in contemporary travel writing: imaginative geographies of a traveller's frontier. *Social and Cultural Geography* 7: 299–317.

Taylor, A. 2000: 'The sun always shines in Perth': a post-colonial geography of identity, memory and place. *Australian Geographical Studies* 38(1): 27–35.

Taylor, C. 1995a: *Philosophical arguments*. Cambridge, MA: Harvard University Press.

Taylor, D.R.F. 2003: The concept of cybercartography. In M.P. Peterson, ed., *Maps and the Internet*. Amsterdam: Elsevier, 405–20.

Taylor, D.R.F., ed., 2006a: *Cybercartography: theory and practice*. Amsterdam: Elsevier.

Taylor, E.G.R. 1930: *Tudor geography*. London: Methuen.

Taylor, F.W. 1911: *The principles of scientific management*. New York: Harper.

Taylor, J. 2006b: Mapping adventure: a historical geography of Yosemite Valley climbing landscapes. *Journal of Historical Geography* 32: 190–219.

Taylor, M.J. 1986: The product life cycle: a critique. *Environment and Planning A* 18: 751–61.

Taylor, P. 1994a: The state as a container: territoriality in the modern world system. *Progress in Human Geography* 18: 151–62.

Taylor, P. 1996: *The way the modern world works: world hegemony to world impasse*. Chichester: Wiley.

Taylor, P.J. 1971: Distance transformation and distance decay functions. *Geographical Analysis* 3: 221–38.

Taylor, P.J. 1976: An interpretation of the quantification debate in British geography. *Transactions of the Institute of British Geographers*, NS 1: 129–42.

Taylor, P.J. 1981: Geographical scales within the world-economy approach. *Review* 5: 3–11.

Taylor, P.J. 1985: *Political geography: world-economy, nation-state and locality*. London: Longman.

Taylor, P.J. 1989: The error of developmentalism in human geography. In R. Walford and D. Gregory, eds, *New horizons in human geography*. London: Macmillan, 303–19.

Taylor, P.J. 1994b: Decolonization. In T. Unwin, ed., *Atlas of world development*. Chichester: Wiley, 22–3.

Taylor, P.J. 1994c: The state as container: territoriality in the modern world-system. *Progress in Human Geography* 18: 151–62.

Taylor, P.J. 1995b: Beyond containers: internationality, interstateness, interterritoriality. *Progress in Human Geography* 19: 1–15.

Taylor, P.J. 1999: *Modernities: a geohistorical interpretation*. Minneapolis: University of Minnesota Press.

Taylor, P.J. 2004a: *Homo geographicus*: a geohistorical manifesto for cities. *Review* XXVII: 37–60.

Taylor, P.J. 2004b: *World city network: a global urban analysis*. London: Routledge.

Taylor, P.J. and Johnston, R.J., eds, 1979: *The geography of elections*. London: Penguin.

Taylor, T. Griffith, ed., 1953: *Geography in the Twentieth Century*, 2nd edn. New York: New York Philosophical Library.

Teivainen, T. 2002: The World Social Forum and global democratization. *Third World Quarterly* 23(4): 621–32.

Teo, P. 1996: Aging in Singapore. *Journal of Cross-Cultural Gerontology* 11: 269–86.

Teschke, B. 2003: *The myth of 1648: class, geopolitics and the making of modern international relations*. London: Verso.

Tester, K., ed., 1994: *The* flâneur. London: Routledge.

Testfatsion, L. and Judd, K.L. 2006: *Handbook of computational economics*, vol. 2: *Agent-based computational economics*. Amsterdam: Elsevier.

Thabit, W. 2003: *How east New York became a ghetto*. New York: New York University Press.

Thacker, A. 2005–6: The idea of a critical literary geography. *New Formations* 57: 56–73.

Thampapillai, D. 2002: *Environmental economics: concepts, methods, and policies*. Melbourne: Oxford University Press.

Thapar, R. 1966: *A history of India*, vol. 1. London: Penguin.

Theil, H. 1967: *Economics and information theory*. Amsterdam: North-Holland.

Theodorson, G., ed., 1961: *Studies in human ecology*. New York: Harper & Row.

Theranian, M., ed., 1999: *Worlds apart: human security and global governance*. London: I.B. Tauris.

Theweleit, K. 1987: *Male fantasies*, trans. S. Conway. Minneapolis: University of Minnesota Press.

Thom, R. 1975: *Structural stability and morphogenesis*. Reading, MA: W.A. Benjamin.

Thomas, G.S. 1989: Micropolitan America. *American Demographics* 11(5): 20–4.

Thomas, I. 2005: *Environmental management: processes and practices for Australia*. Sydney: The Federation Press.

Thomas, I. and Elliot, M. 2005: *Environmental impact assessment in Australia: theory and practice*. 4th edn. Sydney: The Federation Press.

Thomas, K. 1996 [1983]: *Man and the natural world: changing attitudes in England, 1500–1800*. London: Allen Lane.

Thomas, M.D. 1980: Explanatory frameworks for growth and change in multiregional firms. *Economic Geography* 56: 1–17.

Thomas, N. 1991: *Entangled objects: exchange, material culture, and colonialism in the Pacific*. Cambridge, MA: Harvard University Press.

Thomas, N. 1993: *Colonialism's culture: anthropology, travel and government*. Princeton, NJ: Princeton University Press.

Thomas, R.W. and Huggett, R.J. 1980: *Modelling in geography: a mathematical approach*. New York: Harper & Row.

Thomas, W.L. Jr, ed., 1956: *Man's role in changing the face of the Earth*. Chicago: The University of Chicago Press.

Thompson, D'Arcy Wentworth 1992 [1917]: *On growth and form*, rev. edn. New York: Dover.

Thompson, E.P. 1975a: *Whigs and hunters: the origin of the Black Act*. New York: Pantheon.

Thompson, E.P. 1991: *Customs in common*. London: Penguin.

Thompson, E.T. 1975b: *Plantation societies, race relations and the South: the regimentation of populations*. Durham, NC: Duke University Press.

Thompson, J.B. 1990: *Ideology and modern culture*. Cambridge, UK: Polity Press.

Thompson, J.B. 1995: *Media and modernity: a social theory of the media*. Cambridge, UK: Polity Press.

Thompson, J.B. 1996: Hermeneutics. In A. Kuper and J. Kuper, eds, *The social science encyclopedia*. London: Routledge, 360–1.

Thompson, S.K. and Seber, G.A.F. 2002: *Adaptive sampling*. New York: Wiley.

Thompson, W.R. 1968: Internal and external factors in urban economies. In H.S. Perloff and L. Wingo, eds, *Issues in urban economics*. Baltimore, MD: The Johns Hopkins University Press, 43–62.

Thornton, J. 1901: *Advanced physiography*. London: Longman Green and Co.

Thornton, R. 1990: *American Indian Holocaust and survival: a population history since 1492*. Norman, OK: University of Oklahoma Press.

Thrift, N.J. 1983: On the determination of social action in space and time. *Environment and Planning D: Society and Space* 1: 23–57.

Thrift, N.J. 1993: The urban impasse? *Theory, Culture & Society* 10: 229.

Thrift, N.J. 1994a: On the social and cultural determinants of international financial centres: the case of the City of London. In S. Corbridge, R. Martin and N.J. Thrift, eds. *Money, power and space*. Oxford, Blackwell, 327–55.

Thrift, N.J. 1994b: Taking aim at the heart of the region. In D. Gregory, R. Martin and G. Smith, eds, *Human geography: society, space, and social science*. London: Macmillan/ Minneapolis: University of Minnesota Press, 200–31.

Thrift, N.J. 1996: *Spatial formations*. London: Sage.

Thrift, N.J. 1997a: New urban eras and old technological fears: reconfiguring the good will of electronic things. In A. Leyshon and N.J. Thrift (eds), *Money/space: geographies of monetary transformation*. London: Routledge, 323–54.

Thrift, N.J. 1997b: The rise of soft capitalism. *Cultural Values* 1: 29–57.

Thrift, N.J. 1997c: The still point: resistance, expressive embodiment and dance. In S. Pile and M. Keith, eds, *Geographies of resistance*. London: Routledge, 124–51.

Thrift, N.J. 1999a: Steps to an ecology of place. In D. Massey, J. Allen and P. Sarre, eds,

Human geography today. Cambridge, UK: Polity Press, 295–322.

Thrift, N.J. 1999b: The place of complexity. *Theory, Culture & Society* 16: 31–69.

Thrift, N.J. 2000a: Afterwords. *Environment and Planning D: Society and Space* 18: 213–55.

Thrift, N.J. 2000b: Entanglements of power: shadows. In J.P. Sharp, P. Routledge, C. Philo and R. Paddison, eds, *Entanglements of power: geographies of domination/resistance.* London: Routledge, 269–78.

Thrift, N.J. 2000c: Performing cultures in the new economy. *Annals of the Association of American Geographers* 90: 674–92.

Thrift, N.J. 2000d: With child to see any strange thing: everyday life in the city. In G. Bridge and S. Watson, eds, *A companion to the city.* Oxford: Blackwell, 398–409.

Thrift, N.J. 2002: The future of geography. *Geoforum* 33: 291–8.

Thrift, N.J. 2003: Space: the fundamental stuff of geography. In S. Holloway, S. Rice and G. Valentine, eds, *Key concepts in geography.* London: Sage, 95–108.

Thrift, N.J. 2004a: Intensities of feeling: towards a spatial politics of affect. *Geografiska Annaler* 86B: 57–78.

Thrift, N.J. 2004b: Movement-space: the changing domain of thinking resulting from the development of new kinds of spatial awareness. *Economy and Society* 33: 582–604.

Thrift, N.J. 2004c: Remembering the technological unconscious by foregrounding knowledges of position. *Environment and Planning D: Society and Space* 22: 175–90.

Thrift, N.J. 2005a: From born to made: technology, biology and space. *Transactions of the Institute of British Geographers* 30(4): 463–76.

Thrift, N.J. 2005b: *Knowing capitalism.* London: Sage.

Thrift, N.J. 2006: Space. *Theory, Culture & Society* 23: 139–55.

Thrift, N.J. 2007: Overcome by space: reworking Foucault. In J. Crampton and S. Elden, eds, *Space, knowledge and power: Foucault and geography.* Aldershot: Ashgate, 53–8.

Thrift, N.J. 2008: *Non-representational theory: space, politics, affect.* London: Routledge.

Thrift, N.J. and French, S. 2003: The automatic production of space. *Transactions of the Institute of British Geographers* 27(3): 309–35.

Thrift, N.J. and Olds, K. 1996: Refiguring the economic in economic geography. *Progress in Human Geography* 20: 31–7.

Tickell, A. and Peck, J. 1992: Accumulation, regulation and the geographies of post-Fordism: missing links in regulationist research. *Progress in Human Geography* 16: 190–218.

Tickell, A., Sheppard, E., Peck, J. and Barnes, T.J., eds, 2007: *Politics and practices in economic geography.* London: Sage.

Tiebout, C.M. 1956: A pure theory of local expenditures. *Journal of Political Economy* 64: 416–24.

Tietenberg, T. 2005: *Environmental and natural resource economics,* 7th edn. Boston: Addison Wesley.

Till, K. 1999: Staging the past: landscape designs, cultural identity and *Erinnerungspolitik* at Berlin's *Neue Wach.* *Ecumene* 6: 251–83.

Till, K. 2001: Reimagining national identity: 'Chapter of life' at the German Historical Museum. In P. Adams, S. Hoelscher and K. Till, eds, *Textures of place.* Minneapolis, MN: University of Minnesota Press, 273–99.

Till, K. 2003: Places of memory. In J. Agnew, K. Mitchell and G. Toal, eds, *A companion to political geography.* Oxford: Blackwell, 289–301.

Till, K. 2005: *The new Berlin: memory, politics and place.* Minneapolis MN: University of Minnesota Press.

Tilley, C. 2004: *The materiality of stone: explorations in landscape phenomenology.* Oxford: Berg.

Tilly, C. 1990a: *Coercion, capital and European states, AD 990–1992.* Oxford: Blackwell.

Tilly, C. 1990b: Transplanted networks. In V. Yans-McLaughlin, ed., *Immigration reconsidered: history, sociology and politics.* New York: Oxford University Press, 79–95.

Timar, J. 2003: Lessons from postsocialism: 'What's left for emerging critical geography to do in Hungary?' *Antipode* 35: 24–3.

Timberlake, M., ed., 1985: *Urbanization in the world-economy.* New York: Academic Press.

Timpanaro, S. 1976: *On materialism.* Atlantic Highlands, NJ: Humanities Press.

Tobler, W.R. 1963: Geographic area and map projections. *Geographical Review* 53: 59–78.

Tobler, W.R. 1970: A computer movie simulating urban growth in the Detroit region. *Economic Geography Supplement* 46: 234–40.

Todes, D.P. 1989: *Darwin without Malthus: the struggle for existence in Russian evolutionary thought.* Oxford: Oxford University Press.

Tolia-Kelly, D. 2004: Locating processes of identification: studying the precipitates of re-memory through artefacts in the British Asian home. *Transactions* 29: 314–29.

Tomich, D. 2004: *Through the prism of slavery.* Lanham, MD: Rowman and Littlefield.

Tönnies, F. 2001 [1887]: *Community and civil society (Gemeinschaft und Gesellschaft),* trans. M. Hollis. Cambridge, UK: Cambridge University Press.

Torgerson, C.J. 2003: *Systematic reviews and meta-analysis.* London: Continuum.

Torgovnick, M. 1991: *Gone primitive: savage intellects, modern lives.* Chicago: The University of Chicago Press.

Torpey, J. 2000: *The invention of the passport: surveillance, citizenship and the state.* Cambridge, UK: Cambridge University Press.

Tosh, J. 1999: *A man's place: masculinity and the middle-class home in Victorian England.* Manchester: Manchester University Press.

Totten, S. and Markusen, E. 2006: Special issue on Darfur. *Genocide Studies and Prevention* 1(1).

Toulmin, S. 1990: What is the problem about modernity? In Toulmin, *Cosmopolis: the hidden agenda of modernity.* New York: The Free Press, 5–44.

Toulmin, S.E. 1970: Does the distinction between normal and revolutionary science hold water? In I. Lakatos and A. Musgrave, eds, *Criticism and the growth of knowledge.* Cambridge, UK: Cambridge University Press, 39–48.

Touraine, A. 1971: *The post-industrial society.* New York: Random House.

Townsend, J. and Momsen, J.H. 1987: Towards a geography of gender in developing market economies. In J.H. Momsen and J. Townsend, eds, *Geography of gender in the Third World.* London: Hutchinson, 27–81.

Townsend, J., Porter, G. and Mawdsley, E. 2004: Creating spaces of resistance: development NGOs and their clients in Ghana, India and Mexico. *Antipode* 36: 871–99.

Toye, J.F.J. 1987: *Dilemmas of development: reflections on the counter-revolution in development theory and policy.* Oxford: Blackwell.

Toynbee, A. 1884: *The Industrial Revolution.* London: Rivingtons.

Trewartha, G. 1953: The case for population geography. *Annals of the Association of American Geographers* 43: 71–97.

Trigger, B. 2003: *Understanding early civilizations: a comparative study.* Cambridge: Cambridge University Press.

Tripp, A.M. 1997: *Changing the rules: the politics of liberalization and the urban informal economy in Tanzania.* Berkeley, CA: University of California Press.

Trouillot, M.-R. 1990: *Haiti: state against nation.* New York: Monthly Review Press.

Tsing, A.L. 2004: *Friction: an ethnography of global connection.* Princeton, NJ: Princeton University Press.

Tuan, Y.-F. 1971: Geography, phenomenology, and the study of human nature. *Canadian Geographer* 15: 181–91.

Tuan, Y.-F. 1974: *Topophilia: a study of environmental perception, attitudes and values.* Englewood Cliffs, NJ: Prentice Hall

Tuan, Y.-F. 1976a: Geopiety: a theme in man's attachment to nature and place. In D. Lowenthal, and M. Bowden, eds, *Geographies of the mind: essays in historical geosophy in honor of John Kirkland Wright.* New York: Oxford University Press, 11–39.

Tuan, Y.-F. 1976b: Humanistic geography. *Annals of the Association of American Geographers* 66(2): 266–76.

Tuan, Y.-F. 1977: *Space and place.* London: Edward Arnold/Minneapolis, MN: University of Minnesota Press.

Tuan, Y.-F. 1978: Sign and metaphor. *Annals of the Association of American Geographers* 68: 363–72.

Tuan, Y.-F. 1984: *Dominance and affection: the making of pets.* New Haven, CT: Yale University Press.

Tuan, Y.-F. 1989: *Morality and imagination: paradoxes of progress.* Madison, WI: University of Wisconsin Press.

Tuan, Y.-F. 1996: *Cosmos and hearth: a cosmopolite's viewpoint.* Minneapolis: University of Minnesota Press.

Tuan, Y.-F. 1999: *Who am I? An autobiography of emotion, mind, and spirit.* Madison, WI: University of Wisconsin Press.

Tuan, Y.-F. 2001: *Space and place: the perspective of experience.* Minneapolis: University of Minnesota Press.

Tuastad, D. 2003: Neo-Orientalism and the new barbarism thesis: aspects of symbolic violence in the Middle East conflict(s). *Third World Quarterly* 24: 591–88.

Tuhkanen, T. 1987: Computer-assisted production of hill shading and hypsometric tints. *International Yearbook of Cartography* 27: 225–32.

Turco, R. 1997: *Earth under siege: from air pollution to global change.* Oxford: Oxford University Press.

Turk, A. 1994: Cogent GIS visualizations. In D. Unwin and H. Hearnshaw, eds, *Visualization in Geographic Information Systems.* Rexdale, Ontario: Wiley.

Turner, A. 2006: *Introduction to neogeography.* Sebastopol, CA: O'Reilly.

Turner, B. 1986: *Citizenship and capitalism.* London: George Allen & Unwin.

Turner, B. 1993: *Citizenship and social theory.* London: Sage.

Turner, B.L. II 2002: Contested identities: human–environment geography and disciplinary implications in a restructuring academy. *Annals of the Association of American Geographers* 92: 52–74.

Turner, B.L., Clark, W.C., Kates, R.W., Richards, J.F. and Mathews, J.T., eds, 1990: *The Earth as transformed by human action: global and regional changes in the biosphere over the past 300 years.* Cambridge, UK: Cambridge University Press.

Turner, F.J. 1893: The significance of the frontier in American history. Reprinted in Turner,

F.J. 1920: *The frontier in American history*. New York: Henry Holt, 1–38.

Turner, K. 1991: Economics and wetland management. *Ambio* 20: 59–63.

Turner, M.E., Beckett, J.V. and Afton, B. 2001: *Farm production in England 1700–1914*. Cambridge, UK: Cambridge University Press.

Turner, R.K. 2007: Limits to CBA in UK and European environmental policy: retrospects and future prospects. *Environmental and Resource Economics* 37: 253–69.

Turner, R.K., Adger, N. and Doktor, P. 1995: Assessing the economic cost of sea level rise. *Environment and Planning A* 27: 1777–96.

Tyner, J.A. 1982: Persuasive cartography. *Journal of Geography* 81: 140–4.

Tyner, J.A. 2008: *The killing of Cambodia: geography, genocide and the unmaking of space*. Aldershot: Ashgate.

Ullman, E.L. 1956: The role of transportation and the bases for interaction. In W.L. Thomas, ed., *Man's role in changing the face of the Earth*. Chicago: The University of Chicago Press, 862–80.

Ullman, E.L. 1980: *Geography as spatial interaction*. Seattle: University of Washington Press.

Underhill-Sem, Y. 2001: Maternities in 'out-of-the-way' places: epistemological possibilities for retheorising population geography. *International Journal of Population Geography* 7: 447–60.

Underkuffler, L.S. 2003: *The idea of property: its meaning and power*. Oxford: Oxford University Press.

United Church of Christ 1987: *Toxic wastes and race in the United States: a national report on the racial and socio-economic characteristics with hazardous waste sites*. New York: United Church of Christ, Commission for Racial Justice.

United Nations 1983: *The law of the sea. Official Text of the United Nations Convention on the Law of the Sea with Annexes and Index; Final Act of the Third United Nations Conference on the Law of the Sea*. New York: United Nations.

United Nations 2005: Global trends: Asia; available at http://www.unhabitat.org/habrdd/asia.html

United Nations 2006: *World drug report 2006*. New York: United Nations.

United Nations n.d.: International Covenant on Civil and Political Rights; available at http://www.unhchr.ch/html/menu3/b/a_ccpr.htm

United Nations Convention to Combat Desertification 1994, available at http://www.unccd.int/main.php

United Nations Development Programme [UNDP] 1994: *Human development report 1994*. New York: UNDP.

United Nations Development Programme [UNDP] 1996: *Human development report 1996*. New York: Oxford University Press.

United Nations Development Programme [UNDP] 2005: *Human development report 2005*. New York: UNDP.

United Nations Development Programme [UNDP] 2006: *Human development report 2006*. Oxford: Oxford University Press.

United Nations Environment Programme [UNEP] 1992: *Convention on biological diversity*. Montreal: UNEP.

United Nations Environment Programme [UNEP] 2006: *Seychelles – post Tsunami environmental assessment*; available at www.unep.org/tsunami.

United Nations High Commissioner for Refugees [UNHCR] 2006: *The state of the world's refugees: human displacement in the new millennium*; available at http://www.unhcr.org/cgibin/texis/vtx/template?page=publ&src=static/sowr2006/toceng.htm

United Nations World Tourism Organisation [UNWTO] 1994: *Recommendations on tourism statistics*. Statistical Papers, series M, No. 83.

United States Committee for Refugees and Immigrants [USCRI] 2008: *World refugee survey 2007*. Washington, DC: USCRI.

Unwin, T. 1992: *The place of geography*. London: Longman.

Urban Studies 2001: Special issue on urban neighbourhoods. *Urban Studies* 38: 2103–16.

Urry, J. 1981: *The anatomy of capitalist societies: the economy, civil society, and the state*. London: Macmillan/Atlantic Highlands.

Urry, J. 2002 [1990]: *The tourist gaze: leisure and travel in contemporary societies*, 2nd edn. London: Sage.

Urry, J. 2003: *Global complexity*. Oxford: Polity Press.

US Census Bureau n.d.: IDB population pyramids. Available at http://www.census.gov/ipc/www/idbpyr.html

Uvin, P. 1998: *Aiding violence: the development enterprise in Rwanda*. West Hartford, CT: Kumarian Press.

Valdivia, G. 2005: On indigeneity, change and representation in the northeastern Ecuadorian Amazon. *Environment and Planning A* 37(2): 285–303.

Valega, A. 1992: *Sea management: a theoretical approach*. Essex: Elsevier Science.

Valega, A. 2001: *Sustainable ocean governance: a geographical perspective*. London: Routledge.

Valentine, G. 1993: (Hetero)sexing space: lesbian perceptions and experiences of everyday spaces. *Environment and Planning D: Society and Space* 11: 395–413.

Valentine, G. 1997: 'Oh yes I can.' 'Oh no you can't.': children and parents' understandings of kids' competence to negotiate public space safely. *Antipode* 29(1): 65–90.

Valentine, G. 1998: 'Sticks and stones may break my bones': a personal geography of harassment. *Antipode* 30: 305–32.

Valentine, G. 1999: Eating in: home, consumption and identity *Sociological Review* 47: 491–524.

Valentine, G. 2001: *Social geography: space and society*. London: Prentice-Hall.

Valentine, G. 2004: *Public space and the culture of childhood*. Aldershot: Ashgate.

Valentine, G. 2005: Tell me about … using interviews as a research methodology In R. Flowerdew and D. Martin, eds, *Methods in human geography: a guide for students doing a research project*, 2nd edn. London: Pearson Education, 110–27.

Van Cott, D.L. 2000: *The friendly liquidation of the past: the politics of diversity in Latin America*. Pittsburgh: University of Pittsburgh Press.

Van Creveld, M.L. 1999: *The rise and decline of the state*. Cambridge, UK: Cambridge University Press.

Van de Kaa, D.J. 1987: Europe's second demographic transition. *Population Bulletin* 42: 1–57.

Van den Berghe, P. 1981: *The ethnic phenomenon*. New York: Elsevier.

van der Leeuw, G. 1986 [1933]: *Religion in Essence and Manifestation*, Princeton, NJ: Princeton University Press.

van der Ploeg, J.D. 1985: Patterns of farming logic: the structuration of labour and the impact of externalization. *Sociologia Ruralis* XXV(1): 5–25.

van Dijk, T.A., ed., 1997: *Discourse as structure and process*. London: Sage.

Van Hear, N. 1998: *New diasporas: the mass exodus, dispersal and regrouping of migrant communities*. Seattle: University of Washington Press.

Van Houtum, H. 2005: The geopolitics of borders and boundaries. *Geopolitics* 10: 672–9.

van Houtum, H., Kramsch O. and Ziefhofer, W., eds, 2005: *B/Ordering space*. Burlington, VT: Ashgate.

van Hoven, B. 2003: *Europe: lives in transition*. London: Pearson/Prentice Hall.

van Paassen, C. 1957: *The classical tradition of geography*. Groningen: J.B. Walters.

Van Valey, T.L. and Roof, W.C. 1976: Measuring residential segregation in American cities: problems of intercity comparison. *Urban Affairs Quarterly* 11: 453–68.

Van Wissen, L.J.G. and Dykstra, P.A., eds, 1999: *Population issues: an interdisciplinary focus*. New York: Kluwer.

Vance, J.E. 1990: *The continuing city: urban morphology in western civilization*. Baltimore, MD: The Johns Hopkins University Press.

Vance, J.E. Jr 1970: *The merchant's world: the geography of wholesaling*. Englewood Cliffs, NJ: Prentice-Hall.

Vanderbeck, R. 2006: Vermont and the imaginative geographies of American whiteness. *Annals of the Association of American Geographers* 96: 641–59.

Varian, H.R. 2005: Copying and copyright. *Journal of Economic Perspectives* 19(2): 121–38.

Varley, A. 2002: Private or public: debating the meaning of tenure legislation. *International Journal of Urban and Regional Research* 26: 449–61.

Varsanyi, M. 2005: The rise and fall (and rise?) of noncitizen voting: immigration and the shifting scales of citizenship and suffrage in the United States. *Space and Polity* 9: 1–22.

Vasishth, A. and Sloane, D. 2002: Returning to ecology: an ecosystem approach to understanding the city. In M. Dear, ed., *From Chicago to L.A.: making sense of urban theory*. Thousand Oaks, CA: Sage, 347–66.

Vasta, E. 2005: *From ethnic minorities to ethnic majority policy: changing identities and the shift to assimilationism in the Netherlands*. Oxford: COMPAS Working Paper #26.

Vasudevan, A. McFarlane, C. and Jeffrey, A. 2008. Spaces of enclosure. *Geoforum* 39: 1641–6.

Veblen, T. 1899: *A theory of the leisure class: an economic study in the evolution of institutions*. New York: Macmillan (now available in the public domain via Project Gutenberg).

Veblen, T. 1919: *The place of science in modern civilisation and other essays*. New York: B.W. Huebsch.

Venn, C. and Featherstone, M. 2006: Modernity. *Theory, Culture & Society* 23(2/3): 457–65.

Venturi, R., Scott Brown, D. and Izenor, S. 1972: *Learning from Las Vegas: the forgotten symbolism of architectural form*. Cambridge. MA: The MIT Press.

Verdery, K. 1996: *What was socialism and what comes next?* Princeton, NJ: Princeton University Press.

Verdery, K. and Humphrey, C., eds, 2004: *Property in question: value transformation in the global economy*. Oxford: Berg.

Verhulst, A. 1989: The origin of towns in the Low Countries and the Pirenne thesis. *Past & Present* 122: 3–35.

Vernon, R. 1966: International investment and international trade in the product cycle. *Quarterly Journal of Economics* 80: 190–207.

Vertovec, S. 1993: Conceiving and researching transnationalism. *Ethnic and Racial Studies* 22: 447–62.

Veseth, M. 2005: *Globaloney: unraveling the myths of globalization*. Lanham, MD: Rowman & Littlefield.

Vidal de la Blache, P. 1903: *Tableau de la géographie de la France*. Paris: Hachette.

Vidal de la Blache, P. 1911: Les genres de vie dans la géographie humaine. *Annales de Géographie* 20: 193–212.

Vidal de la Blache, P. 1917: *La France de l'est (Lorraine-Alsace)*. Paris: A. Colin.

Vidal de la Blache, P. 1926: *Principles of human geography*, trans. M.T. Bingham; ed. E. de Martonne. New York: Henry Holt.

Viles, H. 2005: A divided discipline? In N. Castree, A. Rogers and D. Sherman, eds, *Questioning geography: fundamental debates*. Oxford: Blackwell, 26–38.

Villa, R.H. 2000: *Barrio-logos: space and place in urban Chicano literature and culture*. Austin: University of Texas Press.

Vincent, J.A. 1999: *Politics, power and old age*. Buckingham: Open University Press.

Viola, L. 1996: *Peasant rebels under Stalin: collectivization and the culture of peasant resistance*. Oxford: Oxford University Press.

Visweswaran, K. 1994: Betrayal. In Visweswaran, *Fictions of feminist ethnography*. Minnesota: University of Minnesota Press, 40–59.

Vitalis, R. 2002: Black gold, white crude: an essay on American exceptionalism, hierarchy and hegemony in the Gulf. *Diplomatic History* 26(2): 23–49.

Voas, D. and Williamson, P. 2001: The diversity of diversity: a critique of geodemographic classification. *Area* 33: 63–76.

Vogel, U. 1994: Marriage and the boundaries of citizenship. In B. van Steenbergen, ed., *The condition of citizenship*. London: Sage.

von Bertalanffy, L. 1968: *General systems theory: foundation, development, applications*. New York: G. Berziller/London: Allen Lane.

von Braun, J., Serova, E., tho Seeth, H. and Melyukhina, O. 1996: *Russia's food economy in transition*. Washington, DC: IFPRI Discussion Paper #18.

von Neumann, J. and Morgenstern, O. 1944: *Theory of games and economic behavior*. Princeton, NJ: Princeton University Press.

von Thünen, J. 1966 [1842]: *Isolated state: an English translation of Der isolierte Staat*, trans. C.M. Wartenberg, ed. with intro. by P.G. Hall. Oxford: Pergamon Press (first volume originally published in 1826).

von Weizsacker, E., Lovins, A. and Lovins, L.H. 1997: *Factor 4: doubling wealth – halving resource use*. London: Earthscan.

Vujakovic, P. 1999: 'A new map is unrolling before us': cartography in news media representations of post-Cold War Europe. *Cartographic Journal* 36: 43–57.

Vujakovic, P. and Matthews, M.H. 1994: Contorted, folded, torn: environmental values, cartographic representation and the politics of disability. *Disability and Society* 9: 359–74.

Wachter, K.W. 2005: Spatial demography. *Proceedings of the National Academy of Sciences of the United States of America* 102(43): 15,299–300.

Wacquant, L. 2001: Deadly symbiosis: when ghetto and prison meet and mesh. *Punishment and Society* 3: 95–134.

Wade, R. 1987: *Village republics: economic conditions for collective action*. Cambridge, UK: Cambridge University Press.

Wade, R. 1996: Japan, the World Bank, and the art of paradigm maintenance: the *East Asian Miracle* in political perspective. *New Left Review* 217: 3–36.

Wade, R. 2004: Is globalization reducing poverty and inequality? *World Development* 32: 567–89.

Wagner, P.L. and Mikesell, M.W., eds, 1962: *Readings in cultural geography*. Chicago: The University of Chicago Press.

Walby, S. 1989: Theorising patriarchy. *Sociology* 23: 213–34.

Walby, S. 1994: Is citizenship gendered? *Sociology* 28(2): 379–95.

Waldinger, R. and Feliciano, C. 2004: Will the new second generation experience 'downward assimilation'? Segmented assimilation reassessed. *Ethnic and Racial Studies* 27: 376–402.

Waldorf, B. 2003: Spatial patterns and processes in a longitudinal framework. *International Regional Science Review* 26: 269–88.

Waldorf, B. and Franklin, R. 2002: Spatial dimensions of the Easterlin hypothesis: fertility variations in Italy. *Journal of Regional Science* 42: 549–78.

Walford, R. 2001: *Geography in British schools, 1850–2000: making a world of difference*. London: Woburn Press.

Walker, G., Mitchell, G., Fairburn, J. and Smith, G. 2005: Industrial pollution and social deprivation: evidence and complexity in evaluating and responding to environmental inequality. *Local Environment* 10(4): 361–77.

Walker, R. 1995: Regulation and flexible specialization as theories of capitalist development. Challengers to Marx and Schumpeter? In H. Liggett and D. Perry, eds, *Spatial practices: critical explorations in social/spatial theory*. London: Sage, 167–208.

Walker, R. 1997: California rages: regional capitalism and the politics of renewal. In R. Lee and J. Wills, eds, *Geographies of economies*. London: Arnold, 345–56.

Walker, R. 2001: California's golden road to riches: natural resources and regional capitalism, 1848–1940. *Annals of the Association of American Geographers* 91: 167–99.

Walker, R. 2005: *The conquest of bread*. Boston: The Free Press.

Walker, R. and McDowell, L. 1993: Editorial. *Antipode* 25: 1–3.

Walker, R.A. 1981: A theory of suburbanization: capitalism and the construction of urban space in the United States. In M. Dear and A.J. Scott, eds, *Urbanization and urban planning in capitalist society*. London: Methuen, 383–429.

Walker, R.B.J. 1993: *Inside/outside: international relations as political theory*. Cambridge, UK: Cambridge University Press.

Walks, R.A. 2001: The social ecology of the post-Fordist/global city? Economic restructuring and socio-spatial polarisation in the Toronto urban region. *Urban Studies* 38: 407–47.

Wallach, L. and Woodall, P. 2004: *Whose trade organization: A comprehensive guide to the WTO*. New York: The New Press.

Wallerstein, I. 1974: *The modern world-system. Vol. 1: Capitalist agriculture and the origins of the European world-economy in the sixteenth century*. New York: Academic Press.

Wallerstein, I. 1979: *The capitalist world-economy: essays by Immanuel Wallerstein*. Cambridge, UK: Cambridge University Press.

Wallerstein, I. 1984: *The politics of the world-economy*. Cambridge, UK: Cambridge University Press.

Wallerstein, I. 1991a: *Geopolitics and geoculture*. Cambridge, UK: Cambridge University Press.

Wallerstein, I. 1991b: *Unthinking social science: the limits of nineteenth century paradigms*. Cambridge, UK: Polity Press.

Wallerstein, I. 2004: *World-systems analysis: an introduction*. Durham, NC: Duke University Press.

Wallerstein, I., Juma, C., Keller, E., Kocka, J., Lecourt, D., Mudimbe, V.Y., Mushakoji, K., Prigogine, I., Taylor, P.J. and Trouillot, M. 1996: *Open the social sciences: report of the Gulbenkian Commission on the restructuring of the social sciences*. Stanford, CA: Stanford University Press.

Walmsley, D. and Lewis, G. 1993: *People and environment: behavioural approaches in human geography*. London: Longman.

Walsh, K. 1995: *Public services and market mechanisms: competition, contracting and the new public management*. London: Macmillan.

Walters, C., Korman, J., Stevens, L.E. and Gold, B. 2000: Ecosystem modeling for evaluation of adaptive management policies in the Grand Canyon. *Conservation Ecology* 4(2): 1 [online] http://www.consecol.org/vol4/iss2/art1/

Walters, C.J. and Holling, C.S. 1990: Large-scale management experiments and learning by doing. *Ecology* 71(6): 2060–8.

Walters, W. 2002: Mapping Schengenland: depoliticizing the border. *Environment and Planning D: Society and Space* 20: 561–80.

Walters, W.P. and Larner, W. 2004: *Global governmentality: governing international spaces*. London: Routledge.

Walton-Roberts, M. and Pratt, G. 2005: Mobile modernities: a South Asian family negotiates immigration, gender and class in Canada. *Gender, Place and Culture: a Journal of Feminist Geography* 12(2): 173–95.

Walzer, M. 1984: Liberalism and the art of separation. *Political Theory* 12: 315–30.

Walzer, M. 2000: *Just and unjust wars: a moral argument with historical illustrations*. New York: Basic Books.

Walzer, N. and Jacobs, B.D., eds, 1998: *Public–private partnerships for local, economic development*. Westport, CT: Praeger.

Wanklyn, H. 1961: *Friedrich Ratzel: biographical memoir and bibliography*. Cambridge, UK: Cambridge University Press.

Ward, D. 1971: *Cities and immigrants: a geography of change in nineteenth-century America*. New York: Oxford University Press.

Ward, D. 1976: The Victorian slum: an enduring myth? *Annals of the Association of American Geographers* 66: 323–64.

Ward, D. 1989: *Poverty, ethnicity, and the American city, 1840–1925: changing conceptions of the slum and the ghetto*. New York: Cambridge University Press.

Ward, K. 1996: Rereading urban regime theory: a sympathetic critique. *Geoforum* 27: 427–38.

Ward, K. 2005a: Geography and public policy: a recent history of 'policy relevance'. *Progress in Human Geography* 29(3): 310–19.

Ward, K. 2005b: Making Manchester 'flexible': competition and change in the temporary staffing industry. *Geoforum* 36: 223–40.

Ward, K. 2006: Geography and public policy: towards public geographies. *Progress in Human Geography* 30(4): 495–503.

Ward, K. 2007: 'Public intellectuals', geography, its representations and its publics. *Geoforum* 38: 1058–64.

Ware, V. and Back, L. 2002: *Out of whiteness: color, politics, and culture*. Chicago: The University of Chicago Press.

Warf, B. and Arias, S., eds, 2008: *The spatial turn: interdisciplinary perspectives*. New York: Routledge.

Wark, M. 1994: *Virtual geography: living with global media events*. Bloomington: Indiana University Press.

Warnes, A.M. 1990: Geographical questions in gerontology: needed directions for research, *Progress in Human Geography* 14: 24–56.

Warntz, W. 1965: *Macrogeography and income fronts*. Philadelphia, PA: Regional Science Research Institute.

Warren, L.S., ed., 2003: *American environmental history*. Malden, MA: Blackwell.

Warren, S. 1994: Disneyfication of the metropolis: popular resistance in Seattle. *Journal of Urban Affairs* 16: 89–107.

Warren, S. 2004: The utopian potential of GIS. *Cartographica* 39(1): 5–16.

Wascher, D.M., ed., 2005: *European Landscape Character Areas: typologies, cartography and indicators for the assessment of sustainable landscapes*. Wageningen: Landscape Europe.

Watkins, J.W.N. 1957: Historical explanation in the social sciences. *British Journal for the Philosophy of Science* 8: 104–17.

Watson, J. 1969: *The double helix.* New York: Mentor.

Watson, J., ed., 1997: *Golden arches east: McDonald's in East Asia.* Stanford, CA: Stanford University Press.

Watson, J.W. 1955: Geography: a discipline in distance. *Scottish Geographical Magazine* 71: 1–13.

Watson, J.W. 1957: The sociological aspects of geography. In G. Taylor, ed., *Geography in the twentieth century.* London: Methuen, 463–99.

Watson, N. 2004: The dialectic of disability: a social model for the 21st century. In C. Barnes and G. Mercer, eds, *Implementing the social model of disability: theory and research.* Leeds: Disability Press, 101–17.

Watson, S. 1998: The new Bergsonism. *Radical Philosophy* 92: 1–23.

Watts, I. 1725: *Logick: or the right use of reason in the enquiry after truth.* London: printed for John Clark and Richard Hett, Emanuel Matthews and Richard Ford.

Watts, M.J. 1983a: *Silent violence: food, famine, and peasantry in northern Nigeria.* Berkeley, CA: University of California Press.

Watts, M.J. 1983b: The poverty of theory. In K. Hewitt, ed., *Interpretations of calamity.* London: George Allen & Unwin, 231–63.

Watts, M.J. 1986: Drought, environment and food security. In M. Glantz, ed., *Drought and hunger in Africa.* Cambridge, UK: Cambridge University Press, 171–212.

Watts, M.J. 1991: Mapping meaning, denoting difference, imagining identity: dialectical images and postmodern geographies. *Geografiska Annaler* 73B: 7–16.

Watts, M.J. 1992: The shock of modernity: petroleum, protest, and fast capitalism in an industrializing society. In A. Pred and M.J. Watts, eds., *Reworking modernity: capitalisms and symbolic discontent.* New Brunswick, NJ: Rutgers University Press, 21–63.

Watts, M.J. 1994a: Living under contract: contract farming, agricultural restructuring and flexible accumulation. In P. Little and M. Watts, eds, *Living under contract: contract farming and agrarian transformation of sub-Saharan Africa.* Madison, WI: University of Wisconsin Press, 21–77.

Watts, M.J. 1994b: Oil as money: the devil's excrement and the spectacle of black gold. In S. Corbridge, R.L. Martin and N.J. Thrift, eds, *Money, power and space.* Oxford: Blackwell, 406–45.

Watts, M.J. 1995: A new deal for the emotions. In J. Crush, ed., *Power of development.* London: Routledge, 44–62.

Watts, M.J. 1999: Collective wish images: geographical imaginaries and the crisis of national development. In D. Massey, J. Allen and P. Sarre, eds, *Human geography today.* Cambridge UK: Polity Press, 85–107.

Watts, M.J. 2001: 1968 and all that. *Progress in Human Geography* 25: 157–88.

Watts, M.J. 2003: Development and governmentality. *Singapore Journal of Tropical Geography* 24: 6–34.

Watts, M.J. 2004: Resource curse? Oil, violence and governmentality in the Niger Delta. *Geopolitics* 9(1): 50–80.

Watts, M.J. 2005: Righteous oil? *Annual Review of Environment and Resources* 30: 1–35.

Watts, M.J. 2006: The sinister political life of community: economies of violence and governable spaces in the Niger delta, Nigeria. In G.W. Creed, ed., *The seductions of community emancipations, oppressions, quandaries.* Santa Fe, NM: SAR Press.

Watts, M.J. 2007: Revolutionary Islam: a geography of modern terror. In D. Gregory and A. Pred, eds, *Violent geographies: fear, terror and political violence.* London and New York: Routledge: 175–203.

Waxman, Z. 2006: *Writing the Holocaust: identity, testimony, representation.* Oxford: Oxford University Press.

Webber, M.J. 2001: Finance and the real economy: theoretical implications of the financial crisis in Asia. *Geoforum* 32(1): 1–13.

Webber, M.J. 1972: *The impact of uncertainty on location.* Cambridge, MA: The MIT Press.

Webber, M.J. and Rigby, D.L. 1996: *The golden age illusion: rethinking postwar capitalism.* New York: Guilford Press.

Weber, M. 1949: 'Objectivity' in social science and social policy. In *The methodology of the social sciences,* trans. E.A. Shils and H.A. Finch. Glencoe, IL: The Free Press.

Weber, M. 1958 [1921]: *The city.* New York: The Free Press.

Weber, M. 1968 [1946]: Class, status, party. In *From Max Weber: essays in sociology,* trans. H.H. Gerth and C. Wright Mills. New York: Oxford University Press.

Weber, M. 1978 [1922]: *Economy and society,* ed. G. Roth and C. Wittich. Berkeley, CA: University of California Press.

Weber, M. 2001 [1904–5]: *The Protestant ethic and the spirit of capitalism,* trans. Talcott Parsons. London: Routledge.

Weber, R. 2002: Extracting value from the city: neoliberalism and urban redevelopment. In N. Brenner and N. Theodore, eds, *Spaces of neoliberalism.* Malden, MA: Blackwell, 172–93.

Webster, C., Glasze, G. and Frantz, K., eds, 2002: Theme issue: the global spread of gated communities. *Environment and Planning B: Planning and Design* 29(3): 315–412.

Weeks, J.R. 1999: *Population: an introduction to concepts and issues.* London: Wadsworth.

Weibel, R. 1991: Amplified intelligence and rule-based systems. In B. Buttenfield and R. McMaster, eds, *Map generalization*. London: Longman Scientific and Technical, 172–86.

Weightman, B. 2006: *Dragons and tigers: a geography of South, East and Southeast Asia*. Chichester: Wiley.

Weiner, D.R. 2005: A death-defying attempt to articulate a coherent definition of environmental history. *Environmental History* 10(3): 404–20.

Weiner, M. 1995: *The global migration crisis*. New York: HarperCollins.

Weiner, M. 1996: Ethics, national sovereignty and the control of migration. *International Migration Review* 30: 171–97.

Weiss, M. 2000: *The clustered world: how we live, what we buy, and what it all means about who we are*. New York: Little, Brown.

Weizman, E. 2002: The politics of verticality. Open Democracy, April/May at http//www.openDemocracy.net and in K. Biesenbach, A. Franke, R. Segal and E. Weizman, eds, 2003: *Territories: islands, camps and other states of utopia*. Berlin: KW-Institute for Contemporary Art, 65–118.

Weizman, E. 2004: Strategic points, flexible lines, tense surfaces, political volumes: Ariel Sharon and the geometry of occupation. *The Philosophical Forum* 35: 221–44.

Weizman, E. 2007: *Hollow land: Israel's architecture of occupation*. London: Verso.

Wekerle, G. and Whitzman, C. 1995: *Safe cities: guidelines for planning, design, and management*. New York: Van Nostrand Reinhold.

Wells, M. 1984: The resurgence of sharecropping: historical anomaly or political strategy? *American Journal of Sociology* 90(1): 1–29.

Wells, M. 1996: *Strawberry fields: politics, class and work in California agriculture*. Ithaca, NY: Cornell University Press.

Werlen, B. 1993 [1988]: *Society, action and space: an alternative human geography*. London: Routledge.

West, L. 1992: Feminist nationalist social movements: beyond universalism and towards a gendered cultural relativism. *Women's Studies International Forum* 15: 563–79.

Westcoat, J. 1992: Common themes in the work of Gilbert White and John Dewey: a pragmatic appraisal. *Annals of the Association of American Geographers* 82: 587–607.

Western, J. 1992: *A passage to England*. Minneapolis: University of Minnesota Press.

Wettenhall, R. 2003: The reality of public–private partnerships. *Public Organization Review* 3: 77–107.

Whatmore, S. 1991: *Farming women: gender, work and family enterprise*. London: Macmillan.

Whatmore, S. 1997: Dissecting the autonomous self: hybrid cartographies for a relational ethics. *Environment and Planning D: Society and Space* 15: 37–54.

Whatmore, S. 1999a: Geography's place in the life-science era? *Transactions of the Institute of British Geographers* 24(3): 259–60.

Whatmore, S. 1999b: Hybrid geographies: rethinking the 'human' in human geography. In D. Massey, J. Allen and P. Sarre, eds, *Human geography today*. Cambridge, UK: Polity Press, 22–39.

Whatmore, S. 2002a: From farming to agribusiness: the global agro-food system. In R.J. Johnston, P. Taylor and M. Watts, eds, *Geographies of global change*, 2nd edn. Oxford: Blackwell, 57–67.

Whatmore, S. 2002b: *Hybrid geographies: natures, cultures, spaces*. London: Sage.

Whatmore, S. 2002c: Unsettling Australia: wormholes in territorial governance. In Whatmore, *Hybrid geographies: natures, cultures, spaces*. London: Sage, 63–90.

Whatmore, S. 2003: Generating materials. In M. Pryke, G. Rose and S. Whatmore, eds, *Using social theory*. London: Sage, 89–104.

Whatmore, S. 2004: Humanism's excess: some thoughts on the post-human/ist agenda. *Environment and Planning A* 36: 1360–3.

Whatmore, S., Munton, R., Little, J. and Mardsen, T. 1987: Towards a typology of farm businesses in contemporary British agriculture. *Sociologia Ruralis* 28(1): 21–37.

Whatmore, S., Stassart, P. and Renting, H. 2003: What's alternative about alternative food networks? *Environment and Planning A* 35(3): 389–91.

Whatmore, S. and Thorne, L. 1997: Nourishing networks: alternative geographies of food. In D. Goodman and M.J. Watts, eds, *Globalising food: agrarian questions and global restructuring*. London: Routledge: 287–304.

Wheare, K.C. 1963: *Federal government*, 4th edn. London: Oxford University Press.

Wheatley, P. 1963: 'What the greatness of the city is said to be': reflections on Sjoberg's preindustrial city. *Pacific Viewpoint* 4(2): 1633–89.

Wheatley, P. 1971: *The pivot of the four quarters: a preliminary enquiry into the origins and character of the Ancient Chinese city*. Edinburgh: Edinburgh University Press/ Chicago: Aldine.

Wheatley, P. 1972: Proleptic observations on the origins of urbanism. In R.W. Steel and R. Lawton, eds, *Liverpool essays in geography*. London: Longman, 315–45.

Wheeler, J.O. 2002: Assessing the role of spatial analysis in urban geography in the 1960s. *Urban Geography* 22: 549–58.

Wheeler, J.O., Aoyama, Y. and Warf, B. 2000: *Cities in the telecommunications age: the fracturing of geographies*. New York: Routledge.

Whelan, Y. 2003: *Reinventing modern Dublin: streetscape, iconography and the politics of identity*. Dublin: University College Dublin Press.

Whitbeck, R.H. 1915–16: Economic geography: its growth and possibilities. *Journal of Geography* 14: 284–96.

White, G., Kates, R. and Burton, I. 2001: Knowing better and losing even more: the use of knowledge in hazards management. *Environmental Hazards* 3: 81–92.

White, H. 1978: *Tropics of discourse*. Baltimore, MD: The Johns Hopkins University Press.

White, P. and Jackson, P. 1995: (Re)theorising population geography. *International Journal of Population Geography* 1: 111–23.

White, R. 1980: *Land use, environment, and social change: the shaping of Island County, Washington*. Seattle: University of Washington Press.

White, R. 1985: Environmental history: the development of a new historical field. *Pacific Historical Review* 54: 297–335.

White, R. 1995: *The organic machine: the remaking of the Columbia River*. New York: Hill and Wang.

White, S. 2000: *Sustaining affirmation: the strengths of weak ontology in political theory*. Princeton, NJ: Princeton University Press.

Whitehand, J. 1987: *The changing face of cities: a study of development cycles and urban form*. Oxford: Blackwell.

Whitehand, J.W.R. 1992: *The making of the urban landscape*. Oxford: Blackwell.

Whitehand, J.W.R. 2001: British urban morphology: the Conzenian tradition. *Urban Morphology* 5: 103–9.

Whitehead, A.N. 1929: *Process and reality: an essay in cosmology*. Cambridge, UK: Cambridge University Press.

Whittlesey, D.W. 1929: Sequent occupance. *Annals of the Association of American Geographers* 19: 162–5.

Whyte, W.F. 1943: *Street corner society: the social structure of an Italian slum*. Chicago: the University of Chicago Press.

Wiegand, P. 2002: Analysis of discourse in collaborative cartographic problem solving. *International Research in Geographical and Environmental Education* 11: 138–58.

Wiener, N. 1948: *Cybernetics: or control and communication in the animal and the machine*. Paris: Hermann.

Wilcox, M. and Rines, G. 1917: *Encyclopedia of Latin America*. New York: Encyclopedia Americana Corp.

Wilden, A. 1972: *System and structure*. London: Tavistock.

Willems-Braun, B. 1997: Buried epistemologies: the politics of nature in (post)colonial British Columbia. *Annals of the Association of American Geographers* 87(1): 3–31.

Williams, C.C. 1996: Local exchange and trading systems: a new source of work and credit for the poor and unemployed? *Environment and Planning A* 28(8): 1395–415.

Williams, C.C. 2005a: *A commodified world: mapping the limits of capitalism*. London: Zed Books.

Williams, C.C., Aldridge, T., Lee, R., Leyshon, A., Thrift, N. and Tooke, J. 2001: *Bridges into work? An evaluation of Local Exchange and Trading Schemes (LETS)*. *Policy Studies* 22: 119–32.

Williams, J. 2001: Achieving local sustainability in rural communities. In A. Layard, S. Davoudi and S. Batty, eds, *Planning for a sustainable future*. London: E.&F.N. Spon, 235–52.

Williams, M. 1989: *Americans and their forests: a historical geography*. Cambridge, UK: Cambridge University Press.

Williams, M. 1994a: The relations of environmental history and historical geography. *Journal of Historical Geography* 20: 3–21.

Williams, P. and Hubbard, P. 2001: Who's disadvantaged? Retail change and social exclusion. *International Review of Consumption, Distribution and Retail* 11: 1–20.

Williams, R. 1973: *The country and the city*. New York: Oxford University Press.

Williams, R. 1977: *Marxism and literature*. Oxford: Oxford University Press.

Williams, R. 1981: *Culture*. London: Fontana.

Williams, R. 1983 [1976]: *Keywords: a vocabulary of culture and society*. London: Fontana.

Williams, R. 1985: *The country and the city*. London: Chatto & Windus.

Williams, R. 2005b [1980]: Problems of materialism. In Williams, *Culture and materialism*. London: Verso, 103–24.

Williams, R.M. 1994b: Consenting to whiteness: reflections on race and marxian theories of discrimination. In A. Callari, S. Cullenberg and C. Biewener, eds, *Marxism in the postmodern age: confronting the new world order*. New York: Guilford Press.

Williams, W.A. 1980: *Empire as a way of life: an essay on the causes and character of America's present predicament, along with a few thoughts about an alternative*. New York: Oxford University Press.

Williamson, J.G. 1966: Regional inequality and the process of national development: a description of the patterns. *Economic Development and Cultural Change* 13: 3–45.

Williamson, O.E. 1975: *Markets and hierarchies*. New York: The Free Press.

Williamson, O.E. 1985: *The economic institutions of capitalism*. New York: The Free Press.

Williamson, T. 2002: *The transformation of rural England: farming and the landscape: 1700–1870*. Exeter: University of Exeter Press.

Willis, P. and Trondman, M. 2000: Manifesto for ethnography. *Ethnography* 1: 5–16.

Wills, J. 2002: Political economy III: neo-liberal chickens, Seattle and geography. *Progress in Human Geography* 26(1): 90–100.

Wilson, A. 1992: *The culture of nature*. Oxford: Blackwell.

Wilson, A.G. 1967: A statistical theory of spatial distribution models. *Transportation Research* 1: 253–69.

Wilson, A.G. 1970: *Entropy in urban and regional modelling*. London: Pion.

Wilson, A.G. 1972: Theoretical geography: some speculations. *Transactions of the Institute of British Geographers* 52: 31–44.

Wilson, A.G. 1981: *Catastrophe theory and bifurcation: applications to urban and regional systems*. London: Croom Helm.

Wilson, A.G. 2000: *Complex spatial systems: the modelling foundations of urban and regional analysis*. Chichester: Wiley.

Wilson, A.G. and Bennett, R.J. 1985: *Mathematical methods in human geography and planning*. Chichester: Wiley.

Wilson, C. 1982: *Marital fertility in pre-industrial England*. Unpublished PhD thesis, University of Cambridge.

Wilson, C. and Groth, P. 2003: *Everyday America: cultural landscape studies after J.B. Jackson*. Berkeley, CA: University of California Press.

Wilson, D. and Grammenos, D. 2005: Gentrification, discourse, and the body: Chicago's Humboldt Park. *Environment and Planning D: Society and Space* 23: 295–312.

Wilson, E. 1991: The invisible *flâneur*. *New Left Review* 191: 90–110.

Wilson, J. and Kelling, G. 1982: The police and neighborhood safety. *Atlantic Monthly*, March: 29–38.

Wilson, J.F. and Popp, A., eds, 2003: *Industrial clusters and regional business networks in England, 1750–1970*. Aldershot: Ashgate.

Wilson, K. and van den Dussen, J., eds, 1993: *The history of the idea of Europe*. Milton Keynes: Open University Press.

Wilson, T. and Rees, P. 2005: Recent developments in population projection methodology: a review. *Population, Space and Place* 11: 337–60.

Wilson, W.J. 1987: *The truly disadvantaged: the inner city, the underclass, and public policy*. Chicago: The University of Chicago Press.

Wilton, R. 2003: Locating physical disability in Freudian and Lacanian psychoanalysis: problems and prospects. *Social and Cultural Geography* 4: 369–89.

Winch, D. 1998: *Riches and poverty: an intellectual history of political economy in Britain 1750–1834*. Cambridge, UK: Cambridge University Press.

Winchester, H. 2000: Qualitative research and its place in human geography. In I. Hay, ed., 2000: *Qualitative research methods in human geography*. Oxford/Melbourne: Oxford University Press, 1–22.

Winichakul, T. 1994: *Siam mapped: a history of the geo-body of a nation*. Honolulu: University of Hawaii Press.

Winter, M. 2004: Geographies of food: agro-food geographies – farming, food and politics. *Progress in Human Geography* 28(5): 664–70.

Wintle, M. 1999: Renaissance maps and the construction of the idea of Europe. *Journal of Historical Geography* 25(2): 137–65.

Wintle, M. 2008: *The image of Europe: visualizing Europe in cartography and iconography throughout the ages*. Cambridge, UK: Cambridge University Press.

Wirth, L. 1928: *The ghetto*. Chicago: The University of Chicago Press.

Wirth, L. 1938: Urbanism as a way of life. *American Journal of Sociology* 44: 1–24.

Wise, M.J. 1975: A university teacher of geography. *Transactions of the Institute of British Geographers* 66: 1–16.

Wise, S. 2002: *GIS basics*. London: Taylor & Francis.

Wisner, B. 1986: Geography: war or peace studies? *Antipode* 18: 212–17.

Withers, C.W.J. 1984: *Gaelic in Scotland 1698–1981: the geographical history of a language*. Edinburgh: John Donald.

Withers, C.W.J. 1996: Encyclopaedism, modernism, and the classification of geographical knowledge. *Transactions of the Institute of British Geographers* 21(1): 275–98.

Withers, C.W.J. 1997: Geography, royalty and empire: Scotland and the making of Great Britain, 1603–1661. *Scottish Geographical Magazine* 113: 22–32.

Withers, C.W.J. 2001: *Geography, science and national identity: Scotland since 1520*. Cambridge, UK: Cambridge University Press.

Withers, C.W.J. 2002: Constructing 'the geographical archive'. *Area* 34: 303–11.

Withers, C.W.J. 2004: Mapping the Niger, 1798–1832: trust, testimony and 'ocular demonstration' in the late Enlightenment. *Imago Mundi* 56: 170–93.

Withers, C.W.J. 2006: Eighteenth-century geography: texts, practices, sites. *Progress in Human Geography* 30: 711–29.

Withers, C.W.J. and Finnegan, D. 2003: Natural history societies, fieldwork and local knowledge in nineteenth-century Scotland: toward a historical geography of civic science. *Cultural Geographies* 10(3): 334–53.

Withers, C.W.J. and Mayhew, R.J. 2002: Rethinking 'disciplinary' history: geography in British universities, c. 1580–1887. *Transactions of the Institute of British Geographers* 27: 1–19.

Withers, C.W.J. and Ogborn, M., eds, 2004: *Georgian geographies: essays on space, place and landscape in the eighteenth century*. Manchester: Manchester University Press.

Witt, A. 2005: The utility of regionalism for comparative research on governance: a political science perspective. In L. Hönnighausen et al., eds, *Regionalism in the age of globalism*, vol. 1. Madison, WI: University of Wisconsin Press, 47–66.

Wittgenstein, L. 1969: *On certainty*. Oxford: Blackwell.

Wohl, A.S. 1977: *The eternal slum: housing and social policy in Victorian London*. London: Arnold.

Wolch, J. and Dear, M. 1993: *Malign neglect: homelessness in an American City*. San Francisco, CA: Jossey Bass.

Wolch, J. and Emel, J. 1995: Guest-edited issue: 'Bringing the animals back in'. *Environment and Planning D: Society and Space* 13(6).

Wolch, J. and Emel, J., eds, 1998: *Animal geographies*. London: Verso.

Wolch, J., Pastor, M. Jr and Dreier, P., eds, 2004: *Up against the sprawl: public policy and the making of southern California*. Minneapolis: University of Minnesota Press.

Wolch, J., Pincetl, S. and Pulido, L. 2002: Urban nature and the nature of urbanism. In M. Dear, ed., *From Chicago to L.A.: making sense of urban theory*. Thousand Oaks, CA: Sage, 369–402.

Wolch, J., West, K. and Gaines, T. 1995: Transspecies urban theory. *Environment and Planning D: Society and Space* 13: 735–60.

Wolch, J.R. 1990: *The shadow state: government and voluntary sector in transition*. New York: The Foundation Center.

Wolf, D.L. 1995: *Feminist dilemmas in fieldwork*. Boulder, CO: Westview Press.

Wolf, E. 1966: *Peasants*. New York: Prentice-Hall.

Wolf, E.R. 1982: *Europe and the people without history*. Berkeley, CA: University of California Press.

Wolf, M. 2004: *Why globalization works*. New Haven, CT: Yale University Press.

Wolf, P.R. and Ghilani, C. 2005: *Elementary surveying: an introduction to geomatics*, 12th edn. Upper Saddle River, NJ: Pearson.

Wolfe, C. 2003: In the shadow of Wittgenstein's lion: language, ethics, and the question of the animal. In C. Wolfe, ed., *Zoontologies: the question of the animal*. Minneapolis: University of Minnesota Press, 1–57.

Wolfe, P. 2004: Twentieth-century theories of imperialism. In P. Duara, ed., *Decolonization: perspectives from now and then*. London: Routledge, 101–17.

Wolfe, P. 2006: Settler colonialism and the elimination of the native. *Journal of Genocide Research* 8: 387–409.

Wolff, J. 2006: Gender and the haunting of cities (or, the retirement of the *flâneur*). In A.

D'Souza and T. McDonough, eds, *The invisible* flâneuse*? Gender, public space, and visual culture in nineteenth-century Paris*. Manchester: Manchester University Press, 18–31.

Wolff, L. 1994: *Inventing Eastern Europe: the map of civilization on the mind of the Enlightenment*. Stanford, CA: Stanford University Press.

Wolff, R. and Resnick, S. 1987: *Economics: Marxian versus neoclassical*. Baltimore, MD: The Johns Hopkins University Press.

Wolford, W. 2003: Producing community: geographies of commitment on land reform settlements in Brazil. *Journal of Agrarian Change* 3(4): 500–20.

Wolford, W. 2004: This land is ours now: a new perspective on social movement formation. *Annals of the Association of American Geographers* 94(2): 409–24.

Wöllmann, L. 2003: Schooling resources, educational institutions and student performance: the international evidence. *Oxford Bulletin of Economics and Statistics* 65: 117–70.

Wolpe, H., ed., 1980: *The articulation of modes of production: essays from economy and society*. London: Routledge and Kegan Paul.

Wolpert, J. 1964: The decision process in spatial context. *Annals of the Association of American Geographers* 54: 537–58.

Wolpert, J. 1965: Behavioral aspects of the decision to migrate. *Papers and Proceedings of the Regional Science Association* 15: 159–72.

Wolter, J.A. 1975: Cartography – an emerging discipline. *The Canadian Cartographer* 12(2): 210–16.

Women and Geography Study Group 1997: *Feminist geographies: explorations in diversity and difference*. London: Longman.

Wong, D.W.S. and Lee, J. 2005: *Statistical analysis of geographic information with ArcView GIS and ArcGIS*. New York: Wiley.

Wong, T., Yeoh, B.S.A. and Graham, E. 2003: Spaces of silence: single parenthood and the 'normal family' in Singapore. *Population Space and Place* 10: 45–58.

Wood, C.H. 2000: A descriptive and illustrated guide for type placement on small scale maps. *Cartographic Journal* 37: 5–18.

Wood, D. 1977: Now and then: comparisons of ordinary Americans' symbol conventions with those of past cartographers. *Prologue: the Journal of the National Archives* 9: 151–61.

Wood, D. 1987: I don't feel that about environmental psychology today. But I want to. *Journal of Environmental Psychology* 7(4): 417–23.

Wood, D., with Fels, J. 1992: *The power of maps*. New York: Guilford Press.

Wood, D. and Beck, R.J. 1994: *Home rules*. Baltimore, MD: The Johns Hopkins University Press.

Wood, D.M. 2007: Beyond the panopticon? Foucault and surveillance studies. In J. Crampton and S. Elden, eds, *Space knowledge and power: Foucault and geography*. Aldershot: Ashgate, 245–63.

Wood, M. and Brodlie, K. 1994: ViSc and GIS: some fundamental considerations. In D. Unwin and H. Hearnshaw, eds, *Visualization in Geographic Information Systems*. Rexdale, Ontario: Wiley.

Wood, W. 2001: Geographic aspects of genocide: a comparison of Bosnia and Rwanda. *Transactions of the Institute of British Geographers* 26: 57–75.

Woods, M. 2006: Political articulation: the modalities of new critical politics of rural citizenship. In P. Cloke, T. Marsden and P. Mooney, eds, *Handbook of rural studies*. London: Sage, 457–83.

Woods, M. and Goodwin, M. 2003: Applying the rural: governance and policy in rural areas. In P. Cloke, ed., *Country visions*. London: Pearson.

Woods, R.I. 1982: *Theoretical population geography*. London: Longman.

Woodward, D. 1974: The study of the history of cartography: a suggested framework. *The American Cartographer* 1: 101–15.

Woodward, D., Delano Smith, C. and Yee, C.D.K. 2001: *Plantejaments i Objectius d'una Història Universal de la Cartografia [Approaches and challenges in a worldwide history of cartography]*. Cicle de conferències sobre Història de la Cartografia, 11. Barcelona: Institut Cartogràfic de Catalunya, 2001.

Woodward, D., ed., 2006: *The history of cartography*, vol. 3: *Cartography in the European Renaissance*. Chicago: The University of Chicago Press.

Woodward, R. 2004: *Military geographies*. Oxford: Blackwell.

Woodward, R. 2005: From military geography to militarism's geographies: disciplinary engagements with the geographies of militarism and military activities. *Progress in Human Geography* 29(6): 1–23.

Worboys, M.F. 2005: Relational databases and beyond. In P.A. Longley, M.F. Goodchild, D.J. Maguire and D.W. Rhind, eds, *Geographical Information Systems*, abridged edition. Chichester: Wiley, 163–74.

Wordie, J.R. 1983: The chronology of English enclosure 1500–1915. *Economic History Review* 36: 483–505.

World Bank 1993: *The East Asian miracle: economic growth and public policy*. New York: Oxford University Press.

World Bank 2001: *World development report 2000/2001: attacking poverty*. Washington, DC: The World Bank/Oxford: Oxford University Press.

World Resource Institute 2005: *Ecosystems and human well-being: synthesis report*. Millennium Ecosystem Assessment. Washington, DC: Island Press.

Worster, D. 1983: *The wealth of nature: environmental history and the ecological imagination*. New York: Oxford University Press.

Worster, D. 1990a: The ecology of order and chaos. *Environmental History Review* 14: 1–18.

Worster, D. 1990b: Transformations of the Earth: toward an agroecological perspective in history. *Journal of American History* 76(4): 1087–106.

Worster, D. 1994: *Nature's economy: a history of ecological ideas*. Cambridge, UK: Cambridge University Press.

Wright, D.J., Goodchild, M.F. and Proctor, J.D. 1997: Demystifying the persistent ambiguity of GIS as 'tool' versus 'science'. *Annals of the Association of American Geographers* 87: 346–62.

Wright, E., Levine, A. and Sober, E. 1992: *Reconstructing Marxism*. London: Verso.

Wright, E.O. 1985: *Classes*. London: Verso.

Wright, E.O., ed., 2005: *Approaches to class analysis*. Cambridge, UK: Cambridge University Press.

Wright, E.O. and Martin, B. 1987: The transformation of the American class structure, 1960–1980. *American Journal of Sociology* 87: 1–29.

Wright, J.K. 1947: *Terrae incognitae*: the place of the imagination in geography. *Annals of the Association of American Geographers* 37: 1–15.

Wright, J.K. 1965 [1925]: *The geographical lore of the time of the Crusades: a study in the history of medieval science and tradition in Western Europe*. New York: Dover.

Wright, M.W. 1999a: The dialectics of still life: murder, women and *maquiladoras*. *Public Culture* 11: 453–74.

Wright, M.W. 1999b: The politics of relocation: gender, nationality and value in the Maquiladoras. *Environment and Planning A* 31: 1601–17.

Wright, M.W. 2004: From protests to politics: sex work, women's worth and Ciudad Juárez modernity. *Annals of the Association of American Geographers* 94(2): 369–86.

Wright, M.W. 2005: Paradoxes, protests and the *Mujeres de Negro* of northern Mexico. *Gender, Place and Culture* 12: 277–92.

Wright, R. and Ellis, M. 2006: Mapping others. *Progress in Human Geography* 30(3): 285–88.

Wright, R.A., Houston, S., Ellis, M., Holloway, S. and Hudson, M. 2003: Crossing racial lines: geographies of mixed race partnering and multiraciality in the United States. *Progress in Human Geography* 27: 457–74.

Wrigley, E.A. 1965: Changes in the philosophy of geography. In R.J. Chorley and P. Haggett, eds, *Frontiers in geographical teaching*. London: Methuen, 3–24.

Wrigley, E.A. 1966a: Family reconstitution. In E. A. Wrigley, ed., *An introduction to English historical demography from the sixteenth to the nineteenth century*. London: Weidenfeld and Nicholson, 96–159.

Wrigley, E.A. 1966b: Family limitation in pre-industrial England. *Economic History Review*, 2nd series, xix: 82–109.

Wrigley, E.A. 1969: *Population in history*. London: Weidenfeld and Nicholson.

Wrigley, E.A. 1981: Marriage, fertility and population growth in eighteenth-century England. In R.B. Outhwaite, ed., *Marriage and society: studies in the social history of marriage*. London: Europa Publications, 137–85.

Wrigley, E.A. 1985a: Urban growth and agricultural change: England and the continent in the early modern period. *Journal of Interdisciplinary History* 15: 683–728.

Wrigley, E.A. 1988: *Continuity, chance and change: the character of the Industrial Revolution in England*. Cambridge, UK: Cambridge University Press, 8–17, 34–50.

Wrigley, E.A., Davies, R., Oeppen, J. and Schofield, R.S. 1997: *English population history from family reconstitutions 1580–1837*. Cambridge, UK: Cambridge University Press.

Wrigley, E.A. and Schofield, R.S. 1989 [1981]: *The population history of England 1541–1971: A reconstruction*. Cambridge, UK: Cambridge University Press.

Wrigley, N. 1985b: *Categorical data analysis for geographers and environmental scientists*. London/New York: Longman.

Wrigley, N. 1986: Quantitative methods: the era of longitudinal data analysis. *Progress in Human Geography* 10: 84–102.

Wrigley, N. 1990: Unobserved heterogeneity and the analysis of longitudinal spatial choice data. *European Journal of Population* 6(4): 327–58.

Wrigley, N. 2002: Transforming the corporate landscape of US food retailing: market power, financial re-engineering and regulation. *Tijdschrift voor Economische en Sociale Geografie* 93: 62–82.

Wrigley, N. and Lowe, M., eds, 1996: *Retailing, consumption and capital: towards the new retail geography*. London: Longman.

Wrigley, N. and Lowe, M. 2002: *Reading retail: a geographical perspective on retailing and consumption spaces*. London: Hodder Arnold.

Wylie, J. 2002a: An essay on ascending Glastonbury Tor. *Geoforum* 33: 441–54.

Wylie, J. 2002b: Becoming icy: Scott and Amundsen's South Polar voyages, 1910–1913. *Cultural Geographies* 9: 249–65.

Wylie, J. 2005: A single day's walking: narrating self and landscape on the South West Coast Path. *Transactions of the Institute of British Geographers* 30: 234–47.

Wynn, G. 2007: *Canada and Arctic North America: an environmental history*. Santa Barbara, CA: ABC-Clio.

Wynne, B. 1992: Uncertainty and environmental learning: reconceiving science and policy in the preventive paradigm. *Global Environmental Change* 2: 111–27.

Wynne, B. 1996: May the sheep safely graze? a reflexive view of the expert–lay knowledge divide. In S. Lash, B. Szersynski and B. Wynne, eds, *Risk, environment and modernity: towards a new ecology*. London: Sage, 44–83.

Xiao-me Chen 1995: *Occidentalism: a theory of counter-discourse in post-Mao China*. New York: Oxford University Press.

Yaeger, P., ed., 1996: *The geography of identity*. Ann Arbor: The University of Michigan Press.

Yancey, W.L., Ericksen, E.P. and Juliani, R.N. 1976: Emergent ethnicity: a review and reformulation. *American Sociologist* 41: 391–402.

Yang, X. and Hodler, T. 2000: Visual and statistical comparisons of surface modeling techniques for point-based environmental data. *Cartography and Geographic Information Science* 27: 165–76.

Yanow, D. 2002: *Constructing 'race' and 'ethnicity' in America: category-making in public policy and administration*. Armonk, NY: M.E. Sharpe.

Yapa, L. 1998: The poverty discourse and the poor in Sri Lanka. *Transactions of the Institute of British Geographers*, NS 23: 95–115.

Yapa, L. and Mayfield, R. 1978: Non-adoption of innovations. *Economic Geography* 54: 145–56.

Yegenoglu, M. 1998: *Colonial fantasies: towards a feminist reading of Orientalism*. Cambridge, UK: Cambridge University Press.

Yelling, J. 1986: *Slums and slum clearance in Victorian London*. London: George Allen & Unwin.

Yelling, J. 2000: The incidence of slum clearance in England and Wales, 1955–85. *Urban History* 27: 234–54.

Yeoh, B.S.A. 1999: Global/globalizing cities. *Progress in Human Geography* 23(4): 607–16.

Yeoh, B.S.A. 2001: Postcolonial cities. *Progress in Human Geography* 25(3): 456–68.

Yeoh, B.S.A. 2006: Bifurcated labour: the unequal incorporation of transmigrants in Singapore. *Tijdschrift voor Economische en Sociale Geografie* 97: 26–37.

Yeoh, B.S.A. and Kong, L. 1994: Reading landscape meanings: state constructions and lived experiences in Singapore's Chinatown. *Habitat International* 18(4): 17–35.

Yeoman, M. 2004: *Oil*. Boston: New Press.

Yergin, D. 1991: *The prize*. New York: The Free Press.

Yergin, D. and Stanislaw, J. 1998: *The commanding heights: the battle between government and the market place that is remaking the modern world*. New York: Simon and Schuster.

Yeung, H.W.-C. 1997: Critical realism: a method or a philosophy in search of a method? *Progress in Human Geography* 21: 51–74.

Yeung, H.W.-C. 2002: *Entrepreneurship and the internationalisation of Asian firms: an institutional perspective*. Cheltenham: Edward Elgar.

Yeung, H.W.-C. 2004: *Chinese capitalism in a global era: towards hybrid capitalism*. London: Routledge.

Yiftachel, O. and Ghanem, A. 2004: Understanding ethnocratic regimes: the politics of seizing contested territory. *Political Geography* 22(4): 538–68.

Yinger, J. 1995: *Closed doors, opportunities lost: the continuing costs of housing discrimination*. New York: Russell Sage Foundation.

Yoffee, N. 2005: The meaning of cities in the earliest states and civilizations. In Yoffee, *Myths of the archaic state: evolution of the earliest cities, states and civilizations*. Cambridge: Cambridge University Press, 42–90.

Yoon, K. 2003: Retraditionalizing the mobile: young people's sociality and mobile phone use in Seoul, South Korea. *European Journal of Cultural Studies* 6(3): 327–43.

Young, I.M. 1990a: *Justice and the politics of difference*. Princeton, NJ: Princeton University Press.

Young, I.M. 1997a: House and home: feminist variations on a theme. In *Intersecting voices: dilemmas of gender, political philosophy, and policy*. Princeton, NJ: Princeton University Press, 134–64.

Young, I.M. 1997b: *Intersecting voices: gender, political philosophy, and policy*. Princeton: Princeton University Press.

Young, I.M. 2000: *Democracy and inclusion*. Oxford: Oxford University Press.

Young, I.M. 2003a: The logic of masculinist protection: reflections on the current security state. *Signs: Journal of Women in Culture and Society* 29: 1–25.

Young, R. 1990b: *White mythologies: writing history and the West*. London: Routledge.

Young, R. 2001: *Postcolonialism: an historical introduction*. Oxford: Blackwell.

Young, R. 2003b: *Postcolonialism: a very short introduction*. Oxford: Oxford University Press.

Young, R.M. 1969: Malthus and the evolutionists: the common context of biological and social theory. *Past and Present* 43: 109–45.

Yudice, G. 2003: *The expediency of culture: uses of culture in the global era*. Durham, NC: Duke University Press.

Yuval-Davis, N. 1999: The 'multi-layered' citizen: citizenship in the age of 'glocalization'. *International Feminist Journal of Politics* 1(1): 119–36.

Zacher, M. 2001: The international territorial order: boundaries, the use of force, and normative change. *International Organization* 55: 212–50.

Zacher, M.W. 2001: The territorial integrity norm: international boundaries and the use of force. *International Organization* 55(2): 212–50.

Zafirovski, M. 2007: 'Neo-feudalism' in America? Conservatism in relation to European feudalism. *International Review of Sociology* 17: 393–427.

Zelinsky, W. 1966: *A prologue to population geography*. Englewood Cliffs, NJ: Prentice-Hall.

Zelinsky, W. 1971: The hypothesis of the mobility transition. *Geographical Review* 61: 219–49.

Zellner, A. 1971: *An introduction to Bayesian inference in econometrics*. New York: Wiley.

Zerilli, L. 1998: Doing without knowing: feminism's politics of the ordinary. *Political Theory* 26(4): 435–58.

Zhou, M. 1992: *Chinatown: the socioeconomic potential of an urban enclave*. Philadelphia, PA: Temple University Press.

Zhou, Y. 1998: How do places matter? A comparative study of Chinese ethnic economies in Los Angeles and New York City. *Urban Geography* 19(6): 531–53.

Zhou, Y.X. and Ma, L.J.C. 2000: Economic restructuring and suburbanization in China. *Urban Geography* 21(3): 205–36.

Zimmerer, K.S. 1994a: Human geography and the 'new ecology': the prospect and promise of integration. *Annals of the Association of American Geographers* 84(1): 108–25.

Zimmerer, K.S. 1994b: Integration: the new ecology in human geography. *Annals of the Association of American Geographers* 84: 108–25.

Zimmerer, K.S. 1997: *Changing fortunes: biodiversity and peasant livelihood in the Peruvian Andes*. Berkeley, CA: University of California Press.

Zimmerer, K.S. 2000: The reworking of conservation geographies: nonequilibrium landscapes and nature–society hybrids. *Annals of the Association of American Geographers* 90(2): 356–69.

Zimmerer, K.S. and Bassett, T.J., eds, 2003: *Political ecology: an integrative approach to geography and environment-development studies*. New York: Guilford Press.

Zimmerman, E.W. 1933: *World resources and industries: a functional appraisal of the availability of agricultural and industrial resources*. New York and London: Harper and Brothers.

Žižek, S. 2001: *Did somebody say totalitarianism?* London: Verso.

Zook, M. 2005: *The geography of the Internet industry.* Blackwell: Oxford.

Zoraster, S. 1997: Practical results using simulated annealing for point feature label placement. *Cartography and Geographic Information Systems* 24: 228–38.

Zorbaugh, H. 1929: *The gold coast and the slum: a sociological study of Chicago's Near North Side.* Chicago: The University of Chicago Press.

Zweig, D. 1997: *Freeing China's farmers.* Armonk, NY: M.E. Sharpe.

Index

Note: This index aims to provide a guide to the complex interconnections within human geography. References to particular topics will be found most easily by looking up that particular topic, but extensive sets of subheadings also indicate the various aspects of more general headings. In addition, a network of *see* and *see also* references indicates alternative headings and related topics. Alphabetical arrangement is word-by-word. References to particular authors are included only where their work is quoted or discussed in some detail. Page numbers in **bold** type indicate the main discussion of a topic that is also treated in less detail on the other pages cited. Page numbers in *italics* refer to diagrams.

Managing
Facilities
& Real Estate

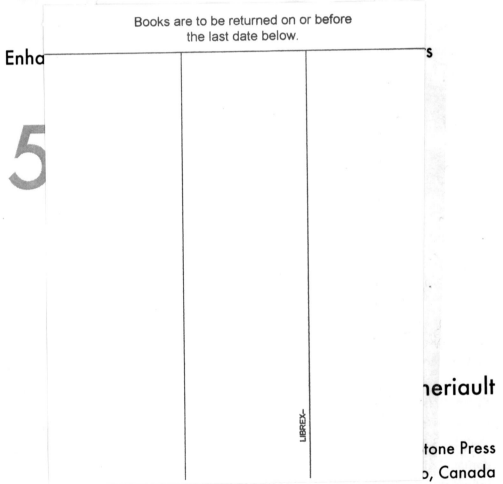

Books are to be returned on or before
the last date below.

Enha   s

5

LIBREX-

heriault

tone Press
, Canada

woodstonepress.com

LIVERPOOL JMU LIBRARY

3 1111 01333 9898

This book is dedicated to my wife, Melanie

Copyright 2010 by Michel Theriault. All Rights Reserved. Except as permitted under the Copyright Act, no part of this publication may be reproduced, distributed or electronically stored in any form or any means without the prior written permission of the publisher.

First Edition

ISBN 978-0-9813374-1-8

Published 2010 by WoodStone Press

This book provides general information on the subject. The reader understands that neither the publisher nor the author are providing specific professional services related to your unique situation or specific requirements, which may differ. It is your responsibility to ensure the information is relevant to your specific situation and apply it appropriately. Neither the author nor publisher shall be liable or responsible to any person or entity with respect to any loss or damage caused, or alleged to be caused, directly or indirectly by using the information in this book.